A

LEXICON,

HEBREW, CHALDEE, AND ENGLISH;

COMPILED FROM THE MOST APPROVED SOURCES,

ORIENTAL AND EUROPEAN, JEWISH AND CHRISTIAN;

CONTAINING

ALL THE WORDS WITH THEIR USUAL INFLEXIONS, IDIOMATIC USAGES, &c.

AS FOUND IN THE

HEBREW AND CHALDEE TEXTS OF THE OLD TESTAMENT,

AND, FOR THE CONVENIENCE OF THE LEARNER,

ARRANGED, AS FAR AS PRACTICABLE,

IN THE ORDER OF THE HEBREW ALPHABET;

MANY HITHERTO OBSCURE TERMS, PHRASES, AND PASSAGES EXPLAINED; AND
MANY ERRORS OF FORMER GRAMMARIANS AND COMMENTATORS
POINTED OUT AND CORRECTED.

TO WHICH ARE ADDED,

THREE APPENDIXES,

THE FIRST, CONTAINING A PLAN WITH TWO SECTIONS, AND A SHORT DESCRIPTION OF THE TEMPLE
OF SOLOMON, ITS COURTS, FURNITURE, &c.
THE SECOND, AN ENGLISH INDEX, ALPHABETICALLY ARRANGED, FORMING A REVERSED DICTIONARY,
ENGLISH, HEBREW, AND CHALDEE.
THE THIRD, PRESENTING CERTAIN ADDITIONS, CORRECTIONS, &c., TO THE LEXICON GENERALLY.

BY SAMUEL LEE, D.D.

REGIUS PROFESSOR OF HEBREW IN THE UNIVERSITY OF CAMBRIDGE;
D.D. of the University of Halle; Honorary Member of the Asiatic Society of Paris, and of the Historical Society of
Rhode Island, America; Member of the Royal Asiatic Society of Great Britain and Ireland, and of its Oriental
Translation Committee; also of the Foreign Translation Committee of the Society for Promoting Christian
Knowledge; Prebendary of Bristol; Rector of Barley, Herts, &c. &c.

WIPF & STOCK · Eugene, Oregon

Wipf and Stock Publishers
199 W 8th Ave, Suite 3
Eugene, OR 97401

A Lexicon, Hebrew, Chaldee and English
By Lee, Samuel
ISBN 13: 978-1-60608-065-8
Publication date 01/16/2009
Previously published by Duncan and Malcolm, 1840

TO THE

MOST REVEREND FATHER IN GOD,

WILLIAM,

BY DIVINE PERMISSION, LORD ARCHBISHOP OF CANTERBURY, PRIMATE
OF ALL ENGLAND, AND METROPOLITAN,

This Work,

INTENDED TO FACILITATE AND PROMOTE THE STUDY OF THE

ORIGINAL SCRIPTURES,

PRIMARILY IN OUR UNIVERSITIES,

AND THENCE GENERALLY

THE ADVANCEMENT OF DIVINE TRUTH IN THE

CHURCH OF CHRIST,

AND PARTICULARLY

IN THAT APOSTOLICAL PART OF IT ESTABLISHED IN THIS KINGDOM,

IS,

BY HIS GRACE'S PERMISSION,

MOST RESPECTFULLY INSCRIBED BY

THE AUTHOR.

PREFACE.

The following work so long promised has, by the Divine aid, now at length been brought to a close. It becomes my duty, therefore, to lay before the reader, in the first place, the causes which led to the apparent delay; and, in the second, the views and principles under which it has been carried on.

In the first place, then, I certainly had formed a very erroneous estimate, as to the amount of thought and labour that would be required. I had very naturally supposed, from the number and pretensions of works of this sort published within the last thirty years, that I should have but little to do beyond the labour of arrangement, abridgement, and correction, to a small extent. I soon, however, had the mortification to discover, that this abundance of materials tended rather to increase my labour, and to multiply my difficulties, than the contrary. I found, or thought I found that, in reality, much less had been done in this way than I had supposed, and had, indeed, a right to expect.

On the works imported from the Continent, and principally from Germany, no reliance could generally be placed: of which examples will presently be given; and, as I was unwilling to omit any thing advanced in them which might be useful to the student, it now became a duty to consult them all, weigh every thing brought forward affecting either the etymology or the sense, and then to judge and act accordingly.

In cases innumerable it was evident that the Biblical text had never been consulted: many of the passages cited had been merely copied from the Concordance of John Buxtorf, where the references are found to be erroneous. To many, therefore, senses had been given which a reference to the context showed to be wrong. A very large number of words, constructions, and phrases, moreover, had, without any notice given of this, been systematically omitted; leaving it, apparently, to the ingenuity of the learner to supply these by the analogy of the Grammar: a work to which the ingenuity of no one could be equal.

In very many cases, moreover, the sense had been made to depend on the translation given of some Oriental word, phrase, or adage, which upon examination turned out to be inaccurate: and of this examples will also be given. In others, the Rationalism of Germany had been allowed to supply the needful; of which numerous instances will be found noticed in the course of the work. Add to these things the business of a parish, attendance on my duties at Cambridge and Bristol, with the unavoidable occurrence of some circumstances of a very afflicting character: the aggregate of which conspired to affect my health to such an extent, as to render the suspension of every thing like literary labour an imperative duty. All which, when duly considered, will, perhaps, account sufficiently for the delay above alluded to.

I now deemed it right to call in assistance, if such could possibly be had. The public were expressing much impatience for the work; the proprietor was necessarily anxious for the fate of his capital already vested in it. All of which tended to press the consideration, that every thing likely to expedite its completion should immediately be had recourse to. My esteemed and learned friend, the Rev. T. Jarrett, Arabic Professor in the University of Cambridge, was so good as to answer the call, and to tender his very timely and valuable aid. This he has most effectually done, commencing at p. 389 of the work, and supplying from that place the greater part of the copy.* All I was able to do, I did; which was, to supply a certain portion of the copy, sustain the office of editor with respect to the rest, and carefully to look over all the proofs before they were put to press.

I may now lay before the reader my statement, as to the views and principles under which this work has been carried on. And I shall premise, that *conciseness* and *precision* have always appeared to me the two great requisites, of which the writers of elementary works should never lose sight; or, to adopt the adage of the Arabs, *The best discourse is that which is* (at once both) *short and clear,* خَيْرُ الْكَلَامِ مَا قَلَّ وَدَلَّ .

For the purpose of ensuring *conciseness*, then, it has been my endeavour to comprehend as much as possible in every individual case, under some general law or principle of grammar: and, in order to *precision*, as it regards particular words, to class every thing, as far as practicable, under some one leading idea or notion, and thence easily and naturally to deduce all the secondary or subsequent ones. The Grammar referred to, as to the first of these, is my own of the edition of 1832, in which the principles, here adverted to, have been uniformly laid down and acted upon.

As to the second, viz., the consideration of single words, my practice has been, as in my Grammar,† to consider the noun, in one or other of its primitive forms, as the root or leading word in each series, both as to form and meaning. Because in the noun, so taken, I could find something simple and tangible; something to which addition might be made in each case; and thence be intelligibly derived all that variety, both as to form and sense, which is found to prevail in every particular part of speech, however simple or com-

---

* It ought to be mentioned here that, in addition to the copy, said above to have been contributed by Mr. Professor Jarrett, the whole of the Index, or reversed part of the Dictionary (Appendix B), has been supplied solely by his industry; as also were many of the particulars contained in the Additions and Corrections (Appendix C) from his suggestions. I will only add, I trust that this will not be the last instance, in which the public will be benefited by his industry, talents, and learning.

† See my Grammar, Lecture x.

pounded it may be. While the verb as such—most commonly taken as the root—is necessarily either a compound term, or at least a simple one, involving at the same time the force of a pronoun, investing it with a precise personal signification.* To take such a word, as a *root*, has seemed to me at variance as well with the nature of things as with the term *root* itself, chosen as it has been to designate the leading and primary word of the several existing series. It should also be borne in mind, that the term *verb* can claim no higher authority than the opinion of those, who have thought proper to adopt it in the technical sense in which it is now used; that it is a mere technicality and nothing more, and, therefore, altogether inadequate to the task of proving the existence of any fact.

Nor will the adoption of the *Infinitive* or *Imperative* form of the *verb*, as presenting a simple form—which some prefer—at all mend the matter; for here, as before, we shall be assuming, that to adopt a mere technicality is the same thing as to determine a philosophical truth; the absurdity of which every one must perceive upon its being once suggested. The truth seems to be, these Infinitives or Imperatives, as they are termed,—conveniently enough for the technical purposes of grammar—present nothing beyond simple primitive segolate nouns, implying the *action, passion, circumstance*, or the like, which the author of language—or, it may be, general convention—has determined they should severally signify; and which usage only has assigned to the particular part of speech, in which Grammarians now class them, and upon which after-times has constructed other forms assignable to other uses. These then are, after all, simple primitive *nouns*, and nothing more; and, as they are found, for the most part, existing also as nouns, the fact that they are so, seems as obvious and certain, as it can be reasonably required it should be.

To those, however, who think differently, this arrangement can present no obstacle either in the Grammar or the Dictionary. They can—if they prefer doing so—as readily refer to the *verb* as the *root*, as they can in any other works constructed on their own principles. Nor will it be of much importance, generally, as to the views to be taken of Holy Writ. As far as my own experience goes—and this has been gained under both systems—I have found the one here recommended much better suited to the genius of language generally, and of this language in particular, than the other; and thence, in cases not a few, sufficient to suggest the means of removing difficulties which nothing else could.

Having thus, then, determined the nature and forms of words, the next thing was to ascertain their *precise* primary force and meaning; and, first, of the primitives. In very many cases no inquiry was necessary. When it was, a comparison of the Hebrew with the Oriental usage—as still existing—of the word in question, together with its cognates, has been instituted; and thence the apparently primitive acceptation elicited.† From this, again, the secondary

---

* See my Grammar, art. 187, seq.
† On this subject, see my Introduction to the Book of Job. London, 1837.

or subsequent significations have been derived, and, as far as practicable, in the order and manner which appeared the most easy and natural. By these means, *certainty*, it has been hoped in the first case, would, to a considerable extent, be ensured; and, in the second, a facility of recollection which was not to be expected under any other. How far success has been attained to, it will be for the reader to judge.

As to the force of combination, as in phrases, sentences, and of the context generally, it has been deemed necessary occasionally to call in the aid of pure Oriental grammar and rhetoric, and this, whenever it could be done, in connexion with the interpretations given in the New Testament; not neglecting, at the same time, those given by other well-received authorities, as the authors of the Septuagint, Aquila, Symmachus, Theodotion, and of the other Hexaplar versions; of the Targums, of the Peschito Syriac, of the Latin Vulgate, and of the Commentaries, Jewish and Christian, generally. But in no instance has it been attempted to elicit or determine from some Oriental word or usage only, the sense and bearing of any word or combination of words. This would be to pervert one of the best means of ascertaining the truth, to one very likely to propagate error. Nor, again, has either orthodoxy or heterodoxy been allowed, as far as I am conscious, imperatively and solely to determine any thing. The endeavour has been to assign to every, and to all of these, the influence to which they seemed severally—or conjointly as the case might be—fairly entitled, and no more. How far I have succeeded in these cases, it is, as before, for the reader to determine.

I have thought it right to make this statement, because, in the first place, those who are not conversant with Oriental literature generally, are very apt to imagine, both that it is of but little value as a help to the study of the Hebrew, and that very unjustifiable liberties have been taken with the Hebrew text from its adoption. To which it may be replied: It only requires an extensive practical knowledge of the languages and usages of the East, to be sufficiently convinced of the perfect futility of the first of these assertions; and, as to the second, although its truth, as a fact, may be admitted to a certain extent, it will by no means follow that the use of this valuable auxiliary is to be condemned, merely because its abuse may have been frequent and extensive.

Again, as to orthodoxy or heterodoxy, singly and respectively, I am well aware how far Grammarians and Interpreters, as such, have been led astray by an overweening and imprudent attachment to considerations connected with one or other of these. The Jews, for example—opposed as they necessarily are to the interpretations of the Old Testament which are found in the New—have spared no pains in the construction of their Grammars, Dictionaries, and Commentaries, tacitly to make every provision against their adoption. And, although they are now found generally among the loudest objectors to the use of the Arabic, time was when the language of Ishmael (לְשׁוֹן יִשְׁמָעֵאל) was appealed to by them for this and other purposes, as one of the safest means they could adopt. To this they added an appeal to *tradition;* which, it is to be regretted, was so readily admitted by the divines of Europe;

but which will be found, upon investigation, to rest on foundations no better than those of conjecture. Matter of this sort will be met with in the richest variety in the writings of Reuchlin, the elder Buxtorfs, our own Pococke, and many others; the influence of which is felt to a very great extent to the present day.

Heterodoxy has produced similar results among the writers of modern Germany. Grammars, Dictionaries, Scholia, Commentaries, evincing very considerable learning, industry, and talent, have been composed in the greatest abundance. In these, appeal is very generally made to Oriental languages and customs, to the opinions of heathen philosophers and poets, to Jewish Grammarians, Targumists, Commentators, Cabbalists, and the like; more for the purpose of adapting the several views and opinions cited to the sacred text, than for that of illustrating mere grammatical, rhetorical, or other usages, and which might fairly be supposed to have been common to writers both sacred and profane. This, I say, is apparent on the face of all the writers of that school; who, nevertheless, are for ever insisting upon it, that they give nothing beyond the legitimate grammatical and historical interpretation! * And, as to their appeals to the Oriental languages and usages, it is the fact that, in the former, they seldom evince a sound practical knowledge, rarely any thing like extensive reading; and, in no case, an acquaintance with the Grammarians and Rhetoricians of the East. In instances not a few they have perpetuated the mistakes of their predecessors, and in others they have advanced many which have originated with themselves; of all which examples will be found in various places throughout this work.

Again, as to orthodoxy in the article of Biblical interpretation, the only authoritative guide and corrective is, beyond all dispute, the New Testament. In this, a system of Theology repugnant to that of the Jews, and directly opposed to the notions of heathen philosophers and poets, is clearly discoverable. Its leading notions and principles are peculiar to itself; they claim an origin and authority super-human; and to this they every where evince an indisputable right. These notions and principles, therefore—connected as they are with theology—cannot fail, in the first place, to exercise a considerable influence on the Grammarian, and thence also on the Interpreter of Scripture, in the second. This, I say, they cannot but do, and that the consequence must necessarily be, a considerable variety discoverable between the interpretations, grammatical as well as theological, of the Jew or Neologian, and of the conscientious and well-informed Christian divine, respectively. And such is indeed the fact. Heathenish principles have here, as in other instances, led to heathenish results; and this, I must affirm, will ever be the case, where the only legitimate and authoritative guide, viz., the New Testament, is systematically disregarded.

It is not, however, intended to be affirmed, that the Grammarian is ever to go

---

* See my Introduction to the Book of Job, p. 101, seq.; Sermons and Dissertations, p. 124, seq.

out of his way, for the purpose of accommodating his rules to the advancement of what he may consider orthodoxy. This would be as dishonest on one hand, as the practice proscribed above is faulty, partial, and unjust, on the other. Nor, if any reliance may be placed on my experience, will this ever be necessary. As far as I have been able to observe or discover, it is certain, the most extensive and deep acquaintance with the Grammarians, Rhetoricians, and usages of the East,—aided by the conclusions arrived at by the best writers of all ages, Jewish as well as Christian; and among the former, the Targumists may be allowed to occupy a distinguished place; among the latter, the fathers of the Church, such as Chrysostom, Theodoret, Jerome, and others,—will show most clearly that the Interpretations of the New Testament are, at once, the most easy, natural, judicious, and acceptable: those which exhibit the greatest agreement both in the letter and spirit with the declarations of the inspired writers whether of patriarchal or ancient Jewish times. One so circumstanced will find, moreover, a sort of family likeness pervading the whole, whether as to language, usages, or doctrines, sufficiently strong to convince him that, as members of the same household, they are the best qualified to explain each other's sentiments and views; and that, as such, they ought never to be separated, much less that their declarations should be interpreted by those, who are utter aliens to their commonwealth.

There is one principle more, not entirely unallied to the foregoing, which I have deemed it my duty never to have recourse to, viz., that of metaphysics, as employed on the one hand by John Calvin and his followers, and on the other by James Arminius, and his. I mean, that of eliciting particular doctrines from the declarations of Scripture, by calling in the acknowledged properties of the Divine mind as helps in the work of interpretation; and thence making deductions as unnecessary to mankind, as they are in reality groundless; but which have, nevertheless, proved the sources of endless dispute and strife. The instances particularly alluded to in the Old Testament, are those in which God is said to have hardened Pharaoh's heart; made blind the eyes, and fat the heart, of the Jewish people; to have made the wicked for the day of evil, and the like. All which originating, as they have, in ignorance of the real import of the original, have invariably been defended on the one hand, or attacked on the other, by an appeal to the metaphysical resources just mentioned. In the New Testament, again, St. Paul has been made a most rigid fatalist, when it is sufficiently evident that all he could have intended was, an appeal to the *particular prophecies*, which had foretold and *predefined* those events, times, and doctrines, which he had been commissioned to unfold, teach, and urge, throughout the world.*

On this last subject, see מַעֲנֶה, פָּעַל, (sign. c.), קָשָׁה, עֵצָה, and שָׁמֵן,†

---

* Rom. viii. ix., &c.

† The reader should be apprized that the Hebrew Bible everywhere referred to, is the stereotyped edition of 1836, published by the proprietor of this work, Mr. James Duncan.

PREFACE. xi

under their proper places in the Dictionary, my Sermons and Dissert. p. lxi., seq., with the notes: also Dissert. i., sect. viii., p. 35, seq.; and Gram. artt. 154. 8; 157. 6, with the notes. Whence it will appear, that the translations themselves are inconsistent with the Oriental idiom in all such cases, and that the defences usually advanced in favour of the doctrines so arrived at, rested solely on principles adopted from the schools of heathen philosophers.

Exemplifications of the other instances of mistake and error, adverted to above, as originating either with the Jews, or the Rationalists of Germany, generally, will be found in the Dictionary, under the terms, אֶבֶן, אִבְחָה, אוּר כַּשְׂדִּים, אוּר, אֲדַרְכּוֹנִים.—See here also the Additions and Corrections appended to the Dictionary:—אָמַד, אִי, אֵל, אַל, אַלְגָּבִישׁ, בְּהֵמוֹת, בְּדֹלַח, בְּאֹשִׁים, אֵת or אֶת. אֲשֵׁרָה, אָשָׁם, אָמִיר, אָלָח, الجَبَسُ, גֹּמֶד, גָּלַשׁ, גִּלָּיוֹן, גּוּר, גָּאַל, בָּשָׁם, בְּרִית, בָּרָא, בֶּצֶר, בָּמָה, בְּחָשְׁמָה, חֶדֶל, הֵידוֹת, הוֹר, on Ezek. xix. 10; דָּם, דּוּדָאִים, דָּנַר, דִּבֵּשׁ, דָּבָר, גֶּרֶב, נְרָא, נָזַה, לִילִית, כֹּהֵן, חַרְגֹּל, حَرْجَل, חַכְלִילִי, חָוֵל, חֹרֶשׁ, to which many others might be added.

Examples, as to the manner in which the primary, secondary, and subsequent senses of words have been ascertained or deduced, will be found under the following, as they occur in the Dictionary, viz.:—אֶבֶן, אָבִיב, אָבַד, אֵת, אָרוֹן, אָסַף, אָנָה, אִם, אֵם, אָכַל, אוּפָז, אָדוֹן, אֲגֻדָּה, or אֶת, also אֵת, pl. אִתִּים, and אִתִּים, בָּא, עֶרֶב, רָגַע, &c.

In determining the sense of the Particles, the Concordance of Noldius, has generally been taken, and the endeavour then made to comprehend his numerous, and in many cases inconsistent, significations under some one primary and leading notion, and then, if necessary, adding as few more as possible, exhibiting at the same time shades of meaning as nearly allied to this, as the nature of the context would, in the several cases, admit of; which, although creating considerable labour in the investigation, never proved, to me at least, unsatisfactory in the end.

As to Noldius,—and the same may be said of lexicographers but too generally,—his practice evinces no endeavour beyond that of offering a signification well suited, as he thought, to each place in which any particle occurred; which eventually resolves itself into a system of mere conjecture; and one, moreover, which takes for granted, that in the particular signification he ascribed to every other word occurring in such passage, as well as the construction which he adopted, was above all suspicion or doubt correct and acceptable; a supposition by no means always true. And of this, proof sufficient will be found in the Dictionary under the Particles אַל or אֶל, אֵל, עַם, אִם, &c. Of this practice, as occurring in lexicographers generally, examples sufficient will be found under the terms already pointed out;* also

---

* One or two examples of this sort, taken from a generally useful and popular writer

in my Sermons and Dissertt. Dissert. i., and my notes on the Book of Job generally.

And it may with truth be affirmed, that we owe to this most plausible and delusive principle, viz., of supplying an *apparently* suitable sense to Hebrew words, phrases, or declarations, instead of investigating their real Oriental import and force, all the difficulties, uncertainties, and ambiguities, which have conspired so abundantly to obscure the declarations of the Old Testament,

---

among ourselves, may not be out of place here. " In Scripture," says the late ingenious Mr. Taylor, in his Fragments to Calmet, vol. iii. p. 628, " בא, BA, signifies not only *coming*, but *going away*, going off, sinking, setting, as the sun sets, &c.," Gen. xxviii. 11 . . . . " because the sun was set, was *gone off*," . . . . Ps. L. 1; "from the rising of the sun to the *going off* of the same (מנאו)." . . . . " In all which places," says he, " there is a clear and indisputable reference to the departure of the solar light." It may be answered, that this is the thing in some sense meant, there need be no dispute, as there can be no doubt about it. But this is not here the point in question; which is, did the sacred writers intend to convey the notion of *departure, going off*, or the like, when they used this word? My own impression is, that it is as certain they meant no such thing, as a question of this sort need be; and, to this effect, the cognate dialects will afford the amplest testimony. Mr. Taylor has here had the misfortune—common to many—to recommend a meaning which the word might in some cases possibly bear; but which it is sufficiently certain no Oriental ever ascribed to it. By מְבָא הַשֶּׁמֶשׁ, they mean *the entering-place of the sun*, i. e. in which it appears to enter the earth, or to set. And, in this acceptation, they oppose בָּא, to יָצָא, i. e. *going in*, to *going out;* which last is the undoubted precise force of this latter term. Comp. Gen. xix. 23; Is. xiii. 10, &c. See also the Dictionary, under בּוֹא, מְבָא, and יָצָא. Here, therefore, by virtue of a very plausible conclusion, we have a signification given to this word directly opposed to its true one! I will only ask, What may not be arrived at from the adoption of a principle such as this?

Once more, Ib. vol. iv. p. 277, seq., the Syriac ܨܒܥ, *intinxit, baptizavit*, is cited to prove that baptism could not have been by immersion; because, it is said, this word is sometimes used to denote variety, as of stripes, spots, &c., in colour; which it is also affirmed could not have been obtained by *dipping*, as had recourse to in dying. In p. 278 of this volume it is also argued on the other hand, that this word is never used in the Syriac New Testament in the sense of *baptizing;* but, that when that sense is intended, עמד, ܥܡܕ, is invariably had recourse to. It is then urged, that as this last word signifies " *stetit*, ita ut stare sit, stare in flumine, illoque *mergi*,"—as Michaelis had, after all, only conjectured—the conclusion drawn is, " having thus investigated the *true* sense of the Syriac words used for baptism, we think," it is added, " the weight of evidence evidently preponderates in favour of immersion."

Here, then, the *true sense* of this Syriac term having been thus fairly established, we may now rest perfectly satisfied that all is right. The truth however is, the whole is palpably wrong. Michaelis was not aware how the verb ܥܡܕ, applied to baptism in the East, nor why the rite itself was styled ܡܥܡܘܕܝܬܐ. The fact is, Confirmation is administered in the Oriental Churches together with baptism; and it is to that rite, rather than to baptism, that these words have been applied. And this the last editor of Calmet ought to have known. See my Sermons and Dissertations, p. 178.— This work is, nevertheless, highly deserving of the attention of the Biblical student, particularly on account of the extracts, &c., collected from travellers and others.

and thence not very slightly to affect many of those contained in the New. To this I feel compelled to ascribe all the difficulty and darkness, which modern times have succeeded in casting over the question of prophecy; and thence, rendering nearly useless one of the most convincing evidences of the truth of Christianity; one which, in the hands of its early apologists, produced the happiest results. To this, too, we owe the plausible, but groundless system proposed some years ago by Mr. John Hutchinson, and which succeeded in carrying along with it some of our best, but not most prudent or well-informed men. To this also, the school of Capellus, Houbigant, Kennicott, Lowth, &c., owed all its beauty and grandeur; and the same may be said of many of the ephemeral and popular writers, male and female, still to be found among us.

It is not, however, intended to be affirmed, that conjecture is never to be had recourse to; this would be to evince both ignorance and folly. All that is meant is, that as we now have easy means of access to every species of Oriental literature, antiquities, and usage, our first duty is to consult these. It is when these, as well as every other aid, such as the ancient versions, commentaries, &c., fail us, that we may fairly have recourse to conjecture, or, which would perhaps be better, leave the matter in doubt, with the hope that the labours of others might be more successful.

As to the order in which the words have been arranged, that of the Hebrew alphabet has been adopted as far as practicable. I say, as far as practicable; because it was clearly impracticable to give *every form of word* occurring in the Hebrew Bible in this order: this would have swollen the work to an enormous extent. In this respect, therefore, Gesenius has generally been followed, except, as observed above, that the primitive noun has usually been made to take the lead; and that words only as they *actually occur*, and these in *all their inflected forms*, full or defective, regular or irregular, have been given; excepting only, as also intimated, those forms of each and every particular person in the verbs, of each and every prefix, or affix in the nouns; of which the learner, but slightly acquainted with the Grammar, could not stand in need. But when the leading word, in order, has *not* been found actually to occur, of this the learner is admonished either by the omission of the vowels, or otherwise. By the insertion of all the forms, of apocope in verbs, of the Infinitives, Participles, and other derivatives, whether masculine, feminine, or common; whether occurring in the singular or plural, the form proper for construction, or, with one or more of the affixes in each case, a very large number of words are presented to the student, which have usually been left, in similar works, to be supplied by his judgment from the analogy of the Grammar; which has appeared to me to be taking too much for granted.* And, as the order adopted is alphabetical, it was deemed unnecessary to present a second, in an analytical index of words either defective in their forms, or otherwise difficult to be found, as in the Lexicons of Gesenius and Winer. These,

---

* I regret that, in a few of the first pages of this work, this full exhibition of all the forms was not adopted. This, however, can present no very serious inconvenience.

therefore, as far as it has been deemed necessary, have been inserted in their proper places in the body of the work.

It has not been thought necessary to say, when speaking of the nouns, whether they were substantive or adjective, both because such description was deemed superfluous,—the learner being supposed to be acquainted with the common usages of Grammar,—and because such designation has not appeared to me strictly applicable to this language.* Nor, of the verbs and verbal nouns, has it been considered necessary to state whether they were Transitive, Intransitive, or Neuter: nor, again, in any instance to introduce the mention of nominative, genitive, accusative, or other case, after the manner of the Latin grammarians; because no such thing as *case*, in that sense, existed in this language. I have thought it more appropriate to say that such verb or noun is construed either immediately (constr. immed.); that is, exerts its influence *immediately* on its object, without any intervening particle, as, *John loves Thomas;* in which case the verb will necessarily be transitive; or, *mediately* (constr. med.); that is, having some particle or particles intervening, as, *John went* TO *London:* where the verb is intransitive; or *absolutely* (constr. abs.), where no subsequent term is necessary; as, *I stand, walk,* &c., where the verb is of necessity neuter. Many verbs, it will be seen, sustain each of these characters: they are by these means, therefore, very readily characterized.

In the verbs, too, the terms pret. (preterite) and pres. (present) have been adopted, in conformity with the usage of my Grammar,† to denote what has usually been styled the *preterite* and *future* tense. Those, however, who prefer terming the latter *the future,* or *the aorist,* will find no inconvenience in my naming it otherwise. I have done so, because I felt that I had the analogy of the language and Oriental usage with me; and was therefore in possession of the principle which did obtain with the sacred writers themselves. ‡ The full rhetorical use of the Apocope, of the Epenthetic ו, and קָטְלָה, and of the Paragogic הָ, was determined, for the first time, in my Hebrew Grammar, Edit. 1832, art. 233, seq. I have since succeeded in ascertaining that of the termination קָה—, as the reader will find under the letter כ, p. 400.

---

* See my Gram. artt. 153. 4; 217. 7, with the notes.

† See my Heb. Gram. Lecture xvii.

‡ On this subject, moreover, see Dictionary, under the letter ו, p. 163. In addition to these and some other particulars, my Grammar presented, for the first time, the laws which regulated the rejection of the אהוי, letters, and ן; enabling the learner to see, in a moment, the real source of every defect occurring in this language. I think it right to say this, because some of my reviewers, who were pleased to speak favourably of my work, had no hesitation in saying that I was indebted either to Dr. Gesenius, or Mr. Ewald, for every thing new and important: whereas the truth is, my Grammar appeared (in 1827) before a copy of Ewald's had reached this country; and, that not one of the particulars adverted to above ever appeared in that of Gesenius, and the most important of them never in that of Mr. Ewald. The fact is, the doctrine of the Hebrew tenses, with the use of the apocopated, epenthetic, and paragogic forms, was extracted by me from the native grammars of the Arabs; works which it does not appear either of these gentlemen ever consulted.

In most cases all the *constructions* of the verbs and verbal nouns are given in the manner just mentioned. The student ought to be apprized, however, that cases occur in which these are so numerous and various, that it would be almost endless to give them in detail; and of this he is always warned. And, as this work was intended to teach how the Hebrew ought to be read and construed, rather than how it should be written, it has been deemed sufficient, in many cases, merely to say what the construction is, leaving it to the industry of the student to make the due application of this. The same is true of the significations ascribed to words generally, and of the various phraseology cited. Enough has been given, it is hoped, to enable the student to find his way with safety and certainty to a large extent in this field of inquiry; and, eventually, with the helps here and elsewhere pointed out, to arrive at that state of proficiency, which cannot but administer the greatest pleasure to himself, as well as profit to the Church of Christ, in the additional light it will be in his power to throw on the pages of revealed truth.

The proper names, both of persons and places generally, I have thought it right to omit; because, first, it was impossible to do justice to either of these, particularly the latter, within the limits assigned to a Dictionary; and, in the second, it appeared unnecessary. If it be suggested that, without this help from the Dictionary, the learner will be unable to distinguish between a noun used as an appellative, or as a proper name; my answer is, If the learner is here to appeal to authority only, then, that of the authorized, or any other good version, will be equally decisive with that of the Dictionary; but, if he is to proceed as a critic, then this in a mere learner will be absurd; and, if in any other character, the authority of a lexicographer will not be deemed sufficient. And, in any case, treatises written specifically on these subjects, and which are accessible in sufficient abundance, had better be consulted. In my Grammar, indeed, a section, or lecture, has been bestowed on scriptural proper names: but this was intended rather as an introduction to such works, in presenting a systematical development of the *forms* of words usually adopted, than any thing else. My opinion therefore is, that such terms are entitled to no place in a Dictionary, the implied business of which is to teach the language generally. In a few instances, indeed, in which I thought some theological or other interesting particular was involved, and on the explanations usually given of which some obscurity rested, I have departed from this general rule, as in יְרוּשָׁלַיִם, יְהֹוָה, אוּר כַּשְׂדִּים, and some other words.

I have given, moreover, in an Appendix, a short description, with a plan and two sections, of the Temple of Solomon, which may be thought by some to be superfluous. My defence is, the descriptions of this famous edifice have appeared to me extremely faulty; the biblical text having been very generally disregarded by their authors; and thence, Rabbinical conjectures having been made to supply its place. Besides, it has been found so difficult to arrive at just notions of things, their positions, &c., from mere verbal description, and particularly with reference to the Temple, that I conceived it would be both the readiest and safest way to supply at once the short details and plan referred to. For a fuller consideration of these particulars, the student is referred to authors who have discussed this subject more at length, and whose conclusions he will now, it is presumed, be the better able either to appreciate, or to receive with the greater care and caution. I once intended also to append to this work a short tract on the use of the Hebrew and Greek definite article, and a few references will accordingly be found made to it. But, as this would have had the effect both of delaying the publication of the work, and also of enlarging it, I made up my mind to publish this tract separately, as early as convenient.

I have now only to request the reader to attend to the additions and corrections given in the third Appendix (C), and to mark the places in his copy of this work, to which they severally belong, in order the better to ensure their assistance when it shall happen to be wanted. To all other instances of human infirmity, with which he will meet, I have to crave his indulgence, assuring him that, as far as my powers and opportunities would carry me, I am conscious of no case in which these have not been exerted to their fullest extent. To expect perfection in a work, occupying a range of inquiry so great, and involving, in cases innumerable, questions so difficult, and this too in a species of literature which may truly be said to be still in its infancy, would be to expect something the least likely possible to be met with. If, however, I have succeeded in making some additions to the stores collected in this way by the industry and learning of my predecessors,—and this I may, perhaps, hope I have done,—I shall, indeed, have the greatest reason to be thankful and to render all praise to Him, who has so far enabled me to succeed, and to make but the smallest additions to a species of literature, at once so important, and which has been generally so much neglected among us.

ABBREVIATIONS.

These, in the terms of grammar, names of authors, &c., are the same with those generally in use, and need no explanation. The following will be found sufficient, viz., augm., augmented; c. or com., common; comp., compare; compd., compound or compounded; cog. or cogn., cognate; contr., contracted or contraction; dag., dagesh; dim., diminutive; fm., form; it., item, also; n. a., noun of action, or Infinitive; non occ., non occurrit, occurs not; r., root; rel., relative noun; seg., segolate; v., verb. For others, see p. xiv. above.

HEBREW LEXICON.

א

אב

א, *Aleph*, or *Eleph* (אֶלֶף). The first letter of the Alphabet in Hebrew and its sister dialects, the Chaldaic, Syriac, Samaritan, Ethiopic, and Arabic; likewise, in the Persic, Hindoostani, Malay, &c., in which the Arabic Alphabet has obtained. What its origin was, it is impossible now to say with any certainty. Stephanus tells us in his Thesaurus Gr. from Plutarch, Sympos. ix. 2, and after him Gesenius, that it was named after the ox, which in the Phœnician is so called: ὅν φασι τὸ ἄλφα πάντων προτάξαι διὰ τὸ φοίνικας οὕτω καλεῖν τὸν βοῦν; and, is arranged first in the order, because, it is added, it is the *first among necessary things*, πρῶτον .... τῶν ἀναγκαίων. Gesenius, however, tells us that it was so named, because it represented the form of an Ox's head with horns. Whether we are to take the reason assigned by Ammonius in Plutarch, or the conjecture of Dr. Gesenius, I leave it for others to say. I would only suggest, that my good friend's conjecture is quite as likely to be correct, as the guess of the learned Greek. See Prep. Evang. Euseb. x. § v.

The power of this letter is, according to Eastern usage, naturally a consonant; and it is pronounced with a sensible effort as occasionally heard in our A, though something more guttural, in order to avoid confounding it with the aspirated ה, our H. And hence it is, that it is often interchanged with ע in the various readings, and holds a parallel place with it in the Cognate roots; as in אָמַם, and עָמַם; גָּאַל, and גָּעַל; תָּאַב, and תָּעַב; בָּאָא, and בָּעָה, &c., as noticed by Dr. Gesenius; from whom I take these examples.

As some variety of pronunciation would probably prevail, even when the Hebrew was a living language (as is the case with our *a* here in England), it need not seem strange if in the Hebrew also, and particularly in the sister dialects, this letter often inter-changed with others; as, אֶחָד, and יָחַד; אֵם, and רֵים; בּוֹר, and בְּאֵר; אֶלֶף, and ܐܠܦܐ Syr. &c. That is, if its not very sensible power as a consonant, did in some cases fall in with those other consonants, which are occasionally lost in the power of a preceding vowel. See Gram. Art. 37.

It is occasionally prefixed to certain words, without at all altering their force; as, זְרוֹעַ, and אֶזְרוֹעַ, *an arm*, as in our *special* and *especial*. Dr. Gesenius thinks that it is sometimes dropped, as in נַחְנוּ, for אֲנַחְנוּ; שֶׁ, for אֲשֶׁר; חַד, for אֶחָד; &c., but this is problematical, especially in the second case. For first, we have no means of knowing with certainty which of these is the primitive form; and, secondly, as it is allowed that א is occasionally prosthetic, as in אֶזְרוֹעַ above; it seems unnecessary to multiply rules, unless there were reasons for doing so. In the case of שֶׁ, for אֲשֶׁר, moreover, we have also to account for the loss of the ר. This word is, therefore, peculiar. But, what is most strange, Dr. Gesenius makes שׁ the primitive form of this word, in another part of his work; assuming that both the ר and א are adscititious! Lex. c. p. 111, 112.

It is prefixed to nouns termed *Heëmanti*, as אֶזְרָח, &c. See Gram. artt. 157, 158. And hence, perhaps, it is that the augmented species of verbs, in the Chaldaic and Syriac, prefix א, rather than the ה taken by the Hebrews, as in *Aphel*, for *Hiphil*, &c.

It is likewise postfixed to nouns in the Chaldaic and Syriac, in place of the Hebrew definite article; as מַלְכָּא, ܡܠܟܐ; Heb. הַמֶּלֶךְ, *the king*; which has been very constantly and erroneously termed the *Emphatic form*.

אָב, m. constr. אֲבִי. Plur. אָבוֹת, constr. אֲבוֹת. Syr. ܐܒܐ, Arab. اَبٌ, &c. is probably a

B

אב (2) אבד

primitive noun, as it appears as such in most languages in one form or another; as, Gr. ἄππα, παπᾶ; Turk. بَابَا; Malay بَاپ, &c.

I. *A father*, Gen. xliv. 19, 20, &c., applied to God as having adopted his people as children, Is. lxiii. 16; lxiv. 7; Deut. xxxii. 6; comp. with Exod. iv. 22; 2 Sam. vii. 14; Ps. lxxxix. 27, 28, &c. It is true, man's creation is occasionally mentioned in connection with this use of the word; but the language of Scripture will not justify the assumption, that he is therefore necessarily a Father. The first and last cases cited here clearly imply the contrary, e. g. Is. lxiii. 16. אֲבִינוּ is joined in apposition (Gram. art. 217, 4) with גֹּאֲלֵנוּ *our Redeemer*, Deut. l. c. אָבִיךָ קָּנֶךָ, *thy Father*, *He hath acquired*, or made, *thee* (his own); with strict reference to God's redeeming and adopting Israel, not to his having created him; for this he had done for all mankind. The gloss of Abusaid, therefore, viz., خَالِقُكَ, *thy Creator*, approved of by Gesenius, is erroneous. I must here remark, this is a case in which the Judæo-Samaritan, the Jewish, and the modern German, school, are likely to concur. It is one of those plausible things by which they have contrived to strip the Scriptures of their peculiarities, and religion of its value.—Hence, considered as a *defender, supporter, &c.*, Job xxix. 16.

II. Metaph. *An originator, inventor, &c.*, so, ὁ τῆς βίβλου πατήρ, Athen. l. 1; Gen. x. 21; xvii. 4, 5; Josh. xxiv. 3, &c. So the Messiah, Is. ix. 5. אֲבִי־עַד *Originator of an age* (αἰών), or *dispensation*.

III. Meton. *A head, chief*, or *ruler*, applied to Kings, Prophets, Priests, &c., 2 Kings v. 13; vi. 21; 1 Sam. x. 12; 2 Kings ii. 12; xiii. 14; Jud. xvii. 10; xviii. 19; Prov. iv. 1, &c. Hence, Joseph, as managing the chief rule, is termed אָב לְפַרְעֹה, *a father to Pharaoh*, Gen. xlv. 8; so, in the Arab. الوَالِدُ الأَمِين (not الأَمِير as Gesen.) *faithful father*, given by Abulfeda as the signification of the Turkish اَتَابَك, *Atabek*. Annal. Mosl. tom. iii. p. 226. Gesen. Thes. will supply other instances. Aff. אָבִי, אָנְךָ, אֲבִיכֶם, pl. אֲבוֹתֵיכֶם, אֲבוֹתָם, and אֲבוֹתֵיהֶם.

אַב, m. Chald. i. q. Heb. אָב, pl. אֲבָהָן, Dan. ii. 23; Ezr. iv. 15; v. 12, &c. Aff. אֲבִי, אֲבָהִי, אֲבָהָךְ, pl. constr. אֲבָהָת, aff. אֲבָהָתִי, אֲבָהָתְנָא, אֲבָהָתְהוֹן.

אֵב, m. r. אבב, Arab. إِبّ, *gramen, pabulum quodcunque virens*. Syr. ܐܒܐ *fructus*.
I. *Greenness, freshness*, of a herb, Job viii. 12; Cant. vi. 11. Aff. אִבּוֹ, &c.
II. Chald. aff. אִנְבֵּהּ, Dan. iv. 9, 11, 18. *Its fruit*. Cogn. Arab. أَنَب *Melongena*, and عِنَب, *uvæ*.

אָבַד, v. pres. יֹאבַד, in pausa, יֹאבֵד, Syr. ܐܒܕ, *periit, amissus est*. Eth. አብደ: *insanivit*; Arab. أَبَد, *indomitum fugit, aufugit*, animal. I. *Strayed, lost*. II. Meton. *Perished*, applied to men, animals, the human mind, and things, e. g., שֶׂה אֹבֵד *a wandering, straying, sheep*, Ps. cxix. 176. Comp. Jer. L. 6; Ezek. xxxiv. 4, 16; Deut. xxvi. 5; Is. xxvii. 13; Job vi. 18. See my notes on this place.—Is. xxix. 14, אָבְדָה חָכְמָה, *wisdom hath perished*; i. e. is not to be found. Comp. Jer. ix. 11; Amos iii. 15; Ps. ix. 19; cxii. 10. יֹאבַד לֵב, *the heart is lost, strays*, Jer. iv. 9. Comp. Job viii. 13, &c. Constr. *immed.* and *med.* with לְ or מִן.

Pih. אִבֵּד, *Made to stray, considered as such*, meton. *destroyed*. Jer. xxiii. 1; Eccles. iii. 6; vii. 7; Jer. li. 55; Numb. xxxiii. 52; Deut. xii. 2; 2 Kings xix. 18; Est. iii. 9, &c.

Hiph. הֶאֱבִיד, i. q. *Pih*. meton. *Destroyed*. Deut. vii. 10, 24; viii. 20; Job xiv. 19. אֲבִידָה, for אוֹבִידָה, with par. ה, and, as if from cogn. v. יבד, or ובד; Arab. أَبَد, *succensuit*. Jer. xlvi. 8. *Hoph*. הוּבַד. Dan. vii. 11.

אֲבַד, Chald. i. q. Heb. אָבַד: pres. יֵאבַד. Jer. x. ii.
Aph. הוֹבֵד, pres. יְהוֹבֵד Infin. הוֹבָדָה Cogn. v. وبد, as above, i. q. *Hiph*. Heb. Dan. ii. 12, 18, 24.

אֹבֵד, m. part. f. אֹבֶדֶת, v. אָבֵד. *Perishing, about to perish*, Num. xxiv. 20, 24; Prov. xxxi. 6; Is. xxvii. 13.

אַבֵּדָה, (r. אבד), for מַאֲבֵדָה, Ezra xxviii. 16.
אֲבֹד, constr. אֲבֹד, Infin. *Perishing*. Deut. iv. 26, &c. Aff. אֲבָדְךָ, in pausa אֲבָדֶךָ, אֲבָדָם, אֲבָדְכֶם.

אֲבֵדָה, f. *Something lost*. Exod. xxii. 8; Lev. v. 22. Made equivalent to אֲבֵדוֹן by the keri, Prov. xxvii. 20.

אַבְדָן, m. *Destroying, destruction*, Est. ix. 5.

אָבָה, v. pres. יֶאֱבֶה, in Kal only. Arab. أَوِي, teneriore affectu commotus fuit. Cogn. Heb. אהב, אוה, חבב. Arab. حَبَّ. *Desirous, willing*, constr. mostly with the neg. לֹא, either expressed or implied, and with an Infin. or verbal noun, with לְ prefixed, or not; as, לֹא אָבָה לְשַׁלְּחָם, *He was not willing to send them.* Exod. x. 27. הֲיֹאבֶה רֵּים עָבְדֶךָ, *Is the Oryx willing to serve thee?* Job xxxix. 9. Abs. Prov. i. 25. לֹא אֲבִיתֶם, *ye would not.* See Is. i. 19; xxx. 15; xxviii. 12; Prov. i. 10, &c. with אֶל, אָבוֹא, for אָבֹא, as in the Arabic. Part. אֹבִים:—with אֵין, Ezek. iii. 7.

אֵבֶה, m. Arab. أَبَاءٌ, nom. unit. أَبَاءَةٌ *Arundo una.* *A reed*, probably that of the papyrus; once Job ix. 26. אֳנִיּוֹת אֵבֶה *reed-vessels*, i. e. small and very swift-sailing vessels in use on the Euphrates and Nile, occasionally used by robbers. See my notes on the place, and comp. Is. xviii. 2.

אֲבֵחָן } see אב Chald.
אֲבָהָת

אָבוֹא, see אָבָה above.

אֲבוֹי, m. Arab. أَبِيٌّ *fastiditus, despectus,* أَبَاءٌ *fastidium, nausea.* Cogn. أَوَّةٌ *malum, ærumna. Misery,* Prov. xxiii. 29; LXX. θόρυβος; Syr. ܐܳܒܽܘܳܐ *perturbatio.*

אֵבוּס, m. constr. probably for אָבוּס, Gram. art. 73. form אֶתְמוֹל, or אֶתְמוּל, Gram. art. 158. r. בוס; Arab. بَاصَ, بُوص *fugit.* 2. conj. *fructum bonum protulit.* مَبَاص *locus quo quis confugit.* Cogn. أَبَسَ *conclusit;* أَبَشَ *collegit rem;* أَبَشَ *qui ornat atrium; instruitque cibo suo ac potu;* أَبِتَ *potu et ingurgitatione lactis* (camelini) *intumuit, &c.* "Convenit utcunque," says Castell, "cum Heb. אבס *saginare, implere.*" *A Crib*, or *Stall*, in which animals are fed, Is. i. 3; Prov. xiv. 4; Job xxxix. 9. Aff. אֲבוּסְךָ; usually, but without sufficient reason, taken as a plural.

אֲבוּס, m. אֲבוּסִים pl. Part. pass. r. אבס above, *Fed, fattened*, Prov. xv. 17; 1 Kings v. 3; whence מַאֲבוּס, and Jer. L. 26; מַאֲסֻרֶיהָ *her granaries, &c.*

אָבוֹשׁ, see v. בּוֹשׁ.

אִבְחָה, f. constr. אִבְחַת once, Ezek. xxi. 20.

Arab. بَاخَ r. بُوخ *quievit, sedatus fuit* ignis, vel ira; *lassus*, de viro, &c. The Kamoos also gives, وَهُمْ فِي بُوخٍ اَيْ اِخْتِلَاطٌ, i. e., *they are in confusion.*—*Resting*, as after great exertion; *remaining stationary* in any place. Our passage has נְתַתִּי אִבְחַת־חָרֶב, *I have appointed the resting, descent,* or *remaining of the sword*, i. e. for the purposes of slaughter. See נוח Ps. cxxv. 3; Is. xxv. 10, xxx. 32; Ezek. v. 13, xvi. 42. And here, viz. chap. xxi. 22, and xxiv. 13; comp. Is. xxxiv. 5. With this the σφαγία ρομφαίας of the LXX., as well as the קְטִילֵי חַרְבָּא of the Targumist, as cited by Dr. Gesenius, will agree sufficiently well, without changing the reading into מִבְחַת, חָרֶב, as he proposes. Besides, one would hardly expect to find טִבְחָה at the end of the verse, as we now do, were this the original reading. Dr. Gesenius complains here, moreover, of the inaccuracy of Castell in giving اِبَاحَةً, for اِبَاحَةٌ, and this in the sense of *exterminium*, instead of *licentiam.* The error in the vowel, however (if it really be one), is probably an error of the press. As to the sense of the word, the place cited by Castell is 2 Macc. xxvi. 6, where we have اِبَاحَةٌ اليَهُود, which certainly will not bear to be translated by Dr. Gesenius's "*licentia*" Judæorum. This would give utter nonsense. The probability is, that, as بُوخ is made equivalent to أَصْل, the iv. conj. is here used in the sense of the xth, viz. اِسْتَأْصَلَ, *rooting up,* i. e. destroying. In this case, therefore, the اِبَاحَةٌ of Castell will be cognate with the بُوخ, i. e. اِخْتِلَاطٌ of the Kamoos given above, and much more suitable to the place under consideration, than the מִבְחַת of Dr. Gesenius.

אָבִי, for אָבִיא, Gram. Art. 74. Hiph. r. בוא, also aff. 1st pers. sing. of אָב.

אָבִיב, m. Arab. أَبّ *contendit ad, tetendit in.* أَبّ *propositum, gramen, &c.*, أَبَا r. أَبَوَ *educavit, cursus, fluxus, &c.*, cogn. أَبَوَ r. أَبَوَ *educavit, &c.;* lit. *Proceeded on, matured,* applied to corn. I. *Grown*, and in the ear. Exod. ix. 31, הַשְּׂעֹרָה אָבִיב, *the barley* (was) *grown*; not בְּאִבּוֹ as Gesenius proposes, Lev. ii. 14. II. Hence given to the *month,* in which this earing of the barley took place, Exod. xiii. 4, xxiii. 15, &c.

אֲבִי (4) אָבַל

And, as the year was then in all probability solar (see my Sermon on the Sabbath, second edit. with the notes), the observance of this month would be easy and regular.

אֲבִידָה, 1st per. pres. sing. with ה parag. Hiph. r. אבד, of cogn. יבד, Arab. وَبَلَ.

אֶבְיוֹן, m. pl. אֶבְיוֹנִים, constr. אֶבְיוֹנֵי, r. אָבָה, Wishing, desiring; hence wanting, destitute, &c.

I. Poor, needy, Syr. اڪَٓܣܢ, applied to circumstances either temporal, or spiritual. Deut. xv. 4, 7, 11; Ps. ix. 19, lxxii. 4.

II. Miserable, as suffering distress or oppression, Ps. xl. 18; lxx. 6; lxxxvi. 1; cix. 22; Prov. xxx. 14; Jer. ii. 34, &c. Aff. אֶבְיוֹנָךְ, אֶבְיוֹנֶיךָ.

אֲבִיּוֹנָה, f. Desire. Eccl. xii. 5.

אָבִיר, m. constr. אֲבִיר, Syr. اܟܳܒܰ٣ plumbum, comp. כבד, Arab. اَبَرَ bene habuit, probus, beneficus, fuit. Mighty, or powerful. Gen. xlix. 24; Is. i. 24; xlix. 26, &c.

אַבִּיר, m. pl. אַבִּירִים, constr. אַבִּירֵי.

I. Mighty, powerful, courageous, or brave, applied to men, or animals, Jud. v. 22; Jer. xlvi. 15; Lam. i. 15, &c. אַבִּירֵי לֵב, men mighty of heart, i. e. exceedingly courageous, Ps. lxxvi. 6; Is. xlvi. 12. אַבִּירֵי בָשָׁן, mighty ones of Bashan, i. e. strong and furious men compared to bulls, Ps. xxii. 13; applied to horses, Jer. viii. 16; xlvii. 3; L. 11.

II. Chief or head, 1 Sam. xxi. 8.

אָבַד, v. once in Is. ix. 17.

Hithp. יִתְאַבְּדוּ, Arab. اِبَكَ carnosus fuit, cogn. عَبَكَ commiscuit rem rei, عَبَكَ adhæsit ei, بَاتَ pinguis evasit, بَاتِى cinxit, Syr. اܟܰ٣ gallus gallinaccus, superbè incedens, &c.—They swell, as volumes of smoke; it is added, גֵּאוּת עָשָׁן, the glorying, i. e. as the towering, of rising smoke.

אָבָל, m. Arab. اِبِلَ nubes fæcunda, pluviæ gignendæ idonea, cogn. وَبَلَ imbrem effudit, بَلَّ rigavit, propr. I. Weeping. II. Mourning, lamentation, as for the dead, Gen. xxvii. 41; L. 10; with בְּכִי, Deut. xxxiv. 8, compared with the cry of ostriches, Mich. i. 8. Aff. אֶבְלְךָ, אֶבְלָם.

אָבֵל, m. pl. אֲבֵלִים, constr. אֲבֵל, pl. אֲבֵלֵי, pl. f. אֲבֵלוֹת, Lamenting, mourning, Gen. xxxvii. 35; Est. vi. 12; Ps. xxxv. 14; Is. lxi. 3, &c. Aff. אֲבֵלֵי.

אָבַל, v. pres. יֶאֱבָל, Mourned, lamented, constr. med. עַל, Hos. x. 5; Job xiv. 22. Abs. Amos viii. 1; Joel i. 9, 10, &c.

Hiph. הֶאֱבִיל, Made, or caused, to mourn, Ezek. xxxi. 15; Lam. ii. 8.

Hithp. הִתְאַבֵּל, Betook him to mourning, 1 Sam. xv. 35, &c. Imp. f. הִתְאַבְּלִי, betake thee to mourning: וָאֶבְכֶּה וָאֶתְאַבְּלָה, so I weep and mourn, Neh. i. 4.

Part. מִתְאַבֵּל, pl. מִתְאַבְּלִים, f. sing. מִתְאַבֶּלֶת, One betaking him, or her, to mourning, 1 Sam. xvi. 1; 2 Sam. xiv. 2; Is. lxvi. 10; constr. with עַל, or אֶל med.

אֹבֶל, see אוּבָל.

אֲבָל, used as an adv. Certainly, nay rather, &c., Gen. xvii. 19; Ezra x. 13, &c. See Noldius.

אֶבֶן, c. pl. אֲבָנִים, constr. אַבְנֵי; Syr. اܟܶ٣ lapis; Eth. አብን: id. Arab. اِبَن concrevit, ut nodus in ligno: اِبَن spissus; اِبَنة homo durus, pertinax, &c. Cogn. بَنَى ædificavit, &c. A stone, generally, Gen. xi. 3; Is. xxviii. 16, &c. Metaph. הָיָה לְאֶבֶן, became (i. e. his heart) for, i. e. as a stone, as we say astounded, or astonied; i. e. made like a stone, insensible with fright, &c. לֵב הָאֶבֶן, heart of stone; i. e. insensible, Ezra xi. 19. Hence, Rock, Gen. xlix. 24. מִשָּׁם רֹעֶה אֶבֶן יִשְׂרָאֵל, thence a shepherd, the rock of Israel; i. e. the Saviour.—Of offence, 1 Sam. xiv. 33. גֹּלּוּ אֵלַי הַיּוֹם אֶבֶן גְּדוֹלָה, roll upon me this day a great stone; i. e. take it for granted, that a great rock of offence, or weight, has devolved upon me. Comp. Ps. xxii. 9, xxxvii. 5; Prov. xvi. 3.—Hail-stone, אֶבֶן בָּרָד, Is. xxx. 30. Comp. Josh. x. 11.—Precious stone, Is. liv. 12: with the adjuncts חֵפֶץ, חֵן, אֵשׁ, יְקָרָה, Prov. xvii. 8; Ezek. xxviii. 14, 16; Exod. xxviii. 13.—Mineral, Job xxviii. 2.—Of certain weight (as in our stone of wool, &c.) אֶבֶן וָאָבֶן, stone and stone; i. e. diverse weights, Deut. xxv. 13. אַבְנֵי כִיס, stones of (the) bag, Prov. xvi. 11; with מִרְמָה, שַׁלְמָה, צֶדֶק.—Weight of lead, Zech. v. 8.—Of tin, ib. iv. 10, used apparently as a plummet. In Is. xxxiv. 11, אַבְנֵי בֹהוּ stones, or weights, of emptiness; i. e. a measure or rule determining that desolation has taken place. Aff. אֲבָנַי.

אבן, Chald. def. אַבְנָא, id. Dan. ii. 34, 35.

אֹבֶן, Dual. אָבְנָיִם, occ. twice, see Exod. i. 16, and Jer. xviii. 3. The pains taken to make this word suit both places may be seen in Rosenmüller, &c. which, as far as I can see, have been to very little purpose. Nor do I think Gesenius's extract from Abulwalid much better, although he styles him an eye-witness of the thing in question. But the matter in question here is, *the meaning of this term*; and of this Abulwalid knew no more than Gesenius himself. In Jer. l. c. it is evident that the horizontal lathe of a potter is meant; on this, I think, there is no difference of opinion. I take אֲבָנִים here, therefore, to signify just what אָפְנִים would; i. e. *two wheels*, were this substituted in its place. It would then be a cognate term; and it is not improbable this was the very term used by Jeremiah. In Exod. l. c. the case is altogether different. The question is there about childbirth; and the words are וּרְאִיתֶן עַל הָאָבְנָיִם. It is added, אִם־בֵּן הוּא, *if it be a son, &c.* Gesenius gives here, "*Et videbitis super labro.*" He then tells us that this *labrum*, wash-pot, was probably like the potter's wheels; i. e. consisting of two stones, an upper and a lower, the upper of which acted as a *lid, &c.* But Why, let it be asked, are the midwives commanded particularly to cast their eyes on these? Had these the means of determining whether the new-born child was or was not a male? Again, supposing these wash-pots were composed of a lid, and sort of under-tub, Would this make them like the potter's horizontal lathe, which is thought to have consisted of two wheels? All this strikes me as extremely weak and inconclusive. Suidas, indeed, tells us of λοχαῖοι δίφροι, used by women in childbirth; which were, perhaps, couches peculiarly constructed for that purpose; and which, as far as I can see, must have been things as far unlike the *wash-pot* in question, as they were to the *lathe* of Jeremiah's potter. It is truly astonishing that such incongruous matter could ever have been thrown together by a writer of Gesenius's powers. Let me now give my view on this passage. I suppose, then, that אֲבָנִים, is in this place cognate with אֹפֶן; which, dual, would be אָפְנָיִם. See Prov. xxv. 11, where we have אָפְנָיו, *its seasons, occasions, &c.* See this word below. I take the command of Pharaoh, therefore, thus, *Observe, look carefully on, the two occasions*; i. e. in which either a male or female child is born. It is added, *If it be a son, then, &c.* Now, it is curious to observe, that not one of the ancient versions says a word about this *wash-pot, stools,* or the like. The LXX. καὶ ὦσι πρὸς τῷ τίκτειν, Vulg. "*et partus tempus advenerit,*" which is very near the truth. Targ. *videbitis in partu*; Syr. "*cum illæ procumbunt.*" The venerable Saadias Haggaon, indeed, makes the midwives to look at *the pulpit!* عِنْدَ المِنْبَرِ, as does Erpenius's Arab. Gesenius, however, tells us that a MS. at Oxford reads منثبر, in the text of Saadias; and this he translates (Thes. sub voce) by "*locus ubi mulier parit.*" But this might be a mere imitation of the Targum of Onkelos, which has לְתִבְרָא: at any rate the authority of this Jew is of little value.

אַבְנֵט, m. pl. אַבְנֵטִים. According to Hottinger the Pers. بَنْد (Winer writes بند!) *a band* or *bandage*, which Gesenius prefers taking from the Sanscrit *bandha*, with a prosthetic א. Nothing, however, can be less probable than that the Israelites adopted a Persic word immediately after their egress from Egypt. The word is most likely Egyptian, and might be cognate with the Persic بند, and our *band*, although not occurring in the Coptic books as we now have them. From the places in which it occurs, it appears to have been made of fine linen, variously wrought, and used to bind as *a girdle* about the body of persons in authority, especially the Jewish priests, Exod. xxix. 9; xxviii. 39; xxxix. 29; Lev. viii. 13; Is. xxii. 21. Aff. אַבְנֵטוֹ.

אָבָק, m. Sam. א ף ק, *pulvis.* Arab. اَبِقَ *aufugit.* Cogn. عَبِقَ *adhæsit ei odor.* عَبَق *pars, aliquid, adhærens butyri.*—*Dust*, light and easily ascending, Is. v. 24; Ezek. xxvi. 10. Applied to the mist of the clouds, when speaking of God, Neh. i. 3; occ. with עָפָר, Deut. xxviii. 24. The difference seems to be this: the former is so light as to be carried about by the wind; the latter heavy, and adhering to men and things. Aff. אֲבָקָם.

אֲבָקָה, f. once, constr. אַבְקַת רוֹכֵל, *Powder of the merchant*, used as a perfume. Cant. iii. 6. Etym. as the last.

As a verb in Niph. pres. יֵאָבֵק, *Adheres to; wrestles, or strives with;* constr. with עִם, Gen. xxxii. 25. Infin. בְּהֵאָבְקוֹ, *in his wrestling,* ib. ver. 26.

אֵבֶר, m. and אֶבְרָה, f. *A quill*, or larger feather of the wing of any bird, Ps. lv. 7; Is. xl. 31; Ezek. xvii. 3; Job xxxix. 16; pl. אֶבְרוֹת, Ps. lxviii. 14. Aff. אֲבְרָתוֹ, אֶבְרוֹתֶיהָ.

Taken by many to signify the *wing*, in some of these places, and Deut. xxxii. 11; Ps. xci. 4. The context, however, rather makes against this.

אַבְרֵךְ, occ. Gen. xli. 43. It appears to have been the term used in proclaiming the authority of Joseph. A similar thing was done in behalf of Mordecai, Est. vi. 11; where, however, we have several words used for this purpose. The attempts to interpret this word have been very various; some taking it as an imper. of בָּרַךְ in *Hiph.*, and signifying *bow the knee*: others, with Luther at their head, have supposed it to be a compound of אֲבִי־רֵךְ; i. e. *father of the state*, and as of Chaldee origin. Others, again, have had recourse to the Coptic, supposing, which is indeed most likely, that the term is Egyptian: and, of these, the most probable seems to be the solution proposed by De Rossi (Etym. Egyp. p. 1), viz, ⲀⲠⲈⲢⲈⲔ, or ⲀⲠⲢⲈⲔ, i. e. *Incline the head*. Other Egyptian terms certainly are to be found in the Hebrew Bible, as it is likely would be the case; as יְאֹר, for ⲒⲀⲢⲞ, the *Nile*. אָחוּ, ⲀⲬⲒ, LXX. Ἄχει, and Ἄχι, see sub voce: פַּרְעֹה, for πουρο; i. e. *the king*: to which some others may be added.

אֶגְאַלְתִּי, for הִגְאַלְתִּי, *Hiph.* r. גאל.

אֲגָגִי, m. patronym. of אֲגַג, Num. xxiv. 7; 1 Sam. xv. 18, &c. *An Agagite*, Est. iii. 1, 10. Joseph. Antiq. xi. vi. sec. 5, makes Haman to be an *Amalekite*.

אֲגֻדָּה, f. contr. for אֲגוּדָה, Arab. جلّ *obesitas, corpulentia*; جلّ *magnitudo dignitatis*. Kamoos, وكلّ منعقد بعضه في بعض من خيط أو غصن *Anything one part of which is bound within another.*—Generally, *anything bound up together in one mass*.
I. *A bunch* or *bundle* of hyssop, Exod. xii. 22, &c.
II. *A body*, or *band* of men, 2 Sam. ii. 25. אֲגֻדָּתוֹ *his band*, people, or church, Amos ix. 6. So the Targumist here. The arch or vault of heaven, as given by Gesen. and Simon. seems unsuitable.
III. Meton. *knots, bindings*, Is. lviii. 6. מוֹטָה *of the yoke*, LXX. στραγγαλιάς.

אֱגוֹז, m. Arab. جَوْزُ, Pers. گوز, Syr. ܓܘܙܐ, augm. א. *A nut*, generally. The various species will be found recited by Castell, *sub*

voce; in Freytag, in Avicenna, the Medical Dictionary of Ibn Elhosain of Bagdad, &c. See also Celsii Hierobot, i. p. 28.—Occurs but once, Cant. vi. 11.

אֲגוֹרָה, f. Arab. اجر *merces, præmium*. as, אֲגוֹרַת כֶּסֶף, *Reward*, or *wages, of silver*; i. e. of money, LXX. ὀβολός. The Jews suppose it to be equal to the gerah. Talm. Lex. Buxtorf. sub voce מעא, col. 1236.

אֲגַל, m. Arab. اجل v. spec. *collecta fuit aqua*. اجيل *collecta in unum locum aqua*.

אֶגְלֵי־טַל, *The drops of dew*; opp. to מָטָר *rain*, Job xxxviii. 28. See my notes on the place.

אֲגַם, m. Arab. جَمّ *multa fuit*, pec. *aqua in puteo*. Aug. א. contr. for אֲגַמִּים, pl. אֲגַמִּים. I. A *pond* or *pool* of water, Ps. cvii. 35; cxiv. 8; Is. xxxv. 7; xli. 18; &c. Constr. אַגְמֵי, as אַגְמֵיהֶם, Exod. vii. 19; Is. xiv. 23. Cogn. Arab. اجم *alterata fuit aqua*, i. e., from its being stagnant.
II. Meton. *Flags*, or *reeds*, growing in stagnant waters; Jer. li. 32. *The flags* (used, perhaps, in making stockades for defence,) *they burned with fire*. Arab. similarly derived, اجام *asylum, munimentum*. Freyt. sub. اجم. Is. xix. 10. אַגְמֵי נֶפֶשׁ, *of stagnant*, i. e. afflicted *mind*. Cogn. Arab. وجم *tetricus, et æger animi, &c*. Gesenius gives the form here אֲגֵם, and is followed by Winer. If this were allowed, אַגְמֵי, not אַגְמֵי, would be the form of constr. For the אֲגַם, above, too, he gives אֲגֵם, which is also incorrect; see Is. xxxv. 7.

אַגְמוֹן, or אֶגְמֹן, m. augm. of the prec. A *Flag* or *reed*, as before, opp. to כִּפָּה, a *branch*. Is. xix. 15; metaph. The *lowest* and *worst* of the people. Comp. Ib. ix. 13; lviii. 5. The Arabs oppose the head and tail much in the same manner. Hamasa. Freyt. p. ٣—, بنو فلان الذوائب لا الذنائب أي الأعالي لا الأسافل, *The sons of such an one are the forelocks, not the tails; that is, they are the highest, not the lowest*. הֲלָכֹף כְּאַגְמוֹן, *Whether to bow down like a reed?* alluding to its elasticity. Meton. *the staff of a harpoon*, or *of an arrow*, Job xl. 26;—also, as used in making fires, כְּדוּד נָפוּחַ וְאַגְמוֹן, *like a blown fire, with reeds*; because when dry they burned furiously, Job xli. 12. Comp. verse following, and Ps. lviii. 10; where the same usage is alluded to. The Rabbins, and after them most modern writers, suppose this word to signify *a large pot*, or *caldron*, because the Gr. λάκκος, and the Lat. *lacus*, are sometimes used to signify *a large vessel*, and because Solomon's brazen sea was also a large vessel. I doubt whether much reliance can be placed on analogies of this sort, when destitute, as this is, of direct proof. The notion of burning, as above, seems to have obtained in the Arabic, probably for the same reasons; as, تَاجِم. Conj. v. of اجم, *ferbuit dies, accensus fuit, arsit ignis, excanduit in aliquem.* اجم *ardor, ira.* Freytag and Jauhari, sub voce. See Celsii Hierobot. Pars. i. p. 465; and my notes on Job xli. 12.

אַגָּן, m. Arab. اِجَّانَة; Syr. ܐܓܢܐ, אַגָּנוֹת; pl. אַגָּנוֹת. *A bason* or *bowl.* Exod. xxiv. 6; Is. xxii. 24; Cant. vii. 3.

אֲגַפִּים, m. pl. Arab. جفّ جفّ جفّة, *agmen, caterva hominum*, vel *numerus ingens.* Augm. with א. *Hosts, armies*, Ezek. xii. 14, xvii. 20; &c. Dr. Gesenius makes it the same with the Chald. גַּף, or אֲגַף, *wing*: Eichorn, after Schultens, *men clothed in armour*. I prefer taking the Arabic, which is here direct, and quite suitable. With affix. אֲגַפֶּיךָ, אֲגַפָּיו, אֲגַפֶּךָ.

אָגַר, v. pres. יֶאְגֹּר; Arab. اجر, *mercedem dedit*, iv. *locavit*, id. Syr. *He laid up* provision, &c. Deut. xxviii. 39; Prov. vi. 8; x. 5.

אִגֶּרֶת, f. def. אִגַּרְתָּא, Chald.; Syr. ܐܓܪܬܐ, Pers. انكار, انكاز, *An account, narrative.* Meton. *Account book, a letter, edict.* Ezra iv. 8; ii. 5, 6, &c.

אִגְּרוֹת, f. pl. אִגְּרוֹת, i. q. אִגֶּרֶת. Neh. ii. 7, 9; vi. 5, 17, 19. Esth. ix. 26, 29. Hence, as Gesenius thinks, with some probability, we have the ἀγγαρεύειν of St. Matt. v. 41.

אֱגְרוֹף, m. Arab. جرف. Syr. ܐܓܪܘܦܐ, *multum, vel totum cepit, verrendo abstergendoque rejecit,* גרף occurs in this sense, Judg. v. 21: with a prosthetic א, *The fist.* Exod. xxi. 18; Is. lviii. 4.

אֲגַרְטָל, m. compd. of אֲגַר, *Collecting*, and טָל *blood*, or טַל *dew*. Gram. art. 169. 10. LXX. Ψυκτῆρες. Vulg. *Phialæ*. Syr. ܐܓܪܛܠܐ. *Dishes* or *basons*, of gold or silver. Ezra

i. 9. Conjectures of the Jews and others, on the etymology of this word, may be seen in the Thesaurus of Gesenius, p. 22, many of which appear to me to be of little use, and not very well founded.

אֵד, m. cogn. with אֵיד, which see. Arab. اياد *gravis*; اياد *aër, terra, &c.* Comp. Syr. ܐܕܡܐ. *Mist, vapour*, which arising in exhalations from the earth, is again precipitated in the rain, Gen. ii. 6; Job xxxvi. 27. So עָב *a cloud*, from עָבָה *densus fuit, evasit.*

אֶדָּדֵה, for אֶתְדַּדֶּה, Gram. art. 83. 1. Hithp. r. דדה; id. with Aff. אֲדַדֵּם.

אָדוֹן, m. from אָדֵן, *A base* or *pedestal.* Arab. هدن *quievit, inhibuit, continuit eum*; it. وكن *benè curavit adornavitve sponsam*; *percussit fuste.* The Phœnician Ἀδώνις. *Proprietor, master*, or *lord*, applied either to God or man; but, when used of God, is mostly in the plural number, Ps. cxiv. 7; Is. i. 24; Gen. xlv. 8. Frequently with the affix of the first person, אֲדֹנִי, *my lord*, Gen. xxxi. 35; xxxiii. 8, 13, 14, &c.; also joined with יְהוָה; as, יְהוָה צְבָאוֹת הָאָדוֹן, *the Lord, Jehovah of Hosts*, Is. iii. 1. הָאָדוֹן יְהוָה, Exod. xxxiv. 23. Our English Bibles generally translate יְהוָה, by LORD, in capitals; when preceded by הָאָדוֹן, they translate it *God*; when צְבָאוֹת follows, by LORD; as in Is. iii. 1. *The Lord, the* LORD *of Hosts.* The copies now in use, however, are not quite constant in this respect. Plur. אֲדֹנִים, *Lords*, or *Lord*, by way of excellence.—I. Applied to men in authority, as in, אֲדֹנִים קָשֶׁה, Is. xix. 4, *a hard*, or *cruel lord.* אֲדֹנֵי הָאָרֶץ, Gen. xlii. 30, 33, *Lord of the land* (said of Joseph); and ib. xxxix. 2. II. To God; as, אֲדֹנֵי הָאֲדֹנִים, *Lord of Lords*, Deut. x. 17. אִם אֲדֹנִים אָנִי, *if I am Lord*, Mal. i. 6. And consequently with the affixed pronouns, אֲדֹנָי, or אֲדֹנִי, אֲדֹנֶיךָ, אֲדֹנֵיכֶם, &c. In Ps. cx. 1, we have לַאדֹנִי, in the singular, but in ver. 5, אֲדֹנָי, with a plural form. The first exhibits a Jewish gloss, probably as old as the times of our Lord. See Matt. xxii. 42. Gesenius tells us that אֲדֹנָי, is exclusively applied to God. It is applied, however, Gen. xix. 18, by Lot, to the two angels. He thinks too, that this is a plural termination without the affix, although אֲדֹנָי, certainly signifies *my lords*, and has the affix ָי: Lot, however, Gen. xix. 2, addresses the angels by the term אֲדֹנַי; and again, ver. 18, by אֲדֹנָי, as just remarked. How then are we to know that the pronoun is used in the one case, but not in the other? This is a refinement incapable of support.

אֱדַיִן, Chald. adv. Heb. אָז, or אֲדַי: Arab. إِذًا, or إِذَا, and in the comp. حِينَئِذٍ. *Then*, Dan. ii. 15, 25, 48, &c. With the particle בְ, Dan. ii. 14, &c., Ezra iv. 24; and מִן, v. 16, *Thence, from thence*.

אֲדִיקֵם, *Hiph*. r. דקק with Aff.

אַדִּיר, augm. of אָדֵר, Arab. هَدَرَ, *fissâ spathâ, conspicuos flores habuit* palma; *longa plena ac adulta fuit, et luxuriavit*, herba. Golius. The Kamoos adds, هَادِرَة وَأَرْضٌ كَثِيرَةُ العُشْبِ مُتَنَاهِيَة, i. e. *Land* (termed) هَادِرَة, *is that which is exceedingly productive of grass*; comp. هَذَرَ, Syr. ܐܕܘ *cumulus, congeries*, &c., ܐܕܝ *decoravit*. Cogn. Heb. הדר. *Great, powerful, splendid, majestic*, applied to beings animate and inanimate; to men, and to God, Ps. xciii. 4; cxxxvi. 18; Ezek. xxxii. 18; Neh. x. 30; Jer. xxv. 34; 1 Sam. iv. 8; Is. xxxiii. 21, &c.

אָדָם, m. has no plural number. Arab. آدَمُ, *colore fusco præditus*; آدَم *Adam, homo*. Comp. the cogn. دم with its derivatives. Syr. ܐܕܡܬܐ *terra rubra*, ܐܕܡ *homo*. Ludolf takes the Ethiopic አደም: which signifies *formosum*. See his Lexicon, col. 377.

I. *Man*, or *men*, generally; *any man, any one*, especially the *first man*; the appellative becoming a proper name on account of its frequent occurrence, retaining, nevertheless, the definite article mostly in the earlier Hebrew, and hence may be rendered *The man*. Applied to man because he was formed out of the earth, הָאֲדָמָה, Gen. ii. 7; imposed perhaps, to keep him in mind of his frail and mortal character: see Gen. iii. 19; and also Ps. lvi. 12; cxviii. 6; cxliv. 3; Is. xxxi. 3; such also is the term בְּן־אָדָם, *Son of man*; see Num. xxiii. 19; Job xvi. 21, &c.

II. *Other men*, as opposed to the Israelites; Jer. xxxii. 20; comp. Is. xliii. 4; Ps. lxxiii. 5. On the constructions, בְּנֵי בָאָדָם, Prov. xxiii. 28; וּבְנֵי אָדָם, Hos. xiii. 2; אֶבְיוֹנֵי אָדָם, Is. xxix. 19, see my Heb. Gram. art. 224, 4, with the note. The following are in apposition, פֶּרֶא אָדָם, a *wild ass, man*, i. e. *a man of that description*, Gen. xvi. 12; so אָדָם בְּלִיַּעַל, Prov. vi. 12. To this term (אָדָם), are opposed, אִישׁ, i. e. *a man of substance, or consideration*: גֶּבֶר, *a brave or warlike man*: אֱנוֹשׁ, *a man liable to pain and sickness*. See these several words. As this word admits of no plural number, when it is necessary to address a certain number, the phrase בְּנֵי אָדָם, is used, Deut. xxxii. 8; Ps. xi. 4, &c.

אֹדֶם, m. from the above, *A ruby*, or, according to some, *a cornelian*; lxx. σάρδιον, Syr. ܣܡܩܬܐ, Chald. סָמְקָא. Epiphanius, as quoted by Simonis, styles it αἱματοειδής, and compares it with the σάρδιον αἱματόεν of Orpheus. See Braun. de vestitu sacerdot; lib. ii. p. 501, &c.; Exod. xxviii. 17; xxxix. 10; Ezek. xxviii. 13.

אָדַם, fem. אֲדָמָה, augmented by doubling the last radical. See Gram. art. 154, 5. *Red*, or *reddish brown*, Num. xix. 2; Zech. i. 8; vi. 2; Cant. v. 10; Gen. xxv. 30; and hence Esau was named אֱדוֹם *Rufus, Ruddiman*.

אָדֹם, see r. דמם.

אָדַם, v. *Was ruddy, splendid* (rutilans). Meton. *healthy, noble*, Lam. iv. 7; *Her Nazarites were more pure than snow, more pure than* (pure) *milk; they were ruddy— healthy, splendid, &c. — in person above pearls; the sapphire* (was) *their cut*, i. e. *their brilliancy*. See פְּנִינִים. Hence,

מְאָדָּם, pl. מְאָדָּמִים part. Puhal. Anything, as skins, *made or dyed red*, Exod. xxv. 5; xxxv. 7; Nah. ii. 4, &c.

יַאְדִּימוּ, *Hiph*. of the same. *They are red; show* or *impart redness*, Is. i. 18.

יִתְאַדָּם, *Hithp*. *It* (the wine) *becomes*, or *shews itself, red* and *splendid*, Prov. xxiii. 31.

אֲדַמְדָּם, f. אֲדַמְדֶּמֶת, pl. אֲדַמְדַּמּוֹת, redup. Gram. art. 169. 6. *Very red*, or *glowing*. See Bochart. Hieroz. tom. ii. lib. v. cap. vi. according to others, *Inclining to red, reddish*, Lev. xiii. 19; xiv. 37.

אֲדַמָּה, for אִתְדַמָּה, Gram. art. 83. 1. Hithp. r. דמה.

אֲדָמָה, f. אֲדָמוֹת pl. I. *Ground, soil, land*, Gen. ii. 19; Exod. xx. 24, &c. II. Meton. *Fruits, produce, &c.*, as growing out of the earth, Is. i. 7. III. *Region, or country*; as, אַדְמַת נֵכָר, *foreign* or *strange country*, Ps. cxxxvii. 4. אַדְמַת יְהֹוָה, *land of Jehovah*, i. e. Canaan, Is. xiv. 2. הַקֹּדֶשׁ—*holy*, Zech. ii. 16. הָאֲדָמָה, *the land*, ἡ γῆ, by way of eminence, Zeph. i. 2. אַדְמָתִי, *my land*, or *country*, Jon. iv. 2. According to some, the

אדם (9) אדר

whole world, Gen. iv. 11 ; vi. 1, 7, &c. But there appears no good reason for this.—אֶרֶץ, differs from this, in signifying rather the *surface*, than the *substance* of the earth ; and hence is, in the earlier parts of the Bible, opposed to שָׁמַיִם, *heavens*.

אַדְמוֹנִי, or אַדְמֹנִי (Gram. art. 166, 8), *Red-haired*, Gen. xxv. 25, where is added by way of explanation, כְּאַדֶּרֶת שֵׂעָר *like a hairy robe*. See also 1 Sam. xvi. 12 ; xvii. 42 ; LXX. πυρράκης ; Vulg. *rufus*.

אֶדֶן, m. אֲדָנִים, pl. constr. אַדְנֵי. See אָדוֹן. I. *A base*, especially the plates of copper, silver, &c., prepared to receive the tenons (יָדוֹת) of the planks forming the wall of the Tabernacle. Their use apparently was, to preserve the wood from the damp of the earth, Exod. xxvi. 19 ; xxvii. 10, &c. II. Meton. *Any foundation*, Job xxxviii. 6 ; Cant. v. 16. Aff. אֲדָנַי, אַדְנֵיהֶם, &c.

אֲדֹנָי, see אָדוֹן.

אֶדֶר, m. see אַדִּיר above. *Magnificence*, Zech. xi. 13 ; Mich. ii. 8 ; i. q. אַדֶּרֶת.

אָדַר, v. does not occur in Kal.—Niph. נֶאְדָּרִי, for נֶאְדָּרָה הִיא, Gram. art. 193, 6. *It hath become glorious*, or *magnificent*, Exod. xv. 6.

יַאְדִּיר, Hiph. *He makes glorious*, &c., Is. xlii. 21, of the noun אַדִּיר ; for יַאֲדִיר.

אִדַּר, Chald. m. Syr. اَوْ and اَوْرِ, Arab. آذَار *area*. אִדְּרֵי־קַיִט, *Threshing-floors of autumn*, Dan. ii. 35 ; Theod. ἅλων.

אֲדָר, Heb. and Chald. Syr. اَوْ, Arab. آذَارُ أذَارُ أذَارُ *nom. mensis Syromacedonum*. The month *Adar*, beginning with the new moon of March, and ending with that of April ; but, as the Rabbins say, beginning with that of February, and ending with that of March ; which is necessary to make it the twelfth, rather than the first, month. According to the Kamoos, the sixth Roomi month, of the Syro Chaldeans apparently. Among the Persians it was the ninth month of the solar year, and dedicated to آذَر, *fire*. This word also signified the ninth day of any month ; also the angel who had the charge of the sun, and presided over the festivities of every such ninth day, which was a feast. These days were looked upon as fortunate. The name is probably Chaldean ; it occurs only in the latter books of the Bible. Esth.

iii. 7, 13 ; viii. 12 ; Ezra vi. 15 ; 1 Macc. vii. 43, 'Αδάρ. See Scaliger de Emendatione Temporum, pp. 102, 245, 626, &c ; Relandi Antiquitates Sacræ, Par. iv. cap. i. par. ii. ; and the Tracts in Ugolini's Thesaurus, vol. xvii. ; the King of Oude's Pers. Dict. under الْآر.

אֲדַרְגָּזְרַיָּא, and אֲדַרְגָּזְרִין, def. pl. Chald. composed perhaps of the Pers. آذ *fire*, and گُذ *passing* ; or id. and Chald. גְּזַר *cut, decide*. *Certain* officers of state apparently, and perhaps those who presided over the ordeals by fire, and other matters connected with the government of Babylon, Dan. iii. 2, 3. Some prefer taking אַדַּר, *magnificent*, and גָּזְרִין, *deciders*, &c., i. e. *chief judges*. It is of little consequence what etymology is adopted, as it is quite impossible to determine with certainty, what these officers were.

אַדְרַזְדָּא, adv. Chald. of אַדַּר and אֻדְרָא. *Very quickly*, Ezra vii. 3 ; Vulg. *diligenter* ; LXX. ἑτοίμως, according to Gibbs's Gesenius ; but I can find no such thing. Winer, after Bohlen, makes it the Pers. در راست, which, as Kosegarten has well observed, is bad Persian. His conjectural درست, however, is little better ; and the same may be said of درزد, neither of which is ever used in any such sense as אַדְרַזְדָּא. Gesenius's זרו, and זריז, are certainly much better.

אֲדַרְכְּמֹנִים, and דַּרְכְּמֹנִים. If these words signify the same thing, the latter seems to identify itself with the Greek δραχμή, 1 Chron. xxix. 7 ; Ezra viii. 27 ; ii. 69 ; Neh. vii. 70—72. In some of these places, it is manifestly connected with words signifying weights ; in none, with names of coins ; whence I am led to believe, that it is not the δαρεικὸς of the Greeks. The Syr. ودمجن of a writer, Barhebræus, of the 13th century can have no weight in a question of this sort, particularly as nothing is more common than the Syrian practice of adopting Greek words. Winer's remark is, therefore, of little worth. Gesenius, however, gives us *Darig*, and *Dergah*, as the Persic for *court*. I can find no such word as the former. For דרכן *aulicum*, which he thinks represents the Persian form of this word, he then gives, as the last component part, کون *imago*. But this again I can find in no Persian book ! So that apparently no such Persian compound ever existed. Again,

c

under דַּרְכְּמוֹן, he gives دار كمان *regis arcus*. But, if these words meant the same thing, how could this happen? I am inclined, therefore, to think that δραχμή, and hence, with Salmasius, that the Arabic *dirhem* درهم, or درم, presents us with the same word, although I am unable to say what the real origin of either of these is.

אַדְרַמֶּלֶךְ, compd. of אֶדֶר הַמֶּלֶךְ, *glory of the king*; or, perhaps, Pers. آنْك *a weapon, a bow and arrow, spear, &c.* and מֶלֶךְ; put for the Apollo of the Greeks.—The name of an idol to which the Sipharenes made their children pass through the fire, 2 Kings xvii. 31. It is joined with עֲנַמֶּלֶךְ, either as another name for the same idol, or of another such idol. I think the former, i. e. *king of riches*, (ملك الغنم); which might well apply to Apollo. It is no objection to this, that human sacrifices are not expressly said to have been made to Apollo; for it is evident enough, from Macrobius and others, that every deity might be considered as resolvable into Apollo, in one way or other. Prop. name, 2 Kings xix. 37; Is. xxxvii. 38.

אֶדְרָע, Chald. for Heb. אֱזְרוֹעַ, *An arm*, Ezr. iv. 23.

אַדֶּרֶת, see אַדִּיר above.

I. *Abundance*, as of fruit, Ezek. xvii. 8; Zech. xi. 3; with aff. אַדַּרְתָּם, &c.

II. *A robe* worn for the sake of distinction, as, אַדֶּרֶת שִׁנְעָר, *a robe of Shinar*; i. e. richly wrought; LXX. ψιλὴ ποικίλη. See Plin. lib. viii. cap. xlviii. (lxxiv.): "*Colores diversos picturæ intexere Babylon maxime celebravit, et nomen imposuit.... Metellus Scipio triclinaria Babylonica sestertium octingentis millibus venisse jam tunc, posuit in Catonis carminibus*," &c. Hom. Il. iii. 125. Helen is introduced working such robes, which Eustathius says is ἐμποικίλλειν, and ζωγραφεῖν. Whence, as Winer well remarks, will be seen the weakness of the conjectures of Kennicott and Michaelis on Josh. vii. 21. אַדֶּרֶת שֵׂעָר, LXX. μηλωτή, *Hairy robe*, such as is usually worn by the ascetics of the East (comp. 2 Kings i. 8), and is called فرجيه; see my Translation of the Travels of Ibn Batuta, p. 196. From such garment made of wool, the Soofees (صوفى) of Persia have received their name. The بُرْدَة of Mohammed, which his followers say was worn in imitation of Elijah's mantle, was a similar sort of garment; as was the τριβώνιον of the Greek philosophers, which we are told Justin (Martyr) continued to wear, even after he had become a Christian. It is probable, from some places in Irenæus, that many of the early heretics really were the wolves in wool, which our Lord predicted, Matt. vii. 15, &c. Comp. Zech. xiii. 4.—Sackcloth differed from this, in its being worn in mourning, and often next the skin; see 1 Kings xxi. 27; 2 Kings vi. 30; Is. xxxii. 11. How Dr. Gesenius could have seen something in the former resembling the *furcloaks* of Europeans, it is difficult to say. Joseph's coat, Gen. xxxvii. 3, 23, termed כְּתֹנֶת פַּסִּים, was some such garment of distinction. The priestly vest of the Phœnicians too was, we are told, adorned with broad streaks of purple, Univers. Hist., vol. ii. p. 348, ed. 1747. And such, apparently, was the بُرْدَة of Mahommed.

אָדוֹשׁ, abs. noun, r. אדש, cogn. with דּוּשׁ. *Threshing*; i. e. beating out corn, &c. with the wheel, Is. xxviii. 28.

אָהַב, and אָהֵב v. pres. יֶאֱהַב and יֹאהַב, 1st pers. אֹהַב, and אֹהֵב. *Desired, loved.* Cogn. יָהַב, Arab. وَهَبَ, and حَبَّ, Prov. viii. 17; Hos. xiv. 5; constr. *immed.* rarely *med.* with לְ, or בְּ. אֲהֵבַת נַפְשׁוֹ אֲהֵבוֹ, *the love of himself he loved him*; i. e. as himself, 1 Sam. xx. 17.

אֲהֹב, infin. or verb noun, Eccl. iii. 8; *Loving*, opp. to שְׂנֹא.

אֹהֵב, part. or agent, *Loving, friend, companion*. אֹהֵב אֲדָמָה, *fond of agriculture*, 2 Chron. xxvi. 10; Prov. xviii. 24; Esth. v. 10, 14; Is. xli. 8.

אָהַב, see r. אהב.

מְאַהֲבִים, part. Niph. pl. *Lovely*, 2 Sam. i. 23; Pih. מְאַהֲבַי, *my lovers*, Hos. ii. 7; see in its place.

אֲהָבִים, and אֹהָבִים, pl. *Amours, loves*, Prov. v. 9. Meton. *Gifts* or *rewards* for love, Hos. viii. 9; comp. Is. xxiii. 17.

אַהֲבָה, f. inf. or verb noun, with prep. ל, ב, כ, מ. I. *Love* or *loving*, Is. lvi. 6; Deut. vii. 8; x. 15; xi. 13, 22; Hos. iii. 1; &c. Meton. *Person beloved*, Cant. ii. 7; iii. 5, &c.

אֲהָהּ, contr. הָהּ, interj. Ah! alas! Constr. *immed.* and *med.* with ל, Joel i. 15; Ezek.

אהו (11) אהל

xxx. 2; Judg. vi. 22, &c. Arab. اَوْ, اَوْ, اَوْ, or وَاَوْ, id.

אָהוּב, part. pass. of אהב, *Beloved.* אֲהוּבָה fem. id. Neh. xiii. 26; Deut. xxi. 15, 16, opp. to שְׂנוּאָה.

אֲהוּדְפוּ, *Hiph.* See r. ידה.

אֲהִי, for איה per. metath. probably; as, אֲהִי מַלְכְּךָ אֵפוֹא *where is now thy king!* Hos. xiii. 10. Some take it to be the apoc. pres. of אָהָה; but this is suitable neither to the vowels nor the context.

אֳהִי, apoc. pres. 1st pers. v. הָיָה.

אֹהֶל, Arab. أهل, *populus, cœtus hominum. A tent,* pl. abs. אֹהָלִים, for אֲהָלִים. Gesenius, Lehrgeb, pp. 152, 572, terms this a Syriasm. It is an irregularity in the points certainly; and that is all that deserves to be said of it. Simonis and Gesenius make it to differ from מִשְׁכָּן, in that designating the external coating, this the internal. Whereas, the truth seems to be, אֹהֶל signifies the whole tent; מִשְׁכָּן the compartments into which it may be divided. Comp. Exod. xxvi. 1, 7; xxxvi. 8, 14; xl. 2, 18, 19; Job xxi. 28. The אֹהֶל מוֹעֵד, *tent of congregation,* constituted apparently the whole area enclosed: the מִשְׁכָּן, properly so called, the tent representing the ναὸς, and containing the ark, &c. אֹהֶל הָעֵדוּת, *tent of the testimony,* as a smaller enclosure, was probably the same thing, Num. ix. 15; xvii. 23; xviii. 2. With affix אָהֳלֹה. With postpos. אָהֳלָה, which is irregular, for אָהֳלָה, Gen. xviii. 6; pl. constr. אָהֳלֵי, אָהֳלֵיכֶם, אֹהָלָיו.

אהל, v. not used in pret. pres. יֶאֱהַל, *Pitching a tent,* Gen. xiii. 12, 18.

Pih. יַאֲהֵל, contr. יַהֵל (Gram. art. 73), Is. xiii. 20.

Hiph. יָאֲהִיל *it gives out light, splendour,* Job xxv. 5; taking the sense of the cogn. הלל (Gram. art. 202, 4.) See my Translation of the passages, and notes.

אֲהָלִים, m. pl. and אֲהָלוֹת f. pl. The perfumed wood, termed *lign aloes;* by the Greeks, ἀγάλλοχον; Arab. اغالجون, and اغالوجي, more recently ξυλαλόη. We have it in the New Testament, in John xix. 39, μίγμα σμύρνης καὶ ἀλόης: which, a little lower down, is said to be *aromatic.* This wood is exceedingly valuable, even in the East, where alone it is produced. A species of it was in great abundance in Ceylon, in the times of Ibn Batūta. See my Translation of his Travels, p. 184, with the notes; where we find that the Kamāri and Kākuli species are not produced in Hindustan, but in Java. See also p. 201, with the note. In the Medical Dictionary of Ibn Hosein of Bagdad, we have a very particular account of this wood and its properties, sub voce عود. See also the Hierobotanicon of Olavus Celsius, pars. i. p. 135—171; Dioscorides, lib. i. cap. 21. In Ps. xlv. 9, the myrrh, *aloes,* and cassia, mentioned, are said to be from the ivory temples of מִנִּי. In Jer. li. 27, we find that this is the name of *a place;* e. g. מַמְלְכוֹת אֲרָרַט מִנִּי וְאַשְׁכְּנָז, *the kingdoms of Ararat, Minri, and Ashkenaz.*

This Minni is, according to Bochart, that part of Armenia which the Greeks termed Μιννύας, and produced perfumes. See the Phaleg. p. 15—23. Others think that a region in Arabia Felix is meant, in which a people named Minæi resided. See also the Phaleg. p. 135, C — 139; Thes. Gesenii, sub voce, Num. xxiv. 6; Prov. vii. 16; Ps. xlv. 9; Cant. iv. 14.

אָהֳלָה, *Oh*ŏ*lah,* f.(*her tent,* or *tabernacle.*) The allegorical name given to Samaria by Ezekiel, xxiii. 4, in allusion, perhaps, to her having set up a temple of her own. The Mappik required in ה was dropped on purpose, perhaps, in converting the word into a proper name.

אָהֳלִיבָה, *Oholibah,* (my tent (is) in, or with, her.) The name whereby Ezekiel represents idolatrous Jerusalem, ch. xxiii. 4, opposed to the above.

אֲהֵמָיָה, see r. המה.

אוֹ, for אַוָּה, Gram. art. 74. 87. 1, *Desiring, willing,* one or the other of several things; so the Latin *vel,* from *velle.* See Nold.—Arab. أَوْ *aut, &c.* Or, either—or; whether. So Pers. خواه, from خواستن *to desire.*

אוּ, with the vowels suitable to אִי, which is in the margin; better, perhaps, אִי (as above) *desiring, &c.* Prov. xxxi. 4.

אוֹב, pl. אֹבוֹת; the etymology is doubtful. Perhaps we have some remains of it in the Arabic آب used as an imprecation; as

אבו (12) אוד

آبَى اللّٰهُ, *may God reject him!* أَدْبٌ *felix fortuna, &c.* root أوب. See Freytag's Lexicon. Simonis may also be consulted. I. *A spirit of divination,* supposed to possess certain privileged persons, or to be within their call. Such was the young woman, Acts xvi. 16, who had a πνεῦμα Πύθωνος; such was the woman of Endor; 1 Sam. xxviii. 7. אֵשֶׁת בַּעֲלַת־אוֹב:—to whom Saul said, ver. 8. קָסֳמִי־נָא לִי בָּאוֹב *Divine, I pray, for me by a* πνεῦμα Πύθωνος. This spirit was common to both men and women, see Lev. xx. 27. II. *A man or a woman in whom there is a spirit of divination* (אוֹב). Characters of this sort are by no means uncommon at this day in the East; and to these may be compared the witches, wizards, and conjurers, among ourselves; which, however, the light of the Reformation has almost entirely put to flight. The hocus-pocus jargon of our modern conjurers, &c., seems to have been in use in the Biblical times, see Is. viii. 19; xxix. 4. The LXX. mostly translate אוֹבוֹת, by ἐγγαστρι-μύθους, on account of their muttering. On this subject may be consulted the dissertations of David Millius, in the Thesaurus of Ugolini, tom. xii. num. 5; or in the Dissertationibus Selectis, num. xii.; or Leonis Allatii Syntagma de Engastrimytho, in the Critici Sacri, tractatt Bibl. vol. i. p. 331; Van Dale de idololatria, p. 649; and Thes. Gesenii, sub voce.

אֹבוֹת, f. pl. Arab. أَيَابٌ, or إِيَابٌ, root أيب, for authorities differ, *uter. Skins used as bottles for wine,* Job xxxii. 19. These were probably the ἀσκοὶ, Arab. زِقٌّ pl. أَزْقَاقٌ, of the New Testament, Matt. ix. 17, &c. The same custom is alluded to, both in Job and in the Evangelists. Dr. Gesenius and others consider this word as the primitive, from which the preceding has been taken, and used in a translated sense; because, say they, necromancers, &c., speak as if speaking out of a jar. I doubt this, because it presents a most slender thread of connexion, and because the words are apparently derived from different roots. See also my notes, &c., on Job xxxii. 19.

אוּבָל, or אָבֵל (root יבל or ובל, with א *Hĕemanti.* Arab. وَبَلٌ *imber), A river,* according to most authorities; but most probably *a canal,* from יבל, which see, Dan. viii. 2, 3, 6. That canals were made prior to Daniel's time in the kingdom of Babylon, we have the best reason for believing; and of these the shortest, and perhaps best, accounts, with their authorities, will be found in the Ancient Universal History, vol. iv. b. i. chap. ix. § 1, edit. 1747.

אוּד, m. pl. אודים, Syr. ܐܘܼܕܵܐ, perhaps the Arab. عُودٌ *wood.* Bar Bahlul, cited by Gesenius, has ܐܘܼܕܵܐ ܕܬܵܢ *a smoking udo;* which that author says, smokes upon its being extinguished. *A stick of firewood,* taken out of the fire before well kindled, and hence emitting smoke. See Is. vii. 4; also the Targum on Job xii. 5, for לַפִּיד בּוּז; Amos iv. 11; Zech. iii. 2. Scheidius makes it a participial noun, of أَوَلَ, i. e. אוּד, for אָווּד, signifying *bent,* and thence, "lignum per ignem incurvatum."

אוֹדוֹת, pl. f. יָדָה, or ידה. Arab. وَدَى *projecit, &c. Projects, means; cause, account,* &c. Gen. xxi. 11, 25; Exod. xviii. 8, &c., with affix אוֹדוֹתַי.

אוֹדְךָ, *Hiph.* r. ידה.

אַוָּה, fem. Arab. هَوَى أَوَى. Syr. ܐܘܵܐ, cogn. Heb. אבה. I. Natural *desire* for food, &c., Deut. xii. 15; xviii. 6; 1 Sam. xxiii. 20. II. *Lust,* Jer. ii. 24, &c.

אִוָּה, v. *Pih.* generally with נֶפֶשׁ, as נַפְשִׁי אִוִּיתִיךָ, *As to my soul, I have desired thee,* i. e. greatly desired, &c., Is. xxvi. 9; Job xxiii. 13, &c., v. neut. and trans. Constr. *immed.* and *med.* with ב, and ל.

הִתְאַוָּה, *Hith.* pres. יִתְאַוֶּה, 2 Sam. xxiii. 15; Apoc. יִתְאָו, Prov. xxiii. 3, 6; xxiv. 1, *Becoming desirous of, coveting, claiming,* Deut. v. 18; Jer. xvii. 16. וְהִתְאַוִּיתֶם לָכֶם, Num. xxxiv. 10, has given endless trouble to the commentators, some supposing the verb here to be the same with תָּאָה, in vv. 7, 8, which, however, no analogy can reconcile; others say that *describe, mark out,* is the sense to be given to the verb; which, it is affirmed, the word אוה (but is this word derived from either אהה, תאה, or הוה? I think not) will sufficiently establish. For my own part, I see no reason whatever for all this; because, I think, *and claim for yourselves,* or the like, will suit the place sufficiently well. הִתְאַוּוּ תַּאֲוָה, *They became desiring a desire,* i. e. intensely desiring, Num. xi. 4.

אוֹחִילָה, keri הוֹחִילָה, Jer. iv. 19. See r. חול.

אוֹי, and אוֹיָה, interj. Constr. *immed.* and *med.* with לְ, as אוֹי עִיר הַדָּמִים, *Wo, city of much blood!* Lam. v. 16: אוֹיָה־נָא לָנוּ, *Wo now to us!* Ezek. xxiv. 6; Num. xxiv. 23; Ps. cxx. 5, &c. Nearly allied to הוֹי, which see, and may designate *grief, threatening, deprecation*, &c., as the context shall suggest.

אוֹיֵב, m. pl. אוֹיְבִים. See אֵיבָה. An *enemy, adversary*, public or private, Ps. iii. 8, vi. 11, &c.; ib. xlv. 6; cx. 1, &c. אוֹיְבֵי יְהוָֹה, *the enemies of Jehovah*, i. e. of his religion and people, Ps. xxxvii. 20; xcii. 10; with affix אוֹיְבְךָ, אוֹיְבִי, &c., regularly.

אוֹיֶבֶת, f. id. Micah vii. 8, 10. אוֹיַבְתִּי, i. q. אוֹיְבָה אַתִּי, Hos. x. 11. See Gram. art. 175. 15, note.

אוֹכָל, see r. אכל.

אוֹכִיל, m. r. יכל, cogn. τοῦ, אכל. *Provision*, Hos. xi. 4.

אֱוִיל, m. pl. אֱוִילִים, Arab. آل, r. اول, i. q. اِرْتَدَّ *descivit, defecit*, خَلَّ, *incrassuit*, &c. *A fool*, particularly as to religion; opp. to חָכָם, Prov. x. 14; to עָרוּם, ib. xi. 16. It differs from נָבָל, which rather signifies *corrupt*.

אֱוִילִי, id. with relative י, Gram. art. 166. 4, &c. *Foolish*, Zech. xi. 15.

אִוֶּלֶת, f. *Foolishness*, pec. with regard to religion, Prov. v. 23, &c. Ib. xiv. 24, we have, עֲטֶרֶת חֲכָמִים עָשְׁרָם אִוֶּלֶת כְּסִילִים אִוֶּלֶת. To render the last member by, *the folly of fools is folly*, would be to involve the author in the charge of dealing in truisms, and also of transgressing one of the commonest rules of oriental rhetoric; which requires that, when the same word happens to occur twice in the same period, it must be taken in different senses. De Sacy's Hariri, p. ٢٣٣, on التجنيس, Gladwin's Prosody and Rhetoric of the Persians, p. 6. So Rev. xvii. 8, οὐκ ἔστι, καίπερ ἐστίν, i. e. *remains not, although it now is*. See my Expos. on the place. Here, *their wealth (is) the crown of (the) wise; the backsliding, apostasy, of* (the) *confident*, i. e. of fools in this sense, *(is) their folly;* i. e. as עָשְׁרָם may be taken to signify the *acquisition*, or *wealth*, in a good sense, made by the truly wise; so אִוֶּלֶת, taken in its primary sense, *falling off*, &c., may, the loss occasioned to the opposite characters, by their dense ignorance. Comp. 1 Tim. vi. 5, 6, and Prov. xv. 16.

אוּל, m. Arab. أوّل *rectè disponere ac administrare*. So Ps. lxxiii. 4, בְּרִיא אוּלָם, *Fat*, i. e. prosperous, *is their administration*, &c. and, taking an abstract for a concrete (as in עֶבֶד, מֶלֶךְ, &c., Gram. art. 152. 10.), אוּלֵי הָאָרֶץ (Keri has אֵילֵי) *princes*, or *governors*, *of the land*, 2 Kings xxiv. 15.

אוּלַי, compd. of או, and לִי, cogn. τοῦ, לֹא. nearly allied to לוּלֵי, and אוּלָם, which see. A particle implying a negation obviated by some occurrence; nearly corresponding to our *unless, except;* Lat. *si non, nisi;* LXX. εἰ μή, modified as the context shall require. Locus valdè vexatus, is Num. xxii. 33. אוּלַי נָטְתָה מִפָּנַי כִּי עַתָּה גַּם־אֹתְכָה הָרַגְתִּי, *unless she had declined from before me, surely now I had even slain thee;* i. e. had *not* this first event taken place, the second (which has not) surely had. Winer asks, on this place, " Unde negandi vim huic voc. accedere existimemus?" I answer, from the same cause which we do in the last syllable of לוּלֵא, לִי (Gram. art. 86. 3,) being perfectly equivalent to לֹא. So ib. xxxiii. 27, אוּלַי יָשָׁר, lit. *or it will not seem right*, &c., Gen. xvi. 2. בֹּא־נָא אוּלַי אִבָּנֶה .... *Go in now* .... OR *I shall* NOT *bear by her*, &c. In all cases, I think, a preceding condition will be found, so as to allow of some such solution as the preceding. See Nold. *sub voce.*

אוּלָם, compd. أَوْ + كَمْ lit. *Or not, otherwise, nevertheless.* אוּלָם אֲנִי וגו, *otherwise I*, &c. i. e. I betake myself to other considerations. Job ii. 5, v. 8. See Nold. sub voce, and כ. 318.

אוּלָם, or אֻלָם, pl. אֻלַמִּים; also אֵילָם, אֵלָם, pl. אֵילַמִּים, and אֵלַמּוֹת, a name applied to a certain part of the Temple. See הֵיכָל.

אָוֶן, m. seg. prim. אָוְן, Arab. أَيْن or أَوْن *time, delay, occasion*, in either a good or bad sense.—I. אוֹן, *Virtue, manhood*, Gen. xlix. 3, Deut. xxi. 17, &c.; meton. *Power*, Job xviii. 7, 12, &c.; *Wealth*, Hos. xii. 9, Ps. xx. 10, cogn. with הוֹן. From its beauty and fertility, the valley of Damascus, Amos i. 5, בִּקְעַת אָוֶן, now termed *Un*, LXX. Ὤν, and by the Persians گلستان rather أَرْم, as some of their authors tell us. II. *Inconstancy, falsehood, sin, idolatry;* meton. *Idol*, and *sorrow*, Is. xli. 29; Ps. xc. 10; Zech. x. 2, &c. In

אוֹן (14) אוֹפִיר

Hos. iv. 15, &c., בֵּית אֵל *Bethel*, lit. *house of God*, sarcastically styled בֵּית־אָוֶן, *Bethaven*, lit. *house of idolatry, &c.*; with affix אוֹנִי, אוֹנוֹ, אוֹנֵךְ. Phr. מְתֵי אָוֶן; אַנְשֵׁי אָוֶן, *men of iniquity*; פֹּעֲלֵי אָוֶן, *doers of iniquity*, &c.

אוֹן, m. pr. אָוֶן, concr. of the above, pl. אוֹנִים. I. *Powerful*, Is. xl. 26, 29; Ps. lxxviii. 51. II. *Sinners*: meton. *Sorrowful*; לֶחֶם אוֹנִים, *bread*, i. e. usual fare, of such persons, Hos. ix. 4; Prov. xi. 7. Hence v. in Hithp. part. Num. xi. 1, מִתְאוֹנְנִים, *sorrowing, murmuring, &c.*

אֳנִיּוֹת, see אֳנִי, *Ships*.

אוֹסֵף, m. see אסף. *One collecting* any thing, Numb. xix. 10.

אוּפָז, or פָּז, Jer. x. 9; Dan. x. 5; Cant. v. 11. It is neither a different name for אוֹפִיר, nor a different way of writing that name, as some have thought, but a mere epithet signifying *Pure, refined*, or the like. In Jer. x. 9, we have כֶּסֶף מְרֻקָּע ... וְזָהָב מֵאוּפָז, i. e. *beaten silver . . . and refined gold;* supposing מֵאוּפָז here, to be parallel with מְרֻקָּע, not with מִתַּרְשִׁישׁ: which I think extremely probable. Because, not only is this word written מוּפָז, in 1 Kings x. 18, which is sufficient to show that the מ prefixed, is not the prep. מִן; for, this place, as compared with 2 Chron. ix. 7, has טָהוֹר, in the parallel. In this case it will be a derivative from יפו, or ופז; Arab. وفز, أوْفَزَ part. مُوفَزَ i. q. وفض; in conj. v. *disgregavit, &c.*; cogn. with فز, فص, and فض, *dimovit, separavit*. From the last of which we have فِضَّة *silver;* because so refined. On the other hand, see Bochart's Phaleg, p. 161, Canaan, p. 769.

אוֹפִיר, or אֹפִר, the name of a place celebrated for its gold. It probably took its name from אוֹפִר, one of the descendants of Eber, Gen. x. 29, who fixed themselves in Arabia for the most part. The gold of Sheba, Havilah, and Ophir, is often mentioned in Scripture. The two former places certainly were in Arabia. (Gen. xxv. 18, &c.) Seetzen, too, found a place so named near the Persian Gulf. Bochart and others, however, after placing the original Ophir in Arabia, look out for another in the East Indies, or elsewhere; because Arabia seems too near to account for the three years' voyages of Solomon's ships for the purpose of transporting the gold, peacocks, &c., to Palestine. Hence too, the Σοφὶρ, Σώφιρα, or Σώφιρα, of the LXX., has been supposed to be an Egyptian name of the East Indies, which has been thought corroborated by the سوفارة *Sufara* of Abulfeda, situated on the coast of Malabar. *Sōfāla* again, on the Eastern coast of Africa opposite to Madagascar, has also been supposed to be the Ophir of Scripture. See Bochart's Phaleg, p. 147, &c.; Reland's Dissert. Miscel. i. 4; Spicileg. Geogr. Sacr. Michaelis ii. 184, &c. also my notes on Job xxii. 24, &c.

אוֹפָן, pl. אוֹפַנִּים, *The wheel* of a chariot, threshing machine. &c., Gen. xiv. 25; Prov. xx. 26; Arab. أفَنَ *diminuit, &c.*

אוּץ, not in use; v. pret. אָץ, *Pressed, was urgent upon;* constr. with בְּ, לְ, מִן. אָץ לָבֹא, *pressed*, or *hasted, to go down*, Josh. x. 13; אָץ לְךָ, *it pressed upon thee*, ib. xvii. 15; Jer. xvii. 16.

Hiph. pres. יָאִיצוּ, *They pressed, urged*, בְּ, Gen. xix. 15; Is. xxii. 4, with לְ; Syr. ܐܠܨ *compressus;* Sam. הֵעִיץ, *cinxit, constrinxit;* cogn. Arab. عوص, وصّ, وصّ, *difficilis intellectu, &c.*

אוֹצָר, pl. אוֹצָרוֹת, constr. אוֹצְרוֹת. r. אצר, Arab. أصَرَ, cogn. حصر, أسَرَ, حبس, i. q. *continuit in carcere. A treasury;* meton. *a treasure*, Deut. xxviii. 12; 2 Kings xx. 13; Is. ii. 7: with affix, אוֹצְרוֹ, אוֹצְרֹתֶיךָ, אוֹצְרֹתָיו, &c.

יֹאצֵר m. part. of אצר. אוֹצָרָה, f. id.

אוֹר, m. אוֹרָה f. pl. אוֹרִים and אוֹרוֹת. Arab. آوار *durus, torridus, de solo.* أوَار *æstus ignis, solis, &c. Light, lightning*, Gen. i. 3—5; Job xxxviii. 3, 11, &c.; meton. that which gives light, *A luminary, the sun*, i. q. מָאוֹר, *instrument*, or *place, of light*, Ps. cxxxvi. 7. It has been supposed from one or two passages, that this word also signifies certain *green herbs*, as 2 Kings iv. 39. But *herbs* can hardly be meant here, for the context tells us, that the person sent to gather the אֹרֹת, whatever that was, gathered it from a vine, גֶּפֶן. Again, Is. xxvi. 19 has, טַל אוֹרֹת, but it is not necessary that אוֹרֹת, here should signify herbs. *Dew of lights*, i. e. *light-giving*, or *reflecting, dew*, will suit the terms full well. The passage contains, apparently,

אוֹר (15) אוֹר

an allusion to Ps. cx. 3. מִשְׁחָר לְךָ טַל יַלְדֻתֶךָ, i. e. *The dew of thy birth (is) a dawn to thee*, i. e. the period of thy being born into the world, shall exhibit a dawn, from which thy Gospel light shall spread throughout the world: both passages evidently referring to the coming of Christ. Again, Is. xviii. 4, כְּחֹם צַח עֲלֵי אוֹר, *as*, or *while* (the) *clearness warms into light*. It is added כְּעָב טַל בְּחֹם קָצִיר, *as the dense dew in the warmth of* harvest; i. e. as the heavy dew which then falls is gradually warmed by the great power of the sun; so, when the standard of Gospel truth shall be erected in the days of the Messiah, will I, from heaven, contemplate with pleasure its invigorating influences, extending itself by my aid and co-operation to the utmost boundaries of the earth.

As to אֹרֹת, occurring in 2 Kings iv. 39, I take it to be the Arabic (أَرَاكٌ), *spinæ species;* and the intention of the gatherer to have been, to collect either the leaves or berries of this; which is, perhaps, the *Egyptian thorn*, and the leaves of which are, according to Prosper Alpinus, collected when green, and boiled in the broth of fowls, &c. His words are, " De brassica spinosa . . . cum audiveram sponte natam, et in Ægypto, et Judea, et Syria, conspectam fuisse. . . . Folia, ut dictum est, cum virescunt decocta ex aqua, aut jure gallinaceo; ferculi modo comedunt, atque etiam non minus cruda: itidem folia cum sale." De plant. exot., lib. ii. cap. x.—This person, in his progress, collects the *berries* or *grapes* (פַּקֻּעֹת שָׂדֶה) *of the plain*, i. e. wild grapes (not *gourds*), which I take to be a species of عنب الثعلب ' *fox-grape of* the orientals. One of the five species of this, we are told by Ibn Hosein, in his medical dictionary, entitled اختيارات بديع, is poisonous, lit. *killing;* the antidote to which is قند, *sugar-candy*. His words are, عنب الثعلب پنج نوعیست یك نوع از آن کشنده بود ... ومصلح وي قند بود. The prophet, miraculously or not, neutralized the killing property of the berry by throwing a quantity of meal into the broth. —Celsius makes the אֹרֹת, and פַּקֻּעֹת, alluded to, to be the *cucumis sylvestris;* but, how this can be styled *a vine*, גֶּפֶן, I am unable to see. Hierobot. pt. I., pp. 393—459. On the oriental usage of the term *dew;* see my notes on Job xxix. 19.

II. Meton. *Prosperity,* Ps. lvi. 14; Job xxii. 28, &c.

III. *Knowledge;* the mind being supposed to be enlightened, Luke ii. 32; Is. ix. 1, 5; xxxv. 5, &c., opposed to misery and ignorance, Matt. xxii. 13; John iii. 19; Is. viii. 22; Joel ii. 2, &c.

IV. Metaph. applied to *God*, as the source of all spiritual light, prosperity, knowledge, Is. x. 17; xlix. 6, &c. In the New Test. to Christ, John i. 7, 9; iii. 19; viii. 12, &c.

אוֹר, for אָוֹר, Gram. art. 75. form יָכֹל v. *Became light, enlightened, shining, prosperous,* &c., Gen. xliv. 3; 1 Sam. xxix. 10; ib. xiv. 27, 29. Imp. אוֹרִי, *shine* thou, f. Is. lx. 1.

Niph. נָאוֹר, *Became bright, &c.,* Ps. lxxvi. 5, pres. יֵאוֹר, 2 Sam. ii. 32. Infin. לֵאוֹר, Job xxxiii. 30.

Hiph. הֵאִיר, pres. יָאִיר, apoc. יָאֵר, *Made light, enlightened, informed, &c.,* Ps. lxxviii. 19; xviii. 29; Job xli. 24. Meton. *Refreshing, invigorating,* constr. with בְּ, אֶל, עַל, לְ, אֵת, and בְּ, Num. vi. 25; Ps. xxxi. 17; Ps. cxix. 135, &c.; also, *Setting on fire,* Is. xxvii. 11; Mal. i. 10.

אוּר, m. pl. אוּרִים contr. of אָוֹר, *Any thing enlightened* or *inflamed;* hence *Fire,* Is. xxiv. 15; xliv. 16; xlvii. 14; Ezra v. 2. Meton. *The light of fire,* Is. l. 11.

The Urim, worn in the breast-plate of the high priest, which, with the *Thummim*, were perhaps intended to typify the influence and value of revealed religion. Occasionally, by way of distinction, with the article, הָאוּרִים וְהַתֻּמִּים Exod. xxviii. 30; Lev. viii. 8, &c.; LXX. literally, δήλωσις καὶ ἀλήθεια. In Exod. xxviii. 17—21, this breast-plate is particularly described: and, from the circumstance of its being used in obtaining answers from Jehovah, it is there termed, חֹשֶׁן הַמִּשְׁפָּט. One would be disposed to think that the *Urim* and *Thummim* added, as it seems to have been, to this breast-plate (ib. ver. 30), was intended *particularly* to shadow out Him, who was to be *the light, the truth,* and *the life;* and that, from its being attached to the breast-plate, bearing twelve precious stones, representing perhaps the twelve tribes,—as their names were engraven on these,—the whole was intended to represent the true church, and its influence with God, under both Testaments. See Rev. xxi. 11, 12, 13, 14, 19, 20, 23: which seems to me to apply all this to

Christ, and to the Christian Church. Dr. Gesenius, however, as the manner of his school is, finds here nothing beyond mere idols, such as the Egyptians had. Diod. Sic. i. 48, 75, 'Ælian var. Hist. 14, 34. He then goes to Philo's Life of Moses (tom. ii. v. 152, edit. Mangey), where he makes his author style these *Images*, following, in this case, our Spencer. But, why did he not refute the note of Mangey, ib., who shows that the whole is a mistake, founded on a wrong interpretation of the word ἀγαλματοφορῇ? Nor can I see why the accounts of Diodorus, or Ælian, are to be preferred to those of Moses himself, just alluded to; unless, indeed, heathen writers are the only safe expositors of Holy Writ! It is not impossible, indeed, that the Egyptians might have had something representing these instruments of the Hebrew ritual, which they had borrowed from the Jews; and which would, of course, be made to quadrate with their own notions; just as the idolatrous Arabs made the Hebrew כֹּהֵן, كَاهِن, *a magician*, and the תָּמִים, تَمَّ, *amulets* to hang about the necks of children. See Hariri's Second Consessus. The age of Diodorus and Ælian will admit of this.

אוּר כַּשְׂדִּים. The name of a place in Mesopotamia, Gen. xi. 28; xv. 7; Neh. ix. 7, in which the family of Abraham originally resided, usually styled *Ur of the Chaldees*. It has usually been supposed to mean, *The fire of the Chaldees*, on account of the fire-worship supposed to be carried on there. Gesenius, ever ingenious and interesting at least, proposes a new view of this. *Ur*, he tells us, signifies, in the Sanscrit, a *town*, or *place*. This, it is his object to substitute for the *castle*, or *fortification*, of Ammianus Marcellinus (25, 8).—Bochart (Phaleg. pp. 43, 87, 88), and Cellarius in his Geography, had fixed upon this *Ur*, as the birth-place of Abraham. Unfortunately, however, for that theory, ورا, *Ura* is still, in the Persian, a mere appellative, signifying *a castle*, as Meninski will shew. All, therefore, that can be made of the passage in Ammianus is, that the Roman soldiers, asking in their march the name of the fortress, were told that it was *A castle!* Bochart, therefore, who does not appear to have been acquainted with the Persian, was, like them, mistaken; and so, of course, was Cellarius. In the next place, it will, I presume, be no easy task to shew, that

Ur, in the Sanscrit, signifies *a town*, and less easy also to shew that this language ever prevailed, or was even known in Mesopotamia; which this hypothesis requires. In the ixth book of the Prep. Evangel. of Eusebius, we have: Δεκάτῃ δὲ γενεᾷ φησιν (i. e. Eupolemus) ἐν πόλει τῆς Βαβυλωνίας Καμαρίνῃ, ἥν τινας λέγειν πόλιν οὐρίην, εἶναι δὲ μεθερμηνευομένην, χαλδαίων πόλιν, ἐν τρισκαιδεκάτῃ γενέσθαι Ἀβραὰμ γενεᾷ, i. e. He, i. e. Eupolemus, says that Abraham was born in the tenth age (i. e. after the flood) in Camarina, a city of Babylonia, which some name *Ouria*, but, being interpreted, signifies a city of the Chaldeans, &c.—Here Gesenius thinks that Eupolemus must have misunderstood his original; and, as we do not know from other sources the precise situation, &c., of this city, not much reliance can be placed on it. I think differently. It seems to me to agree so well with the accounts given in the Bible, that it is worthy of all acceptation. I suspect, however, that this passage was not fully understood by Gesenius. By πόλις Καμαρίνῃ, was probably meant, a city of priests, as כַּמָּר —כֹּמֶר still,—signifies *a priest* in the Chaldee. χαλδαίων πόλις, signifies the same thing; as it is certain that χαλδαῖος was specially applied to *the learned** among the Babylonians. These were, therefore, synonymous terms. And if this place was principally inhabited by

---

* Diodor. Sicul. lib. i. xxxviii. Τοὺς τε Ἱερεῖς . . . . . οὓς Βαβυλώνιοι καλοῦσι Χαλδαίους. Flamines . . . . quos *Chaldæos* Babylonii nominant. And Strabo, lib. xv. Edit. Casaubon. p. 508 et seq. Ἀφώρισο δ᾽ ἐν τῇ Βαβυλωνίᾳ κατοικία τοῖς ἐπιχωρίοις φιλοσόφοις, τοῖς Χαλδαίοις προσαγορευομένοις, οἱ περὶ ἀστρονομίαν εἰσὶ τὸ πλέον . . . Ἔστι δὲ καὶ τῶν Χαλδαίων τῶν ἀστρονομικῶν γένη πλείω. Καὶ γὰρ Ὀρχηνοί τινες προσαγορεύονται, καὶ Βορσιππινοί, καὶ ἄλλοι πλείους, ὡς ἂν κατὰ αἱρέσεις, ἄλλα καὶ ἄλλα λέγοντες περὶ τῶν αὐτῶν δόγματα. Constituta est habitatio peculiaris in Babylonia philosophis indigenis, plurimum astronomiam tractantibus qui Chaldæi appellantur . . . . Chaldæorum astronomicorum genera sunt aliquot. Nam quidam Orcheni dicuntur, quidam Borsippeni, et alii complures qui (ut in sectarum fieri solet diversitate) eisdem de rebus aliter et aliter statuunt. And, a little lower down we are told, that *Borsippa* is a city sacred to Apollo and Diana: not unlike our Καμαρίνη πόλις perhaps. It is evident that in Dan. ii. 4, הַכַּשְׂדִּים is a generic name for philosophers of this sort. The other names, ver. 2, are probably specific names of sects, such as Strabo mentions above.

heathen priests, whose creed was that of fire worshippers, it is not at all unlikely that οὐρίη, אור, *fire*, was a name given to it; especially as we find that such names were formerly given to places in Persia on the same account. So, in the King of Oude's Persian Dictionary (p. ۸۳) آذر آبادگان نام آتشکدهٔ تبریز است و شهر تبریز است کویند چون در تبریز آتشکدهٔ بسیار بوده است بنابر ان بدین نام موسوم شده. That is, *Adhar Abadgān ... it is the name of a fire-temple of Tebriz; it is also the city of Tebriz. They say, as there were many fire-temples in Tebriz, on that account it was so named.* See also other compounds of آذر *fire.* It should seem, therefore, hardly safe to appeal to the Sanscrit, when no proof can be adduced for its use in these parts, and particularly as the older interpretation had authority so good for its support.

אֻוֹרוֹת, i. q. אֲרָוֹת, f. pl. 2 Chron. xxxii. 28. Syr. ܐܐܘܪܐ, Arab. آرِيٌّ, and أَرِيٌّ, pl. أَوَارِيُّ *stabulum, præsepe.* Stables, or stalls for beasts.

אוֹת, c. for אֲוָה, Gram. art. 75, pl. אֹחוֹת, r. אוה. So Arab. آيَةٌ, for أَوْيَةٌ, or أَوْيَةٌ, r. اوي. Syr. ܐܬܐ, pl. ܐܬܘܬܐ.

I. *A mark of distinction, memorial,* or *warning,* Gen. i. 14; xvii. 11; Num. ii. 2; Exod. xxxi. 13, 17; Ezek. xx. 12, 20. See my Sermons and Dissertations, p. 95, &c. Exod. xiii. 9, 16; Deut. vi. 8; Ezek. xiv. 8; Job xxi. 29, &c. Id. *False* or *counterfeited,* Ps. lxxiv. 4; Is. xliv. 25; Jer. x. 2.

II. *Miraculous signs,* or *wonders,* consisting either in word or deed, whereby the certainty of any thing future is foretold or known; as, I. *Prophecy,* which is at least miraculous, Gen. iv. 15; Exod. iii. 12; iv. 8; 1 Sam. ii. 34; 2 Kings xix. 29; Is. vii. 11—14; xxxvii. 30; Dan. iii. 32, 33: II. *Miraculous events* given as pledges, 2 Kings xx. 8, 9; Is. viii. 18; xxxviii. 7, 22. In this sense it is often joined with מוֹפֵת, and is then equivalent to the Greek σημεῖα καὶ τέρατα, Deut. iv. 34; xiii. 2; Is. xx. 3, &c.

אֵת, i. q. אֵת, and אֶת, which see.

אוֹת, or אוּת, v. Niph. pres. יֵאוֹת, נָאוֹת, יֵאוֹתוּ, constr. with לְ: *Consenting to, agreeing to,* Gen. xxxiv. 15, 22, 23; 2 Kings xii. 9. It is cognate with אָתָה, *came in:* hence, *to agree with.* So Lat. *convenio,* and the 3 conj. Arab. آتى, *convenit, &c.* as Dr. Gesenius has well remarked.

אוֹתִיּוֹת, f. pl. *Things coming,* or *to come.* r. אָתָה, Is. xli. 23; xliv. 7; xlv. 11.

אָז, Arab. إِنْ, part. of excitation, Eng. 'st. *see, behold, &c.* (Nold. אחז, *accendit, &c.* Eth. አኀዘ *jussit,*) used with either of the tenses, or a participle; as, جِئْتُكَ إِنْ إِنْ يَقُومُ زَيْدٌ, or إِنْ قَامَ زَيْدٌ, or زَيْدٌ قَائِمٌ. *I came to thee, behold Zaid stood,* or *Zaid* (was) *standing,* or *Zaid* (then) *stands.* Hence it has obtained the sense of *Then, at that time,* and the usage of an adverb. Used with either of the tenses; as, אָז דִּבַּרְתָּ, *then thou speakest,* Ps. lxxxix. 20. אָז יְדַבֵּר, *then speaks, &c.* Josh. x. 12. From this last usage it has been supposed, that the particle had the power of converting a pres. into a past tense, in the verbs. So all the grammarians from the days of Aben Ezra, up to those of Dr. Gesenius. Noldius, however, found several places in which this notion would not hold; as Josh. i. 8; Is. xli. 1, &c. Annot. et Vind. p. 794, ed. 1734. See lett. ו. The truth appears to be, that these writers were perfectly ignorant of the principles which regulated the use of the Arabic and Hebrew tenses. See Gram. art. 231. 9, et seq. Compd. with מִן; as, מֵאָז, *from that time, since.* מֵאָז הַבֹּקֶר, *from then* (i. e.) *the dawn,* i. e. *since,* Ruth ii. 7; Ps. lxxvi. 8; Exod. iv. 10: *since thy speaking,* with infin. &c. compd. with י pron. So Arab. ذَاكَ, إِنْ, إِنَّاكَ of ذَا and كَ. of ذَاكَ, and كَ. אֱזַי, id. Ps. cxxiv. 3—5.

אָזָא, or אֲזָה, v. Chald. Arab. أَزَّ, *accendit,* cogn. وَزَّ *siccavit,* Dan. iii. 19. מְזָא, for בָּאְזָא, contr. for מְאְזָא infin. Pehil, *To heat,* ib. v. 22. אֲזָה it. Pehil, *he heated,* ib. 19. מֵזֵה, infin. as before with pron. ה; א or ה changing into י, as is usual.

אֲזַד, v. Chald.; Arab. أَصَدَ, وَصَدَ, *occlusit ostium, &c.*; or أَصَدَ, آصَدَ, *cooperuit.* Some make it the same with אֲזַל, *abiit;* hence Dan. ii. 5, 8, the only places in which it occurs;

D

I. *The matter is closed*, i. e. *confirmed, by me*; or, II. *It has gone out from me*, i. e. *has been decreed and published*; or, III. *It is covered, concealed from me.* The context seems to me to require this latter. LXX. ἀπέστη. The form אַזְדָּא, is that of a fem. participial noun.

אֵזוֹב, m. Syr. ܙܘܦܐ; Arab. زُوفَا. *Hyssop*, the ὕσσωπος of the Greeks; much used in sprinkling blood, water, &c., under the law, Exod. xii. 22; Levit. xiv. 4, 6, &c. See Castell under אזב; Bochart Hieroz. i. 587—593. Hierobot. Celsii, i. 407, &c.; Vislingii observ. ad Prosp. Alpinum, de plant. Egypt. p. 32.

אֵזוֹר, m. r. אזר, which see; *A belt, or bandage*, used apparently to *strengthen* the loins, 2 Kings i. 8; Is. v. 27; xi. 5, &c.;—or, *to bind them*, Job xii. 18.

אֲזָין, v. see אזן.

אַזְכָּרָה, r. זכר, *A memorial*, a term much used in the East in a religious sense, as ياد Pers.; نِذْكِر Arab.; LXX. μνημόσυνον, ἀνάμνησις, pec. *A species of offering* so named. See Lev. ii. 2, 9, 16; xxiv. 7; Numb. v. 26.

אָזַל, v. pres. fem. אֹזְלִי, for אָזְלִי, Gram. art. 72; Arab. cogn. زَوَل, *abiit, defecit*, cogn. Heb. et Chald. זור, it. Chald. אֲזַל, *He, or it, went away, departed*, אֲזַל לוֹ, *He goes him away*, comp. Prov. xx. 14, with Gen. xii. 1. This pleonastic use of the pronoun is most frequent in the Syriac and Chaldaic. Heb. Jer. ii. 36; Job xiv. 11; 1 Sam. ix. 7. Chald. Ezra iv. 23; v. 8, 15; Dan. ii. 17, 24, &c. מְאֻזָּל, for מֵאָזַל, Ezek. xxvii. 19, has been taken by some as the participle of Puhál of this verb, and as signifying, *Made to go, going to and fro*, as a company of merchants. Bochart. Schulz, in his edition of the Lex. of Cocceius, and Rosenmüller, prefer considering it as if written מֵאוּזָל, i. e. *from* אוּזָל, *Uzál*, the ancient name of Senaa in Arabia Felix. See under אוּזָל: Gesenius and his followers, as a participial noun, derived from אול,—supposing it to be cognate with the Syr. ܚܙܠ; Arab. عَزَل, whence the Talmudic אָלָא, *textor*, and the Syr. ܐܡܪܠ, *rete*,—signifying *to spin* or *weave*. I prefer Bochart's view of the subject.

אֱזַל, 1st pers. sing. Kal. v. אזל Chald.

אֹזֶן, f. Arab. أُذُن; Syr. ܐܕܢܐ; Gr. οὖς, *The ear*, with affix. אָזְנִי, אָזְנוֹ, constr. אָזְנֵי of dual אָזְנַיִם; with aff. אָזְנֶיךָ, Jer. vi. 10; עָרְלָה אָזְנָם, *uncircumcised is their ear*; comp. Acts vii. 51, equivalent to the Arab. لَبِسْتُ أُذُنِي لَهُ *I have clothed my ear to him*, i. e. will not attend to him; opposed to this is גָּלָה אֹזֶן, *he uncovered, or laid bare* (the) *ear*, 1 Sam. ix. 15; xx. 2; 1 Chron. xvii. 25; Job xxxvi. 10, אָזְנָם פָּרָה: Ps. xl. 7, *he dug out*, i. e. *cleared out the ears*; expressive of the state fit to receive instruction, and thence to obey. See my Prolegomena to Bagster's Polyglot Bible, prol. iv. § iii. par. xvii. Rosenmüller in loc. The symbolical use of circumcision seems to be, to intimate that our mind is to be laid open to God; and that, as nothing can be concealed from him, so we must be ready to hear and obey, under all circumstances.

אָזַן, Pihél. Arab. أَذَن, *aurem, seu ansam fecit*, &c. It occurs only once, Eccles. xii. 9, וְאִזֵּן וְחִקֵּר, *He both attended to and investigated*. The Rabbins have had recourse to the Arabic وَزَن, *he weighed*, here, and in this they have generally been followed; but the Hebrew signification seems sufficient.

הֶאֱזִין, or הַאֲזִין, Hiph. *To attend, or listen to*; meton. *obey.* Constr. either *immed.* as Gen. iv. 23, or *med.* with לְ, Job xxxiv. 2; אֶל, Ps. lxxvii. 2; עַל, Prov. xvii. 4; עַד, Num. xxiii. 18. Hence, *to obey*, Exod. xv. 26; Neh. ix. 30; part. מַאֲזִין, for מַאֲזִין, Gram. art. 72, for מַאֲזִין, Prov. xvii. 4, imp. and infin. הַאֲזֵן or הַאֲזִין: par. ה, הַאֲזִינָה, *attend, I pray*, Num. xxiii. 18, &c.

אָזֵן, m. r. זין or אזן; Arab. زِينَة, زَين, *ornatus*, &c.; Syr. ܙܝܢܐ, *armavit*; Chald. זַיִן, *id. Implement of husbandry, or of war*. It occurs only once, Deut. xxiii. 14, יָתֵד תִּהְיֶה לְךָ עַל־אֲזֵנֶךָ, *Thou shalt have a pin, or pale, over* (and above) *thy implement*. Some MSS. read אָזְנֶךָ, pl., which the versions generally do not countenance.

אֲזִקִּים, m. pl., Arab. زِقّ, *uter*, رِقَاق, *platea angustior*, cogn. زَنَاق, *compedes*, cogn. أَزْق *angustia*, ضِيق *id.*, Chald. זְקַק, *ligavit*: זִקִּים, with a prosthetic א, Gram. art. 84. r. זקק. *Chains or bandages*, particularly for the hands. Comp. Jer. xl. 1, with ib. ver. 4.

אָזַר, v. Arab. أَزَر, *cinxit, roboravit*. *He, or it, bound*; constr. either *immed.* or *med.* with בְּ, 1 Sam. ii. 4; 2 Kings i. 8; Jer.

אזר (19) אח

i. 17; Job xxx. 18; xxxviii. 3; 2 Kings i. 8.

Niph. נֶאֱזַר, with בְּ, Ps. lxv. 7, *Girded.*
Pih. *immed.* pers. and thing (Gram. art. 229. 11); Ps. xviii. 33, 40; xxx. 12; Is. L. 11; sense as in Kal.
Hithp. *Became bound,* Is. viii. 9. Imp. Ps. xciii. 1, *immed.* On the force of the Niphhál and Hithpahél species, when occurring in the same verb, see Gram. art. 157. 16, note, and ib. par. 19.

אֶזְרוֹעַ, i. q. זְרוֹעַ, f. with a prosthetic א, Gram. art. 84. *The arm.* See זְרוֹעַ.

אֶזְרָח, m. See זרח. *Indigenous, home-born.* Lev. xvi. 29; xviii. 26; Ps. xxxvii. 35, כְּאֶזְרָח רַעֲנָן, *like an indigenous* (tree or person) *flourishing.* Most interpreters supply עֵץ, tree; others אֱנוֹשׁ, or אִישׁ. Comp. ver. 36, with Ps. ciii. 16. See Hierbot. Celsii, i. 194, and Rosenmüller on the place. Proper name (זֶרַח, for אֶזְרָח), 1 Chron. ii. 6. Whence—

אֶזְרָחִי, m. patronym. Gram. art. 166, of the foregoing; comp. 1 Kings v. 11; Ps. lxxxviii. 1; lxxxix. 1; with 1 Chron. ii. 6. *Ezrakhite.*

אָח, m. אָחָה, *consuit, consociavit;* Chald. I. *A brother,* whether of the same father, or mother only, or of both. II. *A relation,* generally, whether by affinity or blood, as uncle, cousin, nephew. III. *One of the same country, tribe,* or *neighbourhood.* IV. *A fellow,* or *familiar.* V. *Any person* or *thing like another.* VI. *A term of affection* generally, Gen. iv. 2; xlii. 15; Judg. ix. 1;—Gen. xxiv. 27; 2 Sam. xx. 9; Gen. xiv. 14; xiii. 8; xx. 5; Lev. x. 4; 2 Sam. i. 26;—Num. viii. 26; Ex. ii. 11;—Am. i. 9;—Prov. xviii. 9; Job xxx. 29; Ezek. xviii. 10;—Job xix. 13. Constr. אֲחִי, alt. form, פְּקֹד, or פְּקָד. Gram. art. 86, 4; Gen. x. 21: with aff. אָחִי, for אַחְיִי, Gram. art. 73; Gen. iv. 9. So אֲחִיו, אָחִיךָ, אָחִיךְ, אֲחִינוּ; אֲחִיהֶם: alt. form, with the grave aff. אֲחִיכֶם; אֲחִיהֶם: plur. abs. אַחִים, pl. with aff. אַחַי, in pausa; אֶחָי: אֲחֵינוּ, אַחֶיךָ, אַחֶיךְ, אַחָיו. In all which cases, the first vowel (-, or v) ought to be considered as equivalent to Kaméts; Dagesh being implied. Gram. art. 109, as אֶחָד, or אַחֵי, &c. Chald. pl. with aff. אֲחָךְ, Ezra vii. 18.

אָח, f. *A sort of pot,* or rather *stove,* used in the East to warm their rooms in the winter. Arab. كَانُون, *olla,* Jer. xxxvi. 22, 23. See Jahn's Biblische Archäologie, 1 Theil. p. 236, plate ix. fig. 20.

אָח, interjection, *Ah! alas!* Ezek. vi. 11; xxi. 20.

אֹחִים, m. pl. Is. xiii. 21; Arab. آه, *he cried ah! ah!* Either, I. *Howlings,* as Bochart, Castell, and some of the ancient translators suppose; or, II. *Howling animals, owls, &c.* as others think. I incline to the former.

אֶחָד, m. constr. אַחַד, f. אַחַת, in paus. אֶחָת. Eth. ႠႣႤ: *paucus fuit,* &c. contr. m. חַד, Ezek. xxxiii. 30; Dan. vii. 5; and, according to some, אַח, Ezek. xviii. 10; but Gesenius and Rosenmüller take it to mean, *fellow* (deed); i. e. "si fecerit *socium quid* ex facinoribus illis:" which is preferable. I. Numer. *One,* or, taken as an ordinal, *First,* Gen. i. 5, &c. *Some one* (τις), used as an indefinite article; *a* Eng., un Fren., ein Germ., ⲞⲨⲀ Copt. &c. not merely in the more modern Hebrew, as Gesenius asserts, Gen. xxi. 15; xxii. 2; xxvi. 10, &c. See Nold. Concord. part. p. 750, ed. 1734. II. By way of eminence, *Singular, rare,* 2 Sam. vii. 23; 1 Kings xxii. 13; Zech. iii. 9; xiv. 7. So the Pers. ى, Pers. Gram. ed. 1828, p. 24—28, and Arab. ا, *of unity,* ib. So Eng. "He was *a* man, take him for all in all," &c. III. *The same,* i. e. *one and the same* Gen. xi. 1; xl. 5. IV. Distributively, *The one,* and *the other,* Exod. xvii. 12; xviii. 3, 4. V. *Alone, only, one only,* Gen. xix. 9; Is. li. 2, &c.; Exod. xxxiii. 5.

אָחַד, or cog. יָחַד, Arab. أَحَدَ, or وَحَدَ, *fœdus icit, unicus fuit.* The first not used in Kal. Hithp. הִתְאַחֲדִי, Ezek. xxi. 21. Gesenius, Rosenmüller, &c., *Unite thyself* (spoken of a three-edged sword, v. 19.) Schnurrer, *operam da,* &c. I am inclined to believe, that it is here used for אחז, Chald. אחד, Arab. أَخَذَ. *To take hold, to begin,* &c.: hence הִתְאַחֲדִי הַיְמִינִי, *take* (i. e. *begin*), *take the right hand;* הַשְׁמִילִי *place* (act), *take the left hand, &c.* The second used in Kal and Pihél, Gen. xlix. 6; Is. xiv. 20. יָחֵד, Ps. lxxxvi. 11, for יִיחֵד, Gram. art. 73.

ⲀϨⲞⲨ, Copt. ⲀϨⲞⲨ, Ægyptiacè scribebatur ⲀϢⲀⲒ, Lex. La Croze. Jerome, in his Com. on Is. xix. 7, says, "Audivi ab Ægyptiis hoc nomine lingua eorum *quicquid in palude*

אחו (20) אחז

virens nascitur appellari." *Any green herb growing in marshy land.* The LXX. give ἄχι and ἄχει. Aq. and Symm. ἕλος. Gen. xli. 2, 18; Job viii. 11. Bochart. Hieroz. i. p. 404. Hodius de text. Bib. p. 118. Celsii Hierob. ii. 340—346, and Alb. Schultens, Job, 1. c. who take the Arab. اخِدٌ, *laqueus*, pl. أَوَاخِي, *res pascuales*; while others suppose the Chald. אַחֲוָא *ulva*, to be the etym. These languages do, however, occasionally agree in their words, without its being possible to say which has the priority.

אַחֲוָה, or אֲחֻוָה, f. contr. for אַחֲוָיָה, Chald.; with pron. 1st pers. אַחֲוָתִי, r. חָוָה; *My shewing, reasoning, argument*, Job xiii. 17: Chald. Dan. v. 12.

אַחֲוָה, f. See אָח, Arab. أُخُوَّة and المُوَاخاة (*fraternitas*), *Brotherhood*, Zech. xi. 14. Such was probably the covenant of *brotherhood* made by Mohammed and his companions, in the early stages of his career. See Annales Muslemici Abulfed. tom. i. p. 77, not. Hist. p. 18.

אָחוֹר, m. r. אחר, which see: pl. אֲחוֹרַיִם, opp. to קֶדֶם, both as to time and place: when speaking of a person or thing, to פָּנִים, Ps. cxxxix. 5; Is. ix. 11; 1 Chron. xix. 10; Ezek. ii. 10. I. Any person or thing *behind*, or *coming after* another, as to time, place, &c.; also, II. adv. *Behind, backwards*; hence, *western*; because a person facing the rising sun will have his *back* towards the west. For the same reason the south is termed יָמִין, or תֵּימָן, *right hand*; the north, שְׂמֹאל, *left hand*; and the east, קֶדֶם, *front*. Metaphorically, נָסוֹג אָחוֹר, or הָלַךְ, *he*, or *it fell, went, or receded, backwards*; i. e. *fell from, forsook God, grew worse, &c.* 2 Sam. i. 22, with aff. אֲחוֹרִיהֶם, אֲחוֹרַי. See Nold. Concord. part. sub voce.

אָחוֹת, or אָחַת, sing. for אֲחֹוַת, contr. Gram. art. 75. Arab. أُخْتٌ, *soror. A sister;* the word is used in the same latitude of meaning, as אָח, *brother*, is; which see. Also used of a city, in some respects *like* another, Ezek. xvi. 46; xxiii. 31, 33; Jer. iii. 7, 8. Metaph. Prov. vii. 4; Job xvii. 14. Spoken of things *similar*, and used with אִשָּׁה, Exod. xxvi. 3, 5, 6, &c. In constr. אֲחוֹת, aff. אֲחוֹתוֹ (once, Num. vi. 7, אֲחֹתוֹ), אֲחוֹתֵנוּ, אֲחוֹתְךָ, אֲחוֹתְכֶם, אֲחוֹתָם, אֲחוֹתַיִךְ, אֲחוֹתָה, אֲחוֹתִי, pl. אֲחוֹתַי, אֲחוֹתֵיכֶם, אֲחוֹתָיו.

אָחַז, pres. יֹאחֵז or יֶאֱחֹז, Arab. أَخَذَ, Chald. Syr. אחד *cepit*. Cogn. Heb. אחר. I. *He*, or *it took, took hold of, seized*, or *held*, generally: syn. חָזַק, *held fast*; לָבַד, *took in war*; לָקַח, *took, accepted, took out*. Constr. with בְּ, pers. or thing, Exod. iv. 4, with אֶת־, ־בְּ, pers. of the part seized, 2 Sam. xx. 9. II.—As men in war; as beasts, fishes, &c. Is. v. 29; Eccl. ix. 12; Cant. ii. 15. III.—By choice, Num. xxxi. 30; 1 Chron. xxiv. 6:—as the affections of the mind, Exod. xv. 14; Ps. xlviii. 7; Job xviii. 20. IV. *Held*, in the sense of *bound about, girded*, Est. i. 6; Jer. xiii. 21; Is. xxi. 3; Job xxx. 16; Cant. iii. 8. See חבל. Kamoos, الاَخْذ... العقوبة, *punishment*. V. *Hold to*, *join*, or *unite*, syn. אחר, 1 Kings vi. 6, Ezek. xli. 6: hence, *shut up*, or *close*. Syr. ܐܣܡ, Neh. vii. 3; Job xxvi. 9, as the context manifestly requires. With pron. affixes, Ps. cxix. 53; Jer. xlix. 24; Ps. xlviii. 7. Infin. אֲחֹז, 1 Kings vi. 6, with prep. Ps. lvi. 1; Job xxxviii. 13. Imp. אֱחֹז, Exod. iv. 4; fem. אֶחֱזִי, Ruth iii. 15; pl. אֶחֱזוּ, Cant. ii. 15; *in pausa*, אֵחֹזוּ, Neh. vii. 3; אֹחֲזָה with ה par. Cant. vii. 9; 2 Sam. iv. 10.

Niph. Two forms, נֶאֱחַז, and נאחז; I. *Became taken, held, &c.* Gen. xxii. 13; part. Eccl. ix. 12, or actively (Gram. p. 89, note). II. *Became taking* (possession, &c.); נֹאחֲזוּ (of בְּ and seg. form אָחֻז), Num. xxxii. 30; Josh. xxii. 9; also Gen. xxxiv. 10; xlvii. 27; Josh. xxii. 19—Pih. id. Job xxvi. 9. Hoph. מְאֻחָז, 2 Chron. ix. 18, *joined, united to*.

אֲחֻזָּה, f. *Tenure, possession, &c.* of a country, or land, Gen. xvii. 8; Lev. xxvii. 16:—of slaves, Lev. xxv. 45, &c. אֲחֻזַּת נַחֲלָה, *tenure of an inheritance, &c.* Num. xxvii. 7, &c.

אֱחָז, 1st pers. sing. Kal. apoc. v. חזה.

אֲחַזְמְפָּה, 1st pers. sin. Pih. with ב Epenth. v. חמא, Gen. xxxi. 39.

אֲחִידָה, for אֲחוִידָה, contr. Gram. art. 73. fem. Chald. i. q. Heb. חִידָה, r. חור, *Problem*, or *enigma*, Dan. v. 12. pl. אֲחִידָן.

אֲחָיוֹת, see אָחוֹת.

אַחֲלַי, or אַחֲלֵי, I. n. pl. with aff. I. pers. II. id. in constr. r. אחל, cogn. with יחל, *speravit*. Syr. ܐܘܚܠ, *admiratus est*, cogn. Arab. أَوْخَلَ, *gravavit, afflixit malo. My wishes! hopes!* 2 Kings v. 3; Ps. cxix. 5; used as an interjection, *Would to God!* &c.

אֹחֶל, or אָהָל, r. הלל.

אֲחָלָמָה, Chald. חֲלָם; Syr. ܐܚܠܡܐ solidus, integer. According to the accent, the ה is paragogic, Gram. art. 175. 8; but, little reliance can be placed on the accents. *A precious stone;* according to the LXX. *the amethyst* (not the agate, as Winer says in his edit. of Simonis). So Josephus, Jerome, &c. The Syr. and Chald. have עֵין עֶגְלָא, *calf's eye*, supposed to represent that stone. Some suppose it to be the *emerald;* see Braunius de vest. sacerd. ii. 16; Lud. de Dieu on Exod. xxviii. 18; xxxix. 12.

אַחַר, m. dag. imp. Gram. art. 109, Arab. آخَر, *alter, alius, &c.;* Syr. ܐܚܪܢܐ, *distulit*, &c. pl. constr. אַחֲרֵי, aff. pron. אַחֲרָיו, אַחֲרֵיךָ, &c. used mostly as a preposition, or adverb. *After, behind,* Gen. xxii. 13. Hence, *Western* (see אָחוֹר) Exod. iii. 1; *Afterwards*, Exod. v. 1; Num. v. 26; with pron. pleonasticè, Prov. xxviii. 23: with verbs ידע, שׁלח, דרך, הלך, בוא, זנה, מלא, אֲשֶׁר, יצא, which see; followed by אַחֲרֵי כֵּן Lev. xiv. 8; Ezek. xl. 1; pl. Gen. xvii. 8; Exod. xxxiii. 8, &c. See Nold. concord. part. sub voce. It. Chald. Dan. ii. 29, 45; vii. 24, id.

אַחֵר, m. f. אַחֶרֶת, pl. אֲחֵרִים, אֲחֵרוֹת. *Other,* Chald. אַחֳרִין.—Gen. xxvi. 21; xxix. 7; Exod. xx. 3; Is. xlii. 8; Job xxxi. 10. In Ps. xvi. 4, אַחֵר is more suitable to the context, viz. אַחַר מָהֲרוּ (for אַחֵר), *who hurry,* or *hasten backwards,* i. e. from God. Hence

אָחַר, v. pres. 1st pers. אֵחַר, for אֶאֱחַר, Gram. art. 86. 5; Arab. آخَرَ, *tardavit; Delayed, waited, deferred,* Gen. xxxii. 5.

Pih. אִחֵר, for אֲחֵר, *Cause delay,* Gen. xxiv. 56; Ex. xxii. 28. Constr. with לְ pers. לֹא יְאַחֵר לְשֹׂנְאוֹ, *he makes no delay, as to his hater,* i. e. to punish him. אֶחֱרוּ, Jud. v. 28, with (ָ) instead of (ֳ) on account of the (ֳ) following. Gram. art. 107, מְאַחֲרִים עַל, *delaying over,* Prov. xxiii. 30, with בְּ *in,* i. e. *until,* Is. v. 11, spoken of God by an anthropopathia. Ps. xl. 18; lxx. 6, &c.—יְאוּחַר, keri יוּחַר, 2 Sam. xx. 5, taking יחר, or וחר, for the root, as cognate with אחר, Hiph.

אַחֲרוֹן, m. אַחֲרוֹנָה, f. augm. Gram. art. 168, pl. m. אַחֲרוֹנִים. I. *Latter,* opp. to רִאשׁוֹן, *former,* with respect to either time, place, or order, 2 Chron. ix. 29; Ps. xlviii. 14; lxxviii. 4, 6; Job xix. 25; Is. xli. 4; xliv. 6; Prov. xxxi. 25; Is. xxx. 8. Particularly the *latter days,* or *times,* i. e. those in which Judaism and heathenism were to lose their prevalency, and the Christian Church was to be reared. See my notes on Job xix. 25. Comp Heb. i. 2; 2 Pet. iii. 3; 1 Pet. i. 20; 1 John ii. 8. See also my Sermons and Dissertations on Prophecy, &c., p. 365, &c.—II. *Western,* Deut. xi. 24; xxxiv. 2. See אָחוֹר. Adverbially, Deut. xvii. 7; 1 Sam. xxix. 2, &c.

אַחֲרֵי, for אֲחָרֵי, Pih. v. אחר.

אַחֲרֵי, Chald. f. i. q. אַחֲרִית; the final ם in such words as אַחֲרֵי, מַלְכוּ, is used in Chald. and Syr. for the form of construction. *Another; future,* &c. Dan. ii. 39; viii. 5, 6.

אַחֲרֵין, Chald. attrib. Dan. iv. 5, עַד אָחֳרֵין, *At length.*

אַחֲרִית, *After, latter,* or *distant state,* as to time or place, Deut. xi. 12; Job xlii. 12; Eccl. vii. 8: opposed to רֵאשִׁית: particularly that time in which Judaism and heathenism should cease to be dominant, Gen. xlix. 1; Num. xxiv. 14; Deut. iv. 30; xxxi. 29; Is. ii. 2; Jer. xxiii. 30; Ezek. xxxviii. 8; Dan. viii. 19; x. 14, &c. See אַחֲרוֹן above. It. Chald. Dan. ii. 28. Whether it is to be taken in a good or bad sense, the context will always be sufficient to determine.

אָחֳרָן, Chald. attrib. *Another,* Dan. ii. 11.

אֲחֹרַנִּית, f. used adverbially, *Backwards,* Gen. ix. 23; 1 Kings xviii. 37, &c.

אֲחַשְׁדַּרְפְּנִים, pl. m. foreign compd. See Gram. art. 169. 10, *Chief satraps,* or *chief doorkeepers.* Dr. Gesenius, however, proposes in his Thesaurus a more certain etymology, as he thinks; but he has been misled through a want of knowledge of the Sanscrit, to which he has appealed : "Khschatryapati ordinis bellici dominus." He then goes on to say, "Khschetrao, postea schetrao rex. Ita kschatrap سراب Σατράπης." But, kshatryapati is a compound, signifying *Lord of the field* (i. e. of battle). If, then, khschatrco means *king* in the Pehlair, I do not see how it can be any part of the compound kshetryapati, unless it be a compound of *kshétra, field,* and *áp.,* Pers. آب, *water.* But this would be fanciful. I therefore prefer the former etymology. Est. iii. 12; viii. 9; ix. 3; and with the Chaldee termination, Dan. iii. 2, 3, 27; vi. 2, 3.

אֲחַשְׁתְּרָנִים, m. pl. Est. viii. 10, 14, i. q. בְּנֵי הָרַמָּכִים, ib. See רמך. Compd. of خَش آ, and

אחת (22) אטד

سَتَر, *mule.* See Bochart. Hieroz. tom. i. col. 236; Sup. Lex. Heb. Michaelis, p. 65. Gesenius supposes that سَتَر, was formerly pronounced *shatar* or *kshatar*, and that the Hebrews prefixed an א, to facilitate the pronunciation. This is, perhaps, supposing too much.—*Mules,* produced from a male ass and a mare, which were the swiftest and strongest. See Bochart. l. c. The Cambridge translator of Gesenius, Leo, translates "maulthiere," by *noble mules;* and the explanation " *söhne der stuten,*" by " *sons of dromedaries !*"

אַחַת, see אֶחָד. אֲחֵר, *Aph.* Chald. v. נחת.

אֲחָתָה, *Hiph.* 1st pers. sing. with ה parag. v. חתה.

אַט, 1 per. sing. pres. *Hiph.* apoc. v. נטה.

אַט, pl. אִטִּים, r. אטט; Arab. اِطّ, or وَطّ, *murmur edidit, teneriore affectu ductus fuit, &c.* Persons uttering a low murmuring voice. I. *Necromancers, enchanters,* Is. xix. 3. II. Adv. *gently, softly,* 1 Kings xxi. 27. לְאִטִּי, *at my ease, convenience,* Gen. xxxiii. 14, it. לְאַט, *at ease, gently,* Is. viii. 6. לְאַט־לִי לַנַּעַר, *gently with me, as to the young man,* i. e. deal gently with him for my sake, 2 Sam. xviii. 5. וְדָבָר לְאַט עִמָּךְ, *and a matter* (is) *for gentleness with thee,* i. e. thy circumstances are easy, Job xv. 11.

אָטָד, m. Arab. اَطَلْ, Syr. ܐܛܕܐ, or ܗܛܕܐ, *rhamni nigri species.* A sort of *blackthorn,* said to be plentiful about the walls of Jerusalem, and to be very quick of growth. Comp. Luke viii. 7, with Locman's fable 22, *De Rubo.* (العوسج). And see Jud. ix. 14, 15; where allusion seems to be made to its encroaching and untractable character. It is much used in the East for fences, and even for fortifications; and presents the greatest difficulties to an attacking force. Hence Ps. lviii. 10, may be thus translated : *Before your thorns* (generally) *experience the* (destructive influence of the) *blackthorn, like a powerful* (2 Sam. xxiii. 20; keri, 1 Sam. xxv. 6; Is. xxxviii. 20) *and enraged* (person), *shall he* (God) *tear him* (i. e. your enemies severally) *away;* i. e. in less time than this thorn can grow up and be mischievous, &c. Comp. Jud. l. c. The LXX. Πρὸ τοῦ συνιέναι τὰς ἀκάνθας ὑμῶν τὴν ῥάμνον, ὡσεὶ ζῶντος ὡσεὶ ἐν ὀργῇ καταπίεται ὑμᾶς. The Targum, עַד לָא יְתְעַבְּדוּן רַשִּׁיעַיָּא רַכִּיכֵי אֲטֻנִין הֵיךְ דְהַגּוּן עַד אַמְרִין בַּמֵיבִין כְּבוּסְרָא בְּעַלְיוֹלָא שְׁטִינוּן׃ *So long as the wicked*

become not lenient, they will (be as) *hard* (untractable) *as the blackthorn, while they,— immature* (indeed) *as the unripe* (fruit),—*he destroys them as with a tempest.* Rosenmüller in his Scholia on this place, has given both an incorrect copy and translation of the Chaldee. The Syriac text is here much mutilated. It stands thus : ܢܗܘܘܢ ܐܡܪܝܢ ܒܛܘܒܝܗܘܢ ܕܠܐ ܡܣܬܟܠܝܢ ܟܘܒܝܗܘܢ ܐܝܟ ܗܢܘܢ ܐܢܫܝܢ, *They have not understood: their thorns are* (like) *the blackthorns; and wrath shall disperse them.* This again Rosenmüller has miscopied.—The Syr. ܘܐܦܠܐ ܐܚܝܕ ܠܗܘܢ. ܢܗܘܐ ܕܐܠܡܚܣܕ, is either another translation of the member which immediately follows, or else presents us with a miserable dislocation, and interpolation of the text. Sym. has a sense not very distant from this : viz. Πρὶν ἢ αὐξηθῶσιν αἱ ἄκανθαι ὑμῶν ὥστε γενέσθαι ῥάμνος, ἔτι ζῶντα ὡς ὀλόζηρον λαίλαψ ἀρεῖ. So Jerome : "*Antequam crescant spinæ vestræ in rhamnum, quasi viventes, quasi in ira tempestas rapiet eos.*"—The Vulgate, however, " *Priusquam intelligerent spinæ vestræ rhamnum; sicut viventes, sic in ira absorbet eos.*"—And in his commentary, *Rhamnus, sentium genus est asperrimum aculeis, et flore gratissimum. Unde intelligitur duplam habere virtutem, ultionis, et bonorum retributionis, id est, justis floret ad ornatum, peccatoribus præbet spinas ad confringendum.* As *a hedge* it may be considered as *a defence,* Job i. 10, to the good, or as a hindrance to the bad, Prov. xv. 19; Mic. vii. 4. In all these cases, the Heb. סִירוֹת, is taken to signify *thorns.* Rosenmüller thinks this might be tolerated, had the plural ended in ים; but, in the eleven other places in Scripture, in which the word occurs in this form, it means *pots.* This is not true, for in Amos iv. 2, where this word occurs, he says; " *Sane* סִירוֹת, *feminina pluralis terminatione, alias significat ollas . . . sed spinarum, sive hamorum significatione admissa (ut non sit a* סִירִים *diversum) quam inter Hebræos et Kimchi h. l. agnoscit, eleganter prodit similitudo, et aliis prophetarum locis, uti ostendimus, congrua,*" &c. It should also be borne in mind, that there is no mention in the Bible of this thorn being burnt under pots, &c. If then we can suppose the (אָטָד) *blackthorn,* to have been taken by a metaphor to signify the *lowest* and *worst* of the people, ·(see Josh. xxiii. 13 ; 2 Sam. xxxii. 6,) who, when in power, are always

אמן (23) איב

the most oppressive; and the term to have been used proverbially since the days of Jotham, we shall find no difficulty in seeing how it applies here, and in what sense the ancient translators took it. See Hierob. Celsii, i. p. 199, &c.; Bochart. Phaleg. pt. ii. lib. ii. cap. xv. p. 834; Prosp. Alpin. de Plant. Ægypti, p. 21.—Proper name of a place, Gen. L. 10, 11.

אָמוּן, m. *A cord* or *thread*, apparently of Egyptian manufacture, Prov. vii. 16. The form אמוּן occurs in the Targums, as a translation of the Heb. מֵיתָר, or חֶבֶל, Num. iv. 32; Jos. ii. 15; 1 Kings xx. 32, &c. No satisfactory etymology has yet been offered. Some take ὀθόνη, or ὀθόνιον.

אָמַם, Arab. اَطَمَ, *arctavit, occlusit ostium*, id. Chald. *He shut* or *closed* the lips, Prov. xvii. 28; the ears, ib. xxi. 13; Is. xxxiii. 15; —spoken of windows splayed, i. e. the walls of which verge obliquely towards closing on the outside, 1 Kings vi. 4; Ezek. xl. 16. Jerome says on this place . . . "non directas (habet fenestras) et æquales, sed obliquas et angustas exterius, et se intrinsecus dilatantes," ib. xli. 16, 26. Sym. θυρίδες τοξικαί. "Idcirco," says Jerome, "a sagittis vocabulum perceperunt, quod instar sagittarum angustum in ædes lumen immittant et intrinsecus dilatentur;" ib. LXX δικτυωταὶ, *netted* or *cancellated;* Eng. window, i. e. wound, or cancellated, with twigs, &c.

Hiph. יַאְמֵם אֹזֶן, *He closes* (the) *ear*, Ps. lviii. 5. See אוּן.

אָמַר, v. pres. 3 fem. תֶּאְמַר; Arab. اَطَرَ, *sepiit, nervo obligavit sagittam, &c.;* cogn. Heb. עָצַר *cinxit, &c., Contract, shut* or *close*, constr. with עַל, Ps. lxix. 16.

אָמֵר, m. Arab. اَطِر, *peccatum, &c.*, i. e. faulty; so مَرْبُوط and مُعَقَّد, *alligatus*, but used in the sense of *impotent. Bound, restrained*, from using the right hand, Jud. iii. 15; xx. 16.

אִי, m. pl. אִיִּים and אִין, אֲרִי contr. Gram. art. 73. אִי; Arab. اَيّ for اَوْيّ, r. اَوِي or اَيّ, for اَوْيّ, *mansionem capere.* I. *Inhabiting, residing;* by meton. *Habitation, habitable land,* or *country*, whether that be a *continent* or *island;* hence *land*, as opposed to sea or river. II. *The shore,* or *countries* on the sea shores. Synon. אֲדָמָה, properly signifies *ground* or *land*, with respect to culture.

אֶרֶץ, the *earth,* or *land*, generally, whether cultivated or not; and occasionally the *whole earth*, particularly before Canaan was allotted to the Israelites. תֵּבֵל, signifies the *world* generally, including also the sea:—2 Sam. xxii. 16; Gen. x. 5; Is. xlii. 15; Jer. ii. 10; xiii. 22; L. 39; Est. x. 1; Ezek. xxvi. 15, 18, &c.

Also אִיִּים, contr. for אֲחִיִּים, patron. of the above. III. *Land-animals*, particularly those not subject to man; i. e. frightful *land-monsters generally;* צִיִּים being those peculiar to deserts only; תַּנִּים those to both sea and land; which see. Hence, perhaps, the LXX treated them as fabulous animals, viz. ὀνοκένταυρο‥. See Jerome on Is. xiii. 22. Modern lexicographers have, after Bochart, supposed them to be the shagâls, vulg. jackals, of the Persians; because the ابن أوي, Ibn *Awi* of the Arabs seems to present the same word. In after times, indeed, the Arabs might have confined this word to that animal; but it appears unlikely that this, or any of the words above noticed, was so defined in the times of Isaiah, or Ezekiel: and this view has generally, and I think properly, been taken by the elder translators and commentators. See Is. xxxiv. 14; Jer. L. 39; Bochart. Hieroz. tom. i. p. 842, seq.

Hence IV. interj. אִי, *Fearful! woe! &c.*, Eccl. iv. 10; x. 16, constr. with לְ; comp. הוֹי. Some have supposed this to be a mere ejaculation, as O!

Hence also, V. from the signification of residing, &c. אִי in constr. for אַי, Gram. art. 86. 4. *Where?* q. d. *residence?* or *place?* i. e. name it; as אֵי־זֶה הַדֶּרֶךְ, *where* (is) *this the way?* 2 Kings iii. 8; see 1 Sam. ix. 18; Job xxviii. 12, &c., it. אֵי מִזֶּה, *where, from this,* i. e. *whence?* Gen. xvi. 8, &c., it. אֵי לָזֹאת, *where for this?* i. e. *How?* Jer. v. 7. It. compd. אֵי + כֹּה = אֵיכֹה, *where here?* אֵיכָה + כֹּה = אֵיפֹה, *where thus? how?* It. with אַיֵּה, *where?* Gen. xix. 5, with pron. אַיֶּךָ, or אַיֶּכָּה for אָנָה with parag. ה, Gen. iii. 9, *where* (art) *thou?* אַיּוֹ, Exod. ii. 20, &c., *where* (is) *he?* אַיָּם, Is. xix. 12, *where* (are) *they?* אֵי־כָבֵד of אִי־כָבוֹד, which last see, *how?* Cant. v. 3; Est. viii. 6. And VI. taken interrogatively to imply a strong negation: as אִיכָבוֹד, *where is* (the) *glory?* i. e. *it is departed,* 1 Sam. iv. 21; Job xxii. 30. Some however take this last instance to mean *residence,* or *island, of the innocent.* See my notes on the place.

אֵיבָה, for אֹיְבָה, Gram. art. 86. 3. Arab.

אִיד | | אִיל

اَوِبَ, i. q. غَضِبَ, *iratus fuit*; hinc اَبَهُ اللهُ, *amovit cum Deus*, اَبَكَ, or لَكَ اَبَ, i. q. وَيَلَكَ, *væ tibi. Enmity*, Gen. iii. 16. &c.; constr. אֵיבַת, Ezek. xxv. 15, &c.

אֵיד, m. Arab. آدَ, *durities*, r. اَيِدَ cogn. آبَلَ, *gravis molestus*, r. اَوِلَ, for אֵיד, Gram. art. 86. 3. *Calamity, destruction*, 2 Sam. xxii. 19; Ps. xviii. 19; Jer. xlviii. 16; Job xviii. 12, &c., with aff. אֵידִי.

אַיָּה, f. see אִיִּים above. *An unclean bird*, so called, perhaps, on account of its cry, Lev. xi. 14; Deut. xiv. 13; Job xxviii. 7. The Arab. يُويُو, according to Bochart. Hieroz. par. ii. p. 193, &c., *A sort of hawk* or *vulture*.

אַיֵּה, see אִי art. V.

אֵיךְ, or אֵיכָה, ib.

אֵיכֹה, or its equivalent אֵיכוֹ, ib.

אַיֶּכָּה, of אַי and כָּה, *Where* (art) *thou*?

אֵיכָכָה, see ib.

אַיִל, constr. אֵיל or אֶל, of אַיִל Gram. art. 86. 3. m. seg. pl. אֵילִים or אֵלִים, of concr. form אֵל perhaps, see Gram. art. 75. Arab. آيَّلٌ, *crassus liquor*, اِيَالٌ, *crassescere*, cogn. آلَ of اَوَلَ, *incrassuit liquor; extenuata fuit caro camelæ;* i. e. humore amisso rigida evasit. Eng. ill:—hinc آل, *familia*, &c. It is not used, says the author of the Kamoos, except where excellence is the prevailing idea. لا يستعمل اِلّا فيما شَرُفَ غَالِبًا. *Strength*, Ps. lxxxviii. 5, abstr. for concr., *Powerful* or *mighty one*. Applied,—

I.—*To God*, Arab. اِلٌّ or اِيَلٌ, pl. الاتُ, *a hill, &c.* and *idol* worshipped by the tribe of Bakar. Kāmoos. Eng. *hale, hill*, cogn. خِيل, חוּל, Gen. xiv. 20, 22; Is. vii. 14; comp. viii. 8, 10; ix. 6; comp. x. 20, with affix אֵלִי, Exod. xv. 2. Frequently used in compounds, Is. vii. 14; ll. cc. אֲרִיאֵל, ib. xxix. 1, &c.

II.—*To false*, or *suppositious*, *gods*, Is. xliv. 10; xlv. 20, &c. Hence used as a qualifying term, signifying *the greatest*, or *best*, of any thing: אַרְזֵי אֵל, *mighty cedars*, Ps. lxxx. 11; comp. civ. 16; Ps. xxxvi. 7, with xviii. 16.

III.—*To heroes*, or *mighty men*, Exod. xv. 11; Ps. xxix. 1; lxxxix. 7; Ezek. xxxi.

11. In constr. Exod. xv. 15; Ezek. xvii. 13; xxxii. 21. See Bochart. Hieroz. part i. lib. ii. p. 422, &c. יֶשׁ לְאֵל יָד, lit. *there is of God power*, Gen. xxxi. 29; Prov. iii. 27; Mic. ii. 1; Neh. v. 5; neg. Deut. xxviii. 32; comp. Job xii. 6; Hab. i. 1.

IV.—*To the pine*, or *terebinth*. אֵלָה fem. Gen. xxiv. 5; Jud. vi. 11; masc. pl. Is. i. 29; Ezek. xxxi. 14; Cels. Hierob. part i. pp. 34—58.

V.—*To rams*, as being the strongest of the flock, Gen. xv. 9; Exod. xxix. 15; pl. Gen. xxxi. 38; Exod. xxv. 5, &c.

VI.—*To the lintel*, or *arch*, over a door, or window, which supported the superincumbent wall, 1 Kings vi. 31; Ezek. xl. 14, 16. See הֵיכָל.

אַיָּל, m. אַיָּלָה or אַיֶּלֶת f., *Antelope*, or *gazelle*, Ps. xlii. 2; Deut. xii. 15; xiv. 5; pl. אַיָּלִים, Cant. ii. 9, 17; viii. 13; Lam. i. 6. Fem. Gen. xlix. 21; Jer. xiv. 5, &c., pl. f. אַיָּלוֹת, 2 Sam. xxii. 34; Ps. xviii. 34;—xxix. 9, we have, קוֹל יְהוָה יְחוֹלֵל אַיָּלוֹת, see Auth. Vers. and in the corresponding member, יֶחֱשֹׂף יְעָרוֹת, *he lays bare the woods*. How the former signifying *antelopes*, and the latter *woods*, can agree together, I cannot see; nor, how the thunders can contribute towards making these animals bring forth.* If we take אֵילוֹת, instead of אַיָּלוֹת, we shall have *pines*, instead of *antelopes*; and the context will be consistent; we shall also be able to see how the thunders perforating, or riving up, the stately pines, will keep up the strength of the context. So the Syr. ܐܲܝܠܵܢܹ̈ܐ. Comp. 2 Sam. xviii. 9, 10, 14, where the Heb. has אֵלָה. So also Shakspeare—

"Split'st the unwedgable and gnarled oak, Rather than the soft myrtle."
Measure for Measure.

In constr. אַיְלוֹת, Cant. ii. 7; iii. 5; Bochart. Hieroz. part i. lib. iii. c. xvii. On the title of Ps. xxii. see אַיֶּלֶת.

אֵלוֹן, m. augm. of אֵל above, pl. אֵלוֹנִים, i. q. אֵל, sig. IV. *Pine*, or *terebinth*, Jud. ix. 6, 37; 1 Sam. x. 3; Gen. xiii. 18; xiv. 13; xviii. 1; According to Gesenius Thes. pp. 50, 51, *The oak*.

---

* Dr. French and Mr. Skinner, "*maketh the hinds tremble as in labour*." The note tells us that "this timid animal is named as being one of those most terrified by the thunder." I remark, if this were true it would make the Psalmist a mere driveller. As to the translation, it is nothing beyond a comment.

אֵיל (25) אֵיפ

אֱיָלוּת, f. i. q. אֱיָל, or אַיָל, *Strength*, Ps. xxii. 20, compd. of אֱיָל+הוּת, Gram. art. 86. 2.

אֵילְכָה, v. הלך, or ילך.

אֵילָם, or אֻלָם, see הֵיכָל.

אִילָן, m. Chald. augm. of איל Gram. art. 168, *A tree*, generally, Dan. iv. 7. With the definite article postfixed, אִילָנָא, ib. iv. 8, &c.

אֵים, m. אֲיֻמָּה f. for אֲיוּמָה, Gram. art. 96. 2; Arab. اوم *vocem anhelando edere*, q. d. *querulam ardoris notam*; ايمة *fumum excitare*, cogn. with אום, אמם, הום, המה, המם, which see. *Fearful*, Hab. i. 7, syn. with נורא; *formidable*, Cant. vi. 4, 10, spoken of the Church when arrayed against its enemies.

אֵימָה, f. pl. אֵימִים, m. אֵימוֹת, f. for אֲיֻמָּה, Gram. art. 75. I. *Fearful*, Gen. xv. 12; Job xxxix. 20; xli. 6, &c. Also, II. *Fear*, Deut. xxxii. 25; Prov. xx. 2; Job xxxiii. 7, &c., with the paragogic ה, i. e. *of unity* (Arab. ة), Exod. xv. 16, *singular* or *extraordinary fear*. Aff. אֵימָתִי, Exod. xxiii. 7. Pl. אֵימוֹת Ps. lv. 5, i. e. *great* or *many fears*. Pl. m. אֵימִים or אֵמִים, Job xx. 25; Ps. lxxxviii. 16; *Fears*, or *fearful things*. Meton. *Idols*, as objects of fear to their followers; Jer. L. 38. Also the name of a very warlike people, who once inhabited the land of Moab. Gen. xiv. 5; Deut. ii. 10, 11; identical with the רְפָאִים. See my notes on Job xxvi. 5.

אַיִן, constr. אֵין, it. once אַיִן, (or אִין,) for אֵין; Gram. art. 86. 3, 4; Arab. اَيْن, *tempus idoneum*, hinc اِين, *ubi?* Cogn. اون and اَنِي, *tempus*, اَنِّي *ubicunque, unde?* Hence taken interrogatively to imply *Non-existence, is not*, q. d., *no where to be found*: whereas לֹא negatives *property* or *quality* only; and hence (ע) is termed by the Arabs نفي الجنس, while لَيْسَ, like the Heb. אֵין, negatives the existence of the thing. Comp. אַיֵּה, Mal. i. 6. See אי and אִין. Interrog. *Is there not?* אֵין־פֹּה, *Is not here?* 1 Sam. xxi. 9; *Is not, exists not?* אִם־אַיִן מֵתָה אָנֹכִי, *putting the case* (that) *it exists not*, (then) *I am a dead woman*, i. e. I may be considered as such, having no child to keep my name alive, Gen. xxxi. 1. מַיִם אָיִן, *waters exist not.* אֵין יוֹסֵף בַּבּוֹר, *no (existence of) Joseph in the well*, Gen. xxxvii. 29. Whence it may be seen, that when this word comes last in the context, it will take the absolute form; when otherwise, it takes that proper for construction (Gram. art. 171. 3): and also, that the interrogative sense, implying a negation, will suit it. But this appears more clearly when another interrogative with a negation precedes; as, הַמִבְּלִי אֵין קְבָרִים בְּמִצְרַיִם, lit. *Is it not from* a non-existence *of graves in Egypt?* Exod. xiv. 11. See 1 Kings x. 21; 2 Kings i. 3, 6, 16. The word is otherwise indeclinable, and its tense may be considered as *present* to any time implied by the context. e. g. אֵין בָּאָרוֹן. *There is not* (i. e. at that time) *in the ark*, 1 Kings viii. 8. Constr. with pron. אֵינְךָ, *non-existence of thee*, i. e. thy not being; it. אֵינֵמוֹ, *their not*, Gen. xx. 7, with epenth.; אֵינֶנוּ, *its not, by no means*, &c. Gen. xxx. 33, &c.; אֵין לִי, *non est mihi*, i. e. *non habeo*, Levit. xi. 10, &c.; with prep. בְּאֵין, *in not being*, Prov. xi. 14, &c.; כְּאֵין, *like the not being*, i. e. *was very near being*, Ps. lxxiii. 2; לְאֵין, *to non-existence*, i. e. *to him who has not*, Is. xl. 29. Hence the ὅτι οὐκ εἰσί of the New Test., Matt. ii. 18, which is nevertheless found in classical Greek, Eurip. Hippol. 357; Alcest. 281; and Iliad, β. 641, as quoted by Dr. Gesenius. See Schleusn. sub voce εἰμί.

אֵיפָה, or אֵפָה, f. cogn. אָפַף, *circuivit*; Arab. أَف *paucitas*, q. d. circumscriptum quid. cogn. وفي *æquiponderavit*. *The ephah*, a dry measure so called, containing three seahs, or ten omers; somewhat more than three pecks. See Exod. xvi. 36; Lev. v. 11, &c. Equal to the bath in liquid measure, Ezek. xlv. 11; and according to Josephus, equal to the Attic *medimnus*, Arch. 15. 9. § 2. Also, meton. The vessel used in measuring this quantity, Zech. v. 6; Deut. xxv. 14, אֵיפָה וְאֵיפָה, *ephah and ephah*, i. e. diverse *measures*; rendered variously by the LXX., τρία μέτρα, οἰφεί, οἰφί, οἰφι, ὀφεί, ὀφί. Hence the German lexicographers have been led to suppose that the word is Egyptian, and this, the ⲡⲓⲱⲓⲡⲓ found in the Coptic translations of the Pentateuch, they believe confirms. But it is not improbable that both these present nothing more than the Hebrew word a little deformed. Nor will Dr. Gesenius's Coptic ⲱⲡⲓ (for ⲱⲡⲓ does not occur; the ⲱⲡⲓ, ⲡⲓ, of Lacroze exhibiting the noun with the article ⲡⲓ after it, for the purpose of shewing its

E

gender, not a different form of the root) *numerare*, mend the matter; to enumerate and to measure being two very distinct and different ideas. He also says " Unde חֻוִּי *mensura* dicta est." La Croze, however, gives no such word.

אֵיפֹה, *Where? How?* See under אֵי.

אֵפוֹא, id. See ib. Jud. ix. 38.

אִישׁ, m. אִשָּׁה f. for אֱנֹשׁ, אֱנֹשָׁה for אֲנָשִׁים, pl. אִישִׁים, Ps. cxli. 4; Prov. viii. 4, more usually אֲנָשִׁים, of אֱנוֹשׁ inusit. whence constr. אַנְשֵׁי, or by a periphrasis, בְּנֵי אִישׁ, *sons of man.* For אֵישׁ contr. Gram. art. 75; Arab. اِش, *agilis fuit*, cogn. اِیس, *robur;* Heb. אֲשִׁישׁ, *fundamentum* in Hithp. Heb. and Chald. *corroboratus*, &c. I. *A man of the higher or better sort,* ἀνήρ, *vir,* opposed to אָדָם, *man* generally, 1 Sam. xxvi. 15; 1 Kings ii. 2; Ps. iv. 3; xlix. 3. II. *A husband,* Gen. iii. 6; ib. vr. 16. III. Used distributively either for persons or things. *Each,* Judg. ix. 55; Zech. x. 1, Joel. ii. 7; וְאִישׁ, *one and another,* i. e. different persons, Ps. lxxxvii. 5, with אָח, עָמִית, or רֵעַ, *man and his brother,* &c., i. e. each of them, Gen. xi. 3. Even when speaking of inanimate things, Exod. xxv. 20; *One, any one,* 1 Sam. ix. 9. IV. Combined with either an abstract or concrete noun, will express a person possessed of the character implied by such accompanying word, as אִישׁ הַתֹּאַר, *a man of form,* i. e. handsome; 1 Sam. xvi. 8; אִישׁ שֵׂיבָה, *a man of age,* i. e. aged, Deut. xxxii. 23; אִישׁ שְׂפָתַיִם, *a garrulous man,* Job xi. 2, &c.; Exod. iv. 10; Ps. cxl. 12; Exod. xv. 3; Josh. xvii. 1; Jud. iii. 29; 2 Sam. xvi. 7, &c.; with aff. אִישִׁי, Gen. xxix. 32; אִישֵׁךְ, Gen. iii. 17; Num. v. 10, &c. See אִישׁ in its place. Hence v. in Hithp.

הִתְאוֹשֵׁשׁ, pl. הִתְאֹשָׁשׁוּ, *Become ye men,* i. e. stout, courageous, Is. xlvi. 8; comp. 1 Cor. xvi. 13.

אִישׁוֹן, m. dim. of אִישׁ, see gram. art. 168. *Homunculus, manikin,* signifying the small image of a person, as seen in the eye. So in the Arab. إِنْسَانُ الْعَيْنِ, *man of the eye,* or إِنْسَانُ بِنْتِ الْعَيْنِ, *a man, daughter of the eye.* By a meton. that part of the eye in which the image appears. I. *The pupil;* and generally, II. The *middle of any thing.* I. Adage. هُوَ أَعَزُّ عِنْدِي مِنْ بُؤْبُؤِ عَيْنِي, *He is more dear to me than the pupil of my eye;* constr. with עֵין; see Deut. xxxii. 10; Prov. vii. 2, with בַּת־עַיִן, Ps. xvii. 8; comp. Lam. ii. 18. II. אִישׁוֹן לַיְלָה, *the pupil, middle,* or *darkest point of night,* Prov. vii. 9; comp. xx. 20. So Arab. هُوَ فِي بُؤْبُؤِ الْمَجْدِ, *he is in the* (very) *pupil,* i. e. *midst of glory;* Greek, κόρη, κοράσιον, κορασίδιον, Lat. *pupa, pupula,* or *pupilla*.

אִישׁוּן, see אֲשׁוּן.

אִיתוֹן, m. *keri*, Ezek. xl. 15; sec. *kethiv.* יאתון; Targ. מְצִיעָתָא, *middle,* supposed to be for אֵתִין, from אָתָה, *to come in,* and hence translated *entrance.* But every gate or door is necessarily *an entrance;* besides, neither of these forms can be regularly derived from אָתָה; I prefer, therefore, taking אִית, Syr. ܐܺܝܬ, as the primitive, signifying *existence, essence;* hence ܐܺܝܬܝܳܐ *essential,* cogn. Heb. אֵיתָן *fortis, robustus, &c.,* to which אִיתוֹן is an equivalent form; הַשַּׁעַר הָאִיתוֹן will then be *Essential* or *principal gate.* The second form may be derived from the cogn. יאת, which will then signify *the beautiful gate,* and is perhaps the same with that mentioned Acts iii. 2.

אִיתַי, Chald. i. q. Syr. ܐܺܝܬ; cogn. Heb. יֵשׁ and אִישׁ; Arab. ایس: apparently a plural in constr. for אִיתֵי, q. d. *existences of,* used for the substantive verb in all its persons. אִיתַי גְּבַר, *there is a man,* Dan. v. 11; יָכִל... *he is ... able,* Dan. iii. 17; with pron. אִיתוֹהִי, *he is,* i. e. *his being;* אִיתָךְ, *thou art, &c.* אִיתֵיכוֹן *you are.* See the Chaldee and Syriac Grammars.

אֵיתָם, see v. חמם.

אֵיתָן, or אֵתָן, m. attrib. pl. אֵיתָנִים; Arab. أَیْن, *radicalis, firmus;* أُنْ, *idola;* comp. Is. i. 31; חָסֹן, *strong,* for idol: see אֵיל; cogn. وَن, *idolum;* أَون, *multus fuit, &c.; valida fuit, superstes fuit, res;* cogn. وَن, *perennis fuit:* i. e. אֵיתָן for אֵתָן, Gram. art. 158. I. *Mighty, irresistible, violent,* (men or things); *impregnable* (place); as an abstr. II. *Might, irresistibility,* Mich. vi. 2; Job xii. 19; Prov. xiii. 15. דֶּרֶךְ בֹּגְדִים אֵיתָן, *the way* (manner) *of the perfidious* (is) *violent,* i. e. as

אד (27) אכז

opposed to הֵן, in the preceding member. Job xxxiii. 19. נַחַל אֵיתָן, *an irresistible* stream or torrent, not *perpetual*, for these were occasionally dried up, Deut. xxi. 4; Ps. lxxiv. 15; Amos v. 24; which last I take to mean, *for judgment rolleth* (away) *as the waters* (roll away), *and righteousness* (disappears) *like the mighty torrent* (כְּנַחַל אֵיתָן). Or, taking יֻבָּל as the apocopated pres. of Niphhal, *is laid bare*, i. e., overcome and carried away, as a captive. It appears unnatural to take this verse in a sense antithetical to that of the context. יֶרַח הָאֵיתָנִים, *month of the powerful*, i. e. Tisri, 1 Kings viii. 2. Gesenius, Winer, &c., suppose נְחָלִים is to be supplied here, and that the swelling of the rivers is alluded to; but this cannot be true, because the "former rains" did not begin to fall before the next month. Kimchi, and some of his persuasion, suppose the month to have been so called, on account of the feast of Tabernacles, &c., in which the *heads* (powerful) of the Tribes were assembled. I believe this to be the better explanation. See also Jer. v. 15; xlix. 19; II. Gen. xlix. 24; Exod. xiv. 27.

אַךְ, part.; Arab. اك, *compressit, &c.;* وك, *trusio, impulsio*, i. e. אך, for אכך, *excluding, exclusion*; hence, *Only*, אך נחַ, *only Noah*, Gen. vii. 23. אַךְ הַפַּעַם, *only this occasion*, Exod. x. 17. אַךְ עֲשִׂירִי, *only make for me*, 1 Kings xvii. 13. אַךְ טָרֹף טֹרָף, *he is only* (i. e. nothing else has happened to him) *torn to pieces*, Gen. xliv. 28. אַךְ יָצֹא יָצָא, *he had only quite gone*, i. e. just gone, Gen. xxvii. 30. And so, always excluding every thing but the principal idea. See the examples in Noldius.

אָפוּת, 1st pers. sing. pres. Kal. v. כחת.

אַכְזָב, m. Arab. كذب *albedo*, i. e. nullo distinctus colore; hinc *munda, pura*, mulier, &c.; كذب *fefellit, irritus, vanusque fecit. Deficient, deceptive, unstable*, opp. to מְאֻמָּן, Jer. xv. 18; comp. Is. lviii. 11; Mic. i. 14. Words signifying *lying* in Hebrew, properly imply *deficiency*; comp. כחש, כדב, and Rom. iii. 7.

אַכְזָר, m. Arab. كدر *turbidus, turbida aquæ....vitæ, &c.; Untractable, cruel, fierce*, Job xxx. 21; xli. 2; Lam. iv. 3; Deut. xxxii. 33.

אַכְזָרִי, m. augm. of the preceding, opposed to רחם, Jer. vi. 23; Prov. xii. 10; מַלְאָךְ

אַכְזָרִי, *a very cruel angel*, i. e. to disturb and harass him, Prov. xvii. 11; comp. 2 Sam. xxiv. 16; 1 Chron. xxi. 12, 15; 2 Chron. xxxii. 21, &c.

אַכְזְרִיּוּת, f. of אַכְזָרִי, Gram. art. 87. 2, and 164; *Great cruelty*, i. e. a cruelly destroying state of mind, Prov. xxvii. 4.

אָכַל, m. אָכְלָה, f. Arab. اكل *comestio, erosio*, actively or passively, and in a good or bad sense, Gram. art. 146, 8. *Eating, an eating*, or *consuming*, Gen. xli. 35; Jer. xii. 9; נִתַּן לְאָכְלָה, *it hath been given up to consumption*, Ezek. xv. 4, &c. with aff. אָכְלִי, אָכְלָם, אָכְלָם, בְּכָלָם.

אֹכֵל, m. *an eater*, Jud. xiv. 14; Is. lv. 10; Nah. iii. 12.

אָכוֹל, or אָכֹל, i. q. אֲכֹל, Gen. ii. 16, &c. in constr. אֲכָל, Deut. xii. 23, *Eating, consuming*.

אֲכִילָה, f. *What is eaten, meat*, 1 Kings xix. 8.

אָכַל, v. pres. יֹאכַל, and יֹאכֵל. Either in a good or bad sense. I. *He ate*, hence *he subsisted*; meton. *feasted, enjoyed*. II. *He devoured, consumed*, or *destroyed*, spoken of men or things (particularly of the sword, which is hence said to have a mouth), and construed either absolutely or transitively, and with or without the intermediate particles אֵת and בְ. Hence the following phrases אָכַל לֶחֶם, *eating bread, feasting*, Gen. xliii. 32; Jer. xli. 1; comp. Matt. xv. 2. אָכַל אֵפֶר, *eating ashes*, i. e. living on that which is unprofitable and grievous, Ps. cii. 10; comp. Gen. iii. 14; and Is. lxv. 25; Mic. vii. 17. עָשָׂב תֹאכַל, spoken metaphorically of the Old Serpent, the Devil. אָכַל בָּשָׂר, *eating* or *consuming the flesh*; injuring any one, Ps. xxvii. 2; comp. Job xix. 22; Is. ix. 19; *the flesh of his own arm*, i. e. his own strength. Jer. xv. 16, נִמְצְאוּ דְבָרֶיךָ וָאֹכְלֵם, *thy words have been found* (by me), *and I have eaten them*, i. e. feasted on them; see the rest of the verse. Comp. Ezek. iii. 1, 3; Rev. x. 9—and my exposition on this last passage—and John iv. 32—34; also Job xxi. 25. In a bad sense, III. *Practising fornication*, delighting in the sin, Prov. xxx. 20. תֹּאכֵלֵהוּ, for תֹּאכֲלֵהוּ, usually הַאָכִלֵהוּ, not in Pihél, as some have thought, Gram. art. 86. 5; 199. 4.

Niph. נֶאֱכַל, *Is eaten, may be eaten*, Gen. vi. 21; Exod. xii. 16; Lev. xi. 47.

Puh. אֻכַּל, pres. יְאֻכַּל, *Devoured, consumed*, Exod. iii. 2; Neh. ii. 3; Is. i. 20.

Hiph. הֶאֱכִיל, *Gave, made*, or *caused, to eat*,

אכל (28) אכף

enjoy, devour, &c. Exod. xvi. 32; Ps. lxxx. 6; Is. lviii. 14; xlix. 26; Jer. xix. 9. Once הָכִיל for הַאֲכִיל, Gram. art. 199. 9, but this might be for הַכִיל, of the verb כול, in the sense of אכל, or יכל, as the root. See Ezek. xxi. 33. יֻכְלוּ in Ezek. xlii. 5, has been supposed to be the Hoph. of this verb. But this is also unlikely, as the sense would then be unsuitable to the passage. Dr. Gesenius has "*nam tigna s. columnæ detrahebant inde,*" i. e. as if they bit something off, which is not the Hophhal sense of אכל. I am inclined to think that it is only another way of writing יְכָלוּ, *they were* (the galleries) *completed, finished*, or *terminated* (by these מֵחֶיָה), i. e. chambers; so that the lower story projected out beyond the upper. In this case the verb will be the Hoph. of כָּלָה, not of אָכַל. The Arabic cogn. وكل, or يكل, יכל, *commisit, commendavit rem suam* alteri; *in ejus potestate reliquit fretus ipso.*—Castell. sub voce,—will supply a similar sense. This verb may be considered as in Kal. I doubt, too, whether אוֹכִיל is the 1st pers. sing. Hiph. of אכל. It might, indeed, of יכל. The context, Hos. xi. 4, rather requires that it should be a noun, as *food* or *sustenance*. See, in its place.

אֲכַל, pres. יֵאכֻל. Chald. i. q. Heb. Dan. iv. 30; vii. 5, 7, 19, 23. On the phrase אֲכַל קַרְצוֹהִי, Dan. iii. 8; vi. 25; see קרץ.

אַכֵּל, 1st per. sing. apoc. Pih. v. כלה.

אֲכַלֵּה, id. with aff.

אָכֵן, augm. of כֵּן, for אַכֵּן, r. כון. *aptare.* Syr. ܐܟܢ, *firmavit.* Arab. كون, τὸ εἶναι, or compd. of אַךְ and כֵּן, i. e. אָכֵּן, for אָכֵן. *Surely, certainly, most truly,* Gen. xxviii. 16; Exod. ii. 14; 1 Kings xi. 2, &c. See Noldius sub voce, who gives it more meanings than one, perhaps unnecessarily.

אָכֵף, with aff. אַכְפִּי (form כַּף etym. see) אָכַף, and cogn. כָּפַף) i. q. כַּף. *The palm of the hand,* and by meton. *the hand,* Job xxxiii. 7. Comp. ib. xiii. 21, LXX. ἡ χείρ μου; Targ. and Syr. give *oppositio,* and *onus.* See my Com. on the passage.

אָכַף, v. Arab. اكف *constrinxit,* cogn. كوف, and كَفَّ. Syr. ܐܟܦ, *sedulus fuit,* ܟܒ, *incurvatus.* Compels, bows (one) *down to,* Prov. xvi. 26. *For his mouth compels, or bows* (him), *to it;* i. e. the evil *conversation* (not hunger) of a bad man, forces him to submit to sorrowful labour. (See עָמָל, and compare the context.) So the Targumist, Syriac, and LXX. in the main.

אֶכַּף, 1st pers. sing. pres. Niph. v. כפף.

אִכָּר, m. Arab. اكّار, *fossor terra.* Syr. ܐܟܪ *agricola;* pl. אִכָּרִים, aff. אִכָּרֵיכֶם. *Ploughman* or *husbandman,* Jer. li. 23; Amos v. 16; joined with *vine-dressers,* 2 Chron. xxvi. 10.

אֶכְרָה, see v. כרה.

אַל, part. of prohibition, used much with the apocop. pres. Chald. אֱלֻּ, *exploravit,* or of אֱלָה, *imprecatio,* q. d. *absit!* Arab. إل, *jusjurandum.* Syr. ܐܠ, *deploravit. By no means; not at all.* Used, for the most part, with a pres. tense, occasionally with an imper. and once or twice with a pret., Gen. xxii. 12; *by no means put forth thy hand against the boy:* Exod. xvi. 29. אַל־תִּירָאוּ, *fear not at all,* Gen. xliii. 23. אַל־יִפֹּל דָּמִי, *let not my blood fall!* 1 Sam. xxvi. 20. אַל־אֲדוֹת, or, as some think the reading ought to be, אֶל־אֲדוֹת, or עַל־אֲדוֹת, but neither of these will afford a tolerable sense. Better perhaps thus; supplying the ellipses, and transposing the text into the order in which it is to be construed. (וַתְּהִי) לְשַׁלְּחֵנִי עַל־אֲדוֹת הַזֹּאת (תְּהִי) אַל לוֹ וַתֹּאמֶר הָרָעָה הַגְּדוֹלָה מֵאַחֶרֶת אֲשֶׁר עָשִׂיתָ עִמִּי, *So she says to him; Let not this be: because to send me* (away, so will be) *the evil greater than the other which thou hast done with me.* Or, allowing הַוָּאת, *to keep its place. Let it not* (be); *because this great evil,* (i. e.) *to send me away* (is greater) *than the other which thou hast done with me.* In either of these cases, both אַל and עַל is necessary to the sense; and, as some MSS. have either the one or the other here, על has been omitted inadvertently by the copyists, 2 Sam. xiii. 16. אַל־תּוֹתַר, *excel thou not,* Gen. xlix. 4, where a future circumstance is enounced by an imperative formula. See Gram. art. 239. וְיָשֶׂם לְאַל מִלָּתִי, *and will lay down my speech for* (a) "*by no means;*" i. e. a thing not to be regarded. This mode of speaking is common with the Orientals. See the first two or three sentences of the Anvári Soheili. Job xxiv. 25. אַל פְּשִׁיטְתַּם הַיּוֹם, *by no means make a rush* (or attack) *to-day,* 1 Sam. xxvii. 10; where we have an imperative enounced by the preterite sense. See Gram.

art. 236. 2. Occasionally with the precative particle נָא ; as, אַל־נָא, *by no means, I pray*, Gen. xiii. 8, &c.; whence it will be seen that this particle requires no more than one sense to suit it in every instance. See the examples in Noldius. Gesenius makes it a *negative* particle, like לֹא, &c. Gr. μή, &c. which is incorrect; the μή of the Greeks is plainly *prohibitive*.

אַל, Chald. i. q. Heb. Dan. ii. 24, &c.

אֵל, pl. אֵלִים see אַיִל.

אֵל, pron. pl. for אֵלֶּה, *These*. Gram. art. 176.

אֶל, followed by Makkáph אֶל־. Gram. art. 124. In connexion with the pronouns it takes the plural form of construction; as, 1st pers. אֵלַי, 2nd אֵלֶיךָ, 3d אֵלָיו, &c. אֲלֵיהֶם, אֲלֵיכֶם, &c. apparently from the form אֵלֶה in the first cases. In the second, אֵלַי, of the alternate form פָּקַד. Arab. وَلِيَ, *propinquitas*, v. وَلِيَ, *move towards, from*, &c. pres. يَلِي is *near, over against*: whence إِيَّال, infin. 4th conj. *making towards*, and contr. إِلَى, used as a prep. *usque, versus*. And, still further, contr. لِ, id. and Heb. לְ, prep.—*To, towards, as to, for, against, until*, with respect either to place, time, person, thing, &c., and hence, taking for granted that some such progress has been made, *Near, at, upon, in*, equivalent to עַל, for which it is often used in these senses. In either of these acceptations it is used after a great variety of verbs, as a mediating particle, Gram. art. 217. 5, 8, 9. 228. 4, 5, &c. noticed here under those verbs. Examples may be seen in Noldius: the few following are intended to shew, that there is no necessity for departing from the primitive sense of this particle as constantly done by Noldius and others.—

אֶל־ . . . , יִקָּווּ, *Let them be collected . . . TO*, Gen. i. 9. בָּאוּ מִצְרַיְמָה לִשְׁבֹּר אֶל־יוֹסֵף, *they came to Egypt to buy*, (they came) TO *Joseph*, Gen. xli. 57. This is therefore an instance of the *Epanorthosis*, Gram. art. 216. 4, note, and 241. 16—18; comp. Gen. xxxii. 7; 1 Sam. ii. 34; 1 Kings viii. 42, &c., not *à Josepho*, as Noldius has it. This would be to construe the particle with the verb to which it does not belong. וְנִרְאָה . . . אֶל־הַכֹּהֵן, *let him be seen by* (rather, *shewn to*) *the priest*, Lev.

xiii. 7, 19. הַקְּרוֹבִים וְהָרְחֹקִים אִישׁ אֶל־אָחִיו, *those who are near, and those who are afar off, each man*, AS TO (or with respect to) *his brother*, Jer. xxv. 26; Ezek. xliv. 7. וְאֶל־אָדָם לֹא אֲכַנֶּה, *and towards man* (men) *I use no* (flattering) *titles* (see v. כנה), Job xxxii. 21. אֶל־בְּאֵר הַמַּיִם, *at* (i. e. having come to) *a well of water*, Gen. xxiv. 11; comp. Exod. xxix. 12, &c. וַיָּקָם קַיִן אֶל־הֶבֶל, *and Cain arose* AS TO (i. e. *against*) *Abel*, Gen. iv. 8. לִזְנוֹת אֶל־, *to be whorishly inclined towards*,—Num. xxv. 1. וְשַׁבְתֶּם אֵלַי אֶל־נָכוֹן, *and return ye to me* (return ye) TO (what is) *right*, 1 Sam. xxiii. 23. נִשָּׂא לְבָבֵנוּ אֶל־כַּפַּיִם, *let us lift up our hearts* (in addition) TO *our hands to God*, Lam. iii. 41; Ezek. xlviii. 20, &c. אֶל־מֶלֶךְ אַשּׁוּר, AS TO *the king of Assyria*, 2 Kings xix. 32; Is. xix. 11, &c. אֶל־שַׁעַר הָעִיר, TO *the* (constr. preg. i. e. and beyond it) *of the city*, Deut. xxii. 24; Josh. viii. 29. יִתְעַצֵּב אֶל־לִבּוֹ, *he became pained to his heart*, Gen. vi. 6. וְאֶל־הָאָרֹן, *to* (or *in*) *the ark shalt thou place*, Exod. xxv. 21; Lam. ii. 12; Josh. v. 3; 2 Chron. xxxii. 6. Comp. εἰς, 2 Thess. ii. 4, with Dan. xi. 36, where the prep. is עַל, and my Sermons and Dissertations on Prophecy, &c., pp. 235—239; and Schleusner under εἰς and πρός. וַיִּדְקֹר . . . אֶל־קֳבָתָהּ, *so he pierced . . . into her womb*, Num. xxv. 8; where it may be remarked the same verb (וידקר) is construed with two different particles אֵת and אֶל, in the very same context. See Gram. art. 229. 9. See also Exod. xix. 9; Num. xxxvi. 13, &c. With other particles; as אֶל־מוּל, אֶל־מִבֵּית, אֶל־הֵנָּה, אֶל־בֵּין, אֶל־אַחֲרֵי, אֶל־תַּחַת, אֶל־עֵבֶר, אֶל־מִחוּץ, אֶל־מִ־, as in the Eng. *from-off, to-wards, after-wards*, and the like; in all which cases the latter particle qualifies the former, as any other qualifying term would. So also in the phrases, מֵחַיִל אֶל־חָיִל, *from strength to strength, i. e. from one degree*, or state of strength, to another, Ps. lxxxiv. 8; cxliv. 13; Jer. ix. 2; comp. Rom. i. 17, ἐκ πίστεως εἰς πίστιν, 2 Cor. iii. 18, ἀπὸ δόξης εἰς δόξαν. See also, as to time and place, 1 Chron. ix. 25; xvi. 23; Num. xxx. 15; Ezek. xl. 26, &c. See Noldius, p. 38, &c. I have in the above examples followed Noldius, to show that this particle has really only one meaning; and that, in the cases in which he has endeavoured to establish a variety of meanings, he has misconstrued the passages cited.

אֶלְגָּבִישׁ, m. *The hail*, as it appears from the context, Ezek. xiii. 11, 13; xxxviii. 22. The etymology is doubtful. The rabbins take it as a compound of אֵל, *powerful*, and גָּבִישׁ, *crystal*, i. e. mighty hailstone (Job xxviii. 18). Kimchi tells us, moreover, that it stood in some correct copies written as two words, in others as one. Dr. Gesenius thinks it is compounded of the Arabic article ال, and the word جِبْسٌ, because he finds in the Kāmoos, p. 743, الجِبْسُ given as signifying "*congelatum.*" But he has misunderstood his author, who has الجِبْسُ الجَامِدُ الثَّقِيلُ الرُّوحِ, i. e. *Eljibso, that which is hard* (or inanimate); *one affected with difficulty of breathing, &c.* So in Freytag's Hamasa p. 655, الجِبْسُ الثَّقِيلُ الجَافِي, i. e. *Eljibso, that which is heavy, injurious, &c.* Pareau, as cited by Gesenius, makes the Coptic ⲁⲗ *calculus*, the first component part, but this is unlikely. I am inclined to believe that the word is a compound of גָּבִישׁ as above, of Æth. ורהב *gypso induxit, dealbavit;* cogn. Arab. جبش, or جمش, *he smoothed, polished.* The former part of the compound, viz. אֵל, takes its form and sense probably from أَبَلَ *crassescere*, and then signifies *the aggregate of white or lucid stones*, i. e. *a hail-shower.*

אַלְגּוּמִּים, see אַלְמֻגִּים.

אָלָה, f. pl. constr. אָלוֹת: for אֵלָה, or אֵלָה, Gram. art. 73; Arab. ألا for الو *defecit, tardavit, et trans. decurtavit;* cogn. ولي iv. أُولِي *constrinxit;* الوة *juramentum.* Hence, حلف i. q. آلي يُولي إيلاءً *he swore*, and الأَلِيَّة i. q. اليمين, i. e. *An oath*, a formula couched in terms implying some mulct, damage, ban, or curse. Not from אֵל, as calling *God* to witness, as Dr. Gesenius imagines; this belongs to the verb נִשְׁבַּע or הִשְׁבִּיעַ, which see: and in this respect only, these words differ in sense. Properly, *The terms of damage, or execration, contained in an oath; a curse, execration,* or *imprecation,* and by a meton. *An oath*, Lev. v. 1. קוֹל אָלָה *the sound*, i. e. *words*, or *terms of an oath;* which, if required, and one did not declare,

he was guilty. 1 Kings viii. 31, אָלָה לְהַאֲלֹתוֹ, *the condition* or *terms of an oath to restrain him*, Neh. x. 30. בָּאִים בְּאָלָה וּבִשְׁבוּעָה, *(persons) coming into the terms of an oath* (as it regards an imprecation), *and into an oath* (as sworn by the certainty of the existence of God, Gram. art. 242. 4—10). In Kings, however, וּבָא אָלָה, l. c. is not equivalent to this phraseology in Neh., as Drs. Gesenius and Winer will have it. I have no doubt that אָלָה here is the verb, and the passage to mean, "*and he come* (and) *swear,* i. e. utter the terms of the oath, *before the altar.*" It is added, then hear thou, i. e. the terms so uttered, ib. נָשָׂא בוֹ אָלָה, *one lay upon him, recite the ban of an oath to him;* Deut. xxix. 13; Is. xxiv. 6; Jer. xxiii. 10. הָיָה לְאָלָה, *became for a curse* (Gram. art. 229. 3), Jer. xliv. 12. יִתֵּן לְאָלָה, *let him give up* (or out) *for a curse,* Num. v. 21. As this passage contains the other words used in imposing an oath, it will be worth while to notice it a little farther. *Then the priest shall swear the woman* (הִשְׁבִּיעַ), i. e. in God's name) *with the oath* (שְׁבֻעָה) thus administered) *of execration* (הָאָלָה, expressive of injury or damage), *and the priest shall say to the woman, May Jehovah give thee up* (or out). This refers to the שְׁבֻעָה just mentioned) *for an execration, imprecation* or *curse, and for an oath* (sanctioned by his name, i. e. that similar conduct shall assuredly be similarly visited) *among thy people*. 22. *Then shall these waters, conveying the ban of the curse* (הַמְאָרְרִים), this verb signifying, to do the injury so designated, or to declare that it shall be done. See root ארר), *enter into thy bowels, &c.* Hence Lam. iii. 65, הַאֲלָתְךָ, *thy curse.* See in its place.

אָלָה, v. no pres. *He made an imprecation, laid* (some one) *under a curse,* Jud. xvii. 2; infin. אָלֹה and אָלוֹת, Hos. iv. 2; אָלֹה וְכַחֵשׁ, *lay on an imprecation* (swearing), *and failing* (to perform its conditions); ib. x. 4, דִּבְּרוּ דְבָרִים אָלוֹת שָׁוְא, *they have spoken words, swearing* (or laying on an imprecation by that which is) *vanity,* i. e. which can impose no mulct.

Hiph. וַיֹּאֶל, apoc. pres. (perhaps of Kal), Gram. art. 233. 3, cogn. r. יאל, according to the points; but disregarding these, אלה,—*He swore, laid under a ban;* infin. הַאֲלוֹת, *to curse, &c.,* 1 Kings viii. 31; 2 Chron. vi. 22, Arab. آلي, *jusjurandum dedit.*

אָלָהּ, pl. אֵלִים, see אֵיל, or אֵל.

אֵלֶּה, pron. pl. *These*, com.

אֵלָה, f. The terebinth, or *pine tree* of the East, i. q. אֵלָה. See אֵיל or אֵל, and Hierob. Olavii Celsii, pt. i. pp. 34—57; Josh. xxiv. 26.

אֱלָהּ, m. Chald. *God, any god;* with the def. art. affixed אֱלָהָא, *God*, the true God, pl. אֱלָהִין, *gods*, def. אֱלָהַיָּא, Dan. iii. 25, בַּר־אֱלָהִין, *son of gods*, or rather Son of the great God, κατ᾽ ἐξοχήν. The Babylonians, holding the emanation system, supposed the fourth person, seen to be the first-born or agent produced by the Almighty, and by whom he had formed all things. He is termed Διὸς υἱὸς or Θεοῦ παῖς, by the Greek poets; occasionally Αὐδή, φάτις, or φάμα;* by the philosophers, who are followed by Philo, ὁ λόγος.† This was a mere corruption of the Scriptures, which represent the visible God, or Saviour, as a man, styling him occasionally the *Word*, and at other times speaking of his *outgoings* as being from eternity. With pref. לֶאֱלָהּ, Dan. ii. 19, and aff. בֵּאלָהֵהּ; ib. vi. 24; it. iii. 28; אֱלָהּ יִשְׂרָאֵל, Ezra v. 1; אֱלָהּ אֲבָהָתִי, Dan. ii. 23, &c.

אֲלוּ, Chald. i. q. עֲרוּ, which see; ל and ר, being of the same organ, are interchanged. *See, behold*, Dan. ii. 31, &c.

אִלּוּ, of אִם and לוּ; Arab. اِلَّو; Syr. ܐܠܘ, of اِن and لَو. *Otherwise, unless*, Eccles. vi. 6; Est. vii. 4.

אֱלוֹהַּ, m. אֱלֹהִים, pl. *God, any god.* Arab. اِلَه, for اِلَاه, with def. art. اَلْإِلَاه, contr. اَللّٰه, propr. *adoratio;* infin. iv. conj. of اَلَه, *coluit, adoravit:* cogn. اَلَهَ; by meton. *Object of worship.* Comp. פַּחַד, תְּהִלָּה. So Syr. ܣܓܶܕ, i. q. ܣܓܶܕ; v. ܣܓܶܕ, *deificavit*, &c. The ה, being *radical*, is retained in every case, as in גבה. "Ad imitationem Aramaïsmi formæ singularis usus est nonnisi in *sermone poetico* et in *sequiore Hebraïsmo*," &c., says Dr. Gesenius in his Thesaurus. It occurs, however, in Deut. xxxii. 15, 17. Are we to suppose that Moses has *imitated the Syrians* here, or that this exhibits a specimen of *modern Hebrew*? The word occurs, moreover, again and again in Job, who must have lived as early as the sons of Israel. See my Introduction to that book, § iii. Is it necessary also to suppose, that we have here nothing but *modern Hebrew?* אֱלוֹהַּ נֵכָר, *a strange god*, Dan. xi. 39; כָּל־אֱלוֹהַּ, *every god*, i. e. *any god;* ib. 37, אֱלוֹהַּ מָעֻזִּים, *god of fortifications*, ib. 38; spoken of the latter Roman heathen emperors, from Domitian perhaps to the death of Dioclesian. Of the first, Eutropius says, "*Dominum se et Deum primus appellari jussit: nullam sibi nisi auream et argenteam statuam in Capitolio poni passus est; superbia quoque in eo execrabilis fuit.*" Of the last, "*Diocletianus moratus callidè fuit, sagax præterea, et admodum subtilis ingenio, et qui severitatem suam alienâ invidiâ vellet explere, diligentissimus tamen et solertissimus princeps; et qui in imperio Romano primus regiæ consuetudinis formam, magis quam Romanæ libertatis, invexit; adorarique se jussit, cum ante eum cuncti salutarentur.*" See also Suidas sub voce Διοκλητιανός, and 2 Thess. ii. 3—11. Modestius, too, tells us that the first cohort in the Roman armies carried, with the eagles, images of the emperors, which the soldiers worshipped.*

The pl. אֱלֹהִים, used for the *True God*, has given rise to various speculations; some supposing, particularly the elder divines and Hutchinsonians, that the notion of a Trinity in Unity lay concealed in this word; others, again, particularly the Rationalists of modern Germany, have thought that vestiges of a very ancient polytheism were discoverable in it.† Both seem, in this case, to have taken too much for granted, viz., that the ancients were guided in their writings by the technical rules of modern grammarians; and also that they were complete metaphysicians: neither of which can be maintained; hence both are probably false. On the former, see Gram. art. 215. 6, 216, &c. The latter needs no refutation. The Rationalists, too, suppose that, from the occurrence of this word in

---

* Sophocl. Œdip. Tyr. 151, 162. See also Schol.

† It is quite impossible, as some of the early fathers of the Church clearly saw, to give any reasonable account of these things which does not originate in the declarations of Holy Writ. Euseb. Prep. Evang. lib. vii. Justin Martyr to the Greeks. Cyril. Alexand. contra Julian. lib. i. Lactantius De Vera et Falsa Sapientia, &c. &c.

---

* Modestius de Vocab. Militar. in the edit. of 1613 of Ælian's Tactics.

† So think Dr. Gesenius, Ewald, &c. The plural form seems intended to intimate excellence. See Gram. art. 223. 3.

אֵלִי (32) אֵלִי

conjunction with, or separated from, that of יְהֹוָה, they can ascertain the fact that the book of Genesis was originally composed out of two or more documents: one containing the one word, another the other, &c. Gesenius has applied this theory to the book of Psalms also; and has actually ascertained that, in some instances, the one word occurs more frequently than the other! See his Thesaurus sub voce. This theory, as applied to Genesis, must necessarily be false, for we are expressly informed, Exod. vi. 2, 3, (see also my Prolegomena to Mr. Bagster's Poly. Bib. Prol. i. § iii. par. ii.) that the word יְהֹוָה was unknown to the patriarchs: and the probability is, that if this book is really patriarchal, which I believe to be the case, the introduction of this word must have been the work of Moses, its authorised editor. In all the other cases, the inquiry can afford no useful result.—When defined, either by the article (הָאֱלֹהִים), or the context, mostly The true God, Gen. i. 1; Deut. vii. 9; 1 Kings xviii. 21, &c.: but not universally so with the article, Exod. xviii. 11.

It has been supposed occasionally to signify Angels,* but there is no real necessity for this. Ps. viii. 6, וַתְּחַסְּרֵהוּ מְּעַט מֵאֱלֹהִים, which the LXX. and St. Paul, Heb. ii. 7, take thus: Ἠλάττωσας αὐτόν βραχύ τι παρ' ἀγγέλους, i. e. thou hast lowered him, in some degree, as it respects the angels, is applicable to Christ, and manifestly relates to his sufferings on earth. "The angels" here, are probably those who only sustained the messages, and spoke in the words, of Jehovah, Acts vii. 53; Gal. iii. 19. St. Paul then comments only here. In Ps. lxxxii. 1, אֱלֹהִים, God hath been (i. e. surely shall be) set up in the congregation of the mighty one, (אֵל, God): in the midst of gods (inferior deities) doth he give judgment,—is manifestly a prophecy relating to the victories of Christianity. Ib. vr. 6, I have said ye are gods (אֱלֹהִים, rather, supply בְּנֵי from the next hemistich, and read God's, i. e. children), and sons of the Most High are ye

all; i. e. I have declared that this is your proper designation, comp. Gen. vi. 2; Job i. 6: it is added, but as Adam ye die, i. e. ye fall by your heathenish sins. Ps. xcvii. 7, worship him all gods (כָּל־אֱלֹהִים), i. e. all ye heathen deities, fall down before him,—by a personification), is clearly a prediction of the victories of Christ. See also Ps. cxxxviii. 1. It is not necessary, therefore, to suppose with Gesenius, that בְּנֵי אֱלֹהִים (Ps. lxxxii. 1, 6), must mean kings. Nor is it true that خُدَا, in Persian, signifies "Dominus," in the sense of rex or princeps; nor that خُدَا and خُدَاوَنْد are equivalent in this respect: this notion must have grown out of a want of knowledge of Persian usage.

Nor does the word אֱלֹהִים, signify judges or magistrates, in Exod. xxi. 6; xxii. 7, 8, &c. Comp. Deut. xix. 17, where לִפְנֵי יְהֹוָה, before Jehovah, is followed by לִפְנֵי הַכֹּהֲנִים וְהַשֹּׁפְטִים, before the priests and judges; who all assembled before God, from Him to receive, and for Him to pronounce, the judgment.

In the instances in which a negative is used with this word, its primitive and proper sense seems to suit the context best, as 2 Kings xix. 18. לֹא אֱלֹהִים הֵמָּה, no objects of worship are they. Comp. Is. xliv. 6; xlv. 5, &c.

It is occasionally used (like אֵל) to form phrases expressive of goodness, plenty, or greatness; as הַר־הָאֱלֹהִים, mountain of God, i. e. of great plenty, Ps. lxviii. 16; comp. Ps. xxxvi. 7. כְּהַרְרֵי אֵל, as the hills of God, i. e. abundant, see the context. So Ps. lxv. 10, פֶּלֶג אֱלֹהִים, God's river, i. e. מָלֵא מָיִם, full of water, comp. Exod. iii. 1. חִתַּת אֱלֹהִים, the fear of God, i. e. great fear, Gen. xxxv. 5, see ib. xxx. 8; 1 Sam. xiv. 15; Ps. lxxx. 11; Job vi. 4. לֵאלֹהִים, Jon. iii. 3, עִיר־גְּדוֹלָה לֵאלֹהִים, a great city of God, i. e. God allowing it to be so, as in לְאֵל, of God (is) the hand, or power, sub voce אֵל, comp. לַיהוָה, Jud. xvii. 2.

So the Arabs, لِلَّهِ مَا فِي ٱلسَّمَوَاتِ, God's (is) what (is) in the heavens; لِلَّهِ دَرَّكَ, God's (is) thy good fortune, i. e. it is of God. So also Acts vii. 20, ἀστεῖος τῷ Θεῷ, comp. 2 Cor. x. 4. On the same analogy, אִישׁ אֱלֹהִים,* &c., בְּנֵי אֱלֹהִים, בֶּן אֱלֹהִים, where the context

---

* The Jewish commentators and translators of the Scriptures, as well as their Samaritan neighbours, filled as they were with metaphysical notions of the Deity, (which Dr. Gesenius terms puriores) have constantly had recourse to this interpretation, whenever the appearance of God was mentioned in the Scriptures. The way in which they have managed Gen. iii. 22, will be seen in my Proleg. to Mr. Bagster's Polyg. Bible, Prol. ii. § 3. par. xi.

* Winer, in his edition of Simonis, makes these expressions equal to King of Israel, in a secular sense. He then cites Ps. ii. 7; lxxxii. 6; lxxxix. 27, to be comp. with 2 Sam. vii. 14,

אלו (33) אלה

must determine the theological sense. With prefixes and affixes, בֵּאלֹהִים, לֵאלֹהִים, לֵאלֹהַּ, &c., contr. Gram. art. 87. 5. אֱלֹהַי, אֱלֹהֶיךָ, &c.: constr. אֱלֹהֵי. In app. אֱלֹהִים אֱמֶת, God, truth, i. e. *the source of truth*, for *true God*, i. q. אֱלֹהֵי אֱמֶת, 2 Chron. xv. 3; Jer. x. 10. So אֱלֹהִים חַיִּים, ib. Gram. art. 219; it. אֱלֹהֵי יִשְׂרָאֵל, *God of Israel*; אֱלֹהֵי יַעֲקֹב, *God of Jacob*, &c.

אֱלוּל, m. The sixth ecclesiastical month of the Hebrew year, answering nearly to our September, Neh. vi. 15. See Scaliger de Emendatione Temporum, pp. 121, 625; Reland Antiq. Heb. Pars. iv. &c.

אֵלוֹן, see אֵל or אֵלָה. *The pine tree*; Gesenius, *the oak*, Thes. p. 50, 51; Gen. xii. 6, &c.

אַלּוֹן, m. *The oak*, Gen. xxxv. 8. אַלּוֹנִים, pl. Ezek. xxvii. 6. Hierob. Olav. Celssii, i. p. 58, &c.

אַלּוּף, m. pl. אַלּוּפִים. Arab. اَلِفَ *socius consuetudine junctus;* hence اَلْف *a thousand, &c.* verb, اَلَّفَ *he gave a thousand, &c.; conjunxit, sociavit, mansuefactus fuit;* اَلِيف *familiaris socius;* اَلُوف *consuetus, &c.;* cogn. علف, Syr. ܚܢܟ *didicit, &c.* I. *Any person, or thing, to which one is accustomed or rendered familiar;* thence *agreeable,* Jer. xi. 19. וַאֲנִי כְּכֶבֶשׂ אַלּוּף, *but I* (am) *like a gentle lamb,* see Bochart. Hieroz. tom. i. lib. ii. cap. xlvi. Ps. lv. 14, אַלּוּפִי וּמְיֻדָּעִי, *my familiar and known* (friend). Mic. vii. 5, *Trust not in a familiar,* מֵאַלּוּף, comp. רֵעַ in the corresponding member of the parallel. Zech. ix. 7, *and he shall be as a familiar* friend, כְּאַלֻּף, *with Judah*, i. e. when God shall have overcome him, as the former part of the verse declares. Jer. xiii. 21, *what wilt thou say when he* (i. e. some one) *shall appoint* (them) *for a head* (לְרֹאשׁ) *over thee; since thou hast schooled them* (only to serve as) *familiars for thyself?* i. e. when God shall bring upon thee the Babylonians, whom thou hast endeavoured to make thy friends. Hence *A spouse,* Prov. ii. 17; Jer. iii. 4, comp. ver. 20.

---

and with the heathenish διογενής, διοτρεφής βασιλεύς, in Hom. This is in the true spirit of Rationalism. See my Sermons and Dissertations, Diss. i. part. ii. When nothing can be more clear from the context than that Christ's spiritual kingdom is meant.

II. *Confided in* (see נְשׂוּא פָנִים, קְרִיאֵי), because known to be trustworthy: hence, *A head, leader,* like the صَاحِب, of the Arabs, see Jer. xiii. 21, where this connexion is playfully recognised. Ps. cxliv. 14, אַלּוּפֵינוּ מְסֻבָּלִים, *our leaders honoured; no schism, no defection* (out-going lit.), *and no crying out in our squares* (market, or other open places). I take מְסֻבָּלִים here, to be equivalent to נִכְבָּדִים, Ps. cxlix. 8, &c., or to מְכֻבָּדִים, did it occur. The word is nowhere applied to beasts, but always to men (and certainly men are referred to, and not *beasts,* in the latter part of this verse), and seems occasionally to refer to posts of honour. See 2 Chron. xxxiv. 13, where סַבָּלִים is joined with מְנַצְּחִים; and, in 1 Kings xi. 28, Jeroboam was appointed לְכָל־סֵבֶל, *over the whole charge* (tax or revenue perhaps) *of the house of Joseph.* He might, therefore, here be styled מְסֻבָּל, i. e. the person so charged or placed in office, comp. Is. xli. 19, מְשֻׁלָּם, with ib. vi. 7. So φόρος, vectigal, a φέρω; com. and super. φέρτερος, φέρτατος, potentior, excellentior, &c. Τέλος vectigal, et dignitas, qualis est ejus qui magistratu fungitur. Steph. Thes. See Gen. xxxvi. 15, 16, &c.; and Zech. xii. 5, 6, where *leaders* or *magistrates* seem to be meant.

אלח, v. Niph. נֶאֱלָח, *Corrupt, base;* Arab. اِنْتَنَ, *in acrorem versum fuit lac.* See Gram. art. 157. 16, note. Applied only in a moral sense, and perhaps nearly equivalent to נִתְעָב. See Job xv. 16; Ps. xiv. 3; liii. 4. Comp. בַּל.

אַלְיָה, f. Arab. اَلْي, *beneficium.* اَلْيَة, *cauda ovis, vel arietis pinguis et adiposa. The tail of the sheep of the East,* which is large and fat, weighing, as Golius says, from ten to forty pounds weight. It is fixed, during the life of the animal, upon a sort of little waggon to preserve it from injury. The fat when melted is used to lay up preserves, as lard is with us, or to make into candles, Exod. xxix. 22; Lev. iii. 9; vii. 3; viii. 25; ix. 19. See Bochart. Hieroz. tom. i. p. 494, &c., and Dr. Russell's Hist. of Aleppo, p. 51, where every thing necessary to be known on this subject will be found. Plates representing this little waggon will be found in Ludolf's Com. Hist. Æthiop., Jahn's Biblische Archäologie, Calmet's Dict. of the Bible, by Taylor.

אֱלִיל, m. pl. אֱלִילִים, Arab. اَلَّ, *cito ivit;*

אלל (34) נאל

אָלַל, *fœtore corruptus fuit;* أَلِيل, *gemitus, sonus fluentis aquæ.* Syr. اجْمَلْ *debilis, Any thing unstable, perishing, and worthless,* particularly *idols,* Ps. xcvi. 5; 1 Chron. xvi. 26. אֱלִילֵי כַסְפּוֹ, *vain things,* lit. *idols* (of) *his silver,* Is. ii. 20; xxxi. 7, &c. רֹפְאֵי אֱלִל, *healers of a perishing thing, or man,* i. e. you are throwing away your labour. An adage, apparently, Job xiii. 4. רֹעִי הָאֱלִיל, *shepherd,* or feeder, *of that which is vain,* Zech. xi. 17.—So, *mortuis mederi: aquam infundere cineri,* Adag. Erasmi, p. 477.

אַלְלַי, interj. lit. *My woes!* Arab. أَلِ, *gemuit;* cogn. ילל.—אַלְלַי לִי, *woe to me, or woe is mine,* Job x. 15; Mic. vii. 1.

אִלֵּין, or אִלֵּן, Chald. pron. pl. com. *These,* Dan. ii. 44; vi. 7.

אִלֵּךְ, id. Chald. *Those,* Dan. iii. 12, 13.

אָלַם, m. in the Arab. the sense is only a secondary one. أَلِمَ, *dolor,* like חֶבֶל, *dolor,* from חָבַל, *funis;* pain being supposed to result from constriction or narrowness of circumstances; hence צור and רחב כלא and פלט, צרה and ישע, Arab. وَسِعَ, are constantly opposed to each other. *The being dumb, silent;* hence, *silence,* Ps. lviii. 2. הַאֻמְנָם אֵלֶם צֶדֶק תְּדַבֵּרוּן, *is there truly silence?* i. e. is there an entire silence? *speak ye truth, &c.* This I think is the exact force of this passage, although it militates against the construction suggested by the accents, which is to this effect—*Is it true;* i. e. really so, (that) *justice* (is) *silence* (i. e. silent)? *speak ye, &c.* In either of which the paragogic ן, in the verb, has the force of an imperative. See Gram. art. 235, &c. The word occurs only once more, Ps. lvi. 1, עַל־יוֹנַת אֵלֶם רְחֹקִים, which may be translated, " *on the dove of silence of distant*" (ones) : and hence, the Psalm may perhaps be referred to the pain experienced by David at the court of the king of Gath, (see 1 Sam. xxi. 11), as the occasion which suggested it. I believe, too, that the word יוֹנָה, *dove,* notwithstanding Bochart's authority to the contrary (tom. ii. Hieroz. p. i. &c.) is expressive of the *murmuring* or *complaining tone* of this bird, derived from יה, or cogn. אנה, *doluit, &c.* We have a similar heading to Ps. xxii. viz. עַל־אַיֶּלֶת הַשַּׁחַר, i. e. *on the gazelle of the dawn.* That this psalm refers to the sufferings of our Lord is beyond doubt.

In the Song of Solomon, the Beloved, i. e. Christ, is assimilated to the *zebi* or *gazelle,* chap. ii. 8, 9. The term *dawn* (הַשַּׁחַר) probably refers to the eternity of his existence. See Ps. cx. 3. Comp. Is. xli. 2; xliii. 13; Mic. v. 1; Prov. viii. 22 et seq.—In these cases, the titles seem to designate the nature of the context; and, in the last, the allusion is mystical. It is worth remarking, that the Persians have a sort of ode which they term the *gazel* (غَزَل), and a species of composition styled سَجَع, which signifies " *the cooing of doves:*" another, مُسَجَّع, lit, *dove-cooed:* to which some others may be added of a similar description : some of which might have been derived from a very high antiquity, and others fabricated to suit the whims of modern Orientals; such, perhaps, are the رُقْتَا, *rukta, a species of sheep of a grey colour;* and خُيَفَا, *khyfa, a horse, one eye of which is black, the other blue.* See Gladwin's Dissertations on the Rhetoric and Prosody of the Persians, pp. 2, 18, 28, &c.

נֶאֱלַם, v. Niph. *Became* or *remained silent,* Is. liii. 7; Ezek. iii. 26; xxxiii. 22; xxiv. 27; Ps. xxxi. 19; xxxix. 3; Dan. x. 15.

Pih. part. act. מְאַלְּמִים, *Persons binding up;* אֲלֻמִּים (for אֲלוּמִים) *things bound;* i. e. *bundles,* sheaves of corn, or the like, Gen. xxxvii. 7.

אִלֵּם, m. אִלְּמִים, pl. *Dumb* person, i. e. *tongue-bound,* Exod. iv. 11; Ps. xxxviii. 14; Is. xxxv. 6; lvi. 10.

אֻלָם, see אוּלָם.

אַלְמֻגִּים, m. pl. i. q. אַלְגוּמִּים, metath. The word is apparently foreign, and occurs only in 1 Kings x. 11, 12; 2 Chron. ii. 7; ix. 10, 11. It is, perhaps, the Sanscrit अगम: *ăgămah, a tree;* and, as the Hebrews have no short syllables in their language (Gram. art. 31, note), the ל may have been introduced, just as the ר is in דַּרְמֶשֶׂק (Arab. دِمَشْق) for the purpose of obviating this difficulty.* If this be true, the Hebrews, ignorant of the

---

* In all such cases, as the liquid readily blends itself with the preceding vowel, the short vowel may now be considered equivalent to a long, or perfect one. Hence the implied dagesh in all such instances as בֶּרֶךְ, for בֶּרְךְ.

אלם (35) אלם

real meaning of this word, took it to signify a certain sort of *precious wood* brought from Ophir; just, perhaps, as the Roman soldiers, and after them many learned men, supposed *Ur*, to be the name of a place, when it signified *a castle* only. (See אוּר כַּשְׂדִּים). If then the Ophir from which this wood, together with certain precious stones, was brought, was Ceylon, as Bochart seems to have shown (Canaan, lib. i. xlvi.); let us see whether we can find any such wood there. Ibn Batūta (my Translation p. 184) tells us, that " the whole of its (the region of Battāla) shore abounded with *cinnamon wood, bakam*, and the *kalanji aloe* (العود الكلنجي).... The merchants of Malabar and of the Maabar districts, transport it without any other price than a few articles of clothing, &c." These precious woods, therefore, were in great plenty, were cheap, and were transported accordingly in great abundance by the merchants. That precious stones, particularly the *ruby*, abounded in Ceylon, the same author attests p. 187, and that pearls abounded in the pearl-fisheries. If, then, Solomon and Hiram's merchants traded to this place, they would readily obtain these articles in exchange for others. Now we are told (1 Kings x. 12) that the king made out of this wood, whatever it was, מִסְעָד לְבֵית יְהֹוָה, וּלְבֵית הַמֶּלֶךְ וְכִנֹּרוֹת וּנְבָלִים לַשָּׁרִים, A MISHAD, or *support, &c., for the house of Jehovah, and for the king's house, also lyres and nablia for the singers.* This is given again in 2 Chron. ix. 11, except that instead of מִסְעָד, we have מְסִלּוֹת, which, in other places, seems to signify *a way thrown up*, or made artificially. In Ps. lxxxiv. 6, it seems equivalent to מְסִלָּה, in the sense of *support*, or *supporter*. The first is rendered ὑποστηρίγματα by the LXX., the second by ἀναβάσεις. The first, the Syriac renders by ܨܒܬܐ, *ornament*, the Targumist by סָעִיד, *fulcimentum;* the second by מַסְקְלָן, *seats, or benches;* and כְּבֵשַׁיָּא לְסָעֵיד, *steps to ascend;* but, with no claim to probability, can either of them be rendered *pillars.* Our auth. version gives *terraces* for the second. If then, we are here to understand benches, brackets, terraces, or something similar, we need not suppose the timber to have been very large which was brought from the East; for this sort of wood very rarely grows large, but is very hard, and admirable for constructing brackets, or other furniture, such as would be wanted in the temple and the palace.

In the next place, *lyres* and *nablia* are also made out of this wood, on account perhaps of its hard, and hence sonorous, quality. We have seen above, that the *kalanji aloe* (عُود), was one of the precious woods found in Ceylon. We now remark, that the Eastern lyre is,—because perhaps made of this sort of wood,—termed the عُود, ŪD, the very word which designates the wood in question! And the author of the Kamoos tells us, that *it is the name of a stringed instrument, the player upon which is termed* عَوَّاد, *awwād.* His words are, وآلة من المعازف وضاربها عَوَّاد. In the King of Oude's Persian Dictionary, too, we are told that it is the name of a certain musical instrument, ونام سازی هم هست. In Mininski, under عُود, we have the following remarkable play upon the word, which serves to shew that its scent as a perfume, no less than its tone as an instrument of music, is considered a great luxury in the East: اول مجلس نشاط وسرور نغمهٔ عود ايله وبوی عود, *that assembly delightful and joyful with the music of the* ŪD, *and with the scent of the aloe.* The Medical Dictionary of Ibn El Hosein of Bagdad gives a very detailed account of the عود, and of its several species and properties. The following will suffice for our purpose. عود انجوج ویلنجوج نیز کویند وان انواعست وشیخ الرئیس کوید نیکوترین عود صندلی بود که از وسط بلاد هند می آرند وبعد از آن عود هندی که آن جبلی بود وفاضلتر از صندلی بود از بهر آنکه شپش در جامه رها کند وبعضی از مردمان فرق میان صندلی وهندی نکنند وبك نوع سمندوری بود و آن از سفالهٔ هند خیزد وان فاضلترین بود بعد از آن قماری وان نوعی از سفالی وبعد از ان قاقلی وبری That is, ŪD *is also named* ANJŪJ *and* YA-LANJŪJ, *and it is of various sorts.* Sheikh

El Rais (i. e. Avicenna) *says, the best of the* ūD *is that sort of sandal-wood, which they bring from the middle regions of Hindustan; after that comes the mountain* ūD, *which is still better than the Mandalī, because it will drive away the moths from clothes. Some make no difference between the Mandalī and Hindī* ūD. *Another species is the Samandūrī, which is brought from the Safāla of India; it is the best. After this comes the Komāri, which is a species of the Safālī. After this comes the Kākulī and the wild* ūD." Whence it appears, that there are several sorts of this wood, and that of these *the sandal-wood* of Hindustan is one of the best. He goes on to say, واین مولف کوید بهترین عود عودیست که آنرا کلمک خوانند وآن از بندر چته خیزد ۰۰ وآن بغایت عزیز الوجود است وبهم سنك وزر فروشند *And the author says, the best* ūD *is that which they name* KALMAK (Is not this our אַלְמֻגִּי?), *and this is brought from the port of Chata ... It is extremely precious, and sells for its weight in gold.* And again, در منطاي جنسي است که آنرا اشبا کویند وآن دو نوع بود ۰۰۰۰۰۰ وبسیار خوشبوي نبود اما از براي زینتها شاید از آلات مجلس وشانه وشطرنج ودستهاي کارد وغیره *Among the Mantai there is a sort which they call Ashbā, and this is of two kinds ... It is not very sweet-scented, but is proper for* (making) *ornaments, such as instruments* (or furniture) *for sitting-parlours, combs, chess-boards, knife-handles, &c.* Here, then, we have a species of this wood converted, apparently, to the very purposes for which Solomon purchased his; which must amount to little short of demonstration, that a species of the ūD (عود) was the wood used by Solomon; but whether it was the *sandal wood* of India, or the Kalanji אַלְ of Ceylon, &c. it is impossible to determine; but, that it is one or other species of this wood, I think there can be no doubt.

In 2 Chron. ii. 7, Solomon desires that these trees be sent him, with others from Lebanon; whence some have imagined, that they must all have grown there. This does not follow from the context: the request only being to send timber, the algum, which might have been at Tyre and Zidon for sale, with other timber, the produce of Lebanon. The Arabs, indeed, attest that the sandal grows in Syria (Hierob. Cels. pt. i. p. 182); but to this Accosta gives a flat denial. See the whole of this article by Celsius. The term πεύκινα *pitchy* or *gummy*, used here by the LXX., may perhaps be accounted for from the circumstance, that the gum obtained from some of the trees of this species, is used as incense to perfume apartments like the frankincense.

אֲלֻמָּה, f. for אֲלוּמָּה, pl. אֲלֻמּוֹת, *Any thing bound up; a bundle, sheaf*, Gen. xxxvii. 7; Ps. cxxvi. 6.

אַלְמָן, m. אַלְמָנָה, f. r. אָלַם, aug. ן, Gram. art. 168. pl. אַלְמָנוֹת: with aff. אַלְמְנֹתָיו, אַלְמְנוֹתָיו, &c., *A widower*, or f. a *widow*, Jer. li. 5, לֹא אַלְמָן יִשְׂרָאֵל—מֵאֱלֹהָיו, *Israel is not* (left) *as a widower by his God .... for their land is filled* (with) *sin*, i. e. he is not systematically forsaken; his sins are the cause of his chastisement. So Rom. xi. 1—13; 2 Sam. xiv. 5. אִשָּׁה אַלְמָנָה אָנִי וַיָּמָת אִישִׁי, *a widow woman am I, for my husband is dead*, Gen. xxxviii. 11; Exod. xxii. 21, &c. Cities and people are often personified by the figure of a woman, as in our Britannia. So Babylon, Is. xlvii., is represented as one who should be *no widow*. So in the Rev. chap. xvii. 1—8, Babylon is represented as the great whore, sitting upon many waters: by which is evidently meant heathen Rome; and accordingly, in Vaillant's Book of Coins, p. 30, we have the figure of a woman sitting upon the seven hills of Rome, with a wolf at her feet, and two babies, representing Romulus and Remus, its founders. The coin was struck in the reign of Vespasian, had probably been seen by St. John, and perhaps induced him thus to designate the last of the four great kingdoms, which was to make war upon the church. See my Exposition of the Rev., p. 335, &c. In Ezek. xix. 7, this word is used for אַרְמְנוֹתָיו, the letters ר and ל, of the same organ being interchanged. Some MSS. have the latter reading.

אַלְמֹן, m. aug. Gram. art. 168, *Widowhood*, Is. xlvii. 9.

אַלְמָנוּת, f. i. q. אַלְמֹן, aug. Gram. 87. 2; 2 Sam. xx. 3, &c., with aff. אַלְמְנוּתָהּ, אַלְמְנוּתֵךְ, Gen. xxxviii. 14; Is. liv. 4.

אַלְמֹנִי, m. aug. of י + אַלְמֹן, Gram. art. 166. *An undefined*, or *nondescript person, somebody;* of אָלַם: always occurring with פְּלֹנִי,

אלן (37) אלק

which see, 1 Sam. xxi. 3; 2 Kings vi. 8; Ruth iv. 1.

אִלֵּין, pron. Chald. see אֵלֶּין. *Those.*

אלף, v. pres. יֶאֱלַף, Etym. See אלוף, Col*lect, receive, become familiar with.* Hence, I. *Learn,* Prov. xxii. 25.

Pih. II. *Teach,* Job xxxv. 11 ; מַלְּפֵנוּ, for מְאַלְּפֵנוּ, Gram. artt. 72, 73, *He who teaches, teacher;* יְאַלֵּף, *renders familiar,* Job xv. 5 ; אֲאַלֶּפְךָ, *I will render familiar, teach,* ib. xxxiii. 33.

Hiph. מַאֲלִיפוֹת, III. *Producing thousands,* from the numeral אֶלֶף, *a thousand,* Ps. cxliv. 13.

אֶלֶף, m. du. אֲלָפַיִם, pl. אֲלָפִים; constr. אַלְפֵי, Etym. See אלף. *Aggregation;* hence *any great indefinite number.* Deut. i. 11 ; vii. 9 ; xxxii. 30, &c. So also Rev. xx. 2, with my Exposition, pp. 339, 361—365. Numeral, *A thousand,* Gen. xx. 16 ; Num. i. 21, &c. *A large military division of the people,* made by God's appointment when the Israelites left Egypt, Num. i. 2, &c. where we find that they were numbered, and a chief appointed over a whole tribe. He was termed רֹאשׁ אַלְפֵי, *a head of thousands,* and pl. רָאשֵׁי אַלְפֵי יִשְׂרָאֵל. Those who presided over a single thousand seem to have been termed שָׂרֵי הָאֲלָפִים, *princes of thousands;* those over hundreds, שָׂרֵי הַמֵּאוֹת, *princes of hundreds,* Num. xxxi. 14 ; 1 Sam. xvii. 18. *Captains of fifties* existed in the times of the kings, 2 Kings i. 9, 11, and probably in the days of Moses. Thus the word אֶלֶף, was probably applied *indefinitely,* as Ps. L. 10; xc. 4, &c.; or to signify *a tribe* or *family* only, Jud. vi. 15 ; 1 Sam. x. 19; xxiii. 23; Micah v. 1. So the Arab. عَشَر, عَشِيرَة, and مَعْشَر, from the numeral عَشَر, *ten;* and, as a verb, *decimavit;* in iii. conj. *consuevit, consortio junctus fuit,* &c.— This word will either precede or follow that signifying the thing numbered, as the intention of the writer, and the general rules of the syntax may require. See 2 Kings xxiv. 16; xv. 19; and Gram. artt. 181, 226, 227.

אֶלֶף, or אֲלַף, pl. אַלְפִין, sec. קְרִי אַלְפִין, Chald. i. q. prec. אֶלֶף. Dan. v. 1 ; vii. 10.

אלץ, v. Pih. pres. aff. תְּאַלְצֵהוּ, f. Syr. ܐܠܨ, *coegit, ursit;* Arab. cogn. ألص, *coagmentavit,* &c., Dagesh imp. Gram. artt. 109, 113. *She presses* or *urges him,* Jud. xvi. 16.

אַלְקוּם, m. Arab. القم, *width of way;* as a verb, *stopped up;* id. viii. conj., *cause one to swallow down;* and hence, القام, *cibatio.* Prov. xxx. 31, וּמֶלֶךְ אַלְקוּם עִמּוֹ, *and a king* (having) *provision with him,* i. e. that abundance of wealth, subjects, &c., which are necessary to support his dignity and state. See also ib. xiv. 28 ; 1 Sam. ii. 10; xxv. 36. Gesenius and his followers suppose this word to be a compound of the Arabic قوم, *people,* and ال, *the,* i. e. def. article. But this is improbable, and unnecessary. Improbable, because no instance occurs in the whole of the Hebrew language, requiring the Arabic article. It is unnecessary, because the above interpretation suits the context better. The LXX., Chald., and Syr. take the passage to signify, *a king appearing amongst his people.* They seem, therefore, to have taken this term in the sense of subjects, which my etymology will very well bear. See also Gram. art. 180. 2, 3.

אֵם, f. r. אָמַם, seg. Arab. أُمّ, *radix, principium;* hinc أَمَام, *coram;* إِمَام, *antistes;* أُمَّة, *constitutio, religio;* أُمَّة, *cœtus;* pl. אִמּוֹת, it. with affix, sing. אִמּוֹ, אִמָּה, &c. I. *A mother* generally; occasionally *stepmother,* as Gen. xxxvii. 10, sometimes restricted by אֵשֶׁת אָב *father's wife,* Lev. xviii. 8; or *grandmother,* as 1 Kings xv. 10. 13. II. *A mother-city,* or *metropolis.* 2 Sam. xx. 19. Hence a whole people, Hos. ii. 4, Is. L. 1, supposed to diverge as from a common origin or source. See Is. liv. 3 ; Ps. lxxii. 16. Hence in the style of Scripture, *Jerusalem,* which is above, is said to be *the mother of us all,* i. e. the source from which our privilege of sonship springs. So also Babylon (i. e. the plains of Shinar) is the "*mother of harlots and of abominations,* Rev. xvii. 5 ; אֵם הַדֶּרֶךְ, i. q. רֹאשׁ שְׁנֵי הַדְּרָכִים, *the head of two ways,* i. e. whence they diverge, Ezek. xxi. 26; metaph. Job xvii. 14, applied to the worm, as housekeeper of the grave. So Shakspeare, "With worms that are my chambermaids," Rom. and Jul.; and in King John, "And ring these fingers with thy household worms." See my notes on l. c.

אֲמָסָא, see v. מאס.

אִם, part. אָמֵן, contr. Gram. artt. 77.

אִם (38) אִם

242, 5. Arab. اَمْنٌ, *securitas, rectitudo*, &c. Synon. אָמְנָם, *certainty*, &c.; hence adv. I. *Certainly, truly, really;* and, in oaths or vows, which are laid down hypothetically, as *putting a case, if,* Sax. *gif,* i. e. *grant:* stating the matter as a fact taken for granted, or, as sure to take effect as some other certain fact which is introduced for the mere sake of comparison, and to dispel all doubt, on the principle advanced by the apostle, Heb. vi. 17, 18. The force of this particle is identical with that of the Arabic اِنْ, or اَنْ, which the grammarians affirm is equivalent to حَقًّا, *truly;* it is used تَوْكِيدًا, i. e. for the purpose of *confirmation*. It is used, moreover, in two acceptations, the one *positive*, the other *negative*. As I. אִם־שָׁכֹחַ תִּשְׁכַּח אֶת־יְהֹוָה ... הַעִדֹתִי, *really*, or, *putting the case as a fact, that thou entirely disregardest Jehovah,* .. then, in that case, *I have attested,* &c., Deut. viii. 19; אִם־הֹלְכִי עִמִּי וְהָלָכְתִּי, *Putting the case that thou go with me, then I have gone* (i. e. will certainly go). See Gram. art. 233, notes, and ib. *negatively*, on the same principle. וְאִם־לֹא תֵלְכִי עִמִּי לֹא אֵלֵךְ : *And, putting the case, thou goest not with me, I go not,* Jud. iv. 8. It sometimes seems to be interrogative, but this must depend entirely on the context. אִם־פָּרְחָה הַגֶּפֶן, *Hath the vine really blossomed?* Cant. vii. 13. So Gen. xxvii. 21, הַאַתָּה זֶה בְּנִי עֵשָׂו אִם־לֹא, *Art thou this* (person, I mean) *my son Esau,* (or art thou) *really not?* Such is the construction of the Arab. اِنْ and اَمْ, e. g. اَزَيْدٌ فِي الدَّارِ اَمْ عَمْرٌو, *is Zaid in the house, or* (is) *Omr?* اِنَّهَا لَإِبِلٌ اَمْ شَاءٌ, *as to it, is it really a camel, or* (is it) *a sheep?* In which last case, according to Jauhari, the supposition following, اَمْ, certifies what the thing, which was before doubtful, really is. In this instance, he adds, اَمْ is equivalent to بَلْ, *rather;* except that *certainty* does not necessarily follow بَلْ, nor *doubt* the particle اَمْ. In other interrogative instances, doubt may follow اَمْ, but not universally. In some cases, too, it precedes هَلْ, *whether?* as in اَمْ هَلْ عِنْدَكَ عَمْرٌو, where it must have

been added for the purpose of making the question more intensively; as, *is Omr really with you?* I cite these passages, for the purpose of shewing what force the Orientals themselves attach to these particles, and to obviate the necessity of multiplying significations, as Noldius and others have done. So with אִם, in the parallel member, Hos. xii. 12, *Truly Gilead is sin: only vanity (vain or false) have they* (its inhabitants) *been*.

II. In negative sentences, Job xxii. 20, אִם־לֹא נִכְחַד קִימָנוּ וְיִתְרָם אָכְלָה אֵשׁ, (saying) *Hath not our substance been kept back,* i. e. *by injury? but* (as to) *their excess, the fire hath consumed it;* Prov. xxiv. 11, אִם־תַּחְשׂוֹךְ, *keep thou surely* (i. e. without fail) *back,* i. e. corresponding, with some additional force, to the preceding imperative; Neh. xiii. 25, וָאַשְׁבִּיעֵם בֵּאלֹהִים אִם־תִּתְּנוּ בְנוֹתֵיכֶם לִבְנֵיהֶם וגו׳, *Then I swear them in God*('s name); *putting the case* (that) *you give your daughters to their sons, &c.* i. e. as surely as that God liveth, do this, and the curse of the covenant shall fall upon you. No negative is here expressed in the original; the context is, by a sort of σιώπησις, elliptical only. Ezek. xiv. 20, אִם־בֵּן אִם־בַּת יַצִּילוּ, *Shall they assuredly* (i. e. as certainly as I live) *save son or daughter?* Ps. cxxxii. 2, 3, *He swore to Jehovah* (and to his covenant, which involved a curse), *putting the case that, I enter, &c. . . . . until I find out, &c.* (then let me suffer the curse, &c.) And so in every case, involving some ellipsis to be supplied from the matter intimated by the context. With לֹא expressed, which is, perhaps, often interrogative; and, if so, is equivalent to the Arabic اَلَا, *is it not?* rather than اِلَّا, or اَلَّا, e. g. Num. xiv. 35, אִם־לֹא זֹאת אֶעֱשֶׂה, *Shall I not do this?* with a strong asseveration growing out of the particle אִם, q. d. *shall I not certainly do this?* Comp. Josh. xiv. 9; 1 Kings xx. 23; Job i. 11, &c. With an oath, Num. xiv. 28; Ezek. xvii. 19. Comp. Gen. iv. 7, הֲלוֹא אִם־תֵּיטִיב שְׂאֵת וְאִם לֹא, *Is it not* (that) *putting the case thou do well,* (there is) *acceptance : but, putting the case, thou do not, &c.,* ib. xviii. 21, &c., where the אִם לֹא, is manifestly the negative form of אִם; which, put in an interrogatory tone, will suit all the instances in question. See Nold. pp. 70, 71. When no interrogation is necessary, the particle identifies itself with the اِلَّا, اَلَّا, or اَنْ, of the Arabs and Syrians,

אמה (39) אמו

and will correspond to the 'Αλλά, or εἰ μή, of the Greeks, or our *otherwise*, or *if not*.

My endeavour here has been, to ascertain the Hebrew idiomatic force of this particle, not to determine how it may best be translated into any other language. This may be left to the taste of the translator. Grammarians, however, have generally attempted nothing farther than to shew, how they thought this particle might generally be translated, which they could do only by having recourse to critical conjecture; in many instances of which, they would almost necessarily be wrong, because the bearing of the passage ought to be determined rather by the idiomatic force of the particle, than the contrary. A striking case of this sort is exhibited by Dr. Gesenius, in making אִם equivalent to "*o si, utinam,*" &c., in Ps. lxviii. 14; lxxxi. 9; xcv. 7; cxxxix. 19; 1 Chron. iv. 10; Exod. xxxii. 32; and Gen. xxx. 27, where we have אִם־נָא. It is extremely doubtful, however, whether this does not put a sense on these passages, quite foreign to that intended by their authors: nor is it necessary to suppose, in the last, that the precative particle, נָא, exerts any such influence over אִם, as to give it an entirely new meaning. The truth is, this sort of attempt to make the Hebrew and Arabic idioms square, in every case, with those of the modern European dialects, cannot but be very greatly to mistake the business of the grammarian.

אַמָּה, f. pl. אַמּוֹת, Etym. אָם, *prævivit*, &c. I. *The former part of the arm, cubitus* or *ulna;* hence applied as a measure, the *Cubit*, Deut. iii. 11; Gen. vi. 15, &c. Dual. אַמָּתַיִם, *two cubits,* Exod. xxv. 10, &c. II. *A basis* or *pedestal*, Is. vi. 4. As a measure, it is often construed with בְּ, as, מֵאָה בָאַמָּה *one hundred by the cubit*, i. e. one hundred of such measures, Exod. xxvii. 9. It is calculated by Dr. Arbuthnot to contain 21 inches, and 888 decimals. See also Capt. Jervis's Essay on a Primitive Universal Standard, &c.

אָמָה, f. אֲמָהוֹת, pl. Arab. اَمَةٌ, *ancilla*. *Maid-servant*, Jud. xix. 19; 1 Sam. i. 11, &c. aff. אֲמָתְךָ, אֲמָתִי, אֲמָתוֹ, אֲמָהָה, pl. אֲמָהֹתַי, &c.

אֻמָּה, f. pl. אֻמּוֹת, and אֻמִּים, Arab. اُمَّةٌ, *cœtus. Families,* or *tribes*, Gen. xxv. 16; Num. xxv. 15; Ps. cxvii. 2.

It. Chald. pl. אֻמַּיָּא: definite form אֻמַּיָּא, Dan. iii. 4. 7. 29. 31, &c. id.

אָמוֹן, m. Etym. see אמן. Prov. viii. 30, LXX. ἁρμόζουσα. So the ancient Verss. generally; others, *Child* or *pupil*; others, *Artist.* The parallelism, i. e. with יוֹם יוֹם, and פְּלִעֵת, seems to require *Constant, unvarying,* or the like; which the usage of the root (אמן, which see) will very well bear. In Jer. lii. 15, הָאָמוֹן, for הֶהָמוֹן, *the multitude;* see הָמוֹן, אָ for ה, Gram. artt. 23. 202. 4. The name too, apparently of an Egyptian idol in the compd. נֹא אָמוֹן, Jer. xlvi. 25; Nah. iii. 8. As it is a fact very well known, that the nations, in apostatizing from the patriarchal faith, carried with them very many notions, and probably some terms which belonged to that dispersation, this word as applied to the Saviour, in the Proverbs, was perhaps given to an idol, considered as a *constant* and *sure* deliverer or redeemer, in the opinion of its votaries. Apparently the Ἄμμων of the Greeks, Herod. ii. 42; Diod. Sic. i. 13, &c.

אָמוֹן, m. אֲמוּנָה, f. (··), for (τ), by Gram. art. 96. 2. Etym. אמן: pl. אֱמוּנִים, and אֱמוּנוֹת. I. *Faithful,* or *constant,* person or thing, such as may be relied on. Deut. xxxii. 21, לֹא אֵמֻן בָּם, *no faithful* (person) *among them.* Ps. xii. 2; xxxi. 24; צִיר אֱמוּנִים, *a messenger of faithful men,* i. e. one of that description. Prov. xiii. 17. See Gram. art. 219. 4, note. Prov. xx. 6: שֹׁמֵר אֱמוּנִים, *keeping, regarding, faithful things,* Is. xxvi. 2; אֹמְרֵי שְׁלֹמֵי יִשְׂרָאֵל, *I* (am) *of the devoted, faithful* (people) *of Israel.* 2 Sam. xx. 19. Also, objectively, that upon which care has been bestowed. II. *Educated, brought up,* Lam. iv. 5; *upon scarlet,* i. e. delicately. Adverb, בֶּאֱמוּנָה עִנִּיתָנִי, *and faithfully hast thou afflicted me,* i. e. having a constant and kind regard towards me, Ps. cxix. 75. Comp. Ps. xxxiii. 4, &c. This word differs from אֱמֶת, in this respect, that אֱמֶת, signifies *truth,* or *faithfulness*, in the abstract; this, whatever is true or faithful, either as retained in the mind, or reduced to practice, and is therefore nearly equivalent to the English *sincere*.

אַמִּיצִים, m. pl. Arab. أَبُوضٌ, *perquem velox. Powerful, swift,* Zech. vi. 3.

אַמִּיץ, m. Etym. see אמן. *Strong, powerful, prevailing.* Job ix. 4, חֲכַם לֵבָב וְאַמִּיץ כֹּחַ וגו״, *the wise of heart, and powerful of strength,* &c. Is. xxviii. 2; xl. 26.

אָמִיר, m. Arab. أَمِيرٌ, or إِبَارٌ, *punctura.* v. *fœcundavit, palmam fœminam.* Hinc. إِبْرٌ, *prominentior,* velut mucronata, rei ex-

אמל

tremitas. Dimin. اُبَيْر: Hinc quoque, مابور, *aspersione palmæ maris curatus seu fœcundatus.* אָמִיר, perhaps for אָבִיר, מ, for ב, Gram. art. 23.—*The caul, or pod, containing the fruit of the palm tree.* " Ramus enim," says Prosper Alpinus, "quodam involucro oblongo, vesicæ modo, ad ver usque clauso, et tunc aperto præditus, flores emittit parvos . . . . . a quibus dactili parvi virides, uvarum racemos imitantes producuntur, qui autumno maturantur (p. 24). Is. xvii. 6, שְׁנַיִם שְׁלֹשָׁה גַּרְגְּרִים בְּרֹאשׁ אָמִיר אַרְבָּעָה חֲמִשָּׁה בִּסְעִפֶיהָ, *two* (or) *three berries* in the head (or upper part) of the caul (or pod); four (or) five in its fissures. סָעִיף, signifies *any fissure* (see the word), and is also applied to those of rocks. If, therefore, אָמִיר, signifies *this caul* or *pod,* the word סָעִיף, in the following context, applies well to its opening; but is quite unintelligible in any other sense. עָמִיר, (which see,) is probably cognate with אָמִיר,† Ib. vr. 9, *like the leaving of the culture* (i. e. harvest) *and the palm pods* (generally); i. e. the whole culture of the land, and of the fruit trees. It is no objection to this sense of the word, that mention of the olive precedes; which has, perhaps, been made, merely to intimate the manner in which the country should be stripped. The same may be said of the occurrence of reaping and gleaning in the preceding verse. It has been usual to suppose this word derived from the Arab. أمر, and to have taken its signification from أَمِير, signifying *a General,* or *Emir,* and hence to imply, l. c. the *higher* or *upper branches;* all which seems to me extremely forced and unnatural.

אֲמֵלָה, f. أَمَل, *spes, timor,* cogn. אבל, Arab. أبل, *luxit;* metath. ל, et מ, ut in כֶּשֶׂב, et כֶּבֶשׂ; ألم, *dolor, passio.*—*Insatiable, pained,*

---

* The same word, in the Arabic, viz. جَرْجَر, signifies, according to the author of the Kamoos, i. q. فول, i. e. *a bean,* which it might, perhaps, have been termed, on account of its being produced in a sort of pod.

† If so, مابور, *curatus, &c.,* and عَمِير, *cultus, habitatus,* are synonymous; عَمَر, too, is a name for the *palma sacchari,* and for *good Date fruit.* See the Kamoos.

אמל

sick. Ezek. xvi. 30, מָה אֲמֻלָה לִבָּתֵךְ, *How insatiable is thy heart;* comp. the end of preceding verse, and the Targum.

אָמְלַל, m. אֲמֵלָה, fem. אֲמֵלָה, in pausâ. augm. Gram. art. 169. 7. *Sick, pained, wasting, declining,* Hos. iv. 3; Ps. vi. 3; Is. xvi. 8; xxiv. 4. 7; xxxiii. 9; Jer. xv. 9; Joel i. 10, 12; Nahum i. 4, &c.; and hence, as a verb, Gram. art. 197.—

אֻמְלְלוּ, 3 pers. pl. Is. xxiv. 4; Jer. xiv. 2; In pausâ, Gram. art. 120. 7. אֻמְלָלוּ, Is. xix. 8; Lam. ii. 8, *Have become sick.*

אֲמֵלָלִים, m. pl. *Wasted, feeble* (men). Neh. iii. 34.

אָמֻן, see אמון.

אֹמֶן, m. אֲמָנָה, f. seg. Arab. أَمْن, *securitas, integritas.*—*Fidelity,* adv. *with fidelity, truly.* (Gram. art. 210, note.) Is. xxv. 1; Gen. xx. 12; Josh. vii. 20: Est. ii. 20; see Syr. Hence, אָמְנָם, or אֻמְנָם, augm. מ; Gram. art. 167. Id. Gen. xviii. 13; Num. xxii. 37; Ruth iii. 12, &c.

אֹמְנוֹת, f. pl. LXX. ἐστηριγμένα. Targ. סְקוּפַיָא.—*Beams,* or *lintels,* placed perhaps to bear the superincumbent weight over the doors, q. d. *securers;* 2 Kings xviii. 16.

אֹמֵן, m. אֹמֶנֶת, f. *A tutor, tutoress;* i. e. hired to nurse, and bring up another person's child, Num. xi. 12; 2 Sam. iv. 4; 2 Kings x. 1, 5; Ruth iv. 16. Obj. אֵמוּן, Lam. iv. 5. See גדל, and רום; pl. m. אֹמְנִים. Aff. f. אֹמַנְתּוֹ.

אָמֵן, m. Arab. أَمِين. *Faithful, constant,* Is. lxv. 16, adv. *Certainly;* formula of acquiescence, *Amen;* LXX. γένοιτο, Vulg. *fiat.* Deut. xxvii. 15; Neh. v. 13; Ps. xli. 14, &c.

אָמָן, m. Syr. ܐܘܡܢܐ. *Artificer,* Cant. vii. 2.

אֲמָנָה, f. Any thing confirmed or ratified, as, 1. *A covenant,* or *contract.* Arab. أَمَان, or أَمَانَة, *securitatis libellus,* Neh. x. 1; xi. 23. Also, II. The name of a hill in the Libanus chain, and of a river which flows from it. Cant. iv. 8; 2 Kings v. 12, Keri. Hence, as a verb in *Niph.* and *Hiph.*

נֶאֱמָן, Niph. opp. to אכזב, Jer. xv. 18, and applied to either persons or things. *Known,* or *believed to be Stable, constant, never-failing, faithful.* Jer. xlii. 5, עֵד אֱמֶת וְנֶאֱמָן, *A witness of the truth* (abstractedly), *and* (one who is) *constant,* Neh. xiii. 13; Prov. xxvii.

הָאַם (41) אמץ

6; 1 Sam. iii. 20; 2 Sam. vii. 16; Ps. lxxviii. 8, 37; xciii. 5, &c.; f. נֶאֱמָנָה, and נֶאֱמָנֶת, Is. i. 21; Ps. xix. 8; lxxxix. 29; pl. m. נֶאֱמָנִים, Is. viii. 2; xxxiii. 16; constr. נֶאֶמְנֵי, Ps. ci. 6.

הֶאֱמִין, Hiph. constr. abs. or with לְ, or בְּ, and applied to either persons or things. I. *Ascribing stability, firmness, &c.*, to any person or thing; hence, II. *Confiding to, or in him, &c.; as such, believing, trusting to, relying on, &c.*, as the context shall require, Gen. xv. 6; i. e. Abram did not merely believe that God existed, but he trusted in his word; he staggered not at his promises. Comp. Exod. iv. 8; Is. liii. 1; 2 Kings xvii. 14; Ps. lxxviii. 22, 32. In some instances mere credence to a statement or report seems to be implied; but here, *reliance* on the thing reported is rather intended; 1 Kings x. 7; 2 Chron. ix. 6; Ps. cvi. 24; Lam. iv. 12. In Jud. xi. 20, *But Sihon confided not to Israel the passing over of his boundary;* i. e. entrusted him not with that privilege. Job xxxix. 24, לֹא יַאֲמִין, *he confides not;* i. e. does not believe *himself safe* (comp. Deut. xxviii. 66); but scents, as it were, the distant battle, and hurries away to the attack. Is. xxx. 21, הַאֲמִינוּ, for הַיְמִינוּ, (mut. ', in א, Gram. art. 23, if the noun יָמִין, is not really conjugated here). See Gen. xiii. 9, *ye go towards the right hand*. Verb formed of יָמִין, *the right hand, &c.* We have in Is. vii. 9, a very remarkable instance, in which the significations of this word in *Hiph.* and *Niph.* is very apparent, אִם לֹא תַאֲמִינוּ כִּי לֹא תֵאָמֵנוּ, *Putting the case* (that) *ye have no confidence* (i. e. in what has just been related, and elsewhere promised); *surely ye shall find no stability;* i. e. under the immediate government of Jehovah there is nothing like permanent prosperity to be found, except in an unshaken confidence in his word. Is. xxviii. 16, הַמַּאֲמִין לֹא יָחִישׁ, *He who is confident* (faithful) *shall not hurry;* i. e. the believer shall experience no such disappointment as usually attends *hurry*. Comp. Is. lii. 12; Prov. xix. 2. Hence Job xx. 2, 3, חוּשִׁי, *my haste*, and כְּלִמָּתִי, *my reproach*, refer to the same thing. Hence too, the Apostles Paul and Peter, Rom. ix. 33; 1 Pet. ii. 6, have cited the passage in this sense, viz. *" shall not be ashamed."* See my Proleg. to Bagster's Polyglott Bible, Proleg. iv. § iii. par. xiii.

אֹמֶץ, m. אִמְצָה, f. Arab. أَبِصَ, *alacer*, أَبْص, *ligatio, obfirmatio*. Cogn. אוּץ, *coegit*,

&c., it. מָצָא, *invenit*. Syr. and Chald. *potuit*. *Power*, Job xvii. 9; Zech. xii. 5. Hence

אָמֵץ, v. pres. יֶאֱמַץ, *Was powerful, courageous, prevailing*, constr. abs. and with מִן. אָמְצוּ מִמֶּנִּי, *They are stronger than I*, Ps. xviii. 18. חֲזַק וֶאֱמָץ, *Be firm and courageous*, Deut. xxxi. 7. *Fear not, neither be broken* (i. e. in resolution); *be firm and courageous*, Josh. x. 25. יֶאֶמְצוּ בְנֵי יְהוּדָה, *The children of Judah prevail*, 2 Chron. xiii. 18.

Pih. אִמֵּץ, pres. יְאַמֵּץ, *Made strong, courageous*, &c., either, I. In fact; or, II. In declaration only. I. אֲמַצְתִּיךָ, *I will make thee strong*, i. e. will supply thee with power, Is. xli. 10; מְאַמֵּץ כֹּחַ, *prevailing* (in or as to) *strength*, Prov. xxiv. 5; Ps. lxxx. 16, 18; Prov. viii. 28, &c. II. רָוָה אִמֵּץ אֶת־לְבָבוֹ, לָמָה תִּתֵּן וגו׳, *Jehovah ... hath made* (declared) *his heart to be firm; therefore* (because this is the fact, is) *his giving up*, &c., Deut. ii. 30. See Gram. artt. 154. 8; 157. 6, with the notes; Job xvi. 5.

Hiph. pres. יַאֲמִץ, *He strengthens, confirms*, Ps. xxvii. 14; xxxi. 25; not intrans. as Gesenius thinks.

Hithp. הִתְאַמֵּץ, *Acquired power, took courage*, 1 Kings xii. 18; 2 Chron. x. 18; xiii. 7; Ruth i. 18.

אֲמֻצִּים, m. pl. *Powerful, swift*, Zech. vi. 3. 7.

אַמְצָה, f. *Power*, see אֹמֶץ, above.

אֹמֶר, m. Arab. أَمْر, *edictum*. I. *Enouncement, expression*. Ps. xix. 3, 4; xxix. 9; lxviii. 12; constr. with לְ, אֶל, or immed. With aff. אָמְרִי, *my saying*, Josh. vi. 10; Job ix. 27; Ez. iii. 17; אָמְרָם, *their saying*, Ps. xlii. 11; Est. i. 17; iii. 4.

אָמָר, m. אֲמָרָה, once אֶמְרָה, f. constr. אִמְרַת, pl. אִמְרֵי, m. אֲמָרוֹת, fem. אֲמָרִים, m. אֲמָרוֹת f. abs. fm. פֶּקַד, Arab. أَمْر, *mandatum*. *Word*, or *declaration*; meton. *appointment*, or *sentiment*, Hos. vi. 5: Prov. xix. 7; xxii. 21; Gen. xlix. 21; *Naphtali ...* הַנֹּתֵן אִמְרֵי שָׁפֶר, *who giveth pleasant words.* אָמְרֵי אֵל, *the words*, or *appointments of God*, Num. xxiv. 4. 16; Josh. xxiv. 27; Prov. vi. 2; Job vi. 10; with aff. אֲמָרַי, Job xxxiii. 3; אֲמָרַי, Job xxii. 22; אֲמָרָתִי, Jud. v. 29; אִמְרָכֶם, Job

* In Leo's translation of Gesenius, *"which brings forth pretty young ones !"* Ges. *"(und) redet schöne worte."*—A very pretty translation surely !

G

אמר (42) אמר

xxxii. 14. Fem. אִמְרָתִי, Gen. iv. 23. אִמְרָתֵךְ, Deut. xxxiii. 9. אִמְרָתֶךָ, Is. xxix. 4. אִמְרָתוֹ, Ps. cxlvii. 15. אֲמָרָתוֹ, Lam. ii. 17, Gram. art. 96. 2.

אָמוֹר, constr. אֱמֹר, or אֲמֹר, and, without the accent, אֱמֹר, m. *Saying*, i. e. the act of doing so; abstr. אִם־אָמֹר יֹאמַר, *Putting the case*, (that) *saying he shall say*, i. e. shall persevere in saying, Exod. xxi. 5; Gram. art. 222, ib. seq.; Jud. xv. 2, &c. Constr. בֶּאֱמֹר יְהֹוָה, *In Jehovah's saying*, Deut. iv. 10; Ezek. xxxvi. 20, with ל following, Gram. art. 224. 12. So Prov. xxv. 7. טוֹב אֲמָר־לְךָ, *Good is the saying of—to thee*, i. e. the saying of, *Go up, &c.* Gram. art. 224. 9, and note. So Job xxxiv. 18. Hence, with prep. בֶּאֱמֹר, *in saying*, Ps. xlii. 4. כֶּאֱמֹר, Josh. vi. 8; and, by contraction, לֶאֱמֹר, for לֶאֱמוֹר, Gram. art. 87. 5, *for to say*, i. e. *saying*. With aff. אֲמָרְךָ, Ezek. xxxv. 10. אָמְרָם, Jer. xxiii. 38, and בְּאָמְרָכֶם, *In your saying*, Mal. i. 8. 12.

אֹמֶר, אֵמֶר, m. אִמְרָה, or אֹמֶרֶת, f. pl. m. אֹמְרִים, f. אֲמָרוֹת. *Person saying, declaring, &c.* often found parallel in the context with a pres. tense, Gram. art. 231. 10. So 1 Kings xxii. 20. וַיֹּאמֶר זֶה בְּכֹה וְזֶה אֹמֵר בְּכֹה, *And this says, in this* (manner), *and this* (is) *saying in this.* With pron. is equal to a pres. אַתָּה אֹמֵר, *Art thou saying?* sayest thou? Exod. ii. 14. Pron. often understood: שָׁמַעְתִּי אֹמְרִים, *I heard* (them) *saying*, Gen. xxxvii. 17, Exod. v. 16. הָאֹמְרִים, *Those who say*, Job xxii. 17: where the def. art. has the force of אֲשֶׁר, Gram. art. 179. 3, and note. See f. Is. xlvii. 8; Mich. vii. 10, &c.: and without the art. 1 Kings iii. 22, 23; pl. Jer. xxxviii. 22; Amos iv. 1.

אָמוּר, m. *Said, named*, once only, Mich. ii. 7.

אָמַר, pres. יֹאמַר, and יֹאמֶר, Gram. art. 199. 4. *Said, declared*, and, from a superior, *commanded, &c.* The subject matter of such declaration generally following. דְּבַר differs from it in this, that it signifies *spake* only, without regard to the thing said; as, *The Lord* SPAKE *unto Moses*, i. e. he simply addressed him: it is generally added, *saying, &c.* It must be remembered however, that, according to the usage of the Oriental languages, it is neither necessary nor constant, that such complementary terms follow. (See Gram. art. 228. 3, note.) Dr. Gesenius, Thes. p. 119, thinks that such omissions savour of modern Hebraism, he finds, nevertheless, an instance of this sort in Exod. xix. 25, וַיֹּאמֶר אֲלֵהֶם . . . . *So he says*, or *declares, to them*, i. e. the matter mentioned in the preceding context. So Gen. iv. 8, וַיֹּאמֶר קַיִן אֶל־הֶבֶל אָחִיו, *so Cain declares* (the matter) *to Abel, his brother*, i. e. that immediately preceding. The use of the ו, with the apocopated pres. requires this. See Gram. art. 233. 3, with the notes. The same connection of the context is also visible in the following וַיְהִי, so *it comes to pass;* and in וַיָּקָם, *and*, ACCORDINGLY, *he arises, &c.;* manifestly shewing, that the whole of the context is in the closest connection, as to sense; and, that the whole depends upon what is given in the 6th and 7th verses preceding.—How Dr. Gesenius could have so much given in to the mere technicalities of European grammar, as to suppose that an *accusative* case could lie hidden in the particle כֹּה, in the phrase כֹּה אָמַר הָאִישׁ, 1 Sam. ix. 9, I am perfectly at a loss to conceive; particularly as the subject matter of the declaration follows. It is construed with ל, אֶל, *to*, or *of*; עַל, *concerning*, or *against*, Gen. iii. 16, 17; xiii. 14; xx. 5. 16, 2 Kings xix. 32; Jer. xxii. 18; xxvii. 19. לְנַפְשִׁי, *of my person*, Ps. iii. 3; lxxi. 10: with עַל, Ezek. xxxv. 12.—Metaph. Job xxxix. 15.— In the sense *of commanding*, Esth. iv. 13; ix. 14; Neh. xiii. 9; 2 Chron. xxiv. 8; Ps. xxxiii. 9, &c. With בְּלִבּוֹ, *Said in his heart*, i. e. *considered, mused*, Gen. xvii. 17; Ps. x. 6. 11. לְלִבָּם, *to*, or *of, their heart*, Hos. vii. 2.

Niph. נֶאֱמַר, pres. יֵאָמֵר, and יֵאָמֶר, *Became declared, said, named*, Dan. viii. 26, אֲשֶׁר יֵאָמֵר הַיּוֹם, *Which is* (even) *at this day said, recited, &c.* Gen. xxii. 14; Is. lxi. 6; lxii. 4; Jer. iv. 11. לֹא יֵאָמֵר עוֹד, *shall not again be recited*, i. e. the formula of the oath following, because a far greater thing shall have been done. See the following verses to the end of the chapter, which intimate that the whole Gentile world shall also be saved. Comp. Hos. i. 10.

Hiph. הֶאֱמִיר, *Hath made declared*, Deut. xxvi. 17, 18, Auth. vers. *avouched:* which see. Dr. Gesenius has discussed this passage at some length in his Thesaurus; his conclusion agrees with the text of our authorized version.

Hithp. יִתְאַמְּרוּ, *They are declared, published, made famous*, i. e. אַנְשֵׁי הַשֵּׁם. Comp. Gen. iv. 4; Ps. xciv. 4: comp. also Ps. xlix. 12.

אָמַר, or אֲמַר, Chald. pres. יֵאמַר, i. q. Heb. constr. with לְ.—Infin. or verbal noun מֵאמַר, or מֵמַר, 3 pret. f. אֲמֶרֶת, for אֲמַרַת, i. e. another f. form of the noun is here taken, Dan. ii. 5. 12; iii. 9; iv. 23; vi. 24, &c.

אִמַּר, m. pl. אִמְּרִין, Chald. Arab. إِمَّر, et إِمَّرَة, *imbecillis, parvus agnus.* Syr. ܐܶܡܪܳܐ, *agnus. A lamb,* Ezr. vi. 9. 17; vii. 17.

אֶמֶשׁ, m. Arab. أَمْسِ—اَلْيَوْمُ الَّذِي قَبْلَ يَوْمِكَ بِلَيْلَةٍ, *The day, prior to thy day,* (i. e. the day from which you refer,) *by a night,* i. e. اَلْبَارِحَة, *(yesterday,* and *evening). Yesterday, including the following night,* Gen. xix. 34; xxxi. 29. 42; 2 Kings ix. 26, &c.; Job xxx. 3. אֶמֶשׁ שׁוֹאָה וּמְשֹׁאָה, *(who have experienced,) the evening* (dreary night) *of desolation and destruction.* Light and darkness are often put to signify prosperity and misfortune, respectively. See Ps. xcvii. 11; Is. viii. 22, 23; ix. 1. In Winer's edition of Simonis we have, for the etymology of this word, and to fix its sense, مَسَّا أَمْسِ, *heri vesperi,* which is bad Arabic! It is not allowed to give a *tanween* to the first of any two words in construction; and it is irregular to give one to the last of these, as the author of the Kamoos has shewn.

אֱמֶת, f. r. אמן, with aff. אֲמִתְּךָ, and אֲמִתּוֹ. *Truth,* pec. religious, and, as such, including the notions of *justice, right, fairness, sincerity, fidelity, integrity, permanency,* or the like, as the context may require; as, אַנְשֵׁי אֱמֶת יִרְאֵי אֱלֹהִים, i. e. *Men who fear God;* i. e. *men of truth,* who are not to be moved by the consideration of gain, Exod. xviii. 21. See Jer. xlii. 5; Ps. cxix. 142; Neh. vii. 2; ix. 33; חֶסֶד וֶאֱמֶת, *Favour and justice,* i. e. have met, in the mediatorial work of Christ, Ps. lxxxv. 11; joined occasionally with טוֹב, אוֹר, שָׁלוֹם, מִשְׁפָּט, צְדָקָה, תָּמִים, יָשָׁר, 2 Chron. xxxi. 20; Jud. ix. 16; 1 Kings iii. 6; 2 Kings xx. 3; Esth. ix. 30; Ps. xliii. 3. Applied particularly to God and his Word, as the sources of all saving knowledge, Jer. x. 10; xxvi. 15; 2 Sam. vii. 28; Ps. cxix. 151, &c.

אַמְתַּחַת, f. Arab. مَنْح, *elatio,* i. e. *ex-* *tensio diei;* مَتُوح, i. q. بَعِيدَة, *distant;* مِنْتَاح, *long.* Syr. ܡܬܚ, *extendit,* it. Chald. See מתח, pl. constr. אַמְתְּחוֹת, *Sack* or *bag,* i. q. שַׂק, Gen. xlii. 27; xliv. 1, 2. 12; with aff. אַמְתְּחֹתֵיכֶם, אַמְתַּחְתֵּנוּ, אַמְתַּחְתּוֹ, אֲמִתַּחְתִּי, Gen. xlii. 28, 27; xliii. 21, 12.

אֲמִתָּנִי, f. Chald. r. מתן; Arab. مَتِين, *firmus, solidus;* Eth. ደ·ት·ሰ, *ligatura articulorum. Powerful, mighty,* Dan. vii. 7. The lexicographers tell us, that it is put for אֲמִתָּנִין: but this is erroneous; the ת being added to words ending in י, and ו, in Chaldee and Syriac, to mark the *state of construction,* which is not the case here.

אָן, אָנָה, and אָנֶה. Arab. أَيُّ, *tempus, hinc* أَيُّ, *ubicunque, unde, &c.* Cogn. أَوْنُ, et أَيْنَ, *unde?* أَيْنَ, *ubi?* مِنْ أَيْنَ, *unde?* applied to both time and place. See אין. I. *When,* or II. *Where,* interrogatively or not, it. III. *Whither?* or IV. *How long?* as to place or time. Also, V. *Whence?* as the context shall require, Is. x. 3. *And where will you leave?* It. Ruth ii. 19. With verbs of motion, Gen. xvi. 8; Josh. ii. 5; Jud. xix. 17; 1 Sam. x. 14; (אָן) 2 Sam. ii. 1; Neh. i. 16. *Whither?* with prep. מִן, מֵאָן, keri מֵאָיִן, *whence?* 2 Kings v. 25: *How long?* Exod. xvi. 28; Jer. xlvii. 6; Hab. i. 2; Job viii. 2; xviii. 2: comp. אָנֶה וָאָנָה, *hither* or *thither,* 1 Kings ii. 36; 2 Kings v. 25. Whence it must appear, that the Lexicographers have been wrong in supposing, that the terminating ה signified *motion towards a place;* it is nothing more than a part of the primitive word, which, in other cases, submits to apocopation. אָן, evidently signifying *whither,* and אָנָה, *where,* in the passages above cited. See Nold. p. 73.

אֲנָא, or אֲנָה, Chald. pron. 1 pers. sing. I.

אַנָּא, or אָנָּה, partic. Arab. أَنَى, i. q. حَايِن, *waiting, delaying;* أَنَاة, *mildness;* i. e. disposed to delay, or forbearance. Hence, رَجُلُ آنٍ, *a man of great mildness.* Cogn. نَوُ, *donum.* أُونْ, *obsecro.* Eth. ቄዕ·, *ecce. Forbear! gently! I pray!* or the like, Gen. L. 17; Exod. xxxii. 31; 2 Kings xx. 3; Ps.

cxviii. 25: and cogn. with אָ, Gram. art. 243, with note.—With אָנָה, Ps. cxxxix. 7, with which it is also cognate.

אֲנָבָה, see אֵב.

אֱנְדַּע, Chald. v. ידע.

אָנָה, v. pres. non. occ. Arab. اَنَّ, anhelavit. اَنَّى, toleravit. Cogn. اَوْن, quies. اَيْن, lassitudo. اَنِين, gemitus. Syn. τοῦ, אָבַל, Is. iii. 26. וְאָנוּ וְאָבְלוּ, They both suffer and mourn, Ib. xix. 8.

Pih. Exod. xxi. 13, וְהָאֱלֹהִים אִנָּה לְיָדוֹ, God hath given, or caused, pain (to him) by his hand, or means, i. e. the accident is to be ascribed to God's allowing, or rather causing, it to be so, for the purpose of punishing the sufferer.

Puh. Prov. xii. 21, לֹא יְאֻנֶּה, It is not made to suffer (i. e. impers.) to the just (i. e.) any evil. It is added, But the wicked (ones) are full of calamity, Ps. xci. 10, לֹא תְאֻנֶּה אֵלֶיךָ רָעָה, Calamity shall not be made (allowed) to give pain to thee: nor shall a stroke approach thy tent.

Hithp. 2 Kings v. 7, מִתְאַנֶּה הוּא לִי, He affects irritation (pain) at me; i. e. I perceive that, by this extraordinary message, he is enraged at me. Targ. לְאִתְגְּרָאָה בִּי, Syr. ܒ̇ܓ̇ܚ̇ܐ ܟ̇ܕ̇ܗ̇ܘ̇ ܓ̇ܒ̇ܕ̇, In order to appear provoked at me. On this force of the Hithpahel form, see Gram. art. 157. 14. This verb, therefore, has in reality one principal signification, and no more.

אֲנָה, or אָנָה, see אָן above.

אָנָה, see אָנָא.

אָנוּ, Kethib, אֲנַחְנוּ, keri. We; once only, Jer. xlii. 6.

אִפּוּן, m. אִנֵּן, f. Chald. dem. pron. pl. Those, Dan. ii. 4; vii. 17.

אֱנוֹשׁ, m. pl. אֲנָשִׁים, constr. אַנְשֵׁי. I. Arab. اَنَس, consuetudo, familiaritas. اِنْس, genus humanum. II. Chald. et Syr. אֲנַס, coegit, vi compressit, violentiam intulit. Cogn. Syr. ܢ, ægrotavit. Notio sc. arctandi à societate ducta. Syr. ܐܢܫ, homo, pr. plebeius, opp. τῷ, ܒܪܢܫܐ et syn. τῷ, אָדָם, "vocab. mere poeticum," inquit Winer, quamvis sexcenties in pedestri oratione occurrit! Vid. Concord. Man, as a member of society generally, and liable to misfortune, misery, and death. It differs from אָדָם, in that this has respect to his origin: from אִישׁ, in that this respects his superiority: and from גֶּבֶר, or גִּבּוֹר, Chald., in that these respect his courage. With aff. אֲנָשַׁי, אֲנָשֶׁיךָ, אֲנָשֵׁינוּ, &c. It forms certain idioms; as, אַנְשֵׁי הַשֵּׁם, Men of name, famous men, Gen. vi. 4. See Ib. xvii. 27; 1 Kings ix. 22, 27; Is. xxviii. 14; Joel ii. 7; Obad. vr. 7; Neh. vii. 26, &c. See Concord., and אִישׁ above.

אָנוּשׁ, m. אֲנוּשָׁה, f. Grievous, incurable, mortal. Syn. נַחְלָה: applied to a wound, a weapon, the heart, affliction; also to time, Jer. xv. 18; Job xxxiv. 6; Mich. i. 9; Jer. xvii. 9. 16. Comp. יוֹם נַחְלָה, Is. xvii. 11. אֲנוּשָׁה, Ps. lxix. 21, will, according to the vowels, be the 1 pers. pres. Kal. with ה parag. of the cogn. root נוּשׁ, Syr. ܢ. See אֲנוֹשׁ above, as some think; or, it may be the contracted form of מַאֲנוּשָׁה, (root אנשׁ). See Gram. artt. 199. 3. 234. As a verb, also, in Niph. וַיֵּאָנַשׁ, So he becomes mortally sick, 2 Sam. xii. 15.

אֲנָחָה, f. pl. constr. אַנְחוֹת. Arab. اَى, anhelatio. Cogn. اَنّ, Chald. אֲנַח, gemitus. Syr. augm. ܒܢܚܬܐ, id. Sighing, sobbing, Ps. xxxi. 11; cii. 6; Is. xxxv. 10; Job iii. 24. With affix. אַנְחָתִי, אַנְחָתָה, Is. xxi. 2. So many of the mss. and editions, with Mappik—pl. אַנְחוֹתַי. Hence

נֶאֱנַח, v. in Niph., Lam. i. 8, נֶאֶנְחָה, 3 pers. sing. fem. Is. xxiv. 7, נֶאֱנָחָה, They have (surely shall have) been reduced to sighing.

Pres. יֵאָנַח, He, or it, is reduced to sighing, Prov. xxix. 2; תֵּאָנַח, Ezek. xxi. 11; pl. וַיֵּאָנְחוּ, Exod. ii. 23; Imper. הֵאָנַח, Ezek. xxi. 11. And, as a participial noun,—

נֶאֱנָח, m. נֶאֱנָחָה. f. נֶאֱנָחִים, pl. m. Reduced to sighing, Ezek. xxi. 12; Lam. i. 4. 8. 11. 21; Joel i. 18; Ezek. ix. 4.

אֲנַחְנָא, Chald. i. q. Heb. אֲנַחְנוּ.

אֲנַחְנוּ, pron. 1 pers. pl. com. i. q. נַחְנוּ, (Arab. نَحْنُ, nos.) See Gram. art. 145. 2. 5.

אֲנִי, or, with a pause accent, אָנִי, pron. 1 pers. sing. com. i. q. אָנֹכִי. (Arab. اَنَا,

אני (45) אנף

ego. Syr. אֲנָו֗, or אֲנָו֗, id.) Whence the affixes יִ֗, and ִי֗. See Gram. artt. 145. 2. 5; 206 et seq.

אָנְכִי, m. אֲנִיָּה, f. once אוֹנִיָּה, 2 Chron. viii. 18; pl. אֲנִיּוֹת. Arab. إِنَاءٌ, *vas,* pl. آنِيَةٌ, *vasa,* v. آنِي, *retinuit, &c.* I. *Vessels, ships.* Comp. כְּלִי גֹמֶא, Is. xviii. 2. and sing. II. *A fleet.* Dr. Gesenius thinks that אֲנִיָּה exhibits the noun of unity, as in the Arabic تِبْنَةٌ, &c.: but this is improbable, because in that case *singularity,* i. e. in excellence, would be intended, as in the Arab. عَلَامَةٌ, or Heb. יְשׁוּעָתָה. Besides, we have the pl. of the fem. form, 1 Kings ix. 26, 27; Is. ii. 16; Prov. xxx. 19; Jon. i. 3. 5; Gen. xlix. 13. אֲנִיּוֹת סוֹחֵר, *Ships of the merchant,* Prov. xxxi. 14. אֲנִיּוֹת תַּרְשִׁישׁ, *Ships trading to Tartessus,* Is. xxiii. 1. אַנְשֵׁי אֲנִיּוֹת, *Ship-men, seafaring men,* or *sailors,* 1 Kings ix. 27. Aff. אֳנִיּוֹתֵיהֶם, Ezek. xxvii. 29.

אֲנִיָּה, f. of אנה above. *Suffering pain,* Is. xxix. 2. הַאֲנִיָּה וַאֲנִיָּה, *Painful and suffering pain,* i. e. suffering grievously, Gram. art. 223.

אֲנָךְ, m. Arab. أَنُكٌ, *plumbum. Lead,* meton. *a plummet,* as made of that metal, Amos vii. 7, 8, ib. שָׂם אֲנָךְ, *Applying the plummet,* i. e. shewing symbolically that there is none upright.

אָנֹכִי, pron. 1 pers. com. sing. See Gram. art. 145. 2. 5.

אָנֵס, m. See אָנוֹשׁ. *Applying violence, forcing,* Esth. i. 8. Hence, as a verb,—

אֲנַס, *Has pressed, troubled, proved difficult,* Chald. Dan. iv. 6.

אָנַף, Kal. pres. יֶאֱנַף. See אַף. *He breathed violently through the nose:* hence, *was irritated, angry, enraged.* Comp. רוּחַ, Job iv. 9. קָצַף, Ps. x. 5, constr. abs. and with בְּ, Ps. ii. 12; lx. 3; 1 Kings viii. 46; Is. xii. 1; Ps. lxxxv. 6: in Hithp. הִתְאַנַּף, *he became angry,* Deut. i. 37; iv. 21, &c.: pres. יִתְאַנַּף, Ib. ix. 8, &c.

אַנְפַּיִן, Chald. dual. i. q. Heb. אַפַּיִם, Dan. ii. 46; iii. 19. With affix. אַנְפּוֹהִי, *his face.* Gesenius thinks it ought to be taken as a pl. No proof, however, can be given. The Heb. אַפַּיִם, seems to be for the dual.

אֲנָפָה, f. Name of an unclean bird, of which there were probably many species. The LXX. give χαραδριός, Auth. Vers. *the Heron.* See the Hierozoïcon of Bochart, tom. ii. p. 335, et seq.

אָנַק, v. pres. יֶאֱנַק, Kal. Syr. ܐܢܩ, *suspiravit ex angustia.* Arab. عَنَقَ, et أَعْنَقَ, mut. א et ע, *calamitas. Crying out,* from the pain of a wound, &c. Jer. li. 52; Ezek. xxvi. 15. Infin. אֲנֹק.—אֲנַח, signifies *sighing,* from mental agony; שָׁוַע, *crying out in prayer*: שָׁאַג, *roaring,* as a lion : הָמָה, *raging,* as the sea; הָגָה, *muttering,* as in meditation; or in *cooing,* as a dove : רִיעַ, *shouting,* as in exultation.

Niph. הֵאָנֵק דֹּם, *Be thou reduced to lamentation* (in) *silence,* i. e. not with howlings, as is the practice of heathens, but in silence and decency, Ezek. xxiv. 17. Part. נֶאֱנָקִים, *persons so reduced,* syn. with נֶאֱנָחִים, Ezek. ix. 4.

אֲנָקָה, f. constr. אֶנְקַת. I. *Crying out,* from pain, bodily or mental, Mal. ii. 13; Ps. lxxix. 11, &c. Also, II. The name of a reptile; so called, perhaps, from *its cry,* Lev. xi. 30. Auth. Vers. *the ferret;* a sort of lizard, according to Bochart. Hieroz. tom. i. col. 1068, et seq.

אֲנַקְתָה, Chald. i. q. Heb. אַתָּה.

אַנְתּוּן, Chald. i. q. Heb. אַתֶּם, Dan. ii. 8.

אָסוּךְ, m. for אָסוּק, contr. Gram. art. 75, Etym. See סוּךְ, *A vessel,* or *cup,* for holding the common anointing-oil, 2 Kings iv. 2.

אָסוֹן, m. for אָסוֹן, contr. Gram. art. 75. Arab. أَصِيلَانٌ, i. q. أَصِيلٌ, *exitium, mors.* Dicitur لَقِيتُهُ أَصِيَانًا Freytag's Gol. sub voce أَصِيٌّ; unde أَصِيدَةٌ, *malum, fatale. Injury, accidental death,* Gen. xlii. 4. 38; Exod. xxi. 22, 23.

אָסוּר, m. pl. אֲסוּרִים, r. אסר, i. q.

אֲסוּר, m. Chald. Dan. iv. 12; Ezra vii. 26, pl. אֱסוּרִין; and אָסוּר, or אָסִיר, *Bound, fettered,* as a captive, or other prisoner: meton. applied to the thing which binds or ties, just as we say, "The rope is tied, as well as the thing tied by it," Jud. xv. 14. Affix. אֲסוּרָיו, *His bandages,* i. e. tied ropes, Eccl. vii. 26; Jer. xxxvii. 15.

אסו (46) אסף

בֵּית הָאָסוּר, which, pl. is בֵּית הָאֲסוּרִים, Jud. xvi. 21, and Ib. 25, according to the *keri*, and equivalent to the Syr. ܒܶܝܬ ܐܰܣܺܝܪ̈ܶܐ, i. e. *domus vinctorum*, not *domus vinculorum*, as Dr. Gesenius has made it. Nor is there any vestige of *Syriasm* in this word (אָסוּר), as he thinks; nor any Syriac word, from the same root, corresponding to its form.

אָסוּר, m. אֲסוּרִים, m. pl. אֲסוּרוֹת, f. pl. i. q. אָסוּר, preced.

אָסוֹר, or אָסֹר, m. constr. אֱסוֹר, or אֱסֹר, *Binding*, Jud. xv. 13, &c.

אָסִיף, or אָסֻף, m. r. אסף, *Any thing collected*. *Harvest*, Exod. xxiii. 16; xxxiv. 22. This word differs from קָצִיר, in this respect, that קָצִיר, i. e. *crop*, has reference to the reaping, or cutting down; אָסִיף, to the same as collected.

אָסִיר, m. אֲסִירִים, pl. With affix. אֲסִירָיו, אֲסִירֶיךָ, constr. אֲסִירֵי, i. q. אָסוּר. Dr. Gesenius tells us that אָסוּר retains the force of a participle; אָסִיר of a substantive; and, hence he says, the אֲסִירֵי, of the *Keri*, is the true reading in Gen. xxxix. 20. This decision, however, is unsound; for participial nouns are regularly used as substantives; and אָסוּר occurs so used in Ps. cxlvi. 7. In Eccles. iv. 14, we have הָסוּרִים, for הָאֲסוּרִים; Is. xlix. 9, and lxi. 1. The passage in Gen. will be correct, therefore, read it which way we will: although אֲסִירֵי, in the first place, is preferable, for the sake of variety.

אַסִּיר, m. *Bound*, habitually, constantly, or securely; *prisoner*, *captive*, Is. x. 4; xxiv. 22; xlii. 7, &c. On the form, see Gram. art. 154. 12, note.

אָסָם, m. occ. twice, Deut. xxviii. 8; Prov. iii. 10: thus, אֲסָמֶיךָ, *Thy stores*, or *storehouses*, as the context seems to require. Targ אוֹצָרָךְ; LXX. ταμεῖά σοῦ; sing. אָסָם, seg. abstr. or, perhaps, אֶסֶם, concr. Etym. cogn. τοῦ, ܣܰܟ̣, *obturavit*, unde; ܣܝܳܡܶܐ, *custodiæ*, *excubiarum locus*. שׂוּם, Heb. Chald. et Syr. ܣܳܡ, *posuit*. These storehouses, as well as other treasuries of wealth, were occasionally under ground, and so concealed and strengthened as not to be easily discovered or broken into. Some remains of such places are still visible in Greece.

אַסְעָרָם, see r. סער.

אָסֹף, or אָסוֹף, constr. אֱסֹף, with affix.

from אסף, Is. xxxii. 10, &c. אֲסָפְכֶם, אֲסָפְכֶם, Gram. artt. 152. 2. 190. 8, Arab. cogn.

ضَافَ r. ضَوْف, *hospitio excepit*, iv. conj. *addidit*, &c. *Collecting*, Jer. viii. 13; Mich. ii. 12; Is. x. 14, &c.

אָסַף, v. pres. יֶאֱסֹף, *Collecting*, for the purpose of *acquiring*, *taking away*, *preserving*, or *destroying*; as *fruits*, Exod. xxiii. 10; Is. xvii. 5; *ears of corn*, Ruth ii. 7; *money*, 2 Kings xxii. 4; *men*, Exod. iii. 16; iv. 29, &c.: constr. with אֶל, or עַל, designating the place, &c. to which, Gen. xlix. 33; Deut. xxii. 2; Josh. xx. 4; 1 Sam. xiv. 52; Ezek. xxiv. 4; 2 Kings xxii. 20: constr. with מִן, *Collecting*, or *taking away*, 2 Kings v. 3. So also, Gen. xxx. 23; 1 Sam. xiv. 20; Joel ii. 10; Ps. civ. 29; Job xxxiv. 14; Is. iv. 1, &c. "*Taking off*," as by famine or death, Jud. xviii. 25; 1 Sam. xv. 6; Jer. viii. 13; Ezek. xxxiv. 29; Zeph. i. 2. With affix. יַאַסְפֵהוּ, יַאַסְפָה, יַאַסְפֵנִי, יַאַסְפֵךְ, from the segolate form, אֶסֶף; whence יַאַסְפוּ, 3 pers. pl. masc. We also have יֹסֵף, for יֹאסֵף, or יֵאסֵף, of the form of יֹאמַר. See Gram. art. 199. 4.

Niph. נֶאֱסַף, pres. יֵאָסֵף, constr. with אֶל, לְ, or עַל, in which last case *Collected against*, is sometimes meant. See Lev. xxvi. 25; 2 Chron. xii. 5; xxx. 3; Gen. xxxiv. 30. אֶל־עַמּוֹ, or אֶל־עַמָּיו, *collected to his people*; אֶל־אֲבוֹתָיו, *to his fathers*, Gen. xxv. 8; xlix. 29; Num. xxvii. 13; Jud. ii. 10; and, without these adjuncts, Num. xx. 26. Comp. Gen. xv. 15. Not "*de introïtu in orcum*," as Dr. Gesenius supposes, because no one can shew that the orthodox Hebrews ever entertained any such notion, as is sufficiently clear from the ingenious and learned attempt of Schrœder, in his "Dissertatio Inauguralis ad Canticum Hiskiæ," p. 12. Lugd. Batav. 1765. See my notes on Job vii. 9, &c. Comp. Jer. viii. 2; xxv. 33; Ezek. xxix. 5; Job xxvii. 19; Num. xii. 14; comp. with 2 Kings v. 3; suprà.—Jer. xlvii. 6; xlviii. 33; Is. xvi. 10; lx. 20; with what has been said under Kal, in the sense of taking away collectively.

Pih. *Collecting*, for the purpose of preserving, Num. x. 25; Jud. xix. 15. 18; Is. lxii. 9; Jer. ix. 21.

Puh. *Collected*, &c. as in the last, Is. xxiv. 22; xxxiii. 4; Hos. x. 10; Zech. xiv. 14.

Hiphh. Exod. v. 7, הַאֲסִיפוּן, for תֹּאסְפוּן, from cogn. root יסף; so אֱסֹפְךָ, 2 Kings xxii. 20, and 2 Chron. xxxiv. 28, *Add*, *collect*.

(47)

Hithp. Deut. xxxiii. 5, Infin. *Being collected* (together),—is the only instance.

אֲסֻפָּה, f. *A collection*, or *gathering*, Is. xxiv. 22.

אֲסֻפִּים, m. pl. and אֲסֻפוֹת, fem. constr. אֲסֻפֵּי, form פְּקוּד, compens. י, dagesh in last rad. *Collections*, i. e. of stores or money : or, as some think, *storehouses*. The Lat. Vulg. *a council*, or assembly of persons, Eccl. xii. 11 ; 1 Chron. xxvi. 15. 17; Neh. xii. 25.

אֹסְפָה, see v. אסף.

אֲסַפְסֻף, m. redup. of אסף, Gram. art. 169. 6. *Mixed multitude*, or *collection*, Num. xi. 4, with the article, הָאסַפְסֻף, contr. for הָאֲסַפְסֻף, Gram. art. 86. 5. It is not necessary, therefore, to suppose with Dr. Gesenius, that we have a Syriasm here. Comp. Exod. xii. 38.

אֲסְפַּרְנָא, Chald. (compd. of א+ספר+נא, hëemanti. See ספר), q. d. *ad numerum. Exactly, carefully, expeditiously*, Ezr. v. 8; vi. 8. 12, 13; vii. 17. 21. 26. It is not, therefore, a foreign word.

אֱסוֹר, and alt. אִסּוּר, m. i. q. אָסוּר. Arab. اِسْر, *lorum;* اُسْر, *captivitas*. Syr. ܐܣܪ *cingulum;* it. Chald. et Æth. *Tying, binding, taking captive;* constr. abs. with אֶת, בְּ, or עַל, and with לְ, or בְּ, prefixed, Num. xxx. 3 ; Jud. xv. 10. 12; Ps. cv. 22; cxlix. 8.

אִסָּר, m. *An obligation*, either to do, or to forbear doing, something vowed : it differs from נֶדֶר, which respects the terms, or subject matter, of the vow; this, the *obligation*, or *ban*, to be submitted to, in case of its not being performed. See Num. xxx. 11. 14, where this word is connected with שְׁבֻעָה. Dr. Gesenius is mistaken, therefore, in supposing that נֶדֶר is positive, and אִסָּר negative, in its bearing. See l. c. vv. 3, 4, 5. 11, 12. 14. The second occurs in the plural: with affix. ib. verses 6. 8. 15.

אֱסָר, Heb. and Chald. m. אֱסָרָא, with defin. art. postfixed, i. q. Heb. אִסָּר, *An obligation*, Dan. vi. 8—10. 13, 14. 16. Buxtorf and Gesenius prefer the Rabbinic acceptation, viz. *interdict :* but there is no good ground for it. Heb. Num. xxx. 3, &c.

אָסַר, v. pres. יֶאֱסֹר, and אָסוֹר, with affix. יַאַסְרֶהוּ, יַאַסְרֵם, יַאַסְרִי, תַּאַסְרֵהוּ, יַאַסְרֻהוּ, as in אסף. I. *Tying, binding*, as a captive or prisoner ; as horses to a chariot, or vice versâ, a cart to the oxen : one's self by a vow. II. *Urging the lines* to the attack, or rather, perhaps, taking care to preserve order during its continuance. Comp. עָרַךְ, 2 Chron. xiii. 3, with יָאֱסֹר, ib. Constr. abs.—also with בְּ, לְ, or עַל, Gen. xlix. 11. אֹסֵר, part. with י, relat. or parag. Gram. p. 161 ; Ps. cxviii. 27 ;— Gen. xlii. 24; Jud. xvi. 5; 2 Kings xvii. 4 ; xxiii. 33 ; 1 Sam. vi. 7. 10 ; 1 Kings xviii. 44 ; 1 Kings xx. 14; 2 Chron. xiii. 3 ; Num. xxx. 3. 10.

Niph. נֶאֱסַר, תֵּאָסֵר, הָאָסְרוּ, *Becoming bound*, Gen. xlii. 16. 19; Jud. xvi. 6. 13.

Puh. אֻסְּרוּ, in pausâ, אֻסָּרוּ, Is. xxii. 3. By means of the bow they *have been reduced to bondage*, מִקֶּשֶׁת אֻסָּרוּ.

אֲסָרַם, see r. יסר.

אַע, m. Chald. i. q. Heb. עֵץ. The letters having undergone the usual changes. *Wood, timber*, Ezra v. 8; vi. 4. 11. With def. art. postfixed, אָעָא, Dan. v. 4. 23.

אַף, conj. Gram. art. 77. See אסף. Arab. syn. وَافِي, *integer, totus, completus;* hinc fortassis, فَ, *itaque, ergo, &c.* Syr. ܐܦ, lit. *embracing, including ;* hence, *Also, moreover, nay, indeed, &c.* as the context may require; taking care that the precise force of the word never be lost, Deut. xv. 17 ; Num. xvi. 14; Job xv. 4 ; Eccl. ii. 9 ; Est. v. 12.

It is occasionally joined with וְ, כִּי, בַּל, גַּם, אִם, אָמְנָם, and the interrogative הֲ; and will then form an expression compounded of the sense of both. See the examples in Noldius, pp. 92—94. Ed. 1734. It is sometimes repeated, as in Is. xl. 24, where the force is sufficiently apparent : at others, it is omitted by the ellipsis, as in Prov. xvii. 26, according to Noldius. Gesenius's remark, that this word takes place of גַּם in the poetical style, and, in the more recent Hebrew, will be found to be groundless upon a mere inspection of the passages cited in Noldius.

אַף, m. for אַנְף, Gram. art. 76. Arab. أَنْف, *nasus*, it. Eth. Syr. ܐܦ, for نَفْ, *facies*. Dual, אַפַּיִם, sing. with affix. אַפִּי, אַפֶּיךָ, אַפּוֹ, אַפֵּךְ, pl. אַפֵּיהֶם אַפָּם, אַפְּכֶם. *The nostril*. Meton. *The nose*, Num. xi. 20 ; Is. iii. 21 ; Ezek. xxiii. 25, &c.—of animals, Job. xl. 24 ; Prov. xi. 22; Cant. vii. 5.—

אֲפֹו (48) אָפָא

And, as certain affections of the mind, are believed to be visible in the nose; as Eng. vulg. *he turned up his nose:* so גֹּבַהּ אַף, *height of nose*, i. e. *haughtiness*, or *disdain* of countenance, Ps. x. 4. So again, "his nose swelled," for he became enraged. Comp. Prov. xxii. 24; xxix. 22. Used also when speaking of God, Deut. xxix. 19; xxxii. 22; Zeph. ii. 2, 3; Job xxxvi. 13; hence the phrase חָרָה אַף, *The nose* (anger) *became hot;* so also עָלָה אַף, *the nose* (anger) *arose*, Ps. lxxviii. 31; Prov. xv. 1. To which is opposed שָׁב אַף, *the anger returned*, or was assuaged, Gen. xxvii. 45. In the dual, *nostrils*, Gen. ii. 7; vii. 22; Lam. iv. 20; implying anger, Exod. xv. 8. Hence the phrases אֶרֶךְ אַפַּיִם, *The delaying of anger*, i. e. long suffering, קְצַר אַפַּיִם, *Short of anger*, i. e. *hasty*. By a meton. *The face, countenance*, and hence *person*, like the Greek πρόσωπον; Gen. iii. 19; xlii. 6; Neh. viii. 6; 1 Sam. xxv. 23. אַחַת אַפַּיִם, *One of two persons*, i. e. a double portion, 1 Sam. i. 5.

אַפְאֵיהֶם, see v. פאה.

אָפַד, v. pres. יֶאְפֹּד, *Putting on the ephod*, Exod. xxix. 5; Lev. viii. 7. See אֵפוֹד.

אֲפֻדָּה, f. q. d. *Ephodized*, i. e. made like an ephod: clothing so made, Exod. xxviii. 8; xxxix. 5; Is. xxx. 22. From this last passage, it should seem that some such clothing was put upon the idols.

אַפֶּדֶן, m. Arab. فَدَن, *arx firma*. Syr. ܟ݂ܦ݂ܢܳܐ, pl. ܟ݂ܦ݂ܢܺܝ݂ܢ, and with ܐ, prost., اكفدن, *Arces, palatia.* A palace, or rather, *camp*: hence אָהֳלֵי אַפַּדְנוֹ, *The tents of his camp*, Dan. xi. 45.

אֹפֶה, m. אֹפָה, f. for אֹפֶהָם, contr. Gram. art. 73. Arab. وفي, unde ميفى, *fornax lateraria* ... qui paratur coquendo pani. Castell. Syr. ܐܦ̣ܳܐ, *coxit*; pl. m. אֹפִים, fem. אֹפוֹת, *Baker*, Gen. xl. 1, &c.; Hos. vii. 4. 6; 1 Sam. viii. 13. With affix אֹפֵיהֶם. Hence—

אָפָה, v. pres. יֹאפֶה, *Baking*, Gen. xix. 3; Is. xliv. 15. תֹּאפֶה, *she bakes* (for) *him*, 1 Sam. xxviii. 24. om. א, Gram. art. 72. יֵאפוּ, *they bake*, Ezek. xliv. 20. Niph. תֵּאָפֶה, Lev. vi. 10; Ib. vii. 9; and xxiii. 17.

אֵפוֹ, אֵפוֹא, or אֵיפוֹא, i. q. אֵיפֹה. (See א), except that this is used relatively, not interrogatively; and is, therefore, equivalent to the Latin, *quidem, equidem, quandoquidem, demùm, igitur*, or the like. *Now, then, now then*, &c., used occasionally with interrogatives; as, מִי הוּא אֵפוֹא, *Who is he then?* Gen. xxvii. 33; it. v. 37; Is. xix. 12; Job ix. 24; xvii. 15; xxiv. 25. See also Gen. xxvii. 37; Exod. xxxiii. 16: and with אִם־כֵּן, Gen. xliii. 11. Concesso demùm, quod ita se res habet: *If so then, do this, &c.*

אָפוּ, see v. אפה.

אֵפוֹד, m. Cogn. פָּדָה, Arab. فدى, *redemit ex servitute*, &c. So named, perhaps, to keep the Israelites in mind (see Exod. xxviii. 12) of the *great redemption* wrought for them under the leading of Moses; the value of which seems to have been intimated by the costliness of its materials and workmanship. *The ephod*, as worn by Aaron, and after him by the Jewish High Priests. See Exod. xxviii. 6—12. 31—35; xxix. 5; Lev. viii. 7, 8. LXX. ἐπωλίς. Braun. de vestit. Sacerdot. p. 463. 478. Joseph. Antiq. lib. iii. vii. § 5. Jahn Arch. Bib. iii. Theil. p. 351, &c. Epit. p. 189.

II. An inferior sort of *ephod* made of fine linen (בַּד) was also used by Samuel even when a child, by the priests, and David, when engaged in divine service. See 1 Sam. ii. 18. 28; xiv. 3; xxiii. 6. 9, et seq.; 2 Sam. vi. 14.

Idols seem also to have been ornamented with an *ephod*; see אֲפֻדָּה, preced.: and hence, to have been so styled; see Jud. xvii. 5; xviii. 14. 17. 18. 20; Hos. iii. 4.

אָפִיל, or אָפֵל, m. אֲפֵלָה, f. אֲפֵלוֹת, and אֲפִלוֹת, f. pl. See אפל. I. *Concealed*; hence, II. *Quite dark*, or *obscure*: according to some, *Late*, Exod. ix. 32. אֲפִלוֹת, *concealed* (as under ground), i. e. *not yet sprung up*, seems to suit the passage, unless we suppose the term *later* to signify the same thing. In the other acceptation, see Exod. x. 22; Deut. xxviii. 29; Is. viii. 22; Joel ii. 2; Zeph. i. 15; Amos v. 20; Prov. vii. 9. It is more intense in signification than חֹשֶׁךְ. See Exod. x. 21, 22.

אָפִיק, m. Arab. أفَق, see אפק. Cogn. فَاقَ فَوْق, *superior fuit, surrexit, et hinc*, فَائِق, *egregius, eminens.* Any thing rising, swelling; as, I. *Torrents*, or *rivers*, by the

אֹפֶל (49) אֶפַע

rains, &c., Job vi. 15; xl. 17; Ezek. xxxii. 6; xxxiv. 13; Ps. cxxvi. 4. II. *The embossings of shields*, Job xli. 7. In 2 Sam. xxii. 16, and Ps. xviii. 16, אֲפִיקֵי, ought, I think, to be taken as *the swellings of the sea*, or of some great waters, so agitated by the storm described as to be brought upon the lands, and that their beds may be said to be discovered. III. *Mighty*, or *eminent men*, Job xii. 21.

אֹפֶל, m. Arab. اَفَلَ, as in اَفَلَتِ الشَمْس, i. q. غَابَت, *It set*, as the sun, i. q. *became concealed*. Jauhari ... "Falsissima quæque legantur in Castelli et Giggeii Lexicis," inquit Doctiss. Gesenius, in Thes. sub voce; but not a word has he given in proof. *Concealment;* hence, I. *Thick darkness*, Is. xxix. 18; Ps. xi. 2; xci. 6; Job iii. 6; x. 22. Metaph. II. *Misery*, or *sorrow*, Job xxiii. 17; xxx. 26.

אָפְנָיו, m. pl. or dual. Once only. Prov. xxv. 11, *Its time*, or *season;* occasion. Arab. اَوَانٌ, or اَفَانٌ, *tempestas*. See אֹבֶן.

אֶפֶס, m. cogn. פֶּסַס, *deficit*. it. אסף, which see; dual אֲפָסִים, constr. אַפְסֵי. I. *Termination, extremity*. II. *Deficiency, wanting*, Is. xl. 17; xli. 12, 29; xxxiv. 12; Prov. xxvi. 20; Job. vii. 6; 1 Sam. ii. 10; Ps. ii. 8; Prov. xxx. 4. אַפְסַיִם, *Two extremities*, i. e. extremities of both feet; the soles, or ancles, Ezek. xlvii. 3.

Used also as a particle of negation, Is. v. 8; Amos. vi. 10; Deut. xxxii. 36, וְאֶפֶס כָּמוֹנִי, *Nor any one like me*, Is. xlvi. 9; ib. xlv. 14; אֵין עוֹד אֶפֶס אֱלֹהִים, (There) *still exists not;* (there) *is wanting, a God;* comp. 2 Sam. ix. 3. וְאַפְסִי עוֹד, *I am*, or *exist;* and *my not existing*, i. e. putting this as a case, still (there would be no other), Zeph. ii. 15. Comp. Is. xlv. 6; xlvii. 10; אֶפֶס כִּי, *bating that,—excepting that*, Num. xiii. 28; Deut. xv. 4, &c. See Nold. p. 96.

אֶפַע, m. i. q. אֶפְעֶה, Arab. فَعَى, whence الْفَاعِي, i. q. الْغَضْبَان الْمُزْبِد, *The angry, the foaming*, i. e. exceedingly angry. *An adder;* once, Is. xli. 24, וּפָעָלְכֶם מֵאָפַע, *And your doing* (is) *of the adder;* i. e. of an injurious and Satanic sort.—Serpents, scorpions, and indeed every thing injurious, are, in the Scriptures, referred more or less directly to the work of the evil spirit. See Gen. xlix. 17: Ps. lviii. 5; xci. 13; cxl. 4. Comp. with Luke x. 19; Rev. ix. 3. Idolators made all these, in one case or other, objects of worship, perhaps to conciliate their supposed chief. Moor's Hindu Pantheon, *passim*. Prep. Evangel. Euseb. lib. 1, near the end, &c.— Some of the ancient translators seem to have read אֶפֶס here, which Gesenius prefers. But, if they supposed this word to refer to idolatry, or some idol—as it was usual to consider idols as *nothing*—and occasionally to style them אַל, שָׁוְא, אָוֶן, אֱלִיל, and the like; it is perhaps unnecessary to call the reading in question, although we have אַיִן, in the parallel. In ancient times images of serpents, &c. were certainly worn as amulets. See *Schrœder, de Vestitu mulierum passim*. The Kamoos tells us too, under الْاَفْعَى, that الْمِفْعَاة signifies a mark made in the form of *an adder*, and that جَمَلٌ مَفْعِي means, *a camel so marked*. To preserve it probably from the evil eye, &c.—an evident vestige of ancient idolatry.

אֶפְעֶה, m. i. q. אֶפַע, *An adder*, or *viper*. Job. xx. 16; Is. xxx. 6; lix. 5. Hieroz Boch. II. lib. iii. c. 1.

אָפַף, v. occ. 3 pers. m. pl. only, and then without any elision; as Ps. xviii. 5, אֲפָפוּנִי, *They have enclosed*, or *hemmed me in*. Arab. اَفَّ, *mærore gravatus fuit*. اَفَّ, Cogn. r. اَوِفَ, *noxa affecit;* اَيْفَ, *perniciem passus fuit*. Always in a bad sense, Ps. xl. 13; 2 Sam. xxii. 5; Jon. ii. 6.

אָפַק, v. in Hithp. only. Arab. اَفَقَ, and اُفُق, *concinnavit inspissando corium; vicit, superavit; in varias regiones iter habuit vir. Going on*, proceeding to some object or end, Gen. xlv. 1. לֹא־יָכֹל לְהִתְאַפֵּק, *He was unable to go on*. Ib. xliii. 31; 1 Sam. xiii. 12; Is. lxiv. 11. רַחֲמֶיךָ אֵלַי הִתְאַפָּקוּ, Is. lxiii. 15, *They mercies towards me proceeded?* i. e. *Have they proceeded?* &c. LXX. ἀνέχομαι, ἐγκρατεύομαι, Targ. אתחסן.

אֵפֶר, m. generic. Arab. اَفْر, *confusio, absumptio*. I. *Ashes;* often used with עָפָר *dust*, when speaking of mourning, Jer. vi. 26; Lam. iii. 16; Ps. cii. 10; with שַׂק, Est. iv. 1. Metaph. II. *Any thing worthless*, Job xiii. 12; See my notes on this place. Is. xliv. 20, &c.

H

אֵפֶר, m. Cogn. Syr. ܟܘܒܥܐ, et ܟܘܒܥܐ, *tegumentum, cidaris.* Cogn. Arab. غَفَرَ, *texit, &c.* *A fillet* or *tiara* for the head, 1 Kings xx. 38. 41. LXX. τελαμών.

אֶפְרֹחִים, m. pl. r. פרח. Aff. אֶפְרֹחֶיהָ, אֶפְרֹחָיו. The sing. does not occur. Arab. فَرْخ, *Pullis avis. The young of birds,* as found in the nest, Deut. xxii. 6; Job xxxix. 30, &c.; Ps. lxxxiv. 4, has been generally misunderstood by the translators and commentators. It stands thus, vr. 3. נִכְסְפָה, *My soul longeth, yea even,* וְגַם, *fainteth for the courts of Jehovah; my heart and my flesh sing to the living God.* It is added, גַּם־צִפּוֹר, *Even* (as) *a sparrow* (that) *hath found a house, and a swallow a nest for herself* . . . . אֶת־מִזְבְּחוֹתֶיךָ i. e. *as to, with reference,* or *respect to, thine altars, &c.* That is, just as the bird has been anxiously desirous for a place in which to deposit its young; so, in like manner, have I been desirous for the courts and altars of my God, and have sung my songs to him with particular reference to these. If, therefore, we read the passage, beginning with גַּם־צִפּוֹר, and ending with אֶפְרֹחֶיהָ, as if included in a parenthesis and given by way of illustration, we shall discover a clear and consistent interpretation to it. For similar passages see Gram. art. 241. 18. The omission of the כ of similitude is very common.

אַפִּרְיוֹן, m. once, Cant. iii. 9, where (see too vr. 10,) it appears to have been a sort of *moveable,* or *chariot-throne,* not unlike, perhaps, the تَخْتِ رَوَان, *moveable,* or *running-throne* of the Persians. If so, the Arab. أَفَرَ, *cucurrit,* أَفَرَ, *incitatius currere,* will afford a suitable etymology. LXX. Castell, and Gesenius, φορεῖον, *ferculum.* (Cogn. Heb. פרח.) Syr. ܦܘܪܝܐ, *cella, lectus, &c.* which Gesenius very unnecessarily calls in question.

אֲפַרְסְיָא, m. pl. def. Chald. A people so called, Ezra iv. 9. Hiller supposes them to be the Parrhasii of Polybius and Strabo; others take them to have been Persians. (Heb. פרס, *Persa.*) LXX. Ἀφαρσαῖοι.

אֲפַרְסְכָיֵא, m. pl. def. Chald. It. Ezra v. 6, with which occurs—

אֲפַרְסַתְכָיֵא, m. pl. def. Chald. Names of people subject to the Assyrians. Some have supposed them to be the *Parasitaceni,* or *Parætaceni,* people of Media.

אֶפְרָתִי, m. Patron. of אֶפְרָת, Gen. xlviii. 7. *An Ephrathite,* Ruth i. 2, &c.

אָפַת, see v. פתה, *Niph.*

אֶפְתַח, Chald. once, Ezra iv. 13, a compd. perhaps of אַף, and תַּם, for שָׁם, *there* or *then. Thus then, then moreover, &c.* LXX. καὶ τοῦτο. Syr. ܗܟܢܐ. *And so it* (is), &c.

אֶצְבַּע, f. Heb. et Chald. Arab. صَبَعَ, *intendit digitum in aliquem* vituperii ergo pl. אֶצְבָּעֹת, constr. אֶצְבְּעֹת. I. *A finger,* the *fore-finger.* II. *A toe.* III. Synechd. *The hand.* IV. *A digit;* as the context shall require.—שְׁלַח אֶצְבַּע וְדַבֶּר־אָוֶן, *The putting forth of the finger and speaking evil.* The finger is here, perhaps, put for *the hand,* (which the verb שׁלח, seems to require.) If so, the sense may be, *The putting forth,* or *striking with, the fist,* Is. lviii. 9. Comp. Exod. viii. 15; Ps. viii. 4; cxliv. 1; Is. ii. 8; xvii. 8; Luke xi. 20; 2 Sam. xxi. 20. *A digit,* measure so called, Jer. lii. 21. Affix. אֶצְבָּעוֹ, אֶצְבָּעֵךְ, אֶצְבְּעֹתֵיכֶם, אֶצְבְּעֹתֶיךָ, אֶצְבְּעֹתָיו.

אָצִיל, m. r. אצל. Arab. أَصِيل, *radicatus, firmus.* Cogn. وَصِيل, *conjunctus, familiaris.* I. *Connected, attached,* in laws, society, &c. Hence, II. *Adjoining, &c.,* Exod. xxiv. 11. וְאֶל־אֲצִילֵי וגו׳, *And, upon the connected,* i. e. those joined in covenant with them, *of the children of Israel, He sent not forth the hand:* the divine appearance did not strike them dead. II. Is. xli. 9, מִקְצוֹת הָאָרֶץ וּמֵאֲצִילֶיהָ, *From the extremities of the land, and from its adjoining people;* i. e. from Chaldea, and its inhabitants.

אַצִּיל, m. and f. Arab. وَصَلَ, *bene conjunxit, &c.* Syr. ܐܨܝܠܐ, *cubitus, junctura cubiti;* pl. אַצִּילִים, and אַצִּילוֹת.—*Conjuncture* of the hand, arm; or of a chamber, &c. to any building, Jer. xxxviii. 12. אַצִּילוֹת יָדֶיךָ, *The junctures of thy hands,* i. e. the wrists, Ezek. xiii. 18. אַצִּילֵי יָדַי (for יָדַיִם), id. Ib. xli. 8. שֵׁשׁ אַמּוֹת אַצִּילָה (where the ה seems to be paragogic), *Six cubits, the conjuncture,* i. e. the additional *chamber,* or *wing,* as some think.

אַצִּיעָה, see v. יצע.

אֵצֶל (51) אקח

אֵ֫צֶל, m. Arab. viii. conj. اِتِّصَال,
i. q. عِنْدَ. Lat. apud.—*Near, at, &c.* Gen.
xxxix. 10. אֶצְלָהּ, *Near her, with her*, Lev.
x. 12. אֵצֶל הַמִּזְבֵּחַ, *Near the altar, &c.* See
the places in Noldius, p. 97. With pref. and
affix.—Mich. i. 11. בֵּית הָאֵצֶל, House *which is
near;* meaning apparently either Samaria,
or Philistia. מֵאֵצֶל, Ezek. xl. 7. מֵאֶצְלִי,
1 Kings iii. 20. מֵאֶצְלוֹ, 1 Sam. xvii. 30.
מֵאֶצְלָם, Ezek. x. 16. *From with, &c.*

אָצַל, v. in Kal, Niph. and Hiph.
Laying up with self; and hence, *holding
back,* or *withholding,* from others; or, for the
purpose of bestowing upon others, constr.
immed. or med. with לְ, or מִן, as the sense
may require, Gen. xxvii. 36. הֲלֹא־אָצַלְתָּ לִּי
בְּרָכָה׃, *Hast thou not laid up* (with thee) *a
blessing for me?* See also Num. xi. 17;
Eccl. ii. 10. Niph. Ezek. xlii. 6, נֶאֱצַל
subtracted from, or *contracted.* Hiph.
Num. xi. 25, וַיָּאצֶל, contr. for וַיַּאֲצֵל, sense
as in Kal.

אֶצְעָדָה, f. r. צעד, i. q. צְעָדָה. *A bracelet,*
or *clasp,* for the arm, Num. xxxi. 50; 2 Sam.
i. 10.

אֲצַק, see v. יצק.

אָצַר, v. see אוֹצָר. *Treasuring* any thing
up; *keeping, preserving,* as precious, Kal.
2 Kings xx. 17; Is. xxxix. 6.
Niph. Is. xxiii. 1. 18, לֹא יֵאָצֵר, *Shall not be
laid up.*
Hiph. וָאוֹצְרָה, with ה, parag. *So I appoint
as treasurer,* Neh. xiii. 13. Cogn. r. יצר.
Arab. وَصَرَ, i. q. أَصَرَ, *pactum, contractus.*
Part. אוֹצֵר, pl. אוֹצְרִים, Amos iii. 10.

אֶצֶר, r. יצר.

אֶקְדָּח, m. see קדח, *A precious stone*
so called, probably the carbuncle, Is. liv. 12.
LXX. λίθους κρυστάλλου. So the Syr.

אֲקוֹ, m. for אֲנָקוֹחַ, Gram. artt. 76. 74.
r. נקה. According to the Kâmoos, بنات
النقا, is دُوَيْبَّة تَسْكُن الرَّمَل, *A small beast
which lives among the sands* in the deserts:
it is also named شَحْمَة النَّقَا, *Fat of the
sands.* A sort of wild goat, or gazelle.
Hieroz. i. lib. iii. c. xix. Some have thought
that the word is identical with *ounce,* and
that the animal is the *Oryx.* It was a clean
animal, Deut. xiv. 5. Syr. and Chald. יַעְלָא.
Arab. وَعَل, *mountain-goat.*

אָקְחָה }
אֶקָּחָה } see v. לקח.

אֶקְרָאָה, see v. קרא.

אֹר, for יְאֹר, or אוֹר, which see.

אֶרְאֵלָם, occ. once, Is. xxxiii. 7. By
some supposed a compd. of אֲרִי+אֵל+ם. The
ם as in חָם, intensive: and hence to signify
Great heroes collectively. The LXX. seem
to have read אראלם, either in Pih. or Hiph. of
the verb רעל, *terrify:* the text of which, as
it now stands, evidently gives two versions of
this place. The Chald. and Syr. read either
אֶתְגְּלִי לְהוֹן, or נִרְאֹה לָהֶם; the former, יֵרָאֶה לָהֶם,
the latter, ܢܬܚܙܐ ܠܗܘܢ, *He shall appear
to them.* Comp. Is. lxvi. 5. The Vulg. *Ecce
videntes, &c.* Sym. and Theod. Ὀφθήσομαι
αὐτοῖς; Aquil. ὁραθήσομαι αὐτοῖς. If we
may rely on these versions, אֵרָאֶה לָהֶם, *I will
be seen,* or *appear, to them,* was perhaps the
textual reading of their times. And this
seems to me to bid fair for being the true
reading; for in the phraseology of S. S., *to
see,* (see רָאָה), is sometimes the same thing
as *to animadvert, &c.* Hence Christ is said
to appear in flaming fire, &c. So here, this
expression is followed by צָעֲקוּ, *They shall cry
out, &c.* This is an answer sufficient for
Rosenmüller's " Quid sibi vult; ecce ap-
paebo illis?" Schol. in loc.

אֶרֶב, m. Job xxxvii. 8; xxxviii. 40, i. q.
אָרַב, m. Arab. إِرْب, *fallacia, insidiæ-
que,* cogn. وَرْب, *latibulum feræ.* I. *Lying
in wait;* or II. meton. *place* of id. Jer. ix. 7;
Hos. vii. 6, with aff. אָרְבּוֹ. אָרְבָּם.

אֹרֵב, m. pl. אֹרְבִים, *An ambuscader,*
Josh. viii. 2. 12. 14. שִׂים־לְךָ אֹרֵב, *Place thy
ambuscader,* Jud. xx. 29. 33; Jer. li. 12.
הָכִינוּ הָאֹרְבִים, *Set in order the ambuscaders,*
Lam. iii. 10, &c. Much used in Oriental
tactics, and are termed by the Arabs,
كَمِين, pl. كُمَنَاء.

אָרַב, v. pres. אֱרֹב, with ה, parag. אֶאֶרְבָה
Lying in wait, or *ambush,* constr. with לְ pers.
place; עַל pers. or place, Deut. xix. 11; Ps.
x. 9, &c.
Pih. part. מְאָרְבִים, Jud. ix. 25; 2 Chron.
xx. 22.

Hiph. וַיָּרֶב, for וַיַּאֲרֵב, apoc. *So he places an ambush*, 1 Sam. xv. 5.

אַרְבֶּה, m. r. רבה. Arab. رَبْوٌ, *cœtus, agmen, A species of the locust* so called, Exod. x. 4; Lev. xi. 22; Joel i. 4, &c. See Bochart. Hieroz. tom. ii. p. 441, &c. Ludolf's Comment. Hist. Æth. passim. It seems to me that, in the last instance, the locusts are introduced merely to describe the ravages of an invading army. Comp. chap. ii. throughout and Rev. chap. ix.

אֲרֻבָּה, f. of אָרֵב, pl. constr. אֲרֻבוֹת. Is. xxv. 11, אֲרֻבוֹת יָדָיו, *The machinations, or insidious doings, of his hands.* So Saadias, Jarchi, &c.

אֲרֻבָּה, f. pl. אֲרֻבּוֹת: i.e. אֲרֻבָה, for אֲרוּבָה, r. רבב. Arab. رَبَّ, *auxit. Any thing cancellated*, or *woven up*, like wicker work, to guard the aperture so wrought, from the ingress of persons, birds, &c.; such were *windows* (so called, perhaps, from twigs thus *wound together*) before the use of glass. Hence, *A window*, generally, Eccl. xii. 3; 2 Kings vii. 19; applied to the heavens, Gen. vii. 11; viii. 2;—to a dove-cott, Is. lx. 8. In Hos. xiii. 3, it is supposed to signify *a chimney*; but there seems to be no necessity for this. With aff. אֲרֻבֹּתֵיהֶם.

אַרְבַּע, m. and אַרְבָּעָה, constr. אַרְבַּעַת, f. Heb. and Chald. r. רבע. Arab. رَبَعَ, *being the fourth in order, &c. The numeral four.* See Gram. art. 181, 2. With aff. אַרְבַּעְתָּם masc. אַרְבַּעְתָּן, fem. dual, אַרְבָּעָתַיִם, *fourfold.* In the pl. it is put for *forty*, אַרְבָּעִים. This number is, according to Dr. Gesenius, used for a round number like the numbers *seven*, and *seventy*: and, in proof of this, he cites Gen. vii. 17; Jon. iii. 3; Ezek. iv. 6; Matt. iv. 2; and the Persian *chil minár*. My remark is, Several numbers, as, *three, four, six, seven, &c.*, are occasionally used indefinitely in Hebrew, which the context must determine, as in Amos, chapters i. ii., &c. In the places, however, cited by Dr. Gesenius, it is by no means clear that this is the case.

אֶרֶג, m. Cogn. Arab. أَرَكَ, أَرَاكَ, et أَرَاكٌ, مُوتَرَكٌ i. q. مُلْتَفٌّ كَثِيرٌ, i. e. *valdè implexæ* (arbores ita dictæ). *A weaving.* Meton. *Texture, web,* or *woof,* of any thing woven. Job. vii. 6, יָמַי קַלּוּ מִנִּי־אָרֶג, *My days are more swift than the woof*, i. e. as thrown into the *warp* by the weaver's shuttle: in other words, my web of life is more rapidly filled up, than the web of the weaver. Jud. xvi. 14, הַיְתַד הָאֶרֶג, *The pin* (i. e. of) *the woof*, i. e. the machine,—in some respects, not unlike a comb,—by which it is beaten firmly together.

אֹרֵג, m. pl. m. אֹרְגִים, f. אֹרְגוֹת. *A weaver*, Exod. xxviii. 32; 1 Sam. xvii. 7; 2 Kings xxiii. 7, &c.

אָרַג, v. pres. יֶאֱרֹג, f. 2 pers. תַּאַרְגִי. *Weaving,* Is. lix. 5; Jud. xvi. 13, occurs not elsewhere.

אַרְגְּוָן, m. Chald. i. q. Heb. אַרְגָּמָן, 2 Chron. ii. 6.

אַרְגָּז, m. r. רגז. Arab. رَجَزَ, *lentiore motu, ob aquæ copiam, agitata fuit* nubes. *A sort of bag,* or *wallet,* appended to the side of the ark, 1 Sam. vi. 8. 11. 15. It is apparently the same, or nearly the same thing, with the Arabian رِجَازَةٌ, which is thus described by Jauhari, الرِّجَازَةُ مركب اصغر من الهودج ويقال هو كساء يجعل فيه احجار يعلق باحد جانبي الهودج اذا مال i. i. *The rijāza is a thing to ride in, smaller than the haudaj. It is also said to be a sort of purse into which stones are put; it is hung to one of the two sides of the haudaj, when it inclines (towards the other).* Syr. ܪܓܳܙܐ. Com. Ephrem loc. cit. ܐܘܓܳܙܐ, which must mean the same thing.

אַרְגָּמָן, m. Apparently a foreign compound, i. q. ارغوان, or ارجوان as the Persians write it. Compd. of آر, *pretium, valor, imperium, &c.* and گون, or گونة, *color, species, &c.* q. d. *color pretiosus, sive imperialis.* Hinc. Syr. ܐܪܓܘܢܐ, *purpura.* The Heb. מ being a letter of the same organ with ו, has been substituted for it. Bochart, however (Hieroz. pars. ii. lib. v. cap. xi.), thinks that the word originated on the shores of Phœnicia, where the *murex* or *conchylium,* with which they dyed purple, was found in great abundance. If so, the compound might be of Syr. ܐܘܓ, *desiring,* and ܚܡ, or ܓܘܢܐ, *colour;* the whole meaning *desirable, precious, &c. colour.* Similar compounds are ܚܡܓܘܢܐ, *color hysginus;* and Pers. آسمانجون, *cœruleus color,*

ארה   (53)   ארו

&c. The shell from which the dye was extracted was termed πορφύρα by the Greeks; and, as it was found in Phœnicia, the colour obtained from it (purple) was named φοῖνιξ. See Steph. Thes. or Scapula, sub voce, Exod. xxv. 4; Num. iv. 13; Cant. vii. 6. In 2 Chron. ii. 6, we have the Syriac form אַרְגְּוָן, which—as Solomon was writing to a Tyrian king—was most suitable. See Braun. de Vestitu. Sacerd. lib. i. p. 211; Plin. Hist. Nat. lib. ix. 60.

אָרָה, v. Arab. أَرَى, mellificavit apis, &c. *Cropping, or plucking off,* as fruits, &c., Ps. lxxx. 13; Cant. v. 1. The elder lexicographers made מְאִירוֹת, Is. xxvii. 11, a Hiph. part. from this root. It is now generally derived from אור, *setting on fire.*

אָרָה, see v. ארו.

אֲרוּ, Chald. i. q. Heb. רְאוּ, *See, behold;* i. q. Arab. أَرَى, id. to which it approaches in form. אֲלוּ, id. exhibits a change only of ר to ל, being letters of the same organ, Dan. vii. 5—7. 13; Ib. ii. 31.

אָרוּז, pl. אֲרֻזִים. Arab. أَرُوز, *firmus, colligens se et contrahens. Firmly bound,* or *packed,* package, bale, &c. Ezek. xxvii. 24. See ארז.

אֲרוּכָה, or אֲרֻכָה, f. Arab. أَرِيكَة, Ἴασις, *sanitas, abductio vulneris, &c.* I. *Repairing, setting in order,* a wall, health, &c. Is. lviii. 8; Jer. viii. 22; xxx. 17, &c. II. *Lengthening out* (see אָרךְ), as to time, or space, Jer. xxix. 28; Job xi. 9; constr. אֲרֻכַת, aff. אֲרֻכָתֵךְ.

אֲרוֹמָם, see רום.

אָרוֹן, m. r. Arab. أَرُون, whence أَرُون, and إِرَان, i. e. according to Jauhari, تَابُوتٌ, خَشَبٌ, *a wooden chest.* Firozabadi gives سَرِيرُ المَيِّتِ أَو تَابُوتُهُ, *The bier,* or *chest,* i. e. coffin, *of a dead body.* I. *A coffin,* Gen. l. 26. II. *The sacred chest,* or *ark,* of the covenant, Num x. 33; xiv. 44, &c. III. *A money-box* or *chest,* 2 Kings xii. 10, 11. Some modern lexicographers reject the root أَرَنَ, *dentibus apprehendit,* as the etym. "Because, "says one of them, "Cujus . . . in diall. non est commoda significatio." They then propose אָרָה, *decerpsit.* But why, it may be asked, is not the signification of the one just as good as that of the other? For the same reason, I suppose, Freytag has, in his edition of the lexicon of Golius, cancelled the excellent note of that author on this word!

אָרוֹר, m. *Cursing.* r. ארר, Jud. v. 23; infin. or verbal noun.

אָרוּר, m. *Cursed.* r. id. Gen. iii. 14, &c. Part. pass.

אֲרוֹת, f. pl. constr. אֻרְוֹת, it, אֲרָיוֹת, constr. אֻרְוֹת. The last radical being either ו or י, Gram. art. 202. 3. Arab. آرِي, or آرِي, *stabulum, præsepe.* Chald. אֻרְיָה, or אֻרְיָא. Syr. ܐܽܘܪܝܳܐ. I. *Stalls,* for horses or other beasts. II. Synecd. *A stable,* 1 Kings v. 6; 2 Chron. ix. 25; xxxii. 28.

אֶרֶז, m. Arab. أَرْز, or أَرْز, *arbor conifera, cedrus.* Syr. et Chald. אַרְזָא; Æth. ኣርዝ; pl. אֲרָזִים; constr. אַרְזֵי. *The cedar tree,* or *wood,* pec. of Libanus. Celsius, Hierobot. I. p. 106, supposes the *pine* must be meant, merely because the Arabic word signifies both *cedar* and *pine.* This is weak and futile, both because the trees on the Libanus are known still to be cedars, and because the authors of the ancient Versions, who take the word to signify the cedar—could hardly have been ignorant as to what tree was meant. See Bochart's Canaan, p. 706. Jud. ix. 15; 2 Sam. v. 11, &c. Aff. pl. אֲרָזַי, אֲרָזָיו.

אַרְזָה, f. *Cedar-work,* Zeph. ii. 14. The terminating ה is, perhaps, i. q. Arab. ة, of unity,—as in علامة, *a singularly learned man,*—implying singularity of workmanship, i. e. singularly good. See also אִשָּׁה.

אֹרַח, m. אֹרְחָה, f. אֳרָחוֹת, pl. constr. אָרְחוֹת, אֳרָחוֹת, id. Chald. ܐܽܘܪܚܳܐ, Syr. via. I. *A way, road,* or *path.* II. Metaph. *Mode, manner, custom.* III. Meton. *Wayfaring man*; as traveller, merchant, &c. Mostly used in the elevated style, except in the last acceptation, Gen. xlix. 17; Jud. v. 6; Ps. xvii. 4; Prov. i. 19; Job viii. 13; Gen. xxxvii. 25; Is. iii. 12, &c. Phr. אִישׁ אֹרַח, i. q. Arab. إبْنُ السَّبِيلِ. See דרך. Aff. אָרְחוֹתָם, אָרְחוֹתַי, אָרְחוֹתֶיךָ, אָרְחוֹתָיו, אָרְחוֹתֶיהָ, אָרְחֹתֵי.

אֹרַח, id. Chald. pl. אָרְחָן, Dan. iv. 34; v. 23.

אָרְחָא, f. pl. Chald. id. *Ways.* Aff. אָרְחָתֵהּ, אָרְחָתָהּ, Dan. iv. 34; v. 23.

אֹרַח, m. אֹרְחִים, pl. *Travelling,* or *traveller,* Jud. xix. 17; 2 Sam. xii. 4; Jer. ix. 1.

אָרַח, v. Kal. occ. Job xxxiv. 8, אֹרַח לְחֶבְרָה, *He goeth to associate, herd with,* &c.

אֲרֻחָה, f. constr. אֲרֻחַת, *Usual, accustomed,* allowance or provision, 2 Kings xxv. 30; Jer. xl. 5; lii. 34; Prov. xv. 17. אֲרֻחַת יָרָק, *Accustomed* (portion) *of green* (herbs). Aff. אֲרֻחָתוֹ.

אֲרִי, and אַרְיֵה, Syr. ܐܪܝܐ, *leo.* Arab. أَرْي, *fervor, æstus;* v. أَرِيَ, *æstuavit irâ.* Cogn. Heb. אָרָה; *decerpsit,* pl. אֲרָיִים, and f. אֲרָיוֹת. I. *A lion,* generally, Num. xxiii. 24; 1 Sam. xvii. 34, &c. II. Metaph. *Any cruel,* or *bloody man,* Ps. xxii. 22; Prov. xxviii. 15; Job iv. 10; Dan. vii. 4. Comp. 1 Pet. v. 8; 2 Tim. iv. 17. III. *Any warlike, brave,* or *invincible man.* Comp. Gen. xlix. 9, with Rev. v. 5. So Is. xxi. 8, וַיִּקְרָא אַרְיֵה, *So a warrior cries,* i. e., placed on the watch-tower. See Boch. Hieroz. I. lib. iii. c. 1.

אֲרִיָה, see v. רוה.

אַרְיָוָן, pl. m. Chald. Def. אַרְיָוָתָא, f. Dan. vi. 8, *Lions.*

אֲרִיאֵל, or אַרְאֵל, m. of אֵל+אֲרִי, lit. *Lion of God,* applied as an epithet to any warlike person, like the Arab. أَسَدُ اللّٰهِ الغَالِبُ, *The Lion of God the conqueror,* as applied to Ali and others.—2 Sam. xxiii. 20; 1 Chron. xi. 22. To *Jerusalem,* as victorious under God, Is. xxix. 1, 2. To the altar *of burnt offerings* in Ezekiel's temple, Ezek. xliii. 15, 16. הַרְאֵל, vr. 15, is perhaps incorrect, for אֲרִיאֵל. In this place some lexicographers give אֲרִי, *focus,* with אֵל for the etym., but unnecessarily. See Hieroz. I. lib. iii. cap. 1.

אֲרִיךְ, m. Chald. See אָרַךְ.—*Delay.* Syr. ܐܪܝܟܐ, *longus.* Some take the Talmudic *Convenient.* Buxtorf. Lex. Talm. col. 217; occ. Ezra iv. 14.

אָרֵךְ, m. Arab. أَرَكَ, *tardavit. Length* as of forbearance, in the phrases אֶרֶךְ אַפַּיִם, *Length* (tardiness) *of anger :* אֶרֶךְ רוּחַ, *Length of spirit,* i. e. in each case, *forbearance,* Exod. xxxiv. 6; Eccl. vii. 8, &c. Jer. xv. 15,

אַל־לְאֶרֶךְ אַפְּךָ תִּקָּחֵנִי, *Take me not away, for* (the sake of) *thy long-suffering;* not, by being long-suffering (towards my enemies) as Gesenius proposes. He was, perhaps, led astray here by the parenthetical character of the passage. See Gram. art. 241. 18. He also writes this word, אָרֵךְ; but, in this case, it could never have taken the form אֶרֶךְ, in construction. The whole is, therefore, erroneous.

אֹרֶךְ, m. *Length,* as to time, or space, Gen. vi. 15; Exod. xxvi. 2; Ps. xxi. 5. Aff. אָרְכּוֹ, אָרְכָּהּ, אָרְכָּם, אָרְכָּן.

אָרַךְ, v. *Lengthening* out, as to time, place, thing. Constr. med. ל, עַל, אֵת, it. immed. pres. יַאֲרִכוּ, pl. f. תַּאֲרַכְנָה, Gen. xxvi. 8; Ezek. xii. 22, xxxi. 5.

Hiph. הֶאֱרִיךְ, *Cause delay.*—Inf. Num. ix. 19. 22, &c. *Forbear,* as to anger, Prov. xix. 11. *Prolong,* as *days, life,* Deut. iv. 26; 1 Kings iii. 14, &c. *Making long,* the tongue, Is. lvii. 4. Part. Eccl. vii. 16, imp. f. הַאֲרִיכִי, *Lengthen out,* Is. liv. 2; אַאֲרִיךְ, *I lengthen out,* נַפְשִׁי, *my desire,* Job. vi. 11. See my notes, ib. 1 Kings viii. 8, הַבַּדִּים, *the staves.*

אַרְכָּא, f. Chald.
and
אַרְכָּה, f. Heb.
} *Length, prolonging,* as to time, Dan. iv. 24; vii. 12.

אַרְכֻּבָּה, f. Chald. r. רכב. Arab. رَكَبَ, *percussit in genu,* &c. The Kāmoos has, sub voce, الرُّكْبَةُ ... مَوْصِلُ مَا بَيْنَ اسَافِلِ اطْرَافِ الغَجَلِ وَاَعَالِي السَّاقِ. *Rakbat* is the juncture between the lower parts of the thigh, and the upper of the leg. Gol. *Genu.* The Persians, too, have the phrase بر زانو نشستن, i. e. *to sit upon the knee,* for *kneel.* We need not, therefore, suppose any metathesis of אברוך here. Occ. once, Dan. v. 6; with aff. אַרְכֻּבָּתֵהּ, *His knees.*

אַרְכִּי, m. and אַרְכַּוִי, Chald. Patronym. of *Erek.* Gen. x. 10. See Bochart's Phaleg. iv. 16. Occ. Josh. xvi. 2; 2 Sam. xv. 32; xvi. 16; and pl. Chald. אַרְכְּוָיֵא, Ezra iv. 9; keri.

אֲרָם, m. *Syria.* Meton. *Syrians,* Is. vii. 2. 5, &c. On this country, see Bochart's Phaleg. lib. ii. 6; Reland's Palestine, lib. i. c. 24; The Ancient Universal Hist. vol. ii. p. 254. ed. 1747, with the authors referred to.

אֲרָמִי, m. אֲרַמִיָּה, f. and אֲרָמִית, pl. אֲרַמִּים. Patron. of אֲרָם, *Syrian, Syriac.* Once הָרַמִּים for הָאֲרַמִּים (Gram. art. 86. 5), 2 Chron. xxii. 5. Once אֲרוֹמִים, where the keri has אֲדוֹמִים, 2 Kings xvi. 6. אֲרָמִית, used adverbially, Heb. and Chald. 2 Kings xviii. 26; Is. xxxvi. 11; Dan. ii. 4; Ezra iv. 7. *In Syriac, Syriacè;* i. e. in the Syriac language.

אַרְמוֹן, m. pl. f. constr. אַרְמְנוֹת, r. רָמָה. Arab. رَمَى, *superiorum reddidit.* Cogn. Heb. רוּם. In Amos iv. 3, הַרְמוֹן. Sometimes in the form אַלְמוֹן; mut. ל, ר, Is. xiii. 22: pl. אַלְמְנוֹת. *A palace*, Is. xxv. 2; Jer. xxx. 18, &c. Gesenius takes it to mean a part of the royal citadel, and probably *the harem.* The former might be true; but for the latter there is not a shadow of ground in the Hebrew Bible. With aff. אַרְמְנוֹתָיו—וְתֵיךָ, וְתֵיהֶם—וְתֵיהָ.

אֶרֶן, m. Arab. أَرَان. The name of a thorny tree which grows in Arabia Petræa, according to Abul Fazl. Celsius Hierobot. i. p. 192. It is mostly found in vallies, or on plains. The wood is good for cleaning the teeth; the berries it produces are in clusters like those of the grape, and are used for medicinal purposes. The word occurs once, Is. xliv. 14, and has generally been supposed to be the same with the Latin *ornus,* or mountain-ash.

אַרְנֶבֶת, f. Arab. أَرْنَب, *lepus, A hare,* Lev. xi. 6; Deut. xiv. 7. Bochart's Hieroz. i. 994. Canaan, p. 430.

אַרְעָא, f. Chald. def. art. א postfixed, i. q. Heb. אֶרֶץ, mut. צ in ע, more Chaldaïco. Syr. ܐܪܥܐ. Arab. أَرْض, i. q. كُلُّ مَا سَفَلَ, *quicquid humile, inferum et depressum.* opp. τῷ, سَمَاء, i. e. quicquid altum est. I. *The earth,* Dan. ii. 35; iii. 31; Ezra v. 11; II. as an epithet; fem. *Low, inferior,* Dan. ii. 39. אַרְעָא מִנָּךְ, *Lower than thee,* i. e. less elevated.

אַרְעִית, f. Chald. (See Gram. artt. 166. 136. 5), *Low,* or *lower,* part. Dan. vi. 25.

אֶרֶץ, f. see אַרְעָא, pl. אֲרָצוֹת, constr. אַרְצוֹת. I. *The earth,* generally, as opposed to *the heaven,* Gen. i. 1, &c. II. *Any land, or country;* as, אֶרֶץ הַחֲוִילָה, *Land of the Havilah.* אֶרֶץ כּוּשׁ, *Land of Cush,* Ib. ii. vv. 11, 13.

III. Meton. *The inhabitants of the earth.* Gen. vi. 11; xi. 1, &c.; or of any part of it, Jud. xviii. 30; Is. xxiii. 13, &c. κατ᾽ ἐξοχήν, הָאָרֶץ, *Judea,* Lev. xxv. 23, &c. Often used without the definite article, even when the sense seems to require it, Gen. i. 24; ii. 4, &c. See Gram. art. 221. 3—5, in particular. Pl. *Lands, countries,* Gen. x. 20; xxvi. 3, &c. different from that of the Jews; and therefore, during the times of the theocracy, IV. *Heathen nations,* 2 Kings xviii. 35; 2 Chron. xiii. 9, &c. With aff. אַרְצִי, אַרְצוֹ, &c.

אַרְקָא, Chald. ארק, i. q. ארע, or ארץ, def. art. postfixed. In this case the guttural ע seems to have degenerated into the deeper guttural ק, *The earth,* once, Jer. x. 11.

אָרַר, v. Arab. أَرَّ, *Driving, inflaming, injuring.* Cogn. هَرَّ, *abhorruit.* Comp. وَقَرَ. Syr. ܗܪ, aph. *læsit, nocuit.* Gr. ἀρά ἀράομαι. Constr. immed. *Cursing; declaring, denouncing,* or *causing, that injury overtake some one.* Used of God, of a prophet as authorized by him to do so; or, of a false prophet as assuming this power. אָרוֹתִי, *I have denounced,* Mal. ii. 2. Part. אֹרְרַי, *denouncers of,* Job iii. 8; Gen. xxvii. 29; Num. xxiv. 9. In the first passage is added, הָעֲתִידִים עֹרֵר לִוְיָתָן, *Those who are about to stir up a Leviathan,* i. e. whose case is so desperate as to stir up the great sea monster to battle. See my notes on the place. Pres. 1 pers. אָאֹר, Gen. xii. 3, as אָסֹב, for אָסֹבֹב; תָּאֹר, Exod. xxii. 27; Num. xxii. 6. 12. Imp. אֹר, with ה, parag. אָרָה, *Denounce,* or *curse, I pray,* Num. xxii. 6; xxiii. 7: pl. אֹרוּ, *Denounce ye,* Judg. v. 23. The first of these from the cogn. אָרָה, perhaps. Part. אָרוּר, *Denounced,* person or thing, Gen. iii. 14; iv. 11; ix. 25, &c.; pl. Josh. ix. 23; 1 Sam. xxvi. 19.

Niph. Part. נְאָרִים, *Persons subjected to a curse, denounced,* Mal. iii. 9.

Piħ. אֵרָה, (Jehovah) *hath denounced it,* Gen. v. 29. Part. מְאָרְרִים, (waters) *bringing on the curse,* Num. v. 18, &c.

Hoph. יוּאָר, *Is made accursed,* Num. xxii. 6.

אָרַשׁ, v. Piħ. Arab. أَرْش, *mulcta; donum quo conciliatur gratia judici.* Pres. הֵאָרֵשׂ, *Espousing a wife,* by entering into a contract under a fine or mulct; the sum of which is paid over to the father of the bride

ארשׁ (56) אשׁה

as a dower, on the nuptials taking place. Constr. *med.* with לְ, pers. and בְּ, of the price, 2 Sam. iii. 14; Hos. ii. 21, 22. *Immed.* Deut. xx. 7; xxviii. 30.

Puh. f. אֹרְשָׂה; in pausâ, אֹרָשָׂה, *Espoused*, Exod. xxii. 15; Deut. xxii. 28; part. f. מְאֹרָשָׂה, *One espoused*, Deut. xxii. 23. 25. 27.

אֲרֶשֶׁת, f. Arab. أَرَسَ, *operam alicujus expetivit*. *Petition*, or *request*, for assistance or favours generally, Ps. xxi. 3. See the context immediately following. LXX. Δέησις.

אֵשׁ, com. Syr. ܐܶܫܳܐ, *ignis.* Arab. أَسَ, and آسَ, nom. unit. r. اوس, *reliquiæ cinerum in camino*; et ita *cinis omnis*. Angl. *ashes*, ab. Heb. אֵשׁ, Castell. I. *Fire*, generally, Gen. xv. 17; Exod. xii. 8. When coming from God. II. *The lightning*, 1 Kings xviii. 38; 2 Kings i. 10. 12. 14; Job i. 16. Applied to the appearance of God, as revealed on Sinai, &c., Exod. xix. 18; xxiv. 17; It. Exod. iii. 2. Hence, meton. III. Expressive of His *fierce anger*, Deut. xxxii. 22; Jer. xxi. 12. IV. The *ardent* state of mind, under prophetic inspiration, Jer. xx. 9; Ps. xxxix. 3, 4. V. *War*, as a consumer, Num. xxi. 28; Jud. ix. 15. 20; Jer. xlviii. 45; Joel ii. 3. 5. Hence, VI. meton. *Great tribulations*, as in passing through fire and water, Ps. lxvi. 12; Is. xliii. 2;—It. from the heat of the sun, Joel i. 19, 20. Phr. אַבְנֵי אֵשׁ, *stones of fire*, i. e. live coals, sparkling like precious stones, Ezek. xxviii. 14. 16. With aff. אִשּׁוֹ, אֶשְׁכֶם, אֶשָּׁתָם, f. once אִשָּׁתָם, *kethiv.* Jer. vi. 29 (for אִשָּׁתָם), keri תַּם אֵשׁ.

אֶשָּׁא, Chald. אֶשָּׁא, def. i. q. Heb. Dan. vii. 11.

אִשׁ, for אִישׁ, m. Arab. أَيْسَ, *vis, violentia;*—unde إِيسَانْ, *homo*, and آيِسَة, *mulier*, i. q. אִישׁ, and אִשָּׁה, which see.—Syr. ܐܺܝܬ. i. q. יֵשׁ. *Substance;* and, with the substantive verb, or rather the logical copula understood, *There is*, or the like, 2 Sam. xiv. 19; Mic. vi. 10.

אֹשׁ, Chald. m. pl. אֻשַּׁיָּא, def. with aff. אֻשּׁוֹהִי. Arab. أُسّ, أُسَّ وَإِسَّ, أُسَّ, *fundamentum*. *The foundation* of any building, Ezra iv. 12; v. 16; vi. 3.

אֶשֶׁד, m. אֲשֵׁדָה, f. f. constr. אַשְׁדּוֹת. Chald. אֻשָּׁא, f. *fulcrum, sustentaculum*, Buxtorf Lex. Talmud, col. 234. Arab. شَلَّ, *The being firm*, and r. شَلَّ, *cucurrit, impetum*

faciens, &c.; pl. f. אֲשֵׁדוֹת, constr. אַשְׁדּוֹת. *The foot of a mountain* at which torrents imbed themselves, and thence occasionally form rivers. אֲשֵׁדֵי נְחָלִים, *Bed of the torrents*, Num. xxi. 15. אַשְׁדּוֹת הַפִּסְגָּה, *The feet of the* (mount) *Pisgah*, Deut. iii. 17; Jos. xii. 3; xiii. 20. Eichhorn's edition of Simonis makes it also signify *nomadum bubile*, sc. *ovile*, in Josh. x. 40; xii. 8; but without reason.

אִשֶּׁה, m. constr. אִשֵּׁה, pl. abs. אִשִּׁים, constr. אִשֵּׁי. See אֵשׁ. The שׁ, i. e. הַ, is often added to nouns in the Arabic, for the purpose of giving the force of a *substantive*, to an *adjective* noun. See Freytag's Hamāsa, p. ٣٠: so far the ה parag. is accounted for. *Any thing set on fire;* pec. *the offerings made by fire under the law*, Exod. xxix. 18. 25. 41; Lev. ii. 11; xxiv. 7; Num. xv. 3. *The burning of incense*, Lev. ii. 2. Gesenius thinks that, in Lev. xxiv. 7, it is applied to incense scattered on the shew-bread, though not burnt. And ib. ver. 9, he says, that the shew-bread itself is reckoned among the אִשֵּׁי יְהוָֹה; but why? Because probably, in both cases, it was perfumed by the smoke of *burning incense*, Lev. ii. 2. 10.

אִשָּׁה, constr. אֵשֶׁת, f. of אִישׁ, which see —for אִישָׁה, and אֱנָשָׁה. Comp. Gen. ii. 23, which Gesenius tells us,—Thes. sub voce,—is not sufficiently accurate. The truth, however, is, אִשָּׁה is only another mode of writing אִישָׁה, just as אֲגוּדָה is of אֲנוּדָה, &c. In Deut. xxi. 11; 1 Sam. xxviii. 7; Ps. lviii. 9, אֵשֶׁת occurs as the absolute form. Gesenius, moreover, confounds the etymology of this word, as he does in its masc. with that of נָשִׁים, and אֲנוֹשׁ: when it is evident, that they are derived from totally different roots, although often substituted the one for the other. I. *Woman*, generally, Gen. xii. 11; Exod. iii. 22; xxi. 29, &c. II. *Wife*, Gen. xxi. 21; xxiv. 3. *Betrothed*, Gen. xxix. 21, &c. III. *Concubine*, Gen. xxv. 1; xxx. 4, &c. Hence, in apposition, אִשָּׁה זוֹנָה, *a harlot;* אִ׳ פִּלֶגֶשׁ, *a concubine;* אִ׳ אַלְמָנָה, *a widow;* אִ׳ נְבִיאָה, *a prophetess;* אִ׳ יִשְׂרְאֵלִית, *an Israelitess*. In construction, אֵשֶׁת חַיִל, *a woman of ability*. אֵ׳ מִדְיָנִים, *disputatious*. אֵ׳ זְנוּנִים, *a harlot;* אֵ׳ אָב, *father's wife*, i. e. step-mother, opposed to אֵם, *mother*, Lev. xx. 11; 1 Cor. v. 1. It forms certain idioms with אָחוֹת, and רְעוּת, as, Exod. xxvi. 3. 5, 6. 17, &c.; and Is. xxxiv. 15, 16; Jer. ix. 19, as in אִישׁ. See also אָחוֹת, and רְעוּת. Used also *distributively*, Exod. iii. 22;

אשו (57) אשי

Amos iv. 3, &c. *Each, every, &c.* Plur. אִשּׁוֹת, once, Ezek. xxiii. 44, for which נָשִׁים, abs. and נְשֵׁי, constr. is usually substituted, Gen. xxxi. 35; 2 Sam. i. 26, &c. and Gen. vii. 13, &c. See נָשִׁים. With aff. אִשְׁתּוֹ, אִשְׁתְּךָ, once, Ps. cxxviii. 3; אִשְׁתְּךָ, Gram. art. 96. 2. IV. Also applied to men by way of reproach, Is. iii. 12; Jer. li. 30; Neh. iii. 13. See also Gram. artt. 215. 9; 216. 7. 9, and notes.

אֱשׁוּן, keri, אִישׁוֹן, kethiv, occurs only once, Prov. xx. 20. It is very evident, I think, that this is nothing more than another, and perhaps erroneous, mode of pointing אִישׁוֹן, which see. In this place we have אֱשׁוּן חֹשֶׁךְ, and Ib. vii. 9, אִישׁוֹן לַיְלָה וַאֲפֵלָה. Can any one doubt, that these expressions are equivalent? or that, as the vowels have but little authority, this authority ought here to be set at nought? See also איתון, which is only the Chaldaic way of writing the same word. The Targumist prefers the form אֲתוּן, which is still the same word. It is remarkable that Gesenius should not have seen this; as it is certain that *caligo*, which he gives as its sense, is erroneous. Winer is equally dark, as to its Chaldee form.

אָשׁוּר m. r. אשר. Arab. أَشَرَ, *secuit,* אָשׁוּר *reciprocato exultu corruscavit fulmen, &c.* Hence, perhaps, the notion of *direct, straight, &c.* Cogn. יָסַר, *castigavit, corrected,* אָסַר. Arab. أَسَرَ, *confined, bound, &c.;* يَسَرَ, *se arbitrio alterius permisit;* يَسَرَ, *direxit, &c.* I. *Footstep;* and by a meton. II. *The track* of id., Ps. xxxvii. 31; xliv. 19; lxxiii. 2; Job xxxi. 7. Plur. אֲשׁוּרִים, With aff. אֲשׁוּרָי, אֲשׁוּרַי, plur. אֲשׁוּרַי, אֲשׁוּרֵנוּ. It. אַשּׁוּר, or אַשֻּׁר, *Assyria.*

אֲשׁוִיתֶיהָ, or, according to the keri, אֲשׁיוֹתֶיהָ, once, Jer. l. 15, *Her foundations.* r. שׁית or שׁות, *ponere.* Whence שֵׁת, *fundamentum,* שָׁתוֹת, &c. Syr. ܐܫܬܐ, *antiquitas, firmatio;* it. ܐܫܬܐ, *spissitudo, paries.* Cogn. שָׁתַת, *fundavit.* Arab. شَتَّ, *firmitas.* Chald. שְׁתִיָּה, *fundatio.* Arab. أُسِّ, *columna, fulcimentum.*

אֲשִׁימָא.—The name of an idol made, and worshipped, by the inhabitants of Hamath, 2 Kings xvii. 30. Gesenius makes it the same with the Persic آسمان, *āsmān,* heaven. It is very unlikely, however, that the people of Hamath in Syria, should fabricate a deity, and call it by a Persic name, when the Syriac or Chaldaic must have been vernacular to them. For the same reason, it could hardly be of Zend origin. The termination א, moreover, seems to declare for the Syriac or Chaldaic. Selden, de Diis Syris, Syntag. ii. cap. ix. confesses his ignorance as to what it was. The Jews generally take it to have been the image of *a he goat.* I think it not unlikely that it was an idol representing the devil; particularly, as אָשָׁם signifies *reatus, &c.,* for such deities the heathen had, and still have; as the *Mahā Deva* of the Hindoos, &c.

אֲשֵׁירָה, see אֲשֵׁרָה.

אֲשִׁישָׁה, f. pl. אֲשִׁישׁוֹת, and m. אֲשִׁישִׁים, constr. אֲשִׁישֵׁי. Syr. ܐܫܝ, *innatavit.* Arab. أُشّ, *panis siccus,* i. e. *panis simplex citra obsonium.* It. أَشَّ, *agilis fuit, exultavit.* I. *Food, affording support, nourishment, delight, &c.* What it was no one can now say particularly. It probably was a sort of cake soaked either in honey or wine. See 2 Sam. vi. 19; 1 Chron. xvi. 3; Cant. ii. 5; Hos. iii. 1; in Exod. xvi. 31, the Targum of Jonathan has אשישי, for the Heb. צפיחית, which Castell renders by "*Laganum melle obductum,*" on the authority of the Arabic صَغَ, *expandit* in latum, *obduxit, lamina texit:* صَفِيحَة, *lamina, &c.* From the passage in Hosea, it seems probable that these were offered to idols. The distinctions which Gesenius makes between this word, בִּמֹּק, and דְּבֵלָה, cannot, I think, be maintained. II. אֲשִׁישֵׁי, *foundations of,* according to some. De Dieu thinks *lagenæ, bottles,* or *jars,* must be the sense, Is. xvi. 7, to suit נְאָנָם, following, which he translates "*Utique confractæ sunt*" I see no reason for departing from the sense first given; for, if we may consider this a sort of food given for *support* (Cant. ii. 5)—or, as bread is spoken of in Is. iii. 1—there can be no impropriety in speaking of its being broken to pieces; אֲשִׁישֵׁי קִיר־חֲרָשֶׂת, may, therefore signify the *supports, refreshments, &c. of kir khareseth;* and may mean, *the men of that* place, as Jeremiah seems to have paraphrased it, Ch. xlviii. 31. In this respect

אשד (58) אשם

Gesenius's remark is good; while his interpretation of the word by *foundations*, as well as his appeal to Is. lviii. 12, is quite groundless.

אֶ֫שֶׁד, m. *The testicle*, Lev. xxi. 20. Syr. ܐܫܕܐ, *testiculus*. Æth. ቀንተ: *indicio fuit*. Arab. شكّ, *exhibuit statum sum Deo*, &c. So *testis*, in the Latin, as Gesenius has well remarked.

אֲשֻׁפִּים, see v. שכם.

אֶשְׁכֹּל, m. pl. אֶשְׁכֹּלוֹת, and אַשְׁכֻּלוֹת, f. in pausâ, אַשְׁכֻּלוֹת. I. *A cluster* or *bunch* of grapes, or flowers. The primitive notion seems to consist in *binding* or *packing together*; as, شكل, *ligavit, innodavit*; شكّل, *utrinque a fronte comam plexuit mulier—crines ejus ad dextram, et sinistram partem conglobati flavi fuerunt*. Hence, أشكل, *maturuit uva, dactylus*, &c., i. e. it formed bunches and ripened. Comp. Gen. xl. 10. So also the Arabic عنقود, and عنقاد, *botrus, uvarum, palmæ*, &c. from the root عقد, *nodavit, nexuit, &c.* Gesenius, therefore, mistakes greatly when he tells us that, by this word the *branch* is properly meant. See Num. xiii. 23, 24; Cant. i. 14; vii. 8, 9; Is. lxv. 8, &c. II. Also the name of a place, Num. xiii. 23, 24; xxxii. 9, &c.

אֶשְׁכָּר, m. *A rich gift*, or *present*, such as is usually presented to Oriental monarchs, Ezek. xxvii. 15; Ps. lxii. 10. Comp. ver. 15. Arab. شكر, *præmio, mercede donavit, liberalem se præbuit*. شاكر, *gratitudinem commonstravit*: and شكر, *præmium, beneficii agnitio, &c.* Cogn. שָׂכָר, *mercede conduxit*.

אֵ֫שֶׁל, m. I. Properly, *A species of the Tamarisk tree*. Tamarix orientalis, Linn. It is well described by Golius, and after him by Castell, sub voce أثل; and again by Abulwalid as given by Gesenius. Thes. p. 159. II. A name for *Any tree*, generally. So Abulwalid, l. c. وربّما كان اسمًا عامًّا

للشجر كلّه. Hence, הָאֵ֫שֶׁל, 1 Sam. xxii. 6, is explained, 1 Chron. x. 12, by הָאֵלָה, *The turpentine tree*. See too, Gen. xxi. 33, where *A plantation* is probably meant.

אָשָׁם, m. אַשְׁמָה, f. pl. אֲשָׁמִים, and אֲשָׁמוֹת. I. *Guilt*: or, II. by a meton. *An offering to expiate it*. Arab. إثم, *reatus, crimen*. Much has been said by Michaelis and others, on the difference between this word, and חַטָּאת, *sin*, or *sin-offering*: one affirming, that the former must have meant sin of omission; the latter, sin of commission, and *vice versâ*: all of which Gesenius very properly pronounces fanciful and false. Yet, it is evident enough, from his mode of treating them, that he is not very clear on the subject himself. He tells us, e. g. Thes. sub. voce, that חַטָּאת implied *a greater sin*; אָשָׁם, *a less*; and, again, that not only different rites were had recourse to with respect to each of these, but that these rites were frequently joined together; which affords proof sufficient, that he had no correct notions on the subject. Every one will I think see, upon reading over Lev. iv. 5, &c., that the terms חטא, עון, and אשם, are so used, as to make all such distinctions as these fruitless. The true distinctions seem to me to be, that חַטָּאת signifies any *act of sin*, or *error*; עָוֹן, its *turpitude*; אָשָׁם, its *guilt*, as affecting the mind of the sinner, e. g. Lev. iv. 3. אִם־יֶחֱטָא לְאַשְׁמַת הָעָם, *If—he commit sin* (so as) *to implicate the people in guilt*; let him bring for his sin חַטָּאתוֹ, which he has sinned (committed), חָטָא, &c. Again, vr. 13, וְיָשִׁ֫מוּ—וְיָשׁ֫וּ, *And have done—and are guilty*. Again, vr. 22, נָשִׂיא יֶחֱטָא וְעָשָׂה—וְאָשֵׁם, *A ruler sinneth, and doeth—and is guilty, &c.* And so in other instances, making it quite impossible to keep up any such distinctions as those pointed out by Michaelis (Suppl. Lex. Heb.), Gesenius, and others. On my view of the case, the offering brought might be termed either אָשָׁם, חַטָּאת, עָוֹן, or the like: but the two first only are in use. When, therefore, the first, viz. אָשָׁם, is used, respect is had to the *guilt* of the person bringing his offering; its object being to purge his conscience from a sense of this, by securing a complete pardon from God. When חַטָּאת is used, respect is had to the *sinful act*, by which God's law has been transgressed; and pardon from this transgression is accordingly the boon sought.

אשם (59) אשמם

Comp. Heb. x. 1—3. It will be observed, that the appointments alluded to, are made with respect to certain individuals; who, it is presumed, had been made *conscious* of their *guilt*. These offerings were, therefore, public and individual recognitions of this. But, as sins innumerable must have still been committed,—not with *a high hand*, for these were unpardonable; see Num. xv. 30, and xvi.— the daily and other sacrifices for *sin*, must have been intended—not unlike our Indemnity Acts of Parliament—to meet them. See Ps. xix. 13. And, indeed, if these were intended to be types and shadows of the great sacrifice once to be made for sin, the case could scarcely be otherwise. On this view, it will be found that Josephus, Antiq. iii. 9, § 3, and Philo de victimis ii. p. 247. Ed. Mang. were not wholly wrong.

אָשֵׁם, m. pl. אֲשֵׁמִים, *Guilty*. Arab. آثِم, أَثِيم, *criminis reus*, Gen. xlii. 21; 2 Sam. xiv. 13. Gesenius makes אֲשֵׁמִים, Ezra x. 19, to signify *persons offering an* אָשָׁם, or *guilt-offering*, which is an unnecessary refinement. It is difficult to say, whether this word stands as a noun or a verb in Lev. v. 4. See Gram. art. 182. 2.

אָשֵׁם, v, and אָשַׁם, pres. יֶאְשַׁם. I. *Being, or becoming, guilty*. II. meton. *Made subject to its consequences*, i. e. *to destruction, excision*. I. Lev. v. 19. אָשֹׁם אָשַׁם, *He is wholly guilty*, Num. v. 7. לוֹ אָשַׁם אֲשֶׁר, *With respect to whom he is guilty*, Prov. xxx. 10; Ezek. xxii. 4. II. With its consequence, *death*, Hos. xiii. 1. Meton. or, what is termed *sensus prægnans* implying the general consequence, Hos. xiv. 1. שֹׁמְרוֹן תֶּאְשַׁם, *Samaria is* (or shall be) *found guilty*, בַּחֶרֶב *by the sword, &c.*, Is. xxiv. 6, Ezek. vi. 6; xxv. 12, &c.

Niph. נָאְשְׁמוּ, *Are become so desolated*, i. e. subject to the consequences of guilt, *destruction*, Joel i. 18.

Hiph. הַאֲשִׁימֵם, *Bring on them the consequences of guilt*; יִפְּלוּ, *let them fall, &c.*, Ps. v. 11.

אַשְׁמָה, infin. of אָשַׁם, above, Lev. v. 26, &c.

אַשְׁמַנִּים, once, Is. lix. 10, which has been variously interpreted. The ancients generally took, *The sepulchre;* the Jews, *Darkness;* Castell (sub voce שמן) proposes *fertile fields*, which Gesenius has finally adopted. From the context which speaks of *darkness* and the like, one would hardly expect this. Our Auth. Vers. has taken "*desolate places;*" in which, I think, they are borne out by the Syr. ܐܫܡܕܬܐ, *desertum*, and the Heb. שִׁימוֹן, Ps. lxviii. 8, &c., and יְשִׁימוֹת, Ib. lv. 16; Cogn. Arab. أَشِمَ, وَيَشِمُ, *doluit*. See يَشِبُ, وَيَشِبُ. Cogn. Heb. אָשָׁם. Syr. ܐܫܡ. Arab. أَثَمَ, *laceravit, &c.*

אַשְׁמֹרֶת, or אַשְׁמוּרָה, f. constr. אַשְׁמֶרֶת, pl. אַשְׁמֻרוֹת, *Night-watch*,—r. שָׁמַר, also,

אַשְׁמֹרָה, constr. אַשְׁמֶרֶת ..... properly *the time of it*. Under the Theocracy generally, the night was divided into three such watches. I. called רֹאשׁ אַשְׁמֻרוֹת, Lam. ii. 19. II. הָאַשְׁמֹרֶת הַתִּיכוֹנָה, *The middle watch*, Jud. vii. 19. III. אַשְׁמֹרֶת הַבֹּקֶר, *Watch of the dawn*, Exod. xiv. 24, &c. Under the N. T. times, four were adopted after the Roman usage.

אֶשְׁנָב, m. *A Latticed window*. Occurs Jud. v. 28, and Prov. vii. 6, parallel in each case with חַלּוֹן; so called, perhaps, either from its being used to ventilate and cool the house, or, because its bars represented well-arranged teeth. Arab. أَشْنَب, *having a cool mouth, and well-set teeth*.

אַשָּׁף, m. pl. אַשָּׁפִים, *Enchanter*, Dan. ii. 10; i. 20; ii. 2. Also Chald.—

אָשְׁפִין, and def. art. suff. אָשְׁפַיָּא, id. Dan. ii. 27; iv. 4; v. 7. 11. 15, as if from the sing. אָשֵׁף, (not אַשָּׁף, as Gesenius gives; for then the plur. would be אַשָּׁפִין, &c.); Syr. ܐܫܦܐ, *Incantator*.

אַשְׁפָּה, f. with affix, אַשְׁפָּתוֹ. *A quiver*. Syr. ܐܫܦܬܐ, *tegens*; ܐܫܦ, *plenus redundans*. Comp. Ps. cxxvii. 5, and Is. xlix. 2, בְּנֵי אַשְׁפָּתוֹ a periphrasis for הַצִּי, Lam. iii. 13.

אֶשְׁפָּר, occ. 2 Sam. vi. 19; 1 Chron. xvi. 3. Various interpretations have been given, which may be seen in Poole, &c.: I prefer that proposed by Gesenius. De Dieu had suggested the Æthiop. ፲ፀጸ, *mensuravit*, and taken the word to mean *A certain portion*, or *measure*, of the sacrifice. Gesenius thinks a measure, as *A cup* of wine, the most suitable. The Syr. gives, in each place, ܐܫܦܐ, which Bar Serushoi says, signifies *A cup of wine;* and, in the former place, the Arabic

אשפ (60) אשר

of the Polyglott renders this by كَاسٌ خَمْرٍ, *a full cup of wine*. Cogn. Arab. اِصْبَار, *ad summa repletum vas*. Cogn. شَبَّر, *spithamis dimensus fuit*. اَشْبَار, *spithama, dodrans*. Heb. סָפַר, *numeravit*.

אַשְׁפֹּת, m. r. שָׁפַת, *Disposing, &c*. I. *Dung*; and meton. II. *A dunghill*, Neh. ii. 13. שַׁעַר הָאַשְׁפֹּת, *The Dung-gate*, and Ib. iii. 13. הָשְׁפֹּת, the א, being dropped; and—as the miserable poor often house with their cattle—applied to extreme poverty, 1 Sam. ii. 8; Ps. cxiii. 7. Arab. تَفِثَ, *mundavit*.

אַשְׁפַּתּוֹת, f. pl. either the plural of the preceding, or of some cognate form. The Talmudic writers, to whom Dr. Gesenius is perpetually referring on words of this sort, deserve not a moment's notice. *Dunghills*, Lam. iv. 5, only.

אֹשֶׁר, m. once, Gen. xxx. 13, with prep. and affix, בְּאָשְׁרִי, *In my happiness*. Arab. أَشَرَ, *valdè alacris et lætus fuit. Lætitia exultavit. Lætior in altum sese extulit planta*. Cogn. وَشَّرَ, id. وَشَّر, *res difficilis*, &c. Cogn. Heb. יָשַׁר. Arab. يَسَرَ, *opulentus fuit*. يَسَرَ, *direxit*. Heb. יָשַׁר, *correxit*, &c. The progress of thought seems to have been, and which is constant in the S. S. that, whatever is good is difficult of attainment (χαλεπὰ τὰ καλά), is unaccommodating (as truth, see צדק); so this, under Divine Providence, brings prosperity, and a quiet conscience. So also, with us, *rectitude, integrity, straight-forward-ness, &c*. are similarly derived, and are attended with similar consequences.

אֲשֶׁר, Seg. occ. only pl. constr. אַשְׁרֵי. Arab. أَشَرَ, *lætitia exultantes, &c*.—used apparently as an ejaculation, *O happy! O how happy!* or the like. The most usual equivalent in the Arabic is طُوبَى, *very good! very happy!* Ps. i. 1, &c. Various have been the ways in which the apparent ellipsis has been supplied. I prefer considering the word as a plural of excellence, and the form of construction to have respect to the immediately following context: as, אַשְׁרֵי הָאִישׁ, *Rich blessings of the man! &c*. nothing being more common among Oriental writers, than thus to take whole sentences, or periods. See also Gram. art. 224. 12, 13. With suff. אַשְׁרֶיךָ, Deut. xxxiii. 29. אַשְׁרֶיהָ, fem. Eccl. x. 17. אַשְׁרָיו, Prov. xiv. 21. אַשְׁרֵיהוּ, Ib. xxix. 18. אַשְׁרֵיכֶם, Is. xxxii. 20, &c.

אָשַׁר, v. or אָשֵׁר, Imper. אִשְׁרוּ, *Proceed directly, straight-forward*, Prov. ix. 6. Comp. ch. iv. 26, 27. Etym. in יָשַׁר, above.

אִשֵּׁר, Pih. I. *Make direct, cause to proceed directly, &c*. Prov. iv. 14; xxiii. 19. II. *Consider*, hence *pronounce, right, good, happy*, Gen. xxx. 13; Job xxix. 11; Mal iii. 12, &c. Particip. מְאַשְּׁרִים, constr. מְאַשְּׁרֵי, Is. iii. 12; ix. 15; Mal. iii. 15.

Puh. אֻשַּׁר, *He shall be made happy*, Ps. xli. 3. Particip. מְאֻשָּׁר, *Made happy*, Prov. iii. 18. Is. ix. 15, *Pronounced, considered so*.

אֲשֶׁר, Rel. pron. of every gen. and num. See Gram. artt. 177. 216. 13—16. 230. 5—8 *He who, she who, it which, &c*. It never receives any affix; but, when the sense requires this, it is added to a preposition immediately following; e. g. אֲשֶׁר לוֹ, אֲשֶׁר בּוֹ, &c. which will necessarily refer to some preceding noun and agree with it in gender, number, &c. Its place is sometimes occupied by the demonstrative pronouns זֶה, הוּא, or זוֹ. See Gram. art. 177. 3, and note. In the cognate dialects אֲשֶׁר is unknown, and its place supplied by one form or other of this pronoun as Syr. ܕ, Chald. דִּ, Sam. ܙ, Arab. اَلَّذِي —Heb. הַלָּזֶה, Jer. xlix. 19.—Æthiop. **H** or **ʽH** : It is considered in Arabic as making the noun to which it is attached *definite*: and this is certainly sometimes the case in the Hebrew, although the rule is less constant than in the Arabic. Gram. art 220. 6.—In participial nouns, and occasionally in preterites, its place is supplied by the definite article. Gram. art. 179. 3, and note An abundance of examples is given by Noldius. Concord. Partic. pp. 214, 215, Ed 1734. Preceded by any separable or inseparable particle, it will form a sense, and may be considered as a phrase, compounded of both; as, בַּאֲשֶׁר, *In, by, through, &c*. the *which, &c*. So מֵאֲשֶׁר, לְמַעַן אֲשֶׁר אֲשֶׁר, &c. examples of all which will be found in Noldius; as also of cases, in which ellipses or redundancies, of either of these are thought to have taken place. I deem unnecessary, therefore, to epitomize them here.

אשר (61) אשר

As to the etymology of this word, very various have been the endeavours of the learned to ascertain it; yet, I think it possible, and even probable, that, in one sense or other, few of them have been wrong. Gesenius prefers setting out with the usage of the dialects, and gets from the Syr. &c. ךְ, דִי, **H** : to the Greek τὸ, Goth, *tho, the;* Sancr. *tad;* Goth. *that;* Anglo-Sax. *thaere,* &c.; supposing, apparently, that the שׁ, of אֲשֶׁר, forms the primitive vocable, and that it has been changed into ח, ד, ז, τό, &c. But this is not accounting for the word in question; it is only an endeavour to identify it with certain others, the result of which might be either true or false. If, then, we take this word as a verbal noun (form פֶּקַד), used either imperatively, or as a gerund, we shall have some such sense as, *go on* (Gr. φέρε, Lat. *age*), *go to, mark, observe, rightly, well, to the point: as to; with regard to,* &c. equivalent, or nearly so, to אֶת, or כִּי, which see; e. g. אַשְׁרֵי הָאִישׁ אֲשֶׁר וגו׳, *Rich blessings of the man! proceed, add,* &c. *he walketh not,* &c. Take now the cognate, اَذٍ, *rem rei subjunxit, prædicavit, allegavit,* &c. imperatively or otherwise as before, and we shall have, *add, affirm, allege,* and so on. Again, if we take Ewald's אָסַר, *ligavit,* which is another cognate, and apply it in the same way, the result will be much the same; and a sense will be supplied intelligible enough in all the cases; and quite as much so as many now in use in the modern languages. With us, indeed, such relative is naturally *retrospective,* bringing the speaker or hearer back to some antecedent. In the Oriental languages, according to the analysis just given, it will be *prospective* only. And hence perhaps it is, that when reference is made to the antecedent, this is done by the addition of some pronoun, such as, agreeing with it in gender, number, &c. will bring the mind back instantly to the antecedent. E. g. כְּמֹץ אֲשֶׁר תִּדְּפֶנּוּ, *As chaff, adding,* &c. *the wind scatters* IT, i. e. *the chaff.* Hence it is, perhaps, that the Arabian grammarians term this word (i. e. الذي, its equivalent), *A conjunction.* مَوْصُولٌ, Gram. art. 177. 3, note: and hence too perhaps, as the antecedent is in a manner described and so far defined, the demonstrative pronoun, זֶה, זוּ, זוֹ, or the definite article ה, may occasionally take its place: e. g. as above, אַשְׁרֵי הָאִישׁ זוּ לֹא הָלַךְ, i. e. *this hath not walked:* with ה, הָאִישׁ לֹא הֲהָלַךְ, or לֹא הָהֹלֵךְ, participially; leaving on the reader's mind an impression quite of a piece with the preceding; which seems to shew that this analysis is not incorrect. I may add, I am very much of opinion, that our own relative and demonstrative pronouns may be traced to some such primitive usage as this, and perhaps to usages common to the languages of the East; yet, I cannot think with Dr. Gesenius, that the Hebrew אֲשֶׁר, and the Greek τὸ, &c. were once the same identical word; this exceeds my powers of credence.

אֲשֵׁירָה, once אֲשֵׁירָה, pl. אֲשֵׁרִים, and אֲשֵׁרוֹת. lit. *Set up, erected; an erection,* &c. Gesenius, Winer, &c., consider this word as equivalent to עַשְׁתֹּרֶת, pl. עַשְׁתָּרוֹת; and signifying, generally, *Any idol.* It had been shown by Kimchi,* Procopius of Gaza,† Castell,‡ Spencer,§ Selden,∥ Lette,¶ and some others, long ago, that it could not signify *a grove* in many passages in which it was found. Gesenius, in his Comm. on Is. ch. lxv. 11, and again, in his Thesaurus, p. 162, renews the inquiry, as if these his worthy predecessors had done nothing. And it may be doubted whether he has at all settled the question, or, indeed, added any thing to their lucubrations on the subject. If, for example, אֲשֵׁרָה, and עַשְׁתֹּרֶת, really mean the same thing, Why are they completely different words? From the various passages and combinations in which אֲשֵׁרָה is found, we are sure that it was something that could *be made, set up, placed in a building, cut down, put away, burnt, reduced to powder.* Hence, as Selden, and after him Gesenius, has well remarked, it could not possibly be *a grove.* Again, from its occurring with צְבָא הַשָּׁמַיִם, בַּעַל, פֶּסֶל, מַצֵּבָה, עָצָב, פְּסִילָה, חַמָּנִים; it should seem to be something differing from either of them, if, at least, there is any precision in the language. Now, what could this be? Among the important, and almost necessary, parts of an idol was its *Shrine,* or *chapel;* and this, I think it probable, the אֲשֵׁרָה was. For, I. It is evident from

* In his Heb. Dict. sub voce אשר.
† Comment on 2 Kings xvii. 16; xxiii. 7.
‡ Sub voce אֲשֵׁרָה and עַשְׁתֹּרֶת.
§ De Legib. Heb. p. 506, &c.
∥ Selden de Diis Syris Syntag. ii.
¶ Lette in Biblioth. nov. Bremen. Cel. i. p. 58.

Jud. vi. 26, that it was constructed *of wood;* and this, sufficient in quantity to make a fire, such as would consume a heifer offered in sacrifice. II. It appears, ib. vr. 28, that this wooden *erection,* or *frame*—whatever else it was—stood *over* the image of בַּעַל. III. Ib. vr. 30: it was something different from the altar of Baal, and was likewise *over it.* The altar too, was, we are told, *broken down;* but the אֲשֵׁרָה, was *cut down;* a term very proper for an *erection* made of wood. Again, IV. We are told, 1 Kings xv. 13, that Maachah had made an idol (מִפְלֶצֶת) for the אֲשֵׁרָה; which would seem to intimate, that this idol was to be attached to it in one way or other. In like manner, 2 Kings xxiii. 4, we are told of vessels (כֵּלִים), made for Baal, and for the אֲשֵׁרָה. Again, Ib. vr. 7, we read of *houses* (בָּתִּים) woven for the אֲשֵׁרָה, which, from the preceding verse, should seem to consist of compartments in the Temple, divided from one another merely by curtains, and in which the idolatrous priests (הַכְּמָרִים, vr. 5, but here termed הַקְּדֵשִׁים,) used to reside. Now it is certain, that such *Shrines* were in use under the Old Testament; for in Amos v. 26, we are told of the סִכּוּת, lit. *Covering* of a certain idol; for which the LXX. give σκηνὴν τοῦ Μολόχ, &c. The Syr. ܡܫܟܢܗ ܕܡܠܟܘܡ, *The tabernacle of Malcum.* The Arabic of the Polyglott, خَيْمَةُ مُولُوخَ, *The tent of Moloch.* So also the Vulgate. In Acts vii. 43, this passage is cited thus—Καὶ ἀνελάβετε τὴν σκηνὴν τοῦ Μολόχ, καὶ τὸν ἄστρον τοῦ θεοῦ ὑμῶν Ῥεμφάν, τοὺς τύπους οὓς ἐποιήσατε προσκυνεῖν αὐτοῖς. Observe, it is expressly said here, that both the σκηνὴ and ἄστρον were made for the *purpose of worship,* as if the former was as necessary as the latter, to the usages of idolatry. Again, Acts xix. 24, Demetrius the silversmith made *silver* (temples or) *shrines of Diana;* which the Arabic translator renders by هَيَاكِلَ زُهْرَة, *Temples of Venus.* It is evident I think from this, that these *Shrines, temples,* or *chapels,* were considered important parts of idolatry. They are evidently alluded to in other parts of S.S. See Gram. art. 223, and the places referred to.* The most complete accounts of them, however, out of S.S. is perhaps to be found in the Dabistān, a work usually ascribed to Mohammed Mohsin Fāni, and written in the Persic. It occurs in the section on the religion of the ancient Persians. I can notice only a few instances. Speaking of these *temples* generally, the author tells us, that belonging to the planets they were of seven sorts ..... هياكل سياره هفتگانه. We are next told, that the image of Saturn was of black stone, ... پيكر شت كيوان را از سنك سياه; then, that his *shrine,* or *temple,* پيكر كده, was also of black stone; that the image of *Hormuz*—Jupiter—was of earth-colour, &c., and that the worshippers of this *temple,* پرستاران اين كده, had clothes of the same colour, &c.; that both *the house* (خانه) and image (پيكر) of *Behram* —Mars—were of red stone: again, that the *temple,* هيكل, of the Sun was the greatest of temples, عظيمتر از هياكل بود; that it was a sort of dome, made of golden bricks, set within with rubies, diamonds, &c., and that the image was of red gold, پيكر نير اعظم را از طلاي احمر ساخته بودند, and so on, of the rest. From all which, it must appear, that the *Shrine,* or *temple,* of the idol, was considered an important appendage to

---

Angels; because angels were supposed to descend and reside in them after consecration. If so,—and I think the author of the Dabistan speaks somewhere to the same effect,—what the idol was to the angel, the shrine was to the idol, and the temple generally to the shrine. The *Fanum* of the Latins seems to me to have been to them, just what the אֲשֵׁרָה was to the idolaters. These shrines often accompany Hindoo idols—that of Juggernaut is regularly exhibited in one—and pictures of them may be seen in abundance in Major Moore's excellent work, "The Hindoo Pantheon." One often witnesses in London, on May-day, a custom which I think, will illustrate this subject. It is this: one of the chimney-sweeping boys is inclosed in a large conical case, bedecked with various flowers; this he carries from place to place for exhibition, which consists in turning round as swiftly as he well can; the rest of his companions dancing about him. No one can doubt that this is a remnant of the Pagan *floralia,* and the continuance of a practice once in use among idolaters. The thing itself is trivial, but is instructive in this respect.

---

* According to Pococke, idols were called هياكل الملائك (الملائكة), *temples of the*

the idol, while it differed entirely from it. Mention is also made in this work of the *houses*, of those who served the idol, as situated near it; which is equivalent, perhaps, to the *houses* spoken of above: and, perhaps, "*the worshippers of the temple*," mentioned just above, is a good parallel to the נְבִיאֵי הָאֲשֵׁרָה, of S.S., 1 Kings xviii. 19. From these considerations, I am induced to believe that, by the term אֲשֵׁרָה, the *Shrine* of an idol, and not the idol itself, was meant.

אָשַׁרְנָא, Chald. *An erection, wall*, or, perhaps, *building* generally, Ezra v. 3. Etym. as אֲשֵׁרָה.

אֶשְׁתִּיו, see v. שתה.

הִתְאוֹשֵׁשׁ, under אִישׁ.

אֶשְׁתַּדּוּר, Chald. *Rebellion, commotion;* r. שדר, cogn. صدر, *commovit*, &c., Ezra iv. 15. 19. Comp. Dan. vi. 15, מְשַׁתַּדֵּר, part. Ithpa.

אָת, Chald. i. q. Heb. אוֹת, Dan. iii. 32, &c.

אַתְּ, i. q. אַתָּה, pron. 2 pers. Gram. art. 145, et seq.

אַתְּ, id. f. Gram. ib.

אֵת, with Makkaph אֶת־, pointed also אוֹת, and אֶת.—See Gram. artt. 171. 11, 12. 229. 8—10, with the note;—which is accounted for on the supposition, that different cognate roots have been taken: Ib. art. 171. 11. As to the usage of this particle, it may be said to be regulated by the principle which governs composition generally. See Gram. art. 228 et seq. When words are used for the purpose of qualifying one another, all the possible modes of combination are reducible to three only; as, I. *Apposition*; i. e. when two, or more words, signify the same thing, as יְהֹוָה אֱלֹהִים. II. *The definite state of construction*; i. e. the relation of the genitive case; as דְּבַר יְהֹוָה. III. *Independent*, or, what I have elsewhere termed, *specific*, construction, Gram. artt. 219 and 225, notes. In this latter instance, in languages admitting of declensions of nouns, an *accusative case* will often express this relation; as Lat. "*Os humerosque Deo similis;*" Arab. حَسَنُ وَجْهٍ, *formosus faciem*; which may also be expressed by using a particle; as حَسَنٌ بِوَجْهٍ, *formosus vultu*, or, *in facie*. We may here conclude, therefore, that such accusative case is only another way of expressing something which might be expressed by a particle; that is, by inserting some additional *qualifying* word. Now, such qualifying word or particle here, is אֵת, no matter how pointed.

The influence exerted by one word upon another, will moreover necessarily be either *direct*, or *indirect*. (Gram. artt. 228. 5. 229.) *Indirect influence* may be marked by various particles, as לְ, בְּ, עַל, אֶל, אֵת, &c., as the sense shall require. (Gram. Ib. par. 2, &c.) *Direct influence* needs not generally to be marked at all, except only where some ambiguity might otherwise arise,* (Gram. art. 171. 11), and in this case it is that the use of אֵת is imperative, to show that such word is to be considered as influenced, in one way or other, by some word preceding, either expressed or implied. It has been shewn (Gram. art. 229. 9), that the real signification of אֵת is, *as to, with reference to, touching*, or the like. It is also worth remarking, that the Arabic particle which is used for the same purpose, has not only precisely the same power, but is derived in the very same way. This particle is إِيَّا, which is the Masdar, or infinitive form, of the ivth conj., equivalent to the Hebrew *Hiphhil*. of the verb أَوَى, *Se recepit*—ad locum—*commorandi ergo, &c.* إِيَّاكَ, therefore, will signify, *betaking to, coming to*, &c., just as אֵת does. (Gram. art. 171. 11.) It is very remarkable, that آيٌ,—another form of this word,—has the precise sense and usage of the Heb. אוֹת, *miracle;* which is one of the forms of the particle under consideration. Now, as the Arabs have in nouns an accusative form, no such particle as this will be necessary to mark the *direct* influence of any preceding word; because this accusative form will mark it sufficiently. In the pronouns, however, they have no such accusative form; here, the particle is,

---

* Hence all those instances in Noldius, in which it is said to be wanting, p. 133, &c. And, as to multiply words, is the same thing generally as to weaken the style, the highly impassioned often omits this particle: e. g. it occurs not so much as once in the exquisitely beautiful song of Hannah, 1 Sam. ii. 1—10. The same is the case, for the most part, with the Persian particle را. See the ninth ed. of Sir Wm. Jones's Persian Gram. artt. 233, 234, 236.

את (64) את

therefore, necessary; and here only it is used, as, אִיָּי, אוֹתָךְ, אֵיָּךְ, אוֹתִי, אִיָּיִ, אוֹתוֹ, &c., which is in most cases *direct*. The influence will necessarily be *direct* after all transitive verbs, either expressed or implied; as, בָּרָא אֶת־הַשָּׁמַיִם, *creavit cœlos*, Gen. i. 1. וַיַּרְאֵהוּ—אֶת־הַגִּלְעָד, *ostendit ei—Gilead*, Deut. xxxiv. 1.

In combining this particle with the pronouns, it often takes the form אֵת, as אִתִּי, אִתּוֹ, אִתְּךָ, &c., which has usually been translated, *with me, him, thee*, &c., and hence, the influence would seem to be *indirect*; the particle is, nevertheless, precisely what it was before: e. g. וְאוֹתָנוּ עַל־הַמְּרוֹדוּ, *And, as to us, rebel not*: i. e. against us, Josh. xxii. 19. אֵין־יוּכַל־אֶתְכֶם דָּבָר, *He cannot* (do) *any thing, as it respects you*, Jer. xxxviii. 5. הָאָרִיב אֶת־רִיב אִתָּךְ, *He shall contend a contention*, i. e. greatly contend, *as to thee*, Prov. xxiii. 11. רַבִּים אֲשֶׁר אִתָּנוּ מֵאֲשֶׁר אֹתָם, *More who* (are), *touching—respecting—us, than* (are) *touching them;* i. e. on our part, than on theirs, 2 Kings vi. 16, &c. It is evident, I think, that no alteration in sense in the particle, is here made by an alteration in the vowels; the same will hold good in all other instances.

In many cases, this particle seems to have the force and usage of certain prepositions; as, מֵאֵל אָבִיךָ וְיַעְזְרֶךָּ וְאֵת שַׁדַּי וִיבָרֲכֶךָּ, *From the God of thy father; for he shall surely help thee: and touching* (the) *Almighty; for he shall certainly bless thee*, Gen. xlix. 25. Where it is evident that מ, in the first member is, in some respects, equivalent to אֵת in the second. Instances innumerable of this sort will be found in Noldius, and in which he has substituted one or other of the Latin prepositions; which is sufficient to show that this particle exerts that sort of *mediating* influence generally, which other particles, and indeed all qualifying words do.

Its principal use however is, to impress on the reader or hearer's mind, the *importance*, or *prominence*, intended to be attached to the word or words which it immediately precedes; and hence perhaps it is, that such word is, for the most part, *definite**: and it always

marks either the main, or else a subordinate, *subject* of the discourse; as, אֶת־עַמּוּד הֶעָנָן לֹא־סָר, *as to, touching, &c., the pillar of the cloud, it departed not*, Gram. art. 229, 9. Hence too, it will be used in cases of *Epanorthosis*: e. g. אֶת־יוֹסֵף אֶת־כֻּתָּנְתּוֹ אֶת־כְּתֹנֶת וגו׳, *They strip Joseph* (i. e.), *his coat* (i. e.), *the coat, &c.*, Gen. xxxvii. 23. Gram. art. 216, 4. Occasionally, after a long parenthesis; as, יָבִיא יְהֹוָה עָלֶיךָ....יָמִים....אֶת מֶלֶךְ אַשּׁוּר, *Jehovah will bring upon thee.... days....* (i. e.) *the King of Assyria*, Is. vii. 17. On this principle, Gen. xlix. 25, cited above, may be explained, as also Deut. xxxiv. 1, and innumerable others.

One word now, on the manner in which the Orientals themselves speak of this sort of construction, and of the use of the particle إِيَّا, equivalent to our אֵת, אֹת, אֶת. When a word is, they say, *the subject matter of discourse*, (المبتدأ, Gram. art. 212. 3. note,) it will exhibit a nominative case, (رفع), i. e. will be unaffected by any subsequent word, and may be preceded by إِذَا, وَامَّا, فَامَّا, امَّا, &c., *As to, touching, so as to, and as to, when, &c.;* as is the case with our אֶת־עַמּוּד, above cited: so ל, in לִקְדוֹשִׁים, Ps. xvi. 3, &c. Gram. art. 216. 15. And in this case, such nominative may contain the *subject of discourse*, or the subjective case to one or more verbs following: such terms they style مرفوعات. But, in all cases in which a word, or phrase, is affected by the influence of any other word, &c., it is termed منصوب or مفعول, and, in these cases too, it may likewise be preceded by certain particles, such as our prepositions. If any of the personal pronouns happen to be so circumstanced, its abridged form will often be taken, preceded by the particle إِيَّا; e. g. إِيَّاكَ نَعْبُدُ, *Thee we serve;* إِيَّاكَ وَالاسد, *Thee* (I warn) *of the lion, &c.* In all other cases, when the influence of the verb is *direct*,

---

* Schrœderus affirms that it is always definite. Gesenius however has found a few instances in which it is not, viz., Prov. xiii. 21; Ezek. xliii. 10; Exod. xxi. 28. This will suggest another consideration of great importance to the criticism of the New Testament, it is this; it is on this principle that the use of the

Greek article, ὁ, ἡ, τὸ, is often regulated. The definiteness of a word, phrase, or sentence, will, as here with אֵת, be much connected with the *importance*, or *prominence*, of the word or passage, as intended by its author; and, hence, it is, that ὁ Θεὸς, and Θεὸς; ὁ Κύριος, and Κύριος, &c., often occur in the very same chapter, for which Dr. Middleton could render no good account. See on the def. art. ה below, where this question will be more particularly discussed.

and this is either expressed, or implied, this objective case will be marked by an accusative form, (اَلنَّصْبُ), as, قَتَلْتُ رَجُلًا, occidi virum. زَيْدًا ضَرَبْتُهُ, Zeidum (percussi) percussi eum. جَاءَ زَيْدٌ رَاكِبًا, venit Zaidus, (vidi eum, commemmoro eum, &c.), equitantem. The first consideration, therefore, ought always to be, whether the context, with which we are concerned, presents *subjective*, or *objective* matter to our consideration; the second, what the *precise force* of the terms used is: whether any parentheses intervene; whether the language is in the natural order, or inverted; and, again, whether such *subjective* term, or terms, exert *one* only, or *more than one*, sort of influence on the following context: and lastly, whether it appears to be the intention of our author to give particular *prominence* or not, to any part of his context. Were these things duly considered, my own opinion is, we should find Hebrew words quite as precise as those of any other language, and the context as unambiguous. But more of this under the def. art. ה. I have been the more particular here, because I find in our Orientalists generally, particularly the Baron de Sacy* and his pupils, Dr. Gesenius and others, that, if they can find an European word or usage, which will supply *something like* the sense of their author, or a tolerable sense at least, they never think of making any further inquiry; when the great thing required is, not what this, or that, ingenious person may think on this, or that, passage of an Oriental writer, but what *the precise notion* is, which he himself attached to it. Among the Oriental writers themselves, the attention paid to these subjects is next to miraculous, as their very elaborate works on grammar are sufficient to prove.* And if this be deemed necessary among them, who have been brought up in the use of their idioms, usages, &c., how much more must it be among us, whose idioms and modes of thinking are the most distant possible from theirs?

אֵת, (for אֵיָה, Gram. art. 75.), pl. אִתִּים, and אִתִּים, (by a compensation-dagesh, as in פְּקֻדָּה for פְּקוּדָה). With affix אִתּוֹ. The LXX. translate it by σκεῦος, *instrument*, and ἄροτρα, *ploughs*. The Syr. by ܦܰܕܳܢܳܐ, and pl. ܦܰܕܳܢ̈ܐ, *plough-shares*. Arab. سِكِّي, *vomis aratri*. Arab. أَنَتَ, *molle fuit ferrum:* أَنِيتٌ, *molle ferrum.* According to Jauhari *iron,* as distinguished from *steel*. Hence cogn. אֵיָה, whence אֵיתָן, *fortis, robustus,* the σιδηρόφρων of Eschylus. *A plough-iron,* as our agriculturists term both the *coulter* and *share;* and plur. *plough-irons,* 1 Sam. xiii. 20, 21; Is. ii. 4; Joel iv. 10; Mich. iv. 3. The ancient *plough-iron,* seems to have been a sort of hook only, which, when drawn along by oxen, tore up the ground in furrows; and

---

* See Jāmi's Commentary on the كَافِيَة of Ibn. Ulhājib on this subject, from p. ٢٣ to p. ٣٠ and the Sihāh of Jauhari on the particle وَإِيَّا, whose definition of it is this, إِيَّا اسم مبهم و يتصل به جميع المضمرات المتصلة التي لننصب تقول إِيَّاكَ ... وجعلت الكاف بيانًا عن المقصود ليعلم الخاطب من الغايب ولا موضع لها من الاعراب. &c. I. e. إِيَّا, *is an indefinite noun, to which may be attached any of the personal pronouns, as affixed, to express an accusative case. You may say,* إِيَّاكَ, *thee, &c. Now the* كَ, *&c., are affixed to define the object, in order that the person addressed (i. e. the 2d pers.), may be known from the third, since they carry no mark of declension with them.* I. e. إِيَّا, *is prefixed in order to restrict the pronoun following to the objective case, which its own vowels could not do.*

---

* And, accordingly, he gives us in his Grammaire Arabe, both a *subjunctive*, and a *conditional*, mode in the verbs; things of which no Arab ever so much as dreamt; not to mention innumerable other things of the same sort. And Dr. Gesenius here (sub voce אֵת) tells us, that this particle is the *demonstrative pronoun* αὐτός *of the Greeks*. He also tells us that the Arabic إِيَّا, is used *reflexively*, as in إِيَّايَ, which is true enough in that particular case, but most untrue when spoken generally of its use. So, again, the Syriac ܝܳܬ, may be supplied occasionally by נֶפֶשׁ, or its equivalent; and so it may be by a preposition. The question is, as before, not what this particle might *be paraphrased by,* but, what its *precise force* and *usage is?* Which certainly is not that of either αὐτός, or נֶפֶשׁ.

K

אתא (66) אתו

was not unlike an anchor with one side or hook only. And hence it was, perhaps, that an *anchor* was termed by the Arabs سِكّي, a word differing but little from the سِكّي given above. See Virgil. Georgic. lib. i. 19. 162. 170. 494. &c., where it is so described; and "Description de l'Egypte," pll. 70. 71.

אָתָא, and אָתָה, plur. אָתוּ; pres. יֶאֱתֶה, contr. תֵּאתֶה, Mich. iv. 8. יֶאֱתֶא, Deut. xxxiii. 21. Apoc. יָאָה, Is. xli. 25. יֶאֱתָיוּן, Is. xli. 5. Imper. plur. אֱתָיוּ, Is. xxi. 12, &c. Heb. and Chald. I. *Coming into*, or *upon*; more generally, *coming*, i. q. בוא, constr with לְ and עַד, *to*, *even to*. מִן, *from*, &c., Jer. iii. 23; Is. lvi. 9; Job xxxvii. 22; Prov. i. 27, and *immediate* constr. Job iii. 25.—שֻׁבוּ אֵתָיוּ, *return*, i. e. *repent, come in*. The prophet seems to say to the people of the South, the descendants of Esau, you have long enough been immersed in the night of ignorance; come now back, return, and *come in* again among us; for salvation is of the Jews. Idiomat. אֵתָיוּ, *come ye*; Eng. *go to, up, &c.,* Is. xxi. 12; lvi. 12. Arab. أَتَى. Syr. ܐܬܐ, id.

Hiph. הֵתָיוּ, i. q. הֵבִיאוּ, *They brought*, Is. xxi. 14; Jer. xii. 9: as an imper. Chald. הַיְתָיוּ (cogn. יתה), Dan. v. 3. 23; vi. 17. 25, i. q. Syr. ܐܝܬܝܘ, i. e. 3 pers. plur. masc., not sing., as Gesenius has erroneously made it. Nor is הֵיתָיוּ, Ib. vi. 18; or הֵיתָיוּ, Ib. iii. 13, in the *Hoph*, but *Hiph*. form; in the latter, too, the sense is clearly, *they brought*; in the former, the usage seems to be impersonal.

אַתָּה, or אַתְּ, pron. 2 pers. sing. masc. *Thou*, Gram. 145. 2. 3. Arab. أَنْتَ. Syr. ܐܢܬ, f. אַתְּ, or אַתִּי. Arab. أَنْتِ. Syr. ܐܢܬܝ.

אֶתְוָדַע, see v. ידע.

אָתוֹן, fem. Arab. أَتَان, *Stepping shortly*. أَتَان, *asina*. Syr. ܐܬܢܐ, id. plur. אֲתֹנוֹת; with affix אֲתֹנוֹ. *A she ass*, Gen. xii. 16; xlix. 11; Num. xxii. 23, &c. Jud. v. 10, אֲתֹנוֹת צְחֹרוֹת, *white, shining*, or *splendid, she asses*. From these two last places it is evident, that it was usual for dignified persons to ride on this animal. Comp. Zech. ix. 9. The same is the case still in the East.

אַתּוּן, Chald. Syr. ܐܬܘܢܐ. Arab. أَتُون, it. Æth. et Sam. *A furnace*, or *oven heated with fire*. Cogn. ܐܬܘܢ, *fumavit, &c.*, Dan. iii. 6. 11. 15.

אֲתָיוֹ, see v. אתה.

אַתּוּקֵיהָא } Ezek. xli. 15, and
אַתִּיק } Ib. xlii. 3; for אַנְתִּיקָהּ. The final א is adscititious and irregular; it has possibly arisen out of the Arabic affixed pron. هَا, *its, hers*. הָ is, therefore, the pron. f. affixed to the plur. אַתִּיקֵי, plur. abs. אַתִּיקִים, ib. vr. 5, r. Arab. نتق; whence, Kāmoos, انتق شال حجر الاشداء وبنى داره نِتَاق غيره, i. e. אנתק, *He raised hard stones, and built his house opposite* (نِتَاق) *to the house of another*. It. حمل مظلة من الشمس, *He carried a shade* (to cover him) *from the sun*. Whence it should seem that, as نِتَاق, signifies one house, or the like, opposite to another; and, as انتق, means *to construct such houses out of hard stones*; and also, *carrying an umbrella*, and so *forming a shade*; our אַתִּיק, very probably signifies such edifices, vr. 3, chap. xlii. אַתִּיק אֶל־פְּנֵי־אַתִּיק, seems to say just the same thing. It is said, moreover, vr. 6, אֵין לָהֶן עַמּוּדִים, that *they had no pillars*; whence it should also seem, that περίστυλον, as given by the LXX., is any thing but correct. They were, probably, nothing more than chambers, so called because facing one another, and constructed, perhaps, of stone, in a peculiar manner. Auth. Vers. *gallery*, suits the places extremely well.

אַתֶּם, pron. 2 pers. m. pl. *You*. Gram. art. 145. 2—5.

אֶתְמוֹל, and אֶתְמוּל, once, אִתְמוֹל, 1 Sam. x. 11, i. q. תְּמוֹל. I. *Yesterday*, as appears evident from 1 Sam. xx. 27. And, II. generally, *Any indefinite time past*, Job viii. 9; Ps. xc. 4. It is often combined with שִׁלְשׁוֹם, which see. *Heri* (et) *nudius tertius*, Exod. v. 8; 2 Sam. v. 9; and also with כְּ, or מִ, prefixed to the first, Gen. xxxi. 2, *as*

אתן (67) אתר

yesterday and sometime before; i. e. *as formerly.* Deut. xix. 6, *from, since, for, any length of time past.* Syr. ܥܕܡܐܝܬ, id. Arab. اِتمال, *longus, durus, fuit,* &c. Cogn. ثمل, and ثمل, *mora.*

אֵתָן, i. q. אֵיתָן.

אַתֵּן, pron. 2 pers. f. pl. *You,* Gram. art. 145. 2—5.

אֶתְנָה, f. *A gift, reward, fee,* of prostitution, Hos. ii. 14 (al. 11), i. q. אֶתְנַן. r. תָּנָה. Arab. مثني, *portiones quæ aliis liberaliter, donantur,* &c.

אֶתְנַנוּ, see v. אתה.

אֶתְנַן, and אֶתְנַן, r. תָּנָה, with intensit. ן, and א, affixed. Gram. art. 168. *A rich gift, reward, &c.* pec. for prostitution, Ezek. xvi. 31. 34; Deut. xxiii. 19, &c.; with וֹנָה. Affix אֶתְנַנָּה, and pl. אֶתְנַנֶּיהָ, Is. xxiii. 17, 18; Mic. i. 7.

אֶתְקַנְדָּ, see v. נתק.

אֲתַר, Chald. *A place.* With affix אַתְרֵהּ, Ezr. v. 15; vi. 5; Dan. ii. 35, &c. Syr. and Samar. ܐܬܪ, and ܐܬܪ, id. Gesenius makes בָּאתַר, Dan. vii. 6, 7, to consist of this word, with the prep. ב, and hence equivalent to the Arabic علي اثر, or في اثر, *in vestigio;* i. e. *immediately* following; which is altogether erroneous. For, I. The Syr. ܐܬܪ, is no where used in the sense of the Arab. اثر: and, if it were, still it would remain to be shewn, that the idiomatic use of the Arab. في اثر, &c. had obtained in the Syriac. The fact is, however, no such thing exists. And, II. בָּאתַר, Chald. with ܒܐܬܪ, Syr. is a regular triliteral word, used as a preposition. בָּאתַר therefore, Dan. vii. 6, 7, is nothing more than this preposition with the *mater lectionis* (א) inserted, as it often happens in other cases. Dan. ii. 39, moreover, he gives in the form בָּתְרָךְ. It occurs in the text, however, בָּתְרָךְ. Surely Dr. Gesenius never imagined that this variety in the vowels alone, could justify an usage otherwise wholly unprecedented.

ב

The second letter of the Hebrew alphabet, termed *Beth,* or *Baith;* whence the Greek Βῆτα. So called, as it has been thought, because it represented the form of an ancient Hebrew house or tent (בֵּיִת, or בַּיִת). Its power is that of a B or V, just as the point, termed Dagésh, is inserted or not. Gram. art. 10. 109. et seq. Not unlike this is the pronunciation of the letter د *dāl,* by the Persians; which, in certain cases, is sounded like ن; as, گنبد, read گُنْبُذ. See Sir W. Jones's Pers. Gram. ed. 9. art. 14: whence it should seem probable, that this variety is not a mere rabbinic fancy, as some have thought.

It is a letter of the same organ with ב, ו, מ, פ, technically named בּוּמַף. See Gram. art. 23, which are, therefore, occasionally changed one for another. Gram. art. 78. 1. et seq.

When used as a preposition, it is prefixed to nouns,—with which it forms a sort of compound,—with (:) *Sheva,* unless there be some special reason to the contrary, Gram. art. 174. 3, et seq. It may then take (ּ) (ֹ) (ֻ) (ָ) (ֵ), as the nature of the case may require.

As to its origin, it is probably a fragment of the verbal noun בּוֹא, or בּוֹא; Gram. art. 174, implying, *entering into;* thence, *coming, drawing,* or *being, near;* and, by a metonymy, *in, at, on, upon,* any place, person, or thing. The Arabic cognates are, بَاء, *reversus fuit; in mansione locavit; diversatus fuit* in loco: and, taking the opposite view, i. e. from the place or part left, *separatus fuit, discessit; divulsus fuit;* which will serve to shew that the apparent contradictory senses found in some words, have grown rather out of their various usage than out of the words themselves. So, in English we say, one thing is near *to* another; but in Arabic the phrase is, it is near *from* another (قَرِيبٌ عَنْ). Again, the precise or prevailing notion, belonging to words, or, which is much the same thing, the idiomatic usage of them, will necessarily exercise considerable influence on the prepo-

ب (68) ب

sitions, or other particles attending them. Hence بَاءٌ, or بَاءٌ, *congressus, it. mansio; locus in quem quis descendit, &c.;* بَاءَ, *coivit;* بَاءَ, *congressus. It.* بَوَىَ, *descendit in locum; ibique* (meton.) *substititi. Metath.* أَوَي, *se recepit commorandi ergo, &c.*

Jauhari's account of the use of this preposition is the most philosophical that I have seen; which is this, الباء حرف من حروف الشفة بنيت علي الكسر لاستحالة الابتداء بالموقوف وهي من عوامل الجر و تختصّ بالدخول علي الاسماء فهي لاصاق الفعل بالمفعول به تقول مررت بزيد كانّك الصقت المرور به وكل فعل لا يتعدّي فلك ان تعدّيه بالباء والالف والتشديد تقول طار به واطاره وطيّره. *Ba is one of the labial letters, and it receives the vowel kesra (◌ِ), because of the impossibility of commencing a word with a silent letter* (i. e. for special reasons, as in the Hebrew, it does not commence a word—now compounded with it,— with a sheva [:].) *It is one of those particles which govern a following word as if in the state of construction. Its peculiar power is, the influence which it exerts on nouns, for the purpose of uniting the word so influenced* (as an accusative, &c. case, with us) *with the verb influencing it. You may say* (e. g.) "I PASSED BY (بِ, ZAID;" *implying that you had made the act of passing touch Zaid:* (i. e. the action, included in this verb, was thus united with the term signifying Zaid's person, so that *passing* (المرور) here was made to respect, i. e. to *influence* (بالدخول) him. *Any intransitive verb too, may, by adding this letter to a noun following, be made transitive, as well as by the* א *prefixed* (as in the Heb. Hiph.), *or by the middle radical letter doubled* (as in the Heb. Pih.): *as,* طَارَ بِهِ, *He flew away with him;* i. e. أَطَارَهُ, *or* طَيَّرَهُ, *He caused him to fly away.* This includes Gesenius's בְּ, נָשָׂה בּ, and עָבַד בּ; the latter of which he makes equal to הֶעֱבִיד.

On this connecting or modifying usage of particles, and indeed of words generally, see Gram. art. 228, et seq., particularly art. 229, et seq., with the observations, beginning at par. 7. From which it must appear, that the word—or verb, it may be—chosen by the writer or speaker, is the first thing to be considered; that is, whether its action, or influence, be direct, or otherwise, on the subsequent term or terms. If it be *direct*, no preposition generally will be wanted; as in נַעֲשֶׂה אָדָם, *Let us make man; if indirect*, then such mediating preposition must be used, as will convey this indirect action conveniently to its complementary term, as in בִּמְגִלַּת־סֵפֶר כָּתוּב עָלָי, In *the volume of the book it is written* CONCERNING ME, Ps. xl. 8; where it will be seen that, as the influence of the term כָּתוּב, is various with respect to מְגִלָּה, and the 1st pers. following; this is provided for by the prepositions בְּ, and עַל, which will suffice, as to the law regulating the use of the preposition בְּ, generally.

As to the particular meaning of this particle, it must have appeared from what has been said, that it will, according to our idiom, seem various; although, in fact, not more than one general signification may attend it in the estimation of an Oriental. I object to the method adopted by Noldius, Gesenius, and others, of introducing the Latin cases of the *ablative, accusative*, &c., when speaking of these particles, because no such cases exist at all in the Hebrew; and because the consideration of them is, in practice, both useless and cumbrous.

From the primitive signification—*entering in,* or *into*, we may then readily conceive, that *in*, or *at;* as *in*, or *at*, any *place, time, person,* or *thing;* and, in the two last cases, *with*,—as connection with any thing, may also be understood of *association with* it,—may in many cases express its meaning: and this appears to be the case; as, עָמְתוּ *בַּבּוֹר, They shut up* IN *the pit,* Lam. iii. 53. בְּעֵת רָצוֹן, *In*

---

* In Ps. lxxii. 3, we have a most odd instance of this sort of construction, which will be obviated by taking בִּצְדָקָה for the first word of vr. 4, parallel to יָדִין עַמְּךָ בְּצֶדֶק, commencing the second. And so the LXX. have taken it. The cause of this dislocation seems to have been this. It was not seen how וּגְבָעוֹת, could end a sentence; whereas a little knowledge would have shewn, that such construction was considered an elegance. Not unlike this is the case of the number 666, Rev. xiii. 18. See my Exposition, p. 328, 9.

ב (69) ב

an acceptable time, Is. xlix. 8. בְּעֵת רָצוֹן וּבְקַשְׁתּוֹ כִּלָּה, AT, or WITH, *the great he began, and* AT, or WITH, *the small he ended.* So, אֲדֹנִי צֻוָּה בַּיהֹוָה לָתֵת, *My Lord was commanded with* (i. e. *by* here) *Jehovah, to give, &c.* Gen. xliv. 12; Num. xxxvi. 2.

Hence the use of this particle, denoting *the instrument with* which any thing is done; as בַּחִצִּים וּבַקֶּשֶׁת, *With the arrows and with the bow,* Is. vii. 24; the material, as בַּצֶּמֶר, *with wool,* Lev. xiii. 52; בַּנְּחֹשֶׁת, *with brass,* 1 Kings vii. 14, &c. Hence prefixed to verbal nouns, the combined force will be not unlike that of the Latin gerunds in *do ;* as בְּפִגְעוֹ, *In his meeting,* Nold. *incurrendo,* Num. xxxv. 19. בְּהַלֵּל וּבְהוֹדוֹת, *laudando et celebrando,* Ezr. iii. 11. Hence, too, many of these combinations may be construed as adverbs; as, בִּקְרִי, *In accident,* i. e. *accidentally,* Lev. xxvi. 24, &c.; Nold., pp. 139. 151. 153. The time or tense of all which will be regulated by the context.

In, said of things about which the mind is conversant, will be equivalent to our *on, upon, about,* &c., as בַּדָּבָר הַזֶּה .. דַּבֵּר, *Speaking in* (i. e. on, about, &c.) *this matter,* Deut. iii. 26. Comp. Jer. xxxviii. 24; Ps. lxxxvii. 3; Job xxvi. 14, &c; Nold. sign. 12.

Gesenius, after Noldius, makes this preposition occasionally equal to כ, *like,* &c., but without any good reason, e. g. בְּצַלְמֵנוּ כִּדְמוּתֵנוּ, *secundum imaginem* nostram, secundum similitudinem nostram, Gen. i. 26; which, although not far from the exegetical sense, or at least from a tolerable sense, is, nevertheless, not the grammatical sense of the passage, for these reasons; viz., *according to, like,* &c., will afford a much less definite sense here than the preposition ב. They may signify, in some respects similar, on the same analogy, or the like; while ב, signifying *in,* or *on,* will imply *identically* the same. So, in another example, viz., Lev. v. 15; בְּעֶרְכְּךָ, will signify *on,* or *in, thy estimation,* i. e. which *thou determinest;* whereas כְּעֶרְכְּךָ might signify, an estimation made by any other person, in some respects similar to, or analogous, with that usually made by the priests. The same will hold good with regard to Num. xiv. 34; Est. i. 12; Ps. lxxxix. 18; Nold. sign. 27.—I must be excused in dwelling here on what may appear trifling to some; because I am convinced, that it is in unidiomatic substitutions such as these, not only that Scripture is often misunderstood and misapplied, but also, that false principles of interpretation are recommended and adopted.

If many persons or things are spoken of, *among* will be the sense of our *with,* or *at,* in these connexions; as הַיָּפָה בַּנָּשִׁים, *The beautiful with, or among, women,* Cant. i. 8. Comp. Lam. i. 1. 3; Josh. xiv. 15; Jer. xlix. 15; Ps. liv. 6; cxviii. 7, &c. In a similar way it seems to be used in oaths; as נִשְׁבַּע יְהֹוָה בִּימִינוֹ וּבִזְרוֹעַ עֻזּוֹ, *Jehovah hath sworn* BY *or* WITH, *his right hand* (i. e. as an instrument to avenge), *and* BY, *or* WITH, *the arm of his might,* Is. lxii. 8. Comp. Cant ii. 7, &c.

Again, *entering into* may be taken as implying our *into, to, towards,* i. e. motion towards any thing, person, &c. So, לִטּוּ בְדִבְרֵי, *They have respect* TO, *or* TOWARDS, *words of vanity,* Exod. v. 9. שָׁלַח מַאֲשֵׁר, *He sent to Asher,* Jud. vi. 35; comp. 1 Sam. xvi. 3, &c. Nold. sign. 3. In a hostile sense, *against;* as, יָדוֹ בַכֹּל, *His hand against all,* Gen. xvi. 12; comp. Lev. xvii. 10; Num. xxi. 7; and Nold. sign. 8 and 15. So also, progress; as, יוֹם בְּיוֹם, *day to day;* i. e. day after day, *daily,* 1 Sam. xviii. 10. חֹדֶשׁ בַּחֹדֶשׁ, *month to month,* 1 Chron. xxvii. 1; Comp. Is. lxvi. 23; Nold. p. 148. *For,* in a friendly, or affectionate, sense; as אֶעֱבָדְךָ בְרָחֵל..., *I will serve thee* FOR, *with respect to, Rachel,* Gen. xxix. 18. So נֶפֶשׁ בְּנֶפֶשׁ, *life, for, with regard to,* or *in lieu of, life, &c.,* Deut. xix. 21; comp. Cant. viii. 7, &c. Nold. sign. 22—24. So Ger. xxxvii. 34. *For,* in a friendly, or affectionate, שָׂם שַׂק בְּמָתְנָיו, *he placed sackcloth on to his loins, &c.*

The construction and force of this particle with verbs, will be found noticed with them; which will give every sort of usage connected with this particle.

One word, now, on some of the doctrines of Dr. Gesenius respecting it. He tells us (Lex. Manuale, p. 122. and Thes. p. 174), that the *Beth of essence,** (Arab. يَا الزِّيَادة) is of uncertain origin; and that the Arabs

---

* This term seems to have originated from the opinion that, in such phrases as, مَا اللهُ غَافِلًا, *God is not negligent,* the verb كَانَ, or some such verb signifying *existence,* must have been understood. But this is a fallacy; the truth being, that after any verb or noun whatsoever, completing a sentence, an accusative case will follow; as, حَسَنَ وَجْهَهَا ، حَسَنَ وَجْهَهَا . *The thing is therefore a mere fiction.*

prefix it to a predicate, principally when that consists of a participle or adjective; rarely to a substantive, and never to a subjective case. In the first place, the Arab Grammarians never speak, to the best of my knowledge, of any such *letter of essence*. In the second, their ذَةٌ بِا زَاَىٌٔ is circumscribed by no such rules as those of Dr. Gesenius. Jauhari tells us that قد تزاد الباء في الكلام كقولهم ‏.حسبك قال الشاعر ‏.حسبك في‏, &c. القوم ان تعلموا بانك فيهم غنى‏...‏وقال تعالى كفى بربك هاديًا ونصيرًا وغيره *Ba is redundant in speech, as in their saying* حسبك, *as the Poet, It concerns thee with the people, that they know thee to be rich among them:* and, in the Koran, *It is sufficient* IN MY LORD (as to), *leader* and *helper*. Here, be it remembered, the ب, is prefixed to a substantive, and that in each case in a *subjective* situation.* We are told, however, in the Thesaurus, "*non reddenda est, sufficit Deus in directorem, sed sufficit in Deo* (an Gott.) *habere directorem.*" Suppose we allow this; then is the ب any thing but *redundant* (زَاَىٌٔ); and all Gesenius's rules about its use vanish at once! Again, his distinction about participles and adjectives is futile: the Arabs considering all participles either as *agents*, or *patients* (detur venia verbo). Gram. art. 217. 7. note.

Dr. Gesenius next proceeds to certain Hebrew examples, as he thinks of this usage, e. g. Exod. vi. 3, בְּאֵל שַׁדַּי, "*tanquam Deus omnipotens*." Here he makes בְּ, i. q. כְּ, which totally destroys its character as a mere expletive. The Arabic بِا الزِيادَةِ, of redundancy, therefore, has nothing to do here. Why not take the passage thus, *In* (the name) of *El Shaddai?* So Is. xl. 10,

---

* See the Moolla Jāmi's Commentary on the *Kafia* of Ibn Ulhajib. p. ۲۲٦. Dr. Gesenius was led into this mistake by the deficiencies of Mr. de Sacy's Gram. Arabe. The truth seems to be, these constructions, viz. بِقَادِرٍ بِغَافِلٍ, &c. are elliptical, for كَحَالِ غَافِلٍ, i. e. *in the state of a negligent person, &c.*

בְּחָזָק יָבוֹא, "*venit tanquam robustus.*" Why not, *In* (the situation, state, &c., of) *a strong one?* Exod. xxxii. 22, בְּרַע הוּא, *In* (a state &c. of) *evil is he.* Prov. iii. 26, יְהוָה יִהְיֶה בְכִסְלֶךָ, *Jehovah will be* IN (i. e. his constancy, faithfulness, promises, shall rest in thy mind, and so be the source of) *thy confidence.* Again, Ps. lxviii. 5, בְּיָהּ שְׁמוֹ, *In Jah* (is) *his name;* i. e. under this has He been known to us, as a God working wonders for his people. In Hos. xiii. 9, we have, apparently, an epanorthosis שִׁחֶתְךָ יִשְׂרָאֵל כִּי־בִי בְעֶזְרֶךָ, *It* (i. e. their rebellion spoken of) *hath destroyed thee, O Israel, because* (it was) *against me, against thy help* (i. e. helper; an abstract used for a concrete). We have here, therefore, no redundancy in the letter בּ; nor further is it necessary to suppose, that, because in the three following passages, viz. Ezra iii. 3; 1 Chron. ix. 33, and vii. 23, בּ is found with the subjective; this savours of modern Hebrew (*sequioris Hebraismi*), nor that the בּ is altogether redundant. See also Gram. art. 219. 4. with the note.

This particle sustains the same offices in the Chaldee and Syriac.

בָּא, pret. Kal. or part. of v. בוֹא.

בִּאָה, f. *An entrance,* r. בוא, Ezek. viii. 5.

בְּאֻשׁ, m. בְּאוּשְׁתָּא, f. def. *Wicked, base,* r. באש. Ezra iv. 12.

בְּאֵר, m. בְּאֵרוֹת, pl. f. בְּאֵרוֹת, constr. Arab. بِئْر, *puteus;* بَأَرَ, *fodit puteum.* Syr. ܒܐܙܐ, id. I. *A well* of water, Gen. xxi. 19. 25; בְּאֵר מַיִם חַיִּים, *A well of living waters,* i. e. springing up strongly or abundantly. Synon. with עַיִן. Comp. Gen. xvi. 7, with ib. vr. 14, &c.—*Of bitumen,* Ibid. xiv. 10. II. *Pit, or dungeon* used as prisons, from the safety and ease with which prisoners might be confined there. Such was the celebrated black hole at Calcutta, and such may be seen delineated in most of the ornamented copies of the Shah Namah. Jer. xxxvi. 5; Ps. lv. 24; lxix. 16. Syn. בּוֹר, for *grave.* The *den* (בּוֹר, Arab. جُبّ, *puteus*) of lions, into which Daniel was cast (ch. vi. 8. 13, &c.), was a similar place. On. Gen. xvi. See חַי.

בְּאֵר, see בּוֹר.

בֵּאֵר, v. Pih. of the preceding, constr. עַל, in the parall. with כתב. *Dig, cut upon,* or *into,* i. e. I. *Define well* (הֵיטֵב), Deut. xxvii. 8), Hab. ii. 2. Infin. בָּאֵר, or בַּאֵר

באש (71) באת

Hence, meton. II. *Make clear, publish*, Deut. i. 5, pret. Comp. מלל, ברה, חקק. Arab. قاطع.

בְּאֵשׁ, m. Arab. بَأْس, *vehementia, pœna, malum*, بُوس, id. Cogn. بُوس, id. Syr. Aph. اخْبَاءَ, *malum intulit, &c. Evil, affliction*; pec. *Evil savour*, par. with צַחֲנָה, Joel ii. 20;—Amos iv. 10 ; Is. xxxiv. 3. Aff. בָּאְשׁוֹ, בָּאְשָׁם.

בְּאֵשׁ, v. Chald. *Was evil*; constr. עַל, Dan. vi. 15.

בָּאַשׁ, v. pres. יִבְאַשׁ, *Was bad*; pec. *corrupt, stinking*, Exod. vii. 18. 21. The notions of good, and good savour; bad, and bad savour, are almost inseparable in the idioms of this class of languages.

Niph. נִבְאַשׁ, *Became bad, pec. in bad odour*, 1 Sam. xiii. 4 ; 2 Sam. x. 6; xvi. 21; constr. ב, אֶת.

Hiph. הִבְאִישׁ, *Rendered, made bad*, pec. *fetid*. Meton. *odious*, Ps. xxxviii. 6, with נִמְקוּ, Exod. v. 21, with רֵיחַ, Prov. xiii. 5; Eccl. x. 1. הַבְאֵשׁ, or הִבְאִישׁ, Infin. 1 Sam. xxvii. 12, Gen. xxxiv. 30, constr. ב, *med.* and *immed.*

Hithp. הִתְבָּאֵשׁ, i. q. Niph. constr. עִם, 1 Chron. xix. 6.

בְּאֻשִׁים, (for בְּאוּשִׁים, plen. בָּאוּשִׁים, pl. of בָּאוּשׁ, part. of preced. באש), occ. Is. v. 2. 4, only; but, according to some, Job xxxi. 40. In Is. l. c. certainly nothing beyond *bad, corrupt, odious*, grapes or berries, seems to be intended; and so Kimchi, Saadias Haggaon, Symmachus, and some others, appear, according to Celsius, to have understood it. Hierob. ii. 199, et seq. Gesenius, after Jerome, &c., takes it to be the *labrusca, wild-vine*, or عنب الثعلب, *fox-vine* of the Orientals.—See אוּר above;—which is, perhaps, more than either the etymology of the word, or the context, will bear.

בָּאְשָׁה, f. Job. xxxi. 40. *Useless herb*, or *weed*, according to Gesenius and Winer; but, as it is compared here with שְׂעֹרָה, and in connexion with חוֹחַ, and דַּפָּה, some specific herb or shrub, must be meant; most likely the بيش, of Avicenna, Abu'l Fadl, and Kazwini, as cited by Celsius, l. c. which they say is *a killing poison*, سم قاتل our *hemlock*, probably. Winer says, (Lex Sim.) after Golius, that this word is *Persic*; which,

however, is more than either Golius or he can prove. Both Jauhari and Firozabadi, moreover, give it as *Arabic*; besides, it is of no consequence here, whether it be derived from the v. באש or not; the question is only about its meaning; it is possible indeed that, even in the Persic, words cognate with those of the Hebrew and Arabic are to be found.

בְּאַתַר, see בתר.

בָּבָה, f. constr. בַּבַּת, contr. בַּת. Syr. ܒܒܬܐ ܕܥܝܢܐ, *pupilla oculi*. Arab. بَابَا, *celer fuit*. بَابَا, *intelligens*; whence بُوبَو عَيْنِي, *pupilla oculi mei*. The pupil, or crystalline lens of the eye, Zech. ii. 12; Lam. ii. 18: Ps. xvii. 8. See אִישׁוֹן, above.

בַּג, m. occ. mostly in the compd. פַּתְבַּג, which see. Once Ezek. xxv. 7, לְבַּג, where the *keri* has לְבַז, which seems to be the better reading, as it is more conformable with usage, and the ancient versions. A similar error, perhaps of some copyist, is בַּה for בַּז, ib. xlvii. 13, as pointed out by Gesenius. Comp. Jer. xv. 13; xvii. 3; Ezek. xxvi. 5; xxxiv. 23. Others take it to be the same with the Pers. باج, *meat, victuals*. Cogn. Arab. بج, *distendit, &c.*

בֶּגֶד, m. בְּגָדִים, pl. בִּגְדֵי, constr. once fem. aff. בִּגְדוֹתֶיךָ, of pl. בְּגָדוֹת; Ps. xlv. 9. Arab. بجد, *cœtus, turba, virorum, &c.*; جدّة, *solitudo, desertum.* Phr. ابن جدّة, *pollens peritia. Extent, spreading out*, seems the leading notion. I. *Any large piece of cloth*, used either to cover or to wrap up something, Num. iv. 6—13 ; 1 Sam. xix. 13 ; Amos ii. 8. *Cover-lit*, or *blanket*, apparently, 1 Sam. xix. 13 ; 1 Kings i. 1. (Arab. جاد, *tapetium, amiculi genus striatum*.) II. *A cloak* or *mantle*, Gen. xxxix. 13; Lev. xiii. 53, &c., of *woollen-cloth*, as liable to be moth-eaten, Job xiii. 28, and Lev. xiii. 47; also of *linen*, Lev. xiii. 47. פִּשְׁתִּים, it. שֵׁשׁ, בַּד, כִּלְאַיִם, Gen. xli. 42; Lev. xvi. 23; xix. 19, &c.; as to *colour*, תּוֹלַעַת, Num. iv. 8. אַרְגָּמָן, ib. 13; *workmanship*, רִקְמָה, Ezek. xxvi. 16; *use*, קֹדֶשׁ, Exod. xxviii. 2; אֵבֶל, 2 Sam. xiv. 2; *character*, עֲדִים, Is. lxiv. 5; *of office*, 1 Kings xxii. 10; Zech. iii. 5, κατ᾽ ἐξοχήν. III. Metaph. *Dissimulation, perfidy*, Jer. xii. 1. Meton.

בגד (72) בדא

Rapine, violence, Is. xxiv. 16. Aff. בִּגְדִי, בְּגָדָיו, בִּגְדָהּ, בְּגָדֵיהֶם, בִּגְדֵנוּ, בִּגְדְךָ, בִּגְדֵךְ, בִּגְדֵיכֶם. בָּגַד, v. pres. יִבְגֹּד, 1 pers. pl. נִבְגְּדָ, Mal. ii. 10; of בֶּגֶד, sig. III. So Arab. لَبِسَ, *dissimulavit. Dissembled, acted perfidiously.* Abs. 1 Sam. xiv. 33; Job vi. 15 : *med.* ב pers. Judg. ix. 23 ; Lam. i. 2 : *med.* מִן, Jer. iii. 20 : *immed.* Ps. lxxiii. 15.

Part. agent. בּוֹגֵד, pl. בּוֹגְדִים, Ps. cxix. 158; Prov. ii. 22; xi. 3, &c. Infin. בָּגוֹד, Is. xlviii. 8; בָּגוֹד, Is. xxxiii. 1. Aff. בִּגְדוֹ, (of בֶּגֶד) Exod. xxi. 8.

בִּגְדוֹת, i. q. בְּגָדוֹת, *Great perfidy*, pl. of excel., which was probably its ancient and original form, Zeph. iii. 4.

בָּגוּדָה, f. (fm. equiv. פְּקֻדָה=פְּקוּדָה, Gram. art. 154. 11, 12, implying habit.) *Perfidious*, Jer. iii. 7. 10.

בַּד, m. pl. בַּדִּים. Arab. بَكّ, *separatio*; بَكّ, id. *The being alone, separate, apart*; hence, I. *Part, portion.* בַּד בְּבַד, *part for part, &c.*, Exod. xxx. 34. With לְ, adverb. לְבַד, lit. *for part*, i. e. *severally*, Exod. xxvi. 9 ; xxxvi. 16. With aff. לְבַדּוֹ, *for, in, his being alone*, Gen. ii. 18 ; xxx. 40, &c., לְבַדְּהֶן, Ib. xxi. 28. לְבַדִּי, Num. xi. 14. לְבַדָּהּ, Exod. xviii. 14. לְבַדָּם, 1 Kings xi. 29. With מִן following; *excepting, exclusive of, &c.*, Exod. xii. 37 ; Num. xxix. 39. With עַל, id. Ezra i. 6. Also with מ prefixed, id. Gen. xxvi. 1 ; Num. vi. 21 ; Deut. iv. 35. Gesenius says, " Adv. restringendi ; *solum, tantummodo*, in sequiore Hebraïsmo, Eccles. vii. 29 ; Is. xxvi. 13." I am quite unable to see either the force of this distinction here, or the necessity of it. The exception is here clearly made from the matter just mentioned, as it is in other places. In such passages as, לְךָ לְבַדֶּךָ, Ps. li. 6 ; lxxi. 16, the repetition is made for the sake of emphasis, Gram. art. 223. 2 ; Nold. p. 428, &c.

From *the being alone*, perhaps, originated the notion of *going out*, as it were, from society into solitude. Arab. بَكَا, *exivit in campum, desertum.* Whence the term بَدَوِيّ, *a Badaween;* i. e. an inhabitant of the desert. Hence, pl. בַּדִּים, II. *Shoots, branches*, of trees, &c., Ezek. xvii. 6; xix. 14. III. Meton. *Bars, staves of wood*, Exod. xxv. 13; Num. iv. 6. IV. Metaph. *Limbs, or members* of the body, Job xli. 4, &c. V. Metaph. *Bars*, or *defences* of a city, i. e. *Princes*,

Hos. xi. 6, &c. VI. בַּדִּים, *Lies*, (cogn. Syr. ܟܕܒ, *commentus est.* Arab. بَدَا, *excessit patria, modum*) either as *singular*, and thence *incredible, things;* or else, as *extravagancies* exceeding belief, Is. xvi. 6 ; Jer. xlviii. 30, &c. Applied also to persons, *Liars, &c.* Is. xliv. 25; Jer. L. 36; but בְּגוֹרֶיהָ, in the parallel in this last instance, rather requires sign. v. Once more : as things *singular* or *rare* are usually considered excellent, so, perhaps, VII. בַּד, and בַּדִּים, was applied to *fine-linen*, as, Exod. xxviii. 42 ; xxxix. 28 ; Lev. vi. 3, &c. In Job xvii. 16, בַּדֵּי שְׁאוֹל, probably signifies *grave-clothes.* See my notes on the place, and ch. xviii. 13. Arab. بُزّ, i. q. Chald. בּוּץ, *byssus, pannus lineus, &c.* It is not impossible, however, that in this case it is a foreign word. See Steph. Thes. Gr. under βύσσος. In other cases the Copt. ⲂⲎⲦ, *ramus palmæ*, seems to be cognate.

בָּדָא, v. Syr. ܟܕܒ, *effutivit, commentus est.* Arab. بَدَا, i. q. أَبْدَعَ, *novum protulit. Originated*, in a bad sense *innovated*, constr. מ, 1 Kings xii. 33. See my sermon on the Sabbath, p. 28. notes. Part. aff. בֹּדְאָם, for בּוֹדְאָם, Gram. art. 63 ; Neh. vi. 8.

בָּדָד, m. concr. see בַּד. *Separate, alone, solitary*, Lev. xiii. 46 ; Deut. xxxii. 12; Is. xxvii. 10, with ל prefixed, *id.* לְבָדָד, Num. xxiii. 9 ; Ps. iv. 9 ; Mich. vii. 14, unless ל in these instances has the power of imparting *certainty*, and thence, *emphasis*, to the context as it has in the Arabic, which they term لام التوكيد, *lam of confirmation.* See Mr. de Sacy's Gram. Arab. I. p. 371—2. ed. 1810.

בְּדִי, see דַי.

בְּדִיל, m. *Tin*, Num. xxxi. 22 ; Ezek. xxvii. 12, &c. Pl. with aff. Is. i. 25, בְּדִילָיִךְ, where it seems to mean every sort of inferior *separable* alloy ; taking its point from the verb Hiph. הִבְדִּיל, alluding perhaps to the circumstance that *tin* is a base alloy of silver. Comp. vr. 22 ; Ch. xlviii. 10 ; Jer. vi. 30. In Zech. iv. 10, הָאֶבֶן הַבְּדִיל, *The stone* (weight), *the tin,* i. e. *the plummet.*

בָּדַל, m. Amos iii. 12. בְּדַל־אֹזֶן, *A division*, or *portion*, of the *ear*. Hence, as a verb—

Niph. *Be, become, divided, separated*, constr. מ, Num. xvi. 21 ; 1 Chron. xii. 8;

בדל (73) בדק

Ezra vi. 21; ix. 1, &c., with לְ, *to*, or *for* something, 1 Chron. xxiii. 13.

Hiph. *Made,* or *caused division, separation;* constr. בֵּין—וּבֵין, בֵּין—לְ, מ—לְ, אֶת—לְ, מֵעַל, &c., Gen. i. 4. 6; Num. xvi. 9; Deut. xxix. 20; x. 8; Neh. xiii. 3; Is. lvi. 3, &c. Infin. הַבְדֵּל, or הַבְדִּיל. Part. מַבְדִּיל.

בְּדֹלַח, occ. Gen. ii. 12; Num. xi. 7. In the former in connection with *gold,* and the *onyx stone;* in the latter, taken to compare the manna with. What, then, is most likely here to occur with *gold,* and a certain *precious stone?* Some mineral, one would think.— And to some mineral the manna might probably have been compared, as to appearance; for in appearance only the comparison seems to be, especially as mention of the hoar frost is made in immediate connection with it (Exod. xvi. 14). Now this production was not found in Paradise, as Celsius says (Hierobot. i. 324): but in the land of Havilah, which was situated somewhere in the deserts of Arabia. See my Introd. to Job, sect. v. p. 55, note. In those parts, too, the gold termed ἄπυρος, (ib. in Gen. טוֹב, good) was found. (Diodor. Sic. lib. ii. § 1.) We are told, moreover, (ib. § 52) that *precious* stones of all sorts were found, *crystals like the purest water congealed by freezing:* emeralds, beryls, chrysolites, &c.* The *crystal* seems here to answer the description (Exod. xvi. 14, and Num. xi. 7,) best; while the term *beryl* approaches nearest to our word. I myself prefer the former. Bochart. Hieroz. ii. p. 674 et seq. contends for the pearl; because pearl-fisheries have long existed on the Persian Gulph. But, can this be termed "the land of Havilah?" Surely not. Celsius, Gesenius, Winer, &c. suppose it to be the same with the *bdellium* of Pliny (H. N. lib. xii. xix. (ix.),) which is a sort of Arabian gum. But, who would expect to find *gum* mentioned in connection with gold or precious stones? Besides, when mention of the precious gums, &c. is made (Gen. xliii. 11, &c.), no such word as this occurs. It is true, the LXX., Josephus, Aquila, Theodotion, Symmachus, Jerome, &c. are unanimous in rendering this word by *bdellium.* I answer, this has little weight. I know how easily and pertina-ciously error is persevered in when once adopted, as I also do, that the time which had elapsed between the oldest of these translators and the times of Moses, was quite sufficient to put it out of their power to say with precision what this word meant. As to Gesenius's appeal to Burckhardt's Travels in Syria, nothing can be less conclusive. Unless, indeed, he had first shewn,—which he could not do,—that the בְּדֹלַח of the Pentateuch, and the Arabian *gum,* described by the traveller, was the same thing. Besides, it is quite clear that the *manna* of Moses was considered a new and strange thing; and, hence, it was particularly described; while the description given is quite sufficient to shew that the *gum* or *manna** of the Arabian desert was altogether a different thing. But the frosty or icy appearance of the real manna, could not be unlike the crystal of Diodorus. The probability is therefore strong, that some precious stone was meant, and that it was either the crystal or the beryl.

בָּדַק, m. Aff. בִּדְקָךְ, Syr. ܒܕܩ, cogn. ܒܘܩ, *sparsit, contrivit.* Arab. بَذَقَ, *levis, parvus.* Cogn. بَثَّ, *laceravit, fidit.* Cogn. Heb. בצק. *Injury, decay,* as in a building, ship, &c.; requiring repair, 2 Kings xii. 6 et seq.; Ezek. xxvii. 9. 27: with the v. חזק.

בָּדוֹק, Infin. sens. prægn. *Repairing injury, decay,* &c. 2 Chron. xxxiv. 10. Sc

---

* Strabo tells us, too, lib. xvi. that the *emerald* and *beryl* are found in the gold mines of Arabia. Ed. Casaub. p. 536.

* Since Burckhardt's time, Mr. Rich (Residence in Koordistan, vol. i. pp. 142, 143,) gives the following accounts of the Oriental manna "Manna is found on the dwarf oak, though several other plants are said to produce it. . . . It is collected by gathering the leaves of the tree, letting them dry, and then gently threshing them on a cloth. . . . It is afterwards cleared by boiling. There is another kind of manna found on rocks and stones, which is quite pure of a white colour, and it is much more esteemed than the tree manna. The manna season begins in the latter end of June, at which period, when a night is more than usually cool, the Koords say it rains manna, and maintain, that the greatest quantity is always found in the morning after such a night."—All that can be said of this is, it is a sort of *honeydew,* falling at a certain season, and most abundantly under certain circumstances, not altogether unlike that occasionally found on the leaves of some trees among ourselves; but in no one particular is it like the manna described by Moses.

בדר (74) בהמ

also the Syr. ܟ݁ܰܒ݂, *restituit, reparavit.* Synon. here with חָזַק, *making firm.*

בָּדַר, v. Chald. Pah. i. q. Heb. בֵּוֵר, פּוּר. Syr. ܒ݁ܰܕ݂ܪ. Arab. بَذَرَ, *Dispersit,* Dan. iv. 11.

בֹּדוּ, m. for בֹּהוּ, Seg. Gram. art. 87. 2. Syr. ܒ݁ܳܗܘ, *inanitas.* Arab. بَاغ, *inanis;* هَبّ, *ampla res quævis; cavitas pectoris. Emptiness, vacuity, destitution,* as to culture, inhabitants, &c., Gen. i. 2; with synon. תֹּהוּ, for emphasis. Is. xxxiv. 11; Jer. iv. 23 : both alluding to Gen. i. 2.

בָּהַט, m. Est. i. 6, רִצְפַּת בַּהַט. Arab. بَهِتَ, i. q. حَجَر, *Stone.* Cogn. بَهَط, v. *validè conculcavit, densum effecit : commodè disposuit* lectum. Hence, *Firm, well, handsomely laid pavement.* LXX. Σμαραγδίτης. Ges. *Marmor adulterinum.* Castell. *Porphyrites,* al. *Parius,* al. *Crystallum;* al. *Smaragdus.* Syr. Vers. simply ܘܿܕ݂ܝܳܪܳܐ, *of marble;* which is probably the most correct.

בְּהִילוּ, f. Chald. *Hurry, haste,* Ezr. iv. 23, r. בהל. " Per apocopen pro בְּהִילוּת," says Winer, which is wrong ; the ת being adscititious, and forming the state of construction.

בָּהִיר, m. of בּ + הִיר. Arab. بَهَرَ, *diruit aggeris partem.* הִיר, for הִיר, or הִיר, seg. *Breaking through*: here, *in breaking* through, viz. the light. בַּשְּׁחָקִים, *the clouds,* Job xxxvii. 21. See my note, ib.

בָּהֲכִין, 2 Chron. i. 4. Infin. Hiph. v. כּוּן, with prep. בּ, and art. ה. Comp. 2 Chron. xxix. 36.

בֶּהָלָה, f. בַּהֲלוּת, pl. Arab. بَهَلَ, *malemisit ei Deus, execratus fuit.* Cogn. بَهَر, *anhelatio. Fear, terror, astonishment,* Lev. xxvi. 16 ; Is. lxv. 23 ; Jer. xv. 8. Hence the verb—

Niph. נִבְהַל, *Became terrified, astonished.* Meton, *cast down, ruined.* Constr. מִ, *from ;* ל, *at,* 1 Sam. xxviii. 21 ; Ps. vi. 4 ; Zeph. i. 18 ; Is. xxi. 3, &c.

Pih. I. *Make* or *cause to hurry, hasten,* Eccl. v. 1 ; vii. 9 ; Est. ii. 9. Meton. II. *Astonish, confound, ruin,* Job xxii. 10 ; Ps. ii. 5 ; Dan. xi. 44.

Infin. I. 2 Chron. xxxv. 21. II. Ib. xxxii. 18. Part. Ezra iv. 4.

Puh. Part. f. מְבֹהֶלֶת, *keri. Hurried, gotten too speedily;* i. e. by bad means, Prov. xx. 21. Mas. pl. מְבֹהָלִים, Est. viii. 14.

Hiph. i. q. Pih. I. Est. vi. 14 ; 2 Chron. xxvi. 20. II. Job xxiii. 16.

בְּהֵמָה, f. pl. בְּהֵמוֹת, constr. בֶּהֱמַת, pl. בַּהֲמוֹת. Arab. بَهِيمَة, *bestia, &c.* I. *Any quadruped* generally, pec., the gramenivorous, as the *ox, sheep, goat, camel, ass, &c.* Occasionally opposed to *men,* to *wild beasts, birds, reptiles, flocks.* In the more elevated style, sometimes, II. *A wild beast;* as 1 Sam. xvii. 44 ; Is. xviii. 6 ; Jer. vii. 33.

The plural, Job xl. 15, has been usually taken as a pl. of excellence, signifying some stupendously large animal. Bochart will have it to be the *hippopotamus,* and so the moderns generally. Others have supposed it to be the elephant; as Drusius, Grotius, &c. I see no grounds for either. The place seems to speak of the beasts generally, with the view of magnifying the wisdom and power of their Creator. See my notes on the place. Gesenius and Winer, after Jablonski, suppose the word to be Egyptian ; viz., the Coptic ⲡ+ⲉϩⲉ+ⲙⲱⲟⲩⲧ, making altogether ⲡⲉϩⲉⲙⲙⲱⲟⲩⲧ, and signifying *Bomarino,* or *bos aquatilis.* There are some objections to this. I. ⲉϩⲉ is fem. and requires the prefix ϯ or ⲧ, not ⲡ; which would make ϯⲉϩⲉⲙⲙⲱⲟⲩⲧ. And so the identity of the word would vanish ! II. ⲙⲱⲟⲩ, not ⲙⲙⲱⲟⲩⲧ, is the Coptic term for *water.* ⲙⲙⲱⲟⲩⲧ, signifies *mori, to die,* not *water.* III. The construction had recourse to here, would require the insertion of ⲙⲙ, before ⲙⲙⲱⲟⲩⲧ ; which would further destroy the identity of this word with our בְּהֵמוֹת. I take the Coptic as I find it in the Grammar of Schultz, and the Dictionary of La Croze. I know of no other books on which reliance can be placed. And if any can be placed on these, surely this Coptic device is ungrounded, and perfectly worthless. Besides, as the languages of this class afford a root, viz., بَهَمَ, from which our word might be derived, according to our German critics themselves; it never can be likely the sacred writers would have recourse to so clumsy a periphrasis for it, as at best this Coptic compound is. Constr. בֶּהֱמְתּוֹ, &c.

בחן (75) בוד

בֹּהֶן, m. בְּהוֹנוֹת, pl. constr. (of a sing. בְּהֹן, or בְּהוֹן), *The thumb*, or *the great toe*, as the context may require, Lev. viii. 23; xiv. 14; Judg. i. 6, 7. Etymon. unknown.

בֹּהַק, m. occ. only Lev. xiii. 39, preceded by a sort of explanation; and followed by a declaration that the person on whom it appears is clean, i. e. free from the leprosy. *A sort of scurvy.* Arab. بَهَقٌ, *Leuce, vitiligo,* Avicen. Castell sub voce. Syr. ܒܗܩܐ, *fulgens.*

בְּהָרֵג, Ezek. xxvi. 15, for בְּהָרֵג. Infin. Niph. r. הרג.

בַּהֶרֶת, f. pl. בֶּהָרוֹת. Arab. بَهَرَ, *admodum luxit*. *The shining,* or *whitish scurfy, pustule* of the leprosy; which, being brighter than the preceding (בֹּהַק), sinking deeper into the flesh, and having white hair in it, is the sure symptom of the leprosy, Lev. xiii. 2—4; 18—23, 24—28.

בְּהִשַּׁמָּה, Lev. xxvi. 43. Gesenius says is the Infin. of Hoph. r. שמם. But this ought to be בְּהוּשַׁם, see Parad. Winer will have it to be for הֻשַׁמָּה. But this is no part of Hoph. Is it not more likely to be for בְּהַשַּׁמָּה, i. e. the def. art. retained, without the usual contraction into בַּ, with שַׁמָּה, *desolation,* &c.? 2 Chron. xxx. 9, &c.

בּוֹא, or בָּא, m. Infin. See sub. ב, above. *The entering,* or *coming in,* to any place, thing, &c. Aff. בּוֹאִי; בּוֹאֲךָ or בֹּאֲךָ; בּוֹאוֹ; בָּאֲנוּ, בָּאֲכֶם, בֹּאָן, בָּאָה. Hence—

בָּא, v. pres. יָבוֹא, Gram. art. 205. 10. opp. יָצָא. *Entered, came,* or *went, in, to, for,* &c., constr. בְּ, לְ, עַד, אֶל, and *immed.* Lev. xvi. 3; Gen. xix. 31; xxix. 23; Is. iii. 14; lii. 1; Jer. xxxiv. 10; Deut. i. 20; xxiv. 31. בָּא בַיָּמִים, *He entered into days,* i. e. grew old, Gen. xviii. 11. Ellip. 1 Sam. vi. 14. בָּא וְיָצָא לִפְנֵי, *Went in and out before*—i. e. his conduct was open and approved, 1 Sam. xxix. 6; 1 Kings iii. 7; Num. xxvii. 17. בָּאוּ בַבְּרִית, *They entered into,* i. e. received, *the covenant,* Jer. xxxiv. 10. לָבוֹא לַמִּשְׁפָּט...., *To enter into judgment,* 2 Sam. xv. 2. בַּמִּשְׁפָּט, Ps. cxliii. 2. בְּרִיב, *Into contention,* Prov. xviii. 6. בְדָמִים, *Into blood;* i. e. to put one to death. בְּאָלָה וּבִשְׁבֻעָה, *Into a curse and oath,* Neh. x. 30. אֶל־אֲבוֹת, *To* (one's) *fathers,* i. e. to be buried with them, Gen. xv. 15. אֶל־אִשָּׁה, or אֶל אִשָּׁה, *To a wife,* Deut. xxii. 13, &c. הַשֶּׁמֶשׁ בָּאָה, *The sun had entered;* i. e. apparently, *the earth;* had set, Gen. xv. 17, opp. יָצָא, Ps. xix. 6, 7. בִּעֹלוֹת...., *I will enter....with burnt-offerings,* Ps. lxvi. 13; lxxi. 16. Used also of things inanimate, as *a chariot,* the *ark of the covenant, an epistle, assistance, dreams, time,* &c., 1 Sam. vi. 14; iv. 5; v. 10; 2 Kings x. 2. 7; Ps. cxxi. 1; Eccl. v. 2; Gen. xli. 35, &c. In 1 Sam. xxv. 34, תָּבֹאתִי, for תָּבֹא אַתְּ, i. e. a repetition of the pron. for the sake of emphasis.

Part. בָּא pl. בָּאִים, constr. בָּאֵי.
Imper. בּוֹא, with ה paragog. בֹּאָה.
Hiph. הֵבִיא, pres. יָבִיא. Gram. art. 205. 11. *Caused, made, induced ....to enter, bring, come in,* &c. Constr. *immed.* pers. and *immed.* לְ, ־ָה, versus, עַל, בְּ, אֶל, מִן; and *immed.* as to place, time, person to, or from, whom, &c., Gen. iv. 4; xxxix. 14; xlvi. 7; 1 Kings ix. 9; Lev. xvi. 12; 2 Chron. xxxvi. 18, &c. הַמּוֹצִיא וְהַמֵּבִיא, *The bringer out, and leader in;* i. e. the chief general, king, 1 Chron. xi. 2. תָּבִיא בְמִשְׁפָּט, *Thou bringest into judgment,* Job xiv. 3. בַּמִּשְׁפָּט, *Into the judgment,* Eccl. xi. 9. הֵבֵאתִי הַשֶּׁמֶשׁ, *I have caused* (will surely cause), *the sun to enter* (set), Amos viii. 9. Occasionally has an adscititious י, in the conjugation, as הֲבִיאוֹתִים, *I have brought them,* Jer. xxv. 9; Ezek. xxxiv. 13, and without, as הֲבֵאתִים. See Gram. art. 201. 8; Num. xx. 4; 1 Sam. xvi. 17.

Infin. הָבִיא, or הָבֹא; constr. once הָבִי, Ruth iii. 15. It. with prep. לָבִיא, (לְהָבִיא, Gram. art. 73;) 2 Chron. xxxi. 10; Jer. xxxix. 7. Aff. הֲבִיאִי, *My bringing,* Ezek. xx. 42; xxxii. 9. הֲבִיאֲכֶם, הֲבִיאָם, הֲבִיאֲךָ.
Imper. הָבֵא, or הָבִיא. With ה parag. הֲבִיאָה, &c.
Part. מֵבִיא, מְבִי, pl. מְבִיאִים, constr. כְּבִיאֵי. Aff. מְבִיאֲךָ, pl. מְבִיאֶיהָ.
Hoph. הוּבָא, pres. יוּבָא. Passive of Hiph. Gen. xliii. 18; Lev. x. 18; xvi. 17, &c. הֻבָאת, 3 pers. sing. f. præt. Chald. form, Gen. xxxiii. 11. I have thought it superfluous here, as elsewhere, to give every possible shade of meaning, in every place, which a translator may think best for this word. This must be left to his judgment.

בּוֹדֵד, Part. and agent of בדד.

בּוּז, f. בּוּזָה (seg. בֻּזָּה, Gram. art. 86. 2), abstr. Arab. بَوْزٌ, *Enmity,* بَزَّ, id. Syr. ܒܙ, *spoliavit. Contempt,* Job xii. 5. 21; Ps. cvii. 40; Neh. iii. 36, &c. Hence—

בָּז, or בַּז, v. pres. יָבוּז. Cogn. בָּנָה בָּזָה, *Contemned, despised;* constr. *immed.* and

בוד (76) בון

med. ל, Prov. i. 7; xi. 12; xiii. 13; xiv. 21; xxiii. 9. 22; Zech. iv. 10, &c.

Infin. בּוֹז (contr. בְּוֹז, Gram. art. 75), Cant. viii. 7.

בוּד, Not in use. Arab. بَوْكَ, *confusio.* Cogn. بُوخ, id. See أفك, أبك. נָבוֹכָה, Niph. Est. iii. 15, *Confused, perplexed.* Part. נְבֻכִים, pl. Exod. xiv. 3. Deriv. מְבוּכָה, in its place.

בּוּל, contr. for יְבוּל, Gram. art. 76. Cogn. Arab. بَلَّ, *seminavit terram;* conj. iv. *fructum, protulit, &c.* See my note on Job xl. 20. I. *Produce, increase.* In Is. xlix. 19, applied to *timber,* i. e. the produce of a tree out of which an idol had been made. II. The name of a month, 1 Kings vi. 37, which is there said to be the 8th, i. e. our October, or thereabouts. So called, perhaps, because the produce of the year was then all to be gathered in. The months were at this time most probably solar. See my Sermon on the Sabbath with the notes.

בּוּלִים, m. Arab. بَلَس, *ficus,* pec. *alba.* Æth. ባሕ : *ficus,* arbor et fructus. Gesenius adds, "*etiam sycamorus,*" for which I can find no authority. From the form of our word, as well as of that preceding it (בּוֹקֵר, Amos vii. 14), it must imply an agent. Here, a person concerned about figs, in one way or other. According to Theophrastus, Hist. Plant iv. 2; Plin. Hist. Nat. lib. xiii. vii.—xiv. ed. Valpy; and Prosper Alpin. de Plant. Egypt. cap. vi. p. 20; a sort of fig or sycamore fruit is produced in Egypt from the trunk of the tree (comp. 1 Kings x. 27; Luke xix. 4; Ps. lxxviii. 47), which, unless it be scratched or cut open, so as to let out some of its juice, will not ripen. This is not unlike the Jack-fruit of India, and of the islands in the Eastern Archipelago. See my Travels of Ibn Batuta, p. 104, with the notes. I am inclined to think, therefore, that both בּוֹקֵר here, and בּוּלִם, refer to the treatment of this sort of fig. The former, to the act of *scratching,* or *cutting it open* (Arab. بَقَّ. *fidit, dilatavit;* hence בּוֹקֵר, is the dawn or *opening of day*); the latter, to the collecting of them, lit. *figging,* or gathering the figs of, these fig-trees (שִׁקְמִים). Prosper Alpin. tells us, l. c. that it is never without fruit. See Matt. xxi. 19; Mark xi. 13. And again, ib. "*Tumores*

omnes calidos, atque duros ficubus emplastri modo usi sanant." Comp. Is. xxxviii. 21.

בוּן, see בין.

בּוּס, v. Infin. not in use. Hence—Pres. יָבוּס. Cogn. בּוּז, בָּזָה, בָּזַה. Constr. immed. and med. עַל, *Trampling, treading on,* or *down, despising,* Ps. lx. 14; cviii. 14; Is. xiv. 25; Prov. xxvii. 7. Pih. pret. בּוֹסְסוּ, id. Is. lxiii. 18; Jer. xii. 10. Hoph. part. מוּבָס, *Trampled on,* Is. xiv. 19. Hithp. part. f. מִתְבּוֹסֶסֶת, *Become trodden down, &c.,* Ezek. xvi. 6. 22. Particip. noun. pl. בּוֹסִים, *Treading down, &c.,* Zech. x. 5; as if from Cogn. בסה. Syr. ܒܣܐ, *sprevit, aspernatus est.* Arab. بَسَأَ, *vilipendit* rem.

בּוּץ, m. Arab. بَزّ, *byssus.* Cogn. بَيْض, *præstantia candoris.* Syr. ܒܘܨܐ, *byssus.* See בַּד, sign. vii. *A fine sort of linen so called,* Gr. βύσσος. See Thes. Steph. sub vocc. According to Pliny, H. N. lib. xix. 2, the linen cloth of Egypt was far from strong, but very dear. It was of four sorts, named after the places in which it was made, *Taniticum, Pelusiacum, Buticum,* and *Tentyriticum.* He adds, "Superior pars Ægypti in Arabiam vergens gignit fruticem, quem aliqui gossipion* vocant, plures xylon, et ideo lina inde facta xylina. . . . . . Nec ulla sunt eis candore mollitiave præferenda. Vestes inde sacerdotibus Ægypti gratissimæ. Quartum genus Orchomenium appellant. Fit e palustri velut arundine." Our word occurs only in the latter Hebrew; viz. Ezek. xxvii. 16; Est. i. 6; viii. 15; 1 Chron. iv. 21; xv. 27; 2 Chron. ii. 13; iii. 14; v. 12, which induces me to believe both that the term is Syriac, and that the thing meant, is the same with that implied by בַּד. See above. From the places above cited, it appears to have been worn by kings, priests, and persons in authority generally: and from Ezek. xxvii. 16, that it was a Syrian article of merchandise. See Celsii Hierobot. ii. p. 169; Forskal Flor. Ægypt. p. 125; Hiller in Hierophyt, ii. p. 132; R. Forster de Bysso Antiq. Lond. 1776. 8. and Rev. xix. 8. 14.

בּוּקָה, f. Arab. بَوْق, *impetus* pluviæ *vehementior.* بَاقَة, *malum, calamitas.* Cogn.

---

* The notion of *cotton* here, which seems to have originated with the Greek and Latin writers, is warmly opposed by Celsius, l. c.

בוק (77) בות

בקק. *Emptiness, devastation,* Neh. ii. 11, with מְבוּקָה, and מְבֻלָּקָה, for emphasis sake. Gram. art. 223. 2.

בּוֹקֵר, m. Arab. بَاقِرٌ, *agmen boum cum suis bubulcis;* r. בקר. *A cowherd,* or, more generally, *a herdsman,* Amos vii. 16.

בּוֹר, pl. בּוֹרוֹת Syr. ܟܳܒܐ, *expers alicujus rei necessariæ.* Arab. بُورٌ, *terra non consita.* بَايِرَة, *inculta deserta.* Cogn. بِئْر, *puteus.* See באר. Generally any thing excavated, as, I. *A well,* or *cistern,* digged or cut out for water, Deut. vi. 11; 1 Sam. xiii. 6; Gen. xxxvii. 20. II. *A prison* (see באר) Is. xxiv. 22, termed בֵּית הַבּוֹר; Jer. xxxvii. 16; Exod. xii. 29, &c. III. *A sepulchre,* Ps. xxviii. 1; xxx. 4; lxxxviii. 5; Is. xxxvii. 18; hence the phrase, יוֹרְדֵי בוֹר, *Descenders of the pit,* and אַבְנֵי בוֹר, *Stones of the pit,* Is. xiv. 19; יַרְכְּתֵי בוֹר, *Thighs,* i. e. *sides,* *of the pit,* Ib. vr. 15. עַד בּוֹר, *Even to the pit,* Prov. xxviii. 17, &c., בֵּיר, *keri,* Jer. vi. 7, id. See also בֹּר. Hence v—

בּוּר, Infin. *Digging out, exploring,* Eccl. ix. 1; of which it is not improbable, as Gesenius has suggested, that בֵּי, ib. iii. 18, in לִבְרָם, is the pret.—or, perhaps, is another form of the Infin.

בּוּשָׁה, f. Arab. بُوشٌ, بُوشٌ بَايِشٌ, *miscella, hominum turba. tumultus hominum inter se mixtorum.* بَوْشِيٌّ, *inops, magna onustus familia, &c.* Cogn. بَهَتَ.

بُوش. Secondary sense, *Shame, ignominy,* Ps. lxxxix. 46; Ezek. vii. 18; Obad. 10; Mich. vii. 10. Synon. בּוֹשָׁה. Hence—

בּוֹשׁ, v. (for בּוּשׁ, fm. יבל) pres. יָבוֹשׁ, *Ashamed, put to shame,* or *confusion, blushed.* constr. מ, and abs. Found with בָּהַל, חָפֵר, or נִכְלָם, occasionally. Sometimes without the י, as בֹּשׁ, Jer. xlviii. 13; בֹּשׁוּ, Job vi. 20, &c.; Jer. xv. 9; Ps. lxxi. 24; lxxxiii. 18, &c.: pec. when hope, expectation, strength, &c. fail, Is. xix. 9; Jer. xiv. 3, 4; Job vi. 20; Ps. vi. 11, &c. מְקוֹרוֹ יָבוֹשׁ, *He shall be ashamed, be put to confusion* (as to) *his spring;* the reason is added.—It is not necessary therefore to suppose here, that we have the sense of יָבֵשׁ.—Infin. בּוֹשׁ, *Blushing,* Jud. iii. 25; 2 Kings ii. 17; viii. 11.

Imp. f. בּוֹשִׁי, pl. בּוֹשׁוּ, Is. xxiii. 4; Ezek. xxxvi. 22.

Part. ag. pl. בּוֹשִׁים, Ezek. xxxii. 30.

Pih. *Sensu prægnanti. Put to a stand, delayed;* i. e. because confused, &c. Jud. v. 28; Exod. xxxii. 1.

Hiph. הוֹבִישׁ, הֵבִישׁ, and it. הוֹבַשְׁתְּ (from cogn. יבשׁ); pres. תַּבִישׁ, Ps. xiv. 6. Aff. הֱבִישַׁנִי, Ps. cxix. 31. 116. *Brought to shame, confusion,* Jer. x. 14; Is. xxx. 5; constr. עַל, and *immed.* 2 Sam. xix. 6; Ps. xiv. 6; xliv. 8. Part. מֵבִישׁ, f. מְבִישָׁה, *Bringing shame;* not intrans. as Gesenius thinks, Prov. x. 5; xii. 4; xiv. 35; xvii. 2.

Hithp. יִתְבּוֹשֵׁשׁ, *Become ashamed,* Gen. ii. 25. The (ֵ) is here on account of the pause; not because the conjug. is anomalous, as Gesenius thinks. Gram. art. 120. 2.

בּוּת, Infin. not in use. Syr. ܟܳܬ, *pernoctavit.* Arab. بَيَّتَ, *pernoctatio.* Æth. ዐደ: *mansio.* Hence, v. Chald. pret. בָּת, *passed the night,* Dan. vi. 19.

בַּז, m. r. בזז. Syr. ܒܰܙ, *diripuit.* Arab. بَزَّ, *rapuit. Spoil,* taken in war. Aff. בִּזָּה, *Her spoil,* Ezek. xxix. 19, from a different seg. fm. Num. xiv. 30; Jer. xv. 13, &c. Often used after its verb (בָּזַז) for emphasis sake, Is. x. 6; xxxiii. 23, &c. Phrase, הָיָה לָבַז, *Was for a spoil,* Num. xiv. 31, &c. It. נָתַן לָבַז, *Gave for a spoil,* Jer. xvii. 3, &c.

בָּזְאוּ, pl. pret. Kal. of בּוּא, otherwise occurs not, Is. xviii. 2. Cogn. בָּזָה, בָּזָא; Syr. ܒܙ, *diripuit;* Arab. بَزَّ, *subjecit sibi.* "Significatur Æthiopia," says Gesenius. But it appears to be from Æthiopia that messengers are to be sent on the waters, to some other people, whose land the rivers (בּוּאוּ) *have spoiled.* From the several descriptions here given, however, viz. גּוֹי קַו קָו, Comp. ch. xxviii. 10, נוֹרָא, *fearful,* כְּמוּסָה, Comp. ch. v. 5; xxviii. 18; lxiii. 18; Jer. xii. 10; Lam. i. 15, &c. The overflowing of rivers figuratively, ch. viii. 7, 8; xxviii. 18; xxx. 28, &c. The raising of a standard for the Gentiles among them (vv. 3, 4. 7, &c.); the Jewish nation is apparently meant. It is true, the people of Æthiopia appear to be called upon to look (vr. 3) when the standard shall be thus lifted up. Comp. Ps. lxviii. 32. But it is not that people whose land the rivers are here said to have affected. The ancient versions, viz. Syr. ܒܙ; Chald.

בזה (78) בחו

בּוֹ; Vulg. *diripuerant*, &c. are correct—and Hartmann and Gesenius, who make this verb to signify *cutting, intersecting*, &c., are wrong.

בִּזֹּה, Infin. taken passively, Gram. art. 146. 8, note. *Despised*, or *being despised*, Is. xlix. 7. לְ has evidently the sense here of *as to, with respect to*; not of *to*; the context being about Christ. See my Sermons and Dissertations, p. 203; and comp. ch. liii. 3, with Ps. xxii. 7, בְּזוּי עָם. Hence,—

בָּזָה, v. pres. יִבְזֶה, apoc. יִבֶז; cogn. בוז, בוּז; Arab. بَزَا, r. بَزَو, *extulit sese superbius*, &c. *Despised, spurned, contemned.* Constr. *immed.* rarely with לְ, *med.* Num. xv. 31; 2 Kings xix. 21; Is. xxxviii. 22; Gen. xxv. 34; Est. iii. 6; Ps. li. 19.
Part. בּוֹזֶה, Prov. xv. 20. Aff. xiv. 2; pl. 2 Chron. xxxvi. 16; בֹּזַי, constr. Mal. i. 6. Aff. pl. בֹּזַי, 1 Sam. ii. 30.
Passive, בָּזוּי, Jer. xlix. 15; Ps. xxii. 7, &c. f. בְּזוּיָה, Eccl. ix. 16.
Niph. נִבְזֶה, *Despised*, i. e. made so, Ps. xv. 4; Is. liii. 3, &c. Part. id. Ps. cxix. 141; pl. נִבְזִים, Mal. ii. 9.
Hiph. Infin. הַבְזוֹת, *Render*, or *make, despised*, Est. i. 17.

בָּזַז, v. pres. יָבֹז, conj. בְזוּ, בַּזּוּנוּ; once, Deut. iii. 7, בּוֹזֵנוּ, like סב. See בוּז. Constr. *immed.* and *med.* לְ. *Took the spoil*, or *prey*, Num. xxxi. 32; Josh. viii. 28; Deut. ii. 35. With בְ, or שָׁלָל, Is. xxxiii. 23; 2 Chron. xxviii. 8; Infin. בֹּז, 2 Chron. xx. 25; Est. iii. 13, &c.
Imp. p. בֹּזּוּ, Nahum ii. 10.
Part. ag. pl. בֹּזְזִים, Is. xlii. 24; 2 Chron. xx. 25; aff. Ezek. xxxix. 10.
Niph. נָבֹז, pl. נָבֹזּוּ, pres. יִבֹּז, *Became spoiled*, &c., Amos iii. 11; Is. xxiv. 3.
Infin. הִבּוֹז, ib. emphat.
Puh. בֻּזּוּ, *They shall* (surely) *be spoiled*, Jer. l. 37.

בִּזָּיוֹן, m. *Great contempt*, Est. i. 18.

בָּזָק, m. Syr. ܒܙܩ, *dispersio, contritio*. Cogn. בָּרַק, *celeritas* in *incessu*. Cogn. בָּרָק. *Lightning*, Ezek. i. 14.

בָּזַר, v. pres. יִבְזוֹר, Arab. بَزَرَ, *seminavit*. Cogn. بَذَرَ, id. Syr. ܒܕܪ, id. *Dispersed, scattered*, Dan. xi. 24.
Pih. בִּזַּר, id. Ps. lxviii. 31.

בָּחוֹן, m. Syr. ܒܚܢܐ, *investigatio*; Arab. cogn. بَحْن. id. *Trial, experiment, essaying*, as of metals, abstr. for concr., Jer. vi. 27, referring, too, to בְּחַנְתִּי, following, as in נָחוּן תִּתֵּן, Num. xxvii. 7. Comp. ib. xx. 21.

בַּחוּן, m. Dag. impl. Gram. art. 109, *Fortress, watch-tower*, or the like. Is. xxiii. 13. keri. cogn. Arab. بَحْل, *impulsus validus*; بَحْون, *arena accumulata*. Some take it to signify a tower constructed of wood, and placed near the walls of a town for the purpose of harassing the men within. It might, however, mean *an artificial mound* raised up for that purpose; and hence, perhaps, the verb הֵקִימוּ is used here.

בָּחוּר, m. pl. בַּחוּרִים, constr. בַּחוּרֵי, Dag. impl. Arab. بَاحُور, *summus æstus et ardor mediæ ætatis. A youth*, unmarried, pec. as chosen, engaged for war, 1 Sam. xxiv. 3, &c. Sometimes joined with בְּתוּלָה, Deut. xxxii. 25; Lam. i. 18, &c.; Ruth iii. 10; Is. lxii. 5; ix. 16; Jer. xviii. 21, &c. See v. בָּחַר.

בָּחִין, kethiv, of בָּחוּן above.

בָּחִיר, m. Syr. ܒܚܝܪ, *electus. Elect, chosen*, Ἐκλεκτός. Constr. בְּחִיר. Applied to Moses, Ps. cvi. 23; Saul, xxi. 6; to the Israelites, Is. xlv. 4; 1 Chron. xvi. 13; to Christ, Is. xlii. 1; to Christians, Is. xliii. 20; lxv. 9. 15. 22. And hence the use of the term in the New Test. See my Sermons and Dissertations, p. 35 et seq.; not because any metaphysical view of the case has ever been put forth by any sacred writer. ן

בָּחַל, v. f. בָּחֲלָה, Zech. xi. 8, only. Arab. بَحَل, *parcus, talemque se præbuit*, cc. علي, p. et ب, r. Cogn. بَحَل, *penuria laboravit*; Kāmoos, الإدفاع الشديد, *Violently driving back*, or the like. *Greedy, niggard*, l. c. בָּחֲלָה בִּי, opp. to שֹׂמְרִים אֹתִי, vr. 11. In vr. 12, *Thirty pieces of silver*—termed ironically אֶדֶר הַיְקָר, vr. 13,—is the utmost they would give. Comp. Mal. iii. 7, et seq., where לֹא שְׁמַרְתֶּם, is explained by an *avaricious* withholding from God his due. Castell prefers *rugiit*, as given by the ancient versions—Gesenius the usual *fastidiverat* "*lothed.*" Puh. Part. מְבֹחָלָה, *Coveted*. Meton. *Gotten by covetousness*, Prov. xx. 21, kethiv; the

בחן (79) בטח

keri has מבהלה. Adage Arab. خُلَّة. الولد سَجِدَة, *proles res est cujus tenaces, et de qua solliciti sumus.*

בֹּחַן, m. Synon. τοῦ, בָּחוֹן, *Trial, experiment*, &c., Ezek. xxi. 18. Meton. *Tried*, Is. xxviii. 16.

בַּחַן, m. once, Is. xxxii. 14; עֹפֶל וָבַחַן Gesen. *Hill and watch-tower.* Auth. Vers. *Forts and towers. Height and mound*, in a military sense is, perhaps, the real meaning of the passage. See בּ, above, and comp. Neh. iii. 27, חוֹמַת הָעֹפֶל.

בָּחַן, v. pres. יִבְחַן. See בָּחוֹן. I. *Examined, tried, essayed,* as metals. Constr. *immed.* בּ, instr. Zech. xiii. 9, with צָרַף, Jer. ix. 6, as if following upon that process, — II. Metaph. applied to men, as taking place by affliction, Job xxiii. 10; Ps. xvii. 3; Jer. xii. 3:—to God, by men impiously prescribing his duty, Mal. iii. 15; Ps. xcv. 9;—to God, as one who tries the heart, &c., Jer. xi. 20; xvii. 10; xx. 12; Ps. vii. 10; xxvi. 2, &c.— to the ear, as trying assertions, Job xii. 11; xxxiv. 3:—to the eyelids, as judging of character, Ps. xi. 34.

Infin. בְּחֹן, part. בֹּחֵן, Imp. בְּחָ. Niph. pres. יִבָּחֵן, pl. יִבָּחֲנוּ. II. *Be, or become tried, proved.* Gen: xlii. 15, 16; Job xxxiv. 36.

בָּחַר, v. pres. יִבְחַר. See בָּחִיר. *Chose, elected, selected.* Constr. *immed.* and *med.* בּ, ל, once עַל, as Abraham, Neh. ix. 7; kings, as Saul and David, 1 Sam. x. 24; 2 Sam. xxi. 6: Jerusalem, 1 Kings xi. 13, 32: Jacob, as a people, Deut. xiv. 2; Is. xli. 8: *ways, manners,* Is. lxvi. 3 : *fear of God,* Prov. i. 29 : *gardens* of idolatry, &c. Is. i. 29 ; 2 Sam. xix. 39 : *words,* Job ix. 14 : *sensu prægnanti,* תִּבְחָר עָלַי, *Shalt choose* (and lay) *upon me.* There appears no good reason for admitting either the I. or III. senses given by Gesenius, viz. I. *try*; III. *love, desire.*

Infin. בָּחוֹר, constr. בְּחוֹר, aff. בָּחֲרִי, (seg.) בֹּחֶר. Imp. בְּחַר, pl. בַּחֲרוּ. Niph. pres. נִבְחָר, part. *Chosen, eligible,* &c. Jer. viii. 3; Prov. viii. 10, 19; x. 20, &c.

בְּטָא, or בטח, v. part. בּוֹטֶה. Arab. بَطَّ, *calcavit.* Cogn. بَطِيط, *mendacium.* *Speaking wrongfully, falsely,* Prov. xii. 18. Pih. יְבַטֵּא, *Speaks falsely, wrongfully, &c.* Lev. v. 4; Ps. cvi. 33. Infin. בַּטֵּא, Lev.

v. 4. From these places it is sufficiently evident, that something worse than speaking inconsiderately must be meant. I think Gesenius is right in making this word a cognate with בדד, although I doubt the accuracy of his deduction. See also בדא above, and בד, sig. vi. So بَطِيط, *res miranda, mendacium.*

בֶּטַח, m. בִּטְחָה, f. Arab. اَلْبَطِيحَة, i. e. مَسِيلٌ وَاسِعٌ فِيهِ دَقَاقُ الْحَصَى, i. e. *A wide stream in which is small sand.* Hence the phrase, تَبَطَّحَ السَّيْلُ اتَّسَعَ فِي الْبَطْحَاءِ, *A torrent,* or *stream,* תּבטח, i. e. *it spread out into lakes.* Hence, perhaps, the notion of *plenty, security, confidence,* &c. *Confidence;* adv. *in confidence, confidently,* Is. xxxii. 17 ; Gen. xxxiv. 25. Often with לְ, and the verbs הָיָה, יָלַךְ, רָבַץ, נָתַן, בָּחָה, שָׁכַב, שָׁכַן, יָשַׁב, Lev. xxv. 18; Deut. xxxiii. 12; Job xi. 18; xxiv. 23; Ps. lxxviii. 53; Prov. iii. 23; Is. xv. 3; Ezek. xxxiv. 27 ; f. Is. xxx. 16.

בָּטַח, v. pres. יִבְטַח, constr. *med.* בּ, עַל, אֶל, ל, and *abs. Confided, trusted, in, to, on,* Ps. xxviii. 7; Ezek. xxxiii. 13; Ps. xxxi. 7 ; 2 Kings xviii. 21; Job vi. 20; xi. 18 ; xl. 23, &c.

Infin. בְּטֹחַ, Ps. cxviii. 8; Imp. בְּטַח ib. xxxvii. 3; pl. בִּטְחוּ. Part. ag. בּוֹטֵחַ, Deut. xxviii. 52; pl. בּוֹטְחִים; f. בּוֹטְחָה, pl. בּוֹטְחוֹת. Pass. בָּטוּחַ, Ps. cxii. 7.

Hiph. הִבְטִיחַ, pres. יַבְטַח, *Made to confide, trust,* Jer. xxviii. 15 ; Is. xxxvi. 15 ; Jer. xxix. 31.

Part. מַבְטִיחִים, Ps. xxii. 10.

בִּטָּחוֹן, m. *Great confidence,* Is xxxvi. 4 ; Eccl. ix. 4. Gram. art. 168.

בַּטֻּחוֹת, f. pl. *Securities, things confided in. Great confidence,* pl. excel. Job xii. 6.

בָּטֵל, v. Arab. بَطَلَ, *vanus, frustrà fuit.* Syr. ܒܛܠ, *irritum fecit,* Eccl. xii. 3, *unemployed; ceased.* בְּטֵל, id. Chald. Ezra iv. 24.

Pah. Chald. *Caused,* or *made to cease,* Ezra iv. 21. 23; v. 5; vi. 8.

בֶּטֶן, f. Arab. بَطْن, *Excavation, hollowness,* seems to be the primitive idea: hence بَطْنُ الثَّرَى, *sepulchra: medium et intimum alicujus rei: venter.* Syr. ܟܗܢ, *prægnans.*

I. *The belly*, of man or beast, Cant. vii. 3; Job xl. 16: as filled with food, Prov. xiii. 25; xviii. 20; Job xx. 20; Eccl. xi. 5: or, as pregnant, synon. with רֶחֶם, Gen. xxv. 24; xxxviii. 27; Job iii. 11. Hence the phraseology, מִן־הַבֶּטֶן, Jud. xiii. 6, 7; מִבֶּטֶן, Is. xlviii. 8, &c.; מִבֶּטֶן אִמִּי, Ps. xxii. 10; Job xxxi. 18: פְּרִי־בֶטֶן, *offspring*, Gen. xxx. 2; Deut. vii. 13 : בַּר־בִּטְנִי, Prov. xxxi. 2: בְּנֵי בִטְנִי, Job xix. 17, my own children, "the mere effusion of (my) proper loins." Not Job's brethren, but his children. See my notes on the place. It. בֶּטֶן שְׁאוֹל, *cavity of the sepulchre*, Jon. ii. 3. חַדְרֵי־בָטֶן, lit. *recesses, chambers, of the belly;* i. e. the inmost mind, Prov. xviii. 8; xx. 27, &c. תִּרְגְּזוּ בִטְנִי, *my viscera trembled;* i. e. my mind was agitated, Hab. iii. 16. Architecturally, the bellying, or swelling of columns, 1 Kings vii. 20. Aff. בִּטְנִי, בִּטְנוֹ, בִּטְנוֹ, בִּטְנֵךְ, בְּבִטְנָהּ, בְּטָנָם, pl. non occ.

בָּטְנִים, pl. Gen. xliii. 11. *Nuts,* the *pistacia vera* of Linnæus; a tree much abounding in Palestine, but unknown in Egypt. Hierob. Olav. Celsius. i. p. 24, et seq. Plin. Hist. Nat. lib. xiii. x. Bochart. Canaan, lib. i. x.

בִּי, An interjection, used to excite pity or compassion. See Gen. xliii. 20, &c. Nold. p. 175. Gesenius takes it as an abbreviation of בְּעִי, *petitio*, &c. r. בעה. But, if this were the case, such passages as בִּי אֲדֹנִי, would rather imply, *request* or *petition* (me) *Lord,* than favour sought for such person. There can be no doubt, therefore, Noldius and others were correct in appealing to the Arab. بَيَّاكَ اللّٰه, and the Syr. ܒܳܐ, *consolatus est,* for the just interpretation of the word. Gram. art. 243. 2, note. *O favour, pity, be gracious,* or the like.

בֵּין, constr. prim. בַּן, seg. Gram. 147. 10; 171. 3, note. Dual. בֵּינַיִם, pl. בִּינוֹת. Arab. بَيْن, *intervallum, separatio.* I. *Interval, midst.* בְּבֵין, Is. xliv. 4. מִבֵּין, Gen. xlix. 10. אִישׁ בֵּינַיִם, lit. *man of two intervals;* spoken of Goliath, as placed between the two armies, 1 Sam. xvii. 4. II. Hence, used as a preposition. Arab. بَيْن, *Between, among, within;* as, בֵּין אָחִים, *Between brethren*, Prov. vi. 19; Job xxx. 7. בֵּין הָעַרְבַּיִם, *Between the two evenings;* i. e. the period between sunset on two successive days. See my sermon on the Sabbath. Exod. xxix. 39, &c. בֵּין עֲשֶׂרֶת יָמִים

During, within, the space of ten days, Neh. v. 18. בֵּין יָדַיִם, *Between;* i. e. *within, the two hands,* Zech. xiii. 6. בֵּין שׁוּרוֹתָם, *Between, within, their walls,* Job xxiv. 11.

When two things are spoken of, בֵּין....וּבֵין, Gen. xxvi. 28; Exod. xi. 7. Occasionally בֵּין....לְ, Gen. i. 6; Lev. xx. 25. בֵּין....לְבֵין, Is. lix. 2. בֵּין....ל, Joel ii. 17.

Used with other prepositions, as, אֶל־בֵּין, Ez. xxxi. 10. 14. אֶל־בֵּינוֹת, Ib. x. 2. עַל־בֵּין, Ib. xix. 11. מִבֵּין, Zech. vi. 1; Ps. civ. 12; Jer. xlviii. 45. מִבֵּין סִיחוֹן, ellip. for מִבֵּין עַם סִיחוֹן. מִבֵּין רַגְלָיו, *From between the feet*, i. q. מִבֶּטֶן or מֵרֶחֶם, Deut. xxviii. 57. מִבֵּין רַגְלָיו ellip. for מֵאֲשֶׁר מִבֵּין רַגְלָיו, Gen. xlix. 10, *from his posterity*. It. rep. מִבֵּין....מִבֵּין, 2 Kings xvi. 14; Ezek. xlvii. 18. מִבֵּינוֹת לְ, and אֶל־בֵּינוֹת, Ib. x. 2. מִבֵּינוֹת vv. 6, 7. Aff. בֵּינִי, בֵּינְךָ, &c.

בֵּין, Chald. id. Dan. vii. 5. Aff. pl. בֵּינֵיהֶן, v. 8; *keri* בֵּינֵיהוֹן.

בִּין, v. conj. בַּן, and בִּינוֹת, Dan. ix. 2, pres. יָבִין, apoc. יָבֵן, and יָבֶן. Arab. بَانَ, *Distitit, et segregata fuit* res a re. I. *Distinguished, discerned;* meton. *perceived, understood:* constr. לְ, Ps. cxxxix. 2, &c. בְּ, Neh. xiii. 7. אֶל, Ps. xxviii. 5. עַל, Dan. xi. 30; abs. Ps. xciv. 7; *immed*. Prov. vii. 7, &c.

Infin. בִּין, Prov. xxiii. 1; Imp. Dan. ix. 23; x. 1.

Part. pl. בָּנִים, Jer. xlix. 7.

Niph. נָבוֹן, *Became discerning, &c.* Is. x. 13; pres. non occ. Part. נָבוֹן, pl. נְבוֹנִים. Aff. נְבוֹנָי, Gen. xli. 33. 39; Deut. i. 13; Is. v. 21; xxix. 14.

Pih. יְבוֹנְנֵהוּ, *Made him discerning, gave him intelligence,* Deut. xxxii. 10.

Hiph. הֵבִין, pres. non. occ. or is very doubtful. Constr. *immed.* לְ and בְּ, Job xxxv. 23; Is. xxix. 16; Dan. i. 17. I. *Made to know, understand, &c.* II. Occasionally in the sense of Kal, Is. xxviii. 19; Dan. i. 4; ix. 23; Job xxviii. 23; Prov. i. 2, &c. Infin. הָבִין, Imp. הָבֵן, Part. מֵבִין, pl. מְבִינִים, constr. מְבִינֵי.

Hithp. הִתְבּוֹנֵן, pres. יִתְבּוֹנֵן, i. q. Niph. constr. abs.—with עַד, בְּ, אֶל, לְ, מִן. Imp. הִתְבּוֹנֵן, Job xxxvii. 14; pl. Jer. ii. 10; ix. 16.

בִּינָה, f. pl. בִּינוֹת, *Intelligence, discernment, prudence, knowledge*, Job xxviii. 12. 20; Prov. iv. 5; viii. 14; ix. 6. אֵין בִּינָה, *ignorance*, Is. xxxiii. 19. Seems to be used *adverbially*, Job xxxviii. 4; Jer. xxviii. 20. Pl. of excell. בִּינוֹת עַם, *people of great discern-*

בִּיץ (81) בֵּית

ment, Is. xxvii. 11; constr. בִּינַת. Aff. בִּינָתִי, בִּינַתְכֶם, בִּינָתְךָ.
Chald. id. Dan. ii. 21.

בֵּיצִים, pl. m. *Eggs*. Arab. بَيْضٌ, *præstantia candoris*. بَيْضَةٌ, *ovum*. Chald. בִּיעֲתָא. Syr. ܒܥܬܐ, id. Deut. xxii. 6; Is. x. 14; lix. 5; Job xxxix. 14. Aff. בֵּיצֶיהָ, בֵּיצֵיהֶם.

בִּיקְרוֹתֶיךָ, Ps. xlv. 10. See יָקַר.

בַּיִר, i. q. בְּאֵר, Jer. vi. 7, *keri*.

בִּירָה, f. or dub. Arab. بَارَّة, *Thesaurus*. Pers. بَارَهْ, or بَارُو, *fortification, &c.* I. *A palace* with the adjacent city, Est. i. 5; ii. 5, &c. II. *The temple* at Jerusalem, Neh. ii. 8; 1 Chron. xxix. 1. 19. Gesenius makes this *sequioris Hebraïsmi vox*; yet in these two last instances, the sacred writer puts it into the mouth of David. Nor is it in the other instances found, as he intimates, apart from שׁוּשַׁן.

בִּירְתָה, Chald. id. defin. בִּירְתָא. Syr. ܒܝܪܬܐ, Ezra vi. 2.

בִּירָנִיּוֹת, f. pl. *Palaces*, 2 Chron. xvii. 12; xxvii. 4; sing. non occ. Gram. 140. 3.

בַּיִת, m. constr. בֵּית, aff. בֵּיתִי, &c. Seg. r. בית, pl. בָּתִּים; constr. בָּתֵּי; aff. בָּתֵּינוּ, &c. Cogn. r. בות, for בִּיוֹתִים, (sing. בָּיוֹת, fm. פָּקוֹד) contr. Gram. art. 73. בּוֹתִים, and with Dag. compens. בָּתִּים, &c. Gesenius first supposes בָּתָּה to be the sing., but this would supply the pl. בָּתִּים, as in קָדָשִׁים, קֹדֶשׁ. He next proposes בָּנָה i. q. בְּנֵה, from the root בנה; which would give the pl. בְּנָתִים, not בָּתִּים and thence בָּנוֹת! It is astonishing that a grammarian of so much experience, should so grievously forget the analogy of words. Arab. بَيْتٌ, *domus*, pl. بُيُوتٌ (Heb. בָּיוֹת, as above), hence بُيُوتَاتٌ, which is the full and regular pl. Syr. ܒܝܬܐ, *pernoctatio*. ܒܬܐ; constr. ܒܝܬ, pl. ܒܬܐ, for ܒܬܬܐ. Cogn. r. בנה. *A house*, or *residence*: I. Whether of God, or of idols, as *the Temple, &c.*— II. Of the King, as his *Palace*: III. Of men, or beasts, generally, as *House, tent, cave, &c.*: IV. Of the dead, as *the Sepulchre*.—I. 1 Kings vi. 5; xxxviii. 7. 12; Is. lxvi. 1; xxxvii. 38; xliv. 13, &c. II. 2 Sam. xi. 2. 9; 1 Kings ix. 31, &c. III. Job xvii. 13; xxxix. 6; Ps.

lxxxiv. 4, &c. Job viii. 4. Hence also V. *The receptacle* of any thing, Is. iii. 20. בָּתֵּי נֶפֶשׁ *Perfume-boxes*, according to Schrœder, *de Vestitu mulierum*. Comp. Exod. xxvi. 29; xxxvi. 34, &c.; *A prison*, Gen. xxxix. 20, 21, &c.

Hence, Meton. VI. *House*, in the sense of *family*; as, בֵּית פַּרְעֹה; Gen. l. 4. בֵּית אַבְרָהָם, Ib. xvii. 23. בֵּית אָב, Ib. xxiv. 23. בֵּית אָבִיו, Ib. xxxiv. 19. בֵּית יוֹסֵף, Ps. xliii. 18, &c. Also *God's people*, or *family*, Num. xii. 7; Hos. viii. 1. Comp. 1 Tim. iii. 15. Hence also applied to the *Raising of a family*, Ruth iv. 11; Deut. xxv. 9; 1 Sam. ii. 35; xxv. 28; 2 Sam. vii. 27. Comp. Ib. vii. 11. Also, to the *Goods, &c. of a house*, Est. viii. 1, 2; Gen. xv. 2; Exod. i. 21. Also, VII. *The interior* of any thing, opp. חוּץ, Exod. xxviii. 26. מִבַּיִת, Gen. iv. 14, opp. מִחוּץ. With ה, parag. *Intus, introrsum, inwards*, Ezek. xliv. 17; Exod. xxviii. 26, &c. See Nold. p. 182. Cogn. בוא. It is found compounded with many names of places, as, בֵּית אָוֶן, בֵּית אֵל, &c. See Reland's Palestine, and Gram. 170, 24.

בַּיִת, def. בַּיְתָא, בַּיְתָה, constr. בֵּית, pl. בָּתִּין, aff. בַּיְתֵהּ, Chald. i. q. Heb. Dan. ii. 5; iv. 27; Ezra v. 2; vi. 4, &c.

בִּיתָן, m. constr. בִּיתַן, *Great house, palace*, Est. i. 5; vii. 7, 8.

בָּכָא, m. Arab. بَكَاءٌ, بُكَاءٌ, *fletus*. Syr. ܒܟܐ, id. Æth. ብከየ, *flevit*, Ps. lxxxiv. 7. עֵמֶק הַבָּכָא, *Vale of weeping*, applied apparently to this state of things, on account of the various trials experienced in it.

בְּכָאִים, pl. 2 Sam. v. 23, 24; 1 Chron. xiv. 14, 15. The Arab. بَكَاءٌ. According to Celsius Hierob. I. p. 335, et seq. i. e. *a Tree giving out (weeping)* a white sort of gum, the medicinal properties of which are dry and acrid, and good for the tooth-ache.

בְּכֶה, m. Arab. بَكَاءٌ, *fletus. Weeping*, Ezra x. 1.

בָּכָה, v. pres. יִבְכֶּה, apoc. יֵבְךְ. Arab. بَكَى. Syr. ܒܟܐ. Æth. ብከየ: *flevit. Wept*, meton. *Mourned*, on account of loss or injury of any description. Constr. עַל, אֶל, לְ, אַחֲרֵי, and abs. Gen. xlv. 14; Ezek. xxvii. 31; Job xxx. 25; Deut. xxi. 13; Num. xi. 18; Ps. cxxxvii. 1.

Infin. בְּכוֹ, Jer. xxii. 10. בָּכוֹ בָכוֹ, *Weep exceedingly*.

M

Part. גֹּבֶה, Exod. ii. 7; Num. xi. 10, pl. בּוֹכִים, Ib. xxv. 6; Jud. ii. 5, f. בּוֹכִיָּה, Lam. i. 16.

Pih. part. f. מְבַכָּה, pl. מְבַכּוֹת, *Mourning, deploring*, Jer. xxxi. 15; Ezek. viii. 14.

בְּכִי, m. in pause, בֶּכִי. *Weeping, lamentation*, Deut. xxxiv. 8; 2 Sam. xiii. 36; מִבְּכִי, *from weeping*, i. e. emitting so much as a teardrop, Job xxviii. 11. See my note on the place. Aff. בִּכְיִי, *My lamentation*, Ps. vi. 9.

בְּכוֹר, m. pl. בְּכוֹרִים. Arab. بَكُور, *Being, or rising, early*. بَكُورَة, *primogenita*. Syr. ܒܟܘܪܐ, *primogenitus*. Æth. ስም : id. I. *The first-born* of man or beast, Gen. xxv. 13; Exod. xi. 5, &c. And, because certain considerations were attached to these, II. Taken as a superlative, as in בְּכוֹר דַּלִּים, *first-born of the poor*; i. e. the most poor, Is. xiv. 30. בְּכוֹר מָוֶת, *a killing disease*, according to Gesenius, Winer, &c.; but most probably a periphrasis for *the worm*, Job xviii. 13. See my note on the place. The Arabs have, indeed, the phrase, ضَرَبَهُ, signifying *a deadly blow*; which, however, is far from deciding this usage in the sense alluded to: much less is the بنات المنية, of Schultens.

בְּכוֹרָה, f. pl. בְּכוֹרוֹת, *Primogeniture, the being first-born*, either of man or beast, Gen. xxv. 32. 34; Deut. xxi. 17; xii. 6. 17: Gen. iv. 4. Aff. בְּכֹרָתוֹ, בְּכֹרָתְךָ, בְּכֹרָתִי.

בִּכּוּר, m. pl. בִּכּוּרִים, בִּכֻּרִים, *First-fruits*, of the fields, trees, &c. commanded to be offered up, Lev. ii. 14; xxiii. 17; Neh. x. 36, &c. רֵאשִׁית sometimes precedes, which may be taken adverbially, Exod. xxiii. 19; xxxiv. 26. לֶחֶם הַבִּכֻּרִים, *bread* of the first-fruits; i. e. made of the first wheat. יוֹם הַבִּכּוּרִים, *day of the first fruits*: i. e. of Pentecost, on which they were offered, Num. xxviii. 26; occ. sing. only in Is. xxviii. 4. With aff. בִּכּוּרָהּ, which certainly seems to be erroneous, for בִּכּוּרָה, f.

בִּכּוּרָה, f. pl. בִּכּוּרוֹת (for בַּכּוּרוֹת), *Precocious, immaturely ripe, fruit*, Micah vii. 1; Hos. ix. 10; Jer. xxiv. 2. Arab. بَكِير, *præcox palma, &c.*

בְּכִירָה, f. opp. צְעִירָה, *First-born*, or *eldest daughter*, Gen. xix. 31. et seq. xxix. 26.

בָּכִית, r. בכה, f. *Mourning*, Gen. ל. 4.

בָּכַר, v. Pih. pres. יְבַכֵּר, *Brings forth early*, or *first-fruits*; not *fructus præcoces*, as Gesenius and Winer give: this is manifestly at variance with the context.

Infin. בַּכֵּר, *Appointing*, or *constituting as first-born, giving the rights of primogeniture*, Deut. xxi. 16.

Puh. pass. of Pih. Lev. xxvii. 26.

Hiph. part. מַבְכִּירָה, f. *A woman bringing forth her first child; bearing a first-born*, Jer. iv. 13.

בִּכְרָה, f. Arab. بَكَارَة بَكْر, *parvus camelus, vel juvencus*. *A young she camel*, Jer. ii. 23, בִּכְרָה קַלָּה. Pl. constr. m. בִּכְרֵי, Is. lx. 6. Hieroz. Bochart. i. lib. ii. cap. 3.

בַּל, partic. Arab. بَلِي or بَلَا, *usu vetustus evadens, consumpta fuit*, vestis. Syr. ܒܠܐ. Heb. בָּלָה, id. Hence, meton. *Being wanting, &c.* Arab. هو بذي بَلِي, *longius abest, ut ubi sit nescias*. Synon. with לֹא, comp. Ps. lviii. 9; Job iii. 16; Prov. x. 30; Ps. lxii. 3, &c. *Not, by no means*, Is. xxvi. 14; Ps. xlix. 13; Prov. xxiv. 3. In Ps. xxxii. 9, i. q. אֵין, *Is not*; i. e. negatives the existence of its object. *There is no approach* (i. e. of them) to thee, בַּל קָרוֹב אֵלֶיךָ. With other particles, אַף־בַּל, Is. xl. 24; בַּל־עַל, Ps. xvi. 2; בַּל־עִם, Prov. xxiii. 7. See Noldius, p. 183, &c.

בַּל, Chald. m. Arab. بَال, *cura, animus*, Syr. ܒܠ, id.—pec. Care. meton. *The heart, mind*, Dan. vi. 15.

בֵּל, i. q. בַּעַל, apparently. The former was probably the Chaldee, the latter, the Phœnician or Hebrew, form of this word. Selden de Diis Syris. Syntag. ii. cap. i. Servius ad Æneid i., "Lingua Punica *Bal* dicitur, apud Assyrios autem *Bel* dicitur, quadam sacrorum ratione *et Saturnus et Sol*." According to the Greeks and Latins, Βῆλος, and *Balus*. The supreme Deity with the Babylonians; and, according to Cedrenus, *Thurus*, a successor of Ninus, deified in the character of Mars. See Selden l. c. where every necessary information will be found.

בְּלָא, v. Pah. r. בלא, Chald. i. q. Heb. בָּלָה, pres. יְבַלֵּא, *Destroy, make to disappear*, &c. Dan. vii. 25. Comp. Pih. בלה.

בלג, non. occ. Arab. بَلَج, *aperuit*; hence, *nituit, fulsit*, aurora. Conj. iv.—*Hiph*. Heb.—*manifestum reddidit, diduxit*; it. *Lætitia perfudit*; i. e. as having received light.

בלי (83) בלה

Hiph. pres. with ה parag. אַבְלִיגָה, *Let me be glad*, Job ix. 27; x. 20; Ps. xxxix. 13.

Part. מַבְלִיג, *Making manifest, opening upon;* i. e. *bringing on*, Amos v. 9. So the Arab. الحَقّ ابلج والباطل يَجْلِج, *veritas supernatat*, s. *apparet, futilia* a. *merguntur.* Hence, augm. מבליגית, which see in its place.

בָּלָה, Pih. Cogn. בהל, Part. pl. מְבַלֲהִים, *Harassing*; keri מבהלים, Ezra iv. 4. Syr. ܟܠܗܕ̈, *consternavit*.

בָּלָה, f. *Old, worn out.* בָּלֶה נֹאפִים, *Old, worn out*, with *adulteries*, Ezek. xxiii. 43; pl. בָּלוֹת, m. בָּלִים, id. Josh. ix. 4, 5.

בָּלָה, v. pres. יִבְלֶה. Arab. بَلِيَ, *usu vetusta evasit.* Syr. ܒܠܐ. Æth. ՈԱՀ: id. I. *Grow old.* II. meton. *Perish*; applied especially to garments: constr. מִן, and abs. Deut. viii. 4; xxix. 5; Josh. ix. 13; Is. l. 9; li. 6:—to person, or its parts, Job iii. 4; xiii. 28; Ps. cii. 27:—to time, works, &c. Job. xxi. 13; Is. lxv. 22.

Infin. בְּלוֹתִי, aff. Gen. xviii. 12.

Pih. *Made old*, Lam. iii. 4; pres. Job xxi. 13; Is. lxv. 22.

Infin. בַּלּוֹת, Ps. xlix. 15; 1 Chron. xvii. 9.

בַּלָּהָה, f. r. בלה, pl. בַּלָּהוֹת. I. *Terror, consternation*, Is. xvii. 14; Job xviii. 11. 14; xxvii. 20, &c. Ib. xviii. 14, תַּצְעִידֵהוּ לְמֶלֶךְ בַּלָּהוֹת. Gesenius takes the latter word as nom. to the verb, and ל in the sense of כ, which is fanciful. See my note on the passage. II. meton. The efficient cause of this, *Violence, calamity*, or the like. LXX. ἀπώλειαν, Ezek. xxvi. 21; xxvii. 36; xxviii. 19; Ps. lxxiii. 19. Job xxiv. 17, בַּלָּהוֹת, probably for בַּלָּהוֹת, id.

בְּלוֹ, m. Chald. *Custom, tax*, r. בלה. See הֲלָךְ: not because it was imposed on *consumable* articles, or was *oppressive*; for nothing of the sort appears. Most probably *ground-rents*, as was always the case under the feudal system, and as is now the practice in the East, Ezra iv. 13. 20; vii. 24.

בְּלוֹאֵי, pl. constr. m. defect. בְּלֹיֵ, Jer. xxxviii. 11, 12 (sing. בְּלוֹא, fem. פְּקוּד), *Growing old, worn*, pieces of cloth, rags. See סחב, and מלה.

בְּלִי, m. r. בלה. I. *Loss, destruction*, Is. xxxviii. 17. II. *Wanting*: as a prefix, *Without*, בְּלִי מָקוֹם, *Wanting, or without place*, Is. xxviii. 8; בְּלִי נִשְׁמָע, *Without being heard*, Ps. xix. 4; Job xviii. 11; xxx. 8. III. Adverb, i. q. לֹא, *not*, Gen. xxxi. 2; Hos. viii. 7; Is. xiv. 6; xxxii. 10; compd. with prepp. בִּבְלִי, Deut. iv. 42; xix. 4, &c.; לִבְלִי, Jcb xxxviii. 41; xli. 25; Is. v. 14; מִבְּלִי, *From want of*, Deut. ix. 28; Is. v. 18; Lam. i. 4; Job xviii. 15. מִבְּלִי אֵין, for emphasis, Exod. xiv. 11; 2 Kings i. 3. 6. 16, מִבְּלִי אֲשֶׁר לֹא, *without, excepting that not, &c.* Eccl. iii. 11. עַד בְּלִי, *until want of*; i. e. the ceasing of the moon, as long as it shall endure, Mal. iii. 10. See Nold. p. 185, &c.

בְּלִיל, m. r. בלל. Arab. بَلِيل, *humidus*, بَلَل, *recens humiditas plantæ*. *Grass, fodder*; green, and not made into hay, Jcb vi. 5; xxiv. 6; Is. xxx. 24; in this last place, a sort of seed apparently, *vetches* perhaps, or *clover.* Gesenius, and others usually, *mixtum* (r. בלל), a mixture of several sorts of vegetables. Varro de re rustica, and Plin. Hist. Nat. lib. xviii. 41. Pliny, however, Ib. 42, has, "*Apud antiquos* erat pabuli genus, quod Cato ocinum vocat, quo sistebant alvum bubus. Id erat e pabulis, *segete viridi desecta*, antequam gelaret." Which also seems to have been a sort of mixture used while green: or, as Varro has, "Id genus (ocymum) pabuli sunt segetes sectæ virides antequam gerant *siliquas*." This last place will, perhaps, explain the passage cited above from Isaiah.

בְּלִימָה, compd. of בְּלִי and מָה, lit. *Without any thing, not any thing*, Job xxvi. 7. See my note on the place.

בְּלִיַּעַל, compd. of בְּלִי, and יַעַל *Useful.* Arab. وَعَلَ, *prominuit. Useless*; meton. *wickedness, sin, injury.* Whence the phrases, אִישׁ בְּלִיַּעַל, 1 Sam. xxv. 25; אָדָם בְּלִיַּעַל, Prov. vi. 12; בֶּן־בְּלִיַּעַל, 1 Sam. xxv. 17; בְּנֵי בְלִיַּעַל, 1 Sam. ii. 12; Deut. xiii. 14; Judges xix. 22; xx. 13; בַּת בְּלִיַּעַל, 1 Sam. i. 16; דְּבַר בְּלִיַּעַל, Ps. xli. 9; ci. 3; Deut. xv. 9; יֹעֵץ בְּלִיַּעַל, *councillor of sin*, Nahum i. 11; נַחֲלֵי בְלִיַּעַל, *torrents of iniquity*; overspreading oppressions of the wicked, Ps. xviii. 5. Ellipt. בְּלִיַּעַל, for אִישׁ בְּלִיַּעַל, 2 Sam. xxiii. 6; Nahum ii. 1; Job xxxiv. 13, for דְּבַר בְּ, probably.

בָּלַל, v. pres. apoc. יָבֶל (kethiv יָבוֹל). Arab. بَلَّ, *rigavit.* بَلْبَلَ, *confusus et commistus fuit*, sermo. Syr. ܒܠܒܠ, *confudit.* I. *Suffused*, Ps. xcii. 3. II. *Confused*, or *confounded*, Gen. xi. 9. Ib. 7, נָבְלָה, with ה, parag. for נָבֹלָה, *Let us confound.* Part. בָּלִיל, f.

בְּלֻלָּה, pl. בְּלֻלֹת, *confused, or mixed.* It. בְּלִיל. See above: whence בְּלִיל, *He gives fodder,* Judg. xix. 21.

Hithp. pres. יִתְבּוֹלָל, *becomes confounded, mixed with.* Constr. בְּ, Hos. vii. 8. Hence בְּלֻל, for בַּלְבֻּל, *confusion.*

בלם, non occ. Syr. ܟܣܡ, *clausit, constrinxit,* ܟܣܡܐ, *capistrum.* Infin. בְּלֹם, *Constriction, bridling,* Ps. xxxii. 8.

בֶּלַע, m. Arab. بَلْعٌ, *deglutitio.* Syr. et Æth. id. I. *Swallowing up;* meton. II. *destroying,* Jer. li. 44; Ps. lii. 6. Aff. בִּלְעִי, Job vii. 19. בִּלְעוֹ, Jer. l. c.

בָּלַע, v. pres. יִבְלַע, constr. immed. I. *Swallowed, devoured.* Meton. II. *Destroyed,* Job xx. 15. 18; Jer. li. 34; Exod. vii. 12; Is. xxviii. 4, &c.; Num. xvi. 30; Ps. cxxiv. 3; cvi. 17; Prov. i. 12, &c. Infin. בְּלוֹעַ, Jon. ii. 1.

Niph. *Became swallowed up, lost,* Hos. viii. 8; Is. xxviii. 7.

Pih. בִּלַּע, pres. יְבַלַּע, i. q. Kal. intensitive, perhaps, Is. xxv. 8; Lam. ii. 2. 5; 2 Sam. xx. 20; Is. xix. 3.

Infin. בַּלַּע, aff. בִּלְעוֹ. Imp. id. Ps. lv. 10. Part. pl. מְבַלְּעֶיךָ, Is. xlix. 19, aff.

Puh. pres. יְבֻלַּע, passive of Pih. impers. 2 Sam. xvii. 16; Job xxxvii. 20.

Part. pl. מְבֻלָּעִים, Is. ix. 15.

Hithp. i. q. Niph. Ps. cvii. 27.

בִּלְעֲדֵי, aff. בִּלְעָדֶיךָ, בִּלְעֲדֵי, compd. of בַּל and עַד, or עֲדֵי. I. *Besides, without,* Gen. xli. 44; Job xxxiv. 32; where אֲשֶׁר is omitted by the ellipsis, Is. xlv. 6. II. *Not concerning, nothing to, or, as it respects,* Gen. xiv. 24; xli. 16. Compd. with מִן, מִבַּלְעֲדֵי, i. q. I. Is. xxxvi. 10; Jer. xliv. 19; Ps. xviii. 32, &c.

בְּלָק, v. Arab. بَلُوقَةٌ, *desertum, solitudo.* Cogn. بَلَقٌ, *terra vacua, inculta.* Syr. ܒܠܩܬܐ, *egestas.* Part. בּוֹלְקָה, aff. *devastating, ruining it.* Part. Puh. מְבֻלָּקָה, *made desert,* Nahum ii. 11.

בִּלְתִּי, r. בלת. Arab. بَلَتَ, *sectio, præcisio.* Cogn. بَلَتَى, *secuit, præcidit.* Gesenius gives בְּלֵה, as בְּסָה from בָּסָה. But, is בְּסָה *a cushion,* naturally derived from בָּסָה, *concealing?* I doubt it. The same may be said of his other examples, דָּלָה, and קָשָׁה. For the latter, in his Lex. Man. he gives קוֹשׁ, as the root!—Used as a prep. I. *Without* (i. e. excluding, &c.), מַכַּת בִּלְתִּי סָרָה, *a stroke without turning away,* i. e. constant. II. *Besides, except;* אֵין כֹּל בִּלְתִּי, *There is not anything besides, &c.* Num. xi. 6; Josh. xi. 19. So Is. x. 4, בִּלְתִּי כָרַע, for אֵין בִּלְתִּי כָרַע, *There is, or shall be, none besides* (him who אֲשֶׁר) *bows down,* Hos. xiii. 4; Exod. xxii. 19. (אֲשֶׁר) בִּלְתִּי חֶרְפָּתוֹ, *Except (that) his reproach,* Dan. xi. 18; Gen. xliii. 3. III. Adverb, *Not* (i. e. excluding the action of the verb). בִּלְתִּי טָהוֹר, *not clean;* i. e. anything but clean, 1 Sam. xx. 26. עַד־בִּלְתִּי, *until he had not left,* Num. xxi. 35; Job xiv. 12; Deut. iii. 3; Josh. viii. 22, &c. IV. *Unless, except, but,* בִּלְתִּי אִם־חֶרֶב, *But the sword of —,* Jud. vii. 14; Amos iii. 3, 4; Gen. xlvii. 18. Compd. with prepp. לְבִלְתִּי, מִבִּלְתִּי, pron. בִּלְתֶּךָ, partic. אֵין בִּלְתִּי, בִּלְתִּי אִם, בִּלְתִּי אֶל. See Nold. p. 186, &c.

בָּמָה, f. pl. בָּמוֹת, constr. בָּמוֹתֵי, and בָּמֳתֵי defect. Aff. בָּמוֹתַי, &c. Pers. بَامْ, *supremum cujusque rei.* Cogn. Syr. ܒܣܡ. Gr. βῆμα, *suggestum, et* βωμὸς, *ara idolis concremata; tumulus.* Hence the first (ā) is immutable. Gesenius tells us that, in the ancient religion of the Jews, as well as among other nations, HIGH PLACES going under this name were much frequented. I remark, the true ancient religion of the Jews, as well as that of the patriarchs, recognized no such places, except as idolatrous: among the Jews the mention of them is rare: the tabernacle of Moses was evidently in one of them, 1 Chron. xvi. 39. Among the ancient idolators, as their own best writers allow, the heavenly bodies first, and secondly, dead kings and heroes, were considered as gods, and worshipped as such. See Diodor. Sic. lib. i. passim. Marshami Chron. Can. Ægypt. p. 54, &c. After this, the sepulchres of these men, raised in great heaps, tumuli, pyramids, &c., afforded places which seemed the best suited to the worship of such beings. See Clemens Alexandrinus, as cited by Eusebius, Prep. Evangel. lib. ii. on this subject. According to Mr. Rich, in his work entitled "A Residence in Koordistan," &c. very many such places are still to be seen in that country, particularly in the neighbourhood of ancient Nineveh, some of which are of enormous dimensions and height, and are still frequented as places of worship. Gesenius, too, has no doubt that mention of such sepulchral tumuli is to be found in the Bible: e. g.

בְּמוֹ (85) בְּנִי

Ezech. xliii. 7. "*Non profanabunt*" (is his reading of the passage), "*in posterum filii Israëlis nomen meum sanctum, ipsi et reges eorum, scortatione et cadaveribus regum eorum,*" (pro בְּמוֹתָם) *in tumulis* s. sepulcris *eorum,*" &c. Hence perhaps hills, as dedicated to some deity, also became objects of veneration, and were considered as well suited to the service of such gods. Solomon, we are told, set up idols on some of the mounts about Jerusalem, 2 Kings xxiii. 13. 15; and, in these, Josiah spied certain *sepulchres* (ib. ver. 16), which he destroyed. See my note on Job xxi. 33. The word has two significations. I. *High places*, as idolatrous *Places of worship*, Is. xv. 2; xvi. 12; Jer. xlviii. 35. Also of the true God, before the building of the temple, 1 Sam. ix. 12, et seq. 1 Kings iii. 4. But these, in 2 Kings xii. 4, are condemned as error. Is. xxxvi. 7, &c. The priests of these idolatrous places were styled כֹּהֲנֵי הַבָּמוֹת, 1 Kings xii. 32; xiii. 2; 2 Kings xvii. 32. The chapel was termed בֵּית הַבָּמוֹת, pl.—בָּתֵּי הב־, 2 Kings xvii. 29. 32; 1 Kings xiii. 32. On this heathen usage among the Persians, see Herod. i. 131, Xenoph. Cyrop. lib. viii.:—the Greeks, Xenoph. Memorab. iii. 8, § 10. II. *Heights*, in a military sense, as places of strength, 2 Sam. i. 19. 25; Jer. xxvi. 18; Mich. iii. 12; Ezek. xxxvi. 2; Num. xxi. 28. So Ps. xviii. 34; Hab. iii. 19; Amos iv. 13; Mich. i. 3; Deut. xxxiii. 29. And, by a metaphor, applied to the *Waves* of a stormy sea, Job ix. 8; to the *Clouds*, Is. xiv. 14. We may, therefore, get rid of Gesenius's "*arces maris,*" and "*arces nubium,*" as things not unlike castles built in the air.

בְּמוֹ, see מוֹ.

בָּמָתִי, see בָּמָה.

בֵּן, r. בָּנָה, Syr. ܒܢܐ, Arab. بَنَى, *ædificavit.* act. بَنِي. Cogn. בות. See בֵּית, sig. vi. constr.—בֶּן, rarely בִּן, Prov. xxx. 1, &c. pl. בָּנִים; constr. בְּנֵי, with י and ו, parag. Gen. xlix. 11; Num. xxiv. 3. 15. I. *A child*, generally, of either sex, Gen. iii. 16; xxi. 7; xxx. 1, &c. בֶּן־זָכָר, *male child*, Jer. xx. 15. Comp. Rev. xii. 5; Amos ix. 7; Ps. lxxii. 4. II. propr. *A son*, Gen. iv. 25, 26; xvi. 11, &c.
III. *Any descendant*, as *grandson*, &c. Gen. xxix. 5; xxxi. 28; xxxii. 1: occasionally termed בְּנֵי בָנִים, Exod. xxxiv. 7; Prov. xiii. 22, &c. Hence the phrases בְּנֵי יְהוּדָה, בְּנֵי יִשְׂרָאֵל, synon. בֵּית יִשְׂרָאֵל, &c. or אַנְשֵׁי יִשְׂרָאֵל, &c.
IV. A term of affection applied to juniors, Gen. xxxvii. 18; Josh. vii. 19; 1 Sam. iii. 6, &c.
V. Any one educated as a child, Exod. ii. 10. Comp. Acts vii. 21. Hence applied to pupils; teachers being considered as spiritual fathers, 1 Kings xx. 35; 2 Kings ii. 3. 5. 7. iv. 38; Prov. ii. 1; iii. 1, &c.
VI. Hence, metaphorically applied to designate character; as, (*a*) בֶּן־מָוֶת, *child of death;* i. e. worthy of death, 1 Sam. xx. 31. 2 Sam. xii. 5; Deut. xxv. 2. Comp. υἱὸς γεέννης, Matt. xxiii. 15.—τῆς ἀπωλείας; τοῖ φωτός, John xvii. 12; Luke xvi. 8, &c. So also (*b*) בֶּן־חַיִל, *Child of strength*, strong man. בֶּן־בְּלִיַּעַל, *Vain, sinful man.* בֶּן־עַוְלָה, בְּנֵי שַׁחַץ, It. Prov. xxxi. 5; Gen. xv. 2. 2 Kings xiv. 14; Is. xiv. 12; xix. 11; Zech iv. 14. Comp. Eph. ii. 2; 1 Pet. i. 14. (*c*) Applied to inanimate things, Job v. 7; xli 20; Zech. iv. 14; Lam. iii. 13. (*d*) *Sons of God*, בְּנֵי הָאֱלֹהִים, Gen. vi. 2. 4. *Pious persons.* Hos. ii. 1; Ps. lxxxii. 6; lxxiii. 15; xi 1, &c. Comp. John i. 12; Rom. viii. 14, &c Also (*e*) *Angels*, apparently; Job i. 6; xxxviii. 7. (*f*) *Kings*, as God's vicegerents, Ps. lxxxix. 28; and, as inspired by Him, 1 Sam. x. 6. 9; xi. 6; xvi. 13, 14; 2 Sam. vii. 14; Is. xi. 1, 2. So Christ, in his human nature, anointed *king* over all, Ps. ii. 7, as he was also priest, Ps. cx. 4. Followed immediately by a noun signifying place. (*g*) *A native of such place*, or belonging in some respect to it: as *Sons of Zion; of Babylon; of the East; of the province; of foreign land; of the house*, i. e. home born; *of the womb*, i. e. uterine brother; *of the people*, i. e. plebeian; *of my people*, i. e. of the same nation; so used of brutes, Deut. xxxii. 14, &c. Followed by a noun signifying time (*h*), implying a person then born, or *of a certain age;* as, *son of age*, i. e. of an aged father, Gen. xxxvii. 3; *of youth*, Ps. cxxvii. 4, i. e. of time specified, Gen. v. 32; Exod. xii. 5; Jon. iv. 10, &c. Applied also (*i*) to the *young of brutes*, and (*k*) to *the branches*, or *shoots of trees*, Ps. cxiv. 4; Gen. xlix. 11; Lev. xii. 6;—Gen. xlix. 22. Comp. Is. xvii. 6. On similar idiomatic usages in the Arabic, see Golius, or Castell, sub r. بني.

בָּנִין, pl. m. constr. בְּנֵי, Chald. i. q. Heb. Dan. ii. 25; Ezra vi. 9. Sing. בַּר, which see.

בנה (86) בסר

בָּנָה, or בְּנָא, v. Chald. i. q. Heb. בָּנָה, Built. 1st pers. with aff. בְּנֵיתַהּ, Dan. iv. 27. 3d pers. with aff. בְּנָהִי, built it, Ezra v. 11. Part. Peh. בָּנֵה, built, ib. Part. pres. pl. בָּנַיִן, ib. בָּנָא, whence לְבְנָא, to build, verbal noun, Ezra v. 3. 13; מִבְנָא, whence לְמִבְנֵא. Infin. f. לְמִבְנְיָה, Ib. vv. 2. 17. 9.

Ithpe. תִּתְבְּנֵא, pres. 3 pers. f. Ezra iv. 13. 21. Part. מִתְבְּנֵא, Ib. ver. 8.

בָּנָה, pres. יִבְנֶה, apoc. יִבֶן. Syr. ܟܠܐ. Arab. بَنَى, ædificavit. Built, erected, a house, &c., I. really, or II. metaphorically. Constr. immed. or med. with לְ, בְּ, עַל, as the sense may require. I. Ezek. iv. 2; xxvii. 5; Gen. viii. 20; Jer. vii. 31; 1 Kings vi. 1. In this sense, too, it is used to signify repaired, restored, Josh. vi. 26; 1 Kings xvi. 34; Amos ix. 14; Ps. cxxii. 3; cxlvii. 2, &c. Applied to man, Gen. ii. 22. Constr. with לְ.

II. Built up, as raising a family, increasing it, &c., Jer. xxiv. 6; xxxi. 4; Ps. xxviii. 5. Hence, applied spiritually in the New Testament, Edify, Acts xx. 32; Eph. ii. 21, &c.

Part. בָּנָה בּוֹנֶה, pl. בּוֹנִים, contr. בֹּנֵי; aff. בּוֹנָיִךְ; id. pass. בָּנוּי, f. בְּנוּיָה, pl. m. בְּנוּיִים. Infin. בָּנֹה, constr. בְּנוֹת. Imp. בְּנֵה, pl. בְּנוּ.

Niph. נִבְנָה, pres. יִבָּנֶה אֶבָּנֶה, &c. Infin. הִבָּנוֹת, Became built, Num. xiii. 22; Deut. xiii. 17; 1 Kings vi. 7. Rebuilt, Is. xliv. 28.

Metaph. Jer. xii. 16; Mal. iii. 15; Job xxii. 23; Gen. xvi. 2. Constr. with מִן.

בָּנוּ, for בָּאנוּ, r. בוא, 1 Sam. xxv. 8; Gram. art. 72.

בָּנוֹת, pl. of בַּת.

בְּנוֹתַיִךְ, Ezek. xvi. 31. Read בְּנוֹתֵךְ, Infin. r. בָּנָה,—with prep. בְּ.

בִּנְיָה, f. Arab. بِنْيَة, structura. A structure, or edifice, Ezek. xli. 13.

בִּנְיָן, m. Heb. and Chald. Arab. بِنْيَان, ædificium. Syr. id. I. Structure, or edifice, Ezek. xli. 12; Ezra v. 4. II. Wall, Ezek. xl. 5.

בְּנַס, v. Chald. Was angry, &c. Dan. ii. 12. Cogn. Arab. بَنَس, alacritas. Engl. menace, Gr. μηνίω, μηνιάω, irascor.

בָּסַר, aff. בְּסָרוֹ, Job xv. 33, with גֶּפֶן, i. q. בֹּסֶר.

בֹּסֶר, m. Arab. بُسْر, dactyli immaturi jam adulti. LXX. ὄμφαξ. Unripe grape, or, perhaps, precocious, Is. xviii. 5; Jer. xxxi. 29, 30; Ezek. xviii. 2.

בְּעָא, v. pres. יִבְעֵא, Chald. Syr. ܟܥܐ, petiit. Arab. بَغَى, id. Requested, prayed; constr. with מִן, קֳדָם, מִן קֳדָם, pers. and immed. as to thing, Dan. ii. 13, &c.

Part. בָּעֵא, Dan. vi. 14; id. pl. בָּעַיִן, Ib. 5; Infin. מִבְעֵא, Ib. ii. 18.

Pah. Dan. iv. 13; id. i. q. Heb. בָּעָה.

בְּעַד, and בַּעַד. Arab. بَعْدَ, post. Prep. After, behind, as to time or place, or some shade of this slightly varied; as, בְּעַד חַטֹּאתְכֶם, After your sins; i. e. in order to expiate them when so committed, Exod. xxxii. 30; יִסְגְּרוּ בַעֲדָם, They closed (the doors) after them, Judg. ix. 51; Gen. vii. 16; Judg. iii. 22. II. בְּעַד יִשְׂרָאֵל, After, i. e. for the sake of, Israel, 1 Sam. vii. 9; Gen. xx. 7; 2 Kings xix. 4; Jer. xi. 14; xxi. 2; Ezek. xxii. 30; Job. vi. 22, &c. III. Behind, as it were behind one's back, and so unperceived. גָּדַר בַּעֲדִי, Built a wall behind me, Lam. iii. 7; Jon. ii. 7; Ps. cxxxix. 11; Job i. 20; Joel. ii. 8. So, בְּעַד הַחַלּוֹן, Behind the window, i. e. being so placed, &c., he looked down, Gen. xxvi. 8; Josh. ii. 15; 1 Sam. iv. 18; 2 Kings i. 2; 2 Sam. xx. 21; Joel ii. 9. IV. בְּעַד אִשָּׁה, After (associating with) a whorish woman, Prov. vi. 26, &c. In most of which מִבַּעַד would, perhaps, more fully express the sense.

In this sort of acceptation, we shall have none of the redundancies proposed by Noldius (p. 193, &c.) as בַּעֲדֵינוּ הָרָעָה, After us; i. e. as pursuing, evil shall neither come near, nor overtake us, Amos ix. 10. So 1 Sam. i. 6; Zech. viii. 8; Job ix. 7, as in one or other of the examples above. Constr. with לְ, Cant. iv. 1. 3; vi. 7. Aff. בַּעֲדִי, בַּעֲדָךְ, or in pause, בַּעֲדֶךָ, f. בַּעֲדֵךְ, בַּעֲדוֹ, בַּעֲדָהּ, בַּעֲדֵנוּ, בַּעַדְכֶם, בַּעֲדָם.

בָּעָה, v. pres. יִבְעֶה. Arab. بَغَى, modum transgressus fuit, insultavit, intumuit, petiit. I. Pressed forward, obtruded, ran over. II. Sought, requested, importuned. I. מַיִם תִּבְעֶה אֵשׁ, Fire runs—causes to run—over; i. e. makes water to boil, Is. lxiv. 1. II. With וְ par. תִּבְעָיוּן, You really, truly, seek, Is. xxi. 12. Constr. abs.

בעו (87) בעל

Niph. נִבְעָה, *Became obtruded*, i. e. swelling outwards, Is. xxx. 13. II. *Be, become, sought out*, Obad. vr. 6.

בָּעוּ, f. Chald. *Petition, prayer*, Dan. vi. 8. 14; aff. בָּעוּתֵהּ. Winer says here "pro בָּעוּת." He does not appear to be aware, that the ת, is added both in Syr. and Chald. to nouns terminating in י, in all cases of constr.

בָּעַט, v. pres. יִבְעַט. Syr. ܟܒܫ, *calcavit, recalcitravit*. ܡܟܒܫܐ, *conculcatio*, not ܟܒܫ, and ܡܟܒܫܐ, as Winer and Gesenius have it. *Trample on, kick at*. Meton. *Despise, reject*, Deut. xxxii. 15; 1 Sam. ii. 29; constr. abs. and with בְּ, alib. non occ.

בְּעִי. f. i. q. בְּעוּ, above, Job xxx. 24. אַךְ לֹא־בְעִי יִשְׁלַח־יָד,) *Surely only on prayer* (for וּבְנִי,) *He sends not forth* (his) *hand*: i. e. to injure or punish. See my Commentary here, alib. non occ.

בְּעִיר, m. Syr. ܒܥܝܪܐ, *animal, jumentum*. Arab. بَعِير, id. I. *Beast*, or *Cattle* generally, Exod. xxii. 4; Num. xx. 4. 8. 11; Ps. lxxviii. 48. II.—*Of burden*, Gen. xlv. 17. Aff. בְּעִירָם, בְּעִירְכֶם, בְּעִירֵנוּ, בְּעִירֹה.

בַּעַל, m. pl. בְּעָלִים, constr. בַּעֲלֵי. Arab. بَعَل, *dominus, possessor, maritus*; id. Æth. Gesenius adds the Sanscrit, Pála, पाल: but this signifies *nourisher*. The true Sanscrit synonyme is *Bala*, बल: *strong, stout*: BALA-DĒVA, the elder brother of KRISHNA, and the third of the three incarnations termed RAMAS, &c. Wilson's Sanscr. Dict. p. 599. ed. sec. Sir. G. C. Haughton's Do. p. 1931. Abstr. used for a concr. as in עֶבֶד מֶלֶךְ, &c. Gram. art. 152. 10. I. *Lord, master*, or *possessor*, generally, Exod. xxii. 7; Jud. xix. 22; Job xxxi. 39; Is. i. 3; xvi. 8, &c., and hence, II. *A husband*, Exod. xxi. 3. 22; 2 Sam. xi. 26; Joel i. 8. See בְּתוּלָה, here, &c. III. *Possessor*; it is much used like the Arab. ذُو, أُولُو, pl. أُولُو, صَاحِب, and the Heb. אִישׁ, אָב, בֵּן, בַּת, אַנְשֵׁי, to form certain phrases; as, בַּעֲלֵי יְרִיחוֹ, Josh. xxiv. 11. שְׁכֶם— Judg. ix. 2, et seq. בַּעַל פִּעֹר—2 Sam. ii. 4, 5, comp. with ib. xxi. 12, as well remarked by Gesenius. So also, בַּעַל הַקְּרָנַיִם, *horned*, Dan. viii. 6. 20, for אַיִל, *ram*. Comp. Eccl. x. 20; and for similar phraseology see 2 Kings i. 8; Gen. xiv. 13; xxxvii. 19; Exod. xxiv. 14;

Neh. vi. 18; Eccl. x. 11; Prov. xxiii. 2; comp. with Ib. xxix. 2; xvi. 2; Eccl. viii. 8, &c. IV. Also the name of an idol very extensively worshipped in the East; probably the same with the *Bala*, or *Baladéva*, of the Hindoos, noticed above. See also בֵּל.

בְּעֵל, Chald. i. q. Heb. בַּעַל. On the phrase בְּעֵל טְעֵם, Ezra iv. 8, &c. see טְעֵם.

בַּעֲלָה, f. of בַּעַל, above; and used in phraseology like that under No. III. as בַּעֲלַת הַבַּיִת, *Mistress of the house*, 1 Kings xvii. 17. אוֹב—*of a familiar spirit*, 1 Sam. xxviii. 7. כְּשָׁפִים, *of divinations*, Nahum iii. 4.

בַּעַר, m. abstr. for concr. Arab. بَعَر, *stercus, summa paupertas*. *Stupid, ignorant, brutish*. See בְּעִיר, Ps. xlix. 11; lxxiii. 22; Prov. xii. 1; xxx. 2.

בָּעַר, v. pres. יִבְעַר. r. בער. See בְּעִיר. I.—*jured, consumed, &c.*, pec. 1. *By fire*, Is. lxxxiii. 15; cvi. 18; Job i. 16; Is. xlii. 25; lxii. 1; Mal. iii. 19. occ. *with* בָּאֵשׁ, Judg. xv. 14; Hos. vii. 4; constr. with בְּ, מִן. II. Metaph.—*Anger*, Ps. ii. 12; lxxix. 5; Is. xxx. 27. Comp. Ps. xxxix. 4. III. abs. *Burn, consume*, Is. i. 31; Exod. iii. 3; Deut. iv. 11. IV. *Injurious, brutish*. Part. בֹּעֲרִים, Ps. xciv. 8; Ezek. xxi. 31. Sing. בַּעַר: signn. II. III. f. בֹּעֵרָה, Jer. xx. 9, pl. בֹּעֲרוֹת.

Niph. נִבְעַר, *Became brutish*, Jer. x. 14, 21; li. 17; Is. xix. 11.

Pih. בִּעֵר, pres. יְבַעֵר. I. *Injured, destroyed, II. Consumed* by fire, constr. with בְּ, מִן, אַחֲרֵי. I. Is. iii. 14; v. 5; Exod. xxii. 4; 1 Kings xxii. 47; Deut. xxvi. 13, 14; 2 Sam. iv. 11, &c. II. Exod. xxxv. 3; Lev. vi. 5; Neh. x. 35; Is. xliv. 15, &c.

Infin. בָּעֵר, id. Is. iv. 4. Sign. I. Num. xxiv. 22.

Puh. *Made to burn, burning*, Jer. xxxvi. 22.

Hiph. הִבְעִיר, pres. יַבְעִיר, apoc. יַבְעֵר, i. q. Pih. constr. with בְּ, אַחֲרֵי, and immed. Nahum ii. 14; Ezek. v. 2; Exod. xxii. 4; Judg. xv. 5; 2 Chron. xxviii. 3.

Part. מַבְעִיר, Exod. xxii. 5; 1 Kings xvi. 3.

בְּעֵרָה, f. *A burning*, Exod. xxii. 5.

בָּעַת, v. pres. יְבַעֵת, Pih. Syr. ܒܥܬ, *horruit*. Arab. بَعَتَ, *excitavit*; cogn. بَغَتَ, *de improviso accidit, vel supervenit*. Const. immed. and with אֵת. I. *Affrighted, alarmed, terrified*. II. *Excited, stimulated*; *suddenly come upon*. I. Is. xxi. 4; Job

בעת (83) בצק

iii. 5; vii. 14; ix. 34; xiii. 11. 21; xv. 24; xxxiii. 7; Ps. xviii. 5. II. 1 Sam. xvi. 14, 15. Part. מְבַעֵת.

Niph. נִבְעַת, *Became terrified.* Constr. with מִן, Esth. vii. 6; Dan. viii. 17; 1 Chron. xxi. 30.

בְּעָתָה, f. *Fright, terror,* Jer. viii. 15; xiv. 19.

בִּעוּתִים, m. pl. *Terrors.* Ps. lxxxviii. 17; Job vi. 4. Const. בִּעוּתֵי; aff. בִּעוּתֶיךָ.

בֹּץ, m. r. בצץ. Arab. بَضّ, *pauca aqua. Mud, mire,* Jer. xxxviii. 22.

בִּצָּה, f. i. q. בֹּץ, Job viii. 11; xl. 21; pl. aff. בִּצֹּאתָיו, for בִּצוֹתָיו, Ezek. xlvii. 11. The א seems to intimate, that the form is rather Chaldaïc.

בָּצוּר, m. בְּצוּרָה, f. בְּצוּרוֹת, pl.; see בֶּצֶר below. *Strong, fortified,* walls, cities, &c., Num. xiii. 28; Deut. iii. 5; Josh. xiv. 12; Is. ii. 15; xxv. 2; xxvii. 10, &c.

בָּצִיר, m. r. בצר, which see; synon. קָצִיר. I. *The vintage,* Lev. xxvi. 5; Is. xxiv. 13; xxxii. 10; Jer. xlviii. 32. II. i. q. בָּצוּר, *Fortified, strengthened,* Zech. xi. 2, kethiv. cogn. מָצוֹר.

בָּצָל, m. pl. בְּצָלִים. Syr. ܒܨܠܐ. Arab. بَصَل, *cepe. Onions,* Num. xi. 5; alib. non occ.

בֶּצַע, m. Arab. بَضْع, or بِضْعَة, *pars resecta.* بِضَاعَة, *pars opum. Gain, profit,* in a good, or bad sense. I. Judg. v. 19; Job xxii. 3; Ps. xxx. 10; Mal. iii. 14. II. בֶּצַע רָע, *Wicked gain, filthy lucre,* Hab. ii. 9; Exod. xviii. 21; Ps. cxix. 36; Prov. i. 19; xv. 27; xxviii. 16, &c. Gesenius finds the *rapine of kings, &c.* in Jer. xxii. 17; Ezek. xxii. 18; and thence deduces the sense of *filthy lucre.* Is not this an ungrounded refinement? Aff. בִּצְעוֹ, בִּצְעָם, בִּצְעֵךְ, &c.

בָּצַע, v. pres. יִבְצַע. Arab. بَضَع, *amputavit partem, partitus fuit.* Syr. ܒܨܥ, *in frusta concidit.* I. *Cut off parts,* or *pieces.* בְּצַעַם רֹאשׁ, (for בְּצָעֵם), *Cut them off in the head,* i. e. in the leaders or nobles; Amos ix. 1. Comp. Is. vii. 8, 9; ix. 14, and as the following context requires. II. *Acquired gain,* in a bad sense, Job xxvii. 8. Infin. בְּצֹעַ. Part. בּוֹצֵעַ, both generally followed by בֶּצַע, Ezek. xxii. 27; Prov. i. 19.

Pih. בִּצַּע, pres. יְבַצַּע. I. *Cutting off,* or *out,* as a weaver does his web from the loom, Is. xxxviii. 12; Job vi. 12. Hence, II. *Finishing, completing,* Is. x. 12; Zech. iv. 9; Lam. ii. 17. III. *Acquiring filthy lucre,* Ezek. xxii. 12.

בָּצֵק, Arab. بَصْقَة, *vicus urbis elatior.* Cogn. بَزَغ, *extulit se* dens, germen بَرَق, IV. *lac præbuit camela. Dough,* so called, apparently, from its heaving and swelling, although not yet leavened, Exod. xii. 34. 39; 2 Sam. xiii. 8; Jer. vii. 18; Hos. vii. 4. Aff. בְּצֵקוֹ.

בָּצֵק, v. pres. non occ. *Swelled,* applied to the foot, Deut. viii. 4; Neh. ix. 21. "*De pede discalceato,*" says Gesenius; but there is no ground for this. And again, "*Callo obductus est ... optime.*" LXX. in Deut. ἐτυλώθησαν, which is also groundless. The Persians have a phrase, viz., قدم رجي, *foot-pain,* which they apply to *walking, visiting, &c.*; and hence, perhaps, رنجا, *incessus delicatus et affectatus.* If this may be depended upon, our usage here will signify generally, *trouble, difficulty,* or the like.

בֶּצֶר, m. pl. aff. בְּצָרֶיךָ, alt. בְּצִי, Job xxii. 24; xxxvi. 19; *alib. non occ.* Arab. بَصْر, *abscissio.* Lexicographers have generally made this word to signify *gold,* or *gold* or *silver ore*; because,—and for no other reason,— אוֹפִיר, *Ophir,* in the parallel, Job xxii. 24, signifies, as it is thought, *the gold of Ophir.* Gesenius takes for granted that he has settled this point, by an extract from *Rabbi Jonah;* who tells us, that it is the same thing as the Arab. تَبَر, "i. q." says Gesenius, "שָׁבַר, *fregit, &c.* Germ brechen, &c." But, if we allow that تَبَر, and שבר, are the same word, it will by no means follow, either that they mean the same thing, or, that *gold* or *silver,* is meant by בֶּצֶר, which is a totally different one. "Plerique interpretes," adds Gesenius, "conjecturis indulgent utcunque ex orationis serie ductis." And, it may be asked, Is this any thing beyond a conjecture of the said Rabbi Jonah, adorned by another or two of Dr. Gesenius? Winer's attempts are still worse, as Gesenius has shown. I prefer having recourse to the usage of the verb בָּצַר, *vindemiavit, &c.,* which is only another form of our word; and, then to suppose that,

בָּצַר (89) בָּקַע

as wealth much consisted in the produce of the earth, as in the *vintage, &c.*, this word, properly signifying *vintage, crop, &c.*, was by a meton. taken to designate *wealth*, generally, and thence *strength*, which will make it answer sufficiently well to the term אוֹפִיר, following. See my note on Job xxii. 24.

בָּצַר, v. pres. יִבְצֹר. Syr. ܒܨܰܪ, *diminuit.* Arab. بَصَرَ, *vidit, secuit, dissecuit, amputavit caput.* Freytag Lex. Cogn. בצע, בוא, מצה, &c. *Cut, cropped,* off. Hence, I. *Gathered the vintage,* Lev. xxv. 5. 11. II. *Pruned* the vine, Deut. xxiv. 21; Judg. ix. 27. Part. בּוֹצֵר; pl. בּוֹצְרִים, Jer. vi. 9. Metaph. of enemies, Ib. xlix. 9; Obad. vr. 5. Hence, Ps. lxxvi. 13, יִבְצֹר רוּחַ, *Crops the spirit;* i. e. *lowers the pride.* Hence—

Niph. pres. יִבָּצֵר, *Is,* or *becomes cut short, withholden,* Gen. xi. 6; Job xlii. 2.

Pih. pres. f. תְּבַצֵּר, *Makes strong, fortifies,* Jer. li. 53. Infin. בַּצֵּר, *Fortifying, &c.* Is. xxii. 10.

בִּצָּרוֹן, m. *A very strong place, fortification,* Zech. ix. 12. LXX. ὀχύρωμα.

בַּצֹּרֶת, f. Syr. ܒܨܺܝܪ, *defectus, imminutio, Withholding, need.* LXX. ἀβροχία, Jer. xvii. 8. Targ. בְּצִירְתָּא.

בַּקְבֻּק, m. Arab. بَقْبَقَة and بَعْبَع, *bombus aquæ;* i. e. issuing from a narrow-necked vessel. Syr. ܒܰܩܒܽܘܩ, *such vessel. A narrow-necked vessel, jar,* or *guglet,* 1 Kings xiv. 3; Jer. xix. 1. 10.

בְּקִיעִים, m. pl. sing. non occ. *Fissures, rendings;* r. בקע, Amos vi. 11; Is. xxii. 9.

בֶּקַע, m. lit. *A slip, cutting,* pec. *half shekel,* Gen. xxiv. 22; Exod. xxxviii. 26.

בָּקַע, v. pres. יִבְקַע. Syr. ܦܣܰܩ, *scissus est.* Chald. id. Cogn. Heb. פָּקַע, בָּצַר. I. *Cut, cleft, divided.* II. *Laid open* (like the Arab. فَتَحَ, and Pers. گشادن); i. e. *Subdued, took,* as towns, cities, &c. III. *Let go,* as young from eggs; *hatched;* or as water from its confinement. Constr. immed. and with בְּ. I. Exod. xiv. 16; Eccl. x. 9; Ps. lxxviii. 13; cxli. 7; Neh. ix. 11; Ezek. xxix. 7. II. 2 Chron. xxi. 17; xxxii. 1; 2 Sam. xxiii. 16; 1 Chron. xi. 18. III. Is. xxxiv. 15; Ps. lxxiv. 15. Infin. aff. בִּקְעָם, *Their cutting, laying open,* Amos i. 13; 2 Chron. xxxii. 1. Part. בֹּקְעֵ, Imp. בְּקַע.

Niph. נִבְקַע, pres. יִבָּקַע. I. *Became cut, cleft, ruined, destroyed.* II. *Laid open, subdued.* III. *Let go,* as young when brought forth; as waters, or light, when released from confinement. I. Num. xvi. 31; 1 Kings i. 40; Prov. iii. 20; Gen. vii. 11; Job xxxii. 19, &c. II. 2 Kings xxv. 4; Jer. lii. 7. III. Is. lix. 5; lviii. 8. Infin. הִבָּקֵעַ. Sign. I. Ezek. xxx. 16.

Pih. בִּקַּע, pres. יְבַקַּע, as Kal, if not intersitive. I. Gen. xxii. 3; 2 Kings viii. 12; xv. 16; Job xxviii. 10; Ps. lxxviii. 15. III. Is. lix. 5; Ezek. xiii. 13; Hab. iii. 9.

Puh. pres. pl. יְבֻקָּעוּ; part. f. מְבֻקָּעָה, pl. m. מְבֻקָּעִים; sign. I. Josh. ix. 4; Hos. xiv. 1. II. Ezek. xxvi. 10.

Hiph. pres. 2 pers. pl. aff. נַבְקִעֶנָּה, *Let us cause it to be subdued;* with epenth. נ. Gram. art. 235. Infin. הַבְקִיעַ. Sign. III. metaph. *To send forth,* constr. with אֶל, 2 Kings iii. 26.

Hoph. הָבְקְעָה, pass. of Sign. II. Jer. xxxix. 2.

Hithp. הִתְבַּקֵּעַ, i. q. Niph. intens. Sign. I. Josh. ix. 13; pres. יִתְבַּקֵּעַ, id. Mich. i. 4.

בִּקְעָא, Chald. f. i. q. Heb. בִּקְעָה, Dan. iii. 1.

בִּקְעָה, f. pl. בְּקָעוֹת. Lit. *Cutting,* or *cleaving.* Syr. ܦܩܰܥܬܳܐ, *campus.* Arab. بُقْعَة, *vallis, regio.* I. *A valley,* as opposed to mountains, Deut. viii. 7; xi. 11; Is. xli. 18; lxiii. 14; Ps. civ. 8. II. Also, *Any open country,* Gen. xi. 2; comp. Ezek. iii. 23; xxxvii. 1, 2; Josh. xi. 17; xii. 7.

בָּקַק, v. pres. non. occ. Arab. بَقَّ, *multum pluviæ fudit cœlum.* Cogn. بَقْبَقَ, بَعْبَع. See בַּקְבֻּק, above. Cogn. بَقَّ (r. بوق), *malum attulit;* بَاقَة, *calamitas.* I. *Threw,* or *cast off,* or *out,* as fruit from a tree. Part. בּוֹקֵק יִשְׂרָאֵל, *A* (fruit) *casting vine is Israel,* Hos. x. 1. Comp. Jer. xix. 7; Nahum ii. 3. II. Meton. *Evacuated, made void,* or *empty,* Is. xxiv. 1.

Niph. נָבֹק, pres. תִּבּוֹק, *Become void, of no effect,* Is. xix. 3; xxiv. 3. Ib. Infin. הִבּוֹק.

Pih. pres. pl. יְבַקְקוּ, *Making empty, void,* Jer. li. 2.

בֹּקֶר, m. pl. בְּקָרִים (for בְּקָרִים). Arab. بَقَر, *Cutting, laying open.* Cogn. بَكَر, *matutinum tempus—opening-day.* بَكَر, *primum cujuslibet rei.* I. *Dawn, morning,* Gen. i. 5, &c.; 2 Sam. xxiii. 4; Ps. v. 4; lxxiii. 14; ci. 8. בַּבֹּקֶר בַּבֹּקֶר, *Morning after*

N

morning, Exod. xvi. 21. לַבֹּקֶר בַּבֹּקֶר, id. 1 Chron. ix. 27. לִבְקָרִים, lit. *For mornings*, as we say in English, *for days, years, &c.*, i. e. many days; but here rather taken distributively, *every single morning*, Job vii. 8. "Spec vespertina lux," says Dr. Gesenius; but this is groundless: the word, considered in itself, can have no such sense; but, when preceded by עַד, *until*, or the like, must of necessity signify *the next* succeeding morning; i. e. that of the morrow. II. *Early, soon*, Ps. xlix. 15; xc. 14; cxliii. 8.

בָּקָר, c. pl. בְּקָרִים. (See בֹּקֶר.) Lit. *Cutter, layer open*, applied to oxen as used for the plough, Job i. 14. So Lat. "*armentum* for *aramentum*, ab arando dictus, teste Varrone." Gesen. *Ox*, and collect. *oxen*; as, צֹאן וּבָקָר, *flock and oxen*, Gen. xii. 16; xxxiii. 13; Deut. xxxii. 14. Hence, בְּנֵי בָקָר, pl. בְּנֵי בָקָר, *A calf*, Gen. xviii. 7; Exod. xxix. 1, &c. When unity is intended, שׁוֹר is used, as, Num. vii. 3. 17. Hence, as some think, בּוֹקֵר, Amos vii. 14. See בֹּקֶר. Aff. בְּקָרֵךְ, בְּקָרֵנוּ, &c.

בִּקֵּר, v. pres. יְבַקֵּר, Pih. *Cut*, or *laid open*. Hence, Meton. I. *Look, inquire—into*, or *after*. II. *Observe*. III. *Care for*. Constr. *immed*. and with לְ, בְּ, בֵּין, *med.* I. 2 Kings xv. 15; Prov. xx. 25; Ps. xxvii. 4. II. Lev. xiii. 36; xxvii. 33. III. Ezek. xxxiv. 11, 12.

בַּקַּר, v. Chald. pres. יְבַקַּר, Pah. i. q. Heb. sign. I. constr. with בְּ, עַל, Ezra iv. 15. 19; vi. 1; vii. 14.

בַּקָּרָה, f. *Inquiring after, seeking*, Ezek. xxxiv. 12.

בִּקֹּרֶת, f. *Observation, animadversion*, Lev. xix. 20.

בִּקֵּשׁ, v. pres. יְבַקֵּשׁ, Pih. *Sought, sought out, after*, or *into*. Constr. abs. *immed. med.* אֶל, מִן, עַל, לְ, as the different circumstances of the context may require, 2 Kings ii. 17; Gen. xxvii. 15, 16; 1 Sam. x. 14; Job x. 6. פְּנֵי ס׳, *The countenance;* i. e. the favour of any one, 1 Kings x. 24; Prov. xxix. 26. אֶת־הָאֱלֹהִים —אֶת־יְהוָה, *God* for aid, &c., 2 Sam. xii. 16; Exod. xxxiii. 7; 2 Chron. xx. 4. Hence, מְבַקְשֵׁי יְהוָה, *Seekers of Jehovah*; i. e. his worshippers, 1 Chron. xvi. 10; Ps. xl. 17. Comp. נֶפֶשׁ ס׳, הָיָה דָּרַשׁ, *The soul*, or *life of any one*, to injure or destroy it, Exod. iv. 19; 1 Sam. xx. 1, &c.—to preserve it, Prov. xxix. 10. רָעַת ס׳, *The evil of some one*, 1 Sam. xxiv. 10; Ps. lxxi. 13. 24. Comp. Exod. ii. 15; iv. 24; 1 Sam. xix. 2. דַּם ס׳, *The blood of some one*,

2 Sam. iv. 11. Comp. 1 Sam. xx. 16; Ezek. iii. 18, &c. Infin. בַּקֵּשׁ. Imp. בַּקֵּשׁ, pl. בַּקְּשׁוּ. Puh. pres. יְבֻקַּשׁ, Pass. of Pih. Jer. L. 20; Est. ii. 23; Ezek. xxvi. 21.

בַּקָּשָׁה, f. *Petition, request*, Est. v. 3; vii. 8; Ezra vii. 6. Aff. בַּקָּשָׁתִי, בַּקָּשָׁתְךָ, בַּקָּשָׁתוֹ.

בַּר, m. Arab. اِبْن, r. برو. Cogn. بَرَّ, Heb. בָּרָא. Cogn. בָּנָה. Whence בֵּן, see above. Heb. and Chald. *A son*, Prov. xxxi. 2; Ps. ii. 12, נַשְּׁקוּ־בַר, *Kiss the son*. The Christ, ver. 2; the Son of God, ver. 7. Neither David, nor David's mere natural son, ver. 8, under whose rule the nations never came, and never could come. Nor could vv. 10, 11, ever apply to the temporal subjection of kings only. Comp. ver. 12. Aff. בְּרִי. Chald. pl. בְּנֵי of בֵּן, Dan. v. 22; vi. 1. בַּר־אֱלָהִין, Ib. iii. 25, *Son of gods*; but taking this as a pl. of excellence, *Son of God*. So Hom. &c. Διὸς υἱός.—Ezra v. 1, 2; vi. 14. Aff. בְּרֵהּ. Syr. ܒ݁ܰܪ, ܒ݁ܶܢ.

בַּר, m. בָּרָה, f. r. ברר. *Choice, select*. Meton. I. *Beloved*, Cant. vi. 9. II. *Pure, clean*, Ib. vi. 10; Ps. xxiv. 4; lxxiii. 1. III. *Empty, void*, Prov. xiv. 4. IV. *Corn*, as purified from the chaff; comp. Jer. v. 11. Gen. xli. 35. 49; Prov. xi. 26; Joel ii. 24:—as growing, Ps. lxv. 14. Arab. بَرّ, Lat. *far*. V. *Without;* i. e. *in the open country*, Job xxxix. 4. Arab. بَرِّيّ, *externus, agrestis*.

בֹּר, m. r. ברר. I. *Cleanness, purity*, 2 Sam. xxii. 25. Often followed by יָדַיִם, or כַּפַּיִם; as, בְּבֹר יָדַי, *According to the cleanness of my hands;* i. e. my innocency, 2 Sam. xxii. 21. בְּבֹר כַּפֶּיךָ, *By*, id. Job xxii. 30; Ps. xviii. 21. 25. II. Meton. *Material* used for cleansing, as *Soap* (i. q. בְּרִית), Job ix. 30. In Is. i. 25, אֶצְרֹף כַּבֹּר סִיגֶיךָ, *I will purify as* (with) *soap*, (or) *as soap* (cleanses) *thy dross;* i. e. I will purge away thy dross, as soap cleanses the hands, &c. It is not necessary to suppose here therefore, as many have done, that the thing meant has any thing to do with the purifying of metals. All the ancient Versions are to the same effect. See בְּרִית.

בָּרָא, v. pres. יִבְרָא. Arab. بَرَأَ, *creavit, recreavit*. Cogn. برى (r.) برو) *præcidit, præsecando et asciando aptavit*. Syr. ܒ݁ܪܳܐ, *creavit*. "*Ex nihilo*," says Castell, after the Jews, &c. generally; but this is groundless and fanciful; and greatly is it to be regretted that any such notion was ever entertained,

ברא (91) ברב

and applied in defence of revealed religion. It is, I think, quite obvious that the Bible was never intended to teach philosophy of any sort; and hence, it supplies no explanations, and offers no reasons for its doctrines. It deals solely in facts or doctrines. And these it proposes as authoritative. We are no where told, whether matter previously existed or not; and certainly the merely supposed signification of a word must afford but little towards determining such a question, and particularly when we find the usage of the Arabs taking part against us. Of late the study of geology has again called up this question, and various have been the means had recourse to for its solution. I prefer taking the view which considers the account of the creation in Genesis, as referring to the present state of things only, leaving the question, as to any previous creation, untouched. I am then at liberty to believe, that other creations might also have existed, in many respects perhaps totally unlike this, and that these were destroyed; and hence the strange fossil remains now found in the bowels of the earth, and at such surprising depths. If there are no human remains,—and this appears to be the fact,—this might be accounted for on the supposition, that, if men actually existed, they did not become subject to death, as our progenitor did; and hence might have been translated to some happier and more glorified state, as it was the case with Enoch and Elijah, even in this of ours. Nor is it necessary to suppose, that former creations were lighted by the same sun that ours is. With them clouds of light, such as those which are now believed to cover the disk of the sun, might have enveloped the earth itself; or light might have been supplied in some other way. Nor is it necessary to suppose that, even in this our system, the disk of the sun was necessary to the purpose of affording light. If indeed *light* was created on the first day, and suspended some where in the heavens, and a rotatory motion communicated to the earth, evening and morning would necessarily be produced, and the period of the natural day be defined. On the fourth day, when the disk of the sun was created, this light might have been located on it, as its permanent place of habitation. And, it is worth remarking that, in this case, not *light*, but *place of light*, is the term in the original. This will suffice, perhaps, to solve some of the difficulties, and to remove some of the doubts, usually felt on this question; and will, perhaps, guard the philosophical reader from adopting the silly theory that בָּרָא, signifies *created out of nothing;* and the equally silly one, that the *days* of creation, as found in the early parts of Genesis, constituted periods of indefinite length, like the Yōgs of the Hindoos.

Constr. immed. *Created;* i. e. *formed, made*, any thing newly, or anew, Gen. i. 1. 21. 26. 27; comp. ii. 22, Is. xlv. 7, &c., where בָּרָא, is syn. with עָשָׂה, בָּנָה. Jer. xxxi. 22, בָּרָא יְהֹוָה חֲדָשָׁה, *Will create a new thing.* בָּרָא לַעֲשׂוֹת lit. *Created for making; formed* (asciavit) *for completely making,* Gen. ii. 3; comp. Is. xlv. 12, 18. Part. בּוֹרֵא, *Creator, Maker,* pl. excell. aff. בּוֹרְאֶיךָ, *Thy great Creator,* Eccl. xii. 1. Infin. constr. בְּרֹא, Gen. v. 1. Imp. בְּרָא.

Niph. נִבְרָא, pres. יִבָּרֵא, *Became* or *was created,* or *made,* Ezek. xxi. 30; Exod. xxxiv. 10; Is. xlviii. 7; Ps. cxlviii. 5; cii. 19. Infin. הִבָּרְאָ, *Being created,* Gen. v. 2, &c.

Pih. בֵּרֵא, pres. non. occ. *Cut,* as with a sword or axe, Josh. xvii. 15. 18. Infin. בָּרֵא, Ezek. xxiii. 47. Imp. בָּרֵא, *Make, form,* Ib. xxi. 24.

Hiph. הִבְרִיא, Infin. from the noun, בָּרִיא, *Fat, making fat,* 1 Sam. ii. 29.

בָּרְבֻּרִים, m. pl. redup. r. ברר. *Most choice, select,* i. e. fed beasts, 1 Kings v. 3. The Rabbins, and after them, Gesenius, &c. will have this word to signify *birds,* as *geese, capons, &c.* Gesenius prefers *geese* from the whiteness, &c. of their feathers. Bochart has very ably shown, Hieroz. II. lib. i. cap. xix. that there is not the least necessity or ground for introducing any mention of birds here at all; that בַּרְבֻּרִים אֲבוּסִים must, according to Biblical phraseology, signify *fed beasts* of some sort, the term אבוס being applied to nothing else; and ברברים, being a reduplication of בר, *pure, choice,* can hardly signify anything but *most choice,* or the like. Comp. Neh. v. 18; so one of the Greek Versions ἐκλεκτῶν σιτευτά. It is marvellous indeed, that these *stalled-birds* of the Rabbins should have kept their ground so long!

בָּרָד, m. Arab. بَرَد, *grando.* Æth. id. Syr. ܒܪܕ, id. ܒܪܕ, *grandinatus, albo et rubro distinctus, maculosus.* Arab. بَرَد, *vestis striata. Hail,* Exod. ix. 18. 22, 23; x. 5; Ps. xviii. 13, 14; Job. xxxviii. 22, &c. Hence,

בְּרֻדִּים, for בְּרוּדִים, pl. m. *Spotted,*

בְּרָה (92) בְּרוּ

probably with white on some dark ground, see בָּזָּן, last art. Applied to goats and horses, Gen. xxxi. 10, 12; Zech. vi. 3. 6. נְקֻדִּים, *marked with small points or spots;* עֲקֻדִּים, probably, with *knots;* i. e. in which many such spots were clustered, as it were, together. Hence, according to Gesenius, Syr. ܟ݁ܳܢܡܳܐ, *pardus,* and Gall. *broder.* Comp. Eurip. Iphig. in Aul. lin. 221. et seq. Τοὺς .... λευκοστίκτῳ τριχὶ βαλίους, κ. τ. λ.

בָּרָה, v. pres. אָבְרָה. Arab. cogn. بَرّ, *triticum.* بُورَنِيَّة, r. بور, *cibi genus.* I. *Ate,* 2 Sam. xii. 17; xiii. 6. 10. Constr. *abs.* and *immed.* II. i. q. ברו; בְּרוּ לָכֶם, *Choose for you,* 1 Sam. xvii. 8.

Pih. בָּרוֹת, Infin. *Eating,* Lam. iv. 10, בָּרוֹת id. Ps. lxix. 22.

Hiph. pres. 2 pers. f. aff. תַּבְרֵנִי, *Give me to eat,* 2 Sam. xiii. 5. Infin. הַבְרוֹת, Ib. iii. 35.

בָּרוּךְ, m. *Blessed.* See r. בָּרַךְ.

בְּרוֹמִים, m. pl. Arab. بُرْم, and مُبْرَم, *ex duabus aut pluribus partibus in unum contortum filum: vestis ejusmodi: tænia, et linea gemmis ornata, talis qua medium corporis, vel brachium fœminæ, circumcingunt. Costly clothing,* probably such as the Persic زرّ بَفْت, *interwoven with gold,* Ezek. xxvii. 24.

בְּרוֹשׁ, m. pl. בְּרוֹשִׁים. Arab. بَرُوث, *abies.* Syr. id. I. One of the five species of the cedar, according to Celsius, I. p. 74, et seq. which he renders by *abies, Fir-tree.* Gesenius, on the other hand, argues largely for the *Cypress.*—Thes. and Heb. Lex. sub voce. I am inclined to think that the latter is right, Is. xiv. 8; xxxvii. 24; lv. 13; Hos. xiv. 9; Zech. xi. 2. The timber of which was applied to building, to musical instruments, &c., 1 Kings v. 22. 24; vi. 15. 34; 2 Sam. vi. 5; Ezek. xxvii. 5. Meton. II. Any thing made of this wood, as *the staff of a lance,* Nah. ii. 4; *a musical instrument,* 2 Sam. vi. 5. It is perhaps worth remarking that, from the durability of the cypress, mummy-coffins were made of it by the Egyptians; and, on this account, perhaps, it was used in constructing the temple at Jerusalem. In 1 Kings vi. 34, we find the gates of this building were made of it. Those of St. Peter's at Rome were originally made of it; and they are said to have been sound and good after the space of 600 years, when they were removed by Pope

Eugenius IV., and brazen ones substituted for them.

בָּרוֹת, m. pl. בְּרוֹתִים, Chald. i. q. בְּרוֹשׁ, preceding, Cant. i. 17.

בַּרְזֶל, m. Syr. ܦܰܪܙܠܳܐ. Arab. فِرْزِل, *forfex,* quâ ferrum incîdit *faber ferrarius. Iron,* Gen. iv. 22; Ezek. xxvii. 12, &c. Metaph. II. *Hard and ungiving,* Ps. ii. 9; Is. xlviii. 4. III. Meton. *Instrument of iron,* Num. xxxv. 16; Deut. xxvii. 5; Josh. viii. 31; Ps. cv. 18; cxlix. 8.

בָּרַח, v. pres. יִבְרַח. Arab. بَرَح, *obvertit latus corporis—recessit, discessit.* I. *Passed on,* from one part or place towards another; pec. *in flight.* Constr. abs. with מִן, אַחֲרֵי, אֶל, לְ, מֵאֵת, מִיַּד, מִפְּנֵי, מִלִּפְנֵי, Exod. xxxvi. 33; Gen. xxxi. 22. 27; 1 Sam. xix. 18; xxvii. 4, &c. "Obvertit latus sinistrum," says Winer, "quo modo milites fugere solebant." I was not aware till I saw this, that soldiers usually turned the left side when they ran away; nor that Gen. xxxi. 22. 27; Neh. vi. 11, &c., required this sort of interpretation! Part. בֹּרֵחַ, f. בֹּרַחַת. Infin. בְּרוֹחַ. Constr. בְּרֹחַ. Imp. בְּרַח.

Hiph. pl. הִבְרִיחוּ, *Made, caused to pass,* or *fly,* pres. יַבְרִיחַ, Exod. xxvi. 28; 1 Chron. viii. 13; Neh. xiii. 28; Prov. xix. 26, &c. Part. מַבְרִיחַ. Infin. הַבְרִיחַ.

בְּרִי, Job xxxvii. 11. See רִי.

בָּרִיא, m. בְּרִיאָה, f. pl. בְּרִיאִים, בְּרִיאוֹת, constr. m. בְּרִיאֵי, r. ברא. From the notion of *making, recreating,* comp. ברה, we readily arrive at that of *health, plumpness, &c.* Hence I. *Fat,* applied to men, beasts, food, ears of corn, &c., Judg. iii. 17; Ps. lxxiii. 4; Dan. i. 15; Gen. xli. 2. 4, 5; 1 Kings iv. 23; Hab. i. 16; Ezek. xxxiv. 3; Zech. xi. 17, &c. II. *Extraordinary thing, something,* as it were, *newly created,* Num. xvi. 30. Comp. Jer. xxxi. 22; and the καινὴ κτίσις of Paul, 2 Cor. v. 17; Gal. vi. 15.

בְּרִיָה, f. r. ברה. *Eating, eatable,* Ezek. xxxiv. 20. שָׂה בְרִיָה, in appos. q. d. fit for the table, 2 Sam. xiii. 5. 7. 10. There is no necessity here, therefore, for supposing, either that בְּרִיָה, ought to be read בָּרִיא, or, that the word in each place above cited, is not really the same.

בָּרִיחַ, or בָּרִחַ, m. pl. בְּרִיחִים, (form פָּקִיד, implying *habit,*) r. בָּרַח. *Passing on from place to place:* pec. *fleeing, fugitive,* Is. xxvii. 1; Job xxvi. 13; the pl. Is. xliii. 14,

בְּרִי (93) בְּרִי

is taken by the LXX., Syr., and Arab. to signify *fugitives*; by others, *vectes, bars*; and thence was read בְּרִיחִים. See too, Is. xv. 5.

בְּרִיחַ, m. pl. בְּרִיחִים, r. ברח. I. *Tranverse bar*, laid across the upright planks which formed the sides of the Tabernacle, Exod. xxvi. 26—28, &c; xxxv. 11; xxxvi. 31, &c.; Num. iii. 36; iv. 31. II. *Bars* used for making fast the gates of a city, Judg. xvi. 3; Neh. iii. 3; Ps. cxlvii. 13. Sometimes made of *iron*, or *brass*, Ps. cvii. 16; Is. xlv. 2; 1 Kings iv. 13. Metaph. Jon. ii. 7. So some take בְּרִיחֶהָ, Is. xv. 5, as signifying *Princes, rulers*, and hence *defences* of the land. It is, however, more consonant to the context to read בְּרִיחֶהָ, *Her fugitives*, as intimated above, which seems justified by the mention of עֶגְלַת following; and so the Targumist has taken it.

בְּרִית, f. lit. i. q. בָּרוּת, בָּרוֹת, r. ברה. "*Fœdus*, dictum a secando," says Gesenius and others. I can find no proof however for this, beyond the consideration that بَرَىٰ, r. بَرَعَ, Arab. signifies *asciavit, præcîdit, &c.* which is cognate with بَرَىٰ, Heb. ברא. I know, indeed, that this word often follows the verb בָּרָה, which signifies *cut;* but this can determine nothing to our purpose. I also know that an animal was usually *cut* or *divided*, when such *Fœdus* or *covenant* was made, Gen xv. 10, (but even here the birds were not divided). Still, this will by no means determine the sense of our word. In other cases, as that of the bow in the cloud, Gen. ix. 8, et seq., we hear nothing of the *cutting* or *dividing* of animals. The same may be said of the covenant of circumcision, Gen. xvii. 7, et seq., although this act was performed by a sort of *cutting*. I am inclined to think therefore, that *eating, feasting;* and thence *agreement*, or *covenant*, is meant: because *eating together* always has been, and now is, in the East, considered as the mark by which men are known to be friendly. In the times of Noah, Gen. ix. 9, מֵקִים אֶת־בְּרִיתִי, *Establishing my covenant*, seems clearly to intimate, that covenants of this sort were no new things in the world. I suppose, therefore, that Noah's sacrifice, Ib. viii. 20, was a recognition of some such covenant previously existing: and, if so, that of Abel, Ib. iv. 4, recognized a still earlier one: and this, St. Paul assures us, Heb. xi. 4, was offered *in faith:* which implies, at least, that some Divine appointment previously existed. Now, in all these cases, it is but reasonable to suppose, that the sacrifice *was eaten* as a sort of feast. In Jacob and Laban's covenant, Ib. xxxi. 46, et seq., certainly this was the case. The heap of stones here afforded a mark or witness of *the covenant;* and the covenant itself was ratified by the parties *eating together* upon it. At a later period, *eating* the Paschal-lamb, was a sign of the covenant between God and the Jews: and, out of this, joined with patriarchal appointments of a similar nature, grew the whole Jewish ritual. This view of the subject seems to me to be confirmed by this covenant's being termed *a covenant of salt*, בְּרִית מֶלַח. Not because salt alone was ever offered, nor yet because sacred salt was eaten alone on any occasion (as Gesenius seems to urge, "*Quoniam in tali fœdere pangendo sale sacro vesci solebant*"); but because it was commanded that the offerings should be salted with salt, with the view, as it appears to me, of their being eaten. "*Ut cibi sapidi sint. Sacrificia erant convivia Dei*," says Menochius and Oleaster, as cited by Poole, Synops. on Lev. ii. 13. Among the heathen, too, as Pliny tells us, H. N. lib. xxxi. c. xli. "*Maxime tamen in sacris intelligitur* (salis) *auctoritas, quando nulla conficiuntur sine mola salsa*. See, too, Ovid. Fast. i. 127, and 337: a custom, in all probability, continued among them, as sacrifice itself was, from patriarchal times. Comp. Num. xviii. 19; 2 Chron. xiii. 5; Ezek. xliii. 24; Mark ix. 49, 50; Matt. v. 13. It is an error therefore to suppose, as Gesenius does, that *a covenant of salt* was in any respect more sacred than *the covenant* generally: the fact being that the covenant with God was so called, in order to distinguish it from ordinary covenants with men, and because salt was always used in the sacrifices belonging to it. Under the New Testament the same, in principle and spirit, is continued in Christians as one family, and as reconciled to God in the Redeemer, spiritually *eating* the flesh, and drinking the blood of Christ. Comp. John vi. 32, et seq.; 1 Cor. v. 7; Heb. x. 16, &c.—I am induced to believe therefore that, as *cutting off* an animal implied *the punishment* to be inflicted on the party transgressing the covenant; i. e. for the commission of sin, and hence *the death* of the vicarious sacrifice, which was completed in that of Christ; so the feasting together on its flesh—and hence spiritually on the flesh and blood of Christ—intimated, and now intimates, the *agreement*,

i. e. *covenant* thus made, and maintained, between God and man. On this account we are told by our Lord himself, John vi. 53, that unless we *eat his flesh* and *drink his blood*, we have no life remaining in us: that is to say: the sacrifice might indeed have been made to good purpose; but, unless we partake in the feast, we have no part in the covenant intended. — I. *Any agreement*, or *covenant*. II. pec. That made by God with the patriarchs, and ratified in the person of the Messiah. I. Josh. ix. 6, et seq.; Judg. ii. 2; 1 Sam. xviii. 3; xxiii. 18; Mal. ii. 14. Metaph. of inanimate things, Job v. 23. See my notes on the place. Whence the phrases בַּעֲלֵי בְרִית, Gen. xiv. 13 : אַנְשֵׁי בְרִית, Obad. 7 : נְגִיד בְּרִית, Dan. xi. 22 : אֵל בְּרִית, Judg. ix. 46 : בְּרִית עוֹלָם, Amos i. 9; i. q. Arab. موالخاة, Annal. Muslem. I. p. 77, בְּרִית שָׁלוֹם, Ezek. xxxiv. 25, &c.: בְּרִית רִאשׁוֹנִים, Deut. iv. 31 : בְּרִית אֲבוֹתֶיךָ, Ib. 23 : בְּרִית יְהוָה. II. *The covenant* made by God, Gen. xv. 17; Exod. xxiv. 7, 8; xxxiv. 27; Deut. v. 2; Is. xlii. 6; Mal. iii. 1. The sacrificial blood of which was termed דַּם הַבְּרִית, Exod. xxiv. 8; Zech. ix. 11, which clearly had respect to the blood of Christ. Comp. Matt. xxvi. 28; Mark xiv. 24; Heb. xiii. 20. Hence, בְּרִית קֹדֶשׁ, Dan. xi. 28. 30.; מַלְאַךְ הַבְּרִית, Mal. iii. 1. *The Messiah*, ὁ μεσίτης. Hence, too, with reference to the conditions, &c. of this covenant, we have דִּבְרֵי הַבְּרִית, סֵפֶר הַבְּרִית, בְּרִית מֶלַח, בְּרִית עוֹלָם, אֲרוֹן הַבְּרִית, לוּחוֹת הַבְּרִית, אוֹת בְּרִית, בְּרִית הַלֵּוִי. Constr. with כָּרַת, נָתַן, שָׂם, בּוֹא בְ, שָׁמַר, as to *making, establishing, keeping it*; with עָבַר בְּ, הֵפֵר, חִלֵּל, עָבַר, כִּפֵּר בְּ, שָׁקַר בְּ, when speaking of *transgressing, breaking, profaning, forsaking, falsifying, &c.* this covenant. In the LXX. and New Test. Διαθήκη is made to represent this word; but, as it should seem, having a very different etymological sense, viz. *a laying down; something laid down*, or the like: which, in the purer Greek, was generally taken to signify a *will*, or *testament*: in that of the LXX. *an agreement*, or *covenant*. Those who wish to consider the controversy on this subject, can have recourse to the authorities referred to by Schleusner *sub voce*. Generally speaking, however, there is only one place in the New Testament, viz. Heb. ix. 16, in which the sense of the Heb. בְּרִית may not be properly given to the term Διαθήκη. Certainly in many no other can be given, e. g. Matt. xxvi. 28; Mark xiv. 24; Luke i. 72; xxii. 20;

Acts iii. 25; vii. 8, &c. In these the sense of *will*, or *testament*, must be altogether foreign. And, from the context, in Heb. ix., the same is certainly the case. Let us then consider the difficult passage itself, which runs thus : Ὅπου γὰρ διαθήκη, θάνατου ἀνάγκη φέρεσθαι τοῦ διαθεμένου. The only difficulty here, seems to lie in the term διαθέμενου, signifying *the person laying down* the matter of the διαθήκη, i. e. *the Covenanter:* and which, as it has an active sense, can hardly be applied to the *animal* slain as a vicarious sacrifice. If, however, we have recourse to what is termed the *sensus prægnans*, or a meton. by which a word is taken in the sense of its natural consequent, this term may at once be referred to Christ, as the Covenanter and finisher of sacrificial observances; which will unite this verse, in sense, with the preceding. We may then thus translate it. *For where (there is) a covenant, the death of the covenanter (is) necessary to be borne** (in mind): i. e. ultimately, the death of Christ : for about this the argument is. It is then added, Διαθήκη γὰρ ἐπὶ νεκροῖς βεβαιά, κ. τ. λ.: i. e. *a covenant* (made) *on dead beings* (generally); on Christ and his substitutes primarily; secondarily, on *the implied death* of those who are his, *is firm*. Hence, ver. 18, the first covenant was confirmed by shedding the blood of an animal—which had respect to Christ; for without the shedding of this blood there was no remission (ver. 22), taken as it ought to be in all the bearings intended in Scripture. If, then, we take Christ here to be the διαθέμενος, or High Priest of his Church, proposing himself as the sacrifice by which the καινὴ διαθήκη was confirmed, we reconcile St. Paul's reasoning at once with the rites to which it referred, and the whole of this context, with the rest of this epistle. But, introduce the notion of a *Will* and *Testator*, and then we have what is wholly repugnant to the context, and allusions, to which the Hebrews were perfect strangers : the mention of *Will*, *Testator*, or anything of the sort, never so much as once occurring in any of their writings.

בָּרִית, f. i. q. בֹּר, sign. II. *Soap*. Arab. بَرَا, *vacuus a vitiis*. The salt obtained

---

* That is, in the sense of φέρεσθαι διὰ μνήμης .... *tenere memoria*. See Steph. Thes. Græc....sub voce φέρω.

from the ashes of certain plants, &c. mixed with oil, used in cleansing garments, &c. Hieroz. ii. p. 45, et seq. Celsii Hierobot. i. 449, et seq. " *Fit*," says Pliny, " *ex sevo, et cinere. Optimus fagino et caprino.*" H. N. xxviii. 51. It was also made with *Natrum* (נֶתֶר, Jer. ii. 22), which is a fixed native salt, or alkali, instead of the salt of ashes. This was much used by the ancients, Mal. iii. 2.

בֶּרֶךְ, c. du. בִּרְכַּיִם, constr. בִּרְכֵּי. Arab. بَرْك, *cameli. pec decumbentes.* بَرْكَة, *procubitûs cameli modus.* Propr. *The act of kneeling.* Meton. *The knee*, Is. xlv. 23; Job iii. 11; Ezek. vii. 17; xlvii. 4, &c. Aff. בִּרְכֵּיהֶם, בִּרְכֶּיךָ, בִּרְכָּיו, בִּרְכֵּי, Chald. id. Dan. vi. 11.

בָּרַךְ, v. pres. יִבְרַךְ. Arab. بَرَك, *genua flexit, et sic in pectore procubuit* camelus, id. Syr. et Æth. I. *Knelt*, worshipping, 2 Chron. vi. 13; Ps. xcv. 6; Dan. vi. 11. II. Meton. Part. בָּרוּךְ, f. בְּרוּכָה, pl. m. בְּרוּכִים, constr. בְּרוּכֵי. *Worshipped, blessed,* often applied to God as the object of worship, Gen. ix. 26; xiv. 19, &c. occasionally to men, by a further Meton. as hence receiving favours from Him, 2 Sam. ii. 5; xxiii. 21; Ps. cxv. 15; Is. lxv. 23; Ruth iii. 10, constr. with לְ, *as it respects, &c.*

Niph. נִבְרְכוּ, *They shall be,* or *become, blessed*, Gen. xii. 3; xviii. 18; xxviii. 14. " *Reflex . . . benedixit sibi,*" says Gesenius, which is groundless in grammar, and untrue in theology. The blessing was to come from God.

Pih. בֵּרַךְ, pres. יְבָרֵךְ, *Pronounced, or made blessed, holy,* or *prosperous,* used either of God or man. Constr. *immed.* Gen. xxiv. 1. 35; xxviii. 3. 5; xlix. 28, &c. In Job i. 5; ii. 9; and 1 Kings xxi. 10, this word has been thought to signify *cursing;* but for this there is no good ground. For, Job i. 5, אֱלֹהִים, may be taken to signify *idols:* and, if so, the verb בֵּרְכוּ, will retain its proper sense. The same may be said of Ib. ii. 9, and of 1 Kings xxii. 10, 13. Besides, if we allow אֱלֹהִים, in this last place to signify the true God, yet the ascription of blessedness to the king by Naboth, could be nothing short of blasphemy. But, if we take אֱלֹהִים, to signify heathenish deities, the act ascribed to Naboth will be truly heathenish. See my note on Job i. 5. To these passages Gesenius adds Job xxxi. 30: but the verb occurs not there. He also adds Ps. x. 3; but here no such sense as *cursing* is necessary, as a moment's inspection of the passage will shew. He cites likewise the Arab. ابترك, and Æth. ተባረከ: but in no such sense are these verbs to be found. The analogy of these languages, therefore, to which he appeals in the end of his article, will stand him in no stead. The senses, *salutavit, valedixit,* and the like, are often substituted for *bless, &c.* especially by the German lexicographers, which I think a great fault; because, I cannot think the terms *the Lord bless thee, &c.* by any means equivalent to our *how do ye do?* the Arab. سلام عليك, &c. Surely it is better, as certainly it is more honest, to retain with the use of ancient terms the ancient notions which accompanied them, and not to soften every thing, so as to make it square with modern or heathenish usages.

Infin. בָּרֵךְ, and בָּרוֹךְ, if the vowels may be depended on, Gen. xxviii. 6; 1 Sam. xi i. 10, &c. Imp. בָּרֵךְ, part. מְבָרֵךְ, pl. aff. מְבָרְכֶיךָ. Puh. pres. יְבֹרַךְ, *Be,* or *become blessed,* 2 Sam. vii. 29; Ps. cxii. 2; cxxviii. 4; Prov. xii. 9, &c. Part. מְבֹרָךְ, f. מְבֹרֶכֶת, pl. m. aff. מְבֹרָכָיו.

Hiph. pres. יַבְרֵךְ, *He makes kneel down,* Gen. xxiv. 11. Arab. أَبْرَك, *fecit ut genua flectens procumberet* camelus.

Hithp. הִתְבָּרֵךְ, pres. יִתְבָּרֵךְ, i. q. Niph. et Puh., Deut. xxix. 18, *in his own estimation,* בִּלְבָבוֹ, Gen. xxii. 18; xxvi. 4; Jer. iv. 2; Ps. lxxii. 17. Part. מִתְבָּרֵךְ, Is. lxv. 16, constr. with בְּ. I must warn the learner here against the " *benedicens sibi,* and *benedicent sibi, et prosperabuntur,*" *&c.* of some commentators, as giving neither the etymological nor the theological sense of this form.

בְּרַךְ, v. Chald. i. q. Heb. Kal. I. *Knelt,* Dan. vi. 11. II. בְּרִיךְ, part. i. q. Heb. בָּרוּךְ, Dan. iii. 28.

Pah. בָּרֵךְ, for בֵּרַךְ, i. q. Heb. Pih. constr. with לְ, Dan. ii. 19; iv. 31. Part. pass. מְבָרַךְ, Ib. ii. 20.

בְּרָכָה, once בְּרֵכָה, constr. בִּרְכַּת, pl. בְּרָכוֹת, constr. בִּרְכוֹת. I. *A blessing,* or ascription of praise to God, Neh. ix. 5; Ps. cix. 17. II. *Id.* also as received from Him, Gen. xii. 2; xxvii. 35—38; Exod. xxxii. 29; Prov. xi. 11; opp. to קְלָלָה, Deut. xi. 26; Gen. xxvii. 12. III. Also *any favour,* or *present,* received from man, Judg. i. 15; 2 Kings v. 15; xviii. 31; Gen. xxxiii. 11. Aff. בִּרְכָתִי, בִּרְכָתְךָ, בִּרְכָתוֹ, pl. בִּרְכוֹתֵיהֶם.

בְּרֵכָה, f. constr. בְּרֵכַת. Arab. بِرْكَة, *piscina. A pool of water.* בְּרֵכַת מַיִם, Nahum ii. 9 ; 2 Sam. ii. 13 ; iv. 12. Two of such pools were at Jerusalem, termed *the upper*, 2 Kings xviii. 17; Is. vii. 3; *old*, Ib. xxii. 11 ; Neh. ii. 14; iii. 15; and the *lower*, Is. xxii. 9.

בְּרַם, Chald. adv. Syr. ܒܪܰܡ, *profecto. But,* Dan. ii. 28 ; iv. 12 ; v. 17 ; Ezra v. 13.

בְּרָם, Eccl. iii. 18. לְבָרָם Infin. Kal, r. ברר, with aff. and prep. לְ.

בָּרָק, m. pl. בְּרָקִים. Arab. بَرْق, *splendor, fulgur.* I. *Flashing, glittering,* as of a (bright) weapon, or lightning, Ezek. xxi. 15. 33; Deut. xxxii. 41 ; Neh. iii. 3 ; Hab. iii. 11. II. Meton. (a) *a sword*, or (b) *lightning,* Job xx. 35; 2 Sam. xxii. 15; Ezek. i. 13; Job xxxviii. 35, &c. Used apparently as a verb, with Infin. בְּרוֹק, Ps. cxliv. 6.

בַּרְקָנִים, m. pl. occ. Judg. viii. 7. 16, only. A sort of sledge according to some, having on its under-side sharp stones (*pyrites*), which, when drawn over the corn on the threshing-floor, separated the corn from the ear. The *Pyrites* seems to have been had recourse to here, in order to suit the etymology of this word. I think it is far more probable, that the חֲרִיצֵי הַבַּרְזֶל, *Sharp points of iron,* mentioned 2 Sam. xii. 31 ; 1 Chron. xx. 3, by which David is said to have punished the children of Ammon, are meant. In Judg. the parallel has קוֹצֵי הַמִּדְבָּר, *Thorns of the desert,* which might indeed have been set as teeth in the inferior threshing instruments. If then we may understand חֲרִיצֵי הַבַּרְזֶל here, we shall have no difficulty in seeing why these were termed בַּרְקָנִים. See sign. I. immed. above.

בָּרֶקֶת, f. it. בָּרְקַת. Lit. *flashing.* A sort of *precious stone*, Exod. xxviii. 17; Ezek. xxviii. 13, according to some, *the Emerald.* The Syr. ܒܰܪܩܳܐ, Exod. is, however, according to Castell, *a carbuncle.* So Lud. de Dieu. Grotius makes it the Chrysolite. See Braun. de Vestitu Sacerd. p. 548.

בָּרַר, v. pres. non occ. Arab. بَرَّ, *pium se gessit.* Syr. ܒܪܰܪ, *purus.* Cogn. ברה, בור, בחר. I. *Examined* whether pure, Eccl. iii. 18; comp. ix. 1. לָבוּר Arab. اِسْتَبَرَّ. Meton. II. *Separated, selected, chose,* Ezek. xx. 38. Part. בָּרוּר, f. בְּרוּרָה, pl. בְּרוּרִים, f. בְּרוּרוֹת, 1

Chron. vii. 40; ix. 22; Is. xlix. 2; Job xxxiii. 3, &c.
Niph. Part. נָבַר, *Became pure,* 2 Sam. xxii. 27 ; Ps. xviii. 27.
Imp. הִבָּרוּ, *Become ye clean, pure,* Is. lii. 11.
Pih. Infin. בָּרֵר, Dan. xi. 35.
Hiph. Imp. הָבֵרוּ, *Making clean, polish,* Jer. li. 11. Inf. הָבֵר, *Making clean,* Ib. iv. 11.
Hithp. pres. תִּתְבָּרַר. *Thou becomest—appearest—pure,* Ps. xviii. 27. Contr. תִּתָּבָר, 2 Sam. xxii. 27, pointed as if it were the Niph. of הבר. Arab. تَبَرَّرَ, conj. viii. *separatus fuit, &c.* Pl. Dan. xii. 10. Nothing is to be found either here or in the Niph. justifying the reflective sense, "*purgavit se*," &c., of the lexicographers.

בְּשׂוֹרָה, and בְּשֹׂרָה, f. Arab. بُشُور, and بُشْرَى, *Announcing good news.* بِشَارَة, *pulchritudo ;* r. בשׂר. I. *Good news*, 2 Sam. xviii. 22. 25. 27, with טוֹבָה. II. Meton. *Reward for good news,* Ib. iv. 10.

בֶּשֶׂם, and בֹּשֶׂם, m. pl. בְּשָׂמִים. Syr. ܒܶܣܡܳܐ, *aroma.* I. *Scent of perfume,* Exod. xxx. 23 ; Is. iii. 24 ; Cant. iv. 17. II. Meton. *Perfume, aromatic substance,* Exod. xxxv. 28 ; 1 Kings x. 10 ; Ezek. xxvii. 22, &c. הָרֵי בְשָׂמִים, Cant. viii. 14, *Hills bearing aromatic plants, &c.* בְּשָׂמִים רֹאשׁ, *Head perfumes,* i. e. the most valuable, Exod. xxx. 23.

בָּשָׂם, m. occ. once Cant. v. 1, aff. בְּשָׂמִי. Arab. بَشَام, *Nom.* Fruticis odorati, qui formam arboris balsamiferæ refert, crescens prope Meccam. *Amyrum opobalsamum,* Sprengel. Hist. rei Herb. p. 257. de qua disseruit Forsk. in Flora Ægyptiaco-Arabica, p. 79. Freytag. Lex. sub voce. So, apparently, Majus, in Observ. S. L. ii. pp. 37, 38, Winer. Gesenius tells us that, by inserting 1 here, we have in the Arabic بلسام, بلسان , بلسم, or, βάλσαμος, *arbor balsamifera.* But in the Arabic, we have no such word as بلسام, or, بلسم, with any thing like this sense ; and, as to بلسان, it is a totally different word. Freytag, indeed, gives بلسمين, *Balsami arbor.* But I doubt whether he has any good authority for it.

בָּשַׂר, v. Pih. pres. תְּבַשֵּׂר. See בְּשׂוֹרָה. *Announced,* I. any thing generally, Ps. xl.

בָּשָׂר (97) בּוֹשׁ

10; 2 Sam. xviii. 20; 1 Sam. iv. 17. Comp. 1 Kings i. 42; Is. lii. 7, 11. *Good news*, or *tidings*, 2 Sam. xviii. 19; Ps. lxviii. 12; 1 Sam. xxxi. 9; Is. xl. 9, &c. Imp. בַּשְּׂרוּ. Infin. בַּשֵּׂר. Part. מְבַשֵּׂר, f. מְבַשֶּׂרֶת, pl. מְבַשְּׂרוֹת, Ps. lxviii. 12. Persons, such as Miriam and her damsels, announcing the victory. See Exod. xv. Constr. *immed.* and *abs.*

Hithp. pres. יִתְבַּשֵּׂר, *Is* or *becomes informed*, 2 Sam. xviii. 31.

בָּשָׂר, m. pl. בְּשָׂרִים. Arab. بَشَر, *externa hominis cutis*; meton. *homo*; *caro*. I. *Flesh*, generally; as (a) *Man and beast*, Gen. vi. 13. 17. 19; vii. 15, &c.; (b) pec. *Mankind*, Gen. vi. 12; Ps. lxv. 3; cxlv. 21; Is. xl. 5, 6; opposed as weak to *spirit*, *God*, Gen. vi. 5; Job x. 4; Is. xxxi. 3; Ps. lvi. 5, &c., comp. Matt. xvi. 17; Gal. i. 16. (c) Often used of *persons of the same family*, as *relations*, &c., Gen. xxix. 14; Judg. ix. 2; 2 Sam. v. 1; Is. lviii. 7. (d) *The body*, as opp. to נֶפֶשׁ, Is. x. 18; Job xiv. 22; Prov. xiv. 30; (e) and, as inclining to sin, Eccl. ii. 3; v. 5; comp. Matt. xxvi. 41. (f) *The flesh* of either man or beast, Job xxxiii. 21. 25; Gen. xli. 2. 19. (g) Sometimes, apparently, *The skin*, Ps. cii. 5; Job xix. 20. *Flesh*, as eaten, Exod. xvi. 12; Lev. vii. 19, &c. (h) As applied to the *pudenda*. Gen. xvii. 11; Exod. xxviii. 42; Lev. xv. 2: Ezek. xxiii. 20, &c. Aff. בְּשָׂרִי, בְּשָׂרְךָ, בְּשָׂרֵנוּ, בְּשָׂרָם, בְּשָׂרָה, בְּשָׂרוֹ.

בְּשַׂר, m. Chald. i. q. Heb. בָּשָׂר. I. (a) *Flesh*, Dan. vii. 5. (b) *Mankind*, Ib. iv. 9; ii. 11; Defin. בִּשְׂרָא.

בְּשַׂגָּם, Gen. vi. 3. Compd. of בְּ, שֶׁ, for אֲשֶׁר, and גַּם, *In eo quod etiam. In that also.*

בָּשֵׁל, m. f. בְּשֵׁלָה. Syr. ܒܫܠ, *coctus. Boiled, cooked,* Exod. xii. 9; Num. vi. 19.

בָּשַׁל, v. pres. non. occ. Syr. ܒܫܠ, *maturuit.* I. *Matured, ripened,* Joel iv. 13. II. *Boiled, cooked,* Ezek. xxiv. 5.

Pih. בִּשֵּׁל, pres. יְבַשֵּׁל. Syr. Pah. ܒܫܠ, *coxit. Boiled, cooked,* in a pot, Num. xi. 8; 2 Chron. xxxv. 13; 2 Kings iv. 38; Lam. iv. 10, &c. Infin. בַּשֵּׁל, 1 Sam. ii. 13; Exod. xvi. 23. Part. pl. מְבַשְּׁלִים, Ezek. xlvi. 24; f. מְבַשְּׁלוֹת, Ib. ver. 23, applied to *cooking-materials.*

Puh. בֻּשַּׁל, pres. תְּבֻשַּׁל, Exod. xii. 9; Lev. vi. 21; 1 Sam. ii. 15. Part. מְבֻשָּׁל.

Hiph. הִבְשִׁילוּ; *They matured, ripened,* i. e. the עֲנָבִים, just mentioned, Gen xl. 10.

בִּשְׁלִי, see under שֶׁל.

בָּשְׁנָה, f. occ. once Hos. x. 6; r. בוש.

Shame. The termination נָה has created some difficulty here. Gesenius compares it with the Chald. and Æthiop. נָא. Its occurring but once, however, makes this more than doubtful. Winer says, "Formæ est insolitæ (sed i. q. בֹּשׁ)." But what is בֹּשׁ? This difficulty he leaves untouched. I am disposed to think that the word is a compound, as נְאָדְרִי, for נְאָדְרָה הִיא. See r. אדר; and affording an example similar to עֶדְנָה, עֹדְיָה. See in their places, although the vowels slightly disagree; but this may be accounted for on the ground, that the punctuists did not see the analogy of the word: בָּשְׁנָה will, therefore, stand for בֹּשׁ נָה, i. q. בֹּשׁ הֵנָּה, *Shame thus far, there* &c., doth Ephraim receive. See the place.

בּוּשִׁים, m. nom. act. cogn. בּוֹשֵׁם. Arab بَتَّ, *dispersit*, بَتَّ, *commovit.* Cogn بَتَّ, *secuit, abrupit.* Aff. בּוּשֵׁיכֶם, *Your trampling on, injuring,* Amos v. 11.

בֹּשֶׁת, f. r. בוש, contr. for בּוֹשֶׁת, as פְּקַחַת. lit. *Putting to shame.* I. *Shame, blushing.* פָּנִים, Jer. vii. 19; Ps. xliv. 16; Dan. ix. 7, 8. (a) As put on like a garment, i. e. covered with it, Ps. xxxv. 26; cix. 29; Job viii. 22. Hence, Meton. II. *Ignominy, baseness,* Is. liv. 4; lxi. 7; Mich. i. 11; Hab. ii. 10. It. III. *An idol,* as causing shame, ignominy, &c., Jer. iii. 24; xi. 13; Hos. ix. 10. Aff. בָּשְׁתִּי, בָּשְׁתְּךָ, בָּשְׁתָּם, בָּשְׁתָּם.

בַּת, f. contr. for בֶּנֶת, or בִּנְת. Arab. بَتّ. Syr. ܒܪܬܐ. See בֵּן, r. בנה, pl. בָּנוֹת. I. *Daughter,* real, or adopted; and more laxly, as in בֵּן, II. *Uterine sister, niece,* or any female descendant. I. Gen. xi. 29; xxiv. 24; Est. ii. 7. 15, &c. II. Gen. xx. 12; xxiv. 48; xxxvi. 2; xxviii. 6; xxxv. 1; Num. xxv. 1; Deut. xxiii. 17. III. *Women,* as natives, residents, or professing the religion, of certain places. Is. iii. 17; Cant. i. 5; 2 Sam. i. 20; Ezek. xiii. 17; Ps. xlviii. 12, &c. So בַּת אֵל נֵכָר, Mal. ii. 11. בְּנוֹת הָאָדָם, *Carnal women,* Gen. vi. 2. IV. Metaph. *Daughters,* or smaller *cities,* as derived from larger ones or metropoles, Num. xxi. 25. 32; Judg. xi. 26; Josh. xv. 45. V. When used in the singular, and followed in constr. by the name of any place, *The people* generally of that place; as, בַּת יְרוּשָׁלַיִם, *People of Jerusalem,* Is. xxxvii. 22; Zech. iii. 14. So Jer. xlvi. 19; Ps. xlv. 13; Lam. iv. 22; Is. x. 30; Ps. cxxxvii. 8, &c. It being customary to represent countries, cities, &c., *metaph.* by

בַּת—גּ (98) בַּת—גא

the figure of a woman. VI. בַּת, followed by a numeral, signifies a woman of the age intimated by the numeral, Gen. xvii. 17. VII. Followed by עַיִן, for בַּת עַיִן, see אִישׁוֹן. VIII. Applied to the produce of animals, trees, or places; as, בַּת הַיַעֲנָה, *The female ostrich*, Lev. xi. 16, &c. See יַעֲנָה.—*Branches*, Gen. xlix. 22; בַּת אֲשׁוּרִים, *Ivory*, Ezek. xxvii. 6. Aff. בִּתִּי, בִּתּוֹ, בִּתָּהּ, בִּתְּךָ, &c.

בַּת, c. pl. בַּתִּים. Arab. بَتّ, *secuit, &c.* A certain measure of fluids so called, *A bath;* containing one-tenth of the Homer; i. e. seven gallons four pints and 15.2. dec. cubic inches, Ezek. xlv. 10. 11. 14; 1 Kings vii. 26; Is. v. 10, &c. Joseph. Arch. lib. viii. c. ii. §. 9. ὁ δὲ βάδος δύναται χωρῆσαι ξέστας ἐβδομήκοντα δύο. Chald. id. pl. בַּתִּין, Ezra vii. 22. See Capt. Jervis's Essay, p. 9, &c.

בַּתּוֹת, f. occ. once, Is. vii. 19. Arab. بَتّ, *secuit, abrupit;* بَتَّة, *sectio una. Clefts, fissures,* i. e. abrupt, inaccessible places, as in the parall. נְקִיקֵי הַסְּלָעִים.

בָּתָה, f. occ. once, Is. v. 6. Arab. بَاتَ, *disjecit, dispersitue* supellectilia. Cogn. باش, *tumultum addidit;* بَتّ, *secuit. A desolation, excision.*

בְּתוּלָה, f. pl. בְּתוּלוֹת. Arab. بَتُول, *virgo pura.* Syr. ܒܬܘܠܬܐ, id. I. *A virgin,* Gen. xxiv. 16; 2 Sam. xiii. 2. 18. In Joel i. 8, it has been thought to signify *a young widow:* but, בַּעַל נְעוּרֶיהָ, *Lord of her youth,* might here mean, the *spouse of her youth;* i. e. the person who had espoused her from her very childhood. II. By a personification, put for any people; as, בְּתוּלַת יִשְׂרָאֵל. See בַּת, sign. v. Jer. xviii. 13; xxxi. 4. 21; Amos v. 2; Lam. ii. 13, *Israel;* Is. xlvii. 1, *Babylon;* Jer. xlvi. 11, *Egypt.* Aff. בְּתוּלוֹתַי, בְּתוּלוֹתֶיהָ, בְּתוּלוֹתָיו.

בְּתוּלִים, m. pl. Arab. بُتُولِيَّة, Syr. ܒܬܘܠܘܬܐ, *virginitas.* Propr. *The vouchers for virginity* in women: the entire hymen. Deut. xxii. 14, et seq.; Lev. xxi. 13. Comp. Ezek. xxiii. 3. 8, where its rupture is intimated.

בָּתִּים, m. pl. see בַּיִת.

בְּתִיקוּ, v. pret. pl. m. Pih. once, Ezek. xvi. 40. Aff. cogn. Arab. بَتَّكَ, *secuit.* Æth. *rupit, dirupit, &c. They shall cut thee.* LXX. κατασφάξουσί σε.

בֶּתֶר, c. pl. בְּתָרִים, constr. בִּתְרֵי. Arab. بَتَر, *resectio. A section, part cut off,* Gen. xv. 10; Jer. xxxiv. 19. Aff. בִּתְרוֹ, בְּתָרָיו.

בָּתַר, v. pres. non. occ. Arab. بَتَر, *resecuit. Dissected, divided* by incision, Gen. xv. 10; Ib. Pih. pres. יְבַתֵּר, id.

ג

ג, or גּ, *Gimel.* The third letter of the Hebrew alphabet. Without the point it was probably pronounced like our *gh;* with it, like our *g,* as in *gird,* Gram. artt. 4. 11. 31. 47. 109. Its equivalent in the Arabic, ج is, in Egypt and on the banks of the Tigris, pronounced in the latter manner: in other places generally like our *j.* As to form, it is thought to represent the neck of a camel (גָּמָל); and thence also to take its name. The Syr. ܓ, the Æth. ግ, and Greek Γ, are evidently copied from the Hebrew letter.

It frequently interchanges in the etymology, with letters of the same organ, Gram. art. 23; as, גָּדִישׁ, جَدَسَ, كَدَسَ; גִּזְרִית, גַּם, פֶּנֶה, כَنَز; כِبْرِيت, ܟܒܪܝܬܐ, &c.

גָּא, contr. for גֵּאֶה, Gram. art. 73, i. q.

גֵּאָה, m. pl. גֵּאִים. Syr. ܓܐܐ, *decorus, superbus.* Arab. جاي, *retinuit.* Cogn. جَاءَ, *vi retinuit.* conj. ii. iv. *ad dignitatem evexit.* Pers. جَاه, *dignitas.* Angl. *gay. High, lofty, exulting, proud, insolent,* Is. xvi. 6; ii. 12; with רָם, Job xl. 11, 12; Ps. xciv. 2; cxl. 6; Prov. xv. 25; xvi. 19.

גֵּאָה, contr. for גֵּאֲוָה, f. *Loftiness, pride,* Prov. viii. 13.

גָּאָה, v. pres. יִגְאֶה. I. *Arising, growing high,* as a plant, Job viii. 11; as waters, Ezek. xlvii. 5. II. *Becoming lofty, powerful, proud,* as men, Job x. 16. See my notes. *Victorious,* with reference to God, Exod. xv. 1. 21.

גָּאֹה, Infin. of id. *Triumphing, overcoming*, ib.

גַּאֲוָה, f. constr. גַּאֲוַת. I. *Rising, embossing*, as of a shield, Job xli. 7: comp. Ib. xv. 26. II. Metaph. *Loftiness, majesty*, as of God, Deut. xxxiii. 26; Ps. lxviii. 35. *Elevation, glory*, Deut. xxxiii. 29; Is. xiii. 3. III. *Haughtiness, pride, insolence*, Ps. xxxi. 19. 24; xxxvi. 12; lxxiii. 6; Prov. xiv. 3; Is. ix. 8, &c. Aff. גַּאֲוָתִי, גַּאֲוָתְךָ, גַּאֲוָתָם, גַּאֲוָתוֹ.

גְּאוּלִים, constr. גְּאוּלֵי, r. גאל, *Redeemed*, Is. xxxv. 9; li. 10; Ps. cvii. 2; Is. lxii. 12; lxiii. 4. Aff. גְּאוּלַי. Gesenius makes this word to signify *redemptiones*. But, how this can hold in such places as Is. xxxv. 9, it is out of my power to see.

גָּאוֹן, m. constr. גְּאוֹן, pl. גְּאוֹנִים, Ezek. xvi. 56. Comp. Ps. cxxiii. 4, גֵּאיוֹנִים, intens. of גַּאֲוָה. I. *Sublimity, majesty*, of God, Exod. xv. 7; Is. ii. 10; xxiv. 14; Job xxxvii. 4; xl. 10; Mich. v. 3. II. *Glory, pride*, in either a good or bad sense, Is. iv. 2; xiii. 19; xiv. 11; lx. 15; Ps. xlvii. 5; opp. to שִׁפְלוֹן, Prov. xvi. 18. Comp. Ib. viii. 13; Amos vi. 8. Applied also, III. to the *rising* and *swelling* of waters, Job xxxviii. 11; Jer. xii. 5; xlix. 19; L. 44. Aff. גְּאוֹנְךָ, גְּאוֹנָם, גְּאוֹנוֹ, גְּאוֹנֵךְ.

גֵּאוּת, f. r. גאה. I. *Ascending, towering up*, as smoke, Is. ix. 17. II. *Excellency, majesty*, as of God, Ps. xciii. 1; Is. vi. 10. III. *Haughtiness, pride*, as of men, Is. xxviii. 1. 3. IV. Adverbially, Is. xii. 5, *magnificently, &c.*: Ps. xvii. 10; xxxix. 10, *proudly, insolently*: Ib. lxxxix. 10, *gloriously, &c.*

גֵּאָיוֹת, f. pl. *Valleys*. See גיא.

גֹּאֵל, pl. constr. גֹּאֲלֵי, Neh. xiii. 29, *Pollutings, desecratings of*—

גְּאֵל, or גּוֹאֵל, m. pl. גֹּאֲלִים. Arab.

جَالَ, *ivit, venitque*. Cogn. جول, r. جَالَ *obivit; elegit*. part. جَائِل, *perambulans*. Syr. ܓܳܐܶܠ, *misertus est, protexit*. Cogn.

جَوَار, *vicinitatem inivit: in fidem et clientelam recepit*, conj. iv. أَجَار, *protexit, liberavit ab injustitia*. Comp. جيل, and

جير.

The leading notion here seems to be, as *association* implies the friendly relation of *hospitality*, and as this in the East calls for a participation in repelling the assaults of enemies, as well as in social enjoyments; the person so named was considered, as having a supreme regard for the interests of the society, with which he was thus connected, as—

I. *A near relative*, Lev. xxv. 25; 1 Kings xvi. 11; Ruth ii. 20; iii. 9. 12.

Hence, II. Bound by this consideration, and the law of retaliation, as *An avenger*, to vindicate any injury done to the family, particularly that of man-slaughter; and hence he was styled the *Avenger of blood*, גֹּאֵל הַדָּם, Num. xxxv. 19. 21, &c.

III. Applied to God, as *accompanying* and *avenging* his people, as *Redeemer*, Job xix. 25. גֹּאֲלִי חַי, *My Redeemer*, i. e. avenging Redeemer, *liveth*. Gen. xlviii. 16, joined with מַלְאָךְ, *Angel*. Comp. Is. xliv. 6, with Rev. i. 8; ii. 8; xxi. 6, which will shew that it is a title of Christ. Is. xlix. 7; Ps. ciii. 4, &c.

As such very near relative—the senior usually—was supposed to have at heart the interests of the family, he was also supposed to have *their blood upon him*, until it was duly avenged; hence this expression. Comp. Is. lxiii. 1—7, where our Lord, *as avenging Redeemer*, is thus represented. See also Is. lix. 16—21. Hence the idea of *pollution* in the verb. See also פדה. Aff. גֹּאֲלִי, אָלֵף, אָלֵף, &c.

גָּאַל, v. pres. יִגְאַל. See גאל above: constr. abs. and with מִן. *Par pari referre, Rendering like for like* by the law of retaliation, as the nearest relative or friend. Hence *Redeeming*.

I. By paying like value, *land, &c.* Lev. xxv. 25; Ruth iv. 4—6; Ps. cxix. 154; lxix. 19; xxv. 48, 49; xxvii. 13. 15, &c. Imp. Ruth iv. 4. 6. Infin. גְּאֹל, and גְּאָל, Lev. xxvii. 13; Ruth iv. 6. Aff. גְּאָלָהּ, Ib. iii. 13.

II. *Redeeming* by taking vengeance on injustice, and so repaying it, Exod. vi. 6. Comp. Is. xliii. 1—3; xiv. 22, 23; xlvii. 20; lii. 9; Jer. xxxi. 11. Particularly the shedding of blood. See גֹּאֵל הַדָּם above.

III. *Polluting*; i. e. the being attached with guilt from the neglect of some duty. See גֹּאֵל above; which Gesenius tells us is a *modern Hebræism*; non occ. in Kal.

Niph. I. נִגְאַל, and pl. נִגְאָלוּ, pres. יִגָּאֵל, Lev. xxv. 30. 49. 54; Is. lii. 3.

III. Zeph. iii. 1, with blood, Is. lix. 3; Lam. iv. 14.

Pih. גֵּאַלְנוּךָ, *Have we polluted thee?* i. e. so acted as to have injured thy honour, Mal. i. 7.

גאל (100) גב

Puh. יְגֹאֲלוּ, *Are polluted,* Ezr. ii. 62; Neh. vii. 64, which seems to be a sort of pres. of the Niph. נִגְאַל above. The fact is, the noun גאל is here conjugated. Gram. artt. 182. 193. 6. The sense will be the same in either case.

Hiph. אֶגְאַלְתִּי, Is. lxiii. 3, Gram. art. 195. 5, for הִגְאַלְתִּי, interchanged א with ה.

Hithp. יִתְגָּאַל, i. q. Niph. Dan. i. 8.

גְּאֻלָּה, f. constr. גְאֻלַּת. See גאל. I. *Relationship,* as brotherhood; אֶחָיו גֹאֲלֵי נְאֻלָּתְךָ, Ezek. xi. 15. Hence

II. *Right, duty, of redemption,* מִשְׁפַּט הַגְּאֻלָּה, Jer. xxxii. 7, 8; Lev. xxv. 29. 31. 48. גְּאֻלַּת עוֹלָם, *perpetual id.* Ib. xxv. 32. The property of the Levites being unalienable. Hence, Meton.

III. *Price of redemption,* Lev. xxv. 24. 26. 51, 52. Also, Meton.

IV. *The thing, field, &c. to be so redeemed,* Ruth iv. 6. Aff. גְּאֻלָּתִי, גְאֻלָּתְךָ, גְאֻלָּתוֹ.

גַּב, m. pl. גַּבִּים, and f. גַּבּוֹת, r. גבב. Arab. جَبَّ, *vicit, superavit,* conj. iv. *condensatum, pingue fuit lac,* &c. جَبَبٌ, *sectio gibbi camelini.* Cogn. جَبَنَ, *coagulatum fuit lac. Any curvilinear protuberance;* as,

I. *The back* of man or animal, Ezek. x. 12; Ps. cxxix. 3; or exterior *curvature of wheels,* 1 Kings vii. 33; Ezek. i. 18; or, upper part *of the altar,* Ezek. xliii. 13; or, *embossings* of a shield, Job xv. 26. Comp. xli. 7. Arab. جَوْبٌ, مِجَنٌّ, and مُجَنٌّ, *scutum.* Hence,

II. *Defence,* as *a mound,* Job xiii. 12. Also,

III. *Places elevated* apparently, and set apart for prostitution, Ezek. xvi. 24. 31. 39; *arched,* perhaps, as *the vaults* in use for this purpose among the Romans, termed, *Fornices;* whence *Fornicatio,* i. e. *a vaulting,* or *arching over:* and our *fornication.* Also,

IV. *The arch of the eye-brow,* Lev. xiv. 9.

גַּב, Chald. i. q. Heb. *The back,* Dan. vii. 6.

גֵּב, m. pl. גֵּבִים, as קָם, קָמִים, of קום. By the LXX. γαβίν, or γηβείν, Kethiv, גֵּבִים, r. גוב; Arab. جُوبٌ, or جَيِبٌ, جَابٌ, جَبَّ, *secuit.* lit. *Cutters:* occ. with כֹּרְמִים, *vine-dressers. Ploughmen,* 2 Kings xxv. 12. Comp. Is. lxi. 6. So the ancient verss. The root, however, might be גבה. Arab. جَبَى, *collegit tributum;* whence جُبَاةٌ, *exactores tributorum:* but this is less likely. So our *agriculture,* of *ager,* field; and *culter,* cutter, knife.

גֵּב, m. גֵּבִים, pl. r. as in the last. I. *A locust,* Is. xxxiii. 4. II. *A board* or *plank,* 1 Kings vi. 9. Syr. ܓܒܐ, *lignum sectile, tabula.* III. *A well,* Jer. xiv. 3. Syr. ܓܘܒܐ, *fovea, cisterna.* ܓܘܒܐ, *sepulcrum.* So our *grave.* Germ. *graben,* to dig.

גֹּב, m. def. גֻּבָּא, Syr. ܓܘܒܐ, *A well* used as a prison; and hence, as *a den,* for lions. See בור, and באר, Dan. vi. 8. 17.

גֶּבֶא, m. pl. גְּבָאִים. Arab. جَبَا, cogn. جَبَى, *congregavit, deduxit* aqua in aquarium, جَبًا, جَبْوَةٌ, جَبَاوَةٌ, *aqua in aquario,* ex lapidibus structo, &c. Æth. ኀባእ, *congregatio, &c.* Syr. ܓܒܐ, *collegit. A cistern,* or *pit,* Is. xxx. 14; Ezek. xlvii. 11. Aff. pl. גְּבָאָיו.

גִּבְחָה, m. pl. constr. גִּבְחֵי. Arab. جَبَاهَ, *frons hominis.* جَبْهَة, *latitudo frontis:* hence, Metaph. *Dominus familiæ, populi princeps: despectus*—looking down on one as from *a height.* See cogn. גב above. The ה is here radical, and therefore not subject to elision, Gram. art. 202. 6. I. *Height,* as of the heavens, trees, buildings, &c. Job xxii. 12; Ezek. i. 18; xl. 42; 1 Sam. xvii. 4; Amos ii. 9; pl. constr. Job xi. 8. II. Metaph. as of carriage, deportment, *Pride, haughtiness,* Jer. xlviii. 29, with syn. גֵּאָה, &c. Prov. xvi. 18; Ps. x. 4, with רוּחַ, לֵב, אַף. III. As of dignity, *Majesty,* Job xl. 10, with גָּאוֹן. Aff. גָּבְהָם, גָּבְהוֹ.

גָּבֹהַּ, or גָּבוֹהַּ, m. גְּבֹהָה, f. constr. m. גְּבֹהַּ; pl. m. גְּבֹהִים, f. גְּבֹהוֹת. I. *High,* as a mountain, tower, tree; (a) *Tall* as a man, Is. xxx. 25; xl. 9; Gen. vii. 19; Ezek. xvii. 24; 1 Sam. ix. 2; xvi. 7; as an abstract, (b) *Height,* fem. Deut. iii. 5; 1 Sam. ii. 3. גְּבֹהָה גְבֹהָה, *very high;* i. e. *Speak* not much of any very high thing; or adverbially, *proudly,* 1 Kings xiv. 23; 2 Kings xvii. 10; Dan. viii. 3; Deut. xxviii. 52; Jer. xvii. 2.

II. Metaph. *Lofty, proud,* Is. v. 15; Eccl.

גבה (101) גבו

v. 7. מֵעַל גָּבֹהַּ, *above* the *proud*, i. e. oppressive, Ps. cxxxviii. 6; Ezek. xxi. 31 (26). In some of the preceding cases, as Is. xxx. 25; Ezek. xvii. 24; 1 Sam. ii. 3, &c. the language is evidently metaphorical.

גָּבֵהַּ, m. constr. גְּבֵהַ, in which form only it occurs: i. q. גָּבֹהַּ. I. *High, tall,* as in stature, Ezek. xxxi. 3. II. *Lofty, proud:* with רוּחַ, לֵב, עֵינַיִם. See גָּבַהּ. Ps. ci. 5; Prov. xvi. 5; Eccl. vii. 8.

גָּבַהּ, v. pres. יִגְבַּהּ, 3d pl. fem. תִּגְבְּהֶינָה, Ezek. xvi. 50. Etym. in גֹּבַהּ. I. *Was high, lofty,* as the heavens, trees, stature, Ps. ciii. 11; Is. lv. 9; Job xxxv. 5; Ezek. xix. 11; 1 Sam. x. 23; Ezek. xxxi. 5. גְּבָהָא, for גָּבְהָה, i. e. the Chald. for the Heb. form.
II. *Exalted,* as in dignity and honour, Is. v. 16; lii. 13; Job xxxvi. 7: in a bad sense, *haughty,* Jer. xiii. 15; Is. iii. 16. Constr. with לֵב. (a) In *courage,* 2 Chron. xvii. 6, *His heart was raised, elevated, made bold,* &c. (b) In *insolence, Was lofty, proud, contemptuous,* Ps. cxxxi. 1; Prov. xviii. 12; 2 Chron. xxvi. 16; xxxii. 25; Ezek. xxviii. 2. 17, &c. constr. abs. and med. with עַל, בְּ, מִן, Job xxxv. 5; Ezek. xxviii. 17; Ps. ciii. 11.
Infin. גְּבֹהַּ, and f. גָּבְהָה, Ps. ciii. 11; Zeph. iii. 11.
Hiph. הִגְבִּיהַ, pres. יַגְבִּיהַ, *Raise, exalt,* or *make high,* Ezek. xvii. 24; xxi. 3; Jer. xlix. 16. יַגְבִּיהוּ עוּף, *They make ascend* in *flight,* Job v. 7. See my notes on the place. Comp. ib. xxxix. 27, as used of the eagle. Aff. יַגְבִּיהֶהָ, *He raised it,* 2 Chron. xxxiii. 14.
Imp. or *Infin.* הַגְבֵּהַ, Is. vii. 10; Ezek. xxi. 31.
Part. מַגְבִּיהַ, *Raising, exalting,* Prov. xvii. 19. With the relative ('): הַמַּגְבִּיהִי, *Whose property it is to raise one* לָשֶׁבֶת, *to dwell, reside,* live in circumstances of affluence, &c. Ps. cxiii. 5. Comp. Job v. 11; and see Gram. art. 175. 16.

גַּבְהוּת, f. Gram. art. 87. 2, *Loftiness, pride,* Is. ii. 11. 17.

גְּבוּל, or גְּבֻל, f. גְּבוּלָה, m. pl. גְּבוּלִים and fem. גְּבוּלוֹת. Arab. جَبَلَ, *formavit,* i. e. defined as to form. جَبَلَ, *atrium, agger ad munimentum: mons,*—a natural muniment and boundary. Comp. Gr. ὅρος, and ὅρος. Syr. ܓܒܠ, *formavit.* Cogn. حَبَلَ, *fune adstrinxit, fœdus inivit, securitatem invenit,* حَبَلَ, *coercuit,* &c. I. *Limit, boundary,* of either sea or land, Ps. civ. 9. Comp. Job xxxviii. 10; Jer. v. 22; Deut. xix. 14; xxvii. 17; Prov. xxii. 28. גְּבוּל יָם, *sea-boundary,* i. e. as limited by the sea: *western, id.* Num. xxxiv. 3. 6: formed sometimes by rivers or mountains, Num. xxii. 36; Deut. iii. 16; Josh. xviii. 12, &c.: sometimes by line—rope—geographically, Ps. lxxviii. 55. II. Meton. *The space,* or *country,* so bounded, or defined, Gen. x. 19; Exod. x. 14. 19; 1 Sam. xi. 3. 7; 2 Sam. xxi. 5; 1 Kings i. 3, &c. So pl. Jer. xv. 13, &c. Fem. pl. Deut. xxxii. 8; Ps. lxxiv. 17; Job xxiv. 2; Num. xxxii. 33; Is. x. 13. Aff. גְּבוּלִי, &c. Aff. fem. גְּבֻלֹתַי, pl. גְּבֻלֹתֶיהָ, Is. xxviii. 25; Num. xxxiv. 2, &c.

גִּבּוֹר, or גִּבֹּר, m. pl. גִּבּוֹרִים. Arab. جَبْر, *adolescens, fortis, audax.* Augm. جَبَّار, *magnus, gigas.* جَبِير, *admodum superbus.* Hence the verb, conjugation v. جَبَّر, *invaluit, superbivit,* &c. Æthiop. ኀየለ: *coegit, impulit.* Syr. ܓܒܪ, *id.* I. *Mighty, brave, intrepid:* applied to men as warriors, wealthy, &c. Gen. x. 8, 9, Judg. vi. 12; xi. 1; Ruth iii. 1. In Dan. xi. 3, to Alexander. In Ps. xxiv. 8; lxxviii. 65; Is. xlii. 13; Zeph. iii. 17, &c. to God, as most powerful in war. To Christ, Ps. xlv. 4. 6: comp. ib. cxx. 4; Is. ix. 5: comp. ib. x. 20, et seq. with Rom. ix. 27—29. Gesenius, as the manner of his school is, refers us to Ezek. xxxii. 11, for proof that nothing more than *heros strenuus* can be meant. But in that place the word does not occur. In ver. 12, however, we have, גִּבּוֹרִים, in a context which has nothing in common with ours. II. Meton. *Distinguished* for valour, prowess, 2 Sam. xxiii. 8; 1 Kings i. 8; 1 Chron. xi. 26; xxix. 24: for fidelity, 1 Chron. ix. 26; and thence put into office. Comp. Ezek. xxxix. 20:—for faith, Ps. cxii. 2. Metaph. applied to lions, Prov. xxx. 30. Aff. גִּבּוֹרֵיהֶם, גִּבּוֹרֶיהָ, גִּבּוֹרָיו, גִּבּוֹרֶיךָ, גִּבּוֹרָי.

גְּבוּרָה, f. Arab. جَبْرِيَّة, *fortitudo, robur.* See גִּבּוֹר. I. *Power,* generally; with כֹּחַ, 1 Chron. xxix. 12; 2 Chron. xx. 6: with בִּינָה, Prov. viii. 14. חָכְמָה, Job xii. 13; Eccl. ix. 16. עֵצָה, 2 Kings xviii. 20; Is. xi. 2; xxxvi. 5: with יְיָ, or וְרוֹעַ, Jer. xvi. 21; Es. lxxxix. 14. מַלְכוּת, 1 Chron. xxix. 30. So the Arabic, speaking of God, تَبَرَّنَ

بِالْمَلَكُوتِ - تَوْحَدٍ بِالْجَبَرُوتِ, *alone in kingdom—one in power.* Pref. Kuleini on the Shiah. With גְּבוּר, Jer. ix. 22. Particularly as applied to warlike, or other dangerous, undertakings—

II. *Courage, prowess,* 2 Kings xviii. 20; Is. xxxvi. 5; 1 Chron. xxix. 11; Is. iii. 25, &c. applied either to God or man:—to a prophet in announcing the sins of the people, Mich. iii. 8:—to the war horse, Job xxxix. 19.

III. Meton.—To *acts of power or courage,* 1 Kings xv. 23; xvi. 27; xxii. 46, of Men. It. of God, Deut. iii. 24; Ps. cvi. 2. Gesenius takes עֲנוֹת גְּבוּרָה, Exod. xxxii. 18, to signify *victory.* But, as the context relates to a certain noise made in idolatrous rites, the literal meaning of the phrase seems to be, *the answering of might;* i. e. the shouting of armies drawing near for the conflict. See the rest of the verse: LXX. ἐξαρχόντων κατ' ἰσχύν. Targ. Onk. *fortium prævalentium in pugna.*

Chald. id. def. גְּבוּרְתָּא, Dan. ii. 20. Syr. ܓܢܒܪܘܬܐ, *virilitas.*

גֶּבַח, m. occ. once, Lev. xiii. 41. Arab. كَمَحَ, *necessaria illis negavit.* Cogn. كَاحَ r. كُوحٌ, *vile demonstravit.* كَوْخَةٌ, *domus fenestrâ carens.* قَمَحَ, *deformis fuit.* قَاحَ r. قَوْحٌ *contabuit morbo, &c. want, defect, deformity, from disease, apparently.—Bald,* from disease. Comp. נִמְרָט. Gesenius tells us that it is, i. q. גָּבַהּ, *altum fuit;* and that the word means, "*qui frontem habet nimis altum.*" I can find nothing whatever about the forehead; nor can I see what the forehead can have particularly to do with this disease. This baldness, for all we know, might have occurred any where else.

גַּבַּחַת, f. of גִּבֵּחַ, occ. with קָרַחַת. I. *Baldness* in man, Lev. xiii. 42, 43.

II. *Loss of the knap,* probably marking the existence of an infectious disease in cloth, Ib. vr. 55. Aff. גַּבַּחְתּוֹ. Gesenius says, this word signifies *baldness* in the forehead, קָרַחַת, *baldness* in the back part of the head. But this cannot be true: for, 1st, we read of קָרְחָה (syn.) being *between the eyes,* Deut. xiv. 1; and, 2d, of the whole head being קָרְחָה, Is. xv. 2; Jer. xlviii. 37; Ezek. vii. 18. The truth seems to be, that the former signifies *partial baldness* from disease; this *entire*

baldness from shaving, &c. Arab. قَرَحَ, *vulneravit, &c.* قِرَاحٌ, *campus consitus, arborum, omnisque structuræ expers.* قُرْحَةٌ, *macula alba in fronte equi, &c.*

גְּבִי, see גּוּבַי.

גְּבִינָה, f. Syr. ܓܒܝܢܬܐ, *coagulatio;* ܓܒܢܐ, *caseus;* ܐܬܓܒܢ, it. ܐܬܓܒܢ, 2 Sam. xvi. 2; omisit Castell. r. جبن, *coagulatus est,* &c. Arab. جُبْنٌ, *caseus.* Æth. ይጅብን: id. occ. Job x. 10, only. *Cheese.*

גָּבִיעַ, m. גְּבִיעִים, pl. Arab. جُبَّاعٌ, *mulier statura brevis.* Cogn. قَبَعَة, *calyx florum;* it. *mitra,* Heb. כבע, and קובע, it. قَبَاءٌ, *potu repetus fuit.* I. *A chalice,* or sort of *jug,* for wine, &c. Gen. xliv. 2. 12, &c.; filled with wine, Jer. xxxv. 5. Hence, II. The *Cup* or *Bell* of flowers, as exhibited artificially, Exod. xxv. 31, et seq.; xxxvii. 17. 19. Aff. גְּבִיעָהָ, גְּבִיעֵי.

גָּבִיר, m. pl. non occ. See גְּבוּר, *Potentate, Lord,* occ. only Gen. xxvii. 29. 37.

גְּבִירָה, f. of the last, *Powerful woman:* pec. *Queen,* consort, or mother, 1 Kings xi. 19; 2 Kings x. 13; Jer. xxix. 2; 1 Kings xv. 13; 2 Chron. xv. 16.

גָּבִישׁ, m. usually, *Crystal, a gem,* or *pearl.* From the context in which it occurs, however, viz. Job xxviii. 18, I am inclined to believe that it rather signifies, *massive, heavy;* hence, most valuable metal, or the like. Arab. جِبْسٌ, *inanimatum, ut lapis, gravis lingua.* See my note on the place, and אלגבישׁ above.

גָּבַל, v. pres. יִגְבּוֹל. See גְּבוּל above. *Limiting, determining the boundary* of, any place, Deut. xix. 14; Josh. xviii. 20; Zech. ix. 2. Constr. abs. med. with את and בְּ.

Hiph. הִגְבִּיל, and Imp. הַגְבֵּל, *Make limited, set bounds to,* Exod. xix. 12. 23; constr. אֶת.

גַּבְלוּת, f. Syr. ܓܒܠܘܬܐ, *fictio, plasmatio.* Arab. جِبْلَةٌ, *plasma, figmentum.* Cogn. Æth. ገብር: *opus, &c.* lit. *Formation;* i. e. *Artificial work* or *device.* Occurs only twice, Exod. xxviii. 22; xxxix. 15, in the phrase שַׁרְשְׁרוֹת גַּבְלֻת, and contr.

שַׁרְשֹׁת גַּבְלֻת; explained in both cases by מַעֲשֵׂה עֲבֹת; where מַעֲשֵׂה is evidently the rendering intended for גַּבְלֻת, and עֲבֹת, for שַׁרְשְׁרֹת. For, עֲבֹת signifies *ropes*, Ps. ii. 3, to which שַׁרְשְׁרֹת, *chains*, i. e., woven work representing *chains*, sufficiently well corresponds. See r. עבד. Gesenius, therefore, is wrong in making גַּבְלֻת and עֲבֹת synonymous. Nor does גבל signify *torsit*, either in Heb. or in any one of the dialects: his *opus tortile*, therefore, as given to explain this word, is manifestly erroneous. Nor does Exod. xxviii. 14, nor the rendering of the LXX. tend in the least to confirm his view of the question. The whole is therefore groundless.

גִּבֵּן, m. occ. once, Lev. xxi. 20. Syr. ܓܒܢ, *coagulatus est*. Arab. جَبَّن, id. Cogn. جَبَل, *crassus, grossusque*, it. كَبَن, *pinguis et crassus fuit* digitus. *Bunch-backed.*

גִּבְּנִים, m. pl. Words signifying *colour, deformity,* and the like, augm. by doubling the second radical letter in the Arab. See גֵּבֶן above. *Risings,* as of a hill or hillock; as we say of *Clapham-rise, &c.* Ps. lxviii. 16. הַר גַּבְנֻנִּים הַרְבָּשָׁן, *The hill of Bashan* is a *hill of risings, eminences;* i. e. fit for a place of defence. In the par. הַר אֱלֹהִים, *hill of God;* i. e. place of strength, invincible. It is added, ver. 17, *Why do you leap ye hills, eminences;* i. e. strong invincible places? Intimating their capture or levelling, &c.; comp. Is. xl. 4. Comp. also ver. 19 with Eph. iv. 8; foretelling that such apparently strong places should at Christ's coming entirely give way. See also Is. xxx. 25.

גִּבְעָה, f. pl. גְּבָעוֹת, constr. גִּבְעַת, גִּבְעוֹת, of seg. גִּבְעִי. Arab. جِبَاعَة, *dorsi* pars prior. Cogn. قَبَا, r. قبو, *extulit ædificium, rem rei ingessit.* قَبَع, *gibbosus fuit.* Comp. קָמַע I. *A hill,* 2 Sam. ii. 25; Is. xxx. 25; Jer. ii. 20; Job xv. 7; Ps. lxv. 13; Gen. xlix. 26; Deut. xxxiii. 15. גִּבְעָתִי, *My hill;* i. e. God's hill, *Zion,* Ezek. xxxiv. 26. So גִּבְעָתָהּ, *her hill, Zion's hill,* Is. xxxi. 4. And, II. because cities were often built on hills, for security against attacking parties, many places take this word in a compound as their name; as in our *burgh,* and the German

berg, hill; Edinburgh, Königsberg, &c. So according to Gesenius, the ancient *dunum*, as, *Augustodunum, Lugdunum, &c.* Heb. גִּבְעַת בִּנְיָמִין, 1 Sam. xiii. 15. See also 2 Sam. xxiii. 29; 1 Sam. x. 5; xi. 4; Hos. v. 8; ix. 9; x. 9, &c.

גִּבְעָתִי, m. Patronym. 1 Chron. xii. 3.

גִּבְעֹל, m. compd. perhaps, of גָּבִיעַ, sign. II. above, and גֹּל. See גַּבְלֻת; i. e. *Cup*, or *flower-forming,* spoken of flax, once Exod. ix. 31. Gram. art. 169. 2, et seq. In this case, we need not suppose with Dr. Gesenius, that ב *in,* has been omitted by the ellipsis; nor that we have a compound of גָּבִיעַ, and the Syr. ܦܠ, *flos, &c.*: nor need we regard the very abstruse dissertations of the learned Jews, alluded to by him and partly cited in his Thesaurus, about this word, as they do not afford us one syllable of real knowledge on the subject.

גֶּבֶר, m. pl. גְּבָרִים. See גִּבּוֹר. Seg. propr. *vis,* pl. *vires;* whence *vir.* Abstr. for concrete, as in מֶלֶךְ, &c. Gram. art. 152. 10. I. *A man,* i. q. אִישׁ, generally. See Deut. xxii. 5; 1 Chron. xxiv. 4; xxvi. 12: and comp. Ps. i. 1 with Ib. xxxiv. 9; xciv. 12.

II. *A husband,* Prov. vi. 34; Ps. cxxviii. 5.

III. *Warlike man,* Judg. v. 30; Jer. xxx. 6; xli. 16. Hence, generally carrying with it the notion of *strength, courage, violence,* or the like. See Is. xxii. 17; Job xxxviii. 3; xl. 7; Ps. lxxxviii. 5, &c.

IV. Used distributively, like אִישׁ, *Man by man;* לַגְּבָרִים, *viritim,* Josh. xvii. 14. 17. it, *Each,* Joel ii. 8; Lam. iii. 19.

גָּבַר, m. i. q. גֶּבֶר, in the Chaldee form Ps. xviii. 26; 2 Sam. xxii. 6. So Dan. i. 25; v. 11.

Pl. גֻּבְרִין, def. גֻּבְרַיָּא, *Men:* taking a different seg. form, Dan. iii. 8; vi. 6, &c.

גָּבֵר, or גָּבַר, v. pres. יִגְבַּר. See גִּבּוֹר. Cogn. כבר. Arab. كَبَرَ. *Was powerful, mighty;* hence, meton. *prevailed,* spoken of the flood, of an enemy, wealth, blessings, &c. Gen. vii. 18; Exod. xvii. 11; Job xxi. 7; Gen. xlix. 26: constr. abs. and with מִן or עַל when comparison is instituted, Gen. xlix. 26; 2 Sam. i. 23; xi. 23; Ps. lxv. 4. With ב of instrument or place, 1 Sam. ii. 9; Jer. ix. 2.

Pih. גִּבֵּר, pres. יְגַבֵּר, *Making strong, powerful,* Zech. x. 6. 12; Eccl. x. 10: constr. immed. with ב instr.

גבר

Hiph. הִגְבִּיר, pres. יַגְבִּיר. I. as in Kal, Ps. xii. 5. With לְ instr.

II. *Cause to prevail; confirm, ratify,* Dan. ix. 27, immed.:—i. e. during the last week of the seventy, and in the first portion of this, emphatically termed the *last time, latter day, &c.* by the apostles, God shall make His covenant of grace to prevail far and near by their preaching. See my Exposition of the Revelation, p. 357.

Hithp. יִתְגַּבֵּר, *Become powerful, victorious,* Job xv. 25; xxxvi. 9; Is. xlii. 13: abs. and with עַל and אֶל, of person against whom.

גִּבָּר, m. pl. constr. גִּבֹּרֵי, Chald. i. q. Heb. גִּבּוֹר, *Hero, warlike man,* Dan. iii. 20.

גְּבֶרֶת, f. "pro גְּבִירָה," says Gesenius, as if derived from גְּבִיר (but the fem. here is גְּבִירָה). I doubt this, because I know of no instance in which an *immutable* (י) is thus disposed of, Gram. art. 153. 7. It is most likely a fem. of גֶּבֶר, or גְּבִר: i. e. גְּבֶרֶת for גְּבַרְתְּ: and, by an *oblique* correspondence, Ib. art. 96. 2. גְּבִרְתִּי, aff. גְּבִרְתִּי, &c. *Lady, mistress,* Is. xlvii. 5. 7, Gen. xvi. 4. 8, 9; 2 Kings v. 3; Ps. cxxiii. 2; Prov. xxx. 23.

גַּג, m. constr. גַּג, pl. of גַּגּוֹת. Arab. cogn. جَاج, *constitit.* مسجاج, *angustiatus,* it. جَاجَا, *coercuit, finivit.* it. وَجَحَّ, *operuit* domum, tentoriumve. it. الجِيح, *the expanding of any thing,* Kāmoos. Gesenius here accuses Golius and Castell with giving جَح, when جَح is the true root. The error is due to Golius, for even Giggeius has it not; yet it ought to be mentioned, that each of these great Lexicographers has the true root in its proper place. I. *The covering* or *roof* of a house, &c. which is flat in the East, and used for various purposes, Josh. ii. 6. 8; 1 Sam. ix. 25, 26; Prov. xxi. 9; Judg. ix. 51; xvi. 27. II. Of the altar, Exod. xxx. 3; xxxvii. 26. With ה, versus גָּגָה, err. for גָּגָּה, or with Dag. impl. Aff. גַּגֵּךְ, גַּגּוֹ, גַּגּוֹתָיו, גַּגּוֹתָם.

גַּד, m. r. גוד, *Coriander seed.* See Celsii Hierobot. ii. p. 78, et seq. ib. 81, " .... Γοίδ, quod Africanis coriandrum est, ut docet auctor ignotus, sed utilissimus, qui Dioscoridem synonymis exoticis auxit et illustravit. 'Αιγύπτιοι, inquit. Οχιον, Αφροί γοίδ," Dioscor. p. 364. This author Gesenius makes to be Dioscorides himself; these

גד

Africans, Phœnicians, Exod. xvi. 31; Num. xi. 7. See גדלח, Is. lxv. 11. See גַּד following.

גַּד, m. Arab. جَدّ, *avus paternus; felicitas.* Cogn. جَوَال, *liberalis.* Syr. ܓܰܕ, *fortuna,* Gen. xxx. 11. גַּד, *in happiness, good fortune,* if we take the *kethiv;* but if the *keri,* בָּא גָד, *felicity, &c. cometh.* Comp. Job iii. 25, 26. The LXX. ἐν τύχῃ, Vulg. *feliciter,* take the *kethiv.* The Targ. Onkel. and Syr. the *keri.* In Gen. xlix. 19, as Jacob had heavy tidings to announce, certain to befal the Jews in *the latter* days, another signification deduced from this root is alluded to. Hence the name of a tribe. In Is. lxv. 11, *a deity, Baal* most likely. In the parall. מְנִי, perhaps, the *Manu* of the Hindoos. See also Selden de Diis Syris, Syntag. cap. i.

גָּדַד, v. pres. יָגֹד. Arab. جَدّ, *resecuit vestem, putavit palmam, &c.* جَدُود, *succisa res.* Syr. ܓܕ, *abscidit;* hence, ܓܕܐ, *acies militaris:* i. e. section or detachment of an army. Arab. جَاد, r. جود, *egregio incessu et cursu polluit* equus, & جاد بنفس, *incessivit vicitque* eum *amor. Assault, attack,* as of an army, Ps. xciv. 21: constr. עַל. Comp. Gen. xlix. 19; Heb. iii. 16; i. q. גוד.

Hithp. יִתְגּוֹדֵד. I. *Cutting, making incisions* in the flesh, on account of sorrow, shame, &c. Deut. xiv. 1; 1 Kings xviii. 28; Jer. xvi. 6; xli. 5; xlvii. 5.

II. *Assembling,* or *attacking,* as troops, Jer. v. 7; Mich. iv. 14.

גְּדַד, v. Chald. *Cut,* or *cut down,* as a tree. Imp. גֹּדּוּ, Dan. iv. 11. 20.

גְּדוּד, m. pl. גְּדוּדִים, and גְּדוּדוֹת, constr. גְּדוּדֵי. I. *Cutting,* or *incision,* in the flesh, Jer. xlviii. 37; in the ground, *furrows,* Ps. lxv. 11.

II. *Section,* or *detachment,* of an army, mostly for the purposes of foraging, Gen. xlix. 19; 2 Kings v. 2, &c. Phr. רָאשֵׁי הַגְּדוּד, *Heads, commanders, of the detachment,* 1 Chron. xii. 18. Comp. 1 Kings xi. 24. בְּנֵי הַגְּדוּד, *lads of the detachment;* i. e. the men composing it, 2 Chron. xxv. 13. בַּת גְּדוּד, *daughter of a troop;* i. e. possessing great power, Mich. iv. 14. גְּדוּדֵי יְהֹוָה, *troops of Jehovah;* i. e. the heavenly hosts and earthly powers at His command, Job xix. 12; xxv. 3. Aff. גְּדוּדַי.

גָּדוֹל , גָּדֹל , m. constr. גְּדוֹל , or גְּדָל־ thrice in the keri, גְּדָל־ , according to Gesenius: pl. גְּדוֹלִים, גְּדֹלִים, constr. גְּדוֹלֵי, f. גְּדוֹלָה, גְּדֹלָה, pl. גְּדוֹלוֹת, or גְּדֹלוֹת. Syr. ࡓࡁ, contorsit, implicavit. Arab. جَدَلَ, firmiter torsit. Cogn. جِذْل, rei cujusque radix, spec. magna arboris.

Great, in extent, number, quantity, age, dignity, joy, sorrow, operation, &c. as the context may require, Num. xxxiv. 6; Gen. xii. 2; Exod. xv. 16; Gen. x. 21; xxvii. 1; Exod. xi. 3; 2 Kings v. 1; Job i. 3; Hag. i. 1. 12. 14; Prov. xviii. 16; 2 Kings x. 6. 11; Neh. viii. 12; Gen. L. 10; xxxix. 9, &c. Aff. גְּדוֹלָיו, &c.

גְּדוּלָה, or גְּדֻלָּה, f. constr. גְּדֻלַּת, pl. גְּדֻלּוֹת. See גָּדֹל, fm. פָּקַד; hence, I. concr. Great deed or act, &c. 2 Sam. vii. 23; 1 Chron. xvii. 19. Pl. Ps. cxlv. 6: 1 Chron. xvii. 19. 21.

II. Abstr. Greatness, majesty, magnificence, of God, Ps. cxlv. 3; of the king, Ps. lxxi. 21; Esth. i. 4.

גְּדוּפִים, m. pl. and גְּדוּפוֹת, f. Syr. ࡂࡃࡐ , maledictis insectatus est. Arab. جَدَفَ, blasphemavit. Reproaches, Is. xliii. 28; li. 7; Zeph. ii. 8. Syn. חֲרָפָה.

גְּדוּדוֹת, f. pl. sing. non occ. Arab. جَذَّ, avulsit. Cogn. جَذَّ, fregit, secuit, abrupit. Æth. ኀፀነ: pulsavit, feriit, pectus. Syr. ࡂࡃࡏ, abscidit, traxit. it. Sam. The banks of a river, Josh. iii. 15; iv. 18; Is. viii. 7. Aff. גְּדוֹתָיו, 1 Chron. xii. 15. גְּדִיתָיו, a mere error of some copyist.

גָּדִי, m. Patronym. of גָּד, A Gadite, 2 Kings xv. 14.

גְּדִי, m. pl. גְּדָיִים, constr. גְּדָיֵי. Seg. fm. פְּקָד, or פָּקָד. Arab. جَدْيٌ, hædus. Syr. ࡂࡃࡉࡀ, id. saliens, ascendens q. capræ saltu delectantur multum, et ascensa. Castell. Arab. cogn. جَدَّ, firmus constitit. A kid of the goats, Exod. xxiii. 19; xxxiv. 26; Deut. xiv. 21; Is. xi. 6. Occasionally in constr. with עִזִּים, Gen. xxxviii. 17. 20; Judg. vi. 19; 1 Sam. x. 3; Gen. xxvii. 9. 16.

גְּדִיּוֹת, f. pl. of גְּדִיָּה, f. of גְּדִי: once only, Cant. i. 8; with aff. גְּדִיֹּתַיִךְ, thy female kids.

גְּדִילִים, m. pl. sing. non occ. Syr. ࡂࡃࡉࡋ, flexuosus. Arab. جَدُول, contorsic. Plattings not unlike chain-work. So 1 Kings vii. 17, גְּדִלִים מַעֲשֵׂה שַׁרְשְׁרוֹת, in con. with שְׁנָה. Comp. Deut. xxii. 12. Iterum non occ. Gesenius makes it equivalent to the French Feston: for which I can discover no good grounds.

גָּדִישׁ, m. pl. non occ. Syr. ࡂࡃࡉࡔࡀ, acervus tritici, &c. Arab. جَدَشَ, ambivit rem. Cogn. جَدِيس, acervus frumenti, tumulus lapidum. It. جَدَث, sepulchrum, monumentum, A heap of any thing, pec. I. Of corn, probably a stack or mow, Exod. xxii. 5, וְנֶאֱכַל גָּדִישׁ אוֹ הַקָּמָה, And a stack or the standing corn be consumed. Comp. Judg. xv. 5; Job v. 26. II. A monumental tumulus; the best sort of which were constructed of stone, or marble, as the pyramids of Egypt, and the tomb of Cyrus, in Persia. See my note on Job xxi. 32; the worst, of heaps of earth, as in the tumuli often seen in this country, and the much larger ones in Koordistan, as shewn in the note just referred to, Job xxi. 32.

גֹּדֶל, c. pl. non occ. See גָּדוֹל, Greatness, magnificence, might, glory; either in a good or bad sense, as the context shall require:— of God, Deut. iii. 24; v. 21; xxxii. 3, &c. In a bad sense, Is. ix. 8; x. 12; Ezek. xxxi. 2. 7. 18. Aff. גָּדְלוֹ, once. גָּדְלֶךָ, גָּדְלְךָ, גָּדְלִי.

גָּדַל, see גָּדוֹל.

גָּדַל, m. i. q. גָּבַל, Increasing, growing: occ. with הָלַךְ, implying gradual progress, Gen. xxvi. 13; 1 Sam. ii. 26; 2 Chron. xvii. 12.

גְּדֵלִים, m. pl. constr. (of גָּדֵל, not in use,) not of גָּדוֹל, as Gesenius thinks: this would give גְּדוֹלֵי, Gram. art. 153. 5; Ezek. xvi. 26. Great.

גָּדַל, v. pres. יִגְדַּל. See גָּדוֹל, Was, or grew, great, in (stature,) wealth, dignity, estimation, extent, &c. Gen. xxi. 8; xxv. 35; xxv. 27; xxvi. 13; xxxviii. 14; xli. 40; Exod. ii. 10, 11; Ezra ix. 6; Job xxxi. 18, גְּדֵלַנִי כְאָב, "adolevit mihi orphanus sicut patri." Gesenius and others. But, on

P

גדל (106) גדף

what these datives, viz. "*mihi*" and "*patri*" are grounded, it will be difficult to say. If, however, we take the antecedent to be *God*, as implied in vr. 15, and the verb as in Pih. גַּמְלֵנִי, we shall have an obvious and consistent sense. See my notes on the passage. Constr. abs. it. med. בְּ, אֶת, לְ, עַד, מִן.

Pih. גִּדֵּל, and גִּדֵּל, pres. יְגַדֵּל, *Made great*, i. e. *brought up, trained, educated, made wealthy, powerful; pronounced great*, i. e. magnified, applied to persons, or things. 2 Kings x. 6; Is. i. 2; xxiii. 4; xliv. 14; Ezek. xxxi. 4; Josh. iv. 14; Esth. iii. 1; v. 11; x. 2; Gen. xii. 2; Ps. xxxiv. 4; lxix. 31. Constr. *immed. med.* אֶת, בְּ, לְ, instr. מִן, comp.

Infin. גַּדֵּל, Num. vi. 5; 1 Chron. xxix. 12; Josh. iii. 7.

Imp. pl. גַּדְּלוּ, Ps. xxxiv. 4.

Part. pl. מְגַדְּלִים, 2 Kings x. 6.

Puh. part. pl. מְגֻדָּלִים, passive of Pih. Ps. cxliv. 12.

Hiph. הִגְדִּיל, pres. יַגְדִּיל. I. *Became*, or *grew great*, either in a good or bad sense, Ps. lv. 13; Jer. xlviii. 26; Dan. viii. 8. 11. So the phrases, הִגְדִּיל תּוּשִׁיָּה, *He hath become great*, shewn himself to be so, *substantially*, Is. xxviii. 29. הִגְדִּיל לַעֲשׂוֹת,—*for, in, operation*, Ps. cxxvi. 2, 3; Joel ii. 20, 21; Dan. viii. 25; Ezek. xxxv. 13, &c.

II. *Made great*, הִגְדִּיל עִמָּכֶם, *made great with you*; i. e. done magnificently, 1 Sam. xii. 24; Is. ix. 2; xlii. 21; Eccl. ii. 4; Gen. xix. 19; Ps. cxxxviii. 2. הִגְדַּלְתָּ עַל־כָּל־שִׁמְךָ אִמְרָתֶךָ, *Thou hast made* (i. e. surely shalt make) *great thy name, thy word, above all*. I take שִׁמְךָ, and אִמְרָתֶךָ, to be in apposition, signifying the same thing: here Christ as being both the *name* and *word* of God. See vv. 4, 5, et seq. Constr. עִם, לְ, עַל, עַד, בְּ, instr. *immed.* and abs.

Infin. 1 Chron. xxii. 5.

Part. מַגְדִּיל, 2 Sam. xxii. 51; pl. Ps. xxxv. 26.

Hithp. הִתְגַּדַּלְתִּי, pres. יִתְגַּדָּל, i. q. Hiph. sign. I. Ezek. xxxviii. 23; Is. x. 15; Dan. xi. 36, 37. Constr. *abs.* and *med.* עַל.

גְּדֻלָּה, see גְּדוּלָה.

גָּדַע, v. pres. יִגְדַּע. Arab. جَدَعَ, *amputavit*. Cogn. جَلَعَ, *separavit*. جَرَعَ, *sorpsit*. جَزَّ, *resecuit*. جَزَا, *partitus fuit*. جَزَّا, *pensavit*. جَزَعَ, *secuit*. Syr. ܓܰܕ, *abscidit*.

ܓܰܕ, *totondit*. ܓܕܥ, *amputavit*, &c. Syr. גדד, גוּז, גּוּעַ, גּוּר, גוּח, גּוּז, Chald. גּוּז, &c. *Cut off*, or *down*, as an arm, bar, tree, staff, horn, i. e. strength, images, shrines; constr. *immed.* and with אֶת; בְּ instr. Lam. ii. 3; 1 Sam. ii. 31; Judg. xxi. 6; Zech. xi. 10. 14.

Niph. נִגְדַּע, pres. non occ. *Became cut off*, or *down*, Jer. L. 23; xlviii. 25; Is. xxii. 25; xiv. 12; Ezek. vi. 6; Amos iii. 14.

Pih. גִּדַּע, or גִּדֵּעַ, pres. יְגַדֵּעַ, 1st pers. אֲגַדֵּעַ, *Cut off*, or *caused to be cut off*, or *down*, 2 Chron. xxxi. 1; xxxiv. 4. 7; xiv. 2; Deut. vii. 5; xii. 3; Is. xlv. 2; Ps. lxxv. 11; cvii. 16; 2 Chron. xiv. 2; xxxi. 1; xxxiv. 4. 7.

Puh. גֻּדָּעוּ, *They have been cut down*, Is. ix. 9.

גָּדַף, v. Pih. Kal non occ. See גִּדּוּפִים, above, occ. with חֵרֵף. *Blasphemed*, 2 Kings xix. 22; Is. xxxvii. 23; pl. 2 Kings xix. 6; Is. xxxvii. 6; Ezek. xx. 27, pres. non occ. Constr. *med.* אֵת.

Part. מְגַדֵּף, Num. xv. 30; Ps. xliv. 17, with. מְחָרֵף.

גֶּדֶר, m. abstr. Arab. جَدْر, *paries*. Syr. ܓܕܪ *inclusio*. Cogn. Arab. كَدَر, *turbidus fuit*. كَدَر, *juvenis compactus corpore*. Syr. ܟܕܪ, *superfluè in verba provectus*. Heb. כִּדּוּר, *globus*. כִּדּוּר, *Compacting, driving together*, hence *attack*. See my note on Job xv. 24. Cogn. כד, whence כַּד, *cadus, urceus*. Arab. كداء, *collis*. قَدَر, *valuit, magni æstimavit*. II. conj. *justa magnitudine secuit; coxit in olla*. قِدْرَة, *olla, because containing something*: hence the notion of *blackness* in Heb. קדר. Cogn. כתר, כשר, קשר. Syr. ܩܕܪ, Arab. كدر; and, as Gesenius thinks, Germ. *gatter, gitter, &c.*, and perhaps, our *gard, garden, ward, warden, gather*, &c. lit. *A walling*; i. e. *Wall, fence*, apparently of stone, Ezek. xlii. 10; Prov. xxiv. 31.

גָּדֵר, m. גְּדֵרָה, f. concr. pl. גְּדֵרִים, and גְּדֵרוֹת, constr. גִּדְרוֹת. I. *A wall* or *fence*. See גֵּדֶר, i. q. מְשׂוּכָה, Is. v. 5, i. e. of a garden, city, &c. Num. xxii. 24; Ezek. xlii. 7; Ps. lxii. 4; lxxxix. 41.

II. Meton. *Walled* or *fenced* place, city, sheep-fold, &c. Num. xxxii. 16. 24. 36; Ezra ix. 9. Aff. גְּדֵרוֹ, גְּדֵרֲךָ, גְּדֵרַי, pl. f. גְּדֵרוֹתָי.

גָּדַר, v. pres. pl. תִּגְדְּרוּ. See גֶּדֶר. *Walled*

גדר (107) גוד

or *fenced up*. Constr. *med.* אֶת and בְּ, instr. it. עַל, and *immed.* Hos. ii. 8; Amos ix. 11; Lam. iii. 7. 9; Job xix. 8.

Part. ac. גֹּדֵר, pl. גֹּדְרִים, *Waller up*, Is. lviii. 12; Ezek. xxii. 30; 2 Kings xii. 13.

גְּדֵרִי, m. Patronym. of בֵּית־גָּדֵר, or גֵּדֶר, 1 Chron. xxvii. 28.

גֵּה, for זֶה probably, Ezek. xlvii. 13. Comp. vr. 15. So 14 MSS. the LXX. Chald. and Vulg.

גֵּהָה, f. Cogn. גֵּאָה, which see. Syr. ܓܗܐ, *libertas*. Arab. جَهِيٌّ, *patuit*. Conj. II. *Dilatavit*. III. *Gloriatus fuit*. *Health, elevation* of spirit, &c. Prov. xvii. 22. Hence—

גָּהָה, v. not in use; pres. יִגְהֶה, Hos. v. 12. לֹא יִגְהֶה מִכֶּם מָזוֹר, *He* (Assyria) *cannot raise, take up, from you* (the) *pressure*, difficulty.

גהר, pret. non occ. pres. יִגְהַר. Cogn. Syr. ܓܗܪ, *procubuit*. Arab. جَهَنَ, *appropinquavit*. *Bowed*, or *bent*, *downwards*, 1 Kings xviii. 42; 2 Kings iv. 34, 35. Constr. med. עַל, and ה, versus.

גֵּו, or גֵּו, m. גֵּוָה, f. Arab. جَوٌّ, *apposito assumento resarcivit* utrem. جَوٌّ, *depressior terræ locus*: it. *interior* pars *domûs*. جَوَاءٌ, *ampla terra vallisve*. Syr. ܓܘܐ, *medium, pars intima*. ܓܘܐ, *communitas*. Cogn. Heb. גַּב. The first having the root גוו, hence aff. פָּן, &c.; the second, גוו, or גִּיו: hence aff. גֵּו, &c. Generally *the Body*, which when viewed externally,

I. *The back*, Prov. x. 13; xxvi. 3; Is. xxxviii. 17; L. 6; li. 23; f. Job xx. 25; 1 Kings xiv. 9; Ezek. xxiii. 35; viewed internally, II. *The midst*. מָן גֵּו, from *the midst*; i. e. society, *are they driven*, Job xxx. 5. It. Chald. בְּגוֹ נוּרָא, *in the midst of the fire*; i. e. בְּ, resolved into וֹ, Gram. art. 87. 1; Dan. iii. 25; iv. 7, &c. Aff. גֵּוָה, *in it*, Ezra iv. 15. With א, otiose גֵּוָא, Dan. iii. 6. 26, &c.

גּוֹב, m. Arab. جَابَ, r. جوب, *secuit*, &c. See גבה, *A locust*, Nah. iii. 17; pl. גּוֹבַי, for גּוֹבַי, Gram. art. 17. 3; constr. for abs. form. it. גֹּבַי, id. Amos vii. 1; Nah. iii. 17. גּוֹב גּוֹבַי, *locust of locusts*; i. e. a great cloud of them.

גּוּד, v. pres. יָגוּד. Cogn. גדד, which see. Arab. جَالَ, *velox* in actionibus. اَجَالَ, *equum cursu præstantem habuit*. With בְּ, epenth. יְגוּדֶנּוּ, *shall rush (on) him*, Gen. xlix. 19; Hab. iii. 16. Constr. *abs.* and *immed.*

גֵּוָה, f. see גֵּו. Syn. τοῦ. גֵּאָה, or גֵּאָה. I. *Elevation*, success, victory, Job xxii. 29. II. *Haughtiness*, pride, Job xxxiii. 17. Chald. id. Dan. iv. 34.

גּוּז, v. pret. גָּז, pres. יָגֹז. Syr. ܓܙ, *consumptus est*, *defecit*, *transiit*. Arab. جَازَ, r. جوز, *abivit*, *transivit*. Comp. جَزَى, جَزَاءٌ, جَزَاءً.—Ps. xc. 10, כִּי גָז חִישׁ וַנָּעֻפָה, *For it fails, passes away, quickly, and accordingly we fly* (as it were birds) *away*; i. e. *their pride*, ib. רָהְבָּם, *fails*, &c. See too Gram. art. 234. Num. xi. 31. וַיָּגָז שַׂלְוִים וג״י, *So quails passed*, &c. There exists no necessity here, therefore, for making the verb causative, as Gesenius, &c. have supposed. They have mistaken the nominative.

גּוֹזָל, m. pl. Aff. גּוֹזָלָיו. Arab. جَوْزَلٌ, *adolescens, pullus columbinus*. Syr. metath. ܓܘܙܠܐ, *pulli columbarum*. *A young pigeon*, Gen. xv. 9; Deut. xxxii. 11.

גוח see גיח.

גּוֹי, m. pl. גּוֹיִים, for גּוֹיִם, Gram. art. 72. Constr. גּוֹיֵי. Cogn. Heb. גֵּו, גֵּוָה, גֵּאָה, גֵּא. Syr. ܓܘܐ, *communitas*. Arabic جَاوَى, جَوَاءٌ, *ampla terra*. جَاوَى, *castra*. *A nation*, generally; especially, I. *Foreign*, as opposed to Israel; like the Greek βάρβαροι, and Arab. عجم, Gen. xxxv. 11; Deut. iv. 7, 8. 34; xxviii. 36. 49, 50; Jer. xxxi. 10; Ezek. xxiii. 30; Ps. ii. 1; ix. 6, &c. II. Applied to Israel, as partaking of their practices, Is. i. 4; ix. 2: to the nations, as receiving Christianity, Ib. xxvi. 2; xlix. 7. Here גּוֹי לְמָתָעֵב, *Of, respecting* (not *to*) the abhorred *of a nation*; i. e. of the Jews. Comp. Ib. xlii. 6. Where it is evidently synonymous with עַם. So Ps. xxxiii. 12, &c.; Zeph. ii. 9, 10, &c. גְּלִיל הַגּוֹיִם, Is. viii. 23, *Galilee*, in which our Lord first manifested himself. Comp. Is. lxi. 1, with Luke iv. 18. Metaph. applied to the locusts, Joel i. 6; to other animals, Zeph. ii. 14. Comp. Prov. xxx. 25. In Gen. xiv. 1, comp. and Josh. xii. 23.

גּוֹיִם seems to be the proper name of a place. Aff. גּוֹיֵךְ, גּוֹיַיִךְ, and גּוֹיֵהֶם, גּוֹיֵךְ.

גְּוִיָּה, f. constr. גְּוִיַּת, pl. גְּוִיּוֹת. See גֵּו, גַּו, and גֵּו. *The body*, either of man or beast, alive or dead, Gen. xlvii. 18; Ezek. i. 11. 23; Dan. x. 6; Neh. ix. 37; 1 Sam. xxxi. 10. 12; Nah. iii. 3; Ps. cx. 6; Jud. xiv. 8, 9. Aff. גְּוִיָּתוֹ, גְּוִיָּתָם, גְּוִיָּתֵנוּ, pl. גְּוִיּוֹתֵינוּ, גְּוִיָּתְהֶם, גְּוִיָּתְהֶנָה.

גּוּל, see גִּיל.

גּוֹלָה, f. pl. non occ. *Captivity*, applied I. either to the event, or, II. meton. to the people subject to it; and, in this case may be a fem. seg. fm. פְּקֻדָּה, of m. פָּקֻד; גָּלְתָה, and contr. Gram. art. 73. גּוֹלָה, the perfect vowel וֹ returning in order to sustain the first syllable. Syr. ◌, *revelavit*. Arab. جَلِي, id. Hence, meton. as what is laid open, is also laid bare; applied to towns and countries, the defences of which have been broken down, and so exposed to an attacking enemy. So the Arab. فَتَح, and Pers. گشادن. See also גָּלָה. Synon. with שְׁבִי, Ezek. xii. 11; Ezra ii. 1; viii. 35; Neh. vii. 6; Jer. xxix. i. 4; Zech. vi. 10, &c. Also, Part. גֹּלָה, f. גּוֹלָה, for גֹּלָה, Gram. art. 73; 2 Sam. xv. 19; pl. m. Amos vi. 7; occ. f. only once, Is. xlix. 21.

גּוּמָץ, m. Syr. ܓܘܡܨܐ, *fossa*, *fovea*. Chald. גּוּמְצָא, קוּמְצָא, קוּמְצָא, id. cogn. Syr. ܐܨܕܟܠܐ, *decipulum*, r. ثَكِل, *profundavit*. Chald. גּוּמָא, גּוּמְתָא, *fovea*, occ. once, Eccl. x. 8. *A pit*, or *well*, as a snare.

גָּוַע, v. pres. יִגְוַע. Arab. جَاع, r. جُوع, *fame laboravit, sitivit, vehementer* : hence, perhaps, sensu prægnanti, *gasping* in the agonies of death: usually, *Expired*, Gen. vi. 17; vii. 21; Num. xvii. 27; xx. 3. 29; Job iii. 10; x. 18. With יָמָה, syn. Gen. xxv. 8. 17, &c. See my note on Job xiii. 19. Comp. Ps. civ. 29, רוּחָם. Constr. abs. Infin. גְּוֹעַ, and גָּוַע, Num. xvii. 28; xx. 3. Part. גֹּוֵעַ, Ps. lxxxviii. 16.

גּוּף, v. occ. once only, in Hiph. יָגִיף, Neh. vii. 3; opp. τῳ̂, פָּתַח. Syr. ◌ܦ, *rete*. ◌ܐܦ, *clausus est*. Arab.

جَاف, conj. iv. *clausit* portam. *They shut the doors*, constr. immed.

גּוּפָה, f. pl. גּוּפֹת, constr. sing. גּוּפַת. Cogn. גֵּו, גַּו, גַּף. Arab. جِيفَة, *morticinium*, v. جَاف, r. جِيف, *fœtuit* corpus mortuum. *A corpse, dead body*, 1 Chron. x. 12. Comp. 1 Sam. xxxi. 12, where we have גְּוִיָּה, and גְּוִיּוֹת, as equivalents, al. non occ.

גּוּר, m. seg. גֵּר, Gram. art. 87. 1, 2; pl. constr. גֵּרֵי, aff. גֵּרוֹתָיו, also—

גּוּר, m. seg. גּוּר, Gram. art. 87. 1, 2; pl. abs. גּוּרִים, contr. גֻּרֵי, aff. גּוּרֶיהָ, &c.—

Arab. جَار, *vicinus*. See cogn. جول, وجر, وجل, وجبل. The leading notion seems to be, *the being* or *coming near*, either (a) for friendly, or (b) unfriendly purposes. So, *consors* in mercatura, *conjux* viri, &c. : and the verb جَار, *deflexit* a via, scopo, &c. (c) *Vicinus fuit*, *accrevit* planta. Hence, vicinitatem inivit, in fidem recepit : and, on the other hand, i. conj. *exorbitavit* a via, &c. *injustus* fuit, &c. Here an abstr. for concr. *violence*, &c.; but as in use, *A lion's whelp*, Jer. li. 38; Nah. ii. 3; Gen. xlix. 9; Deut. xxxiii. 22; Ezek. xix. 2, 3. 5. It is evident from the two last verses here, that גּוּר signifies a younger animal than כְּפִיר.

גּוּר, v. pret. גָּר, גַּרְתָּה, &c. pres. יָגוּר, constr. immed. and med. בּ of place, עִם pers. אֶת obj.

I. *Sojourned, resided, dwelt*, as a stranger, said of individuals, a people, or, metaph. of brutes, Gen. xii. 10; xix. 9; xx. 1; Judg. xvii. 7; Exod. vi. 4; Ps. cv. 23; Ezra i. 4; Is. xi. 6. In Is. xxxiii. 14, we have, מִי יָגוּר לָנוּ אֵשׁ אוֹכֵלָה מִי־יָגוּר לָנוּ מוֹקְדֵי עוֹלָם, *Which of us* (can) *dwell* (with, or abide,) *consuming fire?* *Which of us* (can) *dwell* (with) *burnings of eternity?* " Vox est peccatorum in vicinia stragium a Jehova in Assyrios immissarum (comm. 12, 13), sibi metuentium," says Dr. Gesenius. I can find no mention whatever of Assyrians here. The beginning of the verse says, *Sinners in Zion shall fear* .... (לֵאמֹר), *saying*), *which, &c.* The words are evidently addressed to the unbelieving Jews, and the burnings here threatened, those foretold by Moses, Deut. xxxii. 22, 23, and alluded to by Peter, 2 Ep. ii. 6; iii. 10, et seq., and others. Comp. Job xviii. 15; xx. 26, and my note on the last.

גוּר (109) גִּישׁ

II. Cogn. τοῦ, עָוַר. Arab. وَجَرَ, وَجِلَ, *Withdrew from, avoided.* See גוּר above: hence, *Feared;* constr. immed. and with מִן, מִפְּנֵי of obj. *from* which; and לְ, אֶל of subj. *for* which, Job xix. 29; xli. 17; Num. xxii. 3; Deut. i. 17; xviii. 22; xxxii. 27; 1 Sam. xviii. 15; Hos. x. 5; *for the* calves, &c., not *they fear the calves,* as Gesenius thinks. Ps. xxii. 24; xxxiii. 8. Pres. once יָגוֹר, Prov. xxi. 7. שֹׁד רְשָׁעִים יְגוֹרֵם, *The violence of the wicked shall* (make) *them fear :* if indeed this is not a contracted form of Pih. for יְגוֹרְרֵם.

III. *Came together, congregated,* for unfriendly purposes, as war, &c. Constr. abs. and with עַל, אֶת, of pers. &c. against whom, Ps. lvi. 7; lix. 4; cxl. 3; Is. liv. 15, &c. But, in all these cases, *acting violently, unjustly, outrageously,* or the like (see גוּר above), may be all that is meant.

Infin. גּוּר, Gen. xii. 10; xix. 9, &c. Imp. id. Ib. xxvi. 3; fem. גּוּרִי, 2 Kings viii. 1.

Part. גֵּר, pl. גֵּרִים, f. גֵּרַת, constr. pl. m. גֵּרֵי, Job xxviii. 4. See my note. Exod. iii. 22; xii. 49, &c.; 2 Sam. iv. 3; Jer. xxxv. 7; Job xix. 15.

Hithp. יִתְגּוֹרָרוּ, *They become withdrawn, withdraw themselves:* it is added, by way of explanation apparently, יָסוּרוּ בִי, *they recede* (acting) *against me :* i. e. for the purposes of idolatry, from which they believe they shall obtain their corn and wine. Comp. Jer. xliv. 17.

Part. מִתְגּוֹרֵר, *becoming, being, a sojourner,* 1 Kings xvii. 20; Jer. xxx. 23, *Violent, destroying.* LXX. τρεφομένη. Targ. מִתְכַּנֵּשׁ collecta.

גּוֹרָל, m. pl. f. גּוֹרָלוֹת. Arab. جَرَلَ, *lapides, it. quod manus eo, quod portare potest, impleta est.* Propr. the *stone,* κλῆρος, ψῆφος, by which the *lot* was determined. and meton. I. *The lot* so determined; with the verbs נָתַן, יָרַד, הִשְׁלִיךְ, הֵטִיל, הוֹטַל, נָפַל, הִפִּיל; also, as to the result, עָלָה, יָצָא, הָיָה, which see. Lev. xvi. 8. 9; Jon. i. 7; Ezek. xxiv. 6; Joel iv. 3; Obad. 11; Prov. xviii. 18; Josh. xix. 10; Numb. xxxiii. 54, &c. used in dividing land, Josh. xv. xvii., &c.— the spoil, Ps. xxii. 19; Joel iv. 3; Nah. iii. 10 —determining a guilty person, Josh. vii. 14; 1 Sam. xiv. 42, apparently; Jon. i. 7,— appointing to office, 1 Chron. xxiv. 5; xxv. 8; Acts i. 26.

II. Meton. *The thing obtained by lot,* Judges i. 3; Is. lvii. 6; Ps. cxxv. 3.

Metaph. of favours received from God, Ps xvi. 5; Dan. xii. 13. Comp. Rev. xx. 6; Is. xvii. 14; Jer. xiii. 25. Aff. גּוֹרָלִי, גּוֹרָלִי, &c. Gesenius gives גּוֹרָלִים, as a pl. I can find no such plural.

גּוּשׁ, or גִּישׁ, m. occ. once, Job vii. 5 לָבַשׁ בְּשָׂרִי רִמָּה וְגוּשׁ עָפָר, *My flesh hath put on* (as a garment) the *worm with the clod of dust:* or prophetically, *shall surely put on &c.* It can hardly be said, that worms were now in Job's flesh: nor, for the same reason that גוּשׁ עָפָר, had now been placed upon him. This, therefore, had nothing to do with his disease, but is spoken with reference to death, which he expected soon to submit to. See my translation of the place with the note, and Castell sub voce, col. 521. The Arab. جَيْشٌ, *Exercitum collegit,* contains perhaps the primitive notion of *collecting* in a mass hence, *clod, &c.*

גֵּז m, pl. constr. גִּזֵּי. Syr. ܓܙܐ *tonsura* Arab. جَزَّ, *lana secta.* جَزٌّ, *tonsura, &c* Lit. a *cropping* or *shearing.* I. *The fleece* of sheep or lambs, Deut. xviii. 4; Job xxxi. 20.

II. Meton. *Young grass after the mowing,* vulg. *aftermath,* Ps. lxxii. 6. But Amos vii. 1, גִּזֵּי הַמֶּלֶךְ, *the king's mowings,* seems to intimate that the king, as supreme feudal lord, took a first cutting of the grass.

גָּזָה, non occ. Cogn. جَزَّ, supra جَزَّ, *partitus fuit.* Syriac ܓܙܐ *amputavit.* r. جَرَى, *pensavit.*

Part. aff. גֹּזִי. Lit. *My hewer out;* the Hebrews sometimes speaking of a birth as of a thing hewn out of a stone-quarry. See Is. li. 1; Ps. lxxi. 6.

גָּנַח, f. i. q. גּוּ, sig. I. Judges vi. 39, 40.

גָּזַז, v. pres. apoc. יָגֵז. Syr. ܓܙ *totondit.* جَزَّ, *resecuit, totondit* oves, caput. Cogn. גוּז, גָּרַע, גּוּעַ, גָּזַם, גּוּר, גּוֹל, גְּרַע, &c. Constr. immed. אֵת, בְּ of place in which, לְ of pers. for whom, מִן from which. *Sheared,* or *cut off,* as wool, hair, birds,—as the quails,—from a certain district, Gen. xxxi. 19; xxxviii. 12; 1 Sam. xxv. 4. 7.—Job i. 20; Mich. i. 16. —Num. xi. 31, וַיָּגָז שַׂלְוִים מִן הַיָּם, *And cut off the quails from the* (region of) *the sea :* i. e. separated them from those parts, and drove them towards the camp.

Infin. constr. גֹּז

גזי (110) גזר

Imp. f. גְּזִי.
Part. גֹּזֵו, pl. גֹּזְזִים, constr. גֹּזְזֵי. Aff. גֹּזְזָיהָ גֹּזְזֵי.
Niph. נָגוֹז, Nah. i. 12, *They are* (shall be) *cut off.*

גָּזִית, f. r. גזה. Lit. *Cutting, hewing;* with syn. חָצוּב, 1 Chron. xxii. 2. Meton. *Hewn*, or *squared stone*. Hence אַבְנֵי גָזִית, *Stones of hewing*, i. e. hewn stones, 1 Kings v. 31, and מוּסְרֵי גָזִית, *Rows of* do. Ib. vi. 36; vii. 9. 11, 12; Exod. xx. 25; Is. ix. 9. Once with בְּ, Lam. iii. 9. Elsewhere as a specificative, Gram. art. 219.

גָּזַל, m. seg. Arab. جَزْلٌ, جَزَلَ, *sectio, segmentum, portio*. Syr. ܓܙܶܠ, *vis damnum:* lit. *cutting away*. *Abstracting forcibly, rapine*, Ezek. xviii. 18 ; Eccl. v. 7.

גָּזֵל, m. גְּזֵלָה constr. גְּזֵלַת, pl. גְּזֵלוֹת, concr. Any thing *Forcibly taken away, rapine*, Lev. v. 21; Is. lxi. 8; Ezek. xxii. 29; Ps. lxii. 11; Syn. עֹשֶׁק, f. Lev. v. 23; Is. iii. 14; Ezek. xviii. 7. 12. 16, &c.

גָּזַל, v. pres. יִגְזֹל. See גֹּזֵל. Lit. *Cut away*, or *off, injuriously; snatched*, or *took away*, or *injured*, violently, as by stealth, robbery, or rapine. Constr. immed. and abs. Gen. xxxi. 31; Deut. xxviii. 31; Judg. ix. 25; xxi. 23; 2 Sam. xxiii. 21; 1 Chron. xi. 23; Ps. xxxv. 10; Job xxiv. 9, &c. Ib. 19, יִגְזְלוּ מֵימֵי־שֶׁלֶג, *They bear violently away* (as, or like) *the snow waters*. See my note on the place.
Infin. גְּזֹל, Is. x. 2.
Part. agent. גּוֹזֵל, constr. pl. גֹּזְלֵי. Aff. גֹּזְלוֹ.
Part. patient. גָּזוּל, Deut. xxviii. 29. 31; Jer. xxi. 12, &c.
Niph. f. נִגְזְלָה, *Becomes, is, taken away*, Prov. iv. 16.

גֶּזַם, m. Arab. جَزْمٌ, *amputatio, excidium*. Syr. ܓܙܰܡ, *incidit*. Æth. id. *A species of the locust*, so called from its destructive character, occ. with אַרְבֶּה, חָסִיל, Joel i. 4; יֶלֶק, ii. 25; Amos iv. 9. Some think, in consequence of the rendering of the Targumist and Syriac, that it was a creeping, wingless, locust: but no reliance can be placed on this.

גֶּזַע, m. Arab. جَزْعٌ, جَدْعٌ, *amputatio*, جَدَعَ, *truncus palmæ*. Cogn. גזה, &c., *The stock* or *trunk of a tree*, Is. xi. 1; xl. 24; Job xiv. 8. Aff. גִּזְעוֹ, גִּזְעָם, al. non. occ.

גֶּזֶר, m. sing. non occ. pl. גְּזָרִים. Syr. ܓܙܳܪܳܐ, *abscissio*, Arab. جَزْرٌ, id. Cogn. جَزْع, &c., *Divisions, sections, parts*, Gen. xv. 17; Ps. cxxxvi. 13.

גָּזַר, v. pres. יִגְזֹר and יָגְזֹר. Constr. immed. עַל, כֵּן, אֶת. I. *Cut off*, or *down*, as men, flocks, trees. II. *In two parts, divided*, as the sea, &c. III. *Decided*, as judgment, sentence. I. 2 Kings vi. 4; Is. ix. 19; Hab. iii. 17. II. Ps. cxxxvi. 13; 1 Kings iii. 25, 26. III. Job xxii. 28. See גְּזֵרָה, sig. II.
Imp. גְּזֹר, in pause גְּזֹרוּ.
Part. גֹּזֵר.
Niph. נִגְזַר, *Became, was, cut off*. Constr. med. מִן, עַל, לְ. Sign. I. Is. liii. 8 ; Ps. lxxxviii. 6; Lam. iii. 54; Ezek. xxxvii. 11. Sign. III. *Determined, decided*, Est. ii. 1.

גזר, v. Chald. non occ. — Part. pl. sign. III. גָּזְרִין, def. גָּזְרַיָּא. Persons *determining, deciding*, on the fate of others astrologically, Dan. ii. 27 ; iv. 4 ; v. 7. 11.
Ithpe. 3 pers. f. אִתְגְּזֶרֶת and הִתְגְּזֶרֶת, *Became, was, cut out*. Constr. מִן, Dan. ii. 45, 34, al. non. occ.

גְּזֵרָה, f. constr. גְּזֵרַת, lit. *cut off*. I. *Part* or *place cut off*, or *separated* from some other. Lev. xvi. 22, i. q. מִדְבָּר, in the last member. Comp. vv. 10. 21. So Syr. ܓܙܶܪܬܳܐ. Arab. جَزِيرَةٌ —the same word apparently—*insula*. Not because, "*herba carentem*, a comedendi significatu," as Gesenius thinks.
II. *Cut*, i. e. *decided; decree, determination*. Chald. Dan. iv. 14. 21. it. Syr. ܓܙܶܪܬܳܐ, *decisio judicis*, v. ܓܙܰܪ, *decrevit*.

גִּזְרָה, f. See גזה. I. *Cut*, hence, *brilliancy*, as applied to precious stones. Lam. iv. 7, סַפִּיר גִּזְרָתָם, As *a sapphire (was) their cut:* i. e. brilliancy, beauty. II. *Insulated*, i. e. *separated*, spoken of a certain inclosure of the temple, Ezek. xli. 12—15; xlii. 1. 10. 13. LXX. τὸ ἀπόλοιπον; in the last place, διαστήματα. See הֵיכָל.

גִּזְרִי, m. Patronym. 1 Sam. xxvii. 8, *keri* of the city גֶּזֶר.

בָּחוֹן, m. pl. non occ. جَحِين, *angustia cordis*. Chald. בְּחַן, *inclinavit, se*. Syr. ܒܚܶܢ, id. *The belly of any reptile*, Lev. xi. 42; of the serpent, Gen. iii. 14, al. non occ.

בֶּחָלֹת, (f. of prim. נַחָל, seg. נֶחָל) pl. m. נְחָלִים, for נַחָלִים, constr. נַחֲלֵי, *Coals*

גיא (111) גיח

thoroughly ignited (פֶּחָם, Prov. xxvi. 21, seems, as Gesenius has well observed, to signify charcoal unkindled): sometimes applied to the thunder-bolt, 2 Sam. xxii. 9. 13. Comp. Ps. xviii. 9; cxl. 11.—Lev. xvi. 12; Is. xliv. 19; Prov. vi. 28, &c. Ib. xxv. 22, גֶּחָלִים אַתָּה חֹתֶה עַל־רֹאשׁוֹ, *Burning coals thou takest* (and placest) *on his head*. Apparently proverbial, comp. Rom. xii. 20. It was usual among the Hebrews to speak of persons being placed in the furnace of affliction. See Is. i. 25; Jer. ix. 7; Zech. xiii. 9; Mal. iii. 3; Ps. xii. 6; 1 Cor. iii. 13; 1 Pet. i. 7. Whence it should appear that fire, considered as purifying metals, is spoken of metaphorically as purifying the mind: which is evidently the intention of this passage.— Metaph. of an only son, as the *fire*, or *life*, of the family, 2 Sam. xiv. 7.

גַּיְא, גֵּיְא, גֵּיא, or גַּי, m. Gram. art. 87. 3. 74. Constr. גֵּיא or גֵּי, pl. f. גֵּאָיוֹת metath. for גְּיָאוֹת. See *kethiv.* 2 Kings ii. 16; Ezek. vi. 3. Aff. גֵּאוֹתֶיךָ. Arab. جَوَا, *depressior terræ locus, vallisve*, جِبَا, *locus in quo colligitur, ac restagnat aqua*, 'جَبِدَة جَبِدَة, *receptaculum aquæ*. *A valley* or *combe*, i.e. of the smaller sort; and, in this respect, differs from עֵמֶק and בִּקְעָה, which are extensive:—from נַחַל, which is watered by the mountain torrents; this not, Numb. xxi. 20; Deut. iii. 29; iv. 46; Is. xxii. 1; Josh. viii. 11; xix. 27; Ezek. xxxi. 12; xxxv. 8. Occ. in many names of places, as גֵּיא בֶן־הִנֹּם, *The valley of the son of Hinnom*, i. q. תֹּפֶת, Jer. vii. 32; xix. 2. 6. Comp. Josh. xv. 8; 2 Kings xxiii. 10. Ib. גֵּי חֲרָשִׁים, Neh. xi. 35. Others in Josh. xix. 14. 27; Ps. lx. 2; 1 Sam. xiii. 18; 2 Sam. viii. 13; Ezek. xxxix. 11; 2 Chron. xiv. 9.

גִּיד, m. pl. גִּידִים, constr. גִּידֵי, (contr. of גֶּוֶד or גָּיֵד, Gram. art. 75.) Arab. جَادَ, r. جُود, *firmius evasit*. Syr. ܓܝܕܐ, *nervus.* Chald. id. *A sinew*, or *nerve*, Gen. xxxii. 33; Is. xlviii. 4 (Arab. جِيد, *cervix*); Ezek. xxxvii. 6. 8; Job x. 11; xl. 17.

גִּיחַ, v. pres. יָגִיחַ, apoc. יָגַח. Syr. ܓܚ, *erupit aqua*. Arab. جَاحَ, r. جَوْح, *eradicavit*. Cogn. جَاخَ, *abrupit*. I. *Drew out*, *in*, or *into*, (a) *as a child from the womb*, &c. (b) *into the mouth*, &c. II. *In length*, i. e.

extended. Constr. med. מִן, from which, בְּ *place in which*, אֶל *to which*, and abs. Ezek. xxxii. 2, "de milite ad pugnam prorumpente," says Gesenius. But, גְּנַהֲרוֹתֶיךָ, *in thy rivers*, immediately follows. I do not see, therefore, how this sense can apply. *Drawest out*, i. e. *extendest* thy length, seems rather to be the sense intended here: not a syllable occurs suggesting the notion of *rushing out* of these rivers. Job xl. 23, " de flumine e fontibus erumpente" he also says. But, as אֶל־פִּיהוּ *into his mouth* follows, *drawing into*: not *rushing out*, must be the sense. Ib. xxxviii. 8, " de infante de utero prodeunte." But the aff. וֹ in גִּיחוֹ (infin.) would rather refer to the nominative in יָצֹךְ preceding. *In his drawing forth*, or *out*, would, therefore, suit the context better. Besides, generally, children neither *rush*, nor *come out* from the womb, without aid. Comp. Ps. xxii. 10. Part. גֹּחִי, *My extractor, &c*. See גֹּחִי above. Mich. iv. 10. Imp. f. גֹּחִי, *bring forth*.

Hiph. Part. מֵגִיחַ, *Drawing out*, i. e. extending the lines (military), Jud. xx. 33. Comp. Cogn. Arab. جَحَّ, *extendit rem*; جَحَا, *gravida fuit mulier*, جَحَّى, r. جَحَو, *eradicavit*.

Aph. Chald. pl. מְגִיחָן, in the Syriac acceptation, *Rushing out*, Dan. vii. 2. constr. לְ, *towards, &c.*

גִּיחוֹן. Arab. جَيْحُون, and جَيْحَان. The Orientals often speak of rivers as the daughters, &c., of certain places. Comp. Job xl. 23. The name of a certain river, Gen. ii. 13. Ib. of a fountain, &c., sometimes termed Shiloh. שִׁלֹחַ, 1 Kings i. 33. 38; 2 Chron. xxxii. 30; xxxiii. 14. See שִׁלֹחַ.

גִּיל, m. f. גִּילָה, constr. f. גִּילַת. Arab. جَالَ, *ivit venitque; claudicavit.* Cogn. جَال, r. جول, conj. iii. *distribuit in orbem.* جيل, *generatio*: Æth. ⴳⵡⴽ: *revolvit*. Syr. ܓܘܠܬܐ, *elatio*. The leading notion seems to consist in, *going round*, thence *dancing in a ring*, as Derveishes in the East, or peasants round a May-pole. *Exultation, rejoicing*: with שְׂמָחִים, Job iii. 21. שִׂמְחָה, Is. xvi. 10; Jer. xlviii. 33; Joel i. 16; Ps. xlv. 16. כְּעַמִּים, Hos. ix. 1; Ps. lxv. 13; Is. xxxv. 2. גִּילַת for גִּילָה, lxv. 18. Aff. גִּילִי, Ps. xliii. 4.

גִּיל (112) גַּל

גִּיל, m. Chald. Arab. جِيلٌ, *gens, natio;* as in the phrase, اَبْنَاءُ الجِنْسِ, *Equals,* persons of the same rank, age, &c. Dan. i. 10.

גִּיל, v. pret. גַּלְתִּי, pres. יָגִיל, apoc. יָגֵל, constr. בּ in the pers. or thing. עֲרֵי, *till.* עֲלֵי, *upon,* and abs. *Exult, leap, rejoice,* applied occasionally to inanimate things. See גִּיל above, Is. lxv. 18, 19; lxvi. 10; Joel ii. 21. 23; Ps. ix. 15; xiii. 6; xiv. 7; xxi. 2; xxxi. 8; Hab. iii. 18; Prov. xxiii. 24. Gesenius finds two places, in which he thinks this verb signifies *trepidare,* viz., Ps. ii. 11; Hos. x. 5. The first has עִבְדוּ...בְּיִרְאָה וְגִילוּ בִּרְעָדָה i. e. *serve...with fear,* and *exult,* or *rejoice, with trembling:* but, as he thinks, *tremble with trembling:* which looks very much like a tautology. We know that religious rejoicing was sometimes attended with dancing, see Exod. xv. 22; Jud. xi. 34; 2 Sam. vi. 16; Ps. cxlix. 3, &c. And all that seems to be intended here is, Let this rejoicing be accompanied with solemnity, religious fear, and reverence. The second place has, וּכְמָרָיו עָלָיו יָגִילוּ, which will, perhaps, be best explained by comparing 2 Sam. vi. 16, with 1 Kings xviii. 26; where we learn that David's exultation was accompanied with *leaping,* in the first place, as was the supplication of Baal's worshippers in the second, when their case appeared to be desperate. Such here was apparently the case with the prophets of Samaria. Comp. Lam. v. 15.

Infin. גִּיל.
Imp. f. גִּילִי, pl. m. גִּילוּ.

גִּיר, or גִּר, m. Arab. جَيَّارٌ, *calx viva. Burnt lime stone,* Is. xxvii. 9. כְּאַבְנֵי־גִר מְנֻפָּצוֹת *As stones of burnt lime dissolved,* or slaked; i. e. so that such altars shall be no more reared. See the rest of the verse.

בִּירָא, Chald. def. id. meton. *Plaister* made of lime, Dan. v. 5.

גִּיר, m. pl. גֵּירִים, i. q. גֵּר, 2 Chron. ii. 16.

גִּישׁ, see גּוּשׁ.

גַּל, m. pl. גַּלִּים, constr. גַּלֵּי, r. גלל. Syr. ܓܰܠ, *fluctus, unda.* Arab. جَلَّ, *magnus fuit.* Lit. *any thing heaped up:* applied to stones, ruins, as I. *Heaps,* Gen. xxxi. 46; Josh. vii. 26; Is. xxv. 2; Jer. ix. 10; li. 37, &c.: — to waters, II. as *Waves, rollers, breakers,* Is. xlviii. 18; li. 15; Jer. v. 22; Jonah ii. 4; Job xxxviii. 18; it. viii. 17. See my notes on this place: it. Cant. iv. 12, as also noticed there; it being customary in the East to bring rivulets into the gardens. See Ps. i. 3; xlii. 8; lxxxix. 10; cvii. 25. Aff. גַּלְּךָ, גַּלָּיו, גַּלֵּיהֶם.

גֹּל, m. Aff. גֻּלָּה, *Its bowl, bason;* i. q. גֻּלָּה, which see.

גַּלָּב, m. pl. גַּלָּבִים. Arab. جَلَبَ, *traxit.* Cogn. جَزَبَ, id. جَزَمَ, *resecuit.* جَلَفَ, id. occ. once, Ezek. v. 1. *A barber, sheaver.* See Gram. art. 154. 12.

גַּלְגַּל, m. pl. גַּלְגַּלִּים, r. גלל. Lit. any thing *round, revolving.* I. *The wheel* of a chariot, Is. v. 28; Ezek. x. 2. 6; xxiii. 24; xxvi. 10; or *The wheel* used at a well, Eccl. xii. 6.

II. *A whirlwind.* Syr. ܓܰܠܓܠܳܐ, Ps. lxxvii. 19; Ezek. x. 13.

III. *Chaff,* &c. as carried before the wind: perhaps *the gossimer,* Is. xvii. 13; Ps. lxxxiii. 14. Syr. ܓܠܠܐ. Arab. جلّ, *stipula.* Aff. גַּלְגַּלָּיו.

Chald. id. sign. I. Dan. vii. 9. Aff. גַּלְגִּלּוֹהִי, *Its wheels.*

גִּלְגָּל, m. occ. once, Is. xxviii. 28. *A cart-wheel;* i. e. such as was used in beating out, or threshing, corn, &c. Also the name of a place, Josh. iv. 19, &c.

גֻּלְגֹּלֶת, f. pl. גֻּלְגְּלֹת. Syr. ܓܳܓܽܘܠܬܳܐ, *cranium.* Arab. جَلَجَةٌ, id. الجَاجَلَةُ, *Golgotha,* Mark xv. 12, &c. *The skull,* 2 Kings ix. 35; Jud. ix. 53. Used mostly in numbering persons, as we say of cattle, so many *head,* &c., Exod. xvi. 16; xxxviii. 26; Num. i. 2. 18. 20. 22; iii. 47; 1 Chron. x. 10, &c. Aff. גֻּלְגְּלֹתָם, גֻּלְגַּלְתּוֹ.

גֶּלֶד, m. occ. once, Job xvi. 15. Arab. جِلْدٌ, *cutis,* of جَلَدَ, *glacies, pruina,* i. e. covering or skinning, as it were, over. *The skin.* Aff. גִּלְדִּי.

גָּלַח, v. pres. יִגְלַח, apoc. יָגַל. Syr. ܓܠܰܚ, *retexit.* Arab. جَلَا, i. q. جَلَّ, *defluvium comæ.* جَلَا, *abstersiva vis, exilium;* v.

גלה (113) גלה

جَلَا, *comptam, sublato velo, conspexit sponsam.* Cogn. جلح, *rasit*; propr. *Throwing off the covering, and so laying bare,* applied in various ways.

I. *Laid bare* or *open,* as the ear to receive information, instruction, 1 Sam. ix. 15; xx. 2. 12, 13; xxii. 8. 17; Job xxxvi. 10. 15. Meton. *Laid open, made known,* a secret, Amos iii. 7; Prov. xx. 19; spoken of a legal instrument סֵפֶר, *unclosed,* גָּלוּי, Jer. xxxii. 11. 14. Constr. immed. and med. with אֵת; לְ, for which: בְ by which. Comp. פָּדָה אָזְנַיִם Ps. xl. 7.

II. *Laid bare, open,* a city, country, (Arab. فَتَحَ, Pers. گشان), and so conquered it: hence, meton. *Went into captivity.* See Is. xxii. 8; Mic. i. 6. According to Gesenius, *Laid the country bare* of people: *nudavit terram incolis*:—i. e. *emigravit,* willingly, 2 Sam. xv. 19, unwillingly, 2 Kings xvii. 23; xxiv. 14; xxv. 21; Amos i. 5; vi. 7. Spoken of inanimate things, Is. xxiv. 11; Job xx. 28; Prov. xxvii. 5. Constr. med. מִן, מֵעַל, *from* which. בְ, *for,* on account of, in place, station. לְ, *as to.*

Imp. גְּלֵה, Ezek. xii. 3.
Infin. גְּלוֹת, constr. גְּלוֹת, Amos v. 5; Jud. xviii. 30.
Part. גּוֹלֶה, f. גּוֹלָה, pl. m. גּוֹלִים, 2 Sam. xv. 19; Is. xlix. 21; Amos vi. 7. Pass. גָּלוּי, Num. xxiv. 4, &c.

Niph. *Became* or *was laid open:* as I. (a) *The pudenda,* Exod. xx. 26; Is. xlvii. 3; Ezek. xvi. 36; xxiii. 29. (b) *Sin,* the cloak being removed, Jer. xiii. 22; Hos. vii. 1; Ezek. xxi. 29; xvi. 57; Prov. xxvi. 26, &c. (c) *Righteousness,* Is. lvi. 1. (d) *Revealed,* as God, i. e. *appeared,* Gen. xxxv. 7; 1 Sam. ii. 27; iii. 21; xiv. 8. 11. (e) as God's word, glory, or arm, 1 Sam. iii. 7; Dan. x. 1; Is. xl. 5; liii. 1. (f) as things unknown before, Is. xlix. 9; Hos. vii. 1; Job xxxviii. 17; Deut. xxix. 28; Is. xxiii. 1, &c. Constr. לְ, עַל, אֶל.

II. *Migrated, gone into captivity,* Is. xxxviii. 12. Constr. מִן.
Infin. נִגְלֹה, constr. נִגְלוֹת, and הִגָּלוֹת, 1 Sam. ii. 27; 2 Sam. vi. 20.

Pih. i. q. Kal. *Laid bare, naked.* (a) *The pudenda mulieris*: meton. *rem habuit cum eâ,* Lev. xviii. 8; xx. 17; Hos. ii. 11. Ib. *Pudenda viri,* eo tamen sensu ut rem haberi censeatur cum uxore ejus, Lev. xviii. 8; xx.

11. 20, 21. Comp. Deut. xxiii. 1; xxvii. 20. (b) *The feet,* Ruth iii. 4. 7. (c) *The foundation of a house,* &c., Mich. i. 6: *the curtain,* &c. being removed, Is. xxii. 8; xlvii. 2; Nah. iii. 5; Job xli. 5. (d) *The veil* from the eyes, Num. xxii. 31; xxiv. 4. 16; Ps. cxix. 18. (e) *Something hidden or secret,* Job xx. 27; Prov. xi. 13. (f) *Exposing a fugitive,* Is. xvi. 3. (g) *Making known* (God), *His righteousness,* &c. Jer. xxxiii. 6; Ps. xcviii. 2. *Sin,* Ezek. xxiii. 18; Lam. ii. 14; iv. 22. Comp. Is. xxvi. 21; Job xx. 27. Constr. immed. it. עַל, אֶת, מִן, לְ, אֶל.

Part. מְגַלֶּה.
Infin. גַּלֹּה. Imp. גַּל, f. גַּלִּי.
Puh. גֻּלְּתָה, *Has been laid bare,* Nah. ii. 8.
Hiph. הִגְלָה, and הִגְלִיא, pres. יַגְלֶה, apoc. יֶגֶל, *Made captive, led captive,* 2 Kings xv. 29; xvii. 6. 11; xviii. 11, &c.
Infin. הַגְלוֹת.
Hoph. הָגְלָה, *Was made captive,* Est. ii. 6; Jer. xiii. 19, &c.
Part. pl. m. מֻגְלִים, Jer. xl. 1. Constr. med. מִן, בְ.
Hithp. pret. non occ. pres. apoc. *Became bare, exposed.* יִתְגַּל, Gen. ix. 21. Constr. בְּתוֹךְ.
Infin. constr. הִתְגַּלּוֹת, Prov. xviii. 2.

בְּלָה, and בְּלָא, Part. act. Chald. i. q. Heb. sign. I. Dan. ii. 22. 28, 29. Id. Pass. גְּלִי, and גְּלִי, for גְּלִיה, &c. (Gram. art. 74). Ib. vv. 19. 30.
Infin. מִגְלֵא, ib. vr. 47.
Aph. הַגְלִי, i. q. Heb. Hiph. *Led away captive,* Ezra iv. 10; v. 12, al. non occ.

גָּלָה, f. i. q. גּוֹלָה. *Captivity.*

גֻּלָּה, f. pl. גֻּלּוֹת, constr. גֻּלֹּת. See גֹּל above.
(a) *A bason* or *bowl.* גֻּלַּת הַזָּהָב, *bowl of gold,* Eccl. xii. 6. Applied apparently to the heart in the agonies of death. So Shakspeare's Hamlet, "Now bursts the cordage of a noble heart." The Persians say, شيشهٔ دلهای ایشان را شکستن, *to break the glass* (bowl or bottle) *of their hearts.* Gesenius thinks the figure is taken from a gilded lamp, which, being hung up by a silken thread (silver cord), is supposed to fall and break to pieces. I doubt whether the several particulars mentioned, as the כַּד and גֻּלָּה, following, ought not to be considered as separate figures, all applying to the same thing, viz., the heart, as believed to be the seat of life. Bowls of the candlestick, Zech.

גְלוּ

iv. 3. (b) *Basons, pools,* or *wells of water,* Josh. xv. 19; Judg. i. 15. (c) *Basons,* cups of flowers, perhaps, carved on the capitals of the columns, 1 Kings vii. 41; 2 Chron. iv. 12, 13. Syr. ܠܩܢܐ, *basons,* it. Chald.

גִּלּוּלִים, m. pl.—sing. non occ. Constr. גִּלּוּלֵי. The elder Lexicographers, *Idola, dii stercorii.* Gesen., &c. *Trunci, caudices,* both, "*a volvendo dicti per contemptum.*" Arab. جلول and جليل, *glorious.* Comp. Is. i. 31. חָסֹן. Arab. حصين, *strong,* may also be proposed as synonymous here. *Idols,* Lev. xxvi. 30; Deut. xxix. 16; 1 Kings xxi. 26, &c. Aff. גִּלּוּלַי, גִּלּוּלָיו, גִּלּוּלֵיכֶם, &c.

גִּלּוּמֵי, m. pl. constr.—sing. non occ.— once only, Ezek. xxvii. 24. Arab. جلاب, *stragula.* Cogn. جلبة, *operimentum,* &c. it.

جلباب, *palla mulieris ferè linea candidaque,* quam capiti impositam Arabicæ et Persicæ mulieres ad talos demittunt, foras *prodeuntes.* See also Freytag's Golius, p. 291. It.

جلوبة, *res quæ aliunde adducitur asportaturve vænum.* Castell. and Gesen. χλαμύς. *Cloaks, mantles.* Cogn. جلم, *shearing* of wool. How Gesenius could arrive at "*a convolvendo dictum,*" I cannot see.

גָּלוּת, once, גָּלֻת, Obad. ver. 20, f. r. גלה. I. *Carrying* (away) *captive,* 2 Kings xxv. 27; Jer. lii. 31; Ezek. i. 2; xxxiii. 21, &c.

II. Meton. *Captivity,* i. e. persons of it, Jer. xxiv. 5; xxviii. 4; xxix. 22; Is. xlv. 13. Aff. גָּלוּתִי, גָּלוּתֵינוּ, Ezek. xxxiii. 21. גָּלוּתֵנוּ, Ib. xl. 1.

גָּלוּת, defin. גָּלוּתָא, f. Chald. Syr. id. sign. II. Dan. ii. 25; v. 13; Ezra vi. 16.

גָּלַח, v. pres. יִגְלַח, and יְגַלֵּחַ. Pih. constr. abs. immed. אֶת, and בְּ instr. Arab.

جلع, *rasit caput.* أجلع, *anteriore capitis parte calvus.* Cogn. جلح, *secuit terram.* *Shaved,* the head, beard, hair, Gen. xli. 14; Num. vi. 9; Deut. xxi. 12, &c. Metaph. Is. vii. 20, of the devastations of war. Infin. גַּלְּחוֹ. Aff. 2 Sam. xiv. 26.

Puh. גֻּלַּח, pres. non occ. *Was shaven,* Judg. xvi. 17. 22.

גְלִי

Part. constr. pl. מְגַלְּחֵי, Jer. xli. 5.

Hithp. הִתְגַּלַּח, (sense propr. for Kal), *He shaved,* Lev. xiii. 33; to which הִסְפִּיר corresponds in the paral. it.

Infin. aff. הִתְגַּלְּחוֹ, *His shaving;* to which נְזִרוֹ is manifestly the objective case: the *se, sibi,* introduced here, therefore, by the Lexicographers, is erroneous. Gesenius refers us to his Lehrg. p. 248, but no instance there given will bear out his theory; and the same may be said of Ewald's: § 242, Nicholson's Transl. See Gram. art. 157. 13, where the views of the Orientals themselves are given on this question.

גִּלָּיוֹן, m. occ. once, Is. viii. 1, r. גלה, fm. גִּלְיָה, r. כלה. Lit. *an exposer, revealer:* and may signify either, *A tablet,* or *a Book.* Comp. Is. xxx. 8. Targ. לוּחַ, *tabula.* LXX. τόμον (χάρτου) καινοῦ. Syr. ܟܬܒܐ, *volumen.* Cogn. מְגִלָּה. Gesenius makes גִּלְיוֹנִים the pl. of this, which sets both the analogy and signification of the word perfectly at nought. The prophet is here commanded to make a certain record relating to future events, and alluding, from the name following, to a sudden *taking of the spoil,* &c. His wife then conceives; and it is foretold, that before the child shall be able to discern between its father and mother, so as to call them by name, this spoil, &c., i. e. of Damascus and Samaria, shall be taken. The same thing is foretold in ch. vii. and there, before *Shear Jashub,* another son of the prophet, shall know to refuse the evil and choose the good, this event is to happen. See my Sermons and Dissertations, p. 273, et seq. Again, ch. viii. 18, we are told that the prophet and his *children* (הַיְלָדִים) were given for signs in Israel. IMMANUEL, therefore (ch. vii. 14), is a person altogether different from these children. And, as it is usual with the sacred writers to pass on from one to another kindred subject; so here, the mention of Isaiah's children, afforded an opportunity to touch on a more mysterious child promised to Israel, and to a conquest, much greater than that here had in view, in their favour. Comp. ch. viii. 9, et seq.

גִּלְיוֹנִים, m. pl. occ. once, Is. iii. 23, with הַשְּׂרִינִים, and other articles of dress. See Schrœderus de vestitu mulierum, p. 311, et seq. LXX. διαφανῆ λακωνικά, which Hesychius explains by λακωνικὸς χιτών, λεπτὴ ἐσθής. But it is not quite certain, that this is the word so rendered by them. Perhaps, the Syr.

גְּלִי (115) גְלַל

גְּלִי, *indumentum:* גֶּלְמָהּ, suits the form better: *retectio, &c.* Arab. جلوة, *vestes pellucidæ,* Freytag's Lex. *A sort of thin transparent dress,* worn by the lewd women of Judea in Isaiah's times, as occasionally among us, through which their nakedness is almost exposed. Gesenius takes them to be *looking-glasses:* but without any good reason for doing so.

גָּלִיל, m. pl. גְּלִילִים, constr. גְּלִילֵי, r. גלל. Syr. ܓܠܝܠܐ, *fluctus, torrens, vallis,* جَمَل, *rotundus.* Arab. جُلّ, *tegumentum jumenti,* it. *cingulum.* Castell. Cogn. جول, جيل. Lit. any thing *round* or *circular:* hence, I. i. q. כִּכָּר, as גְּלִיל הַגּוֹיִם, lit. *Circuit of nations,* because perhaps adjoining them: usually, הַגָּלִיל. Lit. *the circuit,—Galilee,* Josh. xx. 7; xxi. 32, &c. LXX. ἡ γαλιλαία. Also—

II. Applied to *folding* doors, as *revolving* on their hinges, 1 Kings vi. 34. Used participially, see מוּסַבּוֹת, Ezek. xli. 24, i. e. *turned,* or *turning.*

III. *Rings,* as, גְּלִילֵי זָהָב, rings of gold, Cant. v. 14, i. e. *His hands* (are as) *rings of gold inlaid with* (gems of) *Tartessus.* Comp. Est. i. 6.

גְּלִילָה, f. pl. גְּלִילוֹת, i. q. גָּלִיל. Sign. I. *Circuit, region.* Comp. Arab. طَرَف, اَطْرَاف, Josh. xiii. 2; xxii. 10, 11; i. q. כִּכַּר הַיַּרְדֵּן, now termed الغَوْر, *El Ghaur,* Gen. xiii. 12.

גָּלָל, m. pl. גְּלָלִים, constr. גְּלָלֵי. Aff. גְּלָלַי. Arab. جُلّة, *stercus animalis globosum.* Dung, Job xx. 7; Ezek. iv. 12. 15; Zeph. i. 17.

גָּלָל, m. I. i. q. גֵּלֶל, pl. non occ. 1 Kings xiv. 10.

II. Constr. with בְּ prefixed, prep. derived like our *about,* and Arab. أَجْل, lit. *bounding, limiting;* whence, בִּגְלָלֶךָ, or לְאִגְלָךְ,—it. مِن أَجْلِكَ *tui causa, about,* or *concerning thee:* it. مِن جَلَالِكَ but this last usage is probably a solecism. See Freytag under جَل. *About, concerning, for the sake of,* Gen. xii. 13; Deut. xviii. 12; 1 Kings xiv. 16, &c. See Nold. p. 172. Aff. בִּגְלָלְךָ, בִּגְלָלֶךָ; בִּגְלַלְכֶם.

גָּלַל, v. pres. non occ. 1 pers. גַּלּוֹתִי: pl. גַּלּוּ. Constr. immed. and with אֶת—מֵעַל from, אֶל or עַל to which. See גַּל. I. *Rolled* as a stone, Gen xxix. 3. 8; Prov. xxvi. 27; Josh. x. 18. In 1 Sam. xiv. 33, גֹּלּוּ אֵלַי, *Roll ye to me this day a great stone;* i. e. *a heap of stones,* apparently to build an altar with, see vr. 35, following or, as in the case of Jacob and Laban, for the purpose of setting up *a permanent sign of a covenant* then made. Comp. Gen. xxxi. 45. לָקְחוּ אֲבָנִים, it. 44 and 46: the first most probably.

II. Metaph.—any thing morally *heavy* or *afflicting,* as reproach, חֶרְפָּה, Josh. v. 8. דַּרְכֶּךָ, *thy way;* i. e. thy circumstances when afflicting, i. q. בִּטַח עָלָיו, *trust on Him* immediately following, Ps. xxxvii. 5. מַעֲשֶׂיךָ, *thy works,* undertakings, Prov. xvi. 3. In Ps. xxii. 9. ellip. גֹּל אֶל־יְהוָֹה, (saying) *Roll,* i. e. *confide thou* (thy way, work, &c.) *to Jehovah.* We have not here, therefore, either the third pers. imper. (a thing which does not exist), nor yet an infinitive for a finite form of the verb as Gesenius thinks, but a mere imper. as an exhortation.

Part. גּוֹלֵל. Imp. גֹּל or גּוֹל, pl. גֹּלּוּ.

Niph. נָגֹל, *They are,* or *become rolled up* as a book, Is. xxxiv. 4, pres. apoc. יִגֹּל becomes *rolling* away as water, Amos v. 24 See the last member of the verse.

Puh. Part. מְגוֹלָלָה, constr. בְ. *Rolled as* garments in blood, Is. ix. 4.

Hiph. pres. apoc. יָגֶל, *He rolls* the stone Gen. xxix. 10.

Hithp. הִתְגּוֹלֵל, Infin. *To become, set about rolling:* i. e. as a great stone, עָלֵינוּ, i. q. הִתְנַפֵּל following. Comp. Prov. xxvi. 27. Part. מִתְגּוֹלֵל, *Rolling* in blood; 2 Sam. xx. 12.

גִּלְגַּלְתִּי, v. redup. Gram. 197. 2. 3. seq used apparently instead of the Pihel spec. Constr. מִן from which. *I have rolled* thee &c., Jer. li. 25. Comp. Job xiv. 18; Rev. viii. 8.

הִתְגַּלְגֵּל, a sort of Hithp. of prec. *They roll on* as waters, violently, Job xxx. 14. See my note here.

גְּלַל, m. Chald. Cogn. Arab. جَلّ, *magnus illustris;* it. جَلَال, *negotium magnum, grave.* Great, *heavy,* applied to stones. Ezra v. 8; vi. 4.

גלם, v. occ. once only, pres. יִגְלֹם, 2 Kings ii. 8. See גְּלוֹמֵי above. *Wrapped* together, as a mantle.

גָּלְמִי, m. seg. fm. גֹּלֶם, once aff. Ps. cxxxix. 16. Cogn. Arab. perhaps, جَلْمٌ, *sagitta nuda absque alis.* جَلْمَة, *sarmentum, et quicquid supervacuum de ramis arboris resecatur.* Lit. *My shooting, branching;* i. e. the striking out of my, members in their first formation. See the rest of the vr. and comp. Job x. 10. The *embryo*, as Gesenius thinks, could hardly have been meant here: if so, the גָּלָם following would be worse than senseless. Comp. Arab. cogn. جَلَبَ, *de loco in locum eduxit; cuticula obductum fuit, dum sanaretur vulnus:* جَلْبَة, *frutex silvestris virescens.*

גַּלְמוּד, m. גַּלְמוּדָה, f.—pl. non occ. Arab. جَلْمُودٌ, *saxum, vir durus.* Cogn. جَلْمَد, *spissus,* it. جَلْفَدَة, i. e. الجَلْبَة الَّتِي لَاغِنَاءَ لها, *sounds in which there is no song, or music:* the "*clamor inutilis*" of Freytag is, therefore, incorrect. *Hard, sterile, unproductive,* Job iii. 7—of joy, song, as جَلْفَدَة. See my note on the place. Ib. xv. 34; xxx. 3, *desolate.* Is. xlix. 21, *sterile, barren.*

גלע, non occ. in Kal.

Hithp. יִתְגַּלָּע, occ. thrice only. Arab. جَلَعَ, *impudens; patuit os.* جَالَعَ, *pugnavit....* *in potu et alea.* اِجْلَعَ, *conspectui patuit.* The leading signification seems to be, *impudence,* thence, *insolent, intermeddling, dispute, strife, &c.,* as natural consequences. Prov. xviii. 1, *As to* (the) *desire, one alone* (private individual) *may seek* (it): but *in,* or *on, every thing substantial* (valuable, wealthy) *will be intermeddling, dispute,* יִתְגַּלָּע: i. e. an individual may quietly follow his own will and way; but when *public* honour, wealth, &c. are sought, there will be sharp contest. And so, unless I am greatly mistaken, both the Targum and Syriac of the Polyglott have taken it. Ib. xx. 3, וְכָל־אֱוִיל יִתְגַּלָּע, *but every base* (man) *will be meddling:* LXX. συμπλέκεται. The opp. here is, to the respect which he obtains who avoids dispute.

Infin. הִתְגַּלַּע, Prov. xvii. 14. Here פּוֹטֵר, as *a person letting out water* (is) *the beginning of contention: so before* (the act of) intermeddling, לִפְנֵי הִתְגַּלַּע, (is) the *being remiss:* i. e. the suffering the mind to be in an uncontrolled, vagrant, state. Vulg. *judicium deserit.*

גָּלַשׁ, v. occ. twice. Cant. iv. 1; vi. 5, Ges. " i. q. جَلَسَ, *sedit,*" &c.... " discumbunt qs. pendentes e monte," &c., in order to account, as it should seem, for its construction with מִן. But certainly no such sort of sitting, and no such sort of construction as this, is to be found in any Oriental writer whatsoever. I prefer taking the Cognates, جَلَزَ, *deposuit,* كَلَزَ, *collegit,* كَلَدَ, and قَلَدَ, id. قَلَصَ, *accrevit.* Sam. ᛉᛆ᛭, *amplexus.* Syr. ܓܠܘܣܢ, *barba,* and then supposing that *procuring, obtaining,* or the like, is the sense of the verb. These passages will then mean: *Thy hair* (is) *like* (that of the) *flock of the goats, which they obtain from Mount Gilead:* where the construction with מִן will be easy and natural. This hair was probably not dissimilar to that which is obtained from the goat of Angora, or the *bouc de Iuda,* long, silkly, and beautifully curled.

גַּם. Lit. *accumulation, adding.* Arab. جَمّ, *explevit, auxitve adjecto cumulo:* جَمًّا, *confertim, cumulatè:* used as a particle: *Moreover, also, &c.* with such slight variation of either of these as the context may require. Noldius and Gesenius, &c. tell us, that it is used for emphasis' sake: but this would almost necessarily be true of any such word as *moreover:* the *accumulation* of words is perhaps never had recourse to for any other purpose. Noldius too makes it equivalent to the Latin *An;* or numquid? But no such power is discernible in the passages cited by him. The truth is, it will depend generally on the context—interrogative particles being but rarely introduced—whether a question is asked or not. And, on the whole, there appears to be nothing peculiar in the use of this particle, beyond that of our *moreover, even,* or *also.* See the places in Noldius at length, p. 201. et seq. or examine these following, in the Heb. Bible, Exod. xi. 3; Gen. xlvi. 4; 1 Sam. i. 6; Lev. xxvi. 24; Gen. xx. 6. In, Gen. vi. 3, בְּשַׁגַּם, *In that also he is flesh.—*

גמא (117) גמר

Ps. xcv. 9; 1 Sam. xii. 16. It is found in connexion with other particles, as גַּם, whether also? 1 Kings xvii. 20, וְגַם, and also: גַּם אֵין, גַּם עַד, גַּם כִּי, אַף גַּם, לֹא גַּם, גַּם לֹא, גַּם אֵין, אֲשֶׁר גַּם, גַּם אִם, אִם גַּם, גַּם אֶל, גַּם אַל, &c. See Nold. p. 204, &c., in all taking the sense which such combination would naturally suggest. See also Gram. art. 242, et seq.

גֹּמֶא, m. pl. non occ. *The reed* as generally found in lakes: also the *Paper reed of the Nile*, termed by the Latins *Bibula papyrus*, from its requiring much moisture for its growth. Plin. H. N. lib. xiii. c. xi. xii., where its several uses are enumerated (it. Facciolati sub v. papyrus): Lucan iv. 135, &c. Hence, תֵּבַת גֹּמֶא, *ark* or *chest of reed*, i. e. made of that material, Exod. ii. 3. כְּלִי־גֹמֶא, *vessel of do.*, Is. xviii. 2; xxxv. 7; Job viii. 11. See my note.

גמא, v. non occ. in Kal.—Arab. جمي, *cepit, et occultavit* quid. Cogn. جمع.

Pih. pres. יְגַמֵּא, *He takes, drinks, in* the earth; i. e. seems, from the swiftness of his course, to swallow it. Occurs in Job xxix. 24, only. See my note on the passage, Schultens, ib., and Bochart. Hieroz. I. p. 142, et seq.

Hiph. הַגְמִיאִינִי, Imp. f. aff. *make me drink*, i. e. *give me, &c.* Gen. xxiv. 17.

גֹּמֶד, m.—pl. non occ. once Judg. iii. 16, גֹּמֶד אָרְכָּהּ, *a גֹּמֶד—whatever that was—was its length*. Gesenius seems to think that this is the same word as the Chald. and Syr. ܐܟܡܕܐ and, that all the Philologians up to his time have been in the dark concerning it. He also tells us that, גָּמַע, i. e. גמד, *per metathesin*, signifies *truncavit*: and hence he goes on from a *branch, staff, &c.* so cut off, to *ulna, a cubit*; because a staff *(stab)* is taken as a measure in Germany. He does not seem at all to be aware that أكمدا is compounded of عظم, *bone*, and أيد, *the hand*, and hence signifies *a cubit*; although Castell had plainly told him so, at col. 618 of his Lexicon: and, of this, the כּוּרְמִיזָא, *baculus* of Buxtorf, and ܐܟܡܕܐ, of Norberg, cited by him, are in all probability mere corruptions! Again, it is any thing but certain, that the ܟܡܕ, of the Syriac version,—which Castell renders by *pugillus*,—is rightly translated in the Arabic of the Polyglott by ذراع, *a cubit.*—أكمدا and أكمدا, are no doubt corruptions of أكمدا; but then they are corruptions common enough with the Syrians;—see Kürsch's Preface to his Syriac Pentateuch—and no greater than those mentioned above, found in Buxtorf and Norberg. The whole of Gesenius's note is, therefore, founded on the most palpable mistake, and is consequently useless. From the context it should seem, that a weapon a cubit in length could scarcely have been used. I am disposed to think, therefore, that the σπιθαμῆς τὸ μῆκος αὐτοῦ of the LXX., the "*longitudinis palmæ manus*," of the Vulg., and the ܟܡܕ, *pugilles longituda ejus*, of the Syr., are right; and that the Targumist and Arab. are wrong in giving *cubitus, &c.* As to the etymology, as جمل, *to cut*, and جَمَّال, *a cutting sword* (and perhaps Pers. جمدهر, *a dagger*) claim an origin agreeing with that of our גֹּמֶד, I cannot help thinking that some cutting instrument (lit. *a cutter*) is intended by this word: perhaps *a pruning knife*. If so, the place will read thus:—*Ehud made himself a weapon* (sort of sword חֶרֶב), *and it had two edges, (a cutter) pruning knife* (was) *its length*. The blade of which would probably be *a span* in length, or thereabouts. The verb is much used in the Æthiopic to signify the *pruning of trees:* and so עָסִים: is *putator arborum*, Lud. col. 523. If this may be relied on, our word does not signify any specific measure: which is very probable. If it had, most likely it would have so occurred again, as we have so many places in the Bible in which measures are given.

גְּמָדִים, m. pl.—sing. non occ. Once Ezek. xxvii. 11. From the form of the word, *habit, profession*, is evidently meant. Gram. art. 154. 12. And, if we may rely on what has just been said of גֹּמֶד (last art.) *Short-swordsmen* would seem to be intended: such perhaps as those of the Roman armies, who did so much execution in close combat; the mention of *their shields* countenances this. Gesenius, "*bellatores fortes, hostes arborum instar* CÆDENTES," i. e. as derived from جمل, *amputavit;* which, to me, seems too general.

גָּמוּל, m. גְּמֻלָה, f. pl. aff. m. גְּמוּלָיו, f.

גְּמִי (118) גַּן

וּמְגִלּוֹת. Arab. جَمَال, *pulchritudo.* جُمْل, *summam facere.* Cogn. تَجْمِير, *collectio.* جَبَل, *consolidavit*, جَبَّر, id. Heb. גָּמַר. Æth. ⟨ססמ⟩: *perfecit.* Syr. id. Lit. *Completed, finished*, either well or ill. Hence, as the *lex talionis* required *par pari referre*, like for like; this word came to be used for *Retribution* either (a) of good, or (b) of bad actions. (a) With חַיִּים, Judg. ix. 16; Prov. xii. 14; 2 Sam. xix. 37; Ps. ciii. 2. (b) Is. iii. 11; Ps. xxviii. 4; Prov. xii. 14, &c. Aff. גְּמֻלָם, גְּמֻלְךָ, גְּמוּלָם, גְּמוּלוֹ.

גָּמִיר, m. Chald. part. גמר. *Complete, learned*, Ezra vii. 12.

גָּמָל, c. pl. גְּמַלִּים. Syr. ܓܰܡܠܐ, *camelus.* Arab. جَمَل, id. So called, perhaps, on account of its great value and usefulness, from جَمَال, *beautiful.* Cogn. جَبَّل, *formatio.* جَبَّر, *consolidatio.* Comp. جمر, كبر, كبل. *A camel*—Bochart. Hieroz. I. p. 75, et seq.—male or female, Gen. xxxi. 34; xxxii. 16; xxiv. 64; Lev. xi. 4, &c. Constr. גְּמַלֵי. Aff. גְּמַלֶּיךָ, גְּמַלֵּיהֶם, גְּמַלָּיו.

גָּמַל, v. pres. יִגְמֹל. See גְּמוּל. Lit. *Increasing, consolidating, perfecting.* Hence, I. *Recompensing, repaying, rendering like for like*, either (a) in a good, or (b) a bad sense. Constr. med. אֶל, עַל, לְ, and immed. pers.—immed. thing, it. with בְּ of comparison. 1 Sam. xxiv. 18; Ps. xiii. 6; ciii. 10; cvi. 7; Prov. xxxi. 12, &c.; (b) Prov. iii. 30; Ps. vii. 5; Gen. L. 15. 17, &c.

Part. גֹּמֵל, pl. גֹּמְלִים, Prov. xi. 17; Joel iv. 4; 2 Chron. xx. 11.

Imp. גְּמֹל, Ps. cxix. 17.

II. *Mature, ripen*, as fruits, Num. xvii. 23; Is. xviii. 5; Constr. abs. Part. גֹּמֵל.

III. *Weaning*, as a child. Constr. immed. 1 Sam. i. 23, 24; Hos. i. 8; 1 Kings xi. 20.
Part. pass. גָּמוּל, גָּמֻל, or גְּמוּלֵי חָלָב Phrases גְּמוּלֵי מֵחָלָב *Weaned from the milk*, Is. xxviii. 9. כְּגָמֻל עֲלֵי אִמּוֹ: אָמוֹ כַּגָּמֻל עָלַי נַפְשִׁי, *As a weaned* (child) *with his mother; so* (even) *as the weaned* (child), *with me* (is) *my soul.*

Infin. aff. גָּמְלָה, *her weaning* (him), 1 Sam. i. 23. גָּמְלָךְ, *thy weaning* (him), ib.

Niph. יִגָּמֵל, *Become, be, weaned*, Gen. xxi. 8. יִגָּמַל, 1 Sam. i. 22.

Infin. הִגָּמֵל, Gen. xxi. 8.

גָּמַר, v. pres. יִגְמֹר, constr. abs. it. with עַל, and גְּעַר, pers. Arab. جَمَر. Cogn. τῶν

גָּבַל, כָּבַר, גָּבַר. Heb. גָּמַל, &c. propr. *completing, finishing, &c.*

Hence I. *Bring to good effect*, Ps. lvii. 3; cxxxviii. 8.

II. *Finish, come to an end, fail*, Ps. vii. 10; xii. 2; lxxvii. 9.

גַּן, (a) m. pl. גַּנִּים, constr. גַּנֵּי ⎫ Syr.
גַּנָּה, (b) f. pl. גַּנּוֹת, ⎬ ܓܰܢܬܐ,
גִּנָּה, (c) f. pl. גִּנּוֹת, constr. גִּנּוֹת ⎭ *hortus, viridarium.* גָּנַן, *protexit.* Arab. جَنّ, id.—גַּנָּה, *hortus* vinearum, et arboribus consitus. Gesenius tells us that גַּנָּה occurs only in poetry; yet גַּן also occurs in the Prophets. גִּנָּה too, he says, is found only in the more modern Hebrew *(sequiore Hebraismo)*, and Chaldaism. It is found nevertheless in Job viii. 16, and Cant. vi. 11, which certainly are not written in modern Hebrew. *A garden* or *orchard*, either for trees, herbs, fruits, or flowers. (a) Gen. ii. 8. 15; Deut. xi. 10; 2 Kings xxix. 4; Jer. xxxix. 4; lii. 7; Ezek. xxxvi. 35; Joel ii. 3; Is. li. 3; Cant. iv. 12. See my note on Job viii. 17. (b) Is. i. 29, 30; lxi. 11; lxv. 3; Jer. xxix. 5. 28; Num. xxiv. 6, &c. (c) Job viii. 16; Cant. vi. 11; Est. i. 5; vii. 7. 8. Aff. (a) גַּנִּי, גַּנּוֹ. (b) גַּנּוֹתֵיהֶם. (c) גִּנָּתוֹ.

גַּנָּב, m. pl. גַּנָּבִים. Syr. ܓܰܢܳܒܐ, *fur.* Arab. جَنِيب, *qui extra viam se continet, veritus ne quis in ipsum incidat hospes. A thief*, Exod. xxii. 1; Deut. xxiv. 7; Ps. L. 18; Is. i. 23.

גָּנַב, v. pres. יִגְנֹב. Constr. abs. and immed. it. med. אֶת. See גַּנָּב. Prop. *moving*, or *removing* from one side, or part, to another; hence, I. *Stole, took, away secretly*, Gen. xxxi. 19. 30. 32; Exod. xx. 15: Josh. vii. 12; 2 Sam. xix. 42.—*forcibly*, applied to the wind; Job xxi. 18. Abs. with אֶת, יִגְנֹב, יַעֲקֹב אֶת־לֵב לָבָן, *Jacob stole away, as to the heart* (i. e. without the knowledge) *of Laban:* the heart being supposed to be the seat of knowledge, thought, &c., Gen. xxxi. 20. 26, 27. The sense here, therefore, is not *fefellit.* Comp. נִדָּחַם in the paral. vr. 27. The same may be said of the Greek κλέπτω. See Steph. sub voce. The ἔκλεψε νόον, therefore of Homer Il. xiv. 217, as well as the other examples cited in the Thes. of Gesenius are all against his etym.

Part. גֹּנֵב, *stealing*, Deut. xxiv. 7; Zech. v. 3.

גנב (119) געל

Pass. גָּנֻב, *Stolen*, pl. גְּנוּבִים, Prov. ix. 17. So Philostr., as cited by Steph., πᾶν δὲ τερπνότερον τὸ κεκλεμμένον; i. e. τὸ ἀπόρρητον τῆς ἡδονῆς. Fem. with parag. י, גְּנֻבְתִי, *thing stolen*, Gen. xxxi. 39.

Infin. גְּנֹב, Exod. xxii. 11; Hos. iv. 2.

Niph. pres. יִגָּנֵב, Exod. xxii. 11.

Pih. pres. יְגַנֵּב, *Steals*, i. e. *fraudulently appropriates to himself*: not *fefellit*, as Gesenius thinks, 2 Sam. xv. 6.

Part. pl. constr. מְגַנְּבֵי, *Fraudulent takers away of*, Jer. xxiii. 30.

Puh. גֻּנַּב, pres. יְגֻנַּב, *Became stolen*, Exod. xxii. 6; Gen. xl. 15: constr. מִן, of place, Job iv. 12, with אֶל, pers.

Infin. גֻּנֹּב, Gen. xl. 15.

Hithp. יִתְגַּנֵּב. pres. *Act in secret, steal*, 2 Sam. xix. 4. So Philo. l. c. Steph. κλέπτοντα τὴν εἴσοδον: it. κλέπτω τὴν νίκην, κ. τ. λ.

גְּנֵבָה, f. Aff. גְּנֵבָתוֹ, *Stolen thing*, Exod. xxii. 2, 3, al. non occ.

גִּנְזֵי, m. pl. constr. Heb. and Chald., also—

גִּנְזַיָּא, m. pl. def. Chald.—

Arab. جَنَزَ , كَنَزَ , *texit*. Æth. ሕዝ፡ id. Syr. ܓܢܙܐ, *absconditus*; ܓܢܙܐ, *thesaurus*. Pers. گنج, *Treasure*. Cogn. Heb. כנס. And, according to Mr. Bopp, the Sanscrit *Cosha*,

कोष:—*Treasures*, of money, merchandise, &c. Est. iii. 9; iv. 7; Ezek. xxvii. 24; Ezra v. 17; vi. 1; vii. 20.

גִּנְזַבָּיו, m. pl. aff. 1 Chron. xxviii. 11, only, *His treasuries*. Gesenius thinks the final ו here, might have been the Persic diminutive, as in مَرْدَك, *manikin*; which is very doubtful. The LXX. retains the word untranslated (ζακχων). The Vulg. *cellariorum*. Syr. ܓܙܒܬܐ, *gallery, &c.*

גָּנַן, pres. non occ. constr. med. עַל, or אֶל. See גַּן, גִּנָּה above. גְּנוֹתִי, *I have guarded*, (proph.) *will guard, protect*, 2 Kings xix. 34; xx. 6; Is. xxxvii. 35; xxxviii. 6.

Infin. גָּנוֹן, Is. xxxi. 5.

Hiph. pres. יָגֵן, constr. עַל, בְּעַד, i. q. Kal, Is. xxxi. 5; Zech. ix. 15; xii. 8.

געה non occ. pres. יִגְעֶה, constr. עַל, of thing, it. abs. Syr. ܓܥܐ, *clamavit. Lowing*, as oxen, Job vi. 5.

Infin. גְּעוֹ, 1 Sam. vi. 12. From this *lowing* voice, as Gesenius observes, the *cow* took its name, as in the Pers. گاو, *gāv*, Sanscr. *goh*, &c. Comp. Gr. γοάω, and Sanscr. गि, *gi, sing*.

גֹּעַל, m. once, Ezek. xvi. 5. Syr. ܓܥܠ, *deposuit, &c.* Arab. اِسْتَجْعَلَ, اَجْعَلَ, id. *libidinis fervore arrepta fuit canicula, &c.* جُعْل, *donum quo corrumpitur judex*. Hence the notions of *rejection, abhorrence. Abhorrence, loathing*.

גָּעַל, v. pres. תִּגְעַל, constr. immed. it. med. אֶת, בְּ, לְ. See גֹּעַל. *Loathed, abhorred*, Lev. xxvi. 11. 15. 30. 43, 44: often with נֶפֶשׁ, Ezek. xvi. 45.

Part. f. גֹּעֶלֶת, Ezek. xvi. 45.

Niph. נִגְעַל, *Became, was, rejected, cast away*, 2 Sam. i. 21. LXX. προσωχθίσθη.

Hiph. לֹא יַגְעִל, *Casts not*, as we say, "a cow casts not her calf," i. e. *prematurely*, Job xxi. 10. LXX. οὐκ ὠμοτόκησε.

גָּעַר, v. pres. יִגְעַר, constr. immed. it. med. בְּ, pers. it. לְ, pers. בְּ, or אֶת, thing. Syr. ܓܥܪ, *increpavit*. Æth. *gemuit*. Arab. جَأَر, *mugivit bos*. Cogn. جرو, *animosus fuit. Rebuked, reproved*, Gen. xxxvii. 10; Is. xvii. 13; Jer. xxix. 27; Ps. ix. 6; cxix. 21; Mal. iii. 11; Zech. iii. 2.

Imp. גְּעַר, Ps. lxviii. 31.

Part. גּוֹעֵר, Nah. i. 4; גֹּעֵר, Mal. ii. 3.

גְּעָרָה, f. constr. גַּעֲרַת. *Rebuke, chiding, reproof*, Prov. xiii. 1. 8; xvii. 10; Eccl. vii. 5; Is. xxx. 17; li. 20; Ps. lxxvi. 7; lxxx. 17; civ. 7. Aff. גַּעֲרָתְךָ, גַּעֲרָתִי.

געש, v. non occ.—pres. תִּגְעַשׁ. Syr. ܓܥܫ, *cornu petiit*. Arab. cogn. جاش, *commotus fuit*. جوت, *territus*. Syn. רעשׁ. Constr. abs. *Shook, trembled*, Ps. xviii. 8.

Puh. גֹּעֲשׁוּ, *Became, were, moved, shaken, perplexed*, Job xxxiv. 20.

Hithp. הִתְגָּעֲשׁוּ, id. Jer. xxv. 16. Gram. art. 196. 5.

Hithp. it. הִתְגָּעַשׁ, 2 Sam. xxii. 8, which seems to be only a various reading of Ps. xviii. 8, above cited, pl. m. יִתְגָּעֲשׁוּ, id. Jer. v. 22; xlvi. 7, 8; Ps. xviii. 8.

גַּעַת, see געה.

גַּף, m. r. גּוּף. Arab. جفّ, agmen hominum, &c. Syr. ܓܦ, eminuit. Cogn. גב. Whole body; hence, I. Person, self, only, as, בְּגַפּוֹ, in, or with, himself only; i. e. without family, Exod. xxi. 3, 4. II. Back, i. e. hillock, or eminence, Prov. ix. 3 : constr. pl. גַּפֵּי. III. Chald. גַּפִּין. Syr. ܓܦܐ, ala. Wings, Dan. vii. 4. 6. Comp. אֲגַפִּים.

גֶּפֶן, c. pl. גְּפָנִים, constr. גַּפְנֵי. Arab. جفن, radix vitis, vel palmes (vitis). Cogn. جفل, celeriter incessit; جفلة, multa folia habens arbor. I. A vine, generally. גֶּפֶן הַיַּיִן, Wine-grape, Num. vi. 4; Judg. ix. 13; xiii. 14; Gen. xl. 9; Is. vii. 23; xxiv. 7; xxxii. 12, &c. II. The wild vine, גֶּפֶן שָׂדֶה, 2 Kings iv. 39. See אוּר, p. 15 above. In Jer. ii. 21, גֶּפֶן נָכְרִיָּה, foreign vine : i. e. producing corrupt fruit. Comp. Is. v. 2; Deut. xxxii. 32; Matt. vii. 16. Aff. גַּפְנִי, גַּפְנוֹ, &c.

גֹּפֶר, m. occ. once, Gen. vi. 14. עֲצֵי גֹפֶר, Trees or wood of Gopher. Arab. كفر, pix. Cogn. غفر, texit, obduxit. Hence, as Gesenius well observes, most probably some such wood as pitch-pine. See Bochart. Phaleg. lib. iv., Olav. Cels. Hierobot. i. 328, who thinks it was the cypress.

גָּפְרִית, f. pl. non occ. Syr. ܟܒܪܝܬܐ, sulphur. Arab. كبريت, id. Brimstone, sulphur : applied to the lightning, apparently, Gen. xix. 24; Job xviii. 15. See my note on this place, Ezek. xxxviii. 22; Ps. xi. 6. In Is. xxx. 33, נַחַל גָּפְרִית, as a torrent of sulphur, i. e. a rushing stream of lightning poured down upon it, Deut. xxix. 22; Is. xxxiv. 9; with זֶפֶת, pitch.

גֵּר, m. גֵּרָה, f. Dweller, &c. See גור.

גֵּר, m. pl. גֵּרִים. See גור. Arab. جار, r. جور, contr. for גּוֵּר, or גַּוִיר, Gram. artt. 72. 75. A sojourner, i. e. a foreigner residing in the land of Israel, as the Israelites did in Egypt, or as Abraham did in the land of Canaan. Opp. to אֶזְרָח, Exod. xii. 19, &c.; to אָח, Deut. xxiv. 14. Comp. Gen. xv. 13; Exod. ii. 22; xviii. 3, &c. occasionally found with תּוֹשָׁב, which see, Gen. xxiii. 4; Lev. xxv. 35. 47. "Jes. v. 17. גֵּרִים," says Gesenius, "videntur pastores....

quales olim Hebræi," &c. But this is an error: the word is גָּרִים, (not גֵּרִים) Dwellers (then) in the land; i. e. natives not carried into captivity, is probably meant. Metaph. taking the life of man as a sojourning in a foreign country, Ps. xxxix. 13; 1 Chron. xxix. 5. Comp. Gen. xlvii. 9; Ps. cxix. 54. Aff. גֵּרְךָ. גֵּרוֹ.

גֵּר, see נִיר.

גֹּר, see גּוּר.

גָּרָב, m.—pl. non occ.—Syr. ܓܪܒܐ, lepra, et leprosus. جرب, scabiosus. Scurvied person : i. e. infected with a malignant sort of itch. Not scurvy, &c., scabies, abs. as Gesenius makes it, Lev. xxi. 20; xxii. 22. LXX. Ἄνθρωπος ᾧ ἂν ᾖ ἐν αὐτῷ ψώρα ἀγρία: not ψώρα ἀγρία only, Targ. גַּרְבָּן, Vulg. habens....jugem scabiem. Gesenius well remarks that several cognate words seem to have originated from the noise made in scratching or scraping. Our term scurvy is evidently one of these.

גַּרְגְּרִים, m. pl.—sing. non occ. Berries, Is. xvii. 6, al. non occ. See also אָמִיר, pp. 39, 40, above, with the note.

גַּרְגְּרוֹתֶיהָ, pl. m. aff.—sing. non occ. Syr. ܓܪܓ, attraxit; ܓܪܓ, ruminavit. ܓܪܓܪܬܐ, Guttur. Arab. جر, traxit; اجترّ, ruminatio; جرجر, cum murmure per guttur demisit potum. جرجر, murmur aquæ delabentis in gutture. Æth. ጕርጕር : murmuratio. Germ. Gurgel. French and Engl. Gorge. Cogn. Heb. גָּרוֹן.—The neck, or parts in front of it, perhaps, where the ornaments of women, and gorgets of military officers are usually hung. Prov. i. 9; iii. 3. 22; vi. 21, al. non occ.

גרד, v. Kal non occ. Hithp. הִתְגָּרֵד, Infin. Syr. ܓܪܕ, erasit; ܓܪܕ, erasit se. Arab. جرد, avulsit, velut decorticando rem. To scrape, or scratch, himself, Job ii. 8, al. non occ.

גָּרָה, v. in Kal. non occ. Pih. גֵּרָה, constr. immed. ܓܪܐ, trahit. Pah. جرى, litigavit. Æthp. ܐܓܪܝ, insolens fuit. Arab. جرى, cucurrit, processit, audax fuit. استجرى, audacem se

גרה (121) גרז

ostendit. Cogn. جَرُوَ, *ausus est*. it. جَرَّ, conj. iii. *vexavit, inimicus fuit*; iv. *confodit hasta*. Hence, from *proceeding, drawing out, &c.* seems to have followed as a consequence, *contention, attack, &c.* And, it is remarkable, all these notions are here found in the same verb.—Comp. Prov. xxx. 33, and xvii. 14. It is doubtful, too, whether all the words cited here by Gesenius in his Thesaurus (p. 301), have not originally some such signification. See his remarks, sub voce גרר. *Produces, excites.* יְגָרֶה מָדוֹן, *produces contention*, Prov. xv. 18; xxviii. 25; xxix. 22.

Hithp. הִתְגָּרִית, pres. תִּתְגָּרֶה. Apoc. תִּתְגָּר. Constr. med. ב pers. immed. thing; it. ב, or ל, thing. *Hast become drawn out, drawn out thyself*, for contention, attack, Jer. L. 24. הִתְגָּרָה בְרָעָה, *contendest with evil*, 2 Kings xiv. 10; 2 Chron. xxv. 19; Deut. ii. 5. 9. 19; Dan. x. 25; Ib. ver. 10, ellip.; Prov. xxviii. 4, &c.

Imp. הִתְגָּר, Deut. ii. 24.

גֵּרָה, f. Arab. جِرَّة, *trahendi modus, cibus ruminis*. I. *The cud*, as brought up and chewed by certain animals: hence found with the verb. הֶעֱלָה, Lev. xi. 3; Deut. xiv. 6, 7, also with יָרַר, r. גרר, Lev. xi. 7.

II. *The Gerah*, a certain weight, equal to one-twentieth part of a shekel, Exod. xxx. 13; Lev. xxvii. 25; Num. iii. 47; xviii. 16; Ezek. xlv. 12. Derived, as Gesenius thinks, from גַּרְגֵּר, *a bean* or *berry*, used at first just as a barley-corn or pepper-corn was among ourselves, to determine certain measures, or as the *carat*, among the Greeks and Romans.

גָּרוֹן, m. constr. גְּרוֹן. See גֵּרָה. Arab. جَرَيَان, *cursus*. Hence, as with us, *a course*, meton. applied to a place *of passage*: hence, too, the throat, as being open is compared to the grave, Ps. v. 10; and in Is. lviii. 1, to the tube of a trumpet. Comp. Lat. *guttur*. *The throat*, either internal or external, Ps. lxix. 4; cxv. 7; cxlix. 6; Is. iii. 16; Ezek. xvi. 11.

גֵּרוּת, f. Syr. ܓܶܪܘܬܐ, *peregrinitas*. Arab. جَارَة, *protectio*: i. e. from being received as a neighbour. So جِوَار, the being near some one, and received under his protection. *Sojourning, residing*, Jer. xli. 17. גֵּרוּת כִּמְהָם, *In the sojourning*, i. e. the residence, or estate of *Chimham*, in which he enjoyed the protection of David. See 2 Sam. xix. 37, 38, and Targ.

גרז, v. in Kal non occ. Arab. جَزَّ, *amputavit*, i. q. جَزَر.

Niph. נִגְרַזְתִּי, *I am*, or *am become, cut off*, Ps. xxxi. 23, constr. מִנֶּגֶד it. נִגְזָרוּ, Ib lxxxviii. 6; in some MSS. נִגְרָתִי.

גַּרְזֶן, m. Arab. كَرْزَن, كَرْزَن, &c. *securis. An axe*, Deut. xix. 5; xx. 19; Is. x. 15. In 1 Kings vi. 7, that of a stonemason, according to Gesenius, which is by no means certain: the כְּלִי־בַרְזֶל following will hardly allow of this.

גָּרָל, m. kethiv. Prov. xix. 19, for which the keri gives גָּדֹל, and this all the versions follow. Gesenius prefers the kethiv, because, as the Arab. جَرَل, means *locus glareosus*, the grating disagreeable sound made by treading on gravel will, he thinks, supply a more pointed sense. I can see no ground for such a supposition, nor do I know of any such analogy in this family of languages.

גֶּרֶם, m. pl. גְּרָמַי, aff. Syr. ܓܪܡܐ, *abscissio*; ܓܪܡܐ, *excissio*. Arab. جَرَم, *Cutting away, taking away; committing crime*. The primitive notion seems to consist in cutting, deeply injuring, &c. Comp. cogn. גרב, جلف; جلم, جرب, *decorticavit*; when applied to the palm-tree, cutting away the bunches and branches, so as to make the stem quite naked: so when applied to the shearing of sheep. Hence the notion of laid open to the very BODY, or BONE: so Syr. ܓܠܡ, *revelatio*. Arab. جَلَم, *pecude= longis pedibus et crine nudis*. Comp. جَلَمَة, so also, جَرَم, *dactyli sicci; ossa dactylorum magnus corpore*. Hence—

I. *The bone*, Prov. xvii. 22; xxv. 15; Job xl. 18. See my note here.

II. Meton. *Powerful, strong*, Gen. xlix. 14. See جَرِيم; pl. excel. جَرَمَاء, *jumentum eximium*.

III. Hence, *Frame-work*, perhaps, i. e. a sort of pulpit (the مِنْبَر, or publishing pulpit

R

גרם (122) גרף

of the Mohammedans. See my note on Job xxix. 7.), 2 Kings ix. 13; 2 Chron. ix. 18.

גֶּרֶם, m. Chald. *The bone*, Dan. vi. 25: pl. aff. גַּרְמֵיהוֹן.

גָּרְמוּ, v. pl. Zeph. iii. 3. *They cut, injure, spoil*, not לַבֹּקֶר, *at the dawn:* i. e. in the light, but by night; being זְאֵבֵי עֶרֶב. Comp. Job xxiv. 14, and see my note on the place.

Pih גֵּרְמוּ, f. תְּגָרְמִי. *Shall utterly cut away, destroy,* Num. xxiv. 8, *their bones,* i. e. strength; Ezek. xxiii. 34, חֲרָשֶׂיהָ, *her vessels,* i. e. of wine. How the "*reposuit,*" "*derodit,*" rodes, i. e. "lambes," of Gesenius in these several places, can either be derived or defended, I know not.

גֹּרֶן, m. pl. f. גְּרָנוֹת (for גָּרְנוֹת), constr. גָּרְנוֹת. Arab. جرن, *locus ubi siccantur dactyli; area.* I. *An area,* or open court of judicature in the gates of a city, in which public questions were discussed. Gesenius says, "alibi רֹחַב dicta:" which may be doubted. 1 Kings xxii. 10; 2 Chron. xviii. 9. II. pec. *The area,* or *floor,* in which the corn was trodden or threshed out, Judg. vi. 37; Ruth iii. 2; Num. xviii. 30; Is. xxi. 10. בֶּן־גָּרְנִי, *Son of my threshing floor:* i. e. one who has suffered, as if by the wheel of the threshing instrument, &c. Comp. Micah iv. 12, 13. III. Meton. *Corn of the floor,* Job xxxix. 12. Aff. גָּרְנִי, גָּרְנְךָ. He parag. גָּרְנָה.

גָּרַס, v. pres. non occ. Syr. ܓܪܣ, *periit.* Arab. cogn. جرس, *secuit; infelix fuit.* جرش, *in grossiores partes contudit.*

جرض, *mærore affectus fuit. Greatly pained, overwhelmed,* as it were with desire; not unlike the Latin *periit,* perhaps. Constr. med. ל, Ps. cxix. 20.

Hiph. יַגְרֵס, *He breaks, destroys,* Lam. iii. 16. With ב of the thing. See cogn. גֶּרֶשׂ.

גָּרַע, v. pret. non occ. pres. יִגְרַע, constr. immed. med. מִן, אֶל, לִפְנֵי. Syr. ܓܪܥ, *rasit, abrasit.* Arab. جرع, *sorpsit.* Cogn. جدع, *amputavit;* جذع, *separavit.* Heb. גדע, גוע, גור, &c. *Cutting off* or *away;* hence, *taking away, reserving* to self, Deut. xiii. 1. לֹא תִגְרַע, *Thou shalt not take away:* opp. τῷ תֹּסֵף, Jer. xxvi. 2; Job xv. 4: with חָסַר, Ib. ver. 8. תִּגְרַע אֵלֶיךָ, *reservest to thyself,* Ib.

xxxvi. 7. עֵינָיו, for עֵינֵי חָפֵץ, it. Exod. xxi. 10; Ezek. v. 11; xvi. 27, &c.
Infin. גְּרֹעַ, Eccl. iii. 14.
Part. pass. f. גְּרֻעָה, Jer. xlviii. 37.
Niph. נִגְרַע, pres. יִגָּרַע. *Became, was, taken away; subtracted,* Num. xxxvi. 3: opp. נוֹסָף, xxvii. 4; xxxvi. 3, 4; ix. 7.
Part. נִגְרָע, Exod. v. 11.
Pih. יְגָרַע, *Draws off,* of the rain, Job xxxvi. 27.

גָּרַף, v. occ. once, Judg. v. 21. · Syr. ܓܪܦ, *alluvione, corripuit.* Arab. جرف, *totum abstulit.* Cogn. جدب, *abstulit;* جذب, *traxit.* Comp. جرم, جذب, &c. *Swept away,* as mighty waters. Aff. גְּרָפָם.

גרר, v. pres. יָגֹר, and יִגֹּר, constr. immed. it. ב, instr. Syr. ܓܪ. Arab. جر, *traxit, abripuit. Drawing, dragging,* along or *away.* יְגֹרֵהוּ, *He drags him,* Hab. i. 15. יְגוֹרֵם, it *drags them,* Prov. xxi. 7. יֵרֶה .... גֵּרָה, *draws* (up) *the cud,* Lev. xi. 7, of the cognate נגר. Syr. ܓܪ, *tardavit.* Arab. جر, *propulit,* &c.

Niph. נִגְרִים, and נִגְרוֹת (of the latter), *Things drawn forth,* i. e. *dispersed* as waters, 2 Sam. xiv. 14; Job xx. 28. See נגר.
Pih. part. pl. f. מְגֹרָרוֹת, *Sawed,* i. e. stones: so called either from the action—drawing to and fro—of sawing, or from the scraping noise so made, 1 Kings vii. 9.
Hithp. part. מִתְגּוֹרֵר, *Sweeping away,* i. e. assuming that character, as a whirlwind, Jer. xxx. 23.

גֶּרֶשׂ, m. Syr. ܓܪܣ, *contusus, comminutus.* See גרס. Lit. *Beating* or *pounding:* and, meton. *corn,* either *thrashed,* or *reduced to flour,* Lev. ii. 14. 16, al. non occ. Aff. גִּרְשָׂהּ.

גֶּרֶשׂ, m.—pl. non occ. Arab. جرش, *lente cucurrit.* Cogn. جلز, *extendit.* Lit. *putting forth. Produce, fruit, &c.,* Deut. xxxiii. 14, al. non occ.

גרשׁ, v. pret. non occ. pres. יְגָרֵשׁ. *Putting* or *casting forth,* or *out.* Constr. immed. it. med. כְּן, Is. lvii. 20. יְגָרְשׁוּ מֵימָיו, *Its waters cast forth.*
Part. גֹּרֵשׁ, Exod. xxxiv. 11.
Part. pass. f. גְּרוּשָׁה, pl. גְּרוּשׁוֹת, *Cast out,* i. e. *repudiated,* Lev. xxi. 7. 14; xxii. 13; Num.

xxx. 10; Ezek. xlv. 9. Comp. Mic. ii. 9, here.

Niph. נִגְרְשׁוּ, *Cast*, or *driven out*, Is. lvii. 20; Jon. ii. 5; Amos viii. 8, *as by a flood*.

Pih. גֵּרַשְׁתָּ, גֵּרְשָׁה, pres. יְגָרֵשׁ, constr. immed. it. med. אֶת, מִן. *Cast, thrust out, expel*, Gen. iii. 24; iv. 14; xxi. 10; Exod. xi. 1; Judg. xi. 7; Ezek. xxxi. 11.

Infin. גָּרֵשׁ, Exod. xi. 1; Prov. xxii. 10. Imp. גָּרֵשׁ, Gen. xxi. 10.

Puh. גֹּרְשׁוּ, pres. יְגֹרְשׁוּ, *Were, became cast, thrust out*, Exod. xii. 39; Job xxx. 5.

גֶּשֶׁם, גֹּשׁוּ, גֻּשׁוּ, גָּשׂחַ, גַּשׁ, גֵּשׁ. See נָגַשׁ.

גֶּשֶׁם, m. pl. גְּשָׁמִים, constr. גִּשְׁמֵי. Syr. ܓܫܡܐ, *corpus*. Arab. جِشْم, *gravitas ponderis, pinguedo*. Cogn. جسم, *corpus*. *Shower* of rain, gushing as it were down in a body, heavily. See Zech. x. 1; Job xxxvii. 6. See my note here. With גָּדוֹל, 1 Kings xviii. 45. שׁוֹטֵף, Ezek. xiii. 11. Comp. Job xxxviii. 34. Aff. גִּשְׁמֵיכֶם. Hence the verb—

Puh. גֻּשְּׁמָה, more regularly גֻּשָּׁמָה, *rained on*. The Masora, however, has particularly marked this reading, as is to be seen in the lower margin of the common Bibles. Hence, some have taken the word as a noun, of גֶּשֶׁם, with aff. הָ, *its rain* is not.

Hiph. part. pl. מַגְשִׁמִים, *Those who cause or give rain*, Jer. xiv. 22.

גְּשֵׁם, m. Chald. *Body*, Dan. iii. 27; iv. 30; v. 21; vii. 11. Aff. גִּשְׁמֵהּ, גִּשְׁמְהוֹן.

גשׁשׁ, v. in Kal. non occ. Syr. ܓܫ, *palpavit exploravit*. Arab. جَسَّ, id. See my Sermons and Dissertations, p. 181.

Pih. נְגַשְׁשָׁה, 1st. pers. pl. with ה parag. t. ib. נְגַשֵּׁשָׁה. In the first case the Dagesh is omitted, by mistake most likely; in the second, we have (··) under the first שׁ, on account of the pause accent. *We feel, grope about*, Is. lix. 10.

גֶּשֶׁת, see נָגַשׁ.

גַּת, f. pl. גִּתּוֹת (for גִּנֹת), contr. גְּנַת, r. יגן, or יגן. Arab. وَجَنَ, *contudit subegitve fullo pannum, &c. Lit. bruising. Meton. The vat* in which grapes are trodden before they are pressed. Hence, metaph. applied to any place in which war or bloodshed is carried on, Joel iv. 13; Neh. xiii. 15; Judg. vi. 11; Lam. i. 15; Is. lxiii. 2.

גִּתִּי, m. patronym. of גַּת, a city of the Philistines, in which Goliath was born, Josh. xiii. 3, &c. A Gittite, 2 Sam. vi. 10, &c. Hence, perhaps,—

גִּתִּית, found in the titles of certain Psalms, viz.—viii., lxxxi., lxxxiv., and thought by some to be the name of a musical instrument.

ד

ד, *Daleth*, the fourth letter of the Hebrew alphabet, so named, because, as it should seem, it originally represented one of *a pair of folding doors*, which the word signifies. See דֶּלֶת below. In the Samaritan the form is still ᛋ; in the ancient Phœnician it was ꓷ, or ◁; whence we have the Greek Δ, both as to form and name. On its pronunciation, see Gram. art. 11 and 4; in the last of which its numerical power, viz. iv., is given. As its pronunciation originally was,—as that of the Persian د now is, see Sir Wm. Jones's Gram., edit. 9, art. 14,—twofold, and therefore the more easily assimilated to several others of the same organ; it is occasionally found interchanged with ז, Arab. ذ, ز; Chald. and Syr. ט and ܛ; and, as

Gesenius thinks with ת, Arab. ث, and Heb. ל, which may perhaps be doubted; as, in דּוּד; זוּד; נֶדֶר, דָּבַר; נֶטֶף, דָּטַף; פֶּגַע, or جزع. So Pers. گذشتن, or گرشتن, l. c. art. 15. דָּפָּה, Chald. מְבָא. Syr. ܣ, it. בָּטַל, Arab. بَطَل, cogn. בָּתַק, בָּטֵם, Arab. بَتَك, Arab. بَدَن, &c.; but these three last cases are doubtful, as is אֵד, and אוּל. It. with ר, דָּאָה, רָאָה, דִּיפָה, רִיפָה, &c.

דָּא, Chald. i. q. Heb. זֶה, זֹה, or וֹאת; occurring also in the forms דְּנָה, דֵּךְ, דֵּן, דֵּי, all apparently the same with the rel. pron. דִּי, contr. דְּ, Syr. ܕ; but terminating

דאב (124) דב

with an additional letter. *This,* Dan. iv. 27; v. 6, &c.

דְּאָבָה, f. Arab. دَأَبَ, *lassus fuit;* دَأَبَ, *festinavit;* دَأَبَ, *vituperium.* Cogn. דּוּב, *fluxit;* Chald. דּוּב; Syr. ܕܽܘܒ; id. Arab. دَأَبَ, *liquidum evasit;* Lat. *tabes;* lit. *dissolving, melting, &c.:* hence, *Distress, sorrow,* as proceeding from extreme exhaustion or want, Job xli. 14, al. non occ.

דְּאָבָה, f. *Languid, failing,* Ps. lxxxviii. 10. Comp. vi. 8, and Deut. xxxiv. 7, &c., as applied to the eye. With נֶפֶשׁ, Jer. xxxi. 25, it. vr. 12, ib. with לֹ and the verb יוֹסִיפוּ. *They shall no more be, or become languid.*

דְּאָבוֹן, m. augm. *Extreme languor, fainting,* Deut. xxviii. 65, with כִּלְיוֹן עֵינַיִם, in the paral. al. non occ.

דָּאַג, i. q. דָּג.

דָּאַב, v. pres. יִדְאַג. Arab. دَأَجَ, *inflavit in utrem, eumque implevit;* دَوْج, *potatio.* Syr. ܕܽܘܒ, *lac acidum;* ܕܽܘܒ, *mutus.* Arab. cogn. دَوْخ, *lac agitatum:* hence, دَاخَ, *universali morbo laboravit.* Comp. دَاقَ, r. دوق; originating perhaps in an opinion current in the East, that drinking bad milk brings on weakness. See my Job, pp. 191. 219, &c. *Being very anxious, alarmed;* hence,

II. Meton. *Languishing,* constr. abs. it. with אֶת, לֹ, pers. and מִן, of the thing. I. 1 Sam. ix. 5; x. 2; Is. lvii. 11; Ps. xxxviii. 19. II. Jer. xvii. 8.

Part. דֹּאֵג, pl. דֹּאֲגִים, Jer. xxxviii. 19; xlii. 16.

דְּאָגָה, f. *Anxiety, alarm, dread;* with שִׂמְחָה, רִנָּה, as Syn. Ezek. xii. 18, 19; Josh. xxii. 24; Prov. xii. 25; Jer. xlix. 23; Ezek. iv. 16.

דָּאָה, f. Lev. xi. 14; which Deut. xiv. 13, is רָאָה. See p. 123, let. ר; al. non occ. The name of a certain bird. LXX. γύψ. Vulg. *Milvus.* So Bochart. Hieroz. 2. p. 191.

דָּאָה, v. pret. non occ. pres. יִדְאֶה, apoc. יֵדֶא. *Flying,* as an eagle, i. e. swiftly, Deut. xxviii. 49; Jer. xlviii. 40; xlix. 22; Ps. xviii. 11.

דֹּב, or דּוֹב, c. pl. דֻּבִּים. Syr. ܕܶܒܳܐ, *ursus,* vel *ursa.* Æth. ድብ: id. Arab. دُبٌّ, دُبَّة, id. lit. *creeping, crawling.* r. دبّ. *A bear,* he or she: occasionally applied metaphorically to men, 1 Sam. xvii. 34. 36, 37; 2 Sam. xvii. 8; 2 Kings ii. 24; Is. xi. 7; Hos. xiii. 8; Lam. iii. 10; Prov. xvii. 12, &c.

דֹּב, Chald. i. q. Heb. Dan. vii. 5.

דֵּבֶא, m. once, Deut. xxxiii. 25. Aff. דָּנְאָךְ. Auth. Vers. "*thy strength.*" LXX. ἡ ἰσχύς σου. So the Syriac and Targ. Vulg. *senectus tua.* Sam. *Doctores tui.* Gesen. *magnificentia tua.* He objects to the "*senectus*" of the Vulgate, because he says this word can form no opposition to יָמֶיךָ; while he equally improperly proposes *languor, quies,* poët. *mons tua,* to this word. But, on what grounds can he make a word, which he says is the same with دَبَّ, *reptitavit,* signify *languor, quies, mors?* I can see no connecting link between these several notions. Hottinger had proposed the Arab. دَبِّي, *lentus, incessus, &c.;* but these, he says, are metaphorical senses, taken from دَبَّ. Still this can be no objection here; because it may also be argued, that even many Hebrew words may be shewn to be derived from a metaphorical acceptation of others. But, if this were true, how then should we account for دَبَّى, n. a. تَدْبِيَة, *operatus est;* أَدْبَى, *produxit quid simile locustis parvis, &c.?* Is it not full as likely, that such locusts received their name from the notion of *production,* as that this verb was formed from the name of the locust? and hence the phrases, دَبًا دَبِّي, sing. and دَبَّيْن, *multæ opes.* The passage evidently contains a blessing promised to Asher; and, if we may rely on the etymologies just offered, it ought to mean, *as thy days* (shall be), i. e. as the circumstances of thy life, thy trials, wants, &c. See my notes on Job, p. 301, &c. (so shall) be *thy produce, wealth, power.* The opposition here is complete; and the ancient translators have rightly interpreted the place.

דִּבָּה, f. constr. דִּבַּת. Arab. دَبَّة, *reptatio,* hence دَبُوب, *obtrectator.* Syr. ܐܶܡܰܕ ,

דבו (125) דבק

diffamavit; lit. *creeping*, applied to secret scandalous reports; hence, I. *Infamy, ill report.* II. Meton. *infamous character.* I. Gen. xxxvii. 2; Num. xiii. 32; xiv. 36, 37; Ps. xxxi. 14, &c. II. Prov. xxv. 10. Aff. דִּבָּתָם, דִּבָּתְךָ.

דְּבוֹרָה, f. pl. דְּבֹרִים. Syr. ܕܶܒܳܪܐ, *vespa.* Arab. دَبْر, دَبُور, *examen apum.* Cogn. زَنْبُور, *vespa.* A *bee*, Is. vii. 18; Judg. xiv. 8; Deut. i. 44; Ps. cxviii. 12; al. non occ. Gesenius takes the singular as a noun of unity, as in the Arab. عَلَامَة. The passage, Is. vii. 18, in which it occurs, does not countenance this.

דִּבְחִין, m. pl. Chald. *Sacrifices*, Ezra vi. 3; al. non occ. See זבח.

דָּבְחִין, m. pl. Chald. part. r. דבח. Persons *sacrificing*, Ezra vi. 3.

דִּבְיוֹנִים, m. pl. *keri*, 2 Kings vi. 25, al. non occ. for חריונים, which is in the text. Compd. of דב. Arab. دَبَّ, *paulatim fluxit,* i. e. *excrementum;* and יוֹנִים, *pigeons,* i. e. *pigeons' dung.*

דְּבִיר, m. *The oracle,* i. e. that part of the Temple, and of *the most holy place,* in which responses were given from above the Cherubim, and in which the ark of the covenant was placed: so called, as it has been usually thought, because *the word of Jehovah,* דְּבַר יְהֹוָה, was thence received by the chief priest. So Jerome, and, after him, divines generally. Gesenius, after Simonis and Ikenius, thinks it is derived from دُبُر, or دِبَر, *postica pars rei;* meaning *the western part;* because in this part of the Temple the דְּבִיר was; which is perhaps more ingenious than sound, 1 Kings vi. 5. 19—22. 31; viii. 6—8; 2 Chron. iii. 16; iv. 20; v. 7. 9. See under הֵיכָל below.

דְּבֵלָה, f. constr. דְּבֶלֶת, pl. m. דְּבֵלִים. Syr. ܒܟܣ, pl. ܕܒܠܟܣ, *palatha,* παλάθη, *massa caricarum.* Arab. دَبَلَ, *in unum coëgit rem, ac rotundiore forma, ut buccellam.* دُبْلَة, *buccella magna; res quævis buccellæ formam habens.* A *cake* of dried figs, 1 Sam. xxv. 18; xxx. 12; 2 Kings xx. 7; Is. xxxviii. 21; 1 Chron. xii. 40. Celsii Hierob. ii. 377, et seq., where every necessary information on this subject will be found.

דֶּבֶק, m. pl. דְּבָקִים. Syr. ܕܶܒܩܳܐ, *viscus.* Arab. دِبْق, id. *Joining, juncture; soldering* of metals, Is. xli. 7; 1 Kings xxii. 34; 2 Chron. xviii. 33, *rivets,* perhaps, or *rings* connecting the different parts of the armour.

דָּבֵק, m. pl. דְּבֵקִים, Person *adhering to,*
דִּבְקָה, f. 2 Kings iii. 3; Deut. iv. 4: with מ of comp. Prov. xviii. 24. Fem. thing *adhering, touching,* לְ, 2 Chron. iii. 12, p. non occ.

דָּבַק, and דָּבֵק, v. pres. יִדְבַּק, constr. בְּ, אֶל, אַחֲרֵי, and abs. *Adhering, cleaving, sticking to, arriving at,* any person or thing, Gen. ii. 24; xix. 19; xxxiv. 3; Deut. xii. 18; Jer. xiii. 11; Lam. iv. 4; Ps. lxiii. 9; cxxxvii. 6; Job xxxi. 7, &c.

Puh. pres. יְדֻבָּק, *Made to adhere, stick to,* &c. Job xxxviii. 38; xli. 9.

Hiph. הִדְבִּיק, pres. יַדְבִּיק, constr. immed. it. with אֶל, בְּ, אֶת, אַחֲרֵי, *Causing* or *making adhere, stick, come up to,* Jer. xiii. 11; Ezek. iii. 26; xxxix. 4; Judg. xviii. 22; xx. 42. 45; 1 Sam. xiv. 22; 2 Sam. i. 6, &c.

Hoph. part. מֻדְבָּק, *Made to adhere, stick to,* Ps. xxii. 16.

דָּבְקִין, m. pl. part. Chald. *Adhering,* Dan. ii. 43, constr. לְ, al. non occ.

דָּבָר, m. pl. part. דְּבָרִים, Hos. xiii. 14. Arab. كَبَر, *examen apum;* it. *multæ opes;* it. *arvum ejusve partes;* it. *mors;* دِبْر, id. et *fœtus locustæ;* it. *aqua ingens.* Comp. cogn. دَبَر, دِبَل: دَبَل, *postica pars;* غَابِر, *exiens e scopo sagitta;* دَبَار, *agri pars,* &c. *fossulæ inter sata factæ, ut iisdem rigentur.* Syr. et Chald. ܕܒܰܪ, *duxit, eduxit;* ܘܰܕܒܰܪ, *ductus regimen,* i. q. Arabic تَدْبِير. The primitive notion in all which evidently is, *putting forth,* either in a good or bad sense: hence, in the first, *wealth, multitude,* &c.; in the second, *death, injury,* &c.; and, as to the action itself, *coming after, going out of the way; leading, ruling:* hence, meton. places in which this is done, as *part of a field,* &c.: *ditches* for conducting water, &c. Hence, too, applied to speech, as something *put forth, given out, enounced, fluent, fluency.* Gr. ῥέω. Lat. *fluo,* whence *fleo.*

Hence, also, דְּבִיר above, *place of enouncement, oracle.* Lat. *dico, dixit;* cogn. τοῦ, *duco, duxit; verba protulit, &c.* Here, *a Pestilence,* affecting either man, beast, or tillage, occ. with חרב, דם, רעב, מלחמה, Exod. ix. 3; Lev. xxvi. 25; 2 Sam. xxiv. 13. 15; 2 Chron. vi. 28; Ezek. xxviii. 23. Personified, Hab. iii. 5; Ezek. vii. 15, &c.

דֶּבֶר, m. with aff. only, דָּבְרָם, דָּבְרוֹ, Micah ii. 12; Is. v. 17. Lit. *His* or *their driving;* which some take to signify *place of do.;* i. e. *pasture.* Arab. كَلأ, *arvum;* others, *manner of do.* Arab. كَبُور, *habitus, &c.*

דְּבָרוֹת, f. pl. of do. *Things driven along;* i. e. *floats* of timber, 1 Kings v. 23, al. non occ.

דָּבָר, m. pl. דְּבָרִים, constr. דְּבַר, pl. דִּבְרֵי. Gr. ῥῆμα, πρᾶγμα. I. *Something, some matter, any thing;* i. e. which may be put forth, and about which inquiry may be made. דָּבָר גָּדוֹל, *great thing, &c.;* Lev. iv. 3; 1 Sam. xx. 2; 2 Sam. iii. 13. הַדָּבָר הַזֶּה *this matter,* Gen. xx. 8. 10; xxi. 11; xxiv. 28. דְּבַר הַתּוֹעֵבָה, *of abomination,* Jer. xliv. 4. See Exod. v. 13. 19, &c.; 1 Sam. x. 2; Ps. lxv. 4. Occ. with כָּל, אֵין, לֹא, Gen. xviii. 14; Num. xxxi. 23; 1 Sam. xx. 21, &c.

II. More specifically, *The matter in hand, cause;* (a) common, or (b) forensic: as, (a) עַל דְּבַר, *on account, because of,* Gen. xii. 17; xx. 11, &c.; pl. עַל דִּבְרֵי, Deut. iv. 21; Jer. vii. 22, &c.; (b) Exod. xviii. 16. 22; xxii. 8; xxiv. 14, &c.

III. *Matter,* or *thing,* enouncing or enounced; *A word.* Gr. λόγος, &c., either human or divine, Gen. xxix. 13; xxxiv. 18; Exod. iv. 28, &c. Hence, *sentence, promise, matter of promise, precept,* vain *word,* or *words, &c.,* as the context shall require. Hence the phrases, בַּעַל דְּבָרִים, *man of words.* דְּבַר שְׂפָתַיִם, *word of lips,* i. e. *vain words.* דִּבְרֵי רוּחַ, id. Job xvi. 3. דָּבָר טוֹב, *good,* i. e. *elegant word.* דְּבַר יְהוָֹה, *word of Jehovah,* Jer. i. 4. 11; ii. 1; xiii. 8, &c. Hence, *an oracle, &c.* as the passage may require. Aff. דְּבָרִי, דְּבָרֶי, &c. pl. דְּבָרֶיךָ, &c.

There is another use of this term and its equivalents, קוֹל; Chald. פִּתְגָם, מֵימְרָא, and Gr. λόγος, which ought to be noticed, and particularly as certain Lexicographers, &c. make no very orthodox use of it. A difficulty would, no doubt, always be felt, particularly when metaphysics had made some progress in the world, in speaking of the Deity with reference to a Divine revelation. Because, here something was advanced as matter of testimony, and that, too, upon which the whole fabric of revealed religion rested. Now, in this case, something specific must have been meant; and, it should follow, that well defined notions would be formed respecting it. The Metaphysicians would object to any and every particular designation of the person of God, as it is the case with infidel philosophers at this day. How, then, was this to be met? I know of no other way than by revelation itself affording good grounds for the answer. The Deity is omnipresent, say the philosophers; so also says the Scripture. How then, says the objector, can we conceive of a particular revelation of Him, who is thus determined to be incomprehensible?

I answer,—If we can conceive of a time at which there was no creation, and consequently no creatures, at such a time a particular and personal revelation of the Deity could have had no object, as there could be none to whom it could have been made; but, if we conceive of a creation taking place, in which there would be rational agents; as these must necessarily be subordinate beings, and dependent on the Creator, it would be absolutely necessary to their welfare, that they should have information of this sort: and such they could never have as certain by any means short of a particular revelation of God, and that made by Himself. Hence, we read of His goings forth being from everlasting;[*] that He was the first born of every creature,[†] brought forth before the hills;[‡] of the dew of His birth being of the womb of the morning;[§] intimating, as it should seem, that even prior to the work of creation, and with reference to that event, the Deity assumed, and existed in, His personal and individual character.— All of which has been given for the purpose, apparently, of meeting the question abovementioned, and of ensuring the reverence due to the Son from His intelligent creatures.

Hence, perhaps, this personal revelation of God was termed by believers, יְהוָֹה, (*the*)

---

[*] Micah v. 2.
[†] Col. i. 15—19. Comp. Heb. i. 2—6; Rom. viii. 29.
[‡] Job xv. 7. See my note. Comp. Prov. viii. 22—30.
[§] Ps. cx. 3; lxxxix. 27.

דבר (127) דבר

essence, being, or the like, in contradistinction to His incomprehensible character, as filling eternity, &c.: and hence we read in the Old Testament of His frequently appearing in the *form of a man,* and of *man* being created in His image; without in the least affecting, or intending to affect, His all-pervading, upholding, and incomprehensible character and attributes. Now, if we can conceive of this essence *proceeding, coming forth;* i. e. being revealed, for the purposes above-mentioned, from the invisible and incomprehensible ocean of divinity; the term דָּבָר, would, from what has been seen of its original signification above, viz. *going forth, &c.,* not be an inappropriate term to be used as descriptive of His person. *Son of God,** for the same reason,—although capable of suggesting considerations quite foreign to this question,—would also be suitable; as would *the Wisdom of God, express image of His person,* or the like; all of which are, first or last, given to Christ.

Now it is perfectly certain that the heathen, from the most ancient times up to the present, have entertained the notion,—which I think they must have had from Holy Writ,—that such a divine person was primarily revealed, and thence became author of the whole creation; and whom they hence termed, *the second cause, the first intellect, &c. &c.* as may be seen in my notes on Job xi. 6; xv. 7. Euseb. Prep. Evang. lib. xi. capp. xii.—xviii., where will be found passages quoted from Plato, Plotinus, Numenius, Philo, &c., all to this effect. And ib. cap. xix. John i. 1, et seq. is also adduced. See also Viger's notes to his Edit. of Euseb. p. 51, &c., and Theodoret's Sermones de Principio; also Cyrill of Alexandria against Julian, libb. i. viii., and Kuinoels' Prolegom. to St. John's Gospel § vii., who, as the manner of his school is, takes heathenism as the original, and Holy Scripture as the copy; the absurdity of which is too great to deserve refutation.

By all of which I understand, that Divine revelation intended so far to enlighten us on this subject, as to leave us without excuse respecting the particular personal revelation of the Deity: and that the heathen, attached as they were, and still are, exclusively to the emanation system of philosophy, availed themselves at a very early period of these declarations of Scripture, and on them grounded a considerable part of their foolish metaphysico-theological system. On these Scriptures, too, the Jews, and also the early fathers of the Church, founded their use of the term λόγος: and, hence, the latter, the doctrine of *the eternal generation of the Son Homoousian, &c.;* terms neither very intelligible, nor very applicable to this subject. In this respect, however, they were right viz., in maintaining, as they did, the equal Godhead of the Son; which, if the view now taken be correct, could be no less Divine after its particular and personal revelation, and even incarnation, than it was before: no less God because proceeding and coming forth of the Father,* than it was before, when enjoying equal glory in His bosom, and was thus united with His incomprehensible being:† although, as it regarded only the manhood assumed, the Son may truly be said to be inferior to the Father. This usage of the term דָּבָר, (to which may be added, קוֹל, אִמְרָה, &c., as noticed above: comp. Job iv. 12; 1 Chron. xvii. 3; Ps. ciii. 20; cvii. 20; cxxxviii. 2, &c.) originated perhaps in a metonymy, thus: as the *Word* of God, and hence *God* himself could be revealed only by him who was named the Son (Matt. xi. 27; Luke x. 22); hence the person himself, making this revelation, received the name of the *revelation,* or *Word,* so brought to light; and was styled the *Word,* and hence the *Wisdom,* of God. Hence, too, as being the bearer of a communication from the Father, he was styled *The Angel, of Jehovah,* or *Jehovah;* and, also, מֵלִיץ, *Mediator.* See my notes on Job xxxiii. 23, &c.—I have thought it desirable to say thus much on this question; because, although it is not unfrequently touched upon by Commentators, and in some cases not very scripturally, it has never, as far as I

---

* Dan. iii. 25; Ps. ii. 7, and often in the New Testament.

---

* John viii. 42. Comp. ib. xiv. 7—10. Very nearly so Amelius, as cited by Euseb. l. c. 'Αμέλει καὶ ἀναλυθέντα πάλιν ἀποθεοῦσθαι, καὶ Θεὸν εἶναι, οἶος ἦν πρὸ τοῦ εἰς τὸ σῶμα, καὶ τὴν σάρκα, καὶ τὸν ἄνθρωπον καταχθῆναι. "*Adeoque solutum ubi jam fuerit, Dei locum denuò capessere, ac Deum rursus eundem esse, qui erat, priusquam in corpus atque in carnem hominemque descenderet.*"

† Ib. xvii. 5. 8. 11. 13.

have seen, received the explanation of which it was capable, and which Holy Writ itself seemed clearly to suggest.

דָבַר, v.—pret. pres. non occ. Part. דֹּבֵר, m. דֹּבְרִים, constr. דֹּבְרֵי, pl. f. דֹּבְרוֹת, sing. non occ. *Speaking, speaker,* Exod. vi. 29; Num. xxxii. 27; xxxvi. 5; Ps. v. 7; xxxi. 18, &c. Phrase, דֹּבֵר בְּאָזְנֵיכֶם, *speaking in your ears,* Deut. v. 1.

Id. pass. דָּבֻר, m. *Spoken,* Prov. xxv. 11, al. non occ.

Infin. aff. דָּבְרְךָ, *Thy speaking,* Ps. li. 6, al. non occ.

Niph. נִדְבָּר, pres. נִדְבַּרְנוּ, *Became speaking,* i. e. set about doing so: "recipr. Pih.," says Gesenius. But no such reciprocity is latent in the verb: this lies in the אִישׁ אֶל־רֵעֵהוּ, Mal. iii. 16; Ezek. xxxiii. 30; which would otherwise be tautology. Psalm cxix. 23, יָשְׁבוּ—נִדְבָּרוּ, *They sat, they became,* i. e. set about, *speaking, &c.* seems sufficiently to point out the force of this form here. Mal. iii. 13; constr. med בְּ, עַל.

Part. נִדְבָּרִים, Ezek. xxxiii. 30.

Pih. דִּבֶּר, and, remot. accent, דַּבֶּר, pres. יְדַבֵּר, constr. abs. med. אֶל, לְ, עִם, אֵת, אֶת, עַל, *Speaking, enouncing, addressing;* i. e. with reference to the act; not to the thing said. See אָמַר; and, hence, as the subsequent context may require; *promising, threatening, commanding, admonishing, reciting* or *singing.* Gen. xii. 4, כַּאֲשֶׁר דִּבֶּר יְהוָֹה אֵלָיו, *as Jehovah had spoken to him;* i. e. had commanded him. Ib. xvii. 23, דִּבֶּר אִתּוֹ אֱלֹהִים, *God had spoken with him;* id. Ib. xxi. 1, כַּאֲשֶׁר דִּבֵּר, *as He had spoken;* i. e. promised: and so on, in places innumerable. In many cases, however, this verb is used in the sense of אָמַר, as Exod. xvi. 23, הוּא אֲשֶׁר דִּבֶּר יְהוָֹה, *This is that which Jehovah hath said;* where *hath spoken* would be unsuitable. See, also, Ib. xxiii. 7; xxxiv. 32; Lev. x. 3, &c. As to other shades of its meaning, see Exod. xxxii. 14; Judg. v. 12; xiv. 7; 1 Sam. xxv. 39; Ruth iv. 1.

The following are idiomatical usages: דִּבֶּר דְּבָרִים, *spake words;* i. e. without regard to their fulfilment, Hos. x. 4. דָּבָר—דִּבֶּר, *the word — he spake,* Gen. xliv. 2; Exod. iv. 30. דִּבֶּר בְּיַד, *He spake by means of —,* Exod. ix. 35. דִּבֶּר לַעֲשׂוֹת, *He enounced to do;* i. e. threatened to do, Ib. xxxii. 14. דִּבֶּר פָּנִים בְּפָנִים, *face to face He spake,* Deut. v. 4. דִּבֶּר אֶת־הַטּוֹבָה, *spoken good;* i. e. foretold prosperity, 1 Sam. xxv. 30. בִּנְטֹשׁוֹ דִּבֶּר *against himself hath he spoken;* i. e. against his own life, 1 Kings ii. 23. דִּבֶּר בְּפִיו, *spake with his mouth;* an archaism, Ib. viii. 15. עַל־לֵב—אֶל־לֵב, *to the heart;* affectionately: it. *to self,* Gen. xxiv. 25; xxxiv. 3; 1 Sam. i. 13, עִם־לִבּוֹ, מִלִּבּוֹ, id. Eccl. i. 16; ii. 15; Ps. xv. 2: comp. Num. x. 29; 1 Sam. xxv. 30; Jer. xviii. 20. דִּבֶּר רָעָה עַל, *spoken evil respecting,* 1 Kings xx. 23; Jer. xi. 17; xix. 25, &c. דִּבֶּר שָׁלוֹם עִם, *spake peace with;* i. e. peaceably with, Ps. xxviii. 3. אֵת —, Jer. ix. 7. אֶל —, Ps. lxxxv. 9. בְּ —, Ib. cxxii. 8. לְ —, Esth. x. 3. מְשֻׁפָּטִים אֵת —, *adjudged,* Jer. i. 16; xii. 1, &c. It. seq. סָרָה, מִרְמָה, שָׁוְא, שֶׁקֶר, כָּזָב, צֶדֶק, לְ, at the pleasure of the writer. Gesenius makes this verb signify moreover, "*insidias struxit;* dein *perdidit*," and cites Ps. cxxvii. 5, for the first, and 2 Chron. xxii. 10, comp. with 2 Kings xi. 1, for the second; which is groundless: the first signifying clearly nothing more than *addressing, impleading* enemies in the gate; i. e. in a man so circumstanced *defending* his own cause publicly: the second being elliptical, viz. תְּדַבֵּר, for תְּדַבֵּר רָעָה, *she denounced,* or *condemned;* equivalent eventually to תְּאַבֵּד, 2 Kings xi. 1, it being, moreover, unnecessary to suppose either that such parallel passages are strict and literal interpretations of one another, or even that the latter necessarily means any thing beyond the former, signifying *denounced.* See Gram. art. 154. 8.

Infin. דַּבֵּר, Gen. xxiv. 50, &c. it. דַּבֶּר, or דִּבֶּר, Jer. v. 13; Exod. xxv. 28, &c. aff. דַּבְּרוֹ, Gen. xxxvii. 4, &c.

Imp. דַּבֵּר, or דַּבֶּר, pl. דַּבְּרוּ, f. דַּבֵּרִי, Gen. xxiv. 33; L. 4; 2 Sam. xiv. 12.

Part. מְדַבֵּר, f. מְדַבֶּרֶת, pl. מְדַבְּרִים, f. מְדַבְּרוֹת, Gen. xxvii. 6; 1 Sam. i. 13; Is. lxv. 24; xix. 18.

Puh. pres. יְדֻבַּר בָּהּ, *It shall be spoken concerning her;* i. e. shall be asked for in marriage, Cant. viii. 8.

Part. מְדֻבָּר, *Said, enounced,* Ps. lxxxvii. 3. Hithp. מִדַּבֵּר, part. for מִתְדַּבֵּר, Gram. art. 83. 1. i. q. Niph. *One setting about to speak, &c.,* Num. vii. 89; 2 Sam. xiv. 13; Ezek. ii. 2.

דַּבְּרָתֶיךָ, f. pl. aff. *Thy sayings,* precepts, Deut. xxxiii. 3, is probably a mere f. p. of the verbal noun, or infin. Pih. דַּבֵּר, preceding, al. non occ.

דִּבְרָה, f. i. q. דָּבָר, sign. ii. *Cause, account, matter,* עַל דִּבְרַת, *because of, &c.* Eccl.

דבש (129) דבש

iii. 18; viii. 2, it. seq.; שֶׁ, *Because that, &c.*, Ib. vii. 14. *Cause* for adjudication, Job v. 8; It. with (ʼ) parag. Ps. cx. 4. עַל דִּבְרָתִי, *on, according to, the matter, case,* of *Melchizedek.* Chald. id. Dan. ii. 30. Comp. Eccl. vii. 14.

דְּבַשׁ, m. Aff. דִּבְשִׁי. Syr. ܕܶܒܫܳܐ, *mel.* Arab. دِبْس, *Syrup of dates,* or *honey of bees.* *Honey* either, I. of bees; or, II. apparently as found in large quantities in the East, on the leaves of trees—as the *honey-dew* is among ourselves—and even on rocks and stones, and is called *Manna* by our chemists. Mr. Rich (Residence in Koordestan, vol. i. p. 142, 3,) tells us that it "is found on the dwarf oak, though several other plants are found to produce it. It is collected by gathering the leaves of the tree, letting them dry, and then gently threshing them on a cloth. It is thus brought to market in lumps." There is another kind of manna found *on rocks and stones*, which is *quite pure, of a white colour*, and is much more esteemed than the tree manna. "The manna season," adds he, "begins in the latter end of June," &c. Whence it should seem that its produce is looked for like that of any fruit. This was, probably, *the wild honey* of Matt. iii. 4, &c. Μέλι ἄγριον. Syr. ܕܶܒܫܳܐ ܕܰܒܪܳܐ. St. Adaman, abbot of Hii, tells us, in his description of the holy places, that in the place of John's residence in the desert there are locusts which the poor people boil with oil, and a sort of herbs, with large long leaves of a milk white colour, and a taste like that of honey; and that this is what is called in Scripture *wild honey*. Rees's Cyclop., art. Honey. I ask, are not these leaves covered with the *pure white honey-dew* mentioned above? The author of the اختيارات بديع tells us, moreover, that the دِبْس (דבש), *syrup of dates*, mentioned above, is corrected in the stomach by eating *Pure manna* and *the essence of lettuce* after it: his words are, وبعد از آن سكنجبين ساده با مغز كاهو خورند. It is thus used as food.

Of this *rock* and *field-honey*, we have mention, I think, in Deut. xxxii. 13; 1 Sam. xiv. 26, 27; Ps. lxxxi. 17. The land *flowing with milk and honey*, Exod. iii. 8, &c. seems to me to intimate a larger production of this article than could be expected from the honey-bees only.

In other places, as Judg. xiv. 8, &c. the *honey of the bee* must be meant. Gesenius thinks that *syrup of grapes*, "*mel uvarum*," is meant in Gen. xliii. 11; Ezek. xxvii. 17; and refers to Russel's History of Aleppo, p. 20, on the subject. I doubt this. If any reliance can be placed on what has just now been said, it must appear that Burckhardt and the Neologians must have been grievously mistaken in supposing, that this *honey-dew* was the *manna* of Moses; as it now appears that it bore a totally different name.

דַּבֶּשֶׁת, f. Is. xxx. 6, al. non occ. Arab. دَبَش, *supellex domestica vilior*, usually, *The hunch* of a camel, which, according to Dr. Gesenius, the context requires; but it may with equal propriety mean *the furniture*, or pack-saddle, of the camel: and this the Arabic دَبَش, seems to confirm. Comp. Gen. xxxi. 34.

דָּג, m. once, דָּאג, pl. דָּגִים, constr. דְּגֵי—

דָּגָה, f. constr. דַּגַּת, pl. non occ.—

Arabic دَجَّ, *serpsit proprie cum multæ res sunt*. Cogn. دَجَا, *perplexus, et copiosus fuit*. دَجَاج, *profusum* beneficium. دَاجَة, *assecla exercitus. Fish* generally, large or small, of the sea, or of any river, Gen. i. 26. 28; ix. 2; Num. xi. 5. 22; Deut. iv. 18; Jon. ii. 1. 11; Neh. xiii. 16: with reference to their great number, Hab. i. 14; Ezek. xlvii. 10. Aff. דְּגָתָם.

דגה, v. pret. non occ. pres. יִדְגּוּ, *Let them multiply*. See דָּג, Gen. xlviii. 16, al. non occ.

דָּגוֹן, m. *Dagon*, an idol of the Philistines worshipped at Asdod, or Azotus. Δαγών. According to the theology of the Phœnicians, the inventor of agriculture, ἐπειδὴ εὗρε σῖτον καὶ ἄροτρον, ἐκλήθη Ζεὺς Ἀρότριος.... *quod frumentum et aratrum invenisset, aratrius Jupiter nuncupatus est*. Euseb. Prep. Evang. lib. i. c. x. Diod. Sic. tells us that at Ascalon a goddess named Derceto was worshipped, which had the face of a woman, but in every thing else resembled a fish: αὕτη δὲ τὸ μὲν πρόσωπον ἔχει γυναικὸς, τὸ δὲ ἄλλο σῶμα πᾶν ἰχθύος, Bibl., lib. ii. § iv. Which was probably the same deity.

s

דגל (130) דד

See Selden de Diis Syris Syntag. ii. cap. iii. 1 Sam. v. 2—4; Judg. xvi. 23; 1 Chron. x. 10; 1 Macc. x. 83; xi. 4.

דֶּגֶל, m. pl. constr. דִּגְלֵי. Arab. دَجَلَ, texit: obduxit auro, &c. *A banner, standard*, or *flag*, as used in military movements, &c. Num. i. 52; ii. 2. 10. 17, 18. 31, 34; x. 14; Cant. ii. 4.

דגל, v. pret. non occ. pres. 1, pl. נִדְגֹּל, Ps. xx. 6. *We set up a banner.* Comp. Exod. xvii. 15. See נֵס, i. e. our common mark of profession.

Part. דָּגוּל, *Marked, signalized,* constr. מִן, above, more than, Cant. v. 10.

Niph. part. f. pl. נִדְגָּלוֹת, *Things*, armies most likely, *bannered*, i. e. attended with banners and in full array of battle, Cant. vi. 4. 10. Symm. ὡς τάγματα παρεμβολῶν.

דָּגָן, m. constr. דְּגַן, pl. non occ. r. דגה, as Gesenius well remarks. I. *Corn.* II. Meton. *Bread.* I. Gen. xxvii. 28. 37; Num. xviii. 27; Deut. xxviii. 51, &c. II. Lam. ii. 12, &c. Aff. דְּגָנָם, דְּגָנֶךָ, דְּגָנִי, &c.

דָּגַר, pres. non occ. Arab. دَجَرَ, *attonitus mente fuit*: cogn. دَجَنَ, *constitit, consedit loco*: comp. زَاجَلَ, constr. abs. *Hatched*, Is. xxxiv. 15. בָּקְעָה וְדָגְרָה, *has split and hatched*, i. e. her eggs, Jer. xvii. 11. קֹרֵא דָגַר וְלֹא יָלָד, *a partridge hatched, but produced no young*: al. non occ. Alluding, as it has been thought, to the fact of this bird's appropriating the eggs of others; or, to the cuckoo's laying her eggs in the nest of other birds, for them to hatch and bring up. See the Hieroz. of Bochart. ii. lib. 1. c. xii. But the truth of all this is as doubtful as the sense so arrived at is inappropriate to the passages cited. The latter passage—see the whole of the verse—teaches that something is obtained, which, however, proves worthless, i. e. riches gotten by fraud. There might, nevertheless, have been a popular belief of some such bird submitting to the toil of sitting on its eggs, and being unable after all to produce young; which might have passed into an adage. But there is another, and perhaps better, way of viewing this passage, which is this. The sequel of the verse tells us, that he who makes wealth, וְלֹא בְמִשְׁפָּט, *but not after the* (right) *manner*, shall fail. Now, if we supply this to the former member, thus, קֹרֵא דָּגַר לֹא במשפט וְלֹא יָלָד. *As a partridge*

hatched, or sat to hatch, *not after the* (right) *manner, and produced no young*; i. e. her eggs, not having been previously impregnated by the male bird, she produced nothing; or, in other words, she acted independently, when she should have done otherwise, and so failed; so the ungodly candidate for wealth, &c. So in English, *a cock's egg*, or *mare's nest*, are things producing nothing, and are spoken of much in the same way.

דַּד, m. sing. non occ. i. q. שַׁד say Castell and Gesenius. But this is most unlikely. See Ezek. xxiii. 3. 8. 21; Prov. v. 19; the only places in which it is found, and in some of which שַׁד is also found. From the occurrence of בְּתוּלֵיהֶן, in Ezek. one is led to suppose, that something very different from *breast* is meant. The appearances exhibited by the ruptured hymen is certainly the most likely: hence עָשׂוּ דַּדֵּי בְתוּלֵיהֶן, i. e. *they made, produced*, these things by fornication. See ver. 8. 21, where this verb also occurs. Whence it is evident that Gesenius (sub. voce עשה) has likewise mistaken this word. Arab. دَدٌ, *lusus*. Comp. Gen. xxvi. 8. Cogn. دَأْدَأَ, *canalis aquæ amplior*. See Prov. v. 19: it. دَأْدَأَ, *quietavit, sedavit, rem*, &c.

דדה, v. non occ. in Kal. Arab. دَأْدَأَ, *vehementi cursu latus fuit.* Conj. ii. *tardavit, lentè processit, inclinavit in incessu.* Comp. 1 Kings xxi. 27.

Hithp. 1st. pers. sing. אֶדַּדֶּה, for אֶתְדַּדֶּה, Gram. art. 83. 1; Is. xxxviii. 15. *I will proceed gently, submissively.* But, Ps. xlii. 5. אֶדַּדֵּם, for לִפְנֵיהֶם, or עִמָּם, *I will proceed with them*, or *before them*, i. e. with alacrity and joy, al. non occ.

דְּהַב, m. def. דַּהֲבָא, Chald. i. q. Heb. זָהָב. Syriac ܕܰܗܒܳܐ, *aurum.* Arab. ذَهَبٌ, id. *Gold*, Dan. ii. 32; iii. 1. 5. 7; Ezra vii. 15, 16, &c.

דהם, v. in Kal. non occ. Arab. دَهِمَ, *supervenit de improviso.* II. Conj. *denigravit*. IV. *Malè egit adversus aliquem.* دُهِّمَ, *infortunium.* Cogn. ذَهَبَ, *exercitus in fugam conjectus.*

Niph. part. נִדְהָם, *Reduced, impotent*; Gesen. *stupefactus*: to which neither the

דחר (131) דוד

etymology nor the context agrees, Jer. xiv. 9, al. non occ. Syr. כֵּהְמְףּ, *imbecillis.* LXX. ὑπνῶν. Vulg. *vagus.*

דַּהֲרוֹת, f. pl. Judg. v. 22. Arab. دَهُورَ, *trusit* parietem; cogn. نَهْلُول, *generosus equus. Charge, attack,* of cavalry. Hence—

דֹּהֵר, part. pres. *Charging, attacking, horse,* Nahum iii. 2, al. non occ.

דּוֹב, see דֹּב.

דּוֹבֵב, m. part. Arab. دَبَّ, *paulatim fluxit* cruor sanguinis. دَبُوب, *lentè procedens; sanguinem repentem habens,* vulnus, &c. Cant. vii. 10. כְּיֵין....דּוֹבֵב שִׂפְתֵי, *As wine-suffusing the lips of—.* The LXX. Vulg. Syr. seem to have read וְשִׁנַּיִם, or וְשָׂפַי, as the last word here. Gesenius seems to apply יְשֵׁנִים to wines, as *old:* which is any thing but obvious or easy. I would take the whole verse thus: *Thy palate is as wine well moving* (itself), *to, by, my beloved* (taken, considered הָיָה) *as most excellent; suffusing* (agreeably) *the lips of* (the) *slumberers:* that is, *those* who are not sufficiently alive to his beauties (Ps. xlv. 3), in order to excite them: for this book is evidently mystical throughout. But, if the last word be taken with the LXX., &c. comp. Gen. xlix. 12.

דוב, v. in Kal. non occ. i. q. דאב.
Hiph. part. f. pl. מְדִיבֹת, *Things wasting,* Lev. xxvi. 16, al. non occ.

דוג, or דָיג, 3 pers. pl. aff. דִיגוּם, *They shall fish them,* Jer. xvi. 16, al. non occ. The verb is perhaps formed of a noun fm. דָּיִג, see דַּיָּגִים preceding, just as the Chald. pret. fm. קָמֵל: then by contraction, Gram. art. 75: דַּיָּג, see דָּג.

דוג, m. pl. דַּוָּגִים, *Fisherman,* Jer. xvi. 16; Ezek. xlvii. 10, al. non occ.

דוּגָה, f. pl. non occ. *Fishing,* i. e. act of, Amos iv. 2, al. non occ. בְּסִירוֹת דּוּגָה, *with the thorns of fishing;* i. e. with hooks originally made of thorns for that purpose. Comp. Job xl. 26, Ezek. xxix. 4.

דוד, m. pl. דּוֹדִים, constr. דּוֹדֵי. Syr. ܕܳܕ, *turbavit.* Arab. دَاد, *lusit,* sc. fune agitando. Cogn. دَاد, *propulit.* دَدَّ, *lusus.* it. وَدَّ, *amavit;* وَدُّون, *celer fuit.* I. *Love,* meton. *Offices* of it, Cant. i. 2. 4; iv. 10; v. 1;

Ezek. xvi. 6; xxiii. 17. מִשְׁכַּב דּוֹדִים, *bed of,* Prov. vii. 18, &c. In this sense always pl. Aff. דֹּדֶיךָ, דֹּדַיִךְ. II. Meton. *Beloved,* i. e. object of love, Cant. i. 13, 14. 16; ii. 3. 8, 9, 10. 16, 17; iv. 16; v. 2, &c.; Is. v. 1.

III. *Uncle,* f. *Aunt,* Lev. x. 4; xx. 20; xxv. 49; 1 Sam. x. 14, &c. Aff. דֹּדִי, דּוֹדְךָ, דּוֹדָתוֹ, דּוֹדָתְךָ, f. דֹּדְךָ.

דּוּד, m. (seg. דֶּוֶד, Gram. 87. 2, hence) pl. דְּוָדִים, it. דּוּדִים, Lit. *agitation:* meton. that in which it takes place. I. *A pot,* or *caldron,* Job xli. 11; 1 Sam. ii. 14; 2 Chron. xxxv. 13.

II. *A basket,* Jer. xxiv. 2; 2 Kings x. 7; and, as some think, Ps. lxxxi. 7.

דּוּדָאִים, m. pl. constr. דּוּדָאֵי, i. q. דּוּד. I. *A basket* or *pot,* Jer. xxiv. 1, constr.

II. *A root* or *herb* of some sort, found in the fields in the time of wheat-harvest by Reuben the son of Israel, by Leah, Gen. xxx. 14—16. Whence it has been very generally supposed, that it was used in making a philter or love-potion; and that it was so used on this occasion. But, a moment's consideration of the place will shew, that nothing can be less probable than such a supposition; for here Rachel actually gives up the society of her husband for that night, on the condition that *she* shall have Reuben's roots, or *mandrakes.* On this occasion, too, Leah conceives, not Rachel: so that the mandrakes had nothing whatever to do in the matter of this conception: they had only been taken by Rachel in lieu of Jacob's society.

But the word occurs again in Cant. vii. 14, and seems there to have something to do with love; or, rather, that they are laid up for the beloved. They are said to be fragrant,*

* According to the اختبارات بديع, the لفاح is the fruit of the يبروج, *mandrake;* which, in the Persic, is styled سايبرج. The best, he says, is that which is large, has a pungent smell, and is yellow in colour. Its nature is cold and moist. His words are, لفاح ثمر يبروج است بپارسي سايبرج خوانند .... ونيكوترين آن بزرك تيز بوي رسيده زرد بود وطبيعت آن سرد وتر بود. See also Celsii Hierobot. i. 1, where the opinions of the Greeks, Latins, Jews, &c. will be found cited with a liberal hand.

moreover: whence it should seem that they were, for one cause or other, very highly prized. This is all, perhaps, that can be made of these passages of Scripture: the latter of which, I think, evidently alludes to the former: that is, as in the one case, they were given to secure the society of the object beloved, so would they in the other.

If it be said that the etymology here favours the notion of a philter; it may be answered: This word (דּוּדָאִים) is formed on דּוּד, which contains no part of the notion of love: and, if דּוֹדָאִים were the true punctuation, still, as the notion of *love* is here secondary, it cannot be argued that this word has any thing to do with it. And, again, as the primary notion is evidently *agitation*, *excitement*, or the like, if our word designates something applied to medicinal purposes, as will presently appear; no term could perhaps be more suitable to it than this.

It seems to be generally agreed, that these דּוּדָאִים, mean the same thing with the Syriac ܡܲܕܪܘܼܟܵܐ, Chald. יַבְרוּחִין, and Arabic يبروج, or يبروج. (Gesen., erroneously, تبروج, which is faithfully copied by his American translator.) If we can rely on this,—and I think we may,—we can ascertain what these דּוּדָאִים were. Of this there can be no doubt, that they were *mandrakes*, or the *mandragora*, of Linnæus, &c. According to the authorities consulted by Castell, then, and of the اختيارات بديع, it was of two sorts, viz. that cultivated in gardens, and that found to grow wild. Of the latter sort, apparently, were the mandrakes of Reuben. Their medical use is, to discussing tumors, wens, bubos. When taken inwardly they will render one insensible to the pain of even cutting off a limb, and generally have much the same effect as opium. The words of the latter are, يبروج دو نوع است يكنوع را بيخ لفاح گويند ويكي را يبروج الفم خوانند وآن بيخ لفاح بري بري .... وبر ورمهاي صلب ودنبلات وخنازير طلا كردن نافع بود ويبروج چون بكوبند وبر مفاصل كند (كنند) واگر كسي را احتياج بود بقطع عضو در شراب بياشامند بيخود شود از خوردن وي

همان عارض شود كه از خوردن افيون.

In this last case *Mandrake-wine* is evidently meant: which is prepared by suspending some slices of the mandrake root in a certain quantity of white wine. The other properties of this root, as mentioned by our author, correspond with those given by Dr. Cullen and others, and shew that the medical practitioners, both of the East and West, have arrived at the same general results in this respect.

My author notices the love-properties usually ascribed to this root, as also the danger attending its pulling up;—so faithfully depicted by Shakspeare in his Romeo and Juliet,—to which, however, he seems to give no credit. It shews, however, that these notions are common to the East and West. If I were allowed to hazard a conjecture on this, I should say: the truth probably is, that the mistaken view of Scripture just mentioned—like many others which may be adduced *—is of a very ancient date; and, hence, has made its way over a considerable portion of the civilized world. That it is grossly superstitious, and the effect of ignorance, is quite obvious; and, the wonder is, how it has so long passed without consideration and correction. We may now, therefore, dismiss entirely the "*amatoria poma,*" with the form דּוּדַי, of Gesenius, &c. &c., with many other such very learned attempts to fasten this ancient piece of superstitious nonsense on the text of Scripture, as the waking dreams of very learned, but greatly mistaken men.

דָּוָה, m. דָּוָה, f. Syr. ܘܕܳܐ, ܘܕܳܐ, *anxit, afflixit.* Æth. ደወየ: *infirmus fuit.* Arab.

---

* Of this sort are the βαιτύλια of the Phœnicians, stones set up as Jacob's pillar was at *Bethel,* and, hence, so named; many of which are still to be found in the East. Euseb. Prep. Evang. lib. i. c. x. Ibn Batuta's Travels, p. 25. Eusebius tells us, in the same chapter, that *Israel* was the Phœnician name for Saturn, and that he had a son named *Ieud,* Ιεούδ: evidently taken from Scripture. Moses speaks of the Jewish state being destroyed by fire, Deut. xxxii. To this St. Peter alludes, which has given birth to a general notion that the world is to be destroyed by fire! The rites of *sacrificing,* and of observing the Sunday, have, in like manner, originated in Holy Writ, and been generally misapplied by the heathen, as many other such things have.

דות (133) דום

دَوِيَ, id. meton. دَوَاءٌ, *medicamentum*. I. *Sick, diseased*, Lam. i. 13; v. 17. Applied particularly to women in their menstrual courses, Lev. xv. 33; xx. 18; Is. xxx. 22, usually supposed to apply to *a garment, &c.*: but it may just as well apply to the person. II. Meton. *Unclean, polluted*. (דְּוָי), דְּוֵי לַחֲמִי, contr. for דְּוֵיִי, fm. דְּוָי, Gram. art. 73, i. e. ה being elided, the word becomes דְּוֵי; but [·] was put for [·], Gram. art. 106. The original [·] will now therefore return, and the true pl. is דְּוָיִ), lit. *polluted things of my bread;* polluted bread or food: i. e. considered as such, Job vi. 6. See too my note.

דָּוָה, with aff. דְּוֹתָהּ, *Her sickness;* a sort of infin. fm. גְּלוֹה, Lev. xii. 2, al. non occ.

דְּוָי, in pause for דְּוָי. Arab. دَوِيَ, *morbus. Sickness, disease*, Ps. xl. 4, al. non occ.

דַּוָּי, m. *Habitual* or *great sickness* (Gram. 154. 9. 12), Is. i. 5; Jer. viii. 18; Lam. i. 22, al. non occ.

דוך, v. in Kal non occ. Arab. دَوَخَ, *dispersit.* Cogn. أَدَاخَ, *abjecit;* نَوَخَ, *dissipavit.*

Hiph. הֵדִיךְ, pres. יָדִיךְ. I. *Expelled*, Jer. li. 34. II. *Dispelled, forced off,* or *away,* as by scouring with a brush, Is. iv. 4; 2 Chron. iv. 6; Ezek. xl. 38. The primitive notion is therefore preserved.

דוּךְ, v. דָּכוּ, *They beat, pounded,* Num. xi. 8, al. non occ. i. q. דכך, דכא. Arab. دَاكَ, *trivit* in tenuem substantiam. Cogn. دَقَّ, דַּק, id.

דוּכִיפַת, f. The name of a certain unclean bird, Lev. xi. 19; Deut. xiv. 18. Bochart. Hieroz. ii. col. 334, proposes the Arabic دِيك, *Cock,* and Chald. or Syr. כֵּפָא, *rock,* i. e. *cock of the rock;* by which he seems to mean *a wood-cock* twice the size of the common one; and for this he cites several Rabbinic writers. The LXX. give ἔποπα, Lat. *upupa:* and, after them, the Arabic versions, الهدهد. Gesenius proposes + דו כֵּפָא: i. e. Arab. *Lord,* and Chald. *rock;* i. e. *Lord of the rock;* which he says is the same thing as *gallus montanus.* But, is the particle ذو, ever found in any shape whatever compounded with either Hebrew or Syriac words? And, if it were, are we at last any more certain about this word, than we were before? I think not.

דוּמָה, f. Arab. دَوْمُ, *quiescens, restagnans.* Syn. שְׁכִינָה. Words signifying *quiescence, silence,* often imply *death:* comp. צמת. *Quiet, silent, dead,* Ps. xciv. 17. Meton. *place of the dead,* the grave, Ib cxv. 17.

דוּמִיָּה, f. Arab. دَائِمَة, *res perennis,* ac *diu durans,* pec. *pluvia continua et tranquilla.* I. *Remaining, abiding.* לְךָ דֻמִיָּה תְהִלָּה, *for thee,* i. e. *thine, remains praise,* Ps. lxv. 2; Ib. lxii. 2. *Only for God, remains,* i. e. *waits my soul.* דוּמִיָּה נַפְשִׁי. II. *Quietness, silence,* Ib. xxii. 3; xxxix. 3. נֶאֱלַמְתִּי דוּמִיָּה, lit. *I became bound* (in) *silence,* i. e. utterly silent. Where the latter word may be considered adverbial or specificative, Gram. art. 219, note. The form here is that of a possessive or patronymic in the fem. gen. Gram. artt. 136. 5; 166. — of דום.

דוּמָם, augm. of דום, Gram. art. 167, a termination not unlike the Arab. ٌ, and often marking adverbial constructions. I. *Very quiet, silent;* or adv. *very quietly,* Is. xlvii. 5; Hab. ii. 19. II. וְדוּמָם, Lam. iii. 26: thus, *good* (is Jehovah, i. e. parallel with טוֹב יְהֹוָה, commencing the preceding verse), *so let one trust,* וְדוּמָם, i. e. *very quietly,* for the salvation, &c. al. non occ.

דין, or דִין, v. pret. דָּן, pres. יָדִין, or יָדֵין. Syr. ܕ݂ܳܢ, *judicavit.* Arab. دَانَ, *inferior fuit.* دَوَّنَ, *scripsit in albo* nomina, milites. Æth. ደየነ: *judicavit.* The pres. יָדוֹן, occ. once, Gen. vi. 3. לֹא יָדוֹן רוּחִי בָאָדָם לְעֹלָם, which Gesenius renders, *"non in perpetuum spiritus meus* (i. e. *superior et divina natura) in hominibus humiliabitur,* i. e. *corpore mortali habitabit,* &c., taking the signification of the Arab. يَدُونُ as that of יָדוֹן, apparently. But, if this were the case, surely the تَحَلَّ رُوحِي, *descendet spiritus meus* (the *non habitabit* of the Polyg. being erroneous) of Saadias Hagaon would express the sense of the passage: not the καταμείνη of the LXX. or the ܠܐ ܬܟܫܢ, *non habitabit* of the Syr.— this is having recourse to a laxness of interpretation, which would soon put an end to

דּוּן (134) דּוּר

 ־very thing like precision in language. Besides, the sentiment here expressed is both without parallel in the Bible, and without point in the passage. The cogn. verb, moreover, دَانَ , يَدِينُ , *judicabit, &c.* agrees sufficiently well with the passage and the usual interpretation, to satisfy the requirements of criticism, as does the Syriac ܕܳܢ . *Contend, strive,* or the like, is therefore by far the better rendering. Constr. immed. occ. with דָּן—דָּן דִּינְעָנִי וְאֶבְיוֹן , *He judged the cause of the poor and needy,* Jer. xxii. 16; it. v. 28. Used imp. Gen. xxx. 6. Pres. דָּין , constr. בְּ , *with,* or *among,* it. med. אֶת , and immed., Gen. xlix. 16; Zech. iii. 7; Ps. liv. 3; Job xxxvi. 31. See my note. With עִם , Eccl. vi. 10.

Part. דָּן , *Judging,* Gen. xv. 14; Jer. xxx. 13.

Infin. דִּין , with לְ , לָדִין , *To judge,* Ps. L. 4, &c.

Imp. דִּין , pl. דִּינוּ , Prov. xxxi. 9; Jer. xxi. 12.

Niph. נָדוֹן , *Became contending, disputing,* 2 Sam. xix. 10, al. non occ.

הֻדָּן , Job xix. 29; *keri.* i. q. דִּין , *kethiv.* which see.

דּוֹנַג , or דּוֹנֵג , m. pl. non occ. Arab. دِنَاخ, *stabilitio rei ac firma tractatio. Wax,* Ps. xxii. 15; lxviii. 3; xcvii. 5; Mich. i. 4.

דּוּץ , v. pres. f. תָּדוּץ , Job xli. 14, al. non occ. Syr. ܕܽܘܨ , *exultavit.* Arab. دَاصَ , r. دِيص , *alacris fuit.* Cogn. دَاسَ , r. دوس , *calcavit pedibus terram.* Heb. דּוּשׁ . Syr. ܕܽܘܨ , id. *Leaps, exults.* Engl. *Dance?* So Gesenius thinks.

דֻּקַּק , v. Chald. דָּקוּ , Dan. ii. 35. See דקק .

דּוּר , m. Arab. دُور , *gyrus, orbis.* Lit. *circle,* as of society: hence, perhaps, the notion of *residing with, inhabiting* a place. See גאל . I. *Dwelling, residing,* Ps. lxxxiv. 11. Infin. or verbal noun. II. id. used imperatively, Ezek. xxiv. 5. וְגַם דּוּר הָעֲצָמִים and *also encircling the bones, &c.* i. e. place the bones *round about* the bottom of the caldron beneath the flesh. Vulg. *Compone... strues ossium sub ea:* which is perhaps not far from the exegetical sense. The LXX. ὑπόκαιε, and Syr. ܣܶܕ̈ܝ , are no translations of the text as we now have it. בְּדוּר , see r. כדר .

דּוּר , v. Chald. pret. non occ.; pres. f. תְּדוּר , pl. יְדֻרוּן , *Dwell, reside,* Dan. iv. 18; Ib. 9.

Part. pl. m. דָּאֲרִין , and דָּיְרִין , ir. דָּאר , דִּיר . Constr. דָּאֲרֵי , דָּיְרֵי , Dan. ii. 38; iii. 31; iv. 32; vi. 26.

דּוֹר , or דֹּר , m. pl. דּוֹרִים , and f. דּוֹרוֹת . Lit. *revolution.* So the Arab. جِيل , r. جول . I. *Age, generation;* hence, II. *Race;* applied to the period of man's life generally: and hence, to character, as being of a certain race or progeny, good or bad. I. דּוֹר הֹלֵךְ וג׳ , *a* (one) *generation goeth off, and a* (another) *generation cometh on,* Eccl. i. 4. דּוֹר עֲשִׂירִי , *tenth generation,* Deut. xxiii. 3, 4. דּוֹר אַחֵר , *another generation,* or *race,* Judg. ii. 10; Num. xxxii. 13; Deut. xxxii. 5. 20; Ps. xxiv. 6; lxxviii. 8, &c. Phrases, דֹּר וָדֹר , *age and age,* i. e. forever, Ps. lxi. 7; Joel ii. 2. עַד־שְׁנֵי דֹר וָדֹר *to the years of do.* Ps. xlv. 18. בְּכָל־דּוֹר וָדוֹר , *throughout all ages,* Ps. xlv. 18, id. Exod. iii. 15; Joel iv. 20. לְדֹר וָדֹר , Ps. x. 6; xxxiii. 11; xlix. 12. עַד־דֹּר וָדֹר , Ps. c. 5; Is. xiii. 20. מִדֹּר דֹּר , *from generation* (after) *generation,* Exod. xvii. 16. תָּמִים הָיָה בְּדֹרֹתָיו , *was complete in his generations;* i. e. throughout the periods in which he lived. Gesen. "*inter æquales suos,*" exhibits an unnecessary refinement. So Job is said to have lived through several generations, Job xlii. 16. Comp. Is. xxxviii. 12.

The second signification grows naturally out of the theological consideration, viz. of either good or bad men being always found in bodies; and this, either as to nations, or families. See Ps. lxxviii. 8; cxii. 2; Prov. xxx. 11—14; Jer. vii. 29, &c. Id. metaph. as passed off, and now in the grave, Ps. xlix. 20.

The pl. דּוֹרִים is found only in the phrase דּוֹר דּוֹרִים , *age of ages;* i. e. forever, Ps. lxxii. 5; cii. 25; Is. li. 8. The f. דֹּרוֹת , meton. for the *persons, events, &c.* of ages: as, יֵדְעוּ דֹרֹתֵיכֶם , *your generations may know,* Lev. xxiii. 43. See Judg. iii. 2; Job xlii. 17; xli. 4; Is. li. 9, &c. Aff. דֹּרוֹ דֹּרוֹתֵינוּ , דֹּרֹתָיו , דֹּרֹתָם ; דֹּרֹתֵיכֶם .

דּוּשׁ , and דִּישׁ , v. pret. דָּשׁ , pres. דָּישׁ , constr. immed. אֶת , and abs. Syr. ܕܽܘܫ , *calcavit, trituravit.* Arab. دَاسَ , r. دوس ,

דוש (135) דחי

trivit in area, subegit regionem. Cogn. דוץ.
I. *Tread, trample on,* Job xxxix. 15; 2 Kings xiii. 7, &c.
II. *Tread out,* as the corn on the floor; which was done by a sort of dray being drawn over it by oxen, in the wheels of which iron teeth were fixed, Hosea x. 11; Is. xxviii. 28. אָדוֹשׁ יְדֻשֶׁנּוּ, *will he continually triturate it:* where אָדוֹשׁ is an infin. of a cogn. r. אדשׁ, now lost:—applied also to the person attending to this, 1 Chron. xxi. 20.
III. Metaph. applied to the reduction of enemies, Judg. viii. 7; Jer. L. 11; Amos i. 3; Mich. iv. 13; Is. xli. 15; Hab. iii. 12.
Part. f. דָּשָׁה, for דָּשָׁה, Jer. L. 11.
Infin. דּוּשׁ, 2 Kings xiii. 7. Aff. דִּישׁוֹ, Amos i. 3. It. דִּישׁ, Deut. xxv. 4. Imp. f. דּוֹשִׁי, Mich. iv. 13.
Niph. נָדוֹשׁ, *Become trampled, beaten down,* Is. xxv. 10.
Infin. הִדּוֹשׁ, *Being trampled, &c.* Is. xxv. 10.
Hoph. יוּדַשׁ, *It is, becomes, trodden, &c.* Is. xxviii. 27.

דוּשׁ, v. Chald. pres. f. aff. תְּדוּשִׁנַּהּ, *Shall trample it, &c.,* Dan. vii. 23.

דָּחָה, v. pres. non occ. Arab. دَحَا, et دَحَّا, *impulit, propulit.* Syr. ܕܚܐ, id. Constr. immed. abs. *Driving, urging, on,* to a fall. דָּחֹה דְחִיתַנִי לִנְפֹּל, *Thou hast grievously urged me on to fall,* Ps. cxviii. 13.
Infin. constr. דְּחוֹת, Ps. cxl. 5.
Part. דּוֹחֶה, Ps. xxxv. 5.
Part. pass. f. דְּחוּיָה, Ps. lxii. 4.
Niph. pret. non occ. pres. יִדָּחֶה, *Is urged on, impelled,* Prov. xiv. 32; Jer. xxiii. 12.
Part. pl. constr. מֻדָּחֵי, *The driven,* or *cast, out of* Israel, Is. xi. 12; lvi. 8; Ps. cxlvii. 2.
Puh. i. q. Niph. דֹּחוּ, *They are driven.*

דְּחִי, m. seg. *The being urged, driven on,* Ps. lvi. 14; cxvi. 8. Synon. τοῦ, שָׁלַח. See my note on Job xii. 5.

דְּחָוָן, f. pl. Chald. *Concubines,* according to the modern German Lexicographers, as if derived from the Arabic دَحَا, *subegit fœminam. Instruments of music,* according to the Jews, from דָּחָה, *drive, &c.* as if they produced their notes by forcing. But the verb never occurs in this usage. I think it more probable that *Abundance,* in the sense of *luxuries* is meant, from the Arab. دَحَا, *expandit,* إِنْدَحَوَى, *expansus fuit, &c.*

especially, as רחב, ישׁע, and the like, are thus used in opposition to צר, and to imply *happiness, delight, &c.* Some of the Jews, hence perhaps, give שִׂמְחוֹת; Theodotion, and the Syr. *meats.*—occ. once, Dan. vi. 19. The בַּת מֶרֶה preceding seems to confirm this. Besides, *to bring concubines before a king,* seems strange language, and certainly is not very suitable to this context.

دَحِيل, m. דְּחִילָה, f. Syr. ܕܚܝܠ, ܕܚܝܠܐ, *terribilis. Fearful,* Dan. ii. 31; vii. 7.
دَحْلِين, m. pl. part. Chald. Syr. ܕܚܠܝܢ, *timor.* Arab. دَحَل, *fugit* (timore perculsus). *Fearing,* Dan. v. 19.
Pah. יְדַחֲלִנַּנִי, *Affrights me,* Dan. iv. 2.

دُحَن, m. Arab. دُخْن, a species of *The millet plant;* of which the author of the اختيارات بديع tells us there are three, viz. I. The جَاوَرْس, Pers. كاورس; Shirazi, ذُرَة, or كال. II. The جَاوَرْس هندي Pers. زُرَة. III. The دخن Pers. رزن; Shirāzi. الم. Its medicinal properties are cold and dry, bringing on costiveness; but are diuretic. It affords but a small quantity of food unless boiled in new milk; it is then more plentiful. Its astringent properties are corrected by the use of sugar candy.* The same things are said of it by our own physicians. See also Cels. Hierobot. i. 453, et seq. occ. once, Ezek. iv. 9.

* His words are, under سه — جاورس نوعست يكنوع دخن كويند بپارسي ارزن ويشيرازي الم — يكنوع جاورس هندي خوانند وآن ذره است بپارسي زره خوانند ويكنوع جاورس كويند وبپارسي كاورس وبشيرازي كال — Under دخن طبيعت آن سرد وخشكست در دوم وكيند در سوم — شكم را براند وبول بيندد; which is manifestly an error, I read, شكم را ببندد وبول براند — وغذاي اندكي دهد واكر بشير تازه بپزند خشكي وي كمتر بود غذا بسيار دهد — ومصلح وي قند بود .

דחף   (136)   דיג

דחף, v. Arab. cogn. دَقَفَ, دُقُوفٌ, impetus. دَخَو, impulsus.

Part. pl. m. דְּחוּפִים, *Hurried, hastened,* Esth. iii. 15 ; viii. 14.

Niph. נִדְחָף, *Became, was hurried, urged,* 2 Chron. xxvi. 20; Esth. vi. 12. "*Impulit se,*" says Gesenius ; but our first passage declares that יַבְהִלוּהוּ מִשָּׁם, *They disturbed him from that place* ; i. e. forced him out; which is most unpropitious to the *se* of this writer. Al. non occ.

דָּחַק, v. Syr. ܕܚܩ, *repulit.* Arab. دَحَقَ, id. Pres. יִדְחָקוּן, *They press upon,* Joel ii. 8, al. non occ.

Part. aff. דֹּחֲקֵיהֶם, with לוֹחֲצֵיהֶם, Judg. ii. 18. *Their oppressors.*

דִּי, constr. דֵּי. Arab. دَوِيَ, conj. iii. *remedio concinnavit, restauravit rem.* مَدْو, *multus cibus ;* cogn. אֲדוֹ, r. ادو, *opem tulit ;* أَدَي, *incrassuit; multus evasit.* See רַב.

A sufficiency, enough, Esth. i. 18. עַד־בְּלִי־דָי, *Until not enough ;* i. e. exceeding that quantity ; unto excess, Mal. iii. 10. Comp. Ps. lxxii. 17, *unto the failing of the moon, and beyond that;* i. e. forever. דֵּי שֶׂה, *Enough of* (here, *for the purchase of*) *a sheep,* Lev. v. 7 ; it. xii. 8; xxv. 28. דֵּי מַחְסֹרוֹ, *enough for his want,* Deut. xv. 8. So דֵּי עוֹלָה, Is. xl. 16 ; Exod. xxxvi. 5. With ב following, כְּדֵי בָנוּ, *as* (it were) *enough for us,* Neh. v. 8. Aff. דַּיֶּךָ, *thy sufficiency ;* i. e. enough for thee, Prov. xxv. 16. דַּיָּם, Exod. xxxvi. 7; Obad. 5 ; Jer. xlix. 9. דֵּי חֲלֵב, *enough of milk,* Prov. xxvii. 27. Frequently compounded with prepp. כְּ, בְּ, מִן ; which will supply a corresponding sense. See Judg. vi. 5 ; vii. 12; Deut. xxv. 2 ; 1 Sam. xviii. 30; 1 Kings xiv. 28 ; Is. lxvi. 23 ; Nah. ii. 13 ; Jer. li. 58. Note, however, דְּ is, in some cases, a mere expletive, as Bochart has well remarked, Hieroz. i., p. 150. It may fairly be doubted, moreover, whether we have any form of construction in it : דְּ and דֵּי being equivalent sounds, as in חַי and חֵי, by Gram. art. 87. 3.

דִּי, Chald. The relative pronoun *Who, which, what,* i. q. Heb. אֲשֶׁר. It is, apparently, nothing more than the Chaldaic form of the Heb. demonstrative pronoun זֶה, Gram. art. 177. 3 ; and so it will often bear to be rendered: e. g. Dan. ii. 23. דִּי חָכְמְתָא...יְהַבְתְּ לִי, *that hast given me wisdom,* for *who hast, &c.* and so in the rest of the verse. Sometimes preceded by מָה, which seems to refer to the preceding context ; דִּי to the following, as in our *that that,* for *that which,* Dan. ii. 28, 29. 45.

It seems often to stand for our *of ;* but may always be resolved by *that, which,* or the like : e. g. חֶזְוָא דִי־לֵילְיָא, *vision of the night ;* i. e. *vision that* (of) *the night,* Ib. vr. 19. See Ib. 14, 15. Often with a pronoun preceding ; as, שְׁמֵהּ דִּי־אֱלָהָא, *His name, that* (of) *God ;* God's name, &c. Ib. 20. See vr. 32, 33. Also with the definite form preceding, גָּלוּתָא דִי יְהוּד, *the captivity, that* (of) *Judah ; Judah's captivity,* Ib. vr. 25. The same holds good in the Syriac.

It often stands as *a conjunction,* like אֲשֶׁר, or the English *that ;* Lat. *quòd, eo quòd,* Gr. ὅτι, &c. Dan. ii. 8, 9; 16. 18, &c. Preceded immediately by other words, as עַל, Ib. iii. 19. פֱּ, Ib. iii. 7 ; לְקָבֵל, Ib., vr. 40, 41. 45, &c. מִן, Ib. iv. 12, &c. We have here, therefore, in every case, nothing beyond certain idiomatic usages of the demonstrative pronoun זֶה, *that.*

דַּגִּים, i. q. דָּגִים, *Fishermen,* Is. xix. 8 ; Jer. xvi. 16, *keri.*

דַּיָּה, f. pl. דַּיּוֹת. The name of a certain bird, Deut. xiv. 13 ; Is. xxxiv. 15; according to Bochart. Hieroz. ii. lib. ii. c. ix. col. 195, *vultur niger.* LXX. ἰκτῖνος. Vulg. *milvus.*

דְּיוֹ, m. seg. fm. פֶּקַד, for דְּיֵי, Gram. art. 87. 1. Arab. دَوَاة, *atramentarium.* Syr. ܕܝܘܬܐ, *atramentum. Ink,* Jer. xxxvi. 18, al. non occ.

דִּין, see דּוּן. Infin. or verbal noun, m. The act of judging, i. e. I. *Judgment,* Ps. lxxvi. 9 ; Prov. xx. 8; cxl. 13 ; Esth. i. 13. II. Meton. *The cause* for judgment, Deut. xvii. 8 ; Prov. xxix. 7 : by a further meton. *Contention,* Prov. xxii. 10. Aff. דִּינִי, דִּינְךָ.

דִּין, Chald. i. q. Heb. *Judgment,* Dan. iv. 34 ; vii. 22: meton. *punishment,* Ezra vii. 26. Further meton. *court* of judgment, vii. 10. Comp. vr. 26.

דִּינָיֵא, pl. Chald. m. The name of a certain people, Ezra iv. 9.

דַּיָּן, m. pl. non occ. See דּוּן, דִּין. *A judge,* 1 Sam. xxiv. 16 ; Ps. lxviii. 6. It. Chald. id. pl. דַּיָּנִין, Ezra vii. 25.

דִּיק , m. pl. non occ. Syr. ܕܝܩܐ, *speculator*. Arab. اَدَاقَ , *cinxit* ; مَدَاقَ , *circus, pugnæ locus*. From the places in which it occurs, something had recourse to in carrying on sieges, 2 Kings xxv. 1 ; Jer. lii. 4 ; Ezek. iv. 2 ; xvii. 17; xxi. 27; xxvi. 8: and apparently surrounding the whole place, as the first two passages seem to shew. With the vv. בָּנָה , נָתַן . Gesen. *specula, turris oppugnatoria*, i. q. בַּחַן . But, as the word occurs with סֹלְלָה , and סָבִיב , which could hardly be the case, if *watch-towers* were meant, it seems more natural to suppose that *entrenchment* and *breast-work* are meant. If so, our *dyke* is not far from the mark. LXX. 2 Kings, περίτειχος.

דִּישׁ , m. see דּוּשׁ , lit. *Treading out* corn. Meton. *the time of* do., Lev. xxvi. 5, al. non occ.

דִּישׁוֹן , m. Syr. ܕܝܫܢܐ , *ibex ; hircus sylvestris*, id. Chald. Cogn. دُشَ , *exultavit*. Cogn. Heb. דוש. Arab. دَاسَ , r. دوس , *calcavit pedibus terram*, &c. LXX. πύγαργος. Syr. et Targ. ܕܝܫܐ. Arab. verss. الاروي . *A sort of deer*, apparently, Deut. xiv. 5, al. non occ. See Hieroz. i., lib. iii., c. xx., p. 903.

דַּךְ , m. pl. aff. דַּכָּי , r. דכך . Arab. دَكَّ , it. دَاكَ , r. دوك , *comminuit*. Cogn. Heb. דכא , דכה , דקק . Arab. دَقَّ . Lit. *reduced:* hence *poor, mean*, Ps. ix. 10 ; x. 18 ; lxxiv. 21. In Prov. xxvi. 28, we have לְשׁוֹן־שֶׁקֶר יִשְׂנָא דַכָּיו , which Gesenius translates "*Lingua*, i. e. *homo, mendax...edit castigantes eam:*" giving an active sense to דַּךְ . But this is at variance with the usage of this word, and with the context in this place, which seems to require, that, as פֶּה , the *mouth*, produces some injurious effect, so does the tongue. I would read the verb, therefore, in Pih. or Hiph. יְשַׂנֵּא , or יַשְׂנִא , *makes hated, represents* as *hateful*, its *poor*, or *reduced* objects of attack.

דֵּךְ , m. } דָּךְ , f. } Chald. Arab. ذَاكَ , compd. of pron. dem. זֶה , Chald. ד , and pron. 2d per. *This*, Ezra iv. 15 ; v. 8. 16 ; vi. 7, 8, &c.

דָּכָא , v. in Kal non occ. Niph. part. pl. m. נִדְכָּאִים , men *Beaten, injured*, or *oppressed*, Is. lvii. 15, al. non occ. Pih. דִּכָּא , 2d pers. דִּכִּאתָ , for דִּכֵּאתָ , as if the root were דכה : pres. יְדַכֵּא , constr. abs. immed. it. with ל, תְּדַכֵּא . *Beat small, down, break* ; Lam. iii. 34. With the feet, i. e. *trample on*, Ps. lxxii. 4 ; lxxxix. 11 ; cxliii. 3 ; Job vi. 9 ; xix. 2 ; Is. iii. 15 ; Prov. xxii. 22, &c.

Infin. דַּכֵּא , aff. דַּכְּאוֹ , *His striking*, i. e. being stricken, Is. liii. 10. See Gram. art. 146. 8, note. Gesenius here makes the dagesh euphonic ; which seems quite unnecessary. Puh. דֻּכְּאוּ , m. pl. pres. יְדֻכָּא , *Become stricken, broken*, in spirit, *contrite :* in strength, &c. constr. abs. it. with מִן , Jer. xliv. 10 ; Is. xix. 10 ; liii. 5 ; Job xxii. 9.

Part. מְדֻכָּא , pl. מְדֻכָּאִים .

Hith. pres. יַדַּכָּא , for יִתְדַּכָּא , Gram. art. 83. 1. i. q. Puh. Job v. 4 ; xxxiv. 25, al. non occ.

דַּכָּא , m. pl. constr. דַּכְּאֵי , *Greatly, habitually, broken*, in spirit, &c. Ps. xc. 3. (הוּא) תָּשֵׁב אֱנוֹשׁ עַד־דַּכָּא , *thou turnest man back until* (he falls) *broken, &c.* Gesenius here takes the Arab. ذَكَا , *pulvis*, as the sense of דַּכָּא . But, according to the Lexicographers, it has no such meaning, Is. lvii. 15 ; Ps. xxxiv. 19.

דָּכָה , pret. non occ. pres. יִדְכֶּה , keri, Ps. x. 10, i. q. דכא . Here, *He seems, appears, broken*, i. e. in spirit, humble, al. non occ.

Niph. נִדְכֶּה , נִדְכֵּיתִי , i. q. Niph. or Puh. of דכא , Ps. xxxviii. 9 ; li. 19, al. non occ.

Pih. 2d. pers. pret. דִּכִּיתָ , id. aff. דִּכִּיתָנוּ , i. q. Pih. דכא , Ps. xliv. 20 ; li. 10.

דָּכָה , m. i. q. דַּכָּא , Deut. xxiii. 2, al. non occ. Gesenius thinks the injuring of the testicles is meant, as effected in the East by a certain process of bruising, which makes them waste away.

דֳּכִי , aff. דָּכְיָם , once, Ps. xciii. 3, r. דכה . *Their beating* or *dashing* noise. Seg. n. fm. פְּקֹד . See דַּךְ .

דִּכֵּן , Chald. i. q. דֵּךְ , *This*, Dan. ii. 31 ; vii. 20.

דְּכַר , m. pl. דִּכְרִין , Chald. prop. Heb. זָכָר , *male*. *Rams*, Ezra vi. 9. 17 ; vii. 17, sing. non occ.

דִּכְרוֹנָה , f. r. דכר Heb. זכר . Syr. ܕܘܟܪܢܐ . Arab. ذَكَرَ , *meminit*. *A memorial, record*. Gesenius, &c. make the final ־ָה a substitute for ־ָא , i. e. the definite article, usually

T

דכר (138) דלה

termed the emphatic form: there is perhaps no necessity for this, Ezra vi. 2, al. non occ.

דָכְרָנַיָא, f. Syr. ܘܽܘܟ݂ܪܳܢܳܐ, *memoria*. Memory, record, Ezra iv. 15, al. non occ.

דַּל, m. pl. דַּלִּים, f. דַּלּוֹת. Syr. ܕܰܠ, *diminuit*. Arab. دَلَّ. Conj. iv. *macie, laboravit*.

تَدَلْدَلَ, *pendula, ac laxa fuit res*. Cogn. دَلَّ, *abjectus fuit*. Cogn. زَلَّ, *cæspitavit*. Æth. ደለወ : *pendulus*.

I. *Poor, weak*, Lev. xiv. 21; xix. 15; Ruth iii. 10; 1 Sam. ii. 8; 2 Sam. xiii. 4; Job xxxiv. 19: Pl. ib. xx. 10. 19; xxxi. 16; Prov. xxviii. 3. 8; Is. x. 2; Jer. xxxix. 10: f. Gen. xli. 19; Jer. lii. 15, 16. See דָּלָה.

II. Ps. cxli. 3, דַּל שְׂפָתַי, i. q. דֶּלֶת שְׂפָתַי, *Door of my lips*, according to Gesenius: comp. Mic. vii. 5, which is probable. The Arab. دَلَّ, moreover, signifies *indicavit, monstravit*; and دَالٌ, *argumentum*. Cogn. دَلو, is also used in the sense of *exeruit linguam*; it. *turpia locutus est*, in one form or other.

דלב, v. in Kal non occ. Arab. دَلَجَ, undè دَالِجٌ, *mane surgens*. Cogn. دَلَقَ, *eduxit e vagina* gladium.

Part. דּוֹלֵג, Person *skipping, leaping*, Zeph. i. 9. Comp. 1 Sam. v. 5. Constr. with עַל. Pih. pret. non occ. pres. יְדַלֵּג, *Leaping, skipping*, like a hart, Is. xxxv. 6; 2 Sam. xxii. 30; Ps. xviii. 30. Constr. abs. Part. מְדַלֵּג, *Skipping*, Cant. ii. 8, with עַל.

דָּלָה, v. pres. יִדְלֶה. Arab. دَلَو, et دَلَى, *hausit aquam* e puteo. Syriac ܕܠܳܐ, id. I. *Drawing water* from a well. Constr. abs. immed. and with לְ, pers. Exod. ii. 16. 19. Metaph. Prov. xx. 5, *brings up* or *out*.

II. *Tottering, vacillating*. Arab. دَلَو, *leniter propulit* camelum, effecitque ut lentè incederet; conj. iv. *laxus pependit*; it. دَالَية, *morbi genus, quod pedi humano accidere solet*. Prov. xxvi. 7, דַּלְיוּ שֹׁקַיִם מִפִּסֵּחַ, both legs of the lame man *totter, vacillate, are infirm*: such (is) a parable in the mouth of fools. Gesenius takes דלל as the root, and supposes that, as certain French and other words sometimes change a double *l* into *le*, as *famille, familia*; so here we have דַּלְיוּ, for דַּלְלוּ. Of this, too, he thinks he finds an example in the Arab. كَبْيُوب, for كَبُّوب, *calumniator*. But neither كَبْيُوب, nor كَبِيُوب, occurs in the Arabic: these he has probably mistaken for كَبُّوب, and كَبِيُّوب. — The truth is, the radical י (for which ה is a substitute) is here retained contrary to the usual practice.

Infin. דְּלֹה, *Drawing up*, Exod. xvi. 19. Pih. דִּלִּיתָנִי, *Thou hast drawn me up* or *out of the well*, i. e. hast liberated me: wells being used in ancient times as prisons. See בְאֵר, Ps. xxx. 2. Comp. vr. 4.

דַּלָּה, f. constr. דַּלַּת, pl. דַּלּוֹת. *Smallness, poverty*. See דַּל, 2 Kings xxiv. 14; xxv. 12; Jer. xl. 7; Gen. xli. 19; Jer. lii. 15, 16: used as a concrete, which indeed the word may be; the fem. being often used to denote *weakness*, Gram. art. 216. 7. 9. In Is. xxxviii. 12, we have כְדַלָּה יְבַצְּעֵנִי, which Gesenius translates, after others, "*a licio me abscindet*;" i. e. he shall cut me from the thrum (of the web); as if דַּלָּה meant *small thread* here. The passage is an allusion to Job vi. 9. See my note. From the following מִיּוֹם עַד־לַיְלָה in the parallel, מִדַּלָּה would rather seem to signify *lentè*. See דָּלָה, sign. ii. See also the last members of vv. 13 and 14 here. Or it may mean *by* or *from weakness, wasting, &c*. Nor in this case need the notion of *the web* be excluded: the term אֶרֶג, and יְבַצְּעֵנִי, seem sufficiently to imply this. Gesenius, too, gives the Chald. דַּלִּיל, *tela*. But, as this is a citation from the Talmud, which might have originated in a misunderstanding of this passage, no reliance can be placed on it. Again, Cant. vii. 6, we have דַּלַּת רֹאשֵׁךְ, which is said to be כָּאַרְגָּמָן, *like purple*, or, it may be, *something dyed purple*.

We have in the Arab. دَلَال, which is perhaps our very word, *fastus, superbia*. See Freytag's Lex. sub voce دلو; if so, taking this in a good sense, *elegance, grandeur*, or *dignity*, will be meant; and, hence the comparison be made with *purple*, which marked the dignity of kings; hence, too, perhaps, the following מֶלֶךְ אָסוּר, (the) *king is bound, captivated*, as a prisoner. Gesenius takes *coma* pendula: the elder Grammarians, *cin-*

דלח (139) דלק

cinnus; but I do not see how either of these can agree with the context.

דלח, v. pret. non occ. pres. תִּדְלַח; constr. immed. pers. בּ instr. Syr. ܕܠܚ, *perturbavit*. Arab. دلج, *contractu gradu incessit, &c. Disturb, make foul, muddy*, as water, Ezek. xxxii. 2. 13.

דְּלִי, m. (fm. פָקַד, seg.) lit. *drawing;* meton. instr. of do. *A bucket*, as used to draw water from a well, Is. xl. 15, al. non occ. See דלה.

דָּלְיוּ, see דלה.

דָּלְיוּ, m. pl. aff. for דָּלְיָיו, r. דלה (fm. פָּקַד), lit. *His drawings up* or *forth;* meton. *buckets*, as in the last art., Num. xxiv. 7; alluding to much offspring. Comp. Is. xlviii. 1; Prov. v. 15—20.

דָּלִיּוֹת, f. pl. sing. non occ. Syr. ܕܠܝܬܐ, *germina, palmites*. Arab. دالية *vitis*. See דָּלָה, *Boughs* or *branches* of any trees. With aff. דָּלִיּוֹתָיו, Jer. xi. 16; Ezek. xvii. 6. 23; xxxi. 7. 9. 12.

דָּלַל, v. דַּלּוֹתִי, pl. דַּלּוּ, and דַּלּוּ, pres. non occ. *Wasted, reduced, weakened*. See דַּל, Ps. lxxix. 8; cxvi. 6; cxlii. 7; Is. xix. 6; xxxviii. 14; Job xxviii. 4.

Niph. דַּל, pres. constr. abs. it. with מִפְּנֵי *Becomes, is, wasted, reduced, &c*. Judg. vi. 6; Is. xvii. 4.

דֶּלֶף, m. pl. non occ. Syr. ܕܠܦܐ, *stillicidium:* cogn. ܕܠܦ, *effusio*. Æth. ደለወ : *corripuit;* conj. iv. *continuavit*; ደለወ : *contumeliosus*. *Rain-drop*, Prov. xix. 13; xxvii. 15. The notion seems to originate in the close and continuous consecution of the rain-drops, and thence to imply annoyance. See ll. c.

דָּלַף, v. pres. יִדְלֹף, See דֶּלֶף, constr. abs. it. with אֶל, pers. מִן, cause. *Drop, emit, tears*, Job xvi. 20; Ps. cxix. 28. In Eccl. x. 18, יִדְלֹף הַבָּיִת. Gesen. "*pluviam per tecti rimas intromittit*. One would rather suppose that some moral truth was here intended; if so, בַּיִת should seem to signify *house*, in the sense of *family;* i. e. by lowness, want of energy of (the) hands, the house weeps; i. e. is reduced to distress, al. non occ.

דָּלַק, v. pres. יִדְלֹק. Syr. ܕܠܩ, *arsit, flagravit*. Arab. دلق, *eduxit e vagina*

gladium. Cogn. ذلق, *irrequieta fuit, splenduit lucerna*. I. *Burning, consuming.* Ps. vii. 14, הִצָּיו לְדֹלְקִים יִפְעָל, ellip. for חִצָּיו לִהְיוֹת לְדֹלְקִים, *He shall make his arrows to become fiery, consuming*, i. e. he shall send his lightnings upon them. See חֵץ, Obad vr. 18.   II. Applied metaphorically to the affections of the mind, and implying, (a) שְׂפָתַיִם דֹּלְקִים, *burning lips*, i. e. dissembling the warmest friendship, Prov. xxvi. 23. (b) *Burns* with rage, anger, Ps. x. 2. Comp Is. xiii. 8; Gen. xxxi. 36: constr. med אַחֲרֵי, 1 Sam. xvii. 53; where some part of the verb רדף seems to be understood. Comp Lam. iv. 19.

Infin. דְּלֹק, constr.
Part. m. pl. דֹּלְקִים.
Hiph. הִדְלִיק, imp. *Kindle fire, inflame*, pres. aff. יַדְלִיקֵם, Ezek. xxiv. 10; Is. v. 11, constr. immed. al. non occ.

דְּלַק, Chald. i. q. Heb. part. Dan. vii. 9, al. non occ.

דַּלֶּקֶת, f. Arab. ذلقة, *enectus prope fuit siti*. *Burning fever*, Deut. xxviii. 22, al. non occ.

דֶּלֶת, f. du. דְּלָתַיִם, constr. דַּלְתֵי, pl. דְּלָתוֹת, constr. דַּלְתוֹת. See דַּל, דלח, it. Arab. cogn. دلث, conj. viii. اندلث, *contexit, involvit*, rem. Cogn. دلظ, *portæ palatii regii custos*. Propr. I. *The valve*, or *leaf*, of a pair of folding doors. II. Meton. *A door*, generally, Prov. xxvi. 14; Gen. xix. 9, 10; 1 Kings vi. 34; 2 Kings iv. 4; ix. 3. In Ezek. xli. 23, 24, these distinctions seem to be confounded. It runs thus: *and* (there were) *two pair* (of) *folding doors to the temple, and the sanctuary; and two folding doors to the doors* (i. e. to each of these door-ways); *two doors made to revolve* (turn on hinges); *two to one door, and a pair of doors to the other*. Simply, the temple and sanctuary had each a pair of folding doors; and these severally consisted of pairs turning on hinges, Neh. vi. 1; Judg. iii. 23, &c. Metaph. (a) *The leaf* of a book, Jer. xxxvi. 33; (b) of the clouds, as *doors of heaven*, Ps. lxxviii. 23; (c) of the face, *jaws*, Job xli. 6; (d) of the womb, Ib. iii. 10; (d) of the sea, i. e. limits, Ib. xxxviii. 8. 10; (e) of the people, i. e. Israel, by way of eminence, Ezek. xxvi. 2. Aff. דַּלְתּוֹ, דַּלְתִּי, דְּלָתַי, דְּלָתֶיךָ, דַּלְתוֹתֵיהֶם, דַּלְתוֹתָיו, דַּלְתִי, דְּלָתֶיהָ.

דָּם, m. constr. דַּם, pl. דָּמִים, constr. דְּמֵי. Arab. دَم, pl. دِمَاءٌ (*de sanguine multo, et sanguine multorum usurpatur*). Syr. ܕܡܐ, *sanguis*. I. *Blood* of man, or of any animal, Gen. xxxvii. 22; Exod. vii. 19; Lev. iii. 17, &c.

II. Meton. *Blood-shedding,* i. e. the crime of murder, or of manslaughter. Comp. αἷμα, Matt. xxvii. 24; Gen. xxxvii. 26; Josh. xx. 3, &c.

(a) It. *The punishment due* to this, Exod. xxii. 1, 2; Lev. xx. 9; 2 Sam. i. 16; 1 Kings ii. 37; Ezek. xxxiii. 4, 5. Hence the phrases דָּם נָקִי, *innocent blood,* 2 Kings xxi. 16; Ps. cvi. 38; xciv. 21, &c. אִישׁ דָּמִים, *man of much blood.* See دِمَاءٌ, above, Ps. v. 7; xxvi. 9; lv. 24. עִיר דָּמִים, בֵּית דָּמִים, *Bloody house, city,* 2 Sam. xxi. 1; Ezek. xxii. 2; xxiv. 6. דָּמָיו בּוֹ, *His blood-guiltiness is upon him.* דְּמֵיהֶם בָּם,—*upon them,* Lev. xx. 9; Ezek. xviii. 13; Lev. xx. 11, &c.

(b) It. *The impurity of blood,* Lev. xv. 19; Is. i. 15; lix. 3; Ezek. xvi. 22, &c.

Metaph. applied *to wine,* as the Gr. αἷμα τῆς σταφυλῆς. Sir. xxxix. 29. Eustath. ad Hom. Il. ii. 636. Comp. Rev. xiv. 20; and hence taken to represent the blood of Christ in the eucharist, Gen. xlix. 11; Deut. xxxii. 14. Aff. דָּמִי, דָּמָה, דָּמוֹ, דָּמָם, דִּמְכֶם, דְּמֵיהֶם, דָּמַי, דָּמֶיךָ, דָּמֶיהָ, דָּמֵיךָ.

We have, in Ezek. xix. 10, בְּדָמְךָ, which has given much trouble to translators, &c. Gesenius proposes דָּם here to be taken as a derivative from דָּמָה, and in the sense of דְּמוּת, after Kimchi. Yet no one can fail to observe, that this makes the place not one whit easier than it was before. Some think רִמּוֹן, the ῥοά of the lxx., is the true reading: others prefer בְּרֻמְּךָ, *in thy exaltation,* as found in one of De Rossi's mss. Calmet thinks בְּכַרְמְךָ, is the true reading: but all, as far as I can see, without the least necessity or reason; for, if we suppose בְּדָמְךָ, *in thy blood,* to refer to the first state of Israel, when taken up by God; see ch. xvi. 6—14, and the place to read thus, *Thy mother* (was) *like a vine*—(I mean when thou wast) *in* (the state of) *thy blood,—planted by* (the) *waters, &c.,* I think we shall find no difficulty in it. The transition, or rather the allusion to a former description of Israel, is indeed abrupt; but not more so than in many other places in the Bible. See also Dathe, and Rosenmüller on the passage.

דָּמָה, v. pres. יִדְמֶה, constr. med. לְ, אֶל. Syr. ܘܕܡܝ, *similis fuit.* Arab. دَمَى, *idolum.* I. *Was like to, resembled,* Ps. lxxxix. 7; cii. 7; cxliv. 4; Cant. vii. 8; Ezek. xxxi. 8; Is. xlvi. 5.

Imp. דְּמֵה, Cant. ii. 17; viii. 14.

Part. דּוֹמֶה, Cant. ii. 9.

Niph. נִדְמָה, pres. non occ. constr. med. לְ. *Be, become, assimilated,* Ps. xlix. 13. 21; Ezek. xxxii. 2; Hos. x. 7. This last Gesenius places under sign. ii. which is plainly wrong, as it is constr. with לְ, which is never the case in that sense.

Pih. דִּמָּה, pres. יְדַמֶּה, constr. med. אֶל, לְ, I. *Assimilate, compare,* Is. xl. 18. 25; xlvi. 5; Cant. i. 9; Lam. ii. 13. Abs. Hos. xii. 11. אֲדַמֶּה, *I assimilate,* i. e. by symbols, parables, &c.

II. Cogn. τοῦ, זָמַם, *Imagined, thought, meditated,* either in a good or bad sense, Ps. xlviii. 10; L. 21; Is. x. 7; Esth. iv. 13; Num. xxxiii. 56; Judg. xx. 5, &c. Constr. immed. abs. it. med. לְ, בְּ.

Hithp. אֶדַּמֶּה, for אֶתְדַּמֶּה, Gram. art. 83. 1, i. q. Niph. Is. xiv. 14.

II. Kal. Cogn. דָּמַם, דּוּם. Arab. دَمَّ, *vulneravit, perdidit.* Cogn. دَسَى, *sanguinem emisit.* Comp. דָּם; conj. ii. *vulneravit.* دَوَّمَ, *quietum fecit.* Constr. abs. Propr. *Silent, quiet,* Jer. xiv. 17; Lam. iii. 49. Meton. *Reduced to silence, ruined, destroyed.* Constr. immed. Hos. iv. 5; Jer. vi. 2.

Niph. *Was, became, silent, ruined, &c.* Hos. iv. 6; x. 15; Is. vi. 5; xv. 1; Jer. xlvii. 5, constr. abs.

Infin. נִדְמֹה, Hos. x. 15.

דְּמָה, Chald. i. q. Heb. דָּמָה, sign. i. Dan. iii. 25; vii. 5, constr. med. לְ.

דֻּמָה, f. keri דָּמָה, occ. Ezek. xxvii. 32, only, מִי כְצוֹר כְּדֻמָה בְּתוֹךְ הַיָּם. If we take דָּמָה, for דּוּמָה, *silence;* we may thus render the passage: *Who* (is) *as Tyre, as silence, in the midst of the sea?* i. e. her trade, wealth, glory, at an end. Gesenius takes this word as derived from דָּמַם, and as signifying *vastatio.* But Dagesh in the מ would regularly compensate for the loss of the ו; we need not, therefore, suppose this to be a double radical letter. Besides, *silence,* see דָּמָה, sign. ii. will readily enough supply a sense consonant with *vastatio.* Or this word might be a sort of participle of the root כרם.

דמו (141) דמן

Arab. كدم, *propulit, persecutus fuit,* prædam. The translation would then be, *Who* (is) *as Tyre, pursued, driven, in the midst of the sea?* The former is sufficiently obvious, and therefore the better rendering.

דְּמוּת, f. r. דָּמָה, sign. i. Syr. ܕܡܘܬܐ, *similitudo. Similitude, likeness,* Gen. i. 26; v. 1. 3; 2 Chron. iv. 3; Is. xl. 18. In 2 Kings xvi. 10. Synon. תַּבְנִית, *pattern;* which is only a shade of "*likeness.*"—Ezek. i. 5. 16; Dan. x. 16, &c. Aff. דְּמוּתֵנוּ, דְּמוּתוֹ.

דֳּמִי, m. } r. דָּמָה, sign. ii. *Silence, quiet-*
דְּמִי, m. } *ness, rest.* The former, viz. דֳּמִי, Is. xxxviii. 10, in בִּדְמִי יָמַי, should, from the context, seem to signify, *In the silence,* i. e. reduction to silence, closing, ending, *of my days, let me walk in the gates of the grave:* i. e. as if my life were now gone, vexed as I am with disease. The latter, דֳּמִי, Ps. lxxxiii. 2; Is. lxii. 6, 7, occ. with חָשָׁה, and חָרָשׁ, *silence,* &c. in their proper acceptations.

דִּמְיוֹן, m. r. דָּמָה, sign. i., i. q. דְּמוּת, *Likeness, &c.* Ps. xvii. 12. Aff. דִּמְיוֹנוּ, al. non occ.

דָּמַם, v. pres. יִדֹּם, pl. יִדְּמוּ, as in the Chaldaic. Cogn. דָּמָה, sign. ii. Syr. ܕܡܡ, *spectavit* cum animi studio. Æth. ደመመ : *obstupuit.* Arab. دَنَا, *onustum reddidit; perdidit.* نَال, *malè affecit. Was dumb, silent, quiet, inactive,* in consequence of some strong affection of the mind. Constr. abs. it. med. לְ, Job xxix. 21; xxx. 27; xxxi. 34; Ps. xxxv. 15; Exod. xv. 16; Lev. x. 3; Josh. x. 13, synon. עָמַד, Jer. xlviii. 2; Lam. ii. 10; iii. 28. 49; Amos v. 13, &c.

Imp. דֹּם, Ezek. xxiv. 17; pl. דֹּמּוּ, Is. xxiii. 2; f. דֹּמִּי, Jer. xlvii. 6. It. דּוֹם, m. sing. Josh. x. 12, *stand still.* Comp. Arab. كَامَ دوم, 1 Sam. xiv. 9, pl.

Niph. נָדַם, pl. נָדַמּוּ, Jer. xxv. 37, pres. יִדַּמּוּ, 1 Sam. ii. 9; Jer. xlix. 26; L. 30; li. 6; xlviii. 2. תִּדְּמִי, f. pres. It. viii. 14. All in the sense of דָּמָה, sign. ii. *Become silent, ruined, destroyed.*

Pih. דּוֹמַמְתִּי, *I have made silent, quiet,* Ps. cxxxi. 2. Constr. immed. al. non occ.

Hiph. הֲדֻמָּנוּ, aff. *Hath reduced us to silence,* ruined us, Jer. viii. 14, al. non occ.

דְּמָמָה, f. *Silence,* 1 Kings xix. 12. קוֹל דְּמָמָה דַקָּה, lit. *a voice, silence, small;* i. e. as I understand, *a small voice, (then) silence;* as if these were alternate; or as if a sort of whisper broke the silence, which followed the thunder and lightning just mentioned. Comp. Job iv. 16, from which this passage in Kings was principally worded, and Ps. cvii. 29, which is perfectly similar; al. non occ.

דֹּמֶן, m. Arab. دِمَن, *stercoratio;* دِمْن, *stercus. Dung,* 2 Kings ix. 37; Jer. viii. 2; ix. 21; xvi. 4; xxv. 33; Ps. lxxxiii. 11.

דֶּמַע, prim. seg. fm. פֶּקַד, aff. דִּמְעֲךָ, Exod. xxii. 29. Lit. *Tear.* Arab. دَمْع. Syr. ܕܡܥܐ, *lacryma.* Metaph. *juice* of the grape, &c. *Wine,* and perhaps the *precious gums* and *oil.* So the "*arboram lacrymas,* and, τῶν δένδρων τὰ δάκρυα, of Pliny and Theophrastus, respectively, Eich. Sim. sub voce. Whence—

דִּמְעָה, f. cònstr. דִּמְעַת, pl. דְּמָעוֹת, *A tear.* Meton. *Weeping,* Ps. cxvi. 8; Is. xxv. 8; Jer. viii. 23; ix. 16; Eccl. iv. 1; Ps. xxxix. 13; Lam. i. 2, &c. Aff. דִּמְעָתֶךָ, דִּמְעָתִי in pausâ, דִּמְעָתָהּ.

דַּמֶּשֶׂק, m. But דַּמֶּשֶׁק, according to many MSS. See Coll. de Rossi, and Schol. crit. *A sort of fine cloth,* or *silk,* as some think, so called because made at Damascus; so our *Damask.* But why then is the שׂ changed to שׁ? And why is not the noun in the patronymic form דמשקי? The parallelism, moreover, manifestly requires that this word be taken as a proper name. Amos iii. 12, and nowhere else does it occur—הַיֹּשְׁבִים בְּשֹׁמְרוֹן בִּפְאַת מִטָּה וּבִדְמֶשֶׁק עָרֶשׂ, *Those who sit in Samaria, on the side of the couch, and in Damascus* (on the) *bed.* So the LXX. Vulgate, Syr. Targ. and Arab. of the Polyglott; which is, no doubt, correct.

דֵּן, Chald. Def. דְּנָה, pron. demons. i. q. Heb. זֶה, זאת, *This,* Dan. ii. 18. 28, &c. כִּדְנָה, *as this, thus,* Ezra v. 7; Jer. x. 11; Dan. ii. 10. עַל דְּנָה, *upon this, thereupon,* Dan. iii. 16; Ezra iv. 14, 15. אַחֲרֵי דְנָה, *after this, afterwards,* Dan. ii. 29.

דַּע, m. pl. דֵּעִים r. ידע, } rejected by
דֵּעָה, f. pl. דֵּעוֹת } Gram. art. 76. *Knowing, recognizing;* meton. *knowledge, science, opinion,* Job xxxii. 6. 10. 17. 36. תְּמִים דֵּעִים Job xxxvi. 4; it. תְּמִים דֵּעוֹת Ib. xxxvii. 16, *perfect of knowledge,* i. e. *persons thoroughly informed,* in the first case; in the second,

דֵעָה (142) דק

things perfectly true, i. e. known as such. דֵעָה אֶת־יְהוָה, *recognizing Jehovah*, 1 Sam. ii. 3; Is. xi. 9; xxviii. 9; Ps. lxxiii. 11, i. q. דַּעַת. Aff. דֵּעִי.

דְּעָה, Imp. v. יָדַע, Prov. xxiv. 14.

דָּעַךְ, v. pres. יִדְעַךְ. Syr. ܕܥܟ, وَدَكَ, *extinctus est*. *Put out, extinguish*, as a lamp. Metaph. making circumstances worse, Job xviii. 5, 6; xxi. 17; Prov. xiii. 9; xx. 20; xxiv. 20; Is. xliii. 17.

Niph. נִדְעָכוּ, *They* are, or *become, extinguished*, ruined, Job vi. 17. See my note, al. non occ.

Puh. דֹעֲכוּ, i. q. Niph. Ps. cxviii. 12, al. non occ.

דַּעַת, f. for יָדַעַת, Gram. art. 76, i. q. דֵּעַ, or דֵּעָה, *Knowing, recognizing.* Meton. *knowledge, science, opinion*, Hos. iv. 1; vi. 6; Deut. iv. 42; xix. 4; Josh. xx. 5; Hos. iv. 6; Prov. i. 4; ii. 6; xxiv. 5; Job xxxv. 16; xxxvi. 12; xxxviii. 2; xlii. 3. Phrases פְּלִיאָה דַעַת, *wonderful of knowledge*, i. e. exceeding one's knowledge, Ps. cxxxix. 6. Comp. תְּמִים דֵּעוֹת, Job xxxvii. 16. It. אִישׁ דַּעַת, *man of knowledge*, Prov. xxiv. 5. דַּעַת רוּחַ, *knowledge of wind*, i. e. *vanity*, Job xv. 2. See my note. יֹדְעֵי דַעַת, *knowers of knowledge, informed*, Dan. i. 4. הַדַּעַת אֹתִי, *the knowing, recognizing, me*, Jer. xxii. 16.

דֳּפִי, m. seg. fm. פֹּקֶר, Gram. art. 87. 4, Ps. l. 20, al. non occ. LXX. σκάνδαλον. Arab. دَفَوَ, *overwhelming, slaying.* Æth. ደፍአ: *expulit.* Cogn. دَفَّ, *sensim* in *hostem tetendit.* Comp. cogn. دَفَعَ: *stroke, blow*, as given by the slanderous tongue. Comp. Ps. lvii. 5; lxiv. 4.

דָּפַק, v. pres. non occ. Arab. دَفَقَ, *celer.* Kam. دَفَقَ اللهُ رُوحَهُ, *God forced out his spirit*; brought on death. *Beating*, meton. *driving*, as cattle, Gen. xxxiii. 13. Part. דּוֹפֵק, *Beating, knocking*, at a door, Cant. v. 2.

Hithp. part. pl. מִתְדַּפְּקִים, *persons becoming, setting about, knocking* at a door. Constr. med. עַל, Judg. xix. 22. Gesenius thinks *certatim* is included in the force of this participle. I can discover no grounds for this.

דַּק, m. דַּקָּה, f. pl. דַּקּוֹת, r. דָּקַק. Syr. ܕܩ, *comminuit.* Arab. دَقَّ, *exilis*; دُقّ,

pulvis, tenuis. Small, thin, as of dust, hair, cattle, corn, sound, sickly person, Is. xxix. 5; xl. 15; see Gram. art. 217. 7: Exod. xvi. 14; xxxii. 20; Lev. xvi. 12. It. xiii. 30; Gen. xli. 3. 6, &c.; Lev. xxi. 20; 1 Kings xix. 12.

דֹּק, m. Arab. دُقّ, *ornamenti species mulieribus Meccæ propria:* probably *A sort of thin vail*, such as the גִּלְיוֹנִים of Isaiah, ch. iii. 23. See sub voce, Is. xl. 22.

דָּקַק, pret. non occ. pres. יָדֹק. See דַּק above. *Beat*, or *grind small*, Is. xli. 15; Ib. xxviii. 28. This verb and דּוּשׁ are opposed; as, לֶחֶם יוּדָק כִּי לֹא לָנֶצַח אָדוֹשׁ יְדוּשֶׁנּוּ, *Bread* (corn) *is ground, for he will not continually thrash it;* i. e. a more severe regimen is applied, when the nature of the case makes that necessary. It is added, *For the beating of the wheel of his cart, and of his horsemen, will not reduce it to powder.* דָּק, Exod. xxxii. 20, and Deut. ix. 21, is manifestly the noun, not the verb,—al. non occ.

Hiph. הֵדֵק, pres. יָדִיק, apoc. יָדֵק, constr. immed. med. ?, of thing compared. *Reduced to dust* or *powder*, Exod. xxx. 36; 2 Kings xxiii. 6. 15; Mich. iv. 13; 2 Chron. xv. 16; xxxiv. 4.

Infin. הָדֵק, and הָדֵק, Exod. xxx. 36; 2 Chron. xxxiv. 7.

Hoph. יוּדַק, pret. non occ. *Becomes ground, powdered*, Is. xxviii. 28, al. non occ.

דְּקַק, v. Chald. i. q. Heb. דָּקַק, pl. in Dan. ii. 35, for דָּקִּי, Dagesh being compensated by the perfect vowel (ִ), al. non occ.

Aph. 3 pers. pret. f. הַדֶּקֶת, Dan. ii. 34. 45; pl. m. הַדִּקוּ, Ib. vi. 25: pres. תַּדִּק, Dan. ii. 40; vii. 23. Constr. immed.

Part. מְהַדֵּק, f. מַדְּקָה, Dan. ii. 40; vii. 7. 19.

דָּקַר, v. pres. יִדְקֹר. Constr. immed. Syr. ܕܩܪ, *pupugit.* Cogn. Arab. دَغَرَ, *invasit, immisit se* in hostem. *Pierce, run through,* Num. xxv. 8; Judg. ix. 54; Zech. xii. 10; xiii. 3.

Imp. aff. דָּקְרֵנִי, 1 Sam. xxxi. 4; 1 Chron. x. 4.

Niph. pres. יִדָּקֵר, *Shall be thrust through*, Is. xiii. 15, al. non occ.

Hoph. part. pl. מְדֻקָּרִים. *Persons pierced through*, Jer. xxxvii. 10; li. 4. In Lam. iv. 9. Metaph. by want. So Luke ii. 35. See Kuinœl's note,—*by sorrow.*

דָּר, m. Arab. دُرّ, coll. *uniones*. *The union pearl*, perhaps, or a marble stone, resembling this, Est. i. 6, al. non occ. Some take it to signify Parian marble, others white marble; but nothing certain is known about it. See Hieroz. Boch., ii., lib. v., c. viii., col. 708.

דָּר, m. Chald. i. q. Heb. דּוֹר, *Generation*, &c. Dan. iii. 33; iv. 31.

דָּר, see דּוֹר.

דִּרְאוֹן, constr. Dan. xii. 2, probably of—

דֵּרָאוֹן, m. Is. lxvi. 24. Arab. دَرْءٌ, *impulsus*; *excitatio mali*. *Abhorring, contempt*, al. non occ.

דָּרְבֹנוֹת, f. pl. Arab. دِرَابَة, *acies*, *acumen*. Æth. ፀናፍ: *emisit lanceam*. *Goads, stimuli*, Eccl. xii. 11, al. non occ.

דָּרְבָן, m. sing. i. q. דָּרְבֹנוֹת, prec. 1 Sam. xiii. 21, al. non occ.

דַּרְדַּר, m. pl. non occ. Arab. دَرْدَر, *tribulus, spina*. Syr. ܕܪܕܪܐ, see Lud. de Dieu, Gen. iii. 18; Heb. vi. 8. LXX. τρίβολος. *Brambles*, Gen. iii. 18; Hos. x. 8, al. non occ. Hieroz. Bochart. ii. col. 712. Hierob. Celsii. ii. 128.

דָּרוֹם, m. Arab. دَرُومٌ, *pravo modo incedens*; r. دَرَمَ, *propinquis passibus incessit, festinans*. So named, perhaps, because tempests usually came on from that quarter, Job xxxvii. 9; Is. xxi. 1, &c. *The country south of Judea*, Job xxxvii. 17; Deut. xxxiii. 23; Ezek. xxi. 2; xl. 24; Eccl. i. 6, &c.

דְּרוֹר, m. pl. non occ. Arab. دَرّ, *lactis copia; aptitudo ad cursum*. Cogn. دَارَ, r. دور, *circumivit*. Applied to a certain bird, according to some—

I. *The swallow: a sort of wild pigeon*, or *dove*, according to Bochart, Hieroz. ii. lib. i. c. vii. col. 51, &c.; Ps. lxxxiv. 4; Prov. xxvi. 2.

II. מָר־דְּרוֹר, *Spontaneously flowing myrrh. Nativa, quæ vel sponte sudat ex arboribus, priusquam incidantur, cui nulla præfertur*. Hierob. Celsii. i. p. 523. Onkelos and the Syriac Vers. מורא דכיא, *myrrha pura*. LXX. ἐκλεκτή, *electa*. Celsii p. 525, &c. which see. Exod. xxx. 23, al. non occ. And from the notion of plenty, &c.—

III. *Liberty*, as obtained in the year of Jubilee, &c. Lev. xxv. 10; Ezek. xlvi. 17; Is. lxi. 1; Jer. xxxiv. 8. 15. 17. With קרא, constr. med. לְ, בְּ.

דֶּרֶךְ, m. du. דְּרָכַיִם, pl. דְּרָכִים, constr. דַּרְכֵי. Syr. ܕܪܟ, *calcavit*; cogn. دَرَجَ, *gradatim incessit*. Arab. دَرَكَ, *persecutus fuit*; cogn. دَرَجَ, *gradatim progressus fuit*. Prop. *stepping* perhaps. Hence, meton. I. *A way, road*, Gen. iii. 34; xxxviii. 14; xlix. 17; Exod. xiii. 17, 18; Num. xiv. 28; all in construction with the qualifying word immediately following, or that word having ה versus attached to it. So Hos. vi. 9, דֶּרֶךְ יְרַצְּחוּ שֶׁכְמָה, (in the) *way to Shechem they slay*. Gesenius makes this sort of construction equivalent to *ad, versus*; as דֶּרֶךְ הַדָּרוֹם, *the way of the south*, "austrum versus." But what necessity is there for this technicality? The one mode of expression is quite as intelligible as the other. It. דֶּרֶךְ הַמֶּלֶךְ, *the king's road*; i. e. *high way*, Num. xx. 17; xxi. 22; Deut. xi. 30. By a further meton.—

II. *Journey*; as, דֶּרֶךְ שְׁלֹשֶׁת יָמִים, *a journey of three days*, Gen. xxx. 36; xxxi. 23; Exod. iii. 18, &c. לַעֲשׂוֹת דַּרְכּוֹ, *to make, pursue, his journey*, Judg. xvii. 8. הָלַךְ בְּדֶרֶךְ, *has walked in* (the) *way*, i. e. *taken a journey*, Prov. vii. 19. דֶּרֶךְ לוֹ, *he has a journey before him*, 1 Kings xviii. 27; Gen. xix. 2; xxxii. 2; Num. xxiv. 25, &c. It. Meton.

III. *Way, manner, custom*. It. Arab. طَرِيقٌ, سَبِيلٌ, مَمْشًى, مِنْهَاجٌ, Pers. راه, id. דֶּרֶךְ כָּל־הָאָרֶץ, *the way, manner, of all the earth*, Gen. xix. 31. Comp. Prov. xi. 15; 1 Sam. xviii. 14; 2 Kings xxii. 2; Is. viii. 11. Applied also to God's doings, Ps. xviii. 31; Deut. xxxii. 4; Job xxvi. 14; Prov. viii. 22. יְהוָה קָנָנִי רֵאשִׁית דַּרְכּוֹ, is thus rendered by Gesenius, "*Jehova creavit me ab initio creationis*." Which I humbly conceive is utterly incorrect. The thing spoken of here is *wisdom*; which the very next member tells us was *before His works*. קֶדֶם מִפְעָלָיו. It could not, therefore, be one of His works of creation. This the next verse confirms; which declares that this existed, מֵעוֹלָם, *from everlasting, &c*. Besides, קָנָנִי does not signify *created*, but *possessed, enjoyed as his own*. *Jehovah possessed me*,

דרך (144) דרכ

i. e. wisdom; *the first of His ways* is therefore the literal meaning of the passage. And this is apparently imitated in Job xl. 19 (14).— See my Commentary on the place,—speaking of the creation of the powerful graminivorous beasts, as the production of God's *wisdom;* of which, therefore, I take רֵאשִׁית דַּרְכּוֹ to be a periphrasis. The pl. is perhaps always used in this III. sense; and is, as in other cases, applied either to God or man. Phrases, פְּרִדַרְכֶּם, Prov. i. 31. דֶּרֶךְ נָשִׁים, Gen. xxxi. 35. דֶּרֶךְ יְהֹוָה, *Way,* religion, *of Jehovah,* Judg. ii. 22. דֶּרֶךְ חֹל, common, profane, *usage,* 1 Sam. xxi. 6. דֶּרֶךְ אַרְצָם, *manner of their country,* 1 Kings viii. 48; Amos viii. 14; Ps. cxxxix. 24. Comp. Jer. xviii. 15, &c. And, by a further meton.,

IV. *The trials, difficulties, fruits, of one's ways, conduct, &c.,* Is. x. 24; Ps. xxxvii. 5; Job iii. 23; Amos ii. 7.

Aff. דַּרְכִּי, דַּרְכְּךָ, דַּרְכֵּךְ, דַּרְכּוֹ, דַּרְכָּהּ, &c. pl. דְּרָכַי, דְּרָכֵינוּ, &c.

דָּרַךְ, v. pres. יִדְרֹךְ, see דֶּרֶךְ, constr. כִּי, from which; בְּ, *in;* לְ, *for;* עַל, *on;* immed. *Step on, tread,* (a) as grapes in the wine-vat, Job xxiv. 11; Jer. xxv. 30; Lam. i. 15; Is. xvi. 10; lxiii. 2; Mic. vi. 15.

(b) *Tread down,* i. e. injure, destroy, Deut. xxxiii. 29; Judg. v. 21; ix. 27; Mic. i. 3; v. 4; Is. lxiii. 3; Ps. xci. 13.

(c) *Treading the bow;* i. e. planting the left foot against, in order to make the aim the more certain. Diod. Sic. iii. 8. Arrian Ind. xvi. Καὶ τοῦτο (τὸ τόξον) κάτω ἐπὶ τὴν γῆν θέντες, καὶ τῷ ποδὶ τῷ ἀριστερῷ ἀντιβάντες, οὕτως ἐκτοξεύουσι, τὴν νευρὴν ἐπὶ μέγα ὀπίσω ἀπαγαγόντες. Ps. vii. 13; xi. 2; xxxvii. 14; 1 Chron. v. 18; viii. 40; 2 Chron. xiv. 7; Is. v. 28. Applied also to the arrow, Ps. lviii. 8; lxiv. 4. Metaph. Zech. ix. 13.

(d) *Stepping onward, coming forth, proceeding,* Num. xxiv. 17; Hab. iii. 14. Hence, *enter, take possession of,* Deut. xi. 24, 25; Josh. i. 3; xiv. 9; Is. lix. 8; Mic. v. 5; 1 Sam. v. 5.

(e) *Walking in state,* as a king, Mic. i. 3; Job ix. 8.

Part. דּוֹרֵךְ, pl. דּוֹרְכִים. Passiv. f. דְּרוּכָה, pl. דְּרוּכוֹת.

Hiph. הִדְרִיךְ, pres. יַדְרִיךְ, יַדְרֵךְ, *Caused to tread, proceed;* hence *led,* Is. xi. 15; xlii. 16; xlviii. 17; Ps. cvii. 7; cxix. 35; Prov. iv. 11, &c.

(b) Infin. Jer. li. 33. Time of *her treading* (being trodden) *down.*

(c) Jer. ix. 2. וַיַּדְרִיכוּ אֶת־לְשׁוֹנָם קַשְׁתָּם, *They cause their tongue to be trodden,* (which is) *their bow, &c.*

(e) *Cause to enter, take possession of,* Judg. xx. 43; Job xxviii. 8.

Infin. הַדְרִיךְ, Jer. li. 33.

Part. מַדְרִיךְ, Is. xlviii. 17.

דַּרְכְּמֹנִים, m. pl. See אֲדַרְכּוֹנִים, p. 9, above.

דְּרָעוֹהִי, m. pl. Aff. Chald. i. q. Heb. זְרוֹעַ, *His arms,* Dan. ii. 32, i. q. אֶדְרָע.

דָּרַשׁ, v. pres. יִדְרֹשׁ. Constr. med. אַחַר, בְּ, לְ, אֶל, אֵת, it. immed. of the object; it. med. עַל, *about* whom; כִּי, מֵעַל, מֵעִם, מֵאֵת, מִיַּד, *from, &c.* it. abs. Syr. ܕܪܫ, *trivit, disputavit, inquisivit.* Æth. ደረሰ : *composuit, concinnavit.* Arab. درس, *trivit; trivit librum, perlegit.* Propr. perhaps, *went over;* hence, *Sought, inquired,* after, of, from, into, &c., Lev. x. 16; 1 Chron. x. 14; 2 Chron. xvi. 12; xvii. 3, 4; xxiv. 6; Prov. xxxi. 13; Deut. xiii. 15, with synon. שָׁאַלְתָּ חָקַרְתָּ, xvii. 4. 9; 2 Kings viii. 8; Ps. xxxiv. 5; 1 Chron. xxviii. 9; Is. xxxiv. 16. Phrases, יִדְרֹשׁ דָּם מִיַּד, *Shall seek blood* (whether shed) *by means of, &c.* Gen. ix. 5. מֵעִם, *from,* Deut. xviii. 19, &c. דְּרֹשׁ לְשָׁלוֹם, *seeking the peace,* Jer. xxxviii. 4; Deut. xxiii. 7.

(b) In the sense of *Caring for,* Job iii. 4; Ps. cxlii. 5; Ezek. xxxiv. 5.

דָּרוֹשׁ. Imp. and Infin. דְּרוֹשׁ, דָּרוֹשׁ, Lev. x. 16; Deut. xxiii. 21; 1 Kings xxii. 5, &c. Once דָּרְיוֹשׁ, Ezra x. 16.

Part. דֹּרֵשׁ, pl. דֹּרְשִׁים. Aff. דֹּרְשֶׁיךָ, &c. Passiv. f. דְּרוּשָׁה, m. pl. דְּרוּשִׁים.

Niph. נִדְרַשׁ, pres. אִדָּרֵשׁ. Constr. לְ, *Became, was, sought, inquired,* after, Gen. xlii. 22; Is. lxv. 1; 1 Chron. xxvi. 31; Ezek. xiv. 3; xx. 3. 31; xxxvi. 37.

Infin. abs. אִדָּרוֹשׁ, Ezek. xiv. 3.

דֶּשֶׁא, m. Chald. דִּתְאָה. Syr. metath. ܕܬܐܐ. Arab. دثأ, *primum terræ germen.* Gesen. *The first blades of grass; tender herbage:* in this respect differing from עֵשֶׂב, *grass,* generally, and חָצִיר, *ripe,* do., Gen. i. 11, 12; Deut. xxxii. 2; 2 Sam. xxiii. 4; 2 Kings xix. 26; Job vi. 5; Ps. xxiii. 2; Is. lxvi. 14, &c. pl. non occ.

דָּשָׁא, v. pres. non occ. *Be, become, grassy,* Joel ii. 22.

Hiph. f. pres. תַּדְשֵׁא, *Let it send forth*

דשן—ה (145) דשן—ה

young grass, Gen. i. 11; with עֹשֶׂה פְּרִי, *producing fruit*, in the parall. and תּוֹצֵא—דֶּשֶׁא, *it sent forth young grass*, vr. 12.

דֶּשֶׁן, m. pl. non occ. Aff. דִּשְׁנִי, constr. דִּשְׁנֵי. Syr. ܕܽܘܫܢܳܐ, *facultas*, it. ܕܽܘܫܢܳܐ, *donum*.

Pers. دُشْن, *donum; munus* altaris: it. cogn. Arab. دَسَم, *pinguedo cibi*: دُسُومَة, *fimus*, *pinguedo*. I. *Fatness* of meat, Judg. ix. 9; Is. lv. 2; Jer. xxxi. 14; Ps. lxiii. 6; abs. for concr. Ps. xxii. 30; Job xxxvi. 16. Hence applied to, II. *Ashes*, particularly those of the burnt offerings, and of dead bodies as used in manuring the lands. See Pliny, lib. xvii. c. ix. [v.] His words are, "*Transpadanis cineris usus adeo placet, ut anteponant fimo jumentorum: quod quia levissimum est, ob id exurunt.*" Virgil. Georg. 1. 80. Hence, Ps. lxv. 12. *Fatness, fertility*, Lev. i. 16; iv. 12; vi. 3, 4; 1 Kings xiii. 3; Jer. xxxi. 40. Hence—

דִּשְּׁנְתָּ, v. Pih. pres. תְדַשֵּׁן. I. *Make fat*, Prov. xv. 30. (b) *Anoint*, Ps. xxiii. 5. (c) *Consider fat, good*, Ib. xx. 4. See Gram. art. 154. 8.

II. *Cleansed of ashes*, Num. iv. 13. Infin. aff. דַּשְּׁנוֹ, *Cleansing it* of ashes, Exod. xxvii. 3.

Puh. pres. תְדֻשַּׁן, *Is made fat*, satisfied, Prov. xiii. 4; xxviii. 25.

Hithp. obj. הַדַּשְׁנָה, Gram. art. 186, for הִתְדַשְּׁנָה, Gram. art. 83. 1, according to Gesenius: which will require Dagesh in שׁ. It might, moreover, be Hophhal, הֻדְשְׁנָה, or הָדְשְׁנָה, if we suppose an error to exist in the vowels. In the first case, *Became fat*; in the second, *made fat*, will be the sense; either of which will suit the context, Is. xxxiv. 6, al. non occ.

דָּשֵׁן, m. pl. דְּשֵׁנִים, *Fat, fruitful*, Is. xxx. 23; Ps. xcii. 15, al. non occ.

דָּת, f. constr. דַּת, pl. m. דָּתִים, constr. דָּתֵי. Syr. ܕܳܬܳܐ, ܕܳܬܳܐ, *placitum*. Pers. داد, *justice, Edict, mandate, law*, Esth. i. 13. 15. 19; ii. 12; iii. 14; viii. 13; ix. 14. Phrases, דַּת הַיּוֹם, *law of to-day;* i. e. existing law, Esth. ix. 13. אֵשׁ דָּת לָמוֹ, Deut. xxxiii. 2. Usually, *a fiery law for them*. Gesen. *columna ignea*. I am disposed to think that דָּת here, is the same as the Arab. دَكّ, i. q. دَفْ, *a stroke, ictus dolorem inferens, &c.* and that it alludes to those instances of the lightning, &c. in which God had interposed, and would still interpose, *for his people*. See the whole verse.

דָּת, Chald. f. Def. דָּתָא, pl. constr. דָּתֵי, i. q. Heb. *Law, edict, &c.* Dan. ii. 13. 15; vi. 9. 13. 16; Ezra vii. 12. 21. Dan. ii. 9, *consilium*, according to Gesenius. I can see no necessity for this. He also makes דָּת אֱלָהֵהּ, *law of his God*, to mean *religio*, or *religionis disciplina*. But religion, or the rites of religion, differs widely from the law, i. e. the grounds of religion.

דִּתְאָא, m. Def. דִּתְאָה, דִּתְאָא, Chald. i. q. Heb. דֶּשֶׁא, *Young grass*, Dan. iv. 12, 20.

דְּתָבְרַיָּא, m. pl. Def. of דְּתָבַר. Pers. probably, دادور, for دادآور, or دادآور, *Justice bringing* or *bearing*. *Justices, judges*, or *lawyers*, Dan. iii. 2. 3.

ה

ה, *He*. The fifth letter of the Hebrew alphabet, which, therefore as a numeral, represents that number, Gram. art. 4. It is enounced with a deep breathing and the larynx distended; contrary to ח, *kheth*, which very much contracts that organ. It sustains various offices, I. in the etymology, and II. syntax of the Hebrew language.

I. (a) In the etymology, it is found to designate the feminine gender, Gram. artt. 135. 6; 136. 2, et seq. So also in the Chaldee. And in this case it may be said to have some affinity with the letter ת.

(b) When added to nouns, having this feminine termination, it supplies a sort of superlative power; as, יְשׁוּעָה, *salvation*; יְשׁוּעָתָה, *singular, great, salvation*, Gram. art. 175. 8. So the Arab. ة, in عَلَّامَة, *a singularly learned man*. In the Chaldee it often stands for the definite article א; as in דְּנָה, פְּשָׁרָה, &c.

(c) It is prefixed to certain forms, and then supplies a sort of causative force, Gram. art. 157. 2. 4. 10.

(d) It is also found combined with ח, הִיה,

U

ה (146) הא

and prefixed to other forms, Gram. art. 157. 12, 13, et seq. In both these last cases, either in the Hebrew, or in its sister dialects, it claims some affinity with א.

(e) It often interchanges in the sister dialects with ח, as Syr. ܚܡ݂ܶܐ for Heb. פַּח, in Heb. rarely; as, גָּבַה, for גָּבָהּ. More frequently with י, as the middle radical; as, בּוּשׁ. Syr. Chald. דְּחַת, ܟܗܰܬ: דּוֹר. Arab. دَهَل مُول, Chald. רוּץ; נְהַר, נוּר, כָּהָל. ܢܕܗܐ. Gesen.

Its origin, as a letter, I leave to the writers on hieroglyphics to determine. Its application, in forming the feminine gender, originated perhaps in the notion of softness, which seems to be implied in the breathing accompanying its enunciation: as, טוֹב, *bonus*, טוֹבָה, *bona*, &c., which has, probably for a similar reason, prevailed to a great extent in many other languages. In this respect it claims, as already noticed, in this family of languages, some affinity with ח, $, ע, Gram. art. 143. 4.

II. Its offices in the syntax are,—

(a) When affixed to certain words, names of places, &c. its power seems to be equivalent to the Latin *versus*; as, אַרְצָה, *to* (the) *earth*; מִצְרַיְמָה, *to, towards, Egypt, &c.* Gram. artt. 175. 8; 180. 15—17. Occasionally so when prefixed; as, הָעִיר, *to the city*, Josh. viii. 19; 1 Sam. ix. 13. Nold. p. 212, seq.

(b) It is also affixed to imperatives and present tenses of verbs; as, לְכָה, *go to*, for לֵךְ, &c. Gram. art. 175. 5. אֲסַפְּרָה, Ib. par. 6, &c. Ib. art. 234, seq.

(c) It is also used as the affixed pronoun of the fem. gen. ־ָהּ, ־ֶהָ, ־ְהָ, Gram. art. 145. 5, et seq.

(d) It also occupies the place of זֶה, זוּ, אֲשֶׁר, Gram. art. 177. 3, and note. הָהֲלִכוּא, *Who went*, Josh. x. 24. הַיּוּלָד, *who is born*, Judg. xiii. 8, &c. See Nold. ed. 1734, p. 214, &c. Which seems to intimate that the pron. הוּא, *He*, or some such word, was the original term, abbreviated now to ה simply. In the Arabic ال, *el*, the definite article occasionally occupies this situation; as in ال ترضي, *who art agreed*; المَعَى, *who* (is) *with him, &c.* See De Sacy's Gram. Arab. art. 793, ed. 1810. Here perhaps the pron. אַל,—which is now a pl. of זֶה, זוּ,—was the original vocable.

(e) Hence, perhaps, it has obtained the force and usage of the definite article, *the*; Gr. ὁ, ἡ, τό; formerly the demonstrative ὅς, ἥ, ὅ; as grammarians generally allow. For the vowels, usually accompanying this particle as the definite article, see Gram. art. 180. 4, et seq.; for its usage in syntax, see art. 221, et seq.; Nold. p. 211, &c. For further particulars on this subject, see the Appendix.

(f) הֲ, הַ, הָ, prefixed to nouns, pronouns, &c. supplies the force of an interrogative; occasionally used also indefinitely, Gram. art. 179, seq. In this case it seems to claim affinity with the Arabic هل, and أ, *num, anne? &c.* With אִם in the subsequent member, Ib. par. 3, and note; Nold. p. 214, et seq., and the Appendix to this work.

הָא, Chald. interj. Syr. ܗܳܐ. Arab. ها, *Behold! lo!* Dan. iii. 25.

הָא, Heb. and Chald. i. q. הָא, Gen. xlvii. 23; Ezek. xvi. 43. With כְּדִי, *Behold like that*, i. e. *like as*, Dan. ii. 43. LXX. καθώς.

הֶאֱזְנִיחוּ, Hiph. r. זנח.

הֶאָח, Interj. Gram. art. 243, expressive of exultation; insult. *Aha! bravo!* &c. Ps. xxxv. 21. 25; Job xxxix. 25; Is. xliv. 16; Ezek. xxv. 3, &c.

הַב, Imp. of v. יָהַב.

הַב, הָבָה, Imp. r. יָהַב.

הֹבְאִישׁ, see באשׁ.

הַבְהָבַי, m. pl. aff. Hos. viii. 13, al. non occ. redup. of r. יהב, contr. for יְהַבְהָבַי. See יהב, lit. *My gifts*, synon. מִנְחָה, which see. The force of the passage seems to be, *sacrifices of my gifts, or Minkhas! They sacrifice flesh and eat it!* i. e. Instead of bringing in the flour, oil, &c. of which the מִנְחָה was composed, and which was intended for the support of the priests (Lev. ii. 3), they brought the animal only, and this they sacrificed and ate. The point of the passage consists, I think, in the terms זִבְחֵי הַבְהָבַי, uttered with a degree of surprise, as if the מִנְחָה had been converted into a bloody sacrifice, for the bringers themselves only to feed upon.

הָבוּ, see r. יהב.

חבו   (147)   הבל

הִבּוֹק, Inf. Niph. בָּקַק.

הֶבֶל, m. pl. הֲבָלִים, constr. הַבְלֵי. Cogn. חבל Arab. المهبّل — اللحيم المورّم الوجه i. e. conj. ii. part. *Fleshy; swoln of face*, اهتبل كذبًا كثيرًا, *he lied greatly; deceived.* Hence, الصيّد بغاه, *he entrapped, took by deception, something hunted.* Hence, also, الهبتال الكاسب المحتال والصيّاد i. e. הבאל, i. q. *cunning gainer; hunter.* It. conj. iv. اَهْبَل, i. q. اَسْرَع, *he hasted.* It. هبل, *he lost* (a son) *by death.* Kāmoos. The prevailing notion therefore seems to be, *want of stability:* thence *hurry, deception, loss, &c.* And hence, perhaps, applied to the breath in the Syriac, as ܗܒܠ, *halitus.*

Vanity, instability, deception, Job vii. 16; Prov. xiii. 11. הוֹן מֵהֶבֶל יִמְעָט, *wealth diminishes, fails, from instability, although, &c.* So Ib. xxxi. 30, שֶׁקֶר הַחֵן וְהֶבֶל הַיֹּפִי, *Deception is gracefulness, and instability is beauty;* i. e. *deceiving, and unstable.* Comp. Is. xlix. 4.

(b) Applied to idols, as of this character; meton. 2 Kings xvii. 15; Jer. ii. 5; Jon. ii. 9; Ps. xxxi. 7.

(c)—To *Abortions,* Eccl. vi. 4; and thence to men generally, Ib. xi. 8, &c. In both of these places Gesenius makes הֶבֶל, i. q. *nebula:* because, perhaps, חֹשֶׁךְ is in the parallel; but, חֹשֶׁךְ is often taken to signify *distress, &c.* Here, then, the place will mean, *he enters* (the world) *in weakness, and leaves* (it) *in distress, sorrow, &c.* The last he renders by "*Futurum quodque est nebula,*" i. e. "*tenebris obvolutum;*" no doubt with the sentiment of Horace in his mind, "*Prudens futuri temporis exitum, Caliginosa nocte premit Deus.*" Which, however, is quite out of place here. In Is. lvii. 13, too, he makes this word signify *aura lenis:* because, apparently, רוּחַ is in the parallel. Which is also unnecessary: besides, the remaining portion of the verse clearly to oppose *stability* (in ארץ, and הַר קָדְשִׁי) to the *passing character of the wind,* and the instability intimated in הָבֶל. Hence we may see why this word is taken to signify *breath* in the Syriac.

(d) Used adverbially, Job ix. 29; xxi. 34; xxxv. 16; Is. xxx. 7; Ps. xxxix. 7, &c.

הֶבְלֵיהֶם, הַבְלוֹ, הֶבְלְךָ, הֲבָלוֹ. Aff.

הֶבֶל, m. constr. alt. of. fin. פֶּקֶד, Gram. art. 150; pl. הֲבָלִים, i. q. הֶבֶל, Eccl. i. 2; xii. 8, al. non occ.

הָבַל, v. pret. non occ. pres. יֶהְבָּלוּ, pl. m. תֶּהְבָּלוּ, constr. abs. *Do, or act, vainly, foolishly, sinfully,* 2 Kings xvii. 15; Jer. ii. 5; Ps. lxii. 11; Job xxvii. 12, al. non occ.

Hiph. part. pl. m. מַהְבִּלִים, *Persons causing* do., Jer. xxiii. 16, al. non occ.

הוֹבְנִים, *kethiv;* הָבְנִים, *keri;* Ezek. xxvii. 15, al. non occ. Arab. cogn. ابن, *coaluit et ater evasit* sanguis in vulnere: *concrevit ut nodus in ligno.* Whence, apparently, the Greek Ἔβενος, ἐβένη, ἔβελος: the Lat. *ebenus, evenus, hebenus, hebenum;* and our *ebony.* The term אֶבֶן, *lapis,* of Gesenius is evidently a secondary sense. *Ebony.* Used here in the *plural,* either because brought from the East in pieces, or because two sorts of it existed: hence styled *ebonies.* See Boch. Hieroz. ii. p. 140.

הָבַר, Inf. Hiph. r. בור.

הֹבְרֵי, constr. pl. m. Is. xlvii. 13, in הֹבְרֵי שָׁמַיִם (*kethiv,* הברו). Arab. جابر, *Penetrans, amputansque, acutus* ensis. *Astrologers* who *cut* and *parcelled out* the heavens, as we have them now on our celestial globes. Lit. *sectioners, dividers,* of the heavens. LXX. οἱ ἀστρολόγοι τοῦ οὐρανοῦ. Syr. ܒܚܙܝ̈ܝ ܫܡܝܐ, *who gaze on the heavens.*

הֶגֶה, m. pl. non occ. Syr. ܗܓܐ, *gemitus, clamor, meditatio.* Arab. هجا, هجو, *verborum contumelia, &c.* Cogn. وجي. Heb. יָגָה. ὀνοματοποιητικόν.

I. The *murmur* of complaint, lamentation, Ezek. ii. 9: (b) of thunder, Job xxxvii. 2; Ps. xc. 9. כְּמוֹ הֶגֶה, *as a murmur,* i. e. *gradually decline, and fail.* Targ. "*tanquam vaporem oris in hyeme.*" Comp. Eccl. xii. 4, al. non occ.

הָגָה, v. pres. יֶהְגֶּה. Constr. abs. it. med. בְּ; אֶל, כְּ; כְּמוֹ, of thing compared. See הָגָה. I. *Murmuring,* (a) as a dove, Is. xxxviii. 14; lix. 11: (b) as men lamenting, Is. xvi. 7; Jer. xlviii. 31: (c) as a lion over the prey, i. e. *growling,* Is. xxxi. 4.

חגו (148) חד

II. *Meditating*, (a) in a good sense, i. e. murmuring or speaking as it were in the mind (as in אָמַר בְּלִבּוֹ), Josh. i. 8; Ps. i. 2; lxiii. 7; lxxvii. 13; cxliii. 5; Prov. xv. 28: (b) in a bad one, Ps. ii. 1; Prov. xxiv. 2; Is. lix. 13.

III. Meton. *Declaring* one's meditations, suggestions of the heart, &c. Comp. Ps. xlv. 2, where מַעֲשַׂי refers to רָחַשׁ לִבִּי, Is. lix. 3; Ps. xxxv. 28; xxxvii. 30; cxv. 7; Prov. viii. 7; Job xxvii. 4.

Infin. הָגֹה, הָגוֹ, הֶגוּ.

IV. Hence, by a further meton. *Discerning, separating*, i. e. after consideration had, Prov. xxv. 4, 5, following חֲקֹר in the preceding verse, and apparently in some connection with it. It. Is. xxvii. 8, with סַאסְּאָה in the parallel; i. e. *shall sift*. Comp. ch. xxx. 28; Amos ix. 9; Luke xxii. 31.

הֹגוּ, Inf. r. הָגָה.

הָגוּת, f.—pl. non occ. *Meditation*, Ps. xlix. 4, al. non occ.

הָגִיב, m. r. הגב. Cogn. τοῦ, הָגָה. Syr. ܗܓܐ, *imaginatus est*. Arab. هَجَّ, *homo sui cerebri, vehemens*. Aff. הָגִיגִי, Ps. v. 2; xxxix. 4, al. non occ. *Deep, ardent, meditation*.

הִגָּיוֹן } m. Aff. הֶגְיוֹנִי, &c. vowels immu-
הִגָּיוֹן } table; r. הגה. Synon. τοῦ, הֶמְיָה,
The murmuring, as of the lute or lyre, Ps. xix. 15; xcii. 4; Lam. iii. 62. In Ps. ix. 17, we have הִגָּיוֹן סֶלָה. lxx. ᾠδὴ διαψάλματος: as if this was the title of another composition. "Neque aliter," says Gesenius, Symm. Aq. Vulg. But, Aquila has ᾠδὴ ἀεί. Symm. μέλος διαψάλματος. Theod. φθογγῇ ἀεί. The other translators, μελῳδήμα ἀεί. Which amount, however, to much the same thing. The Vulg. and Syr. have not noticed it. The Targ. "*Gaudebunt justi in æternum*:" which is, perhaps, not a bad comment on the passage.

הֲגִינָה, f. occ. once, Ezek. xlii. 12. Arab. هَجِين, *præstans et nobilis camelus*. Chald. הָגוּן, *rectum, &c. Straight, direct, commodious*, as it should seem.

הָגְלַת, Hoph. r. גָּלָה.

הַגְרִים and הַגְרִיאִים, m. pl. Ps. lxxxiii. 7; 1 Chron. v. 10. 19, 20. A people so called, because, perhaps, descended from הָגָר, Gen. xvi. 1, termed by the Greeks, Ἀγραῖοι, Ἀγρέες. Boch. Phaleg., p. 255. هَجَر and هَاجَر, the primary city of Bahrein, Castell. sub voce.

הַד, m. i. q. הֵידָד, r. הדד. Arab. هَدَّ, et هَدَّدَ, *vox gravis et crassa*. *Shouting of the grape-gatherers, soldiery*, &c. Ezek. vii. 7, al. non occ.

הַדָּבְרַיָּא, m. pl. def. Chald. Gesenius takes the ה to be the Heb. def. article, prefixed, as אֵל (Arab. ال) is in other cases: but for this there is no good reason, Gram. art. 180. 2. Besides, the Heb. art. cannot be prefixed to the first of two nouns in construction, as in הַדָּבְרֵי מַלְכָּא, Dan. iii. 27. It is not the Heb. art. therefore. It may be compd. of הדר, and דבר, equivalent to the Gr. εὐποιία, εὐεργία, or the like. *The title of certain* officers in the court of Babylon, Dan. iii. 24; iv. 33; vi. 8, &c.

הָדָה, v. occ. once, Is. xi. 8. Arab. هَدَى, *recta duxit, bene direxit*. *Guided*, i. e. his hand.

הָדָה, v. imp. once occ., Job xl. 12. *Break down, overturn*. See my Commentary on the place.

הַדָּמִין, m. Chald.—sing. non occ. Syr. ܗܕܡܐ, *membrum*. *Pieces, fragments*; with הִתְעַבֵד, *become made*, Dan. ii. 5; iii. 29, al. non occ., i. e. *torn limb from limb*. Comp. 2 Maccab. i. 16, it. Syr. ܐܬܦܠܓ, *membratim discerptus est*.

הֲדֹם, m.—pl. non occ. Arab. هَدْم, *destructio*. Every where with רַגְלַיִם. *Foot-stool*. Metaph. implying subjection of enemies, Ps. cx. 1; Is. lxvi. 1. The place in which Jehovah was said to dwell, Lam. ii. 1; Ps. xcix. 5; cxxxii. 7; 1 Chron. xxviii. 2.

הֲדַס, m. pl. הֲדַסִּים. Arab. هَدَس, *myrtus*. *The myrtle*. See Celsii Hierobot. ii., p. 17, seq., Is. xli. 19; lv. 13; Zech. i. 8. 10, 11; Neh. viii. 15.

הָדַף, v. pres. יֶהְדֹּף. Constr. immed. it. אֵת, it. בְּ, *instrument*; מִן, *from*; אֶל, *to, any place*, &c. Arab. هَذَف, *celeriter quid egit*. Cogn. هَدَم, conj. v. *irruit in aliquem*,

חדר   (149)   חדר

&c. Comp. هَذَبَ. *Drive, thrust* out, back, &c., Num. xxxv. 20. 22; Deut. vi. 19; Is. xxii. 10; Jer. xlvi. 15; Ezek. xxxiv. 21; Job xviii. 18; Prov. x. 3, &c. Infin. הֲדֹף, Deut. ix. 4. Aff. הָדְפָה, 2 Kings iv. 27.

הֶדֶר, m. Syr. ܣܳܐܪܳ, *honor, decus.* Arab. هَدَرَ, *ferbuit; luxuriavit* herba. Cogn. هَدَرَ, *multus, vanusque fuit. Honour, glory, dignity,* Dan. xi. 20, only. נֹגֵשׂ הֶדֶר מַלְכוּת. Lit. *an exactor of the dignity, &c. of the kingdom,* i. e. as Gesenius thinks, of the best part of it, viz. Palestine. Comp. vr. 16, and Zech. viii. 6 (Thes.—ix. 8); 2 Maccab. iii. 1; and his History of the Heb. Language, p. 64: as some others think, *Tax, tribute,* like the Greek usage of τιμή, τέλος. But, if Zech. ix. 8 affords a parallel to this place, the meaning must be *an oppressor, exactor* of taxes, or the like; and הֶדֶר must mean *tax.*

הָדָר, m. constr. הֲדַר, pl. הֲדָרִי, concr.— with הוֹד, and כָּבוֹד, as synon. Any thing *Glorious, honourable, dignified.* פְּרִי עֵץ הָדָר *fruit of* (the) *tree, glorious,* i. e. ripe and good. Comp. Deut. xxxiii. 17: applied to *clothing,* Ps. civ. 1; Prov. xxxi. 22; Job xl. 10; *to person,* Is. liii. 2; Ps. cxlix. 9. Comp. Ib. viii. 6; xxi. 6; xcvi. 6; cxi. 3; Ib. xxix. 4. בְּהַדְרִי, *in that which is glorious,* i. e. in bringing it about, is effective. See the context following. In constr. הֲדַר כְּבוֹד *the dignity of*—, Ps. cxlv. 5. 12; Is. ii. 10. 19. 21; xxxv. 2; Prov. xx. 29. Aff. הֲדָרִי, in pause, הֲדָרֵךְ, &c. In this view this word differs from הֶדֶר, in that it is not an abstract. הֵדֶר, too, and הֲדַר, are only different forms of the same word; of which, also,

הַדָרַת, is the fem. constr. of הֲדָרָה, i. q. הֲדָר, Prov. xiv. 28; Ps. xxix. 2; xcvi. 9; 1 Chron. xvi. 29; 2 Chron. xx. 21, appears— as in Ps. civ. 1, &c. above—to be applied to *clothing.*

הָדַר, v. pres. תֶּהְדַּר. Constr. immed. *Honour,* Lev. xix. 32; Exod. xxiii. 3; Lev. xix. 15.

Part. הָדוּר, *Honoured, dignified,* בִּלְבוּשׁוֹ, *in his clothing,* Is. lxiii. 1. LXX. ὡραῖος ἐν στολῇ. Metaph. *clad with zeal,* Ib. lix. 17. Niph. pl. m. נֶהְדָּרוּ, *Were, became, honoured,* Lam. v. 12.

Hithp. תִּתְהַדַּר, *Be, become, glorious,* Prov. xxv. 6.

הֲדַר, v. Chald. i. q. Heb. *Honour,* constr. לְ, Dan. iv. 31; v. 23. Part. Pah. מְהַדַּר, *Honouring,* Dan. iv. 34.

הַדַשְׁנָה, Hithp. r. דָּשֵׁן.

הָהּ, Interj. expressive of grief. *Ah!* once, Ezek. xxx. 2.

הוֹ, i. q. הָהּ, once, Amos v. 16. הוֹי contr.

הוּא, m. הִיא, f. pron. 3d pers. sing.—pl. הֵמָּה, f. הֵנָּה, הֵן, הֵמָּה, הֵם, Gram. art. 142. 2, et seq. Arab. هُوَ, هِيَ. Syr. ܗܘ, ܗܝ. Cogn. apparently with the verb هَوَى, *decidit, delapsus fuit.* Anglice *fell;* hence, *fell out, happened;* Heb. הָיָה, *fuit, exstitit.* Cogn. הָיָה, *vixit;* some derivative or part of which might not unaptly be taken to represent the third person, *He, she,* and, when applied to things, *it.* So the Greek, ἐκεῖνος, ἐκείνη, ἐκεῖνο, i. e. *one there,* of ἐκεῖ, and the termination νος. Αὐτός, αὐτή, αὐτό, is, perhaps, our very word הוּא, αὐ, with the termination τος, &c. Hence the א will be radical; not because it is slightly pronounced in the vulgar Arabic, for on that pronunciation no reliance can be placed, but because it seems to have formed a part of the root. This will explain *Lennep's* remark, which Middleton has mistaken, viz., "*Articulus vicinitatem habere propriè videtur cum participio verbi* εἰμι *vel* ἐὼ *sum*" (on the Greek article, Ed. 1828), sect. v.; i. e. it seems to have a common origin, and hence to have some affinity with that verb; just as our הוּא has to the Arab. verb هَوَى. Used as,—

(a) *The personal pronoun;* as, הוּא הָיָה, *He, he was,* Gen. iv. 20. יְהוָֹה הוּא הַהֹלֵךְ, *Jehovah, he* (is) *the* (person who) *walks, &c.* Deut. xxxi. 8. אַיֵּה הוּא, *Where* (is) *he?* Esth. vii. 5. Fem. אֶת־אָבִיהָ הִיא, *her father, she, &c.,* Lev. xxi. 9. Taken to represent *things,* as in the Arab.—Gram. art. 216. 7. So מִנְחָה הִיא, *a minkha* (is) *it,* Lev. ii. 15. But here, and, for the most part, in the Pentateuch, written הוּא. So also, as Gesenius has remarked, 1 Kings xvii. 15; Job xxxi. 11; Is. xxx. 33, which is usually termed an Archaïsm. The places written הִיא in the Pentateuch, are only eleven, as noticed in the Masora on Gen. xxxviii. 25.

הוא (150) הוא

Both Noldius and Gesenius have made it equal to the Latin *ipse*, as, Gen. iv. 20; xiv. 15, &c. But this will depend entirely upon the context, which may, indeed, occasionally require it to be so translated, as Is. vii. 14, &c.: but it depends not on the word itself. In some cases, נֶפֶשׁ, גֶּרֶם, or עֶצֶם, are introduced for this purpose. See under these words.

(b) *The demonstrative pronoun, this;* as, הוּא אֲשֶׁר דִּבֶּר, *This* (is the word) *which he spake*, Lev. x. 3. הוּא שְׁמוֹ, *this* (is) *its name*, Gen. ii. 19. So fem. הִיא־צֹעַר, *this* (is) *Zoar*, Gen. xiv. 2. Pl. הֵם הַמְדַבְּרִים, *these* (are) *the speakers, &c.*, Exod. vi. 27. הֵמָּה הַגִּבֹּרִים, *these* (are) *the giants, &c.*, Gen. vi. 4. הֵן is used only after a prefix, and does not occur, perhaps, more than once or twice in this sense. See Ruth i. 13. הֵנָּה, Exod. xxxix. 14, &c.

As the Latin *hic* and *ille*.—אֶחָד הַזֶּה—וְאֶחָד הַזֶּה, *one* (of) *these;* one (of) *those*, Dan. xii. 5. Comp. 1 Sam. xx. 21; 2 Kings iv. 35.

When occurring with זֶה, or אֵלֶּה, it will form a correlative to them, e. g. Judg. vii. 4. זֶה יֵלֵךְ אִתָּךְ הוּא יֵלֵךְ עִמָּךְ... זֶה לֹא־יֵלֵךְ אִתָּךְ הוּא לֹא יֵלֵךְ, i. e. THIS *shall go with thee;* (then) HE *shall go with thee;*...THIS *shall not go with thee;* (then) HE *shall not go with thee*. So, again, Ps. xx. 8, אֵלֶּה בָרֶכֶב וְאֵלֶּה בַסּוּסִים... הֵמָּה כָרְעוּ וְנָפָלוּ וגו', *these in chariots, and these in horses; ... they have bowed and fallen, &c.* LXX. οὗτοι ἐν ἅρμασι καὶ οὗτοι ἐν ἵπποις.... Ἀυτοὶ συνεποδίσθησαν καὶ ἔπεσαν. In this respect, therefore, its *retrospective reference* is precisely of a piece with that of the *definite article*. Gesenius's distinctions of "*sine emphasi*," and "*cum emphasi quadam*," Thes. p. 368, are, as the passages there adduced will sufficiently shew, perfectly useless.

Hence, in all probability, ה was taken,—as the Greek ὁ was of ὅς,—to constitute the *definite article*. See under ה. Hence it is used—

(c) *As an attributive* with the article prefixed; as, הָאִישׁ הַהוּא, *The man, the this* (same), Job i. 1. Comp. Gen. xxi. 31; Is. ii. 11, &c.

(d) As including *the logical copula*, Lat. *sum*. Gr. εἰμι, not *the substantive verb*, as Gesenius says; for then הָיָה must be either expressed or implied. See Gram. art. 213. 7; e. g. נָבִיא הוּא, *he* (is) *a prophet*. See Nold. Annotationes et Vindiciæ, note 1119, where similar examples with all the personal pronouns will be found; who remarks, "Potest tamen ad hæc etiam subintelligi *verbum substantivum*." It should be remembered, however, that the *substantive verb*, הָיָה, will mean, *exstitit, factus est*, or the like, rather than *fuit*. The same is true of the Arabic كَانَ. In the Syriac, indeed, the real substantive verb, ܗܘܐ, has been deprived of this power, by drawing a line under it, thus, ܗܼܘܐ, in which case it may include,—as may the pron. ܗܿܘ, ܗܼܘ, not ܗܘ, or ܗܼܘ,—*the copula*. Dr. Gesenius, however, seems to make a distinction between *verbum substantivum*, and *ipsum verbum substantivum;* for, in this latter case, he says, it is more rarely used: yet the example which he has given, Gen. xvii. 12, אֲשֶׁר לֹא מִזַּרְעֲךָ הוּא, *qui non de semine tuo est*," does not carry us one step beyond his other cases. In the Thesaurus he gives several others; as, אֲשֶׁר לֹא טְהֹרָה הִוא, *quæ non munda erant*, Gen. vii. 2. I would only ask, Who does not see, that this is a very different thing from saying אֲשֶׁר לֹא הָיְתָה טְהֹרָה, which would give the true substantive verb? So the LXX. here, ἀπὸ τῶν κτηνῶν τῶν μὴ καθαρῶν; not ἅτινα οὐκ ἐγένετο καθαρά. Faesius, therefore, to whose doctrine he so strongly objects, is, after all, right.

When this pronoun refers to God, however, it frequently does involve the *substantive verb* (הָיָה); i. e. when it evidently implies *previous existence;* as, Is. xliii. 13, פַּס־מִיּוֹם אֲנִי הוּא, h. e. אֲנִי הָיִיתִי אֲנִי הוּא, *exstiti ego ille*, i. e. qui omnia fecit. So, negatively, Jer. v. 12, לוֹא־הוּא, h. e. לוֹא הָיָה הוּא, οὐκ ἦν, or ἐγένετο, αὐτός. Arab. هُوَ. Syr. ܗܘ. But, in all such cases, *positive existence*, not *mere assertion*, must be intended. See Is. xlviii. 12; Ps. cii. 28, which are totally different, in this respect, from the examples alluded to.

In these cases, too, יְהוָֹה, יָהּ, הָאֱלֹהִים, or some other name of the true God, will be implied. Hence, in numerous cases, some name of God will be understood; as, הוּא אָמַר, Ps. xxxiii. 9. Comp. Ps. xliv. 22; Job v. 18; Is. xxxiii. 16, &c. And so هُوَ, in the Arabic is often used; as, هُوَ الحَيِّ القَيُّوم

(151)

הוּא, Chald. i. q. Heb. Dan. ii. 21, &c.

הֲוָא, Chald. i. q. הָיָה, which see.

הוֹבַד, Hoph. Chald. r. אבד.

הוֹבָדָה, Infin. Aph. Chald. r. אבד.

הוֹד, m.—pl. non occ. Synon. הָדָר, כָּבוֹד, opp. τῷ, מַשְׁחִית. Arab. هَوْد, opus bonum; هَوَادَة, quies, tranquillitas. Glory, dignity, majesty, Num. xxvii. 20; Is. xxx. 30; Ps. xxi. 6; xcvi. 6; civ. 1; Prov. v. 9; Job xxxvii. 22; Hos. xiv. 7, &c. Aff. הוֹדִי, הוֹדוֹ, &c.

הוֹדָה, Hiph. r. יָדָה.

הֹוָה, f.—pl. non occ. Arab. هَوًى, lapsus, ruina. Syr. ܗܘܐ, accidit, fuit. Accident, injury, Is. xlvii. 11; Ezek. vii. 26.

הָוָה, or הָוָא, v. pres. apoc. יְהוּא (for יְהוּ, Gram. art. 87. 2, יְהוּ with א, for ה, otiose), i. q. הָיָה. I. Fall, descend. Imp. הֱוֵא־אָרֶץ, fall (to) earth, Job xxxvii. 6. See my note on the place, Eccl. xi. 3.
Imp. it. הֱוֵה, f. הֱוִי, Gen. xxvii. 29; Is. xvi. 4.
Part. הוֹיָה, Neh. vi. 6; Eccl. ii. 22.

הָוָה, or הָוָא, pres. יֶהֱוֵא, and יְהוֹא, i. q. Heb. הָוָה, הָיָה, Existed, became, was. Constr. abs. it. med. לְ, impl. change, Dan. ii. 35; vii. 13; Ezra v. 5, &c.
With participles of other verbs it forms a sort of imperfect tense; as, הֲוָא עָבֵד, he was doing, i. e. in the habit of, Dan. vi. 11; Ib. iv. 7. 10; vii. 2. 4, &c.
Imp. and Infin. הֱוָא, with לְ prefixed, Dan. ii. 20, &c.
It. הֱוֹן, with לְ also prefixed, Dan. ii. 43; vi. 2, &c.
It. הֱוֹן, with לְ, Dan. v. 17. In these cases Gesenius thinks, after Winer, that these two last forms are mere abbreviations of the pres. with the preformative rejected, and ל added, signifying "ut;" "לֶהֱוֹן, ut sint." But this is a mere figment, and is just as unnecessary as it is groundless.

הַוָּה, f. constr. הַוַּת, pl. הַוּוֹת. Arab. هَوَى, هَوِيَّة, amor, cupido; هَوَى, decidit, &c. So our falling in love; or, perhaps, because desire, love, is precipitate. I. Intense desire, lust, Prov. x. 3; xix. 13; Ps. lii. 4. 9.
II. Meton. Accident, injury, ruin, Mic.

vii. 3; Prov. xi. 6; Job vi. 2. 30; xxx. 13, keri, Ps. v. 10; xxxviii. 13, &c. Aff. הַוָּתִי (for הַוָּתִי), הַוָּתוֹ.

הוֹי, Interj. expressive of Exhortation, threatening, grief, Is. i. 24; Zech. ii. 10; Is. v. 8; Jer. xxiii. 1; Ezek. xiii. 18; Mic ii. 1; 1 Kings xiii. 30; Jer. xxii. 18 xxxiv. 5. Comp. Matt. xviii. 7, &c., Gram art. 243; Nold. p. 253, &c. "Sq. acc. Is i. 4," says Gesenius. I am unable to see how he discovers an accusative case here In his Thesaurus, " sq. nominat. (qui pro vocativo est, &c.) Is. i. 4," &c., whence it should seem that his criterion of these cases is not a very sure one.

הוּךְ, v. Chald. pret. non occ. pres. יֵהַךְ, i. q. הָלַךְ, or יֵלֵךְ, Proceed, go, Ezra v. 5; vi. 5; vii. 13.
Infin. מְהָךְ.

הוֹלֶדֶת, Inf. Hoph. r. ילד.

הוֹלְלוּ, see r. הלל.

הוֹלֵלוֹת, f. pl.—sing. non occ. See הלל. Lit. vain-glorious, &c. things. Glory, folly, Eccl. i. 17; ii. 12.

הוֹלֵלוּת, f. abstr. once, Eccl. x. 13. Glory, folly.

הוֹלֵם, m. for הוֹלֵם, apparently from the parallelism, once, Is. xli. 7. See הלם.

הוּם, or הִים, v. pret. Aff. הָמָם. Arab. هَوَّمَ, nutavit capite; هَامَ, vagatus fuit, furibundi instar. He shall perturb, harass them, Deut. vii. 23, al. non occ.
Niph. pres. תֵּהֹם, f. It was, became perturbed, disturbed, excited, 1 Sam. iv. 5; 1 Kings i. 45; Ruth i. 19, al. non occ.
Hiph. pres. par. אָהִימָה, Ps. lv. 3, I heave, swell, i. e. like the ocean (תְּהוֹם) in my distress. LXX. ἐταράχθην, Mic. ii. 12. תְּהִימֶנָה, they (i. e. the flock, with which the comparison is here made) shall be tumultuous, from the great number of individuals, אִישׁ־מֵאָדָם, is, in like manner, sometimes applied to animals, Gen. vii. 2.

הוּן, or הִין, v. in Kal non occ.
Hiph. הָהִינוּ, constr. לְ. Syr. ܗܘܢ, mente præditus fuit. Part. confirmatus, &c. Arab. هَانَ, r. هون, levis fuit res. Conj. iv. contempsit. They made light of the matter, i. e. despised the consequences, Deut. i. 41. Comp. Num. xiv. 44. LXX. συναθροισθέντες

הוֹן, m. (fm. פֶּךְ, Gram. art. 87. 1), pl. הוֹנִים. Arab. هون, *lenitas, commoditas.* Synon. עֹשֶׁר, Ps. cxii. 3. *Wealth, plenty,* Ps. xliv. 13; Prov. i. 13; vi. 31; viii. 18; xxx. 15, 16; Cant. viii. 7, &c. Aff. הוֹנוֹ, הוֹנְךָ; in pause; f. הוֹנֵךְ; pl. הוֹנֵיכֶם, Ezek. xxvii. 33.

הוֹר, or הַר, m. pl. Aff. הוֹרַי, once only, Gen. xlix. 26; "i. q. הַר, *mons,*" says Gesenius. LXX. ὀρέων μονίμων. Who read, perhaps, הַרְרֵי־עַד. See Hab. iii. 6. But, in this case, the difficulty is, to extract any tolerable sense from the place. The Jewish interpretation, "*progenitors,*" labours under this defect, that the verb הרה appears never to be applied in any other sense except that of *conception* by the female: which in this place is incongruous. Both, therefore, seem unsuitable here. Now we have in the Arabic هور (הור), signifying *Grex ovium,* pec. *ubi præ multitudine aliæ in alias prolabuntur:* Kāmoos. If, then, we apply this to our passage, we shall have, *the blessings of thy father have been great above the blessings of my numerous flocks, even to the desire of the everlasting hills:* i. e. the blessings, which have attended me, are far greater than the wealth which God gave me during the times of my hard servitude with Laban: they extended to the desire for him, who is emphatically styled *the stone, the rock, of Israel,* (vr. 24, it. Ps. xciv. 4; cxxi. 1; cxxv. 2), *the everlasting hills.* תְּדָיֵן, such blessings, i. e. greater than those bestowed upon Joseph during his servitude (נְזִיר אֶחָיו) in Egypt, shall also rest upon him. This seems to me to suit the place well, comparing the circumstances of the father with those of the son, and carrying the blessing to an extent beyond that of mere temporal things. Comp. vr. 18, and Deut. xxxiii. 15; where, מֵרֹאשׁ הַרְרֵי־קֶדֶם וּמִמֶּגֶד גִּבְעוֹת עוֹלָם, *from the* HEAD *of the eternal mountains, and from the* MAJESTY *of the everlasting hills,* i. e. from GOD himself, seems to supply the best interpretation possible to the place in question.

הוֹשַׁבְתִּים, Hiph. r. יָשַׁב.

הוּתַל, see r. הָתַל.

הֻזְדָה, Aph. Chald. r. זִיד, זוּד.

הִזְדַּמִּנְתּוּן, Hithp. Chald. r. זמן.

הִזִּילוּ, Hiph. r. זלל, cogn. נזל.

הֹזִים, m. pl. part. v. הזה, not in use,

once, Is. lvi. 10, with שֹׁכְבִים. Arab. هَزَّ, *movit* (Angl. *nod.*) *caput; ad occasum declinavit* stella. Cogn. أَزَّ, *mortuus est;* هَدَأَ, *quievit;* هَدَلَ, *torpidus, stupidusque;* هَذَى, *alienatio mentis. Nodding, dozing;* it is added, apparently by way of explanation, אֹהֲבֵי לָנוּם, *lovers of slumbering,* i. e. *stupid, regardless;* which, as applied to *watchmen,* is a grievous crime.

הִזַּפּוּ, Hithp. r. נָזָה.

הִזָּרֹתִיכֶם, Inf. Niph. r. חדל.

הֶחָדַלְתִּי, see r. חדל.

הֶחְבֵּאתָהּ, see r. חבא.

הֶחֱטִיא, see r. חטא.

הָחֵל, Inf. Hiph. r. חלל.

הַט, Imp. apoc. r. נטה.

הֻפַּתּוּ, see r. נפה.

הֻטַּמָּא, see r. טמא.

הִי, once, Ezek. ii. 10. Synon. הֶגֶה, קִינָה, Ib. for הְיִי (Gram. art. 76), which see. *Lamentation, woe.*

הִיא, pron. 3d pers. f. sing. See הוּא, Chald. id. Dan. ii. 9, &c.

הַיְדוֹת, pl. f. once, Neh. xii. 8. For הוֹדוֹת, no doubt. See 1 Chron. xxv. 3, where we have, עַל הוֹדוֹת, the identical expression. The error seems to be of long standing, for the LXX. have ἐπὶ τῶν χειρῶν, if this passage has not been corrupted from that in 1 Chron. above cited, which also has עַל יְדֵי. The Syr. has ܗܽܘܕܺܝܬ݂, *Hūdith,* as a proper name. The truth seems to be, the *punctuists* not knowing what to make of this word, when the ו had been written by some slumbering copyist a little too short, ׳, applied the vowels at random, and so favoured the grammarians with a *new form,* a monster hitherto unparalleled: "Ortum," says Gesenius, "vocab. ex הוֹדָה, *celebravit,* pari signif. atque הוֹדוּת." I doubt whether it is desirable to cover so palpable a blunder, by so much ingenious critical conjecture.

הֵידָד, m.—pl. non occ. i. q. הֵד; which see. *The shouting* of those who gather and tread the grapes, Jer. xxv. 30; xlviii. 33. Metaph.—of an attacking army, Jer. li. 14; Is. xvi. 9, 10.

חיה (153) חיה

הָיָה, v. pres. יִהְיֶה, apoc. 1st pers. אֱהִי, 3d, יְהִי. See Gram. art. 205. 12. My notes on Job xxxvii. 6, and sub voce הוה above. Arab. هَوَىٰ, decidit. Syr. ܗܘܳܐ, exstitit, fuit. Fell out, happened, existed, was: but never as the logical copula, is, was, &c., with the Greeks, Latins, and ourselves, Gen. i. 2, et seq. הָאָרֶץ הָיְתָה תֹהוּ, THE earth was, existed, remained, empty, &c. Comp. Ib. ii. 18; iii. 1. 20; iv. 8, &c. in all which cases this verb implies existence, and not the mere logical copula as Gesenius thinks. Winer has a curious remark here: "Sed longe frequentius, ubi solam copulam constituit, omittitur." In other words, when this verb is used as the logical copula, it is not used at all! See under the pron. הוא.

In certain idiomatic expressions, constr. med. לְ, not unlike the Latin Dative case, in est, fuit, mihi, tibi, &c.

(a) יְהִי לְךָ, Is to, or for, thee, Exod. iv. 16; xx. 3; Num. x. 31; Deut. xxi. 15, &c.

(b) With לְ also attached to a second term, nearly equivalent to כְּ in sense, Exod. ii. 10. וַיְהִי לָהּ לְבֵן, And was to her for, or as, a son, Ib. iv. 16; Num. x. 31, &c.

(c) With לְ in the second case only. הָיָה יְהֹוָה לְמֶלֶךְ, Jehovah shall be for king; i. e. shall become king, &c., Zech. xiv. 9. Comp. Gen. xxviii. 21; Is. xliv. 15.

(d) With Infinitives, וַיְהִי הַשֶּׁמֶשׁ לָבוֹא, The sun was for setting; i. e. about to set, Gen. xv. 12. Comp. Josh. ii. 5; Num. viii. 11; 2 Chron. xxvi. 5.

(e) With כְּ. הִיִיתֶם כֵּאלֹהִים, Gen. iii. 5. Comp. Ruth ii. 13; 2 Sam. xiv. 2, &c.

(f) With כְּ repeated. הָיָה כַצַּדִּיק כָּרָשָׁע; It Shall be, as the righteous, so the wicked, Gen. xviii. 25. Comp. Is. xvii. 3; xxiv. 2.

(g) So with עִם, With, i. e. agreeing with, in one sense or other, 1 Kings i. 8; 2 Sam. xiii. 20; 1 Kings xi. 11. Comp. 2 Chron. i. 11; vi. 8.

(h) אַחֲרֵי, 1 Kings xii. 20.

(i) לִפְנֵי, Num. xvi. 16. Comp. vv. 18, 19. And, in all cases partaking of that shade of the primitive meaning which such combination, with the rest of the context, shall require.

Used occasionally with participles, giving a sense equivalent to our imperfect past tense; as, Gen. iv. 17. יְהִי בֹנֶה, He was building. So Job i. 14; Neh. i. 4, &c., which Gesenius takes to be a mark of modern writing, and which I only wish to see proved.

Niph. נִהְיָה, נִהְיְתָה, נִהְיֵיתִי, pres. נהם occ. Came to be, took effect, &c. Synon. בּוֹא. Constr. med. לְ. Deut. xxvii. 9, הַיּוֹם הַזֶּה נִהְיֵיתָ לְעָם וגו׳, This day thou camest to be a people, &c. i. e. thou hast this day become what thou wast not before. See on the force of Niphhal, Gram. art. 157. 19. But, if it had been said, הָיָה לְעָם וגו׳, it would not so clearly have appeared that this change of circumstance had taken place. Hence, occurring with בּוֹא, Ezek. xxi. 12, הִנֵּה בָאָה וְנִהְיָתָה, Behold it has come, and has taken effect. It. xxxix. 8. (This use of בּוֹא, occ. first in Job iv. 5.) Comp. Prov. xiii. 19, with Ib. vr. 12. So Deut. xv. 32; Judg. xix. 30; xx. 3. 12; 1 Kings i. 27; xii. 24; Neh. vi. 8.

In Dan. ii. 1, שְׁנָתוֹ נִהְיְתָה עָלָיו, His sleep had fallen on him. (See Kal.) It is said above, that he had dreamt dreams, חֲלֹם חֲלֹמוֹת; this is added merely by way of explanation, to intimate that it was in the ordinary course of sleep. So the Syr. ܫܶܢܬܗ ܗܘܳܬ ܥܠܰܘܗܝ, For his sleep was (had been) upon him; not "perduravit in eo somnus ejus," as the Polyglott has it. LXX. ἀπ' αὐτοῦ; perhaps, originally, ἐπ' αὐτοῦ, Ib. ch. viii. 27. וְנִהְיֵיתִי וְנֶחֱלֵיתִי, I became fallen (prostrated of strength, collapsed) and sick.

חָיָה, for הֻוָּה, Keri, Job vi. 2; xxx. 13, which see, sign. ii.

הֵיךְ, Interrog. i. q. אֵיךְ, apparently; see Nold. p. 261, note. Dan. x. 17; 1 Chron. xiii. 12.

הֵיכָל, com. pl. הֵיכָלוֹת, constr. הֵיכְלֵי. Syr. ܗܰܝܟܠܳܐ, ܗܰܝܟܠܶܗ. Arab. هَيْكَل. Æth. ሀይከል: Ædificium sublime, templum.

I. Any great and splendid edifice, a palace, 1 Kings xxi. 1; 2 Kings ii. 18; Is. lix. 7; Dan. i. 4; Ps. xlv. 9; Is. xiii. 22; Hos. viii. 14; Joel iv. 5, &c.

II. The Temple of Jehovah built by Solomon, also termed בֵּית יְהֹוָה, The House of Jehovah, 1 Kings iii. 1, &c.; הַבַּיִת, The House, Ib. vi. 37, &c.; בֵּית הָאֱלֹהִים, The House of God, 1 Chron. ix. 11, &c. names previously given to the Tabernacle, Exod. xxiii. 19; xxxiv. 26; Josh. ix. 23; Judg. xviii. 31, &c. And this last was even before that time in use, Gen. xxviii. 17. 22. Also, הֵיכַל קָדְשֶׁךָ, Thy Holy Temple, Ps. v. 7; xi. 4;

x

חיך (154) הכד

lxv. 5, &c. הַקֹּדֶשׁ, *The Holy* place, 1 Chron. xxiii. 32; 2 Chron. xxix. 5, &c. Aff. הֵיכָלוֹ, הֵיכְלֵכֶם, הֵיכָלָם. On the form, see Gram. art. 155. See Plan in the Appendix.

This Temple was built by Solomon, on Mount Moriah, 2 Chron. iii. 1, with the materials partly collected by David his father, and partly by himself, 1 Chron. xxviii. 11—20; xxx. 2, &c.; 2 Chron. ii. 3, et seq., in the space of seven years and six months, 1 Kings vi. 37, 38. After this it was repaired by Josiah, 2 Chron. xxxiv. 8, et seq.; and soon after it was destroyed by the army of Nebuchadnezzar, king of Babylon, Ib. xxxvi. 19, et seq.; 2 Kings xxv. 9, &c.

הֵיכַל, m. Chald. def. הֵיכְלָא, i. q. Heb. I. *A Palace, &c.*, Dan. iv. 1. 26; Ezra iv. 14; v. 14, &c. II. *The Temple* at Jerusalem, i. q. בֵּית אֱלָהָא, Dan. v. 2, 3; Ezra vi. 5, &c. Aff. הֵיכְלֵהּ, הֵיכְלִי.

הֵילֵל, m. lit. *Resplendent, glorious*, r. הלל, i. q. בְּן־שַׁחַר, once, Is. xiv. 12. See the next verse; whence it should seem that it is the name either of a star or of a constellation, to which this king had been elevated, as it was the case in other instances. *Lucifer*, generally, i. e. the morning-star, supposed by some to be the planet Venus. LXX. Ἑωσφόρος. Syriac, as if derived from ילל ܐܝܠܠ ܟܝ ܨܦܪܐ, *ejula in matutino*. Targ. "*Qui eras splendidus*," as derived from הלל and a mere attributive. The usual acceptation is the most probable. Comp. Rev. xxii. 16. On the form, see Gram. art. 155.

הִים, see הוּם.

הֵימָן, Chald. Aph. r. אמן.

הִין, m. the *Hin*, a certain measure of liquids, containing one-sixth part of the *bath*, and = to 12 *logs*, or 1 gall. 2 pints, 2·5 solid inch. According to Josephus, Antiq. lib. iii. c. ix. § 4; δύναται .... δύο χόας Ἀττικοὺς ποιῆσαι. LXX. εἰν, ἱν, ὕν. Etym. unknown, Exod. xxx. 24; Num. xv. 4, et seq.; xxviii. 5. 7. 14; Ezek. iv. 11, &c.

חַיְתִי, Chald. Hiph. r. חיה.

הַיְתָיָה, Infin. do. v. אתה, Chald. Dan. iii. 13; v. 2, &c.

הַד, Imp. Hiph. apoc. r. נכה.

הֲכִי, Interrog. הֲ, with particle כִּי, which see.

הָכִיל, see rr. אכל, כול.

הִכָּה, see r. נכה, aff. Hiph.

הִכָּם, aff. Hiph. r. נכה.

הֵכַנּוּ, see r. כון, Hiph.

הִכְפַּנִי, aff. Hiph. r. נכה.

הכר, v. pret. non occ. pres. תַּהְכִּרוּ, once, Job xix. 3. See my note. *Ye contemn, treat contemptuously*. Constr. לְ.

הַכָּרַת, f. once, constr. הַכָּרַת, Is. iii. 9. If from the r. הכר. Arab. هَكَرَ. *Astonishment*, i. e. the expression of a consciousness of guilt; if from נכר, for הַנְכָּרָה, Gram. art. 76, *Notification, recognition* of it, as expressed in the countenance. LXX. ἡ αἰσχύνη τοῦ προσώπου.

הלא, v. non occ. Kal.

Niph. part. f. נַהֲלָאָה. Cogn. Arab. هَلَّ, *abscessit*. Syr. ܗܠܐ, *elongavit*, once, Mic. iv. 7. Something *removed, cast away*. LXX. ἀπωσμένην. Hence—

הָלְאָה, particle. See Noldius, p. 264, terminating with a paragogic ה. Syr. ܗܠ, and ܗܠܟ, *illuc, deinceps*.

Thence, farther, onward, as to time or place, Lev. xxii. 27; Num. xv. 23; Is. xviii. 2, &c. It. Gen. xix. 9. גֶּשׁ־הָלְאָה, *come on; come more near*, i. e. to the dispute. LXX. ἀπόστα ἐκεῖ, which has been usually followed, although at variance with the etymology, and the apparent sense of the place. Onkelos, correctly, קְרִיב לְהַלָּא, which the translation of the Polyglott gives, nevertheless, "*Recede illuc!*" So Saadias, تَقَدَّمْ عَنِ الْبَابِ, which is also falsely translated, "*Recede à janua!*" Constr. with מִן, from; לְ, towards, which, Is. xviii. 2; 1 Sam. x. 3; xx. 22; Num. xxxii. 19; Amos v. 27, &c.

הֶלְאַת, see Hiph. r. לאה.

הִלּוּלִים, m. pl. r. הלל, twice only, Lev. xix. 24; Judg. ix. 27. *Great* or *habitual praise*; and meton. *matter of* do. For fm. Gram. art. 154. 10. II. It. art. 223. 3. LXX. αἰνετὸς, ἐλλοολίμ. Syr. ܫܘܒܚܐ. Saadias, هَلُّول, *dignum*.

הֲלוֹם, see הֲלֹם.

הַלָּז, com. pron. *This*, Gram. art. 176. 2.

חלז (155) חלך

Noldius, p. 265; Judg. vi. 20; 2 Kings iv. 25; Zech. ii. 8; Dan. viii. 16, &c. Also—

הַלָּזֶה, id. Gram. ib. Noldius, ib. compd. of הַ+לְ+זֶה, i. q. Arab. اَلَّذِي, as to etym. but differs in sense; the Arabic term signifying, *who, which, what.* Gen. xxiv. 65; xxxvii. 19. *This.*

הַלֵּזוּ, Job xxix. 3. See הֲלֹא.

הַלָּזוּ, *This*, once, Ezek. xxxvi. 35, compd. of הַ+לְ+זוּ. The (־) has resulted probably from the mere fancy of the punctuists.

הֲלִיךְ, m.—

הֲלִיכָה, f.—

Aff. pl. הֲלִיכַי, Job xxix. 6, al. non occ.— Pl. f. הֲלִיכוֹת. Aff. הֲלִיכוֹתָיו הֲלִיכוֹתָם. See הָלַךְ. I. *Step;* II. Meton. *Way;* III. By a further meton. *Proceeding, procedure.* I. Job xxix. 6. lxx. αἱ ὁδοί μου. II. f. Job vi. 19; Nah. ii. 6. III. Hab. iii. 6; Ps. lxviii. 25; Prov. xxxi. 27.

הֶלֶךְ, m.—pl. non occ. Syr. ܗܶܠܟܳܐ, *gressus.* Arab. هَلَكَ, *exitium;* i. e. *a going out*, or *away;* perishing. So we say, *going to destruction;* and of a person dying, *departing:* so also the Arab. ذَهَبَ. And even the Latin *pereo*, compd. of *per + eo:* It. *depereo, intereo. Proceeding, flowing,* 1 Sam. xiv. 26. In 2 Sam. xii. 4, we have הֵלֶךְ, for אִישׁ הֵלֶךְ, like the Arab. اِبْن سَبِيل, *man of the way,* i. e. *Traveller;* unless, indeed, we have an abstract used for a concrete, as in עֶבֶד, מֶלֶךְ, &c. Gram. art. 152. 10.

הֲלָךְ, m. Chald.—pl. non occ. lit. *proceed;* so with us *proceeds*, for expenses. *Proceeds* of the State; *taxation*, Ezra iv. 13. 20; vii. 24, al. non occ.

הָלַךְ, v. pres. יֵלֵךְ, cogn. דָּרַךְ, אָרַח, יָלַךְ. See הָלַךְ. Constr. med. אֶל, עַל, עִם, אֶת, לְ, בְּ, כְּ, כֵּן, מִן, מֵעִם, לִפְנֵי, מִדֵּי, אַחֲרֵי, אַחַר, אָנָה, it. immed. and abs.

I. *Walked, went, proceeded;* man, beast, or thing inanimate, Gen. vii. 18; 2 Chron. xxvi. 8; Josh. vi. 8; Neh. vi. 17; 1 Sam. xxiii. 13; 2 Sam. xv. 20, &c. Irreg. pl. m. הַלְכוּא, Josh x. 24, which seems to have arisen out of the Arab. fm. نَصَرُوا, &c.

II. Meton. *Made way, progress;* i. e. increased as it were step by step. Pers. رَفتَه رَفتَه, *gradatim,* Gen. viii. 3. 5; xxvi. 13; Judg. iv. 24; 1 Sam. ii. 26; xiv. 19; 2 Sam. iii. 1; v. 10; xviii. 25; Is. viii. 7; Esth. ix. 4; Jon. i. 11; Prov. iv. 18; 2 Chron. xvii. 12. So Virg. "*Vires acquirit eundo.*"

III. It. Meton. *Proceeded, went on,* morally or otherwise, either in a good or bad sense, Deut. xix. 9; xxviii. 9; Ps. i. 1; xv. 2; lxxxi. 14; 1 Kings ix. 4; Is. xxxiii. 15; Mic. ii. 11; Prov. vi. 12, &c. In which cases the qualifying, or rather *specifying* terms accompanying, may be construed either with בְּ med. or *absolutely*. See Gram. art. 219, note, and ib. par. 4, note. Prov. iv. 18; Ezek. vii. 17; xxi. 12, &c.

IV. It. Meton. *Went off; disappeared; departed,* Gen. xii. 1; xxii. 2; xxv. 32; Ps. lxxviii. 39; Job xiv. 20. See my note, Cant. ii. 11; iv. 6. *Died,* Gen. xv. 2; Ps. xxxix. 14, &c.

Idiomatic usages, הָלַךְ בְּכָל־לְבָבוֹ, *He walked,* i. e. obeyed, with *all his heart*, 1 Kings xiv. 8. לִבִּי הָלַךְ, *my heart went,* I was well aware, 2 Kings v. 26. הָלַךְ הַצֵּל, *the shadow shall proceed,* 2 Kings xx. 9. הָלַךְ הָאֱלֹהִים, *God hath proceeded to—,* 1 Chron. xvii. 21. אַחַר עֵינַי הָלַךְ לִבִּי, *my eyes have strayed after my lust,* Job xxxi. 7. הָלַךְ בַּעֲצַת, *has gone on in the counsel of—,* 2 Chron. xxii. 5. Comp. Ezek. xviii. 17, &c. הָלַךְ לוֹ, as we say, *has walked itself off,* Cant. ii. 4; iv. 6; a Syriasm. הָלַךְ חֲשֵׁכִים, *walked, gone on,* in *great darkness,* Is. L. 10, &c. בַּגּוֹלָה, *into captivity,* Jer. xlviii. 11. בִּשְׁבִי, id. Nah. iii. 10; Lam. i. 5. 18, &c. בְּחֻמִּי, Ps. xxvi. 1. כַּפָּם בַּחֲמַת־קֶרִי, *with you in the heat—fierceness—of resistance,* Lev. xxvi. 28. 40, &c. בִּפְלִצָּה, *in contempt*, Is. xlv. 16. שְׁחוֹחַ, *humbly,* Is. lx. 14. Comp. Ps. xxxviii. 7, to which many similar ones might be added, were it necessary.

Infin. הָלֹךְ. Constr. הֲלֶךְ, Num. xxii. 14. Imp. pl. m. הַלְכוּ, Jer. li. 50.

Part. הוֹלֵךְ, pl. הוֹלְכִים, contr. הוֹלְכֵי. Phrase, הוֹלְכֵי רָכִיל, lit. *Itinerants of merchandize,* i. e. puffers of their own goods, liars, Jer. vi. 28. הֹלֶכֶת, f. pl. הֹלְכוֹת, Lev. xi. 27. עַל־אַרְבַּע, —*On four feet.*

Niph. נֶהֱלַכְתִּי, once, Ps. cix. 23, *I became, set about, departing.* LXX. ἀνταναιρέθην.

Pih. הִלֵּךְ, pres. יְהַלֵּךְ. Constr. med. בְּ, בְּלִי, עַל, בֵּין, מִן, לִפְנֵי, תַּחַת, it. abs. i. q. Kal. I. III.; if not also implying habit, Job xxiv. 10; xxx. 28; Ps. xxxviii. 7; civ. 26; Lam. v. 18. In Ps. civ. 3; Prov. vi. 11, in the

חלך (156) הלל

sense of attacking : where the accompanying terms are manifestly military.

Idioms, קֹדֵר, *in gloom*, Job xxx. 28 ; Ps. xxxviii. 7 ; cxxxi. 1. בְּדַרְכֵי לִבֶּךָ, *In the ways of thy heart*, after thy own will, Eccl. xi. 9. בַּאֲמִתֶּךָ, *in thy truth*, i. e. according to its requirements, Ps. lxxxvi. 11. Comp. Ps. cxlii. 4 ; Prov. viii. 20 ; Ezek. xviii. 9 ; Is. lix. 9 ; Ps. lxxxix. 16. Metaph. Ps. lxxxv. 14. אַט, *softly, humbly*, 1 Kings xxi. 27. In Hab. iii. 10, לְאוֹר חִצֶּיךָ יְהַלֵּכוּ, lit. *for light thy arrows proceeded;* i. e. the flashings of thy lightning gave light. Comp. Ps. lxxvii. 18, 19 ; xcvii. 4.

Imp. הֲלַךְ, Eccl. xi. 9.

Part. הֹלֵךְ, pl. הֹלְכִים.

Hiph. part. m. pl. מַהְלְכִים, once, Zech. iii. 7. LXX. ἀναστρεφομένους. Syriac ܕܡܗܠܟܝܢ, *those who walk*, i. e. take their part among —.

Hithp. הִתְהַלֵּךְ, pres. יִתְהַלֵּךְ. Constr. אֵת, לִפְנֵי, מִי, בְּתוֹךְ, סָבִיב, it. abs. *Became walking, proceeding, going on*. See Hiph. if habit is not also implied, Gen. iii. 8 ; Sam. xi. 2 ; Exod. xxi. 19 ; Job i. 7 ; Zech. i. 10, 11 ; vi. 7 ; Ps. xxxv. 14, &c.

Idioms, אֶת־הָאֱלֹהִים הִתְהַלֵּךְ, *He went on—he lived—with reference to God*, i. e. godly, Gen. vi. 9. בְּחֵקֶר הִתְהַלָּכְתָּ, *hast proceeded to investigate*, Job xxxviii. 16. בַּאֲמִתֶּךָ, *in thy truth*, according to it, Ps. xxvi. 3. Comp. Is. L. 10; Ps. lxxxii. 5 ; lxviii. 22 ; Prov. xx. 7 ; Ps. ci. 2, &c. קֹדֵר אֶתְהַלֵּךְ, *I proceed gloomily*, Ps. xliii. 2. בִּרְחָבָה, *in width*, i. e. plenty, Ps. cxix. 45. עַל־שְׂבָכָה, *upon the snare*, Job xviii. 8. חוּג שָׁמַיִם, *circuit of* (the) *heavens*, Ib. xxii. 14. בְּצֶלֶם, *in a shade*, i. e. in instability, Ps. xxxix. 7. בְּמֵישָׁרִים, *rightly*, Prov. xxiii. 31. וְחִצָּיו יִתְהַלָּכוּ, *thine arrows—lightnings—went on*, Ps. lxxvii. 18, &c.

Infin. הִתְהַלֵּךְ, Zech. i. 10 ; vi. 7.

Imp. id. Gen. xiii. 17 ; xvii. 1.

Part. מִתְהַלֵּךְ, f. מִתְהַלֶּכֶת, pl. m. מִתְהַלְּכִים, Prov. xxiv. 34, in a military sense. See Pih.

הֲלַךְ, v. Chald. Pah. i. q. Heb. Pih. pret. non occ.

Part. מְהַלֵּךְ, *Walking, proceeding*, Dan. iv. 26. Constr. med. עַל. Aph. Part. m. pl. מַהְלְכִין. Constr. בְּ. *Walking, &c.*, Dan. iii. 25 ; iv. 34, al. non occ.

הָלַל, v. pret. non occ. pres. pl. m. יָהֵלּוּ, Is. xiii. 10 ; f. sing. תָּהֵל, Job xli. 10. (See Parad. Kal, Gram. art. 211, page 256, יָטֹב ; here fm. סָב.) Arab. هَلَّ, *splendere cœpit ;* conj. ii. هَلَّلَ, *laudavit*, q. d. splendere fecit, splendidum prædicavit. Cogn. أَهَلَّ, *dignus fuit :* conj. ii. أَهَلَّ, *dignum habuit*. *Shine, give out light :* with אוֹר, immed.

Infin. aff. הֲלוֹ, *His shining, giving out light*, with נֵר, Job xxix. 3. See also my note.

Part. pl. m. הוֹלְלִים, lit. *shiners*. Eng. vulg. *sparks*, i. e. *Vain-glorious, foolish, &c.* Ps. v. 6 ; lxxiii. 3 ; lxxv. 5, al. non occ. See הוֹלֵלוֹת, which is very nearly allied to this participle.

Pih. הִלֵּל, pres. יְהַלֵּל, and יְהוֹלֵל, constr. immed. it. abs. it. med. אֶת, אֶל, לְ, בְּ, instr. Syr. ܗܰܠܶܠ, *laudavit*.

I. *Praised*, Gen. xii. 15 ; Is. lxiv. 9, 10 ; Joel ii. 26 ; Ps. cxvii. 1 ; cxix. 164 ; Prov. xxvii. 2, &c.

II. *Gloried*. Constr. בְּ, עַל, Ps. x. 3 ; xliv. 9 ; lvi. 5. See הִתְהַלֵּל, הוֹלֵל, הַתְהוֹלֵל. The *Dagesh* characteristic of this species is often omitted, Gram. art. 113. The second fm. pres. always in this, or some cognate sense, Ps. lxxv. 5. אַל־תָּהֹלּוּ, contr. for תְּהוֹלְלוּ, *I said to the* (vain) *glorious, glory not*. It. meton.

III. *Pronounces* (vain) *glorious, foolish, mad*, Job xii. 17 ; Eccl. vii. 7 ; Is. xliv. 25.

Puh. pret. f. הֻלְּלָה, pres. יְהֻלַּל, Ezek. xxvi. 17. הָעִיר הַהֻלָּלָה, *the city which has been lauded ;* where הַ stands for אֲשֶׁר, unless we have the very noun here on which the verb is formed, Gram. art. 182. 2, &c., Ps. lxxviii. 63. " Celebrabantur," says Dr. Gesenius, " carminibus *nuptialibus*." But we read of no such *nuptial songs* in the Bible ! This, nevertheless, he dislikes, and proposes another reading. *Praised*, i. e. spoken of by way of approbation, however, will suit the passage well. So the Targumist, אִשְׁתַּבְּחָן.—יְהֻלָּל, *is praised*, Prov. xii. 8.

Part. מְהֻלָּל, *Praised ;* and, as in Niph. generally, Gram. art. 157. 20. *Worthy to be praised*, 2 Sam. xxii. 4 ; Ps. xviii. 4 ; xlviii. 2 ; xcvi. 4 ; 1 Chron. xvi. 25, &c.

Hithp. of fm. הִלֵּל, pret. non occ. pres. יִתְהַלֵּל. I. *Set about, become, glorying, boasting*, 1 Kings xx. 11 ; Ps. xxxiv. 3 ; lxiii. 12 ; Jer. ix. 22, 23 ; Prov. xx. 14.

II. *Become, be, praised*, Prov. xxxi. 30, &c.

Infin. הִתְהַלֵּל, Ps. cvi. 5.

Imp. Ps. cv. 3 ; 1 Chron. xvi. 10.

Part. מִתְהַלֵּל, pl. מִתְהַלְלִים, Prov. xxv. 14 ; Jer. ix. 23 ; Ps. xcvii. 7.

Hithp. of fm. הוֹלֵל, pret. הִתְהוֹלֵל, pres. יִתְהוֹלֵל, *Became vain-glorious, foolish, mad*,

הלם (157) המה

Jer. xxv. 16; L. 38; li. 7; Nahum ii. 5; only in appearance, *dissembled madness*, 1 Sam. xxi. 14.

הֲלֹם, adv. *Hither, thus far*, Gen. xvi. 13; Exod. iii. 5; Judg. xviii. 3, &c. See Noldius, p. 265. Arab. هَلُمَّ, *adesdum, &c.*

הֲלֹם, m. seg. lit. *contusion, beating*, abstr. for concrete, 1 Sam. xiv. 16; Ps. lxxiii. 10. *Broken, stricken, beaten to pieces.* Hence—

הָלַם, v. pres. יַהֲלֹם. Aff. יַהַלְמֵנִי, Ps. cxli. 5. Constr. immed. it. abs. it. med. בְּ, instr. *Struck, beat*, Judg. v. 22. 26; Is. xvi. 8; Prov. xxiii. 35; Ps. lxxv. 6.

Part. pass. pl. m. constr. הֲלוּמֵי, *The beaten of*—i. e. intoxicated with—*wine*, Is. xxviii. 1. Infin. הֲלֹם, above.

Part. הוֹלֵם, for הֹלֵם, Is. xli. 7.

הַלְמוּת, f. A workman's *hammer* or *mallet*, Judg. v. 26, abstr. for concr.

הֵם, הֵמָּה, pron. 3d pers. masc. pl. See הוּא, Nold. p. 266; Gram. art. 145. 2. *They, them.* Is capable of receiving the def. art. See הוּא, and the Appendix. Acts also as the logical copula, Gen. xxv. 16; 1 Kings viii. 40; ix. 20, &c. With fem. pred. Cant. vi. 8. In Zeph. ii. 12, belonging to the 2d pers. according to Gesenius; but the truth is, the place is inverted and abrupt, and should be read thus, גַּם־אַתֶּם הַלְלֵי חַרְבִּי כּוּשִׁים הֵמָּה, *Even ye (are) (the) wounded of my sword,—they are Cushites.*

הָמָה, v. pres. יֶהֱמֶה, apoc. תֶּהֱמִי, with ה, parag. in pause. אֶהֱמָיָה, Ps. lxxvii. 4. With ן parag. יֶהֱמָיוּן, Is. xvii. 12; constr. abs. it. עַל, לְ, med. Arab. هَمَى, *huc illuc pastum vagatus est* grex. Cogn. هَمَّ, *cogitavit solicito* animo; هَامَ, r. هَيْم, *vagatus fuit furibundi instar.* Syr. ܗܡܟ, *avertit* oculos. Cogn. Heb. הָם. Syr. ܚܡܪ. Arab. حَمِيَ, *fervefecit.* *Boil*, seems to be the primitive notion. Hence—

I. *Ferment* as wine (comp. חמרמר), Zech. ix. 15; Prov. xx. 1; Ps. xlvi. 4. Meton. *troubled.*

II. *Moved*, as the bowels, by pain, affection, grief, anger, &c. Cant. v. 4; Jer. xxxi. 20; Ps. lxxvii. 4; xlii. 6. 12; Jer. xlviii. 36, &c.

III. Meton. *Roar, rage*, (a) as the sea; (b) as an enraged people; (c) *growl*, as a bear, dog; (d) *moan*, as a lute or dove : (a) Jer. v. 22; vi. 23; xxxi. 35; li. 55; Is. li. 15: (b) Is. xvii. 12; Ps. xlvi. 7; lv. 18; 1 Kings i. 41; Ps. xxxix. 7: (c) Is. lix. 11; Ps. lix. 7. 15 : (d) Is. xvi. 11; Ezek. vii. 16. Infin. הֲמוֹת, Is. xvii. 12.

Part. הֹמֶה, Prov. xx. 1; Jer. iv. 19.
הֹמִיָּה, } id. f. pl. הֹמוֹת, Ezek. vii. 16.
הֹמִיָּה, } Prov. vii. 11; ix. 13, Gram. art. 136. 5; pl. הֹמִיּוֹת, places *emitting noise*, *tumultuous*, i. e. abounding with people, Prov. i. 21.

הֵמָה, see הֵם.

הֶמְיָהֶם, for הֶמְיָתָם, m. pl. aff. r. המה, cogn. המם. Arab. هَمّ, *cura, angor, solicitudo.* Meton. *Their riches, abundance*, once, Ezek. vii. 11.

הֵמוֹ, and הֵמוֹן, Chald. pron. 3d. pers. masc. pl. *They, them*. Heb. הֵם, Dan. ii. 34, 35; Ezra iv. 10. 23; Nold. p. 276.

הָמוֹן, r. הָמָה, m. (In Job xxxi. 34, fm. according to Gesenius; but, if רֻבָּה is to be taken adverbially, — see my note on the place,—the remark of Gesenius is groundless.) pl. הֲמֹנִים, Joel iv. 14.

I. *Moving of the bowels*, affection, Is. lxii. 15. LXX. τὸ πλῆθος τοῦ ἐλέους σου.

II. *Musical sounds* expressive of joy, Ezek. xxvi. 13; Amos v. 23. See the parallelism

III. *Multitude*, as in commotion, Is. xiii. 4; xxxiii. 3; Dan. x. 6.
(a) Of nations, Gen. xvii. 4, 5; people, Is. xvii. 12.
(b) Of women, 2 Chron. xi. 23.
(c) Of soldiery, Judg. iv. 7; Dan. xi. 11—13.
(d) Of waters, Jer. x. 13; li. 16.
(e) Of wealth, riches, Ps. xxxvii. 16; Eccl. v. 9; Is. lx. 5, &c. Aff. הֲמוֹנֵךְ, הֲמוֹנָהּ, הֲמוֹנָיו, pl. הֲמוֹנֶיהָ.

הָמוֹן, see הֵמוֹ.

הֲמוֹנָה, f. The mystical name of a city, Ezek. xxxix. 16;—see the preceding verse—probably heathen Rome.

הֶמְיָה, f. *Sound, murmuring* of the lute, Is. xiv. 11, r. הָמָה, al. non occ.

הֱמִין, see ימן.

הֻמְכוּ, Job xxiv. 24. Hoph. r. מכך, according to Gesenius. But, see my note. Puh. of המך.

חמל   (158)   חמר

הֲמֻלָּה, and הֲמוּלָה, f.—pl. non occ. Arab. هَمَلَ, continuè pluit cœlum, liberè dimissi sunt cameli. Cogn. حَمَلَ, impetum fecit. Commotion; agitation: or, meton. the sound, thence proceeding, of a multitude, Jer. xi. 16. Of the wings of the cherubim, Ezek. i. 24. Gesenius, i. q. הָמוֹן, which is very doubtful.

הָמַם, v. pres. הוּם. Aff. יְהֻמֵּם, in pause, יְהֹמֵּם, Josh. x. 10; 2 Sam. xxii. 15. Synon. נָכָה, אָכַל, אָבַד. Cogn. הָמָה, הוּם. Arab. هَمَّ, tabescere fecit, exedit morbus; impulit ad citatiorem incessum camelum. Put in motion, commotion; to the route, destruction, Is. xxviii. 28; 2 Chron. xv. 6; Exod. xiv. 24; xxiii. 27; Josh. x. 10; Ps. xviii. 15; cxliv. 6; Deut. ii. 15; Esth. ix. 24; Jer. xxxi. 34.

הָמֹן, not הֲמֹן, as Gesenius gives it. Once, Ezek. v. 7. Aff. הֲמֹנְכֶם, Your abundance, excess, i. e. transgression. Comp. vr. 6, ib. i. q. רִשְׁעָה. LXX. ἀφορμή.

הַמְנִיךְ, m. kethiv, הַמְוֻנְכָא; keri, הַמְנִיכָא, defin. Dan. v. 7. 16. 29. Syr. ܗܶܡܢܺܝܟܳܐ, ܗܶܡܢܺܝܟܳܐ. Torques, spira, murænula. Castell. Pers. همیان, Targum. הֲמָן,—baltheus, zona. Castell. With the Pers. termination, ك, forming a diminutive, A collar for the neck, or a bracelet or ring for the hands, perhaps; al. non occ.

הָמַס, for הָמַם, Infin. Niph. r. מסס.

הִמְסִיו, for הֲמַסּוּ, r. מסה, Josh. xiv. 8.

הֲמַסִּים, pl. m.—sing. non occ. Is. lxiv. 1, only. כִּקְדֹחַ אֵשׁ הֲמָסִים, As the kindling of fire (excites) Slight noises; and as fire stirs up—makes to boil—waters; so shall God by almost silent means (comp. ch. xlii. 2, seq.) so make known thy name, that nations shall eventually shake and tremble at it. The prediction relates to the spread of Christianity. Arab. هَمَسَ, lenis submissusque strepitus pedum, &c. Cogn. هَمْشَة, strepitus rerum commistarum inter sese, ac moventium. Gesen. &c. "sarmentorum et ramorum," &c. Whence הֲמָסִים is next made to signify sarmenta! I ask, and why not, all the varia genera euntium, &c. &c. and so propose a most abundant choice? Castell is not a whit better. "Quidni," says he, "devorationes?" ab هَمَس, mandi. But هَمَس has no such sense. The LXX. &c. seem to have read כִּקְדֹחַ אֵשׁ הַמָּסִים. (See מַס.) ὡς κηρὸς ἀπὸ προσώπου πυρὸς τήκεται.

הֲמָרוֹתָם, r. מָרָה, Infin. Hiph. with Dagesh Euphon, Ges. See my note on Job xvii. 2, r. המר. Their embitterings.

הֵן, pron. 3d pers. pl. fem. always after some preposition, as בָּהֵן, or בָּהֶן, מֵהֵן, לָהֵן. Otherwise, הֵנָּה, which see. On certain idiomatic usages of this pronoun after prepositions, see my note on Job xxx. 24.

הֵן, or הֶן, with ה parag. הִנֵּה, which see. Arab. إِنْ, إِنَّ, siquando, siquidem. Syr. ܐܶܢ. Gr. ἐάν, ἤν. Cogn. אִם, which see; it. Noldius, p. 276, et seq.

I. Behold, see; observe, Gen. iii. 22; Num. xxiii. 24; Is. xxiii. 13; Job xxxi. 35, &c.

II. If, whether? (a) interrogatively, Jer. ii. 10; Ezra v. 17, &c.: it. (b) implying negation, as in אִם, p. 38, above, Dan. iii. 17.

(c) Whether, distributively, Ezra vii. 26.

(d) ——, conditionally, Exod. iv. 1; Dan. iv. 24.

(e) ——, hypothetically, i. e. putting some case, as a fact, and then reasoning from it, Lev. xxv. 20; Is. L. 11; Exod. viii. 22; Jer. iii. 1; Job xiii. 11, &c.

This usage (II.) is not unknown to the Greek; and appears to have originated in that language, just as it has in the Hebrew, by speaking of facts, rather than of opinions. Hoogeveen (under Εἰ, ed. 1813), p. 151, has well remarked, "Cæterum . . . ." " nec conditionem proponi, sed casum verius poni de re præterita." So, Ib. § xii. p. 152. " Si conditio rem certam indicat, accipit εἰ vim αἰτιολογικήν, causamque consequentiæ infert, ut apud, Hom. Il. φ. v. 216. Ἀλεὶ γάρ τοι ἀμύνουσιν θεοὶ αὐτοί,

Εἴ τοι Τρῶας ἔδωκε Κρόνου παῖς πάντας ὀλέσσειν.

" Tibi enim dii ipsi opem ferunt, quoniam dedit tibi Saturni filius omnes Trojanos perdere." " Similiter . . . . Rom. viii. 17. Εἰ δὲ τέκνα, καὶ κληρονόμοι ubi τὸ τέκνα εἶναι rem certam esse nec dubiam," &c. Ib. § xiii. " Interrogationibus quoque inservit, &c. e. g. Εἰ δ᾽ ἀμφοῖν μεταξὺ κεῖται…..Inter utramque sit media? Plat. de Repub. lib. v.; Hom. Odyss. A. v. 158, &c. See also Vigerus de

הֵן (159) הֵנִי

Idiotismis, by Herman. Lond. 1824. p. 504, et seq. cap. viii. sect. vi. par. iii. et seq. These are, therefore, not mere Hebraisms: they are natural constructions growing out of the nature of the case.

הֵן, Chald. i. q. Heb. Dan. iii. 17, *Behold, see, if, whether?* &c., Ezra v. 17; Dan. ii. 5, 6, &c. It. Distributively, Ezra vii. 26, &c.

הֵנָּה, I. Pron. 3d pers. pl. fem. *They, them,* and Dem. *these,* Gram. art. 145. 2; Nold. p. 275, et seq. Gen. xli. 19; xxxiii. 6; xxi. 29. With def. art. 1 Sam. xvii. 28. Often includes the logical copula, as in הוּא הֵמָּה, Gen. vi. 2, &c. With prepp. בָּהֵנָּה, מֵהֵנָּה, לָהֵנָּה, כָּהֵנָּה, Lev. v. 22; iv. 2; Ezek. i. 5; Gen. xli. 19, &c. See Nold. l. c.

הֵנָּה. II. Arab. هُنَّ, هَاهُنَّا, هُنَا, هُنَاكَ, *hic, huc.* Compd. of הֵ־, *versus,* and הֵן, *See, behold. Hither, thus far,* of (a) place or (b) time; (a) Gen. xlv. 8; Josh. iii. 9, &c. הֵנָּה וְהֵנָּה, *hither and thither,* Josh. viii. 20; 1 Sam. xx. 21. עַד־הֵנָּה, *thus far,* Num. xiv. 19; 1 Sam. vii. 12, &c. It. *Here,* Dan. xii. 5; 1 Kings xx. 40.

(b) With עַד, Gen. xv. 16; 1 Sam. i. 16. Contr. עֲדֶנָּה, עֲדֶן. See עַד. And Nold. pp. 281. 2.

הִנֵּה, rarely הִנֵּה, i. q. הֵן. Of which it is compd. with def. art. affixed. *Behold, see, lo:* to excite (a) *attention,* Gen. i. 29; Exod. i. 9; Num. xviii. 6; Josh. ix. 12, &c.

(b) With intimation of something important and unusual, Gen. vi. 17; Exod. xxxii. 34; xxxiv. 10; Is. vii. 14.

(c) With promptness, Num. xiv. 40; 1 Sam. iii. 8; Is. lviii. 9; Ps. xl. 8, &c. The signn. *hic,* and *si,* assigned by Noldius, p. 279, are groundless. See Ib. p. 278, seq. With pron. affixed, הִנֵּנִי, for הִנְּנִי: in pause, הִנֵּנִי, Gen. xxii. 1. 11; xxvii. 1, &c.

הִנְּךָ, הִנֵּךְ, f. הִנָּךְ, Gen. xvi. 11; xx. 3, &c. הִנּוֹ, Num. xxiii. 17; 1 Chron. xi. 25, &c. הִנֶּנּוּ, in pause, הִנֵּנוּ, Job xxxviii. 35. הִנָּה Gen. xvi. 16; Josh. ix. 26, &c. הִנְּכֶם, Deut. i. 10; Jer. xvi. 12. הִנָּם, Gen. xlvii. 1; 1 Sam. xii. 2, &c. It. הִנֵּה אֲשֶׁר, הִנֵּה אֵין, הִנֵּה הַדְּרִיאָה, הַהִדְוָה, &c. See Nold. p. 280, &c.

הֲנָחָה, f. once, Esth. ii. 18, r. נוח, cogn. ינח, *Rest, peace.* LXX. ἄφεσιν.

הֻפַּח, see r. נוח, and ינח.

הֵפִיחַ, pret. Hiph. r. נוח, cogn. ינח.

הֵפִיחַ, Hoph. ib.

הֻנְעַל, pret. Aph. r. עלל, Chald.

הֲנָפָה, Infin. Hiph. Chald. r. נוף.

הסה, v. non occ. in Kal. Arab. هَسِيسُ, *sermo occultus:* ὀνοματοποιητικόν.

Pih. הַס, imp. apoc. *Hush, be silent,* constr. abs. it. med. מִפְּנֵי, Hab. ii. 20; Zeph. i. 7; Zech. ii. 17: it. Judg. iii. 19; Amos vi. 10. Pl. הַסּוּ, Neh. viii. 11.—Used adverbially, Amos viii. 3.

Hiph. pres. apoc. יַהַס, *Made, caused to be silent,* Num. xiii. 30.

הֵסִית, Hiph. r. סות, Chald.

הַעַל, Imp. apoc. Hiph. r. עלה.

הַעֲלָה, Hiph. r. עלה.

הָעֳלָה, Hoph. id.

הֲפוּגָה, f. pl. הֲפוּגוֹת, once, Lam. iii. 49; r. פוג, *Remission, intermission.*

הָפַךְ and הָפַךְ, m. Syr. ܗܦܟ, *reversio,* ܗܦܟ, *contorsio.* הֲפֵכָה, f. Arab. مَنْفَكٌ, *multum errans, et se confundens. Perversion, subversion,* Ezek. xvi. 34; Gen. xix. 29.

הָפַךְ, v. pres. יַהֲפֹךְ. Constr. med. לְ, מִן, אֶל, עַל, אֶת, בְּ, instr. it. *in, among;* it. immed. and abs. *Turn* (a) *over,* Judg. vii. 13; Job xxxviii. 9; Hos. vii. 8; 2 Kings xxi. 13; Ps. xli. 4.

(b) *Subvert, ruin,* Gen. xix. 21. 25; Deut. xxix. 22; Jer. xx. 16; Job ix. 5; xxxiv. 25; Amos iv. 11; Hag. ii. 22, &c.

(c) *Turn back,* Exod. x. 19; 1 Kings xxii. 34; 2 Kings v. 26; 2 Chron. xviii. 33; Lam. iii. 3. And give *the back,* as in battle, Josh. vii. 8; Judg. xx. 39—41; Ps. lxxviii. 9.

(d)—*Change,* i. e. from one sort, &c., to another, i. q. הָיָה לְ, Lev. xiii. 3. הָפַךְ לָבָן, *turned white,* Ps. cxiv. 8; Jer. xiii. 23. With לְ, Ps. xxx. 12; lxvi. 6; cv. 25. 29: Jer. xxxi. 13, &c.

(e) *Change,* i. e. *pervert,* Jer. xxiii. 36; Amos v. 7; vi. 12.

(f) *Convert,* 1 Sam. x. 9. Infin. הָפוֹךְ, constr. הֲפֹךְ, Prov. xii. 7; Gen. xix. 29. Aff. הָפְכָה, הָפְכְכֶם. Imp. הֲפֹךְ, 1 Kings xxii. 34. Part. הֹפֵךְ, pl. הֹפְכִים; Relative הֹפְכִי, Ps. cxiv. 8; Gram. art. 175. 16.

Pass. f. הֲפוּכָה, Lam. iv. 6.

חפך

Niph. נֶהְפַּךְ, pres. יֵהָפֵךְ, pret. once, נַהֲפוֹךְ, Esth. ix. 1, *Became, was turned,* (a) *over,* Job xxviii. 5: Metaph. Lam. i. 20; Hos. xi. 8; Ezek. iv. 8, *to; consigned to,* Lam. v. 2.

(b) *Subverted, overturned,* Jonah iii. 4.
(c)—*Back,* Josh. viii. 20.
(d)—From one sort to another; *Changed,* Exod. vii. 15; Lev. xiii. 17; Esth. ix. 22; Lam. v. 15; Job xx. 14. בִּלְשׁוֹנוֹ, *With his tongue;* i. e. says one thing at one time, at another another; *A prævaricator, double-dealer,* Prov. xvii. 23. Comp. Ps. xii. 3.
(e)—For the worse, *perverted,* Exod. xiv. 5. *Turned against,* with בְּ, Job xix. 19.—*Upon,* 1 Sam. iv. 19, with עַל.
(d)—For the better, *converted,* Is. lx. 5; 1 Sam. x. 6, with לְ.

Hoph. נֶהְפַּךְ, with עַל, i. q. Niph. (e) *Turned upon, against,* Job xxx. 15. See my note. al. non occ.

Hithp. pres. f. תִּתְהַפֵּךְ, *Becomes turned, changed,* Job xxxviii. 14. See my note.

Part. מִתְהַפֵּךְ, f. מִתְהַפֶּכֶת, *Becomes, is turning over,* or *about,* Job xxxvii. 12; Judg. vii. 13; Gen. iii. 24.

הֲפַכְפַּךְ, m. once Prov. xxi. 8; opp. τῷ. יָשָׁר, *Turning, twisting, tortuous.*

הַפְרָם, Infin. aff. Hiph. r. פרר.

הַצְמֵיד, Hithp. r. צִיד.

הַצָּלָה, f. r. נצל, *Deliverance,* Esth. iv. 14; al. non occ.

הֹצֶן, m. Some MSS. have הֹצֶן. The LXX. seem to have read מִצָּפוֹן, ἀπὸ βορρᾶ. Cogn. Arab. حصن, *munimentum.* Æth.

הֲרֵא֫ל : *ferrum. An armament,* force, Ezek. xxiii. 24.

הַצְפִּינוֹ, Infin. Hiph. Aff. r. צפן.

הַקְצוֹת, Infin. Hiph. r. קצה.

הַר, m. pl. הָרִים. With def. art. הָהָר; ה par. הָרָה once. הֶהָרָה, *montem versus.* Constr. הַר, and הֲרֵי. Def. art. הֶהָרִים. r. הור. See Arab. هور.

I. *A mountain,* Is. xxx. 25; xl. 4. 9; lvii. 7; Exod. iii. 12; xix. 2; Gen. xiv. 10; xii. 8; xix. 17, &c.

II. Metaph. *Place of strength,* considered as a refuge, or as an obstacle, Is. xl. 4; Zech. iv. 7; Jer. xvi. 16; Ps. xi. 1; xxx. 8.

III. *Men of great power,* Is. xli. 15. Comp. Dan. ii. 35.

הר

IV. Meton. *A mountainous place,* or *country,* Gen. xiv. 10; Josh. x. 40; xi. 16; xv. 48. ἡ ὀρεινή, Luke i. 39. 65. הַר הָאֱלֹהִים, *Mount of God,* Sinai, because God appeared there, Exod. iii. 1; iv. 27; xviii. 5. Also Zion, Ps. xxiv. 2; Is. ii. 3. Frequently with קֹדֶשׁ; as הַר קָדְשִׁי, *mount of my holiness.* הַר קָדְשׁוֹ, of his do. so styled apparently to show that the holiness belonged to God; and to guard against a superstitious reverence for the mere place, Is. xi. 9; lvi. 7; Ps. ii. 6; xv. 1; xliii. 3; Obad. vr. 16; Ezek. xx. 40. Occasionally הַר בֵּית יְהוָה, *mountain of Jehovah's house,* Is. ii. 2; comp. Ps. lxviii. 16, either very high, or very good; i. e. for pasture— comp. Jer. L. 6,—which is most probable. According to Gesen. הַר קָדְשִׁי, Is. lvii. 13, is put for the whole of the Holy Land. Is it not rather by a synechdoche, because Zion, as the principal place, is solely mentioned? Pl. הָרַי, *my mountains,* for my mountainous land; i. e. the whole of Jewry:—as הַר אֶפְרַיִם, is put for Samaria, Jer. iv. 15, &c. Comp. Amos iv. 1; Is. xiv. 25; lxv. 9. Gesenius here tells us, that the ancient religion considered mountains as holy, because they were supposed to be the seats of the divinities. And so of course, the sanctity of Olympus, and that of mount Moriah in Jerusalem, stood on the same footing! The truth, however, seems to be, high places were chosen rather than low ones, because they could be more easily defended. Hence cities, citadels, palaces, temples, would be, and were usually, so situated; and hence, probably, originated the notion, among the heathen—not among the ancient believers in revelation—that the divinities resided in such places:—so הַר הַמַּשְׁחִית, *mount of the destroyer,* Babylon, Jer. li. 25. And hence, their *high place.* See בָּמָה.

Aff. הָרִי, הָרָם, pl. הָרֶיהָ. It. contr. הָרָיו, הָרֵי, הָרַי.

הֹר, see הוֹר.

הַרְאֵל, lit. *Mount of God,* Ezek. xliii. 15. Ib. vr. 16, אֲרִיאֵל, which see, id. A name of *the great, or brazen altar.*

הֶרֶב, Imp. apoc. Hiph. r. רבה.

הַרְבּוֹת, הַרְבָּה, הַרְבֵּה, Infinn. r. רבה.

הֶרֶג, m. } Arab. هرج, *tumultus, cædes.*
הֲרֵגָה, f. } *Slaughter, slaying,* Is. xxvii. 7; xxx. 25; Ezek. xxvi. 15; Esth. ix. 5; Prov. xxiv. 11:—Jer. vii. 32; xii. 3; xix. 6; Zech. xi. 4. 7.

חרג

חָרַג, v. pres. יַחֲרֹג; with ה par. אַחֲרְגָה; aff. אֶחֱרְגֵהוּ. Constr. immed. it. med. אֵת, לְ, בְּ, it. בְּ, instr. Arab. خرج, confusione, aut cæde, misti fuerunt inter se: hence constr. with בְּ, synon. קָטַל, רָצַח. *Kill, slay*, generally in war, &c., by the sword or otherwise; by pestilence, grief, a viper, &c.; of men, beasts, fruit-trees, 1 Kings xix. 10; 2 Kings xix. 18; Esth. ix. 6:—Is. x. 4; xiv. 20, &c.:—Gen. iv. 8; Exod. ii. 14; xxii. 23; 2 Sam. xii. 9; Amos iv. 10; Judg. ix. 54:—Jer. xviii. 21; Job v. 2; xx. 16; Is. xxvii. 1; xxii. 13; Ps. lxxviii. 47; comp. Job xiv. 8.
Inf. חֲרֹג, constr. הָרְגֵךְ, הָרְגוֹ, aff. הָרְגֵךְ, &c.
Imp. חֲרֹג, aff. הָרְגֵנִי, pl. חִרְגוּ, in pause חֲרֹגוּ.
Part. חֹרֵג, pl. חֹרְגִים, aff. sing. הֹרְגֵךְ.
Pass. pl. m. הֲרוּגִים, constr. הַרְגֵי, aff. הֲרוּגָיו, &c.
Niph. pres. יֵחָרֵג, *Is, becomes slain*, Lam. ii. 20; Ezek. xxvi. 6.
Infin. הֵחָרֵג, Ezek. xxvi. 15.
Puh. הֹרַג, Is. xxvii. 7; Ps. xliv. 23, i. q. Hiph.

חָרָה, f. constr. חֲרַת, pl. הָרוֹת. Arab. هر, *multa aqua, lao.* هرج, *aquatum duxit.* Comp. أرى, هور, هري. *With child, pregnant*, Gen. xvi. 11; xxxviii. 24, 25; Exod. xxi. 22; Is. vii. 14; Jer. xx. 17, &c. Aff. pl. הָרוֹתָיו, הָרוֹתֵיהֶם, and הָרִיוֹתָיו, Hos. xiv. 1, Gram. art. 136. 5.

חָרָה, v. pres. apoc. תַּהַר. See הָרָה, above. *Conceived, became pregnant;* constr. abs. it. immed. it. med. אֵת, לְ to or for whom; propr. of women only; metaph. of men, Gen. xvi. 5; Judg. xiii. 3; Num. xi. 12; Metaph. Ps. vii. 15; Is. xxvi. 18; lix. 4; xxxiii. 11; Job xv. 35. Meton. 1 Chron. iv. 17. Pres. apoc. Gen. iv. 1. 17; xvi. 4. תַּהַר לוֹ, to, by, him, Gen. xxxviii. 18.
Infin. הָרֹה, and הָרוֹ.—Gram. art. 72.—It. הֹרוּ, Is. lix. 13, metaph.
Part. f. aff. הוֹרָתִי, הוֹרָם, Cant. iii. 4; Hos. ii. 7.
Puh. הֹרָה, *Has been conceived*, Job iii. 3.

חַרְחֹרִין, m. pl. Chald. compd. of חרה and הוֹר. Arab. هر, above. Metaph. *Conceptions*, various *imaginations*, or the like, Dan. iv. 2; al. non occ. Syr. ܚܪܥܘܬܐ, *imaginatio*.

הֵרוֹן, m. } r. הרה, *Conception*, Gen. iii. חֵרָיוֹן, m. } 16; Ruth iv. 13; Hos. ix. 11. Aff. הֵרוֹנֵךְ.

(161)

חרי

חֲרִיסָה, f. r. הרס, pl. aff. חֲרִיסֹתָיו, *Its houses*, &c., *broken down, ruined*, Amos ix. 11; al. non occ.

חֲרִיסוּת, f. r. הרס, aff. חֲרִיסֻתֵךְ, *Thy destruction, ruin*, Is. xlix. 19; al. non occ.

הַרְמוֹן, m. i. q. אַרְמוֹן, which see. *A palace*, or *citadel*, Amos iv. 3. LXX. καὶ ἀποῤῥιφήσεσθε εἰς τὸ ὄρος τὸ Ῥομμάν, al. Ρεμμάν. Aquila, εἰς Αρμανὰ ὄρος ἀπάγοντες. Sym. Syr. Chald. εἰς Ἑρμηνίαν, al. Ἀρμηνίαν. Quint. Ed. montem Μονά. See also Bochart. Phaleg. lib. i. cap. iii. p. 22, &c. Where we have Theodoret and Theodotion's reading of the passage.

הָרְלְמוֹ, Imp. pl. Niph. r. רמם.

הֶרֶס, m. once, Is. xix. 18, al. חֶרֶם, which see; given as the *mystic* name of a city, and, therefore,—as it should seem—intended to carry a meaning. Usually, "*City of destruction*." See חֶרֶם, below. Ikenius Dissert. Philol. Theol. xvi. takes it to be *Leontopolis*, from هرس, *vehemens et vorax leo*. See Suppl. Lex. Heb. of Michaelis sub voce. According to Gesen. " ex idiomate quodam Jesaiæ *diruetur harum urbium una*:" the soundness of which may be fairly doubted. From the context, however, it should rather seem that, as one of the five cities professing the true religion, something better than destruction should be predicated of it. If the prediction relates to Christian times,—and of this there can be no doubt,—and if the term is to be taken as signifying *a lion*, why may the interpretation not be, *City of the Lion*? The great altar in Ezekiel's temple is termed אֲרִיאֵל, and הַרְאֵל, which see; which are perhaps other similar *mystical names* belonging to the same period. See also vr. 19 here, et seq. In the Syriac, too, ܚܪܣ signifies *redemptio, salus, &c.*, and, if this may be taken here, we shall have *city of redemption*; i. e. one of these five cities shall excel the rest in this respect: which will be intended if the Lion of the tribe of Judah, in the other case, is meant. This will make the context easy and obvious, and takes no more for granted, perhaps, than such usages really require. It is truly marvellous, that such a writer as Ikenius could see nothing here beyond the Temple of Onias, and Alexander's invasion of Egypt; how *the altar to be erected to Jehovah*, vr. 19, et seq. is its being *a sign and testimony to Him*, that the Egyptians should cry to him, and that He should send them *a Saviour*: that Jeho-

Y

vah should be *known to them*, and that they should *recognize Him*; should *serve Him*; should *vow* and *pay their vows*; should *turn to Him, and be healed*, and so on; if, after all, the whole thing meant was, an event of no moment whatsoever to posterity, and the terms just noticed,—all occurring in this chapter,—were entirely destitute of meaning! It is not to be wondered at, indeed, that he should object to Vitringa's patch-work attempt to make this prophecy fit both these events. The favourite double interpretation system has committed greater havoc than this on Holy Scripture. This Ikenius ought to have seen and exploded. See my Sermons and Dissertations, p. 216, et seq.

הָרַס, v. pres. יֶהֱרֹס, it. יַהֲרֹס, constr. immed. it. med. אֶת, rarely אֶל, לְ; בְּ, instr. Arab. هَرَسَ, *contudit vehementius*. *Broke down* (a) as houses, walls, towers, altars, cities, &c.; opp. τῷ, בָּנָה. Synon. נָתַץ, נָתַשׁ, הֶאֱבִיד, Judg. vi. 25; Is. xiv. 17; Ezek. xiii. 14; Mic. v. 10; 1 Kings xix. 10. 14; Jer. xxiv. 6; xlii. 10; Mal. i. 4; Job xii. 14; Prov. xiv. 1.

(b) *Men;* i. e. put down, reduce, &c., Exod. xv. 7; Is. xxii. 19; Ps. xxviii. 5; it. *Injure, hurt,* Prov. xxix. 4; as if a country were built up by justice, but broken down by flatterers.

(c) *The teeth,* Ps. lviii. 7.
Infin. הָרוֹס, Jer. i. 10; xxxi. 28.
Imp. הֲרֹס, aff. הָרְסָה, 2 Sam. xi. 25.
Part. הֹרֵס, Jer. xlv. 4.
Pass. הָרוּס, 1 Kings xviii. 30.
Niph. f. נֶהֱרָסָה, pres. יֵהָרֵס, *Became, was, broken down,* Prov. xi. 11; xxiv. 31; Jer. xxxi. 40; L. 15; Joel i. 17; Ezek. xxx. 4; xxxviii. 20; Ps. xi. 3.
Part. נֶהֱרָסוֹת, f. pl. Ezek. xxxvi. 35, 36.
Pih. pres. תֶּהֱרֹס, i. q. Kal. Exod. xxiii. 24.
Infin. הָרֵס, Ib.
Part. pl. m. aff. מְהָרְסַיִךְ, Is. xlix. 17.

הֶרֶף, Imp. apoc. Hiph. r. רפה.
הִרְצָת, Hiph. 3 pret. f. r. רצה, Lev. xxvi. 34.

הֲרָרִי, see הר: it. Patronym. *An inhabitant of the mountains* or *mountainous country,* 2 Sam. xxiii. 33.

הָשֵׁב, Imp. Hiph. r. שׁוּב, Is. xlii. 22.
הָשֵׁם, for הוֹשֵׁם, or הֻשַּׁם, Hoph. r. שׁמם.

הַשְׁמָעוּת, f. r. שׁמע, Gram. art. 160. fm. IV. *Hearing,* Ezek. xxiv. 26, al. non occ.

הוֹשַׁע, Imp. apoc. Hiph. r. שָׁעָה, or שָׁעַע.
הִשְׁתַּחֲוָה, Hithp. r. שָׁחָה.
הִשְׁתַּעְשַׁע, Hithp. r. שָׁעַע.
הֲתָבוּתָךְ, Inf. Aph. aff. Chald. r. תוב.
הִתּוּךְ, m. r. נתך, *Melting,* as metal in the fire, Ezek. xxii. 22, al. non occ.
הִתְחַל, Imp. Hithp. apoc. r. חָלָה.
הֵתָיו, Imp. Hiph. r. אָתָה.
הֲתִיסָךְ, Inf. Hiph. aff. r. תָּמַם.
הֵתֵל, v. pres. יַהְתֵל and תֵּהֲתֵלּוּ, constr. med. בְּ, it. abs. Cognn. Arab. خَتَلَ, *decepit.* حَتَلَ, *conditionem illius depravavit.* هَتَرَ, *amentem reddidit.* هِتْرٌ, *mendacium.* عَتَلَ, *violenter traxit.* عَطَلَ, *otiosus fuit.*

See also my note on Job xvii. 2. Much dispute exists as to what the form and origin of this verb is, all originating solely from its irregular punctuation. The elder grammarians took it as in Pihel. Gesenius and Ewald will have it to be a new Hiphhilic form, derived from חלל, *cast* or *throw.* Still it is irregular, and nothing is gained by this roundabout process. If we suppose the root to be هَتَلَ, see my note l. c., and point the word afresh, as if in Kal, all will be regular enough. *Deluded, deceived,* Gen. xxxi. 7; Judg. xvi. 10. 15; 1 Kings xviii. 27; Job xii. 9; Jer. ix. 4.
Infin. הָתֵל, Exod. viii. 25; Job xiii. 9.
Part. pass. pl. m. הֲתֻלִּים, or הֲתָלִים, Job xvii. 2. See my note. *Tears, weeping;* usually *delusions, "provocation."*
Puh. הוּתַל, for הֻתַּל, *Deceived,* r. Arab. تَالَ, *infortunium,* تَوْلٌ, تَالٌ, *desipuit, fatuus fuit.* In this case, Hoph. Is. xliv. 20.

הִתְנַבּוּת, Inf. Hithp. r. נבא.

הֵתַר, v. pres. Pih. 2d pers. pl. m. תְּהוֹתָתוּ, once, Ps. lxii. 4. Arab. هَتَّ, *promptè et egregiè retulit dictum; effudit.* هَتَنَت, *volubili lingua fuit.* هَتَنَ, *celeriter effudit nubes pluviam; iniquus fuit.* LXX. ἐπιτίθεσθε. Syr. ܐܢܕܠܘ, *concitamini.* Targ. מִתְרַגְּשִׁין, *fremitis. Attack unjustly,* either in words or deeds.

ו

ו, *Waw, vaw*, or *vav*, the sixth letter of the Hebrew alphabet; the ἐπίσημον βαῦ, or digamma (ϝ) of the Greeks; also, as a numeral, the number *Six*, Gram. art. 4. Its ancient pronunciation — as is that of its Arabian equivalent (و) — was most probably that of our *W;* which will account for several changes which take place with this letter in the etymology. See Gram. artt. 87. 1, 2. On its etymology and usage, see Gram. art. 173, et seq.; 175. 12, et seq.; 242. 11, et seq.

As being of the same organ with ב, פ, מ, it will occasionally represent one of them in cognate words, Gram. artt. 23; 78. 1, &c.

It will, as well as certain other letters, occasionally lose its power as a consonant, coalescing with the sound of the preceding vowel, Gram. artt. 37—39; 87. 1, 2.

Its copulative powers, as a conjunction, will be found abundantly exemplified in Noldius, p. 282, et seq., while it must appear to every one, capable of generalizing in any degree, that it never could have been necessary to assign *seventy-four* different meanings to this little word!

The modern Jewish Grammarians—from whom all our early grammars were mere transcripts—with whom is Gesenius, M. the Baron de Sacy, &c. assign, moreover, to this letter, as a conjunction, the power also of *converting the preterite tense* of a verb into *the future;* and *the future* (as they term it), i. e. the present, *into the preterite*. Gesenius tells us, after Michaelis, that וַיִּקְטֹל, is only an abbreviated form of הָיָה יִקְטֹל; that the first ה is, like the Syr. in ܩܛܠ ܗܘܐ, suppressed; it is then וָה יִקְטֹל; which, again, as וָה is contracted into מָה, we have, accordingly, וַיִּקְטֹל. The appeal to the Syriac here is inadmissible, because it is only in certain idiomatic cases that the ܗ, ה, is so suppressed; and these do not exist in the Hebrew: besides, this specific combination is quite unknown to the Syriac. And, again, if this be the true solution of the case with יִקְטֹל, how will it also account for that in which the preterite is said to be converted into a future? e. g. Is, וְקָטַל, put for הָיָה קָטַל? And, once more, הָיָה, not הָוָה, is the true Hebrew form!

This theory, too, takes it for granted that יִקְטֹל is a real future tense; which is false. See Gram. art. 231. 10, et seq.; and אָמוּת, יָנִיחַ, אֶשְׁקוֹשׁ, אֵינֶךָ, אֶעֱנָק, Job iii. 11, et seq. To which a multitude of others might be added. The same may be said of the corresponding tense in all the dialects.

Nor, again, will the context in very many instances bear the application of any such conversive power in this particle, even supposing this tense to be a future. So תְּהִי הַמִּשְׂרָה, Is. ix. 5; ib. וַיִּקְרָא: it. 10, וַיֵּשֶׁב: 11, וַיִּתְאַבְּכוּ, וַתִּצַּת, 15; וַיְהִי, וַיִּכְרֵת, 13; וַיֹּאכַל מָגוֹר, 18; וַיְהִי, 19: all of which must be preterites if this doctrine be true; while it is obvious, from the context, that they are all to be taken as futures. Innumerable instances of this description may be adduced, which cannot be desired by those who prefer truth to prejudiced notions: to others they will be useless.

Again, if this particle has the power of thus absolutely altering the tenses of verbs, the same must of necessity be true, perhaps, of every one of the conjunctions, and many of the adverbs; which, it is remarkable, has never occurred to these Grammarians. E. g. אוֹ, in אוֹ יַבְדִּיל, אוֹ יַגֵּר, Deut. iv. 41. Josh. x. 12, &c. אַחַר, Num. iii. 23. אֲשֶׁר, Gen. vi. 4. אַחַת, 1 Kings x. 22, with תָּבוֹא, &c. אֵיכָה יַעֲבְדוּ, Deut. xii. 30, &c. &c. The Concordance of Noldius will supply instances innumerable.

Nor is the preterite tense, preceded by ו, always to be taken in the sense of a future; e. g. וְאָמַרְתִּי, Job vii. 4; וְשָׁבַעְתִּי, &c. The truth is, these usages depend upon principles altogether different from those proposed by these Grammarians.

Mr. Ewald has taken a better view of this subject. He has made this particle both *conjunctive* and *relative* in its application; but, as he has left the usage of the tenses quite undefined, these *conjunctive* and *relative* powers of the particle labour under great uncertainty. Still, he has had good sense and courage enough to get rid of Michaelis's הָיָה יִקְטֹל, together with the *conversive* system of the rabbies; which is doing much. The main fault under which he labours is, that not daring to avow the real *Oriental usage* of the tenses, he has been forced to have recourse to reasoning of a most involved and indecisive description, where the simplest statements would otherwise have served his purpose.

If any reliance, then, can be placed either on the inductions of Mr. Ewald, or of myself, the distinctions hitherto observed between וְ and וַ, are of no essential value : the context always sufficing to show,—or else the forms of the verbs,—when the particle is to be taken as a simple conjunction, or otherwise. For, even, if we have recourse to the Arabic, and suppose that וְ is ‏ = to ‏وَ; and וַ = to ‏فَ: still it is the fact, that either of these particles may be used *relatively*, if not also as simple conjunctions.

As it is now placed beyond doubt, that the Hebrew tense, formerly termed *the future*, is an indefinite, or unlimited, *present ; i. e.* expresses the action, &c. of the verb as *present* with any time intimated by the context; and, as the preterite does, according to Oriental usage, even now, imply *futurity* in prophetical and other similar enouncements; no possible difficulty can remain in discovering—as it is the case with the Arabic, &c.—how the tenses ought to be taken, or how this particle is to be applied. And, if our *indefinite present* should happen to be connected by it with a preceding preterite, and so make its action, &c. contemporaneous with that of this preterite; then, indeed, and in that acceptation, it might fairly be called *conversive* of such present tense, to that of such preterite : but even then, *restrictive* would be a better term. Ewald prefers *relative*.

Now, unless I am greatly mistaken, THIS is the sense in which David Kimchi uses the term וָו הַהִפּוּךְ, *vaw conversivum*, in the Mikhlol, or Hebrew Grammar, composed by him.*   And, it is remarkable, he there

---

* The passage of Kimchi is this (fol. מה verso)—.... ועתיד במקום עבר כמו אָז יָשִׁיר משֶׁה וכתב החכם רבי אברהם אבן עזרא כי כן המשפט בלשון ישמעאל וכתב כי כן יתכן לדבר בהם בלשון העומד והוא כדרך יְכַסֶּה פָנָיו׳ וַיְנוּעוּ אַמּוֹת הַסִּפִּים׳ בעבור כי אין בלשון סימן לזמן אמצעי ידברו בו בלשון עבר ועתיד בלשון לעו פרי״אה והוא זמן עומד לעבר או פרי״אה הוא לזמן עומד לעתיד.   De Balmes, too, speaks very much in the style of Ewald, on the use of the future (our present tense) when used as an imperfect, and cites Is. vi. 4, הַבַּיִת יִמָּלֵא עָשָׁן; and Job i. 5, כָּכָה יַעֲשֶׂה אִיּוֹב כָּל־הַיָּמִים, in neither of which is the *conversive vaw* to be found !

appeals to Aben Ezra, as comparing its usage with that of the Arabic : and to his own native language, the Spanish, as having a similar one.   It is, moreover, extremely doubtful whether De Balmes, who lived about two centuries after Kimchi, had ever heard of the absolute *conversive vaw*, of, the modern Jews, Dr. Gesenius, &c.   The truth apparently is, the modern Jews, with their very learned and laborious follower, John Buxtorf, and others, had the misfortune not to understand Kimchi; and hence all the turmoil about this little troublesome particle ! For, certain it is, that if Aben Ezra and Kimchi understood this particle, as their words above imply, all they could have intended must have been, that it had a sort of *relative*, but *no positive, conversive power* whatsoever.   See also Gram. art. 173. 10. Ewald's " Kritische Grammatik," edit. 1827, p. 539, note.   It. Nicholson's Translation, pp. 166, et seq.; 374, et seq.

Generally, this particle is used—

(a) To couple together words, phrases,

It is, moreover, a very extraordinary thing that neither the Arabs—who write everlastingly on grammar,—the Syrians, the Samaritans, or Æthiopians—all of whom have constructions and usages parallel to this of the Hebrews—should ever have so much as once dreamt of this *conversive vaw*.   And, if it be argued that the *Arabic* ‏لَمْ, ‏لَمَّا, and ‏لَا, exercise a similar conversive power ; my answer will be, Yes ; and so does almost every other adverb, pronoun, &c. of the language,—*relatively*, not *absolutely*—just as it does in the Hebrew, as a very little inquiry will prove.   E. g. ‏كَانُوا يَكْفُرُونَ وَيَقْتُلُونَ ‏النَّبِيِّينَ, *they disbelieved and slew the prophets.* ‏كَفَرُوا فَيَقُولُونَ, *they disbelieved and said.* ‏ثُمَّ يُحَرِّفُونَهُ, *then they corrupted it.* ‏لَا تَهْوَى أَنْفُسُكُمْ, *your souls desired not.* ‏وَ, ‏فَ, ‏لَمْ يَرَ, *he saw not.*   Where we have ‏ثُمَّ, ‏لَا, ‏لَمْ, as good *conversive* particles as ever was the favoured וְ of the Hebrews: and yet the blindness of the Arabs has been such as never to have seen this,—as the good modern Jews have.   As to ‏لَمْ and ‏لَمَّا — when the ‏مُضَارِع, or *relative present tense* following, is to be taken as a preterite (which is by no means universal) — some intimation is always given in the context, that the time of the action, &c. is past, not present.

sentences, periods, paragraphs, &c. either similar, or similarly intended. See Gen. xiv. 18; Exod. xxv. 4; Ps. cxix. 120, &c. &c. See Nold. p. 282, et seq. It.—

(b) To mark the subsequent members of conditional, subjunctive, hypothetical, or other similar, constructions with verbs apocopated, or having the paragogic ה, or ן, or not. See Gram. artt. 233, et seq.; 234, et seq.; 235. 3. And under one or other of these heads may every instance occurring be placed; giving such slight variation of meaning to the particle, viz. *and, moreover, but, then; so, &c.* as the context may require.

וָהֵב, Num. xxi. 14. LXX. Ζωόβ. The Syr. seems to have read לַהַב, *flame*. The passage seems to be a citation from a book now lost, given in illustration of what is there said about the gift of a well. וְהֵב, Arab. وَهَبَ, *dedit*, is therefore probably the name given to the place in which this well was situated, and, as Clericus thinks, the same with מַתָּן, ib. v. 18. Some MSS. have אתחב in one word: but this is manifestly erroneous. See the Schol. Crit. p. 15, of De Rossi, it. Rosenm. in loco. In the Kāmoos we have وَهْبِين, given as the name of a place, and, مَوْهَبَة, as the name of a fortress in *Senaa*: whence it should seem that it was not unusual to give such names to places.

וָו, m. pl. וָוִים, constr. וָוֵי, *Hooks*, or *pins*, affixed to the heads of the standards or pillars of the Tabernacle, Exod. xxvii. 10, 11. 17; xxxviii. 10—12. 17. 28. Aff. וָוֵיהֶם, ib. xxvi. 32. 37. LXX. varie, οἱ κρίκοι, αἱ ἀγκύλαι, αἱ κεφαλίδες.

וָזָר, m. once, Prov. xxi. 8. Arab. وَزَرَ, *crimine gravatus est*. Act. *commisit crimen, &c*. Lit. *loaded*. Comp. Is. i. 4; liii. 11; Ps. xxxviii. 5. *Grievous, heavily, laden, sinner*. Formerly taken as if זָר+ן, *and a foreigner*, and hence *a sinner*.

וָלָד, see יֶלֶד, m. *Son, progeny*, Gen. xi. 30; 2 Sam. vi. 23, keri; kethiv. יֶלֶד: al. non occ.

ז

ז, *Zayin*, the seventh letter of the Hebrew alphabet; as a numeral also the number *seven*, Gram. art. 4; pronounced as our z. Arab. and Pers. ز. Of the same organ with ס, שׁ, שׂ, צ, Gram. art. 23. 4: with most, or all, of which it is found to interchange in cognate words. Ib. art. 78. 4.

זְאֵב, m. pl. זְאֵבִים, constr. זְאֵבֵי. Syr. ܕܐܒܐ. Arab. ذِئْب, *lupus*, Hieroz. Bochart. i. lib. iii. c. x. *A wolf*, Gen. xlix. 27; Is. xi. 6; lxv. 25; Jer. v. 6; Ezek. xxii. 27. זְאֵבֵי עֶרֶב, *of the evening*, because accustomed to prowl and destroy during the night, Hab. i. 8; Zeph. iii. 3. The λύκοι νυκτερινοί, or νυκτιπόροι, &c. of the Greeks. See Bochart. l. c.

זֹאת, pron. f. of זֶה, which see.

זָבַד, m. once, Gen. xxx. 20. Arab. زَبَدَ الزَّبَدُ مَحْرَكَةً للماء وغيره, with a vowel on the middle rad. (used) *of water, &c*. it is also used signifying the *foam* of milk, water, the sea, &c.; also, *donum, munus*. Whence it is probable that allusion is made to *Conception*. Comp. Job x. 10; Num. xxiv. 7; Is. xlviii. 1; Prov. v. 15—18. *A gift*.

זֶבֶד, v. aff. זְבָדַנִי, *Hath given me, endowed me with*; once, Gen. xxx. 30; with זֵד, which see. Constr. immed. LXX. Δεδώρηται ὁ θεός μοι δῶρον καλόν. Syr. ܝܗܒ ܠܝ ܐܠܗܐ, *dotavit me Deus dote*. Hence often occurring in proper names, as in 1 Chron. ii. 36, &c. *Zebedee, &c*.

זְבוּב, m. pl. constr. זְבוּבֵי. Arab. ذُبَاب, *musca; apis*. Syr. ܕܒܒܐ, *musca*. *A fly, bee*, Is. vii. 18. זְבוּבֵי מָוֶת, *flies of death*. Dead flies, according to some; flies inflicting death, i. e. poisonous, as others think, Eccl. x. 1. בַּעַל זְבוּב, lit. *fly-god*, *Baalzebub*, a deity worshipped at Ekron, 2 Kings i. 2. Josephus, as cited by Selden. de Diis Syris, p. 301, et seq. τὸν Ἀκκάρων θεὸν Μυίαν. The Μυίαγρος, Ἀπόμυιος, and Μυοκτόνος of heathen writers. Plin. H. N. lib. x. c. xxviii. " Cyreniaci *Achorem* Deum (invocant) muscarum multitudine pestilentiam afferente, quæ protinus intereunt postquam litatum est illi Deo." So Selden. But the Delph. Ed. Valpy, "Invocant"... et Elei Myiagron Deum, muscarum, &c. See also the note.

זְבוּל, and זְבֻל, m. ⎫
זְבֻלָה, f. ⎭ pl. non occ.

Cogn. Arab. دَوَل, pret. دَالَ, i. q. דָּאַר, conversa fuit; vi. conj. تَدَاوَلَ, ultro, citroque versavit. Comp. دَارْ, whence دَارْ, domus, it. Syr. ܥܰܠ, ingressus est. Lit. inhabited. Habitation; place of residence, 1 Kings viii. 13; 2 Chron. vi. 2; Ps. xlix. 15; Is. lxiii. 15; Hab. iii. 11. עָמַד וְזָבֻלָה stood fast, or still (in its) habitation. If ה is the aff. pron. fem. here—as usually taken—it ought to have mappik הּ: and then a difficulty will arise, as to what it refers as its antecedent.

זֶבַח, m. pl. זְבָחִים, once, f. זְבָחוֹת; constr. וְזִבְחֵי. Syr. ܕܶܒܚܳܐ, sacrificium. Arab. فَجَع, quod mactatur. I. Slaughter. II. Meton. The thing slaughtered, and offered in sacrifice, the flesh of which was in many cases eaten as a feast. See בְּרִית. Hence, I. applied to the slaughter of men, Is. xxxiv. 6; Jer. xlvi. 10; Ezek. xxxix. 17. II. These sacrifices were of various kinds: (a) עֹלָה, or כָּלִיל, which was raised to the altar, and entirely burnt. This was expiatory, Gen. viii. 20; xxii. 3. 6; xlvi. 1; Exod. xxix. 18; Lev. i. 13, &c. often added in this case, לְרֵיחַ נִיחֹחַ, for a placatory savour; i. e. to propitiate God. Such were offered even by the patriarchs, Job i. 5; xlii. 8, &c. as cited above. See Outram on the Sacrifices. Comp. Gen. iv. 4; Heb. xi. 4.

(b) זֶבַח־פֶּסַח, Paschal sacrifice, which was roasted and eaten, Exod. xii. 27; xxxiv. 28, &c.

(c) זֶבַח שְׁלָמִים, Peace-offering, part of which was burnt, Lev. iii. 1, et seq. which was also propitiatory.

(d) Sometimes Eucharistical, עַל תּוֹדָה Lev. vii. 11, 12, et seq.; xxii. 28, &c. where it will be seen that certain cakes and unleavened bread were superadded.

(e) A vow, or free-will offering, נֶדֶר אוֹ נְדָבָה of this sort was that of Jephtha, Judg. xi. 30, et seq.; styled, תְּרוּמָה, קָרְבָּן, or קָרְבָּנוּ, זֶבַח

offering, or sacrifice of his offering, Lev. vii. 15, 16. 32, &c.

(f) זֶבַח מִשְׁפָּחָה, Of a family, 1 Sam. xx. 29. Comp. Ib. ix. 12, 13; xvi. 5.

(g) זֶבַח הַיָּמִים, Of the days; probably of the seven days appointed to be observed in each of the great feasts.

In early times the מִנְחָה, and זֶבַח, seem to have meant the same thing, Gen. iv. 4; in after times the former was restricted to unbloody offerings. See sub voce, and Jahn, Archaeologia Biblica, cap. iv. § 373, et seq. Aff. זְבָחֶיךָ, זְבָחֵימוֹ, זִבְחֵיהֶם, וּזְבָחָיו.

זָבַח, v. pres. יִזְבַּח, constr. immed. it. abs. it. med. לְ, to whom, עַל, upon which, מִן, of, from, which. I. Slaughtered, as for sacrifice, Gen. xxxi. 54; 1 Sam. xxviii. 24; 1 Kings xix. 21; Ezek. xxxix. 17. II. Sacrificed, 1 Kings viii. 63; xiii. 2; Exod. xx. 24; Deut. xii. 21; xvi. 2; Gen. xlvi. 1; Num. xxii. 40; 1 Kings xix. 21; Ps. cvi. 37, &c.

Infin. זְבֹחַ, 1 Sam. xv. 15, &c. Aff. זִבְחוֹ, 2 Sam. xv. 12.

Imp. זְבַח, Ps. L. 14: pl. זִבְחוּ, Exod. viii. 21.

Part. זֹבֵחַ, pl. זֹבְחִים, 1 Sam. ii. 15; Lev. xvii. 5.

Pih. זִבַּח, and זִבֵּחַ, pres. יְזַבֵּחַ, Sacrificed, habitually, 2 Chron. xxxiii. 22; Ps. cvi. 38; Hos. xii. 12; Heb. i. 16; 2 Kings xvi. 4; Hos. iv. 13, &c.

Infin. זַבֵּחַ, 1 Kings xii. 32.

Part. מְזַבֵּחַ, 1 Kings iii. 3. מְזַבְּחִים, Ib. 2, &c.: pl. f. מְזַבְּחוֹת, Ib. xi. 8.

זָבַל, v. pret. non occ. pres. aff. יִזְבְּלֵנִי, He will reside (with) me, Gen. xxx. 20. See וְזָבַל above. See also זְבוּל, al. non occ.

זְבֻל, see וְזָבַל.

זָבְנִין, m. pl. Chald. part. Syr. ܙܒܢ, vendidit. Usually, Gaining, i. e. the time, Dan. ii. 8, al. non occ. But, as ܙܒܢ, also signifies time, Whiling away, i. e. delaying, the time might be the meaning of the passage.

זָג, m. Num. vi. 4, al. non occ. Samar. זגנ, puritas. Arab. زُجَاج, vitrum. The pellucid skin of the grape.

זֵד, m. pl. זֵדִים, r. זוד. Arab. زَيْد, accessio, for זָוֵד, or זֵיד, Gram. art. 75, and hence (··) is immutable. Lit. excessive. Proud, haughty, Prov. xxi. 24; Is. xiii. 11; Jer. xliii. 2; Ps. xix. 14; cxix. 21, &c.

זדו (167) זהם

זָדוֹן, m. constr. זְדוֹן, *Pride, haughtiness;* meton. *Insolence.* See זֵד; or, from a cogn. זדה, if the vowels may be depended on, Jer. xlix. 16; Prov. xi. 2; xiii. 10; xxi. 24; Obad. vr. 3; Deut. xvii. 12. Meton. Jer. L. 31, 32. Aff. זְדֹנְךָ, 1 Sam. xvii. 28.

זֶה
זֹה } m. pron. demons. f. זֹאת. *This,*
זוֹ   Gram. art. 176. With prepp. בָּזֶה,
זֻ   כָּזֶה, לָזֶה, מִזֶּה; art. הַזֶּה. See Nold.,
     p. 331, et seq.; applied either to
     persons or things.

(a) Used as *the subject* of a proposition, זֶה יְנַחֲמֵנוּ, this (man) *will comfort us,* Gen. v. 9; Exod. xv. 2; Judg. iv. 14, &c. Emphatic, when the predicate has the article, as, זֶה הַדָּבָר, *This* (is) THE *word,* Exod. xxxv. 4. LXX. τοῦτο τὸ ῥῆμα, 2 Kings vi. 19; Ps. cxviii. 20, &c. With הוּא, 1 Chron. xxii. 1.

(b) *Distributively, hoc, illud.* Esth. iv. 5; Exod. xiv. 20; 1 Kings xxii. 10; Is. vi. 3; Ps. lxxv. 8, &c. When occurring once only in such cases, *This, hic,* i. e. the nearest, or last mentioned, 1 Sam. xvii. 34. וְנָשָׂא זֶה, *and this,* (i. e. the bear) *took.* Comp. Ib. xvii. 12, where הַזֶּה refers to אֲמָרְתִּי, not to דָּוִד.

(c) Emph. *This same, very.* זֶה סִינַי, Judg. v. 5, &c. It. by way of contempt, Exod. xxxii. 1; 1 Kings xx. 7, &c.

(d) For אֲשֶׁר, Is. lxiii. 1; Ps. lxxiv. 2; civ. 8; Prov. xxiii. 22; Job xxxviii. 2, &c. Gram. art. 177. 2.

(e) May be translated occasionally by *such,* Deut. v. 26; Dan. x. 17, &c.

(f) Implying time, Gen. xxxi. 41; Num. xiv. 22; Judg. xvi. 15, &c.

(g) Time or place, *adverbially.* וְהָיָה זֶה שָׁלוֹם, *And* (there) *shall be at this* (time), i. e. NOW, *peace,* Mic. v. 4. See 1 Kings xviii. 24. Comp. Ruth ii. 7; 1 Kings xvii. 24; Gen. xxvii. 6; Judg. xviii. 4; 2 Sam. xi. 25, &c. בָּזֶה, *in this,* i. e. place, Gen. xxviii. 17; Num. xiii. 17. מִזֶּה, *hence,* Gen. xxxvii. 17; Exod. xi. 1. מִזֶּה וּמִזֶּה, *from this, and from that* part, quarter, Num. xxii. 24; Josh. viii. 33.

זָהָב, m.—pl. non occ. constr. זְהַב, once, זָהָב. Arab. ذَهَبٌ. Syr. ܕܗܒܐ, *aurum.* Gold, Gen. ii. 12; probably that termed ἄπυρος, by the Greeks. See my Job, p. 55; Gen. xxiv. 22. 53. With a numeral preceding, עֶשְׂרָה זָהָב, *twenty* (shekels of) *gold,*

Ib. Gram. art. 227. 6. In Job xxxvii. 22, taken usually to signify *fair weather,* by some the *sun.* See my note on this place. In Zech. iv. 12, supposed to signify pure and brilliant oil; but, הַזָּהָב, here, more likely refers to *the candlestick* generally, i. e. הַמְּנוֹרָה, in vr. 11 preceding; and vr. 12 to this place is perhaps parenthetical. See Gram. art. 241. 18. Aff. זְהָבִי, זְהָבְךָ, זְהָבוֹ, זְהָבָם.

זָהַם, v. in Kal. non occ.
Pih. זִהַם, in זִהֲמַתּוּ, for זִהֲמַתְהוּ, Gram. art. 208; Job xxxiii. 20. *Abhorreth it.* Arab. زَهِمَ, *fœtuit.* See my note on the place.

זֹהַר, m.—pl. non occ. Arab. زُهَرَةٌ, *candor; stella* veneris. Syr. ܙܗܪܐ, *lux. splendor. Brightness, brilliancy,* as of a precious stone, or the heavens in the full effulgence of the sun, Ezek. viii. 2; Dan. xii. 3.

זָהַר, v. non occ. in Kal.
Hiph. הִזְהִיר, pres. pl. m. יַזְהִירוּ, constr. immed. it. med. אֶת; it. מִן, from what, whom. I. *Enlighten, give light;* hence, II. *admonish, warn.* I. Exod. xviii. 20; 2 Chron. xix. 10: II. Lev. xv. 31; 2 Kings vi. 10; Ezek. iii. 17—20; xxxiii. 9. In Dan. xii. 3, יַזְהִרוּ, *shall give light,* not "*shine.*" Comp. Gen. i. 16; Ps. cxxxvi. 9. Comp. Matt. xiii. 43.... ὡς ὁ ἥλιος.
Infin. הַזְהִיר, Ezek. iii. 18; xxxiii. 8.
Niph. נִזְהָר, pres. non occ. *Became, was, admonished, warned,* Ps. xix. 12. Constr. בְּ, instr. it. abs., Ezek. iii. 21; xxxiii. 4—6; in pause, נִזְהָר, in these last instances.
Infin. הִזָּהֵר, Eccl. iv. 13.
Imp. הִזָּהֵר, Ib. xii. 12.

זְהִירִין, Chald. m. pl. *Admonished, cautioned,* Ezra iv. 22.

זִו, m. i. q. זִיו, which see. The name of the second month of the Hebrew year, 1 Kings vi. 1. 37. The same with אִיָּר, Syr. ܐܝܪ, and Arab. أَيَّار. And, if the year was with the Hebrews originally solar—of which perhaps there can be no doubt (see my Sermon on the Sabbath, 2d edit. notes, p. 26)—this month would regularly commence on the thirty-first day after the sun had entered Aries. On the Jewish mode of calculating time, see Scaliger, de Emendatione Temporum, or Relandi Antiquitates, Vet. Heb., Pars. iv., and under חֹדֶשׁ below.

זוּ } See זֶה, and Nold. p. 336.
זוּ }
זוּ }

זוֹב, m.—pl. non occ. Seg. for זָוָב, Gram. art. 87. 1. Arab. زَوْبٌ, *fluxus* aquæ. Cogn. ذَوْبٌ, *liquefactio*. Syr. ܕܘܒܐ, id. *Issue, discharge*, of blood, &c. Lev. xv. 2, 3. 13. 15. 25. 30. Aff. זוֹבוֹ, זוֹבָהּ.

זוּב, v. pret. non occ. pres. יָזוּב, r. זוב. Constr. abs. it. med. עַל. *Issues, flows*, (a) as water, Ps. lxxviii. 20; cv. 41; Is. xlviii. 21.
(b) Blood, Lev. xv. 19. 25.
(c) Semen virile, Lev. xv. 2. 4; xxii. 4; Num. v. 2, &c.
(d) Meton. *Waste away, expire*, Lam. iv. 9.
(e) It. meton. *Abound, overflow with*, Exod. iii. 8: *milk and honey*, Ib. 17; xiii. 5; xxxiii. 3, &c.
Part. זָב, f. זָבָה, constr. זָבַת, Lev. xv. 2; xxii. 4; Num. v. 2, &c.; Lev. xv. 15; f. particularly in the phrase, זָבַת חָלָב וּדְבָשׁ, Exod. iii. 8, &c.

זָדָה, pret. f.—pres. non. occ. Arab. زَيَدَ, *accessio*, &c.: and hence, perhaps, the notion of *boiling*; the same word as *seethe*, as both Castell and Gesenius think. Comp. נבע. Arab. نَبَعَ, and نَبَغَ. Constr. med. עַל, אֶל. *Swell, act insolently*, against, Exod. xviii. 11; Jer. l. 29.
Hiph. הֵזִיד, pres. יָזִיד. Constr. abs. it. med. עַל, i. q. Kal. I. *Behave, act, insolently; swell*, against; *presume*, Neh. ix. 10. 16. 29; Exod. xxi. 14; Deut. i. 43; xvii. 13; xviii. 20.
II. *Boiled*, apoc. וַיָּזֶד יַעֲקֹב נָזִיד, Gen. xxv. 29. On נָזִיד, see in its place.
Aph. Chald. הַזִדָה, Infin. i. q. Heb. Dan. v. 20.

זָוִיּוֹת, pl. f.—sing. non occ. Syr. ܙܘܝܬܐ, *angulus*. Arab. زَاوِيَة, id. r. זוה. *An angle*, or *corner*, of any thing built, as of the altar or Temple, Zech. ix. 15; Ps. cxliv. 12. *Our daughters*, זָוִיּוֹת מְחֻטָּבוֹת, *like the hewn corners*, &c. i. e. as the angles were so bound together as at once to supply both strength and beauty to the edifice, so may our daughters be the patterns of *virtue* and beauty. Comp. אֵשֶׁת חַיִל, Ruth iii. 11; and Gram. art. 216. 9; it.

Prov. xii. 4; xxxi. 10: not imitating the sculptured Caryatides of the Grecian buildings, as Gesenius thinks; for these represented that people as in slavery, supporting the heavy entablatures of their structures. Much less like those of the Egyptians, which manifestly represented heathenish notions, al. non occ.

זוּלַת, f. in constr. of זוּלָה. Arab. زَوَال, *removing, setting aside*. Prep. *Besides, except*, זוּלַת דַּלַּת עַם, *besides the small* (poor) *of the people*, 2 Kings xxiv. 14. Aff. זוּלָתִי, Is. xlv. 5; Hos. xiii. 4. With י parag. Deut. i. 36; iv. 12, &c.; זוּלָתְךָ, in pause; זוּלָתָהּ, Ruth iv. 4; 2 Sam. vii. 21, &c. See Nold., p. 336, et seq.

זוֹנָה, f. pl. זֹנוֹת. } Syr. Chald. ܙܢܝ, *ciba-*
זוּנָה, m. pl. זוּנִים. } *vit; aluit*. Cogn. ارمۦ, *armavit*. Arab. زَانَ, r. زين, *ornavit, compsit*. Chald. זְנָה, *negotiatus est*. Pah. *scortatus est*. Syr. id. Arab. زَنَى, *scortatus est*. The progress of the notion here is, from feeding, to adorning; thence to fornication. Comp. Prov. ix. 17; Jer. v. 7, 8. Hence, I. *An innkeeper, hostess*, Josh. ii. 1. So from περάω, *vendo*, πόρνη; *fæmina quæ corpus suum prostituit et veluti vendit*. Fornication is, therefore, a secondary sense in each case. See also Thes. Steph. under πόρνος; and אֶתְנָן above.
II. *A woman addicted to prostitution*, (a) in the proper sense of that term, Gen. xxxviii. 15; Deut. xxiii. 19; Lev. xxi. 7; Judg. xi. 1; Num. xxv. 1.
(b) Metaph. *Man, woman, &c*. spiritually; i. e. *given to idolatry*, Hos. iv. 15; Lev. xvii. 7; xx. 5; Num. xv. 39; Ezek. vi. 9; xx. 30; Ps. lxxiii. 27.

זוּנָח, for זָנָה. Puh. r. זָנָה.

זָוָעָה, f.—pl. non occ. r. זוע. Syr. ܙܘ, *movit, commovit*. Arab. زَاعَ, r. زوع, *inflexit rem*; cogn. زَاغَ, *deflexit*; زَعْزَعَ, *jactura. Agitation, commotion*, Is. xxviii. 19; Deut. xxviii. 25; Jer. xv. 4; xxiv. 9; xxix. 18; xxxiv. 17. With בְּ, Ezek. xxiii. 46. "Keri ubique exhibet formam זַעֲוָה," Gesenius, which is incorrect.

זוּע, v. pret. זָע, pres. pl. m. יָזוּעַ, *Moved, was agitated*, Esth. v. 9; Eccl. xii. 3. Constr. abs. it. med. מִן, by whom, al. non occ.

Part. וְאָזְנִים, and וְזָעִים, m. pl. *moving*, in commotion, Dan. v. 19; vi. 27, al. non occ. Pih. redup. part. pl. m. Aff. מְזַעְזְעָיִךְ, *Thy agitators: persons vexing thee*, Hab. ii. 7.

זֹרְחָה, f.—for זוּרְחָה, r. זור. Part. fm. פְּקֻדָה, or it might be, for זָרָה, seg. Gram. art. 87. 2, signifying *Compression*; in the other case, *Compressed, broken*. That הָ‍־ is an error, for הַ‍־, there can be no doubt, as Gesenius has also remarked (and as in לָנָה, Zech. v. 4)—once only, Is. lix. 5.

זוּר, v. pret. non occ. pres. זָר (as if r. זור), it. f. aff. תְּזוּרָה. Cogn. צוּר, צרר. Syr. ܐܘܙ, ܐܘܙ, *manu cepit.* Arab. زَوَرَ, i. q. جَوْر, *iniquitas, violentia.* Cogn. زَيْر, *labio presso equum stitit.*

I. *Compressed, squeezed;* meton. *broke*, Judg. vi. 38; Job xxxix. 15. See my note on this place. Constr. abs. it. med. אֶת.

Puh. (cogn. r. זָרָה), Gram. art. 109, *Have been compressed, bound* up as wounds, Is. i. 6. See, too, the verbs immediately following here, al. non occ.

II. pret. זָר, pres. non occ. Synon. τοῦ, סור, *Depart, recede:* comp. Arab. سَارَ, r. سور, *ascendit, &c.:* and, as violence and injury are generally supposed to be inflicted by strangers, so, perhaps, here, this word was applied to them. Comp. זָרָה, Prov. ii. 16; vii. 5, with נָכְרִיָה, ib. v. 20; vi. 24, &c. Constr. med. מִן, ל.

(a) *Departed, receded.* Synon. רחק, Job xix. 13; Ps. lxxviii. 30; Is. xxx. 24, and Ps. lviii. 4. זָרָה, and זוּר, perhaps. Puh. as above, Is. i. 6, *have been separated* as strangers. תָּעָה, *have wandered* in error, &c. al. non occ. as a verb.

(b) Part. זָר, f. זָרָה, once זָרָא, Num. xi. 20, *Strange, abominable; departing, receding,* hence, meton. *A stranger, foreigner; hostile:* pl. זָרִים, f. זָרוֹת, Exod. xxx. 33; Lev. xxii. 10. 12, 13, &c.

(d) As opposed to self, or to something belonging to self. לֹא זָר, *not a foreigner,* i. e. another person, Job xix. 15. 27; Prov. v. 10; xxvii. 2; Hos. viii. 12. Hence, זָר אֶל, *strange, foreign, god,* Ps. xliv. 21; lxxxi. 10.

(e) Hostile, Is. i. 7; xxv. 2. 5; lxi. 5; Jer. v. 19; li. 2, by *a Paranomasia*.

(f) *Adulterous, idolatrous,* Prov. ii. 16; v. 3; vii. 5; xxii. 14, &c.; Exod. xxx. 9; Lev. x. 1; Num. iii. 4; xxvi. 61; Hos. v. 7, &c.

(g) *Strange, unusual, new,* Is. xxviii. 21; Job xix. 17.

Niph. pl. m. זֹרוּ, *Been, became, receding falling off*, Is. i. 4, al. non occ.

Pih. pres. יְזוֹרֵר, *Sneezed.* "Sternutavit," says Gesenius, "quod fit muci particulas e naribus *dispergendo.*" 2 Kings iv. 35. Vulg oscitavit, yawned. So the Targ. and Syr LXX. συνέκαμψεν.

Hoph. part. מוּזָר, *Made separate;* allusion seems to be made to Gen. xlix. 26, נְזִיר אֶחָיו, Ps. lxix. 9.

זחח, v. in Kal, non occ. Arab. زَحَّ, زَحْزَحَ, *removit.* Cogn. نَزَحَ, *exhausit.*

Niph. pres. יִזַּח, *Be, become, removed, separated*, Exod. xxviii. 28; xxxix. 21, al. non occ.

זחל, v. pret. זָחַלְתִּי, Job xxxii. 6, only. Arab. زَحَلَ, *declinavit; retromansit in incessu camela. Withdrew, hesitated, tarried,* al. non occ. Cogn. Chald. דְחַל. Syr ܒܫܠ, *reveritus est.*

Part. pl. constr. m. זֹחֲלֵי, *Creepers, crawlers of —,* applied to serpents, Deut. xxxii. 24 Mic. vii. 17, al. non occ.

זֵידוֹנִים, m. pl. Synon. τοῦ, זָדוֹן; see also cogn. זָרָה, *Excessive, overwhelming,* Ps cxxiv. 5, al. non occ.

זִיו, m. Chald. Syr ܐܦܝܐ, *majestas.* Arab. زِيّ, *forma, habitus externus* rei *Majesty, splendour:* pl. *clear, healthy, appearance,* Dan. ii. 31; iv. 33; v. 6. 9, 10; vii. 28. Comp. הוֹדִי, Ib. x. 8. Aff. זִיוִי, וְזִיוַי, pl. זִיוַיָּא, דְּנָה, דִּי.

זִיו, m. Syr ܐܘܣܝܐ, *essentia.* οὐσία; ܐܘܣܝܐ, *superbia.* Arab. زَوْزِي, *contempsit* ; زَوْزَى, *vir prudens. Abundance, riches,* Is. lxvi. 11. Syr ܚܰܝܠܳܐ, *strength, power.* וְזִיו שָׂדַי, lit. *wealth of the plain,* for beasts *pasturing there,* Ps. L. 11. See vr. 9, et seq It. Ps. lxxx. 14, put metaph. apparently for the more powerful inhabitants of the country al. non occ.

זִיקוֹת, f. and זִיקִים, some MSS. וְזִיקִים, i. e. Dagesh resolved into a preceding perfect vowel, or *vice versâ.* Syr ܐܙܩܐ, *stellæ cadentes; lanceæ igneæ;* ܐܙܩܐ, *stellæ*

z

זית (170) זכח

volans. Arab. تَرَنَّى, *ornavit.* Cogn. زِرِنّ, *collare indusii.* See my note on Job xxx. 18. I. *Sparkling ornaments*, precious stones, perhaps, glittering like fire, worn probably as appendages of idolatry, Is. L. 11. מְאֻזָּרֵי זִיקוֹת, *cinctured with sparklings*, i. e. *ornaments*; hence, ib. assimilated to fire, אֵשׁ. Comp. Is. iii. 24; Prov. xxvi. 18. זִקִים חִצִים, perhaps the *lanceæ igneæ*, of the Syriac, *ignited*, or else *highly polished*, *missiles.* Comp. ברק, and דלק.
II. *Bonds, fetters*, Ps. cxlix. 8; Is. xlv. 14; Nahum iii. 10; Job xxxvi. 8. See my note. Gesenius gives here "Syr. ܐܡܕ, *telum, fulmen.*" On what authority? This question might be put in many other cases, without, as I suspect, any prospect of having a satisfactory answer.

זַיִת, m. constr. זֵית, pl. זֵיתִים. Syr. ܙܝܬܐ, *olea.* Æth. ዘይት: id. Arab. زَيت, *oleum*, pec. olivarum; زيتون, *oliva.* Originally from زبي, *splenduit.* زَيّ, *splendor*, according to Gesenius; but I can find no such words. زبي, indeed, occurs for *formam habuit;* but, what this can have to do with the origin of oil, I cannot see. See Cels. Hierob. ii. p. 331.
I. *The olive tree*, Gen. viii. 11; Exod. xxvii. 20; xxx. 24; Judg. ix. 9, &c. זֵית שֶׁמֶן, *Oil-olive*, Deut. viii. 8. שֶׁמֶן זַיִת, *oil of the olive tree*, Exod. ll. c. הַר הַזֵּיתִים, *Mount of Olives.* "Jam in V. T. sacer habitus," says Gesenius: but How is this to be proved? 2 Sam. xv. 30; 1 Kings xi. 7. In this latter place, indeed, Solomon made a high place, בָּמָה, here; but this was mere idolatry. עֵץ הַזַּיִת, *olive tree*, Hag. ii. 19; Zech. iv. 12. See שבל.
II. Meton. *The olive* fruit, Mic. vi. 15; מַעֲשֵׂה זַיִת, *produce of the olive*, Hab. iii. 17. It. נִצָּתוֹ, Job xv. 33. הוֹדוֹ, Hos. xiv. 7. Phr. יֶחֱטָב זָיִת, Deut. xxiv. 20. See חבט. נֹקֶף זַיִת, Is. xvii. 6; xxiv. 12. See נקף, Deut. xxviii. 40. See נשל. Aff. זֵיתֶךָ, in pause זֵיתָם, זֵיתֵיכֶם, זֵיתָם.

זַךְ, זָךְ, m.) r. זכך, which see. *Pure*, זַכָּה, f.) (a) as oil, frankincense, Exod. xxvii. 20; xxx. 34; Lev. xxiv. 2. 7.
(b) Metaph.—as the mind, conduct, &c. Job viii. 6; xi. 4; xvi. 17; xxxiii. 9; Prov. xvi. 2; xx. 11; xxi. 8.

זכה, v. pres. יִזְכֶּה, pret. non occ. Constr. abs. it. med. בְּ. Syr. ܙܟܐ, *justus est.* Cogn. زَكَا, *purus.* Arab. زَكَا, id. Applied, metaph. only. *Pure, just.* הַאֻמְנָם, *shall I be pure with*, &c., Mic. vi. 11; Ps. li. 6; Job xv. 14; xxv. 4.
Piḥ. *Make pure, clean.* זִכִּיתִי, 1st pers. pret. pres. יְזַכֶּה. Constr. immed. Ps. lxxiii. 13; Prov. xx. 9; Ps. cxix. 9, al. non occ.
Hithp. הִזַּכּוּ, Imp. for הִתְזַכּוּ, Gram. art. 83. 3. *Be, become, clean*, Is. i. 16.

זָכוּ, f. Chald. *Purity, innocence*, Dan. vi. 23, al. non occ. r. זכה.

זְכוּכִית, f. once, Job xxviii. 17. Syr. ܙܓܘܓܝܬܐ, *vitrum.* Arab. زُجَاج, id. See my note on the place. *Glass*, or *crystal*, r. זכך. Syr. and Arab. are mere corruptions.

זָכוּר, m. with aff. only, זְכוּרְךָ, r. זכר. *Male*, of man only, Exod. xxiii. 17; xxxiv. 23; Deut. xvi. 16; xx. 13.

זָכַךְ, v. נֻפוּ, 3 pers. pl. m. only. Cogn. זכה. Constr. abs. Lam. iv. 7; Job xv. 15; xxv. 5. See my note, *Are pure, clean, clear*, al. non occ.
Hiph. הֲזִכּוֹתִי, once, Job ix. 30. *Have cleansed.*

זֵכֶר, and זֶכֶר, m.—pl. non occ. prim. זָכַר. Arab. ذَكَرَ, *recordatio.* Syr. ܕܟܪ, *meminit.* Samar. id. Æth. ዘከረ: id. I. *Memory*, Exod. xvii. 14; Deut. xxv. 19; xxxii. 26; Ps. ix. 7, &c.
II. Meton. *Memorial, record*, Ps. xxx. 5; cxi. 4; cxlv. 7; Prov. x. 7; Exod. iii. 15, &c. Aff. זִכְרִי, זִכְרְךָ, זִכְרָם.

זָכָר, m. pl. זְכָרִים. Arab. ذَكَر, *mas.* Syr. ܕܟܪܐ, id. See זֵכֶר; either because the man keeps up the *memory* of a family, or because his mental retentive powers are great.
Male, of either man or beast, Gen. i. 26; v. 2; xvii. 10; xxxiv. 15, &c.—Gen. vii. 3. 9. 16; Exod. xii. 8; xiii. 12. 15; Ezra viii. 4. Opp. τῷ, נְקֵבָה, Gen. i. 26; v. 2; vi. 19, &c.

Membrum virile (Arab. it. ذَكَر) apparently, Gen. xvii. 14; xxxiv. 15. 22, &c. And, hence, perhaps, the term is applied to the male.

זָכַר, v. pres. יִזְכֹּר. Constr. immed. it. med. לְ, בְּ, בְּי, אֶת, it. immed. et med. אֶת אִתּךָ, וְזָכַרְתִּי אִתְּךָ, Gen. xl. 14. מִן, from time. מֵרָחוֹק, מִקֶּדֶם, מֵעוֹלָם, place, מֵאֶרֶץ. Ps. xlii. 7, לְעוֹלָם, עוֹד. Syr. ܕܟܪ. Arab. ذَكَرَ, meminit. Æth. id. I. Remember, i. e. retain in memory, call to mind, be mindful of, Gen. viii. 1; ix. 15; xl. 14. 23; Exod. xiii. 3; 1 Sam. i. 11; Is. xvii. 10: opp. τῷ, שָׁכַח, Jer. xliv. 21. Synon. הֶעֱלָה עַל־לֵב, Ezek. xvi. 22. 61, &c.

II. With the additional notion of meditating on, doing religious service. בִּדְרָכֶיךָ יְזַכְּרוּךָ, In thy (appointed) ways they meditate on thee, call thy law to mind, saying, &c. Is. lxiv. 4; Jon. ii. 8; Ps. lxiii. 7; lxxviii. 42; cxix. 55; Judg. viii. 34; Nehem. ix. 17; Ezek. vi. 9, &c. So the Arab. ذَكَرَ, and Pers. ياد كرد.

III.—Of rewarding, avenging; consequence, &c. Neh. v. 19; vi. 14; xiii. 22. xiii. 29; Is. xlvii. 7; Job xl. 32. But, in all these cases, the context is the safest and only guide.

Imp. זְכוֹר, זְכָר, זְכֹר, with ־ה, parag. זָכְרָה, Exod. xiii. 3; Deut. ix. 7; Mic. vi. 5; 2 Chron. vi. 42, &c.

זִכְרוּ, pl. in pause, זְכֹרוּ, 1 Chron. xvi. 12; Neh. iv. 8. Aff. זָכְרֵנִי, Judg. xvi. 28, &c.

Part. pl. m. constr. זֹכְרֵי, Ps. ciii. 18.

Niph. נִזְכַּר, pres. יִזָּכֵר. I. Be, become, remembered, recollected, memorialized. Constr. לִפְנֵי, לְ, it. abs. immed., Num. x. 9; Is. xxiii. 16; Ezek. xviii. 22; xxi. 37; Job xxiv. 20; xxviii. 18; Ps. lxxxiii. 5; cix. 14, opp. τῷ, תִּמָּחֶה, Jer. xi. 19, &c.

II.—Born a male. See זָכָר, once, Exod. xxxiv. 19.

Infin. aff. הִזָּכַרְכֶם, Ezek. xxi. 29.

Part. pl. m. נִזְכָּרִים, Esth. ix. 28.

Hiph. הִזְכִּיר, pres. יַזְכִּיר. Constr. immed. and med. אֶל, it. אֶת, בְּ, Ps. xx. 8; Is. xxvi. 13, &c. Memorialize, make mention of; record, either in a good or bad sense, Gen. xl. 14; Is. xlix. 1; xix. 17; xxvi. 13. בְּךָ מַזְכִּיר שְׁמֶךָ, in thee,—i. e. in thy ordinances, בִּדְרָכֶיךָ. See II. above,—will we memorialize thy name. Comp. Ps. xx. 8; Cant. i. 4. מַזְכִּירָה, rejoicing — let us commemorate, &c. more than (in) wine; i. e. the נְגִילָה, and נַשְׂמְחָה preceding, here influencing our verb; hence the constr. with מִן, Josh. xxiii. 7; Exod. xx. 24; xxiii. 13; Is. xlviii. 1.

Infin. הַזְכִּיר, Memorializing, recording, 2 Sam. xviii. 18. With לְ, pref. לְהַזְכִּיר, to record, &c., 1 Kings xvii. 18; Amos vi. 10, &c. So the titles of some of the Psalms, xxxviii. 1; lxx. 1. Aff. הַזְכִּירְכֶם, Ezek. xx. 29. It. prep. כְּ. כְּהַזְכִּירוֹ, as he mentioned, 1 Sam. iv. 18.

Imp. aff. הַזְכִּירֵנִי, Put me in mind, Is. xliii. 26; Pl. lb. xii. 4.

Part. מַזְכִּיר, pl. מַזְכִּירִים. Calling to mind, mentioning, Gen. xli. 9; Is. lxii. 6. Those who memorialize. It. Recorder, 2 Sam. viii. 16; xx. 24, &c. מַזְכֶּרֶת, id. f., Num. v. 15.

זִכָּרוֹן, m. constr. pl. non occ. A memorial, record, Exod. xvii. 14; xxviii. 12; xxxix. 7; Num. v. 15; Eccl. i. 11; Mal. iii. 16; Neh. ii. 20, &c.

זִכְרוֹן, m. pl. זִכְרוֹנִים, it. f. זִכְרֹנוֹת, i. q. זִכָּרוֹן. Memorial, record; but זִכְרוֹן is not constr. of זִכָּרוֹן. Comp. Eccl. i. 11, and ii. 16. Nor can the plurals here given be formed of זִכָּרוֹן; this would set all analogy at nought, nor is it necessary. Lev. xxiii. 24; Job xiii. 12; Esth. vi. 1. Aff. זִכְרֹנֶךָ.

זֻלּוּת, f. r. זלל. Syr. ܙ, despectui fui; obscænitas. Arab. زَلُول, Lightness, shortness, of weight. Baseness, lightness, i. e. want of principle, Ps. xii. 9. When baseness is elevated among men, wicked men walk about on every side, i. e. they are now freed from the shackles which religion would lay on them; and accordingly they injure, oppress, destroy, without even the necessity of an excuse. On the force of יִתְהַלָּכוּן, see my Job i. 7; ii. 2. Nothing can be more true to nature than the sentiment here delivered; and it may be laid down as a corollary to it: That the prime aim and object of such is, to disseminate debasing principles.

זַלְזַלִּים, m. pl. once, Is. xviii. 5. Arab. زَلْزَل, زُلْزُل, supellex, facultas, levitas; زَلْزَال, tremor. Cogn. زَلَّ, lubricus. Applied, apparently, to the things of life, on account of their very uncertain tenure; and, in Is. l. c. to the branches, as the feeble supporters of the produce of a tree. Tender branches, shoots. Cogn. סַלְסִלּוֹת, סַנְסִנִּים, זַלְזַלִּים, Gesen.

זַלִּים, m. pl. part. r. זול. See זֶלֶת, and

זלל (172) זמו

cogn. זלל. Syr. ‏ܐܙܠ, *ascendens.* Arab. زَوَلَ, *amovit.* Cogn. ذَالَ, r. ذيل, *vilipensa fuit* res; it. *verrens lacinia humum superbè incessit.* Cogn. נזל, once, Is. xlvi. 6. הַזָּלִים זָהָב מִכִּיס, *Those who pour forth* (lavishly) *gold from the purse.* LXX. οἱ συμβαλλόμενοι χρυσίον ἐκ μαρσυππίου.

זלל, in Kal non occ.

Part. זוֹלֵל, f. זוֹלֵלָה, in pause, pl. m. זוֹלְלִים, constr. זוֹלְלֵי. Syr. ‏ܐܚܡܠ, *luxurians, obscœnus.* Arab. زَلَّ, *peccavit.* Cogn. فَلِيل, *abjectus. Acting basely, with profligacy, obscenity.* Synon. סוֹרֵר מֹרֶה, Deut. xxi. 20; with סֹבֵא, Prov. xxiii. 21; opp. τῷ, יָקָר, Jer. xv. 19; Prov. xxiii. 20; זוֹלֵל בָּשָׂר לָמוֹ, *debased, of fleshly* gratifications, obscenities. Comp. Ezek. xvi. 26; xxiii. 20; Prov. xxviii. 7; Lam. i. 11.

Niph. pl. m. נָזֹלּוּ, *Were, became, debased,* i. e. *mountains:* metaph. perhaps, for the forces of Egypt and Canaan, Is. lxiv. 2; taken from Judg. v. 5, where we have the cogn. נָזְלוּ, if any reliance can be placed on the vowels. Arab. نَزَلَ, *descendit.* The LXX. take the Arab. زَلْزَلَ, *tremefecit.*

Hiph. הִזִילוּהָ, *They debased her.* Cogn. נזל, which see, Lam. i. 8; it. Is. xlviii. 21. הִזִיל, *made to flow down*, of waters.

זַלְעָפָה, f. pl. זַלְעָפוֹת, constr. זַלְעֲפוֹת. Arab. أَزْلَغَبَ, *extulit se ignis.* Compd. of أَكْثَل, *expulsio*, and أَحْكَل, *effusio.* Apparently the poisonous wind of the East, termed السموم, the *Samum*, Ps. cxix. 53; applied to the mind in a state of great perturbation: it., Lam. v. 10, to a famishing person. Metaph. Comp. Ps. lv. 9; lxxxiii. 16; Ps. xi. 6, al. non occ.

זִמָּה, f. pl. זִמּוֹת, constr. זִמַּת. r. זמם. Arab. زَعَم, *Object, end;* زَعِيم, *malum odorem habens. Intention, imagination,* Job xvii. 11. See my note here. Hence, *evil, sin,* as originating with self, Prov. xxi. 27; xxiv. 8; Ps. xxvi. 10; cxix. 150; particularly with reference to fornication, adultery, or incest, Lev. xviii. 17; xix. 29; Job xxxi. 11; Ezek. xvi. 27; xxii. 9. 11. Synon. נְבָלָה, Judg. xx. 7; Prov. xxiv. 9. זִמַּת אֱוִלֶת, *the imagination of folly* is *sin;* i. e. projects not regulated by the fear of God. With תּוֹעֵבוֹת, Ezek. xvi. 58. Aff. זִמָּתֵךְ, זַמּוֹתִי.—זִמֹּתַי, זִמַּתְכֶנָה, Ps. xvii. 3 is, by Gesen. i. q. זְמוֹתִי. See also the verb זמם.

זְמוֹרָה, f. pl. constr. m. זְמֹרֵי, sing. זְמֹרַת, r. זמר. Lit. *a pruning.* I. *A branch* generally, pec. of the vine, Num. xiii. 23; Ezek. xv. 2; Is. xvii. 10. זְמֹרַת זָר, *branch of a stranger;* allud. to Num. l. c.: but here intimating the introduction of idolatry, Ezek. viii. 17, as some think alluding to the *Phallus* of the Egyptians and Greeks; the *Lingam* of the Hindoos, Engl. *the rod.* See also Facciolati, under *Fascinum:* others, that the rite of using a small bundle of rods when worshipping the sun, as in ancient Persia, is intended. See Strabo, lib. xv. p. 733, Ed. Casaub. Hyde de Relig. Pers. lib. i. c. xxvii. p. 350; others, that the ἰκτήριοι κλάδοι. Œdip. Tyrann. l. 3, &c. are meant. The passage cited from Is. above is sufficient to shew, that some heathenish practice is alluded to; but what that is, it is impossible to say. Aff. זְמֹרֵיהֶם, Nah. ii. 3.

זְמוֹתִי, see r. זמם, and זִמָּה.

זָמִיר, m. once, Cant. ii. 12, r. זמר, *Pruning.* LXX. καιρὸς τῆς τομῆς. Aquila and Symmachus, τῆς κλαδεύσεως. Some, *Singing,* Auth. Vers. &c.

זָמִיר, m.—pl. f. זְמִירוֹת, *Song, hymn,* of success or triumph, Is. xxiv. 7; xxv. 9; Job xxxv. 10;—of prayer, praise, as an exercise of religion, 2 Sam. xxiii. 1; Ps. cxix. 54, al. non occ.

זָמַם, v. זָמַמְתִּי, it. זַמּוֹתִי, pres. pl. יָזֹמּוּ, as if pret. of cogn. זֹם. See זָמָה, i. q. قَصَدَ, it. cogn. سَمَّ, i. q. قَصَدَ, *intendit, proposuit sibi; exploravit.* Constr. abs. it. med. בְּ. *Intended, determined,* Gen. xi. 6; Deut. viii. 14; xix. 19; Jer. iv. 28; li. 12; Lam. ii. 17; Zech. i. 6; viii. 14, 15; Ps. xvii. 3; xxxi. 14; Prov. xxx. 32. אִם־זַמּוֹתָ יָד לְפֶה, *if thou hast determined* (erroneously, i. e. with too much confidence, as the preceding member intimates) (lay thy) *hand to* (thy) *mouth;* i. e. be silent; do not go on to defend this. See Job xxi. 5, from which the sentiment seems to be taken, with my note. Comp. Is. li. 17; Prov. xxxi. 16. *Determined upon, considered.*

Part. זֹמֵם, *Determines, plots against,* Ps. xxxvii. 12. LXX. παρατηρήσεται.

זָמַם, m. Aff. זְמָמוֹ, *His determination, will, project*, Ps. cxl. 9, al. non occ.

זְמָן, m. pl. זְמַנִּים, for זְמָנִים, *its equivalent*. Arab. زَمَان, or زَمَن, *tempus*. Syr. ܘܰܟ, id. *Time, season*, pec. appointed, Eccl. iii. 1; Neh. ii. 6. Aff. זְמַנָּם, Esth. ix. 27; pl. זְמַנֵּיהֶם, Ib. ix. 31, al. non occ. "Non .... temporis spatium notat," says Gesenius, " .... sed temporis momentum ; " which the passages above cited are sufficient to shew will not hold good.

זְמָן, and זְמַן, m. Chald. Defin. זִמְנָא, pl. זִמְנִין, Def. זִמְנַיָּא, i. q. Heb. *Time, season*, pec. appointed, Dan. ii. 16. 21; vi. 11; vii. 12. 22. 25; iii. 7. 8; iv. 33; Ezra v. 3.

זָמַן, v. non occ. in Kal. Arab. زَامَنَ, *tempus præfinivit*. Puh. part. pl. m. מְזֻמָּנִים, and f. מְזֻמָּנוֹת, with עִתִּים, i. e. *Predetermined, times, seasons,* Ezra x. 14; Neh. x. 35; xiii. 31, al. non occ.

זְמַן, r. Chald. occ. once— Aph. הִזְדְּמִנְתּוּן, sec. *keri*: but, Hithp. הִזְדַּמִּנְתּוּן, sec. *kethiv*. Syr. Pah. ܐܙܡ, *præparavit, apparavit. Previously determined, concerted*, Dan. ii. 9.

זָמַר, v. pret. non occ. pres. יִזְמֹר, constr. immed. Arab. زَمَرَ, *pede percussit, calcitravit, inhumanus fuit*, &c. conj. ii. زَمَّرَ, ob iram. s. *iratus, cantavit*; زَمَار, *vox struthiocameli maris; psallendi actus*. The progress of the notion seems to be, from violence or injury received, to crying out in consequence; thence to singing, i. q. from *howling* at a funeral, as practised in Ireland, the transition to *singing* Psalms is easy and natural. It is remarkable, too, that in the Hebrew, as in the Arabic, the secondary notion is confined to the Pih. conjug. and its equivalent.

I. *Cut, prune*, Lev. xxv. 3, 4. Niph. pres. יִזָּמֵר, Is. v. 6.
Hiph. part. pl. f. only. מַזְמֵרוֹת, *Pruning instruments*, Is. ii. 4; xviii. 5; Mic. iv. 3. Aff. מַזְמְרוֹתֵיהֶם, Joel iv. 10.

II. Pih. pret. non occ. pres. pl. יְזַמְּרוּ, *Sing, hymn,* in praise, &c. Constr. immed. abs. it. med. לְ, בְּ, instr. it. among, כִּי, cause, Judg. v. 3; 2 Sam. xxii. 50; Ps. ix. 3; xviii. 50; xxx. 13; lxi. 14, &c.

Infin. זַמֵּר, Ps. xcii. 2.
Imp. pl. זַמְּרוּ, Ps. ix. 12; 1 Chron. xvi. 9 &c.

זַמָּר, m. Chald. pl. def. זַמָּרַיָּא, *Singers*, Ezra vii. 24, al. non occ.

זֶמֶר, m. once, Deut. xiv. 5. *A sort of mountain-goat*, so called according to Boch. Hieroz. i. p. 903, et seq. from its leaping. Arab. زَمَرَ, *fugit cervus*.

זִמְרָא, m. Chald. Def. *Music, song*, Dan. iii. 5. 7. 10. 15, al. non occ.

זִמְרָה, f. constr. זִמְרַת, pl. זִמְרוֹת, pl. non occ. *Song, praise, music*, Ps. lxxxi. 3; xcviii. 5; Is. li. 3; Amos v. 23. זִמְרָת יָהּ, Exod. xv. 2, adopted, Is. xii. 2; Ps. cxviii. 14, is perhaps elliptical for זִמְרָתִי יָהּ, *my song is the Lord*; i. e. the subject of it. זִמְרַת הָאָרֶץ, Gen. xliii. 11, *the cropping, gathering,* i. e. *produce, of the land*, rather than "*cantus terræ,* i. e. laudatissimi proventus ejus," of Gesenius.

זַן, m. pl. זִנִים. Syr. ܙܢܐ, ܙܢܐ, pl. ܙܢܐ, زِنّ, *species*; pl. *multarum specierum*. Hence, probably, أَزْنَم, *scortator*, because addicted to variety; and, hence, the propriety of its application to idolatry. Arab. زَنَى, *scortatus est*. Cogn. زَنَا, *aluit*; زَنَى, *armavit*. Arab. زِين, *ornamentum*. See زَونَة. Cogn. Arab. سَنَا, *terram rigavit aquæ*; سَنَّ, *formavit*. Æth. ᎂᎨᎨ: *proficuum, decorum, fuit*.

Sort, kind, of wealth, Ps. cxliv. 13. מְפִיקִים מִזַּן אֶל זַן, *putting forth from sort to sort*, i. e. things precious from one kind to another. The Arabic equivalent, جِنْس, is still used in the same way in the East; e. g. بازارهاى متعدد مشحون به نعمتها واجناس واشياى گوناگون, *numerous market-places filled with favours* (eatables), SORTS, i. e. *wares, and various things*. And in the same context, a derivative of our word, viz. اقسام زيب وزينت, *various sorts of beauty and* ORNAMENT. From the قواعد سلطنت شاهجهان, in Gladwin's Pers. Moonshee, Ed. Lond. p. ٢٩ — 2 Chron. xvi. 4, בְּשָׂמִים זוּנִים, *perfumes, and varieties* of precious cloth apparently, and the same is

זנב (174) זנו

perhaps intended, Ps. l. c. above. Comp. שְׁנֵי, אַרְגָּמָן, Chald. id. Constr. זְנֵי, Dan. iii. 5. 7. 10. 15, al. non occ.

זָנָב, m.—pl. f. זְנָבוֹת, constr. זַנְבוֹת. Syr. ܙܢܒܐ, cauda. Arab. ذَنَب, id. *The tail* of an animal, Judg. xv. 4. Comp. Is. vii. 4; Is. ix. 13. See under אַגְמוֹן above, Is. xix. 15; Deut. xxviii. 13; Job xl. 17. Aff. זְנָבוֹ. Hence—

Pih. זִנֵּב, v. pres. יְזַנֵּב. Constr. med. אֵת, בְּ, among.—lit. *tail*, i. e. *Cut off*, *smite*, those in the rear, as if they were the tail of the host, &c. Deut. xxv. 18; Josh. x. 19, al. non occ. Verbs, formed from the names of substances, are usually found either in the Pih. or Hiph. form.

זָנָה, v. pres. יִזְנֶה, apoc. f. תֵּזֶן. See וֹנָה and זֵן, above. Constr. abs. immed. אֶל אַחֲרֵי, מֵאַחֲרֵי, עַל, תַּחַת, מִתַּחַת. I. *Playing the whore*, Gen. xxxviii. 24; Lev. xix. 29; Hos. iii. 3; Jer. iii. 1; Amos vii. 17, &c.

II. Metaph. *Becoming, being, idolatrous*, God being supposed to be the husband of Israel, Is. liv. 5, &c. Comp. Hos. i. 2; Ezek. xvi. 22, &c.; Lev. xvii. 7; xx. 5, 6; Deut. xxxi. 16; Judg. ii. 17; Ezek. xxiii. 30. In Is. xxiii. 17, the primitive usage, see זֵן, וֹנָה, seems to be recurred to. Comp. Nah. iii. 4, occ. with מֹכֶרֶת.

Infin. זְנֹה, constr. זְנוֹת, Hos. i. 2; Lev. xx. 5. Aff. זְנוֹתָהּ.

Part. see זוֹנָה, m. זוֹנָה, f.

Puh. זוּנָּה, *Is whoredom committed*, impers. Ezek. xvi. 34.

Hiph. הִזְנָה, pres. f. תַּזְנֶה, apoc. יַזְן, *Caused to commit whoredom*, Exod. xxxiv. 16; 2 Chron. xxi. 11. 13.

As in Kal. Hos. iv. 10. 18; v. 3.

Infin. הַזְנֵה, constr. הַזְנוֹת, 2 Chron. xxi. 13. Aff. הַזְנוֹתָהּ, Lev. xix. 29.

זְנוּנִים, m. pl. constr. זְנוּנֵי, r. זנן, cogn. τοῦ, זנה. Arab. زَنَى, *aqua dubia*; lit. things *prostituted*, or, taking the prim. notion, *varied*, *bartered*. This participial form is adopted in זְקֻנִים, נְעוּרִים, in like manner. I. *Whoredom*, or things pertaining to it, Gen. xxxviii. 24; Hos. i. 2; ii. 6; iv. 12; v. 4; i. q. נְאֻפִים, Hos. ii. 4, &c.

II. Metaph. *Idolatry*. See זָנָה, sign. ii. 2 Kings ix. 22; Ezek. xxiii. 11. 29.

In Nah. iii. 4, comp. Is. xxiii. 17, the primitive sense of *bartering* seems to be recurred to; as remarked under זָנָה, sign. ii.

"De commercio," &c. Gesenius, i. e. זְנוּנֵי זוֹנָה. And yet he tells us, under זָנָה, that "neque audiendi, qui nonnullis in locis, ut Jos. l. c." i. e. אִשָּׁה זוֹנָה, *cauponam hospitam* intelligunt." Yet we have Dr. Gesenius himself here, ascribing either that sense, or one very like it, to this word! Aff. זְנוּנֶיהָ, זְנוּנָיו.

זְנוּת, f. pl. זְנוּתִים, r. זנה, i. q. זְנוּנִים, sign. ii. *Whoredom* of idolatry, Jer. iii. 2. 9; xiii. 27; Ezek. xxiii. 27; xliii. 7. 9; Hos. iv. 11; vi. 10; Num. xiv. 33. Meton. *the vengeance due* to it. Aff. זְנוּתֵךְ, זְנוּתָהּ, זְנוּתָם, זְנוּתְכֶם, זְנוּתָיִךְ.

זָנַח, v. pres. יִזְנַח. Constr. abs. immed. med. מִן of thing. Arab. زَنِخَ, cogn. سَنِخَ, *corruptum, rancidumve fuit, et fœtuit*.

Cogn. زَرَخ, *pepulit*. I. *Is stinking, ill-savoured*; metaph. Hos. viii. 5. Meton.—

II. *Rejecting* as corrupt and worthless, Hos. viii. 3; Lam. ii. 7; Ps. xliii. 2; xliv. 10; lx. 3. 12; lxxiv. 1; lxxxix. 39; cviii. 12; Zech. x. 6. With לְעוֹלָם, and לְעוֹלָם, Lam. iii. 31; Ps. lxxvii. 8: it. לָנֶצַח, Ps. xliv. 24.

Hiph. הִזְנִיחַ, pres. יַזְנִיחַ, i. q. Kal. I. Is. xix. 6, הֶאֱזְנִיחוּ נְהָרוֹת, *The rivers*—of Egypt—*shall stink*, alluding to Exod. vii. 18, בָּאַשׁ הַיְאֹר. If the reading הֶאֱזְנִיחוּ may be relied on, it probably exhibits a Hiph. of the augmented form, אוּנָה, Gram. art. 195. 6.

II. *Rejected*, 1 Chron. xxviii. 9, with לָעַד, 2 Chron. xi. 14, with מִן, Ib. xxix. 19, *laid aside, profaned*.

זנק, v. in Kal. non occ. Syr. ܙܢܩ, *jecit, ejecit; coercuit*. Arab. زَنَقَ, *annulo frœnavit*, &c. once—

Pih. יְזַנֵּק, pres. Deut. xxxiii. 22. יְזַנֵּק מִן־הַבָּשָׁן can hardly mean *prosiliit, leaps out from Bashan*, as Gesenius thinks; because no precise sense can be collected from it; besides, his etymology, giving this notion, is groundless. More agreeably to Oriental usage, *Strikes, injures*, and hence, *restrains*.

זֵעָה, f. r. זוע, once, Gen. iii. 19, constr. זֵעַת, *Sweat of*—. Meton. effect of agitation, &c.

זְוָעָה, f. i. q. וְעָוָה, either by Metath. or from cogn. r. זָעָה. Arab. زَعَا, r. زَعَو, *justè egit*, &c. *Agitation, commotion, vexation*, Deut. xxviii. 25; Jer. xv. 4; xxiv. 9; xxix.

זֵעִי (175) זָעַף

18: Keri. it. xxxiv. 17; Ezek. xxiii. 46; 2 Chron. xxix. 8, Keri.

זָעִיר, m. r. זער. Cogn. צָעִיר. Syr. ‎‏ܙܥܘܪ‎, parvus. Arab. زَعِر, paucis præditus pilis. Cogn. صَغِير, parvus. A little, small, portion, of any thing, Is. xxviii. 10; Job xxxvi. 2.

It. Chald. Dan. vii. 8, f. זְעֵירָה, al. non occ.

זעך, v. in Kal non occ. i. q. דעך, usually, occ. once, Job xvii. 1. See my note. Arab. زَعْكُوك, brevis, &c. Cogn. زَعَج, contrivit; زَعَق, acriter egit jumentum, اِنْزَعَق, cito incesserunt, &c.

Niph. נִזְעֲכוּ, They are swift, pass rapidly away, seem few. Comp. ch. vii. 6.

זָעַם, m. pl. non occ. Arab. زَعَم, concupivit; زَاعَم, mutuo ursit; مُزَاعَمَة, disceptatio. Cogn. تَزَعَّم, cum ira locutus fuit; ضَغَم, momordit. Syr. ‎‏ܐܟܡ‎, reprehendit. Cogn. Heb. זעם.

Indignation, anger, Is. x. 5. 25; xxvi. 20; xxx. 27; Jer. xv. 17; Ezek. xxii. 24; Dan. xi. 36. With עֶבְרָה, Ps. lxxviii. 49. With אַף, Lam. ii. 6. With קֶצֶף, cii. 11, &c. Aff. זַעֲמוֹ, זַעֲמְךָ, זַעֲמִי.

זָעַם, v. pres. יִזְעַם, 1st pers. אֶזְעֹם, constr. immed. abs. it. med. אֵת, r. עַל. Be indignant, angry, Num. xxiii. 8. לֹא זָעַם יְהֹוָה—Why should I be indignant? Jehovah is not indignant, i. e. at Israel, Mal. i. 4: at, or with, Is. lxvi. 14; Dan. xi. 30; Zech. i. 13, suppl. עֲלֵיהֶם, Prov. xxiv. 24.

Imp. זְעָמָה, with ה parag. Num. xxiii. 7. Part. זֹעֵם, Ps. vii. 12.

Pass. constr. זְעוּם f. זְעוּמִים, object of anger, Despised, Prov. xxii. 14; Mic. vi. 10.

Niph. part. pl. m. נִזְעָמִים, Become, made, indignant, angry, Prov. xxv. 23.

זַעַף, m. pl. non occ. Syr. ‎‏ܐܟܦ‎, expulsio; ‎‏ܐܟܦ‎, indignabundus. Arab. زَعَف, interemit. Cogn. صعف and ضعف. Cogn. Heb. זעם. Indignation, anger, Prov. xix. 12; Mic. vii. 9; Is. xxx. 30; 2 Chron. xvi. 10; xxviii. 9.

Metaph. Raging of the sea, Jonah i. 15; 2 Chron. xxi. 19. Aff. זַעְפּוֹ. Infin. of—

זָעַף, v. pret. non occ. pres. יִזְעַף. I. Indignant, enraged. Constr. abs. it. med. עִם, עַל, see נַעַף, Prov. xix. 3; 2 Chron. xxvi. 19. Infin. זְעֹף, above.

II. Part. pl. m. זֹעֲפִים, Mentally excited, wretched, Gen. xl. 6; Dan. i. 10. Theodotion, σκυθρωπά. Comp. Matth. vi. 16.

זָעֵף, m. Indignant, angry, 1 Kings xx. 43; xxi. 4.

זַעַק, m. } Aff. וַיַּעֲקֵךְ, Is. xxx. 19, only. זְעָקָה, f. } constr. זַעֲקַת, pl. non occ. Syr. ‎‏ܐܟܬܐ‎, vociferatio, clamor. Arab. زَعَق, id. Cogn. نَعَق, inclamavit illum. Cogn. Heb. צָעַק. Arab. صَعَق, id. A cry, shout, for help in distress, &c. Is. xv. 5. 8; lxv. 19; Jer. xviii. 22; xx. 16; xlviii. 4. 34; li. 54; Ezek. xxvii. 28; Job xvi. 18, &c. Often subjectively, Gen. xviii. 20; objectively, i. e. cry caused by Sodom, or against Sodom. Aff. וַיְעֲקָתָם, וַיְעֲקָתִי.

זָעַק, v. pres. יִזְעַק. Constr. abs. it. med. אֶל, לְ, אֵת, to whom; עַל, about, or against whom, which; בְּ, in, with; מִלִּפְנֵי, from. See צָעַק. Cry out, for help in distress, &c. 2 Sam. xiii. 19; Judg. vi. 7; 1 Sam. viii. 18; 1 Chron. v. 20; Ps. xxii. 6; cxlii. 2. 6; Is. xxx. 19; lvii. 13; Jer. xi. 11, 12; Hab. i. 2. חָמָס, of violence. Specif. or adv. Gram. art. 219, note.

Infin. זְעֹק } 1 Sam. vii. 8; 2 Sam. xix. 29. זַעֲק } Aff. זַעֲקָה, i. q. זעק above, Is. xxx. 19; lvii. 13.

Imp. זְעַק, Ezek. xxi. 12.

זַעֲקִי, f. Is. xv. 4; Jer. xlviii. 20.

זַעֲקוּ, pl. m. Judg. x. 14, &c.

Niph. נִזְעַק, pres. יִזָּעֵק, Became, betook them to, crying out. Constr. abs. it. med. אַחֲרֵי, Judg. xviii. 22, 23; vi. 34, 35; 1 Sam. xiv. 20.

Hiph. pret. non occ. pres. יַזְעִיק. Constr. abs. it. med. אֵת, מִן, from, cause. Called for, summoned, perhaps by proclamation, Judg. iv. 10. 13; Zech. vi. 8. Proclaimed, Jonah iii. 7. Id. q. Kal, Job xxxv. 9.

Imp. הַזְעֵק, Summon, 2 Sam. xx. 4. Infin. הַזְעִיק, Ib. 5.

זְעִק, v. Chald. constr. לְ, Called to, Dan. vi. 21, al. non occ.

זֶפֶת, fm. Syr. ‎‏ܐܙܦܬܐ‎. Arab. زِفْت, pix; زَفَت, excandescentia. Pitch. Synon.

זָקִי (176) זָקַף

τοῦ, חֹמֶר, נָפְרִית, כֹּפֶר, (a) used as *a coating*, Exod. ii. 3. Comp. Gen. vi. 14. (b) as in its *liquid* or *burning* state, Is. xxxiv. 9.

זְקִים, see זִיקוֹת above.

זְקִיף, Chald. part. m. See זָקַף, *Erected, set up*, Ezra vi. 11, al. non occ.

זָקָן, m. Syr. ܙܩܢܐ, *barba*. Arab. ذَقَن, *mentum*. Pers. ریش سفید, *white hair*, for *old man, age*. *Age*, Gen. xlviii. 10, al. non occ.

זָקָן, m. constr. זְקַן, pl. non occ. I. *The beard*, Lev. xix. 27; 2 Sam. x. 5; Is. vii. 20; xv. 7, Jer. xli. 5; Ps. cxxxiii. 2, &c. II. Meton. *The chin*, Lev. xiii. 29, 30; Ezra ix. 3, &c. Aff. זְקָנִי, זְקָנְךָ, זְקָנוֹ, זְקָנְכֶם, זְקָנָם.

זָקֵן, m. constr. זְקַן, pl. זְקֵנִים, f. זְקֵנוֹת; constr. m. זִקְנֵי. See זָקֵן, opp. τῷ, נַעַר. Syn. יָשֵׁישׁ. *Old, aged*, Gen. xv. 4; xxv. 8; xxxv. 29; Lev. xix. 32; Josh. vi. 21; Zech. viii. 4, &c., זְקַן הַבַּיִת, *the senior of the house*, i. e. principal servant, Gen. xxiv. 2. זְקֵנִים־כָּמוֹהוּ, *his* (a) *seniors*, Job xxxii. 4. לְיָמִים, *as to days*; the specificative having לְ. In the pl. (b) often *The seniors*, or *senators*, as rulers, Job xii. 20; Ps. cvii. 32; Exod. xxiv. 14; Num. xi. 25; xxii. 4; Deut. xxii. 16; xxv. 7—9; xxxi. 28; Josh. xxiv. 31; Judg. ii. 7; 2 Kings x. 1, &c.

(c) *Heads of tribes* or families, Exod. iii. 16; iv. 29; xii. 21; Lev. iv. 15; Num. xi. 16; Ruth iv. 4; Ezra iii. 12, &c. Aff. זְקֵנַי, זְקֵנֶיךָ, זְקֵנַיִךְ, זְקֵנֵינוּ, זְקֵנֵיהֶם, זְקֵנֵיכֶם.

זָקֵן, v. pres. יִזְקַן, constr. abs. i. q. בָּא בַיָּמִים, *Growing old*, Gen. xviii. 12, 13; xix. 31; xxiv. 1; xxvii. 1; Prov. xxiii. 22; 1 Sam. viii. 5; 2 Chron. xxiv. 16; Ruth i. 12. זָקַנְתִּי מִהְיוֹת לְאִישׁ, *I am too old for a husband*, i. e. to be married. Hiph. i. q. Kal זָקֵן, Prov. xxii. 6; Job xiv. 8.

זִקְנָה, f. i. q. שֵׂיבָה, זֹקֶן, constr. זִקְנַת, often with עֵת, *Growing old, becoming aged*, Ps. lxxi. 9. 18; Is. xlvi. 4; 1 Kings xi. 4; xv. 23. Aff. זִקְנָתָה, זִקְנָתוֹ.

זְקֻנִים, pl. m. sing. non occ. *Age*, as some have thought, *days, times, of age*, Gram. art. 142. 4, 5; Gen. xxxvii. 3; xliv. 20. Aff. זְקֻנָיו, Ib. xxi. 2. 7.

זָקַף, m. part. Syr. ܙܩܦ, *erexit*. Arab. ذَرَقَفَ, *rapidè* (manu) *cepit quid*. Cogn. صَقَبَ, *extulit*. Constr. immed. it. med. לְ, *Erects, lifts up*, persons bowed down as it were with some great weight, Ps. cxliv. 14; cxlvi. 8, al. non occ.

זָקַק, v. pret. non occ. pres. יָזֹק, pl. m. Cogn. צוק, יצק, זכה. Arab. زَقَّ, *vinum*; زِقّ, *uter, in quo vinum et alia reconduntur*. Gr. ἀσκός. *Fuse, pour out*, Job xxviii. 1; xxxvi. 27. See my notes. Pih. זִקֵּק, *Melt, fuse*, as metals, in order to purify them, Mal. iii. 3. Puh. part. מְזֻקָּק, pl. מְזֻקָּקִים, *Fused, purified*, as metals, 1 Chron. xxviii. 18; xxix. 4; Ps. xii. 7: as wine, Is. xxv. 6.

זָר, m. see זור.

זֵר, m. pl. non occ. Syr. ܐܶܡܪ̈ܐ, *torques, collare*. Arab. زِيَارَات, *funiculi*. *A sort of binding*, or *border* which surmounted a kind of parapet of a hand-breadth, enclosing the top of the altar of incense, Exod. xxv. 11. 24, 25; xxx. 3, 4; xxxvii. 2. 12. 26. 27. Aff. זֵרוֹ.

זָרָא, see זור, sign. ii. (a).

זָרַב, v. Syr. ܙܪܒ, *strinxit*. Arab. زَرَبَ, *septum, fecit, &c*. Puh. pres. pl. m. יְזֹרְבוּ, *They are bound, oppressed*, Job vi. 17. See my note, al. non occ.

זָרַח, v. pret. non occ. pres. apoc. יָזַר. Aff. תִּזְרַם. Constr. immed. abs. it. med. אֶת, בְּ, instr. לְ, *to which*; עַל, *on which*. Æth. ሠረቀ፡ *sparsit*. Arab. ذَرَّ, *sparsit*. Cogn. زَرَعَ, it. ذَرَا, *expandit rem*. Syr. ܙܪܝ, *asportavit*. I. *Spread, disperse*, as the wind, the dust, &c., Ezek. v. 2; Is. xl. 16. Synon. תָּפִיץ, Exod. xxxii. 20; Jer. xv. 7. אֶזְרֵם בַּמִּזְרֶה, *I will disperse them with a disperser*: meton. *will winnow them with a fan*. LXX. διασπερῶ αὐτοὺς ἐν διασπορᾷ, Is. xxx. 22; by a further meton. *cast away, reject*, as worthless and polluted. Infin. זְרוֹת, Jer. iv. 11. Imp. זְרֵה, Num. xvii. 2. Part. זֹרֶה, Ruth iii. 2.

זרז (177) זרו

Niph. pres. pl. זֹרוּ, *They become dispersed*, Ezek. xxvi. 19.
Infin. pl. aff. הִזָּרוֹתֵיכֶם, *Your dispersions*, Ib. vi. 8.
Pih. pret. aff. זֵרָם, זֵרִיתָנִי; זֵרִיתִי, pres. pl. יְזָרוּ. Constr. immed. it. med. אֶת, בְּ, לְ, in; ?, to. I. *Disperse* entirely, Lev. xxvi. 33; 1 Kings xiv. 16; Ps. xliv. 12; Ezek. v. 10; vi. 5; xii. 15; synon. τοῦ, הֵפִיץ, xxx. 26; Mal. ii. 3; Prov. xx. 8, &c.; as seed, Ib. xv. 7. It. meton.—
II. *Discern, sift* as it were, *observe*, Ps. cxxxix. 3.
Infin. זָרוֹת, Ezek. xx. 23. Aff. זָרוֹתָהּ, Zech. ii. 4; ־ָם, Ps. cvi. 27.
Part. מְזָרֶה, Jer. xxxi. 10: meton. *Discerning, sifting*, Prov. xx. 8. 26.
Puh. pres. יֹרֶה, Job xviii. 15.
Part. מְזֹרָה, Prov. i. 17, *Spread out*.

זְרוֹעַ, or זְרֹעַ, f. constr. m., Is. xvii. 5; li. 5; Dan. xi. 15. 22. See Gram. art. 216. 9, pl. m. זְרוֹעִים, constr. זְרוֹעֵי; f. זְרוֹעוֹת, זְלֹחָת, or זְרוֹעוֹת, i. q. אֶזְרוֹעַ. Syr. ܕܪܥܐ, *Brachium*. Arab. ذِرَاع, id.
I. *The arm*, pr. the fore-arm, *cubitum, ulna*. Of an animal, *the shoulder*, Deut. iv. 34; xxx. 20; Job xxvi. 2; xl. 9; Ps. x. 15; Num. vi. 19; Deut. xviii. 3.
II. Meton. *Strength, power, violence*, for help, or the contrary, 2 Chron. xxxii. 8. זְרוֹעַ בָּשָׂר, *an arm of flesh*; i. e. human strength, Ps. x. 15. זְרוֹעַ רָשָׁע, *of* (the) *wicked*, Ib. lxxxiii. 9. Comp. lxxxix. 11. 14; Is. li. 9; lii. 10; lxiii. 12; Gen. xlix. 24. זְרֹעֵי יָדָיו, *the powers of his hands*. אִישׁ זְרוֹעַ *man of power*, or *violence*, Job xxii. 8. See my note. זְרוֹעוֹת הַנֶּגֶב, *powers of the south*, Dan. xi. 15. See vr. 22. Comp. 1 Sam. ii. 31; Is. liii. 1, with 1 Cor. i. 24. And, by a further meton. *associate*, Is. ix. 19. Comp. with Jer. xix. 9. Aff. זְרוֹעִי, זְרוֹעֵךְ, זְרוֹעוֹ, זְרוֹעָם, pl. זְרוֹעָיו. f. זְרוֹעוֹתָי, זְרוֹעוֹתֶיךָ, זְרוֹעוֹתָם. With א prost. אֶזְרוֹעִי, Job xxxi. 22.

זֶרַע, m. pl. aff. זֵרוּעֶיהָ. Syr. ܙܪܘܥܐ, *semen*. Arab. زَرِيع, *sativus*. *Seed*, for sowing, as seed-corn, &c., Lev. xi. 37; Is. lxi. 11.

זַרְזִיף, m. compd. Syr. ܙܪܙܝܦܐ, *imber vehemens*; and זֹב, *sparsit, stillavit*; once, Ps. lxxii. 6. כִּרְבִיבִים זַרְזִיף אָרֶץ, *As showering rains abundantly sprinkling*, i. e. *saturating* (the) *earth*.

זַרְזִיר, m. compd. Syr. זִן, *accinxit*, and Arab. زَرَّ, *nodo connexuit*; or, of זוּר, reduplicated. זַרְזִיר מָתְנַיִם, *firmly bound, compact, of loins*, implying great strength, once, Prov. xxx. 31. *Bellator equus, The war-horse*, according to Gesenius. Comp. Job xl. 16. פֹּחוּ בְּמָתְנָיו, which is a perfectly similar periphrasis; and might, among other things, signify the *war-horse*. See my notes, also Boch. Hieroz. i., p. 102, and Schultens on Prov. l. c.

זֶרַח, m. Syr. ܙܪܚܐ, *ortus*; hence, אוֹרָה. Aff. זַרְחֵךְ, *Thy rising*, once, Is. lx. 3.

זַרְחִי, m. patronym. of זֶרַח, Num. xxvi. 13. 20.

זָרַח, v. pres. יִזְרַח. Constr. abs. it. med. בְּ, in; לְ, for; עַל; upon. *Rising*, as the sun, light, glory, leprosy, &c., Gen. xxxii. 32; Exod. xxii. 2; 2 Kings iii. 22; Nahum iii. 17; Mal. iii. 20; Job ix. 7; Ps. cxii. 4; Is. lviii. 10; lx. 1, 2; 2 Chron. xxvi. 19.
Infin. זְרֹחַ, Jud. ix. 33; Jonah iv. 8. It. זָרֵחַ above.
Part. זֹרֵחַ, Eccl. i. 5.

זָרַם, m. Arab. زَرَمَ, *abrupta fuit urina, lacryma*; اِزْرَامْ, *iratus*. *Inundation* of waters, either in rain or otherwise, Is. xxviii. 2. זֶרֶם מַיִם כַּבִּירִים, *an inundation of mighty waters* overflowing. Comp. Hab. i. 10; Is. xxv. 4; xxxii. 2; iv. 6; xxx. 30; Job xxiv. 8.

זָרַם, v. 2d pers. aff. זְרַמְתָּם, *Thou overwhelmest them*, as with a flood, i. e. *destroyest* them, Ps. xc. 5.
Puh. pl. m. 3d pers. זֹרְמוּ, *They are made to inundate*, *pour down* waters, Ps. lxxvii. 18, al. non occ.

זִרְמָה, f. constr. זִרְמַת, *Copious, outpouring, emission*, Ezek. xxiii. 20. Aff. זִרְמָתָם, al. non occ.

זֶרַע, m. pl. aff. זַרְעֵיכֶם, once, 1 Sam. viii. 15, al. pl. non occ. Constr. sing. זֶרַע, once, Num. xi. 7, for זֶרַע. Syr. ܙܪܥܐ, *semen*. Arab. زَرْع, id. Properly, perhaps, the *Act of sowing* seed. Hence, meton. (a) *seed* of corn, plants, trees, &c., Gen. i. 11, 12. 29; xlvii. 19; Lev. xi. 37; xxvi. 5; 1 Sam. viii. 15; Job xxxix. 12, &c.

A A

זרע (178) זרע

(b) Meton. *Time of sowing*, Gen. viii. 22; Lev. xxvi. 5, &c.
(c) *Seed of man*, or other animals, Lev. xvi. 16—18; xix. 20, &c.
(d) Meton. *Issue, progeny*, Gen. xix. 32. 34; xxi. 12; xxxviii. 8; 1 Sam. ii. 20; Gen. vii. 3, &c. Hence the phraseology, זֶרַע הַמַּמְלָכָה, *seed of the rule*, i. e. royal, 2 Kings xi. 1. זֶרַע יִשְׂרָאֵל, progeny of Israel, Ib. xvii. 20, &c. זֶרַע הַקֹּדֶשׁ, — *of holiness*, i. e. of the holy people, Ezra ix. 2. זֶרַע יַעֲקֹב, — *of Jacob*. Comp. Neh. ix. 2. זֶרַע מְרֵעִים, — *of evil doers*, Is. i. 4. זֶרַע שִׁחוֹר, — *of the Nile*, i. e. sown in its neighbourhood, Ib. xxiii. 3. זֶרַע מְנָאֵף, — *of* (the) *adulterer*. שֶׁקֶר, — *of falsehood*, Ib. lvii. 3, 4. אֱמֶת, — *of truth*, Jer. ii. 21. זֶרַע אָדָם וְזֶרַע בְּהֵמָה, — *of man and of beast*, Ib. xxxi. 27. בְּרוּכֵי יְהוָֹה, — *of the blessed of Jehovah*, Is. lxv. 23. זֶרַע אֱלֹהִים, — *of God*, i. e. his adopted children, Mal. ii. 15. הַשָּׁלוֹם, — *of peace*, Zech. viii. 12. אֲנָשִׁים, — *male*, 1 Sam. i. 11. It. abs. זֶרַע, *a progeny, race*, Ps. xxii. 31. Comp. Is. liii. 10. זֶרַע וַרְעֲךָ, *the progeny of thy progeny*, Ib. lix. 21, &c.
Aff. זַרְעִי, זַרְעֲךָ, זַרְעוֹ, &c.

זְרַע, Chald. m. i. q. Heb. זֶרַע, Dan. ii. 43.

זָרַע, v. pres. יִזְרַע. Constr. abs. immed. it. med. אֵת, of obj. of time, Lev. xxv. 22, i. q. בְּ, in, with ; אֶל, on, near ; לְ, to, for. Syr. ܙܪܥ. Arab. زَرَعَ, *seminavit*. Æth. ሐረሠ : id. See זֶרַע.

Sowing, as seed, Gen. xxvi. 12; xlvii. 23; Lev. xxv. 20; xxvi. 16; Jer. iv. 3; xxxv. 7 ; Ps. cvii. 37 : as salt, Judg. ix. 45, &c.: and, by a slight variation, *planting*, Is. xvii. 10 : with זְמוֹרָה. And, perhaps, Zech. x. 9, opp. Ps. lxxx. 9. 16.
Metaph. Wickedness, righteousness, light, &c., Prov. xi. 18; xxii. 8; Job iv. 8; Ps. xcvii. 11 ; Hos. x. 12. *Sow for yourselves to righteousness*, (and) *ye shall reap of grace*, i. e. according to its announcements. Comp. ch. viii. 7.

Infin. זְרֹעַ, Is. xxviii. 24. It. זֶרַע above.
Imp. זְרַע, pl. זִרְעוּ, Eccl. xi. 6 ; 2 Kings xix. 29, &c.
Part. זֹרֵעַ, and זוֹרֵעַ, Gen. i. 29, &c., pl. זוֹרְעִים. Constr. זֹרְעֵי.
Pass. זָרוּעַ, f. זְרוּעָה, Jer. ii. 2; Ps. l. c.
Niph. נִזְרַע, pres. יִזָּרַע. I. *Be, become, sown*, of seed, Lev. xi. 37 ; of name, fame, reputation, i. e. name, &c. *be propagated* as a plant, Nah. i. 14. Comp. Is. xiv. 20. Of place, as receiving seed, Deut. xxi. 4 ; xxix. 22 : of a woman conceiving, Num. v. 28.
II. *Be dispersed*, as seed sown, Ezek. xxxvi. 9. Comp. זָרוּ, vr. 19.
Puh. זֹרַע, *Shall they be, become, sown*, i. e. so as to take root and increase, Is. xl. 24.
Hiph. pres. f. תַּזְרִיעַ, lit. *Produces seed*, as a herb, &c. i. e. bears, or is capable of doing so, Lev. xii. 2.
Part. מַזְרִיעַ, Gen. i. 11, 12.

זֵרְעִים } m. pl. i. q. זֵרוּעִים, Is. lxi. 11.
זֵרְעֹנִים } m. pl. Syr. ܙܶܪܥܽܘܢܳܐ, *legumina*.
Vegetables, Dan. i. 12. 16, al. non occ.

זָרַק, v. pres. יִזְרֹק. Syr. ܙܪܩ, *sparsit*. Arab. زَرَقَ, *effudit*. Constr. immed. it. med. אֵת, obj. בְּ, עַל, on ; ־ָה, towards ; as, הַמִּזְבֵּחָה, towards the altar; מִן, instr. 2 Chron. xxxv. 11. מַיִם. *Scatter, sprinkle*, as dust, ashes, embers: also, water, blood, Job ii. 12 ; 2 Chron. xxxiv. 4 ; Exod. ix. 8. 10 ; xxiv. 6 ; xxix. 16. 20 ; Lev. i. 5. 11 ; iii. 2. Of grey hairs, Hos. vii. 9. זָרְקָה בּוֹ, *scatters upon him*, i. e. the symptoms of age.
Infin. זְרֹק, Ezek. xliii. 18.
Imp. זְרֹק, Ib. x. 2.
Part. זֹרֵק, pl. זֹרְקִים, Lev. vii. 14 ; 2 Chron. xxx. 16.
Puh. זֹרַק, *Was, became, sprinkled*, Num. xix. 13. 20.

זֶרֶת, f. Syr. ܙܪܬ, ܙܪܬܐ, *spithama*. *A span* = 10 inches, 944 dec., Exod. xxviii. 16 ; xxxix. 9 ; 1 Sam. xvii. 4 ; Ezek. xliii. 13 ; Is. xl. 12. See r. זרה.

ח

ח, The eighth letter of the Hebrew alphabet; as a numeral, the number *eight*, Gram. art. 4. Pronounced with the larynx more contracted than in ה, — see that letter; — less than in the Arab. ح: equal to that observed in خ. It is probable that the Hebrew ח had originally both these sounds, and equally so, that some mark was used to designate either the one or the other of these, which has now long been lost, Gram. art. 13. Expressed by the LXX. and other Greek writers, in proper names, &c. by χ, κ, or one or other of the vowels; and so by the Latins: as, חָם, χάμ, חָרָן, χαρράν; פֶּסַח, φασέκ; טֶבַח, ταβέκ; חֶרְמוֹן, 'Αερμών; חַוָּה, Αὐραυῖτις; חַוָּה, Εὖα. It. רָחָב, 'Ραχάβ, and 'Ραάβ, &c. Comp. Vulg. Lat., and see Thesaur. Gesen., p. 436. It interchanges in cognate words, and the dialects, with letters of the same organ, Gram. art. 23, as in חָנָק, עָנָק; it. with other letters in some respects similar in sound; as, חָיִל, גִּיל, חָדַר, גָּבַר, חָבַל, כָּבַל, נָבֵל, גָּבַר, כָּבַר, חָבַר, פָּתַח, &c. In the dialects, חָשַׁק. Arab. عشق; חָבַה, شرق, &c., which will be seen under the several roots and other words, as they occur. Gesenius finds the origin of its name (חֵית) in the Arab. and Syr. ܚܳܛ, حاط, *he bound about*, and thence signifying *inclosure*, as its Phœnician and Samaritan form seems to imply. Ewald, in ܚܰܝܬܳܐ, Talm. חַיְתָא, *pera*, from حات, *circumdare*. It may be suggested that, as the aspiration is stronger here than in ה, anciently א, — whence the Gr. E. Gesenius's *septum, inclosure*, might be nothing more than this doubled, thus, 吕, or Samaritan Ǝ, and present a mere double *hh*,—just as the Gr. ω, may be resolved into a double o; or н, into єз: and so Gesenius himself represents it = *hh*. If this may be relied on, the name might have originated in the Arab. حوى, *collegit, congregavit, comprehendit*: and signify *comprehension*, implying the union of both these letters. Cogn. حي, *vixit.*, ii. conj. *uberem, fœcundamque comperit terram*. Whence the proper name חַוָּה, *Eve*, כִּי הִוא הָיְתָה אֵם כָּל־חָי, *because she became the mother* (container. Arab. أحبي, *uterus*) *of all living*, Gen. iii. 20. Besides, the change of ח into ם in Gesenius's etymology is objectionable, as there is no apparent reason for supposing that the ח, in חַיָּה, is radical.

חֹב, m. Aff. חֻבִּי, once, Job xxxi. 33. Samar. חוב, *sinus*. Syr. ܚܽܘܒܳܐ, *amor, as resting in the breast or heart. The breast, bosom.* Cogn. חָבָא. Syr. ܚܒܳܐ, *caligo*. Arab. خبأ. Æth. ኀብአ: Arab. خفي, *occultavit*.

חבא, non occ. pret. pres., &c. Imp. חֲבִי, Is. xxvi. 20, r. cogn. חבה, *Hide, be in concealment*. LXX. ἀποκρύβηθι. Niph. נֶחְבָּא, pres. יֵחָבֵא, *Became, was, hidden, concealed*. Constr. abs. it. med. ב, with, among, בְּ, in; לְ, with Infin., Gen. iii. 10; xxxi. 27; Judg. ix. 5; 1 Sam. x. 27; Job xxix. 8. 10. See my notes, Dan. x. 7, &c.

Infin. הֵחָבֵא Dan. x. 7, &c. It. Gram. art. 202. 4.
הֵחָבֵה 1 Kings xxii. 25; 2 Kings vii. 12.

Part. נֶחְבָּא, Jer. xlix. 10. Pl. m. נֶחְבָּאִים, Josh. x. 17. Puh. חֻבָּא, i. q. Niph. Job xxiv. 4, al. non occ. Hiph. הֶחְבִּיאָה, f. it. with ה parag. הֶחְבְּאָתָה, Josh. vi. 17. 25, pres. יַחְבִּיא, *Hide, conceal*, Is. xlix. 2. Comp. Job xxxvi. 32, and my note. אַחְבִּא, 1st pers. 1 Kings xviii. 13—4. Hoph. הָחְבָּא, i. q. Niph. Is. xlii. 22, only. Hithp. הִתְחַבֵּא, pres. יִתְחַבֵּא, i. q. Niph. 1 Sam. xiii. 6; xiv. 11; xxiii. 23; Gen. iii. 8; Job xxxviii. 30. Part. מִתְחַבֵּא, pl. מִתְחַבְּאִים, 1 Sam. xiv. 22; 2 Kings xi. 3, &c.

חֹבֵב, part. r. חבב. Arab. حبّ, *amavit*. Syr. ܚܒܒ, *accendit*; ܐܚܒ, *amore accensus est*. Cogn. חָבָא. Arab. خبأ, *concealed*, i. e. in order to protect. *Loving, cherishing*, once, Deut. xxxiii. 3.

חבו (180) חבל

lxx. καὶ ἐφείσατο τοῦ λαοῦ αὐτοῦ. See the context.

חֲבוּלָא, f. once, Dan. vi. 23. *Corrupt thing*, part. pass. r. חבל, which see.

חַבּוּרָה f. r. חבר, which see. Lit.
חֲבוּרָה } *closed, a closing;* hence, *The seam, scar,* or *cicatrix, of a wound,* or other injury. Arab. حَبَرَ, *recruduit vulnus;* حِبْرٌ, *vestigium, cicatrix;* حِبَرَةٌ, *vestis striata.* Cogn. خُبْرٌ, *notitia,* pl. חַבּוּרֹת, Gen. iv. 23; Exod. xxi. 25; Is. i. 6; Ps. xxxviii. 6; Prov. xx. 30. Aff. חַבּוּרָתִי, חַבּוּרוֹתַי, and once, חַבְרָתוֹ, Is. liii. 5.

חבט, v. pret. non occ. pres. יַחְבֹּט. Constr. abs. immed. it. med. אֶת. Syr. ܚܒܰܛ, *concussit.* Arab. خَبَطَ, *fuste excussit oleas. Beat off,* or *out,* as fruit from a tree, or corn from the ear, Deut. xxiv. 20; Is. xxvii. 12; Ruth ii. 17.

Part. חֹבֵט, Judg. vi. 11.

Niph. pres. יֵחָבֵט, *Is, becomes, beaten out,* Is. xxviii. 27, al. non occ.

חֶבְיוֹן, m. once, Hab. iii. 4, r. חָבָה, cogn. τοῦ, חָבָא, which see. *A covering,* or *vail.* lxx. ἀγάπησιν, as if from r. חבב.

חֵבֶל, once, חַבָל, Is. lxvi. 7, m. constr. once, f. Zeph. ii. 6; pl. חֲבָלִים, constr. חַבְלֵי, and חֶבְלֵי. Syr. ܚܰܒܠܳܐ, *funis.* Arab. حَبْلٌ, id. Æth. ሐብል : id. Eng. *cable.* Gr. κάμιλος. See Hieroz. Boch. i. lib. ii. c. v. p. 91, seq. *A rope,* or *cord,* Josh. ii. 15; Jer. xxxviii. 6. 11. 13; Job xl. 20; Hos. xi. 4; Esth. i. 6. Metaph. Eccl. xii. 6. Hence, meton. (a) *a gin, snare,* Job xviii. 10; Ps. cxl. 6:—*fatal,* Ps. xviii. 5, 6; cxvi. 3, &c.

It. meton. (b) *Cord* or *line* with which land is measured, 2 Sam. viii. 2; Amos vii. 17; Zech. ii. 1, &c. It.—

Meton. (c) *A lot,* or *portion,* of land so measured, Deut. iii. 4. 13, 14; Josh. xvii. 14; 1 Kings iv. 13; 1 Chron. xvi. 18; Ps. xvi. 6; cv. 11; Mic. ii. 5. 10, &c.

(d) Also *The person* possessing such portion or lot, Deut. xxxii. 9; Ezek. xlvii. 13. See נַחֲלָה. It.—

(e) *A company,* or *band,* of men, 1 Sam. x. 5. 10. It.—

Metaph. (f). As from the notion of *constriction* (see צר), *narrowness* of circumstances, follows that of *difficulty, penury, pain;* so here, *pain,* as of child-birth, &c. is occasionally intended, Is. xiii. 8; lxvi. 7; Jer. xiii. 21; xxii. 23; Hos. xiii. 13; Job xxxix. 3. *Pains,* generally, Job xxi. 17. But this might mean *portions* (c) above. So the Gr. ὠδῖνες. See Æschyl. Agam. 1427. Eurip. Ion. 45, Gesen. See Steph. Thesaur. Gr. sub. ὀδύνη; ὠδίν; ὠδίνω.

Aff. חַבְלִי, חֲבָלַי, חֲבָלָיו, חַבְלֵיהֶם. On the variety (-), (ִ), in the vowels here, and constr., see Gram. art. 96. 2.

חֲבֹל, m. } pl. non occ. Lit. *binding,*
חֲבֹלָה, f. } hence, *A pledge,* Ezek. xviii. 12. 16; xxxiii. 15; f. once. Aff. חֲבֹלָתוֹ, *his pledge,* Ib. xviii. 7.

חֹבֵל, m. constr. pl. חֹבְלֵי, r. חָבַל. Lit. *roper. Seafaring,* or *ship man, sailor,* Jonah i. 6; Ezek. xxvii. 8. 27—29. Aff. חֹבְלָיו.

חֲבָל, and חֲבָלָא, m. Chald. (see חבל, f., above). *Injury, hurt,* Dan. iii. 25; Ezra iv. 22.

חָבַל, v. pres. יַחְבֹּל, it. תַּחְבֹּל, אֶחְבֹּל, r. חָבַל, above. Constr. abs. immed. med. עַל, on; לְ, to. I. *Bind,* (a) as with *a rope.*

Part. חֹבְלִים, Zech. xi. 7. 14. *Binders,* or *bands:* a mystical name given to a shepherd's staff, representing the union of *brotherhood,* vr. 14, ib.

Metaph. (b) as with *A pledge,* Job xxii. 6. Meton. by taking something *in pledge,* Deut. xxiv. 6. 17; Job xxiv. 3. 9. See my notes.

Infin. חֲבֹל, and חָבֹל, Exod. xxii. 25; Ezek. xviii. 16.

Imp. aff. חַבְלֵהוּ, Prov. xx. 16; xxvii. 13.

Part. pass. חֲבֻלִים, Amos ii. 8.

Pih. חִבֵּל, pres. יְחַבֵּל, *Bringing forth* with pain, Cant. viii. 5. In Ps. vii. 15, *conceiving,* perhaps. Arab. حَبِلَ, *concepit.* In Syr. however, ܚܰܒܠܰܬ, *parturivit.*

II. Kal, *Inflicting pain, oppressing, doing wrong,* Neh. i. 7; Job xxxiv. 31.

Niph. יֵחָבֵל, *Shall suffer pain, loss,* Prov. xiii. 13. Gr. ΑΛΛ. καταφθαρήσεται. See Targ. and Syr.

Pih. חִבֵּל, pres. תְּחַבֵּל, *Injure, corrupt,* Eccl. v. 5; Mic. ii. 10.

Infin. חַבֵּל, Is. xiii. 5; xxxii. 7; liv. 16. Part. pl. m. מְחַבְּלִים, Cant. ii. 15.

Puh. חֻבַּל, *Bound, injured, undone,* Job xvii. 1. See my note, Is. x. 27. Lit. the

חבל (181) חבק

yoke shall be injured, broken, i. e. its galling effects overcome by fatness, i. e. prosperity.

חֲבַל, Chald. Paḥ. non occ.

Paḥ. pret. aff. חַבְּלוּנִי, *Have injured me*, Dan. ii. 23.

Imp. aff. חַבְּלוּהִי, *Destroy it*, Ib. iv. 20.

Inf. חַבָּלָה, Ezra vi. 12.

Ithpaḥ. תִּתְחַבַּל, *Shall be, become, destroyed*, Dan. ii. 44; vi. 27; vii. 14.

חֶבֶל, m. once, Prov. xxiii. 34. According to Gesenius, *the cable-rope* attached to an anchor; and, בְּרֹאשׁ חִבֵּל, at *its extremity*, i. e. I suppose, where it is connected with the anchor, when a ship is moored, i. q. בְּלָרָיִם, in the former member. Ewald prefers "*orcus*," as a destroyer. Now, we have in Syr. ܚܒܠ ܣܘܠܩܐ, *sulcus maris*, according to Castell; and, in the Arab. حَبْلٌ, *arenæ cumulus, instar funis terræ incumbens;* so that, in either case, the *top* or *head* of this may be taken to signify *a ridge*, generally; in the sea, *a wave* or *billow*. In Job ix. 8, see my note, the stability of God is marked by saying that *he treads on the high places of the sea*. Here, perhaps, a similar expression is used to shew the absence of all stability and safety in man: i. e. that *he lies*, as it were, on *the head* or top *of the billow*, or *breaker;* for this last the form חִבֵּל seems to intimate, Gram. art. 154. 4, fm. i. and note, ib. par. 12, i. e. implying habit. LXX. ἐν πολλῷ κλύδωνι. So the Syr. and Arab. This word has usually been taken to signify the *mast of a ship*, but evidently on grounds of the weakest probability.

חֲבַצֶּלֶת, f. Cant. ii. 1; Is. xxxv. 1, only. See Cels. Hierob. i., p. 488, seq. Compd. of حَبَصَ, *protrusit, strinxit*, (cogn. مَحْضٌ, *acidus factus, erubuit*) and بَصَلٌ, *cepa:* and perhaps the same thing with سَقَنْجَبِيلٌ, *narcissus, lilium*, according to Castell; but according to Gesenius, *colchicum autumnale*, a wild autumnal flower not unlike saffron, having a bulbous root. To my mind, however, it is far more probable that the *lily* is meant, which has a bulbous root; partly because we have in Cant. ii. 1, שׁוֹשַׁנָּה in the parallel; because it seems to correspond to the κρίνα τοῦ ἀγροῦ, of the Evangelists, Matt. vi. 28; Luke xii. 27; and because Judea abounded with it. This seems to be the true Shemitic word:

the other, viz. שׁוּשָׁן, to have been a foreign word, imported from Σοῦσα, in Persia. See Cels. Hierob. i., p. 383, seq. and the LXX.

חבק, v. in Kal non occ. Syr. ܚܒܩ, *amplexus*. Arab. حَبَقَ, *congessit simul* &c.

Infin. חֲבוֹק, *Embracing*, Eccl. iii. 5.

Part. חֹבֵק, *Folding together*, Ib. iv. 5.

חֹבֶקֶת, f. *embracing*, 2 Kings iv. 16, al. non occ.

Pih. חִבֵּק, pres. יְחַבֵּק. Constr. immed. it. abs. it. med. לְ. *Embracing*, Gen. xxix. 13; xxxiii. 4; xlviii. 10; Prov. iv. 8; v. 20. Of inanimate things, Job xxiv. 8. See my note, Lam. iv. 5, implying distress.

Infin. חַבֵּק, Eccl. iii. 5. It.

חִבֻּק, *Folding together* of the hands, Prov. vi. 10; xxiv. 33, Gram. art. 154. 10, fm. ii.

חָבֵר, m. ⎫ pl. non occ. Syr.
חֶבְרָה, f. ⎭ ܚܒܪܐ, *societas*. Arab. حَبْرٌ, *concentus in horto Paradisi*. *Associating*, for good or bad, Hos. vi. 9; Prov. xxi. 9; xxv. 24; f. Job xxxiv. 8, al. non occ.

חָבֵר, m. ⎫ pl. m. חֲבֵרִים, constr. חַבְרֵי.
חֲבֵרָה, f. ⎭ *Associate, companion*, Judg. xx. 11; Is. i. 23; xliv. 11; xxxvii. 16. 19; Ps. xlv. 8; cxix. 63; Prov. xxviii. 24; Eccl. iv. 10, &c.; f. Mal. ii. 14. Aff. חֲבֵרְךָ, *Thy companion*.

Aff. חֲבֵרָיו, חֲבֵרֶיךָ, חֲבֵרוֹ.

חַבְרוֹהִי, m. pl. Chald. aff. *His companions*, Dan. ii. 13. 17, 18.

חַבְרָתָהּ, id. f. Chald. *Its companion*, Dan. vii. 20.

חַבָּר, m. pl. חַבָּרִים, once only, Job xl. 31. *Persons* habitually *associated*, i. e. fellows of a society; or, perhaps, companies of such. See my note on l. c.

חָבַר, v. pret. pl. חָבְרוּ, *They joined, assembled*, Gen. xiv. 3, al. non occ.

Part. f. pl. חֹבְרֹת, *Joining*. Constr. med אֶל, לְ, עַל, Exod. xxvi. 3; xxviii. 7; xxxix. 4; Ezek. i. 9. 11.

Pass. חָבוּר, constr. Hos. iv. 17, constr.

Pih. חִבֵּר, pres. יְחַבֵּר, constr. abs. immed. it. med. אֵת, it. אֶל, עִם, to whom. *Joining, attaching*, Exod. xxvi. 6. 9. 11; xxxvi. 10. 13. 16; 2 Chron. xx. 36.

Infin. חַבֵּר, Exod. xxxvi. 18.

Puh. חֻבַּר, pres. יְחֻבַּר, *Was, became, joined,*

Exod. xxviii. 7; xxxix. 4; Ps. cxxii. 3; once, יֶחְבָּרְךָ, Ps. xciv. 20. The characteristic Dagesh being omitted, Eccl. ix. 4. Keri.

Hiph. אַחְבִּירָה, Job xvi. 4, *I might compose, put together.* See my note.

Hithp. אֶתְחַבַּר, for הִתְחַבֵּר, Syriasm. יִתְחַבָּרוּ, *Become associated, be joined,* 2 Chron. xx. 35; Dan. xi. 6.

Infin. aff. הִתְחֶבְרְךָ, *Thy being associated,* 2 Chron. xx. 37.

חֶבְרִי, m. patronym. of חֶבֶר, Num. xxvi. 45.

חֹבֶרֶת, f. of חָבֵר, *Conjunction, joining,* Exod. xxvi. 4. 10.

חָבַשׁ, v. pres. יַחְבֹּשׁ, יֶחְבָּשׁ. Constr. abs. it. immed. thing or pers. med. לְ, עַל, pers. it. בְּ, instr. it. med. אֵת. Syr. ܚܒܫ, *obstrinxit.* Arab. حَبَسَ, *congregavit;* حَبَّسَ, *continuit.* Cogn. خَبَسَ, *cepit manu sua;* خَبَشَ, *colligit. Bind* about, as a wound or fracture, the head with a tiara, an ass with a saddle, &c., Gen. xxii. 3; Exod. xxix. 9; Lev. viii. 13; Ezek. xvi. 10; xxxiv. 4. 16; 2 Sam. xvii. 23. In Job v. 18; xxxiv. 17, *Bind,* in the sense of rule, govern. So Is. iii. 7. Part. as a skilful physician, restoring the health of the State, Gesen. Hos. vi. 1.

Infin. חֲבֹשׁ, Is. xxx. 26; lxi. 1. Aff. חָבְשָׁה, Ezek. xxx. 21.

Imp. חֲבוֹשׁ, Job xl. 8; Ezek. xxiv. 17, pl. m. חִבְשׁוּ, 1 Kings xiii. 13.

Part. pass. חָבוּשׁ, *Bound,* Jonah ii. 6. חֲבֻשִׁים, pl. Judg. xix. 10, &c.

Pih. חִבֵּשׁ, *Restrain,* Job xxviii. 11. See my note.

Part. מְחַבֵּשׁ, *Binding up,* Ps. cxlvii. 3.

Puh. חֻבָּשָׁה, חֻבָּשׁוּ, *Was, became, bound up,* Is. i. 6; Ezek. xxx. 21.

חֲבִתִּים, m. pl. once, 1 Chron. ix. 31. Syr. ܚܒܬܐ, *inflammatus.* Arab. خَبَا, r. خبر, *arsit, accendit.* Baked cakes or pastry, made perhaps in a מַחֲבַת, *frying pan.*

חָג, m. pl. חַגִּים. Syr. ܚܓܐ, *festus dies.* Arab. حَج, *solemnitas,* pec. *peregrinatio Meccana. The festival* appointed under the law to be holden on certain occasions, Exod. x. 9; xii. 14; xiii. 6; xxiii. 15, &c. There were three principal ones: I. That of the *Passover,* commencing on the fourteenth night of the month Abib: II. That of the *Pentecost,* on the fiftieth day afterwards: III. That of *Tabernacles,* seven weeks after the Pentecost. For the manner in which these were anciently calculated, see the notes to my Sermon on the Sabbath, 2d edit. "Κατ' ἐξοχὴν," says Gesenius, "de scenopegia." But this is not true; it is applied to each of the other festivals with equal emphasis.

Meton. *The sacrifice,* or *any part of it,* offered up on such occasions, Ps. cxviii. 27; Exod. xxiii. 18; Mal. ii. 3.

Aff. חַגֵּכֶם, חַגְּכֶם, חַגְּנוּ, חַגֶּךָ, חַגֶּךְ, חַגִּי.

חָגָא, f. Some MSS. read חָגָה, once, Is. xix. 17. *A refuge,* as some think. Arab. حَجَا, *confugit.* Syr. ܚܓܐ, *rupes.*

According to others, *Fear.* Arab. خَجَا, *erubuit.* So the context seems to require, and so the LXX. εἰς φόβητρον; it. Syr. Targ. Aquila, εἰς γύρωσιν.

חָגָב, m. pl. חֲגָבִים, *A sort of locust,* so called, perhaps, because their flight is said to conceal the sun (حَجَبَ, *velavit*); but this is extremely doubtful, Lev. xi. 22; Num. xiii. 33; Is. xl. 22; Eccl. xii. 5; 2 Chron. vii. 13.

חָגַג, v. pret. non occ. pres. יָחֹג, pl. once, יָחֹגּוּ. Constr. immed. it. abs. it. med. אֵת, thing or time in which; לְ, pers. בְּ, in, of place. Syr. ܚܓ, *festum celebravit.* Arab. حَج, id. Cogn. Heb. חוג. *Feasting, revelling,* either in a good or bad sense, Exod. v. 1; 1 Sam. xxx. 16; Ps. cvii. 27. Gesenius sees in these places, *dancing, moving round in a circle, &c.,* which is perhaps fanciful. Pec. *keeping the festivals* prescribed by the law; hence constr. with חַג, as, חַגֹּתֶם חַג, ye shall feast a feast, Num. xxix. 12; Exod. xii. 14; Lev. xxiii. 41; med. אֵת, Deut. xvi. 15.

Infin. חֹג, Zech. xiv. 16. 18, 19.

Imp. f. חָגִּי, Nahum i. 15.

Part. חוֹגֵג, pl. חֹגְגִים, Ps. xlii. 5; 1 Sam. l. c.

חַגְוֵי, pl. m. constr. of חֲגָוִים, perhaps Syr. ܚܓܐ, *rupes.* Arab. حَجَا, *confugit,* it. حَجَا, *tractus pars,* r. حجر. Phr.

בְּחַגְוֵי הַסֶּלַע. In *the fastnesses of the rock*, Jer. xlix. 16; Obad. vr. 3; Cant. ii. 14.

חָגוֹר, m.
חֲגוֹרָה, f. } pl. f. חֲגֹרוֹת. Infin. of v. חָגַר, *binding about*; hence, *A girdle, belt*, 1 Sam. xviii. 4; 2 Sam. xx. 8; Prov. xxxi. 24:—f. Gen. iii. 7; 2 Sam. xviii. 11; 2 Kings iii. 21; Is. iii. 24; xxxii. 11. Aff. חֲגֹרָתוֹ, 1 Kings ii. 5. Aff. m. חֲגוֹרוֹ.

חָגַר, v. pres. יַחְגֹּר, constr. immed. it. med. אֶת, obj.—med. בְּ, with which,—it. in the place which. It. immed. thing; med. עַל, on which. Arab. حَجَرَ, *impedivit*; حَجَر, *circulo tenui circumdata fuit luna*.

I. *Gird, bind about*, as a tiara, ephod, sackcloth, armour, sword, the garment about the loins, &c., Exod. xxix. 9; Is. xv. 3; Ezek. vii. 18; xxvii. 31; Lam. ii. 10; Lev. viii. 7. 13; xvi. 4; Judg. iii. 16; 1 Sam. xvii. 39. Metaph. Ps. lxv. 13; Prov. xxxi. 17.

II. *Withhold, restrain*, 2 Sam. xxii. 46; Ps. lxxvi. 11. See Arab. above.

Infin. חֲגֹר, Is. xxii. 12.
Imp. חֲגֹר, 2 Kings iv. 29; ix. 1; Ps. xlv. 4; pl. הִגְרוּ, 2 Sam. iii. 31: f. חִגְרִי, Jer. vi. 26; pl. חֲגֹרְנָה, Ib. xlix. 3.
Part. חֹגֵר, 1 Kings xx. 11, &c.
Pass. חָגוּר, pl. חֲגוּרִים, Judg. xviii. 11; Exod. xii. 11, &c.: f. constr. חֲגוּרַת, Joel i. 8.

חַד, m. } Chald. i. q. Heb.
חֲדָא, or חֲדָה, f. } אֶחָד, Gram. art. 181. 9. *One*, Dan. vi. 3; vii. 5, &c. Used occasionally as the indefinite article, *a, an*, Dan. ii. 31; vi. 18; Ezra iv. 8: to express the ordinal, Gram. art. 181. 4. *First*, Ezra v. 13; vi. 3; Dan. vii. 1. Prefixed to any other number will imply *once* that number of times; as, חַד־שִׁבְעָה, *one seven times*, or *seven fold*, Dan. iii. 19. With כ prefixed, *as one*, i. e. *together*, Dan. ii. 35. It. Heb. Ezek. xxxiii. 30.

חַד, m. non occ. } Arab. حَدّ, *acies*
חַדָּה, f. }
gladii. Cogn. خَدّ, *fovea, sulcus*. *Sharp as a sword*, Is. xlix. 2. See my note on Job xxxvi. 32; Ezek. v. 1; Ps. lvii. 5; Prov. v. 4.

חָדַד, v. pres. non occ.—pl. m. חַדּוּ, *They are keen, fierce*, Hab. i. 8.

Hiph. pres. יָחֵד, *Makes sharp, sharpens*, Prov. xxvii. 17. The following יָחַד is manifestly the pres. Hiph. apoc. of חָדָה, which see; and the passage exhibits an elegant play on these words—a very common thing in adages in all languages—*Iron sharpens iron; so a man delights—enlivens—the face of his friend.* The LXX. elegantly, παροξύνει πρόσωπον ἑταίρου.

Hoph. f. הוּחַדָּה, *Made sharp, sharpened*, Ezek. xxi. 14—16.

חָדָה, v. pret. non occ.—pres. apoc. יָחְדְּ. Constr. med. עַל. Syr. ܚܕܝ, *gavisus est*. Æth. ኀደየ: *tranquillus factus est*. Exod. xviii. 9, *Was glad, rejoiced*. On Job iii. 6, which is usually cited here, see my note. I more than doubt whether "*gaudeat inter dies anni*," can be said to present anything like Hebrew usage. See too the latter member; which seems to determine the question. Sym. μηδὲ συναφθείη.

Pih. 2 pers. aff. תְּחַדֵּהוּ, *Makest him glad*, Ps. xxi. 7, al. non occ.

Hiph. apoc. יָחַד, *Delights, makes glad*, Prov. xxvii. 17. See חוּד above.

חִדּוּד, m. pl. constr. חִדּוּדֵי, *Very sharp things of* —, once, Job xli. 22. See my note on the place, r. חוּד. The form implies intensity, Gram. art. 154. 9, seq.

חֶדְוָה, f. constr. חֶדְוַת, r. חדה, *Joy, gladness*, Neh. viii. 10; 1 Chron. xvi. 27. Chald. id., Ezra vi. 16, al. non occ.

חַדִּין, m. pl. Chald. sing. non occ. once, aff. חֲדוֹהִי, *His breasts*, Dan. ii. 32, i. q. Heb. חָזֶה.

חֶדֶל, m. once, Is. xxxviii. 11. "*Orcus*," according to Gesenius. But no such notion can be shewn to have been entertained by the ancient Hebrews: see my notes on Job xxi. 13; xxvi. 6, with the note also on vr. 5, which will suffice for his appeals to Scheidius (Thes. sub voce) and the term רְפָאִים. Besides, the passage says, לֹא אַבִּיט וגו׳, *I shall* NOT *look upon*, &c. How, then, can *orcus*, propr. *locus quietis*,—supposing Hezekiah to be now hasting thither,—quadrate with this context? Surely this is an oversight. Aquila and Theod. seem to have read חָדֵל here, and this as commencing the next verse. Aq. ἐπαύσατο γενεά μου. Th. ἐξέλιπεν ἡ γενεά μου. The phrase, יוֹשְׁבֵי חֶדֶל, evidently means *the possessors of leisure*, i. e. persons at rest in their possessions. Of these Hezekiah

חדל (184) חדר

says, he shall no longer be one. We have a similar phrase in Ps. xxii. 4, viz. יוֹשֵׁב תְּהִלּוֹת יִשְׂרָאֵל, *Possessor of the praises of Israel.* Comp. Job xiii. 26. Arab. حَدَلَ,

حَدَلَ, *inclinatio;* خِذْلَ, *desertus fuit;* خَذَلَ, *deseruit.* Cogn. عَطَلَ. Engl. *idle.*

חָדֵל, m. — pl. non occ. See חָדֵל. Constr. חֲדַל. *Ceasing, wanting, failing,* Ps. xxxix. 5; Ezek. iii. 27; Is. liii. 3, חֲדַל אִישִׁים, LXX. ἐκλεῖπον (εἶδος) παρὰ τοὺς υἱοὺς τῶν ἀνθρώπων. *Failing* (of the respect) *of men,* i. e. of being a favourite. Comp. Job xix. 14. Arab. حَذَلَ, *declinavit, a. re. constr.*

خَذَلَ عَنْ, *desertus fuit.*

חָדַל, and חָדֵל, pres. יָחְדַּל, יֶחְדַּל, Constr. abs. med. ל, מִן, with Infin., Job iii. 17. וּמִן, specif. it. Is. i. 16—med. ל, מִן, pers. it. מִן, of thing, it. אֶת, obj. *Cease, desist, forbear, fail,* Gen. xi. 8; xviii. 11; xli. 49; Exod. ix. 34; xxiii. 5; Ps. xxxvi. 4; Is. xxiv. 8; Judg. v. 6, 7; xv. 7; Job xvi. 6; Deut. xv. 11; 1 Sam. ix. 5; Job x. 20, &c.
Infin. חֲדֹל, 1 Sam. xii. 23.
Imp. חֲדַל, חִדְלוּ, Exod. xiv. 12, &c.
Pl. חָדְלוּ, Is. i. 16. 22; pause, חָדֵלוּ, Zech. xi. 12.
Part. חָדֵל above.

חֲדַלְתִּי, see הֶחֱדַלְתִּי above.

חֵדֶק, and חֶדֶק, m. Arab. حَدَقٌ, *melongena spinosa.* See Cels. Hierob. ii., p. 35, seq. *A sort of thorn* with which they make fences, Prov. xv. 19. See my note on Job v. 5.

חֶדֶר, m. pl. חֲדָרִים, constr. חַדְרֵי. Syr. ܚܶܕܪܳܐ, *ambitus.* Arab. حَدَرَ, *circumvallavit* urbem. Castell. Cogn. خَدَرَ, *post velamentum; catuit.* Cogn. خِدْرٌ, *penetrale.* Æth. ኀደረ: *habitavit.* Cogn. חצר. Arab. حَضَرَ, حِصْرٌ, lit. *an inclosure,* here, *A chamber,* or other *inner apartment,* Gen. xliii. 30; Judg. xv. 1; xvi. 9. 12; 2 Sam. iv. 7; xiii. 10; Joel ii. 16; Cant. i. 4; iii. 4. Metaph. Job ix. 9. See my note, Prov. xviii. 8; xxvi. 22. חַדְרֵי־בָטֶן, *chambers* or *cellulæ* of the *viscera;* the inner parts of the person, Ib. vii. 27. חַדְרֵי־שְׁאוֹל, — *of the*

grave, i. e. the niches prepared to receive the several coffins. Comp. Is. xiv. 15. 18. אִישׁ בְּבֵיתוֹ. Here, again, Gesenius finds the "*orcus*" of the poets. See חָדֵל above, and the places referred to.

חֲדַר, constr. sing. is either erroneously pointed, or belongs to another form, חֲדָר, perhaps. Syr. ܚܶܕܪܳܐ, *ambitus,* Judg. iii. 24; 2 Sam. iv. 7, &c. Aff. חֲדָרָיו, חֲדָרֶיךָ, חֲדָרָיו.

חֹדֶרֶת, f. part. constr. ל, once, Ezek. xxi. 19. *Inclosing, laying siege to.*

חֹדֶשׁ, m. pl. חֳדָשִׁים, constr. חָדְשֵׁי. Syr. ܚܰܕܬܳܐ, *nova.* Æth. ሐዲስ: *novus.* Arab. حَدَثَ, *res de novo existens.* Lit. *renewing* or *renewal,* hence, *the Commencement of the Hebrew months:* and, meton., *the Month itself;* or space of time assigned to it; styled also *the new moon;* and hence, certain *feasts,* which were holden at the beginning of the month. Gesenius tells us here—what indeed every one has long believed to be true — "*mensis lunaris* calendæ." It is, however, extremely doubtful whether the ancient Hebrews had ever any thing to do with *lunar computation.* The appointments of Moses took it for granted that, at the recurrence of certain feasts, the produce of the earth would always be in a specific state of maturity; which could not be the case if the year was lunar: and certainly no provision whatever was made to correct this. In Egypt, too, the first appointment of this sort was made (see Exod. xii. 1); and among the Egyptians the year was purely *solar.* See my Sermon on the Sabbath, p. 26, seq. If then this computation was originally *solar,* all would be plain, easy, and regular, the feasts and festivals all duly recurring, as there shewn; and this, I believe, was the fact.

It appears also from the most ancient Jewish respectable writers now extant, that the feast of the passover—the first and leading rite of the Jews—did, in their times, regularly take place at the *vernal equinox;* and this must have been regulated by *solar,* not *lunar,* computation, of necessity. Anatolius, as cited by Beveridge, in Canon. vii. Apost. p. 464, vol. i. Patr. Apost. Amst. 1724, informs us, " ex antiquioribus Judæorum Magistris, duobus Agathobulis et Aristobulo (qui unus fuit ex LXX. senioribus, qui Biblia Græca verterant) asserit δεῖν τὰ διαβατήρια θύειν ἐπίσης ἅπαντας μετὰ

חדש (185) חדש

ἰσημερίαν ἐαρινὴν, μεσοῦντος τοῦ πρώτου μηνὸς, apud Euseb. Hist. Eccl. l. 7, c. 32, p. 287, Edit. Vales. Addit insuper ibidem Aristobulus in celebrando paschate requiri, μὴ μονὸν τὸν ἥλιον τὸ ἰσημερινὸν διαπορεύεσθαι τμῆμα καὶ τὴν σελήνην δέ, nimirum, ut cum Pascha peragatur, *sol vernum æquinoctiale segmentum obtineat, et luna autumnale ei oppositum*, sive hæc Libræ, ille Arietis. Idem docet Josephus, τῷ δὲ μηνὶ τῷ ξανθικῷ, ὃς νισσὰν παρ' ἡμῖν καλεῖται, καὶ τοῦ ἔτους ἐστὶν ἀρχὴ, τεσσαρεσκαιδεκάτῃ κατὰ σελήνην, ἐν κριῷ τοῦ ἡλίου καθεστῶτος. Joseph. Antiq. Jud. l. 3, c. 10, p. 93, l. A. edit. Rovier. 1611, unde patet annum Judaicum ita tunc temporis ordinatum fuisse, ut xiv. luna mensis Nisan celebraretur, cum sol arietem ingressus est. Hisce suffragatur et Philo Judæus ἑκατέρα γὰρ τῶν ἰσημεριῶν ἑβδόμῳ γίνεται μηνὶ, καθ' ἃς καὶ ἑορτάζειν διείρηται νόμῳ τὰς μεγίστας καὶ δημοτελεστάτας ἑορτάς. Phil. Jud. de Mundi Opific. p. 27, l. B. edit. Paris, 1640. Ex his enim Philonis verbis liquidissimè constat, Pascha celebrari κατ' ἰσημερίαν ἐαρινὴν, non minus quàm festum Tabernaculorum κατὰ μεταπωρινή." Beveridge concludes, " Quapropter, etiamsi Judæi nonnunquam Pascha antè vernum æquinoctium obierint : *hoc tamen non ex majorum, nedum Mosis . . . . instituto ; sed potius ex periodorum, quibus usi sunt, labe ac vitio accidit.*"

When the lunar computation was first introduced by the Jews, it is perhaps impossible now to say. The cycle of nineteen years was, according to Selden (my Serm. on Sab., p. 29), introduced by Hillel, about A.D. 358. It is clear, therefore, from the testimony of the most ancient and respectable Jewish writers, that the Jewish year was in their days determined by *solar*, and not by *lunar, computation.*

It is true, indeed, that both the term *moon* (σελήνη), and *month* (μηνί, ἑβδόμῳ), occur in each of these places ; while it is obvious, from the context, that it is impossible the period itself could have been regulated by the course of the moon. In like manner, the term *month* (μὴν), occurs in the LXX. for the Hebrew חדש, and occasionally for ירח, *moon*. But, as the moon is said generally to have been given, with the sun (Gen. i. 14), for *signs, seasons, &c.*, the term might here have been used in a lax sense, rather to designate the period of a month, than to affirm any thing about the mode of its chronological calculation or recurrence. In like manner, I think the terms *νεομηνία* and *νουμηνία, new-moon*, were taken, both in the Old Testament and in the New, as translations of חדש, אחד לחדש, and ראש לחדש, Num. xxix. 6 ; Exod. xl. 2 ; Num. x. 10 : Coloss. ii. 16, &c. In this way too, ירח, and pl. ירחים, Deut. xxi. 13 ; Exod. ii. 2, &c. were probably used ; just as the term *month* has in Europe, ever since the adoption of the *solar year* under Julius Cæsar, — thence termed Julian, — without having any thing whatever to do with its calculation.

Now, if the Hebrew year was originally *solar* only, its commencement would regularly take place when the sun entered Aries ; this would constitute the ראש חדשים, ראש השנה, and ראשון לחדשי השנה; see Exod. xii. 1. This, then, and every succeeding *month*, חדש, or ירח, would consist probably of thirty days, as the patriarchal year apparently did,* and as also did that of the Egyptians ; making in the whole, 360 days. The Egyptians, moreover, according both to Herodotus † and Diodorus Siculus, ‡ added either the remaining five days, or five days and a fraction, at the end of every twelfth month, and so completed the *solar year*. And such addition might have been made in times much more remote, by the Patriarchs. For, if they could ascertain the time at which the sun entered Aries, they also must have known that twelve months, of thirty days each,

---

* In Gen. vii. 11—13, we find that Noah entered the ark on the 17th day of the second month. Ib. viii. 4, the ark rested upon the mountains of Ararat, on the 17th day of the 7th month ; making exactly five months since Noah had entered it. Again, Ib. vr. 3, we are told that this continued during 150 days ; which makes exactly five months of thirty days each. Serm. on the Sabbath, p. 27.

† Herod. Lib. ii. c. iv. πρώτους Αἰγυπτίους ἀνθρώπων ἁπάντων ἐξευρέειν τὸν ἐνιαυτὸν, δυώδεκα μέρεα δασαμένους τῶν ὡρέων ἐς αὐτόν. ταῦτα δὲ ἐξευρέειν ἐκ τῶν ἀστρων ἔλεγον . . . . Αἰγύπτιοι δὲ τριηκοντημέρους ἄγοντες τοὺς δυώδεκα μῆνας, ἐπάγουσι ἀνὰ πᾶν ἔτος πέντε ἡμέρας πάρεξ τοῦ ἀριθμοῦ, κ. τ. λ.

‡ The testimony of Diodorus Siculus is, Lib. i. c. L. οἱ δὲ Θηβαῖοι . . . . ἰδίως . . . . καὶ τὰ περὶ τοὺς μῆνας αὐτοῖς καὶ τοὺς ἐνιαυτοὺς διατετάχθαι. τὰς γὰρ ἡμέρας οὐκ ἄγουσι κατὰ σελήνην, ἀλλὰ κατὰ τὸν ἥλιον, τριακονθημέρους μὲν τιθέμενοι τοὺς μῆνας, πέντε δὲ ἡμέρας καὶ τέταρτον τοῖς δώδεκα μησὶν ἐπάγουσι, καὶ τούτῳ τῷ τρόπῳ τὸν ἐνιαύσιον κύκλον ἀναπληροῦσιν.

B B

would never complete the year. I will only add, that, if any reliance can be placed on what has been said, it will follow, that the Jews have lost every trace of the true Sabbath appointed by Moses, and of every other festival depending thereon, just as they also have of the distinction of their tribes. On the methods of calculating time, adopted by the modern Jews, see Scaliger de Emendatione Temporum, p. 194, &c. D. Petavius de Doctrina Temp. p. 234, &c.

— חֹדֶשׁ, signifying, (a) 1*st of the month*, Num. xxix. 6; 1 Sam. xx. 5; xviii. 24.

(b) *A month* in duration generally, Lev. xxvii. 3; Num. iii. 15; ix. 22, &c.

(c) *Feast* or *festival*, held at certain periods of the month, Num. xxviii. 14; Deut. xvi. 1; 1 Sam. xx. 5. 18; 2 Kings iv. 23; Is. i. 13, &c. Phrases, אֹדְשֵׁי יָמִים *whether a month, or some days*, Num. ix. 22. חֹדֶשׁ יָמִים, *a month of days*, i. e. thirty days, or a month's space, Ib. xi. 20, 21. בְּחָדְשׁוֹ *son, i. e. age, of a month*, Ib. xviii. 16. חָדְשׁוֹ בְּחָדְשׁוֹ לְחָדְשֵׁי הַשָּׁנָה, *feast in its feast, of the feasts of the year*, i. e. in every yearly feast, see vr. 11, Ib. xxviii. 14. Comp. Is. lxvi. 23. יֹאכְלֵם חֹדֶשׁ, *a feast shall devour them*, Hos. v. 7. Comp. vr. 6. 8, et seq., and Is. xxxiv. 6, seq. בְּרֹאשׁוֹן בְּאֶחָד לַחֹדֶשׁ, *in the first month, in the first day of the month*, Gen. viii. 13. The months were generally numbered, as, *first, second, &c.* Gen. viii. 13, &c.; occasionally the name was added, as אָבִיב, Exod. ix. 31, &c.

חֳדָשִׁ, m. pl. חֳדָשִׁים) constr. non occ.
חֲדָשָׁה, f. pl. חֲדָשׁוֹת) *New, recent, fresh*, applied either to persons or things, Exod. i. 5; Lev. xxvi. 10; Deut. xx. 5; xxii. 8; Job xxix. 20; Ps. xxxiii. 3; xl. 4; Is. xliii. 19. חֲדָשָׁה, *something fresh, strange*. Comp. Eccl. i. 10; Is. lxii. 2; Jer. xxxi. 22; Ezek. xi. 19, &c. חֲגוֹר חֲדָשָׁה, *girded* (lit.) *newly; recently accoutred*, i. e. with new weapons, &c.; perhaps, LXX. περιεζωσμένος κορύνην. אֱלֹהִים חֲדָשִׁים, *fresh, newly made, gods*, Deut. xxxii. 17; Judg. v. 8. It. *heavens and earth*, Is. lxv. 17; lxvi. 22. Comp. Rev. xxi. 1. Plainly alluding to Christian times.

חָדַשׁ, v. non occ. in Kal. See חֹדֶשׁ.
Pih. חִדֵּשׁ, pres. יְחַדֵּשׁ. Constr. immed. it. med. אֶת. *Renew, restore*, Is. lxi. 4; 1 Sam. xi. 14; Job x. 17; 2 Chron. xv. 8.
Imp. חַדֵּשׁ, Ps. li. 12; Lam. v. 21. It. Infin. 2 Chron. xxiv. 4.

Hithp. תִּתְחַדֵּשׁ, *It becomes renewed, restored*, i. e. נְעוּרָיְכִי, *thy youth*, Ps. ciii. 5, al. non occ.

חֲדַת, m. Chald. i. q. Heb. חָדָשׁ, *New*, Ezra vi. 4.

חִיָּא, see חָיָה.

חוֹב, m. seg. חוּב, Gram. art. 87. 1. Syr. ܚܰܘܒܳܐ, *debitum*. Arab. حَوْب, *peccatum*. Cogn. خُوب, *reducing to poverty. Debt, what is owing*, Ezek. xviii. 7, al. non occ. Hence the verb—

Pih. חִיַּבְתָּה, *You will render due, forfeit*, Dan. i. 10, al. non occ.

חוּג, m. Syr. ܚܽܘܓܳܐ, *ambitus*. LXX. γύρον. Sym. περιγραφήν. *Spherical surface, form*, Job xxii. 14. See my note. Is. xl. 22; Prov. viii. 27, are perhaps imitations of the place in Job, al. non occ. Hence the verb—

חָג, pret. Kal, *He circumscribed*, Job xxvi. 10. See my note. LXX. ἐγύρωσεν. Sym. περιέγραψεν.

חוּד, v. pret. חַדְתָּה, 2 pers. sing. m.— pres. parag. אָחוּדָה. Constr. immed. thing med. ל, pers. Arab. cogn. حَادَ, حيد, *declinavit, deflexit*, a re. حَبَّك, *fecit nodos in loro*; حبك, "*nodus in cornu capri montani; costa valde curva*;" it. المِثَل والنّظير, *similis:*" *similitudo* rather. Kāmoos. See חִידָה. *Proposing an enigma, or riddle*, Judg. xiv. 12. LXX. πρόβλημα ὑμῖν προβάλλομαι, Ib. vr. 16. Synon. מָשָׁל, Ezek. xvii. 2.
Imp. חוּד, parag. ה, חוּדָה, Ezek. xvii. 2; Judg. xiv. 13.

חוה, v. non occ. in Kal.
Pih. pres. יְחַוֶּה, constr. immed. it. med. אֶת. pers. to whom. Syr. ܚܰܘܺܝ, ܚܰܘܳܐ, *indicavit*. Arab. حَوَى, *comprehendit*. Cogn. خوى, *praebuit* mulieri puerperae *cibum*. Its usage is rather Chaldee than Heb. Synon. הִגִּיד. *Shewing, declaring*, proof or demonstration, Job xxxii. 10. 17; xv. 17; xxxvi. 2; Ps. xix. 3.
Infin. חַוֹּת, Job xxxii. 6. It. Chald.—
Pah. pres. אֲחַוֵּא, &c. i. q. Heb. Dan. ii. 4. 11. 24; v. 7.
Aph. pres. יְהַחֲוֵה, &c. i. q. Pah. Dan. v. 12; ii. 6, 7. 9.

חוֹח (187) חוּל

Infin. הַחֲוָיָה, Dan. ii. 10. 16. 27; v. 15.
Imp. aff. הַחֲוֻנִי, Shew ye me, Dan. ii. 6.

חוֹחַ, m. pl. חוֹחִים, and seg. חֲוָחִים. Syr. ܚܘܳܚܳܐ, pruna persica, it. olus. Arab. خُوخ, malum persicum, each of which Gesenius also makes *pruna spinosa!* I. *Thorn* or *bramble*, generally, 2 Kings xiv. 9; 2 Chron. xxv. 18; Is. xxxiv. 13; Hos. ix. 6; Prov. xxvi. 9; Job xxxi. 40; Cant. ii. 2; seg. pl. 1 Sam. xiii. 6.

II. *A fish-hook* made of a thorn, or it may be *an arrow* pointed with a thorn, Job xl. 26 (21). LXX. ψελλίῳ. See חָח.

חוּט, m. pl. non occ. Syr. ܚܘܛܐ, *filum, linea.* Arab. خَوْط, *binding*; خُوط, *filum ex duobus coloribus, &c. A thread*, or *line*, Josh. ii. 18; Judg. xvi. 12; 1 Kings vii. 15; Jer. lii. 21; Eccl. iv. 12; Cant. iv. 3; Gen. xiv. 23. מֵחוּט וְעַד שְׂרוֹךְ, *from thread*, i. e. tie, *even to shoe-latchet*, is evidently proverbial. So the Scholiast on the Hamāsa, Freytag's edit., p. ۳٤٥.

يضرب المثل بها في حقارة الشيء

a proverb is formed on it, on the worthlessness of any thing. Gesen. complains in his Thes., p. 452, that both Giggeius and Castell have erroneously stated this in the Lexicons. See Castell, under فتل. But Gesenius is wrong: not they. The passage in the Kāmoos is,

وَمَا أَغْنَى عَنْكَ فَتِيلًا وَلَا فَتِيلَةً

I am not, or he is not enriched, by thee in a *thread, not even* in *a single thread.* Gesen. "ne hilum quidem lucrati sunt a te." Where *hilum* is not a literal translation of فتيل, nor is the verb in the plural number. Castell. and Gig. "*nihil lucratus est*," citing only part of the passage. See also Freytag's Lex., under فتيل. Hence the verb—

חוּט, Chald. v. Kal non occ.

Aph. יְחִיטוּ, *They conjoin, make continuous*, as a thread, so as to enclose the city, Ezra v. 12. Syr. ܡܫܰܚܠܶܦ, *circumdedit*.

חִוִּי, m. patronym. a *Hivite*, Gen. xxxiv. 2, &c.

חוּל, חִיל, v. pret. חָל, דִּלְתִּי, pres. תָּחוּל, apoc. תָּחָל, it. יָחִיל, apoc. יָחֵל. Constr.

abs. it. med. לְ, for which; מִן, מִפְּנֵי, *from, by*, do.; בְּ, in. Syr. ܡܚܝܠܐ, *imbecillus*. Arab. حَال, r. حول, *præteriit navis, versus, mutatusque fuit, vi polluit.*

I. *Being in pain*, as of child-birth, Deut. ii. 25; 1 Sam. xxxi. 3; 1 Chron. x. 3; Is. xiii. 8; xxiii. 4; xxvi. 17; liv. 1; lxvi. 7, 8; Jer. v. 3. 22; Hos. viii. 10; Joel ii. 6; Mic. i. 12. *Pained for*, לְמוֹב, *prosperity*, Zech. ix. 5. Meton. *bringing forth*, Is. xlv. 10.

(b) Metaph. applied to lands, mountains, &c. *Shaking, trembling*, as if suffering the pains of child-birth, Ps. x. 5; lxxvii. 17; xcvii. 4; Jer. li. 29; Hab. iii. 10.

(c) יָחִילוּ, *They wait*, Judg. iii. 25; apoc יָחֵל, Gen. viii. 10, taking the sense of r. יָחַל. Gram. art. 202. 4.

Infin. חוּל, Ezek. xxx. 17, *Being in pain*.
Imp. f. חוּלִי, Mic. iv. 10; Ps. cxiv. 7; pl. m. חִילוּ, Ps. xciv. 9.

Pih. חוֹלֵל, pres. תְּחוֹלֵל, *Bringing forth, producing*, as by birth. Meton. Ps. xc. 2; Is. li. 2; Job xxvi. 13.

Infin. חֹלֵל, Job xxxix. 1. And by a further meton.—

(d) *Forming, fashioning.* Part. aff. מְחוֹלְלֶךָ, Deut. xxxii. 18.

(e) תְּחוֹלֵל, *Wait than*—r. יָחַל as above— Job xxxv. 14.

Part. מְחוֹלֵל, Prov. xxvi. 10. רַב מְחוֹלֵל־כֹּל. If רַב were here the nominative, constituting the subject of a particular proposition, it would regularly have the definite article. Nor does it ever signify in pure Hebrew, *a master*, or *teacher*, generally, as Gesenius will have it. Besides, it would be out of place to speak of such an one, *producing*, as by birth, *all things*; although it would not, when God is the subject of the discourse. And, again, רַב is never put for *God* in the Bible. The usual rendering, therefore, as well as that proposed by Gesenius, is erroneous. I take כֹּל, therefore, as the subject, and nominative, here, thus: *all expecting much*, (are) *as he who hires a fool, or hires transgressors;* i. e. will find themselves mistaken in the end.

(e) יְחוֹלֵל, pl. יְחוֹלְלוּ, Ps. xxix. 9. See אֵל above. Job xxvi. 5, it.

Part. מְחוֹלְלָה, f. Is. li. 9; liii. 5. *Wounding*, *cutting*, take the sense of the r. חלל.

(d) Puh. חוֹלָל, *Became, was, brought forth, fashioned*, Job xv. 7; Ps. li. 7; Prov. viii. 24, 25.

Hoph. i. q. Puh. יוּחַל, Is. lxvi. 8.

חוּל (188) חוּם

(c) Hithp. Imp. הִתְחוֹלֵל, *Be expecting*, Ps. xxxvii. 7, r. יָחַל.
Part. מִתְחוֹלֵל, *Suffering pain*, Job xv. 2. See my note.
It. redup. fm. f. תִּתְחַלְחַל, *She is pained*, Esth. iv. 4.

II. Kal. Arab. حَالَ, r. حول, *retinuit, insidias struxit*. Cogn. حَلَّ, *descendit, substitit*. Æth. cogn. ⲚⲰϨ: *mansit*; ⲰⲠⲈ: *fuit*. *Fall upon, rest, remain*, 2 Sam. iii. 29; Hos. xi. 6; Jer. xxiii. 19; xxx. 23; Lam. iv. 7.
Hithp. part. מִתְחוֹלֵל, *Falling, descending*, Jer. xxiii. 19.

III. Arab. حَالَ, r. حول, *mota fuit, vacillavit res: commotus fuit* homo : حَوَّلَ, *insilivit* in equum : *distortus fuit*. Cog. جيل , جول. Heb. גִיל.
Infin. חֻל, *Dancing*, probably moving round in a circle, and leaping, Judg. xxi. 21.
Part. f. pl. מְחֹלְלוֹת, *Dancing women*, Judg. xxi. 23.
It. pl. m. מְחֹלְלִים, of. Cogn. r. חלל, *Dancing*, 1 Kings i. 40.
Hiph. יָחִיל, pres. *Shall exult*. Cogn. גִיל, Job xx. 21. Meton.

חוֹל, m. Syr. ܚܳܠܐ, *arena*. Arab. حَالَ, *lutum*. *Sand*, Exod. ii. 12 ; Deut. xxxiii. 19; Jer. v. 22. Often used to intimate *abundance*, Gen. xxxii. 13; xli. 9; Judg. vii. 12. *Weight*, Job vi. 3; Prov. xxvii. 3. *Measure, number*, Jer. xxxiii. 22; Hos. ii. 1; Job xxix. 18.

חוּם, masc. pl. non occ. Arab. خَام, *pannus gossipinus, crudus, non dealbatus lotione*, &c. Cogn. حَام, *Æthiops* homo. Syr. ܚܳܡ, *incaluit*. Cogn. Heb. חמם. Arab. حَمَّ, *niger fuit*. *Dark* in colour, of flocks, Gen. xxx. 32, 33. 35. 40. LXX. φαιόν.

חוֹמָה, f. constr. חוֹמַת, pl. חוֹמוֹת. Dual. חֹמָתַיִם, r. חָמָה. Arab. حَمِي, *præsidio custodivit*: cogn. حَمَى, *prohibuit* ; حَام, r. حرم, *obivit, rem circumlatus fuit*. *A wall*, Lev. xxv. 30, 31. Of a city, Deut. iii. 5; xxviii. 52; Is. xxii. 10; xxxvi. 11, 12; Ps. li. 20; Neh. iii. 8. 33, &c. Metaph. Cant. viii. 9, 10; Jer. i. 18. So Horace, "*Hic murus aëneus esto*," &c. Applied to waters, Exod. xiv. 22; 1 Sam. xxv. 16. Dual. 2 Kings xxv. 4; Jer. xxxix. 4; lii. 7. A place to the west of Jerusalem, containing the fountain of Siloa, and the king's gardens, enclosed, as it should seem, with a second wall. Comp. 2 Chron. xxxiii. 14; Neh. iii. 15. Aff. חוֹמָתָהּ, חוֹמָתֵךְ, חוֹמָתָיִךְ.

חוּס, v. pret. f. חָסָה, חַסְתְּ, pres. יָחוּס. Constr. med. עַל, it. abs. Syr. ܚܳܣ, *pepercit*. *Spare, pity, be affected for*, frequently with עַיִן, *the eye*, Gen. xlv. 20; Deut. vii. 16; xiii. 9; xix. 13; Is. xiii. 18; Jer. xiii. 14; Ezek. v. 11; xxiv. 14; Jon. iv. 11; Ps. lxxii. 13, &c.

חוּף, חֹף, m.—pl. non occ. Arab. خَوْف, *succinctorium* ; حَافَة, *ripa*. *Shore* of the sea, Gen. xlix. 13; Deut. i. 7; Josh. ix. 1; Judg. v. 17; Jer. xlvii. 7; Ezek. xxv. 16.

חוּץ, m.—pl. f. חוּצוֹת, with ה, parag. חוּצָה, or חֻצָה. Syr. ܚܳܨ, *strinxit, coarctavit*, Arab. حَاصَ, r. حوص, id. cogn. Syr. ܚܳܫ, *circumdedit*. Arab. حَاطَ, r. حوط, id. Any thing or place surrounding or inclosing another, as—

(a) *An open place round about*, or *without, a house*, &c., Is. v. 25; x. 6; li. 23; Jer. xxxvii. 21; Lam. ii. 19. 21; iv. 1, &c. Hence—

(b) *Out fields, lands*, &c., with respect to any city or country; and, in the last case, *deserts*, Job v. 10; Prov. viii. 26. Comp. Mark i. 45. With ה, parag. חוּצָה, Prov. v. 16. Phrases, מַיִם הַחוּצוֹת, *mire of places without*, Mic. vii. 10; Zech. ix. 3; x. 5; Ps. xviii. 43. בְּרֹאשׁ כָּל־חוּצוֹת, *at the head of all open places*, Is. li. 20; Nahum iii. 10, &c. חוּצוֹת תָּשִׂים לְךָ, *open places* (not unlike our *squares* perhaps) *thou shalt appoint* (make) *for thyself*, 1 Kings xx. 34. פְּנֵי חוּץ, *the face of* (lands) *without*, i. e. distant, Job xviii. 17. פְּנֵי הַחוּצוֹת, id., Ib. v. 10. Comp. Prov. viii. 26. Hence—

(d) Adv. or prep. *Without*, opp. to *within*, either as to house or country. מוֹלֶדֶת חוּץ *born without*, not home-born, Deut. xxiii. 14; Lev. xviii. 9; Is. xxxiii. 7; 1 Kings vi. 6, &c. It.—

חוק (189) חור

(e) *Outwards,* Exod. xii. 46; 2 Chron. xxiv. 8; xxix. 16. Also with def. art. prefixed, הַחוּץ, Judg. xix. 25; Nehem. xiii. 8. It. הַחוּצָה, id., Gen. xv. 5; xix. 17; 2 Sam. xiii. 17; 1 Kings viii. 8, &c. With prep. בַּחוּץ, Gen. ix. 22; Exod. xxi. 19, &c. לַחוּץ, Ps. xli. 7; Ezek. xli. 17. לָחוּצָה, 2 Chron. xxxii. 5. מִחוּץ, Deut. xxxii. 25; Lam. i. 20. מֵחוּץ, Ezek. xli. 25. Constr. med. לְ, with respect to which, &c., Gen. xix. 16; xxiv. 11, &c. It. לְמִחוּצָה, Ezek. xl. 40. 44. It. אֶל הַחוּצָה, Ezek. xxxiv. 21. לְ מִחוּץ, Lev. iv. 12. 21; vi. 4, &c. Hence, also—

(f) Prep. *Besides, except,* Eccl. ii. 25. LXX. παρέξ. See also Nold., p. 337, &c.

חוֹק, Ps. lxxiv. 11, Kethiv. See חִיק.

חֻקְנוּ, for חָקְקוּ, r. חקק. See חֹק.

חוּר, m. ⎫
חוֹר, m. ⎬ pl. חוֹרִים, and once חוֹרֵי, Is. xix. 9. Constr. חוֹרֵי. Syr. ܚܶܘܳܪ, *albus.* Arab. حَارّ, r. حور, *candida fuit* vestis. Cogn. حُرّ, *ingenuus fuit.* I. *White* (fine) linen, Esth. i. 6; viii. 15; Is. xix. 9. LXX. τὴν βύσσον, al. *net-works.* On this pl. see Gram. art. 139. 6.

II. Meton. *Nobles,* as arrayed in white and splendid robes. See Esth. viii. 15; Dan. vii. 9, and my note on Job vi. 16;—1 Kings xxi. 8. 11; Jer. xxvii. 19; xxxix. 6; Neh. ii. 16; iv. 14; v. 7; vi. 17; vii. 5; xiii. 17; Eccl. x. 17. Aff. חֹרֶיהָ, Is. xxxiv. 12. The first fm. is contr. for חָווּר, the second for חָוֹור, perhaps, Gram. art. 75.

III. Either from another primitive, or from a highly metaphorical usage of this; as, حَوْر, *ima pars, profunditas.* Cogn. خَوْر, *depressa terra; ostium fluminis, &c.* and hence, perhaps, *an aperture* in the ground, &c. by which the light enters.

(a) *The aperture, hole,* (a) of a *viper,* Is. xi. 8: (b) in a wall, &c. as of a window, &c. Ezek. viii. 7; 2 Kings xii. 10; Cant. v. 4.

(b) *A den,* or *cavern,* Job xxx. 6; 1 Sam. xiv. 11; Nahum ii. 13. Used as *a prison.* See בְּאֵר, pl. חוֹרִים, Is. xlii. 22. Aff. חֹרָיו. *His eye-sockets,* or cavities, חֹרָיו, Zech. xiv. 12. Hence, probably, הַחֹרִי, *the Horite,* Gen. xiv. 6, who appear to have resided in *caverns* in the mountains, which are still to be seen in Idumea. LXX. χορραίους.

חִוָּר, m. Chald. i. q. Heb. חוּר; I. above, *White,* Dan. vii. 9.

חוּר, v. pres. m. pl. יֶחֱוָרוּ, *Shall they be white, pale,* Is. xxix. 22, al. non occ. See חוּר above.

חוֹרִי, see חֹרִי.

חוּשׁ, v. pret. חָשׁ, pres. יָחוּשׁ, apoc. f. תָּחַשׁ. Constr. abs. it. med. לְ, עַל. Æth. ሐወሠ: *movit, agitavit.* Arab. حَاشَ, r. حوش, *concitavit, cinctam undique ut in retia ageret, prædam.* Engl. haste, hasten. *Hurrying, hastening,* Deut. xxxii. 35; 1 Sam. xx. 38; Is. viii. 1. 3. This passage is sometimes misunderstood. The prophet was commanded to write down in the presence of certain witnesses, named in the next verse, לְמַהֵר שָׁלָל חָשׁ בַּז, *As to the hastening of* (the) *spoil,* (the) *contempt shall hurry.* This is a prediction; and to this, as such, were the witnesses cited to bear testimony. Soon after this the prophet has a son by his wife, and this prediction,—that it might be the more prominent,—is taken and made his name, vr. 3, 4. Neither with the conception of the child, nor the imposition of this name, had the witnesses any thing to do; but only to attest the fact of the prediction. Comp. Is. xliii. 9, 10.—Hab. i. 8; Ps. xxii. 20; xxxviii. 22; xl. 14; LXX. 2. 6; Job xxxi. 5. Applied to *the hurry,* visible in a highly excited state of mind, Job xx. 2. And to the lusts, according to Gesenius, Eccl. ii. 25. וּמִי יָחוּשׁ, "*quis genio indulsit?*" LXX. τίς πίεται. It is certain that both אכל, and שׂחה, are so occasionally applied.

Infin. חוּשׁ; aff. חוּשִׁי; *My haste,* Job xx. 2. See my note.

חוּשָׁה, with ה, parag. Ps. xxii. 20, &c. *Hasten, I pray,* Gram. art. 234.

Hiph. pl. m. הֵחִישׁוּ, pres. יָחִישׁ. *Hasten, accelerate,* Judg. xx. 37; Is. v. 19; lx. 22; Ps. lv. 9. And, by meton. *stumble,* as the consequence of hurry, *fail,* Is. xxviii. 16. Comp. Rom. ix. 33; x. 11. LXX. καταισχυνθῇ, by a further meton.

חוֹתָם, m. r. חתם, which see. Properly a *seal-ring,* i. e. a ring for the finger, in which *a seal* is set. Comp. Jer. xxii. 24; Job xli. 7, with Cant. viii. 6, whence it should seem that *a seal on the heart* must mean one fixed there; not hung with a string from the neck, and so resting over the heart, as Gesenius thinks;—and hence *a seal,* by meton. Exod. xxviii. 11. 21; Job xxxvii. 14; Hag. ii. 23. Aff. חוֹתָמְךָ, חֹתָמוֹ.

חזה   (190)   חזו

חָזָה, v. pres. יֶחֱזֶה, apoc. אָחַז, תַּחַז. Constr. immed. it. abs. it. med. עַל, concerning which; בְּ, in, on; לְ, for; מִן, from. Syr. ܚܙܐ, consideravit, it. Samar. Arab. خَزَى, conjecturâ æstimavit; occulta indicavit. See also my note on Job xxiii. 9. Cogn. אָחַז. Arab. أخذ, apprehendit. Beholding, viewing, looking upon, observing: hence, considering, discovering, meditating on, and announcing.

(a) — visions, as a prophet, and hence termed חֹזֶה, Is. i. 1; ii. 1; xiii. 1; Amos i. 1; Ezek. xiii. 6; Hab. i. 1; Zech. x. 2; Num. xxiv. 4; Lam. ii. 14.

(b) — any thing with pleasure, Ps. xxvii. 4; Cant. vii. 1; Mic. iv. 11; Job xxxvi. 25.

(c) Looking out any person for office, Exod. xviii. 21; Is. lvii. 8.

(d) — at the Divine appearance, Exod. xxiv. 11; Job xix. 26; Ps. xi. 7; xvii. 15; lxiii. 3.

(e) — any thing, by way of investigation, Job xv. 17; xxiv. 1; xxvii. 12; Ib. viii. 17, apparently in the sense of אָחַז.

Imp. חֲזֵה, Is. xxxiii. 20.

חֲזוּ, pl. Ps. xlvi. 9.

Infin. חֲזוֹת, Ezek. xxi. 34; Ps. xxvii. 4.

Part. חֹזֶה, 2 Sam. xxiv. 11; 2 Kings xvii. 13. Seer, prophet.

חֹזִים, pl. Ezek. xxii. 28, &c. Aff. חֹזַי.

חֲזָה, and חֲזָא, v. Chald. i. q. Heb. Dan. iv. 6. 20; vii. 1, &c.

Infin. מֶחֱזָא, Ezra iv. 14.

Part. חָזֵה, Seeing, Dan. ii. 31, &c.

חָזַיִן, pl. Dan. iii. 27, &c.

חָזֶה, m. constr. חֲזֵה, pl. f. חֲזוֹת. Syr. ܚܕܝܐ, pectus. Arab. حَدًى, carnis frustum. The breast of an animal when cut up, Exod. xxix. 26, 27; Lev. vii. 30, 31; ix. 20, 21, &c. LXX. στηθύνιον.

חֲזוּ, m. Chald. def. חֶזְוָא, pl. חֶזְוִין, constr. חֶזְוֵי. Syr. ܚܙܘܐ, visio. A vision, Dan. ii. 28; iv. 2. 7; vii. 7. 13. Meton. appearance, Dan. vii. 20. Aff. חֶזְוִי, חֶזְוֵהּ, r. חזה.

חִזָּיוֹן, m.—pl. non occ. Constr. חֶזְיוֹן, r. חזה. A vision, or revelation, Dan. i. 17; viii. 1; ix. 24; 1 Sam. iii. 1; Prov. xxix. 18; Lam. ii. 9; 1 Chron. xvii. 15; Is. i. 1, &c.

חָזוּת, f. Vision, revelation, Infin. abs. r. חזה, 2 Chron. ix. 29. Aff. חֲזוּתָהּ, Chald. Dan. iv. 8. 17. Meton. its appearance.

חָזוּת, f. r. חזה, Vision, revelation. Meton. matter of do., Is. xxi. 2; xxix. 11. In Dan. viii. 5, קֶרֶן חָזוּת, "cornu conspicuum, magnum," according to Gesenius. But, horn of vision, i. e. a horn appeared in (the) vision. Again, vr. 8, חָזוּת אַרְבַּע, he makes "quattuor conspicua." All I can see, however, is, they arose (in) vision, four (in) place of it. Aff. חֲזוּתְכֶם, Is. xxviii. 18.

חִזָּיוֹן, m.—pl. f. חֶזְיוֹנוֹת, r. חזה. A vision, as afforded in a dream, Job xxxiii. 15. בַּחֲלוֹם חֶזְיוֹן לַיְלָה, in a dream, a vision of the night, Ib. xx. 8; iv. 13; vii. 14; Joel iii. 1; Zech. xiii. 4. Gesenius makes this word the construct. form of חִזָּיוֹן, contrary to all analogy.

חִזָּיוֹן, m. r. חזה. Continued or habitual vision, revelation; so the form seems to imply. Comp. 2 Sam. vii. 17. It occurs elsewhere only twice, viz. Is. xxii. 1. 5, in the phrase, גֵּיא, or גֵּיא חִזָּיוֹן, valley of frequent vision, revelation, i. e. Jerusalem, to which the context certainly alludes.

חָזִיז, or חָזִיז, m. pl. חֲזִיזִים. Arab. حَزَّ, secuit. Cogn. خَزَّ, transfodit. See my notes on Job xxviii. 26; xxxviii. 25. Lit. cutting, piercing. The lightning or thunderbolt, it. Zech. x. 1. al. non occ.

חֲזִיר, m. Arab. خِنزِير, porcus. Swine, hog, pig, either domestic or wild, Lev. xi. 7; Deut. xiv. 8; Is. lxv. 4; lxvi. 3. 17; Ps. lxxx. 14; Prov. xi. 22.

חָזָק, m. Aff. חָזְקִי, Ps. xviii. 2. —

חָזְקָה, f. Aff. חֶזְקַת, constr. Is. viii. 12.— Arabic حَزَّ, rei tenax. Syr. ܚܣܢܐ, zona. Strength, firmness; the first occ. only, l. c. the second, l. c. and, aff. חֶזְקָתוֹ, 2 Chron. xii. 1; xxvi. 16; Dan. xi. 2.

חָזָק, m. pl. חֲזָקִים, constr. חִזְקֵי ⎫ Strong,
חֲזָקָה, f.—pl. non occ. . . . ⎭ mighty,
unyielding, prevailing, applied to persons or things, in either a good or bad sense. Masc. Exod. xix. 19; xviii. 16; Num. xiii. 31; Josh. xiv. 11, &c.: pl. Judg. xviii. 26; Job xxxvii. 18; Ezek. ii. 4; iii. 7, 8. Fem. often used with יָד, Exod. iii. 19; vi. 1; xiii. 9; xxxii. 11, &c. With זְרוֹעַ, Jer. xxi. 5; Ezek. xx. 34; Deut. iv. 34; v. 15;

חזק (191) חזק

vii. 19. With מִלְחָמָה, 1 Sam. xiv. 54; 2 Sam. xi. 15, &c.

חֹזֶק, m. } i. q. חֵזֶק } Strength, force,
חָזְקָה, f. } and חֶזְקָה } vehemence.
Infin. v. חזק below. Masc., Exod. xiii. 3. 14. 16; Amos vi. 13. Fem., 1 Sam. ii. 16; Ezek. xxxiv. 4; Judg. iv. 3; viii. 1; Jon. iii. 8. Aff. m. חָזְקֵנוּ, Amos l. c.

חָזַק, m. i. q. חָזַק, occ. only in the phrase הוֹלֵךְ וְחָזֵק, proceeding and strong, i. e. gradually stronger, Exod. xix. 19; 2 Sam. iii. 1. See Gram. art. 146. 2, and note.

חָזָק, v. pres. יֶחֱזַק. See חֵזֶק above. Synon. אמץ. Constr. abs. it. immed. בְּ, in; אֶל, עַל, on, to; מִן, more than; לְ, to, for. Applied to persons, mind, or things. Being, becoming, strong, firm, powerful, unyielding, prevailing, Gen. xli. 56, 57; xlvii. 20; Exod. vii. 13; Judg. i. 28; 2 Kings iii. 26; xiv. 5; 2 Chron. xxv. 3; Ezek. iii. 14. In 2 Sam. xviii. 9, not "firmiter adhærebat," as Gesenius thinks; but, became firm, fast: nor Is. xxviii. 22, " constrictus est," but, your bands become firm, unyielding; and so in other places.

Infin. חָזְקָה, Strengthening, 2 Kings xii. 13; Ezek. xxx. 21.

Imp. חֲזַק, Deut. xii. 23; xxxi. 7, &c.

חִזְקוּ, pl. Ib. xxxi. 6, &c.

Pih. חִזַּק, pres. יְחַזֵּק. Constr. immed. it. med. אֶת, בְּ, עַל, לְ, once with דְּ, Ezra i. 6, with בְּ instr. מִן, more than. Making strong, firm, &c.; variously applied, to persons, mind, things, as—

(a) — the hands, loins, arms, i. e. to administer help in one way or other, Judg. ix. 24; Ezra i. 6; Jer. xxiii. 14; Ezek. xiii. 22; Neh. vi. 2 :— Ezek. xxx. 24; Hos. vii. 15; Nah. ii. 2: it. pers. 2 Kings xii. 7; Dan. x. 19.

(b) — the heart, or face, i. e. harden it, or declare it to be so, Exod. ix. 12; x. 20. 27; xi. 10; Judg. iii. 12, &c.; Jer. v. 3.

(c) — any one in evil, Ps. lxiv. 6. Comp. Jer. xxiii. 14: it. for good, Neh. ii. 18; 2 Chron. xxxv. 2.

(f) — by restoration, or repair, pers. Ezek. xxxiv. 16: thing, 2 Kings xii. 9. 13. 15; xxii. 5; 2 Chron. xxxiv. 10: by other means, Is. xli. 7; Jer. x. 4.

(g) — by confirmation, as in office, rule, &c., Is. xxii. 21; 2 Chron. xi. 17.

(h) — by fortifying, or the like, Ps. cxlvii. 13; Is. liv. 2; Nahum iii. 14; 2 Chron. xi. 11; xxxii. 5.

Infin. חַזֵּק, Josh. xi. 20, &c.

Imp. חַזֵּק, Deut. i. 38, &c. Aff. חַזְּקֵהוּ, חַזְּקֵהוּ.

חַזְּקִי, in pause, חַזְּקִי, f.

חַזְּקוּ, pl. m.

Part. מְחַזֵּק, pl. מְחַזְּקִים, Exod. xiv. 17; 2 Kings xii. 8.

Hiph. הֶחֱזִיק, pres. יַחֲזִיק, apoc. יַחֲזֵק. Constr. immed. abs.: it. med. אֶת, בְּ, לְ, עַל, עַד, as follows. I. Taking fast hold of, obtaining, retaining. II. Causing, applying, strength, firmness, &c., as, I.—

(a) — the hand, arm, &c.; i. e. helping, &c. Constr. עַל, בְּ, Exod. iv. 4; Neh. iii. 4—10. 17, &c.: it. immed. Zech. xiv. 13. מִימִינִי, Is. xli. 13: it. med. בְּ, Ib. xlv. 1; li. 18; Judg. xvi. 26; 2 Kings xv. 19; Jer. xxxi. 32. — by the beard, 1 Sam. xvii. 35.

(b) — any one; hold with or to him; it. take hold of, &c. med. בְּ, Deut. xxii. 25; xxv. 11: med. לְ, 2 Sam. xv. 5. עַל, Job xviii. 9: immed. Is. xli. 9: med. מִן, Jer. vi. 23, 24, &c.; Judg. vii. 8, &c.: med. בְּ, Jer. L. 33.

(c) — any thing, as power, deceit, &c., Dan. xi. 21; Mic. vii. 18; Jer. viii. 5; Job ii. 3. 9; xxvii. 6; Is. lvi. 4. 23; Prov. xxvi. 17. Comprehending, perhaps, 2 Chron. iv. 5.

(d) — of pain, &c. seizing one, Mic. iv. 9; Jer. vi. 24; xlix. 24, immed.

II. Applying strength to, i. e. repairing, or the like, abs., Neh. v. 16; Ezek. xxvi. 9. 27; xxx. 25: — to self, becoming powerful, 2 Chron. xxvi. 8: med. עַד, Dan. xi. 32. Confirming, 2 Kings xv. 19.

Infin. הַחֲזִיק, Is. lxiv. 6.

Imp. הַחֲזֵק, m. הַחֲזִיקִי, f., 2 Sam. xi. 25; Nahum iii. 14.

הַחֲזִיקוּ, pl. m. Jer. li. 12.

Part. מַחֲזִיק, pl. מַחֲזִיקִים, Exod. ix. 2; Is. lvi. 4, &c.

מַחֲזֶקֶת, f., Neh. iv. 11.

Hithp. הִתְחַזֵּק, pres. יִתְחַזֵּק, constr. abs. it. med. לִפְנֵי, עַל, against; עִם, with; בְּ, in; בְּעַד, for. Becoming, waxing, strong, generally; pec.—

(a) Received strength, Gen. xlviii. 2; Num. xiii. 20; Judg. xx. 22; 1 Sam. xxx. 6: med. בְּ, 2 Chron. xv. 8; xxiii. 1; xxv. 11; xxxii. 5, &c. Synon. חֲזַק, 2 Sam. x. 12;—2 Chron. xiii. 7, 8; med. לִפְנֵי, against.

(b) — for, or with, another; 2 Sam. iii. 6;

חח (192) חטא

med. ַ, 1 Chron. xi. 10; 2 Chron. xvi. 9; Dan. x. 21, med. עִם.
(c) — in office, i. e. confirmed, 2 Chron. i. 1; xvii. 1; med. עַל, over, xii. 13; med. ַ, in; xiii. 21; xxi. 4, abs.
Infin. הִתְחַזֵּק, 2 Chron. xiii. 8, &c.
Imp. הִתְחַזֵּק, 1 Kings xx. 22.
הִתְחַזְּקוּ, 1 Sam. iv. 9.
Part. מִתְחַזֵּק, pl. מִתְחַזְּקִים, 2 Sam. iii. 6; 1 Chron. xi. 10.

חָח, m. p. חַחִים, with dagesh implic., Gram. art. 109, i. q. חוֹחַ. Of הַחָח, according to Gesen. But no such word exists. *A thorn*, generally; pec. *a hook*, or *ring*, originally a mere thorn probably, fixed in the nose of a beast, to which a string was applied, and by this the animal was led along. Hence, metaph. *a nose jewel*, Exod. xxxv. 22: it. applied as above, but with men, 2 Kings xix. 28; Is. xxxvii. 29; Ezek. xix. 4. 9; xxix. 4. חַחִים, kethiv. for חַחִים. Comp. Job xl. 26. See חוֹחַ. Aff. חַחִי.

חֲטָא, m. pl. חַטָּאִים, constr. חַטָּאֵי. Seg. Gram. art. 148. 2. Arab. خَطَأ, *error*. Æth. **ኀጥእ**: *defuit*; pr. either missing, or falling short of, the mark. Meton. *Sin, wickedness*; for the difference between this word and אָשָׁם, עָוֹן, see under אָשַׁם, p. 58. Yet, by meton., this word may take the sense of either, or of *punishment* due to either, (a) Lev. xxiv. 15; Num. ix. 13; xxvii. 3; Deut. xxiv. 16; 2 Kings xiv. 6, &c. So the phrases, חֵטְא לָמוּת, *sin unto death*, worthy of it, Num. xviii. 22; 1 John v. 16, ἁμαρτία πρὸς θάνατον. Comp. Deut. xxii. 26; xxi. 22.
(b) It. *Object of sin*, Is. xxxi. 7.
(c) *State of* do., Ps. li. 7.
(d) *Offence of* do., Eccl. x. 4. Aff. חֶטְאִי, חֶטְאָם, pl. חֲטָאַי, in pause, חֲטָאָי, חֲטָאֵינוּ, חֲטָאֵיהֶם, חֲטָאָיו.

חַטָּא, m. pl. חַטָּאִים, sing. non occ. *Sinners*, retrospectively, (a) as to acts, or (b) prospectively, as to punishment, Num. xxxii. 14; Ps. i. 1; xxvi. 8; xxvi. 9, &c.: (b) 1 Kings i. 21; Ps. civ. 35; Prov. xiii. 21, &c. Aff. חַטָּאַי, Is. xiii. 9.

חַטָּאָה, f. of do., Amos ix. 8, al. non occ.

חֲטָאָה, f. i. q. חֵטְא, Num. xv. 28.

חֲטָאָה, f. id., Gen. xx. 9.

חַטָּאָה, and חַטָּאת, constr. חַטַּאת, pl. חַטֹּאות, i. q. חֵטְא. *Sin, wickedness*, variously applied; viz.

חַטָּאָה, *Sin*, Exod. xxxiv. 7. But, Is. v. 18, its *punishment*, according to Gesenius; which is far from certain, al. non occ.

חַטָּאת, (a) *Sin*, Num. xii. 11; Deut. xix. 15; Prov. xxiv. 9; Mic. i. 13; Job xiii. 23.
(b) Meton. *Sin-offering*, Gen. iv. 6; Exod. xxix. 14. 36; Lev. iv. 24; v. 9, &c. in very many places. Phr. מֵי חַטָּאת, *Water of*—i. e. *cleansing from—sin*, Num. viii. 7.
(c) It. Meton. *Idol*, Deut. ix. 21; Hos. x. 8.
(d) It. Meton. *Punishment* of do., Zech. xiv. 19, to which Gesenius adds, Lam. iii. 39, which is doubtful. Comp. Is. xl. 2; Prov. x. 16. Aff. חַטָּאתִי, Gen. xxxi. 36, &c. חַטָּאתָם, חַטָּאתֵנוּ, חַטָּאתוֹ, חַטָּאתְךָ.

חָטָא, v. pres. יֶחֱטָא, see חֵטְא, constr. abs. it. med. ְ, עַל, against; ְ, by, in, which; מִן, of, short of; it. with חַטָּאת, Lev. iv. 23; 1 Kings xv. 30. חַטָּא, Deut. xix. 15, &c. Propr. *falling short of*, or *missing, the mark*; hence, (a) *Erring, wandering* away from; opp. τῷ, מצא, Prov. viii. 35, 36; Job v. 24.
(a) Meton. *Sinning*, i. e. falling short of, overstepping (transgressing), or neglecting, any positive law or known duty, Gen. xx. 6. 9; Exod. xxxii. 31. 33; Lev. iv. 3; v. 5. 15, 16; Num. vi. 11; 1 Sam. xix. 4; Neh. ix. 29; 1 Kings viii. 31: opp. τῷ, עֲשׂוֹת טוֹב, Eccl. vii. 20. With שְׁגָגָה, Lev. iv. 2; Num. xv. 27, &c. for which expiation might be made. Comp. Num. xv. 30. See אָשַׁם, for the distinctions between חָטָא, עָוֹן, &c. Gesenius confounds these.
Infin. חֲטֹא, Ezek. iii. 20: it. חֲטוֹ, Gen. xx. 6.
חֲטָאתוֹ, aff. Ezek. xxxiii. 12.
Part. חוֹטֵא, Prov. xiii. 22, &c.; pl. חוֹטְאִים, 1 Sam. xiv. 34.
חוֹטֵאת, f. (for חֹטֵאת, contr.) Ezek. xiv. 4.
Pih. חִטֵּא, pres. יְחַטֵּא, constr. immed. it. med. אֶת, עַל, ְ. Propr. *offered a piacular sacrifice*: hence, meton. *Expiated; cleansed*, or *freed from, sin*. Synon. τοῦ, כִּפֵּר, of men, vessels, altar, houses, &c. Gen. xxxi. 39; Lev. xiv. 52; ix. 15; Num. xix. 19; Ps. li. 9; Ezek. xl. 20; xlv. 18.
Infin. חַטֵּא, Lev. xiv. 49; Ezek. xliii. 23.
Part. מְחַטֵּא, Lev. vi. 19.
Hiph. הֶחֱטִיא, pres. יַחֲטִיא. Constr. immed. it. med. אֶת, with חַטָּאת, 2 Kings xvii. 21, (a) *Miss the mark*, as an archer, Judg. xx. 16; if this ought not to be pointed, יַחֲטִא,

חטב (193) חטר

which is most probable. (b) *Cause, induce* (another) *to sin*, Exod. xxiii. 33 ; 1 Kings xv. 26 ; xvi. 26 ; 2 Kings iii. 3 ; x. 29, &c. Infin. הַחֲטִיא, 1 Kings xvi. 9 ; Eccl. v. 5. Part. pl. m. constr. מַחֲטִיאֵי, Is. xxix. 21, which Gesenius makes equal to מַרְשִׁיעֵי, but this is doubtful. Comp. Job vi. 18, seq. ; Ps. cvii. 4, seq.

Hithp. pret. non occ. — pres. יִתְחַטָּא. Constr. med. בְּ, it. abs. (a) *Be, become, erring*, Job xli. 17. (b) *Be, become, expiated, cleansed* from sin, Num. xix. 12, 13. 20 ; xxxi. 20, &c.

חָטַב, v. pret. non occ. pres. יַחְטְבוּ. Constr. immed. it. med. מִן, from, of place. Arab. خَطَبَ, *lignatus est*. Cogn. חצב, קצב. *Cutting* wood, Ezek. xxxix. 10. Infin. חֲטֹב (for חֲטֹב), Deut. xix. 5. Part. חוֹטֵב, pl. חוֹטְבִים, constr. חֹטְבֵי, Deut. xxix. 11 ; 2 Chron. ii. 10 ; Josh. ix. 21. 23. 27, &c.

Pass. pl. f. חֲטֻבוֹת, Prov. vii. 16. Metaph. *Striped*, variegated. Arab. خَطَبَ, *colore rubro et flavo, cinericeo et terreo, mixtis, præditus fuit*, al. non occ.

Puh. part. pl. f. מְחֻטָּבוֹת, *Hewn, cut*, stones, Ps. cxliv. 12.

חִטָּה, f. pl. m. חִטִּים, once, חִטֵּי, Ezek. iv. 9. Constr. חִטֵּי, r. חנט. Arab. حِنْطَة, *triticum*. Propr. *Grain* of wheat: thence, meton., *wheat*, Exod. ix. 32 ; Deut. viii. 8 ; Job xxxi. 40 ; Is. xxviii. 25 ; Jer. xii. 13 ; Joel i. 11 ; 1 Chron. xxi. 20 ; 2 Chron. xxvii. 5. קְצִיר חִטִּים, *wheat-harvest*, Gen. xxx. 14. בְּבִכּוּרֵי קְצִיר חִטִּים, *first-fruits of* (the) *wheat-harvest* ; lit.—*crop of wheat-grains*, Exod. xxxiv. 22. סֹלֶת חִטִּים, *flour of wheat*, Ib. xxix. 2. חֵלֶב חִטָּה, *fat of wheat*, i. e. its nutriment, Ps. lxxxi. 17 : i. q. חֵלֶב חִטִּים, Ib. cxlvii. 14. חֵלֶב כִּלְיוֹת חִטָּה, *fat of kidneys of wheat*, Deut. xxxii. 14, comparing the grains of wheat with the kidneys of beasts.

חֲטָי, m. Chald. aff. חֲטָיָךְ, al. חֲטָאָךְ, *Thy sin*, Dan. iv. 24, i. q. Heb. חֵטְא.

חָטַם, v. pret. non occ. pres. once. אֶחֱטָם־לָךְ, Is. xlviii. 9. Arab. خَطَمَ, *percussit in naso, capistravit* camelum. *I will restrain* (my anger) for thee, i. e. in thy favour.

חָטַף, v. pres. יַחְטֹף. Constr. immed.

it. med. לְ, *for* whom. Arab. خَطَفَ, *abripuit*. *Rob, take away by violence*, Judg. xxi. 21 ; Ps. x. 9. Infin. חֲטֹף, Ps. x. 9.

חֹטֶר, m.—pl. non occ. Syr. ﺣﻮﻃﺮﺍ, *virga*. *A shoot*, or *rod*, growing out of the stem of a tree ;—applied to the back of a fool by way of chastisement, Prov. xiv. 3. Metaph. to offspring, Is. xi. 1. Synon. נֵצֶר.

חַי, and חֵי, m.—pl. חַיִּים, constr. חַיֵּי.—

חַיָּה, f. constr. חַיַּת, pl. חַיּוֹת.—

r. חיי, opp. to, מֵת, 1 Kings xxi. 15, &c. Arab. حَيَّ, *vivus*. Syr. ﺣﻴﺎ, id. I. *Living, alive*, Gen. iii. 20 ; viii. 21 ; ix. 3 ; xlii. 27. 28 ; xlv. 28 ; Deut. xxxiii. 40, &c. Pl. Exod. iv. 18 ; Num. xvi. 30. 32 ; Deut. iv. 4. &c. Applied *in oaths*; as, חֵי הָעוֹלָם, Dan xii. 7. חֵי־יְהוָֹה, Ruth iii. 13. חֵי אֱלֹהִים 2 Sam. ii. 27. חַי־אֵל, Job xxvii. 2. חַי־אָנִי Num. xiv. 21. 28; Jer. xlvi. 18. The distinctions attempted by the Jews between חַי and חֵי, i. e. that the former applies to animate, the latter to inanimate things, are plainly fictitious ; these exhibiting nothing beyond different modes of writing the same sounds. Nor does this formula signify, *by the life, &c.*; but, as *he* (is) *living*, i. e. as surely as this, &c. Gram. art. 87. 3, and my notes on Job xxvii. 2 ; xxxiii. 30. Phr. אֶרֶץ חַיִּים, *land of* (the) *living*, opposed to the *grave*, Ezek. xxvi. 20 ; Ps. cxvi. 9, &c. בְּאֵר לַחַי רֹאִי, *well of the living* (God) *my seer*, Gen. xvi. 14. In pause, לֶחָי, *for living*, or *vigorous*, i. e. saluting one, wishing him to be so, 1 Sam. xx. v. 6. Comp. לְשָׁלוֹם, ib. vr. 5. See next art. חַי.

II. *Lively, vigorous*, 2 Sam. xxiii. 20, (see kethiv), 1 Sam. xxv. 6 ; Ps. xxxviii. 20 ; Exod. i. 19. חָיוֹת, for חַיּוֹת, in which (ּ) is, for the sake of euphony, perhaps, a mere compensation for the rejected dagesh. So Gen. xviii. 10. 14. כָּעֵת חַיָּה, *as* (at) *the season, period, of a vigorous woman*, 2 Kings iv. 16, 17. The "*tempus reviviscens*," i. e. " *ad idem punctum trahens*," of Eichorn, &c. is erroneous, as are the glosses of the LXX. Hence, meton.—

(a) *Animal*, i. e. living thing, generally, Gen. i. 28 ; vii. 14 ; viii. 1. 17. 19 ; ix. 5 ; Lev. xi. 10. 27 ; xvii. 13 ; Is. xlvi. 1. Phr. חַיָּה טְמֵאָה, Lev. v. 2. רָעָה, Gen. xxxvii. 20. 33. חַיַּת קָנֶה, *beast of the reed*, i. e. loaded with sweet (sugar cane) reed for offerings,

e c

Ps. lxviii. 31. Comp. Is. xliii. 24; Jer. vi. 20. חַיַּת הָאָרֶץ, and הַשָּׂדֶה —, Gen. i. 30; ix. 2. 10. *Beast of the earth or plain*, i. e. wild, opp. to בְּהֵמָה. It. חַיְתוֹ־שָׂדַי —, אֶרֶץ —, יַעַר —, Gen. i. 24; Ps. civ. 11; L. 10. It. בְּעַר —, Is. lvi. 9. It. חַיְתוֹ גוֹי —, *gregarious*, Zeph. ii. 14. On this paragogic vaw, see Gram. art. 175. 12.

(b) *Tribe, company, &c.* Arab. حَيّ, *tribus*, &c. חַיַּת פְּלִשְׁתִּים, *company of Philistines*, 2 Sam. xxiii. 11. 13. Comp. 1 Sam. xvii. 1; 1 Chron. xi. 15; Ps. lxviii. 11. To which Gesenius adds, חַיִּי, *my people, relatives*, 1 Sam. xviii. 18; and to this, חַיַּת קָנֶה above, (a) may also be referred.

(c) i. q. חַיִּים, *Life*, Job xxxiii. 18. 22. 28; Ps. cxliii. 3; Ezek. vii. 13. Hence, meton. the *properties* of —, as, *vigor*, Is. lvii. 10. See II. above. *Mind, desire, &c.* i. q. נֶפֶשׁ, Job xxxviii. 39; xxxiii. 20. Comp. vv. 18. 22. 28; Ps. xxvii. 12; xli. 5. To this Gesenius refers, חַיָּה, Ps. lxxiv. 19. But, *beast*, i. e. fierce beast, applied to men, see (a) above, seems more appropriate. Comp. Ps. xxii. 13, 14. 17. 21, &c. Aff. חַיָּתִי, חַיְתוֹ, חַיָּתָם.

III. *Fresh*, as of a plant, of springing, or running, water, Ps. lviii. 10. See אֲפֵשׁ above. Gen. xxvi. 19; Lev. xiv. 5, 6. 50; xv. 13, &c. Opposed to stagnant, as in the الماء الميت, *dead water*, of the Arabs; Dead Sea, &c.

IV. *Raw*, of flesh, i. e. uncooked, Lev. xiii. 14; 1 Sam. ii. 15.

V. *Life*, i. e. taking the concrete as an abstract noun; but always, perhaps, in the pl. num. חַיִּים, once חַיִּין, Job xxiv. 22;—Gen. ii. 7; iii. 14; vii. 15; Ps. xxxiv. 13, &c. Phr. רוּחַ חַיִּים, or נִשְׁמַת חַיִּים, *breath of life*, or *of living men*, Gen. ii. 7; vi. 17. עֵץ הַחַיִּים, *tree of* do., Gen. ii. 9. Comp. iii. 22. 24. שְׁנֵי חַיֵּי שָׂרָה, *years of the life of Sarah*, Gen. xxiii. 1, &c. Meton. (a) *provision*, or *living*, hence, *prosperity*, Prov. xxvii. 27. Comp. ib. iv. 22, 23; xii. 28; xiii. 14; xiv. 27, &c. Phr. אֹרַח חַיִּים, or דֶּרֶךְ —, *way of* —, Prov. ii. 19; v. 6; xv. 24. מְקוֹר חַיִּים, *fountain of* —, Ps. xxxvi. 10. Aff. חַיֶּיךָ, חַיָּיו, חַיֵּינוּ, חַיָּי, חַיָּיו, &c.

חַי, m. Chald. def. חַיָּא, pl. חַיִּין, def. חַיַּיָּא, i. q. Heb. I. *Living, alive*. חַי עָלְמָא, Dan. iv. 31, i. q. Heb. חֵי הָעוֹלָם, Ib. xii. 7. אֱלָהָא חַיָּא, *the living God*, Ib. vi. 21. 27; ii. 30; iv. 14.

II. i. q. Heb. v. חַיִּין, *Life*, Dan. vii. 12; Ezra vi. 10.

חִידָה, f. pl. חִידוֹת, r. חוּד. Arab. حَوْن, حَال, *superavit* negotii *difficultatem; contraxit in unum;* أَحْوَانِي, *acutus*. Cogn. جِدّ, *similitudo, comparatio*. An *enigma*, or *parable*, i. e. something conveyed in figurative language, intended to exercise the ingenuity of the reader or hearer, Judg. xiv. 12—19; Ezek. xvii. 2: with מָשָׁל, it. Ps. xlix. 5; lxxviii. 2; Prov. i. 6; Hab. ii. 6;—Dan. viii. 23. Gesen. *calliditas, fraus*, without any authority. Num. xii. 8; 1 Kings x. 1; 2 Chron. ix. 1. LXX. αἴνιγμα, διήγημα, διήγησις, πρόβλημα. Aff. חִידָתִי, חִידוֹתָם, חִידָתְךָ.

חָיָה, for חָיַי, v. pres. יִחְיֶה, f. once, תְּחִי, 2 Kings iv. 7; apoc. יְחִי, f. תְּחִי; in pause, יֶחִי. Constr. abs. it. med. בְּ, in; עַל, on; בְּגִלַל, by; opp. to מוּת. Arab. حَيَّ, *vixit*. Syr. ܚܝܐ, id.

Living in health, vigour, safety, &c. as the context shall intimate, Gen. v. 3. 6; xii. 13; xvii. 18; Exod. i. 16; Deut. xxx. 16; Num. iv. 19; xiv. 38; 2 Kings i. 2; Ezek. xviii. 23; xxxiii. 11; Ps. cxviii. 17; Job vii. 16, &c.

Infin. חֲיוֹת, Ezek. xxxiii. 12, &c. It. חָיֹה, חָיוֹ, Ib. xviii. 9; iii. 21, &c. Aff. חֲיוֹתָם, Josh. v. 8.

Imper. חֲיֵה, pl. חֲיוּ, Gen. xx. 7; xlii. 18, &c.

חֱיִי, f. Ezek. xvi. 6.

Pih. חִיָּה, pres. יְחַיֶּה. Constr. immed. it. med. בְּ, instr. it. אֵת. I. *Giving, preserving, restoring, healthy life*, Ps. xxii. 30; xxx. 4; cxix. 50; Num. xxxi. 15; Deut. xx. 16; xxxii. 39; Jer. xlix. 11; Exod. xxii. 17; 1 Sam. ii. 6; xxvii. 9. 11; Job xxxvi. 6. Of seed, conceived or sown, Gen. vii. 3; xix. 32. 34; Hos. xiv. 8.

II.—*Strength, efficiency*, to any person, work, &c. Hab. iii. 2; Hos. vi. 2; Eccl. vii. 12; 1 Chron. xi. 8. Comp. Neh. iii. 34; iv. 1.

Infin. חַיּוֹת, Gen. vii. 3; Ezek. xiii. 19. Aff. חַיֹּתְנוּ, Deut. vi. 24; Josh. ix. 15; Ezek. iii. 18.

Imp. aff. חַיֵּנִי, Ps. cxix. 25, &c. חַיֵּה Hab. iii. 2.

Part. מְחַיֶּה, 1 Sam. ii. 6.

Hiph. הֶחֱיָה, pres. non occ. i. q. Pih. I.

חיה (195) חיל

Gen. vi. 19, 20; Num. xxii. 33; xxxi. 18; Josh. ii. 13; vi. 25; 2 Kings v. 7; viii. 1. 5; Is. xxxviii. 16, &c.
Infin. הֱיֹת, Josh. ix. 20.
הַחַיּוֹת, Gen. vi. 19, &c. Aff. הַחִיתוֹ, Ezek. xiii. 22; Is. lvii. 15.
Imp. pl. m. הַחֲיוּ, Num. xxxi. 18.

חיה, and חיא, v. Chald. pret. et pres. non occ. i. q. Heb. חָיָה, *Living, &c.*
Imp. חֱיִי, Dan. ii. 4. *Let the king live for ever*, Ib. iii. 9; v. 10, &c.
Aph. part. מְחֵא, Dan. v. 19; i. q. Syr. ܡܚܐ, *giving life*.

חֵיוָא, f. def. חֵיוְתָא, and חֵיוָתָא, pl. חֵיוָן, def. חֵיוָתָא. Chald. i. q. Heb. חַיָּה. *A living creature, beast, animal*, Dan. iv. 12; vii. 3. 12. 17.

חַיּוּת, f. r. חיה, *Life*, 2 Sam. xx. 3.

חיי, v. pret. חַי, or חֵי (fm. סָב, for סָבַב), another form of הָיָה, or חָיָה, fm. פָּעֵר, Gram. art. 77; Gen. v. 5. אֲשֶׁר חַי, *which he lived*, Ib. iii. 22. וַחַי לְעוֹלָם, *and he lived for ever*. To one or other of these forms, viz. חַי, or חֵי, may also be referred all those forms of swearing noticed under חַי above, as Dan. xii. 7, &c., which will also account for the fm. חֵי, occasionally occurring, 1 Sam. xx. 3; xxv. 26, &c. It. וְחִי אָחִיךָ עִמָּךְ, *and thy brother live with thee*. It. 1 Sam. xxv. 6. וְחָיִי, *let him certainly live*, or, *for, that he lived;* a form of salutation. With the Arab. ل, of certainty, termed, التأكيدي, Gram. Arabe. Mr. de Sacy, i. p. 371, Edit. 1810. "Cave," says Dr. Gesenius, "ne huc referas exempla, in quibus חַי est adjectivum, ut הַעוֹד אֲבִיכֶם חַי, *vivusne adhuc pater vester?*" Gen. xliii. 7. But why not, *vivitne adhuc pater vester?* Certainly, if the verb is nothing more than the attributive conjugated, Gram. art. 182. 2, et seq., which is apparently the case, it can signify but little as to how these are taken; the sense remaining the same in either case. I have, however, given these examples under this head also, in order to suit them to the common notions of grammar.

חִיל, see חול.

חַיִל, m. constr. חֵיל, pl. חֲיָלִים. Synon. פַּח. Syr. ܚܝܠܐ, *vis, virtus*. Arab. خيلة, *superbia*. *Strength, power, generally;*

variously applied, (a) as for war or any great exploit, Is. xliii. 17; 2 Sam. xxii. 33; 2 Chron. xxvi. 11; xiii. 3; xiv. 7, &c. Phr. אִישׁ גִּבּוֹר חַיִל, גִּבּוֹר חַיִל, אִישׁ חַיִל, אַנְשֵׁי־חַיִל; pl. בְּנֵי־חַיִל, בֶּן־חַיִל; גִּבּוֹרֵי חַיִל, &c. *Men of might*, Exod. xviii. 21. *Man of do.*, Judg. iii. 29. *Hero of might*, Ib. xi. 1. *Man, hero of might*, Ruth ii. 1; pl. 1 Chron. v. 24. — *of might; son, child, of might*, 1 Sam. xiv. 52. *Sons of* do., Deut. iii. 18. It. שַׂר־הַחַיִל, *Head of the force, General*, 2 Sam. xxiv. 2. Hence, (b) *military force*, 2 Kings vi. 15; vii. 6; 2 Chron. xvii. 2; xxiv. 24; Ps. xxxiii. 16, &c.

(c) *Power*, i. e. wealth, Gen. xxxiv. 29; Job xx. 15; Deut. viii. 17, 18; Ruth iv. 11; Prov. xxxi. 29. מֵחַיִל אֶל־חָיִל, *from strength to strength*, Ps. lxxxiv. 8.

(d) *Virtue, integrity*, Gen. xlvii. 6; Exod. xviii. 21. 25; Ruth iii. 11. אֵשֶׁת חַיִל, Prov. xii. 4; xxxi. 10.

(e) *Wealth, fruit*, Joel ii. 22. Comp. כֹּחַ, Job xxxi. 39. Sometimes adverbially, in the phrr. עֹשֶׂה חַיִל, *doing mightily*, Num. xxiv. 18. לַעֲשׂוֹת חַיִל, Deut. viii. 18. אָזְרוּ חַיִל, *have girded* (them) *mightily*, or *with might*, 1 Sam. ii. 4; 2 Sam. xxii. 40; Ps. xviii. 33.

(f) חֵיל, and חֵל (only a different way of expressing the primitive word חַיִל, Gram. artt. 148. 10; 87. 3; here חֵיל, i. q. (b) *Force, army*, 2 Kings xviii. 17; Obad. vr. 20; Ps. x. 8. חֶלְכָה, *keri*, חֵל פָּאִים, *host, or multitude of afflicted ones*. פָּאִים. Arab. كَافٍ, *imbecillis*. See חָלָה.

(g) *Fortification*, pec. *a rampart*, or *breast work*, perhaps, 2 Sam. xx. 15; Is. xxvi. 1; Nahum iii. 8; Lam. ii. 8; 1 Kings xxi. 23: a sort of Pomœrium, perhaps. Comp. 2 Kings ix. 36. The LXX. occasionally, προτείχισμα; once περίτειχος. Vulg. *antemurale*. It. חֵילָה, f. id. Ps. xlviii. 14, al. חֵילָה. Aff. LXX. Vulg. Syr. Chald. Jerome, and 18 MSS. which Gesenius prefers, Ps. cxxii. 7. חֵילָךְ, according to the Rabbins, A space, or sort of *pomœrium*, attached to the court of the Temple. See Lightfoot. Prospect of the Temple service; but, on this no reliance can be placed.

Aff. חֵילִי, חֵילְךָ, חֵילוֹ, חֵילָהּ, חֵילָם, חֵילֵיהֶם.

Chald. i. q. Heb. (a) Dan. iii. 4; iv. 11; v. 7; Ezra iv. 23.

(b) *Force, army*, Dan. iii. 20; iv. 32. Phr. גִּבָּרֵי־חַיִל, *heroes of might*, Dan. iii. 20, i. q. Heb. גִּבּוֹרֵי חַיִל.

חִיל (196) חֵךְ

חִיל, m. ⎱ r. חוּל. I. *Pain*, as of child-
חִילָה, f. ⎰ birth, Ps. xlviii. 7; Jer. vi.
24; xxii. 23; L. 43; Mic. iv. 9; Job vi.
10. II. *Fear, trembling*, Exod. xv. 14.

חִין, m. once, Job xli. 4. Usually,
Favour, beauty; i. q. חֵן. It will be difficult to see how this can suit the terrific
character of the animal there described. I
take it to be i. q. Arab. حَيْن, *exitium,
pernicies. Destructiveness.* See my note.

חַיִץ, m. r. חוּץ. *A wall*, once, Ezek.
xiii. 10.

חִיצוֹן, m. ⎱ pl. non occ. r. חוּץ, opp. to
חִיצוֹנָה, f. ⎰ פְּנִימִי, פָּנִים, פְּנִימָה, *Outer*,
exterior, external, Ezek. xli. 17; xliv. 1;
1 Kings vi. 29, 30; 2 Kings xvi. 18; Ezek.
x. 5; xl. 17, &c.; Esth. vi. 4; Neh. xi. 16,
&c.

חֵיק, and חֵק, pl. non occ. Arab.
حَاقَ, r. حيق, *cinxit*. Æth. ሐቀፈ :
ripa. The primitive notion seems to have
consisted in *surrounding*, thence, *embracing*;
thence, as a noun, applied to, (a) *The bosom*,
Gen. xvi. 5; Exod. iv. 6, 7; Prov. vi. 27:
(b) — of mothers, nurses, &c., and their
children, Num. xi. 12; 1 Kings iii. 20; xvii.
19; Ruth iv. 16; Lam. ii. 12, &c.; thence,
(c) used as expressive of endearment, Is. xl.
11; 2 Sam. xii. 3. (d) In a conjugal
acceptation, Deut. xiii. 7; xxviii. 54;
1 Kings i. 2; 2 Sam. xii. 8; Mic. vii. 5,
&c.; and, (e) hence, in a dishonest sense,
Prov. v. 20—

(f) id. in a moral sense, supposing it to be
the seat of the affections, feelings, &c., Eccl.
vii. 9; Ps. xxxv. 13; lxxxix. 51; Job xix.
27. Hence, with הֵשִׁיב שָׁלֵם, *recompensing,
repaying, into the bosom*, i. e. so as to be
effectual, Ps. lxxix. 12; Jer. xxxii. 18.
Comp. Judg. ix. 57.

(g) — to the bosom, as a place of deposit.
בְּחֵיק יוּטַל, *is cast into the bosom*, i. e. the fold
or lap of it, Prov. xvi. 33: it. שֹׁחַד בְּחֵיק, *a
bribe in the bosom*, Ib. xxi. 14; xvii. 23,
מֵחֵק. Hence—

(h) — to certain things as containers, as
of a chariot, 1 Kings xxii. 35; the border of
the altar, Ezek. xliii. 13, 14. 17.
Aff. הֵיקָם, הֵיקָה, הֵיקוֹ, הֵיקִי.

חִישׁ, cogn. v. חוּשׁ. Adv. *Hastily*, Ps.
xc. 10.

חִישָׁה, Kethiv, for חוּשָׁה, Keri, Ps.
lxxi. 12. Imp. with ה, parag. *Haste,
hasten.*

חֵךְ, m. Syr. ܚܶܟܳܐ, *palatum*. Arab.
حَنَك, id. r. חנך. *The palate*, or upper
part of the mouth, Ezek. iii. 26; Lam. iv. 4;
Job xxix. 10. As the *seat of taste*, Job xiv.
11; xxxiv. 3; Cant. ii. 3; Prov. xxiv. 13.
Hence, as sending forth sweet things, Cant.
vii. 10; v. 16; originating *smooth do.*, Prov.
v. 3, Hence—

Metaph. Morally, as the *seat of percep-
tion*, Prov. viii. 7. Gesenius, "loquitur
palatum meum," rather *shall meditate, consider*; and, hence, *originate, put forth*, Job
vi. 30; xxxi. 30; Ps. cxix. 103. Aff. חִכִּי,
חִכָּם, חִכָּה, חִכּוֹ, חִכֵּךְ, הֵחִךְ.

חכה, v. pret. et pres. non occ. Arab.
حَكَى, and cogn. حَكَا, r. حكي, *astrinxit
nodum*. The primary notion seems to
consist in *making fast*; thence would follow,
Holding out, waiting, or the like.
Part. pl. m. constr. חוֹכֵי, *Persons waiting*,
constr. לְ, for, Is. xxx. 18.
Pih. חִכָּה, pres. יְחַכֶּה. Constr. abs. 2 Kings
ix. 3; it. med. אֶת, of object; לְ, for, of pers.
or thing; עַד, until. *Tarrying*, or *waiting,
for, expecting*, 2 Kings vii. 9; Is. viii. 17;
xxx. 18; lxiv. 4; Ps. xxxii. 20; cvi. 14;
Job xxxii. 4, &c.
Infin. חַכִּי (for חַכֵּה, constr.), Chaldæism,
כְּחַכֵּי אִישׁ, as a man's *expecting, waiting for*,
Hos. vi. 9.
Imp. חַכֵּה, Hab. ii. 3, pl. חַכּוּ, Zeph. iii. 8.
Part. מְחַכֶּה, pl. מְחַכִּים, Dan. xii. 12; Job
iii. 20.

חַכָּה, f. — pl. non occ. See Arab.
حَكَا, and cogn. حَكَى, above. Lit. a *binder,
fastener*, Gram. art. 154. 12, as to form.
Gesen. "ita dictus, quod piscium palato
infigitur." *A fishing-hook*, Is. xix. 8; Hab.
i. 15; Job xl. 25, al. non occ.

חכים, m. Chald. sing. non occ. — pl.
חַכִּימִין, constr. חַכִּימֵי, def. חַכִּימַיָּא. *Wise
man*: professor of philosophy and religion:
magician, Dan. ii. 12, 13. 18. 21. 27. 48;
iv. 3; v. 15, &c. These were the χαλδαῖοι
of the Greeks. See אוּר כַּשְׂדִּים above, p. 16,
as they are now the حُكَمَاء, *Hukamā*. See
my notes on Job, pp. 262. 269. 282. They
might have been styled *Chaldeans*, from חָלַד,

—as *observers of time*, as they were—דֹּבְרֵי, which see—for other reasons.

חַכְלִילִי, m. once, Gen. xlix. 12. "De oculo caligante ebrii," Gesen. who has here corrected Schultens, on Prov. xxiii. 29, in a translation made by him of a passage from the Kāmoos. But, Gesenius is here wrong himself, as to the particular part connected with this word; which is this, حَاكِل, *ebrius vino*. The Kāmoos has الحَاكِلُ المُخَمَّر, i. e. الحَاكِل, *The person refreshed with wine*. So Gol., Castell, &c. *vino recreatus non prorsus ebrius*. The phr., therefore, חַכְלִילִי עֵינַיִם מִיָּיִן, means, *the refreshed of eyes*, i. e. he whose eyes evince the refreshment received *from wine*, as taken moderately and for this purpose, and thence fitted for great undertakings. Comp. 1 Tim. v. 23; Ps. lxxviii. 65; civ. 15; not from the *half blinded eyes of the drunkard*,—as Gesenius thinks,—merely to show the fruitfulness of the land. Revealed religion, I think, no where has recourse to expedients so filthy as this. The LXX. χαροποιοὶ οἱ ὀφθαλμοὶ αὐτοῦ ὑπὲρ οἶνον. Aquila, κατάκοροι. Others, καθάκαροι, θερμοί, διαπυροί, φοβεροί: all which seem to have been arrived at much in the same way.

חַכְלִלוּת, f. once, Prov. xxiii. 29, in the phr. חַכְלִלוּת עֵינַיִם, the *fierceness of eyes*; i. e. aspect of those who indulge in the over frequent, and excessive, excitements of wine: see the context: nothing tending so much to stir up contention, and thence to brutalize the man.

חָכָם, m. constr. חֲכַם, pl. חֲכָמִים, constr. חַכְמֵי—

חָכְמָה, f. constr. חָכְמַת, pl. חָכְמוֹת, constr. חַכְמוֹת—

Arabic حَكَم, *firmiter solideque fecit* quid: hence *frænavit*: and, hence, as power seems to imply knowledge, *sapiens, doctus, medicus, &c.* fuit. *Wise*, generally, pec. (a) as to *religion*, Deut. i. 13. 15; iv. 6; 1 Kings iii. 12: with נָבוֹן, opp. בְּסִיל, Ib. xxxii. 6: more generally, perhaps, Gen. xli. 33. 39; opp. בְּסִיל, Eccl. vi. 8. חֲכַם לֵב, *wise of heart*: the heart being considered the seat of thought, Job ix. 4; Prov. x. 8: opp. τῷ, אֱוִיל, Ib. xi. 29; xvi. 21:—Job xvii. 11; xxxiv. 34; Ps. cvii. 43; Prov. i. 5; xvi. 23, &c. With reference to the primitive notion of strength, &c., Prov. xxiv. 5; xxi. 22; Eccl. vii. 19. *Wise as an angel*, 2 Sam. xiv. 20.

(b) *Teacher* of religion, Prov. i. 6; xi. 30; xii. 18; xiii. 14; xv. 2. 7; xxv. 12; Job xv. 18, &c.

(c) *Wise, intelligent, clever*, as to the arts, &c., Exod. vii. 11; xxxi. 6; xxxv. 10; xxxvi. 1, 2. 8; 2 Sam. xiii. 3; 1 Kings ii. 9; 2 Kings iii. 12. Synon. נָבוֹן. Comp. ch. v. 10—14; 1 Chron. xxii. 15; 2 Chron. ii. 6. 11, 12: pl. Deut. xvi. 19; Ps. xlix. 11. In a bad sense, *crafty*, &c., Job v. 13; Is. v. 21; xliv. 25; Jer. iv. 22; Obad. 8; Esth. i. 13, &c. See חַיִּים, Chald. above. Aff. חֲכָמַי, חֲכָמָיו, &c.

Fem. (a) *Wise, religious*, Exod. xxxv. 25; Prov. xiv. 1. (b) *Intelligent, clever*, 2 Sam. xiv. 2; xx. 16; Jer. ix. 16; Judg. v. 29.

חָכְמָה, f. constr. חָכְמַת, pl. חָכְמוֹת, of seg. fm. חָכְמ. Arab. حِكْمَة, *sapientia, philosophia, &c. Wisdom*, generally, רוּחַ חָכְמָה, *spirit of wisdom*, Exod. xxviii. 3; Deut. xxxiv. 9, &c. with גְּבוּרָה, Job xii. 13. Pec. (a) *as to religion*, Job xxviii. 28; xxxii. 13; xxxiii. 33; Ps. xxxvii. 30; cxi. 10, &c.

(b) *Ingenuity, cleverness*, as to the arts, &c., Exod. xxviii. 3; xxxi. 6; xxxvi. 1, 2, &c.

(c) *Instruction*, Job xv. 8; xxvi. 3; Prov. i. 2. 7, with מוּסָר, *discipline*, and nearly synon. with תּוֹרָה, Ib. iv. 5. 7; xv. 33. Comp. ix. 10; Ps. cxi. 10; Prov. xxix. 15, &c. Originating with God, and hence his gift in every case, Job xii. 13; xxviii. 12; Prov. viii. 11; Exod. xxviii. 3; xxxi. 6, &c. Pl. חָכְמוֹת, pl. of excellence, Gram. art. 223. 3. *Great* or *real wisdom*. Gesenius prefers considering this noun as a singular ("ut עוֹלָלוֹת," as he says), because, perhaps, the fm. should have regularly been חָכָמוֹת, and the verbs connected with it in the pl. number. But no reliance can be placed on either of these considerations: the vowels occasionally being contrary to analogy, from the errors of the copyists perhaps; and the verbs being regulated rather by the sense than the grammatical forms, Gram. art. 215. 5, seq. In Ps. xlix. 4, we have תְּבוּנוֹת in the paral., Prov. i. 20, the verb is in the pl., Ib. xxiv. 7. רָאמוֹת, evidently a pl. is to be construed with it. The only remaining place, viz., Ib. ix. 1, the verb agrees with a sing., i. e. person so denominated.

חכם (198) חלא

Chald. id. Dan. ii. 30, &c. Def. חָכְמְתָא, Ib. ii. 20, &c.

חָכַם, v. pres. יֶחְכַּם, constr. abs. it. med. לְ, to, for, whom; מִן, more than. See חָכָם above. Be, or become, wise, instructed, generally, Deut. xxxii. 29. Synon. הִשְׂכִּיל, 1 Kings v. 11 ; Job xxxii. 9 ; Zech. ix. 2 : Prov. ix. 12, חָכַמְתָּ לָּךְ, thou hast become wise for thyself: Eccl. vii. 23, אֶחְכָּמָה, let me become wise, &c.: Ib. ii. 19, שֶׁחֻכַּמְתִּי, in which I became wise, i. e. gathered instruction.
Imp. חֲכַם, pl. חֲכָמוּ, Be wise, instructed, Prov. xxvii. 11 ; viii. 33, &c.
Pih. pret. non occ. pres. יְחַכֵּם. Constr. immed. Make wise, instruct, Ps. cv. 22 ; cxix. 98 ; Job xxxv. 11, al. non occ.
Puh. part. m. מְחֻכָּם, pl. מְחֻכָּמִים, Made, rendered, wise, Ps. lviii. 6 ; Prov. xxx. 24.
Hiph. part. f. constr. מַחְכִּימַת, Making wise, Ps. xix. 8.
Hithp. pres. only, תִּתְחַכַּם, Be not, become not, i. e. set not up thyself as, over wise, Eccl. vii. 16. Let us be wise, &c.: acting with discretion as to it, i. e. the people, Exod. i. 10, al. non occ.

חֵל, see חַיִל.

חֹל, m. r. חלל, which see, pl. non occ. Profane, common, opp. to sacred or holy, 1 Sam. xxi. 5, 6 ; Lev. x. 10 ; Ezek. xxii. 26 ; xlii. 20 ; xliv. 23 ; xlviii. 15.

חֶלְאָה, f. pl. non occ. Arab. حَلِيٌّ, crustulæ ex labiis post febrem exeuntes; حَلِيٌّ, res ipsa subtiliter trita, vel excoriando detracta; حَلِيٌّ, pars pellis cultro scalpta; i. e. rejectanea, "aerugo ollæ cupreae," says Gesenius. But why? The etymology says nothing about either rust or copper: and the context speaks not of the pot, but of that which is put into it. Propr. Refuse, filth ; hence scum, uncleanness, Ezek. xxiv. 6. עִיר הַדָּמִים סִיר אֲשֶׁר חֶלְאָתָהּ (חֶלְאָתָה) בָהּ, city of much blood: pot, whose filth, scum, is within itself : where the comparison is between the uncleanness visible in Jerusalem, viz. that of blood guiltiness, and the filth in the contents of this pot. See the remainder of the verse, and Ib. vv. 11, 12, al. non occ. In vr. 11, the brass is said to be made hot; but then this is done in order to consume the filth still remaining in it.

חֹלֵא, as a verb, 2 Chron. xvi. 12. See חָלָה.

חֲלָאִים, see חֲלִי below.

חָלָב, and חֵלֶב, m. pl. חֲלָבִים, constr. חֶלְבֵי. Arab. حَلَبٌ, lac, recens, &c.; hence, Syr. ܚܰܠܒܳܐ, adeps, i. e. apparently as cream (חָלָב) becomes the exterior coating of new milk, so does fat of the flesh, &c. of an animal generally: hence, Fat, fatness, Gen. iv. 4 ; Lev. iii. 3, 4 ; iv. 8. 31. 35, &c. Metaph. of land, its best produce, Gen. xlv. 18 ;—Ps. lxxxi. 17 ; cxli. 14. Best of the wheat, it., Deut. xxxii. 14. Comp. Is. xxxiv. 6. It. metaph. applied to the heart, intimates its being veiled, coated, (as the cream of milk, or the fat of the animal: hence, made fat. Comp. Is. vi. 10 ; Matt. xiii. 15, &c.; and hence the terms, "uncircumcised of heart," Ezek. xliv. 7 ; Acts vii. 51. Comp. Jer. iv. 4, and Is. iii. 23, with 2 Cor. iii. 13, 14)—thence impervious to impression and hard, impenitent, Ps. xvii. 10. Comp. lxxiii. 8. Aff. חֶלְבּוֹ, חֶלְבָּהּ, חֶלְבָּם, &c., pl. חֶלְבֵּיהֶן.

חָלָב, m. constr. חֲלֵב (of prim. חָלַב. Arab. حَلِيبٌ, lac recens), pl. non occ. I. New milk, or the cream of it: hence, II. meton. Cheese, probably something like our cream cheese, Prov. xxx. 33. מִיץ חָלָב יוֹצִיא חֶמְאָה, the pressing of cream bringeth forth butter, i. e. that process by which the one is extracted from the other: with us, churning, 1 Sam. xvii. 18. עֲשֶׂרֶת חֲרִיצֵי הֶחָלָב, ten cuttings of cream cheese, perhaps. Often in the phr. אֶרֶץ זָבַת חָלָב וּדְבָשׁ, a land flowing with rich milk and honey, Exod. iii. 8. 17, &c., i. e. abounding with the most delicious produce. Opp. to מַיִם, Judg. v. 25. Comp. iv. 19 ; 1 Sam. vii. 9. מְלֵה חָלָב, lit. milk-lamb, i. e. fed on new milk, Is. vii. 22 ; Joel iv. 18 ; Job x. 10. Mothers' milk, Is. xxviii. 9, &c., Exod. xxiii. 19, &c. Aff. חֲלֵבִי, חֲלֵבְךָ.

חֶלְבְּנָה, f. once, Exod. xxx. 34. Galbanum, which is apparently the original Oriental term. A sort of gum, emitting a rich perfume. Cels. Hierobot. i. p. 267, seq.

חֶלֶד, m. pl. non occ. Arab. خُلْدٌ, perennitas. Duration; hence, time, pec. of this life, as passing away, Job xi. 17. See my note. Ps. xlix. 2, כָּל־יֹשְׁבֵי חָלֶד, all inhabitants of time, all mortal men, Ib. lxxxix.

חלד (199) חלה

48. מֶה־חָדֶל, *how transient!* Ib. xvii. 14. מְתִים מֶחֶלֶד, *men of time*, i. e. attached to present enjoyments. Aff. חֶלְדִּי, *my duration*, Ib. xxxix. 6, al. non occ.

חֹלֶד, m. once, Lev. xi. 29. *The mole.* Syriac ܚܘܠܕܐ, *talpa.* Arabic خلد, id., Bochart. Hieroz. i., lib. iii., cap. xxxv.

חָלָה, v. pres. יֶחֱלֶא, for יֶחֱלֶה, Gram. art. 202. 4. Apoc. יֵחַל. Arab. خلا, *pustulis correptum fuit labium*, ut morbi reliquiis. Cogn. خلا, *defecit*, &c. Constr. abs. it. med. אֶת, *as to*, 1 Kings xv. 23: לְ, *to, for*; עַל, *for*, on account of. *Sick, weak, afflicted:* opp. τῷ, רפא, Ezek. xxxiv. 4; τῷ, חזק, Ib. 16; with מִפְּנֵי, Mal. i. 8. 13; — 1 Sam. xxii. 8; 1 Kings xiv. 1; xvii. 17; 2 Kings xiii. 14; xx. 1, &c.
Infin. חֲלוֹת. Aff. חֲלֹתוֹ, Is. xxxviii. 9. חֲלוֹתָם, Ps. xxxv. 13.
Part. חֹלֶה, חֹלָה, Gen. xlviii. 1, &c. חוֹלַת, constr. חוֹלָה, f., Eccl. v. 12; Cant. ii. 5.
Niph. נַחֲלֵיתִי, 1st pers. and נַחְלוּ, 3d pl. *Became sick, weak, afflicted*, Dan. viii. 27; Jer. xii. 13; Amos vi. 6. Constr. med. עַל, *for*, al. non occ.
Part. f. נַחְלָה (for נֶחֱלָה), pl. נַחֲלוֹת. Synon. אָנוּשׁ, Jer. xxx. 12. מַכָּה, Nahum iii. 19. חֹלִי, Ezek. xxxiv. 4; with שֶׁבֶר, מַכָּה, *Become diseased, infirm, incurable*, Is. xvii. 11; Jer. x. 19; xiv. 17; Ezek. xxxiv. 21.
Pih. חִלָּה, pres. apoc. יְחַל, constr. immed. med. בְּ, instr. I. *Afflicted, made sick*, Deut. xxix. 21. Infin. aff. חַלּוֹתִי, Ps. lxxvii. 11.
II. From a different primitive, viz. Syr. ܚܠܝ, *edulcavit.* Arab. حلا, r. حلي *suavis fuit.* Conj. ii. *rem dulcem effecit.*
Cogn. حلي. See my notes on Job xi. 19; xxix. 21. *Make propitious, conciliate the favour of —, satisfy*, Ps. cxix. 58. חִלִּיתִי פָנֶיךָ בְּכָל־לֵב, *I have rendered, made, thy countenance propitious with all my heart*; i. e. I have laboured to effect this. This usage occurs often, and it applies either to God or man, Exod. xxxii. 18; 1 Sam. xiii. 12; 2 Kings xiii. 4; Dan. ix. 13; Prov. xix. 3, &c.
Infin. חַלּוֹת, Zech. vii. 2, &c.

Imp. חַל, 1 Kings xiii. 6. חַלּוּ, pl. Mal. i. 9.
Puh. I. חֳלֵיתָ, *Thou art become infirm*, &c., Is. xiv. 10, al. non occ. "De umbra in orco," says Dr. Gesenius. The Hebrews, however, do not appear ever to have heard of such a place. See my notes on Job xxi. 13; xxvi. 6. The context here shows that the grave is meant, and that the language involves a personification.
Hiph. הֶחֱלִי (rad. י retained), pres. non occ. i. q. Pih. *Afflicted, made sick, infirm*, Is. liii. 10; Hos. vii. 5; Mic. vi. 13.
Part. f. מַחֲלָה, Prov. xiii. 12.
Hoph. הָחֳלֵיתִי, 1st pers. *I am made sick, wounded*, 1 Kings xxii. 34; 2 Chron. xviii. 33; xxxv. 23, al. non occ.
Hithp. pres. apoc. יִתְחַל, *Became, feigned that he was, sick*, 2 Sam. xiii. 6.
Infin. הִתְחַלּוֹת, *Being, becoming, sick*, 2 Sam. xiii. 2.
Imp. הִתְחַל, *Be, feign that thou art, sick*, Ib. vr. 5, al. non occ.

חַלָּה, f. pl. חַלּוֹת, r. חלל, which see. *A cake*, round and perforated with holes, used principally in sacred rites, Exod. xxix. 23; ii. 4; Lev. viii. 26; xxiv. 5; Num. vi. 15. 19, &c.

חֲלוֹם, m.—pl. f. חֲלֹמוֹת, r. חלם. Syr. ܚܠܡܐ, *somnium.* Arab. حلم, id. *A dream*, Gen. xx. 3; xxxvii. 5, &c. In which visions were sometimes given, Ger. xx. 6; xxxi. 10, 11; Num. xii. 6; 1 Kings iii. 5. Comp. Deut. xiii. 2, &c. "Somnia pro nugis," says Gesen. on Eccl. v. 6. Comp. with vr. 2. But this place will justify no such acceptation. Common *dreams* are here spoken of and nothing else.

חַלּוֹן, m. pl. חַלֹּנִים, it. f. חַלּוֹנוֹת. Lit. *openings, holes*, r. חלל. *A window*, or. *casement* of do., Gen. viii. 6. Comp. 2 Kings xiii. 17; Gen. xxvi. 8. See צֹהַר, it. Josh. ii. 15. 18. 21; Ezek. xl. 25; xli. 16. 26. Aff. חַלּוֹנִי, חַלּוֹנוֹ, חַלּוֹנֵינוּ.

חֲלוֹף, m. once, Prov. xxxi. 8—in the phr. בְּנֵי חֲלוֹף.—Infin. or verbal noun of v. חלף. See Is. xxi. 1. *Passing by, or away.* Phr. lit. *children of* such an event; i. e. *orphans.* Symm. υἱῶν ἀποιχομένων. The usage is purely Hebrew therefore.

חָלוּץ, see v. חָלַץ.

חֲלוּשָׁה, f. once, Exod. xxxii. 18, r.

חלח (200) חלי

חֲלֹשׁ. Syr. ܚܠܳܫܳܐ, *abjectio. Discomfiture.*

חַלְחָלָה, f. pl. non occ. r. חול, Gram. art. 169. 5. *Grievous* or *great pain*, Is. xxi. 3. "*Dolor parturientis,*" says Gesenius here: but this is by no means apparent, Nah. ii. 11; Ezek. xxx. 4. 9, al. non occ.

חלט, v. pres. pl. m. יַחְלְטוּ, *once*, 1 Kings xx. 33. Arab. خَلِطَ, *festinus in re fuit; studio usus fuit.* The passage will then read (Gram. art. 222. 4), *so the men observed and hasted greatly,* i. e. by an hypallage (Gram. art. 214. 7), *were very quick, keen, to observe what* (fell) *from him.* הַמִמֶנּוּ, should perhaps be pointed הַמִמֶנּוּ, making ה the def. art. in the sense of אֲשֶׁר. See lett. ה above, p. 146, (d). Gesen. after the usage of the Mishna, "*declarare jusserunt;*" but, how this can be made to suit either the etymology or the context, it is beyond my power to discover. LXX. ἀνελέξαντο τὸν λόγον ἐκ τοῦ στόματος αὐτοῦ; which is a comment.

חֲלִי, m. ⎫ seg. fm. פֶּקֶד, pl. חֳלָאִים,
חֶלְיָה, f. ⎭ for חֶלְיִים. Gesen. Arab. حَلْيٌ, *monile gemmeum;* v. حَلِيَ, *ornavit monilibus mulierum.* The primitive notion consisted perhaps, in *sweetness,* thence, *pleasing.* See حلو, Arab. *An ornament, necklace,* perhaps, Prov. xxv. 12; Cant. vii. 15. The LXX. σάρδιον. Others, πίνωσις. See Schleusn. Lex. ad. Vet. Test., al non occ. Fem., Hos. ii. 15. Aff. חֶלְיָתָה, al. non occ.

חֳלִי, m. in pause, חֹלִי, pl. חֳלָיִים. Seg. fm. פֶּקֶד, r. חָלָה, *Sickness, disease,* generally, internal or external, of the bowels, head, &c., Dan. vii. 15; xxviii. 61; Is. i. 5; liii. 3; 1 Kings xvii. 17; 2 Kings xiii. 14. Phr. חֳלָיִים רָעִים וְנֶאֱמָנִים, *diseases evil and permanent,* Deut. xxviii. 59. לְחֳלִי לְאֵין מַרְפֵּא, *for a disease, for none to heal,* 2 Chron. xxi. 18. חֳלִי־רֹאשׁ, *every head for disease,* Is. i. 5. עַד־לְמַעְלָה חָלְיוֹ, *until* (the) *rise* (i. e. excess in) *his disease,* 2 Chron. xvi. 12. Meton. *evil, calamity,* Eccl. vi. 2, &c. Aff. חָלְיֵנוּ.

חָלִיל, m. pl. חֲלִלִים, r. חלל. Lit. *perforated. A pipe* or *flute,* as used in feasts, dances, &c., 1 Kings i. 40; Is. v. 12; xxx. 29; Jer. xlviii. 36, al. non occ.

חֲלִילָה, r. חלל, with ה, parag. according to the accents; but most probably a fem. noun; lit. *profane thing,* used, however, as an Interjection, *Profane! fie! forbid it!* or the like. LXX. μὴ γένοιτο, μὴ εἴη, ἵλεως, μηδαμῶς. Arabic حَلَّ, et حَلَّ, *vox increpantis camelam* حَلَّلَ, *juramenti solutio, cum quis juramento obstrictus negat.* Often with לְ, מִן, Gen. xviii. 25; xliv. 7. 17: it. with an oath, or some strong negative asseveration, 1 Sam. xiv. 45; xx. 9; xxiv. 7: it. 1 Kings xxi. 3; 1 Chron. xi. 19; Job xxxiv. 10, &c.

חֲלִיפָה, f. pl. חֲלִיפוֹת, r. חלף. Arab. خَلِيفٌ, *resarcita vestis;* خَلِيفَة, *successor. Change, fresh supply,* to be substituted for something else: (a) of clothes, raiment, Gen. xlv. 22; Judg. xiv. 12, 13. 19, ellip.; 1 Kings v. 14; 2 Kings v. 5, &c.

(b) In a military sense, *Reinforcement,* or *relief of guard,* Job x. 17; xiv. 14. See my notes on these passages, and comp. Ps. xxxviii. 16, which is, perhaps, an imitation of the last. Gesenius finds "orcus" here, as in other places innumerable. See, on חֲלִיפוֹת above, r. חלף. It. Ps. lv. 20, most probably, i. e. they have succeeding troops to support them. LXX. ἀντάλλαγμα. Aq. οἷς οὐκ εἰσὶν ἀλλαγαὶ αὐτοῖς. Symm. οὐ γὰρ ἀλάσσονται. Others, ὅτι ὁ δόλος ἀντάλλαγμα αὐτοῖς. Vers. Syr. ܚܘܠܦܐ, *compensatio.*

(c) — of *workmen,* 1 Kings v. 28. Aff. sing. חֲלִיפָתִי.

חֲלִיצָה, f. pl. חֲלִיצוֹת, r. חלץ. Lit. *stripping,* or *thing stripped off,* the slain; hence, *Spoil,* Judg. xiv. 19; 2 Sam. ii. 21.

חֶלְכָה, m. with ה, parag. of unity. See lett. ה above, p. 145, (b). Ps. x. 8; in vr. 14. חֵלְכָה, in pause; the situation of the accent marking the ה, as parag. Arab. حُلْكَة, *summa nigredo;* where the ﺿ is, apparently, the ﺿ of unity, implying singularity; &c. And, as *blackness, darkness,* and the like, are usually put for *misery* (see my note on Job vi. 16), so here, *Very miserable,* afflicted, &c.; pl. vr. 10. חֵלְכָאִים, Keri, חל כאים, see under חל above, al. non occ.

חָלָל, m. ⎫
חֲלָלָה, f. ⎭ pl. חֲלָלִים. Constr. חַלְלֵי.

חלל (201) חלם

Arab. خَلّ, *telum, et spatium inter confossum telo, et confodientem.* Cogn. خَليل, *hasta;* خَلّة, *foramen quodcunque.* Syr. ܡܚܠܐ, *dissolutio, scissura, rima.*
I. (a) *Pierced, wounded:* (b) meton. *slain.* (a) Job xxiv. 12; Ps. lxix. 27; Jer. li. 52: (b) Deut. xxi. 1—3. 6. Phr. חֲלַל חֶרֶב, *slain of the sword,* Num. xix. 16. Metaph. of famine, Lam. iv. 9. Comp. Is. xxii. 2.
II. *Profane, common,* Ezek. xxi. 30: of a prostitute, Lev. xxi. 7. 14. Aff. חֲלָלָיו, חֲלָלֶיהָ, &c.

חָלַל, v. pres. non occ. Apparently nothing more than the preceding noun חָלָל. I. *Pierced, wounded,* Gram. art. 182. 2, seq. Ps. cix. 22. Comp. Luke ii. 35.
Niph. נָחַל, נֶחֱלָף, pres. יֵחַל. Constr. abs. בְּ, by, in, בְּתוֹךְ, לְעֵינֵי. II. *Be, become, profane, common,* Lev. xxi. 9; Is. xlviii. 11; Ezek. vii. 24; xxii. 16. 26.
Infin. הֵחֵל, Ezek. xx. 9. 14. 22. Aff. הֵחֵלּוֹ, Lev. xxi. 4.
Pih. חִלֵּל, pres. יְחַלֵּל. Constr. immed. med. לְ, אֶת, מִן, abs. once, Gen. xlix. 4. II. *Make, render profane, common,* variously applied, Exod. xix. 22; xxx. 14; Lev. xix. 8. 12. 29; xxi. 9; Is. xliii. 28; Ps. lxxxix. 40. חִלַּלְתָּ לָאָרֶץ נִזְרוֹ, *Thou hast profaned his crown to the earth.* Gesen. "projiciendo *in terram.*" But this is not necessary; for *profaning to the earth* may signify, making it equally common and worthless; i. e. putting an end to its choice and sacred character. Comp. vr. 45. The Ps. evidently refers to the times of Christ, and the rejection of the Jews, on account of their infidelity. See vr. 20, seq., and Ps. lxxiv. 7.
Applied to the produce of a tree, Deut. xx. 6. וְלֹא חִלְּלוֹ, *and has not made,* i. e. *used it as common.* For the three first years the fruit of a tree was considered as in a state of uncircumcision. In the fourth, it was made sacred, i. e. destined to the service of God. After that time it was the propagator's own. See Lev. xix. 23—25; Deut. xxviii. 30; Jer. xxxi. 3; Ezek. xxviii. 16, &c.
To a covenant, i. e. causing it to lose its sacred and binding character, Ps. lv. 21; lxxxix. 35: to statutes, חֻקֹּתַי, Ps. lxxxix. 32, &c.
Infin. חַלֵּל, Is. xxiii. 9; Mal. ii. 10; Amos ii. 7, &c. Aff. חַלְּלוֹ, 1 Chron. v. 1, &c. חַלְּלָם, Jer. xvii. 18.

Part. מְחַלֵּל, pl. מְחַלְּלִים. Aff. מְחַלְּלֶיהָ, Ezek. xxiv. 21, &c. *Piping,* 1 Kings i. 40. See חָלִיל.
It. מְחוֹלֶלֶת, f. *Wounding,* Is. li. 9.
Pass. מְחֹלָל, Is. liii. 5.
Puh. *Was, became wounded,* Ezek. xxxii. 26. *Profaned, made common,* Ib. xxxvi. 23.
Hiph. הֵחֵל, pres. יָחֵל, יַחֵל, i. q. Pih. I. *Make profane,* Ezek. xxxix. 7. Of a covenant or vow, Num. xxx. 3: hence, II. *Loose, set free,* Hos. viii. 10; constr. med. מִן: hence also, III. *Begin,* constr. abs. it. med. בְּ. Opp. τῷ, כלה, 1 Sam. iii. 12;—Gen. vi. 1; x. 8; xli. 54; Deut. iii. 27; Judg. xx. 40;—Gen. ix. 20, יָחֵל נֹחַ אִישׁ, ellip. for לִהְיוֹת אִישׁ, &c. With Infin. simply, Deut. ii. 25. 31.
Infin. הָחֵל, 1 Sam. iii. 12, &c. Aff. הַחִלּוֹ, Gen. xi. 6.
Imp. הָחֵל, Deut. ii. 24. 31.
Part. מֵחֵל, Jer. xxv. 29.
Hoph. הוּחַל. Impers. *It was begun, cœptum est,* Gen. iv. 26. LXX. οὗτος ἤλπισεν, r. יחל. Aq. τότε ἤρχθη, &c. Some take the sense of *profane,* here, as Maimonides; as if the name of יהוה was then first applied to idolatrous purposes.

חֲלַם, m. def. חֶלְמָא, pl. חֶלְמִין. Chald. i. q. Heb. חֲלוֹם. *A dream;* meton. *a vision,* as seen in a dream, Dan. iv. 2; vii. 1; Def. ii. 4—7; v. 12, &c. Aff. חֶלְמִי, חֶלְמָךְ, Ps. cxxvi. 1.

חָלַם, v. pres. יַחֲלֹם. See חֲלוֹם. Constr. immed. it. abs. it. med. לְ. Cogn. חָלַב.
Arab. حَلَمَ, *pinguis fuit.* Syr. ܡܚܠܡ, *somniavit, convaluit.* Comp. John xi. 12. εἰ κεκοίμηται, σωθήσεται: so naturally do the notions of sleep and health run together. *Sleeping,* perhaps originally: hence, meton. I. *Dreaming,* Gen. xxxvii. 6. 9; xli. 11. 15; xlii. 9. חָלַם לָהֶם, *he dreamt of* (as to) *them,* Judg. vii. 13; Is. xxix. 8; Jer. xxiii. 25; Dan. ii. 1. 3; Joel iii. 1, &c.
II. *Be, become, stout, fat.* Synon. יְבוּ, Job xxxix. 4. See my note on the place.
Part. חֹלֵם, *Dreaming,* Gen. xli. 1. And, as visions were oft afforded in dreams, i. q. נָבִיא, Deut. xiii. 2. 4. 6. Comp. Num. xii. 6; pl. חֹלְמִים, Ps. cxxvi. 1.
Hiph. pres. aff. תַּחֲלִימֵנִי, *Thou wilt make me strong, stout, &c.,* Is. xxxviii. 16.
Part. pl. m. מַחֲלִמִים, *Causing to give out as dreams, visions,* as if the people called for, and encouraged, these things, Jer. xxix. 8. Comp. Ib. v. 31.

חַלָּמוּת, f. once, Job vi. 6. Gesen.us,

D D

חלם

in his Thes., p. 480, contends, in the first place, for the *white of an egg;* insisting mainly on the opinions of the Jews; in the second, for *purslain,* because the Syriac ܣܲܟܚܲܕܬܳܐ, seems to require this; which his Arabic interpreter renders, by رِبَقٌ الكَمْقَاء, *saliva portulacæ.* As to the first, no reliance can be placed on the opinions of the Jews, grounded on passages of the Talmud; because the whole is modern, and rests on no good assignable foundation: as to the second, the Arabic translation of the Syr. ܣܲܟܚܲܕܬܳܐ, is destitute of every thing like authority: not to insist on its disagreement with the best Syrian Lexicographers. And, again, could we rely on this translation, still would Gesenius's gloss on it be inadmissible, as if this herb were " *iners et sine sapore:*" the Arabs themselves giving a very different one; i. e. as if the herb were foolish for refusing to grow in any but running water. So Jauhari, لانها لا تنبت الا فى مسيل: which, however, Dr. Gesenius has pronounced to be wrong. But, as to the fact. Is the juice of purslain *without taste?* He seems to have some doubt of this, and, accordingly, has recourse to a second solution: " Nec deest probabile etymon, sive *a foliis pinguibus* dictam existimabis portulacam (cf. ⵎⴻⵏⵜ: ⵟⴱⴰ: genus oleris a pinguedine dictum), sive a *fatuitate;* potest enim חֲלָמוּת, *somnolentia* reddi, hinc *fatuitas*" (cf. Eccl. v. 2. 6. But neither of these places will justify any such notion as remarked above). And, once more, Are the leaves of purslain fat in any sense? But if they were, and if we may rely on the Æthiopic etymology here adduced, would fatness of leaf necessarily imply *somnolency,* and thence *fatuity?* All I can say is, if this congeries of unconnected matter evinces great learning, it certainly does very bad argument. In the last place, Dr. Gesenius objects to the sense derived from the Arab. حَالُومٌ, *lac coagulatum,* because it receives no countenance from the ancients: " veterum auctoritate destituitur;" as if Dr. Gesenius universally considered this of any weight. See my notes on this passage.

חַלָּמִישׁ, masc. pl. non occ. Arab.

الخَلَابِيسُ, which is explained by the author of the Kamoos — among other things — by الخُلْنْبُوسُ, (Giggeius, Golius, and Castell. خُلْنْبُوسْ, which, if خلب is the root, as Jauhari thinks, and as Gesenius partly allows, and if ن, is here introduced, as in some other instances, in lieu of (ّ) *teshdeed,* or *dagesh,* this punctuation must be the correct one; that of the Calcutta Kāmoos false; and of this I have no doubt), حجر القدّاح. *Fire-striking stone, flint, pyrites. Flint,* or *other hard stone,* Deut. viii. 15; xxxii. 13; Is. l. 7; Ps. cxiv. 8; Job xxviii. 9, al. non occ.

חֵלֶף, m. Syr. ܚܠܦ, *loco, vice.* Arab. خَلْف, *ponè, post; post veniens, &c. For, instead of, &c.,* prep., Num. xviii. 21. 31, al. non occ.

חָלַף, v. pres. יַחֲלֹף, " poët. pro עָבַר," says Gesenius. But the truth is, the *precise* sense of each is any thing but identical; this verb signifying, *pass in succession:* that, *pass over.* Arab. خَلَف, *venit post,* vel *ponè alium.* Syr. ܚܠܦ, *alternavit.* Constr. abs. it. med. בְּ, מִן, עַל עִם, it. immed. *Pass by* or *away,* (a) as *the wind,* Hab. i. 11; Is. xxi. 1: (b) as *a spirit,* Job iv. 15: (c) as the *verdure of herbage,* Ps. xc. 5, 6;— *season of rain, &c.,* Cant. ii. 11; Job ix. 26: (d) — *a person from,* or *through,* any place, 1 Sam. x. 3; Is. viii. 8; Job ix. 11; xi. 10: (e) — *over, transgress,* i. q. עָבַר, Is. xxiv. 5: (f) —, *pierce through,* i. q. חָלַל, Judg. v. 26; Job xx. 24. It should be observed, that words originally differing widely in signification, will often agree in their secondary senses. Meton. i. q. Hiph. *Change,* put away, Is. ii. 18. Comp. vr. 20; it., Ps. cii. 27. Infin. חֲלוֹף.

Pih. pres. יְחַלֵּף, constr. immed. *Change,* as clothes, Gen. xli. 14; 2 Sam. xii. 20, al. non occ.

Hiph. pres. הֶחֱלִיף, pres. יַחֲלִיף, פַּתְחָף. Constr. immed. it. med. אֶת, i. q. Pih.

I. *Change,* as clothes, &c., Gen. xxxi. 7. 41; xxxv. 2; Ps. cii. 27; Lev. xxvii. 10; Is. ix. 9.

II. Meton. *Renew,* i. e. be succeeded by a better state, Job xiv. 7; xxix. 20; Is. xl.

חלף (203) חלק

31; xli. 1. See my notes on the two former places.

חָלַף, v. Chald. pres. יַחְלְפוּן, constr. עַל. *Pass by*, or *away*, (c. Heb. above), Dan. iv. 13. 20. 22. 29.

חָלָץ, m. sing. non occ.—dual. חֲלָצַיִם. Arab. خَلَاص, *sincerus, integerrimus*: hence, the notions of strength, power, liberty, &c. Syr. ܚܡܣܢ, *accinctus ad opus*; it. ܚܡܣܝ, losing the ܢ, and doubling ܙ, *lumbi*. Synon. מָתְנַיִם. *The loins*, as the seat of strength. Hence, *covering*, or *binding, the loins*, to give strength, Job xxxi. 20; xxxviii. 3; xl. 7; Is. v. 27; xi. 5; xxxii. 11. To come forth of *the loins*, to be begotten, Gen. xxxv. 11; 1 Kings viii. 19; 2 Chron. vi. 9. Comp. Jer. xxx. 6, al. non occ. Aff. חֲלָצָיו, חֲלָצֶיךָ.

חָלַץ, v. pres. יֶחֱלַץ. Constr. immed. it. med. מִן. See חָלָץ. I. (a) *Deliver, free self, of*; *put off*, or *away, a people, shoe, &c.* Hos. v. 6; Deut. xxv. 9. Comp. vr. 10; Is. xx. 2.

(b) *Deliver, give* the breast, Lam. iv. 3. Part. חֲלוּצִים, Deut. xxv. 10; pl. חֲלוּצִים, Ib. iii. 18.

II. *Girded* or otherwise *equipped* (soldier) for battle, Num. xxxii. 21. 29; Josh. vi. 7. 9. 13; pl. Num. xxxii. 30. 32, &c. Hence, Phrr. הֶחָלוּץ לַצָּבָא, 1 Chron. xii. 23. חֲלוּצֵי צָבָא, Num. xxxii. 27. חֲלוּצֵי צָבָא, Ib. xxxi. 5. *Man*, or *men, of the army, equipped, armed*. Niph. נֶחֱלַץ, pres. יֵחָלְצוּ, pl. constr. abs. it. med. מִן, לִפְנֵי, ל, I. *Be, become, delivered, freed from*, Prov. xi. 8. 9; Ps. lx. 7; cviii. 7.

II. *Equip, arm, &c.*, Num. xxxi. 3. נֵחָלֵץ חֻשִׁים, we will quickly *be armed, equipped*, Ib. xxxii. 17. 20. Comp. vr. 21.

Pih. חִלֵּץ, pres. יְחַלֵּץ. Constr. immed. it. med. אֶת, it. מִן. I. *Deliver, free*, from, Ps. vi. 5; vii. 5; cxvi. 8; cxl. 11; cxix. 153; Job xxxvi. 19, &c.

II. *Set free*, as a stone from a wall; i. e. take out, Lev. xiv. 40, 43.

Hiph. pres. יַחֲלִץ, *Make strong, firm*, Is. lviii. 11. Comp. Job xl. 18, to which this place probably alludes: also Ps. xxxiv. 21. The LXX. and, after them, the translators of the authorized version, have extracted, *make fat*, from the preceding and following context, rather than from this verb.

חֵלֶק, m. } pl. m. חֲלָקִים, f. חֲלָקוֹת, חֶלְקָה, f. } Constr. sing. f. חֶלְקַת, pl.

m. חֶלְקִי, once חַלְקִי, with an euphonic Dagesh. Syr. ܚܘܠܩܐ, *sors, portio*. Arab. خَلْق, *rasio capitis; opes*; it. *lævum*, et *infaustum esse; mors*, v. خَلَق, *metitus fuit rem*. Cogn. خَلَق, *quantitate suâ rem, et mensurâ definivit; lævigavit et æquabilem reddidit*. I. *Part, portion, lot*, (a) of *land, wealth*; with נַחֲלָה, Gen. xxxi. 14; Deut. x. 9; xii. 12; xiv. 27, &c. Hence, *Interest, right*, Josh. xxii. 25. 27; 2 Sam. xx. 1; 1 Kings xii. 16; 2 Chron. x. 16; Neh. ii. 20, &c. Applied to God, Deut. xxxii. 9; Josh. ll. cc. עִם אֵל, Job xxvii. 13. Comp. xxxi. 2. See my note here, and Jer. x. 16; li. 19; Ps. xvi. 5, &c.

(b) *Field*, as a portion of land. Arab. cogn. حَقْل, Syr. ܚܩܠܐ, *ager*; and, hence, the ἀκελδαμά of the New Test., Acts i. 19. Syr. ܚܩܠ ܕܡܐ. Arab. حَقْل الدِّمَاء, i. e. *ager sanguinum*, 2 Kings ix. 10. 36, 37.

(c) *Portion*, as of the sacrifice, Lev. x. 10. — of the prey, Gen. xiv. 24; Num. xxxi. 36; 1 Sam. xxx. 24. Hence, *The prey*, itself, Job xvii. 5. Metaph. morally, Is. lvii. 6; Ps. L. 18; Eccl. ii. 10; iii. 22; Prov. vii. 21. בְּחֶלְקָה שְׂפָתֶיהָ, usually, *with the smoothness, flattery, of her lips*; but, it may be, *with the portion*, i. e. that which the lips had to give over as a prey. Comp. נִיב שְׂפָתָיִם, Is. lvii. 19, and Prov. x. 31. In like manner, Is. lvii. 6, is taken to signify, Gesen. "*cum lævioribus torrentis*, (i. e. *lapidibus glabris torrentis, ex quibus idola facitis.*) But, what can this possibly mean? Did they make idols out of the pebbles found in the mountain torrents? Comp. 1 Sam. xvii. 40. Who ever heard of such a thing? An Hexaplar reading is, ἐν μερέσι φάραγγος; which seems to me well founded; it being certain that *streams* and *rivers* were often dedicated to the deities; and, that hence, we have the *river-nymphs, &c.* Syr. *thy portion and inheritance* is *with the portion of the torrents*. In this view, the idols might be said to be the portion of idolaters, just as Jehovah was, to *be the portion of his people*; and, as these torrents failed (in Heb. phr. *lied*, see under כזב), so did their portion. Phr. חֵלֶק כְּחֵלֶק, *portion as portion*, i. e. equal portions, Deut. xviii. 8. חֵלֶק בְּ, *portion,*

חלק (204) חלק

interest in any one, Josh. ll. cc. חֵלֶק מִמַּעַל, *portion*, *gift from above*, Job xxxi. 2. חֵלֶק לְשִׁבְעָה, *portion to seven;* Eccl. xi. 2, *seven fold.* שִׁבְעָה חֲלָקִים, *seven portions, or parts*, Josh. xviii. 5, seq. Aff. חֶלְקִי, חֶלְקְךָ, &c. pl. חֶלְקֵיהֶם. Fem. (a) Deut. xxxiii. 21; Jer. xii. 10; Job xxiv. 18, &c. (b) *Field*, 2 Sam. xxiii. 11, 12; 2 Kings iii. 19; 1 Chron. xi. 14; 2 Kings ix. 21. 25, 26, &c. II. *Smooth*, Gen. xxvii. 16; Ps. lxxiii. 18; Is. xxx. 10. Comp. Prov. vi. 24; Ps. xiii. 3, 4. Aff. חֶלְקָתָם, חֶלְקָתִי.

חֲלָק, m. Chald. *Part, portion*, Dan. iv. 12. 20; Ezra iv. 16. Aff. חֲלָקֵהּ.

חֲלָקוֹת, pl. f. Chald. *Blandishments, flattering things*, Dan. xi. 32.

חָלָק, m.—pl. non occ. *Smooth, slippery*, opp. to hairy, Gen. xxvii. 11; *fallacious*, Ezek. xii. 24. Synon. שָׁוְא, xiii. 7. מֵב, *flattering*, Prov. v. 3; xxvi. 28. Applied as a proper name, perhaps, to a mountain, Josh. xi. 17; xii. 7.

חָלַק, v. pres. יַחֲלֹק. Constr. immed. it. med. לְ, אֶת, בְּתוֹךְ, עִם, it. abs. I. *Apportion*, as land, wealth, spoil, &c., Josh. xviii. 2; xiv. 5; Deut. iv. 19; xxix. 25; 2 Sam. xix. 30; 2 Chron. xxiii. 18; xxviii. 21; Job xxvii. 17; xxxix. 17; Prov. xvii. 2; xxix. 24, &c.

II. *Smooth, fallacious*, Hos. x. 2; Ps. lv. 22.

Infin. חֲלֹק, Neh. xiii. 13.

Imp. pl. חִלְקוּ, Josh. xxii. 8.

Part. חוֹלֵק, Prov. xxix. l. c.

Niph. pres. יֵחָלֵק, pret. non occ. *Be, become, apportioned*, Gen. xiv. 15; Num. xxvi. 53. 55, 56; Job xxxviii. 24.

Pih. חִלֵּק, pres. יְחַלֵּק; constr. immed. it. med. לְ, pers. בְּ, instr. it. in; אֶת, as to, with. *Apportion*, (a) as in Kal, *divide*, Gen. xlix. 27; Josh. xviii. 10; Judg. v. 30; 2 Sam. vi. 19; 1 Kings xviii. 6; Is. xxxiv. 17; Ezek. v. 1; Joel iv. 2, &c. (b) *Disperse*, Gen. xlix. 7; Lam. iv. 16.—Phr. יְחַלְּקוּ בְגָדַי לָהֶם, *they divided among themselves my garments*, Ps. xxii. 19. חֲבָלִים יְחַלֵּק, *he apportions pains*, Job xxi. 17. See my note. יַחְלְקֵם מַחְלְקוֹת, *he divides them into divisions*, 1 Chron. xxiii. 6. יְחַלֵּק בִּמְחִיר, *he divides, apportions, by price*, Dan. xi. 39. אֲחַלְּקֵלוֹ בָרַבִּים, *I will apportion to him among the mighty*, Is. liii. 12.

Infin. חַלֵּק, Josh. xix. 51, &c.

Imp. חַלֵּק, Ib. xiii. 7.

Puh. חֻלַּק, pres. f. תְּחֻלַּק. *Be, become, divided, apportioned*, Is. xxxiii. 23; Amos vii. 17; Zech. xiv. 1, al. non occ.

Hiph. הֶחֱלִיק, pres. pl. יַחֲלִיקוּן, with ן parag. of sign. II. Kal. constr. immed. it. med. עַל, אֶל, pers. בְּ, instr. *Make smooth, flattering*, Ps. v. 10; xxxvi. 3; Prov. ii. 16; vii. 5; xxviii. 23; xxix. 5.

Infin. חֲלֹק, *Taking portion*, Jer. xxxvii. 12. Sign. I. Kal.

Part. מַחֲלִיק, *Smoothing*, Is. xli. 7.

Hithp. הִתְחַלֵּק, m. pl. *Let them be dividing, apportioning*, Josh. xviii. 5, al. non occ.

חַלָּק, m. pl. constr. חַלֻּקֵי, *Smooth (pieces) of stones*, 1 Sam. xvii. 40, al. non occ. Arab. حَالِق, *acutus, radere aptus.*

חֶלְקָה, constr. חֶלְקַת, f. (for חֲלוּקָה, part. pass. v. חלק), lit. *Divided (portion) of* —, 2 Chron. xxxv. 5.

חֲלַקְלַקּוֹת, pl. f. compd. Gram. art. 169, *Exceedingly slippery* (way), Ps. xxxv. 6; Jer. xxiii. 12; (ways, means, devices) Dan. xi. 21. 34, al. non occ.

חלש, v. pret. non occ.—pres. יַחֲלֹשׁ, act. יֶחֱלַשׁ, neut. Constr. med. אֶת, עַל, it. abs. *Discomfit, reduce*, Exod. xvii. 13; Job xiv. 10. וַיָּמָת וַיֶּחֱלַשׁ, *Dies and grows feeble*, by an hypallage, for, *grows feeble and dies*, Gram. art. 224. 7. See חֲלוּשָׁה, it. Arab. خلس, *rapuit, abripuit, &c.*

Part. חוֹלֵשׁ, Is. xiv. 12, al. non occ.

חַלָּשׁ, m. opp. τῷ, גִּבּוֹר, Joel iv. 10. *Pusillanimous, weak, person.* LXX. ἀδύνατος.

חֹם, m.—pl. non occ. r. חמם. Syr. ܚܘܡܐ, *æstus, calor.* Arab. حَمّ, id. Infin. or verbal noun. *Being, or growing, hot;* of the sun, day, bread, &c., Gen. xviii. 1; 1 Sam. xi. 9. 11; xxi. 7; 2 Sam. iv. 5; Is. xviii. 4; Hagg. i. 6; Job xxiv. 19, &c. Aff. חֻמּוֹ, Job vi. 17. חֻמָּם, Jer. li. 39.

חָם, m. pl. חַמִּים, r. חמם. *Hot*, of bread, Josh. ix. 12. — clothes, Job xxxvii. 17. See my note, al. non occ. Also the original name for Egypt, apparently; styled by the Copts, ⲬⲎⲘⲒ; and, by Plutarach, de Is. et Osir. χημία. He adds, as if to supply the etymon, θερμὴ γάρ ἐστιν καὶ ὑγρά. So the Copt. ϢⲎⲘ, *fervere.* It. Hieronym. quæst., Gen. ix.; Ps. cv. 23. 27; cvi. 22.

חמא (205) חמד

אֶרֶץ חָם, *land of Ham.* See also Ps. lxxviii. 51, and the LXX.

חֵמָא }
חֶמְאָ } f. Chald. Syr. ܚܡܐ, *incaluit.*
חֵמָא } Arab. حَمَا, and حَمَا, r. حمو, *incaluit.* *Heat.* Metaph. *anger,* Dan. iii. 13. 19; xi. 44. This variety in the vowels may be ascribed either to the punctuists or the copyists, and is of no moment.

חֶמְאָה, f. once חֵמָה, Job xxix. 6. Constr. חֶמְאַת. Arab. حَمَأ, r. حمو, *spissum fuit lac. Butter,* or *cheese,* as produced from חָלָב, which see, and Prov. xxx. 33;— Gen. xviii. 8; Judg. v. 25. Joseph. Arch. lib. v. cap. v. γάλα διεφθορὸς ἤδη, *lac jam corruptum,* 2 Sam. xvii. 29; Is. vii. 15. 22; Job xx. 17; xxix. 6; Deut. xxxii. 14. "De quovis lacte," according to Gesenius, in the last three places: but this does not appear. חֲמָאוֹת, in מַחֲמָאוֹת (for מֵחֲמָאוֹת), Ps. lv. 22, is, as Gesenius thinks, the pl. of this. See מַחֲמָאוֹת. Probably, i. q. חָלָב, or חֲלֻמוֹת. See my note on Job vi. 6, and חֲלֻמוֹת above.

חֶמֶד, m.—pl. non occ. }
חֶמְדָּה, f. constr. חֶמְדַּת } Arab. حمد, *laus;* εὐδοκία. *Desire;* m. only in the phrases, שְׂדֵי חֶמֶד, *fields of desire,* i. e. desirable, Is. xxxii. 12. בַּחוּרֵי חֶמֶד, *youths of desire,* Ezek. xxiii. 6, &c.; and כַּרְמֵי חֶמֶד, *vineyards* of do., Amos v. 11. Fem. בְּלֹא חֶמְדָּה, *he departed*—died—*without desire,* i. e. for his life. Applied to the *Holy Land,* Ps. cvi. 24; Jer. iii. 19; xii. 10; Zech. vii. 14:—to vessels, implements of war, &c., as valuable, 2 Chron. xxxii. 27; xxxvi. 10; Jer. xxv. 34; Hos. xiii. 15; Nahum ii. 10; Dan. xi. 8; Is. ii. 16. Phr. חֶמְדַּת כָּל-הַגּוֹיִם, *the desire of all the nations,* i. e. *Him* whom all nations shall receive, and very highly prize, Hag. ii. 7. *The Messiah,* as the context sufficiently shews. The final ת is here, probably, the ה of unity. See letter ה (b) above, p. 145. In that case the pl. בָּאוּ is used to mark the dignity of the person; or, by a *zeugma,* with הַגּוֹיִם, Gram. art. 215. 12. In Dan. xi. 37, חֶמְדַּת נָשִׁים, *desire of women.* Comp. אַהֲבַת נָשִׁים, 2 Sam. i. 26, i. e. *the love of women* to a son. In Dan. l. c. some deity—from the context—as Gesenius has no doubt. *The Messiah,* who was to be born of a virgin, and thence, *the desire of women.* Aff. חֶמְדָּתִי, חֶמְדָּתָם, חֶמְדָּתֵךְ,

חָמַד, v. pres. יַחְמֹד, 1st pers. pl. aff. נֶחְמְדֵהוּ, Is. liii. 2. Constr. immed. it. med. לְ, אֶת. *Desire, covet,* in a good, or a bad sense, Exod. xx. 17; xxxiv. 24; Deut. v. 21; vii. 25; Josh. vii. 21; Is. i. 29; Mic. ii. 2; Ps. lxviii. 17; Prov. i. 22; vi. 25; xii. 12.

Part. aff. חֲמוּדוֹ, *His desirable* matter, store, Job xx. 20; Ps. xxxix. 12. Pl. aff. חֲמוּדֵיהֶם, Is. xliv. 9, *their idols.* Comp. Ib. i. 29.

Pl. f. חֲמוּדוֹת, applied to vessels and other valuables, Gen. xxvii. 15; 2 Chron. xx. 25; Ezra viii. 27; Dan. x. 3; xi. 38. 43: to the prophet Daniel, Dan. ix. 23; x. 11. 19: pl. of excellence here, Gram. art. 223. 3.

Niph. part. נֶחְמָד, pl. נֶחְמָדִים, *Desirable,* Gen. iii. 6; Ps. xix. 11, &c.

Pih. חִמַּדְתִּי, *I have greatly desired,* Cant. ii. 3.

חֵמָה, see חֶמְאָה above.

חֵמָה, f. constr. חֲמַת, pl. חֵמוֹת, r. חמה. Cogn. יחם. Syr. ܚܡ, *incaluit.* Arab. حَمَا, *impura ex conturbatione fuit aqua iratus fuit.* Cogn. حَمَا, r. حمو, *incaluit;* hence, from warmth of affection (comp רחם), *praesidio custodivit, auxilium tulit, &c.* Hence, חוֹמָה, *wall.* I. *Heat,* applied to wine, as exciting, Jer. xxv. 15; li. 17; Hos. vii. 5. Comp. Rev. xvi. 19; Job xxi. 20: to poison, Deut. xxxii. 24. 33; Ps. lviii. 5: and, in each case, indicating the *anger* of Jehovah. Hence, metaph. II. *anger, fury* of a heated or excited mind, Esth. iii. 5; v. 9; Job xxxvi. 18. See my note, Prov. xv. 1. 18. With אַף, Is. xlii. 25; Jer. xxxii. 27, &c. קִנְאָה, Ezek. xvi. 38. With fire Jer. iv. 4; xxi. 12, &c. Said to be poured out;—hence, the phials, Rev. xvi. 1;— Ezek. vii. 8; xiv. 18; Ps. lxxix. 6. Phr. אִישׁ חֵמָה, *a man of heat,* i. e. *angry,* Prov. xv. 18. בַּעַל חֵמָה. id. synon. אִישׁ אַף, Ib. xxix. 22. חֵמָה עֲווֹנוֹת, Job xix. 29. See my note. כּוֹס הַיַּיִן הַחֵמָה, *full cup of the wine—the fury,* Jer. xxv. 15. Hence, the phrr. יִשְׁפֹּךְ חֵמָה *pours out anger,* Is. xlii. 25; Ezek. xx. 33; 34. חֲמַת תַּנִּינִים, *poison of monsters,* Deut. xxxii. 33. Comp. vr. 24. With the v. נָתַךְ, 2 Chron. xii. 7; xxxiv. 25, &c. From its comp. with fire, with יָצָא, 2 Kings xxii. 17, &c.: it. with יָצָא, Jer. xxi. 12, &c.: with נוח, Ezek. v. 13; and, from its abundance,

חֲמוּ

with בְּלֹה, Ib., &c. Aff. חֲמָתוּ, חֲמָתְךָ, חֲמָתִי, חֲמָתָם.

חָמוּץ, m. once, Is. i. 17, r. חמץ; חָמוּץ, perhaps, more properly, as the passage seems to require a passive sense. LXX. ἀδικούμενος. Lit. *soured*, or *fermented*. *Injured, oppressed, vexed*. Or, if taken actively, *lead rightly on* (by) *exciting, encouraging*. See Hieroz. Boch. i. lib. ii. cap. vii. col. 112.

חַמּוּק, m. once, phr. חַמּוּקֵי יְרֵכָיִךְ, *how beautiful* (are) *the surroundings—clothings—of thy thighs*, they are like, &c. Cant. vii. 2. Comp. Ps. xlv. 14. The bridal ornaments of the spouse of Christ. Gesen. "pingitur puella, καλλίπυγος!"

חֲמוֹר, חֲמֹר, m. pl. חֲמֹרִים. Syr. ܚܡܳܪܳܐ. Arab. حِمَار, *asinus*. Boch. Hieroz. i. lib. ii. cap. xii. *An ass*, Gen. xlix. 14; Exod. xiii. 13; xxi. 33; Judg. xix. 3, &c.

In Judg. xv. 16, i. q. חֲמוֹרָה, *heap*. So the interpreters generally; which, however, is unnecessary, as the place may be rendered, *With the jaw of the* ass,—*of an ass!—two fold heaps!* with, &c. And, as asses are in the East much more powerful and valuable than they are with us, they were often used for riding by great men. Comp. Judg. x. 4; xii. 14, &c.; it. Zech. ix. 9, with Matt. xxi. 5; John xii. 15. And, hence, the second Chalif received the title of حِمَار الجَزِيرَة, Ass of the Island, i. e. of Mesopotamia. Gesen.

Aff. חֲמֹרוּ, חֲמֹרְךָ, חֲמֹרֵינוּ, חֲמֹרֵיכֶם, חֲמֹרֵיהֶם.

חֲמוֹרָה, f. once, dual. חֲמֹרָתָיִם, Judg. xv. 16. *Two heaps*. Syr. ܚܡܳܪܬܳܐ, and f. ܚܡܳܪܬܳܐ, *granum perforatum*; which is, perhaps, the very word here used. And, as the Philistines seem to have been eminent in growing corn—and hence probably derived much of their wealth,—see Ib. vr. 1; it. vr. 5, et seq.; it is not unlikely that this term, *twice pierced grain*, was here given to them by way of contempt: the dual number being used to intimate, perhaps, the lying of one carcase upon another. See חֲמוֹר above.

Arab. cogn. خُمْر, *hominum, multitudo, densa turba*.

חָמוֹת, f. sing.—pl. non occ. with aff. only, חֲמוֹתֵךְ, חֲמוֹתָהּ. *Thy, her, mother-in-*

חָמַט

law. Syr. ܚܡܳܬܳܐ. Æth. ሐሞት:
Arab. حَمَاة, *socrus*, Ruth i. 14; ii. 11. 18, 19, &c.

חֹמֶט, m. once, Lev. xi. 30. See Hieroz. Boch. i. lib. iv. cap. v. LXX. σαύρα. A sort of *lizard*, apparently. No satisfactory etymology has been found. The modern Jews, translators, &c. *the snail*.

חָמִי, m. with aff. only, חָמִיךְ, חָמִיהָ. Arab. حَمُو, *socer*. Syr. ܚܡܳܐ. Æth. ሐሙ: id. *Thy, her, Father-in-law*, Gen. xxxviii. 13. 25; 1 Sam. iv. 19. 21, al. non occ.

חָמִיץ, m. once, Is. xxx. 24, in the phr. בְּלִיל חָמִיץ יֹאכֵלוּ, Auth. Vers. "*Shall eat clean provender*." LXX. ἄχυρα. Arab. حَمَض, *acidus fuit*; it. *depasta fuit camelus amaram et salsam plantam*; حَمَض, *dictam*; حَامِضَة, *comedens herbas tales camela*. The Arabs have a proverb, الخُلَّة خُبْز الإبل والحَمَض فاكهتها, i. e. *Elkhulla* (a sort of sweet herb) *is the bread of the camel; but Elhamz* (a salt, sour plant, חמץ,) *is its fruit*; i. e. desert, greater dainty. Jauhari. בְּלִיל חָמִיץ, *provender, fodder*, of this *sharp, sour herbage*; i. e. *the most choice fodder*. See חליל above, p. 83.

חֲמִישִׁי, and חֲמִשִּׁי, m. ⎫ pl. irreg.
חֲמִישִׁית, and חֲמִשִּׁית, f. ⎭ once, חֲמִישִׁתָיו, Lev. v. 24. *Fifth*, ordinal. Gram. art. 181. 2. Arab. خَامِس, *quintus*. Gen. i. 23; xxx. 17; Num. vii. 36, &c. Fem. Gen. xlvii. 24; Lev. xxvii. 15. 19, &c.

Aff. חֲמִישִׁיתוֹ, with masc. non occ.

חָמַל, v. pres. יַחְמֹל. Constr. abs. it. med. עַל, אֶת: occasionally with vv. הוּם, or רחם. Arab. حَمَل, *portavit; tulit, pertulitque patienter*. *Bear* with, *forbear* with. Meton. *spare*, 1 Sam. xv. 15; 2 Sam. xii. 6; 2 Chron. xxxvi. 15, 16; Lam. ii. 2. 17, with הום: Jer. xiii. 14; Ezek. vii. 4; Job vi. 10, &c. Applied to *God's name*, Ezek. xxxvi. 21, meaning perhaps *the Messiah*.

Infin. f. חֶמְלָה, Ezek. xvi. 5.

חמם (207) חמס

It. חֶמְלָה, Is. lxiii. 9 ; Gen. xix. 16. Aff. חֶמְלָתוֹ.

חמם, v. pret. חַם, pres. יָחֹם, apoc. יֵחַם, it. pl. m. יֵחַמּוּ. See חֹם. Constr. abs. it. med. ן. *Be*, or *grow hot*, of the day, the excitement of wine, or lust, Exod. xvi. 21 ; Is. xliv. 16. Impers. 1 Kings i. 2 ; Eccl. iv. 11 ; Jer. li. 39 ; Hos. vii. 7 ; Ps. xxxix. 4.

Infin. חֹם, Is. xlvii. 14 ; it. חֹם, see in its place above.

Niph. part. pl. m. נֵחַמִּים. *Being, becoming, hot, inflamed*, Is. lvii. 5, med. ב, al. non occ.

Pih. תְּחַמֵּם, *She warms*, i. e. *hatches*, once, Job xxxix. 14.

Hithp. יִתְחַמָּם, *Is, becomes, warm*, once, Job xxxi. 20.

חַמָּן, m. pl. חַמָּנִים, sing. non occ. r. חמם, cognn. יחם, חמה, from Arab. خَمَّان. Heb. וחמן, &c. Pers. خماناي, *similitudo*. Castell. Polyg. *Images*, dedicated to the sun, apparently, and which, according to Spencer, de leg. Hebr. lib. ii. cap. xxv. § iii. were of a conical form : " κωνοειδὲς αὐτῷ σχῆμα, μελαινά τε ἡ χροία." See the Thesaurus of Gesenius, p. 489, et seq., who cites this, with certain Phœnician inscriptions containing this word. See also " Henrici Arentii Hamaker, ... Miscellanea Phœnicia, Lugdun. Batav. 1828," pp. 49—54, and also his " Diatribe Philologico-critica, aliquot monumentorum Punicorum," &c. Ib. 1822, with Selden de Diis Syris Syntag. ii. cap. viii. and the authors severally cited in each. Upon the whole, I am disposed to believe, that the term חמן, is rather derived from חָם, *Ham*, the Father of Canaan, of Mitsraim, &c. ; and, hence, the progenitor of the Egyptians, &c., Gen. x. 6—20 : and hence, by the latter, worshipped as presiding angel of the sun, under the title of 'Αμοῦν, Gr. "Αμμων ; which is probably our very word. Hence too, Egypt, seems to have been named χημία. Copt. ⲬⲎⲘⲒ. See חָם above, and Plutarch, de Iside et Osiride ; Lev. xxvi. 30 ; Is. xvii. 8 ; xxvii. 9 ; Ezek. vi. 4. 6 ; 2 Chron. xiv. 4 ; xxxvi. 4. 7, al. non occ. Aff. הַמָּנֵיכֶם.

חָמָס, m. pl. חֲמָסִים, constr. sing. חֲמַס, pl. non occ. Arab. حَمَس, *fortis, durusque*. Syr. ܚܡܣܐ, *patientia. Violence*; meton.

Injury, as either given or received, Ps. vii. 17 ; Ezek. xii. 19 ;—Gen. xvi. 5 ; Judg. ix. 24 ; Jer. li. 35 ; Joel iv. 19 ; Obad. vr. 10 ; Hab. ii. 8. 17. Phrr. אִישׁ חָמָס, *man of violence*, Ps. xviii. 49. אִישׁ חֲמָסִים, id. if not intensitive, 2 Sam. xxii. 49 ; Ps. cxl. 2. 5. עֵד חָמָס, *witness of violence*, i. e. *injurious, false*. חֲמַס יְדֵיכֶם, *the violence of your hands*, Ps. lviii. 3. אוֹצְרִים חָמָס, Amos iii. 10, is, according to Gesenius, "quod vi et injuria partum est," i. e. *treasuring up what is obtained by violence* : but this is not certain : "*who store up violence*," with the Auth. Vers. in the sense of laying it up to prey upon themselves—metaph.—might be the intention of the writer. Comp. Rom. ii. 5 ; which is perhaps an imitation of this place. See the LXX. Aff. חֲמָסִי, חֲמָסוֹ.

חָמַס, v. pres. יַחְמֹס. Constr. immed. it. med. ע, pers. Arab. حَمَس, *vehemens fuit*, in religione, *strenuus* valdè in prælio. Syr. ܚܡܣ, *arripuit*; cogn. עָמַס. *Doing violence, injury, wrong*, to any person or thing, Job xv. 33 ; xxi. 27. See my notes, Prov. viii. 36 ; Jer. xxii. 3 ; Ezek. xxii. 26 ; Zeph. iii. 4.

Niph. pl. m. נֶחְמְסוּ, *Violated, suffered violence*, Jer. xiii. 22. παραδειγματισθῆναι. Comp. Matt. i. 19.

חֹמֶץ, m. — pl. non occ. seg. Syr. ܚܡܥ, *fermentavit*. Cogn. حَمُضَ, *acidus factus est*. Arab. حَمُوض, *subacidus humor*. *Vinegar*, either of wine or any other intoxicating liquor, Num. vi. 3 ; Prov. x. 26 ; xxv. 20 ; Ruth ii. 14. In Ps. lxix. 22. וְלִצְמָאִי יַשְׁקוּנִי חֹמֶץ, *for my thirst they made me drink vinegar*. Comp. Matt. xxvii. 34. 48 ; Mark xv. 23 ; Luke xxiii. 36 ; John xix. 29. See Poole Synop. Kuinoel, &c. on these places.

חָמֵץ, m.—pl. non occ. See חֹמֶץ. *Any thing fermented*, particularly bread, *leavened*, Lev. ii. 11 ; Exod. xii. 15 ; xiii. 3. 7 ; Lev. vii. 13 ; xxiii. 17, &c. ; Amos iv. 5. קַטֵּר מֵחָמֵץ תּוֹדָה, *fumigate*, i. e. with incense *a thank-offering of* that which is *leavened*; i. e. contrary to God's appointments, as may be seen from the places cited in the last article.

חָמֵץ, v. pres. יֶחְמַץ. Constr. abs. See חָמֵץ above. *Fermenting*; of bread, *leavening*; *being, becoming, leavened*, Exod. xii. 34. 39.

חמק (208) חמר

Infin. aff. הִמָּצָתוֹ, *Its being leavened*, Hos. vii. 4.

Part. pass. חָמוּץ. Metaph. from the sharpness affecting the taste in vinegar, applied to the brilliancy of scarlet, or the like, as supposed similarly to affect the sight. Boch. Hieroz. i. lib. ii. cap. vii. coll. 113, seq. "Ergo, ut pinguis est color, et acer, et amarus, et austerus; ita etiam acutus.... ita ὀξύ dici, quod *clarum* est, et *vegetum*, et *multo lumine* excitatum, quales sunt læti omnes et floridi colores.... Et ῥόδα ὀξυφέγγη .... πορφύραι διαφόραι, καὶ ὀξύταται.... χρώματος ὀξέως, καὶ λευκοῦ." So Is. lxiii. 1. חֲמוּץ בְּגָדִים, *splendid of clothing*. Synon. הָדוּר בִּלְבוּשׁוֹ, in the next member. Comp. vr. 2.

Hiph. part. f. מַחְמֶצֶת, lit. *Fermenting; leaven*, Exod. xii. 19, 20. LXX. ζυμωτόν.

Hithp. יִתְחַמֵּץ, *Is, becomes, excited, perturbed*, once, Ps. lxxiii. 21.

חָמַק, v. pres. non occ. See הִמּוּק above, once, Cant. v. 6. LXX. παρῆλθε. Aquil. ἔκλινεν, παρῆλθεν. Sym. ἀπονεύσας παρῆλθεν. Syr. ܐܘܢܟ ܕܒܠ, *se subducens præterierat*. *Withdrew, disappeared*, seem to suit the context. All that can be gathered from the etymology appears to be, that, as حَمَقَ, in the Arabic, signifies "*mente laboravit*," so *defect, non-appearance, disappearing*, may have then obtained in the use of this word, as in the "*ignis fatuus*" of the present day.

Hithp. f. תִּתְחַמָּקִין, Jer. xxxi. 22. LXX. ἀποστρέψεις. Sym. *demergeris in profundum*." He seems to have read תָּעְמָק. Syr. well, ܝܐܢܠ ܟܐܒܒܠ܏, *dubia eris*. See Arab. حَمَقَ above. *Actest undecidedly*, perhaps, *loiterest*. Comp. 1 Kings xviii. 21.

חֶמֶר, m.—pl. non occ. Syr. ܚܡܪܐ, *vinum*. Arab. حَمَرَ, *rubuit facies*, as if from excitement; حَامِرَة, *vehementia æstus*. Cogn. خَمَرَ, *fermentavit; pudore affectus fuit*; خَمْر, *vinum bibit;* خَمْر, *vinum*. *Wine*, Deut. xxxii. 14; Is. xxvii. 2, al. non occ.

חֲמַר, m. Chald. Def. חַמְרָא, pl. non occ. i. q. Heb. חֶמֶר, *Wine*, Dan. v. 1, 2. 4. 23; Ezra vi. 9; vii. 22.

חֹמֶר, m. sing. only. I. *Clay*, or *earth*, as used by the potter; from its redness, perhaps. Comp. אָדָם, אֲדָמָה, Is. xlv. 9; lxiv. 7; Jer. xviii. 4, &c. :—by builders, Exod. i. 14; Job iv. 19; Nah. iii. 14; Gen. xi. 3:—as in forming mounds, Job xiii. 12: —to receive impression, or form, as wax, Job xxxviii. 14: — out of which man was formed, Job x. 9; xxxiii. 6:—as (a) mire of the street, or (b) of the bottom of the sea; (a) Job xxx. 19; Is. x. 6; xli. 25: (b) Hab. iii. 15:— from its cheapness or abundance, Job xxvii. 16. Hence, from the notion of quantity, perhaps, II. (a) *a measure*, so called; the *Homer*, containing ten baths; dry measure, Lev. xxvii. 16; Num. xi. 32; Ezek. xlv. 11. 13, 14. In this sense, pl. חֳמָרִים, (b) *heaps*, Exod. viii. 10.

חֵמָר, m. Arab. حُمَر, *bitumen judaïcum*. *Pitch*, or rather, *a sort of tar*, found to issue from the earth about Babylon and elsewhere, Gen. xiv. 10; and used as a cement, Ib. xi. 3; Exod. ii. 3. This is the ἄσφαλτος of Herodotus, which he says, Clio. clxxix., was used as cement in constructing the walls of Babylon. So Justin from Trogus Pompeius, lib. i. cap. ii. "Hæc (Semiramis) Babyloniam condidit, murumque urbi cocto latere circumdedit, arenæ vice *bitumine* interstrato; quæ materia in illis locis passim e terra *excæstuat:*" and, hence probably so called, see חֶמֶר. See also Tacit. Hist. v. 6. Strabo lib. xvi. Ed. Casaub. p. 743; Diod. Sic. ii. 48; xix. 98, 99. Quint. Curt. v. 16. Dioscor. i. 99, &c. Gesen.

חָמַר, v. pres. יֶחְמְרוּ, constr. abs. See חֶמֶר above. *Fermenting, being* in an *excited state*, Ps. xlvi. 4; lxxv. 9. Comp. חֵמָה. For—

Puh. redup. fm. חֳמַרְמָרָה, (a) *They are excited, become red, inflamed*, Lam. ii. 11; Job xvi. 16. See my note : (b) *perturbed*, Lam. i. 20.

Hiph. pres. aff. f. תַּחְמְרָה (תַּחְמִרָה?) *She cemented it*, i. e. so applied the חֵמָר, as to make it proof against water. Constr. med. בְּ.

חֹמֶשׁ, m.—pl. non occ. Syr. ܣܥܕܟܐ, *inguen, ilia*. Æth. ሐምስ: *matrix*. Arab. حَمِيش, *adeps*. I. *The abdomen*, perhaps, from its fat and fleshy character, 2 Sam. ii. 23; iii. 27; iv. 6; xx. 10.

II. *The fifth part*. Arab. خُمْس, *pars quinta*. See חָמֵשׁ, Gen. xlvii. 26.

חמש (209) חמת

חָמֵשׁ, m. constr. חֲמֵשׁ }
חֲמִשָּׁה, f. constr. חֲמֵשֶׁת } Arab.
خَمْسٌ, f. خَمْسَةٌ, quinque. The numeral *Five*, taken, perhaps, as a *full* (fat, Arab. حَمِيشٌ, *adeps*) or *round* number, from the five digits of the hand; which, being repeated, presents the ground-work of our decimal arithmetic. "Ut numerus septenarius sæpe sacer est et rotundus, ita nonnunquam et quinquenarius," says Gesenius. He then cites Is. xvii. 6; xxx. 17; by way of proof. But, in the first of these places, the numerals, *two, three, four,* also occur; in the second, *one,* and *one-thousand,* are also found. But, are these also sacred numbers, the context being evidently as much for each of them, as for that? "Maxime," he adds, "in rebus Ægyptiacis," Gen. xliii. 34, &c. But all that can be said of these places is, that a *round*, rather than a *sacred,* number, is clearly intended. He next appeals to the πεντάδα of the Basilidian Gnostics, as noticed by Irenæus adv. Hæres. i. 23, and Epiphan. i. p. 68, Colon. But, can the usages of heretics be taken as truly illustrative of the intentions of the sacred writers? I think not. See my Sermons and Dissertations, Dissert. i., Introd. to Job, § ii. et seq., where these principles are fully considered, Gen. v. 6; ii. 15. 17, &c., in places innumerable. Gram. artt. 181. 226.

Pl. חֲמִשִּׁים, f. non occ., Gen. vi. 15; vii. 24; viii. 3, &c. Aff. חֲמִשֵּׁי, חֲמִשֵּׁי, חֲמִשֵּׁיהֶם, 2 Kings i. 10. 12. 14, &c. *Fifty.* Hence—

חִמֵּשׁ, v. Pih. *Divided into fifth parts.* Meton. *took a fifth part.* Arab. خَمَسَ, *quintavit opes populi... quintam cepit partem,* once, Gen. xli. 34. And, as a participial noun of Kal—

חֲמֻשִׁים, m. pl. cogn. חמש, which see. Arab. خَمِسٌ, *fortis, durusque. Firm, compact*, in array of battle, Exod. xiii. 18; Josh. i. 14; iv. 12; Judg. vii. 11. Comp. חֲלוּצֵי הַצָּבָא, Josh. iv. 13, &c. See חלץ above.

חֹמֶת, m. constr. חֵמַת. As the (··) is here immutable, the root is probably חום, which we have perhaps in the Arab. خَيَّمَ, *operuit*, and خَيْمَةٌ, *tentorium*, as something covered, enclosed. Cogn. حَامَ, r. حوم, *obivit, rem circumlatus fuit. A vessel,* most probably a bottle made of skin, see אוֹב, Gen. xxi. 14, 15. 19, al. non occ.

חֲמָתִי, m. Patronym. of חֲמָת, *Hamath,* a city of Syria, Gen. x. 18.

חֵן, m. seg. for חֵן, Gram. artt. 77; 148. 11, and art. 96. 2, pl. non occ. Aff. חִנּוֹ. Syr. ܚܢܢܐ, *gratia.* Arab. حَنٌّ, *benevolentia*. Cogn. خَنَانٌ, *commoditas* vitæ. (a) *Grace, favour.* Phr. מָצָא חֵן בְּעֵינֵי, *he found, obtained, favour in the eyes of —,* Gen. vi. 3, &c.; נָתַתִּי אֶת־חֵן־בְּעֵינֵי, *I have given favour — in the eyes of —,* Exod. iii. 21; xi. 3, &c. It. מָצָא חֵן לִפְנֵי, Esth. viii. 5. הוּצַק חֵן, *grace, favour, is diffused,* Ps. xlv. 3. Comp. Luke iv. 22; Prov. xxii. 11; Eccl. x. 12. With נָשָׂא, *bore, received,* Esth. ii. 15. 17; v. 2; with כָּבוֹד, Ps. lxxxiv. 12; Prov. xi. 16 : with שֵׂכֶל טוֹב, Prov. iii. 4, &c. Meton. accepted, considered, as such, i. e. (b) *Grace, elegance,* Prov. i. 9; iv. 9: hence, phr. יַעֲלַת חֵן, as *a graceful antelope,* Prov. v. 19. (c) *Worth,* אֶבֶן חֵן, *precious stone,* Prov. xvii. 8. Comp. xxii. 1. To this usage may be referred the passage, viz. Zech. iv. 7, הוֹצִיא אֶת־הָאֶבֶן הָרֹאשָׁה תְּשֻׁאוֹת חֵן חֵן לָהּ, *for* (one) *shall bring forth the principal stone ;* (the) *shoutings to it* (shall be) *precious, precious!* i. e. very precious is it. In which it is a strict parallel to Is. xxviii. 16, and 1 Pet. ii. 6; Rev. xxi. 19, &c., which see, and Job xxxviii. 7, with my note. The אֶבֶן פִּנָּה, with יָרִיעַ, of Job, seems sufficiently to identify itself with the אֶבֶן הָרֹאשָׁה, and תְּשֻׁאוֹת, of Zechariah; and to shew, that to this place in Job allusion is made, intimating that the rejoicing at the new creation shall not be unlike that at the completion of the old. Comp. Rev. xi. 17; xix. 1. 6, et seq.; xxi. 3. See my Exposition on these places, Sermons and Dissert. 1830. (d) By a further meton., *petition for favour, grace,* with תַּחֲנוּנִים, Zech. xii. 10.

חָנָה, v. pres. יַחֲנֶה, apoc. יִחַן. Cogn. חנן. Arab. حَنَا, r. حنو, *inclinavit, flexit.* Constr. abs. it. med. עַל, *against;* לְ, *for, at;* בְּ, *in;* סָבִיב, לִפְנֵי, אֶת־פְּנֵי, *before;* לְ מֵחוּץ, *out with respect to —;* סָבִיב לְ, *round about with respect to —. Inclining;* hence, *laying down,* or *pitching,* as a tent, Gen. xxvi. 17; xxxiii. 18; Num. i. 52; ii. 34; Is. xxix. 3; Ps. xxvii. 3; Zech. ix. 8. In Is. xxix. 1, קִרְיַת חָנָה דָוִד, *city* (where) *David pitched his tent*), ellip.

E E

Infin. חֲנוֹת, *inclining*, of the day, Judg. xix. 9. *Pitching*, as a tent, Num. i. 51, &c. Aff. חֲנֹתֵנוּ, Ib. x. 30. חֲנֹתְכֶם, *your pitching*, Deut. i. 33.

Imp. חֲנֵה, 2 Sam. xii. 28; pl. חֲנוּ, Num. xxxi. 19, &c.

Part. חֹנֶה, Exod. xviii. 5; Ps. xxxiv. 8: f. חֹנָה, 2 Sam. xxiii. 13, &c.: pl. חֹנִים, Exod. xiv. 9, &c. Aff. חֹנְךָ, for חֹנֶה עָלֶיךָ. Aq. παρεμβεβληκότων σου. Sym. παρεμβαλλόντων περί σε, Ps. lii. 6.

חַנּוֹת, either a f. pl. of חַנָּה, r. חנן, or, an Infin. of that root. In the first case, *Entreaties* for pity, favour, Job xix. 17. See my note. In the second, *showing favour, pity*, Ps. lxx. 10. In the first case, חַנּוֹתִי, Job l. c. should be read חַנּוֹתַי.

חַפּוּן, m.—pl. non occ. r. חנן, fm. intens. Gram. art. 154. 9. *Very gracious*, applied to God only, Exod. xxii. 26; xxxiv. 6; Ps. lxxxvi. 15, &c.

חֲנִיוֹת, f. pl. once, Jer. xxxvii. 16. Arab. جَنُوة, *puteus*. It is singular that Freytag should omit to give this signification, when both Giggeïus and Castell had given it from the Kamoos. In this case it is synonymous with the בּוֹר, of Jeremiah, used in the same context. See this word. *Wells*, used as dungeons, al. non occ.

חָנַט, v. pres. pl. יַחְנְטוּ, constr. immed. it med. אֵת. Arab. حَنَطَ, *rubuit corium; maturuit*; hence, حَنَطَ, *bonis odoribus condivit mortuum*; as if an embalmed body were *ripened*, or *matured* like something *cooked*. I. *Ripened*, Cant. ii. 13. II. *Embalmed*, Gen. L. 2. 26.

Infin. חֲנֹט, *Embalm*, Gen. L. 2.

Part. m. pl. חֲנֻטִים. Persons *embalmed*, Gen. L. 3. Aq. τῶν ἀρωματιζομένων. Nothing can be more natural than the application of a process something like that of tanning leather to the maturing of fruit. (See בשׁל, which is applied both to cooking, and to the ripening of fruit.) In vulgar English, too, one is said to be *tanned in the sun*, when the colour of his skin has been, in some respects, changed by exposure to the sun's heat. The surface of a mummy has much the appearance of leather. Ewald was wrong, therefore, when he supposed that the "*rubuit*" of the Arab. حَنَطَ, had any thing to do with the ripening of fruit: a change of state, not of colour, being intended. Certain sorts of leather might indeed become red when tanned; and this is all the Arab. Lexicographers mean. Hence, too, we may see what reliance is to be placed on etymologies derived from the Talmud, and other Jewish sources, as dwelt on here and elsewhere by Gesenius.

חִנְטִין, m. pl. Chald. i. q. Heb. חִטִּים. *Wheat*, Ezra vi. 9; vii. 22, al. non occ.

חֲנִיכָיו, m. pl. aff. *His trained* men, r. חנך, which see, Gen. xiv. 14, al. non occ.

חֲנִינָה, f. once, Jer. xvi. 13, r. חנן, i. q. חֵן. *Grace, favour*.

חֲנִית, pl. חֲנִיתִים, and חֲנִיתוֹת, r. חנה, from its flexibility. *A spear*, or *lance*, 1 Sam. xiii. 19; xxi. 9; Ps. lvii. 5, with חִצִּים: comp. 1 Sam. xviii. 11, and Job xli. 18, whence it should seem that this was a missile; and, in this respect differed from פִּידוֹן, which was a sort of halbert. Pl. 2 Chron. xxiii. 9; Is. ii. 4; Mic. iv. 3. Aff. חֲנִיתְךָ, חֲנִיתֶךָ, in pause, Hab. iii. 10, חֲנִיתוֹתֵיהֶם.

חָנַךְ, v. pres. יַחְנְכוּ, יַחְנְכֻּנוּ, parag. aff. constr. immed. it med. לְ, pers. it. med. אֶת. Arab. حَنَكَ, *expertem reddidit; firmavit, intellexit* rem. *Imbue; adapt*, person or thing, so as to become fitted for certain ends: as (a) *a child*, Prov. xxii. 6: (b) *a house*, for residence, Deut. xx. 5. *The Temple* for divine service by prayer, &c., i. e. dedicating it, 1 Kings viii. 63; 2 Chron. vii. 5. Comp. Acts ii. 2, seq.

Imp. חֲנֹךְ, Prov. l. c.

Part. pass. f. חֲנֻכָּה, constr. חֲנֻכַּת, concr. for abstr. *Dedication*, Neh. xii. 27; Num. vii. 10, 11; Ps. xxx. 1, &c.—

Chald. id. Dan. iii. 2, 3; Ezra vi. 16, 17.

חִנָּם, adv. augm. of חֵן, Gram. art. 167; if the terminating ־ָם in these adverbial forms is not the same with the Arab. اً, *an*, which is also used in forming adverbs: lit. *graciously*. (a) *Gratis*, i. e. without fee or reward, Gen. xxix. 15; Exod. xxi. 2; Is. lii. 3; Jer. xxii. 13, &c. (b) *Gratuitously, fruitlessly, in vain*, Mal. i. 10; Prov. i. 17; Job i. 9, &c. (c) *For nothing*, i. e. there being no just cause, *undeservedly*, &c., 1 Sam. xix. 5; Lam. iii. 52; Ps. xxxv. 7; Prov. i. 11. Gr. δωρεάν. It.

חנמ (211) חנן

Ezek. vi. 10. אֱלֵיהֶם, Job l. c. הַחֲנָם, Ps. l. c. Nold., p. 338, &c. לֹא הִנָּם פְּרִיחָם, Ezek. xiv. 23. See Phr. קְלֹת חִנָּם, *gratuitous*, — i. e. taking no effect, — *vileness*, Prov. xxvi. 2. דְּמֵי חִנָּם, *faultless*, innocent, *blood*, 1 Kings ii. 31.

חֲנָמָל, m. once, Ps. lxxviii. 47. *Frost*, usually after the Jews; and which they seem to have arrived at from conjecture, grounded on the parallelism. Gesenius takes the Arab. نَمل, *an ant*. But how *an ant* could destroy certain trees, as the hailstones did, it is difficult to say. Nor can any reliance be placed on the supposition that ח here, and in certain other instances, has been prefixed as a servile letter. It seems probable to me that נ has here been inserted, as in אַנְפֶּה, for אַפֶּה, &c. See under letter נ. If so, the vowels should probably be חֲנַמָל. Now we have in the Arab. cogn. حَابِل, * *vescens arboris spinosæ fructu;* which would well apply to *the locust*. Again, حُبَيْلِيل, is *animalculum quod moritur, deinde ob pluviam*

---

* The more usual form, from which such words are derived, is حَبَّال, or حَبَال, Gram. art. 154: 12, seq. It is worth remarking, that حَبَلَة, signifies *a vineyard, a vine, one of its roots; the fruit* of the trees named عِضَاة: and also a certain herb, سَلَم , سَيَّال , سَمُر , and which last, *the Libyan lizard*, hence named ضَبّ حَابِل, devours; شَجَر الحَبَل, too, signifies *a grape-tree*, العِنَب. The sycamore of Scripture is, indeed, rather *a fig-tree* than *a vine;* see Celsii Hierobot. i. p. 310, seq. It has been remarked by Jerome, and others, in commendation of the term *frost* in this place, that the sycamore-tree is much injured by the cold. It should be remembered, however, that *frost* and *cold* are nowhere mentioned as forming any part of the plagues of Egypt, to which the passage in question evidently relates. Besides, these plagues are spoken of as miraculous; but, as it is usual for the occasional cold winds of Egypt to injure the sycamores, this could have been no miracle. And, again, Exod. x. 5. 15, we are expressly told that the locusts, succeeding the hail-stones, devoured all the fruits, &c., which the hail had left: and in this order the Psalmist speaks, placing this *destroyer* after the hail.

reviviscit; which looks very like the nature of those insects which infest fruit trees. We have, moreover, all but our Hebrew word in the Arab. الحُنْبُل, חנבל, which the author of the Kamoos tells us, is the fruit of the *ghaf-tree*, ثمر الغاف, and of اللوبيا, *a sort of pulse;* whence is formed the verb, حَنْبَل, i. e. *he ate it*. From which a noun of agency would signify *a consumer, devourer, &c.* of such fruit. If it be said, still this does not come home to the fruit of the sycamore, it may be answered that, Consumer of fruit is all this is contended for; besides, corresponding words in these dialects have not universally precisely the same signification; nor have they always, even in the same dialect, at different periods and places. In the preceding verse, be it observed, two of the names of the *locust* do occur; which inclines me to believe, that this is another name of the same animal; and so some of the rabbins, as cited by Bochart have thought. *Consumer* (comp. Mal. iii. 11), perhaps, or *destroyer*, would be the best translation, as preserving the force of حَابِل, Heb. חבל, sufficiently exact, and, at the same time, not venturing to be too specific. Sym. ἐν σκώληκι, *by the worm*. Aq. ἐν κρύει. LXX. πάχνῃ. See Bochart. Hieroz. ii. lib. iv. cap. i. col. 444.

חָנַן, v. pres. יָחֹן, apoc. יָחֵן, it. יָחֻנַן, Amos v. 15. Aff. יְחָנְנִי, parag. ה, יְחָנֵּנִי, Is. xxvi. 11; it. aff. יָחֻנְךָ, for יְחָנְךָ, if it is not Hoph. Gen. xliii. 29. Constr. abs. it. immed. it. med. אֶת, לְ. Syr. ܚܢܢ, *gratiam fecit*. Arab. حن, *misertus fuit*. Cogn. חנה. *Being or acting favourably, graciously, kindly, to any one*, Gen. xxxiii. 5. אֲשֶׁר חָנַן אֱלֹהִים אֶת־עַבְדְּךָ, in which *God hath shewn favour to thy servant*, Exod. xxxiii. 19; Lam. iv. 16; Ps. lix. 6; Deut. xxviii. 50. Apoc. 2 Kings xiii. 23. Aff. חַנֵּנִי, Gen. xxxiii. 11. חָנֵנִי, Deut. vii. 2. יְחָנֵנוּ, Ps. lxvii. 2. יְחֻנְךָ, Num. vi. 25. יְחָנְנוּ, Is. xxvii. 11; Job xxxiii. 24. Infin. חָנֹן, abs. Is. xxx. 19, it. constr.— חַנּוֹת, Ps. lxxvii. 10, it. aff.—Job xix. 17, חַנּוֹתִי.

חֲנַנְכֶם, Is. xxx. 18. Imp. aff. חָנֵּנִי, Ps. iv. 2. חָנְנֵנִי, once, Ps. ix. 14, &c. חָנֵּנוּ, Ps. cxxiii. 3, &c. Pl. חָנֵּנִי, Job xix. 21. חָנּוּנוּ, Judg. xxi. 22.

חנן (212) חסד

Part. חוֹנֵן, Ps. xxxvii. 21, &c. pl. non occ.
Niph. נֵחַנְתְּ, 3d pers. sing. fem. *Hast become graceful*; some, *pitiable*, Jer. xxii. 23, al. non occ.
Pih. pret. non occ. pres. יְחַנֵּן, and חוֹנֵן, i. q. Kal. *Be favourable, gracious to*, Ps. cii. 15; Prov. xxvi. 25.
Infin. aff. חֲנֶנָּהּ, Ps. cii. 14.
Part. מְחוֹנֵן, Prov. xiv. 21.
Hoph. pres. only, יֻחַן, *Be favoured, find favour*, Is. xxvi. 10; Prov. xxi. 10.
Hithp. הִתְחַנֲנְתָּה, &c. pres. יִתְחַנֵּן; אֶתְחַנַּן: constr. med. לְ, אֶל, לִפְנֵי, pers. *Implore, supplicate, favour*, 1 Kings ix. 3; viii. 33. 59; 2 Chron. vi. 24; Job xix. 16; ix. 15; Ps. xxx. 9, &c.
Infin. הִתְחַנֵּן, Esth. iv. 8. Aff. הִתְחַנְנִי, Gen. xlii. 21.

חנן, v. Chald. pret. pres. non occ.
Infin. מִחַן, *Showing favour*, Dan. iv. 24.
Ithpa. part. מִתְחַנַּן, Dan. vi. 12. *Imploring favour*.

חֹנֶף, m. once, Is. xxxii. 6. Syr. ܚܲܢܦܘܼܬܐ, *gentilismus*. Arabic خانف, *fastidiosus. Heathenism; ungodliness*.

חָנֵף, m. pl. חֲנֵפִים, constr. חַנְפֵי. Syr. ܚܲܢܦܐ, *gentilis. Heathenish, ungodly*, person, Is. ix. 16; xxxiii. 14; Ps. xxxv. 16; Prov. xi. 9; Job viii. 13, &c.

חָנֵף, v. pres. תֶּחֱנָף. See חֹנֶף. Constr. abs. it. med. בְּ, instr. it. in, place. *Being heathenish, profane, ungodly*, Is. xxiv. 5; Jer. xxiii. 11; iii. 1; Ps. cvi. 38; Jer. iii. 9; i. q. Hiph. probably erroneously pointed.
Infin. abs. חָנוֹף. Jer. iii. 1; Mic. iv. 11.
Hiph. pres. only, יַחֲנִיף, תַּחֲנִיפִי, constr. immed. it. med. אֶת, בְּ, instr. Num. xxxv. 33; Jer. iii. 2; Dan. xi. 32.

חֲנֻפָּה, f. once, Jer. xxiii. 15, concr. for abs. i. q. חֹנֶף. *Heathenism, impiety*.

חנק, v. in Kal non occ. Syr. ܚܢܩ, *suffocavit, strangulavit*. Æth. ḤNQ: id. Arab. خنق, id.
Niph. pres. יֵחָנַק, *Became hanged*, here *hanged himself*, 2 Sam. xvii. 23, al. non occ.
Pih. part. מְחַנֵּק, *Suffocating, killing*, once, Nahum ii. 13.

חֶסֶד, m. pl. חֲסָדִים, constr. חַסְדֵי. Syr. ܚܣܕܐ, *probrum*; it. *gratia*. Arab.

حَسَد, *invidia*. Cogn. حَصَد, *demessæ segetes; contorsio vehemens; firmitas in chordis, &c*. Hence, as *the reaping of corn, twisting, firmness*, may be applied either in a good or bad sense, i. e. either as implying favour or the contrary; so perhaps this word has taken the signification of *favour*, or *the contrary*; and, in this latter acceptation we have the famous traditionary expression, viz. حصائد الالسنة, *the reapings* (cuttings) *of tongues*, i. e. their malignity. شر كلامها وقطعها في اعراض الناس, *The evil of their sayings, and their cutting* (up) *the reputation of men* (Sharishi, and to the same effect Motarazzi, on the pref. to Hariri,) which has been erroneously rendered by Golius and Castell, while Giggeïus is correct. Gesenius finds " *studium erga aliquem*" here: but without authority. I. *Favour, kindness, benevolence*, with אֶמֶת, Exod. xxxiv. 6; Josh. ii. 14; 2 Sam. ii. 6, &c. Phrr. עָשָׂה חֶסֶד עִם, *do favour with, to*,—Gen. xxiv. 12. 14. 49, &c. יַט אֵלָיו חֶסֶד, *he laid favour on, to, him*, Ib. xxxix. 21: comp. Ezra vii. 28, &c. — לְ נֹצֵר חֶסֶד, *preserving, keeping, favour for* —, Exod. xxxiv. 7; Ps. lxi. 8, &c. It. — לְ עָשָׂה, Deut. v. 10, &c. with עַל, 1 Sam. xx. 8. תִּשָּׂא חֶסֶד לְפָנָיו, *she obtained favour before him*, Esth. ii. 9. 17. חֶסֶד יְסוֹבְבֶנּוּ, *favour, mercy, shall surround him*, Ps. xxxii. 10. אָשִׁירָה —; *let me sing*,—Ps. ci. 1. וֶאֱמֶת יְקַדְּמוּ פָנֶיךָ, — *and truth go before thy face*, Ps. lxxxix. 15; lix. 11. — הַמְעַטְּרֵכִי, *who crowneth thee with* —, Ps. ciii. 4. — מֹשֵׁךְ, *drawing out, extending to* —, Ps. cix. 12; Jer. xxxi. 3. אַל־יַעַזְבֻךָ, *let them not leave thee*, Prov. iii. 3, &c. חָפַצְתִּי, *I have willed*,—Hos. vi. 6; Mic. vii. 18. — שָׁמֹר, *keep*,—Ib. xii. 7; Neh. i. 5. — רֹדֵף, *following up*,—Prov. xxi. 21; Ps. xxiii. 6. With art. הַחֶסֶד, Deut. vii. 12; 2 Sam. ii. 5; Ps. cxxx. 7, &c. בְּ בָּטַחְתִּי, *I trusted in* —, Ps. lii. 10. בְּ יְכֻסֶּה, — *is iniquity covered*, Prov. xvi. 6. בְּ סָעַד, — *is supported by* —, Prov. xx. 28; Ps. xciv. 18. הוּכַן בְּ id., Is. xvi. 5. יָסוּר מִן, —, *pass away from*, 2 Sam. vii. 15; 1 Chron. xvii. 13. אָסִיר מֵעִם —, *will I not annul with*, Ps. lxxxix. 34. יָמוּשׁ מֵאֵת —, *move away from*, Is. liv. 10. מֵעִם תַּכְרִית אֶת —, *wilt cut off from*, 1 Sam. xx. 15. — פְּדָחִיתִי, *I have withholden*, Ps. xl. 11. — דִּמִּיתִי, Ps. xlviii. 10. — אֲרַנֵּן, lix. 17. For other

חסד (213) חסו

constructions, Ps. lxxxv. 8; lxxxviii. 12; lxxxix. 3; xc. 14; xcii. 3; cxix. 41. 64; cxliii. 8. 12; xxxi. 8. 17. 22; xlii. 9; lvii. 4; lxxvii. 9; xcviii. 3; xxxiii. 18, &c.; Neh. xiii. 14. We have, moreover, the following combinations, viz., מַלְכֵי חֶסֶד 1 Kings xx. 31, gracious kings. חֶסֶד גָּדוֹל 2 Chron. i. 8. חֶסֶד יְהוָֹה, Ps. xxxiii. 5. חֶסֶד אֵל, Ps. lii. 3. רַב־חֶסֶד, great of favour, i. e. very gracious, lxxxvi. 5. 15; Joel ii. 13, &c. תּוֹרַת־חֶסֶד, the law of grace, Prov. xxx. 26. אַנְשֵׁי חֶסֶד, gracious, good, men, Is. lvii. 1. חֶסֶד נְעוּרָיִךְ, grace of thy youth, Jer. ii. 2. לְמִי חֶסֶד, for the purpose of mercy, Hos. x. 12. אַהֲבַת חֶסֶד, the love of mercy, Mic. vi. 8. חַסְדֵי־אֱלֹהִים, the favour of God, Ps. lii. 10; xxi. 8. חֶסֶד עוֹלָם, everlasting favour, Is. liv. 8. אֱלֹהֵי חַסְדִּי, God of my favour, Ps. lix. 18. גֹּדֶל חַסְדֶּךָ, the greatness of thy favour, Num. xiv. 19. רֹב חַסְדֶּךָ, the multitude of thy mercy, Neh. xiii. 22; Ps. v. 8. יְקַר חַסְדְּךָ, precious is thy favour, Ps. xxxvi. 8. טוֹב חַסְדְּךָ, good is thy favour, Ps. lxiii. 4, &c. חַסְדֵי יְהוָֹה, the favours of Jehovah, Ps. lxxxix. 2. חַסְדֵי דָוִד, — of David, Is. lv. 3; 2 Chron. vi. 42.

II. Piety, goodness. Sym. ὄνειδος, by an irony, Prov. xiv. 34, i. e. baseness or impiety: so Lev. xx. 17. So also Job vi. 14, according to some. Aff. חַסְדִּי, חַסְדּוֹ; f. חַסְדִּי; pl. חַסְדִּי, חֲסָדַי, חֲסָדִים.

חסד, v. in Kal non occ.

Pih. pres. aff. יְחַסֶּדְךָ, Accuse thee of baseness, impiety. See sign. ii. above, Prov. xxv. 10, al. non occ.

Hithp. pres. תִּתְחַסָּד, Thou becomest (appearest) gracious: sign. i. above, al. non occ.

חָסָה, v. pres. יֶחֱסֶה, יֶחְסֶה, constr. med. בְּ, pers. thing, it. תַּחַת. In one case, seems abs. viz. Ps. xvii. 7: and so usually taken, but the construction is, מוֹשִׁיעַ חוֹסִים—בִּימִינֶךָ, Saving those who trust in thy right hand. Arab. خَسَا, securus se in protectionem recepit. Castell. Æth. ḥWP: gavisus fuit. Cogn. Arab. حَاسَ, r. حوس, strenuus et audax fuit. Comp. حَاسَ, r. حيس. Cogn. Heb. חוש, חוּשׁ. Syr. ܚܣܐ, propitius fuit. Trust, confide, in, Deut. xxxii. 37; Judg. ix. 15; 2 Sam. xxii. 3. 31; Is. lvii. 13; Nah. i. 7; Ps. vii. 2, &c.

Infin. חֲסוֹת, Ps. cxviii. 8; Is. xxx. 2.
Part. חֹסֶה, Prov. xiv. 32, &c. pl. חוֹסִים, Ps.

xviii. 31. Constr. חֹסֵי, with בְּ following, Ps. ii. 12; v. 12, &c.

חָסוֹן, m.—pl. non occ. r. חסן. Strong, powerful, Amos ii. 9. הֶחָסֹן, Is. i. 31. The powerful, i. e. thing thought to be so, the idol.

חָסוּת, f. once, Is. xxx. 3, הָסוּת, The confidence, r. חסה. Gesenius finds refugium here, and fugit in the verb: which is any thing but obvious.

חָסִיד, m. pl. חֲסִידִים, r. חסד. Gracious, either subjectively, or objectively; i. e. either (a) the giver, or (b) the receiver of favour, grace, &c., Jer. iii. 12; Ps. cxlv. 17; 2 Sam. xxii. 26,; Ps. xviii. 26; xii. 2, &c.: (b) Deut. xxxii. 8; Ps. xvi. 10; lxxxvi. 2; cxlix. 1. 5, &c.

Aff. חֲסִידָה, חֲסִידָיו, חֲסִידָךְ, חֲסִידִי, חֲסִידֶיךָ.

חֲסִידָה, f. pl. non occ. The stork, r. חסד; termed pious by the ancients, because kind to the parent and young. See Bochart. Hieroz. ii. lib. ii. cap. xxix. An unclean bird according to the law, Lev. xi. 19; Deut. xiv. 18;—Jer. viii. 7; Zech. v. 9; Ps. civ. 17. In Job xxxix. 13, we have—speaking of the ostrich—אִם־אֶבְרָה חֲסִידָה וְנֹצָה, which Gesenius translates, "at num etiam pia est penna et pluma ejus?" i. e. "sed non (ciconiæ instar) pia est erga pullos, contra eos impie tractat:" which strikes me as far-fetched in the extreme. I prefer taking חֲסִידָה, as qualifying אֶבְרָה, in apposition, Gram. art. 217. 4, seq., and this combination to signify choice, enviable, feather : see חֶסֶד above, and the place in my Job.

חָסִיל, m.—pl. non occ. r. חסל, which see ; lit. devourer. A species of locust, but which it is impossible to say, 1 Kings viii. 37; Is. xxxiii. 4; Joel i. 4; ii. 25; Ps. lxxviii. 46; 2 Chron. vi. 28. Gesen. "LXX. βροῦχος:" but the LXX. give τῇ ἐρυσίβῃ; Aquila, τῷ βρούχῳ. Sym. τῷ μυλήτῃ. See Schleusn. Lex. in Vet. Test. Boch. Hieroz. ii. lib. iv. cap. i. col. 445.

חָסִין, m. once, Ps. lxxxix. 9, r. חסן. Mighty, powerful.

חַסִּיר, m. Chald. once, Dan. v. 27, r. חסר. Deficient, wanting, in weight.

חסל, v. pres. parag. יַחְסְלֶנּוּ, once, Deut. xxviii. 38. Arab. cogn. خرل, secuit, resecuit. Sam. חסל, consumptus fuit. Arab.

חסם (214) חסר

cogn. حَصَلَ, *collegit. Crop off, devour, destroy.*

חסם, v. pret. non occ. pres. תַּחְסֹם, constr. immed. it. med. אֶת. Arab. حسم, *præsectum* membrum, aut venam *cauteris ustulavit* ne efflueret sanguis. Cogn. حزم, *cingulo strinxit. Bind, tie up, stop,* the mouth, Deut. xxv. 4. LXX. οὐ φιμώσεις βοῦν ἀλοῶντα. Comp. 1 Cor. ix. 9; 1 Tim. v. 18, al. non occ.

Part. f. חֹסֶמֶת, once, Ezek. xxxix. 11. Here, I think, *Shut up, stop, stay,* so that Gog, mentioned in the context, should fall there; for it is added, וְקָבְרוּ וּג׳, *and they shall bury Gog there, &c.* See the LXX. and Syr.

חֹסֶן, m.—pl. non occ. Arab. حصن, *munimentum, arx. Strength, power,* Is. xxxiii. 6; Jer. xx. 5; Ezek. xxii. 25. Meton. *wealth,* Prov. xv. 6; xxvii. 24.

חסן, Chald. def. חִסְנָא, *Strength, power,* Dan. ii. 37. Aff. חִסְנִי, *my power,* Ib. iv. 27, al. non occ.

חסן, v.

Niph. יֵחָסֵן, *Be, become, strong, powerful,* once, Is. xxiii. 18.

Chald. Aph. pl. הַחְסִנוּ, pres. יַחְסְנוּן, *Confirm, make strong,* Dan. vii. 18. 22. Theod. κατέσχον καθέξουσιν. The prophecy evidently alludes to that period when Christianity should be *established* in the world. See my Sermons and Dissertations, pp. 345. 359.

חֲסַף, m. def. חַסְפָּא. Chald. pl. non occ. *Clay,* of the potter, Dan. ii. 41. 33—35. 42, 43. 45. Theod. ὀστράκινον, ὄστρακον. Etym. doubtful; perhaps, Arab. حسيفة, *quod vile, &c.*

חֶסֶר, m.—pl. non occ. Syr. ܡܚܣܪ, *detrimentum passus est.* Arab. خسر, *lassus, fuit, defecit* camelus: cogn. خسر, *damnum passus est;* خُسْر, خَسَر, *jactura. Deficiency, want,* Prov. xxviii. 22; Job xxx. 3, al. non occ.

חֹסֶר, m. id. Deut. xxviii. 57; Amos iv. 6, only.

חָסֵר, m. constr. חֲסַר, pl. non occ. Syr. ܡܚܣܪ, *vacuus, expers.* Arab. خاسر, id.

1 Kings xi. 22; Eccl. vi. 2; x. 3. חֲסַר מְשֻׁגָּעִים, *wanting madmen,* 1 Sam. xxi. 16. חֲסַר־לֵב, *wanting* in *sense,* i. e. foolish, Prov. vi. 32; vii. 7; ix. 4, &c. חֲסַר תְּבוּנוֹת, *wanting* in *discrimination,* Ib. xxviii. 16. חַסְרֵי־לָחֶם, *wanting bread,* 2 Sam. iii. 29; Prov. xii. 9.

חָסֵר, v. pres. יֶחְסַר, pl. יַחְסְרוּ, constr. abs. it. immed. it. med. לְ, pers. See חָסֵר. *Want, lack, be in need,* Gen. viii. 3; xviii. 28; Deut. ii. 7; viii. 7; xv. 8; Prov. xxxi. 11; Eccl. ix. 8; Ps. xxiii. 1, &c. Infin. abs. חָסוֹר, Gen. viii. 5.

Pih. pres. תְּחַסְּרֵהוּ, *Thou diminishest him,* makest him fall short of, constr. מִן, Ps. viii. 6. LXX. ἠλάττωσας αὐτόν. Comp. Heb. ii. 7, seq., al. non occ. Part. מְחַסֵּר, *depriving of, withholding from,* Eccl. iv. 8, only.

Hiph. הֶחְסִיר, pres. יַחְסִיר. *Cause to fall short, want,* Exod. xvi. 18; Is. xxxii. 6.

חֶסְרוֹן, m. r. חסר. *Much want, great deficiency,* Eccl. i. 15, only.

חַף, m. *Pure, faultless,* Job xxxiii. 9. See the parallel member, and my note on the passage, al. non occ.

חָפָה, v. once חפא, pres. non occ. Syr. ܚܦܐ, *operuit.* Arab. خفى, *occultavit,* constr. immed. *Covered, veiled,* the head, face, 2 Sam. xv. 30; Jer. xiv. 3, 4; Esth. vii. 8.

Part. pass. חָפוּי, constr. חֲפוּי, 2 Sam. xv. 30; Esth. vi. 12.

Niph. נֶחְפָּה, *Covered, overlaid,* with, constr. בְּ, Ps. lxviii. 14, only.

Pih. חִפָּה, pres. apoc. יְחַף, constr. immed. it. med. אֶת. *Overlay, case,* with gold or wood, 2 Chron. iii. 7—9. Aff. יְחַפֵּהוּ, ll. c. once, יְחַפֵּאוּ, 2 Kings xvii. 9. *Acted secretly, clandestinely.*

Puh. חֻפָּה, according to Gesenius,—Is. iv. 5, which he thus renders,—" *omnes res magnificæ obteguntur.*" LXX. σκεπαθήσεται. His translation, however, is any thing but faithful; the " *omnes res magnificæ* " can hardly be found in the Prophet. The allusion evidently is to the cloud and flame of fire which accompanied, lead, and protected, the Israelites in their march out of Egypt. We may, then, take the passage thus: *For upon the whole (all), glory shall be a covering,* i. e. shall act as a defence, עַל כָּל־מְכוֹן הַר־צִיּוֹן, *upon the whole place, or every place, of Mount Zion.* In this case it

חפה (215) חפץ

amounts to the same thing, whether we take this word as a noun or a verb: the first is most obvious.

חֻפָּה, f. r. חפף, pl. non occ. Arab. خفا, operimentum, velum, &c. Bride-chamber, Ps. xix. 6; Joel ii. 16. LXX. ἐκ παστοῦ αὐτοῦ: hardly, the "*torus nuptialis*" of Gesenius.

חפז, v. pret. non occ. pres. יַחְפּוֹז, pl. תַּחְפְּזוּ, with ירא, בהל, שרץ. Constr. abs. Arab. حفز, *trusit, festinare fecit;* كفر, *pavit, metuit. Affright, alarm;* meton. *hurry,* Deut. xx. 3; Job xl. 23.

Infin. aff. חָפְזִי, *My alarm, hurry,* Ps. xxxi. 23; cxvi. 11. חָפְזָה, 2 Sam. iv. 4. חָפְזָם, 2 Kings vii. 15.

Niph. pl. m. נֶחְפָּזִים, pres. יֵחָפְזוּ, *Be, become, hurried,* Ps. xlviii. 6; civ. 7.

Part. נֶחְפָּז, *Hurried,* 1 Sam. xxiii. 26, al. non occ.

חִפָּזוֹן, m. pl. non occ. *Haste, hurry,* Exod. xii. 11; Deut. xvi. 3; Is. lii. 12, al. non occ.

חֹפֶן, m. dual. חָפְנַיִם, constr. חָפְנֵי. Syr. ܚܦܢܐ. Æth. ᏎᎳᏃ: Arab. حفن, *pugillus;* حفنة, *mensura duarum manuum, quantum iis capi potest. Both closed hands,* i. e. so as to hold something between them, Exod. ix. 8; Lev. xvi. 12; Ezek. x. 2. 7; Prov. xxx. 4. Comp. עַל־כַּפַּיִם, Job xxxvi. 32, with my note. Aff. חָפְנָיו, חָפְנֵיכֶם, חָפְנָךְ

חֹפֵף, part. r. חפף, i. q. חפה, which see. Constr. עַל. *Cover, protect, shield,* Deut. xxxiii. 12, only. LXX. σκιάσει. Aquila. παστώσει. Theod. σκεπάσει.

חֵפֶץ, m. pl. חֲפָצִים. Arab. حفص, *collegit;* whence, أم حفصة, *mater collectionis, quæ pullos sub alas congregat;* i. e. *gallina.* Cogn. حفض, *commodè ac quiete egit vitam. Will, good-will, desire, mind, delight.* Meton. *Thing, matter, affair,* producing, or proceeding from, —, 1 Sam. xi. 25; 2 Sam. xxiii. 5; Eccl. iii. 1. 17; v. 3; viii. 6; xii. 1. 10; Is. lviii. 3; Jer. xxii. 28; Mal. i. 10. אֶרֶץ חֵפֶץ, *land of delight,* Ib. iii. 12. חֵפֶץ יְהוָה, *the will of Jehovah,* Is. liii. 10. חֵפֶץ לַיהוָה, id. 1 Sam. xv. 22. לְשַׁדַּי

of the Almighty, Job xxii. 3. כַּפָּיו, — *of her hands,* Prov. xxxi. 13; viii. 11; iii. 15; Ps. cxi. 2, &c. Aff. חֶפְצִי, חֶפְצוֹ, חֶפְצְךָ, חֶפְצָהּ, חֶפְצָם, חֶפְצֵיהֶם, חֶפְצֵיכֶם.

חָפֵץ, m. r. חפץ, pl. חֲפֵצִים, constr. חֲפֵצֵי. חֲפֵצָה, f. ∫ חֲפֵצֵי. *Willing, delighting, acquiescing,* in, 1 Kings xxi. 6; Ps. v. 5; Mal. iii. 3; Neh. i. 11; Ps. xxxv. 27; xl. 15, &c. Fem. 1 Chron. xxviii. 9, only.

חָפֵץ, v. pres. יַחְפֹּץ, יֶחְפָּץ, pl. יַחְפְּצוּ, pause יֶחְפָּצוּ, it. אֶחְפֹּץ, pause, אֶחְפָּץ, r. חָפֵץ. Constr. abs. it. med. בְ, לְמַעַן, it. immed. it. לְ, with infin. I. *Delight in, be pleased with, acquiesce in; desire, will,* Gen. xxxiv. 19; Num. xiv. 8; Judg. xiii. 23; 1 Sam. xviii. 22; 1 Kings xiii. 33; Ps. xxxiv. 13; xxxv. 27; Job xiii. 3; Ezek. xviii. 23; Deut. xxv. 7; Ps. xxxvii. 23, &c.

II. Arab. حفض, *inflexit, contorsit. Bend, move,* Job xl. 17.

Infin. abs. חָפֹץ, Ezek. xviii. 23. Part. חָפֵץ, f. חֲפֵצָה, see above.

חָפַר, v. pres. יַחְפֹּר, constr. immed. it. med. אֵת, מִן, בְ, in, &c. instr. לְ, for, pers. Arab. حفر, *fodit.* Syr. ܚܦܪ, id. I. *Dig,* as a well, &c., Deut. xxxiii. 14; Gen. xxi. 30; xxvi. 15. 18; Num. xxi. 18; Job xxxix. 21, &c.; and hence, so to make a snare, Ps. xxxv. 7; vii. 16. II. *Dig into.* Metaph. *Search, investigate, seek out,* Josh. ii. 2, 3; Job xxxix. 29.

חָפֵר, pres. יַחְפִּיר. III. Syr. ܚܦܪ, *erubuit.* Æth. ᏎᎬ: id. Arabic حفر, *pudore ductus fuit.* Syn. בוש. Constr. abs. it. med. מִן. *Blush;* meton. *be ashamed, confounded,* Is. i. 29; xxiv. 23; Jer. xv. 9; L. 12; Mic. iii. 7; Ps. xxxiv. 6; xxxv. 4; Job xi. 18: see my note.

Infin. II. חֲפֹר, Josh. ll. c. Part. I. חֹפֵר, Eccl. x. 8. Hiph. III. הֶחְפִּיר, pres. יַחְפִּיר, i. q. Kal. (a) *Blush, &c.,* Is. liv. 4; xxxiii. 9: (כ) *cause, put to the blush, shame,* Prov. xiii. 5. Part. מַחְפִּיר, Prov. xix. 26.

חֲפַר פֵּרוֹת, once, Is. ii. 20: better read as one word, חֲפַרְפָּרוֹת. *Moles,* usually. Gesenius prefers taking it as *a larger mouse,* or *rat.* See Bochart. Hieroz. i. pp. 63. 411. 1026, 1031, 1032, a redup., perhaps, of חפר, leaving out ח in the second place, for

חפש (216) חפש

euphony's sake; as, הִפוּשָׂה, for הפרה+חפר. Of course no reliance can be placed on the present vowels, as they were manifestly intended for two distinct and separate words. Constant, habitual, digger, or the like, would seem to be its literal meaning; to which, Mole answers well.

חֵפֶשׂ, m. once, Ps. lxiv. 7. Arab. حَفَش, insectatio et rei eductio. Chald. Samar. חֲפַס, fodit, scrutatus est, as in חפר. Investigation, search, inquiry.

חפש, v. pret. non occ. pres. pl. יַחְפְּשׂוּ, constr. immed. Search, investigate, Ps. lxiv. 7; Prov. ii. 4; Lam. iii. 40.

Part. חֹפֵשׂ, Prov. xx. 27.

Niph. נֶחְפְּשׂוּ, Shall they be sought out, i. e. Esau, as a people, Obad. vr. 6.

Pih. חִפֵּשׂ, pres. יְחַפֵּשׂ. Constr. abs. it. med. אֶת, כָּן, from. Search diligently, carefully, Gen. xxxi. 35; xliv. 12; 1 Sam. xxiii. 23; 1 Kings xx. 6; 2 Kings x. 23; Amos ix. 3; Zeph. i. 12; Ps. lxxvii. 7.

Puh. pres. יְחֻפָּשׂ, Is searched; i. e. tried grievously, Prov. xxviii. 12. Comp. Luke xxii. 31; σινιάσαι, Amos ix. 9, and v. בחן. LXX. ἁλίσκονται.

Part. מְחֻפָּשׂ, diligently, carefully, searched, Ps. lxiv. 7.

Hithp. הִתְחַפֵּשׂ, pres. יִתְחַפֵּשׂ, constr. abs. it. med. עַל, on, בְּ, of thing; it. לְ, with Infin. Cogn. Heb. חָבַשׁ, which see. Arab. حِبس, peristroma, quod strato superponitur; حَبَس, cingulum ad cohibendos equos. Syr. ܡܚܒܫ, obstrinxit. Cogn. ܡܚܛ, strinxit. Chald. חבץ. See my note on Job xxx. 18. This part of the verb is evidently no derivative from the above חפש, unless, indeed, it was also used in the sense of one or more of its cognates; it has, therefore, given endless trouble to the Lexicographers and Grammarians, who, after all, appear to have succeeded but badly in their decisions. Be, become, clothed, bound, as with any covering, armour, &c. Hence, meton. Equipped, accoutred. See my note on Job xxviii. 14; 1 Kings xx. 38, יִתְחַפֵּשׂ בָּאֲפֵר עַל־עֵינָיו, he became bound, or, he bound himself, with a fillet over his eyes. Job xxx. 18, יִתְחַפֵּשׂ לְבוּשִׁי, is my clothing bound, i. e. about me. 2 Chron. xxxv. 22, לְהִלָּחֶם־בּוֹ הִתְחַפֵּשׂ, to fight with him was he equipped. Comp. last member, and 1 Kings xxii. 30,

with vr. 34, where the armour is mentioned; and 2 Chron. xviii. 29, with vr. 33;—1 Sam. xxviii. 8, וַיִּתְחַפֵּשׂ שָׁאוּל וַיִּלְבַּשׁ בְּגָדִים אֲחֵרִים, so Saul equipped—attired—himself, for he put on other clothes; i. e. he equipped himself suitably to the occasion. Sym. μετεσχημάτισεν ἑαυτόν, al. μετεσχηματίσατο. Αλ. ἠλλοιώθη. See LXX. Comp. also the other places above cited; and it will appear, I think, that we have now arrived at the real force of this word.

חֹפֶשׁ, m. once, Ezek. xxvii. 20. Arab. حَفْش, rei eductio. בִּגְדֵי חֹפֶשׁ, clothes, cloths? of liberation, lit.; i. e. Spreading out freely to the view of the purchaser.

חָפְשָׁה, f. of the last; once, Lev. xix. 20. Freedom, liberty.

חפש, v. Kal non occ.

Puh. f. חֻפָּשָׁה, She was freed, once, Lev. xix. 20.

חָפְשִׁי, m. ⎱ relat. of חֹפֶשׁ above, pl. m.
חָפְשִׁית, f. ⎰ חָפְשִׁים, Gram. artt. 139; 136. 5. Free, from servitude, &c. אֵצֵא חָפְשִׁי, I go out—from servitude—free, Exod. xxi. 5. תְּשַׁלְּחֶנּוּ חָפְשִׁי, thou shalt send him from thee free, Deut. xv. 12, 13. 18. יַעֲשֶׂה חָפְשִׁי, shall make free, 1 Sam. xvii. 25; Job iii. 18, &c. בַּמֵּתִים חָפְשִׁי, free among the dead, Ps. lxxxviii. 6, i. e. dead, and so liberated from the various difficulties and labours, to which captives, and others subject to restraint and slavery, are exposed. In vr. 4, these general evils are alluded to; in vr. 5, a comparison is made with persons descending to the pit, i. e. the prison. See בור in its place; and to a hero who has lost his power, and hence, as it should seem, made captive, Exod. xxi. 2. יֵצֵא לַחָפְשִׁי, he shall go out, for (as) a free man, Ib. vr. 26. לַחָפְשִׁי יְשַׁלְּחֶנּוּ, he shall send him out for—. Pl. Is. lviii. 6; Jer. xxxiv. 9. 11. 16. Fem. 1 Kings xv. 5.

חָפְשׁוּת, Keri, חָפְשִׁית, f. once, 2 Chron. xxvi. 21. Freedom; i. e. retirement from the business of public life. So 2 Kings xv. 5. בֵּית הַחָפְשִׁית, house of liberation, freedom, from public service. There is neither necessity, therefore, nor authority, for the "nosocomium," infirmary, of Gesen., &c. Aquila, ἐν οἴκῳ ἐλευθερίας. Sym. καὶ ᾤκει ἐγκεκλεισμένος, less exactly. Vulg. in domo libera.

חֵץ, m. pl. חִצִּים, constr. חִצֵּי. Arab. خَصَّ, celeriter ivit; حِصَّة, portio. Cogn. خُصّ, domus ex arundine, &c. r. חצץ. An arrow, 2 Kings xix. 15, &c. Phrr. חֵץ תְּשׁוּעָה, arrow of victory, 2 Kings xiii. 17. חֵץ פִּתְאֹם sudden arrow, Ps. lxiv. 8. חֵץ שׁוֹחֵט, a slaughtering arrow; keri, שָׁחוּט — of (the) slaughtered. חֲנִיתוֹ חֵץ, arrow, i. e. staff of his spear, 1 Sam. xvii. 7, where the keri has עֵץ, wood, meaning the same thing. שָׁנוּן —, sharp do., Prov. xxv. 18. חֵץ בָּרוּר, a polished do., Is. xlix. 2. אַנְשֵׁי חִצֵּי, mortal is my arrow, i. e. inflicting death, Job xxxiv. 6. See my note. בַּעֲלֵי חִצִּים, Lords of —, i. e. archers, Gen. xlix. 23. חִצֵּי שַׁדַּי, — of the Almighty, i. e. plagues inflicted by him, Job vi. 4. חִצֵּי גִבּוֹר, — of a hero, Ps. cxx. 4. רָעָב, — of famine, Ezek. v. 16. With verbs, יוֹרֶה חֵץ, he shoots an arrow, 1 Kings xix. 32; Is. xxxvii. 33. יְפַלַּח חֵץ, an arrow pierce, Prov. vii. 23. יָעוּף, — flieth, Ps. xci. 5. יֵצֵא חִצּוֹ, His arrow shall go forth, Zech. ix. 14. כּוֹנְנוּ חִצָּם, they fix their arrow, Ps. xi. 2. דָּרְכוּ חִצָּם, they tread—direct, their arrow, Ps. lxiv. 4. — שָׁלַח, he sends forth arrows, 2 Sam. xxii. 15. מָצָא אֶת הַחִצִּים, find the arrows, 1 Sam. xx. 21. קַח הַחִצִּים, take the arrows, 2 Kings xiii. 18. הָבֵרוּ הַחִצִּים, polish ye the arrows, Jer. li. 11. לִירוֹא בַּחִצִּים, to cast with arrows, 2 Chron. xxvi. 15. בַּחִצִּים יָבוֹא, with arrows shall (one) come; i. e. he shall bring them, Is. vii. 24. קִלְקַל בַּחִצִּים, he shook, agitated, the arrows, i. e. of divination, Ezek. xxi. 26. הַשִּׂיקוּ בְחִצִּים, they set on fire with arrows, Ezek. xxxix. 9. Comp. Is. xliv. 16, and Ps. vii. 14; and my notes on Job v. 7; vi. 4. אֲכַלֶּה, — I will finish, i. e. exhaust, Deut. xxxii. 23. אַשְׁכִּיר, — I will saturate, Ib. vr. 42. נִחֲתוּ, — have descended on me, Ps. xxxviii. 3. יְהַלֵּכוּ לְאוֹר, to the giving of light—they proceeded forth, i. e. the lightnings did so, Hab. iii. 11. אַפִּיל, — I will make to fall, Ezek. xxxix. 3. יְמַגֵּר, — His arrows break to pieces, destroy, Num. xxiv. 8. Aff. חִצִּי, חִצּוֹ, &c. pl. חִצַּי, חִצֶּיךָ, &c.

חָצַב, חָצֵב, v. pres. יַחְצֹב. Constr. immed. it. בְּ, pers. בְּ, in, of place; by, pers. Arab. حَطَبَ, lignatus fuit. Cut, hew out, wood or stone, metal out of the mines, wells, &c., Deut. vi. 11; viii. 9; Is. v. 2; xxii. 16; Prov. ix. 1; 2 Chron. xxvi. 10. Metaph. applied to the prophets, Hos. vi. 5.

Infin. constr. חֲצוֹב, 1 Chron. xxii. 2; Jer. ii. 13. Part. חֹצֵב, 1 Kings v. 29, &c., Ps. xxix., applied to the lightning, pl. חֹצְבִים, 1 Chron. xxii. 2. 15. Constr. חֹצְבֵי, 2 Kings xii. 13. Part. pass. pl. m. חֲצוּבִים, Hewn, cut, out, Deut. vi. 11; Neh. ix. 25. Niph. pres. יֵחָצְבוּן, Be cut, engraven, Job xix. 24, only. Puh. pl. חֻצַּבְתֶּם, Ye have been hewn, cut, out; comparing the procreation of children, to the hewing of any thing out. See גּוֹיִ above, p. 109, Is. li. 1, al. non occ. Hiph. part. f. מַחְצֶבֶת, Causing to cut to pieces, or, perhaps, i. q. Kal. See Hos. l. c. חֹצְבִי, m. part. with (י) rel., Gram. art. 166, seq. Hewer-like, Is. xxii. 16 only.

חָצָה, v. pres. יֶחֱצֶה, apoc. יַחַץ. Constr. immed. it. med. אֶת, it. abs. med. לְ, for. Arab. حَصَّ, divulsit; iii. حَاصَّ, portionem cum alio partitus fuit. Cogn. Heb. חצץ. Divide, apportion, in equal parts or not, Exod. xxi. 35; Num. xxxi. 27. 42; Is. xxx. 28; Gen. xxxii. 8; xxxiii. 1; Judg. vii. 16; ix. 43; Ps. lv. 24, &c. Niph. pres. f. apoc. תֵּחָץ, It becomes divided, Dan. xi. 4, pl. יֵחָצוּ, Ezek. xxxvii. 22; 2 Kings ii. 8. 14.

חֲצוֹצְרָה, see חֲצֹצְרָה.

חֲצוֹת, f. infin. constr. of חָצָה. Division portion, not necessarily, middle; applied to the night watch, perhaps. See my note on Job xxxiv. 20; Exod. xi. 4; Ps. cxix. 62.

חֲצִי, or חֵצִי, m. constr. חֲצִי, pl. non occ. r. חצה. Arab. حِصَّة, portio. I. Part, portion, half, of any thing, Exod. xxiv. 6; xxv. 10; xxvi. 12; xxvii. 5; xxxvii. 1; Num. xii. 12; 1 Kings x. 7; Ezek. xl. 42, &c. Aff. חֶצְיוֹ, חֶצְיָהּ, חֶצְיָם, חֶצְיֵנוּ.

II. חֵצִי, pl. non occ. i. q. חֵץ. An arrow, 1 Sam. xx. 36—38; 2 Kings ix. 24.

חָצִיר, m. i. q. חָצֵר, constr. חֲצִיר, pl. non occ. Arab. حَصَر, surrounding. Cogn. حَضَر, locus habitatus. I. Court, inclosure, habitable place, Is. xxxiv. 13; xxxv. 7, only.

II. Arab. خَضَر, viruit arvum; secuit, succidit; whence, خُضْرَة, olus viride; gramen. (a) Green herbage, generally, as cut for fodder, 1 Kings xviii. 5; Job xl. 15;

F F

חצן (218) חצץ

Ps. civ. 14; cxlvii. 8; Prov. xxvii. 25; Is. xv. 6; xliv. 4, &c. From its soon withering in the sun like the fate of the wicked, Ps. cxxix. 6; xxxvii. 2; Job viii. 12; Is. xl. 6. 8, &c. Phr. חֲצִיר גַּגּוֹת, *grass of house-tops*, 2 Kings xix. 26; Is. xxxvii. 27.

(b) *Leeks* generally, which are said to resemble grass, and to abound in Egypt. LXX. πράσα. See Juv. Sat. xv. 9. Prudent. Hymn. περὶ στεφ. x. 261. 267, and contra Symmach. l. ii. p. 250. Martial. l. xiii. Ep. 18, it. x. Ep. 4. 8. iii. Ep. 47. Cels. Hierob. ii. p. 263. Num. xi. 5.

חֹצֶן, and חֵצֶן, m. pl. non occ. Arab. حِضْن, *pars corporis sub axillis—aut pectore et brachiis, et id quod inter brachia est;* حُضْن, *latibulum* hyænæ, v. حَضَن, in *ulnas cepit et amplexus fuit* puerum. Æth. ሕፅን: *sinus. The bosom, or arms,* as occupied by a child, or anything so holden, when carried, Ps. cxxix. 7, of sheaves; Is. xlix. 22, of children; Neh. v. 13, lap of do., as containing something valuable. Comp. Acts xviii. 6, where Paul, as Nehemiah had done before him, symbolically shook off the Jews, thus expressing their being cast off.

חֲצַף, v. Chald. pret. non occ. Aph. part. f. מַחְצְפָה, and, retaining the ה of Heb. Hiph. מְהַחְצִפָה. Arab. خَسَف, *spina, fluxus, &c.* Cogn. خَاسِف, *velox in incessu*. Cogn. Heb. חצב, i. e. sharp, quick, cutting. *Urgent, pressing, hurrying,* Dan. ii. 15; iii. 22, al. non occ.

חָצַץ, v. in. Kal. non occ. cogn. חצה. Part. חֹצֵץ, in the phr. חֹצְצֵי כֻּלִי, Prov. xxx. 27, only. If we take حَصَّ, *celeriter ivit,* we shall have, *Each rushing on;* i. e. making the attack as an army: if חָצָה, then, *each apportioning, dividing*, as it were, the prey. Gesen. "*omnes divisi*," i. e. agmine partito; but this would require חָצְצִי, not חֹצֵץ. I prefer the first.

Pih. part. pl. m. מְחַצְּצִים. Persons *taking part or portion,* once, Judg. v. 11. r. חָצָה, for מְחַצִּים. The passage calls upon the people to praise Jehovah for the victory lately given, and particularly wherever they are found together in numbers: see vv. 9, 10. So again, vr. 11, where they are said to go down to the gates, a place of public resort, because questions of law were tried there. Here we have, מִקּוֹל מְחַצְצִים בֵּין מַשְׁאַבִּים, *with* (the) *voice of those who take* (their) *portion among the watering-places,* i. e. at the wells and cisterns at which people often meet in numbers, for the purpose of drawing water. The last of the interpretations of Rab. Tanchum, as given by Gesenius, Thes. p. 511, as well as that of Schnurrer, is not far from this. LXX. ἀπὸ φωνῆς ἀνακρουομένων ἀναμέσον ὑδρευομένων.

Puh. pl. m. חֻצָּצוּ, *Are cut, decided,* Job xxi. 21. See my note, al. non occ.

חָצָץ, m. pl. חֲצָצִים. Syr. ܚܨܨܐ, *lapillus, glarea*. Arab. حَصَّي, id. I. *Gravel, small stones*, Prov. xx. 7; Lam. iii. 16.

II. i. q. חֵץ, *An arrow*; metaph. *lightning*, Ps. lxxvii. 18.

חֲצוֹצְרָה, and חֲצֹצְרָה, f. pl. חֲצוֹצְרוֹת, redup. חצר. Arab. حَصَر, *arctè circumdedit;* whence, حَصُور, *angustus animo; flatus venti a re cohibens; gravis difficilis loquela.* Where the Arab. conj. xii. would make, as a verb, احصوصر; and, eliding the ו, which has no vowel of its own, and adding צ, in order to form a noun, we have حصوصر, which is as near as possible to our word. *A trumpet*, as seen in the engravings of the Arch of Titus in Reland's Palestine, &c.: and so differs from שׁוֹפָר, which was a curved horn. See Joseph. Antiq. lib. iii. 12. 6, who says, στενὴ δ' ἐστὶ σύριγξ, sed *fistula ejus angusta est;* and from this circumstance it probably received its name, Num. x. 2, seq.; xxxi. 6; 2 Kings xii. 14; Hos. v. 1, &c. Hence—

מְחַצְּרִים, keri, kethiv, מַחְצְצְרִים. Part. pl. m. as if from Pih. of חצר. *Persons blowing trumpets,* 1 Chron. xv. 24; 2 Chron. v. 13; vii. 6; xiii. 14; xxix. 28. In 2 Chron. v. 12, מַחְצְצְרִים. The Masora tells us we have יתיר ר, a resh too much.

חָצֵר, m. constr. חֲצַר, pl. חֲצֵרִים, and חֲצֵרוֹת. Constr. m. חַצְרֵי, f. חַצְרוֹת. See חָצִיר No. I. above. (a) *Inclosure, area;* (b) *village:* (a) Exod. xxvii. 12, 13. 17—19; 1 Kings vii. 8, 9. 12; viii. 64; Esth. iv. 11: Ezek. x. 3. 5, &c.: (b) Is. xlii. 11; Neh. xii. 29; Lev. xxv. 31; Josh. xix. 8, &c. Fem.

חֹק (219) חֲקֹק

pl. (a) Ezek. ix. 7; xlvi. 22; 1 Chron. xxiii. 28: (b) Exod. viii. 9.
Aff. חֻקָּרִיהֶם, חֻקָּרֶיהָ, חֻקָּרֶיךָ, חֻקָּרַי, חֲקָרוֹ, חֻקְרַיְכֶן. Fem. חֲקוּקֹתַי, חֲקוּקֹתָיו, חֲקוּקֹתָם.

חֵק, see חֵיק.

חֹק, m. pl. חֻקִּים, constr. חֻקֵי, al. חִקֵּי, pl. חֻקֵי, once חוּקֵי—

חֻקָּה, f. pl. חֻקוֹת, constr. חֻקֹּת, al. חֻקֵי, pl. חֻקֵי, once חֻקוֹת—

Infin. of חָקַק. Arab. خَقّ, *fissura terræ*; خَقّ, *verum, jus.* Cogn. حَلَّ, *scalpsit;* lit. *engraven, defined, fixed;* v. חָקַק, *exaravit*, &c. Hence, *Statute, law, custom, duty, privilege,* as previously fixed and published, variously applied: (a) Exod. xv. 25 ; Josh. xxiv. 25; Ezra vii. 10, &c.: (b) in a physical sense, Job xxvi. 10; xxviii. 26; Prov. viii. 29 : (c) *defined portion* of labour, Exod. v. 14; Prov. xxxi. 15: of food, Gen. xlvii. 22; Lev. x. 13, 14; Prov. xxx. 8: of time, Job xiv. 13; Mic. vii. 11; of oil, Ezek. xlv. 14. In the sense of *limit,* as of place, Job xxvi. 10; xxxviii. 10; of *determination,* Job xxiii. 12. 14. See my notes on these last three places. In Ezek. xx. 25, נָתַתִּי לָהֶם חֻקִּים לֹא טוֹבִים, *I gave to them,* i. e. *I pronounced their, laws not good:* it is added, vr. 26, וָאֲטַמֵּא אוֹתָם, *I made them,* i. e. said they were, *unclean.* See Gram. art. 154. 8, with the note, and Job xxxvi. 3, with the note. Synon. with דָּבָר, מִשְׁפָּט, עֵדָה, מִצְוֹת, מִצְוָה, תּוֹרָה. With the verbs, שָׂם, לְמַד, חָקַק, עָשָׂה, סִפֵּר, חָג, שָׁת, &c. as the Concordance will show. Phr. לִבְלִי־חֹק, *without measure,* Is. v. 14. חֹק עוֹלָם, *perpetual statute,* so also, חֻקַּת עוֹלָם. Fem. found with many of the same verbs and nouns as חֹק is; with מַעֲלָה, Lev. xxvi. 43. עָב, 2 Chron. vii. 19. חַיָּל, Ps. lxxxix. 31. אֲשִׁיתְמַעֲשֵׂע, Ib. cxix. 16. In a physical sense, (b) Job xxxviii. 33; Jer. v. 24; xxxi. 35; xxxiii. 25: generally, *Law, appointment, observance,* either sacred or not, Num. ix. 14; xv. 15; Exod. xii. 14. 17. 43 ; Jer. x. 3 ; Lev. xx. 23; 2 Kings xvii. 8, &c. Aff. m. חֻקִּי, חֻקֶּךָ, חֻקָּם חֻקָּיו, omm. dagesh.—pl. חֻקָּי, חֻקֶּיךָ, חֻקָּיו. Fem. pl. חֻקֹתַם, חֻקֹתֶיךָ, חֻקֹתַי, חֻקוֹתָיו and חֻקֹתֵיהֶם.

חֹקָה, v. in Kal non occ. i. q. חָקַק.

Puh. part. מְחֻקֶּה, *Engraven, carved, delineated,* Ezek. viii. 10; xxiii. 14 ; 1 Kings vi. 35 ; constr. med. עַל.

Hithp. תִּתְחַקֶּה, once, Job xiii. 27. *It is impressed, marked, furrowed;* i. e. the punishment of the stocks : the iron, as in the case of Joseph, had seemed to enter into his person. See my note. *"Terram* rastro *effodit*—significatu primario." But whence has this primary signification been had? From mere fancy? Once more, Is it likely that a grave was digged with a *rastrum?* rake or hoe?

חָקַק, v. see חֹק, pres. non occ. חָקוֹת, &c. constr. immed. obj. and med. עַל, on which, it. בְּ. *Cut, carve, engrave, picture,* Ezek. iv. 1; Is. xlix. 16.

Infin. aff. חֻקִי, *His cutting, inscribing,* Prov. viii. 27; it. חֻקּוֹ, *his determining,* Is. 29.

Imper. aff. חֻקָּהּ, *Engrave, inscribe, it,* Is. xxx. 8.

Part. rel. (׳) חֹקְקִי, *Cutting.* See חֹצְבִי, Is. xxii. 16.

Pl. חֹקְקִים, Is. x. 1; constr. חוֹקְקֵי, *Legislators of* —, Judg. v. 9.

Pass. pl. חֲקֻקִים, *Carved, pictured,* Ezek. xxiii. 14.

Pih. pret. non occ. pres. pl. יְחוֹקְקוּ, *Decree, decreed,* Prov. viii. 15.

Part. מְחֹקֵק, *Decider, legislator,* Gen. xlix. 10; Num. xxi. 18, &c.

Pl. מְחֹקְקִים, Judg. v. 14; Ps. lx. 9, &c.

Puh. Part. מְחֻקָּק, *Decided decree, statute,* Prov. xxxi. 5.

Hoph. pres. pl. יֻחָקוּ, omm. dag. compensated by (־). *They be engraven, inscribed,* Job xix. 23, com. vr. 24.

חִקְקֵי, m. seg. constr. I. *Impressions, imaginations,* Judg. v. 15. Comp. Acts v. 33. II. *Decrees, statutes,* Is. x. 1.

חֵקֶר, m. pl. constr. חִקְרֵי. Arab. حَكَر cogn. حَكَر, *litigatio. Investigation, search, inquiry,* Judg. v. 16; Is. xl. 28; Prov. xxv. 3; Job v. 9, &c. Phr. אֵין חֵקֶר, *and* לֹא חֵקֶר, *no investigating,* Job ix. 10 ; xxxvi. 26, &c. חֵקֶר כְּבֹדָם, *searching of their own glory* is (not real) glory, i. e. to be hunting out matter for self-gratification is an evil, Prov. xxv. 27. חֵקֶר אֱלוֹהַּ, Job xi. 7: "i. q. τὰ βάθεα τοῦ θεοῦ," says Gesenius: but this is to mistake the construction, which is, הַחֵקֶר תִּמְצָא אֱלוֹהַּ, *whether* (by) *searching dost* (canst) *thou find God?* which the following member sufficiently proves: and so the LXX. חֵקֶר תְּהוֹם, *searching of the deep,* Ib. xxxviii.

16. חִקְרֵי לֵב, Judg. v. 16, *searchings of heart*, i. q. חִקְקֵי לֵב, vr. 15. See חָקֵק above.

חָמַר, v. pres. יַחְקֹר. Constr. abs. it. immed. it. med. לְ, אֶת. *Search, investigate, try*, of what sort any person or thing is, Deut. xiii. 15; 1 Sam. xx. 12; Prov. xviii. 17; xxviii. 11; Ps. cxxxix. 1; Job v. 27; xiii. 9; xxviii. 27, &c.

Infin. חֲקֹר, 2 Sam. x. 3, &c. Aff. חָקְרָהּ, Judg. xviii. 2.

Imp. pl. חִקְרוּ, Judg. xviii. 2. Aff. חָקְרֵנִי, Ps. cxxxix. 23.

Part. חֹקֵר, Job xxviii. 3, see my note. Jer. xvii. 10.

Niph. נֶחְקַר, pres. יֵחָקֵר. *May, can, be searched out, investigated*, 1 Kings vii. 43; 2 Chron. iv. 18; Jer. xxxi. 37; xlvi. 23.

Pih. חִקֵּר, pres. non occ. i. q. Kal, Eccl. xii. 9.

חֹר, m. sing. non occ. pl. חֹרִים, חוֹרִים, constr. חֹרֵי. r. חוּר. Syr. ܚܺܐܪܳܐ, *liber, ingenuus*. Arab. حُرّ, id. *Nobles*, 1 Kings xxi. 8. 11; Jer. xxvii. 19; xxxix. 6; Eccl. x. 17; Neh. iv. 13, &c. Aff. חֹרֶיהָ, Is. xxxiv. 12.

חֹר, see חוּר.

חֵר, see חוּר.

חֲרָאִים, m. pl. sing. non occ. Arab. خُرْء, *merda*. *Dung*, once, aff. Is. xxxvi. 12, where we have, חֹרְאֵיהֶם, with the vowels of the keri, צוֹאָתָם. The true vowels of this word are therefore unknown. "In margine honestius vc. צוֹאָה, legitur," says Gesenius; a very common, but groundless method, as I think, of accounting for this variety.

חֶרֶב, c. pl. f. חֲרָבוֹת, constr. חַרְבוֹת. Syr. ܚܰܪܒܳܐ, *gladius*. Arab. حَرْبَة, *hasta brevis*; *lancea*. Engl. *harpoon*. Gr. ἅρπη. See my note on Job xl. 19. *A weapon, sword*, Gen. xxxi. 26; Exod. v. 21, &c. in places innumerable; found with קֶשֶׁת, דֶּבֶר, מִלְחָמָה, רָעָב, &c. as destroyers. From its being said to consume, eat up, אָכַל, we have פִּי חֶרֶב, *mouth of the sword*, Exod. xvii. 13, &c.; as a means of injury, יְדֵי חֶרֶב, Job v. 20; as an enemy, פְּנֵי חֶרֶב, *face of the sword*, Job xxxix. 22, &c. Its combinations, both with nouns and verbs, are almost innumerable: a few of the most common with verbs are, — הֵבִיא עַל he *brought upon* —, Lev. xxvi. 25. הָרִיק

emptied, lit. i. e. exhausted, Ib. 33. נָסוּ, *they fled*, the flight of —, Ib. 36. הֵפִיץ, *shalt* smite —, Deut. xx. 13. — שָׁלַף, *drawing the* —, Judg. viii. 10, &c. Pl. Ps. lix. 8; Prov. xxx. 14, &c. Meton. for any cutting instrument, as, *a knife*, Josh. v. 2, 3; *a razor*, Ezek. v. 1; *a graver*, Exod. xx. 25; *axes*, Ezek. xxvi. 9. Whence it should seem that the original idea stood in *cutting*. Meton. as a destroyer, *drought*, Deut. xxviii. 22. Aff. חַרְבִּי, חַרְבְּךָ, חַרְבּוֹ, &c.; pl. חַרְבוֹתָיו, &c.

חֹרֶב, m.
חָרְבָּה, f. } pl. חֳרָבוֹת, constr. חָרְבוֹת. Arab. خَرِيب, *spoliatus*; cogn. خَرَب, *desertus*. *Heat, drought*. Meton. *Desolation, devastation*, m. Gen. xxxi. 40; Job xxx. 30; Is. lxi. 4; Ezek. xxix. 10. Fem. meton. Lev. xxvi. 31; Is. xlviii. 21; lviii. 12; lxi. 4; Ezek. xxxvi. 10. 33; xxxviii. 12; Mal. i. 4; Job iii. 14. See my note. Comp. Is. v. 17; xliv. 26. With שׂוּם, נָתַן or שִׂים, Ezek. xxv. 13; xxxv. 4. — הָיָה לְ, Is. lxiv. 10, &c. תָּמַם, Ps. ix. 7. בָּנָה, Mal. i. 4. יָשַׁב, Ezek. xxxiii. 24. Aff. חָרְבוֹתֵינוּ, חָרְבוֹתָם, חָרְבֹתֶיהָ, חָרְבֹתַיִךְ.

חָרֵב, m.
חֲרֵבָה, f. } pl. f. חֲרֵבוֹת, for חֲרֵבוֹת. I. *Dry*, rather, perhaps, *solitary*; i. e. unaccompanied by anything else, Lev. vii. 10. LXX. μὴ ἀναπεποιημένη, Prov. xvii. 1. Theod. καθ' ἑαυτόν. II. *Desolate, devastated*, Jer. xxxiii. 10. 12; Neh. ii. 3. 17; Ezek. xxxvi. 4; Hag. i. 4. 9.

חָרַב, and חָרֵב, v. pres. יֶחֱרַב. Constr. abs. Arab. حَرِبَ, *irâ accendit, percitus, fuit; exacuit* cuspides. Hence, apparently, the notion of *heat, sharpness, injury*, as well as of *fissus, foramen*, &c. in خَرَب. I. *Was, became, dry*, Gen. viii. 13: *dried up*, of water, Is. xix. 6; Job xiv. 11; Is. xix. 5; Hos. xiii. 15; Ps. cvi. 9.

Imp. f. חִרְבִי, Is. xliv. 27.
Pl. m. חָרְבוּ, Jer. ii. 12.

II. Meton. *Desolate, ruined*, Is. xxxiv. 10; lx. 12; Jer. xxvi. 9; Ezek. vi. 6; xii. 20; Amos vii. 9.

Infin. חֲרֹב, Is. lx. 12.
Imp. חֲרֹב, Jer. L. 21.

Niph. II. pl. נֶחֶרְבוּ, *They are ruined*, destroyed, 2 Kings iii. 23. See Hoph. II.

חרב

Part. f. נֶחֱרָבָת, pl. נֶחֱרָבוֹת, *Ruined, devastated*, Ezek. xxvi. 19; xxx. 7.

Puh. I. חֹרְבוּ, *They have been dried*, Judg. xvi. 7, 8.

Hiph. I. הֶחֱרַבְתִּי, pres. אַחֲרִיב, אַחֲרִב. Constr. immed. it. med. אֶת, בְּ, instr. *Dry up, waters*, Is. xxxvii. 25; L. 2; Jer. li. 36.

Part. f. מַחֲרֶבֶת, Is. li. 10.

II. Constr. immed. it. med. אֶת, *Ruin, lay waste*, 2 Kings xix. 17; Is. xlii. 15; xxxvii. 18; Ezek. xix. 7; Zeph. iii. 6.

Part. מַחֲרִיב, Judg. xvi. 24; pl. aff. מַחֲרִיבַיִךְ, *Thy destroyers, wasters*, Is. xlix. 17.

Hoph. II. f. הָחֳרָבָה, *It is wasted, destroyed*, Ezek. xxvi. 2.

Infin. הֶחֱרֵב, 2 Kings iii. 23. Phr. הַחֲרֵב נֶחֱרְבוּ, *By wasting they are wasted, ruined*, i. e. utterly wasted.

Part. f. pl. מָחֳרָבוֹת, *Wasted*, Ezek. xxix. 12. Chald. הָחֳרְבַת. Hoph. f. *Is wasted*, Ezra iv. 15, al. non occ.

חָרָבָה, f. pl. non occ. *Dry land*, i. q. יַבָּשָׁה, Gen. vii. 22; Exod. xiv. 21; Josh. iii. 17; iv. 18; 2 Kings ii. 8; Hag. ii. 6.

חָרְבֹנֵי, m. pl. constr. once, Ps. xxxii. 4. *Great, excessive, droughts of —*. Aquila. ἐν ἐρημώσει θερείᾳ. Sym. ὡς καῦσος θερινόν. E. ἐν τῷ ἐρημωθῆναι ὀπώραν. LXX. and Theod. ἐν τῷ ἐμπαγῆναι ἄκανθαν.

חָרַג, v. pres. יֶחֱרְגוּ, once, Ps. xviii. 46. In parall., 2 Sam. xxii. 46, יַחְגְּרוּ —. Arab. حَرِج, *angustia pressum fuit; vetitus, prohibitusque fuit*. Cogn. חָגַר. Arab. حَجَرَ, *impedivit. They suffer pressure, trouble, ruin*. Comp. צַר. מִמִּסְגְּרוֹתֵיהֶם, *From*, i. e. *by means of, their own inclosures*; i. e. the very means of defence which they themselves have set up, shall prove the cause of their overthrow: a sentiment occurring often in the Psalms. In this view, both the places mean, in the main, the same thing. Sym. ἐντραπήσονται. LXX. ἐχώλαναν.

חַרְגֹּל, m. once, Lev. xi. 22. Arab. حَرْجَوَان, Ch. הוּרגְלָה, *locustæ genus impenne*, ἀσίρακος. Diosc. ii. 57. Castell. "Arab. حَرْجَلَ, *saliit, saltitavit equus*"—" a saltando dicta," Gesenius. But the Arabic word has no such sense. *A locust*, having no wings, Hieroz. Bochart. ii. lib. iv. c. ii. p. 457, where the error, now adverted to, was probably first committed.

חרד

חָרֵד, m. pl. חֲרֵדִים. Arabic حَرِذ, *iracundus*; حَارِذ, id. *quem timent. Timid, fearing*; meton. *trembling*, Judg. vii. 3; 1 Sam. iv. 13; Is. lxvi. 2. 8; Ezra ix. 4; x. 3: followed by עַל, אֶל, בְּ, *on account of, for*, &c.

חָרַד, v. pres. יֶחֱרַד. Constr. abs. it. med. אַחֲרֵי, לְ, *at, of time*; לִקְרַאת, אֶל, *towards*; מִן, *from, of place*. See חָרֵד. *Fear*; meton. *tremble*, Gen. xxvii. 33; Exod. xix. 16; Ruth iii. 8, &c. Constr. prægnans, Gram. art. 230, implying also, looked, followed, went, &c., as the context may require, 1 Sam. xiii. 7; xvi. 4; xxi. 2; Gen. xli. 28; 2 Kings iv. 13; and hence the prep. אַחֲרֵי, &c.

Metaph. applied to places, Exod. xix. 18; Is. x. 29; xli. 5; Ezek. xxvi. 18.

Imp. חִרְדוּ, Is. xxxii. 11.

Hiph. הֶחֱרִיד, pres. non occ. Constr. abs. it. med. אֶת. *Cause to fear, affright*, Judg. viii. 12; 2 Sam. xvii. 2.

Infin. הַחֲרִיד, Ezek. xxx. 9; Zech. ii. 4.

Part. מַחֲרִיד, Lev. xxvi. 6, &c. In the phr. אֵין מַחֲרִיד, *None alarming*.

חֲרָדָה, f. constr. חֶרְדַּת (f. of seg. חָרֵד), pl. חֲרָדוֹת. *Fear*; meton. *trembling*, Gen. xxvii. 33; 1 Sam. xiv. 15; Is. xxi. 4: metaph. Ezek. xxvi. 16. Either subjectively or objectively, Gram. art. 224. 10; Prov. xxix. 25; 1 Sam. xiv. 15.

חָרָה, v. pres. יֶחֱרֶה, apoc. יִחַר. Constr. abs. it. med. בְּ, *against; in, of time*; לְ, *to self*, impers.— בְּעֵינֵי, אֶל, עַל, *at, against*. Arab. حَرَى, *ardor in gula*, حَرَّة, *inflammatio*. Syr. ܚܳܡܬܳܐ, *litigiosus*. Cogn. ܚܡܺܝ, *aruit præ calore*. Arab. حَرَّ, *ferbuit. Be, become, hot*; meton. *angry* (often with אַף), Num. xi. 33; xxiv. 10; Deut. vii. 4; Zech. x. 3. With לְ, the constr. is impers. חָרָה לוֹ, *it* (i. e. anger) *became hot to him, for, he was angry*, Gen. xviii. 30. 32; 2 Sam. xxii. 8; Ib. xix. 43, &c. It. בְּעֵינֵי, *in the eyes of —*, Gen. xxxi. 35; xlv. 5. But, as *heat* may also imply perturbation of any kind, occurring in this last case with הִתְעַצֵּב, it rather means *be vexed, grieved*, &c. Comp. Gen. iv. 5; Jonah iv. 4. 9; Neh. v. 6.

Infin. abs. חָרֹה, 1 Sam. xx. 7.

Constr. חֲרוֹת, Ps. cxxiv. 3.

חרו (222) חרה

Niph. Part. pl. נֶחֱרִים, Persons, *becoming enraged, angered,* Is. xli. 11 ; xlv. 24.

Hiph. הֶחֱרָה, pres. apoc. יַחַר. I. *Made hot* his anger, Job xix. 11, with עַל. II. *Became warm, zealous,* Neh. iii. 20.

Hithp. pres. apoc. 2 pers. תִּחַר, *Be thou hot, vexed, fretted;* with בְּ, it. לְ, Infin. Ps. xxxvii. 1. 7, 8; Prov. xxiv. 19. In Jer. xii. 5, we have, תִּתְחָרֶה ; and, as a part, xxii. 15, מְתַחֲרֶה, which has induced the Grammarians to frame an additional species of the conjugation, in order to suit them. If, however, we point them, תִּחֲרֶה, and מִחֲרֶה, they become regular forms of Hithp. And, as the Syr. synon. ܚܶܪܝܳܐ, and ܐܶܬܚܪܺܝ, signify, *contendit, litigavit, pugnavit. Contend, dispute, &c.*, which will suit our passages extremely well; I can see no reason why we should put ourselves out of the way here, merely to accommodate these irregular vowels.

חֲרוּזִים, m. pl. Syr. ܚܪܽܘܙܳܐ, *series margaritarum.* Arab. خَرَز, *monile ex variis gemmis, s. baccis simul confertis.* A *necklace of precious stones,* once, Cant. i. 10.

חָרוּל, m. pl. חֲרֻלִּים. According to Celsius Hierobot ii. p. 166, the *Paliurus* of the Greeks and Latins, which is a large sort of thorny shrub, and grows in desolate places. See my note on Job xxx. 7. Gesenius takes it to be the *urtica,* or *nettle,* and makes חרל, as the root, equal to חרר, *burning:* but, how it can be said that people congregated *under the nettle,* as in Job, l. c. it is difficult to conceive, Zech. ii. 9; Prov. xxiv. 31, al. non occ.

חָרוֹן, m. constr. חֲרוֹן, pl. חֲרוֹנִים, r. חָרָה. *Heat* of anger, often occurring, חֲרוֹן אַף, Num. xxv. 4 ; xxxii. 14; 1 Sam. xxviii. 18. And alone, חָרוֹן, Neh. xiii. 18 ; Ps. ii. 5 ; lxxxviii. 17; Ezek. vii. 12. Also for *an angry person,* Ps. lviii. 10. See under אָפֵד. With v. שׁוּב, עָשָׂה, שָׁלַח, שָׁפַךְ, הֵשִׁיב, &c. Aff. חֲרוֹנִי, חֲרוֹנוֹ, חֲרוֹנְךָ, pl. חֲרוֹנֶיךָ.

חָרוּץ, m. pl. חֲרוּצִים, and חֲרוּצוֹת. Arab. حِرْص, *fissura;* حَرِيص, *discissa* vestis.

Æth. ሐረፀ : *moluit, comminuit.* The primary notion seems to consist in *sharpness, cutting.* (a) *Ditch, foss,* rather, *rampart,* Dan. ix. 26, i. q. Chald. חָרִיץ. LXX. τεῖχος. It can hardly be said of a ditch, that it shall be built, נִבְנְתָה.

(b) *Made sharp, sharpened,* applied to the pikes fixed in the wheels of a thrashing machine or dray, Is. xxviii. 27 ; Amos i. 3; pl. f. more fully, מוֹרַג חָרוּץ, Is. xli. 15.

(c) *Cut, decided, determined,* Job xix. 5: meton. *judgment, punishment,* Joel iv. 14 : the allusion is evidently to the times when God shall take up the cause of his Church, which I take to mean those of Constantine. See my Exposition of the Revelation, Sermons and Dissertations.

(d) *Sharpened, instructed* (see שׁנן), *prudent,* Prov. x. 4 ; xii. 24 ; xiii. 4 ; xxi. 5.

(e) *Gold,* apparently, but why so called it is not easy to say. Some think, because its brightness may be said to *cut the* eyes, dazzle them ; others, because it is cut into various forms for ornament's sake : others think it signifies *desired.* Arab. حَرَص, *avidè cupivit.* If so, it is not unlike our term *mammon.* It may, however, be so called, because *cut* or *digged up* out of the earth. Comp. χρυσὸς, χαράσσω, with it : and this seems the more probable opinion, Ps. lxviii. 14 ; Prov. iii. 14; viii. 10. 19 ; xvi. 16 ; Zech. ix. 3.

חַרְחַר, m. pl. non occ. r. חרר, redup. once, Deut. xxviii. 22 ; lit. *intense burning,* or *heat.* *Inflammation, fever.* Aquila, περιφλευσμῷ. Sym. Theod. περιφλογισμῷ. LXX. ἐρεθισμῷ.

חֶרֶט, m. pl. non occ. Syr. ܚܪܳܛܳܐ, *incisio.* Arab. خَرْط, *sectio* gemmarum ; خَارِط, *sculptor.* Cogn. Heb. חרץ. (a) *A graving tool :* (b) *writing style* ; such, perhaps, as are still used in some parts of the East. (a) Exod. xxxii. 4 : (b) Is. viii. 1. חֶרֶט אֱנוֹשׁ, *man's writing style ;* i. e. as commonly used. LXX. γραφίδι ἀνθρώπου.

חַרְטֻמִּים, pl. m. only. Constr. חַרְטֻמֵּי.— חַרְטֻמִּין, id. Chald.— *Sacred scribes,* i. e. those Egyptian priests, according to Gesenius, who took care of the hieroglyphical records: compd. Heb. חֶרֶט, and חָרַם ; or, an augmented form of חֶרֶט ; as פִּדְיוֹם is of פָּדָה, or הָדוֹם, of הֲדַר. Others have recourse to the Coptic; on which, however, very little reliance can be placed. We have, too, in the Arab. خُرْطُم, *nasus;* pl. خَرَاطِيم, *principes* populi; it. خُرْطُوم, *vinum*

חרי

idque cito inebrians, aut quod fluit, antequam calcata sit uva; it. cogn. حَرْبَنَةٌ, *pertinacia.* From which, *deficiency, elevation,* and thence *authority,* seem derivable. And persons of this sort, the ancient teachers of religion were, whether *priests** among the Egyptians, or *Chaldeans* (χαλδαῖοι), among the Babylonians and Assyrians, or *Magi, Druids, &c.* among the Persians, Gauls, and other nations: and such are the حُكَمَاءُ, *hukamā,* or عُلَمَاءُ, *ulamā,* still in the East. It was the modesty of Pythagoras that first suggested the less assuming title of *Philosopher* (φιλόσοφος), *lover of wisdom,* for that of *wise.* And, it should not be forgotten, that of *philosophy* alone the religion of the heathen consisted. "*Magicians,*" according to our Auth. Vers.: *wise men,* or *doctors,* would be more appropriate; as the *Magi* rather belonged to Persia, Gen. xli. 8. 24; Exod. vii. 11. 22; viii. 3. 14, 15; ix. 11. Also applied to the *wise men* of Babylon, Dan. i. 20; ii. 2.

חָרִי, m. pl. non occ.—always with אַף, r. חרה, fm. seg. apparently פֶּקֶר, for פֹּקֶר: which would regularly be חֳרִי, Gram. art. 87. 4; but, as this would also be derivable from פֻּקֶר; it is probable the (ֳ) has here been made to supply the place of *kholém*. *Heat, burning,* Exod. xi. 8; Deut. xxix. 23; 1 Sam. xx. 34; Is. vii. 4; Lam. ii. 3; 2 Chron. xxv. 10, al. non occ.

חֹרִי, m. once, Gen. xl. 16, in, סַלֵּי חֹרִי r. חוֹר, which see. Arab. حَوَارِي, *edulia alba,* pec. *panis albus. White* bread. LXX. κανᾶ χονδριτῶν.

חֹרִי, m. *A Horite,* or person residing in a cavern cut in the rock, r. חוֹר, *a hole,* patronym. Gen. xiv. 6.

חֲרִי, for חֲרָאִי, followed by יוֹנִים kethiv, 2 Kings vi. 25, r. חרא, see above. *Pigeon's dung;* which, it is probable enough, might have been sold as food during a close siege. Bochart, "*non minus probabile,*"—says Gesenius,—imagined that this was the name of some vegetable, Hieroz. ii. lib. i. p. 31; which Celsius, Hierob. ii. 30, seq. has shewn to be groundless. It might have occurred both to Bochart and Gesenius, that it was not very likely to get any sort of vegetable in a closely besieged city. LXX. κόπρου περιστερῶν.

חֲרִיטִים, m. pl. sing. non occ. Arab. خَرِيطَةٌ, *loculus ex corio aliave re. Pockets, purses,* 2 Kings v. 23; Is. iii. 22. On this last, see Schroederus de Vestitu Mulierum, c. xvii. Not unlike the *reticules,* perhaps, used by ladies now.

חֲרִיצֵי, m. pl. constr. r. חרץ, lit. *A cutting,* actively or passively: as, I. חֲרִיצֵי הֶחָלָב, *cuttings of new cheese,* as prepared for the table, perhaps, 1 Sam. xvii. 18. LXX. τρυφαλίδες. See Schleusn. Lex. in Vet Test. under τρυφαλίς. II. *Pikes,* or *points* of iron, constr. with בַּרְזֶל, 2 Sam. xii. 31; 1 Chron. xx. 3, al. non occ. See LXX.

חָרִישׁ, m. pl. non occ. r. חָרַשׁ. *Ploughing, tilling,* the land, Gen. xlv. 6; Exod. xxxiv. 21; 1 Sam. viii. 12. Aff. חֲרִישׁוֹ.

חֲרִישִׁית, f. once, Jonah iv. 8. Gesen. &c. *silens, quietus.* LXX. συγκαίοντι. Castell *vehementer aridus, arefaciens, Very drying, withering;* he adds, suffragantur senes, Syr. et uterque Arab. Which certainly suits the context much better.

חרך, v. pres. יַחֲרֹךְ, once, Prov. xii. 27. Arab. مِحْرَاكٌ, *rutabulum quo movetur ignis.* Cogn. حَرَقَ, *ussit.* Comp. حَرْكَلَ, niל cepit venator, et frustra fuit: compd. perhaps, of حَرَكَ, and رَكَلَ. Syr. ܚܡܛ, *torruit, adussit.* לֹא יַחֲרֹךְ רְמִיָּה צֵידוֹ, lit. *Deceitfulness roasts not,* i. e. appropriates not to its possessor's satisfaction, *his own hunting;* i. e. earnings. LXX. οὐκ ἐπιτεύξεται δόλιος θήρας: giving very nearly the sense of the original: and so the Syr. רְמִיָּה, is either personified here, or else is put for אִישׁ רְמִיָּה, which comes to the same thing.

Hithp. Chald. הִתְחָרַךְ, *Was, became, burnt,* Dan. iii. 27, only.

חֲרַכִּים, m. pl. once, Cant. ii. 9. Chald. חֲרַךְ, *foramen. Lattice,* or *cancellated window.* LXX. διὰ τῶν δικτύων.

חֵרֶם, and חָרֶם, m. pl. חֲרָמִים. Arab. حَرَمَ, *vetitum; sacrum.* Syr. ܚܶܪܡܳܐ, *devotio*

---

* See the Proëmium to the lives of the Philosophers, by Diogenes Laertius.

חרם   (224)   חרס

dira; anathema. The leading notion seems to consist in *stopping, stopping up; restraining,* and thence *forbidding under a curse* or *ban;* thence, meton. the *thing forbidden* considered as *devoted* either *to destruction,* or, to some *sacred use;* and hence, as bringing with it. a curse, if applied to common uses.

I. *A net,* of fisherman, or hunter, Hab. i. 16, 17; Ezek. xxvi. 5. 14; xlvii. 10; Zech. xiv. 11, &c. pl. Metaph. *Entanglements, allurements,* of women, Eccl. vii. 26.

II. *Devotion,* of something to destruction, &c.: also, meton. *anything* so devoted, Lev. xxvii. 28, 29; Num. xviii. 14; Deut. vii. 26; Josh. vi. 17; Mal. iii. 24, &c. LXX. ἄγκιστρον, ἀμφίβληστρον; ἀνάθεμα, ἀνάθημα, ἀνατεθεμισμένον, &c. Aff. חָרְמִי, חֶרְמוֹ.

חרם, v. in Kal. non occ. See חֵרֶם.
Part. pass. חָרוּם, m. once, Lev. xxi. 18. Arab. خَرَم, *simitas;* خَرَمَة, *sedes,* in qua *simitas nasi constituitur. Flat-nosed.*

Hiph. הֶחֱרִים, הֶחֱרִימָה, &c. pres. יַחֲרִים, יַחֲרֵם, constr. immed. it. med. אֶת, obj. it. לְ, to, for, whom, &c.; it. אַחֲרֵי, obj. עַד, till, of time. (a) *Devote* to destruction, any person, thing, &c. Meton. (b) *Apply* the person, thing, &c. to sacred uses;—to God, &c., Josh. viii. 26; x. 28. 35. 40; i. q. וְתָנַם לַפָּח, Is. xxxiv. 2, &c. Applied to the Red Sea, *shall destroy it* as such; dry it up (cogn. החריב), alluding to the passage of the Israelites: the deliverance of whom is often glanced at when the victories of Christianity are foretold, as is the case here, Is. xi. 15: (b) Lev. xxvii. 28; Mic. iv. 13, &c. Phr. הַחֲרֵם—, לְפִי חֶרֶב, 1 Sam. xv. 8. הַחֲרֵם אַחֲרֵיהֶם, *destroy after them,* i. e. supposing them to be flying before the sword, Jer. L. 21.

Infin. הַחֲרֵם, Deut. vii. 2, &c.; it. הַחֲרִים, Josh. xi. 12. Aff. הַחֲרִימָם, Ib. 20.
Imp. הַחֲרֵם, Deut. xiii. 16.
Pl. הַחֲרִימוּ, aff. הַחֲרִימוּהָ, Jer. li. 3; L. 26.
Hoph. pres. יָחֳרָם, *Be, become, devoted* to destruction, &c., Exod. xxii. 19; Lev. xxvii. 29; Ezra x. 8.

חֶרְמֵשׁ, m.—pl. non occ. Compd. خَرَم, *succidit;* and, مَشّ, *luxuries pabuli;* v. مَشّ, *fronduit arbor. Sickle,* or *reaping-hook,* Deut. xvi. 9; xxiii. 26.

חֶרֶס, masc.—plur. non occ. Arab. خَرْش, *scratching;* خَرِش, *qui præ fame dormire non potest.* I. *The itch,* Deut. xxviii. 27, al. non occ.

II. Arab. خَرَس, *seculum;* خَرَس, *princeps;* خَرَس, *custodivit, servavit.* Cogn. قُرْص, *orbis solis. The sun,* Judg. viii. 13; Job ix. 7. With ה, parag., Judg. xiv. 18. In Is. xix. 18 we have, חֶרֶס, and, in some copies, חֶרֶס, in the phrase עִיר הַחֶרֶס. See חֶרֶס above. The passage evidently relates to the times of Christianity; and, as the word includes the sense of *watching, protecting, saving; city of safety,* or *salvation,* might have been intended by the Prophet. Nor will the case be varied much, if we take, *city of the sun,* this latter term being also applied to Christ, as the *Sun of Righteousness,* Mal. iii. 20, where the same times are foretold. Sym. πόλις ἡλίου. Gesenius thinks *Heliopolis,* i. e. אֹן, or בֵּית שֶׁמֶשׁ, is meant: but this is unlikely; as the intention of the Prophet is evidently to give a mystical name, implying—as verbs of naming often do—that the thing named, *salvation,* shall be there.

הַחַרְסוּת, f. keri, חַרְסִית, once, Jer. xix. 2, in the phr. שַׁעַר הַחַרְסוּת, "*porta figlinæ,*" according to Gesenius: taking חֶרֶשׂ, *potsherd,* as the root. Auth. Vers. *east,* or *sun, gate,* Aquil. Sym. Theod. ἀροίθ. LXX. χαρσείθ, leaving the word untranslated. Targ. *dunggate.* Gesenius thinks that הַיּוֹצֵר, Zech. xi. 13, has something to do with this gate; but the context speaks of this as being in the Temple. In another place, too, he thinks this יוֹצֵר is, i. q. אוֹצָר, *treasurer.* Lex. Man. p. 416. The truth is, nothing very certain can now be known of the ancient localities of Jerusalem.

חֹרֶף, masc.—plur. non occ. Arab. خَرَف, *collecting the autumn-fruits;* خَرِيف, *tempus exeundi ad poma legenda;* خَرِيف, *tres autumni menses,* quod tunc arborum poma legantur. *The autumn:* for the most part including the winter, according to Gesenius: but no passage adduced by him will bear this out. Gen. viii. 22, evidently marks the four seasons, viz., winter, summer, spring, and autumn. Nor is בֵּית חֹרֶף, Amos iii. 15, necessarily *a winter-house.* See also

חרף

Jer. xxxvi. 22, where the *ninth month* is mentioned, which must have been either October or November, Ps. lxxiv. 17; Zech. xiv. 8; Prov. xx. 4. Metaph. *Vigour* of youth, Job xxix. 4. See my note; because the autumn in the year—as the evening in the day—was considered its commencement. Aff. חָרְפִּי.

חרף, v. pres. יֶחֱרַף. I. *Keep the season of autumn; shall autumn* on it; i. e. eat up its produce, Is. xviii. 6.

II. As plucking or cropping deprives a tree, &c. of its fruit; so, when applied metaphorically to men, this term will signify *stripping of honour, value*; hence, *reproach, utter reproaches*, Job xxvii. 6, here, apparently, *blasphemy* against God.

Infin. aff. חָרְפָם, *Their reproaching; despising*, 2 Sam. xxiii. 9.

Part. aff. חֹרְפִי, *My despiser, reproacher*, Ps. cxix. 42, &c.

Pl. חוֹרְפֶיךָ, *Thy reproachers*, Ib. lxix. 10.

Niph. Part. f. נֶחֱרֶפֶת, *Espoused*, i. e. deprived of all right in self, and assigned to another: so the Arab. مُحَاجَرْ, *Eliminatus vir, cujus consortio uti prohibearis*. Kāmoos, مَحْدُودٌ، مَحْرُوم.

Pih. חֵרֵף, pres. יְחָרֵף. Constr. immed. obj. and לְ, *to, which, what*; it. med. אֶת, בְּ. I. *Reproach, blaspheme*, 1 Sam. xvii. 26. 36; 2 Kings xix. 22, 23; Ps. xlii. 11; cii. 9; 2 Chron. xxxii. 17; 2 Sam. xxiii. 9; Ps. xlii. 11; lxxix. 12; cii. 9, &c.

II. *Expose to reproach, danger*, Judg. v. 18.

Infin. חָרֵף, 1 Sam. xvii. 25, &c.

Part. מְחָרֵף, Ps. xliv. 17.

חֶרְפָּה, f. constr. חֶרְפַּת, pl. חֲרָפוֹת. See v. חרף. *Reproach, contempt*, act. or pass. Synon. with כְּלִמָּה, בּוּז, גְּדוּפָה, Gen. xxx. 23; xxxiv. 14; Josh. v. 9; 1 Sam. xi. 2; xvii. 26; Ps. xxxix. 9; lxix. 11; lxxix. 12; Dan. xii. 2; Is. xxv. 8; liv. 4; Jer. xxxi. 19; Mic. vi. 16; Job xvi. 10, &c. Meton. *Person* or *thing* reproached, Neh. ii. 17; Ps. xxii. 7; Joel ii. 17. 19. Gesenius makes it signify "*pudenda*," in Is. xlvii. 3; because, perhaps, it is in the parallel with עֶרְוָתֵךְ; but this word is manifestly used metaphorically here, for *lewdness*: the other must, therefore, take its proper sense. Aff. חֶרְפָּתוֹ, חֶרְפָּתִי, &c.

חרץ, m. once, Dan. v. 6. Aff. חַרְצֵהּ. *His loins*, i. q. Heb. חֲלָצַיִם; ל and ר being interchangeable letters. Syr. ܚܰܨܶܗ, id. where the צ is doubled by way of compersation.

חָרַץ, v. pres. יֶחֱרַץ. Constr. abs. it. immed. it. med. לְ. Arab. خَرَصَ, *superior pars cuspidis in hasta*; it. *ipsa hasta*; خَرِيصٌ ; مَخْرَصٌ, *hasta, lancea*. It. خَرْصٌ, *fissura; solicitudo, aviditas, audacia*; it. خَرَصَ, *avide cupidus fuit; in arte solicitus et solers*. The first notion seems to rest in *sharpness*; thence, *excitement, diligence, &c.*; and, lastly, from *sharpness* or *cutting, decision*, as if engraven as a law. I. *Be sharp, active, courageous*, 2 Sam. v. 24. אָז תֶּחֱרָץ, *then be sharp, quick, &c.*, Josh. x. 21, *sharpened*; the tongue being compared to a sharp sword, Exod. xi. 7, where it is evident that both the *men* and *beasts* of Egypt are compared to dogs: the usage is metaphorical therefore. Hence, Part. חָרוּץ, see above, in its place.

II. *Decided, determined*, 1 Kings xx. 40. Part. חָרוּץ, see above. Phr. חָרוּץ אוֹ־יֻבָּל, *gelded*, or *corrupting*, Lev. xxii. 22. כִּלָּיוֹן חָרוּץ, *a decided, determined, consummation*, i. e. the predestinated establishment of Christianity. The same thing is had in view, Joel iv. 14. Pl. חֲרוּצִים יָמָיו, Job xiv. 5. See my note.

Niph. part. f. נֶחֱרָצָה, נֶחֱרֶצֶת, *Is, has, become, decided, determined*. In the phr. כָּלָה וְנֶחֱרָצָה, *completed, and determined*, i. e. completely, fully, determined, Is. x. 23; xxviii. 22; Dan. ix. 27; xi. 36. It. נֶחֱרֶצֶת שֹׁמֵמוֹת, *a determined thing is, desolations*, Ib. ix. 26.

חַרְצֻבּוֹת, pl. f. Arab. transp. ܒܪ, حَضْرَبَة, *anxia tenacitas; angustia*. Cogn. حَصْرَمَة, *cupiditas, avaritia*. Compd. חצר and חצב. *Bonds, bandages, galling and paining the person*: thence, meton. *grievous, biting, pains*. Comp. חבל. חול. Twice only, Is. lviii. 6; Ps. lxxiii. 4: applied in the latter case to the mind, by metaph.

חַרְצַנִּים, m. pl. once, Num. vi. 4, r.

חָרֻק. Arab. حِصْرِم, *fructus acerbus vitis,* aliusve arboris, *omphaces. Unripe, or sour grapes.* LXX. στεμφύλων.

חָרַק, v. pres. יַחֲרֹק. Constr. עַל, pers. immed. and med. בְּ, thing. Syr. ܚܰܪܶܩ, *frenduit;* ܚܽܘܪܳܩܳܐ, *stridor dentium.* Arab. حَرَقَ, *collisit inter se dentes* præ ira, &c. ὀνοματοποιητικόν. *Gnashing, grinding, the teeth,* from hatred, &c., Job xvi. 9; Ps. cxii. 10; Lam. ii. 16.

Infin. abs. חָרֹק, Ps. xxxv. 16.

Part. חֹרֵק, Ps. xxxvii. 12.

חָרַר, v. f. חָרָה, pl. חָרוּ (Dagesh being compensated by ּ). Arab. حَرَّ, *caluit, ferbuit.* Syr. ܚܰܡ, *aruit præ calore. Being hot:* meton. *dry,* Ezek. xxiv. 11; Is. xxiv. 6; Job xxx. 30.

Niph. נָחַר, and נִחַר, pres. יֵחַר. *Becoming hot, dry,* Jer. vi. 29; Ezek. xv. 5; Ps. lxix. 4; cii. 4; Ezek. xv. 5; xxiv. 10.

Pih. redup. חִרְחַר. Infin. *Make hot, kindle* as fire, Prov. xxvi. 21.

חֲרֵרִים, m. pl. once, Jer. xvii. 6. *Dry, parched,* places. LXX. ἐν ἁλίμοις.

חָרֶשׂ, i. q. חרק.

חֶרֶשׂ, m. pl. aff. חֲרָשֶׂיהָ. Constr. חַרְשֵׂי. Arab. خَرَسٌ, *seria, vas fictile vinarium. Earthenware,* i. e. *a pot, &c.,* made of dried and burnt earth. Meton. *Potsherd,* Ps. xxii. 16; Is. xlv. 9; Lam. iv. 2, &c. Phr. כְּלִי־חֶרֶשׂ, *vessel of earthenware,* to boil any thing in, or to melt and refine metal, as a crucible, Lev. vi. 21; Prov. xxvi. 23. To hold water, Num. v. 17. נִבְלֵי־חֶרֶשׂ, Lam. iv. 2, *jars of earthenware,* as of little worth, and soon broken. Hence the phr. "*earthen vessels,*" ἐν ὀστρακίνοις σκεύεσιν, 2 Cor. iv. 7. LXX. ἀγγεῖα ὀστράκινα. Liable to be broken, Is. xxx. 14; and, hence, *potsherd,* Job ii. 8; sharp and cutting in some degree, Ib. xli. 22.

חֶרֶשׁ, m. pl. חֲרָשִׁים. Arab. حَرْشٌ, *vestigium.* Syr. ܢܚܰܪ, *jugulavit.* Cogn. ܚܪܰܡ, *aravit.* Arab. حَرَثَ, *aratio.* Lit. *cutting, carving, &c.:* hence, (a) *art,* as of the artist; (b) *artifice,* in a bad sense: (a) 1 Chron. iv. 14; Neh. xi. 35; (b) Is. iii. 3. In Josh. ii. 1, (c) *silence,* adv. *silently,* Josh. ii. 1; see חָרֵשׁ: but this may mean, *artfully, prudently,* in a good sense.

חֹרֶשׁ, m. pl. חֳרָשִׁים, with ה parag. חֹרְשָׁה. Lat. *silva* à silendo, as some think: so this word, perhaps, see חָרֵשׁ; as others, from ὕλη, *material;* so here, see חֶרֶשׁ, and חָרָשׁ, as used by the artificer. *A wood,* or *forest,* 1 Sam. xxiii. 15, 16. 18, 19; Is. xvii. 9; Ezek. xxxi. 3; 2 Chron. xxvii. 4.

חָרָשׁ, m. (for חַרָּשׁ, Gram. art. 154. 12), constr. חֲרַשׁ, pl. חָרָשִׁים, constr. חָרָשֵׁי. Lit. *cutter, sculptor. Worker, artificer,* in stone, wood, iron, brass (copper). Phr. חָרַשׁ אֶבֶן, Exod. xxviii. 11. חָרָשׁ עֵצִים, Is. xliv. 13. חָרַשׁ בַּרְזֶל, Ib. 12; xlv. 16; Ezek. xxi. 36; 2 Sam. v. 11; 2 Kings xii. 12; 1 Chron. xiv. 1; xxii. 15; xxiv. 12; Exod. xxxviii. 23; Deut. xxvii. 15; Is. xl. 19; Ezra iii. 7, &c.

חֵרֵשׁ, m. pl. חֵרְשִׁים. Arab. خَرَسَ, *obsurduit.* Syr. ܚܪܶܫ, id. أَخْرَسُ, *mutus;* it. *nulla resonans echo* uhons, locusve alius; *crassum* lac, ut cujus agitati sonus non auditur. The primitive notion seems to exist in *denseness, softness,* as of butter, &c., and incapable of producing sound. See חָמוּד above. *Deaf,* Exod. iv. 11; Lev. xix. 14; Ps. xxxviii. 14; Is. xlii. 18, 19; xxxv. 5. Metaph. of persons unwilling to hear, Is. xxix. 18; xliii. 8, &c.

חָרַשׁ, v. pres. יַחֲרֹשׁ, constr. immed. it. med. בְּ, instr. it. in; עַל, on, against; לְ, for, it. abs. see חֶרֶשׁ, חָרָשׁ. I. (a) *Cut, plough,* the land, Job i. 14; Deut. xxii. 10; Judg. xiv. 18; Ps. cxxix. 3; Hos. x. 11. 13; Prov. xx. 4; Amos vi. 12, &c.

(b) *Cut, fabricate, work,* in brass (copper), &c. Metaph. *Evil,* Prov. vi. 14; xii. 20; Ib. 22.

Infin. חֲרֹשׁ, 1 Sam. viii. 12.

Part. חֹרֵשׁ, pl. חֹרְשִׁים, constr. חֹרְשֵׁי, f. חֹרְשׁוֹת, (a) Is. xxviii. 24; Ps. cxxix. 3; Job i. 14; iv. 8: (b) Gen. iv. 22; 1 Kings vii. 14; Prov. iii. 29.

Pass. f. חֲרוּשָׁה, *Cut, engraven,* Jer. xvii. 1.

II. Pret. non occ. pres. יֶחֱרַשׁ. Constr. abs. it. med. מִן, on account of. See חָרֵשׁ above. (a) *Being deaf,* Mic. vii. 16.

(b) *Dumb, silent,* Ps. xxviii. 1; xxxv. 22; xxxix. 13; lxxxiii. 2; cxix. 1.

Niph. I. f. pres. תֵּחָרֵשׁ, *Is, becomes, ploughed,* Jer. xxvi. 18; Mic. iii. 12.

חרש (227) חשב

Hiph. I. הֶחֱרִישׁ, pres. יַחֲרִישׁ, יַחֲרֵשׁ. *Fabricate* evil, once, 1 Sam. xxiii. 9. II. i. q. Kal, (b) Gen. xxxiv. 5; Ps. xxxii. 3; L. 21; Num. xxx. 5. 8. 12; 1 Sam. vii. 8; x. 27, &c. *Be still, or quiet*, Exod. xiv. 14; 1 Sam. vii. 8; Jer. xxxviii. 27.

Infin. הַחֲרֵשׁ, Num. xxx. 15, &c.
Imp. הַחֲרֵשׁ, Judg. xviii. 19, &c.
Pl. הַחֲרִישׁוּ, f. הַחֲרִישִׁי, Job xiii. 13; 2 Sam. xiii. 20.
Part. מַחֲרִישׁ, Gen. xxiv. 21, &c.

חֲרֹשֶׁת, f. r. חרש. I. (b) above. *Cutting, working*, of wood or stone, Exod. xxxi. 5; xxxv. 33, al. non occ. Also the name of a place, Judg. iv. 2, &c.

חרת, v. i. q. חרש. I. above, in Kal non occ.
Part. pass. חָרוּת. *Cut, engraven*, Exod. xxxii. 16.

חֲשִׂיפֵי, m. pl. constr. r. חשׂף. Arab. حَسَف, *gregum actio. Flocks of* —, 1 Kings xx. 27, only. LXX. δύο ποίμνια αἰγῶν.

חָשַׂךְ, v. pres. יַחֲשֹׂךְ. Constr. immed. it. abs. it. med. אֵת, מִן, from; לְ, for. Syr. ܡܣܟ, *cohibuit. Keep back, withhold, restrain*, Gen. xxii. 12; xxxix. 9; 1 Sam. xxv. 39; 2 Sam. xviii. 16; Job vii. 11; xxxviii. 23; Ps. lxxviii. 50; Prov. xxiv. 11; Is. xiv. 6. בְּלִי חָשַׂךְ, *without holding back, sparing*; ellip. for, בְּלִי אֲשֶׁר הוּא חָשַׂךְ, Job xxx. 10. חָשַׂכְתִּי רֹק, *refrained* (from) *spitting*.
Imp. חֲשֹׂךְ, Ps. xix. 14.
Part. חוֹשֵׂךְ, Prov. xiii. 24, &c.
Niph. pres. יֵחָשֵׂךְ. *Is, becomes, restrained, kept back*, Job xvi. 6; xxi. 30.

חָשַׂף, v. pres. יַחֲשֹׂף. Constr. immed. it. med. אֵת. Arab. حَسَف, *decussit*. Cogn. خسف, *laceravit rem*. I. *Lay bare, denudate, expose*, Is. lii. 10; Jer. xiii. 26; xlix. 10; Ps. xxix. 9; Joel i. 7.
Infin. abs. חָשֹׂף, Joel i. 7.
Constr. חֲשֹׂף. II. *Drawing*, as water, &c. Is. xxx. 14; Hagg. ii. 16. Arab. خسف, *fodit puteum*.
Imp. f. חֶשְׂפִּי, *Lay bare*, constr. præ gn. Is. xlvii. 2.
Part. pass. f. חֲשׂוּפָה, Ezek. iv. 7.
Masc. constr. חֲשׂוּפֵי, *Laid bare of* —, Is. xx. 4.

חֵשֶׂב, m. pl. non occ. Æth. ሐሰበ: *reputavit*. Arab. حَسَبَ, id. حَسِبَ, *putavit, opinatus fuit*. Lit. *thought, device*. The belt, or girdle, of the ephod; so called, probably, from its being richly wrought with devices in needle-work, Exod. xxviii. 27, 28; xxix. 5; xxxix. 20, 21; Lev. viii. 7, &c. Comp. Exod. xxvi. 1. Joseph. Antiq. lib. iii. cap. vii. § 4, ζώνη περισφίγγεται βάμμασιν.... διαπεποικιλμένη, χρυσοῦ συνυφασμένου.

חָשַׁב, v. pres. יַחְשֹׁב, with Maccaph. ־יַחֲשָׁב־. Constr. immed. med. עַל, pers. לְ, instr. לְ, to, for; pers. or thing, i. q. לְ, Job xli. 19; xix. 11; it. abs.
(a) *Think, devise, meditate*, variously applied, Gen. L. 20; Exod. xxxi. 4; xxxv. 35; Is. x. 7; Amos vi. 5; 2 Chron. xxvi. 15; Ps. x. 2; xxi. 12; xxxv. 20; Mic. ii. 3; Nah. i. 11: often with מַחֲשָׁבוֹת, for emphasis, Jer. xi. 19, &c.
(b) *Consider, esteem, reckon, impute*, as, constr. med. לְ, לְ, it. immed. Gen. xv. 6; xxxviii. 15; 1 Sam. i. 13; Job xiii. 24; xix. 15; Is. xiii. 17; xxxiii. 8; liii. 3; Mal. iii. 16; Ps. xxxii. 2; 2 Sam. xix. 20, &c.
Infin. חֲשֹׁב, and חְשֹׁב, Exod. xxxi. 4; Prov. xvi. 30, &c.
Part. חֹשֵׁב, *Deviser, artificer*, pl. חֹשְׁבִים, constr. חֹשְׁבֵי, Exod. xxvi. 1; Neh. vi. 2; Ps. xxxv. 4, &c.
Niph. נֶחְשַׁב, pres. יֵחָשֵׁב. Constr. med. בְּ, לְ, עַל, עִם. *Be, become, thought, considered, esteemed, reckoned* as, *imputed*, Gen. xxxi. 15; Lev. vii. 18; xvii. 4; xxv. 31; Num. xviii. 27. 30; Deut. ii. 20; 1 Kings x. 21; Ps. xliv. 23; cvi. 31; Prov. xvii. 28; Job xviii. 3, &c.
Pih. חִשֵּׁב, pres. יְחַשֵּׁב, constr. immed. med. אֶת, לְ, אֶל, pers. כְּ, פִּי, thing; מִן, from, time. *Think, consider, esteem; compute, reckon*. Lev. xxv. 27. 50. 52; xxvii. 18; 2 Kings xii. 16; Hos. vii. 15; Dan. xi. 24, 25; Ps. lxxiii. 16; lxxvii. 6; cxix. 59; Prov. xvi. 9, &c.; Jonah i. 4. חִשְּׁבָה הָאֳנִיָּה לְהִשָּׁבֵר, lit. *the ship reckoned on being broken*: metaph. for, the persons in the ship reckoned on being wrecked.
Part. מְחַשֵּׁב, *One thinking, projecting*, &c., Prov. xxiv. 8.
Hithp. pres. יִתְחַשָּׁב, once, Num. xxiii. 9, i. q. Niph.

חֲשַׁב, v. Chald. Part. pass. pl. חֲשִׁיבִין. *Considered, esteemed*, once, Dan. iv. 32.

חֶשְׁבּוֹן, pl. f. with Dag. Euphon.

חִשָּׁה (228) חשׁד

חִשְׁבֹּנוֹת, r. חשׁב. *Device*, of art or science, discovery, Eccl. vii. 25. 27. 29: whence it must appear that these words, although taken separately by Gesenius, were considered as having the same signification, Ib. ix. 10. In 2 Chron. xxvi. 15, put for *devices of war*, i. e. warlike *machines*. LXX. μηχανὰς μεμηχανευμένας λογιστοῦ.

חָשָׁה, v. pres. יֶחֱשֶׁה. Constr. abs. it. med. ן׳, pers. Cogn. חסה. Synon. חרשׁ. Engl. *hush*. Arab. خَشِيَ, *dificilius spiritum duxit:* حَاشَا, *absit*. Cogn. خَشِيَ, *timuit, abhorruit.* Syr. ܚܳܫܶܐ, *passio*. *Be silent*, Is. lxii. 1. 6; lxiv. 11; lxv. 6; Ps. xxviii. 1; cvii. 29.
Infin. חֲשׁוֹת, Eccl. iii. 7, opp. τῷ דַּבֵּר.
Hiph. הֶחֱשֵׁיתִי, *Be*, or *make, silent*. Constr. abs. it. med. ן׳, from ל׳, obj., Is. xlii. 14; Ps. xxxix. 3; Neh. viii. 11.
Imp. הַחֲשׁוּ, 2 Kings ii. 3. 5.
Part. מַחֲשֶׁה, pl. מַחְשִׁים, Is. lvii. 11; Judg. xviii. 9, &c.

חֲשִׁיךְ, Chald. def. חֲשׁוֹכָא, *Darkness*, r. חשׁך, i. q. Heb. הַחֹשֶׁךְ, once, Dan. ii. 22.

חֲשׁוּקִים, see חָשֻׁקִים.

חַשְׁחָן, f. pl. ⎫ sing. non occ. Syr. ܚܫܚܢ
חַשְׁחִין, m. pl. ⎭ ܚܫܚܝܢ, *usus.* fem. Things *wanting*, Ezra vi. 9: m. persons *desiring, wanting*, Dan. iii. 16, al. non occ.

חַשְׁחוּת, f. *Want, necessity*, i. e. thing necessary, once, Ezra vii. 20.

חֲשִׁיכָה, see חֲשֵׁכָה.

חָשִׁים, see חוּשִׁים.

חָשַׁךְ, m. pl. non occ. Syr. ܚܫܟ, *obscurus fuit*. Cogn. ܚܫܟ, *prohibuit*. Heb. חֹשֶׁךְ; lit. *withholding*, i. e. light, &c.: on the same analogy, see כחד, כחש, and my note on Job xxxiv. 6. I. *Darkness*, Gen. i. 2, seq.: Exod. x. 21, 22; Deut. iv. 11, &c. Phr. אֶרֶץ חֹשֶׁךְ, *land of darkness*, Job x. 21, &c. Ellip. Job xvii. 13; Ps. lxxxviii. 13, &c. for the *grave:* hence *any place of darkness*, Job xii. 22; xxxiv. 22. יֹשְׁבֵי חֹשֶׁךְ, *inhabiters of* (places of) *darkness*, Is. xlii. 7, &c., *prisons*, &c., אוֹצְרוֹת חֹשֶׁךְ *treasurers of* —, xlv. 3. Metaph. II. *Ignorance*, Job xxxvii. 19. Comp. xii. 24, 25. Meton. of this, III. *Calamity, misery, destruction*, Is. ix. 1; Job xv. 22, 23. 30; xx. 26; xxiii. 17; Mic. vii. 8; Amos v. 18.

20; Ps. xviii. 29; Eccl. xi. 8. Phr. יְמֵי הַחֹשֶׁךְ, *days of* —. Comp. Job iii. 3, 4; v. 14; xv. 23, &c. See my note on Job vi. 16. Aff. חָשְׁכִּי, Ps. xviii. 29.
Part. pl. m. חֲשֻׁכִּים, *Obscure persons*, Prov. xxii. 29, opp. τῷ מְלָכִים.

חָשַׁךְ, v. pres. f. תֶּחְשַׁךְ, pl. m. יֶחְשְׁכוּ. Constr. abs. *Be, become, obscure, dark*, variously applied, Exod. x. 15; Is. v. 30; xiii. 10; Lam. iv. 8; v. 17; Ezek. xxx. 18; Mic. iii. 6. Gesenius prefers reading חֲשֵׁכָה here, as a f. noun, *"tenebræ,"* for no good reason, however, and to gain nothing, Job iii. 9; Ps. lxix. 24.
Hiph. הֶחְשִׁיךְ, pres. יַחְשִׁיךְ. Constr. immed. it. med. ל׳. *Make dark, obscure*, Amos v. 8; it. metaph. Ib. viii. 9; Jer. xiii. 16; Ps. cxxxix. 12. Sensu prægnante. כִּמְעַט יַחְשִׁיךְ, *makes dark* (and conceals) *from thee*, Gram. art. 230. יַחְשִׁךְ, Ps. cv. 28, &c.
Part. מַחְשִׁיךְ, Job xxxviii. 2.

חֲשֵׁיכָה, f. it. חֲשִׁיכָה, Ps. cxxxix. 12.—
חֲשֵׁכִים, pl. m. i. q. חֲשֻׁכִּים, propr.— Participial noun. — *Obscured, darkened:* so, perhaps, Gen. xv. 12, אֵימָה חֲשֵׁכָה גְדֹלָה, *a great darkened (distressing) fear*. LXX. φόβος σκοτεινὸς μέγας. Concr. for abstr. i. q. חֹשֶׁךְ, Is. viii. 22; Ps. lxxxii. 5. So pl. m. once, Is. l. 10; or, as a concrete, הָלַךְ חֲשֵׁכִים, *walks, proceeds, goes on, greatly distressed*, as a pl. of excellence, Gram. art. 223. 3.

חֶשְׁכַת, constr. f. of obs. חָשֵׁךְ, i. q. חֹשֶׁךְ, *Darkness, obscurity*, once, Ps. xviii. 12.

חָשַׁל, v. non occ. in Kal. Arab. خَشَلَ, *trita fuit* vestis; خَشِلَ, *imbecillus*.
Niph. Part. m. pl. נֶחְשָׁלִים, persons, *debilitated, infirm*, once, Deut. xxv. 18.

חַשְׁמַל, m. pl. non occ. Compd. of נְחשׁ+מַל (dropping the ן), lit. *cut brass* (copper), i. q. נְחֹשֶׁת קָלָל, Ezek. i. 16: according to some, נְחשׁ+מַל, *copper, gold:* the latter being taken as a Chaldee word; on which, however, no reliance can be placed; and thence the χαλκὸς χρυσοειδής, of Diodorus Siculus, Bochart. Hieroz. ii. p. 877, &c. *a sort of brilliant* white *native gold* as some think, out of which drinking cups and other utensils were made. Hence the *auricalcum* of the Latins, thought to be a mixture of *gold* and *brass*, has been supposed to have been formed. But this is evidently erroneous, as Bochart has well shewn in the article referred to; for this word is written by the Greeks, ὀρείχαλκον, or ὀρίχαλκον, and, occasionally by the Latins, *orichalcum*: signifying *mountain-brass*, as some think. From the context, viz., Ezek. i. 4. 27; and viii. 2, with ה parag. הַחֻשְׁמַלָה, it is supposed to be the χαλκολίβανος, of Rev. i. 15, which Bochart, l. c. conjectures might be taken for the Heb. נְחֹשֶׁת לְבָנָה, *white brass;* or, the latter part of the compd. might be לְבֻן, *white* with heat; which would require the true reading to be χαλκολιβάνῳ....πεπυρωμένῳ, as some copies have it. Gesenius proposes χαλκολίπαρον, *æs splendidum*. But it is unfortunate for both these conjectures, that the former is not Hebrew, and the latter is not Greek. Nothing, however, can be more probable than that our חַשְׁמַל, and χαλκολίβανον, are the same thing: and the latter is a sort of *brilliant electrum* — see LXX.—i. e. according to Suidas, as cited by Bochart, τιμιώτερον χρυσοῦ. ἔστι δὲ τὸ ἤλεκτρον ἀλλότυπον χρυσίον μεμιγμένον ὑέλῳ καὶ λιθείᾳ. " *Auro pretiosius. Est autem electrum ex alienis conflatum, vitro et gemmis mixtum.*" Hesiod, too, terms it φαεινόν: whence it may well be represented by the נְחֹשֶׁת קָלָל of Ezekiel, l. c. It is here construed with עֵין, *eye, look, appearance of —*. Comp. Num. xi. 7; Ezek. i. 22; x. 9.

חַשְׁמַנִּים, m. pl. once, Ps. lxviii. 32, in יֶאֱתָיוּ חַשְׁמַנִּים מִנִּי מִצְרָיִם; and hence some have supposed the word to be the name of a people residing in Egypt, in a city named اشمونين, *Ashmūnīn*, the ⲤⲘⲞⲨⲚ, of the Coptic. Others,—better, perhaps, from the Arab. حَشِيم, *vir magni famulitiæ*,— take it to mean, *Rich, powerful,* men. LXX. πρέσβεις. Aquila, ἐσπευσμένως, from the r. חוש. Sym. ἐκφάνοντες.

חֹשֶׁן, masc. — pl. non occ. Arab. خشن, *asper* mons. Comp. חסן above; as *justice, truth,* and the like, were by the Hebrews considered as *unbending, &c.* See צדק; so here, perhaps, the *breast-plate of justice,*—termed חֹשֶׁן הַמִּשְׁפָּט,—received this name. It was composed of twelve precious stones, representing the twelve tribes of Israel, and was also styled אוּרִים, which see. It was worn, by the high priest, on the breast of the ephod. See Braunius de Vestit.

Sacerd. ii. cap. vii. Exod. xxviii. 4. 15. 22, seq.; xxxv. 27; xxxix. 8, seq.; Lev. viii. 8, &c. Philo, Aq. Theod. Sym. LXX. λόγιον, or λογεῖον; λόγιον τῆς κρίσεως (See Sirach. xlv. 10). From חֹשֶׁב, r. חָשַׁב, λογίζομαι, we have, Vulg. *rationale judicii*, as Gesenius well supposes. The LXX. also give περιστήθιον, and ποδήρης. Josephus Antiq. lib. iii. cap. vii. § 5, says, Ἐσσήνης μὲν καλεῖται: he then particularly describes it.

חֲשֻׁקָה, c. pl. non occ. Cogn. Arab. عشق, *amor quo animus flagrat. Desire, delight,* 1 Kings ix. 1. 19; Is. xxi. 4; 2 Chron. viii. 6, al. non occ.

חָשַׁק, v. pres. non occ. Constr. immed. it. med. בְּ, it. לְ, Infin. Arab. عشق, *amore puellæ flagravit; adhæsit* illi. Constr. med. בְּ. *Desire, delight* in, any person or thing, Gen. xxxiv. 8; Deut. vii. 7; x. 15; xxi. 11; 1 Kings ix. 19; 2 Chron. viii. 6. In Is. xxxviii. 17, חָשַׁקְתָּ נַפְשִׁי מִשַּׁחַת בְּלִי, *thou hast desired my soul* ('s salvation) *from the pit of destruction,* i. e. to save it.

Part. pl. aff. חֲשֻׁקֵיהֶם, or חֲשֻׁקִים, *Their attached, adhering,* parts, *junctures,* Exod. xxvii. 10, 11; xxxviii. 10, &c.

Pih. *Made adhere, attached to,* once Exod. xxxviii. 28.

Puh. Part. pl. m. מְחֻשָּׁקִים, *Made adhere attached,* Exod. xxvii. 17.

חִשֻּׁקֵיהֶם, masc. pl. aff. Lit. *their attachers, joiners,* i. e. spokes, which attach the fellies to the stock of chariot and other wheels, once, 1 Kings vii. 33.

חַשְׁרַת, f. constr. once, 2 Sam. xxii. 12. Arab. حشر, *collegit. Collection, mass,* of waters. Parall. Ps. xviii. 12, חַשְׁרַת־מַיִם. Hence—

חִשֻּׁרִים, aff. חִשֻּׁרֵיהֶם, once, 1 Kings vii. 33. Lit. *their collectors,* i. e. *Naves,* or *stocks,* of wheels, in which the spokes are collected, as in a point.

חֲשַׁשׁ, masc. — pl. non occ. Arab. حشيش, *fœnum. Dried grass, hay,* Is. v. 24; xxxiii. 11.

חַת, pause, חָת, m. pl. חַתִּים } Arab.
חִתָּה, f. r. חתת. Synon. כתת } خت, *cum quis transfoditur apprehensus.*

חתה (230) חתל

Conj. iv. اُخْتَ‎, *erubuit. Broken, spoiled;* applied to persons or things, 1 Sam. ii. 4; Gram. 215. 12; Jer. xiv. 4; xlvi. 5; xlviii. 1. 20. 39; Job xli. 25, בְּלִי־חָת, *unbroken, untameable,* once. Aff. חִתְּכֶם, Gen. ix. 2; synon. τοῦ, מוֹרַאֲכֶם, *your fear, terror.* In some of these places it may be considered as the verb.

חָתָה, v. pret. non occ. pres. יַחְתֶּה. Constr. immed. med. מִן, *from, out of;* בְּ, *into;* עַל, *on.* Arab. حَثَى, i. q. حَثَا, r. حَثْو, *sparsit terram ; super illum terram congessit:* constr. med. بِ, عَلَى. *Take,* usually; better perhaps, *cast out, into, on, &c.,* as the construction shall require, Prov. vi. 27; Ps. lii. 7. Infin. חֲתוֹת, Is. xxx. 14. Part. חֹתֶה, Prov. xxv. 22. LXX. σωρεύσεις. We have not here, therefore, an instance of the *constructio prægnans.*

חֲתָה, f. r. חתת, constr. חִתַּת, *Fear of* ——, once, Gen. xxxv. 5.

חִתּוּל, m. r. חתל, *A bandage* for a wound, once, Ezek. xxx. 21.

חֲתַחְתִּים, m. pl. r. חתת, redup. Gram. art. 169. 3, seq. Persons *entirely broken down* with fear, &c., Eccl. xii. 5. LXX. θάμβοι, al. θάμβος. Aquila, τρόμῳ τρομήσουσι. He seems to have read חַת חִתִּים, in two words.

חִתִּי, m. *A Hittite,* a descendant of חֵת, Gen. x. 15; xv. 20, &c.

חִתִּית, f. r. חתת. *Fear, terror, dread,* Ezek. xxxii. 23. 26. Aff. חִתִּיתִי, Ib. 32. חִתִּיתָם, Ib. 24, &c.

חָתַךְ, v. Kal, non occ. Arabic حَتَكَ, *investigavit, disposuit.*

Niph. נֶחְתַּךְ, *Has been, become, determined,* once, Dan. ix. 24; constr. med. עַל. Theod. συνετμήθησαν, al. ἐκρίθησαν, al. ἐδοκιμάσθησαν.

חָתַל, v. Kal, non occ. Arabic خَتَلَ, *ex occulto et versutè captavit prædam ; decepit.* Words signifying *cloaking, covering ;* as they imply concealing, so do they deception, &c. See בגד לבש.

Puh. pret. 2 pers. f. חֻתַּלְתְּ, *Wert bandaged,* i. e. with swaddling bands, once, Ezek. xvi. 4.

Hoph. Infin. הָחְתֵּל, (by) *being bandaged,* once, Ib.

חֲתֻלָּתוֹ, f. aff. for חֲתוּלָתוֹ. Part. pass. f. Kal. *Its swaddling bandage,* Job xxxviii. 9.

חתם, v. pret. non occ. pres. יַחְתֹּם. Constr. abs. it. immed. med. בְּ, instr. means, *for,* בְּעַד, of thing. Arab. خَتَمَ, *sigillavit, obsignavit.* Cogn. خَتَمَ, *inspiravit, firmum effecit.* Syr. ܚܬܡ. Æth. ኀተመ: id. I. *Seal, seal up :* II. meton. *conclude, finish;* either, because sealing any thing up, may be said to put an end to further inquiry about it; or, because the application of the seal to a letter, in the East, may be considered as its completion. I. 1 Kings xxi. 8; Esth. viii. 8. 10; Deut. xxxii. 34; Jer. xxxii. 10; Cant. iv. 12: see my note on Job viii. 17: Job ix. 7; xiv. 17; Dan. xii. 4, &c. By a further meton., *decree, determine.* Arab. خَتْم, *decretum judiciumque firmum ;*—because a sealed document, issuing from authority, may be supposed to contain some edict, Job xxxiii. 16. בְּמֹסְרָם יַחְתֹּם, *he seals, determines on, their punishment.* See my Comment. on this place, Ib. xxxvii. 7. בְּיַד־כָּל־אָדָם יַחְתּוֹם, *for the good—sake—of every man he seals, determines* (this). See my Comment. II. *Conclude, &c.,* Dan. ix. 24. In the last member here, Keri, חָתֵם, r. תמם, the vowels of which are applied to חתם, in the text.

Infin. abs. חָתוֹם, Jer. xxxii. 44. Constr. חְתֹם, Dan. ix. 24. Imp. חֲתוֹם, Is. viii. 16; Dan. xii. 4. Pl. חִתְמוּ, Esth. viii. 8. Part. חֹתֵם, Ezek. xxviii. 12. Pass. חָתוּם, Deut. xxxii. 34 : pl. חֲתוּמִים, Neh. x. 2.

Niph. נֶחְתַּם, *Was, became, sealed,* Esth. iii. 12. It. נַחְתּוֹם, id. Ib. viii. 8. Gram. art. 193. 4.

Pih. pl. חִתְּמוּ, *They sealed, determined on,* Job xxiv. 16.

Hiph. הֶחְתִּים, *It seals, closes,* or *shuts up,* Lev. xv. 3.

חַתְמָהּ, v. Chald. aff. *He sealed it,* Dan. vi. 18.

חֹתָם, see חוֹתָם.

חתם

חֹתֶמֶת, f. *A seal*, once, Gen. xxxviii. 25.

חָתָן, m. constr. חֲתַן, pl. חֲתָנִים, occ. aff. only, חֲתָנָי, Gen. xix. 14. Arab. خَتَن, conj. iii. *junxit connubium cum aliquo.* Cogn. حَتَن, conj. vi. *alter alteri par æqualisque fuit*. The primitive notion seems to consist in the contracting *of affinity* by means of some agreement or covenant. Comp. גָּאַל, p. 99: particularly marriage with the *daughter of any one*. Hence, I. *A relative*, generally, 2 Kings viii. 27. II. *A son-in-law*, Gen. xix. 12; 1 Sam. xviii. 18; Neh. vi. 18; xiii. 28, &c. III. Meton. *A bridegroom*, person newly added to a family by means of marriage, Ps. xix. 6; Is. lxi. 10; lxii. 5; Jer. vii. 34, &c. IV. *Relative, child*, adopted by means of the covenant of circumcision. Hence, חֲתַן־דָּמִים, *relative, child, of—by blood*, i. e. introduced to the commonwealth of Israel by that means: applied by the wife of Moses to her child, Exod. iv. 25, 26.

חתן, v. Kal, non occ. See חָתָן. Part. חֹתֵן. Lit. a person sanctioning the contracting of affinity by marriage with a daughter. *A father-in-law*, Exod. xviii. 1, 2. 5. 12, seq.; Num. x. 29; Judg. i. 16; iv. 11, &c. Aff. חֹתְנוֹ, Exod. xviii. 8; חֹתַנְךָ, Ib. 6, &c. Fem. aff. חֹתַנְתּוֹ, *his mother-in-law*, Deut. xxvii. 23, al. non occ. Hithp. הִתְחַתֵּן, pres. יִתְחַתֵּן. Constr. med. בְּ, אֶת, לְ, *Being, becoming, joined in affinity with*, particularly *by marriage with a daughter*, Josh. xxiii. 12; Deut. vii. 3; 1 Sam. xviii. 21; 1 Kings iii. 1; 2 Chron. xviii. 1, &c. Infin. הִתְחַתֵּן, 1 Sam. xviii. 23. 26; Ezra ix. 14. Imp. הִתְחַתֵּן, 1 Sam. xviii. 22. Pl. הִתְחַתְּנוּ, Gen. xxxiv. 9.

חֲתֻנָּה, f. aff. once, חֲתֻנָּתוֹ (for חֲתוּנָתוֹ, part. pass. fem.), his being joined in affinity, &c., i. e. *his being married*: his marriage, Cant. iii. 11.

חתף

חֶתֶף, m. once, Prov. xxiii. 28, abs. for concrete. Arab. خَتْف, *profligatio, exitium*. Rapine, for אִישׁ חָתֶף. *Man—practiser—of rapine*.

חתף, v. pres. יַחְתֹּף, i. q. חָטַף, occ. once, Job ix. 12. *Snatch, tear, away*.

חָתַר, v. pres. אֶחְתֹּר, יַחְתֹּר. Constr. immed. it. med. בְּ, לְ, pers. it. abs. See my note on Job xxiv. 16. *Dig, delve*, into any thing; pec. I. into, and through, the wall of a house, Ezek. viii. 8; xii. 5. 7. 12; Amos ix. 2; Job xxiv. 16. II. — into the waters, prop. *Row*, with oars, Jonah i. 13.

חֲתַת, m. once, Job vi. 21. See חַת above. *Breaking down, ruinous stroke*. τραῦμα.

חתת, v. pret. חַת, pl. חַתּוּ, pres. nem occ. Syn. כתת. See חַת above. Constr. abs. *Be, become, broken*, with shame, fear, &c., with רוּעַ, בּוֹשׁ, 2 Kings xix. 26; Is. xxxvii. 27; xx. 5; Jer. viii. 9; L. 2. 36; Obad. 9. Fem. either the verb, or the noun, חַת above, Jer. xlviii. 1. 20. 39, &c. Imper. pl. m. חֹתּוּ, Is. viii. 9. Niph. נָחַת, f. נִחֲתָה, pl. נְחָתוּ; pres. יֵחַת, or יֵחָת, 1st pers. parag. ה, אֵחָתָּה, i. q. Kal, variously applied, Deut. xxxi. 8; Josh. i. 9; viii. 1; x. 25; Is. vii. 8; li. 6. With מִן, מִפְּנֵי, of person, Jer. i. 17; Ezek. ii. 6; iii. 9; Is. xxx. 31; xxxi. 4; Jer. x. 2; Mal. ii. 5. Pih. f. הִתְּתָה, Jer. li. 56, i. q. Kal, but apparently intensive. *Broken to pieces, shivered*. Aff. הִתְּתַנִי, *hast greatly confounded, affrighted, me*, Job vii. 14. See my note. Hiph. pret. 2 pers. הַחְתֹּתָ, 1st, הַחְתֹּתִי; pres. aff. 1st pers. אֲחִתְּךָ, 3d, יְחִתֵּנִי; it. יָחִיתַן, for יְחִתֵן, aff. them, f. *Break to pieces, ruin*, Jer. i. 17; xlix. 37; Job xxxi. 34; Is. ix. 3.

ט

ט, *Téth*, is the ninth letter of the Hebrew alphabet, and therefore stands for the numeral 9, Gram. art. 4. Its pronunciation is very nearly allied to that of our own T, Ib. art. 14; and hence it is that English proper names having this letter, when written by the Orientals, give for it the Arabic ط, which is equivalent to our ט. It is usually written and pronounced טֵית, *Teth*. Gesenius, however, says, "Nomen ipsum hujus elementi *serpentem* denotat" (Arab. طَبِيط, i. e. טֵית), which,—if any reliance can be placed on the rabbinic mode of writing the word,*—must be wrong: and طَبِيَّة, *modus plicandi*, from the r. طوي, or طبي, will afford a more probable origin of its name; and, particularly, as *a fold*, or *wrapping up*, of something will present a tolerable idea of its form, which in the Samaritan is ᐁ. See Gram. art. 4, from which its present Hebrew, Syriac, and Arabic, form is apparently derived. Ewald's notion of its being equivalent to the Greek θ, and pronounced like it, is obviously at variance both with the general practice of the ancient translators of the Scriptures, and of the usage and notions of modern Orientals; and affords a good illustration of the danger of relying on theory, without, at the same time, appealing to fact.

It is a letter of the same organ with ד and ת, Gram. art. 23; it is also cognate with צ; and, with all these, it is found to interchange in cognate words: as in חָטַף, and קָטַל: Arab. قتل: טָעָה, תָּעָה: Syr. ܐܠܒ: Arab. طَبِي: טָבַב, רָבַב, Gesen.

טָאַב, Chald. v. pres. non occ. Syr. ܛܐܒ, *hilaratus est. Was glad, pleased.* Constr. עַל, once, Dan. vi. 24. Heb. טוב.

טָב, m.—pl. non occ. Chald. i. q. Heb. טוב. Syr. ܛܒ, *bonus. Good, excellent,* Dan. ii. 32; Ezra v. 17.

טְבוּלִים, m. pl. once, Ezek. xxiii. 15, r. טבל. The *mitræ pictæ* of Ovid; Eichhorn's Simonis; in the phrase, סְרוּחֵי טְבוּלִים, *luxuriant of coloured, dyed,* (things, mitres, bonnets), *on their heads.* He prefers, however, as does Gesenius after him, taking the Æthiop. ጠብል, ጠበለ: *obvolvit.* Hence, *Turbans, tiaras,* or the like.

טַבּוּר, m.—pl. non occ. Sam. מבג. Æth. ደብር: *mons,* occ. twice, Judg. ix. 37, and Ezek. xxxviii. 12. In the first, מֵרָאשֵׁי הֶהָרִים, *from the heads of the mountains,* is in the parallel in the preceding verse: and hence, *high,* or *eminent, place,* is probably meant. In the other, יֹשְׁבֵי עַל טַבּוּר הָאָרֶץ, evidently implies the same thing; as such places were usually chosen, because they were easily defended. The Rabbins with the LXX. find "*umbilicus*," navel, here: but this is, perhaps, a mere fancy. The allusion is clearly to Jerusalem in the latter place, although the prediction relates to Christian times. A similar prediction will be found in Ps. xlviii., where God's holy hill (הַר־קָדְשׁוֹ) is termed, vr. 2, 3, יְפֵה נוֹף מְשׂוֹשׂ כָּל־הָאָרֶץ וגו׳. Comp. vr. 13, 14, which will throw much light on this otherwise obscure passage.

טֶבַח, m. ⎫ — plur. non occ. Syr.
טִבְחָה, f. ⎭ ܛܒܚܬܐ, *mactatio;* v. ܛܒܚ. Æth. ጠብሕ: *mactavit.* Arab. طبخ, *coctio.* Cogn. Heb. זבח. Arab. ذبح, *jugulavit. Slaughter,* pec. of animals, Prov. vii. 22: it.—for feasting, Gen. xliii. 16. Fem. 1 Sam. xxv. 11; Prov. ix. 2. Metaph. — of men, Is. xxxiv. 2. 6; liii. 7; Jer. xlviii. 15; L. 7, &c. It. fem. Ps. xliv. 23; Jer. xii. 3. Aff. טִבְחָתִי, m. טִבְחָתוֹ.

טָבַח, v. pres. non occ. Constr. immed. it. med. לְ, for, it. abs. *Slay,* pec. of animals for eating, Exod. xxi. 37; 1 Sam. xxv. 11; Prov. ix. 2. Metaph. —, of men,

---

* The Syrians, too, write this word ܐܠܒ, or ܐܠܒܐ, and, as early as the times of Eusebius, it was written Τήθ, Prep. Evang. lib. x. Edit. Viger. p. 474. Have the Germans altered the orthography of this word, in order to make it square with their notions of its etymology? I suspect this certainly.

טבח (233) טבת

Ps. xxxvii. 14; Lam. ii. 21; Ezek. xxi. 15, &c.
Infin. טְבֹחַ, Ezek. xxi. 26, &c.
Imp. טְבֹחַ, Gen. xliii. 16.
Part. pass. טָבוּחַ, Deut. xxviii. 31.

טַבָּח, m.
טִבְחָה, f. } pl. טַבָּחִים, f. טַבָּחוֹת. Arab. طَبَّاخ, coquus. Syr. ܛܒܳܚܳܐ. id. propr. *A butcher*. Meton. *a cook*, 1 Sam. ix. 23, 24. Fem. 1 Sam. viii. 13. Hence, in the courts of kings,—as servants of the household, perhaps,—*keepers*, and probably like our sheriffs, *executioners* of *criminals*, Gen. xxxvii. 36; xxxix. 1; xl. 3, 4; xli. 10. 12. Employed as *officers* of state, in other respects, 2 Kings xxv. 8. 10—12, seq.; Jer. xxxix. 9, 10, &c.; but this officer is styled, רַב־טַבָּחִים, or שַׂר הַטַּבָּחִים, *Chief of* —. It. Chald. def.—

רַב־טַבָּחַיָּא, once, Dan. ii. 14, id.

טָבַל, v. pres. יִטְבֹּל. Arab. طَمَلَ, *colorem imbibere curavit* vestem. Constr. immed. it. med. אֶת, בְּ, with, of thing. (a) *Dip*, *plunge*, in order to cleanse, &c.: hence, (b) *stain*, any person or thing. (a) Lev. xiv. 6. 51; Num. xix. 18; 1 Sam. xiv. 27; 2 Kings v. 14; viii. 15; Job ix. 31; Ruth ii. 14, &c. (b) Gen. xxxvii. 31.
Part. טֹבֵל, Deut. xxxiii. 24.
Pass. pl. טְבוּלִים. See in its place above.
Niph. pl. m. נִטְבְּלוּ. *Were*, *became*, *dipped*, once, Josh. iii. 15.

טָבַע, v. pres. יִטְבַּע. Constr. abs. it. med. בְּ, in, into, of thing. Syr. ܛܒܰܥ, *impressit*. Arab. طَبَعَ, *infixit*. *Sink down*, as into mud, or anything penetrable, 1 Sam. xvi. 49; Jer. xxxviii. 6; Lam. ii. 9; Ps. ix. 16; lxix. 3. 15.
Puh. טֻבְּעוּ, *They were*, *became*, *immerged*, Exod. xv. 4.
Hoph. הָטְבְּעוּ, i. q. Puh. Jer. xxxviii. 22, it. as pillars, &c., on their bases so as to be firm, Job xxxviii. 6; Prov. viii. 25. See my note on the first of these two passages.

טַבַּעַת, f. pl. טַבָּעוֹת, constr. טַבְּעוֹת. Arab. طَبَع, *impressum argillæ*, &c. *sigillum*. Propr. (a) *A seal-ring*, Gen. xli. 42; Esth. iii. 10. 12; viii. 8. 10. (b) *Any ring*, gene-

rally, Exod. xxv. 12; xxvi. 24; xxxviii. 3, &c. Aff. טַבְּעֹתָיו, טַבְּעֹתָם, טַבְּעֹתֵיהֶם.

טֵבֵת, m. once, Esth. ii. 16. *The tenth month* of the Hebrew year, which at that period was *solar:* see חֹרֶשׁ above. It would answer, therefore, very nearly to our *December;* which, according to Plutarch (Quæstiones Romanæ), was so called, because it was in ancient times the *tenth* in order from March when the sun entered Aries, which was the primitive commencement of the year. The name is, perhaps, the same with the Coptic ⲦⲰⲂⲒ, which, according to La Croze, was that of the fifth month of the Egyptians; sometimes written Τύβι, or Τηβι, and, by the Arabs, طوبة.

טָהוֹר, m. constr. טְהוֹר, with Maccáph, טְהָר־, pl. טְהוֹרִים.—
טְהוֹרָה, fem. plur. טְהוֹרוֹת. Arab. طَهَرَ, *mundus*, *purus*, *sanctus*, fuit. Æth. id. (a) *Clean*, free from filth, disease, &c., Zech. iii. 5; Exod. xxxvii. 29; Lev. vii. 19; x. 14; xi. 36, &c.: as animals, Gen. vii. 2; viii. 20. (b) *Pure*, unalloyed, as metal, Exod. xxv. 11. 17. 24; Deut. xiv. 11, &c. (c) — morally, i. e. *holy*, Ps. xii. 7; xix. 10; li. 12, לֵב טָהוֹר, *a pure*, *holy*, *heart*. דּוֹר טָהוֹר, *a generation* (as we say, *school*) *clean*, *holy*, Prov. xxx. 12. טְהָר־לֵב, *pure of heart;* which Gesenius unnecessarily makes *purity*.

טֹהַר, m. aff. טָהֳרוֹ.—

טָהֳרָה, f. constr. טָהֳרַת. Aff. טָהֳרָתוֹ.—Arabic طَهَارَة, *mundities*, *puritas*. There is a slight irregularity in טָהֳרוֹ, which would be regularly, טָהְרוֹ, as in the other cases; but this is an irregularity often occurring in the earlier editions of the Hebrew Bibles and Grammars. (a) *Purification, cleansing*, Lev. xii. 4—6; xiii. 35; xiv. 2. 32; Num. vi. 9; Ezek. xliv. 26, &c. (b) Metaph. *Clearness, brightness, glory*, Exod. xxiv. 10; Ps. lxxxix. 45.

טָהַר, v. pres. יִטְהַר. Constr. abs. it. med. מִן, from, of thing, it. עוֹד, of time; and Jer. xiii. 27. אַחֲרֵי מָתַי עֹד, *not unlike* the Latin *tandem aliquando;* but lit. *Yet after how long?* (a) *Be, become, clean, pure*, from disease, 2 Kings v. 12, 13: (b) legal uncleanness, Lev. xi. 32; xvii. 15; xxii. 8:

H H

טאט (234) טוב

(c) — moral impurity, Job iv. 17; Prov. xx. 9, &c.
Imp. טְהָר, 2 Kings v. 10.
Pih. טִהַר, pres. יְטַהֵר. Constr. immed. it. med. אֶת, it. מִן, of thing.
I. *Cleanse, purify*, from filth generally, 2 Chron. xxix. 15. 18; xxxiv. 8: — from dead bodies, Ezek. xxxix. 18: — the heavens of clouds, Job xxxvii. 21: — metals from dross, Mal. iii. 3. Metaph. — from idolatry, Ezek. xxxvii. 23: — from sin, Mal. iii. 3; Jer. xxxiii. 8.
II. *Declare clean*, either person or thing, Lev. xiii. 6, seq.; xiv. 11; xvi. 30, &c.
Infin. טַהֵר, Ezek. xxxix. 12; Lev. xvi. 30, &c. Aff. טַהֲרִי, *my cleansing*, Ezek. xxxvi. 33, &c.
Imp. aff. טַהֲרֵנִי, Ps. li. 4.
Part. מְטַהֵר, Lev. xiv. 11; Mal. iii. 3.
Puh. part. f. מְטֹהָרָה, Ezek. xxii. 24.
Hithp. pl. הִטַּהֲרוּ, for הִתְטַהֲרוּ, (ע) Euphon. as in הֵרַע, it. הִטַּהֲרוּ, not in pause, pres. יִטַּהֲרוּ. Constr. abs. it. med. מִן, of thing. *Be, become, clean, purified*, legally, &c., Num. viii. 7; Josh. xxii. 17; Neh. xii. 30; Ezra vi. 20.
Imp. pl. הִטַּהֲרוּ, Gen. xxxv. 2.
Part. מִטַּהֵר, *Person to be cleansed*, Lev. xiv. 4. 7, &c.
Pl. מְטֹהָרִים, Neh. xiii. 22; Is. lxvi. 17.

טאטא, v. aff. once, מֵאמֵאתִיהָ, Is. xiv. 23. Gesen. prob. *lutosus fuit*, unde Arab. طَالَ, *lutum*, inde.... *lutum everrit*. But, it will be difficult to discover what *clay*, or the removal of *clay*, can have to do with this passage; or, as this very verb occurs in the Arabic, how *the sweeping away of clay* can be connected with it. The truth is, all this has been had recourse to, merely to give a little authority to a silly Rabbinical story which tells us, that, had not a famous Rabbi heard his servant-maid apply this word to the act of sweeping the house, he never should have discovered what it meant. See the Porta Mosis of Pococke, notes. Arab.
II. *depressus, humilis fuit*, de terra, طَاطَأَ. *terra depressa ac humilis*. *I will humble, debase, it with the humiliation, debasing, of destruction*. Or, if כִּמְאַמֵּא be a participle, *the debaser, subduer*, &c. of destruction. In this sense, the opposition to קוּם, in the two preceding verses, is pointed, as is the agreement with שָׁחַח, in vr. 20.

טוֹב, m. — pl. non occ. seg. fm. פָּקָד, Gram. art. 87. 2. Syr. ܛܳܒܳܐ, *beatitudo*. Arab. طَوْبٌ, it. طُوبَى, id. *Goodness*, variously applied to person or thing. (a) — to the produce of the earth, *fruits, wealth*, &c., Gen. xxiv. 10; xlv. 18. 20. 23; Deut. vi. 11; 2 Kings viii. 9; Ezra ix. 12; Neh. ix. 36. Hence, meton. (b) *Prosperity, happiness*, Is. lxiii. 7; Ps. cxxviii. 8; Prov. xi. 10; Job xx. 21; xxi. 16. Phr. טוּב לֵבָב, Deut. xxviii. 47. טוּב לֵב, Is. lxv. 14, *happiness, delight, of heart*. Hence, (c) goodness of appearance, *beauty*, Hos. x. 11; Zech. ix. 17: *glory, majesty*, Exod. xxxiii. 19.
Metaph. of mind. (c) טוּב טַעַם, *goodness of discernment*. (d) *God*, as the source of all wealth, temporal and spiritual, Jer. xxxi. 12. 14; Ps. xxv. 7; xxvii. 13; xxxi. 20; lxv. 5; cxlv. 7; Neh. ix. 25. 35; Hos. iii. 5. Aff. טוּבִי, טוּבוֹ, טוּבָהּ, טוּבְךָ, טוּבָם.

טוֹב, m. pl. טוֹבִים, טֹבִים.—
טוֹבָה, fem. constr. טוֹבַת, pl. טוֹבוֹת.— Concr. fm. פָּקוֹד, for טָווֹב, Gram. art. 75. *Good*, variously applied. (a) — to land, its produce, fruits, minerals, and wealth, generally, Gen. ii. 9. 12: ἄπυρος, probably. See my Job, p. 55, note. Gen. iii. 6; Exod. iii. 8; Deut. v. 37; Job xxii. 18; Ps. xxxiv. 11; lxxxiv. 12; cvii. 9; Prov. iii. 27, &c. Hence, (b) *happy, prosperous*, Gen. ii. 18; xxix. 10; xxx. 20; Exod. xiv. 12; Num. xi. 18, &c. Hence, (c) *valuable, precious, desirable*, suitable also to Gen. ii. 12, above; 2 Chron. iii. 5; Gen. xlix. 15; Judg. viii. 2; xi. 25; 1 Sam. i. 8; xv. 22; xix. 4, &c. Hence, phr. עָשָׂה טוֹב, Ps. xxxvii. 3. יוֹם טוֹב, *happy day*, 1 Sam. xxv. 8. 36; Esth. viii. 17. אִישׁ טוֹב, 2 Sam. xviii. 27; Prov. xiv. 14. Ib. בְּשׂוֹרָה טוֹבָה. דָּבָר טוֹב, 1 Kings xiv. 13. טוֹב בְּעֵינֵי, Num. xxiv. 1; יִתְנַבֵּא טוֹב, 1 Kings xxii. 8. Comp. Homer's μάντι κακῶν. Comp. vr. 13. 18. לֹא טוֹב, i. q. רַע. (d) *Good*, in appearance, *handsome*. טוֹבַת מַרְאֶה, Gen. xxiv. 16; Esth. i. 11, &c. טוֹב־הֹאַר, 1 Kings i. 6; Gen. vi. 2; Exod. ii. 2. Comp. Acts vii. 20, ἀστεῖος τῷ θεῷ. Hence, phr. טוֹב־עַיִן, *good of eye*, i. e. of gentle, kind, disposition, Prov. xxii. 9; i. q. עֵינַיִם רַכּוֹת. See Gen. xxix. 17, opp. עַיִן רַע. (e) *Kind, benign*, Gen. xxiv. 50; xxvi. 9; Lam. iii. 25; Ps. xxiii. 6; xxxiv. 9; lxxiii. 1, &c. (f) Adv. 2 Sam. iii. 13; Ruth iii. 13, &c. And, as *thing, matter*, is supplied in this sort

טוֹב (235) טוּל

of attributives (Gram. artt. 153. 4; 217. 8; 220. 4), the concrete will often be used in the sense of the abstract: here i. q. טוֹב, Ps. civ. 28; cxxii. 9; Prov. xii. 14; xvii. 13, &c.

Metaph. applied morally, Gen. ii. 17; iii. 5; Deut. i. 39; 2 Sam. xix. 36. Phr. שֵׂכֶל טוֹב, Ps. cxi. 10; Prov. iii. 4, &c.

Aff. טוֹבְךָ, טוֹבִי, &c.

טוֹב, v. pret. pl. טֹבוּ, for טָווּבוּ, or טָוֹבוּ. See טוֹב above, and cogn. יָטַב. Phr. מַה־טֹּבוּ, *How good, desirable, are!* Num. xxiv. 5; Cant. iv. 10. Arab. مَا أَحْسَنَ, *how very good!* al. non occ. The numerous instances, beyond these, given by Gesenius, contain exemplifications of the usage of the noun טוֹב only, as illustrated above.

Hiph. pret. הֵטִיבוֹתָ, and הֵטִיבוּ, pres. יֵטִיב. Constr. abs. it. immed. *Do well*, (a) *wisely*, 1 Kings viii. 18; 2 Chron. vi. 8; 2 Kings x. 30: (b) *liberally, abundantly*, Ezek. xxxvi. 11: (c) *make good, beautiful*, Hos. x. 1: (d) *happy, delighted*, Eccl. xi. 9, al. non occ.

טָוָה, v. pret. שָׁוָה. Arab. طَوَى, *complicuit, convolvit*. Engl. *twine*. *Net*, or *plat*. Auth. Vers. *spin*, Exod. xxxv. 25, 26. LXX. νήθειν.

טוּחַ, v. pret. טָח, טָחָה. Constr. immed. it. med. לְ, pers. אֶת, it. כִּן. Arab. cogn. طَاحَ, r. طَبَخَ, *re fœda contaminatus fuit; contaminavit re fœda aliquem.* (a) *Plaister, daub, paint*, Lev. xiv. 42; Is. xliv. 18; Ezek. xiii. 12. 14; xxii. 28.

Infin. טוּחַ, 1 Chron. xxix. 4. (b) *Case, cover, over.*

Part. pl. m. טָחִים, Ezek. xiii. 10. 15. Constr. טָחֵי, *Daubers of* —, Ib. vr. 11.

טוֹטָפוֹת, f. pl. compd. טוּף, or טפף, Gram. art. 169, seq. Arab. طَافَ, *constrinxit pedibus camelam*; طَافَ, *circumivit*. *Bandages*, perhaps the folds of the turban. *Phylacteries*, as some think; see Matt. xxiii. 5. But there is not the least probability that these were in existence in the days of Moses; they were most probably invented in later times in order to enable the Jews to follow out their favourite system of literal interpretation. Gesenius imagines, too, that the word is the same with the Chald. טוֹטָפְתָא, טוֹטָפָא, *armilla, frontale*. If so, the Syr. ܛܘܛܦܐ, *crepitus lucernæ*, is cognate with it; and the thing was so called from its brilliant, sparkling appearance: *A gem*, perhaps, suspended between the eyes: and such are still used in the East. The notion, that these contained sentences of the Law written on parchment, is, in my opinion, a modern figment of the Jews: all the text appears to me to say is, that the Law shall be *for*, or *as*, i. e. considered as the precious ornaments of the head. Comp. Is. lxi. 10; Mal. iii. 17; Is. xxviii. 5; lxii. 3;—Exod. xiii. 16; Deut. vi. 8; xi. 18. The latter passage of which is perhaps wholly—as a part certainly is—figurative See a similar expression, Is. xlix. 16 Aquila, εἰς ἀτίνακτα. Sym. Theod. LXX ἀσαλεύτον, Deut. vi. 8. Sym. διεσταλμένα al. ἀσάλευτα. LXX. ἀσάλευτον. See also the Vulg. and Syr. Not one of all which Translators seems to have had the least idea whatever of the *Phylacteries* of the Jews For the best of all reasons, no doubt because no such notion then existed. Of the Jewish notions and uses of these תְּפִלִּין, as they term them, see Buxtorf's Talmudic Lexicon, col. 1743, under פלל. The "Philologus Hebræo mixtus," of Leusden, p. 130, seq.

טוּל, v. Kal, non occ.

Hiph. הֵטִיל, pres. אָטִילְךָ, apoc. sing. יָטֵל. Constr. immed. med. אֶת, כִּן, אֶל, עַל. Arab. طَوَّلَ, *in longum extendit*. *Cast forth, out, into*, &c., 1 Sam. xviii. 11; xx. 33; Jer. xvi. 13; xxii. 26; Ezek. xxxii. 4; Jonah i. 4, 5. 12. 16.

Hoph. pl. הוּטְלוּ, pres. יֻטַל, יֻטָל. *Was, became, cast* out, forth, &c., Jer. xxii. 28; Ps. xxxvii. 24; Prov. xvi. 33; Job xli. 1.

Pih. redup. part. aff. מְטַלְטֶלְךָ,—of כִּטַלְטֵלָה below, Is. xxii. 17.—*Casting thee out, forth*, &c. al. non occ.

טוּר, m. pl. טוּרִים, constr. טוּרֵי. Arab. طُور, *atrium domus*: طُور, *modus, formæ, rei; vicis una, modo hoc, modo illud*. *Series, order, range*, of precious stones, or of timber in the walls of an edifice, &c., Exod. xxviii. 17, seq.; xxxix. 10, seq.; 1 Kings vi. 36; vii. 2—4. 12, seq.; 2 Chron. iv. 3. 13. In Ezek. xlvi. 23, Gesenius makes this word to signify *"paries circumductus."* I can discover no necessity for this. The description appears to me merely to say, that, in each of the four corners of the court, there was a *range*, or *series*, i. e. of offices, round about, i. e. following the boundary wall; and that here the sacrifices were boiled. See the plan of the Temple in the Appendix.

טוּר, m. Chald. def. טוּרָא. Syr. ܛܽܘܪܳܐ, *mons.* Arab. طُور, id. Cogn. طُول, *longitudo*; which seems also to be inherent in the foregoing word. *A mountain*, Dan. ii. 35. 45. Cogn. Heb. צוּר.

טוּשׂ, v. pres. יָטוּשׂ. Constr. med. עַל, once, Job ix. 26. Syr. ܛܳܣ, *volavit.* Gesenius finds the English "*to toss*" here. *Dash upon*, would suit the passage much better. Cogn. Heb. דוּשׁ. Syr. ܕܳܫ. *Fly swiftly upon the prey.* Comp. the first member.

טְוָת, m.—pl. non occ. Syr. v. ܛܘܳܐ, *complicuit*: hence,—as in the Arab. طَوٰى *complicuit* (i. e. viscera sua), *fame laboravit*—*jejunus. Fasting*, once, Dan. vi. 19.

טחה, v. Kal non occ. Arab. طَحَا, r. طحو, *expandit.* Part. مَطْحُوٌّ, *amplum umbraculum.* Pih. Part. constr. m. מְטַחֲוֵי, lit. *Extenders of—drawers of—the bow,* i. e. *archers,* once, Gen. xxi. 16.

טְחוֹת, f. pl. for מְחוֹת, r. מוּחַ, sign. (b) Lit. *things covered, cased* over, i. e. unseen, secret. *The inward parts,* viscera, as the seat of sense:—comp. לֵב, בֶּטֶן, כִּלְיוֹת:—when applied to men, Ps. li. 8; where we have סָתַם, in the next member. When applied to the heavenly bodies, as, Job xxxviii. 36. Meton. their *active unseen* energies—as a metaphor of the preceding,—is probably meant. See my note on this place; al. non occ. LXX. Ps. l. c. τὰ ἄδηλα καὶ τὰ κρύφια τῆς σοφίας, κ.τ.λ. The Jews prefer *the reins*; because, as Gesenius says, "adipe obducti sunt:" but this may be said, perhaps, of every other part of the body.

טְחוֹן, m. once, Lam. v. 13. Infin. r. טחן, according to some, i. e. *The act of grinding* with the hand-mill. Comp. Deut. ix. 21. Others, *the hand-mill,* as a noun. LXX κλαυθμόν.

טְחוֹרִים, m. pl. constr. טְחוֹרֵי. Syr. ܛܚܽܘܪ̈ܶܐ, *anus, et nisus exonerantis ventrem,* i. q. עֳפָלִים, which see, and which according to the Lexicographers is the more obscene word; and hence this has been most frequently substituted for it in the *Keri:* which strikes me as great nonsense. *Tumors* in the anus, as of. *hæmorrhoids, &c.,* 1 Sam. v. 6. 9. 12; vi. 4, 5. 11; Deut. xxviii. 27. Aff. מְחוֹרֵיהֶם, מְחוֹרֵיכֶם. LXX. ἕδρας.

טָחַן, v. pres. יִטְחַן. Constr. immed. abs. it. med. בְּ, instr. it. in, place; לְ, to; for; עַד, even to, of degree. Syr. ܛܚܰܢ, *moluit.* Arab. طَحَنَ, id. I. *Grind,* with a hand-mill, Num. xi. 8; Exod. xxxii. 20; Job xxxi. 10, 11. Metaph. *Bruise, oppress;* with דכה, Is. iii. 15. Infin. טְחוֹן, Deut. ix. 21. See טְחוֹן above. Imp. f. טַחֲנִי, Is. xlvii. 2. Part. טֹחֵן, f. pl. טֹחֲנוֹת, Judg. xvi. 21; Eccl. xii. 3, which Gesenius, rather unaccountably, renders "*dentes molares!*" *grinders, teeth so called.*

טַחֲנָה, f. once, Eccl. xii. 4. See טָחַן.

טִיחַ, m. once, Ezek. xiii. 12, r. טוּחַ, for טִיחַ, Gram. art. 73. *Plaistering,* or, *thing plaistered,* perhaps. LXX. ἀλοιφή.

טִיט, masc.—plur. non occ. Arab. طَوَطَ, *congregavit*; ضُوَيْطَة, *lutum in imo piscinæ* (for טִיט, Gram. art. 73). *Mud, mire,* as collected in the streets, the bottom of a well, &c., 2 Sam. xxii. 43; Is. lvii. 20; Jer. xxxviii. 6; Mic. vii. 10; Zech. ix. 3; Ps. xl. 3; Job xli. 22, &c.

טִין, m. Chald. def. טִינָא. Syr. ܛܺܝܢܳܐ, *cænum.* Arab. طِين, id. *Clay,* pec. of the potter; in the phr. חֲסַף טִינָא, Dan. ii. 41. 43, only: lit. *pottery,* or *potter's work,* of clay. Comp. חֲסַף דִּיפְחָר, Ib. 41.

טִירָה, f. constr. טִירַת, pl. טִירוֹת, r. טוּר above (for טִירָה,—Gram. art. 73,—perhaps), lit. *thing arranged, set in order.* Arab. طُور, *tota area domus cum atrio; cum circa rem aliquid ad arcendum ponis.* Any *arrangement of building,* or *buildings,* pec. (a) *certain chambers of the Temple,* Ezek. xlvi. 23. (b) *Palace* generally, enclosed and fortified, perhaps, Gen. xxv. 16: with טִירוֹתָם, Num. xxxi. 10; Ezek. xxv. 4; Ps. lxix. 26; 1 Chron. vi. 39. Id. richly adorned with silver, Cant. viii. 9. Aff. מִיוּחָתָם, מִיוּתָם, מְיוּחָתָם. See LXX.

טַל, m.—pl. non occ. r. טלל. Arab. طَلّ, ros. Æth. id. Dew, Gen. xxvii. 28. 39; Exod. xvi. 13, 14; Deut. xxxii. 2; Is. xxvi. 19; Zech. viii. 12; Ps. cx. 3; Prov. iii. 20; Job xxix. 19. See my note. Mic. v. 6, &c. Aff. טַלֵּךְ, טַלָם. Chald. id., Dan. iv. 12, seq.; v. 21.

טלא, v. Kal, non occ. Syr. ܛܠܳܐ, obduxit. Arab. طَلَا, r. طلي, id. i. e. laid on, patched; طِلَاءٌ, epithema.

Part. pass. טָלוּא, pl. טְלֻאִים, f. טְלֻאוֹת, lit. Plaistered, patched, cattle having large patches, as it were, of different colours, as contradistinguished from such as had spots, נְקֻדּוֹת, נָקֹד, Gen. xxx. 32, 33. 35; Ezek. xvi. 16, בָּמוֹת טְלֻאוֹת, variegated high places, i. e. variously adorned, dedicated, perhaps to various deities; it being customary still in the East to ascribe one colour to one deity, another to another. See the extracts from the Dabistan, given under אֲשֵׁרָה, p. 62, above.

Puh. pl. f. מְטֻלָּאוֹת, Patched, Josh. ix. 5.

טְלָאִים, see טָלֶה.

טֶלֶה, m. constr. טְלֵה, pl. טְלָאִים; taking the א (instead of ה) of the Syr. ܛܠܶܐ, infans; v. ܛܠܶܐ, recens fuit. A young lamb, 1 Sam. vii. 9; Is. xl. 11; lxv. 25.

טַלְטֵל, f. once, Is. xxii. 17, redup. of טול, Gram. art. 169. 5. Great, entire, casting out.

טלל, v. Kal, non occ. Arab. طَلّ, umbrosa fuit dies; operuit, texit.
Pih. aff. pres. יְטַלְּלוּ, once, Neh. iii. 15. He covered, roofed, it. LXX. ἐστέγασεν αὐτήν.
Aph. Chald. pres. f. תַּטְלֵל, Takes shade, Dan. iv. 9.

טָמֵא, m. constr. טְמֵא, pl. טְמֵאִים.—
טֻמְאָה, f. constr. טֻמְאַת, pl. non occ.—
Syr. ܛܰܡܐܐ, inquinatus, pollutus. Arab. مطمي, polluens. Castell. Unclean, polluted, of men, animals, or things, used either in a legal, or a moral sense, Lev. v. 2; vii. 19. 21, &c.; xxii. 4; Is. vi. 5, &c. Pl. Lev. xi. 8. 26, 27, &c. Fem. Ezek. xxii. 5. טְמֵאַת הַשֵּׁם, polluted of name, infamous.

טָמֵא, v. 2 pers. f. טָמֵאת (evidently from the noun טְמֵא above, Gram. art. 182. 2), Ezek. xxii. 4; pres. יִטְמָא. Constr. abs. it. med. עַד, until, it. בְּ, instr. לְ, pers. See טְמֵא above. Be, become, unclean, polluted,—opp. טָהֹר,—of men, animals, or things, either in a legal or a moral sense, Lev. xii. 2. 5; xviii. 25; xxii. 6; Ps. cvi. 39, &c.
Infin. טָמְאָה, f. of fm. פֹּקֶד. Pollution, being polluted, Mic. ii. 10; Lev. xv. 32, &c.; with לְ prefixed. It. cogn. fm.—
טֻמְאָה, Num. v. 19, &c.; it. thing polluted: meton. Judg. xiii. 7. 14, &c. Constr. טֻמְאַת. Aff. טֻמְאָתוֹ, Lev. v. 3; Ezek. xxii. 15, &c.: pl. טֻמְאוֹת, Lev. xvi. 19.

Niph. נִטְמָא, 2 pers. f. נִטְמֵאת, 1st, נִטְמֵאתִי, it. נִטְמֵאתֶם, &c. pres. יִטַּמָּא. But this is evidently the pres. of Hithp., the characteristic ה being assimilated to the ט of the root, Gram. art. 83. 1. Constr. abs. it. med. בְּ, לְ, instr. in, among, it. לְ, to, for, pers. Be, become, polluted, unclean, as in Kal, Lev. xi. 43; xviii. 24; Num. v. 20. 29; Hos. v. 3; vi. 10; Job xviii. 3. נִטְמֵינוּ. See Gram. art. 202. 4. 5. Pres. Lev. xxi. 1. 3, 4, &c.
Part. pl. m. נִטְמָאִים, Ezek. xx. 30, 31.
Pih. טִמֵּא, 2 pers. f. טִמֵּאת, pres. יְטַמֵּא. Constr. immed. it. med. אֶת, it. בְּ, instr. (a) Pollute, defile, Gen. xxxiv. 5. 13; Num. xix. 13. 20; 2 Kings xxiii. 8, &c. (b) Pronounce unclean, polluted, Gram. art. 154. 3; Lev. xiii. 3. 22. 25. 30. 44, &c.
Infin. טַמֵּא, Lev. xiii. 45, &c. Aff. טַמְּאוֹ, Lev. xiii. 59, &c. טַמְּאֲכֶם, Ib. xviii. 28. See xv. 31.
Imp. pl. טַמְּאוּ, Ezek. ix. 7.
Puh. part. f. מְטֻמָּאָה, Made unclean, Ezek. iv. 14.
Hothp. pret. f. הֻטַּמָּאָה, for הִתְטַמְּאָה, in pause, Gram. artt. 83. 1; 185. 2. Once, Deut. xxiv. 4.

טָמַן, v. pres. יִטְמֹן. Constr. immed. med. אֶת; לְ, for, pers. thing; בְּ, in, place. Arab. طَمَنَ, securitatem præstitit viro. Conceal, hide, securely, in the earth, &c., Gen. xxxv. 4; Exod. ii. 12; Josh. ii. 6; vii. 21, 22; Jer. xliii. 10; Ps. cxl. 6; cxlii. 4, &c.
Infin. טְמֹן, Job xxxi. 33; Ps. lxiv. 6. Aff. טָמְנוּ, Jer. xiii. 6.
Imp. aff. טָמְנֵהוּ, Jer. xiii. 4. See Job xl. 13.
Part. pass. טָמוּן, Job iii. 15; xviii. 10, &c.

טנא (238) טעם

Pl. טְמֻמִים, const. טְמוּגֵי, Josh. vii. 21; Deut. xxxiii. 19.

F. טְמוּנָה, Josh. vii. 22.

Niph. Imp. הִטָּמֵן, Be, become, concealed, once, Is. ii. 10.

Hiph. pres. pl. יַטְמִנוּ, They hide, i. q. Kal, 2 Kings vii. 8, al. non occ.

טֶנֶא, m.—pl. non occ. Aff. טַנְאֲךָ. Arab. ضِن, fiscella plicatilis in qua reponitur panis; صِنَّة, canistra; it. مِيضَانَة, corbis, v. cogn. وَضَن, plexuit rem. A basket, Deut. xxvi. 2. 4; xxviii. 5. 17, al. non occ.

טָנַף, v. Kal, non occ. Syr. ܛܢܦ, inquinatus est. Arab. طَنِفَ, inquinavit.

Pih. pres. aff. once, אֲטַנְּפֵם, Shall I soil them? i. e. my feet, Cant. v. 3.

טָעָה, v. Kal, non occ. i. q. תָּעָה.

Hiph. pl. m. הִטְעוּ, They have made err, once, Ezek. xiii. 10.

טַעַם, masc.— plur. non occ. Arab. طَعْم, expetitus, de cibo; طَعْمَة, modus lucrandi; طَاعِم, modestè se gerens cum comedit vir. Syr. ܛܥܡܐ, ratio, sensus. The leading notion seems to consist in desiring, thence selecting and discriminating what is best. (a) Discrimination; thence, meton. judgment, mind, edict: (b) Taste, as to meats, &c. (a) 1 Sam. xxv. 33; Jonah iii. 7; Ps. cxix. 66; Job xii. 20; Prov. xi. 22, אִשָּׁה סָרַת טָעַם, a woman perverse, froward, of judgment. Ps. xxxiv. 1, בְּשַׁנּוֹתוֹ אֶת־טַעְמוֹ, in his changing his mind, i. e. putting on an appearance of idiotcy, 1 Sam. xxi. 14; xxv. 33; Prov. xxvi. 16. מְשִׁיבֵי טָעַם returners of a judgment, i. e. in a difficult question: (b) Exod. xvi. 31; Num. xi. 8; Jer. xlviii. 11; Job vi. 6, &c. Aff. טַעֲמִי, טַעְמְךָ, טַעְמוֹ.

טָעַם, v. pres. יִטְעַם. See טַעַם above. Constr. immed. it. med. בְּ, it. לְ, pers. (a) Discriminate, perceive, judge, Ps. xxxiv. 9; Prov. xxxi. 18. (b) — of food, taste, Job xii. 11; xxxiv. 3; 1 Sam. xiv. 24. 29; Jonah iii. 7; 2 Sam. xix. 36.

Infin. abs. טָעֹם, 1 Sam. xiv. 43.

טְעֵם, v. Chald. Peal non occ.

Paḥ. pres. pl. m. יְטַעֲמוּן, They shall make thee eat, Dan. iv. 22; v. 21.

טְעֵם, m. Chald. def. טַעְמָא, טַעֲמָא, pl. non occ. (a) Consideration, reason, judgment; thence edict, Dan. ii. 14; iii. 12; vi. 3;— Ib. iii. 10. 12. 29; Ezra iv. 19. 21; v. 3. 9. 13; vi. 1; vii. 13. Phr. בְּעֵל טְעֵם, author of an edict; supreme legislator, Ezra iv. 8, 9. 17. (b) Taste, Dan. v. 2.

טְעֵן, v. pres. non occ. I. טַעֲנוּ. Imp. pl. Load ye your beasts, once Gen. xlv. 17. Syr. ܛܥܢ, oneravit. Arab. ظَعَن, migravit; ظَعُون, camelus onus gestans.

II. Puh. part. pl. m. constr. מְטֹעֲנֵי. Persons pierced through of —, once, Is. xiv. 19. Sam. טען, doluit qs. transfixus. Arab. طَعَن, confodit.

טְעַת, Infin. Kal, v. נְטַע.

טַף, masc.— plur. non occ. Arab. طَفَافَة, paucum quid; طَافّ, paucus, modicus, quælibet imperfecta res. Cogn. صَفّ, qui tenui est, et afflicto statu: صَفَف, infirmitas; familiæ multitudo. Generic noun. Infant, child; generally, children, infants, Gen. xxxiv. 29; xliii. 8; xlv. 19; xlvi. 5, &c. Put for the whole family, excepting only the father, as Gesenius thinks. But this is not well grounded. The passage, לְפִי הַטָּף, according to the children, Gen. xlvii. 12, only says, that Joseph provided for the whole house of his father; i. e. each family separately, according to the number of children in each. For this was criterion sufficient: not that the children really constituted each family. Besides, there is generally a marked distinction made between the children טַף, or הַטָּף, and parents, as in Deut. ii. 34: iii. 6; xx. 14; xxxi. 12; Jer. xli. 16; Ezek. ix. 6, &c. The passage, 2 Chron. xx. 13, גַּם טַפָּם נְשֵׁיהֶם וּבְנֵיהֶם, all Judah—even their infants, wives, and children, is added merely to show, that no part of the families was absent, from the woman with her infant to the more advanced child. Aff. טַפֵּנוּ, טַפְּכֶם, טַפָּם.

טֶפַח, m.—pl. non occ. Syr. ܛܦܚܐ, extensio. Arab. cogn. صَفَع, complosit ma-

טפח (239) טפל

manus; rem *dilatavit*; صَفْحَة, applied to the balances, see the Dictionaries. Lit. *Extent*, pec. as measured by that of the hand, *a palm*, or *hand-breadth*; 3 inches, 684 decimals of an inch, according to Dr. Arbuthnot. Captain Jervis, in his very valuable little work on "The Primitive Universal Standard of Weights and Measures," Calcutta, 1835, makes it 3 inches 2581, decimals, &c., p. 29, &c., Exod. xxv. 24; xxxvii. 12; 1 Kings vii. 26; Ezek. xl. 5. 43, &c.

טֶפַח, m. i. q. טֹפַח, pl. טְפָחוֹת, 1 Kings vii. 26; 2 Chron. iv. 5. Comp. Jer. lii. 21. In 1 Kings vii. 9, Auth. Vers. "*Coping*." LXX. ἕως τῶν γεισῶν. Aquila. τῶν παλαιστωμάτων. Sym. τῶν ἀπαρτισμάτων. See Schleusneri Lex. in LXX. Intt. sub vocibus. Metaph. applied to time, Ps. xxxix. 6, pl. excel. for, *a very short space*, or *period*. See LXX. and Schleusn. sub voce, παλαιός, p. 628, vol. ii. Ed. Lond.

טפח, v. Kal non occ. Syr. ܛܦܚ, *expandit*, *aptavit*. Chald. טְפַח, *palmo aliquid collegit*, vel *abstersit*. Arab. cogn. صَفَح, *expandit* ferrum : *complosit manus*.

Pih. f. טִפַּח, pres. non occ. Constr. immed. *Spread out, dilate, extend*, any thing with the hand, as the limbs of an infant before the swaddling bands are applied, &c., Lam. ii. 22. Metaph. applied to the stretching out of the heavens, Is. xlviii. 13. Comp. Ib. li. 13; it. xl. 22; Ps. civ. 2, al. non occ.

טִפֻּחִים, m. pl. once, Lam. ii. 20, in the phr. עֹלְלֵי טִפֻּחִים, where the LXX.—which is followed by the Arabic—has two different renderings, one of which is probably taken from one of the other Hexaplar versions, viz. ἐπιφυλλίδα ἐποίησε μάγειρος, and νήπια θηλάζοντα μαστούς. The Targ. takes the latter word as a noun of (habitual) agency, Gram. art. 154, signifying, *persons who palmed* (i. e. stroked out and distended the limbs with the palms of their hands), and applied the swaddling bandages to *infants*: lit. *infants of the palmers, &c.* See the margin of the Auth. Vers. Gesenius gives "*Gestatio* puerorum." Castell. *educationes*, qs. *palmationes*. But it is difficult to see how a noun of this form can have either of these significations. According to the view given above, the place may be read thus,—*their own fruit—infants of the swaddlers*, i. e. palmed and swaddled infants.

תִּטְפֹּל, v. pres. 2d pers. תִּטְפֹּל. See my notes on Job xiii. 4; xiv. 17. Constr. immed. it. med. עַל, pers. or thing. *Lay on*, or *over*: meton. *Cover, conceal*, Ps. cxix. 69; Job ll. cc. al. non occ. See LXX.

Part. pl. constr. טֹפְלֵי.

מִטְפָּסָר, m. pl. aff. מִטְפְּסָרַיִךְ, twice only, Jer. li. 27; Nahum iii. 17. Pers. تاوسر, *dux bellicus*, according to Bohlen, Gesenius, &c. Ewald prefers تابسر, *altitudinis princeps*; but both these compounds signify precisely the same thing; تاو, and تاب, being different forms only of the same word. No such compound, however, occurs in the Persic, in any thing like these senses. Why not take the Chald. טָב, *egregius, &c.,* and שַׂר, *dux, &c.?* Compd. טַבְשַׂר, *good, great, prince. Prince*, or *leader*.

טפף, v. Arab. طَفَّ, *agilis fuit* equus; *sublimis fuit* res. Comp. دَفَّ, and ذَبَّ. Cogn. Syr. ܛܦܦ, *crepitavit* flamma. Gr. τυφόμενον, Matt. xii. 20. Castell.

Infin. טָפוֹף, once, Is. iii. 16. *Tripping* wantonly along; or, as Hamlet is made to say, "*They amble and jig,....and make their wantonness their ignorance.*" And, Rich. III., "To strut before *a wanton, ambling nymph.*" See Schrœder. de Vestitu Mulierum, p. 127.

טִפְרִין, m. pl. Chald. aff. טִפְרוֹהִי, Dan. iv. 30; *His nails*, Ib. vii. 19. טִפְרַיָּה, do. See Keri, al. non occ. i. q. Heb. צִפֹּרֶן. Syr. ܛܦܪܐ, *unguis*. Arab. ظُفْر, id.

טָפַשׁ, v. or noun, once, Ps. cxix. 70. Arab. طَفَشَ, *sordes*; طَفَشَة, *pinguis, crassa natio*. Syr. ܛܦܫܘܬܐ, *fœditas. Fat, gross, stupid.* Comp. שָׁמֵן, in Hiph.

טֹרַד, m. Part. v. טרד. Syr. ܛܪܕ, *detrusit.* Arab. طَرَدَ, id. Lat. *trudo.* Hor. "*truditur dies die.*" Ephrem Syrus, ܡܣܩܒܠ ܒܥܩܒܐ. *Following closely, treading, as it were on the heels of* —,

טרו

driving out; twice only, Prov. xix. 13; xxvii. 15.

— Part. Chald. pl. m. טָרְדִין, *Driving* out, Dan. iv. 22; xxix. 30.

— pass. טְרִיד, *Driven* out, Dan. iv. 30; v. 21.

טרום, Ruth iii. 14, i. q. טֶרֶם, as in the Keri.

טֹרַח, m. seg. twice only, Deut. i. 12; Is. i. 14. Arab. مَطْرُوح, *prostratus.* *Pressure, wearying.* Aff. טׇרְחֲכֶם.

טרח, v. Kal non occ.

Hiph. pres. יַטְרִיחַ, *One stretches out.* בְּרִי, for, or in giving, water, i. e. irrigation. See my note on Job xxxvii. 11, where alone this verb occurs. Sym. καὶ καρπῷ ἐπιβρίσει νεφέλη. Arab. طَرَح, *longè removit;* ii. conj. *longè protendit ædificium.*

טְרִיָּה, fem. — plur. non occ. Arab. طَرُو, *recens evenit. Fresh, moist,* Judg. xv. 15; Is. i. 6.

טֶרֶם, adv. Arab. صَرَم, *resecuit*, i. e. cutting off, excluding, negativing, the performance of the action of the accompanying verb, with reference to either past, present, or future, time, i. q. עַד לֹא. *Not yet, before that.* See Nold. sub voce, p. 339, seq., with the notes, Gen. ii. 5; Exod. x. 7; Josh. ii. 8; 1 Sam. iii. 3: — it. Exod. xii. 34; Josh. iii. 1; Is. lxv. 24; Ps. cxix. 67, &c. With the negative, further expressed by לֹא, Zeph. ii. 2, twice. Compd. with other particles, as, בְּטֶרֶם, Exod. x. 7; בְּטֶרֶם, Zeph. l. c. מִטֶּרֶם, Hag. ii. 15, &c.

טֶרֶף, masc. — plur. constr. טַרְפֵי. Syr. ܠܗܲܓ݁ܵܐ, *perturbatio.* Arab. طَرْف, cogn. صَرَف, *reduxit, repulitque; impegit in oculum, læsitve:* lit. *rending, tearing,* to pieces. Meton. *Prey,* taken in hunting, or otherwise, pec. by wild beasts, Gen. xlix. 9; Num. xxiii. 3, 4; Ezek. xxii. 25; Nahum

טרף

ii. 13. Metaph. — by violent men, Ps. cxxiv. 6; Is. v. 29; Ezek. xix. 3; Nahum iii. 1, &c. By another metaph. *Provision, food*, Mal. iii. 10; Prov. xxxi. 15. In Ezek. xvii. 9, כָּל־טַרְפֵּי צִמְחָהּ, *all the provisions of her shoot, growth;* i. e. the fruits produced by her, not merely the leaves; for these could be but of little moment. LXX. πάντα τὰ προανατέλλοντα αὐτῆς. Phr. הַרְרֵי־טָרֶף, *mountains of prey*, i. e. powerful robbers.

Aff. טַרְפּוֹ, טַרְפִּי.

טָרָף, m. lit. *Thing taken* forcibly: applied to a leaf, Gen. viii. 11, *plucked.* Gesen. *recens, fresh;* which seems to me a refinement.

טָרַף, v. pres. יִטְרֹף, once, Gen. xlix. 27. יִטְרָף, probably at first, יִטְרַף־בַּבֹּקֶר, when the vowel would be (o) not (a) regularly. Constr. immed. it. abs. See טֶרֶף above. *Taking the prey,* as a wild beast. Meton. *Tearing in pieces; wounding, injuring,* Gen. xlix. 27; Deut. xxxiii. 20; Mic. v. 7; Ezek. xxii. 25; Nahum ii. 13, &c. Metaph. — of violent men, Ps. vii. 3; xxii. 14; Ezek. xxii. 27; Amos i. 11; Job xviii. 4: — of powerful persons — God, Hos. v. 14; vi. 1; Ps. L. 22; Job xvi. 9: — of men, Gen. xlix. 27, &c.

Infin. abs. טָרֹף, Gen. xxxvii. 33, &c. Constr. טְרֹף, and טָרֹף, Ps. xvii. 12; Ezek. xix. 3.

Part. טֹרֵף, Job xviii. 4, &c.

— pl. constr. טֹרְפֵי, Ezek. xxii. 27.

Niph. pres. יִטָּרֵף, *Be, become, torn in pieces,* Exod. xxii. 12; Jer. v. 6.

Puh. טֹרַף, in pause טֹרָף (for טֻרַף, Gram. art. 109), i. q. Niph. Gen. xxxvii. 33; xliv. 28.

Hiph. Imp. aff. הַטְרִיפֵנִי, *Feed me, provide for me,* Prov. xxx. 8.

טְרֵפָה, f. — pl. non occ. *Any thing torn,* pec. *animal* (of the flock) *torn by a wild beast,* Gen. xxxi. 39; Exod. xxii. 30; Lev. vii. 24; Nahum ii. 13: hence considered as unclean and unfit for eating, Ezek. iv. 14; xliv. 31, &c.

טַרְפְּלָיֵא, m. pl. def. Chald. *A people so called,* Ezra iv. 9. LXX. Ταρφαλαῖοι.

י

י, *Yod*, the tenth letter of the Hebrew alphabet, see Gram. artt. 4. 15; and which, when used as a numeral, represents that number. It was, perhaps, at first, a hieroglyphical representation of the hand (יָד), and thence received its name. This figure it is still found to retain, in some degree, in the alphabet of the Samaritans (see Gram. art. 4), in the Phenician inscriptions yet extant, and in the coins of the Maccabees, as Dr. Gesenius has well remarked. But, when he tells us, in order to account for the variety of forms, יוֹד, and יָד; that יָמִים, *days*, is derived from an obsolete form, viz. יָם, i. q. יוֹם; he seems not to be aware that יָמִים is a mere contraction of יְמָמִים, the regular plural of יוֹם, Gram. art. 73. It is not improbable that it was originally written יַ; and that, out of the mixed sound approaching to that of (o), given by the Jews to Kamets (ָ), grew the form יוֹד.

Its power, as a consonant, is that of our Y, Gram. artt. 4. 15; it is of the palatal class, Ib. art. 22. When it loses this power, it is said either to quiesce, or to form a diphthong with the vowel immediately preceding it, Ib. artt. 37—39. In some cases it appears only in the vowel (ִ) Khirik, Ib. artt. 72. 200. 4.

In the etymology it sustains various offices: I. In forming the dual and plural numbers masc. as, מְלָכִים, and מִלְכַיִם: and constr. in each case, מַלְכֵי. II. Either as prefixed, inserted, or affixed, in forming certain nouns, viz. פְּקִיד, Gram. artt. 153. 6; 154. 10: פֶּקֶד, art. 155. Nouns termed *Heëmanti*, artt. 157. 159; and of this class, Patronymic or relative nouns, art. 166, seq., also those said to have received the Paragogic (ִי), Ib. art. 175. 15, seq., which is occasionally a fragment of the pron. fem. אַתִּי, Ib. art. 175. 16, note; or of הִיא, Ib. art. 193. 6. On its use in forming proper names, see Ib. art. 170, seq. Affixed also to imply excess, art. 166. 17; and to the ordinals of numerals, art. 181. 2.

In the roots of words it often interchanges with ו, as וְלַד, or יֶלֶד; בִּין, or בֵּין: with ה, as גִּלָּה, גָּלָה. Arab. جلي.

In the conjugation of verbs it is regularly prefixed with (ִ) to the 3d pers. pres. masc. sing. and pl.; and is also affixed to the 2d pers. fem. sing. and to the 1st pers. com. sing.: also to the 2d pers. sing. Imp. It is also found inserted in the Hiphhil conj. See the paradigm., Gram. art. 211.

יאב, v. יָאַבְתִּי, once, Ps. cxix. 131, constr. med. ל. Syr. ܡܐܒ, *avidè desideravit*. Cogn. Heb. אָבָה, אִוָּה. Arab. أَوَى, *teneriore affectu propensus fuit*. Intensely, greatly, desiring.

יאה, v. once, Jer. x. 7. יָאֲתָה, impers. *It becometh* thee, i. e. to be feared. Syr. ܡܠܐ, *convenit*.

יְאוֹר, see יאר.

יאל, v. Kal non occ. Arab. وَأَل, *confugit ad alium*; iii. conj. *properavit ad locum aliquem*. Cogn. آل, r. أول, *confugit; it. descivit, defecit; it. incrassuit liquor; it. rectè disposuit*. Cogn. وَكِي, *amicus fuit*, &c. The primary notion seems to have consisted in *betaking* one's self to any person or thing for safety; thence, to *commence, begin*, any thing. Again, as haste seems implied in the first place, *hurry, incaution, foolishness*. Comp. חלל, might have followed by way of meton. And again, from *commencing, beginning, taking in hand*, or the like, the being *well disposed, agreeable*, to any person or thing, might have also followed: therefore—

Niph. pl. נוֹאֲלוּ, נוֹאַלְנוּ, pres. non occ. *Be, become, foolish*, Num. xii. 11; Is. xix. 13; Jer. v. 4; L. 36.

Hiph. הוֹאִיל, pres. יוֹאֵל, and יֹאֶל. Constr. abs. it. med. ל, Infin. *Betaking one's self to, undertaking, beginning*, anything with alacrity, willingness, Gen. xviii. 27; Exod. ii. 21; Deut. i. 5; 1 Sam. xii. 22; Hos. v. 10; 1 Chron. xvii. 27; Josh. vii. 7; xvii. 12. In 1 Sam. xvii. 39, יֹאֶל לָלֶכֶת כִּי־לֹא נִסָּה, seems to require a negative; *so he undertook not to go*, for he *had not made proof*: see the remainder of the verse. If so, it was perhaps intended — as in many similar instances — that לֹא should be understood as also applying to יֹאֶל; and so the Syr. ܥܠ ܕܠܐ ܡܟܐܕܘ,

I I

יְאֹר (242) יָבַל

but he was unwilling to go; and the Targ. Job vi. 9. See my note.

Imp. הוֹאֵל, הוֹאֶל־, pl. הוֹאִילוּ, 2 Sam. vii. 29; Judg. xix. 6; Job vi. 28. See my note.

יְאֹר, m. pl. יְאֹרִים. Constr. יְאֹרֵי. Copt. ⲒⲀⲢⲞ, *fluvius.* But we need not confine ourselves to the Egyptian for this word. We have, Arab. آرَ, r. أَوَرَ, *aufugerunt per planiciem et æquabilem locum cameli;* it. أَوَرُ, *torridus, siccus,* de solo. Cogn. Heb. אוֹר, *light, &c.* The application of the term to water, as *running, translucid, &c.,* is easy. Cogn. Gr. ῥέω, ῥύω, *fluo.* Lat. *ruo.* A river, the Nile, or any other large stream, Gen. xli. 1, 2. 18; 2 Kings xix. 24; Dan. xii. 5—7; Is. xix. 8; xxiii. 10; xxxiii. 21; Jer. xlvi. 7, 8; Amos ix. 5; Job xxviii. 10, &c. Aff. יְאֹרִי, Ezek. xxix. 3; pl. יְאֹרַיִךְ, יְאֹרָיו, יְאֹרֵיהֶם.

יָאַשׁ, v. Kal non occ. Arab. يَئِسَ, *desperavit.*

Niph. נוֹאָשׁ, pres. non occ. *Hopeless, desperate; in vain.* וְנוֹאָשׁ מִמֶּנִּי, *so he will become hopeless of me,* 1 Sam. xxvii. 1;—Is. lvii. 10; Jer. ii. 25; xviii. 12; Job vi. 26.

Pih. Infin. יָאֵשׁ, *Rendering hopeless,* once, Eccl. ii. 20.

יָבַב, v. Kal non occ. Syr. ܝܒܒ, *vociferatus est.* Æth. ⲎⲚⲚ : id. Arab. أَبَّ, id.

Pih. 3d pers. f. תְּיַבֵּב, *She cried out, shouted,* once, Judg. v. 28.

יְבוּל, m.—pl. non occ. Syr. ܝܒܠ, *gramen, alga;* v. ܝܒܠ, *deduxit.* Arab. وَبَلَة, *gravitas pabuli;* v. وَبَلَ, *acriter propulit; imbrem effudit copiosè, &c.* Lit. *draw out.* See v. יבל: hence, (a) *Produce* (Lat. *produco*) of the earth, of trees, &c. (b) Meton. *Provision, wealth,* Lev. xxvi. 4. 20; Deut. xi. 17; xxxii. 22; Judg. vi. 4; Ps. lxvii. 7; lxxxv. 13; Hab. iii. 17; Job xx. 28. Aff. יְבוּלָהּ, יְבֻלָם.

יְבוּסִי, m. Patronym. A Jebusite, of יְבוּס, Judg. xix. 10, 11, &c.

יָבֵישׁ, see יָבֵשׁ.

יבל, v. Kal non occ. See יָבַל above. Hiph. pret. non occ. pres. יוֹבִיל, and יֹבֵל.

Syr. ܝܒܠ, *attulit, &c.* constr. immed. it. med. בְּ, instr. לְ, to, pers. *Bear, carry, lead,* along, any person, Ps. lx. 11; cviii. 11 :—or thing, as an offering, Ps. lxviii. 30; lxxvi. 12; Zeph. iii. 10.

Hoph. pres. יוּבַל, pret. non occ. *Be, become, borne, carried, lead,* along, person, thing, &c., as above, Ps. xlv. 15, 16; Is. xviii. 7; liii. 7; lv. 12; Jer. xi. 19; Hos. x. 6; xii. 2; Job x. 19; xxi. 30. 32.

Aph. Chald. הֵיבֵל, i. q. Heb. Ezra v. 14. Infin. הֵיבָלָה, Ib. vii. 15.

יָבָל, m. pl. constr. יִבְלֵי, *Streams* of water, Is. xxx. 25; xliv. 4, only. Sym. ἀγωγῶν ὑδάτων. See יבל.

יַבֶּלֶת, m. f. יַבֶּלֶת, once, Lev. xxii. 22. *Issue,* or *running* disease. See יבל, Auth. Vers. *a wen.* Vulg. *papulas habens.* LXX. μυρμηκιῶντα.

יָבָם, m. aff. יְבָמִי, יְבָמָהּ, pl. non occ. *Husband's brother,* who, if the husband died without issue, was bound to marry his widow, in order to raise up seed to his brother, Deut. xxv. 5—9.

יְבֵמֶת, f. of do. Aff. יְבִמְתֵּךְ, יְבִמְתּוֹ. *Brother's wife,* Deut. xxv. 7. 9; Ruth i. 15. Hence the verb—

Pih. יִבֵּם, aff. יִבְּמָהּ, *He shall* (by the law here laid down) *marry her,* Deut. xxv. 5.

Infin. aff. יַבְּמִי, *To marry me,* Ib. 7.

Imp. יַבֵּם, *Marry thou,* Gen. xxxviii. 8.

יָבֵשׁ, m. pl. יְבֵשִׁים | יְבֵשָׁה, f. pl. יְבֵשׁוֹת } Arab. يَبِسَ, *siccus, aridus.* *Dry,* of wood, stubble, &c., Is. lvi. 3; Ezek. xvii. 24; xxxvii. 2. 4; Nahum i. 10; Num. vi. 3; — of men, *suffering drought,* Num. xi. 6.

יָבֵשׁ, v. pres. יִיבַשׁ, יָבַשׁ. See יָבֵשׁ above. Constr. abs. Synon. חָרֵב. *Was,* or *became, dry, dried up, arid.* Meton. *Withered,* occasionally; of waters, streams, land, grass, trees, &c., 1 Kings xvii. 7; Is. xix. 5. 7; Job viii. 12; xiv. 12; Gen. viii. 7. 14; Jer. L. 38; xii. 4, &c. Metaph. applied to the strength, heart, *failed,* Ps. xxii. 16; cii. 5. To the hand, *withered,* and became inflexible, 1 Kings xiii. 4. Comp. Is. xl. 24. Once, יָבוֹשׁ, Hos. xiii. 15. Comp. Jer. li. 36. See, also, under בּוֹשׁ.

Infin. abs. יָבֹשׁ, Ezek. xvii. 10.
— constr. יְבֹשׁ, Is. xxvii. 11.
It. יָבְשָׁה, f. Gen. viii. 7.

יבש (243) יגו

Pih. pres. יַבֵּשׁ, for יְיַבֵּשׁ, it. תְּיַבֵּשׁ, f. Nahum i. 4; Prov. xvii. 22; Job xv. 30, al. non occ. *Dry up*, as of the sea, green shoot, &c. Hiph. הוֹבִישׁ, pres. אוֹבִישׁ. Constr. immed. it. med. אֶת. I. *Dry up, make to wither*. Of waters, rivers, wine, fruits, grass, &c., Josh. ii. 10; iv. 23; Is. xlii. 15; xliv. 27; Ezek. xix. 12; Joel i. 10; Ps. lxxiv. 15, &c. II. Taking the sense of the cognate בּוֹשׁ; by way of meton., because perhaps dryness in the mouth may be said to indicate great excitement of the mind. (a) *Be, become, ashamed, confounded*, Jer. ii. 26; vi. 15; viii. 12:—*hopeless*, Jer. x. 14; Joel i. 11; Zech. ix. 5. Metaph. applied to cities, Jer. xlviii. 1. 20; L. 2, 3. (b) *Make ashamed*, 2 Sam. xix. 6. *Made shame*, i. e. done shamefully, Hos. ii. 7.

יַבָּשָׁה, f. } pl. non occ. See יָבֵשׁ
יַבֶּשֶׁת, f. } above. Lit. habitually, constantly, usually, *Dry*, applied to the land, as opp. to the sea; so we may say, *the dry*, and the Gr. ἡ ξηρά, and τὸ ξηρόν, opp. τῷ ἡ θάλασσα, as Gesenius has well remarked; and so the Arab. يَبْسُ, *ariditas*, opp. τῷ بَحْرُ, as noted by Castell, and يَابِسَةٌ, *sicca terra*, Gen. i. 9, 10; Exod. iv. 9; xiv. 16; Jonah i. 9. 13; ii. 11; Ps. lxvi. 6; xcv. 5, &c.

יַבֶּשְׁתָּא, f. Chald. id. def. once, Dan. ii. 10.

יֹגְבִים, masc. pl. Arab. وَاجِبٌ, r. وَجَبَ, *cæsus, occisus*; conj. x. *adjudicavit*; i. e. *decided*: whence it should seem that *cutting*, or the like, was among the primitive notions contained in this root. Lit. cutters, *Ploughmen*, agriculturists, 2 Kings xxv. 12, keri. See r. גוב, Jer. lii. 16, occ. with כֹּרְמִים.

יְגֵבִים, m. pl. once only, Jer. xxxix. 10. *Ploughed lands*, apparently, i. q. the feodal term *carrucate*, perhaps; occ. with כְּרָמִים. Theod. ὑδρεύματα, read גֻּבִּים, or considered this word as having that sense. *Fossas, puteos*. Schleusn. Lex. in LXX.

יגה, v. Kal non occ. Arab. وَجِيَ, *malè habuit, doluitve* ungula. Cogn. وَجَعَ, *doluit*. Heb. יגע, — iv. أَوْجَى, *procul a se amovit* illum. Syr. ܐܘܓܝ, *expulit*. Cogn. Æth. ጎሠዐ : *punxit; impulit.*

Niph. part. constr. pl. נוּגֵי } The more — f. pl. נוּגוֹת } usual form would give נוֹגֵי. See Gram. art. 200. 15; but here the ground form seems to have been נָגָה, not מָגָה, Gram. art. 87. 2. 3. *Pained*, usually; but *ejected, expelled, cast out*, suits the etymology and context better, Zeph. iii. 18; Lam. i. 4, only.

Pih. pres. יַגֶּה, for יְיַגֶּה, Gram. art. 87. 5; constr. immed. *Afflict, pain*, Lam. iii. 33, only.

Hiph. הוֹגָה, pres. 2 pers. pl. with ן parag. תּוֹגְיוּן. Constr. immed. it. abs. I. *Afflict, pain*, as in Pih. הוֹגָה, *Hath afflicted her*, constr. Lam. i. 5. 12; iii. 32; Job xix. 2. II. *Removed*, 2 Sam. xx. 13. Constr. med. מִן.

Part. pl. aff. מוֹגַיִךְ, *Thy afflictors*, Is. li. 23. Hence—

יָגוֹן, m. constr. יְגוֹן, pl. non occ. *Affliction*: meton. *sorrow, grief*, Gen. xlii. 38; xliv. 31; Is. xxxv. 10; li. 11; Jer. viii. 18; xxxi. 13; Ezek. xxiii. 33; Ps. xxxi. 11, &c. Aff. יְגוֹנָם.

יָגִיעַ, m. constr. יְגִיעַ, pl. יְגִיעֵי } r. יגע,
יְגִיעָה, f. constr. יְגִיעַת, for יְגִיעָה } which see. I. Person *wearied, fatigued*, with labour, Job iii. 17. See my note. II. Meton. *Labour* bringing weariness, Gen. xxxi. 42; Job x. 3; xxxix. 19. And, III. by a further meton., *Fruits of the earth, Wealth*, acquired by labour, Is. xlv. 14; lv. 2; Jer. iii. 24; Ezek. xxiii. 29; Hag. i. 11; Ps. cix. 11; Eccl. xii. 12, &c. Aff. יְגִיעָם, יְגִיעֲכֶם, יְגִיעָהּ, יְגִיעוֹ, יְגִיעֶךָ.

יָגֵעַ, m. once, Job xx. 18, i. q. יָגִיעַ, sign. iii.

יָגֵעַ, m. pl. יְגֵעִים, i. q. יָגִיעַ, sign. i., Deut. xxv. 18; 2 Sam. xvii. 2; Eccl. i. 8. הַדְּבָרִים יְגֵעִים, *Words* are *wearying*, bringing weariness, where this word evidently has an active sense. Aquila, κοπιῶσι. Sym. κοπώδεις. LXX. ἔγκοποι.

יגע, v. pres. יִיגַע, יִיגְעוּ, and יִיגָע. Arab. وَجِعَ, *doluit*. See יגה. Constr. abs. it. med. בְּ; in, for, &c., לְ, for. *Labour to weariness*, Josh. xxiv. 13; Is. xlvii. 12; xlix. 4; lxii. 8; lxv. 23; Jer. xlv. 3; Ps. lxix. 4; Prov. xxiii. 4; Job ix. 29, &c.

יגר (244) יד

Piḥ. pres. תִּיגַע, *Make one labour to weariness*, Josh. vii. 3; Eccl. x. 15.

Hiph. הוֹגִע, pres. non occ. Constr. immed. it. med. בְּ, instr. i. q. Piḥ. Is. xliii. 23, 24; Mal. ii. 17, al. non occ.

יְגָר, m. Chald. once, Gen. xxxi. 47. Syr. ܝܓܪܐ, *acervus*. Æth. ⲰⲄⲒⲢ : *collis*. Cogn. Heb. אגר. *Heap, mount*.

יָגֹר, v. pret. יָגֹרְתִּי, יָגֹרְתָּ, pres. non occ. Arab. وَجَرَ, *metuit*. Cogn. وَجَلَ, id. Constr. immed. med. מִפְּנֵי. Cogn. גור. *Fear, be afraid of*, Deut. ix. 19; xxviii. 60; Job iii. 24; ix. 28; Ps. cxix. 39.

יָגֹר, m. The noun or root, on which the v. יגר is formed. *Fearing, afraid of*, Jer. xxii. 25; xxxix. 17.

יָד, c. constr. יַד, dual יָדַיִם, constr. יְדֵי, f. יָדוֹת, lit. *putting forth*. Aff. יָדֵנוּ, יָדִי, יָדְךָ, יָדֶךָ, יָדֵךְ, יָדוֹ, יָדָהּ, יָדֵנוּ, יָדְכֶם, יָדָם, יָדַיִם, dual, יְדֵי, &c., r. יָדָה, *cast, throw*. Æth. ⲰⲈⲢⲔ : id. Arab. يَدَي, *contigit, læsitve* in manu, &c. يَدٌ, *manus*. Syr. ܐܺܝܕܳܐ, id. *The hand* of man, or *the paw* or *fore-foot* of a beast, 1 Sam. xvii. 37; Prov. xxx. 28; Gen. ix. 5; xxxviii. 28, &c. And, as the hand is the instrument by which men effect most of their purposes, the word has been variously applied. See under אֶחַז, יָצָא, כָּבֵד, מָחָא, מָלֵא, שׁוּב, עָמַד, חָזַק, רָפָה, רָחַץ, נָשָׂא, נָפַח, מָצָא, &c.; it. תְּמָכָה, חָגַר, קָצַר, רָם, תְּשׂוּמֶת, שׂוּם, רוּם, &c. (a) יָד, *Power, ability, authority, help, aid,* &c.; the hand being considered as the instrument, or means, by which these are acquired and exerted; as, in the phrr. הִשִּׂיג יָד, *(the) hand come up to*, i. e. is equal to, Lev. xxvii. 8. אָזְלַת יָד, *power has departed*, Deut. xxxii. 6. תִּגַּע בּוֹ יָד, *hand touch it*, i. e. person, Exod. xix. 13; Dan. vi. 6. יִתְמֹךְ יָד, *he sustained the hand*, Gen. xlviii. 17. ‎—יַד־יְהֹוָה הוֹיָה בְּ, *the hand—power—of Jehovah* (lit.) *falling on —*, Exod. ix. 3; it. with הָיָה, Deut. xvii. 7; Josh. ii. 19, &c. בְּחֹזֶק יָד, *with strength of hand*, Exod. xiii. 14, &c. בְּאֶבֶן יָד, *with stone of hand*, i. e. thrown by the hand, Num. xxxv. 17; it. 18. Comp. Ezek. xxix. 9, בִּכְלִי עֵצִי יָד, *with instrument of wood of do,* i. e. any wooden tool, &c. used by the hand. In Neh. x. 32, כָּלְיָד, *every hand*, i. e. every person, by meton.

(b) Applied to God, *His power*, or *property;* occasionally, His *Spirit* or *Word;* as, יַד הָאֱלֹהִים, יַד יְהֹוָה, 1 Sam. v. 11, &c.; Exod. ix. 3; Deut. ii. 19, &c.; Ezek. i. 3: we have יַד יְהֹוָה, in the parallel with דְּבַר יְהֹוָה, Ib. iii. 14, occ. with רוּחַ. Comp. viii. 1, with xi. 5; 1 Kings xviii. 46, &c.; Is. viii. 11, from אֵלַי to לֵאמֹר, is parenthetical, and cannot apply here. Gesenius is wrong, therefore, in this instance,—Jer. xv. 17; Ezek. iii. 22; xxxvii. 1, &c., in many of which places,— as it is the case often with the terms, *word, glory, arm*, is probably meant the *Son of God*. See under כָּבוֹד, דְּבַר, זְרוֹעַ; as is also the case occasionally with יָמִין, *right hand*, Ps. cx. 1. שֵׁב לִימִינִי, *sit for*, or, *as, my right hand*, i. e. the instrument or receptacle of my power. Comp. the following context, and Exod. xv. 6; Ps. xlvii. 7; xx. 7, particularly Ps. xliv. 3, 4, where several equivalent terms occur, and Mark xiv. 62, ὄψεσθε τὸν υἱὸν τοῦ ἀνθρώπου καθήμενον ἐκ δεξιῶν τῆς δυνάμεως, κ. τ. λ., alluding to Dan. vii. 13, 14; and, in all such places intimating the investiture of the Divine power in the manhood of Christ, and intended to inculcate his Divinity. See also Heb. i. 3, seq., and 1 Pet. iii. 22, all tending to the same point. צֹאן יָדוֹ, *his own flock*, Ps. xcv. 7. Comp. Ezek. xxxiv. 10; Gen. xxxix. 6; Deut. xxxii. 36; Judg. i. 35; 1 Kings ii. 46; Is. xix. 25, &c. And, by a meton., it. *power*, of man, Judg. iv. 24, with מֶלֶךְ, Deut. xxxii. 36: Gen. xli. 35, &c.

(c) *God's mercy, favour*, or, on the contrary, *punishment*, inflicted by Him, Ezra vii. 9; Neh. ii. 8; Ps. cxxiii. 2; Is. xiv. 26; xxv. 10: with verbs, הָיָה, כָּבֵד, נָטָה, &c., Job xii. 6, however, does not apply to God's hand or power, as Gesenius supposes: see my note. In like manner, this term is used, and applied to men, *passim*, as in the following usages, Exod. ix. 3; Deut. ii. 15, &c.

(d) Implying also, *Index, memorial, monument,* 1 Sam. xv. 12; 2 Sam. xviii. 18; Is. lvi. 5, with שֵׁם; because, perhaps, on such monuments the *name* was usually written. The Phenician monuments, it should seem, had sculptured on them the form of a hand raised up on an arm, and on this the inscription was engraven. See " Hamackeri Diatribe de Monumentis Punicis," p. 20, with Professor Reuven's work on it, p. 5. Gesen.

(e) Also metaph. *The tenons* of the planks which inclosed the sanctuary, as *hands* or *holders*, Exod. xxvi. 17. 19; xxxvi. 22. 24. Also *the axle-trees* of carriage wheels, 1 Kings vii. 32, 33.

(f) Occurring with עִם, or אֵת, *With*, i. e. in favour of —, 1 Sam. xxii. 17; 2 Sam. iii. 12; 2 Kings xv. 19.

(g) — with בְּ‏־הָיְתָה, i. e. *Against, opposing*, Gen. xxxvii. 27; 1 Sam. xviii. 17, &c.

(h) — with עַל, or אֶל, or תַּחַת, after verbs signifying *giving up, over, &c.*, will imply, *possession, dominion, power, &c.*, Gen. xlii. 37; Judg. iii. 30; 1 Sam. xvii. 22, &c. Metaph. — *of the sword*, Ps. lxiii. 11; Jer. xviii. 21: in the sense of בְּיַד, with נָתַן, *Superiority*, 2 Kings v. 18; vii. 2. 17. On the contrary, *service*, 2 Kings iii. 11. Hence, with לֹא, or אֶפֶס, *not* (human, but Divine) *power*, Job xxxiv. 20; Dan. viii. 25; it. dual. Ib. ii. 34, 45. Comp. Lam. iv. 6. Also, in the sense of receiving *into hand*, Gen. xxxii. 14, &c.

(i) — *by means of —*, Jer. v. 31, &c. i. q. בְּיַד (j). Prov. xiii. 11, &c.

(j) Id. בְּיַד מֹשֶׁה, *by the hand*, instrumentality, means, of, *Moses*, Num. xv. 23; 1 Kings xii. 15; Is. xx. 2, &c. *On account of —*, Job xxxvii. 7. See my note on this place.

(k) יָד לְפֶה, or עַל פֶּה, — *to*, or *on* (the) *mouth*, implying silence, Job xxi. 5. See my note, Ib. xxix. 9; Prov. xxx. 2; Mic. vii. 16.

(l) יָד לְיָד, lit. *hand in hand*, as in striking a bargain. See my note on Job xvii. 2; Prov. xi. 21. Not *generation after generation*, as Gesenius and others imagine, from the Persic دست بدست; which, however, this Persic phrase does not mean; but, from hand to hand, by way of receiving in succession. See under תָּקַע.

(m) עַל־רֹאשׁ, — *on* (the) *head*; implying intense grief, 2 Sam. xiii. 19; Jer. ii. 37, &c. In Exod. xvii. 16, עַל־כֵּס יָהּ, — *on*, or *against, the throne* of God, as erected in Israel, i. e. the *hand*, or *power*, of Amalek. See my note on Job xii. 6, and marginal reading of the Auth. Vers.

(n) נָתַן יָד, *He gave, put forth the hand*, implying *submission, agreement, fidelity, &c.*, 2 Kings x. 15; 1 Chron. xxix. 24; Jer. L. 15; Lam. v. 6, &c., it. with שִׂים, in administering an oath, Gen. xxiv. 2; xlvii. 29. And probably in the first acceptation here, Ib. xxxii. 25, with נָגַע, Jacob requiring a blessing from the angel, as a testimony perhaps of their agreement. Comp. 2 Kings, l. c. It should seem that *placing the hand under the thigh*, Gen. ll. cc. is much the same thing as taking hold of the skirt 1 Sam. xv. 27, where *agreement* is evidently sought: and, should the superior be sitting— which is the position of authority—this could hardly be done without placing the hand somewhere under the thigh; so that *laying hold of the skirt* would be nearly equivalent to *placing the hand under the thigh :* the robe, so touched, being considered indicative of authority. Hence the notion, too, of casting the mantle, skirts, shadow, &c., over any one : also *of covering*, implying favour, defence, &c., of honorary dresses, and the like. Comp. 1 Kings xix. 19; 2 Kings ii. 8. 13, 14; Ruth iii. 9; Ezek. xvi. 8; Zech. viii. 23; Mal. iii. 20 (iv. 2), *wings*, person being designated, implying his *skirts*. Comp. Ps. xvii. 8; xxxvi. 8; lxiii. 8 : it. Judg. ix. 15; it. *covering*, i. q. protection, Gen. xx. 16. Connected with *hand*, Is. xlix. 2. To *rend the mantle, make naked, uncover*, and the like, imply, on the contrary, *disagreement, woe, disgrace*, Job i. 20, &c., 1 Sam. xv. 27; xxiv. 5; Deut. xxii. 30, &c.

(o) לְיָד, *According to the hand :* wealth, power : thence, meton. *liberality*, 1 Kings x. 13; Esth. i. 7; ii. 18, &c.

(p) מִתַּחַת יַד, or מִיַּד, *Out of* the *hand*, or *from under —*, i. e. with verbs implying *taking from, &c.* *Deliverance*, rebellion, &c., as the context may require, Gen. ix. 5; xxxi. 39; Exod. xviii. 10; 1 Sam. xvii. 37; 2 Kings viii. 20. 22; xiii. 5, &c.

(q) And, as *the hand is near to*, and, on each side, of the person ; (יָד) is used in the sense of, I. *At hand, near*, Job xv. 23; 1 Sam. xxi. 14; i. q. בְּעֵינֵיהֶם. Comp. Job i. 14; Zech. viii. 6, &c. II. *This*, or *that side, part*, of a river, &c., Exod. xxxviii. 15; and, omitting יָד, by the ellipsis (see מַיִם, שְׂמֹאל), Deut. xxxiii. 2; 1 Kings ii. 19; 2 Kings xxiii. 13. Hence, the usages, רְחַב יָדַיִם, *extensive of both hands ;* i. e. of parts, limit, &c, Gen. xxxiv. 21; Ps. civ. 25; Is. xxxiii. 21, &c. יָד הַיְאֹר, Exod. ii. 5; Deut. ii. 37, &c. בְּעֶבֶר יָד, 1 Sam. iv. 18. יָד, 2 Sam. xiv. 30; xviii. 4. עַל יָד, Josh. xv. 46, &c. עַל יְדֵי, Num. xxxiv. 3; Judg. xi. 26, &c. pl. f.—

יָדוֹת, *Hands*, or, as we say, *arms* or *elbows*, *of a chair*, 1 Kings x. 19. Gesenius makes these the *legs* of the chair or throne: but these could hardly be said to be עַל רֹאשׁ הַמִּכְנָה, *on the head* or *top, &c.* See Ib. vii. 34, 35. And without רֹחַב.

(r) *Space, place,* Num. ii. 17; Deut. xxiii. 13; Is. lvi. 5; lvii. 8; Ezek. xxi. 24: Dual, Josh. viii. 20; it. יָדוֹת, f. pl. *hands:* by meton. *handfulls,* thence, applied as a measure, *Parts, portions,* or the like, Jer. vi. 3; Dan. xii. 7; 2 Kings xv. 7; Gen. xlvii. 24; 2 Sam. xix. 44; Neh. xi. 1; Dan. i. 20, &c. Similar usages in the Syriac and Arabic will be found in the Lexicons of Castell, Schaaf, Golius, Freytag, &c., which it would be tedious to copy out.

יַד, c. Chald. i. q. Heb. יָד. Def. יְדָא. Dual, יְדִין. Aff. יְדָךְ, יְדֵהּ, יְדֵהוֹן; pl. יְדַי, יְדֵי, מִן יַד, 24: i. q. Heb. כְּמִי; בְּיַד, i. q. Heb. בְּיַד, Dan. ii. 34. 45; v. 5. 23; vi. 28; Ezra v. 8; vii. 14. 25.

יְדָא, v. Chald. i. q. Heb. יָדָה. Peal non occ.

Aph. Part. מְהוֹדֵא, contr. מוֹדֵא, Dan. ii. 23; vi. 11, al. non occ.

יָדָה, v. pret. pl. יָדוּ, once only, pres. non occ. Cogn. יָדָד. Arab. يَدَّ, and thence v. يَدَى, *contigit manu, &c.* Æth. ⲱⲈⲠ: *jecit.* Arab. وَدَى, *emisit aliquid,* &c. Cogn. וָדָא, *exeruit,* &c. it. Cogn. وضع ،ودع. Generally, *Put forth,* qualified by the context, i. e. as, *casting stones; giving praise,* thanks, making confession, &c., Jer. L. 14. *They cast,* i. e. at her, constr. med. אֶל.

Pih. pres. יְדוּ, for יְיַדוּ, Gram. art. 87. 5, i. q. Kal, *Cast,* as stones, or the lot: constr. immed. med. אֶל, בְּ, עַל, pers. Joel iv. 3; Obad. vr. 11; Nahum iii. 10; Lam. iii. 53.

Infin. יָדוֹת, *Cast forth, disperse.*

Hiph. הוֹדָה, 1st pers. pl. הוֹדֵינוּ, pres. יוֹדֶה, or יְהוֹדֶה. Constr. immed. it. med. אֶת, ל, עַל, pers. בְּ, instr. *Praise, celebrate.* Synon. הַלֵּל, הַזְכִּיר, 1 Chron. xvi. 4; 2 Chron. v. 13: by recounting, commemorating, God's goodness, truth, &c., Gen. xxix. 35; xlix. 8; 1 Kings viii. 33; Ps. vii. 18; xxviii. 7; xxx. 13; xlv. 18; Prov. xxviii. 13, &c.

Infin. הוֹדוֹת, 1 Chron. xxv. 3; 2 Chron. vii. 3, &c., it. with בְּ, ל, prefixed, Ezra iii. 11; 1 Chron. xvi. 7; Ps. xcii. 2; cvi. 47, &c.

Imp. pl. הוֹדוּ, Ps. xxxiii. 2; c. 4, &c.

Part. מוֹדֶה, Prov. xxviii. 13.

Pl. מוֹדִים, 1 Chron. xxix. 13.

Hithp. הִתְוַדָּה, pres. אֶתְוַדֶּה, יִתְוַדּוּ. Constr. immed. it. med. אֶת, עַל, it. abs. it. ל, pers.

Became, set about, was, putting forth, i. e. *confessing,* sins, Lev. v. 5; xvi. 21; xxvi. 40; Num. v. 7; Dan. ix. 4; Neh. ix. 2.

Infin. aff. הִתְוַדּוֹתוֹ, *His confessing,* Ezra x. 1.

Part. מִתְוַדֶּה, Neh. i. 6, &c.

Pl. מִתְוַדִּים, Ib. ix. 3, &c.

יָדִיד, m. pl. m. aff. יְדִידָךְ, f. יְדִידוֹת. Arab. وَدِيد, *amicus.* Syr. ܝܕܝܕܐ, id. *Beloved,* applied to God's scriptural children as beloved of Him, Deut. xxxiii. 12. יְדִיד יְהוָֹה, Ps. cxxvii. 2. To the Israelites, Is. v. 1; Jer. xi. 15; Ps. lx. 7; cviii. 7: prophetically to Christian privileges, Ps. xlv. 1: to places of worship, lxxxiv. 2.

יְדִידוּת, f. once, Jer. xii. 7, abstr. for concr. *Love.* יְדִדוּת נַפְשִׁי, *my soul's love,* for *beloved.*

יָדַע, v. pres. יֵדַע, once יֶֽאֱדַע: so that יֵדַע,— of which דֵּעֶה is a contracted f. form,—is the ground-form. Syr. ܝܕܥ, *novit, &c.* Cogn. Gr. εἴδω, εἰδέω. Lat. *video.* Angl. *to wot.* Castell. Constr. abs. it. med. אֶת, בְּ, instr. מִן, of time. By the means of seeing, hearing, &c. (a) *Perceiving, becoming informed, aware, conscious, assured of —, feel:* hence, (b) *Know, be acquainted with,* sexually, &c. Hence, (c) meton. *Recognise, acknowledge, allow, own:* and by a further meton. (d) *Regard;* also *animadvert on, punish,* person or thing, &c., as the context may require. (a) Gen. xix. 33; Exod. iii. 4; Lev. v. 1; 1 Sam. xxii. 3; Is. vi. 9; Judg. xiii. 21: with עִם לֵבָב, Deut. viii. 5. Comp. Gen. xv. 8; xxiv. 14; Exod. vi. 7; vii. 17; Gen. ix. 24; Deut. xi. 2; Ezek. vi. 7, &c. Metaph. Ps. cv. 19; Is. i. 3, &c.

(b) Gen. xxix. 5; xxx. 29; Exod. xxxiii. 12. 17; Deut. xxxiv. 10; Is. i. 3. Sexually, Gen. iv. 17. 25; 1 Sam. i. 19. Of catamites, Gen. xix. 5. Of a woman, יֹדְעָה אִישׁ, Gen. xix. 8; Judg. xi. 39; Num. xxxi. 17, &c.

(c) Num. xiv. 31; Deut. ix. 24; Exod. vii. 5; xiv. 4; Ezek. xx. 20; xxix. 46; Job ix. 21; xxxiv. 4, &c.

(d) Gen. xviii. 19; xxxix. 6; Hos. viii. 2; xiii. 4; Ps. xxxvi. 11; Prov. ix. 13; xxvii. 23, &c.; Job xxxv. 15; Judg. viii. 16; Jer. xxix. 23, Keri. Ezek. xix. 7, &c.

Phrr. יָדַע בְּשֵׁם, Exod. xxxiii. 12. פָּנִים אֶל־פָּנִים, Deut. xxxiv. 10. בִּינָה — , דַּעַת — ,

ידע (247) ידע

distinctly, assuredly, Prov. xvii. 27; Job xxxviii. 4. אֲכַנֶּה —, how *I may give titles,* i. e. flatter, Job xxxii. 22. לְךָ —, for thyself, Job v. 27. טוֹב וָרָע —, good, i. e. distinguish good from evil, Gen. iii. 5, &c. נַפְשִׁי —, *my self,* Cant. vi. 12. בֵּינֵינוּ —, *among ourselves,* Job xxxiv. 4. שִׁמְךָ —, *thy name,* person, authority, Ps. ix. 11, &c. לְבָבְךָ —, *thy heart,* 1 Kings ii. 44. סֵפֶר —, *book,* i. e. the contents of —, Is. xxix. 12. בֵּין יְמִינוֹ —, *distinction of his right hand* from —Jon. iv. 11.

Infin. abs. יָדֹעַ, Gen. xv. 13, &c.

Constr. דַּעַת, Josh. iv. 24, &c. לָדַעַת, Gen. iii. 22, &c. Aff. דַּעְתִּי, דַּעְתּוֹ, דַּעְתָּהּ, &c. it. דֵּעָה, Is. xi. 9, &c. דְּעֹה, Prov. xxiv. 14.

Imp. דַּע, Gen. xx. 7, &c.; pl. דְּעוּ, Judg. xviii. 14, &c.

—, f. דְּעִי, 1 Sam. xxv. 17, &c.

Part. יֹדֵעַ, Gen. iii. 5, &c.

Pl. יֹדְעִים, 2 Kings xvii. 26. Constr. יֹדְעֵי, Gen. iii. 5, &c. Aff. יוֹדְעַי, יוֹדְעֶיךָ, &c.

— passive, יָדֻעַ, Is. liii. 3.

Pl. יְדֻעִים, Deut. i. 13. 15.

Niph. נוֹדַע, pres. יִוָּדַע, יִוָּדֵעַ, of pers. or thing. Constr. abs. it. med. בְּ, among, pers. in, place, לְ, אֶל, pers. *Be, become known, apparent:* meton. *recognised,* Gen. xli. 21. 31; Exod. ii. 14; xxi. 36; Ps. ix. 17; lxxvi. 2; Prov. xxxi. 23; Is. xix. 21; lxi. 9; lxvi. 14. נוֹדְעָה יַד־יְהֹוָה, *the hand of Jehovah shall become known;* recognised as powerful and gracious, *as to* (with) *his servants.* See עִם, in the parallel, Exod. vi. 3. לֹא נוֹדַעְתִּי לָהֶם, *I became not known to them;* i. e. by *my name Jehovah.* Comp. Ezek. xx. 9. Constr. med. אֶל, and לְ, Ib. xxxv. 11; Ps. lxxix. 10. Gesenius makes Prov. x. 9, to signify, *shall be punished;* but there seems to be no good reason for this. LXX. γνωσθήσεται, — to which the other ancient versions correspond,—seems to express the true sense. Comp. Jer. xxxi. 19.

Pih. יִדַּע, *Hast made to know,* observe, Job xxxviii. 12. See Keri, 1 pers. יֹדַעְתִּי, better perhaps, Hiph. הוֹדַעְתִּי, Gesen., 1 Sam. xxi. 3. Symm. συνεταξάμην. LXX. διαμεμαρτύρημαι.

Puh. Part. aff. מְיֻדָּעִי, *My known,* i. e. my familiar, Ps. lv. 14: pl. מְיֻדָּעַי, Ps. xxxi. 12; lxxxviii. 9. 19; Job xix. 14. מְיֻדָּעָיו, 2 Kings x. 11.

Hiph. הוֹדִיעַ, pres. יוֹדִיעַ, יֹדַע. Constr. immed. it. med. בְּ, אֶת, in, among; לְ, pers. עַל, on, because of. *Make known, apparent; confess, show; inform, teach, &c.;* as the context may require, Exod. xviii. 16. 20; xxxiii. 12; Num. xvi. 5; Deut. iv. 9; Josh. iv. 22; 1 Sam. xvi. 3; Is. xxxviii. 19. In Judg. viii. 16. וַיֹּדַע בָּהֶם, *and he taught with them;* i. e. made to feel with these instruments of punishment, it. Jer. xvi. 21. אוֹדִיעֵם אֶת־יָדִי, Targ. "*ultionem meam.*"

Infin. הוֹדִיעַ, Gen. xli. 39, &c. Aff. הוֹדִיעֵנִי, הוֹדִיעָם, הוֹדִיעֲךָ, 1 Sam. xxviii. 15; Deut. viii. 3; Ps. xxv. 14.

Imp. הוֹדַע, pl. הוֹדִיעוּ. Aff. הוֹדִיעֵנִי, &c., Ps. xc. 12; Is. xii. 4; Exod. xxxiii. 13; Job xxxvii. 19, &c.

Part. aff. מוֹדִיעֲךָ, מוֹדִיעָם, pl. מוֹדִיעִים, Dan. viii. 19; Jer. xvi. 21; Is. xlvii. 13, &c.

Hoph. הוּדַע (for הוּיְדַע, which would be regular), *Be, become, made, known, &c.,* Lev. iv. 23. 28.

Part. f. מוּדַעַת, Is. xii. 5. Keri.

Hithp. pres. אֶתְוַדַּע, *I will become known,* once, Num. xii. 6. Constr. med. אֶל, pers. pret. non occ.

Infin. הִתְוַדַּע, *Becoming known,* i. e. making himself so, Gen. xlv. 1, al. non occ.

יְדַע, v. Chald. pres. יִנְדַּע, i. q. Heb. יָדַע. Constr. immed. it. abs. *Know, understand, perceive,* Dan. ii. 9. 30; iv. 6. 14. 22; vi. 11; Ezra iv. 15, &c.

Imp. דַּע, Dan. vi. 16.

Part. act. יָדַע, Dan. ii. 8. 22; Ezra vii. 25: pl. יָדְעִין, constr. יָדְעֵי, Dan. v. 23; Ezra vii. 25.

— pass. יְדִיעַ; Dan. iii. 18; Ezra iv. 12. Phr. יְדִיעַ לֶהֱוֵא לְ, *let it be known to—*

Aph. i. q. Heb. Hiph. הוֹדַע, pres. יְהוֹדַע. Constr. immed. it. med. לְ, pers. it. abs. *Make known, show, teach,* Dan. ii. 15. 17. 23. 25. 28, 29. 45; vii. 16; Ezra vii. 27, &c.

Infin. הוֹדָעָה, Dan. v. 8.

It. הוֹדָעוּת, Dan. ii. 26; iv. 15; Ezra v. 10, with aff.

Part. pl. מְהוֹדְעִין, Dan. iv. 4; Ezra iv. 16, &c.

יִדְּעֹנִי, m. pl. יִדְּעֹנִים. Dimin. of ידע (Gram. art. 168), with the relative termination (י), Ib. art. 166. Lit. *Sciolist,* applied to false prophets, prognosticators, Lev. xix. 31; xx. 6; Deut. xviii. 11; 1 Sam. xxviii. 3. 9: frequently with אוֹב, which see, the sense of which is taken, as Gesenius thinks, Lev. xx. 27: but for this there is no good reason. LXX. ἐγγαστρίμυθος, ἢ ἐπαοιδός, θελητής ἢ γνώστης.

יָה, m. i. q. יְהֹוָה, of which it is perhaps an abbreviation, as it has generally been

יחב

thought. Gesenius thinks it is derived from a more ancient pronunciation of יהוה, as יֲהֶוֶה, whence יָהוּ —, in certain proper names; as, אֵלִיָה, abbrev. אֱלִיָּה; and so of others: or, as in the apocopated form יִשְׁתַּחוּ, for יִשְׁתַּחֲוֶה: but this is for יִשְׁתַּחֲוּ, Gram. art. 87. 2: the vowel (ֲ) being drawn back. And, if so, יָהוּ — must have been written for יָהוּ. No reliance can be placed on this sort of reasoning. The root is evidently הוה, from which יהוה, יהו, however pointed, are derived: and of these יָהּ is clearly an abbreviation, unless indeed יה is the root. Æth. ፪ፙሀ: or ፪ፙሖ: *mitis, mansuetus fuit*, &c., of which the Arab. interjections, وَهْ, وَهْيَ, are also abbreviated forms. Syr. ܡܚܰܘ, — as crying out for *mercy*, &c. — It occurs frequently in the phr. הַלְלוּ־יָהּ, Ps. civ. 35; cv. 45; cvi. 1. 48, &c. In other combinations, Ps. lxxxix. 9; xciv. 7. 12; Is. xxxviii. 11;—Exod. xv. 2; Ps. cxviii. 14; Is. xii. 2. עָזִּי וְזִמְרָת יָהּ, *my strength, and my song, is Jah*; or, *my strength is even the song (praise) of Jehovah*, i. e. as if his greatest strength consisted in praising his God, Ps. lxviii. 5. בְּיָהּ שְׁמוֹ, *in Jah his name*, Is. xxiv. 4. בְּיָהּ יְהֹוָה, *in Jah, Jehovah*, &c. In one of the Hexaplar readings we have Is. xii. 2, *iá*; otherwise usually κύριος, or ὁ κύριος. The Syrians have adopted the term ܝܳܐ, from the Heb. just as we have *Jah*.

יהב, once, aff. יָהֵבְךָ, Ps. lv. 23, in הַשְׁלֵךְ עַל־יְהֹוָה יְהָבְךָ, *Cast*, i. e. *give up to Jehovah thy burden*, according to some: others, *thy gift*, i. e. the wealth given to thee by him. But יהב might here be equivalent to the Arab. وَهْب, or وَهَّاب, *great*, or *munificent, giver*; to which the verb יִתֵּן, in the next member, seems to respond. The passage would then read, *cast* (thyself) *on Jehovah thy benefactor, and he will sustain thee*, &c.

יהב, v. non occ. pret. pres. Syr. ܝܗܒ, *dedit*. Arab. وَهَبَ. Æth. ፙሀ: id. Constr. abs. it. immed. thing and med. ל, pers. it. med. אֶת. Imp. הַב, it. with הָ, parag. הָבָה, pl. הָבוּ, f. sing. הָבִי. (a) *Give, concede, allow*, Gen. xxix. 21; xxx. 1; xxxviii. 16; xlvii. 15. Pl. Gen. xlvii. 16; 1 Chron. xvi. 28, 29; Job vi. 22; Ps. xxix. 1, &c.

(b) Meton. *Appoint, place*, Josh. xviii. 4; Deut. i. 13; 2 Sam. xi. 15. Used also in exhorting, as in our *come, go to*, or the like; as, הָבָה נִבְנֶה, *come, let us build*, Gen. xi. 4; Ib. vr. 3. 7; Exod. i. 10, &c.; 1 Sam. xiv. 41, הָבָה תָמִים. LXX. δὸς δήλους. Ἀλλ. δὸς δήλωσιν. From the context, vr. 36, seq., as the parties were brought before the Lord, it should seem that the *Thummim* were had recourse to. See אוּרִים, p. 15. The phrase here used would, in that case, perhaps imply this, although *the lot* might also have been cast. Comp. Deut. xxxii. 3: Ruth iii. 15, הָבִי הַמִּטְפַּחַת, *give, hold out, the veil*. Repeated apparently for emphasis, Prov. xxx. 15. הֵבוּ, Hos. iv. 18, is evidently an abstract noun,—as ܡܰܘܗܰܒܬܳܐ, in Syr.; whence, constr. ܡܰܘܗܰܒܬ,—signifying *gift*, either from this, or some cognate root.

יְהַב, v. Chald. pres. non occ. constr. immed. it. med. ל, pers. (a) *Give, give up*, Dan. ii. 23. 37, 38. 48; iii. 28; v. 18, 19, &c. (b) *Place, lay*, as a foundation, Ezra v. 16.
Imp. הַב, Dan. v. 17.
Part. act. יָהֵב, Dan. ii. 21, pl. יָהֲבִין, Ib. vi. 3.
— pass. יְהִב, Dan. vii. 4. 6. 14.
F. יְהִיבַת, Ib. vii. 12. 27. Conjugated as a verb, pl. m.
יְהִיבוּ, Ezra v. 14, al. non occ.
Ithp. pret. non occ. pres. יִתְיְהִב, Dan. iv. 13; vii. 25; Ezra vi. 4. תְּתִיהֵב, *Became, was, given*, &c.
Part. מִתְיְהֵב, Ezra iv. 20; vi. 9. Def. מִתְיַהֲבָא, Ezra vi. 8.
— pl. מִתְיַהֲבִין, Ib. vii. 19.

יהד, v. Kal non occ.
Hithp. Part. pl. מִתְיַהֲדִים, once, Esth. viii. 17. Arab. تَيَهَّدَ, *Judæus factus est*. *Becoming Jews*, i. e. proselytes to Judaism. I doubt, nevertheless, whether this is the sense of the term. It is hardly conceivable that the Jews could, generally, receive these Gentiles as proselytes on such grounds. We have also the Arab. تَوَهَّدَ, in the sense of *subegit*; and وَهْد, *terra depressa*. *Being, becoming, depressed, humiliated*, seems to me to suit the place much better, as opposed to the שִׂמְחָה, and שָׂשׂוֹן, of the Jews.

יְהוּדִי, m.) pl. יְהוּדִים, and יְהוּדִיִּים.
יְהוּדִיָּה, f. } Patronym. of יְהוּדָה. A
יְהוּדִית, f.) Jew; f. Jewess, 2 Kings xvi. 6; xxv. 25; Esth. iv. 7; viii. 1; 1 Chron. iv. 18, &c. Pl. Chald. יְהוּדָאִין. Def. יְהוּדָיֵא, Dan. iii. 8. 12; Ezra iv. 2; v. 1. 5. The last, יְהוּדִית, is used as an adverb, *Judaicè, in the Jewish language*, 2 Kings xviii. 26; Neh. xiii. 24.

יְהוָה, r. הָיָה, or הָוָה: see יָהּ above. The most sacred and unalienable name of God; unknown, however, to the patriarchs, Exod. vi. 3. It is not, therefore, more ancient in all probability than the times of Moses. It may, consequently, be termed the Israelitish designation of the true God; among whom generally it was held blasphemy—up to a considerable antiquity—even to pronounce it, from a mistaken view, perhaps, of Exod. xx. 7; Lev. xxiv. 11. Philo in Vitam Mosis, tom. iii. pp. 519. 529. On this account it has received the vowels either of אֲדֹנָי, or אֱלֹהִים; as, יְהֹוָה, יֱהֹוִה. This latter punctuation takes place whenever the combination אֲדֹנָי יְהוָה occurs; for then, instead of reading אֲדֹנָי twice over, it has been usual to read אֲדֹנָי אֱלֹהִים. See Gram. art. 159. 2. Whether either of these, or what really was, the ancient pronunciation of this word, it is utterly impossible now to say: nor is it of much importance either to the critic or the theologian, how this question is determined. Gesenius has industriously collected all that is worth attention on this subject from the Greeks and Latins, of which the following is the sum. According to Diodorus Siculus, lib. i. 94, Moses gave the name ΙΑΩ to God. Ἱστοροῦσι—Μωσῆν τὸν ΙΑΩ ἐπικαλούμενον θεόν—. Macrob. Sat. i. 18; Hesych. v. Ὀζείας, Intp. ad Clem. Alex. Strom. v. p. 666. Theod. quæst. 15, ad Exod. καλοῦσι δὲ αὐτὸ Σαμαρεῖται, ΙΑΒΕ (יָהֶוֶה) Ἰουδαῖοι δὲ ΙΑΩ. The same form is found on the gems of the Egyptian Gnostics (Irenæus adv. Hæres, i. 34; ii. 26. See Bellermann über die Gemmen der alten mit dem Abraxasbilde i. ii.) Philo Byblius, Prep. Evangel. Euseb. i. 9, gives the form ΙΕΥΩ. Clem. Alexand. Strom. v. p. 562. ΙΑΟΥ (יָהוּ) Reland—De vera pronunciatione nominis Jehovah, Traj. ad Rhen. 1707—with others following the Samaritan form, יְהֹוָה, takes his stand generally on the abbreviated form יָהוּ, and יָהּ. The controversy, too, of Nicolas Fuller, and Drusias, may be consulted on this subject. Gesenius next tells us his own opinion is, that this word is of the most remote antiquity:—(not, one would think from Exod. vi. 3, cited above, more ancient than the times of Moses; to which the testimony of Diodorus Siculus well agrees)—and he doubts whether it is not of the same origin with the Latin *Jovis, Jupiter*, which might have passed over from the Egyptians to the Hebrews, and have been moulded into a Shemitic form, in order to secure to it the appearance of Shemitic origin and usage. We are then referred to the terms מֹשֶׁה, and בְּהֵמוֹת, as of similar character; which, under these terms, will be seen to be quite groundless. That, אֶהְיֶה אֲשֶׁר אֶהְיֶה, Exod. iii. 14, has reference to this term, I think there can be no doubt; and that the Apocalyptic (Ch. i. 4. 8), ὁ ὢν καὶ ὁ ἦν καὶ ὁ ἐρχόμενος, refers to it likewise is, perhaps, equally certain. But these relate to its interpretation; not to its form, nor to its pronunciation. And, as this is manifestly the most important part of the inquiry, let us see what can be deduced from it.

It is quite certain, then, that the latter place in the Apocalypse applies to Christ; comp. vv. 7, 8.17, 18. A similar passage occurs, Heb. xiii. 8, Ἰησοῦς Χριστὸς χθὲς καὶ σήμερον ὁ αὐτὸς, καὶ εἰς τοὺς αἰῶνας: both these, therefore, cannot but refer to Christ. Again, reference (Rev. i. 17) is certainly made to Is. xli. 4; and there יְהוָה is the person designated *the First, &c.;* and, in truth, the theology of the Hebrews will admit of this term being applied to no other.*

Now, the spirit of the Scriptures goes principally to the point of a *revealed, manifested,* and *known God:* not to a mere theoretical, or metaphysically imagined, deity. See under דָּבָר, p. 126, above: to a Θεὸς ὃς ἐφανερώθη (1 Tim. iii. 16. Comp. 1 John i. 2; iii. 8; 1 Pet. i. 20): and, as the term אֱלֹהִים, had, before the time of Moses (Gen. xxxi. 30, &c.) been applied to idols, the representatives of these metaphysical non-entities, it seems to me that the terms אֶהְיֶה, and יְהוָה — more particularly the latter — were chosen in order to keep up this marked

---

* From an extended inquiry, instituted on comparisons of this sort, the most irrefragable proofs of the divinity of Christ might be collected. And it will be found eventually that it is quite impossible to understand innumerable passages of the Old Testament on any other view.

and very important distinction; and, above all, to keep up the memorial of his promised manifestation in the flesh. Comp. Is. vii. 14, with Ib. ix. 5, 6, and Mic. v. 2—4; which was apparently had in view in the passages cited above from the Epistle to the Hebrews, the Revelation of St. John, &c., and to show that in Jesus of Nazareth the person named יְהֹוָה, in the Old Testament, was manifested to the world.

That the term יְהֹוָה occurs occasionally in books older than the times of Moses, is obvious enough; but, in all those places, the term might have been inserted by Moses himself, as it is certain other names — of places for example — have also been inserted in the book of Genesis. See my Proleg. to Mr. Bagster's Polyglott Bible, I. § iii. 2. . . . As to the usage of the Egyptians, Latins, &c., of any name or names allied to this, or to any other, found in the ancient Scriptures; if such usage can be found, *its antiquity* must be proved before the insinuation of Gesenius, and others of his school, as given above, can be admitted. But, as no such proof can be made out; and, as it is notorious that the heathen of all ages have borrowed largely from revelation; if any use can be made of resemblances of that sort, it must be to show, that the heathen have been the borrowers, and not the sacred writers. Gesenius tells us, moreover, that this was the Θεὸς ἐπιχώριος of the Old Testament. But this is not true. The ancient orthodox Hebrews never held any such notion. Their doctrine was, that יְהֹוָה made the heavens, the earth, the sea, and all that therein was: and that although not recognised, yet He was in truth the God, and the only God, of all nations under heaven. It is astonishing to witness the blindness with which these heathenish notions are constantly ascribed to the writers of both Testaments, by this very enlightened school of divines.

As to the grammatical application of this term: It is subject to no variety, either in its vowels or form, for the state of construction. It has no plural number, and never receives any affixed pronoun. The prepositions it does receive, as, בִּיהוָֹה, לַיהוָֹה, מֵיהוָֹה; read לַאדֹנָי, &c. It is found in construction with other nouns; as, נְאֻם יְהוָֹה, *dictum Domini.* עַם יְהוָֹה, *people of Jehovah.* הֵיכַל יְהוָֹה, רוּחַ יְהוָֹה, יְהוָֹה, &c. In like manner, first in the construction, as, יְהוָֹה צְבָאוֹת; but this is elliptical for יְהוָֹה אֱלֹהֵי צְבָאוֹת, *Jehovah,*

God of Hosts; where יְהוָֹה is in apposition with the following terms: so in יְהוָֹה אֱלֹהִים, יְהוָֹה הָאֱלֹהִים, *Jehovah, God:* but, here, should the context require it, the first might be the subject; the last, the predicate, of a sentence. So also in the phrr. יְהוָֹה אֱלֹהֵי יִשְׂרָאֵל, *Jehovah, God of Israel,* Josh. vii. 13, &c. יְהוָֹה אֱלֹהֵי אֲבוֹתֶיךָ, *Jehovah, the God of thy fathers,* Deut. i. 21, &c. יְהוָֹה אֱלֹהַי, *Jehovah, my God.* יְהוָֹה אֱלֹהֶיךָ, *Jehovah, thy God, &c.,* Deut. i. 1. 31, &c. In אֲדֹנָי יְהוִֹה, where the latter word is read אֱלֹהִים,—see above,—the combination is that of apposition.

יָחִיר, m. pl. non occ. r. יהר. Arab. يَهَر, *locus amplus;* يَبْهَر, *durus lapis;* r. تَبَهَّر, v. اِسْتَيْهَر, *dementatus fuit.* Cogn. وَهَر, *ardor, ex radiis solis in terra repercussis, ita ut vapor aliquis huc illuc motitari appareat.* Engl. vulg. *swell.* *Haughty, conceited, vain,* person, Prov. xxi. 24; Hab. ii. 5, al. non occ.

יַחֲלֹם, m. pl. non occ. r. הלם, lit. *malleable,* i. e. here, will not give way at the stroke of the hammer. Some precious stone. *The adamant,* or, as the ancient versions occasionally have, the *emerald,* or the *jasper;* the former most likely, Exod. xxviii. 18; xxxix. 11; Ezek. xxviii. 13, al. non occ.

יוֹבֵל, masc. pl. יוֹבְלִים. Arab. وَبَلَ, *acriter persecutus fuit; imbrem effudit, &c.* Syr. ܢܒܠ, *deduxit, adduxit;* whence יוֹבֵל, *processus aquarum, rivus.* See r. יבל. *Drawing out* at length, seems to be the primary sense: the secondary, *running, flowing out,* as waters. Gesenius here gives us an elaborate comparison of this word with יְלִל, אלל; Arabic ولول, انتحب; Gr. ὀλολύζειν, &c. Lat. *ejulare, &c.* Germ. *jauchzen;* Sweed. *iolen—jâl, jobl, jodl, &c.,* to shew that this word, and תְּרוּעָה, *shout,* mean the same thing. For my own part, I can see no connexion whatever, either between these two words, or this one word, and his synonymes, or cognates; while, *drawing out, lengthening,* as in the course of a river, the processions of the Jubilee, or the sound of a horn, seem obvious and natural enough.—*The Jubilee,* a feast of the Jews, announced by the sounding of horns, on the seventh day of the seventh month in the year, immediately succeeding every period of seven times seven years; i. e. on this day of this month, every recurring *fiftieth year*, Lev. xxv. 9—11. 13. 15. 31. 40. Josephus Antiq. lib. iii. 12. And, at this period, the person and property of every Israelite, in any way incumbered with servitude or debt, became free. Hence, the ἔτος ἀφέσεως, and ἄφεσις, of the LXX. Phr. בִּמְשֹׁךְ בְּקֶרֶן הַיּוֹבֵל, *in the lengthening out, continuing the sound, with the horn of the Jubilee, &c.*, or, more literally, *of the Jubilee-er*, i. e. of the person usually announcing the Jubilee with it, Josh. vi. 5; Exod. xix. 13, בִּמְשֹׁךְ הַיֹּבֵל. In Josh. vi. 6, שׁוֹפְרוֹת יוֹבְלִים; Ib. 4. 8. 13. שׁוֹפְרוֹת הַיּוֹבְלִים, not etymologically the same thing with שׁוֹפָר תְּרוּעָה, Lev. xxv. 9, as Gesenius will have it; although exegetically there is no essential difference between them. The same may be said of תָּקַע בַּשּׁוֹפָרוֹת, Josh. vi. 4, 5. A similar mistake has been made by the Jews in the phr. קֶרֶן הַיּוֹבֵל, where, from the consideration that this horn was a ram's horn, they came to the conclusion that יֹבֵל here meant a ram!

The note of Gesenius here, in which he tells us that the usage of both יֹבֵל, and יוֹבְלִים, rests on an idiom not generally understood, and which is found in three different forms; means only, that, as a singular noun may be taken generically signifying all or many of the class to which it belongs, so the singular or plural may be used either in the first or second word in the construction, or both: a thing well known to the Grammarians. See Gram. artt. 142; 215. 5, &c.

יוּבַל, m. once, Jer. xvii. 8, i. q. אוּבָל, which see. In all probability, an artificial *streamlet* or *channel*, by which water *is drawn* from rivers, &c., into gardens and other plantations, i. q. פֶּלֶג מַיִם, Ps. i. 3. See Wisdom of Sirach. xxiv. 30 (41 Polygl.), ὡς διῶρυξ ἀπὸ ποταμοῦ, καὶ ὡς ὑδραγωγὸς ἐξῆλθον εἰς παράδεισον.

יוֹם, c. dual. יוֹמַיִם, pl. יָמִים (for יוֹמִים, Gram. art. 73). Constr. יְמֵי (for יָמֵי, of יוֹמֵי). Arab. وَآم, *domus calida.* Cogn. وَآب, *iratus est*; ܐܷܬ݂ܚܰܡܰܬ݂, *ferbuit dies.* Taking its name apparently from the warmth of day, as contradistinguished from the cold of the night. So also, Gesen. Arab. يَوْم Syr. ܝܰܘܡܳܐ, *dies.* (a) *The natural day*, from sunset to sunset, including the space of twenty-four hours, Gen. i. 5. 8. 13, &c. (b) *The day*, as distinguished from *night*, Ib. vv. 4, 5. 14. 16. 18, &c. Meton. (c) *Any period* of time, as made up of days; as, שְׁנֵי חַיֶּיךָ, *the days of the years of thy life*, i. e. its whole space, Gen. xlvii. 8. בִּימֵי אַבְרָהָם, *in the days of Abraham*, Gen. xxvi. 1. So 2 Sam. xxi. 1, &c. בַּיָּמִים הָהֵם, *in those days*, Exod. ii. 11. כָּל־הַיָּמִים, *the whole of the, or those, days*, i. e. continually. הֶאֱרִיךְ יָמָיו, *he prolonged his days*, Deut. iv. 26. 40; v. 30, &c. בָּא בַיָּמִים, *he had entered into days*, i. e. had grown old, Gen. xxiv. 1. Metaph. יָמִים יְדַבֵּרוּ, *let days speak*, i. e. the experienced, Job xxxii. 7. — מִיָּמִים, *from*, i. e. *since thy days*, times of thy life, Job xxxviii. 12. שְׁנָתַיִם יָמִים, *two years, days*, i. e. period of —, Gen. xli. 1, &c. חֹדֶשׁ יָמִים, *a month, days*, i. e. days, period, of a month, Gen. xxix. 14, Id. שְׁלֹשָׁה שָׁבֻעִים יָמִים, יָח יָמִים, Deut. xxi. 13, &c. *three weeks, days*, i. e. period of —, Dan. x. 2, 3. Comp. Amos iv. 4. In the singular, (d) Distribution, repetition, or the like, seems to be intended; as, כָּל־הַיּוֹם, lit. *the whole of this day*, i. e. as if this, or the present, day were to be repeated distributively, Ps. xlii. 4. 11; xliv. 23; lii. 3, &c. not unlike, לַבְּקָרִים, Ib. lxxiv. 22; lxxxvi. 3, &c. LXX. καθ᾽ ἑκάστην ἡμέραν. When so limited by the context, (e) *The whole of this present day*, Is. lxii. 6; opp. כָּל־הַלַּיְלָה, Ps. xxxii. 3, &c. LXX. ὅλην τὴν ἡμέραν. יָמִים עַל־שְׁנָה, Exod. xiii. 10. יָמִים עַל־שָׁנָה, lit. *days upon year*, i. e. for an indefinite period, Is. xxxii. 10. יָמִים שְׁנַיִם, *days, period, of two years*, 2 Chron. xxi. 19. So the following combinations applied, viz.

(α) הַיּוֹם, *This day, to-day*, i. e. in it, on it, during it, Gen. iv. 14; Exod. xii. 14; xxxiv. 11, &c. opp. הַלַּיְלָה, Neh. iv. 16; Hos. iv. 5. Synon. τοῦ, יוֹמָם. Arab. اليَوْم, or يَوْمًا. In many cases, *the day*, either *absolutely*, or *relatively*, present, i. e. present to the time of the writer or speaker, or to any other time introduced into the narrative, Gram. art. 231. 7; as, 1 Sam. i. 4; xiv. 1, &c. In like manner—

(β) כַּיּוֹם, or כְּהַיּוֹם, *As, on this day*, i. e. as if the thing mentioned should happen *to-day.* See my note on Job i. 6;—Gen. xxv. 31. 33; 1 Kings i. 51; Is. lviii. 4; it. כַּיּוֹם הַזֶּה, *as on this to-day*, i. e. very day, 1 Sam. xxii. 8. 13; Deut. viii. 18; Ezra ix. 7, &c.

(252)

(γ) בְּיוֹם, *On this day*, Jer. xxxvi. 30; Prov. xii. 16, &c.

(δ) מִיּוֹם, *From the day, time*, Exod. x. 6; Deut. ix. 24, &c. So—

(ε) יוֹם יוֹם, *Day*, after *day*. Arab. يَوْمًا فَيَوْمًا, בְּכָל־יוֹם וָיוֹם, יוֹם וָיוֹם, Esth. iii. 4; ii. 11; it. יוֹם בְּיוֹם, id. Neh. viii. 18. בְּיוֹם בְּיוֹם, 1 Sam. xviii. 10. לְיוֹם בְּיוֹם, 2 Chron. xxiv. 11. יוֹם לַשָּׁנָה, Num. xiv. 34. מִיּוֹם אֶל־יוֹם, Ib. xxx. 15, &c.

(f) Applied to any *Particular day*, i. e. on which some remarkable *event* took place; and, Meton.,—to such event as, יוֹם מַלְכֵּנוּ, *the day of our king*, i. e. of his prosperity, Hos. vii. 5: "*natalis*," says Gesenius. But it does not appear that birth-days were ever kept as feasts by the Hebrews; Job iii. 1, is mentioned on a very different account. Comp. Hos. ii. 2. 17; Obad. vr. 12, *Jehovah's day*, i. e. on which his judgments are executed, Is. ix. 3; ii. 12; Joel i. 15; Ezek. xiii. 5; Job xxiv. 1; xxvii. 6, &c. See my note here. In the New Test., 1 Cor. v. 5; 2 Cor. i. 14, &c.: it. Rom. xiv. 5, &c.: it. 1 Cor. iv. 3, &c. Phrr. יוֹם טוֹב, 1 Sam. xxv. 8. יוֹם צָרָה, 2 Kings xix. 3. יוֹם אֵידָם, Deut. xxxii. 35, &c.

(g) — of the great feasts, Judg. xvii. 10. זֶבַח הַיָּמִים, *Sacrifice of the days*, i. e. of the seven or eight so appointed to be kept. Comp. 1 Sam. ii. 19; Exod. xii. 15, &c.

(h) Dual, יוֹמַיִם, *Two days*, Exod. xvi. 29, &c. In Hos. vi. 2, יְחַיֵּנוּ מִיֹּמַיִם בַּיּוֹם הַשְּׁלִישִׁי יְקִמֵנוּ, *from* (after) *two days he will revive us; on the third day he will raise us up;* or, as we say in English, *after two or three days*, i. e. a short indefinite period. It may, however, possibly refer to the periods of the great persecutions, mystically designated by "*times times and a half*," "*three days and a half*," &c. See the concluding remarks to my Exposition of the Book of the Revelation, "Sermons and Dissertations."—It would be almost endless to recite every sort of phrase in which this word is found: the instances given, however, will supply analogies, enabling the learner to see the force of the rest.—Some, who are perhaps better Geologists than Biblical critics, have imagined, that, because the term *day* (יוֹם), is sometimes taken to designate *a period* of time, it might therefore signify such period in the account of the creation; and so give them time sufficient to account for certain formations of the earth; but, in these cases, the terms *evening* and *morning* are added, which makes these places look very much like descriptions of natural days. Besides, one might as well expect an account of the laws of rectilinear motion, electricity, &c., as of the phenomena of geology: and something like this John Hutchinson and his followers vainly imagined they found in the Bible. See under בָּרָא. Aff. יוֹמְךָ, יוֹמְךָ, יוֹמָם, pl. יָמַי, יָמֶיךָ, יָמֶיךָ, יָמָיו, יְמֵיכֶם, יָמָיו, &c.

יוֹם, c. Def. יוֹמָא, i. q. Heb. הַיּוֹם, pl. יוֹמִין, def. יוֹמַיָּא. Constr. יוֹמֵי, and יְמֵי. Constr. יוֹמָת. *Day*, as in the Heb. So, יוֹם בְּיוֹם, Ezra vi. 9. יוֹמִין תְּלָתָא, Dan. vi. 8. עַתִּיק יוֹמַיָּא, *the Ancient of days*, Dan. vii. 13. 22; vr. 9, יוֹמִין —. In the former case the combination is that of apposition; or, the second term may be considered as absolute, as in the Arab. حَسَنُ وَجْهٍ, or the Lat. *nuda pedem*. Aff. בְּיוֹמֵיהוֹן, Dan. ii. 44.

יוֹמָם, indecl., Gram. art. 167, adv. *By day*; opp. τῷ, לַיְלָה, Lev. viii. 35; Num. ix. 21; x. 34; xiv. 14, &c. It. constr. i. q. יוֹם, Jer. xxxiii. 20. הֲיוֹת יוֹמָם־וָלַיְלָה, Ib. vr. 25; Ezek. xxx. 16. צָרֵי יוֹמָם, *daily enemies*, or, perhaps, *enemies of that period*, i. e. such as were suitable to it. In Neh. ix. 19, with prep. בְּיוֹמָם: but here יוֹמָם is, perhaps, aff., and cited from Exodus, where the original account of the egress is given; and the prep. prefixed accordingly.

יָוָן, m. The name of one of the sons of Japhet (Gr. Ἴων, son of Xythos), Gen. x. 2; and, hence, of the country possessed by his posterity. See Bochart. Phaleg. lib. iii. c. iii. p. 174. And, from the context in which it is afterwards found, *Greece* generally, Is. lxvi. 19; Ezek. xxvii. 13; Zech. ix. 13; Dan. viii. 21. In Ezek. xxvii. 19, Gesenius takes it to designate يَوَن, or يَوَن, a place in Arabia Felix; but, as it occurs there with the same accompanying term as it does elsewhere, there can be no reason for supposing it to imply a different place. Gr. Ἰωνία, Æschyl. Pers. 773, it. Schol. 176. 563.

יְוָנִי, m. pl. יְוָנִים, for יְוָנִיִּים. Patronym. of יָוָן. *Greeks*, Ἴωνες. Phr. בְּנֵי הַיְוָנִים, Joel iv. 6.

יָוֵן, m. constr. יְוֵן, pl. non occ. Arab. وَنِي *torpor;* v. وَنِي *torpuit:* fin. קֵץ,

יוֹנֵק (253) יוֹרֶה

Gram. art. 159, rejecting ي fin. lit. something which retards, clogs, hinders. *Mire, clay*, Ps. xl. 3; lxix. 3. Comp. Dan. ii. 41, al. non occ.

יוֹנָה, f.—pl. m. יוֹנִים, r. יָנָה, which see. A *dove*, or *pigeon*, so called perhaps from its cooing, as a *cry of oppression*. Comp. Is. xxxviii. 14; lix. 11; Nahum ii. 7; as flying away from this, Ps. lv. 7; Jer. xlviii. 25; Ezek. xvi. 7;—Gen. viii. 8—10; Lev. v. 7; xii. 8, &c. Phr. בְּנֵי יוֹנָה, *young of doves.*— Applied to the Church as the spouse of Christ, Cant. ii. 14; v. 2; vi. 9. Phr. עֵינַיִךְ יוֹנִים, *thy two eyes* are as *doves*, i. e. expressive of sorrow and gentleness, Ib. i. 15. Constr. once, Ps. lvi. 1. יוֹנַת, it. pl. once, יוֹנַי, Ezek. vii. 16. Aff. יוֹנָתִי, Cant. ii. 14, &c.

יוֹנֵק, m. pl. יוֹנְקִים, particip. of יָנַק, which see. (a) *Suckling;* or (b) as applied to the shoots of trees, *sucker;* and, in this acceptation, f. aff. יוֹנַקְתּוֹ, &c.; pl. יוֹנְקוֹת. (a) Deut. xxxii. 25; 1 Sam. xv. 3; Is. xi. 8, &c. (b) Comp. Is. liii. 2; Job viii. 16; xiv. 7; xv. 30; Ezek. xvii. 22; Hos. xiv. 7; Ps. lxxx. 12.

יוֹצֵר, m. pl. יוֹצְרִים, particip. of יָצַר, which see. Lit. one who forms, shapes; or, meton., devises any thing. Applied to God, or man. *Maker, former, deviser, &c.,* synon. τοῦ בָּרָא, Is. xlv. 7. 18; Jer. x. 15; li. 19; Amos iv. 13, &c.; Jer. xix. 1. Hence, pec. *a potter*, Ps. ii. 9; Is. xli. 25; Lam. iv. 2, &c. In Zech. xi. 13, Gesenius thinks that אוֹצָר is either the true reading, or else that this word, by a sort of Chaldaism, ought to take its sense: and he cites the Syriac, as giving this, for the true sense. Every other authority, however, is against him. See LXX. Aquila, πρὸς τὸν πλάστην. The place is cited in Matt. xxvii. 10, and there ascribed to Jeremiah; which is either an error of the Greek copyists, or else may be considered as a proof, that the passage once existed in Jeremiah: it being perfectly incredible that an evangelist could so have exposed himself to the sneers of the Jews, as to have made a citation so erroneous. And, it appears to be the fact, that the Jews of that day never made such objection to the text of any of the evangelists. The citation is, εἰς τὸν ἀγρὸν τοῦ κεραμέως. It should be observed here, that, הִשְׁלִיכֵהוּ, and אַשְׁלִיךְ, must of necessity be taken

in the sense of *declare that it shall be cast, &c.* See Gram. art. 157. 6; the prophet being commissioned to make this declaration: the theological sense only of which the evangelist cites. Again, it is evident, from the context, that *Jehovah's price* is the price had in view, not that of the prophet; or, in other words, that of *Jehovah's fellow*, Zech. xiii. 7. Examine this place, which clearly foretels slaughter with the sword. The price predicted, therefore, is *the price of blood*. And the rabbies, themselves, of the evangelist's day, determined, l. c. vr. 6—9, that it was *unlawful to lay up such money in the treasury;* an authority to which Dr. Gesenius will never object. The evangelist is, therefore, right in giving the sense above cited; and Gesenius, with the Syriac translator, is clearly wrong.

יוֹרֶה, m. pl. יוֹרִים, particip. r. יָרָה. Æth. **ⱷⰄⱷ** : *projectus fuit*. Arab. وَرَى, *ignem emisit;* وَرِي, *ulcus emittens saniem*. (a) *Casting forth*, or *about*, missiles, &c., Prov. xxvi. 18. Hence, *Archer*, 1 Chron. x. 3; 2 Chron. xxxv. 23. (b) — *water, sprinkling, watering*, as by rain, Hos. vi. 3. Pec. *the former rain*, i. e. of the ancient Hebrew year.—But see Part. of v. יָרָה below,—Deut. xi. 14; Jer. v. 24, al. non occ.

יֶתֶר, יוֹתֵר, m. } plur. non occ.
יוֹתֶרֶת, f. } particip. r. יתר.

Syr. ܝܰܬܰܪ, *lucratus est*. Arab. وَتَرَ, *imminuit*, i. e. by taking away some supposed excess; hence, *discretam effecit* rem: iii. *unum post alium produxit liberos*. Cogn. وَتْر, lit. *exceeding; excess*. Hence, (a) *Abundance, profit*, Eccl. vi. 8: (b) adv. *move, further*, Eccl. ii. 15; vii. 11; xii. 12; Esth. vi. 6: with מִן, Ib. vii. 16, *excessively*, i. e. in things beyond thy reach. — וְיֹתֵר שֶׁ, *and moreover, since, because*, Eccl. xii. 9. See also Nold., p. 341.

Fem. *Exceeding, redundant*, constr. med. יֹתֶרֶת, with עַל, Exod. xxix. 43; Lev. iii. 19; immed. Exod. xxix. 22; Lev. viii. 16. 25, &c.: but always in similar construction. See LXX. *The lobe*, or *excess, of the liver*.

יוֹזְבָח, m. for אֲחִרְחִי, 1 Chron. xxvii. 8.

יָזַע, m. i. q. זֵעָה, once, Ezek. xliv. 18.

יחד (254) יחי

Gesen. "Amhar. Ⲙ፡ pro, ⲘⲎⲞ፡ sudavit." But this is nothing more than the Æthiop. ⲘⲀⲎ፡ ⲘⲐⲎ፡ or ⲘⲐⲞ፡ i. q. Heb. יָצָא. *Out-going, &c.* Better, Arab. cogn. وَزَغَ, *sparsim excrevit* urinam; وَزَغَ, id. Of which וַיֵּצֵא is clearly a derivative, not greatly differing in sense from צֵאָה.

יָחַד, m. Aff. יַחְדָּיו, or יַחְדָּו. Cogn. אֶחָד. Syr. Ethpa. ܐܶܬܚܰܝܰܕ, *unitus est. Union, agreement,* 1 Chron. xii. 17. Adv. (a) *As one:* hence, (b) *singly; at once:* (c) *wholly, together, altogether, entirely, &c.*, וַיִּקְבְּצוּ...יָחַד, 1 Sam. xi. 11; Is. l. 8; xxii. 3; l. 8; Ps. cxxxiii. 1; Job iii. 18: (b) Job xxxiv. 29; Ezra iv. 3;—Job x. 8; 2 Sam. xiv. 6; Ps. xxxiii. 15: (c) Job iii. 18; Deut. xxxiii. 5; Mic. ii. 12; Is. xxiv. 7, &c. Where it will be observed that the signification will vary, without affecting essentially the exegetical sense, according as we view the subject matter, either distributively, or in the aggregate. With aff. we have a pleonasm of the pronoun; which, as far as reference can take place, refers to the main subject preceding; as, לָשֶׁבֶת יַחְדָּו, *for his,* i. e. the people's, *dwelling as one,* or *together,* Gen. xiii. 6. It signifies nothing that this subject be occasionally a plural, because the very introduction of this term compels the reader to view the whole as *a whole,* or *singly,* Deut. xii. 22; 1 Kings iii. 18; 1 Chron. x. 6; Is. xviii. 6, &c. See Nold., p. 342, seq.

יָחַד, v. pret. non occ. pres. יֵחַד, r. יחד above. Constr. med. אֶת, בְּ, pers. *Unite, be as one,* Gen. xlix. 6; Is. xiv. 20.

Pih. once, יַחֵד (for יִיַחֵד, Gram. art. 73). *Unite, make as one,* Ps. lxxxvi. 11.

יָחִיד, m. pl. יְחִידִים } Participial noun. יְחִידָה, f. pl. non occ. } Lit. *reduced to one, deserted, &c. Only,* or *solitary,* one, Ps. xxv. 16; Prov. iv. 3: pl. Ps. lxviii. 7, al. non occ. Pec. an *only child,* Gen. xxii. 2. 12. 16; Jer. vi. 26; Amos viii. 10: fem. Judg. xi. 34. Aff. יְחִידָתִי, with נַפְשִׁי, Ps. xxii. 21; xxxv. 17: where Gesenius thinks it means *life,* " *pro vita.*" *My only one* is the literal sense, which can hardly be applied to the life of any one, and never is, as far as my knowledge goes, in any Oriental usage whatever. The sense here is, most likely mystical, and, if so, "*king's daughter*" (בַּת־מֶלֶךְ), of Ps. xlv. 14; afterwards (vr. 15, seq.), *the king's spouse,* representing Christ's Church, is meant; and the times of the great persecution are probably referred to. Comp. 2 Tim. iv. 17. Aquila, μοναχήν. Sym. μονότητα. LXX. μονογενῆ. It is natural enough, indeed, to find nothing beyond generals in the declarations of the Bible, when its theology is neglected.

יָחִיל, m. once, Lam. iii. 26, r. יחל. One *expecting, waiting for.*

יָחַל, v. Kal non occ. Cogn. τοῦ, הוֹל (c). Syr. ܣܰܟܺܝ, *desperavit.* Arab. حَال, r. حول, *uno extitit anno;* حَال, *tempus.* Æth. ⲘⲞⲚ፡ *diem transegit.*

Pih. יִחֵל, pres. יְיַחֵל. Contr. and apoc. יָחֵל, Gen. viii. 10. Constr. abs. it. immed. it. med. עַל, לְ, אֶל. (a) *Expect, wait, hope for* —, Ps. xxxiii. 22; cxix. 43. 74. 91. 114. 147; Job vi. 11; xiii. 15; xxix. 23; Ezek. xiii. 6; Mic. v. 6, &c.: (b) *Cause to hope,* Ps. cxix. 49. יַחֵלוּ, see חָלָה.

Imper. יַחֵל, Ps. cxxx. 7.
Part. מְיַחֵל, pl. מְיַחֲלִים, Ps. lxix. 4; xxxi. 25, &c.

Niph. נוֹחֲלָה, f. pres. יִיָּחֵל, i. q. Pih. (a) Ezek. xix. 5; Gen. viii. 12.

Hiph. הוֹחִיל, pres. אוֹחִיל, it. יֹחֵל. Constr. med. לְ, person and thing, it. abs. i. q. Pih. 1 Sam. x. 8; xiii. 8; 2 Sam. xviii. 14; Job xxxii. 11; Ps. xlii. 6, &c.

יָחַם, pret. non occ. pres. יֵחַם, for יִיחַם, Gram. art. 200. 4, 5. יְחֵמָה, m. by an Arabism. Arab. وَحَم, *appetitus,* pec. *venerei congressus.* Cogn. חמם. (a) *Be warm, in heat,* as animals for the male: hence, (b) meton. *conceive:* (c) *be hot* with anger. (a) *Be, become, warm,* 1 Kings i. 1; Eccl. iv. 11: as animals, (b) *conceive, &c.,* Gen. xxx. 38, 39. Metaph. of a lewd woman, compared with a heated pot, Ezek. xxiv. 11. (c) *Be hot* with anger, Deut. xix. 6. All of which, however, might be pres. Niph. of חמם, as many have remarked: still the same would be the same.

Niph. Part. pl. m. נֵחָמִים, *Persons becoming heated* with idolatrous fornication. Metaph. Is. lvii. 5.

Pih. pret. f. aff. יֶחֱמַתְנִי. Meton. *She conceived me,* Ps. li. 7.

Infin. יַחֵם, Gen. xxx. 41. בְּכָל־יַחֵם הַצֹּאן, *In, at, every conception* of the flock. Comp.

יחם (255) יטב

xxxi. 10. Aff. יַחְמָה, *their conception*, Ib. xxx. 41.

יַחְמוּר, masc.—plur. non occ. Arab. كَمُور, *A sort of goat or gazelle*, of a brownish colour. See Bochart. Hieroz. i. p. 913. The *cervus dama* of Linnæus, according to Oedmann, Deut. xiv. 5; 1 Kings v. 3.

יָחֵף, masc.—plur. non occ. Arab. خَفِي, *nudis pedibus fuit.* Syr. ܚܦܝ, *nudipes. Bare-footed*, 2 Sam. xv. 30; Is. xx. 2—4; Jer. ii. 25. מְיָחֵף, ellip. for מִהְיוֹת יָחֵף, *from being bare*, exposed.

יחר, v. pres. יֵיחַר, or יֵחַר, once, 2 Sam. xx. 5, i. q. אחר. *Tarrying.* The Keri reads יוֹחֵר. Hiph. al. non occ.

יחש, v. Kal, non occ. Arab. وخش, conj. ii. *projecit; protendit cum brachio manum; miscuit.*
Hithp. הִתְיַחֵשׂ, pres. non occ. *Being, becoming, registered*, as to pedigree. Constr. abs. med. בְּ, in, of time, לְ, thing, 1 Chron. v. 1. 7. 17; ix. 1; Ezra viii. 3, &c.
Infin. הִתְיַחֵשׂ, *Being registered, registration*, 1 Chron. v. 1; 2 Chron. xii. 15, &c.
Aff. הִתְיַחְשָׂם, 1 Chron. vii. 5. 7, &c.
Part. pl. m. מִתְיַחְשִׂים, *Registered* persons, Ezra ii. 62: Neh. vii. 64, al. non occ.

יטב, v. pret. non occ. Cogn. טוֹב, pres. יֵיטַב, יִיטַב. Constr. abs. it. med. בְּ, instr. לְ, pers. it. לִפְנֵי, בְּעֵינֵי, *Be*, or *seem, good, happy*. יִיטַב לֵב, *the heart be happy, glad*, Eccl. vii. 3; Judg. xix. 6, &c. יִיטַב לִפְנֶיךָ — עֶבֶדְךָ, *thy servant seems good to thy presence*; impers. Neh. ii. 5. יִיטַב בְּעֵינֶיךָ, *it seem good in thy eyes*, 1 Sam. xxiv. 5. יִיטַב לָכֶם, Jer. vii. 23; Esth. ii. 4. Constr. med. מִן, of comparison, *be, seem, better*. תִּיטַב לַיהוָה מִשּׁוֹר, *shall seem good to Jehovah, rather than*, i. e. *better, than an ox*, Ps. lxix. 32. Gesenius places תִּיטְבִי, Nahum iii. 8, here; but it manifestly belongs to Hiph.
Hiph. הֵיטִיב, pres. יֵיטִיב, f. תֵּיטִבִי. Constr. abs. it. immed. it. med. עִם, אֶל, pers. אֶת, pers. thing, it. לְ, pers. or Infin. בְּ, Instr. (a) *Do good, well, to* —, Gen. iv. 7; xii. 16; xxxii. 10; Josh. xxiv. 20; 1 Sam. xxv. 31; Deut. xxx. 5. הֵיטַבְתָּ לִרְאוֹת, *thou hast done well to see*, i. e. *hast well, rightly, seen*, Jer. ii. 12.
Pres. f. תֵּיטִבִי, and תֵּיטְבִי, Jer. ii. 33;

Nahum iii. 8. The slight irregularity in the vowels of the last, is owing, probably, to the copyists.
(b) *Make good, ready; prepare.* Syr. ܛܒ, Exod. xxx. 7; 2 Kings ix. 30; Hos. x. 1.
Infin. הֵיטֵב, הֵיטִיב, *Doing well, thoroughly, effectually.* הֵיטֵב אֵיטִיב, *I will do thoroughly well* with thee, Gen. xxxii. 13. הֵיטֵב טָחוֹן, *grinding thoroughly*, Deut. ix. 21. Comp. xiii. 15; xvii. 4; xix. 18; Is. i. 17; Jer. vii. 5; Jonah iv. 4, &c. With לְ, pref., Lev. v. 4; Deut. xxviii. 43, &c. It. aff. xxxii. 40; Deut. viii. 16; Exod. xxx. 7. (b)
Imp. הֵיטִיבָה, parag. ה, f. הֵיטִיבִי, pl. m. הֵיטִיבוּ, Ps. li. 20; cxxv. 4; Is. xxxiii. 16; Ps. xxxiii. 3; Jer. vii. 3, &c.
Part. מֵיטִיב, מֵיטִב, מֵטִב, pl. מֵיטִבִים. Constr. מֵיטִבֵי, מֵיטִיבֵי, 1 Sam. xvi. 17; Ps. cxix. 68; Ezek. xxxiii. 32; Judg. xix. 22; Prov. xxx. 29.

יְטַב, v. Chald. pres. יִיטַב, i. q. Kal Heb. Ezra vii. 18.

יַיִן, constr. יֵין, pl. non occ. Æth. ወይን: *vitis, vinea, vinum.* Engl. *a vine.* Arab. وَيْن, unit; وَيْنَة. Gr. οἶνος; *vinum; uvæ nigricantes. Wine.* Ph?r. בֵּית הַיַּיִן, Cant. ii. 4. בֵּית מִשְׁתֵּה הַיַּיִן, Esth. vii. 8. *Banquetting wine-house.* Metan. *Drunkenness* by wine, Gen. ix. 24; 1 Sam. i. 14; xxv. 37. Hence the idioms, יַיִן תַּרְעֵלָה, apposition. *Wine, trembling*, i. e. causing trembling instead of intoxication, Ps. lx. 5. חֲלוּמֵי יַיִן, *the beaten, bruised, of wine*, Is. xxviii. 1. נִבְלְעוּ מִן הַיַּיִן, *they are swallowed up of wine*, i. e. ruined by it, Ib. 7. Wine of Lebanon, &c., Hos. xiv. 8; Ezek. xxvii. 18. Metaph. perhaps, in every case in the Canticles. So Deut. xxxii. 33, &c.

יָן, for יָד, 1 Sam. iv. 13, by an error of the copyists. See the Keri.

יכח, v. Kal non occ. Arab. وكح, *validè conculcavit* pede suo; cogn. وكح, *pugno percussit*; كوح, r. كوح, *pugnando vicit*, &c. Æth. ጦሐቀ: *disceptavit.*
Hiph. הוֹכִיחַ, pres. יוֹכִיחַ. Constr. abs. it. immed. it. med. אֶת, לְ, עִם, אֶל, בֵּין, it. בְּ, instr. מִן, by, of pers. (a) *Shew, evince, argue, convince*, Gen. xxi. 25; xxiv. 14. 44;

יכי (256) ילד

Prov. ix. 25; Job vi. 25; xiii. 10. 15; xv. 3. (b) Meton. *Convict, chastise, punish*, 2 Sam. vii. 14; 2 Kings xix. 4; Is. ii. 4; xi. 4; xxxvi. 4; Mic. iv. 3; Hab. i. 12; Ps. vi. 2; Job v. 17; Prov. iii. 12, &c.

Infin. הוֹכֵחַ, Lev. xix. 17, &c.

Imp. הוֹכַח, Prov. ix. 5.

Part. מוֹכִיחַ, pl. מוֹכִיחִים, Job ix. 33; Prov. xxiv. 25.

Hoph. הוּכַח, once, Job xxxiii. 19. *Is, becomes reproved, chastised*.

Niph. נוֹכַח, pres. 1st pers. pl. with ה, parag. נִוָּכְחָה. *Be, become, contending*, Is. i. 18.

Part. נוֹכָח, Job xxiii. 7: f. נֹכַחַת, Gen. xx. 16. See r. נכח.

Hithp. once, pres. יִתְוַכַּח, i. q. Niph. Mic. vi. 2.

יָכִיל, m. pl. יְכִלִין. Chald. r. יכל. *Able, powerful, capable of*, Dan. iii. 17; iv. 34: pl. Ib. ii. 27; iv. 16.

יָכִינִי, m. Patron. of יָכִין, Num. xxvi. 12.

יָכֹל, rarely יָכוֹל, v.—pres. of Hoph. אֻכַּל, אוּכַל, יַל, יוּכַל. See Gram. art. 188. 2. 3. Constr. abs. it. immed. it. med. לְ, מִן, עִם. Cogn. כוֹל, כִּיל, כָּלָה, כֹּל. Arab. وَكَلَ, *commisit rem suam alteri, in ejus potestate reliquit fretus ipso. Being, becoming, capable of, able, for, or equal to, any action, pers.,* &c., *so as to succeed, prevail, overcome,* &c. וַיַּרְא כִּי לֹא יָכֹל לוֹ, *and he saw that he was not able for him*, i. e. prevailed not against him, Gen. xxx. 8; xxxii. 26. 28; 1 Sam. xvii. 9; Ps. cxxix. 2; Obad. i. 7; Jer. xxxviii. 22, &c;—Gen. xxxvi. 7. לֹא יָכְלוּ—מִגּוּרֵיהֶם, *was not capable of, able for, their residings*. So with Infin., Gen. xxxvii. 4; Judg. viii. 3; Ps. xxxvi. 13, &c. With pers., Ps. xiii. 5: thing, Is. i. 13; xlvi. 2. Med. לְ, Infin., Gen. xlv. 1; Exod. xl. 35; 1 Kings iv. 15, &c.: it. med. or immed., Job xxxi. 23; Deut. i. 9; xiv. 24, &c. Abs., Exod. viii. 14; 2 Kings iii. 26; Jonah i. 13; Jer. iii. 5; Hos. viii. 5. לֹא יוּכְלוּ נְקֹיוֹן, *shall they be incapable of innocency*, Ps. xxi. 12. בַּל־יוּכְלוּ, *they are by no means capable of*. Comp. Jer. v. 22; xx. 11.

Infin. abs. יָכוֹל, יָכֹל, Num. xiii. 30; 1 Sam. xxvi. 25.

— constr. יְכֹלֶת, Num. xiv. 16; Deut. ix. 28.

יְכֵל, יָכִל f. יָכְלָה, v. Chald. of יָכֹל above. Constr. med. לְ, pres. יִכַּל, תִּכַּל, it. יוּכַל, Dan. ii. 47; vi. 21; vii. 21: pres. v. 16. Kethiv, תוכל, see keri, Ib. iii. 29; ii. 6.

Part. יָכִל, pl. יָכְלִין (of יְכַל). See above.

יֶלֶד, m. pl. יְלָדִים, constr. יַלְדֵי, once, erroneously no doubt, יִלְדֵי, Is. lvii. 4, i. q. בֵּן. וָלָד, וֶלֶד. Arab. وَلَدٌ, *proles*; وَلَدٌ, *filius*. Æth. ወልድ: id. Gr. υἱός. The primitive notion seems to have existed in *putting forth;* thence, *increase*. Comp. وَلَد, conj. vi. *numerosi evaserunt;* and Heb. צֶאֱצָא, צֶאֱצָאִים, propr. abstr. *parturition, &c*. Hence, *Child, boy*. Engl. *lad*, or *young man*, Gen. xxi. 8. 14—16; xxxvii. 30; 1 Kings xii. 8. 10. 14, &c.; Is. ix. 5. "κατ' ἐξοχὴν *de regis filio*," says Gesenius; but it will be difficult to find the son of any earthly king, of whom it may be said, that, to the increase of his government and peace, there shall be no end; not to insist on the other things there said of him, which cannot apply to any mortal whatsoever. The translation of Aquila is, ὅτι παιδίον ἐγεννήθη ἡμῖν, υἱὸς ἐδόθη ἡμῖν, καὶ ἐγένετο τὸ μέτρον ἐπ' ὤμου αὐτοῦ· καὶ ἐκλήθη (al. ἐκάλεσε) τὸ ὄνομα αὐτοῦ θαυμαστός, σύμβουλος, ἰσχυρός, δυνατός, πατὴρ ἔτι, ἄρχων εἰρήνης. Sym.... υἱὸς ἐδόθη ἡμῖν, καὶ ἔσται ἡ παιδεία αὐτοῦ ἐπὶ τοῦ ὤμου αὐτοῦ, καὶ κληθήσεται τὸ ὄνομα αὐτοῦ παραδοξασμός, βουλευτικός, ἰσχυρός, δυνατός, πατὴρ αἰῶνος, ἄρχων εἰρήνης. Theod..... καὶ ἔσται ἡ παιδεία αὐτοῦ ἐπὶ τοῦ ὤμου αὐτοῦ, καὶ ἐκάλεσε τὸ ὄνομα αὐτοῦ θαυμαστῶς βουλεύων, ἰσχυρός, δυνάστης, πατὴρ αἰῶνος, ἄρχων εἰρήνης.. Where the πατὴρ ἔτι of Aquila may be remarked as an instance of his κακοζηλία: the πατὴρ αἰῶνος, of the two latter translators, as evincing a singular insight into this very important passage of Holy Writ. Phrr. יֶלֶד שַׁעֲשׁוּעִים, *child of great delights;* very delightful child, Jer. xxxi. 20. יֶלֶד זְקֻנִים, *child of age*, Gen. xliv. 20. נֶפֶשׁ־הַיֶּלֶד, *the soul of the child*, 1 Kings xvii. 21; plainly indicating the separation of the soul from the body, in death. יַלְדֵי־פֶשַׁע, *children of vice*, Is. lvii. 4. Comp. Hos. i. 2, and Is. ii. 6. Of the produce of beasts, Is. xi. 7; Job xxxviii. 41. Aff. pl. יְלָדַי, יְלָדָיו, יְלָדֶיהָ, יַלְדֵיהֶם, יַלְדֵיהֶן.

יַלְדָּה, f. pl. יְלָדוֹת, *Female child, girl*, Gen. xxxiv. 4; Joel iv. 3; Zech. viii. 5, al. non occ.

יָלַד

יָלַד, v. pres. יֵלֵד.—In Ps. ii. 7; Jer. xv. 10; ii. 27, with (·) on the second rad. after the Chaldee manner, by error of the copyists most likely. See יֵלֵד above. Constr. immed. it. med. אֵת, לְ, to whom. Lit. *put forth*,— see יָצָא, מִלֵּט, פָּלַט,—seems to be the primitive notion. Hence—

(a) *Bring forth* as a mother, Gen. iv. 1. 22; xvi. 1. 15, &c. Of beasts, Gen. xxx. 39. Of birds, producing eggs, Jer. xvii. 11. Metaph. of wickedness, Job xv. 35; Ps. vii. 15. Comp. Is. xxxiii. 11; Prov. xxvii. 1. Of the day, Zeph. ii. 2.

(b) — as a father, *beget*,— comp. Gen. xxxv. 11—Gen. iv. 18; x. 8. 13, &c. Of God, Deut. xxxii. 18, as *Creator*. Of idols, Jer. ii. 27. From which places Gesenius thinks he has found a solution for the difficulty in Ps. ii. 7, "*This day have I begotten thee*," i. e. says he, "*te regem creavi*," "*constitui*, nimirum spiritum divinum tibi tribuens." But, does any such sense as either of these occur in the passages above cited? And, is not the simple notion of begetting, or of creating, widely different from that of creating, i. e. constituting any one *a king?* as also from that of *giving the Spirit?* The truth seems to be, the incarnation and mysterious birth of Christ, as of the house and lineage of David, is rather had in view in these particular words than any thing else: nor can I see how they can be applied to the eternal generation of the Son, in any other sense than that in which "*his outgoings were*" predetermined "*from everlasting.*" 1 Cor. iv. 15, therefore can have nothing whatever to do with them.

Infin. יָלֹד, abs. Job xv. 35.

— fem. לֵדָה, Jer. xiii. 21; 2 Kings xix. 3, &c.; not constr., as Gesenius erroneously makes it.

— constr. לֶדֶת, for יַלְדֶת, Gen. xvi. 2. 16; iv. 2; xxv. 26, &c.: once, לַת, 1 Sam. iv. 19. Aff. לִדְתִּי, לִדְתָּהּ, לִדְתָּה, 1 Kings iii. 18; Gen. xxxviii. 27, &c.; Job xxxix. 2.

Part. יֹלֵד, יֵלֵד, Jer. xxx. 6; Prov. xvii. 21, &c. Aff. pl. יֹלְדָיו, Zech. xiii. 3.

— f. יוֹלֶדֶת, יֹלֵדָה, Gen. xvii. 19; Jer. xv. 9. יֹלַדְתְּ, constr. for יוֹלֶדֶת אַנְתְּ, Gen. xvi. 11; Judg. xiii. 5. 7; as, in the first, קָרָאת is also for קָרָאת אַנְתְּ, i. e. taking the pret. as a participial noun, Gram. art. 182. 2, &c. Aff. יוֹלַדְתְּךָ, יוֹלַדְתֶּךָ, יוֹלַדְתָּהּ, יוֹלַדְתּוֹ.

— pl. יֹלְדוֹת, once, Jer. xvi. 3.

— pass. יָלוּד, 1 Kings iii. 26, 27. Constr. יְלוּד, Job xiv. 1; xv. 14; xxv. 4.

— pl. יְלִידִים, once, 1 Chron. xiv. 4.

Niph. נוֹלַד, pres. יִוָּלֵד. Constr. abs. it. med. לְ, to, בְּ, in, of time or place. *Be, become born*, 1 Chron. ii. 3. 9; iii. 1. 4; xxvi. 6. In the last four places the constr. is either impers. or to be taken distributively. With pl. Ib. iii. 5; xx. 8. Pres. Job iii. 2; xv. 7; xxxviii. 21, &c. Applied to animals, Lev. xxii. 27; Deut. xv. 19. נוּלְדוּ, for נוֹלְדוּ, 1 Chron. iii. 5; xx. 8, by a manifest error of the copyists.

Infin. הִוָּלֵד, Gen. xxi. 5. Aff. הִוָּלְדוֹ, הִוָּלְדָהּ, Eccl. vii. 1; Hos. ii. 5.

Pih. pret. pres. non occ.

Infin. aff. יַלֶּדְכֶן, *Your making bring forth*, i. e. aiding, once, Exod. i. 16.

Part. f. מְיַלֶּדֶת, *Midwife*, Gen. xxxv. 17; xxxviii. 28, &c.

— pl. מְיַלְּדוֹת, Exod. i. 17. 19. 21, &c.

Puh. pret. יֻלַּד; יֻלָּד, יֻלַד, pres. non occ. i. q. Niph. Gen. iv. 26; x. 21. Ib. 25. יֻלַּד שְׁנֵי בָנִים, *Was there born two sons:* impers. as in Niph. Comp. xxxv. 26; xlvi. 22. 27, &c. Metaph. *Spiritually born*, Ps. lxxxvii. 4—6: evidently referring to the conversions to take place in the first Christian times; and which, in vr. 7, is made the song of the redeemed; it. of things inanimate, Ps. xc. 2. הָרִים יֻלָּדוּ, *mountains were brought forth*, i. e. into existence.

Hiph. הוֹלִיד, הֹלִיד, pres. יוֹלִיד, apoc. יוֹלֶד, יֹלֶד. Constr. immed. it. med. אֵת, pers. בְּ, in, of thing, place; בְּתוֹךְ, amongst, it. abs. *Make, cause, to bring forth*, as *children, vegetation, dew*: it. metaph. *vice*; never used of the female, Is. lxvi. 9; 1 Chron. ii. 18; viii. 8; Is. lv. 10. Of a father, *begat*, Gen. v. 4. 7. 10. 13, seq.; xi. 11, seq. Metaph. Is. lix. 4; Job xxxviii. 28.

Infin. הוֹלִיד,—once, הוֹלִד, Is. lix. 4.—Aff. הוֹלִידוֹ, Gen. ll. cc. &c.

Part. מוֹלִיד, pl. מוֹלִידִים, Is. lxvi. 9; Jer. xvi. 3, al. non occ.

Hoph. Infin. f. only, הֻלֶּדֶת, הֻלֶּדֶת. *Being born*, Gen. xl. 20; Ezek. xvi. 4, 5, al. non occ.

Hiph. once, pres. pl. יִתְיַלְדוּ, *They are* (recited in the genealogies, as) *begotten*, Num. i. 18, i. q. יִתְיַחֲשׂוּ, in the later books. Gesen.

יַלְדוּת, f. r. יֶלֶד, (b) *Youth*, Eccl. xi. 9. 10. (a) *Birth, forth coming*, Ps. cx. 3. See my note on Job xxix. 19. The "*pubes*,

L L

juventus," of Gesenius here, is a precious specimen of the new and enlightened theology surely!

יָלוּד, pl. יְלוּדִים, i. q. יֶלֶד above. Person *born, offspring, son,* Exod. i. 22; 2 Sam. v. 14; xii. 14; Josh. v. 5; Jer. xvi. 3, al. non occ.

יָלִיד, constr. (of יְלִיד), pl. constr. יְלִידֵי, r. יֶלֶד, i. q. יָלוּד. *Offspring, born, son,* Gen. xiv. 14; xvii. 12, 13. 23. 27; Lev. xxii. 11; Num. xiii. 22. 28; 2 Sam. xxi. 16. 18, where we have רָפָה, i. q. רָפָא, in רְפָאִים. See my note on Job xxvi. 5, 6.

ילך, v. (pret. הָלַךְ, is in use, which see), pres. יֵלֵךְ, cogn. הָלַךְ, &c. Arab. cogn. وَلَكَ, *properavit.* Constr. abs. it. med. אֶל, אַחֲרֵי, עוֹד, אַחַר, עִים, מֵעַל, מֵאֵת, עִם, אֶת, עַל, בְּ, מִן, אָנָה, לְנֶגֶד, לִפְנֵי, ־ָה, versus, לְ, adv., &c. See הָלַךְ, it. i. q. הָלַךְ. (a) *Walk, go, proceed,* pers. or thing, Gen. xxiv. 58; Exod. iii. 11; Lev. xxvi. 41; Num. x. 30; Jer. xlvi. 22; Hab. iii. 5; Job vii. 9, &c. (b) — morally, or the contrary, Deut. xxix. 18; Prov. x. 9; Ps. xxvi. 11; 1 Kings xi. 5; Exod. xvi. 4, &c. So in the phrr. בְּתָמִי אֵלֵךְ, Ps. xxvi. 11. תֵּלֶךְ בְּדַרְכֵי, 1 Kings iii. 14. בְּחֻקּוֹתַי —, Ib. vi. 12. לְפָנַי —, Ib. ix. 4. תֵּלֶךְ בְּתוּחָתִי —, Exod. xvi. 4; constr. See 1 Kings xvi. 2; xviii. 18, &c. (c) — *prosperously or not,* 1 Sam. xxviii. 22; 2 Sam. iii. 21, 22; Prov. ii. 20; x. 9; Ps. xlii. 10. In the following phrr. אֵלֵךְ חֹשֶׁךְ, Job xxix. 3: comp. Eccl. vi. 4; Lam. iii. 2. בְּגֵיא צַלְמָוֶת —, Ps. xxiii. 4. קֹדֵר אֵלֵךְ —, Ib. xlii. 10. בְּקֶרֶב צָרָה —, Ib. cxxxviii. 7. אֵלֵךְ מַר —, Ezek. iii. 14. אֵילֵךְ שׁוֹלָל —, Mic. i. 8. בְּשַׁעֲרֵי שְׁאוֹל —, Is. xxxviii. 10, &c.

The following are reflective, as in our *I will go me,* Cant. iv. 6; Exod. xviii. 27; Gen. xii. 1, &c. With ־ָה, versus, Gen. xxviii. 5. 7. 10, &c. i. q. אֶל. It is also much used like our *go to, up,* i. e. betake yourself to, set about, &c., in אֵלֵךְ אָשׁוּבָה, Hos. v. 14. אָקוּמָה וְאֵלְכָה וגו׳, 2 Sam. iii. 21. See קוּם, as used in the same way, &c., particularly with the Imperative, Exod. iv. 16; xix. 24; xxxii. 7. 34, &c. With Infin. abs. הָלוֹךְ, Ps. cxxvi. 6. הָלוֹךְ יֵלֵךְ וּבָכֹה, *proceeds, going on* (i. e. gradually strengthening in his progress, see הָלוֹךְ above, p. 155), *even weeping:* to which many similar usages may be added.

Infin. לֶכֶת, לָכֶת (for יָלֶכֶת), Gen. xi. 31; xii. 5; Prov. xv. 21; Ruth iii. 10, &c. Aff. לֶכְתּוֹ, לֶכְתְּךָ, לֶכְתְּךָ, לֶכְתִּי, &c. Imp. לֵךְ, לְךָ; with ה parag. לְכָה; pl. לְכוּ, Gen. xii. 1; xix. 32; xxxvii. 20, &c.

— f. לְכִי, pl. לֵכְנָה, לֵכְןָ, Judg. ix. 10. 12; Ruth i. 8. 12.

Part. under הָלַךְ, which see, it. Niph., &c.

Hiph. הוֹלִיךְ, pres. יֹלִיךְ, it. יֹלֵךְ, יֹלֶךְ. Constr. immed. it. med. בְּ, כִּן, עַל, לְ, instr. ־ָה, versus, אֶל, אֶת, אָנָה. *Cause, make, to walk, go; bring, lead, drive,* Deut. viii. 2; 2 Kings xxiv. 15; Prov. xvi. 29; Is. xlii. 16; xlviii. 21; Ezek. xxxvi. 12. Pres. Lev. xxvi. 13; Deut. xxviii. 36; 2 Sam. xiii. 13; Ezek. xxxii. 14; Exod. xiv. 21; 2 Kings vi. 19, &c.

Infin. הוֹלִיךְ, 2 Chron. xxxvi. 6, al. non occ. Imp. הוֹלֵךְ, Num. xvii. 11; pl. הוֹלִימוּ, 2 Kings xvii. 27, al. non occ.

— f. הֵילִיכִי (retaining the rad. י), Exod. ii. 9, al. non occ.

Part. מוֹלִיךְ, pl. f. מוֹלִכוֹת, Job xii. 17; Zech. v. 10. Aff. מוֹלִיכְךָ, מוֹלִיכָם, מוֹלִיכֵם; Jer. ii. 17; Deut. viii. 15; Is. lxiii. 3.

יָלַל, m. once, Deut. xxxii. 10. Aq. ἐν κενώματι ὀλολυγμοῦ ἠφανισμένης. Arab. وَلْوَلَ, *inaequalitas* dentium. Cogn. وَلْوَلَ, *ejulavit.* Syr. ܐܝܠܠ, *gemuit.* The notion seems to have originated in *disorder,* and thence to have designated *discord, dissonance;* and, perhaps, the original notion is still preserved in our passage; for we have, בְּאֶרֶץ מִדְבָּר וּבְתֹהוּ יְלֵל יְשִׁמֹן, *in a desert land, and in a waste, disordered,* i. e. uncultivated, *wilderness.* See LXX. Syriac ܟܕܡܣܕܢܟܠ ܘܕܗܡܣܕܟܝ, *and in the desolation of Ashimun.* See also Targ. and Arab. The term לַיִל, *night,* is probably cognate with this.

יָלַל, v. Kal non occ.

Hiph. הֵילִיל, pres. יְיֵלִיל, once, יְהֵילִילוּ, Is. lii. 5. Constr. abs. it. med. עַל, for, occ. with נָעַק, סָפַד. *Wail, howl, cry, mourn.* The cry of Eastern women in great affliction is often a sort of repetition of the syllable *lil, lil.*—Jer. xlvii. 2; Zech. xi. 2; Ezek. xxi. 13. Pres. Jer. xlviii. 31; Mic. i. 8; Is. xv. 2, 3; xvi. 7; lxv. 14; Hos. vii. 14. In Is. lii. 5, *shout,* as of victory. Gesen. But this is very doubtful. Gesenius makes לֹא הוּלְלוּ (for הוּלְלוּ), Ps. lxxviii. 63, a passive form of this word: but, apparently, without either necessity or grounds for doing so. The word

יָלַל (259) יָם

is a regular Puh. of r. הלל, and so Aquila, Sym. and Theod. have taken it. Aq. οὐχ ὑμνήθησαν: S. T. οὐκ ἐπῃνέθησαν. So the Targ. and apparently the Syriac. LXX. ἐπένθησαν.
Imp. הֵילֵל, Ezek. xxi. 17, pl. הֵילִילוּ, Is. xiii. 6; Jer. iv. 8; Amos viii. 3, &c.
— f. הֵילִלִי, Jer. xlviii. 30; xlix. 3.

יְלָלָה, f. constr. יִלְלַת (of a lost fm. יָלַל perhaps). *Wailing, lamenting,* Is. xv. 8; Jer. xxv. 36; Zech. xi. 3. Aff. יִלְלָתָהּ (of יִלְלָה), Zeph. i. 10, al. non occ.

יָלַע, v. once, Prov. xx. 25. Arab. ولع, *mentitus fuit, retinuit, abstulit.* Cogn. ولع. Cogn. Heb. לוע. Arab. لاع, r. لوع, &c. The sense of the place seems to be, *'Tis a snare to a man, that he retain (fraudulently) what is holy:* a good comment on which is Mal. iii. 8—12. The v. is therefore synon. τοῦ, קָבַע. Comp. Prov. xxii. 23. Aq. σκῶλον ἀνθρώπου καταπίεται ἡγιασμένος.

יַלֶּפֶת, f. Lev. xxi. 20; xxii. 22; with גָּרָב. Arab. ولف, *venerunt homines alii post alios. A sort of herpes,* or *itching, creeping scurvy.* LXX. λειχήν.

יֶלֶק, m.—pl. non occ. *A sort of hairy, winged locust,* Jer. li. 27; Nahum iii. 16; Ps. cv. 34; Joel i. 4; ii. 25. See Hieroz. Bochart. ii. p. 443. Arab. ولق, *properavit, agilis fuit.*

יַלְקוּט, m. once, 1 Sam. xvii. 40, r. לקט. *A bag or purse.*

יָם, m. constr. יָם. In such cases as, יָם־כִּנֶּרֶת, the combination is that of apposition (Gram. art. 217. 4), pl. יַמִּים, r. ימם. Cogn. הָמָה, *rage, roar, &c.* Arab. يَمّ, *mare, &c.* Syr. ܝܡܐ, id. *Any great collection* of water, as, I. *The sea.* II. *Any great lake.* III. *Any large river.* I. Josh. xv. 12. הַיָּדוֹל — פְּלִשְׁתִּים, xviii. 14; Exod. xxiii. 31; 2 Chron. ii. 15; viii. 18; Job ix. 8; xi. 9; xxxviii. 8. 16; xli. 23, &c. Pec. יַם־סוּף (see סוּף), *Red Sea,* Num. xiv. 25, &c., מִצְרַיִם —, Is. xi. 15: alluding to Exod. xv. 8. 10, &c.
II. (a) יָם־כִּנֶּרֶת, *Sea of Gennesaret,* or *Tiberias,* Num. xxxiv. 11; Josh. xii. 3, &c. (b) יָם־הַמֶּלַח, *Salt Sea,* i. e. *Sea of Sodom,* or *Dead Sea,* Num. xxxiv. 3. 12; Deut. iii. 17; Josh. iii. 16; xii. 3, &c. Called also, יָם הָעֲרָבָה, Deut. iii. 17; iv. 49; Josh. iii. 16; xii. 3: also, הַיָּם הַקַּדְמֹנִי, *Eastern Sea,* Joel ii. 20: it. Zech. xiv. 8, where it is opposed to הַיָּם הָאַחֲרוֹן. *The Western,* or *Mediterranean, Sea,* i. q. מִפְּאַת־יָם, Ezek. xlv. 7. (c) Metaph. *The brazen sea* of Solomon, 2 Kings xxv. 13; 1 Chron. xviii. 8.
III. *Large river.* (a) The Nile, Is. xix. 5; Nah. iii. 8: termed also by the Arabs, يَمّ, and بحر. Pl. *branches of the Nile,* Ezek. xxxii. 2. (b) The Euphrates, Is. xxvii. 1; Jer. li. 36. Hence—
Taken as a limit or boundary, will, in various phrr., signify the quarter in which such *sea* lies; as, רוּחַ יָם, *sea wind,* i. e. blowing from the west, Exod. x. 19. פְּאַת־יָם, *sea quarter,* i. e. western, Exod. xxvii. 13; xxxviii. 12. יָמָּה, *sea-wards, westward,* Gen. xxviii. 14; Exod. xxvi. 22. הַיָּמָּה, id., Exod. x. 19. מִיָּם, *from the sea the west,* Gen. xii. 8. — לְיָם, *from the west, with respect to* —, Josh. viii. 9; xii. 13. Comp. Ps. cvii. 3; Is. xlix. 12. מִיָּם עַד־יָם, *from sea to sea,* Amos viii. 12. Hence the phrr. הֲמוֹן יָם, i. q. גּוֹיִם, Is. lx. 5; i. q. שְׁפַע יַמִּים, Deut. xxxiii. 19. שִׁפְעַת גְּמַלִּים, Is. lx. 6. Not the riches, as Gesenius thinks, but the multitudes of the nations, as the prediction is evidently of the conversion of the nations to Christianity. לֵב־יָם, *heart of the sea,* Exod. xv. 8. כֶּתֶף יָם, *shoulder, side of the sea,* Num. xxxiv. 11. קְצֵה יָם, *limit of the sea,* Josh. xiii. 27, &c. לְשׁוֹן יָם, *tongue of*—point of—Josh. xviii. 19. Comp. Is. xi. 15. בְּמָתֳרֵי־יָם, Job ix. 8. See my note. מִשְׁבְּרֵי־יָם, *breakers of the sea,* Ps. xciii. 4. כְּחוֹל הַיָּם, *as the sand of the sea,* i. e. for multitude, Gen. xxxii. 12. Comp. 2 Sam. xvii. 11. שְׂפַת הַיָּם, *lip, side, of the sea,* Gen. xxii. 17; i. q. חוֹף יָמִּים, Deut. i. 7. אִיֵּי הַיָּם, Esth. x. 1, &c. Metaph. Ps. cxiv. 3. 5, &c. To which many other similar usages may be added; all regulated, however, by the same analogies.

יָם, m. Chald. id. Def. יַמָּא, Dan. vii. 2, 3.

יַמּוֹת, pl. f. of יוֹם.

יָמִים, pl. m. of יוֹם.

יֵמִים, m. pl. once, Gen. xxxvi. 24.

יְמִי (260) יְמִי

According to the Vulgate, *warm waters*. See also Jerome's Quæst. on the place; which Gesenius thinks, both from the etymologies of יוֹם, יָמָה, and from the fact that hot springs are still found to the east of the Dead Sea, is correct. The Greek translators generally preserve the Heb. word Ιαμείμ: not venturing to meddle with it. ὁ Σύρος λέγει πηγὴν αὐτὸν εὑρηκέναι. Bahrdt's Hexapla. The Syriac Version, however, reads simply ܡܰܝ̈ܳܐ, *waters*. And this is, perhaps, the true sense of the passage; as, in those early times the finding of springs was of immense importance, both to the rearing of cattle, and the accommodation of travellers.

יָמִין, m. — constr. יְמִין, pl. non occ. Arab. يَمْن, *dexter*; يَمِين, id. (a) *The right* side, hand, leg, eye, &c., as the context may require, 1 Kings vii. 39; 2 Kings xii. 10; Zech. iv. 11; Ezek. x. 3;—2 Sam. xx. 9; Ps. lxxiii. 23; Jer. xxii. 24;—Exod. xxix. 22; Lev. vii. 32, &c.;—1 Sam. xi. 2; Zech. xi. 17. For the most part elliptically, as, עַל־יָמִין אוֹ עַל־שְׂמֹאל, *to the right* (hand), *or to the left*, Gen. xxiv. 49, &c.: and often adverbially, לֹא אָסוּר יָמִין וּשְׂמֹאל, Deut. ii. 27; Num. xx. 16. Metaph. Deut. v. 29; xvii. 11, &c. Hence the phrr. עַל יָמִין, Job xxx. 12. אֶל יָמִין, 1 Sam. xxiii. 24. לִימִין, Ps. cix. 31, &c. מִימִין, Gen. xlviii. 13. לְמִימִין, 2 Kings xxiii. 13. אִישׁ יְמִינֶךָ, *man of thy right hand*, i. e. whom thou protectest, Ps. lxxx. 18. Hence, *being*, or *standing*, at the right hand, will imply *protection, favour, aiding*, Ps. xvi. 8; cix. 31; cx. 5; cxxi. 5. Comp. 1 Kings ii. 19; Ps. xlv. 10; cx. 1. And, as יָד, is often either expressed or implied (see under that word). (b) *Power*, by meton., will be intended, as יְמִין יְהוָֹה עֹשָׂה חָיִל, *the right* hand *of Jehovah doing* (producing, giving) *might*, Ps. cxviii. 16. Comp. Ps. lxxiii. 23; lxxiv. 11; lxxvii. 11; Hab. ii. 16; Is. xli. 10, &c. Hence, יְמִינָם שֶׁקֶר, *their right* hand (i. e. power) *is the right* hand *of falsehood*, i. e. of deception, promising strength, but giving only weakness, Ps. cliv. 8. Hence the phrr. תִּשָּׁכַח יְמִינִי, *shall my right* hand disregard, i. e. fail me, Ps. cxxxviii. 5. And, perhaps, to this usage may be referred Jonah iv. 11. In this sense, too, i. q. זְרוֹעַ, Ps. xliv. 4. Comp. Is. xli. 13; Exod. xv. 6, &c. In many of these places the person, or angel, of Jehovah, i. e.

Christ, is probably meant. Comp. Heb. xi. 26; 1 Pet. i. 11, &c.

(c) *The southern* quarter, or country; because a man facing the rising sun will have this country on his right hand, or side. See אָחוֹר, p. 20 above, 1 Sam. xxiii. 19. 24; 2 Sam. xxiv. 5; Ps. lxxxix. 13. And so when applied to buildings, 1 Kings vii. 39; 2 Kings xii. 10, &c.

Gesenius makes this term ominous of good luck, "pariter atque (apud) Græcos." But this is erroneous. The *hand*, and hence the *right hand* (b, above) often implied *power*, thence *success*, and particularly with reference to God's assistance. Aff. יְמִינִי, יְמִינוּ, יְמִינְךָ, &c.

יְמִינִי, m. patron. or rel. noun, of יָמִין, 2 Chron. iii. 17; Ezek. iv. 6, i. q. יְמִינִי. See the Keri. With בֶּן, אִישׁ, &c., *Benjamite*, Judg. xix. 16; 1 Sam. ix. 1, &c., Gram. artt. 166. 11; 170. 9. Once, יְמִינִי, Num. xxvi. 12.

יָמַן, v. Kal non occ. See יָמִין above, from which we have—

Hiph. pret. non occ. pres. 1st pers. with ה parag. אֵימִנָה, *I take*, proceed towards, *the right hand*, or *southward*, Gen. xiii. 9. תַּאֲמִינוּ, *ye take the right hand* path, Is. xxx. 21, al. non occ.

Infin. הֵמִין, 2 Sam. xiv. 19.

Imp. f. הַיְמִינִי, Ezek. xxi. 21.

Part. pl. m. מֵימִינִים, *Using the right hand*, 1 Chron. xii. 2, al. non occ.

יָמָנִי, m. ⎫ pl. non occ. i. q. יְמִינִי.
יְמָנִית, f. ⎭ Arabic يَمَنِي, *dextra manus*, &c. Attrib. *Right* hand, side, &c., 1 Kings vii. 21; 2 Chron. iii. 17: F. Exod. xxix. 20; Lev. viii. 23, 24, &c.

יָמַר, v. Kal non occ. Cogn. מוּר. Arab. أَمَرَ, *imperavit*.

Hiph. הֵמִיר, *Change, exchange*, for other; constr. immed. it. med. בְּ, for, Jer. ii. 11, al. non occ.

Hithp. תִּתְמָרוּ, "*substituemini*," Gesen. Which seems hardly suitable to the passage, Is. lxi. 6. *Ye shall obtain rule*, i. e. the sovereignty, is easily deduced from the Arab. أَمَرَ; whence, أَمِير, *Emir, commander;* and is a direct prophecy of the universal prevalence of Christianity. Comp. Ps. xlv. 17; Is. lx. 10, &c. al. non occ. Aquila,

ימר (261) ינש

καὶ ἐν δόξῃ αὐτῶν πορφύρᾳ ἐνδύσεσθε. See LXX.

יָמֵר, see מור.

אָמַר .r ,יֽאָמְרוּךָ for ,יַאֲמִירוּךָ.

יָמַשׁ, v. Kal non occ. Cogn. מָשַׁשׁ, מוּשׁ.

Hiph. Imp. aff. הֲיְמִשֵׁנִי, pointed, however, in the text as if the Hiph. of מוּשׁ, once, Judg. xvi. 26. *Let me grope, feel.*

יָנָא .r ,Syriasm ,יָנָאץ for ,יְנָאֵץ.

יָנְדַּע, pres. Chald. r. ידע.

יָנָה, v. pret. non occ. pres. 1st pers. pl. aff. נִינָם. Cogn. אנה. Arab. وَنِي, *torpuit.* Cogn. عَنَّ, *debilitas. Oppress, vex, ruin,* Ps. lxxiv. 8. נִינָם יָחַד, *let us ruin them altogether.*

Part. f. יוֹנָה, of anger, the sword, &c., Jer. xxv. 38; xlvi. 16; L. 16; Zeph. iii. 1, al. non occ.

Hiph. הוֹנָה, pres. יוֹנֶה, i. q. Kal. Constr. immed. it. med. אֶת, Ezek. xviii. 7. 12. 16; xxii. 7. 29;—Exod. xxii. 21; Deut. xxiii. 17; Lev. xix. 33, &c.

Infin. הוֹנֹת, Ezek. xlvi. 18, al. non occ.

Part. pl. aff. מוֹנַיִךְ, *Thy oppressors,* Is. xlix. 27.

יָנַי, for יָנִיא, pres. Hiph. r. נוא.

יָנִיחַ, pres. Hiph. r. נוח.

יְנִיקָה, f. pl. aff. יְנִיקוֹתָיו, i. q. יוֹנְקוֹת, see יוֹנֵק, r. ינק. *Its suckers,* i. e. tender branches: once, Ezek. xvii. 4.

יָנַק, v. pres. יִינַק. Syr. ܝܢܩ, *suxit.* Arab. يَنَعَ, *coagulum.* Constr. immed. it. abs. *Suck in,* milk as an infant, poison, &c. Metaph. *Wealth,* Is. lx. 16; lxvi. 11, 12; Deut. xxxiii. 15; Job iii. 11; xx. 16.

Part. יוֹנֵק, f. יוֹנֶקֶת, Deut. xxxii. 28; Ps. viii. 3, &c.

Pl. יוֹנְקִים, f. יוֹנְקוֹת, Job viii. 16; Ezek. xvii. 22.

Constr. m. יוֹנְקֵי, Joel ii. 16. Aff. f. יוֹנְקוֹתָיו, יוֹנְקוֹתָיו. Fem. applied only to the *suckers* or *tender branches* of trees.

Hiph. הֵינִיק, pres. יָנִיק, הֵינִיק. Apoc. הָנֵק. Constr. immed. it. med. אֶת, it. לְ, pers. *Give suck, suckle,* as a mother, &c., Gen. xxi. 7; Lam. iv. 3; Exod. ii. 7; Deut. xxxii. 13; 1 Sam. i. 23.

Infin. הֵינִיק, 1 Kings iii. 22.

Imp. aff. הֵינִקִהוּ, Exod. ii. 9.

Part. f. מֵינֶקֶת, *A nurse,* Gen. xxxviii. 8; Exod. ii. 7. Aff. מֵינִקְתּוֹ, 2 Kings xi. 2: it. מֵינִקְתָּהּ, מֵינִקְתּוֹ, 2 Chron. xxii. 11; Gen. xxiv. 59.

— pl. מֵינִיקוֹת, Gen. xxxii. 16. Aff. מֵינִיקוֹתַיִךְ, Is. xlix. 23.

יַנְשׁוּף, once, יַנְשׁוֹף, Is. xxxiv. 11—pl. non occ. According to Bochart, Hieroz. ii. p. 281, seq. Chald. and Syr. *The owl.* LXX. and Vulg. *the Ibis.* Gesenius, *the common crane* or *heron* ("der Trompeter-vogel", from its cry, as derived from נָשַׁף, *blew.* Bochart, on the other hand, takes נֶשֶׁף, as the root. One thing only is certain, that it was proscribed as unclean, Lev. xi. 17; Deut. xiv. 16; Is. xxxiv. 11, al. non occ.

יָסֹב, pres. Kal r. סבב. Chaldæism, for יָסֹב.

יָסֵב, pres. Hiph. r. סבב. Chaldæism, for יָסֵב.

יָסַד, pres. non occ. Arab. وَسَدَ, *posuit illi sub capite rem pro cervicali.* Constr. immed. it. med. לְ, for, בְּ, or אֶת. *Founding,* i. e. *laying the foundation of any edifice,* Is. liv. 11; Ezra iii. 12, &c. Hence, metaph. applied to the earth, *establishing it in its present order,* Ps. cii. 26; civ. 5. 8; Prov. iii. 19; Ps. lxxviii. 69; Is. xlviii. 13, &c. It. to countries, Is. xxiii. 13; — *place,* as appointed for anything, Ps. civ. 8;— powers, forces, for rule, Amos ix. 6;—for chastisement, Hab. i. 12. *Fix, lay up, for use,* the heap of grain, 2 Chron. xxxi. 7.

Part. יֹסֵד, Is. li. 13; Zech. xii. 1, al. non occ.

Infin. יְסֹד, Is. li. 16. לִיסוֹד, *irregularly,* 2 Chron. xxxi. 7.

— aff. יָסְדוֹ, Job xxxviii. 4. יָסְדוּ, Ezra iii. 12. See Gram. art. 152. 2.

Niph. pl. m. נוֹסְדוּ, pres. f. תִּוָּסֵד, once. *Be, become, fixing, projecting, plotting,* i. e. laying the ground-work of something, Ps. ii. 2. —*founded,* i. e. its foundations laid, Is. xliv. 28.

Infin. הִוָּסְדָהּ, aff. *Its being founded,* Exod. ix. 18. הִוָּסְדָם, *their plotting, &c.,* Ps. xxxi. 14.

Pih. יִסֵּד, pres. aff. parag. יְסַדְנָה, once, Josh. vi. 26. Constr. immed. it. med. עַל, בְּ, in, אֶת, i. q. Kal, usually; but, more probably, *causative* of it. *Cause to found, fix, establish,* 1 Chron. ix. 22; Esth. i. 8; Is.

יְסַד

xiv. 32; xxviii. 16; 1 Kings xvi. 34; Ps. viii. 3; Zech. iv. 9; Ezra iii. 10.

Infin. יְסֹד, 1 Kings v. 31 (17).

Puh. יֻסַּד, pres. non occ. *Was, became, founded,* i. e. the foundations laid, 1 Kings vi. 37; Ezra iii. 6; Hag. ii. 18; Zech. viii. 9.

Part. מְיֻסָּד, pl. מְיֻסָּדִים, 1 Kings vii. 10; Cant. v. 15.

Hoph. Infin. הוּסַד, Ezra iii. 11; 2 Chron. iii. 3.

Part. מוּסָד, f. מוּסָדָה, pl. מוּסָדוֹת, 2 Chron. viii. 16; Is. xxx. 32; Ezek. xli. 8; Is. xxviii. 16. מוּסָד מוּסָּד, *Founded foundation,* i. e. most secure foundation, or establishment. On this sort of repetition, see Gram. art. 223, seq. Comp. הֻפַּשׁ מִדְחָפֵשׂ, Ps. lxiv. 7. בְּצֵל מְצֻלָּל, Exod. xii. 9. Gesen.

יָסֻד, m. Part. constr. for יָסוֹד, lit. *fixed matter of —*, i. e. *beginning, commencement,* Ezra vii. 9, i. e. speaking as of a foundation being the commencement of an edifice.

יְסוּדָתוֹ, f. aff. of the above. *Its foundation,* Ps. lxxxvii. 1, al. non occ.

יְסוֹד, m. pl. aff. יְסֹדֶיהָ, it. f. יְסֹדוֹתֶיהָ. *Foundation,* Exod. xxix. 12; Lev. iv. 7; 2 Chron. xxiv. 27; Job iv. 19, &c. Morally, metaph. Prov. x. 25: politically, of princes, apparently, Ezek. xxx. 4. To *lay bare the foundation,* is to take away its power; strip it of *its curtain,* as we may say of a modern fortification. See Hab. iii. 13; Ezek. xiii. 14; Mic. i. 6, &c., and גַּלֵּה above, p. 113.

יְסוֹר, Gesen. *Castigator.* So Rosenmüller and others of a modern date. More probably, 3d pers. sing. pres. masc. of יָסַר. Comp. 1st pers. aff. אֶסְרֵם, Hos. x. 10; which would give for the 3d pers. יְסֹר, or יְסוֹר; the (') of the root being compensated by the insertion of Dagesh, as in instances innumerable. See my note on Job xl. 2, the only place in which it occurs.

יְסוּרַי, m. pl. Aff. for יִסּוּרַי, according to the Keri. Lit. *And my decliners,* for, *and persons declining from me;* once, Jer. xvii. 13. Gesenius treats this word as literally correct, and derived as יָרַי is from רִיב. But, in this case, it would regularly be a part. pass. of יָסַר, and the sense be *my chastised ones,* i. e. persons chastised by me. The Keri is no doubt right, and the r. סוּר.

יסך, v. pres. יָסֵךְ, once, Exod. xxx. 32.

יסף

The context, however, seems to require יֻסַּךְ, *Be poured out.* Cogn. נסך.

יָסַף, v. pres. Hiph. in use. Syr. ࠀࠌࠎࠐ̈, *addidit.* Constr. abs. it. as an auxiliary verb with an Infin. following, or with an Infin. with לְ, it. med. עַל, on, or to, it. לְ, or אֶל, to, בְּ, in. *Added, repeated,* Deut. xix. 9; Num. xi. 25, &c. As an auxiliary; see Gen. viii. 12; xxxviii. 26; 1 Sam. xxvii. 4; Is. xxxvii. 31. In most which cases, our term *again* will express the intention of the writer. See Gram. art. 222. 4. With עַל, אֶל, לְ, *upon, to, &c.,* i. e. *increase, make more, &c.,* as the place may require, Lev. xxii. 14; xxvii. 13. 15. 19. 27, &c.; Is. xxvi. 15; Deut. xix. 9, &c. Immed. בְּ. יָסְפוּ—שִׂמְחָה־בְ, they *shall increase—joy in—*Is. xxix. 19.

Infin. סְפוֹת, Is. xxx. 1.

Imp. pl. סְפוּ, Is. xxix. 1; Jer. vii. 21; but both these forms may be derived from the cogn. סָפָה.

Part. יֹסֵף, for יוֹסֵף, *Adding, repeating,* Is. xxix. 14; xxxviii. 5.

— pl. יֹסְפִים, Deut. v. 22.

Niph. נוֹסַף, pres. non occ. *Was, became, added, repeated,* Jer. xxxvi. 32; Exod. i. 10; Num. xxxvi. 3.

Part. נוֹסָף, f. נוֹסָפָה, pl. f. נוֹסָפוֹת, Prov. xi. 24; Num. xxxvi. 4; Is. xv. 9.

Hiph. הוֹסִיף, pres. יוֹסִיף, יֹסִיף, יֹסֵף, occasionally יֹאסֵף, Exod. v. 7. Apoc. יֹסֵף, i. q. Kal, 2 Kings xx. 6; xxiv. 7; Ps. lxxi. 14; Eccl. i. 16. Pres. Gen. viii. 21; xxx. 24; Exod. x. 28, 29; Josh. vii. 12; Deut. iii. 26; xxv. 3, &c.; Joel ii. 2, לֹא יֹסֵף, for לֹא יֹסִיף. Comp. Job xx. 9. In Is. xlvii. 1, תוֹסִיפִי יִקְרְאוּ־לָךְ, thou (f) *shalt not add* (so that בַּאֲשֶׁר), they *call thee,* i. e. thou shalt no more obtain this privilege.—*Increase,* Job xlii. 10, &c.

Infin. הוֹסִיף, הֹסִיף, Lev. xix. 25; 2 Chron. xxviii. 13, &c.

Part. pl. m. מוֹסִיפִים, Neh. xiii. 18.

יסף, v. Chald. Kal non occ.

Hoph. Heb. הוּסַף, *Became, was, added,* Dan. iv. 33.

יסר, v. pret. non occ. pres. Aff. אֶסְרֵם, Hos. x. 10. See יָסוֹר above. Arab. وَصَرَ, *pactum, contractus.* Cogn. Heb. אָסַר, אָצַר—אָצֹר. Lit. *restrain, constrain.* Hence, *Chastise, correct,* as parents do their children, for the purpose of reducing them to rule and order, Hos. x. 10; Job xl. 2. See my note.

Part. יֹסֵר, Prov. ix. 7; Ps. xciv. 10, al. non occ.

Niph. pret. non occ. יִוָּסֵר, *Be, become, chastised, corrected*, Lev. xxvi. 23; Prov. xxix. 19; Jer. xxxi. 18; Ezek. xxiii. 48. נְסְרוּ, for נְתוֹסְרוּ, as Gesenius thinks. See Gram. art. 193. 4; but a regular pret. if pointed נוֹסְרוּ, which is most likely.

Imp. Ps. ii. 10; pl. הִוָּסְרוּ, f. הִוָּסְרִי, Jer. vi. 8.

Pih. יִסַּר, pres. יְיַסֵּר, i. q. Kal, if not also intensitive. *Chastise, correct*, with words, stripes, &c., of parents, God, &c., 1 Kings xii. 11. 14; 2 Chron. x. 11; Ps. cxviii. 18; Is. viii. 12; xxviii. 26; Job iv. 3. Pres. 1 Kings xii. 11. 14; Ps. vi. 2; xxxviii. 2; Deut. viii. 5; Jer. ii. 19. Metaph. Ps. xvi. 7.

Infin. יַסֹּר, Ps. cxviii. 18; it. יִסְּרָה, Lev. xxvi. 18. Aff. יַסֶּרְךָ, Deut. iv. 36.

Imp. יַסֵּר, Prov. xix. 18; xxix. 17.

Part. aff. מְיַסֶּרְךָ, Deut. viii. 5.

Hiph. pres. aff. אַיְסִירֵם, Hos. vii. 12, only, *I will chastise them*.

יָע, m. sing. non occ. pl. יָעִים, r. יָעָה. Arab. وِعَاء, *loculus, theca*, ubi aliquid reconditur. Usually a *shovel*; but, from the etymology, as well as the accompanying words in the context, it should rather signify *a sort of Vessel*, or *box*, perhaps, used either for bringing fuel to the fire on the altar, or for carrying the ashes away from it. LXX. θέρμαι, καλυπτήρ, κρεάγρα, πυρεῖον, φιάλη, Exod. xxvii. 3; xxxviii. 3; Num. iv. 14; 1 Kings vii. 40. 45; 2 Kings xxv. 14, &c. Aff. יָעָיו.

יָעַד, v. pres. aff. parag. יִעֲדֶנָּה. Constr. immed. it. med. לְ, to, pers. Syr. ܥܰܕ, *condixit, constituit*, locum vel tempus. Arab. وَعَدَ, *promisit*; e contrario, *minatus est*. *Appoint, determine*, variously, 2 Sam. xx. 5; Jer. xlvii. 7; Mic. vi. 9. שִׁמְעוּ מַטֶּה וּמִי יְעָדָהּ *Hear* (there is) *a rod; and, Who hath appointed it?* Applied to the espousing of a wife, Exod. xxi. 8, 9. Always aff.

Niph. נוֹעַד, pres. pl. יִוָּעֲדוּ. Constr. abs. it. med. לְ, אֶל, עַל. *Be, become, appointed, &c.* Meton. (a) *Brought together, assembled, met*: and, by a further meton., (b) *agreed*; either for friendly or unfriendly purposes.

(a) Exod. xxv. 22; xxix. 42, 43; xxx. 6. 36; Num. xvii. 19, &c. (b) Ps. xlviii. 5; Amos iii. 3; Num. x. 4; Job ii. 11, &c.

Part. pl. m. נוֹעָדִים. (b) Num. xiv. 35; xvi. 11, &c.

Hiph. pret. non occ. pres. aff. יוֹעִידֵנִי. Constr. immed. pers. med. לְ, thing, i. q. Kal, if not also causative. *Appoint*, time or place, usually: but there seem to be no good grounds for this addition, Job ix. 19. Parag. and aff. 1st pers. Jer. xlix. 19; L. 44. See Gram. art. 235, al. non occ.

יַעַד, pres. apoc. Hiph. r. עוּד.

Hoph. Part. pl. m. מוּעָדִים, *Appointed, fixed, set up*, Jer. xxiv. 1.

— f. מְעָרוֹת, *Fixed*, Ezek. xxi. 21, al. non occ.

יָעָה, v. once, Is. xxviii. 17. Arab. وَعَى, *asservavit*; conj. iv. *totam peregit truncationem*, nullâ relictâ parte. Cogn. وَعَع, *concussit illos*. Æth. ᎥᎠᎦ : *cremavit, ussit*, &c. As, אָסַף, p. 46, above, signifies, *laying up* either to preserve or destroy; so apparently this verb, lit. *lay up*. Meton. *Carry off, destroy*. Theod. καὶ ταράξει χάλαζα ἐλπίδα ψεύδους.

יְעוֹרִים, m. pl. i. q. יְעָרִים. See יַעַר. Kethiv, Ezek. xxxiv. 25. *Woods*.

יָעַז, v. Kal non occ. Cogn. עוּז.

Niph. part. נוֹעָז, *Powerful, formidable*, once, Is. xxxiii. 19. Sym. τὸν λαὸν τὸν ἀναιδῆ. LXX. καὶ μέγαν λαόν. Jerome, "*impudens*."

יָעַט, v. Aff. יְעָטָנִי, *Hath clothed me*, Is. lxi. 10, only. i. q. cogn. עָטָה. See, too, הִלְבִּישַׁנִי, in the parallel.

יָעַט, יַעַט, pres. apoc. r. עוּט.

יעט, v. Chald. Pehal non occ. Heb. i. q. יָעַץ.

Part. pl. m. aff. יָעֲטוֹהִי, *His advisers, counsellors*, Ezra vii. 14, 15, al. non occ.

Ithp. pl. m. אִתְיָעַטוּ, *They counselled, advised*, Dan. vi. 8, only.

יָעֵל, m. pl. יְעֵלִים, constr. יַעֲלֵי. } Arab. יַעֲלָה, f. constr. pl. non occ. } وَعِل, *caper montanus*. Syr. ܝܰܥܠܳܐ, *rupicapra*. See Bochart. Hieroz. i. p. 915, it. p. 899. So called, apparently from its propensity to climbing the rocks. Cogn. r. עָלָה. *A sort of mountain antelope* or *goat*, probably much the same with the *Chamois* of the Alps. 1 Sam. xxiv. 3, צוּרֵי הַיְּעֵלִים, lit. *rocks of the mountain goats*; name of a place on the desert of En-gedi. Gesen.—Ps. civ. 18; Job xxxix. 1. See my note. Fem. Prov. v. 19, יַעֲלַת חֵן, *antelope of grace*, i. e. graceful: with אַיֶּלֶת, i. q. *gazelle*, in the paral. So the Arabs. Bochart. i. 899, أَزْهَى مِنَ الْوَعِلِ , *more splendid than the antelope*; applied to a lovely woman. Hence—

יָעַל, v. Kal non occ. Cogn. עָלָה, *Rise, be high*, &c. Hence—

Hiph. הוֹעִיל, pres. יוֹעִיל. Constr. abs. it. med. כְּ, of thing, בְּ, instr. it. לְ, pers. it. immed. *Be profitable, advantageous*, &c., 1 Sam. xii. 21; Is. xxx. 5, 6; xliv. 9; Jer. ii. 11; xii. 13; Hab. ii. 18; Job xv. 3; Prov. xi. 4, &c.; Jer. ii. 8, ellipt. אַחֲרֵי לֹא יוֹעִילוּ, *after* gods which *profit not* —, Job xxx. 13. See my translation and note.

Infin. הוֹעִיל, Is. xliv. 10; Jer. xxiii. 31, &c.

Part. m. מוֹעִיל, once, Jer. xvi. 19.

יַעֲמֹדְנָה, for תַּעֲמֹדְנָה, r. עמד.

יַעַן, Apocope of v. pres. יַעֲנֶה, lit. *it, he, answers to, means*, &c. Arab. يَعْنِي, and يَعْنِي, id. Applied as a particle, *Because, because of*, Num. xx. 12; 1 Kings xx. 42; 2 Kings xxii. 19; Is. xxxvii. 29; Jer. v. 14; Ezek. v. 9, &c. With other particles; as, יַעַן אֲשֶׁר, *because that, since that*, &c., 1 Sam. xxx. 22, &c. יַעַן כִּי, id., Num. xi. 20; Is. vii. 5. יַעַן וּבְיַעַן, *because, yea because*, emphatically, Lev. xxvi. 43; Ezek. xiii. 10: and omitting the וְ, Ib. xxxvi. 3. יַעַן מָה, *For what cause, reason?* Hag. i. 9. כִּי יַעַן, Jer. xlviii. 7. כִּי יַעַן אֲשֶׁר, Gen. xxii. 16 : as the apocope of יַעֲנֶה, Gen. xxvii. 39, &c. See r. עָנָה, it. Nold. p. 344, seq., with the notes.

יָעֵן, pl. m. יְעֵנִים, once, Lam. iv. 3. Keri. *Ostriches*. So called according to Gesenius, because *voracious*. Syr. ܝܰܥܢܳܐ, *vorax fuit*; but there appears no ground for this in nature. Bochart, under יענה Hieroz. i. p. 65, " quasi *clamosam* dicas, aut *filiam clamoris*. Clamosum enim est animal."

יַעֲנָה, f. of the last above; always as a compound, בַּת יַעֲנָה, i. e. *daughter of the female ostrich*, for *female ostrich*, pl. בְּנוֹת יַעֲנָה; which, according to Gesen., is put for both sexes, Is. xiii. 21; xxxiv. 13; Mic. i. 8; Job xxx. 29 : opp. to יַחְמָס, *the male ostrich*, Bochart, Hieroz. ii. p. 235; Lev. xi. 16; Deut. xiv. 15. Forbidden by the law as unclean.

יַעְעָרוּ, see under עוּר.

יָעֵף, masc.—plur. non occ. Arab. وَغْفٌ, and وُغُوفٌ, *debilitas* visûs. Cogn. Heb. עוּף. The primitive notion consisted perhaps in *running*, &c. Arab. وَغَفَ, *celeriter cucurrit*: thence, meton., *Weary, fatigued*, Is. xl. 29; L. 4.

יְעַף, m. Chald. once, Dan. ix. 21, בִּיעָף, *In hasting, flight*, perhaps.

יָעַף, v. pres. יִיעַף, יָעֵף. See יָעֵף above. Constr. abs. *Be weary, fatigued*, Is. xl. 31. יֵלְכוּ וְלֹא יִיעָפוּ, *They shall walk and not be weary*: synon. τοῦ, יָעַט, with יָרוּץ, preceding; which justifies the etymology above given, Ib. xxviii. 30; xliv. 12; Jer. ii. 24; li. 58. 64; Hab. ii. 13, al. non occ.

יָעַץ, v. pres. יִיעַץ. Arab. وَعَظَ, *monuit*. Constr. abs. it. immed. it. med. עַל, pers. אֶל. *Advise, admonish, counsel*, either self or others, 2 Sam. xvi. 23; xvii. 7. 15. 21; Is. vii. 5; xiv. 27; xix. 12; xxxii. 8, &c. Pres. Exod. xviii. 19; Num. xxiv. 14. Gesen. "*prædixit*," which is groundless; so on, Is. xli. 28. Phr. יָעַץ מִדְבָּרוֹת, Is. xxxii. 8. יָעַצְףָ בֹּשֶׁת לְ-, 1 Kings i. 12. אִיעָצְךָ נָא עֵצָה Hab. ii. 10. אִיעֲצָה עָלֶיךָ עֵינִי, prægn. Gesen. for אִיעָצָה וְאָשִׂימָה וְגוּ, *I will advise and place*, &c. ; but, perhaps, used here in the sense of the Arab. cogn. وَضَعَ, *posuit, collocavit*, i. e. *I will place my eye upon thee*.

Imp. pl. m. עֻצוּ, of the cogn. r. עוּץ, Judg. xix. 30 : Is. viii. 10.

Part. יֹעֵץ, יָעֵץ, pl. יוֹעֲצִים. Constr. יוֹעֲצֵי, 2 Sam. xv. 12; Nahum i. 11; Prov. xv. 22, &c.

— f. aff. יוֹעַצְתּוֹ, of יוֹעֶצֶת, 2 Chron. xxii. 4, only.

— pass. f. יְעוּצָה, Is. xiv. 26, only.

Niph. נוֹעַץ, pres. יִוָּעֵץ. Constr. abs. it. med. עִם, עַל, אֶל, לְ, Infin. *Be, become, advising, counselling, consulting*, Is. xl. 14; xlv. 21; Ps. lxxi. 10; lxxxiii. 6; 1 Kings xii. 6. 8. 28; 2 Kings vi. 8; 1 Chron. xiii. 1; 2 Chron. x. 6. 8; Neh. vi. 7, &c.

Part. pl. m. נוֹעָצִים, 1 Kings xii. 6. 9, &c.

יער (265) יפה

Hithp. pres. pl. יִתְיָעֲצוּ, once, Ps. lxxxiii. 4, i. q. Niph.

יַעַר, masc. pl. יְעָרִים, f. יְעָרוֹת. Arab. وَعْر, وَعَرَ ,وَعِرَ ,وَعُرَ ; Infin. v. وَعَر, difficilis superatu; salebrosus fuit, mons, locus; impedivit. Syr. ܐܓܒܐ, dumus, &c.; hence, as something impassable. I. *A wood, forest,* Eccl. ii. 6. יַעַר צוֹמֵחַ עֵצִים, *a wood,* or *forest, producing trees,* 1 Sam. xxii. 5; 2 Kings xix. 23; Is. vii. 2; xliv. 23; Ps. L. 10; lxxxiii. 15; Ezek. xxxiv. 25, Keri; xxxix. 10; Ps. xxix. 9. בֵּית יַעַר הַלְּבָנוֹן, *house of the forest of Lebanon,* 1 Kings vii. 2; x. 17. So called from being built with cedar wood: styled עֶשֶׁת, Neh. iii. 19. An armoury of Solomon. Aff. יַעֲרִי, יַעֲרָה.

II. יַעַר, it. f. יַעְרָה. Arab. وَغْر, *fervor, æstus. Honey,* the purest and best, as obtained from bees. Pliny, H. N., xi. 15. "In omne melle, quod per se fluxit, ut mustum et oleum, appellatur acetum." Palladius in Junio, tit. 7. "Mella conficimus expressis diligenter favis. Mel recens paucis diebus apertis vasculis habendum est, atque in summitate purgandum, donec refrigerato calore, musti more, deferveat. Nobilius mel erit, quod ante expressionem secundam velut sponte profluxerit." The *mel acetum* is the Gr. μέλι ἀσκητόν; and, according to Hesychius κράτιστον, *the best.* Our chemists purify it by exposing it to a warm bath heat: they then term it, "*mel despumatum.*" The honey obtained from trees, "quæ vocentur occhi, ex quibus defluat mel horis matutinis duabus." Pliny, H. N. xii. 19, was a different thing. See דְּבַשׁ above, p. 129. So called, therefore, from its being purified by fermentation or heat. Twice only, Cant. v. 1, אָכַלְתִּי יַעְרִי עִם דִּבְשִׁי, *I have eaten my pure, with my wild, honey.* 1 Sam. xiv. 27, בְּיַעְרַת הַדְּבָשׁ, *in the pure* (best) *of the field-honey.* This makes a real distinction between these two words.

יָעַר, pres. Hiph. r. עוּר.

יָפֶה, m. constr. יְפֵה.—

יָפָה, f. constr. יְפַת, pl. יָפוֹת. Constr. יְפוֹת. Arab. وَفِي, *servavit pactum;* conj. iii. *eminuit:* hence applied to appearance, &c. (a) *Beautiful, handsome,* man, woman, animal; voice, region, &c. (b) *Excellent,* Gen. xii. 14; xli. 2; 2 Sam. xiii. 1; xiv. 25; Cant. i. 8; v. 9: with the addition of תֹּאַר, עֵינַיִם, נוֹף, מַרְאֶה, 1 Sam. xvii. 42; xvi. 12; Ps. xlviii. 3; Gen. xxix. 17; Ps. xlviii. 3; Ezek. xxxiii. 32; Eccl. iii. 11 v. 17, &c. Fem. Cant. i. 8; v. 9; Gen. xii 11; xxix. 17, &c. Pl. Gen. xli. 2. 4. 18 Job xlii. 15; Amos viii. 13. Aff. יָפָתִי, Cant. ii. 10. 13.

יָפָה, v. pres. apoc. יִיף (of יָפָה). Constr. abs. *Beautiful, handsome,* Cant. iv. 10; vii 2. 7; Ezek. xvi. 13; xxxi. 7, al. non occ. Pih. pres. aff. יִפֵּהוּ, *Beautified it,* Jer. x. 4. only.—Redup. pret. יָפְיָפִיתָ, *Thou art exceedingly beautiful,* Ps. xlv. 3, only. Gesenius has great doubts whether this does not exhibit an erroneous reading. "Cæterum," says he, "hæc forma analogiâ prorsus caret; neque ullum extat exemplum *primarum* radicalium geminatarum." Because no example is to be found doubling the first radical letters. But we have חַרְחַר, from חָרָה, *he inflamed, &c.,* Gram. art. 197. 3, seq. There can, therefore, be no reason on this ground for suspecting this reading: and the truth is, it is perfectly consistent with the genius of the language. See also art. 169. 3, seq.

Hithp. 2d pers. f. תִּתְיַפִּי, *Thou becomest beautified,* i. e. beautifiest thyself, Jer. iv. 30, only.

יְפֵה־פִיָּה, f. compd., which would more regularly be written יְפֵהפִיָּה, or rather יְפֵיפִית, and so be the ground form of יְפֵיפִית above. The vowels in יְפֵהפִיָּה, have evidently been made to suit the supposition, that the first portion of the compound is in the state of construction with the second; which has the effect of leaving the second in a form not to be accounted for. *Very beautiful,* once, Jer. xlvi. 20.

יֶפַח, m. constr. יְפֵחַ. Cogn. פּוּחַ, נָפַח, ὀνοματοποιητικόν. *Breathing, panting,* for, i. e. longing for, Hab. ii. 3, יָפֵחַ לַקֵּץ, *the vision—breathing for the* (time of the) *end,* i. e. having respect continually to it. Ps. xxvii. 12, וִיפֵחַ חָמָס, *and* (the) *breather out of violence,* taken generically as all such, al. non occ. Hence—

יפח, v. Hithp. תִּתְיַפֵּחַ, *She becomes panting,* in breathless agitation, as in the greatest agonies; once, Jer. iv. 30.

יֳפִי, masc. constr. יְפִי (for יָפְיִ, which does not occur, although given as occurring by Gesen.) See יָפֶה above. (a) *Beauty,* of woman, Ps. xlv. 12; Is. iii. 24; Ezek. xvi.

M M

יפע (266) יצא

25. (b) *Excellency, majesty*, of a king, Is. xxxiii. 17. — of a city, Ps. L. 2; Ezek. xxvii. 3, 4. 11. Aff. יָפְיֵךְ, יָפְיִי, יָפְיֵךְ, יָפְיָה.

יִפְעָה, f. r. יפע, non occ. Aff. only, יִפְעָתֵךְ. Arab. وَفِعَ, *structura elata*, et *excelsa*, and hence applied to a full grown youth (وَفَعَ, f. وَفَعَة): hence also, cogn. יפה. *Beauty, brilliancy*, Ezek. xxviii. 7. 17, only; with יְפִי in the paral. Hence—

יפע, v. Hiph. only, הוֹפִיעַ, f. תּוֹפַע. Constr. immed. it. abs. it. med. מִן, עַל. (a) *Exhibit brilliancy: shine* forth, Deut. xxxiii. 2; Ps. L. 2; lxxx. 2; Job iii. 4; x. 3. 22.

Infin. הוֹפִיעַ, *Causing to shine forth*, Job xxxvii. 15. See my note.

Imp. הוֹפִיעַ, Ps. xciv. 1. With ה parag. Ps. lxxx. 2.

יֵפֶר, pres. apoc. Hiph. r. פרה.

יָפְתְּ, pres. apoc. Hiph. r. פתה.

יָצָא, v. pres. יֵצֵא. Æth. ፃአ: *exivit*. Constr. abs. it. med. מִן, *from*, *because of*, כְּפִי; *from between*; אֶל, עַל, *against*; לְ, *to, for*; לִפְנֵי, *before*; ב, *in*, *against*; עִם, *with*; מִלִּפְנֵי, *from before*; אֶל־מִחוּץ לְ, Deut. xxiii. 11. אֶל־מִנֶּגֶב לְ, ־ה parag., Josh. xv. 3, &c. *Go out, forth*, variously applied, of men, (a) as of a land, city, house, place, &c., Gen. viii. 19; xliv. 4; Exod. xvi. 29; Num. xii. 5, &c.; 1 Kings xi. 29; Eccl. iv. 14; Jer. iv. 7; xxii. 11, &c. (b) — from the womb, the loins, &c., as children, with מִמְּעֵי, מֵחֶם, מִמֵּי, מִכֶּרֶשׁ מִשְׁפַּט, Gen. xxiv. 6; xxv. 26; xlvi. 26; 2 Sam. xvi. 11; Job i. 21; Is. xlviii. 1; Jer. xx. 18, &c. (c) — from a people, as the original stock, 1 Chron. i. 12; ii. 53; Gen. x. 11. (d) — simply, or for the purpose of doing something, Judg. iii. 24; Exod. xvi. 4; Lev. xvi. 24; 1 Sam. xxiii. 15, &c. — to make war, 2 Kings xix. 9; Is. xxxvii. 9. — God to protect; or king to lead, &c., Judg. iv. 14; 2 Sam. v. 2; 1 Chron. xiv. 15, &c. (e) — bondman from bondage, Lev. xxv. 41. 54. חָפְשִׁי, Exod. xxi. 5. לְחָפְשִׁי, Ib. 2, &c. (f) — shepherds against wild beasts, 1 Sam. xvii. 35. (g) — men into captivity, &c., Jer. xlviii. 7; Zech. xiv. 2; Job xxxix. 4, &c. (h) — for peace, or war, לְמִלְחָמָה — לְשָׁלוֹם, Judg. iii. 10; xx. 14; 1 Kings xx. 18, &c.

Metaph. (i) — of the shoot of a tree as of a son, Is. xi. 1. — of the cold, Job xxxviii. 29. — of the soul, as of a person going forth, Cant. v. 6, &c.

Of things inanimate. (k) The sun's rising, as if coming out of the earth, Gen. xix. 23; Ps. xix. 6: — stars, Neh. iv. 15: the morning, Hos. vi. 3. (l) — of plants, 1 Kings v. 13: flowers, Job xiv. 2. (m) — waters, as issuing from a spring, &c., Gen. ii. 10; Deut. viii. 7; Is. xli. 18: metal, in a liquid state, Job xxviii. 1. (n) — of a boundary running out, &c., Josh. xv. 3, 4. 9. 11, &c. (o) — of money expended (outgoing), 2 Kings xii. 13. (p) — of an edict, or word going forth, Hab. i. 4; Is. xlv. 23; Ps. xvii. 2; xix. 5; Esth. vii. 8; Dan. ix. 23. (q) — of the eye protruding with fat, Ps. lxxiii. 7. (r) — of fire, Num. xvi. 35; xxi. 28; Jer. xlviii. 45. (s) — the hand, horn, arrows, &c., Ruth i. 13; Dan. viii. 8; Zech. ix. 14: — breath, Job xxvi. 4; to which many similar usages may be added. Phr. בְּחֵמָא גְדוֹלָה, *with great wrath*, Dan. xi. 44. כַּבָּרָק —, *like lightning*, Zech. ix. 14. נִצָּבִים —, *setting themselves up*, Num. xvi. 27. לְמֵאוֹת —, *for, as, hundreds*, 2 Sam. xviii. 4. גְדוּדִים —, *by troops, detachments*, 2 Kings v. 2. מִתְהַלֵּל, Esth. viii. 14, &c.

Infin. יָצֹא, יָצוֹא, abs., Gen. viii. 7; xxvii. 30, &c.

— constr. צֵאת (for יְצֵאת), Gen. xxiv. 11, &c. Aff. צֵאתִי, &c., Exod. xiii. 8, &c.

Imp. צֵא, Gen. viii. 16, &c. ־ה, parag. Judg. ix. 29.

Pl. צְאוּ, Gen. xix. 14, &c.

F. צְאִי, Cant. i. 8; pl. צְאֶינָה, Ib. iii. 11.

Part. יָצֵא, יוֹצֵא, Gen. ii. 10, &c.: pl. יוֹצְאִים יוֹצְאִים, Exod. xiii. 4, &c. Aff. constr. יוֹצְאֵי, Gen. ix. 10, &c.

— f. יוֹצֵאת יֹצֵאת (for יוֹצְאָה), Gen. xxiv. 15, &c.; once, יֹצֵא, Eccl. x. 5, for יֹצְאָה, once, יֹצְאָה, Deut. xxviii. 57.

Pl. יֹצְאוֹת יוֹצְאוֹת, 1 Sam. ix. 11, &c.

Hiph. הוֹצִיא, pres. יוֹצִיא, יוֹצֵא, יֹצֵא. Constr. immed. it. med. אֶת, מִן, pers. med. ב, place; ב, instr. in; אֶל מִחוּץ, *outwards*; לְ, *to, for*. *Cause to come*, or *go, out; bring out:* of (a) persons, or (b) things, as in Kal. (a) Exod. iii. 11; xii. 51: xiii. 3; Deut. vi. 23; vii. 8, &c. (b) Gen. i. 12. 24; xiv. 18; Lev. iv. 12; vi. 4; xiv. 45; Deut. xxii. 19; Is. lxi. 11; Zech. iv. 7; Job xxviii. 11; Ps. xxv. 15; xxxvii. 6; Prov. xxx. 33, &c. — of tribute exacted, with עַל, 2 Kings xv. 20.

Infin. הוֹצִיא, Exod. vi. 13. 27, &c. Aff.

יצא (267) יצה

הוֹצִיאִי, Jer. vii. 22, Keri. See also Exod. xiv. 11; iii. 12; Deut. xxix. 24; Jer. xxxix. 14; 2 Chron. xxxiv. 14.

Imp. הוֹצִיא הוֹצֵא, Gen. xix. 12; Is. xliii. 8: ה parag. הוֹצִיאָה, Ps. cxlii. 8, &c.
— pl. הוֹצִיאוּ, Gen. xlv. 1, &c.
— f. הוֹצִיאִי, Josh. ii. 3.

Part. מוֹצִיא. מוֹצִא. Aff. מוֹצִיאִי, 2 Sam. xxii. 49, &c.
— pl. מוֹצִיאִים, constr. מוֹצִאֵי, Neh. vi. 19; Num. xiv. 37.

Hoph. pret. f. הוּצְאָה, pres. non occ. *Was, became, brought forth, out, &c.*, Ezek. xxxviii. 8, only.

Part. pl. masc. מוּצָאִים, Ezek. xiv. 22; xlvii. 8.
— f. מוּצֵאת (for מוּצֵאָה), Gen. xxxviii. 25.
— pl. מוּצָאוֹת, Jer. xxxviii. 22.

יצא, Chald. Pehal. non occ.
Shaph. שֵׁיצִיא, *Made out, wrought out, finished*, Ezra vi. 15, only, i. q. Hoph.

יצב, v. cogn. נצב. Arab. وَصَبَ, *firma ac constans fuit* res. Cogn. وَصَبَ.

Hithp. only, constr. abs. it. med. עִם, בְּתַחְתִּית, מֵרָחֹק, בְּתוֹךְ, בִּפְנֵי, לִנְגֶד, מִנֶּגֶד, בְּ, לִפְנֵי, הִתְיַצְּבוּ, pl. m. pres. יִתְיַצֵּב. *Be, become, set up, stand fast*, variously applied: simply, abs., Exod. xiv. 13; 1 Sam. xii. 16; 2 Chron. xx. 17, &c. — in the presence of —, Job i. 6; ii. 1; Zech. vi. 5; 1 Sam. x. 23. — near —, Num. xxiii. 3. 15; 2 Sam. xviii. 13. — on, Ps. xxxvi. 5; Hab. ii. 1. — with —, Num. xi. 16; 2 Chron. xx. 6; Ps. xciv. 16, &c. — among, 1 Sam. x. 23; 2 Sam. xxiii. 12. — far from, הִתְעַצֵּב, for הִתְעַצֵּב, Exod. ii. 4. — against, Ps. ii. 2. — accoutred for war, Jer. xlvi. 4; Job xxxviii. 14, &c.

Infin. הִתְיַצֵּב, 2 Sam. xxi. 5, &c.
Imp. הִתְיַצֵּב, 2 Sam. xviii. 30, &c., ה parag., Job xxxiii. 5.
— pl. הִתְיַצְּבוּ, 1 Sam. x. 19, &c.

יצג, v. Kal non occ. Syr. cogn. ܝܰܨܶܓ, *cætus*: synon. יצב, נצב.

Hiph. הִצִּיג, pres. יַצִּיג, יַצֵּג. Apoc. יַצֵּג. Constr. immed. it. med. לְ, לִפְנֵי, בְּ, עַל, עִם, בְּתוֹךְ, אֵצֶל, אֶת. *Set up, make stand up*, Gen. xxx. 38; xxxiii. 15; xliii. 9; xlvii. 2; Judg. vii. 5; viii. 27; 1 Sam. v. 2; 2 Sam. vi. 17; Hos. ii. 5; 1 Chron. xvi. 1.

Imp. הַצֵּג, Deut. xxviii. 56.
— pl. הַצִּיגוּ, Amos v. 15.
Part. מַצִּיג, Judg. vi. 37.

Hoph. pret. only, יֻצַּג, *Be stayed;* remain unmoved, Exod. x. 24, al. non occ.

יִצְהָר, m. — pl. non occ. Aff. צִהֲרָהּ, once, יִצְהָרְךָ, Deut. vii. 13, where (ʻ)—see Keri—is a mere mater lectionis, (ּ) is therefore immutable, r. צהר. Arab. طَهَرَ, *mundus, purus fuit*. Cogn. ظَهَرَ, *conspicua fuit* res; صَهَرَ, *liquavit* rem; *unxit caput liquamine. Fine oil*, of olives probably, Num. xviii. 12; 2 Kings xviii. 32; Jer. xxxi. 12; Joel i. 10; 2 Chron. xxxi. 5, &c.; Zech. iv. 14. שְׁנֵי בְנֵי-הַיִּצְהָר, *two sons of the* (holy) *oil*. Mystically of the law and Gospel, considered as God's two clear witnesses. Comp. Rev. xi. 3. And see my Exposition on the place, Sermons and Dissertations, Lond., 1830.

יִצְטַבַּע, pres. Ithp. Chald. r. צבע.
יִצְטַיָּרוּ, pres. pl. Hithp. v. ציר.

יְצִיאַי, m. pl. constr. with מִן, pref. מִיצִיאֵי, *From, by, "the effusion of his....loins,"* (his sons) there they felled him, 2 Chron. xxxii. 21, al. non occ.

יַצִּיב, m.   ⎫ pl. non occ. r. יצב. Chald.
יַצִּיבָא, f. ⎭ *Firm, fixed, settled*, matter, Dan. ii. 8. 45; iii. 24; vi. 13; vii. 16. 19, al. non occ.

יצע, v. Kal non occ. Arab. وَضَعَ, *posuit*.

Part. pass. יָצוּעַ, m. I. lit. *laid, placed*, i. e. *bed, couch*. Aff. יְצוּעִי, Gen. xlix. 4; pl. constr. יְצוּעֵי, 1 Chron. v. 1: aff. יְצוּעָי, pl. of excellence, Job xvii. 13; Ps. lxiii. 7; cxxxii. 3, al. non occ. II. יָצִיעַ, Keri, יָצוּעַ, c. pl. non occ. lit. *lien, laid to. The series of small chambers* (otherwise termed צְלָעוֹת) built against each side of the Temple of Solomon; marked (o) in the plan in the Appendix: 1 Kings vi. 5, 6. 10.

Hiph. pret. non occ. pres. יַצִּיעַ, אַצִּיעָה, with ה parag. *Place, strew*, as a bed or couch, Is. lviii. 5; Ps. cxxxix. 8. "*Et orcum mihi substernerem*." Gesen. But, of this "*orcus,*" as often remarked before, it is most probable the ancient Hebrews knew nothing. The deep and dark chambers of the grave was evidently all they meant. See my note on Job xxi. 13; xxvi. 6.

Hoph. pret. יֻצַּע, *Been, become, strewed,*

יצק (268) יצר

spread, as a couch, Is. xiv. 11 ; Esth. iv. 3, al. non occ.

יָצַק, v. pres. יִצֹק. יָצָק (for יִיצָק), once, 1 Kings xxii. 35. אֶצֹּק, אֶצָּק־. Constr. immed. of thing, med. לִפְנֵי, עַל, מִן, לְ. (a) *Pour out*, as water, blood, oil. (b) *Fuse*, as metals. (a) Gen. xxxv. 14; Lev. viii. 15; ix. 9; xiv. 26; Num. v. 15; 2 Sam. xiii. 9; 2 Kings iii. 11, i. e. *served, waited on*; iv. 4. 41, &c. (b) 1 Kings vii. 46; 2 Chron. iv. 17; Exod. xxv. 12; xxvi. 37; xxxvi. 36; Job xxviii. 2, &c. Hence, meton., (c) *Firm, unyielding*, as any thing molten (cogn. צוק), Job xxxviii. 38. See my note, xli. 15, 16.—Metaph. Ps. xli. 9. In sign. (a), Is. xliv. 3, applied to the spirit. Josh. vii. 23, i. q. יָצִיג.

Infin. צֶקֶת, Exod. xxxviii. 27.

Imp. צֹק, 2 Kings iv. 41. יְצֹק, Ezek. xxiv. 3.

Part. pass. יָצוּק, Job xxviii. 2, &c.

— pl. יְצֻקִים, 1 Kings vii. 24 ; f. יְצֻקָה, aff. יְצֻקָתוֹ, *Its being fused*, Ib. pl. יְצֻקוֹת, 1 Kings vii. 30.

Hoph. הוּצַק, pres. יוּצַק, *Be, become, poured out, suffused*. Metaph. Ps. xlv. 3;—Lev. xxi. 10; Job xxii. 16.

Part. מוּצָק, מֻצָּק, 1 Kings vii. 16. 23. 33. Sign. (c) Job xi. 15; xxxvii. 10; xxxviii. 38.

— f. aff. מֻצָקְתּוֹ, 2 Chron. iv. 3. מוּצֶקֶת more properly, מְיֻצָּקָה. Pih. as Gesenius has observed, 2 Kings iv. 5. *The pouring out, &c.*

— pl. מוּצָקוֹת, Zech. iv. 2, noun of instr. lit. *pourers out, canals, tubes*, or *spouts*, perhaps.

יֵצֶר, pl. non occ. Aff. יִצְרוֹ, יִצְרֵנוּ. See v. following. *Formation, imagination, figment* (metaph.) of the mind. Often with לֵב, מַחְשְׁבוֹת, Gen. vi. 5; viii. 21; Deut. xxxi. 21; 1 Chron. xxviii. 9; xxix. 18; Hab. ii. 18; Is. xxvi. 3, יֵצֶר סָמוּךְ, *a* (well) *sustained imagination* (thought). Thou wilt keep, &c., i. e. grounded on thy support, Ib. xxix. 16, וַיֹּאמֶר אָמַר לְיֹצְרוֹ, *or, a thought, imagination* (of man) *say to his Maker, &c.*

יֵצֶר, pres. apoc. Kal. r. צוּר.

יָצַר, v. pres. יִיצֹר. יֹצֵר, aff. יְצָרוֹ, אֶצָּרְךָ. Synon. עָשָׂה, בָּרָא. Arab. وَصَرَ, *pactum*. Cogn. صَار, r. صور, *condidit*. Syr. ܨܪ, *arctavit*; ܨܘܪܬܐ, *imago*. Constr. immed.

it. med. אֶת, לְ, for; עַל, on, against; מִן, from; בְּ, in. *Form, fashion, make*, Gen. ii. 7, 8. 19; Is. xxvii. 11; xxix. 16; xliii. 21; Jer. i. 5; Amos iv. 13; Hab. ii. 18, &c. Metaph. 2 Kings xix. 25 ; Ps. xciv. 20.

Part. יוֹצֵר, יֹצֵר, pl. constr. יֹצְרֵי, Is. xlv. 7. 9 ; Ps. xciv. 9. Aff. יֹצְרִי, &c., Is. xlix. 5, &c. Metaph. Jer. xviii. 11. See under יוֹצֵר above. Applied to God, artificer, &c., as the context shall determine.

— pass. pl. m. aff. יְצֻרַי, lit. things *formed, members*, Job xvii. 7, only. Comp. Ps. cxxxix. 16.

Niph. נוֹצַר, pres. non occ. *Became, was, formed, made*, once, Is. xliii. 10.

Puh. pret. pl. יֻצְּרוּ, i. q. Niph. Metaph. perhaps, Ps. cxxxix. 16, only.

Hoph. pres. יוּצָר, i. q. Niph., Is. liv. 17, only.

יָצַת, v. pret. non occ. pres. f. תִּצַּת, pl. m. יִצְּתוּ, for יִצַּתוּ, f. pl. תִּצַּתְנָה. Constr. med. בְּ, of obj. or instr. (a) *Burn*, Is. ix. 17. (b) *Be set on fire, burnt*, Is. xxxiii. 12 ; Jer. xlix. 2; li. 8.

Niph. f. נִצְּתָה, pres. non occ. *Be, become, set on fire, burning*; it. *burnt*, 2 Kings xxii. 13. 17; Jer. ii. 16; ix. 9. 12; xlvi. 19; Neh. i. 3; ii. 17.

Hiph. הִצִּית, pres. apoc. יַצֵּת, pl. יַצִּיתוּ. Constr. immed. instr. med. עַל, obj. it. בְּ; it. בְּ, instr. אֶת, obj., 2 Sam. xiv. 31 : it. immed. obj., Jer. li. 30: i. q. Kal, if not causative of it, Jer. xi. 16. 1st pers. pret. הִצַּתִּי, Jer. xvii. 27 ; xxi. 14 ; xxxii. 29; 2 Sam. xiv. 30. הוֹצִיתִיהָ, Kethiv, read הוֹצִיתִוּתָהּ. See Keri. Lam. iv. 11; Josh. viii. 8. 19, &c.

Part. מַצִּית, Ezek. xxi. 3, only.

יֶקֶב, m. pl. יְקָבִים, constr. יִקְבֵי. Seg. fm. פָּקַד. Arab. وَقْب, *fovea in monte*, vel *saxo, in quo restagnat aqua*. I. *Wine* —, or *oil-vat*, so placed under the press as to receive the wine, or oil, when expressed from the fruit. LXX. ὑπολήνιον, Joel ii. 24 ; iv. 13. Hewn out of a solid stone, apparently; hence v. חָצַב, Is. v. 2. Comp. Jer. ii. 13 ; 2 Chron. xxvi. 10:—and the term צוּר, *rock*, i. e. stone, Job xxix. 6. See my note. Not that it was a mere well dug in the earth, or cavity in the mountain rock, as Gesenius will have it. Num. xviii. 27. 30 ; 2 Kings vi. 27 ; Zech. xiv. 10, &c. II. Job xxiv. 11. *The trough*, or *cistern*, in which the grapes were trodden, or bruised for the press. Aff. יְקָבֶךָ, pl. יְקָבֶיךָ.

יקד

יָקַד, v. pret. non occ. pres. יֵקַד, יֵקָד. Arab. وَقَدَ, accensus fuit ignis. Syr. ܡܶܬ݂, id. Constr. abs. it. med. עַד, even to. *Burn as fire*, Deut. xxxii. 22; Is. x. 16. Infin. יְקֹד, Ib. Part. f. יֹקֶדֶת, Is. lxv. 5. Hoph. pres. תּוּקַד. Constr. med. בְּ, it. עַל, on; עַד, even to. *Become, be made, burning*, Lev. vi. 2. 5, 6; Jer. xv. 14; xvii. 4, al. non occ.

יְקֵדָא, f. r. יקד, constr. יְקֵדַת. *Burning*, once, Dan. vii. 11. Chald.

יָקִדְתָּא, and יְקִידְתָּא, part. f. r. יקד. *Heated, burning*, Dan. iii. 6. 11. 15. 17. 20, 21. 23. 26, al. non occ. Chald.

יְקֵהַת, f. constr. (With an Euphonic Dagesh.) Arab. يَقِهَ, præcepti admissio. Cogn. وَقَفَ, paruit dicto. *Obedience*, Gen. xlix. 10; Prov. xxx. 17.

יְקוֹד, Infin. v. יקד.

יְקוּם, m.—pl. non occ. r. קוּם. Arab. قَامَ, r. قوم, constitit, erectus fuit. "Quicquid (in terra) vivit," says Gesenius. But neither does the context nor the primitive usage of this word justify this. *Whatever has been raised, made to exist*, or the like, as men, beasts, birds, trees, herbage, flowers, edifices, &c., is clearly comprehended in both, Gen. vii. 4. 23; Deut. xi. 6, only.

יָקוֹשׁ, and יָקֻשׁ, m.—pl. יְקוֹשִׁים. r. יקשׁ. Arab. وَقَشَ; whence, مِيقَاش, forcipes. Castell. *One who snares birds, a fowler*, Ps. xci. 3; Prov. vi. 5; Hos. ix. 8; Jer. v. 26, al. non occ.

יָקַח, and יָקֹד, r. לָקַח, which see.

יַקִּיר, m. r. יקר, once, Jer. xxxi. 20. *Dear, precious, honoured.* Def. Chald. יַקִּירָא, Ezra iv. 10.

יַקִּירָה, f. *Grave, of great import*, Dan. ii. 11, only.

יָקַע, v. pres. f. תֵּקַע. Cogn. נָקַע. Arab. وَقَعَ, cecidit, concidit. Conj. ii. afflixit exercuitque malis. I. *It fell, became dislocated*, the thigh joint, Gen. xxxii. 26. II. *Fall away from,*—of the mind,—affections.

יקץ

Constr. med. מִן, from, by, מֵעַל, Jer. vi. 8; Ezek. xxiii. 17, 18, al. non occ. See נֶבַע.

Hiph. pret. aff. הוֹקִיעֲנוּם, once, 2 Sam. xxi. 6. Constr. לְ, pers. בְּ, in. *We will cause them to drop, fall*, i. e. hang them; pres. aff. יֹקִיעֵם, *they hang them*, Ib. 9. Gesenius finds "*palo afflixit*," empaled, here; but on no ground beyond that of mere fancy.

Imp. הוֹקַע, Num. xxv. 4. Hoph. part. pl. m. מוּקָעִים, *Persons hanged*, 2 Sam. xxi. 13, only.

יָקַץ, v. pres. only, יִיקַץ, יֶקֶץ, once, יָקַץ, Gen. ix. 24. Constr. abs. it. med. מִן. Arab. يَقَظَ, وَقَصَ, *evigilavit, excitatus, fuit*. Cogn. وَقَصَ, *fregit*; it. *fracta fuit* cervix. *Awake from sleep*, Gen. xxviii. 16; xli. 4. 7. 21; Judg. xvi. 14. 20; 1 Kings iii. 15; Ps. lxxviii. 65; Hab. ii. 7; Gen. ix. 24. מִיֵּינוֹ—, *from his wine*, i. e. from his sleep brought on by wine.

יֶקֶר, m. Seg. fm. יִקְרוֹ, pl. non occ.—

יְקָרָה, f. Seg. fm. יִקְרַת, pl. יְקָרוֹת.— Syr. ܐܝܩܪܐ, *gravitas, honorabilitas*. Arab. وَقَرَ, *gravavit; gravis moribus fuit*. *Weight, preciousness, value; honour, glory*. Applied to persons or things, m., Jer. xx. 5; Ezek. xxii. 25; Prov. xx. 15; Job xxviii. 10; Ps. xxxvii. 20; xlix. 13. 21; Esth. i. 4; vi. 6, &c. Aff. יְקָרוֹ. Fem. 1 Kings v. 31 (17); vii. 9—11; Is. xxviii. 16; Zech. xiv. 6, al. non occ. Chald. יְקָר, def. יְקָרָא, once, יְקָרָה, id., Dan. ii. 6; iv. 27. 33; v. 18. 20; vii. 14.

יָקָר, m. pl. יְקָרִים. Constr. sing. יְקַר. יְקָרָה, f. pl. יְקָרוֹת, as in יְקָרָה above: and to this fm. are those plurals referred by Gesen., &c. *Precious, dear; honourable, glorious*, of persons or things, Job xxviii. 16; Ps. xxxvi. 8; cxvi. 15; Prov. i. 13, &c. Hence, *rare, scarce*, 1 Sam. iii. 1. Pl., Lam. iv. 2. Fem., 2 Sam. xii. 30; 1 Kings x. 2. 10, 11; 2 Chron. iii. 6; ix. 1. 9. 10; Prov. vi. 26, &c.; Ps. xlv. 10: pl. aff. with Dagesh euphonic, and prep. בְּ. בִּיקָרוֹתֶיךָ, *among thy honourable women*.

יָקַר, v. pres. יִיקַר, יֵקַר. Constr. abs. it. med. בְּ, in; מֵעַל, by; לְ, pers. *Be, become precious, prized, valued*, of person or thing, 1 Sam. xviii. 30; xxvi. 21; 2 Kings i. 13

יקר (270) ירב

14; Is. xliii. 4; Zech. xi. 13. אֲשֶׁר יְקַרְתִּי מֵעֲלֵיהֶם, in *which I was prized, valued, by them*, ironically, Ps. xlix. 9; lxxii. 14; cxxxix. 17, al. non occ.

Hiph. הֹקַר, pres. 1st pers. אוֹקִיר. Constr. immed. med. מִן. Lit. *make precious*. Meton. *Rare, scarce*, Prov. xxv. 17; Is. xiii. 12, only.

יָקְרָה, r. קָרָה, which see.

יָקֹשׁ, v. יָקֹשְׁתִּי, pl. יָקְשׁוּ, Gram. art. 188. 3. Constr. med. לְ, Jer. l. 24; Ps. cxli. 9, al. non occ. *Snaring, taking as a fowler*. See קוּשׁ.

Part. pl. m. יוֹקְשִׁים, Ps. cxxiv. 7.

Niph. נוֹקַשׁ, 2d pers. pres. תִּנָּקֵשׁ. Constr. abs. it. בְּ, instr. *Be, become, taken, ensnared as a bird*, Is. viii. 15; xxviii. 13. Metaph. Deut. vii. 25; Ps. ix. 17; Prov. vi. 2, al. non occ.

Puh. Part. m. pl. יוּקָּשִׁים, i. e. the ground-form of the pret., applied as if a participial noun (מוֹקְשִׁים), Gram. art. 182. 2, Eccl. ix. 12.

יָקֵשׁ, see r. קָשָׁה,—it. יָקֹשׁ, Hiph. of do.

יָרֵא, m. constr. יְרֵא, pl. יְרֵאִים, constr. יִרְאֵי.—

יִרְאַת, f. constr. pl. non occ.—

Participial noun (Gram. artt. 155. 5. 6; 192). *Fearing*, (a) God; or (b) man; mostly with pronouns, and hence equivalent to the verb, as in the Syriac. Constr. immed. it. abs. it. med. אֵת, מִן, לְ, with Infin., Gen. xlii. 18; Deut. xxv. 18; Judg. vii. 6; Eccl. viii. 13; Jer. xxvi. 19; Jonah i. 9: — the word, &c. (a) of God, Exod. ix. 20; Prov. xiii. 13. In constr. יְרֵא אֱלֹהִים, *fearer of God*, Gen. xxii. 12; Job i. 8, &c. Pl., Exod. xviii. 21; Ps. xv. 4, &c. — of his name, Mal. iii. 20. Comp. 16. — an oath, Eccl. ix. 2. — the sword, Jer. xlii. 16. (b) — of man, Gen. xxxii. 12; Deut. vii. 19; xx. 8. Constr. distinct. יְרֵא וְרַךְ לֵבָב, 1 Sam. xxiii. 3, abs., Jer. xlii. 11, &c.; Eccl. ix. 2. Fem., Prov. xxxi. 30. Aff. יְרֵאָיו, יְרֵאַי.

יָרָא, it. יָרָא, r. רָאָה.

יָרָא, v. pres. יִרָא, יָרֵא. Arab. cogn. وَرِعَ, *præ metu attonitus fuit*; وَرَعَ, *timidus fuit*. Constr. abs. it. immed. it. med. אֵת, מִן, לְ, Infin. it. for, בְּ, in. *Fear* (a) God, (b) man, (c) thing. (a) Lev. xix. 14. 32; xxv. 17. 36; 1 Kings xviii. 3, &c. (b) Gen. xix. 30; xxvi. 7; xlvi. 3; Judg. vi. 27; vii. 3; viii. 20; 1 Kings i. 50, &c. (c)

1 Sam. xiv. 26; Ps. cxix. 120; Deut. xxviii. 58; Ps. xxiii. 4; lxxxvi. 11; Is. xxxvii. 6, &c. יְרָאתֶם, irreg. for יְרֵאתֶם, Josh. iv. 24, by error of the copyists, no doubt.

Infin. יְרֹא, with לְ, לְרָא, for לִירֹא, Josh. xxii. 25; 1 Sam. xviii. 29.

— it. יִרְאָה, f. constr. יִרְאַת. Aff. יִרְאָתִי, &c., Deut. iv. 10; v. 29; Gen. xx. 11; 2 Sam. xxiii. 3; Jer. xxxii. 40, &c. Meton. *True religion*, as consisting of the fear of God, Ps. xix. 10; Job iv. 6; xv. 4, &c.

Imp. יְרָא, pl. יְראוּ, Prov. iii. 7; Josh. xxiv. 14, &c. The ר partaking, in some degree, of the character of the letters אהוי, takes the (ִ) in the pl. here, with the first, rather than the second letter of the word. Not unlike this is the analogy of Gram. art. 73.

Niph. pret. non occ. pres. once, תִּוָּרֵא, 2d pers. sing., Ps. cxxx. 4, *Thou art to be feared, reverenced*.

Part. נוֹרָא, pl. non occ. (m.) applied to (a) God, (b) man, or (c) things. *Fearful*, f. נוֹרָאָה, pl. נוֹרָאוֹת, aff. נוֹרְאֹתֶיךָ, *terrible*, (a) Exod. xv. 11; Ps. xlvi. 3. Constr. distinct., Gram. art. 225. נוֹרָא עֲלִילָה, *terrible* (in frequent, reiterated) *operation*. Comp. Exod. xv. 11; Deut. x. 17; Neh. i. 5, &c. — the name, i. e. person, of God, Christ, i. q. מַלְאַךְ הָאֱלֹהִים, Judg. xiii. 6, to whom this epithet is applied: מַלְאַךְ יְהוָה, Ib. vr. 13. 15, 16. 18, פֶּלֶא. Comp. Is. ix. 5;—and here vv. 22, 23;—Mal. i. 14; Ps. xcix. 3; cxi. 9, &c. (b) Is. xviii. 2. 7, &c. (c) — day of God, i. e. of his marvellous works, Joel ii. 21; iii. 4; Mal. iii. 23. — place in which God appeared, Gen. xxviii. 17. — God's works generally, Exod. xxxiv. 10; Ps. lxvi. 3;—xlv. 5, תּוֹרֵךָ נוֹרָאוֹת יְמִינֶךָ, for תּוֹרְךָ יְמִינְךָ בְּשַׂמֵּחַ נוֹרָאוֹת, *thy right hand shall teach thee*, i. e. instruct people what thou art, *by thy doing wonders*, wonderfully. See Is. lxiv. 2. Similar phraseology is that in Eph. iv. 20, ὑμεῖς δὲ οὐχ οὕτως ἐμάθετε τὸν Χριστόν; Ps. lxv. 6; cvi. 22, &c.

Pih. pret. pl. aff. יֵרְאֻנִי, *They made, caused, me to fear*, 2 Sam. xiv. 15, pres. non occ.

Infin. aff. יָרְאֻנִי, *To make me fear*, Neh. vi. 19. יָרְאָם, 2 Chron. xxxii. 18, al. non occ.

Part. pl. m. מְיָרְאִים, Neh. vi. 9. 14, al. non occ.

יָרֵב, for יָאֱרַב, r. אָרַב, apoc. pres. Hiph.

יָרֵב, see v. רִיב.

יֵרַד, v. pres. יֵרֵד, apoc. יֵרְדְּ, in pause, יֵרַד,

ירד

it. f. תֵּרֵד, not in pause, Lam. iii. 48, by mistake of the copyists probably. Arab. وَرَدَ, descendit in stomachum humor. Æth.

ⲱⲈⲢ: descendit. Cogn. وَرَطَ, præcipitem dedit. Constr. abs. it. med. עַל, אֶל ה, לִקְרַאת, בְּ, in, to; לִפְנֵי, לְ, Infin. it. to, place; מִן, from; מֵאֵת, it. immed. elliptically. Descend, of things animate, and inanimate, from a higher place, state, &c., to a lower, either properly or conventionally, Gen. xxiv. 16. 45; Exod. ii. 5; Josh. xvii. 9; 1 Kings xviii. 40; Is. xlii. 10; Ps. cvii. 23; Ezek. xxvii. 29; Ruth iii. 3. 6; 1 Sam. ix. 27; 2 Kings vi. 18. — from a metropolis, as usually built on elevated places, Gen. xii. 10; xxvi. 2; xlvi. 3; 1 Sam. xiii. 20; xxiii. 6. See Auth. Vers., xxv. 1; xxvi. 2, &c. Hence the usage of the New Test., go up to Jerusalem, John vii. 8; Acts xv. 2. — of rivers, rain, &c., Deut. ix. 21; Ps. lxxii. 6; Num. xxxiv. 11, 12; Josh. xviii. 13. — of tears, Lam. i. 16; iii. 48; Jer. ix. 17, &c. — of the day declining, Judg. xix. 11; but here we have רַד, for יָרַד, if it is not the Infin. of רָדָה, or a derivative of רָדָה, or רוּד. — of men, beasts, or things, to death, ruin, &c., Ps. lv. 16; Job vii. 9; xvii. 16; xxxiii. 24; Is. xxxii. 19; xxxiv. 7; Deut. xx. 20; xxviii. 52; Zech. xi. 2. Metaph. Deut. xxviii. 43.

Infin. abs. יָרֹד, Gen. xliii. 20. Aff. יָרְדִי, Ps. xxx. 4. Keri.

— it. f. רְדָה, Gen. xlvi. 3.

— it. f. רֶדֶת, Deut. xxviii. 52; Num. xi. 9, &c. Aff. רִדְתִּי, &c., Ps. xxx. 10, &c.

Imp. רֵד, Exod. xix. 21, ה parag., Gen. xlv. 9; in pause, רֵדָה, 2 Kings i. 9, &c.

— pl. רְדוּ, Gen. xlii. 2, &c.

— f. רְדִי, Is. xlvii. 1, &c.

Part. יֹרֵד, pl. יֹרְדִים, יֹרְדֵי, Judg. ix. 36, 37; 1 Sam. x. 8, &c. Constr. יֹרְדֵי, Ps. cxv. 17, &c.

— f. יֹרֶדֶת, יֹרְדָה, pl. יֹרְדוֹת, Lam. i. 16; Eccl. iii. 21; Prov. v. 5, &c.

Hiph. הוֹרִיד, הֹרִד, pres. יוֹרִיד, apoc. יֹרֵד, it. יָרֵד. Constr. immed. it. med. פַּתַח, אֶת, מֵעַל, from; עַל, on; בְּ, instr. לְ, to; ה parag. Make descend, bring down, cast down, &c., of persons or things, Gen. xlv. 13; Josh. ii. 18; 2 Kings xvi. 17; Is. x. 13; xliii. 14; lxiii. 6; Ezek. xxxiv. 26; Lam. ii. 10; Ps. lxxviii. 16; Prov. xxi. 22, &c. Once, 1 Kings vi. 32, יָרַד (for וַיֹּרֶד = יוֹרֵד; compensating the loss of the ו, by [ֹ]).

ירד

Phrr. שְׁאוֹל — "in orcum," says Gesenius—to the grave, however, is all that is meant, 1 Sam. ii. 6; and Ezek. xxxi. 16. שְׁאֹלָה —, id. Ps. lv. 24, לִבְאֵר שַׁחַת, to the pit of destruction. Comp. Ezek. xxviii. 8. 1 Kings ii. 9, הוֹרַדְתָּ אֶת־שֵׂיבָתוֹ בְדָם, bring thou down his grey hair with blood to the grave. Comp. Gen. xlii. 38; xliv. 29; Ezek. xxvi. 20; Lam. ii. 18, פַּלְגֵי דִמְעָה —, tears as a stream. כַּדָּהּ עָלֶיהָ —, her pitcher on her hand, Gen. xxiv. 18. וְרִירוֹ אֶל־זְקָנוֹ —, his saliva on his beard, 1 Sam. xxi. 14.

Infin. הוֹרִיד, Gen. xxxvii. 25. Aff. הוֹרִדִי, Ezek. xxxi. 16.

Imp. הוֹרֵד, Exod. xxxiii. 5, &c.

— pl. הוֹרִידוּ, Gen. xliii. 11.

— f. הוֹרִידִי, Lam. ii. 18.

Part. מוֹרִיד, 1 Sam. ii. 6; 2 Sam. xxii. 48.

Hoph. הוּרַד, pres. 2 pers. תּוּרָד. Be brought down, lowered, Gen. xxxix. 1; Num. x. 17; Is. xiv. 11. 15; Zech. x. 11; Ezek. xxxi. 18.

יַרְדֵּן, m. in mere narrative, generally with the article, הַיַּרְדֵּן, The Jordan, r. יָרַד, cogn. רדה. Syr. ܢܰܪܕܳܢ, lit. runner, river. Pers. رَفْتَن, proceed, go. Where رَوْ, for رَفْ, is the root. So the German, Rhyn, Rhein, from the v. rinnen, as Gesenius has observed, Gen. xiii. 10, 11; xxxii. 11, &c. In Job xl. 23, for any large river, as many have thought; but this has resulted from a mistaken view of that place. See my notes. As well might the Euphrates be taken for any large river. "Quod sane," says Gesenius, "scriptorem in Palæstina degertem prodit." But, has any writer of Palestine ever used the word יַרְדֵּן, in this loose sense? No such thing. And, could no writer out of Palestine speak of the Jordan? Surely any one on the east side of that river might speak of it just as naturally as one on the west could.

יַרְדֹּף, see r. רָדַף.

יָרֹה, v. pres. 1st pers. pl. aff. נִירָם, once, Num. xxi. 30. Gesenius gives יֵרֶה; but it never occurs. Æth. ⲱⲢⲱ: projectus fuit. Arab. وَرَى, affecit læsitve eum in pulmone; وَرَى, ignem scintillasve emisit. Constr. immed. it. med. בְּ, in, לְ, for. (1) Cast out, shoot, send forth, armed force, the lot, arrows, stones, &c., Exod. xv. 4; 1 Sam.

ירה

xx. 36, 37; Josh. xviii. 6; Prov. xxvi. 18; 2 Chron. xxvi. 15, &c. (b) *Cast, lay*, as a foundation, Job xxxviii. 6; Gen. xxxi. 51.

Infin. abs. יָרֹה, Exod. xix. 13. With לְ, לִירוֹא, 2 Chron. xxvi. 15, it. לִירוֹת, Ps. xi. 2; lxiv. 5.

Imp. יְרֵה, 2 Kings xiii. 17.

Part. יוֹרֶה, pl. יוֹרִים, *Casting forth*; pl. *archers*,—Prov. xxvi. 18; 1 Chron. x. 3; 2 Chron. xxxv. 23. In Hos. vi. 3, כְּמַלְקוֹשׁ יוֹרֶה אָרֶץ, *as the former rain sprinkling the earth*; but this is by no means well founded. Much better take יוֹרֶה here, as in Hiph. i. q. מוֹרֶה, i. e. *causing the earth to send forth, shoot out, &c.*, an expression very suitable to the rain supposed to fall immediately after the sowing of the seed. Comp. Deut. xi. 14; Jer. v. 24, where it also occurs. In Prov. xi. 25, יוֹרֶא, often classed with this word, ought evidently to be read יוֹרֶה, or יוּרָא, Hoph. or Niph. יֵרֶה, *Shall be, become, watered, satiated*. Arab. cogn. روي, *satiavit, irrigavit*. Syr. ܪܘܝ, *madefactus fuit*. Æth. ሮዐየ: id.

Niph. pres. יֵרֶה, *Shall be shot*, Exod. xix. 13, al. non occ.

Hiph. הוֹרָה, pres. יוֹרֶה, apoc. יֹר. Constr. immed. it. med. לְ, בְּ, אֶל, עַל, מֵעַל, i. q. Kal. (a) *Cast forth, shoot*, as arrows, rain, &c. (b) *Put forth*, as instruction, i. e. *teach, instruct*. (a) Job xxx. 19; 1 Sam. xx. 20; 2 Sam. xi. 20; 2 Kings xix. 32; Is. xxxvii. 33; 2 Kings xiii. 17; Ps. lxiv. 4. 8; 2 Chron. xxxv. 23: rain, Hos. x. 12; as the context seems to suggest; but (sign. b) *teach*, is perhaps also intended, by a play on the word not unusual with the prophets. יוֹרֶא, Prov. xi. 25, is usually put under Hiph., but see under the Part. above, Joel ii. 23; Ps. lxxxiv. 7. Part.

(b) *Teach, instruct*, Exod. iv. 12. 15; 1 Sam. xii. 23; 1 Kings viii. 36; Ps. xxv. 8; Job xxvii. 11, &c.

Infin. הוֹרוֹת, (b) Gen. xlvi. 28, &c. Aff. הוֹרוֹתָם, Exod. xxiv. 12.

Imp. aff. הֹרֵנִי, Job xxxiv. 32, &c.

— pl. הוֹרוּנִי, Ib. vi. 24.

Part. מוֹרֶה, pl. מוֹרִים, (a) 1 Sam. xx. 37; xxxi. 3, &c. (b) Job xxxvi. 22; Is. xxx. 20, &c. Aff. מוֹרֶיךָ, מוֹרֶךָ.

ירה, with ה rad. once, pres. pl. תִּרְהוּ, Is. xliv. 8. Arab. ورى, *præ metu attonitus fuit. Be astounded* with fear. Usually classed under יָרֵא, *feared*. LXX. μὴ πλανᾶσθε. Gesenius.

ירו

יָרוּן, r. רָנַן.

יָרוּץ, r. רָצַץ.

יָרוֹק, m. once, Job xxxix. 8, r. ירק *Green* herb, shoot.

יְרוּשָׁלַם, rarely יְרוּשָׁלֵם, 1 Chron. iii. 5. *Jerusalem*, so called after the times of David; in whose days it became the place, in which it had been predicted God would cause his name to dwell, and which should, therefore, be *the chosen* place. In earlier times it was styled שָׁלֵם, Gr. Σόλυμα, Gen. xiv. 18; Ps. lxxvi. 3: and יְבוּס, *Jebus*, Judg. xix. 10, &c. So that it had once both these names; which, if compounded, would read יְבוּשָׁלֵם, or יְבוּשָׁלַם; and, omitting the Dagesh, as being irregular after a perfect vowel (here וּ), we should have יְרוּשָׁלֵם, &c., which would signify something like, *the trampling or treading down of peace*; so named, perhaps, on account of the warlike character of its ancient idolatrous inhabitants; but most unsuitably as the city, which God himself had chosen for his own. If then we take ירוּ, as a part. pass. of ירה above, in the sense of *founded*, i. e. *house, &c.*, we shall have the دار السلام, *house, mansion, of peace*, of Saadias Haggaon, i. q. مدينة السلام, *city of peace*. Or, if we take either of the other significations of that verb, an equally suitable denomination will be the result. In this case, the transition from the old to the new name would be easy, and quickly adopted. It is true we find no such compound as that supposed above; yet this new name looks so like a compound of the two old ones, that it seems very likely to have been chosen for the purpose of intimating the existence of them both, with the altered character which this city was ever after to sustain. It is no uncommon thing, moreover, for eastern cities to receive a new name on such occasions as that mentioned above. So *Bagdad* (باغ داد, *garden of justice*,) received the title of مدينة المنصور, *city of Mansur*, Abulfed. Ann. Moslem., tom. ii. 103: and, part of it, that of مدينة السلام, *city of peace*, Ib. p. 789. The dual marked by the vowels in יְרוּשָׁלַם, &c., is, in all probability, a

ירח (273) ירך

mere figment of the Jews. In the Chald. of Daniel and Ezra, it is still יְרוּשְׁלֵם, or יְרוּשְׁלַם, Dan. v. 2; vi. 11; Ezra vi. 8. Gr. Ἱερουσαλήμ, and Ἱεροσόλυμα. See Anot. et Vind. Noldii. n. 791, p. 825.

יָרֵחַ, m. pl. יְרָחִים, constr. יַרְחֵי. Arab. وَرَخ, mollis, ac tenuis fuit. Conj. ii. i. q. اَرَخَ, temporis adscriptione notavit epistolam. Whence, our term era, and, as some think, year. Month of the ancient Hebrews. See under חֹדֶשׁ. A lax description—as with ourselves—of the period in which the moon performs its revolution round the earth: time being reckoned among them, in all probability, by solar computation, 1 Kings vi. 37, 38; viii. 2; Zech. xi. 8. Pl., Exod. ii. 2; Deut. xxxiii. 14; Job iii. 6; xxix. 2, &c. Phr. יֶרַח יָמִים, a month of days, i. e. its space; if small space (the primitive notion apparently) is not here meant, Deut. xxi. 13; 2 Kings xv. 13.

יָרֵחַ, m.—pl. non occ. Aff. יְרֵחִי, Is. lx. 20. Concr. noun of agency. The moon, Gen. xxxvii. 9; Ps. viii. 4; civ. 19. Phr. לִפְנֵי יָרֵחַ, i. q. עַד בְּלִי דּוֹר דּוֹרִים, Ps. lxxii. 5. יָרֵחַ, id. Ib. vr. 7. יָרֵחַ יָקָר הֹלֵךְ, the moon gloriously proceeding on, Job xxxi. 26.

יְרַח, m. Chald. i. q. Heb. יֶרַח, Ezra vi. 15.

יָרַט, v. pres. aff. once, יִרְטֵנִי, for יִירְטֵנִי. Arab. وَرَط, præcipitem dedit in exitium; conj. v. lapsus fuit in exitium. Precipitating into ruin, Job xvi. 11. See my note. Num. xxii. 32, יָרַט הַדֶּרֶךְ לְנֶגְדִּי, ellip. for וגו׳ יָרַט אַף, thou art lost as to way, i. e. art in a ruinous state: taking יָרַט as a verbal noun. LXX. οὐκ ἀστεία ἡ ὁδός σου ἐναντίον μου.

יָרִיב, m. aff. sing. יְרִיבֵךְ, pl. יְרִיבַי, r. רִיב. Contender, opposer, adversary, Is. xlix. 25; Jer. xviii. 19; Ps. xxxv. 1, al. non occ.

יְרִיעָה, fem. plur. יְרִיעוֹת, יְרִיעָה. Syr. ܝܪܺܝܥܳܐ, velum tentorii. Veil, or curtain, of a tent, &c., Exod. xxvi. 1—5; xxxvi. 9; Is. liv. 2; Ps. civ. 2, &c.; Hab. iii. 7. Meton. Pavilions. Aff. יְרִיעֹתַי, יְרִיעֹתֵיהֶם.

יָרֵךְ, pres. Niph. r. רָכַךְ.

יָרֵךְ, c. constr. יֶרֶךְ, dual, יְרֵכַיִם. Aff.

יְרֵכִי, &c. Arab. وَرِك, femur, clunes.. (a) The thigh, Num. v. 21, 22; Gen. xxiv. 2. 9; xxxii. 26. 32; Exod. xxviii. 42, &c. Phr. שׁוֹק עַל יָרֵךְ, Judg. xv. 8, leg upon thigh, i. e. wholly, Vulg. Eng. "hip and thigh." סָפַק אֶל יָרֵךְ, strike upon the thigh, in token of distress, Ezek. xxi. 17. כַּף הַיָּרֵךְ, the joint of the thigh, at which it is united with the pelvis, Gen. xxxii. 33. יֹצְאֵי יֶרֶךְ יַעֲקֹב, offspring of the thigh of Jacob, Exod. i. 5. On the practice of laying the hand under the thigh in making oaths, see under יָד. The sword usually hung upon the right thigh, Judg. iii. 21; Ps. xlv. 4. And—as with the hand (יָד)—used to designate (b) side, part, Exod. xl. 22. 24; Lev. i. 11; Num. iii. 29. 35; 2 Kings xvi. 14.

(c) Used also to designate the standard of the candlestick of the sanctuary, out of which the branches on each side proceeded, Exod. xxv. 31; xxxvii. 17: "forma feminea יָרֵכָה," says Gesen. But the latter place has יְרֵכָהּ, with the pron. f., and nothing can be more certain than that the former ought to be so written; and so the older editions read it. The omission is, I suspect, a mere error of the press in Van der Hooght's edition, which has been carefully continued by subsequent editors; and here it has been made by Gesenius the basis of a rule! LXX. ὁ καυλὸς αὐτῆς. Gesenius finds "nates" signified by this word, Num. v. 21. 27. I can find no such sense there; nor does Ez. xxiv. 4, exhibit any new sense.

יַרְכָה, f. aff. יַרְכָתוֹ, once, Gen. xlix. 13, dual, יַרְכָתַיִם, i. q. יָרֵךְ, sign. (b). Side, part, quarter, Exod. xxvi. 23; 1 Kings vi. 16; Ezek. xlvi. 10. In all which Gesenius gets from "nates, clunes"—which are groundless—"pars postica," &c., which is equally so. In Ps. cxxviii. 3; Jon. i. 5; 1 Sam. xxiv. 4; Is. xiv. 15; Ezek. xxxii. 23, he finds "partes postremæ," "penetralia," &c., for all which there is not the least ground whatsoever. And so of Is. xxxvii. 24; Judg. xix. 1. 18, &c., which, whether they have such signification or not, must depend on the circumstances of the context. See Exod. xxvi. 23; xxxvi. 28; Ps. xlviii. 3, &c., where such qualifying words are given.

יַרְכָה, f. Chald. i. q. Heb. יָרֵךְ. The thigh. Aff. יַרְכָתַהּ, Its thigh, generically, thighs, Dan. ii. 32. Where Gesen. again finds "clunes!" Theod. οἱ μηροί.

N N

יָרַע, r. רָעָה, or רָעַע.

יָרַע, v. pres. יֵרַע. Constr. abs. it. med. לְ, pers. בְּ, in. Cogn. רֵעַ רוּעַ. Arab. ورع, *timidus, it. debilis fuit*. Be in *afflicted, evil, condition; grieved, pained*, Is. xv. 4. נַפְשׁוֹ יָרְעָה לּוֹ, lit. *his soul was to him afflicted*; he possessed it in evil plight. "*Contremiscit ei*." Gesen. But nothing intimating fear or trembling is to be found here, Neh. ii. 10. יֵרַע לָהֶם רָעָה גְדֹלָה, *it afflicted them* (with) *a great evil*, Gen. xxi. 12; Deut. xv. 10; 1 Sam. i. 8; Job xx. 26. See my note. — *of the evil eye*, Deut. xxviii. 54. 56.

יֶרֶק, m. pl. non occ. Arab. ورق, *frons folium*. Syr. id. ورق, *frondes avulsit*; ورق, *fronduit* arbor. The primary notion seems to have consisted in *throwing, shooting, out*. See יצא, and ירה; hence applied I., to *green herbs*, as shoots out of the earth; II. to *spitting*, as shot out of the mouth. Æth. ⲞⲢⲔ: *spuit, expuit. Freshness, greenness*, i. e. *herbage*, as grass, Gen. i. 30; ix. 3; Num. xxii. 4; Ps. xxxvii. 2; Is. xv. 6. — *produce of trees*, Exod. x. 15. In the last instance, *fruit* is evidently meant; examine the previous member: whence it should seem, that *greenness* is not necessarily meant by this word.

יָרָק, m. constr. יְרַק, pl. non occ. *Fresh, green, herb*, Deut. xi. 10; 1 Kings xxi. 2; 2 Kings xix. 26; Is. xxxvii. 27; Prov. xv. 17. Syr. ܝܰܪܩܳܐ, *olus*.

יָרַק, v. pres. non occ. Cogn. רקק רוק. See יֶרֶק, sign. ii. above. *Spit*, — בִּפְנֵי, in the presence of —, Num. xii. 14; Deut. xxv. 9. See my note on Job xxx. 10.

Infin. יָרֹק, Num. l. c.

יִרְקוֹן, m. pl. non occ. See יֶרֶק above: whence, ⲞⲢⲔ: *expuit*: hence, meton. Syr. ܡܰܪܩܳܐ, *attenuatus est, macruit*, i. e. from, casting, throwing, out, we have the notion of *exhaustion*; thence, *wasting, &c.*

Syr. ܡܰܪܩܳܢܳܐ, *pallor*. Arab. يرقان, *rubigo*; mostly with שִׁדָּפוֹן דֶּבֶר. *Wasting, blasting*; perhaps (a) *the smut* in corn, Deut. xxviii. 22; 1 Kings viii. 37; Amos iv. 9; Hag. ii. 17. (b) *Withering, wrinkling, wasting*, in the face, Jer. xxx. 6. Aquila, ἰκτέρῳ. LXX. ὤχρα, ἴκτερον, ἀνεμοφθορία. Theod. ὠχρι-άσει. "*Smut*, or *ustilage*" (in corn), when the distempered ear comes out of its covering formed by the blades, looks *lank* and *meagre*; the common, and immediate covering of the grains, are in this case so very *slight* and *thin*, that the black powder is seen through them," &c. Rees's Encyclop. sub voce. I quote this to show how exactly the description of the disease agrees with the etymology given above. The *yellowness*, &c., of the Greek and other translators, gave a name of this disease formed on other considerations. The "*rubigo*," of Pliny is evidently of this sort. H. N., lib. xviii. 44.

יְרַקְרַק, m. pl. fem. יְרַקְרַקֹּת, redup. of רקק. LXX. χλωρίζουσα, χλωρότητι. Arab. برّاق, *ensis multo fulgore*. *Greenish*, or *yellowish*, occurring with אֲדַמְדָּם, *shining, bright*, is, most likely, its true meaning. It is one of the symptoms of *the leprosy*, Lev. xiii. 49; xiv. 36, i. e. of the *lepra vulgaris*, which is thus described. "The *lepra* vulgaris shews itself in small *reddish* (אֲדַמְדָּמוֹת), and *shining* (יְרַקְרַקּוֹת) elevations of the cuticle. These patches.... are surrounded by a *red* border." Again, on the progress towards a cure. "The scales being farther and farther removed, a circle of red shining cuticle.... appears within the original patch," &c. Rees's Encyclop. sub voce. Applied to gold, Ps. lxviii. 14, al. non occ.

יָרַשׁ, v. pres. יִירַשׁ, יֵרַשׁ. Constr. abs. it. immed. it. med. אֶת, עִם, לְ. Arab. ورث, *hæreditate accepit*. Syr. ܝܺܪܶܬ, ܡܺܬ, id. (a) *Possess, inherit, succeed in possession*: and, meton. (b) *Dispossess* others, supposing *possession* thus to have been obtained: hence, by a further meton., (c) *Be, become poor*: of person or thing, Num. xxvii. 11; Deut. vi. 18; xii. 29; Ib. xix. 1; xxx. 5; xxxi. 3: יְרֵשְׁתָּם, it. יְרַשְׁתָּם, Ib. iv. 1, &c., taken from the Arab. ورث, perhaps, Gram. art. 188. 28, note; Ps. lxix. 36, &c. Pres. Gen. xv. 8; xxii. 17; Ps. xxxvii. 9, &c. (b) Deut. ii. 12. 21. 22; ix. 1; xi. 23, &c.

Infin. רֶשֶׁת (for יְרֶשֶׁת), Lev. xx. 24, &c. Aff. רִשְׁתְּךָ, &c., Gen. xxviii. 4; xv. 7; 1 Kings xxi. 16, &c. It. aff. יִירָשֵׁנוּ, Judg. xiv. 15.

Imp. parag. יְרָשָׁה, Deut. xxxiii. 23.

ירש (275) ישר

Imp. רֵשׁ, Deut. i. 21; in pause, רָשׁ, Ib. ii. 24, &c.
— pl. רְשׁוּ, Deut. i. 8, &c.
Part. יוֹרֵשׁ, Gen. xv. 3; Deut. xviii. 14.
— pl. יוֹרְשִׁים, Deut. xii. 2, &c. Aff. יוֹרְשָׁיו, Jer. xlix. 2.
— f. יֹרֶשֶׁת, Num. xxxvi. 8, only.
Niph. pres. יִוָּרֵשׁ, sign. (c) above. *Be, become, poor.* Cogn. רוּשׁ, Gen. xlv. 11; Prov. xx. 13; xxiii. 21; xxx. 9, al. non occ.
Pih. pres. יָרֵשׁ, Gesen. "*pauperem reddidit,*" Deut. xxviii. 42. But the things here mentioned are the fruits of the country: how these can be made poor I cannot see. They may be *taken in possession,* and that it is perhaps the intention of the writer to say. Hither Gesenius also refers. הֹלַירְשֵׁנִי, Judg. xiv. 15. How, then, are we to account for the prefixed ל? He says the Infinitive would be לְרִשְׁנוּ. It is true this would be an Infinitive of this verb; but it is not certain, nevertheless, that the other word is not also an Infinitive, as more Infinitives than one are often found with verbs: and, as the construction requires that this be considered as an Infinitive, I take for granted that it is so.
Hiph. הוֹרִישׁ, pres. יוֹרִישׁ; apoc. יוֹרֵשׁ. Constr. immed. abs. it. med. אֶת, מִפְּנֵי. (a) *Make, cause, to possess, succeed in possession,* Num. xiv. 24; Josh. viii. 7; xvii. 12; Judg. i. 19; Job xiii. 26; 2 Chron. xx. 11, &c. (b) *Dispossess, drive from possession,* Exod. xxxiv. 24; Num. xxxii. 21; xxxiii. 52; Deut. iv. 38; Judg. xi. 24; Job xx. 15; 1 Sam. ii. 7. (c) *Make poor,* 1 Sam. ii. 7. Meton. *Desolate,* Num. xiv. 12, &c.
Infin. הוֹרִשׁ, once, הוֹרִישׁ, Judg. i. 28; Deut. iv. 38; Josh. iii. 10, &c. Aff. הוֹרִישׁוֹ, Num. xxxii. 21; Judg. ii. 23.
Part. מוֹרִישׁ, Deut. xviii. 12, &c. Aff. מוֹרִשָׁם, Deut. ix. 4.

יְרֵשָׁה, f. pl. non occ. *A possession,* Num. xxiv. 18, only.

יְרֻשָּׁה, f. (for יְרוּשָׁה. Part. pass. lit. *thing possessed*), constr. יְרֻשַּׁת. *A possession,* Deut. ii. 5. 9. 19; Judg. xxi. 17, &c. Aff. יְרֻשָּׁתְךָ, יְרֻשַּׁתְכֶם, יְרֻשָּׁתוֹ.

ישם, v. i. q. שׂום, pres. only, 1st pers. parag. אָשִׂימָה, Judg. xii. 3. Kethiv. See Keri. Gen. xxiv. 33. יָשֵׂם, or יָשֶׂם, Kethiv. Keri, יָשִׂים, Ib. l. 26. יָשֵׂם.

יִשְׂרָאֵל, m. compd. The name given to Jacob on the occasion of the angel's wrestling with him (Gen. xxxii. 29. Comp. Hos. xii. 5), intimating the esteem in which he was held by God. Arab. سَرْو, *elatio gloriæ et nobilitatis*; it. سَرَاة, *superior pars, &c.*— of Heb. שַׂר, *Prince, leader*; and אֵל, *God, Prince of God.* Comp. שָׂרָה, Gen. xi. 29. Hence, he was, after Abraham, the head of God's chosen people, and bore this name as a voucher that, as he had prevailed with the angel, so should he with men, עִם־אֲנָשִׁים תּוּכָל. Hence, too, Exod. iv. 22, "*Israel is my son,*" &c. Hence, the *true Israelite,* ἀληθῶς Ἰσραηλίτης, John i. 48. Comp. Rom. ix. 6; Is. xlix. 3; Ps. lxxiii. 1, &c.; is God's adopted child (Eph. i. 5); reigns with Christ (Rom. v. 17, &c.); and, through him, is more than a conqueror (Ib. viii. 37). Under the New Covenant, to be called by a *New Name,* Is. lxii. 2. Comp. Jer. xxxiii. 16; Acts xi. 26; χρηματίσαι τε πρῶτον.... τοὺς μαθητὰς χριστιανούς. Where χρηματίσαι is evidently to be taken in the sense of *made known by revelation,* as in Heb. xii. 5. See Schleusner. Lex. N. Test. sub voce. By this name of *Israel* was the whole nation, by meton., afterwards called: but, as the house of Judah became very prominent in the days of David, and a sort of division took place between him and the family of Saul, the terms *Judah* and *Israel* were adopted by the followers of them respectively. See 2 Sam. ii. 9, seq. Again, in the days of Rehoboam (1 Kings xii.), this was likewise done by the adherents to the House of Solomon and of Jeroboam, which continued to the Babylonian captivity. After that time the terms *Israel* and *Judah* were used of the whole nation.

יִשְׂרְאֵלִי, m. patronym. of יִשְׂרָאֵל, 2 Sam. xvii. 25, &c.

יִשְׂרְאֵלִית, f. id., Lev. xxiv. 10.

יֵשׁ, and ־יֶשׁ. According to some, אִשׁ, 2 Sam. xiv. 19; Mic. vi. 10: but this may be read אִישׁ. Whence תּוּשִׁיָּה. An indeclinable word. Seg.—Cogn. ישׁשׁ. See יֵשִׁי,— שָׂה, fm. פֶּקַר, Gram. artt. 74; 150. Arab. ر. وَشِي, *progenie multiplicati, &c.* See my note on Job v. 12. وَشَاء, *opulentia.* Cogn. شِيَّ, أَسِيَ, *res, &c.* Syr. ܐܝܬ. Chald. אִית, *est, sunt.* Cogn. Heb.

אֱלִישָׁה: אִישׁ. In all which, *existence, real being*, thence *substance, firmness, wealth, &c.*, have resulted as secondary significations. Abstr. or sort of Infinitive, (a) *existing, being*, propr. *existence* (opp. τῷ, אַיִן), the logical copula being understood, Gen. xxviii. 16; xxxix. 4, 5. 8; Deut. xxix. 17; Ruth i. 12; iii. 12; Lam. i. 12, &c. With pl. 2 Kings ii. 16; Ezra xiv. 44; 2 Chron. xvi. 9, &c. The following are idioms, אִם־יֵשׁ אֶת־נַפְשְׁכֶם לְ־, *if* (there) *exists, as to you*, i. e. *with you* (the will) *for burying, &c.*, i. e. putting the case that you are not averse. Comp. 1 Kings ii. 16, &c.; Gen. xxiii. 8. יֵשׁ לְ־, *he exists, is, to*, as in the Latin, *est mihi, tibi, &c.*, for *habeo, &c.*, Eccl. iv. 9; viii. 6, &c. יֵשׁ תַּחַת יָדְךָ, 1 Sam. xxi. 4. וְיֵשׁ, *it is, yea it is*, 2 Kings x. 15. וְעֵינַיִם יֵשׁ, *but eyes really exist!* i. e. blind people, having eyes nevertheless, Is. xliii. 8. אֹהֲבֵי יֵשׁ, *the lovers of substance*, i. e. real wealth, Prov. viii. 21. Comp. xxiii. 18. With לֹא, *were, existed*, Job xvi. 4; Num. xxii. 29. וְיֵשׁ אֲשֶׁר, *and it is, because that, &c.*, Num. ix. 20, 21. הֲיֵשׁ, *Is there?* Gen. xxiv. 23, &c. יֶשְׁךָ, Eccl. ii. 13. Aff. יֶשְׁךָ, lit. *thy being, existing*—thou art, Judg. vi. 36. יֶשְׁכֶם, Gen. xxiv. 49. יֶשְׁנוּ, with single parag. נ, Gram. art. 235. Arab. note. Comp. Deut. xxxi. 10, where the single נ is found in other cases, Deut. xxix. 14; Esth. iii. 8, &c. See also the "Lexicon particularum," &c., of Christian Koerber, attached to that of Noldius, p. 21, seq.

יָשַׁב, v. pres. יֵשֵׁב. Arab. وَثَبَ, *saliit*. In the dialect of the Himyarites, *sit*. Syr. ܝܬܒ, id. Constr. abs. it. immed. it. med. מֵחוּץ לְ־, עִם, תַּחַת, לְ־, כֵּן, עַל, אֶל, בֵּין, אֵצֶל, אֶת, בְּ־ (a) *Sit, remain, dwell, reside*, 1 Kings i. 46; ii. 12; 2 Kings xiii. 13, &c.;—Lev. xiv. 8; 1 Kings xi. 16; 2 Sam. vii. 1, &c.—Gen. xiii. 12; xix. 29; Judg. v. 17; 1 Sam. xxvii. 11, &c. (b) By *sitting*, as by *rising up*, the performance of certain actions generally, is sometimes meant. See Ps. cxxxix. 2; Deut. vi. 7. Pec. for judgment, rule, Zech. vi. 13; Ps. ix. 5. 8; lxxx. 2; xcix. 1; cxxii. 5; Is. xiv. 13; xxxvii. 16. Hence, *(as) a king*, Ps. xxix. 10. — *a purifier*, Mal. iii. 3, &c. — chief, Job xxix. 25. — as in ambush, to waylay, Ps. x. 8; xvii. 12; Job xxxviii. 40 (xxix. 2); Jer. iii. 2. — in distress, ruin, weeping, &c., Is. iii. 26; xlvii. 5; Job ii. 13. — in idleness,

quiet, prosperity, &c., Is. xxx. 7; xxxii. 18; Jer. xxii. 23. See Gram. art. 194. 13; Jer. L. 12; Zech. xiv. 10, &c.
Metaph. of things, Gen. xliv. 24; Ps. xxii. 4. *Inhabiting the praises, &c.*, rather, *but thou remainest, continuest, holy;* or, *remainest* (the) *holy one;* (object, proprietor) *of the praises of Israel.* Aq. Sym. Theod. ὕμνος. LXX. ἔπαινος: reading תְּהִלַּת, sing. probably. By meton. *praise*, for *object of* do. Comp. Jer. xvii. 14. We may, too, take תְּהִלּוֹת, as a pl. of excellency.
Infin. abs. יָשׁוֹב, 1 Sam. xx. 5. שֶׁבֶת, Deut. i. 6, &c. Aff. שִׁבְתִּי, שִׁבְתּוֹ, &c., Ps. cxxxix. 2; xxxiii. 14, &c.
Imp. שֵׁב, Gen. xx. 15, parag. ה, שְׁבָה, Ib. xxvii. 19, &c. With י, rel. שְׁבִי, Ps. cxxiii. 1.
— pl. שְׁבוּ, Ib. xxii. 5, &c.
F. שְׁבִי, Ib. xxxviii. 11, &c.
Part. יוֹשֵׁב, pl. יוֹשְׁבִים, constr. יוֹשְׁבֵי, Gen. iv. 20; Num. xxxiii. 55; Gen. xix. 25, with aff. regularly.
— f. יוֹשֶׁבֶת, Lev. xv. 23.
— pl. יוֹשְׁבוֹת, 1 Sam. xxvii. 8.
Niph. נוֹשַׁב, pres. non occ. *Be, become, inhabited*, Jer. vi. 8; xxii. 6; Ezek. xxvi. 19; xxxvi. 10.
Part. f. נוֹשֶׁבֶת, Ezek. xxvi. 17, &c.
— pl. נוֹשָׁבוֹת, Ib. xxxviii. 12.
Pih. pl. m. pret. יִשְּׁבוּ, *They shall make, cause, to remain*, Ezek. xxvi. 4.
Hiph. הוֹשִׁיב, pres. יוֹשִׁיב, apoc. יוֹשֵׁב, *Make, cause, to sit, dwell, reside, in, with; inhabit,* 1 Sam. ii. 8; 1 Kings xxi. 9; Ps. lxviii. 7; cxiii. 7; Ezek. xxxvi. 33; Is. liv. 3.
Infin. הוֹשִׁיב, 1 Sam. ii. 8: with rel. י־, הוֹשִׁיבִי, Ps. cxiii. 8.
Imp. הוֹשֵׁב, Gen. xlvii. 6.
— pl. הוֹשִׁיבוּ, 1 Kings xxi. 9.
Part. מוֹשִׁיב, Ps. lxviii. 7: with rel. י־, מוֹשִׁיבִי, Ps. cxiii. 9.
Hoph. הוּשַׁב, pres. יוּשַׁב. *Made, caused, to dwell, &c.*, Is. v. 8; xliv. 26, al. non occ.

יָשׁוּד, r. שָׁדַד.

יֵשׁוּעַ, propr. name; i. q. יְהוֹשֻׁעַ, usually: but this may fairly be questioned, i. q. Gr. Ἰησοῦς, r. ישׁע. Arab. وَسِعَ, *ampla fuit res*, opposed to צַר, *straitness, &c.* Generally, *Saviour;* αὐτὸς γὰρ σώσει τὸν λαὸν αὐτοῦ ἀπὸ τῶν ἁμαρτιῶν αὐτῶν, Matt. i. 21. The fm. is that of a pres. answering to the σώσει of the angel: lit. *He shall save:* of the ground fm. פָּקוֹד, Gram. art. 189. 6. יֵשׁוּעַ,

for יֵשׁוּעַ, which would be the full form. It is not strictly, therefore, i. q. יְהוֹשֻׁעַ, although the *general sense* differs not essentially. It occurs, Neh. viii. 17, &c., for Joshua, &c. Hence—

יְשׁוּעָה, f. constr. יְשׁוּעַת, pl. יְשׁוּעוֹת, r. ישׁע. And with ה of *unity* יְשׁוּעָתָה. See ה, (b) p. 145, above. Lit. amplitude, space: thence, meton., *Freedom, safety, salvation*. With ה of unity, or pl. *singular, great, salvation*, Exod. xiv. 13; xv. 2; 1 Sam. xiv. 47; 2 Sam. x. 11; Job xiii. 16; Ps. cxviii. 14. 21, &c. With ה of unity, Ps. iii. 3; lxxx. 3; Jonah ii. 10. Pl., 2 Sam. xxii. 51; Ps. xviii. 51; xxviii. 8, &c. Metaph. יְשׁוּעָה חוֹמוֹת יָשִׁית, *He shall place salvation* (as) *walls*, &c., Is. xxvi. 1. כּוֹבַע יְשׁוּעָה, Ib. lix. 17. Comp. lx. 18; xxxiii. 6; Hab. iii. 7. מַעַיְנֵי יְשׁוּעָה, *springs, fountains, of salvation*, Is. xii. 3. לִישׁוּעָתְךָ קִוִּיתִי, *for our singular, perfect, salvation*, Ps. lxxx. 3. Aff. יְשׁוּעָתִי, יְשׁוּעָתוֹ, &c. Pl. and ה unity, have no aff.

יֵשַׁח, m. once, Mic. vi. 14. Aff. יִשְׁחֲךָ.
Arab. وَشَخَ, *sequior, et imbecillis*. Cogn.

وَشِيخَة, *induit fasciam*, &c.; it. cogn. وَشِيخَة, *vilior sequiorque hominum turba. Baseness, hypocrisy.* Sym. καὶ διαφθερεῖς εἰς τὰ ἐντός σου. LXX. καὶ συσκοτάσει ἐν σοί. Syr. ܡܰܟܺܐܒܘ, *et dysenteria*. Targ. לִמְרַע, *in infirmitatem*. The writer evidently means, that, because there is something like an evil disease within, nothing eaten will satisfy. Gesenius's etym. وحش, is indirect, and his interpretation supplies a weak and frigid tautology: viz. "*fames*," hunger.

יְשׁוּחוּ, r. שָׁחַח.

יָשַׁט, v. Kal non occ.
Hiph. pres. יוֹשִׁיט, apoc. יוֹשֶׁט. Constr. med. לְ, pers. אֶת, thing. Syr. aph. ܐܘܫܛ, *extendit. Extend, stretch* out, Esth. iv. 11; v. 2; viii. 4, al. non occ.

יַשִׂי, r. נָשָׂא.

יָשִׂים, pres. Hiph. r. שָׂמַם.

יְשִׁימוֹן, m.—pl. non occ. r. ישׁם. Syr. ܐܫܺܝܡܘܢ, *solitudo. Any great desert*, 1 Sam. xxiii. 19. 24; Is. xliii. 19, 20, &c.: pec. that of Arabia in which the Israelites sojourned under Moses, Num. xxi. 20; xxiii.

28; Ps. lxviii. 8; lxxviii. 40; cvi. 14; cvii. 4; Deut. xxxii. 10.

יְשִׁימוֹת, f. pl. once, Ps. lv. 16. Kethiv. See Keri. *Desolations*. Elsewhere the name of a place.

יָשִׁישׁ, once, יֵשֵׁשׁ, 2 Chron. xxxvi. 17; pl. יְשִׁישִׁים, r. ישׁשׁ. Cogn. ישׁ. Arab. الأَسَاسُ, *fundamentum structuræ*. Synon. τοῦ, שָׂב, זָקֵן. *Old, aged, elderly, person*, Job xii. 12; xv. 10; xxix. 8; xxxii. 6; 2 Chron. l. c.

יִשְׁאַל, r. שָׁאַל.

יָשַׁם, v. pres. only, f. תֵּשַׁם, pl. תִּשַּׁמְנָה. Cogn. τοῦ, שָׁמַם. Comp. אָשַׁם. Arab. وَشَمَ, *probra et convitia effudit* in famam alterius. Constr. abs. *Be, become, desolate, ruined*, Gen. xlvii. 19; Ezek. xii. 19; xix. 7. Pl., Ib. vi. 6, al. non occ.

יִשַּׁם, r. שָׁמֵם.

יִשָּׁמֵם, r. שָׁמֵם.

יָשֵׁן, masc. plur. יְשֵׁנִים, constr. יְשֵׁנֵי.—
יְשֵׁנָה, f.—pl. non occ.—
Arab. وَشَن, *crassus* camelus: hence the notion of *heavy*, thence sleepy. Cogn. وَسَن, *proclivis in somnum fuit*. Participial noun. *Sleeping, slumbering, dozing*, 1 Sam. xxvi. 7. 12; 1 Kings iii. 20; xviii. 27; Cant. v. 2; vii. 10; Dan. xii. 2; Ps. lxxiv. 65.

יָשָׁן, m. — pl. יְשָׁנִים ⎱ opp. חָדָשׁ, חֹדֶשׁ,
יְשָׁנָה, f.—pl. non occ. ⎰ Lev. xxvi. 10.
From the notion of *heaviness, sleepiness, inactivity*, that of *age*, would naturally follow. *Old*, of things only, Lev. xxv. 22; Cant. vii. 14; Neh. iii. 6; xii. 39; Is. xxii. 11.

יָשֵׁן, v. pres. יִישַׁן, pl. יִישְׁנוּ. See יָשֵׁן above. Constr. abs. it. med. בְּ, in, of place; תַּחַת, under. *Sleep, slumber, doze*, Gen. ii. 21; xli. 5; Job iii. 12; Ezek. xxxiv. 25; Ps. iii. 6; iv. 9; cxxi. 4; Is. v. 27; 1 Kings xix. 5; Prov. iv. 16. Metaph. — of death, immed. שְׁנַת־עוֹלָם, Jer. li. 39, &c. — תַּרְדֵּמָה, Ps. xiii. 4. — of inactivity, Ps. xliv. 24.
Infin. יְשׁוֹן, Eccl. v. 11, al. non occ.
Part. יָשֵׁן above.
Niph. יִוָּשֵׁן, pres. non occ.—of יָשֵׁן above.

ישׁב (278) ישׁפ

Be, become, grow, old, as inhabitants of any place, Deut. iv. 25, al. non occ.
Part. נוֹשָׁן ⎫ *Grown old, dry,* Lev. xxvi.
— f. נוֹשָׁנָה ⎭ 10: f. Ib. xiii. 11, al. non occ.
Pih. f. aff. pres. תְּיַשְּׁנֵהוּ, *She made him sleep,* Judg. xvi. 19, only.

יִשְׁנוּ, r. שֵׁן.

יָשַׁע, r. שָׁעָה.

יֶשַׁע, and יֵשַׁע, m. abstr. or Infin. Constr. immed. it. med. אֶת. Seg. fm. פֶּךָ, pl. non occ. See יְשׁוּעַ, and יְשׁוּעָה, above. Lit. amplitude, space: opp. to straitness, constriction. Meton. *Deliverance, freedom, safety, salvation,* Ps. xx. 7; xii. 6; L. 23; Job v. 11; Hab. iii. 12; Is. xlv. 8; lxi. 10. Particularly as derived from God: hence the phrr. אֱלֹהֵי יִשְׁעִי, Ps. xviii. 46: comp. vr. 3; lxii. 8; Is. li. 5. מָגֵן יִשְׁעֲךָ, *shield of thy salvation,* Ps. xviii. 36. יְשׁוּעָה יִשְׁעֶךָ Ib. li. 14. אִמְרַת יִשְׁעֶךָ, Ib. lxix. 14. אַלְבִּישׁ יֶשַׁע, *I will clothe* with *salvation,* Ps. cxxxii. 16. Aff. יִשְׁעִי, &c. Hence the verb—

Hiph. הוֹשִׁיעַ, pres. יוֹשִׁיעַ, twice, יְהוֹשִׁיעַ, after the Chaldee manner, 1 Sam. xvii. 47; Ps. cxvi. 6. יוֹשִׁיעַ, apoc. יֹשַׁע, יוֹשַׁע. Constr. abs. immed. it. med. אֶת, לְ, from; בְּ, in, by, of person, rarely of things. *Deliver, set free, save,* as the context shall require, Judg. ii. 18. מְיָד, Ib. הוֹשִׁיעָה לִּי יָדִי, *my own hand hath delivered me:* comp. Judg. vi. 36: Ps. xliv. 4. זְרוֹעָם, *their arm,* Ib. xcviii. 1. יְמִינִי, *His right hand.* Comp. Is. lix. 1; lxiii. 9; Job xxvi. 2; 1 Sam. xxiii. 2; abs., Is. xliii. 12; — Prov. xx. 22; Job v. 15. With תְּשׁוּעָה גְדוֹלָה, by *a great salvation,* 1 Chron. xi. 14.

Infin. הוֹשִׁיעַ, 2 Sam. iii. 18. With לְ prefixed 'mostly, Deut. xx. 4, &c., it. Aff. לְהוֹשִׁיעֵנִי, Ps. xxxi. 3, &c.

Imp. הוֹשַׁע, Jer. xxxi. 7. With ה parag. הוֹשִׁיעָה, 2 Sam. xiv. 4; Ps. cxviii. 25. הוֹשִׁיעָה נָא, whence the term *"Hosanna,"* Matt. xxi. 9, &c., pl. non occ.

Part. מוֹשִׁיעַ, Deut. xxii. 27, &c. Aff. reg. מוֹשִׁיעִי, 2 Sam. xxii. 3, &c.

— pl. מוֹשִׁיעִים, Obad. vr. 21; Neh. ix. 27.

Niph. נוֹשַׁע, pres. יִוָּשַׁע, *Be, become, delivered, saved.* Constr. abs. it. med. בְּ, in, by; מִן, from; Num. x. 9; Deut. xxxiii. 29; 2 Sam. xxii. 4; Jer. viii. 20; xvii. 14; Is. xlv. 17. 22; Ps. lxxx. 4. 8, &c. In Zech. ix. 9, צַדִּיק וְנוֹשָׁע הוּא, *righteous, and one who has been, become, saved,*—i. e. prægn. has obtained salvation,—*is He,* i. e. for himself and others. LXX. σώζων.

Imp. pl. הִוָּשְׁעוּ, *Be, become ye, saved,* Is. xlv. 22.

Part. נוֹשָׁע, Zech. l. c., al. non occ.

יָשְׁפֶה, and יַשְׁפֵה, masc. Arab. يَصَب, يَشُم, يَشْبُ, يَشِف, it. يَصَب. Syr. ܝܫܦܐ. Æth. ያስፕ፡

Jaspis. The Jasper stone, Exod. xxviii. 20; xxxix. 13; Ezek. xxviii. 13, al. non occ.

יֹשֶׁר, and יוֹשֶׁר, m.—pl. non occ. Aff. יָשְׁרוֹ, Job xxxiii. 23. See my note. Cogn. אֹשֶׁר, which see, p. 60, above. *Rectitude, integrity,* Deut. ix. 5; Job vi. 25; Prov. ii. 13; iv. 11; Job xxxiii. 3; Ps. cxix. 7; 1 Chron. xxix. 17, &c.

יָשָׁר, m. constr. יְשַׁר, pl. יְשָׁרִים. Constr. יִשְׁרֵי.

יְשָׁרָה, f. constr. יִשְׁרַת, pl. יְשָׁרוֹת.— See יָשַׁר above. Synon. תָּם, כֵּן, צַדִּיק, opp. עָקֵשׁ. *Right, upright, righteous, true.* Applied to God, man, and things, Ps. xcii. 16; xxv. 8; Deut. xxxii. 4;—Job i. 1. 8; ii. 3;—Ps. cxi. 8; cxix. 137. With the article, Deut. vi. 18; xii. 25, סֵפֶר הַיָּשָׁר, *the book of right,* i. e. of truth. Some book written, apparently, under inspiration. The word cannot be a proper name here; if it were, the article could not have been regularly prefixed, Josh. x. 13; 2 Sam. i. 18;—Prov. xxix. 27: pl. Num. xxiii. 10; Job iv. 7, &c.; Ps. vii. 11, &c.: fem., Ezra viii. 21; Ps. cvii. 7; Mic. iii. 9; opp. τῷ, עִקֵּשׁ, 1 Kings iii. 6. Pl., Ezek. i. 23. Phrr. יָשָׁר בְּעֵינָיו, *right in his own eyes,* Judg. xvii. 6. Comp. Deut. xii. 25. 28; Prov. xiv. 12. יִשְׁרֵי לֵב Ps. vii. 11. דֶּרֶךְ, xxxvii. 14. Adv., Is. xxvi. 7. תְּפַלֵּס...יָשָׁר, *thou shalt rightly, truly, weigh.*

יָשַׁר, v. pres. יִישַׁר, pl. f. יִשְׁרָנָה, once. See יָשַׁר above. Constr. med. בְּ, בְּעֵינֵי. (a) *Be right, upright, good.* (b) *Go, proceed, right,* i. e. directly onwards. (a) Jer. xviii. 4; xxvii. 4; Judg. xiv. 3. 7; Hab. ii. 4; 1 Sam. xviii. 2. 26; 1 Kings ix. 12; 1 Chron. xiii. 4. (b) 1 Sam. vi. 12, יִשַּׁרְנָה for יִישַׁרְנָה. Dagesh compensating for the loss of the י. The form (differing here from the common paradigm) is that in use among the Arabs. See the Grammars. "*Maxime de via,*" says Gesenius: but only one

יִשַׁר

instance—the last here—occurs, and that manifestly in the sense of אֲשֶׁר.

Pih. pret. יִשַּׁרְתִּי, pres. יְיַשֵּׁר. Constr. immed. it. med. לְ. *Make right, good, direct.* כָּל יִשַּׁרְתִּי, *I have made wholly right, good, direct,* Ps. cxix. 128. דְּרָכָיו אֲיַשֵּׁר, *his ways will I make direct,* Is. xlv. 13. Comp. vr. 2. See Keri, Prov. iii. 6. יְשָׁר־לָכַת, *proceeds straight forward,* Prov. xv. 21. See xi. 5; 2 Chron. xxxii. 30. So יִשְּׁרוּ, Job xxxvii. 3, according to Gesenius: but no mark of Pih. is to be found here. See my note on the place.

Imp. pl. יַשְּׁרוּ, Is. xl. 3, only.

Part. pl. m. מְיַשְּׁרִים, Prov. ix. 15, only.

Puh. Part. מְיֻשָּׁר, once, 1 Kings vi. 35. *Made direct, plain; laid flat; smooth,* perhaps. LXX. χρυσίῳ καταγομένῳ, al. non occ.

Hiph. pres. יְיַשִּׁירוּ, used imperatively. *Be they made direct,* straightforward, Prov. iv. 25.

Imp. הַיְשֵׁר, for הַיְשִׁיר, where the rad. י is retained. The more usual form would be הוֹשֵׁר. See Gram. art. 87. 1. *Make direct,* Ps. v. 9.

יְשֻׁרוּן, m.—pl. non occ. A periphrastic name of Jacob or Israel, applied to the whole people generally, Deut. xxxii. 15; xxxiii. 5. 26; Is. xliv. 2, al. non occ. Augm. of יָשׁוּר. See Gram. art. 168. Intensively, *Entirely, fully, right, righteous.* Comp. Num. xxiii. 21, with Ib. vr. 10, where יְשָׁרִים = יְשֻׁרוּן, is evidently applied to *Israel,* יִשְׂרָאֵל, a word not very greatly differing from it, particularly if שַׁר, and שָׁר, were originally supposed to be cognates. The יִשְׂרָאֵלוּן of Gesenius is the most clumsy attempt at etymological conjecture I have ever seen from him.—So Aq. Sym. Theod. εὐθύς: sed "Obstare videtur, Jes. l. c." Gesen. I think quite the contrary. If chosen by Jehovah, and, hence, is considered as his servant, this יְשֻׁרוּן must have been pardoned, i. e. justified by him likewise.

יִשָּׁרְנָה, r. יָשַׁר.

יָשַׁשׁ, see שׁוּשׁ above.

יִשְׁתַּחֲו, r. שָׁחָה.

יִשְׂתַּקְשְׁקוּ, r. שָׁקַק. Hithp.

יָת, Chald. i. q. Heb. אֵת. Syr. ܝܳܬ. Aff. יָתְהוֹן, Dan. iii. 12.

יְתָא, r. אָתָה.

יתב

יְתִב, v. Chald. pret. יְתִיב, יְתִב, i. q. Heb. יָשַׁב. Syr. ܝܺܬܶܒ. Arab. dialect. Himyar. وَثَبَ. Constr. abs. it. med. בְּ, in. (ו) *Sit,* Dan. vii. 9, 10. 26.

Part. pl. m. יָתְבִין. (b) *Residing,* Ezra iv. 17, al. non occ.

Aph. הוֹתֵב, pres. non occ. Constr. immed. pers. med. בְּ, in, of place, Ezra iv. 10, only.

יָתֵד, c. constr. יְתַד, pl. f. יְתֵדוֹת, constr. יִתְדוֹת. Arab. وَتِد, *palus, paxillus.* Cogn. وَطِد, *stabilis, firmus.* A pin (of wood probably, see Ezek. xv. 3) on which to hang any thing; or by which any thing may be fastened, Ezek. l. c. Is. xxii. 23—25. Tent-pin, Judg. iv. 21, 22; v. 26. — of the loom, Ib. xvi. 14. See LXX. and אֶרֶג above. — of the Tabernacle, Exod. xxvii. 19; xxxv. 18; Num. iii. 37; iv. 32; Is. xxxiii. 20; liv. 2, &c.: and from the stability hence derived, metaph., *powerful and wise princes,* Is. xxii. 20—25, evidently shadowing out the person of Christ, with the decay of the former powers in Jewry. Comp. Ezra ix. 8; Zech. x. 4. — to bore a hole in the earth with, Deut. xxxiii. 14. Not *a spade,* or the like, but a sort of *pin,* such as is used by gardeners for setting potatoes, &c. Aff. יְתֵדֹתָי, יְתֵדוֹתָיו, &c.

יָתוֹם, masc. pl. יְתוֹמִים, r. יתם. Arab. يَتَمَ, *solitarius, orphanus, fuit;* يَتِيم, *orphanus.* Syr. ܝܰܬܡܳܐ, id. *An orphan,* Exod. xxii. 21. 23; Deut. x. 18; Is. i. 17, &c. Aff. pl. יְתֹמֶיךָ, יְתֹמָיו, Jer. xlix. 11; Is. ix. 16, &c.

יִתְוַקַּח, r. יָבַח. Hithp.

יָתְגָּר, m. constr. of יֶתֶר, Part. of יָתַר below. *Abundance,* once Job xxxix. 8. See my note. LXX. νομὴν αὐτοῦ. Syr. ܒܣܘܓܐܐ ܕܛܘܪܐ, *in multitudine montium*

יִתְזִין, see זוּן above.

יָתִיר, m.—f. יְתִירָה, once, יַתִּירָא, pl. non occ. Chald. r. יְתַר. *Excellent, extraordinary,* Dan. ii. 31; iv. 33; v. 12. 14. Adv. Ib. iii. 22; vii. 7. 19.

יִתְכַּס, pres. apoc. Hithp. r. כָּסָה.

יִתַּם, pl. יִתְּמוּ, r. תָּמַם.

יִתַּמּוּ, pl. pres. Niph. of do.

יָתֵר, c. seq. fm. פְּתֵר, pl. non occ. Syr. ܝܬܰܪ, *lucratus est*. Æth. ⲞⲦⲌ: *tetendit*. Arab. وَتَرَ, id. وَاتَرَ, *unum post alterum produxit*, &c. Cogn. وَتَرَ, conj. x. *multum petiit de re*. Hence, I. *Excellence, abundance, residue, remainder*, or *the rest* of —, Gen. xlix. 3. Metaph. Prov. xvii. 7; Ps. xvii. 14; Job xxii. 20. Adv. Is. lvi. 12; Dan. viii. 9: id. עַל יֶתֶר, Ps. xxxi. 24;—Deut. iii. 11; Judg. vii. 6; 2 Sam. x. 10; 1 Kings xi. 41; Joel i. 4, &c. And from the notion of drawing out as a bow, &c. Comp. Is. v. 18. II. *String*, or *cord*, pl. יְתָרִים, Ps. xi. 2; Job xxx. 11, see my note; Judg. xvi. 7—9, al. non occ. Aff. (I.) יִתְרוֹ, יִתְרָם.

יִתְרָה, f. of יֶתֶר (I.) above. Constr. יִתְרַת, *Abundance, excess*, Is. xv. 7; Jer. xlviii. 36, al. non occ.

יתר, v. Kal non occ.
Part. יוֹתֵר, see in its place above.
Niph. נוֹתַר, pres. יִוָּתֵר, *Be left, remain*. Constr. abs. it. med. מִן, of; לְ, to; בְּ, in, with; אַחֲרֵי, after; כְּ, as, like; עַד, until; אֶת, Gen. xxxii. 25; Exod. x. 15; xxix. 34; Num. xxvi. 65; Josh. xi. 11; 1 Kings xvii. 17; xix. 10, &c.; Dan. x. 13. Gesenius makes נוֹתַרְתִּי, "*victoriam reportavi*," from the Syr. Æth. *præstans, excellens fuit*: rather, *I excelled, prevailed with*. See נוֹשַׁע above.
Part. נוֹתָר, pl. נוֹתָרִים, 2 Kings iv. 7; Exod. xxviii. 10, &c.
— f. נוֹתֶרֶת, pl. נוֹתָרוֹת, Lev. ii. 3; Gen. xxx. 36, &c.
Hiph. הוֹתִיר, pres. יוֹתִיר, f. pause, הוֹתֵר. Constr. abs. it. immed. it. med. עַד, מִן, לְ, בְּ, instr. (a) *Cause to remain, leave*; (b) *to abound, be wealthy*. (a) Exod. x. 15; xii. 10; Is. i. 9; Ezek. vi. 8: (b) Deut. xxviii. 11; xxx. 9. Gen. xlix. 4, אַל־הוֹתַר. The final vowel (-) here, and in Ruth ii. 14, is nothing more than what the following ר occasionally causes elsewhere; it being in some respects considered as allied to the gutturals, Gram. art. 109.
Infin. הוֹתִיר הוֹתֵר, Exod. xxxvi. 7; Jer. xliv. 7, &c.
Imp. הוֹתֵר, Ps. lxxix. 11.

יִתְרוֹן, m.—pl. non occ. r. יתר. *Gain, profit, good*, Eccl. i. 3; ii. 11. 13; iii. 9; v. 8. 15; vii. 12; x. 10.

יִתְעֵם, Ithp. Chald. pres. r. שׂוּם.

כ

כ, The eleventh letter of the Hebrew alphabet; and, used as a numeral, represents the number twenty, Gram. art. 4. See its etymology under כה below. On its pronunciation, see Gram. artt. 16. 47; its classification, and interchanging with other letters, artt. 23. 2; 78. 2. 5. Gesenius makes it interchangeable with even י, as he also does י, with ק. But no reliance can be placed on an analogy so doubtful as this, when כָּשֵׁר, and יָשַׁר; יָשִׁישׁ, and ܟ݂ܰܫܺܝܪ, may be shown to be derived from primitive roots, having totally different significations. See these words in Castell. And it is extremely important that we guard, in this particular, against the danger of creating too great a latitude of interpretation, which may be turned eventually to the worst possible accounts.

On the etymology, and mode of prefixing this letter, as *a particle*, to certain words, see Gram. art. 174. 2, seq.; and on its application and force, Nold. Concord. partic. p. 349, seq., with the references there made. But, as Noldius, like Gesenius, is more diffuse than is suitable to the business of the Grammarian, I will endeavour to give such a general view of the case, as may embody all that seems necessary of their observations.

With *nouns*, then, of whatever sort, *affixed pronouns*, and *many particles*, this particle has the effect of instituting *comparison* with something signified by some other term or terms following, expressed, it may be, or implied; and thence, of pointing out *similitude, relationship*, or the like. With verbs (i. e. as conjugated in their several persons) this is never done: but, when such similitude, &c., is required, the needful is supplied, either by a separate word, or particle; and occasionally with this particle prefixed to it: as, כֹּה, כֵּן, כַּאֲשֶׁר, &c. And, be it remembered, that, in such comparisons, &c. the things compared are supposed to be

כ (281) כ

placed *positively* in juxta-position with each other, so that the one may be substituted *for* the other, and considered as standing in its place: and that this holds good, whether the comparison be simple or complex, single or double, &c. Which will cover all the varieties of signification given to this particle by Noldius, as well as all the cases, proposed by Gesenius and others, as to its usages.

Examples (from Nold.) כִּימֵי נִדָּתָהּ, *As* (in) *the days of her uncleanness, &c.*; i. e. considering her now positively as such, then &c., Lev. xv. 25. כַּמַּטָּרָה, *as*, i. e. in the situation of *a mark*, Lam. iii. 12. כְּאָכֹל, *as the consuming of* —, i. e. supposing this positively to take place,—כ, *so* — &c., Is. v. 24. כַּאֲבָנִים, *as the stones*, i. e. what the stones positively were as to number, 2 Chron. ix. 27. — כַּאֲשֶׁר אֵינְךָ, *as thou art not*... *so*, &c., i. e. what thy ignorance is in the one case, that it also is in every other to which the comparison extends, Eccl. xi. 5. כַּיּוֹם, and כְּעֵת, כְּהַיּוֹם, כְּיוֹם הַזֶּה, &c., i. e. laying down the time thus specified, as that with which the comparison is made. And so in every other case, of number, measure, quantity, space, &c., which must be translated, of necessity, as the idiom of the language shall require into which the translation is made. In many places, indeed, either this particle, or some other word, is omitted by the ellipsis: and this constitutes the main difficulty, as to its use and force. When the Infinitives of verbs are used, some such word as עֵת, יוֹם, &c., seems to be omitted: as, כְּבוֹא הַשֶּׁמֶשׁ, for כְּעֵת בּוֹא וגו', Deut. xvi. 6; or, in such cases, the *event so implied* may, in its progress, be considered as constituting the leading member of the comparison. Which is, perhaps, the more simple and easy way of viewing these cases.

Gesenius finds, in some instances, a singular idiom, in which this particle is used, observed by no one, as far as he knows, before him. The following are examples: Neh. vii. 2, כִּי הוּא כְּאִישׁ אֱמֶת, *for he* was, *as a man of truth*, lit. i. e. such as a man, guided solely by truth, would necessarily be. According to Gesenius, "*quam maxime fidus.*" So 1 Sam. xi. 27, כְּמַחֲרִישׁ, "*quam quietissime se gessit.*" Prov. x. 20, כִּמְעָט, "*quam paucissime;*" more literally and correctly, *as little*, or nothing, in value. Is. i. 9, שָׂרִיד כִּמְעָט, *a remnant* (esteemed) *as little*; i. e. as nothing. According to the Oriental proverb, النَّادِرُ كَالْمَعْدُومِ, *That, which is rare, is as the non-entity.* The passage is cited by the Apostle, Rom. ix. 29, and is there referred to the remnant of the true believers among the Jews of his day, which was indeed small with reference to the Jews generally; but constituted, nevertheless, the first fruits to God under the new dispensation. There is nothing important, therefore, in the remark of Gesenius: nothing of any real use, that could not have been arrived at without it, by means of the considerations offered above.

The cases, in which this particle itself is omitted, are very numerous; and, to an European reader, they often seem very abrupt. In some instances the mistakes which have originated in these ellipses have involved the most serious consequences. They require, therefore, particular attention, such as hitherto they certainly have not received. Many of the instances given as elliptical, by Noldius and others, may be resolved on other grounds* (p. 358, &c.) So far, therefore, their labour has tended rather to mislead than the contrary.

I. In all cases, then, in which something is predicated of any person, or thing, which is *naturally incongruous* with it (i. e. metaphorically), this particle, or its equivalent, must be supplied by the ellipsis, e. g. אִישׁ (אֲשֶׁר הוּא) כְּמָה — כְּתוֹלֵעָה, for רִמָּה וּבֶן־אָדָם תּוֹלֵעָה, Job xxv. 6. Ib. xvii. 14, כְּאָבִי אַתָּה, &c. Comp. Is. xl. 6; xli. 14, &c. And so, in all such passages, as, *I am the way, the truth, the life, the door, the good shepherd*, or God is said to be *a strong tower, light, rock*, and so on. Which, however, may also be expressed by prefixing the prep. ל; due regard being had to the preceding construction; e. g. הָיִיתָ לְאָב וגו', *thou shalt be for*, i. e. in the place of, *a father, &c.* Comp. Is. xl. 4; xli. 15; Amos v. 7; 2 Sam. vii. 14, &c. This metaphorical usage is said, by St. Paul, to speak of things that are not, as though

---

* E. g., Num. ix. 16, הֶעָנָן יְכַסֶּנּוּ וּמַרְאֵה־אֵשׁ לָיְלָה, *the cloud covers it accordingly* (by day), *and the appearance of fire by night*, i. e. also covers it: the particle of comparison consisting in the preceding כֵּן. The כ need not, therefore, be supplied from the preceding context. Again, Lam. iv. 9, שֶׁהֵם יָזֻבוּ מְדֻקָּרִים וגו', *since they waste away, being pierced*, i. e. *diseased, &c.*, and so of most of the rest.

כ (282) כ

they were (Rom. iv. 17), Θεοῦ, τοῦ ζωοποιοῦντος τοὺς νεκροὺς, καὶ καλοῦντος τὰ μὴ ὄντα ὡς ὄντα. God, *who makes the dead alive*, i. e. representing them as such, *and calls things having no existence (in nature), as though they had*. Let this be carefully remembered, and many apparent difficulties connected with this subject will be easily overcome.

In this way, therefore, believers are said to be, *the sons of God, children of the Most High*, because they are also the reputed *members of Christ; He being the vine, they the branches*, and so on. In like manner, but in a much higher sense, *the child* to be born, Is. ix. 5, was to be named *Wonderful, Counsellor, Mighty God, &c.*, comp. Luke i. 35; i. e. the manhood of the Redeemer, should, by the divine unction which he should receive (John iii. 34), be put into the situation to be thus justly and truly esteemed, and believed on.* Hence, Is. liv. 5, אֱלֹהֵי כָל־הָאָרֶץ יִקָּרֵא, *God of the whole*

---

* An equivalent to this is found variously expressed in the New Test., e. g. John xix. 7, ἑαυτὸν υἱὸν τοῦ Θεοῦ ἐποίησεν: he laid it down that he was positively so. Comp. ch. x. 3. 6, ὅτι εἶπον, υἱὸς τοῦ Θεοῦ εἰμι. On this principle, see Gram. artt. 151. 8, with the notes; 157. 6, also with the notes. 1 Cor. i. 30, ὃς ἐγενήθη ἡμῖν σοφία ἀπὸ Θεοῦ, κ.τ.λ.

In determining the exegetical interpretation of such passages, great care ought to be taken; otherwise we shall be in danger of falling into blasphemy, or perhaps heathenism, on the one hand; or, into the most ridiculous fanaticism on the other. E. g., the manhood of Christ cannot be considered *really* and *naturally* as being the *son of God, wisdom of God, &c.*, except in the general and low sense—which is after all metaphorical — of *creature*. It was by the assumption of the manhood into the deity that this sonship, in its exalted sense, was brought about and established. He was, as man, therefore, thus *made the son of God;* put into the situation to be esteemed, considered, and believed on, as such. In the Eucharist, the bread and wine, in their proper and natural character as elements, are, as far as the purposes of faith require, spiritually taken; i. e. are metaphorically *considered, as the representatives of the real and true body and blood of Christ*. So, in the justification of a sinner, he is *considered* by God, as now holding a situation—exempt from the charge of sin—to which he had no natural right or title; but which had been secured to him by grace, through the instrumentality of faith. I have thus, at the risk of being thought tedious, deemed it my duty, so far to touch on this most essential part of the Hebrew Grammar.

---

earth shall he be called, i. e. be considered such, and that justly: and again, Ib. xl. 9, הִנֵּה אֱלֹהֵיכֶם, *Behold, your God!* Hence, too, the עִמָּנוּאֵל, *Immanuel* of Is. vii. 14, and Matt. i. 23. Comp. Zech. xiii. 7; Ps. ii. 7; cx. 1; Matt. xxii. 44, &c. Is. xi. 10, read, "*the root*," not "*a root;*" with Rev. xxii. 16—ἡ ῥίζα καὶ τὸ γένος τοῦ Δαβίδ, i. e. the origin, *Creator*, and, at the same time, as it regards the manhood, his lineal descendant. On his revelation under the Old Test., see under דָּבָר above.

Hence the usages in the New Test., δίκαιον —ἐνώπιον τοῦ Θεοῦ, Acts iv. 19: δίκαιοι παρὰ τῷ Θεῷ, Rom. ii. 13, i. e. esteemed, reputed, as such by Him: and, therefore, really just, and thence, justified by imputation: and hence also the usage, ἐλογίσθη αὐτῷ εἰς δικαιοσύνην, Ib. iv. 3, &c.: whence the verb, δικαιόω, Ib. iii. 30: comp. 21, 22, &c. Hence may be solved a difficulty occurring in the genealogy of our Lord, Luke iii. 23, ὡς ἐνομίζετο υἱὸς Ἰωσήφ, κ. τ. λ. *As he was considered*, esteemed (i. e. by the law, ὁ νόμος, whence the verb) *the son of Joseph*. He was made such by the law, which determined that man and wife (Joseph having previously legally taken Mary to wife) should be held *as one flesh* (הָיוּ לְבָשָׂר אֶחָד), Gen. ii. 24). Joseph, therefore, being lineally descended from David—as both the genealogies show—Mary was now legally in the same situation: and so, consequently, was the child now born of her. In all these, therefore, and all similar cases, something, having no real existence, is *reckoned and acted upon, as if it truly had:* a principle extending very far in the usages of the Hebrew language: see under אִם above; it. Gram. art. 236, seq. Hence, it contains no subjunctive, or conditional, mood; every thing being put positively as a condition, and the result calculated upon accordingly. It would be endless to enumerate every sort of expression coming under this category in both Testaments. This must be left, therefore, to the industry of the student. I will now offer a few examples, in which the *incongruity* of circumstance, mentioned at the outset of this article does not appear, and yet the rule holds good.

II. In many cases in which an incongruity is not apparent, yet wherein it is evident that metaphor is had recourse to, this particle, or its equivalent, must be supplied by the ellipsis: e. g. וְאֵת פְּצָעַי, *this* (is) *the reward of* —, i. e. is rendered *as a reward* usually is, Ps. cix. 20; Ib. cxlix. 9. הֲדַר הוּא, *it is* (as) *glory, splendour to* —, Is. lviii. 6. הֲלֹא זֶה צוֹם, *is not* (such as) *this the fast?* See vr. 5 above. הַמָּה, Jer. ii. 7. אֶרֶץ הַכַּרְמֶל, *a land* (such as) *Carmel,* בַּכַּרְמֶל, i. e. for fruitfulness. Ib. with לְ, לְתוֹעֵבָה, *for an abomination,* i. e. that it should be considered as such. Exod. xv. 19, הָלְכוּ בַיַּבָּשָׁה, *they walked on dry land,* rather (as) *on the dry land.* 1 Kings xxii. 11, בְּאֵלֶּה תְּנַגַּח, (as) *with these thou shalt butt,* or *push,* as an ox. And so, in visions, Ib. vr. 17, רָאִיתִי אֶת־כָּל־יִשְׂרָאֵל, *I saw* (as it were) *all Israel;* which is compensated in the כַּצֹּאן following. So in vr. 19, where, as Theodoret has observed in other similar instances, it is not necessary to suppose that Jehovah really so appeared, but only, that such a vision actually appeared to the mind of the prophet. See my note on Job i. 6.

These ellipses, it should be observed, occasionally take place with reference to verbs, as well as to nouns; and also to verbal, and nominal sentences. With verbs, פֹּה, כֵּן, כַּאֲשֶׁר, and the like, are the terms to be supplied. See under כַּאֲשֶׁר below.

Under one or other of the preceding heads —the first undoubtedly—must be classed the terms used by our Lord and his apostle, with reference to the institution of the Holy Sacrament. These are, Matt. xxvi. 26, τοῦτό ἐστι τὸ σῶμά μου. See also Mark xiv. 22; Luke xxii. 19. In 1 Cor. xi. 24, τοῦτό μου ἐστὶ τὸ σῶμα τὸ ὑπὲρ ὑμῶν κλώμενον, &c. It is argued here, by Romanists, from a rigidly literal interpretation of these passages, that on the occasion of the blessing mentioned, an actual and real change took place in the elements used, so that they became the real flesh and blood of Christ. Which is absurd; for, first, it is expressly said, that these elements were mere *bread* and *wine*; and no such real change is necessarily intimated in the language here used; because the thing is incongruous, on several accounts. First,—to make such addition to Christ's body and blood, which were then entire. Secondly, for his disciples to feast on his living flesh and blood, would be cannibalism; and the latter of which is expressly forbidden by the law: the former, an abomination too great to need forbidding. Thirdly, to suppose that this was instituted as a sacrificial rite, as the Romanists do, is to make it unlike all other sacrificial rites, which were typically representative of the flesh and blood of Christ: but not presenting his flesh and blood in reality. Fourthly, to suppose that the body, said to be really broken, and the blood to be really shed, are to be considered also as really eaten and drunk, respectively, is absurd; and particularly so when the apostle tells us that, by thus eating and drinking, we *commemoratively announce* the death of our Lord; that is, as in the ancient sacrifices on which believers feasted, the sufferings of Christ were symbolically foretold; so in this, are those sufferings now—also symbolically —commemorated; the terms are, therefore, necessarily to be taken metaphorically.

Again, 1 Cor. xi. 25, τοῦτο τὸ ποτήριον ἡ καινὴ διαθήκη ἐστὶν ἐν τῷ ἐμῷ αἵματι. *This cup is,* according to the apostle—if we insist on a literal interpretation—really and truly *the New Testament itself,* in this place, as much as it is the *real blood* of Christ in the other. The *cup,* I say, is now the main subject of the discourse, the *blood* a subordinate one: which is also absurd. Apply this literal sort of interpretation now to all those passages in John vi., in which the eating of Christ's flesh and drinking of his blood is mentioned or alluded to, and the incongruity, nay, the grossness of the absurdity, will be too great to escape the ridicule of the merest rustic. E. g., the Jews really died who ate of the manna; but those who should eat of Christ's flesh and drink of his blood, should, according to this view, never so die. The intention, therefore, of the sacred writer, in every case, here, is to impress on the mind of his reader, that this *bread* and *wine* are to be *considered* and *viewed as standing for,* or *representing,* the *real body and blood of Christ,* and nothing else; which,—by taking and uniting them with his own,—are publicly to attest the believer's union with Christ; and, at the same time, his spiritual support, as drawn from Him: and hence also to attest his concurrence, and continuance, in the covenant of His grace. See under בְּרִית above. It is my intention to consider this subject more at length hereafter, in answer to Dr. Wiseman. I considered it my duty, in the mean time, to turn the attention of the student to this peculiar sort of construction, more particularly than it has hitherto been done in works of this nature. See Schleusner, under the Gr. particle ὡς.

כאש (284) כאר

This particle has the same power in the Chald., Dan. ii. 10; vi. 1; Ezra v. 7, &c.

כַּאֲשֶׁר, compd. of כְּ + אֲשֶׁר, lit. *As, like, according to, that which,* applied to thing, event, time, &c., but never to person; and to be variously translated, as the context may require, by *as, even as, just as, like as, as though; when; as much as; because, &c.* See Nold., p. 361, seq.; and, Gen. vii. 9; Num. ii. 17; Zech. x. 6; Job x. 19; Exod. xxxii. 19; Deut. ii. 16; Gen. xxxiv. 12; 1 Sam. ii. 16; Num. xxvii. 14; 1 Sam. viii. 6; Exod. xxxix. 43, &c.

It serves, with כְּ, to mark the protasis and apodosis of hypothetical sentences, as in Num. ii. 17; Is. xxxi. 4; Judg. i. 7, &c. With a double protasis, Is. x. 10, 11. With a double apodosis, Exod. i. 12. Occasionally omitted by the ellipsis, Is. lv. 9; Jer. iii. 20: and having ו in the apodosis, Amos ix. 7, &c. See Nold. p. 364.

With other words and particles, see Nold. p. 360, seq., which are generally noticed, in this work, under such words or particles.

כְּאֵב, m. it. constr.—pl. non occ. Syr. ܟܐܒ, *dolor.* Arab. كَأْبٌ, *mœror; v.* كَئِبَ, *mœstitia et dolore languit. Pain,* either of the body or mind, Job ii. 13; xvi. 6; Jer. xv. 18; Is. xvii. 11; lxv. 14. Aff. כְּאֵבִי.

כאב, v. pret. non occ. pres. יִכְאַב, pause, יִכְאָב. *Be pained,* either in body or mind, Job xiv. 22; Prov. xiv. 13. Part. כֹּאֵב, pl. כֹּאֲבִים, Ps. lxix. 30; Gen. xxxiv. 25.

Hiph. pret. aff. הִכְאַבְתִּי, pres. יַכְאִיב. Constr. abs. it. immed. *Cause pain, make pained,* either of body or mind, Ezek. xiii. 22.

Meton. *Make useless, ruin,* 2 Kings iii. 19. Cogn. פָּנָה.

Part. מַכְאִב, Ezek. xxviii. 24.

כְּאֵה, m. pl. כָּאִים—see v. כאה with חִיל Keri, Ps. x. 10. See חִיל (f) above, p. 195, it. חֶלְכָה, p. 200. *Afflicted, helpless,* people, al. non occ.

כאה, v. Kal non occ. Syr. ܟܐܐ, *increpavit.* Arab. كَأَى, *male habuit.* Cognn. כָּאַי, *sermone excruciavit;* كَأَى, *decrepitus fuit;* كَهِيَ, *imbecillis fuit.*

Hiph. Infin. הַכְאוֹת, *Paining, enfeebling,* the heart, Ezek. xiii. 22, al. non occ. Aquila, ἐχειμάζετε. LXX. διεστρέφετε.

Niph. נִכְאָה, pret. or part. *Be, become, pained, enfeebled,* Dan. xi. 30. נִכְאָה לֵבָב, Ps. cix. 16, is usually given here; but, if we may rely on the vowels, נִכְאָה, constr. must come from נָכֵא, which would rather be a noun. Still, this cannot greatly affect the sense, as the verb is, in all probability, nothing more. Gesenius places נִכְאָה here, Job xxx. 8, making Dagesh euphonic. It is, however, much more probably, Pih. of נכא,

Syr. ܢܓܒ, *læsit.* Arab. نَكَأَ, *percussit.* See my note.

כְּאָרִי, Ps. xxii. 17. See כור, r.

כָּבֵד, m.—pl. non occ. Æth. ኀጣዕ: *grave esse.* Syr. ܝܩܝܪ, *iratus est.* Arab. كَبَدَ, *vir medio obesas fuit; it. torsit, cruciavit, &c. Weight,* of a burden, stone, war; *abundance,* as of carcases. Prov. xxvii. 3; Is. xxx. 27; xxi. 15; Nahum iii. 3, al. non occ.

כֹּבֶד, id. once, Is. i. 4, עַם כֶּבֶד, *people of weight,* of sin, i. e. grievously sinful. LXX. πλήρης. Other verss. βεβαρημένον.

כָּבֵד, constr. כְּבַד (of כָּבֵד, see the v. below), pl. כְּבֵדִים, pl. constr. כִּבְדֵי (of כָּבֵד). I. *Heavy,* of pers. or thing, in either a good or bad sense. (a) 1 Sam. iv. 18. (b) *Weighty, rich,* Gen. xiii. 2. (c) *Numerous,* Gen. L. 9; Num. xi. 14; 1 Kings iii. 9; x. 2; 2 Kings vi. 14; xviii. 17, &c. (d) *Heavy,* i. e. *stupid, sullen* of mind, Exod. vii. 14; Prov. xxvii. 3. *Of things,* (e) heavy, i. e. *grievous, oppressive,* famine, &c., Gen. xii. 10; xli. 31; xliii. 1; L. 10, 11; Exod. viii. 20; ix. 3. 18. 24; xvii. 12, see note on Job xxiii. 2; 2 Sam. xiv. 26; Ps. xxxviii. 5, &c. (f) —, *dense,* Exod. xix. 16. (g) *Heavy,* i. e. *slow, difficult,* of utterance, Exod. iv. 10. (h) —, hence difficult to be understood, &c., Ezek. iii. 5; Exod. xviii. 18, &c. Aff. non occ.

II. *The liver,* as being the largest of the viscera. Arab. كَبِد, *jecur,* pl. non occ., Exod. xxix. 13. 22; Lev. iii. 4, &c. Aff. כְּבֵדִי, Lam. ii. 11. Comp. Job xvi. 13 (and see my note), of which this passage is perhaps an imitation. כְּבֵדוֹ, Prov. vii. 23, is a similar passage.

כבד   (285)   כבד

כָּבֵד, and כָּבַד, pres. יִכְבַּד. See כָּבֵד above. Constr. abs. it. med. עַל, אֶל, מִן, on account of; it. than. *Be heavy,* (a) grievous, of things: sin, Gen. xviii. 20; Is. xxiv. 20. —, servitude, Exod. v. 9; Neh. v. 18. Comp. Job xxxiii. 7. —, war, Judg. xx. 34; 1 Sam. xxxi. 3, &c. —, the hand, variously, Job xxiii. 2; Ps. xxxii. 4; Judg. i. 35; 1 Sam. v. 6. 11. —, the ear, of hearing, Is. lix. 1. —, the eye, of sight, Gen. xlviii. 10. —, the heart, of kindness; sullen, obdurate, Exod. ix. 7. Comp. —, more than, Job vi. 4. (b) *Be grave, respectable, honourable,* Job xiv. 21; Is. lxvi. 5. So with us, person *of weight,* or, on the contrary, *light character;* this usage obtains in many languages.

Infin. כָּבוֹד, or כָּבֹד. See כָּבוֹד, in its place below.

Part. pass. f. כְּבוּדָה, m. non occ. *Glorious, noble, honoured,* Ps. xlv. 14; Ezek. xxiii. 41; Judg. xviii. 21. *Wealth.* Theod. LXX. ἔνδοξον: al. τὸ βάρος. The true form is, no doubt, כְּבוּדָה: but here, as in other cases innumerable, the omission of the ו, occasioned the doubling of the ד by Dagesh, which was continued after the ו had been restored, contrary to the analogy of the language.

Niph. נִכְבַּד, pres. אֶכָּבֵד, with ה parag. אִכָּבְדָה, in pause, אִכָּבֵדָה. *Be, become, honourable, glorious.* Constr. abs. it. med. בְּ, pers. Exod. xiv. 4. 17; Lev. x. 3; 2 Sam. vi. 20. 22; Is. xlix. 5; Ezek. xxviii. 22.

Infin. Aff. הִכָּבְדִי, Exod. xiv. 18; Ezek. xxxix. 13.

Imp. הִכָּבֵד, 2 Kings xiv. 10.

Part. נִכְבָּד, pl. נִכְבָּדִים, Gen. xxxiv. 19; Num. xxii. 15, &c. Constr. נִכְבְּדֵי, with Dagesh euphon., Prov. viii. 24, *of waters, abounding:* of pers., Is. xxiii. 8, &c. Aff. Nahum iii. 10, &c.

— f. pl. נִכְבָּדוֹת, Ps. lxxxvii. 3, only.

Pih. כִּבֵּד, pres. יְכַבֵּד. Constr. immed. it. med. אֶת. (a) *Make heavy, sullen, unrelenting,* of heart, 1 Sam. vi. 6. (b) *Make honourable, honour,* Judg. xiii. 17; Is. xxix. 13; xliii. 23; lviii. 13. Pres. 1 Sam. ii. 30; Is. lx. 13; Ps. xv. 4; lxxxvi. 12; xci. 15. &c.

Infin. כַּבֵּד, Num. xxii. 17. Aff. כַּבְּדֵךְ, Ib. xxii. 37.

Imp. כַּבֵּד, Exod. xx. 12, &c. Aff. כַּבְּדֵנִי, 1 Sam. xv. 30.

— pl. כַּבְּדוּ, Is. xxiv. 15, &c.

Part. מְכַבֵּד, aff. מְכַבְּדוֹ, 2 Sam. x. 3; Prov. xiv. 31.

— plur. aff. מְכַבְּדַי, 1 Sam. ii. 30; Lam. i. 8.

Hiph. הִכְבִּיד, pres. יַכְבֵּד. Constr. immed. it. med. אֶת, עַל, מִן. *Make heavy,* (a) grievous, 1 Kings xii. 10. 14; Is. xlvii. 6; Lam. iii. 7. —, the ear, of hearing, Zech. vii. 11; Is. vi. 10. —, the heart, sullen, unrelenting, Exod. viii. 27 (32); ix. 34. —, pronounced it to be so, Exod. x. 1. See Gram. art. 157. 6.

(b) *Make honourable, glorious,* Is. viii. 23; Jer. xxx. 19.

Infin. הַכְבִּיד, הַכְבִּד, Exod. viii. 11; 2 Chron. xxv. 19, abs.

Imp. הַכְבֵּד, Is. vi. 10. *Pronounce hard,* Gram. art. 157. 6.

Hithp. Part. מִתְכַּבֵּד, *Becoming, feigning himself, honourable,* once, Prov. xii. 9. *More happy the base* (despised person) *and* (who is) *servant to himself, than the self honouring, &c.*

כְּבֵדוּת, f. once, r. כבד, Exod. xiv. 25, adv. *Heavily;* with difficulty.

כָּבָה, v. pres. יִכְבֶּה. Arab. كَبَا, cineribus tectus fuit ignis; fefellit igniarium non excutiens ignem. Cogn. كفا, avertit rem; كف, id. Syr. ܟܒܐ, abscondit. Cogn. Heb. חפה. Constr. abs. Lit. Kept back, concealed: thence, *Be extinguished, put out,* as fire, Lev. vi. 5, 6; Prov. xxvi. 20. בְּאֶפֶס עֵצִים תִּכְבֶּה אֵשׁ, *in the lack of wood the fire is kept back; is extinguished,* Is. xxxiv. 10; lxvi. 24, &c. Of light, 1 Sam. iii. 3; Prov. xxxi. 18. Metaph. Of anger, 2 Kings xxii. 17. Of persons perishing, Is. xliii. 17, &c.

Pih. pl. m. כִּבּוּ, pres. 2d pers. תְּכַבֶּה. Constr. abs. it. immed. it. med. אֶת, לְ. *Extinguished, put out,* 2 Sam. xxi. 17; Jer. iv. 4, &c.

Metaph. 2 Sam. xiv. 7, &c.

Infin. כַּבּוֹת, Cant. viii. 7; Ezek. xxxii. 7. Aff.

Part. מְכַבֶּה, Is. i. 31, &c.

כָּבוֹד, and כָּבֹד, m. constr. כְּבוֹד. Infin. of v. כבד above. Lit. The being heavy. Hence, meton., *Glory, splendour, majesty,* of animate or inanimate things. — of God, Ps. xix. 2; xxiv. 7—9; lxxix. 9; xcvi. 8. In many instances the person of Christ, apparently, Is. xxxv. 2, seq.; lxvi. 18, 19; Ezek. xxxix. 21. Synon. τοῦ, יָד, here, or with זְרוֹעַ, Is. liii. 1, &c. — of man, Ps. viii. 6; Job xix. 9; 1 Sam. iv. 21, &c. — of things, 1 Sam. ii. 8; Is. xxxv. 2; lx. 13. *Abundance, wealth*, Ps. xlix. 17; Is. x. 3; lxvi. 12. *Multitude*, as of an army, Is. viii. 7; xvii. 3, 4, &c. Metaph. *The mind, soul* (from כָּבֵד, *the liver*, perhaps, as in לֵב in the parallel here, בְּפָלֵץ, הֲלָץ, &c., as being of the viscera), Ps. xvi. 9; lvii. 9; cviii. 2. In Gen. xlix. 6, *honour, glory*, as of the whole house of Israel, or true Church, seems rather to be meant, than the "*animus*" of Gesenius, which appears to me to give no distinct sense. So also, perhaps, Mic. i. 15. Comp. Is. v. 13, &c. Aff. כְּבוֹדִי, כְּבֹרִי, &c.

כַּבִּיר, m. pl. כַּבִּירִים. Arab. كَبِير, *magnus*. *Mighty, powerful, great*, of pers. or thing, Job xv. 10. כַּבִּיר מֵאָבִיךָ יָמִים, *greater than thy father* as to *days*; older, Ib. xxxi. 25; xxxiv. 17. 24; xxxvi. 5; Is. xvi. 14; opp. מְעַט מִזְעָר. —, of the wind, Job viii. 2. — *waters*, Is. xvii. 12; xxviii. 2.

כְּבִיר, m. — pl. non occ. Cogn. כָּבַר, *texit*. Arab. كَفَرَ, id. Cogn. كَفَل, *stragulum*. *A sort of cushion*, or *pillow*, covered or cased with goat's skin, 1 Sam. xix. 13. 16. See Montfauc. Hexapla, Aq. μορφώματα, καὶ τὸ ἧπαρ τῶν αἰγῶν καὶ στρογγύλωμα τριχῶν. Two versions, manifestly of the same passage. See Schleusn. Lex. LXX. Vet. Test. under ἧπαρ, and στρογγύλωμα.

כֶּבֶל, m. seg. fm. פַּחֲדְּךָ, pl. constr. כַּבְלֵי. Cogn. חָבַל. Syr. ܟܒܠܐ, *compes*. Arab. كَبْل, id. *Foot-lock*, or *fetter*, of iron, Ps. cv. 18; cxlix. 8, al. non occ. See my note on Job xiii. 27. Comp. Æsch. Prom. vinct. l. 76, and the scholiast.

כבס, v. Kal non occ. Syr. cogn. ܟܒܫ. Heb. כָּבַשׁ, *subegit, &c*. Cogn. בוס.

Part. m. כֹּבֵס, pl. non occ. *Fuller, cleanser*, of clothes, 2 Kings xviii. 17; Is. vii. 3; xxxvi. 2, in the phr. שְׂדֵה כוֹבֵס, only.

Pih. כִּבֵּס, כַּבֵּס, pres. יְכַבֵּס. Constr. immed. it. med. אֶת, it. abs. it. בְּ, instr. מִן, from, of. Propr. *Wash, cleanse*, clothes and the like: not the body, for then, רָחַץ is used. See Lev. xvii. 16; Num. xix. 19, &c., which was done with נִדָּה, Jer. ii. 22; or, בֹּרִית, Mal. iii. 2; — Gen. xlix. 11; xiii. 6. 34. 54; xi. 28. 40, &c. Metaph. from sin, &c. Ps. li. 4. 9; Jer. iv. 14, &c. On these lustral, or baptismal, washings away of moral or legal uncleanness, see Selden, de Synedriis Veterum Ebræorum, lib. i. cap. iii.

Imp. f. כַּבְּסִי, Jer. iv. 14. Aff. כַּבְּסֵנִי, Ps. li. 4.

·Part. pl. m. מְכַבְּסִים, Mal. iii. 2.

Puh. כֻּבַּס, pres. non occ. *Be, become, washed, cleansed*, Lev. xiii. 58; xv. 17.

Hothp. Infin. הַכַּבֵּס (for הִתְכַּבֵּס, Gram. artt. 185. 2; 82. 3, i. q. Puh. Lev. xiii. 55, 56, al. non occ.

כְּבָר, adv. r. כבר. Syr. ܟܒܪ, *forsan, jam, olim, &c*. Arab. كَبِرَ, *annositas, &c*; v. كَبُرَ, *excessit* eum uno *ætatis* anno. Expressive, for the most part, of time past. *Already, now, &c*., Eccl. i. 10; iii. 15; vi. 10. With other particles, כִּי כְבָר, Eccl. ix. 7. בְּשֶׁכְּבָר, Ib. ii. 16; iv. 2. Also the name of a certain river, Ezek. i. 1, &c., i. q. חָבוֹר, 2 Kings xvii. 6, &c.

כבר, v. Kal non occ. See כַּבִּיר above. Hiph. pret. non occ. pres. יַכְבִּר. Constr. immed. *Multiplies*, Job xxxv. 16, only. Part. מַכְבִּיר, *Abundance*, Job xxxvi. 31, only.

כְּבָרָה, f. once, Amos ix. 9. *A sieve*, used to separate the *wheat* from the *chaff*, or the *larger* from the smaller *grain*; and, on this last account, so called perhaps. Aqu. Sym. κοσκίνῳ. LXX. λικμῷ. Comp. Luke xxii. 31.

כִּבְרָה, f. constr. כִּבְרַת, in which form only it occurs, r. כבר. *A certain measure of extent* in length, but what, it is impossible to say, Gen. xxxv. 16. See De Dieu on this place. Aquila, καθ' ὁδὸν τῆς γῆς. LXX. χαβραθά, Ib. xlviii. 7. LXX. κατὰ τὸν ἱππόδρομον χαβραθὰ τῆς γῆς; two versions apparently of the same passage, 2 Kings v. 19: where the Greek translators leave the word as they found it. See "Hodius de Bibliorum textibus," &c., p. 115. The شَوْطُ الفَرَس, *course of the horse*, of the Arabs, about three parasangs, according to Gesenius; but no reliance can be placed on this, as we have no means of connecting either its etymology, or its extent, with that of the Hebrew word

כבש (287) כד

in question. And perhaps, after all, no positive measure is meant, but indefinitely, *some extent, some distance*, and nothing more: and this I have no doubt is the truth. And so, apparently, the Targum.

כֶּבֶשׂ, m. seg. pl. כְּבָשִׂים. Aff. pl. כְּבָשָׂי.—

כִּבְשָׂה and כַּבְשָׂה, f. constr. כִּבְשַׂת, pl. כְּבָשׂוֹת.—

Arab. كَبَسَ, *depressit.* Syr. ܟܒܫ.

Heb. כָּבַשׁ, *subegit.* Cogn. Arab. كَبْش, *agnus anniculus; aries.* A *lamb* from one to three years old; so called, perhaps, on account of its great gentleness, Exod. xii. 5; xxix. 39; Lev. iii. 7; iv. 32; xii. 6. בֶּן־שְׁנָתוֹ, *the young of its year*; not more than a year old, Ib. xiv. 24. הָאָשָׁם —, of the *sin* (guilt) *offering*, Num. vi. 12; vii. 17, &c. Metaph. Is. xi. 6. According to Gesen., Gen. xxi. 28, any sheep: so Simonis, Lev. iv. 32: for neither of which, however, are there any good grounds. Fem., Lev. xiv. 10; Num. vi. 14; 2 Sam. xii. 3, 4. 6: Gen. xxi. 29, 30.

כֶּבֶשׁ, m. once, 2 Chron. ix. 18. Syr. ܟܒܫܐ, *compressio;* ܟܘܒܫܐ, *scabellum.* A *footstool.*

כָּבַשׁ, v. pres. יִכְבּוֹשׁ. Constr. immed. it. med. אֵת, לְ, for, to. Cogn. τοῦ, כבס. *Reduce, subdue, humble,* Jer. xxxiv. 11. 16; Neh. v. 5; 2 Chron. xxviii. 10. — *force,* Esth. vii. 8. Metaph., Zech. ix. 15, אַבְנֵי־קֶלַע —, *the stones of the sling,* i. e. ward them off, see יָבֵן, preceding. Mic. vii. 19. עֲוֹנוֹתֵינוּ —, *our iniquities,* i. e. as men, who would rise up against us, Gen. i. 28, of the creatures of the earth generally.

Infin. כְּבֹשׁ, 2 Chron. l. c. כָּבוֹשׁ, Esth. l. c.
Imp. pl. aff. כִּבְשֻׁהָ, Gen. l. c.
Part. pl. m. כֹּבְשִׁים, Neh. l. c.
Niph. f. נִכְבָּשָׁה, pres. non occ. *Be, become, subdued, humbled, &c.* Constr. abs. it. med. לִפְנֵי, Num. xxxii. 22. 29; Josh. xviii. 1; 1 Chron. xxii. 18.
Part. pl. f. נִכְבָּשׁוֹת, Neh. v. 5, al. non occ.
Pih. כִּבֵּשׁ, once, 2 Sam. viii. 11, i. q. Kal, if not causative. Aquila, Sym. ὑπέταξεν. LXX. κατεδυνάστευσεν.

כִּבְשָׁן, masc. — plur. non occ. Arab. قَبَسَ, *accendit ignem.* Gesen. cogn. Syr. ܟܒܫ, *strinxit, contraxit.* Probably the large *ovens*, *kilns*, or *furnaces*, in which bricks, &c. were burnt in Egypt: in which ore or metals were fused, according to some. Hence, differing from תַּנּוּר, Gen. xix. 28; Exod. ix. 8. 10; xix. 18. See LXX. The point of the expression, perhaps, consists in this, that the gain derived from the labour of the Israelites, should be more than equalled by the diseases made thus to originate from the ashes of the brick-kilns.

כַּד, masc., plur. כַּדִּים, r. כדד. Arab. كَدّ, *angustia; mortarium;* كَدُوٌّ, *difficilis puteus, cujus aqua magno labore hauriri debet.* Gr. κάδος. Lat. *cadus.* A sort of *Earthen jar,* or *vessel,* used for drawing water out of wells, Gen. xxiv. 14. 16. 18. 20. 43. 45. Carried usually on the shoulder, by persons of station, Ib. vr. 15; 1 Kings xvii. 34; Judg. vii. 16: — liable to be broken, Eccl. xii. 6. Also used for holding flour, 1 Kings xvii. 12. 14. 16. Aff. כַּדָּהּ, כַּדָּךְ.

כִּדְבָה, f. Chald. *Lying, false,* r. Heb. כזב, which see, Dan. ii. 9, only.

כַּדּוּר, see r. כדר below.

כְּדִי, see דִּי.

כְּדִי, see דִּי.

כַּדְכֹּד, masc. — plur. non occ. Arab. كَذْكَذ, *ingens rubedo.* Chald. כַּדְכּוֹדִין, כַּרְכּוּדִין, *Calcedonius.* Castell. Some precious stone, probably the *Ruby,* Is. liv. 12; Ezek. xxvii. 16, only. Sym. καρχηδόνιος.

כדר, non occ. whence, perhaps, as a root, the terms כַּדּוּר, and כְּדוּר. See this last in its place below.—

כַּדּוּר, m. augm. fm. פָּקוּד, Gram. art. 154. 10, pl. non occ.—only twice, Is. xxii. 18; xxix. 3. It has of late been usual to take this word as compd. of בְּ +דּוּר, *as,* or *like, a ball,* or *sphere;* which is any thing but suitable to the context in either case. In the first, there is a parenthesis—not usually observed—which should be read thus, vr. 17, הִנֵּה יְהוָה מְטַלְטֶלְךָ טַלְטֵלָה גָּבֶר...אֶל־אֶרֶץ רַחֲבַת יָדַיִם וגו׳, *Behold, Jehovah* (is) *casting thee out* (about to do so) *as the casting out of a warrior... into a land of extensive districts.* The parenthesis,—*And investing* (in a military sense) *shall invest thee; binding shall bind thee about* with *a binding* (constriction), *a warlike inclosure* (כַּדּוּר). In the latter place, וְחָנִיתִי עָלַיִךְ כַּדּוּר וְצַרְתִּי וגו׳, *and I will set up* (as a camp) *an inclosure, investment, against*

כה (288) כחה

thee, and I will press upon thee, &c.: see the rest of the verse. Whence it will be evident that some warlike apparatus must be intended. See the Targum in both places. The introduction of כְּ, as the particle of comparison, is weak and frigid. See my note on Job xv. 24, where the probable etymology of the word will be found.

כֹּה, Particle, adv. see under כ. It is probably a contraction of כֹּוָה, Infin. r. כוה, Gram. art. 75; further contracted into כְּ: of which we have a remnant in the Syr. ܟ̈ܐܢܐ‎, *naturam indidit, creavit, plasmavit*, i. q. ܟܐܣ‎, r. כסם; whence כֵּן having the same signification. (a) *So, thus, in this form, manner*, or the like. כֹּה תֹאמְרוּן, *thus say ye*; כֹּה אָמַר, *thus hath said, &c.*, i. e. in this manner used this form of words, giving the very words used, Gen. xxxii. 5, &c.; Gram. art. 231. 13; Nold. p. 365, seq. So, Gen. xxxi. 37, שִׂים כֹּה, *place thus*, i. e. in the manner shown by the gesture of the speaker, equivalent to (b) *here*. So the Syr. ܗܟܢܐ‎, *here*, as opposed to ܬܡܢ‎, *there*; it being evident that ܗ‎, and ܬ‎, are here the principal constituents of the compounds. From the same root is the Syr. ܟܐܡ‎, *nimirum, scilicet*. See Lex. Syr. Michaelis, p. 412. Which must be fatal to the "כָּהוּ contr. כֹּה, *sicut hoc*," of Gesenius. See also Lex. Syr. Schaaf, p. 256. The Syr. ܟܡܐ‎, *ne, num?* and Heb. כִּי, are probably descended from the same root. Exod. ii. 12, &c. With other particles, בְּכֹה, 1 Kings xxii. 20. עַד־כֹּה, Exod. vii. 16; Gen. xxii. 5; Josh. xvii. 14; 1 Kings xviii. 45. It. אִם־כֹּה; הֵנָּה־כֹה; כִּי כֹה; לָכֵן כֹּה, Nold. in their places.

כָּה, Chald. i. q. Heb. כֹּה. (b) Dan. vii. 28. עַד־כָּה, *Thus far*, al. non occ.

כֵּהָה, f. (concr. or Participial noun of כָּהָה, for כֵּהֲהָה, Gram. art. 73), pl. כֵּהוֹת (for כְּהֵהוֹת). Arab. كَاهٍ, *imbecillis, languidus*. Cogn. كَبِي, id. كَاهّ, *decrepitus fuit*. Syr. ܟܐܒ‎, *exhalavit spiritum frigidum*. Weak, *languid, infirm*. Of the eyes, 1 Sam. iii. 2, עֵינָיו הֵחֵלּוּ כֵהוֹת, *his eyes began* (to be, לִהְיוֹת) *weak*. Of the mind, Is. lxi. 3, רוּחַ כֵּהָה *languid, infirm, mind*. Of a light, Ib. xlii. 3.

Of a disease abating, losing its virulence, Lev. xiii. 6. 21. 39, &c. Of a breach, Nahum iii. 19, אֵין־כֵּהָה, *not weak, languid*, ruinous, i. e. vigorous, by a Litotes: but used here apparently as an abstr. if *matter*, (דָּבָר) or the like is not omitted by the ellipsis.

כָּהָה, v. pres. יִכְהֶה. Constr. abs. See כֵּהָה above. *Be, become, weak, languid*, of the eyes, Gen. xxvii. 1; Deut. xxxiv. 7; Zech. xi. 17; Job xvii. 7. See my note. Of the mind, or person, Is. xlii. 4. Infin. כֵּהוֹה, abs. Zech. xi. 17. Pih. כִּהָה, pres. non occ. i. q. Kal, Ezek. xxi. 12. Gesenius places here, Lev. xiii. 6. 21. 26. 28. 56. But it is evident, from a moment's inspection, that כֵּהָה, in these places, is the mere concrete noun noticed above. The truth is, none of the Lexicographers have seen the real character of that word, and hence their mistakes, 1 Sam. iii. 13, v. active, לֹא כִהָה בָּם, *he made them not weak*, i. e. he contributed not to abate their *violence, rapacity, &c*. See ch. ii. 15, seq. See cogn. כָּאָה, with the etymon. Aquila, καὶ οὐκ ἠμαύρωσεν ἐν αὐτοῖς.

כָּהָל, m. Chald. pl. כָּהֲלִין. Part. noun. Æth. ከህለ፡ *potuit*. Arab. كَمَّلَ, *provectiore ætate fuit*; *plene adulta fuit planta*. Cogn. Heb. כלה, כל, יכל, &c. *Able, adequate* to any task, Dan. ii. 26; iv. 15; v. 8. 15. al. non occ.

כֹּהֵן, m. pl. כֹּהֲנִים, constr. כֹּהֲנֵי. Arab. كَاهِن, *administrator alieni negotii*; *operam viro deferens in necessitate*. Castell. The primary notion seems to have consisted in *doing the business of*, or *acting as a mediator for, another*: whence derived it is impossible now to say. Thence, secondarily, acting as *a priest*: thirdly, after idolatry had been introduced, as *a diviner*; Arab. *Ariolus*, i. e. *heathen priests*: and, fourthly, from their wealth and influence, Syr. ܟܗܢ‎, *beatus fuit*; *magnarum divitiarum* (opum) *possessor*. *A priest*, or secondary mediator between God and man, both under the patriarchal and Jewish dispensations, Gen. xiv. 18; xli. 45. 50; xlvi. 2; Exod. ii. 16; iii. 1; xix. 6; Josh. vi. 4; 1 Sam. xxii. 17; Ps. cx. 4. In 2 Sam. viii. 18. Comp. 1 Chron. xviii. 17; some have supposed the word to signify *minister*, in a political sense; which would be to take the usage here as grounded on the primary notion noticed above: which to me is more probable than the opinion of Gesenius, who holds that *priests* in the true sense of that term are meant: because in that case, priests, not of the tribe of Levi, would be acknowledged. Aff. pl. כֹּהֲנֵי, כֹּהֲנֵינוּ, &c.

כֹּהֵן, Chald. def. כַּהֲנָא, pl. כַּהֲנַיָּא, i. q. Heb. הַכֹּהֵן. See כֹּהֵן above, Ezra vii. 12. 21; ix. 16. 18, &c. Aff. כַּהֲנוֹהִי. Hence the verb—

כִּהֵן, v. Pih. pres. יְכַהֵן, Dagesh being implied, Gram. art. 109. Constr. abs. it. med. לְ, to; בְּ, in, of place; תַּחַת, in place of. Syr. ܟܗܢ, *sacerdotem egit*. Æth. ኩህነ: id. *Act, officiate, as priest*, Exod. xxviii. 1. 3, 4. 41; xl. 13; Lev. xvi. 32; Num. iii. 4; Is. lxi. 10. יְכַהֵן יְכַהֵן פְּאֵר, כִּהֵן which seems highly parenthetical; ought evidently to be construed with שׂוֹשׂ אָשִׂישׂ וגו׳, preceding: and הִלְבִּישַׁנִי, or יַעְטָנִי, with יְכַהֵן פְּאֵר. It will then read thus: *I will greatly rejoice in Jehovah; my soul shall exult in my God, as the bridegroom does over the bride* (comp. Ib. lxii. 5): *for he hath clothed me with the garments of salvation*.... (As the priest, כַּכֹּהֵן, who) *officiates adornedly*, i. e. in rich vestments (comp. Exod. xxviii. 41), *or as the bride, &c.* This will make every thing regular and obvious, which, it is astonishing, no one has seen.

Infin. כַּהֵן, with לְ, pref., Exod. xxix. 1, &c. מִכַּהֵן, Hos. iv. 6. Aff. לְכַהֲנוֹ, Exod. xxviii. 1, &c.

כְּהֻנָּה, f. constr. כְּהֻנַּת, pl. כְּהֻנּוֹת. Syr. ܟܗܢܘܬܐ, *sacerdotium*. Arab. كهنوت, id. *The priesthood*, or *office of priest*, Exod. xxix. 9; Num. xvi. 10; Ezra ii. 62; Num. xxv. 13; Josh. xviii. 7. Pl., 1 Sam. ii. 36. Aff. כְּהֻנַּתְכֶם, כְּהֻנָּתָם.

כו, masc. Chald. plur. כַּוִּין. Arab. كُو, *fenestra*; كُوّ, *foramen magnum in pariete*. Syr. ܟܘܐ, *fenestra*, once, Dan. vi. 11. *Windows; casements.*

כּוֹבַע, m. constr. כּוֹבַע, pl. כּוֹבָעִים, i. q. cogn. קוֹבַע. Syr. ܟܘܒܥܐ, *pileus*. Arab. قَبَعَة, *calyx florum*. Gesenius has a long note here to show that this word partakes of the form of a segolate or abstract noun, having occasionally the accent on the ultimate, or penultimate, syllable. But, on these accents no reliance can be placed: and, after all, the vowels are irregular even on this view. But, if we suppose כּוֹבַע to have been written for כְּבָע, or כֲּבָא, as in the Arab. قَبَّاع above, and the (וֹ) of the pl. to stand for the alif (ا) of the Arabic, the vowels will be regular enough. The Syr. above is formed on the same analogy. It is strange that Gesenius did not see this. *A helmet*, 1 Sam. xvii. 5; Ezek. xxvii. 10; xxxviii. 5. Metaph. Is. lix. 17. Pl., Jer. xlvi. 4; 2 Chron. xxvi. 14, al. non occ.

כוה, v. Kal non occ. Syr. ܟܕ݂ܐ, *adussit*. Arab. كَوَى, *cauterizavit*.

Niph. pres. 2d pers. sing. תִּכָּוֶה, *Be, become, burnt*, Is. xliii. 2: pl. f., Prov. vi. 28, al. non occ.

כּוֹה, m. i. q. כֹּה, Dan. xi. 6.

כְּוִיָּה, f. once, Exod. xxi. 25. *Burning, branding*, of the body. Synon. τοῦ, כִּי. Arab. كَيّ, *inustio*.

כּוֹכָב, m. constr. כּוֹכַב, pl. כּוֹכָבִים, constr. כּוֹכְבֵי. Arab. كَوْكَب. Syr. ܟܘܟܒܐ, *stella*; it. Æth. Of Arab. كَبّ; whence, كَبَب, *pilulæ*. Cogn. كُوب, *calix rotunda*. Engl. *Cup*. Compd., perhaps, of كُوب + كَب, and hence the (וֹ) retained in the pl. abs. *Star*, Num. xxiv. 17; Amos v. 26; Gen. xxxvii. 9; Job iii. 9. Metaph. Job xxxviii. 7. See my note. Comp. Ps. cxlviii. 3; Num. l. c. Of constellations, Is. xiii. 10; Obad. vr. 4. Pl., taken as intimating multitude, Gen. xxii. 17, &c. צֵאת הַכּוֹכָבִים, *outgoing*, i. e. *rising of the stars*, Neh. iv. 15. Aff. כּוֹכָבֶיךָ, Ezek. xxxii. 7.

כול, v. Kal pret. כָּל, once, Is. xl. 12, constr. immed. obj. it. med. בְּ, instr. Arab. كَيْل, r. كَالَ, *mensuratum fuit*; كُول, *mensuravit*. Syr. ܐܟܝܠ, id. *Measured*.

Pih. redup. כִּלְכֵּל, pres. יְכַלְכֵּל. Constr. immed. it. med. אֶת. (a) *Contain* as in a vessel, 1 Kings viii. 27; 2 Chron. ii. 5; vi.

P P

כּוּם (290) כּוּן

18. (b) *Sustain*, as with provision, Gen. xlv. 11; xlvii. 12; l. 21; 1 Kings iv. 7, &c. — with firmness, Mal. iii. 2; Jer. xx. 9; Prov. xviii. 14; Ps. lv. 23; cxii. 5, &c.

Infin. כַּלְכֵּל, Ruth iv. 15, &c. Aff. כִּלְכֶּלְךָ, 1 Kings xvii. 4.

Part. מְכַלְכֵּל, Mal. l. c.

Puh. pl. m. כֻּלְכְּלוּ, *Were sustained, provided for*, 1 Kings xx. 27.

Hiph. pres. יָכִיל. Constr. immed. (a) *Contain*, 1 Kings vii. 26. 38. (b) *Sustain, bear, support*, Jer. x. 10; Joel ii. 11.

Infin. הָכִיל, (a) Ezek. xxii. 32: (b) Jer. vi. 11; Amos vii. 10.

כּוּמָז, masc. — plur. non occ. Arab. كُمْرَة, *conglobata dactylorum massa*, i. q. جُمْرَة. According to some, a *Sort of golden beads*, worn about the wrists and neck of Arabian women. Diod. Sic. lib. iii. c. xliv. Strabo. lib. xvi. Others suppose it to signify a belt or girdle ornamented with such beads, or the "*baccatum monile*," of Virgil. Exod. xxxv. 22; Num. xxxi. 50, only.

כּוּן, v. Cogn. תכן. הקן. Syr. ܟ, *cœpit esse*. Æth. ᎢᏛᎥ : *contigit*. Arab. كَانَ, *fuit*. Existence seems to be the primary notion: thence *order, &c.* Kal, once, Job xxxi. 15. Aff. parag. וַיְכֻנְנֵהוּ, *formed, fashioned*, set *him* in order.

Niph. נָכוֹן, pres. יִכּוֹן. *Be, become, disposed, set in order, fixed, established*, of person or thing, Gen. xli. 32; Exod. viii. 22; xxxiv. 2; Judg. xvi. 26. 29; Ps. lxxxix. 38; ci. 7; Prov. xxv. 5, &c. Phrr. נְכוֹן הַיּוֹם, Prov. iv. 18, *established* (state) *of the day*, i. e. full noon. Arab. قَائِمَةُ النَّهَارِ, id. Gr. σταθερὸν ἦμαρ, σταθερὰ μεσημβρία. Gesen. שַׁחַר נָכוֹן, Hos. vi. 3, *established dawn*, i. e. full day; or *true dawn*, as opposed to *the false*, i. e. الصُّبْحُ الصَّادِقِ, opp. τῷ, الصُّبْحُ الكَاذِبِ. *The false dawn* in the East, is a sort of premature twilight, which entirely disappears before the true dawn commences. The passage implies that the outgoing of Jehovah is clear and certain.—רוּחַ נָכוֹן, *spirit, mind, so regulated.* So Ps. lvii. 8, נָכוֹן לִבִּי, *my heart is disposed, fixed.* נָכוֹן הַדָּבָר, *the matter is fixed*, Gen. xli. 32. אֱל־נָכוֹן, *for a fixed thing, for certain*, 1 Sam. xxiii. 23; xxvi. 4: Exod. xix. 11,—הָיוּ, *let them be ready.* Ps. xxxviii. 18, לְצֶלַע נָכוֹן, *ready for stumbling.* Comp. Job xii. 5; xviii. 12; Prov. xix. 29. Fem. נְכוֹנָה, *thing fixed, established, truth*, &c., Ps. v. 10; Job xlii. 7, 8. שָׁדַיִם נָכֹנוּ, *both breasts were fixed*, i. e. fully grown, Ezek. xvi. 7.

Imp. הִכּוֹן, הֵכֹּן, *Be, become, fixed, disposed, prepared*, Ezek. xxxviii. 7; Amos iv. 12.

Hiph. הֵכִין, pres. יָכִין, apoc. יָכֵן. Constr. immed. it. med. אֶת, obj. לְ, אֶל, to, for, pers. or thing, בְּ, in, of place. *Dispose, prepare, fix, establish*, Josh. iv. 4; 1 Sam. xiii. 13; 1 Kings vi. 19; 1 Chron. xvi. 3; Job xxix. 7; Ps. lxxxix. 3. 5; x. 17; lxv. 10; lxviii. 11; 2 Chron. xvii. 5, &c. Phrr. הֵכִין לִבּוֹ, *prepared his heart*, disposed it, 2 Chron. xii. 14. הֵכִין דְּרָכָיו, *disposed* (aright) *his ways*, Ib. xxvii. 6. כְּלֵי־מָוֶת—, *weapons of death*, i. e. deadly, Ps. vii. 14. כִּסְאוֹ—, *his throne*, Ib. ciii. 19. אֲשֶׁר הֵכִין, for הֵכִין, *that he prepared*, 2 Chron. xxix. 36. See letter ה above, p. 146, (d). אֶת־פָּנָיו—, *thy face*, i. e. direct, turn it.

Infin. הָכִין, הָכֵן, Josh. iv. 3; iii. 17, &c. Aff. הֲכִינֵנוּ, Nah. ii. 4; Prov. viii. 27, &c.

Imp. הָכֵן, Ps. cxix. 133; Prov. xxiv. 27, &c.

— pl. הָכִינוּ, Josh. i. 11, &c.

Part. מֵכִין, Ps. lxv. 7; Jer. x. 12, &c.

Hoph. הוּכַן, pres. non occ. *Be, become, disposed, prepared, fixed*, Is. xvi. 5; xxx. 33; Zech. v. 11: Nah. ii. 6, הֻכַן.

Part. מוּכָן, pl. מוּכָנִים, Prov. xxi. 31; Ezek. xl. 43.

Pih. כּוֹנֵן, pres. יְכוֹנֵן. Constr. immed. it. med. לְ, בְּ, instr. אֶת, obj. עַל, עַד. *Dispose, prepare, fix, establish*, Ps. ix. 5; xxiv. 2; xl. 3; cvii. 36; Prov. xix. 19; Is. li. 13; lxii. 7; Deut. xxxii. 7, &c.

Imp. כּוֹנֵן, Job viii. 8. With ה parag., Ps. xc. 17. Aff. כּוֹנְנֵהוּ, Ib.

Puh. pl. m. כּוֹנָנוּ, i. q. Niph. Ps. xxxvii. 23; Ezek. xxviii. 13.

Hithp. pres. יִתְכּוֹנֵן, Prov. xxiv. 3: pl. יְכוֹנָנוּ, Ps. lix. 5: f. תִּכּוֹן, Num. xxi. 27: 2d pers. תִּכּוֹנָנִי, Is. liv. 14. In all which places, except the first, ה is assimilated to the rad. כ, in Dagesh, Gram. art. 82. 3. Sense, i. q. Niph.

כּוּן, masc. pl. כַּוָּנִים, twice, Jer. vii. 18; xliv. 19. LXX. χαυῶνας, which represents the Hebrew word merely in Greek letters. According to some, r. כָּוָה, thence *cakes*, as having been exposed to heat in cooking. Gr. πόπανον. Gesenius takes כן as the root. Pih. כֵּן, thence, *preparations* of cookery. It is of no importance, as to which etymon. is taken. It is not unlikely they were round flat cakes, made to represent the disk of the moon.

כּוֹס, masc. plur.—f. כֹּסוֹת. Syr. ܟܳܣܳܐ, *calix*. Cogn. ܟܒ, *collegit*, it.; ܟܡܣܐ, *loculus*. Arab. كِيس, *crumena*. Cogn.

كُوز, lit. *coacervatio*, thence, *calix*. I. *Drinking cup*, Gen. xl. 11. 13; 1 Kings vii. 26; 2 Chron. iv. 5. Often, *full cup*, Jer. xxv. 15; Ezek. xxiii. 32; Ps. xxiii. 5, &c. Thence, metaph. כּוֹס יְשׁוּעוֹת, Ps. cxvi. 13, *cup of great salvation*, from that used at the Paschal feast. חֲמָתוֹ —, *of his fury.* הַתַּרְעֵלָה —, *of trembling*, Is. li. 17. 22. Comp. Ps. xi. 6; xvi. 5; lxxv. 9; Jer. xvi. 7; li. 7; Lam. iv. 21; Ezek. xxiii. 33; Hab. ii. 16. Pl., Jer. xxxv. 5. Aff. כּוֹסִי, &c.

II. Pl. non occ. A certain unclean bird, most likely *the rough-billed pelican*, which has a sort of bag attached to the lower part of his bill. See Boch. Hieroz. ii. p. 275; Lev. xi. 17; Deut. xiv. 16; Ps. cii. 7.

כּוּר, masc.—plur. non occ. Syr. ܟܽܘܪܳܐ, *fornax*. Arab. كُور, *fossio terræ;* كُور, *foculus*, aut *fornax ex luto structa*. A *furnace* for melting and refining metals; often metaph., Deut. iv. 20; 1 Kings viii. 51; Is. xlviii. 10; Jer. xi. 4; Ezek. xxii. 18. 20. 22; Prov. xvii. 3; xxvi. 21. Hence the verb—

כּוּר, whence the pl. participial form, כָּאֲרִי, once, Ps. xxii. 17 (as Chald. קָאֵם of קוּם, and pl. as מֵי, for מַיִם, Ps. xlv. 9), persons *Digging, piercing into, or through.* So Gesenius thinks the word may possibly be taken. Two manuscripts, however, read כָּארוּ, for כָּרוּ, as he also shows. He should likewise have shown—which he has omitted to do— that this really is the reading of the Masora.* It is, therefore, the authorized reading of the Jews; and no doubt can exist as to its sense. Aquila gives ᾔσχυναν, which clearly shows that he read this as a verb, and most likely this very verb; verbs signifying *digging* often implying *shame* also: see חפר. The LXX. ὤρυξαν, proves the same thing: and, hence, that the reading of the Masora is the true one; and also, that recourse need not be had to Gesenius's Chald. reasons for its form; the א being a mere *mater lectionis*, as in קָאם, for קָם, Hos. x. 14. Gesenius tells us, that the most simple interpretation would be, taking the vulgar acceptation of the terms, "*sicut leones inhiant. s. imminent, manibus pedibusque meis*," i. e. *omnia membra lacerare minantur.*" Why, then, it may fairly be asked, is the term כָּאֲרִי, introduced at all? That implying *dogs*, used just before, and again vr. 21, would have answered the purpose full as well, if this had been the sense intended. But, if the term *lion* is introduced for the greater strength, how are we to reconcile this with the notions of dividing the garments, and casting lots, as in vr. 19? Once more, Is it usual to put the hands and feet for all the members? I think not: certainly good proof of this ought to have been given. Nor are the grounds, on which "*inhiant,*" and *imminent* are assumed, at all better. Nor is the assumption good, that David only is meant here. The terms just mentioned are not at all applicable to him in any case; much less are the predictions of the prevalence of true religion, with which the Psalm closes. Nor, indeed, is there any person except Christ, to which this Psalm can be fairly applied, as every candid inquirer must see. There certainly is a remarkable agreement visible between this Psalm, and the fifty-third chapter of Isaiah, which can leave no doubt on the mind of any one, that David could have been intended by neither; or, that the New Testament view of both is not the correct one.

כּוֹר, see כֹּר.

כּוּשִׁי, m. pl. כּוּשִׁיִּים, כּוּשִׁים. Patronym. of כּוּשׁ, *Native of Cush*, a *Cushite*, Jer. xiii. 23; xxxviii. 7. 10. 12; pl. 2 Chron. xxi. 16.

כּוּשִׁית, f. Num. xii. 1, &c.

כּוּשָׁן, m. i. q. כּוּשׁ, *Cush*, apparently, Hab. iii. 7.

כּוֹשָׁרוֹת, f. pl. once, Ps. lxviii. 7; r. כָּשַׁר. *Great prosperity, wealth.* LXX. ἐν ἀνδρείᾳ. Symm. εἰς ἀπόλυσιν. Theod. ἐν εὐθύτησιν.

---

* Masora, on Num. xxiv. 9. See the other authorities to the same point, given on this place in Jahn's Heb. Bib.

כות (292) כחד

פּוֹתֶרֶת, see פָּתַר.

כָּזָב, m. pl. כְּזָבִים. Syr. ܟ݁ܽܘܫ, *mentitus est*. Arab. كَذَبَ, *mendacium*. The primitive notion exists in *falling short, failing, deficiency*: hence, كَذَبَ, as a verb. *Non duravit; per incuriam erravit.* Conj. ii. *fefellit, vanusque fuit, &c.*; and Heb. applied to waters which occasionally fail. Comp. כָּחַד, and כָּחַשׁ. Hence Paul's lie to God's glory, Rom. iii. 7, is his inadequate * preaching of it: not his falsehood in doing so. *Falsehood, lying*, something falling short of the truth, Ps. iv. 3; v. 7; Prov. vi. 19. — *of idols*, Ps. xl. 5; Amos ii. 4. — *false oracles*, Ezek. xiii. 6. Aff. כֻּזְבֵיהֶם, Amos, l. c.

כזב, v. See כּוּב above, Kal non occ. except—
Part. כֻּזָב, once, Ps. cxvi. 11. *Deficient, falling short, false.*
Pih. כִּזֵּב, pres. יְכַזֵּב, constr. abs. it. med. לְ, בְּ, עַל, *Advance what is short of the truth*, *lie, deceive*, Mic. ii. 11; Ezek. xiii. 19; Job vi. 28; xxiv. 6; Ps. lxxxix. 36, &c. Metaph. of waters, *failing, deceiving* the expectations, Is. lviii. 11.
Infin. aff. כַּזֶּבְכֶם, *Your deceiving, lying to* —, Ezek. xiii. 19.
Niph. f. נִכְזָבָה, *Is, becomes, fallacious; fails*, Job xli. 1. נִכְזָב, *thou fail; art proved deficient, false*, Prov. xxx. 6, al. non occ.
Hiph. pres. aff. יְכַזִּיבֵנִי, *Convicts me of falsehood;* pronounces me false, once, Job xxiv. 25.

כֹּחַ, rarely כּוֹחַ, plur. non occ. Arab. كَاحَ, r. كَوَح, *pugnando vicit.* Infin. كَوْح. كَاح, *crassities.* I. *Strength, vigour, power*, applied to things animate and inanimate. — *of God*, Num. xiv. 17; Job xxiii. 6; xxx. 18. — *of men*, Judg. xvi. 6. 30; Job xxvi. 2. Meton. Gen. xlix. 3. אַתָּה כֹּחִי *thou art* (the result of) *my strength.* In much the same way of the produce of the earth, Gen. iv. 12; Job xxxi. 39. *Ability, fitness*, Dan. i. 4. *Wealth*, Job vi. 22; xxxvi. 19; Prov. v. 10. II. *A lizard*, so called from its great strength. Bochart.

* And hence the point in the term, ἐπερίσσευσεν following.

Hieroz. i., p. 1069; only, Lev. xi. 30. Aff. כֹּחִי, &c.

כחד, v. Kal non occ. Æth. ᎦᎰᎠ፡ *negavit.* Arab. جَحَدَ, id. See כחש.
Niph. נִכְחַד, pres. יִכָּחֵד. I. *Be withholden, concealed*, Ps. lxix. 6; cxxxix. 15; 2 Sam. xviii. 13; Hos. v. 3. II. — *made useless, destroyed*, Job iv. 7; xxii. 20; Zech. xi. 9; Exod. ix. 15.
Part. f. נִכְחֶדֶת, pl. נִכְחָדוֹת, ii. sign., Zech. xi. 9. 16; Job xv. 28.
Pih. כִּחֵד, pres. יְכַחֵד. Constr. abs. it. immed. it. med. מִן, לְ. *Keep back, withhold, conceal*, Gen. xlvii. 18; Josh. vii. 19; 1 Sam. iii. 17, 18; 2 Sam. xiv. 18; Is. iii. 9; Jer. l. 2; Ps. xl. 11; Job vi. 10, &c.
Hiph. pret. 1st pers. הִכְחַדְתִּי, pres. יַכְחִיד. Constr. immed. it. med. אֶת, מִן. I. *Hold back, conceal*, Job xx. 12. II. *Bring to nought, destroy*, as in אסף, Exod. xxiii. 23; Zech. xi. 8; Ps. lxxxiii. 5; 2 Chron. xxxii. 21.
Infin. הַכְחִיד, with מֵעַל, 1 Kings xiii. 34.

כָּחַל, v. once only, Ezek. xxiii. 40. כָּחַלְתְּ עֵינַיִךְ, *thou hast anointed thy eyes*, i. e. with (الكُحْل, alcohol) a composition of certain black powder, for the purpose of giving more brilliancy to its expression. Arab. كَحَلَ, *illevit stibio oculos.*

כַּחַשׁ, m.—pl. aff. כַּחֲשֵׁיהֶם. (a) *Deficiency;* (b) *failure, falsehood.* (a) Job xvi. 8: (b) Hos. x. 13; xii. 1; Nah. iii. 2; Ps. lix. 13. Hence—

כָּחַשׁ, v. Synon. כזב כוב, *Fail, be wanting, deficient*, once, Ps. cix. 24, with מִן, of.
Pih. כִּחֵשׁ, pres. יְכַחֵשׁ. Constr. abs. it. immed. thing; it. med. בְּ, לְ. *Hold back, withhold;* thence, *fail, deceive, deny, lie*, Josh. vii. 11; xxiv. 27; Jer. v. 12; Ps. xviii. 48; lxvi. 3; lxxxi. 16;—Gen. xviii. 15. In 1 Kings xiii. 18, לוֹ כִּחֵשׁ, *he lied to him*, is to be referred to מַלְאָךְ preceding: there being no reason for supposing that the old prophet had here recourse to falsehood. A vision had probably been afforded, in which—as in the case of Micaiah, 1 Kings xxii. 20, seq.— a spirit had been allowed thus to act upon his mind, for the purpose of trying the man of God. Applied, metaph.,

(293)

to inanimate things, Hab. iii. 16; Job viii. 18; Hos. ix. 2.

Infin. כַּחֵשׁ, Zech. xiii. 4; Is. lix. 13, &c.

Niph. pres. pl. יִכָּחֲשׁוּ, *Be, become* (convicted as), *false, liars*, only, Deut. xxxiii. 29, with לְ.

Hithp. יִתְכַּחֲשׁוּ, once, 2 Sam. xxii. 45, i. q. Niph.

כָּחָשׁ, m. pl. כְּחָשִׁים, *Deficient, wanting, lying*, Is. xxx. 9, only.

כִּי, Particle, thus derived apparently. Arab. كوي, whence كَي, *inustio, stigma*; i. e. *a mark*, intended pointedly to indicate something. Whence the particle كِي, *ut, ita, &c.*, the double letter being got rid of, in consequence of the frequency of its use, and the word itself used to excite attention to something following; as, *mark, observe*, or the like, as in our own *because*, i. e. *mark* as such; much in the manner of all imperatives, i. e. as verbal primitive nouns uttered with emphasis. In Syr. ܟܐ, *Ne, num?* interrogatively, and occasionally expressing doubt. In the Æth. ከ: is only found prefixed to the pronouns; as, ከያ: i. q. Heb. אֹתִי, Arab. إِيَّايَ. And, for the purpose of exciting attention, or the like, these Heb. and Arab. particles are always used. See under אֵת. I conclude, therefore, that כִּי is also a particle of this sort, and, therefore, liable to a similar diversity of sense, according to the situations in which it is found; and not unlike the Pers. کی, the Latin *quia, quippe, &c.* Examples: see Nold., p. 367, כִּי בַדָּבָר, *observe, mark, in the matter, &c.*, Exod. xviii. 11, i. e. *for, because, &c.*, כִּי גֹאֵל, Deut. xxiii. 8. Ruth iii. 9, &c. Nold. 2. "*An utrum:*" *whether*. כִּי כֵנִים, Gen. xlii. 33, *mark, ye are just*, i. e. represent yourselves as such; equivalent to our *that*. 3. *Annon, nonne?* כִּי הֶעֱלִתִיךָ, *mark,—is it not so?—I have brought thee up, &c.* 4. *Certè, omnino: surely*, Num. xxii. 33; Ruth i. 10, &c. And so, with some slight variety, either as the terms of the context, or as the position in it of the particle, may require, in all the nine-and-twenty significations which Noldius ascribes to it. And let it be borne in mind, as noticed under אִם, that, in the languages

of this family, all enouncements are *positive*; conditional, or subjunctive, or similar, expressions are formed, only by words introduced for that purpose, Gram. art. 232, sec. So much on the etymology and primitive force of this particle: let us now examine more particularly the usage and force of it.

This particle is had recourse to for *two* specific purposes: I.—which is not very frequent—for pointing out the first member of an hypothetical, conditional, or subjunctive sentence: II.—which is frequent—for marking the latter member of such sentence, as depending, in one way or other upon a preceding one, either expressed or implied. Examples of the first case, in which, nevertheless, relation to some preceding declaration is evident, 1 Sam. xxiv. 20, כִּי־יִמְצָא אִישׁ אֶת־אֹיְבוֹ....וַיהוָה, *if*, or *when, a man finds his enemy, &c.—so Jehovah, &c.* Exod. xxii. 22, כִּי אִם־צָעֹק יִצְעַק אֵלַי וגו׳, *for, when, if, he certainly cries to me, I will surely hear, &c.* Deut. vii. 17, כִּי תֹאמַר בִּלְבָבְךָ וגו׳, *when, if, thou sayest in thy heart, &c.* In all which cases, כִּי is as nearly synonymous with אִם as can be imagined: in some of which, indeed, it is introduced, apparently for the purpose of strengthening, — giving certainty, as in oaths,—to the protasis, or leading term of category. The precise term by which it is to be rendered by the translator, will entirely depend on the manner in which he views the whole. Examples of the second case:—these are innumerable—we can here give only a few, by way of specimen. In this case the construction of the protasis may be various: and the relation of the apodosis be various also, as being deduced from various views of the subject. Deut. הוּא אָחִיךָ כִּי, *for, because, he is thy brother*. Gen. xlii. 33, כִּי כֵנִים אַתֶּם, — *that* —, i. e. the thing in question, *you are just* men. 2 Kings xviii 34, כִּי הִצִּילוּ אֶת־שֹׁמְרוֹן, — *that, they should deliver Samaria?* i. e. imagining them to be so circumstanced as to do this. Job xxxi 18, כִּי מִנְּעוּרַי, *seeing that, because that, &c. from my youth*. Num. xxii. 33, כִּי עַתָּה גַּם וגו׳, *surely, without doubt, as a consequence, I had now slain even thee*. Here אוּלַי is in the protasis, implying negation. 1 Sam. ii. 21, כִּי־פָקַד יְהוָה וגו׳, *consequently, therefore, accordingly*, i. e. from the blessing mentioned in vr. 20, *Jehovah visited Hannah, &c.* In 1 Kings xviii. 27, it obtains, in both these usages, קִרְאוּ־כִי־אֱלֹהִים הוּא כִּי־שִׂיחַ וְכִי־שִׂיג לוֹ וְכִי־דֶרֶךְ לוֹ אוּלַי וגו׳, *cry—because, for, he is a God:*

put the case (i. q. אִם) he is *meditating, or he is pursuing, or he has a journey* before him: perhaps he slumbers, (in every case) *then be he excited.* And so in innumerable instances which may be cited.

Gesenius labours, ineffectually, I think, in endeavouring to make this particle quadrate in every case with the Latin, *qui, quæ, quod.* Something like a similar sense may, certainly, thus be extracted from very many passages; but, the real question is, will these be genuine counterparts of their originals? It must surely be obvious to every one that they will not, because they exhibit undoubted infractions of the oriental idiom: and, as necessarily convey to the mind of the learner any thing but their true import. The principle, too, on which this conjectural mode of rendering is conducted, is most pernicious to the mind; leading it to imagine, that if a sense can be extracted, that will, of necessity, be the true sense; than which nothing can be more fallacious, e. g. Gen. iii. 19, כִּי מִמֶּנָּה לֻקָּחְתָּ, "*de qua sumptus es.*" (LXX. ἐξ ἧς ἐλήφθης, &c.) But, if this were the sense, the expression would be equivalent, אֲשֶׁר לֻקַּח מִשָּׁם, as in vr. 23, or אֲשֶׁר לָקַח מִמֶּנָּה. Besides, it is evident, from the antithetic character of the construction, that this passage is intended to be considered as intimating a consequence of that which immediately precedes it; and of this, the following member also, commencing with כִּי, affords an illustration. This one instance only, is, therefore, quite sufficient to show, that, however this mode of proceeding may satisfy, or suit, certain translators and commentators, it is not that which is calculated to elicit the true sense of the original. It is true, indeed, that כִּי is a relative particle, as Dr. Gesenius affirms; still, it is by no means equivalent in its use — whatever might be said as to its origin — with the Latin *qui, quæ, quod.*

It is found in connexion with other particles, the compound then partaking of the sense of the whole, as in other combinations, as, כִּי אִם, Gen. xxxii. 27, לֹא אֲשַׁלֵּחֲךָ כִּי אִם־בֵּרַכְתָּנִי, lit. *I send not, will not send, thee away, for surely thou shalt bless me,* i. e. until thou do so. In like manner, Lev. xxii. 6; Ruth iii. 18, &c.; Nold., p. 378, it. numm. 2, 3, 4; num. 5; Gen. xviii. 7, אֵין זֶה כִּי אִם־בֵּית אֱלֹהִים, *this is not, for, but, surely God's house,* i. e. nothing else. So also Esth. ii. 15; Josh. xiv. 4, &c.

In 1 Sam. xxv. 34, it is in the apodosis of a hypothetical construction. כִּי אִם...לוּלֵי מִהַרְתְּ נוֹתַר וּגו׳, *unless thou hadst hasted, there had (not) surely remained, &c.* The negative contained in לוּלֵי, is, as it is usual, supplied by the ellipsis to the second member or apodosis. So Num. xiv. 30; 1 Sam. xxx. 17; 2 Sam. xii. 3, &c.; Nold., num. 7—9; Gen. xlvii. 18, כִּי אִם, *for, but, surely, &c.* So Ruth iii. 12; 1 Sam. viii. 9; 1 Kings xviii. 18; 2 Chron. xviii. 17, &c. And so, with some slight variation, all the other examples, however, compounded, as כִּי אִם־לִפְנֵי, 2 Sam. iii. 13. כִּי גַם, Eccl. vii. 12; iv. 14; viii. 12, &c.; Nold., p. 380. And, p. 381, כִּי כֵן, Esth. i. 8; 1 Kings ii. 7, &c. כִּי עַל, Jer. lii. 3. כִּי עַל־כֵּן, Gen. xviii. 5; Num. x. 31, &c.

כִּי, masc. plur. non occ. Arab. كِيٌّ, *inustio,* once, Is. iii. 24. *Branding, as a mark of infamy.*

כִּיד, masc. once, Job xxi. 20. Arab. كِيدٌ, كَيْدٌ, *fraus; ira inimici, &c. Ruin, destruction.*

כִּידֹדֵי, pl. m. constr. once, Job xli. 11, r. כדד. Arab. كَدٌّ, *excussio ignis. Sparks of fire.*

כִּידוֹן, masc.— plur. non occ. Arab. كَيْدٌ, *fraus, stratagema, bellum.* Augm. וֹן, *of,* or *belonging to, war. Lance,* or *spear, a missile* perhaps, Josh. viii. 18. 26; 1 Sam. xvii. 6. 45; Jer. vi. 23; L. 42; Job xxxix. 23; xli. 20.

כִּידוֹר, m. once, Job xv. 24, r. כדר (fm. פִּיקוֹד, for פָּקוּד, the dagesh being compensated perhaps by a perfect vowel. Arab. كَدَرَ, *agitata fuit* nubes; *effudit* aquam. Conj. vii. *præceps ruit, effususque fuit* in aliquem. *Attack, onset.* See my note on the place.

כִּיּוּן, m. once, Amos v. 26. Arab. Pers. كَيْوَانُ, *Saturn,* Acts vii. 43, καὶ τὸ ἄστρον τοῦ Θεοῦ ὑμῶν Ῥεμφὰν (al. Ῥαιφὰν, Ῥεφφὰν, Ῥεφὰν, Ῥαφὰν, Ῥομφὰ, &c.), the Coptic ⲠϨⲢⲈϤⲪⲒ, ⲠϨⲪⲀⲚ, &c. probably an ancient Egyptian name of Saturn, Kirch. Ling. Ægypt., p. 49; Jablonsk. Opusc. ii. p. i.; Mich. Supplem., p. 1225, seq. Gesen. The image, or symbol, of the planet is necessarily the thing meant here. See also אֲשֵׁרָה above.

כִּיּוֹר, and כִּיֹר, m. pl. כִּיֹּרִים, and f. כִּיּוֹרָה. Arab. كَوْر, *fossio terræ;* كَار, *dimidiatus uter, &c.* See כור, primarily a hole or pit digged in the earth: thence, meton. I. *A sort of pot,* or *brazier,* in which fire was kept, Zech. xii. 6. II. *Lavers* of brass, in which the sacrifices were washed; five of these were placed on each side of the house, exclusive of the great brazen sea: and each containing forty baths. Also a *laver* for the use of the priests in the Tabernacle; for which, the *brazen sea* was a substitute in the Temple of Solomon, Exod. xxx. 18. 28; xxxi. 9; xxxv. 16; xxxix. 39;—1 Kings vii. 38. 40; 2 Chron. iv. 6, &c.: the latter marked (k) in the plan of the Temple given in the Appendix. III. *A fire-pan* for cooking meat, 1 Sam. ii. 14. IV. *A pulpit,* from its resembling a vessel of this sort. Auth. Vers. *A scaffold,* 2 Chron. vi. 13. See my note on Job xxix. 7.

כִּילַי, it. כֵּלַי, m. Is. xxxii. 5. 7, only, opp. τῷ, שׁוֹעַ. Arab. كَيُول, *meticulosus;* كَيُول, id. it. *postrema aciei homo.* Cogn. خَيِل, *superbus.* Cogn. Heb. נכל. Syr. ܢܟܠ, *decepit.* The termination, being plural, implies excess, Gram. artt. 139. 6; 223. 3. *Avaricious, oppressive.*

כִּילַפּוֹת, f. pl. once, Ps. lxxiv. 6. Syr. ܟܠܦܐ, *securis, malleus.* Lat. *clavus.* Engl. *club;* Arab. كَلَب, *compunxit* (stimulavit) *calcari.* Cogn. كَلَف, *compulit.* *Hammers,* or *axes.*

כִּימָה, f.—pl. non occ. Syr. ܟܣܬܐ. *Pleiades.* Arab. كُومَة, *cumulus.* The *constellation of the Pleiades,* Amos v. 8; Job ix. 9; xxxviii. 31. See my note, Job ix. 9. Hyde on the Tables of Ulugh Beigh, p. 32.

כִּיס, masc.—plur. non occ. Arab. كِيس, *crumena.* Cogn. Heb. כוס. Arab. كَاس, *poculum;* تَكَاوُس, *congestio;* v. كَاس, *convolvit se serpens.* The primary notion seems to have existed in surrounding comprehending; thence, *A purse* or *bag,* wherein to keep money, Prov. i. 14; Is. xlvi. 6: or *weights,* Deut. xxv. 13; Mic. vi. 11; Prov. xvi. 11.

כִּיר, m. dual, כִּירַיִם, r. כור, once, Lev. xi. 35. *A pot,* or *jar,* earthen apparently, as liable to being broken. If reliance is to be placed on the dual form, having, perhaps, *two* compartments; but, if taken as a plural, more than two.

כִּישׁוֹר, m. once, Prov. xxxi. 19, r. כשר. *A distaff.* Aquila, Symm. Theod. ἀνδρεῖα (or ἀνδρεία). LXX. τὰ συμφέροντα.

כִּיתְרוֹן, for כִּיתְרוֹן, Eccl. ii. 15.

כָּכָה, Particle, compd., according to Gesenius, of כָּה + כָּ, i. q. פֹּה + כְּ, sic: rather, perhaps, of כְּ, part. and ךְ, af. pron. as in the Arabic ذَاكَ, and ذَلِك, lit. *hic,* vel *hoc, tibi,* where the pronoun is pleonastic. And so Schultens, on Job i. 5. This will account for the accent's being found on the penultimate, Exod. xii. 11; Num. viii. 26; Deut. xxix. 23; Josh. x. 25, &c. For אָנֹכִי, see under אִי, p. 28, above.

כִּכָּר, c. compd. of כַּר + כְּ, of r. בור. Arab. كَوْر, *in gyrum ambiens caput* cidaris: cf كَرْكَر, *convertit molam;* lit. any thing flat and round; as, (a) *A cake* of bread, כִּכַּר לֶחֶם, Exod. xxix. 23; 1 Sam. ii. 26; Prov. vi. 26: pl. כִּכְּרוֹת לֶחֶם, Judg. viii. 5; 1 Sam. x. 3. (b) *A talent,* of gold, silver, or lead, Exod. xxxviii. 25, 26; 1 Kings ix. 14; x. 10. 14; Zech. v. 7, 8: Dual, כִּכָּרַיִם, 2 Kings v. 23: pl. כִּכָּרִים, constr. כִּכְּרֵי, 2 Kings v. 5; 1 Chron. xxii. 14; xxix. 7; Ezra viii. 26. (c) *Tract of country,* appearing to the eye as limited within a circle; particularly that adjoining the western banks of the Jordan. Arab. الغَوْر, Gen. xiii. 12; xix. 17; 2 Sam. xviii. 23. ἡ περίχωρος τοῦ Ἰορδάνου, Matt. iii. 6. Chald. pl. כַּכְּרִין, i. q. Heb. (b) Ezra vii. 22.

כֹּל, once, כּוֹל, with makkáph following, כָּל; with aff. כֻּלּוֹ, pl. non occ. r. כול, cogn. כלה, יכל, כלל, &c. Syr. ܟܠ, *mensura.* Arab. كُول, *mensuratum fuit.* Cogn. كَيِل, *mea-*

כל (296) כל

sura. Comprehending, limiting, seems to be the primitive notion; thence, cogn. כָּלָא. Syr. ܟ݁ܠܳܐ; Arab. كَلَأَ, *detinuit, &c.;* ڪَفَّ,

كُلّ, *omnis;* propr. subst. (a) *The whole,* or *all,* taken collectively; Lat. *totus,* Gen. xiii. 10; xix. 17. 25; Exod. xxix. 18; Is. xxviii. 24; Job xxxiv. 13; Dan. vi. 4, &c. Often with aff. pron. כֻּלְּךָ, Is. xxii. 1, &c. כֻּלָּךְ, Ib. xiv. 29. כֻּלֹּה, Gen. xxv. 25. כֻּלֹּה 2 Sam. ii. 9. כֻּלָּהּ, Ezek. xxix. 2, &c.; Gen. xlii. 11; Deut. i. 22; Eccl. ii. 14; 2 Sam. xxiii. 6; Gen. xlii. 36; 1 Kings vii. 37, &c.

Hence, (b) *Complete, perfect, entire.* כָּל־הֶבֶל, *entire, mere, vanity,* Ps. xxxix. 6; Deut. vi. 5. Gr. πᾶς, Rom. xv. 13, &c.

(c) *Distributively. All, every,* Gen. ii. 2; Exod. xiii. 2; 1 Kings xix. 18. *Each* one, Is. xv. 3; Neh. iv. 10; Exod. xii. 6, &c. When two only are mentioned, *both,* Eccl. ii. 14; Prov. xxii. 2. Indefinitely, *any* one, Exod. xx. 4; Lev. iv. 2; Num. xxxv. 22; Judg. xix. 19; Jer. xiii. 7; Prov. xxx. 30, &c. Which, however, may be implied in any indefinite noun, as, דָּבָר, Gen. xviii. 14; מִזְמָּה, Job xlii. 2; וּכְמַסְתֵּר, Is. liii. 3. The Arab. *tanween,* ٌ, has the same effect in the Arabic. Occasionally with the article, as in הַבְּהֵמָה, Gen. vii. 2, &c.

(d) — laxly, *Many, most* of, Exod. xxxii. 26; Gen. xli. 57; Num. xvi. 32; 1 Kings i. 39, 40; Ps. ix. 2, &c. So, πᾶς, Matt. iii. 5; viii. 34, &c.; which may be expressed by our term *generally, generally speaking, &c.* So Judg. xvi. 17; Exod. i. 14; Deut. vii. 7, &c. Hence, equivalent to πάντως, adverbially.

This word appears occasionally to be redundant, as in כָּל־עוֹד, Job xxvii. 3; but this is not the case: on the contrary, it has its use in all, imparting the whole force of its meaning in every such construction. In l. c. כָּל, is to be construed with וְנִשְׁמָתִי, *for still the whole of my breath is within me;* or, it may be taken adverbially,—*is wholly within me.* Comp. Gen. viii. 22; xxxix. 23, כָּל־מְאוּמָה, lit. *every something,* i. e. *any thing whatsoever.* So 2 Sam. iii. 35. Compd. with prepositions, בְּכֹל, or בַּכֹּל, Gen. xxxix. 5; Deut. i. 31, &c. See Nold. p. 385, § 11. With aff. as noticed above, Ib. Construed with other particles, כָּל־אֲשֶׁר, אֵין כֹּל, אֵין כָּל, &c. p. 386, seq. It receives the article like other attributes, when used substantively; as, הַכֹּל, Eccl. ix. 1; Dan. xi. 2, &c., with prep. בַּכֹּל, Gen. xvi. 12; כַּכֹּל, Job xxiv. 24; לַכֹּל, Jer. xiii. 7, &c.

כֹּל, or כָּל־, Chald. i. q. Heb. (a) Ezra vi. 11, 12; vii. 16; Dan. iii. 2. 5. 7. Aff. כָּלְהוֹן, Dan. ii. 38, &c. Def. כֹּלָּא, i. q. Heb. כַּכֹּל, Dan. ii. 40; iv. 9. (c) Dan. vi. 8, &c. Compd. with other particles, כָּל־דִּי, *All, every one, who* —, Dan. vi. 8; Ezra vii. 21: i. q. Heb. כָּל־אֲשֶׁר.—כָּל־קֳבֵל־דִּי, i. q. Heb. כָּל־עֻמַּת שֶׁ, lit. *all before that,* i. e. *obvious that;* hence, *because, that, forasmuch as, &c.,* Dan. vi. 5. 23, &c.—כָּל־קֳבֵל דְּנָה, id., Dan. ii. 14; Ezra vii. 17, &c. Nold., p. 388.

כֶּלֶא, masc. plur. כְּלָאִים. Syr. ܟ݁ܠܳܐ, *prohibitio.* Æth. ⵉⵍⴰⵜ: id. Arab. كَلَأ, *custodia.* Lit. *restraint. Confinement, prison.* Aff. כִּלְאוֹ, in the phr. בִּגְדֵי כִלְאוֹ, *his prison-clothes,* 2 Kings xxv. 29; Jer. lii. 33. It. בֵּית כֶּלֶא, and בֵּית הַכֶּלֶא, *prison-house,* 2 Kings xvii. 4; Jer. xxxvii. 15, &c. Pl. בָּתֵּי כְלָאִים, Is. xlii. 22. Hence—

כָּלָא, v. pres. יִכְלָא. Constr. immed. it. med. מִן, *from;* בְּ, *in;* it. abs. *Restrain, confine, withhold,* Jer. xxxii. 3; Hagg. i. 10; 1 Sam. xxv. 33, כְּלִיתִי, for כְּלִיתִיו. Ps. cxix. 101, כָּלִאתִי, *I have restrained, withholden.* 1 Sam. vi. 10, כְּלוּ. The last three of r. כָּלָה, see Gram. art. 202. 4. Pres. Ps. xl. 10. 12; Is. xliii. 6; Gen. xliii. 6. יִכְלֶה, of כלה. Infin. כְּלוֹא, Eccl. viii. 8.

Part. pass. כָּלוּא, it. כָּלֻא, Jer. xxxii. 2; Ps. lxxxviii. 9. See under כלוא.

Niph. pres. יִכָּלֵא, *Be, become, restrained, withholden.* Constr. abs. it. med. מִן, Gen. viii. 20; Exod. xxxvi. 6; Ezek. xxxi. 15.

Pih. Infin. כַּלֵּא, Dan. ix. 24; but better referred perhaps to כלה, כִּלָּה, *finishing.* See under כלה.

כִּלְאַיִם, m. dual, usually as i. q. Arab. كِلَا, *ambo.* Æth. ⵉⵍⴰ: *duplicis generis. Of two sorts* or *kinds:* but the root may possibly be כָּלָא, *restraint,* in the sense of *disallowed, improper, unsuitable:* and hence, Lev. xix. 19, mean, *thou shalt not cause thy cattle to gender with an unsuitable kind; thy field thou shalt not sow* with *two improper, incongruous sorts* (of seed); *nor shall a garment of two disagreeing sorts, &c.* See שַׁעַטְנֵז, — *come upon thee.* In which, something like the "*simplex munditiis,*" of Horace, seems to be inculcated, i. e. that the Israelites should be *pure, simple, plain,*

כלב (297) כלה

unostentatious, in their habits and practices. That a field should not simply be sown with diverse seed, or a garment composed of diverse sorts of cloth, seems to have no adequate object here: but, that *incongruities* should not be practised in these respects, although involving, perhaps, nothing beyond a question of taste, is of considerable importance as it regards morality: a vitiated taste, in the one respect seldom being unaccompanied with a similar one in the other.

כֶּלֶב, m. pl. כְּלָבִים, constr. כַּלְבֵי. Arab. كَلْبٌ. Syr. ܟܰܠܒܳܐ, *canis.* *A dog*, considered as an unclean, ferocious animal: and hence (كَلْبٌ, *kelb*) used as a term of reproach by Mohammedans towards Christians generally, Exod. xi. 7; Judg. vii. 5; Prov. xxvi. 11; Ps. lix. 7. 15; Is. lvi. 10; 1 Kings xiv. 11, &c. Metaph. applied to fierce, or otherwise bad men, 2 Sam. xvi. 9; 1 Sam. xxiv. 14. Comp. 2 Sam. iii. 8; Ps. xxii. 17. 21; Job xxx. 1. See my note. Ps. lxviii. 24. Aff. כְּלָבֶיךָ. In Deut. xxiii. 18, in the sense of קְדֵשִׁים, as Gesenius thinks: and, in the same, κύνες, Rev. xxii. 15. Damm, in his Homeric Lexicon (sub. κύων), endeavours to soften down some of these passages. He seems to have forgotten, that among the Hebrews this animal was considered as *unclean,* much more so when dead; which he takes to imply *harmlessness!* 1 Sam. xxiv. 15. So very liable are mere classical scholars to misunderstand and misrepresent Holy Writ. Yet even Homer is not without expressions of abhorrence as to the character of the dog, Il. A. 225; Z. 344. 356, &c., as also given by Damm.

כָּלָה, f.—pl. כָּלוֹת. Cogn. כול, כלל, יכל, כלא. Syr. ܟܽܠ, *omnis.* Used much as the Arab. تَمَامٌ, is. *Complete, finished, determined* upon, thing, &c. (for כָּלְתָה, i. e. fem. of concrete fm. כָּלֶה.) With נֶחֱרָצָה, Is. x. 23; xxviii. 22; Dan. ix. 27. נִכְהֲלָה, Zeph. i. 18; Dan. xi. 16. וְכָלְתָה בְיָדוֹ, for הָיְתָה בְיָדוֹ, if the word is not really the verb: in either case, *it shall be finished,* or, meton. *wasted, destroyed.* So Deut. xxviii. 32, of the eyes. Very frequently with עָשָׂה, and then used adverbially, as in the Arab. تَمَامًا. *Completely, entirely,* and occasionally, *even to*

destruction, Gen. xviii. 21; Jer. v. 19; xxx. 11; xlvi. 28, &c. With גֶּרֶשׁ, Exod. xi. 1; it. לְכָלָה, Ezek. xiii. 13; 2 Chron. xii. 12. Gesenius gives it as construed with בְּ, Jer. xxx. 11: אֵת, Jer. v. 18, &c. But this is a mistake, these particles clearly referring to the verb עָשָׂה, not to this word.

כָּלָה, v. pres. יִכְלֶה, apoc. יִכֶל. Constr. abs. it. med. לְ, אֶל, עַל, to, for, according to; מִן, מֵעִם, בְּ, (a) *Be complete, finished, determined.* (b) Meton. *wasted, decayed, ruined.* (a) Gen. xlv. 53; Exod. xxxix. 32; 1 Kings vi. 38; Is. x. 25; xvi. 4; xxiv. 13; xxxii. 10; Jer. viii. 20; Ezek. v. 13;—1 Sam. xx. 7. 9; Prov. xxii. 8, &c. (b) Gen. xxi. 15; 1 Kings xvii. 14; Lam. ii. 11; Job vii. 9. With נַפְשִׁי, Ps. lxxxiv. 3; רוּחַ, cxliii. 7; כָּלַי, lxix. 4; כִּלְיוֹתַי, Job xix. 27; שְׁאֵרִי וּלְבָבִי, Ps. lxxiii. 26; בְּעֶצֶם —, Ps. xxxvii. 20: cii. 4, &c. With ן parag. in pause, יִכְלָיוּן, Is. xxxi. 3.

Infin. כְּלוֹת, Ruth ii. 23, &c.; Prov. v. 11. Aff. כְּלוֹתָם, Jer. xliv. 27.

Pih. כִּלָּה, pres. יְכַלֶּה, apoc. יְכַל. תְּכַל. Constr. abs. it. immed. it. med. לְ, בְּ, אֵת, מִן, (a) *Complete, finish, determine.* (b) Meton. *Waste, ruin, destroy.* (a) Gen. xliv. 12; Ruth iii. 18; 1 Chron. xxvii. 24. Often with an Infin. having לְ prefixed. *Finished, ceased to —,* Gen. xxiv. 15; xliii. 1; Num. vii. 1; Deut. xxxi. 4, &c. In Gen. ii. 2, and Ps. lxxviii. 33, *pronounce finished, &c.* See Gram. art. 154. 8, which affords a complete solution of the difficulty so long felt in Gen. ii. 2. It should be observed, that יְכַל, and יְכַלֵּשׁ, following, have necessarily the same force, and are also in Pih. (b) Is. xxvii. 10; xlix. 4; — Gen. xli. 30; Jer. xv. 12; 2 Sam. xxi. 15; Ps. xc. 9.

Infin. abs. כַּלֵּה, 2 Kings xiii. 17. 19, &c., it. כַּלָּא, of cogn. r. Dan. ix. 24.

— constr. כַּלּוֹת, Num. vii. 1; Deut. xxxi. 24, &c. Aff. כַּלּוֹתִי, Jer. xix. 15, &c.

Imp. כַּלֵּה, Ps. lix. 14; pl. כַּלּוּ, Exod. v. 13.

Part. מְכַלֶּה, pl. f. מְכַלּוֹת, Job ix. 22; Lev. xxvi. 16.

Puh. כֻּלָּה, pl. m. pret. כֻּלּוּ, pres. pl. *Were, became, finished, completed,* Gen. ii. 1; Ps. lxxii. 20, al. non occ.

כַּלָּה, f. pl. כַּלּוֹת, r. כלל, "a coronando dicta." Gesen. But no instance occurs in which *a spouse*, or *bride*, is said to be crowned. The word seems primarily to have marked some sort of *affinity*, as in the

Q Q

כלה (298) כלי

Arab. كَلّ, *orphanus, domestici ; qui prole ac parente caret*; كَلَالَة, *longinquior cognatio, uti patruelium*, &c.; كُلَّة, *velum muliebre*. Comp. כְּלַיָה, Is. lxi. 10. See also חָתָן above. I. A *daughter-in-law* (as a person adopted into a family), Gen. xi. 31; xxxviii. 11. 16; Lev. xx. 12, &c. II. A *spouse*, i. e. a female under an engagement to marry, Is. xlix. 18; lxi. 10; lxii. 5; Joel ii. 16, &c.; apparently, *a newly married wife*, Jer. vii. 34; xvi. 9, &c. And, hence, perhaps, *a wife* of some standing, Mic. vii. 6; Cant. iv. 8—12, &c. Aff. כַּלָּתוֹ, Gen. ll. cc.: כַּלָּתֶךָ, Lev. xviii. 15, &c.: pl. כַּלּוֹתֶיהֶם, Hos. iv. 14: כַּלּוֹתֶיהָ, Ruth i. 7, &c.

כְּלָהֶם, of כָּל + הֶם, i. e. with the full form of the affix., instead of the more usual ־ָם.

כְּלָהֵנָה, id. fem.

כְּלוּא, m. i. q. כְּלָא, see r. כלא above, and Keri, Jer. xxxvii. 4; lii. 31, al. non occ.

כְּלוּב, masc.—plur. non occ. lit. *woven, platted*, as a basket-work. Syr. ܟܠܘܒܐ, *corbis*. Arab. كَلَب, *inserto loro inter duas corii partes, &c.* I. A *fruit-basket*, Amos viii. 1, 2. II. A *bird-cage*, Lev. v. 27, al. non occ. Gr. κλωβὸς, κλουβὸς, κλοβός. Boch. Hieroz. ii. p. 90, which see.

כְּלוּלוֹת, f.—pl. once, aff., Jer. ii. 2, כְּלוּלֹתָיִךְ, *Thine espousals*, i. e. state in which these were entered into; so, נְעוּרַיִךְ, in the same context.

כֶּלַח, m.—pl. non occ. Cogn. כלה as in קשה, קשח; twice only, Job v. 26; xxx. 2. *Wealth, honour*. Meton. *Contempt, insolence*. See my Translations, and notes on these places. Cogn. Arab. قلح, *invaluit planta*. Cogn. قلخ, id. Symm. πᾶν τὸ πρὸς ζωήν. LXX. Hexap. συντέλεια. This is, therefore, probably a rendering of some other of the Hexaplar versions. In the former place the LXX. has ἐν τάφῳ, for בְּכֶלַח, with a twofold translation of the rest of the verse.

כְּלִי, m. in pause, כֶּלִי, pl. כֵּלִים; constr. כְּלֵי, r. כול; see above, or Arab. كِيل. *Contain, measure, &c.* and hence we have the vowels in the penult. (ֵ), and (ֶ), which, no doubt, ought to have been retained in every case. So aff. כֶּלְיָךְ, כֵּלֵינוּ, כֵּלָיו, כְּלֵיכֶם; but כְּלֵיהֶם again takes (ֵ). I. (a) *Vessel* (as a container) of earthenware, gold, silver, &c., Gen. xxxi. 37; xlv. 20; Ezek. iii. 22; xi. 2; Jer. xlvi. 19; in various constructions qualifying the sense. (b) *Ship*, or *boat*, Is. xviii. 2. (c) *Musical instrument*, 2 Chron. xxxiv. 12; Amos vi. 5; because made, perhaps, in the shape of a jar or vessel. כְּלֵי־נֶבֶל, Psalm lxxi. 22. Metaph. vessels pouring out poisonous draughts. See חֵמָה, Is. xiii. 5; Jer. l. 25. Comp. Is. xxxii. 7. Hence, (d) *Arms*, i. e. instruments of war, Judg. xviii. 11. 16: of death, Ps. vii. 14. Phr. *arms-bearer*, armiger, כֵּלִים נֹשֵׂא, 1 Sam. i. 6, 7, seq.; xxxi. 4—6: and בֵּית כֵּלִים, *an armoury*, Is. xxxix. 2. Hence, (e) *Implements* of husbandry, pec. the furniture of the ox, 2 Sam. xxiv. 22. Hence, also, (f) *Clothing*, indicative of condition, &c., as, כְּלִי־גֶבֶר, *man's clothing*, Deut. xxii. 5. — of the bride, Is. lxi. 10. See כַּלָּה, and מהן above. Phr. כְּלִי אֵין חֵפֶץ בּוֹ, *unfavoured vessel*, i. e. person so designated, Jer. xxii. 28; xlviii. 58, &c. So כְּלִי אֹבֵד, *perishing vessel*, Ps. xxxi. 13: on the contrary, כְּלִי חֶמְדָּה, *vessel of desire*, Jer. xxv. 34. כְּלִי יָקָר, Prov. xx. 15. Whence St. Paul's *vessels to honour and dishonour*, Rom. ix. 21; 2 Tim. ii. 21, &c. כְּלִי יוֹצֵר, *vessel* of the *artificer*, 2 Sam. xvii. 28; Jer. xix. 11, &c. כְּלִי רֹעֶה, *implement of a shepherd*, Zech. xi. 15. שֹׁמֵר הַכֵּלִים, *keeper of do.*, 1 Sam. xvii. 22, &c., to which many more may be added.

כְּלִיא, i. q. כְּלוּא, r. כלא. Kethiv, Jer. xxxvii. 4; lii. 31.

כִּלְיָה, fem. plur. כְּלָיוֹת. Constr. כִּלְיוֹת, of seg. fm. כִּלְיָה. Often with שְׁתֵי. Arab. كُلْيَة, كِلْيَة, كُلْوَة, *ren*; of كلا, *ambo*, as some think, because *in pairs*: others, of כִּלְאַיִם, *of two sorts*. The *reins* of man or beast, Exod. xxix. 13. 22; Lev. iii. 4. 10; Job xvi. 13; Is. xxxiv. 6, &c. Metaph. xxxii. 14. Meton. considered as the seat of sense, thence of the feelings, Jer. xi. 20: with לֵב, Ib. xvii. 10; xx. 12; Ps. vii. 10; Job xix. 27, כָּלוּ כִלְיֹתַי בְּחֵקִי, *my reins have been wasted, consumed, within me*. Ps. lxxiii. 21; Prov. xxiii. 16. Aff. כִּלְיוֹתַי, כִּלְיוֹתֵיהֶם.

כִּלָּיוֹן, m. r. כלה, once, Deut. xxviii. 65. *Wasting away* of the eyes.

כְּלָיוֹן, m. r. כלה, once, Is. x. 22. *Con-summation.* LXX. συντελῶν. Gesenius and others make the first of these two words to be in the state of construction to the second, as above, in בִּלְיוֹן. The analogy of the language will not admit of this.

כָּלִיל, m. ⎫ constr. כְּלִיל, pl. non occ. r.
כְּלִילָה, f. ⎭ כלל, i. q. כֹּל. *Whole, entire;* adv. *wholly, entirely;* of beauty, Ezek. xvi. 14; xxvii. 3; xxviii. 12; Lam. ii. 15; Judg. xx. 40. *Whole of the city,* Exod. xxviii. 31, &c. *Wholly purple*—of sacrifices, *the whole, all,* as a holocaust, Deut. xxxiii. 10; Ps. li. 21. Of spoil, Deut. xiii. 13. Adv. Is. ii. 18; Lev. vi. 15 (22).

כָּלַל, v. pret. only, pl. כָּלְלוּ, *They per-fected,* Ezek. xxvii. 4. 11, only. Cogn. כלה, כול, &c. LXX. συνετέλεσαν.
Pih. redup. כִּלְכֵּל. See under r. כול above.

כְּלַל, v. Chald. Shaf. aff. שַׁכְלִלֵּה, *Finished, completed, it,* Ezra v. 11: pl. שַׁכְלִלוּ, Ib. iv. 12; vi. 14, al. non occ.
Infin. לְשַׁכְלָלָה, Dan. v. 3. 9, only.
Pass. pres. pl. יִשְׁתַּכְלְלוּן, Ezra iv. 13. In vr. 12, we have שׁוּרַיָּא אֶשְׁכְלִלוּ, which the Keri directs to be read שׁוּרַיָּא שַׁכְלִלוּ, and very naturally restores the true reading. Gesen., however, thinks that ח has been thrown out of the verb; and so, in order to account for a manifest blunder, he makes no hesitation in creating an anomaly!

כלם, r. Kal non occ. Arab. كَلَمَ, *vulneravit;* كَلَّمَ, *disputavit;* كَالَمَ, asperos sermones.—*Hurt, &c.,* by words, seems to be the primary notion. Thence the noun—

כְּלִמָּה, f. constr. כְּלִמַּת, pl. כְּלִמּוֹת. Synon. בֹּשֶׁת, חֶרְפָּה, Ps. xxxv. 26; lxxi. 13. *Shame, confusion, ignominy,* Prov. xviii. 13; Is. xlv. 16; xxx. 3: and, as it has the property of suffusing the countenance, Ps. lxix. 8, the word is used, metaph., to express *clothing,* as with a garment, Ps. cix. 29; Ps. xxxv. 26; lxxi. 13, &c. Constr. Lev. xx. 11, &c. Pl., Mic. ii. 6, &c. Aff. כְּלִמָּתִי, &c.

כְּלִמּוּת, f. *State, circumstance,* of shame, &c., Jer. xxiii. 40. Hence the verb—
Niph. נִכְלַם, pres. יִכָּלֵם. Constr. abs. it. med. מִן, by, from; לְ, of; עַד, till. *Be, become, ashamed, confounded,* with בּוֹשׁ occasionally, Num. xii. 14; 1 Chron. xix. 5; Ps. xxxv. 4; xl. 15, &c.

Infin. הִכָּלֵם, Jer. iii. 3; viii. 12.
Part. נִכְלָמִים, pl. נִכְלָמִים, Ps. lxxiv. 21; 2 Sam. x. 5: f. נִכְלָמוֹת, Ezek. xvi. 27.
Hiph. הִכְלִים, and הָכְלִים, pres. יַכְלִים. Constr. immed. it. abs. it. med. אֶת. *Put to shame, make ashamed, injure,* 1 Sam. xx. 34; xxv. 7; Job xix. 3; Ps. xliv. 10; Is. xlv. 16, &c.
Infin. הַכְלִים, Jer. vi. 15; Prov. xxv. 8.
Part. מַכְלִים, Judg. xviii. 7; Job xi. 3.
Hoph. הָכְלַם, pres. non occ. i. q. Niph. Jer. xiv. 3; 1 Sam. xxv. 15, al. non occ.

כָּמַהּ, v. once, Ps. lxiii. 2. Constr. med. לְ. Syr. ܟܡܗ, *caligine offusus est.* Arab. كَمِهَ, *cæcutivit, mente debilitatus fuit,* with אְמָא in the parallel. *Desired* intensely, even to fainting. Aquila, ἐπετάθη σοι ἡ σάρξ μου. Symm. ἱμείρεταί σε ἡ σάρξ μου.

כָּמָה, see מָה.

כְּמוֹ, Particle, i. q. כְּ, compd. of כְּ + מוֹ, lit. *as,* or *like, that which.* This substitution of מוֹ, for מָה, has apparently arisen from the circumstance of (־), i. e. ׀, alif preceded by the vowel *fatah,* being pronounced in a manner approaching to וֹ. This particle, therefore, is, as Gesenius has well remarked, equivalent to the Arab. كَمَا, and Syr. ܐܝܟܕ, which are similarly compounded. We have a similar case in the pronunciation of מוֹאָב; which, fully written, would be, מָא אָב; Syr. ܐܒܐ ܐܝܟ; Arab. مَاءُ اَبٍ, lit. *water of the father;* an Oriental method of expressing *seed of the Father.* This substitution must have been very ancient. We find a similar difference even now existing between the Oriental and Occidental Syrians. The former would say, with Paul, *maran-atha;* the latter, *moranetho.* Syr. ܡܪܢ ܝ̇ܢ, *our Lord cometh.* The literal sense of this particle is, therefore, as given above, and is synonymous with כַּאֲשֶׁר: comp. Is. xli. 25: but is mostly used in the elevated style. For examples of its usage, see Nold. p. 389, seq.; which may be thus classed and abridged.

I. Whether used *singly,* or *doubly,* it always implies comparison, as to *persons, things, time,* circumstances, events, &c.

Used singly, הָאִישׁ כָּמוֹנִי, *Whether a man*

such as I am? &c., Neh. vi. 11. לֹא הָיָה כָמֹהוּ, *there was not its like*, Exod. ix. 18. כְּמוֹ תַנּוּר, *as an oven* (heated), Hos. vii. 4. Sometimes adverbially, as, אֲסַפְּרָה כְּמוֹ, *I should thus recount*, Ps. lxxiii. 15. כְּמוֹ יָלָדְנוּ, *as though*, or *as that, we had brought forth*, Is. xxvi. 18. כְּמוֹ־לֶאֱכֹל, *as though* (it were) *to eat up*, Hab. iii. 14. כְּמוֹ הַשַּׁחַר עָלָה, as (at the time) *the dawn arose*, i. e. *as when*, or at that period, Gen. xix. 15. Comp. Ezek. xvi. 57, &c.

II. Used doubly, or with other similar terms of comparison. כְּמוֹהוּ כְּאַיִן, lit. *its as though*, i. e. its comparison, (is) *as nothing*, i. e. taking the phrase used for the comparison intended by it; a thing common enough in the Arabic and Persic, Hag. ii. 3. So also, כְּמוֹךְ כְּמוֹהֶם, lit. *thy as though*, (is) *as their as though*, i. e. *thy comparison* or *likeness* (is) *as theirs*, Judg. viii. 18. Comp. Gen. xliv. 18; Ps. lviii. 10. See אֲשֶׁר above, p. 22.

Noldius makes כְּמוֹ, redundant in כְּמוֹ כֵן, Is. li. 6; but this is unnecessary, as it refers to the first word in the construction, כֵן, so יְמוּתוּן, thus. *And thus*, or, *in like manner, its inhabitants shall so die*, i. e. and this, or thus, I say, or speak, of its inhabitants, they shall so die, viz., כְּעָשָׁן, and כַּבֶּגֶד, just mentioned. Nor is it omitted by the ellipsis in Jer. xv. 18, which may thus be rendered, *as*, or *like, the most false*, inconstant thing, (i. e) *waters not to be trusted*, i. e. as a constant, unfailing supply. In such places as Ps. lviii. 9, it is to be supplied, as is usual in most elliptical expressions; and in כְּ, כַּאֲשֶׁר, &c., is, as noted in their places, and Gram. art. 230, seq.

This particle, as in some instances above, receives the affixed pronouns, as, כָּמוֹנִי, כָּמוֹךָ, or כְּמוֹהֶם, כְּמוֹהוּ, כָּמוֹהֶם, כָּמוֹהוּ, כָּמוֹנוּ, כָּמָהּ. It is also construed with other particles, as, כְּמוֹ אֲשֶׁר, מִי כְמוֹ, אֵין כְּמוֹ, the combination necessarily partaking of the sense of both. See Noldius in their places.

כְּמוֹשׁ, m.—pl. non occ. the proper name of an idol of the Moabites and Ammonites. Syr. ܟܡܘܫ, *incubus, suppressio nocturna.* Cogn. Heb. כבש. Arab. كَمَشَ, *properus fuit; extrema amputavit, &c.* Probably the Mahā Devā, or destroying deity, of the Hindoos, 1 Kings xi. 7; 2 Kings xxiii. 13; Jer. xlviii. 7. Phr. עַם־כְּמוֹשׁ, *people of Chemosh*, i. q. מוֹאָב, preceding, Num. xxi. 29.

כַּמֹּן, masc.— plur. non occ. Arab.

كَمُّون. Gr. κύμινον. *The cummin*, herb or seed, twice only, Is. xxviii. 25. 27. Plin. H. N. xix. c. viii.

כָּמַס, m. once, Deut. xxxii. 34. Part. pass. of r. כמס, extant in the Arab. كَمَسَ, whence أَكْمَسُ, or أَكْمَسُ, *qui vix videri possit.* Synon. τοῦ חָתוּם, in the parallel. *Withdrawn from sight, secreted, laid, or treasured, up.* Symm. ἀπόκειται. LXX. συνῆκται.

כמר, pl. only, כְּמָרִים. Syr. ܟܘܡܪܐ, *sacrificulus;* v. ܟܡܪ, *tristatus est. Idolatrous priests*, from their ascetic character, as Gesenius thinks; but from the Pers. كَمَر, belt, worn by the Magi, as Ikenius thinks. See his Dissertation on the כְּמָרִים. 2 Kings xxiii. 5; Hos. x. 5; Zech. i. 4. Hence the verb—

Niph. נִכְמַר, pres. non occ. See ܟܡܪ above. Generally, *Became affected, warmed*, (comp. Lam. v. 10) *with intense feeling*, as, *compassion, love :* with רַחֲמַי, Gen. xliii. 30; 1 Kings iii. 26. Constr. with אֶל, עַל, med., Hos. xi. 8; abs., Lam. v. 10. *Become, made black*, with heat. Syr. ܟܡܪ, *atratus*, al. non occ.

כַּמְרִירֵי, pl. m. constr. of sing. כִּמְרִיר, cogn. fm. שַׂפְרִיר, סָרִיר, and, with י, parag. חַכְלִילִי, Prov. xxvii. 15; Jer. xliii. 10; Gen. xlix. 12. A sort of superlative of ܟܡܪ; whence, ܟܡܪ, *atratus:* and, as things rather than persons constitute the rest of the context, *The blackest, most gloomy, afflicting*, &c., *things* of day, of time, &c., once, Job iii. 5. See my note on the place. Aquila, ὡς πικραμμοί, i. e. taking כְּ, as the particle of comparison.

כֵּן, masc. pl. בָּנִים. Arab. كَون, *esse*, כֵּן, fm. כֵּנָה, contr. כֵּן כֵּן, and thence the (־) immutable in בָּנִים, lit. I. *Being;* thence *Substantial, true.* Comp. יֵשׁ, and the Gr. ὤν, ὄντως, οὐσία, implying *reality, certainty*, &c., Gen. xlii. 11. 19. 31; Is. xvi. 6. With לֹא, *false, fallacious.* Hence the particle—

כֵּן, lit. II. *Real, true;* adv. *really, truly;* but admitting of being variously rendered, according to the context in which it is found, which exhibits this particle,

כן (301) כן

universally standing either, I. *absolutely*, or II. so as to form *comparison*.

I. *Absolutely.* כֵּן מִשְׁפָּטֶךָ, *real, true, just,* is *thy decision,* 1 Kings xx. 40. לֹא יֵעָשֶׂה כֵן, *it should not really be done,* or, *so* be done, Gen. xxix. 26. וַיַּעַשׂ דָּוִד כֵּן, *so David really did, &c.,* 2 Sam. v. 25. יְהִי לְךָ כֵן, 2 Kings ii. 10. Comp. Jer. v. 31; Exod. x. 29; Num. xxvii. 7; xxxvi. 5; 2 Kings vii. 9. Occasionally to be rendered by, *so, such,* Jer. xiv. 10; Ps. cxxvii. 2; Nah. i. 12;—Exod. x. 14; Num. xiii. 33; 2 Sam. xxiii. 5, &c.

II. *In comparisons.* Generally in the ἀπόδοσις of hypothetical sentences; the πρότασις, having כְּ, כִּי, אִיכָה, כְּמוֹ, כַּאֲשֶׁר, אֲשֶׁר, שֶׁ, כְּלֹעֻמָּה, either expressed or implied. כְּרֻבָּם כֵּן חָטְאוּ־לִי, *according as their increase was, so, really,* i. e. in the same degree, *they sinned against me,* Hos. iv. 7. כַּאֲשֶׁר יְעַנּוּ אֹתוֹ כֵּן יִרְבֶּה, *even as they afflicted* him : *so, verily, &c., he increased,* Exod. i. 12. Comp. Is. liv. 9; Jer. xxxii. 12;—Is. xxvi. 17;—Deut. xii. 30;—Num. vi. 21;—Eccl. v. 15. Sometimes, adversatively, *nevertheless,* Is. lii. 15. כֵּן יַזֶּה, *nevertheless* he *shall sprinkle, &c.,* i. e. even as in the one case the depression was great, so in the other shall the result be good and extensive. The same is the force in Exod. i. 12; Hos. iv. 7; xi. 2; Ps. xlviii. 6. Noldius (p. 393) thinks it redundant, in אַחֲרֵי־כֵן, אַחַר כֵּן, and כִּי־כֵן; but, upon a close examination of the places, it will be found to be otherwise. See Lev. xiv. 36; 1 Sam. x. 5;—Gen. vi. 4; Exod. iii. 20, &c.;—Esth. i. 8; 1 Kings ii. 7, &c., as given in their places in his Concordance. Nor is it omitted necessarily by the ellipsis, in many places so noted down by him: as, Neh. v. 5, כִּבְשַׂר אַחֵינוּ בְּשָׂרֵנוּ כִּבְנֵיהֶם בָּנֵינוּ, *as the flesh of our brethren is our flesh, as their children are our children;* and so in most of the other instances: see p. 393.

In the combinations, אַחֲרֵי־כֵן, אַחַר כֵּן, אָכֵן, מֵאַחֲרֵי־כֵן, כְּמוֹ־כֵן, כִּי עַל־כֵּן, לָכֵן, כִּי־כֵן, וָכֵן, לָבֵן, לֹא־כֵן, אֲשֶׁר־כֵן, אִם־כֵּן, עֲדֵי־כֵן, the sense is such as the compound, with the adjoining context, shall require: all which will be found in their places in Noldius; the above expositions, however, will suffice to point it out generally.

III. כֵּן, m. } aff. כֵּנִי, כֵּנוֹ, r. כנן. Arab.
כַּנָּה, fem. }

כֵּן, *servavit, custodivit*; كِنٌّ, *involucrum, monimentum* rei; *omne id sub, in, quo quid reconditur, custoditur.* (a) *Place, station,* Gen. xl. 13; xli. 13; Dan. xi. 7. 20, 21. 38: thence, (b) *Base, foot,* of the laver, Exod. xxx. 18. 28; xxxi. 9; xxxv. 16; xxxviii. 8; Lev. viii. 11. Of the mast of a ship, Is. xxxiii. 23. (c) f. *Stock, root,* Ps. lxxx. 16, as the v. נְטִיעָה following requires. Comp. vr. 8. The "*protege*" of Gesenius affords no sense.

כֵּן, pl. כִּנִּים. LXX. σκνῖφες. Vulg. *sciniphes.* (Gesenius, σκνῖφες? which he makes "species culicum pungendo molestorum... Culex reptans Linn.; culex molestus Forsk.") A sort of troublesome *musquito,* according to some: others, with Bochart, take it to signify *lice.* According to some, Is. li. 6: but see כְּמוֹ, II. above. Pl., Exod. viii. 12, 13; Ps. cv. 31, al. non occ. The sister dialects supply nothing beyond the cogn. قُنْقُن, *mus campestris major.* See Bochart. Hieroz. ii. p. 572, seq., where the question is argued at length.

כנה, verb, Kal non occ. Arab. كَنَى, *dignavit nomine per se significante* rem *aliam.* Syr. ܟܢܳܐ, *cognominavit.*

Pih. pret. non occ. pres. יְכַנֶּה. Constr. abs. it. immed. it. med. בְּ, אֶל. I. Call *by name,* Is. xliv. 5; xlv. 4. II. Call *by flattering names, titles,* i. e. *flatter,* Job xxxii. 21, 22. See my notes.

כַּנָּה, Ps. lxxx. 16. See כֵּן, Num. iii.

כְּנָוֹת, see כֵּנָה.

כִּנָּן, Chald. See כֵּן.

כִּנּוֹר, m. pl. כִּנֹּרִים, Ezek. xxvi. 13: f. כִּנֹּרוֹת, 1 Kings x. 12. Syr. ܟܶܢܳܪܐ, *cithara.* Arab. كِنَّارَة, كِنَّار, id. Gr. κινύρα, and κιννύρα; according to Joseph. Antiq. lib. vii. cap. xii. § 3. *A musical instrument of ten strings, played with a plectrum.* But, in 1 Sam. xvi. 23; xviii. 10; xix. 9, played with the *hand;* which, generally speaking, may signify the same thing. Gesenius's objection to Josephus, therefore, has not much weight. *A lute,* or *lyre,* Gen. iv. 21; 1 Sam. xvi. 16. 23; Is. v. 12; xvi. 11; Ps. xxxii. 2; xliii. 4; xlix. 5; lxxi. 22; Job xxxi. 31, &c. Aff. כִּנֹּרִי, כִּנּוֹרֶיךָ, כִּנֹּרוֹתֵינוּ.

כַּנְלוֹתְךָ, see r. כלה.

כַּנָּם, more correctly, perhaps, כִּנָּם, i. q.

כנם (302) כנע

פָּנִים above. Comp. Exod. viii. 12, with vr. 13. In the first place, we have כִּנִּם; in the second, כִּנָּם. Why not כִּנִּים? The LXX. has σκνίφες, in each case, and the other Greek translators evidently read the same word in all; and no doubt has existed that in each case the sense must be the same. I have no hesitation, therefore, in supposing that the vowels should be the same in each.

כִּנְמָא, m. — pl. non occ. Chald. for כְּנִאֲמַר, according as it is said, as some think; others, כֵּן אָמַר. But in each of these cases the final ר is changed into א in a most unaccountable way. The Talmudic usage, appealed to by Gesenius, is of too late a date to be worthy of notice. The term occurs only in Ezra iv. 8; v. 4. 9. 11; vi. 13. A more probable derivation would be, the Persic نَمَا, نِمَا, showing, exhibiting; and the particle כְּ, as, like, &c. As the showing, i. e. as the example, or copy following; or it may be a Chaldaic form of the Heb. נָאֵם, said; the א‍ָ being the definite article, e. g. נְאֵמָא, and, by contr. נְמָא; adding כְּ, כְּנֵמָא, as, according to, the saying, i. e. following. In the Arab. we have, نِيَم, vox debilis; which seems sufficient to establish this.

כָּנַס, v. pres. non occ. Æth. ሐነሰ : congregavit. Arab. كَنَسَ, congregatio. Cogn. كنز, recondidit. Syr. ܟܢܫ, i. q. Æth. constr. immed. it. med. לְ, pers. אֶת. Gather, collect, together, gold, silver, stones, water, men, &c., Eccl. ii. 8.
Infin. כְּנוֹס, Eccl. ii. 26; iii. 5; Neh. xii. 44; 1 Chron. xxii. 2.
Imp. כִּנוֹס, Esth. iv. 16.
Part. כֹּנֵס, Ps. xxxiii. 7.
Pih. כִּנַּסְתִּי, i. q. Kal, if not causative, Ezek. xxii. 21; xxxix. 28: with אֶל, pres. יְכַנֵּס, Ps. cxlvii. 2.
Hithp. Infin. כְּהִתְכַּנֵּס, When, being, becoming, collecting, comprehending, Is. xxviii. 20. Symm. τὸ μὴ εἰσελθεῖν. Theod. τοῦ μὴ συναχθῆναι, al. συναφθῆναι.

כנע, v. Kal non occ. Arab. كَنَعَ, humilis fuit. Samar. id.
Niph. נִכְנַע, pres. יִכָּנַע. Constr. abs. it. med. מִפְּנֵי, לִפְנֵי, מִלִּפְנֵי. תַּחַת. Be, become, humbled, debased, 1 Kings xxi. 29; 2 Chron. xxxiii. 23; xxxvi. 12;—Lev. xxvi. 41; Judg. iii. 30; viii. 28; xi. 33, &c.
Infin. הִכָּנֵעַ, 2 Chron. xxxiii. 23. Aff. הִכָּנְעוֹ, 2 Chron. xxxiii. 19, &c.
Hiph. הִכְנִיעַ, pres. יַכְנִיעַ, יַכְנַע. Constr. immed. it. med. אֵת, לִפְנֵי, בְּ, instr. it. in. Humble, debase, bring down, 2 Sam. viii. 1; Ps. lxxxi. 15; cvii. 12; Is. xxv. 5; Job xl. 12; 1 Chron. xvii. 10.

כְּנֵעָה, f. aff. כִּנְעָתֵךְ, once, Jer. x. 17. Arab. كنع, cum congregatur res. Thy package, bale, of merchandize, wealth. LXX. τὴν ὑπόστασίν σου.

כְּנַעֲנִי, masc. plur. כְּנַעֲנִים, aff. כְּנַעֲנָיו. Patronym. I. Canaanite, or descendant of כְּנַעַן Canaan, a son of Ham, Gen. x. 6: so called, apparently, long before the land—afterwards so called—was possessed by his posterity. It is groundless, therefore, to suppose with Gesenius, that this land was so called because some parts of it were depressed and low, " pr. regio depressa," a rad. כָּנַע. The greater probability is, that this name was prophetically given to the grandson of Noah, for the purpose of pointing out his future degradation. Comp. Gen. ix. 25, and see Gram. art. 170. 23; Gen. xxiv. 3; Judg. i. 1, &c. And, because the people so called traded much in merchandize. II. A merchant, Job xl. 30 (25); Prov. xxxi. 24: just as כַּשְׂדִּי, Chaldean, is for Astrologer, as Gesenius has well remarked.

כָּנָף, c. constr. כְּנַף, dual, כְּנָפַיִם, constr. כַּנְפֵי. Syr. ܟܢܦܐ, ala. Arab. كنف, ala avis; v. كَنَفَ, sub alis tutatus est. Comp. Matt. xxiii. 37. I. The wing of a bird, &c.: thence termed, (a) בַּעַל כָּנָף, bird of wing, Gen. i. 21. צִפּוֹר..., vii. 14; Deut. iv. 17. בַּעַל כָּנָף, possessor of wing, Prov. i. 17. בּוֹדֵד כָּנָף, wanderer of wing, Is. x. 14. — of the Cherubim, 1 Kings vi. 27, &c. Metaph. (b) כַּנְפֵי־רוּחַ, Ps. xviii. 11; civ. 3. שַׁחַר, of the morning, cxxxix. 9: (c) as the means of protection, Ps. xvii. 8; xxxvi. 8; lvii. 2, &c.: (d) the extreme parts (wings) of an army, Is. viii. 8; i. q. אֲגַפִּים, according to Gesenius, but see sub voce: (d) the skirts of the loose flowing upper garment, Deut. xxii. 12; 1 Sam. xxiv. 5. 12; Num. xv. 38, &c. Ellip. כְּנַף אִישׁ יְהוּדִי, Zech. viii. 23; Ezek. v. 3; Hag. ii. 12. And, by a meton., (e) the wing implied protection, so here

כנף (303) כסא

the *person protected,* i. e. *wife, &c.* כְּנַף אָבִיו, *wing (skirt) of his father,* i. e. wife, Deut. xxiii. 1. Comp. xxvii. 20; Ezek. xvi. 8; Ruth iii. 9. Hence, with reference to the mysterious conception of Christ, ἐπισκιάσει, Luke i. 35. And so, generally. Abraham is said to be a *covering of the eyes* of Sarah, Gen. xx. 16 : (f) extreme part of the earth, or land, Is. xxiv. 16. Pl., Job xxxvii. 3; xxxviii. 13; Is. xi. 12; Ezek. vii. 2 : (g) — of abominations, Dan. ix. 27. Phrr. שֵׁשׁ כְּנָפַיִם, *six two-fold wings,* i. e. six wings, taken by two and two, Is. vi. 2. Comp. Ezek. i. 6; x. 21. In Mal. iii. 20, מַרְפֵּא בִּכְנָפֶיהָ, lit. *a healer in his wings,* i. e. He is, by the sending forth of his beams, a dispenser of light, warmth, and consequently of health ; referring to Christ.

כנף, v. Kal non occ. See כָּנָף above. Niph. once, Is. xx. 20, pres. יִכָּנֵף. Gesen. "*operuit, occultavit se.*" Arab. كَنَفَ, *texit.* But in the sense of *protection,* and, therefore, quite unsuitable to this place. The Arabic root signifies also, *deflexit, secessit,* constr. with عَنْ, from : the sense will then be nearly that of the Auth. Vers. and suit the acceptation of the noun כָּנָף, in that of *extreme part.* The context, however, requires rather the Pih. יְכַנֵּף, which is very probably the true reading. *Put away, remove to a distant part.*

כנש, v. Chald. i. q. Heb. כנס. *Collect, gather together.* Infin. מִכְנַשׁ, Dan. iii. 2, only. Ithp. Part. m. מִתְכַּנְּשִׁין. *Being, becoming, assembled, &c.,* Dan. iii. 3. 27, only, pl.

כְּנָת, fem. Aff. כְּנָתֵהּ, כְּנָוָתְהוֹן. Syr. ܟܢܬܐ, pl. ܟܢܘܬܐ, *socius, socii;* r. כֻּם, *titulo appellavit.* See בָּנָה above. Lit. *a naming,* or *calling;* meton. *company, society:* and abstr. for concr. Person of the same calling or society : thence, *Companion, associate.* Pl. כְּנָוָת, aff. כְּנָוָתֵהּ, Ezra iv. 9. 17. 23; v. 3. 6; vi. 6. 13. Gesenius makes all these aff. of כְּנָוָן, pl. of כְּנָת: but no such pl. occurs : nor is it necessary, for the sake of analogy, to suppose any such thing.

כֵּס, m. once, Exod. xvii. 16, in the phrase כֵּס יָהּ, *throne of Jah,* i. e. as erected among the Israelites. Gesenius thinks the reading suspicious here, and proposes נֵס, from נִסִּי, preceding : which would be mean and frigid.

כְּסָא, and כְּסֶה, masc.—pl. non occ. synon. τοῦ, חֹדֶשׁ, Ps. lxxxi. 4. Syr. ܟܣܐ, *primus dies plenilunii, &c.* Gesen. from Bar Ali, &c. Arab. كَسَا, *induit pulchritudinem;* اكسي, *dignitate conspicuus.* So the moon, Job xxxi. 26, יָרֵחַ הֹלֵךְ, *gloriously walking on,* proceeding, i. e. as if gorgeously appareled. Comp. Cant. vi. 10. It is not improbable, therefore, that ܟܣܐ, *operuit, induit,* is the root, especially as it never could have been unknown that the moon received its brightness, as a coating, from another. Twice only, Ps. l. c. and Prov. vii. 20. *The new moon :* thence meton., *feast* of do.

כִּסֵּא, twice, כִּסֶּה, pl. כִּסְאוֹת (for כִּסָּאוֹת), masc. Syr. ܟܘܪܣܝܐ, *cathedra.* Arab. كُرْسِيّ, id. v. كَرَّسَ, *fundamentum jecit domûs;* تكريس, *cum res super aliam congeritur.* The primitive notion seems to consist in *placing* one thing upon another; thence *stability,* as in the foundations of an edifice : and hence applied to *a regal chair,* or *throne.* Comp. Prov. xvi. 12 ; xxv. 5 ; as the seat of power. "*Velo pensili coperta*" (taking the root as כסא, or כסה), Gesenius. But thrones were not so—necessarily—veiled. The throne of God, necessarily is (Job xxvi. 9); but not so earthly kings who personally appeared to give judgment. The insertion of ר too in all the dialects, is perhaps too much to be supposed a mere compensation of Dagesh, Job xxxvi. 7; 2 Sam. iii. 10.

כסה, v. pres. non occ. Syr. ܟܣܐ, *operuit.* Arab. كَسَا, id. *Cover, conceal.* Part. כֹּסֶה, Prov. xii. 16. 23, only. — pass. constr. כְּסוּי, *covered,* Num. iv. 6. 14 ; Ps. xxxii. 1 : in the phr. כְּסוּי חֲטָאָה, *covered,* as to *sin:* i. e. pardoned. See כפר. The notion seems to have originated in our first parents requiring clothing, when they had discovered that nakedness was shameful. Hence cleanliness of garments, white garments, &c. denoting purity. Comp. Eccl. ix. 8 ; Rev. iii. 4 ; xvi. 15, &c. Niph. f. נִכְסְתָה, *Been, became, covered, concealed,* Jer. li. 42, only.

כסה (304) כסח

Infin. הִכָּסוֹת, the *being covered, concealed*, Ezek. xxiv. 8, only.

Pih. כִּסָּה, pres. יְכַסֶּה, apoc. יְכַס. Constr. immed. it. med. אֶת, עַל, on, upon, it; לְ, it. בְּ, instr. so עַל, אֶל, Ps. cxliii. 9; it. מִן, from; i. q. Kal. *Cover, conceal*, Num. ix. 15; xxii. 5; Job xv. 27; xxiii. 17;—Ezek. xvi. 10; xviii. 7. 16; Jonah iii. 6, ellip., Gram. art. 220;—Gen. xxxviii. 14; Exod. x. 15; Jer. xlvi. 8; Ezek. xvi. 8. Covering the head, Is. xxix. 10, bringing into circumstances of distress. Comp. 2 Sam. xv. 30; v. חָפָה. Ellip. of נֶפֶשׁ, or עֶצֶם, Deut. xxii. 12. Metaph. *covering* sin, i. e. blotting it out, Ps. lxxxv. 3; Prov. x. 12; Neh. iii. 37. Synon. τοῦ, כִּפֶּר. Phr. אֶת־עֵין הָאָרֶץ, lit. *the eye of the land*, i. e. the very land, or *the land itself*, as Arab. عَيْن, Num. xxii. 5. Metaph. כִּסְּתָה כְלִמָּה פָנָי, *reproach has covered*, suffused, *my face*, Ps. lxix. 8; Jer. li. 51. אֹתָם פַּלָּצוּת —, *horror hath covered them*, Ezek. vii. 18. בִּשֵּׁת —, Ps. xliv. 16. חָמָס —, *violence*, i. e. dissemble, Prov. x. 11, &c. Comp. Job xxxi. 33; Ps. xxxii. 5. Meton. *clothe*, Is. lviii. 7; Ps. civ. 6, &c. In Ps. cxliii. 9, אֵלֶיךָ כִסִּתִי, i. q. עָלֶיךָ. See my note on Job xxxvi. 32. Comp. Mal. ii. 16, i. e. *by thee I conceal* me: am safely guarded. LXX. πρὸς σὲ κατέφυγον. Ezek. xxxi. 15, כִּסֵּתִי עָלָיו, *I covered*, i. e. restrained the deep on his account. Comp. Job xxxviii., from which, perhaps, this figure is borrowed. LXX. ἐπέστησα.

Infin. כַּסּוֹת, Exod. xxviii. 42; Mal. ii. 13, &c. Aff. כַּסֹּתוֹ, Exod. xxvi. 13.

Imper. pl. aff. כַּסּוּנוּ, *Cover us*, Hos. x. 8.

Part. מְכַסֶּה, Gen. xviii. 17, &c.: pl. מְכַסִּים, f. מְכַסּוֹת, Is. xi. 9; Ezek. i. 11. Aff. מְכַסְּךָ, Ezek. xxvii. 7: pl. מְכַסֶּיךָ, Is. xiv. 11.

Puh. pl. m. כֻּסּוּ (for כֻּסּוּ), i. q. Niph., Ps. lxxx. 11; Prov. xxiv. 31.

Pres. יְכֻסֶּה, Eccl. vi. 4; plur., Gen. vii. 19, 20.

Part. pl. m. מְכֻסִּים, 1 Chron. xxi. 16.
— f. מְכֻסּוֹת, Ezek. xli. 16.

Hiph. pres. apoc. יְתַכַּס, i. q. Niph. Puh. Gen. xxiv. 65; 2 Kings xix. 1; Is. xxxvii. 1. Pl., Is. lix. 6; Jonah iii. 8.

Part. מִתְכַּסֶּה, pl. מִתְכַּסִּים, 1 Kings xi. 29; 2 Kings xix. 2; Is. xxxvii. 2.

כָּסָה, i. q. כָּסָא.

כַּסּוּחָה, Is. v. 25. See סוּחָה.

כְּסוּת, f.—pl. non occ. r. כסה. Syr. ܟܣܘܬܐ, *absconsio*. Arab. كِسْوَة, *indumentum*. (a) *Covering*: meton. (b) *clothing*. (a) Gen. xx. 16, הוּא לָךְ כְּסוּת עֵינַיִם, *he, or it, is to thee a covering of the eyes*. According to Gesenius, the thousand shekels just mentioned, were to be considered as a mulct, or fine, from the king of Gerar, to induce Sarah to connive at his fault: and this he argues is the meaning of the LXX. ταῦτα ἔσται σοι εἰς τιμὴν τοῦ προσώπου σου, καὶ πάσαις ταῖς μετὰ σοῦ. Which any ordinary reader of Greek would, perhaps, take to mean, *these shall be for the honour of thy person, &c.*, i. e. those shekels were to be considered as a present of honour, just as dresses of honour are now, when given by princes in the East. The *covering of the eyes* here seems to intimate much the same thing as St. Paul's *covering* for the woman, 1 Cor. xi. 5, seq., i. e. to procure the respect due to her, Job xxvi. 6. (b) Job xxiv. 7; xxxi. 19; Exod. xxii. 26; Deut. xxii. 12; Is. L. 3. Aff. כְּסוּתָם, כְּסוּתֹה, כְּסוּתְךָ.

כסח, v. pret. pres. non occ. Arab. كَسَحَ, *amputavit* rem. Syr. ܟܣܚ, id.

Part. pass. f. כְּסוּחָה, *Cut off*, as a branch, &c., Ps. lxxx. 17.
— pl. m. כְּסוּחִים, Is. xxxiii. 12, al. non occ.

כְּסִיל, masc. pl. כְּסִילִים. Arab. كَسِيل, *iners, piger*. As *firmness, inflexibility*, or the like, are usually found affording the primary notion to *wisdom, justice, truth, &c.*, *weight* to respectability: see כבד, צדק, אמן; so laxness, instability, lightness, &c., to *folly, falsehood, baseness*. Synon. אֱוִיל, opp. τῷ, חָכָם, Eccl. vi. 8. I. *A fool*, particularly as to religion, Prov. i. 32; x. 1; xiii. 19, 20; Ps. xlix. 11, &c. II. The name of a certain constellation, apparently *Orion*. See my note on Job ix. 9; xxxviii. 31;—Amos v. 8. Pl. aff. כְּסִילֵיהֶם, *their orions*, lit. i. e. constellations similar to that. The term probably originated in the contempt shewn by believers to the practice of elevating heathen heroes into deities, and giving them a place among the constellations.

כְּסִילוּת, f. once, Prov. ix. 13, in אֵשֶׁת כְּסִילוּת, *Woman of* FOOLISHNESS, i. e. foolish woman or wife.

כֶּסֶל, pl. כְּסָלִים. See כסל above. From the notion of inactivity, naturally arose that of fatness, denseness: hence (a) *The loins*,

Job xv. 27; Lev. iii. 4. 10. 15; iv. 9; vii. 4. (b) *The viscera* (as in לֵב, בֶּטֶן, חֵלֶב), Ps. xxxviii. 8. See Bochart. Hieroz. i. p. 506. Thence *slowness*, whence (c) *expectation, confidence*, Ps. lxxviii. 7; Prov. iii. 26; Job viii. 14;. xxxi. 24. (d) *Foolishness*, Eccl. vii. 25. Aff. כִּסְלִי, &c.

כִּסְלָה, f. of כֶּסֶל. (a) *Confidence, hope,* Job iv. 6. (b) *Foolishness,* vain fruitless confidence, Ps. lxxxv. 9, al. non occ.

כִּסְלֵו, m.—pl. non occ. The ninth month of the Hebrew year so called, but why it cannot now be discovered, Zech. vii. 1; Neh. i. 1; 1 Maccab. i. 57. χασελεῦ.

כַּסְלֻחִים, m. pl. A people so called, Gen. x. 14; 1 Chron. i. 12. *The Colchii,* according to Bochart. (Phaleg. lib. iv. c. xxxi.)

כסם, v. pret. non occ. pres. pl. m. יִכְסְמוּ, once, Ezek. xliv. 20. Castell. i. q. κοσμέω, *adorn*: for which he cites several of the versions as favourable. Gesen. i. q. עם, *crop, cut*: but even this may here mean, *cutting to adorn, &c.* Infin. abs. כָּסוֹם, Ib. al. non occ.

כָּסֶמֶת, fem.—plur. masc. כֻּסְּמִים. Arab. كِرْسَنَة, *ervinæ*. Cogn. كُسوم, *confertis herbis hortus. A kind of corn, spelt* apparently. See Cels. Hierob. ii. p. 98, seq.; Exod. ix. 32; Is. xxviii. 25; Ezek. iv. 9. Aquila, ζέα. LXX. Theod. ὄλυρα.

כָּסַס, v. pret. non occ. pres. 2 pl. תָּכֹסּוּ Arab. كَسَّ, *validè contudit comminuitque*: whence كَسِيس, *caro quæ super lapides siccata contunditur et redacta in polentæ formam, reservatur in itineris commeatum.* Hence, *To apportion,* i. e. determine the fractional part, rather than *to number,* as usually taken; once, Exod. xii. 4. LXX. συναριθμήσεται.

כָּסַף, c. pl. aff. כַּסְפֵּיהֶם: as a verb, כָּסַף, *desire*: thence, *grow pale* with desire: and thence, *pale*; and so applied (a) to *silver* (so ἄργυρος, from ἀργὸς, *albus, white,* Gesen.): thence (b) to *money,* generally. (a) Gen. xxiii. 15. שֶׁקֶל־כֶּסֶף, *shekel,* or *weight, of silver, money. Shekel,* however, is mostly omitted, as, Gen. xx. 16; xxxvii. 28; Deut. xxii. 19. 29; Hos. iii. 2, &c. (b) *Money,* Gen. xxiii. 13; Deut. xxiii. 20; Exod. xxi.

21. בְּכַסְפּוֹ הוּא, for בְּכַסְפּוֹ וגו'. In Gen. xl. i. 25. 36, Gesenius thinks *silver bars,* or *bullion,* is rather meant. The distinction is of no importance. Aff. כַּסְפִּי, כַּסְפּוֹ, &c.

כְּסַף, c. Def. כַּסְפָּא, Chald. i. q. Heb. כֶּסֶף, Dan. ii. 32. 35. 45; v. 23; Ezra vii. 15, &c.

כסף, v. pret. non occ. pres. יִכְסוֹף, תִּכְסֹף. Arab. كَشَبَ, *avidè voravit carnes.* See cogn. كَشَبَ, كَشَفَ. *Desire* intensely, constr. med. לְ, Job xiv. 15; Ps. xvii. 12. Niph. f. נִכְסְפָה, *Be, become, intensely desirous.* Constr. med. לְ, for, Ps. lxxxiv. 3; Gen. xxxi. 30. Infin. abs. נִכְסֹף, Gen. l. c. Part. נִכְסָף, *Not desiring intensely for....* Supply the ellipsis from Ps. lxxxiv. 3, לְחַצְרוֹת יְהוָה, *the courts of Jehovah,* i. e. by an elegantly inserted litotes, *irreligious nation,* Zeph. ii. 1. LXX. ἀπαίδευτον, *unlearned, ignorant,* intending, apparently, the same thing. Gesen. *"gens sine pudore,"* i. e. not growing pale with shame. But this is unexampled in these dialects: al. non occ.

כסת, f. pl. כְּסָתוֹת, aff. כְּסָתוֹתֵיכֶנָה, Ezek. xiii. 18. 20, only. Hence the sing. ought to be כְּסָתָה, of the seg. m. כֶּסֶת, or r. כסת, not כסה, as Gesenius thinks: nor do the examples דֶּלֶת, and קֶשֶׁת, bear him out here, as a fem. form may have been the ground-form of the pl. as in some other instances. Syr. ܟܣܬܐ, *gibbus* (bunch, or pod, perhaps). Cogn. ܟܣܬܐ, *stramen. Cushions,* commonly: but, most probably, some sort of ornaments placed on the idols. ὁ Ἑβραῖος, φυλακτήρια. Sym. ὑπαγκώνια. LXX. προσκεφάλαια.

כְּעַל, see עַל, Is. lix. 18.

כְּעַן, Chald. adv. compd. of כְּ + עַן, r. Heb. עָנָה, *answered;* and of this כְּעֶנֶה,—of which כְּעֶת, Ezra iv. 17, is a contraction—is a fem. form: lit. *according to, as, answer, purpose, &c.,* not differing greatly from Heb. לְמַעַן. *So, therefore,* Dan. iv. 34; Ezra iv. 21, &c. But, *accordingly,* Ezra iv. 13. *Now, but,* Dan. ii. 23; Ezra iv. 14, &c. וּכְעֶנֶת, Dan. ii. 23; v. 15; Ezra v. 17. Ib. vr. 16. Not unlike the צְרִי־כְעַן, of the Heb., 1 Kings xxii. 16; in sense, synon. Heb. צְרִי־כֵן. See Nold., p. 394.

כְּעֶנֶת, fem. of the last. *So on.* Lit.

R R

כעס (306) כף

according to, as, object, intention, &c. כְּעֵת, id. contr., Ezra iv. 17;—Ib. iv. 10, 11; vii. 12.

כַּעַס, masc. plur. כְּעָסִים. Arab. v. اَكْمَسَ, *abiit tumidus irâ.* Cogn. وَعَاسَ, شَدِيد, *violent.* (a) *Vexation, sadness,* opp. τῷ, שְׂחוֹק, Eccl. vii. 3. Meton. (b) *Anger, indignation,* (a) Eccl. i. 18; ii. 23; xi. 10; Prov. xvii. 25; xxi. 19: (b) Deut. xxxii. 19; Ezek. xx. 28; 2 Kings xxiii. 26. Aff. בַּעַסְךָ, בַּעֲסִי, &c.

כָּעֵשׂ, m. in Job only, i. q. כַּעַס, Heb. Job v. 2; vi. 2; x. 17; xvii. 7. Aff. בַּעֲשִׂי &c.

כַּף, f. dual, כַּפַּיִם, pl. כַּפּוֹת. Syr. ܟܦܐ, *incurvatio.* Arab. كَفّ, *manus usque carpum:* pec. *vola.* Hence (a) *the palm of the hand;* or (b) meton. *the hand:* (c) *the sole of the foot:* (d) *the foot* of a beast: (e) *a bason* or *phial,* for oil, &c.: (f) *cup* or *receptacle* for the stone of a sling, &c.: (g) *bending,* or *curved,* palm-branches. (a) Lev. ix. 17; 1 Kings xvii. 12, &c. (b) i. q. יָד, and used much in the same way. See יָד, Gen. xl. 11. 21; Lev. xiv. 15. 26. With נָכָה, *clapping the hands,* 2 Kings xi. 12; Ezek. xxi. 19: it. with סָפַק, Num. xxiv. 10. תָּקַע, Nah. iii. 19; Ps. xlvii. 2. מָחָא, Is. lv. 12, &c. בְּכַף, *in the power of* —, with various verbs, Prov. vi. 3; Is. lxii. 3; Jer. xii. 7, &c. With שׂוּם, followed by נַפְשִׁי, *putting the life in jeopardy,* i. e. into a situation easily to be lost, Judg. xii. 3; 1 Sam. xxviii. 21; Job xiii. 14, &c. By לְפִי, — *hand on the mouth,* implying silence, Job xxix. 9. It. מִכַּף, *out of the power,* Judg. vi. 14; 1 Sam. iv. 3; 2 Sam. xiv. 16, &c. With עַל following, *keep, protect, &c.,* Exod. xxxiii. 22; Ps. cxxxix. 5; Job xxxvi. 32, &c. See my note, and comp. Is. xlix. 2. 16; li. 16; Hab. iii. 4; Zech. ix. 14. With עַל preceding, i. q. בְּ, Lev. xiv. 28;—Ps. xci. 12, &c. אֶל־כַּפַּיִם, *to,* in addition to, Lam. iii. 41: into, Judg. xiv. 9. With פָּרַשׂ, *spreading out the hands* in prayer, Exod. ix. 29; Ps. xliv. 21; Ezra ix. 5, &c. With נָשָׂא, *lift up—to obey, honour, &c.,* Ps. cxix. 48; cxli. 2; lxxxviii. 10, &c. With רָחַץ, נָקָה, *cleanse, purify,* Job ix. 30. Comp. Is. xxxiii. 15; Ps. xxvi. 6, &c. Opp. נִגְאָל, Is. lix. 3. Phrr. יְגִיעַ כַּף, *labour of the hands,* Ps. cxxviii. 2. נְקִי כַּפַּיִם, *pure of hands;* innocent, Ps. xxiv. 4. נְקִיוֹן כַּפַּי, *cleanness of my hands;* my innocency, Gen. xx. 5; Ps. lxxiii. 13. בֹּר כַּפַּי, Job xxii. 30. חָמָס בְּכַפַּי, *violence in my hands;* am violent, Job xvi. 17; 1 Chron. xii. 17. עֲלֵי —, Ps. vii. 4. מֵאוּם, Job xxxi. 7. See my note. פֹּעַל כַּפָּיו, *work of his hands,* Ps. ix. 17. חֵפֶץ כַּפֶּיהָ, *will of her hands;* labour willingly performed, Prov. xxxi. 13. פְּרִי כַפֶּיהָ, *fruit of* —, Ib. vr. 16. תָּמְכוּ פָלֶךְ, *hold, recline on, the distaff,* Ib. vr. 19.

(c) *Of the sole* of the foot, Deut. ii. 5; xi. 24; xxviii. 65. מָנוֹחַ לְכַף רַגְלָהּ, *rest to the sole of thy foot.* Comp. Gen. viii. 9; for rest generally. Pl., Josh. iii. 13; iv. 18; Is. lx. 14. כַּף פְּעָמַי, — *of my footsteps,* 2 Kings xix. 24. Hence the usage, מִכַּף רַגְלְךָ וְעַד —, *from the sole of thy foot to thy crown,* Deut. xxviii. 35; 2 Sam. xiv. 25. וְעַד רֹאשׁ — Is. i. 6 — תַּחַת כַּפּוֹת, *beneath the soles* —, 1 Kings v. 17 (3). עַל —, *at the soles* —, Is. lx. 14. *Place of* —, Ezek. xliii. 7.

(d) *Foot* of a beast, Lev. xi. 27. See יָד.

(e) *Bason* or *phial,* Num. vii. 14. 20, &c. Pl., Exod. xxv. 29; Num. vii. 84, &c.

(f) *Cup* — of the sling, &c., 1 Sam. xxv. 29. כַּף הַיָּרֵךְ, — *of the thigh* joint at the hip, Gen. xxxii. 26. 33.

(g) *Bending,* or *curved,* branches, &c., Lev. xxiii. 40.

Aff. כַּפִּי, כַּפָּי, &c.

כֹּף, m.—pl. only, כֵּפִים, Jer. iv. 29; Job xxx. 6, only. Syr. Chald. ܟܐܦܐ, *rupes. Rocks;* whence the κηφᾶς, *cephas,* i. q. πέτρος of the N. T. Gesen.

כפה, v. pres. only, יִכְפֶּה. Arab. كفى, *retro vertit.* Cogn. كفى, *sufficit.* Cogn. كفّ, *clausit astrictis vinculis.* Syr. ܟܦܐ, *abscondit.* כִּפְחָה־אַף, *averts, satisfies, anger;* once, Prov. xxi. 14. Sym. σβέσει ὀργήν. LXX. ἀνατρέπει ὀργάς.

כִּפָּה, f.—pl. non occ. Aff. כַּפָּתוֹ, i. q. כַּף, (g) above. (a) *Bent,* or *curved, branch,* Is. ix. 13; xix. 15. In the phr. כִּפָּה וְאַגְמוֹן lit. *curved branch and reed,* i. e. the old and young: the old and venerable, elder (רֹאשׁ preceding) as bent with age; the young as straight, shooting up as a bulrush. Aq. Incurvum καὶ στρεβλοῦντα. Sym. LXX. ἀρχὴν καὶ τέλος. Theod. κεπφὰ καὶ ἀγμόν. (b) *Branch,* generally, Job xv. 32.

כְּפוֹר, masc. — pl. constr. כְּפוֹרֵי. Æth.

כפי (307) כפל

ከፈሮ : *modius.* Arab. كَفَر, *vas dactylorum;* كَوَافِر, *cadi magni, lagenæ prælongæ.* (a) *A vessel or cup,* covered, as Gesenius thinks, r. כָּפַר, Ezra i. 10; viii. 27; 1 Chron. xxviii. 17. (b) *Hoar frost,* as covering every thing, according to Simonis, Exod. xvi. 14; Ps. cxlvii. 16; Job xxxviii. 29.

כָּפִיס, m. once, Hab. ii. 11. Syr. ܟܦܣ, *contraxit, connexuit.* Arab. كَفَس, *fasciæ infantis.* A *tie-beam,* i. e. *a beam* reaching from wall to wall, and so confining them as not to allow them to bulge outwards, according to some. See Castell, sub voce. But the context seems to require something more; it declares that the stone shall cry out of the wall, and that the כָּפִיס, from the timber (עֵץ), shall answer it. It must signify, therefore, *something in the timber,* not the timber itself; just as the stone is something within the wall. And, if the word—as the Syriac implies—signifies *tie* or *ligature; Cramp, holdfast, tenon,* or some such word, will give its true sense. Some Gr. versions, "σκώληξ de ligno." LXX. κάνθαρος ἐκ ξύλου. Aq. μάζα ἐκ ξύλου. Sym. σύνδεσμος οἰκοδομῆς ξύλινος. Theod. and vers. E. σύνδεσμος ξύλου.

כְּפִיר, m. pl. כְּפִירִים. (a) *A young, newly weaned lion.* See Ezek. xix. 2, 3. The different Heb. names for the lion, Bochart. after the rabbins, thus arranges, as to their age, 1. גור, 2. כפיר, 3. ארי, or אריה, 4. שחל, 5. שחץ, 6. לביא, 7. ליש; agreeing with Shakspeare's seven ages in man, Hieroz. i. p. 713, seq.; Ps. xvii. 12; civ. 21; Judg. xiv. 5. Metaph. (b) applied to *fierce and cruel men,* Ps. xxxiv. 11; xxxv. 17; lviii. 7. Comp. Jer. ii. 15; Ezek. xxxii. 2. (c) Also to men bold in a good cause, Prov. xxviii. 1; Mic. v. 7; applied to the "*remnant,*" in the apostolic times, who were the means of subduing heathenism. (d) Also to *powerful* or *leading men,* Ezek. xxxviii. 13; Nah. ii. 14. Aff. כְּפִירָיִךְ, כְּפִירָיו.

כֶּפֶל, masc. dual, כִּפְלַיִם. Arab. كِفل, *par, tantundem.* Æth. ከፈለ : *pars, portio.* Syr. cogn. ܟܦܠܐ, *complexio brachii.* בְּכֶפֶל רִסְנוֹ, *for the* DOUBLING *of his curb,* Job xli. 5. See my translation. *Doubling, twofold,* Job xi. 6; Is. xl. 2: this last passage is probably an imitation of a certain part of the book of Job. See my Job, Introd. p. 25, seq. Gesenius makes Job xi. 6, to mean, "*complicationes sapientiæ,*" i. e. the wisdom of God as inexplicable!

כָּפַל, v. pres. non occ. See כֶּפֶל. *Double,* i. e. add like to like, constr. med. אֶת, Exod. xxvi. 9. Synon. τοῦ, חָבַר.

Part. pass. כָּפוּל, *Doubled,* Exod. xxviii. 16; xxxix. 9.

Niph. pres. f. תִּכָּפֵל, *Be, become, doubled, repeated,* once, Ezek. xxi. 19.

כָּפָן, m.—pl. non occ. Syr. ܟܦܢܐ, *famelicus. Hunger, want,* Job v. 22; xxx. 3.

כפן, v. f. pret. only, כָּפְנָה, *Became languid, wasted, wanting,* Ezek. xvii. 7.

כָּפַף, v. pres. non occ. See כַּף above. *Bend, bow down,* once, Ps. lvii. 7.

Infin. כֹּף, once, Is. lviii. 5.

Part. pass. pl. כְּפוּפִים. *Persons bent, bowed down,* with distress, Ps. cxlv. 14; cxlvi. 8.

Niph. pres. 1st pers. אִכַּף, *Shall I be, become, bowed down;* here, bow myself, Mic. vi. 6, al. non occ.

כֹּפֶר, masc.—plur. non occ. Arab. كَفَر, — act. كَفَر, — *texit,* operuit. Angl. To cover. Castell. Hence, in a theological sense, Syr. ܟܦܪ, *abstersit, purgavit.* It is peculiar to the Scriptures to consider sin, not as entirely done away, so that absolute perfection now becomes man's character—which would involve impossibilities, taking him as he is,—but as *covered, concealed,* or the like, by virtue of God's favour through Christ; so that righteousness — which really exists in none—is *imputed, counted on,* as belonging, and attaching, to the true believer. Comp. Ps. xxxii. 1, with Rom. iv. 7, seq.; Ps. lxxxv. 2, &c., and see under letter כ above. Hence, I. *A propitiation, expiation, price of redemption,* i. e. made the means of taking away sin, and rendering man acceptable to God: such were various rites under the law, all which received their completion in the sacrifice of Christ, Exod. xxi. 30; xxx. 12; Job xxxiii. 24. See my note. Used also in a secular sense, as redeeming from punishment, &c., Num. xxxv. 31, 32, &c. — as a bribe, 1 Sam. xii. 3; Job xxxvi. 18, &c.

II. *Pitch.* Arab. كَفَر, *pix quâ picantur*

כפר (308) כפש

naves. Syr. ܟܽܘܦܪܳܐ, *bitumen*—as used in smearing over ships, &c., Gen. vi. 14, only.

III. *A village.* Arab. كَفْرٌ, *pagus, vicus,* i. e. a number of buildings erected nearly together for the purpose of mutual protection and safety: not unlike *cover,* i. e. protection for game, as in the phrase of sportsmen, 1 Sam. vi. 18, only.

IV. *A shrub,* so named. Gr. κύπρος; Lat. *cyprus*: transplanted perhaps from the Island so called. Its leaves, when dried and reduced to powder, compose the Henna, حِنَّاء, of the Arabs, with which their women colour their eye-brows, &c. See Cels. Hierobot. i. p. 222, seq. Its flowers grow like the clusters of the grape: hence, Cant. i. 14, אֶשְׁכֹּל הַכֹּפֶר, *cluster of the cyprus:* pl. כְּפָרִים, Ib. iv. 13, al. non occ. So named, according to Simonis, because used for anointing.

כָּפָר, m. pl. כְּפָרִים, i. q. כֹּפֶר, sign. iii. *A village,* Josh. xviii. 24, constr.; Neh. vi. 2; Cant. vii. 12; 1 Chron. xxvii. 25, al. non occ.

כִּפֻּרִים, m. pl. used, apparently, by way of excellence, Gram. art. 223. 3. *Efficient,* or *great, expiation,* Exod. xxix. 36; xxx. 10. חַטָּאת הַכִּפֻּרִים, *sin (offering) of expiation,* Ib. vr. 16. כֶּסֶף הַכִּפֻּרִים, *money of—,* Num. v. 8. אֵיל הַכִּפֻּרִים, *ram of—,* Lev. xxv. 9. יוֹם הַכִּפֻּרִים, *day of—.*

כַּפֹּרֶת, f. Lit. *covering,* i. e. of the ark of the covenant; a plate of pure gold laid flat on the top of it; and usually termed *The mercy seat.* LXX. ἱλαστήριον, and καταπέτασμα. Others, βλῆμα. Exod. xxv. 17, seq.; xxvi. 34; xxx. 6; xxxi. 7, &c. Phr. בֵּית הַכַּפֹּרֶת, *house of the propitiatory,* i. e. the Holy of holies, 1 Chron. xxviii. 11.

כָּפַר, v. once only, Gen. vi. 14. See כֹּפֶר above, sign. ii. *Pitch, smear with pitch,* or *bitumen.*

Pih. כִּפֶּר, pres. יְכַפֵּר. See כֹּפֶר above, sign. i. Arab. كَفَرَ, *expiavit crimen.* Constr. med. בְּ, instr. עַל, לְ, בְּעַד, אֶת, it. immed., Deut. xxxii. 43; Ps. lxv. 4; lxxviii. 38. *Cover,* i. e. *expiate sin.* Meton. *The person guilty of sin.* Ps. ll. cc., Exod. xxx. 10; Lev. iv. 20. 26. 31, &c. — or *thing* subject to uncleanness, &c., Deut. l. c.; Lev. xiv. 53; xvi. 16. 33; Ezek. xlv. 20;—Ib. vr. 17. 24; Num. v. 8; 2 Sam. xxi. 3; 2 Chron. xxx. 18, ellip. The more full expression is, according to Gesenius, to be found in Lev. iv. 26, and v. 18. And, in a secular sense, *Appease, assuage, anger,* Gen. xxxii. 21; Prov. xvi. 14. *Avert, purchase, bribe off, calamity,* Is. xlvii. 11. See כֹּפֶר above, sign. i. Infin. Exod. xxx. 15, 16, &c. Aff. כַּפְּרִי, *my expiating,* Ezek. xvi. 63. See Exod. xxix. 36; Is. xlvii. 11.

Imp. כַּפֵּר, Deut. xxi. 8; Lev. ix. 7, &c.

Puh. כֻּפַּר, pres. יְכֻפַּר. *Be, become, expiated,* Is. vi. 7; xxii. 14; xxvii. 9; Prov. xvi. 6; Num. xxxv. 33: with לְ, for, implying cause; it. בְּ, instr., Exod. xxix. 33. (b) *Blot out,* i. e. *abolish,* a covenant, Is. xxviii. 18.

Hithp. pres. יִתְכַּפֵּר, i. q. Puh. 1 Sam. iii. 14; it. נִכַּפֵּר (for נִתְכַּפֵּר, Gram. art. 193. 4), Deut. xxi. 8.

כָּפַשׁ, v. Kal non occ. Cogn. כָּבַשׁ, and כָּבַס. Arab. اِنْكَفَسَ, *contortus fuit.* Cogn. كَبَسَ, *obruit* domum ejus, *depressit;* كَفَتَ, *propulit vehementius.*

Hiph. aff. הִכְפִּישַׁנִי, *He hath overwhelmed, covered, me,* in the dust; once, Lam. iii. 16.

כְּפַת, v. Chald. pres. non occ. כַּפְּתוּ, once, Dan. iii. 21. Arab. كَفَتَ, ad *pectus adstrinxit* infantem. Sam. כפת, *cohibuit;* כסף, *constrinxit.* Cogn. Heb. קפץ. *They bound.*

Pah. Infin. כַּפָּתָה, Dan. iii. 20. Part. pl. m. מְכַפְּתִין, *Bound,* Ib. 23, 24, al. non occ.

כַּפְתֹּר, m. pl. כַּפְתֹּרִים. Compd. of כפר, *texit,* and פתר, *coronavit.* Gesen. Rather, perhaps, كُور, *spira* cidaris *obvolutæ; in gyrum ambiens caput* cidaris; it. *circulus in gyrum circumvolutus,* and פתר, *coronavit.* I. *Twisted capitals* of columns, Amos ix. 1; Zeph. ii. 14. II. *Ornamented heads* or *bowls*—similar perhaps to such capitals—of the golden candlestick, Exod. xxv. 31. 33, 34, seq.; xxxvii. 17, &c. LXX. σφαιρωτήρ, Vulg. *spærula;* Josephus Antiq. lib. iii. cap. vi. § vii.: and, after him, interpreters generally, *Pomegranates.* Aff. plur. כַּפְתֹּרֶיהָ, כַּפְתֹּרֵיהֶם.

כַּפְתֹּרִים, m. pl. *People of Caphtor.* See Gen. x. 14; Jer. xlvii. 4; Amos ix. 7.

כר (309) כרה

פַּר, m. pl. פָּרִים. Arab. كَرّ, *iteravit*, &c., from playfulness. I. *Fatted* or *pasture lamb*, Deut. xxxii. 14; 1 Sam. xv. 9; 2 Kings iii. 4; Ps. xxxvii. 20; Is. xvi. 1; xxxiv. 6, &c.

II. By a meton., *The place*, or *pasture*, of their feeding. Arab. اَكْرَار, *campus*, Is. xxx. 23; Ps. lxv. 14. לָבְשׁוּ כָרִים הַצֹּאן, *the flocks clothe* the *pastures*, i. e. cover and adorn them by their numbers. But, see Schult. animadv. ad Ps. lxv. 14.

III. *Battering rams*, Ezek. iv. 2; xxi. 27. Gr. κριός. Arab. كبش, *aries*; pec. *machina bellica*. So the Gr. See Bochart. Hieroz. i. 429.

IV. כַּר הַגָּמָל, Gen. xxxi. 34. *The haudaj*, or *small portable chamber*, in which the Eastern women ride on the backs of camels; furnished with curtains and a shade to skreen them from inquisitive eyes, and from the burning rays of the sun. Arab. كُور, it. مَكْوَر, *sella camelina*.

כֹּר, m. pl. כֹּרִים. Arab. كَرّ, *corus tritici*; كَرّ, id. it. *genus mensuræ aridorum Babylonicum*, &c. Both a *liquid* and *dry measure*, containing ten ephahs or baths; and equal to the חֹמֶר. See Captain Jervis's Essay on the Primitive Universal standard of weights and measures, p. 10, seq.; 1 Kings v. 2. 25; Ezek. xlv. 14. Pl., 2 Chron. ii. 9; xxvii. 5, al. non occ.

כרא, v. Chald. in—
Ithp. אֶתְכְּרִיַּת, Dan. vii. 15, only. Syr. and Chald. כְּאִב, *doluit*. *Was, became, pained, afflicted.*

כרבל, v. i. q. according to Gesenius, כְּבֵל, כָּבַל, *accinxit, induit*; but found only as a pass. part. מְכֻרְבָּל, in 1 Chron. xv. 27. *Equipped, clothed*, or the like, as the context requires. LXX. περιεζωσμένος. In Gram. art. 197. 2, is given the analogy of its conjugation, from Kimchi. Arab. جَا يَمْشِي مُكَرْبَلًا, *venit languidè incedens*. *Slightly girded*, perhaps, as is usual with the flowing upper garments of the Orientals.

כַּרְבְּלָא, f. Chald. Aff. בְּכַרְבְּלָתְהוֹן. Their *mantles*, i. e. loose flowing upper garments;

once, Dan. iii. 21. Theod. περικνημίσιν, al. non occ.

כרה, f. pl. constr. כְּרוֹת. Arab. كَرَى, *fodit* puteum, &c. Æth. ከረየ: *fodit*; lit. *a digging*, once, Zeph. ii. 6, in כְּרֹת רֹעִים, *diggings*, or *wells, of shepherds*. Comp. Gen. xxvi. 25. LXX. Κρήτη νομὴ ποιμνίων.

כרה, v. pres. יִכְרֶה. See כרה above. Constr. immed. it. med. לְ, pers. it. Infin. it. עַל, against. I. *Dig*, as a well, pit, &c., Gen. xxvi. 25; L. 5; Exod. xxi. 33; Num. xxi. 18; Jer. xviii. 20. 22; Ps. vii. 16; xl. 7. אָזְנַיִם כָּרִיתָ לִּי, lit. *ears hast thou digged*, i. e. *opened*, as a well, &c., *for me*. LXX. it. Heb. x. 9, σῶμα δὲ κατηρτίσω μοι. Aquila, ὠτία δὲ ἔσκαψάς μοι. LXX. in some MSS. Theod. Edd. v. vi. ὠτία δὲ κατηρτίσω μοι. The Heb. seems to say, thou hast given me open ears, i. e. given me the means of obedience. See אֹזֶן above. The Apostle transfers this to the *body*—as the interpretation probably then in use—which afforded the same theological sense in the main, although differently worded.—Ps. lvii. 7; cxix. 85. And, as the toil of digging may have been compared with that of bargaining, i. e. making a purchase with apparent strife, as in the Eastern markets; hence—

II.—(a) *Buying, purchasing.* Arabic كَرَى, *conduxit*, Deut. ii. 6; Hos. iii. 2; Job xl. 30. See my note. And, as bargaining, covenant making, was often carried on with feasting—hence (b) 2 Kings vi. 23. Hence also—

כֵּרָה, f. *A feast*, Ib., al. non occ.

כְּרוּב, masc. plur. כְּרוּבִים. *Cherub*, plur. *Cherubim*. Certain symbolical figures, described, Ezek. i. 6, seq., and apparently intended to represent the Deity. Each figure had four faces, that of a man, of a lion, of an ox, and of an eagle; symbolizing, perhaps, the wisdom, fearfulness, power, and ubiquity, of God. Of this sort are many of the symbols given in the Revelation, and particularly the τέσσαρα ζῶα, mentioned in the fourth chapter. Such also are the horses of Zechariah (chap. vi.). See my Exposition of the Rev. l. c. It would be idle to offer anything on the etymology; nothing satisfactory having yet been discovered. Castell, Simonis, Gesenius, &c., may be consulted by those who wish to see what has been said on this subject, Exod. xxv. 19; xxxvi. 8; 2 Sam. xxii. 11; 1 Kings vi. 24—26; Ps. xviii. 11; Ezek. xxviii. 14, &c. Pl., Gen. iii. 24; Exod. xxv. 19, 20. 22; xxxvii. 8, &c.

כָּרוֹז, m. Chald. Def. כָּרוֹזָא. Syr. ܟܪܘܙܐ, præco. Arab. كَارِز, id. *A proclaimer, crier,* or *herald,* once, Dan. iii. 4.

כרז, v. Chald. Syr. ܟܪܙ, prædicavit. Arab. كَرَزَ, id. occ. only in—

Aph. pl. m. הַכְרִזוּ. *They proclaimed;* once, Dan. v. 29.

כָּרִי, m. Pl. according to some; but it may be a mere generic noun denoting a whole class, or even a patronym. The keri has for it, 2 Sam. xx. 23, כְּרֵתִי. A title given to a certain officer in the army, a captain of an hundred; of the same rank, apparently, with the רָצִים, or *couriers,* 2 Kings xi. 4. 19. In 2 Sam. xx. 23. Aq. ἐπὶ τοῦ χερηθὶ, καὶ ἐπὶ τοῦ φελήθι. Sym. ἐπὶ τῶν χερηθαίων, καὶ ἐπὶ τῶν φελεθαίων. Theod. ἐπὶ τοῦ πλινθίου καὶ ἐπὶ τοὺς δυνατούς. In Kings ll. cc. LXX. and Theod. τὸν χορρὶ καὶ τὸν ρασείμ. Which shows that nothing specific was known of this word when these translations were made.

כְּרִיתוּת, and כְּרִיתָת, fem. plur. aff. כְּרִיתֶהָ, r. כרת, *secuit, amputavit;* lit. *Cutting asunder, divorce;* always with סֵפֶר preceding. *Writing, bill of divorce,* Deut. xxiv. 1. 3; Is. L. 1; Jer. iii. 8. Aq. βιβλίον κοπῆς. Sym. βιβλίον διακονῆς. Theod. βιβλίον ἐξολοθρεύσεως. LXX. ἀποστασίου.

כַּרְכֹּב, m. aff. כַּרְכֻּבּוֹ, twice only, Exod. xxvii. 5; xxxviii. 4. Compd. of كَرَكَ, *munimentum.* (Syr. ܟܪܟܐ, *orbis, volumen,* &c.) and كُرْز, *vinculum.* (Æth. ᐱᐸᐳ : sporta viminea.) *A sort of brazier,* or *basket,* placed on the grating of the altar, for the purpose apparently of containing the fire, and keeping it from falling over. LXX. ἐσχάραν. ΑΛΛ. σύνθεσιν.

כַּרְכֹּם, m. once, Cant. iv. 14. Arab. كُرْكُم, *crocus,* vulgo *curcuma;* unde et crocus indicus dicitur, et ab formam *Cyperus indicus* esse Dioscor. i. 4, putatur. Castell.

sub voce. Syr. ܟܘܪܟܡܐ, id. Castell. The word is an augment. fm. of כרך, perhaps, if not a foreign word. See Cels. Hierobot. ii. p. 11, seq.; Auth. Vers. *Saffron.* Arab. زَعْفَرَان, Avicen. and Abul Fadl. LXX. κρόκος.

כַּרְכָּרוֹת, f. pl. once, Is. lxvi. 20. Arab. كَرَّ, *regressus fuit, recurrit,* &c. Whence, كَرْكَرَ, *huc illuc convertit se,* &c. *Dromedaries* (Gr. Δρομὰς, *cursitans, velox*), so called from their agility and swiftness in travelling. See Herod. lib. iii. c. 103.

כֶּרֶם, m. (f. Is. xxvii. 2, 3), pl. כְּרָמִים. Constr. כַּרְמֵי. Arab. كَرَم, *generositate indolis superavit alium,* &c. Act. كَرْم, it. *vitis, vinea.* I. *A vineyard,* Exod. xxii. 4; Deut. xx. 6; xxviii. 30. 39; Amos v. ii. כַּרְמֵי־חֶמֶד, *vineyards of desire;* desirable, Is. xxvii. 2. כֶּרֶם חֶמֶר, *vineyard of wine;* recent. edd. read חֶמֶר, here also. To which the Jewish people, as planted in a fruitful land, by the interposition of Divine power, are often assimilated. Comp. Ps. xliv. 3; Is. iii. 14; v. 1, seq.; xxvii. 2, seq.; li. 3. Comp. Matt. xx. 1, seq; xxi. 28; Luke xx. 9. II. *Orchard,* planted with any valuable trees, Judg. xv. 5; Job xxiv. 18. See my note here. Aff. כַּרְמִי, כַּרְמְךָ, &c. Hence—

כֹּרְמִים, m. pl. כֹּרְמִים, sing. non occ. *Vinedressers,* Joel i. 11; Is. lxi. 5, &c. Aff. כֹּרְמֵיכֶם.

כַּרְמִי, m. patronym., Num. xxvi. 6.

כַּרְמִיל, masc.—plur. non occ. i. q. שָׁנִי, תּוֹלַעַת. *Crimson,* as it should seem from the etymology. Compd. Pers. كِرْم; Sanscr. *krimi. A worm,* and آل, *bright red.* Gesen. Arab. قِرْمِز, *coccus baphica,* hinc *kermes,* 𝕮𝖗𝖎𝖒𝖘𝖔𝖓. كُرْمُزَل, *coccineus vermiculatus;* vox armen. Castell. So, *vermillion,* of the French *vermeil,* Gesen., 2 Chron. ii. 6. 13; iii. 14, al. non occ.

כַּרְמֶל, masc.—pl. non occ. Aff. כַּרְמִלּוֹ, 2 Kings xix. 23. Compd. of כֶּרֶם+אֵל. The Dagesh in ל, in כַּרְמִלּוֹ, may be considered as a compensation for the loss of א. Lit. *vine-*

כרם (311) כרף

yard of God, i. e. *best vineyard.* See under אֵל above, p. 24, sign. ii. I. *Carmel,* a very fruitful hill, situated on the south of the tribe of Asher, and not far from the Mediterranean sea. Mostly with the definite article, 1 Sam. xv. 12; xxv. 40; 1 Kings xviii. 19, 20. 42; Jer. iv. 26; Cant. vii. 6; Amos i. 2, &c. Hence—

II. *Any well cultivated,* or *fruitful place,* as an orchard, field, &c., abounding with fruit trees, &c., opp. to woods, deserts, mountains, Is. x. 18; xvi. 10; xxix. 17; xxxii. 15, 16; Jer. iv. 26; xlviii. 33; 2 Chron. xxvi. 10; Mic. vii. 14, &c.

III. Meton. *First produce,* or *fruits,* as obtained from the best cultivated grounds, Lev. ii. 14, גֶּרֶשׂ כַּרְמֶל ... מִנְחַת בִּכּוּרִים, *an offering of first fruits...the produce of a fruitful field,* i. e. as being the best. Aquila. Symm. ἁπαλὰ λάχανα ὀσπριώδη. LXX. χίδρα ἐρικτά. Theod. πίονα ἄλφιτα. Lev. xxiii. 14; 2 Kings iv. 42, וְכַרְמֶל, seems to signify, *and first fruits generally, without specifying further.* LXX. καὶ παλάθας.

כַּרְמְלִי, m. Patronym. of כַּרְמֶל, sign. i., 1 Sam. xxx. 5, &c.

כַּרְמְלִית, f. 1 Sam. xxvii. 3.

כָּרְסְאָ, fem. plur. כָּרְסָן, Chald. Arab. كُرْسِيّ, *solium.* Syr. ܟܘܪܣܝܐ, id. *A throne,* i. q. Heb. כִּסֵּא, Dan. v. 20; vii. 9. Aff. כָּרְסְיֵהּ, Ib.

כרסם, v. pres. aff. only, יְכַרְסְמֶנָּה, once, Ps. lxxx. 14. Arab. كَرْسَم, *toto ore validè momordit,* al. non occ. *Devours it.*

כרע, m. dual, כְּרָעַיִם, sing. non occ. Arab. كُرَاع, كِرَاع, *crura animalium.* Syr. ܟܪܥܐ, *crus, tibia.* Both the legs, or leg bones, Exod. xii. 9; Lev. i. 13; viii. 21; ix. 14; Amos iii. 12. Of the springing legs of the locust, Lev. xi. 21, &c. Aff. כְּרָעָיו.

כָּרַע, v. pres. יִכְרַע. Constr. abs. it. med. בְּ, *in, of place;* עַל, *on;* לְ, *to;* לִפְנֵי, *before;* תַּחַת, *under.* Arab. ركع, metaph. *incurvatus est inter precandum. Bowing down,* as an animal by folding the legs; whence the usages, כָּרַע רָבַץ כְּאַרְיֵה, *he bowed, lay down, as a lion,* Gen. xlix. 9. See Num. xxiv. 9, כָּרְעוּ עַל בִּרְכֵיהֶם, *they bowed down on their knees,* Judg. vii. 6. Comp. Is. xlv. 23. (a)

for worship, 1 Kings xix. 18; Ps. xxii. 30; lxxii. 9; xcv. 6; 2 Chron. vii. 3: (b) indicative of weakness, Judg. v. 27; 2 Kings ix. 24; Ps. xx. 9; Is. x. 4; xlvi. 1, 2; lxv. 12: (c) — to lie down, Gen. l. c. Num. l. c.: (d) — as animals to bring forth their young, Job xxxix. 3: hence of women, 1 Sam. iv. 19: (e) — for adulterous purposes, Job xxxi. 10.

Infin. כְּרֹעַ, 1 Kings viii. 54.

Part. כֹּרֵעַ, Esth. iii. 5.

— pl. m. כֹּרְעִים, Ib. iii. 2.

— f. כֹּרְעוֹת, Job iv. 4.

Hiph. הִכְרִיעַ, pres. 2d pers. תַּכְרִיעַ. *Make, cause, to bow down.* Constr. immed. it. med. תַּחַת, Ps. xvii. 13; xviii. 40; 2 Sam. xxii. 40; lxxviii. 31. Meton. *Depress, afflict,* Judg. xi. 35.

Infin. הַכְרִיעַ, Ib.

כַּרְפַּס, m. once, Esth. i. 6. Arab. كَرْفَاس, كُرْفُس, كِرْبَاس; Lat. *carbasus;* Gr. κυρβασίας. *A very fine and precious sort of cotton,* either white or of any colour, as purple. Cels. Hierobot. ii. 161, has a passage from Strabo, illustrating well the place above mentioned: "Et mox," says Celsius, ' de Rege Indorum;' "*aurea lectica margaritis circumpendentibus recubat; distincta sunt auro et purpura carbasa, quæ indutus est.*" See the whole of the article. It. Schrœder. de ornatu mulierum, p. 108, seq.

כרר, v. Kal non occ. Arab. كَرّ, *recurrit.* Æth. አንቀርቀረ: *volvit.*

Pih. redup. כִּרְכֵּר. Arab. كَرْكَر, *huc illuc nubem egit ventus.*

Part. m. only, מְכַרְכֵּר, Synon. τοῦ, מְפַזֵּז, 2 Sam. vi. 14. 16. *Leaping about, dancing.* Aquila. καρχαρούμενον. Sym. καγκάζοντε. LXX. ἀνακρουόμενον. Comp. 1 Chron. xv. 29, where מְשַׂחֵק seems to be put for it,—al. non occ.

כָּרֵשׂ, m.—pl. non occ. once, Jer. li. 34. Syr. ܟܪܣܐ, *venter.* Chald. Æth. id. Arab. كِرْش, *ventriculus animalis ruminantis.* Aff. כְּרֵשׂוֹ, *his stomach.*

כָּרַת, v. pres. יִכְרֹת. Arab. كَرَتَ. Metaph. *Pressit* eum, *afflixit, mœror,* con. vii., in the primary sense, *dissectus fuit*

כרת (312) כרת

Constr. immed. it. med. אֶת, עִם, לִפְנֵי, לְ, pers. מִן, of thing; בְּ, in, of place. I. *Cut off*, or *down*, as trees, branches, idols, shrines, the head, foreskin, skirt of the garment, &c., Deut. xix. 5; Is. xiv. 8; xliv. 14; Jer. x. 3; xxii. 7; xlvi. 23; 2 Chron. ii. 9;—Num. xiii. 23, 24;—Exod. xxxiv. 13; Judg. vi. 25, 26. 30;—1 Sam. xvii. 51; v. 4;—Exod. iv. 25;—1 Sam. xxiv. 5. 12.

II. Meton. *Kill* men, Jer. xi. 19.

III. Pec. in the phr. כָּרַת בְּרִית, equivalent to the Gr. ὅρκια τέμνειν, τέμνειν σπονδάς. Lat. *icere, ferire, percutere fœdus.* Gesen. Engl. *Strike a bargain,* from cutting up, and dissecting, the parts of animals sacrificed, or otherwise slaughtered, on such occasions. But, as בְּרִית signifies *the feast* joined in on these occasions — see p. 93 above — the division of the parts of the animal among the guests, over which agreement was evinced, was perhaps rather meant. So the apostle, " *Christ our passover is sacrificed for us, therefore, let us keep the feast,*" &c., 1 Cor. v. 7, 8. And, on the slaughtering, &c. of the animal, see Hieroz. i. lib. ii. c. xxxiii. p. 323, seq. Gen. xv. 10; Jer. xxxiv. 18, 19; —Deut. iv. 23; v. 3, &c. Job xxxi. 1, בְּרִית כָּרַתִּי לְעֵינַי: see my note on the place. בְּרִית is sometimes omitted by the ellipsis: as, 1 Sam. xi. 2; xx. 16; xxii. 8; 2 Chron. vii. 18; Is. lvii. 8. דָּבָר, as Hag. ii. 5; and אֲמָנָה, as, Neh. x. 1, is put for it.

Infin. כָּרוֹת, Hos. x. 4, &c. Constr. כְּרוֹת, Jer. xxxiv. 8. With Makkáph, כְּרָת־, 1 Sam. xxii. 8. Aff. כָּרְתִי, 1 Sam. xxiv. 12.

Imp. pl. כִּרְתוּ, Josh. ix. 6, &c.

Part. כֹּרֵת, pl. כֹּרְתִים, Is. xiv. 8; Neh. x. 1. Constr. כֹּרְתֵי, Ps. l. 5.

— pass. כָּרוּת, constr. כְּרוּת, Lev. xxii. 24; Deut. xxiii. 2.

— pl. f. כְּרֻתוֹת, 1 Kings vii. 2.

Niph. נִכְרַת, pres. יִכָּרֵת, *Be, become, cut down, off,* of a tree, Job xiv. 7; Is. lv. 13. — of man, Gen. ix. 11; Ps. xxxvii. 9, &c. מִן־הָעִיר, from the city, Zech. xiv. 2: it. מֵעַמֶּיהָ, *from its people,* Gen. xvii. 14. מִקֶּרֶב עַמּוֹ —, Lev. xvii. 4. 9; xviii. 29; xx. 18. מִיִּשְׂרָאֵל, Exod. xii. 15. מִתּוֹךְ הַקָּהָל Num. xix. 20. מֵעֲדַת יִשְׂרָאֵל, Exod. xii. 19, &c. Metaph. of a land, by famine, Gen. xli. 36: of a name, Ruth iv. 10: of hope, Prov. xxiii. 18; xxiv. 14:—of faith, Jer. vii. 28;—Josh. ix. 23, מִכֶּם עֶבֶד —, *a servant from among you,* i. e. your being servants shall continue. Comp. 2 Sam. iii. 29. — of waters, *divided,* Josh. iii. 13; iv. 7. —

of meat cut between the teeth, Num. xi. 33. — of wine, Joel i. 5. — of the bow, Zech. ix. 10, &c.

Puh. f. כֹּרָתָה, Judg. vi. 28, m. כֹּרַת, Ezek. xvi. 4, where the Keri directs כָּרֹת to be read; i. q. Niph. al. non occ.

Hiph. הִכְרִית, pres. יַכְרִית. Constr. immed. it. med. אֶת; obj. it. מִן, מִקֶּרֶב, מֵעִיר, מִחוּץ, מִדֶּרֶךְ, לְ, i. q. Kal. *Cut off,* as men, nations, beasts, &c., Lev. xvii. 10; Josh. xxiii. 4; Zeph. iii. 6; Ezek. xxv. 7. — name, Is. xiv. 22; Zech. xiii. 2. — memory, Ps. cix. 15. — idols, Lev. xxvi. 30; Mic. v. 12. — sustenance, Nahum ii. 14. — chariots, Zech. ix. 10. — flattering lips, Ps. xii. 4, &c.

Infin. הַכְרִית, Exod. viii. 5, &c. Aff. הַכְרִיתְךָ, Is. xlviii. 9. הַכְרִיתוֹ, Jer. li. 62.

Hoph. הָכְרַת, once, Joel i. 9, i. q. Niph. *Cut off,* made to cease.

כְּרֻתוֹת, f. pl. part. pass. r. כָּרַת, above. Lit. *Things cut,* beams, 1 Kings vi. 36; vii. 12.

כְּרֵתִי, masc. plur. כְּרֵתִים. I. Name of a portion of the Philistines, residing on the south-west shore of Judea, derived from the island of Crete, as some think; but without any good foundation, 1 Sam. xxx. 14; Ezek. xxv. 16; Zeph. ii. 5. Comp. with Amos ix. 7; Jer. xlvii. 4; Deut. ii. 23: out of all which we only learn that certain Philistines came from כַּפְתּוֹר: but not a word to identify *Caphtor* with *Crete.* If, moreover, this people was so called, after the name of their country, they would here have been termed, כַּפְתֹּרִים, not כְּרֵתִים. No reliance can, therefore, be placed on this reasoning. See, also, Gen. x. 13, 14. LXX. χελεθί, κρῆτας, κρητῶν, in these places respectively, and vr. 6, in the last, has κρήτη, for Heb. כְּרֻת, which clearly evinces the ignorance of the translator.

II. The style and title of certain brave soldiers in David's army, 2 Sam. viii. 18; xv. 18; xx. 7. 23, occurring with הַפְּלֵתִי, according to Gesenius, *Executioners* (" *carnifices*") and *couriers.* Of the first of these interpretations however no adequate authority can be adduced, and the second offers no very strong probability. So called, most likely, after the tribes of the Philistines, out of which they may have been hired as mercenary soldiers: a thing always common in the East. See also under כָּרִי.

כֶּשֶׂב, m. } i. q. כֶּבֶשׂ, which see—pl. m.
כִּשְׂבָּה, f. } כְּשָׂבִים. *A lamb*, from the
first to the third year, Lev. iii. 7; iv. 35;
xvii. 3, &c. Pl., Gen. xxx. 32, 33. 35, &c.
Fem., Lev. v. 6.

כַּשְׂדִּי, pl. כַּשְׂדִּים, *Patronym. Descendant
of* כֶּשֶׂד, Gen. xxii. 22. *Chaldean*, i. e. an
inhabitant of Chaldea or Babylonia. See
my Introduction to the book of Job, sect. iii.
p. 28. Is. xliii. 14; xlviii. 20; Jer. xxiv. 5;
xxv. 12, &c. Also put for Chaldea, אֶרֶץ being
omitted by the ellipsis, Jer. L. 10; Ezek.
xvi. 29, &c. See under אוּר כַּשְׂדִּים, p. 16
above. It. Chald. Def. כַּשְׂדָּאָה, pl. כַּשְׂדָּאִין.
Def. כַּשְׂדָּיֵא, i. q. Heb. Dan. iii. 8. Also, *an
astrologer, magician*, Ib. ii. 10; iv. 4; v. 30,
&c. See also אוּר כַּשְׂדִּים above.

כָּשָׂה, v. פָּשִׁיט, once, Deut. xxxii. 15,
i. q. כָּסָה, which see. Arab. كَسَا, *induit
pulchritudinem;* conj. viii. *indutus fuit aries
pinguedine*. *Thou coveredst*, i. e. thyself
with fatness: and this the order of the context evidently requires. LXX. ἐπλατύνθη.

כַּשִׂיל, m. once, Ps. lxxiv. 6. Arab.
كَتَلَ, *coegit in unum;* كَاتَلَ, *profligavit;* r.
כָּשַׁל, *corruit.* LXX. ἐν πελέκει. *An ax*.
Targ. in Jer. xlvi. 22.

כָּשַׁל, v. pres. non occ. See כַּשִׂיל above.
Constr. abs. it. med. בְּ, instr. it. in, among,
&c.; מִן, from, because of; אָחוֹר, backwards.
Totter, stagger, (a) from weakness, Ps. cix.
24, of the knees. See my note on Job xii. 5,
on this sort of expression, Is. lviii. 3; Job
iv. 4. Synon. τοῦ, כרע, &c. (b) *Stumble*,
from striking against something, Lam. v. 13;
Hos. xiv. 2; iv. 5; Jer. vi. 21; xlvi. 12;
Lev. xxvi. 37; Is. viii. 15. Hence, generally,
(c) *Stumble* to fall, Ps. xxvii. 2; Jer. xlvi. 6;
Is. xxviii. 13, &c. Metaph. Is. lix. 14.
Infin. abs. כָּשׁוֹל, Is. xl. 30, only.
Part. כּוֹשֵׁל, Is. viii. 27, &c., pl. f. כּשְׁלוֹת, Is.
xxxv. 3.
Niph. נִכְשַׁל, pres. יִכָּשֵׁל. *Be, become,
tottering, stumbling*, from weakness, &c., Is.
xl. 30; Dan. xi. 14. 19. 33; Prov. iv. 14.
19; xxiv. 16; Ezek. xxxiii. 12; Ps. ix. 4;
Hos. v. 5, &c.
Infin. aff. הִפָּשְׁלָם, Dan. xi. 34; and, ה
omitted, with prep. בְּהִכָּשְׁלוֹ, for בְּהִכָּשְׁלוֹ. *In his
fall taking place*, Prov. xxiv. 17.

Part. נִכְשָׁל, Zech. xii. 8, pl. נִכְשָׁלִים, 1 Sam.
ii. 4.
Pih. pres. once, f. תְּכַשֵּׁל, Ezek. xxxvi. 14,
i. q. Kal.
Hiph. הִכְשִׁיל, pres. יַכְשִׁיל. *Cause, make, to
stumble,* Mal. ii. 8; Ps. lxiv. 9; Jer. xviii.
15; Prov. iv. 16: Keri. 2 Chron. xxv. 8;
xxviii. 23. Meton. *fail*, become weak, Lam.
i. 14, &c.
Infin. הַכְשִׁיל, 2 Chron. xxv. 8; xxviii. 23,
aff.
Hoph. part. pl. only, מֻכְשָׁלִים, *Made to
stumble,* Jer. xviii. 23.

כִּשָּׁלוֹן, m. once, Prov. xvi. 18. *An
entire fall,* i. e. ruin.

כֶּשֶׁף, masc. plur. only, כְּשָׁפִים. Arab.
كشف, *manifestavit, &c.* Hence, مكاشف,
discoverer, revealer, a title given to certain
interpreters of dreams, &c., still in the East.
See my Travels of Ibn Batuta, p. 9, note.
Certain *magical rites,* as, *incantations*,
2 Kings ix. 22; Is. xlvii. 9. 12; Jer.
xxvii. 8; Mic. v. 11; Nah. iii. 4, בַּעֲלַת כְּשָׁפִים,
lady, possessor, of witchcrafts. LXX. ἡγουμένη
φαρμάκων. Aff. כְּשָׁפַיִךְ, &c. ll. cc. Hence
the verb—
Pih. כִּשֵּׁף, *Acted the magician,* used witchcraft, 2 Chron. xxxiii. 6, only.
Part. מְכַשֵּׁף } pl. m. מְכַשְׁפִים. *Magician*,
— f. מְכַשֵּׁפָה } *wizard;* f. *witch,* Exod. vii.
11; Deut. xviii. 10; Dan. ii. 2; Mal. iii. 5:
fem., Exod. xxii. 17.

כֶּשֶׁף, m. pl. aff. כַּשְׁפֵיכֶם, *Your magicians*,
once, Jer. xxvii. 9.

כָּשֵׁר, v. pres. יִכְשַׁר. Syr. ܟܫܪ,
prosperatus est. Pah. *prosperavit.* Arab.
كشر, *levior risus.* Cogn. אשר, ישר. Gesen.
Do well, be acceptable, Esth. viii. 5. Constr.
לִפְנֵי, Eccl. xi. 6, al. non occ.
Hiph. Infin. הַכְשִׁיר, *The giving of prosperity*, Eccl. x. 10, only. Symm. ὁ γοργευσάμενος.

כִּשְׁרוֹן, masc. sing. only. *Prosperity,
profit,* Eccl. ii. 21; iv. 4. Symm. ἐν γοργότητι. LXX. ἐν ἀνδρίᾳ.

כְּתָב, masc.—pl. non occ. Syr. ܟܬܒܐ,
scriptura. Arab. كَتَبَ and كِتَاب,
id. Lit. (a) *writing;* thence, (b) *Epistle,
letter;* (c) *register, record;* (d) *Scripture*.
Differs from סֵפֶר, in this particular, that כתב

כתב (314) כתי

has respect to the *manner* of writing (Arab. كَتَبَ, *decrevit; consuit* utrem, &c., as if engraving, cutting into something were the primitive notion), סֵפֶר, to the *matter*, or things enumerated. Gesenius's "pro antiquiore סֵפֶר," is, therefore, groundless. See Esth. i. 22; iii. 14; iv. 5; viii. 13. פַּתְשֶׁגֶן כְּתָב, *copy,* exemplar, *of the writing,* Ib. iii. 12; viii. 8, 9, &c. (b) 2 Chron. ii. 10. (c) 2 Chron. xxxv. 4; Ezek. xiii. 9; Ezra ii. 62; Neh. vii. 64; Esth. ix. 27. (d) Dan. x. 21. Aff. כְּתָבָם, כְּתָבָם.

כְּתָב, Chald. i. q. Heb. Def. כְּתָבָא, and כְּתָבָה, pl. non occ., Ezra vi. 18; vii. 22; Dan. v. 7, 8. 15—17. 24, 25; vi. 9—11.

כָּתַב, v. pres. יִכְתֹּב. See כָּתַב above. Constr. immed. it. med. אֵת, obj. it. ל, pers. to, for; it. עַל, to, on, against; אֶל, to, on; מִן, from; בְּ, in, with. *Write, engrave,* (a) as in a book or table, Exod. xxxiv. 1; Deut. vi. 9; xi. 20; xxvii. 3. 8; Jer. xxxvi. 2. (b) *Epistles, letters, &c.,* 2 Chron. xxx. 1; Ezra iv. 7; Job xxxi. 35; Exod. xxxii. 32; Deut. xvii. 18; xxiv. 1. 3; Jer. xxxvi. 17. (c) *Register, enrol,* Ps. lxix. 29; lxxxvii. 6; Is. iv. 3; Jer. xxii. 30. (d) — *as a law, decree,* Is. lxv. 6; Job xiii. 26.

Infin. כָּתוֹב, Jer. xxxii. 44. Constr. Deut. xxxi. 24; Ps. lxxxvii. 6, &c. Aff. כָּתְבוֹ, Jer. xlv. 1.

Imp. כְּתֹב, Exod. xvii. 14, &c. With Makkáph, כְּתָב, Ib. xxxiv. 27, &c. it. Aff. כָּתְבָה, Is. xxx. 8, &c. Pl. כִּתְבוּ, Deut. xxxi. 19, &c.

Part. כֹּתֵב, Jer. xxxvi. 18; pl. כֹּתְבִים, Ib. xxxii. 12.

— pass. כָּתוּב, Deut. xxviii. 61, &c.: pl. כְּתוּבִים, כְּתֻבִים, Exod. xxxi. 18, &c.

— f. כְּתוּבָה, 2 Sam. i. 18, &c.: pl. כְּתֻבוֹת, 2 Chron. xxxiv. 24.

כְּתַב, v. Chald. pres. 1st pers. pl. נִכְתָּב, i. q. Heb. Dan. v. 5; vi. 26; vii. 1; Ezra iv. 8; v. 7, &c.

Part. כְּתִיב, Ezra vi. 2, &c.

כְּתֹבֶת, f. once, Lev. xix. 28. *Writing.*

כִּתִּים, and כִּתִּיִּים, pl. m. Name of a people so called: not a colony of the Phenicians, as Gesenius will have it: for these were the descendants of Ham; but a tribe descended from Japhet, Gen. x. 4. Inhabitants of Cyprus, as some think, from a city named, Gr. κίτιον, or κίττιον, Joseph. Antiq. lib. i. cap. vi. § 1; Epiphan. adv. Hær. xxx. § 25. But here both have been deceived in one instance, viz., 2 Kings vii. 6, as Bochart. has shown, Phaleg. i. p. 178, by taking חתים, for כתים. Generally, the people inhabiting the shores of the Mediterranean, Num. xxiv. 24; Jer. ii. 10; Dan. xi. 30, &c. See Bochart. l. c. Michaelis Spicileg. i. p. 103, seq.

כָּתִית, masc.— plur. non occ., r. כתת. Usually, *beaten oil,* from olives beaten in a mortar, according to Rabbi Solomon, from which the oil distils without being subjected to the press; and thence, the *most pure.* But this, as is often the case with the rabbies, has been fabricated for the mere purpose of fitting the thing. It is most likely, that, as *fine* powder is obtained, in many instances, by *beating* in a mortar, or the like, *fine oil* has, by way of comparison, been termed כָּתִית; lit. *beaten small,* Exod. xxvii. 20; xxix. 40; Lev. xxiv. 2; Num. xxviii. 5; 1 Kings v. 25. Comp. Arab. دَقَّ, دَكَّ.

כֹּתֶל, masc. once only, aff. כָּתְלֵנוּ, Cant. ii. 9. Arab. كَتْل, *massa luti.* Our wall. LXX. τοῦ τοίχου ἡμῶν; it. Chald. pl. def. כָּתְלַיָּא, Ezra v. 8, al. non occ.

כְּתַל, masc. once, Dan. v. 5, i. q. Heb. כֹּתֶל.

כֶּתֶם, m.—pl. non occ. *The finest gold.* See my note on Job xxxviii. 16. Arab. كَتَمَ, *abdidit;* lit. *a laying,* or *treasuring up,* Job, l. c. 19; xxxi. 24; Prov. xxv. 12; Dan. x. 5; Cant. v. 11; Ps. xlv. 10. Meton. *Dress* ornamented with such gold. Hence the verb, Kal non occ.—

Niph. נִכְתַּם, part. Lit. *laid, treasured, up,* constr. לִפְנֵי, *before me,* i. e. with me; has not been washed, or blotted, out. Usually, *Spotted, defiled, &c.,* of the Syr. ܟܬܡ, *maculavit;* but this is, probably, a secondary sense, taken from vestments spotted with fine gold ornaments (see כֶּתֶם above): once, Jer. ii. 22.

כְּתֹנֶת, f. pl. aff. כֻּתֳּנֹתָם, constr. כָּתְנוֹת.—

כֻּתֹּנֶת, f. pl. כֻּתֳּנוֹת, כָּתְנוֹת.—

Arab. كَتَّان, *filum lineum.* Eng. *Cotton.*

כתף (315) כתר

Syr. ܟܬܦܐ, *tunica, indusium. A sort of under garment*, or *shirt*, worn by the priests and others, Exod. xxix. 5 ; Lev. viii. 7; xvi. 4; reaching occasionally to the ancles: see under פס, Gen. xxxvii. 3. 23, seq.: worn also by women, Cant. v. 3; 2 Sam. xiii. 18, 19. See Jahn's Biblische Archäologie, 1 Theil. ii. Band. p. 73, seq. Pl., Gen. iii. 21 ; Exod. xxviii. 40; xxix. 8 ; Lev. viii. 13, &c. Aff. כְּתֻנְתִּי, Job xxx. 18. כֻּתָּנְתְּךָ, Is. xxii. 21, &c.

כָּתֵף, c. constr. כֶּתֶף, is the form taken; pl. m. aff. כְּתֵפָיו, of כְּתֵפִים, and f. כְּתֵפוֹת, constr. כִּתְפוֹת. Arab. كَتِف, كَنِف, *humerus*. Syr. ܟܬܦܐ, id. (a) *The shoulder*, as bearing burdens, Is. xlvi. 7 ; xlix. 22; Ezek. xii. 6, 7. 12, &c. As a place of attack, *the back*, Is. xi. 14. Comp. 1 Sam. xvii. 6. — of an animal, Ezek. xxiv. 4 ; Is. xxx. 6. (b) Applied to *the side* of an edifice, see יָד, 1 Kings vi. 8; vii. 39. — of the sea, Num. xxxiv. 11. — of a town or region, Josh. xv. 8. 10, 11; xviii. 12, seq. So, according to Gesenius, Is. xi. 14. Pl., *shoulders* of a garment, Exod. xxviii. 7. 12 ; xxxix. 4. 7. 18. 20. (b) *Sides of gates*, Ezek. xli. 2. 26. (c) *Shoulders* of axles, or pivots, 1 Kings vii. 30. 34. See Braun. de Vestitu Sacerd. p. 467, seq.

כֶּתֶר, masc. — plur. non occ. Pers. كتر, *dignity, estimation*. Greek κίταρις, κίδαρις. See Thes. Gr. Steph. Ed. Valp. Vol. i. p. ccccxvii. *Persian diadem* or *crown*, Esth. i. 11; ii. 17; vi. 8, al. non occ. Hence the verb —

Pih. plur. כִּתְּרוּ, pres. non occ. Constr. immed. it. med. אֵת. *Surround, encompass*, in a hostile manner, Judg. xx. 43 ; Ps. xxii. 13, al. non occ.

Hiph. pret. non occ. pres. pl. m. יַכְתִּירוּ. Constr. immed. it. med. אֵת, בְּ. (ε) *Surround, come about*, in a friendly sense, Ps. cxlii. 8. (b) *Comprehend*, Prov. xiv. 18, וַעֲרוּמִים יַכְתִּירוּ דָעַת, *but the subtile comprehend knowledge*. Aquila, ἀναμενοῦσι γνῶσιν. LXX. κρατήσουσιν αἰσθήσεως. Theod. στεφθήσονται γνῶσιν.

Part. מַכְתִּיר, *Surrounding*, as an enemy, Hab. i. 4, al. non occ.

כֹּתֶרֶת, fem. plur. כֹּתָרוֹת. *Cincture*, or *capital*, of a column, 1 Kings vii. 16. 19, 20, &c.

כתש, pret. non occ. pres. תִּכְתּוֹשׁ. Syr. ܟܬܫ, *percussit*. Cogn. Heb. כתח. Constr. med. אֵת. *Break, bruise*. Metaph. of chastisement, once, Prov. xxvii. 22. Aquila, Theod. ἐὰν κόπτῃς τὸν ἄφρονα, κ.τ.λ. LXX. ἐὰν μαστιγοῖς, κ.τ.λ.

כָּתַת, v. pres. אָכֹּת, 1st pers. Arab. كَتَّ, *invitem coegit*. Cogn. كَنْكَتَ, كَتَّ, *id in quo minutiores partes lapidum*; كَتَّ, *id in quo quid contunditur*. Constr. immed. it. med. בְּ, מִן, אֵת. (a) *Beat*, or *break*, to pieces, synon. שָׁבַר, Is. xxx. 14, as a vessel, generally, Lev. xxii. 24 ; Deut. ix. 21. (b) *Beat* out, as iron by a smith, Joel iv. 10. (c) — *down*, as enemies, Ps. lxxxix. 24. Synon. τοῦ, נָגַף, al. non occ.

Part. pass. כָּתוּת, Is. Lev. ll. cc.

Pih. כִּתָּה, pres. non occ. i. q. Kal. (a) 2 Kings xviii. 4 ; 2 Chron. xxxiv. 7. (b) Is. ii. 4 ; Mic. iv. 3. (c) Zech. xi. 6.

Puh. כֻּתַּתוּ, pl. m. *Be, become, broken, beaten* to pieces. Constr. בְּ, instr. once, 2 Chron. xv. 6.

Hiph. pret. non occ. pres. pl. יַכִּתוּ. Constr. immed. it. med. אֵת, Num. xiv. 45 ; Deut i. 44, al. non occ.

Hoph. pret. non occ. pres. יֻכַּת, pl. יֻכַּתּוּ, i. q. Puh. (a) Is. xxiv. 12 ; Mic. i. 7. (c) Jer. xlvi. 5, al. non occ.

ל

ל, *Lamed*, is the twelfth letter of the Hebrew alphabet, Gram. art. 4: and, as a numeral, stands for thirty, Ib. It occasionally interchanges with letters of the same class, Ib. artt. 24; 79. 2: and as noticed in their several places in this work. Gesenius makes it also interchangeable with ד, in אֲדַר, i. q. אֲלַל; but this is doubtful. See under the former, p. 17, seq. above. He also thinks that, when occurring as the last of a quadri-literal word, as in חַרְגֹּל, &c., it forms a sort of *diminutive*, as in the Greek, Latin, &c. But of this no good proof can be made out.

As to its etymology, it may be either an abridged form of אֶל, Arab. إِلَي, *ad, versus*, &c.; v. وَلَى, *avertit* faciem, *amicus fuit, &c.*—See under אֶל, p. 29 above;—and signify, *to, towards, as to, &c.*: or it may be a contraction of the cogn. לוי, Gram. art. 171. 5. Arab. لوي, *plicuit, contorsit*, membrum; *propensus fuit* in rem. And hence imply, *connexion with, adherence to*, any thing, &c. Which will amount to much the same thing.

The vowels proper for this particle, when connected with other words, are shown, Gram. artt. 107; 119. 12; 121. 3; 174. 3, seq.

This particle, which is always inseparable, Gram. art. 172, is used as a preposition, implying—

I. (a) Motion, progress, &c., towards any place. *To, towards*, Gen. xxvi. 20; Is. li. 6; Job x. 19; xx. 6; Dan. iv. 9; Ps. lxviii. 19; Ruth i. 8, &c.

And thence, by a meton. (i. e. having come to —), *At, in*, any place, or thing. So the Gr. εἰς, ἐς, for ἐν. לְפֶתַח אֹהֲלוֹ, *at, in, the door of his tent*, Num. xi. 10. לְפִי חֶרֶב, Prov. viii. 3. לְחוֹף יַמִּים, Gen. xlix. 13. לְיָמִין, Ps. cix. 31; Is. lxiii. 12. Comp. Ps. cx. 1. So לְעֵינֵי לִפְנֵי, passim. So also, לַחַיִּים, Ps. xli. 7. לַחוּצָה, 2 Chron. xxxii. 5. לְמִצְפֶּה, Hos. v. 1. לָשַׁחַת, Is. li. 14. In all which places it is synonymous with the prep. בְּ.

(b — *to person*, Gen. xxiv. 54, &c.

(c) — *or thing*, 1 Sam. xvi. 7; 2 Kings x. 21; xxi. 16; Is. liii. 7; Jer. xii. 15, &c.

(d) — or time, *To, till, until*, Lev. xxiv. 12; Deut. xvi. 4; Is. xxv. 8, &c.

And thence, by a meton., as above. (a) *At, in*, any time, season, &c. לַבֹּקֶר, Ps. xxx. 6; lix. 17. לָאוֹר, Job xxiv. 14. לָעֶרֶב, Gen. xlix. 27; Ps. xc. 6: fully, לְעֵת עֶרֶב, Gen. viii. 11. So also, לִבְקָר וְלָעֶרֶב, לְעֵת בֹּא הַשֶּׁמֶשׁ, Josh. x. 27. So also, לִבְקָר וְלָעֶרֶב, 1 Chron. xvi. 40; 2 Chron. ii. 3.—Period, or season. לִשְׁלֹשֶׁת הַיָּמִים, Ezra x. 8. אַחַת לְשָׁלֹשׁ שָׁנִים, 1 Kings x. 22. In passages such as Gen. vii. 4; Amos iv. 4; 2 Sam. xiii. 23, &c. our *for, till*, or some such word will be most suitable, as coming under the first head here. The instances given by Gesenius ("*de conditione*")—in which the sense of *in* seems to be intended, as in לְבַד, "*in separatione*," i. e. alone; לְבֶטַח, "*in securitate*," will come more properly under a following head (f). לְרִקְמוֹת, Ps. xlv. 15, comes not under this head, but ought, evidently, to be construed with מִמִּשְׁבְּצוֹת, preceding; thus, מִמִּשְׁבְּצוֹת זָהָב לְרִקְמוֹת לְבוּשָׁהּ, *of interwoven* (materials) *of various* (sorts) *with gold is her clothing*; such as the زَرْ بَافْ, *gold-woven* of the Persians at the present day. The text here, therefore, as in many other cases, has been disjointed by the punctuists.

(e) — metaph. or relation, fitness, propriety, &c. to action, event, circumstance, &c. *To, for, in order to, for the purpose of, &c.*, as the context may especially require. Josh. xxii. 29, לִבְנוֹת מִזְבֵּחַ לְעֹלָה לְמִנְחָה וּלְזָבַח, TO *build an altar* FOR *offering*, FOR *mincha, and* FOR *sacrifice*. Neh. viii. 4, עָשׂוּ לַדָּבָר, *they made* FOR *the matter*, occasion. Exod. xii. 13, נֶגֶף לְמַשְׁחִית, *disease* TO *destroy*. And such, as in the first and last examples here, is the construction of Infinitives or verbal nouns generally.*

(f) — also to person, thing. *To, for, as to, belonging to, with respect to, &c.* Lam. iii. 12, לַחֵץ ....יַצִּיבֵנִי, *he hath set me up*.... FOR *the arrow*, i. e. as a mark. Ps. v. 3, הַקְשִׁיבָה לְקוֹל, *attend* TO *the voice*. 1 Kings

---

* תִּתֵּן, 1 Kings vi. 19, as also Ib. xvii. 14. Kethiv, ought, no doubt, to be taken as an unusual form of the Infinitive, as Gesenius and Ewald have observed. In this case the usage will be regular.

ל (317) ל

vi. 12, אֲשֶׁר לַדְּבִיר, *which* was TO, BELONGING TO, *the oracle*. Comp. 2 Chron. i. 6. אֹסְרִי לַגֶּפֶן, *tying to the vine*, Gen. xlix. 11. מִסָּבִיב לְמִשְׁכַּן, — *on all sides* AS TO *the tent*, Num. xvi. 14. So the obscure passage, Ps. xii. 7, צָרוּף בַּעֲלִיל לָאָרֶץ, *purified in the crucible, as to the earth,* i. e. as to the earth, or earthy particles contained in it. לְרֵעֵהוּ יְשֻׂנָּא, TO, or AS TO, *his friend, is he hateful,* Prov. xiv. 20. In all which cases words *not* directly influencing their complementary terms (Gram. art. 228. 5, seq.) will necessarily be used. And so in all those cases in which ל is made to precede a nominative absolute, Gram. art. 216. 15. לִקְדוֹשִׁים, *as to the saints,* Ps. xvi. 3. לַעָם, *as to the afflicted,* Job vi. 14, &c. And so generally the places in which Gesenius proposes the Latin *"adeo,"* as an equivalent to this particle, viz., Deut. xxiv. 5; 2 Chron. vii. 21; Eccl. ix. 4; 2 Chron. v. 12, which exhibits a large number of instances of this sort, e. g. לְכָלָם לְאָסָף לְהֵימָן לִידוּתוּן וְלִבְנֵיהֶם, —, AS TO *the whole of them,* TO *Asaph,* TO *Heman,* TO *Jeduthun,* TO *their children, &c.:* and so also, a large number of those interpreted both by him and Noldius, by the Latin "*à, ab,*" expressing anything but the *real* sense of this particle; as, מִזְמוֹר לְדָוִד, *Psalm belonging to* (or of) *David,* Ps. iii. 1, &c. אָנֹכִי כְּפִיךָ לָאֵל, *I am, according to thy mouth* (word), *God's,* i. e. for, or belonging to God; standing on his part; as the context manifestly requires. So, לַאֲדֹרָיִם, Hos. vi. 10; יוֹם לַיהוָֹה, *Jehovah's day,* i. e. in which he will do some great thing, Is. ii. 12. Comp. Ps. lxxxi. 5; Jonah iii. 3; עִיר גְּדוֹלָה לֵאלֹהִים, *a great city,* AS TO *God* (i. e. taking God as the measure of comparison, which is the greatest that can be imagined. For similar instances of comparison with ל, see Gram. art. 241. 12—14). 1 Kings x. 1. Comp. Ps. xviii. 45; Job xxxvii. 1, &c. Ps. iii. 9, לַיהוָֹה הַיְשׁוּעָה, TO *Jehovah* belongs *salvation,* i. e. to him it is to be ascribed; or, in another point of view, *of him it comes.* Comp. Judg. vii. 18. In 2 Sam. iii. 2, viz., בְּכֹרוֹ אַמְנוֹן לַאֲחִינֹעַם, which Gesenius translates, *" primogenitus ejus* (Davidis) *erat Amnon ab Ahinoam."* He has not seen the construction, which is this (see the beginning of the verse), וַיִּוָּלְדוּ לְדָוִד, *and there were born* TO *David....*and his firstborn Amnon (was born) TO *Ahinoam,* i. e. continuing the same construction, and understanding the verb as repeated. And so of innumerable other instances, which it would be tedious to give.

In many cases this particle gives a sense nearly equivalent to that supplied by כְּ. See under this letter: and this may be expressed in English, by *for,* e. g. Gen. ii. 22, לְאִשָּׁה, FOR *a woman,* i. e. he so constructed it as to become a woman, 2 Sam. v. 3. לְמֶלֶךְ, *for king,* i. e. to be king; which may be written, לִהְיוֹת לְמֶלֶךְ. See under the v. הָיָה. Comp. Gen. ii. 7; Job xiii. 12; xvii. 12; Lam. iv. 3; v. 15; Joel iii. 4, &c.

In such passages as דִּבְרֵי הַיָּמִים לְמַלְכֵי יִשְׂרָאֵל, 1 Kings xv. 31, the construction is not adopted merely because the *" status constructus minus placebat,"* the state of construction pleased less, as Gesenius says, for then יְמֵי שְׁנֵי־חַיֵּי אַבְרָהָם, Gen. xxv. 7, could scarcely have been allowed. No: in such cases the introduction of ל, as in the Arabic, may be said to supply the place of the definite article to the last governing noun (here יִשְׂרָאֵל); which the term אַבְרָהָם, as a proper name, could not receive. There is, therefore, a substantial reason (not a *"minus placebat"*) for taking this construction here.

Those instances in which ל may be said to mark an accusative case after a transitive verb, may be thus resolved—ל, *as to, with respect, reference, to, &c.,* is perfectly equivalent to the particle אֵת. See under that term, p. 63, above. It is but reasonable, therefore, that it should be found occupying precisely the same situation in many cases in the Hebrew, and very commonly in the Syriac and Chaldaic; and this is the fact. See Jer. xl. 2; Lam. iv. 5; Job v. 2, &c. Is. viii. 1; which Gesenius gives here, should be rendered, *as to the hasting of the* spoil, *the hurrying of* the *contempt, &c.* See under the verb חוּשׁ, p. 189 above. Or, the ל preceding מַהֵר, here may be taken as the Arabic ل, *lam* of corroboration, signifying, *surely, certainly,* or the like. The passage will then read—surely (there shall be יִהְיֶה) *a hasting of* the *spoil, a hurrying of* the *contempt.* The latter appears to me the best interpretation of this place. See also Nold., p. 395, seq. In p. 415, seq. a large number of instances of its omission is given.

The same usages of this particle obtain, for the most part in the Chaldee. A few places only need be enumerated, Dan. ii. 5. 17; iv. 19; vi. 11; vii. 2. Equivalent to the Heb. אֵת (f. above), Dan. ii. 10. 23—25; v. 4, &c. Often prefixed to Infinitives, as, Dan. ii. 9, 10. 12, &c. Gesenius and Winer

לֹא (318) לֹא

make it, in certain cases, equivalent to the Latin *ut*, and as giving a sense not unlike the Latin *optative, imperative, &c.*, e. g. ——לֶהֱוֵא מְבָרַךְ, *benedictus sit*; in all which cases the preformative of the future (our present) is supposed to be rejected. But this is the same thing as to say, that we have, in these cases, the mere naked form of the Infinitive or Imperative (Gram. artt. 182. 10; 189, &c.): and, if so, in the case of the Infinitive, the usage is identical with that of the Heb. (f. above). In that of the Imperative, the ל, will be that of corroboration, as noticed in the last article; which will suit every case so occurring.

A very large number of instances will be found in Noldius (pp. 418, seq., 434, seq.), in which this particle is prefixed to other words or particles. In all which cases the sense will be found such, as the compound—duly observing what has been delivered above—should naturally give.

לֹא, sometimes לוֹא, rarely לֹי, r. לוא.

Arab. لَوَى, *difficultus*. Heb. לָאָה. See my note on Job vi. 21. A particle (a) of *negation*; and occasionally (b) of *prohibition*, i. q. Arab. لا. Syr. ܠܐ, *non*. Engl. *No, not; by no means, &c.* Used with every part of speech except the Imperative of verbs: while אַל is used mostly with the present tense. See אַל, p. 28, above. It differs from אַיִן, in that this negatives the existence of anything; לֹא, its *properties, qualities, action, &c.* See אַיִן above, p. 25. (a) Of negation. לֹא הִמְטִיר, *he had not caused rain*, Gen. ii. 5. לֹא יֻסָּד, *had not been founded*, Ezra iii. 6. לֹא נָדוּ, *they removed not away*, Ps. lxxviii. 30. לֹא זָכַר, *is not borne in mind*; mentioned, Job xxviii. 18. לֹא יֵעָצֵר, *is not, may not be, withholden*, Gen. xi. 6, &c. And, carrying the present tense on into the future, the particle becomes (b) *prohibitive*; as, לֹא תַעֲשׂוּ, *you may not, shall not, make*, Lev. xix. 4. לֹא תוֹנוּ, *you shall not afflict*, Ib. xxv. 17. לֹא תָבוֹא, *come not in*, Prov. xxii. 24, &c. In all which cases לֹא is perfectly equivalent to אַל. "*Differt ab אַל*," says Gesenius, "*quod est dehortantis*:" which our last example from the Proverbs is sufficient to annihilate. See the whole verse. Gesenius places לֹא יֵקַר, Exod. xxviii. 32, under this head: which is clearly erroneous: לֹא being there plainly negative,

signifying, *it shall not be torn*, or rather *tearable* (detur venia verbo), i. e. such as not to admit of tearing or rending.

When the sentence is intended to be interrogative, לֹא will be equivalent to הֲלֹא; as, לֹא לִבִּי הָלַךְ, *Did not my heart go?* 2 Kings v. 26. לֹא יַשְׁאִירוּ, *Will they not leave?* Jer. xlix. 9. לֹא אֶחוּס, *Shall I not spare?* Jonah iv. 11, &c. הֲלֹא, Gen. iv. 7; xx. 5, &c. Often used affirmatively; as, 1 Sam. xx. 37; 2 Sam. xv. 35, &c.

When joined with attributives, it negatives their *quality* or *property* (Gram. art. 241. 4); as, לֹא חָכָם, *not wise*, i. e. unwise, Deut. xxxii. 6; Hos. xiii. 13. לֹא־טוֹב, *not good, unsuitable*, Gen. ii. 18. לֹא־עַז, *not strong, weak*, Prov. xxx. 25. Comp. Ps. xliii. 1; Deut. xxxii. 21; Jer. v. 7; Is. x. 15; xxxi. 8, &c. בַּל, as in בְּלִי־טוֹב, Prov. xxiv. 23, seems to be more emphatic. The expression nearly equivalent to this in the English is, *anything but*, i. e. the thing is anything else but what its name implies. So לֹא אֶחָד, lit. *not any one, none*, 2 Sam. xiii. 20; Job xiv. 4, &c. Nold. p. 425. It should be remembered that, in these cases, *the quality*, not *the existence of the thing*, is negatived.* In most such cases, therefore, *not any*, or some such expression is to be understood as implied in the term לֹא: *any, some*, or the like, being occasionally expressed by־בְּל, as Exod. x. 15; or, by the noun's wanting the definite article.

Often compounded with בְּ, as, בְּלֹא יוֹמוֹ, Job xv. 32. Comp. Num. xxxv. 23; Is. lv. 1; Ezek. xxii. 29: and other instances given by Noldius, p. 184, seq., from which it will be evident that all such constructions are elliptical; † e. g. בְּלֹא יוֹמוֹ, i. q. בְּעֵת שֶׁהוּא לֹא יוֹמוֹ, *at a time, which is not his day*. So, in the next case, בְּלֹא רְאוֹת, lit. *in not seeing*: more fully, בַּאֲשֶׁר לֹא הָיְתָה רְאוֹת לוֹ, or the like: and so in every similar case. The construction, לֹא בְ, as in לֹא בְיָד, לֹא בְכֶסֶף, joined with the last by Gesenius, as being of the same character, is of a totally different kind; for here the particle לֹא negatives some *action* or

---

* And hence this particle is termed by the Arabian Grammarians, لا لنفي الجنس, i. e. לֹא, *for negativing the quality*. See also Gram. art. 233. 3, note.

† And so Gesenius makes לְלֹא, equivalent to לַאֲשֶׁר לֹא, Lex. Man. p. 517.

property preceding, with which the preposition בְּ has nothing to do. This usage, therefore, comes under one or other of the cases noted above. And one passage in Job, viz., xxx. 28, בְּלֹא חַמָּה, "*non sole* atratus," he has, clearly, misunderstood: the *gloom, blackness, &c.* implied in קֹדֵר preceding, never being said to be the result of a hot sun: on the contrary, the light and warmth of the sun are universally appealed to as sources of delight and comfort. See my note on Job vi. 15. Nor can Cant. i. 6, be cited as opposing this. The meaning of Job plainly is, that he goes on in gloom (metaph. misery), because the light and warmth of the sun (metaph. usual sources of comfort) have been withholden from him. Mistakes of this sort will, of necessity, often be made where the ingenuity of conjecture is unrestrained by a due regard to usage.

In many cases, לֹא is found written (*kethiv*) where the *keri* and the context require that לוֹ, *to, for, him,* be read. The mistake has probably originated in the copyists' writing after some one reading the text to them. See Exod. xxi. 8; Lev. xi. 21; 1 Sam. ii. 3, &c., as cited by Noldius, p. 422, seq., and noticed, p. 1444, in the "Annotationes et Vindiciæ."

A large list of combinations of this particle, with other words and particles, will also be found in Noldius, p. 425, seq., and in their proper places; which, it will be seen, require the significations which their single component parts duly understood would naturally give.

In the Chald. לָא, once לֵהּ, Dan. iv. 32, i. q. Heb. *No, not, &c.,* Dan. ii. 5. 9—11; iii. 12. 14, &c. With the interrogative ה, הֲלָא, Ib. iii. 24; iv. 27. Ib. 32, מְלָה, *as not,* supp. existing. The place is clearly elliptical; the particle, therefore, retains its usual sense.

לַאֲדִיב, for לְהַאֲדִיב, Hiph. Infin. r. ארב, i. q. דאב, 1 Sam. ii. 33.

לָאָה, v. pres. תִּלְאֶה, 2d pers. apoc. תֵּלֶא. Constr. abs. it. med. לְ, Infin. Syr. ܠܐܝ *laboravit.* Arab. لأى, *coarctatus fuit.* See לֹא above, and my note on Job iv. 2. *Be weary, faint;* meton. *vexed,* Gen. xix. 11; Job iv. 2. 5, al. non occ.

Niph. נִלְאָה, נִלְאֵת, &c. pres. non occ. Constr. med. בְּ, instr. עַל, upon; לְ, Infin. and with Infin. immed. *Become weary,* *faint;* meton. *pained, vexed,* Is. xvi. 12; Jer. ix. 4; xx. 9;—Is. xlvii. 13;—Is. i. 14; Jer. vi. 11; xv. 6; Prov. xxvi. 15:—it. *dislike, loathe,* Exod. vii. 18. LXX. οὐ δυνήσονται. Part. Ps. lxviii. 10.

Hiph. הֶלְאָה, pres. pl. m. יַלְאוּ. Constr. immed. it. med. אֶת. *Make weary, vex:* meton. *ruin,* Ezek. xxiv. 12; Is. vii. 13; Mic. vi. 3; Jer. xii. 5. Meton. Job xvi. 7: see my note. Symm. ἐκόπωσέ με.

לְהָאוֹר, for לְהַאוֹר, Infin. Niph. r. אור.

לָאַט, v. once, 2 Sam. xix. 5; constr. med. אֶת, i. q. לוט. *Vail,* or *cover the face.* For לְאַט, Job xv. 11. See אַט above, and my note on the place.

לָאַט, see אַט.

לָאָט, see לוט.

לְאֹם, and לְאוֹם, masc. pl. לְאֻמִּים, it. f. לְאֻמּוֹת. Arab. لأم, *consolidatio;* لِئَم, *concordia hominum. A family, tribe,* or *nation,* i. q. אֻמָּה, synon. τοῦ, גוי, Gen. xxv. 16. 23; xxvii. 29; Prov. xi. 26; xiv. 28. *God's people,* Is. li. 4, &c. *The heathen,* Ps. vii. 8; ix. 9; xliv. 3, &c. Aff. לְאוּמִי, Is. l. c. Also the name of a certain people, Gen. xxv. 3.

לֵב, c. with makkáph, לֶב־, pl. f. לִבּוֹת. Aff. לִבִּי, לִבְּךָ, &c. A contraction (Gram. art. 77) of—

לֵבָב, c. constr. לְבַב, pl. לְבָבוֹת. "לֵב, *cavus fuit,*" says Gesenius: which is groundless. Arab. لُبّ, *consistens; cor, mens, &c.* Firmness, solidity, or the like, seems to be the primary notion: thence applied to the heart, as the principal organ of life: and thence is supposed to be the seat of the thoughts, feelings, &c. So the verb لَبَّ, *substitit, mansitque aliquo loco: nucleo prædita fuit* bacca: *polluit intellectu, &c.* (a) *The heart,* of man generally: of beasts, rarely, Dan. iv. 13 (16);—2 Sam. xviii. 14; Ps. xlv. 6, &c. (b) i. q. נֶפֶשׁ, the *seat of life,* Ps. lxxiii. 21; lxxxiv. 3; cii. 5; Jer. iv. 18. Hence said to live, be sick, to sleep, be sustained by food, &c., Ps. xxii. 27; Is. i. 5; Eccl. ii. 23; Gen. xviii. 5; Ps. civ. 15, &c. (c) The seat of the various affections, Judg. xvi. 15; Deut. iv. 29; vi. 5; Prov. v. 12; xxxi. 11; lvii. 8; lxxiii. 21; cix. 16; Eccl. ii. 20, &c. Hence said to be *sad, sorry,*

לב (320) לבב

wounded, grieving, &c., Prov. xiii. 12; xiv. 13; Is. lxi. 1. And hence, again, melted, hardened, uncircumcised, Is. xiii. 7; Deut. xx. 8; Ezek. xi. 19; xxxvi. 26. Hence also certain actions are ascribed to it, Hos. vii. 14; Is. xxxiii. 18; Ps. xxxviii. 9; Lam. ii. 19. And, hence, said to be vested with moral qualities, as *pure, &c.*, Ps. li. 12; ci. 4; lxiv. 7; 1 Kings iii. 6; ix. 4; Neh. ix. 8; Prov. vii. 10; Job xxxvi. 13. And hence the phrr. בְּלֵב וָלֵב, *in heart and heart*, i. e. saying one thing, but intending another, Ps. xii. 3. Comp. 1 Chron. xii. 38. רְחַב —, *broad*, assuming; easy, Prov. xxi. 4; Is. lx. 5. גֹּדֶל —, greatness of —, Is. ix. 9. גֹּבַהּ —, *highness*, haughtiness of —, Ezek. xxviii. 5. אֲשֶׁר בִּלְבָבְךָ, *What is in thy heart*; i. e. intention, will, &c., 1 Sam. xiv. 7; xiii. 14; Is. x. 7; lxiii. 4. חֲכַם לֵב, *wise of heart*, Job ix. 4. Comp. 1 Kings x. 24. חֲסַר־לֵב, *deficient of heart*, i. e. of understanding, Prov. vii. 7; ix. 4. אַנְשֵׁי לֵב, *men of heart*, i. e. of understanding, Job xxxiv. 10. לִי לֵבָב, *to me is heart*, i. e. intelligence, Ib. xii. 3. פַּח לֵב, *might of heart*; prevailing wisdom, Ib. xxxvi. 5. See my note. יִגְנֹב אֶת־לֵב, *he stole, as to the heart*, i. e. he stole away secretly, not having spoken of it, Gen. xxxi. 20. יְדַבֵּר עַל לֵב, he spoke to *the heart of* —, i. e. kindly, affectionately, 2 Chron. xxxii. 6, &c. בֹּחֵן לֵב, *trying, examining, the heart*, 1 Chron. xxix. 17, &c. To which a very great variety may still be added; which, however, the student will profitably collect for himself.

Metaph. *The middle*, or *interior, part of anything*, Exod. xv. 8; Ps. xlvi. 2. Of the sea, Deut. iv. 11: of heaven, 2 Sam. xviii. 14: of a certain tree. Aff. לְבָבִי, לְבָבְנוּ, לְבָבְךָ, לְבָבוֹ, &c.

לְבַב, לֵב, Chald. i. q. Heb. Aff. לִבִּי, לִבְבָךְ, לִבְבֵהּ, Dan. ii. 30; iv. 13; vii. 4. 28, &c. Hence the verb—

Niph. pres. יִלָּבֵב, once, Job xi. 12. *Takes heart, becomes bold, daring.* Arab.

لَبَّ, conj. iv. *incessu vehementi fuit.* Syr. ܠܒܒ, *audax fuit.* See my note on the passage. Symm. διακενής θρασύνεται. LXX. νήχεται λόγοις. See Schleusn. Lex. Vet. Test. sub voce νήχω.

Pih. לִבֵּב, pres. f. תְּלַבֵּב, constr. immed. lit. I. *Gave heart* to any one; *encouraged, emboldened,* Cant. iv. 9. Symm. and vers. E. ἐθάρσυνάς με. LXX. ἐκαρδίωσας ἡμᾶς. "*Ab-stulit* alicui *cor.*" Gesen. A notion foreign to Biblical usage, but common enough to modern balladmakers.

II. *Make* certain *cakes*, termed לִבְבוֹת: a sort of pancakes, apparently, 2 Sam. xiii. 6. 8, al. non occ.

לְבִבוֹת, fem. pl. sing. non occ. Arab. لُبَابٌ, *sinceritas* rei: *simila* (perfectissimum) tritici; *medulla* panis. *A sort of pancakes*, made perhaps of the finest wheat flour, 2 Sam. xiii. 6—8. 10. LXX. κολλυρίδας.

לַבָּה, f. contr. of לֶהָבָה, Gram. art. 73, constr. לַבַּת, once, Exod. iii. 2. בְּלַבַּת אֵשׁ, *in a flame of fire*.

לִבָּה, f. of לֵב; whence the pl. לִבּוֹת, once, Ezek. xvi. 30. Aff. f. לִבָּתֵךְ, *thy heart*. Pl., Ps. vii. 10; Prov. xv. 11, &c. See לֵב, above.

לְבוֹנָה, see לְבָנָה, below.

לְבוּשׁ, and לְבֻשׁ, masc. pl. non occ. r. לבשׁ. *Upper*, or *outer, garment*, 2 Kings x. 22; Esth. vi. 8; Is. xiv. 19; Job xiv. 7. 10; xxxi. 19; xxxviii. 14; and xli. 5. See my notes. In Mal. ii. 16. This term has of late much been taken to signify *a wife*. The passage seems obscure; but, after mature consideration, will, I think, be found to contain no such sense. The context manifestly treats on the inhumanity then shown by the Israelites to their wives. The verse under consideration thus proceeds, *when* one *hates, he dismisses* (saying) *Jehovah, the God of Israel, has* (so) *commanded. And so he conceals violence with his cloak*, i. e. when any one chooses to dislike his wife, he divorces her at once, citing the precept (Deut. xxiv. 1) of divorce; and by this means he cloaks over his violent conduct. It is very true the Arab. لِبَاسٌ, is used to imply either wife or husband, as Pococke (on this place), Schultens (on Ps. lxv. 14), and Michaelis (sup. Lex. Heb. n. 1272), have shown; but, then, the Arabian usage is anything but this of the prophet; which is quite direct. Besides, the construction of פָּשָׂה עַל (see under the verb above) cannot be fairly applied in any such sense: which was not then known. I am compelled to conclude, therefore, that the whole is founded on mistake.

לְבֻשׁ, m. Chald. pl. aff. לְבֻשֵׁיהוֹן, i. q. Heb. occ. only, Dan. iii. 21; vii. 9.

לָבַט, v. Kal non occ. Syr. ܠܒܛ, concitavit. Arab. لَبَطَ, festinavit, &c. Hurry, generally implying failure. See v. חוּשׁ, p. 189.

Niph. pret. non occ. pres. יִלָּבֵט, Stumbles, falls, Prov. x. 8. 10; Hos. iv. 14. Aquila, δαρήσεται. Symm. βασανισθήσεται. Theod. φυρήσεται. LXX. ὑποσκαλισθήσεται.

לְבִי, c. (i. q. לָבִיא, see Gram. art. 74), pl. לְבָאִים, f. לְבָאוֹת. Lion, generally, Nah. ii. 13. Metaph., Ps. lvii. 5. Arab. لَبِيَ, multum expetivit cibi. Cogn. لَبّ. Syr. ܠܒܒ, was bold, &c. See לבב above. לָבִיא, "a rugiendo dictus," says Gesenius. On what authority he does not say. I can find none. Aff. לְבָאָיו, Nah. l. c.

לָבִיא, m. pl., see לְבִי. A fierce she lion, according to Bochart. Hieroz. i. p. 719. Gesenius objects, because Ezek. xix. 2, on which the argument of Bochart. rests, is written לָבִיא. Bochart. saw this, and objected to the punctuation of the word there, declaring that it was contrary to analogy, "contra analogiam." Probably Bochart. is right. Arab. لَبْوَة, لَبَاة, لَبُوَة, &c. Lœna. See Lex. Arab. Freytag. sub v. لَبَا, Gen. xlix. 9; Num. xxiii. 24; xxiv. 9; Deut. xxxiii. 20; Job iv. 11; xxxviii. 39; Is. v. 29; xxx. 6, &c. LXX. λέων, σκύμνος.

לְבִיָּא, f. Ezek. xix. 2. See לָבִיא above. LXX. σκύμνος. Ἀλλ. λέαινα.

לָבָן, m. pl. לְבָנִים } constr. sing. m. לְבָן, לְבָנָה, f. pl. לְבֵנוֹת } once, Gen. xlix. 12. Arab. لَبَن, lac. (a) White, Gen. xxx. 35; Exod. xvi. 31; Zech. vi. 3; Lev. xiii. 4. 10; Gen. xxx. 37, &c. (b) Proper name, Laban, Gen. xxiv. 29, &c. (c) לְבָנָה, used in the more emphatic style, to signify the moon (from its whiteness), as חַמָּה is for the sun (from its heat). So Arab. قَمَر, albus fuit, of قَمَر, the moon. Gesen. Is. xxiv. 23; xxx. 26; Cant. vi. 10, al. non occ.

לָבֵן, v. pres. 2 pers. pl. with ה parag. נִלְבְּנָה (of לָבֵן below). Let us make bricks or tiles, Gen. xi. 3, only.

Infin. לְבֹן, with prep. ל, Exod. v. 7. 14, only. Arab. لَبَّن, lateres formavit e luto, coxitque.

Hiph. הִלְבִּין, pres. יַלְבִּין, constr. abs. et. immed. (a) Be, become, white, pure, Is. i. 18; Joel i. 7; Ps. li. 9. (b) Make white, clean, Dan. xi. 35, al. non occ.

Hith. pres. יִתְחַלְּבוּ, They shall be, become, white, clean, Dan. xii. 10, only.

לְבֵנָה, fem.—pl. masc. לְבֵנִים, constr. לְבְנֵי, Exod. v. 19. Arab. لَبِن, later e luto coctus. Brick, or tile, as made of chalky or white earth, according to Vitruvius. ii. 3, and Harmer. observ. 15, ch. iii. vol. i. edit. 1816..... Gen. xi. 3; Exod. v. 16. 18; Is. ix. 9; Ezek. iv. 1, &c.

לִבְנֶה, m. twice, Gen. xxx. 37; Hos. iv. 13. The white poplar. Arab. لُبْنَى. See Celsius, Hierobot. i. p. 292, seq. See ll. cc. in the Gr. of the LXX.

לִבְנָה, f. once, constr. לִבְנַת, Exod. xxiv. 10. Whiteness, according to some: others take the word as derived from לְבֵנָה, as signifying tiled, or paved, work. See LXX.

לְבוֹנָה, and לְבֹנָה. Aff. לְבֹנָתָהּ. Gr. λίβανος, λιβανωτός. The purest frankincense, so called from its whiteness. Plin. H. N. lib. xii. c. xiv.; Lev. ii. 1. 15; v. 11; xxiv. 7; Num. v. 15; Is. lx. 6; Jer. vi. 20; Cant. iv. 6. 14, &c. The tree which produces it, is, according to Ibn Batuta (see my Translation, p. 61), termed الكُنْدُر, El Kondor. It "has a thin leaf, which, when scarified, produces a fluid like milk; this turns into gum, and then is called lobān." Whence, no doubt, with the article el, we have the "olibanum" of the druggists.

לְבָנוֹן, m. The Libanus, or Lebanon; so called from the whiteness of the snow always resting on its highest eastern point. In simple prose, always with the definite article, הַלְּבָנוֹן, according to Gesenius, 1 Kings v. 6. 9, &c. In the more lofty style, always without it, Ps. xxix. 6; Is. xiv. 8, &c. It may here be remarked that, generally, the lofty style excludes all particles, as much as is consistent with perspicuity: of which the student will satisfy himself by comparing a Psalm, or

T T

לבש (322) לבש

a passage in the middle part of the book of Job, with the same quantity of context in the style of mere narrative.

לָבַשׁ, and לָבֵשׁ, pres. יִלְבַּשׁ, constr. abs. it. immed. it. med. אֶת, it. בְּ, instr., Esth. vi. 8, &c. Syr. ܠܒܫ, vestivit se. Samar. Æth. id. Arab. لَبِسَ, id. it. obscuram, et confusam illi effecit, proposuitque rem. Put on clothing; cloak, &c., Lev. vi. 3, 4; xvi. 23, &c. Metaph. as clothing is supposed to cover the body, so certain qualities are also supposed to affect it: as, majesty, &c., Ps. civ. 1. — power, Is. li. 9. — the worm, Job vii. 5. — slain, men, Is. xiv. 19. — ignominy, Job viii. 22; Ps. xxxv. 26; cix. 29. — justice, Job xxix. 14. — righteousness, &c., Is. lix. 17. — terror, Ezek. xxvi. 16. — ruin, Ezek. vii. 27. — salvation, 2 Chron. vi. 41. Applied also to the fields, as covered with flocks, Ps. lxv. 14. See בַּד, above. — to the influences of the Holy Spirit, as overshadowing (Luke i. 35), and actuating the whole man, Judg. vi. 34; 1 Chron. xii. 18; 2 Chron. xxiv. 20. Hence the virtues of the mantle of Elisha, 1 Kings xix. 20: comp. v. 16. — of the handkerchiefs and aprons taken from the body of Paul, Acts xix. 12. — of touching the garment of Christ, Matt. ix. 20, &c. — of the shadow of Peter, Acts v. 15.

Infin. לָבוֹשׁ, abs., Hag. i. 6: it. לִלְבֹּשׁ, Gen. xxviii. 20; Lev. xxi. 10.

Imp. לְבַשׁ, 1 Kings xxii. 30: f. לִבְשִׁי, 2 Sam. xiv. 2: pl. לִבְשׁוּ, Jer. xlvi. 4.

Part. pl. m. לֹבְשִׁים, Zeph. i. 8.
— pass. לָבוּשׁ, constr. לְבוּשׁ, 1 Sam. xvii. 5; Prov. xxxi. 21, &c.

Puh. Part. masc. pl. only, מְלֻבָּשִׁים, Being, becoming, clothed, 1 Kings xxii. 10, &c.

Hiph. הִלְבִּישׁ, pres. יַלְבִּישׁ. Constr. immed. it. med. אֶת, it. med. עַל, on, upon, Gen. xxvii. 16: כְּ, of. Clothe any one, Is. lxi. 10: the בְּ of instr. being understood, Gram. art. 220. On this place, see also under letter ב above, Gen. xli. 42; Exod. xxviii. 41, &c. Metaph. — with salvation, Ps. cxxxii. 16; Is. l. c. — shame, Ps. cxxxii. 18. — scorn, of the neck of the horse, Job xxxix. 19. See my note. — heaven with blackness, Is. L. 3.

Infin. הַלְבִּישׁ, Esth. iv. 4.
Imp. הַלְבֵּשׁ, Zech. iii. 4.
Part. aff. מַלְבִּשְׁכֶם, Clothing you, 2 Sam. i. 24.

לְבֵשׁ, v. Chald. pres. יִלְבַּשׁ, i. q. Heb. Dan. v. 7. 16, only.
Aph. pl. masc. הַלְבִּישׁוּ, i. q. Heb. Hiph. Dan. v. 29, med. לְ, pers. immed. thing, al. non occ.

לְבוּשׁ, לָבוּשׁ, see לָבַשׁ, and לְבוּשׁ.

לֹג, m.—pl. non occ. The Log, a liquid measure among the Jews, containing, according to Dr. Aubuthnot, 24·3 dec. solid inches. Syr. ܠܓܬܐ, pelvis, Lev. xiv. 10. 12. 15. 21. 24, al. non occ.

לַח, Chald. i. q. לֹא, Heb. לֹא.
לֹח, i. q. לֹא, Kethiv, Deut. iii. 11.
לַהַב, m. pl. לְהָבִים, constr. לַהֲבֵי. Arab. لهب, lingua ignis, flamma. Flame—

לֶהָבָה, f. pl. לְהָבוֹת, constr. לַהֲבוֹת, constr. sing. לַהֶבֶת, pointed like a tongue, and hence, perhaps, applied to weapons, the lightning, &c.; or the comparison might have originated in the brightness or flashing of each, Judg. xiii. 20; Is. xiii. 8; lxvi. 15. — of lightning, Joel ii. 5; Is. xxix. 6. — of a sword, Nah. iii. 3; Job xxxix. 23, &c. Meton. the weapon itself, Judg. iii. 22. See under גָּבַר, p. 117, above. Fem., Num. xxi. 28; Ps. cvi. 18; Is. iv. 5; Dan. xi. 33; Ezek. xxi. 3; Ps. cv. 32; xxix. 7, &c.

לַהַג, masc. once, Eccl. xii. 12. Arab. لهج, Act. v. لهج, addictus fuit rei. Intense occupation, study. Jauhari, اللهجة اللسان وقد يحرك فلان فصيح اللهجة, i. e. اللهجة the tongue; and, with a vowel, eloquent of tongue. See סְפָרִים in the preceding member.

לָהַה, v. cogn. לאה, once, pres. f. apoc. תֵּלַהּ. Faint, feeble, languishing, Gen. xlvii. 13. LXX. ἐξέλιπε.
Hithp. redup. part. מִתְלַהְלֵהַּ, once, Prov. xxvi. 18. Syr. ܐܬܠܗܠܗ, obstupuit. Arab. لهلهة, terra ampla nebulæ obnoxia; i. e. subject to the mirage. Insane, mad, person. Aquila, κακοθιζόμενοι. Symm. πειρώμετοι. LXX. ὥσπερ οἱ ἰωμένοι.

לְהֱוֵן, Chald. r. הוא, under הָיָה.

לחט (323) לו

לָהַט, masc. i. q. לַהַב, once, Gen. iii. 24.
Syr. ܠܰܗܛܳܐ, *flamma.* Hence—

להט, v. pret. pres. non occ.
Part. לֹהֵט, pl. לֹהֲטִים, *Flaming* fire, Ps. civ. 4. *Inflamed,* furious men, Ib. lvii. 5.
Pih. לִהֵט, pres. f. תְּלַהֵט, *Set on fire, inflame.* Constr. immed., Deut. xxxii. 22; Is. xlii. 25; Joel i. 19; ii. 3; Ps. lxxxiii. 15; xcvii. 3; cvi. 18; Job xli. 13.

לַהֲטֵיהֶם, masc. plur. aff. of לַהַט, once, Exod. vii. 11: lit. *their flames.* Meton. *Dazzlings,* i. e. specious tricks, such as to deceive and amaze the ignorant: usually, *their enchantments.* Aquila, ἐν ἠρεμαίοις αὐτῶν. Symm. ἀποκρύφων αὐτῶν. Theod. φαρμακείαις αὐτῶν. See LXX. Or, for לָאֲטִים, r. לאט, or לוט, *covered, secret.*

להם, v. Kal non occ. Arab. لَهَمَ, *insinuavit, imbuit, &c.*
Hithp. part. m. pl. מִתְלַהֲמִים, twice, Prov. xviii. 8; xxvi. 22. *Enchanting, fascinating* (things), i. e. *insinuating themselves.* Gesen. " Quæ avidè deglutiuntur, *buccellæ dulces.*" But, whence these *buccellæ dulces?* Some moral effect is evidently had in view by the sacred writer. חַדְרֵי בָטֶן, must, therefore, signify the inmost recesses of the mind: and מִתְלַהֲמִים cannot signify any eatable. Aquila, γοητικοί, well. Theod. ἐξαπλούμενοι.

לָהֵן, compd. of הֵן + לְ. See הֵן above. *Therefore, on that account,* Ruth i. 13; Dan. ii. 6. *But,* Dan. ii. 30; Ezra v. 12. *Besides, except* (compd. of הֵן + לֹא), Dan. ii. 11; iii. 28; vi. 8. See Nold. p. 431. And, *Annotationes et Vindiciæ.*

לַהֲקַת, f. constr. once, 1 Sam. xix. 20, transposed, for קְהִלַּת *congregation,* as some think, i. e. f. of קָהָל. Others, after de Dieu, *senate,* or *presbytery,* from the Æth. ᎡᎮ: *princeps, &c.* Aquila, ὅμιλον. Symm. συστροφήν. Theod. σύστημα. LXX. ἐκκλησίαν.

לַהֲשׂוֹת, Infin. Hiph. with לְ pref. r. שָׁעָה.

לוֹ, thrice for לֹא, which see.
לוּ, and thrice לוּא, 1 Sam. xiv. 30; Is. xlviii. 18; lxiii. 19, once, לֻא, *kethiv,* 2 Sam. xviii. 12, r. לוה. Arab. لَوَى, *flexit, &c.* Not unlike אִם, or כִּי, except that negation is always implied: and, therefore, cognate in some respects with לֹא, לוֹא. A particle implying *conditionality* with *negation,* and requiring the verb (either expressed or implied) to be taken in *a past,* or *relatively past,* tense. See my note on Job vi. 2. As the Hebrew and sister dialects have neither *Conditional* nor *Subjunctive* moods, all oblique modes of expression must be made, either by the introduction of particles adequate to that purpose, or by such forms of the verb as custom might have allowed to have that effect. But here this (i. e. apocope, paragoge, &c., Gram. art. 233, seq.) implies nothing beyond relation to something preceding. Obliquity, therefore, or indirectness of expression can be had only by means of particles: of which this (לוּ) is one; and is used with verbs either in the pret. pres. or participle active: to be construed nevertheless always in the past, or relatively past tense; e. g. לוּ חָכְמוּ, HAD *they been* (which they were not) *wise,* then—Deut. xxxii. 29, לוּ הַחֲיתֶם אוֹתָם, *had you* (but you did not) *saved them alive,* Judg. viii. 19. לוּ....אַעֲבִיר בָּאָרֶץ, *should I cause to pass* (which I do not) *over the land,* Ezek. xiv. 15. —— כִּי אִישׁ הֹלֵךְ רוּחַ, *should a man vagrant of spirit,* i. e. whose mind is vagrant and uncertain as the wind, Mic. ii. 11. לוּ יְשִׁמְּמֵנוּ, *should Joseph deal cruelly with us,* Gen. L. 15, &c.

In certain situations it implies a wish, intimating negation, nevertheless, at the same time. לוּ יִשְׁמָעֵאל יִחְיֶה, *would Ishmael might live! &c.,* i. e. in the sense implied by the context, Gen. xvii. 18. Such is the ηὐχόμην (supp. ἄν) of Paul, Rom. ix. 3. See my note above-mentioned. Of this sort is the ἂν δυνητική of the Attics, by which obliquity of expression is often intimated with verbs in the Indicative mood. See Vigerus de idiot. Græc. cap. v., sect. ii., Ed. 1824, p. 195, seq. Hoogeveen, Doctr. partic. Glasg. 1813, p. 30, seq. Thes. Steph., Ed. Valpy, sub voce, p. 1978, seq. Num. xiv. 2; Josh. vii. 7; Ps. lxxxi. 14, &c. See Nold., p. 431, seq. In some of which cases futurity seems implied; still, as the speaker in every case places himself in time farther future, the action, &c. of the verbs will be relatively in the past tense, and always in estimation negatived. Here, therefore, as in אִם, and כִּי, a fact is put as a case: but, unlike those particles, a negation is inherent in the supposition.

This particle is occasionally omitted by the

לוה (324) לוט

ellipsis, Cant. i. 2; Ps. cxxii. 6, &c. Nold. p. 432.

לָוָה, v. pres. 2d pers. תִּלְוֶה. Arab. لَوَى, contorsit membrum; inficiatus fuit quod deberet; protraxit solvendi moram. Constr. immed. it. med. לְ, for; it. abs. Borrow at usury, &c., Neh. v. 4; Deut. xxviii. 12. Meton. Get, obtain, Eccl. viii. 15.

Part. לֹוֶה, Borrower, borrowing, Ps. xxxvii. 21; Prov. xxii. 7; Is. xxiv. 2.

Niph. נִלְוָה, pres. יִלָּוֶה. Constr. med. עִם, אֶל, עַל. Be, become, turned, attached, joined, to any one, Gen. xxix. 34; Num. xviii. 2. 4; Is. xiv. 1; Ps. lxxxiii. 9; Jer. L. 5; Dan. xi. 34; Zech. ii. 15.

Part. נִלְוֶה, Is. lvi. 3: pl. נִלְוִים, Is. lvi. 6; Esth. ix. 27.

Hiph. הִלְוָה, pres. 2d pers. תַּלְוֶה. Constr. immed. it. abs. Make, cause, to borrow. Meton. Lend, Exod. xxii. 24; Deut. xxviii. 12. 44.

Part. מַלְוֶה, Is. xxiv. 2; Ps. cxii. 5; Prov. xix. 17; xxii. 7.

לוּז, m. once, Gen. xxx. 7. The almond tree. Arab. لَوْز, of which there are three sorts, the sweet (الحلو), the bitter (المر), both cultivated in orchards: the wild (البري), or mountain (الجبلي); probably that mentioned here. It grows into a large tree, the leaves of which are soft. Cels. Hierobot. i., p. 253, seq. Its medical properties are described at length in the Medical Dictionary of Ibn Hosein, of Bagdad, entitled, اختيارات بديعي, occasionally cited in this work.

לוּז, v. pres. only, pl. יָלֻזוּ. Constr. med. מִן. Arab. لَانَ, r. لون, confugit. Escape, depart, from, Prov. iii. 21.

Niph. Part. נָלוֹז, constr. נְלוֹז, pl. נְלוֹזִים. Arab. لَانَ, r. لون, perversus, contumax fuit. Perverse, incorrigible, Prov. iii. 32; xiv. 2; Is. xxx. 12. בְּעֹשֶׁק וְנָלוֹז, in oppression, and the perverse man, in any person, opposed to God's laws. Pl., Prov. ii. 14.

Hiph. pres. only, יַלִּיזוּ, Prov. iv. 21, i. q. Kal, above, if the cognate ליז is not the root.

לוּחַ, m.—pl. f. לוּחֹת, לֻחֹת, dual, לֻחֹתַיִם. Syr. ܠܘܚܐ, tabula. Arab. لَوْح, id. A tablet of stone or wood, Deut. ix. 9: hence, Ib. לוּחֹת הַבְּרִית, tables of the covenant, Ib. vr. 10, 11. 15; x. 1. הָעֵדוּת —, of the testimony, Exod. xxxi. 18; xxxiv. 29. — of wood, 1 Kings vii. 36. The leaf of a folding-door, Cant. viii. 9. The deck of a ship, dual, Ezek. xxvii. 5. Hence, apparently, the leaf of a book, Is. xxx. 8. Metaph. of the heart, Jer. xvii. 1; Prov. iii. 3. Comp. 2 Cor. iii. 3.

לוֹט, masc. once, Is. xxv. 7. Arab. لَوْط, pallium, &c. Covering, vail, i. e. means of blinding. Comp. 2 Cor. iii. 13, seq. Aquila, Theod. πρόσωπον τῆς σκοτίας. Symm. πρόσωπον τοῦ ἐξουσιαστοῦ.

לוּט, v. i. q. לאט, above, Kal non occ. except—

Infin. abs. לוֹט (for לָווֹט, fm. פָקוֹד, Gram. art. 75), Vailing, acting as a cover, &c. once, Is. xxv. 7.

Part. לָט, Covering, concealing, i. e. secret, covert, manner, Ruth iii. 7; 1 Sam. xviii. 22; xxiv. 5: it. לָאט, as קָאם, for קָם, Hos. x. 14;—Judg. iv. 21.

— pl. m. aff. לְטֵיהֶם, Their covered, i. e. secret arts, Exod. vii. 22; viii. 3. 14, al. non occ. See under להט above.

— pass. f. לוּטָה (for לָווּטָה, Gram. art. 75). Covered, wrapt up, 1 Sam. xxi. 10.

לֵוִי, masc. (for לִוְיִי, Gram. art. 75), A Levite, pl. לְוִיִם: of the proper name לֵוִי, Exod. iv. 14; vi. 25, &c. Chald. sing. id. pl. def. לֵוָיֵא, Ezra vi. 16, &c.

לִוְיָה, f. constr. לִוְיַת, pl. non occ. r. לָוָה, above, non occ. r. לָוָה, above, non occ. r. לָוָה, above. A wreath, or chaplet, for the head, Prov. i. 9; iv. 9, al. non occ. Aquila, προσθήκη. LXX. στέφανον. More literally, δέμα, or δῆμα; whence διάδημα.

לִוְיָתָן, masc. sing. only, r. לָוָה. On the termination, see Gram. art. 168, and my notes on Job iii. 8; xl. 25. Any sea monster, generally, the whale, or the sea serpent, as the context may require. Bochart. Hieroz. ii. lib. v. cap. xvi., and Ib. cap. xviii. makes it to signify the crocodile; which has generally been followed. His view is, nevertheless, groundless. See my notes above cited. I. Any sea-monster, generally, Ps. lxxiv. 14; civ. 26. Comp. תַּנִּין, Is. li. 9; Ezek. xxix. 3; xxxii. 2, 3.

לוּל

II. *The sea-serpent*, applied as a symbol of the king of Babylon, Is. xxvii. 1. III. *The whale*, of the fiercer sort, Job iii. 8; xl. 25, seq. LXX. μέγα κῆτος. Theod. δράκοντα, Job iii. 8. LXX. δράκοντα, cap. xli. 1.

לוּל, m. pl. לוּלִים, once, 1 Kings vi. 8. Gesenius traces an affinity here with the German *rollen*; our *roll*. *The winding stairs* leading from the lower to the upper chambers of the Temple. See Plan of the Temple in the Appendix. LXX. ἑλικτὴ ἀνάβασις: See Schleusn. Lex. in LXX. sub voce ἑλικτός.

לְלָאוֹת, and לֻלָאוֹת, constr. לֻלְאֹת, pl. f. sing. non occ. Arab. لُولَاءُ, *angustia*. *Loops*, or *loop-holes* perhaps, made in the edges of the curtains of the Tabernacle, into which the golden hooks of the next succeeding curtain were inserted, Exod. xxvi. 4, seq.; xxxvi. 11, seq. LXX. συμβολή. See Schleusn. Lex. in LXX. sub voce.

לוּלֵי, and לוּלֵא, compd. of לֹא + לוּ or of לוּ + לֵי (לִי), Syr. ܠܘܠܐ; the final ן being taken as a mark of construction, as, ܡܠܟܬܐ, for ܡܠܟܬܐ, Syr. for אִמָּא, אִמָּא being also an augmented fm. of אֵם, cogn. הָיָה. Whence the Arab. أَيْ, *id est, nimirum, &c.* And the Syr. ܐܝܕܐ, *quæ illa*. It was shown under לוּ above, that לוּ always implied *negation*. The addition of the second negative here, has the effect of making the sense *positive* in the second member of the sentence, which is hypothetically negatived in the first; as, ... לוּלֵי אֱלֹהֵי אָבִי הָיָה לִי כִּי .... וַיְקָם שִׁלַּחְתָּנִי, *had not the God of my father been for me; surely thou hadst dismissed me empty*, Gen. xxxi. 42; Deut. xxxii. 27; 1 Sam. xxv. 34; Is. i. 9; Ps. xciv. 17; cvi. 23, &c. Both the composition of this conj. particle, with its usage and sense, is very nearly allied to the English *unless*. LXX. εἰ μή. With כִּי Nold. כִּי, §. 33, p. 377: and, for the word itself, Ib. p. 432.

לוּן, and לִין, v. pret. לָן, 1st pers. pl. לַנּוּ, pres. יָלִין, apoc. יָלֶן, constr. abs. it. med. בְּ, in, of time or place, or state; בְּתוֹךְ, *in the midst*; בְּדוּדִי, *without*; פֹּה, *here*; לְ, *to, until*; אֶת, *with*; עַל, *near, on*; בֵּין, *between*. Arab.

(325)

לוּץ

لَانَ, r. لِين, *placidus fuit*; لَيَانٌ, *placiditas*; سَكَنَ, *procrastinatio*. In like manner, سَكَنَ, *quietus fuit*; thence, *habitavit*: and so also the English *lie*, *rest*; remain fixed, reside, &c. *Lodge, remain*, during the night, Gen. xxxii. 22; 2 Sam. xii. 16; Judg. xix. 13. Fem. לָנָה, for לִינָה, Zech. v. 4: so הַלִּינָה, for הַלִּינָה, Is. lix. 5. Pres., Exod. xxiii. 18; xxxiv. 25; Deut. xvi. 4; Job xxix. 19; xli. 14, &c., of things inanimate: weeping, Ps. xxx. 6: righteousness, Is. i. 21. Apoc., Gen. xxviii. 11; xxxii. 14, &c.: vain thoughts, Jer. iv. 14: verb fem. sing. with pl., Gram. art. 216. 7.

Infin. לוּן, with לְ, לָלִין, Gen. xxiv. 25; Judg. xix. 10, &c.

It. לִין? — לְלִין, Gen. xxiv. 23.

Imp. לִין, Judg. xix. 6. 9.

— f. לִינִי, Ruth iii. 13.

— plur. לִינוּ, Num. xxii. 8; Judg. xix. 9, &c.

Part. pl. m. לָנִים (for לוֹנִים, or לָנִים, Gram. art. 75), Neh. xiii. 21, only.

Niph. pres. pl. only, יִלּוֹנוּ, constr. med. עַל, *against*. Arab. لَوَّنَ, *colore infecit; mutavit animi affectum*. *Complain, murmur*, Exod. xv. 24; xvi. 2; Num. xiv. 2; xvii. 6; Josh. ix. 18.

Hiph. plur. 2d pers. הֲלִינֹתֶם, pres. pl. הַלִּינוּ, (ה עֵלִינוּ) being compensated by Dagesh, in order to preserve a difference from Kal); but, apoc. יָלֶן, as before. Constr. עַל, i. q. Niph. *complain, murmur*, Exod. xvi. 7; Num. xiv. 29. 36; xvi. 11. Apoc., Exod. xvii. 3.

Part. pl. m. מַלִּינִים מַלִּינָם, Exod. xvi. 8; Num. xiv. 27; xvii. 20.

לוּץ, v. pret. לָץ, once, Prov. ix. 12. Arab. لَاصَ, r. لوص, *aspexit per rimas portæ; ænigmaticè locutus est;* conj. iii. *aspexit veluti meditabundus* ad bonum,—ad malum. *Deride, scorn*.

Part. לֵץ (for לָיֵץ, or Gram. art. 75), pl. לֵצִים (the [-] immutable, because compensating for the loss of ־י). *Scorner; deriding, insulting*, person, Prov. ix. 7, 8; xiv. 6; xv. 12, &c. Pl., Ps. i. 1; Prov. i. 22, &c. It. לֵצִים, of the cogn. לִיץ, for מְלִיצִים, Pih. of לוּץ, as Gesenius thinks.

Hiph. plur. aff. הֱלִיצֻנִי, *They have derided me*, Ps. cxix. 51, only, pres. יָלִיץ, Prov. iii.

34; xiv. 9; xix. 28. Constr. immed. it. med. לֹ.

Part. מֵלִיץ, pl. constr. מְלִיצֵי. *Advocate, or person undertaking, explaining, &c.* the business of another, Job xxxiii. 23. מַלְאָךְ מֵלִיץ, *interceding angel, mediator.* Comp. xvi. 20. See my notes. Such generally were all angels appearing on the business of the Almighty. Gen. xlii. 23, *Interpreter. Ambassadors, orators*, 2 Chron. xxxii. 31; Is. xliii. 27. LXX. ἄρχων, ἑρμηνευτής; πρεσβύτης, θανατοφόρος. Aff. מְלִיצֶיךָ מְלִיצַי.

Hithp. תִּתְלוֹצָצוּ, *Be mocking, deriding*, once, Is. xxviii. 22. Aquila, χλευάζετε. LXX. εὐφρανθείητε.

לוּשׁ, v. pret. non occ. pres. f. תָּלָשׁ, constr. immed. Syr. ܠܫ, *depsit* farinam. Æth. ᎓᎐Ꮎ : id. *Knead dough,* 1 Sam. xxviii. 24; 2 Sam. xiij. 8.

Infin. לוּשׁ, Hos. vii. 4, only.

Imp. f. לוּשִׁי, Gen. xviii. 6.

Part. fem. pl. לָשׁוֹת, *Women kneading,* Jer. vii. 18.

לְוָת, Chald. Syr. ܠܘܬ, *ad, apud*; v. ܠܘܬ, *conjunxit.* Cogn. Heb. לָוָה. Prep. aff. לְוָתָךְ, once, Ezra iv. 12. *With thee.*

לָז, see הַלָּז.

לָזֶה, see הַלָּזֶה.

לָזוּ, see הַלָּזוּ.

לְזוּת, f. r. לוּז, cogn. לוּץ לִיץ; which see: once, Prov. iv. 24: with עִקְּשׁוּת in the paral. Cogn. Arab. لصا, *conviciis incessivit. Perverseness.*

לַח, masc. pl. לַחִים, with *dagesh* implied, Gram. art. 109. Æthiopic ᎃᎀᎻᎀᎻ : *madefacere* panem. Arab. لخ, *lacrymosus fuit* oculus: cogn. لخيان, *aqua modica a monte fluens. Moist, fresh* (green), opp. τῷ, יבש. Comp. Judg. xvi. 7; Ezek. xxi. 3; xvii. 24; Gen. xxx. 37, of wood. Num. vi. 3, of grapes. Judg. xvi. 7, 8, of *new ropes,* made probably of the fibres of the cocoa-nut tree: hence, said to be *not dried,* אל חרבו. See my Travels of Ibn Batuta, pp. 177, 178, with the notes, and Rees's Cyclopædia, art. *cocos.*

לֵחַ, m. once, Deut. xxxiv. 7. *Freshness, vigour,* of youth. Aff. לֵחֹה, for לֵחוֹ.

LXX. χελώνια, al. χελύνια, αὐτοῦ. Ἄλλως χελύνια αὐτοῦ, ὁ δέ Εβραῖος, τὰ χλωρὰ αὐτοῦ. Bahrdt's Hexapla.

לָחוּם, aff. and prep. בִּלְחוּמוֹ, Job xx. 23. *In his eating, feasting.* Comp. Ps. lxxviii. 30, 31; and see my note on the place: r. לָחֶם. Arab. لحم, *carnis appetens; carnivorus;* לָחוּם is used, Prov. xxiii. 1, in the same sense; the variety in the pointing is of little authority. See v. לָחֶם. In Zeph. i. 17; aff. לְחֻמָם, *their flesh;* opp. τῷ, דָּמָם, *their blood.* Arab. لحم, *caro,* al. non occ.

לְחִי, in pause לֶחִי, f. dual, לְחָיַיִם, constr. לְחָיֵי. Arab. لحى, *mandibula, maxilla;* لحيه, *barba.* *The cheek,* or *cheek-bone,* or *jaw-bone,* Judg. xv. 15—17; Job xl. 26; Is. xxx. 28; Ezek. xxix. 4; Hos. xi. 4. And, as the beard (growing thereon) was reverenced, *striking* any one on the *cheek,* or *jaw,* was considered peculiarly reproachful, 1 Kings xxii. 24; Mic. iv. 14; Is. L. 6; Job xvi. 10; Lam. iii. 30: in Ps. iii. 8, the reader is carried on to the breaking even of the teeth. Aff. לֶחְיִי, לְחָיַי, לְחֵיהֶם. See LXX.

לָחַח, v. Kal non occ., except Infin. Syr. ܠܚܟ, *linxit.* Engl. *lick.* Sanscrit, लिह्, id.—

Infin. constr. לְחֹךְ, *Licking up,* as an ox in eating, Num. xxii. 4, only.

Pih. fem. לִחֲכָה, *Licked,* or *lapped, up,* as a dog does water, 1 Kings xviii. 38. Pres. pl. m. יְלַחֲכוּ, Num. xxii. 4; Mic. vii. 17: in pause, יְלַחֵכוּ, Ps. lxxii. 9; Is. xlix. 23. Constr. immed., al. non occ.

לֶחֶם, c. pl. non occ. Seg. fm. שֶׁקֶר, prim. *eating, devouring:* hence, (a) *Eatable, provision,* generally: thence, (b) *feast:* pec. (c) *bread,* Exod. xvi. 22. 29; Ps. xli. 10; cii. 5; Job xx. 14. (b) לֶחֶם אֱלֹהִים, — of God, i. e. sacrificial, Lev. xxi. 8. 17;—Jer. xi. 19, עֵץ בְּלַחְמוֹ, *tree with its eatable,* i. e. its fruit : לֶחֶם הַפֶּחָה, *provision of the governor,* Neh. v. 18. Comp. vr. 15; Obad. vr. 7. לַחְמִי, ellipt. for אַנְשֵׁי לַחְמִי, *men who eat of thy provision,* Eccl. x. 19, &c. (c) *Bread,* Exod. xxv. 50; xxxv. 13; xxxix. 6; in the phr. לֶחֶם הַפָּנִים, *bread of the presence,* i. e. of God; Vulg. *shew-bread.* 1 Sam. x. 4,

לְחֵם (327) לחץ

שְׁתֵּי לָחֶם, *a couple of loaves.* כִּכַּר לָחֶם, *cake of bread,* Exod. xxix. 23. חַלַּת לֶחֶם, id. Id. לֶחֶם אִשֶּׁה, *bread of fire,* i. e. offered in burnt-offering, Lev. iii. 11. לֶחֶם חָמֵץ, *bread of leaven,* i. e. leavened, Ib. vii. 13. — *of wave-offering,* Ib. xxii. 17: *staff of* —, Ib. xxvi. 26. Meton. (d) once, *Bread-corn,* Is. xxviii. 28. Aff. לַחְמִי, לַחְמוֹ, &c.

לְחֵם, Chald. c. *Eating; a feast,* Dan. v. 1, only.

לָחַם, v. pres. יִלְחַם. Constr. immed. it. med. בְּ, אֶת, with. Arab. لَحِمَ, *abrosit os, et edendo nudavit carne.* I. *Eat, feast upon,* Prov. iv. 18; Ps. cxli. 4; Prov. xxiii. 6. Infin. לְחוֹם, Prov. xxiii. 1 : it. לָחוּם (or לָחוּם), Job xx. 23. See לָחוּם above.

Part. pass. pl. m. constr. לְחוּמֵי (for לְחוּמֵי), *Devoured of* —, Deut. xxxii. 24.

II. As eating involves the notions of devouring, consuming, and the like; so this verb has been made to imply *war,* as a consumer. Comp. Num. xiv. 9. See also under אָכַל. Hence—

Imp. לְחַם, *Wage war, impugn,* Ps. xxxv. 1, only.

Part. לֹחֵם, pl. לֹחֲמִים, Ps. lvi. 2, 3. Aff. לֹחֲמָי, Ps. xxxv. 1.

Niph. נִלְחַם, pres. יִלָּחֵם. Constr. immed. it. med. בְּ, עִם, אֶל, עַל, לְ, אֶת, מִן, from, of place. *Make, wage, war,* Josh. x. 25; 1 Sam. xvii. 10; Exod. i. 10; 2 Kings xiii. 12; xiv. 15; Jer. i. 19; xv. 20; Neh. iv. 8, &c.

Infin. abs. נִלְחֹם, Judg. xi. 25.

It. הִלָּחֵם, Exod. xvii. 10; Num. xxii. 11, &c.

Imp. הִלָּחֵם, 1 Sam. xviii. 17; Judg. ix. 38.

— pl. הִלָּחֲמוּ, 2 Kings x. 3.

Part. נִלְחָם, pl. נִלְחָמִים, Exod. xiv. 25; Josh. x. 25, &c.

לָחֶם, m. once, Judg. v. 8, in the phrase לֶחֶם שְׁעָרִים, *War of the gates,* i. e. at the gates, for the purpose of taking the city. See LXX. ἀλλ. ὡς ἄρτον κρίθινον, i. e. לֶחֶם שְׂעֹרִים, with other vowels.

לַחְמִי, m. Patronym. of בֵּית לֶחֶם. See Gram. art. 166. 7. *Bethlehemite,* 2 Sam. xxi. 19; 1 Chron. xx. 5, &c.

לְחֻמָם, Infin. with לְ pref. r. חמם.

לְחֵנָה, fem. plur. לְחֵנָת, Chald. Arab. لَجْن, *corrupta fuit* nux ; لَجْنَة, *fœtens pudendis ancilla. A concubine,* Dan. v. 2, 3. 23.

לַחַץ, masc.— plur. non occ. Arab. لَحْص, *infortunium, calamitas. Oppression, affliction,* Exod. iii. 9; 1 Kings xxii. 27; 2 Kings xiii. 4, &c. Phrr. שָׁחַק לַחַץ וּמַיִם לַחַץ, 2 Chron. xviii. 26. Comp. Is. xxx. 20. לַחַץ אוֹיֵב, Ps. xlii. 10. Comp. Job xxxvi. 15. With עַל, Deut. xxvi. 7. Aff. לַחֲצֵנוּ.

לָחַץ, v. pres. יִלְחַץ, constr. immed. it. med. אֶת, it. abs. *Oppress, afflict,* Exod. xxii. 20; xxiii. 9; Num. xxii. 25; Judg. iv. 3; x. 12; 2 Kings xiii. 4. 22; Amos vi. 14, &c.

Part. plur. masc. לֹחֲצִים, Exod. iii. 9. Aff. לֹחֲצָיו, &c., Jer. xxx. 20.

Niph. pres. f. תִּלָּחֵץ, *Became, was, pressed, injured,* Num. xxii. 25, only.

לָחַשׁ, m. pl. לְחָשִׁים. Syr. ܠܚܫܐ, *musitatio, incantatio.* Æth. ለሐሰ: *musitavit, submisse locutus est.* (a) *Murmur, whisper* (of prayers apparently), Is. xxvi. 16. LXX. ἐν θλίψει μικρᾷ. Syr. "*In carcere susurraverunt* (ܠܚܫ) *correptionem tuam.* (b) *Incantation, charm,* Jer. viii. 17 ; Eccl. x. 11; Is. iii. 3. נְבוֹן לַחַשׁ, *intelligent of whisper, soft, winning, address,* i. e. the cunning courtier. Aquila, συνετὸν ψιθυρισμῷ. Symm. (συνετὸν) ὁμιλίᾳ μυθτικῇ. Theod. ἐπῳδῇ. LXX. ἀκροατὴν. (c) Pl., Is. iii. 20. *Charms:* meton. *amulets,* supposed to have certain protecting virtues ; — see Schrœder, de Vestitu Mulierum, cap. xi. pp. 172, 173 ;—made perhaps in the shape of serpents, and suspended from the neck, between the breasts. See also Rosenmüller, ad locum.

לחש, v. see לָחַשׁ, Kal non occ.

Pih. part. pl. m. מְלַחֲשִׁים, once; Ps. lviii. 6. *Enchanters.* Aquila, Theod. ἐπᾳδόντων. Sym. ψιθυριζόντων. ἈΛΛ. ἐπαοιδῶν, al. non occ.

Hithp. pres. יִתְלַחֲשׁוּ, constr. med. עַל, Ps. xli. 8. *Muse of, secretly consider, discuss.* LXX. Sym. ἐψιθύριζον.

Part. m. pl. מִתְלַחֲשִׁים, 2 Sam. xii. 19, only. *Whispering* persons.

לָט, m. part. r. לוט.

לָט, masc. — plur. non occ. Arab.

לטא (328) ליל

لاَدَنْ, Lat. *ladanum*. Gr. λήδανον. See Herodot. iii. cvii. cxii. A sort of laudanum, found adhering to the stem and leaves of certain shrubs, not unlike the honey-dew among ourselves. It forms a sort of resin, which is burnt as incense, and hence used as a perfume. See Cels. Hierobot. i., p. 280, seq. In the اختيارات بديعي of Ibn Hosein (sub voce), the best (لادن نيكوترين), forms a perfumed ointment, inclining to a yellowish colour, in which there is no sandy particle: it dissolves in butter, and has no sediment. His words are,—

نيكوترين آن چرب خوشبوي بود
كه لون آن بزردي زند وهيچ ريگ
در وي نبود ودر روغن حل شود
وهيچ ثفلي نداشته باشد. See also Rees's Cyclopædia, under LADANUM. Twice, viz., Gen. xxxvii. 25; xliii. 11. So called, according to Gesenius, because of its *covering* (see v. לוט; comp. לֹּטֶף) the shrubs, &c. on which it is found.

לְטָאָה, f. once, Lev. xi. 30. According to Bochart. Hieroz. i., p. 1073, seq., i. q. the Arab. وحَرٌ. A sort of lizard, adhering to the ground (r. لطا, *adhæsit terræ*), and poisoning every thing it touches. LXX. χαλαβώτης. Vulg. *stellio*.

לָטַשׁ, v. pres. יִלְטוֹשׁ, pret. non occ. Constr. immed. it. med. אֶת. Syr. ܠܛܫ, *acuit, polivit*. Cogn. Arab. لَطَسَ, *illisit, contudit*; مِلطَس, *malleus*. Sharpen, tool, weapon, &c., Ps. vii. 13; Job xvi. 9. Infin. לְטוֹשׁ, 1 Sam. xiii. 20.
Part. לֹטֵשׁ, Gen. iv. 22. Gesenius prefers "*malleavit*," beat, hammered, out, here. See LXX.
Puh. Part. מְלֻטָּשׁ. *Sharpened*, Ps. lii. 4, only.

לֻיוֹת, pl. f. occ., 1 Kings vii. 29, 30. 36, only, i. q. לִוְיָה, apparently, which see; r. לוה. Ornaments *attached*, rather *attaching*, to certain parts of the Temple. *Garlands*, or *festoons*, according to Gesenius. Perhaps the Arab. لَبَّة, *plicatura*, as a *wreath*, or the like.

לַיִל, m. constr. לֵיל, Exod. xii. 42, &c. With ־ָה, parag. לַיְלָה, in pause, לָיְלָה. So the Arab. لَيْل, *nox*; and, with ة of unity, لَيْلَة, *nox una, singularis*; pl. f. לֵילוֹת; in pause, לֵילוֹת. Syr. ܠܠܝܐ, ܠܠܝܐ, id. Cogn. Sanscrit, नील, *dark blue*. Pers. id. I. *Night*, opp. to day, Is. xvi. 3; Lam. ii. 19; Gen. i. 5. 14; Ps. xix. 3, &c. II. Adverbially, *By night*, Gen. xiv. 15; Exod. xiii. 21, 22; Num. ix. 21, &c. III. Metaph., *Time of adversity*; light, or whiteness, usually implying prosperity. See my note on Job vi. 16.—Job xxxv. 10; Mic. iii. 6; Is. xxi. 11, &c.

לֵילְיָא, m. Chald. def. *Night*, Dan. ii. 19; v. 30; vii. 2. 7. 13.

לִילִית, f. once, in the phr. הִרְגִּיעָה לִילִית, Is. xxxiv. 14. It is truly amusing to see with what earnestness Dr. Gesenius here urges the fabulous nonsense of the Rabbins; as if nothing but the follies of these men, or the dreams of heathen poets, could at all avail in elucidating the Hebrew Scriptures. Nor is Bochart. Hieroz. ii., p. 831, seq. one whit better; so marvellously has Rabbinism been allowed to impose on the credulity of the Christian world. The question here is, What does this word most probably mean? Dr. Gesenius says, after the Rabbins, "*spectrum nocturnum*," &c. But why *spectrum*? Because, it should seem, the Jews have a story among them of very long standing (see Bochart. l. c.), telling us that there are four mothers of the demons, *Lilith, Naama, &c. &c.*; of whom, Adam, during the 130 years of his separation from Eve, begot them all, &c. &c. And from this it is, as it should seem, heterodoxy to depart! The context, however, evidently speaks of real beings, as a little attention will show. Why may not this, then, be a real being, or creature, likewise? From its being said that it shall *rest* (הִרְגִּיעָה לָהּ מָנוֹחַ, and מָצְאָה שָׁם), one would be tempted to believe that some otherwise *restless* or *wandering* creature, would, in these ruined and neglected places, find safety and repose. The word, as Gesenius allows, signifies "*nocturna*." It is a relative fem. of ליל, *night*, beyond all doubt. If,

לין (329) לכה

then, we drop the notion of *spectrum*, and suppose some *real animal* to be meant, *nightly* (wanderer), whether bird or beast—which we need not determine—will sufficiently define and well express the sense of the place: thus, הַרְפִּיעָה לִּילִית, the *nightly wanderer shall rest, &c.* The word is, moreover, taken to signify a *screech-owl;* which, indeed, it might very well mean, without at all carrying along with it either the Latin fable of the *strix,* or the Jewish one of the Mother of Demons. See also the Syr. of the Polyg. The Arab. لَيْلِي, *nocturnus, qui quid noctu facit*, of which the fem. would be لَيْلَة, will correspond sufficiently well to our לִילִית.

לִין, see לוּן.

לִיסוֹד, for לְיִסוֹד, r. יסד, Infin. Kal, 2 Chron. xxxi. 7; Is. li. 16; p. 261 above.

לִיקְחַת, for לִלְקַחַת, see יָקָה, Prov. xxx. 17.

לַיִשׁ, masc.—plur. non occ. Arab. اَلَيْسُ, *intrepidus;* hinc, *leo.* Cogn. لَيْثٌ, *leo.* Chald. לַיִשׁ, id. See Hieroz. i., pp. 61. 720. A strong *lion,* Is. xxx. 6; Prov. xxx. 30; Job iv. 11.

לֵךְ, Imp. יָלַךְ.

לָכַד, m. once, Prov. iii. 26. Arab. لَكَدَ, *res adhærens;* مَلَاكِدُ, *qui compedibus vinctus, incedens cum alio irritatur. Capture,* by the snare or the like. See LXX. Ἀλλ. ἀγρευθῇς.

לָכַד, v. pres. יִלְכֹּד. Constr. immed. it. med. אֶת. See לָכַד above. *Take,* as a beast in the toils, pit, &c., Amos iii. 5; Ps. xxxv. 8; Jer. xviii. 22. — captives in war, Num. xxi. 32; Josh. xi. 12; Judg. viii. 12. — city or place by siege, &c., Josh. viii. 21; x. 1; xi. 10. Metaph. — the wise by (constr. בְּ) their own cunning, Job v. 13; Prov. v. 22. *Take* by intervention; *intercept.* Constr. med. לְ, Judg. vii. 24. — by lot, Josh. vii. 14. 17.

Infin. abs. לָכֹד, Amos, l. c. Aff. לָכְדָהּ, Jer. xxxii. 24, &c.

Imp. aff. f. לָכְדָהּ, 2 Sam. xii. 28.
— pl. m. לִכְדוּ, Judg. vii. 24.

Part. לֹכֵד, Job, l. c. Prov. xvi. 32.

Niph. נִלְכַּד, pres. יִלָּכֵד, *Be, become, taken,* by (constr. בְּ) the snare, stratagem, &c., Ps. ix. 16; Jer. li. 56; 1 Kings xvi. 18; 1 Sam. x. 20, 21. Metaph. Prov. vi. 2. Comp. Eccl. vii. 26.

Hithp. pres. only, יִתְלַכָּדוּ, pl. *Be, become, adhering* (see לָכַד above), Job xli. 8. See my note. Theod. συνέχονται. It. Ib. xxxviii. 30, id. or, *taken captive.* See my note here also. Ὁ Ἑβραῖος, πήγνυται. LXX. ἔπηξεν. Ἀλλ. ἔπηξεν.

לְכָה, Imp. with ה parag. v. יָלַךְ, which see, p. 258 above. Used not unlike our "*go to,*" as noticed there. Also written לָךְ, Num. xxiii. 13; Judg. xix. 13, &c. See Gram. art. 72. Also for לְךָ, לְכָה, *to,* or *for thee,* Gen. xxvii. 37, &c.; Gram. art. 145. 5.

לָכֵן, Partic. conjunc. of כֵּן + לְ. See כֵּן. Lit. *for so, thus.* Hence, *Therefore,* or the like, Judg. x. 13; 1 Sam. iii. 14, &c. *Nevertheless,* Num. xvi. 11; Jer. v. 2; xvi. 14, &c. See Nold., p. 434, seq., and examine the places cited.

לֶכֶת, Infin. Kal, v. יָלַךְ.

לְלָאוֹת, see לוּלֵי.

לָמַד, v. pres. יִלְמַד, constr. immed. it. med. אֶת, אֶל. Arab. لَمَدَ, *se submisit alicui.* Æth. ᎀᎵᎲ: *assuevit. Accustom to* —. Meton. *Learn,* anything, Deut. v. 1; xiv. 23; xvii. 19; xviii. 9; Is. ii. 4; Jer. x. 2.

Infin. abs. לָמֹד, Jer. xii. 16. Aff. לְמֻדִי, Ps. cxix. 7.

Imp. pl. לִמְדוּ, Is. i. 17.

Part. pass. pl. constr. לִמּוּדֵי, 1 Chron. v. 18.

Pih. לִמַּד, pres. יְלַמֵּד, constr. abs. it. immed. it. אֶת, med. it. בְּ; instr. מִן, of, of thing, it. עַל, over; pers. לְ, to; pers. thing, בְּ, in, place. *Accustom to, teach,* any person, anything, 2 Chron. xvii. 7; Ps. lxxi. 17; Deut. iv. 5. 14; xi. 19; Ps. xviii. 35; Is. xl. 14; Jer. ii. 33; xiii. 21; Job xxi. 22.

Infin. לַמֵּד, Jer. xxxii. 33, &c. Aff. לַמְּדָם, Judg. iii. 2.

Imp. aff. לַמְּדֵנִי, Ps. xxv. 4, &c.

Part. מְלַמֵּד, Deut. iv. 1, &c. Aff. מְלַמְּדָיו, Is. xlviii. 17. Pl. מְלַמְּדַי, Ps. cxix. 99.

Puh. לֻמַּד, pres. non occ. *Be, become, accustomed to, taught,* anything, Jer. xxxi. 18, al. non occ.

Part. מְלֻמָּדָה, f., Is. xxix. 13; Hos. x. 11.
— pl. m. constr. מְלֻמְּדֵי, 1 Chron. xxv. 7.

U U

לָמָה , לָמָה , לָמָה , see מָה.

לָמוֹ , pleon. for לְ, as in כְּמוֹ , בְּמוֹ , Job xxvii. 14; xxix. 21; xxxviii. 40; xl. 4.

לָמוּד , and לָמֻד , pl. לִמּוּדִים , constr. לִמּוּדֵי . Aff. לִמֻּדָי. *Accustomed, trained, taught* (professionally, Gram. art. 154. 10. 12. fm. ii.), Is. l. 4; Jer. ii. 24; xiii. 23. Constr. pl. Is. liv. 13. *Disciples*, Ib. viii. 16.

לְמִן , see מִן.

לְמַעַן , compd. לְ + מַעַן, r. עָנָה . Arab. عَنَىٰ , *voluit, intendit, significavit,* aliquid. Used as a preposition. Lit. *For purpose, cause, &c.* of: hence, *Because of, &c.;* and with a verb following, *In order that, because that,* or the like; retrospectively, or prospectively, i. e. with reference to what precedes, or follows, as the context may require, e. g.

I. *Retrospectively.*

לְמַעַן שְׁמֶךָ , *Because of thy name,* 1 Kings viii. 41, i. e. the journey here mentioned was undertaken on this account. לְמַעַן דָּוִד , *on David's account,* i. e. of the promises made to him, 2 Kings viii. 12. Comp. Is. lxii. 1; 2 Chron. xxi. 7, &c.: examples of which Noldius will supply.

II. *Prospectively,* i. e. with reference to futurity. לְמַעַן תְּבָרְכְךָ נַפְשִׁי , *in order that my soul may bless thee,* i. e. this being done, I will give thee the blessing. So, לְמַעַן יַאֲמִינוּ , *in order that they may believe;* or, *so shall they believe,* i. e. this being repeated before them, they shall then believe thee, Exod. iv. 5. Comp. Deut. iv. 1; Is. xli. 20, &c. Still, in these cases, respect is in some degree had to the past.

It is not to be supposed, however, that this term (לְמַעַן) is intended to imply that one thing, &c. may have been done, in order to ensure the occurrence of another :— this would, in many instances, be productive of manifest absurdities :— but rather to imply, that, as the one thing has taken place, so, for some cause or other—not always named— another will, or shall, also take place. So, Jer. xliv. 8, לְמַעַן הַכְרִית לָכֶם וּלְמַעַן הֱיוֹתְכֶם לִקְלָלָה וגו׳ : not, "*that ye might cut yourselves off, and that ye might be a curse,*" &c; for this would imply that they had done certain things for the express purpose of injuring themselves. The meaning is this, *in order to your cutting off, and in order to your becoming a curse, &c.,* i. e. so that this will be the final conse-

quence. Comp. Hos. viii. 4; Ps. li. 6; Neh. vi. 13. So, Deut. xxix. 18; Is. lxvi. 11; Jer. vii. 10, לְמַעַן עֲשׂוֹת וגו׳ , *because of doing* (having done) *all these* (things, which are) *abominations.* See Nold., p. 442, seq. As to single expressions, לְמַעַן שְׁמוֹ , *because of his name,* Ps. xxiii. 3, &c., is explained by Ps. lxxix. 9, עַל דְּבַר כְּבוֹד שְׁמוֹ , *on account of the glory of his name,* i. e. of the excellency of his attributes, which contain every thing that is great and good. By name, too, *person* is often implied; and by God's name, occasionally, the *person* of the Messiah. Comp. Exod. xxiii. 21; Is. ix. 5; Matt. i. 23; Rev. xix. 13. But here, as we know the person by the attributes only, the result is much the same in either view of the case. So the phr. לְמַעַן חַסְדּוֹ , *because of his favour,* Ps. vi. 5, &c., nearly synonymous with כְּחַסְדּוֹ . Comp. Ps. xxv. 7; li. 3, &c., as Gesenius has well observed. So, לְמַעַן צִדְקוֹ , *because of his righteousness;* in order to make good the truth of his promises, Is. xlii. 21. לְמַעַנְכֶם , *because of you, for your sakes,* Is. xliii. 14. Comp. Ib. vr. 25.

לְמַעַן אֲשֶׁר , lit. *for cause that:* hence, *In order that, because that, &c.* — תֵּדְעוּ , *ye may know,* Josh. iii. 4. Comp. 2 Sam. xiii. 5; Deut. xxvii. 3, &c. יְצַוֶּה , — *he will order,* rule by precept, Gen. xviii. 19. Comp. Lev. xvii. 5. In like manner other combinations, as לְמַעַן אֲשֶׁר לֹא , Num. xvii. 5 : לְמַעַן זֹאת , 1 Kings xi. 39: לְמַעַן לֹא , Ezek. xix. 9, &c.: כִּי לְמַעַן , Josh. xi. 20 : רַק לְמַעַן , Judg. iii. 2, as the combined powers of the terms and context in which they are found shall require. Of which, examples will be found in Noldius, under their proper heads.

לָנָה , for לָנָה , see v. לוּן above.

לֹעַ , masc. once, aff. לֻעֲךָ , *Thy throat,* Prov. xxiii. 2, r. לוּעַ . Syr. ܠܽܘܥܳܐ , *mandibula.*

לָעַב , v. Kal non occ. Arab. لَعِبَ , *lusit impudicè; irrisit.* Syr. ܠܰܥܶܒ , *lascivivit.*

Hiph. part. pl. m. מַלְעִבִים , once, 2 Chron. xxvi. 16. *Ridiculing, deriding,* persons.

לַעַג , m. pl. non occ. Syr. ܠܽܘܥܳܓܳܐ , *audacia.* Arab. لَعَجَ , *agitatio; calor animi.* *Derision, ridicule,* Ps. lxxix. 4; Ezek. xxiii. 32; xxxvi. 4. Meton. *Cause of derision,* Hos. vii. 16. יִשְׁתֶּה־לַעַג , *drinks in derision;*

indulges in it, Job xxxiv. 7; Ps. cxxiii. 4. Aff. לָעֲמוּ, Hos. l. c. Infin. v. לָעֵג.

לָעַג, v. pres. יִלְעַג. See לַעַג above. Constr. med. לְ, pers. בְּ, in, thing. *Deride, ridicule, scorn,* 2 Kings xix. 21; Is. xxxvii. 22; Prov. i. 26; Ps. lix. 9; Job ix. 23; xi. 3; xxii. 19, &c.

Part. לֹעֵג, Prov. xvii. 5; Jer. xx. 7.

Niph. Part. constr. נִלְעֲגֵי, once, Is. xxxiii. 19, in the phr. נִלְעֲגֵי לָשׁוֹן, *stammering,* confused, *of tongue.* Syr. ܠܥܓ, *balbus, blæsus.*

Hiph. pres. יַלְעִיג, הַלְעִיג. Constr. med. לְ, בְּ, i. q. Kal. Ps. xxii. 8; Job xxi. 3; Neh. ii. 19; iii. 33.

Part. m. pl. מַלְעִגִים, 2 Chron. xxx. 10.

לַעַג, m.—pl. m. constr. לַעֲגֵי, *Scoffers, scorners,* in the phr., Ps. xxxv. 16, לַעֲגֵי מָעוֹג, *scoffers, ridiculers, of the cake,* i. e. those who act the parasite at the tables of the great. ψωμοκόλακες and κνισσοκόλακες. Some, however, take מָעוֹג, for מַלְעוֹג, or לָעוֹג, here, and render the phrase by, "*subsannant subsannatione,*" or *subsannando.*

לָעָה, v. pres. non occ. once, Job vi. 3. דְּבָרַי לָעוּ, *my words have been rash.* Arab. لغا, *locutus fuit temere.* See my note. Aquila, ῥήματα μου κατεπατήθησαν. Sym. οἱ λόγοι μου κατάπικροι. Theod. ἔγκοποι. LXX. ἐστὶ φαῦλα. Cogn. לוע.

לָעַז, v. part. only occ. לֹעֵז, Ps. cxiv. 1. Syr. ܠܥܙ, *barbarè, pec.* Ægyptiacè *locutus est.* Cogn. ܚܠܓ, *hæsitavit linguâ. Speaking barbarously:*—a foreign tongue, al. non occ.

לָעַט, v. occ. Hiph. only. Imp. aff. הַלְעִיטֵנִי, Gen. xxv. 30. Arab. لعط, whence, مَلْعَط, *planta quæ pascendo carpitur; pabulum :* لَعْظَم, *avidè voravit. Feed me, give me to eat.* LXX. γεῦσόν με.

לַעֲנָה, fem.—plur. non occ. Arab. لَغَن, *abegit, &c.;* لَعْنَة, *execratio. Wormwood,* Deut. xxix. 17; Jer. ix. 14; xxiii. 15; Lam. iii. 15. 19; Prov. v. 4; Amos v. 7; vi. 12. Applied, metaph., morally generally, implying distress. Comp. Rev. viii. 10. 11.

לַפִּיד, m. pl. לַפִּידִים, constr. לַפִּידֵי. Gr. λαμπάς (the μ being introduced in place of the second פ, Heb.) "Origo est in *lambendo,*" says Gesenius: than which nothing can be more uncertain. The word is probably of Shemitic origin; but how derived it is impossible to say. Syr. ܠܡܦܕܐ, *lampas. A lamp,* or *torch,* Gen. xv. 17; Judg. vii. 16; Job xii. 5. לַפִּיד בּוּז, *lamp of contempt,* i. e. which has lost its brilliancy for want of oil, and is waning to its extinction. (Comp. Matt. xxv. 3, seq.), a lively image of a failing rich man. See my note. Is. lxii. 1; Zech. xii. 6; Job xli. 10; Dan. x. 6, &c.

לִפְנֵי, used as a prep. *Before.* See פָּנִים. 1 Kings vi. 17. לִפְנֵי, for לְפָנִים, or elliptically perhaps.

לִפֵת, v. pres. יִלְפֹּת, constr. med. אֶת Arab. لفت, *inflexit; respexit, &c. Turned to,* or *towards,* Judg. xvi. 29, only. LXX. περιέλαβε.

Niph. pres. יִלָּפֵת, pl. יִלָּפְתוּ. *Be, become turned about, towards, &c.,* Ruth iii. 8; Job vi. 18: see my note: al. non occ.

לְצַבּוֹת, for לְהַצַבּוֹת, Infin. Hiph. v. צבה.

לֵץ, v. cogn. του̂, לוץ, which see. Part. לֵצִים, *Scoffers, scorners,* Hos. vii. 5. Aquila χλευαστῶν. LXX. λοιμῶν.

לֶקַח, m.—pl. non occ. Aff. לִקְחוֹ, לָקְחָה. Arab. لقح, *conceptio, &c.* Lit. *taking, receiving, conceiving :* pec. of *Instruction,* in religion, as something *received,* Deut. xxxii. 2; Is. xxix. 24; Prov. i. 5; iv. 2, &c.; Job xi. 4, &c.

לָקַח, v. pres. יִקַּח, Gram. art. 198. 16.

See لقح, above. Æth. ለቀሐ : *commodavit.* Constr. abs. it. immed. it. med. מִן from; אֵת, לְ, to, for; עִם, with; בְּ, in; מֵעַל from on; עַל. (a) *Take,* generally, Gen. ii. 22; xxvii. 36; xxxi. 1, &c. Idiomatically, as in the English, *take and do so and so.* see יָד, קוּם, שׁוּב, 2 Sam. xviii. 18. וַיִּקַּח וַיַּצֵּב *he took and set up.* Comp. Jer. xxiii. 31, &c. So the Gr. λαβὼν, Viger. Herm. Edit. Lond. 1824, p. 352. Notante Gesenio. *Take to self,* Gen. vii. 2; xv. 10; xx. 2;

לקט (332) לקח

Lev. xv. 14, &c. — a wife, Gen. iv. 19; vi. 2; xii. 19; xix. 14, &c. — to his son, Gen. xxxiv. 4; Exod. xxi. 10; xxxiv. 16: ellip. (b) *Take away*, Gen. xiv. 12; Job i. 21; xii. 20, &c. — the life, Jer. xv. 15. Translate (of Enoch), Gen. v. 24. (c) *Take possession of*, Num. xxi. 25; Deut. iii. 14; xxix. 7. Metaph. Job iii. 6; xv. 12. —, allure, &c., Prov. vi. 25; xi. 30. (d) *Receive*, Num. xxiii. 20. — into favour, Ps. xlix. 16; lxxiii. 24. — into the ear, mind, Job iv. 12. — as prayer, &c., Ps. vi. 10; Prov. ii. 1; iv. 10; xxiv. 32.

Infin. קַח, Ezek. xvii. 5. Aff. קָחָם, Hos. xi. 3.

— It. לָקַח, Deut. xxxi. 26. לָקוֹחַ, Jer. xxxii. 14, &c.

— constr. קַחַת, 2 Kings xii. 9, &c. With לְ, pref., Gen. iv. 11, &c. Constr. immed. it. med. אֶת, &c. Aff. קַחְתִּי, Ezek. xxiv. 25, &c.

Imp. לְקַח, Exod. xxix. 1; Ezek. xxxvii. 16.
— it. קַח, Gen. vi. 21; xii. 19, &c. With ה ָ, parag., Gen. xv. 9. Aff. קָחֵנוּ, 1 Sam. xx. 21, &c.

— pl. קְחוּ, Gen. xlii. 33, &c. Aff. קָחֻהוּ, 1 Kings xx. 33.

Fem. לְקִחִי, 1 Kings xvii. 11.
— it. קְחִי, Ib. vr. 10; Is. xxiii. 16.
Part. לֹקֵחַ, Prov. xi. 30.
— pl. לֹקְחִים, Jer. xxiii. 31. לֹקְחֵי, constr. Gen. xix. 14.
— pass. pl. m. לְקֻחִים, Prov. xxiv. 11.

Niph. נִלְקַח, pres. f. תִּלָּקַח, *Be, become, taken*, 1 Sam. iv. 11. 17; 2 Kings ii. 9; Esth. ii. 8. 16.

Infin. הִלָּקַח, 1 Sam. iv. 19. Aff. הִלָּקְחוֹ, 1 Sam. xxi. 7.

Puh. לֻקַּח, pres. of Hoph. יֻקַּח, i. q. Niph. Gen. ii. 23; iii. 19. 23; xii. 15; xviii. 4; Judg. xvii. 2; 2 Kings ii. 10; Jer. xxix. 22; xlviii. 46: Is. xlix. 25; Job xxviii. 2.

Hithp. part. f. מִתְלַקַּחַת, twice, Exod. ix. 24; Ezek. i. 4: lit. *being, becoming, taken with*, i. e. *Mixed, mingled, with.* Aquila, συναναλαμβανόμενον. Sym. ἐνειλούμενον. LXX. φλογίζον.

לֶקֶט, masc. — plur. non occ. Arab. لَقَطَ, *legit, collegit*; pec. *rem humi positam, vel abjectam. Collecting, gleaning*, Lev. xix. 9; xxiii. 22, only.

לָקַט, v. pres. pl. masc. יְלַקְּטוּ. *Collect, gather, glean.* Constr. immed. it. abs. it.

med. בְּ, in, of place; מִן, from; pers. אֵת, obj., Exod. xvi. 4, 5. 17, 18. 21, 22. 26; Ps. civ. 28.

Infin. לְקֹט, Exod. xvi. 27; Ruth ii. 8; Cant. vi. 2.

Imp. plur. לִקְטוּ, Gen. xxxi. 46; Exod. xvi. 16.

Pih. לִקֵּט, pres. יְלַקֵּט, i. q. Kal, Gen. xlvii. 14; Ruth ii. 2. 7. 16—19; Lev. xix. 9. 10.

Infin. לַקֵּט, Ruth ii. 15. 23, &c.

Part. מְלַקֵּט, plur. מְלַקְּטִים, Is. xvii. 5; Judg. i. 7, &c.

לָקָה, v. pres. יָלָק. Constr. med. אֵת, it. מִן, of thing; בְּ, instr. it. abs. Arab. لَقَّ, *percussit manu.* Lit. *strike: Lick,* as dogs; ὀνοματοποιητικόν, Judg. vii. 5; 1 Kings xxi. 19; xxii. 38. Pret. fully, לָקֵקוּ.

Pih. Part. m. pl. מְלַקְּקִים. *Persons licking up*, Judg. vii. 6. 7. Dagesh omitted, Gram. art. 113, al. non occ.

לֶקֶשׁ, masc. — plur. non occ. Syr. ܠܩܫܐ, *serotinus. Latter grass, aftermath*, i. e. grass growing up immediately after the mowing, Amos vii. 1, only. Aquila, ὄψιμος ὀπίσω τῆς γάζης βασιλέως.

לָקַשׁ, v. Kal non occ.
Pih. pres. pl. m. יְלַקֹּשׁוּ. *They cut, crop,* Job xxiv. 6, only. See my note.

לֵירָא, for לִירָא, Infin. Kal. v. יָרָא.

לְשַׁד, masc. — plur. non occ. Arab. لَسَدَ, *suxit* hœdus; لَسَدٌ, act. of do. *Moisture,* Ps. xxxii. 4. Aff. לְשַׁדִּי. Aquila, εἰς προνομήν μου. Sym. εἰς διαφθοράν. Theod. LXX. εἰς ταλαιπωρίαν. So Edit. E. all taking the לְ here as a prep. Num. xi. 8, כְּטַעַם לְשַׁד הַשָּׁמֶן, "*as the taste of fresh oil.*" Auth. Vers. Aquila, τοῦ μαστοῦ ἐλαίου: taking לְ as a mark of the Gen. case, and שַׁד the breast. Schleusn. Lex. LXX. ἐγκρὶς ἐξ ἐλαίου. *Placenta olei,* Gesen. So also Syr. and Targ. *Oiled bread or cake,* al. non occ.

לָשׁוֹן, fem. constr. לְשׁוֹן, pl. לְשׁוֹנוֹת. Syr. ܠܫܢܐ, *lingua.* Arab. لِسَانٌ, id. it. Æth. Chald. I. *The tongue,* of any animal, Ps. xii. 4; cxx. 3; cxxxvii. 6, &c.

II. Meton. *Language,* as uttered by the tongue, Job xv. 5; Prov. xvi. 1; Esth. i. 22; Dan. i. 4; Gen. x. 5: also, *Nation, family, &c.,* as having a common language, Gen. x. 20; Is. lxvi. 18.

III. Applied also to other things, as, לְשׁוֹן זָהָב, *a tongue* (wedge) *of gold*, Josh. vii. 21. 24. לְשׁוֹן אֵשׁ, *tongue* (flame) *of fire*, Is. v. 24. So the Arab. لسان النار id. Pers. زبانهٔ آتش, or زبان, id.—לְשׁוֹן הַיָּם, *tongue of the sea*, i. e. gulf or estuary. Arab. لسان البحر, id., Josh. xv. 5; xviii. 19; Is. xi. 15: and simply לָשׁוֹן, Josh. xv. 2.

Phrr. תַּחַת לָשׁוֹן, *under the tongue*, i. e. in the mouth, Ps. x. 7; lxvi. 17; Job xx. 12. אִישׁ לָשׁוֹן, *man of* (a slanderous) *tongue*, Ps. cxl. 12. בַּעַל לָשׁוֹן, Eccl. x. 11, id. נַכֵּהוּ בַלָּשׁוֹן, *let us smite him with the tongue; accuse, traduce, him*, Jer. xviii. 18. שׁוֹט לָשׁוֹן, *running on, course, of the tongue*, i. e. in its hurry to injure, Job v. 21. See my note. לְשׁוֹן תַּהְפֻּכוֹת, *tongue of revolvings*, i. e. perverse, Prov. x. 31. —, *of the cunning ones*, Job xv. 5. כְּבַד לָשׁוֹן, *heavy, slow, of tongue*; unfit to be an orator, Exod. iv. 10. רְמִיָּה —, *of deceit*, Ps. cxx. 3. מַרְפֵּא לָשׁוֹן, *healer in tongue*, i. e. one who reconciles differences, Prov. xv. 4. יַד לָשׁוֹן, *hand, power, of the tongue*, Prov. xviii. 21. מְלִיצ לָשׁוֹן, see under v. לָעַג, Is. xxxiii. 19, &c.; to these a very large number may still be added, which the student can collect for himself from the Concordance. Aff. לְשׁוֹנִי, &c.

לִשְׁכָּה, f. constr. לִשְׁכַּת, pl. לִשָׁכוֹת, constr. לִשְׁכוֹת, i. q. נִשְׁכָּה. Gr. λέσχη. Cogn. Arab. لسق, *adhæsit*; لسقة, *junctura*. Cogr. لصق, id. *Chamber*, 1 Sam. ix. 22; Jer. xxxvi. 12: pec. those attached to the sides of the Temple, 2 Kings xxiii. 11; Jer. xxxv. 4; Ezek. xl. 17. 38. 45; Neh. x. 38; xiii. 4, 5; 2 Chron. xxxi. 11, &c.

לֶשֶׁם, masc.— pl. non occ. Twice only, Exod. xxviii. 19; xxxix. 12. Auth. Vers. *Ligure*. LXX. λιγύριον. Vulg. *Ligurius*. "*Hyacinthus*," Castell, who quotes Rev. xxi. 20, where we have the *Jacinth*.

לָשַׁן, v. Kal non occ. See לָשׁוֹן above.
Pih. Part. Aff. מְלָשְׁנִי, Keri; מַלְשִׁינִי (for מְלַשְׁנִי), lit. Vulg. *Tongue-walking; slandering*, once, Ps. ci. 5. So Arab. لسن, *incessivit linguâ suâ*.
Hiph. pres. 2d pers. תַּלְשֵׁן; i. q. Pih. Prov. xxx. 10.

לִשָּׁן, pl. def. לִשָּׁנַיָּא, Chald. *Tongue*; thence, *Family, people* (לָשׁוֹן, II. above), Dan. iii. 4. 7. 31; v. 19; vi. 26; vii. 14.

לַת, with לְ, לַת, Infin. v. ילד, for לֶדֶת, כְּ. 257 above.

לֶתֶךְ, m. once, Hos. iii. 2, in the phr. לֶתֶךְ שְׂעֹרִים. Auth. Vers. *Half-homer*. LXX. γομὸρ κριθῶν—οἱ λοιποὶ—ἡμίκορον. Aquila, κόρου κριθῶν. Sym. θύλακος κριθῶν. Theod. γομὸρ ἀλφίτων. Vulg. *corus dimidius*.

מ

מ, *Mem*, the thirteenth letter of the Hebrew alphabet, equivalent to our *m*. As a numeral it stands for *forty*, Gram. art. 4. It is classed among the *labials*, Ib. art. 23: with which, in the etymology, it often interchanges, Ib. art. 78. 1. Gesenius thinks it took its name from its ancient form resembling the *undulation* of waters (מַיִם), as in the Samaritan ᛗ, *men;* which he also thinks is confirmed by its Æthiopic name *mai*, also signifying *water*.

In the etymology it has various uses, as, I. in its interchanging with letters of the same organ (Gram. art. 78. 1, as above), and as in Heb. אִם, Syr. ܐܢ, Arab. اَنْ, اِنْ, وَاِنْ, وَاِن *If, &c.* Heb. בֹּהֶן, Arab. اِبْهَام, *the thumb;* Heb. בָּמִים, Syr. ܟܠܒܐ; Heb. כֶּשֶׁן, Arab. دسم; Heb. מֹדֶד, Arab. نُور; Heb. שָׁמֶן, שׁמם. The Heb. pl. ־ים, Chald. and Syr. ־ין, (Gesen.) Arab. ون, ین, &c., as noticed under the several roots.

II. In forming a large class of nouns, termed *Hêemanti*, with מ prefixed; as, in מִגְדָּל, מְלָחָמָה, &c., Gram. art. 161; also terminating in ם, Ib. art. 167, as in יָמִים, אֲמָנָם, &c. See also art. 157. 17, where its original form and influence, when prefixed, are pointed out. In this situation it is found forming participial nouns of all the forms of

מֵא (334) מֵאָה

the conjugation of the verb, except *Kal* and *Niphḥál*. See Gram. art. 211.

III. It is found as an abbreviated form of the preposition מִן; as in מִנִּי, מֵנִי, Gram. art. 171. 13. Also art. 172, seq., as, in מִדֶּרֶךְ, for מִן דֶּרֶךְ, &c. And, when followed by a letter not capable of receiving *Dagésh*, with the vowel (-), as מֵאִישׁ, מֵרָשָׁע, &c., Ib. par. 4. And here it is often used as a mediating particle between certain verbs and their complementary terms. See under מִן.

IV. It is also found as an abbreviation of מַה, מָה, מֶה, with (-), מַ, as מַלָּכֶם, *What* is it *to you?* See under מה.

מָא, i. q. Heb. מָה, *What, that which*, relat. דִּי לְמָא, once, Ezra vi. 8.

מַאֲבוּס, m. once, pl. aff. מַאֲבוּסֶיהָ, Jer. L. 26, r. אבס. See אָבוּס above, p. 3. *Her granaries.* LXX. τὰς ἀποθήκας αὐτῆς.

מְאֹד, masc. an indeclinable word, used substantively and adverbially. Arab. مَاَدَ, conj. viii. *acquisivit sibi;* and hence, as a secondary sense, *tener, mollis, &c* Cogn. مَدَّ, *extendit;* مَادَّة, *materia;* مَادِي, *moram concessit*. I. Subst. with aff. *Might, power, excess.* בְּכָל־מְאֹדְךָ, *with all thy might*, Deut. vi. 5; 2 Kings xxiii. 25. With prep. עַד־מְאֹד, *even to excess.* Adv. *exceedingly*, Gen. xxvii. 33; 1 Kings i. 4; Ps. cxix. 51; Dan. viii. 8, &c. Nold., p. 542. עַד־לִמְאֹד, lit. *even to — for excess,* i. e. very exceedingly, 2 Chron. xvi. 14. מְאֹד מְאֹד, *in great excess*, Gen. vii. 19; Num. xiv. 7: with בְּ, Ib. xvii. 2. 6. 20; Ezek. ix. 9. טוֹב מְאֹד, Gen. i. 31. יָפָה הִיא מְאֹד, Ib. xii. 14. Comp. xv. 1; Ps. xlvi. 2. עֶזְרָה נִמְצָא מְאֹד, *is found a powerful help.* תֵּרֵד מְאֹד, 1 Sam. xx. 19, usually, *shall go down quickly;* seems to be meant, *shall omit no effort to do so;* or, as in the margin of our Bibles, *diligently:* fully, perhaps, תֵּרֵד בְּכָל־מְאֹדְךָ.—Gen. iv. 5; Exod. xiv. 10; Num. xiv. 39, &c. See Nold., p. 474, seq. II. Adj. *Excessive*, Is. xlvii. 9; Job xxxv. 15. See my note.

מֵאָה, f. constr. מְאַת. Syr. ܡܐܐ, ܡܐܢ, *centum.* Arab. مِائَة, id. Cogn. مَاَلَ *extendit, &c.;* مَاَي, id. Cogn. مَاَ. مَاَ, *aqua,* water: from which perhaps originated the notion of *great extent,* in number, &c. (a) *A hundred,* dual, מָאתַיִם; in pause, מָאתָיִם, *two hundred;* pl. מֵאוֹת, מֵאֹת, *hundreds.* Qualifying other words, either in opposition, or in the state of construction, as, מֵאָה שָׁנָה, Gen. xvii. 17. מְאַת שָׁנָה, Ib. xxv. 7, Gram. art. 226. Whether this numeral, or the thing numbered, take the precedence, will depend upon the mind of the writer or speaker, Gram. art. 212. 3. More rarely this numeral follows, as, 2 Chron. iii. 16, which Gesenius takes to be a mark of the more modern usage. But no reliance can be placed on this. Dual, Gen. xi. 23. Pl., with other numerals, &c., Gen. v. 7, seq.; Exod. xii. 37; Deut. i. 15, &c. The fm. מֵאיוֹת occasionally occurs, 2 Kings xi. 4. 9, 10. 15: to be read מֵאִיּוֹת, according to Gesenius. With the article, as, אַמּוֹת הַמֵּאָה, lit. *cubits, the hundred*, Ezek. xlii. 2: to make this, as a qualifying term, agree with the preceding two in construction. Dual, Ezek. xiv. 15. Pl., Exod. xxxviii. 28; Num. xxxi. 14, &c. (b) *A hundred times* or *fold*, Prov. xvii. 10; Eccl. viii. 12. (c) *Hundredth,* part of money, &c., Neh. v. 12.

מֵאָה, fem. Chald. id., Dan. vi. 2; Ezra vi. 17; vii. 22. Dual, מָאתַיִן, Ezra vi. 17.

מַאֲוַיֵּי, m. pl. constr. once, Ps. cxl. 9, r. אוה, cogn. אָבָה. *Desires, lusts, of —.*

מְאוּם, masc.—pl. non occ. contr. מוּם, which see; r. אום. Arab. آم, r. أوم, *fumum fecit.* Whence, أَوْمُ لَيَال, *noctes; s. tempora, infelicia, iniqua.* Thence, *Blot, stain,* Job xxxi. 7, see my note; Dan. i. 4.

מְאוּמָה, an indeclinable word, compd. מָה + וּמָה. Lat. *quid + quid, quicquid. Anything,* Num. xxii. 38; Deut. xxiv. 10; 2 Kings xx. 20. With לֹא, or אֵין, *not anything, nothing,* Deut. xiii. 18; 1 Kings xviii. 43; Eccl. v. 13; Jer. xxxix. 10. אֵין כָּל־מְאוּמָה, *not anything whatsoever,* Gen. xxxix. 23. Comp. 1 Sam. xxi. 3.

מָאוֹר, m. constr. מְאוֹר, pl. מְאוֹרִים, and מְאֹרוֹת, r. אור. Lit. *place* of light. See under ברא above. (a) *Luminary,* sun, or moon, Gen. i. 14. 16; Ps. lxxiv. 16. מְאוֹר הַשֶּׁמֶשׁ, *place of light, even the sun,*—is probably the true meaning. — candle, Num. iv. 9. 16. מְנֹרַת הַמָּאוֹר, *the candlestick.* Meton. *Light,* Ps. xc. 8. Metaph. — *of the eyes,* Prov. xv. 30, i. e. favourable look, as a testimony of regard. Aquila, φωστὴρ ὀφθαλμῶν. Sym. φωτισμὸς ὀφθαλμῶν. Pl.

מאו (335) מאן

m. constr. אוֹר מְאוֹרֵי, *luminaries of light*, Ezek. xxxii. 8.

מְאוּרָה, f. constr. once, מְאוּרַת Is. xi. 8. Cogn. Arab. اُرِيّ, *præsepe, stabulum*, r. אוּר, or אָרִי, whence אֻרְיָה, *stabulum*. See p. 53 above. *Den* or *hole* of a serpent, &c. LXX. κοίτην. Cogn. Arab. مَغَارَة, *spelunca*.

מֹאזְנַיִם, m. dual, constr. מֹאזְנֵי, r. אוּן. Arab. cogn. وَزَنَ, *ponderavit*; مِيزَان, *libra, bilanx*. *Balance*, *scales*, Job xxxi. 6; Ps. lxii. 10. Phr. — בְּ לַעֲלוֹת, *apt, ready, to ascend in the balance*, i. e. in attesting lightness, Ib. vanity. שַׁחַק מֹאזְנַיִם, *particle* (of dust) *of the balance*, Is. xl. 15. מֹאזְנֵי צֶדֶק — *of justice*, i. e. just, Lev. xix. 36; opp. τῷ, מֹאזְנֵי מִרְמָה, — *of deceit*, Hos. xii. 8; Amos viii. 5. Comp. Mic. vi. 11.

מֹאזְנַיָא, m. dual, def. Chald. id. Dan. v. 27, only.

מְאִירוֹת, see מְאֵרָה above.

מְאִירוֹת, Part. Hiph. f. pl. v. אוּר, p. 15 above.

מַאֲכָל, m.—pl. non occ. r. אָכַל. *Meat, eatable*, as of corn, fruit, &c., Gen. ii. 9; iii. 6; vi. 21; 1 Chron. xii. 40, &c. Phr. עֵץ מַאֲכָל, *tree of eatable*, fruit tree, Lev. xix. 23. צֹאן מַאֲכָל, *flock of* —, i. e. slaughtered for meat, Ps. xliv. 12. — אוֹצָרוֹת, *treasures of* —, 2 Chron. xi. 11. — *of the table*, 1 Kings x. 5; 2 Chron. ix. 4. Aff. מַאֲכָלְךָ, Ezek. iv. 10, &c.

מַאֲכֹלֶת, f. once in מַאֲכֹלֶת אֵשׁ, Is. ix. 4. *Consumption, devouring, of fire*.

מַאֲכֶלֶת, f. pl. מַאֲכָלוֹת, r. אכל, lit. *devourer*. Comp. Prov. l. c. *Slaughtering knife*, Gen. xxii. 6. 10; Judg. xix. 29. Pl., Prov. xxx. 14, al. non occ.

מַאֲמַצִּים, pl. masc. once, Job xxxvi. 19, in מַאֲמַצֵּי כֹחַ. *Confirmers, strengtheners, of power*. See my note, r. אָמַץ, p. 41 above. Theod. κρατοῦντες ἰσχύν.

מַאֲמָר, m.—pl. non occ. r. אָמַר, *Edict, command*, Esth. i. 15; ii. 20; ix. 32, only.

מֵאמַר, m. Chald. i. q. Heb. מַאֲמָר, Dan. iv. 14; Ezra vi. 9.

מָאן, m. constr. pl. מָאנֵי; def. pl. מָאנַיָא. Syr. ܡܐܢܐ, *vas*, i. q. Heb. כְּלִי. *A vessel*, Dan. v. 2, 3. 23; Ezra v. 14; vii. 19.

Synon. τοῦ, אֲנִי, and perhaps from the same root. أَنِي, conj. iv. *retinuit*; whence, إِنَاء, id. Gesen.

מָאן, v. Kal non occ. Syr. ܥܕܢ, *tædio fuit*. Arab. مَانَ, *toleravit*.

Pih. מֵאֵן, pres. יְמָאֵן, constr. med. לְ, with Infin. it. omitting the לְ; it. abs. *Refuse, be unwilling*, Gen. xxxvii. 35; xxxix. 8; xlviii. 19; Exod. vii. 14; Num. xxii. 13, 14; Deut. xxv. 7; Job vi. 7, &c.
Infin. מָאֵן, Exod. xxii. 16.
Part. מָאֵן, pl. מֵאֲנִים, (for מָאֲנִים), Exod. vii. 27; Jer. xiii. 10, &c. See Gram. art. 192.

מָאַס, v. pres. יִמְאַס. Arab. مَاسَ, *succensuit* illi. Cogn. مَاشَ, *repulit*. Constr. immed. it. med. בְּ, אֶל; it. abs. (a) *Despise, reject*; opp. τῷ, בָּחַר, Is. vii. 15, 16; xli. 9; Job xxxiv. 33; Jer. ii. 37; 1 Sam. xvi. 1; Ps. cxviii. 22, &c. (b) Meton. *Set at naught, lightly esteem*, Prov. xv. 32; Job ix. 21; xix. 18; xxx. 1, &c.
Infin. מְאֹס, Lam. iii. 45.
Part. f. מֹאֶסֶת, Ezek. xxi. 18 (13). LXX. φυλὴ ἀπωσθῇ.
Niph. נִמְאַס, pres. יִמָּאֵס. *Be, become, despised, rejected; lightly esteemed*, Is. liv. 6; Jer. vi. 30; Ps. xv. 4. Also, in the sense of נָמֵס, of the cogn. מָסַס. *Dissolve, waste*, Ps. lviii. 8; Job vii. 5. See my translation.

מַאֲפֶה, m. r. אפה, once, Lev. ii. 4. *A baking; thing baked*.

מַאֲפֵל, m. r. אפל, once, Josh. xxiv. 7. *Darkness*.

מַאְפֵּלְיָה, once, Jerem. ii. 31. Synon. τοῦ, מִדְבָּר, preceding, or, צַלְמָוֶת, Job x. 22. Compd. of יָהּ + מַאֲפֵל (comp. שַׁלְהֶבֶתְיָה, Cant. viii. 6); or, it may be a mere fem. fm. of מַאְפֵּלִי. See Gram. artt. 166. 5; 175. 16. *Dark, gloomy; inhospitable*, Jer. ii. 31.

מָאַר, v. Kal non occ. Arab. مَأَر, *irritavit, recruduit* vulnus.
Hiph. part. מַמְאִיר, f. מַמְאֶרֶת, *Irritating, vexing, paining*, Ezek. xxviii. 24: f. of the leprosy, Lev. xiii. 51, 52; xiv. 44. LXX. ἔμμονος, Ἀλλ. σπανίζουσα, Ἀλλ. φιλόνεικος.

מַאֲרָב, m.—pl. non occ. r. אָרַב. *Place of lying in wait, ambush*, Josh. viii. 9; Judg.

מאר (336) מבח

ix. 35; Ps. x. 8. Meton. *Persons* so doing; *an ambushment*, 2 Chron. xiii. 13.

מְאֵרָה, f. constr. מְאֵרַת, pl. מְאֵרוֹת, r. אָרַר. *A curse, malediction*, Deut. xxviii. 20; Mal. ii. 2; iii. 9; Prov. iii. 33; xxviii. 27, al. non occ.

מֵאֵת, for מִן אֵת, *From with, at, &c.* See אֵת.

מִבְדָּלוֹת, fem. plur.—r. בָּדַל, once, Josh. xvi. 9. LXX. ἀφορισθεῖσαι. They read, perhaps, מָבְדָּלוֹת, in Hoph., which would seem to suit the context better. The present vowels are probably those of the Arab.

مَبْدَلَة, *mutatoria. Separations*, i. e. cities apportioned to, &c.

מָבוֹא, m. constr. מְבוֹא, pl. constr. מְבוֹאֵי, it. pl. fem. מְבוֹאוֹת, r. בּוֹא. Lit. *Place of entering, entry*, 2 Chron. xxiii. 13; Ezek. xlvi. 19; Judg. i. 24; 2 Kings xi. 16; xvi. 18; 2 Chron. xxiii. 15; Ezek. xxvii. 3; xxvi. 10. מְבוֹא הַשֶּׁמֶשׁ, *entering in of the sun*, i. e. place of its setting, Deut. xi. 30, &c.

מְבוּכָה, fem. aff. מְבוּכָתָם, pl. non occ. r. בּוּךְ. *Confusion, perplexity*, Is. xxii. 5; Mic. vii. 4.

מַבּוּל, masc.—pl. non occ. r. יָבַל, or נבל. Cogn. בּוּל, בלל, בלה. *The deluge, flood*, of Noah, Gen. vi. 17; vii. 7. 10. 17; ix. 11. 28, &c., Ps. xxix. 10. "*De cœli oceano,*" says Gesenius. But, who ever heard of anything like an *ocean of heaven*, among the Hebrews? The intention of the passage, obviously, is, *Jehovah sat as king on the flood*, i. e. ruled, even when that catastrophe took place.

מְבוּסָה, fem.—pl. non occ. r. בּוּס. *A treading*, or *trampling, down*, Is. xviii. 2. 7; xxii. 5, only.

מבונים, masc. plur. for מְבִינִים, Kethiv, 2 Chron. xxxv. 3. Part. Hiph. v. בִּין, p. 80, above.

מַבּוּעַ, masc. constr. pl. מַבּוּעֵי, r. נבע. *Spring*, or *fountain, of water*, Eccl. xii. 6; Is. xxxv. 7; xlix. 10, al. non occ. Arab.

مَنْبَع, *profluvium; locus scaturiginis*.

מְבוּקָה, fem. once, Nah. ii. 11, r. בּוּק. *Emptiness, void*.

מֵבִי, for מֵבִיא, Part. Hiph. r. בּוֹא.

מִבְחַר, masc. constr. pl. aff. מִבְחָרָיו, r. בחר. *Choice, best*, &c., of persons or things, Gen. xxiii. 6; Exod. xv. 4; Deut. xii. 11; Is. xxii. 7; xxxvii. 24; Jer. xxii. 7; Ezek. xxiii. 7; Dan. xi. 15, &c.

מִבְחוֹר, m. id. twice only, 2 Kings iii. 19; xix. 23.

מַבָּט, masc. (for מַנְבָּט, r. נָבַט). Aff. מַבָּטָם, it. מִבְּטָה, Zech. ix. 5. Lit. *Expectation; hope.* Meton. *Place*, or *object, of* —, Is. xx. 5. 6, al. non occ.

מִבְטָא, m. r. בָּטָא, twice only, in the phr. מִבְטָא שְׂפָתֶיהָ, Num. xxx. 7. 9. *Rashness, rash utterance, of her lips.*

מִבְטָח, m. pl. מִבְטָחִים, r. בָּטַח. *Trust.* Meton. *Place, person*, or *thing, trusted in*, Prov. xxii. 19; Ps. xl. 5; lxv. 6; lxxi. 5; Job xviii. 14. See my note. Aff. מִבְטָחִי, מִבְטָחוֹ, it. מִבְטָחָה, מִבְטָחָם, where (ּ) takes the place of (-). Pl., מִבְטַחַיִךְ, Jer. ii. 37.

מַבְלִיגִית, f. once, Jer. viii. 18. Aff. r. בלג. *Opening upon; exhilaration*. Arab.

بَلَاجَةً وَجَه, παῤῥησία. Castell. Col. 358.

מִבְנֶה, m. r. בָּנָה, once, Ezek. xl. 2. *Building, erection*.

מִבְעִתְּךָ, Part. aff. Pih. 1 Sam. xvi. 15; for מְבַעִתְּךָ, r. בעת.

מִבְצָר, m. pl. מִבְצָרִים, r. בָּצַר. *Fortification*, Is. xxv. 12, apparently explained by מִשְׂגַּב הֹמוֹתֶיךָ. Whence, עִיר מִבְצָר, Josh. xix. 29. עָרֵי מִבְצָר, Jer. xxxiv. 7. *City*, or *cities, of fortification*, i. e. fortified, Num. xxxii. 36; 1 Sam. vi. 18; 2 Kings iii. 19; Ps. cviii. 11; Is. xvii. 3. With def. art., Num. xxxii. 17; Josh. x. 20, &c. Metaph., Jer. vi. 27. Pl., Dan. xi. 24, &c. Constr. Lam. ii. 2, &c. Aff. מִבְצָרֶיךָ, &c., Jer. v. 16. It. pl. fem. מִבְצָרוֹת, Dan. xi. 15.

מַבָּרִאשׁוֹנָה, f. compd. מַה + בְּ + רִאשׁוֹנָה, *What, at the head!* 1 Chron. xv. 13, r. ראש.

מִבְרָח, masc.—plur. aff. מִבְרָחָו; Keri, מִבְרָחָיו. *His fugitives*, Ezek. xvii. 21, only. r. בָּרַח.

מְבֻשִׁים, masc. pl.—r. בוש. Aff. מְבֻשָׁיו, *pudenda ejus*, once, Deut. xxv. 11. Aquila, ἐν αἰσχύνῃ.

מְבַשְּׁלוֹת, fem. pl.—r. בָּשַׁל. Part. Pih. Lit. *boiling things. Boilers*; once, Ezek. xlvi. 23.

מַג, m. only in the compd. רַב־מָג, the

latter part of which seems to be the Persic مُغ, *Fire-worshipper, magician;* and the compd. to be nearly equivalent to the پِیرِ مُغانٌ, *senior of* —, i. e. *chief of* —, quoted from a Persian poet in Sir Wm. Jones's Pers. Gram., p. 37, edit. 1828. Jer. xxxix. 3.

מִגְבָּלוֹת, fem. pl.—r. גבל, once, Exod. xxviii. 14, i. q. גְּבֻלוֹת, apparently. *Devices.* See גְּבֻלוֹת, p. 102 above.

מִגְבָּעוֹת, fem. pl.—r. גבע. Cogn. Syr. ܡܰܓܒܥܐ, *pileus.* Æth. ቆብዕ : *mitra sacerdotalis,* it. *monachalis. The mitre,* or *bonnet,* worn by the common priests; that of the high priest being termed מִצְנֶפֶת, Exod. xxviii. 40; xxix. 9; xxxix. 28; Lev. viii. 13; Joseph. Antiq., lib. iii. c. vii. § 7.

מֶגֶד, m. pl. מְגָדִים, aff. מְגָדָיו. Arab. مَجْدٌ, *gloria. Excellence, glory,* i. e. any thing so considered, and thence, *the best, most choice;* as in the phrr. מֶגֶד שָׁמַיִם, *glory of the heavens;* here, of the *dew,* Deut. xxxiii. 13: and see my note on Job xxix. 19, p. 413. מֶגֶד תְּבוּאֹת שֶׁמֶשׁ, — *of the incomings of* (from) *the sun.* גֶּרֶשׁ יְרָחִים —, *of the putting forth of* the moons, Ib. vr. 14. גִּבְעוֹת עוֹלָם —, *of the hills of eternity,* Ib. vr. 15. See vr. 16. פְּרִי מְגָדִים, *fruit of* much *choice,* great *excellence,* Cant. iv. 13. 16. In the Syr. we have ܡܰܓܕܐ, for *dry fruit.* But this will not suffice to determine the sense of this word, Ib. vii. 14, occ. with חֲרָשִׁים. Aquila, Deut. xxxiii. 15, τραγημάτων τῶν βουνῶν. Sym. ὀπώρας τῶν βουνῶν.

מִגְדָּל, m. pl. מִגְדָּלִים, f. מִגְדָּלוֹת, r. גדל. (a) *A tower,* from its height, Gen. xi. 4: — for defence, Judg. viii. 9; ix. 46, seq.; 2 Chron. xiv. 16. Meton. (b) *Castle,* as having towers, 1 Chron. xxvii. 25; Prov. xviii. 10. (c) *Watch-tower,* 2 Kings ix. 17; xvii. 9: — of a vineyard, Is. v. 2. Metaph. (d) — of a *powerful man,* Is. ii. 15; xxx. 25. (e) A sort of *pulpit,* Neh. viii. 4. Comp. ix. 4, and see my note on Job xxix. 7, p. 410. In Cant. v. 13, מִגְדְּלוֹת מֶרְקָחִים, lit. *towers of perfumes.* LXX. φύουσαι μυρεψικά, evidently reading מְגַדְּלוֹת, the part. of Pih. Gesen. "areola in horto, eaque in medio assurgens et elatior." But, has not this *elevated enclosure* been fabricated for the sole purpose of accommodating this place? Cocceius makes *elevated beds* here, in which he supposes certain aromatic plants were cultivated. We have in the Arabic, جَدَلٌ, *grana in aristis robustior;* جَدَالٌ, *dactyli immaturi, virentes, et adhuc rotundi:* and, as if taken from one or other of these notions, جَدْوَلَةٌ, *elegantiâ membrorum prædita* puella. If the second member, moreover, is here explanatory of the first, the conjecture of Cocceius is, perhaps, the best.

מִגְדָּנוֹת, fem. pl.—r. מגד, augm. ־ן, Gram. art. 168. *Choice, precious, things,* Gen. xxiv. 53; Ezra i. 6; 2 Chron. xxi. 3; xxxii. 23, al. non occ.

מָגוֹר, m. pl. מְגוּרִים, r. גור, II. p. 109 above. *Fear, terror,* Jer. vi. 25; xx. 3. 10; Lam. ii. 22; Ps. xxxi. 14, &c.

מְגוּרֵי, masc. pl. constr. sing. non occ. r. גור, sign. I. above. *Sojournings,* i. e. *residings* in strange countries, Gen. xvii. 8; xxxvi. 7; xxxvii. 1, &c. Meton. *Residence, habitation,* Ps. lv. 16; Job xviii. 19. Metaph. *Human life,* considered as a sojourning, Gen. xlvii. 9; Ps. cxix. 54. Comp. גֵּר, and תּוֹשָׁב. Aff. מְגוּרֶיךָ, מְגוּרָי, &c.

מְגוֹרָה, f. constr. מְגוֹרַת (of מָגוֹר above), pl. מְגֹרוֹת. I. *Fear, terror,* Prov. x. 24. Pl., Ps. xxxiv. 5; Is. lxvi. 4. Aff. מְגוּרֹתַי, &c.

II. A *granary* (of sign. I. above), Hag. ii. 19. Pl., מְגֻרוֹת, Joel i. 17, al. non occ.

מְגֵזרוֹת, pl. f.—r. גזר, once, 2 Sam. xii. 31. *Axes.* Syr. ܡܰܓܙܪܐ, *scalprum.*

מַגָּל, masc.—pl. non occ. *Sickle,* for reaping, Jer. L. 16; Joel iv. 13, al. non occ. Arab. مِنْجَلٌ *falx messoria.* Syr. ܡܰܓܠܐ, id.

מְגַמַּת, f. constr. r. גמם, once, Hab. i. 9, in the phr. מְגַמַּת פְּנֵיהֶם, which Gesenius makes to signify, "*turba facierum eorum;*" but which is anything but Hebrew phraseology. Kimchi's "*desiderium,*" "*anhelitus,*" noticed by him, is far better, and is equally well derived from the Arab. جَمَّ, *appetebat. Desire.* Meton. *Object.* Sym. ἡ πρόσοψις.

מגן, v. Kal non occ. Arab. مَجَّانًا, qui sæpè rependit beneficia.

Pih. מִגֵּן, pres. aff. תְּמַגְּנֶךָ, אֲמַגְּנֵךְ. I. Give freely, gratis, Gen. xiv. 20; Prov. iv. 9. II. I. q. נָתַן, or שׂוּם. Give, put into such or such situation: esteem, consider, as such, Hos. xi. 8. Sym. ἐκδώσω σε.

מָגֵן, masc. plur. מָגִנִּים, constr. מָגִנֵּי, it. f. מָגִנּוֹת, 2 Chron. xxiii. 9. Arab. جَنَّ, texit; مِجَنٌّ, clypeus. A shield, Deut. xxxiii. 29; Judg. v. 8; 2 Sam. i. 21; xxii. 31. 36; 2 Kings xix. 32. Less in weight than the צִנָּה: see 1 Kings x. 16. Phr. אִישׁ מָגֵן, man of shield, i. e. armed with one, Prov. vi. 11; xxiv. 34. נֹשְׂאֵי מָגֵן, bearers of shields, 1 Chron. v. 18. הַחֲזֵק מָגֵן וְצִנָּה, take hold of the small and larger shield, Ps. xxxv. 2. מִמְשְׁחוּ מָגֵן, anoint the shield; prepare it for battle, Is. xxi. 5. Metaph. of God as a protector, Gen. xv. 1; Ps. iii. 4; xviii. 3. 31, &c. Ps. vii. 11, מָגִנִּי עַל־אֱלֹהִים, my shield is on (rests on) God; has its protecting power from him. Comp. Ps. cxliv. 2, מָגִנֵּי אֶרֶץ, shields of the earth, i. e. all things protecting it, whether princes—as in the first member—or any other source of strength, are God's. Aquila, θυρεοὶ γῆς. Sym. οἱ ὑπερασπισμοὶ τῆς γῆς, it. vers. E. See LXX. Aff. מָגִנֵּי, &c.

מְגִנָּה, f. constr. מִגְנַּת, in, מִגְנַּת־לֵב, Veiling, covering, of heart. Comp. κάλυμμα, 2 Cor. iii. 15. So the Koran, اكنّةً علي القلوب. Sur. vi. 25, &c. Gesen. Once, Lam. iii. 65.

מִגְעֶרֶת, f.—r. גָּעַר, once, Deut. xxviii. 20. Rebuke. Meton. Calamity. Aquila, ἐπιτίμησιν. LXX. ἀνάλωσιν.

מַגֵּפָה, f. constr. מַגֵּפַת, pl. aff. מַגֵּפֹתַי, r. נָגַף. Lit. a stroke, smiting. Hence, I. A plague, or pestilence, Exod. ix. 14; Num. xiv. 37; xvii. 13; xxv. 18; xxxi. 16; 1 Sam. vi. 4; 2 Sam. xxiv. 21; Zech. xiv. 12. 15. Pl., Exod. ix. 14. II. A beating, defeat, in battle, 1 Sam. iv. 17; 2 Sam. xvii. 9.

מגר, v. Syr. ܡܓܪ, cecidit. Arab. جَرّ, pedes jumenti ligavit.

Part. pass. pl. m. constr. מְגוּרֵי. Fallen, delivered up, Ezek. xxi. 17 (12). See LXX. Pih. מִגַּרְתָּה, Thou hast made to fall, cast down. Constr. med. ל, Ps. lxxxix. 45. Pres. יְמַגֵּר, Chald. id., Ezra vi. 12.

מְגֵרָה, f. pl. מְגֵרוֹת, r. גָּרַר. A saw, 2 Sam. xii. 31; 1 Kings vii. 9; 1 Chron. xx. 3. Syr. ܓܪ, rapuit, attraxit; imitative of the sound of such action, p. 122 above.

מִגְרָעוֹת, f. pl.—r. גָּרַע. Offsets, i. e. steps which take place in a wall where reduced in thickness, as in the chambers attached to the Temple, &c., 1 Kings vi. 6.

מגרפה, f. pl.—aff. מַגְרְפֹתֵיהֶם, r. גָּרַף. Lit. their turnings, harrowings, up. Syr. ܓܪܦ, converrit, convertit. Their furrows, once, Joel i. 17. Gesenius gives, Syr. ܡܓܪܦܐ, Arab. مِغْرَفَة, pala ipsa. But no such words are to be found.

מִגְרָשׁ, m. pl. מִגְרָשִׁים, constr. מִגְרְשֵׁי, it. f. מִגְרְשׁוֹת, r. גָּרַשׁ. Lit. out-place, as in our out-houses, &c. Hence the phrr. מִגְרָשׁ לָעִיר, Ezek. xlviii. 17. Comp. Num. xxxv. 2; and Ezek. xlv. 2. I. Suburbs, or suburban lands, assigned to the Levites, for the support of themselves and cattle, Num. xxxv. 2, seq.; Josh. xxi. 11, seq.; 1 Chron. vi. 40, seq. Whence these cities are styled, עָרֵי מִגְרָשִׁים, 1 Chron. xiii. 2. On the extent of these lands, see my Third Letter to Dr. Pye Smith, pp. 82, seq.: 192, seq. Hence, II. Pastures, generally, 1 Chron. v. 16; Ezek. xlviii. 15. III. Any lands surrounding a city or edifice, Ezek. xxvii. 28; xlv. 2; xlviii. 17. Aff. מִגְרְשֵׁיהֶם, מִגְרָשֶׁיהָ, &c.

מַד, c. pl. מַדִּים, and מִדִּין, according to Gesenius; r. מדד. I. Upper garment, or tunic, Ps. cix. 18; Lev. vi. 3. II. Rich coating, or covering, of the seats of the nobles (Hiller., Gesen., &c.), Judg. v. 10. III. Measure, extent, Job xi. 9. Jer. xiii. 25, מְנָת־מִדַּיִךְ, portion of thy measures, from me, &c. Aff. מַדּוּ, Ps. l. c. מַדָּיו, Judg. iii. 16. מִדָּה, Job, l. c.

מַדְבַּח, m. Chald. r. דבח, Heb. זבח. An altar, Ezra vii. 17, al. non occ.

מִדְבָּר, pl. non occ. r. דָּבַר, p. 121 above. I. Any large plain into which cattle are driven to pasture. Syr. ܡܕܒܪܐ, arvum. Arab. بَرّ, id. pec. virescentis segetis, quæque resecta equis in pabulum præberi solet, Jer. xxiij. 10; Ps. lxv. 13; Joel i. 19; ii. 22;

מדד (339) מרה

Is. xlii. 11. II. *A desert*, or *wilderness*, properly so called, Is. xxxii. 15; xxxv. 1; l. 2; Jer. iv. 11; l. 12. מִדְבַּר שְׁמָמָה, Joel ii. 3; iv. 19; Job xxxviii. 26; Ps. cvii. 35. Often the great desert of Arabia, through which the Israelites passed; particularly with the def. art., Gen. xiv. 6; xvi. 7; Exod. iii. 1; xiii. 18; Deut. xi. 24. — מִדְבַּר יְהוּדָה *of Judah*, Judg. i. 16; Ps. lxiii. 1. Applied, metaph., Hos. ii. 5; Jer. ii. 31. With ה parag. הַמִּדְבָּרָה, Exod. iv. 27. Aff. מִדְבָּרֶךָ, Is. li. 3. III. Cant. iv. 3, מִדְבָּרֵךְ נָאוֶה. Sym. διάλεξίς σου καλή. LXX. ἡ λαλιά σου ὡραῖα. Syr. ܡܡܠܠܟܝ, id. *Thy speech, address, &c.*

מָדַד, v. מַדּוֹתִי, and fully, מְדָדוֹ, pl. מָדְדוּ, pres. יָמֹד, תָּמוֹד, Ezek. xlv. 3: apoc. יָמַד. Constr. immed. it. med. אֶת, אֶל, it. בְּ, it. instr. Arab. مَدَّ, *extendit*. *Measure*, i. e. extend the measuring line, &c. on any thing, Deut. xxi. 2; Is. xl. 12; lxv. 7; Ezek. xl. 20; xlii. 16—19, &c.: pres. Exod. xvi. 18. Ezek. xl. 5, 6. 8, 9, &c. Metaph. Is. lxv. 7, *apportion*, i. e. as they have deserved. Infin. מֹד, with ל, pref., Zech. ii. 6.

Niph. pres. only, יִמַּד. *Be, become, can be, measured*, Jer. xxxi. 37; xxxiii. 22; Hos. ii. 1, al. non occ.

Pih. מִדֵּד, pres. יְמַדֵּד, it. יְמֹדֵד. Aff. יְמַדְּדֵם, constr. immed. i. q. Kal, 2 Sam. viii. 2; Hab. iii. 6, meton., viewed its extent, *measure*. Comp. Job xxviii. 24: and see my preliminary remarks on this chapter, and LXX. who took the r. מוּד, cogn. מוּשׁ. Arab. مَاكَ, r. ميد, *agitata fuit res*. Ἀλλ. διεμέτρησε, Ps. lx. 8; cviii. 8.

Hithp. pres. only, יִתְמֹדֵד. *Be, become, extended, stretched out*, in the prim. sense, 1 Kings xvii. 21.

מֹדַד, m. r. מָדַד, once, Job vii. 4. *Flight*, usually: but see my note. *Time of wandering, distraction*. Some take it to be the pret. Pih. of מָדַד.

מִדָּה, f. constr. מִדַּת, pl. מִדּוֹת. Aff. מִדּוֹתֶיהָ, &c., r. מָדַד. I. *Extent, measure; it. height*, Exod. xxvi. 2; xxxvi. 9. Phrr. אִישׁ מִדָּה, *man of height*, tall man, 1 Chron. xi. 23. אַנְשֵׁי מִדָּה, Is. xlv. 14. אַנְשֵׁי מִדּוֹת Num. xiii. 32; Jer. xxii. 14. בֵּית מִדּוֹת, *house of great extent*. חֶבֶל מִדָּה, *rope of measure*, i. e. measuring line, Zech. ii. 5; ii. i. q. מַד, *Vesture, coat*, Ps. cxxxiii. 2. III. *Tribute*, as taken by measure, Neh. v. 4.

Chald., Ezra iv. 20; vi. 8: with ב inserted in place of dagesh. מִנְדָּה, Ezra iv. 13; vii. 24. Syr. ܡܕܐܬܐ, id.

מַדְהֵבָה, f. once, Is. xiv. 4, applied, as an epithet to Babylon. Lit. *place of gold*. Syr. ܡܕܗܒܐ, *auratus, inauratus*. Arab. مَذَهَب, id. Babylon was always famous for its wealth in *gold*, and thence styled by Æschylus, Persæ. l. 53, "Βαβυλῶν δ᾽ ἡ πολύχρυσος. Babylon vero auro dives." Comp. Rev. xviii. 12; Herodot. i. clxxxiii.; Diod. Sic. ii. ix. Gesenius doubts whether מַרְהֵבָה is not the true reading; but he adduces no good reason for this. Aquila, indeed, probably had this reading before him, as he gives λιμός: but the LXX. have ἐπισπουδαστής.

מִדְהֵרוֹת, f. pl.—r. דָּהַר, see דַּהֲרוֹת, p. 131 above, which has here כֵּן, pref. *Charges, attacks*, of cavalry, Judg. v. 22.

מדו, m. pl. aff. מַדְוֵיהֶם, *Their garments*, i. q. מַד, r. מָדָה, i. q. מָדַד, 2 Sam. x. 4; 1 Chron. xix. 4, al. non occ.

מַדְוֶה, m. pl. constr. מַדְוֵי, r. דָּוָה. Lit. *wasting*. *Consuming disease*, Deut. vii. 15; xxviii. 60, al. non occ.

מַדּוּחִים, m. pl.—r. נָדַח, once, Lam. ii. 14. Lit. *expulsions, drivings out*. Auth. Vers. *Causes of banishment*. LXX. ἐξώσματα.

מָדוֹן, m.—pl. non occ. r. דִּין, cogn. דָּר. Arab. ديوان, *mandatum*; whence, ديوان, *tribunal*. I. *Dispute, contention*, Hab. i. 3; Prov. xv. 18; xvi. 28; xvii. 14; xxii. 10. Phr. אִישׁ מָדוֹן, *man of contention*, i. e. contentious. Meton. *Cause, subject, of contention*, Ps. lxxx. 7. II. מָדוֹן, Keri (מִדְיָן Gesen.), Kethiv, in the phr. אִישׁ מָדוֹן, i. q. אִישׁ מִדָּה, *man of height*, tall in stature, 2 Sam. xxi. 20. Comp. 1 Chron. xx. 6, r. מדד.

מִדְיָנִים, constr. מִדְיָנִים, מִדְיָנִים, it. מִדְיָנִים, r. דִּין, cogn. דָּן, sing. non occ. *Disputes, strifes, contentions*, Prov. xxiii. 29; xviii. 18, 19; vi. 14. 19; x. 12. Phrr. אֵשֶׁת מִדְיָנִים, *wife of —*, i. e. contenticus. Keri, מִדְיָנִים, Prov. xxi. 9. 19; xxvii. 15. אִישׁ מִדְיָנִים, Ib. xxvi. 21. מִדְיָנֵי אִשָּׁה, *scoldings of a wife*, Ib. xix. 13.

מַדּוּעַ, compd. מָה + יָדוּעַ. Gr. τί μαθών, τί βουλόμενος; Interrog. *Why then? Why*,

מדוּ (340) מדנ

Indeed? referring generally to something preceding, Josh. xvii. 14; 2 Sam. xix. 42; Jer. viii. 19; Job xviii. 3, &c. Relatively, Exod. iii. 3. *Why, how,* Job xxi. 7, &c. See my note. Nold., p. 483. On Job xxi. 4, see also my note.

מָדוֹר, masc. Chald. r. דור, pl. non occ. *Habitation, dwelling,* Dan. iv. 22. 29; v. 21. Aff. מְדוֹרָךְ, מְדוֹרֵהּ, ll. cc.

מְדוּרָה, fem.—pl. non occ. r. דור. *Pile of fire,* Ezek. xxiv. 9; Is. xxx. 33. Aff. מְדֻרָתָהּ.

מְדוּשָׁה, f. once, aff. מְדֻשָׁתִי, Is. xxi. 10. *My treading,* or *bruising out,* of corn. Metaph. of Babylon, thence to be trodden down.

מַדְחֶה, m. r. דחה, once, Prov. xxvi. 28. *Casting, driving out; ruin.* Sym. ὀλίσθημα. LXX. ἀκαταστασίας.

מַדְחֵפוֹת, f. pl.—r. דחף, once, Ps. cxl. 12. With prep. לְ, adverbially. *Swiftly, hastily.* LXX. εἰς καταφθοράν.

מָדְיָא, m. it. מָדָא. Keri, m. patronym. of מָדַי, *Media.* Chald. def. *A Median,* Dan. vi. 1.

מַדַּי, compd. דַּי + מַה. *What* (is, was) *sufficient;* adv. *sufficiently,* once, 2 Chron. xxx. 3.

מִדַּי, compd. דֵּי + מִן. See under דַּי, p. 136 above.

מִדִּין, pl. m., see מַד above.

מִדְיָנִים, see מְדָנִים above.

מִדְיָנִי, m. pl. מִדְיָנִים, patronym. of מִדְיָן. *A Midianite,* Num. x. 29; Gen. xxxvii. 28.

מִדְיָנִית, f. of do., Num. xxv. 15.

מְדִינָה, f. constr. מְדִינַת, pl. מְדִינוֹת, r. דין. Lit. *Jurisdiction:* hence, I. *Province.* Syr. ܡܕܝܢܬܐ, Arab. مَدِينَة, id., Esth. i. 1. 22; ii. 1; iii. 12. 14; Neh. vii. 6. II. *Region* or *country,* Dan. xi. 24; Lam. i. 1; Ezek. xix. 8; Eccl. ii. 8; v. 7.

מְדִינָה, f. Chald. constr. מְדִינַת, def. מְדִינְתָּא, pl. מְדִינָן, def. מְדִינָתָא, i. q. Heb. I. Dan. iii. 2. 3. II. Dan. ii. 48, 49; iii. 1. 12. 30; Ezra v. 8, &c.

מְדֹכָה, f. once, Num. xi. 8. Lit. place of pounding. *A mortar,* r. דוך.

מְדָנִים, m. pl. for מִדְיָנִים, or מְדִינִים, by Gram. art. 73. See מְדָנִים above.

מִדְיָנַי, m. for מִדְיָנֵי, Gram. art. 73, pl. מִדְיָנִים, *Midianites,* Gen. xxxvii. 36. See vr. 28.

מַדָּע, and מַדָּע, r. ידע, pl. non occ. I. *Knowledge, experience,* 2 Chron. i. 10—12; Dan. i. 4. 17. II. *Mind.* LXX. συνείδησις, Eccl. x. 20. Aff. מַדָּעֲךָ.

מוֹדָע, see מוֹדָע.

מַדְקָרוֹת, f. pl.—r. דקר. *Piercings of the sword,* once, Prov. xii. 18.

מְדָר, m. aff. מְדָרְהוֹן, r. דור, i. q. מָדוֹר, which it will still represent if we take (ָ) for Kametz Khatuph; once, Dan. ii. 11. *Their habitation, dwelling.*

מַדְרֵגָה, f. pl. מַדְרֵגוֹת, r. דרג. Syr. ܕܪܓܐ, *gradus.* Arab. دَرَجَة, id. مُدْرَج, *via, qua quis incedit. Precipitous ascent,* as in the clefts of rocks. LXX. φάραγγες. Syr. and Targ. ܒܪܓܐ, *turres,* Ezek. xxxviii. 20; Cant. ii. 14, al. non occ.

מִדְרָךְ, m. r. דרך, once, Deut. ii. 5, in מִדְרַךְ־רָגֶל, *treading-place of the sole of the foot,* i. e. its extent.

מִדְרָשׁ, m. once, 2 Chron. xiii. 22. Syr. ܕܪܫ, *studuit,* &c. Arab. دَرَسَ, *trivit librum, perlegit studiosè;* مُدَرِّس, *liber commentarius.* The Discourses, or Sermons, of Ephrem Syrus are termed ܡܕܪܫܐ. *Book, work, commentary,* or some such general term, seems most suitable. LXX. ἐπὶ βιβλίῳ.

מָה, מַה, מֶה, and contr. מַ, מֶ, Pron. interrog., &c. Syr. ܡܐ, Arab. مَا, *quid, &c.* On its application, see Gram. art. 178. 2, seq. Interrog. *What?* מֶה עָשִׂיתָ, *What hast thou done?* Gen. iv. 10. Comp. Exod. iii. 13; Judg. i. 14; Zech. i. 9, &c. Without interrog. מַה־יֵּעָשֶׂה לוֹ, *What may be done to him,* Exod. ii. 4. Comp. Num. xxiii. 3; Judg. ix. 48; 1 Kings xiv. 3, &c. Interrog. with expostulation, *What!* מַה־פִּשְׁעִי, *What is my wickedness!* Gen. xxxi. 36. Comp. 1 Sam. xx. 1; 1 Kings xii. 16; Job vi. 11, &c. Interrog. with wonder, מַה־נּוֹרָא, *How fearful!* Gen. xxviii. 17. מַה־טּוֹבוּ, *How good are —!* Num. xxiv. 5; 2 Sam. vi. 20; Cant. vii. 2, &c. Interrog. with comparison,

מה (341) מהו

What? מַה־דּוֹדֵךְ מִדּוֹד, *What is thy love more than, rather than —?* Comp. Eccl. xi. 2; Mal. i. 13; Ps. xxxix. 5, &c. *How, how much?* Interrog. with admiration, מָה־אָהַבְתִּי תוֹרָתֶךָ, *How, or how much, have I loved thy law!* Ps. cxix. 97. Comp. Job xxvi. 2, 3, &c. Interrog. with reference to object, end, &c., *For what? Why?* מַה־תִּצְעַק אֵלָי, *Why, for what, criest thou to me?* Exod. xiv. 15. Comp. Gen. xxi. 29; Josh. iv. 6; Judg. viii. 1; 2 Kings vi. 33, &c. Interrog. as to manner, *How? In what way, manner, &c.?* מַה־נְּדַבֵּר וגו׳, *How shall we speak, &c.?* Gen. xliv. 16. Comp. Exod. x. 26; 1 Sam. x. 27; 2 Kings iv. 43, &c. Interrog. with insult. מַה־נַּחֲנִי, *How graceful shalt thou be!* Jer. xxii. 23. — with extenuation; comparatively small, מַהדִיא, *What is that!* i. e. how *trifling*, Gen. xxiii. 15; Eccl. ii. 22; 1 Kings ix. 13; 2 Kings viii. 13; Ps. viii. 5, &c. Interrog. or relatively, *What, what sort, character, &c.* מַהדִיא, *What it is,* Num. xiii. 18. Comp. 1 Sam. xxviii. 14; Hag. ii. 3. When taken relatively, this particle appears to be equivalent to our *something, anything, anything whatever, &c.,* and is frequently found in this sense at the end of a sentence, as, וְיַעֲבֹר עָלַי מָה, *then come over me anything whatever,* what will, Job xiii. 13. See my note here, and the places cited, it. Nold. § 9, p. 487.

When compounded with prepositions, &c., the force will be that which such compound would — the above usages being borne in mind—naturally supply, as, וּמָה, Judg. xviii. 3. 24; בַּמָּה, 1 Kings xxii. 21: בַּמֶּה, 2 Chron. vii. 21; Nold., p. 187: כַּמָּה, Gen. xlvii. 8; Ps. cxix. 84, &c.; Nold., p. 388: מַדּוּעַ, p. 497: לָמָה, לָמָּה. p. 439, seq.; מָה דִּי, Ib., p. 495: מַהדִיָה, Ib.; מַהדֻּאת, Ib. So, also, עַד־מָה, צַד־מָה, &c. in their proper places.

מָה, once, מָא, Chald. i. q. Heb. Dan. ii. 22; iv. 32. וּמָה, *and why?* Ezra vi. 9. מָה דִּי, i. q. Heb. מַהדֻּשׁ, *that which,* Dan. ii. 28, 29. כְּמָה, *How, how much?* Dan. iii. 33. לְמָה, *For what, why?* Ezra iv. 22. עַל־מָה, id. Dan. ii. 15. לְמָא דִי, *as to what,* Ezra vi. 8. דִּי לְמָה, Ib. vii. 23.

מהמה, v. Kal non occ., a mere reduplication of the pron. מָה, *what,* occ. in— Hithp. הִתְמַהְמְהַּ, pres. יִתְמַהְמֵהַּ. Cogn. תמה (Is. xxix. 9), which is probably of the same origin. Syr. ܡܗܡܗ, *bullivit.* Arab. ܐܰܟ݂, *consistere fecit;* red. ܡܰܗܡܶܗ, *increpando prohibuit; destitit.* Constr. abs. it. med. יַ. *Delay, tarry, wait,* Gen. xix. 16; xliii. 10; Judg. xix. 8; Ps. cxix. 60; Hab. ii. 3. Infin. הִתְמַהְמֵהַּ, Exod. xii. 39. Aff. הִתְמַהְמְהָם, Judg. iii. 26. Part. מִתְמַהְמֵהַּ, 2 Sam. xv. 28.

מְהוּמָה, f. constr. מְהוּמַת, pl. מְהוּמוֹת. Arab. هَوَّمَ, *nutavit capite.* Cogn. هَامَ, r. هيم, *amore mulieris captus fuit;—vagatus fuit;* هَمَّ, *anxit res. Perturbation, tumult, vexation,* Deut. vii. 23; xxviii. 20; 1 Sam. v. 9. 11; Is. xxii. 5; Ezek. xxii. 5; Zech. xiv. 13; Amos iii. 9; Prov. xv. 16. "De vita turbulenta et voluptuosa divitis." Gesen. But does this appear? LXX. μετὰ ἀφοβίας. The Auth. Vers. is more correct.

מָהִיר, and מַהֵר, masc.—pl. non occ. r. מהר. Syr. ܡܗܺܝܪ, *festinus.* Arab. مَاهِر, *acutus, solers. Ready, quick, skilful,* Prov. xxii. 29; Is. xvi. 5; Ps. xlv. 2; Ezra vii. 6.

מָהוּל, m. once, Is. i. 22. Part. of r. מהל, Chald. i. q. Heb. מול. Usually, *cut,* i. e. as among the Arabs, *wine cut with water,* i. e. mixed with it, and so injured. Schultens. Animadv. in loc. Who saw, nevertheless, that this would not necessarily signify *adulterate, make worse;* as the Orientals usually mix their wine with water. Rather the cogn. مهن, *molestiâ affecit; vexavit;* it. مهرات, r. مهر, *effusa, abjecta, aqua.* And cogn. Syr. ܡܚܰܠ, *imbecillis, miser.* It. ܡܚܰܢ, *subegit mulierem:* whence the notion of *polluting* or *adulterating. Debased, adulterated.*

מְהֵימַן, part. Aph. r. אָמַן, Dan. ii. 45; vi. 5. *Faithful, sure.*

מְהַחֲתִין, Part. masc. pl. Chald. Aph. r. נְחַת, once, Ezra vi. 1.

מְהָךְ, Chald. Infin. הוך, p. 151 above.

מַהֲלָךְ, m.—pl. non occ. r. הָלַךְ. I. *A walk,* Ezek. xlii. 4. II. *Journey,* Neh. ii. 6; Jonah iii. 3, 4. Aff. מַהֲלָכְךָ. Pl. מַהְלְכִים. Part. Hiph. See p. 156 above.

מַהֲלָל, m. once, Prov. xxvii. 21. Aff. מַהֲלָלוֹ. *Praising him;* a sort of participial noun. (Hiph.) It may signify *praise*, i. e. *so let a man be according to*, or as is, *his praise*; i. e. what the crucible is to silver, &c.; in other words, let his praise act as a stimulus to his further excelling. See also the LXX.

מַהֲלֻמוֹת, fem. pl.—r. הָלַם. *Beatings, stripes*, Prov. xviii. 6; xix. 29, only.

מַהֲמֹרוֹת, f. pl.—r. המר, once, Ps. cxl. 11. Arab. هَمَّ, *impulit; effudit aquam*; هَمَّار وهَمَّال, *verbosus*; i. e. from the notion of the *flowing* of waters; and thence, as injurious. Heb. retains, apparently, the primitive sense. *Flowings, torrents, floods*, carrying ruin with them. Symm. Theod. βοθύνους. LXX. ταλαιπωρίαις.

מַהְפֵּכָה, f. constr. מַהְפֶּכַת, pl. non occ. r. הָפַךְ. *Overthrow, subversion*, Deut. xxix. 22; Is. i. 7; xiii. 19; Jer. xlix. 18; L. 40; Amos iv. 11.

מַהְפֶּכֶת, f.—pl. non occ. r. הָפַךְ. Syr. ܡܗܦܟܬܐ, *contorsio, oppositio;* ܗܦܟ, *rejecit.* Lit. *overthrow, ruin. Imprisonment; stocks*, Jer. xx. 2, 3; xxix. 26; 2 Chron. xvi. 10. Symm. βασανιστήριον ἢ στρεβλωτήριον. LXX. Theod. τον καταρράκτην. See Schleus. Lex. in LXX. Probably *the torture*, such as was formerly used in our prisons. Hence, בֵּית הַמַּהְפֶּכֶת, 2 Chron. l. c.

מָהֵר, m. ⎫ pl. non occ. Arab. مَهَر,
מְהֵרָה, f. ⎭ *solers fuit.* (a) *Quick, ready*, Zeph. i. 14. Adv. (b) *Quickly, readily*, Exod. xxxii. 8; Deut. iv. 26; vii. 4. 22; Josh. ii. 5; Prov. xxv. 8, &c. Fem. id. Num. xvii. 11; Deut. xi. 17; Josh. viii. 19. בִּמְהֵרָה, id. Eccl. iv. 12. עַד־מְהֵרָה, *even to swiftness*, very swiftly, Ps. cxlvii. 15. מְהֵרָה חוּשָׁה, *quickly! haste!* 1 Sam. xx. 38.

מֹהַר, masc.—plur. non occ. Arab. مَهْر, *donum sponsalitium.* Synon. מַתָּן. *A gift*, or *price*, tendered to the parents by a young man wishing to marry a daughter, Gen. xxxiv. 12; Exod. xxii. 16; 1 Sam. xviii. 25. In lieu of which, *service* was sometimes given and taken, as in Jacob's case, Gen. xxix. 18. The hundred foreskins exacted by Saul from David, 1 Sam. l. c. was an ancient Phenician custom. See my Travels of Ibn Batuta, p. 17, note. The word probably signifies *ready, quick*, or the like; because, perhaps, the price was, on such occasions, *promptly* given. LXX. Gen. Exod. ll. cc. φερνή; 1 Sam. ἐν δόματι.

מָהַר, v. Kal, once, Ps. xvi. 4. I. *Hasten, hurry.* See מָהִיר above.

Niph. part. נִמְהָר ⎫ plur. נִמְהָרִים, constr.
— fem. נִמְהָרָה ⎭ נִמְהֲרֵי. *Being, becoming, hasty, hurried, precipitous*, Hab. i. 6; Job v. 13; Is. xxxii. 4. לֵב נִמְהָרִים, *heart of the hurried*, inconsiderate, Ib. xxxv. 4. נִמְהֲרֵי־לֵב, *hurried of heart*; timorous, alarmed.

Pih. מִהַר, pres. יְמַהֵר (dagesh being implied, Gram. art. 109), i. q. Kal. Constr. abs. it. med. ל, Infin. and immed. it. med. אֶל, *to*, it. אֵת, of object. *Hasten, hurry*, Gen. xxvii. 20; 1 Sam. iv. 14; xxv. 34; Is. li. 14. Used much as an auxiliary verb, as, מִהֲרוּ שָׁכְחוּ, *they hasted, they forgot*, i. e. *they quickly forgat*, Ps. cvi. 13. Comp. Gen. xix. 22; xlv. 13; Exod. ii. 18, &c. The second verb in such cases often omitted by the ellipse, Gen. xviii. 6. מַהֲרִי שְׁלֹשׁ, *hasten (bring) three*, &c., Nahum ii. 6; 2 Chron. xviii. 8, &c. With ה parag. מַהֲרָה וּלְכָה, *hasten, and go, I pray*, 1 Sam. xxiii. 27.

Infin. מַהֵר, Prov. vii. 23; Exod. xii. 33, &c.

Imp. מַהֵר, Gen. xix. 22, &c. With ה parag., 1 Sam. xxiii. 27 above.
— fem. מַהֲרִי, Gen. xviii. 6; pl. m. מַהֲרוּ, Gen. xlv. 9, &c.

Part. מְמַהֵר, Gen. xli. 32.
F. pl. מְמַהֲרוֹת, Prov. vi. 18.

II. Kal. See מֹהַר above, pres. f. aff. יִמְהָרֶנָּה. *Let him pay the price of marriage for her*, Exod. xxii. 15.

Infin. מָהוֹר, Ib., al. non occ.

מַהֲתַלּוֹת, f. pl.—r. התל, once, Is. xxx. 10. *Delusions.* See my note on Job xvii. 2, as to the etymology. Symm. πλάνας. LXX. πλάνησιν.

מוֹ, a syllabic adjunct, never found alone, i. q. מָה; Syr. ܡܐ; Arab. مَا. See under כְּמוֹ, p. 299, above, attached also occasionally to the prepp. בְּ, לְ, as in בְּמוֹ, לְמוֹ, without affecting their significations in any sensible degree. It is in the more elevated style only that it is had recourse to; as, בְּמוֹ, Is. xxv. 10; xliii. 2; xliv. 16; Ps. xi. 2; Job xvi. 4, 5, &c. See Nold., p. 188, לְמוֹ. See in its place above, and Nold., p. 438.

מוֹאָבִי, מוֹאָבִיָּה, f. and מוֹאָבִית. m., Patronym. of מוֹאָב. *Moab*. See p. 299, above. *A Moabite*, Ruth iv. 5; 2 Chron. xxiv. 26.

מוּאָל, partic. i. q. מוּל, or מוֹל. See Keri. Once, Neh. xii. 38. *Over against*.

מוֹבָא, m. pl. aff. מוֹבָאָיו, r. בוא, twice only, 2 Sam. iii. 25; Ezek. xliii. 11. For the more regular form מָבוֹא; but so written—as Gesenius has well observed—to correspond with מוֹצָא. Slight irregularities of this sort often occur in the Arabic.

מוּג, v. pres. only in Kal. f. תָּמוּג, it. תָּמוֹג. Aff. תְּמוּגֶנּוּ. Arab. مَاجَ, r. موج, *fluctuavit*. Cogn. مَجَّ, *ejecit vinum, &c. ex ore*; IV. *aqua fluxit* in lignum. *Dissolve, melt*. Meton. *Flow*; indicating weakness, dissolution. See פָּחַו, Ps. xlvi. 7; Amos ix. 5; Is. lxiv. 6.

Infin. מוֹג, Ezek. xxi. 20.

Niph. נָמוֹג, *Be, become, dissolved; undone*. Constr. abs. Exod. xv. 15; Josh. ii. 9. 24; 1 Sam. xiv. 16; Is. xv. 4; Nah. ii. 7; Jer. xlix. 23.

Part. masc. plur. נְמוֹגִים, Ps. lxxv. 4. LXX. ἐτάκη.

Piḥ. pres. aff. תְּמוּגֵנִי, *Thou dissolvest me: makest me waste away*, Job xxx. 22. תְּמוּגְגֶנָּה, *dissolvest it*, i. e. by raining plentifully on it, Ps. lxv. 11.

Hithp. pl. m. הִתְמוֹגְגוּ, pres. תִתְמוֹגָג, pl. f. תִּתְמוֹגַגְנָה, i. q. Niph. Nahum i. 5; Ps. cvii. 26; Amos ix. 13, al. non occ.

מוּד, v. cogn. מדד, once, Hab. iii. 6. Piḥ. יְמֹדֵד, "*commovit*," of the cogn. מוּט, מוּד, נוּד. So LXX. ἐσαλεύθη ἡ γῆ. Ἀλλ. διεμέτρησε τὴν γῆν. Auth. Vers. *Measured the earth*. Rather, metaph., *he viewed*, i. e. measured with his eye. Not unlike the Arab. قَدْرَ مَدِّ البَصَرِ, *far as the extent of the sight*. See מדד above.

מוֹדָע, מֹדָע, m. f. aff. מֹדַעְתָּנוּ, r. יָדַע. *Familiar*, i. e. *known, kinsman* or *friend*, Prov. vii. 4; Ruth ii. 1; iii. 2, al. non occ.

מוּזָנִים, m. pl. Part. Hoph. r. זון, once, Jer. v. 8. *Fed, fattened*. Keri, מְיֻזָּנִים.

מוֹט, masc. — plur. non occ. Syr. ܡܰܘܬܳܐ, ܡܰܘܬܶܐ, *declinatio, deflexus*. Arab. مَاطَ, r. ميط, *pepulit, &c.* I. *Moving, tottering, vacillating*, from weakness; opp. to stability. Synon. τοῦ, מָעַד, Job xii. 5; Ps. xxxviii. 17; xlvi. 3; lv. 23; lxvi. 9; cxxi. 3; Is. xxiv. 19. II. *A pole*, or *staff*, on which anything may be carried, Num. iv. 10. 12; xiii. 23. Also, III., *A yoke* for the neck, on which to carry burdens, Nah. i. 12.

מוֹטָה, fem. of the last, pl. מוֹטוֹת, מֹטוֹת, i. q. מוֹט, sign. II., 1 Chron. xv. 15; III. Lev. xxvi. 13; Jer. xxvii. 1; xxviii. 10. 13; Ezek. xxx. 18; Is. lviii. 6. 9.

מוֹט, v. pret. מָט, pres. תָּמוֹט. See מוּט above. Constr. abs. it. med. עִם, with לְ, בְּ, in, into. *Totter, to a fall*, of men or things, Prov. xxv. 26: applied often to the foot. Synon. τοῦ, מָעַד. See my note on Job xii. 5; Ps. xciv. 18; Deut. xxxii. 35. Metaph. of the earth, Ps. xlvi. 7; lx. 4: of mountains, Ps. xlvi. 3; Is. liv. 10: of a man becoming poor, Lev. xxv. 35. מָטָה יָדוֹ עִמָּךְ, *his hand* (power) *fail with thee*.

Infin. מוֹט, Ps. lv. 23; Is. xxiv. 19. בְּמוֹט Ps. xxxviii. 17, &c. מוֹט above.

Part. מָט, Prov. l. c. It may also be the pret.

Niph. plur. masc. נָמוֹטוּ, pres. יִמּוֹטוּ. *Be, become, moved, tottering*, Ps. xvii. 5; x. 7; xiii. 5; xxi. 8; lxxxii. 5; Job xli. 14, &c.

Hiph. pres. pl. יָמִישׁוּ. *They make, cause, to fall, come down*, Ps. lv. 4; cxl. 11. Kethiv; Keri in Kal.

Hithp. f. הִתְמוֹטְטָה, once only, Is. xxiv. 19, i. q. Niph.

מוּךְ, v. pret. מָךְ, pres. יָמוּךְ. Syr. ܡܟ, *tenuis factus*. Cogn. Arab. مَكَّ, *diminuit*. Syr. ܡܟ, *dejectus*. Cogn. Heb. מכך. Lit. *waste. Be, become, indigent, poor*, Lev. xxv. 25. 35. 39. 47; xxvii. 8. Constr. abs.

מוּל, Partic. once, מוֹל, Deut. i. 1; מוּאָל, Neh. xii. 38, r. אָלַל. Cogn. אוּל, אֵל. Ewald and Gesenius, i. q. Arab. أَوَّلَ, *præcessit, &c*: The word, however, has very much the appearance of a primitive, or segolate, form, viz., מֹל, or מוּל, Gram. ar. 87. And, if this be the fact, מל is probably the root, i. q. Arab. مَالَ, r. ميل, *inclinavit, propensus fuit*, ad aliquid: *propinqua fuit domo via*. Whence, *Near, over against, opposite*, would be regularly

מוֹל   (344)   מוּם

and easily deduced. Again, this word may very well be the root of that signifying *circumcision;* and, accordingly, this Arabic verb is found to signify (conj. iv.) *removit, avertit, rem,* i. e. the removal of something injurious. I take it, therefore, for the root of both. (a) *Near, with,* Exod. xviii. 19; Josh. xix. 46; Deut. iii. 29. Comp. Ib. ii. 19. (b) *Opposite, over against,* Deut. xi. 30; 1 Sam. xiv. 9; Deut. iv. 46; xxxiv. 6, &c. מוּל, Deut. i. 1. Compd. with other particles, וּמִמּוּל, 1 Kings vii. 5. אֶל־מוּל, Josh. viii. 33, &c.; Nold., p. 61. לְמוּאֵל, id. Neh. xii. 38. אֶל־מוּל פְּנֵי, Num. viii. 2; Ib. p. 61. פְּנֵי—, Exod. xxviii. 25; Ib. p. 62. מִמּוּל, aff. מִמֻּלִי, Num. xxii. 5; Ib. p. 506. פְּנֵי—, Exod. xxviii. 27; Ib.

מוּל, v. pret. מָל, pres. apoc. יָמֶל. See מוּל above. Lit. *put away* something. *Circumcise.* Constr. immed. it. med. אֵת, Exod. xii. 44; Josh. v. 4. 7, &c. Pres. Gen. xvii. 23; xxi. 4; Josh. v. 3. Metaph. Deut. x. 16; xxx. 6. Comp. Rom. ii. 29.

Imp. מָל, Josh. v. 2.

Part. pass. מוּל, Jer. ix. 24.

— pl. מֻלִים, Josh. v. 5.

Niph. pres. יִמּוֹל, *Be, become, circumcised,* Gen. xvii. 12—14; xxxiv. 24; Lev. xii. 3. Infin. הִמּוֹל, Gen. xvii. 10. 13; Exod. xii. 48. בְּהִמּוֹל, Gen. xxxiv. 22. Aff. Ib. xvii. 24. לְהִמּוֹל, Gen. xxxiv. 15, &c.

Imp. pl. הִמֹּלוּ, Jer. iv. 4.

Pih. pres. יְמוֹלֵל. One, some one, impers. *Cuts off,* as grass, &c., Ps. xc. 6, only.

Niph. pres. aff. אֲמִילַם, *I will cut them off,* or *down,* Ps. cxviii. 10—12.

Hithp. pres. יִתְמֹלָלוּ. *They* (persons) are *cut off,* or *down,* Ps. lviii. 8.

מוֹלֶדֶת, f. pl. aff. מוֹלְדוֹתֶךָ, r. יָלַד. (a) *Nativity, birth,* Esth. ii. 10. 20; Ezek. xvi. 3, 4. Meton. (b) *Place of birth,* Gen. xii. 1; xxiv. 4: for אֶרֶץ מוֹלֶדֶת, Gen. xi. 28; xxiv. 7; Jer. xlvi. 16. It. (c) *Person born,* Gen. xlviii. 6; Lev. xviii. 9. 11. It. (d) *Persons of the same family; relatives,* Gen. xxxi. 3; Esth. viii. 6, &c. Aff. מוֹלַדְתֵּנוּ מוֹלַדְתִּי, &c.

מוּלָה, f. pl. once, מוּלֹת. *Circumcisions,* i. e. rites of, Exod. iv. 26.

מוּם, m. — pl. non occ. Syr. ܡܘܡܐ, *macula.* Arab. مُوم, *variolæ plumbei coloris.* *Spot; blemish,* from disease, &c.,

Lev. xxi. 17, seq.; xxii. 20, 21. 25. Comp. 2 Sam. xiv. 25; Cant. iv. 7. Metaph. Deut. xxxii. 5; Job xi. 15; xxxi. 7; Dan. i. 4. מאוּם. Aff. מוּמָם, מוּמוֹ.

מוּמַת, part. Hoph. r. מות.

מוּן, see מִין.

מוּסָב, masc.—plur. non occ. r. סבב, fm. Part. Hoph. concr. for abs. *A surrounding, winding about,* once, Ezek. xli. 7. See LXX.

מוּסָב, part. Hoph. r. סבב.

מוֹסָד, m. pl. constr. מוֹסְדֵי, pl. abs. non occ.—

מוֹסָדָה, fem. pl. מוֹסָדוֹת, pause; constr. מוֹסְדוֹת—

r. יסד, p. 261. *Foundations,* propr. of an edifice. Metaph. — of the mountains, heaven, earth, &c., Deut. xxxii. 22; Ps. xviii. 8; lxxxii. 5; Prov. viii. 29; Is. xxiv. 18, &c. Mic. vi. 2, הָאֵתָנִים מוֹסְדֵי אָרֶץ, *the powerful ones, foundations* (supports, peers), *of the land:* where the metaph. is carried still farther, see LXX. Is. lviii. 12, מוֹסְדֵי דוֹר־וָדוֹר, *foundations of age after age,* i. e. of ancient times. Fem., Jer. li. 26; 2 Sam. xxii. 8. 16; Ps. xviii. 16; Is. xl. 21.

מוּסָד, m.   ⎫ r. יָסַד. (a) Part. Hoph.
מוּסָדָה, f. ⎭ See p. 262 above.

מוּסָךְ, m. r. סכך, once, 2 Kings xvi. 18. Lit. *Covering, porch.* Kethiv, מיסך.

מוֹסֵר, sing. non occ. plur. masc. constr. מוֹסְרֵי. Aff. pause, מוֹסְרָי. Fem. pause, מוֹסְרוֹת. Constr. מוֹסְרוֹת, r. יסר, in the sense of the cogn. אָסַר. *Bonds,* of prisoners, slaves, &c., Is. xxviii. 22; lii. 2; Jer. ii. 20; v. 5; xxvii. 2; Job xxxix. 5; Nahum i. 13; Ps. ii. 3; cvii. 14; cxvi. 16. Aff. מוֹסְרוֹתַיִךְ, מוֹסְרוֹתֵימוֹ, &c. Job xxxiii. 16, מֹסָרָם, for (מוּסָרָם). See מוּסָר.

מוּסָר, masc. — plur. non occ. r. יָסַר. (a) *Chastisement, discipline,* as of children, subjects, &c., Ps. L. 7; Prov. v. 12. 23; viii. 33; xii. 1, &c. Phrr. שֵׁבֶט מוּסָר, *rod of chastisement,* Prov. xxii. 15. תּוֹכְחוֹת מוּסָר, *arguings, rebukes, of discipline,* Ib. vi. 23. פּוֹרֵעַ מוּסָר, *rejector of discipline,* Ib. xiii. 18. קַחַת מוּסָר, *the receiving of discipline,* Jer. v. 3. Metaph. אֲנִי מוּסַר, *I am* (the cause, means, of) *chastisement,* Hos. v. 2. מוּסַר יְהוָה, *discipline of Jehovah,* Deut. xi. 2. מוּסַר הַשְׂכֵּל, *discipline of intelligence,* i. e. for acquiring it, Prov. i. 3. Comp. Ib. xv. 33.

מוע (345) מוע

מוּסַר הֲבָלִים, *discipline of vanities*, Jer. x. 8, &c. (b) Meton. *Learning, erudition*, occ. with דַּעַת, or חָכְמָה, Prov. i. 2. 7; xii. 1; xv. 33; xxiii. 23. Aff. מוּסָרִי, מוּסָרְךָ, מוּסָרָם, for כְּסָרָם, Job xxxiii. 16.

מוֹעֵד, m. pl. מוֹעֲדִים, constr. מוֹעֲדֵי, r. יָעַד. (a) *Coming together, convention*. In the phr. אֹהֶל מוֹעֵד, *tent of assembly*, or *congregation*, Exod. xxvii. 21; xl. 22. 24; Num. xvii. 19, &c. See LXX. Is. xxxiii. 20; Ib. xiv. 13, הַר־מוֹעֵד, *mountain of assembly*. Whether some particular place in the constellations, or mountain on earth supposed to be sacred, it will be difficult to determine. But, as sacred places were generally on heights, in imitation perhaps of the sacred place of Sinai, or, of the Temple at Jerusalem (comp. Ps. xlviii. 3), this appears most probable here. It is not unlikely that some place among the constellations might have been so called; particularly as Temples among the Idolaters were all supposed to be inferior habitations of certain demons, holding their supreme courts in some star. See under אֲשֵׁרָה, p. 61, seq. above. Job xxx. 23, בֵּית מוֹעֵד, *house of meeting* of all living, i. e. the grave. Gesenius finds here his favourite "*orcus;*" without any necessity apparently. Meton. *Sign, signal, of coming together*, Judg. xx. 38. It. *Assembly, congregation*, Is. xiv. 31. Aff. pl. מוֹעֲדָיו.

(b) Meton. *Time, season;* or, (c) *place, appointed*: (b) Gen. xvii. 21; 1 Sam. xiii. 8. 11; 2 Sam. xx. 5; xxiv. 15; Jer. viii. 7. Hab. ii. 3, חָזוֹן לַמּוֹעֵד, the *vision* (is) *for* THE *appointed time*, i. e. to be fulfilled when that period, afterwards named *the fulness of time*, should come; intimated here by the term קֵץ. Comp. Dan. viii. 19; xi. 27. 35. Meton. *Festivals*, Lam. i. 4; ii. 6. יוֹם מוֹעֵד, Hos. ix. 5; xii. 10. מוֹעֲדֵי יְהֹוָה, Lev. xxiii. 2. 4. 37. 44. It. fem. plur. מוֹעֲדוֹת, 2 Chron. viii. 13. Meton. *Victim* slaughtered on the occasion, 2 Chron. xxx. 22.—*Time, season*, of certain duration, Gen. i. 14; Dan. xii. 7; *year* perhaps. On this last usage, see my Exposition of the Rev. London, 1830, p. 356, seq.

(c) *Place appointed*. מוֹעֵד אֵל, — *of God*, i. e. place of worship, Josh. viii. 14; Lam. ii. 6; Ps. lxxiv. 8. כָּל־מוֹעֲדֵי־אֵל, *the whole of God's appointed* places, i. e. *his synagogues*, and places of prayer, προσευχαί, scattered throughout the Holy Land. See my third Letter to Dr. Pye Smith, p. 87, with the note. Aff. מוֹעֲדוֹ, מוֹעֲדָהּ, &c.

מוּעָדָה, f.—pl. non occ. Lit. *Being appointed*, fm. part. Hoph. It is said, לָנוּס שָׁמָּה, *to flee thither*, i. e. *cities of refuge*, Josh. xx. 9.

מוּעֶדֶת, see r. מָעַד.

מוּעֶדֶת, part. Kal. r. מָעַד.

מוּעָף, m. fm. Part. Hoph. r. עוּף, once, Is. viii. 23. *Darkness:* metaph. *misery*, usually; but it may be doubted whether עָיֵף, is not the root. If so, *weakness:* meton. *wretchedness*, or the like, will be the better interpretation. See Rosenm. ad locum.

מוֹעֵצוֹת, f. pl. Aff. מוֹעֲצוֹתָם, sing. non occ. r. יָעַץ. *Counsels; devices,* either in a good or bad sense, as the context may require, Prov. i. 31; xxii. 20; Jer. vii. 24; Mich. vi. 16; Ps. v. 11; lxxxi. 13; Hos. xi. 6.

מוּעָקָה, f. once, Ps. lxvi. 11, r. עוּק, or עִיק. *Pressure;* meton. *pain*.

מוֹפֵת, masculine plur. מוֹפְתִים. Arab. وَنَى, *integer, completus fuit:* III. *venit, advenit*. Cogn. وَنَدَ, it. cogn. يَفَعَ, *ascendit; prominens fuit*. Whence, Heb. יָפָה, *pulcher, venustus, &c.*, as something, perfect, complete; rare. Syr. (in a bad sense) ܐܣܟ, *consumptus, destructus est.* Comp. תמם, Heb., and نَّامَ, Arab. And, as אוֹת, with which it is often used, is cogn. with אָתָה, so this seems to imply the *coming, happening*, of something *rare, strange, &c.* (a) *Sign, wonder:* (b) meton. *mark, intimation, portent*, of something fearful to come to pass. LXX. variously, ῥῆμα, σημεῖον, σκληρότης, τέρας: which last seems the most correct; אוֹת, implying a sign, intimation, &c., more generally. So Symm. on Ps. lxx. 7, and Aquila, Zech. iii. 8. And generally the τέρατα, and σημεῖα, of the New Test., correspond to the מוֹפְתִים, and אוֹתוֹת, of the Old. (a) Exod. iv. 21; vii. 3. 9; xi. 9; Ps. lxxviii. 43; cv. 5. Often with אוֹתוֹת, for emphasis, perhaps, Deut. iv. 34; vii. 19; xxvi. 8; xxix. 2; Ps. cxxxv. 9, &c. With verbs, עָשָׂה, שָׂלַח, בּוֹא, הָיָה, שׂוּם, נָתַן. Metaph. sometimes applied to the prophets, &c., Ezek. xii. 6; xxiv. 27; Zech. iii. 8; Ps.

Y Y

מוֹץ (346) מוּק

lxxi. 7, &c. (b) Deut. xiii. 2, 3 ; 1 Kings xiii. 3. 5 ; Is. viii. 18, &c. Aff. מוֹפְתַי, מוֹפְתָיו.

מוֹץ, and מֹץ, m.—pl. non occ. Syr. ܡܘܨܐ, emunxit. Cogn. Heb. מִיץ, מִצָּה. Lit. extract, as the worst part, refuse: pec. Chaff, of corn, as carried by the wind from the floor, Hos. xiii. 3 ;— Is. xvii. 13 ; xxix. 5; xli. 15; Zeph. ii. 2 ; Ps. i. 4 ; xxxv. 5 ; Job xxi. 18.

מוֹצָא, it. מֹצָא, masc. pl. constr. מוֹצָאֵי.— .... f. pl. מוֹצָאוֹת..... r. יָצָא.— Out-going, i. e. time or place of, generally, Gram. art. 157. 17; Numbers xxxiii. 2. (a) Time of —, pec., Dan. ix. 25. (b) Place of —, Job xxviii. 1, see my note here ; Is. xli. 18; lviii. 11 ; Ezek. xliii. 11; xliv. 5 ; Ps. cvii. 33. 35. (c) The east, from which the sun seems to go out, Ps. lxxv. 7, in the combination, מִמּוֹצָא וּמִמַּעֲרָב, lit. from the place of out-going, and of growing dark, i. e. of the east and west. Comp. Ps. xix. 10 ; Hos. vi. 3. (c) Thing going out, production, speech, &c., Num. xxx. 13 ; Deut. viii. 3 ; xxiii. 24; Jer. xvii. 16 ; Ps. lxxxix. 35. (d) Circumstances of —, 2 Sam. iii. 25; Ps. lxv. 9 ; Ezek. xii. 4 : and, perhaps, Num. xxxiii. 2; Hos. vi. 3. Under this head I would place 1 Kings x. 28; 2 Chron. i. 16, מוֹצָא הַסּוּסִים, the out-goings of the horses, i. e. circumstances attending their origin, &c. See LXX. In all such circumlocutions, the idiom into which a translation is to be made, must, of necessity, be primarily regarded. Feminine, מוֹצָאוֹת, Keri ; מֹצָאוֹת, Kethiv ; 2 Kings x. 27. Dunghill. Auth. Vers., draught-house. Comp. Mark vii. 9, ἀφεδρῶνα. LXX. λυτρῶνα.

מוּצָא, part. Hoph. r. יָצָא.

מוּצָק, מוּצַק, m. } r. יָצַק. Lit. Fused
מֻצָקָה, f.   } metal, 1 Kings vii. 37; Ib. vr. 16. Meton. Hard, solid, substance, Job xxxviii. 38 : al. non occ. Fem. aff. מֻצָקְתוֹ, its being cast, fused, 2 Chron. iv. 3.

מוּצָק, m. r. צוּק. Part. Hoph. Lit. Thing compressed, constrained; abstr. constraint, Job xxxvii. 10 ; xxxvi. 16. See my notes.

מוּצָקָה, fem. pl. מֻצָקוֹת. Lit. Things fused ; pipes, tubes : r. יָצַק, Zech. iv. 2, only. LXX. ἐπαρυστρίδες.

מוּק, v. Kal non occ. Syr. ܡܘܩ, derisit. Arab. مَاقَ, r. موق, vecors fuit. Angl. To mock. Castell. Cogn. מקק. Arab. مَقَّ, conj. viii. hinniendo ad extremum guttur vocem allidens equus, vel verba loquendo vir. Gr. μωκίζω. Hiph. pres. pl. יָמִיקוּ, They mock, insult, Ps. lxxiii. 8, only.

מוֹקֵד, m. pl. constr. מוֹקְדֵי, r. יָקַד. Lit. Burning, Is. xxxiii. 14. Meton. Fuel, fire brand, Ps. cii. 4, al. non occ.

מוֹקְדָה, f. once, Lev. vi. 2 (9), r. יָקַד. Place of burning, hearth, i. e. on which the burnt-offerings were consumed on the altar.

מוֹקֵשׁ, m. pl. מוֹקְשִׁים, constr. מוֹקְשֵׁי, once, f. מֹקְשׁוֹת, Ps. cxli. 9, r. יָקַשׁ, i. q. פַּח, Josh. xxiii. 13, &c. Snare, or trap, to take birds or beasts withal, Amos iii. 5. Mostly, metaph., as, מוֹקְשֵׁי מָוֶת, snares of death, Ps. xviii. 6. Comp. Exod. x. 7; xxiii. 33 ; xxxiv. 12; Deut. vii. 16 ; Prov. xii. 13 ; Is. viii. 15 ; Ps. lxiv. 6 ; cxl. 6, &c. מֹקְשֵׁי עַם Job xxxiv. 30. See my note. בְּמוֹקְשִׁים יִקֳּבֶנּוּ־אָף, bore through his nose in the toils, snares, i. e. when so taken, Job xl. 24. See my note.

מוֹר, see מֹר.

מוּר, v. Kal non occ. Syr. ܡܘܪ, emit. Aph. vendidit. Arab. مَارَ, r. مور, huc illuc commota fuit res: transivit, i. q. Heb. אמר. Hiph. הֵמִיר, pres. יָמִיר, יָמֵר. Constr. immed. it. med. בְּ, for. (a) Change, alter, state, relation, &c., Ps. xv. 4 ; xlvi. 3, constr. abs. (b) Exchange, as, one thing for another, Lev. xxvii. 10. 33 ; Ps. cvi. 20; Jer. ii. 11; Hos. iv. 7; Mic. ii. 4 ; Ezek. xlviii. 14. Infin. abs. הָמֵר הָמִיר, Ps. xlvi. 3 ; Lev. xxiii. 10. Niph. נָמַר, Be, become, changed, once, Jer. xlviii. 11, r. cogn. Arab. مَرَّ, transivit.

מוֹרָא, m. pl. מוֹרָאִים, r. יָרֵא, i. q. פַּחַד, חַת. (a) Fear, Gen. ix. 2 ; Deut. xi. 25 ; Is. viii. 12. (b) Reverence, Mal. i. 6. (c) Meton. Object of fear, reverence God, &c., Is. viii. 13 ; Mal. ii. 5 ; Ps. lxxvi. 12. (d) Fearful, stupendous, act, &c., Deut. iv. 34 ; xxvi. 8 ; xxxiv. 12 ; Jer. xxxii. 21. Aff. מוֹרָאִי, מוֹרָאֲכֶם.

מור (347) מוש

מוֹרַג, masc. plur. מוֹרִגִים, מוֹרִיגִים, r. מרג. Arab. مرج, *miscuit, confudit, &c.;* conj. iv. *evacuavit.* Cogn. مرخ, id. Comp. مرغ. نورج, نَوْرَج, *tribulum quo fruges in area teruntur.* A sort of wain, or cart, in which are inserted wooden rollers instead of wheels, and in these are fixed teeth of iron, &c. A seat is also placed above these, for the driver to sit upon. A couple of oxen is attached to this machine, for the purpose of drawing it to and fro over the corn on the thrashing-floor; and, by this means, is the grain beaten out. In Jahn's Biblische Archäologie, 1 Theil. 1 Band. Tab. iv. fig. vii., we have a tolerably good representation of it, Is. xli. 15; 2 Sam. xxiv. 22; 1 Chron. xxi. 23, al. non occ. Comp. Varo de re Rustica, 1. 52; Niehbuhr, tom. i. p. 151. Gesen.

מוֹרָד, m.—pl. non occ. r. יָרַד. *Descent, declivity,* Josh. vii. 5; x. 11; Jer. xlviii. 5; Mic. i. 4;—1 Kings vii. 29, מַעֲשֵׂה מוֹרָד, "*opus pendens, pensile,* Festons.," Gesen. More probably, *sloping,* i. e. in manner of a declivity.

מוֹרָה, m. pl. מוֹרִים, r. יָרָה, which see. Part. Hiph. Lit. casting, putting forth, (a) instruction, *Teacher, doctor,* Is. ix. 14; xxx. 20; Hab. ii. 18; Job xxxvi. 22, &c. (b) *Arrows, &c., Archer,* 1 Sam. xx. 37; xxxi. 3, &c. *Herbage, &c.* (c) *Former rain.* See יוֹרֶה, p. 272 above, Joel ii. 23. Aff. מוֹרַי Prov. v. 13, —מוֹרָיִךְ.

מוֹרָה, masc.—plur. non occ. r. מָרָה. *A razor,* Judg. xiii. 5; xvi. 7; 1 Sam. i. 11, only. Ps. ix. 21, for מוֹרָא. See the Keri.

מוֹרָט, m. twice, Is. xviii. 2. 7, r. מָרַט. *Ruin, ruinous.* Gesenius. The elder grammarians took the r. מָרַט, thence, *Made bald; peeled,* Auth. Vers. Others, part. Puh. r. מָרַט, *swift, ready.*

מוֹרִיגִים, pl. of מוֹרַג, which see.

מוֹרָשׁ, m. ⎫ p. aff. מוֹרָשֵׁיהֶם, constr.
מוֹרָשָׁה, f. ⎭ מוֹרָשֵׁי, r. יָרַשׁ. *Possession,* Exod. vi. 8; Is. xiv. 23; Obad. vr. 17; Ezek. xi. 15. Metaph. Job xvii. 11, *Prepossessions,* see my note: Deut. xxxiii. 4; Ezek. xxxvi. 3.

מוֹרַשְׁתִּי, m. Patronym. of בַּת מוֹרֶשֶׁת Mic. i. 14;—Mic. i. 1; Jer. xxvi. 18, *Native of Moresheth.*

מוּשׁ, v. pret. מָשׁ, pres. יָמוּשׁ, תָּמֻשׁ. Constr. abs. it. med. אֵת, מִן, from. Cogn. Arab. مشى, *incessit, repsit.* (a) *Move, depart,* Zech. xiv. 4; Num. xiv. 44; Judg. vi. 18; Josh. i. 8; Is. liv. 10; lix. 21; Jer. xxxi. 36. (b) *Remove, put away,* Zech. iii. 9.

Hiph. pres. יָמִישׁ, constr. abs. it. med. מִן, from; it. immed. it. med. לְ. (a) i. q. Kal. (a) *Move, depart,* Exod. xiii. 22; xxxiii. 11; Ps. lv. 12; Is. xlvi. 7; Mic. ii. 3. (b) *Remove, put away,* Job xxiii. 12; Nah. iii. 1; Mic. ii. 4. (c) *Cease, desist,* Jer. xvii. 8. But, observe, if we suppose מִישׁ to have been taken also as the root, no necessity for the Hiph. would exist. And this is, most likely, the fact. It—

מוּשׁ, for the cogn. מָשַׁשׁ, which see. Pret. Kal non occ.

Pres. aff. אֲמֻשְׁךָ, Gen. xxvii. 21. *I would feel thee,* Ib. xxvii. 22; xxviii. 12.

Hiph. pres. i. q. Kal, יָמִישׁוּן, Ps. cxv. 7. Apoc. יָמֵשׁ, in יְמַשֵּׁשׁ הֹשֶׁךְ, *so that one may feel, grope,* in *darkness:* not, *may be felt:* the ellipsis of בְּ being very common in such cases, Gram. art. 219, 220.

Imp. aff. הֲמִישֵׁנִי, *Cause, let, me, feel,* Judg. xvi. 24.

מוֹשָׁב, m. pl. constr. מוֹשְׁבֵי, it. f. מוֹשָׁבוֹת, r. יָשַׁב. (a) *Residence, dwelling,* Gen. xxvii. 39; Exod. xii. 20; Ps. cxxxii. 13; Ezek. xlviii. 15. Whence the phrr. בֵּית מוֹשָׁב, Lev. xxv. 29. עִיר מוֹשָׁב, Ps. cvii. 4. 7. 36, &c. (b) *Seat,* 1 Sam. xx. 18. 25; Job xxix. 7. See my note here. (c) Meton. *Time of residing, dwelling,* Exod. xii. 40. (d) —, *act, manner, of sitting,* 1 Kings x. 5; 2 Chron. ix. 4. (e) *Dwellers, inhabitants,* 2 Sam. ix. 12. Aff. מוֹשָׁבוֹ, &c. Fem. מוֹשְׁבֹתֵכֶם, &c.

מוֹשְׁכוֹת, f. pl. r. מָשַׁךְ, which see.

מוֹשָׁעוֹת, fem. plur. r. יָשַׁע. Pl. excell., Gram. art. 223. 3. *Great, singular, salvation,* once, Ps. lxviii. 21.

מוּת, twice, Ps. xlviii. 15; ix. 1.

מָוֶת, masc. constr. מוֹת. Seg. fm. שֶׁקֶר, Gram. art. 148. 9. Pl. constr. מוֹתֵי, Ezek. xxviii. 10. Arab. موت, *mors.* See verb following, (a) *Death,* 2 Kings ii. 21; Ps.

מוֹת (348) מוּת

lxxxix. 49, &c.; opp. τῷ, חַיִּים, Jer. viii. 3. Personified, Ps. xlix. 15; Job xxviii. 22; Jer. ix. 20; xviii. 21. Meton. (b) *Persons dead*, Is. xxxviii. 18. It. (c) *The grave*, not "*orcus*," as Gesenius thinks. Prov. ii. 18; Ps. ix. 14, שַׁעֲרֵי מָוֶת, *gates of* —. Prov. vii. 27, חַדְרֵי מָוֶת. (d) *Mortal disease, pestilence*, Jer. xv. 2; 2 Kings iv. 40; xliii. 11; Job xxvii. 15. (e) *Destruction, ruin*, Prov. xi. 19; xii. 28; Is. xxv. 8; Exod. x. 17. Phrr. מִשְׁפַּט מָוֶת, *sentence of death*, Deut. xix. 6. חֲטֵא מָוֶת, Ib. xxii. 26. מְהוּמַת מָוֶת, 1 Sam. v. 11. בְּדִמְיָה, Ib. xx. 31; pl. xxvi. 16. אַנְשֵׁי מָוֶת, 2 Sam. xix. 29. Comp. 1 Kings ii. 26. מִשְׁבְּרֵי מָוֶת, 2 Sam. xxii. 5. מֹקְשֵׁי־מָוֶת, Ib. vr. 6. בְּכוֹר מָוֶת, Job xviii. 13. See my note. כְּלֵי־מָוֶת, Ps. vii. 14. To which many more might be added. With ה parag. הַמָּוְתָה, Ps. cxvi. 15. Aff. מוֹתוֹ, Judg. xvii. 30, &c. Pl. מוֹתֵי, Is. liii. 9.

מוֹת, m. Chald. id., Ezra vii. 26.

מוּת, v. pret. מֵת (for מָוֵת, Gram. art. 75. It is also the participial noun), pl. מֵתִי, מַתְנוּ, 1st pers. מַתִּי, pres. יָמוּת, it. apoc. יָמָת. Arab. مَاتَ, r. مَوت, *defer buit calor: quievit ventus; interiit*. Syr. ܡܝܬ, *mortuus est*. Æth. ᎾᎱᎮ: id. Constr. abs. *Die*, of man or beast, Exod. xi. 5; Eccl. ix. 4: naturally, or by violence, Exod. xxi. 12. 15; Deut. xiii. 10; xix. 11, 12; xxi. 21; Job i. 19: med. בְּ, instr. or cause, Josh. x. 11. בְּאַזְנֵי הַבָּדָד Judg. xv. 18. בַּצָּמָא —, Ezek. v. 12. בַּדֶּבֶר —, in, Num. xxvii. 3: med. מִפְּנֵי, Jer. xxxviii. 9. תַּחַת, Exod. xxi. 20. Metaph. — of the heart, 1 Sam. xxv. 37. — trunk of a tree, Job xiv. 8. — a land, not cultivated, Gen. xlvii. 19: i. q. חֵשֵׁשׁ, seq. עִם xii. 2, עִמָּכֶם תָּמוּת הָכְמָה, ironically. Meton. *Perish*, of a city, Amos ii. 2; Hos. xiii. 1.

Infin. מוּת, Gen. ii. 17; iii. 4, &c. Aff. מוֹתִי, &c. It. מוּה, with לְ, pref. always, Gen. xxv. 32, &c.

Aff. מָתָן, 2 Sam. xx. 3. מֻתֵנוּ, Exod. xiv. 12. Imp. מֻת, Deut. xxxii. 50; Job ii. 9. Part. מֵת, pl. מֵתִים, constr. מֵתֵי, Gen. xlviii. 21; Exod. xii. 33; Is. xxii. 2.

Fem. מֵתָה, plur. non occ., Gen. xxx. 1; xlviii. 7, &c. Aff. m. מֵתְךָ, &c.

Pih. pret. aff. מוֹתְתַנִי, *Put me to death*, Jer. xx. 17. מֹתַתִּי, *I have put to death*, 2 Sam.

i. 16. Pres. יְמוֹתֵת, 1 Sam. xvii. 51; 2 Sam. i. 10; Ps. xxxiv. 22.

Infin. לְמוֹתֵת, with לְ, pref., Ps. cix. 16. Imp. aff. מוֹתְתֵנִי, *Put me to death*, Judg. ix. 54; 2 Sam. i. 9.

Hiph. הֵמִית, pres. יָמִית, i. q. Pih. 2 pers. pret. הֵמַתָּה, 1st, הֵמַתִּי. Aff. הֲמִיתִּיךָ, הֲמִיתִּיו, Num. xiv. 15; Hos. ix. 16; 1 Sam. xvii. 35; Hos. ii. 5. Constr. med. בְּ, instr. Judg. xvi. 30; it. אֶת, 2 Sam. iii. 30; it. immed., Exod. xxi. 29, &c. Often, by pestilence, &c., as sent by God, Is. lxv. 15; Hos. ii. 5; Exod. xvi. 3; xvii. 3; Num. xiv. 15, &c.

Infin. הָמִית, Lev. xx. 4. הָמֵת, Jer. xxxviii. 15, &c. Aff. הֲמִיתוֹ, Exod. iv. 24.

Imp. aff. הֲמִיתֵנִי, 1 Sam. xx. 8: pl. הָמִיתוּ, Ib. xxii. 17.

Part. מֵמִית, plur. מְמִיתִים, 1 Sam. ii. 6; 2 Kings xvii. 26. מְמִתִים, Jer. xxvi. 15; Job xxxiii. 22.

Hoph. הוּמַת, pres. יוּמַת, *Be, become, put to death*, 2 Kings xi. 2; Deut. xxi. 22; Gen. xxvi. 11; Exod. xix. 12, &c. Part. masc. מוּמָת, 1 Sam. xix. 11: plur. מוּמָתִים, מֻמָתִים, 2 Kings xi. 2; 2 Chron. xxii. 11.

מוֹתָר, masc. — pl. non occ., r. יָתַר. (a) *Increase, abundance*, Prov. xiv. 23; xxi. 5. (b) *Excellence, preference*, Eccl. iii. 19, al. non occ. Symm. τί πλέον; Theod. τίς περίσσεια;

מְזָא, see r. אוֹא.

מִזְבֵּחַ, masc. constr. מִזְבַּח, plur. מִזְבְּחוֹת. With ה parag. מִזְבְּחָה, r. זָבַח. *An altar*, idolatrous, or not, Lev. i. 9. 13. 15; 2 Chron. xxix. 22. — of burnt-offering, הָעֹלָה, Exod. xxx. 28. נְחֹשֶׁת —, Ib. xxxix. 39. הַקְּטֹרֶת Ib. xxx. 27. Pl., Num. xxiii. 1. 29, &c. Aff. מִזְבְּחִי, Exod. xx. 26. מִזְבְּחֶךָ, Deut. xxxiii. 10; pl. מִזְבְּחוֹתָיו, 1 Kings xix. 10, &c.

מֶזֶג, m. once, Cant. vii. 3. Syr. ܡܙܓܐ, *mistura*. Arab. مَزْج, id. Lit. *Mixture*. Meton. *Mixed wine*. LXX. κρᾶμα.

מַדֻּעַ, for מַה־דֻּעַ, see מָה.

מָזָה, r. non occ. Arab. مَزَّ, *auxit*, redup; مَزْمَزَ, *huc illuc novit, et agitavit*. Whence, pl. constr. מְזֵי רָעָב, *Exhausted, reduced*, of (by) *famine*; or, *agitated, perplexed*, &c., once, Deut. xxxii. 24. LXX. τηκόμενοι λιμῷ.

מְזָוֵינוּ, m. pl. aff. once, Ps. cxliv. 13.

(349)

LXX. τὰ ταμεῖα αὐτῶν. Arab. زَاوِيَةٌ, *angulus*: often used to signify the cell of a devotee. *Store-room; cellar.* See זויה, p. 168 above.

מְזוּזָה, f. constr. מְזוּזַת, pl. מְזוּזוֹת, r. זוז. *Door-post*, or *jamb*, in which the hinges are fixed, Exod. xxi. 6; Is. lvii. 5; 1 Sam. i. 9; Deut. vi. 9; xi. 20, &c. Aff. מְזוּזָתָם, מְזוּזָתִי.

מָזוֹן, masc.—pl. non occ., r. זון. Syr. ܡܳܙܘܿܢܳܐ, *alimentum*. *Food, meat*, Gen. xlv. 23; 2 Chron. xi. 23. It. Chald., Dan. iv. 9. 18.

מָזוֹר, m.—pl. non occ., r. זור. *Binding, pressing together*, of a wound. Comp. חֲבוּרָה, Is. i. 6, where we have לֹא זֹרוּ, &c. Meton. *Bandaged wound*, Hos. v. 12, twice; in the latter of which, וְלֹא יִגְהֶה מִכֶּם מָזוֹר, *nor can he take up from you the wound, affliction.* Aquila, ἐπίδεσις, vel σύνδεσμος. LXX. ὀδύνη, Jer. xxx. 13. לְמָזוֹר, *to a binding, bandaging*, i. e. for healing. See the rest of the context. Obad. vr. 7, יָשִׂימוּ מָזוֹר, they place as, i. e. make, *a binding;* wound, affliction. LXX. ἔνεδρα, al. non occ.

מֵזַח, m. ⎱ pl. non occ. Syr. ܐܣܡܐ, מָזִיחַ, m. ⎰ *extulit;* ܐܣܡܐ, *elatio, pompa.* Arab. مَرَحَ, *lætificatus est.* See also my note on Job xii. 21. *A girdle*, as giving strength: thence, meton., *pride, insolence, &c.*, Ps. cix. 19; Is. xxiii. 10. *Pride, &c.* Targ. תְּקוֹף, *fortitudo*, Job xii. 21, insolence, &c., al. non occ.

מֵזִין, for מְאָזִין, part. Hiph. r. אזן.

מַזָּלוֹת, fem. plur., r. נזל. Arab. مَنْزِلٌ, *mansio, domus.* The Arabian name for *the signs of the zodiac* generally. The فلك البروج is not the "*circulum palatiorum*," or signs of the zodiac, as Gesenius erroneously states; but that orb (supposing, on the Ptolemæan system, that there are many, "*orbs on orbs*") in which they are found. Once, 2 Kings xxiii. 5. But here, as the context seems to intimate, *the planets.* LXX. τοῖς μαζουρώθ. See my note on Job xxxvii. 9, and מַזָּרוֹת below.

מַזְלֵג, masc. plur. fem. מִזְלָגוֹת. Arab. زَلَجَ, *acutum reddidit* ferrum. Cogn. زَلَقَ, *avarus, tenax.* *A fork* having three teeth, שְׁלֹשׁ הַשִּׁנַּיִם, 1 Sam. ii. 13, 14; Exod. xxxviii. 3; Num. iv. 14; 1 Chron. xxviii. 17; 2 Chron. iv. 16. Aff. מִזְלְגֹתָיו, Exod. xxvii. 3.

מְזִמָּה, f. pl. מְזִמּוֹת, r. זמם, which see. (a) *Thought, invention*, generally, Jer. xxiii. 20; Job xlii. 2: (b) for *good*, Prov. i. 4; iii. 21; v. 2; viii. 12: (c) — for *evil, fraud, violence, &c.*, Ps. x. 2. 4; xxi. 12; xxxvii. 7; cxxxix. 20; Jer. li. 11; Prov. xii. 2; xiv. 17; xxiv. 8; Job xxi. 27. With ־ה, of unity, singularity. See let. ה, p. 145, (b) above. הַמְּזִמָּתָה, *the great, singular* (here bad), *imagination*, Jer. xi. 15. Aff. מְזִמּוֹתָי.

מִזְמוֹר, m.—pl. non occ., r. זמר. See p. 173 above. *Psalm*, or *hymn*, as a title often prefixed to the Psalms, Ps. iii. 1; iv. 1; v. 1; vi. 1, &c. Occasionally found with שִׁיר, Ps. xxx. 1; xlviii. 1; xlii. 1; xlviii. 1, &c.

מְזַמְּרוֹת, f. pl. fm. Part. Piḥ. *Snuffers*, Gesenius. Others, and much more likely, *Psalteries*, 1 Kings vii. 50; 2 Kings xii. 14; 2 Chron. iv. 22; Jer. lii. 18. Arab. مِزْمَارٌ, *psalterium*, al. non occ.

מַזְמֵרוֹת, fem. pl., r. זמר, p. 173 above. *Pruning instruments*, Is. ii. 4; xviii. 5; Mic. iv. 3; Joel iv. 10. Aff. מַזְמְרֹתֵיכֶם.

מִזְעָר, m.—pl. non occ., r. זער. Synon. τοῦ, מְעַט, לֹא כַבִּיר, Is. xvi. 14. *A little*, of time, Is. x. 25; xxix. 17. — of number, Is. l. c. and xxiv. 6.

מָזֹרוֹ, see מָזוֹר above.

מְזָרִים, m. pl. ⎱ r. זרה, זור, or אור. See מְזָרוֹת, f. pl. ⎰ my notes on Job xxxvii. 9; xxxviii. 32. Names, apparently, of some *northern constellation*, or stars (Simonis). Opp. τῷ, חֶדֶר, in the former passage. According to Gesenius, with Eichorn, *dispersing northern winds*. See the Lat. Vulg. and LXX. The fem. מְזָרוֹת. Gesen. makes, i. q. מַזָּלוֹת, which see. It should be observed, that, in the former passage, מְזָרִים is opposed to חֶדֶר, not to סוּפָה; which is sufficient to show that Gesenius and Eichorn's view is groundless. Nor, in the second passage, can מְזָרוֹת, in the sense of winds, be opposed to עָשׁ, &c. Eichorn is, therefore, wrong in each case. For the first, Aquila has μαζούρ. Theod. and LXX. ἀπὸ δὲ ἀκροτηρίων. See also the Targum on each place.

מִזְרֶה, m.—pl. non occ., r. זָרָה. Lit. *Disperser; a fan*, used to winnow corn, Is. xxx. 24; Jer. xv. 7, al. non occ.

מִזְרָח, m. constr. מִזְרַח, pl. non occ., r. זרח. Lit. *Place of rising*, i. e. of the sun. *The East*, opp. τῷ, מַעֲרָב, Is. xlv. 6, &c.; or *eastern part, quarter, &c.*, Num. xxi. 11; Deut. iv. 47; Josh. i. 15; iv. 19; xiii. 5. Opp. τῷ, מָבוֹא, Ps. cxiii. 3, &c. With ־ָה, parag. *towards*, Exod. xxvii. 13; Deut. iv. 41; Josh. xii. 1, &c.: it. with pref. לְ, 2 Chron. xxxi. 14; Ellipt. Neh. xii. 37 (accus. according to Gesen.); but this is unnecessary, as מִזְרָח may be in construction with the two preceding words: rather, with the signification of them both, Gram. art. 224. 5.

מִזְרָע, m. constr. once, Is. xix. 7, r. זָרַע. Arab. مَزْرَعَة, *locus in quo semen jacitur. Sown, cultivated, field*, or *place*.

מִזְרָק, m. pl. מִזְרָקִים, constr. מִזְרְקֵי, it. f. מִזְרָקוֹת, r. זָרַק. Lit. *instrument, &c.* of sprinkling. *Bowl*, or *cup*, either for sacrificial purposes, or for drinking, Exod. xxxviii. 3; Num. iv. 14; vii. 13. 19. 25, &c.; Amos vi. 6. Aff. מִזְרְקֹתָיו.

מֹחַ, m. once, in מֹחַ עַצְמוֹתָיו וגו׳, Job xxi. 24. With *marrow his bones, &c.* Arab. مَحّ, *albumen ovi*. Syr. ܥܕܡܐ, *medulla*. Cogn. Arab. مُخّ, *medulla; vitellus*; r. מיח. Whence, מֵחִים. See in its place below. And—

מֵיחִים, and מְחִים, m. pl. (for מְיִחִים, fm. פָּרָה), Gram. art. 73. *Fat* ones, Is. v. 17; Ps. lxvi. 15, al. non occ.

מָחָא, v. pret. non occ. pres. pl. יִמְחֲאוּ, twice, Is. lv. 12; Ps. xcviii. 8, in the phr. יִמְחֲאוּ כָף, *they strike, clap, the hands*, exultingly. Syr. ܥܕܡ, *percussit*. Piħ. Infin. aff. מַחְאֲךָ, *Thy clapping the* hands, Ezek. xxv. 6.

It. Chald. Paħ. f. מְחָה, constr. med. לְ. *Struck, smote*, Dan. ii. 34, 35. Paħ. יִמְחָא, pres. in דִּי־יִמְחֵא בִידֵהּ, *who can clap with his hand*, and say,—i. e. exultingly with such question,—Dan. iv. 32 (35). Gesen. "*non est qui manum Dei percutiat.*"

With which he compares the Arab. ضرب علي يديه. But it is far from certain that this is the true meaning of this Arabic phrase. The greater probability is, that, *striking upon his hands*, here in the Arabic, signifies agreeing, bargaining, &c., against some one. The full phrase is, ضرב ידא علي ידיה, &c. See my note on Job xvii. 3. If so, this Arabic phraseology agrees with that in question; but not under the view taken by Gesen. The same may be said of the same phr. in the Targ., Eccl. viii. 3. The question in each case is, whether בִּידֵהּ should be rendered by "manum ejus," or "manum suam:" I hold the latter.

Ithp. יִתְמְחֵא, once, Ezra vi. 11. *Be, become, smitten, stricken*, i. e. destroyed. Cogn. מחה.

מָחֵא, part. Aph. Chald. r. חיא.

מַחֲבֵא, m. once, Is. xxxii. 2, r. חבא. *Covering, concealment; hiding-place*. Aquila, κρύπτων πνεῦμα. Symm. ἀποκρυφή.

מַחֲבֹאִים, m. pl. (for מַחֲבָאִים, perhaps), *Hiding-places*, 1 Sam. xxiii. 23, only.

מַחֲבַת, m.—pl. non occ., r. חבת. *A frying-pan*, Lev. ii. 5; vi. 14; vii. 9; Ezek. iv. 3; 1 Chron. xxiii. 29.

מַחְגֹּרֶת, f. once, Is. iii. 24, r. חָגַר. *A girding*.

מָחָה, v. pres. יִמְחֶה. Constr. immed. it. med. אֶת,—עַל, אֶל, it. abs. Cogn. מָחָא. Arab. محا, *delevit. Strike, wipe, out* or *away*, of person or thing. Men, Gen. vi. 7; vii. 4. — name, memory, Exod. xvii. 14; Deut. ix. 14. — city, 2 Kings xxi. 13. — writing, Exod. xxxii. 32, 33. — sins, Ps. li. 3. 11; Is. xliii. 25; xliv. 22. — tears, Is. xxv. 8. — the mouth, Prov. xxx. 20. *Strike, touch to; arrive at*, Num. xxxiv. 11.

Infin. abs. מָחֹה, Exod. xvii. 14. Constr. מְחוֹת, 2 Kings xiv. 27.
Imp. מְחֵה, Ps. ll. cc. Aff. מְחֵנִי, Exod. l. c.
Part. מֹחֶה, Is. l. c.
Niph. pl. m. נִמְחוּ, pres. יִמָּחֶה, apoc. יִמָּח. *Be, become, wiped, blotted, out*, Ezek. vi. 6; Gen. vii. 23; Deut. xxv. 6; Judg. xxi. 17; Ps. cxix. 13; Prov. vi. 33, &c.
Hiph. pres. apoc. תֶּמַח, fem. תַּמְחִי, i. q. Kal, Jer. xviii. 23; Neh. xiii. 14.

מחי (351) מחו

Infin. מְחוֹת, with ל, pref. Lit. *For wiping out, destroying,* Prov. xxxi. 3. The passage is elliptical, and may be supplied thus: אַל־תִּתֵּן לַנָּשִׁים חֵילֶךָ וּדְרָכֶיךָ (יִהְיוּ) לַמְחוֹת מְלָכִין *give not thy strength to women, so that thy ways (may be) for the wiping out,* destroying, *of kings,* i. e. he being a king, let him take care not to indulge in certain lusts; to which Solomon was manifestly given, and which would end in his ruin. Comp. 1 Kings xi. 1, seq.; Prov. xxii. 14; xxiii. 33. LXX. εἰς ὑστεροβουλίαν. Theod. εἰς μεταμέλειαν. See the Targum.

מְחוּגָה, fem. once, Is. xliv. 13, r. חוג. *A pair of compasses,* as used by mechanics.

מָחוֹז, masc. constr. r. חוז, once, Ps. cvii. 30. Syr. ܡܚܘܙܐ, *oppidum.* Arab. حَوْز, *ora regionis*; v. حَازَ, *collegit; obtinuit rem,* &c. Cogn. חָזָה, *congregavit.* Here, *place of* —, i. e. *Port, haven, harbour.*

מַחֲוִים, m. pl. *Mahavites.* Patronym. otherwise unknown, 1 Chron. xi. 46.

מָחוֹל, m. constr. מְחוֹל.—

מְחוֹלַת, femin. constr. plur. מְחוֹלוֹת.— r. חוּל, sign. iii., p. 188 above. *Dance, dancing;* which is extemporaneous usually in the East; the most dignified person leading, occasionally with tabrets, &c., the rest following, and imitating the leader's steps, &c. See Harmer's Observ. lii. p. 423, vol. ii., edit. 1816; Exod. xv. 20; 1 Sam. xviii. 6; Ps. xxx. 12; cxlix. 3; cl. 4; Jer. xxxi. 4. 13; Cant. vii. 1. Occasionally in circles, as with the Eastern Derveishes, Exod. xxxii. 19. During the dance, a song was uttered by the leader, and responded to by the followers, as in Exod. xv. 20;—1 Sam. xxi. 12; xxix. 5. Aff. מְחוֹלֵנוּ, Lam. v. 15.

מַחֲזֶה, masc.—pl. non occ., r. חָזָה. *A vision,* Gen. xv. 1; Num. xxiv. 4. 16; Ezek. xiii. 7.

מֶחֱזֶה, m.—pl. non occ., r. חזה. *Place of seeing. Window,* 1 Kings vii. 4, 5.

מְחִי, m., r. מָחָה, once, Ezek. xxvi. 9. Lit. *A striking,* i. e. of Balistas, battering-rams, &c.

מִחְיָה, fem., r. חָיָה, constr. מִחְיַת, pl. non occ. *Means of living; living* (like the Arab. مَعِيشَة) *food,* &c., Gen. xlv. 5; Judg. vi. 4; 2 Chron. xiv. 12; Ezra ix. 8, 9. Also, *Crude, raw* (sign. iv., p. 194 above), i. e. unsound, diseased, Lev. xiii. 10; which is proved sufficiently by the חָי following. See LXX. Ἀλλ. ὡς ὁμοίωμα σαρκὸς ζώσης, 1b. vr. 24 only.

מְחִיר, m. pl. aff. מְחִירֵיהֶם, r. מחר, cogn. מָכַר. Syr. ܡܚܝܪܐ, *mensura, estimatio. Price,* 1 Kings xxi. 2; Prov. xvii. 16; xxvii. 26. בִּמְחִיר, *with a price,* 2 Sam. xxiv. 24, &c. בְּלֹא מְחִיר, *without price,* i. e. that which cannot be said to be a price, so little is it. See under לא, Is. lv. 1. לֹא בִמְחִיר, *not with price,* i. e. for nothing. This phr. is not strictly equivalent to the last, Is. xlv. 13. Meton. *Wages, reward,* Mic. iii. 11; Deut. xxiii. 19. Aff. מְחִירָהּ, Job xxviii. 15.

מַחֲלָה, m. constr. מַחֲלֵה, pl. non occ., r. חָלָה. *Sickness, disease,* Prov. xviii. 14; 2 Chron. xxi. 15. Aff. מַחֲלֵהוּ, Prov. l. c.

מַחֲלָה, f. i. q. מַחֲלֶה, Exod. xv. 26; xxiii. 25, &c.

מְחֹלָה, see מְחוֹלָה.

מְחִלָּה, fem. plur. מְחִלּוֹת, only, Is. ii. 19, r. חָלַל, p. 200 above. Arab. خَلَّ, *foramen quodcunque. Holes, caverns,* of the earth.

מַחֲלָיִים, m. pl. r. חלה, once, 2 Chron. xxiv. 25, of מַחֲלוּיִי. Relat. n. of part., Gram. art. 175. 15, 16. *Circumstances of disease, sickness.*

מַחֲלָף, masc. plur. מַחֲלָפִים, r. חָלַף, in the sense of חָלַל, p. 202 above, (f.) Syr. ܡܚܠܦܐ, *culter,* once, Ezra i. 9. *Slaughtering-knives.*

מַחְלָפוֹת, f. pl., r. חָלַף. Syr. ܡܚܠܦܬܐ, *germen, circulus; nodus laxior.* Arab. خِلْف, *quæ rapit crines post se* mulier; *crinibus nudata ad occiput. Locks,* of hair, Judg. xvi. 13. 19, only.

מַחֲלָצוֹת, f. pl., r. חָלַץ, p. 203 above. Lit. *Things put off.* Comp. Arab. خَلَعَ, whence خِلْعَة, *pretiosa vestis:* dress of honour. *Rich dress, mantle,* Is. iii. 22; Zech. iii. 4. See Schrœd. de Vest. Mulier. c. xiv.

מַחֲלֹקֶת, fem. pl. מַחְלְקוֹת, r. חָלַק. *Apportionment, distribution:* meton. *Order, course,* so distributed; of land, Josh. xi. 23; xii. 7; xviii. 10: pec. of the priests' service, 1 Chron. xxvii. 1, seq.; xxvi. 12. 19; xxviii. 21; 2 Chron. viii. 14; xxxi. 15; Neh. xi. 36; Ezek. xlviii. 29, &c. Aff. מַחְלֻקְתּוֹ, 1 Chron. xxvii. 2: pl. מַחְלְקוֹתָם, מַחְלְקֹתֵיהֶם. LXX. διαίρεσις, διαμερισμός, διάταξις; ἐφημερία, κλῆρος.

מַחֲלֻקָּה, f. Aff. מַחְלֻקָּתְהוֹן, *Their distribution, order,* Ezra vi. 18, only.

מַחֲלַת, In some titles of the Psalms only, liii., lxxxviii. "*Cithara.*" *Lute,* or *lyre,* according to Gesenius. But no dependence can be placed on this.

מְחֹלָתִי, masc. Patronym. of אָבֵל מְחוֹלָה, 2 Sam. xxi. 8. Person of Abel Meholah. *Meholathite.*

מַחֲמָאֹת, f. pl. once, Ps. lv. 22, r. חמא read מֶחֱמָאֹת, the (-) under מ, being, no doubt, a mere error of the copyists. See חֶמְאָה, p. 205 above. Lit. *Than Butters;* which, as generally liquid from heat in the East, may be often rendered *Oil; oils.* So the ghee of the Hindoostanies. מִשֶּׁמֶן, in the following parallel, is sufficient to show that מֶחֱמָאֹת is the true reading. So Symm. λειότερα βουτύρου.

מַחְמָד, m. constr. מַחְמַד, pl. מַחֲמַדִּים, r. חמד. Lit. *Desirable,* person or thing; often with עַיִן:— of the eye, "lust of the eye," 1 John ii. 16; 1 Kings xx. 6; Ezek. xxiv. 16. 21. 25; Hos. ix. 6. Pl., Lam. ii. 4. מַחֲמַדֵּי בִטְנָם, — of their womb, children, Hos. ix. 16. Pl. excell., Cant. v. 16, i. e. *very desirable.* Comp. Joel iv. 5; 2 Chron. xxxvi. 19. Aff. מַחֲמַדֶּיהָ, Is. lxiv. 10; מַחֲמַדֵּינוּ.

מַחֲמַדִּים, id. Aff. מַחֲמַדֶּיהָ, Lam. i. 7; מַחֲמַדֵּיהֶם, Ib. vr. 11. Kethiv, al. non occ.

מַחְמָל, m. r. חמל, p. 206 above; once, Ezek. xxiv. 21, in the phr. מַחְמַל נַפְשְׁכֶם, with מַחְמַד עֵינֵיכֶם, in the paral. Arab. مَحْمِل, *quo quis sustinetur et fretus est. The support,* confidence, *of your soul.* LXX. ὑπὲρ ὧν φείδονται αἱ ψυχαὶ ὑμῶν. Or, *the pity of* —, i. e. thing tenderly regarded. *Desire.* Gesen.

מַחֲמֶצֶת, f. pl. non occ. See r. חָמֵץ, p. 208 above.

מְחֹן, Infin. Peh. Chald. r. חנן.

מַחֲנֶה, m. constr. מַחֲנֵה; dual, מַחֲנַיִם, pl. m. מַחֲנִים, f. מַחֲנוֹת, r. חָנָה. *A camp,* generally, (a) of soldiers, Josh. vi. 11; 1 Sam. xiv. 15. Meton. (b) *An army,* Exod. xiv. 24; Judg. iv. 16. (c) *Large body* of people, Gen. l. 9. — of the Israelites in the Desert, Exod. xvi. 13; Num. iv. 5. 15; v. 2; x. 34; xi. 1. 9. 30, 31. — in the Temple, 2 Chron. xxxi. 2, &c. (d) — flocks, Gen. xxxiii. 8. (e) — of locusts, Joel ii. 11. — of angels, termed, מַחֲנֵה אֱלֹהִים, Gen. xxxii. 2, 3. Comp. Job xxxviii. 7, from the circumstance of their (angels) being engaged in the service of God as leader and king. See my note on the latter place. And, dual, Cant. vii. 1, מַחֲנָיִם, *two camps,* i. e. companies of dancers. (בִּמְחֹלַת הַמַּחֲנָיִם, lit. *as the dance of two camps.*) Then follows, מַה־יָּפוּ פְעָמַיִךְ, *how beautiful are thy footsteps, &c.* See under מָחוֹל above. See LXX. here. Ἀλλ. διερχομένην ὡς χορὸν τῶν παρεμβολῶν. Reference is, perhaps, made here to Gen. xxxii. 2, 3, cited above. If so, a beautiful comment is supplied to that place. Such, too, was apparently the πλῆθος στρατιᾶς οὐρανίου of Luke ii. 13.

מַחֲנַק, masc. r. חָנַק, once, Job vii. 15. *Strangling, suffocation.* See my note on the place. Aquila, ἀγχόνην.

מַחְסֶה, and מַחֲסֶה, constr. מַחְסֵה, pl. non occ., r. חָסָה. Lit. *Place of trust, confidence.* Meton. *Refuge,* Job xxiv. 8; Ps. xlvi. 2; civ. 19; Is. iv. 6; xxv. 4. Applied to God (as جناب , مأنوس , ميمنة , &c. are to great men in the East), Ps. xlvi. 2, above, &c.; lxii. 8; lxxi. 7, &c. Metaph. Is. xxviii. 17, מַחְסֵה כָזָב, *refuge* of lies, Ib. vr. 15. Aff. מַחְסֵנוּ. It. מַחְסִי, for מַחְסֵהִי, Gram. art. 73.

מַחְסוֹם, m. once, Ps. xxxix. 2, r. חָסַם. *Bridle, curb.* Symm. φίμῳ. LXX. φυλακήν.

מַחְסוֹר, m. pl. aff. once, מַחְסוֹרֶיךָ, Prov. xxiv. 34, r. חָסֵר. *Want, lack, need,* Judg. xviii. 10; xix. 19; Ps. xxxiv. 10; Prov. xxi. 17, אִישׁ מַחְסוֹר, *man of* —, i. e. poor man. Ib. xxviii. 27, כָּל־מַחְסוֹרָיו עָלַי, *all thy need* (rests) *on me,* i. e. becoming my guest, I shall provide as the laws of hospitality require, Judg. xix. 20. Aff. it. מַחְסֹרוֹ.

מַחַץ, m. r. once, Is. xxx. 26. מַחַץ מַכָּתוֹ, *Contusion, bruise, of his stroke.* Arab.

مחץ (353) מחר

مَخَصَ, concussit terram pede: cogn.

مَخَصَ, contudit, concussit, conquassavit.

מָחַץ, v. pres. יִמְחַץ. See מַחַץ above. Constr. immed. it. abs. it. med. בְּ, in, into; עַל, upon. *Dash* violently, the foot into blood, Ps. lxviii. 24. — arrows at one, Num. xxiv. 8. — *the head*, &c. to pieces, Judg. v. 26; Ps. xviii. 39; lxviii. 22; cx. 5, 6; Deut. xxxii. 39; Num. xxiv. 17; Hab. iii. 13; Job v. 18; xxvi. 12. See my note.
Imp. מְחַץ, Deut. xxxiii. 11.

מַחֲצֵב, m. r. חָצַב. *Cutting*, in the phr. אַבְנֵי מַחְצֵב, *stones of —*, i. e. *hewn stones*, 2 Kings xii. 13; xxii. 6; 2 Chron. xxxiv. 11, al. non occ.

מֶחֱצָה, f. constr. מֶחֱצַת, r. חָצָה, p. 217 above. *Portion, apportionment; half*, Num. xxxi. 36. 43, only. LXX. ἡμίσευμα.

מַחֲצִית, f. id., Exod. xxx. 13; xxxviii. 26; 1 Kings xvi. 9; Neh. viii. 3; 1 Chron. vi. 55, &c. Aff. מַחֲצִיתָה, מַחֲצִיתָם, מַחֲצִיתוֹ. LXX. ἡμίσευμα, ἥμισυ.

מַחְצְרִים, and מְחַצְצְרִים. See r. חֲצֹצְרָה, p. 218 above.

מָחָה, v. pret. f. מָחֲקָה, once, Judg. v. 26. Sam. צצץ, *delevit, perdidit*. Arab. مَحَقَ, id. *Destroyed*. LXX. διήλωσε. Theod. ἀπέτεμεν. Symm. διήλασε.

מֶחְקָר, m. pl. constr. מֶחְקְרֵי, once, Ps. xcv. 4. r. חָקַר. Comp. חֵקֶר תְּהוֹם, Job xxxviii. 16. Lit. *places of search, or research*. *Depths*: opp. τῷ, תּוֹעֲפוֹת following. Aquila, ἐξιχνιασμοὶ γῆς. Symm. κατώτατα γῆς.

מָחָר, m.
מָחֳרָת, f. } plur. non occ. constr. fem.

מָחֲרָה. Arab. مَخَرَ, *lata per mare fuit navis*; viii. *autrorsum excepit naso suo ventum*. The primitive notion seems to consist in *proceeding forwards*; which, applied to time, may designate the (a) *Morrow*, or day following some other day previously expressed or implied. Syr. ܡܚܪ, id., 1 Sam. xx. 5; Is. xxii. 13. יוֹם מָחָר, Is. lvi. 12; Prov. xxvii. 1. לְמָחָר, *to, for, on*, Num. xi. 18; Exod. viii. 6. 19, &c. כָּעֵת מָחָר 1 Kings xix. 2. Comp. Josh. xi. 6; 1 Sam. ix. 16. פַּעַם מָחָר הַשְּׁלִישִׁית, *as* (at) *this time to-morrow, or third day*, i. e. or the day after to-morrow. Gesen. More literally, as (at) this time to-morrow third day, i. e. the third day hence, beginning with the present, 1 Sam. xx. 12. LXX. ὡς ἂν ὁ καιρὸς, τρισσῶς. More generally, (b) *Hereafter, henceforward*, Gen. xxx. 33; Exod. xiii. 14; Deut. vi. 20; Josh. iv. 6. 21: so Matt. vi. 34, εἰς τὴν αὔριον. John i. 29. 35, τῇ ἐπαύριον. בַּמָּחָר, Esth. ix. 13. Comp. v. 12. פִּי מָחָר, Judg. xx. 28, &c.; Nold. p. 500. Fem., Num. xi. 32; Jonah iv. 7; Nold., ib. With other partic. מִמָּחֳרָת, Gen. xix. 34; Exod. ix. 6. עַד מִמָּחֳרָת, Lev. xxiii. 16. מָחֳרַת הַיּוֹם, 1 Chron. xxix. 21, &c. מִמָּחֳרַת הַפֶּסַח, Num. xxxiii. 3. Comp. 1 Sam. xx. 27. Aff. מָחֳרָתָם, 1 Sam. xxx. 17; but with כְּ, as in יוֹם. Gesen.

מַחֲרָאוֹת, fem. pl., r. חָרָא, once, 1 Kings x. 27. Kethiv, i. q. Keri, מוֹצָאוֹת, which see above.

מַחֲרֶשֶׁת, and מַחֲרֶשֶׁת, f. pl. מַחֲרֵשׁוֹת, r. חָרַשׁ, p. 226 above. Arab. مِحْرَاث, *aratrum*. Lit. *Cutter*. Aff. 1 Sam. xiii. 20, מַחֲרֵשָׁתוֹ, and מַחֲרֵשָׁתוֹ. Auth. Vers. " *his share, and his coulter*." So Gesen. LXX. δρέπανον and θεριστήριον. Tromm. Sym. τὴν ὕννιν (al. ὕνιν), καὶ τὴν δίκελλαν. Aquila, for the first, τριόδοντα. Theod. βούκεντρον. As אֵתוֹ, occurring here, signifies a part of the plough, it is not very probable that these our words have anything to do with that instrument. The Greek Translators are probably the most correct. Pl., Ib. vr. 21, al. non occ.

מַחְשׂוֹף, m. once, Gen. xxx. 37, r. חָשַׂף. Lit. *Laying bare*, i. e. by peeling.

מַחְשָׁבָה, fem. plur.—מַחֲשָׁבוֹת.

מַחֲשֶׁבֶת, fem. it. constr.—מַחְשְׁבוֹת. r. חָשַׁב. (a) *Thought, design, project*, in either a good or bad sense, as the context may require, Gen. vi. 5; 2 Sam. xiv. 14; Job v. 12; Prov. xii. 5; xv. 22; xix. 21; Esth. viii. 3. 5; ix. 25; Ezek. xxxviii. 10. (b) *Work of art, ingenuity*, Exod. xxxi. 4; xxxv. 33. 35. Aff. מַחֲשַׁבְתּוֹ, pl. מַחְשְׁבוֹנוֹ, &c.

מַחְשָׁךְ, m. pl. מַחֲשַׁכִּים, constr. מַחֲשַׁכֵּי, r. חָשַׁךְ. *Darkness*, Is. xxix. 15; xlii. 16. Metaph. *Adversity*, Ps. lxxxviii. 19. Pl., lxxxviii. 7; cxliii. 3; Lam. iii. 6. Constr. Ps. lxxiv. 20, — *of the earth*, i. e. places of ignorance.

מַחְתָּה, fem. pl. מַחְתּוֹת, r. חָתָה. Æth. ႗ተወ : (αἴθω), succensus, accensus fuit. (a) A shovel, or pan, for removing coals of fire, Exod. xxvii. 3; xxxviii. 3. (b) A censer, Lev. x. 1; Num. xvi. 6. 17, 18; xvii. 11, &c. (c) Dishes or pans, for receiving the snuffs of the lamps, Exod. xxv. 38; xxxvii. 23; 2 Kings xxv. 15, &c. Aff. מַחְתָּתוֹ, pl. מַחְתֹּתָיו, &c.

מִחְתָּה, f. constr. מְחִתַּת, r. חָתַת. Lit. (a) breaking. A stroke, injury, ruin, Prov. x. 14. 29; xiii. 3; xviii. 7; Jer. xvii. 17; Ps. lxxxix. 41. Meton. (b) Fear, terror, Prov. x. 15; xxi. 15; Is. liv. 14, &c.

מַחְתֶּרֶת, f.—pl. non occ., r. חָתַר. Lit. Digging through, or into, walls, &c. See my note on Job xxiv. 16. Exod. xxii. 1; Jer. ii. 34, only.

מָט, see מַטֶּה.

מָטָא, and מָטָה, pres. יִמְטֵא, constr. abs. it. med. אֶל, לְ, עַל, עַד. Syr. ܡܛܐ, advenit. Arab. مضى, præteriit. Cogn. Heb. מָצָא. Come on, to, arrive at, any person, or place, Dan. iv. 8. 17. 19. 21. 25; vi. 25; vii. 13: of time, Ib. vr. 22.

מַטְאֲטֵא, masc. once, Is. xiv. 23. See מאטא, p. 234 above, and LXX.

מַטְבֵּחַ, masc., r. טָבַח, once, Is. xiv. 21. Slaughter.

מַטֶּה, m. (once, f. Mic. vi. 9; Gesen.: not so necessarily, ה ָ following, may intimate thing.) Constr. מַטֵּה, pl. f. מַטּוֹת, it. m. aff. מַטִּי. (a) Branch, of a tree, Ezek. xix. 11, seq. Thence, meton., (b) A staff, Exod. iv. 2. 4. 17; Num. xx. 9. Whence, metaph., מַטֵּה־לֶחֶם, staff, i. e. support, of bread, Lev. xxvi. 26; Ps. cv. 16; Ezek. iv. 16, &c. (c) Staff, stick, or rod, of chastisement, Is. ix. 3. מַטֶּה שִׁכְמוֹ, rod of his shoulder, i. e. applied to it, Is. ix. 3; Ib. x. 5. 24; Nah. i. 13; Ezek. vii. 10. מַטֵּה רְשָׁעִים, — of the wicked, Is. xiv. 5, &c. Hence, (d) meton., as the symbol of asserting rights, A sceptre, or mace, Ps. cx. 2, מַטֵּה עֻזְּךָ, sceptre of thy power, i. e. vindicating it, see seq., Ezek. xix. 12. 14, i. q. שֵׁבֶט מֹשֵׁל, where the primary notion is mixed up with this. Also, a spear; but a sceptre, or mace, will suit the places, viz., Hab. iii. 9. 14; 1 Sam. xiv. 27. Hence, also, (e) from the sceptre borne by its chief, A tribe, pec. as descended from the patriarchs of Israel, Num. i. 4. 16; xvii. 17. 21; xxxi. 4, 5; xxxiv. 18; xxxvi. 7, &c. Phr. רָאשֵׁי הַמַּטּוֹת, heads of —, 1 Kings viii. 1, i. q. נְשִׂיאֵי הַמַּטּוֹת, Num. vii. 2, &c. Aff. מַטָּם, masc. Hab. l. c.

מַטָּה, r. נָטָה, adv. opp. τῷ, מַעְלָה. Downwards, Deut. xxviii. 43; Prov. xv. 24. לְמַטָּה, for לְמַטָּה מַטָּה, opp. τῷ, לְמַעְלָה, preceding, to be read thus, מִשְּׁאוֹל שָׁאוֹל לְמַטָּה, from (inclining) downwards (to the) grave. See LXX. With לְ, Deut. xxviii. 13; Ezek. i. 27; 1 Chron. xxvii. 23; Jer. xxxi. 37; Eccl. iii. 21; opp. τῷ, לְמַעְלָה, 2 Kings xix. 30. Phr. לְמַטָּה מֵעֲוֹנֵנוּ, downwards from our sin, i. e. in a lower degree than it deserved, Ezra ix. 13. With לְ, and מִן, לְמַטָּה מִן, opp. τῷ, לְמַעְלָה. Lit. from downwards, i. e. from below, Exod. xxvi. 24; xxvii. 5; xxviii. 27, &c.

מִטָּה, fem. constr. מִטַּת, pl. מִטּוֹת, r. נָטָה. A couch, bed, to recline or sleep on, Gen. xlvii. 31; xlviii. 2; xlix. 33; Exod. vii. 28; Amos iii. 12; vi. 4. — on which they recline at table, Esth. i. 6; Ezek. xxiii. 41: Cant. iii. 7, " sella gestatoria." Gesen. For which there appears to be no good reason. LXX. κλίνη. Used as a bier for the dead, 2 Sam. iii. 31. Aff. מִטָּתוֹ, מִטָּתִי, &c.

מֻטֶּה, masc. pl. מֻטּוֹת, r. נָטָה, twice, Is. viii. 8; Ezek. ix. 9. Extending, extension, on, over, throughout.

מִטַּהֵר, for מִתְטַהֵר, part. Hithp. r. טהר.

מַטְוֶה, m. r. טוה, once, Exod. xxxv. 25. Lit. spinning. Thing spun, yarn. LXX. νενησμένα.

מְטִיל, m. r. מטל. Arab. مطل, ferrum cudit et extendit. A bar of iron. Once, Job xl. 18. See my note.

מַטְמוֹן, m. pl. מַטְמוֹנִים, constr. מַטְמְנֵי, r. טָמַן. Thing, or place, securely hidden. Treasure, Gen. xliii. 23; Jer. xli. 8; Is. xlv. 3; Prov. ii. 4; Job iii. 21.

מַטָּע, masc. plur. constr. מַטְּעֵי, r. נָטַע. Planting. Meton. Plant, Ezek. xvii. 7; xxxi. 4; xxxiv. 29; Is. lx. 21; lxi. 3; Mic. i. 6. Aff. מַטָּעָהּ, מַטָּעֵי.

מַטְעַמִּים, masc. pl.
מַטְעַמּוֹת, fem. pl. } r. טָעַם. Arab. مطعم, cupediæ. Savoury, dainty, meats,

Gen. xxvii. 4. 7. 9, seq.; Prov. xxiii. 3. 6. Aff. מַטְעַמּוֹתָיו, al. non occ. Aquila, Symm. ἐδέσματα.

מִטְפַּחַת, f. pl. מִטְפָּחוֹת. r. טָפַח. *Large upper garment; mantle*, Ruth iii. 15; Is. iii. 22. See Schrœd. de Vestitu Mulierum, c. xvi.

מָטָר, masc.—plur. fem. מְטָרוֹת. Arab. مَطَر, *pluvia.* Syr. ܡܶܛܪܳܐ, id. *Rain*, Exod. ix. 33; Deut. xi. 17; Is. xxx. 23; Job xxxvii. 6. Phr. מְטַר הַשָּׁמַיִם, — *of heaven*, Deut. xi. 11. מְטַר גֶּשֶׁם, — *of the shower*, Zech. x. 1. אַרְצֶךָ, — *of thy land*, Deut. xxviii. 24. זַרְעֶךָ, — *of thy seed*, Is. xxx. 23. Hence the verb—

Hiph. הִמְטִיר, pres. apoc. יַמְטֵר; תַּמְטִיר. Constr. immed. it. med. עַל, בְּ. *Rain; cause, give, rain,* of showers, hail, lightning, fire and brimstone, manna, bread, Gen. ii. 5; Exod. ix. 18. 23;—Ps. xi. 6; Gen. xix. 24; Ezek. xxxviii. 22;— Exod. xvi. 4; Ps. lxxviii. 24; Job xx. 23.

Infin. הַמְטִיר, Job xxxviii. 26; Is. v. 6.
Part. מַמְטִיר, Gen. vii. 4, &c.
Niph. pres. f. תִּמָּטֵר, *Be, become, rained* on, Amos iv. 7, only.

מַטָּרָה, f.—pl. non occ. r. נָטַר. Arab. نَطَرَ, *custodem egit.* Cogn. نَظَرَ, *vidit.* (a) *Custody;* or *prison*, Neh. iii. 25; xii. 39; Jer. xxxii. 2. 8; xxxiii. 1. (b) *Mark, object, butt*, 1 Sam. xx. 20; Job xvi. 12; Lam. iii. 12: in the Chaldaic form, מַטָּרָא.

מִי, see מַיִם below.

מִי, c. Interrogative pron. *Who? what?* sing. or pl. Æth. መኑ : Syr. ܡܰܢ. Arab. مَا, *What?* מִי הָאִישׁ הַלָּזֶה, *Who is this man?* Gen. xxiv. 65. מִי־אָתְּ, *Who art thou?* Ruth iii. 9. Comp. Esth. vi. 4; Judg. i. 1, &c. Sometimes after the thing or person inquired about; as, בַּת־מִי, *Daughter of whom?* Gen. xxiv. 23. 47. שׁוֹר־מִי, *Ox of whom?* חֲמוֹר מִי, *Whose ass?* 1 Sam. xii. 3. דְּבָר־מִי, *Whose word?* Jer. xliv. 28. Used also, as in other languages, to imply a strong *negation, paucity, difficulty,* or the like, as the term affected by it may require: as, מִי שָׂמְךָ, *Who placed*, appointed, *thee?* Exod. ii. 14. מִי מָנָה עֲפַר, *Who has counted the dust?* Num. xxiii. 10. מִי יֹאמַר, *Who shall say?* Prov. xx. 9. Implying that no one has done, or can do so. So τίς, Matt. vi. 27; Rom. viii. 34. In like manner with nouns, מִי־אֵל, *What God?* Deut. iii. 24. מִי אָדוֹן, *What Lord,* or *who is Lord?* Ps. xii. 5. מִי יְהוָה, *What Jehovah?* or, *who, what, is Jehovah?* Exod. v. 2. Comp. Judg. ix. 28. 38. מִי אָנֹכִי, *What am I?* Exod. iii. 11. מִי עַמִּי, — *my people?* 1 Chron. xxix. 14. Comp. 1 Sam. ii. 25; Is. li. 19; liii. 1; Prov. xxxi. 10, &c.; Nold., p. 501.

Hence the phrr. מִי יוֹדֵעַ, *Who knows?* i. e. no one can say whether —, 2 Sam. xii. 22. יְחָנֵּנִי, *he may be gracious to me:* Joel ii. 14. יָשׁוּב, *he may turn.* Comp. Esth. iv. 14; Jonah iii. 9; Eccl. ii. 19; Ps. xc. 11, &c.— מִי יִתֵּן, *Who can, shall, give, grant,* that such or such a thing may be? Nearly equivalent to, would it were! Exod. xvi. 3; Num. xi. 29; Deut. v. 26; Cant. viii. 1, &c.; Nold., p. 904. Not unlike this are the following usages: מִי פֶשַׁע יַעֲקֹב, *Whose?* or *what!* is *the sin of Jacob?* מִי בָּמוֹת יְהוּדָה, *Whose? What!* are *the high places of Judah?* Mic. i. 5. מִי שְׁמֶךָ, *Whose is thy name?* i. e. to what personage belongs thy name? A delicate mode of asking, who art thou? Judg. xiii. 17. So also, Amos vii. 2. 5, מִי יָקוּם יַעֲקֹב, *Who? What! shall,* or *can, Jacob arise?* Is. li. 19, מִי אֲנַחְמֵךְ, *Who? shall,* or *can, I pity thee?* Gesenius thus, מִי אָנֹכִי כִּי אֲנַחְמֵךְ, *Who am I, that I should pity thee?* But this implies *weakness, inability,* in the person speaking; which cannot be predicated of the speaker here. It is, therefore, erroneous. These usages are in some degree analogous to that of the Arab. مَا, of admiration, *How! What!* or to the Latin *Quid!* So Gen. xxxiii. 8, מִי לְךָ וגו', *What! Whose?* Is *thine, &c.?*

Used also without an Interrogation, Lat. *qui,* מִי שָׂם, *who put*, Gen. xliii. 22. מִי הָלַךְ, *who is gone,* 1 Sam. xiv. 17. Comp. 1 Kings i. 20; Ps. xxxix. 7, &c. Repeated, like the Lat. *quisquis,* Exod. x. 8. מִי וָמִי, *whoever.* Lit. *who and who.* So unrepeated, מִי־בַעַל דְּבָרִים וגו', *whoever has questions, &c.* Lit. who is master of words, pleadings, Exod. xxiv. 14. Comp. Eccl. v. 9; Judg. vii. 3; Is. liv. 15, &c.; Nold., p. 501.

Compounded with other particles: לְמִי, *To whom, whose?* Gen. xxxii. 18. *For whom?* Exod. xxxii. 24. אֶת־מִי, *As to whom?* 1 Sam. xii. 3. מִמִּי, Ezek. xxxii. 19. בְּמִי, 1 Kings xx. 14. עַל־מִי, see Nold. in its place. So, מִי אֲשֶׁר, מִי זֶה, מִי זֹאת, מִי אוֹ,

מִי (356) מַיִם

מִי הוּא, מִי גַם, אֲשֶׁר מִי, אַחֲרֵי מִי, אֱלֹמִי, מִי אֵפוֹא הוּא, מִי הוּא זֶה, &c., Ib. p. 502, &c.

With לֹא.—As an interrogation may strongly negative, &c., so with לֹא, מִי will strongly affirm. Jer. x. 7, מִי לֹא יִרָאֲךָ, *Who shall not fear thee?* Job xii. 9, מִי לֹא יָדַע, *Who has not known?* that is, all shall, &c. Comp. Amos iii. 8; Nah. iii. 19; Job xxv. 3.

מְיֻנִּים, m. pl. once, Jer. v. 8. Keri; Kethiv, מְיֻזָּנִים, r. יזן, according to some. See זוּנָה, p. 168 above. Part. Hoph. *Fed.*— Others, r. יון. Arab. وَزَنَ, *ponderavit. Heavy*, as stallions well formed. So Schult. Others, cogn. Syr. ܐܰܙܶܢ, *armavit.* Arab. زَانَ, *compsit. Appointed, accoutered*, as for war. LXX. ἵπποι θηλυμανεῖς.

מֵיטָב, m.—pl. non occ., r. יָטַב. *Good, choice; best*, place or part: in the phrr. Exod. xxii. 4, מֵיטַב שָׂדֵהוּ וּמֵיטַב כַּרְמוֹ, *best of his field, and best of his vineyard.* 1 Sam. xv. 19, מֵיטַב הַצֹּאן וְהַבָּקָר, *best of the flock and of the oxen.* מֵיטַב הָאָרֶץ, *best of the land*, Gen. xlvii. 6. 11.

מִיכָל, masc. once, 2 Sam. xvii. 20, in מִיכַל הַמָּיִם. Usually, *brook of water.* Gesen. "*parvus rivus aquæ;*" from the Arab. مَكَلَ, *parum aquæ continuit* (puteus). But, both seem incongruous; for, if מִיכָל contains the notion of water at all, to add הַמַּיִם, must have been superfluous; as much so as in *brook of waters* with us. The Arabic term, however, seems to apply to *a well* only. How then it can apply to a brook, does not seem very obvious. In the Arabic we have, وَكَلَ, *lassus fuit;* وَكَال, *segnities et tarditas equi.* And, supposing a noun of place thence formed, as مَوْكَل, or مَكَّل, from the cogn. يَكِلُ, we shall have our term מִיכָל, *place of inactivity*, or *stagnation*: and, with הַמַּיִם following, *stagnant place, pit*, or *lake, of waters.* Which might have been some lake or morass in the Desert, between Jerusalem and the Jordan. Some have proposed to read מִיבַל here, r. יבל, i. e. *stream.* So Capellus. Buxtorf's answer is, "No such word is to be found: but, that מִיכָל may be derived from יכל, signifying, *vehementia aquæ*, for *river*, or the Jordan. The Jews, in the days of Jerome, certainly understood *the Jordan.*" See his Questions on the place.

מַיִם, masc. pl. constr. מֵי, מֵימֵי. Æth. ᎣᎤᎤᎠ: *liquescere.* Arab. مَهَّ, *multa aqua imbuit.* Cogn. مَاء, *aquâ scatuit puteus.* Æth. ᎣᎠᏓ: Arab. مَاء, مَآءَة. Syr. ܡܰܝܳܐ, *aqua. Water*, generally, Gen. viii. 9; xviii. 4; Exod. xv. 19; Num. v. 18; —Exod. vii. 19; viii. 2, &c. With attributives, in the pl. מַיִם חַיִּים, *living*, i. e. fresh, springing, *waters*, Gen. xxvi. 19; Lev. xiv. 5, &c. קְדֹשִׁים —, *holy*, Num. v. 17. רַבִּים —, *many*, Ps. xviii. 17. With pl. verbs, Gen. vii. 19; viii. 5; 2 Kings ii. 19; Ezek. xlvii. 1; formally, Gram. art. 215. 5. With sing. verbs, Gen. ix. 15; Num. xx. 2; xxiv. 7, &c.: logically, Gram. ib. With the name of a town, &c., denoting a river, lake, &c., in its neighbourhood: as, מֵי מִגְדּוֹ, of the torrent Kishon, Judg. v. 19. מֵי נִמְרִים, Jer. xlviii. 34. So מְרִיבָה, — נִפְתּוֹחַ, — עֵין שֶׁמֶשׁ, Num. xx. 13; Josh. xv. 7. 9. Of certain springs, מֵי יְרִיחוֹ, Josh. xvi. 1. מֵי דִימוֹן, Is. xv. 9. Of a river, מֵי מֵרוֹם, Josh. xi. 5. מֵי מִצְרַיִם, *lakes of Egypt*, Exod. vii. 19; viii. 2. כָּל־מֵימֵי יִשְׂרָאֵל, *waters of Israel*, 2 Kings v. 12. Comp. 2 Chron. xxxii. 3; Job xxiv. 19. מֵי נֹחַ, — *of Noah*, i. q. הַמַּבּוּל —: of the deluge, Is. liv. 9. מֵי רֹאשׁ — *of the poppy*, opium. Gesen. מֵי רַגְלַיִם, — *of both feet*, urine; Keri, Is. xxxvi. 12. אָפְסַיִם, — of extremities, Ezek. xlvii. 3. מֵי מָתְנַיִם, — *of*—up to— *both loins*, Ib. vr. 4. *Seed*, Is. xlviii. 1. Comp. Num. xxiv. 7; Ps. lxviii. 27. So Arab. مَاء. הַמָּרִים הַמְאָרֲרִים, — *of great bitterness, bringing the curse*, Num. v. 18. חַטָּאת, — *of expiation*, Ib. viii. 7. נִדָּה, — of, id., Ib. xix. 13. מֵי מָלֵא, — *of filling*, fulness, Ps. lxxiii. 10, &c.

Metaph. implying *Abundance*, Ps. lxxix. 3; lxxxviii. 18; Is. xi. 9; Hab. ii. 14: also, *great perils*, Ps. xviii. 17; xxxii. 6; lxix. 2, 3; Job xxvii. 20: *weakness*, Josh. vii. 5: *incontinence*, Gen. xlix. 4.

Aff. מֵימַי, 1 Sam. xxv. 11: מֵימֵינוּ, Lam. v. 4: מֵימֶיךָ, Exod. xxiii. 25: מֵימָיו, Num. xx. 8, &c.

מִין, masc. pl. constr. מִינֵי. Syr. ܓܶܢܣܳܐ, *stirps, familia. Kind, species.* Always with לְ prefixed, and pron. aff., as, לְמִינוֹ, לְמִינֵהוּ,

לְמִינֵהֶם, לְמִינָה, *according to his*, or *its, hers, their, species* or *kind*, Gen. i. 11, 12. 21. 24, 25; Lev. xi. 15, 16, &c.

מֵינֶקֶת, f. r. יָנַק. *A nurse*, Gen. xxxv. 8, &c. Part. Hiph., p. 261 above.

מֵיסַךְ, Kethiv, for מוּסָךְ, 2 Kings xvi. 18. r. סכך.

מֵיץ, masc.—plur. non occ. Arab. مَاصَ, r. موص, *confricuit manu*. Syr. ܡܨܐ, *emunxit. Pressing, squeezing*, Prov. xxx. 33. מִיץ חָלָב, *squeezing, pressing, of milk*, i. e. *churning*; which is done by putting the milk or cream into a skin prepared for the purpose; and then squeezing and agitating the skin repeatedly with the hand. Harmer's Observ. vol. i., p. 500, Edit. 1816. This gives point to the rest of the context.

מִישׁוֹר, מִישֹׁר, masc.—pl. non occ. r. יָשַׁר. Lit. *straight, even, place*. (a) *A plain*, generally, Is. xl. 4; xlii. 16. Pec. that situate in the tribe of Reuben. With def. art. ה, Deut. iii. 10; iv. 43; Josh. xiii. 9. 16, 17, &c. Metaph. (b) *Truth, righteousness*, Ps. xxvii. 11; xlv. 7; cxliii. 10; Is. xi. 4. (c) Adv. *Truly, righteously*, Ps. lxvii. 5.

מֵישָׁרִים, מִישָׁרִים, m. pl., r. יָשַׁר. Lit. (a) *True, direct, persons*, Cant. i. 4. Pl. excell., *very true, &c.* Hence, as an abstract, (b) *Very truth, righteousness*, Ps. xvii. 2; xcix. 4; Prov. viii. 6; xxiii. 16; Is. xxvi. 7. With צֶדֶק וּמִישָׁפָּט, Prov. i. 3. (c) Adv. *Truly, righteously*, Ps. lviii. 2; lxxv. 3. It. with בְּ, pref. Ps. ix. 9; xcvi. 10; xcviii. 9; Prov. xxiii. 31. It. with לְ, Cant. vii. 10. Phr. לַעֲשׂוֹת מֵישָׁרִים, *to make straight, direct, things*; or, Vulg. Eng. make things straight, restore order, peace, Dan. xi. 6. Comp. vr. 17, and Mal. ii. 6, with cogn. מִישׁוֹר.

מֵיתָר, masc. pl. aff. מֵיתָרַי, מֵיתָרֶיךָ, &c. r. יָתַר, p. 280 above. Arab. وَتَر, *nervus, chorda, arcus*, &c. (a) *Bow-strings*, Ps. xxi. 13. (b) *Cords, ropes*, of a tent, &c., Exod. xxxix. 40; Num. iii. 37; iv. 32; Is. liv. 2; Jer. x. 20, &c.

מַכְאוֹב, and מַכְאָב, masc. pl. מַכְאוֹבִים, מַכְאֹבִים, it. f. מַכְאֹבוֹת, once, Is. liii. 3. See r. פָּאַב, p. 284 above. (a) *Pain*, Ps. lxix. 27; Job xxxiii. 19; Is. liii. 4; Jer. xlv. 3; 2 Chron. vi. 29. Meton. (b) *Cause, source, of pain*, as a wound, &c., Jer. xxx. 15; Lam. i. 18; Ps. xxxviii. 18. Metaph. (c) *Grief, sorrow*, Exod. iii. 7; Lam. i. 12. Aff. מַכְאוֹבוֹ, מַכְאֹבוֹ, מַכְאֹבֶךָ, &c.; pl. מַכְאוֹבֵינוּ, מַכְאֹבָי, &c.

מַכְבִּיר, m. once, Job xxxvi. 31, r. כָּבַר. *Abundance*.

מִכְבָּר, masc. constr. מִכְבַּר. See כְּבָרָה, *a sieve*, p. 286 above. *Thing* or *place—of a sieve*, or *sifting. Brazen net work* for the altar, Exod. xxvii. 4; xxxv. 16; xxxviii. 4. 30; xxxix. 39, &c.

מַכְבֵּר, masc. once, 2 Kings viii. 15. *Carpet*, or other *coarse cloth*. We find a similar thing recorded in the Persian history, entitled, خلاصة الاخبار, *Kholasat El Akhbar*. (In my copy, p. 162, verso). The words are these, آنگاه مالك فرمان داد که مفرشی بر دهان عبد الله نهادند تا نفسش منقطع کشت. *The Malik ordered that they should place a carpet on Abdallah's mouth, so that his life was cut off.*

מַכָּה, f. constr. מַכַּת, pl. מַכּוֹת; it. m. pl. מַכִּים, 2 Kings viii. 29; ix. 15: r. נָכָה. (a) *A stroke* or *blow*, Deut. xxv. 3; 2 Chron. ii. 9. חִטִּים מַכּוֹת, lit. *wheat of beatings out:* but comp. 1 Kings v. 25. (b) Meton. *Wound*, 1 Kings xxii. 35; Is. i. 6. (c) *Slaughter* in war, Josh. x. 10. 20; Judg. xi. 33; xv. 8. (d) *Calamity* from God, Num. xi. 33; Lev. xxvi. 21; Deut. xxviii. 59. 61; xxix. 21;—1 Sam. vi. 19. Aff. מַכָּתִי, מַכָּתֶךָ, מַכָּתָךְ, &c.; pl. מַכּוֹתֶךָ, &c.

מִכְוָה, fem. constr. מִכְוַת, pl. non occ. r. כָּוָה. Lit. *place of burning. Inflamed part*, Lev. xiii. 24, 25. 28. Phr. מִכְוַת־אֵשׁ, *burning* (as) *of fire*, l. c. al. non occ.

מָכוֹן, m. constr. מְכוֹן. Pl. aff. מְכוֹנָיו, r. כּוּן. Arab. مَكَان, *locus*. Æth. id. lit. *place of setting in order, establishing*. (a) *Establishment, habitation, place*, Exod. xv. 17; 1 Kings viii. 13. 39. 43. Often in the phrr. מָכוֹן לְשִׁבְתֶּךָ, מְכוֹן שִׁבְתְּךָ, ll. cc. 1 Kings ll. cc. Comp. Is. iv. 5; Ps. xxxiii. 14;—Is. xviii. 4, אַבִּיטָה בִמְכוֹנִי, *let me look* (with complacency) *on my habitation*, i. e. on the place which God had chosen for his service in Jerusalem. (b) *Base, foundation*, Ps. lxxxix. 15; xcvii. 2; Dan. viii. 11. Aff. מְכוֹנוֹ, &c.

מכו (358) מכל

מְכוֹנָה, מְכֻנָה, f. pl. מְכֹנוֹת. Fem. of the above מָכוֹן. (a) *Place*, Ezra iii. 3 : but, (b) *Base*, will suit the place equally well, as in all other places, 1 Kings vii. 27, seq.; 2 Kings xvi. 17; xxv. 13. 16; Jer. xxvii. 19; lii. 17. 20. Aff. pl. מְכוֹנֹתָיו.

מְכֻרָה, מְכוּרָה, fem. pl. Aff. מְכֹרֹתַיִךְ, מְכֹרֹתָיִךְ, Ezek. xxi. 35; xvi. 3. Sing. מְכוּרָתָם, Ib. xxix. 14: r. כּוּר. Lit. place of digging; mine, &c. *Place of origin, birth, nativity*. Comp. Is. li. 1.

מְכִירִי, masc. Patronym. of מָכִיר, Num. xxvi. 29.

מָךְ, see v. מוּךְ.

מכך, v. cognn. מוּךְ, מָקַק. Syr. ܡܟܟ, *stratus, dejectus, est*. Arab. مَكّ, *diminuit, consumpsit*. Kal non occ.

Niph. pres. יִמַּךְ, *Becomes attenuated, weak*, once, Eccl. x. 15.

Hoph. pl. הֻמָּכוּ, *They fall, perish*: Gesen. But see my note on Job xxiv. 24, where it occurs.

מִכְלָה, fem. pl. מִכְלוֹת. I. *Perfections*, r. כָּלָה, once, 2 Chron. iv. 21. LXX. χρυσίου καθαροῦ. II. for מִכְלָא, Gram. art. 202. 4 : r. כָּלָא, once, Hab. iii. 17. *Fold*, or *other place for confining* the flocks. Pl. מִכְלָאוֹת, Ps. lxxviii. 70. Aff. מִכְלְאוֹתָיִךְ, Ps. L. 9, al. non occ.

מִכְלוֹל, masc. twice, Ezek. xxiii. 12; xxxviii. 4, in the phrr. לְבֻשֵׁי מִכְלוֹל. Lit. *Persons clothed of perfection*, i. e. richly clothed. LXX. ἐνδεδυκότας εὐπάρυφα. See Schleusn. Lex. in LXX.

מִכְלָל, masc. once, Ps. L. 2, r. כָּלַל, in מִכְלַל־יֹפִי, *Perfection of beauty*. Aquila, τετελεσμένης κάλλει. See LXX.

מַכְלֻלִים, m. pl. once, Ezek. xxvii. 24. Lit. *perfections*, usually: thence, *Splendid, precious, garments*. The term is still used in this sense in the East. The author of the "*Kowayîd us Sultanet Shahjehan*," speaking of the rich trappings of the elephant, says,

فيلان نامي .... با سازهاي مكمل ومكلل وغيرة

"Renowned elephants .... decked in *complete trappings*," &c.; where مكلل is evidently synonymous with مكمل *complete, perfect*. Gladwin's Moonsh. Edit.

1801, p. ۳۲.—"*Gemmis vel rosarum figuris contextus* (a Pers. كل, rosa)." Freytag.

מַאֲכֶלֶת, fem. for מַאֲכֶלֶת, r. אָכַל, once, 1 Kings v. 25. *Food*.

מִכְמַנִּים, masc. pl. r. כָּמַן, once, Dan. xi. 43, in the phr. מִכְמַנֵּי הַזָּהָב, *Hidden* (treasures) *of gold*. LXX. ἐν τοῖς ἀποκρύφοις τοῦ χρυσοῦ.

מִכְמָר, m. ⎫ plur. aff. מַכְמָרָיו, r. כָּמַר.
מִכְמֹר, m. ⎭ Æth. ሀዐሀ : *cumulavit*. *A net*, or *toil*, used by hunters, Is. li. 20; Ps. cxli. 10, al. non occ. Symm. ἐν ἀμφιβλήστρῳ, ἠμφιβληστρευμένος. Aquila, Theod. συνειλημένος. See LXX.

מִכְמֶרֶת, fem. aff. מִכְמַרְתּוֹ, pl. non occ., r. כָּמַר. *A net* used by fishermen, Is. xix. 8; Hab. i. 15, 16.

מִכְנְסֵי, m. pl. constr. r. כָּנַס, only in the phrr. מִכְנְסֵי־בָד, מִכְנָסַיִם פִּשְׁתִּים, *Trousers*, or *breeches, of linen*, Exod. xxviii. 42; xxxix. 28; Lev. vi. 3; xvi. 4; Ezek. xliv. 18, only. LXX. περισκελές. Josephus describes these, Antiq. Lib. iii. c. vii. § 1, πρῶτον, says he, μὲν περιτίθεται τὸν μαναχασὴν (μεχνασὴν?) λεγόμενον, βούλεται δὲ συνακτῆρα μὲν δηλοῦν, διάζωμα δ᾽ ἐστὶ περὶ τὰ αἰδοῖα ῥαπτὸν ἐκ βύσσου, κ.τ.λ.

מֶכֶס, m. r. כָּסַס, p. 304 above. Contr. of מִכְסָס, and, dropping the last radical, and drawing back the accent, מֶכֶס, *Fractional part* or *number*. Meton. *Price, tribute*, Num. xxxi. 28. 37, 38—41. Syr. ܡܟܣܐ, *vectigal*. Aff. מִכְסוֹ.

מִכְסַת, fem. constr. of מֶכֶס, *Number, proportional*, Exod. xii. 4; Lev. xxvii. 23, only.

מִכְסֵה, m. constr. מִכְסֵה, pl. non occ., r. כָּסָה. *Covering* of the ark, a tent, &c., Gen. viii. 13; Exod. xxvi. 14; xxxvi. 19; xxxix. 34; Num. iv. 25, &c. Aff. מִכְסֵהוּ.

מְכַסֶּה, masc. Part. Piħ. r. כָּסָה, p. 304 above. *Thing, &c., Covering*, Is. xiv. 11, &c.

מֶכֶר, masc. aff. מִכְרָה, מִכְרָם, pl. non occ. Arab. مَكَرَ, *par rependit* Deus. The primary notion seems to consist in *equality, barter*, or the like. Whence, (a) *Equal, value, price*, Prov. xxxi. 10; Num. xx. 19. (b) *Valuable, saleable*, article, Neh. xiii. 16.

מָכַר, v. pres. יִמְכֹּר. See מָכַר above. Cogn. מָהַר, מוּר, מָהַר, יָמַר. Constr. immed. it. med. אֶת, ל, מִן, בְּ, it. abs. Propr. *Barter, exchange*, for something else. (a) *Sell*, Gen. xxxvii. 27, 28; Lev. xxv. 25; xxvii. 20; Joel iv. 3, &c. (b) — or *give* a daughter in marriage, in consideration of something previously given. See מֹהַר, Gen. xxxi. 15; Exod. xxi. 7. (c) — or *give* men *up*, into the power of others, Deut. xxxii. 30; Judg. ii. 14; iii. 8; iv. 2, &c.

Infin. abs. מָכֹר, Deut. xiv. 21. Constr. מְכֹר, Neh. x. 32. Aff. מָכְרָהּ, Exod. xxi. 8. It. מִכְרָם,—of מֶכֶר above—Amos ii. 6, &c.

Imp. with ־ה parag. מִכְרָה, Gen. xxv. 31: f. מִכְרִי, 2 Kings iv. 7.

Part. m. מֹכֵר ‫}‬ pl. מוֹכְרִים. Constr. מֹכְרֵי.
— f. מֹכְרָה ‫}‬ Aff. מֹכְרֵיהֶן, Lev. xxv. 16; Neh. xiii. 16. 20; Zech. xi. 5. Fem., Nah. iii. 4.

Niph. נִמְכַּר, pres. יִמָּכֵר. *Be, become, sold,* Lev. xxv. 34. 42. 48; Ps. cv. 17, &c.

Infin. aff. הִמָּכְרוֹ, Lev. xxv. 50.
Part. pl. m. נִמְכָּרִים, Neh. v. 8.
Hithp. הִתְמַכֵּר, pres. יִתְמַכְּרוּ, i. q. Niph. Deut. xxviii. 68. — or *given up*, 1 Kings xxi. 25; 2 Kings xvii. 17.

Infin. aff. הִתְמַכֶּרְךָ, 1 Kings xxi. 20.

מַכָּר, m. pl. aff. מַכָּרָיו, r. נָכַר. *Known person, relative, friend,* or *neighbour,* 2 Kings xii. 6. 8, only.

מִכְרֶה, m., r. פָּרָה, once, Zeph. ii. 9, in the phr. מִכְרֵה־מֶלַח, *Pit of salt.*

מְכֵרָה, fem. once, pl. aff. מְכֵרֹתֵיהֶם, once, Gen. xlix. 5; r. כּוּר: thence, *Swords.* Gr. μάχαιρα. But, De Dieu, ad loc., and Ludolf. Lex. Æthiop., p. 87, from the Arab. مَكَرَ, *machinatus est. Machinations, devices.* Aquila, σκεύη ἀδικίας ἀνάσκαφε. The preceding כְּלֵי חָמָס, however, seems to require some *instrument* here, rather than *device.* If so, some instrument used for digging through, or sapping, a foundation, was probably intended. In Job xxiv. 16, a similar practice is mentioned. See my note. Aquila evidently entertained this view, obscure as his version of the place is. In Gen. xxxv. 25, we have חַרְבוֹ אִישׁ. But, as in the Lat. *ferrum,* any other *cutting,* or · *graving, tool* might have been meant.

מְכֵרָתִי, m. Patronym. 1 Chron. xi. 36.

מִכְשׁוֹל, m. pl. מִכְשֹׁלִים, r. כָּשַׁל. *Place, instr.* or *cause of stumbling,* Lev. xix. 14; Is. viii. 14. — צוּר, *rock* or *stone of* —, Ib. lvii. 14; Jer. vi. 21; Ezek. iii. 20; xviii. 30; xliv. 12; Ps. cxix. 165. Metaph. *Offence; delusion,* Ezek. vii. 19. עָוֹן, — *of their sin,* i. e. tempting them to it, Ib. xiv. 3. 7. — *of the mind* or *conscience,* לֵב —, 1 Sam. xxv. 31.

מַכְשֵׁלָה, fem. plur. מַכְשֵׁלוֹת, r. כָּשַׁל. *Stumbling, fall, ruin,* Is. iii. 6; Zeph. i. 3: of idols, apparently. Symm. καὶ τὰ σκάνδαλα σὺν ἀσέβεσι, al. non occ. And such is the use of the term σκάνδαλον, in the New Test.

מִכְתָּב, m.—pl. non occ., r. כָּתַב. (a) *Writing,* Exod. xxxii. 16; xxxix. 30; Deut. x. 4. (b) Meton. *Thing written; epistle, letter,* 2 Chron. xxi. 12; xxxvi. 22; Ezra i. 1: *composition, ode,* Is. xxxviii. 9: *ordinance,* 2 Chron. xxxv. 4.

מְכִתָּה, f. once, aff. מְכִתָּתוֹ, Is. xxx. 14: r. כָּתַת. *Its breaking,* i. e. *being broken to pieces.*

מִכְתָּם, m.—pl. non occ. "i. q. מִכְתָּב," says Gesenius, "*scriptum,* spec. *carmen:* b. in ore vulgi sensim in m mutato." All of which is much more plausible than sound. Why, it may be asked, had vulgar usage so much influence as to change the letter b into m in this word in particular? Or, why should it bring about a change, in which there is no reason for believing it ever had any thing to do? Besides, if we are at liberty thus to alter the text, the consequence will be, that no part of it will long have much authority. It is true we have no means of knowing with certainty what the titles of many of the Psalms were intended to convey (see under אִלֵּם, p. 34 above); still it is better to confess our ignorance, than to have recourse to alterations of this sort. At present my own opinion is, that כתם is the root: and that something *hidden, mysterious,* and perhaps *precious,* is intended by this word. It is found, Ps. xvi. lvi. lvii. lviii. lix. lx.

מַכְתֵּשׁ, m.—pl. non occ., r. כָּתַשׁ, Prov. xxvii. 22. *A mortar.* Aquila, Theod. ἐν ὄλμῳ. On Judg. xv. 19, see Bochart. Hieroz. i., p. 202, seq., who thinks that the sockets of the teeth, in the jaw bone, styled in the Gr. ὀλμίσκους, *mortariola,* or *little mortars,* are meant: so also Gesen. All of which is grounded on an apparent similarity of terms in the Greek only; and which,

מלא (360) מלא

therefore, appears scarcely worthy of belief. There is, however, enough in the context, I think, to make all clear. Whatever הַמַּכְתֵּשׁ may mean here, certain it is that the place from which the waters flowed, was situated in (the place called) *Lehi*, and received the name of "*Fountain of the Caller,*" or "*Crier out,*" עֵין הַקּוֹרֵא. It is also certain, that this *fountain* or *spring* was in *Lehi* up to the time in which this event was recorded: it is added, אֲשֶׁר בַּלֶּחִי עַד הַיּוֹם הַזֶּה. If then this fountain had a local habitation and a name, independent of the jaw-bone, so must also הַמַּכְתֵּשׁ, the substitute of which it became, and ever afterwards remained. The text, moreover, says, הַמַּכְתֵּשׁ אֲשֶׁר בַּלֶּחִי, the *Maktesh which, &c.*, which could hardly signify such a thing situate in the jaw-bone; particularly as the *spring* above-mentioned remained permanent. But, if some *tank, pond, well*, or *bason*, was called "*the mortar,*" from its resembling that vessel; and God caused water to flow from it on that occasion, all will be clear and easy; and this, I think, was the case. In Zeph. i. 11, we have a place so called, no doubt, from its resemblance to a mortar.

מְלוֹא, מִלֹּא, once, מְלוֹ, Ezek. xli. 8. Syr. ܡܠܐ, ܡܠܐܐ, *plenitudo*. Arab. ملا. Æth. ሞልአ : id. (a) *Filling, fulness*. מְלֹא כַף, *palm-full*, 1 Kings xvii. 12. מְלֹא חָפְנֵיכֶם, *both closed hands full*, Exod. ix. 8. מְלֹא בֵיתוֹ כֶּסֶף, *the filling of his house* with *silver*, Num. xxii. 18. Comp. Judg. vi. 38, where the thing filling, has not the prep. בְּ. In some cases, however, מִן supplies its place. See Exod. xvi. 32, 33, מְלֹא קוֹמָתוֹ, his *full*, entire, *stature*, 1 Kings xxviii. 20. מְלֹא בִגְדוֹ, his *garment full*, 2 Kings iv. 39. מְלֹא רֹחַב, *fulness of width*, i. e. *full width*, Is. viii. 8. Comp. 2 Sam. viii. 2; Ezek. xli. 8. מְלֹא רֹעִים, *fulness of shepherds;* their entire body, Is. xxxi. 4. הַיָּם וּמְלֹאוֹ, *the sea and its fulness*, Ps. xcvi. 11. Comp. Amos vi. 3. Thence, meton. (b) *Multitude*, Gen. xlviii. 19. מְלֹא הַגּוֹיִם. N. Test. τὸ πλήρωμα τῶν ἐθνῶν. Aff. מְלֹאוֹ, מְלֹאָה.

מָלֵא, מָלָא, v. occasionally contr. מָלְתִי Job xxxii. 18. מְלוּ, Ezek. xxviii. 16. Pres. יִמְלָא. See מָלֵא above. Constr. immed. it. med. אֶת, עַל, over, above; לְ, to; מִן, of, the thing, &c., *with* which anything, &c. is filled, is often put, abs. as, מָלֵא מַיִם, *is full* of *water*, Ps. lxv. 10. Comp. Job xxxvi. 16; Ps. x. 7, &c. *Fill*, Gen. i. 22; Exod. xl. 34, 35; 1 Kings viii. 10, 11; Jer. li. 11: *fill the shields*, i. e. appoint them so as to cover you, Ezek. viii. 17; xxviii. 16; Job xxxvi. 17: *executed fully, thoroughly.* See my note. In these cases the verb may be said to be transitive. In the following instances, or to require some mediating particle, either expressed or understood, Gen. vi. 13; Josh. iii. 15; Judg. xvi. 27; Job xxxii. 18; Ps. x. 7; xxvi. 10, &c. *Fulfil*, of time, Gen. xxv. 24; xxix. 21; L. 3; Lev. viii. 38, &c. Phrr. מָלְאָה נַפְשִׁי, Exod. xv. 9, *my soul is full*, i. e. *satisfied*. Exod. xxxii. 29, מִלְאוּ יֶדְכֶם, *fill your hands;* take office, usually; but here, be active, *fulfil it*. מָלֵא לֵב, *the heart is full*, i. e. intent, Eccl. viii. 11. Comp. Ib. ix. 3; Esth. vii. 5. Metaph. חֶרֶב מָלְאָה דָם, *the sword filled* (as a devourer) *with blood*, Is. xxxiv. 6. מָלְאָה צְבָאָהּ, *her warfare is fulfilled*, accomplished, Ib. xl. 2.

Infin. מְלֹאת, Lev. viii. 33; xii. 4, &c. Imp. pl. מִלְאוּ, Exod. xxxii. 29, &c. Part. masc. מָלֵא, constr. מְלֵא, pl. מְלֵאִים, 2 Kings iv. 4; Jer. vi. 11; Num. vii. 13, &c.

— f. מְלֵאָה, pl. מְלֵאוֹת, Num. vii. 14; Gen. xli. 22, &c.

Niph. נִמְלָא, pres. יִמָּלֵא, constr. abs. it. med. אֶת, מִן, לְ. *Be, become, full*, or *filled*. נִמְלָא-טָל, *filled* with *dew*, Cant. v. 2; Gen. vi. 11; Exod. i. 7; 1 Kings vii. 14; 2 Kings iii. 17, &c.—Of the mind, Eccl. vi. 7.—*Fulfil*, of time, Exod. vii. 25; Job xv. 32. Of weapons, i. e. fully provided with, 2 Sam. xxiii. 7.

Pih. מִלֵּא, once, Jer. li. 34; pres. יְמַלֵּא, once יְמַלֶּה, Job viii. 21. Constr. immed. it. med. אֶת, אַחֲרֵי, בְּ, instr. in. The thing, &c. *with* which, abs. as in Kal, it. med. מִן, i. q. Kal. (a) *Fill*, of time, &c. *Fulfil*, Exod. xxxv. 35; 1 Kings xviii. 35; Ps. cvii. 9. מִלֵּאתִי אֶת-דְּבָרֶיךָ, *I will fulfil thy words*, 1 Kings i. 14. So of promises, &c. 1 Kings ii. 27; viii. 15; 2 Chron. vi. 4. (b) *The hand*, i. e. consecrate to the priests' office by taking certain parts of the sacrifice into it, Lev. xxi. 10; Num. iii. 3; Exod. xxix. 9. (c) Used with other verbs, implying perseverance, full performance, &c. קָרְאוּ מַלֵּאוּ, *cry out, fill*, i. e. fully, with energy, Jer. iv. 5; Gram. art. 222. 4. So with אַחֲרֵי, i. e. thoroughly, entirely, follow, &c., Deut. i. 36; Josh. xiv. 8, 9. 14; 1 Kings xi. 6, &c.

מלא (361) מלא

(d) Of the gems in the breast-plate. *Inserting, filling* them *in*, Exod. xxviii. 17. (e) Of the bow, i. e. *fully drawing it*, 2 Kings ix. 24; Zech. ix. 13. A usage common to the Arabs, as shown by Schultens; Opp. Min. pp. 176. 355, in اَمْلاً فِي الْقَوس, and فِي الْقَوسِ اَمْلاَ النزع, it. Syr. ܥܕܠܐ. (f) Of time, *fulfilled*, Gen. xxix. 27; Job xxxix. 2; Dan. ix. 2, &c. (g) Of number, Is. lxv. 20; 1 Sam. xviii. 27. (h) Of the appetite, Job xxxviii. 39; Prov. vi. 30. (i) Of libations, fully, heartily, Is. lxv. 11. (k) Of the Jordan, מִמַּלֵּא עַל־כָּל־גְּדוֹתָיו, *above all its banks*, 1 Chron. xii. 15.

Infin. מַלֵּא, Exod. xxix. 33, &c. : it. מַלֹּאות, מַלֹּאת, Exod. xxxi. 5; 1 Chron. xxix. 5.

Imp. מַלֵּא, Gen. xxix. 27: pl. מַלְאוּ, Jer. iv. 5.

Part. מְמַלֵּא, Jer. xiii. 13: pl. מְמַלְאִים, Job iii. 15.

Puh. Part. pl. מְמֻלָּאִים, once, Cant. v. 14. *Filled*, with gems. Symm. πλήρεις ὑακίνθων. Ed. vi. πλήρεις χρυσολίθων. See LXX.

Hithp. pres. יִתְמַלְאָן, once, Job xvi. 10. *They are fully* set against me. LXX. κατέδραμον.

מְלָא, v. Chald. pres. non occ. i. q. Heb. *Filled*, Dan. ii. 35, only.

Ithp. הִתְמְלִי, i. q. Niph. or Hithp. Heb. Dan. iii. 19, only.

מָלֵא, masc., fem. מְלֵאָה, &c. Part. of מָלֵא above, and applied either transitively or not, as the verb is; of which, indeed, it is the leading form. Phrr. רוּחַ מָלֵא, *a full wind*, i. e. complete tempest, Jer. iv. 12. כֶּסֶף מָלֵא *full silver*, i. e. weight of it, Gen. xxiii. 9. מְלֵא יָמִים, person *full of days*; of full age, Jer. vi. 11. הַמְלֵאָה לָהּ, lit. *the full to its self*, i. e. its full load, Amos ii. 13. מְלֵאִים מְרֻמָּה, *full* with *deceit*, Jer. v. 27, where the combination is that of apposition, Gram. art. 219, or, what the Arabs term تَمييز, *specification*, Ib. note. The mediating particles, as with the verb, are often used, as, מְלֵאִים אֶת־הַהֵיכָל Is. vi. 1, &c. The fem., viz. מְלֵאָה, is used to signify either the *fully ripe* fruits, &c. (comp. Mark iv. 28), as offered to God, or, the *overplus*, *excess*, of these. The Jews, as Kimchi, &c., have taken this first acceptation: some other interpreters, the last. See Bochart. Canaan, p. 452, Exod. xxii. 28; Num. xviii. 27; Deut. xxii. 9. See LXX.

מִלְאָה, fem. constr. מִלְאַת, pl. aff. מִלּוּאתָם. *Filling in*, *insertion*, of precious stones in the priest's breast-plate. See מָלֵא (d) above. Or, it may be, *consecrating* with these (b. ib.), Exod. xxviii. 17. 20; xxxix. 13. Aquila, Symm. Theod. καὶ πληρώσεις ἐν αὐτῷ πληρώματα λίθων.

מִלֻּאִים, masc. plur. (a) i. q. מִלּוּאת above, Exod. xxv. 7; xxxv. 9. 27; 1 Chron. xxix. 2. (b) *Inauguration, consecration.* See מָלֵא (d) above. With — אֵיל, Exod. xxix. 22. 26, 27. 31; Lev. viii. 33. (c) Parts of the offerings used in —, Lev. vii. 37; viii. 28; Ib. 31. בְּסַל הַמִּלֻּאִים, *in the basket of consecrations*, i. e. for carrying those portions of certain offerings which belonged to the priests.

מַלְאָךְ, masc. constr. מַלְאַךְ, plur. מַלְאָכִים, constr. מַלְאֲכֵי, r. לאך. Æth. ꝉꝉꝉ : *misit, ministravit*. Arab. لَأَكَ, id. Syriac ܡܠܐܟܐ, *angelus*. Lit. messenger, missionary, or the like. *Person sent*, or *commissioned*, on any errand, either by (a) God or (b) man. (a) *Angel*. As man is incapable of receiving any communication from God in His abstract and incomprehensible character of Deity, if a revelation was ever to be made to man by any visible personage, it must have been by the intervention of some *being* fitted to sustain such office: and such (1) was the person emphatically styled the *Angel of Jehovah*, מַלְאַךְ יְהוָה. This person is described in Exod. xxiii. 20, seq., and to him are ascribed the acts and reverence attributable to none but God himself. For, it is added, v. 21, *my name* (person) is *within him*, כִּי שְׁמִי בְּקִרְבּוֹ. Examine the context, and Ib. vr. 23; xxxii. 34; also, Gen. xxii. 12. 15; xxxi. 11; xlviii. 16; Exod. iii. 2; xiv. 19; Judg. ii. 1. 4; vi. 11, 12. 22, &c. From which, and the accompanying context, it must appear that this angel was God himself; or, in other words, that person, who is in other places emphatically called *The Word*. See under דָּבָר, p. 126, above. Comp. 1 Cor. x. 4. 9; Heb. xi. 26; John viii. 56. 58. Such *Messenger*, or *Angel*, was necessarily *a Mediator*, as intervening between God and man. See Job xxxiii. 23, and my note on the place. (b) In a lower sense, *Angel* of God, created spiritual being, employed occasionally by him, Num. xxii. 22, seq.; 1 Kings xix. 7; 1 Chron. xxi. 16, &c.

3 A

מלא (362) מלו

(c) *Messenger, ambassador, &c.*, Job i. 14; 1 Sam. xvi. 19; xix. 11; 1 Kings xix. 2. (d) — as a prophet, Is. xlii. 19 : see my Sermons and Dissert., p. 161, seq. : Hag. i. 13; Mal. iii. 1. (e) *Priest*, Eccl. v. 5; Mal. ii. 7. Aff. מַלְאָכִי, מַלְאָכוֹ, מַלְאָכֶךָ; pl. מַלְאָכָיו, מַלְאָכֶיהָ.

מְלָאכָה, fem. constr. מְלֶאכֶת, pl. מַלְאֲכוֹת, constr. מַלְאֲכוֹת, r. לאך. Lit. *ministry, mission*; but used in the sense of (a) *Work*, or (b) *making*. (a) Gen. xxxix. 11; Exod. xx. 9, 10; xxxi. 14, 15; xxxv. 2; Lev. xxiii. 7. — *of the artificer*, Exod. xxxi. 3 ; xxxv. 35. מְלֶאכֶת עוֹר, — *of, in, skin*, Lev. xiii. 48. — *of the house of Jehovah*, 1 Chron. xxiii. 4; Ezra iii. 8. עֹשֵׂי הַמְּלָאכָה, *doers of the work*, 2 Kings xii. 12; Esth. iii. 9; ix. 3. אֲשֶׁר עַל־הַמְּלָאכָה, *who were over the work*, 1 Kings v. 30. — *of God*, Gen. ii. 2 ; Ps. lxxiii. 28, &c. (b) Meton. *Making, acquisition; wealth*, made by work, Exod. xxii. 7. 10. — *flocks*, Gen. xxxiii. 14 ; 1 Sam. xv. 9. Aff. מְלַאכְתּוֹ, Gen. ii. 2. מְלַאכְתְּךָ, Exod. xx. 9. Pl. מְלַאכוֹתֶיךָ, Ps. lxxiii. 28.

מַלְאֲכוּת, f. constr. מַלְאֲכוּת, once, Hag. i. 13. *Message, embassy.*

מַלְאָכִים, 2 Sam. xi. 1, for מְלָכִים.

מְלֵאת, f. once, Cant. v. 12, in the phr. יֹשְׁבוֹת עַל מִלֵּאת, *standing upon fulness*, i. e. a complete inlaying, as of jewels; i. q. מִלֻּאָה above. Others, *place abounding, filled* with, every good. LXX. καθήμεναι ἐπὶ πληρώματα.

מַלְבּוּשׁ, masc. plur. aff. מַלְבּוּשֵׁי, r. לָבַשׁ. *Clothing, raiment*, 2 Kings x. 22; Is. lxiii. 3; Zeph. i. 8; Job xxvii. 16; Ezek. xvi. 13; 2 Chron. ix. 4, &c. Aff. מַלְבּוּשֵׁיהֶם, 1 Kings x. 5.

מַלְבֵּן, masc.—pl. non occ., r. לבן. Lit. *brick-place*; and may signify either a *brickyard*, or *brick-kiln*. The former seems most likely, 2 Sam. xii. 31; Jer. xliii. 9; Nah. iii. 14. LXX. διὰ τοῦ πλινθίου.

מִלָּה, fem. constr. מִלַּת, def. מִלָּתָה, Dan. ii. 5. מִלָּתָא, plur. masc. מִלִּין, מִלִּים, Heb. and Chald. r. מָלַל. Cogn. נמל, מול. See my note on Job iv. 2, &c. Syr. ܡܶܠܬܳܐ, *sermo*. (a) *Saying, word;* thence, meton., *argument*, as the context may suggest: a term more of Chaldean than Hebrew usage: hence occurring so frequently in Job vi., 26; viii. 10; xiii. 17; xxiii. 5; xxxii. 15; xxxvi. 2, &c. Hence, as that book seems always to

have been much imitated in the lofty style, our word often occurs in that kind of composition in other books. (See my Introduction to the book of Job, p. 108.) Ps. xix. 5 ; cxxxix. 4 ; 2 Sam. xxiii. 2 ; Prov. xxiii. 9, &c. Chald., Dan. iv. 28. 30 ; v. 15, &c. Meton. (b) *person or thing spoken of*, Job xxx. 9 ; xxxii. 11. Chald., Dan. ii. 8. 15. 17. Aff. מִלָּתִי, pl. מִלַּי, Job xiii. 17 ; xix. 23, &c. מִלֵּךְ, Ib. iv. 4. מִלֵּיהֶם, Ps. xix. 5.

מִלֻּא, מִלּוֹא, Infin. v. מָלֵא.

מָלֻא, for מָלֻאוּ, r. מָלֵא.

מִלֻּאִים, v. מִלֻּאִים.

מִלּוֹא, masc. (a) the name given to a certain part of the citadel of Jerusalem, 2 Sam. v. 9; 1 Kings ix. 15, &c.; termed בֵּית מִלּוֹא, apparently, 2 Kings xii. 21. Also, (b) — to a fortress of the Sichemites, Judg. ix. 6. 20; of which בֵּית מִלּוֹא, signifies the inhabitants.

מַלּוּחַ, m. r. מָלַח. *The salt plant*, or *shrub*, i. q. the ἅλιμον of the Greeks, and the ܡܰܠܽܘܚܳܐ, or ملوخ, of the Syrians. So, as far as the etymology goes, our *salad*. A shrub not unlike the bramble and with which fences are made : its tops are eaten by the poorer sort of people when fresh. Athenæus iv. 6, ἐν τῇ χαράδρᾳ τρώγοντες ἅλιμα, καὶ κακὰ τοιαῦτα συλλέγοντες. See Bochart. Hieroz. i. iii. ch. xvi., and my note on Job xxx. 4, the only place in which it is found; also, Bochart. Hieroz. i., p. 872. Symm. ἀποκνίζοντες φλοιοὺς φυτῶν. LXX. περικυκλοῦντες ἅλιμα ἐπὶ ἠχοῦντι.

מְלָכָה, מְלוּכָה, fem.—pl. non occ., r. מָלַךְ. *Rule, government; royalty*, 1 Sam. x. 16. 25 ; xi. 14. — עִיר, *city of* —, 2 Sam. xii. 26. — כִּסֵּא, *throne of* —, 1 Kings i. 46. Abs. הַמְּלוּכָה, *the* —, Ib. ii. 19. — זֶרַע, *seed of* —, 2 Kings xxv. 25. With עָשָׂה, *rule, govern ;* עַל, *over* —, 1 Kings xxi. 7.

מַלּוּכִי, masc. Patronym. of מַלּוּךְ, Neh. xii. 14.

מָלוֹן, m. } plur. non occ. constr. מְלוֹן,
מְלוּנָה, f. } r. לוּן. *Lodging-house, inn*, Gen. xlii. 27; xliii. 21; Exod. iv. 24; Josh. iv. 3; Jer. ix. 1. *Quarters*, as of soldiers, Is. x. 29. Fem., *Tent, cot*, of a garden-keeper, Is. i. 8; xxiv. 20.

מֶלַח, m.—pl. non occ. Syr. ܡܶܠܚܳܐ,

מלח (363) מלח

sal. Arab. مَلَح, id. it. *pulchritudo;* مَلَح, *albedo mista cum nigredini.* From *whiteness,* or *light,* Happiness seems to have been metaphorically expressed often by the Orientals. See my note on Job vi. 16, pp. 225—227. The appearance of salt, with its agreeable properties, succeeded perhaps in giving it the sense of *beauty, &c.,* to which its cognates, חָמַל, &c., noticed by Gesenius, afford some corroboration: and thence, probably, the application of this term to *savour, raciness,* &c. of speech. *Salt,* Lev. ii. 13, &c. Phr. בְּרִית מֶלַח, *covenant of salt,* i. e. salted. See בְּרִית above, Num. xviii. 19. יָם הַמֶּלַח, *salt sea,* Gen. xiv. 3, i. e. the Dead Sea. —— , or גֵּיא הַמֶּלַח, *valley of* —, 2 Chron. xxv. 11; Ps. lx. 2. נְצִיב מֶלַח, *pillar, statue, of* —, Gen. xix. 26. According to some, *ruinous portion,* or the like, from the usages, *sowing with salt,* יִזְרָעֶהָ מֶלַח, Judg. ix. 45; *being given to salt,* לִמְלָח נְתֻנוּ, Ezek. xlvii. 11, i. e. to ruin. Hence the verb—

מְלַח, m. Chald. id. Ezra iv. 14; vi. 9; vii. 22.

מלח, pres. only, Lev. ii. 13. בְּמֶלַח תִּמְלָח *thou shalt salt with salt.*

Niph. pl. m. נִמְלָחוּ, once, Is. li. 6. Arab. مَلَح, *celeriter alas agitavit volando avis.* Cogn. مَلَح, *validè incessit, et longè abierunt per terram. Shall pass away, vanish.* To this last etymology, the words of St. Peter, 2 Epist. iii. 10, seem to agree, οἱ οὐρανοὶ ῥοιζηδὸν παρελεύσονται. There can perhaps be no doubt, the whole ought to be taken metaphorically, as signifying that the state of things then existing, both among the Jews and Heathens, should pass away, and be succeeded by another, the character of which should be, *to make all things new.* See Rev. iii. 12; xxi. 1. 5; and my Exposition of that book.

Puh. Part. מְמֻלָּח, Exod. xxx. 35. *Salted.*
Hoph. in the phr. הָמְלֵחַ לֹא הֻמְלַחַתְּ, Ezek. xvi. 4. Lit. *Thou wast not salted by being salted,* i. e. "wast not salted at all." Auth. Vers. The first word here being the Infin. abs. Salt, it should seem, was used in the water in which infants were washed for the first time.

מְלַח, v. Chald. 1st pers. pl. pret. מְלַחְנָא

Lit. *We salt;* for we *eat the salt,* i. e. feed on, Ezra iv. 14, al. non occ.

מֶלַח, masc. plur. מְלָחִים, with בְּלוֹיֵ, Jer. xxxviii. 11, 12. *Decaying, passing away, rotting.* See مَلَح, above. r. מָלַח. Theod. κατὰ μαλεείν; the Hebrew word itself clearly showing that he knew not how to translate it. See LXX.

מַלָּח, m. occ. only in plur. מַלָּחִים. Syr. ‎‎ܡܠܚܐ, Arab. مَلَّاح, *nauta.* Sea-faring men, *sailors,* Ezek. xxvii. 29; Jonah i. 5. Aff. מַלָּחַיִךְ מַלָּחֶיהֶם, Ezek. xxvii. 9. 27, r. מָלַח, from the saltness of the sea.

מְלֵחָה, f.—pl. non occ. Lit. *salty,* or *mare-ish, sea-ish,* contr. *marsh;* אֶרֶץ, being omitted by the ellipse. *Salt, barren,* land, Job xxxix. 6; Jer. xvii. 6; Ps. cvii. 34. Plin. H. N. lib. xxxi. 7, cited by Bochart. Hieroz. i., p. 872, "Omnis locus, in quo reperitur sal, sterilis est, nihilque gignit." Virgil. Georgic. ii. 238. Termed by the Greeks, ἁλίσπαρτον.

מִלְחָמָה, f. once, מִלְחֶמֶת, f. pl. מִלְחָמוֹת, constr. מִלְחֲמוֹת. r. לָחַם. Lit. *consuming, devouring, thing. Battle, war,* Gen. xiv. 2; Deut. xx. 12. 20; 2 Sam. xxi. 15. 20. Phrr. לְמִלְחָמָה עָלֶיהָ, *for war against her,* i. e. for the purpose of —, Is. vii. 1. עָשָׂה מִלְחָמָה, *made war,* Gen. l. c. אִישׁ מִלְחָמָה, *man of war, warrior,* Exod. xv. 3. אַנְשֵׁי מִלְחָמָה, or עַם מִלְחָמָה, *of wars,* Is. xlii. 13. *people of* —, i. e. soldiers, Josh. viii. 1; xi. 7; Joel ii. 7. קֶשֶׁת מִלְחָמָה, — *bow* —, *instruments of* —, *weapons,* 1 Chron. xii. 33; Ps. lxxvi. 4; Zech. x. 4. Comp. Hos. i. 7; ii. 20.

Meton. *Event of war,* victory, Eccl. ix. 11. Aff. מִלְחַמְתָּהּ, מִלְחַמְתּוֹ, מִלְחַמְתִּי. Pl. מִלְחֲמוֹתָיו.

מֶלֶט, masc. once, Jer. xliii. 9. Syr. ‎‎ܡܠܛܐ, Arab. مَلَاط, *lutum, quo in ædificando lapidum strues continentur,* it. *quo oblinitur paries. Clay,* or the like, used as mortar, either for building or plaistering walls, l. c. The prophet was commanded, apparently, to build, and perhaps to plaister over, a sort of pedestal on which a throne might be set. If this was to be done in a *brick-yard,*—see מַלְבֵּן above,—such material

מלט (364) מלך

would be in plenty. Syr. ܒܸܚܠܵܐ, ܒܓܿܒܠܵܐ, *in argilla in officina lateritia.*

מלט, v. Kal non occ. Syr. ܥܲܕ݂ܠܵܐ, *linivit.* Arab. id. The primary notion seems to have implied *smoothness, slipperiness*: whence, as a verb in—

Pih. מִלֵּט, מִלַּט, pres. יְמַלֵּט. Constr. immed. it. med. אֶת, obj. med. מִן, from; pers. בְּ, instr. *Make one escape*, or *slip*, from any person or thing. *Deliver, save*, 2 Sam. xix. 10; Is. xlvi. 4; Jer. xxxix. 18; Job xx. 20; xxii. 30; see my notes here : Eccl. ix. 15. Of eggs, or young, *bring forth*, Is. xxxiv. 15.

Infin. מַלֵּט, Is. xlvi. 2; Jer. xxxix. 18.

Imp. with ה parag. מַלְּטָה, Ps. cxvi. 4, pl. m. מַלְּטוּ, Jer. xlviii. 6.

Fem. מַלְּטִי, 1 Kings i. 12.

Part. מְמַלֵּט, pl. מְמַלְּטִים, 1 Sam. xix. 11; 2 Sam. xix. 6.

Niph. נִמְלַט; יִמָּלֵט, *Be, become, delivered, set at liberty*; it. *saved*, 1 Sam. xxx. 17; Prov. xi. 21; Ps. xxii. 6; 1 Sam. xx. 29.

Infin. הִמָּלֵט, Gen. xix. 19.

Imp. הִמָּלֵט, Ib. 17.

Part. נִמְלָט, 1 Kings xix. 17, &c.

Hiph. הִמְלִיט, pres. non occ., Is. xxxi. 3; lxvi. 7, only, i. q. Pih.

Hithp. pres. only, אֶהְמַלְּטָה, with ה parag. יִתְמַלְּטוּ, Job xix. 20; xli. 11; i. q. Niph. See my notes.

מְלִילֹת, fem. plur. once, Deut. xxiii. 26, r. מלל. Lit. *things cut* or *cropped off. Ears of corn.*

מְלִינִים, m. pl. Part. Hiph. r. לון, which see. The dagesh is euphonic.

מֵלִיץ, m. Part. Hiph. r. ליץ.

מְלִיצָה, fem.—pl. non occ., r. ליץ, with מָשָׁל, and חִידוֹת. Lit. *interpretation.* Hence, *Saying, composition*, or the like, having an enigmatic, esoteric, or recondite, meaning. Twice only, Prov. i. 6; Hab. ii. 6. LXX. σκοτεινὸν λόγον, πρόβλημα.

מֶלֶךְ, m. pl. מְלָכִים, once, מְלָאכִים, 2 Sam. xi. 1; it. מְלָכִין, Prov. xxxi. 3. Constr. מַלְכֵי. Syr. ܡܲܠܟܵܐ, *consilium*: thence applied to *rule*, in ܡܠܟ, *rex*: just as سُلْطَان, *sultan, rule, power*, is to *emperor.* So Arab. مَلَكَ, *rule*, for مَلِكَ, *king*,

Gram. art. 152. 10. Lit. *rule*: thence, *King, ruler.* Applied (a) — *to God*, as king of all the earth, Ps. xlvii. 3. 8. — of Israel, and every Israelite, Ps. v. 3 ; x. 16 ; xliv. 5; xlviii. 3, &c. — of Jacob, Is. xli. 21. — Israel, Ib. xliv. 6. (b) — *to idols*, by their followers, Is. viii. 21; Amos v. 26; Zeph. i. 5. (c) — *to men*, Gen. xiv. 1, 2, &c. With def. art. *The king*, הַמֶּלֶךְ, Gen. xiv. 17; xxxix. 20, &c. Phrr. מֶלֶךְ מְלָכִים, Ezek. xxvi. 7, —, of the king of Babylon, as an emperor. הַמֶּלֶךְ הַגָּדוֹל, Is. xxxvi. 4, of the king of Assyria. (d) As *leaders* of armies, Job xv. 24; xviii. 14. Aff. מַלְכִּי; מַלְכְּךָ, pl. מְלָכֵינוּ, &c., Gram. art. 148. 6.

מֶלֶךְ, masc. def. מַלְכָּא, מַלְכָּה; pl. מַלְכִין, ; def. מַלְכַיָּא. Chald. i. q. Heb. Dan. ii. 10. 37; vii. 1. מֶלֶךְ מַלְכַיָּא, Ezra vii. 12. מֶלֶךְ לְיִשְׂרָאֵל רַב, *a great king of Israel*, Ezra v. 11. מָרֵא מַלְכִין, *Lord of kings*, Dan. ii. 47.

מִלְכָה, aff. מִלְכִּי. *My counsel*, once, Dan. iv. 24. Syr. ܡܸܠܟܵܐ, *consilium.*

מֹלֶךְ, masc. always with art. הַמֹּלֶךְ. *Molech, Moloch*: Gr. Μολόχ: i. q. מַלְכָּם, מִלְכָּם. The name of an idol of the Ammonites often worshipped by the Hebrews, Lev. xviii. 21; xx. 2, seq.; 1 Kings xi. 7; 2 Kings xxiii. 10; — 1 Kings xi. 5. 33; 2 Kings xxiii. 13. The same, apparently, with כִּיּוּן, see p. 294 above, or *the planet Saturn*, as generally supposed. See Selden de Diis Syris, Syntag i. cap. vi.; Michaelis Supp. p. 1514. According to the author of the Dabistan (on the ancient Persians), the image of Saturn was made of black stone. It had the head of a monkey, the body of a man, and the tail of a pig. On his head was a crown, in his right hand a hair-sieve, in his left a serpent. On his shrine, see p. 62 above. It was probably the same with the *Mahadeva*, or destroying deity of the Hindoos : and, hence, was to be placated by the sacrifice of children, &c. See, too, Diodorus Siculus, lib. xx. 14, on the worship paid to Saturn by the Carthaginians, as quoted by Gesenius.

מַלְכֻּדְתּוֹ, f. aff. r. לָכַד, once, Job xviii. 10. *His snare*, or *trap.* LXX. ἡ σύλληψις αὐτοῦ.

מַלְכָּה, f. constr. מַלְכַּת, pl. מְלָכוֹת, fem. of מֶלֶךְ. *A queen, consort*, or *regnant*, Esth. i. 9. 11, seq.; 1 Kings x. 1. 4. 10; 2 Chron. ix. 1. 3. 9. Pl., Cant. vi. 8. Opp. to

מלך (365) מלם

concubines, Ib. 9. Id. Chald. Dan. v. 10. Def. מַלְכְּתָא.

מְלִכָה, see מְלוּכָה.

מַלְכוּ, fem. constr. מַלְכוּת, def. מַלְכוּתָא, pl. constr. מַלְכְוָת. Chald. pl. def. מַלְכְוָתָא, Syr. ܡܰܠܟܽܘܬܳܐ, def. ܡܰܠܟܽܘܬܳܐ, regnum. Rule, pec. of a king, Dan. ii. 39; iii. 33; vii. 14; ii. 37. 42; iv. 26. Pl., Ib. ii. 44; vii. 27. Kingdom, Dan. vi. 29; Ezra iv. 24, &c. Aff. מַלְכוּתֵהּ, מַלְכוּתָךְ, מַלְכוּתִי, &c.

מַלְכוּת, f. i. q. מַלְכוּ. Chald.; whence the pl. מַלְכָיוֹת, once, Dan. viii. 22. Rule, kingdom, 1 Chron. xxviii. 5; xxix. 25; Ezra iv. 5; Neh. xii. 22, &c. Phrr. מַלְכוּת שָׁאוּל 1 Chron. xii. 23. Comp. Dan. i. 1. בֵּית הַמַּלְכוּת, house of rule, royal palace, Esth. i. 9, i. q. בֵּית הַמֶּלֶךְ. בִּגְדֵי מַלְכוּת אֲשֶׁר תֶּתֶר מַלְכוּת (for), Esther put on (robes of) royalty, Esth. v. 1. מַלְכוּת יְהוּדָה, kingdom of Judah, 2 Chron. xi. 17. Comp. Dan. ix. 1. Aff. מַלְכוּתֵךְ, מַלְכוּת, &c.

מַלְכָּם — מִלְכֹּם, מַלְכָּם } i. q. מֹלֶךְ, Molech, above, Jer. xlix. 1. 3; Amos i. 15; Zeph. i. 5. מֶלֶךְ, with aff. But, 1 Chron. viii. 9, a proper name, pl. non occ.

מַלְכַּת, f. of מֶלֶךְ, i. q. מַלְכָּה, pl. non occ. A queen, occ. only, Jer. vii. 18; xliv. 17—19. 25, in the phr. מְלֶכֶת הַשָּׁמַיִם, queen of the heavens. Astarte of the Phenicians, or Diana,—or perhaps the Venus,—of the Greeks, &c. The word is found in some MSS. written מְלֶאכֶת; whence some have supposed that work, service, host, was meant. So the LXX. τῇ στρατιᾷ τοῦ οὐρανοῦ. Syr. ܠܟܰܘܟ̈ܒܰܝ ܫܡܰܝܳܐ. Syr. once, xliv. 19. ܠܡܰܠܟܰܬ ܫܡܰܝܳܐ, reginæ cœli. Targ. Syderi cœli.

מלל, v. Syr. ܡܰܠܶܠ, locutus est. Cogn. נָמַל. See my notes on Job iv. 2; xii. 11, &c.: the primitive notion being, perhaps, cutting, deciding: thence applied generally to the delivery of opinions, or judgments.

Part. only, מוֹלֵל, Speaking (his sentiments), Prov. vi. 13.

Pih., מִלֵּל, pres. יְמַלֵּל. Constr. immed. it. med. לְ, to. Announce, tell, Gen. xxi. 7; Job xxxiii. 3; Ps. cvi. 2; Job viii. 2.

מלל, v. Chald. non occ. in Peḥal.

Pah., מַלִּל, pres. יְמַלִּל. Speak, announce.

Constr. immed. obj. it. med. pers. עִם, לְ, Dan. vi. 22; vii. 25.

Part. מְמַלֵּל, Dan. vii. 8. 20.

Fem. מְמַלְּלָא, Ib. 11, al. non occ.

מַלְמַד, m. once, in מַלְמַד הַבָּקָר, Judg. iii. 31. Lit. corrector, trainer, of the oxen, i. e. A goad, or other such instrument. Aquila, ἐν διδακτῆρι. Symm. ἐχέτλη τῶν βοῶν.

מַלֵּף, contr. for מְאַלֵּף, Part. Pih., r. אָלַף.

מלץ, v. Kal non occ. Cogn. מלש. Arab. مَلَصَ, lubricitas. Cogn. مَلَسَ, demulsit suâ linguâ. Whence the notion of smoothness, agreeableness, &c.

Niph. pl. נִמְלְצוּ, Are become smooth, agreeable, delightful, Ps. cxix. 103, al. non occ. LXX. γλυκέα.

מֶלְצַר, m.—plur. non occ. twice, Dan. i. 11. 16. A certain officer in the king of Babylon's palace; but what, it is impossible to say. Some suppose the word a compd. of مُل + سَر, prefect of the wine: others of مَال + سَر, — of the treasure. But no reliance can be placed on these. LXX. Αμελσάδ, as if it were a proper name, and so the Syr. and Targ.: but this cannot be correct.

מָלַק, v. pres. non occ. Arab. مَلَقَ, delevit; percussit fuste: twice only, Lev. i. 15; v. 8; in the phrase מָלַק אֶת־רֹאשׁוֹ, Break, or bruise, alluding perhaps to יְשׁוּפְךָ רֹאשׁ, Gen. iii. 15; and thence shadowing out the bruising of the tempter's head, and perhaps the deserving of this in the person offering. LXX. ἀποκνίσει. Τὸ Σαμαρ. ἀνακλάσει. ΑΛΛ. λεπτίσει, ΑΛΛ. μαδίσει. Bahrdt's Hexapla.

מַלְקוֹחַ, masc. dual, or plur. aff. מַלְקוֹחָי, r. לָקַח. I. Instrument of taking. The jaws, as in eating, Ps. xxii. 16. II. Meton. Thing taken (as being devoured), Prey, spoil, Num. xxxi. 11, 12. 27. 32; Is. xlix. 24. Phrr. רֹאשׁ מַלְקוֹחַ, capital, i. e. sum, amount, of prey, Num. xxxi. 25. מַלְקוֹחַ עָרִיץ prey of the powerful, Is. xlix. 25 : here, and vr. 24. Gesenius includes captives.

מַלְקוֹשׁ, m.—pl. non occ., r. לָקַשׁ. Lit. collecting. Applied to what is termed The latter rain, i. e. the last falling immediately before the harvest; or, because, perhaps, the

מלק (366) ממד

Autumn was considered (in a *civil* sense) the *former* part of the year, the Spring the *latter*, Deut. xi. 14; Jer. iii. 3; v. 24; Joel ii. 23; Hos. vi. 3; Prov. xvi. 15. In its proper sense, Zech. x. 1. מָטָר בְּעֵת מַלְקוֹשׁ, *in the time of collecting;* or, *for the time, &c.,* Job xxix. 23: compared to the enouncements of an acceptable speech. See my note, and the LXX.

מֶלְקָחַיִם } m. dual, r. לֶקַח. (a) *Pair of*
מַלְקָחַיִם } *tongs,* Is. vi. 6. (b) *Pair of snuffers,* Exod. xxv. 38; xxxvii. 23; 1 Kings vii. 49; 2 Chron. iv. 21. Aff. מַלְקָחֶיהָ, Num. iv. 9, &c. LXX. ἐπαρυστῆρα. οἱ λοιποι, λαβίδες. Bahrdt's Hexapla. Exod. xxv. LXX. Num. l. c. λαβίδας.

מֶלְתָּחָה, f. r. לחח. Æth. 𐩡𐩡𐩡𐩫𐩠: species quædam est *tunicæ*. Ludolf. Lex. col. 329, "vestis byssina: Castell. Once, 2 Kings x. 22. *A vestry;* or *wardrobe,* perhaps.

מַלְתִּי, for מַלְאָתִי, r. מלא.

מַלְתָּעוֹת, fem. pl. constr. i. q. מְתַלְעוֹת. Metath. r. לתע. Arab. لَتَّ, *momordit*. Æth. 𐩫𐩡𐩠𐩫: *mala, maxilla*. Once, Ps. lviii. 7. *Jaws,* perhaps; according to some, *grinding teeth,* or *great teeth*. LXX. τὰς μύλας.

מַמְּגֻרוֹת, f. pl. once, Joel. i. 17, r. מגר. Lit. *place of (something) cast or laid down,* i. e. *repository* of corn, according to the context: *Granary*.

מְמַדִּים, plur. masc., r. מדד, once, Job xxxviii. 5. Aff. מִמַּדֶּיהָ, *Its extents, measures*. See my note.

מָמוֹת, fem. plur. constr. מְמוֹתֵי, r. מות. *Deaths,* Jer. xvi. 4; Ezek. xxviii. 8, al. non occ.

מַמְזֵר, masc.—plur. non occ. Probably compd. of זָר + עַם + מִן, contr. מַמְזָר, מְמַזְעָר, *Of a foreign people:* or, if the vowels of the last member are to be attended to, מַמְזִיר, *of a bordering,* neighbouring, *people :* hence, not of true Hebrew descent: (a) *A foreigner,* or (b) *Bastard*. (a) Zech. ix. 6: (b) Deut. xxiii. 3. See LXX., al. non occ. No satisfactory etymology can be extracted from the sister dialects.

מִמְּךָ, aff. prep. מִן, which see.

מִמְכָּר, m. } plur. aff. מִמְכָּרָיו, Deut.
מִמְכֶּרֶת, f. } xviii. 8, r. מָכַר. *Sale;* or, meton. *Thing sold,* Lev. xxv. 25. 27—29. 33. 42. 50; Ezek. vii. 13; Neh. xiii. 20.

מַמְלָכָה, fem. constr. מַמְלֶכֶת, pl. מַמְלָכוֹת. Constr. מַמְלְכוֹת, r. מָלַךְ. *Rule, regal government,* Exod. xix. 6; Deut. iii. 10; 1 Kings xi. 11; xiv. 8; 1 Sam. xxviii. 17; 2 Chron. ix. 19, &c. *City of —,* Josh. x. 2. *House of —,* Amos vii. 13. Also, place of —, *Kingdom,* Deut. xxviii. 25; Is. xix. 2; Jer. xviii. 7. 9, &c. Aff. מַמְלַכְתְּךָ, מַמְלַכְתִּי, &c.

מִמְסָךְ, masc., r. מָסַךְ. Lit. mixture. *Mixed wine,* i. q. מֶסֶךְ, מָזַג, Prov. xxiii. 30; Is. lxv. 11, al. non occ. Theod. κεράσματα. LXX. Is. l. c. κέρασμα.

מִמֶּן, with aff. See מִן.

מֶמֶר, masc. once, Prov. xvii. 25, r. מָרַר. *Bitterness*. Metaph. *Grief*.

מְמֹרָה, f. in מְמֹרָתוֹ. Aff. r. מָרַר, once, Job xx. 25. Lit. his bitterness. Meton. *Gall,* or *gall bladder*. See my note.

מַמְרֹרִים, m. pl., r. מָרַר, once, Job ix. 18. *Bitter things.* See my note. Gesenius doubts of the genuineness of the reading; but for no good reason. The insertion of Dagesh in the second מ cannot stand for much in any case: and this seems to be the only ground of his suspicion. See LXX.

מִמְשַׁח, m. once, Ezek. xxviii. 14. Syr. ܡܡܫܚܐ, *mensuratus*. Arab. مَسَحَ, *pectore prominente;* r. מָשַׁח. Cogn. مَسَّ, *manum duxit super re liquida, &c*. Hence, *dimensus fuit*. Lit. *Extent, extension*. Concr. *Extended, stretched out,* i. e. as the wings which overshadowed the mercy-seat. Which is confirmed by the following הַסּוֹכֵךְ. The description is here of the king of Tyre; which will be made easy by supposing the particle כְּ, or כַּאֲשֶׁר, to have been omitted by the ellipsis. Symm. τοῦ χερουβ καταμεμετρημένου. Theod. τοῦ κατασκηνοῦντος. See LXX.

מִמְשָׁל, masc. plur. מִמְשָׁלִים, r. מָשַׁל.—

מֶמְשָׁלָה, f. constr. מֶמְשֶׁלֶת, pl. מֶמְשָׁלוֹת.— *Dominion, rule,* Dan. xi. 3. 5. Pl. meton. *Lords, rulers,* once, 1 Chron. vi. 6. Fem., Gen. i. 16; Ps. cxxxvi. 8; Mic. iv. 8; Jer. xxxiv. 1, &c. Pl., once, aff. מַמְשְׁלוֹתָיו, Ps.

cxiv. 2. Pl. of excellence here, *his peculiar, &c., dominion.* LXX. ἐξουσία αὐτοῦ. Aff. מֶמְשַׁלְתֶּךָ, Ps. cxlv. 13; Is. xxii. 21. מֶמְשַׁלְתּוֹ, 1 Kings ix. 19; 2 Kings xx. 13, &c.

מִמְשָׁק, m. once in מִמְשַׁק חָרוּל, Zeph. ii. 9. Arab. مَشَقَ, *in longum latumve traxit.* Cogn. Heb. משק. Lit. *Overspreading of —.* On the latter term, see my note on Job xxx. 7. The meaning seems to be, *over-running of brambles;* the חָרוּל being a wild shrub, is here taken *generally,* perhaps. The LXX. read ומשק here.

מַמְתַקִּים, m. plur. twice only, Neh. viii. 10, opp. τῷ, מַשְׁמַנִּים; and Cant. v. 16, opp. τῷ, מַחֲמַדִּים, r. מָתַק. Lit. *Sweetnesses.* Meton. *Sweet* things.

מָן, plur. non occ. Aff. מִנּוֹ; once, Neh. ix. 20. It is difficult to say what the true etymology of this word is. It appears to have originated in the expression, מָן הוּא, Exod. xvi. 15. Comp. vr. 31. Auth. Vers. marg., "*What is this?*" Taking the Chaldaic signification of מָן, *Who? what?* or, "*It is a portion:*" taking מָנָה as the root, or Arab. مَنِيَ, *convenit, aptum fuit.* According to which, מָן הוּא would signify, *It is convenient, suitable, opportune;* and this would suit the context. Or the root might be مَنَّ, *benevolus, benignus, fuit;* and, in this case, *He is kind, gracious,* or the like, would be the meaning; which seems to me the most suitable to the whole of the preceding context. It has been assumed by modern Lexicographers, and other writers in Germany generally, that the *manna* here spoken of is a *sort of gum* still found in certain parts of the deserts of Arabia, and elsewhere in the East. But nothing can be more improbable than this: for, I. had this been the case, the Israelites could not have been ignorant as to what it was (see vr. 15). II. It would not have bred worms, nor have stunk (vv. 20. 24). III. It would not have been found in a double portion on the day preceding the Sabbath, and not at all on that day (vr. 22. 26, 27). IV. Its being a *small round thing,* like *coriander seed* (vv. 14. 31), is proof sufficient that it was not the *gum* above-mentioned: as is the fact—V. That it continued to fall during the whole forty years of the sojourning of the Israelites in the desert (vr. 35), and ceased on the morrow after they had entered Canaan (Josh. v. 12). See under בּוּלַח above, p. 73, with the note: Exod. ll. cc. it. xvi. 33; Deut. viii. 16; Ps. lxxviii. 24; Num. xi. 6. 9, &c.

מָן, or מַן, with Makkáph, sing. or pl. Syr. ܡܢ, مَن, *Quis? quid?* Interrog. (a) *Who?* (b) *What?* (a) Ezra v. 3. 9; Dan. iii. 15. Also relatively, with דִי following, *Whoever, whosoever,* Dan. iii. 6. 10. Also with לְ, pref., Dan. iv. 14. 22. 29; v. 21. (b) Ezra v. 4, מַרְאֲנוּן שְׁמָהָת, *what are the names of —?* See also under מִי, Judg. xiii. 17.

מָן, with נ parag. מִנִּי, Judg. v. 14; Is. xlvi. 3, &c.; and מְנֵי, id., Is. xxx. 11; and contr. מִ, or מֵ with a guttural following, generally. See also Gram. artt. 171. 13; 172. 2—4. Of the Arab. مَنَّ, *præcidit,* signifying *a portion* or *part cut off;* and, as a prep. *apart, apart from, &c.* Cogn. Syr. ܥܕܢܐ, *pars portio;* v. ܥܕܢ, *numeravit.* Arab. مَنِي, *certâ quantitate quid definivit.* Heb. מָנָה. Whence prep. مِن, ܡܢ, *e, ex, &c.* A preposition of various application, carrying along with it nevertheless in every case, its primary notion, modified as the circumstances under which—or the point from which — it is viewed, may specially require. Examples will be found in Noldius, from p. 457 to p. 474, of which the following is a reduction, or abridgment. (a) *From, apart from.* מִכָּל־מְלַאכְתּוֹ, he rested *from all his work,* Gen. ii. 2. שֶׁבֶת מֵרִיב, *residing from, apart from, contention,* Prov. xx. 3. Comp. Num. xv. 24; Is. xiv. 19; Jer. xlviii. 45, &c. Hence, meton. (b) *From out of, out of, of,* of person, thing, time, place, &c. as denoting some portion, aliquot part; the material, proceeding, &c. (c) מִזִּקְנֵי הָעִיר, — *of the elders of the city,* Ruth iv. 2; Exod. xvii. 5. מִבְּנֵי הַנְּבִיאִים, — *of the sons of the prophets,* 2 Kings ii. 7. Comp. Neh. i. 2; Job v. 1, &c.

(d) Hence, *of the agent, author, &c.,* of anything: or, בְּעֵרָה מֵאֹפֶה, *heated by the baker,* Hos. vii. 4. Comp. Jer. xliv. 28; Ezek. xix. 10; Gen. xix. 36. אוּלַי אִבָּנֶה מִמֶּנָּה, *perhaps I shall be built up by her,* Gen. xvi. 2. Comp. Ps. xxxvii. 23; Job iv. 17; Ps. xviii. 22; Num. xxxii. 22; Jer. li. 5, &c.

מִן (368) מִן

(e) *Originator,* as, וּבָנוּ מִמְּךָ, *and those originating of thee shall build,* Is. lviii. 12. Comp. Judg. xiii. 2; xvii. 7, &c.

(f) *Thing, material.* מֵעֲצֵי הַלְּבָנוֹן, — *of the trees of Lebanon,* Cant. iii. 9. עֶצֶם מֵעֲצָמַי, *bone of my bones,* Gen. ii. 23. Comp. Hos. xiii. 2; Job xxxiii. 6. So the Gr. ἀπὸ, Matt. iii. 4: ἐκ, Matt. iii. 9, &c. In such cases the latter noun may occasionally be construed, either as a genitive case, or as an adjective: as, אַרְיֵה מִיַּעַר, *a lion of the forest,* or *forest lion,* Jer. v. 6. Comp. Ps. lxxx. 14; Jer. xxiii. 23, &c.

(g) *Object;* with verbs implying, *eating, filling, taking, giving, narrating, sprinkling, &c.* e. g. וּמֵעֵץ הַדַּעַת לֹא תֹאכַל, *and of the tree of knowledge—thou shalt not eat,* Gen. ii. 17. Comp. xiii. 2, &c. So the Gr. ἀπὸ, Matt. v. 18, &c. *Filling, &c.,* Ps. cxxvii. 5; 1 Kings xii. 9:— *of taking,* Deut. xxxiii. 3:— *of giving, narrating,* Ps. lix. 13; Is. ii. 3, &c.: *of sprinkling,* Lev. vi. 20; 2 Kings ix. 33, &c. But these constructions will be found given with such several verbs.

Hence, (h) *of instruments,* as the thing with which anything is effected; as, מֵחֶזְיֹנוֹת תְּבַעֲתַנִּי, *from, by, visions thou affrightest me,* Job vii. 14. Comp. Ib. iv. 9. מִמֵּי הַמַּבּוּל, *by the waters of the flood,* Gen. ix. 11. Comp. Ps. xxviii. 7; lxxvi. 7; lxxviii. 6; Is. xxii. 3; xxviii. 7, &c. Hence—

(i) Of the *cause, reason, &c.:* as, מִפִּשְׁעֵינוּ *because of our sins,* Is. liii. 5. Comp. Deut. vii. 7; Ps. lxviii. 30; Cant. iii. 8; Esth. v. 9. And hence with the particles, מִבִּלְתִּי, מִבְּלִי. See under בַּל, בְּלִי. Also used after verbs generally requiring such complementary terms. Also after Infinitives: as, מֵאַהֲבַת יְהֹוָה אֶתְכֶם, lit. *from Jehovah's loving you,* i. e. because, &c., Deut. vii. 8. מִן־שָׁלְחוֹ אֹתָם, *from his sending them,* i. e. after, &c., 1 Chron. viii. 8. Comp. 2 Chron. xxxi. 10.

(k) And, as the being *apart from,* or *from,* anything, implying a negation as to the *presence* of the person or thing so spoken of; so this particle may, after certain preceding terms, be interpreted as intimating such negation; as, Num. xxxii. 7, מֵעֲבֹר אֶל, *from passing over to* —, i. e. that this may *not* be done, Gen. xxvii. 1. מֵרְאוֹת, *from seeing,* i. e. that he might not see, Is. xliv. 18. Comp. Ib. liv. 9. In some cases the Infin. of הָיָה, viz. הְיוֹת, seems to be omitted by the ellipse, as in מִמֶּלֶךְ, for מִהְיוֹת מֶלֶךְ, *from being king,* 1 Sam. xv. 23. Comp. 1 Kings xv. 13; Jer. xlviii. 2. 42; Is. lii. 14, &c. So

also, מִן־יְקוּמוּן, *from their rising,* i. e. that they may not rise, Deut. xxxiii. 11.

(l) In like manner, מִן is prefixed to other prepositions, when a sense compounded of the two will be the result; as, מֵאַחֲרֵי, מֵאַחַר, *from after;* מִבֵּין, *from between:* so, מִבְּעַד, מִתַּחַת, מֵאֵת, מֵעִם, מֵעַל, מִלִּפְנֵי. In all which cases it will very much depend on the nature of the preceding terms; these acting as *mediating* ones, Gram. artt. 224. 2; 228, &c.

(m) The following, as connected with verbs, are usually found as *adverbs,* מִבַּיִת, מֵהַבַּיִת, מִקֶּדֶם, מִקָּרוֹב, מִפָּנִים, מִפְּנֵי, מֵעֵבֶר, מִזֶּה, מֵרָחוֹק, מִתּוֹךְ. So the Gr. ἐκ δευτέρου, ἐκ τρίτου, Matt. xxvi. 42. 44, &c.; which see in Noldius in their places respectively.

(n) In the compounds מִבַּלְעֲדֵי, and לְמִן, Gesenius thinks that, in construing, מִן and לְ, ought to be transposed, and read מִן בַּלְעֲדֵי, and מִן לְ: but this is unnecessary in either case, and manifestly erroneous in the latter. Instances of the first are, Num. v. 20; 2 Sam. xxii. 32; Josh. xxii. 19, &c. See Nold., p. 482, and בַּלְעֲדֵי above, p. 84. The Syriac has this transposition, indeed, in ܒܠܥܕ ܡܢ; but this affects not our question. The real sense of the compound is, *from, out of, of, excepting; besides;* e. g. in the phr. מִבַּלְעֲדֵי אִישֵׁךְ, *I speak of, from, besides thy husband,* i. e. *of* or *about* any one excepting thy husband. The same is true of the particle לְ prefixed, signifying *as to, with respect, reference, to,* the sentiment, &c., following. See Job xxxvi. 3, with my note; and Gram. art. 241. 13.

(o) In some cases the construction is evidently elliptical; *Part, portion, something, some,* or the like being understood; as, מִדָּם, *some of the blood,* Lev. iv. 9. מֵהֵנָּה מֵאַחַת, *some of one of these,* Lev. iv. 2. מֵאַחַד אַחֶיךָ, *some of one of thy brethren,* Deut. xv. 7. In Gen. vii. 22, the construction is, כֹּל־מִכֹּל אֲשֶׁר וגו׳, *the whole—of all that, &c.,* i. e. none were excepted. The terms מֵאֵין, and מֵאֶפֶס, Is. xl. 17; xli. 24; come under another head (e. g. of origin), as מֵאֲצַל, in the latter place, is sufficient to show. These two usages are termed by the Arabs,

تَبْعِيض, *apportioning;* and تَفْسِير, or بَيَان, *explanation,* respectively. See Jauhari, sub voce, مِن, and the Kāmoos, Edit. Calcutt. p. ١٨٠٩ — So in the examples

מִן (369) מִן

cited by Gesenius, ما من اله الا الله, *there is not* anything *of a God, except the God*, i. e. nothing that can be so considered. ما من احد, *Not of one*, i. e. *not of so much as one*. ما لهم من علم, *There is not to them of knowledge*, i. e. they have nothing, not a particle, of it. But, when he tells us that, Syr. ܢ ܥܡ ܡܕܥܡ, signifies *"non a quoquam," "et contr.* ܢ ܡܕܥܡܐ, *nequaquam,"* he greatly mistakes, both meaning precisely the same thing, viz. *nunquam*. Lit. *not of any ever*, i. e. time.

(p) *Of time*, as מִשְּׁנַת הַיֹּבֵל, *from the year of Jubilee*, Lev. xxvii. 17. מִיּוֹם עַד לַיְלָה, *from day to night*, Is. xxxviii. 12. מִיָּמָיו, Job xxxviii. 12. מִיּוֹם, *from day*, i. e. its first existence, Is. xliii. 13. So מִמָּחֳרָת, *from the morrow*, i. e. the commencement of the next day, Gen. xix. 34; Exod. ix. 6. מֵעוֹלָם, *from an age*, i. e. an indefinitely long time, Is. xlii. 16. So, מֵרֵאשִׁית קֶדֶם, *from the beginning*, Is. xlvi. 10. מִקַּדְמֵי אָרֶץ, Prov. viii. 23. מִיָּמִים, *from*, i. e. immediately after, *two days*, Hos. vi. 2. מִיָּמִים, *from*, after, *some days*, Judg. xi. 4; xiv. 8. מִיָּמִים רַבִּים, *from*, after, *many days*, Josh. xxi. 3; Is. xxiv. 22. מִשְּׁלֹשׁ חֳדָשִׁים —, *after three months*, Gen. xxxviii. 24. Comp. Num. xxiv. 23; Hos. vii. 4; Is. xliv. 7. The term implying time is occasionally omitted, as, מִנְּעוּרִים, *from youth*, 1 Sam. xii. 2; 1 Kings xviii. 12. מִבֶּטֶן אִמִּי, *from the womb of my mother*, Judg. xvi. 17, i. e. the *time of* birth and youth, respectively.

(q) *Of place*, מִשָּׁמַיִם, *from heaven*, Is. xiv. 12, &c. Comp. Judg. ii. 12; Jer. xxxvi. 9; 1 Sam. ii. 8, &c.—with any verbs, &c. requiring such construction. Comp. Job i. 21; Judg. xi. 36; Exod. xii. 42; Ps. xviii. 7; xl. 3, &c. Also with אֶל, עַד, וְיַד, or ־ה parag. in the following member, either of place, persons, or things; as, מִתֵּימָן—וְדְדָנָה, *from Teman—even to Dedan*, Ezek. xxv. 13. מִגְּדוֹלָם וְעַד־קְטַנָּם, Jonah iii. 5. Comp. Gen. xiv. 23; Exod. xxii. 3; Lev. xiii. 2; 1 Kings vi. 24; Is. i. 6; Ps. cxliv. 13. מִין אֶל־מִין, *from sort to sort*, Ib. lxxxiv. 8. מֵחַיִל אֶל־חָיִל, *from strength to strength*. Hence also—

(r) As some person or thing, selected *from* others, is considered the most eligible or *best*, as in the phrase *one of a thousand*, i. e. one better than all the others remaining; so this particle is often (meton.) employed for this purpose; as, עַם סְגֻלָּה מִכֹּל הָעַמִּים, *a people peculiar from all people*, more choice than, Deut. xiv. 2. גָּבֹהַּ מִכָּל־הָעָם, *high, tall, from all the people;* taller *than* —, 1 Sam. x. 23. Comp. Gen. iii. 1; Jer. xvii. 9; 1 Sam. xviii. 30; 2 Kings x. 3; 2 Chron. ix. 22; Ezek. xxxi. 5, &c. Verbs, being attributive, will have the same construction; as, הִשְׁחִיתוּ מֵאֲבוֹתָם, *they acted basely from* (beyond) *their fathers*, i. e. more basely *than* —, Judg. ii. 19. Comp. Gen. xix. 9; xxix. 30; xxxviii. 26; Jer. v. 3. So, יִרְבֶּה מִמְּךָ הַדֶּרֶךְ, *the way, journey, is greater than thee*, i. e. than thy power is to perform it, Deut. xiv. 24. Comp. Gen. xviii. 14; Job xv. 11. See Gram. art. 241. 9. As this sort of comparison implies something like diminution, with reference to one of the things compared, it is occasionally made by introducing the particle לֹא, or אַל; as, חֶסֶד חָפַצְתִּי וְלֹא זָבַח, *I have willed piety, and not sacrifice*, Hos. vi. 6; Prov. viii. 10. קְחוּ מוּסָרִי וְאַל־כָּסֶף, *accept my discipline, and not silver*, i. e. *rather than* —; the comparison being continued in the following member, in each case by מִן.*

Also with Infinitives following; as, גָּדוֹל .... מִנְּשֹׂא, lit. *greater than to bear*, i. e. intolerable, Gen. iv. 13. Comp. Gen. xxix. 19; 1 Kings viii. 64; Prov. xvi. 19, &c.

In Ps. lxviii. 30, מֵהֵיכָלֶךָ עַל יְרוּשָׁלָיִם, "*ad templum tuum in Hierusalem*." But, in all probability, מֵהֵיכָלֶךָ ought to be read with the preceding verse, thus: זוּ פָּעַלְתָּ לָנוּ מֵהֵיכָלֶךָ, *which thou hast wrought for us from thy Temple:* the Temple being considered the place in which God dwelt, to which prayer was to be directed, and from which deliverance was to be had. And in this way the text of the LXX. ought manifestly to be read, ὁ κατηρτίσω ἐν ἡμῖν ἀπὸ τοῦ ναοῦ σου. Then, Ἐπὶ Ἰερουσαλὴμ σοὶ οἴσουσι βασιλεῖς δῶρα. The same may be said of the

---

* A few instances, occurring in Noldius, still require notice and correction. In 2 Sam. vi. 12, he makes this particle signify *ad, to*. But, מִבַּעֲלֵי יְהוּדָה, ought to be referred to הָעָם, preceding, and rendered *so David went, and all the people of the princes of Judah who were with him*. And so the ancient versions generally have taken it. Not, "*ad Baalim Judæ*," as if it were the name of a place. The Auth. Vers. is erroneous here in like manner.

3 B

מִן (370) מִנָא

Æthiopic and Syriac Versions in this place, which have all probably been thus altered to suit the present division of the Masoretic text. The text, as it stands, will moreover admit of a different rendering, viz., *from, because of* (as the *cause, &c.* above), *thy Temple, &c.* i. e. of the religion thence propagated; for the Ps. is certainly prophetic. The former is the more natural acceptation.

Deut. xxviii. 47, מֵרֹב כֹּל, i. e. *From, on account of, the abundance of all,* that God had given them. Not, "*ad omnem abundantiam.*" And so of the rest, p. 458.

Ib. Ruth ii. 14, וַתֵּשֶׁב מִצַּד, *so she sat from, apart from, the side, &c.;* the circumstances of the case requiring, that the distance be *not great,* i. e. *near.* So the Arab. قَرِيبٌ مِنْ, *near from;* our, *near to.* So 1 Sam. xx. 21, מִמְּךָ וָהֵנָּה, *apart from thee, and hitherwards,* i. e. not far from thee on this side. So also Ps. xliii. 1, רִיבָה רִיבִי מִגּוֹי לֹא חָסִיד, *contend my contention apart from,* i. e. on the other side, not as one with, *a nation* anything but pious. Comp. Dan. xi. 8, כִּמִּפְּךָ: and, on the contrary, מֵהֶם, Ezek. lvii. 8, *of them,* i. e. as one *of them.* The context, therefore, must be carefully considered in every case, otherwise nothing but error will be the result.

Aff. מִמְּךָ, מִמֶּךָ, מִמֶּנִּי, מִמֵּנוּ, מִמְּפֶּה, מִמְּנָה; it. מֶנְהוּ, מֶנְהָ: 1st pl. מִמֵּנוּ; 2d, מִכֶּם, מִכֶּן; מֵהֶן, מֵהֶם.

מִן, Chald. i. q. Heb. מִן. (a) *Out of, from,* Dan. iii. 26؛ thence *Of* (b) *author, originator,* Ezra iv. 21. (c) *Cause, reason, &c.,* Dan. v. 19; Ezra vi. 14. Phrr. מִן קְשֹׁט *verily;* מִן יַצִּיב, *certainly,* Dan. ii. 8. 47. מִן־דִּי, *because that,* Dan. iii. 22. (c) Elliptically (Heb. [o] above), *Part, portion,* or the like being understood, Dan. ii. 33. And the same is the case in the Syriac of 2 Tim. ii. 20, appealed to by Gesenius here. The particle, therefore, has no new signification, l. c. (d) *From,* of person, time, place, &c., Dan. ii. 16; iii. 22. 26; ii. 20. מִן־וְעַד, (e) with other particles, מִן לְוָת, *from with;* מִן קֳדָם, *from before;* מִן אֲרַע, *from then, thence.* Also implying (e) negation (Heb. [k] above), מִן אֲנָשָׁא, *from man,* i. e. from being human, Dan. iv. 13. (f) Used also in making comparisons, *Than, more than* (Heb. [r]), Dan. ii. 30. (g) Also used as a mediating particle, with certain verbs, Dan. iv. 28; v. 3. 19, &c. Aff. מִנִּי, מִנָּךְ, מִנֵּהּ, מִנָּה, מִנְּהוֹן, מִנְּהֵן.

מְנָא, Chald. see מְנָה.
מְנָאוֹת, pl. of מְנָת.
מַנְגִּינָה, f. aff. מַנְגִּינָתָם, r. נָגַן, i. q. נְגִינָה. *Song,* of ridicule, Lam. iii. 63, only.

מִנְדָּה, fem. Chald. i. q. מִדָּה; the נ being inserted, as in other cases, to compensate for the *dagesh forte.*

מַנְדַּע, m. Chald. i. q. Heb. מַדָּע, r. יָדַע. Def. מַנְדְּעָא. Aff. מַנְדְּעִי. (a) *Knowledge, wisdom,* Dan. ii. 21; v. 12. (b) *Intelligence, understanding,* Ib. iv. 31. 33.

מָנֶה, masc. plur. מָנִים. Syr. ܡܢܐ, *mina, mna.* Arab. مَنَا, and مَنٌّ, id. Lit. *number.* A certain *Weight,* thought, from a comparison of 1 Kings x. 17, with 2 Chron. ix. 16, to consist *of one hundred shekels.* But in Ezek. xlv. 12, it appears to have consisted of the various weights of 20, 25, and 15, shekels, ll. cc. it. Ezra ii. 69; Neh. vii. 71, 72. Castell, however, makes the מָנֶה equal to 60 shekels of the sanctuary,—to 100 of those in common use. The new מָנֶה of Ezekiel equal to 60—i. e. adding up together the different values noticed above— of the sanctuary, to 120 common shekels. He also gives 25 shekels, or 100 zuzin, as its value. Hence the verb below.

מָנָה, f. constr. מְנַת, מְנָה (see מִנָּה below), pl. מָנוֹת, i. q. חֵלֶק. *Part, portion,* Exod. xxix. 26; Lev. vii. 33; 1 Sam. i. 4; Neh. viii. 10. 12; Jer. xiii. 25: with גּוֹרָל, Ps. xi. 6; xvi. 5; lxiii. 11; Esth. ix. 19, &c.

מֹנֶה, m. pl. מֹנִים, pl. of part. מֹנֶה, apparently. Lit. *numberers.* Meton. *Occasions, times,* Gen. xxxi. 7. 41, only.

מָנָה, v. pres. תִּמְנֶה. Constr. immed. it. med. אֶת, בְּ, לְ. Arab. مَنَى, *certâ quantitate definivit.* Cogn. r. مَنَّ, وَمَنُو. (a) *Number,* Num. xxiii. 10; 1 Chron. xxi. 1; xxvii. 24. Meton. (b) *Appoint, constitute,* Is. lxv. 12; 1 Kings xx. 25.

Infin. מְנוֹת, Gen. xiii. 16, &c.
Imp. מְנֵה, 2 Sam. xxiv. 1.
Part. מוֹנֶה, Ps. cxlvii. 4; Jer. xxxiii. 13.
Niph. נִמְנָה, pres. יִמָּנֶה. *Be, become, numbered,* Gen. xiii. 16; Is. liii. 12; 2 Chron. v. 6.
Infin. הִמָּנוֹת, Eccl. i. 15.
Pih. מִנָּה, pres. apoc. יְמַן, i. q. Kal. (b)

Appoint, constitute, Job vii. 3; Jonah ii. 1; iv. 6—8; Dan. i. 5. 10, 11, with med. עַל.
Imp. מַן, Ps. lxi. 8, only.
Puh. Part. pl. masc. מְמֻנִּים. Persons *appointed, constituted,* 1 Chron. ix. 29, only.

מְנָה, מנא, v. Chald. pres. non occ. See Heb. מָנָה. Syr. ܡܢܐ, *numeravit, supputavit.* Arab. مَنَى, *experimento probavit. Numbered, tried,* Dan. v. 26.
Part: Heb. מְנֵא, Dan. v. 25, al. non occ.
Pah. מַי, pres. non occ. Constr. immed. it. med. עַל, Heb. (b) *Constituted, appointed,* Dan. ii. 24. 49; iii. 12.
Imp. מֱנִי, Ezra vii. 25.

מִנְהָג, masc. pl. non occ., r. נָהַג. Arab. مِنْهَاج, *way, &c. Driving* along, of horses, &c., 2 Kings ix. 20, only. Aquila, ἔλασις. Theod. Symm. ἀγωγή.

מִנְהָרוֹת, f. pl. r. נָהַר, once, Judg. vi. 2. Arab. مَنْهَر, *locus in fluvii alveo excavatus ab aqua. Valleys* flowing with water. Gesen. More probably, *Clefts* in the mountains, serving as canals to the mountain torrents; and hence, as difficult of access, likely to be occupied by a conquered people. LXX. Theod. μάνδρας. LXX. ἄλλως, τρυμαλιάς.

מָנוֹד, masc. constr. in the phr. מְנוֹד רֹאשׁ once, Ps. xliv. 15. *A shaking of the head,* r. נוּד.

מָנוֹחַ, m. r. נוּחַ, pl. aff. once, מְנוּחָיְךָ, Ps. cxvi. 7. *Place of rest,* Gen. viii. 9; Deut. xxviii. 65; Is. xxxiv. 14; Lam. i. 3; Ruth iii. 1:—of a woman's finding a home after marriage. 1 Chron. vi. 17, מִמְּנוּחַ הָאָרוֹן, *from, since, the ark's resting-place,* i. e. after it had been placed there.

מְנוּחָה, מְנֻחָה, fem. of the last, plur. מְנוּחוֹת. *Rest, quiet,* Gen. xlix. 15; Judg. xx. 43; Is. xi. 10; xxviii. 12; Jer. xlv. 3. Meton. *Place of rest,* Num. x. 33; Is. xxxii. 18; Mic. ii. 10. Metaph. *The Holy Land,* or rather *the comforts of true religion,* to be had there, Ps. xcv. 11. See Heb. iv. 1, seq. and my Sermon on the Sabbath, 2d Edit., p. 46, seq. Phr. מֵי מְנֻחוֹת, *waters of great rest,* pl. excell., Ps. xxiii. 2. Aff. מְנוּחָתִי, מְנוּחָתוֹ, &c.

מָנוֹן, m. once, Prov. xxix. 21. Arab. مَنُون, *multum exprobrans beneficia.* Syr. ܡܥܕܠ, *contemptus;* r. מֵן. Heb. מן. Symm. γογγυσμός. LXX. ὀδυνηθήσεται. Lit. *One brings up his slave delicately from* (his) *youth, and in* (the) *end he becomes a despiser of the favour.* The intention seems to be to show to the Hebrews, that the favours often conferred by them on strangers (i. e. heathen slaves as favourites: comp. Is. ii. 6), would ever be returned, as it was but right they should, by ingratitude and contempt. Æsop's countryman and the frozen viper, has a similar bearing; to which may be compared tale 4, book i., of Saadi's Gulistan: where we have a story with this distich, which will afford a good illustration to our passage.

پرتو نیکان نگیرد هرکه بنیادش بد
تربیت نا اهل را چون گردگان بر گنبذ است.

Whoever is of bad origin, he will receive none of the light of the good. The indulgent bringing up of the worthless, is just as a walnut (thrown) *upon a dome.* And a proverb in Mr. Roebuck's Collection, Calcut. 1824, p. 303, عاقبت گرگ زاده گرگ شد, *the wolf's whelp becomes a wolf at last.* Usually, *seed, son,* r. נוּן, or נִין: but this would rather signify *posterity,* or the like. See my note on Job xviii. 19; and therefore could not apply here. Besides, that a man must adopt a pampered slave as a son finally, seems as far remote from reason, as it is from the facts of all such cases.

מָנוֹס, masc. aff. מְנוּסִי ⎫ pl. non occ., r.
מְנוּסָה, f. constr. מְנֻסַת ⎭ נוּס. (a) *Flight,* Jer. xlvi. 5. Fem., Lev. xxvi. 36; Is. lii. 12. (b) Meton. *Place of flight; refuge,* Ps. cxlii. 5; Job xi. 20, &c. Arab. مَنَاص, *refugi locus.*

מָנוֹר, m. in the phr. מְנוֹר אֹרְגִים, *Weavers' beam.* Syr. ܢܽܘܠܳܐ, *jugum textorium, et servile.* Arab. نِير, id. Cogn. נֹעַל, مِنْوَال, id. 1 Sam. xvii. 7; 2 Sam. xxi. 19.

מְנוֹרָה, constr. מְנוֹרַת, pl. מְנוֹרוֹת, r. נוּר. Arab. مَنَار, *locus lucis;* مَنَارَة, id. it. *candelabrum. The candlestick* used in the Tabernacle and Temple, Exod. xxv. 31, seq.; xxx. 27; xxxi. 8; 1 Kings vii. 49; Zech. iv. 2. 11, &c.

מִנְזָרִים, m. pl. aff. מִנְזָרַיִךְ; with Dagesh euphon. r. נָזַר, i. q. נְזִירִים, once, Nah. iii. 17. *Nobles, princes.*

מִפָּח, r. נוּח, or יָנַח.

מִנְחָה, f. constr. מִנְחַת, pl. מִנְחֹת. Arab. مَنَحَ, *donavit. A gift* offered to (a) men, or (b) God. (a) Gen. xxxii. 14. 19. 21; xliii. 11. 15. 25, 26; Judg. iii. 15 : — in tribute, 2 Sam. viii. 2. 6; 1 Kings v. 1; 2 Kings xvii. 4; Ps. lxxii. 10, &c. (b) — to God in sacrifice, Gen. iv. 3—5. Generally unbloody, and consisting of various fruits, flour, oil, &c. opp. τῷ, זֶבַח, Lev. ii. 1. 4—6; vi. 7, seq.; vii. 9. Phr. זֶבַח וּמִנְחָה, Ps. xl. 7; Jer. xvii. 26; Dan. ix. 27. נֹשְׂאֵי מִנְחָה, *bearers of* —, 2 Sam. viii. 6. עַד לַעֲלוֹת הַמִּנְחָה, *up to the* (time of) *offering the Minkha,* 1 Kings xviii. 29. These appear to have been offered in Divine service; 1st, about half-past 12 o'clock, P.M.; 2d, about half-past 3, P.M. Castell. sub voce. Aff. מִנְחָתְךָ, מִנְחָתִי, &c.

מִנְחָה, f. Chald. i. q. Heb. Dan. ii. 46. Aff. מִנְחָתְהוֹן, Ezra vii. 17, al. non occ.

מְנִי, m. pl. non occ., r. מָנָה. The name of an idol worshipped occasionally by the Jews, Is. lxv. 11; alluded to in vr. 12, in the verb מָנִיתִי. As if, *numbering, portion, fortune,* or the like, were its meaning. And to this, the Arab. مَنِيَّة, *fatum;* مَنَا, *mors,* correspond sufficiently well. The ancient Arabs had an idol, termed مَنَاة, *Manāt,* which Pococke thinks was so named from مَكَى, *fluere,* intimating the shedding of human blood in sacrifice to it (Specimen. Hist. Arab. p. 93, seq.), and believes to be the מְנִי of Isaiah. But, if we may rely on similarity of name, the Hindoo *Menū,* said to be the son of Brahma; supposed, too, to be the same with the lawgiver of Crete, *Minos,* and of the Egyptians *Mneuis;* or of *Menes,* the first Egyptian king; all of which, according to Sir Wm. Jones (preface to his Laws of Menu., p. xv., Haughton's edition), may be interpreted to mean *mind,* like *menes, mens;* from the Sanscrit root *men,* to understand. If so, this idol appears to identify itself with the *Buddh,* of the Buddhists, the حِكْمَة, and عقل اول, *first intellect,* of the mystical Arabs and Persians : and to be a mere copy of the חָכְמָה of the Hebrews. (Prov. viii.) See my note on Job xi. 6, with the additional references at p. 553, and sub voce דָּבָר, above, p. 126. See also Selden de Diis Syris, Syntag. i., cap. 1.

מְנִי, m. once, Jer. li. 27, occurring with אֲרָרָט, and supposed to signify *Armenia* generally (see Bochart.'s Phaleg. lib. i., cap. iii., pp. 19, 20), which is again thought to be a compd. of מְנִי + הַר.

מִנִּי, m.—pl. non occ., once, Ps. xlv. 9, which may be thus translated. *The myrrh,* and *aloes,* and *Cassia,* (perfuming) *the whole of thy garments,* (brought) *from the ivory temples of the Minæi, shall delight thee.* These *Minni,* or *Minæi,* according to the Greeks and Latins, were a people inhabiting spicy Arabia: and of the spices there produced, myrrh was one. Bochart. speaks of them, thus, in his Phaleg., lib. ii. cap. xxii. p. 135, " Minæos plurimum nobilitavit thuris ex Atramitis advecti frequens cum Syris commercium. Plinius, lib. xii. cap. 14, *Hi primi commercium thuris fecere, maximeque exercent, a quibus et Minæum dictum est.* Nempe ex quatuor populis Arabiæ aromatiferæ, hi primi se offerebant ex Syriâ venientibus....Quin etiam ipsi Minæi thus et alia aromata ex locis remotioribus in Arabiam Petræam et Palestinam usque vehebant. Agatharcides, cap. 44....Γερραῖοι καὶ Μιναῖοι....τόντε λιβανωτὸν....καὶ τὰ φορτία τὰ πρὸς εὐωδίαν ἀνήκοντα ἀπὸ τῆς χώρας τῆς ἄνω κατάγουσιν (εἰς τὴν παλαιστίνην)....Sed et in ipsa Minæâ felix fuit myrrhæ proventus." Which, according to Galen, was termed *the Minæan myrrh,* by some; ἔννιοι δ' αὐτὴν ὀνομάζουσι Μιναίαν, κ.τ.λ. from the place producing it. See the remainder of the article, and the Hierobotanicon of Ol. Celsius, under the words designating these several perfumes: where it will be seen that Arabia produces them all. The הֵיכְלֵי שֵׁן were either temples or palaces, not built with, but adorned most probably with ivory. (Comp. 1 Kings x. 18; Ezek. xxvii. 6;

מִנִי (373) מִנְעָל

Amos vi. 4.) Such a palace Ahab had, 1 Kings xxii. 39, termed, בֵּית הַשֵּׁן, which was no doubt a foreign luxury. Comp. Amos iii. 15, where many of these are denounced. In Arabia, too, elephants were, according to Strabo, lib. xvi., in great abundance: and the palaces of the nobles were most richly built and adorned. There can be no doubt, therefore, I think, that it is to presents of this sort, to be brought from Arabia, that the Psalmist alludes. Comp. Ps. lxviii. 30, seq.; it. Ps. lxxii. 10. See also the LXX.

מִנִּים, masc. plur., r. מן, once, Ps. cl. 4. Syr. ܡܢܐ, *chordæ*. Strings of the harp or other instrument. Aquila, LXX. ἐν χορδαῖς. Ἀλλ. διὰ χορδῶν. Gesenius makes the מִנִּי of Ps. xlv. 9, to be this word, which he renders, "*fides* (i. e. concentus musici) *te exhilarant*." With what propriety the reader will judge when he has carefully considered the last article but one.

מִנִּי, and מִנֵּי, under מִן, with ׳ parag.

מְנָיוֹת, pl. see מָנָה.

מֵנִיחַ, Part. Hiph. v. נוּחַ, or יָנַח.

מִנְיָן, m. constr. מִנְיַן, once, Ezra vi. 17; r. מָנָה. Syr. ܡܢܝܢܐ, *numerus*. Number.

מִנְלָם, m. Aff. r. Arab. نَوَلٌ, *giving*, *presenting*; نَيْلٌ, *quod quis consequitur*, *opes*. Syr. ܢܨܠ, *deprehendens*; once, Job xv. 29. *Their wealth*. See my note on the place. Without the aff. מִנְלָה, perhaps. Gesenius doubts of the genuineness of the reading, probably unnecessarily.

מָנַע, v. pres. יִמְנַע. Constr. immed. obj. med. מִן, from; לְ, *as, to*; it. med. אֶת, obj. Arab. مَنَعَ, *recusavit, denegavit*. Keep back, withhold, Gen. xxx. 2; Num. xxiv. 11; 1 Sam. xxv. 26. 34; Eccl. ii. 10; Amos iv. 7; Ezek. xxxi. 15. Imp. מְנַע, fem. מִנְעִי, Jer. ii. 25. מִנְעִי רַגְלֵךְ, *withhold thy foot from (being) bare*, i. e. from immodest exposure. Comp. Prov. i. 15; Jer. xxxi. 16. Part. מֹנֵעַ, Prov. xi. 26; Jer. xlviii. 10. Niph. נִמְנַע, pres. יִמָּנַע. Be, become, withholden, kept back, Joel i. 13; Num. xxii. 16; Job xxxviii. 15; Jer. iii. 3.

מַנְעוּל, m. pl. מַנְעוּלִים, r. נָעַל, with בְּרִיחַ.

Arab. نَعَلَ, *calceis donavit*; conj. ii. *laminâ ferreâ munivit*: hence the notion of defence. A bolt, or lock, of a gate, &c., Cant. v. 5; Neh. iii. 3, seq. Aff. מַנְעֻלָיו.

מִנְעָל, masc. id., Deut. xxxiii. 26, or Defence, perhaps, generally. LXX. ὑπόδημα.

מַנְעַמִּים, m. pl. r. נָעֵם, once, Ps. cxli. 4. Delicacies.

מְנַעְנְעִים, masc. pl. r. נוּע, redup. Lit. Agitatings. Vulg. *sistra*; Sistrums. So Gr. σεῖστρον, from σείω. Gesen. Once, 2 Sam. vi. 5. LXX. ἐν κυμβάλοις. With cymbals. Aquila, Symm. ἐν σείστροις.

מְנַקִּיּוֹת, f. pl. r. נָקָה. Syr. ܡܢܩܝܬܐ, *pateræ libatoriæ*. Bowls used in making libations, Num. iv. 7; Jer. lii. 19. Aff. מְנַקִּיֹּתָיו, Exod. xxv. 29; xxxvii. 16, al. non occ.

מֵינֶקֶת, or מִינֶקֶת, f. See Hiph. r. יָנַק. A nurse. Aff. מֵנִקְתּוֹ, 2 Kings xi. 2, &c.

מְנַשִּׁי, m. Patronym. of מְנַשֶּׁה, Deut. iv. 43, &c.

מְנָת, fem. contr. מְנָאת, r. מָנָא; i. q. מָנָה; pl. מְנָאוֹת, מְנָיוֹת, Neh. xii. 44. 47; xiii. 10; i. q. מָנָה above. Part, portion, Ps. xi. 6; xvi. 5; lxiii. 11; 2 Chron. xxxi. 3, 4. It will amount to the same thing, if we suppose מְנָת to have been written for מְנַת, constr. sing. See מָנָה above.

מָס, m. once, Job vi. 14. See my note. Wasting, necessitous, miserable, r. מסס. Arab. مَسٌّ, *vehemens necessitas*.

מַס, m. מַס in pause, pl. מִסִּים. For מֶכֶס, according to Gesen., and so *ks*, or Gr. ξ at the end of words occasionally loses the *k*, as in *aiax*, *aias*, &c.; which is inapplicable in this case. For here ב, in the *middle* of a word, is rejected; not to insist on the impropriety of determining the forms of Hebrew words from Latin and Greek usage. The root, however, might be Syr. ܡܟܣ, from which we have ܡܟܣܐ, *statera*, *trutina*. Arab. مَسَا, *æris alieni oblitus fuit*, *idque solvere distulit*. Cogn. نَسَا; whence, نَسَاء, *debitum aliquo post tempore præstandum*: thence, Tribute, tax, 1 Kings iv. 6; v. 13; Phrr. הָיָה לָמַס, lit. became of, to,

מסב (374) מסה

tribute; tributary, Deut. xx. 11; Judg. i. 30, &c. With עֶבֶד added, — *of a slave, or servant*, Gen. xlix. 15; Josh. xvi. 10. With נָתַן, שָׂם, or עָלָה, in the place of הָיָה, Josh. xvii. 13; Judg. i. 28; 1 Kings ix. 21. שָׂם מַס עַל, laid *tribute, tax, upon*—, Esth. x. 1. אֲשֶׁר עַל הַמַּס, *Who was over the tribute*, 2 Sam. xx. 24, &c. שָׂרֵי מִסִּים, *princes of taxes;* chief collectors, Exod. i. 11.

מֵסַב, m. pl. constr. מְסִבֵּי, it. pl. of מְסִבּוֹת, r. סבב. Lit. *round about* place, thing. (a) *Seats* arranged round any place, thing, &c., for reclining on, Cant. i. 12. (b) *Places surrounding*, 2 Kings xxiii. 5. Pl. fem. *turnings about, revolutions, &c.*, Job xxxvii. 12. See my note. Symm. αὐτὸς δὲ κυκληδὸν ἀναστρέφεται. LXX. Theod. καὶ αὐτὸς κυκλώματα διαστρέψει. (c) Adv. *round about*, 1 Kings vi. 29. Aff. מְסִבָּי, Ps. cxl. 10, is more properly the Part. pl. Hiph. persons *surrounding me*. See Rosenmüller, on the place.

מַסְגֵּר, m.—pl. non occ., r. סָגַר. Part. Hiph. lit. one who closes anything. (a) *Joiner*, perhaps, 2 Kings xxiv. 14. 16; Jer. xxiv. 1; xxix. 2; always with חָרָשׁ. (b) Meton. *Place, thing, closed. Confinement, prison*, Is. xxiv. 22; xlii. 7; Ps. cxlii. 8.

מִסְגֶּרֶת, fem. plur. מִסְגְּרוֹת, r. סָגַר. Lit. *Closing, inclosure.* (a) *Inclosure*, considered as a place of safety, Mic. vii. 17; Ps. xviii. 46; 2 Sam. xxii. 46. (b) *Border* of any thing, as its inclosure, Exod. xxv. 25, seq.; xxxvii. 14, &c. (c) — of the bases of the brazen sea, 1 Kings vii. 28, 29. 31, 32. 35, 36; 2 Kings xvi. 17. Aff. מִסְגְּרוֹתֶיהָ, מִסְגְּרֹתָם, it. מִסְגְּרֹתָם.

מַסַּד, masc. once, 1 Kings vii. 9, r. יָסַד. *Foundation.*

מִסְדְּרוֹן, m. r. סדר, cogn. שׁוּרָה, with ה parag. once, Judg. iii. 23. *A portico,* or *porch*, so called from the rows of columns in its front. Aquila, παραστάδα. Symm. πρόθυρα. LXX. προστάδα.

מסה, v. cogn. מאס, מסס. Syr. ܡܣܐ, *contabuit.* Aph. *humectavit.* Kal non occ. Hiph. pl. הִמְסִיו, fm. Chald. for הִמְסוּ, pres. 1st pers. אֶמְסֶה; 2d, apoc. תֵּמֵס (for תַּמְסֶה); 3d, aff. יְמָסֵם. (a) *Dissolve, liquify*, Ps. cxlvii. 18. Meton. (b) *Waste, consume*, Ps. xxxix. 12. (c) *Relax, unnerve, weaken*, Josh. xiv. 8. (d) *Water, suffuse*, with tears,

Ps. vi. 7, al. non occ., unless תֵּמַס, Ps. lviii. 9, may so be taken.

מַסָּה, fem. constr. מַסַּת, pl. מַסּוֹת, r. נָסָה, which see. *Trial, experiment, proof.* Meton. *Temptation*, by trial. Whence the proper name of a place, *Massa*, Exod. xvii. 7, &c.; Ps. xcv. 8. כְּיוֹם מַסָּה, *as the day of trial*, i. e. of tempting God. It is added, by way of explanation, אֲשֶׁר נִסּוּנִי... בְּחָנוּנִי, *in which, they tried me ... they proved me*, Deut. vi. 16; xxxiii. 8. מַסַּת, Job ix. 23; but see my translation and note. Pl., *Temptations*, i. e. the wonderful works of God, by which the faith of believers is proved, Deut. iv. 34; vii. 19; xxix. 2, al. non occ.

מְסַת, fem. constr. מִסַּת, once, Deut. xvi. 10, f. τοῦ, מַס, which see. *Tribute; offering.* Phr. מִסַּת נִדְבַת יָדְךָ, *offering of freewill of thy hand.* Aquila, ἔπαρσιν ἑκουσίων. Gesen. "*numerus*:" "*pro ratione, prout.*" See LXX. Syr.

מָסוֶה, m.—pl. non occ., r. סוה, non occ. Arab. سَوِيَ et سُوِيَ, مَكَان, medius locus. Jauhari gives, سَوَاءُ الشَّيْءِ وَسَطُهُ, i. e. סוא, *of anything, is its middle*. Applied to the *veil* of Moses, as something placed *in the midst*, and intervening, Exod. xxxiv. 33, 34, 35, al. non occ.

מְשׂוּכָה, fem. constr. מְשֻׂכַת, pl. non occ., r. שׂוּךְ. *Fence, hedge*, Is. v. 5; Mic. vii. 4; Prov. xv. 19. Aff. מְשׂוּכָתוֹ.

מַסָּח, masc. r. נָסַח, once, 2 Kings xi. 6. Arab. نَسَخَ, *dispersit* terram; مِنْسَخ, *res quâ dispergitur terra.* Lit. *Disperser, driver away, &c.* As a *dispersing* detachment, i. e. to disperse disorderly or inquisitive people. Syr. ܡܢ ܢܣܚ, *a damno*.

מִסְחָר, once, 1 Kings x. 15, r. סָחַר. *Merchandise, traffic.*

מֶסֶךְ, masc. once, Ps. lxx. 9. Cogn. מֶזֶג. *Mixture.* Arab. مَزَجَ. Syr. ܡܙܓܐ, *misture.* Hence—

מָסַךְ, v. pres. non occ. Constr. immed. it. med. בְּ. *Mix*, generally of drink, Prov. ix. 2. 5; Ps. cii. 10. —, of spirit, Is. xix. 14. Infin. מְסֹךְ, constr. Is. v. 22, al. non occ.

מָסָךְ, masc. constr. מָסַךְ, plur. non occ.,

מסך (375) מסל

r. סָכַךְ. *Covering*, pec. of the Tabernacle or its parts, Exod. xxvi. 36, seq.; xxxv. 17; xxxix. 38. 40; xl. 5. With פָּרֹכֶת, *veil, curtain*, Ib. xxxv. 12; xxxix. 34; xl. 21. וַיְגַל אֵת מָסַךְ יְהוּדָה, *so he laid open the curtain of Judah:* used here apparently in the sense of *curtain*, in fortification, Is. xxii. 8. See under גָּלָה above.

מִסְפָּד, f. once, Ezek. xxviii. 13. Aff. מְסֻכָתְךָ, i. q. מָסָךְ, r. סָכַךְ above.

מַסֵּכָה, f. constr. מַסֶּכֶת, pl. מַסֵּכוֹת, r. נָסַךְ. Lit. *fusing*, as of metals: hence, meton. (a) *Molten* image, idol, Exod. xxxiv. 17; Lev. xix. 4; Deut. ix. 12, &c. (b) *Libation*, Is. xxx. 1. It. in the sense of the cogn. r. סָכַךְ. (c) *Covering*, Is. xxv. 7; xxviii. 20. Aff. מַסֵּכְתָּם, Num. xxxiii. 52.

מִסְכֵּן, m.—pl. non occ., r. סָכַן. Arab. مِسْكِين, *pauper*. Æth. Syr. id. *Poor, destitute*, Eccl. iv. 13; ix. 15, 16, al. non occ.

מִסְכֵּנֻת, f. r. סָכַן. *Poverty, want*, once, Deut. viii. 9.

מִסְכְּנוֹת, fem. pl. only, r. סָכַן. Gesen. סֹכֵן, by transposition. But, as سَكَنَ, *being quiet*, may supply the notions of both *riches* and *poverty*; rest, in the one case implying *ease, plenty*; in the other, want of employment, idleness, and thence *poverty*: there is perhaps not sufficient reason for this metathesis. So in the Arab. سَكَنَ, *quietus fuit;* سَكَنٌ, *alimentum;* سَكَّنَ, *stabilivit;* سَكَنٌ, *misericordia, benedictio;* and, on the other hand, مَسْكَنَة, *paupertas, miseria.—Treasuries* of corn, &c., Exod. i. 11; 1 Kings ix. 19; 2 Chron. viii. 4; xvi. 4; xvii. 12; xxxii. 28, al. non occ.

מַסֶּכֶת, f. in pause, מָסָכֶת,—pl. non occ., r. נָסַךְ. Cogn. Arab. نَسَجَ, *texuit.* The *web*, as connected with the weaving machine, Judg. xvi. 13, 14, only. Aquila, Symm. LXX. διάσμα. LXX. it. ὕφασμα.

מְסִלָּה, fem. constr. מְסִלַּת, מְסִלּוֹת, r. סָלַל. (a) *A raised*, or *high way*, as a breastwork in fortification, Is. lxii. 10; Judg. v. 20. (b) *Highway, road*, or *path*, Num. xx. 19; 2 Sam. xx. 12, 13; Is. xi. 16; xix. 23, &c.

(d) *Elevations; terraces* perhaps. See under אֻלַמִּים, p. 34, seq. above. Gesen. *scala:* but without authority or probability. Metaph. (e) *Way, manner*, of life. See דֶּרֶךְ, Prov. xvi. 17; Ps. lxxxiv. 6. Aff. מְסִלָּתוֹ, מְסִלֹּתַי, מְסִלֹּתָם.

מַסְלוּל, m. once, Is. xxxv. 8. *A raised highway.*

מַסְמְרִים, m. sing. non occ., r. סָמַר.
מַסְמְרוֹת, f. Cogn. שָׁמַר. Arab. مِسْمَار, *clavus. Nails*, Is. xli. 7; Jer. x. 4; Eccl. xii. 11; 1 Chron. xxii. 3; 2 Chron. iii. 9.

מסס, v. see מַס above. Cogn. מָסָה, מָאַס. Arab. مَسَّ, conj. iii. *liquefecit;* cogn. مَسِيَ, iv. *liquefactum fuit.* Comp. مَاتَ, r. مَوتَ.

Infin. Kal, מְסֹס. *Dissolving, melting; fainting*, Is. x. 18.
Niph. נָמֵס, pres. יִמַּס. *Be, become, dissolved, melted*, as wax, &c., Exod. xvi. 21; Ps. lxviii. 3. Metaph. of mountains, Is. xxxiv. 3: of bonds, as falling off, Judg. xv. 14: of flocks, as *wasting*, 1 Sam. xv. 9. Metaph. as *enervated* by fear, 2 Sam. xvii. 10; — the heart, Deut. xx. 8; Josh. ii. 11; v. 1; Josh. vii. 5; Ezek. xxi. 12: — by grief, pain, Ps. xxii. 15; cxii. 10, &c.
Infin. הִמֵּס, 2 Sam. l. c., &c.
Hiph. pl. הִמַסּוּ, *They have caused to melt; faint*, Deut. i. 28.

מַסָּע, masc. pl. constr. מַסְעֵי, aff. מַסְעֵיהֶם, r. נָסַע. Arab. نَسَعَ, *abiit* per terram. Cogn. نَسَغَ, *petivit, ussitque dictis; punxit* acu manum, &c. (a) *A missile* weapon, Job xli. 18. (b) *March, journey*, as of an army, &c., Gen. xiii. 3; Exod. xl. 36; Num. x. 2. 6. 12. 28; xxxiii. 1, 2;—Deut. x. 11. In 1 Kings vi. 7, we have, אֶבֶן שְׁלֵמָה מַסָּע Auth. Vers., *stone made ready....brought*. Gesen. *Lapicidinæ*, i. e. *of the quarry*. But on what authority? This does not appear. The *"lapides dolati"* of the Vulgate is not without some probability of being correct. Syr. Polyg. ܕܡܣܩܠܐ, *of carrying*, i. e. *removing*, &c., as the Auth. Vers., which is the best rendering.

מִסְעָד, m., r. סָעַד, once, 1 Kings x. 12. *Prop, support.*

מִסְפֵּד, masc. constr. מִסְפַּד, pl. non occ. r. סָפַד. *Lamentation, wailing*, Gen. L. 10; Jer. xlviii. 38; Ezek. xxvii. 31; Mic. i. 11, &c. Aff. מִסְפְּדִי, Ps. xxx. 12.

מִסְפּוֹא, m.—pl. non occ., r. סָפָא. Syr. ܡܶܣܦܳܐ ܡܶܣܦܳܐ, *plenus redundans.* Cogn. ܣܦܰܩ, *concessit.* Arab. شَفَا, r. شَفَو, *satiavit; præbuit illi* rem. *Provender, fodder*, Gen. xxiv. 25. 32; xlii. 27; xliii. 24; Judg. xix. 19, al. non occ.

מִסְפַּחַת, fem. sing. only, r. סָפַח, i. q. סַפַּחַת. *Scurf, scab*, Lev. xiii. 6—8. Aquila, ἐξανάδοσις. Symm. ἔκβρασμα, ἔκφυμα. LXX. σημασία.

מִסְפָּחוֹת, f. pl. only, r. סָפַח. *Pillows, cushions*, Ezek. xiii. 18. 21, only. Gesen. "*pulvilli, culcitræ*;" but the etymology requires something *spread out, extended*. Auth. Vers. *Kerchiefs*. It is evident that idolatrous practices are here had in view, and we read in 2 Kings xxiii. 7, of women weaving, בָּתִּים,—for the pl.: see p. 61. 2, above—a sort of chapel, perhaps, enclosed with *curtains*, in imitation of the place in which the ark of the testimony once stood. (See 2 Sam. vii. 2; 1 Chron. xvii. 1.) This was the work of idolatrous *priestesses*, see vr. 17, who seem to have employed themselves in decorating the heads of their *erections*, רָאשׁ כָּל־קוֹמָה, vr. 8, for the purpose of making them the more alluring. Symm. ὑπαυχένια. LXX. ἐπιβόλαια. See Schleusn. Lex. in LXX. sub voce, ἐπίβλημα.

מִסְפָּר, masc. constr. מִסְפַּר, constr. pl. מִסְפְּרֵי, once, 1 Chron. xii. 23, r. סָפַר. *Number*, Num. i. 2; ix. 20, &c. With the ellipsis of כְּ, or בְּ, as, מִסְפָּר נַפְשֹׁתֵיכֶם, *according to*, or *in*, *the number of your persons*, Exod. xvi. 16. So עֶשְׂרִים וְאַרְבַּע מִסְפָּר, four and *twenty, in*, or *according to, number*, 2 Sam. xxi. 20. And, as number is readily ascertained, this term will designate *few* or *many*, as the accompanying words shall require; as, מְתֵי מִסְפָּר, *men of number*, i. e. few, Gen. xxxiv. 30; Deut. iv. 27, &c. יָמִים מִסְפָּר, *few days*, Num. ix. 20. So שָׁנוֹת מִסְפָּר, *a few years*, Job xvi. 22. In like manner, אֵין מִסְפָּר, *want of number*; no *number*; innumerable, Gen. xli. 49. עַד־אֵין מִסְפָּר, *even to —*, Job v. 9; ix. 10. לְאֵין מִסְפָּר, 1 Chron. xxii. 4. In Deut. xxxiii. 6, the negative אַל, is to be repeated before יְהִי: the sense will then be, *and let not his men be few*, i. e. let them be innumerable. With an interrogative also, a negative may be implied, as, הֲיֵשׁ מִסְפָּר לִגְדוּדָיו, *is there any number to his forces?* i. e. they are innumerable. Aff. מִסְפָּרָם, מִסְפָּרְכֶם.

מָסַר, v. non occ. pret. pres. Arab. مَسَرَ, *extraxit; concitavit* ad simultatem: *prodidit* illum. Syr. ܡܰܣܪ, *opus aggressus est; contempsit.* Infin. with לְ, in the phrase לִמְסָר־מַעַל, constr. med. בְּ. *To stir up rebellion* against, &c., or, *to extract, wring out, rebellion*, Num. xxxi. 16. LXX. τοῦ ἀποστῆσαί καὶ ὑπεριδεῖν τὸ ῥῆμα κυρίου. Comp. Num. v. 6; Ezek. xiv. 13; 2 Chron. xxxvi. 14. Whence Gesenius was tempted to suspect the reading as incorrect: which is groundless. Niph. pres. pl. וַיִּמָּסְרוּ, *So there were extracted, selected*, Num. xxxi. 5. LXX. καὶ ἐξηρίθμησαν. *Et electi sunt.* Targ. Onk. and Syr.

מָסֹרֶת, fem. once, Ezek. xx. 37, for מַאֲסֹרֶת, r. אָסַר. *Bond, obligation.*

מֹסָר, m. i. q. מוּסָר, r. יָסַר. *Discipline, correction*, once, Job xxxiii. 16.

מִסְתּוֹר, masc., r. סָתַר, once, Is. iv. 6. *Hiding-place, refuge.*

מִסְתָּר, m. pl. מִסְתָּרִים, r. סָתַר. *Hiding-place*. (a) *Ambush*, Ps. x. 9; xvii. 12; Hab. iii. 13; Lam. iii. 10, &c. (b) *Secret place*, Is. xliv. 3; Jer. xiii. 17; Ps. x. 8, &c. Aff. מִסְתָּרָיו.

מַעְבָּד, m. Chald. pl. aff. מַעְבָּדוֹהִי, once, Dan. iv. 34. *His works, doings*, r. עבד. Heb. מַעַבְדֵיהֶם, *their works*, Job xxxiv. 25, an instance in which a Chaldee word has been adopted. See my Job, p. 50.

מַעֲבֶה, masc., r. עָבָה, once, 1 Kings vii. 46. בְּמַעֲבֵה הָאֲדָמָה, *in the thick* (deep) *of the soil.*

מַעֲבָר, masc. constr. מַעֲבַר, r. עבר . . . —

מַעְבָּרָה, f. pl. מַעְבָּרוֹת, constr. מַעְבְּרוֹת .— *Passage* (a) of a river, &c., Gen. xxxii. 23. Phr. מַעֲבַר מַטֵּה מוּסָדָה, *passage of the established*, i. e. decreed, *staff* of chastisement, &c. (b) *Pass*, 1 Sam. xiii. 23. Fem. (a) מַעְבְּרוֹת, erroneously pointed for מַעֲבָרוֹת, Judg. iii. 28; Is. xvi. 2; Jer. li. 32. (b) Is. x. 29.

מַעֲגָל, masc. once, מַעְגָּל, constr. מַעְגַּל, pl. constr. מַעְגְּלֵי, aff. מַעְגָּלָיו .—

מַעֲגָלָה, f. pl. מַעְגְּלוֹת. Aff. מַעְגְּלוֹתָיו, r. עָגַל.—
Arab. عَجَلَة, rota. Syr. ܟ̈ܪܟ, provolvit.
Lit. Instrument of revolving; a wheel.
Hence, meton. (a) *the track* of a wheel, Ps.
lxv. 12. Thence, (b) *A way, path*, Ps.
cxl. 6; Prov. ii. 18. And metaph. (c)
Way, manner, Ps. xxiii. 3; Prov. ii. 9. 15;
iv. 26. (d) Meton. *Waggon:* and by a
further meton., *Place, fortified*, i. e. barri-
cadoed by *waggons, &c*. Gesen. 1 Sam. xvii.
20; xxvi. 5. 7. Arab. عَجَلَة, *plaustrum*.

מָעַד, v. pres. אֶמְעַד, תִּמְעַד, constr. abs.
Arab. مَعَدَ, *celeriter rapideque traxit.*
Vacillate, totter, 2 Sam. xxii. 37; Ps. xviii.
37; xxvi. 1; xxxvii. 31.
Part. pl. constr. מוֹעֲדֵי רֶגֶל, People, *tottering
of foot*, i. e. whose foot is not firm from
weakness or other causes, Job xii. 5. But
see my notes on the place.
Hiph. Imp. הַמְעֵד, *Make, cause, to vacillate, totter*, once, Ps. lxix. 24. And so,
according to some, הַעֲמָדְךָ, Ezek. xxix. 7, by
transposition for הַמְעָדְךָ.
Hoph. Part. fem. מוּעָדֶת, in pause, מוּעָדֶת,
Made to vacillate, Prov. xxv. 19, al. non
occ.

מַעֲדָן, m. pl. מַעֲדַנִּים: it. f. מַעֲדַנּוֹת. r. עָדַן.
Syr. ܗܢܝܐ, *deliciæ*. Arab. غَدَن, *mollities:
bona, deliciæ*. *Delicacies, delights*, Gen.
xlix. 20; Prov. xxix. 17; Lam. iv. 5. Fem.
pl., Job xxxviii. 31, מַעֲדַנּוֹת כִּימָה *delights of
—*, i. e. influences; by Rosenmüller, Gesen.,
&c., "*vincula pleiadum;*" as if derived from
עָנַד: but this is groundless. See my note on
the place. Adv. מַעֲדַנּוֹת... וַיֵּלֶךְ, *so he walks
(in) greatly delighted*, 1 Sam. xv. 32.
Gesenius gives a pl. מַעֲדָנִים, Jer. li. 34.
The received reading, however, is מֵעֲדָנַי, of
מִן + עֶדֶן.

מַעְדֵּר, masc. once, Is. vii. 25, r. עָדַר.
A rake, or some such agricultural instrument.

מֵעֶה, masc. plur. constr. מְעֵי. Aff. מֵעַי,
מֵעֶיךָ, &c. Arab. مَعْي, *intestinum*; مَعًا,
viscera. (a) *The intestines*, 2 Sam. xx. 10;
Job xxx. 27; Is. xvi. 11; Jer. iv. 19; xxxi.
19; Lam. i. 20, &c. (b) Meton. *The belly*,
internally, Jonah ii. 1, 2; Ps. xxii. 15, &c.:
externally, Cant. v. 14. (c) *The womb*, Is.
xlix. 1; lxiii. 15; Ps. lxxi. 6; Ruth i. 11;
2 Sam. xvi. 11, &c. And, as the seat of
thought was supposed to be the viscera, (d)
The heart, mind. See לֵב, Is. xvi. 11; Ps.
xl. 9; Job xxx. 27; Lam. i. 20; Cant. v. 4.
Chald. sign. (b). Aff. מְעוֹהִי, *His belly*, Dan.
ii. 32, only.

מֵעָה, f. pl. Aff. מֵעוֹתָיו, i. q. מְעֵי above.
Gesen. Is. xlviii. 19, where he takes it to
signify, metaph., *fish*, i. e. as the produce of
the bowels of the ocean. But a better interpretation may be thus obtained. In the first
member the comparison is, with חוֹל, *the sand
of the sea*: in the second, with כִּמְעוֹתָיו,
which, to preserve unity in the passage,
should be something corresponding in sense
with חוֹל, not with מֵעֶה. Now, in the
Arab., the v. مَعَا, r. معو, signifies, among
other things, "*extendit se.*" In the Æth.,
also, from the same root, ፍጥሰም፡
plaga septentrionalis. The passage, therefore, may be rendered, *and thy seed shall be
as the sand* (in number), *and the offspring
of thy bowels as its extent*, or *its vast extent*;
taking the pl. as a pl. of excell., i. e. so extensively spread abroad.

מָעוֹג, masc. sing. only, i. q. עֻגָּה, r. עוּג.
Arab. عُجَّة, *laganum ex ovis in sartagine
coctis*. *A cake*, 1 Kings xvii. 12. Comp.
13; Ps. xxxv. 16. See לַעֵג.

מָעוֹז, מָעֹז, m. pl. מָעֻזִּים, constr. מָעוּזֵי,
r. עוּז. *Place of strength, munition*, Judg.
vi. 26; Dan. xi. 7. 10. 31. Often applied to
persons (see מָנוֹס) as a *refuge*, Jer. xvi. 19;
Is. xxv. 4; xxx. 2; Ps. xxxvii. 39; xliii. 2.
Metaph. מָעוֹז רֹאשִׁי, as *my helmet*, Ps. lx. 9.
צוּר מָעֻזָּךְ, *rock of thy munition*, i. e. he who is
as such a rock, Is. xvii. 10; 2 Sam. xxii. 33,
&c. Phr. מָעוֹז יָם, — *of the sea*, Is. xxiii. 4.
עָרֵי מָעוֹז, *cities of —*, i. e. fortified, Is. xvii. 9.
אֱלֹהַּ מָעֻזִּים *the God of —*, i. e. of war, Dan.
xi. 38. Aff. מָעֻזִּי, &c.

מָעוֹן, masc. constr. מְעוֹן, plur. מְעוֹנִים.—
מְעוֹנָה, fem. aff. מְעוֹנָתוֹ, plur. מְעוֹנוֹת.
r. עוּן. Arab. مَعَن, *statio, sedes*. *Habitation, place of residence,* — of God, i. e. the
Temple, Ps. xxvi. 8. Heaven, Ps. lxxvi. 3;
lxviii. 6; Deut. xxvi. 15. Metaph. *Refuge*,
Ps. xc. 1; Deut. xxxiii. 27.—*Den of beasts*,
Jer. ix. 10; x. 22; li. 37; Ps. civ. 22;
Amos iii. 4; Nah. ii. 12. *Habitation*, gene-

3 c

מְעוֹ (378) מְעַט

rally, Jer. xxi. 13. Aff. מְעוֹנְךָ, מְעוֹנוֹ, &c. pl. f. מְעוֹנוֹתֵינוּ.

מָעוּף, m. constr. מְעוּף, once, Is. viii. 22; r. עוּף. Syr. ܥܘܦ, duplicavit, involvit. Lit. Doubling, involving, of pressure, distress. Arab. مَعُوفة, profundæ. Castell. Gesenius gives under the root, for תְּעֻפָה, Job xi. 17, "caligine tectus....eris sicut mane, or תְּעוּפָה, caligo erit ut mane." But no notion of darkness appears to be inherent in this word, no more than it is in that of the morning or dawn. If the comparison had been with the night, the case would have been different. Still, as distress, is sometimes intimated by darkness or blackness, see קֹדֶר, פָּארוּר, it may be allowable in a translator's so taking the word here by a meton. LXX. θλίψις, καὶ στενοχωρία, which is not far from the matter.

מָעוֹר, m. plur. aff. once, מְעוֹרֵיהֶם, r. עוּר, cogn. עִרָה, Their nakednesses, Hab. ii. 15.

מָעֹז, see מָעוֹז.

מְעַט, once, מְעָט, 2 Chron. xii. 7; pl. מְעַטִּים. Arab. أَمْعَط, calvus; whence the notion of paucity. A little, few, i. e. small quantity, or number; constr. מְעַט מַיִם, — of water, Gen. xviii. 4. Comp. Num. xiii. 18; xxvi. 54, &c. אֹכֶל —, of food, Ib. xliii. 2. As the governing noun, מְתֵי מְעָט, men of fewness, a few, Deut. xxvi. 5. Comp. Dan. xi. 34. In apposition, גּוֹיִם לֹא מְעַט, nations not a few, Is. x. 7. Comp. Neh. ii. 12. Adverbially, Ps. viii. 6: — of time, Ruth ii. 7; Ps. xxvii. 10; Hos. viii. 10; Hag. ii. 6: — of distance, 2 Sam. xvi. 1; constr. med. מִן, from. So, when respect is had to persons or things, הַמְעַט מִכֶּם, lit. Whether a little from you? i. e. Is it a trifle with you? or less than you? your desert? Comp. Ezek. xvi. 20; Ps. viii. 6. Repeated, as, מְעַט מְעַט, by little and little, Exod. xxiii. 30. Comp. Deut. vii. 22. Pl., Ps. cix. 8; Eccl. v. 1. With other particles prefixed, — אִם, 2 Sam. xii. 8: הֲלֹא מְעַט, Job x. 20: פִּי מְעַט, Gen. xxx. 30: מְעַט צְעָר, Is. xvi. 14: lit. little, small, i. e. very small, or few.

With כְּ, (a) As a small thing, trifle, was it, i. e. it was near; but little was wanting that —, Gen. xxvi. 10; 2 Sam. xix. 37; Ps. lxxiii. 2; cxix. 87. עַד —שִׁי —, Cant. iii. 4. (b) Shortly, soon, Ps. lxxxi. 15; xciv. 17. It, Ps. ii. 12; Job xxxii. 22. (c) Lit. As a few, i. e. comparatively speaking, as nothing, a very few, Is. i. 9; Ps. cv. 12; 1 Chron. xvi. 19. See Nold., pp. 517. 390. Hence the verb—

מָעַט, pret. non occ. pres. יִמְעַט, constr. abs. it. med. מָן, לִפְנֵי, pers. אֶת, thing. Be, become, few, small, Exod. xii. 4; Jer. xxix. 6; xxx. 19; Is. xxi. 17; Ps. cvii. 39; Neh. ix. 32; Prov. xiii. 11.
Infin. מְעֹט, Lev. xxv. 16, only.
Pih. pl. מִעֲטוּ, i. q. Kal, Eccl. xii. 3, only.
Hiph. f. הִמְעִיטָה, pres. יַמְעִיט, constr. abs. it. immed. it. med. אֶת. מִן. Make few, small; diminish, Lev. xxv. 16; xxvi. 22; Num. xxvi. 54; xxxii. 54; Jer. x. 24; Ps. cvii. 38, &c. Assign, give, few, little, Exod. xxx. 15; Num. xxxv. 8.
Part. מַמְעִיט, Exod. xvi. 17, 18; Num. xi. 32.

מְעָטָה, f. once, Ezek. xxi. 20. Gesen. "Glaber—politus, acutus, i. q. מֹרָט," v. 15, 16. Auth. Vers. Wrapped up. Arab. مَعَط, evaginavit ensem. Cogn. مَعَط, conj. viii. id., מְעוּטָה, therefore, is for מְעוּטָה, part. Kal. Drawn, naked, sword; and so perhaps, מֹרָט.

מַעֲטֶה, m. constr. מַעֲטֵה, once, Is. lxi. 3. Garment, clothing, of praise. Comp. בִּגְדֵי יֶשַׁע, Ib. lxi. 10, r. עָטָה.

מַעֲטָפָה, f. pl. מַעֲטָפוֹת, r. עָטַף, once, Is. iii. 22. Flowing upper robe, mantle. See Schroeder. de Vest. Mulierum, p. 235. Syr. ܥܛܦ, circumvolutus. Arab. عِطَاف, pallium.

מְעִי, m. once, Is. xvii. 1. Synon. τοῦ, מַפֵּלָה, i. q. עִי, r. עָוָה, or עָיָה. Arab. غَوَى, conj. vii. cecidit. Cogn. مَعَى, defessus. Cogn. عَبَى, pernicie affecta fuit seges.

מְעִיל, m. pl. מְעִילִים, r. מָעַל. Comp. בֶּגֶד. Long and full upper garment, worn by persons of dignity (men or women), robe, mantle, or the like. See Braun. de Vest. Sacerd. ii. 5; Schroed. de Vest. Mulierum, p. 269. It appears to have had a mouth, or neck hole, in the middle, Exod. xxxix. 23, and, four corners, כְּנָפוֹת, LXX. πτέρυγες, Deut. xxii. 12;—1 Sam. xv. 27; xviii. 4; xxiv. 5. 12. Also by the Prophets and Priests, Ib. xxviii. 14:—but under the Ephod; thence termed, מְעִיל הָאֵפוֹד, Exod. xxviii. 31; xxxix.

מֵעִי (379) מַעַל

22: — by women, 2 Sam. xiii. 18. Metaph. Is. lxi. 10; lix. 17. Aff. מֵעָיו, &c.

מָעִין, מֵעִים, Chald. See מְעָה above.

מַעְיָן, constr. מַעְיַן, with ו parag. מַעְיָנוֹ, Ps. cxiv. 8. Aff. מַעְיָנוֹ; pl. מַעְיָנִים; constr. מַעְיְנֵי; it. pl. fem. מַעְיָנוֹת; constr. מַעְיְנוֹת; r. עִין. Syr. ܡܥܝܢܐ, fons; ܡܒܘܥܐ, id. Arab. عَيْن, id. A fountain, well, of water, Gen. vii. 11; viii. 2; Lev. xi. 36; Ps. lxxiv. 15; lxxxiv. 7; Hos. xiii. 15, &c. Metaph. Is. xii. 3; Ps. lxxxvii. 7, &c.

מְעִינִים, 1 Chron. iv. 41. Kethiv for מְעוּנִים. See מָעוֹן.

מָעַךְ, v. occ. Part. only. Syr. cogn. ܡܥܝܟ, angusto pectore fuit. Comp. עוּק. Arab. مَعَقَ, i. q. عَمَقَ, profundus fuit. Pressure being apparently the primary notion. Thence—

Part. מָעוּךְ, fem. מְעוּכָה. (a) Pressed. Meton. (b) Bruised, injured. (a) חֲנִיתוֹ מְעוּכָה־בָאָרֶץ, his spear pressed down, i. e. stuck, into the earth, 1 Sam. xxvi. 7. (b) Lev. xxii. 24, with כָּתוּת, &c. lxx. θλαδίαν. Ἀλλ. σπάδοντα. See Schleusn. Lex. in lxx. Gesen. comminutis testiculis. Al. non occ.

מַעַל, masc.—plur. non occ. Arab. v. مَعَل, properavit, corrupit, &c.: whence مَعَل, corruptio, &c. Cogn. مَغَل, obtrectavit. Perverseness, sin, against God, Job xxi. 34. See my note. Sym. ἀνεπιστημόνως. In other places, Lev. v. 15. 21, &c., as an Infin. with the v. מָעַל, which see. Aff. מַעֲלוֹ, &c.

מַעַל, m. }
מַעֲלָה, f. } used as an adv. r. עָלָה. Lit. ascending. Not used, however, except with מִן prefixed, as, מִמַּעַל. Lit. From above, over, &c., Is. xlv. 8; Job xviii. 16: opp. τῷ, מִתַּחַת, Amos ii. 9; Deut. v. 8: with מִלְמַעְלָה, 1 Kings vii. 20, and apparently synonymous with it. Over against, near, Is. vi. 2: constr. here and elsewhere with לְ, as to, as it respects, &c.; above as to —, Gen. xxii. 9; Lev. xi. 21; Jer. xliii. 10; Dan. xii. 6, &c. See Nold., p. 509. Fem. Above, over, in height, 1 Sam. ix. 2; 1 Kings vii. 31:—in superiority, Deut. xxviii. 43: — as to time, onwards, 1 Sam. xvi. 13; Exod. xxx. 14, &c. — age, Num. i. 20: and so Hag. ii. 15, where Noldius erroneously gives retro, backwards: the prophet plainly directing them to look forward from that day, and from other events mentioned. With לְ, לְמַעְלָה, Upwards, Eccl. iii. 21; Is. vii. 11; Ezek. i. 27; xli. 7. — onwards, as to time, 1 Chron. xxiii. 27; 2 Chron. xxxi. 17. Over, above. Metaph. Ezra ix. 6; Prov. xv. 24. Highly, very much or abundantly, 1 Chron. xxix. 3; 2 Chron. i. 1, &c. See Nold., p. 441. 2. With מִן, מִלְמַעְלָה, from above, Josh. iii. 13. 16. Above, upwards, Gen. vii. 20; Exod. xxv. 21; 1 Kings vii. 25, &c. עַד לְמַעְלָה...., even to superiority, i. e. greater extent, &c., 2 Chron. xvi. 12; xvii. 12, &c. לְמַעְלָה מִן, more than, further than, 1 Chron. xxix. 3. Opp. τῷ, מַטָּה, Prov. xv. 24. לְמַטָּה, Eccl. l. c. וּלְמַעְלָה, 1 Chron. xxiii. 27, &c.

מָעַל, v. pres. יִמְעֹל (there being two Infinn. מַעַל, and מְעֹל). See מַעַל above. Constr. med. בְּ, pers. or thing, it. abs. Ezek. xviii. 24; 2 Chron. xxvi. 18, &c. Do perversely, wickedly, rebel, Lev. vi. 2; xxvi. 40; Num. v. 12, &c. — in some certain thing, Josh. xxii. 20; 1 Chron. ii. 7; Prov. xvi. 10.

Infin. מַעַל, Num. v. 7. 12. 27. Aff. מַעֲלוֹ, מַעֲלָם, 2 Chron. xxix. 19; Ezek. xx. 27.

— מְעוֹל, 2 Chron. xxviii. 19. Constr. מְעֹל, מְעָל, with לְ, pref., Num. v. 6; Neh. xiii. 26; Ezek. xiv. 12.

מַעַל, m. pl. constr. מַעֲלֵי, Chald. r. עלל i. q. Heb. בוא. Lit. enterings in of —. Settings of the sun, Dan. vi. 15, only.

מַעַל, for מִן עַל, see עַל.

מַעַל, masc. constr. once, Neh. viii. 6, r. עלה. Arab. وَعَل, prominuit, eminuit. Cogn. Heb. עלה (מוֹעַל, for מַעַל, Gram. art. 87. 1). Elevating, lifting up of —.

מַעֲלָה, masc. constr. מַעֲלֵה, pl. aff. מַעֲלָיו, r. עלה. Ascent, or place of acclivity, Neh. xii. 37; ix. 4; 1 Sam. ix. 11; Josh. x. 10; Is. xv. 5, &c. Pl., Ezek. xl. 31. Thence, meton., mount, as, מַעֲלֵה הַזֵּיתִים, Mount of Olives, 2 Sam. xv. 30.

מַעֲלָה, f. pl. מַעֲלוֹת, r. עלה. (a) Ascent, going up, from one place to another, Ezra vii. 9. Metaph. מַעֲלוֹת רוּחֲכֶם, suggestions of your own minds, Ezek. xi. 5. Comp. עֲלִי־לֵב, Ib. xxxviii. 10, &c.

(b) Step, as of stairs, &c., 1 Kings x. 19;

מֵעַל (380) מֵעַם

Ezek. xl. 26. 31. 34, &c. (c) Applied, as some think, to the *graduated gnomon* of a sun-dial, 2 Kings xx. 9—11; Is. xxxviii. 8. So Symm. Targ. Jerome, and the rabbins generally. Others, viz., Joseph. Antiq. x. 2, § 1; the LXX. and the Syriac, *the steps* of a staircase. Gesen. (d) This word occurs, too, as a title of certain Psalms, as, Pss. cxx.—cxxxiv., which Gesenius thinks was intended to mark a certain kind of repetition in the composition, intimating a sort of *progress* or *stepping*, e. g. Ps. cxxi. 1, מֵאַיִן יָבֹא עֶזְרִי : שִׂיר מִיָּם יְחֹוָה וגו׳, seq. Of the same sort, he says, is the Song of Deborah; see Judg. v. 3. 5, 6. 9, &c. This distinction, however, is fanciful: not one instance of it occurring in Psalm cxx., pointed out by Gesenius as bearing this title. And, again, instances of it occur in Ps. cxxxv., which has not this title. Bellermann's *trochaïc* character of these Psalms is equally groundless. Others have imagined that the *ascent*, or *going up*, of the Israelites out of captivity was intimated. It is perhaps more likely that these Psalms were so designated, because used in processions in *going up* to the Temple. Comp. Is. xxx. 29; Ps. xlii. 4. Not much reliance, however, can be placed on conjectures of this sort.

מַעֲלִיל, Zech. i. 4, for מַעֲלַל, Keri.

מַעֲלָל, masc. occ. in pl. only, מַעֲלָלִים, constr. מַעַלְלֵי, r. עָלַל. Arab. عَلَّ, *bibendum dedit secunda vice, causam præbuit, &c.* Syr. ܥܰܠ, *effecit, causam præbuit; it. ingressus est, &c.* The primary notion seems to be, *enter into*, thence *do effectually, habitually, &c.* Hence, *Habitual doings*, good or bad, as the context may require; and in this respect differing from פֹּעַל, and מַעֲשֶׂה, 1 Sam. xxv. 3; Ps. lxxvii. 12; lxxviii. 7, &c. Aff. מַעֲלָלֵינוּ, Zech. i. 6: מַעֲלָלֶיךָ, Deut. xxviii. 20 : מַעֲלָלָם, Jer. iv. 18 : מִעַלְלֵיכֶם, Is. i. 16, &c.

מֵעִם, of עִם + מִן.

מַעֲמָד, masc.—pl. non occ. r. עָמַד. (a) *Standing, order,* 1 Kings x. 5; 2 Chron. ix. 4. (b) *Station*, place of standing, 1 Chron. xxiii. 28; 2 Chron. xxxv. 15; Is. xxii. 19. Aff. מַעֲמָדְךָ, *thy station*, or *rank*.

מָעֳמָד, m. Part. Hoph. r. עמד, which see.

מַעֲמָסָה, f. once in the phr. אֶבֶן מַעֲמָסָה, *stone of burden*, Zech. xii. 3, r. עָמַס. Well illustrated by Jerome on the place, who tells us that *large round stones* were kept in the villages, &c., of Palestine, for the purpose of trying the strength of the young men; some being able to lift one of them as high as the knee only, others higher: and hence their strength was known. He also saw, he says, a very heavy brazen ball in the Temple of Minerva, at Athens, which he could scarcely move; with which the comparative strength of the several combatants was adjudged. This custom and this passage were alluded to by our Lord, Matt. xxi. 44; Luke xx. 18; the supposition being, in each case, that such stone would prove so heavy, that it would fall and crush him who may have so far succeeded as to have lifted it up.

מַעֲמַקִּים, masc. pl. constr. מַעֲמַקֵּי, r. עָמַק; the Dagesh in the ק implying, Gram. art. 154. 5, *intensity;* thence *Great depths, very deep places*, Ps. cxxx. 1; Is. li. 10; Ps. lxix. 3. 15; Ezek. xxvii. 34.

מַעַן, r. עָנָה. See מַעֲנֶה. Lit. *intent, purpose, &c.;* but used always with לְ prefixed, as a preposition.

(a) *Because of, on account of,* 1 Kings viii. 41; 2 Kings viii. 19; Is. lxii. 1, &c.; Nold., p. 442.

(b) Adv. *In order that, for the purpose that, so that,* Gen. xxvii. 25; Exod. iv. 5; Deut. iv. 1, &c.

(c) For *thence, so, accordingly,* Jer. xliv. 8; Hos. viii. 4; Ps. li. 6, &c.

(d) *Because that,* Neh. vi. 13, לְמַעַן שָׂכוּר הוּא לְמַעַן וגו׳, *Because that he was an hireling, thence, therefore, I feared, &c.* See Gram. art. 157. 19; Is. lxvi. 11, &c. *Because of,* Jer. vii. 10, &c.

With interrog. הֲ, Job xviii. 4; with וְ conj. Is. lxii. 1, &c.

With aff. לְמַעֲנִי, 2 Kings xix. 34; xx. 6, &c.: לְמַעֲנֶךָ, Job xviii. 4; Dan. ix. 19: לְמַעַנְכֶם, Deut. iii. 26, &c.

With אֲשֶׁר, as, לְמַעַן אֲשֶׁר; it. לְמַעַן אֲשֶׁר לֹא, &c. See Nold., p. 443, seq. always giving the sense which such combination would naturally require.

מַעֲנֶה, m. r. עָנָה, constr. מַעֲנֵה, pl. non occ. *Answer*, Prov. xv. 1. 23; Job xxxii. 3. 5. — of prayer, Prov. xvi. 1. With aff. and prep. לְ, לְמַעֲנֵהוּ, *for his own intent, purpose*, i. e. to answer his own ends. Jehovah hath done (not made) *all for his own purpose* (object, or will); so *even* (the) *wicked* (man) *for the day of evil* (calamity), Prov. xvi. 4.

מען (381) מער

See my Sermons and Dissertations, Lond. 1830, p. lxii. seq. note.

מַעֲנָה, fem. r. עָנָה. Syr. ܚܓܐ, *solicitus fuit*. Arab. عَنِي, id. The primitive notion, *penetrating, cutting,* or the like: thence, meton. *Cutting, furrow,* Ps. cxxix. 3. Kethiv, Keri, מַעֲנִית. Sym. παρέτειναν κακοῦντες. See LXX. 1 Sam. xiv. 14.

מְעֹנָה, see מָעוֹן.

מַעֲצָבָה, fem. once, Is. L. 11, r. עָצַב. *Labour, affliction.* Aquila, εἰς διαπόνησιν. Sym. ἐν ὀδύνῃ κοιμηθήσεσθε. LXX. ἐν λύπῃ.

מַעֲצָד, masc.—plur. non occ. Arab. مِعْضَد, مَعْضَد, *instrumentum ensiforme, quo arbores cæduntur. A sort of axe,* or *other carving tool,* Is. xliv. 12; Jer. x. 3, al. non occ.

מַעֲצוֹר, m. r. עָצַר, once, 1 Sam. xiv. 6. *Restraint, hindrance.* Aquila, ἐπίσχεσις. Symm. ἐποχή. See LXX.

מַעֲצָר, m. r. עָצַר, once, Prov. xxv. 28, i. q. מַעֲצוֹר above.

מַעֲקֶה, m. r. עָקָה, once, Deut. xxii. 8. Arab. عَقَا, *retinuit;* عَقَاةٌ, *area domûs, quodque eam circumstat. A parapet,* or *battlement.*

מַעֲקַשִּׁים, masc. plur. once, Is. xlii. 16, r. עָקַשׁ. *Unlevel, abrupt,* places, opp. τῷ מִישׁוֹר.

מַעַר, masc. r. עָרָה, pl. non occ. *Naked* place; *nudity,* Nah. iii. 5; 1 Kings vii. 36. כְּמַעַר־אִישׁ, *according to the naked* place,—i. e. place barely assignable to, or due space—*of, each.* LXX. κατὰ πρόσωπον ἔσω.

מַעֲרָב, m. }
מַעֲרָבָה, f. } with ה *locale,* מַעֲרָבָה, pl. non occ. r. עָרַב. I. Place of setting (sun). *The west,* Dan. viii. 5; Ps. lxxv. 7; ciii. 12; cvii. 3; Is. xliii. 5; 1 Chron. xii. 15; xxvi. 30, &c. Fem. Is. xlv. 6, al. non occ.

II. Pl. aff. מַעֲרָבֵךְ, *Merchandise, ware,* Ezek. xxvii. 13. 17. 19. 25. 27. 33, 34, al. non occ. Aff. sing. מַעֲרָבֵךְ.

מַעֲרָה, masc. constr. מַעֲרֵה, i. q. מַעַר. *Naked, bare,* place. *Plain,* or *moor,* perhaps, once, Judg. xx. 33. LXX. Μαραγαβέ. Arab. عُرْوَة, *quicquid circumjacet urbem.*

מַעֲרוֹת, pl. f. 1 Sam. xvii. 23. Kethiv, Keri, מַעַרְכוֹת. If the reading be genuine, it may be a fem. of the preceding, *Plains, suburbs,* or the like. The Versions read with the Keri.

מְעָרָה, f. constr. מְעָרַת, pl. מְעָרוֹת, r. עוּר, cogn. עָרָה. Arab. غُور, *descendit in terram;* whence, مَغَارَة, *spelunca. A cave,* Gen. xix. 30; xxiii. 9; xlix. 29; Josh. x. 18; Judg. vi. 2; Is. ii. 19, &c. Josh. xiii. 4, מְעָרָה, is taken by some as a proper name.

מַעֲרִיץ, masc. once, Is. viii. 13, r. עָרַץ, part. Hiph. aff. מַעֲרִצְכֶם, *your terrible,* or *fearful one.*

מערד, masc. plur. constr. מַעַרְכֵי, r. עָרַךְ. *Disposings of* the heart, once, Prov. xvi. 1.

מַעֲרָכָה, f. of the last, constr. מַעֲרֶכֶת, pl. מַעֲרָכוֹת, constr. מַעַרְכוֹת. *Disposition, order, arrangement,* Exod. xxxix. 37. נֵרוֹת הַמַּעֲרָכָה, *lights of the —,* i. e. of the sacred candlestick. *— of wood,* Judg. vi. 26; but see Auth. Vers. *— of shew-bread,* Lev. xxiv. 6; Neh. x. 34; 2 Chron. ii. 3. Applied also to the table of do., Ib. xxix. 18. *— of battle,* 1 Sam. iv. 16; xvii. 8. 22. 48.

מַעֲרֻמִּים, plur. masc. aff. r. עָרַם, once, 2 Chron. xxviii. 15. Lit. *Their nudities,* for concr. *naked ones.*

מַעֲרָצָה, fem. once, Is. x. 33, r. עָרַץ. *Fearfulness, terror.* LXX. μετὰ ἰσχύος.

מַעֲשֶׂה, masc. constr. מַעֲשֵׂה, plur. מַעֲשִׂים, constr. מַעֲשֵׂי, r. עָשָׂה. Lit. *making:* thence, *Work* as of an artificer, &c. מַעֲשֵׂה חֹשֵׁב, Exod. xxvi. 1. 31. מַעֲשֵׂה רֶשֶׁת, *— of network,* Ib. xxvii. 4. Comp. 2 Chron. xvi. 14; Ps. xlv. 2. *— of God,* Ps. viii. 7; xix. 2; ciii. 22; Is. v. 19; x. 12, &c. *— of man* generally, Deut. iv. 28; Ps. cxv. 4; cxxxv. 15, &c. Meton. *Labour, business, occupation,* i. e. performance of work, &c. in which case synon. with פֹּעַל: Gen. xlvii. 3, מַה־מַּעֲשֵׂיכֶם, *What your occupations?* Comp. 1 Chron. xxiii. 28; Exod. v. 4. מִי הַמַּעֲשֶׂה, *days of work, labour,* Ezek. xlvi. 1. And hence, generally, any *performance, act, deed, enterprise,* to be restricted by the context. Comp. דֶּרֶךְ, and Exod. xxiii. 24, כְּמַעֲשֵׂיהֶם, *according to their doings, deeds, &c.:* Ib. xviii. 20; Lev. xviii. 3; Mic. vi. 16; Eccl. iv. 3. On the word, Job xxxiii. 7, see my note. By a further meton., *Wealth,*

(382)

&c., obtained by *labour, occupation,* &c. Comp. מְלָאכָה, Is. xxvi. 12; Exod. xxiii. 16; 1 Sam. xxv. 2. Phrr. יוֹם הַמַּעֲשֶׂה, *day of business,* 1 Sam. xx. 19. מַעֲשֵׂה אֹפֶה, *work of the baker,* confectionary, Gen. xl. 17. מַעֲשֵׂה רֹקֵם, work of the *embroiderer ;* needle-work, Exod. xxvi. 36. Comp. Ib. xxviii. 11. 14. 32; xxx. 25. 35; Num. viii. 4; xxxi. 20, &c. Aff. מַעֲשֵׂהוּ, מַעֲשֵׂינוּ, מַעֲשֶׂךָ, pl. מַעֲשֵׂי, &c.

מַעֲשֵׂר, m. constr. מַעֲשַׂר, pl. f. מַעַשְׂרוֹת, r. עשׂר. *Tithe,* Gen. xiv. 20; Num. xviii. 21. 26; Neh. xii. 44. Phr. הַמַּעֲשֵׂר מִן מַעֲשֵׂר, *tithe of the tithe,* Num. xviii. 26. מַעֲשֵׂר הַמַּעֲשֵׂר, id. Neh. x. 39. שְׁנַת הַמַּעֲשֵׂר, *year of tithing,* Num. xxvi. 12. מַעְשַׂר הָאָרֶץ, *tithe of the land,* Lev. xxvii. 30. Comp. Ib. 32; Num. xviii. 24; Deut. xxiv. 23. 25; Ezek. xlv. 11. 14, &c.; and see Selden's work on Tithes, capp. i. ii.; Hottinger de Decimis Judæorum, Lugdun. Batav. 1713.

מַעֲשַׁקּוֹת, pl. fem. r. עָשַׁק. *Oppressions, exactions,* or, as a pl. of excellence, *great oppression, grievous exaction,* twice, Is. xxxiii. 15; Prov. xxviii. 16.

מֹף, it. נֹף, pr. name. *Memphis,* a city of ancient Egypt, Hos. ix. 6; Is. xix. 13; Jer. ii. 16. The ruins of which are still to be seen on the western shore of the Nile, eastward of Old Kahira. Arab. منف. Plutarch, de Iside et Osiride, says as to its etymology, as quoted by Gesenius, "τὴν μὲν πόλιν Μέμφιν οἱ μὲν ὅρμον ἀγαθῶν ἑρμηνεύουσιν, οἱ δ' ὡς τάφον Ὀσίριδος." On the Coptic derivations, &c. respecting this word—in which, I confess, I can place no faith—see Jablonski Opusc. ed. Water. i. pp. 137. 150. 179; ii. p. 131, &c., as cited by Gesenius.

מִפְגָּע, masc. r. פָּגַע, once, Job vii. 20. *Object of attack,* butt. LXX. κατεντευκτήν. Αλ. ἐναντιοῦσθαι.

מַפָּח, masc. r. נָפַח, once, Job xi. 20, in מַפַּח נֶפֶשׁ, lit. *a puffing of the soul,* which some take to signify *expiring, dying.* To me it rather is the expression of *contempt,* the *being puffed at, despised.* Gesen. compares Jer. xv. 9, נָפְחָה נַפְשָׁהּ; but this is by no means an equivalent expression. Aq. Symm. Theod. LXX. ἀπώλεια. But this may be the sense in either case.

מַפֻּחַ, masc. r. נָפַח, once, Jer. vi. 29. *Bellows* of a smelter, &c.

מֵפִיץ, masc. pl. מְפִיצִים, r. פּוּץ. (a) *Disperser,* Nah. ii. 1; Jer. xxiii. 1. (b) Meton. "*Malleus* bellicus," Gesen. Some warlike instrument, *a balista* perhaps, Prov. xxv. 18. LXX. ῥόπαλον, *a club.* So the Syr.

מְפִיקִים, m. pl. part. Hiph. r. פּוּק.

מַפָּל, masc. plur. constr. מַפְּלֵי, r. נָפַל.—

מַפָּלָה, fem. constr. מַפֶּלֶת.—

מַפֵּלָה, fem.— (a) *Deciduous,* worst of the corn, Amos viii. 6. — *of flesh,* Job xli. 15, the lower and harder parts, *muscles,* perhaps. See my note on the place. LXX. τὰ ἔγκατα. (b) *Fall, ruin,* f. Is. xvii. 1; xxiii. 13; xxv. 2; Ezek. xxvi. 15. 18; xxvii. 27; xxxi. 13. 16; Prov. xxix. 16. (c) Meton. *Carcase* as fallen, ruined, Judg. xiv. 8. Aff. מַפַּלְתְּךָ, מַפַּלְתָּהּ, מַפַּלְתּוֹ.

מִפְלָאוֹת, fem. plur. constr. r. פלא, once, Job xxxvii. 16, synon. τοῦ, נִפְלָאוֹת. *Miracles, wonders.* See my note on the place.

מִפְלַגֹּת, f. pl. once, 2 Chron. xxxv. 12. *Classes, divisions,* r. פָּלַג.

מִפְלָט, masc. once, Ps. lv. 9, r. פָּלַט. *Escape, safety.*

מִפְלֶצֶת, f. in pause, מִפְלָצֶת, pl. non occ. r. פָּלַץ, lit. *feared,* i. e. object of fear. *An idol, image,* 1 Kings xv. 13; 2 Chron. xv. 16, al. non occ. Aff. מִפְלַצְתָּהּ.

מִפְלָשֵׂי, masc. plur. constr. r. פלשׂ. *Poisings, balancings of —,* once, Job xxxvii. 16.

מִפְעָל, m. ⎫ r. פָּעַל, pl. aff. מִפְעָלָיו, Prov.
מִפְעָלָה, f. ⎭ viii. 22. *His works, doings,* fem. plur. מִפְעָלוֹת, *Works,* &c. Ps. xlvi. 9; lxvi. 5.

מַפָּץ, masc. r. נָפַץ. Aff. מַפָּצוֹ. *His breaking down, bruising,* once, Ezek. ix. 2.

מֵפִץ, masc. r. נָפַץ, i. q. מֵפִיץ, apparently, once, Jer. li. 20. *Battle ax,* Auth. Vers. Gesen. *Malleus.*

מִפְקָד, masc.—pl. non occ. r. פָּקַד. (a) *Arrangement, appointment,* 2 Chron. xxxi. 13. (b) *Census,* publicly appointed, 2 Sam. xxiv. 9. Also the pr. name of one of the gates of Jerusalem, Neh. iii. 31, al. non occ.

מִפְרָץ, masc. once, pl. aff. מִפְרָצָיו, Judg. v. 17, r. פָּרַץ. Auth. Vers. *Breaches,* marg.

creeks. From the preceding חוֹף יַמִּים, *the sea-shores,* in some sense or other, must be meant. Gesen. "Arab. فُرْضَة, *sinus fluvii... statio navium.*"

מַפְרֶקֶת, fem. r. פָּרַק. Syr. ܦܘܪܩܐ, *vertebra,* once, 1 Sam. iv. 18. Aff. מַפְרַקְתּוֹ, *The bone,* or *vertebræ, of his neck.* Aquila, τένων. Symm. σπόνδυλον. LXX. νῶτος.

מִפְרָשׂ, m. r. פָּרַשׂ, pl. constr. מִפְרְשֵׂי. (a) *Spreadings, expandings, of* —, Job xxxvi. 29. (b) Meton. sing. *The sail* of a ship, Ezek. xxvii. 7, al. non occ. Aff. מִפְרָשֵׂךְ.

מִפְשָׂעָה, fem. r. פָּשַׂע. Arab. مَفْسُو, *qui dolorem clunium præ se fert.* Syr. ܦܣܥ, *incessit,* once, 1 Chron. xix. 4. *The buttocks.* Comp. שְׁתוֹתֵיהֶם, 2 Sam. x. 4.

מַפְתֵּחַ, m.—pl. non occ. r. פָּתַח. Arab. مِفْتَاح, مَفْتَح, *clavis. A key,* Judg. iii. 25; Is. xxii. 22; 1 Chron. ix. 27. Phr. וְהֵם עַל הַמַּפְתֵּחַ, *and they were over the key;* they had the authority of it, al. non occ.

מִפְתָּח, masc. r. פָּתַח, once, Prov. viii. 6. *Opening* of the lips.

מִפְתָּן, masc. r. פָּתַן, plur. non occ. *The threshold* of a door, gate, house, 1 Sam. v. 4, 5; Ezek. ix. 3; x. 4. 18; Zeph. i. 9, &c.

מֵץ, masc.—pl. non occ. r. מוּץ. Cogn. מָצָה. Syr. ܡܨܝ, *exsuxit.* Participial noun. *One who wrings, presses, out. Oppressor,* once, Is. xvi. 4.

מִיץ, see מוּץ.

מָצָא, v. pres. יִמְצָא. Syr. ܡܛܐ, *advenit, potest;* ܡܛܐ, id. Æth. ООΧ𐌀: *venit.* Arab. مَضَى, r. مضي, *perrexit.* Constr. immed. obj. it. אֶת, it. abs. it. med. בְּ, in. לְ, pers. בְּרֵי, Lev. xxv. 26; כְּ, עַד, מִן, of, any of, Ezra viii. 15. The primary notion seems to be *go, proceed,* or, as in vulgar Engl., *get on :* thence, meton. *obtain, find, &c.*

(a) *Come to, arrive at,* Job xi. 7. (b) *Obtain, acquire,* pers. or thing, Gen. xxvi. 12; 2 Sam. xx. 6; Ezek. iii. 1; Prov. iii. 13; viii. 9. 35; xviii. 22. Frequently with הֵן, Gen. xviii. 3; xxx. 27, &c. ; — Hos. xii. 9; Ruth i. 9. *Vision,* from God, Lam. ii. 9, &c. Of the hand, as the instrument, Lev. xxv. 28; Job xxxi. 25. Abs. 2 Sam. xviii. 22. In a bad sense—*calamity,* i. e. its taking effect, Ps. cxvi. 3; Prov. vi. 33; Hos. xii. 9.

(c) *Find, discover,* pers. or thing, Gen. ii. 20; viii. 9; xi. 2; xviii. 26; 1 Sam. xxix. 3. 6, &c. Phr. תִּמְצָא יָדְךָ, *thy hand shall find,* 1 Sam. x. 7, i. e.—shall be at hand; come in thy way, Ib. xxv. 8; Judg. ix. 33; Eccl. ix. 10. Metaph. of the mind, Eccl. iii. 11; vii. 27; viii. 17. — of solving an enigma, Judg. xiv. 12. *Ability,* as in the Syr. *potest* above, is intimated in these last cases. Comp. Rom. vii. 18.

(d) *Find,* i. e. *meet with, happen to,* Exod. xviii. 8; xxii. 5; Num. xx. 14; xxxii. 23, &c. — of the hand, *prevail,* 1 Sam. xxiii. 17; Is. x. 10; lvii. 10; Ps. xxi. 9; Job xxxi. 25. In Ps. lxxvi. 6, *all the men of might,* i. e. none of — *have prevailed,* (i. e.) *their hands* have not.

(e) Meton. as a consequence of finding, obtaining, *Be sufficient, enough,* Num. xi. 22; Judg. xxi. 14.

Infin. מְצֹא, Ps. xxxii. 6. With לְ, לִמְצֹא, Gen. xix. 11, &c. Aff. מָצְאֵנוּ, Gen. xxxii. 20.

Imper. מְצָא, 1 Sam. xx. 21. Plur. מִצְאוּ, Jer. vi. 16. Fem. מְצֶאןָ, Ruth i. 9.

Part. מוֹצֵא, Ps. cxix. 162. It. מוֹצָא, Eccl. vii. 26. Pl. מֹצְאִים, Num. xv. 33. Aff. מֹצְאִי, &c. Fem. מֹצְאָה, constr. 2 Sam. xviii. 22. Pl. מֹצְאוֹת, Josh. ii. 23.

Niph. נִמְצָא, pres. יִמָּצֵא, constr. abs. it. med. לְ, pers. it. אֶת, בְּ, בְּיַד, עִם, מִן. (a) *Be, become, obtained, acquired,* to, by, any one, Josh. xvii. 16; Jer. xv. 16; Hos. xiv. 9; Job xxviii. 12. (b) *Found, arrived at :* thence (c) *Present, at hand.* (b) Gen. xliv. 16, 17; Exod. xxii. 3; 1 Kings xiv. 13: (c) Gen. xlvii. 14; xix. 15; 1 Chron. xxix. 17; 2 Chron. xxxiv. 32; Ezra viii. 25. — of God, Is. lxv. 1; Jer. xxix. 14; 1 Chron. xxviii. 9. Meton. of words, *Acceptable,* as things sought after, Jer. xv. 16. Comp. 2 Chron. xix. 3; Ps. xlvi. 2. נִמְצָא מְאֹד, *very acceptable,* or, ready to be found.

Infin. הִמָּצֵא, Exod. xxii. 3. Aff. הִמָּצְאוֹ, Is. lv. 6.

Part. נִמְצָא; plur. נִמְצָאִים; pause, נִמְצָאִם. Aff. נִמְצָאָיו, Gen. xlvii. 14; 1 Sam. xiii. 15; Ezra viii. 25; Is. xxii. 3.

מצא

— fem. נִמְצָאָה, pl. נִמְצָאוֹת, 2 Kings xix. 4; Gen. xix. 15.

Hiph. הִמְצִיא, pres. יַמְצִא. *Cause to come, arrive,* i. e. *give, deliver up,* into the hand, power, 2 Sam. iii. 8. — *recompense, repay,* Job xxxiv. 11; xxxvii. 13; Zech. xi. 6. — *present, offer* up, Lev. ix. 12, 13. 18.

Part. מַמְצִיא, Zech. l. c.

מֹצַאֲכֶם, see Infin. above.

מֻצָּב, m. r. נָצַב, cogn. יצב, part. Hoph. once, Is. xxix. 3. Lit. thing set up. Auth. Vers. *A mount.* Gesen. *statio* militum, *præsidium.* Symm. στάσιν. LXX. χάρακα. Arab. مَنْصَبْ, *locus elatus, et ubi quid erectum tenetur.*

מַצָּב, m. ⎫ see מֻצָּב, pl. non occ. (a)
מַצֵּבָה, f. ⎬ *Place of erection, standing,* Josh. iv. 3. 9. (b) Metaph.
מַצָּבָה, f. ⎭ *Station, dignity,* Is. xxii. 19.
(c) *Station* of soldiers, *column* (in a military sense), 1 Sam. xiii. 23; xiv. 1. 4. 6. 11; 2 Sam. xxiii. 14, al. non occ. Aff. מַצָּבְךָ. Fem. 1 Sam. xiv. 12; Zech. ix. 8; i. q. מַצָּב, sign. (c).

מַצֵּבָה, fem. constr. and abs. מַצֶּבֶת, it. מַצֶּבֶת, plur. מַצֵּבוֹת, constr. מַצְּבוֹת; r. נָצַב, cogn. יצב. Sherishi, on the 32 Makamat of Hariri, has the following note, نصب صنم كانوا في الجاهلية ينصبونه ويدعون عليه لأوثانهم, i. e. نصب, *an image which they set up* (נִצְּבוּ) *in the time of ignorance, and over it they prayed to their idols.* This sort of *pillar* seems first to have been erected by Jacob, Gen. xxviii. 18: which seems to have been intended by him as a mere remembrancer of his vow. It there is styled מַצֵּבָה, and he is said to have poured oil upon it. Absalom's *pillar,* מַצֶּבֶת, 2 Sam. xviii. 18, was perhaps the next instance of this sort. And this, we are expressly told, was intended for a memorial. Such *pillars* afterwards became objects of idolatrous worship, and appear still to exist as such in the East. See my Travels of Ibn Batuta, p. 29, note. We are told a little farther on, from Edrisi, that such are worshipped in the Islands of the Indian seas, after oil of fish has been poured upon them. (a) *A pillar* set up as a memorial, Gen. l. c. Exod. xxiv. 4; 2 Sam. xviii. 18. (b) *Image,* or statue, of an idol

מצד

(הַבַּעַל, *of Baal*), 2 Kings iii. 2; x. 26; xviii. 4; xxiii. 14; Mic. v. 12; Hos. x. 1, &c. Forbidden, Deut. xvi. 22, when perhaps first adopted by the Israelites for idolatrous purposes. Aff. מַצְּבוֹתֶיךָ, &c.

מָצָד, masc.—pl. fem. מְצָדוֹת. Primarily, *Place of hunting,* Gesen. Arab. r. صَادَ, *venatus est :* thence *a place of safety.* But comp. cogn. صدّ, *impedivit.* Gesenius, thence, makes it signify "*vertex, cacumen montis;*" which is fanciful and unauthorized. *Fortress, strong place, munition, citadel,* suiting the context much better, 1 Sam. xxiii. 14. 19; 1 Chron. xii. 8. 16; xi. 7; Jer. xlviii. 41; li. 30, &c.

מָצָה, v. pres. apoc. יִמַץ, plur. יִמְצוּ. Cogn. מָצַץ, מָצָה. Arab. مَصَّ, *suxit.* Syr. ܡܨܐ, *exsuxit.* Constr. abs. it. immed. *Suck, drain, wring, out,* Judg. vi. 38; Is. li. 17; Ezek. xxiii. 34; Ps. lxxv. 9, al. non occ.

Niph. נִמְצָה, pres. יִמָּצֶה, *Be, become, sucked, drained, wrung out,* Lev. i. 15; v. 9; Ps. lxxiii. 10, al. non occ.

מַצָּה, fem. plur. מַצּוֹת, r. מָצַץ. *Sweet,* according to Gesenius. Arab. مَصَّ, *suxit.* Syr. ܡܨܝܐ, *exsuccus, extenuatus,* it. Arab. مَصَاص, *sincerus, purus :* thence, I. *Pure,* i. e. *unleavened,* of bread. חַלַּת מַצָּה, *unleavened cake,* Lev. viii. 26; pl. חַלּוֹת מַצּוֹת Num. vi. 15 : and simply, מַצּוֹת, Exod. xii. 15. 18. Phr. חַג מַצּוֹת, *feast of* —, i. e. of the Passover, Exod. xxiii. 15; xxxiv. 18. Opp. τῷ, חָמֵץ, Exod. xii. 39. With לֶחֶם, חַלּוֹת, and רְקִיקֵי, Ib. xxix. 2, where the manner of making them is described, &c. St. Paul evidently alludes to this *unleavened* bread, as if it were intended to shadow out the *sincerity* of those who partook of it, 1 Cor. v. 8, μηδὲ ἐν ζύμῃ κακίας καὶ πονηρίας, ἀλλ' ἐν ἀζύμοις εἰλικρινείας, καὶ ἀληθείας. II. pl. non occ. r. נָצָה. *Contention, quarrel,* Prov. xiii. 10; xvii. 19; Is. lviii. 4, al. non occ. Aquila, Symm. Theod. μαχήν.

מִצְהָלָה, fem. pl. constr. מִצְהֲלוֹת, r. צָהַל. *Neighings,* as of horses, Jer. viii. 16. Aff. מִצְהֲלוֹתֶךָ, Ib. xiii. 27, al. et sing. non occ.

מָצוֹד, m. pl. מְצוֹדִים ⎫ r. צוּד, cogn. צָדַד.
מְצוֹדָה, f. pl. מְצוֹדוֹת ⎬ (a) *Prey* taken in

מצו (385) מצו

the chase, &c. Prov. xii. 12. (b) Meton. מְצוֹדִים, *nets*, for *as nets*, ellip. τοῦ, בְּ, Eccl. vii. 26. (c) i. q. מְצָד, *Fortress, munition, &c.* Is. xxix. 7; Ezek. xix. 9; Eccl. ix. 14. Aff. מְצוֹדָתַהּ, Is. l. c.

מָצוֹד, m. r. צוד. *A hunter's net*, once, Job xix. 6. See my note.

מְצוּדָה, fem. r. id. constr. מְצֻדַת, plur. מְצוּדוֹת. (a) *Prey*, of hunters, &c., Ezek. xiii. 21. (b) *Net* of do., Ezek. xii. 8. (c) i. q. מְצָד, and מְצוּדָה above. *Fortress, munition, &c.*, Job xxxix. 28; 1 Sam. xxii. 4; 2 Sam. v. 7; 1 Chron. xi. 5, &c. Metaph. of God, as a *place of strength, &c.*, Ps. xviii. 3; xxxi. 4; lxxi. 3; xci. 2. Aff. מְצוּדָתִי.

מִצְוָה, f. constr. מִצְוַת, plur. מִצְוֹת, r. צָוָה. *Command, precept*, of man or God, 2 Kings xviii. 36; Prov. vii. 1, 2;—Deut. vi. 1. 25; Josh. xxii. 3; Lev. iv. 27, &c. הַלְוִיִּם —, *respecting the Levites*, Neh. xiii. 5, &c. Aff. מִצְוָתוֹ, מִצְוָתְךָ, &c.

מְצוֹלָה, fem. plur. מְצוֹלוֹת.—
or
מְצוּלָה, fem. plur. מְצוּלוֹת.—
r. צוּל, i. q. צוּלָה. *Depth* of the sea, &c., Exod. xv. 5; Neh. ix. 11; Jonah ii. 4; Mic. vii. 19; Job xli. 22. — of a river, Zech. x. 11. — of mire, Ps. lxix. 3. 16, &c.

מָצוֹק, masc. — plur. non occ. —
מְצוּקָה, fem. plur. מְצוּקוֹת.—
r. צוק. *Restraint, difficulty, trouble*, Ps. cxix. 143; Jer. xix. 9, &c. Fem, Job xv. 24; Zeph. i. 15; Ps. xxv. 17; cvii. 6. 13. 19. 28. Aff. מְצוּקֹתַי, &c.

מָצוּק, m. r. יָצַק, cogn. צוק, *Set up, &c.* (a) *Pillars, supports*, constr. מְצֻקֵי אֶרֶץ, — *of the earth*, 1 Sam. ii. 8: see the following context. (b) *Eminences, projecting parts, as craggs*, of rocks, 1 Sam. xiv. 5. Gesen. "*columna s. rupes prærupta.*"

מָצוֹר, masc. — plur. non occ. —
מְצוּרָה, fem. plur. מְצוּרוֹת.—
r. צוּר. Lit. compression, from being bound about: thence, (a) i. q. מָצוֹק. *Restraint, difficulty*, Deut. xxviii. 53, seq. (b) *Siege*, as being hemmed in, Ezek. iv. 2. 7. Phr. בֹּא בַּמָּצוֹר, *to come into* (the situation of) *siege*, 2 Kings xxiv. 10; xxv. 2, &c. (c) Meton. *Mound*, or *mount*, of besiegers, Deut. xx. 20; Mic. iv. 14. Fem., Is. xxix. 3. (d) *Munition, citadel, &c.*, 2 Chron. xxxii. 10; Hab. ii. 1. Phr. עִיר מָצוֹר, *city bound about*, i. e. with fortification, defence, Ps. xxxi. 22; lx. 11; 2 Chron. viii. 5. So fem., 2 Chron. xi. 11. Phrr. עָרֵי מְצוּרָה, Ib. xiv. 5. עָרֵי מְצוּרוֹת, Ib. xi. 10.

מָצוֹר, masc. i. q. מִצְרַיִם. Arab. مَصَر, a name of *Egypt*, alluding, perhaps, by a sort of play upon words, to its confined and, hence, naturally fortified situation. See the first paragraph in Abdolatiph's Egypt by White; Bochart.'s Phaleg. iv. 24; Diodor. Sic. i. 31. Phr. יְאֹרֵי מָצוֹר, Is. xix. 6; xxxvii. 25; 2 Kings xix. 24;—Mic. vii. 12.

מָצוּת, fem. once, aff. מַצּוּתָךְ, Is. xli. 12, in — אַנְשֵׁי, *men of thy contention, &c.* i. e. who harass thee with contention, i. q. מַצָּה, sign. II. above.

מֵצַח, masc. plur. מִצְחוֹת, r. צחח, perhaps. Arab. صُوح, *mons; murus; vultus arrectus* quasi parieti similis sit. Comp. the passages cited below. *The forehead*, as the seat of impudence, cruelty, &c. מֵצַח אִשָּׁה זוֹנָה, *forehead of a harlot*, Jer. iii. 3. חִזְקֵי־מֵצַח וּקְשֵׁי־לֵב, *unyielding of forehead and hard of heart*, Ezek. iii. 7. מִצְחֲךָ נְחוּשָׁה, *thy forehead is brass*, Is. xlviii. 4; — Exod. xxviii. 38; 1 Sam. xvii. 49; 2 Chron. xxvi. 19, &c. Pl., Ezek. ix. 4. Aff. מִצְחֲךָ, מִצְחוֹ, &c.

מִצְחָה, f. constr. once, 1 Sam. xvii. 6, in מִצְחַת נְחֹשֶׁת, *Guard, greaves, &c. of brass; from the notion of mons or paries, mount or wall*, as noticed above. Fem. of מֵצַח, above. LXX. κνημῖδες χαλκαῖ.

מְצִלָּה, fem. plur. מְצִלּוֹת, dual, מְצִלְתַּיִם (Dagesh om., Gram. art. 113). Syr. ܨܨ, whence ܨܨܝ, *tinnitus acutus*. Arab. صَلَّ, *sonuit cum tinnitu*. Propr. *Ringing instrument*: thence, (a) *Cymbals* (always dual) occ. with other musical instruments, 1 Chron. xiii. 8; xv. 16; Neh. xii. 27; Ezra iii. 10, &c. (b) *Bells* as hung to the necks of horses, Zech. xiv. 20, pl. See also צִלְצַל. Gesenius's מְצִלָּה, is a mere, unnecessary, fiction.

מִצְנֶפֶת, fem.—plur. non occ. r. צָנַף. A sort of *Bonnet* or *mitre*, or rather *turban*, worn by the Jewish chief priest. See Braunius de Vestitu Sacerdot. p. 625, seq. Joseph. Antiq. lib. iii. c. vii. § 3 .... πῖλον ἄκωνον .... καλεῖται μὲν μασναεμφθής. See

3 D

מצע (386) מקב

the rest of this par., and Bell. Jud. lib. v. (vi.) c. v. § 7; Exod. xxviii. 4. 39; xxix. 6, &c. — of a nobleman, Ezek. xxi. 31.

מַצָּע, m.—pl. non occ. r. יָצַע, i. q. יָצוּעַ. *A bed*, or *couch*, once, Is. xxviii. 20.

מִצְעָד, m. pl. constr. מִצְעֲדֵי. Aff. מִצְעָדַי, r. צָעַד. *Steps.* Metaph. *Proceedings*, Ps. xxxvii. 23; Prov. xx. 24;— Dan. xi. 43. בְּמִצְעָדָיו, *in his footsteps*, i. e. attached to his interests. Comp. בְּרַגְלָיו, Judg. iv. 10.

מִצְעִירָה, compd. of מִן+צְעִירָה. *Of a small* sort, kind, Dan. viii. 9.

מִצְעָר, m.—pl. non occ. r. צָעַר. *Little, small*, in size, consideration, Gen. xix. 20; Job viii. 7. — of number, 2 Chron. xxiv. 24. — of time, Is. lxiii. 18. Propr. name of a hill, Ps. xlii. 7.

מִצְפֶּה, m. r. צָפָה, pl. non occ. *Watchplace*, or *tower*, Is. xxi. 8; 2 Chron. xx. 24. Also the pr. name of several towns, Josh. xv. 38, &c.

מַצְפֻּנִים, masc. pl. once, Obad. 6, r. צָפַן. Aff. מַצְפֻּנָיו, *his hidden places*. LXX. τὰ κεκρυμένα αὐτοῦ.

מצץ, v. pres. plur. יָמֹצּוּ, synon. τοῦ, תִּינֹקִי, in the parallel. Arab. مَصَّ, مَزَّ, *suxit.* Cogn. Heb. מָצָה, מָוַץ. Syr. ܥܕܢܓ, *suctio lenis. Suck* as an infant, once, Is. lxvi. 11.

מְצֻקִי, see מָצוּק, above.

מֵצַר, m. plur. מְצָרִים, constr. מְצָרֵי, r. צָרַר. Gesen. as מֵסַב, of סָבַב. Others, cogn. r. צוּר. *Pressure:* thence, *restraint, trouble*, Ps. cxvi. 3; cxviii. 5; Lam. i. 3, al. non occ.

מִצְרַיִם, masc. propr. name of one of the sons of Ham, Gen. x. 5: thence of *Egypt*, probably as named after him: sometimes also styled מָצוֹר. See in its place above. Arab. مِصْر, Syr. ܡܨܪܝܢ. Whence the Patronymic—

מִצְרִי, masc. pl. מִצְרִים ⎫ *Egyptian*, Gen.
מִצְרִית, f. pl. מִצְרִיּוֹת ⎭ xii. 12. 14; xvi. 1; xxxix. 1; Exod. i. 19, &c.

מַצְרֵף, masc.—pl. non occ. r. צָרַף. Lit. *purifying instrument. A crucible*, Prov. xvii. 3; xxvii. 21, al. non occ.

מַק, m.—pl. non occ. r. מָקַק. *Wasting,*

consumption: meton. *Rottenness*, Is. iii. 24; v. 24, al. non occ.

מַקֶּבֶת, fem. plur. מַקָּבוֹת, r. נָקַב. Lit. *Transfixer* or *perforater*: thence, (a) *Hammer*, for driving nails, &c., Judg. vi. 21; 1 Kings vi. 7; Is. xliv. 12; Jer. x. 4. (b) Meton. *Perforation, hole, shaft*, of a well, Is. li. 1, al. non occ.

מִקְדָּשׁ, m. ⎫ pl. מִקְדָּשִׁים, constr. מִקְדְּשֵׁי, or ⎬ r. קָדַשׁ. (a) *Sacred place,*
מִקְדָּשׁ, m. ⎭ *sanctuary;* the *Tabernacle*, or *Temple*, Exod. xxv. 8; Lev. xii. 4; xxi. 12; Num. x. 21; Ezek. xxi. 7; 1 Chron. xxii. 19; 2 Chron. xxix. 21: it. מְקוֹם מִקְדַּשׁ יְהוָֹה, Is. lx. 13: מְכוֹן מִקְדַּשׁ יְהוָֹה, Dan. viii. 11: — מִקְדַּשׁ מֶלֶךְ, — *of* the *king*, as consecrated by him, Amos vii. 13. מִקְדְּשֵׁי בֵית יְהוָֹה, Jer. li. 51, *sacred places of the Temple*. מִקְדְּשֵׁי אֵל, Ps. lxxiii. 17, id. if this last is not a pl. of excellence. מִקְדְּשֵׁי יִשְׂרָאֵל, Amos vii. 9, idolatrous places of worship: see the parallel preceding member. For other usages, see Neh. x. 40; Ezek. xliv. 1; xlv. 4, &c. (b) *Sacred thing, part*, Num. xviii. 29. (c) *An asylum*, as a place of safety, Is. viii. 14; Ezek. xi. 16. Comp. 1 Kings i. 50; ii. 28. Aff. מִקְדָּשׁוֹ, erroneously מִקְדָּשׁוֹ, Num. xviii. 29: מִקְדָּשְׁךָ, &c.

מַקְהֵלִים, pl. m. ⎫ r. קָהַל. *Congregations, assemblies*, Ps.
מַקְהֵלוֹת, plur. f. ⎭ xxvi. 12; lxviii. 27. al. non occ. Fem. also the name of a place, Num. xxxiii. 25.

מִקְוֶה, m. ⎫ r. קָוָה, which see: constr. once ⎬ מִקְוֵה. (a) *Expectation,*
מִקְוָה, f. ⎭ *confidence, hope*, i. q. תִּקְוָה, 1 Chron. xxix. 15; Ezra x. 2. Meton. *Person confided in*, God, Jer. xiv. 8; xvii. 13; L. 7.

(b) *Collection, assemblage* of men, animals, &c., 1 Kings x. 28; 2 Chron. i. 16. מִקְוֵא, — of waters, Gen. i. 10; Exod. vii. 19; Lev. xi. 36. Fem., Is. xxii. 11, al. non occ.

מָקוֹם, masc. constr. מְקוֹם, pl. f. מְקוֹמוֹת, r. קוּם. Lit. place of standing. (a) *Place*, Gen. i. 9; Exod. xxi. 13; Lev. iv. 12, &c. Constr. Gen. xii. 6; xiii. 4. With אֲשֶׁר, Ib. xxxix. 20; xl. 3, &c. Otherwise, Josh. i. 3; Jer. xiii. 7, &c. With זֶה, for אֲשֶׁר, Ps. civ. 8. Also the אֲשֶׁר, om. לֹא (אֲשֶׁר) מְקוֹם, Job xviii. 21, &c. (b) Meton. *Habitation, residence*, Josh. xx. 4; Judg. xviii. 10; 1 Sam. xxvii. 5; 2 Sam. vii. 10; pl., Deut. xii. 2, &c. (c) *Room, space*, Gen. xxiv. 23. 25;

מִקְוּ (387) מִקְנ

1 Sam. xxvi. 13. Comp. Is. v. 8; xxviii. 8; Jer. vii. 32; xix. 11, with negatives. (d) *Place, country, neighbourhood,* of, Gen. xii. 6; xviii. 24, &c. Gesen. "*oppidum, vicus.*" But this the context will not bear. Aff. מְקוֹמוֹ, מְקוֹמָהּ, &c.; pl. מְקוֹמוֹתָם, &c.

מָקוֹר, m. constr. מְקוֹר, plur. non occ. r. קוּר. (a) *Spring, fountain.* Meton. (b) *Origin,* Zech. xiii. 1; Jer. ii. 13; viii. 23; Hos. xiii. 15. Prov. xiii. 14; xiv. 27; xvi. 22; Jer. xvii. 13. In Ps. lxviii. 27, אֲדֹנָי מִמְּקוֹר, ellip. for אֲדֹנָי מִהְיוֹתוֹ מְקוֹר יִשְׂרָאֵל, *Bless the Lord, from His being* (because of His being) *the source, origin, of Israel,* i. e. Israel's adoption as his. (c) *Natura mulieris* per euphemismum, Lev. xii. 7; xx. 18. Meton. of a wife generally, Prov. v. 18. Aff. מְקוֹרָהּ, מְקוֹרְךָ, &c.

מָקָח, m. once, 2 Chron. xix. 7, r. לָקַח. *Receiving, accepting.*

מַקָּחוֹת, f. pl. r. לקח, once, Neh. x. 32. Lit. *acceptable, receivable, things. Goods, merchandise.*

מִקְטָר, m. r. קטר, once, Exod. xxx. 1. *Perfume, incense.*

מִקְטֶרֶת, f. r. קטר. *A censer,* 2 Chron. xxvi. 19; Ezek. viii. 11. Aff. מִקְטַרְתּוֹ.

מַקֵּל, m. id. constr. and מַקֵּל, pl. f. מַקְלוֹת. Arab. cogn. بَقَلَ, *prodiit; herbascere cœpit* terra; بَقَّلَ, *rexit, imperavit.* Æthiopic ⵐⴻⵑ : *planta;* v. ⵀⵁⵑ : *punivit.* Whence *the walking staff,* and, eventually, *the mace,* became a symbol of authority. (a) *Shoot, twig,* Gen. xxx. 37—39. 41; Jer. i. 11. (b) *Walking staff,* Gen. xxxii. 11; 1 Sam. xvii. 40; Zech. xi. 10. 14, &c. (c) *Mace,* instr. of authority, Jer. xlviii. 17. — or *punishment,* Ezek. xxxix. 9; Num. xxii. 27. — of prediction, by *Rabdomantia,* 'Ραβδομαντεία, Hos. iv. 12. With aff. the Dagesh mostly omitted. מַקְלִי; but מַקֶלְכֶם, Exod. xii. 11.

מִקְלָט, m. r. קלט. Arab. قَلْطٌ, *securitas. Place of security, safety, refuge.* עִיר —, or הַמִּקְלָט, or עָרֵי מִקְלָט, *city, or cities, of safety, refuge,* Josh. xxi. 13; Num. xxxv. 11. 13, 14; xxxviii. 6, &c. It. הֶעָרִים לְמִקְלָט, *the cities for security,* Num. xxxv. 12. 15. Comp. Josh. xx. 3. Aff. מִקְלָטוֹ.

מְקַלְלוֹנִי, Jer. xv. 10, for מְקַלְלַוְנִי.

מִקְלַעַת, fem. constr. pl. מִקְלְעוֹת, constr. מִקְלְעוֹת, r. קלע. *Carving, sculpture,* 1 Kings vi. 18; vii. 31; vi. 29. 32, al. non occ.

מִקְנֶה, m. constr. מִקְנֵה, pl. aff. מִקְנֵךְ, &c. r. קנה. Lit. *acquirement:* thence, *Possession, wealth,* as of land, flocks, cattle, Gen. xlix. 32; iv. 20; Deut. iii. 19, &c. Phrr. אַנְשֵׁי מִקְנֶה, *men of cattle,* i. e. having them, Gen. xlvi. 32. שָׂרֵי מִקְנֶה, *chiefs of* —, Ib. xlvii. 6. מְקוֹם מִקְנֶה, *place* —, i. e. *pasture,* Num. xxxii. 1. אֶרֶץ מִקְנֶה, id., Ib. 4. — אֹהֳלֵי, *tents of* —, 2 Chron. xiv. 14. מִקְנֶה וְקִנְיָן, *cattle and wealth,* Ezek. xxviii. 12. צֹאן וּבָקָר, מִקְנֶה כָּבֵד, *flock and cattle, weighty,* i. e. much, *wealth,* Exod. xii. 38. Comp. Gen. xiii. 2. 7; xxvi. 14, &c. Aff. מִקְנִי, מִקְנֶךָ, מִקְנֵנוּ, &c.

מִקְנָה, fem. constr. מִקְנַת, f. of מִקְנֶה, plur. non occ. *Acquirement, purchase, possession.* מִקְנַת־כֶּסֶף, *purchase of silver,* i. e. with silver, Gen. xvii. 12, 13. 23. 27. סֵפֶר הַמִּקְנָה, *book, deed, of purchase,* Jer. xxxii. 11, 12, seq.; Gen. xxiii. 18; Lev. xxv. 16. 51; xxvii. 22. Aff. מִקְנָתוֹ.

מִקְסָם, masc. twice only, Ezek. xii. 24; xiii. 7; r. קסם. *Divination.*

מִקְצוֹעַ, מִקְצֹעַ, m. pl. constr. מִקְצוֹעֵי, it. f. מִקְצֹעוֹת, r. קצע. *Corner, angle,* of any thing, Exod. xxvi. 24; xxxvi. 29; Neh. iii. 19, 20. 24, 25. Aff. מִקְצוֹעֹתָיו, Ezek. xli. 22.

מַקְצֻעוֹת, f. pl. r. קצע. *Carving tools,* once, Is. xliv. 13. Auth. Vers. *Planes.*

מִקְצָת, m. (for מִקְצָה, of מִן קָצֶה, according to Gesen.) r. קצה. But it may be a Heemanti noun, like the Arab. مَقْصَة, *extrema auris parte* mutilus camelus. *Part, limit,* Dan. i. 2. 5. 15; Neh. vii. 70. Aff. מִקְצָתָם.

מָקַק, v. Kal non occ. Cogn. מוּךְ, מָכַךְ, מוּג. Arab. مَقَّ, cogn. viii. *exhausit* omne quod in ubere erat. Cogn. مَقَا, مَقَو, *vehementer suxit.* Comp. مَقِي. Cogn. Lat. *maceo, macer.* Niph. pl. נָמֵקִי, נְמַקֹּתֶם, pres. הִפָּמֵק, pl. יִמַּקּוּ, constr. abs. it. med. בְּ. *Waste away, consume, fail,* Lev. xxvi. 39; Is. xxxiv. 4; Ezek. xxiv. 23; Zech. xiv. 12; Psalm xxxviii. 6. Part. pl. m. נְמַקִּים, Ezek. xxxiii. 10. Hiph. הָמֵק. Infin. abs., Zech. xiv. 12, only. *Making, causing, to waste.*

מִקְרָא, m. pl. constr. מִקְרָאֵי, aff. מִקְרָאֶהָ,

מִקְרָ (388) מֹר

Is. iv. 5, r. קָרָא. Lit. *act*, or *place*, of calling, or reading. (a) *Act of calling, assembling*, together, Num. x. 2. Comp. Is. i. 13. (b) Meton. *Convocation, congregation*, with קֹדֶשׁ, generally, Exod. xii. 16; Lev. xxiii. 2—4. 7, 8. 37, &c. (c) *Reading, reciting*, Neh. viii. 8.

מִקְרֶה, m. constr. מִקְרֵה, aff. מִקְרֵהוּ, r. קָרָה, (a) *Accident*, Deut. xxiii. 11; 1 Sam. vi. 9; xx. 26; Ruth ii. 3. (b) *Event, result*, Eccl. ii. 14, 15; iii. 19; ix. 2, 3.

מְקָרֶה, masc. once, Eccl. x. 18, r. קָרָה. Part. Pih. Lit. *frame, frame-work*. Hence, *Building, edifice*.

מְקֵרָה, fem. twice only, Judg. iii. 20. 24, r. קָרַר. Syr. ܩܰܪ, *frigescere*. Arab. قَرَّ, *friguit dies*; مَقْرُور, *frigore affectus*. *Coolness, refreshing*. LXX. θερινός.

מַחְשָׂה, m. } r. קָשָׂה, plur. non occ.—
מִקְשָׁה, f. } masc. once, Is. iii. 24, opp. τῷ, קָרְחָה. *Wreathing, platting*, of the hair. Arab. قَشَّ, *opere tornatili elaboravit*. Fem. (a) *Embossing; working in relief*, a sort of chequered work, apparently, having the appearance of platted hair: so Jer. x. 5. כְּתֹמֶר מִקְשָׁה הֵמָּה, *as the palm tree* (are) *they a chequered work*, i. e. so carved as to appear like the bark of the palm. Of the candlestick, cherubim, &c., Exod. xxv. 18. 31; xxxvii. 17. 22; Num. viii. 4; x. 2. Phr. מִקְשָׁה אַחַת, *one* (sort of) *wreathed work*, Exod. xxv. 36. Aquila, ἐξημυγδαλωμένη. Symm. ἐκτετορνευμένη. LXX. τορευτή. How lathe-work could be applied to several of these things it is not very easy to see.

(b) *A cucumber*. Arab. مَقْثَاة. Meton. *Place of, garden of* —, once, Is. i. 8.

מַר, masc. plur. מָרִים, constr. מָרֵי.—
מָרָה, fem. constr. מָרַת, plur. non occ.— r. מוּר. (a) *A drop*, once, Is. xl. 15. כְּמַר מִדְּלִי. LXX. ὡς σταγὼν ἀπὸ κάδου. Arab. مَرْمَر, *pluvia*. (b) Arab. مَرَّ, *amara fuit* res. Syr. ܡܰܪ, *amarum fecit*; *exacerbavit*. *Bitter*,—and hence, meton. *Bitterness*,—of mind, &c., 1 Sam. xv. 32; xxii. 2. מַר נֶפֶשׁ, *bitter*, sorrowful, *of soul*. Comp. Judg. xviii. 25; 2 Sam. xvii. 8; Ps.

lxiv. 4. דָּבָר מַר, *a bitter matter*, i. e. afflicting. Opp. τῷ, מָתוֹק, Prov. xxvii. 7. — *of a cry*, Gen. xxvii. 34; Esth. iv. 1; Ezek. xxvii. 31; Zeph. i. 14. — *lamentation*. Metaph. Is. v. 20; Jer. iv. 18. Season of —, יוֹם מָר, Amos viii. 10. — *of waters* bringing the curse, מֵי הַמָּרִים, Num. v. 18, 19. 23, 24. 27. Adv., Is. xxxiii. 7, מַר יִבְכָּיֻן, *bitterly shall they weep*.

Fem. מָרָה, once, מָרָא, Ruth i. 20. Phr. מָרָה נֶפֶשׁ, and מָרַת נֶפֶשׁ, 1 Sam. xxx. 6; 2 Sam. iv. 27; 1 Sam. i. 10. בְּנֶפֶשׁ מָרָה, *in bitterness of soul*, Job xxi. 25. Comp. 2 Sam. ii. 26.

מֹר, and מוֹר, m. with Makkaph. מָר־, pl. non occ. Arab. مُرّ. Gr. μύρρα. *Myrrh*, used as a perfume, &c., Exod. xxx. 23; Ps. xlv. 9; Prov. vii. 17; Cant. iii. 6; iv. 14, &c. "A kind of gum resin, issuing by incision, and sometimes spontaneously, from the trunk and larger branches of a tree growing in Arabia, Egypt, and especially in Abyssinia." "The trees producing myrrh grow on the eastern coast of Arabia Felix, and in that part of Abyssinia which is situated near the Red Sea, and called, by Mr. Bruce, Troglodyte." Rees's Cyclopedia, sub voce. See also Celsius Hierobot i., p. 520, seq., who makes the מָר־דְּרוֹר, of Exod. xxx. 23, i. q. Arab. مر درور, *murru dserori*; the latter word of which he renders by "*pulvis aromaticus*," and adds, "Videtur Moses hunc pulverem innuere, sive Myrrham in pollinem redactam," &c. See also Dioscorides, i. c. 77, 78. Diodor. Sic. v. 41. Theophrastus, lib. ix. 4. Plin. lib. xii. 15, &c. as there cited.

מָרָא, v. Kal non occ. Cogn. מָרָה. Syr. ܡܪܐ, *morosus se opposuit*. Arab. مَرَأَ, *fortis fuit*; تَمَرَّأَ, *fortitudinem præ se tulit*. See my note on Job xxxix. 18.

Part. מוֹרָאָה, fem. *Rebellious*, Zeph. iii. 1, only, and Job l. c.

Hiph. תַּמְרִיא, *she puts forth her courage*, from provocation. LXX. ἐν ὕψει ὑψώσει. Symm. πετομένη. Once, Job l. c.

מָרָא, masc.—pl. non occ. Syr. ܡܳܪܳܐ, *dominus*. See מרא above. Chald. *Lord*, Dan. ii. 47; iv. 16. 21: v. 23. Aff. מָרַאי.

מַרְאֶה, masc. constr. מַרְאֵה, plur. constr. מַרְאֵי, r. רָאָה. Lit. *thing seen*: hence, (a) *Sight, appearance, vision*, Exod. iii. 3; Ezek.

viii. 4; xi. 24; xliii. 3. Phr. יְפַת־מַרְאֶה, *beautiful of appearance, form,* Gen. xii. 11. טוֹבַת מַרְאֶה, *good of* —, Ib. xxiv. 16; xxvi. 7. נֶחְמָד לְמַרְאֶה, *desirable to the sight,* Ib. ii. 9. כְּמַרְאֵה אָדָם, *as the appearance,* similitude, *of a man,* Dan. x. 18. דְּמוּת כְּמַרְאֵה־אֵשׁ, *a similitude as the likeness of fire,* Ezek. viii. 2. Comp. Ib. i. 26. (b) *View, sight,* מַרְאֵה עֵינֵי הַכֹּהֵן, *view of the eyes of the priest,* Lev. xiii. 12. Comp. Deut. xxviii. 34; Is. xi. 3; Ezek. xxiii. 16; Eccl. xi. 9, &c. Aff. מַרְאֵהוּ, מַרְאָהּ, מַרְאֵינוּ, מַרְאֶיךָ, מַרְאָיו, מַרְאֵיהֶם, מַרְאֵיהֶן. Gesenius doubts of any of these being plurals, certainly without any substantial reason.

מַרְאָה, f. of the preceding pl. מַרְאוֹת. (a) *Vision,* as seen by a Seer, &c., Num. xii. 6; 1 Sam. iii. 15; Dan. x. 7, 8. 16. Phr. מַרְאוֹת הָאֱלֹהִים, Ezek. i. 1 : מַרְאֹת הַלַּיְלָה, Gen. xlvi. 2. (b) *Mirror, looking-glass,* Exod. xxxviii. 8. Arab. مِرْآة, *speculum.*

מֻרְאָה, f. Aff. מֻרְאָתוֹ, once, Lev. i. 16. *Its crop,* r. מרא. Arab. مَرِيّ, *Æsophagus.* LXX. τὸν πρόλοβον. Aq. τὴν σιτίζουσαν. Symm. and Theod. τὴν φύσαν. Syr. ܡܘܙܦܚܢܐ.

מְרַאֲשׁוֹת, plur. fem. r. ראש. Lit. *head-places,* or *things:* thence, *At the head.* מְרַאֲשֹׁתָיו, *at his head,* Gen. xxviii. 11. 18; 1 Sam. xix. 13. 16; xxvi. 7. 11. 16; 1 Kings xix. 6. מְרַאֲשֹׁתַי, *from (being) at the head of,* 1 Sam. xxvi. 12. מְרַאֲשׁוֹתֵיכֶם, *the ornaments of your heads,* Jer. xiii. 18. LXX. ἀπὸ κεφαλῆς ὑμῶν. So Syr. and Vulg. Castell, *principatus.*

מַרְבַדִּים, masc. plur. r. רבד. *Coverlets, ornamental coverlets,* Prov. vii. 16; xxxi. 22. LXX. κειρίαις, χλαίνας. Aq. and Theod. περιστρώματα.

מִרְבָּה, f. once, Ezek. xxiii. 32, r. רבה. *Greatness, abundance; much, too much.*

מַרְבֵּה, masc. constr. מַרְבֵּה. *Greatness, extent, abundance,* Is. ix. 6; xxxiii. 23.

מַרְבִּית, fem. (a) *Id.* (b) *Increase, interest.* Arab. رِبًا. Syr. ܪܶܒܝܳܐ, *Id.* (c) *Offspring.* (a) 2 Chron. ix. 6; xxx. 18; מַרְבִּיתָם, 1 Chron. xii. 29. (b) Lev. xxv. 37. (c) 1 Sam. ii. 33.

מַרְבֵּץ, masc. constr. מִרְבַּץ, r. רבץ. *A resting-place* for cattle or wild beasts, Ezek. xxv. 5; Zeph. ii. 15.

מַרְבֵּק, r. רבק. Arab. رَبَقَ, *ligavit, constrinxit; inseruit* caput ejus in laqueum. A place where cattle are tied up to fatten, *A stall,* 1 Sam. xxviii. 24; Jer. xlvi. 21; Amos vi. 4; Mal. iii. 20.

מַרְגּוֹעַ, once, Jer. vi. 16, r. רגע. *Rest, quiet.* LXX. ἁγνισμόν. Syr. ܢܝܳܚܐ.

מַרְגְּלוֹת, pl. f. Aff. מַרְגְּלֹתָיו, r. רגל, *At the feet, any thing at the feet,* Ruth iii. 4. 7, 8. 14; Dan. x. 6. Comp. מראשות above.

מַרְגֵּמָה, f. once, Prov. xxvi. 8, r. רגם. *A heap of stones.* Syr. ܟܡܐܟܠܐ. LXX. ἐν σφενδόνῃ. Vulg. *acervum Mercurii.*

מַרְגֵּעָה, fem. once, Is. xxviii. 12, r. רגע. *Rest, quiet.* LXX. τὸ σύντριμμα. Aq. ἡ ἀνάψυξις. Sym. ἡ ἐρημία. Theod. ὁ ἀγνός. Vulg. *refrigerium.* Syr. ܡܕܟܐ.

מָרַד, v. pres. יִמְרֹד. Syr. ܡܪܰܕ, *rebellis fuit, descivit.* Arab. مَرَدَ and مَرُدَ, *andax et constans fuit in rebellione.* Cogn. מרה. Constr. abs. immed. it. med. בְּ, עַל. *Rebelled,* Num. xiv. 9; Josh. xxii. 18, 19, &c. Part. מֹרְדִים, Neh. ii. 19; Ezek. ii. 3; Job xxiv. 13. Inf. מְרוֹד, Josh. xxii. 29; Neh. vi. 6. מָרְדְּכֶם, Josh. xxii. 16.

מֶרֶד, masc. abstr. *Rebellion,* Josh. xxii. 22.

מְרַד, Chald. m. *Id.* Ezra iv. 19.

מְרַד, Chald. fem. מַרְדָּא, with art. מַרְדְּתָּא. *Rebellious,* Ezra iv. 12. 15.

מַרְדּוּת, f. i. q. מָרָד, 1 Sam. xx. 30.

מָרָה, v. pres. non occ. Arab. مَرَى, *denegavit* quod deberet. III. *Contendit disputando* contra alium. Syr. ܡܰܪ, *amarum fuit.* Cogn. מור, and Arab. مَرَّ, *amarus fuit* de re. II. *Amarum fecit.* III. *Luctatus fuit alteri. Rebelled, rebelled against, disobeyed.* Constr. abs. immed. it. med. בְּ, אֵת, 1 Kings xiii. 21. 26; Num. xx. 24, &c. Part. מֹרֶה, pl. מֹרִים. *Rebelling, rebellious,* Deut. xxi. 18. 20; Ps. lxxviii. 8, &c. Infin. מְרוֹ, Lam. i. 20. Hiph. i. q. Kal, also. *Embittered, angered.* Prct. הֵמְרוּ, Ps. cvi. 33; cvii. 11.

מרה (390) מרו

Pres. יָמֶר, apocop. תֶּמֶר, תַּמֶר, Exod. xxiii. 21; Josh. i. 18, &c.
Part. plur. מַמְרִים, constr. עִם, Deut. ix. 7. 24; xxxi. 27.
Infin. constr. הַמְרוֹת, Ps. lxxviii. 17; Is. iii. 8; Job xvii. 2, according to some copies.

מרה, fem. dual, מְרָתַיִם, Jer. l. 21. According to some, *two-fold rebellion*; taking the words מְרָתַיִם הָאָרֶץ to signify *Babylon*. The LXX. join the words עַל הָאָרֶץ to the preceding verse, and translate מְרָתַיִם עֲלֵה עָלֶיהָ, πικρῶς ἐπίβηθι ἐπ' αὐτήν. The Vulg. translates הָאָרֶץ מְרָתַיִם, *terram dominantium*; the Syr. ܐܢܚܬ ܥܠ ܥܡܕܢ ܐܪܥܐ.

מרה, fem. constr. מָרַת. *Bitterness, vexation, sorrow*, Prov. xiv. 10.

מרה, fem. constr. מֹרַת. *Id.*, Gen. xxvi. 35.

מרוד, plur. מְרוּדִים. Æth. ⲘⲢⲆ: *persequi, insurgere* contra aliquem; ⲘⲢⲆ: *persecutio. Persecuted*, Is. lviii. 7. LXX. ἀστέγους. Vulg. *vagos*. Syr. ܡܪܘܕܐ. מְרוּדִי, *my being persecuted*, Lam. iii. 19. LXX. ἐκ διωγμοῦ μου. Vulg. *transgressionis meæ*. Syr. ܥܨܝܘܬܝ. יְמֵי מְרוּדֶיהָ, *the days of her persecuted ones*, or *of her being persecuted*, Lam. i. 7. LXX. ἀπωσμῶν αὐτῆς. Vulg. *prævaricationis*. Syr. ܥܨܝܢܗ.

מרוח, constr. מְרוֹחַ, once, Lev. xxi. 20. מְרוֹחַ אָשֶׁךְ, *having crushed testicles*, being made an eunuch in this way. LXX. μονόρχις. Syr. *Id.*

מָרוֹם, m. constr. מְרוֹם, pl. מְרוֹמִים, constr. מְרוֹמֵי. Aff. מְרוֹמָיו, r. רום. (a) *High, exalted*. (b) *A high place, exalted situation*. (c) *On high*. (d) *Height, grandeur*. (e) *Haughtiness*. (f) and adv. *Haughtily*. (a) Jer. xvii. 12; Ps. xcii. 9. (b) Is. xxvi. 5; xxxiii. 5, &c. (c) 2 Kings xix. 29; Ps. x. 5; Is. xxii. 16; xxxvii. 33; xl. 25. (d) Ps. lxxi. 19; Mic. vi. 6, &c. (e) Is. xxiv. 4. (f) Ps. lvi. 3. בַּמָרוֹם, *highly, greatly*, Job xxxix. 18; Ps. xciii. 4. לַמָרוֹם, *upwards, on high*, Ps. lxviii. 19. מִמָּרוֹם, *from on high, from above*, 2 Sam. xxii. 17; *contemptuously*, Ps. lxxiii. 8.

מָרוֹץ, r. רוץ. *A race*, Eccl. ix. 11.

מְרוּצָה, (a) r. רוץ, constr. מְרוּצַת. Aff. מְרוּצָתָם, *Their manner of running*. (b) *Course of life*. (c) r. רצץ, *Oppression*. (a) 2 Sam. xviii. 27. (b) Jer. viii. 6; xxiii. 10. (c) Jer. xxii. 17.

מְרוּקִים. Aff. מְרוּקֵיהֶן, r. מרק. *Purification*, Esth. ii. 12.

מִרְזֵחַ, constr. מִרְזַח. Arab. مَرْزَحٌ, *vox*. (a) *Lamentation*, Jer. xvi. 5. (b) according to some, *cry of merriment*, Amos vi. 7. מִרְזַח סְרוּחִים. LXX. χρεμετισμὸς ἵππων. Sym. ἑταιρεία τρυφητῶν. Vulg. *factio lascivientium*. Syr. ܒܝܬ ܫܡܚܐ ܕܢܗܘܐ.

מרה, v. once, Is. xxxviii. 21. Pres. pl. יָמְרְחוּ. *Let them soften and apply* to the diseased part. Cogn. מרק, משח. Arab. مَرَخَ, II. *mundavit frumentum scopio*; *unxit cutem oleo*; مَرْخَ, *apotheca in quâ uvas passas condunt*; مَرَخَ, *inunxit et emollivit corpus oleo*. IV. *Emollivit copiosiore aquâ, atque extenuavit massam*; مَرْخَ, *dactylus immaturus*; مَرَسَ, *abstersit manum*. V. *Se affricuit rei*; مَرَشَ, *maceravit, subegitque; fricuit extremis digitis membrum*. LXX. τρίψον καὶ κατάπλασαι. Vulg. *cataplasmarent*. Syr. ܢܡܫܚܘܢ.

מֶרְחָב, m. r. רחב, pl. contr. מֶרְחֲבֵי. Lit. *Wide places of* —, i. e. abundant room, the freedom of prosperity as opposed to the restraint of adversity. Comp. Arab. مَرْحَبًا ومَسْهَلًا, *amplo et commodo fruaris loco*, 2 Sam. xxii. 20; Ps. xviii. 20; xxxi. 9; cviii. 5; Hos. iv. 16; Hab. i. 6.

מֶרְחָק, pl. מֶרְחַקִּים, constr. מֶרְחַקֵי, r. רחק. *Distance*. אֶרֶץ מֶרְחָק, *a distant land*, Prov. xxv. 25; Is. xiii. 5; xlvi. 11; Jer. vi. 20. אֶרֶץ הַפֻּרְחָק, *Id.* Jer. iv. 16. יַרְכְּתֵי אֶרֶץ, *the distant parts of the earth*, Is. viii. 9. מֶרְחָק, *Id.* Zech. x. 9. מִמֶּרְחָק, (a) *from a distance, from afar*. (b) *At a distance*. (a) Ps. cxxxviii. 6; Prov. xxxi. 14, &c. (b) Jer. xxxi. 10. נָס מִמֶּרְחָק, *he began to flee while at a distance*, Is. xvii. 13.

מֶרְחַקִּים, r. רחק. *Those who are at a distance*, Is. xxxiii. 17; Jer. viii. 19.

מַרְחֶשֶׁת, r. רחש. Arab. رَخَشَ, *motus*,

מרט, *agitatio*; تَرْخَش, *motus fuit.* VIII. *Commotus fuit, vacillavit*; رَخَض, *lavit*; مِرْحَضَة, *vas, in quo lavatur. A pot for boiling,* Lev. ii. 7; vii. 9. LXX. ἐσχάρας.

מרט, v. constr. immed. Arab. مَرَتَ, *glabrum reddidit;* مَرَط, *evulsit è corpore pilos; festinavit.* III. *Evulsit capillos et unguibus vulneravit.* IV. *Delapsis immaturis dactylis nudata fuit* palma. V. *Excidit, defluxit,* de pilis. Syr. ܡܪܛ, *evulsit pilos.* Sam. ᛃᚹᛋ, *Id.* Æth. ОО𐩦: *raptim profectus est, maturavit iter. Plucked out hair:* hence, *made smooth,* as the head or chin after the hair is plucked; *polished.* וָאֶמְרְטָה מִשְּׂעַר רֹאשִׁי, *so I pluck out some of the hair of my head,* in sorrow, Ezra ix. 3. וָאֶמְרְטֵם, *so I plucked the hair of their head,* in reproof, Neh. xiii. 25.

Part. abs. מֹרְטִים, *those who plucked my hair,* in contempt, Is. L. 6.

Part. pass. f. מְרוּטָה, *Polished,* applied to a sword, Ezek. xxi. 14. 33. *Rubbed bare,* applied to the shoulder, Ezek. xxix. 18.

Infin. מָרְטָה, Ezek. xxi. 16.

Niph. pres. יִמָּרֵט, *Becomes bald,* Lev. xiii. 40, 41.

Puh. part. מֹרָט, *Polished,* 1 Kings vii. 45.

— F. מֹרְטָה, *Id.* Ezek. xxi. 15, 16.

מרט, Chald. *Id.* Pih. מְרִיטוּ, *Were plucked,* Dan. vii. 4.

מְרִי, and מֶרִי. Aff. מֶרְיָם, מֶרְיָךְ. (a) r. מור, *Bitterness.* (b) r. מרה, *Rebellion.* (c) *Rebellious.* (a) Job xiii. 2. (b) Prov. xvii. 11; Is. xxx. 9; 1 Sam. xv. 23; Deut. xxxi. 27; Neh. ix. 17. (c) Ezek. ii. 7, 8; xliv. 6. בֵּית מְרִי, *a rebellious family,* Ezek. ii. 5, 6; iii. 9. 26, 27; xii. 3. בֵּית הַמְּרִי, *Id.* Ezek. ii. 8; xii. 2. 9; xvii. 12; xxiv. 3. בְּנֵי מֶרִי, *rebellious,* Num. xvii. 25.

מְרִיא, plur. מְרִיאִים, constr. מְרִיאֵי. Aff. מְרִיאֲכֶם, r. מרא. (a) *Fattened.* (b) pec. *A fatted calf.* (a) Ezek. xxxix. 18. (b) 2 Sam. vi. 13; 1 Kings i. 9. 19. 25; Is. i. 11; xi 6; Amos v. 22.

מְרִיבָה, r. ריב, const. מְרִיבַת, plur. מְרִיבוֹת. *Strife, contention,* Gen. xiii. 8; Num. xxvii. 14, &c.

מְרִירוּת, f. r. מור. *Bitter sorrow,* Ezek. xxi. 11.

מְרִירִי, r. מור. *Bitter,* applied to destruction, Deut. xxxii. 24.

מֹרֶךְ, r. רכך. *Softness, cowardice,* Lev. xxvi. 36.

מֶרְכָּב, r. רכב. Aff. מֶרְכָּבוֹ. (a) *Any thing to sit on while riding,* Lev. xv. 9. (b) *Chariots,* collectively, 1 Kings v. 6.

מֶרְכָּבָה, fem. constr. מִרְכֶּבֶת, aff. מֶרְכַּבְתּוֹ, pl. מַרְכָּבוֹת, constr. מַרְכְּבוֹת. Aff. מַרְכְּבֹתָיו, תִּיהֶם. *A chariot,* 2 Sam. xv. 1; 1 Kings x. 29, &c.

מַרְכֹּלֶת, once, aff. מַרְכֻלְתֵּךְ. *Thy merchandize,* Ezek. xxvii. 24 : r. רכל.

מִרְמָה, fem. pl. מִרְמוֹת, r. רמה. *Deceit, artifice,* 2 Kings ix. 23; Job xv. 35, &c. — אַבְנֵי, *deceitful weights,* Mic. vi. 11. — אִישׁ, *a* — *man,* Ps. xliii. 1; v. 7; lv. 24. — לָשׁוֹן, — *tongue,* Ps. lii. 6. — מֹאזְנֵי — *balance,* Prov. xi. 1; xx. 23; Hos. xii. 8; Amos viii. 5. — פִּי, — *mouth,* Ps. cix. 2. — שִׂפְתֵי, — *lips,* Ps. xvii. 1.

מִרְמָס, r. רמס. *Trampling under foot, a thing trampled under foot,* Is. x. 6; v. 5; vii. 25; xxviii. 18; Ezek. xxxiv. 19; Dan. viii. 13; Mic. vii. 10.

מֵרֵעַ, m. Aff. מֵרֵעֵהוּ. (a) *Friends or companions* collectively, with a plural verb. (b) *A friend or companion.* (a) 2 Sam. iii. 8; Prov. xix. 7. (b) Judg. xiv. 20; xv. 2. 6. Pl. מֵרֵעִים, Jud. xiv. 11.

מִרְעֶה, masc. r. רעה, constr. מִרְעֵה. Aff. מִרְעֵהוּ, מִרְעֲכֶם. *Pasture,* Gen. xlvii. 4; 1 Chron. iv. 39—41, &c.

מַרְעִית, fem. r. רעה. Aff. מַרְעִיתִי, -ךָ, -תוֹ, -תָם. (a) *The act of pasturing cattle.* (b) *Act of feeding,* applied to cattle. (c) *A flock.* (a) Jer. xxiii. 1; Ezek. xxxiv. 31; Ps. lxxiv. 1; lxxix. 13; xcv. 7; Is. xlix. 9. (b) Hos. xiii. 6. (c) Jer. x. 21; xxv. 36.

מַרְפֵּא, masc. r. רפא. (a) *A remedy for* disease, mischief, or calamity. (b) Meton. *Healing.* (c) *Soundness.* (d) r. רפה, *The act of giving way, yielding.* (a) Prov. iv. 22; vi. 15, &c. (b) Jer. xiv. 19; Mal. iii. 20. (c) Prov. xiv. 30; xv. 4. (d) Eccl. x. 4.

מַרְפֵּה, *Id.* Jer. viii. 15.

מִרְפָּשׂ, r. רפש. *What has been trampled*

מרץ (392) מרד

on; *water rendered turbid by trampling*, Ezek. xxxiv. 19.

מרץ, v. Kal non occ. Arab. مَرِضَ, *ægestus fuit.* IV. *In morbum conjecit: prope accessit ad rectam rationem et sententiam;* مَرَضٌ, *morbus, tam animi quam corporis. Being diseased* in body or mind.

Niph. pret. נִמְרְצוּ. *Have become, or been considered, unsound or weak*, Job vi. 25. LXX. ὡς ἔοικε φαῦλα ἀληθινοῦ ῥήματα! See my notes on the place.

Part. נִמְרָץ, f. נִמְרֶצֶת, חֹלֶה נִמְרָץ, *A diseased, polluted, portion*, Mic. ii. 10. קְלָלָה נִמְרֶצֶת, *a foul curse*, 1 Kings ii. 8. LXX. κατάραν ὀδυνηράν.

Hiph. pres. מַה־יַּמְרִיצְךָ, *What urges thee to folly, that thou answerest me?* Job xvi. 3. See notes. LXX. τί παρενοχλήσει σοι ὅτι ἀποκρίνῃ.

מַרְצֵעַ, r. רצע. *An awl* or other *instrument for boring a small hole*, Exod. xxi. 6; Deut. xv. 17.

מַרְצֶפֶת, r. רצף. *A layer* of stones formed as a basis for the brazen sea, 2 Kings xvi. 17.

מָרָק, once. Arab. مَرَقٌ, *jusculum. Broth*, Jud. vi. 19, 20.

מרק, v. Syr. ܡܪܰܩ, aph. *lavit, abstersit;* ܡܶܪܩܳܐ, *detersio, expolitio. Made clean and bright by rubbing.*

Imper. מְרִיקוּ, Jer. xlvi. 4.

Part. pass. מָרוּק, *Polished*, 2 Chr. iv. 16.

Puh. מֹרַק, Lev. vi. 21.

מֶרְקָחָה, fem. r. רקח. (a) *A pot of ointment*, Job xli. 23. (b) *Spices* added to flesh, in order to improve its flavour, Ezek. xxiv. 10.

מֶרְקָחִים, *Perfumes*, Cant. v. 13.

מִרְקַחַת, *Perfumery*, Exod. xxx. 25; 1 Chron. ix. 30; 2 Chron. xvi. 14.

מרר, v. Kal non occ. Arab. مَرَّ, *transivit; amarus fuit; amara et ingrata dixit;* مَرْمَرَ, *iratus fuit.* Syr. ܡܰܪ. Sam. מרר; and Æth. መረረ፡ *amarus fuit. Was bitter* or *disagreeable.* (a) To the senses, or (b) To the mind.

Niph. נָמֵר, *Became offensive*, of an odour, Jer. xlviii. 11.

Pres. יֵמַר, *Becomes bitter*, Is. xxiv. 9.

Piḥ. pres. יְמָרֵר, *Makes bitter; grieves.* אֲמָרֵר בַּבֶּכִי, *I wept bitterly*, Is. xxii. 4. יְמָרְרוּ אֶת־חַיֵּיהֶם, *they embitter their lives*, Exod. i. 14. יְמָרְרֻהוּ, *Id.* Gen. xlix. 23.

Hiph. הֵמַר, i. q. Piḥ. הֵמַר שַׁדַּי לִי, *The Almighty hath made* (my life) *bitter to me*, Ruth i. 20. שַׁדַּי הֵמַר נַפְשִׁי, *Id.* Job xxvii. 2.

Inf. הָמֵר, *Weeping bitterly*, Zech. xii. 10.

Hith. pres. יִתְמַרְמַר, *Is angry*, Dan. viii. 7; xi. 11.

מְרֵרָה, femin. Aff. מְרֵרָתִי. Arab. مَرَارَةٌ, *fel;* مَرَارَةٌ, *folliculus fellis. The gall bladder*, Job xvi. 13.

מְרֹרָה, f. constr. מְרוֹרַת, pl. מְרוֹרוֹת. (a) *The gall.* (b) *Bitterness.* (a) Job xx. 14. (b) Deut. xxxii. 32; Job xiii. 26.

מְרֹרִים, *Bitter herbs*, Exod. xii. 8; Num. ix. 11; Lam. iii. 15.

מִרְשַׁעַת, r. רשע. *Wickedness; wicked*, 2 Chron. xxiv. 7.

מַשָּׂא, m. r. נשא. (a) *Any thing carried, A burden.* (b) *The act of lifting or carrying.* (c) *A load*, as much as can be carried. (d) *Any thing burdensome.* (e) *Tribute.* (f) *Calamity.* (g) *Lifting up the voice in singing.* (h) *Solemn declaration.* (i) *Prophecy concerning.* (a) Num. iv. 15; Is. xxii. 25, &c. (b) Num. iv. 24. 47; 2 Chron. xx. 25; xxxv. 3. (c) 2 Kings v. 17. מַשָּׂא צֶמֶד־פְּרָדִים, 2 Kings viii. 9. (d) Num. xi. 17; 2 Sam. xv. 33, &c. (e) 2 Chron. xvii. 11. (f) Hos. viii. 10. (g) 1 Chron. xv. 22. 27. שַׂר הַמַּשָּׂא, *leader of the burden:* lit. here; meton. — *of the choir of singers.* (h) Prov. xxx. 1; xxxi. 1; Jer. xxiii. 33, 34. 38. (i) Constr. (1) immed. Is. xiii. 1; xv. 1. 6, &c. (2) בְּ, Is. xxi. 13: מַשָּׂא דְּבַר־יְהוָה, Zech. ix. 1. (3) Favourably, אֶל, Mal. i. 1. (4) עַל, Zech. xii. 1. מַשָּׂא נַפְשָׁם, *that on which their affections are set*, Ezek. xxiv. 25. Aff. מַשָּׂאִי, מַשָּׂאָם.

מַשָּׂא, once, פָּנִים מַשָּׂא. *Preference of persons*, 2 Chron. xix. 7 : r. נָשָׂא.

מַשְׂאָה, once, Is. xxx. 27, כֹּבֶד מַשְׂאָה. LXX. μετὰ δόξης τὸ λόγιον. Vulg. *gravis ad portandum.* Syr. ܡܰܫܩܠܳܐ ܕܒܶܣܪܳܐ. According to others, *the rising of flame, burning:* rather, perhaps, *Burden, heavy of burden*, i. e. denouncing heavy things, i. q. מַשָּׂא. See Auth. Vers.

מִשָּׂא (393) מֶשֶׁךְ

מַשְׂאֵת, m. constr. מַשְׂאַת, pl. מַשְׂאוֹת. (a) *The act of lifting up.* (b) *A signal.* (c) *Prophecy.* (d) *Gift.* (e) *Tribute.* (a) Ps. cxli. 2; Jud. xx. 38. 40. (b) Jer. vi. 1. (c) Lam. ii. 14. (d) Est. ii. 18; Jer. xl. 5; Gen. xliii. 34; 2 Sam. xi. 8; Zeph. iii. 18. (e) 2 Chron. xxiv. 6. 9.

מַשְׂאוֹת, f. *The act of lifting or pulling up,* Ezek. xvii. 9.

מִשְׂגָּב, m. r. שׂגב. Constr. מִשְׂגַּב. Aff. מִשְׂגַּבִּי, מִשְׂגַּבּוֹ. *High place.* (a) *A hill,* or other *fortified place affording refuge.* (b) meton. *Refuge, source of safety,* applied to God. (a) Jer. xlviii. 1; Is. xxv. 12; xxxiii. 16. (b) 2 Sam. xxii. 3; Ps. ix. 10; xviii. 3; xlvi. 8. 12; lix. 10. 17, 18; xlviii. 4; lxii. 3. 7; xciv. 22; cxliv. 2.

משׂוכה, f. r. שׂוך, constr. מְשֻׂכַת. Aff. מְשׂוּכָתוֹ. *A fence,* Prov. xv. 19; Is. v. 5.

מַשּׂוֹר, m. r. נשׂר, once. Arab. مِنْشَارٌ, *serra.* Syr. ܡܰܣܳܪܳܐ, *id.* *A saw,* Is. x. 15.

מְשׂוּרָה, f. Arab. مَشَرَ. II. *Divisit, dispersit rem;* مَشَارٌ, *agri pars quæ sextario frumenti conseri potest.* *A measure* for liquids, Lev. xix. 35; 1 Chron. xxiii. 29; Ezek. iv. 11. 16.

מָשׂוֹשׂ, m. r. שׂוש, constr. מְשׂוֹשׂ. Aff. מְשׂוֹשִׂי־שָׂהּ. (a) *Joy.* (b) *Cause of joy.* (c) *Its expression; rejoicing.* (a) Is. xxxii. 13; lxvi. 10, &c. (b) Job viii. 19; Ps. xlviii. 3, &c. (c) Is. xxiv. 8. In Is. viii. 6, מְשׂוֹשׂ is put for שָׂשׂ.

מִשְׂחָק, m. r. שׂחק. Once, *An object of laughter,* Hab. i. 10.

מַשְׂטֵמָה, m. r. שׂטם. *Hatred,* Hos. ix. 7, 8. lxx. μανία. Aq. ἐγκότησις. Ἀλλ. ἔκστασις. Syr. ܡܰܣܛܡܳܐ.

מַשְׂכִּית, f. Chald. סְכָה, *speculatus, contemplatus est, aspexit.* Syr. ܣܟܺܝ, *expectavit, intendit, speravit.* Sam. סכי, *desideravit;* סכוי, *oculus, conspectus.* Æth. ሰቈየ: *fenestra.* Aff. מַשְׂכִּיתוֹ, pl. מַשְׂכִּיּוֹת. Aff. מַשְׂכִּיּוֹתָם. *Figure* (a) external, *image.* (b) Internal, *imagination.* (a) Lev. xxvi. 1; Num. xxxiii. 52; Prov. xxv. 11. (b) Ps. lxxiii. 7; Prov. xviii. 11. Some take מַשְׂכִּיּוֹת, in Prov. xxv. 11, to signify *baskets,* from שׂוּך.

מַשְׂכֹּרֶת, f. aff. מַשְׂכֻּרְתִּי, תֵּךְ, מַשְׂכֻּרְתֵּךְ, r. שׂכר. (a) *Wages.* (b) *Reward.* (a) Gen. xxix. 15; xxxi. 7. 41. (b) Ruth ii. 12.

מַשְׂמְרוֹת, f. once, *Nails,* Eccl. xii. 11. See מַסְמְרוֹת.

מִשְׂפָּח, masc. once, Is. v. 7, r. שׂפח. According to Gesenius, *Shedding of blood.* See Auth. Vers. He compares the Arabic سَفَحَ, *sanguinem profudit.* Had this been the meaning of the prophet, the alliteration with מִשְׁפָּט, would have been more exact if he had used מִשְׁפָּךְ, which would be regularly derived from שָׁפַךְ, a verb of common occurrence. lxx. ἀνομίαν. Aq. διασκέδασιν. Syr. ܡܣܰܦܚܳܐ. Vulg. *iniquitas.* Others make it synonymous with מִסְפַּחַת, *a scab;* but this seems unsuitable. The passage requires some act of injustice, or a combination for that purpose. Arab. سَفَعَ, *colaphos duxit alicui; percussit.* III. *Propellere et abigere studuit alterum.* *Violence.*

מִשְׂרָה, f. r. שׂרה. *Government, authority,* Is. ix. 5, 6.

מִשְׂרְפוֹת, f. r. שׂרף. *Burning.* (a) Of lime. (b) Of perfumes at a funeral. (a) Is. xxxiii. 12. (b) Jer. xxxiv. 5.

מַשְׂרֵת, m. once, 2 Sam. xiii. 9. Probably, *a frying-pan.* lxx. τὸ τήγανον. But Vulg. *quod coxerat,* &c. Syr. ܠܰܓܒܐ. Etymology uncertain.

מַשָּׁא, m. r. נשׁא. *Interest,* Neh. v. 7. lxx. ἀπαιτήσει ἀνὴρ τὸν ἀδελφὸν αὐτοῦ ἃ ὑμεῖς ἀπαιτεῖτε. Vulg. *usuras.*

מַשְׁאַבִּים, m. pl. r. שׁאב, once, Judg. v. 11. lxx. ἀναμέσον ὑδρευομένων. Sym. συμπινόντων. *Watering places.* Arab. شَابَ, r. شِيبَ, *sonitus edit inter bibendum.*

מַשָּׁאָה, f. r. נשׁא, constr. מַשַּׁאת, pl. מַשָּׁאוֹת. *A debt,* Deut. xxiv. 10; Prov. xxii. 26. lxx. ὀφείλημα.

מַשָּׁאוֹן, m. r. נשׁא, once, Prov. xxvi. 26. *Deceit.* lxx. δόλον. According to some the root is שׁאה, and the meaning *solitude.*

משׁאלה, f. r. שׁאל, pl. constr. מִשְׁאֲלוֹת. Aff. מִשְׁאֲלֹתֶיךָ. *Prayers,* Ps. xx. 6; xxxvii. 4.

משׁארת, fem. r. שׁאר, for שׁאר. Aff.

3 E

מִשְׁאַרְתֶּךָ. Pl. aff. תָיך־, מִשְׁאֲרוֹתָם. *Kneading-trough*, Exod. vii. 28; xii. 34; Deut. xxviii. 5. 17.

מִשְׁבְּצוֹת, pl. f. r. שׁבץ, in זָהָב מִשְׁבְּצוֹת. (a) *Gold settings* for precious stones. (b) Probably, *gold cloth*. (a) Exod. xxviii. 11. 13, 14. 25; xxxix. 6. 13. 16. (b) Ps. xlv. 14. LXX. ἐν κροσσωτοῖς χρυσοῖς.

מַשְׁבֵּר, m. r. שׁבר, constr. מִשְׁבַּר, pl. constr. מִשְׁבְּרֵי. Aff. מִשְׁבָּרֶיךָ. (a) *Pains of childbirth*. (b) *Violent pains of any kind*. (c) *Breakers*, of the sea. (a) 2 Kings xix. 3. LXX. ὠδίνων, Is. xxxvii. 3; Hos. xiii. 13, ἐν συντριβῇ τέκνων. (b) 2 Sam. xxii. 5, συντριμμοὶ θανάτου. (c) οἱ μετεωρισμοὶ τῆς θαλάσσης, Ps. xlii. 8; lxxxviii. 8; xciii. 4; Jon. ii. 4, μετεωρισμοί.

מִשְׁבַּת, m. r. שׁבת. Once, pl. aff. מִשְׁבַּתָּה. *Her cessations*, i. e. the entire cessation of the employments and amusements of her inhabitants, Lam. i. 7. LXX. μετοικεσίας, as if from שׁבה. Syr. ܡܶܫܒܰܬ.

מִשְׁגֶּה, m. r. שׁגה. Once, *A mistake, inadvertency*, Gen. xliii. 12.

מָשָׁה, v. In two forms: Kal, מִן הַמַּיִם מְשִׁיתִהוּ, Exod. ii. 10.
— Hiph. יַמְשֵׁנִי מִמַּיִם רַבִּים, 2 Sam. xxii. 17; Ps. xviii. 17. *Drew out* of the water. Syr. ܡܫܐ, and Sam. משה, *Id.* Cogn. Arab. ماش, *prohibuit, repulit* ab aliquâ re; مشى, *gressus fuit, incessit.*

מֹשֶׁה, m. r. נשה. Once, constr. מֹשֵׁה, i. q. מַשָּׁאה. *A debt*, Deut. xv. 2.

מְשׁוּאָה, f. r. שׁאה. Thrice, and each time joined to שֹׁאָה, with which it appears synonymous. *Desolation; a desolate place*, Job xxx. 3; xxxviii. 27; Zeph. i. 15.

מַשְׁאוֹת, and מַשֻׁאוֹת, f. pl. *Id.*, Ps. lxxiii. 18; lxxiv. 3.

מְשׁוּבָה, f. r. שׁוב. מְשׁוּבָה, constr. מְשׁוּבַת. Aff. תִי־, תָם־, מְשׁוּבֵךְ. Pl. aff. תַיִךְ־, תֵינוּ־, מְשׁוּבֹתֵיכֶם. (a) *Turning away, going aside;* pec. *from God's commandments*. (b) As an adjective, *Rebellious, backsliding*. (a) Jer. ii. 19; iii. 22; v. 6; viii. 5; Hos. xi. 7; xiv. 5; Prov. i. 32. (b) Jer. iii. 6. 8. 11, 12.

מְשׁוּגָה, f. r. שׁגג. Once, מְשׁוּגָתִי, i. q. מְשֻׁגָּה. *Error*, Job xix. 4.

מָשׁוֹט, m. r. שׁוט. Pl. aff. מְשׁוֹטָיִךְ (Dagesh euphon.) *An oar*, Ezek. xxvii. 6. 29.

מָשַׁח, v. pres. יִמְשַׁח. Arab. مسح, *manum duxit super rem et abstusit; dimensus fuit;* مساحة, *dimensio;* مسح, *quod illinitur, ut unguentum;* مسّح, *fricuit odoramentis corpus*. Syr. ܡܫܚ, *unxit, mensuravit.* Samar. משח, *Idem.* Æth. መስሐ : *epulatus est.* Constr. immed. it. med. אֶת, with שֶׁמֶן, either with or without בְּ, (a) *Anointed*. (b) *Anointed, setting apart to the office of king or priest*. (c) *Set apart to an office*. (d) *Dedicated an inanimate object by anointing it*. (e) *Anointed himself for a banquet*. (f) *Obtained as the portion set apart for him*. (a) Jer. xxii. 14. (b) Exod. xl. 15; 1 Sam. ix. 16; 1 Kings i. 39, &c. (c) Is. lxi. 1. (d) Gen. xxxi. 13; Exod. xxx. 26; xl. 9—11; Lev. viii. 10; Num. vii. 1. (e) Amos vi. 6.

Part. pl. מְשֻׁחִים, Judg. ix. 15.
Part. pass. מָשׁוּחַ, 2 Sam. iii. 39. Pl. מְשֻׁחִים, Num. iii. 3. (a) Exod. xxix. 2; Lev. ii. 4; vii. 12.
Infin. מְשֹׁחַ, Judg. ix. 8; Dan. ix. 24. מָשְׁחָה, Exod. xxix. 29; (f) Num. xviii. 8. Aff. מָשְׁחִי, 1 Sam. xv. 1. מָשְׁחוֹ, Lev. vii. 36. מָשְׁחָתָם, Exod. xl. 15.
Imp. aff. מְשָׁחֵהוּ, 1 Sam. xvi. 12. מְשָׁחוּ, Is. xxi. 5.
Niph. נִמְשַׁח, 1 Chron. xiv. 8.
Infin. הִמָּשַׁח, Lev. vi. 13; Num. vii. 10. 84. 88.

מְשַׁח, m. Chald. *Oil*, Ezra vi. 9; vii. 22. Syr. ܡܫܚܐ, *Id.*

מִשְׁחָה, f. constr. מִשְׁחַת. Aff. מָשְׁחָתָם. (a) *Anointing*. שֶׁמֶן הַמִּשְׁחָה, Exod. xxv. 6; xxix. 7. 21, &c.: without the article, Exod. xxx. 25. 31; Lev. x. 7; xxi. 12. (b) *A portion*, Lev. vii. 35.

מִשְׁחָר, m. i. q. שׁחר. *The dawn*, Ps. cx. 3.

מָשְׁחָת, m. r. שׁחת. *Injuring*, as an adjective, *disfigured*, Is. lii. 14.

מִשְׁחַת, m. Aff. מָשְׁחָתָם. *Defilement*, Lev. xxii. 25.

מִשְׁטוֹחַ, m. r. שׁטח, constr. מִשְׁטַח. *A place for spreading nets*, Ezek. xxvi. 5. 14; xlvii. 10.

מִשְׁטָר, m. r. שטר. Aff. מִשְׁטָרוֹ. *Authority, influence,* Job xxxviii. 33.

מֶשִׁי, m. twice, Ezek. xvi. 10. 13. Arab. وَشْي, *coloravit pinxitve* pannum; وَاشٍ, *textor;* وَشْي, *color et pictura* vestis; *sericum figuris pictum. Figured silk.*

מָשִׁיחַ, m. r. משח, constr. מְשִׁיחַ, i. q. Gr. χριστός. Aff. יחִי, ךָחֲ, מְשִׁיחוֹ. Pl. aff. מְשִׁיחָי. *Anointed.* Applied, (a) To the high priest. (b) To kings. (c)—As the title of that Divine priest and king whose priesthood is after the order of Melchizedek, and whose kingdom is an everlasting kingdom. (d)—To the Israelites, &c., as the chosen (anointed) people of God. (a) Lev. iv. 3. 5. 16; vi. 15. (b) 1 Sam. ii. 10. 35; xvi. 6, &c.—To Saul, 1 Sam. xii. 3. 5; xxiv. 7. 11; xxvi. 9. 11. 16. 23; 2 Sam. i. 14. 16. 21.—To David, 2 Sam. xix. 22; xxii. 5; xxiii. 1; Ps. xx. 7; xxviii. 8; cxxxii. 17.—To Solomon, 2 Chron. v. 42. To Cyrus, Is. xlv. 1. (c) Ps. ii. 2; Dan. ix. 25, 26. (d) Hab. iii. 13; 1 Chron. xvi. 22; Ps. cv. 15.

מָשַׁךְ, v. pres. יִמְשֹׁךְ. Arab. مَسَكَ, *tenuit, apprehensum, prehendit;* مَسِيكٌ, *cohibuit se et abstinuit;* أَمْسَكَ, *dominatus est.* Æth. חתם: *tetendit* arcum; *jaculatus est* sagittas. Syr. ܡܫܚ, *induruit.* *Took hold of, drew.* (a) *Stretched out* the hand, immed. (b) *Took hold of.* (c) *Seized as* spoil. (d) *Drew.* (e) *Drew* a bow, בְּ. (f) *Drew* a yoke, בְּ. (g) *Drew* a net, בְּ. (h) *Scattered* seed, immed. (i) *Lengthened* a sound. (k) *Continued* in a thing towards a person, with two accus., also with acc. of thing, and לְ, or עַל, before the person. (l) *Kept* or *reckoned* among, עִם. (m) *Cheered.* (a) Hos. vii. 5. (b) Exod. xii. 21. (c) Judg. xx. 37; Ezek. xxxii. 20. (d) Job xxiv. 22; Is. v. 18, &c. (e) 1 Kings xxii. 34; 2 Chron. xviii. 33: immed. Is. lxvi. 19. (f) Deut. xxi. 3. (g) Ps. x. 9. (h) Amos ix. 13. (i) Exod. xix. 13. (k) Ps. x. 11; cix. 12, &c. (l) Ps. xxviii. 3. (m) Eccl. ii. 3.

Part. משֵׁךְ, m. Ps. cix. 12; Amos ix. 13, &c. Plur. fem. מֹשְׁכוֹת, *Attractions, influences,* Job xxxviii. 31.

Inf. מְשֹׁךְ. Aff. מָשְׁכוֹ, Exod. xix. 13; Josh. vi. 15; Ps. x. 9. תַּרְתִּי בְלִבִּי לִמְשׁוֹךְ בַּיַּיִן אֶת־בְּשָׂרִי, Eccl. ii. 3. LXX. κατεσκεψάμην εἰ ἡ καρδία μου ἑλκύσει ὡς οἶνον τὴν σάρκα μου. Vulg. *cogitavi in corde meo abstrahere à vino carnem meam.* Syr. ܢܣܒܬ ܒܠܒܝ ܠܡܓܒܠ ܒܚܡܪܐ, *cogitavi mecum exhilarare vino carnem meum.*

Imp. מְשֹׁךְ, Ps. x. 11. Aff. מָשְׁכֵנִי, Cant. i. 4. Pl. מִשְׁכוּ, Exod. xii. 21.

Niph. pres. יִמָּשֵׁךְ תִּמָּשֵׁךְ. *Shall be protracted, delayed,* Is. xiii. 22; Ezek. xii. 25. 28.

Puh. Part. מְמֻשָּׁךְ, *Spoiled,* Is. xviii. 2. 7: f. מְמֻשָּׁכָה, *obtained,* Prov. xiii. 12.

מֶשֶׁךְ, *Acquiring, laying hold of,* Job xxviii. 18. *Scattering* of seed, Ps. cxxvi. 6.

מִשְׁכָּב, m. r. שכב, constr. מִשְׁכַּב. Aff. מִשְׁכָּבַנְכֶם, מִשְׁכָּבָם, בָהּ, בוֹ, בִּךָ, בִּי. Plur. constr. מִשְׁכְּבֵי. Aff. מִשְׁכְּבוֹתָם. (a) *A bed.* (b) *A bier.* (c) *Lying in bed.* (d) *Lying with.* (a) Lev. xv. 4; 2 Sam. xvii. 28, &c. (b) 2 Chron. xvi. 14. (c) Exod. xxi. 18; vii. 28; 2 Sam. iv. 5; 2 Kings vi. 12; Eccl. x. 20. (d) Num. xxxi. 18; Judg. xxi. 11; Ezek. xxiii. 17.

משכב, m. Chald. Aff. בִּי, בָךְ, מִשְׁכְּבֵהּ. *A bed,* Dan. ii. 28, 29; iv. 2. 7. 10; vii. 1.

מִשְׁכָּן, m. r. שכן, constr. מִשְׁכַּן. Aff. יִ, תֵינוּ, יָךְ, מַךְ, יָיו, תָיו: pl. מִשְׁכָּנוֹת: constr. נוֹת. Aff. מִשְׁכְּנוֹתָם. *A habitation, dwelling.* (a) *Of* men. (b) *Of* beasts. (c) *Of* God. [1] *The tabernacle.* [2] *The temple.* (a) Num. xvi. 24; Job xviii. 21, &c. (b) Job xxxix. 6. (c), [1] Exod. xxv. 9; xxvi. 1, &c.; מִשְׁכַּן הָעֵדֻת, Exod. xxxviii. 21; Num. i. 50, &c.: מִשְׁכַּן יְהֹוָה, Lev. xvii. 4; Num. xvi. 9, &c. [2] 2 Chron. xxix. 6; מִשְׁכַּן בֵּית הָאֱלֹהִים, 2 Chron. vi. 33.

מָשַׁל, v. Pres. יִמְשֹׁל. Arab. مَثَلَ, *similis fuit; assimilavit; exemplum* in eo statuit, c. بِ. p. مَثَّلَ, *erectus constitit; præstans fuit;* مَثَّلَ, *assimilavit; parabolam instituit;* مُثْلَةٌ, *pœna, supplicium;* أَمْثَلُ, *præstans, præstantissimus.* Pl. *Proceres, optimates.* Cogn. بَسَلَ, *strenuus fuit;* بَاسِلٌ, *vir strenuus, heros.* Syr. ܡܬܠܐ, *parabola, similitudo, proverbium.* Æth.

מָשַׁל: *existimavit; similis fuit; comparavit.* The leading idea seems to be, *rule: similarity* would grow out of this, in the circumstance that moral laws, i. e. *rules* of life, consisted very much in teaching by *parables,* or *similitudes:* the word itself thence took *similarity, &c.,* as a secondary meaning. (a) *Ruled,* abs. (b) *Had authority over,* בְּ. (c) *Had authority to do,* לְ. (d) *Uttered a comparison respecting,* עַל, בְּ; in a bad sense, Job xvii. 6. (a) Dan. xi. 3—5; Zech. vi. 13. (b) Gen. iv. 7; Judg. viii. 23, &c. (c) Exod. xxi. 8. (d) Ezek. xii. 23; xvi. 44.

Part. מֹשֵׁל, Gen. xlv. 26; Josh. xii. 2, &c. Inf. מְשֹׁל, aff. מָשְׁלִי, Prov. xxix. 2; Ezek. xix. 14, &c. (e) Job xvii. 6.

Imp. מְשֹׁל, Judg. viii. 22; Ezek. xvii. 1.

Hiph. הִמְשִׁיל, Dan. xi. 39, (b).

Pres. יַמְשִׁיל, Ps. viii. 7, (b). *Make like,* Is. xlvi. 5.

Inf. הַמְשִׁיל, *Giving authority,* Job xxv. 2. See my notes.

Niph. נִמְשַׁל, *Became like,* Ps. xlix. 13. 21; xxviii. 1; cxliii. 7; Is. xiv. 10.

Piħ. Part. מְמַשֵּׁל, *Speaking parables,* Ezek. xxi. 5.

Hith. Pres. אֶתְמַשֵּׁל, *I become like,* Job xxx. 19.

מָשָׁל, m. constr. מְשַׁל; aff. מְשָׁלוֹ; plur. מְשָׁלִים; constr. מִשְׁלֵי. (a) *A solemn, authoritative declaration.* (b) *Decision, rule,* deduced either from revelation, experience, or discussion, *proverb.* (c) *A by-word; subject of a taunting proverb.* (a) Is. xiv. 4; Ps. lxviii. 2, &c. (b) 1 Sam. xxiv. 14; Ezek. xviii. 2, &c. (c) Ps. xliv. 15; Mic. ii. 4, &c.

מֹשֶׁל, aff. מָשְׁלוֹ. (a) *Authority,* Zech. ix. 10. (b) *Any thing like,* Job xli. 25.

מִשְׁלֹחַ, m. r. שׁלח, constr. מִשְׁלַח. (a) *Act of putting out* the hand. (b) *Act of sending out* cattle to graze. (a) Deut. xii. 7; xv. 10; xxiii. 21; xxviii. 8. 20. (b) Is. vii. 25.

מִשְׁלוֹחַ, *Id.* m. (a) Is. xi. 14. (b) Esth. ix. 19. 22.

מִשְׁלַחַת, f. *Id.* (b) Ps. lxxviii. 49; Eccl. viii. 8. Sym. οὐδέ ἐστι παρατάξασθαι εἰς τὸν πόλεμον.

מְשֻׁלָּשׁ, see שָׁלֹשׁ.

מְשַׁמָּה, fem. plur. מְשַׁמּוֹת, r. שׁמם. (a) *Astonishment.* Meton. *Cause of astonishment.* (b) *Desolation.* (a) Ezek. v. 15. (b) Is. xv. 6; Jer. xlviii. 34: with שְׁמָמָה, Ezek. vi. 14; xxxiii. 28, 29; xxxv. 3.

מִשְׁמָן, m. r. שׁמן, pl. מִשְׁמַנִּים, constr. מִשְׁמַנֵּי. Aff. מִשְׁמַנֵּיהֶם, עֵינָיו. (a) Sing. and pl. *Fatness.* (b) Pl. *Fertile places.* (a) Ps. lxxviii. 31; Is. x. 16; xvii. 4. (b) Gen. xxvii. 28, 29; Dan. xi. 24.

מַשְׁמַנִּים, m. pl. *Fattening things, rich food,* Neh. viii. 10. LXX. λιπάσματα.

מִשְׁמָע, m. r. שׁמע. *Act of hearing,* Is. xi. 3.

מִשְׁמַעַת, fem. Aff. מִשְׁמַעְתָּם, -תּוֹ, -תֵּךְ. *Hearing,* both judicial and obedient. (a) *A court of justice for hearing causes, council.* (b) Abst. for concr. *Subjects.* (a) 1 Sam. xxii. 14, שַׂר אֶל־מִשְׁמַעְתְּךָ. LXX. ἄρχων παντὸς παραγγέλματός σου. Syr. ܢܓܠ ܗܦܟܬܐ. 2 Chron. xi. 25; 2 Sam. xxiii. 23. LXX. ἔταξεν αὐτὸν Δαυῒδ πρὸς τὰς ἀκοὰς αὐτοῦ. Syr. ܣܒܪܗܝ ܕܘܝܕ ܠܩܕܡܐ ܕܢܦܩ ܣܒܪܗ. (b) Is. xi. 14.

מִשְׁמָר, m. r. שׁמר, constr. מִשְׁמַר. Aff. מִשְׁמָרוֹ, מִשְׁמָרָיו; pl. aff. מִשְׁמָרָיו. (a) *The act of guarding,* or *watching.* (b) *Keeping guard,* as soldiers. (c) *Imprisonment.* (d) *A prison.* (e) *What should be observed and kept, an appointed duty.* (a) Job vi. 12; Prov. iv. 23. (b) Neh. iv. 3. 16; xii. 25, &c. (c) Gen. xl. 1; xlii. 16, &c. (d) Lev. xxiv. 12; Num. xv. 34.

מִשְׁמֶרֶת, f. Aff. מִשְׁמַרְתָּם, -תּוֹ, -תְּךָ, -תִּי; plur. מִשְׁמָרוֹת, constr. מִשְׁמְרוֹת. Aff. -תָם, מִשְׁמְרוֹתֵיהֶם. *Id.* (c) 2 Sam. xx. 3; 2 Kings xi. 5—7, &c. (a) Num. i. 53; iii. 7, 8. 28, &c. (e) Lev. iii. 36; viii. 35, &c.

מִשְׁנֶה, m. constr. מִשְׁנֵה, aff. מִשְׁנֵהוּ, pl. מִשְׁנִים, r. שׁנה. *The act of repeating.* (a) *Second.* (b) *The second rank.* (c) *Second in rank.* (d) *Double.* (e) *A copy.* (f) *Of an inferior kind.* (g) *A division of Jerusalem so called.* (a) Gen. xliii. 12; 1 Sam. viii. 2. (b) Gen. xli. 43; 2 Kings xxiii. 4. (c) 2 Kings xxv. 18; 2 Chron. xxxi. 12; Neh. xi. 9, &c. (d) Exod. xvi. 5. 22; Is. lxi. 7. (e) Deut. xvii. 18; Josh. viii. 32. (f) According to some, 1 Sam. xv. 9. (g) 2 Kings xxii. 14; 2 Chron. xxxiv. 22.

מְשִׁסָּה, f. pl. מְשִׁסּוֹת, r. שׁסס. *Prey,* 2 Kings xxi. 14; Is. xlii. 22. 24; Jer. xxx. 16; Zeph. i. 13; Hab. ii. 7.

מִשְׁעוֹל, m. r. שעל, once. Arab. مَسْعَل, *fauces, locus ubi tussitur.* Conf. *fauces montium.* *A narrow way*, Num. xxii. 24. בְּמִשְׁעוֹל הַכְּרָמִים. LXX. ἐν ταῖς αὔλαξι τῶν ἀμπέλων. Syr. ܚܡܣܠܐ ܕܟܪܡܐ.

מִשְׁעִי, once, masc. Arab. سَعَي, *operam dedit;* مَسْعَاً, *operatio;* مَسْعَاة, *conatus, studium laudabile.* לְמִשְׁעִי, *carefully*, Ezek. xvi. 4.

מִשְׁעָן, m. constr. מִשְׁעַן, r. שען. *A support:* spoken of God, 2 Sam. xxii. 19; Ps. xviii. 19. Of food, Is. iii. 1.

מַשְׁעֵן, m. מַשְׁעֵנָה, f. *Id.* Is. iii. 1.

מִשְׁעֶנֶת, f. Aff. יְתִּי, יְתּוּ־, יְתָּךְ־, מַשְׁעַנְתָּם־, &c. *A walking-stick, staff,* Num. xxi. 19; Judg. vi. 21, &c.

מִשְׁפָּחָה, f. constr. מִשְׁפַּחַת, aff. מִשְׁפַּחְתִּי, &c.; plur. מִשְׁפָּחוֹת, constr. מִשְׁפְּחוֹת, aff. מִשְׁפְּחוֹתָיו, &c. See שִׁפְחָה. (a) *A household.* (b) *A family or clan.* (c) *A tribe.* (d) *A race, generation.* (e) *A race, sort, of animals.* (a) Lev. xx. 5; Exod. xii. 21. (b) Num. iii. 15; xxvi. 5; Josh. vii. 14, &c. (c) Judg. xviii. 2; Zech. xii. 13. (d) Lev. xxv. 45; Jer. viii. 3; Amos iii. 1, &c. (e) Gen. viii. 19.

מִשְׁפָּט, m. constr. מִשְׁפַּט, aff. מִשְׁפָּטִי, &c.; pl. מִשְׁפָּטִים, constr. מִשְׁפְּטֵי, aff. מִשְׁפָּטֵי, &c. מִשְׁפְּטֵיהֶם, r. שפט. (a) *The act of deciding as a judge.* (b) Meton. *A decision.* (c) *A punishment.* (d) *A court of justice.* (e) *A cause for trial.* (f) *Justice, equity.* (g) *Any positive institution, whether* [1] *religious, or* [2] *civil.* (h) *A right claimed in consequence.* (i) *Custom.* (k) *Manner, appearance.* (a) 1 Kings iii. 28; 2 Chron. xix. 6, &c. (b) Num. xxvii. 11; Deut. xvi. 18; Job xix. 7, &c. (c) Lev. xxiv. 22; Ps. cxix. 84, &c. (d) Deut. xxv. 1. (e) 1 Kings iii. 11; Job xiii. 18; xxiii. 4, &c. (f) Gen. xviii. 25; Deut. xxxii. 4; 2 Sam. viii. 15, &c. (g), [1] Lev. v. 10; Num. xv. 16, &c.: [2] Deut. xvii. 11; 1 Sam. xxx. 25, &c. (h) Exod. xxiii. 6; Deut. xviii. 3, &c. (i) Gen. xl. 13; Josh. vi. 15, &c. (k) 2 Kings i. 7.

מִשְׁפְּתַיִם, dual, Gen. xlix. 14, and quoted Judg. v. 16, רֹבֵץ בֵּין הַמִּשְׁפְּתַיִם. Syr. ܘܪܒܥ ܒܝܬ ܡܣܠܐ. LXX. ἀναπαυόμενος ἀνὰ μέσον τῶν κλήρων. Vulg. *accubans inter terminos.* There is, likewise, an imitation of it in אִם־תִּשְׁכְּבוּן בֵּין שְׁפַתָּיִם, Ps. lxviii. 14, where שְׁפַתָּיִם must mean, either the same, or very nearly the same, thing with the word here. But here the Auth. Vers. has given "*the pots.*" Symm. and the LXX. κλήρων, as above. My own opinion is, that the latter interpretation of the Auth. Vers. is the true one; and it will suit either of the places equally well. Arab. ثَبَتَ, *stabilivit, fixit;* مُثْبَتٌ, تِبَاتٌ, *sella ligata loro;* مُثْبَتٌ, *vir crassus, qui non relinquit pulvinar;* أَنْفَقَة, *chytropus, tripedaneum ollæ sustentaculum; lapides quibus olla imponitur;* مِثْفَاة, *signum tripodis formam habens, quod cervicibus jumentorum inuri solet.* The interpretations given are various. That of our Authorized Version, offered above, is perhaps the best. Gesenius gives *caula, stabula.* Comp. גְּדֵרוֹחִים, Josh. xv. 36. Dathe prefers, *aquarum canales.* Arab. r. سفت, *bibit.* See also Ludolf. Lex. Æth. p. 76.

מֶשֶׁק, m. once, Gen. xv. 2, in בֶּן־מֶשֶׁק בֵּיתִי. LXX. ὁ δὲ υἱὸς Μασὲκ τῆς οἰκογενοῦς μου. Vulg. *filius procuratoris domûs meæ.* The Syriac translator omits the word. The LXX. supposed it to be the name of Eliezer's mother. Some take שקק to be the root, and interpret the words, "*Filius cursitationis domûs meæ:*" others, "*Filius possessionis domûs meæ.*" The latter take מֶשֶׁק to be equivalent to מֶשֶׁךְ. Arab. مَسَكَ, *tenuit.* Cogn. مَشَقَ, *consuit.* Or thus, وَثِقَ, *confisus, et fretus fuit* aliquo. II. *Fidum, fiduciâ dignum esse dixit* aliquem. III: *Fœdus pactumve inivit;* ثِقَة, *fiducia; homo, in quo fiduciam ponis;* مَوْثِق, *fœdus, pactum.* Probably, *A trusty servant born in the house,* and already adopted as a son: a thing, even now, very common in the East. The latter part of the verse deserves notice, viz. הוּא דַּמֶּשֶׂק אֱלִיעֶזֶר, i. e. *he* (is) *Dammesek Eliezer:* he is so named. Not, "*this Eliezer of Damascus:*" the passage says no such thing. Gesenius's "*Elieser Damascenus*" is wrong also. For,

משׁק (398) משׁר

in this case, it ought to have been הוּא אֲשֶׁר הַדַּמֶּשֶׂק. The LXX. is right, therefore, in giving οὗτος Δαμασκὸς Ἐλιέζερ, as a proper name, as also is Jerome, in saying, "Vocaturque *Damascus Eliezer.*" It is not improbable, indeed, that Abraham gave, after all, to this man—if once adopted as a son—a portion of goods among the sons of his concubines, Gen. xxv. 6. And if so, he may have been the founder of *Damascus,* and have called the city after his own name.

מֶשֶׁק, m. constr. מֶשֶׁק, r. שׁקק, once. *Running to and fro,* Is. xxxiii. 4. According to some, *gathering.* Syr. ܐܡܪ ܕܠܗܡ ܘܒܥܢܝ ܘܟܢܫܢ. LXX. ὃν τρόπον ἐάν τις συναγάγῃ ἀκρίδας, οὕτως ἐμπαίξουσιν ὑμῖν. Vulg. *sicut colligitur bruchus, cum fossæ plenæ fuerint de eo.*

מַשְׁקֶה, m. constr. מַשְׁקֵה, pl. מַשְׁקִים, aff. מַשְׁקָיו, r. שׁקה. (a) *One who gives drink, a cup-bearer.* (b) Meton. *The drink* itself. (c) *What has been supplied with drink, a watered country.* (a) Gen. xl. 1. 23, &c. (b) Lev. xi. 34; Is. xxxii. 6. (c) Ezek. xlv. 15.

מִשְׁקוֹל, m. r. שׁקל, once. Arab. مِثْقَال, *pondus quo ponderatur res. Weight,* Ezek. iv. 10.

מַשְׁקוֹף, m. r. שׁקף. Arab. سَكَفَ, *limine instruxit* portam; سَاكِف, *superius limen portæ, in quo cardo circumvertitur. The lintel,* or *beam,* laid over a door-way, Exod. xii. 7. 22, 23, only.

מִשְׁקָל, m. constr. מִשְׁקַל, aff. מִשְׁקָלוֹ, &c.; r. שׁקל. (a) *The act of weighing.* (b) Meton. *Weight.* (a) 2 Kings xxv. 16; Jer. lii. 20, &c. (b) Judg. viii. 26; Gen. xxiv. 22, &c.

מִשְׁקֶלֶת, f. once, Is. xxviii. 17. LXX. εἰς στάθμους.—

מִשְׁקֹלֶת, f. once, 2 Kings xxi. 13. LXX. τὸ στάθμιον.— *A balance.* Syr. ܡܫܩܠܬܐ, *Id.*

מִשְׁקָע, m. r. שׁקע, once. Arab. سَقَع, *ex vase aquam ore hausit.* A place where water settles, *a pond,* Ezek. xxxiv. 18. LXX. τὸ καθεστηκὸς ὕδωρ. Auth. Vers. "*Deep waters.*"

מִשְׂרָה, f. constr. מִשְׂרַת, r. שׂרה. Arab. ثَرِيَ, *humida et humore mollita fuit terra post siccitatem;* ثَرَى, *humor, mador.* Syr. ܨܒܥ, *tinxit, mersit;* ܡܙܓ, *succus ex uvis pressus. Juice,* once, Num. vi. 3, מִשְׁרַת־עֲנָבִים. LXX. ὅσα κατεργάζεται ἐκ σταφυλῆς.

מַשְׁרוֹקִיתָא, f. r. שׁרק, Chald. Apparently, *A shrill wind instrument.* Auth. Vers. *Flute.* LXX. σύριγγος. Vulg. *fistulæ,* Dan. iii. 5—15. Arab. شَرَقَ, *rima :* because perforated.

מָשַׁשׁ, cogn. מוּשׁ. Arab. مَسَّ, *tetigit.* Æth. መሰሰ : *palpando quæsivit instar cæci.* Comp. μάσσω, and Sanscr. पश्, *tangere. Touched, felt.*

Pret. Kal non occ. Pres. aff. אֲמֻשְׁךָ, *Let me touch, feel, thee,* Gen. xxvii. 21. See מוּשׁ, Ib. vv. 12. 22.

Pih. מִשֵּׁשׁ, pres. יְמַשֵּׁשׁ, constr. immed. (a) *Examined by feeling.* (b) *Felt his way, groped.* (a) Gen. xxxi. 34. 36. (b) Deut. xxviii. 29; Job v. 14; xii. 15.

Part. מְמַשֵּׁשׁ, (b) Deut. xxviii. 29.

מִשְׁתֶּה, m. constr. מִשְׁתֵּה, pl. aff. מִשְׁתָּיו, מִשְׁתֵּיהֶם, תֵּיכֶם, r. שׁתה. (a) *The act of drinking.* (b) *A banquet.* Comp. συμπόσιον. (c) Meton. *The drink itself.* (a) Dan. i. 5. 8. (b) Gen. xix. 3; xxi. 8, &c. (c) Ezra iii. 7; Dan. i. 10.

מִשְׁתְּיָא, m. Chald. def. form of the preceding word, *Id.* Dan. v. 10.

מַתְבֵּן, m. r. תבן, once, *A heap of straw,* Is. xxv. 10.

מֶתֶג, m. aff. מִתְגִי. *A bridle,* 2 Kings xix. 28; Ps. xxxii. 9; Prov. xxvi. 3; Is. xxxvii. 29.

מָתוֹק, m., f. מְתוּקָה, pl. מְתוּקִים, r. מתק. (a) *Sweet.* (b) *Sweetness.* (c) *Pleasant.* (a) Ps. xix. 11; Judg. xiv. 18, &c. (b) Judg. xiv. 14; Ezek. iii. 3. (c) Eccl. v. 11; xi. 7, &c.

מתח, v. Syr. ܡܬܚ, *extendit.* Chald. מְתַח, *Id. Stretched out* as a curtain. Once, וַיִּמְתָּחֵם, Is. xl. 22.

מָתַי, partic. Arab. مَتَى, *quando?* مَتَنْ, r. متو, and مَتَى; cogn. مَكّ,

מתד—נ (399) מתן—נא

extendit funem. (a) *When?* (b) *When, without the interrogation.* (c) לְמָתַי, *Until when?* (d) עַד מָתַי, *Id.* (e) אַחֲרֵי מָתַי, *After how long.* (a) Gen. xxx. 30; Ps. xlii. 3, &c. (b) Prov. xxiii. 35; Ps. ci. 2, &c. (c) Exod. viii. 5. (d) 1 Sam. xvi. 1. (e) Jer. xiii. 27.

מַתְכֹּנֶת, f. aff. יתּוֹ, מַתְכֻּנְתָּהּ r. מכן. (a) *A fixed quantity.* (b) *Arrangement, plan, composition.* (a) Exod. v. 8; Ezek. xlv. 11. (b) 2 Chron. xxiv. 13; Exod. xxx. 32. 37.

מְתַלְעוֹת, f. pl. aff. מְתַלְּעֹתָיו. Arab. تلع, and تلع, *fregit contusione* caput. The *grinders, teeth* so called, Job xxix. 17; Prov. xxx. 14; Joel i. 6. LXX. μύλας.

מֹתֶם, m. r. תמם. *Soundness of body,* Ps. xxxviii. 4. 8; Is. i. 6.

מַתָּן, m. aff. מַתָּנָם, r. נתן. *A gift,* Gen. xxxiv. 12; Num. xviii. 1; Prov. xviii. 16; xix. 6; xxi. 14.

מַתְנָא, fem. pl. מַתְּנָן, aff. מַתְּנָתָךְ, Chald. *Id.* Dan. ii. 6. 48; v. 17.

מַתָּנָה, f. constr. מַתְּנַת, pl. מַתָּנוֹת, constr. מַתְּנוֹת, aff. מַתְּנֹתֵיכֶם־תָם. *Id.* Gen. xxv. 6; Num. xviii. 6, &c.

מָתְנַיִם, dual, m. constr. מָתְנֵי, aff. מָתְנָי, &c. Arab. مَتْن, *firmus, robustus fuit*; مَتْن, *pars terræ dura et elata; firmus et constans; latus unum dorsi lumbum circumdans*; مَتْنُنَا الظَّهْر, *lumbi dorsi.* Syr. ܡܬܢܐ, *lumbi.* The *loins,* Ezek. viii. 2; Prov. xxxi. 17, &c.

מֶתֶק, m. Arab. مَطْقَة, *dulcedo*; تَعَطَّقَ, *gustavit* rem *gustûs sentiendi causâ; lingua superiori palato illisa excitavit sonum ob bonum cibi gustum*; مَطَّ, *lambit* mel, aquam; *multum edit.* Syr. ܡܬܩ, *suxit.* *Sweetness,* Prov. xvi. 21; xxvii. 9.

מתק, aff. מָתְקוֹ. *Id.* Job xxiv. 20.

מתק, aff. מָתְקוֹ. *Id.* Judg. ix. 11.

מתק, v. pres. יִמְתַּק. *Were sweet, became sweet,* Exod. xv. 25; Job xxi. 23 (see my notes here); Prov. ix. 17.

Hiph. pres. הַמְתִּיק. (a) I. q. Kal. (b) *Made, or considered, sweet.* (a) Job xx. 12. (b) Ps. lv. 15.

מַתָּת, f. for מַתֶּנֶת, r. נתן. *A gift,* Prov. xxv. 14; Eccl. iii. 13; iv. 17; v. 18; Ezek. xlvi. 5. 11.

נ

נ, *Nun,* the fourteenth letter of the Hebrew alphabet, and equivalent to our *n*. As a numeral, it stands for fifty: its final form denoting 700. It is classed among the liquids, Gram. art. 24. As a prefix, it forms the conjugation Niphḥal, Gram. art. 157. 18, &c.; and the first person plural of the present tense in all the conjugations. As an affix, it forms nouns of an intensitive or frequentitive signification, Ib. art. 168, and gives to verbs the sense of a strong asseveration, Ib. art. 235. When followed by a silent sheva, it is dropped, and its place is supplied by a dagesh in the next letter; but, if this occurs at the beginning of a word, it is omitted without compensation, Ib. art. 76.

נָא, an interjection, indecl., Gr. *vai, vv,* Mat. xv. 27; Rev. xxii. 20: (Arab. gram. حرف تنبيه, *particle of exciting*), Gram. art. 243. Syr. ܢܐ, *quæso;* cogn. آمّ, *equidem.* Æth. ነዒ : cogn. ነዑ፡ *agite:* ነዑ : *veni, age:* it. ንጻ: id. *en, ecce.* Arab. نا, r. نوا, *surrexit* cum labore, &c. Thence as a particle of exciting, as Eng. *Up!* So Schrœder; cogn. نوي Gr. νοέω, *intendit.* Castell. ii. conj. نوّي, *niti jussit* concordante Socio; it. *vocavit.* (a) Used to express *supplication, petition,* or the *contrary,* not unlike the English, *pray,* for I pray, or *prithee,* for I pray thee: as, בֹּא־נָא, *go in, pray,* Gen. xvi. 2. וְעַתָּה שָׂא נָא, *and now, pray, take away,* 1 Sam. xv. 25. Which is sufficient to show, against the rabbins, that it is not equivalent to עַתָּה. וִיהִי־נָא, *let there be, I pray,* 2 Kings ii. 9. Also with the first pers. and often as addressed to self (with ה parag. more generally, Gram. artt. 234. 239). אֵלְכָה נָּא, *pray, let me go*, Exod. iv. 18. Comp. Is. v. 1; 1 Kings i. 12; Num. xx. 17; Cant. iii. 2, &c. — *to self.* אָסֻרָה־נָּא וְאֶרְאֶה, *let me now go away and see*, Exod. iii. 3. Comp. 2 Sam. xiv. 15; Gen. xviii. 21; Jer. v. 24, &c. With a negative, generally, אַל־נָא תַעֲבֹר, *pass not over, I pray*, Gen. xviii. 3; xix. 8; xxxiii. 10; where, and vr. 7. 18, 19, its repeated insertion is emphatical, i. e. here expressive of submission, It.: Ps. cxxiv. 1; Cant. vii. 9. (b) *Exhortation*, or the contrary. שִׁמְעוּ־נָא, *hear, I pray*, Num. xx. 10; Judg. xiii. 4; 1 Kings i. 12; Jer. vii. 12, &c. (c) *Irony*, or *blame.* עִמְדִי־נָא, *pray, stand* (then), Is. xlvii. 12; Jer. xvii. 15; Ps. cxv. 2, &c. Noldius makes it, moreover, equal to *igitur, itaque; omnino, certe; tunc, tum* (pp. 528, 529); apparently, because these words seemed to give, sufficiently near, the meaning of certain passages: an error very common to Lexicographers, whose business it is to determine, not what any passage may loosely be rendered by, but what is the precise and real signification of the terms used. He also considers it as omitted by the ellipsis, in אֶעְבְּרָה, *let me pass*, Num. xxi. 22, &c. But this is unnecessary: the text being sufficiently full.

It is also compounded with other particles, as אַל־נָא, above. אִם־נָא, Gen. xviii. 3, &c. הִגֵּה־נָא, Ib. xii. 11; xvi. 2, &c. אוֹי־נָא, Jer. iv. 31; Lam. v. 16. אָנָּא...נָא, Gen. L. 17; 2 Kings xx. 3; Is. xxxviii. 3, &c., in which a word or more is found to intervene. In נֶגְדָה־נָּא, Ps. cxvi. 14. 18, we have a transposition of the parag. ה with נָא; thus, אֲשַׁלֵּם נְגֶדָה־נָּא for אֶשְׁלָמָה־נָא נֶגֶד. This, which is unusual indeed, makes all perfectly plain. We have, therefore, no ellipsis here. Again, in Judg. v. 26, in יָדָהּ לַיָּתֵד תִּשְׁלַחְנָה, we have the single epenthetic נ joined with the paragogic ה, of which we have instances, with a pronoun, Num. xxiii. 14, in קִרְבֵנוּ: comp. Deut. xxxi. 10; xxix. 14; in יֶשְׁנוֹ, Ps. lxxii. 15; xci. 12. Instances of the doubled נ are given, Gram. art. 235, with their use and force. I was not then aware of those with the single נ. The Arabs, as it will there be seen, term the latter, مُشَكَّدَةٌ, *made strong*; the former, خَفِيفٌ, *making light*, as opposed to heavy. Noldius, therefore, is right in considering this as paragogic, although he could assign neither use

nor force to the form. In the Arabic, it gives *emphasis* or strength; and so it does here, i. e. *she put forth her hand powerfully, with effect*, or the like.

נָא, m. once, Exod. xii. 9. *Raw.* Arab. نِيءٌ, *crudus, semicoctus*, de carne.

נֹאד, m. once, נאוד, Judg. iv. 19. Aff. נֹאדְךָ, pl. נֹאדוֹת. Arab. نَاقَ, *aquam de se emisit terra;* نَاقَ, *aqua è terrâ emanans;* نَدِيَ, *uvidus fuit, maduit. A skin for wine, milk, &c.*, Josh. ix. 4. 13; Judg. iv. 19; 1 Sam. xvi. 20; Ps. lvi. 9, — for tears; cxix. 83; whence it appears that they were hung up in the smoke. Gesen.

נָאוֹת, f. it. נוֹת, plur. constr. of נָאָה, f. part. Niph. of אוה. *Sought after, delighted in, chosen.* Hence, *the best parts of any thing.* נ׳ אֱלֹהִים, *the objects of God's choice*, Ps. lxxxiii. 13. נ׳ מִדְבָּר, *the choice pastures of the desert*, Ps. lxv. 13; Jer. ix. 10; xxiii. 10; Joel i. 19, 20; ii. 22. נ׳ הָרֹעִים, *pastures chosen by the shepherds*, Amos i. 2. נ׳ חָמָס, *the great love of violence;* i. e. *violent pursuits and projects*, Ps. lxxiv. 20. נ׳ הַשָּׁלוֹם, *the delights of peace*, Jer. xxv. 37. נ׳ דֶּשֶׁא, *pleasant places of herbage; agreeable pasture*, Ps. xxiii. 2. But, if أَوَى, *habitavit*, be taken as the root, or the cogn. נָוֶה, *place of abiding, habitation;* — used for fields, — *pasture*, as the residence of the flocks, will be the sense: and this has usually been taken.

נְאֻם, cogn. Arab. نَأْمَةٌ, *phthongus, sonus.* Cogn. نَعَمْ, *bene, maximè, ita;* affirmandi particula; نَعَمَ, *affirmavit rem.* Lit. *Declaration, dictum, of* —. In the phrase, נְאֻם יְהוָֹה, *it is a declaration of Jehovah*, Gen. xxii. 16; Num. xiv. 28, &c. Very common in the prophetical books. נ׳ בִּלְעָם, Num. xxiv. 3. 15. נ׳ דָּוִד, 2 Sam. xxiii. 1. נ׳ פֶּשַׁע, Ps. xxxvi. 2. Used of Agur, Prov. xxx. 1. A verb from the same root occurs in וַיִּנְאֲמוּ, Jer. xxiii. 31, יִנְאֲמוּ נְאָם, *they make a solemn declaration.*

בְּאֵמֻנִים, see אמן, p. 40, above.

נָאַף, v. pres. יִנְאַף. Cogn. Arab. نَافَ, *sitim explevit;* a term occasionally

כאף (401) נאר

applied to sexual intercourse. Cogn. نَابَ,
r. نوب, *vicem subiit, explevitque, vicariam operam præstitit.* Constr. abs. it. med. אֶת.
(a) *Committed adultery.* (b) *Metaph. Worshipped false gods, instead of the true.* (a) Exod. xx. 14; Deut. v. 17; Lev. xx. 10; Jer. v. 7. (b) Jer. iii. 9.
Part. נֹאֵף, f. נֹאֶפֶת, pl. f. נֹאֲפוֹת, Lev. xx. 10; Job xxiv. 15, &c.
Inf. נְאוֹף, Jer. xxiii. 14; Hos. iv. 2.
Pih. *Id.* נִאֵף, Jer. iii. 8. נִאֵף, Ezek. xxiii. 37.
Pres. יְנָאֵף, Jer. xxix. 23. תְּנָאַפְנָה, Hos. iv. 13, 14.
Part. מְנָאֵף, f. מְנָאֶפֶת, pl. מְנָאֲפִים, Ps. L. 18; Prov. xxx. 20; Is. lvii. 3.

נִאֻפִים, m. aff. נִאֻפֶיהָ. *Adulteries.* Metaph. *Acts of idolatry*, Jer. xiii. 27; Ezek. xxiii. 43.

נַאֲפוּפִים, m. aff. נַאֲפוּפֶיהָ. *Her repeated (acts of) adultery*, Hos. ii. 4.

נָאַץ, v. pres. יִנְאַץ. Arab. نَاصَ, *retrocessit, retromansit; declinavit ab aliquo. Turned away from*, through disregard and contempt: meton. *disregarded, despised; rejected, as unworthy of regard.* Constr. immed. it. med. אֶת, it. abs. it. med. בְּ, instr. מִן, of cause, Deut. xxxii. 19; Ps. cvii. 11; Prov. i. 30; v. 12; xv. 8; Jer. xiv. 21; xxxiii. 23; Lam. ii. 6.
Pih. נִאֵץ. *Id.* Num. xvi. 30; Ps. x. 13, &c.
Pres. יְנָאֵץ, Ps. lxxiv. 10.
Part. pl. aff. מְנַאֲצַי, Num. xiv. 23; Is. lx. 14; Jer. xxiii. 17.
Hithp. Part. מְנֹאָץ, for מִתְנֹאָץ. *Contemned*, Is. liv. 5. Or it may be for מְנֹאָץ, which would be the part. of Puhal, with the same signification, but the pointing inaccurate.

נְאָצָה, fem. pl. נֶאָצוֹת, aff. נָאָצוֹתֶיךָ. *Reproach, insult*, 2 Kings xix. 3; Is. xxxvii. 3; Neh. ix. 18. 25; Ezek. xxxv. 12.

נָאַק, v. pres. יִנְאַק, cogn. אנק. Syr. ܐܢܩ, *suspiravit.* Æth. ፈአሐ: *gemitus.* Arab. نَعَقَ, *inclamavit oves et increpuit;* *crocitavit corvus;* نَهَقَ, *rudit asinus. Cried out*, in sorrow, Job xxiv. 12; Ezek. xxx. 24.

נְאָקָה, fem. constr. נַאֲקַת. aff. נַאֲקָתָם, plur.

נַאֲקוֹת. *A cry* of sorrow, Exod. ii. 24; Judg. ii. 18; Ezek. iii. 24.

נאר, Kal non occ. Arab. cogn. نَغَرَ, *adversatus fuit, restitit;* نَغَرَ, *intus æstuavit irâ;* نَهَرَ, *increpuit, repulit;* نَارَ, r. نور, *fugit, abhorruit ab* aliquâ re. Apparently synonymous with נֵחַ, with which it is always connected. Symmachus considered it cognate with ארר.
Pih. נֵאֵר, נֵאַרְתָּה, *Rejected* as worthless, Ps. lxxxix. 40; Lam. ii. 7. LXX. read נֵעֵר, ἀπετίναξε; κατέστρεψας. Sym. εἰς κατάραν ἔδωκας. Syr. ܐܣܠܝ.

נבא, Kal non occ. Arab. نَبَأَ, *annuntiavit;* نَبَاء, *nuntius; res quæ nuntiatur.* Cogn. נָבָה, *animadvertit* rem; נָבָה, *recordatus fuit rei.* Æth. ነበአ: *locutus est.*
Niph. נִבָּא, pres. יִנָּבֵא, constr. abs. it. immed. it. med. אֶת. *Announced* as the will of God, either as to past or future events, *prophesied*, 1 Sam. x. 11; Jer. xx. 1, &c. With אֶל, or לְ, pers. to whom, and עַל, about whom.
Part. נִבָּא, pl. נִבָּאִים, and נְבִאִים, constr. נְבִאֵי, 1 Sam. xix. 21; Jer. xxxii. 3; Ezek. xiii. 2, &c.
Inf. הִנָּבֵא, aff. הִנָּבְאוֹ, Jer. xix. 14; Ezek. xxxvii. 7; xi. 13, &c.
Imp. הִנָּבֵא, Ezek. xi. 4; xiii. 2, &c.
Hith. הִתְנַבֵּא, הִנַּבֵּאתִי, הִנַּבְּאוּ, *Id.* 1 Sam. i. 6; Ezek. xxxvii. 10, &c. In 1 Sam. xviii. 10, the word seems to signify, he went on *prophesying* or *preaching* from the impulse of an evil spirit; just as Virgil's Sibyl is said to have spoken. A similar sort of phrenzy is still put on by pretenders among the heathen, &c., to the present day. That divine impulse which actuated the true prophets was, on the contrary, calm, collected, and rational.
Pres. יִתְנַבֵּא, 1 Kings xxii. 8. 18, &c.
Part. מִתְנַבֵּא, pl. מִתְנַבְּאִים, Num. xi. 27; 2 Chron. xviii. 7; Ezek. xiii. 17.
Inf. הִתְנַבּוֹת, aff. הִנַּבֹּאתוֹ, 1 Sam. x. 13; Zech. xiii. 4.
נבא, Chald. Hith. הִתְנַבִּי, *Prophesied*, Ezra v. 1.

נְבוּאָה, f. constr. נְבוּאַת. (a) *A predic-*

3 F

נבי (402) נבו

tion. (b) Meton. *A prophetical book.* (a) Neh. vi. 12. (b) 2 Chron. ix. 29; xv. 8.

נְבוּאָה, f. constr. נְבוּאַת, Chald. *Id.* Ezra vi. 14.

נָבוּב, m. constr. נְבוּב. Arab. نَبَّ, *mutivit, fremuit caper libidinosus;* نَبَ عَنُدَّ ۚ *magnificè semet extulit, et superbivit.* II. *Internodia produxit planta.* Cogn. أَنَبَ, *ingrato ac duriore modo tractavit; malè accepit, petentem aliquid repulit increpando;* أَنْبُوبٌ, *prominentior pars,* scil. *nodi arundinis; tubulus, fistula, siphon; series arborum.* (a) *Proud, insolent.* (b) *Hollow.* (a) Job xi. 12. See my notes on the place. (b) Exod. xxvii. 8; xxxviii. 7; Jer. lii. 21. LXX. κοῖλον, κύκλῳ. Syr. ܡܫܝ̈ܓ.

נְבִזְבָּה, f. pl. aff. נְבִזְבָּתָךְ, twice, Dan. ii. 6; v. 17. The context requires either *a gift* or some other *mark of honour.* LXX. δόματα, τὴν δωρεὰν τῆς οἰκίας σου. Vulg. *dona, dona domûs tuæ.* Syr. ܐܡܪ ܟܣܦܐ ܘܠܡܘܗܒܬܐ. These versions read נבז ביתך as two words; and, therefore, probably read נבז, in the former passage. The Persian نَوَاخْتَن *to praise, treat kindly and honourably,* from which are derived نَوَازْ, نَوَازِشْ, *act of kindness* and *attention,* may be the origin of this word. So Gesen.

נבח, v. once. Infin. נְבֹחַ. Arab. نَبَحَ, *latravit canis.* Syr. ܢܒܚ, *Id.* To *bark,* as a dog, Is. lvi. 10.

נבט, v. Kal non occ. Arab. نَبَطَ, *scaturivit aqua.* IV. *Ad scaturiginem perduxit fodiendo puteum.* Pass. *Apparuit, prodiit quid, quod ante latebat. Came into sight.*

Hiph. הִבִּיט, pres. יַבִּיט, יַבֵּט, *Brought into sight.* (a) *Looked,* abs. (b) *Looked at,* or *towards,* constr. med. לְ, אֶל, עַל, it. immed. (c) Meton. *Perceived* by looking, constr. immed. (d) *Looked favourably at,* constr. med. אֶל, it. immed. (e) *Looked for, expected to see.* (f) *Looked towards with expectation,* constr. med. אֶל. (g) *Looked at with attention; attended to* a command, constr. med. אֶל, לְ. (h) *Noticed.*

(a) 1 Kings xviii. 43; Ps. xxxiii. 13, &c. (b) Exod. iii. 6; Num. xxi. 9, &c. (c) Num. xxiii. 21; 1 Sam. ii. 32, &c. (d) Is. lxiv. 8; Lam. iv. 16, &c. (e) Job vi. 19. (f) Ps. xxxiv. 6; Is. xxii. 11, &c. (g) 1 Sam. xvi. 7; Ps. lxxiv. 20, &c. (h) Ps. x. 14.

Part. מַבִּיט, Ps. civ. 32.

Inf. הַבִּיט, aff. הַבִּיטָם־, ־מִי, Exod. iii. 6; Ps. cxix. 6; Lam. iv. 16; Jonah ii. 5; Hab. ii. 15.

Imp. הַבֵּט, הַבִּיט, הַבִּיטָה, Job xxxv. 5; Ps. lxxx. 15, &c.

Niph. or Pih. נִבַּט, with לְ, *Looked towards,* Is. v. 30.

נָבִיא, masc. aff. ־אֲךָ, נְבִי־אֲכֶם, plur. נְבִיאִים, constr. נְבִיאֵי, aff. נְבִיאַי, &c.; r. נבא. Arab. نَبِيٌّ, and Syr. ܢܒܝܐ, *propheta. A prophet.* (a) *A person commissioned by God to declare his will to men,* either as to their general conduct, or to any particular or difficult circumstances. (b) Pec. *One commissioned to foretell future events.* (c) *One to whom revelations have been made.* (d) *One who claims to be a prophet,* whether truly or not. (e) *Spokesman,* charged to deliver a divine commission previously communicated to another. (f) *A person devoted to the study of God's revealed will,* and under the instruction of one to whom revelations have been made. (g) These last persons were also called בְּנֵי הַנְּבִיאִים, *sons of the prophets.* (a) Deut. xviii. 15. 18; xxxiv. 10, &c. (b) Is. xxxvii. 2; Jer. xx. 2, &c. (c) Gen. xx. 7; 1 Kings xiii. 11, &c. (d) Deut. xiii. 2; Is. ix. 14, &c. (e) Exod. vii. 1. (f) 1 Sam. x. 5. 10, 11; xix. 21; 1 Kings xviii. 4, &c. (g) 1 Kings xx. 35; 2 Kings ii. 3. 5. 7, &c.

נְבִיא, m. def. נְבִיאָה, pl. def. נְבִיאַיָּא, Chald. *Id.* Ezra v. 1, 2; vi. 14.

נְבִיאָה, fem. of the preceding. (a) *A prophetess.* (b) *A prophet's wife.* (c) Applied to Miriam, either because she was *the sister of Moses the prophet,* or because engaged in celebrating the glorious deliverance from Egypt. (a) Judg. iv. 4; 2 Kings xxii. 14; 2 Chron. xxxiv. 22; Neh. vi. 14. (b) Is. viii. 3. (c) Exod. xv. 20.

נִבְכֵי־יָם, m. once, Job xxxviii. 16. LXX.

נָבָל (403) נָבָל

πηγὴν θαλάσσης. Sym. συνοχῆς πηγῆς. Syr. ܚܣܥܩܕܬ ܘܡܥܕܐ. Vulg. *profunda maris.* Dathe, after Schultens, *maris scopulos.* Arab. نَبَكَةٌ, and نَبَكَةٌ, plur. نَبَكٌ , نَبَكٌ , إِنْتَبَكَ , *collis acuto vertice præditus;*

elatus, editus fuit; بَكَّ , *compressus fuit,* uti in densâ hominum turbâ; *confluxit et tumultuatus fuit;* بَاكَ , r. بوك , *confusum turbatumque fuit* negotium. Either *submarine rocks,* or (reading נְבֻכִים) *labyrinths, mazes, of the sea.* See my notes on the place. Gesenius considers נָבַךְ as a primitive, cognate with נָבַע, نبع, and נָבַךְ, *erupit.*

נָבֵל, v. pres. יִבֹּל, and יָבֵל. (a) *Became shrivelled, and fell,* as flowers, fruits or leaves. Metaph. (b) *Wasted away* with fatigue, sorrow, or misfortune. (c) *Wasted away* and *crumbled to dust.* (d) *Acted as one whose intellect had decayed, acted foolishly.* (a) Ps. i. 3; xxxvii. 2; Is. xl. 7; lxiv. 5, נָבֵל, for נָבֵל; Jer. viii. 13; Ezek. xlvii. 12. (b) Exod. xviii. 18; 2 Sam. xxii. 46; Is. xxiv. 4. (c) Job xiv. 18; Is. xxxiv. 4. (d) Prov. xxx. 32.

Part. נֹבֵל, fem. נֹבֶלֶת (a) Is. i. 30; xxviii. 1. 4; xxxiv. 4.

Inf. נְבֹל, constr. נְבֹל, Exod. xviii. 18; Is. xxxiv. 4.

Pih. Pret. with aff. נִבַּלְתִּךְ, constr. immed. *Treated as worthless, despised,* Nah. iii. 6.

Pres. יְנַבֵּל, Deut. xxxii. 15; Jer. xiv. 21.

Part. מְנַבֵּל, Mic. vii. 6.

נָבָל, f. נְבָלָה, pl. נְבָלִים, f. נְבָלוֹת. *Corrupt, worthless,* in intellect or character. (a) *Foolish.* (b) *Impious.* (a) Deut. xxxii. 6. 21; 2 Sam. iii. 33, &c. (b) Job xxx. 8; Ps. xiv. 1; liii. 2, &c.

נֵבֶל, m. and "נֵ, plur. נְבָלִים, constr. נִבְלֵי, aff. נִבְלֵיהֶם, נִבְלְךָ. *A skin,* as stripped from a dead animal. (a) *A bottle of skin* for containing liquids, *pec.* wine. (b) *Any kind of vessel or jar,* made of earthenware. (c) *A musical instrument:* so called, perhaps, because in the shape of a *wine skin* or *jar.* The LXX. translate the word by ὄργανον, ψαλτήριον, κιθάρα, and νάβλα; but most commonly by the last. The Syriac, by ܟܢܪܐ, and ܟܢܪܐ. Josephus tells us that

the νάβλα had twelve notes (φθόγγους), and was played by the fingers, Ant. vii. 12. 3. Both the instrument and the name were introduced from Asia into Greece by the Corybantes. Strabo x. 3. Among the Romans the name became *Nablia* or *Naulia.* Ovid, addressing a female, says—

" Disce etiam duplici genialia nablia palmâ
Venere: conveniunt dulcibus illa jocis."
Arte Amat. 3. 327.

It is generally considered to be *a kind of lute.* If it was a stringed instrument, which is very probable, the expression נִבְלֵי עֲלָמוֹת, 1 Chron. xv. 20, seems to imply that it was adapted to female voices. In Ps. xxxiii. 2, and cxliv. 9, נֵבֶל עָשׂוֹר, *nablia* or *lute of ten* (strings). (a) 1 Sam. i. 24; x. 3; xxv. 18; 2 Sam. xvi. 1; Is. xxii. 24; Jer. xiii. 12. (b) Is. xxx. 14; Lam. iv. 2. (c) 1 Sam. x. 5; 2 Sam. vi. 5; 1 Kings x. 12; 1 Chron. xiii. 8; xv. 15, 16. 20. 28; xvi. 5; xxv. 1. 6; 2 Chron. v. 12; ix. 11; xx. 28; xxix. 25; Ps. xxxiii. 2; lvii. 9; lxxi. 22; lxxxi. 3; cxliv. 9; Neh. xii. 27; Is. v. 12; xiv. 11; Amos v. 23; vi. 5.

נְבָלָה, f. *Worthlessness.* Hence, *disgrace.* (a) *An act bringing disgrace* on its victim, or the victim's family: *a disgraceful action.* (b) Meton. *Punishment* for such an action. (c) *Impiety.* (d) *Folly.* (a) Applied [1] to crimes of incontinence; and [2] to the covetousness of Achan, which brought disgrace on the Israelites. [1] Gen. xxxiv. 7; Deut. xxii. 21; Judg. xix. 23, 24; xx. 6. 10; 2 Sam. xiii. 12; Jer. xxix. 23: [2] Josh. vii. 15. (b) Job xlii. 8. (c) Is. xxxii. 6. (d) 1 Sam. xxv. 25.

נְבֵלָה, fem. constr. נִבְלַת, aff. נִבְלָתִי, נִבְלָתְךָ, &c. Arab. نَبِيلَةٌ, *cadaver.* (a) *A dead body;* [1] of an animal found dead: [2] of a man. (b) Applied to *idols,* as being equally lifeless and offensive. (c) Sing. for pl. (a), [1] Lev. vii. 24; xvii. 15; xxii. 8; Deut. xiv. 21, &c.: [2] 1 Kings xiii. 24; 2 Kings ix. 37, &c. (b) Jer. xvi. 18, (c) Jer. xvi. 4; xxxiv. 20, &c.

נבלות, fem. aff. נַבְלֻתָהּ, once, *Shame, nakedness,* Hos. ii. 12.

נבע, v. Arab. نَبَعَ, *scaturivit è fonte aqua: apparuit;* نَبَغَ, *apparuit, manifesta*

evasit res. Syr. نَبَعَ, scaturivit. Æth.
ሰጠባእ : lacrymavit. Gushed or bubbled out, like water from a spring: came forth, came to light.
Part. נֹבֵעַ, Prov. xix. 4, נַחַל נֹבֵעַ. A stream gushing out from an unfailing spring.
Hiph. Pret. non occ. Pres. יַבִּיעַ. Constr. immed. with לְ before the person to whom uttered. (a) Brings out, utters, declares. (b) Prepares. (a) Ps. xix. 3; lix. 8; lxxviii. 2; xciv. 4; cxix. 171; Prov. i. 23; xix. 2. (b) Eccl. x. 1, יַבִּיעַ שֶׁמֶן רֹקֵחַ, The ointment of the perfumer gives out. See also Dathe.

נִבְרַשָׁא, Chald. def. נֶבְרַשְׁתָּא, f. once, Dan. v. 5. LXX. τῆς λαμπάδος. Syr. ܢܶܒܪܰܫܬܳܐ. Arab. نِبْرَاس, lucerna. Syr. ܢܶܒܪܰܫܬܳܐ. Id. flamma. A lamp, or other artificial light. According to some, from נוּר, and אֵשׁ.

נֶגֶב, m. Chald. נְגֵב, aruit, exsiccatus est. Syr. and Sam. Id. נגב, siccum. (a) The parched country which lay on the south of Judea. (b) The south. (c) נֶגְבָּה, [1] Towards the south: [2] On the south. (d) מִנֶּגֶב, on the south. (a) Gen. xiii. 1; Ps. cxxvi. 4; Is. xxi. 1, &c. (b) Gen. xx. 1; xxiv. 62; Exod. xxvii. 9, &c. (c), [1] Gen. xiii. 14; xxviii. 14, &c.: [2] Exod. xxvi. 18; xl. 24, &c. (d) Josh. xv. 7; xviii. 13; xix. 34, &c.

נֶגֶד, m. aff. נֶגְדִּי, &c. The fore part of the body. As a preposition, Before. (a) In the presence of. (b) In front of. (c) Opposite to. (d) In comparison with. (e) Before the mind of. (f) Straight forwards. (a) Gen. xxxi. 32. 37; Exod. xxxiv. 10, &c. (b) Josh. viii. 33; Neh. vii. 3, &c. (c) Exod. xix. 2; Josh. iii. 16; viii. 11; Ezek. xl. 13, &c. (d) Is. xl. 17. (e) Ps. xliv. 16; li. 5; Is. xlix. 16. (f) Josh. vi. 5. 20. With ה parag., Ps. cxvi. 14. 18. See under נָא above. כְּנֶגְדּוֹ, lit. like his front, i. e. like him, Gen. ii. 18. 20. לְנֶגֶד, (a) i. q. נֶגֶד, sign. a, b, e. (b) In opposition to. (c) For, appointed to. (d) Before, preceding on a journey. (a), [1] 2 Sam. xxii. 25; 2 Kings i. 13; Job iv. 16, &c.: [2] Neh. iii. 28 : [3] Num. xxii. 32 ; 2 Sam. xxii. 23, &c. (b) Neh. iii. 37; Prov. xxi. 30. (c) Josh. v. 13; Neh. xi. 22. (d) Gen. xxxiii. 12. מִנֶּגֶד, (a) In the presence of. (b) In sight. (c) Out of the sight of. (d) In

front of others, at their head. (e) Over against, opposite to. (f) In opposition to, against. (a) 1 Sam. xxvi. 20. (b) Gen. xxi. 16; 2 Kings ii. 7, &c. (c) Prov. xiv. 7; Jer. xvi. 17; Amos ix. 3, &c. (d) Judg. ix. 17. (e) Judg. xxxiv. 20; Neh. iii. 19, &c. (f) 2 Sam. xviii. 13.

נגד, v. Kal non occ.
Hiph. הִגִּיד, pres. יַגִּיד, apoc. יַגֵּד, יַגֶּד. Brought before; told, declared, or made known in any way. (a) With לְ, pers. to whom. [1] The subject of information not being mentioned. [2] With לֵאמֹר. [3] With כִּי. [4] The subject being mentioned, either with or without אֵת. (b) Without naming the person. [1] The subject not being mentioned. [2] The subject being mentioned either with or without אֵת. (a), [1] 1 Sam. xiv. 1; 2 Kings iv. 27, &c.: [2] Lev. xiv. 35; 1 Sam. xxv. 14, &c.: [3] Gen. xviii. 11; Judg. xiii. 9, &c.: [4] Gen. xli. 25; Judg. xiii. 6, &c. (b), [1] Esth. vi. 2; Is. xli. 26, &c.: [2] Is. xlv. 21; xlviii. 14, &c.

Part. מַגִּיד, fem. מַגֶּדֶת, plur. constr. מַגִּידֵי, Gen. xli. 24; Judg. xiv. 19; Esth. ii. 20, &c.

Inf. הַגִּיד, הַגֵּד, Gen. xliii. 6; Judg. xiv. 12, &c.

Imp. הַגֵּד, הַגֶּד, הַגִּידָה, Gen. xxix. 15; 1 Sam. xxiii. 11; 2 Sam. xviii. 21, &c.; הַגִּידִי, Gen. xxiv. 23; 2 Kings iv. 2. הַגִּידוּ, Gen. xxiv. 49; Ps. ix. 12, &c.

Hoph. הֻגַּד, Pass. of Hiph., Josh. ix. 24; Ruth ii. 11, &c.

Pres. יֻגַּד, Gen. xxii. 20; xxvii. 42, &c.
Inf. הֻגֵּד, Josh. ix. 24; Ruth ii. 11.

נגד, m. Chald. Part. נָגֵד, once, Proceeding, flowing, Dan. vii. 10. Æth. ነገደ : peregrè abiit; profectus est.

נֹגַהּ, m. aff. נָגְהָם. Syr. ܢܽܘܓܗܳܐ, aurora, manè, diluculum crepusculum; ܢܓܰܗ, illuxit. Æth. ነግህ : matutinum tempus, diluculum; ነግህ : manè. (a) The dawn. (b) The light of day. (c) Any light: [1] Of the moon: [2] Of the stars. (d) A brilliant light. (a) Prov. iv. 18; Is. lxii. 1. (b) Is. lx. 3. (c) Is. L. 10; Amos v. 20: [1] Is. lx. 19: [2] Joel ii. 10; iv. 15. (d) 2 Sam. xxii. 13; xxiii. 4; Ps. xviii. 13; Is. iv. 5; Ezek. i. 4. 13. 27, 28; x. 4;—Hab. iii. 4; fem. as a thing, al. m. Ib. 11.

נֹגַהּ, m. Chald. def. נָגְהָא, once, *The dawn*, Dan. vi. 20.

נְגֹהוֹת, pl. f. *Light*, Is. lix. 9.

נָגַהּ, v. pres. יִגַּהּ, *Shined*, as light, Job xviii. 5; xxii. 28; Is. ix. 1.

Hiph. pres. יַגִּיהַּ. (a) *Caused to shine*. (b) *Made light*. (a) Is. xiii. 10. (b) 2 Sam. xxii. 29; Ps. xviii. 29.

נָגַח, v. pres. יִגַּח. Arab. نَجَحَ, *propere evenit res*; نَجَحَ, *gloriatus fuit*; *fodit* puteum; *partem de clivo vallis abruptam in medium aquæ projecit* torrens. VI. *Agitatæ et inter se collisæ sunt undæ* maris; جَاخَ, r. جُوخ. II. *Prostravit*. - Syr. ܢܓܚ, *erupit* aqua. Sam. 𐡀𐡋𐡆, *pugnavit*. Constr. immed. it. med. אֶת. *Attacked, rushed upon in an hostile manner*. Pec. *Pushed with horns*, Exod. xxi. 28. 31, 32.

Pih. pres. יְנַגֵּחַ, *Id*. Deut. xxxiii. 17; 1 Kings xxii. 11; 2 Chron. xviii. 10; Ps. xliv. 6.

Part. מְנַגֵּחַ, Dan. viii. 4.

Hith. pres. יִתְנַגַּח, *Entered into conflict* with, constr. med. עִם, Dan. xi. 49.

נַגָּח, m. *Addicted to pushing with his horns*, Exod. xxi. 29. 36.

נָגִיד, m. constr. נְגִיד, pl. נְגִידִים, constr. נְגִידֵי, r. נגד. Arab. نَجَدَ, *superavit, vicit; manifesta et clara fuit* res; نَجِدَ, *animosus, strenuus fuit*; نَجُدَ, *animosus, strenuus*; *solus dux viæ*; نَجِيد, *fortis, animosus*. *One who goes before*. (a) *A leader* or *principal person*. (b) *Prince*. (c) *Chief of a tribe*. (d) *Chief of any number of persons*. (e) *A person appointed to any charge*. (a) 1 Chron. v. 2; xiii. 1; 2 Chron. xxxii. 21; Is. lv. 4. (b) 2 Sam. vi. 21; vii. 8; 1 Kings i. 35; xiv. 7; xvi. 2, &c. (c) 1 Chron. xxvii. 16; 2 Chron. xix. 11. (d) 1 Chron. ix. 20; xii. 27; xxvii. 4; 2 Chron. xxxi. 12. (e) 1 Chron. xxvi. 24; 2 Chron. xi. 11; Jer. xx. 1. In Dan. xi. 22, נְגִיד בְּרִית, i. q. בַּעַל בְּ", *one who has entered into a covenant*.

נְגִינַת, fem. aff. יָתִי, נְגִינָתָם, pl. נְגִינוֹת, aff. נְגִינוֹתַי, r. נגן. (a) *Music*, either vocal or instrumental. (b) *A song*. (c) Meton. *The subject of a song*. (a) Ps. lxi. 1; lxxvii. 7; Is. xxxviii. 20; Lam. v. 14; Hab. iii. 18. In the titles of Psalms iv., vi., liv., lv., lxvii., lxxvi. (b) Ps. lxix. 13. (c) Job xxx. 9; Lam. iii. 14.

נָגַן, v. pret. pres. Kal non occ. Cogn. נָגַם, נִגֵּם, and תִּנְגֹּם, *leni et submissâ voce usus fuit* in lectione vel cantu; نَغْم, *cantus dulcis*. Arab. غَنَّى. II. *Cecinit* carmen. *Performed in either vocal or instrumental music*.

Part. pl. נֹגְנִים, *Musicians*, Ps. lxviii. 26.

Pih. נִגֵּן, *Played on a stringed instrument*: followed by בְּיַד, 1 Sam. xvi. 16. 23.

Pres. יְנַגֵּן, Is. xxxviii. 20.

Part. מְנַגֵּן, 2 Kings iii. 15: with בְּיַד, 1 Sam. xviii. 10; xix. 9: with בְּכִנּוֹר, 1 Sam. xvi. 16.

Inf. נַגֵּן, 1 Sam. xvi. 17, 18; 2 Kings iii. 15; Ps. xxxiii. 3; Is. lxiii. 16; Ezek. xxxiii. 32.

נָגַע, v. pres. יִגַּע. Cogn. Arab. نَجَعَ, *bene profecit, utilis fuit edenti* cibus: *effectum habuit* oratio. (a) *Touched*, constr. med. בְּ, עַל, אֶל. (b) *Touched gently* so as to awaken, בְּ. (c) Metaph. *Touched the heart*, בְּ. (d) *Touched* so as to injure, immed. it. med. בְּ. (e) *Struck*, בְּ. (f) *Arrived*, spoken of time, abs. (g) *Arrived at*, with בְּ, אֶל, עַד. (h) *Reached*, with בְּ, אֶל, עַד, עַל. (i) *Reached the ears of*, אֶל. (a) Gen. xxxii. 32; Lev. v. 3; Is. vi. 7, &c. (b) 1 Kings xix. 5; Dan. viii. 18; x. 18. (c) 1 Sam. x. 27. (d) Gen. xxvi. 29; 1 Sam. vi. 9; 1 Chron. xvi. 22; Job xix. 21; v. 19; Ps. cv. 15. (e) Job i. 19. (f) Ezra iii. 1; Neh. vii. 73. (g) 2 Sam. v. 8; Is. xvi. 8; Jer. xlviii. 32; Jonah iii. 6. (h) Judg. xx. 41; Job iv. 5; Jer. iv. 10. 18; li. 9; Hos. iv. 2; Mic. i. 9. (i) Jonah iii. 6.

Part. נֹגֵעַ, fem. נֹגַעַת, plur. נֹגְעִים, fem. נֹגְעוֹת, Gen. xxvi. 11; Judg. xx. 34; 1 Kings vi. 27; Jer. xii. 14.

Inf. נְגֹעַ, גַּעַת, aff. גַּעְתּוֹ, נָגְעוֹ, Gen. xx. 6; Lev. xv. 23; Ruth ii. 9; 2 Sam. xiv. 10, &c. Imp. גַּע, Job i. 11; ii. 5; Ps. cxliv. 5.

Part. pass. נָגוּעַ. *Struck*, Ps. lxxiii. 14; Is. liii. 4.

Niph. יִנָּגַע. *Are beaten* in battle, Josh. viii. 15.

Pih. (from נֶגַע, with aff. נִגְעוֹ), pres. יְנַגַּע, constr. med. אֶת. *Struck* with disease, Gen. xii. 17; 2 Kings xv. 15; 2 Chron. xxvi. 20.

Puh. pres. יְנֻגָּע. *Are afflicted,* Psalm lxxiii. 5.

Hiph. הִגִּיעַ. (a) *Made to touch*, immed. and אֶל, לְ, עַד, עַל. (b) *Reached*, immed. it. med. אֶל, לְ, עַד. (c) *Reached the ears of*, אֶל. (d) *Reached its proper time*, לְ. (e) *Came near*, לְ. (f) *Arrived at*, immed. it. med. עַד, אֶל. (g) *Arrived at* a certain rank, לְ. (h) *Arrived at* a certain time, לְ. (i) *Arrived*, spoken of time, abs. (k) *Arrived*, at a place, abs. (a) Exod. iv. 25; xii. 22; Lev. v. 7; Is. vi. 7; xxvi. 5; Jer. i. 9; Lam. ii. 2; Ezek. xiii. 14. (b) 2 Chron. xxviii. 9; Job xx. 6; Ps. xxxii. 6; Is. viii. 9; xxv. 12; Zech. xiv. 5. (c) Esth. ix. 26. (d) Esth. ix. 1. (e) Ps. lxxxviii. 4. (f) 1 Sam. xiv. 9; Ps. cvii. 18; Is. xxx. 4. (g) Esth. iv. 14. (h) Dan. xii. 12. (i) Eccl. xii. 1; Cant. ii. 12; Ezek. vii. 12. (k) Esth. vi. 14.

Part. מַגִּיעַ, f. מַגַּעַת, pl. constr. מַגִּיעֵי, Gen. xxviii. 12; 2 Chron. ii. 11; Is. v. 8, &c.

Inf. הַגִּיעַ, aff. הַגִּיעֵנוּ, 1 Sam. xiv. 9; Esth. ii. 12. 15.

נֶגַע, m. aff. נִגְעִי, נִגְעוֹ, plur. נְגָעִים, constr. נִגְעֵי. (a) *A stroke, blow.* (b) *An infliction of evil.* (c) *Affliction.* (d) *The mark of a blow, a spot.* (a) Deut. xvii. 8; xxi. 5; 2 Sam. vii. 14; Ps. lxxxix. 33; Prov. vi. 33. (b) Gen. xii. 17; Exod. xi. 1; 1 Kings viii. 37; Ps. xxxix. 11; xci. 10. (c) 2 Chron. vi. 29; Ps. xxxviii. 12. (d) Lev. xiii. 3. 9. 29. 31. 42, &c.

נָגַף, v. pres. יִגֹּף. Cogn. נקף, and Arab. نَقَفَ, *percussit, fregit* caput. IV. *Fidit, fregit.* Constr. immed. it. med. אֶת. (a) *Struck.* (b) *Struck so as to wound; wounded.* (c) *Struck so as to kill; killed.* (d) *Struck with panic; caused to be beaten in battle.* (e) *Struck* with disease or calamity. (f) *Struck* against a stone, as the foot in walking, constr. abs. it. med. בְּ. (a) Exod. xxi. 22; Ps. xci. 12. (b) Exod. xxi. 35; Is. xix. 22. (c) 2 Chron. xiii. 15. (d) Judg. xx. 35; 1 Sam. iv. 3; 2 Chron. xiv. 11. (e) Exod. xxxii. 35; Josh. xxiv. 5;

1 Sam. xxv. 38, &c. (f) Ps. xci. 12; Prov. iii. 23.

Part. נֹגֵף, Exod. vii. 27; 2 Chron. xxi. 14.
Inf. נְגֹף, constr. נְגֹף, aff. נָגְפוֹ, Exod. xii. 23. 27; Is. xix. 23.

Niph. נִגַּף, pass. of sign. (d), 2 Sam. x. 15; 2 Chron. xix. 16. 19, &c.

Pres. יִנָּגֵף, 1 Sam. iv. 2. 10; 2 Chron. vi. 24, &c.

Part. נִגָּף, plur. נִגָּפִים, Deut. xxviii. 7. 25; Judg. xx. 32. 39.

Hith. pres. יִתְנַגְּפוּ. *Strike themselves, stumble,* Jer. xiii. 16.

נֶגֶף, m. (a) *An infliction of disease.* (b) *The act of stumbling.* (a) Exod. xii. 13; xxx. 12; Num. viii. 19; xvii. 11, 12; Josh. xxii. 17. (b) Is. viii. 14.

נגר, v. Kal non occ. Arab. نَغَرَ, *multum bibit* aquam; نَغَرَ, *bulliendo efferbuit* olla; نُغَرٌ, *fons aquæ salsæ;* نُغَارٌ, *sanguine manans* vulnus. Cogn. جَرَّ, *propulit; asciavit* lignum. Syr. ܢܓܪ, aph. *produxit, protraxit. Drew forth or along; made to flow over.* See גרר.

Hiph. הִגַּרְתִּי, pres. יַגִּיר. (a) *Dragged away.* (b) *Poured out.* (c) *Scattered.* (a) Ps. lxiii. 11; Ezek. xxxv. 5. (b) Ps. lxxv. 9. (c) Mic. i. 6.

Imp. with aff. הַגִּרֵם, (a) Jer. xviii. 21.
Hoph. Part. מֻגָּרִים. *Poured out,* Mic. i. 4.
Niph. Pret. נִגְּרָה. (a) *Was put forth*, as the hand. (b) *Overflowed,* as the eye. (c) *Was spilt,* as water. (d) *Was scattered,* as wealth. (a) Ps. lxxvii. 3. (b) Lam. iii. 49.
Part. נִגָּרִים, fem. נִגָּרוֹת, (c) 2 Sam. xiv. 14. (d) Job xx. 28.

In Ps. lxxvii. 3, the LXX. have ἐναντίον αὐτοῦ, as if they read נֶגְדִּי; but Symmachus had the present reading, for he gives ἐκτέτατο. In Lam. iii. 49, the LXX. have κατεπόθη, while Sym. has ἐπέμεινε.

נָגַשׁ, v. pres. יַגֹּשׁ, תִּנַּגְּשׂוּ. Arab. نَجَشَ, *excitavit, agitavit* feram, *venandi ergo; compulit dispersos* camelos. Cogn. نَجَشَ, *scrutatus est, inquisivit;* نَقَشَ, *summâ cum curâ perscrutatus fuit* rem, *et detexit.* Æth. ሠርወ: *regnavit;* ሠርጊ: *rex.* Sam.

נגש (407) נדב

נגש, præfecit, præposuit. Constr. med. אֶת, pers. and thing. *Exacted* a task, debt, or tax, Deut. xv. 2, 3; 2 Kings xxiii. 35; Is. lviii. 3.

Part. נֹגֵשׂ, plur. נֹגְשִׂים. *An exactor, taskmaster, slave-driver*, Exod. iii. 7; Job iii. 17; Is. ix. 4; Dan. xi. 20, &c.

נגשׁ, v. Pret. non occ. Pres. יִגַּשׁ. (a) *Came near:* [1] abs.: [2] constr. med. אֶל. (b) *Came up to;* [1] עַד: [2] אֶת. (c) *Came near, so as to touch;* [1] constr. med. בְּ: [2] עַל. (a), [1] Gen. xviii. 23; xxvii. 27; Lev. xxi. 21, &c.: [2] Gen. xxvii. 22; xliv. 18; Exod. xxiv. 15, &c. (b), [1] Judg. ix. 52: [2] 1 Sam. ix. 18. (c), [1] Job xli. 8; Is. lxv. 5: [2] Ezek. ix. 6.

Inf. גֶּשֶׁת, aff. גִּשְׁתּוֹ, גִּשְׁתָּם, Gen. xxxiii. 3; Exod. xxviii. 44; xxxiv. 30, &c.

Imp. גַּשׁ, גֵּשׁ, גְּשָׁה; fem. גְּשִׁי, pl. גְּשׁוּ, Gen. xix. 9; xxvii. 21; xlv. 4; Ruth ii. 14; 2 Sam. i. 15; Josh. iii. 9.

Niph. נִגַּשׁ, is used instead of the pret. of Kal, Gen. xxxiii. 7; Exod. xx. 21, &c.

Part. הַנִּגָּשִׁים. *Those who come near,* Exod. xix. 22.

Hiph. הִגִּישׁ, pres. יַגִּישׁ. *Brought near.* (a) A person. (b) A sacrificial offering. (c) Any thing. (a) Gen. xlviii. 10. 13; Exod. xxi. 6. (b) Lev. ii. 8; viii. 14, &c. (c) Gen. xxvii. 25; 2 Sam. xvii. 29, &c.

Part. מַגִּישׁ, pl. מַגִּישִׁים, constr. מַגִּישֵׁי, Mal. i. 7; ii. 12: iii. 3, &c.

Imp. הַגִּישָׁה, pl. הַגִּישׁוּ, 1 Sam. xiii. 9; xiv. 18, &c.

Hoph. pret. הֻגָּשׁוּ. *Were brought or placed,* 2 Sam. iii. 34.

Part. מֻגָּשׁ. *Brought, offered,* Mal. i. 11.

Hith. Imp. הִתְנַגְּשׁוּ. *Approach,* Is. xlv. 20.

נֵד, m. Arab. نَدّ, *collis in altum assurgens.* (a) *A heap.* (b) *A mound.* (a) Is. xvii. 11. (b) Exod. xv. 8; Josh. iii. 13. 16; Ps. xxxiii. 7; lxxviii. 13.

נָדַב, v. pres. with aff. יִדְּבֶנּוּ. Arab. نَدَبَ, *vocavit* ad rem aliquam; *impulit* ad aliquid; نَدُبَ, *agilis, expeditus pulcher fuit.* IV. *Periculo exposuit* seipsum. Cogn. נדף, constr. immed. it. med. אֶת. *Rendered willing, impelled,* Exod. xxv. 2; xxxv. 21. 29.

Hith. הִתְנַדַּב, הִתְנַדַּבְתִּי, pres. יִתְנַדְּבוּ. *Offered,* or *performed willingly,* 1 Chron. xxix. 6. 9. 17; Ezra ii. 68.

Part. מִתְנַדֵּב, plur. מִתְנַדְּבִים, Judg. v. 9; 1 Chron. xxix. 5; 2 Chron. xvii. 16; Ezra iii. 5; Neh. xi. 2.

Inf. הִתְנַדֵּב, aff. הִתְנַדְּבָם, Judg. v. 2; 1 Chron. xxix. 9. 14. 17; Ezra i. 6.

נדב, v. Chald. Ith. הִתְנַדַּב, *Id.,* Ezra vii. 15.

Part. מִתְנַדֵּב, plur. מִתְנַדְּבִין, Ezra vii. 13. 16. Inf. הִתְנַדָּבוּת, Ezra vii. 16.

נְדָבָה, fem. constr. נִדְבַת, pl. נְדָבוֹת, constr. נִדְבוֹת, aff. נְדִיבָתִי־, נְדִיבָתָם־. (a) *A voluntary offering.* (b) *Free will.* (c) *A ready manifestation of feeling.* (d) Pl. *Abundance, liberality.* (a) Exod. xxxv. 29; xxxvi. 3, &c. (b) Deut. xvi. 10. (c) Hos. xiv. 5. (d) Ps. lxviii. 10. In Ps. cx. 4, עַמְּךָ נְדָבֹת, *thy people* will make *voluntary offerings;* or, it may be, will manifest *readiness of mind.* The LXX. read עִמְּךָ, *with thee* there will be *voluntary offerings.*

נִדְבָּךְ, m. pl. נִדְבָּכִין, Chald. Cogn. דבק, and Arab. دَفَقَ, *effudit* aquam. VII. *Effusa fuit* aqua. *A layer,* Ezra vi. 4. LXX. δόμος.

נדד, v. pret. נָדְדָה, נָדוּ, pres. יִדּוֹד, יָדַד. Arab. نَدَّ, *fugax fuit, aufugit.* II. *Divulgavit: dispersit.* III. *Adversatus fuit.* نَدَأَ, *terruit, agitavit.* Cogn. נוד. (a) *Fled.* (b) *Wandered, walked to and fro.* (c) *Flapped* the wings. (a) Gen. xxxi. 40; Esth. vi. 1; Ps. xxxi. 12; lxviii. 13; Is. x. 31; xxi. 15; xxii. 3; xxxiii. 3; Jer. iv. 25; ix. 9; Hos. vii. 13; Nah. iii. 7.

Part. נֹדֵד, fem. נֹדְדָה, plur. נֹדְדִים. (a) Is. xxi. 14. (b) Job xv. 23; Prov. xxvii. 8; Is. xvi. 2, 3; Jer. xlix. 5; Hos. ix. 17. (c) Is. x. 15.

Inf. נְדֹד, (a) Ps. lv. 8. Puh. נוֹדַד, *Was driven away,* Nah. iii. 17. Hiph. pres. with aff. יְנִדֻהוּ, *They cause him to wander,* Job xviii. 8.

Hoph. pres. יֻדַּד, *He is made to wander,* Job xx. 8.

Part. מֻנָּד, *Driven to and fro,* 2 Sam. xxiii. 6.

Hith. הִתְנוֹדְדָה, *Was shaken to and fro, was agitated,* Is. xxiv. 20.

Pres. תִּתְנוֹדֵד, Jer. xlviii. 27. LXX. ἐπολέμεις. So the Syriac. But the Vulg. *captivus duceris.* יִתְנוֹדְדוּ, Ps. lxiv. 9. LXX. ἐταράχθησαν.

נדד (408) נדי

נָדַד, v. 3 f. נַדַּת, Chald. *Fled,* of sleep, Dan. vi. 19.

נְדֻדִים, m. plur. *Moving to and fro, agitation, restlessness,* either of body or mind, Job vii. 4.

נדה, v. Kal non occ. Arab. نَدَا, r. نَدو, *separatus, dispersus fuit.* It. *Liberalis fuit;* نَدَّ, *increpuit, abegit* camelos. Syr. ܢܰܡ, *nauseavit, abominatus est.* Sam. נדה, *recessit; separatus, dimotus est.* Æth. ᎀᎉᎰ : *egit ante se* pecora.

Pih. Part. plur. מְנַדִּים, aff. מְנַדֵּיכֶם, *Putting aside, separating* as impure; *desiring to avoid,* Is. lxvi. 5; Amos vi. 3.

נֵדֶה, m. *A present,* Ezek. xvi. 32. In the same verse, מָדָנַיִךְ, appears to signify *thy presents,* as if put for נְדַיִךְ, which is the reading of two mss.

נִדָּה, f. constr. נִדַּת, aff. נִדָּתָהּ. (a) *Legal impurity.* (b) *A female in that state.* (c) Moral *impurity.* (d) *Any thing impure and worthless.* (a) Lev. xii. 2. 5; Num. xix. 9. 13. 20, 21, &c. (b) Lam. i. 17; Ezek. xviii. 6; xxii. 10; xxxvi. 17. (c) Lev. xx. 21; Ezra ix. 11; Zech. xiii. 1. (d) Ezek. vii. 19, 20.

נדח, v. pres. יִדַּח. Arab. نَدَخَ, *allisit; appulit* navis ad littus; cogn. دَخَا, r. دخو, *projecit, disjecit,* רדה. *Impelled* or *urged.* (a) *Drove* an axe. (b) *Drove away.* (b) 2 Sam. xiv. 14.

Inf. נְדֹחַ, (a) Deut. xx. 19.

Niph. נִדַּח, (a) *Was impelled,* as the hand in striking with an axe. (b) Was driven away. (c) *Was induced* to an action. (a) Deut. xix. 5. (b) Job vi. 13; Jer. xl. 12; xliii. 5; xlix. 5. (c) Deut. iv. 19; xxx. 17.

Part. נִדָּח, fem. נִדָּחָה, נַדַּחַת, pl. נִדָּחִים. (b) Deut. xxii. 1; xxx. 4; 2 Sam. xiv. 13, 14, &c.

Puh. Part. מְנֻדָּח, *Driven,* Is. viii. 22.

Hiph. הִדִּיחַ, (a) *Brought with violence on,* עַל. (b) *Drove away;* [1] from a country, [2] astray, [3] from office. (c) *Induced to* an action. (a) 2 Sam. xv. 14. (b), [1] Deut. xxx. 1; Jer. xvi. 15; Dan. ix. 7, &c.: [2] 2 Kings xvii. 21; Jer. xxiii. 2; L. 17.

[3] 2 Chron. xiii. 9; Ps. lxii. 5. (c) Prov. vii. 21.

Pres. יַדִּיחַ, וַיַּדַּח, 2 Kings xvii. 21; Jer. xxiv. 9.

Inf. הַדִּיחַ, Ps. lxii. 5.

Hoph. Part. מֻדָּח, *Driven astray,* Is. xiii. 14.

נָדִיב, m. constr. נְדִיב, pl. נְדִיבִים, constr. נְדִיבֵי, aff. נְדִיבָמוֹ, r. נדב. *Ready to give* or *perform.* (a) *Willing, liberal.* (b) *Nobleminded.* (c) *Noble* in rank, *a prince.* (d) *Distinguished* for skill. (e) Probably, *a libertine.* (a) Exod. xxxv. 5. 22; 2 Chron. xxix. 31. (b) Prov. xvii. 7; Is. xxxii. 5. (c) 2 Sam. ii. 8; Job xii. 21; xxxiv. 18, &c. (d) 1 Chron. xxviii. 21. (e) Job xxi. 28. See notes.

נְדִיבָה, fem. aff. נְדִיבָתִי, plur. נְדִיבוֹת. *Liberality, noblemindedness,* Job xxx. 15; Ps. li. 14; Is. xxxii. 8.

נָדָן, aff. נְדָנֵהּ, *Sheath* of a sword, 1 Chron. xxi. 27.

נִדְנֶה, Chald. *Id.* Dan. vii. 15, בְּגוֹ נִדְנֶה. LXX. ἐν τῇ ἕξει μου. Syr. ܚܨܗ ܕܓܘܫܡܗ. According to the common interpretation, the body is considered as the *sheath* of the mind. But is not this a refinement? May not the true reading be בדמה? This might be translated to *the body.* Arab. بَدَن, *corpus, exceptis capite et pedibus necnon manibus* hominis. Æth. ᎀᎄᎅ : *cadaver* humanum.

נדף, v. pres. יִנְדֹּף. Arab. نَدَفَ, *concussit* gossipium, impulso magni arcûs nervo, atque ita *attenuavit et divisit* illud : *violenter propulit* equum. Æth. ᎀᎅᎈ : *percussit; feriit.* (a) *Scattered, drove about,* as smoke or chaff. (b) *Routed* an enemy, *conquered* him. (a) Ps. i. 2; lxviii. 3. (b) Job xxxii. 13.

Niph. נִדַּף, *Is driven away,* Is. xix. 7.

Part. נִדָּף, Lev. xxvi. 36; Job xiii. 25; Prov. xxi. 6; Is. xli. 2.

Inf. הִנָּדֹף, Ps. lxviii. 3.

נָדַר, v. pres. יִדֹּר, יִדַּר. Arab. نَذَر, *devovit* Deo. Syr. ܢܕܰܪ, and Sam. נדר, *idem.* *Made a vow* to God, generally followed by נֶדֶר, and לְ, Gen. xxviii. 20; Num. xxx. 3; 2 Sam. xv. 8; Ps. cxxxii. 2, &c.

Part. נֹדֵר, Lev. xxvii. 8; Mal. i. 14.

Inf. נְדֹר, Num. vi. 2; Deut. xxiii. 23.

נדר (409) נחל

Imp. pl. נִדְרוּ, Ps. lxxvi. 12.

נֶדֶר, and נֵדֶר, m. Aff. נִדְרִי, &c.; pl. נְדָרִים, aff. נְדָרַי, &c. נְדָרֵיכֶם, (a) *A vow; the act of vowing.* (b) *The thing vowed.* (a) Gen. xxviii. 20; Num. vi. 2, &c. (b) Deut. xii. 6. Phrr. נָדַר נֶדֶר, שִׁלֵּם נ׳, עָשָׂה נ׳.

נֹהַּ, m. once, Ezek. vii. 11, *Lamentation,* r. נהה. LXX. ὡραϊσμός. Vulg. *requies.* Two MSS. read נֹחַ. Houbigant takes the Æth. ፈሣዕ: *quies, requies, respiratio,* from ፈሣዕ: *respiravit, requievit, recreatus est.*

נָהַג, v. pres. יִנְהַג. Arab. نهج, *apertam et manifestam reddidit viam; præscripsit quid pro recto tramite; incessit viam; instituit facere;* نهج, *via aperta, et manifesto.* Constr. immed. it. med. אֶת. (a) *Led.* (b) *Conducted* cattle. (c) *Drove* or *led off as spoil.* (d) *Drove* a vehicle. (e) *Led* an army. (f) *Guided.* (a) 1 Sam. xxx. 22; Cant. viii. 2; Lam. iii. 2. (b) Gen. xxxi. 18; Exod. iii. 1; 1 Sam. xxx. 20. (c) 1 Sam. xxx. 2; Job xxiv. 3; Is. xx. 4. (d) 2 Kings ix. 20. (e) 1 Chron. xx. 1; 2 Chron. xxv. 11.

Part. נֹהֵג, pl. נֹהֲגִים, Ps. lxxx. 2. (f) 1 Chron. xiii. 7; Eccl. ii. 3.

Part. Pass. pl. נְהוּגִים, Is. lx. 1.

Imp. נְהַג, 2 Kings iv. 24.

Pih. נִהַג, pres. יְנַהֵג. (a) *Brought* on a wind. (b) *Led* a people. (c) *Led captive.* (d) *Drove* into exile. (e) *Drove* a vehicle. (a) Exod. x. 13; Ps. lxxviii. 26. (b) Ps. xlviii. 15; lxxviii. 52; Is. xlix. 10; lxiii. 14. (c) Gen. xxxi. 26. (d) Deut. iv. 27; xxviii. 37. (e) Exod. xiv. 25.

Part. pl. f. מְנַהֲגוֹת, Nah. ii. 5.

נָהָה, v. pres. non occ. Syr. ܢܗܐ, *ingemuit. Lamented,* Mic. ii. 4.

Imp. נְהֵה, Ezek. xxxii. 18.

Niph. pres. יִנָּהוּ, *Id.* יִנָּהוּ אַחֲרֵי יְהוָֹה, *they mourn after the Lord,* i. e. regret the loss of the symbol of his presence, 1 Sam. vii. 2.

נָהוֹר, m. Chald. def. נְהוֹרָא, i. q. נְהָרָה, *Light,* Dan. ii. 22.

נְהִי, m. in pause, נֶהִי, aff. נִהְיָם, r. נהה, *Lamentation,* Jer. ix. 9. 17—19; xxxi. 15; Ezek. xxvii. 32; Amos v. 16.

נָהִירוּ, f. Chald. r. נהר. Syr. ܢܗܝܪܘܬܐ, *illuminatio. Light.* Metaph. *Wisdom,* Dan. v. 11. 14.

נחל, v. Kal non occ. Arab. نهل, *restinxit sitim;* نهل, *potus, cibus. Drank.*

Pih. 2 m. נִהַלְתָּ, pres. יְנַהֵל. Constr. immed. it. med. לְ. (a) *Led* to water. (b) *Led,* as a flock. (c) *Tended* carefully. (d) *Fed.* (e) *Gave rest to.* (a) Ps. xxiii. 2; Is. xlix. 10. (b) Exod. xv. 13; Ps. xxxi. 4. (c) Is. xl. 11. (d) Gen. xlvii. 17. (e) 2 Chron. xxxii. 22. LXX. κατέπαυσεν αὐτούς. Vulg. *præstitit iis quietem.*

Part. מְנַהֵל, Is. li. 18.

Hith. pres. אֶתְנָהֲלָה, *I proceed with my flock,* Gen. xxxiii. 14.

נַחֲלָלִים, masc. pl. once, Is. vii. 19. According to Gesen., *Pastures.* But three MSS. read

נְחָלִים, m. r. חלל, *Crevices;* and with this agree the Syr., LXX., and Vulgate Versions, which have نخيل, ῥαγάδα, and *foraminibus.*

נָהַם, pret. 2 m. נָהַמְתָּ, pres. יִנְהַם. Syr. ܢܗܡ, *rugiit, fremuit, gemuit.* Arab. نهم, *increpuit inclamando; rugiit* leo; *vehementer anhelavit* vir. (a) *Roared,* as a lion. (b) *Groaned.* (a) Is. v. 29, 30. (b) Prov. v. 11; Ezek. xxiv. 23.

Part. נֹהֵם, *Roaring,* Prov. xxviii. 15.

נַהַם, m. *The roaring* of a lion, Prov. xix. 12; xx. 2.

נְהָמָה, f. constr. נַהֲמַת. (a) *The roaring* of the sea. (b) *Groaning.* Meton. *Sorrow.* (a) Is. v. 30. (b) Ps. xxxviii. 9.

נהק, v. pret. non occ. pres. יִנְהַק. Arab. نهق, *rudit* asinus. *Brayed,* Job vi. 5; xxx. 7.

נָהָר, m. constr. נְהַר, pl. נְהָרִים, constr. נַהֲרֵי; it. נְהָרוֹת, constr. נַהֲרוֹת. Arab. نهر, نهر, *fluvius, flumen.* Syr. ܢܗܪܐ, *Id.* (a) *A river.* (b) Pec. *The Euphrates.* (c) *Any stream.* (d) *The current of the sea.* (a) Gen. ii. 13; xv. 18, &c. (b) Gen. xxxi. 21; Exod. xxiii. 31; Josh. xxiv. 2; 2 Sam. x. 16, &c. (c) Job xx. 17; xxii. 16; Ps. xlvi. 5, &c. (d) Jonah ii. 4.

3 G

נחר, v. pret. 2 m. נָהַרְתָּ, pres. 3 pl. יִנְהֲרוּ. Arab. نَهَرَ, *fluere fecit effodiendo fluvium*; *fluxit aqua*; *interdiu fuit* vel *fecit quid*. Syr. ܢܗܰܪ, *splenduit, illuxit*. *Flowed as a river*. (a) *Assembled themselves*. (b) *The countenance brightened*. (a) Is. ii. 20; Jer. xxxi. 12; li. 44; Mic. iv. 1. (b) Probably, Ps. xxxiv. 6; Is. lx. 5.

נָחָר, m. Chald. def. נַהֲרָא, and נַהֲרָה. *A river*, Ezra iv. 10—20; v. 3—13; Dan. vii. 10, &c.

נְהָרָה, f. once. Arab. نَهَار, *dies*. Syr. ܢܘܽܗܪܳܐ, *lux, luminare*. The light of day, Job iii. 4.

נוא, v. Kal non occ. Arab. نَاءَ, r. نَوَأَ, *abstinuit, noluit, aversus fuit* à re; نَاء r. نَوَء, *surrexit cum labore et molestiâ*. *Surrexit* contra alium; نَهَى, *vetuit*. *Was weak and unable to perform* a thing. Hiph. הֵנִיא, pres. יָנִיא. Constr. immed. it. med. אֶת. *Made weak*. (a) *Discouraged*. (b) *Prohibited*. (c) *Frustrated*. (a) Num. xxxii. 7. (b) Num. xxx. 6. 9. 12. (c) Ps. xxxiii. 10. In Ps. cxli. 5, שֶׁמֶן רֹאשׁ אַל־יָנִי רֹאשִׁי is translated by the lxx. ἔλαιον δὲ ἁμαρτωλοῦ μὴ λιπανάτω τὴν κεφαλήν μου. The Syr. and Vulg. are precisely the same. They read שֶׁמֶן רָשָׁע, and perhaps יָנִיא, for יָנִי.

נוב, v. pres. יָנוּב. (a) *Threw out shoots*. (b) *Produced* as fruit. (c) *Increased*. (a) Ps. xcii. 11. (b) Prov. x. 31. (c) Ps. lxii. 11. Pih. יְנוֹבֵב, *Makes fruitful*, Zech. ix. 17.

נוב, Is. lvii. 19. See נִיב.

נוד, v. pres. יָנוּד. Arab. نَاد, r. نود, *mutavit, vacillavit præ somnolentia*; *movit caput*. V. *Commotus et agitatus fuit* de ramo. Syr. ܢܳܕ, *motus, concussus, territus fuit*. *Was agitated*. (a) *Moved itself to and fro*. (b) *Wandered* as a fugitive. (c) *Departed*. (d) *Shook* his head as an expression of pity, *condoled with*; constr. med. לְ. (a) 1 Kings xiv. 1. (c) Jer. L. 3; iv. 1. (d) Job xlii. 11; Is. li. 19; Jer. xv. 5; xvi. 5; xxii. 10; Nah. iii. 7.

Part. נָד, (b) Gen. iv. 12. 14. Inf. נוּד, (a) Prov. xxvi. 2. (d) Job ii. 11; Ps. lxix. 21. Imp. s. f. נוּדִי, pl. m. נֻדוּ. (c) Ps. xi. 1; Jer. xlviii. 17; xlix. 30; L. 8. (d) Jer. xlviii. 17. Hiph. pres. יָנִיד. (a) *Moved* to and fro. (b) *Caused to wander*. (c) *Disturbed*. (a) Jer. xviii. 16, יָנִיד בְּרֹאשׁוֹ, *shakes his head*, in astonishment or pity. (c) Ps. xxxvi. 12. Inf. הָנִיד, (b) 2 Kings xxi. 8. Hith. part. מִתְנוֹדֵד, *Bemoaning himself*, Jer. xxxi. 18.

נוּד, v. pres. תְּנֻד, Chald. *Departs*, Dan. iv. 11.

נוֹד, m. aff. נֹדִי, *Wandering*, Ps. lvi. 9.

נָוֶה, m. constr. נְוֵה, aff. נָוֶךָ, נָוֵהוּ, נָוָם, נְוֵהֶן. Arab. نَوَى, *intendit, proposuit sibi rem*; *transmigravit ab uno loco in alium*; نَوًى, *animi propositum, intentio*; *domus*. Lit. *The object and end of a journey*; *resting-place, dwelling*. (a) *Resting-place of cattle*. (b) *Dwelling of men*. (c) *Chosen habitation of God*. (a) Is. lxv. 10; Ezek. xxv. 5, &c. (b) Prov. iii. 33; xxi. 10; xxiv. 15, &c. (c) 2 Sam. xv. 25; Jer. xxv. 30.

נָוָה, f. constr. נְוַת, Id. Job viii. 6.

נָוָה, v. pres. יִנְוֶה, *Dwelt, dwelt quietly*, Hab. ii. 5. Part. f. נָוָה, Ps. lxviii. 15. In a passive sense, Jer. vi. 2. Hiph. pres. aff. אַנְוֵהוּ, *I will prepare a dwelling for him*, Exod. xv. 2.

נוּחַ, v. pres. יָנוּחַ, apoc. יָנַח. Arab. نَاخَ, r. نوخ, *in genua decubuit* camelus. Syr. ܢܳܚ, *quievit requievit*; *cessavit*. *Lay down*. (a) *Rested*. (b) *Halted*. (c) *Ceased*. (d) *Took up his quarters and remained in*; with בְּ. (e) *Pitched on*, as a bird; with בְּ. (f) *Came down on, and took possession of*; with עַל. (g) *Settled on*, as a ship in shallow water; with עַל. (h) Impers. יָנוּחַ לִי, *I have rest*. (a) Exod. xxiii. 12; Deut. v. 14; Job iii. 25, &c. (c) Exod. xx. 11; 1 Sam. xxv. 9. (d) Prov. xiv. 33; xxi. 16; Eccl. vii. 9; Is. xxv. 10. (e) Exod. x. 14; Is. vii. 19. (f) Num. xi. 26; 2 Kings ii. 15; Ps. cxxv. 3; Is. xi. 2. (g) Gen. viii. 4. (h) Job iii. 12; Is. xxiii. 12.

נול (411) נוט

Inf. נוֹחַ, (a) Esth. ix. 16—18. (f) Num. xi. 25; Josh. iii. 13. (h) Neh. ix. 28.

נֵיחַ, (b) Num. x. 36. (e) 2 Sam. xxi. 10. Aff. נִיחוֹךְ, 2 Chron. vi. 41.

Hiph. has two forms: I. הֵנִיחַ, pres. יָנִיחַ, apoc. יָנַח. (a) *Gave rest to.* (b) *Gave comfort to,* constr. immed. (c) *Allowed to fall down,* constr. immed. (d) *Caused to rest* upon, with בְּ, אֶל, or עַל. (a) constr. [1] immed. lxiii. 14: [2] med. לְ, Deut. xii. 10; Josh. xxii. 4; xxiii. 1, &c. (b) Prov. xxix. 17. (c) Exod. xvi. 11. (d), [1] with בְּ, Ezek. v. 13; xvi. 42, &c. [2] with אֶל, Ezek. xl. 2: [3] with עַל, Is. xxx. 32.

Part. מֵנִיחַ, Josh. i. 13.

Inf. הָנִיחַ, aff. הֲנִיחִי, Deut. xxv. 19; Is. xiv. 3; Ezek. xxiv. 13; xliv. 3.

Imp. pl. הָנִיחוּ, Is. xxviii. 12.

II. הֵנִיחַ, and הִנִּיחַ, pres. יַנִּיחַ, apoc. וַיַּנַּח. (a) Constr. immed. [1] *Placed.* [2] *Left in a given state.* [3] *Forsook.* [4] *Quitted.* [5] *Allowed to rest.* (b) Imm. of person, and med. לְ, of thing: [1] *Allowed to remain for a purpose.* [2] *Rendered.* (c) Immed. of thing, and med. לְ, of person: [1] *Bequeathed.* [2] *Gave into the power of.* [3] *Cast down* on a place. (d) *Permitted,* immed. it. med. לְ. (e) *Left untouched,* med. לְ. (a), [1] Lev. xvi. 23; Num. xix. 9; Deut. xxvi. 4; 1 Kings viii. 9, &c. [2] Ezek. xvi. 39. [3] Jer. xiv. 9. [4] Eccl. x. 4. [5] Eccl. vii. 18; xi. 6. (b), [1] Gen. xxxix. 16; Lev. vii. 15; Judg. iii. 1; 2 Sam. xvi. 21; xx. 3; Jer. xxvii. 11; xliii. 6. [2] Is. lxv. 15. (c), [1] Ps. xvii. 14; Eccl. ii. 18. [2] Ps. cxix. 121. [3] Is. xxviii. 2; Amos v. 7. (d) 1 Chron. xvi. 21.

Part. מַנִּיחַ, (d) Eccl. v. 11.

Inf. הַנִּיחַ, Num. xxxii. 15; Esth. iii. 8.

Imp. הַנַּח, הַנִּיחָה; pl. הַנִּיחוּ, Exod. xvi. 33; Judg. vi. 20, &c. (d) Exod. xxxii. 10; Judg. xvi. 26; 2 Sam. xvi. 11. (e) 2 Kings xxiii. 18.

Hoph. הוּנַח, *Rest is given,* Lam. v. 5.

הֻנִּיחָה, f. *Was placed,* Zech. v. 11.

Part. מֻנָּח, *Left, remaining,* Ezek. xli. 9. 11.

נוט, v. pres. תָּנוּט, once, Ps. xcix. 1. Probably cognate with נוד, and מוט. *Is agitated,* shaken. LXX. σαλευθήτω. Vulg. *moveatur.* Syr. ܢܙܘܥ, *tremefiat.*

נְוָלוּ, f. Chald. once, Ezra vi. 11, וּבַיְתֵהּ נְוָלוּ יִתְעֲבֵד. LXX. καὶ ὁ οἶκος αὐτοῦ τὸ

κατ' ἐμὲ ποιηθήσεται. Vulg. *domus autem ejus publicetur.* Syr. כֻּזְבֵּל, *fimo.*

נְוָלִי, f. Chald. twice, Dan. ii. 5; iii. 29, וּבָתֵּיכוֹן נְוָלִי יִתְּשָׂמוּן. LXX. καὶ οἱ οἶκοι ὑμῶν διαρπαγήσονται. Syr. Id. Vulg. *domus vestræ publicabuntur;* but in the latter passage, *domus ejus vastetur:* considered as cognate with נָבֵל, and translated, *a dunghill.* But may be cognate with the Arab. نَالَ, r. نَوْل, *præbuit, largitus fuit?* نَوَّلَ, and نَوَّلَ, *donum.* Thence, *A confiscation.*

נום, v. pres. יָנוּם. Arab. نَوْم, *somnus;* نُوَام, *somnolentia;* نَامَ, *dormivit, dormitavit.* Syr. ܢܳܡ. Æth. ႖ႰႫ: *Id. Slept,* Ps. lxxvi. 6; cxxi. 3, 4; Is. v. 27; Nah. iii. 16.

Inf. נוּם, Is. lvi. 10.

נוּמָה, f. *Sleepiness, sluggishness,* Prov. xxiii. 21.

נון, once, v. Niph. pres. יִנּוֹן, *Shall be drawn out, continued, perpetuated,* Ps. lxxii. 17. LXX. διαμενεῖ. Syr. ܢܐܡܪܘܢܝܗܝ. See נין.

נוס, v. pres. יָנוּס, apoc. יָנָס. Cog. נסס. Arab. نَاسَ, r. نَوْس, *ultro, citroque mota et agitata fuit defendens res.* Syr. نَسَ, *trepidavit, timuit.* (a) *Fled:* [1] abs. [2] From a person, place, or thing, with מִן, מִפְּנֵי, or לִפְנֵי. [3] To a place, with אֶל, לְ, or עַד. (b) *Escaped* by fleeing. (c) *Passed away,* as a state of health. (a), [1] Judg. iv. 17; 1 Sam. xix. 10; 2 Sam. xix. 9, &c. [2] Josh. xx. 6; 1 Sam. iv. 16, 17; 2 Sam. i. 4; x. 14, &c. [3] Deut. iv. 42; xix. 11; Josh. xx. 4; Judg. vii. 22, &c. (b) Jer. xlvi. 6. (c) Deut. xxxiv. 7; Is. li. 11; Cant. ii. 17.

Part. נָס, pl. נָסִים, Exod. xiv. 27; Josh. viii. 20, &c.

Inf. נֻס, aff. נָסְךָ, נוּסְכֶם, Gen. xix. 20; Deut. iv. 44; 2 Sam. xxiv. 13, &c.

Imp. pl. נֻסוּ, Jer. xlix. 30; li. 6, &c.

Hiph. הֵנִיס, *Caused to flee for refuge,* Exod. ix. 20.

Pres. יָנִיס, *Put to flight,* Deut. xxxiii. 30.

נוּעַ (412) נוּף

Inf. הָעִים, *To escape the observation of,* Judg. vi. 11.

נוּעַ, v. pres. יָנוּעַ, apoc. יָנַע. Arab. نَاعَ, r. نوع, *commotus, perturbatus fuit.* II. Concussit ramum. (a) *Was shaken.* (b) *Was disturbed, agitated.* (c) *Wandered in distress and agitation; wandered.* (d) *Was changeable, varied.* (e) *Staggered, as a drunken man.* (f) *Moved, as the lips.* (a) Is. vi. 4. (b) Exod. xx. 18; Is. vii. 2; xix. 1. (c) Job xxviii. 4; Ps. lix. 16; cix. 10; Lam. iv. 14, 15; Amos iv. 8; viii. 12. (d) Prov. v. 6. (e) Is. xxiv. 20; xxix. 9.

Part. נָע, pl. נָעִים, נָעוֹת, Gen. iv. 22; Prov. xxii. 19. (f) 1 Sam. i. 13.

Inf. נוּעַ, נוֹעַ, Judg. ix. 9. 11. 13; Ps. cix. 10; Is. xxiv. 20; Jer. xiv. 10. (a) Is. vii. 2.

Niph. pres. יִנּוֹעַ, *Is shaken,* Amos ix. 9; Nah. iii. 12.

Hiph. הֵנִיעַ, pres. יָנִיעַ. (a) *Shook* as the head or hand. (b) *Caused to wander.* (c) *Dispersed,* as fugitives. (a) 2 Kings xix. 21; Job xvi. 4; Ps. xxii. 8; cix. 25; Is. xxxvii. 22; Lam. ii. 15; Zeph. ii. 15. (b) Num. xxxii. 13; 2 Sam. xv. 20; Amos ix. 9. (c) Ps. lix. 12. In Dan. x. 10, הֵנִיעֻנִי, *it set me trembling,* on my hands and feet. LXX. ἤγειρε. Vulg. and Syr. *Id.*

נוּף, v. I. Pret. נַפְתִּי, *I have sprinkled,* Prov. vii. 17. Arab. نَفَى, *effudit nubes aquam.*

Hiph. pres. תָּנִיף, *Thou causest to sprinkle,* Ps. lxviii. 10.

II. Hiph. הֵנִיף, pres. יָנִיף, apoc. יָנֶף. Arab. نَافَ, r. نوف, *eminuit, extititve supra rem.* (a) *Lifted up:* [1] The hand over or against a person or thing, with אֶל, or עַל. [2] — an instrument, with עַל. (b) *Shook to and fro.* (c) *Presented an offering:* applied to [1] Persons, [2] Animals, or [3] Inanimate things. (a), [1] 2 Kings v. 11; Job xxxi. 21; Is. xi. 15, &c. [2] Exod. xx. 20; Deut. xiii. 26; xxvii. 5; Josh. viii. 31, &c. (c), [1] Num. viii. 11. 13. 15. 21. [2] Lev. xiv. 12. 24. [3] Exod. xxxv. 22; Lev. xxiii. 11. 20; Num. v. 25, &c.

Part. מֵנִיף, aff. מְנִיפוֹ, Is. x. 15; xix. 16; Zech. ii. 13.

Inf. הָנִיף, aff. הֲנִיפְכֶם, Lev. vii. 30; x. 15; xxiii. 12; Is. x. 15.

הֵנֵפָה, (b) Is. xxx. 28.

Imp. הָנִיפוּ יָד, *Beckon* with *the hand,* Is. xiii. 2.

Hoph. הוּנַף, *Was offered,* Exod. xxix. 27.

Pih. pres. יְנַפֵּף יָדוֹ, *Beckons* with *his hand,* Is. x. 31.

נוֹף, m. once, *An elevated situation.* יְפֵה נוֹף, *beautiful of,* from *elevated situation,* Ps. xlviii. 3.

נוּץ, v. Hiph. 3 pl. הֵנֵצוּ, pres. יָנֵאץ, for יָנִיץ, or יָנֵץ. *Blossomed,* Eccl. xii. 5; Cant. vi. 11; vii. 13. See נָץ.

נֹצָה, נוֹצָה, f. *Plumage of,* or *for, the head,* Job xxxix. 13; Ezek. xvii. 3. 7. Arab. نَصِي, *coma frontis propendula.* Cogn. نَصَا.

prehendit antias.

נוּר, f. Chald. def. נוּרָא, *Fire,* Dan. iii. 7. 11. 15, &c. Syr. ܢܘܪܐ, and Sam. נור, *Id.*

נוּשׁ, v. i. q. אָנַשׁ, and Syr. ܢܫ, *ægrotavit.* Once, pres. with ה parag. אָנוּשָׁה, *I am diseased,* in mind, Ps. lxix. 21.

נזה, v. pres. יִזֶּה, apoc. יַז, and יִז, constr. med. אֵת, מִן. Arab. نَزَا, r. نزو, *assilivit.* IV. *Effecit ut emitteret sanguinem;* نَضَّ, *leniter, sensimque fluxit aqua.* Æth. ነዝሐ: *respersit. Was sprinkled,* Lev. vi. 20; 2 Kings ix. 33; Is. lxiii. 3.

Hiph. הִזָּה, pres. יַזֶּה, apoc. יַז. *Sprinkled,* pec. with blood, Exod. xxix. 21; Lev. iv. 6. 17; v. 9; Is. lii. 15, &c. The sprinkling of blood on the veil of the Tabernacle, on the altar, and on the mercy-seat, as well as on Aaron, his sons, and their garments, is manifestly alluded to in Is. lii. 15; and this passage cannot fairly be interpreted otherwise, than of a purification through the blood of Christ. See my Sermons, Diss. ii. l. c.

Part. מַזֶּה, constr. מַזֵּה, Num. xix. 21.

Imp. הַזֵּה, Num. viii. 7.

נָזִיד, m. constr. נְזִיד, *Any viand prepared by boiling,* Gen. xxv. 29. 34; 2 Kings iv. 38—40; Hag. ii. 12.

נָזִיר, m. constr. נְזִיר, aff. נְזִירְךָ, pl. נְזִרִים, aff. נְזִירֶיהָ, r. נזר. Cogn. Heb. and Syr. נדר. Arab. نَذَرَ, *devovit Deo. Set apart.* (a)

נזל (413) נזר

Precluded by a vow from certain things allowable to others, *a Nazarite.* (b) Applied to Joseph, either as separated from his brethren, or as distinguished above them by his merit and rank. This application is sometimes derived from נֵזֶר, *a diadem*. (c) Applied to vines, Lev. xxv. 5. 11 : but in what sense is not certain. LXX. τὴν σταφυλὴν τοῦ ἁγιασματός σου—τὰ ἁγιασμένα. Vulg. *uvas primitiarum tuarum ; primitias.* Le Clerc; *vineam non putatam.* (a) Num. vi. 2—21; Judg. xiii. 5. 7. 17; Lam. iv. 7; Amos ii. 11, 12. (b) Gen. xlix. 25; Num. xxxiii. 16. (c) Lev. xxv. 5. 11.

נזל, v. 3 pl. נָזְלוּ, pres. יִזַּל. Arab. نَزَلَ, *descendit loco;* نَزْل, *catarrho laboravit;* نُزْل, *pluvia.* (a) *Sunk down.* (b) *Dropped down,* as water or dew. (c) *Dropped water.* (d) Metaph. *Rained* righteousness. (a) Judg. v. 5. (b) Num. xxiv. 7; Deut. xxxii. 2; Ps. cxlvii. 18; Cant. iv. 17. (c) Job xxxvi. 28; Jer. ix. 18. (d) Is. xlv. 8. Part. נוֹזְלִים, aff. נוֹזְלֵיהֶם, (a) *Flowing.* (b) *Streams.* (a) Jer. xviii. 14. (b) Exod. xv. 8; Ps. lxxviii. 16. 44; Prov. v. 15; Cant. iv. 15; Is. xliv. 3. Hiph. הִזִּיל, *Caused to flow,* Is. xlviii. 21.

נֶזֶם, m. aff. נִזְמִי, pl. נְזָמִים, constr. נִזְמֵי. Arab. cogn. زَمَّ, *ligavit, capistravit;* زِمَام, *funiculus annexus annulo qui per cameli nasum trajicitur.* A *ring,* usually of gold, worn as an ornament. (a) *A nose-jewel.* (b) *An earring.* (a) Gen. xxiv. 22. 30. 47 ; Judg. viii. 24. 28; Prov. xi. 22; xxv. 12, &c. (b) Gen. xxxv. 4.

נֶזֶק, m. once, *Injury, loss,* Esth. vii. 4.

נזק, v. Chald. *Suffered loss.* Part. נָזִק, Dan. vi. 3. Aph. *Caused loss to,* pres. תְּהַנְזִק, Ezra iv. 13. Part. f. constr. מְהַנְזְקַת, Ezra iv. 15. Inf. constr. הַנְזָקַת, Ezra iv. 22.

נֶזֶר, נֵזֶר, m. aff. נִזְרוֹ. (a) *A state of separation and dedication.* (b) *A mark of being dedicated to God:* thence, pec. a plate of gold worn on the head-dress of the high priest, and inscribed קֹדֶשׁ לַיהוָֹה. (c) *A royal diadem.* (d) *Sovereignty.* (e) *The hair of the head,* as shorn by the Nazarite.

(a) Num. vi. 4—21; Lev. xxi. 12. (b) Exod. xxix. 6; xxxix. 30; Lev. viii. 9; Num. vi. 7. (c) 2 Sam. i. 10 ; 2 Kings xi. 12 ; 2 Chron. xxiii. 11 ; Ps. lxxxix. 40; cxxxii. 18; Zech. ix. 16. (d) Prov. xxvii. 24. (e) Jer. vii. 29.

נזר, v. Kal non occ. *Separated, kept from* any thing. Arab. نَاذَر, *impedivit.* Syr. ܢܙܰܪ, *abstinuit.* Niph. pres. יִנָּזֵר. (a) *Restricted himself.* (b) *Abstained from,* with מִן. (c) *Withdrew himself from,* with מֵאַחֲרֵי. (d) *Devoted himself* to a certain practice, as a *Nazarite* was peculiarly devoted to God, with לְ. (b) Lev. xxii. 2. (c) Ezek. xiv. 7. (d) Hos. ix. 10. Inf. הִנָּזֵר, (a) Zech. vii. 3. Hiph. הִזִּיר, pres. יַזִּיר. (a) *Set apart to,* with אֶת, and לְ, (b) *Restrained from,* with אֶת, and מִן. (c) *Restricted himself* from, with מִן. (d) *Devoted himself* to, with לְ. (a) Num. vi. 12. (b) Lev. xv. 31. (c) Num. vi. 3. (d) Num. vi. 5, 6. Inf. הַזִּיר, (d) Num. vi. 2.

נחה, v. pres. non occ. Arab. نَجَا, r. نجو. Cogn. Heb. נחה, נוח. *Contendit versus aliquem.* (a) *Led, conducted, guided,* constr. abs. it. med. אֶת. (b) Apparently, either *Relied on,* or *made peace with,* with עַל. (a) Gen. xxiv. 27 ; Exod. xiii. 17; xv. 13; Ps. lx. 11 ; lxxvii. 21; cviii. 11; Is. lviii. 11. (b) Is. vii. 2. Imp. נְחֵה, Exod. xxxii. 34; Ps. viii. 9; xxvii. 11; cxxxix. 24. Hiph. הִנְחָה, pres. יַנְחֶה. (a) *Led.* (b) *Gave rest to.* (c) *Placed.* (d) *Brought back.* (a) Gen. xxiv. 48 ; Num. xxiii. 7, &c. (b) Ps. lxi. 3; lxvii. 5 ; Is. lvii. 18. (c) 1 Kings x. 26 ; 2 Kings xviii. 11. (d) Job xii. 23. For אַחְחֶם, Job xxxi. 18, and פִּנְחֵם, see my notes. Inf. aff. הַנְחֹתָם, Exod. xiii. 21; Neh. ix. 19.

נִחוּמִים, m. pl. aff. נִחוּמַי, r. נחם. (a) *Consolations.* (b) Meton. *A disposition to impart consolation, pity.* (a) Is. lvii. 18 ; Zech. i. 13. (b) Hos. xi. 8.

נְחוּשׁ, m. *Copper* or *brass,* Job vi. 12. Arab. نُحَاس, *Æs.*

and נְחֻשָׁה, f. *Id.* Lev. xxvi.

נחי (414) נחל

19; 2 Sam. xxii. 35; Job xx. 24; xxviii. 2, &c.

נְחִילוֹת, f. once, Ps. v. 1. Probably, *Instruments of the flute kind*, r. חלל, or חול.

נְחִירִים, m. pl. aff. נְחִירָיו, *Nostrils*, Job xxi. 12. See נחר.

נַחַל, m. dual, נַחֲלַיִם, pl. נְחָלִים, constr. נַחֲלֵי, aff. נַחֲלָיךָ. Cogn. Arab. نَهَلَ, see נחל.
(a) *A stream*, whether *river* or *brook*. (b) *A torrent*, whose bed fills suddenly, and is dry during part of the year. Thence, (c) *A valley*, through which streams run. (a) Gen. xxxii. 24; Lev. xxiii. 40; Deut. ii. 13. 24; iv. 48, &c. (b) 1 Kings xvii. 7; Job vi. 15; xxviii. 4. (c) Num. xiii. 23, 24; xxxii. 9; Deut. i. 24, &c.

נַחֲלָה, f. *Id*. sig. (a) Ps. cxxiv. 4.

נַחֲלָה, f. constr. נַחֲלַת, aff. נַחֲלָתִי, &c.; נַחֲלַתְכֶם, pl. נְחָלוֹת, r. נחל. *The act of taking possession*. (a) *A settlement, dwelling*. (b) *A possession in land, inheritance*. (c) *A possession* of any kind: either, [1] *The object of choice*; thence, *portion*, as the Israelites were the chosen people of God: [2] *The consequence* of conduct: or [3] *Share, portion*. (a) Deut. iv. 38; xv. 4; xx. 16; Judg. xviii. 1, &c. (b) Num. xxvi. 62; xxvii. 7; xxxvi. 7—9, &c. (c), [1] Deut. iv. 20; Is. xix. 25; Joel ii. 17, &c. [2] Job xx. 29; xxvii. 13; xxxi. 2. [3] Gen. xxxi. 14; Josh. xiii. 14; 2 Sam. xx. 1, &c.

נָחַל, v. pres. יִנְחַל, cognate with the Arab. نَحَلَ, *descendit* ex itinere, *diversatus fuit* in loco. (a) *Obtained possession*, constr. abs. (b) Constr. immed. it. med. אֶת. [1] *Took possession of*. [2] *Possessed*. (b) *Took or received as his portion*. (c) *Apportioned*, with לְ, of pers., and אֶת, of thing. (a) Num. xviii. 20; xxvi. 55; Josh. xvi. 4, &c. (b), [1] Exod. xxiii. 20; Josh. xiv. 1; xvii. 6. [2] Exod. xxxii. 13; Num. xviii. 23; xxxv. 8, &c. [3] Exod. xxxiv. 9; Ps. cxix. 111; Prov. iii. 38, &c. (c) Num. xxxiv. 17.

Inf. נְחֹל, Num. xxxiv. 18.

Pih. נִחֵל, *Gave settlements to*, constr. med. אֶת, Josh. xiii. 32; xiv. 1.

Inf. נַחֵל, Num. xxxiv. 29.

Hiph. הִנְחִיל, pres. יַנְחִיל. (a) *Caused to possess*, with אֶת, of person and thing. (b) *Left as an inheritance to*, with לְ, of pers., and אֶת, of things. (c) *Gave an inheritance to*, with אֶת. (a) Deut. i. 38; xix. 3; Josh. i. 6, &c. (b) 1 Chron. xxviii. 8. (c) Ezek. xlvi. 18.

Part. מַנְחִיל, Deut. xii. 10.

Inf. הַנְחִיל, הַנְחֵל, aff. הַנְחִילוֹ, Deut. xxi. 16; xxxii. 8; Prov. viii. 21; Is. xlix. 8.

Hoph. הָנְחַלְתִּי, *I am made to possess*, Job vii. 3.

Hith. הִתְנַחַל, pres. יִתְנַחֲל. (a) *Took*, each for himself. (b) *Left as an inheritance*. (a) Num. xxxiii. 54; xxxiv. 13; Is. xiv. 2; Ezek. xlvii. 13. (b) Lev. xxv. 46.

Inf. הִתְנַחֵל, Num. xxxii. 18.

נַחֲלָת, f. *Portion*, Ps. xvi. 6.

נֹחַם, m. Arab. نَحَمَ, *suspirium*. *Pity*: hence, *Change of purpose*, Hos. xiii. 14. LXX. παράκλησις. Vulg. *consolatio*.

נחם, v. Kal non occ. Arab. نَحَمَ, *gemuit, suspiravit*. *Sighed*.

Niph. נִחַם, pres. יִנָּחֵם, *Became sighing*. (a) *Was grieved*. (b) Meton. *Repented*. constr. [1] Abs. [2] Med. עַל. (c) *Felt pity*. [1] Abs. [2] on account of an infliction, with אֶל, עַל, or מִן. [3] *And withdrew it*, with אֶל, or עַל. (d) *Mourned* over, with אֶל, לְ, or עַל. (e) *Recovered from his grief*, constr. abs. it. med. עַל, or אַחֲרֵי. (f) *Freed himself* from a displeasing person or thing, with מִן. (g) Meton. *Was grieved and changed his conduct*, with regard to promised good, with עַל. (h) *Changed his purpose*. (a) Gen. vi. 6, 7; 1 Sam. xv. 11. 35; Ezek. xxxi. 16. (b), [a] Exod. xiii. 17; Job xlii. 6; Jer. xxxi. 19. [2] Jer. viii. 6. (c), [1] Ps. cvi. 45; Is. lvii. 6; Jer. xx. 16, &c. [2] 2 Sam. xxiv. 16; 1 Chron. xxi. 15, &c. [3] Exod. xxxii. 14; Jer. iv. 28; Ezek. xiv. 22, &c. (d) Judg. xxi. 6. 15; Ezek. xxxii. 31. (e) Gen. xxiv. 67; xxxviii. 12; 2 Sam. xiii. 39. (f) Is. i. 24. (g) Jer. xviii. 10. (h) 1 Sam. xv. 29; Ps. cx. 4.

Inf. הִנָּחֵם, 1 Sam. xv. 29; Ps. lxxvii. 3; xc. 13; Jer. xv. 6.

Pih. נִחֵם, pres. יְנַחֵם. Constr. immed. it. med. אֶת. *Sympathized with, comforted*, Is. xlix. 13; Jer. xxxi. 13; Ezek. xiv. 22, &c.

Part. מְנַחֵם, aff. מְנַחֲמְכֶם, pl. מְנַחֲמִים, constr. מְנַחֲמֵי, 2 Sam. x. 3; Job xvi. 2; Eccl. iv. 1; Is. li. 12, &c.

נחם (415) נחש

Inf. נַחֵם, aff. נַחֲמוֹ, &c., Gen. xxxvii. 35; Is. lxi. 2, &c.

Puh. נֻחַם, 3 f. in pause, נֻחָמָה, Is. liv. 11. Pres. 2 pl. in pause, תִּנֻּחָמוּ, Is. lxvi. 13. Hith. הִנֶּחָמְתִּי, in pause, for הִתְנֶחָמְתִּי, pres. יִתְנֶחָם. (a) *Became comforted, comforted himself.* (b) *Gratified his anger.* (c) *Changed his purpose.* (a) Deut. xxxii. 36; Ps. cxix. 52. (b) Ezek. v. 12. (c) Num. xxiii. 19.

Part. מִתְנַחֵם, (a) Gen. xxvii. 42.

Inf. הִתְנַחֵם, (a) Gen. xxxvii. 35.

נֶחָמָה, f. aff. נֶחָמָתִי, *Consolation*, Job vi. 10; Ps. cxix. 50.

בַּחְנוּ, for אֲנַחְנוּ, *We*, Gen. xlii. 11; Exod. xvi. 7, 8; Num. xxxii. 32; 2 Sam. xvii. 12; Lam. iii. 42.

נחץ, v. once. Part. pass. נָחוּץ, *Urgent*, 1 Sam. xxi. 9. LXX. κατὰ σπουδήν. Cogn. Arab. نَخَسَ, *fodicans trusit jumentum.* Cogn. نَحَشَ, *incitavit.*

נחר, m. Aff. נַחֲרוֹ. Arab. نَخَر, *sonum emisit, spiritumve cum sono eduxit per nares;* نَخَرَة, pl. نَخَر, *extremitas rostri equini, &c.*

נַחֲרָה, f. constr. נַחֲרַת, *Id.*, Jer. viii. 16.

נָחָשׁ, m. constr. נְחַשׁ, pl. נְחָשִׁים. This word is not found, in its Hebrew signification, in the cognate dialects; but it is manifestly the generic name of the *serpent* tribe. (a) For, [1] It was the form assumed by the rod of Moses. [2] It is said to be עַקַלָּתוֹן. [3] Its bite is deadly. [4] It is poisonous. [5] It has a divided tongue. [6] It has a gliding motion. [7] It conceals itself in fences and the holes of walls. [8] Its threatening sound is mentioned. (b) The species mentioned are, [1] the צֶפַע, [2] the צִפְעוֹנִי, [3] שְׁפִיפוֹן, and [4] שָׂרָף. The latter species were sent to plague the Israelites by their deadly bite. (c) It was the instrument made use of by Satan in the temptation of our first parents. And hence, (d) נָחָשׁ בָּרִחַ is an epithet of Satan. See La Cepède, Discours sur la Nature des Serpens, and my Notes on Job xl. 25. 32. (a), [1] Exod. iv. 3; vii. 15. [2] Is. xxvii. 1. [3] Prov. xxiii. 32; Eccl. x. 8. 11; Amos v. 19; ix. 3. [4] Ps. lviii. 5. [5] Ps. cxl. 4. [6] Prov. xxx. 19. [7] Eccl. x. 8; Amos v. 19. [8] Jer. xlvi. 22. (b), [1] Is. xiv. 29. [2] Jer. viii. 17. [3] Gen. xlix. 17. [4] Is. xiv. 29; Num. xxi. 7. 9, 10. (c) Gen. iii. 1—14. (d) Job xxvi. 13; Is. xxvii. 1. The only other passages where the word occurs are, 2 Kings xviii. 4; Is. lxv. 25; Mic. vii. 17. See Hieroz. Bochart., ii. pp. 406. 746, seq.

נָחַשׁ, v. Kal non occ. Arab. نَحَسَ, *sciscitatus fuit* nuncium, *inquisivit* de eo. See Hieroz. Bochart., i. 20.

Pih. נִחֵשׁ, pres. יְנַחֵשׁ. (a) *Used divination.* (b) *Watched, observed.* (a) Gen. xliv. 5. 15; Lev. xv. 26; 2 Kings xvii. 17; xxi. 6. (b) Gen. xxx. 27; 1 Kings xx. 33.

Part. מְנַחֵשׁ, (a) Deut. xviii. 10.

Inf. נַחֵשׁ, (a) Gen. xliv. 5. 15. The connexion between these terms may have arisen, either from the superior instinct said to be possessed by some species of serpents, or the brilliancy of the serpent's eye and the acuteness of its vision. See Bochart. l. c.

נַחַשׁ, m. pl. נְחָשִׁים, *Divination*, Num. xxiii. 23; xxiv. 1.

נְחָשׁ, m. def. נְחָשָׁא, Chald. *Copper or brass*, Dan. ii. 32. 45; iv. 20; v. 4. 23; vii. 19. Syr. ܢܚܫܐ, *Id.*

נְחֹשֶׁת, f. aff. נְחֻשְׁתִּי, יָתָהּ, תֶּךָ, נְחֻשְׁתָּם. (a) *Id.* (b) *A chain, or fetter.* (c) Dual, נְחֻשְׁתַּיִם, *Fetters.* (d) Probably, *Money.* Lat. *æs.* (a) Gen. iv. 22; Exod. xxv. 3, &c. (b) Lam. iii. 7. (c) Judg. xvi. 21; 2 Kings vii. 7; 2 Chron. xxxiii. 11, &c. (d) Ezek. xvi. 36.

נְחֻשְׁתָּן, m. The title given to the brazen serpent made by Moses, and subsequently idolized by the Israelites, 2 Kings xviii. 4.

נָחַת, v. pret. non occ. pres. יֵחַת, and תִּנְחַת. Syr. ܢܚܬ, *descendit.* I. (a) *Came down.* (b) *Came down upon* with violence, with עַל. (c) *Penetrated* the mind, with בְּ. (a) Job xvii. 16. (b) Ps. xxxviii. 3; Jer. xxi. 13. (c) Prov. xvii. 10.

Niph. נִחַתוּ, probably an error for נָחֲתוּ, *Penetrated*, spoken of arrows, with בְּ, Ps. xxxviii. 3.

Pih. Inf. נַחֵת, *Bringing down, levelling,* Ps. lxv. 11.

Hiph. Imp. הַנְחַת, *Cause to come down*, or *depress*, Joel iii. 11. LXX. ὁ πραῢς ἔστω μαχητής. Vulg. *ibi occumbere faciet Dominus robustos tuos.* Syr. ܐܚܬ.

נחת (416) נטי

נחת, v. Chald. *Id.*
Part. נָחֵת, Dan. iv. 10. 20.
Aph. *Placed*, pres. תַּחֵת, Ezra vi. 5.
Part. pl. מְהַחֲתִין, Ezra vi. 1.
Imp. אֲחֵת, Ezra v. 15.
Hoph. הָנְחַת, *Was made to descend*, Dan. v. 20.

נַחַת, f. I. r. נָחַת. (a) *Coming down with violence*. (b) *Being placed*. (a) Is. xxx. 30. (b) Job xxxvi. 16.
II. r. נוּחַ, *Rest, quietness*, Eccl. iv. 6; vi. 5; ix. 17; Is. xxx. 15.

נְחִתִּים, m. pl. *Coming down*, spoken of an army, 2 Kings vi. 9.

נָטָה, v. pres. יִטֶּה, apoc. יֵט. Arab. نَطَ, and نَطَا, r. نطو, *extendit*. Cogn. وَطِئَ, *subegit*. *Stretched, inclined* towards, &c. Constr. immed. it. med. אֶת.
(a) *Stretched out*, [1] The hand; [2] The hand, with a spear; [3] A sword; [4] A rod; [5] A line, for measuring. (b) *Spread*, [1] Itself; [2] A covering; [3] The heavens, as a covering; [4] A tent; [5] *A tent*, abs. (c) *Bowed*, [1] The heavens; [2] Himself. (d) *Went aside*, [1] To lodge with a person, with עִד; [2] To a person, with אֶל; [3] Abs.; [4] *From the right way*; [5] From a person, with מִפְּנֵי, or מִן; [6] From a law, with מִן. (e) The heart *turned* towards, with אַחֲרֵי. (f) *Turned* the heart towards, with אַחֲרֵי, or לְ. (g) *Turned* an attentive ear towards, with אֶל. (h) *Brought* upon or unto, with עַל, or אֶל. (i) *Put forward* the shoulder to a burden, with לְ. (a), [1] Josh. viii. 26; Job xv. 25; Is. xxiii. 11, &c. [2] Josh. viii. 18. [3] Ezek. xxx. 25. [4] Exod. ix. 23; x. 13. [5] 2 Kings xxi. 13; Job xxxviii. 5; Is. xxxiv. 11; xliv. 13; Lam. ii. 8. (b), [1] Job xv. 29; [2] Jer. xliii. 10. [3] Ps. civ. 2; Is. xlv. 12; Jer. x. 12; li. 15, &c. [4] Gen. xxxiii. 19; 2 Sam. vi. 17; 1 Chron. xvi. 1, &c. [5] Exod. xxxiii. 7; Jer. xiv. 8. (c), [1] 2 Sam. xxii. 10; Ps. xviii. 10, &c. [2] Judg. xvi. 30. (d), [1] Gen. xxxviii. 1. [2] Gen. xxxviii. 16. [3] Num. xx. 17; xxi. 15; xxii. 33; 2 Sam. ii. 19, &c. [4] 1 Sam. viii. 3; 1 Kings ii. 28; xi. 9; Ps. lxxiii. 2; Prov. iv. 27, &c. [5] Num. xx. 21; xxii. 23. 33; Job xxxi. 7; Ps. xliv. 19. [6] Ps. cxix. 51. 157; Prov. iv. 5. (f) Ps. cxix. 112. (g) Ps. xl. 2. (h) Gen. xxxix. 21; 1 Chron. xxi. 10; Ps. xxi. 12; Is. lxv. 12, &c. (i) Gen. xlix. 15.

Part. נֹטֶה, aff. נוֹטֵיהֶם, Job ix. 8; xxvi. 7; Is. xlii. 5, &c.
Part. pass. נָטוּי, f. נְטוּיָה, pl. נְטוּיוֹת. (a) *Stretched out*, used of [1] The hand; [2] The arm; [3] The neck; [4] A shadow; [5] A canopy; [6] A sword. (b) *Leaning*, as a wall. (a), [1] Is. v. 25; ix. 11. 16. 20; x. 4, &c. [2] Exod. vi. 6; Num. iv. 34; v. 15, &c. [3] Is. iii. 16. [4] Ps. cii. 12. [5] Ezek. i. 22. [6] 2 Chron. xxi. 16. (b) Ps. lxii. 4.
Inf. נְטוֹת, aff. נְטוֹתוֹ, Exod. xxiii. 2; Josh. viii. 19.
Imp. נְטֵה, Exod. viii. 1. 12; ix. 22, &c.

Niph. נִטָּה, pres. יִנָּטֶה, *Stretched out* as a cord, shadow, or encampment, Zech. i. 16; Jer. vi. 4; Num. xxiv. 6.

Hiph. הִטָּה, pres. יַטֶּה, apoc. יֵט. (a) I. q. Kal, sign. [a, 1], [b, 2], [d, 3], [g], and [h]. (b) *Caused to turn aside*. (c) *Thrust aside*. (d) *Held out*, [1] Food; [2] A drinking vessel. (e) *Perverted* judgment. (f) *Turned*, [1] The ear, or [2] Heart towards, with לְ. (g) *Turned* the heart. (a), [a, 1] Is. xxxi. 3; Jer. vi. 12; xv. 6. [b, 2] 2 Sam. xxi. 10; Is. liv. 2. [d, 3] Job xxiii. 1. [h] Ezra vii. 28; ix. 9. (b) 1 Kings xi. 4; Prov. vii. 25; Is. xliv. 20. (c) Ps. xxvii. 9; Amos v. 12. (d), [1] Hos. xi. 4. (e) Exod. xxiii. 5; Deut. xvi. 15; xxiv. 16, &c. (f), [1] Ps. cxvi. 2; Prov. v. 13; Jer. vii. 24, &c. [2] Ps. cxli. 4; Prov. ii. 22. (g) 2 Sam. xix. 15.
Part. מַטֶּה, pl. מַטִּים, constr. מַטֵּי, Deut. xxvii. 19; Ps. cxxv. 5; Prov. xxiv. 11; Mal. iii. 5.
Inf. הַטּוֹת, Exod. xxiii. 2; 1 Kings viii. 58, &c. (c) Is. x. 2.
Imp. הַטֵּה, or הַט, הַטּוּ, 2 Kings xix. 16; Ps. xvii. 6, &c. (d), [2] Gen. xxiv. 14.

נָטִיל, r. נטל, *Loaded*, Zeph. i. 11.

נְטִפוֹת, נְטִיפוֹת, f. pl. twice, Judg. viii. 26; Is. iii. 19. LXX. τῶν στραγγαλίδων. Αλλ. ὁρμίσκων, τὸ κάθεμα. Aquila, κροκυφάντους. Sym. χαλαστά. Theod. τὰ καθέματα. Vulg. *monilibus*. Syr. ܐܨܕܡܐ. Probably, either *ornamental chains* for the neck, or *ear-rings, ear-drops*. Comp. نُطْفَة, *inauris*. Some suppose them to have been

נטי (417) נטף

perfume boxes: r. נטף. See Schrœder (p. 45) de Vestitu Mulierum.

נְטִישׁוֹת, f. pl. aff. נְטִישׁוֹתָיהָ, ־תֶיךָ, r. נטש. (a) *Shoots* of a vine, Is. xviii. 5; Jer. xlviii. 32. (b) Metaph. *The smaller towns*, considered, probably, as shoots from the capital, Jer. v. 10. Vulg. *auferte propagines ejus.* LXX. ὑπολίπεσθε τὰ ὑποστηρίγματα αὐτῆς, ὅτι τοῦ κυρίου εἰσίν. So likewise the Syr.

נָטַל, v. pres. יִטּוֹל. Syr. ܢܛܠ, *grave fuit.* (a) *Laid* a burden on, with עַל. (b) *Lifted up.* (a) Lam. iii. 25. (b) Is. xl. 15.

Part. נוֹטֵל, (a) 2 Sam. xxiv. 12.

Hiph. הִטַּלְתִּי, *Took up and removed,* Jer. xvi. 13; xxii. 26.

נטל, v. Chald. נְטַלַת, *I lifted up* my eyes, Dan. iv. 31. נְטִילַת, *was lifted up,* Dan. vii. 4.

נֵטֶל, m. once, *A burden,* Prov. xxvii. 3.

נֶטַע, m. constr. נֶטַע, aff. נִטְעֵךְ, pl. נְטָעִים, constr. נִטְעֵי. (a) *A plant.* (b) *A plantation.* (a) Job xiv. 9; Is. xvii. 10. (b) Is. v. 7; xvii. 11.

נָטַע, v. pres. יִטַּע. Constr. immed. (a) *Planted*, [1] A tree, [2] A garden, [3] A people. (b) *Pitched* a tent. (c) *Set up* an idolatrous shrine. (d) *Drove* a nail. (a), [1] Num. xxiv. 6; Ps. civ. 16; Is. xliv. 14, &c. [2] Gen. ii. 8; Deut. xx. 6; Prov. xxxi. 16, &c. [3] Jer. xxxii. 41; xlii. 10; xlv. 4; Ezek. xxxvi. 36, &c. (b) Dan. xi. 45. (d) Deut. xvi. 21.

Part. נֹטֵעַ, pl. נֹטְעִים, Ps. xciv. 9; Jer. xi. 17; xxxi. 8.

Part. pass. נָטוּעַ, pl. נְטוּעִים, Eccl. iii. 2. (c) Eccl. xii. 11.

Inf. נְטוֹעַ, נַטַּע, Eccl. iii. 2; Is. li. 16.

Imp. pl. נִטְעוּ, 2 Kings xix. 29; Is. xxxvii. 30; Jer. xxix. 5. 28.

Niph. נִטְּעוּ, Is. xl. 24.

נְטִעִים, pl. m. *Planted,* Ps. cxliv. 12.

נָטַף, v. pres. יִטֹּף. Arab. نطف. Syr. ܢܛܦ. Æth. ነጠበ: *stillavit;* ነጠፈ: *percolavit.* (a) *Dropped,* as dew. (b) *Let drop* water, myrrh, or wine. (a) Job xxix. 22. (b) Judg. v. 4; Ps. lxviii. 9; Prov. v. 3; Cant. iv. 11; v. 5; Joel iv. 18.

Part. pl. f. נֹטְפוֹת, (b) Cant. v. 13.

Hiph. הִטִּיף, pres. יַטִּיף. (a) *Let drop* water. (b) *Let fall* sentiments, i. e. *uttered* prophetic declarations. (a) Amos ix. 13. (b) Mic. ii. 6. 11; Amos vii. 16.

Part. מַטִּיף, (b) Mic. ii. 11. LXX. καὶ ἔσται ἐκ τῆς σταγόνος τοῦ λαοῦ τούτου. Vulg. *et erit super quem stillatur populus iste.*

Imp. הַטֵּף, (b) Ezek. xxi. 2. 7. LXX. ἐπίβλεψον. Vulg. *stilla.* If the LXX. is a correct translation, this verb may be cognate with the Arab. طاف, r. طوف, *circumivit, obivit.*

נָטָף, m. pl. constr. נִטְפֵי, (a) *A drop,* Job xxxvi. 27. (b) *Myrrh,* Exod. xxx. 23. See Celsii Hierobot., part i., 529.

נָטַר, v. pres. יִנְטוֹר, יִטּוֹר. Arab. نظر, *oculos convertit* ad rem; نطر, *custodem egit.* Syr. ܢܛܪ, *servavit, custodivit.* *Watched.* (a) For good, i. e. *guarded.* (b) For evil, i. e. retained anger. [1] Abs. [2] Med. לְ, אֶת. (a) Cant. i. 6. (b), [1] Jer. iii. 5. 12. [2] Lev. xix. 18.

Part. נוֹטֵר, f. נוֹטֵרָה, pl. נוֹטְרִים. (a) Cant. i. 6; viii. 11, 12. (b) Nah. i. 2.

נטר, v. Chald. נִטְרֵת, *I kept* it in my heart, Dan. vii. 28.

נָטַשׁ, v. pres. יִטּשׁ, (a) *Left.* (b) *Forsook* God. (c) *Forsook* a law. (d) *Left* to itself. (e) *Ceased to think of.* (f) *Allowed.* (g) *Spread.* (h) *Scattered.* (i) *Drew* a sword. (a) Judg. vi. 13; 1 Sam. xii. 22; 2 Kings xxi. 14, &c. (b) Deut. xxxii. 15; Jer. xv. 16. (c) Prov. i. 8; vi. 20. (d) Exod. xxiii. 11; Hos. xii. 15; Num. xi. 31, &c. (e) 1 Sam. x. 2. (f) Gen. xxxi. 28. (g) 1 Sam. iv. 2.

Part. pass. f. נְטוּשָׁה, pl. נְטֻשִׁים. (h) 1 Sam. xxx. 16. (i) Is. xxi. 15.

Inf. נְטֹשׁ, *To neglect,* Prov. xvii. 14.

Niph. נִטַּשׁ, pres. יִנָּטֵשׁ. (a) *Was left, forsaken.* (b) *Spread itself.* (c) *Became loose.* (a) Amos v. 2. (b) Judg. xv. 9; 2 Sam. v. 18. 22; Is. xvi. 8. (c) Is. xxxiii. 23.

Puh. נֻטַּשׁ, for נֻטַּשׁ, *Is forsaken,* Is. xxxii. 14:

נִי, with aff. and prep. בְּ, once, Ezek. xxvii. 32. בְּנִיהֶם. If the punctuation be correct, this word is perhaps used for נְהִי, *lamentation;* but the substitution of נ for ה, for ה, furnishes an interpretation both suiting the context and agreeing with the Syr. and LXX.

נִיב (418) נִיר

נִיב, m. r. נוב. *Produce, fruit,* Mal. i. 12; Is. lvii. 19.

נִיד, m. once, r. נוד. *Moving of the lips,* Job xvi. 5.

נִידָה, for נִדָּה, f. which see, Lam. i. 8.

נִיחֹחַ, m. aff. נִיחוֹחִי, נִיחֹחֲכֶם, pl. aff. נִיחוֹחֵיהֶם, r. נוח. *Satisfaction, approbation.* Used only in the phrase רֵיחַ נִיחֹחַ, *odour of approbation;* applied to sacrifices and offerings. LXX. ὀσμὴ εὐωδίας. Vulg. *odor suavitatis,* Gen. viii. 21; Exod. xxix. 18; Lev. i. 9, &c.

נִיחֹחִין, masc. pl. Chald. id. Meton. *Offerings* to God, Ezra vi. 10 : to man, Dan. ii. 46.

נִין, m. aff. נִינִי, *Posterity,* Gen. xxi. 23; Job xviii. 19; Is. xiv. 22: in each place joined with נֶכֶד. The etymology of this word has been usually traced to نۏن, or نُون, *a fish;* but it is more probably connected with أَنَّ, *effudit, fudit;* أَنَى, *ad extremum et perfectionis terminum pervenit.* IV. *Procrastinavit, distulit;* أَنًى, *tempus;* and أَنَ, r. اون, *Id.* See my Note on Job xviii. 19.

נִיסָן, m. The name of the first month of the Hebrew year, Neh. ii. 1 ; Esth. iii. 7. The origin has been variously referred—to נוס, because it was the month of the flight of the Israelites out of Egypt—to نشأ, *crevit, accrevit;* and to יָצָא, as if it were written נִיצָן, for נִצָּן. These last derivations make the word synonymous with אָבִיב, the other name for the same month.

נִיצוֹץ, m. once, Is. i. 31. *A spark.* Arab. نَائِض, r. نوض, *micuit splenduit fulmen.*

נִיר, v. Inf. נִיר, Imp. pl. נִירוּ. Syr. ܢܺܝܪܳܐ, *jugum aratorium.* Arab. زِيَر, id. Whence the verb. (a) *To clear out* ground *for cultivation.* (b) *To cultivate* it. (a) Jer. iv. 3; Hos. x. 12. (b) Prov. xiii. 23. In Hos. x. 12, instead of נִירוּ לָכֶם נִיר וְעֵת לִדְרוֹשׁ אֶת־יְהוָֹה, the LXX. read נִירוּ לָכֶם נִיר בְּדַעַת דִּרְשׁוּ אֶת־יְהוָֹה, φωτίσατε ἑαυτοῖς φῶς γνώσεως, ἐκζητήσατε τὸν κύριον. The Syriac also translates נִירוּ לָכֶם נִיר, by ܢܘܗܪܐ ܠܟܘܢ.

נִיר, m. i. q. נֵר. Arab. نُور, *lumen.* Aff. נִירָם. *A light.* Metaph. either *prosperity, rank,* or *a representative in one's rank,* 1 Kings xi. 36; xv. 4; 2 Kings viii. 19; 2 Chron. xxi. 7.

נָכָא, v. once. Niph. נִכְאוּ, *Were beaten,* Job xxx. 8. Cogn. נכה.

נָכָא, f. נְכֵאָה, in the phrase רוּחַ נְכֵאָה, *An afflicted mind, broken spirit,* Prov. xv. 13; xvii. 22; xviii. 14.

נְכָאִים, m. pl. *Smitten, distressed,* Is. xvi. 7.

נְכֹאת, f. twice, Gen. xxxvii. 25; xliii. 11. *Storax,* the gum of the styrax-tree. According to Bochart. (Hieroz. ii. 4. 12), both the Hebrew and Greek names are derived from the fact, that the wood was much used for lances. Arab. نَكَتَ, *extremitate virgæ percussit* terram *ita ut vestigium remanserit.* The LXX. consider the word as plural, and as a generic term, θυμιαμάτων; but Aquila translates it by στύραξ. Gesen. takes it to be a verbal noun from נכא, and originally to signify *contusio, pulvis aromaticus,* and subsequently to be applied to a particular species of perfume. From this is derived נְכֹתֹה, *his perfume-house,* 2 Kings xx. 13; Is. xxxix. 2.

נֶכֶד, m. aff. נֶכְדִּי. Nearly synonymous with נִין, with which it is joined in each place where it occurs, Gen. xxi. 23; Job xviii. 19; Is. xiv. 22. For the etymology, see the Note to Job xviii. 19.

נָכָה, v. Kal non occ. Arab. نَكَى, *affecit noxâ, nece, vel vulneribus.* Constr. immed. it. med. אֶת.

Hiph. הִכָּה, pres. יַכֶּה, apoc. יַךְ. (a) *Struck.* (b) *Struck violently, wounded.* (c) *Killed.* (d) *Conquered.* (e) *Struck* with a disease or plague. (f) *Struck* with calamity. (g) *Struck down* a person so as to kill him. (h) *Struck* into, with בְּ. (i) *Struck* its roots. (k) *Struck* out of the hand. (l) The sun, or drought, *struck, injured.* (m) *Struck* with the tongue, taunted. (n) *Struck* the hands

נכה (419) נכח

together in lamentation or disapprobation. (o) *Struck* the hands together in applause. (p) וַיַּךְ לֵב דָּוִד אֹתוֹ, *David's heart smote him, his conscience reproved him.* (a) Exod. xvii. 5; Num. xxii. 32; Ps. lxxviii. 20, &c. (b) Exod. ix. 24; xxi. 18. 20, &c. (c) 1 Sam. xiii. 35; 2 Sam. x. 18; 2 Kings xiii. 25, &c. [1] בַּחֶרֶב, Josh. x. 1; 2 Sam. xii. 9; Jer. xx. 4. [2] לְפִי חֶרֶב, Josh. x. 2; 1 Sam. xxii. 19; 2 Sam. xv. 14. [3] הִכָּהוּ נֶפֶשׁ, Gen. xxxvii. 21; Deut. xix. 6; Jer. xl. 1, &c. (d) Deut. iv. 46; 2 Sam. viii. 1, 2. 9, &c. (e) Exod. iii. 20; xii. 29; Num. xxxiii. 4, &c. (f) 1 Kings xiv. 15; Jer. ii. 30; xiv. 19, &c. (g) 2 Sam. ii. 22; xviii. 11. (h) 1 Sam. xix. 10; ii. 14. (i) Hos. xiv. 6. (k) Ezek. xxxix. 3. (l) Ps. cxxi. 6; Is. xlix. 10; Jonah iv. 7, 8. (m) Jer. xviii. 18. (n) Ezek. xxii. 13. (o) 2 Kings xi. 12. (p) 1 Sam. xxiv. 5; 2 Sam. xxiv. 10.

Part. מַכֶּה, constr. מַכֵּה, aff. מַכֵּךְ, מַכֵּהוּ, pl. מַכִּים, Exod. ii. 11; xxi. 12; Deut. xxv. 11; 1 Sam. iv. 8; Is. xv. 2; L. 7, &c. In 2 Chron. ii. 9, מַכּוֹת, appears to be used in a passive sense, unless the true reading be מָכוֹת, which seems to be that of the LXX., Syriac, and Vulgate.

Inf. הַכֵּה, הַכּוֹת, aff. הַכֹּתִי, &c., Deut. xiii. 16; Gen. viii. 21, &c.

Imp. הַכֵּה, apoc. הַךְ, aff. הַכֵּינִי, pl. הַכּוּ, aff. הַכּוּהוּ, 2 Sam. xiii. 28; 1 Kings xx. 35; 2 Kings vi. 18; ix. 27; x. 28; Ezek. vi. 11, &c.

Hoph. הֻכָּה, הוּכָה, Ps. cii. 5), pres. pl. יֻכּוּ, Passive of Hiphhil, Num. xxv. 14; Ezek. xxxiii. 21; Zech. xiii. 6, &c.

Part. מֻכֶּה, constr. מֻכֵּה, f. מֻכָּה, pl. מֻכִּים, constr. מֻכֵּי, Exod. v. 16; Num. xxv. 14, 15; Is. liii. 4; Jer. xviii. 21, &c.

Niph. נִכָּה, *Was wounded*, 2 Sam. xi. 15.

Puh. נֻכָּה, in pause, נֻכּוּ, *Was beaten down*, Exod. ix. 31, 32.

נָכֶה, m. constr. נְכֵה, (a) *Injured.* (b) *Afflicted.* (a) נְכֵה רַגְלַיִם, 2 Sam. iv. 4; ix. 3. (b) נְכֵה רוּחַ, Is. lvi. 2.

נָכִים, m. pl., Ps. xxxv. 15. According to Dathe this word has a passive sense, and signifies *Wretches*; but Gesenius considers it as having an active signification, and translates it, *Those who smite with the tongue, revilers.* LXX. μάστιγες. Sym. πλῆκται. Vulg. *flagella.* Syr. نَقَبَ, *diu.*

נֹכַח, Partic. *Before.* (a) *Opposite, over against.* (b) *In sight of.* (c) פְּנֵי נֹכַח, *In sight of.* (d) אֶל נֹכַח, *Towards.* (e) עַד נֹכַח, *As far as in front of.* (f) לְנֹכַח, [1] *In front of.* [2] *In behalf of.* [3] *Straight forwards.* (g) יֵצֵא נִכְחוֹ, *Goes straight forwards.* (a) Exod. xxvi. 35; xl. 24; Josh. xv. 7; xviii. 17, &c. (b) Judg. xviii. 6. (c) Jer. xvii. 16; Lam. ii. 19; Ezek. xiv. 2, 3. 6. (d) Num. xix. 4. (e) Judg. xix. 10; xx. 43; Ezek. xlvii. 20. (f), [1] Gen. xxx. 38. [2] Gen. xxv. 21. [3] Prov. iv. 25. (g) Ezek. xlvii. 9.

נֹכַח, m. aff. נִכְחוֹ, *Straightforwardness, uprightness,* Is. lvii. 2.

נְכֹחָה, f. pl. נְכֹחוֹת, *Id.*, Is. xxvi. 10; xxx. 10; lix. 14; Amos iii. 10.

נְכֹחִים, m. pl. Straightforward, *upright*, Prov. xxiv. 27.

נכל, v. Arab. نَكَلَ, *abscessit, retrocessit; timidus abstinuit ab hoste, vel à jurejurando.* Syr. ܢܟܠ, *decepit.* Probably, *Withheld*, and *used artifice for that purpose.*

Kal, Part. נֹכֵל, *Withholding*, Mal. i. 14. The LXX. however derive it from יָכֹל, and translate it δυνατός. Vulg. *dolosus.* The Syriac omits the word altogether.

Pih. נִכֵּל, *Used artifice*, Num. xxv. 18.

Hith. pres. יִתְנַכְּלוּ, *Plotted together against,* Gen. xxxvii. 18. Constr. med. אֶת, or בְּ.

Inf. הִתְנַכֵּל, Ps. cv. 25.

נֹכֶל, m. pl. aff. נִכְלֵיהֶם, *Artifice*, Num. xxv. 18.

נְכָסִים, m. pl. נְכָסִים, *Treasures, wealth,* Josh. xxii. 8; 2 Chron. i. 11, 12; Eccl. v. 18; vi. 2. Apparently cognate with כנס.

נְכָסִים, m. pl. נִכְסִין, constr. נִכְסֵי, Chald. *Id.* Ezra vi. 8; vii. 26.

נֵכָר, constr. נֵכַר. Arab. نَكِرَ, *nescivit, abnegavit; improbavit; subtili ingenio et versutus fuit;* نَكِير, *abnegatio;* نُكْر, *intelligentia. Strange, foreign; a foreigner,* 2 Chron. xiv. 2; Neh. xiii. 10. אַדְמַת נ״, *a foreign land,* Ps. cxxxvii. 4. אֵל נ״, *a foreign*, and therefore *a false god,* Deut. xxxii. 12; Ps. lxxxi. 10; Mal. ii. 11, &c. אֱלֹהֵי נ״, and הַבַּל נַ״, *Id.*, Gen. xxxv. 2; Josh. xxiv. 20. 23; Judg. x. 16, &c. בֶּן נ״, *a foreigner,* Gen. xvii. 12. 27; Exod. xii.

נכר (420) נצב

43 ; 2 Sam. xxii. 45, 46, &c. "נ הַבְלֵי, foreign vanities, idols, Jer. viii. 19.

נֵכֶר, m. Treating as a stranger, dealing harshly with; punishment, Job xxxi. 3.

נָכָר, m. aff. נָכְרוֹ, Id., Obad. 12. Arab. نكر, gravis, molestus, de re.

נכר, v. Kal non occ.
Hiph. הִכִּיר, pres. יַכִּיר, apoc. יַכֵּר. Constr. immed. it. med. אֶת. (a) Recognised an apparent stranger, Recognised. (b) Considered. (c) Knew. (d) Beheld. (e) Acknowledged, regarded the claims of. (f) Acknowledged as right, regarded. (g) Esteemed as like. (h) Took judicial cognizance of. (i) הִכִּיר פָּנִים, Regarded persons, was partial in judgment.
(a) Gen. xxvii. 23; xlii. 8; Judg. xviii. 3; Job ii. 12, &c. (b) Neh. vi. 12. (c) 2 Sam. iii. 36. (d) Gen. xxxvii. 33; Job xxiv. 17. (e) Deut. xxi. 17; xxxiii. 9; Is. lxi. 9; lxiii. 16. (f) Job xxiv. 13. (g) Jer. xxiv. 5. (h) Job xxxiv. 25. (i) Deut. i. 17; xvi. 19.
Part. מַכִּיר, aff. מַכִּירָךְ, pl. מַכִּירִים, Ruth ii. 19; Ezra ii. 13; xiii. 24; Ps. cxlii. 5.
Inf. הַכִּיר, הַכֵּר, aff. הַכִּירֵנוּ, Ruth ii. 10; Prov. xxiv. 23; xxvii. 21.
Imp. הַכֵּר, (b) Gen. xxxi. 32; xxxvii. 32; xxxviii. 25.
Pih. pres. יְנַכֵּר, (a) i. q. Hiph. [a], [b], and [e]. (b) Alienated. (c) Rejected. (a) Job xxi. 29. [b] Deut. xxxii. 27. [e] Job xxxiv. 19. (b) Jer. xix. 4. (c) 1 Sam. xxiii. 7. Gesen. proposes to read מָכַר. LXX. πέπρακεν.
Hith. pres. יִתְנַכֵּר, (a) Made himself strange. (b) Attempted to conceal himself. (c) Was recognised. (a) Gen. xlii. 7. (b) Prov. xxvi. 24. (c) Prov. xx. 11.
Part. f. מִתְנַכְּרָה, (a) 1 Kings xiv. 5, 6.

נָכְרִי, pl. נָכְרִים, fem. נָכְרִיָּה, pl. נָכְרִיּוֹת.
(a) Foreign. (b) A stranger. (c) Strange, singular. (a) Exod. xxi. 8; Deut. xvii. 15; Judg. xix. 12. (b) Ps. lxix. 9; Prov. xxvii. 2; Eccl. vi. 2. (c) Is. xxviii. 21.

נֹלָתָה, see נכא.

נלה, v. once, Is. xxxiii. 1, כְּנַלֹּתְךָ for מְחַנְלֹתְךָ, Hiph. Inf. Arab. نال, r. نيل, consecutus, assecutus fuit. IV. Compotem reddidit. Succeeded, accomplished. Gesen. after Capellus, reads כְּכַלֹּתְךָ, when thou hast finished.

נִמְבְזֶה, for נִבְזֶה, r. בזה, Despised, worthless, 1 Sam. xv. 9.

נמל, v. Cogn. מול. מָלַל. Kal, נְמַלְתֶּם. Cut, pec. in circumcision, circumcised, Gen. xvii. 11.
Niph. נָמוֹל, pres. יִמַּל. (a) Was circumcised. (b) Was nipped, or cropped off. (a) Gen. xvii. 26, 27. (b) Job xiv. 2; xviii. 16; xxiv. 24; Ps. xxxvii. 2.

נְמָלָה, f. pl. נְמָלִים. Arab. نمل, نملة, formica. An ant, Prov. vi. 6; xxx. 28.

נָמֵר, m. pl. נְמֵרִים. Arab. نمر, pardus. Syr. ܢܶܡܪܳܐ, Id. A panther, Cant. iv. 8; Is. xi. 6; Jer. v. 6; xiii. 22; Hos. xiii. 7; Hab. i. 8. See Hieroz., ii., lib. 3, cap. 7.

נְמַר, Chald., Id., Dan. vii. 6.

נֵס, m. aff. נִסִּי. Arab. نصّ, extulit, elevavit, monstravit. Syr. ܢܶܣܳܐ, signum, propositum, scopus. (a) A banner, standard. (b) Meton. The leader to whom the standard belongs. (c) An example. (d) A flag-staff, pole. (e) A sail. (a) Is. v. 26; xi. 12; Jer. vi. 6, &c. (b) Is. xi. 10. (c) Num. xxvi. 10. (d) Num. xxi. 8, 9. (e) Is. xxxiii. 23; Ezek. xxvii. 7.

נסג, v. pres. יַסִּג. Cogn. סוג. Moved himself back. (a) Withdrew from God's service. (b) Avoided by retiring, avoided, constr. immed. (b) Mic. ii. 6.
Inf. נָסוֹג, (a) Is. lix. 13.
Hiph. pres. יַסִּיג, apoc. יַסֵּג. (a) Removed a boundary. (b) Carried away property. (a) Deut. xix. 14; Prov. xxii. 28. (b) Mic. vi. 14.
Part. מַסִּיג, pl. constr. מַסִּיגֵי, (a) Deut. xxvii. 17; Hos. v. 10.
Hoph. הֻסָּג, Was turned back, perverted, Is. lix. 14.

נסה, v. Kal non occ. Arab. نشأ, percepit odorem. Syr. ܢܣܐ, tentavit.
Pih. נִסָּה, pres. יְנַסֶּה. Constr. immed. it. med. אֶת. Tried. (a) Tried the character of a man. (b) Tried, tempted, God. (c) Tried the fitness of armour. (d) Tried persons in a practice. (e) Tried one's own heart. (f) Made a trial, abs. (g) Undertook. (h) Found by trial, experienced. (a) Gen. xxii. 1; Exod. xv. 25; xvi. 4; Deut. xxxiii. 8. (b) Exod. xvii. 2; Deut. vi. 16;

נסח (421) נסע

xiv. 22; Ps. xcv. 9; Is. vii. 12, &c. (c) 1 Sam. xvii. 40. (d) Dan. i. 14. (e) Eccl. ii. 1. (f) Judg. vi. 39. (g) Deut. iv. 34; xxviii. 56; Job iv. 2. (h) Eccl. vii. 23. Part. מַסָּה, Deut. xiii. 3.

Inf. נַסּוֹת, aff. נַסּוֹתוֹ, &c., Exod. xvii. 7; Deut. viii. 2; 1 Kings x. 1, &c.

Imp. נַס, aff. נַסֵּנִי, (d) Dan. i. 12. (a) Ps. xxvi. 2.

נסח, v. pres. יִסַּח. Arab. نَسَخَ, abrupit, dispersit; نَسَخَ, abolevit, abrogavit. Dispersed, scattered, Ps. lii. 7; Prov. xv. 25.

Niph. נִסְּחתֶם, pres. יִסַּח, Pass. of Kal, Deut. xxviii. 63; Prov. ii. 22.

נסח, v. Chald. Ithpe. pres. יִתְנְסַח, Let it be pulled out, Ezra vi. 11.

נסיך, m. aff. נְסִיכָם, pl. constr. נְסִיכֵי, aff. נְסִיכֵמוֹ, r. נסך. (a) A libation. (b) A molten image. (c) An anointed person, a prince. (a) Deut. xxxii. 38. (b) Dan. xi. 8. (c) Josh. xiii. 28; Ps. lxxxiii. 12; Ezek. xxxii. 30; Mic. v. 4.

נֶסֶךְ, once, נֵסֶךְ, m. aff. נִסְכּוֹ, &c., pl. נְסָכִים, aff. נְסָכֶיהָ, נִסְכֵּיהֶם, נִסְכֵּיכֶם. (a) A libation. (b) Meton. A molten image. (a) Gen. xxxv. 14; Num. xxviii. 7; Is. lvii. 6, &c. (b) Is. xli. 29; xlviii. 5; Jer. x. 14; li. 16.

נָסַךְ, v. pres. יִסְכוּ, constr. immed. it. med. אֶת. Cogn. סוּךְ, and סָכַךְ. (a) Poured out. (b) Melted. (c) Anointed. (d) Poured out a libation. (e) Spread as a covering. (a) Is. xxix. 10. (b) Is. xl. 19; xliv. 10. (c) Ps. ii. 6. (d) Exod. xxx. 9; Hos. ix. 4.

Part. pass. f. נְסוּכָה, (c) Is. xxv. 7.

Inf. נְסֹךְ, (d) Is. xxx. 1.

Niph. נִסַּכְתִּי, Pass. of (c), Prov. viii. 23.

Pih. pres. יְנַסֵּךְ, i. q. Kal, sig. (d), 1 Chron. xi. 18.

Hiph. הִסִּיכוּ, pres. יַסִּיךְ, apoc. יַסֵּךְ, Id., Gen. xxxv. 14; Ps. xvi. 4; Jer. xxxii. 29, &c.

Hoph. pres. יֻסַּךְ, Pass. of Hiph., Exod. xxv. 28; xxxvii. 16.

נסך, v. Chald. Pah. Inf. נַסָּכָה, To make an offering, Dan. ii. 46.

נִסְמָן, see סמן.

נסס, v. from נֵס. Raised, or bore, a standard. Part. נֹסֵס, f. נֹסְסָה, Is. x. 18; lix. 19.

Hith. Inf. הִתְנוֹסֵס, To rally round a standard, Ps. lx. 6.

Part. pl. f. מִתְנוֹסְסוֹת, Raising themselves like a standard, Zech. ix. 16.

נָסַע, v. pres. יִסַּע. Arab. نَسَعَ, abiit per terram; نَزَعَ, dimovit, evulsit è loco suo rem. (a) Departed. (b) Set out on a journey. (c) Travelled. (d) Went, of a wind. (e) Removed, in a neuter sense. (f) Pulled up, or out. (a) Gen. xxxiii. 17; xxxvii. 17; 2 Kings xix. 8, &c. (b) Num. ii. 34; x. 5, 6. 17. 21, &c. (c) Gen. xii. 9; Num. ii. 17; xii. 15, &c. (d) Num. xi. 31. (e) Exod. xiv. 19. (f) Judg. xvi. 3. 14; Is. xxxiii. 20.

Part. נֹסֵעַ, pl. נֹסְעִים, Num. x. 29. 33.

Inf. נְסֹעַ, נָסוֹעַ, aff. נָסְעָם, Gen. xi. 2; xii. 9; Num. iv. 5, &c.

Imp. pl. סְעוּ, Num. xiv. 25.

Niph. נִסַּע, Pass. of (f), Is. xxxviii. 12; Job vi. 21. This reading requires יִתְרָם to be rendered their tent-rope; but נָסַע appears a preferable mode of pointing, and in that case יִתְרָם will be rendered their abundance.

Hiph. pres. יַסִּיעַ, apoc. יַסַּע. (a) Causat. of Kal, sign. [a], [c], [d], and [e]. (b) Quarried stone. (a), [a] Exod. xv. 22. [c] Ps. lxxviii. 52. [d] Ps. lxxviii. 26. [e] 2 Kings iv. 4; Job xix. 10; Ps. lxxx. 9. (b) 2 Kings v. 31.

Part. מַסִּיעַ, (b) Eccl. x. 9.

נסק, v. once, pres. אֶסַּק, I go up, Ps. cxxxix. 8. Syr. ܢܣܩ, ascendit.

נסק, v. Chald. Id. Aph. הַסִּק, Lifted up, Dan. iii. 22.

Inf. הַנְסָקָה, Dan. vi. 24.

Hoph. הֻסַּק, Was lifted up, Dan. vi. 24.

נְעוּרִים, m. aff. נְעוּרַי, נְעוּרֶיךָ, &c., r. נער. Youth, early life, Gen. xlvi. 34; Lev. xxii. 13; 1 Sam. xii. 2, &c. נְעוּרוֹת, aff. נְעוּרוֹתַיִךְ, Id., Jer. xxxii. 30.

נָעִים, constr. נְעִים, pl. נְעִימִים, fem. נְעִמוֹת, r. נעם. Pleasant. (a) Sweet music. (b) Pleasant words. (c) Amiable. (d) Becoming, proper. (e) Prosperous. (a) 2 Sam. xxiii. 1; Ps. lxxxi. 3. (b) Prov. xxiii. 8. (c) 2 Sam. i. 23; Cant. i. 16. (d) Ps. cxxxiii. 1; cxxxv. 3; cxlvii. 1; Prov. xxii. 18. (e) Job xxxvi. 11; Ps. xvi. 6; Prov. xxiv. 4.

נַעַל (422) נָעַר

נַעַל, c. aff. נַעֲלִי, נַעֲלוֹ, נַעֲלְךָ; dual, נַעֲלַיִם; pl. נְעָלִים, and נְעָלוֹת, aff. נְעָלָיו, &c., נַעֲלֵיכֶם. Arab. نَعْل, *solea, calceus.* Syr. ܢܥܠܐ, *Id. A sandal, a shoe*, Gen. xiv. 23; Exod. iii. 5; Deut. xxiv. 10, &c. Hence—

נָעַל, v. (a) Pres. aff. אֶנְעָלֵךְ, *I put sandals on thee*, Ezek. xvi. 10. (b) נָעַל הַדֶּלֶת *Bolted, made fast, the door*, Judg. iii. 23; 2 Sam. xiii. 18.

Part. pass. נָעוּל, pl. f. נְעוּלוֹת, (b) Judg. iii. 24; Cant. iv. 12.

Imp. נְעֹל, (b) 2 Sam. xiii. 17.

נֹעַם, m. (a) *Pleasantness.* (b) *Kindness, grace.* (a) Prov. iii. 17; xv. 26; xvi. 24. (b) Ps. xxvii. 4; lxx. 17; Zech. xi. 7. 10.

נָעֵם, v. pres. יִנְעַם. Arab. نَعِمَ, *jucundus, commodus* alicui *fuit.* Constr. abs. it. med. לְ. *Was pleasant, agreeable.* (a) Of things. (b) Of persons. (a) Gen. xlix. 15; Ps. cxli. 6; Prov. ii. 10; ix. 17; xxiv. 25. (b) 2 Sam. i. 26; Cant. vii. 6; Ezek. xxxii. 19.

נַעֲמָנִים, m. i. q. נֹעַם, Is. xvii. 10.

נַעֲצוּץ, m. pl. נַעֲצוּצִים. Arab. نَعَض, *nomen arboris spinosæ in regione hidjas frequentis. A species of thorn*, Is. vii. 19; lv. 13. See Cels. Hierob., part ii., p. 189.

נַעַר, m. aff. נַעֲרִי, נַעֲרְךָ, pl. נְעָרִים, constr. נַעֲרֵי, aff. נְעָרָיו, and נַעֲרֵיהֶם. (a) *A male infant.* (b) *A boy.* (c) *A youth.* (d) *A servant.* (a) Exod. ii. 6; Judg. xiii. 5. 7. 12. 24; 1 Sam. i. 22; 2 Sam. xii. 16. (b) 1 Sam. i. 24; ii. 18; 2 Kings v. 14, &c. (c) Gen. xxxvii. 2; xli. 12; Exod. xxxiii. 11, &c. (d) 1 Sam. ii. 13; xx. 38; xxv. 14; 2 Sam. ix. 9, &c.

נֹעַר, m. *Childhood, youth*, Job xxxiii. 25; xxxvi. 14; Ps. lxxxviii. 16; Prov. xxix. 21.

נָעַר, v. נָעֲרוּ, *Roared*, Jer. li. 38. Arab. نَعَرَ, *sonum emisit per nares.* Syr. ܢܓܢ, *rugiit.* Cogn. נהר.

נָעַר, v. נָעַרְתִּי. Cogn. עור, and עָרָה. *Shook, shook out* or *off, emptied by shaking*, Neh. v. 13.

Part. נֹעֵר, Is. xxxiii. 9. 15.

— pass. נָעוּר, Neh. v. 13.

Niph. נִנְעֲרָה, pres. אִנָּעֵר, יִנָּעֵר. Pass. of Kal, Ps. cix. 23; Job xxxviii. 13.

Pih. נִעֵר, pres. יְנַעֵר, *Threw out*, Exod. xiv. 27; Neh. v. 13; Ps. cxxxvi. 15.

Hith. Imp. הִתְנַעֲרִי, *Shake thyself*, Is. lii. 2.

נַעַר, Arab. نَعَر, *peragravit* regionem, *abiit* in terram; نَعَار, *repulsus, in fugam versus. The act of wandering or of straying.* הַנַּעַר, *that which strays, or is strayed*, Zech. xi. 16. Syr. ܡܒܕܪ. LXX. τὸ ἐσκορπισμένον. Vulg. *dispersum.*

נַעֲרָה, f. pl. נְעָרוֹת, constr. נַעֲרוֹת, aff. נַעֲרוֹתֶיהָ, &c. Written also נַעֲרָ, Gen. xxiv. 14, &c. (a) *A girl.* (b) *A young woman.* (c) *A female servant.* (a) 2 Kings v. 2. 4. (b) Gen. xxiv. 14; Deut. xxii. 23; Ruth ii. 6; 1 Kings i. 2, &c. (c) Ruth ii. 8; 1 Sam. xxv. 42; Esth. iv. 16, &c.

נְעֹרֶת, f. *Stupa, quod ex lino excussa*, Castell. *Tow*, Judg. xvi. 9; Is. i. 31.

נָפָה, f. constr. נְפַת, r. נוף. Probably, *Act of scattering*; but commonly interpreted *a sieve*, Is. xxx. 28. לַהֲנָפָה גוֹיִם בְּנָפַת שָׁוְא, *to scatter the nations so as to leave none remaining.* LXX. τοῦ ταράξαι ἔθνη ἐπὶ πλανήσει ματαίᾳ. Vulg. *ad perdendas gentes in nihilum.*

נָפַח, v. pres. יִפַּח. Arab. نَفَخَ, *spiravit ventus.* Syr. ܢܦܚ, *flavit.* Æth. ነፍሐ ፡ *Id.* (a) *Blew*, constr. immed. (b) *Blew* a fire, immed. (c) *Blew* upon, immed. it. med. בְּ, עַל. (d) *With* נֶפֶשׁ, *Expired.* (a) Gen. i. 7. (c) Ezek. xxii. 21; Hag. i. 9. (d) Jer. xv. 9.

Part. נֹפֵחַ, (c) Is. liv. 16.

Part. Pass. נָפוּחַ, (c) Job xli. 12; Jer. i. 13.

Inf. נְפֹחַ, (b) Ezek. xxii. 20.

Imp. f. פֻּחִי, (c) Ezek. xxxvii. 9.

Puh. נֻפָּח, in pause, Pass. of (b), Job xx. 26.

Hiph. הִפִּחַ, *Puffed at, despised*, constr. immed. either with, or without, נֶפֶשׁ, Job xxxi. 39; Mal. i. 13.

נְפִילִים, m. *A race mentioned only in* Gen. vi. 4, and Num. xiii. 33. The latter were men of gigantic stature, and had distinguished themselves as warriors; and probably the former resembled them in both

נָפַךְ (423) נָפַל

these particulars. For the etymology, see my note to Job xv. 25.

נֹפֶךְ, m. A precious stone, but of what kind is uncertain, Exod. xxviii. 18; xxxix. 11; Ezek. xxvii. 16; xxviii. 13. LXX. ἄνθραξ. Vulg. *carbunculus*.

נֵפֶל, m. Lit. a falling. *An untimely birth*, Job iii. 16; Ps. lviii. 9; Eccl. vi. 3.

נָפַל, v. pres. יִפֹּל. Syr. ܢܦܠ, نَفَلَ, *cecidit*. (a) *Fell*, abs. [1] Of a thing, as a wall, tree, tent, dew, &c. [2] Of a person, tripped and *fell*. [3] *Fell down*, fatally wounded. [4] *Was killed*. [5] *Fell to the ground, came to nothing*. [6] *Dismounted*. [7] —, of a state or city. [8] *Lay down*. [9] —, of the arms, *hung down*, through weakness. [10] Of the countenance, in sorrow or anger. [11] Of an affair, *fell out, terminated*. (b) *Fell upon*, with עַל. [1] —, of a state or feeling, as sleep, fear, &c. [2] —, of reproach. [3] *Fell upon and took possession of*. [4] Mischief *fell upon*. [5] *Fell upon* a sword. [6] *Fell upon* the neck of another. (c) *Fell to*, of an inheritance, with לְ. (d) *Fell on his face*, with or without עַל פָּנָיו, or אֶל פָּנָיו. (e) נ״ לְמִשְׁכָּב, *Was confined to his bed*. (f) *Deserted to, joined*, with עַל, or אֶל. (g) נ״ בְּיַד, *Fell into the hand of*. (h) *Perished*. (i) *Fell into* a pit, or mischief, with בְּ, or אֶל. (k) נ״ בְּעֵינֵי, *Sunk in his own esteem*. (l) נ״ בְּגְדֻלָּה, *Obtained a settlement*. (m) נ״ לֵב, *The heart sunk*. (n) נ״ אַרְצָה, *Perished*. (a), [1] 2 Sam. xvii. 12; Judg. vii. 13; Ezek. xiii. 12; Zech. xi. 2, &c. [2] Is. iii. 8; xxxi. 3; Jer. xlvi. 12. [3] Judg. v. 27; 2 Sam. ii. 23; 2 Kings vi. 6. [4] 2 Sam. i. 4; iii. 38; 1 Chron. xx. 8, &c. בַּחֶרֶב, 2 Sam. i. 12; Is. xxxi. 8; Lam. ii. 21, &c. לַחֶרֶב, Lev. xxvi. 7. [5] Num. vi. 12. נ״ דְּבַר אַרְצָה, 2 Kings x. 10. [6] Gen. xxiv. 64. [7] Is. xxi. 9; Jer. li. 8; Amos v. 2, &c. [8] 1 Sam. xix. 24. [9] Ezek. xxx. 25. [10] Gen. iv. 6. [11] Ruth iii. 18. (b), [1] Gen. xv. 12; Josh. ii. 9; Ps. cv. 38, &c. [2] Ps. lxix. 10. [3] Job i. 15; Eccl. ix. 12; Ezek. viii. 1; xi. 5. [4] Is. xlvii. 11. [5] 1 Sam. xxxi. 4, 5; 1 Chron. x. 4, 5. [6] Gen. xxxiii. 4; xlv. 14; xlvi. 29; L. 1. (c) Num. xxxiv. 2; Judg. xviii. 1; Ps. xvi. 6. (d) Gen. xvii. 3. 17; 2 Sam. xix. 19; 2 Chron. xx. 18, &c. (e) Exod. xxi. 18. (f) With עַל, 2 Kings xxv. 11; 1 Chron. xii. 19; Jer. xxi. 9, &c.

With אֶל, 2 Kings vii. 4; 1 Chron. xii. 19; Jer. xxxviii. 19; lii. 15. (g) Judg. xv. 18; 2 Sam. xxiv. 14; 1 Chron. xxi. 13. (h) Prov. xi. 8. (i) Exod. xxi. 33; Prov. xiii. 17; xxvi. 27; xxviii. 10; Is. xxiv. 18. (k) Neh. vi. 16. (l) Ezek. xlvii. 22. (m) 1 Sam. xvii. 32. (n) 1 Sam. xiv. 45; xxvi. 20; 2 Sam. xiv. 11; 1 Kings i. 52.

Part. נֹפֵל, f. נֹפֶלֶת, pl. נֹפְלִים, Gen. xv. 12; Num. xxiv. 4; Deut. xxii. 14.

Inf. נָפוֹל, נְפֹל, aff. נָפְלִי, and נָפְלוֹ, נָפְלָם, Num. xiv. 3; 1 Sam. xxix. 3; 2 Sam. i. 10; Esth. vi. 13; Jer. xlix. 21.

Imp. pl. נִפְלוּ, Jer. xxv. 27; Hos. x. 8.

Hiph. הִפִּיל, pres. יַפִּיל, apoc. יַפֵּל. Constr. immed. (a) Causat. of Kal, signn. [a, 1], [a, 3], [a, 4], [a, 5], [a, 8], [a, 10], [b, 1], [b, 4], and [c]. (b) *Threw* to the ground. (c) *Knocked out* a tooth. (d) *Overcame*. (e) *Caused to settle* in a country. (f) *Offered* prayers. (g) Probably, *Cast out*. (h) *Forsook*. (i) *Threw* into the fire, with בְּ, or עַל. (a), [a, 1], Esth. iii. 7; ix. 24; Is. xxxiv. 17; Ezek. xxx. 22, &c. [a, 3] Ezek. vi. 4. [a, 4] 2 Kings xix. 7; Is. xxxvii. 7; Jer. xix. 7, &c. [a, 5], 1 Sam. iii. 19; Esth. vi. 10. [a, 8] Deut. xxv. 2. [a, 10] Job xxix. 24. With בְּ, Jer. iii. 12. [b, 1] Gen. ii. 21; Prov. xix. 15. [b, 4] Jer. xv. 8. [c] Josh. xxiii. 4. (b) Dan. viii. 10. (c) Exod. xxi. 27. (d) Prov. vii. 27; Dan. xi. 12. (e) Ps. lxxviii. 55. (g) Is. xxvi. 19. (h) Judg. ii. 19; 2 Chron. xxxii. 21. (i) Ps. cxl. 11; Jer. xxii. 7.

Part. מַפִּיל, pl. מַפִּילִים, *Felling* a tree, 2 Kings vi. 5. (f) Jer. xxxv. 26; Dan. ix. 18. 20.

Inf. הַפִּיל, 1 Sam. xviii. 28. In Num. v. 22, וְלַנְפִּל, for וּלְהַפִּיל.

Imp. pl. הַפִּילוּ, 1 Sam. xiv. 24.

Hith. הִתְנַפַּלְתִּי, pres. אֶתְנַפֵּל, *Prostrated myself*, Deut. ix. 18. 25.

Part. מִתְנַפֵּל, Ezra x. 1.

Inf. הִתְנַפֵּל, *To fall upon with violence*, Gen. xliii. 18.

וְנִפַּל, Ezek. xxviii. 23, is probably an error for וְנָפַל.

נְפַל, v. Chald. pres. יִפֵּל. *Fell*. (a) *Fell down*. (b) *Prostrated himself*. (c) *Was thrown down*. (d) *Came down*, of a voice. (e) *Fell* to a person, became necessary to him. (a) Dan. iv. 28. (b) Dan. ii. 46; iii. 5, 6, 10, 11. 15. (c) Dan. vii. 20. (d) Dan. iii. 23. (e) Ezra vii. 20.

Part. pl. נָפְלִין, (b) Dan. iii. 7.

נֶפֶץ, m. *The act of breaking or dashing*, Is. xxx. 30, נֶפֶץ וָזֶרֶם, *bursting and inundation*, i. e. the bursting out of a flood of water.

נָפַץ, v. pres. non occ. Arab. فَضّ, *fregit rem separatione partium; disgregavit populum*. Cogn. פוּץ. Constr. immed. it. med. אֵת. (a) *Broke*, or *dashed, down*, or *out*. (b) *Dispersed*. (c) *Dispersed itself*. (c) Gen. ix. 19; 1 Sam. xiii. 11; Is. xxxiii. 3.

Part. pass. נָפוּץ, pl. f. נְפֹצוֹת, (a) Jer. xxii. 28. (b) Is. xi. 12.

Inf. נְפוֹץ, (a) Judg. vii. 19.

Pih. נִפֵּץ, pres. יְנַפֵּץ, i. q. Kal, signn. (a), (b). (a) Ps. ii. 9; cxxxvii. 9; Jer. xlviii. 12; li. 20—23. (b) Jer. xiii. 14.

Inf. נַפֵּץ, (b) Dan. xii. 17.

Puh. Part. pl. f. מְנֻפָּצוֹת, Pass. of (a), Is. xxvii. 9.

נְפַק, v. Chald. *Came forth*, Dan. ii. 11. 13, 14; v. 5.

Part. נָפֵק, pl. נָפְקִין, Dan. iii. 26; vii. 10.

Imp. pl. פֻּקוּ, Dan. iii. 26.

Aph. הַנְפֵּק, הַנְפֵּק, *Brought out*, Ezra v. 14; vi. 5; Dan. v. 2, 3.

נִפְקָא, Chald. f. def. נִפְקְתָא, *Outgoings, expense*, Ezra vi. 4. 8.

נֶפֶשׁ, f. aff. נַפְשִׁי, &c. pl. once נְפָשִׁים, and נְפָשׁוֹת, constr. נַפְשׁוֹת, aff. נַפְשׁוֹתֵינוּ, &c. Arab. نَفْس, *spiritus, anhelitus*; نَفْس, *anima, persona*. (a) *Breath*. (b) Meton. Any thing that breathes: *An animal*. (c) *A person*. (d) *The soul*, as the principle of life. (e) *Self*. (f) *Life*. (g) *Livelihood*. (h) *The feelings, spirits*. (i) *The feelings* of an animal. (k) *Desire, inclination*. (l) בַּעַל נ׳, *A person of an unruly appetite*. (m) בָּתֵּי הַנֶּפֶשׁ, *Perfume boxes*. (a) Gen. i. 30. (b) Gen. i. 20, 21. 24; ii. 19; ix. 10, &c. (c) Gen. xlvi. 15. 18. 22; Lev. iv. 2. 27; v. 2, &c. (d) 1 Kings xvii. 21, 22; Ps. lxxxvi. 4; Prov. xix. 2, &c. (e) Job ix. 21; Ps. iii. 3; xxxv. 13; lxix. 11, &c. (f) Gen. ix. 5; xxxvii. 21; Exod. xxi. 23; Lev. xvii. 11, &c. (g) Deut. xxiv. 6. (h) Exod. xxiii. 9; Lev. xxvi. 16; Num. xxi. 5; Deut. xxviii. 65; Judg. xviii. 25; Ruth iv. 15; 1 Sam. xxii. 2. (i) Prov. xii. 10. (k) Deut. xxiii. 25; Job vi. 11; Eccl. vi. 7. (l) Prov. xxiii. 2. (m) Is. iii. 20. See Schrœder *de Vestitu Mulierum*, on this place.

נָפַשׁ, v. Niph. pres. יִנָּפֵשׁ. (a) *Had breathing time, had an interval of rest*. (b) *Rested* after labour. (c) *Rested* after a journey. (a) Exod. xxiii. 12. (b) Exod. xxxi. 17. (c) 2 Sam. xvi. 14.

נֶפֶת, f. once, Josh. xvii. 11. Apparently, *An elevated district*: r. נוּף.

נֹפֶת, f. r. נוּף. No. I. *Any liquid that drips*, pec. *honey*, Ps. xix. 11; Prov. v. 3; xxiv. 13; xxvii. 7; Cant. iv. 11.

נִפְתּוּלִים, pl. m. constr. נַפְתּוּלֵי, r. פתל. *Struggles*, Gen. xxx. 8.

נֵץ, m. *The hawk*, Lev. xi. 16; Deut. xiv. 15; Job xxxix. 26. See Hieroz., part ii., lib. ii., cap. xix.

נֵץ, m. aff. נִצָּהּ, *Blossom*, Gen. xl. 10.

נָצָא, v. Inf. נֹצָא, *Flying*, or *fleeing*, Jer. xlviii. 9. Cogn. Arab. نَاصَ, *fugit*. Heb. נוס.

נָצַב, v. Arab. نَصَب, *posuit*. *Placed*, Kal non occ.

Niph. נִצַּב, (a) *Placed himself, stood*. (b) *Was placed, was appointed*. (a) Gen. xxxvii. 7; Exod. vii. 15; xxxiii. 21; xxxiv. 2; xv. 8; xxxiii. 8; Ps. xlv. 10. Part. נִצָּב, (a) Gen. xxiv. 13. 43; Exod. xvii. 9, &c. (b) Ruth ii. 5, 6; 1 Kings iv. 5. 7; v. 16; xxii. 48.

Hiph. הִצִּיב, pres. יַצִּיב, apoc. יַצֵּב. Constr. immed. it. med. אֵת. *Made to stand*. (a) *Placed*. (b) *Set up*. (c) *Fixed, appointed*. (d) *Set* a trap. (e) *Kept, supported* in a place. (a) Gen. xxi. 28, 29. (b) Gen. xxxv. 14. 20; Josh. vi. 26; 2 Sam. xviii. 18, &c. (c) Deut. xxxii. 8; Ps. lxxiv. 17; Prov. xv. 25. (d) Jer. v. 26. (e) Ps. xli. 13. Part. מַצִּיב, 1 Sam. xv. 12.

Infin. הַצִּיב, 1 Sam. xiii. 21; 1 Chron. xviii. 3.

Imp. f. הַצִּיבִי, Jer. xxxi. 21.

Hoph. part. מֻצָּב, *Set up*, Gen. xxviii. 12.

נִצָּב, m. *The handle* of a knife, Judg. iii. 22. Arab. نِصَاب, *Id.*

נִצְבְּתָא, f. def. Chald. *Firmness, strength*, Dan. ii. 41.

נָצָה, v. I. *Flew, fled*, נָצוּ, Lam. iv. 15. See נצא.

II. Niph. pres. יִנָּצוּ. Arab. نَصّ, *conj*. ii. *instando ursit*. Syr. ܢܨܐ, *rixatus*

נצה (425) נצי

est. Quarrelled, Exod. xxi. 22 ; Lev. xxiv. 10 ; Deut. xxv. 11 ; 2 Sam. xiv. 6.
Part. pl. נִצִּים, Exod. ii. 13.
Hiph. הִצָּה, *Excited to strife*, Num. xxvi. 9.
Inf. aff. הַצֹּתָם, הַצּוֹתוֹ, Num. xxvi. 9 ; Ps. lx. 2.

III. Niph. pres. תִּצֶּינָה, *Are stripped*, Jer. iv. 7. Arab. نَضَا .r نَضَوَ, *detraxit vestem alteri*.
Part. pl. נִצִּים, *Bare*, 2 Kings xix. 28 ; Is. xxxvii. 26.

נִצָּה, f. aff. נִצָּתוֹ, *Blossom*, Job xv. 33 ; Is. xviii. 5 : r. נצץ.

נֹצָה, f. aff. נֹצָתָהּ, *The contents of a bird's crop*, Lev. i. 16. But LXX. σὺν τοῖς πτεροῖς. The feminine affix, however, shows that this cannot be correct : r. נצה.

נֶצַח, and "בְּ, m. aff. נִצְחִי, pl. נְצָחִים. Arab. نَصَحَ, *monuit ; purus et sincerus fuit de re ; verè rectèque se habuit ; plene et ad satietatem hauserunt potum cameli*. Syr. ܢܨܚ, *vicit*. *Completeness, truth, faithfulness*. (a) נֵצַח יִשְׂרָאֵל, A title of the Deity, as a being of *perfection*, and *truth*. (b) *Perpetuity*. (c) *Success; the hope of success*. (d) As an adverb, *without end*. (e) לָנֶצַח : [1] *According to truth*. [2] *Entirely, wholly*. [3] *Continually*. [4] *For ever*. (f) לְנֶצַח נְצָחִים, *Most completely*. (g) עַד נֶצַח : [1] *Thoroughly*. [2] *Without end*. (a) 1 Sam. xv. 29. (b) 1 Chron. xxix. 11 ; Ps. lxxiv. 3 ; Jer. xv. 18. (c) Ps. xiii. 2 ; xvi. 11 ; Am. i. 11. (d) Lam. iii. 18. (e), [1] Prov. xxi. 28 ; Hab. i. 4. [2] Job iv. 20 ; xx. 7 ; xxxvi. 7. [3] 2 Sam. ii. 26 ; Job xiv. 20 ; Is. xxviii. 28. [4] Job xxiii. 7 ; Ps. ix. 7. 19 ; x. 11 ; xliv. 24, &c. (f) Is. xxxiv. 10. (g), [1] Job xxxiv. 36. [2] Ps. xlix. 20.

נָצַח, v. Pih. *Conquered, excelled, presided*.
Part. מְנַצֵּחַ, pl. מְנַצְּחִים, *One who presides*. (a) *A leader* or *chief* in any work. (b) Pec. in music. (a) 2 Chron. ii. 1. 17 ; xxxiv. 13. (b) In the titles of Pss. iv., v., vi., viii., &c.
Inf. נַצֵּחַ, *To preside, direct*, 1 Chron. xv. 21 ; xxiii. 4 ; 2 Chron. xxxiv. 12 ; Ezra iii. 8. 10.

נְצַח, v. Chald. Ithpa. Part. מִתְנַצַּח, *Superior*, with עַל, Dan. vi. 4.

נֶצַח, m. aff. נִצְחָם, *The juice* of grapes,

Is. lxiii. 3. 6. LXX. αἷμα, in both passages. Vulg. *sanguinem*, in v. 3 ; and *virtutem*, in v. 6. Arab. نَضَحَ, *conspersit*. Cogn. נזה.

נָצִיב, m. pl. נְצִיבִים, constr. נְצִיבֵי. r. נצב. Any thing or person *set up* or *appointed*. (a) *A pillar*. (b) *A military station, garrison*. (c) *A chief* or *commander*. (a) Gen. xix. 26. (b) 1 Sam. x. 5 ; xiii. 3, 4 ; 2 Sam. viii. 6. 14 ; 1 Chron. xi. 16 ; xviii. 13 ; 2 Chron. xvii. 2. (c) 1 Kings iv. 19.

נָצַל, v. Kal non occ. Arab. نَصَلَ, *exiit ; liberatus fuit* ab aliquâ re. Æth. ነሥአ፡ *avulsit*. Cogn. נשל. *Drew out, or off*.
Niph. נִצַּל, pres. יִנָּצֵל, *Became, was, drawn out*. (a) *Was delivered, escaped*. (b) With אֶל, *ran away to*. (a) 2 Kings xix. 11 ; Ps. lxix. 15 ; Mic. v. 10. (b) Deut. xxiii. 16.
Inf. הִנָּצֵל, Is. xx. 7 ; Hab. ii. 9.
Imp. הִנָּצֵל, Prov. vi. 3.
Pih. נִצֵּל, pres. יְנַצֵּל. (a) *Delivered*. (b) *Plundered*. (c) *Gained spoil*. (a) Ezek. xiv. 13. (b) Exod. iii. 22 ; xii. 36. (c) 2 Chron. xx. 25.
Hiph. הִצִּיל, pres. יַצִּיל, apoc. יַצֵּל. Constr. immed. it. med. אֶת, and with or without מִן. (a) *Delivered, rescued*. (b) *Took away*. (c) With בֵּין, *Parted*. (d) וְהִצִּיל עֵינֵינוּ, *And* (deliver himself) *escape* (out of) *our sight*. (a) Exod. xii. 27 ; xviii. 10 ; 1 Sam. xxx. 18, &c. (b) Gen. xxxi. 9. 16 ; Ps. cxix. 43. (d) 2 Sam. xx. 6.
Part. מַצִּיל, (c) 2 Sam. xiv. 6. (a) Deut. xxxii. 39 ; Judg. xviii. 28, &c.
Inf. הַצִּיל, הַצֵּל, aff. הַצִּילֵנוּ, &c., Gen. xxxvii. 22 ; 2 Kings xviii. 30, &c. With לְ, for אֶת, Jonah iv. 6.
Imp. הַצֵּל, הַצִּילָה, aff. הַצִּילֵנִי, &c., pl. הַצִּילוּ, Gen. xxxii. 11 ; Ps. xxii. 21 ; lxxxii. 4 ; Prov. xxiv. 11.
Hoph. Pass. of Hiph. Part. מֻצָּל, *Rescued*, Amos iv. 11 ; Zech. iii. 2.
Hith. pres. יִתְנַצְּלוּ, *Strip themselves* (lit. become spoiled) of their ornaments, Exod. xxxiii. 6.

נְצַל, v. Chald. Aph. *Rescued*.
Part. מַצִּל, Dan. vi. 28.
Inf. הַצָּלָה, aff. הַצָּלוּתֵהּ, Dan. iii. 29 ; vi. 15.

נִצָּן, m. pl. נִצָּנִים, i. q. נִצָּה, *A flower*, Cant. ii. 12.

נָצַץ, v. Part. plur. נֹצְצִים, *Glittering*,

3 I

נצר (426) נקב

Ezek. i. 7. Sam. נצץ, *accensus est; scintillavit.*

נָצַר, v. pres. יִצֹּר, and יִנְצָר. Arab. نَصَرَ, *juvit, defendit;* نَطَرَ, *custodem et observatorem egit, pec. palmeti vineæve.* Cogn. נטר. Constr. immed. it. med. אֶת. *Guarded.* (a) *Guarded* a person. (b) *Preserved* from evil, with מִן. (c) *Watched,* in order to preserve. (d) *Watched* his own heart. (e) *Watched, scrutinized.* (f) *Besieged.* (g) *Shut up.* (h) *Observed* a law. (i) *Observed* mercy, truth, &c. (a) Ps. lxiv. 2; Is. xxvi. 3; xxvii. 3; xlii. 6, &c. (b) Ps. xii. 8; xxxii. 7; cxl. 2. (d) Ps. cxix. 129. (h) Ps. cxix. 22. 56. 100; Prov. xxii. 12, &c.

Part. נֹצֵר, pl. נֹצְרִים, constr. נֹצְרֵי. (c) Job xxvii. 18; Ps. cxix. 129; Prov. xiii. 3, &c. (e) Job vii. 20. (f) Is. i. 8; lxv. 4. (g) Ezek. vi. 12. (i) Exod. xxxiv. 7; Ps. xxxi. 24.

Part. pass. נָצוּר, f. נְצוּרָה, constr. נְצֻרַת, pl. נְצֻרוֹת. Prov. vii. 10, נְצֻרַת לֵב, a woman with a heart watchful for evil, *subtile of heart.* Is. xlvii. 6, נְצֻרוֹת, *concealed things.*

Inf. נְצֹר, Prov. ii. 8. Imp. נְצֹר, צֹר, נִצְרָה, Ps. xxxiv. 14; cxli. 3; Is. viii. 17; Nah. ii. 1, &c.

נֵצֶר, m. Arab. نَضَرَ, *nitore fulsit vultus; viruit arbor;* نَضَّارَ, *lignum, tabula, asseres.* A *sucker, branch,* Is. xi. 1; xiv. 19; lx. 21; Dan. xi. 7. LXX. φύτευμα, ἄνθος. Theod. βλαστόν. Sym. ἔκτρωμα. Vulg. *flos, stirps, germen.*

נְקֵא, Chald. *Pure, white,* Dan. vii. 9. Heb. נָקִי.

נָקַב, v. pres. יִקֹּב, and יִנְקֹב. Arab. نَقَبَ, *perfodit.* Syr. ܢܩܒ, and Sam. נקב, *Id.* Constr. immed. it. med. אֶת. (a) *Pierced.* (b) *Bored through.* (c) *Bored* a hole. (d) *Broke* the head with a staff. (e) *Marked out, determined.* (f) *Named.* (g) *Marked as worthless.* [1] *Spoke contemptuously of.* [2] *Pronounced unfortunate.* [3] Expressed a wish that one might be so, *cursed.* (a) 2 Kings xviii. 21; Is. xxxvi. 6. (b) Job xl. 24. 26. (c) 2 Kings xii. 10. (d) Hab. iii. 14. (g), [1] Lev. xxiv. 11. [2] Num. xxiii. 8. 28; Job iii. 8; v. 3; Num. xxiii. 28; Is. lxii. 2. [3] Prov. xi. 26; xxiv. 24.

Part. נֹקֵב, (g) Lev. xxiv. 16. Part. pass. נָקוּב, pl. constr. נְקֻבֵי, (b) Hag. i. 6. (f) Amos vi. 1. Inf. aff. נָקְבוֹ, (g) Lev. xxiv. 16. Imp. נָקְבָה, (e) Gen. xxx. 28. Niph. נִקְּבוּ, *Were marked* by name, Num. i. 17; 1 Chron. xii. 31; xvi. 41; 2 Chron. xxviii. 15; xxxi. 19; Ezra viii. 20.

נֶקֶב, m. pl. aff. נְקָבֶיךָ, *Holes* bored in setting precious stones, Ezek. xxviii. 13.

נְקֵבָה, f. *Female,* used both of women and animals, Gen. i. 26; v. 2; Lev. iv. 28. 32; v. 6, &c.

נָקֹד, pl. נְקֻדּוֹת, f. נְקֻדּוֹת. Chald. נְקַד, *notavit, punctis notavit.* Arab. نَقَدَ, *genus ovium necnon caprarum deforme et brevipes, —ejudem tamen lana optima habetur. An inferior species of sheep and goats,* marked probably with spots. See Hieroz., i., lib. ii., cap. xliv.

נֹקֵד, m. pl. נֹקְדִים. Arab. نَقَّادٌ, *ovium* نَقَّدٍ *appellatarum, pastor. A shepherd, having a flock of* נְקֻדִים; *any shepherd,* 2 Kings iii. 4; Amos i. 1.

נִקֻּדִים, m. pl. (a) Applied to bread, Josh. ix. 5. 12. LXX. εὐρωτιῶν καὶ βεβρωμένος.—γεγόνασι βεβρωμένοι. Vulg. *in frusta comminuti; vetustate nimiâ comminuti.* According to some, *mouldiness;* according to others, *crumbs.* (b) Apparently, *a kind of cake,* 1 Kings xiv. 3. LXX. κολλύρια τοῖς τέκνοις αὐτοῦ. Vulg. *crustulam.*

נְקֻדּוֹת, f. pl. *Studs* of silver, Cant. i. 11. LXX. στιγμάτων. Vulg. murenulas *vermiculatas* argento.

נָקָה, v. Arab. نَقِيَ, *purus, mundus fuit. Was pure.* Inf. נְקֹה, Jer. xlix. 12. Niph. נִקָּה, pres. יִנָּקֶה. (a) *Was innocent, clear,* abs. (b) With מִן, *Was clear,* [1] from guilt, or punishment; [2] from an oath; [3] in reference to a person. (c) *Was cleared away.* [1] *Was swept away.* [2] *Was devastated.* (d) *Was cleared, considered as innocent, escaped punishment.* (a) Exod. xxi. 19; Num. v. 31; 1 Sam. xxvi. 9, &c. (b), [1] Num. v. 31. [2]

נקט (427) נקם

Gen. xxiv. 8. 41. [3] Judg. xv. 3. (c), [1] Zech. v. 3. [2] Is. iii. 26. (d) Prov. vi. 29; xi. 21; Jer. xxv. 29; xlix. 12, &c.
Inf. הַנְקֵה, (d) Jer. xxv. 29.
Imp. f. הַנְקֵה, (d) Num. v. 19.
Pih. נִקִּיתִי, pres. יְנַקֶּה. (a) *Considered innocent.* (b) *Treated as innocent.* (c) *Cleansed.* (a) Exod. xx. 7; Deut. v. 11; 1 Kings ii. 9; Job ix. 28; x. 14. (b) Exod. xxxiv. 7; Num. xiv. 18; Jer. xxx. 11; xlvi. 28; Nah. i. 3. (c) Joel iv. 21.
Inf. נַקֵּה, Exod. xxxiv. 7, &c.

נקט, v. f. נִקְטָה, *Is wearied,* Job x. 1. See קוט, and my note.

נָקִי, m. constr. נְקִי, pl. נְקִיִּים and נְקִיִּם. (a) *Innocent, clear,* abs. (b) With מִן, *Clear,* [1] From an oath, [2] From blood, i. e. the guilt of shedding it. [3] In reference to a person, (c) *Exempt.* (a) Exod. xxi. 28; Deut. xix. 10; 2 Sam. xiv. 9, &c. (b), [1] Gen. xxiv. 41; Josh. ii. 17. 20. [2] 2 Sam. iii. 28. [3] Num. xxxii. 22. (c) 1 Kings xv. 22.

נְקִיא, m. *Id.,* Joel iv. 19; Jonah i. 14.

נִקָּיוֹן, m. for constr. נְקִיוֹן. (a) *Innocency.* (b) *Cleanness* of teeth, i. e. emptiness of the mouth. (a) Gen. xx. 5; Ps. xxvi. 6; lxxiii. 13; Hos. viii. 5. (b) Amos iv. 6.

נָקִיק, m. constr. נְקִיק, pl. constr. נְקִיקֵי, m. *A fissure* in a rock, Is. vii. 19; Jer. xiii. 4; xvi. 16. LXX. τρώγλαις, τρυμαλιᾷ. Vulg. *cavernis, foramine.*

נָקַם, v. pres. יִקֹּם. Arab. نَقَمَ, *se vindicavit ab aliquo.* Syr. ܐܬܢܩܡ, *ultionem sumpsit.* (a) *Avenged, took vengeance for,* constr. immed. (b) *Took revenge on,* constr. immed. it. med. אֵת, לְ. (c) *Punished,* constr. immed. (d) *Revenged* a person (constr. immed.) on another. with מִן. (a) Deut. xxxii. 43. (b) Lev. xix. 18; Josh. x. 13.
Part. נֹקֵם, f. נֹקֶמֶת, (a) Lev. xxvi. 25; Nah. i. 2. (b) Nah. i. 2. (c) Ps. xcix. 8.
Inf. נְקֹם, נְקֹם, (c) Exod. xxi. 20; Ezek. xxiv. 8; xxv. 12.
Imp. נְקֹם, (d) Num. xxxi. 2.
Niph. נִקַּם, pres. יִנָּקֵם. (a) *Revenged himself on,* with בְּ, or מִן. (b) *Was punished.* (a) Judg. xv. 7; 1 Sam. xiv. 25; Is. i. 24; Ezek. xxv. 12. (b) Exod. xxi. 20; Ezek. xxv. 15.
Inf. הִנָּקֵם, (a) 1 Sam. xviii. 25; Esth. viii. 13; Jer. xlvi. 10.

Imp. הִנָּקֵם, Jer. xv. 15, וְהִנָּקֶם לִי מֵרֹדְפַי, *And avenge me of my persecutors.*
Pih. נִקַּמְתִּי, i. q. Kal, (a) 2 Kings ix. 7; Jer. li. 36.
Hoph. pres. יֻקַּם, *Shall be avenged,* Gen. iv. 15. 24; Exod. xxi. 21.
Hith. pres. הִתְנַקֵּם, i. q. Niph. (a), Jer. v. 9. 29; ix. 8.
Part. מִתְנַקֵּם, *One desirous of vengeance,* Ps. viii. 3; xliv. 17.

נָקָם, m. constr. נְקַם. (a) *Vengeance.* (b) *Punishment.* (a) Deut. xxxii. 35. 41; Prov. vi. 34; Is. xlvii. 3, &c. (b) Ps. lviii. 11; Ezek. xxv. 12. 15, &c.

נְקָמָה, f. constr. נִקְמַת, aff. נִקְמָתִי, &c., pl. נְקָמוֹת, f. *Id.* (a) *Vengeance* taken by a person, נִקְמַת פ׳. (b) *Vengeance inflicted on a person,* נְקָמָה מִן. (a) Jer. xx. 10; Ezek. xxv. 14. 16, &c. (b) Jer. L. 28; Ps. lxxix. 10, &c. (c), [1] Ps. cxlix. 7. [2] Num. xxxi. 3; Ezek. xxv. 14. 16. [3] Jer. xx. 10. (d), [1] Judg. xi. 36. [2] 2 Sam. xxii. 48. (e) Ezek. xxv. 15. Phrr. (e) *Inflicted vengeance on,* [1] עָשָׂה נְקָמָה בְּ. [2] נָתַן נ׳ בְּ. [3] לָקַח נ׳ מִן. (d) *Took vengeance for,* [1] עָשָׂה נְקָמוֹת לְ. [2] נָתַן נ׳ לְ. (e) *Acted revengefully,* עָשָׂה בִּנְקָמָה.

נקע, v. נָקְעָה, *Fell away from,* — of the affections, Ezek. xxiii. 18. 22. 28. See יקע.

נקף, v. pres. יִקֹּף. Arab. نَقَفَ, *percussit, pec. caput.* Syr. ܢܩܦ, *conjunxit, applicuit.* Arab. وَقَفَ, *stetit;* وَقَفَ, *limbus ambiens clypeum; armilla.* Cogn. נקב, and נקב. *Struck, struck down, killed,* Is. xxix. 1, יִקֹּפוּ. חַגִּים.—Vulg. *solennitates evolutæ sunt.* Syr. ܢܬܟܪܟܘܢ ܥܐܕܐ, *solennitates celebrentur.*—*Let them kill sacrifices.* By Meton., Auth. Vers., Gesen., "*festa in orbem eant.*" Targ. "*abolebuntur.*"
Pih. נִקֵּף, (a) *Cut down.* (b) *Pierced through.* (a) Is. x. 34. (b) Job xix. 26.
Hiph. הִקִּיף, pres. יַקִּיף, apoc. יַקֵּף. Constr. immed. it. med. אֵת, עַל. (a) *Fixed,* placed around, with עַל. (b) *Surrounded.* (c) *Went round* a place. (d) *Came round,* of time. (e) *Made a circle* of the hair, i. e. cut it into a circular form. (a) Job xix. 6; Lam. iii. 5. (b) 2 Kings vi. 14; xi. 8; 2 Chron. xxiii. 7; Ps. xvii. 9; xxii. 17; lxxxviii. 18. (c) Is. xv. 8. (d) Job i. 5. (e) Lev. xix. 27.

נקף (428) נשא

Part. pl. מַקִּפִים, (b) 1 Kings vii. 24; 2 Chron. iv. 3.
Inf. הַקֵּיף, הַקֵּף, (c) Josh. vi. 3. 11.
Imp. pl. aff. הַקִּיפוּהָ, (c) Ps. xlviii. 13.

נֹקֶף, m. *The shaking* of an olive-tree, in order to make the fruit fall, Is. xvii. 6; xxiv. 13, כְּנֹקֶף זַיִת. LXX. ὡς ῥῶγες ἐλαίας.—ὃν τρόπον ἐάν τις καλαμήσηται ἐλαίαν. Vulg. *sicut excussio oleæ; quomodo si paucæ olivæ quæ remanserunt, excutiantur ex oleâ.*

נִקְפָּה, f. once, Is. iii. 24. LXX. ἀντὶ ζώνης σχοινίῳ ζώσῃ. Vulg. *pro zonâ funiculus.* Interpreters are divided between *a cord*, as a substitute for the elegant girdle usually worn, and *the rending* of garments in mourning.

נקר, v. pres. pl. יִקְּרוּ. Arab. نَقَرَ, *excavavit* saxum; *perfodit* rostro avis. Syr. ܢܩܒ, *fodit, effodit. Pierced, dug.* (a) *Pecked out*, as a bird. (b) *Put out* an eye, by piercing. (a) Prov. xxx. 17.
Inf. נְקוֹר, (b) 1 Sam. xi. 2.
Pih. נִקֵּר, pres. יְנַקֵּר, (a) *Pierced through.* (b) *Put out* an eye. (a) Job xxx. 17. (b) Num. xvi. 14; Judg. xvi. 21.
Puh. נֻקַּרְתֶּם, *Were dug out*, Is. li. 1.

נִקְרָה, f. constr. נִקְרַת, pl. constr. נִקְרוֹת. *A cleft* of a rock, Exod. xxxiii. 22; Is. ii. 21.

נקש, v. i. q. יקש, *Snared*, as a fowler.
Niph. pres. תִּנָּקֵשׁ, *Thou art ensnared, enticed*, Deut. xii. 30.
Pih. pres. יְנַקֵּשׁ, *Spread a snare for*, with לְ, Ps. xxxviii. 13; cix. 11.
Hith. part. מִתְנַקֵּשׁ, *Id.*, with בְּ, 1 Sam. xxviii. 9.

נקש, v. Chald. part. pl. f. נָקְשָׁן, *Knees* were *striking* against each other, Dan. v. 6. Syr. ܢܩܫ, *pulsavit, collisit.*

נֵר, m. aff. נֵרִי, נֵרוֹ, i. q. נִיר. (a) *A light.* Metaph. (b) *Prosperity.* (a) Exod. xxvii. 20; Lev. xxiv. 2; 1 Sam. iii. 3, &c. (b) Job xxix. 3; xviii. 6; Prov. xiii. 9, &c.

נֵר, *Id.*, Prov. xxi. 4.

נִרְגָּן, m. Arab. نَيْرَج, *susurro; celer, ut ultro citroque se convertat. A busybody*, Prov. xvi. 28; xviii. 8; xxvi. 20. 22.

נֵרְדְּ, m. aff. נִרְדִּי, pl. נְרָדִים, *Spikenard*, Cant. i. 12; iv. 13, 14. See Hierobot.,

part. ii., p. 1. Sir W. Jones, Asiat. Res., vol. ii.

נִגְרָה, f. pl. גֵּרוֹת, i. q. גֵּר, Exod. xxx. 7; Lev. xxiv. 4; Prov. xxxi. 18, &c.

נָשָׂא, v. pres. יִשָּׂא. Constr. immed. it. med. אֵת. *Lifted up, took, carried.* (A), (a) *Lifted up.* (b) *Lifted up* his hand, [1] With בְּ, *against.* [2] In a solemn promise. [3] *Beckoning.* (c) *Lifted up* his voice. (d) *Lifted up* his feet. (e) *Lifted up* his eyes, [1] And saw. [2] With אֶל, *Looked towards*, in love or expectation. [3] מָרוֹם, *In pride.* (f) נָשׂוֹא נ", [1] *Lifted up his soul* to God. [2] *Set his heart on.* [3] *Paid regard to.* (g) *Raised* the face, [1] In confidence. [2] *Raised* the face to, *looked towards.* (h) His heart *lifted* him up. (i) His heart *impelled* him. (k) ראשׁ נ", [1] *Raised the head* of another, i. e. *elevated* him. [2] *Raised his own head.* [3] *Took the sum of.* [4] *Examined the case of.* (B), (a) *Took.* (b) *Took* a wife. (c) *Took up*, in order to carry. (d) *Took* into the hand. (e) *Took* into the mouth. (f) *Uttered.* (g) *Offered* prayer. (h) *Received* a precept. (i) *Took away.* (k) *Took hold of*, with בְּ. (l) *Obtained.* (m) פָנִים נ", *Accepted the person, regarded with respect or partiality.* (n) עָוֹן נ", *Took away iniquity, forgave it.* (o) Without עָוֹן, but with לְ, of the person or crime, *forgave.* (C), (a) *Carried.* (b) *Carried away.* (c) *Brought.* (d) *Carried* a yoke. (e) *Endured.* (f) *Bore the punishment or consequences of.* (g) *Supported* dignity. (h) *Assisted, helped forward.* (i) *Encouraged* a report. (k) *Bore* fruit. (l) *Bore* a branch. (m) *Bore fruit*, abs. (n) *Wore.* (o) *Supported, eased*, with בְּ. (p) *Supported* with food. (q) *Laid* on another, with עַל. (r) *Imposed* an oath upon, with בְּ. (s) *Removed itself*, of the earth. (A), (a) Judg. ix. 48; 1 Kings xiii. 29; Amos vi. 10, &c. (b), [1] 2 Sam. xviii. 28; xx. 21. [2] Exod. vi. 8; Num. xiv. 30; Neh. ix. 15, &c. [3] With אֶל, Is. xlix. 22. (c) Gen. xxvii. 38; Ps. xciii. 3; Is. xlii. 2; lii. 8, &c. (d) Gen. xxix. 1. (e), [1] Gen. xxxiii. 1. 5. 29; xxxi. 10; Dan. viii. 3, &c. [2] Ps. cxxi. 1; cxxiii. 1; Ezek. xviii. 6. 12. 15, &c. [3] 2 Kings xix. 22; Is. xxxvii. 23. (f), [1] Ps. xxv. 1; lxxxvi. 4; cxliii. 8. [2] Hos. iv. 8. [3] Prov. xix. 18. (g), [1] Job xi. 15. [2] Num. vi. 26; 2 Sam. ii. 22; 2 Kings ix. 32. (h) 2 Kings xiv. 10; 2 Chron. xxv. 19. (i)

נשא (429) נשא

Exod. xxxv. 21. 26; xxxvi. 2. (k), [1] Gen. xl. 13; 2 Kings xxv. 27; Jer. lii. 31. [2] Job x. 15; Ps. lxxxiii. 3; Zech. ii. 4. [3] Exod. xxx. 12; Num. i. 49; xxxi. 49, &c. [4] Gen. xl. 20. (B), (a) Ps. cxxxix. 9. (b) 2 Chron. xi. 21; Ezra ix. 2; x. 44, &c. (c) Exod. xii. 34; Ruth ii. 18; 1 Sam. xvii. 20; 2 Kings iv. 20. (d) Is. xxxviii. 21; Ps. cxvi. 13. (e) Ps. xvi. 4; L. 16. (f) Exod. xx. 7; Is. xiv. 4; Jer. ix. 9; xi. 14; Ezek. xxvi. 17; xxvii. 32, &c. (g) 2 Kings xix. 4; Is. xxxvii. 4; Jer. vii. 16. (h) Deut. xxxiii. 3. (i) Num. xvi. 15; Job xxxii. 23. (k) Job xxi. 12. (l) Esth. ii. 9; v. 2; Ps. xxiv. 5; Eccl. v. 14, &c. (m) Gen. xix. 21; Job xxxiv. 19; Prov. vi. 35, &c. (n) Ps. xxxii. 8; lxxxv. 3; Ezek. iv. 5. 7. (o) Gen. xviii. 24. 26; Exod. xxiii. 21; Josh. xxiv. 19; Is. ii. 9, &c. (C), (a) Is. xxii. 6; Gen. xxxi. 17; xlviii. 19; Deut. i. 31, &c. (b) Exod. x. 13; 1 Sam. xvii. 34; 2 Kings xxiii. 4, &c. (c) 1 Kings x. 11; 1 Chron. xviii. 11. (d) Lam. iii. 9. (e) Ps. lxix. 8; lxxxviii. 16; Is. liii. 4; Jer. xxxi. 19, &c. (f) Lev. v. 1. 17; xxiv. 15; Is. liii. 12; Ezek. xviii. 19, &c. (g) Zech. vi. 13. (h) Ezra viii. 36. (i) Exod. xxiii. 1. (k) Ezek. xxxvi. 8; Joel ii. 22. (l) Ezek. xvii. 23. (m) Hag. ii. 19. (n) Exod. xxviii. 12. 29, 30. 38. (o) Job vii. 13. (p) Gen. xiii. 6. (q) Is. x. 24. (r) 1 Kings viii. 31. (s) Nah. i. 5.

Part. נֹשֵׂא, f. נֹשֵׂאת נֹשְׂאָה, pl. נֹשְׂאִים, constr. נֹשְׂאֵי, f. נֹשְׂאוֹת, Deut. xxiv. 15; Judg. ix. 24; 1 Chron. xviii. 2. 6; Neh. iv. 11, &c.

Part. pass. constr. נְשׂוּא, נָשׂוּי, נָשׂוּא, pl. נְשׂוּאִים, Supported, forgiven, Ps. xxxii. 1; Is. xxxiii. 24; xlvi. 3.

Inf. נְשׂוֹא, נְשׂא, aff. נָשְׂאִי, שְׂאֵת, aff. שְׂאֵתִי, שְׂאֵתוֹ, Gen. xliv. 1; xlv. 27; Deut. i. 9; Job xli. 17; Ps. xxviii. 2; lxxxix. 10. 51, &c.

Imp. שָׂא, נְשָׂא, fem. שְׂאִי, pl. שְׂאוּ, Gen. xxi. 18; xxvii. 3; Lev. x. 4; Ps. x. 12, &c.

Niph. נִשָּׂא, pres. יִנָּשֵׂא. (a) Was lifted up, was raised. (b) Raised himself. (c) Was carried. (d) Was carried away. (a) Prov. xxx. 13; Is. xl. 4; Ezek. i. 19, &c. (b) Is. xxxiii. 10. (c) Exod. xxv. 28; Is. lxvi. 12; Jer. x. 5, &c. (d) 2 Kings xx. 17; Is. xxxix. 6.

Part. נִשָּׂא, f. נִשָּׂאָה, f. נִשֵּׂאת, pl. f. נִשָּׂאוֹת Lifted up, high, Is. ii. 2. 14; xxx. 25; Zech. v. 7, &c.

Inf. הִנָּשֵׂא, Ezek. i. 19, &c.

Imp. הִנָּשֵׂא, pl. הִנָּשְׂאוּ, Ps. vii. 7; xxiv. 7.

Pih. נִשָּׂא, נִשֵּׂא, pres. יְנַשֵּׂא. (a) Took away. (b) Presented a gift. (c) Carried. (d) Assisted. (e) Raised in rank. (f) נַשּׂוּ'כ, Set his heart. (a) 2 Sam. v. 12; Amos iv. 2. (b) 2 Sam. xix. 43. (c) Is. lxiii. 9. (d) 1 Kings ix. 11; Ezra i. 4. (e) Esth. iii. 1; v. 11.

Part. pl. מְנַשְּׂאִים, (d) Esth. ix. 3. (f) Jer. xxii. 27; xliv. 14.

Imp. aff. נַשְּׂאֵם, Ps. xxviii. 9.

Hiph. הִשִּׂיא, (a) Caused to bear the consequences of. (b) Brought. (a) Lev. xxii. 16. (b) 2 Sam. xvii. 13.

Hith. pres. יִתְנַשֵּׂא, יִנָּשֵׂא. (a) Raised himself, arose. (b) Exalted himself. (c) Was exalted. (a) Num. xxiii. 24. (b) Num. xvi. 3. (c) Num. xxiv. 7; 2 Chron. xxxii. 23; Ezek. xxix. 15.

Part. מִתְנַשֵּׂא, (b) 1 Kings i. 5. (c) 1 Chron. xxix. 11.

Inf. הִתְנַשֵּׂא, (b) Prov. xxx. 32. (c) Ezek. xvii. 14.

נְשָׂא, v. Chald. (a) Carried away. (b) Took. (a) Dan. ii. 35.

Imp. שָׂא, (b) Ezra v. 15.

Ith. Part. f. מִתְנַשְּׂאָה, Exalting itself, Ezra iv. 19.

נְשֻׂאת, Niph. part. f. A gift, 2 Sam. xix. 43.

נשׂב, v. Kal non occ. Cogn. נסכ, סוג.

Hiph. הִשִּׂיג, pres. יַשִּׂיג, apoc. יַשֵּׂג. Constr. immed. it. med. אֶת. Reached. (a) Reached, of time. (b) Attained, obtained. (c) Overtook. (d) Came upon, befel. (e) Reached his hand to his mouth. (f) הִשִּׂיגָה יָדוֹ, Was able to reach, was able. (a) Gen. xlvii. 9; Lev. xxvi. 5. (b) Prov. ii. 19; Is. xxxv. 10; li. 11. (c) Gen. xliv. 4; Deut. xix. 5; 2 Sam. xv. 14; Lam. i. 3, &c. (d) Deut. xxviii. 2. 15. 45; Ps. xl. 13; lxix. 25, &c. (f) Lev. v. 11; xiv. 22; xxv. 49, &c.

Part. מַשִּׂיג, f. מַשֶּׂגֶת, (e) 1 Sam. xiv. 26. (f) Lev. xiv. 21. מַשִּׂיגֵהוּ חֶרֶב, Reached him with a harpoon, Job xli. 18.

Inf. הַשִּׂיג, (c) 1 Sam. xxx. 8.

נְשׂוּאָה, f. pl. aff. נְשֻׂאֹתֵיכֶם, r. נשׂא. A burden, Is. xlvi. 1.

נָשִׂיא, m. constr. נְשִׂיא, pl. נְשִׂיאִים, נְשִׂיאִם, constr. נְשִׂיאֵי, aff. נְשִׂיאַי, &c., r. נשׂא. One who is lifted up, elevated in rank. (a) A chief. (b) Chief of a tribe, among the Israelites. (c) Chief of a subdivision of a tribe. (d) Prince, sovereign, of a people.

נשך (430) נשי

(e) Pl. *Vapours, clouds.* (a) Gen. xxiii. 6.
(b) Num. vii. 11. 24. 30; Josh. xxii. 14, &c.
(c) Num. iii. 32. (d) 1 Kings xi. 34; Ezek. xii. 10; xliv. 3, &c.

נָשַׂק, v. Kal non occ. Cogn. נסק. Probably, *mounted* as flame.
Hiph. הִשִּׂיקוּ, pres. יַשִּׂיק, *Kindled a fire,* Is. xliv. 15; Ezek. xxxix. 9.
Niph. נִשְּׂקָה, *A fire was kindled,* Ps. lxxviii. 21.

נָשָׁא, v. Kal non occ. Cogn. נשׁה. Probably, *erred through forgetfulness.*
Hiph. הִשִּׁיא, pres. יַשִּׁיא, יַשֵּׁי. Constr. immed. it. med. אֶת, לְ, בְּ. *Caused to err.* (a) *Led astray, deceived.* (b) *Came upon unexpectedly.* (c) *Laid a burden on,* with בְּ. (a), [1] Constr. immed. it. med. אֶת, Gen. iii. 13; 2 Kings xix. 10; 2 Chron. xxxii. 15; Is. xxxvii. 10; Jer. xxxvii. 9; xlix. 16; Obad. 3. 7. [2] With לְ, 2 Kings xviii. 29; Is. xxxvi. 14; Jer. iv. 10; xxix. 8. (b) Ps. lv. 16. (c) Ps. lxxxix. 23.

נָשַׁב, v. נָשָׁבָה. Cogn. נשׁף. Arab. اَنْسَبَ, *vehemens fuit* ventus, et pulverem *dispersit. Blew,* of the wind, Is. xl. 7.
Hiph. pres. יַשֵּׁב. (a) *Caused* a wind *to blow.* (b) *Dispersed,* as the wind disperses dust. (a) Ps. cxlvii. 18. (b) Gen. xv. 11.

נָשָׁה, v. I. for נָשָׁא, pres. תִּשֵּׁי, for תִּשִּׂי. Arab. نَسِيَ, *oblitus fuit, neglexit.* Syr. ܢܫܐ, *oblitus fuit.* (a) *Forgot,* Deut. xxxii. 18; Lam. iii. 17. (b) *Neglected, disregarded,* Jer. xxiii. 39.
Niph. pres. aff. תִּנָּשֵׁנִי, Is. xliv. 21, לֹא תִנָּשֵׁנִי, Either, *thou shalt not be forgotten by me,* or *thou shalt not forget me.* Both interpretations suit the context; the latter is the more simple, the former better suited to the vowels. LXX. μὴ ἐπιλανθάνου μου. Vulg. *ne obliviscaris mei.*
Pih. aff. נַשַּׁנִי, *Caused me to forget,* Gen. xli. 51.
Hiph. הִשָּׁה, pres. יַשֶּׁה, *Caused to forget* or *neglect,* Job xxxix. 17. In Job xi. 6, יַשֶּׁה לְךָ אֱלוֹהַּ כִּעֲוֺנֶךָ, *Causes, allows,* or *declares thee to be forgetful through thy iniquity.* But see the notes.
II. *Lent money to* a person, with בְּ, of the person, Jer. xv. 10.
Part. נֹשֶׁה, pl. נֹשִׁים, also נֹשֵׁא, pl. נֹשְׁאִים, aff. נוֹשִׁי, Deut. xxiv. 11; Neh. v. 7. 10, 11; Is. xxiv. 2. Also abs. *a money lender,* Exod. xxii. 24; 2 Kings iv. 1; Ps. cix. 11; 1 Sam. xxii. 2; Is. L. 1.
Hiph. pres. יַשֶּׁה, *Id.,* Deut. xv. 2; xxiv. 10.

נְשִׁי, masc. aff. נִשְׁיֵךְ, *A debt,* 2 Kings iv. 7.

נְשִׁיָּה, f. *Forgetfulness,* Ps. lxxxviii. 13.

נָשֶׁה, m. Arab. نَسًا, *nervus, tendo qui per femur et crus ad talos fertur. The ischiatic nerve,* Gen. xxxii. 33.

נָשִׁים, f. pl. of אִשָּׁה, *Women.*

נְשִׁיקָה, f. pl. נְשִׁיקוֹת, r. נשׁק. *A kiss,* Prov. xxvii. 6; Cant. i. 2.

נָשַׁךְ, v. pres. יִשַּׁךְ. Æth. ነሐከ : *momordit.* Constr. immed. it. med. אֶת. (a) *Bit,* [1] of a serpent. [2] Of a man. (b) *Annoyed.* (c) From נֶשֶׁךְ, *Was lent on interest.* (a), [1] Num. xxi. 9; Prov. xxiii. 32; Eccl. x. 8. 11; Amos v. 19; ix. 3. (c) Deut. xxiii. 20.
Part. נֹשֵׁךְ, pl. נֹשְׁכִים, aff. נֹשְׁכֶיךָ, (a, 1) Gen. xlix. 17. (a, 2) Mic. iii. 5. (b) Hab. ii. 7.
Part. pass. נָשׁוּךְ, (a, 1) Num. xxi. 9.
Pih. נִשֵּׁךְ, pres. יְנַשֵּׁךְ, *Bit,* of a serpent, Num. xxi. 7; Jer. viii. 17.
Hiph. pres. תַּשִּׁיךְ, *Lent on interest to,* with לְ, Deut. xxiii. 20, 21.

נֶשֶׁךְ, m. *Interest;* from its involving an injurious, *biting,* system, Exod. xxii. 24; Deut. xxiii. 19; Prov. xxviii. 8. Phrr. נָתַן בְּנֶשֶׁךְ, *lent on interest,* Lev. xxv. 37; Ps. xv. 5; Ezek. xviii. 8. 13. לָקַח נֶשֶׁךְ, *took interest,* Lev. xxv. 36; Ezek. xviii. 17; xxii. 12.

נִשְׁכָּה, f. aff. נִשְׁכָּתוֹ, pl. נְשָׁכוֹת, for לִשְׁכָּה, נ being substituted for ל, Gram. art. 24. *A chamber,* pec. one of those attached to the sides of the Temple, Neh. iii. 30; xii. 44; xiii. 7.

נָשַׁל, v. pres. יִשַּׁל. Arab. نَسَلَ, *excidit pluma, pilus, lana; defluxit* vestis de corpore; نَشَلَ, *celeriter extraxit, amovit quid.* Cogn. שׁלל. (a) *Fell off,* [1] As unripe fruit; [2] As the head of an axe from the handle. (b) *Pulled off* a shoe. (c) *Stripped* or *deprived of a place, drove out.* Comp. *castris exuere.* (a), [1] Deut. xxviii. 40. [2] Deut. xix. 5. (c) Deut. vii. 22; xix. 5.
Imp. שַׁל, (b) Exod. iii. 5; Josh. v. 15.

נשם (431) נשר

Pih. pres. יְנַשֵּׁל, i. q. Kal. (c) 2 Kings xvi. 6.

נְשָׁמָה, f. constr. נִשְׁמַת, aff. נִשְׁמָתִי, נִשְׁמָתוֹ, pl. נְשָׁמוֹת. Arab. نَسَمَ, leniter spiravit ventus; نَسَمَةٌ, animæ spiritus, halitus; homo. Syr. ܢܫܡ, spiravit. (a) Breath. (b) Life. (c) A human being. (d) The breath of God, [1] His anger. [2] That life of which he is the author. [3] The wind. (a) Gen. ii. 7; vii. 22; Job xxvi. 4; xxvii. 3, &c. (b) 1 Kings xvii. 17; Is. ii. 22; xlii. 5. (c) Deut. xx. 16; Josh. x. 40; xi. 11. 14; 1 Kings xv. 29; Ps. cl. 6. (d), [1] 2 Sam. xxii. 16; Ps. xviii. 16; Is. xxx. 33. [2] Job xxxii. 8; xxxiii. 4; xxxiv. 14; Is. lvii. 16. [3] Job xxxvii. 10.

נִשְׁמָא, f. aff. נִשְׁמְתָךְ, Chald. Breath, life, Dan. v. 23.

נָשַׁף, v. Arab. نَسَفَ, ventilavit flatu motuque frumentum; comminuit, dispersitque; مِنْسَفٌ, ventilabrum. Cogn. נשב. (a) Blew, spoken of God. (b) Blew on, with בְּ. (a) Exod. xv. 10. (b) Is. xl. 24.

נֶשֶׁף, m. aff. נִשְׁפּוֹ, The twilight; probably from the refreshing breezes that blow at this time, and especially in hot countries. (a) The dawn. (b) The evening twilight, dusk. (c) Darkness. (a) 1 Sam. xxx. 17; Job vii. 4; Ps. cxix. 147. (b) Job iii. 9; xxiv. 15; Prov. vii. 9. (c) 2 Kings viii. 5. 7; Is. v. 11; xxi. 4; lix. 10; Jer. xiii. 16.

נֶשֶׁק, and נֵשֶׁק, m. (a) The arrangement of an army; battle. (b) An army drawn up in battle array. (c) Arms. (d) An armoury. (a) Ps. cxl. 8. (b) Job xxxix. 21. (c) 1 Kings x. 25; 2 Chron. ix. 24; Ps. lxxviii. 9; Ezek. xxxix. 9, 10. (d) 1 Kings x. 2; Neh. iii. 19; Is. xxii. 8.

נָשַׁק, v. pres. יִשַּׁק. Syr. ܢܫܩ, osculatus est. Cogn. شَاقَ r. شوق, movit aliquem amor; شَوْق, desiderium; نَسَقَ, ordine disposuit. (a) Kissed, constr. [1] immed. it. med. [2] לְ. [3] אֶל. (b) Pl. Kissed each other. (c) Of the hand, touched the mouth, and was kissed by it, with לְ. (d) Adored, either putting the hand to the mouth, or kissing the idol, constr. [1] immed. it. [2] med. לְ. (e) Arranged, regulated himself. (f) Arranged himself in order of battle, armed himself. (a), [1] Gen. xxxiii. 4; 1 Sam. x. 1; Cant. i. 4; viii. 1. [2] Gen. xxvii. 27; 2 Sam. xv. 5; Prov. vii. 13, &c. [3] 1 Sam. xx. 41. (b) Ps. lxxxv. 11. (c) Job xxxi. 27. (d), [1] Hos. xiii. 2. [2] 1 Kings xix. 18. (e) Gen. xli. 40.

Part. pl. constr. נֹשְׁקֵי, (f) 1 Chron. xii. 2; 2 Chron. xvii. 17; Ps. lxxviii. 9. Inf. נְשֹׁק, (a, 2) 2 Sam. xx. 9. Imp. שְׁקָה, (a, 2) Gen. xxvii. 26. Pih. pres. יְנַשֵּׁק, i. q. Kal, (a, 2) Gen. xxix. 13; xxxii. 1; xlv. 15. Inf. נַשֵּׁק, Gen. xxxi. 28. Imp. pl. נַשְּׁקוּ, I. q. Kal, (d) Ps. ii. 12. Hiph. Part. pl. f. מַשִּׁיקוֹת, Joined, touched, with אֶל, Ezek. iii. 13.

נֶשֶׁר, m. pl. נְשָׁרִים, constr. נִשְׁרֵי. Arab. نِسْرٌ, aquila. Syr. ܢܫܪܐ. Æth. ንስር: Id. The eagle, Lev. xi. 13; Job xxxix. 30; Prov. xxx. 17, &c. See Hieroz., part ii., lib. ii., cap. 1.

נְשַׁר, m. pl. נִשְׁרִין, Chald. Id., Dan. iv. 30; vii. 4.

נשת, v. נָשְׁתָה. (a) Became parched, of the tongue, Is. xli. 17. (b) Wasted away, of strength, Jer. li. 30. Probably, cogn. שׁתה. Niph. נִשְּׁתוּ, Were dried up, of waters, Is. xix. 5.

נִשְׁתְּוָן, m. Pers. نوشتن, To write. A letter, Ezra iv. 7; vii. 11.

נִשְׁתְּוָן, m. def. נִשְׁתְּוָנָא, Chald. Id., Ezra iv. 18. 23; v. 5.

נתח, v. Arab. نَتَحَ, extraxit, evulsit rem; vulsit, carpsitque accipiter carnem. Pih. נִתַּח, pres. יְנַתֵּחַ. Constr. immed. it. med. אֶת. Divided, cut into pieces, a dead animal, Lev. viii. 20; 1 Sam. xi. 7; 1 Kings xviii. 33, &c.

נֵתַח, m. pl. נְתָחִים, aff. נְתָחָיו. A part of an animal, a piece of flesh, Lev. i. 6; ix. 13; Ezek. xxiv. 4, &c.

נָתִיב, m. constr. נְתִיב, and— נְתִיבָה, fem. aff. נְתִיבָתִי, pl. נְתִיבוֹת, aff. נְתִיבוֹתַי, &c.—

נתי (432) נתן

(a) *A path*. (b) *The course* of a vein of metal. (c) *A track* on the sea. (d) Metaph. *Course of life*. (a) Judg. v. 6; Job xviii. 10; xxxviii. 20; Prov. viii. 2, &c. (b) Job xxviii. 7. (c) Job xli. 24. (d) Ps. cxix. 105; cxlii. 4; Prov. i. 15; viii. 20, &c.

נְתִינִים, pl. m. r. נתן. *Servants whose business it was to wait on the Levites*, or the origin of their name, &c. See Num. viii. 19; Josh. ix. 23, seq.; Ezra ii. 58; viii. 20; Neh. vii. 60, &c.

נָתַךְ, v. pres. יִתַּךְ. Cogn. נסך. *Was poured out:* spoken of, [1] Water; [2] Anger; [3] A curse. [1] Job iii. 24. [2] 2 Chron. xii. 7; xxxiv. 25; Jer. xlii. 18; xliv. 6; Dan. ix. 27. [3] Dan. ix. 11.

Niph. נִתַּךְ, (a) *Became, was, Id.* [1] Of water; [2] Of anger. (b) *Was melted.* (a), [1] Exod. ix. 33; 2 Sam. xxi. 10. [2] 2 Chron. xxxiv. 21; Jer. xlii. 18; Nah. i. 6. (b) Jer. xxii. 21.

Part. f. נִתֶּכֶת, (a, 2) Jer. vii. 20.

Hiph. הִתִּיךְ, pres. יַתִּיךְ. Constr. immed. it. med. אֶת. (a) *Poured out.* (b) *Melted.* (a) 2 Kings xxii. 9; 2 Chron. xxxiv. 17; Job x. 10. (b) Ezek. xxii. 20.

Inf. הַנְתִּיךְ, (b) Ezek. xxii. 20.

Hoph. pres. תֻּתְּכוּ, *Shall be melted*, Ezek. xxii. 20.

נָתַן, v. pres. יִתֵּן, יִתֵּן; Judg. xvi. 5, נַתֵּן, for יִתֵּן. Syr. pres. ܢܰܬܠ, *dedit.*—See Gram. art. 154. 8, notes, as occasionally supplying the force of the Piḥel, or Hiphḥil, conjugations. — *Gave, placed, rendered.* Constr. of the thing given, placed, or rendered, immed. it. med. אֶת. (a) *Gave* as a present, [1] with לְ, of person; [2] with אֶל; [3] with אֶת. (b) *Gave in marriage*, with לְ. (c) אִתָּהּ לוֹ לְאִשָּׁה "נ, *Id.* (d) *Gave up to evil*, with לְ. (e) *Produced* fruit. (f) *Emitted* an odour. (g) *Emitted* water. (h) *Ascribed.* (i) *Sold.* (k) *Allowed* to do, Inf. with or without לְ. (l) *Offered* a victim. (m) *Placed*, with אֶל, בְּ, לְ, עַל. (n) *Appointed* to an office. (o) *Appointed* a law, boundary, &c. (p) *Imposed* a tribute, with עַל. (q) *Inflicted*, with בְּ, עַל. (r) *Laid* reproach on —, with לְ, עַל. (s) *Wrought* a miracle. (t) פְּ "נ, [1] *Made, rendered, like.* [2] *Considered as.* (v) *Made, rendered.* [1] Constr. immed. [2] With לְ. Phrr. (a a) בְּיַד "נ, [1] *Gave into the power of.* [2]

Handed to. (a b) יָדוֹ "נ, [1] *Put forth his hand.* [2] *Surrendered himself.* (a c) יָד תַּחַת "נ, *Apparently, submitted to.* (a d) בְּ יָד "נ, *Laid hands on*, to injure. (a e) בְּלֵב "נ, [1] *Put into the heart* to do. [2] *Put into the heart*, a thought, feeling, skill, &c. (a f) אֶל לִבּוֹ "נ, [1] *Put into his heart.* [2] *Laid it to heart.* (a g) לְ לִבּוֹ "נ, [1] *Applied his heart to.* [2] *Attended to.* (a h) בְּנֶשֶׁךְ "נ, *Put out at interest.* (a i) בְּ פָּנֵי "נ, *Set his face against.* (a k) אֶל פָּנֵי "נ, *Turned his face towards.* (a l) לְפָנֶיךָ, *Placed before thee, in thy reach.* (a m), [1] קוֹלוֹ; [2] בְּקוֹלוֹ "נ, *Uttered his voice.* (a n) מִי יִתֵּן, *Who will grant? O that!* (a), [1] Gen. xxv. 6; xxx. 18; xliii. 23; xlv. 22, &c. [2] Gen. xxxi. 14; Exod. xxv. 16. 21; xxxi. 18; Lev. xv. 14, &c. [3] Josh. xv. 19; Judg. i. 15. (b) Josh. xv. 16; Judg. i. 12; 1 Sam. xxv. 44, &c. (c) Gen. xxx. 9; Deut. xxix. 8. (d) Ps. cxviii. 18; cxxiv. 6; Is. xxv. 31; xxxiv. 2, &c. (e) Lev. xxv. 19; xxvi. 4; Ps. lxvii. 7; Ezek. xxxiv. 27. (f) Cant. i. 12; ii. 13; vii. 14, &c. (g) Num. xx. 8. (h) 1 Sam. vi. 5; xviii. 8; Job i. 22, &c. (i) Prov. xxxi. 24. (k) Exod. iii. 19; Num. xxi. 23; 1 Sam. xviii. 2; Ps. lxvi. 9, &c. (l) Lev. xx. 2, 3. (m) 1 Kings vi. 5; vii. 39. 51; xii. 29, &c. (n) 1 Sam. xii. 13; 1 Kings ii. 35; 2 Chron. ii. 10, &c. (o) Exod. xvi. 29; Lev. xxvi. 46; Josh. xxii. 25; Ps. cxlviii. 6. (p) 2 Kings xviii. 17. (q) Ezek. vii. 3. 8; xxiii. 25; xxv. 14. (r) Ps. lxxviii. 66; Jer. xxiii. 40. (s) Deut. xiii. 1; 1 Kings xiii. 3. 5; 2 Chron. xxxii. 24, &c. (t), [1] Lev. xxvi. 19; 1 Kings x. 27; 2 Chron. i. 15. [2] Gen. xlii. 30. (v), [1] Lev. xxvi. 31; Ps. xxxix. 6; cv. 32, &c. [2] Gen. xvii. 20; Deut. xxviii. 13; Ezek. v. 14; Zeph. iii. 20, &c. (a a), [1] Gen. xxxix. 4. 8; Deut. vii. 24; Josh. ii. 24; xxi. 44, &c. [2] Gen. xl. 13; Ezek. xxiii. 31. (a b), [1] Ezek. xvii. 18. [2] Jer. L. 15; Lam. v. 6. (a c) 1 Chron. xxix. 24. (a d) Exod. vii. 4. (a e), [1] Exod. xxxv. 34. [2] 1 Kings x. 24; 2 Chron. ix. 23; Ps. iv. 8; Eccl. iii. 11, &c. (a f), [1] Neh. ii. 12. [2] Eccl. vii. 2. (a g), [1] Eccl. i. 13. 16. [2] Eccl. vii. 21. (a h) Lev. xxv. 37; Ps. xv. 5; Ezek. xviii. 13, &c. (a i) Lev. xvii. 10; xx. 6; xxvi. 17, &c. (a k) Dan. ix. 3. (a l) Deut. i. 21; ii. 36. (a m), [1] Jer. ii. 15; Joel ii. 11; Hab. iii. 9, &c. [2] Ps. xlvi. 7; lxviii. 34;

נתן (433) נתק

Jer. xii. 8. (a n) Lev. xi. 29 ; Deut. v. 29 ; 2 Sam. xix. 1, &c.

Part. נֹתֵן, pl. נֹתְנִים, constr. נֹתְנֵי, Gen. ix. 12 ; Neh. xii. 47 ; Hos. ii. 7, &c.

Part. pass. נָתוּן, pl. נְתוּנִים, f. נְתוּנוֹת, Num. iii. 9 ; Deut. xxviii. 31 ; 2 Chron. i. 12, &c.

Inf. נָתוֹן, נָתֹן, constr. נְתֹן, נְתָךְ, Gen. xxxviii. 9 ; xli. 43 ; Num. xx. 21 ; xxi. 3, &c.

תִּתֵּן, 1 Kings vi. 19. But usually— תֵּת, תֶּת־, aff. תִּתִּי, &c., Gen. iv. 12 ; xv. 7 ; xxix. 19, &c.

Imp. תֵּן, תֶּךָ, תְּנָה, f. תְּנִי, in pause, תֵּנִי, pl. תְּנוּ, Gen. xiv. 21 ; xxiii. 4 ; xxx. 14. 26 ; xlvii. 15 ; Is. xliii. 6, &c.

Niph. נִתַּן, pres. יִנָּתֵן, Pass. of Kal, Gen. xxxviii. 14 ; Lev. xix. 20 ; Is. ix. 5, &c.

Part. נִתָּן, Exod. v. 16 ; 2 Kings xxii. 7 ; Is. xxxiii. 16, &c.

Inf. הִנָּתֵן, Jer. xxxii. 4 ; xxxviii. 3, &c.

Hoph. pres. יֻתַּן, i. q. Niph., Lev. xi. 38 ; Num. xxvi. 54 ; xxxii. 5, &c.

נתן, v. Chald. pres. יִנְתֵּן, תִּנְדַּע, aff. יְתִנְּנַהּ, pl. יִנְתְּנוּן, *Gave*, Ezra iv. 13 ; vii. 20 ; Dan. ii. 16 ; iv. 14. 22. 28.

Inf. מִנְתַּן, Ezra vii. 20.

נתס, v. once, נָתְסוּ, *They break down, cut off*, Job xxx. 13. Arab. نتس, *evulsit spinam.* Syr. ܢܬܣ, *scidit, dilaceravit.*

Cogn. انتض, *protrusit.*

נתע, v. Niph. נִתְּעוּ, once, for נִתְּצוּ, by a common Chaldaism, *They become struck out, broken down*, Job iv. 10.

נתץ, v. pres. יִתֹּץ. Constr. immed. it. med. אֶת. (a) *Broke down, destroyed*, [1] An altar ; [2] A house, or [3] A wall. (b) *Ruined* a person. (c) *Struck out* teeth. (a), [1] Judg. vi. 30 ; xxiii. 15 ; Exod. xxxiv. 13, &c. [2] Lev. xiv. 45 ; 2 Kings xxiii. 7 ; Is. xxii. 10, &c. [3] Jer. xxxix. 8. (b) Job xix. 10 ; Ps. lii. 7.

Part. pass. pl. נְתֻצִים, Jer. xxxiii. 4.

Inf. נְתוֹץ, Jer. i. 10 ; xviii. 7 ; xxxi. 28.

Imp. נְתֹץ, (c) Ps. lviii. 7.

Pih. נִתֵּץ, pres. יְנַתֵּץ, i. q. Kal, Deut. xii. 3 ; 2 Chron. xxxi. 1 ; xxxiv. 4, &c.

Niph. נִתְּצוּ, Pass. of Kal, Jer. iv. 26 ; Nah. i. 6.

Puh. נֻתַּץ, *Id.*, Judg. vi. 28.

Hoph. יֻתַּץ, *Id.*, Lev. xi. 35.

נֶתֶק, m. *Porrigo*, or *scalled head;* so named from the falling off of the hair, Lev. xiii. 30—37 ; xiv. 54.

נתק, v. pret. aff. נְתַקְנִיהוּ, pres. aff. אֶתְּקֶנְךָ.

Arab. نتق, *commovit, quassit ; detraxit de corpore* pellem ; *extraxit è puteo* urnam.

Cogn. עתק, and نتك, *evulsit crines.* *Drew off, plucked away with violence.* Constr. immed. (a) *Drew away* persons *from a place*. (b) *Drew off* a ring from the finger. (a) Judg. xx. 32. (b) Jer. xxii. 24.

Part. pass. נָתוּק, *Castrated*, Lev. xxii. 24.

Niph. נִתַּק, pres. יִנָּתֵק. (a) Pass. of Kal [a]. (b) *Was purged away*, as dross. (c) A string *came out of its place*, by breaking. (d) A cord *was broken.* (e) Metaph. A plan *was broken off*. (a) Josh. iv. 18 ; viii. 16. (b) Jer. vi. 29. (c) Is. v. 27. (d) Judg. xvi. 9 ; Eccl. iv. 12 ; Is. xxxiii. 20. (e) Job xvii. 11 ; xviii. 14.

Pih. נִתֵּק, pres. יְנַתֵּק. (a) *Removed* a yoke. (b) *Pulled up* out of the ground. (c) *Broke* a cord. (d) *Tore* her breasts. (a) Is. lviii. 6. (b) Ezek. xvii. 9. (c) Judg. xvi. 9. 12 ; Ps. ii. 3 ; Jer. ii. 20 ; v. 5, &c. (d) Ezek. xxiii. 34.

Hiph. Inf. aff. הַתִּיקֵנוּ, i. q. Kal [a], Josh. viii. 6.

Imp. aff. הַתִּיקֵם, Jer. xii. 3.

Hoph. הָנְתַּק, Pass. of Hiph., Judg. xx. 31.

נֶתֶר, m. νίτρον. (a) *Nitre, natron*, Prov. xxv. 20. (b) *The soap* made with natron and oil, Jer. ii. 22.

נתר, v. pres. יִתַּר. Æth. ⲞⲦⳆ:, *tetendit, extendit, expandit.* Arab. نتر, *vi et vehementer traxit ;* وتر, *nervus, chorda, sive arcûs sive citharæ ;* وتر, *tetendit* arcum.

Cogn. יתר, sign. II. *Stretched* a string, *rebounded* as a string. Hence, the heart *beat violently*, Job xxxvii. 1.

Pih. Infin. נַתֵּר, *To leap* as locusts, Lev. xi. 21.

Hiph. pres. יַתִּיר, (a) Untied a string, *loosened.* (b) *Stretched out* the hand. (c) *Straightened.* (d) Made to vibrate, *caused to tremble.* (a) Ps. cv. 20. (b) Job vi. 9. (c) 2 Sam. xxii. 33. (d) Hab. iii. 6.

Part. מַתִּיר, (a) Ps. cxlvi. 7.

Inf. הַתֵּר, (a) Is. lviii. 6.

3 K

נתר, v. Chald. *Fell off*, as leaves. Syr. ܢܬܪ, *decidit, defluxit.*

Aph. Imp. pl. אַתְּרוּ, *Shake off* its leaves, Dan. iv. 11.

נָתַשׁ, v. pres. יִתּוֹשׁ. Arab. نتش, *evulsit* spinam. Syr. ܢܬܫ, *dilaceravit; eradicavit.* Constr. immed. it. med. אֶת. *Plucked up*, as a plant; opp. of נטע. (a) *Expelled* a people. (b) *Destroyed* a city, or shrine. (a) Deut. xxix. 28; 1 Kings xiv. 15; Jer. xii. 14. 17; xxiv. 7, &c. (b) Ps. ix. 7; Mic. v. 14.

Part. נֹתֵשׁ, aff. נֹתְשָׁם, Jer. xlv. 4; xii. 14. Inf. נְתוֹשׁ, constr. נְתוֹשׁ, aff. נָתְשִׁי, Jer. i. 10; xii. 15. 17, &c.

Niph. pres. יִנָּתֵשׁ, (a) Pass. of Kal, [a], [b]. (b) *Waters failed.* (a), [a] Jer. xxxi. 9; Amos ix. 15. [b] Dan. xi. 4. (b) Jer. xviii. 14.

Hoph. pres. הֻתַּשׁ, *Was plucked up*, of a tree, Ezek. xix. 12.

ס

ס, *Sámek*, the fifteenth letter of the Hebrew alphabet; as a numeral, stands for *sixty.* See Gram. artt. 4. 17. 23. It is sounded like S, in *Sir*, and closely resembles in sound the letter שׂ, with which it is frequently interchanged, as well as sometimes with שׁ, ז, and צ.

סְאָה, f. dual, סָאתַיִם, pl. סְאִים. A dry measure, being one-third of an Ephah, and containing a little more than a peck, Gen. xviii. 6; 1 Sam. xxv. 18; 1 Kings xviii. 32; 2 Kings vii. 1. 16. 18. LXX. μέτρον, μετρητής. Aquila and Symmachus, σάτον. Is. xxvii. 8, בְּסַאסְאָה, *by seah and seah, with accurate measure.* See also Gram. art. 169. 2. Sym. ἐν σάτῳ σάτον.

סְאוֹן, m. once. Syr. ܣܐܘܢ, *calceavit;* ܣܐܘܢܐ, *caliga, ocrea.* Chald. סֵינָא. Aeth. ሠእን: *Id.* Cogn. Arab. صِوان, *custodia*, r. صون, in a military sense often. Aeth. ኣጽን: *protexit munitionibus,* &c. According to Castell, *pugna, calceamentum, conculcatio, sonus clamor militum.* According to Gesenius, *calceus*, spec. militum, *caliga.* Is. ix. 4, כָל־סְאוֹן סֹאֵן בְּרַעַשׁ. LXX. Ὅτι πᾶσαν στολὴν ἐπισυνηγμένην δόλῳ. Vulg. *quia omnis violenta prædatio cum tumultu.* Syr. ܡܛܠ ܕܟܠ ܬܟܬܘܫܐ ܒܪܓܘܫܝܐ. The signification of the word is uncertain: the context evidently intimates *military action*, and so far the Vulgate has given a good general interpretation of it. Every (military) *defence of* (the) *defender* (is) *in tumult*, would, perhaps, be a more exact translation of it.

סְאן, v. part. סֹאֵן. See the last word.

סַאסְאָה, Is. xxvii. 8. See סְאָה.

סְבָא, masc. aff. סָבְאָם, סָבְאָם. Arab. سِبَاء, *emit* vinum *potandi ergo;* سِبَاء, *vini emptio; emptumve vinum;* سِبَاء, *ingurgitator vini;* سَبَأ, *vinum.* (a) *Wine.* (b) *The act of drinking wine.* (a) Is. i. 22; Hos. iv. 18. (b) Nah. i. 10.

סָבָא, v. *Drank wine, became drunk.* Pres. נִסְבָּאָה, Is. lvi. 12.

Part. סֹבֵא, pl. constr. סֹבְאֵי, Prov. xxiii. 20, 21; Deut. xxi. 20.

Part. pass. pl. סְבוּאִים, Nah. i. 10.

סָבַב, v. pret. סָבַב, סַבֹּתִי, and סַבּוֹתִי, סַבּוּ, and סַבּוּ; pres. יָסֹב, יָסֹבּוּ. Cogn. שׁוב. Aeth. ሠብሐ: *sepimentum ex palis.* Arab. سَبَب, *occasio, causa;* سَبَّب, *causam, occasionemve paravit.* (a) *Turned about.* (b) *Made a circuit,* [1] immed. it. med. אֶת, [2] med. בְּ. (c) *Reached round.* (d) *Surrounded*, [1] With אֶת, [2] With עַל. (e) *Ended a circuit at*, with אֶל, or לְ. (f) *An act overtaken in its consequences*, immed. it. med. אֶת. (g) *Was the cause of mischief to, entrapped*, with בְּ. (h) Metaph. *Went over mentally*, examined in succession. (i) *Arrived at a conclusion, came to a result.* (a) Jer. xli. 14. (b), [1] Judg. xi. 18; 1 Sam. vii. 16; Josh. vi. 3. 15; 2 Kings iii. 9. [2] Eccl. xii. 5; 2 Chron. xvii. 9; xxiii. 2. (c) 1 Kings vii. 15. 23; 2 Chron. iv. 2; Jer. lii. 21. (d),

סבה (435) סבך

[1] Gen. xxxvii. 7; Ps. cxviii. 10. 12; Eccl. ix. 14, &c. [2] 2 Chron. xviii. 31; Job xvi. 13. (e) 2 Chron. xxxiii. 14; Ezek. xlii. 19. (f) Ps. xlix. 6; Hos. vii. 2. (g) 1 Sam. xxii. 22. (h) Eccl. vii. 25. (i) Eccl. ii. 20. In 1 Sam. xvi. 11, לֹא נָסֹב. LXX. οὐ μὴ κατακλιθῶμεν. Syr. ܠܐ ܢܣܬܡܟ, Vulg. *non discumbemus*. Probably, *we will not turn to the object of our meeting, or, it may be, not to any thing else*.

Part. סֹבֵב, 2 Kings vi. 15, &c.; pl. סֹבְבִים, Cant. iii. 3; v. 7.

Inf. סֹב, Deut. ii. 3. סְבֹב, Num. xxi. 4.

Imp. סֹב, סֹבִּי, pl. סֹבּוּ, 1 Sam. xxii. 18; 2 Sam. xviii. 30; 1 Sam. xxii. 17, &c.

Niph. נָסַב, נָסֵבָּה, נְסִבּוּ, pres. יִסֹּב. (a) I. q. Kal, [a], [b], [d]. (b) *Returned*. (c) *Came round in turn*. (d) *Was removed*. (e) *Was changed*. (f) *Changed his conduct*. (g) *An inheritance went away*. (a), [a] 1 Sam. xv. 27; xvii. 30; Ps. cxiv. 3. 5, &c. [b] Num. xxxiv. 4, 5; Josh. xv. 3. 10; xvi. 6, &c. [d] Gen. xix. 4; Josh. vii. 9; Judg. xix. 22. (b) 1 Chron. xvi. 43. (c) Hab. ii. 16. (d) 1 Sam. v. 8. (e) Zech. xiv. 10. (f) Ps. lxxi. 21. (g) Num. xxxvi. 7; 1 Kings ii. 15; Jer. vi. 12, &c.

Pih. pres. סוֹבֵב, i. q. Kal. [b] Ps. lix. 7. 15; lv. 11; Cant. iii. 2. [d] Ps. xxxii. 7. 10; Jon. ii. 4, &c.

Inf. סַבֵּב, *To bring about* a thing, 2 Sam. xiv. 20.

Hiph. הֵסֵב, הֲסִבֹּת, נָסֵבּוּ, pres. יָסֵב. (a) *Causat. of Kal*, [a], [b], [d]. (b) *Causat. of Hiph*. [d], [g]. (c) *Changed a name to*. (a), [a] 1 Kings viii. 14; xviii. 37; 2 Chron. xxxv. 22, &c. [b] Exod. xiii. 18; Josh. vi. 11; Ezek. xlvii. 2. [d] 2 Chron. xiv. 6. (b), [d] 1 Sam. v. 9; 2 Kings xvi. 18; 2 Chron. xiii. 13, &c. [g] 1 Chron. x. 14. (c) 2 Kings xxiii. 34; xxiv. 17; 2 Chron. xxxvi. 4.

Part. מֵסֵב, Jer. xxi. 4.
Inf. הָסֵב, 2 Sam. iii. 12; 1 Chron. xii. 23.
Imp. הָסֵב, הָסִבִּי, 2 Sam. v. 22; 1 Chron. xiv. 4; Cant. vi. 4.

Hoph. pres. יוּסַב, (a) *Was turned round*. (b) *Was inclosed*. (a) Is. xxviii. 27.
Part. pl. f. מוּסַבּוֹת, /מֻס׳, (a) Ezek. xli. 24. (b) Exod. xxxix. 13.

סִבָּה, f. i. q. נְסִבָּה, *A change, a turn* in the course of events, 1 Kings xii. 15.

סָבִיב, m. r. סבב. Constr. סְבִיב; pl. constr. סְבִיבֵי, aff. סְבִיבָיו; it. pl. סְבִיבוֹת, aff. סְבִיבֹתַי, &c. (a) *A circuit*. (b) *As a preposition, Around*, [1] In the sing. [2] In the sing. followed by לְ. [3] סְבִיבָיו. [4] סְבִיבוֹת. [5] סְבִיבֹתַי, &c. (c) מִסָּבִיב, either with or without לְ, [1] *Around*. [2] *From around*. Like אֶל, and עַל, it does not admit a singular affix. (d) In the pl. *Surrounding places*. (a) 1 Chron. xi. 8; Eccl. i. 6. (b), [1] Gen. xxiii. 17; Exod. xvi. 13; xxvi. 24, &c. [2] Exod. xl. 33; Num. i. 53; ii. 2, &c. [3] Ps. xcvi. 2; Jer. xlviii. 17, &c. [4] Num. xi. 31; Judg. vii. 18, &c. [5] 1 Sam. xxvi. 5; Ezek. iii. 7, &c. (c), [1] Deut. xii. 10; xxv. 19; Josh. xxi. 44, &c. [2] Num. xvi. 24. 27. (d) Jer. xvii. 26; xxxiii. 44.

סְבַךְ, m. pl. constr. סִבְכֵי, *An entangled thicket*, Gen. xxii. 13; Is. ix. 17; x. 34.

סָבְכֵּךְ־, סְבֹךְ, *Id*. Ps. lxxiv. 5.

לְסֹבֶךְ, aff. סֻבְּכוֹ, *Id*. Jer. iv. 7.

סָבַךְ, v. Arab. شَبَكَ, *implicuit*. Cogn. שׂוּךְ. Syr. ܣܒܟ, *fixit, infixit*. *Wrapped, folded, coiled, entangled*.

Part. pass. pl. סְבֻכִים, Nah. i. 10.
Puh. pres. in pause, סְבֻכוּ, Pass. of Kal, Job viii. 17.

סַבְּכָא, f. Dan. iii. 5; and שַׂבְּכָא, vers. 7. 10. *A certain stringed instrument so called*. Athen. iv. 23, Σύρων εὕρημα φησιν εἶναι, ὡς καὶ τὸν λυροφοίνικα σαμβύκην. Strabo x. βαρβάρων ὠνόμασται—σαμβύκη. Auth. Vers. *Sackbut*.

סֵבֶל, m. (a) *A burden*. (b) *A task*, a civil burden. (a) Neh. iv. 11; Ps. lxxxi. 7. (b) 1 Kings xi. 28.

סֵבֶל, m. aff. סֻבְּלוֹ, *A burden*, Is. ix. 3; x. 27; xiv. 25.

סָבַל, v. pres. יִסְבֹּל. Constr. immed. Syr. ܣܒܠ, *tulit, portavit*. (a) *Carried* a load. (b) *Supported, carried*, as a child. (c) *Endured the consequences of*. (a) Is. xlvi. 7. (b) Is. xlvi. 4. (c) Is. liii. 4. 11; Lam. v. 7.

Inf. סְבֹל, (a) Gen. xlix. 15.
Puh. part. pl. מְסֻבָּלִים, *Laden*, but according to Bochart, *with young*, Ps. cxliv. 14.

Hith. pres. יִסְתַּבֵּל, *Becomes a burden*, Eccl. xii. 8.

סְבַל, v. Chald. *Id*.
Puh. part. pl. מְסוֹבְלִין, *Brought*, Ezra vi. 3.

סבל (436) סגר

סַבָּל, m. pl. סַבָּלִים, *A porter*, 1 Kings v. 15; 2 Chron. ii. 1. 17; xxxiv. 13.

סִבְלוֹת, pl. f. Aff. סִבְלֹתָם, סִבְלֹתֵיכֶם. *Burdens, labours, tasks*, Exod. i. 11; ii. 11; v. 4; vi. 6, 7.

סְבַר, v. pres. יִסְבַּר, Chald. Syr. ܣܒܪ, *speravit, cogitavit*. *He hopes, purposes*, Dan. vii. 25.

סַגִּים, see סִיגִים.

סָגַד, v. pres. יִסְגֹּד. Constr. med. לְ. Arab. سجد, *adoravit*. Syr. ܣܓܕ, *Id. Worshipped*, Is. xliv. 15. 17. 19; xlvi. 6.

סְגִד, v. pres. יִסְגֻּד. Chald. *Id.* Dan. ii. 46; iii. 6.

סְגוֹר, m. r. סגר. (a) *An inclosure.* (b) *Refined gold.* (a) Hos. xiii. 8. (b) Job xxviii. 15.

סְגֻלָּה, f. constr. סְגֻלַּת, aff. סְגֻלָּתוֹ. Arab. سجل, *aurum, &c.* (a) *A collection of valuables*, such as the precious metals, precious stones, &c. Hence, (b) *An object of special regard*: applied, [1] To the Jews, as a nation. [2] To pious Jews, individually. (a) 1 Chron. xxix. 3; Eccl. ii. 8. (b), [1] Exod. xix. 5; Deut. vii. 6; xiv. 2; xxvi. 18; Ps. cxxxv. 4. [2] Mal. iii. 17.

סְגָנִים, plur. masc. aff. סְגָנֶיהָ. Pers. شحنة, *prætor, præfectus*. *Chiefs*, [1] Among the Babylonians and Persians, inferior to פַּחוֹת. [2] Among the Jews, after the return from Babylon, inferior to שָׂרִים. [1] Jer. li. 23; Ezek. xxiii. 6. 12. 23, &c. [2] Neh. ii. 16; iv. 8. 13; v. 7, &c.

סִגְנִין, pl. m. def. סִגְנַיָּא, Chald. *Id.* Dan. ii. 48; iii. 2. 27; vi. 8.

סָגַר, v. pres. יִסְגֹּר. Constr. immed. it. med. אֶת. Cogn. סכר. Syr. ܣܓܪ, *clausit*. Arab. سجر, *accendit ignem; exemit, vacuavit*. (a) *Shut* a door. (b) *Shut a door upon, shut in*. (c) *Closed* a breach. (a) Gen. xix. 6; Josh. ii. 7; Judg. iii. 23, &c. (b), [1] With עַל, Exod. xiv. 3; Job xii. 14. [2] With בְּעַד, Gen. vii. 16; Judg. iii. 22; ix. 51; 2 Kings iv. 21. (c) 1 Kings xi. 27. Part. סֹגֵר, f. סֹגֶרֶת, Josh. vi. 5; Is. xxii. 22. Part. pass. סָגוּר, (a) Ezek. xliv. 1. 2;

xlvi. 1. (b) Job xli. 6. זָהָב סָגוּר, *refined gold*, 1 Kings vi. 20; vii. 49, 50, &c. See my note on Job xxviii. 15.

Niph. נִסְגַּר, pres. יִסָּגֵר, Pass. of Kal, [a] and [b]. [a] Neh. xiii. 19; Is. xlv. 1, &c. Imp. הִסָּגֵר, *Shut thyself up*, Ezek. iii. 24.

Pih. סִגַּר, pres. יְסַגֵּר, *Delivered up*, 1 Sam. xvii. 46; xxiv. 18; xxvi. 8; 2 Sam. xviii. 28.

Puh. סֻגַּר, *Was shut up*, Eccl. xii. 4; Is. xxiv. 10. 22; Jer. xiii. 19.

Part. f. מְסֻגֶּרֶת, Josh. vi. 1.

Hiph. הִסְגִּיר, pres. יַסְגִּיר. (a) *Shut up* a person. (b) *Delivered up.* (a) Lev. xiii. 4; xiv. 46, &c. (b) Deut. xxxii. 30; Ps. lxxviii. 50; Lam. ii. 7, &c.

Inf. הַסְגִּיר, aff. הַסְגִּירוֹ, 1 Sam. xxiii. 20; Amos i. 6. 9.

סְגַר, v. Chald. *Id.* Dan. vi. 23.

סַגְרִיר, m. Arab. سجر, *aquâ implevit.* Sam. אסגר, *pluvia*. *Rain*, Prov. xxvii. 15.

סַד, m. Arab. سدّ, *obstruxit, occlusit. Fetters*, Job xiii. 27; xxxiii. 11.

סָדִין, m. pl. סְדִינִים. Arab. سَدَن, *lana*; سِدْن, *velum, tegumentum;* cogn. سِدْل, *Id.* سَدَل, *laxavit, dimisit* mulier vestem suam. The lxx. translate the word by σινδόνας, which is manifestly derived from it. Apparently, *Any covering.* (a) *Fine cloth* of Syrian manufacture. (b) *A dress made of it.* (c) *A piece of this cloth* used as a sheet, see Herod. ii. 95. (a) Prov. xxxi. 24. (b) Is. iii. 23. (c) Judg. xiv. 12, 13.

סְדָרִים, pl. m. Syr. ܣܕܪ, *ordinavit, disposuit*. Sam. סדר, *Id.* Arab. سطر, *ordo, series.* Cogn. שְׂדֵרוֹת. *Ranks, orderly arrangement,* Job x. 22.

סַחַר, m. Arab. سهر, *vigilavit;* ساهور, *luna*. *Roundness*, like that of the full moon, Cant. vii. 2.

סֹהַר, m. *Watching, guarding.* בֵּית הַסֹּהַר, *a prison*, Gen. xxxix. 20—23; xl. 3. 5.

סוּג, v. pret. סָג, pres. נָסוֹג. See נסג. *Went*, or *slided, back* from the fear of God, Ps. liii. 4; lxxx. 19. Part. Pass. סוּג, *One who has gone back,* Prov. xiv. 14.

Niph. נָסוֹג, pres. יִסֹּג. (a) *Was driven*

סוּג (437) סוּף

back. (b) *Was induced to go back.* (a) 2 Sam. i. 22; Ps. xxxv. 4; xl. 15, &c. (b) Ps. xliv. 19; lxxviii. 57; Is. L. 5, &c.
Part. pl. נְסוּגִים, (a) Jer. xlvi. 5. (b) Zeph. i. 6.

סוּג, v. Syr. ﺳﻮﺝ, *sepivit. Fenced.* Cognn. סוך, סוך, שׂוּךְ.
Part. pass. f. סוּגָה, Cant. vii. 3.

סוּגַּר, m. r. סגר. *Any place of confinement, Prison,* Ezek. xix. 9.

סוֹד, m. aff. סוֹדִי, r. יסד. *Act of fixing, establishing.* (a) *Setting a fence* about. (b) *Fixed determination, counsel.* (c) *Deliberation.* (d) *Consideration, prudence.* (e) *A meeting for deliberation, assembly.* (f) *Secret.* (a) Job vi. 11. (b) Ps. lxxxiii. 4; Prov. xi. 13; xx. 19, &c. (c) Ps. lv. 15. (d) Prov. xv. 22. (e) Ps. lxxxix. 8; cxi. 1; Jer. vi. 11, &c. (f) Prov. xi. 13; xx. 19, &c.

סוּחָה, f. r. apparently סוח, for סחה, *Filth,* Is. v. 25.

סוּךְ, v. pret. סָךְ, pres. יָסוּךְ. Cogn. נסך. (a) *Anointed* himself, [1] With שֶׁמֶן. [2] Without it. (b) *Anointed* another, constr. immed. (a), [1] Deut. xxviii. 40; 2 Sam. xiv. 12; Mic. vi. 15. [2] Ruth iii. 3; Dan. x. 3. (b) 2 Chron. xxviii. 15; Ezek. xvi. 9. Inf. סוּךְ, (a, 2) Dan. x. 3.
Hiph. pres. apoc. יָסֶךְ, i. q. Kal, (a, 2) 2 Sam. xii. 20.

סוּמְפֹּנְיָה, f. Dan. iii. 5. 15; but in vers. 10, סיפניא. Generally considered to mean some musical instrument; but, may it not be merely a copy of the Greek συμφωνία, and be intended to signify the same thing? The word is omitted by the LXX. in verses 5 and 10, but is expressed by συμφωνίας, in verse 15.

סוּס, m. pl. סוּסִים, and סָסִים, aff. סוּסַי, &c. (a) *A horse.* Syr. ܣܘܣܐ, *Id.* (b) *A swallow,* probably from the rapidity of its flight. See Hieroz., vol. ii. page 60. (a) Gen. xlix. 17; 2 Sam. xv. 1; 1 Kings i. 28; xxii. 4, &c. (b) Is. xxxviii. 14; Jer. viii. 7.

סוּסָה, f. aff. סֻסָתִי, collectively, *Horses,* Cant. i. 9. So the LXX. τῇ ἵππῳ μου, and Vulg. *equitatui meo.*

סוּף, m. Arab. ﺳَﺎﻑ, r. ﺳﻮﻑ, *periit.* Syr. ܣܘܦ, *Id.* Cogn. אסף, אפס.

An end. (a) *The end* of a valley. (b) *The rear* of an army. (c) *The termination* of life. (d) *The completion* of an inquiry. (e) *The result.* (a) 2 Chron. xx. 16. (b) Joel ii. 20. (c) Eccl. vii. 2. (d) Eccl. iii. 11. (e) Eccl. xii. 13.

סוֹף, m. def. סוֹפָא, Chald. *Id.* (a) Dan. iv. 8. 19. (c) Dan. vi. 27. (d) Dan. vii. 28.

סוּף, v. pres. יָסוּף, pl. יָסֻפוּ. *Come to an end, perish,* Esth. ix. 28; Is. lxvi. 17.
Hiph. pres. אָסֵף, aff. אֲסִיפֵם, causat. of Kal, Jer. viii. 13; Zeph. i. 2, 3.

סוּף, v. pret. f. סָפָה, Chald. *Came to an end, was completed,* Dan. iv. 30.
Aph. pres. הֲסֵף, *Brought to an end, destroyed,* Dan. ii. 44.

סוּף, m. Arab. ﺻُﻮﻑ, *lana. Probably, Wool.* Hence, from the woolly appearance of many species, (a) *Sea-weed.* (b) יַם־סוּף, *The Red Sea,* which takes this name from a particular species ("*alga, juncus,*" Castell., &c.) that abounds in it. (c) *Aquatic plants,* growing in the Nile. (a) Jon. ii. 6. (b) Ps. cvi. 7. 9. 22; cxxxvi. 13. 15; Jer. xlix. 21. (c) Exod. ii. 3. 5; Is. xix. 6.

סוּפָה, f. with ה emphatic, סוּפָתָה; aff. סוּפָתוֹ, pl. סוּפוֹת. *A whirlwind, tornado,* from its sweeping away and destroying every thing, Job xxi. 18; Is. xxi. 1; Hos. viii. 7, &c.

סוּר, v. pret. סָר, pres. יָסוּר, apoc. יָסַר. Cogn. סור. Arab. ﺳَﺎﺭ, r. ﺳﻴﺮ, *incessit: recepit se.* Cogn. ﺻﻮﺭ. (a) *Went aside.* (b) *Turned aside* from the road. (c) *Went aside* from a course of life. (d) *Turned aside* from a commandment, [1] With מִן. [2] Immed. (e) *Went away.* [1] Of an inanimate thing. [2] Of God. (f) *Departed* from God. (g) *Was removed.* (h) *It was over, ceased.* (i) *Rebelled* against, with בְּ. (a) Exod. iii. 4. (b) 2 Kings iv. 8. 10; Prov. ix. 4. 16, &c. (c) 1 Kings xxii. 43; 2 Kings iii. 3; x. 29, &c. (d), [1] 1 Kings xv. 5; Ps. cxix. 102. [2] 2 Chron. viii. 15. (e), [1] Lev. xiii. 58; Judg. xvi. 17, &c. [2] Judg. xvii. 20; 1 Sam. xviii. 12; xxviii. 15, &c. (f) 2 Kings xviii. 6; Jer. xvii. 5; Ezek. vi. 9, &c. (g) 1 Kings xv. 14; xxii. 44; 2 Kings xii. 4, &c. (h) 1 Sam. xv. 32; Is. xi. 13. (i) Hos. vii. 14.

סות (438) סחב

Part. סָר, Job i. 1. 8; ii. 3; Prov. xiv. 16.
Inf. סוּר, Deut. xvii. 20; Josh. xxiii. 7;
Prov. xiii. 19, &c. It. סוֹר, Dan. ix. 5. 11.
Imp. סוּר, סוּרָה, pl. סוּרוּ, Gen. xix. 2; Judg.
iv. 18; 2 Sam. ii. 22, &c.
Hiph. הֵסִיר, pres. יָסִיר, apoc. יָסַר, and יָסֵר.
Causat. of Kal. (a) *Removed.* (b) *Laid
aside, gave up.* (c) *Drew off* a ring. (d)
Laid aside a dress. (e) *Laid aside, omitted.*
(f) *Set aside.* (g) *Destroyed.* (a) Lev. i.
16 ; 1 Kings xvii. 23 ; 1 Chron. xiii. 13, &c.
(b) Job xxvii. 5 ; Ps. xviii. 23. (c) Gen.
xli. 42; Esth. iii. 10. (d) Gen. xxxviii. 14.
(e) Josh. xi. 15. (f) Job xxvii. 2 ; xxxiv. 5 ;
Is. xxxi. 2, &c. (g) 1 Sam. xxviii. 3 ;
2 Kings xviii. 4. 22 ; xxiii. 19, &c.
Part. מֵסִיר, Is. iii. 1, &c.
Inf. הָסִיר, הָסֵר, Gen. xxx. 32 ; xlviii. 17,
&c.
Imp. הָסִיר, הָסֵר, f. הָסִירוּ, pl. הָסִירוּ, Gen.
xxxv. 2 ; 1 Sam. i. 14 ; 1 Kings xx. 24 ;
Ezek. xxi. 31, &c.
Hoph. הוּסַר, pres. יוּסַר. Pass. of Hiph.
Lev. iv. 31. 35 ; Dan. xii. 11.
Part. מוּסָר, pl. מוּסָרִים, 1 Sam. xxi. 7 ; Is.
xvii. 1.

סוּת, v. Kal non occ. Arab. سَتِي,
accelerare illum *curavit, ad illud acceleravit;*
وَسَوْطٌ, r. سَوْطٌ, *scuticâ percussit* سَاطَ,
scutica. Probably, *Used a whip, hastened
by whipping.*
Hiph. הֵסִית, pres. יָסִית, apoc. יָסֵת, it. הֵסִית,
pres. יָסֵת. Constr. immed. it. med. אֶת.
Urged, excited, induced, against a person, or
to an action, 1 Sam. xxvi. 19 ; 1 Kings xxi.
25 ; Job xxxvi. 16, &c.
Part. מֵסִית, 2 Chron. xxxii. 11 ; Jer.
xxiii. 3.

סוּת, once, aff. סוּתֹה. According to
Castell, by aphæresis for כְּסוּת ; but more
probably a false reading for that word, as
the Sam. has the full word כסותו, Gen.
xlix. 11.

סָחַב, v. pres. aff. יִסְחָבוּם. Arab.
سَحَبَ, *traxit humi; vehementer edit
bibitque.* Cogn. סחף. Constr. immed. it.
med. אֶת. (a) *Dragged along the ground.*
(b) *Tore in pieces and devoured.* (a) 2 Sam.
xvii. 13. (b) Jer. xlix. 20.
Inf. סָחֹב, סָחוֹב, (a) Jer. xxii. 19. (b) Jer.
xv. 3.

סְחָבָה, f. pl. סְחָבוֹת, *Tearing to pieces,*
Jer. xxxviii. 11, 12.

סָחָה, v. Arab. سَحَا, r. سَحَى, and
سَحِي, *removit verrendo, radendo, &c.,*
lutum. Kal non occ.
Pih. סֵחִיתִי, *Swept away,* Ezek. xxvi. 4.

סְחִי, m. *Off-scouring, filth,* Lam. iii. 45.

סָחִישׁ, m. once, 2 Kings xix. 29, but in
Is. xxxvii. 30, שָׁחִיס. *What is produced
without sowing, spontaneous.* The etymology
is very doubtful. Æth. ረሰየ: *refecit, &c.*

סָחַף, v. Arab. سَحَفَ, *abstulit* ventus
nubem; *rasit.* Syr. ܣܚܦ, *dejecit, de-
turbavit. Beat down, destroyed by beating
down.*
Part. סֹחֵף, A *beating* rain, Prov. xxviii. 3.
Niph. נִסְחָף, Pass. of Kal, Jer. xlvi. 15.

סַחַר, m. constr. סְחַר. (a) *Commerce.*
(b) *Wealth acquired by commerce.* (c) *A
seat of commerce.* (a) Prov. iii. 14. (b) Is.
xlv. 14. (c) Is. xxiii. 3.

סֹחַר, m. aff. סַחְרָהּ, *Id.* (a) and (b)
Prov. iii. 14 ; xxxi. 18 ; Is. xxiii. 18.

סָחַר, v. (a) *Travelled* to a country,
with אֶל. (b) *Travelled over* a country,
without restraint, constr. immed. it. med.
אֶת. (a) Jer. xiv. 18. (b) Gen. xxxiv. 21 ;
xlii. 34.
Imp. aff. סְחָרוּהָ, (b) Gen. xxxiv. 10.
Part. סוֹחֵר, סֹחֵר, f. aff. סֹחַרְתֵּךְ, pl. סוֹחֲרִים,
constr. סֹחֲרֵי. *A traveller,* pec. one who
travels for the purposes of commerce, *a
merchant,* Gen. xxxvii. 28 ; 1 Kings x. 28 ;
Prov. xxxi. 14; Ezek. xxvii. 12, &c. Cogn.
Arab. تَاجِرٌ, *mercator.*
Pih. redup. סְחַרְחַר, *The heart was agitated,*
Ps. xxxviii. 11.

סְחֹרָה, f. constr. סְחֹרַת, *A seat of commerce,* Ezek. xxvii. 15.

סֹחֵרָה, f. Syr. ܣܚܪܬܐ, *turris. A
tower,* Ps. xci. 4. Cogn. סהר.

סֹחֶרֶת, f. once, Esth. i. 6. Usually
taken to signify some kind of valuable stone.
According to some, *black marble:* comp.
שחור, and Syr. ܣܚܘܪܐ, *lapis niger tinc-
torius:* but according to others, *tortoise-shell.*

סמי (439) סכל

LXX. στρωμναὶ διαφανεῖς ποικίλως διηνθισμέναι, κύκλῳ ῥόδα πεπασμένα.

סֵתִים, pl. once, Ps. ci. 3, but in Hos. v. 2, שֵׂטִים (where however some MSS. read סֵטִים), a participial noun of r. סוּט, which does not occur in any other form, and is probably cognate with שָׂטָה. Sinners, those who go aside out of the right way.

סִיג, m. pl. סִיגִים, r. סוג. What is separated from metals by refining them. Dross; also alloy of inferior metals mixed with silver; inferior metals contrasted with silver, Ps. cxix. 19; Prov. xxv. 4; Ezek. xxii. 19, &c.

סִיוָן, m. The third month of the Jewish year, Esth. viii. 9. See חֹדֶשׁ.

סִים, in Jer. viii. 7, Keri, for סוּס. A swallow.

סִיר, com. pl. סִירוֹת. Arab. زِيرٌ, magnum vas; سَارٌ, r. سور, vehementius efferbuit vas. (a) A pot for boiling. (b) A vessel for washing. (c) Pl. סִירִים, Thorns, as being used for fuel. (d) Pl. סִירוֹת, Hooks, for fishing; probably at first made of thorns. (a) 2 Kings iv. 38—41; Ezek. xxiv. 6; Zech. xiv. 21, &c. (b) Ps. lx. 10; cviii. 10. (c) Eccl. vii. 6; Is. xxxiv. 13; Hos. ii. 8; Nah. i. 10. (d) Amos iv. 2.

סָךְ, m. once, Ps. xlii. 5: r. סכך. Arab. شَكِيكَة, turba, agmen. A multitude, crowd.

סֹךְ, m. aff. סֻכּוֹ, סֻכָּה, r. סכך. Thicket, hiding-place, dwelling, Ps. x. 9; Jer. xxv. 38; Ps. xxvii. 5; lxxvi. 3.

סֻכָּה, f. of last, constr. סֻכַּת, aff. סֻכָּתוֹ, pl. סֻכּוֹת. (a) A thicket. (b) A hiding-place. (c) A hut, made of the branches of trees. (d) A dwelling. (a) Job xxxviii. 40. (b) Ps. xxxi. 21. (c) Gen. xxxiii. 17; Lev. xxiii. 42, 43; John iv. 5, &c. (d) 2 Sam. xxii. 12; Job xxxvi. 29; Ps. xviii. 12; Amos ix. 11. Hence, חַג הַסֻּכּוֹת, the Feast of Tabernacles, Lev. xxiii. 34; Deut. xvi. 13. 16, &c.

סְבוּת, f. A shrine, Amos v. 26.

סָכַךְ, v. pret. סַכּוֹת, pres. יָסֹךְ. Arab. شَلَّ, adhæsit, firmiter cohæsit; totum se operuit; سَلَّ, obstruxit. (a) Covered,

[1] Constr. immed. [2] It. med. עַל. [3] Med. לְ. (b) Protected by covering, with לְ. (c) Placed as a covering, with עַל of the thing covered. (d) Compacted, put together, (a), [1] Job xl. 22. [2] 1 Kings viii. 7. [3] Lam. iii. 44. (b) Ps. cxl. 8. (c) Exod. xxxiii. 22; xl. 3. (d) Ps. cxxxix. 13. Part. סוֹכֵךְ, pl. סוֹכְכִים, and סוֹכֵךְ׳, (a, 2) Exod. xxv. 20; xxxvii. 9; 1 Chron. xxviii. 18. Constr. abs., Ezek. xxviii. 14. 16. Hiph. pres. יָסֵךְ, יָסֵךְ, i. q. Kal. (a) Covered, with עַל, Exod. xl. 21. (b) Covered, to protect, with לְ, Ps. xci. 4. (c) Protected, with עַל, Ps. v. 12. (d) Dressed himself, 2 Sam. xii. 20. (e) Shut in, confined, constr. immed., Job xxxviii. 8; it. med. בְּעַד, Job iii. 22.

Pih. redup. סִכְסַכְתִּי, pres. יְסַכְסֵךְ. Arab. شَكَّ, arma. Armed, Is. ix. 10; xix. 2.

סָכָל, m. Syr. ܣܟܠ, stultus factus est. Folly. Abstr. for concrete, Fools, Eccl. x. 6.

סָכָל, m. pl. סְכָלִים. A fool, foolish, Eccl. ii. 19; vii. 17; Jer. iv. 22, &c.

סכל, v. Kal non occ. Pih. pres. יְסַכֵּל, Made foolish, Is. xliv. 25. Imp. סַכֶּל, 2 Sam. xv. 31. Niph. נִסְכַּל, Became foolish, acted foolishly, 1 Sam. xiii. 13; xxiv. 10; 1 Chron. xxi. 8; 2 Chron. xvi. 9. Hiph. הִסְכַּלְתָּ, Acted foolishly, Gen. xxxi. 28; 1 Sam. xxvi. 21.

סִכְלוּת, f. Folly, Eccl. ii. 3. 12, 13; vii. 25; x. 1. 13.

סָכַן, v. pres. יִסְכּוֹן. Arab. سَكَنَ, tranquillus, quietus fuit. Sat still, comfortably, idly, or negligently. (a) Was prosperous. (b) Was beneficial. (c) Was a companion. (a) Job xxxiv. 9. (b) Abs. Job xv. 3. With לְ, or עַל, Job xxii. 2; xxxv. 3. Part. סֹכֵן, f. סֹכֶנֶת, (c) abs. or with לְ, Is. xxii. 15; 1 Kings i. 2, 4. Niph. pres. יִסָּכֵן, Was endangered from negligence, Eccl. x. 9. Puh. Became poor, through idleness. Part. מְסֻכָּן, Is. xl. 20. Hiph. Was familiar with, accustomed to, constr. immed. it. med. עִם, Num. xxii. 30; Ps. cxxxix. 3. Inf. הַסְכֵּן, Num. xxii. 30. Imp. הַסְכֶּן, Job xxii. 21.

סכר, v. Kal non occ. Cogn. סגר. Shut.

Niph. pres. יִסָּכֵר, *Was shut*, Gen. viii. 2; Ps. lxiii. 12.

Pih. סִפַּרְתִּי, *Delivered up*, Is. xix. 4.

סכר, v. once, part. pl. שֹׂכְרִים, for שׂכָרִים. *Hired*, Ezra iv. 5.

סכת, v. Kal non occ. Arab. سَكَتَ, *siluit, tacuit. Was silent.*

Hiph. Imp. הַסְכֵּת, *Keep silence*, Deut. xxvii. 9.

סַל, m. pl. סַלִּים. Arab. سَلّ, *canistrum. A basket*, for bread, Gen. xl. 16—18; Exod. xxix. 3; Lev. viii. 2, &c.: for meat, Judg. vi. 19.

סלא, v. Kal non occ. Probably, *Weighed, estimated by weighing*.

Puh. part. pl. מְסֻלָּאִים, *Valued*, Lam. iv. 2.

סלד, v. once, Job vi. 10.

Pih. pres. אֲסַלְּדָה, *I will harden myself*. Arab. صَلَدَ, *dura fuit* terra. See the notes.

סָלָה, v. *Trampled on*, Ps. cxix. 118.

Pih. סִלָּה, *Id.*, Lam. i. 15.

Puh. i. q. סלא, *Valued, estimated*, Job xxviii. 16. 19.

סֶלָה, A particle, the signification of which it is impossible to determine, from the fact that, wherever it occurs, the sense is complete without it. It is found no less than seventy times in the Psalms, and three times in Habakkuk's prayer; and almost always at the end of a sentence. The different explanations of interpreters may be found in Noldius, Annot., and Vind., num. 1877. In form the word resembles the Arab. صَلْوَة, or صَلاَة, *Dei invocatio*, and may have been used like our *amen*, or the doxology, Gram. art. 243. 2, and note.

סַלּוֹן, m. pl. סַלּוֹנִים. Arab. سَلّان, *spinæ in palmarum ramis. The thorn of any plant*. Metaph. *A person causing annoyance to others*, Ezek. ii. 6; xxviii. 24.

סָלַח, pres. יִסְלַח. Arab. صَلَحَ, *recte se habuit* res. III. *Pacem fecit* cum aliquo. Constr. med. לְ. *Forgave* a person or fault, Exod. xxxiv. 9; Num. xxx. 6; Jer. v. 7, &c.

Part. סֹלֵחַ, Ps. ciii. 3.

Inf. סְלֹחַ, Deut. xxix. 20; 2 Kings xxiv. 4; Is. lv. 7.

Imp. סְלַח, סָלְחָה, Num. xiv. 19; Dan. ix. 19; Amos vii. 2.

Niph. נִסְלַח לוֹ, *He was forgiven*, Lev. iv. 26. 31. 35; v. 13. 16. 18, &c.

סַלָּח, m. *One who forgives, or is disposed to forgive*, Ps. lxxxvi. 5.

סְלִיחָה, f. pl. סְלִיחוֹת, *Forgiveness*, Neh. ix. 17; Ps. cxxx. 4; Dan. ix. 9.

סלל, v. Pret. non occ. Pres. יָסֹלּוּ. Cogn. סָלָה. Syr. ܣܠܐ, *rejecit*. Arab. سَلَى. Heb. שָׁלָה, *tranquillus fuit*. *Threw up* an embankment; *levelled* a road; *made a road*, Job xix. 12; xxx. 12.

Part. pass. f. סְלוּלָה, סֹלּ״י, *Levelled*, Prov. xv. 19; Jer. xviii. 15.

Imp. סֹלּוּ, *Level*, Is. lvii. 14; lxii. 10. In Ps. lxviii. 5, סֹלּוּ לָרֹכֵב בָּעֲרָבוֹת, *make a way for him who rides through the deserts*. Comp. Is. xl. 3.

With aff. סָלּוּהָ, *Level her with the ground*, Jer. l. 26.

Pih. redup. Imp. aff. סַלְסְלֶהָ, *Exalt her*, Prov. iv. 8.

Hith. Part. מִסְתּוֹלֵל, either *opposing himself* as a rampart is opposed to the enemy, or *exalting himself*, with בְּ, Exod. ix. 17.

סֹלְלָה, f. pl. סֹלְלוֹת, *A mound*, 2 Sam. xx. 15; Is. xxxvi. 33; Jer. vi. 6, &c. Phr. שָׁפַךְ סֹלְלָה, *threw up a mound*, ἐχῶσε χῶμα.

סֻלָּם, m. once. Arab. سُلَّم, *scala. A ladder*, Gen. xxviii. 12.

סַלְסִלּוֹת, pl. f. i. q. סַלִּים, *Baskets*, used in gathering grapes, Jer. vi. 9.

סֶלַע, m. aff. סַלְעִי, סַלְעוֹ, pl. סְלָעִים. Arab. سَلَعَ, *fidit, vulneravit*; سِلَع *fissura in monte. A cleft in a rock; a cavern* made use of as a place of security; *a rock*, Num. xxiv. 21; Prov. xxx. 26; 1 Sam. xiii. 6, &c.

סָלְעָם, m. once, Lev. xi. 22. *A species of locust*. According to Bochart. Hieroz., tom. ii., page 446, from the Chaldee סְלַע, *voravit, absumsit*.

סֶלֶף, m. *Capriciousness, perverseness*, Prov. xi. 3; xv. 4.

סלף, v. Kal non occ. Arab. صَلَفَ,

סלק (441) סמל

falso gloriatus fuit. Ingrata fuit, nec placuit marito, quamvis bene se gereret mulier. Probably, *Boasted without foundation, it was treated capriciously.*

Pih. pres. יְסַלֵּף. Constr. immed. (a) *Turns aside, perverts; renders of no avail.* (b) *Overthrows.* (a) Exod. xxiii. 8; Deut. xvi. 19; Prov. xix. 3; xxii. 12. (b) Job xii. 19; Prov. xiii. 6.

Part. מְסַלֵּף, (b) Prov. xxi. 12.

סלק, v. סְלִק, pl. סְלִקוּ, Chald. i. q. Syr. ܣܠܩ, *ascendit. Came up, grew up,* Dan. ii. 29; vii. 8. 20; Ezra iv. 12.

Part. pl. f. סָלְקָן, Dan. vii. 3.

סֹלֶת, f. Arab. سَلْتَ, *detergendo, vel decorticando eduxit; detersit. Cleaning grain by removing the husk. Grain thus cleaned; flour* cleared of the bran, *fine flour,* Gen. xviii. 6; Exod. xxix. 2; Lev. ii. 5, &c.

סַמִּים, m. pl. Arab. شَمَّ, *olfecit rem;* שָׁמָמוֹת, *odores boni. Perfumes,* Exod. xxv. 6; xxx. 7. 34; xxxi. 11, &c.

סְמָדַר, m. coll. *Flowers,* Cant. ii. 13. 15; vii. 13. From the Arab. شَمَّ, *olfecit;* and ذَرَّ, *sparsit. Odour-scatterers.*

סָמַךְ, v. pres. יִסְמֹךְ. Syr. ܣܡܟ, *innixus fuit; appropinquavit.* Arab. سَمَكَ, *extulit. Laid on, pressed on.* (a) סָמַךְ אֶת־יָדָיו עַל, *Laid his hands on.* (b) *Supported with his hands; supported,* constr. immed. (c) *Pressed upon, weighed heavily on,* with עַל. (d) *Advanced towards,* with אֶל. (a) Exod. xxix. 10. 19; Num. xxvii. 23; Deut. xxxiv. 9, &c. (b) Gen. xxvii. 37; Is. lix. 16; lxiii. 5. (c) Ps. lxxxviii. 8. (d) Ezek. xxiv. 2.

Part. סוֹמֵךְ, plur. constr. סֹמְכֵי, (a) *Supporting,* Ps. xxxvii. 17. 24. (b) *Helping,* Ezek. xxx. 6. (c) *Stretching out his hands towards, to help,* with לְ, Ps. cxlv. 14.

Part. pass. סָמוּךְ, pl. סְמוּכִים, *Supported,* Ps. cxi. 8; cxii. 8; Is. xxvi. 3.

Imp. aff. סָמְכֵנִי, *Support me,* Ps. cxix. 116.

Niph. נִסְמַךְ, pres. יִסָּמֵךְ. Constr. med. עַל. (a) *Leaned on,* for support. (b) *Trusted in.* (a) Judg. xvi. 29; 2 Kings xviii. 21; Is. xxxvi. 6. (b) 2 Chron. xxxii. 8; Ps. lxxi. 6; Is. xlviii. 2.

Pih. Imp. pl. aff. סַמְּכוּנִי, *Support me,* Cant. ii. 5.

סֶמֶל, and סֵמֶל, m. Arab. سَمَلَ, *composuit;* part. سَامِل. Comp. شَمَلَ. Whence the Σεμέλη, *Semele,* of the Greeks and Latins. Cogn. צֶלֶם. *Any figure, form,* Deut. iv. 16; 2 Chron. xxxiii. 7. 15; Ezek. viii. 3. 5.

סמן, v. Niph. Part. נִסְמָן, *Appointed,* Is. xxviii. 25, וּשְׂעֹרָה נִסְמָן, *and the barley* in *an appointed place.* So Gesenius. See Castell. LXX. κέγχρος. Vulg. *milium.* Some prefer taking "*hordeum signatum,*" implying *the best,* and to this Castell evidently inclines. He compares זָמַן, and the Talmudic סִמֵּן, *signavit.*

סָמַר, v. Arab. سَمَرَ, *clavis confixit; rem corroboravit. Grew hard, rigid,* as a nail, Ps. cxix. 120.

Pih. pres. תְּסַמֵּר, *Id.* Job iv. 15.

סָמָר, *Rough, bristly,* applied to a species of locust, Jer. li. 27.

סְנֶה, m. The *Bush* in which the angel of the Lord appeared to Moses on Mount Sinai, Exod. iii. 2—4; Deut. xxxiii. 16. According to the LXX. βάτος. Vulg. *rubus.* The bramble. So Celsius, Hierob., ii., page 58.

סַנְוֵרִים, m. pl. twice, Gen. xix. 11; 2 Kings vi. 18. The context requires the word to be interpreted *Blindness,* either temporary or permanent. LXX. ἀορασία. Vulg. *cæcitate.* Various conjectures have been offered respecting the origin of the word; to all these may perhaps be added, with some degree of probability, the Arab. سَمَرَ, *nox, tenebræ.*

סַנְסִנִּים, pl. m. aff. סַנְסִנָּיו, once, Cant. vii. 9. LXX. τῶν ὕψεων αὐτοῦ. Vulg. *fructus ejus.* Arab. سِنْسِن, *extremitas vertebrarum dorsi.* The top of a palm tree, where the fruit is produced, Castell.

סְנַפִּיר, twice, Lev. xi. 9; Deut. xiv. 9. *Fins;* perhaps, *Scales.* The interpreters generally agree in the first signification given here of this word. Comp. Arab.

3 L

סם (442) סער

سَفَرَ, *verrit domum; iter fecit;* سَفَرٌ, *iter;* but see my note on Job xl. 25, p. 531.

סָס, m. once, Is. li. 8. Arab. سُوسٌ, *tinea.* Syr. ܣܳܣܳܐ, and Gr. σής, *Id. The clothes-moth.*

סָעַד, v. pres. יִסְעַד. Constr. abs. it. immed. Arab. سَعِدَ, *felix fuit.* III. *Juvit.* IV. *Beavit.* سَعَّلَ, *felicitas.* (a) *Was prosperous.* (b) *Made prosperous.* (c) *Supported.* (d) *Cheered, refreshed.* (a) Prov. xx. 28. (b) Ps. xx. 3. (c) Ps. xviii. 36; xciv. 18. (d) Ps. xli. 4; civ. 15. Inf. aff. סַעֲדָה, (c) Is. ix. 7. Imp. סְעָד, סְעָדָה, aff. סְעָדֵנִי, pl. סַעֲדוּ. (c) Ps. cxix. 117. (d) Gen. xviii. 5; Judg. xix. 5. 8; 1 Kings xiii. 7.

סעד, v. Chald. Pah. part. pl. מְסָעֲדִין, *Assisting,* with לְ, Ezra v. 2.

סָעָה, v. once, Ps. lv. 9. Part. f. סֹעָה, *Rapid.* Arab. سَعَى, *cucurrit.* But the LXX. translate מֵרוּחַ סֹעָה, ἀπὸ ὀλιγοψυχίας, and the Vulgate, *a pusillanimitate animi.* Comp. Syr. ܣܰܥܝܳܐ, *audacia, &c.* Castell.

סָעִיף, masc. pl. סְעִפִים, constr. סְעִפֵי. Arab. سَعِفَ, *fissuris affecta fuit* manus;

سَعَفٌ, سَعَفَةٌ, *ramus palmæ.* Cogn. شَعَبَ, *dissecuit;* شُعْبَةٌ, *ramus arboris.* (a) *A cleft* in a rock, *a cavern,* Judg. xv. 8. 11; Is. ii. 21; lvii. 5. (b) *A separation, party, sect; opinion,* 1 Kings xviii. 21. (c) *A branch,* Is. xvii. 6; xxvii. 10.

סעף, v. from סָעִיף. Pih. Part. מְסָעֵף, *Pruning down, cutting away,* Is. x. 33.

סעף, pl. סְעִפִים, *Persons of divided minds, of unsteady principles,* Ps. cxix. 113. See שְׂעִפִּים, and my note on Job iv. 13.

סְעַפּוֹת, fem. pl. *Branches,* Ezek. xxxi. 6. 8.

סַעַר, m. aff. סַעֲרֵךְ, and סְעָרָה, f. constr. סַעֲרַת, plur. סְעָרוֹת, constr. סַעֲרוֹת. Arab. سَعَّرَ, *accendit et excitavit* ignem; *circumivit, obivit.* Pass. سُعِّرَ, *vento fervido;* سَمُومٌ, *appellato afflictus fuit* vir; سَعَرٌ,

ardor ignis; furor, insania. Prob. *A pestilential wind,* a violent wind, whirlwind, 2 Kings ii. 1; Ps. lv. 9; John i. 4; Job xxxviii. 1, &c.

סער, v. Part. סֹעֵר, f. סֹעֲרָה, *Tempestuous,* tossed by the wind, John i. 11. 13. Metaph. *Agitated by calamity,* Is. liv. 11. Pres. יִסְעֲרוּ, *Rage as a tempest,* Hab. iii. 13.

Niph. pres. יִסָּעֵר, *Is agitated,* as by a tempest, — of the heart, 2 Kings vi. 11. Pih. pres. aff. אֲסָעֲרֵם, *I scattered,* — as by a tempest, Zech. vii. 14. Puh. pres. יְסֹעָר, *Is scattered,* Hos. xiii. 3.

סַף, m. aff. סִפִּי, pl. סִפִּים, and סִפּוֹת. (a) *A dish, basin, goblet, bowl,* Exod. xii. 22; 2 Sam. xvii. 28; 1 Kings vii. 50; 2 Kings xii. 14; Jer. lii. 19; Zech. xii. 2. (b) *The threshold,* Judg. xix. 27; 1 Kings xiv. 17; Is. vi. 4, &c.

סָפַד, v. pres. יִסְפּוֹד, *Lamented, bewailed.* Constr. (a) abs. Ezek. xxiv. 16. 23; Zech. xii. 12. (b) Med. לְ, 1 Kings xiv. 13; Jer. xvi. 6; xxii. 18, &c. (c) Med. עַל, 2 Sam. i. 12; xi. 26; Zech. xii. 10, &c. Part. pl. סֹפְדִים, *Mourning,* Is. xxxii. 12: *professed mourners,* Eccl. xii. 5. Inf. aff. סְפוֹד, סָפוֹד, Gen. xxiii. 2; Zech. vii. 5, &c. Imp. pl. סִפְדוּ, 2 Sam. iii. 31; Jer. iv. 8, &c. Niph. pres. pl. יִסָּפְדוּ, *Shall be lamented,* Jer. xvi. 4; xxv. 33.

סָפָה, v. pres. יִסְפֶּה. Cogn. with סוּף. (a) *Came to an end, perished.* (b) *Brought to an end, destroyed.* (a) Ps. lxxiii. 19; Jer. xii. 4. (b) Gen. xviii. 23, 24; Is. vii. 20. Inf. aff. סְפוֹתָהּ, (b) Ps. xl. 14. Niph. נִסְפָּה, pres. יִסָּפֶה, i. q. Kal. (a) Gen. xix. 15. 17; 1 Sam. xxvi. 10; xxvii. 1, &c. Part. נִסְפֶּה, *Perishing,* Prov. xiii. 23; 1 Chron. xxi. 12. *Missing,* Is. xiii. 15. In the second of these passages, as Houbigant has remarked, the parallel place requires that we should read נִסְכָּה: see 2 Sam. xxiv. 13. In Deut. xxxii. 23, אַסְפֶּה, is probably a contraction of אֶאֱסֹפֶה, from אָסַף.

ספח, v. Imp. aff. סְפָחֵנִי. Arab. سَفَحَ, *effudit;* صَفَحَ, *transire jussit* ad puteum camelos; *perquisivit* rem. *Poured*

ספח (443) ספר

out, poured into; hence, *spread*, and *admitted into*. *Admitted*, 1 Sam. ii. 36.
Niph. נִסְפְּחוּ, *Were admitted* among, Is. xiv. 1.
Pih. part. מְסַפֵּחַ, *Pouring out* anger, Hab. ii. 15.
Puh. pres. יְסֻפָּחוּ, *Are spread, scattered*, Job xxx. 7.
Hith. Inf. הִסְתַּפֵּחַ, *Obtaining admission*, 1 Sam. xxvi. 19.

סַפַּחַת, f. *A scab, scald*, either from its *spreading* in the flesh, or from the *falling off* of the hair, Lev. xiii. 2. 6—8; xiv. 56.

סָפִיחַ, m. constr. סְפִיחַ, pl. aff. סְפִיחֶיהָ. (a) *The pouring out, rushing* of water. (b) The produce of grain accidentally *spilt* instead of being sown, *self sown grain*. (a) Job xiv. 19. (b) Lev. xxv. 5. 11; 2 Kings xix. 29; Is. xxxvii. 30.

סְפִינָה, f. *A ship*, John i. 5. Arab. سَفِينَة, and Syr. ܣܦܝܢܬܐ, *Id.* Al. non occ.

סַפִּיר, m. pl. סַפִּירִים. *A sapphire*, Exod. xxviii. 19; xxxix. 11; Job xxviii. 6. 16, &c.

סֵפֶל, m. twice, *A bowl*, Judg. v. 25; vi. 38. Comp. Arab. زَبِيل, *vas in quo res portantur aut ponuntur*; صُفْن, *vas coriaceum, quo aqua hauritur*.

סָפַן, v. pres. יִסְפֹּן. Cogn. צפן. *Covered*, pec. *with planks*, 1 Kings vi. 9.
Part. pass. סָפוּן, pl. סְפוּנִים. (a) *Covered*, 1 Kings vii. 3. 7; Jer. xxii. 14; Hag. i. 4. (b) *Secured*, Deut. xxxiii. 21.

סִפֻּן, m. *Ceiling*, 1 Kings vi. 15.

ספף, v. Hith. Inf. הִסְתּוֹפֵף, *To remain at the threshold*, Ps. lxxxiv. 11. See סף.

ספק, m. aff. סִפְקוֹ. *Striking hands* in a bargain; hence, the consequence of a successful bargain, *Abundance, sufficiency*, Job xx. 22. See my note on the place.

סָפַק, v. pres. יִסְפֹּק. Constr. immed. it. med. אֶת. Ὀνοματοποιητικόν. Comp. *Smack*. Arab. صفق, *percussit vehementius ut audiretur sonus*. (a) *Struck* the hands *together*, in sorrow, indignation, or contempt, אֶת־כַּפַּי Num. xxiv. 10; Lam. ii. 15; Job xxvii. 23. (b) *Struck the hand* on the thigh, expressive of the same feelings, Jer. xxxi. 19. (c)

Expressed contempt for, in any way, Job xxxiv. 26. So also Jer. xlviii. 26, impersonally. (d) *Expressed contempt*, Job xxxiv. 37.
Imp. סְפֹק, (b) Ezek. xxi. 17.

סָפַר, m. aff. סִפְרִי, סִפְרָךְ, pl. סְפָרִים, constr. סִפְרֵי. (a) *An enumeration*, Gen. v. 1. (b) *Register record*. (c) *A book*, a written work, Exod. xxiv. 7; Deut. xvii. 18; xxxi. 26, &c. (d) *A book*, — blank book for writing, Exod. xvii. 14; Num. v. 23; Jer. xxxvi. 2. 4. (e) *A letter*, 1 Kings xxi. 8; 2 Kings v. 5; x. 2. 6, 7, &c. (f) *Any writing*, Deut. xxiv. 1. 3; Is. L. 1; Jer. iii. 8, &c. (g) *Writing*, Is. xxix. 11, 12.

סָפַר, v. pres. יִסְפֹּר. Engl. *Cypher*. Syr. ܣܦܪ. Arab. سَفَرَ, *scripsit, &c*. Constr. immed. it. med. אֶת. *Numbered, reckoned*, Lev. xv. 13; 2 Sam. xxiv. 10; Ezek. xliv. 26, &c.
Part. סֹפֵר, and סוֹפֵר. *One who numbers, one who writes*. (a) *A professed writer*, Ps. xlv. 2. (b) *A secretary*, 2 Sam. viii. 17; xx. 25; 2 Kings xii. 11, &c. (c) *A general officer who enrolled the soldiers*, 2 Kings xxv. 19; Jer. lii. 25. (d) *A transcriber of the law*, and one therefore supposed to be familiar with it, Ezra vii. 6. 11; Neh. viii. 1. 4; Jer. viii. 8, &c.
Infin. סְפֹר, Gen. xv. 5; xli. 49; Deut. xvi. 9.
Imp. סְפֹר, pl. סִפְרוּ, Gen. xv. 5; 1 Chron. xxi. 2; Ps. xlviii. 13.
Niph. pres. יִסָּפֵר, Pass. of Kal, Gen. xvi. 10; xxxii. 12; 1 Kings iii. 8, &c.
Pih. סִפַּרְתִּי, pres. יְסַפֵּר. (a) *Counted*, Job xxxviii. 37; Ps. xxii. 18. (b) *Recounted, related*, with אֶת, of the thing, and לְ, or אֶל, of the person, Gen. xxiv. 66; Judg. vi. 13; Ps. lxxi. 15; cxix. 26, &c. (c) *Talked*, Ps. lxix. 27.
Part. מְסַפֵּר, pl. מְסַפְּרִים, (b) Judg. vii. 13; 2 Kings viii. 5, &c.
Inf. סַפֵּר, (b) Ps. L. 16; lxxiii. 28, &c.
Imp. סַפֵּר, סַפְּרָה, pl. סַפְּרוּ, (b) Gen. xl. 8; Is. xliii. 26, &c.
Puh. סֻפַּר, pres. יְסֻפַּר, Pass. of Pih., Job xxxvii. 20; Ps. xxii. 31; Is. lii. 15, &c.

סְפַר, m. pl. סִפְרִין, Chald. i. q. Heb. סֵפֶר, Ezra iv. 15; Dan. vii. 10.

סָפֵר, m. def. סָפְרָא, Chald. i. q. סוֹפֵר, Ezra iv. 8, 9; v. 12. 21, &c.

סָפַר, m. *A numbering*, 2 Chron. ii. 16.

סְפֹרָה, f. aff. סְפֹרָתְךָ, i. q. סֵפֶר, (b) Ps. lvi. 9.

סְפֹרוֹת, fem. pl. *Amount, number*, Ps. lxxi. 15.

סָקַל, v. pres. יִסְקֹל. Constr. immed. it. med. אֶת. *Pelted, pelted with stones;* either as a judicial punishment or in a tumult. [1] With בָּאֲבָנִים, Deut. xiii. 10; xvii. 5; xxii. 21, &c. [2] Without בָּאֲבָנִים, Exod. viii. 21; xvii. 4.

Inf. סְקֹל, aff. סָקְלוּ, Exod. xix. 13; xxi. 28; 1 Sam. xxx. 6.

Imp. pl. aff. סִקְלֻהוּ, 1 Kings xxi. 10.

Niph. pres. יִסָּקֵל. Pass. of Kal, Exod. xix. 13; xxi. 28, 29. 32.

Pih. pres. יְסַקֵּל, i. q. Kal, 2 Sam. xvi. 6. 13; Is. v. 2.

Imp. pl. סַקְּלוּ, with מֵאֶבֶן. *Clear* of stones, Is. lxii. 10.

Puh. סֻקַּל, Pass. of Pih., 1 Kings xxi. 14, 15.

סָר, m. סָרָה, f. r. סוּר. *Averse, disinclined, sad*, 1 Kings xx. 43; xxi. 4, 5; Prov. ix. 22.

סָרָב, m. pl. סָרָבִים. *Rebellious*, Ezek. ii. 6. Al. non occ. Chald. סְרַב, *abnuit, renuit, rebellavit*.

סַרְבָּלִין, masc. pl. aff. סַרְבָּלֵיהוֹן. Arab. سَرَاوِيل, i. q. Pers. شَلْوَار (à شَل, *femur*), *femoralia. Drawers, trowsers*, Dan. iii. 21. 27.

סָרָה, f. r. סוּר. *Turning aside* (a) from God, *rebellion*, Deut. xiii. 6; Is. i. 5; xiv. 6, &c. (b) From the truth, *falsehood*, Deut. xix. 16.

סֶרַח, m. *Being left loose; a portion of* a thing *left loose*, Exod. xxvi. 12.

סָרַח, v. pres. תִּסְרַח. Arab. سَرَح, *libere dimisit. Unconfined, loose*, Exod. xxvi. 12.

Part. f. סֹרַחַת, intrans. *Luxuriant,—of* a vine, Ezek. xvii. 6.

Part. pass. סָרוּחַ, *Left loose*, Exod. xxvi. 13; סְרוּחִים מִגְבָּעוֹת, — *of full turbans*, Ezek. xxiii. 15. סְרוּחִים עַל־עַרְשׂוֹתָם, *stretched negligently, dissolutely, on their couches*, Amos vi. 4. 7.

סִרְיוֹן, m. pl. סִרְיֹנוֹת, i. q. שִׁרְיוֹן. *A corslet*, Jer. xlvi. 4; li. 3.

סָרִיס, m. constr. סְרִיס, pl. סָרִיסִים, constr. סְרִיסֵי, and סָרִיסָיו, aff. סָרִיסָיו. Arab. سَرِس, *impotens ad venerem.* (a) *A eunuch*, Is. lvi. 3, 4; Dan. i. 3. 7. (b) Hence, since such were commonly appointed to offices of trust in Asiatic courts, *Any chief officer*, 1 Kings xxii. 9; 2 Kings viii. 6; xxv. 19, &c. Syr. ܣܪܺܝܣܳܐ, *Id*.

סָרְכִין, m. pl. once, Dan. vi. 3. *Superintendents* of the whole empire. Probably a corruption of the Persian سَرْهَنْگ, *commander-in-chief*, or *one who has the chief direction* of affairs.

סְרָנִים, m. pl. constr. סַרְנֵי. Syr. ܣܰܪܢܳܐ, *apsis, axis, rota.* (a) Apparently, *Axles*, 1 Kings vii. 30. (b) The name of the five *Lords* of the Philistines, Judg. xvi. 30; 1 Sam. vi. 18; xxix. 7, &c. So the Arab. قُطْب, *axis*, it. *Princeps*. Comp. אֶדֶן, and יָחֵד, above.

סַרְעַפָּה, f. pl. aff. סַרְעַפֹּתָיו, for סְעַפֹּתָיו (as שַׁרְבִּים, for שְׁבָטִים). *Branches*, Ezek. xxxi. 5.

סָרַף, v. Kal non occ. Apparently, i. q. שׂרף.

Pih. Part. aff. מְסָרְפוֹ. *Burning; he who burns him*, Amos vi. 10.

סַרְפָּד, m. once, Is. lv. 13. Some kind of shrub growing wild in Judea, and esteemed of little value; but it is impossible to determine more particularly. See Cels. Hierobot. ii., p. 218. According to some, *the nettle*.

סָרַר, v. pres. non occ. Cogn. סוּר. *Was perverse, refractory*, Hos. iv. 16.

Part. סוֹרֵר, f. סוֹרֵרָה, and סוֹרֶרֶת, pl. סוֹרְרִים. *Perverse, refractory*. (a) Of persons, Deut. xxi. 18; Ps. lxxviii. 8; Is. lxv. 2, &c. (b) Of animals, Hos. iv. 16. Phr. כָּתֵף סוֹרָרָה, *a shoulder that will not submit to the yoke*, Neh. ix. 29; Zech. vii. 11.

סְתָו, m. Arab. شِتَاء, *hiems*. Syr. ܣܬܘܐ, *Id. Winter*, Cant. ii. 11.

סָתַם, v. pres. יִסְתְּמוּ. Constr. immed. it. med. אֶת. Arab. سَكَم, *occlusit*. II. *Obturavit os.* (a) *Filled up, blocked up.* (b)

Repaired. (c) *Shut up, concealed.* (a) 2 Kings iii. 19. 25; 2 Chron. xxxii. 4. 3.

Inf. סָתוֹם, (a) 2 Chron. xxxii. 3.

Imp. סְתֹם, (c) Dan. viii. 6; xii. 4.

Part. pass. סָתוּם, pl. סְתֻמִים, (c) Ps. li. 8; Ezek. xxviii. 3; Dan. xii. 9.

Niph. Inf. הִסָּתֵם. Pass. of Kal, (b) Neh. iv. 7.

Pih. סִתְּמוּ, pres. יְסַתְּמוּ. I. q. Kal, (a) Gen. xxvi. 15. 18.

סֵתֶר, m. aff. סִתְרִי, pl. סְתָרִים. *Concealment.* (a) *Secrecy.* (b) בַּסֵּתֶר, *Secretly.* (c) *Secret place.* (d) *Place of concealment.* (e) *Place of security.* (a) Judg. iii. 19; Job xxiv. 15. (b) Deut. xiii. 6; Job xiii. 10; xxxi. 27, &c. (c) Job xxii. 14; Ps. lxxxi. 8; xci. 1. (d) Ps. xviii. 12; Is. xxviii. 17. (e) Ps. xxxii. 7; Is. xvi. 4; xxvii. 5, &c.

סִתְרָה, f. *Shelter, protection,* Deut. xxxii. 38.

סָתַר, v. pres. יִסְתַּר. Arab. سَتَرَ, *texit, obtexit. Covered, concealed; conceals himself,* Prov. xxii. 3.

Niph. נִסְתַּר, pres. יִסָּתֵר. (a) *Concealed himself.* (b) *Was concealed, unknown.* (c) *Was sheltered.* (d) *Was distant, out of sight.* (e) *Was excluded.* (f) *Was disregarded.* (a) 1 Sam. xx. 19; 1 Kings xvii. 13; Job xiii. 20, &c. (b) Num. v. 13; Job iii. 23; xxviii. 21, &c. (c) Zeph. ii. 3. (d) Gen. xxxi. 49. (e) Gen. iv. 14. (f) Ps. xxxviii. 10; Is. xl. 27.

Part. נִסְתָּר, pl. נִסְתָּרִים, f. נִסְתָּרוֹת, Deut. vii. 20; xxix. 29; Ps. xix. 13, &c.

Inf. הִסָּתֵר, Job xxxiv. 22.

Imp. הִסָּתֵר, Jer. xxxvi. 19.

Pih. Imp. fem. סַתְּרִי. *Hide, shelter,* Is. xvi. 3.

Puh. part. fem. מְסֻתָּרָה. *Concealed,* Prov. xxvii. 5.

Hiph. הִסְתִּיר, pres. יַסְתִּיר. (a) *Concealed.* (b) *Sheltered.* (c) *Placed for security.* (d) הִסְתִּיר פָּנָיו מִן, *Turned away his face from.* (a) 1 Sam. xx. 2; Ps. cxix. 19; Jer. xxxvi. 26, &c. (b) Job xiv. 13; Ps. xvii. 8; lxiv. 3, &c. (c) Is. xlix. 2. (d) Ps. x. 21; xxii. 25; xxx. 8, &c.

Part. מַסְתִּיר, Is. viii. 18; liii. 3.

Inf. הַסְתֵּר, Deut. xxxi. 18; Prov. xxv. 2, &c.

Imp. הַסְתֵּר, Ps. li. 11.

Hith. pres. תִּסְתַּתֵּר, *Is concealed, lost,* Is. xxix. 14.

Part. מִסְתַּתֵּר, *Hiding himself,* 1 Sam. xxiii. 19; xxvi. 1; Ps. liv. 2; Is. xlv. 15.

סְתַר, v. Chald. *Id.*

Pah. pret. aff. סַתְרֵהּ, *Put out of sight, destroyed,* Ezra v. 12.

Part. pl. f. def. מְסַתְּרָתָא. *Concealed things,* Dan. ii. 22.

ע

ע, *Ayin,* the sixteenth letter of the Hebrew alphabet; as a numeral, it stands for seventy. This letter had originally, like ד and ח, two sounds, and not improbably these were distinguished by a diacritical point like the Arabic ain and ghain, Gram. artt. 4. 18. As it had some affinity in sound to the letters ג, כ, ק, ר; these are occasionally found occupying the same situation in cognate roots. Comp. עָמַר, כָּתַר, נָבַע, נָבָא; נָבַךְ, נָבָה. Chald. אַרְעָא, אֶרֶק, מָטַט, מרט. It often occupies, in the Chaldee, the situation of the Heb. ץ; as אַרְעָא, אֶרֶץ. So Syr. ܟܢ. Heb. צֹאן; בְּעֶצֶם, וְעִצְן, אֶרֶץ. In the softer pronunciation of the Chaldees it was sometimes omitted, as ה, ו, י, are, Gram. art. 73; as, בַּל, for בְּעַל, Gesen. See p. 82, above. There is, however, no good reason for supposing that the partic. בְּ is for בְּעִי, no such elision taking place in the Hebrew; nor would the sense, so supplied, suit this particle. See p. 80, above, and Gram. art. 243. 2, note.

עָב, com. constr. עַב; pl. עָבִים, and עָבוֹת, constr. עָבֵי, aff. עָבָיו, r. עבה. See עָנָן. Arab. عَبَّ, *bibit;* عَبّ, *aquæ per se effusæ exuberantes.* (a) *A cloud, a thick cloud.* (b) *A covering,* as a cloud covers the sky. (a) 1 Kings xviii. 44; Job xx. 6; Ps. cxlvii. 8; Eccl. xi. 3, &c. (b) Exod. xix. 9.

עָב, m. pl. עָבִים. See עָב, above. Probably, *A covering* of planks, 1 Kings vii. 6; Ezek. xli. 25, 26. Vulg. *epistylia; gros-*

עבד (446) עבד

siora ligna; *latitudinem* parietum. From the places, as well as the etymology, "*freeze*," or "*fascia*"—as used in architecture—is probably the thing meant.

עָבַד, v. pres. יַעֲבֹד. Constr. abs. immed. it. med. אֶת, and sometimes לְ. Arab. عَبَدَ, *servus*; عَبَدَ, *adoravit*. (a) *Served*, [1] A master. [2] As a subject, or vassal. [3] The true God. [4] A false god. (b) *Worked, laboured*. (c) *Tilled* the ground. (d) *Complied with, assented to*. (e) *Performed* a religious service. (f) *Imposed servitude on, made to serve*, with בְּ, of the person. (a), [1] Gen. xxix. 15; Exod. xxi. 6; Deut. xv. 12. 18, &c. [2] Deut. xxviii. 48; 2 Kings xviii. 7; Jer. xxvii. 11, &c. [3] Exod. xxiii. 25; Deut. xxviii. 47; Mal. iii. 18, &c. [4] Deut. iv. 19; xxviii. 36; 2 Kings x. 18; xxi. 21, &c. (b) Exod. xx. 9; xxxii. 21; Deut. v. 13. (c) Gen. iv. 12; 2 Sam. ix. 10; Jer. xxvii. 11, &c. (d) 1 Kings xii. 7. (e) Exod. xiii. 5; Num. iv. 26; xviii. 7, &c. (f) Exod. i. 14; Lev. xxv. 39; Deut. xv. 19; Jer. xxv. 14; xxviii. 7, &c.

Inf. עֲבֹד, aff. עָבְדוֹ, Gen. ii. 5; Exod. xiv. 12; Deut. xi. 13, &c.

Imp. עֲבֹד, aff. עָבְדֵהוּ; pl. עִבְדוּ, aff. עָבְדוּהוּ; Exod. x. 8; 1 Sam. vii. 3; xxvi. 19; 1 Chron. xxviii. 9, &c.

Part. עֹבֵד, plur. עֹבְדִים, constr. עֹבְדֵי, Gen. iv. 2; Num. xviii. 21; 2 Kings x. 19, &c.

Niph. נֶעֱבַד, נֶעֶבְדָתֶם, pres. יֵעָבֵד. Pass. of Kal. (a) *Became, was served*, Eccl. v. 8. (b) *Was tilled*, Deut. xxi. 4; Ezek. xxxvi. 9. 34.

Puh. עֻבַּד, *Labour was imposed on*, with בְּ, Deut. xxi. 3; Is. xiv. 3.

Hiph. הֶעֱבִיד, pres. יַעֲבֵד. וַיַּעֲבִדוּ. Causat. of Kal. (a) *Caused to labour*. (b) *Caused to serve*. (c) *Caused to serve* God. Meton. (d) *Wearied*. (a) Exod. i. 13; Ezek. xxix. 18. (b) Jer. xvii. 4. (c) 2 Chron. xxxiv. 33. (d) Is. xliii. 23, 24.

Part. pl. מַעֲבִדִים, (a) Exod. vi. 5.

Inf. הַעֲבִיד, (a) 2 Chron. ii. 17.

Hoph. pres. aff. הָעֳבָדֵם, and נָעֲבָדֵם, Exod. xx. 5; xxiii. 24. *Be induced to worship them*, according to Gesenius; but, more probably, this is merely a variation of the points, the regular punctuation being תַּעַבְדֵם, and נַעַבְדֵם, Kal. pres.

עֲבַד, v. Chald. pres. pl. יַעַבְדוּן. Syr. ܥܒܕ, *fecit*. (a) *Made*. (b) *Performed, did*. (a) Jer. x. 11; Dan. iii. 1. 15; v. 1. (b) Ezra vi. 13. 16; Dan. iv. 32; vi. 22, &c.

Inf. מֶעְבַּד, Ezra iv. 22.

Part. עָבֵד, f. עַבְדָא, pl. עָבְדִין, Ezra iv. 15; Dan. iv. 32; vii. 21.

Ithpe. pres. יִתְעֲבֵד. Pass. of Kal. *Was made*, Ezra vii. 11. 23; Dan. iii. 29, &c.

Part. מִתְעֲבֵד, f. מִתְעַבְדָא, Ezra v. 8; vii. 26.

עֶבֶד, m. aff. עַבְדִּי, pl. עֲבָדִים, constr. עַבְדֵי, aff. עֲבָדַי, עַבְדֵיכֶם. (a) *A slave, servant*. (b) *A vassal*. (c) *A submissive epithet*, used in addressing a superior, and applied [1] to the speaker himself, and [2] To some one connected with him. (d) *Any one employed in the service of a king*. (e) *A servant* of God, [1] One who worships and serves him, and as such is the object of his especial favour. [2] One commissioned by him for any purpose. (a) Gen. xxxii. 5; Exod. xii. 44; xxi. 2; Lev. xxv. 44, &c. (b) 2 Kings xvi. 7; xvii. 3; xxiv. 1, &c. (c), [1] Gen. xviii. 3; xix. 19; xliv. 33; 2 Sam. xix. 27, &c. [2] Gen. xliv. 27. 30; 1 Sam. xvii. 58, &c. (d) 1 Sam. xxix. 3; 2 Sam. xv. 34; 1 Kings ix. 22; 2 Kings v. 6, &c. (e), [1] Gen. xxvi. 24; 2 Sam. iii. 18; vii. 5; Job xlii. 7, &c. [2] Applied to Moses, Deut. xxxiv. 5; Josh. i. 1. 13. 15, &c. To Joshua, Josh. xxiv. 29; Judg. ii. 8. To David, 2 Sam. vii. 8; 1 Kings iii. 6; Is. xxxvii. 35, &c. To Christ, Is. lii. 13; liii. 11. To Nebuchadnezzar, Jer. xxv. 9; xxvii. 6. תִּהְיֶה עֶבֶד לָעָם הַזֶּה, *thou submittest to this people*, 1 Kings xii. 7.

עֲבֵד, m. pl. aff. עַבְדוֹהִי, *Id*. Chald. *A servant* of God, Ezra v. 11; Dan. iii. 26; vi. 21.

עֲבַד, m. pl. aff. עֲבָדֵיהֶם. *Their works*, Eccl. ix. So the LXX. and Vulg.

עֲבֹדָה, f. constr. עֲבֹדַת, aff. עֲבֹדָתוֹ, עֲבֹדָתֵנוּ. (a) *Servitude, laborious employment*. (b) *Employment of any kind*. (c) *Tillage*. (d) *Service, benefit*. (e) *Service* required by the king. (f) *The services* performed by the Levites. (g) *Religious worship*. (h) *Any religious observance*. (a) Exod. i. 14; Lev. xxiii. 7; Deut. xxvi. 6, &c. (b) Gen. xxix. 27. (c) 1 Chron. xxvii. 26; Neh. x. 38. (d) Ps. civ. 14. (e) 1 Kings xii. 4; 1 Chron. xxvi. 30; 2 Chron. x. 4, &c. (f) Num. iv. 23. 47; viii. 25, 26, &c. (g) Exod. xxxv. 24; xxxvi. 1; 1 Chron. ix. 28, &c. (h) Exod. xii. 25, 26; xiii. 5.

עבד (447) עבי

עֲבֻדָּה, f. *Slaves*, collectively, Gen. xxvi. 14; Job i. 3.

עֲבֹדוּת, f. aff. עַבְדֻתֵנוּ. *Slavery*, Ezra ix. 8, 9.

עָבָה, v. *Became large, thick, stout, heavy*, Deut. xxxii. 15; 1 Kings xii. 10; 2 Chron. x. 10. Syr. ܟܒܫ, *incrassatus est*. Æth. ዐቢየ : *major factus est, crevit*.

עָבוֹט, m. aff. עֲבוֹטוֹ, r. עבט. *A pledge*, Deut. xxiv. 10—13.

עָבוּר, m. constr. עֲבוּר, r. עבר. *Produce* of the ground, Josh. v. 11, 12.

עֲבוּר, r. עבר. Used only with בְּ prefixed, בַּעֲבוּר, as a preposition and conjunction. (a) With a noun or affix, [1] *Because of*. [2] *In return for*. (b) With a verb, [1] *For the purpose that*. [2] *Because*. [3] *While*. (a), [1] Gen. iii. 17; Exod. xiii. 8; 1 Sam. xii. 22, &c. [2] Amos ii. 6; viii. 6. (b), [1] Gen. xxvii. 4; Exod. ix. 14; 2 Sam. x. 3, &c. [2] Mic. ii. 10. [3] 2 Sam. xii. 21. לַעֲבוּר, *for the purpose that*, Exod. xx. 17; 2 Sam. xiv. 20; xvii. 14.

עבט, v. pres. יַעֲבֹט. Syr. ܥܒܛ, *concordavit*. Æth. ዐንመ : *angariavit*. *Gave a pledge*, Deut. xv. 6. Inf. עֲבֹט, Deut. xxiv. 10. Hiph. הַעֲבִיט, pres. תַּעֲבִיט. *Lent on security to* a person, constr. immed. of person, Deut. xv. 6. 8. Pih. pres. יְעַבְּטוּן, Joel ii. 7, וְלֹא יְעַבְּטוּן אֹרְחוֹתָם, either, *they shall not embarrass their paths*, or *they shall not break their ranks*. Comp. Arab. عبط, *fidit rem integram*. See LXX.

עָבְטִיט, m. once, Hab. ii. 6, מַכְבִּיד עָלָיו עַבְטִיט. Vulg. *qui aggravat contra se densum lutum*; as if עב + טיט. LXX. ὁ βαρύνων τὸν κλοιὸν αὐτοῦ στιβαρῶς; reading עֻלּוֹ, and deriving עָבְטִיט from עבט, in the sense of *binding firmly*. Gesenius takes it to signify *copia æris alieni*; but the context appears rather to require *an accumulation of pledges* in the possession of an unfeeling usurer.

עֳבִי, m. r. עבה. *Thickness*, Job xv. 26. בְּעֳבִי הָאֲדָמָה, *in thick* (clayey) *soil*, 2 Chron. iv. 17.

עֳבִי, aff. עָבְיוֹ. The *thickness* of metal, 1 Kings vii. 26; 2 Chron. iv. 5; Jer. lii. 21.

עֲבִידָא, f. Chald. def. עֲבִידְתָּא, constr. עֲבִידַת, r. עבד. (a) *Work, building*. (b) *Worship, service*. (c) *Business*. (a) Ezra iv. 24; v. 8; vi. 7. (b) Ezra vi. 18. (c) Dan. ii. 13. 49.

עָבַר, v. pres. יַעֲבֹר. Arab. عبر, *transivit; lacrymavit*. Constr. abs. immed. it. med. עַל, בְּ, אֶל, אֵת. *Passed*. (a) *Passed on*, abs. (b) *Passed away*, of a season or condition. (c) *Passed away, ceased*. (d) *Passed* a person or place. (e) *Passed* a river, or the sea. (f) *Passed* a limit. (g) *Trespassed, transgressed*. (h) *Exceeded, went beyond*. (i) *Passed through* a country, people, or road. (k) *Passed* from place to place. (l) *Passed over*. (m) *Came upon*. (n) *Passed away, disappeared*, of water, &c. (o) *Passed* as money. (p) *Dropped* as a liquid. (a) Gen. xxxiii. 3; 2 Sam. viii. 8; xx. 13; 2 Kings iv. 43, &c. (b) Job xvii. 11; xxx. 15; Ps. xc. 4; Cant. ii. 11, &c. (c) Esth. i. 19; ix. 27. (d) Judg. iii. 26; xi. 29; Prov. xxiv. 30, &c. (e) Josh. iv. 22; 2 Sam. xvii. 22. 24; xix. 40, &c. (f) Jer. v. 22. (g) Deut. xxvii. 13; Josh. vii. 11; Judg. ii. 20; 1 Sam. xv. 24, &c. (h) Ps. xxxviii. 5; lxxiii. 7. (i) Gen. xxx. 32; Exod. xii. 12; Josh. iii. 4; Job xv. 19, &c. (k) 1 Kings xxii. 24; 2 Chron. xviii. 23. (l) Ps. xliv. 8; cxxiv. 4; Hos. x. 11, &c. (m) Num. v. 14; Deut. xxiv. 5; 1 Chron. xxix. 30; Ps. lxxxviii. 17, &c. (n) Job xi. 16; Ps. xviii. 13.

Inf. עָבוֹר, עֲבוֹר, aff. עָבְרִי, Num. xx. 21; Deut. iv. 21; 2 Sam. xvii. 16, &c. Imp. עֲבֹר, עִבְרִי, pl. עִבְרוּ, Gen. xxxii. 16; Exod. xvii. 5; Is. xxiii. 10, &c. Part. עֹבֵר, pl. עֹבְרִים, constr. עֹבְרֵי. (o) Gen. xxiii. 16. (p) Cant. v. 13; Num. xiv. 41; Job xxi. 29, &c.

Niph. pres. יֵעָבֵר, *Can be passed*, Ezek. xlvii. 5.

Pih. עִבֵּר, pres. יְעַבֵּר. (a) I. q. Chald. עַבַּר, *concepit*. *Conceived*, Job xxi. 10. (b) Probably, *Caused to pass, passed* chains of gold from one side to the other, 1 Kings vi. 21. Arab. غبر. V. *Suscepit prolem, &c.*

Hiph. הֶעֱבִיר, pres. יַעֲבִיר, apoc. יַעֲבֵר. Causat. of Kal. (a) *Caused* or *allowed to pass*. (b) *Allowed* a period *to pass*. (c) *Removed, took*, or *put away*. (d) *Destroyed*. (e) *Removed* guilt, reproach, &c. (f) *Re-*

עבר (448) עבר

moved from one place to another. (g) *Brought across.* (h) *Caused to go through a country.* (i) *Transferred.* (k) *Offered, presented.* (l) *Passed a razor over the beard.* (a) Gen. viii. 1; 2 Kings xvi. 3; Ezek. xx. 37, &c. (b) Jer. xlvi. 17. (c) Jon. iii. 6; Esth. viii. 2. (d) 1 Kings xv. 12; 2 Chron. xv. 8. (e) 2 Sam. xii. 13; Job vii. 21; Zech. iii. 4, &c. (f) Gen. xlvi. 21; Jer. xv. 14. (g) Num. xxxii. 5; Josh. vii. 7; 2 Kings xix. 21, &c. (h) Lev. xxv. 9; Ezra i. 1; Neh. viii. 15, &c. (i) Num. xxvii. 7, 8. (k) Exod. xiii. 12. (l) Ezek. v. 1.

Part. מַעֲבִיר, pl. מַעֲבִרִים, Deut. xviii. 10; 1 Sam. ii. 24; Dan. xi. 20.

Inf. הַעֲבִיר, (a) Deut. ii. 30. (i) 2 Sam. iii. 10.

Imp. הַעֲבֵר, 2 Sam. xxiv. 10; 2 Chron. xxxv. 23; Ps. cxix. 37. 39.

Hith. הִתְעַבֵּר, pres. יִתְעַבֵּר. *Allowed himself to go beyond proper limits,* gave way to his feelings, *was angry,* Deut. iii. 26; Ps. lxxviii. 21. 59; lxxxix. 39.

Part. מִתְעַבֵּר, Prov. xiv. 16; xx. 2; xxvi. 17.

עֵבֶר, m. aff. עֶבְרוֹ, pl. עֲבָרִים, constr. עֶבְרֵי, aff. עֲבָרָיו. עֶבְרֵיהֶם. Arab. عَبْر, *latus, ora;* عبر, *ripa fluvii.* (a) *The passage* of a river, *a ford.* (b) *A mountain pass.* (c) *The passage* of a desert. (d) *The country lying near* a river, on both sides. (e) *A side.* (f) *The opposite side.* [1] With respect to the speaker. [2] With respect to a journey. [3] With respect to the seat of government. (g) The same side. (h) אֶל עֵבֶר, [1] *Towards.* [2] *On the opposite side to.* (i) אֶל עֵ״ פָּנָיו, *Forwards.* (k) עַל עֵ״ פָּנָיו, *In front of it.* (l) עֵבֶר הַ״ מִזְרָחָה, *The east side.* (m) עֵבֶר הַ״ יָמָּה, *The west side.* (n) מֵעֵבֶר, [1] *From the other side.* [2] *On the other side.* (o) מֵעֵבֶר לְ״, [1] *Beyond,* with respect to the speaker. [2] *Beyond,* with respect to Canaan. [3] *Opposite to.* [4] *Across.* (p) מֵעֵבֶר לְ״ מִזְרָחָה, *On the east side.* (q) מֵעֵבֶר לְ״ יָמָּה, *On the west side.* (r) מַעֲבָרָה לְ״, *Id.* (s) אִישׁ לְעֶבְרוֹ, *Each in his own direction.* (t) מִכָּל עֲבָרָיו, *From every side.* (a) Num. xxi. 12; xxvii. 12; Jer. xxii. 20, &c. (b) 1 Sam. xxvi. 13. (c) Job i. 19. (d) Deut. iii. 8; 1 Sam. xxxi. 7; Is. viii. 23, &c. (e) Exod. xxxii. 15; 1 Sam. xiv. 1. 40. 43; Jer. xlviii. 28. (f), [1] Deut. xi. 30; Judg. xi. 18; Josh. ii. 10, &c. [2] Josh. ix. 1. [3] Neh. iii. 7.

(g) 1 Kings v. 4. (h), [1] Exod. xxviii. 26; xxxix. 19. [2] Josh. xxii. 11. (i) Ezek. i. 9. 12. (k) Exod. xxv. 37. (l) Deut. iv. 41. 47. 49; Josh. i. 15; xii. 1, &c. (m) Josh. v. 1; xii. 7. (n), [1] Josh. xxiv. 3. [2] 2 Sam. x. 16; 1 Chron. xix. 16. (o), [1] Num. xxxii. 32; Deut. xxx. 13; Is. xviii. 1, &c. [2] Num. xxxv. 14; Josh. xiv. 3; xvii. 5; 1 Kings xiv. 15, &c. [3] 1 Kings iv. 12. [4] Judg. vii. 25. (p) Num. xxxiv. 15; Josh. xiii. 32; xviii. 7, &c. (q) Josh. xxii. 7. (r) 1 Chron. xxvi. 30. (s) Is. xlvii. 15. (t) Jer. xlix. 32.

עֲבַר, Chald. i. q. עֵבֶר. *Beyond,* with respect to the seat of government, Ezra iv. 10; v. 3; vi. 8, &c.

עֲבָרָה, f. once, 2 Sam. xix. 19, וְעָבְרָה הָעֲבָרָה לַעֲבִיר אֶת־בֵּית הַמֶּלֶךְ. LXX. καὶ διέβη ἡ διάβασις τοῦ ἐξεγεῖραι τὸν οἶκον τοῦ βασιλέως. Vulg. transierunt vada ut traducerent domum regis. Syr. ܘܥܒܕܘ ܡܥܒܪܬܐ ܕܢܥܒܪܘܢ ܒܝܬ ܡܠܟܐ, "*et paravunt vada, ut traducerent familiam regis.*" Either, *A raft,* or *boat,* for crossing the river, or *The passage,* or *ford,* of the river. The nominative of the verb in this case being the thousand Benjamites. Pl. constr. עַבְרוֹת, 2 Sam. xv. 28, for עֲבָרוֹת, which see.

עֶבְרָה, f. constr. עֶבְרַת, aff. עֶבְרָתִי, pl. עֲבָרוֹת, constr. עֶבְרוֹת. Any strong and *unrestrained* feeling, pec. unrestrained anger. *Anger,* Ps. lxxviii. 49; Ezek. vii. 19; Hos. v. 10, &c. Pl. of excess, Job xxi. 30; xl. 6; Ps. vii. 7.

עִבְרִי, fem. עִבְרִיָּה, pl. עִבְרִים, fem. עִבְרִיּוֹת. *Hebrew, a Hebrew.* (a) The national epithet of the posterity of Jacob, Exod. ii. 11. 13; Deut. xv. 12; Exod. i. 15, &c. (b) An epithet of Abraham, Gen. xiv. 13. According to some, the name was given to this patriarch in the land of Canaan, from the circumstance of his being a stranger from *the other side* of the Euphrates. Others think it is derived from עֵבֶר, in whose time, apparently, some important changes took place in the relations existing between the different branches of Shem's posterity, Gen. x. 25, and who is spoken of as being the father of all the בְּנֵי עֵבֶר, Gen. x. 21. The name appears to have belonged originally to all Eber's descendants, although it was afterwards appropriated by the Israelites.

עבשׁ, v. once, עָבְשׁוּ, Joel i. 17. Arab.

עבת (449) עגל

عَبَسَ, *siccus fuit;* عَبَسَ, *urinæ et stercoris sicci partes adhærentes caudæ cameli;*

عِفَاس, *corruptio. Became shrivelled and worthless,* incapable of germination, of seed. See Bochart. Hieroz., tom. ii., p. 471.

עָבַת, fem. עֲבָתָה. Cogn. עָבָה. Arab. عَبَتَ, *miscuit, commiscuit. Thick, entangled,* as the foliage of trees, Lev. xxiii. 40; Neh. viii. 15; Ezek. vi. 13; xx. 28.

עֲבֹת, com. pl. עֲבֹתִים, and עֲבֹתֹת. (a) *Thick branches, entangled foliage.* (b) *A cord, rope,* formed by twisting its threads. (c) *A chain.* (d) *An obligation, restraint.* (a) Ezek. xxxi. 3. 10. 14. (b) Judg. xv. 13, 14; xvi. 12; Ezek. iii. 25, &c. (c) Exod. xxviii. 14. 22. 25; xxxix. 15. 17, 18. (d) Ps. ii. 3; Ezek. iv. 8; Hos. xi. 4. Hence—

עבת, v. Pih. pres. aff. יְעַבְּתוּהָ. *They confirm, establish it,* Mic. vii. 3.

עגב, v. עָגְבָה, pres. תַּעֲגַב. Constr. med. עַל. Arab. عَجِبَ, *miratus, admiratione affectus fuit. Loved, fell in love with,* Ezek. xxiii. 5. 7. 9. 12. 16. 20.

Part. pl. עֹגְבִים, *Lovers,* Jer. iv. 30.

עֲגָבִים, pl. masc. *Love,* Ezek. xxxiii. 31, 32.

עגבה, f. aff. עַגְבָתָהּ, *Id.,* Ezek. xxiii. 11.

עֻגָּה, and עֻגָּה, f. constr. עֻגַת, pl. עֻגוֹת. *A cake baked on the hearth,* Gen. xviii. 6; Exod. xii. 39; Num. xi. 8; 1 Kings xvii. 13; xix. 6; Ezek. iv. 12; Hos. vii. 8.

עָגוּר, m. *A crane,* Is. xxxviii. 14; Jer. viii. 7. See Bochart. Hieroz., tom. ii. p. 57. The name is supposed by Bochart to be derived from the cry of the bird. Gesenius, however, considers the word as a participle from עגר, which he compares with the Arabic عَجَرَ, *flexit, inflexit:* hence, עָגוּר, *turning round, flying in a circle,* as a swallow; and poetically used for *the swallow itself.*

עָגִיל, masc. pl. עֲגִילִים. Syr. ܚܓܠ, *provolvit. A ring, an ear-ring,* Num. xxxi. 50; Ezek. xvi. 11.

עָגוֹל, עָגֹל, pl. fem. עֲגֻלּוֹת. *Round, circular,* 1 Kings vii. 23. 31. 35; x. 19; 2 Chron. iv. 2.

עֵגֶל, m. aff. עֶגְלְךָ, pl. עֲגָלִים, constr. עֶגְלֵי.— and

עֶגְלָה, f. constr. עֶגְלַת, aff. עֶגְלָתִי, pl. עֲגָלוֹת.— Arab. عِجْل, *vitulus;* عِجْلَة, *vitula.* Syr. ܥܓܠܐ, and ܥܓܠܬܐ, *Id.* (a) *A young bullock.* [1] In the first year. [2] In the third year. [3] Shut up to fatten. [4] Trained. [5] Employed in treading corn. [6] Employed in ploughing. [7] Offered in sacrifice. [8] Its image in gold. The object of idolatrous worship among the Israelites. (b) Metaph. *A prince, leader.* (a), [1] Lev. ix. 3; Mic. vii. 5. [2] Gen. xv. 9; Is. xv. 5; Jer. xlviii. 34. [3] 1 Sam. xxviii. 24; Jer. xlvi. 21; Amos vi. 4; Mal. iii. 20. [4] Jer. xxxi. 18; Hos. x. 11. [5] Jer. L. 11. [6] Deut. xxi. 3; Judg. xiv. 18. [7] Lev. ix. 2. 8. [8] Exod. xxxii. 14; 2 Kings xvii. 16, &c. (b) Ps. lxviii. 31. Compare Ps. xxii. 13.

עֲגָלָה, fem. aff. עֶגְלָתוֹ, pl. עֲגָלוֹת, constr. עֶגְלוֹת. Arab. عَجَلَة, *plaustrum.* Syr. ܥܓܠܬܐ, *Id.* (a) *A cart, a wagon,* drawn by two bullocks. (b) *A war-chariot.* (a) Num. vii. 3. 6; 1 Sam. vi. 7; Is. v. 18, &c. (b) Ps. xlvi. 10.

עגם, v. once, עָגְמָה. Constr. med. לְ. Arab. وَجَمَ, *fastidivit, pertæsus fuit;* اَجَمَ, *ingratam habuit* rem. עָגְמָה נַפְשִׁי לָאֶבְיוֹן, *Did my soul despise the poor?* Job xxx. 25. But see my notes.

עגן, v. once. Niph. pres. 2d pl. f. תֵּעָגֵנָה, for תֵּעָגֶנָה. *Will ye be prevented from marrying?* Ruth i. 13. Chald. עגונה, *solitaria orbata viro.*

עַד, m. r. עֵדָה. Properly, *Progress* in time or space.
(A) *Perpetuity, eternity.* Phrr. (a) אֲבִי עַד, *possessing eternity, the eternal.* (b) שֹׁכֵן עַד, *inhabiting eternity.* (c) לָעַד, [1] *for ever, without end.* [2] *Continually, without interruption or change.* (d) עֲדֵי־עַד, i. q. לָעַד. (e) לַעַד עַד־עוֹלָם, *to every period of time.* (f) לָעַד לְעוֹלָם, *Id.* (g) לְעָלְמֵי עַד, *Id.* (h) לְעֹלָם וָעֶד, *Id.* (i) עוֹלָם וָעֶד, *Id.* (a) Is. ix. 6.

3 M

עד (450) עד

(b) Is. lvii. 15. (c), [1] Ps. ix. 19; cxi. 3. 10; Mic. vii. 18, &c. [2] Ps. xxi. 7; xxxvii. 29; lxi. 9, &c. (d) Ps. lxxxiii. 18; xcii. 8; cxxxii. 12. 14; Is. xxvi. 4; lxv. 18. (e) Is. xxx. 8. (f) Is. xlv. 17. (g) Ps. cxi. 8; cxlviii. 6. (h) Exod. xv. 18; Ps. ix. 6; xlv. 15, &c. (i) Ps. x. 16; xxi. 5; xlv. 7, &c.

(B) *Antiquity.* (a) עַד הַרְרֵי, Ancient mountains, Hab. iii. 6. (b) עַד מְנֵי, *From of old,* Job xx. 4.

(C) As a particle, עַד, and עֲדֵי, with aff. עָדַי, עָדֶיךָ, עָדָיו, עָדֶיהָ, עָדֵיכֶם, עֲדֵיהֶם. (a) *As far as,* in place. (b) *Unto* a place or person. (c) *As far as,* in time, *until:* [1] With a noun. [2] With a verb in the past tense. [3] With a verb in the present tense. [4] With an Infinitive. [5] With a particle. (d) *Until, before :* [1] With a noun. [2] With an Infinitive. (e) *While, during.* (f) *Still.* (g) *As far as,* in degree. The usage of this particle is very nearly allied to that of the Greek ἄχρι, ἄχρις, μέχρι, μέχρις, ἕως, in the New Test. See Schleusner, Wahl., &c. (a) Deut. i. 7; 1 Sam. xvii. 52; Ps. xlvi. 10, &c. (b) Gen. ʟ. 10; Deut. i. 31; 1 Sam. ix. 9, &c. (c), [1] Lev. xv. 5; 1 Kings xviii. 26; Ezra iv. 5, &c. [2] Josh. ii. 22; 1 Sam. ii. 5; Ezek. xxxix. 15, &c. [3] Gen. xxxviii. 11; Prov. vii. 23; Hos. x. 12, &c. [4] Num. xxxii. 13; Judg. vi. 18; Ruth i. 19, &c. [5] Gen. xxiv. 19; Deut. ii. 14; Neh. xiii. 19; Ps. xl. 13, &c. (d), [1] 1 Sam. xiv. 24; 2 Chron. xv. 19; Ezek. xlvi. 2, &c. [2] Gen. xix. 22; Lev. xxv. 30; Ps. xviii. 38, &c. (e) Judg. iii. 26; 2 Kings ix. 22; Jonah iv. 2. (f) 1 Sam. xiv. 19; Job i. 18; Hag. ii. 19. (g) Gen. xxvii. 33; Is. lxiv. 8; Ps. lxxix. 5, &c.

עַד, Chald. i. q. Heb. (a) *Until.* (b) *Before.* (a) Dan. ii. 9; iv. 30; vii. 22, &c. (b) Dan. vi. 8. 13. 25.

עַד, m. Arab. عَدَا, r. عدو, *irruit in aliquem. Spoil,* Gen. xlix. 27; Zeph. iii. 8; and, probably, Is. xxxiii. 23.

עֵד, m. Aff. עֵדִי, pl. עֵדִים, constr. עֵדֵי, aff. עֵדַי, עֵדֶיךָ, עֵדֵיהֶם. (a) *An eye or ear witness:* spoken of [1] God; [2] Any person; and [3] metaphorically, of any inanimate thing. (b) *A witness,* one who gives evidence. (c) *Testimony.* (d) *Proof.* (a), [1] Gen. xxxi. 50; 1 Sam. xii. 5; Job xvi. 19, &c. [2] Lev. v. 1; Deut. xxiv. 22; 1 Sam. xii. 5, &c. (b) Exod. xxiii. 1; Deut. xvii. 6; xix. 15, 16, &c. So also in Is. lv. 4. (c) Exod. xx. 16; Deut. v. 20; Prov. xxv. 19. (d) Exod. xxii. 12; Deut. xxxi. 19. 26, &c.

עֹד, see עוֹד.

עָדָה, v. Arab. عَدَا, *præteriit, supersedit;* عَدَّ, IV. *paravit.* Æth. ዐደወ : *perrexit, transivit.*

I. Pret. עָדָה. *Passed* through, with עַל, Job xxviii. 8.

II. Pret. עָדִית, pres. תַּעְדֶּה, apoc. תַּעַד, aff. אֶעְדֶּךְ. (a) *Adorned himself:* [1] *Put on* an ornament. [2] *Put on* as an ornament. (b) *Adorned* another, constr. immed. of person and thing. (a), [1] Is. lxi. 10; Jer. iv. 30; Ezek. xxiii. 40; Hos. ii. 13. [2] Jer. xxxi. 4; Ezek. xvi. 13. (b) Ezek. xvi. 11.

Imp. עֲדֵה, (a, 2) Job xl. 10.

Hiph. part. מַעְדֶּה. *Stripping off* a garment, Prov. xxviii. 8.

עֲדָה, v. Chald. pret. עֲדָה, pres. יֶעְדֵּה, תֶּעְדֵּא. *Passed.* (a) *Passed upon,* with בְּ. (b) *Passed away,* of a kingdom. (c) *Was altered,* of a law. (a) Dan. iii. 27. (b) Dan. iv. 28; vii. 14. (c) Dan. vi. 9. 13.

Aph. pret. הֶעְדִּיו, pres. יְהַעְדּוּן. Causat. of Kal. *Removed, took away,* Dan. v. 20; vii. 26.

Part. מְהַעְדֵּה, Dan. ii. 21.

עֵדָה. I. Fem. of עֵד. (a) *An eye or ear witness.* Metaph. Applied to inanimate things. (b) *Proof.* (a) Gen. xxxi. 52; Josh. xxiv. 27. (b) Gen. xxi. 30. Hence—

II. Constr. עֲדַת, aff. עֲדָתוֹ, &c. Collectively, *An assembly of persons as witnesses.* (a) *Any assembly.* (b) *A party,* a number of persons united for any purpose. (c) *A family.* (d) Pec. הָעֵדָה, *The congregation of Israel.* Called, also, [1] עֲדַת יִשְׂרָאֵל [2] עֲדַת יְהֹוָה, [3] עֲדַת בְּנֵי יִשְׂרָאֵל, and [4] עֲדַת אֵל. (e) Pl. עֵדוֹת, aff. עֵדוֹתַי, &c. *The precepts* given by God to this people. (f) עֲדַת דְּבֹרִים, *A swarm of bees.* (a) Jer. vi. 18. (b) Num. xvi. 11; xxvi. 9; xxvii. 3, &c. (c) Job xv. 34; xvi. 7. (d) Exod. xvi. 22; xxxviii. 25; Lev. iv. 15; Num. xvi. 3, &c. [1] Exod. xii. 3. 6. 47; Josh. xxii. 18, &c. [2] Exod. xvi. 1, 2. 9; xvii. 1, &c. [3] Num. xxvii. 17; xxxi. 16; Josh. xxii. 16, 17. [4] Ps. lxxxii. 1. (e) Deut. iv. 45; vi. 20; Ps. xciii. 5; xcix. 7; cxxxii. 12, &c. (f) Judg. xiv. 8.

עדו (451) עדן

עֵדוּת, and עֵדָה, f. r. יעד. *A covenant.* (a) The terms enjoined by God in the covenant which he made with the Israelites, *the law*. (b) *The book of the law.* (c) *The decalogue*, written by the finger of God on two tables of stone and placed in the ark. Hence, [1] אֲרוֹן הָעֵדוּת, *The ark of the covenant.* [2] אֹהֶל הָעֵדוּת, *The tent of the covenant.* [3] מִשְׁכַּן הָעֵדוּת, *Id.* (d) *Any religious ordinance*. (e) Pl. aff. עֵדְוֹתָיךְ, עֵדְוֹתָיו, *Precepts.* (f) In the titles of Psalms lx. and lxxx. the signification of this word is uncertain, but it is usually interpreted as some kind of musical instrument. (a) Ps. xix. 8; lxxviii. 5; lxxxi. 6; cxix. 88. (b) 2 Kings xi. 12. (c) Exod. xx. 16; xxvii. 21; xxx. 36; xxxi. 18, &c. [1] Exod. xxv. 22; xxvi. 33, 34, &c. [2] Num. ix. 15; x. 11; xvii. 22, &c. [3] Exod. xxxviii. 21; Num. i. 50. 53, &c. (d) Ps. cxxii. 4. (e) 1 Kings ii. 3; Ps. cxix. 14; Jer. xlv. 23, &c.

עֲדִי, m. in pause עֶדְיְ, aff. עֶדְיֵךְ, עֶדְיוֹ, עֶדְיָהּ; pl. עֲדָיִים, r. עדה. *The act of adorning.* (a) *Ornaments.* (b) *Trappings* of a horse. (a) Exod. xxxiii. 4—6; 2 Sam. i. 24; Ezek. vii. 20; xvi. 7. 11, &c. (b) Ps. xxxii. 9. In Ps. xxxii. 9, and ciii. 5, this word has been translated *mouth*, but apparently without any satisfactory reason. Gesenius renders it *life* in the latter passage: probably *thy lot*, what is assigned to thee is not far from the truth. Compare Arab. عِدَّة, *dispositio*.

עֲדִים, pl. m. once, Is. lxiv. 5, בֶּגֶד עִדִּים. LXX. ῥάκος ἀποκαθημένης. Vulg. *pannus menstruatæ.* Arab. عِدَّة, *status mulieris, quo cum eâ rem habere nefas est. The periodic separation of females.*

עדין, f. עֲדִינָה, r. עדן. *Luxurious, delicate,* an epithet of Babylon, Is. xlvii. 8.

עדן, v. Kal non occ. Arab. غَدِنَ, *mollities, teneritas, viror;* غدن, XII. *Præ copiâ humoris multum viruit* planta. Syr. ܟܦܢ, *deliciæ; abundantia.*

Hith. pres. יִתְעַדֵּנוּ. *They live luxuriously,* Neh. ix. 25.

עֵדֶן, m. *Pleasure.* (a) *Eden,* the name of the district in which our first parents were placed by their Creator, and from which they were driven after their disobedience and fall, Gen. ii. 8. 15; iii. 23, 24, &c. (b) Pl. עֲדָנִים, aff. עֲדָנֶךָ. *Pleasures,* 2 Sam. i. 24; Ps. xxxvi. 9.

עֲדֶן, and עֲדֶנָה, i. q. עַד־הֵנָּה. *Hitherto, as yet,* Eccl. iv. 2, 3.

עֶדְנָה, f. *Pleasure,* Gen. xviii. 12.

עִדָּן, m. def. עִדָּנָא, pl. עִדָּנִין, def. עִדָּנַיָּא. Chald. (a) *Time.* (b) *A prophetic period, a time.* (a) Dan. ii. 8, 9. 21; iii. 5. 15. (b) Dan. v. 13. 20. 22. 29; vii. 12. 25. Syr. ܥܶܕܳܢ, *tempus.*

עדף, v. Only in participle, עֹדֵף, f. עֹדֶפֶת, pl. עֹדְפִים. Arab. غَدَفَ, *liberalis erga aliquem, multum largitus fuit.* (a) *Was left over and above.* (b) *Exceeded.* (a) Exod. xvi. 24; xxvi. 12, 13; Lev. xxv. 27. (b) Num. iii. 46. 48, 49.

Hiph. הֶעְדִּיף, *Caused or allowed to exceed,* Exod. xvi. 18.

עֵדֶר, m. aff. עֶדְרוֹ, pl. עֲדָרִים, constr. עֶדְרֵי, aff. עֶדְרֵיהֶם. *A flock or herd,* Gen. xxix. 2; xxx. 40; xxxii. 16; Is. xl. 11, &c.

עדר, v. *Arranged, set in order.* Hence, a body of men,—regulating them as a shepherd his flock.

Part. pl. constr. עֹדְרֵי, 1 Chron. xii. 38.

Inf. עֲדֹר, 1 Chron. xii. 33.

Niph. נֶעְדָּר, and נֶעְדַּר, pres. יֵעָדֵר. (a) *Was missing,* as one out of a flock. (b) *Was left behind.* (c) *Was dilatory, delayed.* (d) *Was cleared out* by raking or hoeing. (a) 1 Sam. xxx. 19; Is. xxxiv. 16; xl. 26. (b) 2 Sam. xxi. 22. (c) Zeph. iii. 5. (d) Is. v. 6; vii. 25.

Part. f. נֶעְדֶּרֶת. *Missing, not to be found, or obtained,* Is. lix. 15.

Pih. pres. יְעַדְּרוּ. *Omitted, neglected,* 1 Kings v. 7.

עדש, m. pl. עֲדָשִׁים. Arab. عَدَس, *lens; lens vulgaris. Lentiles,* Gen. xxv. 34; 2 Sam. xvii. 28; xxiii. 11; Ezek. iv. 9. See Celsii Hierobot., tom. ii., p. 103.

עוב, or עיב, v. Kal non occ. Arab. عَابَ, r. عيب, *vitiosa fuit* merx. II. *Opprobio afficit.* Syr. ܐܚܒ, *contempsit.* Sam. ᛋᛏᚢᚠ, *condemnavit.* Cogn. חוב.

Hiph. pres. יָעִיב. *Treated as worthless,*

עוֹרֵב

rejected, Lam. ii. 1. But LXX. ἐγνόφωσεν, and Vulg. *obtexit caligine.* See עָב. Alibi non occ.

עוּגָב, and עֻגָב, m. aff. עֻגָבִי, r. עגב. Some kind of musical instrument, but its precise character it is impossible to determine. From the signification of the root it seems probable that its notes were soft and plaintive. Gesenius thinks it was a wind instrument, and supposes *breathing, blowing,* to be the original signification of the root. In Gen. iv. 21, כִּנּוֹר וְעוּגָב. LXX. ψαλτήριον καὶ κιθάραν. Vulg. *cithará et organo.* Syr. ܟܢܪܐ ܘܩܝܬܪܐ. Auth. Vers. *The harp and organ.* Luther, *Von dem sind hergekommen die Geiger und Pfeifer.* In Job xxi. 12, כִּנּוֹר — תֹּף — עוּגָב. LXX. ψαλτήριον — κιθάραν — ψαλμοῦ. Vulg. *tympanum — citharam — organi.* See my note. In Job xxx. 31, LXX. ψαλμὸς. Vulg. *organum.* In both these places the Syr. has أعلن. The word occurs also in Ps. cl. 4, where the LXX. has ὀργάνῳ; the Vulg. *organo.* Probably, *A lute.*

עוּד, v. In Kal only as a participle, *Was a witness.* See עֵד.

Hiph. הֵעִיד, pres. יָעִד, apoc. יָעַד. (a) Constr. immed. it. med. אֶת. [1] *Called or took witnesses.* [2] *Bore witness to.* [3] *Bore witness against.* (b) Constr. immed. it. med. אֶת, and בְּ, *Called as a witness to a declaration made to another.* (c) Constr. med. בְּ, [1] *Made a solemn or authoritative declaration.* [2] *Enjoined, commanded.* [3] *Solemnly warned.* [4] *Reproved.* (a), [1] Is. viii. 2; Jer. xxxii. 10. [2] Job xxix. 11. [3] 1 Kings xxi. 10. 13. (b) Deut. iv. 26; xxx. 19; xxxi. 28. (c), [1] Gen. xliii. 3; Deut. viii. 9. [2] Exod. xix. 2, 3; 2 Kings xvii. 15; Neh. ix. 34; Jer. xi. 7, &c. [3] 1 Sam. viii. 9; 1 Kings ii. 42; Neh. ix. 26. 29, 30. [4] Neh. xiii. 15. 21.

Part. מֵעִיד, Deut. xxxii. 46.

Inf. הָעֵד, Gen. xliii. 3; 1 Sam. viii. 9; Jer. xi. 7.

Imp. הָעֵד, pl. הָעִידוּ, Exod. xix. 21; Jer. xxxii. 25. 44; Amos iii. 13.

Hoph. הוּעַד. *Warning or information was given,* with בְּ, Exod. xxi. 29.

עוֹד, v. Pih. aff. עֹדְנִי. *They surrounded me,* Ps. cxix. 61. Æth. ዐጸፈ: *circumire.*

עוֹד

עוּד, v. Arab. عَانَ, r. عون, *confugit ad aliquem. Took refuge with.* See עוז.

Pih. pres. יְעוֹדֵד. *Affords refuge to,* Ps. cxlvi. 9.

Part. מְעוֹדֵד, Ps. cxlvii. 6.

Hith. pres. נִתְעוֹדָד. *We are provided with a refuge, are succoured,* Ps. xx. 9.

עוֹד, and עֹד, aff. עוֹדִי, עוֹדְךָ, עוֹדֶנִי, עוֹדֶנּוּ, עוֹדָם, and הֵם עוֹד. Arab. عَاد, r. عود, *rediit; repetivit rem. The repetition* or *continuance of an action.* As a particle, (a) *Again.* (b) *Besides.* (c) *Still.* (d) *Any longer.* (a) Gen. viii. 10; Judg. xx. 25; 2 Sam. v. 13, &c. (b) 1 Kings xxii. 7; 2 Kings iv. 6; Is. v. 4, &c. (c) Gen. xxix. 7; Num. xi. 33; Esth. vi. 14, &c. (d) Deut. xxxi. 2; 1 Kings x. 5; Joel ii. 19, &c.

עָוָה, v. עָוָה, עָוִינוּ, pres. non occ. Arab. غَوَى, *in latus inflexit rem; torsit;* غَوَى, *erravit. Was bent, crooked, perverse. Did wrong,* Esth. i. 16; Dan. ix. 5.

Niph. נַעֲוֵיתִי. (a) *Was bent* with pain, Is. xxi. 3. (b) *Was bowed down* with sorrow, Ps. xxxviii. 7. (c) *Was perverse* in mind.

Part. constr. נַעֲוֵה, (c) Prov. xii. 8.

Pih. עִוָּה, *Made crooked,* Lam. iii. 9. עִוָּה פָנֶיהָ, *overturned,* Is. xxiv. 1.

Hiph. הֶעֱוָה. (a) *Made crooked* his path. (b) *Perverted* justice. (c) *Walked in a crooked path, acted perversely.* (a) Jer. iii. 21. (b) Job xxxiii. 27. (c) 2 Sam. xix. 20; xxiv. 17; 1 Kings viii. 17; 2 Chron. vi. 37; Ps. cvi. 6.

Inf. הַעֲוֵה, aff. הַעֲוֹתוֹ, 2 Sam. vii. 14; Jer. ix. 5.

עַוָּה, fem. *Being overturned,* Ezek. xxi. 32.

עָווֹן, see עָוֹן.

עוּז, v. Arab. عَانَ, r. عون, *confugit ad aliquem. Took refuge with.*

Inf. עוּז, Is. xxx. 2. This may, however, be derived from עוז, which see.

Hiph. הָעִיזוּ. (a) *Caused to take refuge, collected in a place of safety.* (b) I. q. Kal, Is. x. 30.

Imp. הָעֵז, pl. הָעִיזוּ, and הָעִיזוּ. (a) Exod. ix. 19. (b) Jer. iv. 6; vi. 1.

עִוִי, f. Chald. pl. aff. עֲוָיָתָךְ. *Thy iniquities,* Dan. iv. 24. See עוה.

עֲוִיל, m. pl. עֲוִילִים, aff. עֲוִילֵיהֶם. (a) *Wicked,* r. עָוַל. (b) *A suckling,* r. עוּל. (a) Job xvi. 11; xix. 18. (b) Job xxi. 11.

עָוֶל, and עָוֶל, m. aff. עַוְלוֹ. Arab. غَالَ, *declinavit, pec. à justo, injustus fuit; propendit in alteram partem statera.* Turning or leaning to one side more than the other. (a) *Unfairness, partiality* in judgment. (b) *Injustice.* (c) *Iniquity.* (a) Lev. xix. 15. 35; Ps. lxxxii. 2. (b) Deut. xxv. 16; xxxii. 4; Job xxxiv. 32; Ps. vii. 4, &c. (c) Ezek. xviii. 26; xxxiii. 13. 15, &c. Hence—

עַוָּל, m. One habitually *unfair, unjust, wicked,* Job xviii. 21; xxvii. 7; xxix. 17; xxxi. 3; Zeph. iii. 5.

עוּל, v. Kal non occ.
Pih. pres. יְעַוֵּל. *Acts unjustly,* Is. xxvi. 10. Part. מְעַוֵּל, Ps. lxxi. 4.

עוּל, v. Arab. غَالَ, r. عول, *sustentavit, aluit* familiam suam; غَالَتْ, r. غيل, *gravida, vel cum viro concumbens lactavit* infantem. (a) *Was with young.* (b) *Suckled young ones.*
Part. f. pl. עָלוֹת. (a) Gen. xxxiii. 13; Ps. lxxviii. 71; Is. xl. 11. (b) 1 Sam. vi. 7. 10. Hence—

עוּל, m. aff. עוּלָהּ. *An infant at the breast,* Is. xlix. 15; lxv. 20.

עַוְלָה, f. i. q. עָוֶל. With ה paragogic, עַוְלָתָה, contr. עֹלָתָה, pl. עוֹלוֹת. (a) 2 Chron. xix. 7; Job vi. 29, &c. (b) 2 Sam. iii. 34; vii. 10; Job xi. 14, &c. (c) Job xv. 16; xxii. 23, &c.

עוֹלָה, see עֹלָה.

עוֹלֵל, and עוֹלָל, m. pl. עוֹלְלִים, and עוֹלָלִים, constr. עוֹלְלֵי, aff. עוֹלָלֶךָ, עוֹלָלַיִךְ, עוֹלְלֵיהֶם, r. עוּל. *An infant—at the breast, a young child, a child:* [1] Unborn, Job iii. 16. [2] In arms, Lam. ii. 20. [3] Killed by being dashed on the ground, 2 Kings viii. 12; Ps. cxxxvii. 9, &c. [4] Coupled with יוֹנֵק, 1 Sam. xv. 3; xxii. 19, &c. [5] Playing in the street, Jer. vi. 11; ix. 20, &c. [6] Succeeding to property, Ps. xvii. 14.

עוֹלֵלוֹת, see עֹלֵלוֹת.

עוֹלָם, and עֹלָם, masc. aff. עוֹלָמוֹ, pl. עוֹלָמִים, constr. עוֹלְמֵי, r. עלם. *Duration,* past or future, the extent of which is either *unknown, unlimited,* or *indefinite,* being limited by the necessity of the case. (a) *Antiquity.* (b) *Eternity.* (c) *The duration of the earth, moon, &c.* (d) *The whole life.* (e) *Future duration, indefinite, but not endless;* being limited [α] by decay, [β] by the extinction of a family. Applied, [1] To the sanctions of the law, which was binding on every generation till abrogated by the Lawgiver. [2] To the time for which Canaan was promised to Abraham's posterity. [3] To the time that the Israelites should be God's people. [4] To the time that David's posterity should reign. (f) *Unlimited future time.* Phrr. (g) בְּרִית עוֹלָם, *Perpetual covenant;* that with Noah, that with Abraham, that of circumcision, that with Isaac, that with Jacob, and that with David. (h) מֵעוֹלָם עַד עוֹלָם, *From generation to generation.* (a) Deut. xxxii. 7; Job xxii. 15; Ps. cxxiii. 3, &c. (b) Gen. xxi. 33; Deut. xxxiii. 27; Ps. xc. 2; Is. xl. 28, &c. (c) Gen. ix. 12; xlix. 26; Deut. xxxiii. 15, &c. (d) Deut. xv. 17; 1 Sam. i. 22; Job xl. 28, &c. (e), (a) Josh. iv. 7; 1 Kings ix. 3; 2 Chron. vii. 16, &c. (β) Josh. xiv. 9; 1 Sam. ii. 30; xiii. 13; xx. 15. 42, &c. [1] Exod. xii. 14; xxvii. 21; Deut. xii. 28, &c. [2] Gen. xiii. 15; xvii. 8; xlviii. 4, &c. [3] 2 Sam. vii. 24. 26; 1 Chron. xvii. 22. 24, &c. [4] 2 Sam. vii. 13. 17. 25; xxii. 51, &c. (f) Ps. x. 16; xlv. 7; lxvi. 7, &c. (g) Gen. ix. 16; xvii. 7. 13. 19; 2 Sam. xxiii. 5; 1 Chron. xvi. 17, &c. (h) Ps. ciii. 17, &c.

עוֹנָה, f. aff. עֹנָתָהּ, once, Exod. xxi. 10. Arab. عَانَ, r. عون. II. *Nupta fuit* mulier; عون, *fœmina nupta.* Apparently, *Conjugal rights.* LXX. τὴν ὁμιλίαν αὐτῆς. Vulg. *pretium pudicitiæ.* Syr. ܥܡܕܒܗ.

עָוֹן, and עָווֹן, m. constr. עֲוֹן, aff. עֲוֹנִי, עֲוֹנְךָ, &c., pl. aff. עֲוֹנָיו, עֲוֹנֵינוּ; it. pl. עֲוֹנוֹת, aff. עֲוֹנוֹתַי, עֲוֹנוֹתֶיךָ, &c., r. עוה. (a) *Sin, iniquity.* (b) *Guilt.* (c) *Punishment.* (a) Gen. xv. 16; Exod. xxxiv. 7; 1 Sam. xx. 8, &c. (b) Exod. xxviii. 43; 2 Sam. xiv. 9; Is. i. 4, &c. (c) Gen. xix. 15; 1 Sam. xxviii. 10.

עֲוִעִים, m. pl. r. עוה. Once, Is. xix. 14.

עוֹף (454) עוּר

Giddiness. LXX. πλανήσεως. Vulg. vertiginis.

עוֹף, and עָף, m. pl. non occ. Syr. ܨܦܪܐ, volucris. Collectively, Birds, Gen. i. 21; Lev. xvii. 13; Deut. xiv. 20, &c.

עוּף, I. v. עָפוּ, pres. יָעוּף, apoc. יָעַף, and עָף. (a) Flew. (b) Flew away. (c) Flew upon, as a bird of prey, attacked, with בְּ. (a) Ps. xviii. 11; xci. 5; Prov. xxiii. 5; Is. vi. 6, &c. (b) Ps. lv. 7; xc. 10. (c) Is. xi. 14.

Part. f. עָפָה, pl. עָפוֹת, Is. xxxi. 5; Zech. v. 1, 2.

Inf. עוּף, Job v. 7; Prov. xxvi. 2.

Pih. pres. יְעוֹפֵף. (a) Flew. (b) Caused to fly, brandished a sword. (a) Gen. i. 20; Is. vi. 2.

Part. מְעוֹפֵף. (a) Is. xv. 2; xxx. 6.

Inf. aff. עוּפִי. (b) Ezek. xxxii. 10.

Hiph. pres. הָעִיף. Turned the eyes quickly on, Prov. xxiii. 5.

Hith. pres. יִתְעוֹפֵף, i. q. Kal. (b) Hos. ix. 11.

עוּף, II. v. pres. יָעֻפָה. Syr. ܥܛܦ, duplicavit, involvit; defecit viribus. Was in obscurity, was oppressed with calamity, Job xi. 17. See my note.

עוּץ, v. i. q. יָעַץ, which see. Used only in the Imperative plural עֻצוּ, Judg. xix. 30; Is. viii. 11.

עוּק, v. Kal non occ. A Chaldee form of צוּק, which see. Was straitened, was pressed.

Hiph. pres. תָּעִיק. Presses, crushes, Amos ii. 13.

Part. מֵעִיק. Pressing down, Ibid.

עוּר, v. Aroused himself, awoke, arose.

Imp. עוּרָה, עוּרִי, Judg. v. 12; Ps. xliv. 13; Is. li. 9; Zech. xiii. 7, &c.

Niph. pres. יֵעוֹר. (a) Pass. of Kal, Jer. vi. 22; xxv. 32; Zech. iv. 1, &c. (b) Pass. of Pih. [c], Hab. iii. 9.

Part. נֵעוֹר, Zech. ii. 13.

Pih. עוֹרֵר, pres. יְעוֹרֵר. (a) Roused. (b) Excited, stirred up. (c) Raised a spear, scourge, cry. (a) Is. xiv. 9; Cant. ii. 7; iii. 5, &c. (b) Prov. x. 12; Zech. ix. 13. (c) 2 Sam. xxiii. 18; 1 Chron. xi. 11. 20; Is. x. 26; xv. 5.

Inf. (b) עֹרֵר, Job iii. 8.

Imp. עוֹרְרָה, Ps. lxxx. 3.

Hiph. הֵעִיר, pres. יָעִיר, apoc. יָעַר, and עָר, (a) I. q. Pih. [a] Cant. ii. 7; Is. L. 4; Zech. iv. 1, &c. [b] Deut. xxxii. 11; 2 Chron. xxxv. 22; Is. xli. 2, &c. (b) I. q. Kal, Ps. lvii. 9; cviii. 3.

Part. מֵעִיר. (a) Isa. xiii. 17; Jer. L. 9, &c.

Inf. הָעִיר, Ps. lxxiii. 20, &c.

Imp. הָעִירָה. (b) Ps. xxxv. 23; הָעִירוּ, Joel iv. 9.

Hith. הִתְעוֹרַרְתִּי, pres. יִתְעוֹרֵר, i. q. Kal, Job xvii. 8; xxxi. 29.

Part. מִתְעוֹרֵר, Is. lxiv. 6.

Imp. הִתְעוֹרְרִי, Is. li. 17.

עוּר, v. Kal non occ. Arab. عَوَرَ, monoculus fuit. Syr. ܥܘܪ, exoculavit, excæcavit. Was blind.

Pih. עִוֵּר, pres. יְעַוֵּר. Blinded, Exod. xxiii. 5; Deut. xvi. 19; 2 Kings xxv. 7; Jer. xxxix. 7; lii. 11. See p. 163, Serm. Diss.

עִוֵּר, m. pl. עִוְרִים. (a) Blind. (b) Mentally blind. (a) Exod. iv. 11; Lev. xix. 14; Deut. xxvii. 18; Is. xxix. 18, &c. (b) Is. xlii. 19; xliii. 8.

עִוֵּר, m. Chald. Syr. ܥܘܪܐ, pulvis paleæ. Arab. عَوَار, festuca. Chaff, Dan. ii. 35.

עוֹר, m. aff. עוֹרִי, pl. עוֹרוֹת, aff. עוֹרָם. The skin: [1] Of man. [2] Of animals. [1] Exod. xxxiv. 30; Job ii. 4; xxx. 30, &c. [2] Gen. iii. 30; Exod. xxvi. 14; Lev. xvi. 27, &c.

עִוָּרוֹן, m. Blindness, Deut. xxviii. 28; Zech. xii. 4.

עַוֶּרֶת, f. Id., Lev. xxii. 22.

עוּשׁ, v. Imp. pl. עוּשׁוּ, Joel iv. 11. LXX. συναθροίζεσθε. Vulg. erumpite. Syr. ܐܬܟܢܫܘ. Arab. عَشَّ, quæsivit rem: collegit, conjunxit; غَشَّ, IV. ad festinandum impulit. Either, assemble or hasten. Gesen., after Castell, prefers the latter, and considers the word as synonymous with חוּשׁ.

עוּת, v. Kal non occ. Arab. عَاتَ, r. عوت, avertit, divertit. Bent, made crooked.

Pih. עִוֵּת, pres. יְעַוֵּת. Constr. immed. (a) Made crooked. (b) Made unfair, unequal. (c) Perverted judgment. (d) Treated unjustly. (e) Bowed down. (a) Ps. cxlvi. 9;

עות (455) עזב

Eccl. vii. 13. (c) Job viii. 3; xxxiv. 12. (d) Ps. cxix. 78.
Inf. עֲזֹ. (b) Amos viii. 5. (d) Lam. iii. 37.

עוּת, v. Once, Inf. עוּת, Is. L. 4. Arab. غُوث, r. غوث, *opem tulit.* *To aid.*

עוֹתָה, f. aff. עֻוָּתִי. *Unjust treatment,* Lam. iii. 59.

עַז, m. pl. עַזִּים, f. עַזָּה, pl. עַזּוֹת, r. עזז. (a) *Strong:* applied to [1] Bodily strength and power: [2] Wind and waters: [3] A country: [4] Anger, desire, love. (b) *Harsh.* (c) *Strength.* (a), [1] Num. xiii. 28; Judg. xiv. 4. 18; Prov. xxx. 25, &c. [2] Exod. xiv. 21; Neh. ix. 11; Is. xliii. 16. [3] Num. xxi. 25. [4] Gen. xlix. 7; Prov. xxi. 14; Cant. viii. 6; Is. lvi. 11. (b) Deut. xxviii. 50; Prov. xviii. 23; Is. xix. 4; Dan. viii. 23. (c) Gen. xlix. 3; 2 Sam. xxii. 18.

עֵז, c. plur. עִזִּים, aff. עִזֵּךְ. Arab. عَنْز, *capra.* Syr. ܥܙܐ, *Id.* (a) *A goat.* (b) Pec. *A she-goat.* (c) In the pl. *Goats' hair.* (a) Lev. iv. 23; vii. 23; xvii. 3, &c. (b) Gen. xxxi. 38; xxxii. 14; Num. xv. 27, &c. (c) Exod. xxv. 4; xxxv. 26; Num. xxxi. 20. Castell, after Bochart., compares the Greek αἴξ.

עֵז, pl. עִזִּין, Chald., *Id.*, Ezra vi. 17.

עֹז, m. עָז, aff. עָזִי, עֻזְּךָ, עָזוֹ, עֻזֵּנוּ, עָזְכֶם, &c., it. עֻזִּי, עֻזְּךָ, r. עזז. (a) *Strength, power, might:* [1] Of God. [2] Of a king or nation. [3] Of the body. [4] Of a tower, or city. [5] Of the voice. (b) *Ascription of power, praise.* (c) *Source of strength, refuge.* (a), [1] 1 Chron. xvi. 26; Job xii. 16; Ps. lxxii. 12, &c. [2] Judg. v. 21; 1 Sam. vi. 14; Ps. xxix. 11, &c. [3] Job xli. 14; Prov. xxxi. 17. [4] Judg. ix. 51; Ps. lxi. 4; Is. xxvi. 1, &c. [5] Ps. lxviii. 34. (b) Ps. viii. 3. (c) Ps. xxviii. 7; xlvi. 2; cxviii. 14, &c. בְּכָל, *with all his might,* exerting himself to the utmost, 2 Sam. vi. 14; 1 Chron. xiii. 8. כְּלֵי עֹז, *instruments of praise,* 2 Chron. xxx. 21.

עֲזָאזֵל, thrice only, Lev. xvi. 8. 10. 26. The different interpretations of this word, as well as the arguments for and against them, may be seen in Bochart. Hieroz., tom. i., p. 650. The most natural appears to be *"the goat of departure,"* or *"the scapegoat,"* from עֵז, and אָזַל. The objection urged against this interpretation, that עֵז always signifies *a she-goat,* is manifestly without foundation, as may be seen by the passages quoted above.

עָזַב, v. pres. יַעֲזֹב. Constr. immed. it. med. אֶת. *Left.* (a) *Left behind.* (b) *Allowed to remain.* (c) *Went away from.* (d) *Forsook, neglected:* [1] God. [2] A person. [3] A law or practice. (e) *Failed.* (f) *Allowed to fail, took away.* (g) *Left unrestrained, loosened, gave loose to.* (h) עָזַב בְּיַד, *Left in the hand of.* (a) Gen. xxxix. 12; L. 8; Exod. ii. 20, &c. (b) Judg. ii. 21; Mal. iii. 19. (c) Gen. ii. 24; xliv. 22; Jer. xxv. 35, &c. (d), [1] Deut. xxxi. 16; 1 Kings ix. 9; 2 Chron. xxi. 10, &c. [2] Job xx. 19; Ps. lxxi. 11; Is. xlix. 14, &c. [3] 2 Chron. xii. 1; Is. lviii. 2; Ezek. xxiii. 8, &c. (e) Ps. xxxviii. 11; xl. 13. (f) Gen. xxiv. 27; Ruth ii. 20. (g) Job x. 1. (h) Gen. xxxix. 6; 2 Chron. xii. 8; Neh. ix. 28, &c.

Part., aff. עֹזֵב, fem. עֹזֶבֶת, pl. עֹזְבִים, constr. עֹזְבֵי, Prov. ii. 13; x. 17; Zech. ii. 17, &c.

Part. pass. עָזוּב, f. עֲזוּבָה, constr. עֲזוּבַת, pl. עֲזוּבוֹת, Is. liv. 6. (g) Deut. xxxii. 36; 1 Kings xiv. 10; xxi. 21, &c.

Inf. עֲזֹב, עָזוֹב, aff. עָזְבָה, עָזְבָם, &c., Gen. xliv. 22; 2 Kings viii. 6; Jer. ii. 16; xiv. 8, &c.

Imp. עֲזֹב, and עָזְבָה, pl. עִזְבוּ, aff. עָזְבוּהָ, Ps. xxxvii. 8; Prov. ix. 6; Jer. xlix. 11; li. 9, &c.

Niph. נֶעֱזַב, pres. יֵעָזֵב. Pass. of Kal, Lev. xxvi. 43; Job xviii. 4; Neh. xiii. 11, &c.

Part. נֶעֱזָב, f. pl. נֶעֱזָבוֹת, Ps. xxxvii. 25; Ezek. xxxvi. 4.

Puh. עֻזַּב, עֻזָּבָה, i. q. Niph. Is. xxxii. 14; Jer. xlix. 25.

עִזָּבוֹן, m. pl. aff. עִזְבוֹנַיִךְ, Ezek. xxvii. 12. 14. 16. 19. 22. 27. 33. Apparently, (a) Any thing parted with, *Merchandise:* and (b) A place employed in merchandise, *a market.* LXX. τὴν ἀγοράν σου; ὁ μισθός σου.

עָזוּז, m. r. עזז. *Mighty,* Ps. xxiv. 8. *Mighty men,* Is. xliii. 17.

עֱזוּז, m. aff. עֱזוּזוֹ. *Might,* of God, Ps. lxxviii. 4; cxlv. 6; in war, Is. xlii. 25.

עָזַז, v. pres. יָעֹז, apoc. תָּעֹז. Constr. abs. it. med. עַל. Arab. عَزّ, *potens, honoratus*

עזן (456) עזר

factus est; vicit potentiâ; عَزّ, *potentia, dignitas.* Syr. ܥܰܙ, *fortificatus est, invaluit.* (a) *Was strong.* (b) *Prevailed.* (c) *Considered himself strong, confided in.* (d) *Showed himself strong.* (a) Ps. lxxxix. 14; Eccl. vii. 19. (b) Judg. iii. 10; vi. 20; Ps. ix. 20; Dan. xi. 12. (c) Ps. lii. 9.

Inf. constr. עֲזוֹ, Prov. viii. 28.

Imp. עֻזָּה, (d) Ps. lxviii. 29.

Hiph. הֵעֵז, הֵעֵזָה, *Made strong or bold.* הֵעֵזָה פָנֶיהָ, *put on a bold face,* Prov. vii. 13. הֵעֵז בְּפָנָיו, *Id.,* Prov. xxi. 29.

עָזְנִיָּה, f. twice, Lev. xi. 13; Deut. xiv. 12. An unclean bird: according to the LXX. τὸν ἁλιαίετον, *the sea-eagle.* The Vulgate agrees with this; but Bochart. insists that it is rather *the black eagle,* μελαναίετος, *valeria.* So named, as in Latin, from its strength. See Hieroz., tom. ii., p. 188.

עזק, v. Kal non occ. Arab. عَزَق, *fidit terram;* مِعْزَق, *instrumentum quo terra finditur.* Æth. ОН፦ᎢᎢ: *puteus.*

Pih. pres. aff. יְעַזְּקֵהוּ. *Digged it,* Is. v. 2. Al. non occ.

עִזְקָא, f. Chald. constr. עִזְקַת, aff. עִזְקְתֵהּ. Syr. ܥܶܙܩܬܐ, *annulus. An engraved ring, a seal,* Dan. vi. 18.

עָזַר, v. pres. יַעֲזֹר. Arab. عَزَر, *juvit.* Syr. ܥܰܕܰܪ, *Id. Helped, assisted.* Constr. [1] Immed. it. med. אֶת, Gen. xlix. 25; 1 Sam. vii. 12; Is. xli. 13, &c. [2] Med. לְ, 2 Sam. xxi. 17; Job xxvi. 2; Zech. i. 15, &c. [3] Med. עִם, 1 Chron. xii. 21. [4] Med. אַחֲרֵי, 1 Kings i. 7.

Part. עֹזֵר, pl. constr. עֹזְרֵי, aff. עֹזְרַי, &c., 1 Kings xx. 16; Job ix. 13; Ps. cxviii. 7, &c.

Part. pass. עָזֻר, Is. xxxi. 3.

Inf. constr. עֲזֹר, aff. עָזְרִי, &c., 1 Chron. xii. 17; xv. 26, &c.

Imp. aff. עָזְרֵנִי, pl. aff. עִזְרוּ, Josh. x. 4; Ps. cix. 26, &c.

Niph. נֶעֱזַרְתִּי, pres. יֵעָזֵר, Pass. of Kal, Ps. xxviii. 7; Dan. xi. 34.

Inf. הֵעָזֵר, 2 Chron. xxvi. 15.

Hiph. part. pl. מַעְזְרִים, i. q. Kal, 2 Chron. xxviii. 23.

עֵזֶר, m. aff. עֶזְרִי, עֶזְרוֹ, &c. (a) *Help.* (b) *Helper.* (a) Exod. xviii. 4; Deut.

xxxiii. 26; Ps. xx. 3, &c. (b) Gen. ii. 18; Ps. lxx. 6; cxv. 9, &c.

עֶזְרָה, f. of the last, constr. עֶזְרַת, aff. עֶזְרָתִי, &c. *Id.,* Judg. v. 23; Job vi. 13; Ps. xlvi. 20, &c. With ה paragogic, Ps. xliv. 27; lxiii. 8; xciv. 17. עֶזְרָת, *Id.,* Ps. lx. 3; cviii. 13.

עֲזָרָה, f. i. q. חָצֵר. (a) *A court* of the temple, 2 Chron. iv. 9; vi. 16. (b) *A border,* or *surbase* running round the altar, Ezek. xliii. 14. 17. 20; xlv. 19.

עֵט, m. Arab. غَاط, r. غُوط, *effodit.* (a) *A graver,* Job xix. 24; Jer. xvii. 1. (b) *A pen,* Ps. xlv. 2; Jer. viii. 8.

עֵטָא, fem. Chald. i. q. עֵצָה. *Counsel, wisdom,* Dan. ii. 14.

עָטָה, v. pres. יַעֲטֶה, apoc. יַעַט. Constr. immed. Arab. عَطَا, r. عطو, *manu accepit rem;* غَطَا, r. غطو, *texit* rem. Syr. ܟܣܐ, *delevit.* (a) *Put on, covered himself, wore.* (b) *Covered.* (c) Probably, *Invested,* in a military sense. (d) Probably, *Took possession of, invested himself with:* see Is. xxii. 21. (e) Phr. עָטָה עַל שָׂפָם, *Covered his upper lip.* (a) Ps. lxxi. 13; cix. 19. 29; Is. lix. 17. (b) Ps. lxxxiv. 7. (d) Jer. xliii. 12. (e) As a mark of mourning or shame, Lev. xiii. 45; Ezek. xxiv. 17. 22; Mic. iii. 7.

Part. עֹטֶה, aff. עֹטְךָ. (a) 1 Sam. xxviii. 14; Ps. civ. 2. (c) Is. xxii. 17. In Cant. i. 7, we have כְּעֹטְיָה אַחֲרֵי. Vulg. *vagari incipiam.* Hence, Dathe reads כְּטֹעִיָּה; but Schultens, whom Gesenius follows, translates it by *quasi deliquium animi patiens.* Comp. Arab. غشي عليه, *deliquium animi passus est.*

Inf. עֲטֹה, (c) Is. xxii. 17.

Hiph. הַעֲטִיָה. *Placed as a covering,* Ps. lxxxix. 46.

עֲטִין, masc. pl. aff. עֲטִינָיו. Arab. عَطَن, *maceravit et concinnavit* pellem; عَطِين, *pellis macerata et parata. A skin prepared for holding milk or water, a bottle of skin,* Job xxi. 24. Al. non occ. See the notes.

עֲטִישָׁה, fem. plur. aff. עֲטִישֹׁתָיו, once,

עטל (457) עיט

Job xli. 10. Arab. عَطَسَ, *sternutavit.* Sneezing.

עֲטַלֵּף, m. pl. עֲטַלֵּפִים. *The bat*, Lev. xi. 19; Deut. xiv. 18; Is. ii. 20. According to Bochart., for עטמלּף, which he interprets *avis tenebrarum.* But more probably from عَطَلَ, *nubibus obductum fuit cœlum*, and עָף, for עוֹף: so Gesenius.

עָטַף, v. pres. יַעֲטֹף. Arab. عِطَافٌ, *pallium.* Syr. ܚܠܳܦ, *indutus est.* (a) *Covered*, with לְ. (b) *Covered himself, was covered.* (c) *Covered his face* in sorrow, *was overwhelmed with affliction, was exhausted.* (a) Ps. lxxiii. 6. (b) Job xxiii. 9; Ps. lxv. 14. (c) Ps. cii. 1. In Is. lvii. 16, it may be interpreted either according to (b) or (c).

Part. pass. pl. עֲטוּפִים. *Worn out, exhausted, weak*, Gen. xxx. 42; Lam. ii. 19.

Inf. עֲטֹף, (c) Ps. lxi. 3.

Niph. Infin. הֵעָטֵף, i. q. Kal, (c) Lam. ii. 11.

Hiph. Infin. הַעֲטִיף, *Id.*, Gen. xxx. 42.

Hith. pres. תִּתְעַטֵּף, *Id.*, Ps. lxxvii. 4; cvii. 5; cxliii. 4.

Inf. הִתְעַטֵּף, Ps. cxlii. 4; Lam. ii. 12; Jonah ii. 8.

עָטַר, v. pret. non occ. pres. aff. יַעְטְרֵנוּ. *Encircled.* (a) *Surrounded* in a hostile manner, with אֶל. (b) *Covered*, constr. immed. (b) Ps. v. 13.

Part. pl. עֹטְרִים. (a) 1 Sam. xxiii. 26.

Pih. עִטֵּר, עֲטָרָם, pres. aff. תְּעַטְּרֵהוּ. (a) *Crowned.* (b) *Adorned, blessed.* (a) Cant. iii. 11. (b) Ps. v. 6; lxv. 12.

Part. aff. מְעַטְּרֵי. (b) Ps. ciii. 4.

Hiph. part. f. מַעֲטִירָה. *Giving crowns*, Is. xxiii. 8.

עֲטָרָה, f. constr. עֲטֶרֶת, pl. עֲטָרוֹת. (a) *A crown, royal diadem.* (b) *Whatever adorns*, or *gives dignity.* (a) 2 Sam. xii. 30; Esth. viii. 15; Cant. iii. 11, &c. (b) Prov. xii. 4; xiv. 24; xvi. 31.

עִי, m. pl. עִיִּים, and עִיִּין, r. עוה or עיה. *A ruin, a heap of ruins, a heap*, Ps. lxxix. 1; Jer. xxvi. 18; Mic. i. 6; iii. 12.

עִיט, v. pres. יַעַט, and יָעֵט. Arab. غَاظَ, r. غِيظ, *irritavit, irâ implevit;* غَيْظ, *ira.* Syr. ܐܶܬܚܰܡܰܬ, *indignatus est;* حَمِئَ, *indignatio.* (a) *Was angry* with, with בְּ. (b) *Rushed* on with anger, *pounced* on, with אֶל. (a) 1 Sam. xxv. 14. (b) 1 Sam. xiv. 33; xv. 19.

עַיִט, m. constr. עֵיט, pl. non occ. *Any rapacious animal*, either (a) *Bird*, or (b) *Beast.* (a) Gen. xv. 11; Is. xviii. 6; Ezek. xxxix. 4. (b) Jer. xii. 9. Doubtful, Is. xlvi. 11.

עֵילוֹם, m. 2 Chron. xxxiii. 7, i. q. עוֹלָם, which see.

עָיִם, once. Arab. غَامَ, r. غيم, *sitivit;* غَيْم, *sitis, ira.* Probably, *Drought*, Is. xi. 15. בְּעָיָם רוּחוֹ, *with the drought of his wind* i. e. with a strong drying wind.

עַיִן, f. constr. עֵין, aff. עֵינִי, &c. dual עֵינַיִם, constr. dual and pl. עֵינֵי, aff. עֵינַי, עֵינֵינוּ, &c. Arab. عَيْن, *oculus; fons.* Syr. and Æth. *Id.* (a) *An eye.* (b) *The sight.* (c) *The judgment, feeling.* (d) *Appearance to the eye, colour, sparkling, glitter.* (e) עֵינוֹת, *Outward appearance.* (f) Pl. עֲיָנוֹת, constr. עֵינֹת, *A fountain, spring.* Phrr. (g) עַיִן בְּעַיִן, *Face to face.* (h) עֵין הָאָרֶץ, *The face of the earth.* (i) לְעֵינֵי, *In the sight of, before.* (k) בְּעֵינֵי, *In the judgment of* —, as [1] חֵן בְּעֵינֵי [2] — הָרַע, [3] — הַיָּשָׁר. (a) Gen. xiii. 14; xx. 16; xliv. 21, &c. (b) 2 Sam. xx. 6; Ps. xxxiii. 18. (c) Deut. vi. 16; xv. 9; xxviii. 56, &c. (d) Lev. xiii. 55; Num. xi. 7; Prov. xxiii. 31; Ezek. i. 4. 7, &c. (e) 1 Sam. xvi. 7. (f) Gen. xvi. 7; xxiv. 28; Exod. xv. 27; 2 Chron. xxxii. 3, &c. (g) Num. xiv. 14; Is. lii. 8. (h) Exod. x. 5. 15; Num. xxii. 5. 11. (i) Gen. xxiii. 11; Exod. iv. 30; xix. 11, &c. (k), [1] Gen. vi. 8; xxxiii. 8. 15, &c. [2] Deut. ix. 18; xxxi. 29, &c. [3] Deut. xii. 28; xxi. 9, &c. Hence—

עִין, v. Part. Keri, עוֹיֵן. *Watching*, with an evil eye, 1 Sam. xviii. 9.

עָיֵף, f. עֲיֵפָה, pl. עֲיֵפִים. See יָעֵף. (a) *Weary.* (b) *Parched*, (a) Gen. xxv. 29; Deut. xxv. 18; Judg. viii. 14, &c. (b) Job xxii. 7; Ps. lxiii. 2; cxliii. 6; Prov. xxv. 25; Is. xxxii. 2, &c.

עָיֵף, v. עָיְפָה. *Is weary*, Jer. iv. 31. Al. non occ.

עֵיפָה, f. r. עוּף. (a) *Darkness*, Amos iv. 13. (b) With ה paragogic, עֵיפָתָה, for

3 N

עֲיפָתָה. *Great, singular darkness,* Job x. 22.

עַיִר, masc. aff. עֲירֹה, pl. עֲיָרִים. Arab. عَيْر, *asinus,* tum potissimum *asinus silvester.* (a) *An ass.* (b) Pec. *A male ass.* (c) *A young ass.* (a) Judg. x. 4; xii. 14; Is. xxx. 6. 24. (b) Gen. xxxii. 16. (c) Gen. xlix. 11; Job xi. 12; Zech. ix. 9.

עִיר, f. aff. עִירוֹ, &c. pl. עָרִים (once, Judg. x. 4, עֲיָרִים), constr. עָרֵי, aff. עָרָיו, &c. *A city, town, settlement,* Gen. iv. 17; xi. 4; xxiv. 10, &c. עִיר חוֹמָה, *a walled town,* Lev. xxv. 29. עִיר הַמְּלוּכָה, *the royal residence,* 2 Sam. xii. 26. עִיר דָוִד, *city of David,* i. e. his residence, Zion, 1 Kings iii. 1; 1 Chron. xi. 5, &c. The origin of the word is doubtful: according to Castell, it is related to עִיר, and קִרְיָה.

עִיר, m. Chald. pl. עִירִין, r. עוּר. *A watcher,* applied apparently to an angel, Dan. iv. 10. 14. 20.

עִיר, in Ps. lxxiii. 20; Jer. xv. 8; Hos. vii. 4; and xi. 9, is variously interpreted. Gesenius compares the Arab. غَار, r. غور, *ferbuit æstu dies;* and hence deduces the ideas of *heat, anger,* and *fear.* Others consider the word as equivalent to עַיִר, and to be derived from it. All these passages, however, may be satisfactorily interpreted from the two significations of עִיר, already given, and that of the verb עור.

עֵילָם, and עָרָם, m. pl. עֵירֻמִּים. Arab. عَرَم, *carne nudavit os;* عُرَام, *nudatus carne.* (a) *Naked,* Gen. iii. 7. 10, 11; Ezek. xviii. 7. 16. (b) *Nakedness,* Deut. xxviii. 45. See עָרוֹם.

עַיִשׁ, see עָשׁ.

עַכָּבִישׁ, *The spider,* Job viii. 14; Is. lix. 5. Arab. عَنْكَبُوت, *Id.*

עַכְבָּר, m. pl. constr. עַכְבְּרֵי, aff. עַכְבְּרֵיכֶם. *The jerboa.* Dipus jaculus of Linnæus, Lev. xi. 29; 1 Sam. vi. 4, 5. 11. 18; Is. lxvi. 17. Arab. عَكَابِر, plur. *mares murium, quibus;* يَرْبُوع, *nomen est.*

עֶכֶס, m. pl. עֲכָסִים. Arab. عِكَاس, *funis qui ab anteriore oris parte cameli religatur ad interiorem pedem.* (a) *A fetter,* Prov. vii. 22. (b) Pl. *Ornamental foot-rings,* worn by the Jewish women, Is. iii. 18. Hence—

עָכַס, v. Pih. pres. תְּעַכַּסְנָה. *Wear foot-rings, make their foot-rings sound,* Is. iii. 16.

עָכַר, v. pres. aff. יַעְכָּרְךָ. Constr. immed. it. med. אֶת. Arab. عَكَر, *turbidus, fœculentus fuit.* II. *Fœculentum reddidit. Troubled* water; hence, metaph. *Troubled* in mind, or circumstances, *caused sorrow, vexation,* or *disgrace,* Gen. xxxiv. 30; Josh. vii. 25; 1 Sam. xiv. 30; 1 Kings xviii. 18. Part. עֹכֵר, aff. pl. עֹכְרֵי, Judg. xi. 35; 1 Kings xviii. 17, &c.

Niph. נֶעְכַּר, Pass. of Kal. *Was irritated, excited,* Ps. xxxix. 3.

Part. fem. נֶעְכֶּרֶת, as a subst. *Vexation, trouble,* Prov. xv. 6.

עַכְשׁוּב, once, Ps. cxl. 4. *An asp.* So the Versions generally. Bochart. derives the name from عَكَس, *invertit, præpostere disposuit.*

עַל, and עֲלֵי, prep. aff. עָלַי, עָלֶיךָ, עָלַיִךְ, עָלָיו, עָלֶיהָ, עָלֵינוּ, עֲלֵיכֶם, עֲלֵיהֶם, and עָלֵימוֹ, r. עלה. Arab. عَلَى, *super, supra.* (a) *Upon, on:* denoting, [1] Place, [2] Instrument or means, [3] Manner, [4] Burden, [5] Duty or office. (b) *Above, over:* [1] In place; [2] In rank or power, [3] In quantity or number. (c) *Beside, near, before.* (d) *Besides, over and above.* (e) *In reference to:* [1] *Concerning.* [2] *Towards.* [3] *Against.* (f) *For:* [1] *On account of.* [2] *In behalf of.* (a), [1] Gen. iii. 14; Lev. xvi. 21; 2 Kings iv. 34, &c. [2] Gen. xxvii. 40; Deut. viii. 3; Dan. viii. 25, &c. [3] Ps. cx. 4. [4] Is. i. 14. [5] Ezra x. 4; Neh. xiii. 13. (b), [1] Gen. i. 20; xix. 23; Ps. xxix. 3, &c. [2] Gen. xli. 33; 1 Sam. xv. 17; Ps. xcv. 3, &c. [3] Gen. xlix. 26; Exod. xvi. 5; Num. iii. 46, &c. (c) Gen. xvi. 7; Exod. xviii. 13; Judg. iii. 19, &c. (d) Gen. xxxi. 50; Num. xxviii. 10; Deut. xix. 9, &c. (e), [1] Gen. xviii. 19; 1 Kings v. 13; Is. xxxvii. 9, &c. [2] Gen. xix. 16; 2 Sam. xx. 8; Ps. ciii. 13, &c. [3] Is. xxix. 8; Jer. xi. 19; Amos vii. 9, &c. (f), [1] Gen. xx. 3; Lev. iv. 3; Neh. x. 33, &c. [2] 1 Kings ii. 18; 2 Kings x. 3; Job xlii. 8, &c. מֵעַל, [1]

עַל (459) עָלָה

From upon, Exod. xl. 36. [2] *From above*, Gen. xxvii. 39. מֵעַל לְ, *Above*, Gen. i. 7.

עַל, Chald. aff. עֲלֹיְהִי, עֲלַיָּא, עֲלֵיהוֹן, *Id.*, Ezra iv. 12; v. 3; Dan. vi. 19, &c.

עָל, m. r. עלה. *The Lofty One, the Most High*, Hos. vii. 16; xi. 7.

עֹל, and עוֹל, m. aff. עֻלְּךָ, עֻלּוֹ, עֻלֵּנוּ, עֻלָּם, עֹלָם. Arab. عُلّ, *vinculum cervicis, sive ex ferro sit, sive è loro*. (a) *A yoke*. (b) Metaph. *Servitude*. (a) Num. xix. 2; Deut. xxi. 3; 1 Sam. vi. 7, &c. (b) Deut. xxviii. 48; 1 Kings xii. 4; Is. ix. 3, &c.

עֵלָּא, Chald. with מִן. *Above*, Dan. vi. 3.

עָלֵג, m. pl. עִלְגִים, once, Is. xxxii. 4. Arab. علج, *barbarus, religionem Muhammedis non profitens. A foreigner, stammerer*.

עָלָה, v. pres. יַעֲלֶה, apoc. יַעַל. Constr. abs. it. immed. it. med. אֶל, עַל, בְּ, לְ. (a) *Went up, came up*. (b) *Arose, of the dawn*. (c) *Grew up, grew*. (d) *Increased*. (e) *Produced*. (f) *Was put upon*. (a) Gen. xlix. 4; Exod. xii. 38; xix. 3; Josh. viii. 20; Judg. xxi. 5, &c. (b) Gen. xix. 15; xxxii. 26. (c) Gen. xl. 10; Deut. xxix. 22; Is. v. 6, &c. (d) 2 Chron. xviii. 34. (e) Prov. xxiv. 31. (f) Num. xix. 2; Judg. xvi. 17; Ezek. xliv. 17, &c.

Inf. עֲלוֹת, constr. עֲלוֹת, aff. עֲלֹתִי, &c., Gen. xlvi. 4; Exod. xix. 12; Deut. ix. 9, &c.

Imp. עֲלֵה, עֲלִי, pl. עֲלוּ, Gen. xxxv. 1; 1 Sam. xxv. 35; Jer. xlvi. 4, &c.

Part. עֹלֶה, f. עֹלָה; pl. עֹלִים, f. עֹלוֹת, Gen. xxxviii. 13; Judg. xx. 31; 1 Sam. ix. 11. (c) Gen. xli. 22.

Niph. נַעֲלָה. (a) *Is exalted*, of God, Ps. xlvii. 10; xcvii. 9. (b) *Was lifted up*, Ezek. ix. 3. (c) *Was led away*, 2 Sam. ii. 27. (d) *Was taken up*, Ezek. xxxvi. 3.

Inf. הֵעָלוֹת, (c) Jer. xxxvii. 11.

Hiph. הֶעֱלָה, pres. יַעֲלֶה, apoc. יַעַל. Causat. of Kal. (a) *Caused to go or come up, carried or brought up*. (b) *Offered a burnt-offering*. (c) *Placed a thing on another*. (d) *Placed, set up*. (a) 1 Sam. xii. 6; 2 Kings xvii. 14; Neh. ix. 18, &c. (b) Gen. viii. 20; Lev. xvii. 8; 2 Chron. viii. 12, &c. (c) 1 Kings x. 17; 2 Chron. iii. 14; Lam. ii. 10, &c. (d) Num. viii. 2.

Inf. הַעֲלֹה, constr. הַעֲלוֹת, הַעֲלוֹתִי, &c., Jer. xi. 7; Ezek. xxiii. 46; xxvi. 3, &c.

Imp. הַעַל, f. הַעֲלִי; pl. הַעֲלוּ, 1 Sam. xxviii. 11; Exod. xxxiii. 12; Jer. li. 27, &c.

Part. מַעֲלֶה, constr. מַעֲלֵה, aff. מַעֲלְךָ, f. מַעֲלָה, constr. מַעֲלַת; pl. מַעֲלִים, constr. מַעֲלֵי, Lev. xi. 45; Deut. xiv. 7; xx. 1; Lev. xi. 26; 2 Sam. vi. 15, &c.

Hoph. הֹעֲלָה, הֹעֲלָתָה, Pass. of Hiph. (a) Nah. ii. 7. (b) Judg. vi. 28. (c) 2 Chron. xx. 34.

Hith. pres. apoc. יִתְעָל. *Lifts up himself*, Jer. li. 3.

עָלֶה, masc. constr. עֲלֵה, aff. עָלֵהוּ; pl. constr. עֲלֵי, aff. עָלֶיהָ, עָלָיו, r. עלה. (a) *A leaf*. (b) *Foliage*. (a) Lev. xxvi. 36; Gen. viii. 11, &c. (b) Gen. iii. 7; Jer. xvii. 8, &c.

עִלָּה, f. Chald. r. עלל. Arab. عِلَّة, *causa, prætextus. A pretext, ground for complaint*, Dan. vi. 5, 6.

עֹלָה, and עוֹלָה, f. constr. עֹלַת, aff. עֹלָתִי; pl. עֹלוֹת, aff. עֹלֹתֶיךָ, r. עלה. (a) *A burnt-offering*, Lev. i. 10; vii. 8; xvi. 24, &c. (b) *A step*, Ezek. xl. 26. (c) Contraction of עַוְלָה, Ps. lviii. 3; lxiv. 7.

עִלָּה, pl. fem. עִלָּן, Chald. *Id*. (a) Ezra vi. 9.

עָלְוָה, Hos. x. 9, for עַוְלָה, which see.

עֲלוּמִים, pl. m. aff. עֲלוּמֶיךָ, עֲלוּמַי, עֲלָמֵנוּ, r. עלם. *Youth*, *time of youth*, Job xx. 11; xxxiii. 25; Ps. lxxxix. 46; xc. 8; Is. liv. 4.

עֲלוּקָה, f. once. Arab. عَلَق, *depastus fuit*; عَلِق, *adhæsit, affixus fuit*; عَلَقَة, *hirudo. A leech*, Prov. xxx. 15.

עָלַז, v. pret. non occ. pres. יַעֲלֹז, i. q. עלס, and עלץ. *Rejoiced*, applied occasionally to inanimate things, 2 Sam. i. 20; Ps. lx. 8; xcvi. 12; Prov. xxiii. 9, &c. Constr. abs. it. with עַל, or בְּ, of the subject of joy.

Inf. עֲלֹז, Is. xxiii. 12.

Imp. f. עֲלִי, pl. עֲלוּ, Ps. lxviii. 5.

עָלֵז, m. *Rejoicing, one who rejoices*, Is. v. 14.

עֲלָטָה, f. Arab. غَطَل, *nubibus obductum fuit* cœlum; غَطْلَة, *magna obscuritas noctis. Darkness*, Gen. xv. 17; Ezek. xii. 6, 7. 12.

עֱלִי, m. once. *A pestle*, Prov. xxvii. 22: r. עלה, from its *rising*.

עֲלִי, f. עֲלִיָה, pl. עֲלִיוֹת, r. עלה. *Upper*, Josh. xv. 19; Judg. i. 15.

עֱלִי, m. Chald. def. עִלָּיָא. (a) *High, supreme, of God*, Dan. iii. 26. 32; v. 18. 21. (b) *The supreme God, the Most High*, Dan. iv. 14. 21, 22. 29. 31; vii. 25. See עֶלְיוֹן.

עֲלִיָה, f. עֲלִיַת, aff. עֲלִיָתוֹ; pl. עֲלִיוֹת, aff. עֲלִיּוֹתָיו, r. עלה. Arab. عِلِّيَّة, *cœnaculum*. (a) *An upper room, a chamber*, Judg. iii. 23; 2 Sam. xix. 1; 2 Kings i. 2; Jer. xxii. 14, &c. (b) *An ascent, a stair-case*, 2 Chron. ix. 4.

עֶלְיוֹן, f. עֶלְיוֹנָה, pl. f. עֶלְיוֹנוֹת, r. עלה. *High*, in situation or power. (a) *Lofty*, of a building. (b) *Higher, upper*, in place. (c) *High*, in rank. (d) *Highest, supreme*, of God. (e) *The Most High*. (a) 1 Kings ix. 8; 2 Chron. vii. 21. (b) Gen. xl. 17; Josh. xvi. 5; 2 Kings xviii. 17; Ezek. xlii. 5, &c. (c) Deut. xxvi. 19; xxviii. 1. (d) Gen. xiv. 18—20. 22; Ps. vii. 18; xlvii. 3, &c. (e) Num. xxiv. 16; Deut. xxxii. 8; Ps. ix. 3, &c.

עֶלְיוֹן, Chald. pl. עֶלְיוֹנִין, *Id*. (e) Dan. vii. 22. 25.

עָלִיז, f. עֲלִיזָה, pl. עֲלִיזִים, constr. עֲלִיזֵי, r. עלז. *Rejoicing; habitually rejoicing, or expressing joy*, Is. xiii. 3; xxii. 2; xxiv. 8, &c.

עָלִיל, m. once, *A crucible*, Ps. xii. 7; r. עלל. Comp. Æth. ዐለለ : *separavit, segregavit*.

עֲלִילָה, f. pl. עֲלִילוֹת, aff. עֲלִילֹתָיו, &c., r. עלל. (a) *Action*. (b) *An action*: either, [1] *A noble action*, or [2] *A wicked action*. (a) Ps. xiv. 1; lxvi. 5; cxli. 4. (b) 1 Sam. ii. 3. [1] Ps. lxxvii. 13, &c. [2] Ezek. xx. 43; xxiv. 14; Zeph. iii. 11, &c. שָׂם לָהּ עֲלִילֹת דְּבָרִים, *ascribed actions to her which have no existence except in his words*, Deut. xxii. 14. 17.

עֲלִילִיָּה, fem. r. עלל. *Action*, Jer. xxxii. 19.

עֲלִיצוּת, f. aff. עֲלִיצָתָם, r. עלץ. *Rejoicing, ground of rejoicing*, Hab. iii. 14.

עֲלִית, f. Chald. aff. עֲלִיתֵהּ, i. q. עֲלִיָה. *An upper room, a chamber*, Dan. vi. 11.

עָלַל, v. Kal non occ. Arab. عَلَّ, *bibendum dedit secundâ vice; causam præ-* buit. Syr. ܥܰܠ, *effecit, causam præbuit; it. ingressus est. Entered into; did effectually or habitually.*

Pih. עוֹלֵל, עִלֵּל, pres. יְעוֹלֵל. (a) *Made to enter*. (b) *Treated, acted towards*, with לְ. (c) *Affected, affected painfully*, with לְ. (d) *Repeated an action, went over again, gleaned, immed.* (e) *Acted as a child*. See עוֹלֵל. (a) Job xvi. 15. (b) Lam. i. 22; ii. 20. (c) Lam. iii. 51. (d) Lev. xix. 10; Deut. xxiv. 21; Judg. xx. 45; Jer. vi. 9.
Inf. עֹלֵל, (d) Jer. vi. 9.
Imp. עוֹלֵל, (b) Lam. i. 22.
Part. מְעוֹלֵל, (e) Is. iii. 12.
Puh. עוֹלַל, Pass. of Pih. *Was done or caused*, Lam. i. 12.
Hith. הִתְעַלֵּל, constr. med. בְּ. (a) *Exerted himself in action, put forth his power against*. (b) *Abused his power over, insulted*. (c) *Practised*. (a) Exod. x. 2; 1 Sam. vi. 6. (b) 1 Sam. xxxi. 4; Judg. xix. 25, &c.
Inf. הִתְעֹלֵל, (c) Ps. cxli. 4.

עֲלַל, v. Chald. עַל, עֲלַל. *Entered*, Dan. ii. 16; v. 10. See *Keri*.
Part. pl. עָלִין, Dan. iv. 4; v. 8.
Aph. הַנְעֵל, Causat. of Peḥal. *Brought in*, Dan. ii. 25; vi. 19.
Inf. הַנְעָלָה, Dan. iv. 3. הֶעְלָה, Dan. v. 7.
Imp. aff. הַעֵלְנִי, Dan. ii. 24.
Hoph. הֻעַל, Pass. of Hiph., Dan. v. 13. 15.

עֹלֵלוֹת, pl. fem. constr. עֹלְלוֹת, r. עלל. *What is left for gleaning, gleanings*, Judg. viii. 2; Is. xvii. 6; xxiv. 12; Jer. xlix. 9; Obad. 5; Mic. vii. 1.

עֶלֶם, masc. — plur. non. occ. —

עַלְמָה, fem. — plur. עֲלָמוֹת. —
Arab. غُلَام, *adolescens, juvenis plenæ ætatis*. Syr. ܓܰܕܡܳܐ, fem. ܓܰܕܡܬܳܐ, *id*. The leading notion seems to have consisted in *excitement, impression*, or the like; and thence to have extended itself to *youth*, as the season peculiarly subject to it; thence *growth*. Arab. cogn. اَلَم, *dolor*; اَنَف, conj. v. *benignè tractavit*; اَبَّ, *propulit*; اَبَّة, *cupido*; غَلْمَة, id. Syr. ܕܟܡ, *iratus est*. Cogn. ܕܟܒ, *injuria affecit*. Thence, to *knowledge*, as عَلَم,

עלם (461) עלם

signum, indicium, or mark impressed: meton. عِلْم, *scientia, &c.* Thence to the *world* (עוֹלָם), as containing marks of the Divine wisdom (Ps. xix.) And thence, as this is but partially discoverable to man, probably arose the notion of *hiding, concealing; eternity*, as an indefinite period, &c. Æth. ዐለመ: *æternitati consecravit*. Also the Samaritan, עלם, *connivit*. Masc. but twice, 1 Sam. xvii. 56; xx. 22; i. q. נַעַר, vr. 21. *Youth, young man*. Fem. seven times only, viz., Gen. xxiv. 43; Exod. ii. 8; Is. vii. 14; Ps. lxviii. 26; Prov. xxx. 19; Cant. i. 3; vi. 8. In all of which *a young unmarried*, but *marriageable, woman*, or *virgin*, must necessarily be meant. The place most disputed has been Is. vii. 14, where Gesenius says, with the rashness peculiar to his school, "*de conjuge juvenili, recens nupta*" . . . LXX. male reddunt παρθένος. But, is there any usage justifying this? Certainly he has produced none. בְּתוּלָה, he tells us, would properly express *virgin*. And is this liable to no exception? See Joel i. 8. A parallel to which cannot be found with עַלְמָה occurring in it. This word, therefore, is less decisive than the word עַלְמָה, as to the meaning of *virgin*. If this word, then, signifies *marriageable young woman* only, it cannot be shown also to signify *married young woman*. If Aquila, Symmachus, and Theodotion, rendered it by νεᾶνις, it ought to be remembered that this was done for *a party purpose*, such as that which has influenced Gesenius. Nor will his appeal—with Michaelis—to the usage of the German *jungfrau*, avail any thing here: it is to Hebrew, not to German, usages that the appeal must be made: and no such appeal can be made in this place. Besides, our passage would be without point or meaning, as Michaelis has justly observed, were a *young married woman* only meant (Supp. Lex. Heb. sub voce); much more out of place would the name of *Immanuel* be, as applied to such issue. Comp. Is. viii. 8; Matt. i. 23. Jerome has, on Is. vii. 14, "*Lingua quoque Punica, quæ de Hebræorum fontibus manare dicitur, proprie virgo* ALMA *appellatur.*" Why has Gesenius, who so often appeals to the Punic, omitted to do so on this occasion? On the use of the definite article, as prefixed in this place, see Gram. artt. 180. 14; 221. On the force of the pres. tense in יָתֵן, art. 231. 19, note.

And, on the exegetical sense of the place, see my Sermons and Dissertations (London, 1830), p. 273, seq. In the terms, הָעַלְמָה הָרָה, therefore, i. e. *the virgin*, or *marriageable young woman, shall be with child, a married woman* could not possibly have been meant; neither could an unmarried young woman illegitimately, for this was *folly* and corruption in Israel, and could not have had place here: nor could any other except some *young woman*, of whom intimation had formerly been given, as the addition of the article requires. "*The woman's seed*" (Gen. iii. 15; Gal. iv. 4), as already predicted, and applied by inspired authority, concurs well with every particular connected with this place; while every other attempt to interpret it presents some insuperable difficulty: the usual interpretation, therefore, is the true one.

עָלַם, v. Kal non occ. except part. pass. עָלוּם, aff. pl. עֲלֻמֵנוּ. *Our hidden things, sins*, Ps. xc. 8; but *sins of youth* (Arab. غُلُومَة, *adolescentia*), might as well be meant. Comp. Job xx. 11. See my note here, and comp. Ps. xxv. 7. And so the Targumist. On the etym. see עוֹלָמִים, עָלַם, above.

Niph. נֶעֱלַם, pres. non occ. Constr. med. מִן, it. abs. *Became, was, hidden, concealed*, Lev. iv. 13; v. 2, 3; Num. v. 13; Job xxviii. 21; 2 Chron. ix. 2.

Part. נֶעְלָם, pl. נַעֲלָמִים, 1 Kings x. 3; Eccl. xii. 14; Ps. xxvi. 4.

— f. נַעֲלָמָה, Nah. iii. 11.

Niph. הֶעְלִים, pres. אַעְלִים, תַּעְלִים. Constr. immed. obj. it. with מִן, of person or thing. *Hide, conceal*, 2 Kings iv. 27; Is. i. 15; Ezek. xxii. 26; Job xlii. 3: it. med. בְּ, 1 Sam. xii. 3: לְ, Ps. x. 1; Lam. iii. 56. The context will sufficiently point out the feelings of the writer in each case.

Infin. הַעְלֵם, Lev. xx. 4, only.

Part. מַעְלִים, Prov. xxviii. 27; Job xlii. 3, al. non occ.

Hithp. הִתְעַלֵּם, pres. יִתְעַלֵּם, i. q. Niph. Constr. abs. it. med. מִן, Deut. xxii. 1. 4; Ps. lv. 2; Is. lviii. 7; Job vi. 16. See my note.

עָלַם, def. עָלְמָא, pl. עָלְמִין, def. עָלְמַיָּא, i. q. Heb. עוֹלָם. See עֶלֶם above. An indefinite period of time, either, (a) future, or (b) past. (a) *For ever, eternal*, Dan. iii. 33; iv. 31; vii. 18. 26. Pl., Dan. ii. 4. 44; vi.

עלם (462) עלף

18, &c. (b) *Eternity; everlasting*, Dan. ii. 2; Ezra iv. 15.

עלמות, twice only, Ps. ix. 1, עַל־מוּת; xlvi. 1, עַל־עֲלָמוֹת. Of these, and similar terms, as occurring in the titles of some Psalms, nothing certain is, or can be known. Nor is it likely that they are of any great importance. Rosenmüller's "Explicatio Dictionum nonnullarum, in Psalmorum titulis," need only to be read over to afford sufficient proof of this. It will be found prefixed to his first volume of Scholia on the Psalms. The expression עַל־מוּת, occurs again, Ps. xlviii. 15, where Gesenius tells us the context requires that it should be, "i. q. עוֹלָם, *æternitas* .... *in perpetuum*—LXX. εἰς τοὺς αἰῶνας"—which, perhaps, may be fairly doubted. The Targumist has, "*in diebus pueritiæ nostræ*," reading עלמות, in one word, with a sense deduced from עֶלֶם, above. The Syr. read, עַל־מָוֶת, which is most probably the true reading; to be taken in the sense of אֶל־מָוֶת, *to death, usque ad mortem*, i. e. ever, so long as we live; corresponding in this way to the עוֹלָם preceding. In this case the rendering of the LXX. will be rather paraphrastical: a thing common enough with them.

עֵילָמִי, m. Patronymic of עֵילָם, Chald. def. pl. עֵלְמָיֵא. *Elamite*, Ezra iv. 9.

עלס, v. pres. יַעֲלֹס, cogn. עלץ, עלז. Constr. abs. *Exult, rejoice*, Job xx. 18, only. See my note.

Niph. f. נֶעֱלָסָה. *Becomes exulting*, i. e. in exhibiting its power, Job xxxix. 13, only. The place is elliptical, requiring the repetition of הֶאֱמִין, from the preceding verse, with בְּנִכְרְדָנִים כִּי, &c. See my note. Al. non occ.

Hithp. pres. with ה, parag. נִתְעַלְּסָה, i. q. Niph. *Let us be exulting, rejoicing*, once, Prov. vii. 18.

עלע, v. pres. pl. Pih. יְעַלְּעוּ. *They gulp, swallow down*. This word is probably an ὀνοματοποιητικόν, i. e. so formed as to imitate the sound of the thing meant: once only, Job xxxix. 30. See my note on the place. Arab. عَلّ, *bibendum dedit secunda vice*, &c.; وَلَع, *cupidus fuit;* وَلَغ, *insertâ* n vas linguâ *sorbuit conis*, &c.

עלע, m. pl. עִלְעִין, Chald. i. q. Heb. צֵלָע. *A rib*, once, Dan. vii. 5.

עלף, v. Kal non occ. Arab. غَلِفَ, *operuit*. Comp. עָטָה, עָטַף. (a) *Clothe, cover*. (b) *Faint*.

Puh. עֻלְּפוּ, *Became overwhelmed, faint*, Is. li. 20. The transition from *clothe* to *faint* may have originated in the languor experienced, in hot countries, from too much clothing. Al. non occ.

Part. f. מְעֻלֶּפֶת. *Covered, overlaid*, Cant. v. 14.

Hithp. pres. יִתְעַלָּף. (a) *Become clothed, disguised* (comp. בגד), Gen. xxxviii. 14. (b) *Became faint, swooning*, Jonah iv. 8; Amos viii. 13, al. non occ.

עֻלְפֶּה, m.—pl. non occ., once, Ezek. xxxi. 15.—LXX. ἐξελύθησαν: reading עֻלְּפָה, in Puh.; and so the Syr. Arab. and Vulg. It is probably the true reading.—*Languor, fainting*. See עלף above. Gesenius makes ה‍ָ‍ paragogic, apparently without good ground; the word in its present form is adverse to all analogy.

עָלַץ, v. pres. יַעֲלֹץ, i. q. עלו, עָלַם. Constr. abs. it. med. בְּ, in; לְ, against; לִפְנֵי, before. *Exult, rejoice.* לִפְנֵי בַיהֹוָה —, *my heart exults in Jehovah*, 1 Sam. ii. 1; Ps. v. 12; ix. 3; Prov. xi. 10. לִי אוֹיְבַי —, *mine enemies against me*, Ps. xxv. 2. לִפְנֵי אֱלֹהִים —, —, *before God*, Ps. lxviii. 4. Abs. 1 Chron. xvi. 32.

Infin. עֲלֹץ, constr. Prov. xxviii. 12. Al. non occ.

עַם, m. pl. עַמִּים, rarely עֲמָמִים. Constr. עַמֵּי, rarely עַמְמֵי. r. עמם. Cogn. עמה, גמם, &c. Arab. عَمّ, *cœtus hominum;* v. عَمّ, *communis fuit*. Cogn. جَمّ, غَمّ, *pressit, strinxit*. Comp. צור. Whence, prep. עִם, *with*. Syr. ܥܰܡ, id. And, as some think, the Lat. *con, cum*. Gr. σύν; γάμος; κοινός; ἅμα, ὁμοῦ, &c. Germ. *sammt, &c.* (a) *People*, generally, Is. xl. 7; xlii. 5; xliv. 7: to which Gesenius adds Job xii. 2. See my note on the place. (b) *Any people*, Jew or Gentile, good or bad, as the context may determine: as, עַם יְהֹוָה, — *of Jehovah*, Exod. xv. 3. הַקָּהָל —, *of the congregation*, Lev. xvi. 33. יִשְׂרָאֵל —, *of Israel*, 2 Sam. xviii. 7. יְהוּדָה —, *of Judah*, Ib. xix. 41. הָאָרֶץ —, Gen. xxiii. 12. אֶחָד —, —, Ib. xi. 6. עֲסָרָב —, *great people*, Gen. L. 20. קְשֵׁה־עֹרֶף — *of hard, stiff, neck*. עָנִי —, *afflicted, poor,*

עם (463) עם

2 Sam. xxii. 28. כְּמוֹשׁ, — *of Chemosh*, Num. xxi. 29, &c. Also, as qualified by a periphrasis, בְּנֵי יִשְׂרָאֵל, — *of the children of Israel*, זוּ גָאָלְתָּ, — *whom thou hast avenged* (redeemed), Exod. xv. 13. Comp. vr. 16. אֲשֶׁר לֹא יָדַעְתָּ, — *whom thou knowest not.* Deut. xxviii. 33. נוֹשַׁע בַּיהוָה מָגֵן עֶזְרֶךָ, — *saved by*, or, *in Jehovah the shield of thy help*, Ib. xxxiii. 29. רָב כַּחוֹל, — *numerous as the sand*, &c., Josh. xi. 4. And so with prepp. עַמּוֹ, עַמִּי, *his people, my people, &c.* Hence, applied to the tribes of Israel, עַם זְבֻלוּן, Judg. v. 18, &c. — to the members of a family, either living or dead, Lev. xxi. 1. 4; xix. 16; Gen. xxv. 8. 17, &c. *The people* generally, as distinguished from their leaders, 1 Kings xii. 16; 2 Kings xi. 17, &c. Thence, as *soldiers*, Judg. v. 2, &c. And so the pronouns prefixed, or separate, the definite article, &c. הָעָם הַזֶּה, 2 Sam. xvi. 18. And, indeed, in every case, the qualifying terms sufficiently determine the precise force of this word. Pl., Deut. iv. 27; Ps. ix. 12, &c. Rarer form, Neh. ix. 22. 24; Judg. v. 14. Aff. עַמִּי, &c.; rare form, עֲמָמַי, Judg. l. c.

עָם, m. def. עַמָּא, עַמָּה, pl. def. עַמְמַיָּא. Chald. Dan. iii. 4, 7. 31; v. 19; vi. 26; vii. 14, &c.

עִם, prep. See עַם above. Syr. ܥܰܡ, Arab. metath. مَعَ, *With*; which is universally the meaning of our Hebrew word, with such synonymous shade of difference as its situation may require; e. g. (as compared with Noldius, p. 572, seq.) *With* (cum.) צַדִּיק עִם רָשָׁע, *just with unjust*, Gen. xviii. 23; Cant. iv. 14, &c. (*A, ab*) חֵלֶק... עִם אֵל..., *portion with God*, Job xxvii. 13. (*Ad*) יֵאָמֵן דְּבָרְךָ עִם דָּוִד, *let thy word be established with David*, 2 Chron. i. 9. (*Apud*) יָשַׁבְתָּ עִמּוֹ, *reside thou with him*, Gen. xxvii. 44, &c. (*Contra*) וַיִּלָּחֶם עִם יִשְׂרָאֵל, *he fought with Israel*, Exod. xvii. 8; Num. xx. 3, &c. (*Coram*) יִגְדַּל... עִם יְהוָה, 1 Sam. ii. 21. But, *became great* (i. e. grew up in estimation) *with Jehovah*, may be the true sense here. Comp. Luke ii. 52, παρὰ Θεῷ; 1 Kings xv. 14; Ps. lxxviii. 37, &c. (*Erga*) עֲשִׂיתֶם... עִם בֵּית אֲבִי חֶסֶד, *ye do kindly with the house of my father*, Josh. ii. 12; 2 Sam. iii. 8, &c. (*Et*) וְזִכְרוֹן לֶחָכָם עִם הַכְּסִיל, *memory of a wise man, with* (that of) *a fool*, Eccl. ii. 16. Comp. 1 Sam. xvi. 12, &c. (*Aeque ac*) Much in the same way, Eccl. ii. 16; 1 Chron. xxv. 8, &c. (*In* = בְּ) רוּחַ אַחֶרֶת עִמּוֹ, *another spirit with him*, Num. xiv. 24. Comp. Deut. viii. 5; Josh. xiv. 7, &c. (*Inter*, together *with*) Is. xxxviii. 11; Ps. lxix. 29, &c. (*Nempe*) עִם בְּנִי עִם יִצְחָק, *with my son, with Isaac*, Gen. xxi. 10; 2 Sam. ii. 5; Eccl. vii. 11. Noldius makes עִם equal to Lat. *præ*; but with no good reason. (*Præter*) וְעִמְּךָ, "*præter te*." But this is unnecessary. The Psalmist asks, Whom have I in heaven? The context necessarily supplies the answer, God. He proceeds, *with thee*, I desire none on earth: none *besides thee*. The σύν of St. Luke, xxiv. 21, is not, therefore, in point. (*Pro*) 1 Sam. xiv. 45; Dan. xi. 39: a moment's inspection will show require no such translation; *with* being sufficiently applicable. (*Quamdiu*) Ps. lxxii. 5, עִם שֶׁמֶשׁ, *with* (the duration of) *the sun*. (*Quum, quando*) עִם הָעֲלוֹת, *with the ascending*, Ezra i. 11. (*Sicut*) עִם יְהוָה, *with Jehovah*, i. e. in his estimation, Deut. xviii. 13, &c. The same may be said of *sub*, in 2 Chron. xvii. 14, &c. *Super*, Job xxx. 1. *Usque ad*, Dan. iii. 33: see below. The truth is, in all such cases as these, much must rest upon the taste of the translator; for, although *with*, *along with*, or some such rendering, will always, perhaps, afford an obvious sense: yet, it will not always afford the *exact* and *full* sense which the preceding or following terms, or both, adopted by the translator may particularly require. And, into questions of this sort Lexicographers cannot enter. Nor need they specify the verbs requiring this or that sense in this particle; the discretion of the translator ought to look to this.

With *prefixes* and *affixes*, as these may require, e. g. וְעִם, *and with*, Gen. xxxiii. 1, &c. מֵעִם, *from with Jehovah*, i. e. by his estimation, Ruth ii. 12; 1 Sam. xvi. 14, &c. שָׁעִם, *who with*, 1 Chron. v. 20. שָׁ־עִם, Eccl. i. 11.

עִמִּי, *with me*, Lev. xxvi. 23. 40, &c. עִמְּךָ, Gen. xxi. 22. עִמְּכָה, 1 Sam. i. 26. עִמּוֹ, *with him*, Gen. xiii. 1, &c. עִמָּהּ, *with her*, Gen. iii. 6, &c. עִמָּנוּ, *with us*, Exod. x. 26, &c. עִמָּכֶם, *with you*, Gen. xlii. 38, &c. עִמָּהֶם, *with them*, Num. xxii. 12, &c. The fem. עִמָּדִי, *with me*, may be the aff. with a form from the verb עמד, the insertion of ד, as in this place, being unauthorized by any usage of this family of languages, Job vi. 4; ix. 33, &c., signifying, *my standing*, or the

עמד (464) עמד

like, for *standing, being*, with *me*. See Nold., pp. 576—7, with the " Annotationes et Vindiciæ," p. 937, &c. And, for עִם אֵין, עִם צַקָה, עִם עִם־זֶה, כִּי עִם, בַּל עִם, עִם אֲשֶׁר, אֲשֶׁר עִם, in their proper places in that work; as construed with certain verbs, or with each accompanying particle, severally, as occurring in this. Also—

Chald. i. q. Heb. *With*, Dan. ii. 11. 18. 43; vi. 22; vii. 21. During *with*, עִם לֵילְיָא the *night:* by night, Dan. vii. 2. עִם דָּר וְדָר — *with generation and generation*, i. e. endures with it, Ib. iii. 33; iv. 31. עִם עֲנָנֵי שְׁמַיָּא, together *with the clouds of heaven*, Ib. vii. 13. Aff. עִמֵּי, Dan. iii. 32. עִמָּךְ, Ezra vii. 13. עִמֵּהּ, Dan. ii. 22. עִמְּהוֹן, Ezra v. 2.

עֹמֶד, m. occ. with aff. only, as, עָמְדִי, &c., Jer. xviii. 20, &c.; and is the Infin. or noun of action of the verb עָמַד. Applied, by meton. to *Place of standing, station*, 2 Chron. xxxiv. 31; Dan. viii. 17, 18.

עָמַד, v. pres. יַעֲמֹד, יַעֲמָד. Arab. عَمَدَ, *stabilivit; baptizavit:* so Syriac ܥܡܕ, because *confirmation* is given with baptism in the Eastern Churches. Æth. ዐዐመ: *columnam erexit*. Constr. abs. it. immed. it. med. בְּ, *in;* עַל, *on, over against, near;* נֶגֶד, אֶת־פְּנֵי, אֶת, בִּפְנֵי, לִפְנֵי, *before;* מִן, *from*, &c. *Stood* fast, still; *staid* or *remained,* &c. either absolutely, or for various purposes, as the several qualifying terms may require; used either of men or things, Gen. xxiv. 30, 31; xli. 17; Deut. xxxi. 15; Josh. iii. 16, &c. — in order to serve, &c., Gen. xli. 46; Deut. i. 38; 1 Kings i. 28; x. 8; xviii. 15. — with לְ, Lev. xviii. 23. *Stood over, presided*, with עַל, Num. vii. 2. *Near*, 2 Kings ii. 7; Judg. vi. 31. — *to defend*, Dan. xii. 1; Esth. viii. 11; ix. 16. With לְ, 1 Sam. xix. 3. — *fast*, i. e. endure, Ps. cii. 27; Exod. xviii. 23; Amos ii. 15. — *firm*, continued, Ezek. xiii. 5. — *against*, resisted, Ps. lxxvi. 8; cxxx. 3; cxlvii. 17, &c. With בִּפְנֵי, Josh. xxi. 42; xxiii. 9. נֶגֶד, Eccl. iv. 12. מִן, Dan. xi. 8. With בְּ, *persisted, persevered,* Is. xlvii. 12; Eccl. viii. 3. Immed., Ezek. xvii. 14. *Abide* (it), abs. it. בְּ, Exod. ix. 28; Lev. xiii. 5. 37; Jer. xxxii. 14; xlviii. 11, &c. *Stood* still, 1 Sam. xx. 38; Josh. x. 13; Jonah i. 15; Mic. v. 3. — so as *to cease* from doing something, with מִן, Gen. xxix. 35; xxx. 9. — up, i. q. קוּם, says Gesenius; which may be doubted when made a test of more

modern composition,* Dan. iii. 20; viii. 23; xi. 2; xii. 1. 13; Eccl. iv. 15; 1 Chron. xx. 4. With עַל, — against, *arose against,* Dan. viii. 25; xi. 14; 1 Chron. xxi. 1. In Ezra x. 14, יַעַמְדוּ־נָא, does not necessarily mean any thing beyond, *Let them now stand fast, firmly:* and so Dan. xi. 31. We need not, therefore, have recourse to the " *constituantur*" of Gesenius.

Infin. עֲמֹד, עֲמוֹד, Exod. xviii. 23; Ezra ii. 63, &c. Aff. עָמְדִי (form עָמֹד, see above), Jer. xviii. 20, &c. עָמְדְךָ, Dan. x. 11. עָמְדָךְ, Obad. vr. 11, &c.

Imp. עֲמֹד, Deut. v. 28, &c. עִמְדִי, 2 Sam. i. 9. Pl., עִמְדוּ, in pause, עֲמֹדוּ, Nah. ii. 9. Part. עֹמֵד, עוֹמֵד, pl. עֹמְדִים, Gen. xviii. 8; Exod. xxvi. 15, &c.

— fem. עֹמֶדֶת, עוֹמֶדֶת, plur. עֹמְדוֹת, Ps. xix. 10; cxxii. 2, &c.

Hiph. הֶעֱמִיד, pres. יַעֲמִיד, apoc. יַעֲמֵד. Constr. immed. it. med. אֶת, בְּ, לִפְנֵי, לְ, כֵּן, also with לְ, — לְ, to; for בֵּין — אֵת, &c. Causative of Kal. (a) *Cause to stand.* (b) *Set up, raise.* (c) *Establish:* thence, (d) *Appoint:* (e) *Confirm, accomplish*, &c. (a) Lev. xiv. 11; xvi. 7; xxvii. 11. (b) 1 Kings xii. 32; Neh. iii. 14, 15; 2 Chron. xxxiii. 19; Ps. cvii. 25. (c) Ps. xxxi. 9; 1 Kings xv. 4; Ezra ii. 68; Neh. xiii. 11; Prov. xxix. 4. (d) 1 Chron. xvi. 17; 2 Chron. viii. 14; xxxiii. 8; Ps. cv. 10, &c. (e) Ps. cxlviii. 6; 2 Sam. xxii. 34; Ps. xviii. 34; Dan. xi. 14, &c. With various government, וַיַּעֲמֶד־לוֹ כֹהֲנִים לַבָּמוֹת, so he appointed, set up, *for himself priests for the high places*, 2 Chron. xi. 15. Comp. 2 Chron. xxv. 14; Judg. xvi. 25. In Ezek. xxix. 7, הַעֲמִידָךְ, is manifestly an erroneous reading for הַמְעִידָהּ. Comp. Ps. lxix. 24. LXX. συνέκλασας. Vulg. " *dissolvisti.*" Syr. ܘܙܥܬ, " *concussisti.*"

Infin. הַעֲמֵי, Neh. vii. 3. הַעֲמִיד, Dan. xi. 14. Aff. הַעֲמִידוֹ, 2 Chron. ix. 8. הַעֲמִידָךְ, Ezek. xxiv. 11.

Imp. הַעֲמֵד, Is. xxi. 6.

Part. מַעֲמִיד, 2 Chron. xviii. 34.

Hoph. Pass. of Niph. pres. יָעֳמַד. *Made to stand*, Lev. xvi. 10.

Part. מָעֳמָד, 1 Kings xxii. 35; Ps. lxix. 3.

עֲמִדָּה, fem. r. עמד. Aff. עֲמָדָתוֹ. *His standing, station*, Mic. i. 11, only.

---

* See my Sermons and Dissertations, pp. 176—9.

(465)

עַמּוּד, עַמֻּד, m. עַמֻּדִים, עַמּוּדִים. Arab. عَمُودٌ, columna. Syr. ܟܐܣܕܐ, id. (a) *Pillar* or *column*, as erected either for the Tabernacle or Temple, Exod. xxxv. 11. 17; xxxvi. 38; xl. 18, &c.; 2 Kings xxv. 17; 2 Chron. iii. 15. As in rich furniture, Cant. v. 15. Made of wood, brass, or iron, 1 Kings vii. 2; Jer. lii. 17; i. 18. Meton. (b) *A pulpit*, as supported, perhaps, by a column, 2 Kings xi. 14; xxiii. 3, &c. See my note on Job xxix. 7. (c) Applied also to smoke, from its rising in the form of *a pillar*, Judg. xx. 40. Also to the clouds, for the same reason, Job xxvi. 11. See my note: and particularly to that which led the Israelites as a cloud by day, and a flame of fire by night, Exod. xiii. 22; xiv. 19; xxxiii. 9, 10, &c. In Job ix. 6, by metaph., *Nobles*, *peers*, as the أَرْكَانُ دَوْلَةٍ, PEERS, *pillars*, *of the state*, of the Persians. See my note.

Aff. עַמּוּדָיו, &c.

עֲמִיקָא, def. עֲמִיקְתָא, f. Chald. *The deep*, *profound*, *thing*, Dan. ii. 22, only, r. עמק.

עָמִיר, m.—pl. non occ. i. q. עֹמֶר, r. עמר. Arab. غَمَرَ, *arctius colligavit*; أَغْمَارٌ, *manipuli*. *Sheaf of corn*, Jer. ix. 21; Amos ii. 13; Mic. iv. 12; Zech. xii. 6.

עֲמִית, fem. r. עמה, cogn. τοῦ, עמם. Always sing. with aff., as עֲמִיתִי. *My society*, *company*, *companionship*, or the like, Zech. xiii. 7.; pause עֲמִיתֶךָ, Lev. xviii. 20; xix. 15. 17; xxv. 14, &c.; עֲמִיתוֹ, Ib. v. 21; xxv. 17, &c.; abstr. for concr.

עָמָל, m. constr. עֲמַל, aff. עֲמָלִי, עֲמָלוֹ, &c. plur. non occ. Arab. عَمَلٌ, *opus faciens*. Syr. ܥܡܠܐ, *labor*. Cogn. غَمَرَ, عَمِلَ. (a) *Labour*, *work*, Eccl. ii. 11. 20; iv. 4; vi. 7; x. 15. (b) *Labour*, with the notion of *sorrow*, *vexation*, Gen. xli. 51; Is. liii. 11; Ps. xxv. 18; Deut. xxvi. 7; Job iii. 10; v. 7; vii. 3, &c. (c) — with the notion of *sin* annexed, Num. xxiii. 21; Job iv. 8; xv. 35; Ps. vii. 15; x. 7. 14; xc. 10, &c. (d) — of *weariness*, Jer. xx. 18; Ps. cvii. 12. Meton. *Fruit*, *result*, of labour, Ps. vii. 17; cv. 44; Eccl. v. 18. Phr. מְנַחֲמֵי עָמָל *consolers of misery*, Job xvi. 2, for *miserable consolers*.

עָמֵל, masc. pl. עֲמֵלִים. Arab. عَامِلٌ, *operator*, *mercenarius*. Syr. ܥܡܠܐ, *labore defessus*. *Working*, *labouring*. Meton. *Weary* person, Eccl. iii. 9; iv. 8; ix. 9; Prov. xvi. 26; Job iii. 20. Phr. כָּל־יַד עָמֵל *the whole hand* (power, force) *of the labouring*, wretched —, Job xx. 22. Plur. once, עֲמֵלִים, Judg. v. 26, *workmen*, i. e. those who pitch tents (comp. ch. iv. 21.)

עֲמָלֵקִי, m. Patronym. of עֲמָלֵק, Gen. xiv. 7, &c. On this people see my Introduction to the Book of Job, p. 33.

עמם, v. pres. non occ. See עָם above. From the notion of *association*, *density*; and thence, *obscurity*, *concealment*, seem natural enough. Arab. cogn. غَمَّ, *pressit*, *obstruxit*, *texit*. Cogn. عَبَابٌ, *caterva*;

r. غَابَ, غَيِبَ, *latuit*. *Concealed*, *hid*, Ezek. xxviii. 3. לֹא עֲמָמוּךָ, *do not .conceal* (from) *thee*, Ib. xxxi. 8, al. non occ. Hoph. pres. יֻעַם. *Is* (the gold) *obscured*, Lam. iv. 1.

עֲמָמִיא, and Chald. עֲמֲמַיָא. See עָם, above.

עמס, v. pres. יַעֲמֹס.) Arab. عَمَسَ, עמש, once, Neh. iv. 11. } *difficultas, compressio*. Constr. abs. it. med. לְ, עַל. *Load*, i. e. lay a burden on, Ps. lxviii. 20; Gen. xliv. 13, al. non occ. Part. pl. m. עֹמְסִים, עֲמוּסִים. *Lading*, laying burdens upon, Neh. iv. 11; xiii. 15. Aff. עֲמֻסָיו. *Lading* (themselves with) *it*, Zech. xii. 3. See מַעֲמָסָה, p. 380 above.

— pass. pl. עֲמֻסִים.) *Borne*, *carried*, as f. עֲמוּסוֹת. } a burden. Comp. Exod. xix. 4; Num. xi. 12. Fem. *Burdens*, Is. xlvi. 3. 1, al. non occ.

Niph. הֶעֱמָס, pres. non occ. *Caused lading*, i. e. to be laid on, 1 Kings xii. 11; 2 Chron. x. 11, al. non occ.

עֹמֶק, m. once, Prov. xxv. 3. *Depth*, opp. τῷ, רוּם. Syr. ܥܘܡܩܐ, *profunditas*. Arab. عُمْقٌ, id. Æth. ዐመቀ: id.

עָמֹק, masc. pl. עֲמֻקִים.) See עמק. (a) עֲמֻקָּה, fem. pl. עֲמֻקוֹת. } *Deep*. (b) Meton. *Subtle*, *unsearchable*. (a) Lev. xiii.

3 O

עמק (466) עמר

3. 25. 30, 31, seq.; Ezek. xxiii. 32. (b) Ps. lxiv. 7; Eccl. vii. 27; Job xi. 8; xii. 22. Metaph., Prov. xviii. 4; xx. 5; xxii. 14; xxiii. 27.

עָמֹק, עֲמֻקִי, pl. constr. sing. non occ. i. q. עָמֵק. (a) *Deep* place, Prov. ix. 18. (b) *Unintelligible.* In the phr. עִמְקֵי שָׂפָה, *deep, unintelligible, of lip,* i. e. *of language,* Is. xxxiii. 19; Ezek. iii. 5, 6, al. non occ.

עֵמֶק, m. pl. עֲמָקִים. Aff. עִמְקֵךְ, &c. See עָמַק. *Valley,* or *vale,* as the context may require. This differs from גַּי, בִּקְעָה, and נַחַל, as being of greater extent, and more generally applied—as well as in its etymology—occasionally covered with corn, &c., or as a place of battle, &c. Without the article, and in construction, applied often as a proper name: e. g. עֵמֶק הַשִּׂדִּים, Gen. xiv. 3. עֵמֶק שָׁוֵה, Ib. 17. Comp. Josh. vii. 24. 26; xv. 8; 2 Chron. ii. 26; Hos. ii. 17; Joel iv. 2, &c. With the article, Josh. viii. 13; xiii. 19; xvii. 16. Meton. Inhabitants of —, Jer. xlviii. 8; 2 Chron. xii. 15; Jer. xlvii. 5. In the two last places, Gesenius thinks עֲנָקִים, *anakim,* ought to be read: but without any good reason. Without the art. in constr. עֵמֶק הַמֶּלֶךְ, *the king's vale,* 2 Sam. xviii. 18. עֵמֶק הַבָּכָא, Ps. lxxxiv. 7. Comp. Joel iv. 14. All of which, however, might have been used as proper names.

עָמֵק, v. pl. עָמְקוּ, only, Ps. xcii. 6. Phr. מְאֹד עָמְקוּ, *they are very deep,* i. e. *inscrutable.* LXX. σφόδρα ἐβαθύνθησαν.

Hiph. הֶעֱמִיק, pres. non occ. Causative of Kal. (a) *Make deep,* Is. xxx. 33. הַעֲמִיקוּ לָשֶׁבֶת, *make deep to dwell,* lit. i. e. make your residence secure, either by its *secrecy* in the holes of the rocks, and the like, as appears to have been often the case in Palestine, or by being well entrenched, opp. τῷ, סֹלּוּ, Jer. xlix. 8. 30. (b) Metaph. *Proceed, act, deeply,* i. e. *excessively,* Is. xxxi. 6; Hos. v. 2; ix. 9.

Imp. הַעְמֵק, Is. vii. 11: in הַעְמֵק שְׁאָלָה, which Aquila renders βάθυνον εἰς ᾅδην: evidently reading שְׁאֹלָה, instead of שְׁאָלָה; and this, לְמַעְלָה, in the corresponding member seems to justify. And so Symm. and Theod. See LXX. i. e. let thy request go down either to the depths of the earth, &c.

Part. pl. מַעֲמִיקִים. *Persons acting deeply,* i. e. in secret, as the following context shows, Is. xxix. 15. LXX. οἱ βαθέως βουλὴν ποιοῦντες. Syr. ܡܥܡܩܬܐ, *se distorquentes.*

עֹמֶר, m. pl. עֳמָרִים. See עָמִיר above. (a) *A sheaf of corn,* Lev. xxiii. 10. 15; Job xxiv. 10; Deut. xxiv. 19, &c. Pl., Ruth ii. 7. 15, &c. (b) *The omer,* a dry measure containing one-tenth part of an ephah, Exod. xvi. 36. 22. 32, &c.

עָמַר, v. Kal non occ. See עָמִיר. Pih. part. מְעַמֵּר. *Binding sheaves,* Ps. cxxix. 7.

Hithp. הִתְעַמֵּר, pres. תִּתְעַמֵּר, constr. med. בְּ. Sam. עמר, *subjecit.* Arab. غَمَرَ, *aretius colligavit; eminuerunt* homines; *mersit. Treat as a slave, tyrannize over,* Deut. xxi. 14; xxiv. 7. LXX. ἀθετήσεις. Syr. ܐܙܕ, *make merchandise.* Al. non occ.

עֲמַר, m. Chald. *Wool,* once, Dan. vii. 9. Heb. צֶמֶר.

עמש, see עמס above.

עֻמַּת, f. constr. as if from עֻמָּה, r. עמם, pl. עֻמּוֹת, aff. עֻמָּתִי: and, occasionally, with לְ prefixed: once, לְעֻמַּת, synon. עִם, לִפְנֵי, מִמּוּל, אֶל־פְּנֵי. (a) *Near, at,* Exod. xxv. 27; xxviii. 27; xxxvii. 14; xxxix. 20, &c. (b) *Over against, corresponding to,* Eccl. vii. 14; Ezek. xlii. 7; xlviii. 13. 18. 21, &c.: it. מִלְעֻמַּת, 1 Kings vii. 20. לְעֻמָּתָם, *over against him,* 2 Sam. xvi. 13. לְעֻמָּתָם, Ezek. i. 20, 21; iii. 13; x. 19; xi. 22. So the plur. לְעֻמּוֹת, Ib. xlv. 7. LXX. ὡς. Adv. *Agreeably to, accordingly,* 1 Chron. xxiv. 31; xxvi. 12, &c.; Eccl. v. 15. כָּל־עֻמַּת, *altogether as, accordingly as.* LXX. ὥσπερ, לְעֻמַּת, ἐξισόω, ἐχόμενος, καθώς, &c. Finding it impossible, apparently, as with ourselves, to use a single word exactly giving its sense.

עֵנָב, m. pl. עֲנָבִים, constr. עִנְבֵי, dagesh euph. Arab. عِنَب, *uvæ.* Syr. ܥܢܒܐ, *uva. Grape* (generic noun), Num. vi. 3; xiii. 20. אֶשְׁכּוֹל עֲנָבִים, *bunch of —,* Ib. xiii. 23. Comp. Gen. xl. 10. דַּם עֲנָבִים, *blood of —,* i. e. *wine,* Gen. xlix. 11; Deut. xxxii. 14. עֲשׂוֹת עֲנָבִים, *produce —,* Is. v. 2. 4. עִנְּבֵי רוֹשׁ, Deut. xxxii. 32: i. q. عِنَب الثَّعْلَب; Syr. ܘܒܐܫܐ, *fox grape,* or poisonous berry. See p. 15 above. Castell. *solanum majus:* perhaps, i. q. עֲנָבִים בְּמִדְבָּר. Aff. עֲנָבֵימוֹ, Deut. xxxii. 32.

עֵ֫נֶב, masc.—plur. non occ. Arab. غُنْج, *amatorius fœminæ gestus. Delight, pleasure,* Is. xiii. 22; lviii. 13, only.

עָנֹג, m. } plur. non occ. See עָנֹג, syn.
עֲנֻגָּה, f. } τοῦ, רַךְ. *Delicate, tender,* as brought up in pleasure, Deut. xxviii. 54. 56; Is. xlvii. 1, al. non occ.

עָנֹג, v. Kal non occ. See עָנֹג above.
Puh. part. f. מְעֻנָּה. *Delicately brought up,* and living in pleasure, Jer. vi. 2. Aquil. Theod. τὴν φανεράν. Montfaucon thinks τρυφεράν ought to be read; but this is unnecessary, as φανερὰν equally well expresses the splendour, &c. which may be included in the Heb. as applied to the luxurious rich, al. non occ.
Hithp. plur. הִתְעַנֵּגְנוּ, pres. יִתְעַנָּג. Constr. med. בְּ, *in;* עַל, *on, against;* מִן, *from;* it. abs. See עָנֹג. *Be, become, delighted,* or *delight self* in, on, Ps. xxxvii. 4. 11; Is. lv. 2; lvii. 4; lviii. 15; lxvi. 11; Job xxii. 27; xxvii. 10.
Infin. הִתְעַנֵּג, Deut. xxviii. 56, abs.

עָנָה, v. pres. יַעֲנֶה, apoc. יַעַן. Syr. ܥܢܐ, *curam adhibuit; cecinit, &c.* Arab. عَنَا, r. عَنَو, *eduxit.* Conj. II. *captivum habuit.* IV. *Captivum fecit, humilem reddidit.* Cogn. عَنَى, *protulit, captivus fuit; respondit:* غَنَى, II. *cecinit; uxorem duxit.*
The primary notion seems to be, *lead, bring, out:* thence, *expose, humble, subdue, take captive, &c.,* as in גָּלָה, Arab. جَلَى. From the first of these—as applied to words—we have, *answer, &c.,* as from דבר. Arab. دَبَر, *drive out,* we have דָּבָר, *a word:* דִּבֶּר, *spoke:* from the second, *humility, affliction, &c.*

I. (a) *Spoke, gave, out his mind, opinion:* began speaking, &c. "Max. in recentiore Hebraïsmo," says Gesenius: which is a mere fancy. Abs. Job iii. 2; xxxii. 20; Is. xiv. 10; Zech. i. 10; iii. 4; iv. 11. 12; Cant. ii. 10. *Addressed,* Zech. i. 11: med. אֶת.
(b) *Recite, celebrate* with song, &c., med. לְ, Exod. xv. 21: בְּ, instr. 1 Sam. xxi. 12: לְ, pers. 1 Sam. xxix. 5; Ps. cxlvii. 7.
(c) *Shout,* as in battle, abs. it. med. עַל, Exod. xxxii. 18; Jer. li. 14. (d) *Bellow, bleat,* as a wild bull, Is. xiii. 22: with בְּ, in.
(d) *Announce, answer,* of God, Gen. xli. 16; 1 Sam. ix. 17. — *of a judge giving sentence,* med. עַל, Exod. xxiii. 2. — *of a witness giving testimony for —,* immed. Deut. xix. 16: med. בְּ, for —, metaph. Gen. xxx. 33; 1 Sam. xii. 3: — against, Num. xxxv. 30; Deut. xix. 18; 2 Sam. i. 16.
(e) *Answered,* immed. it. med. אֶת, &c., Job i. 7; Gen. xxiii. 14; Cant. v. 6; Prov. xviii. 23, &c. — *by way of excuse,* Job ix. 14, 15. 32; xvi. 3. — *of refutation,* Job xxxii. 12. — *favourably,* 1 Sam. xiv. 39; Ps. iii. 5, &c.; Ps. xxii. 22. מִקַּרְנֵי רֵמִים עֲנִיתָנִי, — *from the horns of the oryx,* Gesenius thinks, means, answer (hear) *and deliver* me, &c., sensu prægnanti. But why not *answer me* (crying) *from among the horns, &c.?* See the LXX. and Syr. Eccl. x. 19, הַכֶּסֶף יַעֲנֶה אֶת־הַכֹּל, *silver gives a favourable answer as to all,* i. e. "argenteis pugna telis ac omnia vinces." Hos. ii. 23, אֶעֱנֶה אֶת־הַשָּׁמַיִם וְהֵם יַעֲנוּ אֶת־הָאָרֶץ: וְהָאָרֶץ תַּעֲנֶה וגו׳, *I will favourably answer as to the heavens* (making them give rain), *and they shall favourably answer as to the earth, and the earth, &c.* See the following context. LXX. ἐπακούσομαι, &c.
(f) — *of God, to punish, reward, &c.,* i. e. *answer one according to his deeds,* Hos. v. 5. עָנָה גְאוֹן־יִשְׂרָאֵל בְּפָנָיו, *the glory* (i. e. God) *of Israel shall answer to his face.* See following context, Ps. cxviii. 5, &c. Said also of (metaph.) righteousness, sin, &c., Gen. xxx. 33; Is. lix. 12; Jer. xiv. 7.
II. (a) *Humbled, subdued,* passive. (b) *Afflicted,* passive. Constr. immed. it. abs. it. med. בְּ, instr. (applied sometimes to agriculture, apparently, "as in מַעֲנֶה, or מַעֲנִית," Gesen.: see p. 381 above). (a) Is. xxxi. 4; Zech. x. 2. Active, 2 Chron. vi. 26. (b) Ps. cxvi. 10; cxix. 67.
Infin. I. עֲנוֹת, Gen. xlv. 3; Exod. xxxii. 18, &c. II. Eccl. i. 13; iii. 10.
Imp. I. עֲנֵה, Prov. xxvi. 5; Mic. vi. 3. Aff. עֲנֵנִי, 1 Kings xviii. 37, &c.; עֲנֵנוּ, Ib. 26. Pl. עֲנוּ, 1 Sam. xii. 3, &c.
Part. I. עֹנֶה, Judg. xix. 28, &c. Aff. עֹנֵהוּ, Job v. 1; 1 Sam. xiv. 40. Pl. עֹנִים, Jer. xliv. 20.
Niph. I. נַעֲנָה, pres. יֵעָנֶה. *Be, become,* (a) *Answering,* or (b) *Answered.* (a) With לְ, Ezek. xiv. 4. 7. (b) Job xi. 2; xix. 7; Prov. xxi. 13, al. non occ.
Niph. II. (a) *Be, become, humble, humbled*

עָנָה (468) עָנוּ

or *subdued:* with מִפְּנֵי, Exod. x. 3. (b) *Afflicted,* Is. liii. 7; Ps. cxix. 107, al. non occ.

Infin. II. with prep. לְ, לַעֲנוֹת, for לְהַעֲנוֹת, Exod. l. c.

Part. f. נַעֲנָה, Is. lviii. 10.

Pih. I. pres. יְעַנֶּה, once, Job xxxvii. 23: but the context requires that יַעֲנֶה, in Niph. be read. See my note. Aquila, κακουχήσει, *affliget.* Syr. ܟܢܕ, *respondens.*

Infin. עַנּוֹת, i. q. Kal I. (b) Exod. xxxii. 18; Ps. lxxxviii. 1.

Imp. plur. עַנּוּ, Id., Is. xxvii. 2. Al. non occ.

Pih. II. עִנָּה, pres. יְעַנֶּה, i. q. Kal, if not intensitive. (a) *Humble, subdue.* (b) *Afflict.* (a) — a woman, Gen. xxxiv. 2; Deut. xxii. 24. 29; 2 Sam. xiii. 22. — generally, Ps. cii. 24, &c. Immed. it. med. אֶת, it. בְּ, in. (b) Immed. med. בְּ, כֵּן, *Afflict,* Num. xxiv. 24; Ps. xc. 15; xxxv. 13; Nah. i. 12; Ps. lxxxviii. 8. מִשְׁבָּרֶיךָ עִנִּיתָ, with *thy billows* (lit. breakers) *thou hast afflicted* me: ellip. בְּ, and יָד. Symm. ταῖς καταιγίσιν σου ἐκάκωσάς με. See LXX.

Infin. (b) עַנֵּה, Exod. xxii. 22.

עַנּוֹת, Is. lviii. 5. עַנּוֹת, Num. xxx. 14. Aff. Exod. i. 11; Deut. viii. 2, &c.

Imp. (a) pl. עַנּוּ, Judg. xix. 24.

Part. (b) pl. m. aff. מְעַנַּיִךְ. *Thy afflicters,* Is. lx. 14; Zeph. iii. 19, al. non occ.

Puh. II. עֻנֵּיתִי. (b) *I have been afflicted,* Ps. cxix. 71. Pres. I. (a) תְּעֻנֶּה, *is humbled,* Lev. xxiii. 29, al. non occ.

Infin. aff. עֻנּוֹתוֹ. *His being afflicted, suffering affliction,* Ps. cxxxii. 1.

Part. מְעֻנֶּה. *Afflicted,* Is. liii. 4, al. non occ.

Hiph. I. Part. only, מַעֲנֶה, med. בְּ. *Answers,* or *causes answer* favourably, Eccl. v. 19.

Hiph. II. Gesenius makes 1 Kings viii. 35; 2 Chron. vi. 26; i. q. *oppressit, affixit, &c.* And so the Auth. Vers. and LXX. But, the Targ. and Syr. give the sense of *answer.* In either case the verb may be in Kal, and so the older grammarians took it.

Hithp. הִתְעַנָּה, pres. non occ. II. (b) *Be, become, afflicted,* 1 Kings ii. 26.

Infin. הִתְעַנּוֹת. (a) *Be, become, humble, submissive,* Dan. x. 12; Ezra viii. 21.

Imp. f. הִתְעַנִּי, Id., Gen. xvi. 9.

עֲנָה, v. Chald. pres. non occ. f. עֲנָה; pl. m. עֲנוֹ, i. q. Heb. *Spoke out, answered,*

abs. Dan. ii. 7. 10; iii. 9. 16; v. 10; vi. 14. It. med. לְ, ii. 47.

Part. עָנֵה, Dan. ii. 5. 8. 15. 20, &c. Pl. עָנַיִן, Ib. iii. 24.

Part. עָנִין, plur. sign. II. Heb. *Afflicted* persons, Ib. iv. 24 (27).

עָנָו, m. pl. עֲנָוִים, or עֲנָיִים, constr. עַנְוֵי, or עַנְוֵי. The latter form usually in the Keri. It is, however, in reality a different form (עָנִי below). *Humble, meek, poor, afflicted,* as the context may require. Sing. once, Num. xii. 3, Keri עָנִיו. Pl., Ps. ix. 13; x. 12. 17; xxii. 27, &c. Constr., Ps. lxxvi. 10; Zeph. ii. 3; Is. xi. 4, &c.

עֲנָוָה, fem. of עָנָו. ⎫ *Meekness, humility,* עֲנָוָה, f. constr. עַנְוַת. ⎭ Prov. xv. 33; xviii. 12; xxii. 4; Zeph. ii. 3. עַנְוָה, once, Ps. xlv. 5. Eichhorn's Simonis, however, makes the final ה paragogic, and the sing. i. q. עַן, *propter:* while Schultens makes it the Imp., and the sense, "*responde rigorem, vigoremque justissimum.*" The passage is, perhaps, elliptical, and hence these conjectures; and may be supplied thus: עַל דְּבַר־אֱמֶת וְעַנְוָה צֶדֶק, *because of truth and meekness and righteousness.* See LXX. Aff. עַנְוָתְךָ, Ps. xviii. 36, *thy gentleness, kindness.*

עֱנוּת, f. once, phr. עֱנוּת עָנִי, *Affliction of the humble,* Ps. xxii. 25. See LXX. &c.

עֲנֻז, see ע.

עֳנִי, in pause, עֹנִי, it. עוֹנִי, m.—pl. non occ. (Seg.) *Affliction, misery, poverty,* Exod. iii. 7; 2 Kings xiv. 26; Neh. ix. 9, &c. In pause, Deut. xvi. 3; Job xxx. 16; Ps. cvii. 41. Metaph. אֲסִירֵי עֳנִי, *bound of misery,* Ps. cvii. 10; Lam. i. 3, &c. Aff. עָנְיִי, Gen. xxxi. 42. עָנְיֵנוּ, Deut. xxvi. 7. עָנְיֵךְ, Gen. xvi. 11, &c.

עָנִי, masc. plur. עֲנִיִּים, constr. עֲנִיֵי. —

עֲנִיָּה, fem. — plur. non occ. — i. q. עָנָו, which see. *Humble, meek,* Zech. ix. 9. *Poor, afflicted,* Deut. xxiv. 12. 14, 15; 2 Sam. xxii. 28; Job xxiv. 9. Pl., Job xxxiv. 28; xxxvi. 6. עֲנִיִּים, occasionally. See עָנָו above, Ps. ix. 19; Is. xxxii. 7. Constr., Job xxiv. 4, &c.

Fem., Is. x. 30; li. 21; liv. 11, al. non occ. Aff. pl. עֲנִיֶּיךָ, Ps. lxxii. 2; lxxiv. 19. עֲנִיֵּי, for עֲנִיֵּי, Is. xlix. 13.

עֲנִיו, Keri of עָנָו, Num. xii. 3, above.

עִנְיָן, m. constr. עִנְיַן, pl. non occ. r. עָנָה.

עֲנַם (469) עָנַן

Arab. عُنْوَان , عُنْيَان , omnis res, qua altera indicatur; r. عَنَى, voluit. Lit. Word, answer: thence, Thing, matter, business, intent. Comp. Heb. דָּבָר. So Arab. شَيْ, of شَا =, voluit, Eccl. i. 13; ii. 26; iii. 10; iv. 8; v. 2. 13; viii. 16. Aff. עִנְיָנִי, Ib. ii. 23. Al. non occ. The LXX. render it by πειρασμός, περισπασμός; taking sign. ii. as its ground. Aquila, περισπασμός. Symm. ἀσχολία, once ἀνομία.

עֲנַמְמֶלֶךְ. The name of an idol, 2 Kings xvii. 31. See אַדְרַמֶּלֶךְ above, p. 10.

עָנָן, m. constr. עֲנַן, pl. עֲנָנִים. Aff. עֲנָנוֹ.

עֲנָנוּ. Syr. ܥܢܢܐ, nubes. Arab. عَنّ, adparitio rei; pars cœli conspicua. Cogn. عَنَا, r. عَنَو, emisit uter aquam; عَنَّا, tractus cœli, &c. Thence, A cloud. And v. by meton., Cover, conceal, &c. Cogn. عَمِيَ; fluxit; عَمَاء, nubes: and, as a verb, obscurum fuit; texit, &c. Comp. Ezek. xxxviii. 9; Ps. cxlvii. 8, &c.

(a) A cloud, Gen. ix. 14; Exod. xiii. 21; Job xxvi. 8, &c.: with יוֹם, — time, period, of darkness, distress, &c., Ezek. xxx. 3; xxxiv. 12; Joel ii. 2; Zeph. i. 19, &c. So, bright or light cloud, intimates prosperity, Zech. x. 1; Rev. xiv. 14. See my note on Job, p. 226. —, as accompanying the presence of the Deity, Exod. xiv. 24; xix. 9; Num. xii. 5; Nah. i. 3, &c. —, as being God's chariot, Ps. civ. 3. Pec. the pillar of a cloud which led the Israelites, Exod. xiv. 21, &c. See עַמּוּד above. Used by way of comparison, to intimate many, much, Is. xliv. 22; lx. 8; Jer. iv. 13, &c. Comp. Heb. xii. 1. —, a numerous army, Ezek. xxx. 18; xxxviii. 9. Comp. Dan. vii. 13, with Jude, vr. 14; Matt. xxiv. 30, &c. —, height, Job xx. 6; Is. xiv. 14. —, a covering, Job xxxviii. 19. —, as a protection, Ps. cv. 39; Is. iv. 5. —, concealment, Lam. iii. 44, &c. —, as implying instability, sudden, or quick, departure, Hos. vi. 4; xiii. 3. Many of these properties belong to עָב, שַׁחַק. Comp. Jude, vr. 12; Eccl. xii. 2, &c.

עֲנַן, m. Chald. pl. constr. עֲנָנֵי, i. q. Heb. Dan. vii. 13, only.

עָנַן, v. Kal non occ. See עָנָן above.
Pih. Infin. Aff. עַנְנִי, for עַנְּנִי. My clouding, bringing on a cloud, once, Gen. ix. 14. LXX. συννεφεῖν με —.

It. pret. עוֹנֵן, pres. pl. תְּעוֹנֵנוּ. Divine, by the clouds, or appearance of the heavens generally, 2 Kings xxi. 6; 2 Chron. xxxiii. 6. Comp. Is. xlvii. 13, הֹבְרֵי שָׁמַיִם הַחֹזִים בַּכּוֹכָבִים. Comp. Jer. x. 2. Pres. once, Lev. xix. 26. LXX. ὀρνιθοσκοπήσεσθε. Syr. ܠܐ ܬܨܒܘ, Divine, generally. Some, Divine by times, seasons, &c. So Jarchi, Nicholas, Fuller, &c.: but this is groundless. Gesen. thinks, acting secretly, thence divining generally, is meant: but this would rather refer to sacred mysteries than to any sort of divination. See Matt. xvi. 2, 3; Luke xii. 56. Part. מְעוֹנֵן, pl. מְעוֹנְנִים, מְעוֹנְנִים. Diviners, meteorologists, Deut. xviii. 10. 14; Mic. v. 11. Al. non occ. Aquila, κληδονιζόμενοι.

עָנֵן, masc. plur. עֲנָנִים) i. q. מְעוֹנֵן. Diviner, Is. ii. 6; עֲנָנָה, f.—pl. non occ.) Jer. xxvii. 5. Fem., Is. lvii. 3, al. non occ.

עֲנָנָה, f.—pl. non occ. Cloud, collectively, once, Job iii. 5. Aquila, νέφωσις. Symm. ἀχλύς. Theod. συννέφεια.

עָנָף, m. constr. עֲנַף. Aff. pl. עֲנָפֶיהָ. Syr. ܥܢܦܐ, ramus. Arab. عَنَف, movit, agitavit. Castell. The primitive notion is perhaps retained in the terms, عُنْفًا عُنْفًا, unus post alterum, i. e. of produce successively: whence عُنْقُو, and عُنْوَان, principium rei, pec. vigoris juvenilis. A branch of a tree, Ezek. xvii. 8. 23; xxxi. 3; Mal. iii. 19; Lev. xxiii. 40. Pl., Ps. lxxx. 11. Aff. עֲנָפֵכֶם, if the vowels may be relied on, must be derived from עָנֵף, id. Ezek. xxxvi. 8, al. non occ. It. Chald. pl. aff. עֲנָפוֹהִי, its branches, Dan. iv. 9. 11. 18, al. non occ.

עֲנָפָה, f. (of the form עָנָף, now lost). Branching out, Ezek. xix. 10, only. LXX. ὁ βλαστὸς αὐτῆς: evidently reading עֲנָפָהּ.

עָנָק, m. pl. עֲנָקִים, it. fem. עֲנָקוֹת. Arab. عُنْق, collum. Æth. ዐንቀ፡ collo circumdedit torquem. A chain, or other ornament for the neck, Prov. i. 9; Judg. viii. 26; Cant. iv. 9. Aquila, περιτραχήλιον, πλόκαμον. Symm. ὁρμίσκος. Cant. (incertus), κλοιός.

עֲנָק, v. pret. fem. Aff. עֲנָקַתְמוֹ. Pride, haughtiness, (lit.) *Neck-chains them*, i. e. is carried about them as an ornament for the neck, once, Ps. lxxiii. 6. Symm. ἠμφιάσαντο. See עֲנָק.

Hiph. pret. הַעֲנִיק. *Place, lay, on the neck*, i. e. a gift, either as *an ornament of the neck*, or as a burden on the shoulders, once, Deut. xv. 14. See LXX. and Vulg. Arab.

اَعْنَقَ, *collari cinxit canem.*

Infin. הַעֲנֵק, Ib. only.

עֹנֶשׁ, masc. — plur. non occ. Arab.

عَنَشَ, *propulit; exturbavit.* VIII. *Injuria affecit.* Cogn. عَنَتَ, *incidit in damnum.* Cogn. אנש. See אָנוּשׁ, p. 44, above. Comp. עָמַס; עמש. *Mulct, fine, or tax*, levied in money, 2 Kings xxiii. 33; Prov. xix. 19. LXX. ζημιωθήσεται, and so Auth. Vers., al. non occ.

עֲנָשׁ, m. Chald. i. q. Heb. עֹנֶשׁ, once, Ezra vii. 26.

עָנַשׁ, v. עָנוֹשׁ, pres. יַעֲנֹשׁ, constr. immed. it. med. אֶת, לְ. *Mulcted, fined, taxed*, to be levied in money. See עֹנֶשׁ above. Deut. xxii. 19; 2 Chron. xxxvi. 3, al. non occ. LXX. ζημιοῦν.

Infin. עָנוֹשׁ, עֲנָשׁ־, Exod. xxi. 22; Prov. xvii. 26; xxi. 11, al. non. occ.

Part. m. pl. עֲנוּשִׁים, Amos ii. 8, only.

Niph. נֶעֱנָשׁוּ, pres. יֵעָנֵשׁ. *Be, become, mulcted, fined*, Exod. xxi. 22; Prov. xxii. 3; xxvii. 12.

עֶנֶת, see מִעֲנָה, p. 305—6, above.

עֲנָתֹתִי, m. patronymic of עֲנָתוֹת, Jer. i. 1. *Anathothite*, 2 Sam. xxiii. 27, &c.

עָסִיס, m.—pl. non occ. r. עסס. Arab.

عَسَّ, *circumivit.* VIII. *Palpavit*; عَسْعَسَ, *commovit, agitavit.* Lit. *trodden:* by meton. *New wine*, Joel i. 5; iv. 18; Amos ix. 13; Is. xlix. 26. עֲסִיס רִמֹּנִי, *new wine, juice, of the pomegranate*, Cant. viii. 2.

עָסַס, v. See עָסִיס above, once, aff. עִסּוֹתֶם. *You shall tread*, as grapes, Mal. iii. 21.

עָפָה, see עוּפָה.

עֳפָאִים, m. pl. Syr. ܥܦܳܐ, *floruit.*

Aph. *frondes emisit. Branches*, usually; but *leaves* seems to be more correct. Castell, "*potius frondes*, id. Chald. and Syr. suffragantur R. D. Nathan," &c., once, Ps. civ. 12.

עֳפִיָּה, m. pl. Chald. aff. i. q. Heb. עֳפָאִים. *Its leaves, or branches*, Dan. iv. 9. 11. 18, al. non occ. Syr. ܥܦܳܐ, *ramus*; ܥܦܶܐ, *frondes.*

עֹפֶל, m. Arab. عَفَل, *pinguedo circa perinæum capri, &c.*; عَفَلَة, *res in pudendis feminæ vel camelæ herniæ in viris similis.* See Schrœd. Origg. Heb., cap. iv. pp. 54, 55. Schultens. ad Meidanii Prov., p. 23. So also Jauhari, sub voce. (a) *Swelling*, or *tumor*, Deut. xxviii. 27; 1 Sam. v. 6. Pl. עֳפָלִים, read with the vowels of the Keri, viz. טְחוֹרִים. See p. 236, above: but which, as Gesenius has remarked, ought to be read עֳפָלִים. *Tumors* in the anus: *hæmorrhoids*, probably. (b) *Mount, hill*, Is. xxxii. 14; Mic. iv. 8. הָעֹפֶל, an *eminence* on the eastern part of Mount Zion, surrounded by a wall, 2 Kings v. 24; 2 Chron. xxvii. 3; xxxiii. 14; Neh. iii. 26, 27; xi. 21, al. non occ. See Joseph. de Bell. Jud. lib. vi. c. vi. § 3; τὸν Ὀφλᾶν, al. Ὀφελ, καλούμενον ὑφῆψαν. See also Reland's Palestine, p. 855.

עָפֵל, v. See עֹפֶל above. Kal non occ.

Puh. pret. f. עֻפְּלָה. *Swollen, inflated*, Hab. ii. 4. LXX. ὑποστείληται. Aquila, νωχελευομένου, al. non occ.

Hiph. pres. plur. יַעְפִּלוּ. *They swelled, raised*, themselves, i. e. acted in a self-exalting, confident, manner, Num. xiv. 44, only. See LXX. Comp. Deut. i. 43.

עַפְעַפִּים, m. pl. constr. עַפְעַפֵּי, r. עוּף. Syr. ܥܦܥܦܐ, *duplicatio.* Eye-lids, Job xvi. 16; Ps. cxxxii. 4; Jer. ix. 17. Put for *the eyes*, Ps. xi. 4; Prov. iv. 25; vi. 25; xxx. 13; and perhaps some other places. Metaph. עַפְעַפֵּי שַׁחַר, *eye-lids of the dawn*, Job iii. 9; xli. 10. The Arabian poets, as Gesenius observes, name the sun الْعَيْن, *the eye*; to which they give *eye-lids*, in حَوَاجِب الشَّمْس. The Malays generally call the sun, مَاتَ هَارِي, *eye of day*, as the Egyp-

עפר (471) עץ

tians did, *the eye of Horus,* i. e. of Apollo. Aff. עְסְפַּפִינוּ, עְסְפַפַּי, &c.

עְפָר, masc. pl. עֲפָרִים. Arab. يَعْفُورْ, *pullus dorcadis, al. vaccæ sylvestris.* Castell. it. أَعْفَرْ, *ex albo subrubicunda ovis, talis dorcas cum brevi collo. Kid, young goat,* or *gazelle,* Cant. ii. 9. 17; iv. 5; vii. 4; viii. 14. Gesenius, "غْفَرْ, et غُفَرْ, *fœtus rupricapræ.*"

עָפָר, m. constr. עֲפַר, pl. f. constr. עֲפָרוֹת. Syr. ܥܰܦܪܳܐ, *terrenus.* Arab. عَفَرْ, *terra, pulvis.* (a) *Earth, mould:* thence, (b) *Dust.* (a) Gen. ii. 7; iii. 19; Job vii. 5; xxxviii. 38, &c. (b) Josh. vii. 6; Job ii. 12; Lam. ii. 10; Ezek. xxvii. 30, &c. Thence, used to imply *much* in number, quantity, &c., Gen. xiii. 16; Num. xxiii. 10; Job xxvii. 16; Ps. lxxviii. 27, &c. Thence, (c) *The earth,* i. e. face of it, Job xix. 22; xli. 25. *Clay, &c.,* used for plastering, Lev. xiv. 42. 45. — to form *a mound,* Hab. i. 10. (d) *Depths* of the earth, (comp. Ezek. xxvi. 20), as holes, sepulchres, &c., Is. ii. 19; xxvi. 19; Job xvii. 16; xiv. 8; xxviii. 2. 6; xxx. 6; xl. 13, &c. To which may be referred, most properly, perhaps, שׁוּב אֶל־עָפָר, Gen. iii. 19. Comp. יוֹרְדֵי עָפָר, *descenders of the dust,* to the grave, Ps. xxii. 30, &c.—Thence implying *humility,* occasionally *a dead man.* See Eccl. xii. 7; Ps. xxx. 10; cxix. 25. עָפָר מָוֶת, Ps. xxii. 16. עָפָר וָאֵפֶר, Gen. xviii. 27; Ps. ciii. 14, &c. By way of comparison for *smallness,* דַּק לְעָפָר, Deut. ix. 21; 2 Kings xxiii. 6. 15; Ps. xviii. 43. — for *meanness,* Ps. xliv. 26; 1 Sam. ii. 8; Ps. cxiii. 7; Is. lii. 2. Whence the phrr. אָכַל עָפָר, Gen. iii. 14; Is. lxv. 25; Lam. iii. 29. עָפָר יְלַחֵכוּ, Ps. lxxii. 9. Aff. עֲפָרוֹ, עֲפָרָהּ, &c. Whence the verb—

עפר, v. Kal non occ.

Pih. עִפֵּר, once, in the phr. וְעַפֵּר בֶּעָפָר. Lit. *He dusted with dust,* cast dust, 2 Sam. xvi. 16.

עוֹפֶרֶת, עֹפָרֶת, f.—pl. non occ. *Lead,* "*a colore subalbo,*" says Gesenius. (Arab. أَعْفَرْ, *subalbicans*), which is very doubtful, Exod. xv. 10; Num. xxxi. 22; Jer. vi. 29; Ezek. xxii. 18, &c. Phr. אֶבֶן הָעֹפָרֶת, lit.

stone of —, i. e. *weight of* —, because stones were used as weights, Zech. v. 8.

עֵץ, m. pl. עֵצִים, constr. עֲצֵי, r. עָצָה. Cogn. עוּץ. Arab. عَضّْ, *radix, origo.* Cogn. عَصِي, *durus fuit.* Cogn. عَضْ, *ossa dactylorum; arbor crassior; trabs.* Cogn. عَصَا, *baculus.* (a) *Tree,* generally, for fruit or timber, Gen. i. 11. 29; ii. 9. 16; iii. 1. 8; Exod. ix. 25; Num. xiii. 20. (b) *Wood; gallows,* Gen. xl. 19; Deut. xxi. 22; Josh. x. 26, &c. *Idol* of —, Jer. ii. 27. — for burning, *fuel,* Gen. xxii. 3. 9; Lev. i. 7; iv. 12; Is. xxx. 33. — for building, *timber,* Exod. xxv. 10; 1 Kings vi. 23. 31, 32; Ezek. xv. 3. Phrr. כְּלִי־עֵץ, *vessel of* —, Lev. xi. 32. Comp. 2 Sam. vi. 5. הָאָרֶן—, *of cedar,* Ib. xiv. 6. עֵץ אָרוֹן, *chest, ark of* —, Deut. x. 1. עֵץ חָרָשֵׁי, 2 Sam. v. 11. מִגְדַּל־עֵץ, *tower-pulpit of* —, Neh. viii. 4. עֵץ שֶׁמֶן, Ib. 15. עֵץ הַחַיִּים, *tree of life,* Gen. iii. 24. לֹא־עֵץ, *not wood,* i. e. any thing but wood, Is. x. 15. לַח—, יָבֵשׁ—, *green* — *dry,* Ezek. xxi. 3, &c. Aff. עֵצוֹ, Hos. iv. 12. עֶצְיָה—, Deut. xx. 19, &c.: pl. עֵצֵינוּ, עֲצֵי, &c.

עָצָב, and עֶצֶב, m. pl. עֲצָבִים. Arab. عَصَبْ, *tendo, nervus;* عَصْبْ, *præstantiores populi.* (a) *Tendon, sinew,* applied to Coniah, Jer. xxii. 28, in the phr. הַעֶצֶב נִבְזֶה, *whether a despised tendon, sinew,* of the state, i. e. *noble?* The notion of " *vessel,*" has most likely been taken from אִם כְּלִי וגו׳, &c. following. Auth. Vers. " *broken idol.*" Aquila, τὸ στόμα ἐξουδενωμένον. Symm. " Numquid purgamentum, sic quisquiliæ viles atque projectæ?" LXX. omits the word altogether. Symm. took the sense of the Arab. غِضَابْ, *quisquiliæ.* Vulg. " *vas fictile.*" Syr. ܚܶܣܕܳܐ, *despectus.* Targ. id. (b) *Labour.* (c) *Pain,* from the notion of binding, &c. See חֶבֶל. Syr. ܚܒܰܫ, *ligavit.* Æth. ዐሰበ: *difficile, arduum.* Arab. عَصَبْ, *cinxit,* Prov. v. 10; x. 22; xiv. 23. Phr. לֶחֶם הָעֲצָבִים, Ps. cxxvii. 2. (c) *Pain* of child-birth, Gen. iii. 16. — of mind, *provocation,* Prov. xv. 1. Aff. עֶצְבֵּךְ.

עָצָב, m.—pl. non occ. Lit. fabrication. (a) *Idol,* Is. xlviii. 5; Ps. cxxxix. 24. דֶּרֶךְ עֹצֶב, *way of an idol,* idolatry. Gesen. usually, "*way of pain.*" LXX. ἀνομίας. Syr.

עֶצֶב (472) עֶצֶב

מַעְצָד, of falsehood. (b) Pain, grief, 1 Chron. iv. 9; Is. xiv. 3. Aff. עָצְבְּךָ, עָצְבִּי.

עֶצֶב, m. pl. aff. עַצְבְּכֶם. Your labours, pains, i. e. privations and mortifications submitted to for the sake of religion, once, Is. lviii. 3. Schult. nervis vestris. Arab. عِصَاب. Gesen. "operarius." Ellip. בְּ. So LXX. Theod. Sym. "Debitores vestros." The parall. requires labours, or the like. Comp. the preceding members. Syr. and Targ. take idol here.

עֶצֶב, m. pl. עֲצַבִּים, constr. עַצְבֵּי. Arab. عَصَب, vittâ fasciâve revinxit; مَعْصَب, Dominus. (Lit. person, &c. binding.) Idols, Hos. iv. 17; viii. 4; xiii. 2; xiv. 9; Zech. xiii. 2; Ps. cvi. 38; cxxxv. 15, &c. Aff. עֲצַבֵּיהֶם, עֲצַבָּיו, Mic. i. 7; 1 Sam. xxxi. 9, &c.

עָצַב, v. pres. non occ. Constr. immed. See עָצֵב above. Pret. aff. עֲצָבוֹ. He pained, grieved, thwarted, him, 1 Kings i. 6, only. Infin. aff. עָצְבִּי. Giving me pain, 1 Chron. iv. 10, only.
Part. pass. fem. constr. עֲצוּבַת. Pained, grieved, of —, Is. liv. 6, al. non occ.
Niph. נֶעֱצַב, pres. יֵעָצֵב. Constr. abs. it. med. בְּ, cause; אֶל, עַל, for; אֶת, obj. Be, become, affected with pain, grief, Gen. xlv. 5; 1 Sam. xx. 3. 34; 2 Sam. xix. 3; Eccl. x. 9; Neh. viii. 10, 11, al. non occ.
Pih. pret. pl. עִצְּבוּ, pres. יְעַצְּבוּ. Constr. immed. it. med. אֶת. (a) Bound up together, compacted, Job x. 8. See my note. (b) Gave pain, grieved, thwarted, Is. lxiii. 10. Comp. Ephes. iv. 30; Ps. lvi. 6, al. non occ.
Hiph. pres. pl. aff. יַעֲצִיבֻהוּ, immed. i. q. Pih. (b) Ps. lxxviii. 40.
Infin. aff. הַעֲצָבָהּ. Auth. Vers. "To worship her." Arab. conj. ii. عَصَّب, firmiter constrinxit, caput suum, vittâ fasciâve, Dominum, ac caput familiæ constituit: to constitute her lord, Jer. xliv. 19, al. non occ. It is curious to observe how anxious persons professing a false religion, or entertaining false notions of the true, have always been to have a female deity. So the Greeks in the celebrated Helen. See the Encomium of Helen, by Isocrates, Ἑλένης ἐγκωμιον. The Mohammedans in Fatima, the daughter of Mohammed. (See my "Persian Controversies," p. 49, seq.) The Hindoos, in their Parvati, and others. Simon Magus, in his Helen (Grabe's Irenæus, p. 94, col. 2, line 20), which, in some editions, was read "Selenen," i. e. the moon, as here in Jer.! And so the Roman Catholics have the Virgin Mary, honoured even as God! Late editions of the Hebrew Bible read הַעֲצָבָה, with ה' רמה, soft ה, as directed by the Masora; which is no doubt wrong, as the ancient Versions sufficiently prove.
Hithp. pres. pl. יִתְעַצְּבוּ. Constr. abs. it. med. אֶל, i. q. Niph., Gen. vi. 6; xxxiv. 7. The last, Gesen. "iram concepit;" which is erroneous: this being expressed by the יִחַר לָהֶם following. Aquila, διεπονήθη. LXX. διενοήθη, al. non occ.

עִצָּבוֹן, m. constr. עִצְּבוֹן, pl. non occ. Intens. Painful, great labour, Gen. iii. 16; where the pains of child-birth are meant. Comp. חֵבֶל, p. 180, (f) above; Ib. 17; v. 29. Aff. עִצְּבוֹנְךָ, al. non occ.

עַצֶּבֶת, f. constr. עַצֶּבֶת, pl. עַצָּבוֹת. Aff. עַצְּבוֹתַי, &c. (a) Pain, grief, intens., Job ix. 28; Prov. x. 10; xv. 13;—Ps. cxlvii. 3. Meton. for wounds, Ps. xvi. 4. Gesenius, "Idolum." So Rosenmüller (see Scholia on the place) after Symm. (τὰ εἴδωλα αὐτῶν). Aquila (διαπονήματα). Targ., &c. Others, generally with the Auth. Vers. "sorrows:" which, however, can hardly be supported here. Al. non occ.

עָצֶה, m. once, Lev. iii. 9. The spine, usually; but, Bochart. Hieroz., i. p. 497, makes it to signify the "Os coccygis." Arab. عَصْعَص. See the whole article, and עֵץ, above.

עֵצָה, fem. constr. עֲצַת, pl. עֵצוֹת. Aff. עֲצָתִי, pl. עֲצָתְךָ (of עֵצִים), r. יָעַץ. Arab. cogn. عَصَّ, dura, firma, fuit. See עֵץ, which, probably, contains the primary notion inherent in this word, implying firmness, &c. Comp. סוֹד, it. Prov. xxiv. 6. Counsel, either as given or received, 2 Sam. xvi. 20; 1 Kings i. 12; 2 Kings xviii. 20; Is. xix. 3; Hos. x. 6. — of God, Job xxxviii. 2; Is. xiv. 26; xlvi. 11, &c. Phrr. אַנְשֵׁי עֲצָתִי, אִישׁ עֲצָתִי, my counsellor, &c., Ps. cxix. 24, &c. עָשָׂה עֵצָה, Is. xxx. 1. See 1 Kings i. 12; Job xxxviii. 2; xlii. 3, &c.: places too numerous to insert. רוּחַ עֵצָה, spirit, mind, to receive counsel, wisdom, prudence, Is. xi. 2. Comp. Prov. viii. 14; xxi. 30. Phr. גְּדֹל הָעֵצָה, Jer. xxxii. 19. בְּעֵצָה, by counsel, i. e.

עצה (473) עצל

deliberately, 1 Chron. xii. 19, &c. Applied also to prophecy, as resulting from the counsels of the Deity, Is. xliv. 26, &c. Comp. Acts ii. 23, where we have, τῇ ὡρισμένῃ βουλῇ καὶ προγνώσει τοῦ Θεοῦ. Hence, the doctrine of *Predestination*, argued on as fact from prophecy solely, so frequently mistaken, as if taught and urged metaphysically from a consideration of the properties of the Divine mind—a fault common both to Calvinists and Arminians. See my Sermons and Dissertations, p. 35, seq.

עֵצָה, f. collectiv. i. q. עֵץ, cogn. τοῦ, עֵצֶה. *Wood, timber*, once, Jer. vi. 6. Applied also by Eich. Simonis, Gesen. &c., to Prov. xxvii. 9, in מֵעֲצַת נָפֶשׁ, "*de lignis odoratis*," says Gesen.: as if נָפֶשׁ here signified *scent, perfume*: which seems forced and unnatural. All the place seems to say is, *so the sweetness* (value) *of one's friend is, of the advice of the soul*, i. e. from its feeling and sincerity: in other words, as the perfume is grateful to the sense in the one case, so is the advice coming from a sincere heart in the other. Aquila, καὶ γλυκαίνει ἑταῖρον αὐτοῦ βουλῇ ψυχῆς. So Targ. Syr.

עָצָה, Part. Kal, only. Arab. عَصَى, *obligavit vulnus*. Æth. ዐጠወ: *clausit*. Cogn. עץ, עצה, עז, i. e. making *fast, firm*, once, Prov. xvi. 30. *Closing his eyes, &c.*, i. e. resisting the light. Aquila, Theod. στερεῶν. LXX. στηρίζων.

עָצוּם, m. pl. עֲצוּמִים, עֲצֻמִים. Aff. עֲצוּמַי, r. עצם, of which this is the Part. pass. *Powerful*, as to (a) Number, (b) Strength, (c) Greatness. (a) Deut. ix. 14; Ps. xxxv. 18; Is. lx. 22; Joel i. 6. (b) Prov. xxx. 26. (c) Ps. cxxxv. 10; Prov. xviii. 18; Zech. viii. 22; Ps. x. 10. בַּעֲצוּמָיו, *among his great ones*, i. e. into their power. Gesen. "*in ungulas ejus:*" but this is far fetched and unnecessary. Aquila, ἐπιπεσόντος αὐτοῦ μετὰ τῶν ἰσχυρῶν αὐτοῦ. See LXX.

עָצִיב, m. Chald. once, Dan. vi. 21. *Painful, sorrowful*.

עָצֵל, m.—pl. non occ. Arab. عَصَلَ, *tardavit*. Cogn. عَطَلَ, *otiosus fuit*. *Sluggish, tardy*, person, Prov. vi. 6. 9; xiii. 4, &c.; occ. in no other book.

עַצְלָה, f. (of עצל, seg. not in use)—

עַצְלוּת, f.—pl. non occ. r. עצל.—

Dual, עַצְלְתַיִם. *Sluggishness, sloth*, Prov. xix. 15, only. Dual, Eccl. x. 18, intensive, עַצְלוּת, once, Prov. xxxi. 27.

עָצַל, v. Kal non occ. See עָצֵל.

Niph. pres. 2 pers. pl. תֵּעָצֵלוּ. *Be, become, sluggish, slothful*, once, Judg. xviii. 9.

עֶצֶם, m. pl. עֲצָמִים, and עֲצָמוֹת. Aff. עֲצָמַי, pl. עֲצָמֵי, &c. Constr. m. עַצְמֵי, f. עַצְמוֹת. Aff. עַצְמֹתַי, &c. Æth. ዕጽም: *os*. Arab. عَظْم, id. Cogn. عَصَم, عَضَم, *os, radix caudæ equinæ*. (a) *Bone*, Gen. ii. 23; Exod. xii. 46; Num. ix. 12; Ezek. xxxvii. 7, &c. (b) Meton. *The body*, Exod. xxiv. 10. Thence taken to signify *self*, Gen. vii. 13; Exod. xii. 17; Lev. xxiii. 14; Josh. x. 27, &c. (comp. נֶפֶשׁ. Arab. نَفْس, גֶּרֶם, and Arab. عَيْن): but never of persons. So עֶצֶם הַיּוֹם, Arab. ذَاتُ اليَوْم. *The self* (same) *day*. עֶצֶם הַשָּׁמַיִם, Job xxi. 23. בְּעֶצֶם תֻּמּוֹ, *in his integrity's self;* his very, own, entireness, Lam. iv. 7. אָדְמוּ עֶצֶם מִפְּנִינִים, *more ruddy* in *self, person* than —; or, if עֶצֶם refer to the following word, which is not improbable, *more ruddy than coral itself, very coral*. Symm. πυρρότεροι τὴν ἕξιν ὑπέρ τὰ περίβλεπτα. See LXX.

עֹצֶם, m.—pl. non occ. } m. *Strength,*
עָצְמָה, f. constr. עָצְמַת. } *power*, Deut. viii. 17; Job xxx. 21; i. q. עֶצֶם. (b) Ps. cxxxix. 15. Fem., Is. xl. 29; xlvii. 9; it. Meton. *Multitude*, Nah. iii. 9. Aff. masc. עָצְמִי.

עָצַם, v. once, עָצְמוּ, Ps. xxxviii. 20, pres. יַעַצְמוּ. See עֶצֶם, and עֹצֶם, above. I. *Was powerful*, (a) As to number. (b) Strength, might. (c) Greatness. (a) Exod. i. 7. 20; Ps. xl. 6. 13; lxix. 5; Jer. xv. 8, &c. (b) Gen. xxvi. 16; Dan. viii. 8. Comp. ii. 23. (c) See in עָצוּם above.

II. *Make fast, close*, the eyes. See עָצָה above. Arab. أَعْصَم, *firmavit*. Cogn. عَطَم, *clausit oculos*; عَصَب, *cinxit*, Is. xxxiii. 15. Infin. aff. עָצְמוֹ, (b) Dan. viii. 8, only. Part. עֹצֵם, pl. non occ. Is. ll. cc. sign. ii. — pass. עָצוּם, pl. עֲצוּמִים. See above. Pih. pres. יְעַצֵּם. *Binds, closes*, the eyes, once, Is. xxix. 10. Pih. pret. עִצְּמוֹ. Lit. *He bones him*, i. e.

3 P

עצם (474) עקב

breaks his bones, Jer. L. 17, only; of עֶצֶם above, sign. I.

Hiph. pres. aff. יַעֲצִימֵהוּ. *Strengthens him*, constr. כֵּן above, Ps. cv. 24, only.

עֲצֻמוֹת, f. pl. once. Aff. עַצְמוֹתֵיכֶם. See עֶצֶם above. Lit. *Your powers*, i. e. defence, strength, in argument, Is. xli. 21. Arab. عِصْمَة, *defensio*.

עֲצָנוֹ, once, 2 Sam. xxiii. 8, in עֲדִינוֹ הָעֶצְנִי LXX. Ἀδινὼν ὁ Ἀσωναῖος, correctly. יָשַׁב, &c. referring apparently to David. Comp. 1 Chron. xi. 11: and read עִם יָשַׁב.

עָצַר, m.—pl. non occ. Arab. عَصَرَ, *prohibuit*; *pressit* uvas; غَصَرَ, *prohibuit*. Syr. ܟܠܐ, *pressit*. Æth. ዐፀወ: id. (a) *Shutting up, restraining*, the womb from child-bearing, Prov. xxx. 16. Comp. Gen. xvi. 2; xx. 18. (b) — in prison, restraint, or misery, Is. liii. 8. Comp. Jer. xxxiii. 1, &c.; Ps. cvii. 39, al. non occ.

עֶצֶר, masc.—pl. non occ. See עָצַר. Meton. once, Judg. xviii. 7, restraint; *Rule*. Phr. עֶצֶר יוֹרֵשׁ, *one possessing rule, a ruler*. Symm. μηδενὸς ἐνοχλοῦντος.

עָצַר, v. pres. יַעֲצֹר, and יַעֲצוֹר, תַּעְצֹר. See עָצַר above. Constr. abs. it. immed. it. med. אֶת, בְּ, כֵּן, from; לְ, בְּ, מִפְּנֵי. (a) *Shut up, restrain, detain*, Gen. xvi. 2; Deut. xi. 17; Judg. xiii. 16; 1 Kings xviii. 44; Is. lxvi. 9; Jer. xxxiii. 1; 2 Chron. vii. 13; Job iv. 2; xii. 15. (b) Meton. *Rule, reign*. See עָצַר, 1 Sam. ix. 17. — *retain* power, בְּ —, Dan. x. 8. 16; xi. 6; 1 Chron. xxix. 14; 2 Chron. ii. 6; xiii. 20. Also without בַּהּ, ellip. 2 Chron. xiv. 10; xx. 37.

Infin. עֲצֹר, Gen. xx. 18.
—, Job iv. 2. לַעְצֹר, 2 Chron. xxii. 8.
Part. עָצוּר, Deut. xxxii. 36, &c.
— f. עֲצוּרָה, 1 Sam. xxi. 5.

Niph. נֶעֱצַר, pres. הֵעָצֵר. Constr. abs. it. med. מֵעַל. *Be, become, shut up, restrained, detained*, i. e. *congregated, assembled*. — of the heavens, 1 Kings viii. 35; 2 Chron. vi. 26;—Num. xvii. 13. 15, &c.; 2 Sam. xxiv. 21. 25; Ps. cvi. 30. — *assembled*, &c., 1 Sam. xxi. 8. See עֲצָרָה.
Infin. הֵעָצֵר, 1 Kings l. c.
Part. נֶעְצָר, 1 Sam. xxi. 8.

עֲצָרָה } fem. pl. aff. עַצְרֹתֵיכֶם. See עָצַר.
עֲצֶרֶת } Lit. *restraint, shutting up*: applied, (a) to any *Day of assembling*, or con-gregation, as a day of *restraint*. (b) Such assembly or congregation. (a) 2 Kings x. 20; Is. i. 13; Joel i. 14; ii. 15; Jer. ix. 1; Amos v. 21. Pec. (b) *The seventh day* of the feast of the Passover, or *the eighth* of that of Tabernacles: termed also, מִקְרָא קֹדֶשׁ, Lev. xxiii. 36; Num. xxix. 35; Deut. xvi. 8; 2 Chron. vii. 9; Neh. viii. 18; Jer. ix. 1; Amos v. 21. Ikenius, Dissert. Theol., p. 50, seq., thinks the term was so applied, because work was *forbidden* on such days, Deut. xvi. 8, &c. Gesen., on the other hand, thinks the Arab. جُمْعَة, and يَوْمُ الْجُمْعَةِ, *day of coming together*, which, with the Mohammedans, is Friday (*Dies Veneris*), justifies the supposition that *restraint, shutting up, &c.*, is rather the cause of the term. He is, perhaps, right in the end, although it is doubtful whether the Mohammedan usage did not originate in a totally different notion. The real origin of the term is to be sought in consecrating such seasons *apart to religious service*, whence also they were called מִקְרָא קֹדֶשׁ. Hence the phrr. קִדְּשׁוּ עֲצָרָה, and קִרְאוּ עֲצָרָה, 2 Kings x. 20; Joel i. 14. Comp. Is. lviii. 3. 13.

עָקֵב, m.—pl. non occ. Syr. ܥܶܩܒܳܐ, *calx, extrema pars*, &c. Arab. عَقِب, n. of action of, "*percussit in calce pedis, ponè venit*," &c. The primary notion consists in, the *hinder part* of any thing; whence we have, pec. *the heel*; thence, *consequence*; v. *pursuing, punishing*, &c. Adv. and prep. (a) In *consequence that;—of, because that; for the sake of*. Nold. Quia, eo quod, propter. עֵקֶב הָיְתָה, *because there was, in consequence that*, &c., Num. xiv. 24; Deut. viii. 20; Is. v. 23. In Deut. vii. 12, וְהָיָה עֵקֶב תִּשְׁמְעוּן, *and it shall be, in consequence that ye surely hear*, i. e. *if ye hear*: supposing the thing done, then, &c. See under אִם, in which the bearing is similar: the primitive notion prevailing. Ps. xix. עֵקֶב רָב, *a great consequence*; or, Angl. *the consequence is great*, i. e. important and valuable. Comp. Ps. cxix. 112. Prov. xxii. 4, עֵקֶב עֲנָוָה, *the consequence of humility* is the fear of the Lord, &c. i. e. the fear of the Lord, and thence riches, &c. follow upon no other disposition.

(b) Adv. *consequently*, עֵקֶב אֶקְּרָה, *I will surely keep it consequently*, i. e. of thy teaching me, Ps. cxix. 33.

With other particles, עֵקֶב לֹא, Deut. viii. 20.

עֲקֹב (475) עקב

עַל־עָקֵב, Ps. xl. 16; lxx. 4. עֵקֶב אֲשֶׁר, Gen. xxvi. 5; xxii. 18; 2 Sam. xii. 6. עֵקֶב כִּי, 2 Sam. xii. 10; Amos iv. 12.

עָקֹב, m.—pl. non occ. Infin. of v. עקב below. Arab. عَقَبَة, *locus montis difficilis adscensu;* whence, (a) *A steep place,* Gesen., Is. xl. 4. But here the meaning may be that of the Arab. عُقَاب, *lapis intra puteum prominentior, ad quam laceratur urna;* and thence applied to any *prominence* difficult to be overcome, i. e. projecting like *the heel,* and hence presenting an obstacle. Such places, says the prophet, shall be לְמִישׁוֹר, for i. e. converted into a *level,* or *plain,* place: all such obstacles, σκάνδαλα, shall be removed. In other places see under the verb—

עָקֵב, m. constr. עֲקֵב, pl. עִקְבֵי, and occasionally עֲקֵבֵי; dag. euphon. fem. עֲקֵבוֹת. Aff. עֲקֵבוֹ, pl. עֲקֵבֵי, fem. עִקְבוֹתֶיךָ. (a) *The heel* of a man, Gen. iii. 15; xxv. 26; xlix. 17; Judg. v. 22; Jer. xiii. 22; Ps. xli. 10; Job xviii. 9. (b) Meton. *Impression of the heel, track, vestige,* Ps. lxxvii. 20; lxxxix. 52; Cant. i. 8. (c) *The heel,* i. e. *rear* of an army, Gen. xlix. 19; Josh. viii. 13. (d) *Supplanters, enemies; pursuers,* Ps. xlix. 6, in עֲקֵבַי. But this may very well mean *the iniquity of my tracks,* vestiges, ways. Comp. דֶּרֶךְ. Symm. ἀνομία τῶν ἰχνέων μου. lxx. τῆς πτέρνης μου. Eichhorn's Simonis refers עִקְבוֹת, &c. with dagesh, to עָקֵב, as a singular, which however does not occur.

עָקַב, v. pres. יַעְקֹב. Constr. immed. it. med. אֶת, it. abs. See עֵקֶב above. Lit. (a) *Heel, take by the heel,* Hos. xii. 3. Comp. Gen. xxv. 26. Hence, from seizing one from behind, i. e. insidiously. (b) *Circumvent, defraud,* Gen. xxvii. 36; Jer. ix. 3, al. non occ. Arab. عَقَّبَ, *malo incessivit.* Infin. עָקוֹב, Jer. ix. 3. (b)

Part. f. עֲקֻבָּה, for עֲקוּבָה. *Tracked, marked,* Hos. vi. 8. See עָקַב, (b) above. Aquila, περικαμπὴς ἀπὸ αἵματος. Symm. διώκται ἀπὸ αἵματος. Syr. "sanguine conspersa."

Pih. pres. aff. יְעַקְּבֵם. *Does trace them.* Syr. ܥܰܩܶܒ, *inquisivit, investigavit.* Arab. عَقَّبَ, *pressit, vestigia.* Once, Job xxxvii. 4. See my note.

עֲקֻבָּה, fem. once, 2 Kings x. 19, בְּעָקְבָה, *In fraud; insidiously.* See עָקַב, (b) above.

עָקֹד, masc. pl. עֲקֻדִּים. Arab. عَقْد, *baltheus;* عِقْد, *monile colli.* *Stripe, streak,* as seen on the coats of cattle—(see בְּרֻדִּים above, and Bochart. Phaleg., p. 606)— encircling the neck, legs, &c., Gen. xxx. 35. 39. 41; xxxi. 8. 10. 12, al. non occ.

עָקַד, v. pres. יַעֲקֹד. Constr. med. אֶת, once, Gen. xxii. 9. Arab. عَقَدَ, *ligavit.* Binds, ties.

עקה, f. constr. עֲקַת, r. עוק. Syr. ܥܳܩܳܐ, *pressura.* Arab. عُوق, *obstaculum.* *Pressure; oppression,* once, Ps. lv. 4.

עקל, v. Kal non occ. Syr. ܥܩܠ, *pervertit.* Chald. id. Arab. عَقَلَ, *constrinxit.* Puh. Part. מְעֻקָּל. *Been, become, perverted,* once, Hab. i. 4.

עֲקַלְקַלָּה, f. pl. עֲקַלְקַלּוֹת, intensit., Gram. art. 169; Ps. cxxv. 5. *Much perverted, very crooked, devious,* paths, Judg. v. 6. Metaph. id. Ps. cxxv. 5, al. non occ.

עֲקַלָּתוֹן, m. r. עקל, intensit., Gram. art. 168, once, Is. xxvii. 1. Syr. ܥܩܰܠܬܳܢܳܐ, *tortuosus.* *Very tortuous, crooked.* Aquila, ἐσκιρρώμενον, ἢ ἐπειρωμένον. Symm. τοῦ σκολιοῦ. See lxx.

עָקָר, masc. once, Lev. xxv. 47, in גֵּר מִשְׁפַּחַת עָקָר. *Root, nerve, of a strange family,* i. e. its head. Arab. عَقْر, i. q. أَصْل, *radix.* Syr. ܥܶܩܳܪܳܐ, id.

עָקָר, masc.—pl. non occ. ⎫ Syr. ܥܩܰܪ,
עֲקָרָה, fem. constr. עֲקֶרֶת, ⎭ *funditus evertit;* ܥܩܰܪ, *sterilis.* Arab. عَاقِر, *sterilis fuit mulier.* As in Engl. *to skin* may imply either *taking off,* or *putting on a skin;* so here, *the root* may be applied either in a prosperous or contrary sense, as in *take root, root out, &c.* *Barren, sterile,* of man or woman, and perhaps cattle, Exod. xxiii. 26; Deut. vii. 14;—Gen. xi. 30; xxv. 21; xxix. 31, &c. Constr. f. Ps. cxiii. 9.

עקר, v. Kal non occ., except in—

עָקַר (476) עָקַשׁ

Infin. with לְ, לַעֲקוֹר, constr. *To eradicate, root up*, opp. τῷ, נָטַע, Eccl. iii. 2, only. See עָרָה above.

Niph. pres. f. הֵעָקֵר. *Be, become, rooted up;* destroyed, once, Zeph. ii. 4.

Pih. עִקֵּר, pres. יְעַקֵּר. Constr. immed. it. med. אֶת. Arab. عَقَرَ, *pedes incidit. Nerve,* i. e. *cut the nerve, hamstring*, as of men or horses when taken in battle, Josh. xi. 6. 9. Meton. applied to chariots when the horses are, no doubt, meant, 2 Sam. viii. 4; 1 Chron. xviii. 4. — *of an ox*, Gen. xlix. 6. But here *ox* is probably put (metaph.) for a *powerful man*, as in other cases. אִישׁ, in the parallel seems to prove this; alluding to the violater of Dinah, Gen. xxxiv.

עֲקַר, v. Chald. Peḥal non occ. Ithpeh. אֶתְעֲקַרָה, Keri אֶתְעֲקָרָה. *Was, became, rooted up*, Dan. vii. 8, only.

עִקָּר, m.—pl. non occ. *Nerve, stump*, Dan. iv. 12. 20. 23, al. non occ. Syr. ܟܶܣܦܳܐ, *radix, stipes.*

עַקְרָב, m. pl. עֲקְרַבִּים. Arab. عَقْرَب, *scorpio;* it. capistrum, quo solea astringitur *supra pedem; calamitates*; عَقْرَج, *ferrum harpagini simile.* (a) *A scorpion*, Deut. viii. 15; Ezek. ii. 7. (b) In the pl. some instrument of punishment so called. Gesen. "*Flagelli* genus aculeis munitum. . . . Ita Lat. *scorpio* teste Isidoro (Origg. 5. 27) est: *virga nodosa et aculeata.*" See Facciolati, sub voce, where we have, "*scorpiones* rectissimè vocantur, quia arcuato vulnere in corpus infiguntur."—The name also of a certain sort of ballista; and also, meton. of the missiles projected by it:—1 Kings xii. 11. 14; 2 Chron. x. 11. 14, al. non occ.

עָקַשׁ, v. pres. aff. יְעַקְּשֵׁנִי. Arab. عَقَشَ, *inflexit* lignum. Cogn. عَقَصَ, *torsit.* See عَكَسَ, عَكَصَ، عَكَشَ, once, Job ix. 20. *Convict me of perverseness*, corresponding to יַרְשִׁיעֵנִי, in the paral. LXX. σκολιὸς ἀποβήσομαι. Αλλ. καὶ ἐστρέβλωσέ με. Vulg. "*pravum me comprobabit.*"

Niph. Part. constr. נַעֲקָשׁ. *One perverse of* —, once, Prov. xxviii. 18.

Pih. עִקֵּשׁ, pres. יְעַקֵּשׁ. *Make perverse, crooked.* Metaph. Morally, Is. lix. 8; Mic. iii. 9, al. non occ.

Part. מְעֻקָּשׁ, Prov. x. 9, only.

עִקֵּשׁ, m. constr. עִקֵּשׁ, pl. עִקְּשִׁים, constr. עִקְּשֵׁי. See עקש above. *Perverse, tortuous.* Syn. פְּתַלְתֹּל, and נִפְתָּל. Applied to a generation, Deut. xxxii. 5. — *a people*, 2 Sam. xxii. 27; Ps. xviii. 27. — *person*, Prov. viii. 8; xi. 20; xxii. 5. — *the heart*, Ps. ci. 4; Prov. xvii. 20. — *the lips*, Prov. xix. 1. — *ways*, morally, Ib. ii. 15, al. non occ.

עִקְּשׁוּת, f.—pl. non occ. *Perverseness, crookedness.* — *of mouth*, Prov. iv. 24; vi. 12. Comp. Ib. xix. 1, and see לוּחַ, p. 326 above. Aquila, στρεβλότητα στόματος. See LXX. Symm. στρεβλεύμασι στόματος.

עָר, pl. aff. עָרֶיךָ: and, according to some, עָרִים, Ps. ix. 7 : r. עִיר, or עוּר. Arab. غَارَ, r. عور, *cepit, perdidit.* Cogn. غَارَ, *ferbuit* æstu dies. *An enemy*, 1 Sam. xxviii. 16; Ps. cxxxix. 20. It. Chald. עָר, *thine enemies*, Dan. iv. 16. See Keri, al. non occ.

עֶרֶב, m.—pl. f. עֲרָבוֹת; dual עַרְבַּיִם. Arab. عَرَبَ, *profundus fuit.* Cogn. غَرَبَ, *distitit; occidit sol;* it. *niger fuit.* The primitive notion seems to have consisted in, motion towards, or from any place or thing. Arab. عَرِبَ, *alacer, lubens; appetivit, inivit; immiscuit.* Thence, *Agreeableness, concurrence, mixture; woof* of the web; *compact; pledge: whiteness*, as indicating mirth, &c., as opposed to *blackness:* and thence the willow. And, on the other hand, *departure;* thence, *place* or *person without: desert, foreigner, Arabian:* and, applied to the sun, *evening, blackness, darkness; raven* or *crow; dun* or *black fly, &c.* Comp. cogn. Heb. אָרַב, עָרַב. I. *The evening*, a term apparently as indefinite as among ourselves. According to the Samaritans and Caraite Jews, its duration was of two parts: first, beginning with the setting sun; the second, at the end of the twilight. But, according to the rabbins, first, when the sun began to decline towards the West; the second, when it had set. Which has been had recourse to purely for the purpose, in each case, of attaching a favourite interpretation to the dual form, viz. עַרְבַּיִם. Others have, for the same reason, had recourse to the Greek, δείλη πρωία, and δείλη ὀψία. See Bochart. Hieroz., i. p. 559; Rosenmüller on Exod. xvi. 12, &c. All of which, according to my

עֲרָב (477) עֲרָב

notions, is groundless and wrong. See my Sermon on the Sabbath, with the notes: where it is shown that the phrase בֵּין הָעַרְבַּיִם, *between the two evenings*, means between the period termed evening, עֶרֶב, on one day, and the same period on the next, including one whole day: so that the paschal lamb was to be eaten sometime between six o'clock on the 14th of Nisan, and six o'clock on the next day, comprehending the whole day, viz., the 14th day of Nisan; the day commencing with the Hebrews about six o'clock in the afternoon. Our blessed Lord, according to this, both ate the paschal lamb at the due time appointed for that rite, and also suffered on that day so appointed. And hence also it is that we read of some who would not enter the Judgment Hall of Pilate about day-break on the same day, because they had not yet eaten the passover, John xviii. 28. This makes the whole plain and easy. This phrase occurs, Exod. xii. 6; xvi. 12; xxviii. 39. 41; xxx. 8; Lev. xxiii. 5; Num. ix. 3. 5. 11; xxviii. 4. Sing. opp. τῷ, בֹּקֶר, Gen. i. 5. 8; Exod. xviii. 12, &c. It. with mid-day, Ps. lv. 13. Twilight, Prov. vii. 9. Offering of —, Ps. cxli. 2; Dan. ix. 21. Shades of —, Jer. vi. 4. Wolves of —, Zeph. iii. 3; Hab. i. 8. Phrr. לְעֵת עֶרֶב, *at the time of evening*, Gen. viii. 11; xxiv. 11, &c. לִפְנוֹת עֶרֶב, *at the time of even turn*, i. e. as the evening was coming on, Gen. xxiv. 63; Deut. xxiii. 12. עֲרֵי־עֶרֶב, Ps. civ. 23, *until* —, it. — עַד Exod. xviii. 13, it. — עַד עֶרֶב, *until the time of* —, Josh. viii. 29, &c., it. לָעֶרֶב, Job iv. 20, &c. Pl. once, Jer. v. 6.

II. *Distance*: thence, *foreign; foreigner.* Arab. غَرِيب, *exoticus;* of غَرَب, *distitit*; pl. non occ. מַלְכֵי הָעֶרֶב, kings of distance, i. e. foreign, 1 Kings x. 15;—Jer. xxv. 20. 24; L. 37; Ezek. xxx. 5. But, from Jer. xxv. 24, so called, perhaps, because שֹׁכְנִים בַּמִּדְבָּר, i. e. בַּעֲרָבָה, *residing in the desert.*

III. עֶרֶב, pl. non occ. i. q. עֵרֶב. II. (a) *Foreigner, stranger*, Exod. xii. 38. עֶרֶב רַב, *much foreign*, people, Neh. xiii. 3, al. non occ. (b) Arab. غَرَاب, *arboris cujusdam lanugo, ex qua funes conficiuntur*, it. *qui sacculos et crumenos confecit:* whence, perhaps, the notion of *mixture, commixture*, and the like. The *woof* of the web in weaving, Lev. xiii. 48. 52. 56. 59, &c.

IV. Pl. only, עֲרָבִים, constr. עַרְבֵי. Arab. غَرَب, *salix; salix Babylonica.* Osiers, willows, i. q. Greek 'Ιτέα, of Dioscorides. According to Abulfadl, as cited by Celsius, Hierobot., i. p. 304, the word is generic, and comprehends a whole class, Is. xliv. 4; Job xl. 22 (17);—Ps. cxxxvii. 2. German, Trauerweide, Gesen. Phr. נַחַל הָעֲרָבִים, the torrent, or valley of —, Is. xv. 7. Burckhardt notices a *spring*, apparently in the same quarter, termed, صفصاف عين, "*fountain of the willow*," Is. xv. 7; it. עַרְבֵי נַחַל, *willows of the torrent*, Lev. xxiii. 40.

עֲרָב, and עֲרָב, fem. proper name. *Arabia:* so called from its desert, sterile, character. See עֲרָבָה, 2 Chron. ix. 14; Is. xxi. 13. Whence—

עַרְבִי } masc. pl. עַרְבִים, and עַרְבִיִּים, עַרְבִי } 2 Chron. xvii. 11. *Arab, Arabian*, Is. xiii. 20; Jer. iii. 2; Neh. ii. 19; 2 Chron. xxi. 16.

עָרֹב, m.—pl. non occ. Aquila, πάμμυια, πάμμικτος. Symm. κυνόμυια. So LXX. To the latter Bochart. inclines, Hieroz., ii. lib. iv. c. xv. p. 553. *Musca canina*, sive *tabanus.* The *gad-bee, ox-fly*, or *dun-fly.* The Jews, generally, *all manner of noxious animals*, as lions, bears, serpents, &c. Jerome, "omne genus muscarum." Auth. Vers. "swarms of flies." Others, otherwise. The probability is strong, that it is the generic name of *some sort of noxious fly;* but what that is, it is impossible to say. St. John seems to have had his eye on this plague, when he spoke of it as consisting of *locusts* (Rev. ix. 3, seq.) It is true, Exod. x. 4, is usually referred to here; but, it should be observed, in that place the destruction of the produce of the land only is had in view; here the injury of men. It is not improbable the *fly* was so called from its property to injure. Arab. غَرَب, *acutior pars, et nitor dentium; gladii acies; acuitas; alacritas*, Exod. viii. 17, 18. 20. 25, 26; Ps. lxxviii. 45; cv. 31.

עֹרֵב, m. pl. עֹרְבִים, constr. עֹרְבֵי. Arab. غُرَاب, *corvus.* A *raven*, or *crow;* so called, perhaps, from its *blackness.* Gr. κόραξ. See עֶרֶב above; and Hieroz., ii. lib. ii. c. xiii. p. 214. Cant. v. 11: or,

ערב (478) יערב

perhaps, from its croaking as in the Sanscrit, काक, and कारव, *kāka*, and *kārava*, *a crow*, Gen. viii. 7; Lev. xi. 15; Deut. xiv. 14; Ps. cxlvii. 9; Is. xxxiv. 11; Job xxxviii. 41; Prov. xxx. 17, &c. In 1 Kings xvii. 4. 6, some suppose Arabs to be meant. But this is both unnecessary and groundless. For a miracle must have been wrought in any case, and the text, as it now stands, will admit of nothing less. Besides, to have made known generally to the Arabs the place of the prophet's retirement, would have been to have entirely ruined its object. Aquila, Symm., Theod., LXX. here, καὶ οἱ κόρακες, κ.τ.λ. And so the ancient versions, except the Arabic, which possesses no authority.

עָרֵב, m.—pl. non occ. *Agreeable, sweet*, twice, Prov. xx. 17; Cant. ii. 14. See עָרַב above.

עָרַב, v. pres. וַיֶּעֱרַב, pl. יֶעֶרְבוּ. Constr. immed. it. med. עַל, לְ, אֶת, pers. it. abs. (a) *Was agreeable, sweet* (see עָרֵב above), Ps. civ. 34; Ezek. xvi. 37; Prov. iii. 24; xiii. 19; Jer. vi. 20, &c. (b) *Agreed, made compact*, by bartering goods, &c., Ezek. xxvii. 9. 27. (c) *Became surety; pledged; gave pledge*, Gen. xliii. 9; xliv. 32; Job xvii. 3, with עִם, Is. xxxviii. 14; Ps. cxix. 122; Prov. xi. 15; xx. 16; xxvii. 13: with לְ, vi. 1; with לִפְנֵי, xvii. 18; Neh. v. 3, &c. (d) *Became dark, evening came on*, Judg. xix. 9. Metaph. Is. xxiv. 11, עָרְבָה כָּל־שִׂמְחָה, *all joy has grown dark ; its sun is set*.

Infin. עֲרוֹב, Judg. l. c. (d) Ezek. l. c. Ps. l. c. (c).

Imp. aff. עָרְבֵנִי, Job l. c. (c); Is. l. c. (c).

Part. עֹרֵב, Prov. xvii. 18 (c).

— pl. עֹרְבִים, Neh. l. c. (c); Prov. xxii. 26 (c).

Hiph. Infin. הַעֲרֵב, opp. τῷ, הַשְׁכֵּם. (d) *Growing late, &c.*, 1 Sam. xvii. 16, only.

Hithp. הִתְעָרְבוּ, pl. m. pres. non occ. (a) *Be, become, agreeable to, intermixed with*, with בְ, Ezra ix. 4; Prov. xiv. 10; Ps. cvi. 35: with לְ, Prov. xx. 19; עִם, Ib. xxiv. 21. (b) *Agree, make compact with*, אֶת, 2 Kings xviii. 23; Is. xxxvi. 8. Gesen. "*In certamen descendit*." But neither the etymology nor the context will give countenance to this. Eichhorn's Simonis, "*Sponsionem ini*. LXX. καὶ νῦν μίχθητε. Vulg. "*transite*." Syr. ܐܬܚܠܛ, i. q. LXX. Targ. אִתְעָרַב, i. q. Heb.

ערב, v. Chald. Peh. non occ.

Pah. Part. מְעָרַב. *Mixed*, Dan. ii. 43, only.

Ith. Part. m. מִתְעָרַב. *Be, become, mixed, associated, with*, Dan. ii. 43.

— pl. מִתְעָרְבִין, Ib. al. non occ.

עֲרָבָה, f. pl. עֲרָבוֹת, constr. עַרְבוֹת. Aff. עֲרָבָתָה. See עָרָב above. (a) *Any plain, champaign, country*, Josh. iii. 16; 2 Sam. iv. 7, &c. (b) *A desert*, Job xxiv. 5; Is. xxxv. 1; li. 3; Jer. l. 12; li. 43, &c. In Kethiv, 2 Sam. xv. 28; xvii. 16; we have, עֲרָה. Pl. abs., Ps. lxviii. 5. Comp. יְשִׁימוֹן, in. vr. 8, which should shew what particular desert is intended. Some have imagined the clouds to have been meant (metaph.) here. With the article, הָעֲרָבָה, is, according to Gesen., الغور, *El ghaur*, of the Arabs, into which the valley of the Jordan runs, and which extends as far as the Gulf of Ailah, Deut. i. 1; ii. 8; Josh. xii. 1, &c. Whence the phrr. יָם הָעֲרָבָה, *sea of the desert*, i. e. the Dead Sea, Deut. iv. 49, &c. נַחַל הָעֲרָבָה, *torrent of the desert*, i. e. the brook Kidron, Amos vi. 14, &c. עַרְבוֹת יְרִיחוֹ, *plains of Jericho*, Josh. v. 10: and עַרְבוֹת מוֹאָב, — of Moab, Num. xxxi. 12, &c.

עֲרֻבָּה, f. aff. עֲרֻבָּתָם. *Pledge, surety*. See עָרַב above, 1 Sam. xvii. 18; Prov. xvii. 18, only.

עֵרָבוֹן, m.—pl. non occ. See עָרַב above. Arab. عُرْبَان, عَرَبُون. Greek ἀρραβών. *Security, pledge*, Gen. xxxviii. 17, 18. 20, al. non occ.

ערבי, see עָרַב above.

ערבתי, m. Patronym. of עֲרָבָה, 2 Sam. xxiii. 31.

ערג, v. pres. תַּעֲרוֹג. Æth. ዐርገ: *ascendit; preces Deo obtulit*. Arab. عرج, *ascendit;* عَرَج, *inclinatio, propensio* in rem; *cum quis insistit rei;* عِجَّاك, *adaquatio camelorum*. The Jews take this word to signify *lowing, bleating*, as an animal, which, Joel i. 20, בַּהֲמוֹת שָׂדֶה תַּעֲרוֹג, seems to justify, as does the Syriac Version, which every where gives ܓܥܐ, *clamavit*. Bochart. Hieroz. i. p. 884, calls this in question, and prefers the sense of *desiring, longing* for, or the like, after the LXX. and Vulgate. Still,

ערו (479) ערו

both are probably right; the one taking the act by which *desire, &c.* is evinced, viz., *lowing, bleating:* the other (meton.) the cause of such *lowing, &c.,* viz., *desire, longing.* The Æth. and Arab. above seem to reconcile both these views: which differ rather on the use, than on the real meaning, of the word, Ps. xlii. 2, al. non occ.

עֲרֻגַּת, or עֲרֻגָה, Part. f. constr. See ערג, pl. עֲרֻגוֹת, עֲרֻגֹת. Lit. *raised. A raised bed,* or *parterre,* in a garden or orchard, Cant. v. 13; vi. 2; Ezek. xvii. 7. 10, al. non occ. Aquila, Symm. πρασιά.

ערד, m. pl. def. עֲרָדַיָּא. *Wild asses,* once, Dan. v. 21. Syr. ܥܪܕܐ, *effrœnis fuit.* Arab. عَرَدَ, *durus fuit; fugit.* I. q. Heb. עָרוֹד.

ערה, f. pl. עָרוֹת. Arab. عَرِيَ, *nudus fuit;* عُرْيٌ, *nuditas. Naked, bare,* places, i. e. pastures; places in which there are no buildings; synon. τοῦ, מִדְבָּר, once, Is. xix. 7.

עָרָה, v. pres. apoc. תְּעַר, pl. יְעָרוּ. See ערה above. (a) *Make naked,* strip. (b) *Empty.* (c) *Pour out.*

עֵרָה, pres. יְעָרֶה, apoc. תְּעַר, pl. יְעָרוּ. Pih. See ערה above. (a) *Make naked, bare.* (b) *Empty; pour out.* (a) Is. iii. 17; xxii. 6; Zeph. ii. 14; Hab. iii. 13. Comp. גָּלָה, II. above, p. 113. (b) Gen. xxiv. 20; 2 Chron. xxiv. 11; Ps. cxli. 8. Comp. ἐκένωσε, Phil. ii. 7.

Infin. עָרוֹת, Hab. l. c.
Imp. pl. עָרוּ, Ps. cxxxvii. 7.
For עָרֵר, and תִּתְעָרֵר, see under ערר.
Niph. pres. יֵעָרֶה. *Be, become, poured out,* Is. xxxii. 15, only.
Hiph. הֶעֱרָה. (a) *Make naked, lay bare, expose,* Lev. xx. 18, 19. (b) *Poured out,* Is. liii. 12, al. non occ.
Hithp. pres. f. תִּתְעָרִי. (a) *Be, become, stripped, exposed,* Lam. iv. 21.
Part. מִתְעָרֶה. (b) *Being poured forth,* i. e. *diffuse,* and spreading abroad like the branches of a tree, Ps. xxxvii. 35, only.

עֲרֻגַּת, see under ערג above.

עָרוֹד, m. i. q. עֲרָד above. *Wild ass,* Job xxxv. 9, only.

עֶרְיָה, fem. constr. עֶרְיַת, pl. non occ. Arab. عُرْيٌ, *nuditas.* See ערה above. *Naked-ness, exposure.* (a) *Unfortified state of a country:* see גָּלָה, Gen. xlii. 9. 12. (b) —, *nudity of a person,* male or female, Gen. ix. 22, 23; Lev. xviii. 7. 17. (c) Meton. *Shame, disgrace.* עֶרְוַת דָּבָר, *matter of shame, filth,* Deut. xxiii. 15; Ib. xxiv. 1: some uncleanness, perhaps. עֶרְוַת מִצְרַיִם, — *of Egypt,* Is. xx. 4. — *of fornication,* Ezek. xxiii. 29. Aff. עֶרְוָתְךָ, Exod. xx. 26. עֶרְוָתוֹ, Lev. xx. 17, &c.

עֶרְוַת, f. constr. Chald. See ערה above. *Pouring out. Meton. Loss,* Ezra iv. 14, only.

עָרוֹם, עָרֹם, plur. עֲרֻמִּים, masc.—
עֲרֻמָּה, fem.—pl. non occ.—
Arab. عَرَمَ, *carne nudavit os;* it. *lactavit infantem:* whence, عَرَمٌ, *adeps, aggeres:* it. عَرِمَ, *malignus fuit. Naked,* Gen. ii. 25; Eccl. v. 14; Job i. 21; Is. lviii. 7, &c. — *partially.* Gr. γυμνός, James ii. 15, &c.; Job xxii. 6; xxiv. 7. 10. So 1 Sam. xix. 24; Is. xx. 2—4. Fem, Hos. ii. 5, only. — *exposed, spoiled,* Job xxvi. 6; Mic. i. 8; Amos ii. 16.

עָרוּם, m. pl. עֲרוּמִים. See עָרֹם. (a) *Malignant, cunning,* Gen. iii. 1; Job v. 12; xv. 5. Also, (b) *Prudent, cautious,* Prov. xii. 16. 23; xiii. 16, &c.

עָרֹם, see עָרוֹם above.

עֲרוֹעֵר, m. once, Jer. xlviii. 6. Gesen. "probab. i. q. עָרָר, pr. *nudus,* deinde *egenus, propulsus.* (cf. xvii. 6). LXX. ὄνος ἄγριος (עָרוֹד)," &c. Eichhorn's Simonis, "*Meleagris.*" Arab. غَرْغَرْ." Vers. Syr. ܓ݂ܰܒ݂ܣܐ, *stipes: A stump,* or denudated trunk of a tree, perhaps. He seems to have taken the Arab. عَرَا, *radix,* as a key to this word. The context evidently requires either *a person* or *thing,* in a hopeless condition. The Syr. has preferred taking *a thing* so circumstanced; Gesenius, *a person.* To this, عَرَبِيٌّ, *peregrinus, advena;* and the Heb. cogn. עֲרִירִי, *solitary,* may, perhaps, give some support: such person in such situation being in a hopeless condition. Also the name of some cities, Deut. ii. 36; Josh. xiii. 25, &c.

עֵרַע (480) עֲרָךְ

עֲרָעֵרִי, m. Patronym. of עֲרוֹעֵר, or עֹעֵר, 1 Chron. xi. 44.

עָרוּץ, al. עָרוֹץ, m. constr. See עֲרָץ: once, Job xxx. 6. *Abrupt, fearful,* place.

עֶרְיָה, f.—pl. non occ. i. q. עֶרְוָה, and synon. τοῦ, עֵרֹם, Ezek. xvi. 7. 22. 39, &c. *Nudity, nakedness,* Ezek. l. c. it. xxiii. 29; Mic. i. 11. In Hab. iii. 8, used as an Infin. עָרָה הָעוֹר, *thou makest quite bare.*

עֲרִיסוֹת, fem. plur. only with aff. עֲרִיסֹתֵינוּ, "*Massa, mixtio farinæ cum aqua.*" Chald. ערס, *commiscuit.*" Eichhorn's Simonis. Gesen. "*Polenta.*" For which he gives the Syr. ܢܐܣܠ?, id. But the Syr., according to Castell, signifies, "*zythum, ptisana.*" *Dough,* Num. xv. 20, 21; Ezek. xliv. 30; Neh. x. 38, al. non occ.

עֲרִיפִים, m. pl. aff. only, עֲרִיפָיו, once, Is. v. 30, r. ערף, *cœli.* Castell. " Abrav. et Arab. ערף, ערפה, Arab. Oxon. סחאב, *nubes,* sc. *distillantes.*" Which Gesenius follows, adding, Syr. et Vulg. *caligo.* But as אוֹר occurs in the passage,—Arab. غَرِيفَة, *sidera.* Metaph.—*Nobles,* may have been intended: the sun, moon, and stars, being put, Gen. xxxvii. 9, for Jacob, his wife, and sons. And this, I think, is here the case. عَرِيف too, signifies *prince.*

עָרִיץ, m. pl. עֲרִיצִים, constr. עֲרִיצֵי, r. עָרַץ. (a) *Strong, powerful, mighty,* Jer. xx. 11; Is. xxv. 3—5, &c. (b) *Violent, cruel,* Ps. xxxvii. 35; Is. xiii. 11; xxix. 20; Job vi. 23; xv. 20; xxvii. 13; Ezek. xxviii. 7, &c.

עֲרִירִי, m. pl. עֲרִירִים, r. עור, cogn. τοῦ, שרה. Arab. عَارُورَة, *camelus absque gibbo. Destitute,* of children, *childless,* Lev. xx. 20, 21; Jer. xxii. 30; Gen. xv. 2. הֹלֵךְ עֲרִירִי So the Lat. *incedo regina,* al. non occ.

עָרַךְ, m.—pl. non occ. Aff. עֶרְכִּי, &c. Arab. cogn. عَرَّج, II. *intentus fuit* rei; *comparavit;* عَرَّك, *conseruit cum eo manus.* (a) *Order, arrangement, suit, series.* — of the shew-bread, Exod. xl. 23. 44; Judg. xli. 4. — of cloths, Judg. xvii. 10. (b) *Value, estimation,* i. e. one thing being so set against another as to ascertain its worth, Job xxviii. 13. Comp. vr. 16, 17. 19; Lev. v. 15. 18. 25; xxvii. 12; Ps. lv. 14. מֶעֶרְכִּי, *according to my value,* i. e. my equal. So, בְּעֶרְכְּךָ, Lev. l. c., &c. מֵעֶרְכְּךָ, Ib. xxvii. 8, &c.

עָרַךְ, v. pres. יַעֲרֹךְ. See עֶרֶךְ. Cogn. ארך. Constr. immed. it. med. עַל, לְ; אֶת, אֶל, מִפְּנֵי. (a) *Set in order, arrange, dispose.* — a table for a feast, Ps. xxiii. 5; Prov. ix. 2; Is. xxi. 5; lxv. 11. — the altar, candlestick, &c., Gen. xxii. 9; Exod. xxvii. 21; Lev. i. 6; xxiv. 3, 4. 8; Num. xxiii. 4. — the battle, &c., Judg. xx. 20. 22: with עִם, לִקְרַאת, or אֶת, of pers., 2 Sam. x. 9, 10; x. 17; Jer. L. 9. 14. — words in dispute, Job xxxii. 14; xxxvii. 19. מִפְּנֵי חֹשֶׁךְ, *from, on account of, darkness;* ignorance. — cause for trial, Ps. L. 21; Job xiii. 18; xxiii. 4. Phrr. יַעֲרְכוּנִי, for יַעֲרְכוּ עָלַי, Job vi. 4: with עֶרֶךְ, Exod. xl. 4. 23. צִנָּה וָרֹמַח. — shield and spear, 1 Chron. xii. 8. Comp. Jer. xlvi. 3.

(b) — for the purpose of *comparing, valuing, estimating,* Is. xl. 18; Ps. xl. 6; lxxxix. 7; Job xxviii. 17. 19; xxxvi. 19. See my note. Infin. עֲרֹךְ, Is. xxi. 5; עֶרְךָ, Ps. xl. 6, &c. Imp. with ה parag. עֶרְכָה, Job xxxiii. 5. — pl. עִרְכוּ, Jer. xlvi. 3. Part. pl. עֹרְכִים, constr. עֹרְכֵי, Is. lxv. 11; 1 Chron. xii. 33, &c. — pass. עָרוּךְ, constr. עֲרוּךְ, Is. xxx. 33; Joel ii. 5. — f. עֲרוּכָה, 2 Sam. xxiii. 5. — pl. עֲרוּכוֹת, Josh. ii. 6. Hiph. הֶעֱרִיךְ, pres. יַעֲרִיךְ. Constr. immed. it. med. אֶת. (b) *Valued,* (meton.) *set a tax upon,* Lev. xxvii. 8. 12. 14; 2 Kings xxiii. 35.

עָרֵל, f. עֲרֵלָה, constr. עֲרֶלַת, pl. עֲרֵלוֹת, constr. עֲרְלוֹת. Syr. ܟܘܦܕܠܐ, *præputium.* Arab. غُرْل, id. The original notion seems to have consisted in *laxness, excess;* as Arab. غَرِل, *mollis, laxo corpore; hasta longa,* &c.: and, thence, particularly after the times of Abraham, when circumcision had been commanded, was considered as an abomination. *Foreskin:* thence, *uncircumcision,* Gen. xxxiv. 14; Exod. iv. 25; Lev. ix. 24. Phr. בְּשַׂר עָרְלָה, *flesh* of his —, Gen. xvii. 14, seq. With other aff., Gen. xvii. 11. 23: pl., 1 Sam. xviii. 26. Metaph. Because it constitutes a covering, and thence an impediment. עָרְלַת לֵב, — *of heart,* i. e. impenetrableness, hardness, wickedness of —, Deut. x. 16; Jer. iv. 4. עָרְלָתוֹ אֶת־פִּרְיוֹ, *its uncircumcision as to its fruit,* i. e. its first fruits, Lev. xix. 23. Pl., 1 Sam. xviii. 24; 2 Sam. iii. 14, &c.

עָרֵל, m. } constr. עֲרַל, it. עֲרָל, pl. עֲרֵלִים,
עֲרֵלָה, f. } constr. עַרְלֵי. See ערל above.
Uncircumcised person, Exod. xii. 48; Is. liii. 1. Phr. עָרֵל נֵבָר, Gen. xvii. 14: i. q. עֲרַל בָּשָׂר, Ezek. xliv. 9: pl. עַרְלֵי בָשָׂר, &c. As a term of reproach, Judg. xiv. 3; 1 Sam. xvii. 23. 36; Ezek. xxviii. 10; xxxi. 18, &c. Metaph. — of the heart, *coated, hard, &c.,* Ezek. xliv. 7. 9; Jer. ix. 25; Lev. xxvi. 41. Phr. עֲרַל שְׂפָתַיִם, *— of lips,* i. e. *hesitating of speech,* Exod. vi. 12. 30. — *of ears,* i. e. heavy, slow, of hearing, Jer. vi. 10. — *of trees,* forbidden as profane, because the first fruits had not been yet offered, Lev. xix. 23. Hence the verb—

עָרֵל, v. עֲרַלְתֶּם. *Ye shall consider, esteem, uncircumcised,* profane; once, Lev. xix. 23. Pres. non occ.

Niph. Imp. הֵעָרֵל. *Appear, be considered, uncircumcised,* Hab. ii. 16, where allusion is made to Gen. ix. 22, al. non occ.

עָרְמָם, m. aff. עָרְמָם, once, Job v. 13. *Their craftiness, cunning.* See עָרוֹם.

ערם, v. Pret. pres. Kal non occ. See עָרוֹם above.
Infin. עָרוֹם. (a) *Being cunning, subtile,* 1 Sam. xxiii. 22, al. non occ.
Niph. pl. נַעֲרְמוּ. (b) *They became swollen, heaped,* once, Exod. xv. 8. عَرِم, *adeps, aggeres.* See עָרוֹם above, and عَرَمَة, *cumulus, frumenti.*
Hiph. יַעֲרִימוּ, pl. יַעֲרִימוּ. (a) *Act, do, cunningly,* Ps. lxxxiii. 4; 1 Sam. xxiii. 22. (b) — *prudently, wisely,* Prov. xv. 5; xix. 25.

עָרֹם, m. i. q. עָרוֹם.

עָרְמָה, fem. of עָרוֹם, pl. non occ. (a) *Craftiness, cunning,* Exod. xxi. 14; Josh. ix. 4. (b) *Prudence,* Prov. i. 4; viii. 5. 12.

עֲרֵמָה, f. constr. עֲרֵמַת, pl. עֲרֵמוֹת, and masc. עֲרֵמִים. See עָרוֹם. *Heap* of ruins, Jer. l. 26; Neh. iii. 34. — *of corn,* Ruth iii. 7; Cant. vii. 3; Hag. ii. 16, &c.; generally, 2 Chron. xxxi. 6. 7. 9.

עַרְמוֹן, m. pl. עַרְמֹנִים. *The platanus,* or *plane tree.* Cels. Hierobot. i., p. 513, seq., twice, Gen. xxx. 37; Ezek. xxxi. 8. So called, perhaps, from its bushy appearance,

"*patulis diffusa ramis.*" Cic. de. Orat. See עָרוֹם above, and Syr. ܐܪܡ, *coacervavit.*

עַרְעָר, m. — pl. non occ. Cogn. עוּר, עֲרִירִי, עֲרָה. *Naked. Destitute, poor,* Jer. xvii. 6; Ps. cii. 18. Symm. in Jer. l. c. ξύλον ἄκαρπον.

עֹרֶף, m.—pl. non occ. Aff. עָרְפִּי, עָרְפּוֹ, &c. Arab. عُرْف, *juba equi. Back of the neck, shoulders; back,* of a man, opp. τῷ פָּנִים, Jer. xviii. 17. — of a bird, Lev. v. 8. Phrr. קְשֵׁה־עֹרֶף, *hard, stubborn, of neck,* i. e. *not willingly bowing down,* Exod. xxxii. 9; xxxiii. 3, &c. Comp. Prov. xxix. 1; Deut. xxxi. 27; Is. xlviii. 4. יִפְנוּ עֹרֶף, *they turn the back, run away,* Josh. vii. 12; Jer. xxxii. 33, &c. יָדְךָ בְּעֹרֶף, *thy hand on the neck,* i. e. *to chastise.* Comp. Job xvi. 12. נָתַתָּה לִּי עֹרֶף, *thou hast given to me the back* of my enemies, i. e. *made them to flee before me,* Ps. xviii. 41. הָפַךְ עֹרֶף, Josh. vii. 8. Also *to forsake, abandon,* Jer. ii. 27. Hence—

ערף, v. pret. aff. עֲרָפְתּוֹ, pres. יַעֲרֹף. Constr. abs. it. immed. Angl. vulg. (a) *Neck,* i. e. *cut off the head, behead,* Exod. xiii. 13; xxxiv. 20. Pl., Deut. xxi. 4. (b) Meton. *Destroy, ruin,* Hos. x. 2. (c) *Drop, distil,* as the blood from the neck of a decapitated bird, &c., Deut. xxxii. 28. Metaph. applied to speech, as assimilated to the droppings of dew, or of the honey comb, Deut. xxxii. 2. Comp. Ps. xix. 11.
Part. (a) עֹרֵף, Is. lxvi. 3, only.
— pass. f. עֲרוּפָה, Deut. xxi. 6, only.

עֲרָפֶל, masc.—pl. non occ. Comp. of אָרִיךְ + אֹפֶל, *nubes et caliginosus,* Gesenius. Syr. ܥܪܦܠܐ, *nubes.* Arab. عَرَف, conj. xii. *densa fuit ac implicita* palma, and افل, *tenebræ. Thick, intense, darkness,* Deut. iv. 11; Job xxxviii. 9, &c. Metaph. *Gross ignorance,* Is. lx. 2. *Great tribulation,* Joel ii. 2; Zeph. i. 15. Applied to God as *inscrutable,* 1 Kings viii. 12; 2 Chron. vi. 1: and thence *as concealing him,* Exod. xx. 21; Ps. xcvii. 2. Comp. Job xxii. 13; 2 Sam. xxii. 10.

עָרַץ, v. pres. יַעֲרֹץ, constr. immed. it. abs. it. med. מִן. Arab. عَرَض, *conturbatus fuit.* Cogn. عرس, *perculsus fuit.* (a) *Feared, trembled,* Deut. i. 29; vii. 21; xx. 3; xxxi. 6; Josh. i. 9. (b) Trans.

עָרַק

Affright, alarm: meton. *Shake*, Is. ii. 9. 21; xlvii. 12; Ps. x. 18; Job xiii. 25.

Infin. עָרֹץ, Ps. l. c. &c.

Niph. נַעֲרָץ. Part. i. q. נוֹרָא. *Fearful*, Ps. lxxxix. 8, only.

Hiph. pres. pl. הַעֲרִיצוּ, i. q. תִּירָא, Is. viii. 12, i. q. Kal (a). יַעֲרִיצוּ, Is. xxix. 23, id.

Part. מַעֲרִיץ, with aff., Is. viii. 13. *Causing to fear*, object of —, al. non occ.

עָרַק, v. Part. Kal only, pl. עֹרְקִים. Persons *flying, escaping*, Job xxx. 3. Arab. عَرَقَ, *abiit, fugit*. Æth. *decessit*. Ib. vr. 17. Aff. עָרְקִי. *My nerves*. Arab. عِرْق, *arteria, nervus*, al. non occ.

עַרְקִי, m. Patronym., Gen. x. 1, from *Tel Arka*, more fully, *Arca Cæsarea*; a place situate on the north of Tripoli, according to Gesen.

עָרַר, v. pret. pres. non occ. See עֲרִירִי above. Cogn. עוּר, עָרָה.

Imp. parag. עָרָה. *Be, become, naked, stripped*, once, Is. xxxiii. 11.

Pih. עוֹרֵר, pres. הִתְעוֹרֵר, constr. immed. it. med. אֶת, it. לְ, עַל, pers. sign. τοῦ, עוּר, i. q. יְעֵר,—which is another reduplicated form only—for יְעֹרֵר, Is. xv. 5. *Excite, stir up*. See under עוּר, Pih.—Of עֵר, *Made naked, bare, exposed*. Comp. גָּלָה: once, Is. xxiii. 13. — of a fortress. Also in the form—

עַרְעֵר, Infin. עַרְעֵר. *Making naked, exposed*, with—

Hithp. pres. fem. תִּתְעַרְעֵר. *It shall be, become, exposed*, Jer. li. 58, only. Comp. cogn. עָרָה, Ps. cxxxvii. 7; Hab. iii. 13. The same sense might be applied to many of the instances adducible under עוּר, as, 2 Sam. xxiii. 18; 1 Chron. xi. 11. 20, i. e. *drew forth*, as from a sheath or scabbard.

עֶרֶשׂ, fem. pl. עֲרָשׂוֹת. Syr. ܥܰܪܣܳܐ, *lectus*. Arab. عرس, meton. *conjunx*. *Couch, bed*, Deut. iii. 11; Ps. vi. 7; xli. 4; cxxxii. 3. עֶרֶשׂ יְצוּעִי, *couch of my bed*, i. e. reclining place of my rest. Amos iii. 12, ellip. for בְּפַאַת עֶרֶשׂ. See preceding member, Cant. i. 16, &c. Aff. עַרְשׂוֹ, pl. עַרְשׂוֹתָם, &c.

עָשָׂב, c. pl. עֲשָׂבוֹת (dag. euph.), once only. Aff. עֲשָׂבָם, Is. xlii. 15. Arab. عُشْب, *gramen*. Syr. ܥܶܣܒܳܐ, id. *Green herb*, generally, as food for either man or beast: differs from דֶּשֶׁא, which signifies the

עֵשֶׂב

younger shoots of do., Gen. i. 11, 12; ii. 5; iii. 18; Exod. x. 12. 15, &c. Pl., Prov. xxvii. 25.

עֲשַׂב, def. עִשְׂבָּא, i. q. Heb. עֵשֶׂב, Dan. iv. 12. 22. 29; v. 21.

עָשָׂה, f. עָשָׂה, for עָשְׂתָה, once, Lev. xxv. 21; v. pres. יַעֲשֶׂה apoc. יַעַשׂ. Constr. immed. it. abs. it. me אֶת, לְ, בְּ, עִם, &c. Propr. (a) *Work, labour*, hence, (b) meton. *Make, fabricate; produce*. (c) *Do, act, perform*; with such slight shades of one or other of these as the context may require: of which the Arab. عَسَى, *crassa evasit e labore manus, firma, dura evasit* res, seem to be remnants. (a) *Wrought, laboured* in, with בְּ, Exod. v. 9; xxxi. 4; Neh. iv. 15, &c. (b) *Made, fabricated*, Gen. viii. 6; xiii. 4; Exod. v. 16, &c. — of God (see בָּרָא above), Gen. i. 7. 16; ii. 2; iii. 1, &c. Hence, (2) *Made, produced*, as wealth, reward, &c., Gen. xii. 5; xxxi. 1; Deut. viii. 17. 18; Is. xix. 10. — of trees, &c., as fruit, &c., Gen. i. 11, 12; xli. 47; Job xiv. 9; Hos. viii. 7, &c. — war, Gen. xiv. 2; Deut. xx. 12; Josh. xi. 18, &c. — peace, with לְ, Is. xxvii. 5. — oil, unguents, &c., Exod. xxx. 25; Hos. ii. 10; viii. 4. — instruments, &c., Exod. xxv. 39; xxvii. 3; xxxvi. 14; xxxviii. 3, &c. *Make, constitute, appoint*, Exod. xxxii. 10; xxxvi. 24: with תַּחַת, Is. xliv. 17;—1 Kings xii. 31; 1 Sam. xii. 6; Jer. xxxvii. 15, &c.; either immed. or med. לְ, &c., very much at the pleasure of the writer. (c) *Did, performed, made, exercised*, variously. — work, 2 Kings xii. 12, &c. — wonders, Ps. lxxviii. 4. 12; xcviii. 1. — God's commands, &c., Gen. vi. 22; Lev. xx. 22; Deut. xv. 5; Ps. ciii. 20, 21. — regal power, 1 Kings xxi. 7. — what is lawful, just, &c., Gen. xviii. 19. 25; Exod. xviii. 9; Ps. ix. 17; Is. lviii. 2; Gen. xxiv. 12; xl. 14. — what is wrong, wicked, &c., 2 Kings xvii. 22; Is. liii. 9; Gen. xxxiv. 7; Ps. xxxvii. 1. — a present, 2 Kings xviii. 31. *Did*, i. e. *prepared, dressed*, as food, an animal for food, sacrifice, &c., Gen. xviii. 6—8; xxi. 8; Judg. xiii. 15; 2 Sam. xii. 4. Then, meton. *Offered* in sacrifice, Exod. xxix. 36. 38, 39. 41; Lev. ix. 7, &c.; Hos. ii. 10. וְזָהָב עָשׂוּ לַבַּעַל, they *offered gold to Baal*; but it might signify, (b), (2) *they made*, i. e. *acquired gold for* —, 2 Chron. xxiv. 7; Exod. x. 25; 2 Kings xvii. 32. *Did, originated* for —, Jer. ii. 17;

עֹשֶׂה (483) עָשׂוֹר

iv. 18. *Did, dressed* the beard, nails, &c., 2 Sam. xix. 25; Deut. xxi. 12. *Did, performed*, something intended, Is. xxx. 1. Comp. Eccl. viii. 11; Dan. viii. 24; xi. 7. 17. 28. 30. — vows, Judg. xi. 39. — of God, Ps. xxii. 32; xxxvii. 5; lii. 11. *Did, i. e. performed, kept*, the sabbath, feast, &c., Exod. xii. 48; Num. ix. 10. 14; Deut. v. 15. *Passed time*, יָמִים, Eccl. vi. 12: and, omitting the mention of time, Ruth ii. 19, אָנָה עָשִׂית : but this might also come under (b), (2) above.—Phrr. כֹּה יַעֲשֶׂה לִי אֱלֹהִים וגו'׳, *so God do to me, &c.*, 1 Sam. iii. 17, &c. Preceding other verbs for emphasis sake (Gram. art. 222. 4), 1 Kings viii. 32, &c. כֵּן עָשָׂה, *so did he*, Exod. xl. 16, &c. מִי עָשָׂה הַדָּבָר הַזֶּה, *Who did this thing?* Judg. vi. 29. זֹאת, —, Ib. xv. 6. עָשָׂה פֶרֶץ, i. q. פֶרֶץ . . . עָשָׂה תְשׁוּעָה, *wrought salvation*, Judg. xxi. 15; 1 Sam. xi. 13. עָשׂ חַיִל, *did powerfully*, 1 Sam. xiv. 47. בִּגְבוּרָתוֹ, 2 Kings xx. 20, &c. עָשָׂה בְעָקְבָּה, *acted in craftiness*, 2 Kings x. 19, and so in other cases. Infin. עֲשׂוֹ, 1 Sam. xxvi. 25; Jer. vii. 5, &c.: it. עֲשֹׂה, Gen. L. 20: עֲשׂוֹ, Ib. xxxi. 28. Constr. עֲשׂוֹת, Gen. ii. 3, 4, &c. With בְּ, לְ, מִן, Gen. ii. 3; xviii. 25; Ezek. v. 15; xxiii. 21. See Pih. Aff. עֲשֹׂתִי, *my doing*, 2 Sam. xxiii. 17, &c.; Is. lxiv. 2; Ezek. xvi. 30; Jer. vii. 13; Exod. xviii. 18, &c. with other aff.—
Imp. עֲשֵׂה, Gen. vi. 14, &c.: f. עֲשִׂי, Ib. xvi. 6: pl. עֲשׂוּ, Gen. xlii. 18.
Part. m. עֹשֶׂה, Gen. i. 11, &c. Constr. עֹשֵׂה, Exod. xv. 11, &c. Pl. עֹשִׂים, Gen. xxiv. 49, &c. Constr. עֹשֵׂי, Exod. xxxv. 35. Aff. עֹשֵׂנִי, Job xxxi. 15. עֹשֵׂהוּ, Ps. xcv. 6. עֹשָׂף, Is. xliv. 2. הָעֹשׂוּ, עֹשֵׂהוּ, Job xl. 19; Prov. xiv. 31. עֹשֵׂהוּ, Jer. xxxiii. 2. Pl. עֹשֵׂי, Job xxxv. 10. Comp. Is. liv. 5; Ps. cxlix. 2; Is. xxii. 11; Ps. cxi. 10.
— f. עֹשָׂה, Deut. xx. 20, &c. Pl. עֹשׂוֹת Lev. xviii. 29, &c.
— pass. עָשׂוּי, Ezek. xl. 17, &c.: pl. עֲשׂוּיִם, Ps. cxi. 8, &c.
— f. עֲשׂוּיָה, Ezek. xxi. 20. עֲשֻׂיָה, Num. xxviii. 6. Pl. עֲשׂוּיוֹת, 1 Sam. xxv. 18.
Niph. נַעֲשָׂה, pres. יֵעָשֶׂה, apoc. תֵּעָשׂ. *Be, become,* (a) *Made,* (b) *Done, &c.* (a) Ps. xxxiii. 6. (b) *Done, performed*, Judg. xvi. 11; 1 Kings x. 20, &c. *Kept*, as a feast, 2 Kings xxiii. 22, 23. *Done, dressed, cooked*, Lev. vii. 9. — of error, abomination, &c., Num. xv. 24; Deut. xiii. 15; xvii. 4; Mal. ii. 11. — thing predetermined, Dan. xi. 36. — prepared, Neh. v.

18. Pres. often in the sense of Lat. part. in *dus, dum*, as לֹא יֵעָשֶׂה, *non faciendum*; not to be done, ought not, &c., Gen. xxix. 26; xxxiv. 7, &c. יֵעָשֶׂה מְלָאכָה, *work to be done*, Exod. xxxi. 15; Lev. xxiv. 19. Apoc., Esth. v. 6; vii. 2; ix. 12.
Part. נַעֲשׂוֹת, Neh. v. 18: pl. נַעֲשִׂים, Eccl. iv. 1; Esth. ix. 28.
— f. pl. נַעֲשׂוֹת, Ezek. ix. 4.
Infin. הֵעָשׂוֹת, Esth. ix. 1. 14. Aff. הֵעָשׂוֹתוֹ, Ezek. xliii. 18, al. non occ.
Pih. m. pl. עָשׂוּ, twice only, Ezek. xxiii. 3. 8, in עָשׂוּ דַּדֵּי בְתוּלֵיהֶן. See דַּד, p. 130, above.
Chald. עסא, Pah. עַשִּׁי, *pressit, &c.* *Pressed, injured.* See LXX.
Puh. עֻשֵּׂיתִי. *I was made, formed,* Ps. cxxxix. 15, only.

עָשׂר , עָשׂוֹר, m.—pl. non occ. r. עשׂר. Arab. عَاشُور, *dies decimus*. The *number ten, a decade*. So שָׁבוּעַ, *hebdomas*. Gr. δεκάς, ἐννεάς, τετράς. Gesen. יָמִים אוֹ עָשׂוֹר, *some days, or* (it may be) *a decade*, ten, Gen. xxiv. 55. בְּנֵבֶל עָשׂוֹר, *on the nablium of ten strings*, Ps. xxxiii. 2. Comp. xcii. 4; cxliv. 9. Applied also to *the tenth day* of the month, as its decade. בֶּעָשׂוֹר לַחֹדֶשׁ, Exod. xii. 3; Lev. xvi. 29, &c.

עֲשִׂירִי, m. ⎱ plur. non occ. Ordinal
עֲשִׂירִיָּה, f. ⎰ number of עֶשֶׂר, *ten*, Gram. art. 181. 2. The
עֲשִׂירִית, f. *tenth*, applied to periods of time, to persons, things. דּוֹר עֲשִׂירִי, *tenth generation*, Deut. xxiii. 3, 4;—Gen. viii. 5; Num. vii. 66; xxvii. 32; Zech. viii. 19, &c. The fem. עֲשִׂירִיָּה, once, abs. Is. vi. 13. In all cases of constr. f. עֲשִׂירִית. In Exod. xvi. 36; Lev. v. 11: *tenth part* is necessarily meant.

עשק, v. Kal non occ. Syr. ܥܣܩ, *difficilis.* Arab. عَسِق, id. Hence the name of a well, Gen. xxvi. 20. עֵשֶׂק, *difficulty, contention.*
Hith. pl. הִתְעַשְּׂקוּ, with עִם. *They contended with,* Gen. xxvi. 20, only. Comp. רִיבוּ preceding.

עָשָׂר, עֶשֶׂר, masc.—
עֲשָׂרָה, fem.—
עֲשֶׂרֶת fem. plur.—
pl. עֶשְׂרִים. Arab. عَشْر, *decem.* The numeral *ten,* Gram. artt. 181. 2; 226. It need only be remarked here, that עָשׂוֹר and עֲשָׂרָה are

עֲשׂר (484) עֲשׂוֹת

used when some number between *ten* and *twenty* is required to be expressed, e. g. אַחַד עָשָׂר, *eleven*; אַרְבָּעָה עָשָׂר, *fourteen*; when the thing numbered is of the masc. gender: אַחַת עֶשְׂרֵה, שֵׁשׁ עֶשְׂרֵה, &c. when it is of the fem. And that the pl. is used to express *tens*, i. e. *twenty*. See Gram. ll. cc. while the fem. pl. will signify *decades*, Exod. xviii. 21; Deut. i. 15. Examples of the other cases: עֶשֶׂר שָׁנִים, *ten years*, Gen. v. 14; xvi. 3. עֶשֶׂר יְרִיעֹת, *ten curtains*, Exod. xxvi. 1, &c.; the thing numbered being always in the plur. masc. or fem. With בְּ, עֶשֶׂר בָּאַמָּה, *ten by the cubit*, i. e. ten cubits by measure, 1 Kings vi. 26. עֲשָׂרָה, Gen. xviii. 32, *ten men*. עֲשָׂרָה גְמַלִּים, *ten camels*, Ib. xxiv. 10. Comp. Ib. 22: *ten shekels' weight*, xxxii. 15; xlii. 3, &c.: observing that this fem. form has (generally) a *masc.* pl. fm. with it, for variety's sake perhaps, as the constr. is apposition: but a singular in עֲשָׂרָה לֶחֶם, 1 Sam. xvii. 17. So 2 Kings xiii. 7. Comp. Jer. xxxii. 9, עֲשָׂרָה, apposition mostly, as, עֲשָׂרָה מֹנִים, *ten times*, Gen. xxxi. 7. 41; Exod. xxxiv. 28. With sing., Judg. xvii. 10; but שְׁקָלִים is omitted here by the ellipsis. עֶשְׂרִים, Gen. xviii. 31; xxxi. 38, &c. None are found with affixes. Hence—

עֲשַׂר, m. עֲשָׂרָה, f. Chald. i. q. Heb. *Ten*, Dan. iv. 26; vii. 7. 24, &c. Pl. עֶשְׂרִין, *twenty*, Dan. vi. 2, only.

עָשַׂר, v. pres. יַעְשֹׂר, constr. immed. *Decimate, tithe*, 1 Sam. viii. 15. 17, only.
Pih. pres. תְּעַשֵּׂר. *Tithe*, i. e. *take*, or *pay*, *it*, Deut. xiv. 22: with aff., Gen. xxviii. 22, with לְ, pers.
Part. pl. with art. הַמְעַשְּׂרִים. *The persons paying tithe*, Neh. x. 38, only.
Infin. עַשֵּׂר, Gen. xxviii. 22; Deut. xiv. 22.
Hiph. Infin. with prep. לַעְשֵׂר, for לְעַשֵּׂר. *To pay tithe*, Deut. xxvi. 12. בְּעַשֵּׂר, *in paying tithe*, Neh. x. 39, al. non occ.

עֲשָׂרָה, see עֶשֶׂר.

עֲשִׂירָה, see עֶשֶׂר.

עִשָּׂרוֹן, masc. pl. עֶשְׂרוֹנִים, dimin. fm. Gram. art. 168. A dry measure, the *tenth part* of an ephah, apparently, i. q. עֹמֶר. See LXX., Num. xv. 4. Novarius makes the Syr. ܟܣܘܡܐ, the *tenth part* of the *Seah*, Gesen.; Num. xxviii. 13. 21. 29, &c. Pl., Lev. xiv. 10; xxiii. 13. 17; xxiv. 5, &c.

עֲשׂוֹת, see עָשָׂה above.

עָשׁ, masc.—pl. non occ. Arab. عُثٌّ, *tinea lanam erodens*. (a) *A moth*, Job iv. 19; xiii. 28; Is. L. 9; li. 8, &c. (b) עָשׁ, and עַיִשׁ. The name of a constellation, Job ix. 9, and xxxviii. 32; probably that of the Great Bear. The term is apparently the same with the Arab. نَعْشٌ, a *bier* or *litter*. The ἅμαξα of the Greeks, and *wain* of the English. Three stars in the tail of the Bear the Arabs term بَنَاتُ النَّعْشِ, *daughters of the wain*; the בְּנֵי, probably of Job xxxviii. 32. Jauhari, however, gives a passage from an old Arabian poet, styling these بَنُو نَعْشٍ, the very terms of Job. See my note on Job ix. 9, al. non occ. See also Bochart. Hieroz., ii. p. 114; Schult. on Job ll. cc.; Michælis Suppl., p. 190, seq.

עֲשׂוּקָה, m. once, Jer. xxii. 3, r. עשק. Lit. *fraud, oppression*. *Fraudulent, oppressive, person*.

עֲשׁוּקִים, m. pl. of the last. *Frauds, oppressions*, Eccl. iv. 1; Amos iii. 9; Job xxxv. 9; al. pl. Part. v. עָשַׁק, which see.

עָשׂוֹת, m. once, Ezek. xxvii. 19, r. עשה. *Wrought*. LXX. εἰργασμένος.

עָשִׁיר, m. pl. עֲשִׁירִים, constr. עֲשִׁירֵי, aff. עֲשִׁירֶיהָ, r. עשר. Syr. ܥܰܬܝܼܪܳܐ, *dives*. *Rich*, opp. τοῖς, דַּל, רָאשׁ, אֶבְיוֹן, 2 Sam. xii. 1; Job xxvii. 19; Ps. xlix. 3; Prov. x. 15; Ruth iii. 10. Often in a bad sense, as, Prov. xxviii. 11; Jer. ix. 22, &c. In Eccl. ix. 6, the contrary, *humility*—of character—seems intended. Constr., Ps. xlv. 13. Aff., Mic. vi. 12.

עָשָׁן, m.—pl. non occ. constr. עֲשַׁן, aff. עֲשָׁנוֹ. Arab. عَدَنٌ, *fumus*. *Smoke*, Gen. xv. 17; Judg. xx. 40; Ps. lxviii. 3, &c. Metaph. *Fierce anger*, 2 Sam. xxii. 9. Comp. Job xli. 12. — as to its appearance and action, see phrr. Judg. l. c.; xx. 38; Cant. iii. 6; Joel iii. 3; Is. ix. 17. — as *a cloud*, Is. iv. 5, alluding to that which occasionally filled the Tabernacle or Temple. Comp. Ib. vi. 4. Gesenius makes it signify *a cloud of dust*, Ib. xiv. 31. But this is neither necessary nor a customary

עשן (485) עשר

usage of the Hebrews: while *cloud* is often used to convey the notion of a powerful army. Phrr. כָּלוּ בֶעָשָׁן, *they end in smoke*, Ps. xxxvii. 20; cii. 4. Alluding to the consuming of an offering, כְּעָשָׁן, it. Is. li. 6. Prov. x. 26, כֶּעָשָׁן לָעֵינַיִם, *as smoke to the eyes*. Aff., Is. xxxiv. 10; Exod. xix. 18. Hence—

עָשַׁן, v. pres. יֶעְשַׁן. Constr. abs. it. med. בְ. *Smoked*, Exod. xix. 18; Ps. civ. 32; cxliv. 5. — of the *Divine wrath*, Deut. xxix. 19; Ps. lxxiv. 1; lxxx. 5, al. non occ.

עֹשֶׁק, m.—pl. non occ. Syr. ܥܰܣܩܳܐ, *oppressio*. Arab. عَسْقَة, *angustia*. (a) *Oppression, injury*, opp. τῇ, צְדָקָה, Is. liv. 14: with סָרָה, Ib. lix. 13;—Ps. lxxiii. 8; Eccl. v. 7; Jer. vi. 7, &c. (b) Meton. Thing obtained by —, Lev. v. 23; Ps. lxii. 11; Eccl. vii. 7; Is. xxx. 12, &c.

עָשְׁקָה, Is. xxxviii. 14, is given by Gesenius as a fem. noun, signifying *oppression*. It is, more probably, 3d pret f. of the verb עָשַׁק, used impersonally; and signifying, *it oppresses, ruins me*, i. e. my disease. Vulg. "*vim patior.*"

עָשַׁק, v. pres. יַעְשֹׁק. See עֹשֶׁק. Constr. immed. it. abs. it. med. אֶת, לְ. (a) *Oppressed, injured, wronged, defrauded*, Lev. v. 21. 23; xix. 13; Deut. xxiv. 14; Mic. ii. 2. — the poor, Prov. xiv. 31; xxii. 16, &c. — a ruler, his subjects, 1 Sam. xii. 3, 4. — a conqueror, the conquered, Is. lii. 4; Jer. L. 33, &c. — God, man, Job x. 3. (b) *Press upon*, as a river, Job xl. 23. See my note. In the same sense (morally), אָדָם עָשֻׁק בְּדַם נָפֶשׁ, *a man pressed*, in a state of remorse, *by the blood of a person*, i. e. blood-guilty, Prov. xxviii. 17.

Infin. עֲשֹׁק, Hos. xii. 8. Aff. עָשְׁקוֹ, 1 Chron. xvi. 21; Ps. cv. 14.

Part. עֹשֵׁק, עֹשֵׁק, Ps. lxxii. 4; Prov. xiv. 31, &c. Pl. constr. עֹשְׁקֵי, Mal. iii. 5. Aff., Ps. cxix. 121; Eccl. iv. 1. Fem. pl. עֹשְׁקוֹת, Amos iv. 1.

— pass. עָשׁוּק, עָשׁוֹק, Deut. xxviii. 29. 33, &c. Plur. עֲשׁוּקִים, Job xxxv. 9; Ps. ciii. 6, &c.

Puh. Part. fem. מְעֻשָּׁקָה. Person *become oppressed*, Is. xxiii. 12, only. Gesen. "*vi compressa.*" But there is no good ground for this.

עֹשֶׁר, m.—pl. non occ. Aff. עָשְׁרוֹ, &c.

opp. τῷ, רָאשׁ. *Riches*. Syr. ܥܽܘܬܪܳܐ, *divitiæ*. See עָשִׁיר, 1 Sam. xvii. 25; 1 Kings iii. 11. 13, &c. Aff., Prov. xi. 28; xiv. 24, &c.

עָשַׁר, v. pres. יֶעְשַׁר, constr. abs. Syr. ܥܬܰܪ, *ditatus est*. Arab. غَثَرَ, *herbæ abundè rigatæ*; غُثْر, *copia annonæ*. *Was rich, wealthy*, Hos. xii. 9; Job xv. 29.

Pih. once, kethiv, עִשֵּׁר, 1 Kings xxii. 49, which Gesenius makes to signify "*exstruxit*" naves, as cogn. with אשר, כשר, ישר. But here the *keri* has עָשָׂה, and so has the *kethiv*, 2 Chron. xx. 36, 37. The reading therefore is suspicious. But the *kethiv* has not עִשֵּׁר, but עָשַׁר. What then becomes of Gesenius's etymology? If, however, we had had אֳנִיּוֹת עָשַׁר, *was rich* in *ships* would have afforded a tolerable sense; as it is, no good sense is afforded.

Hiph. הֶעֱשַׁרְתִּי, pres. יַעְשִׁיר, יַעֲשִׁיר, constr. immed. (a) *Made rich*, Gen. xiv. 23; 1 Sam. ii. 7; xvii. 25; Ps. lxv. 10; Prov. x. 22. (b) Made self rich, i. e. *was, became, rich*, Ps. xlix. 17; Prov. x. 41; xxi. 17; Dan. xi. 2; Jer. v. 27.

Infin. הַעֲשִׁיר, Prov. xxiii. 4; (b) xxviii. 20. Part. מַעְשִׁיר. (a) 1 Sam. ii. 7.

Hith. part. מִתְעַשֵּׁר. *Becomes, is, rich*, Prov. xiii. 7. See LXX. Comp. 2 Cor. vi. 10.

עֲשֵׁשׁ, v. pret. fem. עָשְׁשָׁה, pl. עָשְׁשׁוּ, pres. non occ. constr. abs. it. med. כֵּן, בְ, of thing. Synon. עתק, Ps. vi. 8. Arab. عَتَّ, *errosit tinea lanam*; عَثَّ, *extenuatum fuit* corpus. *Became old, wasted, languid*, Ps. l. c.; xxxi. 10, 11, al. non occ.

עָשֵׁת, m. once, Cant. v. 14. Gesen. "*fabrifactum, affabre factum.*" Eich. Sim. "*nitor.*" LXX. πυξίον. See my note on Job xii. 5. *Net-work* of ivory, perhaps, such as we see in the Chinese spheres, fans, and the like. Vers. Syr. ܥܒܳܕܳܐ, *work*. Arab. عَتَّ, *errosit*. Cogn. عَتَا, *modum excessit*; عَتَا, *mala dedit, &c.*

עַשְׁתּוֹת, fem. pl. Some copies and editions read עַשְׁתוּת. Arab. عَتَّ, *corripuit*

עֲשֶׁת (486) עֵת

gravibus verbis. Cogn. غَتّ, *vitiosum fuit dictum.* See also עָשָׁה. Whence it should seem, *piercing, rebuking, injuring,* expressions, or the like, were meant. *Tauntings,* or *taunting.* See my Job xii. 5, with the note, al. non occ.

עֲשְׁתֵּי, m. pl. constr. of עֶשֶׂה, apparently; occurs only in the combination, עֲשְׁתֵּי עָשָׂר, and עֲשְׁתֵּי עֶשְׂרֵה, Gram. art. 181. 7. It is perhaps a derivative of غَتّ, *modum excessit,* or of some word cognate with it, signifying *excess,* as being the first number next after the sum of the fingers on both hands, or the first complete decimal product: hence, i. q. אֶחָד עָשָׂר, *eleven.*

עֶשְׁתֹּנוֹת, fem. pl. *Thoughts,* usually, once, Ps. cxlvi. 4. Aff. עֶשְׁתֹּנֹתָיו. LXX. διαλογισμοὶ αὐτῶν. ΑΛΛ. αἱ προθέσεις αὐτοῦ. His *devices, machinations.*

עַשְׁתֹּרֶת, f. pl. עַשְׁתָּרוֹת. Gr. Ἀστάρτη. *Astarte,* a female deity of the Zidonians, having the head of a bull, whence the עַשְׁתְּרוֹת קַרְנַיִם, of Gen. xiv. 5, &c. Worshipped occasionally with *Baal,* Judg. ii. 13; x. 6; — 1 Sam. vii. 3, 4; xii. 10; xxxi. 10; 1 Kings xi. 5. 33; 2 Kings xxiii. 13. Gesenius thinks the origin of the word is Syr. ܒܝܬ ܐܣܬܪܐ, ܐܣܬܪܐ, from the Persic ستارە, *star;* whence the proper name אֶסְתֵּר, which is, perhaps, as probable as other etymologies formerly given: of all which, however, nothing certain can be pronounced. For a full account of this idol, see Selden de Diis Syris. Syntagma. ii.; also Euseb. Prep. Evang., i. 10. A city called after this idol is mentioned, Gen. l. c.; Deut. i. 4; Josh. ix. 10, &c. The pl. is taken to signify *Idols* or *images* of this deity. Aquila, ἀγάλματα ἀστάρτης, Judg. ll. cc.; 1 Sam. ll. cc. Gesen. — rather whimsically perhaps — takes עַשְׁתְּרוֹת צֹאן, Deut. vii. 13, &c., to signify, *" veneres, amores, gregis,"* i. e. *soboles, proles, gregis.* I should prefer the better established —

עַשְׁתְּרֹת, fem. pl. constr. in עַשְׁתְּרוֹת צֹאנֶךָ, Deut. vii. 13; xxviii. 4. 18. 51. Compd. perhaps of غَتّ, *modum excessit.* Cogn. غَتّ; whence, عَتَعَنَة, *hœdus firmior,*

validior; غَنِي, *luxuriavit* herbis terra, and עֹשֶׁר, *wealth;* put for *the produce* of the flock. Eichh. Simon. " comp. ex. 2 Synonymis, עָשֵׁר, *dives fuit;* et ex. עָתַר, Chald. et Syr." *" grex ovium;* aliis *fœmella ovis, a summa fœcunditate."*

עֵת, עֶת, m. pl. עִתִּים, and עִתּוֹת. Aff. עִתִּי, plur. עִתֹּתַי. Arab. عَنِّي, *donec;* r. عَتّ, *repetivit verba, &c.* Cogn. عَتَا, r. عَتَو, *exorbitavit.* The notion of *time,* originating perhaps in *repetition, excess;* and thence *duration.* Cogn. עדה, עדא. Arab. عَدَّ, *numeravit. Time, season;* or, meton. *its consequences, results,* Gen. xxix. 7; Exod. xviii. 22. 26; Josh. viii. 29; Eccl. iii. 1, seq., &c. Constr. as a fem. (sing.), Ib. xi. 6; Jer. li. 33, only. With לֹא, preceding, *out of* (due) *time, season,* Job xxii. 16. *Prosperous* —, Ps. lxxxi. 16. *Unhappy,* &c. —, Is. xiii. 22; Jer. xxvii. 7; Ezek. xxx. 3; Eccl. ix. 11, 12. *Due, usual,* —, Hos. xiii. 13. Phrr. מֵעֵת אֶל־עֵת, 1 Chron. ix. 25, *from time to time.* בְּכָל־עֵת, *at every season, time,* Exod. xviii. 22. עֵת־עֵת, *until the time,* Ps. cv. 19. עֵת רָצוֹן, *acceptable* —, Ps. lxix. 14. עֵת פְּקֻדָּתָם, — of their *visitation,* Jer. xlvi. 21, &c. Pl., Job xxiv. 1; Esth. i. 13; Dan. ix. 25, &c. Fem., Ps. ix. 10; x. 1; xxxi. 16. See also my note on Job xxvii. 6. With prefixes, כָּעֵת, for כְּעֵת, *according to the time, season,* i. e. *this time, now,* as it were, Judg. xiii. 23; Job xxxix. 18, &c. כָּעֵת חַיָּה, Gen. xviii. 10. 14, *as the season,* period, *of a vigorous woman.* See חַי, p. 193 above. מָחָר —, *to-morrow,* Exod. ix. 18, &c. בָּעֵת, Deut. i. 9. לְעֵת, *in, at, the time,* Gen. viii. 11. Often used, too, as a specifying noun, Gram. art. 219, note; Ps. lxix. 14, &c.: it. pl. עִתִּים רַבּוֹת, *many times,* on *many occasions,* Neh. ix. 28.

עָתָ, see עָתָה.

עתד, v. Kal non occ. Arab. عَتَد, *paratus fuit.*

Pih. Imp. aff. עַתְּדָהּ, *Prepare it.* Synon. τοῦ, הָכֵן, Prov. xxiv. 27, only.

Hithp. הִתְעַתָּדוּ. *Have become prepared,* with לְ, Job xv. 28. See my note.

עַתָּה, see עֵת above. Adv. of time, variously applied. (a) *Now,* abs. present

עתו (487) עתי

time, Gram. art. 231. 6. Opp. τῷ, אָז, Gen. xxii. 12; Josh. xiv. 11; Is. xlviii. 7; Hag. ii. 3, &c.: relative pres. i. e. present to any time introduced by the writer or speaker, 1 Sam. ii. 16; ix. 12; xvii. 29, &c. *Now, at length*, 1 Sam. xxvii. 1; 1 Kings xv. 16; Num. xi. 23. Nold., *breve, intra breve tempus* (p. 578). So Is. xliii. 19; Hos. x. 3, &c. *Now, shortly, speedily*, Judg. viii. 6; Hos. viii. 10; Ps. xii. 6, &c. *Now*, precative.—See נָא,—Mic. iv. 14;—2 Chron. vi. 40; Gen. xxxi. 13, &c. *Now*. Engl. *Now then*, inferentially, Exod. vi. 1; 1 Sam. xxv. 7; 2 Sam. xviii. 3, &c. So Gen. xix. 9; Nold. "*itaque:*" Exod. xviii. 19, &c. *Then*, i. e. *now*, with future time, Ezek. xxvi. 18; Is. xxix. 22. And so in all similar cases. *Then*, inferentially, in the ἀπόδοσις, i. e. retributive member of a hypothetical sentence, 2 Kings xviii. 20. עַתָּה עַל מִי בָטַחְתָּ כִּי מָרַדְתָּ בִּי, *then, on whom wilt thou rely, when*, or *since, thou hast rebelled against me*? or *then accordingly*, Jer. xiv. 10; Hos. iv. 16, &c. With prefixes, מֵעַתָּה Is. ix. 6; עַד עַתָּה Gen. xxxii. 5; וְעַתָּה, Gen. iii. 22. With אַךְ, גַּם, כִּי, לֹא, עִם, עַם, רָאֵה, מְהֵרָה, זֶה, רָב, as such combinations would necessarily require. See Nold., p. 580, and in their proper places.

עָתוּד, i. q. עָתִיד, Is. x. 13; Esth. viii. 13. *Kethiv*.

עַתּוּד, m. pl. עַתּוּדִים, constr. עַתּוּדֵי, sing. non occ. Arab. عَتُود, *caper juvencus.* (a) *A he goat*, Gen. xxxi. 10. 12; Num. vii. 17, &c. — as leader of the flock, Jer. l. 8. (b) Hence, metaph. applied to *leaders* of the people, Is. xiv. 9; Zech. x. 3, &c.

עִתִּי, masc. relative n. of עֵת. Hence, "*tempestivus,*" "*opportunus.*" *Seasonable, ready* at hand, once, Lev. xvi. 21. Which seems rather forced. Some derivative of the Arab. غَنِي, *abstulit torrens.*—Castell. gives, *fluvius, viros, armenta deduxit:*—signifying, *Driver, carrier away*, or the like, would perhaps suit the place better. LXX. ἕτοιμος, reading עָתִיד, and so the Syr. and Arab. Verss., unless, indeed, they took עתד to be cogn. with עתר.

עָתִיד, m. pl. עַתִּידִים, and f. עֲתִידוֹת, r. עתד. *Prepared, ready*, Job iii. 7: see my note, xv. 24; Esth. iii. 14; viii. 13. Fem. pl. Things, circumstances, *ready*, or *about to*

take place, Deut. xxxii. 35. LXX. ἕτοιμα, Is. x. 13. עֲתִידֹתֵהֶם. LXX. τὴν ἰσχὺν αὐτῶν: taking the sense from עַתּוּד, (b) above. *Their prepared* (at hand) *wealthy circumstances*, i. e. general wealth, al. non occ.

עַתִּיד, Chald. i. q. Heb. pl. עֲתִידִין, Dan. iii. 15, only.

עָתִיק, m. once, Is. xxiii. 18. Arab. عَتِيق, *manumissus, liber; nitens.* The word stands adverbially, and would in the Arab. be written عَتِيقًا. The sense might then be, *freely, in a state of liberty;* or *splendidly.* The former is the more probable one. Aquila, εἰς ἔσθησιν μεταρσέως. Symm. εἰς τὸ παλαιῶσαι. Theod. εἰς παλαίωσιν. Whence it is evident they all read עָתִיק. What the LXX. read, it may be difficult to say.

עַתִּיקִים, m. pl. constr. עַתִּיקֵי. Arab. عَتَق, *antiquus fuit;* عَتِيق, *antiquus.* (a) *Ancient*, 1 Chron. iv. 22, only. (b) Arab. عَتَق, *libertate donatus fuit. Freed, removed from*, Is. xxviii. 9, only.

עַתִּיק, m.—pl. non occ. i. q. Heb. (a) *Ancient*, Dan. vii. 9. 13. 22, only.

עתם, v. Kal non occ. Arab. غَتَمَ, *æstus ingens, et suffocans.*

Niph. נֶעְתַּם. *Is burnt up, consumed.* See the context, once, Is. ix. 18. LXX. συγκέκαυται. And so the Targum. Some take Arab. غَتَمَ, *obscura evasit :* but this is at variance with the context.

עָתָק, m.—pl. non occ. Arab. عَتَق, *dentibus prehendit;* تَعْتِيق, *morsus.* (a) *Biting, haughty, sarcastic*, word, &c., 1 Sam. ii. 3; Ps. xxxi. 19; xciv. 4. Synon. τῆς, גֻּבְהָה, Ib. lxxv. 6, retain the notion of *lofty*, from the first member, and apply it to צַוָּאר, in the second: then עָתָק תְּדַבְּרוּ may be construed together, al. non occ.

עָתֵק, m. once, Prov. viii. 18. Gesen. *nitidus, pulcher.* LXX. κτῆσις πολλῶν. Aquila, μετ' εἰρήνης. Symm. παλαιός, so Theod. Arab. عِنَاق, *manumissio, libertas. Freedom, liberty.* But, עָתֵק הוֹן may signify *permanent, durable, wealth:* while, taking the terms separately, which is preferable, we have, *wealth, freedom, and righteousness.* Hence—

עָתַק, v. pres. יֶעְתַּק. Arab. عَتَقَ, *festinavit.* (a) *Remove quickly, hurry,* from, with מִן, Job xiv. 18; xviii. 4. (b) *Grow old:* see עָתִיק above: Job xxi. 7; Ps. vi. 8. Hiph. pl. הֶעְתִּיקוּ, pres. יַעְתֵּק, with כֵּן, it. immed. (a) *Cause to move, remove,* Gen. xii. 8; xxvi. 22; Job ix. 5. — *transcribe* from one book to another, Prov. xxv. 1. — *put away,* or, it may be, *took away,* i. e. silenced, Job xxxii. 15, al. non occ.

עָתָר, m. constr. עֲתַר, once, Ezek. viii. 11. Gesen. "*suffitus*" . . . "*ubi rectè,* LXX." —who have, ἡ ἀτμὶς τοῦ θυμιάματος: but ἡ ἀτμὶς here, is the translation of עָנָן, not of עָתָר; which is left untranslated. The Syr. has ܥܛܪܐ, which the translator took as synon. with עתר. In the Arabic we have, indeed, عِطْرٌ, *sphærulæ ex musco aliisque aromatibus formatæ.* Still the usual acceptation, viz. (a) *Abundance.* Syr. ܥܘܬܪܐ, Chald. id. is better grounded. See עֹשֶׁר above.

Pl. aff. עֲתָרַי, Zeph. iii. 10, only. (b) *My suppliants.* See the verb below.

עָתַר, v. pres. יֶעְתַּר, synon. τοῦ, קָטַר. Cogn. Syr. ܥܛܪ, *fumavit odore suavi.* Arab. عَطِبَ, *bonos odores spiravit.* Metaph. *Prayed, supplicated,* constr. med. אֶל, לְ, Gen. xxv. 21; Exod. viii. 26; x. 18; Judg. xiii. 8, al. non occ.

Niph. נֶעְתַּר, pres. יֵעָתֵר, constr. abs. it. med. לְ, pers. *Was, became, prevailed upon* by prayer; *was made propitious,* Gen. xxv. 21; 2 Sam. xxi. 14; xxiv. 25; Is. xix. 22, &c. Infin. הֵעָתֵר, 2 Chron. xxxiii. 19, only. Part. נֶעְתָּר, fem. pl. נַעְתָּרוֹת. *Propitious,* 1 Chron. v. 20. *Seemingly, apparently, propitious,* Prov. xxvii. 6: or, perhaps, here in the primitive sign. *Incensed, perfumed,* or the like. LXX. ἑκούσια. Gesenius makes נַעְתּוֹר a form of the Infin. It is an unusual form in any case: but to me it seems rather to be a participle, as does the fem. form, נַעְתָּרוֹת; which Gesenius makes to signify, *larga, multa:* but this affords no suitable sense. So נַעְתּוֹם, Esth. viii. 8.

Hiph. הֶעְתַּרְתִּי, pres. אַעְתִּיר. Constr. med. אֶל, בְּעַד, לְ, i. q. Kal. (a) *Prayed, &c.,* Exod. viii. 5. 24, 25; ix. 28; x. 17; Job xxii. 27. (b) *Multiplied,*—of the Syr. and Chald. ܥܬܪ, *dives fuit,*—Ezek. xxxv. 13.

עֲתֶרֶת, f. once, Jer. xxxiii. 6. *Riches, abundance.* See עֹשֶׁר above.

פ

פ, or פ, *Pe.* The seventeenth letter of the Hebrew alphabet, and, as a numeral, denoting *eighty.* Without the point it is sounded as *f,* and with it as *p.* It is a radical, and is occasionally interchanged with ב and מ. Gram. artt. 4. 23.

פֹּא, once, Job xxxviii. 11, for פֹּה, which see.

פֵּאָה, f. constr. פְּאַת, pl. פֵּאֹת. (a) *A corner.* (b) *A direction, side;* referring to either of the four cardinal *points.* (a) Of a field, Lev. xix. 9; xxiii. 22: — of a table, Lev. xxvi. 25; xxxvii. 13: — of the hair, or beard, Lev. xix. 27; xxi. 5. Hence, קְצוּצֵי פֵאָה, an epithet applied to certain Nomadic tribes, who cut short a portion of their hair in a manner forbidden to the Israelites, Jer. ix. 25; xxv. 23; xlix. 32.

מִפְּאַת פְּנֵי, *in front,* Lev. xiii. 41. (b) Num. xxxiv. 3; Ezek. xli. 12, &c. In Num. xxiv. 17, we have וּמָחַץ פַּאֲתֵי מוֹאָב, in which פַּאֲתֵי has been taken by some to denote *both sides,* dual constr. i. e. *every part;* several of the Versions translate it by *chiefs, princes,* as being *prominent* persons. Probably, *and shall crush the companies of Moab.* Arab. فِئَةٌ, *agmen hominum.* Hence—

פאה, v. once. Hiph. pres. aff. אַפְאֵיהֶם, *I will scatter them in every direction,* Deut. xxxii. 26.

פָּאַר, m. aff. פְּאֵרְךָ, pl. פְּאֵרִים, constr. פַּאֲרֵי aff. פַּאֲרֵכֶם. Cogn. Arab. فَخْرٌ, *gloria.* Any ornament, pec. *an ornamental head-dress,* worn both by men and women, Exod. xxxix.

פאר (489) פגע

28; Is. iii. 10; lxi. 3. 10; Ezek. xxiv. 17, 18. 23. Hence—

פָאַר, v. Kal non occ.

Pih. פֵּאַר, pres. יְפָאַר. Constr. immed. *Adorned, made beautiful*, Ps. cxlix. 4; Is. lv. 5; lx. 7. 9.

Infin. פָּאֵר, Ezra vii. 27; Is. lx. 13.

Hith. pres. יִתְפָּאֵר. *Adorned himself, prided himself.* (a) *Felt complacency*, constr. abs. it. med. בְּ. (b) *Boasted himself*, with עַל. (a) Is. xliv. 23; xlix. 3. (b) Judg. vii. 2; Is. x. 15.

Infin. הִתְפָּאֵר, (a) Is. lx. 21; lxi. 3.
Imp. הִתְפָּאֵר, (b) Exod. viii. 5.

פָאַר, v. Pih. pres. תְּפָאֵר. *Went over the branches accurately*, Deut. xxiv. 20. Either from Arab. فَارَ, *mus*, or from.

פֹּארָה, fem. pl. פֹּארוֹת, aff. פֹּארֹתָיו. *A branch*, Is. x. 33; Ezek. xvii. 6; xxxi. 5, 6. 8. 12, 13.

פָּארוּר, m. twice, Joel ii. 6, and Nah. ii. 11, in the phrase, פָּנִים קִבְּצוּ פָארוּר. The Versions generally refer the word to פָרוּר, and make it signify either *the heat* or *the blackness of a pot*. Gesen. gives to קבץ the sense of *withdrawing*, and considers פָּארוּר as synonymous with זִיו, *the beauty or brightness of the countenance.* The phrase will therefore be interpreted *faces became black*, with gloom, or *became pale* with terror.

פַּג, m. pl. aff. פַּגֶּיהָ, once, Cant. ii. 13. Arab. فِجّ, *immaturus, de fructu.* An unripe fig.

פִּגּוּל, m. pl. פִּגֻּלִים. *Any thing impure and disgusting*, Lev. vii. 18; xix. 7; Is. lxv. 4; Ezek. iv. 14. Prob. cogn. פֶּגֶר. Gesenius compared the Æth. ፈደለ: *impurus, impudicus fuit.*

פָּגַע, v. pres. יִפְגַּע. Constr. immed. it. med. אֶת, בְּ, אֶל. (a) *Came to* a place, reached. (b) *Met, fell in with.* (c) *Met hostilely, fell upon.* (d) *Waited on*, in supplication, — *entreated.* (e) *Admit favourably.* (a) Gen. xxviii. 11; Josh. xvi. 7; xix. 11. 34, &c. (b) Gen. xxxii. 1; Exod. v. 20; 1 Sam. xxii. 17, &c. (c) Judg. xv. 12; 1 Kings ii. 25. 32, &c. (d) Ruth i. 16; Job xxi. 15; Jer. vii. 16; xxvii. 18. (e) Is. xlvii. 3; lxiv. 4.

Infin. פְּגֹעַ, aff. פִּגְעוֹ, Num. xxxv. 19. 21; 1 Sam. xxii. 17.
Imp. פְּגַע, pl. פִּגְעוּ, Gen. xxiii. 8; Judg. viii. 21, &c.
Hiph. הִפְגִּיעַ, pres. יַפְגִּיעַ. (a) Causat. of Kal. [c] Is. liii. 6. [d] Jer. xv. 11. (b) I. q. Kal, [d] Is. liii. 12; Jer. xxxvi. 25.
Part. מַפְגִּיעַ, i. q. Kal, [c] Job xxxvi. 32. [d] Is. lix. 16.

פֶּגַע, masc. *An occurrence, accident*, 1 Kings v. 4; Eccl. ix. 11.

פֶּגֶר, m. pl. פְּגָרִים, constr. פִּגְרֵי, aff. פִּגְרֵיהֶם. Syr. ܦܓܪ, ﻓَﺠَﺮ, *caro, corpus.* A dead body of man or beast, Gen. xv. 11; 1 Sam. xvii. 46; Jer. xli. 9; Is. xxxiv. 3, &c. Hence—

פָּגַר, v. Pih. pret. pl. פִּגְּרוּ. *Became lifeless, languid, unable to proceed*, 1 Sam. xxx. 10. 21.

פָּגַשׁ, v. pres. יִפְגֹּשׁ. Cogn. פגע. Constr. immed. it. med. אֶת, בְּ. (a) *Met.* (b) *Met hostilely*, fell upon. (a) Gen. xxxii. 17; xxxiii. 8; Is. xxxiv. 14, &c. (b) Hos. xiii. 8.
Infin. פְּגֹשׁ, constr. פְּגֹשׁ, (a) Jer. xli. 6. (b) Prov. xvii. 12.
Niph. pl. נִפְגָּשׁוּ. *Met each other*, Ps. lxxxv. 11; Prov. xxii. 2; xxix. 13.
Pih. pres. plur. יְפַגְּשׁוּ. *Stumble, against, stumble*, Job v. 14.

פָּדָה, v. pres. יִפְדֶּה. Constr. immed. it. med. אֶת. Arab. فدى, r. فدي, *dato lytro redemit.* (a) *Redeemed.* (b) *Delivered.* (a) Exod. xiii. 13. 15; xxxiv. 20; Num. xviii. 15, &c. (b) 2 Sam. iv. 9; Job xxxiii. 28; Is. xxix. 22, &c.
Infin. פְּדֹה, פָּדֹה, Num. xviii. 15; 2 Sam. vii. 23, &c.
Imp. פְּדֵה, aff. פְּדֵנִי, פְּדֵנוּ, Ps. xxv. 22; xxvi. 11; xliv. 27, &c.
Part. פֹּדֶה, aff. פֹּדְךָ, Deut. xiii. 6; Ps. xxxiv. 23.
Part. pass. pl. פְּדֻיִם, constr. פְּדוּיֵי, aff. פְּדוּיָו. Num. iii. 46. 51; xviii. 16, &c.
Niph. pret. f. נִפְדָּתָה, pres. יִפָּדֶה. Pass. of Kal, Lev. xix. 20; xxvii. 29; Is. i. 27.
Hiph. aff. הִפְדָּהּ. *Allowed her to be redeemed*, Exod. xxi. 8.
Hoph. Infin. הָפְדֵּה, i. q. Niph., Lev. xix. 20.

פְּדוּת, f. (a) *Redemption, deliverance*, Ps. cxi. 9; cxxx. 7; Is. l. 2. (b) פְּדֻת, *A*

3 R

separation, distinction, Exod. viii. 19. So the LXX. and Vulg.

פִּדְיוֹם, m. *Redemption-price, ransom,* Num. iii. 49.

פִּדְיוֹן, masc. *Id.,* Exod. xxi. 30; Ps. xlix. 9.

פדע, v. once, pret. or imp. aff. פְּרָעֵהוּ. *Redeem, deliver him,* Job xxxiii. 24, i. q. פדה. See the notes.

פֶּדֶר, m. aff. פִּדְרוֹ. A word of doubtful signification and etymology, occurring only three times, Lev. i. 8. 12; viii. 20. According to some, *the trunk;* but more generally translated, *the fat.* See Bochart. Hieroz., tom. i. p. 471.

פֶּה, m. constr. פִּי, aff. פִּי, פִּיךָ, פִּיו, and פִּיהוּ, פִּיהָ, פִּינוּ, פִּיכֶם, פִּיהֶם, and פִּימוֹ; (c) pl. פִּים, and פִּיּוֹת. Arab. فَمٌ, *os.* (a) *Mouth.* (b) *Any opening,* as of a sack, well, cave, dress, &c. (c) *Edge* of a sword. (d) *Mouthful,—share, portion, part, amount.* (e) *Word,—declaration* or *command.* (f) *Expression, signification, tenor.* (a) Exod. iv. 10, 11; Deut. xxiii. 24; 2 Kings iv. 34, &c. (b) Gen. xxix. 2; xlii. 27; Exod. xxviii. 32; Josh. ix. 14, &c. (c) Gen. xxiv. 36; Exod. xvii. 13; Num. xxi. 25, &c. (d) Deut. xxi. 17; 2 Kings ii. 9; Zech. xiii. 8, &c. (e) Num. xiv. 41; xxii. 18; xxiv. 13, &c. (f) Gen. xliii. 7; Exod. xxxiv. 27. Phrr. פֶּה אֶל־פֶּה, *mouth to mouth,* without the intervention of any other being, Num. xii. 8. פֶּה אֶחָד, *unanimously,* Josh. ix. 2; 1 Kings xxii. 13; 2 Chron. xviii. 12. מִפֶּה אֶל־פֶּה, *from end to end,* Ezra ix. 11. פֶּה לָפֶה, *Id.,* 2 Kings x. 21; xxi. 16. בְּכָל־פֶּה either, *in every direction* or *with open mouth,* Is. ix. 11.

פֹּה, adv. of place. (a) *Here.* (b) *Hither.* (a) Gen. xix. 12; xxii. 5; xl. 15, &c. (b) 1 Sam. xvi. 11; Ezra iv. 2. מִפֹּה —, *on this side — on that side,* Ezek. xl. 10. 41. 48, 49, &c. In this phrase, מִפוֹ is also used for מִפֹּה, Ezek. xl. 10. 39; xli. 1, &c.

פוג, v. pret. non occ. pres. פָּפוּג, apoc. יָפֻג. Syr. ܦܘܓ, *defecit, refriguit. Became chilled, became languid, ceased to act,* Gen. xlv. 26; Ps. lxxvii. 3; Hab. i. 4.

Niph. נְמוּגֹתִי *Id.,* Ps. xxxviii. 9.

פּוּגָה, f. constr. פּוּגַת. *Cessation, intermission,* Lam. ii. 18.

פוח, v. pret. non occ. pres. יָפִיחַ, i. q. נפח. *Blew, — became cool by a breeze,* Cant. ii. 17; iv. 6.

Hiph. pres. יָפִיחַ. (a) *Blew,* of the wind. (b) *Blew up* a fire, with בְּ. (c) *Inflamed,* constr. immed. (d) *Puffed at,* contemptuously, with בְּ. (c) *Uttered,* constr. immed. (f) From פַּח, *Ensnared.* (b) Ezek. xxi. 36. (c) Prov. xxix. 8. (d) Ps. x. 5. (e) Prov. vi. 19; xiv. 5; xix. 5. 9; xii. 17. (f) Ps. xii. 6. (?)

Infin. הָפֵחַ, (f) Is. xlii. 22.

Imp. f. הָפִיחִי, (a) Cant. iv. 16.

פּוּךְ, m. (a) A black powder used for beautifying the eyes; *powdered antimony:* see כחל, 2 Kings ix. 30; Jer. iv. 30. (b) A precious stone, apparently the same as the לֶשֶׁם, 1 Chron. xxix. 2; Is. liv. 11.

פּוֹל, m. Arab. فُولٌ, *fabæ. Beans,* 2 Sam. xvii. 28; Ezek. iv. 9.

פּוּם, פֻּם, m. aff. פֻּמֵּהּ, Chald. i. q. Heb. פֶּה. *A mouth,* signn. (a) Dan. iv. 28; vi. 23; vii. 8. 20. (b) Dan. vi. 18. Arab. فَمٌ, *Id.*

פון, v. once, pres. אָפוּנָה. Probably, *I pine away,* Ps. lxxxviii. 16. Cogn. Arab. فَنِيَ, *evanuit, disparuit.*

פוץ, v. pres. יָפוּצוּ, sing. non occ. Cogn. נפץ. Arab. فَاصَ, r. فَيْصٌ, *abiit, peregrinatus fuit* in terrâ; فَاضَ, r. فَيْضٌ, *effusus fuit.* (a) *Dispersed themselves, were scattered.* (b) *Overflowed.* (a) Gen. xi. 4; Num. x. 35; 1 Sam. xi. 11, &c. (b) Prov. v. 16; Zech. i. 17.

Imp. pl. פֻּצוּ, (a) 1 Sam. xiv. 35.

Part. pass. pl. aff. פוּצַי, Zeph. iii. 10.

Niph. נָפוֹצָה, i. q. Kal, (a) Gen. x. 18; Jer. x. 21; Ezek. xi. 17, &c.

Part. f. נְפוֹצֶת, pl. נְפוֹצִים, 2 Sam. xviii. 8; 1 Kings xxii. 17.

Pih. pres. יְפַצֵּץ. *Shatters,* Jer. xxiii. 29.

Pih. redup. pres. aff. יְפַצְפְּצֵנִי. *Shakes me to pieces,* Job xvi. 12.

Hiph. הֵפִיץ, pres. יָפִיץ, apoc. יָפֵץ, יָפַץ. (a) Causat. of Kal. *Scattered, threw into confusion.* (b) *Poured out.* (c) I. q. Kal, [a],

פוק (491) פזז

(a) Gen. xiii. 8; Deut. iv. 27; Is. xli. 16, &c. (c) 1 Sam. xiii. 8; Job xxxviii. 24.

Infin. הָפִיץ, aff. הֲפִיצִי, Ezek. xii. 15; xx. 23, &c.

Imp. הָפֵץ, Job xl. 11.

Part. מֵפִיץ, pl. מְפִיצִים, Prov. xxv. 18; Jer. xxiii. 1.

Hith. pres. pl. יִתְפֹּצְצוּ, Pass. of Pih. *Are shattered*, Hab. iii. 6.

פּוּק, v. I. i. q. נפק. Kal non occ.

Hiph. pres. פָיִק, apoc. יָפֵק, and יָפִיק, *Brought out*. (a) *Supplied*. (b) *Obtained*. (c) *Brought to a favourable issue, prospered*. (a) Is. lviii. 10. (b) Prov. iii. 13; viii. 36; xii. 2; xviii. 22. (c) Ps. cxl. 9.

Part. pl. מְפִיקִים, (a) Ps. cxliv. 13.
II. Pret. pl. פָּקוּ. *Staggered, stumbled*, Is. xxviii. 7.

יָפִיק, is usually considered as the pres. Hiphhil, the signification being the same as in Kal; but the root is more probably פיק, from which both פָּקוּ, and יָפִיק, are derived, Jer. x. 4.

פּוּקָה, f. once. *A cause of stumbling*, 1 Sam. xxv. 31.

פּוּר, v. Hiph. הֵפִיר. See פרר.

פּוּר, m. pl. פּוּרִים, פֻּרִים. (a) Apparently an old Persian word; interpreted by גּוֹרָל, *a lot*, Esth. iii. 7; ix. 26. (b) Hence, in the plural, the festival observed in commemoration of the deliverance of the Jews from the designs of Haman, Esth. ix. 24. 26. 29. 31, 32. In modern Persian we have, پُو, *Inquiry, search*. پَر, *A wing, feather* (arrows being used in drawing lots). پَار, *A bit, piece; flight*.

פּוּרָה, f. twice, Is. lxiii. 3; Hag. ii. 16. *A wine-press*. Arab. فَار, r. فور, *æstuavit, efferbuit; sanguinem profudit*.

פּוּשׁ, v. פָּשׁוּ, פָּשׁוֹתָם, pres. תְּפוּשׁוּ. Arab. فَشَا, *propagata et multiplicata sunt pecora*. Cogn. פוץ. (a) *Became numerous, flourished*. (b) *Spread themselves*. (a) Jer. L. 11; Mal. iii. 20. (b) Hab. i. 8.

Niph. plur. נָפֹשׁוּ. *Were scattered*, Nah. iii. 18.

פָּז, m. r. פזז. (a) *Refined*. (b) *Refined gold*. (a) Cant. v. 11. (b) Job xxxviii. 17; Ps. xxi. 4; Is. xiii. 12, &c.

פזז, v. Arab. فَزَّ, *exsilivit loco pavit que dorcas; dimovit, exturbavit loco;* فَسَّ, *segregavit;* وَفَزَّ, and وَفَسَّ, *cucurrit, properavit*. Syr. ܚܡܐ, *durus, difficilis*. *Removed,—moved from place to place,—was strong and active*.

Kal, pres. pl. יָפֹזוּ. *Are strong and active*, Gen. xlix. 24.

Pih. part. מְפַזֵּז. *Moving from place to place,—dancing*, 2 Sam. vi. 16.

Hoph. part. מוּפָז. *Having had its impurities removed,—purified*, 1 Kings x. 18.

פזר, v. i. q. בזר, which see. *Scattered, dispersed*.

Part. pass. f. פְּזוּרָה, of sheep, Jer. L. 17.

Niph. נִפְזְרוּ, Pass. of Kal, Ps. cxli. 7.

Pih. פִּזֵּר, pres. יְפַזֵּר, i. q. Kal. (a) *Scattered*, Ps. liii. 6; lxxxix. 11; cxlvii. 16; Joel iv. 2. (b) *Distributed liberally*, Ps. cxii. 9.

Part. מְפַזֵּר, (b) Prov. xi. 24.

Puh. Pass. of Pih. (a) Part. מְפֻזָּר, Esth. iii. 8.

פַּח, pl. פַּחִים, constr. פַּחֵי. Arab. فَخّ, *laqueus*. Syr. ܦܚܐ, *Id*. (a) *A snare, gin*, Job xviii. 9; Ps. cxxiv. 7; Prov. vii. 23; Eccl. ix. 12, &c. (b) Metaph. used of any concealed danger, Ps. cxix. 110; cxl. 6; Jer. xviii. 22, &c. (c) Any thing spread—*a plate* of metal, Exod. xxxix. 3; Num. xvii. 3.

פַּחַד, m. פַּחְדְּךָ, פַּחְדְּכֶם, פַּחְדּוֹ, פַּחְדָּם, pl. פְּחָדִים. (a) *Fear,*—dread or reverence, פַּחְדּוֹ, both *his fear*, and *the fear of him*. (b) The *object of fear*. (a) Deut. ii. 25; 1 Sam. xi. 7; Job xiii. 11; xv. 21, &c. (b) Gen. xxxi. 42. 53.

פָּחַד, v. pres. יִפְחַד. Constr. abs. it. med. מִפְּנֵי, מִן. (a) *Feared,*—dreaded or reverenced. (b) *Was agitated* with wonder and joy. (c) *Hastened* with wonder and joy. (a) Deut. xxviii. 66; Ps. cxix. 161; Is. xix. 16, &c. (b) Is. lx. 5; Jer. xxxiii. 9. (c) Hos. iii. 5.

Pih. pres. תְּפַחֵד. *Feared greatly*, or continually, Is. li. 13.

Part. מְפַחֵד, Prov. xxviii. 14.

Hiph. הִפְחִיד. *Caused to shake, to tremble*, Job iv. 14.

פחד (492) פטי

פַּחַד, masc. plur. aff. פַּחֲדֵי. Arab. فَخِذٌ, femur. *A thigh*, Job xl. 17.

פַּחְדָּה, f. of פַּחַד, *fear;* aff. פַּחְדָּתִי. *The fear of me*, Jer. ii. 19.

פֶּחָה, m. constr. פַּחַת, aff. פֶּחָתְךָ, פֶּחָם; pl. abs. and constr. פַּחוֹת, aff. פַּחוֹתֶיהָ, it. pl. constr. פַּחֲוֺת. A word apparently of Assyrian origin. (a) *A governor of a province.* (b) *A military commander,—captain.* (a) Neh. ii. 7; iii. 7; v. 5. 14; Jer. li. 23. 28, &c. (b) 1 Kings xx. 24.

פֶּחָה, m. Chald. constr. פַּחַת, pl. def. פַּחֲוָתָא. *Id.*, Ezra v. 3. 14; Dan. iii. 2, &c.

פָּחַז, m. Syr. ܦܚܙ, *salax, lascivus fuit.* Arab. فَخَزَ, *superbivit*, vel *falso gloriatus fuit.* Probably *Boiling* or *running over; swelling up.* Wantonness or *pride*, Gen. xlix. 4.

פחז, v. part. pl. פּוֹחֲזִים. (a) *Dissolute*, Judg. ix. 4. (b) *Proud*, Zeph. iii. 4.

פַּחֲזוּת, fem. aff. פַּחֲזוּתָם. *Pride*, Jer. xxiii. 32.

פֶּחָם, m. twice. Arab. فَحَمٌ, and فُحَمٌ, *carbo. Charcoal*, Prov. xxvi. 21; Is. xliv. 12; liv. 16.

פֶּחָר, masc. once, Chald. *A potter*, Dan. ii. 41. Syr. ܦܚܪ, *Id.* Arab. فَخَّارٌ, *lutum quo fictilia vasa finguntur.*

פַּחַת, m. i. q. פֶּחָה, 2 Kings xviii. 24; Is. xxxvi. 9.

פַּחַת, m. pl. פְּחָתִים. Syr. ܦܚܬ, *fodit;* ܦܚܬܐ, *fovea.* Arab. فَحَتَ, *Id. A pit*, 2 Sam. xvii. 9; xviii. 17; Is. xxiv. 17, 18; Jer. xxviii. 28. 43, 44; Lam. iii. 47. It. Infin. Kal, v. נָפַת, p. 422, above.

פְּחֶתֶת, f. once. *Corrosion, fretting into* a garment, Lev. xiii. 55.

פִּטְדָה, f. constr. פִּטְדַת. *A precious stone*: either *the topaz* or *the emerald*, Exod. xxviii. 17; xxx. 19; Job xxviii. 19; Ezek. xxviii. 13.

פַּטִּישׁ, m. Arab. فَطَسَ, *latum fecit cudendo ferrum;* فِطِّيسٌ, *malleus magnus*

fabri ferrarii. *A hammer*, Is. xli. 7; Jer. xxiii. 29; L. 23.

פָּטִישׁ, m. Chald. pl. aff. פַּטִּישֵׁיהוֹן. Syr. ܦܛܝܫܐ, *interula; tunica. A tunic*, Dan. iii. 21, al. non occ.

פָּטַר, m. Arab. فَطَرَ, *fidit; prodiit; incepit, auspicatus fuit; creavit Deus.* Æth. ፈጠረ: *creavit, formavit. Opening; coming forth; beginning.* פֶּטֶר רֶחֶם, *first-born*, Exod. xiii. 2. 12; xiii. 15; xxxiv. 19, &c. And without רֶחֶם, Exod. xiii. 13; xxxiv. 19, 20. See Hieroz., tom. i. p. 296.

פָּטַר, v. pres. יִפְטֹר. (a) *Slipped out* or *away.* (b) *Let out* water. (c) *Exempted from duty.* (a) 1 Sam. xix. 10. (c) 2 Chron. xxiii. 8.

Part. פּוֹטֵר, (b) Prov. xvii. 14. Part. pass. pl. פְּטוּרִים, (c) 1 Chron. ix. 33. פְּטוּרֵי צִצִּים, *open flowers*, 1 Kings vi. 18. 29. 32. 35.

Hiph. pres. יַפְטִירוּ. *Opened wide*, in mockery, with בְּ, Ps. xxii. 8.

פְּטֹרָה, f. constr. פִּטְרַת, i. q. פֶּטֶר, Num. viii. 16.

פִּי, see פֶּה.

פִּיד, m. aff. פִּידוֹ. Arab. فَادَ, r. فيد, *disparuit, mortuus fuit. Destruction*, Job xxx. 24; xxxi. 29; Prov. xxiv. 22.

פִּיָּה, f. pl. פִּיּוֹת. *The edge* of a sword, Judg. iii. 16. See פֶּה.

פִּיחַ, m. r. פוח. *Ashes, dust*, Exod. ix. 8. 10.

פִּילֶגֶשׁ, see פִּלֶּגֶשׁ.

פִּימָה, f. once. Arab. فَيَّمَ, *adipe impletum fuit;* فَيَّمَ, *potens, robustus;* فوم, *allium; triticum; ciceres; panis;* tum de omni frumento, quod coquendo pani inservit. *Food; fatness; strength*, Job xv. 27. See the notes.

פִּיפִיּוֹת, pl. f. r. פֶּה. *Edges*, Is. xli. 15. חֶרֶב פִּיפִיּוֹת, *a two-edged sword*, Ps. cxlix. 6.

פִּיק, m. once, r. פוק. *Staggering*, Nah. ii. 11.

פַּךְ, m. *A flask*, for oil, 1 Sam. x. 1; 2 Kings ix. 1. 3.

פכה, v. Kal non occ. Prob. cogn. בכה.

פלא (493) פלג

Pih. Part. pl. מְפַלְּאִים. *Flowing out*, Ezek. xlvii. 2.

פֶּלֶא, m. aff. פִּלְאֲךָ, pl. פְּלָאִים, and פְּלָאוֹת. *Separation; peculiarity; miraculousness. A miracle*, Exod. xv. 11; Ps. lxxxiv. 6; Is. xxix. 14; Lam. i. 9; Dan. xii. 6, &c. פֶּלֶא יוֹעֵץ, *marvellous in counsel*, Is. ix. 5.

פלא, v. Kal non occ.

Niph. נִפְלָאתָה (for נִפְלְאָה), נִפְלֵיתִי, נִפְלְאוּ; pres. יִפָּלֵא, pl. יִפָּלוּ. (a) *Was marvellous.* (b) With בְּעֵינֵי, *Appeared difficult* or *marvellous.* (c) With מִן, *Was concealed, out of reach, too difficult for.* (d) *Was wonderfully made*, or *was struck with wonder.* (a) 2 Sam. i. 26. (b) 2 Sam. xiii. 2; Neh. vi. 17; Zech. viii. 6. (c) Gen. xviii. 14; Deut. xvii. 8; Prov. xxx. 18; Jer. xxxii. 17. 27. (d) Ps. cxxxix. 14.
Part. fem. נִפְלָאת, and נִפְלָאָה; pl. נִפְלָאִים, fem. נִפְלָאוֹת, constr. נִפְלְאוֹת, aff. נִפְלְאֹתַי, &c. (c) Deut. xxx. 11. *Miraculous; a miracle*, Exod. iii. 20; xxxiv. 10; Job xxxvii. 14; Ps. cxviii. 23, &c.

Pih. Infin. פַּלֵּא. *Set apart*, Lev. xxii. 21; Num. xv. 3. 8.

Hiph. הִפְלִיא, and הִפְלָא, pres. יַפְלִא. (a) *Set apart.* (b) *Made wonderful.* (c) *Acted wonderfully.* (a) Num. vi. 2; Lev. xxvii. 2. (b) Deut. xxviii. 59; Ps. xxxi. 22; Is. xxviii. 29. (c) 2 Chron. xxvi. 15.
Infin. הַפְלִיא, and הַפְלֵא, 2 Chron. ii. 9; Is. xxix. 14; Joel ii. 26.
Part. מַפְלִא, Judg. xiii. 19.
Hith. pres. תִּתְפַּלָּא. *Thou showest thyself marvellous*, Job x. 16.

פִּלְאִי, f. פִּלְאִיָּה. (a) *Secret.* (b) *Out of reach, too difficult for.* (a) Judg. xiii. 18. (b) Ps. cxxxix. 6. See the *Keri.*

פֶּלֶג, m. pl. פְּלָגִים, constr. פַּלְגֵי, aff. פְּלָגָיו. Arab. فَلَج, *diffidit in duas partes; sulcavit terram; partitus fuit rem*; فَلْج, *pars, semissis*; فَلَج, *fluvius parvus.* Syr. and Sam. *divisit.* Æth. ፈለገ: *flumen. Dividing; making a furrow; distributing. A channel* for water, *an* artificial *stream, a brook*, Ps. i. 3; xlvi. 5; lxv. 10; Is. xxx. 25. Of tears, Lam. iii. 48. Of oil, Job xxix. 6.

פלג, v. Kal non occ.

Niph. נִפְלְגָה. *Of the earth, Was divided*, Gen. x. 28; 1 Chron. i. 19.

Pih. פִּלֵּג. *Cut out, formed*, a canal, channel, Job xxxviii. 25.
Imp. פַּלֵּג. *Divide*, Ps. lxv. 10.

פלג, v. Chald. *Divided.* Part. pass. f. פְּלִיגָה, Dan. ii. 41.

פְּלַג, m. Chald. *A half*, Dan. vii. 25.

פְּלַגּוֹת, pl. f. i. q. פֶּלֶג, Judg. v. 15, 16; Job xx. 17.

פְּלֻגּוֹת, pl. f. *Divisions, classes*, 2 Chron. xxxv. 5.

פלג, pl. f. aff. פְּלֻגָּתְהוֹן, Chald. *Id.*, Ezra vi. 18.

פִּלֶגֶשׁ, and פִּילֶגֶשׁ, fem. aff. פִּילַגְשׁוֹ, pl. פִּלַגְשִׁים, and פִּילַגְשִׁים, constr. פַּלְגְשֵׁי, aff. פִּילַגְשָׁיו. *A concubine, secondary wife*, Gen. xxxv. 22; Judg. xix. 2; 2 Sam. iii. 7; v. 13; xvi. 21; 2 Chron. xi. 21, &c. The etymology is doubtful. Castell gives פֶּלֶג אִשָּׁה, *uxor divisa, dimidiata.* Comp. παλλακή.

פְּלָדוֹת, pl. f. once, Nah. ii. 4. A word variously rendered. According to some, it is the plur. of פֶּלֶד, by metathesis for לַפִּיד, *torches.* Others compare Syr. ܦܘܠܕܐ, *ferri præstantissimum genus, chalybs.* Arabic فُولَاذ, Pers. پُولاد, *ferrum durum, chalybs. Iron work* of the chariots; *glittering scythes.*

פלה, v. Kal non occ. Cogn. פלא.

Niph. נִפְלִינוּ. *Are separated*, Exod. xxxiii. 16.

Hiph. הִפְלָה, pres. יַפְלֶה. (a) *Made a separation, separated.* (b) *Set apart.* (a) Exod. viii. 22; ix. 4; xi. 7. (b) Ps. iv. 4.
Imp. הַפְלֵה, (b) Ps. xvii. 7.

פֶּלַח, fem. Arab. فَلَح, *fidit, sulcavit aravit*; فِلْح, *fidit in duas partes*; فَيْح, *mola. Cutting; furrowing.* (a) *A piece.* (b) *A mill-stone.* (a) 1 Sam. xxx. 12; Cant. iv. 3. (b) Judg. ix. 53; 2 Sam. xi. 21; Job xli. 15.

פלח, v. constr. immed. *Cut.* Part. פֹּלֵחַ, Ps. cxli. 7.

Pih. pres. יְפַלַּח, *Intensive of Kal.* (a) *Cut to pieces.* (b) *Disentangle.* (c) *Pierce through.* (d) Metaph. *Harrow.* (a) 2 Kings iv. 39. (b) Job xxxix. 3 : but see the notes. (c) Prov. vii. 23. (d) Job xvi. 13.

פלח, v. Chald. pres. יִפְלְחוּן. Syr.

פלח (494) פלל

فَلَحَ, servivit, coluit. Served, worshipped, Dan. iii. 28; vii. 14. 27.
Part. פְּלַח, pl. פָּלְחִין, constr. פָּלְחֵי, Ezra vii. 24; Dan. iii. 12: vi. 17, &c.

פָּלְחָן, m. Service, worship, Ezra vii. 19.

פלט, v. פַּלֵּט. Arab. فَلَتَ, effugium, liberatio; أَفْلَتَ, liberavit. Syr. ܦܠܛ, evasit, effugit. Escaped, constr. abs., Ezek. vii. 16.
Pih. pres. יְפַלֵּט. Constr. immed. (a) Delivered. (b) Brings forth safely. (a) 2 Sam. xxii. 44; Ps. xxxvii. 40, &c. (b) Job xxi. 10.
Infin. פַּלֵּט. Deliverance, Ps. xxxii. 7; lvi. 8.
Imp. פַּלְּטָה, plur. פַּלְּטוּ, Ps. xvii. 13; lxxxii. 4.
Part. aff. מְפַלְטִי. My deliverer, Ps. xviii. 3; xl. 18; lxx. 6, &c.
Hiph. pres. יַפְלִיט, i. q. Pih. Is. v. 29; Mic. vi. 14.

פָּלִיט, m. pl. פְּלִיטִים, and פְּלֵיטִים, constr. פְּלִיטֵי, aff. פְּלִיטָיו, &c. Having escaped; safe; a fugitive, Gen. xiv. 13; Is. lxvi. 19; Jer. L. 28; Ezek. vi. 8, &c.

פְּלֵיטָה, and פְּלֵטָה, constr. פְּלֵיטַת, f. of preceding. Those that have escaped; remnant, Judg. xxi. 17; Is. x. 20; 2 Chron. xx. 24, &c. In one or two passages it may signify deliverance, but has not necessarily that signification.

פְּלִיל, masc. pl. פְּלִילִים. Arab. بَلِيلٌ, potitus fuit re; tetigit rem, scivit eam; بَلَّ, res communis juris; licitum. A judge; having the knowledge of what is lawful, and the power to decide, Exod. xxi. 22; Deut. xxxii. 31; Job xxxi. 11.

פְּלִילָה, f. Justice, Is. xvi. 3.
פְּלִילִי, m. A thing cognizable by a judge, Job xxxi. 28.

פְּלִילִיָּה, f. Judgment, Is. xxviii. 7.

פֶּלֶךְ, m. פִּלְכוֹ. Arab. فَلَكٌ, rotundus fuit; فَلَكٌ, pars rotunda et maxima; orbis cœlestis; فَلَكَةٌ, res quælibet rotunda; orbiculus fusi muliebris. Any thing round. (a) A spinning-wheel. (b) Circuit, district. (a) 2 Sam. iii. 19; Prov. xxxi. 19. (b) Neh. iii. 9. 12, &c.

פלל, v. Kal non occ. See פלל.
Pih. פִּלֵּל, pres. יְפַלֵּל. (a) Judged, constr. immed. (b) Adjudged punishment, with לְ. (c) Inflicted judicial punishment, abs. (d) Judged probable; expected. (a) 1 Sam. ii. 25. (b) Ezek. xvi. 52. (c) Ps. cvi. 30. (d) Gen. xlviii. 11.
Hith. הִתְפַּלֵּל, pres. יִתְפַּלֵּל. Appealed to a judge; prayed. Constr. [1] abs., 2 Kings vi. 17. [2] Med. לְ, To, Dan. ix. 4. In behalf of, 1 Sam. ii. 25. [3] אֶל, To, Gen. xx. 17; Num. xx. 17; 1 Kings viii. 33. Towards, 1 Kings viii. 30. 35. 42. (Gram. art. 241. 18.) For a thing, 1 Sam. i. 27. [4] בְּעַד, In behalf of, Deut. ix. 21; Jer. vii. 18; xiv. 21, &c. [5] עַל, Id., Job xlii. 8.
Infin. הִתְפַּלֵּל, 1 Sam. i. 12.
Imp. הִתְפַּלֵּל, Num. xxi. 7.
Part. מִתְפַּלֵּל, 1 Kings viii. 28.

פַּלְמוֹנִי, i. q. לְפַלְמוֹנִי, פְּלֹנִי אַלְמֹנִי. To that particular one, Dan. viii. 13.

פְּלֹנִי. Arab. فُلَانٌ, quidam. A certain person. פְּלֹנִי אַלְמֹנִי, a certain person or place, whose name is not mentioned, but is to be supplied. Such a one, such a place, Ruth iv. 1; 1 Sam. xxi. 3; 2 Kings vi. 8.

פֶּלֶס, m. Equalizing, balancing. A steel-yard, Prov. xvi. 11; Is. xl. 12.

פלס, v. Pih. pres. יְפַלֵּס. (a) Pondered, considered. (b) Approved. (c) Planned. (b) Is. xxvi. 7. (c) Ps. lviii. 3; lxxviii. 50; Prov. v. 6.
Imp. פַּלֵּס, (a) Prov. iv. 26.
Part. מְפַלֵּס, (a) Prov. v. 21.

פלץ, v. Kal non occ. Æth. ፈለጠ: migravit de loco in locum. VI. Incertis sedibus vagatus est. Shook, trembled.
Hith. pres. יִתְפַּלָּצוּן, Id., Job ix. 6.

פַּלָּצוּת, f. Trembling, fear, Job xxi. 6; Ps. lv. 6; Is. xxi. 4; Ezek. vii. 18.

פלש, v. only in Hith. pres. יִתְפַּלְּשׁוּ. Cogn. Arab. أَبْلَسَ, fractus animo, tristis et mœstus fuit; بَلَسٌ, cineres alkali. Either, Rolled themselves in, or sprinkled themselves with, dust. Constr. abs. it. בְּאַ, Ezek. xxvii. 30.
Imp. fem. הִתְפַּלְּשִׁי, pl. הִתְפַּלְּשׁוּ, Jer. vi. 26; xxv. 34; Mic. i. 10.

פלת (495) פנה

פְּלֵתִי, m. found with כְּרֵתִי, and גִּתִּים. Probably *A mercenary soldier* of one of the tribes of the Philistines—used collectively—*Pelethites*, 2 Sam. viii. 18; xv. 18; xx. 7. 23. Gesenius compares the Arab. فلت, *celer equus*; فلتان, *audax, robustus, celer.* See כְּרֵתִי.

פֵּן, m. aff. פִּנָּה, pl. פִּנִּים, i. q. פָּנָה. *A corner*, Prov. vii. 8; Zech. xiv. 10.

פֶּן, always with Makkaph, פֶּן־. Cogn. r. פנה. *Seeing, looking towards* and guarding against a consequence: whether that consequence is certain; *seeing* ye shall, or only probable; *seeing* ye may; *lest. Videte ne* —. Usually joined to the present tense, Gen. iii. 4; xxvi. 9; Ps. ii. 12, &c. Twice joined to the preterite, 2 Sam. xx. 6; 2 Kings ii. 16.

פַּנַּג, once, Ezek. xxvii. 17, בְּחִטֵּי מִנִּית וּפַנַּג וּדְבַשׁ; either, like מִנִּית, the name of a place in the Holy Land which traded in wheat with the Syrians, *Pannag;* or some article of traffic, but what it appears impossible to determine. *Millet, cassia, sweet cakes,* and *balsam,* have been conjecturally given as a translation. Possibly, cogn. פנג.

פָּנָה, v. pres. יִפְנֶה, apoc. יִּפֶן, and יָפֶן. *Turned his face, turned himself,* towards or away. Constr. abs. immed. it. med. אֶל, לְ, בְּ, מִן, אַחֲרֵי. (a) *Turned himself,* to look or to go away. (b) *Turned himself towards.* [1] Favourably, *regarded.* [2] Unfavourably, *punished.* [3] For assistance. [4] To worship; to follow a practice; to take a road. (c) Of time, *Changed:* [1] *Declined.* [2] *Began.* (a) Exod. ii. 12; x. 6; Deut. xvi. 7; ix. 15; 2 Kings xxiii. 16, &c. פָּנָה אַחֲרָיו, *looked back,* Exod. xx. 40; 2 Sam. i. 7; ii. 20; 2 Kings ii. 24. (b), [1] Lev. xxvi. 9; 2 Sam. ix. 8; 1 Kings viii. 28, &c. [2] Deut. ix. 27. [3] Job v. 1. [4] Lev. xx. 6; Deut. xxxi. 18. 20; 1 Sam. xiii. 17, 18; Job xxxvi. 21; Ps. xl. 5; Is. liii. 6, &c. (c), [1] Ps. xc. 9; Jer. vi. 4. Infin. פְּנָה, constr. פְּנוֹת, Ezek. xliii. 17; Hag. i. 9. (c), [2] Gen. xxiv. 63; Exod. xiv. 27; Deut. xxiii. 12; Judg. xix. 26; Ps. xlvi. 6. Imp. פְּנֵה, pl. פְּנוּ, Num. xiv. 25; Josh. xxii. 4; Ps. xxv. 16, &c. Part. פֹּנֶה, pl. פֹּנִים, f. פֹּנוֹת, Hos. iii. 1. Of position; *looking* or *lying* towards, 1 Kings vii. 25; Ezek. viii. 3, &c.

Pih. פִּנָּה. (a) *Caused to turn* or *go away, removed.* (b) *Cleared,* a road, or house. (a) Zeph. iii. 15. (b) Gen. xxiv. 31; Lev. xiv. 36; Ps. lxxx. 10; Mal. iii. 1. Imp. plur. פַּנּוּ, (b) Is. xl. 3; lvii. 14; lxii. 10.

Hiph. הִפְנָה, pres. apoc. יֶּפֶן. (a) Causat. of Kal. *Turned.* (b) I. q. Kal, *Turned himself.* (a) Judg. xv. 4; Jer. xlviii. 39. (b) Jer. xlvi. 5. 21; xlvii. 3; xlix. 24. Infin. aff. הַפְנֹתוֹ, (b) 1 Sam. x. 9. Part. מַפְנֶה, (b) Nah. ii. 9.

Hoph. הָפְנָה. *Were caused to turn themselves,* Jer. xlix. 8.

פִּנָּה, f. constr. פִּנַּת, aff. פִּנָּתָהּ; pl. פִּנּוֹת, aff. פִּנּוֹתָם, פִּנּוֹתָיו. (a) *A turning, corner,* of a street or building. (b) *A battlement, parapet.* (c) A person high in rank; *a prince.* (a) Prov. vii. 12; Job i. 19; xxxviii. 6; Jer. li. 26, &c. (b) 2 Chron. xxvi. 15; Prov. xxi. 9; xxv. 24; Zeph. i. 16. (c) Judg. xx. 2; 1 Sam. xiv. 40; Is. xix. 13.

פָּנִים, pl. m. constr. פְּנֵי, aff. פָּנַי, פָּנֶיךָ, פָּנָיו, פָּנֵינוּ, פְּנֵיהֶם, פְּנֵיכֶם. (a) *Face, countenance.* (b) *Person.* (c) *Presence.* (d) *Surface.* (e) *Front; in front.* (f) Phrr. פָּנִים אֶל־פָּנִים, or פָּנִים בְּפָנִים, *face to face.* (g) נָתַן פָּנָיו בְּ, or, *set his face against,* for evil. (h) הִסְתִּיר פָּנָיו מִן, *concealed his face from,* in displeasure. (i) הֵסֵב פָּנָיו מִן, or הֵשִׁיב, *turned away his face.* (k) בִּקֵּשׁ פָּנֶיךָ, *sought thy face,* as a suppliant. (l) חִלָּה פָּנֶיךָ, or כִּפֶּר, *propitiated thee.* (m) נָשָׂא פָּנֶיךָ, *accepted thy person.* (n) הֵשִׁיב פָּנֶיךָ, *turned away thy face, rejected thee.* (o) נָשָׂא פָּנִים אֶל, *looked at,* pec. with confidence or favour. (p) אֶת פְּנֵי, *in the presence of, before.* (q) בִּפְנֵי, *in the face of, against,* an enemy. (r) לִפְנֵי, *before:* [1] In the presence of. [2] In the sight or judgment of. [3] Preceding in place or rank. [4] In front of. [5] *Before* an enemy, or defeat or flight. [6] In opposition to, against. [7] In time. (s) לְפָנִים, [1] *Forwards.* [2] *Formerly.* (t) *The inside* of a covering. (u) לִפְנַי, *within.* (v) מִלְּפָנִים, *Id.* (w) מִלְּפָנִים, *from ancient time.* (x) מִלִּפְנֵי, [1] *In the presence of.* [2] *From the presence of.* [3] *On account of,* (y) בִּשְׁבִיל, [1] *In the presence of.* [2] *From the presence of.* [3] *By means of, on account of.* [4] *From the power of.* (z) מִפָּנִים, *in front.* (aa) עַל פְּנֵי, [1] *In the presence of.* [2] *In preference to.* [3] *Towards.*

פני (496) פנק

[4] *On the surface of.* (a) Gen. xxxi. 2; Exod. xxxiv. 35; Ps. civ. 15; Prov. xv. 13, &c. (b) Deut. i. 17; x. 17; xvi. 19; 2 Chron. xix. 7, &c. (c) Exod. x. 11. (d) Gen. i. 2; ii. 6; vii. 18, &c. (e) Exod. xxvi. 9; Lev. ix. 8; Num. xx. 10, &c.;— 1 Chron. xix. 10; 2 Chron. xiii. 14; Ezek. ii. 10. (f) Gen. xxxii. 31; Exod. xxxiii. 11; Deut. xxxiv. 10, &c.;—Deut. v. 4. (g) Lev. xx. 3. 5; Jer. xliv. 11; Ezek. xiv. 8, &c. (h) Deut. xxxi. 17; xxxii. 20; Is. L. 6, &c. (i) Ezek. vii. 22; xiv. 6. (k) 2 Chron. vii. 14; Ps. xxiv. 6; cv. 4. (l) Gen. xxxii. 20; Exod. xxxii. 18; 1 Sam. xiii. 12; 2 Kings xiii. 4. (m) Gen. xix. 21; 1 Sam. xxv. 35. (n) 1 Kings ii. 16. 20. (o) Num. vi. 27; 2 Sam. ii. 22; Job xxii. 26, &c. (p) Gen. xix. 27; xxvii. 30; xxxiii. 18, &c. (q) Num. xii. 14; Deut. i. 25; Josh. xxiii. 9, &c. (r), [1] Gen. xli. 46; xlvii. 2; Exod. vii. 10, &c. [2] Gen. xliii. 14; Deut. xxiv. 4. 13, &c. [3] Exod. xiv. 19; Deut. iii. 18; Josh. i. 14, &c. [4] Exod. xxix. 10; xxx. 6; xl. 5, &c. [5] Judg. iv. 15. 23; xx. 35; 1 Sam. iv. 2, &c. [6] 2 Kings x. 4; Job xli. 2; Prov. xxvii. 4, &c. [7] Gen. xiii. 10; xxvii. 7; 2 Kings xix. 26, &c. (s), [1] Jer. vii. 24. [2] Deut. ii. 10. 12. 20; Josh. xi. 10, &c. (t) Job xli. 5. (u) 1 Kings vi. 17. (v) 1 Kings vi. 29. (w) Is. xli. 26. (x), [1] 2 Chron. xxxiii. 12. 23; xxxiv. 27, &c. [2] Gen. xli. 46; xlvii. 6; Lev. ix. 24, &c. [3] 1 Sam. xviii. 12. (y), [1] 2 Kings xxii. 19; xxv. 26; Zech. ii. 13, &c. [2] Gen. xvi. 8; xxxv. 1; Exod. ii. 15, &c. [3] Gen. vii. 7; xxvii. 46; xli. 31, &c. [4] Ps. lxi. 4. (z) 2 Sam. x. 9. (a a), [1] Gen. xi. 28; xxv. 18; Lev. x. 3, &c. [2] Deut. xxi. 16. [3] Gen. xviii. 16; Num. xxiii. 28. [4] Gen. i. 2; xi. 4, &c.

פְּנִימָה, from פָּנִים, sign. (u), (a) *Within*, [1] *To the inside.* [2] *On the inside.* (b) לִפְנִימָה, *Id.* (c) מִפְּנִימָה, *On the inside.* (a), [1] Lev. x. 18; 2 Kings vii. 11; 2 Chron. xxix. 18, &c. [2] 1 Kings vi. 17; Ps. xlv. 14. (b) 1 Kings vi. 30; 2 Chron. xxix. 16; Ezek. xl. 16; xli. 3. (c) 1 Kings vi. 19. 21; 2 Chron. iii. 4.

פְּנִימִי, f. פְּנִימִית; pl. פְּנִימִים, f. פְּנִימִיוֹת. *Inner*, 1 Kings vi. 27. 36; 1 Chron. xxviii. 11; 2 Chron. iv. 22, &c.

פְּנִינִים, pl. m. *Pearls*, Job xxviii. 18; Prov. iii. 15; viii. 11; xxviii. 18; xxxi. 10; Lam. iv. 7. Comp. πίννα, *pinna marina.* See Hieroz., tom. ii. p. 681, and 693, where the opinion that the word signifies *coral* is discussed.

פנק, v. Kal non occ. Arab. فَنِقَ, *juvenca et pinguis*, de camelâ; *molliter habita atque educata*, de puellâ; فَنِقَ, *molliter et delicatè habuit educavitque.* Syr. ܦܰܢܶܩ, *oblectatus est, oblectavit se.*
Pih. part. מְפַנֵּק. *Bringing up delicately*, Prov. xxix. 21, al. non occ.

פַּס, m. Chald. def. פַּסָּא. Syr. ܦܰܣܳܐ, *vola* manus, *planta* pedis. Probably *The extremity.* Comp. אֶפֶס, יָד, פַּס, and פַּסָּא דִידָא, *the extremity of the hand*, Dan. v. 5. 24.

פַּס, plur. פַּסִּים. *The extremities;* the hands and feet. כְּתֹנֶת פַּסִּים, apparently, *a long dress*, reaching nearly to the ground, and covering the hands, Gen. xxxvii. 3. 23. 32; 2 Sam. xiii. 18, 19. LXX. χιτῶνα ποικίλον. Sym. χειριδωτόν. Aquila, ἀστραγάλειον.

פסג, v. once. Pih. Imp. פַּסְּגוּ, Ps. xlviii. 14. A word of very doubtful signification. The context appears to require the idea of *counting, observing*, or *admiring.* We have, Chald. פְּסַג, *dividit, dissecuit; fulcivit; exaltavit.* Gesenius takes this as the root, and translates, *dissecate; accuratè contemplamini.* LXX. καταδιέλεσθε. Sym. διαμετρήσατε. Vulg. *distribuite.*

פסח, f. constr. פִּסְחַת, once, Ps. lxxii. 16. Arab. فَشَا, *propagata et multiplicata sunt pecora;* فَشْو, *pecudum progenies et propago.* Probably *An abundant growth* of corn : or, taking the Chald. פַּס as the root, *a handful.* The LXX. and Vulg. translate פִּסַּת־בַּר, by στήριγμα, and *firmamentum.*

פָּסַח, m. pl. פְּסָחִים. Arab. فَسِحَ, *amplus, spatiosus fuit* locus : *amplos passus fecit; scripsit securitatis publicæ literas pro itinere suscipiendo alicui.* II. *Concessit alicui potestatem* rei; فَسَحَ, *literæ securitatis pro itinere suscipiendo;* أَفْصَى, *eximius et liber fuit* ab aliquâ re. *Standing over* to defend. Comp. ἀμφιβέβηκας, Il. A. 27, and see Is. xxxi. 5,

פֶּסַח

giving security. The verb seems to be i. q. עָבַר עַל. Comp. Exod. xii. 23. So Gesenius, and thence cogn. τοῦ, فَسَخَ, *luxavit manuno,* &c. *Passing, hopping, limping, over,* will probably be its exact sense. Thence, (a) *The passover.* (b) *The Paschal lamb.* (a) Exod. xii. 27; xxxiv. 25; Lev. xxiii. 5, &c. (b) Exod. xii. 21; Deut. xvi. 5; 2 Chron. xxxv. 7, 8, &c.

פָּסַח, v. pres. non occ. Constr. med. עַל. *Passed, stood, over* for defence; *defended, protected,* Exod. xii. 13. 23. 27.

Infin. פָּסֹחַ, Is. xxxi. 5.

Part. pl. פֹּסְחִים. Either, *Defending, holding,* two inconsistent opinions, or—see פָּסֵחַ *halting, hesitating,* between them, 1 Kings xviii. 21; and note on Job xx. 2.

פִּסֵּחַ, m. pl. פִּסְחִים. Arab. فَسَخَ, *debilis fuit; dispersit* rem; *luxavit* manum. *Lame,* 2 Sam. ix. 13; Job xxix. 15; Prov. xxvi. 7; Is. xxxiii. 23, &c.

פסח, v. Niph. pres. יִפָּסֵחַ. *Was lamed, became lame,* 2 Sam. iv. 4.

Pih. pres. יְפַסְּחוּ. Probably, *Leaped about,* in a frantic manner, on or by the altar; this being, apparently, their manner of expressing their earnestness in calling upon Baal, 1 Kings xviii. 26.

פְּסִילִים, pl. m. constr. פְּסִילֵי, aff. פְּסִילָיו &c.; r. פָּסַל. *Carved images, idols,* Deut. vii. 25; 2 Kings xvii. 41; Hos. xi. 12, &c. In Judg. iii. 19. 26, הַפְּסִילִים is generally interpreted *quarries;* but there appears no necessity to adopt a second signification for the word. These were probably Moabitish idols; and might mark the extent of the portion of the land of Israel which the Moabites occupied at that time; or at this place there might be a Moabitish station, as Ehud appears to have considered his followers and himself in danger till the place was passed. It is not impossible, however, that the Arab. فَصِيل,—*septum depressius extra moenia urbis vel arcis,*—may furnish the true interpretation.

פֶּסֶל, m. aff. פִּסְלִי, פִּסְלוֹ, פִּסְלָם. Arab. فَصَل, *dissecuit; separavit.* Syr. ܦܣܠ, *dolavit, sculpsit. Hewing, carving.* (a) *A carved image, an idol.* (b) *An idol,* whether carved or molten. (a) Exod. xx. 4; Is. xlv. 20; Hab. ii. 18, &c. (b) Is. xl. 19; Jer. x. 14; li. 17, &c.

פָּסַל, v. pres. יִפְסֹל. Constr. immed. *Hewed, carved,* either stone or wood, Exod. xxxiv. 4; Deut. x. 3; 1 Kings v. 32; Hab. ii. 18.

Imp. פְּסָל, Exod. xxxiv. 1; Deut. x. 1.

פְּסַנְתֵּרִין, and פְּסַנְטֵרִין. A musical instrument, ψαλτήριον, *the Psaltery,* Dan. iii. 5. 7. 10. 15. It is probable that this word was introduced with the instrument; and even if the Babylonians had no previous intercourse with the Greeks, it is likely that about this time, Aryenis, the wife of Astyages, and sister of Crœsus, whose mother was an Ionian, would have introduced the Greek music at the Median courts, and from the Medes it would speedily reach Babylon. See Herod. i. 74. 92.

פסם, v. once, פָּסוּ. Arab. فَاصَ, r. فَيَض, *mortuus* r. فَاصَ, *cessavit;* فِيص, *fuit.* Cogn. אסם. *Ceased, ceased to exist, disappeared,* Ps. xii. 2. LXX. ὠλιγώθησαν. Vulg. *diminutæ sunt.*

פעה, v. once, pres. אֶפְעֶה. Syr. ܦܥܐ, and Chald. פְּעָה, *vociferatus est; balavit* ovis. *Cry out,* as in pain, Is. xlii. 14.

פָּעַל, v. pres. יִפְעַל, and יִפְעָל. Arab. فَعَل, and Syr. ܦܥܠ, *opus fecit, egit.* Constr. abs. it. immed. with לְ, or בְּ, of the person *for* or *against* whom the action is performed. (a) *Worked,* abs. (b) *Made, formed.* (c) *Did, performed.* (d) *Practised.* (a) Is. xliv. 12; xliii. 13. (b) Exod. xv. 17; Ps. vii. 16; Is. xliv. 15, &c. (c) Num. xxiii. 23; Deut. xxxii. 27; Prov. xvi. 4, &c. (d) Job xxxiv. 32; xxxvi. 23; Prov. xxx. 20, &c.

Part. פֹּעֵל, aff. פֹּעֲלִי; pl. constr. פֹּעֲלֵי, Job xxxiv. 8; xxxvi. 3; Ps. xv. 2, &c.

פֹּעַל, m. aff. פָּעֳלִי, פָּעֳלְךָ, and פָּעֳלֶה, פָּעֳלוֹ, and פָּעֳלָם, פָּעֳלֵכֶם, פָּעֳלָם; pl. פְּעָלִים (a) *Work,* [1] Any thing made. [2] Employment. [3] Action. [4] Practice. (b) *Wages,* what is gained by work. (c) *Acquisition.* (a), [1] Ps. ix. 17; Is. xlv. 9. 11; 2 Sam. xxiii. 20. [2] Deut. xxxiii. 11; Job xxiv. 5; Ps. civ. 23, &c. [3] Ps. xliv. 2; xcv. 9; Hab. i. 5, &c. [4] Prov. xx. 11; Is. xli. 24; lix. 6, &c. (b) Job vii. 2; Jer. xxii. 13. (c) Prov. xxi. 6.

3 s

פְּעֻלָּה, f. constr. פְּעֻלַּת, aff. פְּעֻלָּתִי, &c.; plur. פְּעֻלּוֹת. (a) *Work, employment.* (b) *Wages.* (c) *Reward or punishment.* (a) 2 Chron. xv. 7; Jer. xxxi. 16; Ezek. xxix. 20, &c. (b) Lev. xix. 13. (c) Ps. cix. 20; Prov. x. 16; xi. 18, &c.

פַּעַם, fem. dual, פַּעֲמַיִם, pl. פְּעָמִים, constr. פַּעֲמֵי, aff. פְּעָמָיו, פְּעָמָיךָ, &c.; it. sign. (e), פְּעָמוֹתָיו. *Stepping:* hence, by a common figure, *acting;* and, since in stepping we strike the ground, *striking.* (a) In the plural only, *Foot-steps; feet.* (b) *Progress* of a chariot. (c) An act, and the time of its performance; *a time.* [1] פַּעַם אַחַת, *Once;* *at once, at one time.* [2] פַּעַם — פַּעַם, *At one time—at another time.* [3] הַפַּעַם, *This time,* on this occasion; *at once,* immediately. [4] רַק הַפַּעַם, אַךְ הַפַּעַם, *Only this once.* [5] בְּפַעַם הַזֹּאת, *On this occasion.* [6] בְּפַעַם, *At a time.* [7] כְּפַעַם בְּפַעַם, *As before, as usual.* [8] פַּעַם וּשְׁתַּיִם, *Once or twice.* [9] פַּעֲמַיִם *Twice:* שָׁלֹשׁ פְּעָמִים, *Three times, &c.* [10] פַּעֲמַיִם שָׁלֹשׁ, *Twice or even thrice.* [11] מֵאָה פְעָמִים, *A hundred fold.* (d) *An anvil;* or, according to some, *a hammer.* (e) Probably, *The feet* of the ark. (a) 2 Kings xix. 24; Ps. xvii. 5; lviii. 11; Prov. xxix. 5; Is. xxvi. 6, &c. (b) Judg. v. 28. (c), [1] Josh. vi. 3. 11. 14; 1 Sam. xxvi. 8; Josh. x. 42; Is. lxvi. 8. [2] Prov. vii. 12. [3] Gen. xxix. 35; Exod. ix. 27; Judg. xv. 3, &c.; Gen. xlvi. 30. [4] Gen. xviii. 32; Exod. x. 17; Judg. vi. 39, &c. [5] Exod. viii. 27; ix. 14; 2 Sam. xvii. 7, &c. [6] 2 Sam. xxiii. 8. [7] Num. xxiv. 1; Judg. xvi. 20; 1 Sam. iii. 10, &c. [8] Neh. xiii. 20. [9] Gen. xxvii. 36; xli. 32; Exod. xxiii. 17, &c. [10] Job xxxiii. 29. [11] 2 Sam. xxiv. 2. (d) Is. xli. 7. (e) Exod. xxv. 12; xxxvii. 3; 1 Kings vii. 30.

פָּעַם, v. Pih. Infin. aff. פַּעֲמוֹ. *Moved, excited to action,* Judg. xiii. 25.

Niph. נִפְעַמְתִּי, pres. תִּפָּעֵם. *Was moved, was disturbed,* Gen. xli. 8; Ps. lxxvii. 5; Dan. ii. 3.

Hith. pres. תִּתְפָּעֵם, i. q. Niph., Dan. ii. 1.

פַּעֲמֹן, m. pl. פַּעֲמֹנִים, constr. פַּעֲמֹנֵי. *A bell,* the sound being produced by striking, Exod. xxviii. 33, 34; xxxix. 25, 26.

פָּעַר, v. פָּעֲרָה, פָּעַרְתִּי, פָּעֲרוּ. Arab. فغر, *aperuit* os suum; *aperuit* se flos. *Opened* the mouth, with eagerness to swallow, constr. פֶּה, or בְּפֶה, Job xvi. 10; xxix. 23; Ps. cxix. 131; Is. v. 14.

פָּצָה, v. pres. יִפְצֶה. Arab. فصي, *separavit* rem à re. II. *Liberavit* aliquem. Syr. ܦܨܝ, and Sam. ࠐࠎࠄ ࠁ, *liberavit.* Constr. immed. it. med. אֶת. (a) *Opened* the mouth, the lips. (b) *Rescued.* (a) Gen. iv. 11; Judg. xi. 36; Job xxxv. 16, &c. Imp. פְּצֵה, (a) Ezek. ii. 8. (b) Ps. cxliv. 7. 11. Part. פֹּצֶה, (a) Is. x. 14. (b) Ps. cxliv. 10.

פָּצַח, v. פָּצְחוּ, pres. יִפְצְחוּ. Arab. فضح, *contundendo fregit.* VII. *Apertus, fissus fuit; emisit aquam* situla rupta; *vehementer flevit;* فضّ, *effusio* aquæ. *Broke, broke through* all restraint, *burst forth; uttered with eagerness.* Joined to רִנָּה, or רָגַן, Is. xiv. 7; lv. 12. Imp. f. פִּצְחִי, pl. פִּצְחוּ, Is. xliv. 23; liv. 1, &c.

Pih. פִּצֵּחַ. *Broke, broke to pieces,* Mic. iii. 3.

פְּצִירָה, f. once, 1 Sam. xiii. 21. The verse appears corrupt, and the LXX. evidently followed a very different text. Two interpretations are given to פִּצִירָה פִים, [1] *Bluntness of edge:* so the Vulgate, which is followed by Gesenius, Dathe, and several modern Versions. This translation, however, would require פְּצִירָה. [2] *A file:* so the Syriac, which is followed by our Auth. Vers. and Castell. LXX. καὶ ἦν ὁ τρυγητὸς ἕτοιμος τοῦ θερίζειν: r. פצר.

פָּצַל, v. Kal non occ. Cogn. בצל. Arab. فصل, and Syr. ܦܨܠ, *secuit, dissecuit.*

Pih. פִּצֵּל, pres. יְפַצֵּל. *Peeled,* Gen. xxx. 37, 38.

פְּצָלוֹת, pl. fem. once. *Parts peeled, stripped; streaks,* Gen. xxx. 37.

פָּצַם, v. once, pret. aff. פְּצַמְתָּהּ. Arab. فصم, *fregit.* *Broke* the earth, broke its surface, Ps. lx. 4.

פֶּצַע, masc. aff. פִּצְעִי; pl. פְּצָעִים, constr. פִּצְעֵי, aff. פְּצָעַי. Arab. فضع, *fregit* lignum. *Breaking;* breaking the skin, *wounding.* A

פצע (499) פקד

wound, Gen. iv. 23; Job ix. 17; Prov. xxiii. 29; xxvii. 6; Is. i. 6, &c.

פָּצַע, v. pret. aff. פְּצָעוּנִי. *Wounded*, Cant. v. 7.

Infin. פָּצֹעַ, 1 Kings xx. 37.

Part. pass. constr. פְּצוּעַ, Deut. xxiii. 2.

פָּצַר, v. pres. יִפְצַר. Constr. med. בְּ.

Cogn. بَطَرَ, *fidit, diffidit* rem; نَجَّارَ, *petulantem et insolentem se gessit*. IV. *Obtusum fecit; fatigavit*. (a) *Urged, pressed*, to consent. (b) *Pressed upon*, to injure. (a) Gen. xix. 3; xxxiii. 11; Judg. xix. 7; 2 Kings ii. 17; v. 16. (b) Gen. xix. 9.

Hiph. Infin. הַפְצֵר, *Intensive of Kal. Being too urgent, perverse, obstinate*, 1 Sam. xv. 23.

פָּקַד, v. pres. יִפְקֹד. Constr. immed. it. med. אֶת. Arab. فَقَدَ, *quæsivit* rem *perditam. Visited, inquired for* or *into*. (a) *Visited, inquired for.* (b) *Missed, inquired after* and did not find. (c) *Inquired into.* (d) *Inquired after*, for good, *cared for*. (e) *Inquired into judicially, punished.* Constr. immed. of the crime, אֶל, or עַל, of the person, and בְּ, 'of the punishment. (f) *Called to mind.* (g) *Examined* a body of men, and [1] *Numbered* them; [2] *Arranged* them. (h) *Took an account of.* (i) *Arranged* business. (k) *Placed.* (l) *Appointed.* (m) With עַל, *Laid a charge upon, charged*. (a) Judg. xv. 1; 1 Sam. xvii. 18. (b) 1 Sam. xx. 6; xxv. 15; Is. xxxiv. 16. (c) Exod. iii. 16; 1 Sam. xv. 2; Job xxxi. 14, &c. (d) Exod. iv. 31; 1 Sam. ii. 21; Ps. lxv. 10, &c. (e) Exod. xxxii. 34; Ps. lxxxix. 33; Is. xiii. 11, &c. (f) Ezek. xxiii. 21. (g), [1] Num. i. 44; iii. 39; 1 Kings xx. 15, &c. [2] 1 Kings xx. 26; Job xxxiv. 13; Jer. xv. 3, &c. (h) Num. iv. 32. (i) Job v. 24; xxxvi. 23. (k) Gen. xl. 4; 2 Kings v. 24. (l) Gen. xxxix. 4; Num. iii. 10; xxvii. 16. (m) 2 Chron. xxxvi. 23.

Infin. פָּקֹד, constr. פְּקֹד, aff. פָּקְדִי, Gen. L. 24; Exod. xxxii. 34; Ps. lix. 6.

Imp. פְּקֹד, aff. פָּקְדֵנִי, pl. פִּקְדוּ, 1 Sam. xiv. 17; Ps. lxxx. 15; cvi. 4, &c.

Part. פֹּקֵד, Exod. xx. 5.

Part. pass. pl. פְּקֻדִים, const. פְּקוּדֵי, aff. פְּקֻדָיו, &c. (g) Exod. xxx. 13; xxviii. 21; Num. i. 22, &c.

Niph. נִפְקַד, pres. יִפָּקֵד. (a) *Pass. of Kal* [b], [e], and [l]. (b) *Punishment was inflicted.* (c) *Was visited* by evil. (a), [b] Num. xxxi. 49; 1 Sam. xx. 18; xxv. 7, &c. [e] Is. xxiv. 22. [l] Neh. vii. 1; xii. 44. (b) Num. xvi. 29. (c) Prov. xix. 23; Is. xxix. 6.

Infin. הִפָּקֵד, 1 Kings xx. 39.

Pih. part. מְפַקֵּד, i. q. Kal (g) Is. xiii. 4.

Puh. פֻּקַּד, (a) *Pass. of Kal*. [h] Exod. xxxviii. 21. (b) *Was deprived of*, Is. xxxviii. 10.

Hiph. הִפְקִיד, pres. יַפְקִיד, apoc. יַפְקֵד. I. q. Kal (k) and (l). [k] 2 Chron. xii. 10; Jer. xxxvi. 20, &c. [l] Gen. xxxix. 5; 2 Kings vii. 17, &c.

Imp. הַפְקֵד, Num. i. 50.

Hoph. הָפְקַד. *Pass. of Kal* (e), (k), and (l). [e] Jer. vi. 6. [k] Lev. v. 23.

Part. pl. מֻפְקָדִים, (l) 2 Kings xii. 12; xxii. 5, &c.

Hith. הִתְפַּקֵּד, pres. יִתְפַּקֵּד. *Pass. of Kal.* (g) Judg. xx. 15. 17; xxi. 9.

Hoth. הָתְפָּקְדוּ, *Id.*, Num. i. 47; ii. 33; xxvi. 62; 1 Kings xx. 27.

פְּקֻדָּה, f. constr. פְּקֻדַּת, aff. פְּקֻדָּתוֹ, &c.; pl. פְּקֻדּוֹת. *Appointment, arrangement.* (a) *Providence.* (b) *Office.* (c) *Government.* (d) *Class.* (e) *What is laid up, Treasure.* (f) *Examination, punishment.* (a) Job x. 12. (b) Num. iii. 32; iv. 16, &c. (c) 1 Chron. xxvi. 30; 2 Chron. xxiii. 18; xxiv. 11, &c. (d) 1 Chron. xxiii. 11. (e) Is. xv. 7. (f) Is. x. 3; Jer. x. 15; Hos. ix. 7, &c.

פִּקָּדוֹן, m. *A deposit*, Gen. xli. 36; Lev. v. 21. 23.

פְּקִדֻת, fem. once, בַּעַל פְּקִדֻת. *Probably, Captain of the guard* at the gate, Jer. xxxvii. 13.

פִּקּוּדִים, pl. m. constr. פִּקּוּדֵי, aff. פִּקּוּדֶיךָ, פִּקּוּדָיו, &c. *Precepts* of God, Ps. xix. 9; cxi. 7; cxix. 4, &c.

פָּקַח, v. pres. יִפְקַח. Arab. فَقَحَ, *oculos primum aperuit* catulus. Constr. immed. it. med. אֶת. (a) *Opened* his eyes, both lit. and metaph. (b) *Opened* the eyes of another. (c) *Opened* his ears. (a) 2 Kings iv. 35. Job xiv. 3; Zech. xii. 4. (b) Gen. xxi. 19. 2 Kings vi. 17. 20.

Infin. פָּקֹחַ, constr. פְּקֹחַ, (b) Is. xlii. 7. (c) Ib. xlii. 20.

Imp. פְּקַח, (a) 2 Kings xix. 16; Prov. xx. 13; Is. xxxvii. 16; Dan. ix. 18. (b) 2 Kings vi. 17. 20.

פקח (500) פרא

Part. פֹּקֵחַ, (b) Ps. cxlvi. 8.
Part. pass. pl. f. פְּקֻחוֹת, Jer. xxxii. 19.
Niph. נִפְקְחוּ, pres. תִּפָּקַחְנָה, Pass. of Kal, Gen. iii. 6. 8; Is. xxxv. 8.

פִּקֵּחַ, m. pl. פִּקְחִים. *Having the eyes open, able to see*, Exod. iv. 11; xxiii. 8.

פְּקַח־קוֹחַ, once, Is. lxi. 1. This is usually considered as being properly one word, the repetition of the second and third radicals denoting intensity or completeness. *Complete opening of the prison.* There seems, however, reason to doubt the accuracy of this. Grotius takes the latter part of the word to be equivalent to the Chald. קִיחָה, and translates the whole *apertio lori*. De Dieu compares the Æth. ፍትሕ: *compes, vinculum; carcer*, and translates, *apertio carceris*.

פָּקִיד, m. constr. פְּקִיד, aff. פְּקִידוֹ, pl. פְּקִידִים. *Any one appointed; an officer, chief, superintendent,* 2 Kings xxv. 19; Jer. xx. 1; lii. 25, &c. פְּקִידוֹ, *an officer appointed by him*, Judg. ix. 28; 2 Chron. xxiv. 11. פְּקִיד הַלְוִיִּם, *chief of the Levites*, Neh. xi. 22.

פְּקָעִים, pl. m. Architectural ornaments, probably of a globular form, resembling in shape either the *mushroom* or the *wild grape*. Arab. فُقْع, tuberis terrestris species alba et mollis. Syr. ܩܦܣܐ, *grossus*, 1 Kings vi. 18; vii. 24.

פַּקֻּעֹת, pl. fem. once, 2 Kings iv. 39. According to some, *Mushrooms*, found under the wild vine. According to Celsius, *cucumis agrestis*. But more probably *the foxgrape*: عنب الثعلب. See אוֹר, p. 15, and Hierobot., tom. i. p. 393.

פַּר, and פָּר, m. plur. פָּרִים, r. פרה. *A young bull;* a bull from the second year and upwards, Exod. xxix. 1; 1 Sam. i. 24; Judg. xxv. 25; Ps. lxix. 32, &c. Metaph., Ps. xxii. 13. Gesenius says the word is often used of the animal in its first year; but there is no proof of this in the passages he quotes. The German *farr*, fem. *fürse*, to which he refers, appears to resemble the Hebrew word both in sound and signification; but this resemblance is probably merely accidental.

פֶּרֶא, m. pl. פְּרָאִים. Arab. فَرَأ, *onager*. *A wild ass*, Gen. xvi. 12; Job vi. 5; xi. 12; xxiv. 5, &c. See Bochart. Hieroz., tom. i. p. 867.

פרא, v. once. Hiph. pres. יַפְרִיא; apparently for פָּרָה. *Propagate*, Hos. xiii. 15. According to some, however, *resemble the wild-ass*.

פְּרָאת, pl. f. aff. פֹּרֹאתָיו, for פֹּארֹתָיו, Ezek. xxxi. 8: see פֹּארָה.

פַּרְבָּר, only in 1 Chron. xxvi. 18. A place in Jerusalem, but of what description it is impossible to determine. Buxtorf reads פַּרְבָּד. LXX. διαδεχομένους. Vulg. *cellulis*. According to Lightfoot it was a gate on the west side of the Temple. It is usually taken to signify a *suburb*, and as equivalent to פַּרְוָר, which see.

פֶּרֶד, m. aff. פִּרְדוֹ; pl. פְּרָדִים, aff. פִּרְדֵיהֶם. Arab. فَرَدَ, *solus fuit; separatim egit*; فَرْدٌ, *unicus, incomparabilis.* Being alone, being *separate* or *distinguished* from others. *A mule;* either from its hybrid character, according to Bochart., or from its being distinguished for its swiftness, 2 Sam. xiii. 29; xviii. 9; 1 Kings x. 25; Ezra ii. 66, &c. Is there any connexion between this word and the German *pferd, a horse?*

פרד, v. *Separated; spread*, of wings. Only in Part. pass. pl. f. פְּרֻדוֹת, Ezek. i. 11.
Niph. נִפְרְדוּ, pres. יִפָּרֵד. Pass. of Kal. *Was separated, separated himself,* Gen. ii. 10; x. 5. 32; Prov. xix. 4, &c.
Infin. הִפָּרֵד, Gen. xiii. 14.
Imp. הִפָּרֶד, Gen. xiii. 9.
Part. נִפְרָד, pl. נִפְרָדִים, Judg. iv. 11; Neh. iv. 19.
Pih. pres. יְפָרֵד. *Go aside*, Hos. iv. 14.
Puh. part. מְפֹרָד. *Separate*, Esth. iii. 8.
Hiph. הִפְרִיד, pres. יַפְרִיד, i. q. Kal, constr. immed. it. med. בֵּין, Gen. xxx. 40; Ruth i. 17; 2 Kings ii. 11; Prov. xviii. 17.
Infin. aff. הַפְרִידוֹ, Deut. xxxii. 8.
Part. מַפְרִיד, Prov. xvi. 28; xvii. 9.
Hith. הִתְפָּרְדוּ, pres. יִתְפָּרְדוּ, i. q. Niph., Job iv. 11; xli. 9; Ps. xxii. 15; xcii. 10.

פְּרֻדָה, constr. פְּרֻדַת, fem. of פֶּרֶד, 1 Kings i. 33. 38. 44.

פְּרֻדוֹת, pl. fem. once. Syr. ܦܪܕܬܐ, *granum. Distinct, separate portions, grains; seeds, corn sown,* Joel i. 17.

פַּרְדֵּס, m. pl. פַּרְדֵּסִים. *An enclosure; garden, park,* Neh. ii. 8; Cant. iv. 13; Eccl.

פרח (501) פרו

ii. 8. A similar word appears to have been in use among the Persians, from which the Greeks took their παράδεισος. The Arabs and modern Persians have فِرْدَوْس, with the same signification. According to Castell the word is Armenian; but this may be doubted. Is it not connected with פרד? May it not be a slight modification of עֵץ עַד, פֶּרֶד, *an enclosure for trees?*

פָּרָה, v. פָּרוּ, pres. יִפְרֶה. Syr. ܦܪܝ, and Æth. ፈረየ : *fructuosus fuit, fructum edidit.* See פְּרִי. Constr. abs. (a) *Bore fruit,* was fruitful. (b) Applied metaph. to the human race and to animals. (a) Is. xi. 1; xlv. 8. (b) Gen. viii. 17; Exod. xxiii. 30; Jer. xxiii. 3, &c.

Imp. פְּרֵה, pl. פְּרוּ, (b) Gen. i. 22. 28; ix. 1. 7; xxxv. 11.

Part. פֹּרֶה, f. פֹּרִיָּה, and פָּרָת, Gen. xlix. 22; Deut. xxix. 18; Ps. cxxviii. 3; Is. xvii. 6; xxxii. 12; Ezek. xix. 10.

Hiph. aff. הִפְרַנִי, pres. apoc. יֶפֶר. *Made fruitful,* Gen. xvii. 6. 20; xxviii. 3; xli. 52; Lev. xxvi. 9.

Part. aff. מַפְרִךְ, Gen. xlviii. 4.

פָּרָה, fem. of פַּר, aff. פָּרָתוֹ, pl. פָּרוֹת, Gen. xxxii. 15; Job xxi. 10; Hos. iv. 16, &c.

פֶּרֶה, once, Jer. ii. 24, for פֶּרֶא, which see.

פַּרְוָרִים, pl. m. once, 2 Kings xxiii. 11. The LXX., Vulgate, and Syriac leave this word untranslated, the last having a ר for the second ר. Modern interpreters translate it *suburbs,* but on what good authority it does not appear. Gesenius goes to the Persian, and considers it as compounded of بارُو, *a wall, rampart,* and وَار, *possessing.* But surely the Jews would be under no necessity to borrow a word to express what was *outside the wall;* and, besides this, the passage requires a place near the Temple, as Bochart has rightly observed. If it is not a Semitic word, it is probably connected in signification with the Sun or its worship. Now the Persian پَرَوَر, denotes *flying, swift,* and would be a suitable epithet for the horses of the Sun, being dedicated ὡς ταχυτάτοι τῷ ταχυτάτῳ; and we might then translate the clause, אֶל־לִשְׁכַּת נְתַן־מֶלֶךְ הַסָּרִיס אֲשֶׁר בַּפַּרְוָרִים, *at the chamber of Nathan-Melek, the eunuch, who was over the swift* (horses).

פַּרוּר, m. Arab. فَارَ, r. فور, *æstuavit, efferbuit bulliendo olla. A pot* for boiling, Num. xi. 8; Judg. vi. 19; 1 Sam. ii. 14.

פרח, f. pl. פֵּרוֹת, once, Is. ii. 20. If these syllables form a separate word, that word will be equivalent to the Arab. فَأْرَة, fem. of فَأْر, *mus.* But see חֲפֹר פֵּרוֹת.

פרז, masc. pl. aff. פְּרָזָו. Arab. فَرَزَ, *segregavit, discrevit rem ab aliis.* II. *Modum præscripsit, statuit;* فِرْزَة, *pars segregata et à cæteris distincta. Separating, distinguishing, deciding. Ruler,* Hab. iii. 13. LXX. δυναστῶν. Vulg. *bellatorum ejus.* Syr. ܡܓܒܪܢܐ. Dathe translates רֹאשׁ פְּרָזָו, *caput pagorum.*

פְּרָזוֹן, m. aff. פְּרָזוֹנוֹ. *A judicial decision; justice,* Judg. v. 7. 11. Gesenius, however, makes this synonymous with the last. LXX. δυνατοί. Vulg. *fortes.*

פְּרָזוֹת, pl. f. Settlements *apart* from the principal town or city; *unwalled towns, villages,* Esth. ix. 19; Ezek. xxxviii. 11; Zech. ii. 8.

פְּרָזִי, m. *One living in an unwalled town* or *a village,* Deut. iii. 5; 1 Sam. vi. 18; Esth. ix. 19.

פַּרְזֶל, Chald. m. def. פַּרְזְלָא, i. q. Heb. בַּרְזֶל. *Iron,* Dan. ii. 33; iv. 20; vii. 7, &c.

פֶּרַח, m. aff. פִּרְחָם, פִּרְחָה; pl. aff. פְּרָחֶיהָ. Arab. فَرْخ, *pullus avis, tum quoque cæterorum animalium et plantarum; ramus. Shooting up, spreading, propagating.* (a) *A young shoot* of a plant. (b) *A bud.* (c) *An artificial flower-bud.* (a) Is. v. 24; Nah. i. 4. (b) Num. xvii. 23; Is. xviii. 5. (c) Exod. xxv. 33; Num. viii. 4; 1 Kings vii. 26, &c.

פָּרַח, v. pres. יִפְרַח, constr. abs. (ε) *Threw out a shoot, budded.* (b) *Shot up, flourished.* (c) *Spread, extended itself.* (ε) Num. xvii. 23; Cant. vii. 13; Is. xxvii. 6, &c. (b) Ps. lxii. 7; Ezek. vii. 10; Hos. x. 4, &c. (c) Lev. xiii. 20. 25. 39; xiv. 43, &c.

Infin. פָּרוֹחַ, Lev. xiii. 12; Ps. xcii. 8; Is. xxxv. 2.

Part. פֹּרֵחַ, f. פֹּרַחַת, Gen. xl. 10; Exod. ix. 9, 10; Lev. xiii. 42. 57. In Ezek. xiii. 20,

פרח (502) פרם

we have פִרְחוֹח, twice coupled with נְפֻשׂוֹת, and נְפָשִׁים. The passage is very obscure, and has been very differently rendered; but the majority of interpreters have taken the verb in the sense of the Syr. ܦܪܚ, volavit. In the former clause, *flying* to you, and in the latter, *flying away*.

Hiph. הִפְרִיחְתִּי, pres. יַפְרִיחַ. (a) Causat. of Kal, Is. xvii. 11; Ezek. xvii. 24. (b) I. q. Kal, Job xiv. 9; Ps. xcii. 14; Prov. xiv. 11.

פִּרְחָח, m. once, Job xxx. 12. Arab. فَرْخَ, i. q. فَحَّ, *superbivit*. *Insolent, with insult*.

פָּרַט, m. Arab. فَرَطَ, *prævertit, præcessit*; *prodiit res ab aliquo non cogitante in agendo*; فَرْط, *prætermissio occasionis. Omission; what is omitted*, Lev. xix. 10.

פרט, v. only in part. pl. פֹּרְטִים. Probably, *Taking the lead* on instruments of music, as an accompaniment to the dancers, or, *abounding in* —, Amos vi. 5.

פְּרִי, m. in pause פֶּרִי, aff. פִּרְיִי, פִּרְיְךָ, פִּרְיֵךְ, פִּרְיוֹ, פִּרְיָהּ, פִּרְיְכֶם, פִּרְיָם, and פִּרְיָהֶם. r. פרה. *Fruit*. (a) *Fruit* of a tree. (b) *Produce* of the ground. (c) פְּרִי־בֶטֶן, *Offspring*. (d) *Result* of actions, whether good or evil, *reward* or *punishment*. (a) Gen. i. 11; Lev. xxvi. 4; Eccl. ii. 5, &c. (b) Deut. vii. 13; xxvi. 2. 10; Ps. cvii. 34, &c. (c) Gen. xxx. 2; Deut. vii. 13; xxviii. 4. 18, &c. (d) Ps. lviii. 12; Prov. xi. 30; Is. iii. 10; Jer. vi. 19; xvii. 10, &c.

פָּרִיץ, m. constr. פְּרִיץ; pl. פְּרִיצִים, constr. פְּרִיצֵי, r. פרץ. (a) *A violent, lawless, person*. (b) *A wild* beast. (a) Ps. xvii. 4; Jer. vii. 11; Ezek. vii. 22; xviii. 10; Dan. xi. 14. (b) Is. xxxv. 9.

פֶּרֶךְ, m. Arab. فَرَكَ, *confricuit; odit*; فِرْك, *odium*. Chald. פְּרַךְ, *fregit*. *Rubbing, grinding. Harshness, oppression*, Exod. i. 13, 14; Lev. xxv. 43. 46. 53; Ezek. xxxiv. 4.

פָּרֹכֶת, fem. Arab. فَرَقَ, *separavit*; فُرْقَة, *discessus, separatio*. *The veil*, separating the holy from the most holy place in the Tabernacle, Exod. xxvi. 31; Lev. iv. 6; Num. xviii. 7, &c.

פָּרַם, v. pres. יִפְרֹם. Constr. immed. Syr. ܦܪܡ, *scidit*. *Rent* his garments, Lev. x. 6; xxi. 10. Part. pass. pl. פְּרֻמִים. *Rent*, of garments, Lev. xiii. 45.

פֶּרֶם, masc. Arab. فَرَصَ, *secuit, fidit, laceravit. Separating, breaking, distributing. A species of eagle*, according to Bochart. Hieroz., tom. i. p. 185: *The osprey*. Linn. *ossifraga*. Buff. *orfraie*. So named from its habit of *breaking* the bones of its prey; which it does, according to Pliny, by letting the prey fall from a considerable height, Hist. Nat., lib. xxx. cap. 7: but according to Buffon it breaks them with its beak, Lev. xi. 13; Deut. xiv. 12.

פרם, v. pres. יִפְרְסוּ. (a) *Broke, distributed* bread. (b) *Distributed bread*. (b) Jer. xvi. 7.

Infin. פָּרֹם, (a) Is. lviii. 7.

Hiph. הִפְרִיסָה, pres. יַפְרִיס; part. מַפְרִים, fem. מַפְרֶסֶת, pl. constr. מַפְרִיסֵי. Two significations are given to this conjugation, viz. *dividing* the hoof, and *having a hoof*, from פַּרְסָה. It is not improbable, however, that the latter is the only meaning properly belonging to it, Lev. xiii. 3—7. 26; xiv. 6. 78; Ps. lxix. 32.

פרם, v. Chald. *Divided*. Part. pl. פָּרְסִין. They are *dividing*, they divide, Dan. v. 25. Peil, f. פְּרִיסַת. *It is divided*, Dan. v. 28. Part. פָּרֵם, Dan. v. 28.

פַּרְסָה, f. pl. פְּרָסוֹת, constr. פַּרְסוֹת, aff. פַּרְסֹתֵיךָ, and פַּרְסֵיהֶן. Syr. ܦܪܣܬܐ, *ungula*. *A hoof*, Exod. x. 26; Lev. xi. 3; Is. v. 28; Mic. iv. 13; Zech. xi. 16, &c.

פָּרַע, m. Arab. فَرْع, *summum et vertex rei; caput et princeps populi; coma mulieris; perfectus capillus* (totum caput tegens). *The hair of the head*, probably long hair, Num. vi. 5; Ezek. xliv. 20.

פָּרַע, v. pres. יִפְרַע. Constr. immed. Prob. allowed the hair to hang loose. (a) *Uncovered* the head. (b) *Placed in a state of disorder*. (c) *Was in disorder; disregarded*. (d) *Left* a road. (e) *Exempted*. (f) Apparently, *Avenged*. Comp. Syr. ܦܪܥ, *retribuit*. (a) Lev. x. 6; xxi. 10;

פרע (503) פרק

Num. v. 18. (b) Exod. xxxii. 25. (c) Prov. i. 25; viii. 33. (e) Ezek. xxiv. 14.
Infin. פְּרֹעַ, (f) Judg. v. 2.
Imp. פְּרָעֵהוּ, (d) Prov. iv. 15.
Part. פּוֹרֵעַ, (c) Prov. xiii. 18; xv. 32.
Part. pass. פָּרוּעַ, פָּרֻעַ, (a) Lev. xiii. 45. (b) Exod. xxxii. 25.
Niph. pres. יִפָּרַע. *Becomes lawless,* Prov. xxix. 18.
Hiph. הִפְרִיעַ, pres. תַּפְרִיעוּ. Causat. of Kal (e) and (f). (a) *Made idle,* Exod. v. 4. (b) *Brought vengeance on,* 2 Chron. xxviii. 19.

פְּרָעוֹת, pl. f. constr. פַּרְעוֹת. *Revenge,* Deut. xxxii. 42; Judg. v. 2. Gesenius takes the word to mean *chiefs.*

פַּרְעֹשׁ, m. Arab. بُرْغوث, *pulex.* Syr. ܩܰܠܒܕܳܢܳܐ, Id. *A flea,* 1 Sam. xxiv. 15; xxvi. 20.

פָּרַץ, m. pl. פְּרָצִים, and פְּרָצוֹת, aff. פִּרְצֵיהֶן. *Breaking through, overflowing, spreading.* (a) *A breach* in a wall. (b) *Overflowing* of water. (c) *Sudden calamity,* (a) 1 Kings xi. 27; Neh. vi. 1; Is. lviii. 12, &c. (b) 2 Sam. v. 20; 1 Chron. xiv. 11; Job xxx. 14. (c) Judg. xxi. 15; 2 Sam. vi. 8; 1 Chron. xiii. 11; Job xvi. 14.

פָּרַץ, v. pres. יִפְרֹץ. Constr. immed. it. med. בְּ. (a) *Broke down* a wall or fence. (b) *Made a breach* in a wall. (c) *Burst forth,* of water. (d) *Overflowed,* of the vessel. (e) *Broke to pieces.* (f) *Inflicted a sudden calamity, afflicted.* (g) *Urged* a person. (h) *Burst forth* like water, *spread,* through numbers. (i) *Dispersed* an enemy. Comp. *fudit* hostes. (k) *Distributed* persons. (a) Neh. iii. 35; Ps. lxxx. 15; lxxxix. 40, &c. (b) 2 Kings xiv. 13; 2 Chron. xxv. 23. (c) Job xviii. 4. (d) Prov. iii. 10. (e) 2 Chron. xx. 37. (f) Exod. xix. 22. 24; 2 Sam. vi. 8; 1 Chron. xiii. 11, &c. (g) 1 Sam. xxviii. 23; 2 Sam. xiii. 25. 27; 2 Kings v. 23. (h) Gen. xxviii. 14; Exod. i. 12; Job i. 10, &c. (i) 2 Sam. v. 20; 1 Chron. xiv. 11. (k) 2 Chron. xi. 23.
Infin. פְּרֹץ, פְּרוֹץ, Eccl. iii. 3; 2 Chron. xxxi. 5; Is. v. 5.
Part. פֹּרֵץ, Eccl. x. 8; Mic. ii. 13.
Part. pass. f. פְּרוּצָה, pl. m. פְּרוּצִים, 2 Chron. xxxii. 5; Neh. ii. 13; iv. 7; Prov. xxv. 28.
Niph. part. נִפְרָץ. Probably, *Much, frequent;* but, according to some, *Clear, distinct,* 1 Sam. iii. 1.

Puh. part. f. מְפֹרָצָה. *Broken down,* Neh. i. 3.
Hith. part. pl. מִתְפָּרְצִים. *Breaking loose, running away,* 1 Sam. xxv. 10.

פָּרַק, m. Arab. فَرَقَ, *separavit.* Syr. ܦܣܩ, *redemit.* Sam. ܦܣܩ, *redemit; divisit. Separating, tearing asunder, pulling off or away, rescuing.* (a) *Tearing in pieces,* prey, Nah. iii. 1. (b) Either, *What is torn in pieces, prey,* or *a division* in the road, a cross way, Obad. 14.

פָּרַק, v. pres. aff. יִפְרְקֵנִי. Constr. immed. (a) *Tore in pieces.* (b) *Pulled off* a yoke. (c) *Rescued.* (b) Gen. xxvii. 40. (c) Ps. cxxxvi. 24.
Part. פֹּרֵק, (a) Ps. vii. 3. (c) Lam. v. 8.
Pih. pres. יְפָרֵק, i. q. Kal, (a) and (b). (a) Zech. xi. 16.
Imp. pl. פָּרְקוּ, (b) Exod. xxxii. 2.
Part. מְפָרֵק, (a) 1 Kings xix. 1.
Hith. הִתְפָּרְקוּ, pres. יִתְפָּרְקוּ. (a) Pass. of Kal. *Was pulled* or *broken off.* (b) Reflexive of Kal, *Pulled off from themselves.* (a) Ezek. xix. 12. (b) Exod. xxxii. 3.
Imp. הִתְפָּרְקוּ, (b) Exod. xxxii. 24.

פְּרַק, v. Chald. Imp. פְּרֻק. *Break off,* *put an end to,* thy sins, Dan. iv. 24.

פֶּרֶק, masc. constr. פֶּרֶק. *Fragments, portions,* Is. lxv. 4. The Keri is מְרַק, *Broth;* but there is no reason to identify these two words.

פָּרַד, and פּוּר, v. Arab. فَرَّ, *secuit, fidit,* فَرَّ, *disquisivit.* IV. *Fidit;* فَرْفَرَ, *movit, agitavit. Broke, cleft, divided.*
Infin. פּוּר, Is. xxiv. 19.
Pih. פּוֹרֲרָה, i. q. Kal, Ps. lxxiv. 13.
Pih. redup. pres. aff. יְפַרְפְּרֵנִי. Intensitive of Kal. Metaph. *Shatters, agitates,* the mind, Job xvi. 12.
Hiph. הֵפֵר, in pause, הָפֵר, it. הֵפִיר, pres. יָפֵר. Metaph. (a) *Broke* a covenant or command. (b) *Frustrated.* (c) *Annulled.* (d) *Withdrew, broke off.* (a) Gen. xvii. 14; Deut. xxxi. 20; Is. xxxiii. 8, &c. (b) 2 Sam. xv. 34; Ps. xxxiii. 10; Is. xiv. 27, &c. (c) Num. xxx. 9. 13; Judg. ii. 1; Job xl. 8, &c. (d) Job xv. 4; Ps. lxxxix. 34.
Infin. הָפֵר, הָפִיר, aff. הַפְרְכֶם, Lev. xxvi. 15; Num. xxx. 13; Zech. xi. 10, &c.

פרש (504) פרש

Imp. הָפְרֵה, הַפְרֵה, 1 Kings xv. 19; Ps. lxxxv. 5.
Part. מֵפֵר, Job v. 12; Is. xliv. 25.
Hoph. pass. of Hiph. הֻפַר, Is. viii. 11; Jer. xxxiii. 21; Zech. xi. 11.
Hith. הִתְפּוֹרְרָה, Pass. of Kal, Is. xxiv. 19.

פָּרַשׂ, v. pres. יִפְרֹשׂ. Constr. immed. Arab. فَرَشَ, instravit, expandit in terra rem; dispersit. (a) Spread. (b) Stretched out the hands. (c) Metaph. Spread folly. (d) I. q. פָּרַץ, Broke. (a), [1] A cloth, Num. iv. 6. 8; 2 Kings viii. 15, &c. [2] A net, Ps. cxl. 6; Lam. i. 13; Ezek. xii. 13, &c. [3] The wings, Jer. xlviii. 40; Ezek. xvi. 8, &c. [4] A writing, 2 Kings xix. 14; Ezek. ii. 10. [5] A tent, Exod. xl. 19. (b), [1] To seize, Lam. i. 10. [2] In prayer, 1 Kings viii. 38; 2 Chron. vi. 29; Job xi. 13, &c. [3] To give or assist, Prov. xxxi. 19. (c) Prov. xiii. 16. (d) Mic. iii. 3.
Part. פּוֹרֵשׂ, plur. פֹּרְשִׂים, constr. פֹּרְשֵׂי, 1 Kings viii. 7; Prov. xxix. 5; Is. xix. 8, &c.
Part. pass. פָּרוּשׂ, f. פְּרוּשָׂה, פְּרֻשׂוֹת, 1 Kings xviii. 54; Hos. v. 1; Joel ii. 2.
Niph. pres. יִפָּרֵשׂ. Was spread, scattered, Ezek. xvii. 21.
Pih. פֵּרֵשׂ, pres. יְפָרֵשׂ. (a) Spread out the hands, as in swimming. (b) Stretched out the hands, as in earnest entreaty. (c) Scattered. (a) Is. xxv. 11. (b) Ps. cxliii. 6; Is. lxv. 2; Jer. iv. 31; Lam. i. 17. (c) Zech. ii. 10.
Infin. פָּרֵשׂ, aff. פָּרְשְׂכֶם. (b) Is. i. 15. (c) Ps. lxviii. 15.

פרש, v. Syr. ܦܪܫ, definivit, determinavit. Aph. Punxit; ܦܪܫܐ, stimulus. Pointed or marked out distinctly.
Infin. פְּרֹשׁ, Lev. xxiv. 12.
Niph. part. pl. f. נִפְרָשׂוֹת. Scattered; for נִפְרָשׁוֹת, which is the reading of some editions, Ezek. xxxiv. 12.
Puh. פֹּרַשׁ, Pass. of Kal. Was pointed or marked out distinctly, Num. xv. 34.
Part. מְפֹרָשׁ. Made distinct: according to some, by distinctness of reading; according to others, by an interpretation, Neh. viii. 8.
Hiph. pres. יַפְרִישׁ. Stung, Prov. xxiii. 32.
פרש, v. Chald. Pah. part. מְפָרַשׁ, i. q. Heb. מְפֹרָשׁ, Ezra iv. 18.
פָּרָשׁ, m. pl. פָּרָשִׁים, aff. פָּרָשָׁיו. Arab. فَرَس, equus; فَارِس, eques. Syr. ܦܪܫܐ, eques. Æth. ፈረስ: equus. (a) A horseman, Gen. L. 9; Exod. xiv. 26. 28; Jer. iv. 29, &c. (b) According to Bochart. A horse, 1 Sam. viii. 11; 2 Sam. i. 6; Is. xxi. 7. 9; xxviii. 28.

פֶּרֶשׁ, masc. aff. פִּרְשׁוֹ. Arab. فَرْث, fimus. Dung, Exod. xxix. 14; Num. xix. 5; Mal. ii. 3, &c.

פָּרָשָׁה, f. constr. פָּרָשַׁת, r. פרש. A distinct account, Esth. iv. 7; x. 2.

פַּרְשֶׁגֶן, m. A copy of a writing, Ezra iv. 11. 23; v. 6; vii. 11. Syr. ܦܪܫܓܢܐ, Id.

פַּרְשְׁדוֹן, once, Judg. iii. 22, in the phrase וַיֵּצֵא הַפַּרְשְׁדֹנָה. It is not improbable that the true reading is הַפֶּרֶשׁ, which would make the construction regular. The LXX. translate it as if synonymous with הַמִּסְדְּרוֹנָה, in the next clause. Vulg. per secreta naturæ alvi stercora proruperunt. According to some, exiit gladius per podicem. Castell, stercus effusum. Dung.

פַּרְשֵׁז, v. once, Job xxvi. 9. Spreading. A contraction, apparently, of פָּרַשׂ פָּז.

פֹּרָת, see פָּרָה.

פרתם, m. pl. פַּרְתְּמִים. Apparently the Sanscrit प्रथम: pratama. First, chief. Chiefs, nobles, Esth. i. 3; vi. 9; Dan. i. 3.

פָּשָׂה, v. pres. יִפְשֶׂה. Chald. פְּשָׂא, expandit, diffudit se. Arab. فَشَا, dimanavit in publicum. V. Propagatus fuit morbus. Spread itself, of any appearance or eruption on the person, Lev. xiii. 5. 7, 8; xiv. 39, &c.
Infin. פְּשׂה, Lev. xiii. 7. 22. 27. 35.

פָּשַׂע, m. Syr. ܦܫܥ, incessit. A step, in walking, 1 Sam. xx. 3.

פָּשַׂע, v. pres. אֶפְשָׂעָה. Stepped, trod, Is. xxvii. 4, al. non occ.

פשק, v. Opened the mouth. Comp. Syr. ܦܫܩ, abscidit. Pah. dirupit. Cogn. Arab. فَشَق, diduxit ab invicem crura.
Part. פֹּשֵׂק, Prov. xiii. 3.
Pih. pres. תְּפַשֵּׂק. Opened the legs, Ezek. xvi. 25.

פָּשׁ, once, Job xxxv. 15. Arab. فَاشَ, r. فِيشٌ, *expansus fuit*; فَشَّ, and فَشِي, *manavit*. *Spreading, extent*. See the note.

פָּשַׂח, v. Kal non occ. Syr. ܦܫܚ, *discerpsit, divulsit*.
Pih. pres. aff. יְפַשְּׁחֵנִי. *Tore to pieces*, Lam. iii. 11, only.

פָּשַׂט, v. pres. יִפְשֹׁט. Syr. ܦܫܛ, *expandit, extendit*. Cogn. Arab. بَسَطَ, *expandit* stratum. *Spread*, pec. *spread* a garment *on the ground; took off* a garment for that purpose. (a) *Stripped off* his dress. (b) A troop *spread, extended itself*, to plunder or fight. (a) Lev. vi. 4; 1 Sam. xix. 24; Ezek. xxvi. 17, &c. (b) Judg. ix. 33. 44; xx. 37; 1 Sam. xxiii. 27, &c.
Infin. פְּשֹׁט, (a) Is. xxxii. 11.
Part. pl. פּוֹשְׁטִים, (a) Neh. iv. 17.
Pih. *Stripped* another.
Infin. פַּשֵּׁט, 1 Sam. xxxi. 8; 2 Sam. xxiii. 10; 1 Chron. x. 8.
Hiph. הִפְשִׁיט, pres. יַפְשִׁיט. I. q. Pih. (a) *Stripped* another. (b) *Skinned*. (a) Job xix. 9; xxii. 6; Ezek. xvi. 39; xxiii. 26; Hos. ii. 3. (b) Lev. i. 6; Mic. iii. 3.
Infin. הַפְשִׁיט, (b) 2 Chron. xxix. 34.
Imp. הַפְשֵׁט, (a) Num. xx. 26.
Part. pl. מַפְשִׁיטִים, (b) 2 Chron. xxxv. 11.
Hith. pres. יִתְפַּשֵּׁט. *Stripped himself*, 1 Sam. xviii. 4.

פֶּשַׁע, masc. aff. פִּשְׁעִי, פִּשְׁעוֹ; pl. פְּשָׁעִים, constr. פִּשְׁעֵי, aff. פְּשָׁעַי, פִּשְׁעֵיכֶם. *A throwing off of a previously acknowledged authority, a deliberate breach of a known duty*. (a) *Rebellion*. (b) *Transgression*. (c) *Any serious fault*. (d) *Injury*, by the loss of property. (a) 1 Sam. xxiv. 12; Job xxxiv. 37. (b) Job xxxiii. 9; Ps. lix. 4; Is. liii. 5, &c. (c) Gen. xxxi. 36; L. 17; 1 Sam. xxv. 28. (d) Exod. xxii. 8.

פָּשַׁע, v. pres. יִפְשַׁע. Constr. med. בְּ, עַל, מִתַּחַת יַד. (a) *Rebelled* against a sovereign. (b) *Rebelled* against God, *transgressed*. (c) *Transgressed* a law. (a), [1] With בְּ, 1 Kings xii. 19; 2 Kings i. 1; iii. 5. 7. [2] With מִתַּחַת יַד, 2 Kings viii. 20. 22; 2 Chron. x. 19; xxi. 8. 10. (b) 1 Kings viii. 50; Is. i. 2; Jer. iii. 13, &c. (c) Hos. viii. 1.
Infin. פְּשֹׁעַ, פֶּשַׁע, Ezra x. 13; Is. lix. 13; Amos iv. 4.
Imp. pl. פִּשְׁעוּ, Amos iv. 4.
Part. פּוֹשֵׁעַ, plur. פּוֹשְׁעִים, Ps. li. 15; Is. xlviii. 8, &c.
Niph. part. נִפְשָׁע. Pass. of Kal. *Transgressed against*, Prov. xviii. 19.

פָּשַׁר, masc. Arab. فَسَّرَ, *detexit* rem *absconditam, explicuit*. Syr. ܦܫܪ, *Id*. *Interpretation, explanation*, Eccl. viii. 1.

פְּשַׁר, m. Chald. def. פִּשְׁרָא, and פִּשְׁרָה, aff. פִּשְׁרֵהּ, and פִּשְׁרָא, pl. פִּשְׁרִין, *Id*., Dan. ii. 4. 7. 16. 36; v. 16, &c.

פְּשַׁר, v. Chald. *Interpreted, explained*.
Infin. מִפְשַׁר, Dan. v. 16.
Pah. *Id*. Part. מְפַשַּׁר, Dan. v. 12.

פִּשְׁתָּה, f. aff. פִּשְׁתִּי, pl. פִּשְׁתִּים, aff. פִּשְׁתֶּיהָ. In the singular, (a) *The flax plant*. (b) *A lamp-wick*, made of flax. In the plural, (c) *Flax*. (d) *Linen*. (e) פִּשְׁתֵּי הָעֵץ, according to some, *Cotton*. (a) Exod. ix. 31; Hos. ii. 7. 11. (b) Is. xlii. 3; xliii. 17. (c) Judg. xv. 14; Prov. xxxi. 13; Ezek. xl. 3. (d) Lev. xiii. 47; Ezek. xliv. 17, 18, &c. (e) Josh. ii. 6.

פַּת, f. aff. פִּתִּי, פִּתְּךָ, פִּתּוֹ, pl. פִּתִּים, constr. פִּתּוֹתֵי, r. פתת. The origin of the word is uncertain. Arab. فَتَّاتٌ, *frustulum, mica*. *A piece, a piece of bread*, Gen. xviii. 5; Job xxxi. 17; Prov. xxiii. 8; Ps. cxlvii. 17; Ezek. xiii. 19, &c.

פֹּת, aff. פָּתְהֶן. Arab. فَوْتٌ, *interstitium*. —*Pudendum muliebre*, Is. iii. 17. Pl. פֹּתוֹת. *Hinges*, 1 Kings vii. 50.

פְּתָאִים, see פֶּתִי.

פִּתְאֹם פִּתְאוֹם, adv. *Suddenly, immediately*, Num. vi. 9; xii. 4; Job v. 3; 2 Chron. xxix. 36, &c. Gesenius derives the word from פֶּתַע, with which it is joined three times (he says *sæpe*); but it is not improbably a contraction of פֹּה+פֶּה+אֹם, i. q.
فَوْتُ فَمٍ.

פַּתְבַּג, constr. פַּתְבַּג, aff. פַּתְבָּגוֹ, פַּתְבָּגָם. This should probably be written as two words, of which the former פַּת, *a piece*, is to be taken in the sense of *portion, allowance*; and the latter, בָּג, is apparently the Persian بَاغ, *meat, victuals*; so that פַּתְבַּג הַמֶּלֶךְ, will signify *the portion of food* assigned them by

3 T

פתג (506) פתח

command *of the king*. The nature of this food is not stated, but it was perhaps unclean by the law: there is, however, no reason to connect it with idolatrous worship, as some have done. To this the βεκὸς, ἄρτος, of Herodot. ii. 2?

פִּתְגָּם, masc. constr. פִּתְגָם. *A decree, sentence*, Esth. i. 20; Eccl. viii. 11.

פִּתְגָּם, m. Chald. def. פִּתְגָמָא. (a) *A decree.* (b) *A decree communicated in writing, a royal letter.* (c) *Any letter.* (a) Ezra vi. 11; Dan. iii. 16; iv. 14. (b) Ezra iv. 17. (c) Ezra v. 7. 11. This word has been variously derived: by some, from the Pers. پَيْغَام , پَيْغَم , *A message, mission;* which is itself probably a borrowed word: by others, from the Arab. فَتْوَى , *responsum à juriconsulto datum.*

פתח, v. pres. יִפְתֶּה, apoc. יִפְתּ. Arab. فَتِيَ , *juvenile ætate fuit;* فَتًى , *adolescens.* Æth. ፈተወ: *desideravit, concupivit. Was youthful, under the influence of passion; was silly,* Deut. xi. 16; Job xxxi. 27.

Part. פֹּתֶה, f. פֹּתָה. *Silly,* Job v. 2; Prov. xx. 19; Hos. vii. 11.

Pih. פִּתָּה, constr. immed. (a) *Led to folly, persuaded to evil, seduced.* (b) *Persuaded, enticed.* (c) *Deceived.* (d) *Used fair words to.* (a) Exod. xxii. 16. (b) 1 Kings xx. 20—22; 2 Chron. xviii. 19—21; Prov. i. 10. (c) Jer. xx. 7; Ezek. xiv. 9. (d) Ps. lxxviii. 36.

Infin. aff. לְפַתֹּתְךָ, 2 Sam. iii. 25.

Imp. f. פַּתִּי, Judg. xiv. 16; xvi. 5.

Part. pl. aff. מְפַתֶּיהָ, Hos. ii. 14.

Puh. pres. יְפֻתֶּה, Pass. of Pih., Prov. xxv. 15; Jer. xx. 10; Ezek. xiv. 8.

Niph. נִפְתָּה, pres. apoc. אֶפְתּ, Pass. of Pih., Job xxxi. 2; Jer. xx. 7.

Hiph. pres. apoc. יַפְתּ. *Declared foolish,* i. e. idolatrously, with לְ, Gen. ix. 27. See the note on Job xxxi. 27.

פִּתֻגֶן, m. aff. פִּתְגָה, pl. פְּתוּחִים, constr. פְּתוּחֵי, aff. פְּתוּחָיו, r. פתח. *Engraving, carving,* Exod. xxviii. 11; 2 Chron. ii. 5. 13; Ps. lxxiv. 6; Zech. iii. 9, &c.

פֶּתַח, masc. aff. פִּתְחוֹ, פִּתְחָה, pl. פְּתָחִים, constr. פִּתְחֵי, aff. פְּתָחָיו, פְּתָחֵיהֶם. Arab. فتح ,

aperuit portam. Syr. ܦܬܚ, *Id.* Æth. ፈትሐ: *solvit vinctum. Opening, loosing.* (a) *An opening, door-way, gate-way, entrance.* (b) *A door* or *gate.* (a), [1] Of a tent, Gen. xviii. 1; Exod. xxxiii. 8; Num. xii. 5, &c. [2] Of a house, Gen. xix. 11; Deut. xxii. 21; Judg. xix. 26, &c. [3] Of a city, Josh. viii. 29; Judg. ix. 35; 1 Kings xvii. 10, &c. [4] Of a room, 2 Kings iv. 15, &c. [5] Of the mouth, Mic. vii. 5. (b) Judg. ix. 52.

פָּתַח, v. pres. יִפְתַּח. Constr. immed. it. med. אֶת. (a) *Opened,* [1] a door, gate, window. [2] A sack, ark, book, &c. [3] His hand. [4] His mouth. [5] His eyes. (b) *Opened the door.* (c) *Opened the gates,* to a besieger. (d) The earth *opened its mouth.* (e) *Uttered.* (f) Metaph. *Opened* the ears of another. (g) *Opened* a rock, *cleft* it. (h) *Opened* a pit, *dug* it. (i) *Opened* a stream, *let it loose.* (k) *Loosened, untied.* (l) *Brought out for sale.* (m) *Drew* a sword. (a), [1] Gen. viii. 6; Judg. xix. 28; Mal. iii. 10, &c. [2] Gen. xlii. 27; Exod. ii. 6; Neh. viii. 5, &c. [3] Deut. xv. 8; Ps. civ. 28. [4] Job iii. 1; xxxiii. 2; Prov. xxxi. 26, &c. (b) Cant. v. 6. (c) Deut. xx. 11; 2 Kings xv. 16. (d) Ps. cvi. 17; Is. xlv. 8. (e) Ps. xlix. 5. (f) Is. L. 5. (g) Ps. cv. 4. (h) Exod. xxi. 33. (i) Is. xli. 18. (k) Is. xiv. 17. (l) Gen. xli. 56; Amos viii. 5. (m) Ps. xxxvii. 14.

Infin. פְּתֹחַ, פִּתְחִי, aff. פִּתְחִי, Deut. xv. 8; Cant. v. 8; Ezek. xxxvii. 13, &c.

Imp. פְּתַח, f. פִּתְחִי; pl. פִּתְחוּ, Josh. x. 22; 2 Kings xiii. 17; Cant. v. 2, &c.

Part. פֹּתֵחַ, Judg. iii. 25, &c.

Part. pass. פָּתוּחַ, fem. פְּתוּחָה, pl. פְּתוּחוֹת, Num. xix. 15; Josh. viii. 17; (a, 5) Neh. i. 6, &c.

Niph. נִפְתַּח, pres. יִפָּתֵחַ. Pass. of Kal, (a), (f), (i), and (k). [a] Ezek. i. 1; Nah. ii. 7; iii. 13, &c. [f] Is. xxxv. 5. [i] Jer. i. 14. [k] Is. v. 27.

Infin. הִפָּתֵחַ, [k] Is. li. 14.

Part. נִפְתָּח, [i] Zech. xiii. 1.

Pih. פִּתַּח, pres. יְפַתֵּחַ. (a) I. q. Kal, (a), (f), (h), and (k). (b) *Carved, engraved.* (a), [a] Job xli. 6; Cant. vii. 13; Is. lx. 11. [f] Is. xlviii. 8. [h] Is. xxviii. 24. [k] Job xii. 18; xxxix. 5; Ps. xxx. 12, &c. (b) Exod. xxviii. 9. 11. 36; 1 Kings vii. 36.

Infin. פַּתֵּחַ, (k) Ps. cii. 21; lviii. 6. (b) 2 Chron. ii. 6. 13.

Part. מְפַתֵּחַ, (k) 1 Kings xx. 11. (b) Zech. iii. 9.

פתח (507) פתל

Puh. Part. f. pl. מְפֻתָּחוֹת. *Engraven.*
Hith. Imp. f. הִתְפַּתְּחִי. *Loosen thyself,* Is. lii. 2.

פתח, v. Chald. *Id.*
Peil, פְּתִיחוּ, Pass. of (a), Dan. vii. 10.
Part. pl. f. פְּתִיחָן, Dan. vi. 11.

פֶּתַח, m. *Opening, laying open,* metaph. Ps. cxix. 130.

פִּתָּחוֹן, m. constr. פִּתְחוֹן. *Opening of the mouth, power to speak,* Ezek. xvi. 63; xxix. 21.

פְּתִי, masc. pl. פְּתָיִם, פְּתָיִים, and פְּתָאיִם, r. פתה. *A youth.* (a) *Ignorant.* (b) *Foolish.* (c) *Folly.* (a) Ps. xix. 8; cxvi. 6; Prov. ix. 4. 16, &c. (b) Prov. xiv. 15; xix. 25; xxi. 11, &c. (c) Prov. i. 22.

פְּתִי, m. Chald. aff. פְּתָיֵהּ. *Breadth,* Ezra vi. 3; Dan. iii. 1. Syr. ܦܬܐ, *latus fuit;* ܦܬܝܐ, *latitudo.*

פְּתִיגִיל, once, Is. iii. 24. Contrasted with מַחֲגֹרֶת שָׂק. LXX. χιτώνος τοῦ μεσοπορφύρου. Vulg. *fasciâ pectorali.* The significations given to the word, and the derivations proposed, appear equally conjectural. Possibly it may be compounded of פְּתִיל and גִּיל, or גַּל, which last may be compared with the Arab. جلوة, *vestes pellucidæ.* Auth. Vers. *A stomacher.* See Schrœd. de Vest. Mul., p. 138.

פְּתַיּוּת, fem. once, r. פתה. *Folly,* Prov. ix. 13.

פְּתִיחוֹת, pl. f. r. פתח. *Drawn, drawn swords,* Ps. lv. 22. LXX. βολίδες. Vulg. *jacula.*

פָּתִיל, m. constr. פְּתִיל, aff. פְּתִילֶךָ, plur. פְּתִילִים, r. פתל. Arab. فتيل, *funis.* Any thing twisted. (a) *A lace, thread, cord.* (b) *An ornamental string* or *lace* for a seal. (c) *A thin strip* of gold. (d) *A cloth,* as a cover. (a) Exod. xxviii. 28. 37; xxxix. 21.

31; Judg. xvi. 9; Ezek. xl. 3. (b) Gen. xxxviii. 18. 25. (c) Exod. xxxix. 3. (d) Num. xix. 15.

פתל, v. Kal non occ. Arab. فَتَلَ, *torsit funem.* Syr. ܦܬܠ, *Id.* Æth. ፈተለ : *torsit, nevit. Twisted, spun.*
Niph. נִפְתַּלְתִּי. *Was twisted. Was involved with, struggled with* another, Gen. xxx. 8.
Part. נִפְתָּל, pl. נִפְתָּלִים. Metaph. *Twisted, perverse,* Job v. 13; Prov. viii. 8.
Hith. pres. in pause, תִּתְפַּתָּל. *Twisted himself, struggled,* so as to thwart the devices of the perverse, Ps. xviii. 27. In 2 Sam. xxii. 27, we have תִּתַּפָּל, which appears to be an error of the copyist.

פְּתַלְתֹּל, masc. once. *Perverse,* Deut. xxxii. 5.

פֶּתֶן, m. pl. פְּתָנִים. *The asp; vipère d'Egypte,* of Buffon, Deut. xxxii. 33; Job xx. 14. 16; Ps. lviii. 5; xci. 13; Is. xi. 8. Arab. بثن, *coluber,* Forsk. Faun., quoted by Freytag.

פֶּתַע, masc. Arab. فتع, *conculcavit, donec frangeretur;* فتك, *de improviso et fraudulenter obruit atque peremit* aliquem. *Rushing suddenly on.* (a) *Suddenness.* (b) *Suddenly.* (a) Num. vi. 9; xxxv. 22. (b) Hab. ii. 7. In Prov. vi. 15; xxix. 1; Is xxix. 5; xxx. 13; the true signification appears to be *crushing.*

פָּתַר, v. pres. יִפְתָּר. See פֶּשֶׁר. Constr. immed. *Interpreted, explained,* Gen. xl. 16. 22; xli. 12, 13.
Infin. פְּתֹר, Gen. xli. 15.
Part. פֹּתֵר, Gen. xl. 8; xli. 8. 15.

פִּתְרוֹן, m. aff. פִּתְרֹנוֹ, pl. פִּתְרֹנִים. *Interpretation,* Gen. xl. 5. 8. 12. 18; xli. 11.

פתח, v. Arab. فتّ, *contudit, et digitis fregit* rem. *Broke to pieces.*
Infin. פָּתוֹת, Lev. ii. 6.

צ

צ, Tzādé, the eighteenth letter of the Hebrew alphabet, is sounded as *ts* or *tz*, and, as a numeral, stands for *ninety*. It is interchanged occasionally with the other sibilants, ז, ס, and שׁ, and sometimes with ט; as well as in one or two instances with ד. Gram. artt. 78, 79. 83.

צֵאָה, f. constr. צֵאַת, aff. צֵאָתְךָ, r. יצא. *Excrement*, Deut. xxiii. 14; Ezek. ii. 12.

צֶאֱלִים, pl. m. twice, Job xl. 21, 22. Arab. ضَال, *arbor, quæ remota à fluminibus nonnisi pluviâ rigatur, aliis lotus*. See the notes. LXX. παντοδαπὰ δένδρα, δένδρα μεγάλα. Vulg. *umbra*.

צֹאן, com. aff. צֹאנִי, &c. pl. non occ. Arab. ضَائِن, pl. ضَأْن, *ovis*. Syr. ܥܳܢܳܐ, *grex*; *oves, et capræ*. (a) *A sheep or goat*, coll. *sheep or goats*; *a flock* of these animals. (b) When unity is intended, שֶׂה is used. (c) בְּנֵי צֹאן, *Lambs* or *kids*. (d) Metaph. *A people*, as the objects of care, from God, a sovereign, or a prophet. (a) Gen. xii. 16; xxxi. 19. 43; Exod. x. 24, &c. (b) Exod. xxi. 37. (c) Ps. cxiv. 4. 6; Jer. xxxi. 12. (d) 2 Sam. xxiv. 17; Ps. c. 3; Ezek. xxxiv. 2, 3, &c.

צֶאֱצָאִים, pl. m. constr. צֶאֱצָאֵי, aff. צֶאֱצָאַי, &c. r. יצא. (a) *Productions* of the earth. (b) Metaph. *Offspring*. (a) Job xxxi. 8; Is. xxxiv. 1; xlii. 5. (b) Job v. 25; xxvii. 14; Is. xliv. 3, &c. See צפיעה.

צָב, m. pl. צַבִּים. (a) Arab. ضَبّ, *lacertæ species. A kind of lizard: lacerta stellio*, Lev. xi. 29; Bochart. Hieroz., i. 1044. (b) Arab. ضَبّ, IV. *abscondidit rem*; ضَابَ, r. ضوب, *latuit. A covered wagon*, Num. vii. 3; Is. lxvi. 20.

צָבָא, m. (once, f., Dan. viii. 12), constr. צְבָא, aff. צְבָאִי, pl. aff. צְבָאַי; it. pl. צְבָאוֹת, constr. צִבְאוֹת, aff. צִבְאֹתַי. Æth. ፀብእ: *bellum; militia*: ፀብአ: *bellum intulit; oppugnavit*. (a) *An army*. (b) *Any multitude*. (c) שַׂר צָבָא, *Commander-in-chief*.

(d) צְבָא הַשָּׁמַיִם, [1] *The heavenly bodies*. [2] *The angels*. (e), [1] יְהוָֹה צְבָאוֹת: [2] יְהוָֹה אֱלֹהֵי צְבָאוֹת: [3] יְהוָֹה אֱלֹהִים צְבָאוֹת: and, [4] אֱלֹהִים צְבָאוֹת, Titles of Jehovah, as the Creator and Sovereign of the countless multitudes of creatures both in heaven and on earth. (f) *Warfare, military service*. (g) *Any appointed service, duty*, or *trial*. (a) Num. xxxi. 21. 32. 48; 2 Sam. iii. 23; Ps. lxviii. 13, &c. (b) Gen. ii. 1. (c) 2 Sam. ii. 8; xix. 14; 1 Kings xvi. 16, &c. (d), [1] Deut. iv. 19; xvii. 3; 1 Kings xvii. 16; Jer. xxxiii. 22, &c. [2] 1 Kings xxii. 19; Neh. ix. 6; Ps. cxlviii. 2, &c. (e), [1] 1 Sam. i. 3. 11; iv. 4; xvii. 48; 2 Sam. vi. 2, &c. [2] 2 Sam. v. 10; Ps. lxxxix. 9; Jer. v. 14, &c. [3] Ps. lix. 6; lxxx. 5. 20; Is. iii. 15, &c. [4] Ps. lxxx. 8. 15. (f) Num. i. 3. 20. 22. 24; Josh. xxii. 12, &c. (g) Num. iv. 3. 23. 30; Job vii. 1; xiv. 14; Is. xl. 4.

צָבָא, v. צָבָאוּ, pres. יִצְבָּאוּ. (a) *Assembled for war, fought*. (b) *Assembled for any service or duty, performed* it. (a) Num. xxxi. 7; Zech. xiv. 12. (b) Exod. xxxviii. 8. Infin. צְבֹא, (a) Is. xxxi. 4. (b) Num. iv. 23; viii. 24. Part. pl. צֹבְאִים, aff. צֹבְאֶיךָ, fem. צֹבְאוֹת. (a) Num. xxxi. 42; Is. xxix. 7, 8. (b) Exod. xxxviii. 8; 1 Sam. ii. 22.

Hiph. Part. מַצְבִּא. *Marshalled an army*, 2 Kings xxv. 19; Jer. lii. 25.

צְבָא, v. Chald. צְבִית, pres. יִצְבֵּא. Syr. ܨܒܳܐ, *voluit. Wished, was willing*, Dan. iv. 14. 22. 29; v. 21; vii. 19. Infin. aff. מִצְבְּיֵהּ, Dan. iv. 32. Part. צָבֵא, Dan. v. 19.

צְבָאִים, and **צְבָאוֹת**, pl. of צְבִי, which see.

צָבַח, v. צָבְתָה. Arab. صَبَّ, *fudit, effudit; fusus, effusus fuit;* صَابَ, r. صوب, *Id. Burst*, Num. v. 27.

Hiph. Inf. לַצְבּוֹת. *Caused to burst*, Num. v. 22, for לְהַצְבּוֹת.

צְבוּ, f. r. צבא. Syr. ܨܶܒܝܳܢܳܐ, *res, negotium. Determination, resolution*, Dan. vi. 18.

צָבוּעַ, masc. once, Jer. xii. 9. Arab.

צבט (509) צד

ضَبْعٌ, *hyæna.* A *hyæna.* So the LXX. See Bochart. Hieroz., i. 830.

צָבַט, v. once, pres. יִצְבָּט. Arab. ضَبَطَ, *firmiter tenuit;* ضَبَتْ, *prehendit manu.* Took up in his hand, Ruth ii. 14.

צְבִי, masc. in pause, צֶבִי; pl. צְבָיִם, and צְבָאִים; f. צִבְיָה, pl. צְבָאוֹת. Syr. ܛܒܝܐ, *voluit.* Arab. ظَبْيٌ, f. ظَبْيَةٌ, *capreolus dorcas.* Syr. ܛܒܝܐ, *Id.* (a) *Beauty, ornament, honour.* (b) אֶרֶץ הַצְּבִי, and הַצְּבִי, *The beautiful land,* or *the chosen, favoured land.* (c) *An antelope.* Linn. *Antilope dorcas.* See Bochart. Hieroz., i. 924. (a) Is. xiii. 19; xxiii. 9; xxiv. 16; Ezek. xx. 6, &c. (b) Dan. viii. 9; xi. 16. 41. (c) Deut. xii. 15. 22; xiv. 5; 2 Sam. ii. 18; 1 Kings iv. 23, &c.

צָבַע, masc. pl. צְבָעִים. Arab. صَبَغَ, *tinxit pannum; immersit* manum in aquâ. Syr. ܨܒܥ, *Id.* Dipping, dyeing. *A dyed dress,* Judg. v. 30, only.

צְבַע, v. Chald. Pah. Part. pl. מְצַבְּעִין. *Made wet,* Dan. iv. 22. Ithpa. pres. יִצְטַבַּע. Pass. of Pah., Dan. iv. 12. 20. 30; v. 21.

צָבַר, v. pres. יִצְבֹּר. Constr. immed. Arab. صَبَرَ, *disposuit in ordinem.* II. *Collegit.* (a) *Heaped up.* (b) *Laid up, treasured up.* (a) Hab. i. 10. (b) Gen. xli. 35. 49; Exod. viii. 14; Job xxvii. 16; Ps. xxxix. 7; Zech. ix. 3.

צְבָרִים, pl. m. *Heaps,* 2 Kings x. 10.

צְבָתִים, pl. m. Arab. ضَبَتْ, *prehendit manu. Handfuls,* Ruth ii. 16.

צַד, m. aff. צִדִּי, &c.; pl. צִדִּים, constr. צִדֵּי, aff. צִדֵּיכֶם, &c. Arab. صَدَّ, *vultum avertit* ab aliquo; صَدَّ, *fluvii litus;* ضَدَّ, *vicit* in lite; ضِدَّ, *contrarius, hostis.* (a) *The side,* [1] Of a person or animal. [2] Of a thing. (b) מִצַּד, *At the side of.* (c) עַל צַד, *At the side, in the arms.* (d) Probably *An adversary.* וְהָיוּ לָכֶם לְצִדִּים, *and they shall be adversaries to you.* The passage may, however, be interpreted intelligibly without adopting this signification. (a), [1] Num. xxxiii. 55; 2 Sam. ii. 16; Ezek. xxxiv. 21, &c. [2] Gen. vi. 16; Exod. xxvi. 13; xxx. 4, &c. (b) Deut. xxxi. 26; Ruth ii. 14; Ps. xci. 6, &c. (c) Is. lx. 4; lxvi. 12. (d) Judg. ii. 3.

צַד, m. Chald. *Id.* מִצַּד, *On the side of, in reference to,* Dan. vi. 5. לְצַד, *against,* Dan. vii. 25.

צִדָּא, Chald. once, Dan. iii. 14. *Opposition, perverseness,* as opposed to *accident.* But LXX. ἀληθῶς. Vulg. *verè.*

צָדָה, v. Cogn. צוּד. *Lay in wait, laid wait for,* Exod. xxi. 13. Part. צֹדֶה, 1 Sam. xxiv. 12.

צָדָה, v. Syr. ܨܕܝ, *vastatus est; desolavit. Laid waste.* Niph. נִצְדוּ. Pass., Zeph. iii. 6.

צְדָה, see צֵידָה.

צְדִיָּה, f. r. צדה. *Lying in wait,* Num. xxxv. 20. 22.

צַדִּיק, masc. pl. צַדִּיקִים, r. צדק. (a) *Righteous, just,* [1] In character and general conduct. [2] In administering judgment. (b) *Having a just cause.* (c) *Innocent.* (d) Probably *True.* (a), [1] Gen. vi. 9; xviii. 23—25; Ezek. iii. 21, &c. [2] 2 Chron. xii. 6; Ps. vii. 12; Jer. xii. 1; Dan. ix. 14, &c. (b) 2 Chron. vi. 23; Prov. xviii. 5. 17; Is. xxix. 21, &c. (c) Exod. xxiii. 7. 2 Sam. iv. 11; 2 Kings x. 9, &c. (d) Is. xli. 26.

צֶדֶק, masc. aff. צִדְקוֹ, צִדְקִי, &c. Arab. صَدَقَ, *verax, sincerus fuit;* صَدَقٌ, *veritas.* Syr. ܘܢܩܣ, *justum, æquum fuit.* Æth. ጸድቀ: *justus fuit; justificatus est; verax fuit.* (a) *Truth.* (b) *Fairness, correctness,* in weights and measures. (c) *Equity* in the administration of justice. (d) *A just cause.* (e) *Acquittal, justification.* (f) *Righteousness, justice,* of character and conduct. (g) Apparently, *Justification,* i. q. Δικαιοσύνη Θεοῦ, Rom. iii. 22. (a) Ps. lii. 5. (b) Lev. xix. 36; Job xxxi. 6; Ezek. xlv. 10, &c. (c) Deut. i. 16; xvi. 18. 20; Job viii. 3; Ps. ix. 5, &c. (d) Ps. vii. 9; xvii. 1; xviii. 21. 25. (e) Job vi. 29. (f) Ps. xv. 2; xlv. 8; Is. i. 21; xxvi. 10; Jer. xxii. 13; Ezek. iii. 20, &c. (g) Dan. ix. 24.

צְדָקָה, v. צָדְקָה, pres. יִצְדַּק. (a) *Was*

equitable. (b) *Was righteous.* (c) *Acted justly.* (d) *Had a just cause, was in the right.* (e) *Was acknowledged to be just, or in the right.* (a) Ps. xix. 10. (b) Job ix. 15. 20; Ps. xl. 3, &c. (c) Job xxxiii. 12; xxxiv. 5; xxxv. 7, &c. (d) Gen. xxxviii. 26; Job xiii. 18; Ezek. xvi. 52, &c. (e) Job xi. 2; Ps. li. 6; Is. xliii. 27, &c.

Niph. נִצְדַּק. *Was purified,* Dan. viii. 14. So the LXX. and Vulg.

Pih. צִדֵּק, pres. יְצַדֵּק. Constr. immed. *Justified, cleared,* himself or another, Jer. iii. 11; Ezek. xvi. 52.

Infin. aff. צַדְּקֶךָ, צַדְּקוֹ, Job xxxii. 2; xxxiii. 32; Ezek. xvi. 52.

Hiph. הִצְדִּיק, pres. יַצְדִּיק. Constr. immed. it. med. לְ. *Made* or *declared righteous, declared the right.* (a) *Did justice to* a suitor. (b) *Gave judgment in favour of.* (c) *Acquitted.* (d) *Justified,* in a theological sense. (e) *Led to righteousness.* (a) 2 Sam. xv. 4. (b) Deut. xxv. 1; Job xxvii. 5. (c) Exod. xxiii. 7. (d) Is. liii. 11.

Infin. הַצְדִּיק, (b) 1 Kings viii. 32; 2 Chron. vi. 23.

Imp. pl. הַצְדִּיקוּ, (a) Ps. lxxxii. 3.

Part. מַצְדִּיק, aff. מַצְדִּיקִי; pl. constr. מַצְדִּיקֵי. (b) Is. L. 8. (c) Prov. xvii. 15; Is. v. 27. (e) Dan. xii. 3, according to the Vulgate.

Hith. pres. נִצְטַדָּק. *Cleared himself,* Gen. xliv. 6.

צְדָקָה, fem. constr. צִדְקַת, aff. צִדְקָתִי, &c.; pl. צְדָקוֹת, aff. צִדְקֹתָיךָ, i. q. צֶדֶק. (a) *Truth.* (b) *Equity,* pec. in the administration of justice. (c) *A just cause* or *claim.* (d) *Righteousness, justice* of character and conduct. (e) *Favour, approbation; a suitable time* or *quantity.* (a) Is. xlv. 23. (b) Job xxxvii. 23; Is. xxviii. 17; Dan. ix. 7, &c. (c) 2 Sam. xix. 28. (d) Gen. xviii. 19; Deut. xxiv. 13; Ps. cvi. 3, &c. (e) Is. lxi. 10. (f) Joel ii. 23.

צִדְקָה, f. Chald. *Id. Equity, righteousness,* Dan. iv. 24.

צָהֹב, m. Arab. صَهَبٌ, *rubedo,* i. q. شَقَرٌ, *color rubicundus luti rubri. Red,* Lev. xiii. 30. 32. 36. LXX. ξανθίζουσα. Vulg. *flavus.*

צהב, v. Hoph. Part. מֻצְהָב. *Probably Of a gold colour,* Ezra viii. 27, only. Comp. זָהָב. LXX. στίλβοντος. Vulg. *fulgentis.*

צהל, v. צָהֲלָה, pres. יִצְהֲלוּ. Arab. صَهَلَ, *hinnivit equus.* Syr. ܨܗܰܠ, *Id.* (a) *Neighed.* (b) *Uttered a cry of joy, shouted for joy.* (a) Jer. v. 8; L. 11. (b) Esth. viii. 15; Is. xxiv. 14.

Pih. Intens. of Kal. Imp. fem. צַהֲלִי, pl. צַהֲלוּ. (a) *Shouted for joy.* (b) *Lifted up the voice,* in sorrow. (a) Is. xii. 6; liv. 1; Jer. xxxi. 7. (b) Is. x. 30.

Hiph. Infin. הַצְהִיל, apparently for הַזְהִיר, i. q. הִזְהִיר. *Caused to shine,* Ps. civ. 15.

צֹהַר, m. Arab. ظُهْرٌ, *tempus et hora diei statim post meridiem;* ظَهَرَ, *apparuit, manifesta fuit* res. Cogn. זהר. (a) *A light, aperture for light, window,* Gen. vi. 16. (b) Dual, צָהֳרַיִם, *Noon,* Gen. xliii. 16; Deut. xxviii. 29; 2 Sam. iv. 5; Ps. lv. 18, &c.

צהר, v. Arab. ظَهَرَ, *mundus purus fuit;* صَهَرَ, *liquavit rem; unxit caput liquamine.*

Hiph. pres. יַצְהִיר. *Made the fine oil* called יִצְהָר, Job xxiv. 12.

צַו, m. r. צוה. *A precept, command,* Is. xxviii. 10. 13. In Hos. v. 10, we have, הָלַךְ אַחֲרֵי צָו, which the LXX. render πορεύεσθαι ὀπίσω τῶν ματαίων, reading, שָׁוְא, or שָׁו; while the Vulg. has *abire post sordes,* reading צוֹא.

צוֹא, pl. צוֹאִים, צוֹאִים. Syr. ܨܐ, *fœdavit. Filthiness, filthy,* Zech. iii. 3. 4.

צוֹאָה, fem. constr. צֹאַת, aff. צֹאָתוֹ, צֹאָתָם. *Filth,* and, probably, *dung,* Prov. xxx. 12; Is. iv. 4; xxviii. 8; xxxvi. 12.

צַוָּאר, m. constr. צַוַּאר, aff. צַוָּארִי, &c. (צַוְּרֹן, Neh. iii. 5); pl. constr. צַוְּארֵי, aff. צַוָּארָיו, צַוְּארֵיכֶם, and צַוְּארֹתֵיהֶם, צַוְּארֵי. Syr. ܨܰܘܪܳܐ, *collum.* Arab. ظَهْرٌ, *dorsum, tergum.* Æth. አፍ: *portare, gestare, ferre.* (a) *The neck.* (b) *The back of the neck.* (c) *The shoulder* or *back.* (a) Ps. lxxv. 6; Cant. i. 10; iv. 4, &c. (b) Is. lii. 2: Jer. xxvii. 12; xxviii. 10, &c. (c) Job xv. 26. The pl. is sometimes used in the sense of the singular, Gen. xxvii. 16; xxxiii. 4; xlv. 14; xlvi. 29.

צוב, v. Arab. صَابَ, r. صوب, *effudit. Burst.*

צוד (511) צול

Part. f. צָדָה, Num. v. 21.

צוּד, v. pret. צָדוּ, pres. יָצוּד. Constr. immed. Arab. صَادَ, r. صيد, *venatus fuit; piscatus est.* Syr. צֻד, *Id.* See צֵיד. *Hunted, laid wait for, pursued,* either (a) Animals, or (b) Men. (a) Lev. xvii. 13; Job xxxviii. 39. (b) Job x. 16; Jer. xvi. 16; Lam. iv. 18, &c.
Infin. צוּד, צֵיד, (a) Gen. xxvii. 5. (b) Lam. iii. 52.
Imp. צוּדָה, (a) Gen. xxvii. 3.
Part. צָד, (a) Gen. xxvii. 33.
Pih. Pres. הַמְצֹדְדָנָה, i. q. Kal, (b) Ezek. xiii. 18.
Infin. צוֹדֵד, Ezek. xiii. 18.
Part. pl. f. מְצֹדְדוֹת, Ezek. xiii. 20.
Hith. הִצְטַיָּדְנוּ. *Furnished ourselves with provisions,* Josh. ix. 12.

צוה, v. Kal non occ. Cogn. Arab. سَوَى, *intendit, proposuit sibi rem;* شَيَى, voluit; وَضَى, IV. *Testamento mandavit rem alicui; imperavit alicui.* Syr. צְבָא, *voluit.* Probably *Wished.*
Pih. צִוָּה, pres. יְצַוֶּה, apoc. יְצַו. *Declared his will.* (a) *Commanded;* constr. [1] Immed. of person or thing. [2] Abs. [3] עַל, of pers. [4] אֶל, of pers. [5] לְ, of pers. (b) *Gave his last orders,* with אֶל, or לְ, of pers. (c) *Appointed* a person to an office. (d) *Appointed* a thing, *caused* it. (a), [1] Gen. vi. 22; xviii. 19; xxxii. 4, &c. [2] Gen. xlvii. 11; L. 16; Exod. vii. 10, &c. [3] 1 Kings xi. 10; Esth. ii. 10. 20; Jer. xxxv. 6, &c. [4] Exod. xvi. 34; Num. xv. 23. [5] Deut. xxxiii. 4; 1 Sam. xx. 29; Esth. iii. 2, &c. (b) 2 Sam. xvii. 23. (c) Gen. xii. 20; 1 Sam. xxv. 30; 2 Sam. vii. 11, &c. (d) Deut. xxviii. 8; Ps. lxviii. 29; Is. xlv. 12, &c.
Infin. צַוֹּת, aff. צַוֹּתִי, Gen. xlix. 33; Ezek. x. 6, &c.
Imp. צַוֵּה, צַו, pl. צַוּוּ, Lev. vi. 2; Josh. i. 11; iv. 16, &c. (b) 2 Kings xx. 1.
Part. מְצַוֶּה, Gen. xxvii. 8, &c.
Puh. צֻוָּה, pres. יְצֻוֶּה. Pass. of Pih., Exod. xxxiv. 34; Num. iii. 16; Ezek. xii. 7, &c.

צוח, v. pres. in pause, יִצְוָחוּ. Arab. صَاح, r. صيح, *clamavit maximâ voce.* *Shouted* for joy, Is. xlii. 11, only.
צְוָחָה, f. צְוָחַת, aff. צְוָחֵךְ. *A cry of*

sorrow or *regret*, Ps. cxliv. 14; Is. xxiv. 11; Jer. xiv. 2; xlvi. 12.

צוּלָה, f. Cogn. Arab. ضَلّ, *erravit; latuit, abditus est.* See צלל. Probably *Concealment; an unknown depth; the deep,* Is. xliv. 27, only.

צוֹם, m. aff. צֹמְכֶם, pl. צֹמוֹת. Arab. صَوْم, *jejunium;* صَام, *jejunavit.* Syr. צוֹמָא, *Id. A fast,* 2 Sam. xii. 16; Esth. ix. 31; Is. lviii. 3, &c.

צוּם, v. pret. צָמָה, pres. יָצוּם, apoc. צָם. *Fasted,* constr. abs., 2 Sam. xii. 16. 21; 1 Kings xxi. 27; Esth. iv. 16, &c. Once, constr. immed. צַמְתֻּנִי. *Did ye fast to me?* Zech. iii. 5.
Infin. צוּם, Zech. vii. 5.
Imp. pl. צוּמוּ, Esth. iv. 16.
Part. צָם, 2 Sam. xii. 23; Neh. i. 4.

צוּף, m. pl. צוּפִים. Syr. צוּף, *redundavit, supernatavit.* Arab. ضَفَا, *abundavit, de opibus; redundavit, de receptaculo aquæ,* res. Cogn. נטף. *Dripping, overflowing, floating.* A honey-comb, Ps. xix. 11; Prov. xvi. 24.

צוּף, v. pret. צָפוּ. *Flowed,* of water, Lam. iii. 54.
Hiph. הֵצִיף, pres. apoc. יָצֶף. (a) *Caused to flow.* (b) *Caused to float.* (a) Deut. xi. 4. (b) 2 Kings vi. 6.

צוּק, v. pret. צָקוּן, pres. יָצִיק, i. q. יָצַק. *Poured out,* Job xxviii. 2; xxix. 6; xli. 14. Metaph. *Poured out* prayer, Is. xxvi. 16.

צוּק, v. Arab. ضَيْق, *angustia, afflictio;* ضَاقَ, *angustus et arctatus fuit.* Æth. ጾቀ፡ IV. *Coarctavit; angustavit. Was encamped, pressed; was in difficulty.*
Infin. צוֹק, Dan. ix. 25.
Hiph. הֵצִיק, pres. יָצִיק. Causat. of Kal. Constr. immed. it. med. לְ. (a) *Urged, constrained.* (b) *Distressed,* pec. by a siege. (a) Judg. xiv. 17; xvi. 16; Job xxxii. 18. (b) Deut. xxviii. 53; Is. xxix. 2; Jer. xix. 9.
Part. מֵצִיק, plur. מְצִיקִים. (b) Is. xxix. 7; li. 13.
צוּקָה, f. *Distress,* Prov. i. 27; Is. vi. i. 23; xxx. 6.

צוּר, v. pret. צָרַף, pres. יָצוּר, apoc. צַר.

צוּר (512) צחח

Cogn. צרר, יצר. Arab. صُورَة, *forma*; صَوَّرَ, *formavit*; صَرَّ, *constrinxit, nodavit crumenam*; ضَرَّ, *nocuit*; ضَار, r. ضور, *Id.* (a) *Formed, fashioned*, constr. immed. (b) *Tied up* money. (c) *Surrounded.* (d) *Overlaid.* (e) *Acted hostilely.* (f) *Besieged.* (a) Exod. xxxii. 4; 1 Kings vii. 15. (b) Deut. xiv. 28; 2 Kings v. 23; xii. 1. (c) Ps. cxxxix. 5. (d) Cant. v. 9. (e) Exod. xxiii. 22; Deut. ii. 9. 19. (f) Constr. [1] Med. אֶת, 1 Chron. xx. 1. [2] Med. אֶל, Deut. xx. 19. [3] Med. עַל, Deut. xx. 12; 1 Kings xx. 1; Is. xxix. 3, &c.
Infin. צוּר, (f, 2) 1 Sam. xxiii. 8.
Imp. f. צוּרִי, (f) Is. xxi. 2.
Part. צָר, pl. צָרִים, (f, 3) 1 Kings xv. 27; Jer. xxi. 4, &c.

צוּר, m. aff. צוּרִי, &c.; pl. צוּרִים, and צוּרוֹת. Syr. ܛܽܘܪܳܐ, *mons*. Arab. ظُر, *confecit silicem igni excutiendo aptum.* (a) *A rock.* (b) *Pec. A rock* used as a place of security. (c) *A title of God*, as a sure refuge. (d) *A stone.* (e) *A sharp stone used as a knife.* (f) *The edge* of a sword. (g) Probably *Form, figure.* (a) Exod. xvii. 6; xxxiii. 22; Job xviii. 4, &c. (b) Job xxii. 24; Ps. xxxi. 3; lxxiii. 26, &c. (c) Deut. xxxii. 15. 31; 2 Sam. xxii. 47; xxiii. 3, &c. (d) Is. viii. 15. (e) Josh. v. 2, 3. (f) Ps. lxxxix. 44. (g) Ps. xlix. 15. But LXX. βοήθεια. Vulg. *auxilium*.

צוּר, see צָאַר.

צוּרָה, f. constr. צוּרַת, aff. צוּרָתוֹ; pl. aff. צוּרֹתָי. Arab. صُورَة, *forma. Form, figure*, Ezek. xliii. 11.

צוּרֹן, m. pl. aff. צַוְּרֹנָיִךְ. A diminutive of צַוָּאר, expressive of affection, *The neck*, Cant. iv. 9.

צוּת, or צִית, once, pres. aff. Kal or Hiph. אַצִּיתֶנָּה, i. q. יצת. *Set on fire, burned*, Is. xxvii. 4.

צַח, masc. pl. f. צָחוֹת. Arab. ضَحَّ, *sol, et lux ejus; campus patens soli expositus*; ضَحَا, *apparuit, patuit et conspicua fuit via; prodiit* in solem; *apricatus fuit; sudavit*; صَحَّ, *sanus, integer fuit*; صَحِيح, *sanus, integer. Exposed to the sun.* (a) *Hot, burning.* (b) *Bright; clear, white.* (c) In the pl. f. *Clear, distinct things; distinctly, plainly*, or *without fault.* (a) Is. xviii. 4; Jer. iv. 11. (b) Cant. v. 10. (c) Is. xxxii. 4.

צָחָה, masc. constr. צְחֵה. *Parched*, Is. v. 13.

צָחָה, v. pret. צָחוּ. *Was bright; white*, Lam. iv. 7.

צְחִיחִים, m. pl. צְחִיחִים. *Exposed to the sun.* (a) *Dry, bare.* (b) *Open, exposed; high.* (a) Ezek. xxvi. 4. 13, 14. (b) Neh. iv. 7.

צְחִיחָה, f. *A dry, parched land*, Ps. lxviii. 7.

צִחֲנָה, fem. aff. צַחֲנָתוֹ, once, Joel. ii. 20. Arab. سَخَنَ, *caluit, calida fuit aqua*; سُخْنَة, *calor febrilis, vel æstus in corpore. Heat, the heat of putrefaction; stench.*

צַחְצָחוֹת, pl. f. once, Is. lviii. 11. Arab. ضَحْضَاح, *aqua pauca, minimè profunda.* Either, *Dry places* or *drought.*

צָחַק, v. צָחֲקָה, pres. יִצְחָק. Arab. ضَحِكَ, *risit.* Cogn. שׂחק. *Laughed*, const. abs., Gen. xvii. 17; xviii. 12, 13. 15: med. לְ, Gen. xxi. 6.
Pih. pres. יְצַחֵק. (a) *Laughed at; insulted*, med. בְּ. (b) *Made laughter.* (c) *Joked.* (d) *Sported.* (b) Judg. xvi. 25.
Infin. צַחֵק, (a) Gen. xxxix. 14. 17. (d) Exod. xxxii. 6.
Part. מְצַחֵק, (c) Gen. xix. 14. (d) Gen. xxi. 9; xxvi. 8.

צְחֹק, masc. *Laughter, ridicule*, Gen. xxi. 6; Ezek. xxiii. 32.

צַחַר, masc. Cogn. צחר. *Brightness, whiteness*, Ezek. xxvii. 18, only.

צָחֹר, pl. fem. צְחֹרוֹת. Arab. صُحْر, *colorem albo et rubro mixtum habens*, de asinâ. *White*, Judg. v. 10, only.

צִי, m. pl. צִים, and צִיִּים. *A ship*, Num. xxiv. 24; Is. xxxiii. 21; Ezek. xxx. 9; Dan. xi. 30. See צִיָּה.

צַיִד, m. constr. צֵיד, aff. צֵידִי, r. צוד. (a) *Hunting.* (b) *Game, prey.* (c) *Provi-*

(513)

sions, of any kind. (a) Gen. x. 9; xxv. 27; xxvii. 30. (b) Gen. xxvii. 3. 19; Lèv. xvii. 13; Job xxxviii. 41, &c. (c) Josh. ix. 5. 14; Neh. xiii. 15; Ps. cxxxii. 15.

צַיָּד, masc. pl. צַיָּדִים. *A hunter,* Jer. xvi. 16.

צֵידָה, and צָדָה, f. *Provisions* of any kind, Gen. xlii. 25; Judg. ix. 11; 1 Sam. xxii. 10, &c.

צִיָּה, fem. pl. צִיּוֹת. Arab. صَوَى, *exaruit palma;* صَاوٍ, *aridus.* (a) *Drought.* (b) *Parched,* of a land. (c) *A parched land, wilderness.* (a) Job xxiv. 19. (b) Ps. lxiii. 2; cvii. 35; Is. xli. 18, &c. (c) Job xxx. 3; Is. xxxv. 1; Ps. lxxviii. 17; cv. 41.

צִיּוֹן, m. *A parched land,* Is. xxv. 5; xxxii. 2.

צִיּוּן, m. pl. צִיֻּנִים. Arab. صُوًى, *pars terræ altior duriorque; lapis viæ index; sepulcrum.* Syr. ܨܘܢܐ, *cippus, tumulus lapidum. A mound.* (a) *A sepulchral monument.* (b) *A mound or stone as a way-mark.* (a) 2 Kings xxiii. 17; Ezek. xxxix. 15. (b) Jer. xxxi. 21.

צִיִּים, pl. m. *Inhabitants of the desert:* either, (a) Men, or (b) Beasts, but not confined to any particular species. (a) Ps. lxxii. 9; lxxiv. 14; Is. xxiii. 13. (b) Is. xiii. 21; xxxiv. 14; Jer. L. 39.

צִינֹק, m. once, Jer. xxix. 26. Sam. צנק, *coarctavit, clausit.* Arab. زِنَاق, *compedes, quibus quaterni religantur pedes.* Probably *Fetters.*

צִיץ, m. pl. צִיצִים. Cogn. Arab. ضَاءَ, r. ضَوءَ, *luxit, micuit;* نَصَّةُ, *cincinnus vel coma quæ decidit in anteriorem faciei partem;* زِبْرَة, *plumæ.* Cogn. נֵץ, and נצץ. (a) *A flower, blossom.* (b) Any thing of a *bright, shining* appearance, *a polished plate* of metal. (c) *Plumage; wings.* (a) Num. xvii. 23; 1 Kings vi. 18; Is. xxviii. 1; xl. 6—8, &c. (b) Exod. xxviii. 36; xxxix. 30; Lev. viii. 9. (c) Jer. xlviii. 9.

צִיץ, v. pret. צָץ, pres. יָצִיץ, apoc. יָצֵץ. (a) *Flowered.* (b) Metaph. *Flourished.* (a) Num. xvii. 23; Ps. xc. 6; Ezek. vii. 10, &c. (b) Ps. xcii. 8; cxxxii. 18; Is. xxvii. 6.

Hiph. part. מֵצִיץ. Probably *Looked brightly, cheerfully,* Cant. ii. 9.

צִיצָה, fem. constr. צִיצַת. *A flower,* Is. xxviii. 4.

צִיצַת, for צִיצִית, f. (a) *A lock of hair.* (b) *A fringe.* (a) Ezek. viii. 3. (b) Num. xv. 38, 39.

צִיר, v. Hith. pres. in pause, יִצְטַיָּרוּ. Most probably an error of transcribers for יִצְטַיְּרוּ, r. ציר, which see. If the reading be taken as correct, compare Arab. صَارَ, r. صير, *ivit. Prepared themselves for a journey.*

צִיר, m. pl. צִירִים, צִירֶיךָ. (a) *A person sent on a journey; a messenger, an ambassador.* (b) *A hinge,* as that on which a door *moves.* (a) Prov. xiii. 17; xxv. 13; Is. xviii. 2; lvii. 9, &c. (b) Prov. xxvi. 14.

צִירִים, pl. m. constr. צִירֵי, aff. צִירֶיהָ, r. צוּר, or צרר. (a) *Pangs* of a woman in labour. (b) *Distress of mind.* (c) *Figures, images.* See צוּר. (a) 1 Sam. iv. 19; Is. xxi. 3. (b) Is. xiii. 8; xxi. 3; Dan. x. 16. (c) Is. xlv. 16.

צֵל, m. aff. צִלּוֹ, &c., r. צלל. Arab. ظِلّ, *umbra, defectus lucis.* (a) *A shadow.* (b) *Dusk.* (c) *Shade, shelter from the sun.* (d) *Shelter* from danger, *protection.* (a) Judg. iv. 36; Job viii. 9; Is. xxxviii. 8, &c. (b) Job vii. 2. (c) Is. xxv. 4; Jonah iv. 6, &c. (d) Ps. xvii. 8; xci. 1; Eccl. vii. 12, &c.

צָלָא, v. Arab. صَلَا, r. صلو. IL *Precatus fuit.* Syr. ܨܠܝ, Paḥ. *Id.* Paḥ. Part. מְצַלֵּא, pl. מְצַלַּיָּא. *Prayed,* Ezra vi. 10; Dan. vi. 11.

צלה, v. pres. יִצְלֶה. Arab. صَلَى, صلي, *assavit. Roasted,* Is. xliv. 16. 19. Infin. צְלוֹת, 1 Sam. ii. 15.

צָלוּל, or צָלִיל, once, Judg. vii. 13. *A cake.* LXX. μαγίς. Aquila, ἐγκρυφίας. Vulg. *subcinericius* panis: r. either צלל from its being *covered* with ashes while baking, or צלה.

צלח, v. pres. יִצְלַח. Arab. صَلُحَ, *reetè se habuit res; integer, probus fuit* homo.

3 U

צלח

Cogn. سَلَكَ, *ivit, incessit*. Syr. ܣܠܩ. Aph. *descendit, supervenit*. The leading idea seems to be *motion forwards*: hence, *advancement, success*. (a) *Crossed* a river. (b) *Fell upon, took possession of*. (c) *Advanced, prospered, succeeded, flourished*, constr. abs. (d) *Was accomplished*. (e) *Was useful, fit*; with לְ. (a) 2 Sam. xix. 18. (b) Constr. [1] Immed., Amos v. 6. [2] Med. אֶל, 1 Sam. xvi. 13; xviii. 10. [3] Med. עַל, Judg. xiv. 10; 1 Sam. x. 6. 10; xi. 6. (c) Is. liv. 17; Jer. xii. 1; xiii. 10; Ezek. xvii. 9, &c. (d) Is. liii. 10. (e) Jer. xiii. 7. 10; Ezek. xv. 4.

Imp. צְלָח, Ps. xlv. 5.

Hiph. הִצְלִיחַ, pres. יַצְלִיחַ. (a) *Made to prosper*. (b) *Accomplished*. (c) *Was prosperous*. (a), [1] Constr. immed. of thing, Gen. xxiv. 40. 56; 2 Chron. xxvi. 5, &c. [2] Med. לְ, of person, Neh. ii. 20. (b) 2 Chron. vii. 11; Ps. i. 3; Is. xlviii. 15, &c. (c) 1 Chron. xxii. 13; xxix. 23; Prov. xxviii. 13, &c.

Imp. הַצְלִיחָה, הַצְלַח, plur. הַצְלִיחוּ. (a) Neh. i. 11; Ps. cxviii. 25. (c) 1 Kings xxii. 12. 15, &c.

Part. מַצְלִיחַ, Gen. xxiv. 42, &c.

צְלַח, v. Chald. Aph. הַצְלַח. (a) *Made prosperous, advanced*; constr. med. לְ. (b) *Was prosperous*. (a) Dan. iii. 30. (b) Dan. vi. 29.

Part. מַצְלַח, plur. מַצְלְחִין, (b) Ezra v. 8; vi. 14.

צַלַּחַת, fem. pl. צְלָחוֹת. Arab. زَلَفَ, *gustavit*; ڒَلَفَة, *patina*. *A dish*, 2 Kings xxi. 13; 2 Chron. xxxv. 13; Prov. xix. 24; xxvi. 15.

צְלֹחִית, f. *Id.*, 2 Kings ii. 20.

צָלִי, m. constr. צְלִי, r. צלה. *Roasted meat*, Exod. xii. 8, 9; Is. xliv. 16.

צָלָל, m. aff. צִלְלֵי, pl. צְלָלִים, constr. צִלְלֵי, i. q. צֵל. *A shadow*, Job xl. 22; Cant. ii. 17; iv. 6; Jer. vi. 4.

צָלַל, v. צָלְלוּ. Arab. ظَلَّ, II. *obumbravit*; ضَلَّ, *latuit, abditus fuit*. (a) *Became shaded, lost the light*. (b) *Was concealed, sunk* in the water. (a) Neh. xiii. 19. (b) Exod. xv. 10.

Hiph. part. מֵצֵל, *Giving shade*, Ezek. xxxi. 3.

צָלַל, v. צָלִי, pres. תְּצִלֶּינָה, and תְּצַלְנָה.

Arab. صَلَّ, *sonuit res; sonum edidit cum tinnitu ferrum*. Syr. ܨܰܠ, *tinnitus acutus*. (a) *Tingled*, of the ears. (b) *Quivered*, of the lips. (a) 1 Sam. iii. 11; 2 Kings xxi. 12; Jer. xix. 3. (b) Hab. iii. 16.

צֶלֶם, m. aff. צַלְמוֹ, pl. constr. צַלְמֵי, aff. צַלְמֵיהֶם, צְלָמָיו. Arab. ظَلَمَ, *obscurus fuit*. Æth. ጸላም: *Id.* Syr. ܨܰܠܡܳܐ, *figuravit, pinxit*; ܨܰܠܡܳܐ, *simulacrum*. (a) *A shadow*, as opposed to the substance. (b) *An imagination*. (c) *A representation*, either *a picture* or *an image*. (d) *Resemblance*, either mental or bodily. (a) Ps. xxxix. 7. (b) Ps. lxxiii. 20. (c) Num. xxxiii. 52; 1 Sam. vi. 5. 11; Ezek. xxiii. 14, &c. (d) Gen. i. 26, 27; v. 3; ix. 6, &c.

צַלְמָוֶת, i. q. צֵל מָוֶת. *The shadow of death*: applied to the *tomb*, and to any *very thick darkness*, physical or mental, Job x. 22; xii. 22; Is. ix. 1, &c.

צֵלָע, f. constr. צֶלַע, and צַלְעֲ, aff. צַלְעוֹ; pl. צְלָעוֹת, and צְלָעִים, constr. צַלְעוֹת, aff. צַלְעֹתָיו. Arab. ضِلْع, *costa*; ضِلاعَة, *latus*; ضالِع, *claudus*. (a) *A rib*. (b) *A plank used for wainscotting*. (c) *A side*, [1] Of a man. [2] Of any thing. (d) *A side-chamber*, one of a series of rooms running along the wall. (a) Gen. ii. 21, 22. (b) 1 Kings vi. 15. (c), [1] Job xviii. 12. [2] Exod. xxv. 14; xxvi. 26; 2 Sam. xvi. 13; 1 Kings vi. 34, &c. (d) 1 Kings vi. 5. 8; Ezek. xli. 5. 9. 11, &c.

צֶלַע, m. aff. צַלְעִי. *Falling on one side; limping, falling*, Ps. xxxv. 15; xxxviii. 18; Jer. xx. 10.

צָלַע, v. Only as a participle, צֹלֵעַ, fem. צֹלֵעָה. *Halting, lame*, Gen. xxxii. 31; Mic. iv. 6, 7; Zeph. iii. 19.

צֶלְצַל, m. constr. צִלְצַל, pl. צִלְצְלִים, constr. צִלְצְלֵי. (a) *A cymbal*, ὀνοματοποιητ. (b) *A species of locust*, so named either from the noise of their wings or from their *darkening* the sky by their numbers. (c) According to some, *The tumultuous noise* of an army. (d) Some kind of instrument employed in killing the whale; but its exact nature, and the etymology of the word, are uncertain.

צמא (515) צמו

Bochart. refers to ضَالَّة, *arma quævis*, aliis *sagitta*. (a) 2 Sam. vi. 5; Ps. cl. 5. (b) Deut. xxviii. 42. (c) Is. xviii. 1. (d) Job xl. 31.

צָמָא, m. constr. צְמָא, aff. צְמָאִי, צְמָאָם. Arab. ضَامِي, *sitiens*. *Thirst*, Exod. xvii. 3; Ps. lxix. 22; civ. 11, &c.

צָמֵא, m.—f. צְמֵאָה, pl. צְמֵאִים. *Thirsty*, Deut. xxix. 19; Ps. cvii. 5; Is. xxi. 14, &c.

צָמֵא, v. צָמְאָה, 2 fem. צָמֵת, pres. יִצְמָא. (a) *Thirsted*, constr. abs. (b) Metaph. *Earnestly desired*, med. לְ. (a) Exod. xvii. 3; Judg. iv. 19; Ruth ii. 9, &c. (b) Ps. xlii. 3; lxiii. 2.

צִמְאָה, f. *Thirst*, Jer. ii. 25.

צִמָּאוֹן, m. *A thirsty land*, i. e. *a land parched through want of water*, Deut. viii. 15; Ps. cvii. 33; Is. xxxv. 7.

צֶמֶד, masc. aff. צִמְדּוֹ, pl. צְמָדִים, constr. צִמְדֵי. Arab. ضَمَدَ, *vittâ religavit*. Syr. ܨܡܕ, Id. Æth. ጸመደ : *jugum*. *Binding, yoking together*. (a) *A couple of oxen at the plough*. (b) *The quantity of land ploughed in a day by a pair of oxen; an acre*. (c) *A couple*, [1] Of oxen. [2] Of asses. [3] Of mules. [4] Of horsemen. (a) 1 Sam. xiv. 14; 1 Kings xix. 19; Jer. li. 23. (b) Is. v. 10. (c), [1] 1 Sam. xi. 7; 1 Kings xix. 21, &c. [2] Judg. xix. 3. 10; 2 Sam. xvi. 1. [3] 2 Kings v. 17. [4] 2 Kings ix. 25; Is. xxi. 7. 9.

צָמַד, v. Kal non occ. *Tied, bound*.

Niph. pres. יִצָּמֵד. *Was bound, yoked*: used only of the Israelites who had been seduced into the worship of Baal-peor, and probably used contemptuously to denote the slavery into which their passions had led them, Num. xxv. 3; Ps. cvi. 5.

Part. pl. נִצְמָדִים, Num. xxv. 5.

Puh. part. f. מְצֻמֶּדֶת. *Was tied, fastened*, 2 Sam. xx. 8.

Hiph. pres. תַּצְמִיד. Metaph. *Put together, contrived*, Ps. L. 19.

צָמָה, i. q. צָמָא. *Thirst*, Is. v. 13.

צַמָּה, f. aff. צַמָּתֵךְ. Arab. صَمَّ, *obturavit ampullam*; صِمَام, *obturaculum ampullæ*,

epistomium. *A woman's veil*, Cant. iv. 1. 3; vi. 7; Is. xlvii. 2.

צְמֻקִים, and צִמּוּקִים, pl. masc. r. צמק. Ital. "*Simmuki:*" Gesen. Arab. صَامِق, *sitiens*. Eng. vulg. *dry*. *Dried fruits, dried grapes*, 1 Sam. xxv. 18; xxx. 12; 2 Sam. xvi. 1; 1 Chron. xii. 40.

צֶמַח, masc. aff. צִמְחֹה. (a) *Shooting, springing up*. (b) *A shoot*. (c) *Plants*. (d) *The Branch*, a title of Christ. (a) Ps. lxvi. 11; Ezek. xvii. 9, 10. (b) Hos. viii. 7. (c) Gen. xix. 25; Ezek. xvi. 7, &c. (d) Jer. xxiii. 5; xxxiii. 15; Zech. iii. 8; vi. 12. In Is. iv. 2, צֶמַח יְהוָֹה, is by some taken to signify, *a new race springing up in the fear of God and under his protection, after the punishment of their fathers*: by others it is considered as a title of Christ as *the Son of God*; which is undoubtedly the true sense, as the place is manifestly a prophecy relating to the times of Christ. Comp. Ib. xi. 1; Rev. v. 5; xxii. 16.

צָמַח, v. pres. יִצְמַח. (a) *Shot* or *grew up*, [1] Of plants. [2] Of hair. (b) *Flourished*. (c) *Sprung up, arose, began*. (d) *Produced*. (a), [1] Gen. ii. 5. [2] Lev. xiii. 37. (b) Is. xliv. 4; Ezek. xvii. 6; Zech. vi. 12. (c) Job v. 6; Ps. lxxxv. 12; Is. xliii. 19, &c.

Part. צוֹמֵחַ, צֹמֵחַ, pl. f. צֹמְחוֹת. (a) Gen. xli. 6. 23; Exod. x. 5. (d) Eccl. ii. 6.

Pih. צִמַּח, pres. יְצַמֵּחַ. *Grew*, of hair, 2 Sam. x. 5; 1 Chron. xix. 5; Ezek. xvi. 7.

Infin. צַמֵּחַ, Judg. xvi. 22.

Hiph. הִצְמִיחַ, pres. יַצְמִיחַ, apoc. יַצְמַח. Causat. of Kal. Constr. immed. it. abs *Caused to grow, produced*, Gen. iii. 18; Deut. xxix. 23; Is. lxi. 11, &c. Metaph. Is. xlv. 8; lxi. 11; Jer. xxxiii. 15, &c.

Infin. הַצְמִיחַ, Job xxxviii. 27.

Part. מַצְמִיחַ, Ps. civ. 14; cxlvii. 8.

צָמִיד, m. pl. צְמִידִים, r. צמד. (a) *Tied, fastened*. (b) *A band*, pec. *a metallic band for the arm, bracelet*. (a) Num. xix. 15. (b) Gen. xxiv. 22; Num. xxxi. 50; Ezek. xvi. 11, &c.

צַמִּים, m. Arab. ضَمّ, *rem attrahendo cum alterâ conjunxit*. (a) *A noose, knot, snare*. (b) Probably *Destruction*. (a) Job xviii. 9. (b) Job v. 5. But see the notes.

צְמִיתֻת, fem. Apparently, *Perfect silence; completeness*. לִצְמִיתֻת, *completely*,

צָמַק (516) צָנַח

i. e. *without power of redemption*, Lev. xxv. 23. 30.

צָמֵק, v. only part. pl. צְמֻקִים. Arab. اَصْمَقَ, *corruptum habuit saporem lac*; صَمَكِيك, *durus; spissus et viscosus*, de lacte. *Dry*, of the breasts, Hos. ix. 14.

צֶמֶר, masc. aff. צִמְרוֹ. Syr. ܥܲܡܪܵܐ, *lana*. *Wool*, Lev. xiii. 47; Ps. cxlvii. 16; Hos. ii. 5. 9. Comp. Arab. ضَمَرَ, *texit*.

צַמֶּרֶת, f. aff. צַמַּרְתּוֹ. *Foliage*, Ezek. xvii. 3. 22; xxxi. 3. 10. 14. LXX. τὰ ἐπίλεκτα, ἀρκὴ αὐτοῦ. Vulg. *medullam; cacumen ejus*.

צָמַת, v. צָמָה. Arab. صَمَتَ, *siluit, conticuit;* صُمَات, *absolutio rei peragendæ*. Æth. **ጸመተ** : *funditus eversus fuit*. *Silenced, brought to an end, destroyed*, Lam. iii. 53.

Niph. נִצְמָתִי נִצְמָתוּ. *Was put to silence*, Job vi. 17; xxiii. 17.

Pih. aff. צִמְּתַנִי. *Reduced to silence, overwhelmed, took full possession of*, Ps. cxix. 137.

Pih. redup. aff. צְמִתְּתֻנִי (see צְמִיתֻת). *Id.*, Ps. lxxxviii. 17.

Hiph. 2 pers. הִצְמַתָּה, pres. יַצְמִית. *Silenced, brought to an end, destroyed*, Ps. xviii. 41; lxxiii. 27; ci. 5. 8, &c.

צֹנֶא, aff. צֹנְאֲכֶם, for צֹאנְכֶם, Num. xxxii. 24. See צֹאן.

צֹנֶה, i. q. צֹאן. *Sheep*, Ps. viii. 8.

צִנָּה, fem. constr. צִנַּת, pl. צִנּוֹת. Arab. صَانَ, r. صون, *custodivit ab aliquo; recondidit;* صِيَان, *repositorium vestium, in quo asservantur,* صِن, *operculo instructum vas canistro simile, in quo reponitur panis*. Any thing used for *defence* or for *preserving* what is placed in it. (a) *A shield*. (b) *A vessel* for containing snow. (a) 1 Sam. xvii. 7. 41; 1 Kings x. 16; 2 Chron. xi. 12. (b) Prov. xxv. 13.

צִנּוֹת, pl. f. *Hooks*, pointed like thorns, Amos iv. 2.

צִנִּים, pl. m. *A fence of thorns, thorns*, Job v. 5; Prov. xxii. 5.

צִנּוֹר, m. pl. aff. צִנֹּרֶיךָ, twice. *A water-course, cataract*. So the majority of interpreters. In 2 Sam. v. 8, Aquila, κρουνισμῷ. Sym. ἐπάλξεως. LXX. παραξιφίδι. Vulg. *fistulas*. In Ps. xlii. 8, Sym. κρουνῶν. LXX. καταῤῥακτῶν. Vulg. *cataractarum*.

צָנַח, v. pres. תִּצְנַח. (a) *Dismounted*. (b) The nail *went down* into the ground. (a) Josh. xv. 18; Judg. i. 14. (b) Judg. iv. 21. Arab. زَنَحَ, *trusit*.

צְנִינִים, pl. m. i. q. צִנִּים. *Thorns*, Num. xxxiii. 55; Josh. xxiii. 13.

צָנִיף, m. constr. צְנִיף, pl. צְנִיפוֹת, r. צנף. *Something wrapped* round the head; *head-dress, turban*, Job xxix. 14; Is. iii. 23; lxii. 3; Zech. iii. 5.

צְנֻמוֹת, pl. f. once, Gen. xli. 23. The LXX. and Vulg. omit the word. It is usually taken as the Pass. Part. of צנם, which is supposed to have signified, *was hard*. Syr. ܢܫܦܐ, *durities*. But compare Arab. صَنَمَة, *flos, spica plantæ*.

צָנַע, v. Arab. صَنَعَ, *paravit, elaboravit*. Syr. ܐܙܢܥ, *dolose egit*. Æth. **ጸነዐ** : *durus fuit*. The primitive notion seems to consist in readiness, activity, or the like : thence to have taken various shades of these as in the Syr. and Æth. *Humble* is the sense usually given. But, *Ready, apt*, or the like, seems to suit the places better. Prov. l. c. Sym. ἐπιμελέσι. Theod. ἐπιεικῶν. Mic. l. c. LXX. ἕτοιμον εἶναι. Theod. ἀσφαλίζου. Pers. V. καὶ φροντίζειν. Vulg. " et solicitum." Syr. ܡܛܝܒܐ, *paratus*.

Part. Pass. pl. צְנוּעִים, Prov. xi. 2. *Ready, prepared*.

Hiph. *Humbled*. Infin. הַצְנֵעַ, adverbially, Mic. vi. 8. *Being ready, prepared*.

צָנַף, v. pres. יִצְנֹף. (a) *Bound, wrapped round*, immed. (b) *Wrapped round his head*, abs. (a) Is. xxii. 18. (b) Lev. xvi. 4. Infin. צָנוֹף, Is. xxii. 18.

צְנֵפָה, f. *A binding* or *wrapping*, Is. xxii. 18.

צִנְצֶנֶת, f. once, Exod. xvi. 33. Arab. وَصَن, *complicavit, contexuit;* مِصْنَانَة, *cophinus, corbis*. *A basket*.

צַנְתְּרוֹת, pl. fem. constr. once, Zech. iv.

צָעַד (517) צָעַץ

12. *Pipes, tubes.* The etymology is uncertain. Castell gives Syr. ܨܰܕܳܐ, *sulcus.*

צַעַד, masc. aff. צַעֲדִי, pl. צְעָדִים, constr. צַעֲדֵי, aff. צְעָדָי. Arab. صَعَد, *ascendit.* (a) *Stepping, going, motion.* (b) *A step.* (c) Metaph. *Progress, action, conduct.* (a) Prov. xxx. 29. (b) 2 Sam. vi. 13. (c) 2 Sam. xxii. 37; Prov. iv. 12; xvi. 9, &c.

צָעַד, v. צְעָדָה, pres. יִצְעַד. Constr. abs. it. immed. *Went forwards* or *upwards.* (a) *Walked, advanced.* (b) *Walked, proceeded over* or *through* a land. (c) *Shot up.* (a) 2 Sam. vi. 13; Prov. vii. 8; Jer. x. 5. (b) Hab. iii. 12. (c) Gen. xlix. 23.
Infin. aff. צַעְדְךָ, Judg. v. 4; Ps. lxviii. 8.
Hiph. pres. aff. הַצְעִידוּ. Causat. of Kal, Job xviii. 14.

צְעָדָה, f. i. q. צַעַד. *Marching,* 2 Sam. v. 24; 1 Chron. xiv. 15.

צְעָדוֹת, pl. f. Arab. مِصْعَاد, *catena,* quâ captivorum pedes constringuntur, ne amplos passus faciant. *Ornamental chains worn at the ancles,* Is. iii. 20.

צָעָה, v. part. צֹעֶה, fem. צֹעָה, pl. צֹעִים. Arab. ضَيع, r. ضَيع, *periit;* ضَاع, r. ضوع, *movit, commovit; terrore implevit.* Syr. ܛܥܳܐ, *erravit; latuit.* A word variously interpreted. Probably the succession of ideas it conveyed was *travelling, wandering, wandering for plunder, losing one's way, perishing,* Is. li. 14; lxiii. 1; Jer. ii. 20; xlviii. 12.
Pih. aff. צִעָהוּ. Either *Destroyed,* or *plundered,* Jer. xlviii. 12.

צָעִיף, masc. aff. צְעִיפָהּ. Arab. ضَعَّف, *duplicavit.* Cogn. צמק. *A woman's veil,* Gen. xxiv. 65; xxxviii. 14. 19.

צָעִיר, masc. aff. צְעִירוֹ, pl. צְעִירִים, constr. צְעִירֵי, aff. צְעִירָיו, f. צְעִירָה: r. צער. Arab. صَغِير, *parvus.* (a) *Small,* in size or importance. (b) *Young, younger.* (a) Ps. cxix. 141; Jer. xlix. 20; Mic. v. 1, &c. (b) Gen. xix. 31; xxv. 23; Josh. v. 26; Job xxx. 1, &c.

צְעִירָה, f. aff. צְעִירָתוֹ. (a) Fem. of צָעִיר, Gen. xix. 31; xxix. 26, &c. (b) *Smallness; inferiority in age,* Gen. xliii. 33.

צָעַן, v. pres. יִצְעַן, once, Is. xxxiii. 20.

Arab. ظَعَن, *migravit, iter fecit;* زَحَن, *removit è loco. Removed,* either himself or a thing.

צַעֲצֻעִים, pl. m. once, 2 Chron. iii. 10, מַעֲשֵׂה צַעֲצֻעִים. LXX. ἔργον ἐκ ξύλων. Vulg. *opere statuario.* Arab. صَاغ, r. صوغ, *formavit, finxit.* Probably *Carvings.*

צָעַק, v. pres. יִצְעַק. Cogn. זעק. Arab. صَعَق, *vehemens sonus, clamor.* Constr. abs. it. med. אֶל, לְ. *Cried out,* for help, in sorrow, or strife, Gen. xxvii. 34; Exod. xxii. 13; Deut. xxii. 24; 1 Kings xx. 39; 2 Chron. xiii. 14, &c.
Infin. צְעֹק, Exod. xxii. 22; 2 Kings viii. 3.
Imp. f. צַעֲקִי, צְעָקָה, pl. צְעָקוּ, Jer. xxii. 20; xlix. 3.
Part. f. צֹעֶקֶת, pl. צֹעֲקִים, Gen. iv. 10; Exod. v. 8; 2 Kings viii. 5.
Niph. pres. יִצָּעֵק. *Were called, summoned; assembled themselves,* Judg. vii. 23, 24; x. 17; xii. 1; 1 Sam. xiii. 4; 2 Kings iii. 21.
Pih. part. מְצַעֵק. Intensitive or frequentitive of Kal, 2 Kings ii. 12.
Hiph. pres. apoc. יַצְעֵק. *Caused to be summoned,* 1 Sam. x. 17.

צְעָקָה, fem. constr. צַעֲקַת, aff. צַעֲקָתוֹ, &c. *A cry,* for help, in sorrow, or strife, Gen. xxvii. 34; Exod. iii. 9; xxii. 22, &c.

צָעַר, v. pres. pl. יִצְעֲרוּ. Arab. صَغُر, *parvus fuit, tum corporis mole, tum quantitate et pretio. Was* or *became small* or *of little importance,* Job xiv. 21; Jer. xxx. 19; Zech. xiii. 7.

צָפַד, v. once, Lam. iv. 8. Arab. صَفَد, *constrinxit, et ligavit.* Cogn. צמד. *Adhered, cleaved to,* with עַל.

צפה, v. pres. apoc. יִצֶף. Arab. طَاف, r. طوف, *circumivit, obivit rem;* طَايِف, *circuitores et vigiles nocturni.* Probably *Went round* or *turned himself round* in all directions, as a watchman on a tower. (a) *Kept watch,* abs. (b) Metaph. of the tower itself, *Looked.* (c) *Watched, observed,* constr. immed. it. med. בְּ, בְּ. (d) *Looked for, expected.* (e) *Watched,* for evil; *plotted*

צפה (518) צפו

against, with לְ. (c) Gen. xxxi. 49; Ps. lxvi. 7.

Infin. צֹפֶה, (a) Is. xxi. 5.

Part. צֹפֶה, pl. צֹפִים, aff. צֹפְךָ, צֹפַי, f. צוֹפִיָּה, pl. צֹפוֹת. (a) *Keeping watch, a watchman,* 1 Sam. xiv. 16; 2 Sam. xiii. 34; 2 Kings ix. 16, &c. *A prophet,* Ezek. iii. 17; xxxiii. 7. (b) Cant. vii. 5. (c) Prov. xv. 3; xxxi. 27. (d) Hos. ix. 8. (e) Ps. xxxvii. 32.

Part. pass. צָפוּי, for צָפוּי. (e) *Watched, plotted against,* Job xv. 22.

Pih. צִפִּינוּ, pres. אֲצַפֶּה. (a) I. q. Kal [a]. (b) *Looked for, expected help,* constr. abs. it. med. אֶל, בְּ. (b) Ps. v. 4; Lam. iv. 17; Mic. vii. 7.

Imp. צַפֵּה, f. צַפִּי, (a) Jer. xlviii. 19; Nah. ii. 2.

Part. מְצַפֶּה, pl. aff. מְצַפֶּיךָ, (a) 1 Sam. iv. 13; Hab. ii. 1. *A watchman,* Is. xxi. 6; Mic. vii. 4.

II. Pih. צִפָּה, pres. יְצַפֶּה, apoc. יְצַף. Arab. صَفَّ, *ordine ac in seriem disposuit* rem ; صَفَ, *series, ordo. Covered, overlaid,* either with metal or wood ; constr. immed. of the wood or metal, and immed. or med. אֶת, of the thing covered, Exod. xxv. 11 ; xxvii. 2 ; xxxvi. 34 ; 1 Kings vi. 20, &c.

Puh. part. מְצֻפֶּה, plur. מְצֻפִּים. Pass. of Pih. *Was overlaid,* Exod. xxvi. 32 ; Prov. xxvi. 23.

צָפָה, f. aff. צָפָתְךָ, r. צוּף. *Overflowing,* Ezek. xxxii. 6. *I will water the land* (with) *thy overflowing from thy blood up to the mountains* ; or, *I will water the land of thy overflowing,* i. e. whose fertility depends on an annual overflowing, *with thy blood,* instead of the waters of the Nile.

צִפּוּי, m. r. צפה. *A covering or coating,* Num. xvii. 3, 4 ; Is. xxx. 22.

צָפוֹן, m. (Where it appears to be fem. the word רוּחַ is understood, which is in construction with צָפוֹן). (a) *The north :* either from צפן, as the *concealed,* dark part of the heavens ; or from צפה, as that part of the heavens to which those who travel by night must *look,* in order to discover the direction in which they are travelling, Exod. xxvi. 20 ; Num. xxxiv. 7 ; Job xxvi. 7, &c. (b) *The north wind,* Cant. iv. 16 ; Is. xliii. 6. (c) מִצָּפוֹן, *On the north,* 1 Sam. xiv. 5. (d) לְצָפוֹן, *On the north of,* Josh. viii. 11. 13 ; xv. 6, &c.

צְפוֹנִי, m. *Northern,* applied to the army of locusts that devastated the land, Joel ii. 20.

צִפּוֹר, com. plur. צִפֳּרִים. Arab. صَفَرَ, *sibilavit, fistulavit, et hoc modo cecinit* avis ; صَافِر, *sibilans; omnis avis sonum edens;* عُصْفُور, *passer avis.* (a) *A bird,* of any kind. (b) Pec. *A sparrow.* (a) Gen. vii. 14; Deut. iv. 17 ; Ps. viii. 9, &c. (b) Lev. xiv. 5—7, &c.

צַפַּחַת, f. Syr. ܨܰܦܚܳܐ, *patina, scutella.* Arab. صَفَعَ, *latam fecit* rem. Probably *A dish;* and, hence, *any vessel,* 1 Sam. xxvi. 11, 12. 16 ; 1 Kings xvii. 12. 14. 16 ; xix. 6.

צְפִיחָה, f. aff. צְפִיחָתֵנוּ, r. צפה. *A watch-tower,* Lam. iv. 17.

צַפִּיחִת, f. Arab. صَفِيحَة. *lamina. A flat cake, a cake,* Exod. xvi. 31. LXX. ἐγκρίς. Vulg. *similæ.*

צָפִיעַ, pl. constr. צְפִיעֵי. Arab. صَفَعَ, *stercus egessit;* صَفْع, *stercus elephanti.* Æth. ዐፅዐ ፡ *stercus. Dung,* Ezek. iv. 15, only.

צְפִיעָה, f. pl. צְפִעוֹת. Once, Is. xxii. 24. הַצֶּאֱצָאִים וְהַצְּפִעוֹת. These words are omitted by the LXX. ; and Aquila inserts them untranslated. Vulg. *vasorum diversa genera.* Modern interpreters have taken the ordinary meaning of צֶאֱצָאִים, *Offspring;* and have considered צְפִעוֹת as nearly synonymous. It appears, however, most probable that some kind of domestic utensils was intended by the prophet. Comp. Arab. ضَاءَ, r. ضَوَءَ, *luxit, micuit;* ضَوِيّ, *lucidus;* أَسْفَعُ, *niger.* Possibly, *The bright and the dark,* the fine and the coarse, the valuable and those of little value.

צָפִיר, m. constr. צְפִיר, pl. constr. צְפִירֵי. Syr. ܨܦܺܝܪܳܐ, *hircus.* Sam. צפיר, *hædus. A goat, a he-goat,* 2 Chron. xxix. 21 ; Ezra viii. 35 ; Dan. viii. 5. 8. 21.

צפי (519) צפר

צָפִיר, m. Chald. pl. constr. צְפִירֵי, *Id.*, Ezra vi. 17.

צְפִירָה, f. constr. צְפִירַת. Arab. ضَفْر‎ *plexuit comam;* صَفْر‎, *vacuus, inanis fuit.* Æth. ፀፈረ፡ *plexuit coronam, sertum.* Syr. ڞܶܦܳܐ, *manè.* (a) *A crown,* Is. xxviii. 5. (b) According to some, *A morning;* according to others, *Desolation,* Ezek. vii. 7. 10. Theod. ἡ πλοκή. Aquila, ἡ προσκόπησις.

צָפִית, f. r. צפה. *Watching; a watch-tower,* Is. xxi. 5.

צָפַן, v. pres. יִצְפּוֹן. Constr. immed. (a) *Hid, concealed.* (b) *Excluded.* (c) *Laid up, treasured up.* (d) *Lay hid, lay in wait.* (a) Exod. ii. 2; Job x. 13; Prov. xxvii. 16, &c. (b) Job xvii. 4. (c) Job xxiii. 12; Ps. cxix. 11; Ps. xxxi. 20, &c. (d) Ps. x. 8; lvi. 7; Prov. i. 11. 18.

Part. pl. aff. צֹפְנֶיךָ, (a) Prov. xxvii. 16.
Part. pass. צָפוּן, f. צְפוּנָה, aff. צְפוּנְךָ, pl. aff. צְפוּנָיו, צְפוּנֶיךָ, (c) Job xx. 26; Ps. xvii. 14; lxxxiii. 4; Prov. xiii. 22; Hos. xiii. 12.
Niph. נִצְפַּן, נִצְפְּנוּ. Pass. of Kal, Job xv. 20; xxiv. 1; Jer. xvi. 17.
Hiph. pres. aff. תַּצְפִּנֵנִי. I. q. Kal, (a) Job xiv. 13.
Infin. aff. הַצְפִּינוֹ, Exod. ii. 3.

צֶפַע, m. once. *The basilisk,* Is. xiv. 29. See Hieroz., tom. ii. p. 399.

צִפְעוֹנִי, m. pl. צִפְעֹנִים, *Id.,* Prov. xxiii. 32; Is. xi. 8; lix. 5; Jer. viii. 17.

צפף, v. Pih. redup. pres. אֲצַפְצֵף, תְּצַפְצֵף. Arab. صَفْصَفَ‎, *passer;* صَنْصَفَة‎, *pipitus passeris.* (a) *Chirped,* as a bird. (b) *Spoke in a low voice.* (a) Is. xxxviii. 14. (b) Is. xxix. 4.

Part. מְצַפְצֵף, pl. מְצַפְצְפִים. (a) Is. x. 14. (b) Is. viii. 19. In two of these passages the Auth. Vers. uses the ambiguous word *peep,* in the sense of to *chirp.*

צַפְצָפָה, f. once, Ezek. xvii. 5. Usually translated *A willow,* i. e. *as a willow;* כְּ, being understood. Comp. Arab. صَفْصَاف‎, *salix.* Winer, in his edition of Simonis, gives *fluxum copiosum, aquæ copiam;* taking צוף as the root; עַל, being understood. The older interpreters take צפה as the root, and translate, (in) *a conspicuous place.*

צָפַר, v. pres. יִצְפֹּר, once, Judg. vii. 3. Arab. ضَفَر‎, *cucurrit.* Probably *Hastened:* or, taking the Syr. ڞܰܦܰܪ, *manè.* Did a thing in the morning; went away in the morning.

צְפַר, Chald. masc. pl. צִפְּרִין, def. צִפֲּרַיָּא, constr. צִפֲּרֵי. Syr. ܨܶܦܪܳܐ, ڞܶܦܪܐ, i. q. Heb. צִפּוֹר. *A bird,* Dan. iv. 9. 11. 18. 30.

צְפַרְדֵּעַ, masc. collectively, f. pl. צְפַרְדְּעִים. Arab. ضِفْدَع‎, *rana:* compounded, according to Bochart., of ضِفَّة‎, *ripa,* fluvii; and رِدَاع‎, *lutum et aqua, limus.* *A frog; frogs,* Exod. vii. 26. 28, 29; viii. 1—9; Ps. lxxviii. 45; cv. 30.

צִפֹּרֶן, masc. plur. aff. צִפָּרְנֶיהָ. Arab. ظُفْر‎, *unguis.* (a) *A nail* of the finger, Deut. xxi. 12. (b) *The point* of a graver, Jer. xvii. 1.

צֶפֶת, f. once, 2 Chron. iii. 15. Syr. ܨܶܦܬܳܐ, *gemma annuli.* Apparently, Any thing ornamental; the *capital* of a pillar.

צָצִים, see ציץ.

צִקְלֹן, m. aff. צִקְלֹנוֹ, once, 2 Kings iv. 42. The word is omitted by the LXX. Vulg. *perâ.* Syr. ܨܩܠܽܘܢ, *mantile.* Several interpreters translate, *In its husks;* but this is mere divination. *Saccus, pera.* Gesen.

צַר, and צָר, masc. aff. צָרִי, pl. צָרִים (and צָרַי, Jer. xlviii. 5), constr. צָרֵי, r. צור. *A besieger;* an enemy, Esth. vii. 6; Job xvi. 9; Ps. lxxviii. 61. Fem. צרה, aff. צָרָתָהּ, *A rival,* 1 Sam. i. 6.

צֻר, m. i. q. צוּר. *A rock,* Is. v. 25.

צֹר, m. (a) *Id.,* Ezek. iii. 9. (b) *A knife,* Exod. iv. 25.

צַר, and צָר, fem. צָרָה, r. צרר. (a) *Narrow.* (b) *Small.* (c) *Close, closely.* (a) Num. xxii. 26; Is. xxviii. 20. (b) 2 Kings vi. 1; Prov. xxiv. 10; Is. xlix. 10. (c) Job xli. 7.

צַר, and צָר, m. r. צרר. *Difficulty, adversity, distress* of mind or circumstances, Deut. iv. 30; Job xv. 24; xxxvi. 16; Ps. cxix. 143, &c.

צרב, v. Kal non occ. Arab. ضَرَبَ, *percussit; adussit* ignis. Probably cognate with שׂוּף.
Niph. נִצְרְבוּ. *Was struck* by fire, *was scorched*, Ezek. xx. 47.
צָרֶבֶת, fem. (a) *Burning*, of fire. (b) *Inflammation*. (a) Prov. xvi. 27. (b) Lev. xiii. 23. 28.

צָרָה, f. with ה parag. צָרָתָה, Ps. cxx. 1, constr. צָרַת, aff. צָרָתִי, צָרָתְכֶם, pl. צָרוֹת, i. q. צַר, r. צרר, Gen. xxxv. 3; xlii. 21; Judg. x. 14; 1 Sam. xxvi. 24; Job v. 19, &c.

צרח, v. Arab. صَرَخَ, *sonuit, clamavit*. *Shouted, cried out*, either in distress or to alarm an enemy.
Part. צֹרֵחַ, Zeph. i. 14.
Hiph. pres. יַצְרִיחַ, i. q. Kal, Is. xlii. 13.

צְרִי, צֳרִי, in pause, צֶרִי, masc. Arab. ضَرًا, r. ضرو, *sanguine manavit* vulnus; ضَرِيَ, *fluxit;* ضَرْو, *fructus lentisci*. *Mastich*, a gum obtained from the Pistacia Lentiscus, Gen. xxxvii. 25; xliii. 11; Jer. viii. 22; xlvi. 11; li. 8; Ezek. xxvii. 17. See Hierobot., ii. p. 183.

צְרִיחַ, masc. pl. צְרִיחִים. Arab. صَرَّحَ, *clare exposuit, manifestem fecit* rem; صَرْح, *arx, palatium, et omnis excelsior structura*. A lofty, conspicuous, place; *a tower*, Judg. ix. 46. 49; 1 Sam. xiii. 6. LXX. τὴν συνέλευσιν, τὸ ὀχύρωμα, ἄντρον, βόθρους.

צְרִךְ, masc. aff. צָרְכְּךָ. Arab. ضَرِيكٌ, *infelix pauper*. Sam. צרך, *coegit*. Syr. ܐܘܠܨܢܐ, *opus fuit*. *Need, necessity*, 2 Chron. ii. 15, only.

צרע, v. used only in Part. pass. of Kal, צָרוּעַ, and Part. of Puh. מְצֹרָע, f. מְצֹרַעַת, pl. מְצֹרָעִים. *Struck with leprosy*. The etymology is doubtful; but the nearest word in the cognate dialects is the Arab. صَرَعَ, *prostravit*. Pass. *epilepsiâ correptus fuit;* צָרַע, Lev. xiii. 44, 45; xiv. 3; xxii. 4; Num. v. 2. מְצֹרָע, Lev. xiv. 2; 1 Sam. iii. 29; 2 Kings v. 1, &c.

צִרְעָה, f. three times, Exod. xxiii. 28; Deut. vii. 20; Josh. xxiv. 12. LXX. τὰς σφηκίας, τὴν σφηκίαν. Vulg. *crabrones*. Syr. ܙܒܘܪܐ. *Wasps, hornets*. See Hieroz., ii. p. 534.

צָרַעַת, f. aff. צָרַעְתּוֹ. *The leprosy*, Lev. xiii. 2, &c.; 2 Kings v. 3. It is applied to a corrosive appearance in garments and on the walls of houses, Lev. xiii. 47, &c.; xiv. 34, &c.

צָרַף, v. pres. יִצְרֹף. Constr. immed. (a) *Refined* metals. (b) *Purified* a person's character. (c) *Tried* a person's character. (a) Jer. vi. 29. (b) Is. i. 25. (c) Judg. vii. 4; Ps. xvii. 3; lxvi. 10, &c.
Infin. צְרוֹף, (a) Ps. lxvi. 10; Jer. vi. 29. (b) Dan. xi. 35.
Imp. צָרְפָה, Ps. xxvi. 2.
Part. צֹרֵף, aff. צֹרְפָם, pl. צֹרְפִים. *A refiner; a goldsmith, silversmith*, Judg. xvii. 4; Neh. iii. 8; Is. xl. 19.
Part. pass. צְרוּפָה, f. צְרוּפָה. *Purified, pure*, 2 Sam. xxii. 31; Ps. xii. 7; xviii. 31; cxix. 140; Prov. xxx. 5.
Niph. pres. יִצָּרְפוּ. *Shall be purified*, Dan. xii. 10.
Pih. part. מְצָרֵף, i. q. צֹרֵף, Mal. iii. 2, 3.

צָרַר, v. Arab. صَرَّ, *constrinxit, nodavitque crumenam;* صُرَّة, *crumena;* ضَرَّ, *nocuit, noxâ affecit*. (a) *Tied* or *bound up*. (b) *Acted hostilely to, vexed, distressed*. (c) *Was crowded, straightened for room*. (d) Impers. with לְ, *Was distressed, suffered grief, anxiety*, or *doubt*. (a) Pret. צָרַר, Job xxvi. 8; Prov. xxx. 4; Hos. iv. 19. (b) Pret. id., Num. xxxiii. 55; Ps. cxxix. 1, 2. Pres. יָצַר, Is. xi. 13. (c) Pres. תֵּצַר, Prov. iv. 12; Is. xlix. 19. (d) Pret. צַר, pres. יֵצֶר, and הֵצַר, Gen. xxxii. 7; Judg. ii. 15; x. 9; 1 Sam. xxviii. 15, &c.
Infin. צְרוֹר, (a) Prov. xxvi. 8. (b) Lev. xviii. 18; Num. xxv. 17.
Imp. צוּר, (a) Is. viii. 17.
Part. צֹר, aff. צֹרְרֵי, pl. צֹרְרִים, &c. (b) Num. x. 9; Esth. iii. 10; Ps. vii. 5.
Part. pass. צָרוּר, fem. צְרוּרָה, pl. צְרֻרוֹת. (a) Exod. xii. 32; 1 Sam. xxv. 29; 2 Sam. xx. 3; Hos. xiii. 12.
Puh. part. pl. מְצֹרָרִים. Pass. of Kal. (a) Josh. ix. 4.
Hiph. הֵצַר, pres. יָצַר, צָרוּ. With לְ, causat. of Kal. (d) *Distressed*, Deut.

צרו—ק | (521) | צרו—קבו

xxviii. 52; 1 Kings viii. 37; 2 Chron. vi. 28, &c.

Infin. הָצֵר, 2 Chron. xxviii. 22; xxxiii. 12. Part. f. מְצֵרָה. *In labour*, Jer. xlviii. 40; xlix. 22.

צְרוֹר, m. pl. צְרוֹרוֹת. *Tying up.* (a) *A bundle.* (b) *A bundle* or *bag* of money. (c) Dimin. of צור. *A small stone; a particle, grain.* (a) 1 Sam. xxv. 29; Job xiv. 17; Cant. i. 13. (b) Gen. xlii. 35; Prov. vii. 20; Hag. i. 6. (c) 2 Sam. xvii. 13; Amos ix. 9.

ק

ק, *Kóph*, is the nineteenth letter of the Hebrew alphabet, and as a numeral stands for a hundred. It occasionally interchanges with ג, and כ, letters of the same class, and sometimes with ע.

קֹא, m. aff. קֵאוֹ, i. q. קִיא. *A vomit*, Prov. xxvi. 11.

קָאַת, f. with the article הַקָּאַת, constr. קָאַת. The name of a water-bird: according to Bochart. the word is used both for *the pelican* and *the heron*, Lev. xi. 18; Deut. xiv. 17; Ps. cii. 7; Is. xxxiv. 11; Zeph. ii. 14. Hieroz., tom. ii. p. 292.

קַב, m. constr. קַב. A measure, containing, it is said, the sixth part of a סְאָה, 2 Kings vi. 25. Arab. قاب, *quantitas, spatium;* قَوْب, *capax et amplus,* de vase.

קבב, v. pret. aff. קַבֹּה, pres. aff. תִּקֳּבֶנּוּ. Constr. immed. Cogn. נָקַב, i. q. נָקַב, sign. (g). *Cursed,* Num. xxiii. 8. 25. 27.

Infin. לֹב, Num. xxiii. 11. 25; xxiv. 1. Imp. קֳבָה, aff. קָבְנוֹ, Num. xxii. 11. 17; xxiii. 13. With נ parag.

קֵבָה, fem. once, Deut. xviii. 3. Arab. قَبًا, *edit cibum;* قِبَّة, and قَبَّة, *echinus,* i. e. *stomachi pars pelliculata.* The stomach.

קֻבָּה, fem. Arab. قُبَّة, *fornix; tabernaculum.* An alcove; a recess, place of retirement, tent, Num. xxv. 8. In the latter part of the verse we have, אֶל־הַקֻּבָּה, which has generally been interpreted in reference to the person of the Midianitish woman, but most probably refers to the place where both persons were killed, and therefore should be translated *in her tent,* i. e. the tent into which Zimri had brought her.

קִבּוּץ, masc. pl. aff. קִבּוּצַיִךְ, r. קבץ. *An assembly, a company, troop,* Is. lvii. 13.

קְבוּרָה, f. constr. קְבֻרַת, קִבְרָת, aff. קְבֻרָתוֹ, קְבוּרָתָם, קְבוּרָתָהּ, r. קבר. (a) *Burial.* (b) *A burial-place.* (a) 2 Chron. xxvi. 23; Jer. xxii. 19. (b) Gen. xxxv. 20; Deut. xxxiv. 6; 1 Sam. x. 2, &c.

קְבָל, masc. קְבָל, aff. קְבָלוֹ. Arab. قَبَل, and قُبَل, *antica pars et prior;* قَبِلَ, *acceptavit, admisit rem.* The front; before, 2 Kings xv. 10; Ezek. xxvi. 9.

קבל, v. Pih. קִבֵּל, pres. יְקַבֵּל. Constr. immed. *Turned the face towards, looked favourably on.* (a) *Accepted,* a person, a present, or advice. (b) *Received from another, took.* (c) *Took on himself, undertook.* (a) 1 Chron. xii. 18; Esth. iv. 4; Job ii. 10. (b) 2 Chron. xxix. 16. 22; Ezra viii. 30. (c) Esth. ix. 23. 26.

Imp. קַבֵּל, 1 Chron. xxi. 11; Prov. xix. 20. Hiph. part. pl. f. מַקְבִּילוֹת. *Taking hold of,* Exod. xxvi. 5; xxxvi. 12.

קבל, v. Chald. Pah. קַבֵּל, pres. pl. יְקַבְּלוּן, *Id. Received, took,* Dan. ii. 6; vi. 1; vii. 18.

קֳבֵל, קֳבָל, Chald. *The front.* (a) לָקֳבֵל, לְקָבֵל, [1] *In front of.* [2] *In consideration of, in consequence of.* (b) כָּל־קֳבֵל דְּנָה, *All before that,* i. e. *wholly in consequence of that, for this reason, therefore.* (c) כָּל־קֳבֵל דִּי, *Because.* (a), [1] Dan. ii. 31; iii. 3; v. 1. 5. [2] Ezra iv. 16; vi. 13; Dan. v. 10. (b) Ezra vii. 17; Dan. ii. 12. 24, &c. (c) Ezra iv. 14; vii. 14; Dan. ii. 8, &c.

קבע, v. pres. יִקְבַּע. Cogn. חבא. Constr. immed. Arab. قَبَعَ, *abdidit caput suum; reliquit socios vir; abiit in regionem.* Con-

3 X

קבע (522) קבר

cealed himself from another; forsook, neglected him, Prov. xxii. 23; Mal. iii. 8. The LXX. give the word the signification of deceived. Vulg. figet. Syr. ܣܒ, fixit.

Part. pl. קֹבְעִים, aff. קֹבְעֵיהֶם, Prov. xxii. 23; Mal. iii. 8, 9.

קִבְעַת, f. constr. Arab. قَبْعَة, calyx, folliculus florum. A cup, drinking-cup, Is. li. 17. 22.

קָבַץ, v. pres. יִקְבֹּץ. Constr. immed. Arab. قَبَضَ, cepit rem manu. II. Collegit. Took hold of; collected, gathered together, persons or things, Gen. xli. 48; Judg. xii. 4; 1 Kings xx. 1, &c.

Infin. aff. קָבְצִי, Zeph. iii. 8.

Imp. קְבֹץ, pl. קִבְצוּ, 1 Sam. vii. 5; 1 Kings xviii. 19, &c.

Part. קֹבֵץ, Prov. xiii. 11; Ezek. xxii. 19.

Part. pass. pl. קְבוּצִים, Neh. v. 16.

Niph. נִקְבַּץ, pres. יִקָּבֵץ. Pass. of Kal. Was gathered together; they assembled themselves, Josh. x. 6; 1 Sam. vii. 6; Ezek. xxix. 5, &c.

Infin. הִקָּבֵץ, Esth. ii. 8, &c.

Imp. pl. הִקָּבְצוּ, Gen. xlix. 2, &c.

Part. pl. נִקְבָּצִים, aff. נִקְבָּצָיו, Is. lvi. 8; Jer. xl. 15.

Pih. קִבֵּץ, pres. יְקַבֵּץ. (a) I. q. Kal. (b) Acquired. (a) Deut. xxx. 3; Is. xi. 12; xxxiv. 16, &c. (b) Mic. i. 7.

Infin. קַבֵּץ, aff. קַבְּצִי, Is. lxvi. 18; Zeph. iii. 20, &c.

Imp. aff. קַבְּצֵנוּ, Ps. cvi. 47.

Part. מְקַבֵּץ, Is. xiii. 14, &c.

Puh. part. f. מְקֻבֶּצֶת. Pass. of Pih., Ezek. xxxviii. 8.

Hith. הִתְקַבֵּץ, pres. יִתְקַבֵּץ. I. q. Niph. Assembled themselves, Josh. ix. 2; Judg. ix. 47, &c.

Imp. הִתְקַבְּצוּ, Jer. xlix. 14.

קְבֻצָה, fem. constr. קְבֻצַת. A collection, heap, Ezek. xxii. 20.

קָבַר, m. aff. קִבְרוֹ, pl. קְבָרִים, constr. קִבְרֵי, aff. קִבְרֵינוּ, קִבְרֵיהֶם, and קְבָרוֹת, constr. קִבְרוֹת, aff. קִבְרֹתָיו. Arab. قَبَرَ, inhumavit; قَبْرٌ, sepulcrum. Syriac and Æth. Id. Burying. A burial-place, sepulchre, Gen. xxiii. 4. 6; L. 5; Exod. xiv. 11; Neh. iii. 16; Job xxi. 32; Jer. viii. 1, &c.

קָבַר, v. pres. יִקְבֹּר. Constr. immed. Buried, Gen. xxiii. 19; Deut. xxxiv. 6, &c.

Infin. קָבוֹר, קְבֹר, aff. קָבְרִי, Gen. xxiii. 8; L. 14; Deut. xxi. 23, &c.

Imp. קְבֹר, pl. קִבְרוּ, Gen. xxiii. 15; xlix. 29, &c.

Part. קֹבֵר, pl. קֹבְרִים, 2 Kings ix. 10; xiii. 21; Ps. lxxix. 3.

Part. pass. קָבוּר, pl. קְבֻרִים, 1 Kings xiii. 31; Eccl. viii. 10.

Niph. pres. יִקָּבֵר. Pass. of Kal, Jer. xxii. 19; xxv. 33, &c.

Pih. pres. aff. תְּקַבְּרֵם, Hos. ix. 6.

Infin. קַבֵּר, 1 Kings xi. 15.

Part. מְקַבֵּר, pl. מְקַבְּרִים, Num. xxxiii. 4; Jer. xiv. 16, &c.

Puh. קֻבַּר. Pass. of Pih., Gen. xxv. 10.

קָדַד, v. pres. יִקֹּד. See קָדַר. Bowed his head, as a mark of reverence, or in worship, Gen. xxiv. 26; Exod. iv. 31; 1 Kings i. 16. 31, &c.

קִדָּה, f. An aromatic used in the preparation of the sacred oil, and usually interpreted Cassia, Exod. xxx. 27; Ezek. xxvii. 19. See Celsii Hierobot., tom. ii. p. 185.

קַדְמֹנִים, pl. masc. once, Judg. v. 21; r. קדם. The ancients. So the LXX.

קָדוֹשׁ, and קָדֹשׁ, m. constr. קְדוֹשׁ, aff. קְדֹשִׁי, &c.; pl. קְדֹשִׁים. Arab. قَدَسَ, purus fuit. Holy, pure from moral or ceremonial defilement. Applied, (a) To God, who is infinitely holy in himself, and whose will is the standard of holiness in others. (b) To holy spirits. (c) To persons; [1] Holy in their lives. [2] Invested with a sacred character. (d) To things; sacred, set apart to God. (a) Lev. xi. 44, 45; Ps. xxii. 4; xcix. 9; Is. vi. 3, &c. (b) Job v. 1; xv. 15; Dan. viii. 13. (c), [1] Lev. xix. 2; xx. 7; Ps. lxxxix. 6, &c. [2] Exod. xix. 6; Lev. xxi. 8; Deut. xxviii. 9, &c. (d) Exod. xxix. 31; Lev. vi. 9; x. 13, &c. קְדוֹשׁ יִשְׂרָאֵל, a title of Jehovah, as being especially the God of the Israelites; to whose service they were dedicated, and whose name and institutions they were bound to hallow, Ps. lxxi. 22; Is. i. 4; x. 20, &c.

קָדַח, v. קָדְחָה. Arab. قَدَحَ, extundere instituit ignem ex igniario. (a) Struck, or kindled a fire. (b) A fire was kindled. (a) Jer. xvii. 4. (b) Deut. xxxii. 22; Jer. xv. 14.

קדה (523) קדם

Infin. קֹדַח, Is. lxiv. 1.
Part. pl. constr. קֹדְחֵי, Is. l. 11.

קַדַּחַת, f. *A fever,* Lev. xxvi. 16; Deut. xxviii. 22.

קָדִים, masc. r. קדם. *What is before.* Hence (see אָחוֹר), (a) *The east.* (b) *The east wind.* (a) Ezek. xl. 19; xliii. 17; xlvii. 18, &c. (b) קָדִימָה, *Eastward,* Ezek. xi. 1; xlv. 7, &c. (b) Gen. xli. 6; Exod. x. 13; Jer. xviii. 17, &c.

קַדִּישׁ, m. Chald. pl. קַדִּישִׁין, constr. קַדִּישֵׁי, i. q. קָדוֹשׁ. *Holy,* signn. (a), (b), and (c). (a) Dan. iv. 5, 6. 15; v. 11. (b) Ib. iv. 10. 20. (c) Ib. vii. 18. 21, 22. 25. 27.

קֶדֶם, m. Arab. قِدَمْ, *præcessit;* قُدُمٌ, *tempus antiquum.* Syr. ܩܕܡ, *ante, coram.* *What precedes,* in place or time. (a) *Before,* in place. (b) *The east,* [1] מִקֶּדֶם, *On the east.* [2] לְמִקֶּדֶם, *On the east of.* (c) *Former time.* (d) *Antiquity.* (e) יְמֵי קֶדֶם, *Former ages.* (f) יָמִים מִקֶּדֶם, *Id.* (g) *Formerly.* (h) מִקֶּדֶם, [1] *Id.* [2] *From former generations.* (i) מִקַּדְמֵי־אָרֶץ, *From the beginning of the world.* (a) Ps. cxxxix. 5. (b) Gen. x. 30; xxv. 6; Is. ii. 6, &c. [1] Gen. ii. 8; xii. 2, &c. [2] Gen. iii. 24; Josh. vii. 2; Ezek. xi. 23, &c. (c) Job xxix. 2. (d) Deut. xxiii. 15; Ps. lxviii. 34. (e) Ps. xliv. 2; lxxiv. 2; Is. xxiii. 7, &c. (f) Ps. lxxvii. 6; cxliii. 5. (g) Jer. xxx. 20; Lam. v. 21. (h), [1] Neh. xii. 46. [2] Ps. lxxiv. 12; lxxvii. 12; Is. xlv. 21, &c. (i) Prov. viii. 23. Hence, קֵדְמָה, *Eastward,* Gen. xxv. 6; Exod. xxvii. 13; xxxviii. 13, &c.

קדם, v. Kal non occ.
Pih. קִדַּמְתִּי, pres. יְקַדֵּם. Constr. immed. (a) *Preceded,* in place, abs. (b) *Came before,* into the presence of; met with presents or offerings. (c) *Came upon,* or *against,* hostilely. (d) *Came before* a place. (e) *Preceded,* in time. (f) *Hastened, was early.* (a) Ps. lxviii. 26; lxxxix. 15. (b) Deut. xxiii. 5; Neh. xiii. 2; Ps. lxxxviii. 14; Is. xxi. 14; Mic. vi. 6. (c) 2 Sam. xxii. 6. 19; Job xxx. 27. (d) 2 Kings xix. 32. (e) Ps. cxix. 148. (f) Ps. cxix. 147. Imp. קַדְּמָה, (c) Ps. xvii. 13.

קֳדָם, Chald. i. q. קֶדֶם, aff. קֳדָמַי, קֳדָמָךְ, קֳדָמָיִךְ, קֳדָמוֹהִי. (a) *Before:* [1] *In the presence of.* [2] *In the judgment of.* (b) מִן קֳדָם, [1] *From the presence of.* [2] *By command of.* [3] *From the power of.* (a), [1] Dan. ii. 10, 11. 24, 25, &c. [2] Dan. iii. 32; vi. 2. (b), [1] Dan. ii. 15; vii. 10, &c. [2] Ezra vii. 14. [3] Dan. v. 19; vi. 26.

קִדְמָה, fem. constr. קִדְמַת, aff. קִדְמָתָהּ, קִדְמָתָן, קַדְמָתְכֶן; pl. aff. קַדְמוֹתֵיכֶם. (a) *Former condition.* (b) *Beginning, origin.* (c) *Before,* in time. (a) Ezek. xvi. 55; xxxvi. 7. (b) Is. xxiii. 7. (c) Ps. cxxix. 6.

קַדְמָה, f. Chald. קַדְמַת. *Former state* or *time.* מִן קַדְמַת, and מְקַדְמַת. *Before,* Ezra v. 1; Dan. vi. 11.

קֵדְמָה, f. constr. קֵדְמַת, i. q. קֶדֶם. *Eastward of,* Gen. ii. 14; iv. 16; 1 Sam. xiii. 5; Ezek. xxxix. 11.

קַדְמוֹן, fem. קַדְמוֹנָה. *Eastern,* Ezek. xlvii. 8.

קַדְמוֹנִי, m. pl. קַדְמוֹנִים, f. קַדְמוֹנִיּוֹת. (a) *Eastern.* (b) *Former, ancient.* (c) Fem. pl. *Former things.* (a) Ezek. x. 19; xi. 1; xlvii. 18; Joel ii. 20; Zech. xiv. 8. (b) 1 Sam. xxiv. 13; Ezek. xxxviii. 17; Job xviii. 20. (c) Is. xliii. 18; Mal. iii. 4.

קַדְמַי, pl. def. קַדְמָיֵא, fem. def. קַדְמָיְתָא, pl. def. קַדְמָיָתָא. *First, former,* Dan. vii. 4. 8. 24.

קָדְקֹד, m. aff. קָדְקְדֵךְ, קָדְקֳדוֹ, קָדְקֳדוֹ. *The crown of the head,* Deut. xxviii. 35; xxxiii. 20; 2 Sam. xiv. 25, &c. Arab. قَدَّ, *dissecuit; per longum secuit;* مَقَدٌّ, *locus æqualis; pars occipitis inter aures.*

קָדַר, v. Arab. قَذَرَ, *immundus et spercus fuit, sorduit.* Cogn. كَدَرَ, *impurus turbidusque fuit* liquor, color; كَبَرَ, *Id.* *Incommodis et adversæ fortunæ casibus turbata fuit* vita. (a) *Was dark, black, was darkened, was blackened.* (b) Metaph. *Was gloomy, distressed.* (a) Jer. iv. 28; Joel ii. 10; iv. 15; Mic. iii. 6. (b) Jer. viii. 22; xiv. 2. Part. קֹדֵר, pl. קֹדְרִים. (a) Job xxx. 28. (b) Job v. 11; vi. 17; Ps. xxxv. 14; xxxviii. 7; xlii. 10; xliii. 2.

Hiph. הִקְדַּרְתִּי, pres. אַקְדִּיר. Causat. of Kal. *Made dark,* Ezek. xxxi. 15; xxxii. 7, 8.

Hith. הִתְקַדְּרוּ. *Became dark,* 1 Kings xviii. 45.

קדר (524) קדש

קַדְרוּת, f. *Darkness*, Is. L. 3.

קְדֹרַנִּית, adv. *Gloomily, mournfully*, Mal. iii. 14.

קֹדֶשׁ, masc. aff. קָדְשִׁי, קָדְשְׁךָ, קָדְשׁוֹ, קֹדֶשׁ; pl. קָדָשִׁים, and קֳדָשִׁים, constr. קָדְשֵׁי, aff. קָדָשַׁי, קֳדָשֶׁיךָ, and קֳדָשָׁיו, קָדְשֵׁיכֶם, קָדְשֵׁיהֶם. (a) *Holiness*. (b) *Any thing* or *place consecrated* to God, *holy*. (c) *Any person consecrated* to God: as, [1] The priests and Levites; [2] The Israelites. (d) Following a noun in construction, i. q. קָדוֹשׁ, *Holy*. (e) הַקֹּדֶשׁ, *The Holy Place, the Sanctuary*. (f) קֹדֶשׁ הַקֳּדָשִׁים, *The Holy of Holies*, the *Most Holy Place*, [1] in the Tabernacle, [2] In the Temple. (g) קֹדֶשׁ קָדָשִׁים, *Most holy*. (a) Exod. xv. 11; Amos iv. 2, &c. (b) Exod. xxix. 33, 34; xxx. 37; xxxi. 14, &c. (c), [1] 2 Chron. xxiii. 6; Ezra viii. 28. [2] Deut. xxxiii. 2; Jer. ii. 3. (d) Exod. iii. 5; xii. 16; xvi. 23, &c. (e) Exod. xxvi. 33; xxviii. 29. 35, &c. (f), [1] Exod. xxvi. 33; Num. iv. 19; 1 Chron. vi. 34. [2] 1 Kings viii. 6; 2 Chron. iii. 8. 10; v. 7. (g) Exod. xxix. 37; xxx. 10. 29. 36, &c.

קָדַשׁ, v. pres. יִקְדַּשׁ. (a) *Was hallowed, consecrated*, abs. (b) Constr. immed. Either, *Rendered sacred*, by contact, or *was set apart from*. (a) Exod. xxix. 21. 37; Num. xvii. 2; 1 Sam. xxi. 6, &c. (b) Is. lxv. 5. See Exod. xxix. 37.

Niph. נִקְדַּשׁ, pres. יִקָּדֵשׁ. (a) *Was rendered holy*. (b) *Was reverenced*. (a) Exod. xxix. 43. (b) Lev. x. 3; xxii. 32; Ezek. xx. 41, &c.

Infin. aff. הִקָּדְשִׁי, (b) Ezek. xxvi. 23; xxxviii. 16.

Pih. קִדַּשׁ, pres. יְקַדֵּשׁ. Constr. immed. (a) *Hallowed, consecrated, set apart*, a person or thing. (b) *Reverenced*. (c) *Regarded as sacred, kept holy*. (d) *Rendered sacred*, by contact. (e) *Purified*, by religious rites. (f) *Appointed* a religious service. (g) *Prepared* a person or thing. (a) Gen. ii. 3; Exod. xxviii. 41; Lev. xvi. 19; Num. vi. 11, &c. (b) Deut. xxxii. 51. (c) Lev. xxv. 10; Jer. xvii. 22; Ezek. xliv. 24, &c. (d) Ezek. xliv. 19. (e) Exod. xix. 14; 1 Sam. xvi. 5; Job i. 5, &c. (g) Mic. iii. 5. Comp. sign. (e).

Infin. קַדֵּשׁ, aff. קַדְּשׁוֹ, קַדְּשָׁם, Exod. xx. 5; xxix. 1; Lev. viii. 11, &c.

Imp. קַדֵּשׁ, pl. קַדְּשׁוּ, (a) Exod. xiii. 2. (e) Josh. vii. 13. (f) 2 Kings x. 20; Joel i. 14. (g) Jer. vi. 4.

Part. מְקַדֵּשׁ, aff. מְקַדְּשׁוֹ, מְקַדִּשְׁכֶם, Exod. xxxi. 13; Lev. xxi. 15; Ezek. xxxvii. 28, &c.

Puh. Part. מְקֻדָּשׁ, pl. מְקֻדָּשִׁים, aff. מְקֻדָּשָׁי. Pass. of Pih., 2 Chron. xxvi. 18; xxxi. 6; Ezra iii. 5; Is. xiii. 3; Ezek. xlviii. 11.

Hiph. הִקְדִּישׁ, pres. יַקְדִּישׁ. I. q. Pih. signn. (a), (b), (e), and (g). (a) Lev. xxvii. 14; Deut. xv. 19; 2 Sam. viii. 11, &c. (b) Is. viii. 14; xxix. 23. (e) 2 Chron. xxix. 19. (g) Zeph. i. 7.

Infin. הַקְדִּישׁ, הַקְדִּישׁ, aff. הַקְדִּישִׁי, הַקְדִּישׁוֹ, (a) Judg. xvii. 3; 1 Chron. xxiii. 13; 2 Chron. ii. 3. (b) Num. xx. 12; xxvii. 14. (g) Jer. xii. 3.

Part. מַקְדִּישׁ, pl. מַקְדִּישִׁים, (a) Lev. xxii. 2; xxvii. 15.

Hith. הִתְקַדֵּשׁ, pres. יִתְקַדֵּשׁ. (a) *Caused himself to be reverenced*. (a) A religious ceremony *was celebrated*. (c) *Purified himself* by religious rites. (d) *Kept himself from pollution*. (a) Ezek. xxxviii. 23. (c) 2 Chron. v. 11; xxx. 3. 17, &c. (d) Exod. xix. 22; Lev. xiii. 44; xx. 7, &c.

Infin. הִתְקַדֵּשׁ, (b) Is. xxx. 29. (c) 2 Chron. xxix. 34.

Imp. plur. הִתְקַדְּשׁוּ, (c) 1 Chron. xv. 12; xxix. 5.

Part. f. מִתְקַדֶּשֶׁת, pl. מִתְקַדְּשִׁים, (a) Is. lxvi. 17. (c) 2 Sam. xi. 4.

קָדֵשׁ, m. pl. קְדֵשִׁים, fem. קְדֵשָׁה, pl. קְדֵשׁוֹת. (a) *A Catamite*; or, probably, *a priest of Baal-Peor*. (b) Fem. *A prostitute*. (a) Deut. xxiii. 18; 1 Kings xiv. 24; xv. 12; 2 Kings xxii. 46; xxiii. 7; Job xxxvi. 14. (b) Gen. xxxviii. 21, 22; Deut. xxiii. 18; Hos. iv. 14.

קהה, v. pres. תִּקְהֶינָה. Arab. قَهِيَ, *non appetivit, fastidivit* cibum. *Were set on edge*, of the teeth, Jer. xxxi. 29, 30; Ezek. xviii. 2.

Pih. קֵהָה. *Became blunt*, of an instrument, Eccl. x. 10.

קָהָל, masc. constr. קְהַל, aff. קְהָלָה, קְהַלְכֶם. Syr. ܩܗܠܐ, *collegit*. (a) *A meeting*. (b) *An assemblage of persons*. (c) *A multitude*. (d) הַקָּהָל, *The general assembly of the Israelites*; apparently the whole people: called also, [1] קְהַל עַם הָאֱלֹהִים; [2] קְהַל יְהוָה; [3] קְהַל יִשְׂרָאֵל; [4] קְהַל עֲדַת יִשְׂרָאֵל; [5] קְהַל עֲדַת בְּנֵי יִשְׂרָאֵל. (a) Deut. ix. 10; x. 4;

קהל (525) קוב

xviii. 16; Judg. xxi. 8, &c. (b) 1 Kings viii. 65; 2 Chron. xxx. 13; Ezra x. 1, &c. (c) Gen. xxxv. 11; xlviii. 4; Ezek. xxxviii. 4. 15, &c. (d) Lev. iv. 14; xvi. 33; Num. x. 7, &c. [1] Num. xx. 4; xxiii. 2—4, &c. [2] Judg. xx. 2. [3] Lev. xvi. 17; Deut. xxxi. 30, &c. [4] Judg. xii. 6. [5] Num. xiv. 5.

קָהַל, v. Kal non occ.
Niph. נִקְהֲלוּ, pres. יִקָּהֵל. *Assembled themselves,* Exod. xxxii. 1; Num. xvi. 3; Esth. ix. 16, &c.
Infin. הִקָּהֵל, Num. xvii. 7; Esth. viii. 11.
Part. pl. נִקְהָלִים, Ezek. xxxviii. 7.
Hiph. הִקְהִלַת, pres. יַקְהִיל. Causat. of Niph. *Called together, summoned,* Exod. xxv. 1; Num. viii. 9; Job xi. 10, &c.
Infin. הַקְהִיל, Num. x. 7.
Imp. הַקְהֵל, pl. הַקְהִילוּ, Num. xx. 8; Deut. xxxi. 28, &c.

קְהִלָּה, f. constr. קְהִלַּת, i. q. קָהָל, Deut. xxxiii. 4; Neh. v. 7.

קֹהֶלֶת, m. Part. act. of קהל, with ת of unity. See lett. ה (b) above: once, Eccl. vii. 27, as fem.: but which should, perhaps, be read אָמַר הַקֹּהֶלֶת. See lxx. vr. 28. Singular, excellent, *Preacher,* applied to Solomon, Eccl. i. 1, 2. 12, &c.

קָו, and קַו, m. aff. קַוִּם. *A thing stretched out; a line, cord.* (a) *A measuring-line.* (b) *A boundary-line.* (c) *A limit, rule, doctrine,* to direct the conduct. (a) 1 Kings vii. 23; 2 Chron. iv. 2; Ezek. xlvii. 3, &c. (b) Job xxxviii. 5; Is. xxxiv. 17. In Ps. xix. 5, sign. (c), appears quite applicable. Gesenius, however, takes the φθόγγος of the lxx.; and supposes that the word is to be interpreted as *a string of a harp,* and hence its *sound.* But, in this case also, we may take it as a distinct word, and compare the Arab. قَوَّى, *clamavit.* Some suppose that קוֹלָם is the true reading. In Is. xviii. 2. 7, we have גּוֹי קַו־קָו, to which three suitable interpretations may be given. (1) If Egypt is meant, *A land marked out by lines, i. e.* cut up by canals. (2) If Judea is meant, *A land of rule upon rule,* i. e. of precept upon precept. (3) *A land of great desolation.* Comp. Arab. قَوِيَ, *hominibus vacua fuit* domus; قَوَاء, *desertum, deserta* terra. lxx. ἔθνος ἀνέλπιστον. The second

is to be preferred. Aquila, ὑπομένον. Vulg. *gentem expectatam.* See קוה.

קוֹבַע, m. i. q. כּוֹבַע. *A helmet,* 1 Sam. xvii. 38; Ezek. xxiii. 24, al. non occ.

קוה, v. Syr. ܩܘܝ, *expectavit; mansit, permansit.* Arab. قُوَّة, *robur; potentia; auxilium.* *Looked to, for strength or help; hoped in, waited for.* Constr. immed.
Part. plur. constr. קוֹי, aff. קוֹיְ, קֹוֶיךָ, קוֹי, Ps. xxv. 3; xxxvii. 9; lxix. 7; Is. xl. 30; xlix. 23; Lam. iii. 25.
Niph. נִקְוּו, pres. יִקָּוּ. See קו. (a) *Were bounded, limited;* were collected within a boundary. (b) *Were collected.* (a) Gen. i. 9. (b) Jer. iii. 17.
Pih. קִוָּה, pres. יְקַוֶּה, apoc. יְקַו. Constr. immed. it. med. אֶל, לְ. Intens. of Kal. (a) *Looked or hoped for, trusted in, expected.* (b) *Watched,* for evil. (a) Gen. xlix. 18; Job iii. 8; vii. 2; Ps. xxv. 5; cxxx. 5, &c. (b) Ps. lvi. 7; cxix. 95.
Infin. קַוֵּה, and קַוֹּה, Ps. xl. 2; Jer. viii. 15; xiv. 19.
Imp. קַוֵּה, Ps. xxvii. 14; xxxvii. 34; Prov. xx. 22.

קוֹחַ, see פְּקַחְקוֹחַ, Is. lxi. 1.

קוט, v. קָט, pres. אָקוּט. Constr. abs. it. med. בְּ. I. q. קוּץ. *Was wearied of, loathed, scorned,* Ps. xcv. 10; Ezek. xvi. 47.
Niph. נְקוֹטוֹתֶם, נָקֹטוּ. *Were loathed,* Ezek. vi. 9; xx. 43; xxxvi. 31.
Hith. pres. in pause, אֶתְקוֹטָט. I. q. Kal, Ps. cxix. 158; cxxxix. 21.

קוט, v. pres. יָקוּט. Arab. قَبَض, r. قبض, *ruptus fuit.* *Is* (about to be) *broken,* Job viii. 14.

קוֹל, m. aff. קוֹלִי, &c.; pl. קוֹלוֹת. Arab. قَالَ, r. قول, *dixit;* قَوْل, *dictum, verbum.* Syr. ܩܠܐ, *vox.* (a) *Voice:* [1] Of man. [2] Of God. (b) *Sound* or *cry* of animals. (c) *Sound,* [1] Of words. [2] Of inanimate things. [3] Of shouting, rejoicing, or weeping. (d) Pl. קוֹלוֹת, [1] *Thunder.* [2] *Sound* of water. (e) קוֹל גָּדוֹל, *A loud voice or noise.* (f) רָם ק', *Id.* (g) יְהוָֹה ק', *Thunder.* (h) נָתַן ק', *Uttered a sound, lifted up his voice* (i) נָתַן בְּקוֹל, *Id.* (k) שָׁמַע בְּקוֹל, *Listened to the words of.* (l) שָׁמַע לְקוֹל, *Id.* (m) לְ הֶעֱבִיר קוֹל, *Made a proclamation,* in the phrr. [1] נָתַן קוֹל, *Id.* (a),

קוּם (526) קוּם

[1] Gen. xxvii. 2; Judg. xviii. 3; 1 Sam. xxvi. 17, &c. [2] Deut. xviii. 16; xxvi. 4; Is. vi. 8, &c. (b) 1 Sam. xv. 14; Job iv. 10; Cant. ii. 12. (c), [1] Lev. v. 1; Deut. i. 34; v. 28, &c. [2] Exod. xix. 19; Lev. xxvi. 36; 2 Sam. v. 24; 1 Kings xiv. 6, &c. [3] 1 Sam. iv. 6. 14; Is. xxxiii. 11; lxv. 19; Jer. ix. 18, &c. (d), [1] Exod. ix. 23; xix. 16; 1 Sam. xii. 17, &c. [2] Ps. xciii. 4. (e) Deut. v. 22; 2 Sam. xv. 23; xix. 5, &c. (f) Deut. xxvii. 14. (g) Ps. xxix. 3—5. (h) Ps. lxxvii. 18; civ. 12; Lam. ii. 7, &c. (i) Ps. xlvi. 7; lxviii. 34. (k) 1 Sam. viii. 7; xv. 19, &c. (l) Gen. iii. 17; Exod. xv. 26; 1 Sam. ii. 25, &c. (m), [1] Exod. xxxvi. 6; 2 Chron. xxx. 5; xxxvi. 22, &c. [2] 2 Chron. xxiv. 9.

קוּם, v. pret. קָם (once קָאם, Hos. x. 14), pres. יָקוּם, קָם, apoc. יָקֹם. Arab. قَامَ, r. قوم, stetit, surrexit. Syr. and Æth. Id. Arose, stood. Constr. abs. it. med. בְּ, אֶל, עַל. (a) Rose up. (b) Arose from bed. (c) Rose from a place of ambush or secrecy. (d) With עַל, אֶל, or בְּ, Arose against, in anger or hostility. (e) Stood up. (f) Lying down or sitting, being the ordinary position of rest; Arose, denotes the commencement of any undertaking, whether journey or not. (g) Existed, came into being, made his appearance. (h) Took place. (h) Stood. (i) Stood firm against an enemy. (k) Stood, remained firm, was of force, of a promise or resolution. (l) Was secured, was permanent, of property or an office. (m) Was fixed, incapable of action, of the eyes. (a) 2 Sam. xii. 21; 1 Kings viii. 54; Esth. vii. 7; Job vii. 4, &c. (b) 1 Kings iii. 21; Job vii. 4; Eccl. xii. 4, &c. (c) Deut. xix. 11; Josh. viii. 19; 1 Sam. xx. 41, &c. (d) Gen. iv. 8; 2 Sam. xiv. 7; Ps. xxvii. 12; Is. xiv. 22; Mic. vii. 6, &c. (e) Exod. xxxiii. 10; Lev. xix. 32; 2 Kings xiii. 21; Esth. v. 9, &c. (f) Deut. xxvii. 8; xxxi. 16; 1 Sam. xvii. 48; 2 Sam. xxiii. 10, &c. (g) Num. xxiv. 17; Deut. xxxiv. 10; Judg. v. 7; 2 Kings xxiii. 25, &c. (h) Gen. xli. 30; Prov. xxiv. 22. (i) Neh. ix. 4. (k) Lev. xxvii. 14; Num. xxx. 5; Deut. xix. 15; Jer. li. 29, &c. (l) Lev. xxv. 30; xxvii. 19; 1 Sam. xxiv. 20; Job xv. 29, &c. (m) 1 Sam. iv. 15; 1 Kings xiv. 4.

Infin. קוּם, aff. קוּמִי, קוּמְךָ, קוּמוֹ, קוּמָה, קָמָה, Gen. xix. 33. 35; xxxi. 35; Deut. vi. 7; Is. ii. 19; Zeph. iii. 8. (i) Josh. vii. 12, 13.

Imp. קוּם, קָם־, קוּמָה, f. קוּמִי; pl. קוּמוּ, קָמוּ, f. קְמֶנָה, Gen. xiii. 17; xix. 14; xxi. 18; Num. x. 35; Deut. ii. 13; Josh. vii. 10; Is. xxxii. 9, &c.

Part. pl. קָמִים, קוֹמִים, aff. קָמַי, קָמֶיךָ, קָמָיו, קָמֵינוּ, קָמֵיהֶם. Always in sign. (d), either with עַל, or with aff., Exod. xv. 7; xxxii. 25; Deut. xxxiii. 11; 2 Sam. xxii. 40; 2 Kings xvi. 7; Ps. iii. 2; xliv. 6, &c.

Pih. has two forms: I. קִיֵּם, pres. אֲקַיֵּמָה. Causat. of Kal, signn. (i) and (k). (a) Strengthened, supported. (b) Kept a resolution, confirmed an engagement. (c) Fixed a time. (b) Ps. cxix. 106. (c) Esth. ix. 27. 31, 32.

Infin. קַיֵּם, (b) Ruth iv. 7; Ezek. xiii. 6. (c) Esth. ix. 21. 29. 31.

Imp. aff. קַיְּמֵנִי, (a) Ps. cxix. 28.

II. Pres. יְקוֹמֵם. (a) Set up, rebuilt, restored. (b) Set himself up. (a) Is. xliv. 26; lviii. 12; lxi. 4. (b) Mic. ii. 8.

Hiph. הֵקִים, pres. יָקִים, apoc. יָקֵם, יָקֶם. Constr. immed. Causat. of Kal. Caused to arise or stand, raised up, set up. (a) Caused to rise up. (b) Raised up a fallen person or thing. (c) Strengthened. (d) Set up, placed, fixed. (e) Brought into being, brought forward, raised up, appointed. (f) Made or confirmed a covenant. (g) Confirmed, [1] An engagement. [2] In authority. [3] A kingdom, or throne. (k) Put in force. (a) Gen. xlix. 9; 2 Kings ix. 2; Is. xiv. 9, &c. (b) Eccl. iv. 10; Amos x. 11. (c) Ps. lxxxix. 44. (d) Exod. xxvi. 30; xl. 18; Num. xxx. 14, 15; Josh. iv. 9. 20; Prov. xxx. 4; Ezek. xxvi. 8, &c. (e) Josh. v. 7; Judg. ii. 18; 1 Kings xiv. 14; Jer. xxix. 15, &c. (f) Gen. vi. 18; ix. 17; Exod. vi. 4; Ezek. xvi. 60, &c. (g), [1] Num. xxx. 14, 15. [2] 2 Sam. vii. 12; 1 Chron. xvii. 11. [3] 1 Kings ix. 5; 2 Chron. vii. 18. (k) Gen. xxvi. 3; 1 Sam. xv. 11. 13; Jer. xxxiv. 18, &c.

Infin. הָקִים, הָקֵם, aff. הֲקִימוֹ, Num. ix. 15; Deut. xxii. 4; 2 Sam. xii. 17, &c.

Imp. הָקֵם, aff. הֲקִימֵנִי, plur. הָקִימוּ, Gen. xxxv. 8; Ps. xli. 11; Jer. li. 12, &c.

Part. מֵקִים, aff. מְקִימִי, מְקִימָהּ, Gen. ix. 9; Ps. cxiii. 7; Amos v. 2, &c.

Hoph. הֻקַם, הוּקַם, Pass. of Hiph. signn. (d), (e), and (g), Exod. xl. 17; 2 Sam. xxiii. 1; Jer. xxxv. 14.

Hith. part. aff. מִתְקוֹמְמִי, fem. מִתְקוֹמֲמָה; pl. מִתְקוֹמֲמִים, aff. מְתְקוֹמְמֵי. I. q. Kal, sign. (d), Job xx. 27; xxvii. 7; Ps. xvii. 7; lix. 2.

קוֹם, v. Chald. קָם, pres. יְקוּם. I. q. Heb. signn. (a), (b), (f), (g), (h), and (l). (a) Dan. iii. 24. (b) Dan. vi. 20. (f) Ezra v. 2. (g) Dan. ii. 39; vii. 17. 24. (h) Dan. vii. 10. (l) Dan. ii. 44.

Imp. f. קוּמִי, Dan. vii. 5.

Part. קָאֵם, pl. קָאֲמִין, def. קָאֲמַיָּא, Dan. ii. 31; iii. 3; vii. 16.

Pah. Infin. קַיָּמָה. I. q. Pih., (b) Dan. vi. 8.

Aph. הֲקֵים, aff. הֲקִימֵהּ, and אֲקִימֵהּ, pres. יְקִים, and יְהָקִים. I. q. Hiph. (a) Set up. (b) Established. (c) Appointed. (d) Confirmed. (a) Dan. iii. 1—3. 7, &c. (b) Dan. ii. 44. (c) Ezra vi. 18; Dan. iv. 14; v. 11. 21, &c. (d) Dan. vi. 9.

Infin. aff. הֲקָמוּתַהּ, (c) Dan. vi. 4.

Part. מְקִים, (c) Dan. ii. 21.

Hoph. הֳקַמַת. Pass. of Aph. Was set up, Dan. vii. 4.

קוֹמָה, f. constr. קוֹמַת, aff. קוֹמָתְךָ, קוֹמָתוֹ, קוֹמָתָם, קוֹמָתָהּ. Height, [1] Of a person. [2] Of a thing. [1] 1 Sam. xvi. 7; xxviii. 20; Cant. vii. 8. [2] Gen. vi. 15; Exod. xxv. 10; 1 Kings vii. 26; Ezek. xxxi. 14, &c. כָּל־קוֹמָה, persons of all heights, Ezek. xiii. 18.

קוֹמְמִיּוּת, adv. At full height, erect, Lev. xxvi. 13.

קוּן, v. See קִינָה.

Pih. קוֹנֵן, pres. יְקוֹנֵן. Constr. immed. it. med. עַל, אֶל. Uttered a funeral or mourning lamentation; lamented, 2 Sam. i. 17; iii. 33; 2 Chron. xxxv. 25; Ezek. xxvii. 32; xxxii. 16.

Part. pl. fem. מְקוֹנְנוֹת. Mourning women, who were hired at funerals to express, by loud lamentations, the sorrow of the relatives, Jer. ix. 16. See Matt. ix. 23.

קוֹף, m. pl. קוֹפִים. I. q. Sans. कपि. Pers. كپی, and κῆπος. Apes, 1 Kings x. 22; 2 Chron. ix. 21.

קוּץ, v. קַצְתִּי, pres. אָקֻץ, תָּקֹץ, apoc. יָקֹץ. Constr. med. בְּ, מִפְּנֵי. I. q. קוּט. (a) Was wearied of, loathed. (b) Hated. (c) As a ground of dislike, Feared. (a) Gen. xxvii. 46; Lev. xx. 23; Num. xxi. 5; Prov. iii. 11. (b) 1 Kings xi. 25. (c) Exod. i. 12; Num. xxii. 3.

Part. קָץ, (c) Is. vii. 16.

Hiph. pres. aff. נְקִיצֶנָּה, Is. vii. 6.

קוּץ, or קִיץ, v. Kal non occ.

Hiph. הֵקִיץ, pres. יָקִיץ. I. q. יָקַץ. (a) Awoke, intrans. (b) Was awake. (c) Arose from the sleep of death, came to life. (d) Roused himself, was vigilant, active. (a) Ps. iii. 6; Prov. xxiii. 35; Is. xxix. 8, &c. (b) Prov. vi. 22. (c) 2 Kings iv. 31; Job xiv. 12; Jer. li. 39, &c.

Infin. הָקִיץ, Ps. xvii. 15; lxxiii. 20.

Imp. הָקִיצָה, pl. הָקִיצוּ, (b) Ps. xlix. 24; lix. 6; Is. xxvi. 19, &c.

קוֹץ, m. pl. קוֹצִים, constr. קוֹצֵי. According to Celsius, A generic name for thorny plants, a thorn-bush, Gen. iii. 18; Exod. xxii. 5; 2 Sam. xxiii. 6; Judg. viii. 7. 16, &c.; Hierobot., ii. 223.

קוּצּוֹת, pl. f. aff. קְוֻצּוֹתַי. Syr. ܩܵܨ̈ܐ, cincinni. Arab. قُصَّة, capillus frontis. Locks, of hair, Cant. v. 2, only.

קוּר, v. קַרְתִּי. Cogn. נקר, and כור. Dug a well, 2 Kings xix. 24; Is. xxxvii. 25.

Hiph. הֵקִיר. A well threw up water; produced abundantly, Jer. vi. 7.

Infin. הָקִיר, Ibid.

Pih. redup. קִרְקֵר. (a) Dug down a wall. (b) Destroyed a people. (b) Num. xxiv. 17.

Part. מְקַרְקֵר, (a) Is. xxii. 5.

קוֹרֵא, see קרא.

קוֹרָה, f. aff. קֹרָתִי, pl. קֹרוֹת, r. קרה. (a) A beam. (b) A roof. (a) 2 Kings vi. 2. 5; 2 Chron. iii. 7; Cant. i. 17. (b) Gen. xix. 8.

קוּרִים, pl. m. constr. קוּרֵי, constr. קוּרֵיהֶם. Arab. قور, planta gossipii; gossipium novum; funis è gossipio. Threads, Is. lix. 5, 6.

קוֹשׁ, v. pres. יָקוֹשׁוּן, i. q. יקשׁ. Ensnared, Is. xxix. 21, only.

קֶטֶב, m. Cogn. קצב, חצב, חטב. Cutting, cutting down; destruction, Deut. xxxii. 24; Ps. xci. 6; Is. xxviii. 2.

קֶטֶב, m. aff. קָטָבְךָ, Id., Hos. xiii. 14.

קְטוֹרָה, fem. r. קטר. Incense, Deut xxxiii. 10.

קָטַל, masc. Arab. قَتَل, amputavit, succidit. Syr. ܩܛܠ, interfecit. Arab. قتل, and Æth. ፈተለ: Id. Cutting: killing. Slaughter, Obad. 9.

קָטַל, v. pres. תִּקְטֹל. Constr. immed.

קטל (528) קטר

Slew, Job xiii. 15; xxiv. 14; Ps. cxxxix. 19, al. non occ.

קטל, v. Chald. *Id.*

Part. קָטֵל, Dan. v. 19.

Peil, קְטִיל, קְטִילַת, pass. *Was slain*, Dan. v. 30; vii. 11.

Ithpe. Infin. הִתְקְטָלָה, *Id.*, Dan. ii. 13.

Pah. קַטֵּל. I. q. Kal, Dan. iii. 22.

Infin. קַטָּלָה, Dan. ii. 14.

Ithpa. part. plur. מִתְקַטְּלִין. Pass., Dan. ii. 13.

קָטֹן, masc. constr. קְטֹן. *Small*, in size, quantity, or importance; *young*, Gen. xlii. 13; 1 Sam. ii. 19; xv. 17; xx. 35; 1 Kings iii. 7; 2 Chron. xxi. 17; Is. liv. 7, &c.

קָטָן, m. aff. קְטַנָּם, fem. קְטַנָּה, pl. קְטַנִּים, constr. קְטַנֵּי, fem. קְטַנּוֹת. *Id.*, Gen. ix. 24; Num. xxii. 18; 1 Sam. ix. 21; 2 Kings ii. 23; Ps. civ. 25; Jer. vi. 13, &c.

קָטֹן, v. קָטֹנְתִּי, pres. יִקְטֹן. *Was small; was of little importance*, Gen. xxxii. 10; 2 Sam. vii. 19; 1 Chron. xvii. 17.

Hiph. Infin. הַקְטִין. Causat. of Kal. *Made small*, Amos viii. 5.

קֹטֶן, m. aff. קָטְנִי, and קָטְנִּי. *The little finger*, 1 Kings xii. 10; 2 Chron. x. 10.

קָטַף, v. pres. אֶקְטֹף. Cogn. חטף, קטב. Arab. قطف, *vindemiavit, decerpsit uvas.* Syr. ܩܛܦ, *Id. Plucked off*, a branch, ears of corn, Deut. xxiii. 26; Ezek. xvii. 4. 22.

Part. pl. קְטֻפִים, Job xxx. 4.

Niph. pres. יִקָּטֵף. *Was cut off; withered*, Job viii. 12.

קָטַר, v. Kal non occ. Arab. قتر, *nidorem exhalavit assa caro*, &c.; قتار, *nidor, odor.* Cogn. عطر, *aroma. Emitted an odour.* Part. pass. f. pl. קְטֻרוֹת.

In Ezek. xlvi. 22, הַחֲצֵרוֹת קְטֻרוֹת, has been variously translated. (1) Taking קטר in its usual acceptation; *smoky*, from the fires made in them. (2) Taking קטר in its Chaldee sense, i. q. Heb. קשר, *joined, united, covered in.*

Pih. קִטֵּר, pres. יְקַטֵּר. *Raised an odour by burning*. (a) *Burned incense*, constr. abs. it. immed. it. with ל, of the object of worship. (b) *Fumigated*, constr. immed. (c) *Burned* fat, constr. immed. (a) 2 Kings xvi. 4; xxiii. 8; Is. lxv. 7, &c.

Infin. קַטֵּר, Jer. xi. 13. 17, &c. (b) Amos iv. 5. (c) 1 Sam. ii. 16.

Part. plur. מְקַטְּרִים, fem. מְקַטְּרוֹת, 2 Kings xviii. 4; Jer. xliv. 15, &c.

Puh. Part. f. מְקֻטֶּרֶת. Pass. of Pih. *Was perfumed*, Cant. iii. 6.

Hiph. הִקְטִיר, pres. יַקְטִיר, apoc. יַקְטֵר. (a) *Burned* incense. (b) *Burned* a sacrifice. (c) *Burned incense* or *sacrifices.* (a) Exod. xxx. 7; xl. 27; 2 Chron. xxix. 7. (b) Lev. i. 9; ii. 2; ix. 10, &c. (c) 2 Chron. xxviii. 3; Hos. ii. 15.

Infin. הַקְטִיר, Exod. xxx. 20, &c.

Imp. הַקְטֵר, 2 Kings xvi. 15.

Part. מַקְטִיר, pl. מַקְטִירִים, f. מַקְטִירוֹת, 1 Kings iii. 3; xi. 8; xiii. 20, &c.

Hoph. pres. תָּקְטַר. Pass. of Hiph., Lev. vi. 15.

Part. מֻקְטָר, Mal. i. 11.

קְטָר, m. *Incense*, Jer. xliv. 21, only.

קְטַר, masc. pl. קִטְרִין, constr. קִטְרֵי. Syr. ܩܛܪ, *ligavit. Joints, ligatures, knots, difficulties*, Dan. v. 6. 12. 16.

קְטֹרֶת, f. aff. קְטָרְתִּי. *Incense*, whether of (1) Spices, or (2) Fat. (1) Exod. xxx. 1. 7; xxxi. 11; Ezek. xvi. 18, &c. (2) Ps. lxvi. 15.

קִיא, m. aff. קִיאוֹ. Arab. قَيْء, r. قي, *vomuit.* Æth. ፀእከ: *Id. Vomiting. A vomit*, Is. xix. 14; xxviii. 8; Jer. xlviii. 26.

קִיא, v. pret. fem. קָאָה, pres. יָקִיא, תָּקִיא. Constr. immed. it. abs. (a) *Vomited, threw up.* (b) Metaph. *Expelled with disgust.* (a) Job xx. 15; Prov. xxiii. 8; Jonah ii. 11. (b) Lev. xviii. 25. 28; xx. 22.

Imp. pl. קִיוּ, (a) Jer. xxv. 27.

Hiph. pret. aff. הֲקִאֻתוֹ, *Id.*, Prov. xxv. 16.

קַיִט, m. Chald. i. q. Heb. קַיִץ. *Summer*, Dan. ii. 35.

קִיטוֹר, masc. r. קטר. (a) *Smoke.* (b) *Vapour.* (a) Gen. xix. 28; Ps. cxix. 83. (b) Ps. cxlviii. 8.

קִים, m. aff. קִימָנוּ, r. קום. *Rising up. One that rises up; an adversary*, Job xxii. 20. See קום, sign. (d), part.

קְיָם, m. Chald. r. *Id. Any thing established; a decree*, Dan. vi. 8. 16.

קִים, masc.—fem. קָיְמָה, Chald. r. קום. Enduring, steadfast, Dan. iv. 23; vi. 27.

קִימָה, f. aff. קִימָתָם, r. Id. *The act of rising up*, Lam. iii. 63.

קִימוֹשׁ, see קִמּוֹשׁ.

קִין, m. aff. קִינוֹ. Arab. قَنَاة, *canna et hasta.* *A cane, spear made of cane; a spear,* 2 Sam. xxi. 16.

קִינָה, fem. pl. קִינוֹת, aff. קִינוֹתֵיהֶם, r. קון. *A lamentation for the dead*, 2 Sam. i. 17; 2 Chron. xxxv. 25; Ezek. ii. 10; xxxv. 25, &c. Syr. ܩܺܝܢܬܳܐ, *canticum.* Arab. قَانَ, r. قين, *collegit in unum rem dispersam, recteque composuit.* II. *Compsit et adornavit.* The original idea appears to be an enumeration of the excellencies of the deceased, and a setting off of his character to the greatest advantage. The Irish have both the thing and name in their *caoine*, pron. *keene*.

קַיִץ, m. aff. קֵיצֵךְ. Arab. قَاظَ, r. قيظ, *admodum ferbuit*, uti *mediâ æstate dies; æstiva habuit;* قَيْظ, *media æstas*. Syr. ܩܰܝܛܳܐ, *æstas, æstus*. (a) *Summer.* (b) *Summer fruits.* (a) Gen. viii. 22; Ps. xxxii. 4; lxxiv. 17; Prov. vi. 8, &c. (b) 2 Sam. xvi. 1, 2; Is. xvi. 9; Jer. xl. 10. 12, &c.

קִיץ, v. pret. קוץ. *Spent the summer, summered*, Is. xviii. 6, only.

קִיצוֹן, m.—f. קִיצוֹנָה, from קֵץ. *The last,* Exod. xxvi. 4. 10; xxxvi. 11. 17.

קִיקָיוֹן, m. *The Palma Christi, ricinus communis,* called in Egypt κίκι, Jonah iv. 6. 9, 10. See Celsii Hierob., ii. p. 273.

קִיקָלוֹן, m. once, Hab. ii. 16. According to Ewald, for קְלָקְלוֹן, r. קלל, or קלה. *Contempt, shame.* LXX. ἀτιμία. But Vulg. *vomitus ignominiæ,* as if for קִיא קָלוֹן. Auth. Vers. *Shameful spewing.*

קִיר, m. pl. קִירוֹת, aff. קִירוֹתָיו, קִירוֹתֶיהָ. (a) *A wall,* [1] Of a city. [2] Of a house. (b) *Side* of an altar. (c) Pl. *Sides* of the heart. (d) Probably *A city.* See קִרְיָה. (a), [1] Num. xxxv. 4; Josh. ii. 15. [2] 1 Sam. xix. 10; 1 Kings vi. 5; 2 Kings iv. 10; Ezek. xli. 13. 22, &c. (b) Exod. xxx. 3;

Lev. i. 15; v. 9, &c. (c) Jer. iv. 19. (d) Is. xv. 1; xvi. 7. The etymology of this word is doubtful. Possibly it may be derived from קור, i. q. נקר, and כרה, and may originally have meant *a ditch and rampart*, and hence any *wall* of a town, and subsequently the *wall* of a house; just as our word *wall* is derived from *vallum.*

קַיתְרֹס, Chald. i. q. κίθαρις. *A harp,* Dan. iii. 5. 7. 10. 15. Syr. ܩܺܝܬܳܪܳܐ, *Id.*

קַל, m.—fem. קַלָּה, pl. קַלִּים, r. קלל. (a) *Swift,* Job xxiv. 18; Eccl. ix. 11; Is. xix. 1; Jer. ii. 23, &c. (b) *Swiftly,* Is. v. 26; Joel iv. 4. (c) קַל בְּרַגְלָיו, *Swift-footed,* 2 Sam. ii. 18; Amos ii. 15.

קָל, m. Chald. i. q. Heb. קוֹל. (a) *A voice.* (b) *A sound.* (a) Dan. iv. 28; vi. 21. (b) Dan. iii. 5. 7. 10, 11; vii. 11.

קלה, v. Kal non occ. Syr. ܩܠܳܐ, *contempsit.* Arab. قَلَي, *odit.* Cogn. קלל. *Despised, thought lightly of.*

Niph. נִקְלָה. *Was despised,* Deut. xxv. 3; Is. xvi. 14.

Part. נִקְלֶה. *Despised, of little importance, mean,* 1 Sam. xviii. 23; Prov. xii. 9; Is. iii. 5.

Hiph. Part. מַקְלֶה. I. q. Kal, Deut. xxvii. 16.

קָלָה, v. Syr. ܩܠܳܐ, *frixit.* Æth. ፀለወ: and Arab. قَلَي, *Id. Roasted;* burnt alive, Jer. xxix. 22.

Part. pass. קָלוּי, Lev. ii. 14; Josh. v. 11.

Niph. part. נִקְלֶה, Ps. xxxviii. 8. Apparently *A burning disease.*

קָלוֹן, m. constr. קְלוֹן, aff. קְלוֹנֵךְ. (a) *Worthlessness; base conduct.* (b) Consciousness of unworthiness, *shame, confusion.* (c) *Contempt,* from others. (d) *Pudenda.* (a) Prov. xviii. 3; Hos. iv. 18. (b) Job x. 15; Ps. lxxxiii. 17. (c) Prov. iii. 35; vi. 33; ix. 7. (d) Jer. xiii. 26; Nah. iii. 5.

קַלַּחַת, fem. twice, 1 Sam. ii. 14; Mic. iii. 3. *A vessel for boiling, a caldron.* The etymology is uncertain.

קלט, v. only in part. pass. קָלוּט. Arab. قَلَص, *valde brevis;* قَلْط, *deformitas;* قَلَص, *contractus, diminutus fuit.* Either *Dwarfish* or *defective,* Lev. xxii. 23. LXX. κολοβόκερκον.

3 Y

קְלִי (530) קְלָם

קָלִי, masc. r. קלה. *Corn roasted in the ear,* which was a common kind of food, Lev. xxiii. 14; Ruth ii. 14; 1 Sam. xxv. 18; 2 Sam. xvii. 28.

קָלִיא, m. *Id.*, 1 Sam. xvii. 17.

קָלַל, v. קָלוֹת, קֻלִּי, pres. יֵקַל, (sign. b). Arab. قَلَّ, *paucus, imminutus fuit.* Syr. ܩܠ, and Æth. ፀለለ: *Id. Was or became small* in quantity, weight, or importance. (a) *Was diminished, became shallow.* (b) *Was swift.* (c) *Was worthless, unworthy.* (a) Gen. viii. 8. 11. (b) 2 Sam. i. 23; Job vii. 6; ix. 25; Jer. iv. 13; Hab. i. 8. (c) Job xl. 4; Nah. i. 14.

Niph. נָקַל, pres. אֵקַל תֵּקַל. (a) *Was thought a small* or *easy thing.* (b) *Was thought worthless, was despised.* (c) *Lowered himself.* (d) *Became easy.* (a) 2 Kings iii. 18; xx. 10; Is. xlix. 6, &c. (b) Gen. xvi. 4, 5; 1 Sam. ii. 3. (c) 2 Sam. vi. 22. (d) Prov. xiv. 6.

Pih. קִלֵּל, pres. יְקַלֵּל. Constr. immed. it. med. בְּ. *Spoke contemptuously of, reviled, declared worthless, wished ill to,* Lev. xx. 9; 1 Sam. xvii. 43; 2 Sam. xvi. 9. 13; Eccl. vii. 22, &c.

Infin. קַלֵּל, aff. קִלְלִי קִלֶּלְךָ, Deut. xxiii. 5; 2 Sam. xvi. 7; Neh. xiii. 2.

Imp. קַלֵּל, 2 Sam. xvii. 10.

Part. מְקַלֵּל, aff. מְקַלֶּלְךָ, plur. מְקַלְלִים, Gen. xii. 3; Exod. xxi. 17; 1 Sam. iii. 13; Eccl. vii. 21, &c.

Puh. pres. יְקֻלַּל. Pass. of Pih., Job xxiv. 18; Is. lxv. 20.

Part. pl. aff. מְקֻלָּלָיו, Ps. xxxvii. 22.

Pih. redup. קִלְקֵל. (a) I. q. Arab. قَلْقَلَ, *commovit* rem. *Shook* the arrows, in divining, constr. med. בְּ, Ezek. xxi. 26. (b) Probably *Lightened* of rust, *polished ; sharpened,* Eccl. x. 10. But LXX. ἐτάραξε.

Hiph. הֵקַל, pres. יָקֵל. (a) *Slighted, treated as of little weight.* (b) *Lightened,* or *removed* a load. (a) 2 Sam. xix. 44; Ezek. xxii. 7.

Infin. הָקֵל, (b) Jonah i. 5.

Imp. הָקֵל, (b) 1 Kings xii. 4. 9, 10, &c.

Hith. redup. הִתְקַלְקְלוּ. Pass. of Pih. redup. *Was shaken,* Jer. iv. 24.

קָלָל, m. *Polished, shining,* Ezek. i. 7; Dan. x. 6.

קְלָלָה, f. constr. קִלְלַת, aff. קִלְלָתוֹ קִלְלָתְךָ,

pl. קְלָלוֹת. (a) *Reviling.* (b) *A curse.* (c) *The object of reviling* or *cursing.* (a) 2 Sam. xvi. 22; 1 Kings ii. 8. (b) Deut. xxvii. 13; xxviii. 15; xxix. 27, &c. (c) Deut. xxi. 23; Jer. xxvi. 6; Zech. viii. 13, &c.

קֶלֶס, m. *Scorn, contempt,* Ps. xliv. 14; Jer. xx. 8.

קָלַס, v. Kal non occ.

Pih. Infin. קַלֵּס. *Mocked, scorned,* Ezek. xvi. 31.

Hith. pres. יִתְקַלֶּס, plur. יִתְקַלְּסוּ. Constr. med. בְּ. *Id.,* 2 Kings ii. 23; Ezek. xxii. 5; Hab. i. 10.

קַלָּסָה, fem. i. q. קֶלֶס. *Scorn, contempt,* Ezek. xxii. 4.

קֶלַע, m. aff. קַלְעוֹ, pl. קְלָעִים, constr. קַלְעֵי. Arab. قَلَعَ, *loco dimovit, vel extraxit, evulsit;* قَلِعَ, *instabilis fuit ;* قِلْع, *velum navis ;* مِقْلَاع, *funda. Removing, plucking out, whirling.* (a) *A sling.* (b) *A curtain,* from its tremulous motion. (a) 1 Sam. xvii. 40. 50; xxv. 29; 2 Chron. xxvi. 14; Job xli. 19; Zech. ix. 15. (b) Exod. xxvii. 9. 11, 12. 14; xxxv. 17, &c.

קָלַע, v. constr. immed. (a) *Cut out, carved.* (b) *Slung.* (c) Metaph. *Threw out,* as with a sling ; *expelled.* (a) 1 Kings vi. 29. 32. 35.

Part. קֹלֵעַ, (b) Judg. xx. 16. (c) Jer. x. 18.

Pih. pres. יְקַלֵּעַ. *Slung* a stone, 1 Sam. xvii. 49; xxv. 29.

קַלָּע, m. pl. קַלָּעִים. *A slinger,* 2 Kings iii. 25.

קַלְקַל, masc. r. קלל, once, Num. xxi. 5. Either *Worthless,* or *unsubstantial* food.

קִלְּשׁוֹן, masc. once, 1 Sam. xiii. 21. שְׁלֹשׁ קִלְּשׁוֹן, *A pitchfork.* The etymology is uncertain. Some take קלשׁ, to be identical in signification with לקשׁ, *gathered.* Comp. Arab. قَلَشَ, *percussit, jecit ; vestigium impressit.*

קָמָה, fem. constr. קָמַת, pl. קָמוֹת, r. קום. *Standing corn,* pec. *corn in the ear,* Deut. xxiii. 26; Judg. xv. 5; 2 Kings xix. 26; Hos. viii. 7, &c.

קִמּוֹשׁ, and קִימוֹשׁ, m. *The nettle,* Is.

קמח (531) קנא

xxxiv. 13; Hos. ix. 6. See Celsii Hierobot., ii. 206.

קֶמַח, m. Arab. قَمْح, triticum. *Flour*, of any kind, Gen. xviii. 6; Num. v. 15; 2 Sam. xvii. 28; Is. xlvii. 2; Hos. viii. 7, &c.

קמט, v. pres. aff. תְּקַמְּטֵנִי. Syr. ܡܥܟܠ, *corrugatus, maculatus est;* ܡܥܟܠܐ, *ruga, macula.* Arab. قَمَطَ, *constrinxit fune;* قِمْط, *funis.* Either *Covered with wrinkles,* or *bound as a captive* or *criminal,* Job xvi. 8. See my note.

Puh. קֻמְּטוּ. Pass. of Kal. Either *Became wrinkled, withered away,* or *were seized and carried away,* Job xxii. 16, al. non occ.

קָמַל, v. twice, Is. xix. 6; xxxiii. 9. Syr. ܡܥܟܠ, *ægrotavit, infirmatus est;* ܡܥܟܠܐ, *mucor panis. Withered.*

קמץ, masc. aff. קָמְצוֹ, pl. קְמָצִים. Arab. قَمَزَ, *collegit, cepitque extremis digitis;* قُمْزَة, *manipulus. Grasping in the hand.* (a) *The hand.* (b) *A handful.* (c) לִקְמָצִים, *In abundance.* (a) Lev. vi. 8. (b) Lev. ii. 2; v. 12. (c) Gen. xli. 47.

קָמַץ, v. constr. immed. (a) *Grasped, took up in the hand,* Lev. ii. 2; v. 12; Num. v. 26.

קִמְשׁוֹנִים, plur. masc. *Nettles,* Prov. xxiv. 31. Hierobot. Cels., ii. 206.

קֵן, m. קָן, aff. קִנִּי, pl. קִנִּים. (a) *A nest.* (b) *A dwelling.* (c) *Family.* (d) Pl. *Cells, chambers.* (a) Deut. xxii. 6; Job xxxix. 27; Ps. lxxxiv. 4; Is. xvi. 2, &c. (b) Num. xxiv. 21; Jer. xlix. 16, &c. (c) Job xxix. 18. (d) Gen. vi. 14.

קנא, v. Kal non occ.

Pih. קִנֵּא, pres. יְקַנֵּא. (a) *Was jealous of* a wife, constr. immed. (b) *Envied.* (c) *Rendered jealous, provoked.* (d) *Was jealous for.* (a) Num. v. 14. (b), [1] Constr. immed., Gen. xxvi. 14; Is. xi. 13; Ezek. xxxi. 9. [2] Med. בְּ, Gen. xxx. 1; Ps. xxxvii. 7; Prov. iii. 31, &c. [3] Med. לְ, Ps. cvi. 16. (c) Deut. xxxii. 21; 1 Kings xiv. 22. (d) Num. xxv. 13; 1 Kings xix. 10. 14; Zech. i. 14, &c.

Infin. קַנֹּא, aff. קַנְאוֹ, קַנְאוֹ, Num. xxv. 11; 2 Sam. xxi. 2; 1 Kings xix. 10. 14.

Part. מְקַנֵּא, Num. xi. 29.

Hiph. pres. יַקְנִיא. *Make jealous* or *angry,* Deut. xxxii. 16. 21; Ps. lxxviii. 58.

Part. מַקְנִיא, for מַקְנֶה, Ezek. viii. 3.

קנא, v. Chald. pres. תִּקְנֵא, i. q. Heb. קָנָה. *Acquired, procured,* Ezra vii. 17.

קַנָּא, m. *Jealous,* applied to God only, and in reference to idolatry, Exod. xx. 5; xxxiv. 14; Deut. iv. 24; v. 9; vi. 15.

קִנְאָה, fem. constr. קִנְאַת, aff. קִנְאָתִי, pl. קְנָאוֹת. (a) *Jealousy.* (b) *Envy.* (c) *Anger.* (d) *Zeal.* (a), [1] In a husband, Num. v. 14, 15; Prov. vi. 34; Cant. viii. 6. [2] In God, Num. xxv. 11; xxix. 20; Ezek. viii. 3. 5, &c. (b) Job v. 2; Is. xi. 13. (c) Is. xlii. 13; Zeph. iii. 8. 18, &c. (d) 2 Kings x. 16; Ps. lxix. 10; Zech. i. 14, &c.

קָנֶה, m. constr. קְנֵה, pl. קָנִים, constr. קְנֵי. it. fem. aff. קָנָם. Syr. ܩܢܐ, *calamus aromaticus, mensorius,* &c. Arab. قَنَاة, *canna, hasta; siphon, &c.* Engl. *Cane.* (a) *Reed* or *cane,* of lakes, &c., 1 Kings xiv. 15; Is. xix. 6; Job xl. 21. (b) *Sweet* or *aromatic* —, Exod. xxx. 23; Is. xliii. 24; Jer. vi. 20; Ezek. xxvii. 19. In Ps. lxviii. 31, חַיַּת קָנֶה, *beast of the reed,* i. e. bearing the precious article for offerings to God. Comp. the context, and see חַיָּה, p. 193 above. LXX. τοῖς θηρίοις τοῦ καλάμου. (c) *Measuring* —, *rod* or *perch,* of six cubits, Ezek. xl. 3: see Ib. xli. 8. (d) *Rod, beam,* of the balance, Is. xlvi. 6. (e) — *stem, stalk,* of wheat, Gen. xli. 5. 22. (f) *Branch* of the candlestick, Exod. xxv. 31. 36; xxxvii. 19. 22: forming a sort of *canal* for conveying the oil to the burners, i. q. צַנְתְּרוֹת Comp. Zech. iv. 12. (g) Also, *The tibia,* or *arm-bone above the elbow,* Job xxxi. 22: see my note. (h) Used also as *a staff* to lean upon: whence the phr. מִשְׁעֶנֶת הַקָּנֶה, *support of a reed,* 2 Kings xviii. 21; Is. xxxvi. 6; Ezek. xxix. 6. Whence, also, קָנֶה רָצוּץ, *a broken reed,* i. e. metaph. a person broken down by over much pressure, Is. xlii. 3. Aff. קָנֶהָ, Job l. c., &c. Whence—

קָנָה, v. pres. יִקְנֶה, apoc. יָקֶן. Arab. قَنَا, r. *creavit* Deus; *acquisivit* sibi. Syr. ܩܢܐ, *profecit.* Æth. ፈጠረ: *domi-*

קנו (532) קנץ

natus est, possedit. Constr. immed. it. med. אֶת, לְ, pers. it. מִן, from, בְּ, instr. (a) *Create, produce,* of God, Gen. xiv. 19. 22; Deut. xxxii. 6; Prov. viii. 22. See דָּבָר above. Thence, (b) *Make, acquire, appropriate,* to self, Gen. iv. 1; Ps. lxxviii. 54, &c. — *by purchase,* Gen. xxv. 10; xxxiii. 19; xlvii. 23; xlix. 30; Lev. xxv. 14. 28; Josh. xxiv. 32; Prov. xx. 14; 2 Sam. xxiv. 24; Jer. xxxii. 9, &c. — *by redemption,* Exod. xv. 16; Is. xi. 11; Neh. v. 16; Ps. lxxiv. 2, &c.

Infin. קְנֹה, Lev. xxv. 14, &c.: it. קְנֹה, Prov. xvi. 16.

קָנוּ, 2 Sam. xxiv. 24. Constr. קְנוֹת, Prov. l. c., &c. Aff. קְנוֹתְךָ, Ruth iv. 5.

Imp. קְנֵה, Gen. xlvii. 19; with נָּא, Ruth iv. 4, &c.

Part. קֹנֶה, Deut. xxviii. 68, &c. Constr. קֹנֵה, Gen. xiv. 19, &c. Aff. קֹנֵהוּ, Lev. xxv. 50, &c.: pl. קֹנֶיהָ, Zech. xi. 5.

Niph. נִקְנָה, pres. pl. יִקָּנוּ. *Was, became, acquired, purchased,* Jer. xxxii. 15. 43, only.

Hiph. pret. aff. הִקְנַנִי. *Appropriated me as a slave* (עֶבֶד, preced.), Zech. xiii. 5, only.

Part. מַקְנֶה. See r. קָנָא. *Provoking to jealousy,* Ezek. viii. 3, only.

קַנּוֹא, m.—pl. non occ. i. q. קַנָּא. *Jealous,* Josh. xxiv. 19; Nah. ii. 2, only.

קְנִזִּי, masc. Patronym. τοῦ קְנַז, Josh. xiv. 6, &c.

קִנְיָן, constr. קִנְיַן, m.—pl. non occ. (a) *Creature.* See קָנָה, (a) Ps. civ. 24, where we have קִנְיָנֶךָ, for קִנְיָנְךָ, in pause. See foot of the page (Heb. Bib.) LXX. κτίσις. Gesen. (b) *Making, acquisition, possession, wealth,* of merchandise, cattle, &c., Gen. xxxiv. 23; xxxvi. 6; Lev. xxii. 11; Ezek. xxxviii. 12, 13; Ps. cv. 21; Prov. iv. 7. Aff. Ps. l. c. Prov. l. c. קִנְיָנָם.

קִנָּמוֹן, m. constr. קִנְמָן, pl. non occ. Gr. κίνναμον, κιννάμωμον. Lat. *cinnamum, cinnamomum.* Copt. κανάμωμον. Herodot. Thalia., cxi. Theophrast., ix. c. 7. See Cels. Hierobot., ii. p. 350, seq. *Cinnamon,* Exod. xxx. 23; Prov. vii. 17; Cant. iv. 14; Rev. xviii. 13. Etym. unknown.

קָנַן, v. Kal non occ. Cogn. קָנָה. Syr. ܐܩܶܢ, *nidificavit.* Cogn. Arab. قَانَ, r. قين, *concinnavit.* See קֵן, below.

Pih. קִנֵּן, pres. תְּקַנֵּן. Constr. abs. *Build*

a nest, a bird, Is. xxxiv. 15; Jer. xlviii. 28; Ezek. xxxi. 6; Ps. civ. 17, al. non occ.

Puh. Part. with pron. 2 pers. fem. aff. מְקֻנַּנְתִּי, Jer. xxii. 23. See Gram. art. 194. 13.

קְצֵי, constr. pl. for קְצֵי, Job xviii. 2. See קֵץ below.

קֶסֶם, masc. pl. קְסָמִים. Syr. ܩܶܣܡܳܐ, *divinatio.* Arab. قَسْم, *consilium, sententia;* قَسَّام, *divinator.* See Pocock. Spec. Hist. Arab., p. 98, seq. *Divination, enchantment,* which among the Arabs, see l. c., was carried on with arrows, Deut. xviii. 10; 2 Kings xvii. 17; Ezek. xiii. 6. 23; xxi. 26; 1 Sam. xv. 23. Meton. *The reward of —,* Num. xxii. 7. In Prov. xvi. 10, *Oath.* Arab. قَسَم, *jusjurandum,* i. e. duly to administer justice, &c., seems to be the meaning. Gesen. "*oraculum.*" LXX. Μαντεῖον.

קָסַם, v. pres. יִקְסֹם, pause, יִקְסֹמוּ, constr. abs. it. med. בְּ, for, it. לְ, pers. for. See קֶסֶם above. *Divine,* with arrows, &c., Ezek. xxi. 26;—2 Kings xvii. 17; Mic. iii. 11; Ezek. xiii. 23:—with familiar spirit, 1 Sam. xxviii. 8.

Infin. קְסֹם, Mic. iii. 6. With Makkáph, קְסָם־, Ezek. xxi. 26, &c.

Imp. f. קָסֳמִי, 1 Sam. l. c.

Part. קֹסְמִים, Deut. xviii. 10. 14, &c. Aff. קֹסְמֵיכֶם, Jer. xxix. 8.

קֶסֶת, f.—pl. non occ. i. q. קָשָׂה. Gesen. in pl. קְשׂוֹת, Num. iv. 7. Æth. ⵞⵌⵓⵓ : *hydria.* Gesen. *An ink-pot,* usually carried in the girdle of a scribe, Ezek. ix. 2, 3. 11, only.

הַקַּעֲקַע, m. once, Lev. xix. 28. Arab. قَعَّ, *incessivit verbis.* IV. *Fodiendo incidit in aquam —;* تَقَعْقَعَ, *validè manducans* dentibus. Cogn. قَاع, r. قوع, *immisit se, incubuit. Mark, impression.* LXX. στικτά.

קְעָרָה, f. constr. קְעָרַת, pl. קְעָרוֹת, constr. קְעָרֹת, aff. קְעָרֹתָי. Arab. قَعَار, *the being deep, &c.* Lit. *Any thing made deep, hollowed out;* whence, قَعْرَان, *profunda scutella. Deep saucer* or *dish,* Num. vii. 13.

קפא (533) קפץ

19, seq. 85. Pl., Num. iv. 7; vii. 84. Aff. Exod. xxv. 29; xxxvii. 16.

קפא, v. pret. קָפְאָה. Syr. ܩܦܐ, *detentus est.* Cogn. ܩܦܐ, *condensatus est.* Arab. قَفَّ, *contracta fuit* res. Cogn. Heb. גבא. *Became hardened, congealed,* of waters, Exod. xv. 8. Of men, — *hardened, stupid,* i. e. senseless, Zeph. i. 12, al. non occ. LXX. καταφρονοῦντας.

Part. pl. קֹפְאִים, Zeph. l. c. with עַל.

Hiph. pres. aff. תַּקְפִּיאֵנִי. *Thou condensest me,* Job x. 10, only. See my note.

קִפָּאוֹן, masc. once, Zech. xiv. 6. See קפא. LXX. πάγος. *Congealing, hardness, denseness.* The place stands thus, לֹא יִהְיֶה אוֹר יְקָרוֹת וְקִפָּאוֹן, which I would translate, *There shall not be the light of things precious, but* (excessive) *denseness, darkness,* i. e. trouble. The prophecy appears to relate to the fall of Jerusalem and the troubles that should follow. See my Sermons and Dissert., page 360, seq. On this sort of language, see my note on Job vi. 16. See also Suidas, under λευκὴ ἡμέρα.

קִפָּדָה, m. with ה, parag. Syr. ܩܦܕ, *corrugatio.* Arab. قَفَدَ, *leviter in occipite percussit.* Cogn. قَفَرَ, *irruit cum impetu. Destruction, ruin,* Ezek. vii. 25, only. Whence—

קפד, v. Kal non occ.

Pih. קִפַּדְתִּי, once, Is. xxxviii. 12. Arab. قَفَدَ, *peregit* opus. Syr. ܩܦܕ. Ethpe. *præcisus est. I have finished, cut short.* Comp. the following verbs. That is, I am brought into the situation of a web cut out of the loom of the weaver prematurely.

קִפֹּד, m.—pl. non occ. Syr. ܩܦܕܐ, Arab. قُنْفُذ, and قُنْفَذ, *erinaceus.* Æth. *histrix. A hedge hog,* Is. xiv. 23; xxxiv. 11; Zeph. ii. 14. Bochart. Hieroz., i. page 1035.

קִפּוֹז, m. once, Is. xxxiv. 15. Arab. قَفَّاز. See Hieroz., pp. 23. 68. *Serpens jaculus. A sort of serpent* that suddenly darts upon its prey. Others take it to signify a sort of owl. LXX. ἐχῖνος: reading קפד, apparently.

קָפַץ, v. pres. יִקְפֹּץ. Arab. قَفَصَ, *pedibus constrinxit* dorcadem, et *constrictum prehendit.* Constr. immed. it. med. אֶת, עַל. *Shut, close up, constrict,* the mouth, hand, metaph., bowels, Deut. xv. 7; Is. lii. 15; Ps. lxxvii. 10; cvii. 42; Job v. 16.

Niph. pres. יִקָּפְצוּן, once, Job xxiv. 24. *They are,—become, shut up.* See my note. Gesen. "*congregatus est.*"

Pih. Part. מְקַפֵּץ, masc. once, Cant. ii. 8. *Leaping,* usually. Arab. قَفَصَ, *agilitas viri; saltitatio.* Comp. מְדַלֵּג, in the paral.

קֵץ, m. pl. constr. only, קִצֵּי, for קִצֵּי, once, Job xviii. 2. Dagesh being resolved into נ, in the Chaldee manner, r. קצץ. Syr. ܩܨ, *convenit.* Cogn. Arab. قَضَى, *decrevit;* قَصَّ, *totondit, præcidit, secuit.* Samar. *desiit, cessavit. End, extremity, limit.* — of space, Is. xxxvii. 24; Jer. l. 26. — time, Gen. viii. 6; xvi. 3; xli. 1: with לְ, prefixed, 2 Chron. xviii. 2; Dan. xi. 6. 13. — of action, condition, &c., Job xvi. 3; Is. ix. 6; Job xxviii. 3; Eccl. xii. 12; Ezek. xxi. 30. 34; xxxv. 5. Pec. *End, cessation,* of the Jewish polity, &c., elsewhere styled, אַחֲרִית הַיָּמִים, Ezek. vii. 2. 6; Dan. viii. 17. 19; ix. 26; xi. 27. See my Sermons and Dissert., p. 356, seq. *End, termination, ruin,* Gen. vi. 13; Ezek. vii. 12; Eccl. xii. 12; Amos viii. 2; Dan. xi. 45, &c. Aff. קִצּוֹ, &c.

קֶצֶב, masc. pl. constr. קִצְבֵי. Arab. قَصَبَ, *dissecuit, amputavit;* قَصَب, noun of action, thrice only, 1 Kings vi. 25; vii. 37. (a) *Cut, form, character,* Jonah ii. 7. קִצְבֵי הָרִים, (b) *Sections, clefts,* of the mountains.

קצב, v. pres. יִקְצֹב. See קָצַב. Constr. immed. *Cut* wood, 2 Kings vi. 6, al. non occ.

Part. pass. fem. pl. קְצוּבוֹת. *Cut, shorn,* of the flock, Cant. iv. 2, only.

קָצָה, fem. plur. קְצוֹת, constr. Arab. قَصَى, *procul distitit; extremitate sua locum conspexit, &c. Extremity, border,* Exod. xxvi. 4; xxxvi. 11. — *limit, &c.* of space, Exod. xxv. 19; xxviii. 23, 24. 26. הָאָרֶץ,— *of the earth,* Is. xl. 28, &c. הַשָּׁמַיִם, — *of the heavens,* Jer. xlix. 36, &c. Metaph.

קָצֶה

Job xxvi. 14. מִקְצוֹת הָעָם, *of the extremities of the people*, i. e. from the least to the greatest, without any regard to the proper tribe, Levi, 1 Kings xii. 31; xiii. 33. Aff. קְצוֹתָיו, Exod. xxv. 19; xxxvii. 8. קְצוֹתָם, Ps. xix. 7, &c.

קָצֶה, m. constr. קְצֵה, pl. aff. קְצֵיהֶם, i. q. קֵץ. *End, extremity, limit*, of space, Exod. xiii. 20; Num. xi. 1; xxxiii. 37; Is. v. 26; vii. 18; xiii. 5; Ps. xix. 7. — of time, Gen. viii. 3; Josh. iii. 2; ix. 16; 1 Kings ix. 10, &c. — of men, &c., i. e. including the whole, Gen. xix. 4; Num. xxii. 41; Is. lvi. 11; Jer. li. 31, &c. Aff. קְצֵהוּ, Gen. xlvii. 2. 21. מִקְצֵה, Dagesh implied, Gram. art. 109: pl. Ezek. xxxiii. 2.

קֵצֶה, m.—pl. non occ. i. q. קָצֶה, Is. ii. 7; Nah. ii. 10; iii. 3—9, only.

קְצוּ, m. pl. constr. only, קְצוֵי, i. q. קֵץ.—

קָצוּ, f. of קַצ, sing. non occ. pl. קְצוֹת.— Is. xxvi. 15; Ps. xlviii. 11; lxv. 6. Arab. قَصْوَ, *extremitas*: to which, קְצוּתָי, Exod. xxxvii. 8; xxxix. 4, ought perhaps to be referred, and pointed, קְצוּתָי. The editions, however, point קְצוֹתָי, with the Keri, Exod. xxxviii. 5; Ps. lxv. 9, only. *Extremities, borders*.

קָצָה, v. Kal non occ. except Infin. See קֵץ, קָצֶה above.

Infin. constr. קְצוֹת. *Cutting off, destroying*, Hab. ii. 10.

Pih. Infin. קַצּוֹת. *Cutting off, short, down*, 2 Kings x. 33, only.

Part. מְקַצֶּה. *Cutting off*, Prov. xxvi. 6, only, which Gesenius renders, "*cui pedes abscissi sunt, is bibit patitur injuriam, sic qui verba mittit per manus stulti.*" But this makes מְקַצֶּה passive. More exactly thus, perhaps, *He who sends words* (a message of good news) *by the hand of a fool, cuts off the feet as to the injured* (לַחֲמָס שֹׁתֶה), i. e. acts as one who provides a swift messenger to relieve the distressed, but, before he dismisses him, cuts off his feet.

Hiph. הִקְצָה, synon. τοῦ יָקַצֵעַ, prec. *Cut, scraped, off*, Lev. xiv. 41, only.

Infin. הַקְצוֹת, Ib. vr. 43, only.

קֶצַח, m.—pl. non occ. Gr. Μελάνθιον, μελανόσπερμον, it. Σπέρμα μέλαν. Lat. *git, gith, nigella*. A sort of *black seed* used as a condiment, not unlike *black pepper*, perhaps.

קָצִי

See Cels. Hierobot., ii. p. 70, seq.; Is. xxviii. 25. 27, only. Aquila, μελάνθιον. See LXX.

קָצִין, m. constr. קְצִין, pl. constr. קְצִינֵי, r. קָצָה. Arab. قَاضٍ, *decrevit*; قَاضِ, *judex*. *Judge, magistrate*, Is. i. 10; iii. 6, 7. *Governor, leader*, Josh. x. 24; Judg. xi. 6. 11; Mic. iii. 1. 9; Dan. xi. 18. Synon. τοῦ שׁוֹפֵט. *Prince, ruler*, Prov. vi. 7; xxv. 15. Aff. קְצִינֵךְ, Is. xxii. 3.

קְצִיעוֹת, f. pl. once, Ps. xlv. 9. Arab. قَصِيعَة. Greek, κασία. *Cassia*. See Cels. Hierobot., ii. p. 360.

קָצִיר, m. constr. קְצִיר, aff. קְצִירוֹ, r. קָצַר. Lit. *Cut, cropped, off*. Thence, (a) *Crop*, as cut down, Lev. xix. 9; xxiii. 22, &c. *Harvest* generally, Gen. viii. 22; xxx. 14; xlv. 6. יְמֵי קָצִיר, *days of* —, Josh. iii. 15; 2 Sam. xxi. 9;—Prov. xxv. 13. יוֹם קָצִיר, — עֵת, *time of* —, Jer. L. 16, &c. (b) *Branches*, as a produce, Ps. lxxx. 12; Job xiv. 9, &c.

קָצַע, v. Kal non occ. Arab. قَصَعَ, *unguibus fricavit*. Cogn. قَصَعَ, *subjugavit, masticavit*. *Scratch, scrape, off*.

Hiph. pres. יַקְצִעַ. Constr. med. מִן. *Scratches, scrapes off*, once, Lev. xiv. 41.

Hoph. part. fem. pl. מְהֻקְצָעוֹת, once, Ezek. xlvi. 22. Lit. *Scraped off, detached things*, i. e. small courts about the Temple.

קָצַף, m.—pl. non occ. Aff. קִצְפִּי, &c. Arab. قَصَفَ, *fregit*; قَصَفَة, *folia arboris* . . . *tenuia*; قَصِيف, *fractus arboris ramus*. Cogn. قُصَابَة, *quicquid de exterioribus ramis abscissum decidit*; قَصَبَ, *amputavit*. (a) *Broken branch, stick*, as seen floating on the face of water, Hos. x. 7. LXX. and Theod. φρύγανον. Symm. ἐπίζεμα, *spuma*; and so usually. (b) *Anger, wrath*, of God, Josh. ix. 20; xxii. 20; Is. xxxiv. 2; lx. 10; Zech. i. 2, &c. — of man, Eccl. v. 16; Esth. i. 18. Phrr. קֶצֶף שֶׁצֶף, *inundation of anger*, Is. liv. 8. בָּא קֶצֶף עַל, *wrath came in upon* —, 2 Chron. xxxii. 26. With אַף, and חֵמָה, Deut. xxix. 28.

קָצַף, v. pres. יִקְצֹף. See קֶצֶף above.

קצף (535) קצר

Arab. قصف, *vehemens sono fuit ventus, et fragore tonitru.* Constr. abs. it. immed. it. med. עַל, אֶל. *Broke out into anger, was angry, wroth; enraged,* Gen. xl. 2; xli. 10; Exod. xvi. 20; Deut. ix. 19; 2 Kings v. 11; Is. lvii. 16; lxiv. 4; Lam. v. 22; Esth. i. 12, &c.

Infin. קְצֹף, Is. liv. 9, only.
Part. קֹצֵף, Zech. i. 15, only.
Hiph. הִקְצִיףְ, pres. plur. יַקְצִיפוּ. Constr. med. אֶת. *Make angry, provoked to anger,* Deut. ix. 7, 8; Ps. cvi. 32.
Infin. הַקְצִיף, Zech. viii. 14, only.
Part. pl. m. מַקְצִיפִים, Deut. ix. 22, only.
Hithp. הִתְקַצֵּף. *Was, became, angry, wroth,* Is. viii. 21, only.

קְצָפָה, fem. once, Joel i. 7. See קֶצֶף above. "*Fractum, fractura*," Gesen. LXX. συγκλασμός. Arab. قصف, *qui languet cum famescit.* Cogn. قضف, *macie extenuatus fuit. Languor, weakness, wasting.* Comp. Is. xxiv. 7, and vr. 12, here. Syr. Vers. ܩܦܘܫܡܐ, *divulsio.*

קָצַץ, v. pres. non occ. See קֵץ above. Constr. med. אֶת. *Cut off,* the hand, beard, Deut. xxv. 12, only.
Part. pl. constr. קְצוּצֵי. *Persons cut of —,* Jer. ix. 25; xxv. 23; xlix. 32, only.
Pih. קִצֵּץ, pres. יְקַצֵּץ. Constr. immed. it. med. אֶת. *Cut off,* as in Kal, Exod. xxxix. 3; Judg. i. 6; 2 Sam. iv. 12; 2 Kings xvi. 7; xxiv. 13; Ps. xlvi. 10, &c.
Puh. Part. pl. מְקֻצָּצִים, Judg. i. 7, only.

קְצַץ, v. Chald. Pah. Imp. once, Dan. iv. 11. קַצִּצוּ. *Cut down,* of a tree.

קֹצֶר, masc. once, in phr. קֹצֶר רוּחַ. Lit. *Cutting off, short, of spirit,* i. e. *impatience,* Exod. vi. 9.

קָצֵר, m. constr. קְצַר, pl. non occ. i. q. קְצַר־רוּחַ, *impatience,* Prov. xiv. 29; Ib. xiv. 17. קְצַר־אַפַּיִם, id. קְצַר יָמִים, *short of days,* Job xiv. 1. Pl. constr. קִצְרֵי, *persons of short, small, power,* 2 Kings xix. 26; Is. xxxvii. 27. The form is, therefore, most probably, קָצֵר, not קַצָּר, as Gesenius, &c., make it; for which he cites Ezek. xlii. 5; but קְצָרוֹת occurs there. The error originated in Buxtorf's Concord., under the v. where we have קְצֻרוֹת given, as occurring in this place.

קָצַר, v. pres. יִקְצַר, הִקְצִיר. Constr. abs. Arab. قصر, *diminuit, abbreviavit. Is, becomes, short, deficient, unable* for —, Is. xxviii. 20; Mic. ii. 7. Comp. Job xxi. 4. הֲקָצַר רוּחַ, *is the spirit shortened, contracted?* See קְצַר רוּחַ above. With יָד, see קִצְרֶיךָ above, Num. xi. 23; Is. L. 2, &c. With נֶפֶשׁ, Num. xxi. 4; Judg. x. 16; xvi. 16; Zech. xi. 8: *unable to bear up, "discouraged."* So the Arab. قَاصِرُ الْيَدِ, *short of hand, unequal to —;* قَصَرَتْ نَفْسِي, *my mind is deficient; cannot bear —;* قَصِيرُ الذِّرَاعِ, *of arm,* id. opp. to الْيَدِ الطُّولَى, Gesenius. But this last rather means *oppressive hand,* than *powerful hand.*

Infin. קְצוֹר, Is. L. 2, only.
Part. pass. fem. plur. קְצֻרוֹת, Ezek. xlii. 5, only.
Pih. קִצֵּר, trans. of Kal. *Made short,* once, Ps. cii. 24.
Hiph. הִקְצַרְתָּ, i. q. Pih., once, Ps. lxxxix. 46. Pres. יִקְצֹרוּ, *they crop, reap,* Job xxiv. 6, according to the *Kethiv.* See the *Keri.* See קָצִיר.

קְצָת, f. for קְצָאת, from קָצָה, as קָנָה, is from מָנָה, Gesen.: but always with מִן, prefixed, as מִקְצָת, for מִקְצָאת; so that Dagesh is implied, Gram. art. 109. But, as the word occurs always in the state of construction, except where a pronoun is affixed, why may not קְצָת, be for קָצָה? and מְנָת, for מְנָה? by a slight variation of the vowels only: a thing certainly not very uncommon, i. q. קָצֶה above. *End, extremity, limit;* of time, Dan. i. 15. 18. Meton., including *part,* or *the whole* intervening, pers. or thing, as the context may require: so קָצֶה, and קָצָה, above. Dan. i. 2, מִקְצָת כְּלֵי בֵית־הָאֱלֹהִים, *of the limit, whole, of the vessels of the house of God,* i. e. *some* of them. So Ib. vr. 5; Neh. vii. 70. Comp. Gen. xlvii. 2, מִקְצֵה אֶחָיו. Aff. מִקְצָתָם, Dan. i. 5: pl. non occ.

קְצָת, and קְצָה, Chald. id. always in constr. — of time, Dan. iv. 26. 31. Ib. ii. 42, מִן קְצָת מַלְכוּתָא, *of part, the kingdom shall be,* i. e. from one quarter, partly. In two, out of these three instances, קְצָה, is the form: which is sufficient to show the irregularity of the vowels: and, in my estimation, to confirm the remark offered above on the same word, Heb.

קַר, m. once, Gen. viii. 22, r. קרר. Arab. قَرَّ, friguit dies; قَرّ, قَارّ, frigidus dies. Syr. ܩܰܪ, frigescere; ܩܶܦܳܐ, frigus. Cold, season.

קַר, m. pl. קָרִים. See קֹר above. Cold, waters, Jer. xviii. 14; Prov. xxv. 25. — of the mind, cool, quiet, Prov. xvii. 27. So Arab. قَرَّ, quievit, al. non occ.

קֹר, see קוּר.

קָרָא, v. pres. יִקְרָא. Syr. ܩܪܳܐ, clamavit, vocavit, invitavit, legit, cantavit. Arab. قَرَأَ, legit, &c. Constr. abs. it. immed. it. med. אֵת, בְּ, לְ, &c., variously. Eng. cry, crow, synon. τοῦ, צָעַק. — of things animate or inanimate. I. (a) Cried, cried out, called, shouted, &c. generally, abs., &c., Gen. xxxix. 14, 15; xli. 43; xlv. 1; Lev. xiii. 45; Judg. vii. 20; 2 Sam. xx. 16; Is. L. 2; Isv. 12, &c. (b) — to, called to, with אֶל, עַל, לְ, Judg. xviii. 23; 1 Sam. xxvi. 14; 1 Kings xvii. 11; Is. xxxiv. 14, &c. (c) — for some person or thing, immed., Gen. xxvii. 1; Exod. ii. 8; 1 Sam. iii. 16, &c., med. לְ; Gen. xx. 9; Lev. ix. 1; Hos. xi. 1; אֶל, Gen. iii. 9; Exod. iii. 4;—2 Kings viii. 1, with לְ. (d) — after, with אַחֲרֵי, 1 Sam. xx. 37, &c.; Jer. xii. 6. (c) Cry to, call upon, in petition, prayer, abs., Ps. iv. 2; xxii. 3; xxxiv. 7; and with אֶל, Ps. iv. 4; xxviii. 1; xxx. 9, &c., with לְ, לֵאלֹהִים, Ps. lvii. 3, &c.: with עַל, against some one, Deut. xv. 9. — in the name of God, with בְּשֵׁם, Gen. iv. 26; xii. 8; Exod. xxxiii. 19, &c. — of Baal, 1 Kings xviii. 26. (f) — call by name some one, i. e. give, make, him a name; famous; celebrate, Ps. xlix. 12; Is. xliv. 5; Ruth iv. 11. (g) Call, i. e. name, with לְ, pers. or thing named, Gen. xxvi. 18; Ruth iv. 17; Ps. cxlvii. 4, &c. So Gen. i. 5, וַיִּקְרָא...לָאוֹר יוֹם, he called the light, day. Comp. vr. 8. 10, &c., seq.; 1 Sam. iv. 21; Ruth i. 20, &c.: immed. in both places, or with אֵת, Gen. iv. 25, &c. Sometimes impers., Is. ix. 5, וַיִּקְרָא שְׁמוֹ, and one, i. e. men generally, shall call his name —. Ib. vii. 14, קָרָאת שְׁמוֹ, she shall call his name. Comp. מָצָאת, Gram. art. 203. In all similar cases קָרָא may be considered, i. q. הָיָה, be;

the name being supposed to imply what the person or thing really is. (h) — called together, an assembly, congregation, with אֵת, &c., Gen. xli. 8: אֶל, Ib. xlix. 1: immed., Joel i. 14; Is. i. 13;—Lev. xxiii. 2. 4. — invited to a feast, abs., 1 Sam. ix. 13. 22: with אֵת, 1 Kings i. 9, 10; abs., 41. 49, &c. (i) Called into question, litigation, abs., Job v. 1; xiii. 22: with בְּ, Is. lix. 4. (k) —, i. e. appointed one to an office, Is. xlii. 6; xlviii. 12; xlix. 1; li. 2, &c., various. (l) — forth soldiers, Is. xiii. 3, immed. pers. לְ, thing. (m) — proclaim, publish, preach, Exod. xxxiii. 19: with בְּשֵׁם, — of wisdom, Prov. i. 21; viii. 1. Prov. xx. 6, יִקְרָא אִישׁ חַסְדּוֹ, man (one) will proclaim his goodness. Comp. Is. xl. 6; lviii. 1; Zech. i. 14. Phrr. קָרָא וְאֵת, Joel iv. 9. דְּרוֹר ... לְ קְרָא, Jer. xxxiv. 8. צוֹם —, Ib. xxxvi. 9, &c. (m) — read, as in a book, generally, Deut. xvii. 19; 2 Kings v. 9; xix. 14; xxii. 8. (n) — read out, aloud, Exod. xxiv. 7; Josh. viii. 34; Neh. viii. 8. 18; ix. 3, &c., variously, med. בְּ, לִפְנֵי, בְּאָזְנֵי, &c., as the writer or speaker may require.

Infin. קְרֹא, Gen. iv. 26, &c. Aff. קָרְאִי, Ps. iv. 2, &c. קָרְאֵנוּ, Deut. iv. 7. קָרְאָם, 1 Kings viii. 52, &c., it.—

קְרֹאוֹת, Judg. viii. 1, only.

Imp. קְרָא, Deut. xxxi. 14, &c. Aff. קְרָאֵנִי, Ps. L. 15. Comp. Jer. xxxvi. 15.

— pl. קִרְאוּ, Judg. xvi. 25, &c. Pause, קְרָאוּ, Is. xxxiv. 16. Aff. קְרָאֻהָ, Is. lv. 6. Fem. plur. קְרֶאןָ, Exod. ii. 20. קְרֶאןָ, Ruth i. 20.

Part. קֹרֵא, Job xii. 4; Ps. xlii. 8, &c.
— pl. קֹרְאִים, Ps. xcix. 6. Constr. קֹרְאֵי, Ib. Aff. קֹרְאָיו, Ps. lxxxvi. 5. Comp. Ib. cxlv. 18.

— pass. קָרוּא, plur. קְרֻאִים, Esth. v. 12; 2 Sam. xv. 11, &c. Aff. קְרֻאָיו, Zeph. i. 7. Comp. Prov. ix. 18.

Niph. נִקְרָא, pres. יִקָּרֵא. Be, become, called, named. (a) pec. Called for, summoned, Esth. iii. 12; iv. 11; viii. 8. (b) — together, assembled, Is. xxxi. 4; Jer. iv. 20. שֶׁבֶר עַל שֶׁבֶר, breach upon breach is assembled, accumulated, i. e. as if called up by some one; or, made to meet: see II. below. (c) — named, with עַל, pers. or thing named, as, שֵׁם יְהוָה נִקְרָא עָלֶיךָ, the name of Jehovah is named upon thee, Deut. xxviii. 10: with לְ, Gen. ii. 23; Prov. xvii. 21, &c. Comp. 2 Sam. vi. 2; 1 Kings viii. 43; 2 Chron. vi.

קרא (537) קרא

33, &c.: abs., Eccl. vi. 10. נִקְרָא שְׁמוֹ, Dan. x. 1. עַל שֵׁם, Gen. xlviii. 6. With בְּפִי, Lev. xliv. 26. With בְּ, *in*, Deut. xxv. 10, with מִן, *from*, i. e. as the cause, Is. xlviii. 2. — מֵעִיר הַקֹּדֶשׁ, *from the holy city*. And thence, as things are named from their properties, (d) *Being, becoming, the thing so called*, Is. i. 26; Zech. viii. 3. Comp. Is. xlviii. 2, with מִן above: Ib. xliii. 7, &c., where the naming implies the belonging to such person or thing. So, Gen. xxi. 12, בְּיִצְחָק יִקָּרֵא לְךָ זָרַע, *in Isaac shall thy seed be called*, i. e. thy posterity shall be of him, or belonging to him. So also, Ib. xxxv. 10, יִשְׂרָאֵל יִהְיֶה שְׁמֶךָ, *Israel* (prince of God) *shall thy name* (thou) *be*. Hence also, (e) *Become named, be famous*, Is. xiv. 20. Comp. אַנְשֵׁי הַשֵּׁם, Gen. vi. 4; Ruth iv. 14. (e) — *called out; read, recited*, Esth. vi. 1: with בְּ, Neh. xiii. 1.

Part. נִקְרָא, Is. xliii. 7, only.

— pl. נִקְרָאִים, Is. xlviii. 1.

Puh. קֹרָא, pres. non occ. i. q. Niph. (c) *Called, named*, with לְ, Is. xlviii. 8; lviii. 8. 12; lxi. 3; lxii. 2; Ezek. x. 13, with בְּ, Is. lxv. 1.

Part. aff. מְקֹרָאַי. *My called, chosen*, Is. xlviii. 12, only.

קָרָא, pres. יִקְרֶא, for קָרָה. See Gram. art. 202. 4. Arab. قَرَا, r. قرى for قَرَا, *legit.* Freytag. Lex. sub voce. *Hospitio excepit* amicum; *collegit* aquam, &c. Cogn. قَرَا, r. قرو, *tetendit ivit*. II. *Proceed towards —, meet; happen*. Pec. (a) *Verging* or *proceeding towards, over against*, Gen. xv. 10; 1 Sam. iv. 2. In a hostile sense, Josh. viii. 14; xi. 20; Judg. vii. 24, &c. (b) — *meet*, Gen. xlvi. 29; Exod. iv. 27; xviii. 7, &c. Infin. (b) — *happen*. Constr. immed., Gen. xlii. 4. 38; Job iv. 14; Jer. xiii. 22: med. אֶת, Ib. xlix. 1; Lev. x. 19; Deut. xxxi. 29: abs., Exod. i. 10.

Infin. קְרֹאת, for קְרֹאת, for קִרְאָה, always with לְ pref. ll. cc. under (a), (b), &c. In Num. xxiv. 1, לִקְרַאת נְחָשִׁים, lit. *to meet serpents*; to observe perhaps by what he could gather, as a soothsayer, from the fortuitous action, &c., of serpents, what answer he ought to return. LXX. εἰς συνάντησιν τοῖς οἰωνοῖς. Syr. ܩܶܨܡܳܐ, *divinatio.*

Aff. לִקְרָאתִי, לִקְרָאתְךָ, &c., Num. xxii. 34; Gen. xxxii. 6;—Deut. i. 44; Gen. xiv. 17; xxiv. 17.

Part. pl. fem. aff. קֹרְאֹתַיִךְ. *Things meeting* (happening to) *thee*, Is. li. 19, only.

Niph. נִקְרָא, pres. יִקָּרֵא, constr. abs. it. med. עַל, בְּ, לִפְנֵי. (a) *Met; happened to meet*, Exod. v. 3; 2 Sam. xviii. 9; Deut. xxii. 6. (b) *Was, accidentally, happened*, 2 Sam. i. 6; xx. 1.

Infin. נִקְרָא, 2 Sam. i. 6.

Hiph. pres. 2d pers. sing. תַּקְרֵא. *Thou causest to meet, happen to*. Constr. med. אֶת, once, Jer. xxxii. 23.

קְרָא, v. Chald. pres. יִקְרֵא, יִקְרָא. Constr. abs. it. immed. it. med. קֳדָם. *Read, recited*, from a book, Dan. v. 7, 8. 15—17; Ezra iv. 18. 23.

Infin. מִקְרָא, Dan. ll. cc.

Part. קָרֵי, Ezra ll. cc.

Pah. קְרָא, pres. non occ. constr. med. בְּ. *Proclaimed, published*, Dan. iii. 4; iv. 11; v. 7, al. non occ.

Ithp. pres. יִתְקְרֵי. *Be called, summoned*, Dan. v. 12, only.

קֹרֵא, m.—pl. non occ. twice only, viz., 1 Sam. xxvi. 20; Jer. xvii. 11. *A partridge*, so called, as it is thought, from the *crowing* sort of noise it makes. Bochart, however, Hieroz., ii. p. 80. seq., makes it the قَارِيَة, *kāriat*, of the Arabs; which they describe as a green coloured bird with short legs and a long bill, and which Bochart styles, *rusticulæ* seu *gallinaginis genus*. On Jer. l. c. see Ib. p. 84, and דגר, in its place above.

קֶרֶב, masc. pl. aff. once, קִרְבֵי, Ps. ciii. 1. Aff. קִרְבִּי, קִרְבְּךָ, &c. Syr. ܩܪܶܒ, *appropinquavit, tetigit*. Arab. قَرَبَ, id. From the notion of approaching and coming in contact with any thing, that of being *in the midst*, if several were supposed to be present, would necessarily follow. This is the case with this word, which, as Gesenius has remarked, has acquired the usage of a preposition. *The midst*, or *inward part*, of any thing or person. Pec. (a) The *inward part, entrails*, of an animal; *the heart, &c.* (Arab. قَلْب), of man, Gen. xli. 21; Exod. xxix. 13. 22; Lev. i. 13; iii. 3. 9. 14; iv. 8;—Ps. v. 10; lxii. 5. Comp. Ib. xxxix. 4; li. 12; lxiv. 7; Is. xvi. 11, &c. (b) *Amidst, among, &c.*, often with בְּ, or מִן, prefixed, Gen. xlv. 6; xlviii. 16; Exod. viii. 18; Num. v. 27;—

3 z

קרב (538) קרב

Exod. xxxi. 14; Lev. xvii. 4. 10; xviii. 29, &c. — of time, Hab. iii. 2. *In the midst of years*, i. e. during the remainder of the Hebrew polity: that which was to follow having no end, and to which this term קרב could apply no more than that of "*the last days*" could.

קְרָב, masc. pl. fem. קְרָבוֹת. Syr. ܩܪܳܒܐ, *bellum*. Lit. drawing near: thence *contest, &c. Contest, conflict, battle, war*: with מִלְחָמָה, Job xxxviii. 23. Comp. Zech. xiv. 3;—2 Sam. xvii. 11; Ps. lv. 19. 22; lxxviii. 9; cxliv. 1; Eccl. ix. 18: pl., Ps. lxviii. 31. It. Chald., Dan. vii. 21, only.

קָרֵב, masc. pl. קְרֵבִים. See קָרַב above. *Approaching, drawing near*, Num. i. 51; iii. 10, 38; xviii. 7; Deut. xx. 3; Ezek. xl. 46; xlv. 4, &c. Whence—

קָרַב, or קָרֵב, v. pres. יִקְרַב. See קָרֵב above. Constr. abs. it. med. אֶל, לְ, מוּל, בְּ, &c., variously. *Approached, drew near*, generally, of persons, things, or time. (a) *Drew near, approached*, Exod. xiv. 20; xxxii. 19, &c.: with אֶל, Lam. iii. 57; iv. 18; Deut. xv. 9, &c.; abs., Deut. ii. 19: with מוּל, Job xxxii. 22: with לְ, Ps. xci. 10: with בְּ. Pec. (b) — of God, to help, Lam. l. c. Ps. lxix. 19. — men, 1 Kings ii. 7. (c) — of God's priests or people to serve him, Lev. xvi. 1: with לִפְנֵי, Ezek. xl. 46; Zeph. iii. 2. (d) Arab. تَقَرَّبَ. — to a woman or wife, Gen. xx. 4; Is. viii. 3; Ezek. xviii. 6. (e) — for war, to battle, אֶל, לְ, לִקְרַאת, Deut. xx. 2, 3; 1 Sam. xvii. 48. — against a city, אֶל, Deut. xx. 10; Josh. viii. 5. With עַל, against any one, Ps. xxvii. 2. (d) — to thyself, i. e. keep by thyself, with אֶל, Is. lxv. 5. Comp. גֶּשׁ־הָלְאָה, Gen. xix. 9: with הֲלֹם, — *hither*, Exod. iii. 5.

Infin. קֹרֹב, Ps. xxxii. 9. קְרָב, 2 Sam. xv. 5: it. fem. קִרְבָה, Exod. xxxvi. 2; Lev. xvi. 1, &c. It. קוֹב, aff. קָרְבָם, Deut. xx. 2. It. constr. קִרְבַת, Is. lviii. 2; Ps. lxxiii. 28: fem. of קָרֵב.

Imp. קְרַב, Lev. ix. 7. With ה parag. קָרְבָה, Ps. lxix. 19.

— pl. קִרְבוּ, Exod. xvi. 9, &c.

Part. קָרֵב, pl. קְרֵבִים. See this word above. See Gram. art. 192. In the Arab. intransitive verbs have not usually the participial form, فَاعِل. Heb. פּוֹקֵד.

Niph. נִקְרַב, pres. non occ. *Should, ought to, draw near*. See Gram. art. 157. 20, where the reflective sense is taken. Upon further consideration, I think *ought, should*, as in יְעֻשֶּׂה, Ib. is the exact force of this verb, Exod. xxii. 7; Josh. vii. 14, al. non occ. See LXX.

Pih. קֵרֵב, pres. תְּקָרֵב, constr. immed. *Made, caused, to come near*, Is. xlvi. 13; Hos. vii. 6, in sign. (d) above, Ps. lxv. 5;—i. q. Kal, Job xxxi. 37; Ezek. xxxvi. 8.

Imp. קָרֵב, Ezek. xxxvii. 17, only.

— pl. קָרְבוּ, Is. xli. 21, only.

Hiph. הִקְרִיב, הִקְרַב, pres. יַקְרִיב, יַקְרֵב, apoc. יַקְרֵב, constr. immed. it. med. אֵת, obj. לְ, pers. כֵּן, of, from, עַל, on, upon, אֶל, לִפְנֵי, before, &c., i. q. Kal, abs., Exod. xiv. 10; Gen. xii. 11, &c. *Made, caused, bade, approach, draw near*. Men, אֶל, Exod. xxviii. 1; xxix. 4: לִפְנֵי, Num. viii. 9, 10: immed., Jer. xxx. 21. — times, Ezek. xxii. 4. — *present*, gift, sacrifice, Judg. iii. 18; v. 25; Lev. iii. 1; vii. 8; Num. ix. 13, &c. — a cause to the judge, Deut. i. 17. — field to field, Is. v. 8: with בְּ, — from, i. e. *remove*—according to Gesen.—with מִן, 2 Kings xvi. 14. וַיַּקְרֵב מֵאֵת פְּנֵי הַבַּיִת, *so he caused* (it) *to be near—from the front of the house* . . . and placed it—on the side, &c. The passage, however, appears to me to be elliptical and parenthetical. If so, the word has no new meaning here.

Infin. הַקְרִיב, הַקְרֵב, Lev. vii. 38; Num. iii. 4. Aff. הַקְרִיבוֹ, Lev. vii. 16. See Num. xxviii. 26; xxvi. 61.

Imp. הַקְרֵב, Exod. xxviii. 1, &c. Aff. הַקְרִיבֵהוּ, Mal. i. 8.

Part. מַקְרִיב, pl. מַקְרִיבִים, constr. מַקְרִיבֵי, Lev. iii. 1; xxi. 6; Num. xvi. 35.

קְרֵב, v. Chald. i. q. Heb. קָרַב. Constr. abs. it. med. עַל, לְ, pres. non occ. *Approached, drew near*, Deut. iii. 8. 26; vi. 13; vii. 16.

Infin. aff. מִקְרְבַהּ, Dan. vi. 21.

Pah. pres. only, תְּקָרֵב. *Thou offer*, Ezra vii. 17.

Aph. pret. pl. הַקְרִבוּ. *They offered*, Ezra vii. 17. Aff. הַקְרְבוּהִי, *they caused him to approach, brought him near*, with קֳדָם, Dan. vii. 13.

Part. pl. masc. מְהַקְרְבִין. Persons *offering*, Ezra vi. 10, only.

קָרְבָּן, and קֻרְבָּן, constr. קָרְבַּן, pl. קָרְבָּנוֹת, aff. only, קָרְבְּנֵיהֶם, r. קרב. Arab. قُرْبَان,

קרב

sacrificium, &c. Syr. ܡܩܘܪܒܢܐ, id. Æth. id. According to Josephus, contra Apionem, lib. i. 22, δῶρον Θεοῦ; the term itself being used as an oath among the Hebrews and Syrians only; by which *a vow* is probably meant. Comp. Mark vii. 11. See Schleusner and Wahl sub voce. *An offering*, bloody or unbloody, Lev. ii. 4. 12; vi. 13; Num. vii. 10, seq. Aff. קָרְבָּנִי, Num. xxviii. 2, &c.

קִרְבַת, f. constr. Infin. v. קרב above.

קַרְדֹּם, m. pl. קַרְדֻּמִּים, fem. קַרְדֻּמּוֹת, and קַרְדֻּמּוֹת, Judg. ix. 48. Arab. قَدُّوم, *ascia*, *securis*; the dagesh being resolved into ר, as in some other instances. *An axe* for cutting wood, Judg. l. c., Ps. lxxiv. 5; 1 Sam. xiii. 20, 21; Jer. xlvi. 22, al. non occ. Aff. קַרְדֻּמּוֹ.

קָרָה, f.—pl. non occ. aff. קָרָתוֹ, r. קור. *Cold, chilliness*, Nah. iii. 17; Ps. cxlvii. 17; Prov. xxv. 20; Job xxiv. 7; xxxvii. 9, al. non occ.

קְרֵה, m. once, with מִן, pref. constr. in מִקְּרֵה לָיְלָה, *from accident of* the *night*, i. e. accidental pollution during sleep, Deut. xxiii. 11, only. See קרה below.

קרה, v. pres. יִקְרֶה, apoc. יִקַר, of which קָרָא, II. above, is only another form. Constr. immed. it. med. אֶת, לְ, it. abs. Arab. قَرَا, r. قَرَّ, *intendit, contendit, prosequutus fuit; collegit—congessit.* The primitive notion seems to have consisted in *tending towards*; thence, *joining, accumulating, &c.* Whence, *beam, conjoining do., meeting together, city, &c.* *Met, happened*, Gen. xliv. 29; Num. xi. 27; Deut. xxv. 18; Eccl. ii. 15; Esth. iv. 7; vi. 13, &c.; immed. with אֶת, Eccl. ii. 14; ix. 11; with לְ, Dan. x. 14: abs., Ruth ii. 7.

Niph. נִקְרָה, pres. יִקָּרֶה, apoc. יִקָּר. (a) *Was, became, meeting; accidentally met with, dropt in with*, med. עַל, Exod. iii. 18. אֶל, Num. xxiii. 4. 16. פֹּה, Ib. vr. 15. לִקְרַאת, Ib. xxiii. 3. בְּ, in, of place, 2 Sam. i. 6.

Pih. pret. pl. aff. קֵרוּהוּ. *They made it join, framed it together*, as with timbers, Neh. iii. 3. 6, pres. non occ.

Infin. קָרוֹת, Neh. ii. 8; 2 Chron. xxxiv. 11, only.

Part. מְקָרֶה, Ps. civ. 3, only.

Hiph. הִקְרָה, pres. non occ.—with לִפְנֵי

(539)

קרו

Made, caused, to meet, drop in, with me, Gen. xxvii. 20. לְ, for, *Make suitable, convenient*, for, Num. xxxv. 11.

Imp. הַקְרֵה, Gen. xxiv. 12, al. non occ.

—.קָרוֹב, קָרֵב, masc. pl. קְרוֹבִים.— ... , קְרוֹבוֹת, pl. f. קְרוֹבָה, קְרֵבָה, r. קרב. *Near, at hand*, of (a) Person, neighbour: (b) Station: (c) Time: (d) Place: (e) Things. Also, (f) adverbially, with various constructions as in the verb. (a) Of God, Ps. xxxiv. 19, &c. '— man, Gen. xlv. 10; Exod. xiii. 17; Deut. xxii. 2, &c. (b) Ps. xxxviii. 12; Job xix. 14. — *kindred*, Lev. xxi. 2; Num. xxvii. 11; Ps. xxxviii. 12; Ruth ii. 20; iii. 12. (c) Deut. xxxii. 35; Is. xiii. 6; Ezek. vii. 7, &c. (d) Gen. xix. 20; 1 Kings viii. 46; 2 Chron. vi. 36; Deut. xxxii. 17; Ezek. xxii. 5, &c. (e) Deut. xxx. 14. In Job xvii. 12, אוֹר קָרוֹב מִפְּנֵי חֹשֶׁךְ, Gesenius translates, "*lux prope abest a tenebris*," i. e. "mox in tenebras mutabitur." Which gives no very definite sense, and seems irreconcileable with the context. See my translation and note on the place. — of righteousness, Is. li. 5. — distress, destruction, Ps. xxii. 12; Jer. xlviii. 16. — God's name; person named, Ps. lxxv. 2. Comp. Jer. xii. 2. (f) Adv. mostly with מִן, מִקָּרוֹב. Arab. عَنْ قَرِيبٍ, and مِنْ قَرِيبٍ, lit. from *near*, i. e. at hand, not requiring time to arrive at. *Short, shortly, soon*, Job xx. 5; Ezek. vii. 8. Comp. Num. xxiv. 17, קָרוֹב וְלֹא אֲשׁוּרֶנּוּ, *I shall see him, but not shortly*, i. e. in a short time. Comp. עַתָּה, in the parallel. Comp. קְרוֹבָה, Prov. x. 13; Is. lvi. 1. — לָבוֹא קְרוֹבָה, *shortly to come in.* Aff. קֹרְבִי, Exod. xxxii. 27. קְרוֹבַי, Job xix. 14.

קֶרַח, masc.—plur. non occ. (a) *Cold.* Meton. (b) *Frost.* (a) Gen. xxxi. 40; Jer. xxxvi. 20; Job vi. 16. (b) Job xxxvii. 10; xxxviii. 29; Ezek. i. 20. *A precious stone* so called apparently. LXX. κρυστάλλου, al. non occ.

קֶרַח, m. once, aff. קַרְחוֹ. *His frost, ice*, Ps. cxlvii. 17. LXX. κρύσταλλον αὐτοῦ.

קָרְחָה, once, קָרְחָא, f. of the last, pl. non occ. Aff. קָרְחָתְךָ, Mic. i. 16, only. Lit. *Iciness*. See קָרְחָה above: thence, smoothness, *Baldness*, Lev. xxi. 5; Deut. xiv. 1 Is. iii. 24; xv. 2; xxii. 12, &c. Hence—

קָרַח, v. pres. plur. יִקְרְחָה, Lev. xxi. 5. See the *Keri*. *Shave, make bald*, al. non occ.
Imp. f. קָרְחִי. *Make thee bald*, once, Mic. i. 16.
Niph. pres. יִקָּרֵחַ. *Be, become, bald, shorn*, once, Jer. xvi. 6.
Hiph. pl. הִקְרִיחוּ. *They have made* (themselves) *bald, for thee*, with אֶל, once, Ezek. xxvii. 31.
Hoph. Part. מָקְרָח. *Made, become, bald*, once, Ezek. xxix. 18.

קֵרֵחַ, masc.—pl. non occ. See v. קָרַח above. *Bald*, person, opp. τῷ, גִּבֵּחַ, applying rather to the top, than the fore part, of the head, Lev. xiii. 40; 2 Kings ii. 23, only.

קָרְחִי, masc. patronym. of קֹרַח, Num. xxvi. 58; 1 Chron. xii. 6, &c.

קָרַחַת, fem. i. q. קָרְחָה, Lev. xiii. 42, 43, Ib. vr. 53. *Bare*, of the pile or knap of cloth, al. non occ. Aff. קָרַחְתּוֹ.

קְרִי, m.—pl. non occ. r. קָרָה. In pause, קֶרִי. *Meeting, opposing*, in a hostile manner, always with v. הָלַךְ, with בְּ, once, בַּחֲמַת, Lev. xxvi. 28; Ib. xxvi. 24. 27. 40, 41. Adverbially, or בְּ, omitted by the ellipsis, Lev. xxvi. 21. 23, al. non occ.

קְרִיא, masc. pl. constr. קְרִיאֵי. See *Keri*, it. קָרִיא, Num. i. 16; xvi. 2; xxvi. 9, only.

קְרִיאָה, fem. r. קָרָא, once, Jonah iii. 2. *Cry, proclamation*.

קְרִיָּה, f. constr. קִרְיַת, pl. non occ. r. קָרָה. Arab. قَرْيَة. Syr. ܩܪܺܝܬܐ, *urbs*, &c. Lit. meeting, associating. *A town* or *city*, i. q. עִיר, but used *mostly* in the loftier style. See, however, Deut. ii. 36; iii. 4; 1 Kings i. 41. 45;—Is. i. 21. 26; xxii. 2; xxv. 2; xxvi. 5; xxxii. 13; Jer. xlix. 25; Ps. xlviii. 3; Prov. x. 15; Job xxxix. 7, &c. Also used as a proper name, Gen. xxiii. 2, &c.

קִרְיָה, and קִרְיָא, Chald. def. קִרְיְתָא, pl. non occ. i. q. Heb. *A town* or *city*, Ezra iv. 10. 12, 13. 15, 16. 19, al. non occ.

קָרַם, v. pres. יִקְרֹם. Constr. immed. it. med. עַל. Syr. ܩܪܰܡ, *incrustavit*. *Overlaid, cased*, twice, Exod. xxxvii. 6. 8.

קֶרֶן, masc. pause, קָרֶן, dual, קַרְנַיִם, constr. קַרְנֵי, pl. f. קְרָנוֹת, constr. קַרְנוֹת. Aff. קַרְנִי, pl. קַרְנָיו, and קַרְנָיו, it. קַרְנֹתַי. Syr. ܩܰܪܢܳܐ,

Arab. قَرْن, *cornu*. *The horn* of any horned animal, Ps. xxii. 22; xcii. 11. (a) Used as a *vessel* for oil, &c., 1 Sam. xvi. 1. 13; 1 Kings i. 39. (b) — as a *trumpet*, Josh. vi. 5. (c) — apparently for Mount *Tabor*, Is. v. 1, as representing the Holy Land by its fruitfulness. See Lowth's note on the place. (d) — applied also to men and states, signifying *power*—from the strength of oxen butting with their horns, Dan. viii. 3. 5, 6. 9. 20, 21; Mic. iv. 13. See under חָזוּת, p. 190, above. Comp. 1 Kings xxii. 11. Hence, metaph. implying, *Strength, power*, either in a (e) Good, or (f) Bad, sense. (e) With רוּם, 1 Sam. ii. 10; 1 Chron. xxv. 5; Ps. cxxxii. 17, &c. (f) Ps. lxxv. 5; Jer. xlviii. 25. With מָגֵן, as *a weapon*, 2 Sam. xxii. 3; Ps. xviii. 3. The same is probably the sense in Job xvi. 15, "caput meum," says Gesenius, "in quo summum decus summaque gloria." However the term be taken, splendour, glory, or the like, must have been meant. He also thinks Alexander had the title of ذُو الْقَرْنَيْن, *possessing horns*, because he was powerful. The Arabs might, however, have adopted this from the coins of Alexander, which so represent him. In Ezek. xxvii. 15, שֵׁן, קַרְנוֹת שֵׁן, *horns of tooth*, is used for *elephants' teeth* apparently. (g) — applied also to pike-like ornaments placed at each corner of *the altar*, in קַרְנוֹת הַמִּזְבֵּחַ, *horns of the altar*, Lev. iv. 7, seq.; viii. 15; ix. 9; xvi. 18, &c. (h) — also to *rays of light*, or perhaps *streams of lightning*, Hab. iii. 4. See my note on Job xxxvi. 32. Comp. Is. xlix. 2.

קֶרֶן, m. Chald. def. קַרְנָא. Syr. ܩܰܪܢܳܐ, dual, קַרְנַיִן, def. קַרְנַיָּא, i. q. Heb. Dan. vii. 7, 8. 20, 21. 24. Also a musical instrument so called, Dan. iii. 5. 7. 10, &c.

קָרַן, v. pres. non occ. See קֶרֶן, Heb. (h). *Emitted rays, shone*, of the skin of the face of Moses, Exod. xxxiv. 29, 30. 35, only.
Hiph. Part. מַקְרִן. *Producing*, thence, *having horns*, once, Ps. lxix. 32. LXX. κέρατα ἐκφέροντα.

קֶרֶס, masc. pl. קְרָסִים, constr. קַרְסֵי. Aff. קְרָסָיו. Syr. ܩܪܰܣ, *contractus fuit*. *Hook, link, loop*, Exod. xxvi. 6. 11. 33; xxxv. 11; xxxvi. 13; xxxix. 33, &c.

קָרַס, v. pret. pl. קָרְסוּ, once, Is. xlvi. 2.

הרס (541) קרץ

See קרס above. *They were*, or *became bent, bowed*, down : with פְרַע.
Part. קרָס, Ib. vr. 1, only. The Ancient Versions seem to have understood this word as synonymous with קרע. Arab. قرص.

קַרְסֹל, m. aff. twice, קַרְסֻלָי, Ps. xviii. 37; 2 Sam. xxii. 7; in the phr. מַעֲדוּ קַרְסֻלָי *My ancles*. Arab. اقزل, *emaciata crura habens*; v. قزل, *incessit ac si pes truncatus, et huc illuc vacillans*. Cogn. Heb. פָּסַל Gesen. The ר inserted perhaps for euphony, as in some other cases. On usages of this sort, see my note on Job xii. 5.

קָרַע, v. pres. יִקְרַע. Constr. immed. it. abs. it. med. בְּ, מֵעַל, מִן, אֵת. Arab. قرع, *dilaceravit*. *Tore, rent*, as a garment, &c., Lev. xiii. 56; 2 Sam. xiii. 19; 2 Kings v. 8;—Gen. xxxvii. 29; Josh. vii. 6, &c. — the heavens, Is. lxiii. 19. — a kingdom away from some one, 1 Sam. xv. 28; 1 Kings ii. 11—13, &c. Metaph. — *the heart*, Joel ii. 13; Hos. xiii. 8. Once, of the eyes, Jer. iv. 30, תִּקְרְעִי בַפּוּךְ עֵינַיִךְ, lit. *thou rendest thy eyes with stibium*, i. e. *adornest them to such a degree as to inflame them*; or, it may be, *patchest them* with it : from קְרָעִים, — *tearest*, i. e. *cuttest*, with a knife, once, Jer. xxxvi. 23. — *windows in a wall*, Jer. xxii. 14. Metaph. with words or other injurious means, Ps. xxxv. 15.
Infin. קְרֹעַ, 1 Kings xi. 11; Eccl. iii. 7. Aff. קָרְעִי, Ezra ix. 5.
Imp. pl. קִרְעוּ, 2 Sam. iii. 31, &c.
Part. קֹרֵעַ, 1 Kings xi. 31, only.
— pass. קָרוּעַ, 2 Sam. xv. 32: pl. קְרֻעִים, 1 Sam. iv. 12, &c. Constr. קְרוּעֵי, 2 Kings xviii. 37, &c.
Niph. נִקְרַע, pres. יִקָּרֵעַ. *Be, become, torn, rent*, Exod. xxviii. 32; xxxix. 23; 1 Kings xiii. 3. 5, al. non occ.

קְרָעִים, m. pl. only. *Rendings, pieces*. See קָרַע above, 1 Kings xi. 30, 31; 2 Kings ii. 12. — *rags*, Prov. xxiii. 21.

קֶרֶץ, masc. once, Jer. xlvi. 20. Arab. قرص, n. of action of v. قرص, *concidit, proscidit, &c. A cutting off, destruction*.

קָרַץ, v. pret. non occ. pres. יִקְרְצוּ. Arab. قرص, *concidit; digitis prehensum com-

pressit*. (a) *Closing, pressing together*, the lips or eyes, indicating secret fraud, cunning, &c., Prov. xvi. 30; x. 10. Immed. and med. בְּ. Cogn. Arab. قرض, *ruminavit; dixit; exterminavit*.
Part. קוֹרֵץ, Prov. vi. 13, al. non occ.
Puh. קֹרַצְתִּי, once, Job xxxiii. 6. *I have been cut, hewn*, out. Comp. Is. li. 1.

קְרֵץ, masc. Chald. aff. pl. קַרְצוֹהִי, and קַרְצֵיהוֹן, i. q. קְרָצִים, ≈ interchanging with ע in Heb. and Chald. words. *Rendings*; and with אֲכַל, *accusations*, Dan. vi. 25; iii. 8, al. non occ. Comp. קָרַע, in Hos. xiii. 8, and the Syr. ܐܟܠܩܪܨܐ, as applied to Satan, and see my note on Job xiii. 14.

קַרְקַע, m.—pl. non occ. Syr. ܩܪܩܥܐ, *solum, fundum*. Cogn. Arab. قرقر, *terra æquabilis. Bottom, foundation, basis*, of the Tabernacle, Num. v. 17. — of Solomon's Temple, 1 Kings vi. 15, 16. 30; vii. 7. This last place is best explained by Ib. vi. 16. Gesen. "*a fundo ad lacunar s. tegumentum*" . . . i. e. "in omnibus parietibus ab imo ad summum." — of the sea, Amos ix. 3, al. non occ.

קֶרֶשׁ, masc. pl. קְרָשִׁים, constr. קַרְשֵׁי, aff. קְרָשָׁיו. Arab. قرشة, *scissio. A plank*, or *board*, as used in constructing the Tabernacle, &c., Exod. xxvi. 16—22; xxxvi. 22, &c. — benches of a ship, Ezek. xxvii. 6.

קָרֶת, masc.—pl. non occ. r. קָרָה. Lit. *joining, frame-work*: probably *A pulpit*. See my note on Job xxix. 7. Usually, i. q. קִרְיָה, in the more elevated style only. Occ. Job l. c. Prov. viii. 3; ix. 3. 14; xi. 11.

קְשָׂה, f. pl. קְשָׂוֹת, constr. קְשׂוֹת. Arab. قش, *qualus, quasillus. A sort of small vessel, Patten, phial*, or the like, Exod. xxv. 29; xxxvii. 16; Num. iv. 7; 1 Chron. xxviii. 17. LXX. σπονδεῖον.

קְשִׂיטָה, f.—pl. non occ.—thrice only, Gen. xxxiii. 19; Josh. xxiv. 32; Job xlii. 11. A piece of money so called, consisting apparently of a certain *weight* of silver, as the word itself signifies something *weighed*. Arab. قسط, *a pair of scales*. See my note on Job xlii. 11. Gesenius tells us that it was of either *gold* or *silver*: but no mention

קִשָׁה (542) קָשַׁב

of gold occurs in connexion with this word. From a comparison of Gen. xxxiii. 19, with Ib. xxiii. 15, 16, the *kesita* would seem to be of the value of four *shekels*. The notion that this was a coin bearing the impression of a lamb, appears to be entirely without foundation. See Bochart. Hieroz., i. lib. ii. cap. xliii., and Rosenmüller, on Gen. xxxiii. 19. The most recent notice, however, of this coin, is to be found in a communication from Mr. Thomas Yeates to the Numismatic Society, and published in their proceedings of 1837-38, p. 141. But, here, the exploded story of its bearing the impression of a lamb, &c. is trumped up without the least attempt whatever to afford proof of this; not to insist on other matter equally worthless.

הַקַשְׂקֶשֶׂת, f. pl. קַשְׂקְשׂוֹת, and קַשְׂקַשִׂים, aff. קַשְׂקְשׂתָיו. Usually, (a) *The scales* of a fish: thence applied, (b) To *armour*, as resembling these. (a) Lev. xi. 9, 10. 12; Deut. xiv. 9. 10; Ezek. xxix. 4. (b) 1 Sam. xvii. 5. I am inclined to believe, however, that this word signifies *fin*, rather than *scales*, and, also, that סְנַפִּיר,—the word usually translated *fin*,—signifies *scales*, and is but another form of the Coptic ϣⲉⲛϥⲓ, *shenfi, squammæ piscium*. See my note on Job xl. 25, p. 531, and סְנַפִּיר above.

קַשׁ, and קָשָׁה, m.—pl. non occ. Arab. قَشٌّ, *aruit herba*; قَشّ, *stipula*, r. קשש. The whole stalk, with the ear, of corn dried, apparently: whence, (a) *Stubble*, Exod. v. 12; xv. 7; Is. v. 24; xlvii. 14, &c. (b) *Chaff*, Job xiii. 25; Is. xl. 24; xli. 2, &c.

קִשֻּׁא, m. pl. קִשֻּׁאִים. Arab. قِثَّاء. Syr. ܩܛܐ, *cucumis*; ܩܛܐ, *asininus*. Cucumbers, once, Num. xi. 5. See Celsii Hierobot., ii. 247. So called, perhaps, from the difficulty felt in digesting them. See Plin., xix. c. v., and r. קָשָׁה.

קָשֵׁב, m.—pl. non occ. Syr. ܩܫܒ, *notificatio*. Cogn. קצב. Lit. keenness. Attention, 1 Kings xviii. 29; 2 Kings iv. 31; Is. xxi. 7. Phr. הִקְשִׁיב קֶשֶׁב רַב־קָשֶׁב, *he attended* (with) *great attention*, al. non occ.

קַשָּׁב, fem. קַשֶּׁבֶת. See קָשֵׁב. Attentive, Neh. i. 6. 11, only.

קַשֻּׁב, fem. pl. קַשֻּׁבוֹת, i. q. קַשֶּׁבֶת, Ps. cxxx. 2; 2 Chron. vi. 40; vii. 15, al. non occ.

קָשַׁב, v. pres. pl. fem. תִּקְשַׁבְנָה. They attend, listen, once, Is. xxxii. 3.

Hiph. הִקְשִׁיב, pres. יַקְשִׁיב, apoc. יַקְשֵׁב. See קָשַׁב above. Constr. abs. it. immed. it. med. לְ, אֶל, עַל, בְּ, ל. Of person or thing, *Attended to, regarded*, Ps. x. 17; lxvi. 19; Prov. ii. 2; xvii. 4; Is. xxi. 7; xlviii. 18; Jer. vi. 19; xxiii. 18; Job xiii. 6, &c.

Infin. הַקְשִׁיב, 1 Sam. xv. 22, &c.

Imp. הַקְשֵׁב, Job xxxiii. 31. With ה parag. Ps. v. 3, &c.

— f. הַקְשִׁיבִי, Is. x. 30, &c.: pl. הַקְשִׁיבוּ, Is. xxviii. 23, &c.

Part. מַקְשִׁיב, Prov. i. 24, &c.: pl. מַקְשִׁיבִים, Cant. viii. 13.

קָשֶׁה, m. constr. קְשֵׁה, pl. קָשִׁים, constr. קְשֵׁי.—

קָשָׁה, f. constr. קְשַׁת, pl. קָשׁוֹת.—

Syr. ܩܫܐ. Arab. قاسٍ, *durus*. Hard,— either, (a) Actively, or (b) Passively,—(a) *Obdurate, unyielding*, 1 Sam. xxv. 3; 2 Sam. iii. 39; Is. xlviii. 4, &c. — difficulty, Exod. xviii. 26. — vehement, cruel, Gen. xlii. 30; Is. xxi. 2; 2 Sam. ii. 17; 1 Kings xiv. 6; Ps. lx. 5; Cant. viii. 6. Phrr. קְשֵׁה עֹרֶף, *obdurate of neck*, Exod. xxxii. 9; xxxiii. 3, &c. קְשֵׁי פָנִים, — *of face*, impudent, Ezek. ii. 4. קְשֵׁה־לֵב, — *of heart*, Ib. iii. 7. — powerful, irresistible, Is. xix. 4; xxvii. 8. (b) — *hard* of servitude, i. e. subject to such, Exod. i. 14; vi. 9; Deut. xxvi. 6; 1 Kings xii. 4. Phr. קְשֵׁה־יוֹם, — *of day*, i. e. whose days are grievous, Job xxx. 25. Phr. קְשַׁת־רוּחַ, — *of spirit*, overwhelmed, depressed, 1 Sam. i. 15.

קָשָׁה, v. pres. יִקְשֶׁה, apoc. יֵקֶשׁ. Syr. ܩܫܐ. Arab. قَسَا, r. قَسِيَ, *durus fuit*. Constr. abs. it. med. עַל, obj. מִן, of comp. it. בְּ, in, with. Was, became, (a) *Hard*, grievous, overpowering, Gen. xlix. 7; Deut. xv. 18; 1 Sam. v. 7; 2 Sam. xix. 44. (b) *Difficult*, Deut. i. 17.

Niph. נִקְשָׁה, pres. non occ. once, Is. viii. 21. *Subjected to hardship, difficulty.*

Pih. pres. f. apoc. תְּקַשׁ, once, Gen. xxxv. 16, i. q. Hiph. (a) 2, Ib. vr. 17.

Hiph. הִקְשָׁה, pres. אַקְשֶׁה, apoc. יֵקֶשׁ. Constr. immed. it. med. אֶת, obj. אֶל, against. *Made hard, hardened*, either (a) really, or (b) by declaration only, i. e. pronounced to be hard, see Gram. art. 157. 6. (a) I. *Obdurate*, Jer. xix. 15; Neh. ix. 29; Prov.

קָשׁוּ (543) קָשַׁר

xxviii. 14; xxix. 1; 2 Chron. xxxvi. 13; Ps. xcv. 8, &c. 2. *Grievous, difficult*, 1 Kings xxii. 4; 2 Chron. x. 4. Phr. הַקְשָׁה... לִשְׁלֹחֵנוּ, *made* (it) *a difficulty to send us*, Exod. xiii. 15. הִקְשִׁיתָ לִשְׁאוֹל, *thou hast made it hard for request;* hast made a hard, difficult, request, 2 Kings ii. 10. בְּהַקְשֹׁתָהּ בְּלִדְתָּהּ, *in her making* (it) *a difficulty in her bringing forth*, i. e. in her having hard labour, pains, Gen. xxxv. 17. 3. *Difficult, refractory*, Prov. xxviii. 14; Job ix. 4: ellip. לִבּוֹ, or the like. (b) Exod. vii. 3; Deut. ii. 30.

Infin. aff. הַקְשֹׁתָהּ, Gen. l. c.

Part. מַקְשֶׁה, Prov. xxix. 1, &c.

קָשׁוֹט, m. Chald. pl. non occ. i. q. Heb. קְשֹׁט. *Truth*, Dan. iv. 34. Abstr. for concrete, *True*, i. e. according to his own law. Phr. מִן קְשֹׁט, *of a truth, verily*, Dan. ii. 47, al. non occ.

קָשַׁח, v. Kal non occ.

Hiph. הִקְשִׁיחַ, pres. תַּקְשִׁיחַ, constr. immed. Synon. Hiph. τοῦ, קָשָׁה. Arab. قسح, *durus fuit*. I. *Made hard, obdurate*, Is. xliii. 17. II. *Treat hardly*, Job xxxix. 16. The verb, however, is probably impersonal here. If so, some one *considers* (them) *hard*, i. e. her young, as unnaturally unattached to the parent. See my note on the place, al. non occ.

קֹשֶׁט, and קְשֹׁט, masc.—pl. non occ. Arab. قسط. Syr. ܩܘܫܬܐ, *veritas*. Twice only, Ps. lx. 6; Prov. xxii. 21. *Religious truth.*

קֳשִׁי, masc. r. קָשָׁה, once, Deut. ix. 27. *Hardness, obstinacy.*

קֶשֶׁר, m.—pl. non occ. aff. קִשְׁרוֹ. Arab. قشر, *cortex, crusta*, &c.; قاشور, *omnia excorians; malo affectus*. The primitive notion seems to consist in covering, binding, as bark does a tree; thence, uneasiness, evil, &c. See קֹשְׁרִים below. *Covenant;* thence, *Conspiracy, treachery*, or *treason*, 2 Kings xi. 14; xii. 21; xiv. 19; xv. 30; xvii. 4; Is. viii. 12; Jer. xi. 9, &c. Aff., 1 Kings xvi. 20. Thence—

קָשַׁר, v. pres. יִקְשֹׁר, יִקְשָׁר. See קֶשֶׁר above. Æth. ፈጸረ: *clausit, observavit.* Constr. abs. it. immed. it. med. בְּ, עַל, לְ, אֶת. (a) *Tied, bound*, to, or upon, person or thing,

עַל, בְּ, לְ, Gen. xxxviii. 28; Deut. vi. 8; xi. 18; Prov. vii. 3; Jer. li. 63; Job xxxix. 10; xl. 29, &c. Metaph. Gen. xliv. 30; Prov. vi. 21; xxii. 15. (b) *Bound each other, Conspired* against, &c., 1 Kings xv. 27; xvi. 9. 16. 20; 2 Kings x. 9; xv. 15. 30; Amos vii. 10, &c.

Imp. aff. קָשְׁרֵם, (a) Prov. iii. 3, &c.

Part. pl. קֹשְׁרִים, (b) 2 Sam. xv. 31.

— pass. f. קְשׁוּרָה, (a) Gen. xliv. 30, &c.

Niph. fem. נִקְשְׁרָה, pres. f. תִּקָּשֵׁר. *Bound, made sure, firm*, Neh. iii. 38. Metaph., 1 Sam. xviii. 1, al. non occ.

Pih. pret. non occ. Pres. תְּקַשֵּׁר. *Bind* on as ornaments, Is. xlix. 18; Job xxxviii. 31: *secure* to thyself. See my note.

Puh. Part. fem. pl. מְקֻשָּׁרוֹת. Lit. *Bound; compact, strong*, Gen. xxx. 41, only.

Hithp. plur. הִתְקַשְּׁרוּ, pres. יִתְקַשֵּׁר. *Was, became bound in conspiracy, conspired*, 2 Chron. xxiv. 25; 2 Kings ix. 14, only.

Part. pl. מִתְקַשְּׁרִים, 2 Chron. xxiv. 26, only.

קִשֻּׁרִים, m. pl. See קֶשֶׁר, and the verb above. *Bandages, belts*, of women, Jer. ii. 32; Is. iii. 20, only. See Schrœder. de Vest. Mulier., c. ix. Aff. קִשֻּׁרֶיהָ, Jer. l. c.

קָשַׁשׁ, v. Kal non occ. except in—

Imp. plur. קֹשּׁוּ. Arab. قشّ, *collegit. Collect, assemble*, together, Zeph. ii. 1, only.

Pih. Imp. pl. קֹשְׁשׁוּ. *Let them collect, gather*, Exod. v. 7, only.

Infin. שֹׁשׁ, Ib. v. 12, only.

Part. מְקֹשֵׁשׁ, Num. xv. 32, 33, only.

— f. מְקֹשֶׁשֶׁת, 1 Kings xvii. 10. 12, only.

Hithp. Imp. pl. הִתְקוֹשְׁשׁוּ. *Be ye collected, assembled; assemble yourselves*, Zeph. i. 2, only.

קֶשֶׁת, f. pl. קְשָׁתוֹת, constr. קַשְּׁתוֹת. Arab. قوس, *arcus*. Syr. ܩܫܬܐ, id. (a) *A bow* for shooting arrows, Gen. xxi. 16; Is. xii. 18; Job xx. 24, &c. Phrr. נְחוּשָׁה —, *of copper*. See my note, Ib. גִּבֹּרִים —, *of the mighty*, 1 Sam. ii. 4. דֹּרְכֵי קֶשֶׁת, *treaders of the bow*, 1 Chron. viii. 40. See under דַּךְ, p. 144. נֹשְׁקֵי קֶשֶׁת, *equipped* (with) *the bow*, 1 Chron. xii. 2. בֶּן־קֶשֶׁת, *an arrow*, Job xli. 20. רִשְׁפֵי קֶשֶׁת, id., Ps. lxxvi. 4. See my notes on Job v. 7; vi. 4. קֶשֶׁת רְמִיָּה. See note on Job xxiv. 20. Comp. 2 Sam. i. 22. מֹשְׁכֵי קֶשֶׁת, *drawers of the bow*, Is. lxvi. 19. Comp. 2 Kings xxii. 34. מָלֵא יָדוֹ בַקֶּשֶׁת, lit. *filled his hand with the bow;* drew it to its full extent, 2 Kings ix. 24. In 2 Sam. i. 18, קֶשֶׁת, should, according to Gesenius, be construed with וַיֹּאמֶר, and imply a composition respecting the bow, on the event there in question. As to *break the bow*, was to destroy a weapon of war, the phrase, שָׁבַר אֶת־קֶשֶׁת, Hos. i. 5, &c., was used to denote *discomfiture*, and the like. Comp. Gen. xlix. 24. (b) *The rainbow*, Gen. ix. 13, seq.; Ezek. i. 28. Aff. קַשְׁתִּי, קַשְׁתְּךָ, קַשְׁתּוֹ, &c.; pl. קַשְׁתוֹתָיו, &c.

קַשָּׁת, masc. once, Gen. xxi. 20. *An archer.*

קָתְרֹס, m. Chald. *Keri*, for קִיתָרוֹס, which see, Dan. iii. 5, &c.

ר

ר, *Resh*, pronounced like our *r*, is the twentieth letter of the Hebrew alphabet. In the Rabbinic notation it stands for the number 200, see Gram. art. 4. It is classed with the liquids ל, ס, נ, Ib. art. 24. It is considered as incapable of receiving *Dagesh*; and is, therefore, very rarely found with it. When the *Dagesh* is so omitted, a compensation takes place in the preceding vowel, which is said then to be either *expressed*, or *implied*, Ib. art. 109.

In some cases ר is inserted for the purpose of supplying the place of *Dagesh forté*, as in דַּרְמֶשֶׂק, for דַּמֶּשֶׂק, *Damascus*. קַרְדֹּם, for Arab. قَدُوم, *an axe*. פֻּרְסֵא, Chald. for the Heb. כִּסֵּא, *a throne*, &c.

It occasionally interchanges with ל, or נ, being a letter of the same organ, as in אַרְמְנוֹת, and אַלְמְנוֹת, *palaces*. שְׁנַיִם, Chald. תְּרֵין, *two*: as also—but very rarely—with the sibilants ז, ס, as in פָּרַס, פָּנַק, חָרַם, חָסַם, Gesen. But this is any thing but certain.

רֹאֶה, m. constr. רְאֵה, once, Job x. 15. Arab. رَائِي, *videns, spectator*. Person *seeing, looking on*.

רָאָה, v. pres. יִרְאֶה, apoc. יֵרֶא, and יָרָא. Arab. رَأَى, *vidit*. Gr. ὁράω. Constr. abs. immed. it. med. אֵת, בְּ, לְ, אֶל, עַל, &c. (a) *Saw, viewed, observed*, abs., Lev. v. 1; xiii. 56; Ps. x. 11; xl. 4; cxiv. 3; Hab. iii. 5, &c. — favourably, with pleasure, &c. Med. בְּ, Gen. xxix. 32; Ps. xxii. 18; liv. 9; Is. lxvi. 24, &c. — with pain, Gen. xxi. 16; xliv. 34, &c. — down upon, unfavourably, Job xl. 11; xli. 26; Cant. i. 6. — the face, countenance, of any great personage, i. e. be admitted to his presence favourably. — of God, Exod. xxiv. 10; xxxiii. 20.

Comp. Ps. xi. 7; xvii. 15: — otherwise fatal, see Gen. xvi. 13; xxxii. 31. Comp. Esth. iv. 11; v. 2, seq. — of kings, 2 Kings xxv. 19; Jer. lii. 25; Esth. i. 14. (b) — *looked out, provided, chose, cared*, for. Med. לְ, עַל, Gen. xxii. 8. 14; Exod. v. 21. Med. אֵת, Gen. xxxix. 23. Immed., Ib. xli. 33; Deut. xii. 13; 1 Kings xii. 16, &c. — to, Is. xvii. 7, &c.: with אֶל. (c) — *visited*, as a person in sickness, 2 Sam. xiii. 5; 2 Kings viii. 20; Ps. xli. 7. (d) *See* the sun, i. e. *live*, Eccl. vii. 11. Comp. ix. 9; Is. xxxviii. 11. Thence, *See good*, Ps. xxxiv. 13; Jer. xxix. 32; Mic. vii. 9; Eccl. L. 1. — *misery*, Lam. iii. 1. — *evil*, Prov. xxvii. 10; Jer. xliv. 17; Obad. vr. 13, &c. (e) Thence, metaph. *Perceived, discovered, found, felt*, Eccl. i. 16; ii. 12; Jer. ii. 31; xx. 12, &c. — *experienced*, Is. xl. 5; Job iv. 8, &c. With בֵּין, med. (f) *Discern, discriminate*, Mal. iii. 18. (g) — as a prophet, meteorologist, heathen priest, &c., Is. xxx. 10; Eccl. xi. 4; Ezek. xxi. 26. Phrr. בַּאֲרֻבּוֹת —, *through the windows*, Eccl. xii. 3. אֶת שָׁלוֹם —, *the welfare of*, Gen. xxxvii. 14. Followed by a sentence having כִּי prefixed, *Saw, observed, that* —, Gen. vi. 5; Judg. xx. 41; 2 Sam. xvii. 23, &c.

Infin. רְאֹה, רָאֹה, רְאוֹ, רַאֲוָה, Exod. iii. 7; Gen. xxvi. 28; Ezek. xxviii. 17, &c.; it. רְאוֹת, Is. xlii. 20: constr. רְאוֹת, Exod. x. 28, &c.: it. with בְּ, כְּ, לְ, מִן, pref., 1 Chron. xxi. 28; Gen. xxiv. 30; ii. 19; xxvii. 1. Aff. רְאֹתִי, Gen. xlvi. 30. רְאֹתְךָ, Exod. x. 28, &c. רְאֹתוֹ, 2 Sam. xxiv. 17, &c.

Imp. רְאֵה, Gen. xxvii. 27. Used also to excite attention, *Behold, observe*, Gen. xli. 41; Exod. vii. 1, &c.

— f. רְאִי, 1 Sam. xxv. 35, &c.

— pl. m. רְאוּ, Gen. xxxix. 14, &c.; fem. רְאֶינָה, Cant. iii. 11.

Part. רֹאֶה, Gen. xiii. 15; xxxi. 5, &c.,

ראה (545) ראה

i. q. חֹזֶה, *A seer, prophet*, 1 Sam. ix. 9; 1 Chron. ix. 22; xxvi. 28, &c. Also, i. q. רָאִי, *vision*, using the concrete for the abstract, Is. xxviii. 7. Aff. רָאִי, Is. xlvii. 10. רֹאֵנוּ, Is. xxix. 15. Pl. רֹאִים, constr. רֹאֵי, Num. xiv. 22; Esth. i. 14. Aff. רֹאַי, Ps. xxii. 8. רֹאֶיךָ, Is. xiv. 16, &c.

— f. רֹאָה, pl. רֹאוֹת, Prov. xx. 12, &c.; it. רֹאֵת, Deut. iii. 12, &c.

Niph. נִרְאָה, pres. יֵרָאֶה, apoc. יֵרָא. Constr. abs. it. med. אֶל, לְ, בְּ, עַל, אֶת, &c. *Was, became, seen, apparent, appearing*, Gen. xlviii. 3; Exod. iii. 16. Phr. עַיִן בְּעַיִן, *eye to eye*, clearly, Num. xiv. 14. — אֶת פְּנֵי יְהֹוָה, *as to the presence of Jehovah*, i. e. in his presence, Exod. xxxiv. 24; 1 Sam. i. 22 : it. אֶת, omit., Exod. xxiii. 15; xxxiv. 20, &c. : it. with לִפְנֵי, Dan. i. 13. See (a) 4, Kal. לְפָנִים, *in former times*, 2 Chron. ix. 11. *Be provided*, (b) above, in Kal, Gen. xxii. 14.

Infin. הֵרָאֹה, Judg. xiii. 21, &c. : it. הֵרָאוֹת, Lev. xiii. 14. לְהֵרָאוֹת, 2 Sam. xvii. 17, &c. : and רָאוֹת, Deut. xxxi. 11, &c. Aff. הֵרָאֹתוֹ, Lev. xiii. 7.

Imp. הֵרָאֵה, 1 Kings xviii. 1.

Part. נִרְאֶה, Gen. xii. 7; xxxv. 1.

Puh. pret. pl. רֹאוּ, once, Job xxxiii. 21, i. q. Niph. The *Dagesh*,—Gesenius prefers supposing Mappik,—is here implied, Gram. art. 109.

Hiph. הִרְאָה, and הֶרְאָה, pres. יַרְאֶה, apoc. יֵרְא. Constr. immed. it. med. אֶת, בְּ. (a) *Made, caused, to see; showed*, Gen. xli. 28; xlviii. 11; Exod. xxvii. 8; Num. viii. 4; Deut. xxxiv. 4, &c. — of prophets, things, to come, 2 Kings viii. 10. 13; Ezek. xi. 25; Amos vii. 1, &c. 1. Med. בְּ, to see with pleasure, delight, Ps. L. 23; lix. 11; xc. 16 : it. with אֶת, 2 Sam. xv. 25. 2. *See, feel, experience* evil, Ps. lx. 5; lxxi. 20; Hab. i. 3; Eccl. iv. 7. — good, Ps. iv. 7; Eccl. ii. 24.

Infin. הַרְאוֹת, Deut. iii. 24, &c. Aff. הַרְאֹתְךָ, Exod. ix. 16; Ezek. xl. 4, &c.

Imp. aff. הַרְאֵנִי, Exod. xxxiii. 18. הַרְאֵנוּ, Judg. i. 24, &c. : f. aff. הַרְאִינִי, Cant. ii. 14.

Part. מַרְאֶה, Exod. xxv. 9; Ezek. xl. 4, only.

Hoph. הָרְאָה, pres. non occ. (a) i. q. Niph. Lev. xiii. 49. (b) *Was made, caused, to see, was shown*, Exod. xxvi. 30; Deut. iv. 35.

Part. מָרְאֶה, Exod. xxv. 40.

Hithp. pret. non occ. pres. plur. יִתְרָאוּ, הִתְרָאָה תִּתְרָאוּ, *Be, become, looking at, viewing*, each other in uncertainty, Gen. xlii. 1. In anger, or for warlike purposes, i. e. meet for contention, 2 Kings xiv. 8. 11; 2 Chron. xxv. 17. 21. So the Arab. conj. vi. *invicem viderunt*, e regione *fuit*, ex adverso *spectavit*.

VIII. *Deliberavit*; اَرى, *disputare, contendere*.

רֹאָה, see Part. Kal of רָאָה.

רָאָה, f. once, Deut. xiv. 13; the name of an unclean *bird;* which, in the parallel place, Lev. xi. 14, is written דָּאָה, and is most probably the correct reading. See page 124, above. *A sort of vulture*, apparently. Bochart. Hieroz., ii. pp. 191, 192, *milvus;* a kite.

רְאָוָה, an Infin. of רָאָה, see above.

רְאוּת, f. r. רָאָה. *Seeing, viewing*, once, Eccl. v. 10. Keri.

רְאוֹת, f. pl. constr. apparently of some sing. now lost, once, 2 Chron. xxvi. 5. *Visions:* as the context seems to require. Eichh. Simonis, " Proprie est infinitivus nominascens." Gesenius takes no notice of it. LXX. ἐν φόβῳ κυρίου. Ἀλλ'. ἐν ὁράσει κυρίου. Ἀλλ'. ἐν ὁράσει Θεοῦ.

רְאִי, m. once, Job xxxvii. 18. *Mirror*, of polished metal. See my note on the passage.

רֳאִי, m. in pause, רֹאִי, m.—pl. non occ. r. רָאָה. (a) *Vision, revelation*, Gen. xvi. 13, in אֵל רֳאִי, *God of vision, appearance*, i. e. who reveals himself. Followed by, הֲגַם הֲלֹם רָאִיתִי אַחֲרֵי רֹאִי. Have I even thus far seen (lived, see רָאָה, v. above), (d) *after vision*, i. e. revelation? None being able to see God and live. This she mentions as an instance of mercy, it. Ib. 14; xxiv. 62. (b) I. q. מַרְאֶה, *Appearance, view, sight*, 1 Sam. xvi. 12; Job vii. 8; xxxiii. 21. See my note here. (c) *Monstrosity*, παράδειγμα, *example*, Nah. iii. 6, only.

רֵאִים, see רְאֵם.

רִאשׁוֹן, see רִאשׁוֹן.

רְאִית, fem. i. q. רְאוּת, above, Eccl. v. 10. Kethiv.

רְאֵם, v. fem. רְאֵמָה, once, Zech. xiv. 10, r. רוּם, as קָאם, Hos. x. 14, of קוּם. *Was* (prophet. *shall be*), *raised, elevated*. Aquila, Symm., Theod., ὑψωθήσεται.

רְאֵם, רְאֵמִים and רֵמִים, masc.—plur.

4 A

ראם (546) ראש

רֵאֵם, רְאֵמִים, רָאמִים. Arab. رِئْم, *oryx*. And this. Bochart. Hieroz., i. p. 948, seq., argues, is the animal in question here. Gesenius, with A. Schultens, on Job xxxix. 9, 10, will have it to be a sort of wild ox, viz., *the Buffalo*. The LXX. makes it *the unicorn*, μονοκέρωτα, which, although found to exist (see Quarterly Review, No. 47), is not at all likely to be the animal. Gesenius prefers considering it *the buffalo*, from Ps. xxix. 6, where בִּרְאֵמִים, is found in the parallel with עֵגֶל, *a calf*. The word occurs, Num. xxiii. 22; Deut. xxxiii. 17; Job xxxix. 9, 10; Ps. xxii. 22; xxix. 6; xcii. 11; Is. xxxiv. 7. From these passages of Job and Isaiah, too, this animal is manifestly mentioned as one of the ox tribe. Schultens and Gesenius are, therefore, probably right.

רָאמוֹת, f. pl. r. ראם, i. q. רום. Things *high, sublime, above comprehension*, Prov. xxiv. 7. — *high* in value, *most precious*, Job xxviii. 18. See my note. Sym. ὑψηλά, Ezek. xxvii. 16.

רָאשׁ, masc. pl. רָאשִׁים, and רָשִׁים, r. רוּשׁ, i. q. רָשׁ. *Poor*, opp. τῷ, עָשִׁיר, 2 Sam. xii. 1. 4;—Prov. x. 4.

רֵאשׁ, m. i. q. רֵישׁ, r. רוּשׁ,—pl. non occ. *Poverty*, Prov. xxx. 8. Aff. רֵאשְׁךָ, Ib. vi. 11.

רֵאשׁ, m. def. רֵאשָׁה, pl. רֵאשִׁין. Aff. רֵאשִׁי, Chald. i. q. Heb. רֹאשׁ. (a) *The head*, Dan. ii. 38; iii. 27; iv. 2. 7. 10; vii. 1. 6, &c. (b) *Chapter, summary*, Ib. vii. 1. Aff. pl. רָאשֵׁיהוֹם, Ezra v. 10.

רֹאשׁ (for רָאשׁ, Gram. art. 73), masc. רָאשִׁים (for רְאָשִׁים, Ib.), constr. רָאשֵׁי. See also Gram. art. 152. 3, where רֹאשׁ is taken as the primitive form. Aff. רֹאשִׁי, רֹאשְׁךָ, Is. xv. 2. רָאשָׁיו, for רֹאשָׁיו, apparently. So LXX. κεφαλῆς. Pl. רָאשָׁי, רָאשֶׁיהָ, &c. Syr. ܪܺܝܫ. Arab. رَأْس. Æth. ርእስ፡ *caput*. (a) *The head* of [1] Man. [2] Beast, or thing. Metaph. [3] In station, *chief, supreme, prince; city*, &c. [4] *Capital, amount*, or *sum*, in number. [5] *Source, commencement, &c*. (b) The name of a certain plant. According to Celsius, Hierobot., ii. 46, *cicuta*, or *hemlock*. Gesen. contends for the *poppy*. Oedmann for the *colocynth*: and Michaelis (Suppl. Lex. Heb., p. 2220), for the *lolium*, or *tares*. All that is certain is, that it was considered a poison. (a), [1] Gen. xl. 20; xlviii. 14, &c. [2] Gen. iii. 15; Exod. xxix. 15. 19; Lev. iv. 4. 15. 24; v. 8, &c. — of thing, Lev. i. 4; iii. 2. 8; iv. 29. 33, &c. *Head*, or *top* of —, Gen. viii. 5; xi. 4; xlvii. 31; Exod. xvii. 9, 10; xix. 20; xxxiv. 2; Num. xxi. 20, &c. [3] 1 Sam. xv. 17; Is. vii. 8. — of the fathers, families, Exod. vi. 14. 25; Num. vii. 2; xxxii. 28; xxxvi. 1. — of the priests, 2 Chron. xix. 11; xxiv. 6. — *city*, Josh. xi. 10; Is. vii. 8. — *stone of the corner*, Ps. cxviii. 22. — of *perfumes*, Exod. xxx. 23; Cant. iv. 14; Ezek. xxvii. 22, &c. [4] *Sum, amount, &c.*, Lev. v. 24. With נָשָׂא, Exod. xxx. 12; Num. i. 2, בְּמִסְפַּר. Comp. vr. 49; iii. 40. — of *a body of men, detachment*, Judg. vii. 16. 20; ix. 34. 37. 43; 1 Sam. xi. 11; 1 Chron. xii. 23. — of each, Judg. v. 30. — of words, Ps. cxix. 160. Metaph. רֹאשׁ שִׂמְחָתִי, *whole amount of my* (earthly) *joy*, Ps. cxxxvii. 6. [5] *Heads, sources*, Gen. ii. 10. — of the *way, commencement, beginning*, Ezek. xvi. 25. — of the *open* or *outer parts*, Lam. ii. 19. — of *captives, front*, Amos vi. 7. — of *time*, Is. xl. 21; Exod. xii. 2. In Prov. viii. 26, תֵּבֵל עַפְרוֹת רֹאשׁ, Gesenius makes, "prima gleba orbis terrarum," i. e. "quæ prima creata est." As if one part of the earth were supposed to have been created before another. The context, however, excludes every created part. This passage would rather mean, therefore, *the principal of the lands* or *places of the earth*. Phr. בְּרֹאשָׁם נָתַתִּי, *I have laid on their own heads*; *punished them with* —, Ezek. ix. 10, &c. בְּרָאשֵׁינוּ יִפּוֹל, *he will fall upon our heads*; *ruin us*, 1 Chron. xii. 19. אֹשֵׁב רֹאשׁ, Job xxix. 25, *I sit* (as) *chief*, like the Latin, "*incedit regina*." הָיוּ לְרֹאשׁ, *they have become for the head*, i. e. *become chief*,—is a very common usage noted under הָיָה, page 153 above. רֹאשׁ נְזִרוֹ, Num. vi. 9. Comp. vr. 18. הוּא יְשׁוּפְךָ רֹאשׁ, *he shall bruise thee*, *the head*, i. e. *capitally*, Gen. iii. 15. Other idioms will be found under נָשָׂא, נָתַן, &c. רֹאשׁ וְזָנָב, *head and tail*; *high and low*, Is. ix. 13. (b) רֹאשׁ, and רוֹשׁ. *Poison, venom*, Deut. xxix. 17; xxxii. 32; Hos. x. 4; Amos vi. 12; Ps. lxix. 22; Lam. iii. 5. 19. — of *adders*, Deut. xxxii. 33; Job xx. 16. Phr. מֵי־רֹאשׁ, *water* of —, Jer. viii. 14; ix. 14; xxiii. 15: which Gesenius takes to signify, "*opium*."

רֹאשָׁה, fem. once, Ezek. xxxvi. 11, pl. aff. רָאשֵׁתֵיכֶם, *Your beginnings,* i. q. רֹאשׁ [5] above.

רֹאשָׁה, fem. once, Zech. iv. 7. *Chief, principal,* רֹאשׁ, [3] above.

רִאשׁוֹן, m. twice, רִאשִׁי, Josh. xxi. 10, Job xv. 7; once. רִישׁוֹן, Job viii. 9: pl. רִאשֹׁנִים, r. רֹאשׁ.—

רִאשֹׁנָה, and רִאשׁוֹנָה, f. pl. רִאשׁוֹנוֹת and רִאשֹׁנוֹת.—

masc. (a) *First* or *former,* as to [1] Time: [2] Order or place: [3] Dignity. [1] Gen. xxvi. 1; Is. xli. 4; xliv. 6; xlviii. 12, &c.: opp. τῷ, אַחֲרוֹן. So רִאשֹׁנִים, *ancestors,* Deut. xix. 14, &c. Comp. 2 Chron. xvi. 11. [2] Gen. xxv. 25; xxxii. 18; Exod. xii. 2, &c. [3] 1 Chron. xviii. 17. Applied also to persons, things, times, months, day, &c. It. adverb, Jer. L. 17, &c. Fem. [1] Is. xlii. 9; xliii. 9; xlviii. 3, &c. [2] Is. lx. 9; Zech. vi. 2, &c. Adverb, Gen. xxxiii. 2; xxxviii. 28, &c. Phr. בָּרִאשֹׁנָה, *as formerly,* Deut. ix. 18, &c. בָּרִאשֹׁנָה, *in front,* Is. lx. 9. כְּבָרִאשֹׁנָה, *as formerly,* Is. i. 26. לָרִאשֹׁנָה, *as to the first;* at the first, *formerly,* Judg. xviii. 29. So, בָּרִאשֹׁנָה, Gen. xiii. 4. First of all, Deut. xiii. 10, opp. τῷ, אַחֲרֹנָה; לְמַבְּרִאשֹׁנָה, lit. *as to what at the first,* or, *in the first place;* i. q. רֹאשֹׁנָה + הָ + בְּ + לָמָה, 1 Chron. xv. 13.

רִאשֹׁנִית, f. once, Jer. xxv. 1. *First.*

רָאשֹׁתִי, f. constr. מִן pref. once, 1 Sam. xxvi. 12, מֵרָאשֹׁתֵי שָׁאוּל. *From the head* (furniture, implements, or the like) *of Saul.* LXX. ἀπὸ προσκεφαλῆς αὐτοῦ. See מְרַאֲשׁוֹת p. 389, above.

רֵאשִׁית, once, רֵשִׁית, fem.—pl. non. occ. r. רֹאשׁ. Syr. ܪܺܫܺܝܬܳܐ, *initium, principium;* opp. τῷ, אַחֲרִית. *First,* or *former,* (1) *State,* in either order, or dignity. (2) — *time.* (3) — *produce,* fruit, or offspring. (4) — *way, proceedings.* (1) — *first,* or *beginning,* Gen. i. 1; x. 10; Num. xxiv. 20: see my note on Job xl. 15, p. 519: Is. xlvi. 10; Job viii. 7; xlii. 12; Eccl. vii. 8; Hos. ix. 10, &c. (2) *First, beginning,* as to time, period, Deut. xi. 12. (3) — *produce, fruits,* &c., as offered, Lev. ii. 12; xxiii. 10; Num. xv. 20; Deut. xviii. 4; xxvi. 10; Jer. ii. 3. Thence, of *offspring,* Gen. xlix. 3; Ps. lxxviii. 51; cv. 36. Thence, *the best,* 1 Sam. ii. 29; Jer. xlix. 35; Amos vi. 1; Dan. ix. 41, &c.

So, Deut. xxxiii. 21, וַיַּרְא רֵאשִׁית לוֹ, *so he looked out,* provided, *for himself,* a (lit.) *headship,* state of wealth. (4) *First, of way,* proceedings. —, דַּרְכּוֹ, Prov. viii. 22; Job xl. 19. See my note ib. on vr. 15. Aff. רֵאשִׁיתְךָ, Job viii. 7. רֵאשִׁיתוֹ, Ib. xlii. 12. See also Hos. ix. 10; Num. xviii. 12.

רַב, m. pause, רָב, pl. רַבִּים, constr. רַבֵּי.—

רַבָּה, f. constr. רַבַּת, pl. רַבּוֹת.—

Arab. رَبَّ, *auxit, collegit; dominus fuit.* Æth. ረቡሐ: *extendit.* Syr. ܪܰܒ, *magnus.* (a) *Much,* or (b) *Many,* as applied to quantity, or individuality. Also, (c) *Abundant, enough.* (d) *Great, vast,* in extent, station, &c. (a) Gen. xxiv. 25; Exod. xii. 38; 1 Kings x. 2; Ps. xix. 11, &c. Adverb, רַב שָׂבַעְנוּ בוּז, *we are much filled* with *contempt,* Ps. cxxiii. 3; Is. xxi. 7. (b) Gen. xxvi. 14; Deut. xx. 1; Josh. xvii. 14; 1 Kings iii. 8; Job xxxvi. 28; Ps. lxxxix. 51. Phrr. וַיִּפֹּל מִמֶּנּוּ רָב, *and many of them fell,* Exod. xix. 21: opp. τῷ, מְעַט, Num. xiii. 18; 1 Sam. xiv. 6, בְּרַב אוֹ בִמְעָט. Comp. Num. xxvi. 56; 2 Chron. xiv. 10, אֵין בִּן רַב לְאֵין כֹּחַ; Ib. xxxii. 7, עִמָּנוּ רַב מֵעִמּוֹ, *more with us, than with him.* (c) Gen. xxxiii. 9; xlv. 28; Deut. i. 6; iii. 26; 2 Sam. xxiv. 16; 1 Kings xix. 4, &c. (d) — as to space, extent, Gen. vii. 11; Esth. i. 20; 1 Kings xix. 7. — of God's goodness, Ps. xxxi. 20. — of calamity, Num. xi. 33; 2 Chron. xiii. 17. — sin, Ps. xix. 14. — station, dignity, Job xxxv. 9: but see my note here. מַבַּחִים —, 2 Kings xxv. 8. סָרִיסִים —, Dan. i. 3. — מָשָׁל, Dan. xi. 4. לְהוֹשִׁיעַ —, Is. lxiii. 1. — as to birth, Gen. xxv. 23. — *age,* Job xxxii. 9. — in art, Prov. xxvi. 10, &c. So Gesenius: but see מְחוֹלֵל, p. 187, above. Phrr. רַב תְּבוּנָה, *great of* (in) *intelligence,* Prov. xiv. 29. רַבַּת בָּנִים, — *in children,* having many, 1 Sam. ii. 5. רַבָּתִי עָם, — *in people,* Lam. i. 1: with י, parag., Gram. art. 175. 16. Hence—

רִבָּיו, *his arrows,* once, Job xvi. 13. The notion of shooting out being cognate with that of increase, extent. See my note on this place.

רַב, m. Chal. def. רַבָּא, pl. רַבְרְבִין, aff. רַבְרְבָנֵי, &c. Fem. def. רַבְּתָא, pl. רַבְרְבָן, and רַבְרְבָתָא, &c. I. q. Heb. (1) *Great, large,* Dan. ii. 31. 35; v. 1; vii. 7. — in extent,

רב (548) רבה

Dan. vii. 2; iv. 27. — *power*, Dan. vii. 3. 17. (2) *Great*, in station, dignity. — of God, Dan. ii. 45; Ezra v. 8. — of kings, &c., Dan. ii. 10. 14. 48; iv. 6; v. 11; Ezra iv. 10. *Great, important*, Dan. vii. 20. — *fearful*, Dan. iii. 33; vii. 8. 11. *Great* men, *Nobles*, Dan. iv. 33; v. 2. 23; vi. 18, &c.

רַב, see רִיב.

רֹב, רוֹב, or רָבִי, and לִבּ־, plur. constr. רֲבֵי, aff. רֻבָּם רֻבְּכֶם, r. רבב. *Multitude, abundance*, Lev. xxv. 16; Ps. xxxiii. 16; li. 3; and so Job iv. 14: see my note: Is. i. 11. — in extent, Josh. ix. 13. לָרֹב, *to abundance, abundantly*, Gen. xxx. 30; xlviii. 16; Deut. i. 10. Phrr. רֹב שָׁנִים, *abundant in years, old*, Job xxxiii. 7. Comp. Eccl. xi. 1. לֹא יִסָּפֵר מֵרֹב, *shall not be counted from abundance*, Gen. xvi. 10. Comp. 1 Kings iii. 8. רֻבֵּי תּוֹרָתִי, *the abounding of my law*, its abundant provisions, Hos. viii. 12.

רבב, v. pret. רַבּוּ, pres. non occ. See רב above. Cogn. רָבָה. Constr. abs. it med. מִן, than. I. *Be, become many, numerous*, 1 Sam. xxv. 10; Ps. iii. 2; lxix. 5; civ. 24, &c. Infin. רֹב, Gen. vi. 1.

II. Pret. רַב, pl. רַבּוּ. See רַבַּי, under רַב, above. *Shot*, as arrows, lightning, Gen. xlix. 23; Ps. xviii. 11.

Puh. Part. pl. f. מְרֻבָּבוֹת, once, Ps. cxliv. 13. *Made very numerous:* but the occurrence of מֵאֲלִיפוֹת, from Num. אלף, plainly suggests that רָבָבָה, should be considered as the ground form of this word. Lit. *Ten thousanded*, i. e. produced to that extent. LXX. πληθύνοντα.

רְבָבָה, f. pl. רִבְבוֹת,·constr. רִבְבוֹת, r. רבב. Arab. رَبِّيْ, *mille*. Lit. Many, put to express an indefinitely large number, as in רְבָבָה כְּצֶמַח הַשָּׂדֶה, *many as the shoots of the field*, Ezek. xvi. 7, i. e. just as we say, *ten thousand*. Aquila, Symm., μυριὰς, μυριάδες, Deut. xxxiii. 2, i. q., רִבּוֹ, Gen. xxiv. 60; Lev. xxvi. 8; Deut. xxxii. 30; Ps. xci. 7, &c.: Pl., 1 Sam. xviii. 8. Constr., Num. x. 36; Deut. xxxiii. 17, &c. Aff. רִבְבֹתָיו, 1 Sam. xviii. 7.

רבד, v. pret. רָבַדְתִּי, once, Prov. vii. 16, i. q. רַף. See my note on Job xvii. 13. Arab. رَبَدَ, *constitit, substitit:* whence

مِرْبَدْ, κλεισίον, stabulum. See מַרְבַדִּים above, p. 389. *Spread, strewed, made up*. Aq., Theod., περιστρώμασι περιέστρωσα.

רָבָה, v. pres. יִרְבֶּה, apoc. יֶרֶב. תֶּרֶב. Cogn. רבב. See also רַב, opp. τῷ, מֵעַט. Constr. abs. it med. עַל, on; לְ, to, towards; מִן, than. (a) *Be, become, much* or *many, multiply*, Gen. i. 22; viii. 17; xliii. 34; Exod. i. 10. 12. 20; Deut. vi. 3; viii. 13; xxx. 16; 1 Sam. xiv. 30. (b) *Great, powerful*, Job xxxiii. 12; Prov. xxix. 2: but comp. vr. 16.

Infin. רְבוֹת, Exod. xi. 9, &c.

Imp. רְבֵה, pl. רְבוּ, Gen. xxxv. 11; L. 22, &c.

Part. רֹבֶה, Gen. xxi. 20, in יְהִי רֹבֶה קַשָּׁת, *he became increasing* (i. q. יֶרֶד, ib.), i. e. *growing up an archer.* Arab. رَبِي, *adolevit.*

Pih. רִבִּיתִי, once only, Ps. xliv. 13. *Made much*, i. e. obtained great price, or wealth.

Hiph. הִרְבָּה, pres. יַרְבֶּה, apoc. יֶרֶב. Constr. immed. it. med. אֵת, לְ, מִן, than; עַד, בְּ, in; כְּ, as, like. (1) *Multiplied, increased*, Deut. i. 10; Judg. xvi. 24; Job ix. 17; x. 17, &c. (2) *Extended, enlarged*, 1 Chron. iv. 10; Num. xxvi. 54; Ps. lxxi. 21. (3) *Made great*, Ps. xviii. 36;—Job. xxxiv. 37, Gesen. Phrr. הִרְבָּה לְהִתְפַּלֵּל, *she did much to pray*, i. e. prayed much, 1 Sam. i. 12, &c. תַּרְבּוּ תְדַבְּרוּ, *ye speak much*, 1 Sam. ii. 3, Gram. art. 222. יַרְבֶּה, opp. τῷ, יַמְעִיט, Exod. xxx. 15.

Infin. abs. הַרְבּוֹת, Deut. xvii. 16. Constr. הַרְבַּת, 2 Sam. xiv. 11. See Kethiv. adv. הַרְבֵּה, Gen. iii. 16; xvi. 10, &c.: it. הַרְבֶּה variously. הַרְבֵּה מְאֹד, *very much, exceedingly*, Gen. xv. 1; xli. 49; Deut. iii. 5, &c. הַרְבֵּה נָפַל, *much, many, fell*, lit. *multiplyingly*, i. e. in great number, *fell*, 2 Sam. i. 4, opp. τῷ, מְעַט, Eccl. v. 11. צַדִּיק הַרְבֵּה, *lit. multiplying righteousness*, i. e. assuming it to self. Comp. תִּתְחַכַּם in the next member, Eccl. vii. 16: see also vr. 17, &c.

Imp. הַרְבֵּה, Ezek. xxiv. 10, only, apoc. הֶרֶב, Judg. xx. 38: f. הַרְבִּי, Is. xxiii. 16. Pl. הַרְבּוּ, Gen. xxxiv. 12; Amos iv. 4. Part. מַרְבֶּה, Prov. xxviii. 8; Is. xxxiii. 23. Constr. מַרְבֵּה, Lev. xi. 42.

— pl. מַרְבִּים, Exod. xxxvi. 5, &c.

רְבָה, v. Chald. pres. non occ. Arab. رَبِي, *accessione crevit*. Syr. ܪܒܐ, id.

רְבוּ ‎ ‎ (549) ‎ ‎ רִבִּי

constr. abs. *Grew, became great*, in quantity or power, Dan. iv. 8. 19, al. non occ.

Pah. רַבִּי, once, Dan. ii. 48 : med. ל, *made great*, in station.

רִבּוּ, and רִבּוֹא, f. dual, רִבּוֹתַיִם, pl. רִבּוֹת, רִבֹּאוֹת, Neh. vii. 71. Syr. ܪܒܘ. Arab. رَبِّي, *myrias*, i. q. רְבָבָה. An indefinitely large number, *Ten thousand, myriad*, Jonah iv. 11 ; 1 Chron. xxix. 7 ; Ezra ii. 64 ; Neh. vii. 66. Dual, Ps. lxviii. 18. Pl., Ezra ii. 69 ; Dan. xi. 12, al. non occ. It would be as erroneous to suppose—with Gesenius—that the sing. should be regularly רִבּוֹת, as it would, that the Syr. ܪܒܘ, ought to be written ܪܒܘܐ. The truth is, the ת is added for the purpose, apparently, of filling up the hiatus which would otherwise occur in the case, construction, affix, &c. רִבּוֹ, is written, perhaps, for רִבּוּ or רִבִּי. Gram. art. 87. 2.

רִבּוֹ, f. pl. רִבְבָן, *Keri*, רִבְבָן, Chald. Dan. vii. 10, only. I. q. Heb.—r. רבב.

רִבָּה, f.—pl. non occ. Def. רִבּוּתָא. Aff. רְבוּתָךְ, r. רבה. *Greatness*, in station, power. Dan. iv. 19. 33 ; v. 18 ; vii. 27, al. non occ.

רִבּוֹת, see רִבּוּ.

רְבִיבִים, m. pl. r. רבב. Arab. رَبَبٌ, *aqua copiosa*, etiam *salubris*, رَبَابٌ, *nubes alba*, as portending rain, prosperity. See my note on Job vi. 16, throughout. *Showers*, so called from their copiousness, and fertilizing properties, Deut. xxxii. 2 ; Jer. iii. 3 ; xiv. 22 ; Ps. lxv. 11 ; lxxii. 6 ; Mic. v. 6, al. non occ.

רָבִיד, constr. רְבִד, m. r. רָבַד. Arab. رَبَدَ, *impositi invicem dactyli, &c*: it. رَبَدَ, *diversicolores lanæ partes quæ de cameli, aliusve animalis, collo, vel ex aure appenduntur, ornatus ergo*. *A chain*, or other *ornament*, hanged about the neck, Gen. xli. 42 ; Ezek. xvi. 11, only. Aquila, Symm., Gen. μανιάκης ; Ezek. κλοιός. LXX. Theod., κάθεμα.

רְבִיעִי, masc. pl. רְבִיעִים, } Ordinal of the רְבִיעִית, f. pl. non occ. } number *four*. Gram. art. 181. 2. *Fourth*, Gen. i. 19 ; xv. 16, &c. Fem., Lev. xix. 24 ; 1 Kings vi. 1, &c. The thing numbered is often omitted by the ellipsis, Ezek. i. 1, &c. See Gram. art. 227. 6. Phrr. בְּנֵי רְבֵעִים, *sons of the fourth* (fathers in order), i. e. of the fourth generation, 2 Kings x. 30 ; xv. 12. The fem. also signifies *the fourth part*, fractionally, of measure, Exod. xxix. 40 ; Lev. xxiii. 13, &c. — of time, Neh. ix. 3. — of space, *fourfold*, or — *square*, Ezek. xlvii. 20 ; Auth. Vers.

רְבִיעִי, Chald. f. רְבִיעָא, once, רְבִיעָי, *Keri*, רְבִיעָאָה, in every case ; def. רְבִיעָתָא, i. q. Heb., Dan. ii. 40 ; iii. 25 ; vii. 7. 23 : def. Ib. 19. 23.

רָבַךְ, v. occ. in Hoph. Part. f. only. Arab. رَبَكَ, *commiscuit*, pec. *bene paravit jusculo confractum, intritumve* panem.

Hoph. Part. fem. מֻרְבֶּכֶת. *Saturated*, with oil. Synon. τοῦ, בָּלוּל, Lev. vi. 14 ; vii. 11 ; 1 Chron. xxiii. 29, only.

רֶבַע, masc. pl. aff. רִבְעֵיהֶן, רְבָעָיו, רְבָעָיו.—

רֹבַע, m.—pl. non occ.— Arab. رُبْع, *quadrans*, r. רבע. *Fourth part* of any thing, Exod. xxix. 40 ; 1 Sam. ix. 8 ; —Num. xxiii. 10 ; 2 Kings vi. 25, al. non occ. sing. Pl. aff. — *side*, i. e. any one side of four, Ezek. i. 8. 16 ; xliii. 16, 17, al. non occ.

רבע, m. aff. רִבְעִי, once, Ps. cxxxix. 3, in אָרְחִי וְרִבְעִי. *My way*, path, *and my lying down*, reposing, for רִבְעִי, r. רָבַע ; a change peculiar to the Syriac and Chaldaïc. Syr. ܪܒܥ, *cubavit*. See Rosenmüller on the place. Whence—

רבע, I. v. Kal non occ. except— Infin. רִבְעָה, med. ה. *Lying with*, carnally, Lev. xx. 16 ; Ib. xviii. 23. Aff. רִבְעָה, al. non occ.

Hiph. pres. 2d pers. תַּרְבִּיעַ, once, Lev. xix. 19. *Cause, suffer, to lie with*, gender. It.—

רבע, II. v. r. רָבַע, or רוּבַע. Kal non occ. except in— Part. רָבוּעַ, plur. רְבֻעִים. } *Four-sided*, — fem. רְבֻעָה, pl. non occ. } having four sides, Exod. xxvii. 1 ; xxviii. 16 ; Ezek. xliii. 16, &c. Pl., 1 Kings vii. 5, only. Fem., Ezek. xli. 21, only.

Puh. Part. מְרֻבָּע, pl. non occ. } *Made four-* — fem. מְרֻבָּעָה, plur. מְרֻבָּעוֹת. } *sided*, *four-square*, 1 Kings vii. 31 ; Ezek. xl. 47 ; xlv. 2, al. non occ.

רבע (550) רבר

רֶבַע, pl. only, רִבֵּעִים. Men of *the fourth generation*, Exod. xx. 5; xxxiv. 7; Num. xiv. 18; Deut. v. 9, al. non occ.

רֶבֶץ, pl. non occ. Aff. רִבְצוֹ, רִבְעָהּ, רִבְעָם. Arab. رَبَضَ, *cubuit*. Cogn. رَبَعَ, *se incurvavit; prolem genuit*. See רָבַע above. Syr. ܪܒܥ, *cubuit*. *Lying down*, of cattle, properly, Is. lxv. 10; xxxv. 7; Jer. l. 6. Meton. *Place of* —, of man, Prov. xxiv. 15, al. non occ.

רָבַץ, v. pres. יִרְבַּץ. See רֶבֶץ. Constr. abs. it. med. בְּ, in; לְ, at; בֵּין, between; תַּחַת, under; עַל, אֶל, on; עִם, with. *Lie down*, of beasts, Gen. xxix. 2; xlix. 9; Num. xxii. 27, &c. — of a bird brooding over her young, Deut. xxii. 6, only. — of men at ease, Job xi. 19; Is. xiv. 30; xvii. 2. — of the deep, as affording wealth, Gen. xlix. 25. Metaph. — of anger, *lie upon one*, with בְּ, Deut. xxix. 19. — of *sin*, Gen. iv. 7, in חַטָּאת רֹבֵץ, where, however, the concordance is logical, not formal, Gram. art. 215. .5, seq. Hence it has been supposed, that an *animal* of some kind ought to be understood; and thence, that the place should be rendered *sin-offering*. Gesenius thinks that *sin lying*, as a wild beast in ambush, is the sense of the place. It is, however, of but little importance which of these senses is adopted; for *guilt* in every case is implied, and thence punishment and degradation (opp. τῷ, שְׂאֵת). That guilt was to be cancelled only by *sacrifice*, is either implied or positively taught throughout the Bible, and is obvious enough in the case of Abel, as implied here, and reasoned on by St. Paul, Heb. xi. 4; where he tells us that Abel's sacrifice was more *excellent* than Cain's: πλείονα θυσίαν, a FULLER *sacrifice*; the fact being, Cain brought *no proper sacrifice*: it was a mere *offering* of the fruits of his ground. And, hence, it should seem, *he did not well*; the context supplying no other cause for his having done ill. If so, his offering evinced nothing beyond gratitude to his Creator; while that of Abel did this, with the additional consideration of his own unworthiness and guilt, a thing incumbent on all, now that man had fallen.

Part. רֹבֵץ, pl. רֹבְצִים, Exod. xxii. 5; Gen. xxix. 2.

— fem. רֹבֶצֶת, Gen. xlix. 25, &c.—pl. non occ. Hiph. pres. תַּרְבִּיץ, יַרְבִּצוּ. Constr. immed.

med. בְּ, in. (a) *Cause, make, to lie down*, of beasts, Is. xiii. 20; Jer. xxxiii. 12; Cant. i. 7. — of men, Ezek. xxxiv. 15; Ps. xxiii. 2. (b) *Set*, precious stones, Is. liv. 11, only.

Part. מַרְבִּיץ, pl. מַרְבִּצִים, Is. l. c. (b), Jer. l. c. (a), al. non occ.

רַבְרְבִין, pl. m. Chald. of רַב.

רַבְרְבָנִין, pl. See under רַב.

רֶגֶב, masc. pl. רְגָבִים, constr. רִגְבֵי. Arab. مَرْجَب, *stabilis, firmus*. The primary notion seems to have consisted in *firmness, hardness*: thence, cogn. رَجْم, *lapis*. (a) *Clods* of earth, hard from drought, Job xxxviii. 38. See my note, al. non occ. (b) *Stones* set up as monuments, Job xxi. 33, only. See my notes on both places.

רֹגֶז, masc. — plur. non occ. Aff. רָגְזָהּ, fem. רִגְזָךְ. Arab. رَجَز. Syr. ܪܘܓܙܐ, *ira, indignatio*. (a) *Disturbing, vexation, trouble*, Job iii. 17. 26; xiv. 1; Is. xiv. 3. (b) *Neighing*, as expressive of the fierceness of the war-horse, Job xxxix. 24 (27). (c) *Fury, anger*, Hab. iii. 2. (d) *Rage, roar*, of the thunder, Job xxxvii. 2. Fem. once, Ezek. xii. 18. *Perturbation, trembling*.

רָגַז, v. pres. יִרְגַּז. See רֹגֶז. Cogn. רָעַשׁ. Synon. τοῦ, חָרֵד. Constr. abs. it. med. לְ, מִן, בְּ, עַל, לִפְנֵי. (a) *Shook, trembled*, — of things, Joel ii. 10; Amos viii. 8; 2 Sam. xxii. 8; Ps. xviii. 8; Is. v. 25, &c. — persons, Jer. xxxiii. 9; Is. xxxii. 10, 11; Joel ii. 1, &c. (b) — became *disturbed, agitated*, Deut. ii. 25; 2 Sam. vii. 10; xix. 1; Is. xiv. 9; xxviii. 21; lxiv. 1; Hab. iii. 16. תִּרְגַּז, — with anger, Prov. xxix. 9; Ezek. xvi. 43; Ps. iv. 5. Comp. Eph. iv. 26. Phr. יִרְגְּזוּ מִמִּסְגְּרֹתֵיהֶם, *They shall tremble from their close places*: i. e. their fear shall be heard from these, Mic. vii. 17. יִרְגְּזוּן יְרִיעוֹת, *the curtains of* — *shall shake*, i. e. the palaces—thence powers—of which these were a part, Hab. iii. 6. Comp. Is. xxiii. 11.

Imp. pl. רִגְזוּ, Ps. iv. 5, only.

Hiph. pres. אַרְגִּיז, הִרְגִּיז. Constr. immed. it. med. לְ. *Move, agitate*, Is. xiii. 13; xxiii. 11; Jer. l. 34. — *move* to anger, Job xii. 6. — *disturb*, 1 Sam. xxviii. 15; Is. xiv. 16; Job ix. 6. מִמְּקוֹמָהּ —, so that

רגז (551) רגל

it is removed *from its station*, dignity. See my note here.

Part. מַרְגִּיז, pl. constr. מַרְגִּיזֵי, Job ll. cc.

Hithp. Infin. aff. only, הִתְרַגֶּזְךָ. *Thy commotion, excitement*, 2 Kings xix. 27, 28; Is. xxxvii. 28, 29, with אֶל, al. non occ.

רגז, v. Chald. occ. only in—

Aph. pret. pl. הַרְגִּזוּ, with לְ. *Provoked, excited, to anger*, Ezra v. 12, only.

רְגַז, m.—pl. non occ. Chald. *Anger*, Dan. iii. 13.

רָגֶז, m.—pl. non occ. *Trembling*, once, Deut. xxviii. 65.

רֶגֶל, c. dual, רַגְלַיִם, pl. רְגָלִים, constr. רַגְלֵי. Aff. רַגְלִי. Syr. ܪܶܓܠܳܐ. Arab. رِجْل, *pes. The foot*, of either man or beast, Ezek. xxix. 11; Exod. xxi. 24; Lev. xxi. 19; Num. xxii. 25; Is. xxxii. 20; Ezek. i. 7, &c. Sometimes put (meton.) for the whole person, Job xxiii. 11; xxviii. 4; Ps. xxxvi. 12, &c. Phrr. מִכַּף רֶגֶל, *from the sole of the foot to* —, Is. i. 6. שָׁרְשֵׁי רַגְלַי, *soles of my feet*, Job xiii. 27. רֶגֶל מוּעָדֶת, *tottering foot*, Prov. xxv. 19. Comp. Ps. xxxviii. 17; xciv. 18: and see my note on Job xii. 5. עָבְרוּ בְרָגֶל, *they passed over on foot*, Ps. lxvi. 6. לְרַגְלִי, — *for my proceeding*, i. e. on account of me, Gen. xxx. 30. לְרֶגֶל הַמְּלָאכָה, *at the foot*, i. e. according to the pace, of the property, Ib. xxxiii. 14. לְרַגְלָיו, *at his feet*, his person, Hab. iii. 5. Comp. 1 Sam. xxv. 42; Job xviii. 11. בְּרַגְלֶיךָ, *at thy feet*, near thee, at hand, Exod. xi. 8. Comp. Judg. iv. 10; v. 15; viii. 5; 1 Sam. xxv. 27; 2 Sam. xv. 17. הִשְׁקִיתָ בְרַגְלְךָ, *shalt water with thy foot*, i. e. as much ease as the channels in a garden are, which may be turned, &c. with the foot. See פֶּלֶג. — מֵימֵי רַגְלַיִם, *water of the feet*, urine, Is. xxxvi. 12. Keri הַרַגְלַיִם שְׂעַר, *hair of the feet, pubes*, Is. vii. 20. מִבֵּין רַגְלֶיהָ, *from between her feet*, womb, Deut. xxviii. 57. רְגָלִים, *feet*, for strokes of the feet: thence, *times, repetitions*, Exod. xxiii. 14; Numb. xxii. 28. 32, 33. יִשָּׂא רַגְלָיו, Gen. xxix. 1. יָדַיִם אֶת־רַגְלָיו, Ib. xli. 44, shall *lift up his foot*, move. Pers. قدم بر داشتن. מְנַע רַגְלְךָ, *withhold thy foot, go not*, Prov. i. 15. Comp. Jer. ii. 25. שָׁמַר רַגְלְךָ, *shall keep thy foot, preserve thee*, Prov. iii. 26. הֲדֹם רַגְלַי, *stool of my foot*, Is. lxvi. 1. מְקוֹם רַגְלַי, *place of my feet*, dwelling place, Ib. lx. 13. To these many other usages may be added, which the student may take from the Concordance at his leisure.

רְגַל, f. Chald. dual, רַגְלִין, def. רַגְלַיָּא. Aff. רַגְלֵיהּ, רַגְלוֹהִי, i. q. Heb. רֶגֶל, Dan. vii. 4; ii. 41, 42; Ib. 33, 34; vii. 7.

רָגַל, v. pres. non occ. Cogn. רָכַל. Once, Ps. xv. 3, in לֹא רָגַל עַל לְשֹׁנוֹ. Lit. *Walks* (it) *not upon his tongue;* meaning, perhaps, much the same thing as the following context: pec. makes not his tongue a sort of stalking horse, on which to injure his neighbour. Arab. اِرْتَجَلَ, *vituperavit*. Castell.

Pih. pret. non occ. pres. יְרַגֵּל. (a) *Goes about*, as a busybody (comp. 1 Tim. v. 13), calumniating, 2 Sam. xix. 28. (b) — *exploring*, as a spy, &c., Deut. i. 24; Josh. xiv. 7; Judg. xviii. 2. 14. 17.

Infin. רַגֵּל, Num. xxi. 32, &c. Aff. רַגְּלָהּ, 2 Sam. x. 3.

Imp. רַגְּלוּ, Josh. vii. 2.

Part. pl. מְרַגְּלִים, Gen. xlii. 9, &c.

תִּרְגַּלְתִּי, 1st pers. pret. fm. תרגל. Arab. اِرْتَجَلَ, *pedem prehendit*. Gesenius gives, Syr. ܐܰܪܓܶܠ, "*ire docuit*." But upon what authority? The verb is formed on a derivative of רֶגֶל, not now in use, and signifying, apparently, *Being at*, or *near the foot;* or, as we say, *at hand*. See phr. לְרֶגֶל, under רֶגֶל above. So LXX. συνεπόδισα; once, Hos. xi. 3. Syr. ܪܰܒܝܶܬ, *I led:* so the Targum.

רַגְלִי, m. pl. רַגְלִים, m. relative n. of רֶגֶל. *Foot soldier, infantry;* with or without אִישׁ, Exod. xii. 37; Num. xi. 21; Judg. xx. 2, &c. Pl. once, Jer. xii. 5. Syr. ܪܶܓܠܳܐ, Arab. رَاجِل, id.

רגם, v. רָגַם, pres. יִרְגְּמוּ. Constr. immed. it. med. אֶת, בְּ, of pers. or thing, it. עַל, of pers. Syr. ܪܓܰܡ, *lapidibus obruit*. Arab. رَجَم, id. *Overwhelmed with stones, stoned to death*. Phr. בָּאֶבֶן אוֹתָךְ רָגְמוּ, *they shall overwhelm thee with stones*, Ezek. xvi. 40. —, Ib. xxiii. 46. — אֹתוֹ, Lev. xxiv. 14. רָגְמֻהוּ, Deut. xxi. 21. וְרָגְמוּ יִרְגְּמוּ־בוֹ Lev. xxiv. 16. בָּאֲבָנִים, Num. xiv. 10. See, also, Lev. xx. 27; xxiv. 16. 23; Num. xv. 36, &c.

רגם (552) רגשׁ

Infin. רָגוֹם, רְגֹם, Lev. xxiv. 16; Num. xv. 35: it. לִרְגּוֹם, Ib. xiv. 10.

רִגְמָה, f. aff. רִגְמָתָם, once, Ps. lxviii. 28, r. רגם. LXX. ἡγεμόνες. Which suits the passage well. Arab. رَاجِم, jaculando defendit aliquem, hostes propellens; رجمة, cippus; رَجْمَة, signum. Their stone of defence; sign, monument, of power. The final ה, or ח, moreover, may have been added (see קְהִלָּה above) to express singularity or excellence; which will add to the force of the passage. Gesenius gives, "caterva, agmen," which suits neither the etymology nor the context well.

רגן, v. pret. pres. non occ. Arab. رَجَن, puduit alicujus; erubuit. VIII. Confusum turbatumque fuit negotium. Syr. cogn. ܢܓܢ, subduxit se. The primary notion was, perhaps, secret, concealed, disregard or shunning. Thence the expression of this, in murmuring or complaining.

Part. masc. pl. רוֹגְנִים, once, Is. xxix. 24. Murmurers. Symm. γογγυσταί.

Niph. pres. וַיֵּרָגְנוּ. They set about murmuring, with בְּ, Ps. cvi. 25; Deut. i. 27. Aquila, προσηρίσατε. See LXX. Al. non occ.

רֶגַע, m. pl. רְגָעִים. Arab. رِجْع, passus, gressus, jumenti; anteriorumque pedum flexus ac eductus. Thence, perhaps, as in רַגְלַיִם above, the notion of rapid, or momentary, succession or following of action. Thence, Instant, moment, of time. Constr. specif., Gram. art. 219, note; Exod. xxxiii. 5; Job xxxiv. 20; Ps. vi. 11, &c.; it. with בְּ, Is. liv. 7; Job xxi. 13. With כְּ, Num. xvi. 21; Ps. lxxiii. 19. Pl. with לְ. Moment after moment, incessantly, Job vii. 18; Is. xxvii. 3; Ezek. xxvi. 16; xxxii. 10. Phrr. רֶגַע בְּאַפּוֹ, momentary in his anger, Ps. xxx. 6. With מֵעַט, Ezra ix. 8; Is. xxvi. 20: with קָטֹן, for emphasis. עֲדֵי־רָגַע, during a moment, momentary, Job xx. 5.

רָגֵעַ, m. pl. constr. רִגְעֵי, once, Ps. xxxv. 20. The quiet, peaceable of —. Aquila, γῆς, E. συντελεία γῆς. LXX. ἐπ' ὀργῇ δόλους. See the verb below.

רָגַע, v. pres. non occ. constr. abs. it. immed. Arab. رَجَع, rediit, retractavit, iteravit; profecit, bene cessit, convaluit, restitutus fuit. The primary notion seems to have been, gradual progress. See רָגַע above. Thence, coming to the natural result; in certain things, to quick decay; in others, to rest; in others, to restitution of something lost, e. g. (a) Job vi. 5. עוֹרִי רָגַע, my skin proceeds, decays, and —. (b) רֹגַע הַיָּם, he calms the sea, Ib. xxvi. 12. LXX. κατέπαυσε τὴν θάλασσαν. See my note in each case.

Part. רֹגֵעַ, (b) Is. li. 15; Jer. xxxi. 35.

Niph. Imp. f. הֵרָגְעִי, i. q. Hiph. (a) Jer. xlvii. 6.

Hiph. pret. f. הִרְגִּיעַ, pres. אַרְגִּיעַ. Constr. immed. it. med. לְ, to; אֶת, obj. (a) Rest, find rest, Is. xxxiv. 14; Deut. xxviii. 65. (b) Give, restore, or make, to rest, Prov. xii. 19; Jer. xlix. 19; L. 34. 44; Is. li. 4. עַמִּים אַרְגִּיעַ, I will restore rest to the Gentiles. לְאוֹר, will be construed better with the word immediately preceding it.

Infin. (b) aff. הַרְגִּיעוֹ, Ib. xxxi. 2, only.

רֶגֶשׁ, m. } pl. non occ. See v. רָגַשׁ,
רִגְשָׁה, f. } below. Usually, "turba," or "turma." Both the etymology, however, and context seem rather to require tumult either in a good or bad sense, e. g. Ps. lv. 15, בְּבֵית אֱלֹהִים נְהַלֵּךְ בְּרָגֶשׁ, we walked in the house of God in (joyous) tumult, i. e. in the sacred processions. Comp. Is. xxx. 29; 2 Sam. vi. 15. In Ps. xxvi. 6, 7, a similar procession round the altar is mentioned. LXX. ἐν ὁμονοίᾳ. So Syr.—Targ. festinatione. In Ps. lxiv. 3 (al. non occ.), we have, מֵרִגְשַׁת פֹּעֲלֵי אָוֶן —, which Symm. renders, ἀπὸ κυκήσεως ἐργαζομένων ἀδικίαν; "a tumultu," &c.: and so the Targum. Syr. ܬܪܓܫܬܐ, actio, conversatio. Tumult, therefore, suits the context well here; and with this the etymology agrees.

רָגַשׁ, v. pl. רָגְשׁוּ, once only, Ps. ii. 1. Syr. ܪܓܫ, tumultuatus est. Arab. رَجَسَ, tonuit cœlum, concussum fuit cum valido fragore. Cogn. رَجَزَ, fragorem edidit tonitru. Syr. ܪܓܙ, iratus est. Comp. Heb. רֹגֶן; ὀνοματοποιητικόν. Are tumultuous, engaged in uproar. LXX. ἐφρύαξαν. Aquila, ἐθορύβησαν. Symm. κυκᾷ.

רְגַשׁ, v. Chald.

Aph. pl. הַרְגִּשׁוּ, Dan. vi. 7. 12. 16, only. Assembled angrily, tumultuously.

רַד, Imp. of יָרַד.

רַד, m. Infin. (See below) of the r. יָרַד, in the sense of יָרַד, descending, declining, Judg. xix. 11.

רָדַד, v. cogn. רָדָה. Arab. رَدَّ, repulit, reposuit. Kal occ. only in—
Part. רוֹדֵד, once, Ps. cxliv. 2. *Brings down, subdues.*
Infin. רַד, *The bringing down, subduing,* once, Is. xlv. 1.
Hiph. pres. apoc. יְרַד, *He lays down, on;* overlays, once, 1 Kings vi. 32, only. These last two forms might as well be referred to the v. רָדָה.

רָדָה, v. pres. תִּרְדֶּה, pl. יִרְדּוּ, apoc. יֵרְדְּ. Constr. immed. it. med. בְּ, עַל, מִן. Cogn. רוּד, יָרַד. Syr. ܪܕܳܐ, castigavit. Arab. رَكَّى, calcavit terram. (a) *Subdue, rule, govern,* Gen. i. 28; Lev. xxv. 43. 46; xxvi. 17; Numb. xxiv. 19; Ps. lxxii. 8; Jer. v. 31. — *of fire, getting a complete mastery,* Lam. i. 12;—Judg. xiv. 9, יִרְדֵּהוּ אֶל־כַּפָּיו, *took it down into his hands,* seems to have the sense of יָרַד, which see. LXX. ἐξεῖλεν.
Infin. רְדוֹת, Ezek. xxix. 15. Aff. רְדֹתָהּ, Deut. xx. 20, al. non occ.
Imp. רְדֵה, Ps. cx. 2. Pl. רְדוּ, Gen. i. 28, only.
Part. רֹדֶה, pl. רֹדִים, 1 Kings v. 4; ix. 23, &c. Aff. רֹדָם, Ps. lxviii. 28.
Hiph. pres. apoc. once, Is. xli. 2. יְרַדְּ, *cause to rule, govern.*

רָדִיד, m. aff. רְדִידִי, pl. רְדִידִים, r. רדד, *A loose flowing mantle* or *veil,* Is. iii. 23; Cant. v. 7, al. non occ. See Schrœder. de Vestit. Mulier., cap. xxi.

רֹדָם, part. aff. of רָדָה.

רָדַם, v. Kal non occ. Arab. رَدَمَ, *occlusit* ostium; *obturavit* hiatum. The primary notion consisted in *closing up, making fast.* Occ. only in—
Niph. נִרְדַּמְתִּי, pres. יֵרָדַם. Constr. abs. *Became stupified, insensible,* as in deep sleep, Dan. viii. 18; Jon. i. 5.
Part. נִרְדָּם. *Fast asleep,* Judg. iv. 21; Prov. x. 5. *Stupified,* Jon. i. 6; Dan. x. 9. *Dead, destroyed,* Ps. lxxvi. 7.

רָדַף, v. pres. יִרְדֹּף, יִרְדְּפָה. Constr. abs. it. immed. it. med., אֶת, אַחֲרֵי, עַד, לְ, בְּ, with Infin. (a) *Pursued,* in order to come up with, overtake. (b) — *as an enemy, to*

injure, destroy. Syr. ܪܕܰܦ, *secutus* in bonum et malum. Arab. رَدَفَ, *successit* unum negotium alteri. (a) — of persons, Josh. ii. 7; Judg. iii. 28, &c. Avenger of blood, Josh. xx. 5. — of things, righteousness, Prov. xxi. 21. — peace, &c., Ps. xxiii. 6; xxxiv. 15. — wickedness, Ps. cxix. 150. — the wind, Hos. xii. 2. — blood, Ezek. xxxv. 6. For the avenger of, or vengeance due to, blood. (b) — as an enemy, *persecuted, &c.,* Gen. xiv. 14; xxxv. 5; Exod. xiv. 4; Judg. vii. 25; Job xix. 28, &c. — *of a mere sound,* Lev. xxvi. 36.
Infin. רְדֹף, Josh. viii. 16. Aff. רָדְפִי, Ps. xxxviii. 21. תִּרְדֹּף, 1 Sam. xxv. 29. See Amos i. 11; Deut. xi. 4.
Imp. רְדֹף, Gen. xliv. 4. Aff. רָדְפֵהוּ, Ps. xxxiv. 15. Pl. רִדְפוּ, Josh. ii. 5, &c.
Part. רֹדֵף, רֹדֶף, pl. רֹדְפִים; constr. רֹדְפֵי; aff. רֹדְפַי, &c., Lam. i. 6; Lev. xxvi. 17; Josh. ii. 7; Is. li. 1; Ps. vii. 2, &c.
Niph. pret. aff. נִרְדַּפְנוּ, once, Lam. v. 5. *We are pursued, persecuted.*
Part. נִרְדָּף, once, Eccl. iii. 15. Gesen. "*præteritum,* pr. propulsum, elapsum." So Auth. Vers. But perhaps used here in the Arabic sense *of thing, &c., succeeding,* i. e. of the former and latter things God regulates each succeeding one, and assigns to it its time and place. Sym., ἐπιζητήσει ὑπὲρ τῶν ἐκδιωκομένων. So the Syr. and Targum. See LXX. But this reverts to moral considerations, and would rather require הַנִּרְדָּף.
Pih. f. רִדְּפָה, pres. יְרַדֵּף, and יִרְדֹּף, for יְרַדֵּף. Constr. immed. it. med. אֶת. *Followed, pursued,* in order to overtake, obtain, &c. Intensitive perhaps.—Persons, Hos. ii. 9; Ps. vii. 6; Prov. xii. 11; xxviii. 19. — things, — words, Prov. xix. 7. — evil, Ib. xi. 19. — righteousness, xv. 9; — darkness, Nah. i. 8.
Part. מְרַדֵּף, Prov. ll. cc.
Puh. רֻדַּף, *Pursued, driven on,* Is. xvii. 13, only.
Hiph. pl. m. aff. הִרְדִּיפֻהוּ, Judg. xx. 43, only. *They pursued, chased, them.*
Hoph. part. מֻרְדָּף, once, Is. xiv. 6. *Pursued, chased,* i. e. people, nations. Gesenius thinks מִרְדָּה ought to be the reading here; and so Daederlin, in order, perhaps, to correspond with the preceding מַכֵּה. But there seems to be no necessity for this.

רחב (554) רחט

רָחַב, רַחַב, in pause, m. ⎫ plur. non
לֶחֶב, m. ⎭ occ. Syr. ܪܗܒ, *turbatus est;* ܪܗܒܬܐ, *timor, pavor.* Arab. رَهِبَ, *timuit;* رَهْبُوتٌ, *terribilis.* See my note on Job ix. 13. Fearfulness: thence, *Insolence, tyranny,* ostentatious exercise of power. רַחַב, *insolence,* seems to be used to designate Egypt, Ps. lxxxvii. 4, אַזְכִּיר רַהַב וּבָבֶל, *I will call to mind, memorialize, insolence* (Egypt, on account of its tyranny) *and Babel.* Is. li. 9, has תַּנִּין, in the parallel, evidently alluding to Egypt in a similar manner. Comp. Ezek. xxix. 3, 4; xxxii. 2, 3; and my note on Job xl. 25, p. 530, seq. If this be the case, we need not look to the Coptic for this word: and hence, perhaps, no one has been able to find it in that language. Bochart, however, tells us, Phaleg., pp. 66, D. 294, A. that the *delta* is designated by this word, in the compd. Ἀθριβή, of Αθ + ριβί, signifying, *cor pyri.* The Greek passage, taken from the Egyptian Grammarian Orion, is this, "Ἀθριβὴν προσηγόρευσαν, ὅπερ ἐστὶ Ἑλληνιστὶ βούλοιτο φράζειν οὐκ ἄλλως ἔχοι λέξαι, πλὴν καρδίαν ἀπίων (ἀπίου), οὕτως Ὠρίων." See the whole of each article. If this may be relied on, the Heb. רַהַב may have been intended at once to intimate this place, and the character of the whole country, as experienced by the Israelites. A similar play on the name *Jacob* will be found, Gen. xxvii. 36. The word occurs again, Is. xxx. 7, in רַחַב הֵם שָׁבֶת. Gesen. "*insolentia,*" i. e. "*insolentes hi sedent.*" Lit. *Insolence are they* (as to) *residence,* i. e. insolent throughout their habitations, which evidently refers to Egypt. Examine the former part of the verse. Job ix. 13; xxvi. 12; Ps. lxxxix. 11, al. non occ. רָהָב, occ. only, aff. in רָהְבָּם. *Their power* exercised to create fear, &c., ostentatiously, Ps. xc. 10, corresponding to גְּבוּרֹת. Ib. LXX. πλεῖον αὐτῶν.

רַחַב, m. pl. once, רְהָבִים. See רַחַב above. *Insolent, tyrannic,* Ps. xl. 5.

רָהַב, v. pres. pl. יִרְהָבוּ. See רַחַב above. Constr. med. בְּ. (a) *Act insolently, irreverently; insult,* Is. iii. 5.
Imp. רְהַב, Prov. vi. 3, in רְהַב רֵעֶיךָ. LXX. παρόξυνε. Theod. παρορμησον. *Consider him as an object of fear,* danger; deal with him as such. Constr. immed.

Hiph. aff. הִרְהִיבַנִי, pres. it. aff. תַּרְהִיבֵנִי. Constr. immed., Cant. vi. 5. *They excite me to daring, insolency,* i. e. embolden me. LXX. ἀναπτέρωσάν με. Auth. Vers., *overcome me,* pres., Ps. cxxxviii. 3. LXX. πολυωρήσεις. Symm., συνέστησας τῇ ψυχῇ μου δυνάμεις μου. Auth. Vers., *strengthenedst me.* Lit. *makest me daring; emboldenest me,* by placing power within me; giving me assurances of thy favour, al. non occ.

רחט, masc. pl. רְחָטִים. Syr. ܪܗܛܐ, *fluxus.* Arab. رَهْطٌ, *foramen muris campestris.* (a) *A trough* or *channel,* used in watering cattle, Gen. xxx. 38. 41; Exod. ii. 16. (b) Arab. رَهْطٌ, *pellis quæ in ligulas scindatur.* *Thongs,* Cant. vii. 6, in מֶלֶךְ אָסוּר בָּרְהָטִים; which should be read, perhaps, כְּמֶלֶךְ וגו׳, AS, or LIKE, *a king bound in thongs.* If THE *king* had been meant, the article would most likely have been added, as הַמֶּלֶךְ: but, as this is not done, the comparison should apparently be continued. Allusion too seems to be made to the power said to have been lodged in the hair of Sampson. The comparison, therefore, probably consisted in the head, exhibiting a sort of tower or mount, of strength (פַּרְמֶל: comp. Is. v.), amiable and lovely by its extreme gentleness and beauty. Which—if the Church is meant—is most appropriate. Gesen. "*cincinni.*"

רחים, masc. pl. aff. רָהִיטֵנוּ, *Keri;* רָחִיטֵנוּ, Kethiv, Cant. i. 17, only. Arab. رَهْطٌ, *supellex domestica.* Perhaps here,—as קֹרוֹת, preceding, seems to apply to the frame-work of the house,—the *inside-work,* as it is termed, as floors, doors, wainscotting, &c., and their finishings, was intended, in the sense of *furniture,* or furnishings. LXX. φατνώματα. Vulg., Gesen., &c., laquearia. Syr. ܪܗܛܐ, *cinguli, ligamina:* which seems to be applied to the finishings or adornings of the beams.

רו, m. Chald. aff. only, רֵוֵהּ, r. Heb. רָאָה. *Aspect, appearance,* Dan. ii. 31; iii. 25.

רוד, v. pret. רָד, pres. non occ. Arab. رَادَ, r. رود, *discurrit huc illuc mulier apud vicinas suas, &c.* Comp. הִתְהַלֵּךְ, p. 156, above. Constr. med. עִם,

רוח (555) רוח

with; once, Hos. xii. 1, יְהוּדָה עֹד רָד עִם־אֵל, *Judah still walked with* (acted with) *God*. See the rest of the verse. Schrœder, and, after him, Gesen. and some others, take רָד, in the sense of *vagrant, &c.*, manifestly against the tenour of the context. See Rosenmüller on the place. וָרִדְנוּ, Jer. ii. 31, i. q. Hiph. Gen. l. c.

Hiph. pres. only, אָרִיד, תָּרִיד, twice. Ps. lv. 3, אָרִיד בְּשִׂיחִי, *I wander* (mentally) *in my complaint*. See my note on Job xx. 8, יָד. Gen. xxvii. 40, כַּאֲשֶׁר תָּרִיד, *when thou wanderest*, i. e. becomest a free, wandering people—such as the Arab descendants of Esau were—*then, &c.* See Rosenmüller on the place, where the view of Schrœder is probably the correct one.

רָוֶה, masc. }
רָוָה, fem. } pl. non occ. Arab. رَيٌّ,

r. رَوِيَ, n. of action of, *explevit potu*. Syr. ܪܘܝ, *madefactus, inebriatus est*. Æth. ሮዐየ: id. (a) *Soaked, satiated*, with water, as a garden, Is. lviii. 11; Jer. xxxi. 12, al. non occ. (b) Fem. — with drink, *drunken*; or, taking the concrete as an abstract, *drunkenness*: once, Deut. xxix. 18. The passage is evidently proverbial. Lit. *On account of the drunken woman's adding the thirsty man*; which seems to me to signify, *because the fornicating* (idolatrous Church) *multiplies* the thirsting (for such fornication), i. e. is to itself the generator of its own wickedness. See Rosenmüller on the place.

רָוָה, v. pres. pl. יִרְוְיֻן, רָוְיָה. Constr. med. מִן, of thing. Specif. or abs. Gram. artt. 219, 220. *Be, become, satiated*, as with drinking. — with blood, Jer. xlvi. 10. — with fatness, Ps. xxxvi. 9. — unlawful love, lust being assimilated to thirst. See שָׁתָה, צִמְאָה. Prov. vii. 18.

Pih. f. רִוָּה, pres. aff. יְרַוֶּךָ, אֲרַוֶּךָ for אֲרַוְיֶךָ, Is. xvi. 9. Constr. immed. it. med. בְּ, instr. it. in. מִן, of thing; i. q. Kal, but intensive perhaps. (a) *Be, become satiated, filled*, Is. xxxiv. 5. 7. (b) *Active, satiate, fill*. — with fatness, wealth; specif. as in Kal, Jer. xxxi. 14; so, Is. xvi. 9. — with tears. Meton., *delight, satisfy*, Prov. v. 19.

Imp. or Infin. רְוֵה. (b) Ps. lxv. 11.

Hiph. הִרְוָה, pres. non occ. i. q. Pih. (b) constr. immed. med. אֶת, specif. it. abs., Is. xliii. 24; lv. 10; Jer. xxxi. 25; Lam. iii. 15.

Part. מִרְוֶה, Prov. xi. 25, al. non occ.

רֶוַח, m. }
רְוָחָה, f. } plur. non occ. Arab. رَوْحٌ,
רֵוַחָה, f. } *interstitium amplum, &c.*;

رَوْح, *quies*; رَوْحَة id.: it. *iter vespertino tempore factum*. Hence, ريح, *ventus*;

روح, *anhelitus, spiritus*. (a) *Space, distance*, Gen. xxxii. 17. (b) Synon. τοῦ, הַצָּלָה, *Deliverance, quiet*, Esth. iv. 14 : f. רְוָחָה, Exod. viii. 11.: aff. 2d fem. רַוְחָתִי, Lam. iii. 56, al. non occ. The 1st f. of the fm. פֶּקַח, 2d of פָּקַח, and רָוַח, of either.

רוּחַ, f. pl. רוּחוֹת, רֻחוֹת. Aff. רוּחִי, &c. See רָוַח above. Here רוּח, for רֶוַח, Gram. art. 87. 2: properly, *Distance, space, freedom* from restraint, Comp. צַר. Thence, from its *freedom*, or *extent* in space. (a) *The air*, Job xli. 8; Jer. ii. 24; xiv. 6. Phr. רוּחַ הַיּוֹם, *cool air of the day, evening*: or, it may be, *quiet of the day*, period of retiring from labour. Comp. Gen. iii. 8; Cant. ii. 17; iv. 6, &c. So the Arab. برياح — or بروح من العشي, *initio vesperæ*. يوم روح, *lætus dies*. Thence—

II. *Breath*, synon. τῆς, נְשָׁמָה. Arab. نسمة, Job iv. 9; ix. 6; Ps. xviii. 16. — of life, רוּחַ חַיִּים, Gen. vi. 17; vii. 15. Comp. Eccl. iii. 21; viii. 8; xii. 7. Phrr. דְּחֵי רוּחִי, Is. xxxviii. 16. הָיְתָה רוּחִי, Gen. xlv. 27. שָׁבָה רוּחוֹ, Judg. xv. 19; 1 Sam. xxx. 12. אֵין רוּחַ בּוֹ, Ezek. xxxvii. 8; Hab ii. 9; 1 Kings x. 5.

III. *Spirit, soul*, — of man as given by God, termed רוּחַ אֱלוֹהַּ, Job xxvii. 3. הָרוּחַ, Eccl. xii. 7; Ps. civ. 29, &c. — *embodied*, or *disembodied*, Gen. vi. 17; Ezek. xxxvii. 8; Job iv. 15; 1 Kings xxii. 21. — of animals, Eccl. iii. 19. 21, &c.

IV. Thence, *Mind, spirit, disposition, &c.* רוּחַ, simply, Josh. ii. 11; רוּחַ אִישׁ, Prov. xviii. 14. Phrr. תְּחִי רוּחַ, *spirit, mind*, is *enlivened*: opp. τῷ, מָרַת רוּחַ, (comp. Ps. cvi. 33); Gen. xlv. 27; xxvi. 34. קְצַר רוּחַ, *shortness of* —, *impatience*: opp. τῷ, אֶרֶךְ רוּחַ, Exod. vi. 9; Eccl. vii. 8. — קָשַׁת, *hard of* — *sorrowful*, 1 Sam. i. 15; — נְכֵאָה, דַּכָּא, *contrite of* —, Ps. xxxiv.

רוּחַ

19; Prov. xv. 13. נִשְׁבָּרָה —, broken, Ps. li. 19. — גָּבַהּ: opp. τῷ. — שָׁפָל, Prov. xvi. 18, 19. — קַר, cool of —, Ib. xvii. 27. — רַעְיוֹן, evil of, vexation of —, Eccl. i. 14. 17, &c. עָרִיצִים, — of the violent, Is. xxv. 4. מִזֶּה —, Ib. lxi. 3. זְנוּנִים, — of fornication, Hos. iv. 12.— עִוְעִים —, Is. xix. 14. תַּרְדֵּמָה —, Ib. xxix. 10. מִשְׁפָּט —, Ib. xxviii. 6, &c., with verbs. — הֵעִיר אֶת, stirred up, 2 Chron. xxxvi. 22; Ezra i. 1, &c. בְּ —, נָתַן, placed — in, 2 Kings xix. 7. — מְרֵבָה, Exod. xxxv. 21: whence רוּחַ נְדִיבָה, Ps. li. 14. — עָלָה עַל, i. q. עָלָה עַל לֵב, Ezek. xx. 32. הָיָה בְרוּחַ, 1 Chron. xxviii. 12. שָׁבָה רוּחַ, Judg. xv. 19.

V. — of God, simply רוּחַ, or הָרוּחַ, יְהוָֹה, רוּחַ אֱלֹהִים, — טוֹבָה. Aff. רוּחִי, קָדְשׁוֹ, Is. xxxii. 15; Num. xxvii. 18; Gen. xli. 38; Judg. iii. 10; Ps. li. 13; Neh. ix. 20; Hag. ii. 5, &c. Thence—

VI. The invisible, but effectual, source of life, Job xxiii. 9; xxxiii. 4; Ezek. xxxvii. 6. — of animation, existence, rule, Gen. i. 2; Ps. xxxiii. 6; Job xxvi. 13; Is. xxxiv. 16. — wisdom, piety, Job xxxii. 8; Ps. cxlviii. 10. Phrr. תִּשָּׂא אוֹתִי רוּחַ, Ezek. xi. 1. תָּבֹא בִי רוּחַ, Ib. ii. 2. רוּחַ הַחַיָּה, Ezek. i. 21. The absence of the article in some of these passages can be accounted for in no other way, than that the context makes the term sufficiently definite without it. — רוּחַ מִשְׁפָּט בָּעֵר, Is. iv. 4. חָכְמָה —, בִּינָה —, גְּבוּרָה —, דַּעַת —, יִרְאַת יְהוָֹה, Ib. xi. 2. חֵן וְתַחֲנוּנִים, Zech. xii. 10. יְהוָֹה לָבְשָׁה —, of Jehovah covered, as with clothing, Judg. vi. 34; 1 Chron. xii. 18, &c.: whence, perhaps, N. Test., "put on Christ." נָכוֹן —, Ps. li. 12. חֲדָשָׁה —, Ezek. xviii. 31, with לֵב חָדָשׁ — as governing the mind, intellect, dispositions. — of the prophets, Num. xxiv. 2; 1 Sam. x. 6. 10; xix. 20. 23. — of Christ, Is. xlii. 1; lix. 12. Whence, אִישׁ הָרוּחַ, Hos. ix. 7. — in interpreting dreams, Gen. xli. 38. — inspiring artificers, Exod. xxxi. 3; xxxv. 31. — as the source of courage, Judg. iii. 10; vi. 34; xi. 29. — given to some, taken from others, 1 Sam. xvi. 13, 14. — transferred, Num. xi. 17; 2 Kings ii. 15. — to be given to all flesh in Christian times, Joel iii. 1; Is. xliv. 3; lix. 21, &c. — also of evil affections, Judg. ix. 23. רוּחַ רָעָה, even permitted by God himself, and hence occasionally termed, Spirit of or from God, see 2 Kings xix. 7; 1 Sam. xvi. 14, 15. 23: whence the Phrr. רוּחַ שֶׁקֶר, 1 Kings xxii. 22, 23, see 24. כִּזְבִים —,

Jer. li. 1. הֹלֵךְ —, proceeding, increasing in, Mic. ii. 11. קִנְאָה —, Num. v. 14, &c.

VII. As the breath (2) may be considered as wind; hence, The wind, generally, Gen. viii. 1; Exod. x. 19. Tempestuous —, Job i. 19; Ps. cxlviii. 8. Comp. Job xxx. 15; Is. xxviii. 8; xxxii. 12: styled רוּחַ יְהוָֹה, 1 Kings xviii. 12; 2 Kings ii. 16; Is. xl. 7. — or breath of the mouth, (3) word, power, Ps. xxxiii. 6; Is. xi. 4. — as proceeding like steam or smoke from the nose in enraged animals. Anger, wrath: with אַף, Job iv. 9; Ps. xviii. 16: without אַף, Judg. viii. 3; Is. xxx. 28; Zech. vi. 8, &c. And, as the wind is yielding and unstable, (4) vanity or folly, will be its force. Phrr. דִּבְרֵי רוּחַ, Job xvi. 3. דַּעַת רוּחַ, Ib. xv. 2. Comp. Is. xli. 29; Prov. xi. 29. — שֹׁמֵר רוּחַ, observing — (as a vanity), Prov. xi. 4. The whole phraseology, connected with this word, is too extensive to insert here.

רוּחָא, Chald. f. pl. constr. רוּחֵי, def. רוּחָא, i. q. Heb. (1) The wind, Dan. ii. 35; vii. 2. (2) Spirit, mind, Ib. v. 12; vi. 4. (3) — of God, Ib. iv. 5, 6; v. 11, &c.

רָוַח, v. pres. יִרְוַח, constr. med. לְ. See רְוָח above: opp. τῷ, צַר. Was space, delay; relief, 1 Sam. xvi. 23; Job xxxii. 20, al. non occ.

Puh. part. pl. מְרֻוָּחִים, Jer. xxii. 14, only. Spacious, ample.

Hiph. הֵרִיחַ, pres. יָרִיחַ, apoc. יָרַח, plur. parag. ן, יְרִיחוּן. Constr. immed. it. med. אֶת, בְּ, instr. in; מִן, from. Inhaling: thence, (a) Scenting, smelling, Gen. xxvii. 27; Deut. iv. 28; Ps. cxv. 6. — with pleasure, as perfume, or the incense of offerings, med. אֶת, Gen. viii. 21: בְּ, Lev. xxvi. 31; Exod. xxx. 35. Meton. (b) Be satisfied, placated, as with such offering, &c., Amos vi. 21; 1 Sam. xxvi. 19, with בְּ. (c) Causing one to smell, receive with delight; be inspired with, med. בְּ, Is. xi. 3. (d) Scent, feel, touch, the fire, Judg. xiii. 9. — scent, perceive (verbs of sense being occasionally put one for another), Job xxxix. 28, with מִן, al. non occ.

Infin. הָרִיחַ, Exod. l. c. aff. הֲרִיחוֹ, Is. l. c.

רְוָחָה, see רָוַח.

רַוְחָה, Ib.

רוּם, v. pret. רָם, pres. יָרוּם, apoc. יָרָם. Syr. ܐܘܪ܏, sustulit. (a) Was high, lofty. (b) Raised himself, was raised. (c)

רוֹם (557) רוּם

Was high in rank or *power*. (d) *Was lifted up, haughty*, [1] Of the heart. [2] Of the eyes. (a) Job xxii. 12; Ps. lxi. 3. (b) Gen. vii. 17; Is. xlix. 11; Ezek. x. 4, &c. (c) Ps. xviii. 47; xlvi. 11; xcix. 2, &c. (d), [1] Deut. viii. 14; Ezek. xxxi. 10; Hos. xiii. 6, &c. [2] Ps. cxxxi. 1; Prov. xxx. 13.

Infin. רוּם, רָם, aff. רוּמָם, Deut. xvii. 20; Ps. xii. 9; Ezek. x. 17.

Imp. רוּמָה, Ps. xxi. 14, &c.

Part. רָם, pl. רָמִים, constr. רָמֵי, fem. רָמָה, pl. רָמוֹת. (a) *High, lofty*. (b) *Loud*, of the voice. (c) *High in rank* or *power*. (d) *Haughty*. (a) Deut. xii. 2; Is. x. 33; Ezek. vi. 13, &c. (b) Deut. xxvii. 14. (c) Deut. i. 28; Ps. cxiii. 4; Is. lvii. 15, &c. (d) 2 Sam. xxii. 28; Prov. vi. 17; Is. ii. 12, 13, &c.

Pih. רוֹמַמְתִּי, pres. יְרוֹמֵם. Constr. immed. (a) *Lifted up*. (b) *Caused to grow*. (c) *Brought up* children. (d) *Raised in rank* or *power*. (e) *Exalted with praise*. (f) *Raised* a building. (a) Ps. xxvii. 7; cvii. 25. (b) Ezek. xxxi. 4. (c) Is. i. 2; xxiii. 4. (d) 2 Sam. xxii. 49; Job xvii. 4; Ps. xxxvii. 34, &c. (e) Ps. xxx. 2; cxlv. 1; Is. xxv. 1, &c.

Infin. רוֹמֵם, (f) Ezra ix. 9.

Imp. pl. רוֹמְמוּ, (e) Ps. xcix. 5. 9.

Part. מְרוֹמֵם, (d) 1 Sam. ii. 7.

Puh. רוֹמַם, pres. תְּרוֹמַמָה. Pass. of Pih. (a), (d), and (e). (a) Ps. lxxv. 11. (e) Ps. lxvi. 17.

Part. מְרוֹמָם, (d) Neh. ix. 5.

Hiph. הֵרִים, pres. יָרִים, apoc. יָרֵם and יָרָם. (a) *Lifted up*, [1] The hand. [2] The voice. [3] The head. [4] The horn. [5] A rod. [6] The steps. (b) *Took up*. (c) *Took out* of a number or quantity as an offering. (d) *Presented* an offering, *offered*. (e) *Took away, removed*. (f) *Set up*, [1] A standard. [2] A pillar. (g) *Set on high*. (h) *Exalted in rank* or *power*. (a), [1] Gen. xiv. 22; xli. 44; 1 Kings xi. 27, &c. [2] Gen. xxxix. 15; 2 Kings xix. 22; Job xxxviii. 34, &c. [3] Ps. cx. 7. [4] Ps. lxxv. 5, 6. [5] Med. בְּ, Exod. vii. 20. (b) Lev. ii. 9; vi. 10. 15; Num. xvii. 2, &c. (c) Num. xviii. 26; xxxi. 28. 52. (d) 2 Chron. xxx. 24; xxxv. 8, 9; Ezra viii. 25, &c. (f), [1] Is. xlix. 22. [2] Gen. xxxi. 45. (g) Job xxxix. 27; Is. xiv. 14. (h) 1 Kings xiv. 7; xvi. 2; Ps. lxxxix. 20, &c.

Infin. הָרִים, aff. הֲרִימִי, הֲרִימְכֶם, (a, 2) Gen. xxxix. 18. Med. בְּ, 1 Chron. xv. 16. (a, 4) 1 Chron. xxv. 5. (c) Num. xviii. 30. 32. (h) Ps. lxxv. 7.

Imp. הָרֵם, הָרֶם־, הָרִימָה, הָרִימִי, f. הָרִימִי, pl. הָרִימוּ, (a, 2) Is. xiii. 2; xl. 9; lviii. 1. (a, 5) Exod. xiv. 16. (a, 6) Ps. lxxiv. 3. (b) 2 Kings vi. 7. (e) Is. lvii. 14; Ezek. xlv. 9. (f) Is. lxii. 10.

Part. מֵרִים, pl. constr. מְרִימֵי, aff. מְרִימָיו, (a, 3) Ps. iii. 4. (a, 5) Is. x. 15. (d) Exod. xxxv. 24. (e) Hos. xi. 4. (h) Prov. iii. 35.

Hoph. הוּרַם, הֻרַם, pres. יוּרַם. Pass. of Hiph. sign. (d) Exod. xxix. 27. (e) Lev. iv. 10; Dan. viii. 11.

Hith. pres. יִתְרוֹמָם. *Raised, exalted himself*, Dan. xi. 36.

רוּם, v. Chald. *Id*. Pass. רָם. *Was lifted up*, of the heart, Dan. v. 20.

Pah. part. מְרוֹמֵם. *Exalting with praise*, Dan. iv. 34.

Aph. part. מֵרִים. *Exalting in rank* or *power*, Dan. v. 19.

Hith. הִתְרוֹמַמְתָּ. *Exaltedst thyself*, Dan. v. 23.

רוּם, m. רָם. (a) *Height*, Prov. xxv. 3. (b) *Haughtiness*, Prov. xxi. 4; Is. ii. 11. 17; x. 12; Jer. xlviii. 29.

רוּם, Chald. m. aff. רוּמֵהּ. *Height*, Ezra vi. 3; Dan. iii. 1; iv. 17.

רוֹם, m. *Height*; *on high*, Hab. iii. 10.

רוֹמָה, f. *Haughtiness; haughtily*, Mic. ii. 3.

רוֹמְמוֹת, fem. pl. constr. *Extolling* praises, Ps. cxlix. 6.

רוֹמְמוּת, fem. aff. רוֹמְמֻתְךָ. *Exaltation; majesty*, Is. xxxiii. 3.

רוּעַ, v. Arab. رَغَا r. رَغَو, *vociferatus fuit*. Kal non occ., unless we refer רֵעוּ, Is. viii. 9, to this root. Probably *Shout, call together* your forces, *assemble* yourselves. Aquila, Symm., and Theod., συναθροίσθητε. Vulg. *congregamini*. But LXX. γνῶτε, reading דְּעוּ.

Hiph. הֵרִיעַ, pres. יָרִיעַ, apoc. יָרַע. (a) *Shouted*, in joy, alarm, or war. (b) *Sounded* a trumpet, with בְּ. (a) Josh. vi. 20; Judg. xv. 14; Ezra iii. 11; Ps. xli. 12, &c. (b) Num. x. 9.

Infin. הָרִיעַ, 2 Chron. xiii. 12. 15.

Imp. f. הָרִיעִי, pl. הָרִיעוּ, Josh. vi. 10; Zech. ix. 9.

רוּף (558) רזה

Part. pl. מְרִיעִים, Ezra iii. 13.
Puh. pres. יְרֹעָע. *There shall be shouting*, Is. xvi. 10.
Hith. pres. אְתְרוֹעָע, i. q. Hiph. Ps. lxv. 14; cviii. 10.
Imp. f. הִתְרוֹעָעִי, Ps. lx. 10.

רוּף, v. Arab. رَفَّ, *nictavit, palpitavit*.
Syr. ܪܦ, *excussit alis*. *Shook, agitated*.
Puh. pres. יְרוֹפַף. Pass., Job xxvi. 11.

רוּץ, v. pret. רָץ, pres. יָרִיץ, יָרוּץ, apoc. יָרָץ. Æth. ሮጸ፡ *currere*. (a) Constr. abs. it. immed. *Ran*. (b), [1] Med. אֶת, *Ran with*, in a race. [2] Med. אַחֲרֵי, *Ran after*, to overtake. [3] Med. עַל, *Ran against, rushed upon*. [4] Med. אֶל, *Id.* it. *Ran to*. [5] Med. בְּ, *Ran into*, for refuge; *ran on* a rock. (c) *Hastened*. (d) *Did a thing speedily, readily*. (a) Gen. xviii. 7; 1 Sam. viii. 11 ; 2 Sam. xviii. 23, &c. (b), [1] Jer. xii. 5. [2] 1 Kings xix. 20; 2 Kings v. 20. [3] Job xviii. 14. [4] Job xv. 26; Dan. viii. 6; Gen. xxiv. 20. 29; Num. xvii. 12; 1 Sam. iii. 5, &c. [5] Prov. xviii. 10; Amos vi. 12. (c) Ps. cxix. 32; Prov. i. 16; Jer. xxiii. 21, &c. (d) Hab. ii. 2.
Infin. רוּץ, 1 Sam. xx. 6; Ps. xix. 6; Prov. vi. 18.
Imp. רוּץ, רָץ, 1 Sam. xx. 36; 2 Sam. xviii. 23, &c.
Part. רָץ, plur. רָצִים, once, רָצִין, 2 Kings xi. 13. (a) *Running*. (b) *A runner*. (c) *One who rides post*. (a) 2 Sam. xviii. 22. 24. 26, &c. (b) 1 Kings xiv. 27; 2 Kings xi. 11; Job ix. 25, &c. (c) Esth. viii. 10. 14.
Pih. pres. יְרוֹצֵצוּ, Intens. of Kal, Nah. ii. 4.
Hiph. pres. יָרִיץ. (a) *Caused to run*. (b) *Brought* a person or thing *quickly*. (c) *Stretched out* his hands *quickly*. (a) Jer. xlix. 19; L. 44. (b) Gen. xli. 14; 2 Chron. xxxv. 1. 3. (c) Ps. lxviii. 32.
Imp. הָרֵץ, (b) 1 Sam. xvii. 17.

רוֹשׁ, see רֹאשׁ.

רוּשׁ, v. pret. רָשׁוּ, cogn. ירשׁ. *Was poor, in want*, Ps. xxxiv. 11.
Part. רָשׁ, pl. רָשִׁים. *Poor, a poor man*, 1 Sam. xviii. 23; Prov. xiv. 20; xxiii. 7, &c. It. רָאשׁ, pl. רָאשִׁים, 2 Sam. xii. 1. 4; Prov. x. 4; xiii. 23.
Hith. part. מִתְרוֹשֵׁשׁ. *Feigned himself poor*, rov. xiii. 7. See רוּשׁ.

רָז, Chald. m. def. רָזָא, pl. רָזִין, def. רָזַיָּא.

Syr. ܐܪܙܐ, *arcanum fecit*. *A secret, any thing unknown*, Dan. ii. 18—47; iv. 6.

רָזָה, v. constr. med. אָה. Arab. رَزَى, *diminuit* rem; رَذِيَ, *extenuatus, enervatus tritusque fuit* itinere, labore, morbo. *Diminished, brought low; destroyed*, Zeph. ii. 11. LXX. ἐξολοθρεύσει. Vulg. *attenuabit*.
Niph. pres. יֵרָזֶה. *Was diminished; wasted away*, Is. xvii. 4.

רָזֶה, f. רָזָה. (a) *Fat*, of an animal. (b) *Rich*, of soil. (a) Ezek. xxxiv. 20. (b) Num. xiii. 20.

רָזוֹן, m. *Wasting, diminution, destruction*, Ps. cvi. 15; Is. x. 16; Mic. vi. 10.

רָזוֹן, masc. i. q. רֹזֵן. *A prince*, Prov. xiv. 28. But see Gram. art. 152. 10.

רָזִי, masc. once, Is. xxiv. 16, i. q. רָזוֹן, r. רזה.

רָזַם, v. pres. יִרְזְמוּן, once, Job xv. 12. Arab. رَزَمَ, *ita emaciatus fuit ut terræ adhærens surgere non posset* camelus; *cepit, accepit* rem. III. *Diu permansit* in domo. Cogn. رَزَبَ, *firmiter adhæsit loco nec inde prodiit*. *Fixed, fastened, laid hold of*. See my notes.

רֹזֵן, m. pl. רוֹזְנִים. Arab. رَزِين, *gravis pondere* res; *moribus gravis, dignitate et potentiâ pollens*. *Heavy, weighty; a man of weight, a chief, prince*, Judg. v. 3; Ps. ii. 2; Prov. xxxi. 4, &c.

רָחָב, masc. constr. רְחַב, pl. constr. רַחֲבֵי, fem. רְחָבָה, constr. רַחֲבַת. Arab. رَحُبَ, *amplus et spatiosus fuit*. *Broad, large, extensive, capacious*, Gen. xxxiv. 21; Exod. iii. 8; Ps. civ. 25; Is. xxxiii. 21, &c. רְחַב נֶפֶשׁ, *a man of unlimited desires*, Prov. xxviii. 25. לֵבָב —, *Id.*, Ps. ci. 5. לֵב —, *Id.*, Prov. xxi. 4.

רֹחַב, masc. pl. constr. רַחֲבֵי. *Breadth, extent*. Metaph. *Plenty*, Job xxxvi. 16; xxxviii. 18.

רֹחַב, m. aff. רָחְבּוֹ. (a) *Breadth, width*, Gen. vi. 15; Exod. xxvi. 16; xxxvii. 1, &c. (b) *Extent, expanse*, Job xxxvii. 10. (c) רֹחַב לֵב, *Breadth of heart; extent of understanding*, 1 Kings v. 9.

רָחַב, v. *Was broad, wide; was widened,*

רחב (559) רחי

enlarged; was opened; see רָחַב, above: 1 Sam. ii. 1; Is. lx. 5; Ezek. xli. 7.

Niph. part. נִרְחָב. *Enlarged, extended*, Is. xxx. 23.

Hiph. הִרְחִיב, pres. יַרְחִיב. (a) *Made broad, extensive, capacious.* (b) With נֶפֶשׁ, [1] *Extended* his desires. [2] *Enlarged* itself. (c) Without נֶפֶשׁ, *Enlarged itself.* (d) *Opened* his mouth *wide.* (e) *Opened, enlarged* the heart. (f) With לְ, [1] *Freed from restraint.* [2] *Made room for, granted ample room to.* [3] *Made a way for.* (a) Exod. xxxiv. 24; Deut. xii. 20; Is. xxx. 33; lvii. 8, &c. (b), [1] Hab. ii. 5. [2] Is. v. 14. (c) Ps. xxv. 17. (d) Ps. xxxv. 21; Is. lvii. 4. (e) Ps. cxix. 32. (f), [1] 2 Sam. xxii. 37; Ps. iv. 2. [2] Gen. xxvi. 22. [3] Prov. xviii. 16.

Infin. הַרְחִיב, Amos v. 13.

Imp. הַרְחִיב, fem. הַרְחִיבִי, Ps. lxxxi. 11; Is. liv. 2; Mic. i. 16.

Part. מַרְחִיב, Deut. xxxiii. 20.

רֹחַב, and רְחוֹב, fem. aff. רְחֹבָהּ, plur. רְחֹבוֹת, aff. רְחֹבוֹתֵינוּ. *Any broad, open, unenclosed place* in a town, *a square, a street*, Gen. xix. 2; Deut. xiii. 16; 2 Chron. xxxii. 6; Ps. cxliv. 14; Prov. xxii. 13, &c.

רַחוּם, masc. r. רחם. Arab. رَحِيمٌ, *misericors. Merciful*, an epithet applied only to God, Exod. xxxiv. 6; Deut. iv. 31; Ps. lxxviii. 38, &c.

רָחוֹק, and רָחֹק, m. pl. רְחוֹקִים, f. רְחוֹקָה, pl. רְחוֹקוֹת, r. רחק. *A distance, an interval.* (b) *Distant*, in place. Metaph. of God. (c) *Out of reach, unattainable.* (d) *Difficult.* (e) *Distant*, of time. (f) מֵרָחוֹק, [1] *From a distance.* [2] *At a distance.* [3] *At a distant time, long ago.* (g) לְמֵרָחוֹק, [1] *At a distance.* [2] *With regard to what is distant* and difficult to discover. [3] *At a distant time, long ago.* [4] *To a distant time.* (h) עַד מֵרָחוֹק, *To a distance.* (i) עַד לְמֵרָחוֹק, [1] *To a distance.* [2] *At a distance.* (a) Josh. iii. 4; Mic. iv. 3. (b) Deut. xx. 15; Josh. ix. 6. 22; Prov. xxvii. 10, &c.; Ps. x. 1; xxii. 2; Prov. xv. 29, &c. (c) Ps. cxix. 155; Eccl. vii. 23. (d) Prov. xxxi. 10. (e) Ezek. xii. 27. (f), [1] Job xxxix. 25; Is. xliii. 6; xlix. 12, &c. [2] Exod. ii. 4; xx. 21; 1 Sam. xxvi. 13, &c. [3] Is. xxii. 11; xxv. 1. (g), [1] Job xxxix. 29. [2] Job xxxvi. 3. [3] 2 Kings xix. 25; Is. xxxvii. 26. [4] 2 Sam. vii. 19;

1 Chron. xvii. 17. (h) Is. lvii. 9. (i), [1] 2 Chron. xxvi. 15. [2] Ezra iii. 13.

רָחוּט, m. aff. רָחִיטֵנוּ, or רַחִיטֵנוּ, Keri רָחִיטֵנוּ, once, Cant. i. 17. LXX. φατνώματα. Vulg. *laquearia.* According to some, *Ceiling*; others, *Rafters.* Castell prefers the latter. See רחט, above.

רֵחַיִם, dual, m. Arab. رَحًى, and رَحِيَ, dual, رَحَوَانِ, *mola. A pair of millstones;* a mill, Exod. xi. 5; Numb. xi. 8; Deut. xxiv. 6; Is. xlvii. 2; Jer. xxv. 10.

רָחִיק, Chald. pl. רְחִיקִין, i. q. רָחוֹק, *Distant*, Ezra vi. 6.

רָחֵל, f. רְחֵלִים, aff. רְחֵלֶךָ. Arab. رَخِل, *agna, ovis.* (a) *A ewe*, Gen. xxxi. 38; xxxii. 14. (b) *Any sheep*, Cant. vi. 6; Is. liii. 7.

רֶחֶם, m. aff. רַחְמָהּ. Arab. رِحْم, *uterus. The womb*, Gen. xx. 18; xxix. 31; Job xxxi. 15, &c.

רַחַם, (a) *Id.*, Gen. xlix. 28; Prov. xxx. 16; Is. xlvi. 3; Ezek. xx. 26. (b) *A female*, Judg. v. 30.

רָחָם, m. רָחָמָה, f. according to Bochart, i. q. Arab. رَخَم, *avis vulturis forma: corvi magnitudine, collo et corpore albo, sed extremis alarum nigra. The aquiline vulture. Vultur percnopterus*, Linn., Lev. xi. 18; Deut. xiv. 17.

רחם, v. pres. aff. אֲרַחֶמְךָ. Arab. رَحِم, *misericors, clemens, propitius fuit.* رَحَم, *misertus fuit, amavit.* Syr. ܪܚܡ, *amavit.* *Loved*, Ps. xviii. 2.

Pih. רִחַם, pres. יְרַחֵם. Constr. immed. it. med. עַל, *Loved, pitied, had mercy on*, Exod. xxxiii. 19; Ps. ciii. 13; Is. ix. 16, &c.

Infin. רַחֵם, aff. רַחֲמָם, Ps. ciii. 13; Is. xxx. 18, &c.

Part. מְרַחֵם, aff. מְרַחֲמָם, Ps. cxvi. 5; Is. xlix. 10.

Puh. pres. יְרֻחָם, Pass. of Pih., Prov. xxviii. 13; Hos. xiv. 4.

רַחֲמָה, f. dual, רַחֲמָתַיִם, *A female*, Judg. v. 30.

רַחֲמִים, pl. m. constr. רַחֲמֵי, aff. רַחֲמָיו. (a) *The viscera*, considered as the seat of

רחם (560) רחק

the affections. (b) *Pity, mercy.* (a) Gen. xliii. 30; 1 Kings iii. 27. (b) Gen. xliii. 14; Ps. cxlv. 9; Is. xlvii. 6, &c.

רַחֲמִין, Chald. pl. m. *Mercy*, Dan. ii. 18.

רַחֲמָנִי, f. pl. רַחֲמָנִיּוֹת, *Tender, merciful*, Lam. iv. 10.

רחף, v. רָחֲפוּ. Arab. خَفَّ, *mollis, tenuisque fuit massa.* Syr. ܢܫܒ, *incubuit, fovit, motatus fuit* more avium incubantium. *Shook, trembled;* but, according to some, *melted, became soft*, Jer. xxiii. 9. LXX. ἐσαλεύθη. Vulg. *Contremuerunt.*

Pih. pres. יְרַחֵף, *Fluttered, hovered*, Deut. xxxii. 11.

Part. f. מְרַחֶפֶת, *Applied to the Spirit of God moving over the abyss*, Gen. i. 2, al. non occ.

רחץ, m. aff. רַחְצִי. Arab. رَحَضَ, *lavit, de manibus et vestibus. Washing, bathing*, Ps. lx. 10.

רָחַץ, v. pres. יִרְחַץ. Constr. abs. it. immed. it. med. אֶת. (a) *Washed himself.* (b) *Washed* any part of his body. (c) *Washed* another. (d) *Washed* an animal. (e) *Washed away* impurity. (a) Lev. xiv. 8; xv. 5; xvi. 4, &c. (b) Lev. xiv. 8; xvi. 24; xxii. 6, &c. Metaph. Ps. xxvi. 6; lxxiii. 13. (c) Exod. xxix. 4. (d) Exod. xxix. 17; Lev. viii. 21. (e) Is. iv. 4.

Infin. רְחֹץ, רָחְצָה, Gen. xxiv. 32; Exod. xxx. 18, &c.

Imp. רְחַץ, pl. רַחֲצוּ, Gen. xviii. 4; 2 Sam. xi. 8, &c.

Part. f. רֹחֶצֶת, pl. רֹחֲצוֹת, 2 Sam. xi. 2; Cant. v. 12.

Puh. רֻחַץ, Pass. of Kal, Prov. xxx. 12; Ezek. xvi. 4.

Hith. הִתְרַחַצְתִּי, i. q. Kal, (a) Job ix. 30.

רַחְצָה, f. *Washing, a place for washing* sheep, Cant. iv. 2; vi. 6.

רָחַק, v. pres. יִרְחַק. Æth. ርሕቀ፡ *discessit, procul abfuit.* Syr. ܐܢܫܒ, *longè distare fecit.* Constr. med. מִן, it abs. *Was distant, kept at a distance, withdrew himself*, Exod. xxiii. 7; Job xxi. 16; Prov. xix. 7; Jer. ii. 5, &c.

Infin. רְחֹק, רָחֳקָה, Ps. iii. 5; ciii. 12; Ezek. viii. 6.

Imp. f. רַחֲקִי, pl. רַחֲקוּ, Is. liv. 14; Ezek. xi. 15.

Pih. רִחַק, pres. יְרַחֵק, *Placed or kept at a distance, forsook*, Is. vi. 12; xxvi. 15; xxix. 13; Ezek. xliii. 9.

Hiph. הִרְחִיק, pres. יַרְחִיק. (a) *Caused to be distant, removed to a distance.* (b) *Went to a distance;* fully, הִרְחִיק לָלֶכֶת. (a) Job xix. 13; Ps. ciii. 12; Ezek. xi. 16, &c. (b) Gen. xliv. 4; Judg. xviii. 22; Ps. lv. 8, &c.; Exod. viii. 24.

Infin. הַרְחִיק, aff. הַרְחִיקָם. (a) Joel iv. 6. (b) Gen. xxi. 16; Exod. viii. 28, &c.

Imp. הַרְחֵק, aff. הַרְחִיקֵהוּ. (a) Job xi. 14; xiii. 21, &c.

רחק, m. pl. aff. רְחֵקֶיךָ, *One who withdraws himself, forsakes*, Ps. lxxiii. 27.

רחש, v. once. Syr. ܪܚܫ. Aph. *scaturire fecit. Threw up, emitted* as a spring, metaph. of the heart, Ps. xlv. 2. LXX. ἐξηρεύξατο. Sym., ἐκινήθη.

רַחַת, f. r. רוח, once, Is. xxx. 24. *An instrument for winnowing.*

רָטֹב, m. once, Job viii. 16. Arab. رَطْب, *humidus, mollis, recens fuit. Moist, green, fresh.*

רטב, v. pres. יִרְטְבוּ. *Was wet*, from rain, Job xxiv. 8.

רֶטֶט, m. once, Jer. xlix. 24. Chald. רְטַט, *tremuit.* Syr. ܪܛܛ, *Id. Trembling.* See רתת.

רָמַפַּשׁ, v. once, Job xxxiii. 25. *Grew fresh or moist.* Compounded of רָטֹב, and פַּשׁ, r. פוש.

רטש, v. Kal non occ. Arab. رَطَسَ, *percussit interiore volâ aliquem. Struck.*

Pih. pres. תְּרַטֵּשׁ, *Struck so as to kill, killed*, 2 Kings viii. 12; Is. xiii. 18. LXX. ἐνσείσεις, συντρίψουσι. Vulg. *Elides; interficient.*

Puh. רֻטְּשָׁה, pres. יְרֻטְּשׁוּ, Pass. of Pih., Is. xiii. 16; Hos. x. 14; xiv. 1; Nah. iii. 10.

רִי, m. r. רוה, once, Job xxxvii. 11. *Watering, irrigation.* Contr. for רְוִי. Gram. art. 73.

ריב, m. aff. רִיבִי; רִיבְנֶם; pl. constr. רִיבֵי, it. pl. רִיבוֹת. Arab. رَيْب, *dubitatio. A doubt.* (a) *A question of right, controversy, suit.* (b) *A quarrel, strife.* (a) Exod. xxiii. 2; Deut. xxi. 5; 2 Sam. xv. 2, &c. (b) Gen. xiii. 7; Judg. xii. 2; Prov. xv. 18, &c.

ריב (561) ריק

רִיב, v. pret. רָב, רַבְתָּ, and רִיבוֹת, pres. יָרִיב, apoc. יָרֵב, and יָרֶב. Constr. abs. it. immed. it. med. לְ, בְּ, עִם, עַל, אֶל, אֵת. (a) *Disputed, argued.* (b) *Quarrelled.* (c) *Opposed, acted as an adversary.* (d) *Defended* a person or cause. (e) *Decided* a cause *favourably.* (a) Gen. xxvi. 22; xxxi. 36; Job xxxiii. 13; Jer. ii. 9; xii. 1, &c. (b) Exod. xxi. 18. (c) Ps. ciii. 9; Is. xlix. 25; lvii. 16; Hos. v. 13, &c. (e) 1 Sam. xxv. 39; Prov. xxii. 23; Lam. iii. 58, &c.

Infin. רִיב, twice רֹב, Judg. xi. 25; Job ix. 3, &c.

Imp. רִיב, רִיבָה; pl. רִיבוּ, Hos. ii. 4; Mic. vi. 1, &c. (d) Ps. xliii. 1; Is. i. 17.

Part. רָב, Is. xlv. 9; Jer. li. 36.

Hiph. i. q. Kal sign. (c) Part. pl. constr. מְרִיבֵי, aff. מְרִיבָיו, 1 Sam. ii. 10; Hos. iv. 4.

רֵיחַ, m. aff. רֵיחוֹ, רֵיחֲנוּ, r. רוח. *An odour, smell,* Gen. xxvii. 27; Cant. i. 12; ii. 13, &c. Pec. of sacrifices, Gen. viii. 21; Exod. xxix. 18; Lev. i. 9, &c. Metaph. Exod. v. 21; Jer. xlviii. 11.

רֵיחַ, Chald. f. *Id.*, Dan. iii. 27.

רֵים, see רְאֵם.

רֵיעַ, m. aff. רֵעֲכֶם, i. q. רֵעַ, *A friend*, Job vi. 27.

רִיפוֹת, and רִפוֹת, twice, 2 Sam. xvii. 19; Prov. xxvii. 22. Aquila and Sym. πτισάνας, ἐμπτισσομένων. Arab. رَفَتَ, *Fregit, comminuit*, رُفَاتٌ, *Res fracta minutatim. Grain.*

רִיק, m. Arab. رَيْتٌ, *vanus, futilis.* رَاقَ, *Effusa fuit* aqua. (a) *Empty.* (b) *An empty, vain thing.* (c) *In vain.* (d) לָרִיק, לְרִיק, *Id.* (a) Jer. li. 34. (b) Ps. ii. 1; iv. 3; Jer. li. 58; Hab. ii. 13. (c) Ps. lxxiii. 13; Is. xxx. 7. (d) Lev. xxvi. 16. 20; Is. lxv. 23, &c.

רִיק, v. Kal non occ. Prob. *Was empty.*

Hiph. הֵרִיק, pres. יָרִיק, apoc. יָרֶק. (a) *Emptied* a vessel. (b) Metaph. *Made* or *left empty.* (c) *Poured out.* (d) *Drew* a sword. (e) *Made ready* a spear. (f) *Made ready* armed men. (a) Jer. xlviii. 12; Hab. i. 17. (c) Eccl. xi. 3. Metaph. Mal. iii. 10. (d) Exod. xv. 9; Lev. xxvi. 33; Ezek. v. 2, &c. (f) Gen. xiv. 14.

Infin. הָרִיק, (b) Is. xxxii. 6.
Imp. הָרֵק, (e) Ps. xxxv. 3.
Part. pl. מְרִיקִים, (a) Gen. xlii. 35. (c) Zech. iv. 12.

Hoph. הוּרַק, pres. תּוּרַק. *Was poured out,* Cant. i. 3; Jer. xlviii. 11.

רִיק, m. pl. רֵיקִים, f. רֵיקָה, it. רֵק, m. pl. רֵקִים; f. רָקָה. (a) *Empty.* (b) *Hungry.* (c) *Emptied, stripped, poor.* (d) *Unimportant.* (e) *Worthless,* in character. (a) Gen. xxxvii. 24; xli. 27; Judg. vii. 16; Ezek. xxiv. 11, &c. (b) Is. xxix. 5. (c) Neh. v. 13. (d) Deut. xxxii. 47. (e) Judg. ix. 4; xi. 3; 2 Chron. xiii. 7, &c.

רֵיקָם, adv. (a) *Emptily.* (b) *Empty-handed, without an offering, present,* or *property.* (c) *Without cause.* (d) *Without effect.* (a) Jer. xiv. 3. (b) Gen. xxxi. 42; Exod. iii. 21; xxiii. 15; Deut. xv. 13; xvi. 16, &c. (c) Ps. vii. 5; xxv. 3. (d) Is. lv. 11; Jer. L. 9.

רִיר, m. aff. רִירוֹ. Arab. رَيْرٌ, *aqua manans ex ore infantis.* (a) *Spittle,* 1 Sam. xxi. 13. (b) *Whey* of cheese, Job vi. 6.

רִיר, v. pret. רָר. *Ran,* of a liquid; *emitted* a liquid, or humour, Lev. xv. 3.

רִישׁ, and רֵישׁ, m. aff. רֵישׁוֹ, v. רוש. *Poverty,* Prov. x. 15; xiii. 18; xxiv. 34; xxviii. 29; xxxi. 7.

רִישׁוֹן, i. q. רִאשׁוֹן. *First, former,* Job viii. 8, only.

רַךְ, m. pl. רַכִּים, f. רַכָּה, pl. רַכּוֹת, r. רכך. (a) *Tender, young, soft.* (b) *Of tender age.* (c) *An object of tender care.* (d) *Effeminate.* (e) *Of little power.* (f) *Timid.* (g) *Gentle,* of words. (h) *Tender,* of eyes, either *soft* or *weak,* usually interpreted the latter. (a) Gen. xviii. 7; Prov. xxv. 15; Ezek. xvii. 22. (b) Gen. xxxiii. 13; 1 Chron. xxii. 5; xxix. 1. (c) Prov. iv. 3. (d) Deut. xxviii. 54. 56; Is. xlvii. 1. (e) 2 Sam. iii. 39. (f) Deut. xx. 8; 2 Chron. xiii. 7. (g) Job xl. 27; Prov. xv. 1. (h) Gen. xxix. 17.

רֹךְ, m. *Effeminacy,* Deut. xxviii. 56.

רֶכֶב, m. aff. רִכְבּוֹ, רִכְבָּהּ, pl. constr. רִכְבֵי. Arab. رَكِبَ, *vectus fuit, equitavit.* Syr. ܪܟܒ, *Id. Riding.* (a) *A rider.* (b) *An upper millstone.* (c) *A chariot, chariots.* (a) 2 Kings vii. 14; Is. xxi. 7. 9; (b) Deut. xxiv. 6; Judg. ix. 53. (c) 2 Kings

4 c

רכב (562) רכל

ix. 21. 24; x. 16; Josh. xvii. 18; Judg. i. 19; iv. 3, &c.

רָכַב, v. pres. יִרְכַּב. Constr. abs. it. immed. it. med. עַל, בְּ. (a) *Rode*, on a horse, mule, camel, or ass. (b) Metaph. of God. (a) Numb. xxii. 30; 1 Sam. xxx. 17; 2 Sam. xiii. 29; 1 Kings xiii. 13; Esth. vi. 8, &c. Abs. 1 Kings xviii. 45; 2 Kings ix. 16.

Infin. רְכֹב, 2 Sam. xvi. 2; 2 Kings iv. 24. Imp. רְכַב, Ps. xlv. 5.

Part. רֹכֵב, aff. רֹכְבוֹ, f. רֹכֶבֶת, pl. רֹכְבִים, constr. רֹכְבֵי, aff. רֹכְבֵיהֶם, Gen. xlix. 17; Judg. x. 4; 1 Sam. xxv. 20, &c. (b) Deut. xxxiii. 26; Is. xix. 1.

Hiph. הִרְכִּיב, pres. יַרְכִּיב, apoc. יַרְכֵּב. Causat. of Kal. (a) *Caused to ride*. [1] On horseback, &c. [2] In a chariot. [3] Metaph. (b) *Carried in a chariot*. (c) *Placed* upon. (d) *Caused to be ridden*. (a), [1] Exod. iv. 20; 1 Kings i. 33; Esth. vi. 9, &c. [2] Gen. xli. 43; 2 Kings x. 16; 2 Chron. xxxv. 24. [3] Deut. xxxii. 13; Job xxx. 22; Is. lviii. 14. (b) 2 Sam. vi. 3; 2 Kings xiii. 16; 1 Chron. xiii. 7. (d) Hos. x. 11.

Imp. הַרְכֵּב, (c) 2 Kings xiii. 16.

רַכָּב, m. aff. רַכָּבוֹ. (a) *A rider, horseman*. (b) *A driver, charioteer*. (a) 2 Kings ix. 17. (b) 1 Kings xxii. 34; 2 Chron. xviii. 33.

רִכְבָּה, f. *Riding*, Ezek. xxvii. 20.

רְכוּב, m. aff. רְכוּבוֹ. *What is ridden on*, vehicle, chariot, seat, Ps. civ. 3, only.

רְכוּשׁ, and רֶכֶשׁ, m. aff. רְכוּשׁוֹ, &c., pl. aff. רְכוּשֵׁינוּ; r. רכשׁ. *What has been acquired*, property, wealth, Gen. xiv. 11, 21; Numb. xvi. 32; 2 Chron. xxxi. 3; Ezra viii. 21, &c.

רָכִיל, m. r. רכל. *Running to and fro as a busybody, meddling*; slander, Lev. xix. 16; Prov. xi. 13; xx. 19; Jer. vi. 28; ix. 3; Ezek. xxii. 9.

רכך, v. pret. רַךְ, pres. יֵרַךְ. Arab. رَكَّ, subtilis, tenuis fuit. *Was tender*. Metaph. *Was timid, gentle*, of the heart or of words, Deut. xx. 3; 2 Kings xxii. 19; Ps. lv. 22; Is. vii. 4; Jer. li. 46.

Puh. רֻכְּכָה. *Was softened*, Is. i. 6.

Hiph. הֵרַךְ. *Rendered timid*, Job xxiii. 16.

רכל, v. only in part. רֹכֵל, f. רֹכֶלֶת, aff. רֹכַלְתֵּךְ, pl. רֹכְלִים, constr. רֹכְלֵי, aff. רֹכְלֶיךָ.

Cogn. רגל. Arab. رَكَلَ, *percussit pede*. مَرْكَلٌ, via. *Went to and fro, travelled*, pec. *as a merchant*. Part. *A merchant*, 1 Kings x. 15; Cant. iii. 6; Ezek. xxvii. 3. 15. 23, &c.

רְכֻלָּה, f. aff. רְכֻלָּתֵךְ, רְכֻלָּתֶךָ. *Merchandise*, Ezek. xxvi. 12; xxviii. 5. 16. 18.

רכס, v. pres. יִרְכְּסוּ. *Tied, fastened*, Exod. xxviii. 28; xxxix. 21, only. Arab. رَكَسَ, constrinxit vinculo رِكَاسٌ, appellato.

רֶכֶס, m. pl. רְכָסִים. *Entangled, rugged* places, Is. xl. 4.

רֹכֶס, m. pl. constr. רֻכְסֵי. *Combinations, artifices*, Ps. xxxi. 21.

רָכַשׁ, v. constr. immed. *Acquired, gained*, Gen. xii. 5; xxxi. 18; xxxvi. 6; xlvi. 6, al. non occ.

רֶכֶשׁ, m. Arab. رَكْضٌ, *cursus celer*. رَكَضَ, cucurrit. Syr. ܪܶܟܫܳܐ, equus. *Running*; a swift species of horse, a post horse, 1 Kings iv. 28; Esth. viii. 10. 14; Mic. i. 13.

רָם, see רום.

רָם, see רְאֵם.

רָמָה, f. aff. רָמָתֵךְ, pl. aff. רָמֹתֶךָ. r. רום. *A high place*, pec. *a high place used for idolatrous purposes*, Ezek. xvi. 25. 31. 39.

רָמָה, v. constr. immed. Arab. رَمَى, jecit, projecit. Syr. ܪܡܳܐ, Id. (a) *Threw*. (b) *Shot with* a bow. (a) Exod. xv. 1. 21. Part. constr. רֹמֵה, pl. constr. רֹמֵי. (b) Ps. lxxviii. 9; Jer. iv. 29.

Pih. רִמָּה. Probably *Tripped up*, hence *deceived*, Gen. xxix. 25; 1 Sam. xix. 17; Prov. xxvi. 19, &c.

Puh. רֻמּוּ, for רֻמִּיוּ. *Was thrown* or *lifted up*. Cogn. רום, Job xxiv. 24.

Infin. aff. בְּמוֹתַנִי, 1 Chron. xii. 17.

רְמָח, and רְמָא, v. Chald. pret. רְמוֹ, רְמִינָא. Id. (a) *Threw*, Dan. iii. 24; vi. 17. (b) *Imposed* tribute.

Infin. מִרְמֵא, (a) Dan. iii. 20; (b) Ezra vii. 24.

רמה (563) רמש

Peil, רְמִיו. Pass. (a) *Were thrown*, Dan. iii. 21. (b) *Were placed*, Dan. vii. 9.
Ithpe. pres. יִתְרְמֵא, תִּתְרְמוּן, *Was thrown*, Dan. iii. 6. 15.

רִמָּה, f. Arab. رِمّ, *comedit, voravit.* رِمّة, *teredo. A worm, worms*, Exod. xvi. 24; Job vii. 5; xxiv. 20, &c.

רִמּוֹן, m. pl. רִמּוֹנִים, constr. רִמּוֹנֵי. Arab. رُمّان, *malum punicum. A pomegranate*, [1] The tree, 1 Sam. xiv. 2; Cant. vi. 11; Joel i. 12, &c. [2] The fruit, Num. xiii. 23; Cant. iv. 3. [3] An artificial imitation of the fruit, Exod. xxviii. 33, 34; xxxix. 26, &c.

רָמוּת, f. aff. רָמוּתָךְ, r. רום. *Height, pile, heap*, of dead bodies, Ezek. xxxii. 5.

רֹמַח, m. pl. רְמָחִים, aff. רָמְחֵיהֶם. Arab. رُمْح, *lancea quâ utuntur ad percutiendum, non ad conjiciendum. A spear*, Numb. xxv. 7; 1 Kings xviii. 28; Neh. iv. 7, &c.

רְמִיָּה, f. r. רמה. (a) *Deceit.* (b) *Hanging loose, negligence.* Comp. Arab. رَمِيّ. VI. *Laxa, remissa fuit* res. (a) Job xiii. 7; xxvii. 4; Ps. xxxii. 2, &c. (b) Prov. xii. 24; xix. 15. The phrase קֶשֶׁת רְמִיָּה Ps. lxxviii. 57, and Hos. vii. 16, has been variously interpreted: *a deceitful bow*, one whose faulty construction prevents the arrow from doing execution; hence termed *deceitful*. See my note on Job xx. 24.

רֶמֶךְ, plur. רַמָּכִים, once, Esth. viii. 10. Arab. رَمَكَة, *equa. A mare.* בְּנֵי הָרַמָּכִים, *the offspring of mares.*

רמם, v. i. q. רום.
Niph. pres. יֵרֹמּוּ, and יֵרוֹמּוּ. *Was raised*, Ezek. x. 15. 17. 19.
Imp. הֵרֹמּוּ. *Remove yourselves*, Num. xvii. 10.

רמם, v. pres. apoc. יָרֹם. See רָמָה. *Became putrid*, Exod. xvi. 20, only.

רָמַס, v. pres. יִרְמֹס. Constr. immed. *Trampled down* or *on, trod on, walked in*, Ps. xci. 13; Is. lxiii. 3; Mic. v. 7, &c.
Infin. רְמֹס, Is. i. 12.
Imp. f. רִמְסִי, Nah. iii. 14.

Part. רֹמֵס. *One that tramples down; an oppressor*, Is. xvi. 4.
Niph. pres. תֵּרָמַסְנָה, Pass., Is. xxviii. 3.

רמש, v. pres. תִּרְמֹשׂ. Constr. immed. it. med. עַל, בְּ, *Id.*, Gen. ix. 2; Lev. xx. 25; Ps. civ. 20.
Part. רֹמֵשׂ, f. רֹמֶשֶׂת, Gen. i. 21; vii. 8; Ps. lxix. 35, &c.

רֶמֶשׂ, masc. A generic term including *reptiles, and all the smaller land animals*, Gen. i. 24, 25; vi. 7; Ps. cxlviii. 10, &c. Used once of *water animals*, Ps. civ. 25.

רֹן, m. pl. constr. רָנֵי, r. רנן. *Singing; a song*, Ps. xxxii. 7.

רנה, v. pres. תִּרְנֶה. Cogn. רנן. *Rung, rattled*, Job xxxix. 23, only.

רִנָּה, fem. aff. רִנָּתִי, רִנָּתָם, r. רנן. (a) *Singing, a shout of joy.* (b) *A shout* or *cry of any kind.* (c) *A cry for help.* (a) 2 Chron. xx. 22; Ps. xxx. 6; xlii. 5; xlvii. 2; Prov. xi. 10, &c. (b) 1 Kings xxii. 36. (c) 1 Kings viii. 28; Ps. xvii. 1; lxi. 2; xcviii. 3, &c.

רנן, v. pres. יָרֹן, once, יָרִין, Prov. xxix. 6. Constr. abs. Arab. رَنّ, *vociferatus fuit, clamorem edidit; ejulavit; sonuit* arcus. (a) *Sung.* (b) *Shouted*, in surprise or admiration. (c) *Called out* in invitation. (d) *Cried out for help.* (a) Ps. xxxv. 27; Prov. xxix. 6; Is. xxxv. 6, &c. (b) Lev. ix. 24. (c) Prov. i. 20; viii. 3.
Infin. רָן, Job xxxviii. 7.
Imp. f. רָנִּי, pl. רָנּוּ, Is. xii. 6; xliv. 23, &c. (d) Lam. ii. 19.
Pih. רִנֵּנוּ, pres. יְרַנֵּן. Intens. of Kal. (a) *Sung, shouted, rejoiced.* (b) *Sung of, celebrated*, constr. immed. (a) Ps. lxiii. 8; Jer. xxxi. 12; li. 48, &c. (b) Ps. li. 16; lix. 16.
Infin. רַנֵּן, Ps. cxxxii. 16; Is. xxxv. 2.
Imp. pl. רַנְּנוּ, Ps. xxxiii. 1, &c.
Puh. pres. יְרֻנָּן. Pass. of Pih. *There shall be singing*, Is. xvi. 10.
Hiph. pres. יַרְנִין. (a) *Caused to sing* or *rejoice.* (b) *Shouted, rejoiced.* (a) Job xxix. 13; Ps. lxv. 9.
Imp. pl. הַרְנִינוּ, (b) Deut. xxxii. 43; Ps. xxxii. 11; lxxxi. 2.
Hith. part. מִתְרוֹנֵן. *Shouted, rejoiced*, Ps. lxxviii. 65.

רְנָנִים, masc. pl. רְנָנִים, once, Job xxxix. 13. *The ostrich.* See Bochart. Hieroz., tom. ii., page 238.

רנן (564) רעב

רְנָנָה, fem. constr. רִנְּנַת, pl. רְנָנוֹת, r. רנן. Singing, rejoicing, Job iii. 7; xx. 5; Ps. lxiii. 6; c. 2.

רְסִיסִים, masc. pl. constr. רְסִיסֵי, r. רסס. Sprinkling; a drop, Cant. v. 2, only.

רְסִיסִים, m. pl. רְסִיסִים, r. רסס, i. q. רִצּוּץ. Fractures, Amos vi. 11, only.

רֶסֶן, m. aff. רִסְנוֹ. Arab. رَسَنٌ, funis, capistri pars, quæ ad nasum est. A bridle, halter, Job xxx. 11; xli. 5; Ps. xxxii. 9; Is. xxx. 28.

רסס, v. Infin. רֹס. Arab. رَشَّ, conspersit humore. Sprinkled, Ezek. xlvi. 14, only.

רַע, and רָע, masc. pl. רָעִים, constr. רָעֵי, f. רָעָה, pl. רָעוֹת, r. רעע. Evil, bad, wrong. (a) Wicked. (b) Fatal, deadly. (c) Calamitous. (d) Disagreeable, painful. (e) Offensive, displeasing: fully, רַע בְּעֵינֵי–. (f) Sad. (g) Ill favoured. (h) Envious, [1] Of the eye. [2] רַע עַיִן, Of a person. (k) Wickedness. (l) Harm, injury, calamity. (a) Gen. vi. 5; xiii. 13; Ps. ci. 4; cxl. 2, &c. (b) Gen. xxxvii. 20. 33; Lev. xxvi. 6; Ezek. xiv. 14, &c. (c) Gen. xlvii. 9; 1 Kings v. 4; Jer. ii. 19, &c. (d) Deut. xxviii. 35. 59; Job ii. 10. 17, &c. (e) Gen. xxxi. 24; Eccl. ii. 17; Gen. xxxviii. 7; Num. xxii. 34; Josh. xxiv. 15, &c. (f) Gen. xl. 7; Neh. ii. 1, 2. (g) Gen. xli. 21. (h), [1] Deut. xv. 9. [2] Prov. xxiii. 6; xxviii. 22. (k) Neh. ix. 28; Ps. vii. 10; Hab. ii. 9, &c. (l) Gen. xlviii. 16; Ps. xli. 6; Zeph. iii. 15.

רֹעַ, m. r. רעע. Badness, [1] Of actions; wickedness. [2] Of the heart. [3] Of the countenance; sadness. [4] Of the general appearance. [5] Of food. [1] Deut. xxviii. 20; Is. i. 16; Jer. iv. 4, &c. [2] 1 Sam. xvii. 28; Neh. ii. 2. [3] Eccl. vii. 3. [4] Gen. xli. 19. [5] Jer. xxiv. 2, 3. 8. 17; xxix. 17.

רֵעַ, m. aff. רֵעֹה, r. רעע. Shouting, crying out, Exod. xxxii. 17; Mic. iv. 9.

רֵעַ, m. aff. רֵעִי, pl. aff. רֵעֶיךָ. Syr. ܪܶܥܝܳܐ, voluit. Will, desire, Job xxxvi. 33; Ps. cxxxix. 2. 17.

רֵעַ, m. aff. רֵעִי, רֵעֶה and רֵעֵהוּ, רֵעֲהוּ, and רֵעִי, pl. רֵעִים, constr. רֵעֵי, aff. רֵעַי, &c. r. רעה. (a) A companion, friend. (b) A neighbour. (c) Phr. אִישׁ — רֵעֵהוּ, each—his companion, i. e. each other. (a) Gen. xxxviii. 12; 2 Sam. xiii. 3; 1 Chron. xxvii. 33; Prov. xvii. 17, &c. (b) Exod. xx. 17; Lev. xix. 13; Deut. xxiii. 25, &c. (c) Gen. xi. 3. 7; xliii. 33; Exod. xi. 2, &c. Of inanimate things, Gen. xv. 10.

רָעֵב, masc. aff. רְעָבָם. Arab. رَغِبَ, voluit, expetivit. Æth. ርኅበ : esuriit. (a) Hunger. (b) Famine. (a) Deut. xxviii. 48; Jer. xiv. 18; Lam. iv. 9, &c. (b) Gen. xii. 10; xxvi. 1; xli. 27, &c.

רָעֵב, m. pl. רְעֵבִים, fem. רְעֵבָה. Hungry, famishing, 2 Sam. xvii. 29; 2 Kings vii. 12; Ps. cvii. 9; Is. xxxii. 6, &c.

רעב, v. pret. pl. in pause, רָעֵבוּ, pres. יִרְעַב. Constr. abs. it. med. לְ. (a) Was hungry. (b) Hungered for, was famished through want of. (c) Suffered from famine. (a) Ps. xxxiv. 11; Is. viii. 21; xxxv. 13; &c. (b) Jer. xlii. 14. (c) Gen. xli. 55. Hiph. pres. יַרְעִיב. Allowed or caused to suffer hunger, Deut. viii. 3; Prov. x. 3.

רְעָבוֹן, masc. constr. רַעֲבוֹן. Hunger, famine, Gen. xlii. 19. 33; Ps. xxxvii. 19.

רַעַד, m. and רְעָדָה, fem. Æth. ረዐደ : tremuit. Arab. رَعَدَ, tonuit; أَرْعَدَ, correptus tremore fuit. Trembling, awe, Exod. xv. 15; Job iv. 14; Ps. ii. 11; Is. xxxii. 14, &c.

רעד, v. pres. תִּרְעַד. Trembled, Ps. civ. 33. Hiph. part. מַרְעִיד, pl. מַרְעִידִים, Id., Ezra x. 9; Dan. x. 11.

רָעָה, v. pres. יִרְעֶה. Constr. abs. it. immed. Arab. رَعَى, pavit; pastum duxit; rexit. (a) Fed, of cattle. (b) Metaph. Of a nation. (c) Consumed. (d) Devastated. (e) Fed on, delighted in. (f) Associated with. (g) Fed cattle. (h) Metaph. Governed, directed, guarded, provided for a people. (k) Afforded food to, nourished. (l) For רעע, Injured, oppressed. (a) Exod. xxxiv. 3; Is. v. 17; xxvii. 10, &c. (b) Is. xiv. 3; Jer. l. 19; Mic. vii. 14, &c. (c) Ps. xlix. 15; Jer. xxii. 22. (d) Mic. v. 6. (e) Prov. xv. 14; Is. xliv. 20; Hos. xii. 2. (g) Gen. xxx. 31; Is. lxi. 5; Jer. vi. 3, &c. (h) 2 Sam. v. 2; Jer. iii. 15; Ezek. xxxiv. 13. 23; Mic. v. 4, &c. (k) Hos. ix. 2.

רעה (565) רעי

Infin. רְעוֹת, aff. רְעֹתוֹ, Gen. xxxvi. 24; xxxvii. 12, &c.
Imp. רְעֵה, fem. רְעִי, pl. רְעוּ, Gen. xxix. 7; Cant. i. 8; Mic. vii. 14, &c.
Part. רֹעֶה. *Feeding; a shepherd*, Gen. iv. 2; xxix. 9; Jer. vi. 3, &c. Applied metaph. [1] To God, Gen. xlviii. 15; Ps. xxiii. 1; Is. xl. 11, &c. [2] To kings, Is. xliv. 28; Ezek. xxxiv. 23; xxxvii. 24, &c. [3] To prophets, Jer. iii. 15; xxiii. 1, 2, &c. Sign. (f) Prov. xiii. 20; xxviii. 7; xxix. 3. (l) Job xxiv. 21.
Pih. רֵעָה. *Became a companion*, Judg. xiv. 20.
Hiph. pres. aff. יַרְעֶה. *Caused to feed*, metaph. *ruled*, Ps. lxxvii. 72.
Hith. pres. apoc. תִּתְרַע, i. q. Pih. Prov. xxii. 24.

רָעָה, fem. constr. רָעַת, aff. רָעָתִי, &c., pl. רָעוֹת, r. רעע. (a) *Evil, injury, mischief, calamity.* (b) *Wrong, wickedness.* (a) Gen. xxvi. 29; xliv. 4; Exod. x. 10; Deut. xxxi. 17, &c. (b) Gen. vi. 5; Judg. xi. 27; 1 Sam. xxiv. 12; xxix. 6, &c.

רֵעֶה, masc. r. רעה, i. q. רֵעַ. *A friend*, 2 Sam. xv. 37; xvi. 16; 1 Kings iv. 5.

רֵעָה, f. pl. aff. רֵעוֹתֶיהָ, רֵעוֹתַי, fem. of last. *A female friend or companion*, Judg. xi. 37, 38; Ps. xlv. 15.

רֹעָה, fem. r. רעע. *Breaking*, Prov. xxv. 19; Is. xxiv. 19.

רְעוּת, f. aff. רְעוּתָהּ, fem. of רַע. (a) *A companion, friend, neighbour*, Exod. xi. 2; Esth. i. 19; Is. xxxiv. 15, 16; Jer. ix. 19. (b) רְעוּת רוּחַ, Eccl. i. 14; ii. 11; iv. 4, &c. According to some, *Feeding on the wind*, i. e. *emptiness:* so Aquila and Theod. νομὴ ἀνέμου. Symm. βόσκησις ἀνέμου. Others, comparing the Chald. רְעָה, i. q. Heb. רָצָה, *Wish for, delight in the wind.* So LXX. προαίρεσις πνεύματος. Vulg. *afflictio spiritus:* as if from רעע.

רְעוּת, Chald. fem. r. רְעָה, *voluit. Wish, will*, Ezra v. 17; vii. 18.

רְעִי, m. r. רעה. *Pasture*, 1 Kings v. 3, only.

רֹעִי, m. i. q. רֹעֶה, r. רעה. *A shepherd*, Is. xxxviii. 12; Zech. xi. 17.

רֵעִיה, f. aff. רַעְיָתִי, i. q. רְעוּת. *A female companion, friend*, Cant. i. 9; ii. 2; iv. 7, &c.

רַעְיוֹן, m. i. q. רְעוּת. *Desire, pursuit*, Eccl. i. 17; ii. 22; iv. 16, only.

רעיון, Chald. m. pl. constr. רַעְיוֹנֵי, aff. רַעְיוֹנָךְ, רַעְיוֹנֹהִי, r. רְעָה. *Desire, purpose; thought*, Dan. ii. 29; iv. 16; v. 10, &c.

רָעַל, m. Syr. ܪܥܠ, *timuit, tremuit;* ܪܥܠ, *commotio, tremor.* Arab. رَعَلَ, *percussit, feriit gladio;* رَعَل, *species veli.* (a) *Trembling, giddiness*, Zech. xii. 2. (b) Pl. רְעָלוֹת, *Veils*, Is. iii. 15.

רעל, v. Hoph. in pause, הָרְעָלוּ. *Were shaken, thrown*, of spears, javelins, Nah. ii. 4.

רַעַם, masc. aff. רַעְמֵךְ. Syr. ܪܥܡ, *tonuit.* Ethpe. *Iratus est;* ܐܬܪܥܡ, *tonitru.* Arab. رَغْم, *aversatio, ira.* (a) *Thunder.* (b) *Tumult; rage.* (a) Job xxvi. 14; Ps. lxxvii. 19; lxxxi. 8; civ. 7. (b) Job xxxix. 25.

רעם, v. רָעֲמוּ. pres. יִרְעַם. *Thundered.* (a) Metaph. *Resounded, roared*, of the sea. (b) *Was disturbed, excited.* (a) 1 Chron. xvi. 32; Ps. xcvi. 11; xcviii. 7. (b) Ezek. xxvii. 35.
Hiph. הִרְעִים, pres. יַרְעֵם. (a) *Caused thunder, thundered.* (b) *Caused anger or vexation.* (a) 1 Sam. ii. 10; vii. 10; Job xxxvii. 4; Ps. xxix. 3, &c.
Infin. aff. הַרְעִימָהּ, (b) 1 Sam. i. 6.

רַעְמָה, f. *Rage, scorn*, Job xxxix. 19. See the note.

רַעֲנָן, masc. pl. רַעֲנַנִים, fem. רַעֲנַנָּה. (a) *Flourishing*, [1] Of a tree. [2] Of leaves. [3] Of a branch. (b) Metaph. of persons, *Prosperous.* (c) Probably *Surrounded by foliage.* (d) בְּשֶׁמֶן רַעֲנָן, either, *With fresh oil*, or *with the oil of the prosperous.* (a), [1] Deut. xii. 20; 1 Kings xvi. 4; Jer. xi. 16, &c. [2] Jer. xvii. 8. [3] Job xv. 32. (b) Ps. xcii. 15; Dan. iv. 1. (c) Cant. i. 16. (d) Ps. xcii. 11.

רעע, v. I. *Was evil, bad, wrong.* See רַע.
Hiph. הֵרַע, pres. יָרַע. Constr. abs. it. med. אֶת, בְּ, לְ. (a) *Did evil.* (b) *Did evil to, treated ill, afflicted.* (a) 2 Kings xxi. 11; 1 Chron. xxi. 17; Ps. lxxiv. 3, &c. (b) Med. אֶת, Num. xvi. 15; Deut. xxvi. 6.

רעע (566) רפא

Med. אֶ, 1 Chron. xvi. 22. Med. לְ, Exod. v. 23; Josh. xxiv. 20; Ruth i. 21; 1 Sam. xxvi. 21, &c.

Infin. הָרֵעַ, הָרַע, Lev. v. 4; 1 Sam. xii. 25, &c.

Part. מֵרַע, pl. מְרֵעִים. *Doing evil; an evil-doer*, Job viii. 20; Prov. xvii. 4.

II. Pret. רָעַע, pres. יָעַע. Syr. ܪ̈ܥ, *fregit*. Cogn. רצץ. Constr. immed. (a) *Broke, broke to pieces*. (b) *Crushed*. (a) Jer. ii. 16; xii. 16; xv. 12. (b) Job xxxiv. 24; Mic. v. 5.

Niph. pres. יֵרוֹעַ. Pass. of Kal. *Was broken, broken to pieces; was ruined*, Prov. xi. 15; xiii. 20.

Hith. הִתְרֹעֲעָה, *Id.*, Is. xxiv. 19.

Infin. הִתְרוֹעֵעַ, Prov. xviii. 24.

רעע, Chald. v. pres. תֵּרֹעַ, *Id.*, Dan. ii. 40.

Paḥ. part. מְרָעַע, *Id.*, Ibid.

רעף, v. pres. יִרְעֲפוּ. Arab. رَعَفَ, *fluxit sanguis; abundavit uter. Flowed, overflowed; let drop*, Job xxxvi. 28; Ps. lxv. 12, 13; Prov. iii. 20.

Hiph. Imp. pl. הַרְעִיפוּ, *Id.*, Is. xlv. 8.

רעץ, v. pres. יִרְעַץ, i. q. רעע, and רצץ. *Crushed; overpowered, oppressed*, Exod. xv. 6; Judg. x. 8.

רַעַשׁ, m. Arab. رَعَسَ, *trepidavit, tremuit*; رَاعِسٌ, *tremens; alacris*. (a) *Shaking, trembling*. (b) *An earthquake*. (c) *The rumbling* of wheels. (d) Either, *The rattling* of a horse's hoofs, or *his restless eagerness* in rushing to battle. (e) *Any loud noise, tumult*. (f) *The rattling* of a spear. (a) Ezek. xii. 18; xxxviii. 19. (b) 1 Kings xix. 11; Is. xxix. 6; Amos i. 1; Zech. xiv. 5. (c) Jer. xlvii. 3; Ezek. iii. 12, 13; xxxvii. 7; Nah. iii. 2. (d) Job xxxix. 24. (e) Job xli. 21.

רעש, v. רָעֲשָׁה, pres. יִרְעַשׁ. Constr. abs. *Was shaken, trembled*. Applied, [1] To the earth. [2] The heavens. [3] Mountains, islands, &c. [4] Men and animals, under the influence of fear. [5] Trees, standing corn, &c. [1] Judg. v. 4; Ps. lxviii. 9; Is. xiii. 13, &c. [2] Joel ii. 10; iv. 16. [3] Ezek. xxvi. 15; Nah. i. 5. [4] Ezek. xxxviii. 20. [5] Ps. lxxii. 16.

Part. pl. רֹעֲשִׁים, Jer. iv. 24.

Niph. נִרְעֲשָׁה, *Id.* [1] Jer. L. 46.

Hiph. הִרְעַשְׁתִּי, pres. aff. תַּרְעִישׁ. Causat. of Kal. (a) *Caused to tremble, shook*. (b) Either, *Caused to rush on so as to make the earth tremble*, or *filled with restless eagerness*. (a) Ps. lx. 4; Ezek. xxxi. 16; Hag. ii. 7. (b) Job xxxix. 20. But see the note.

Part. מַרְעִישׁ, Is. xiv. 16; Hag. ii. 6. 20.

רָפָא, v. pres. יִרְפָּא. Constr. immed. it. med. אֶת, לְ. Arab. رَفَا, and رَفَو, r. رفو, *reparavit ruptam vestem*. Æth. ረፈአ: *consuit. Bound up* a wound. (a) *Healed* a wound. (b) *Healed* a person. (c) Metaph. of a nation, country, or individual, *Restored to prosperity, delivered from calamity*. (d) *Healed* transgressions, i. e. *removed* their evil consequences. (e) Impers. רָפָא לוֹ, *Was healed*. (a) Is. xxx. 26. (b) Gen. xx. 17; 2 Kings xx. 8. (c) Deut. xxxii. 39; Ps. cvii. 20; Is. xix. 22; Hos. xi. 3, &c. (d) Jer. iii. 22; Hos. xiv. 5. (e) Is. vi. 10.

Infin. רָפוֹא, רָפֹא, aff. רְפָאִי, Eccl. iii. 3; Is. xix. 22; Hos. vii. 1.

Imp. רְפָא, רְפָאָה, aff. רְפָאֵנִי, Num. xii. 13; Ps. vi. 3; xli. 5.

Part. רֹפֵא, aff. רֹפְאֶךָ, pl. רֹפְאִים, constr. רֹפְאֵי. *A healer, physician*, Gen. L. 2; Exod. xv. 26; 2 Kings xx. 5; 2 Chron. xvi. 12; Job xiii. 4, &c.

Niph. נִרְפָּא, pres. יֵרָפֵא. Pass. of Kal. (a) *Was repaired*, of an earthen vessel. (b) *Was healed*, of a wound or disease. (c) *Was healed*, of a person. (d) *Was rendered wholesome*, of water. (e) Metaph. *Was restored to prosperity*. (f) Imp. נֵרָפָא לָנוּ. *We were healed*. (b) Lev. xiii. 37; xiv. 3. 48, &c. (c) 1 Sam. vi. 3. (d) Ezek. xlvii. 8, 9. 11. (e) Jer. xvii. 14; li. 8. (f) Is. liii. 5.

Infin. הֵרָפֵה, Jer. xv. 18. (a) Jer. xix. 11. (b) Deut. xxviii. 27. 35.

Piḥ. רִפֵּאתִי, pres. יְרַפֵּא. (a) *Repaired*. (b) *Healed*. (c) *Caused to be cured*. (d) *Rendered wholesome*. (a) 1 Kings xviii. 30. (b) Ezek. xxxiv. 4; Zech. xi. 16. Metaph. Jer. vi. 14; li. 9. (c) Exod. xxi. 19. (d) 2 Kings ii. 21.

Infin. רַפֹּא, Exod. xxi. 19.

Part. מְרַפֵּא, for מְרַפֶּה, רפה, which see.

Hith. Infin. הִתְרַפֵּא. *To get himself cured*, 2 Kings viii. 29; ix. 15; 2 Chron. xxii. 6.

רְפָאוֹת, pl. f. Probably *Things bound on, bandages; external applications, remedies*, Jer. xxx. 13; xlvi. 11; Ezek. xxx. 21.

רפא (567) רפח

רְפָאוּת, f. once. *Healing, health*, Prov. iii. 8.

רְפָאִים, pl. m. *The Rephaim*, apparently the name of the tribe inhabiting Sodom, Gomorrah, &c., the neighbouring cities of the plain, Gen. xiv. 5; xv. 19; Deut. ii. 11. 20; Josh. xv. 18, &c. The destruction of this people, or of the majority of them, is referred to, Job xxvi. 5, where see the note; Ps. lxxxviii. 11; Is. xiv. 9; xxvi. 14, 15, &c.

רפד, v. pres. יִרְפַּד. Arab. رَفَدَ, *suffulcivit, sustentavit*. Cogn. רבץ רבד. *Supported, rested* himself, Job xli. 22; the construction being יְרַפֵּד נִפְשׁוֹ עֲלֵי־חָרוּץ בַּעֲלֵי־טִיט *He sustains himself upon the pointed things as upon mire*.
Pih. רִפַּדְתִּי. (a) *Supported, constructed*, a couch, Job xvii. 13. (b) *Strengthened, refreshed*.
Imp. pl. aff. רַפְּדוּנִי. (b) Cant. ii. 5.

רָפָה, v. I. pres. יִרְפֶּה, apoc. יֵרֶף. Syr. ܪܦܳܐ, *laxavit*. Aph. *dimisit*. *Sunk down* from weakness or decay. (a) *Hung down*, of the hands. (b) *The day declined*. (c) *Fuel sunk down* in the fire. (d) *Anger diminished, gave way*. (e) *Became weak, dispirited*. (f) *Desisted*. (a) 2 Sam. iv. 1; Jer. vi. 24; Ezek. xxi. 12, &c. (b) Judg. xix. 9. (c) Is. v. 24. (d) Judg. viii. 3. (e) Jer. xlix. 24. (f) Exod. iv. 26; Neh. vi. 9.
Niph. part. pl. נִרְפִּים. *Become idle*, or rather, *unemployed*, Exod. v. 8. 17. LXX. σχολάζουσι. Vulg. *vacant*.
Pih. רִפָּה, pres. תְּרַפֶּינָה. (a) *Allowed to hang down*. (b) *Rendered weak*. (a) Ezek. i. 24, 25.
Part. מְרַפֵּא, for מְרַפֶּה, pl. מְרַפִּים. (b) Ezra iv. 4; Jer. xxxviii. 4.
Hiph. pres. יַרְפֶּה, apoc. יֶרֶף. Constr. abs. it. immed. it. med. ל, מִן. (a) *Withheld* or *withdrew* the hands, either in helping or punishing. (b) *Gave up; ceased to support*. (c) *Let go*. (d) *Withheld the hands from, left undisturbed*. (e) *Ceased from*. (f) *Ceased*, abs. (a) Josh. x. 6. (b) Deut. iv. 31; Josh. i. 5; Ps. cxxxviii. 8, &c. (c) Job xxvii. 6; Prov. iv. 13; Cant. iii. 4. (d) Job vii. 19. (e) Neh. vi. 3.
Imp. הַרְפֵּה, הֶרֶף, pl. הַרְפּוּ. (a) 2 Sam. xxiv. 16; 1 Chron. xxi. 15. (d) Deut. ix. 14; Judg. xi. 37, &c. (e) Ps. xxxvii. 8; (f) 1 Sam. xv. 16; Ps. xlvi. 11.
Hith. הִתְרַפָּה. *Relaxed himself, was slothful*, Prov. xxiv. 10.
Part. מִתְרַפֶּה, pl. מִתְרַפִּים, Josh. xviii. 3; Prov. xviii. 9.
II. For רָפָא, which see. Pres. תִּרְפֶּינָה, Job v. 18.
Imp. רְפָה, Ps. lx. 4.
Niph. נִרְפְּתָה, pres. יֵרָפוּ, 2 Kings ii. 22; Jer. li. 9.
Infin. הֵרָפֵה, Jer. xix. 11.
Pih. pres. יְרַפֵּא, Jer. viii. 11.

רָפֶה, m. constr. רְפֵה, f. pl. רָפוֹת. *Weak*, [1] Of a nation, Num. xiii. 18. [2] Of the hands, 2 Sam. xvii. 2; Job iv. 3; Is. xxxv. 3.

רְפִידָה, f. aff. רְפִידָתוֹ. r. רפד. *A support*. Probably *the sides and back* of the chariot, throne, Cant. iii. 10, only. LXX. ἀνάκλιτον. Vulg. *Reclinatorium*.

רִפְיוֹן, m. r. רפה. *Weakness*, Jer. xlvii. 3, only.

רפס, and רפש, pres. תִּרְפֹּשׂ. Arab. رَفَسَ, *pede percussit*. Cogn. רמס. *Trampled, trampled down*, Ezek. xxxii. 2; xxxiv. 18.
Niph. Pass. of Kal. Part. נִרְפָּשׂ. *Disturbed by trampling*, Prov. xxv. 26.
Hith. *Submitted, humbled himself*.
Imp. הִתְרַפֵּס, Prov. vi. 3.
Part. מִתְרַפֵּס, Ps. lxviii. 31.

רפס, Chald. v. רָפַס, *Id.*, Dan. vii. 7, only.

רַפְסֹדוֹת, pl. f. once, 2 Chron. ii. 15, i. q., דֹּבְרוֹת, 1 Kings v. 23, *Floats, rafts*. The etymology is uncertain.

רפק, v. Kal non occ. Arab. رَفَقَ, *juvit, favit*. مَرْفِق, *cubitus*. VIII. *Innixus fuit*. Probably *Assisted, supported*.
Hith. part. f. מִתְרַפֶּקֶת. *Supporting herself, leaning*, Cant. viii. 5, only.

רפש, see רפס.

רֶפֶשׁ, m. once, Is. lvii. 20, apparently nearly synonymous with טִיט, *Mud*. The LXX. omit the clause. Vulg. *conculcationem*.

רְפָתִים, pl. m. once, Hab. iii. 17. Arab. رُفَة, *stramen*. *Stalls* for oxen. LXX. φάτναις. Vulg. *præsepibus*.

רץ (568) רצח

רץ, m. pl. constr. רַצֵּי, r. רִצֵּי. *A fragment; a small piece* of silver, Ps. lxviii. 31, only.

רָץ, see רוץ.

רצא, v. I. For cogn. רוּץ, Infin. רָצוֹא, Ezek. i. 14.

II. For רצה רָצָאתִי, Ezek. xliii. 27.

רצד, v. Kal non occ. Arab. رَصَدَ, *observavit, rem: insidiatus fuit.*
Pih. pres. תְּרַצְּדוּן, Ps. lxviii. 17. Either *watched enviously*, or *laid wait for*. Aquila and Theod. ἐρίζετε. Symm. περισπουδάζετε. LXX. ὑπολαμβάνετε. Vulg. *suspicamini*.

רָצָה, v. pres. יִרְצֶה, apoc. יִרֶץ. Constr. immed. it. med. אֶת, בְּ, עִם. Arab. رَضِىَ, r. رضو, *vicit placendo.* رِضَي, *gratum habuit;* n. a. رِضْوَانْ. (a) *Approved of, took pleasure in.* (b) *Received favourably* an offering or a person. (c) *Loved.* (d) *Fulfilled.* (e) *Associated* with, constr. med. עִם. (f) *Was received favourably,* med. עִם. (a) 1 Chron. xxviii. 4; Ps. cxlvii. 10; Eccl. ix. 7, &c. (b) Gen. xxxiii. 10; 2 Chron. x. 7; Jer. xiv. 10; Hos. viii. 13, &c. (c) Ps. xliv. 4; cii. 15; Is. xlii. 1, &c. (d) Lev. xxvi. 34. 41. 43; 2 Chron. xxxvi. 21; Job xiv. 6. (e) Ps. L. 18; but LXX. συνέτρεχες αὐτῷ, and Vulg. *currebas*, reading תָּרָץ for תִּרְצֶה.
Infin. רְצוֹת, aff. רְצוֹתִי, רְצוֹתוֹ. (f) Job xxxiv. 9; 1 Chron. xxix. 3; Ps. lxxvii. 8; Prov. xvi. 7.
Imp. רְצֵה, Ps. xl. 14; cxix. 108.
Part. רוֹצֶה, aff. רֹצָם, Ps. cxlvii. 11; cxlix. 4; Jer. xiv. 12.
Part. pass. רָצוּי, constr. רְצוּי, Deut. xxxiii. 24; Esth. x. 3.
Niph. נִרְצָה, pres. יֵרָצֶה. Pass. of Kal, signn. (b) Lev. i. 4; vii. 18; xix. 7, &c. (d) Is. xl. 2.
Pih. pres. יְרַצּוּ. *Gave satisfaction to*, by restitution, Job xx. 10.
Hiph. הִרְצָה (for הִרְצְתָה, which is the reading of the Sam.), i. q. Kal (d) Lev. xxvi. 34.
Hith. pres. הִתְרַצָּה. *Made himself acceptable*, 1 Sam. xxix. 4.

רָצוֹן, m. constr. רְצוֹן, aff. רְצוֹנִי, &c. (a) *Approbation, favour*, whether *approving* or *being approved*. (b) *An object of approbation.* (c) *Will, pleasure, choice.* [1] The *feeling*. [2] The *object*. (d) *Uncontrolled will, violence.* (e) *Enjoyment.* (a) Lev. i. 3; Ps. v. 13; lxix. 14; Prov. viii. 35, &c. Phrr. עֵת רָצוֹן, Ps. lxix. 14; Is. xlix. 8; — יוֹם, Is. lviii. 5. — שְׁנַת, Is. lxi. 2. (b) Prov. xi. 1. 20; xv. 8. (c), [1] Lev. xix. 5; Neh. ix. 24; Dan. viii. 4, &c. [2] Ezra x. 11; Ps. xl. 9; cxliii. 10; cxlv. 19. Phr. בִּכְלִי־רְצוֹנָם. (d) Gen. xlix. 6. (e) Deut. xxxiii. 23; Ps. cxlv. 16.

רָצַח, m. Arab. رَضَخَ, and رَضَّ, *contudit, confregit.* (a) *Crushing.* (b) *Killing, slaughter.* (a) Metaph. Ps. xlii. 11: where, LXX. καταθλᾶσθαι. Aquila, φονεῦσαι. Symm. σφαγήν. Vulg. *confringuntur.* (b) Ezek. xxi. 27.

רָצַח, v. pres. יִרְצַח. Constr. immed. it. med. אֶת. *Struck.* (a) נֶפֶשׁ ר׳. *Struck fatally, killed.* (b) Without נֶפֶשׁ, *killed.* (a) Deut. xxii. 26. (b) Exod. xx. 13; Num. xxxv. 27. 30; Deut. iv. 42, &c.
Infin. רְצֹחַ, (b) Jer. vii. 9; Hos. iv. 2.
Part. רֹצֵחַ. *Killing; one who kills,* whether by accident or through malice, Num. xxxv. 6. 11; Deut. iv. 42; Josh. xx. 3, &c.
Niph. pres. יֵרָצֵחַ, Pass. of Kal, Prov. xxii. 13.
Part. f. נִרְצָחָה, Judg. xx. 4.
Pih. pres. יְרַצְּחוּ. Frequentative of Kal, *Habitually kill*, Ps. xciv. 6; Hos. vi. 9.
Part. מְרַצֵּחַ, pl. מְרַצְּחִים. *A murderer*, 2 Kings vi. 32; Is. i. 21.
Puh. pres. Ps. lxii. 4, תְּרָצְחוּ, or תְּרֻצְּחוּ, for תִּרְצְחוּ. Either, *Ye shall be crushed* or *ye shall be killed.* Another reading, however, is in Pih. תְּרַצְּחוּ. *Ye crush,* or *attempt to crush* or *kill.* So LXX. φονεύετε; and Vulg. *Interficites.*

רָצַע, v. once, Exod. xxi. 6. Constr. med. אֶת. Arab. رَصَعَ, *confodit ita ut cuspis intus abderetur. Pierced, bored.*

רצף, m. pl. רְצָפִים. Arab. رَضْفٌ, *lapis ignitus, quo ignito lac calefit: lapis, cui impositæ assantur carnes.* According to some, *Hot stones* used in baking bread or flesh; others, *burning coals*, 1 Kings xix. 6, only.

רצף, v. only in part. pass. of Kal, רָצוּף.

רצף (569) רקח

Arab. رَصَفَ, *lapillis stravit. Covered, overlaid*, Cant. iii. 10, only.

רִצְפָּה, f. constr. רִצְפַּת. (a) *A burning coal.* (b) *A pavement, floor*, (a) Is. vi. 6. (b) 2 Chron. vii. 3; Esth. i. 6; Ezek. xl. 17, 18; xlii. 3.

רצץ, v. pret. רָצוֹץ, pres. יָרוּץ, תָּרֻץ. Constr. immed. it. med. אֶת. Arab. رَضَّ, *contudit, fregit.* (a) *Bruised, broke, crushed.* (b) Metaph. *Oppressed.* (c) Intrans. *Became broken, burst.* (d) Metaph. *Relaxed himself.* (b) 1 Sam. xii. 3, 4. (c) Eccl. xii. 6. (d) Is. xlii. 3.
Part. pl. f. רְצֻצוֹת, (b) Amos iv. 1.
Part. pass. רָצוּץ, constr. רְצוּץ, pl. רְצוּצִים. (a) 2 Kings xviii. 21; Is. xxxvi. 6; xlii. 3; (b) Deut. xxviii. 33; Is. lviii. 6; Hos. v. 10.
Niph. נָרוֹץ, pres. תֵּרוֹץ. Pass. of Kal sign. (a) Eccl. xii. 6; Ezek. xxix. 7.
Pih. רִצֵּץ, pres. יְרַצֵּץ, and יְרֹצְצוּ. I. q., Kal signn. (a) Ps. lxxiv. 14. (b) Judg. x. 8; 2 Chron. xvi. 10; Job xx. 19.
Hiph. pres. תָּרֻץ. I. q. Kal sign. (a), Judg. ix. 53.
Hith. pres. יִתְרֹצֲצוּ. *Struggled together*, Gen. xxv. 22. LXX. ἐσκίρτων. Vulg. *Collidebantur*.

רַק, m. pl. f. רַקּוֹת. Arab. رَقَّ, *tenuis fuit res.* (a) *Thin, lean*, Gen. xli. 19, 20. 27. (b) Adv. [1] *Only.* [2] *Certainly*, i. e. *this, and this alone.* [3] With a negative, *except.* [1] Gen. vi. 5; Deut. ii. 28; 1 Kings xiv. 8, &c. [2] Gen. xx. 11; Deut. iv. 6; Judg. xiv. 16, &c. [3] 2 Kings xvii. 18; 2 Chron. v. 10; xviii. 15, &c.

רֵק, see רִיק.

רֹק, m. aff. רֻקִּי, r. רקק. *Spitting, spittle*, Job vii. 19; xxx. 10; Is. L. 6.

רָקָב, m. const. רְקַב. *Decay, rottenness*, Job xiii. 28; Prov. xii. 4; xiv. 30; Hos. v. 12; Hab. iii. 16.

רקב, v. pres. יִרְקַב. *Became rotten, decayed*, Prov. x. 7; Is. xl. 20.

רִקָּבוֹן, m. i. q. רָקָב. *Rottenness*, Job xli. 9.

רקד, v. רָקְדוּ, pres. תִּרְקְדוּן. Arab. رَقَدَانٌ, *saltus ob alacritatem factus.* Syr. ܦܳܙ,
saliit, subsiliit præ lætitiâ. Leaped, danced, of persons, animals, and inanimate things, Ps. cxiv. 4. 6.
Infin. רְקוֹד, Eccl. iii. 4.
Pih. pres. יְרַקֵּד, i. q. Kal, Job xxi. 11; Is. xiii. 21; Joel ii. 5.
Part. מְרַקֵּד, f. מְרַקֵּדָה, 1 Chron. xv. 29; Nah. iii. 2.
Hiph. pres. aff. יַרְקִידֵם, causat. of Kal, Ps. xxix. 6.

רַקָּה, f. aff. רַקָּתוֹ, רַקָּתֵךְ, r. רקק. (a) *The temple*, of the head. (b) Probably *the cheek*. (a) Judg. iv. 21, 22; v. 26. (b) Cant. iv. 3; vi. 7.

רָקַח, m. cogn. رَقَّ, *bene curavit ac recte administravit opes.* رَقَاحِي, *mercator. Careful preparation* of any composition for use or sale; pec. *spicing* or *perfuming*, Cant. viii. 2.

רקח, v. pres. יִרְקַח. *Compounded, prepared*, Exod. xxx. 33.
Part. רֹקֵחַ, pl. constr. רֹקְחֵי. *A compounder, apothecary, perfumer*, Exod. xxx. 35; xxxvii. 29; 1 Chron. ix. 30; Eccl. x. 1.
Puh. part. pl. מְרֻקָּחִים. Pass. of Kal, 2 Chron. xvi. 14.
Hiph. Imp. הַרְקַח. *Applied* perfumery, threw in spices, Ezek. xxiv. 10.

רַקָּח, m. pl. רַקָּחִים, f. pl. רַקָּחוֹת. *An apothecary, perfumer*, 1 Sam. viii. 13; Neh. iii. 8.

רֹקַח, m. *An ointment*, Exod. xxx. 25. 35.

רְקָחִים, pl. m. aff. רְקָחָיִךְ. *Ointments, perfumes*, Is. lvii. 9.

רָקִיעַ, m. constr. רְקִיעַ, see רקק. *Any thing stretched or spread out.* (a) *The expanse* of heaven, *the atmosphere, sky.* (b) *A canopy.* (a) Gen. i. 6—8. 14. 20; Ps. xix. 2; cl. 1; Dan. xii. 3. (b) Ezek. i. 22—26; x. 1.

רָקִיק, m. pl. constr. רְקִיקֵי, r. רקק. *A thin cake*, Exod. xxix. 2. 23; Lev. ii. 4; Num. vi. 15, &c.

רקם, v. Arab. رَقَمَ, *scripsit, notavit punctis diacriticis; strias intexuit panno.* رَقْم, *species striatæ pictæque vestis. Embroidered*, or *wove with various colours.*
Part. רֹקֵם. *An embroiderer*, or one who

רקם

weaves with various colours, Exod. xxvi. 36; xxvii. 16; xxviii. 39, &c.

Puh. רֻקַּמְתִּי. Pass. of Kal. Metaph. of the human body, *Wrought with art*, Ps. cxxxix. 15.

רִקְמָה, רִקְמָתָם, רִקְמָתֵךְ, f. aff. רִקְמָה, dual רִקְמָתַיִם, pl. רְקָמוֹת. (a) *Embroidery*. (b) *A variety of colours*, of the plumage of a bird. (c) Dual, either *Two pieces of embroidery*, or *a piece embroidered on both sides*. (a) Judg. v. 30; 1 Chron. xxix. 2; Ps. xlv. 15; Ezek. xvi. 10, &c. (b) Ezek. xvii. 3. (c) Judg. v. 30.

רקע, v. Pres. aff. אֶרְקָעֵם. Arab. رَقَعَ, *reparavit, resarcivit* vestem *partibus panni insertis*. رَقِيع, and رَقِيع, *coelum*. Sam. רקיע, *vestis, vestimentum*. Syr. ܪܩܥ, *firmavit, stabilivit, constrinxit*. Constr. immed. (a) *Stretched out*, of God *stretching out* or *spreading* the earth. (b) *Stamped on* in order to stretch, *stamped on*. (c) *Stamped* with the feet, as an expression of strong feeling, either indignation or joy. (b) 2 Sam. xxii. 43.

Infin. aff. רִקְעֲךָ, (a) Ezek. xxv. 6.
Imp. רְקַע, (c) Ezek. vi. 11.
Part. רֹקַע, (a) Ps. cxxxvi. 6; Is. xlii. 5; xliv. 24.

Pih. pres. יְרַקֵּעַ. (a) *Beat thin, beat into thin plates*. (b) *Covered* with a thin plate of gold. (a) Exod. xxxix. 3; Num. xvi. 30. (b) Is. xl. 19.

Puh. Pass. of Pih. Part. מְרֻקָּע, (a) Jer. x. 9.

Hiph. pres. תַּרְקִיעַ. *Stretched out*, with לְ, Job xxxvii. 18.

רְקֻעִים, pl. masc. constr. רִקֻּעֵי. *Things stretched or beaten out; plates*, Num. xvii. 3.

רקק, v. pres. יָרֹק, i. q. ירק, sign. II. *Spit*, Lev. xv. 8.

רָשׁ, רֵשׁ, see יָרַשׁ, רוּשׁ.

רִשָּׁיוֹן, m. Syr. ܪܫܐ, *dedit, obtulit*. Chald. רְשָׁא, *potuit, licentiam habuit*. *A grant, permission*, Ezra iii. 7.

רֵשִׁית, see רֵאשִׁית.

רשם, v. Arab. رَسَمَ, *scripsit; præscripsit*. *Wrote, decreed*.
Part. pass. רָשׁוּם, Dan. x. 21.
רְשַׁם, Chald. v. pres. תִּרְשֻׁם, *Id.*, Dan. vi. 9—14.

רשע

Peil, רְשִׁים, Pass., Dan. v. 24, 25; vi. 11.

רֶשַׁע, m. aff. רִשְׁעוֹ, רִשְׁעֲךָ, רִשְׁעֵנוּ. Syr. ܪܘܫܥܐ, *peccavit*; ܪܘܫܥܐ, *improbitas*. *Wickedness; impiety, injustice*, Job xxxiv. 8; Ps. xlv. 8; Is. lviii. 4; Mic. vi. 11, &c.

רָשָׁע, m. pl. רְשָׁעִים, constr. רִשְׁעֵי, f. רְשָׁעָה. (a) *Wicked; impious, unjust*. (b) רְ" לָמוּת, *Meriting death*. (c) *Guilty, faulty*. (a) Gen. xviii. 23; Exod. xxiii. 1; Ps. ix. 18; Is. lviii. 7, &c. (b) Num. xxxv. 31. (c) Exod. ii. 13; ix. 27; Deut. xxv. 1, &c.

רָשַׁע, v. pres. יִרְשַׁע. Constr. abs. *Was wicked, impious, unjust; acted wickedly, impiously, unjustly*, 1 Kings viii. 47; Job x. 15; Eccl. vii. 17, &c. לֹא רָשַׁעְתִּי מֵאֱלֹהָי, *I have not sinned* (so as to depart) *from* (the ways of) *my God*, Ps. xviii. 22.

Hiph. הִרְשִׁיעַ, pres. יַרְשִׁיעַ. Constr. immed. it. med. אֶת. (a) *Declared guilty, condemned*. (b) *Proved guilty*. (c) *Overcame in battle*. (d) I. q. Kal, *Acted wickedly*. (e) *Acted wickedly against* —. (a) Deut. xxv. 1; Job xxxiv. 17. 29; Prov. xii. 2, &c. (b) Is. liv. 17. (c) 1 Sam. xiv. 47. (d) 2 Chron. xx. 35; Neh. ix. 33; Dan. xii. 10, &c.

Infin. הַרְשִׁיעַ, 1 Kings viii. 32; 2 Chron. xxii. 3.
Part. מַרְשִׁיעַ, pl. constr. מַרְשִׁיעֵי, (a) Prov. xvii. 15. (e) Dan. xi. 32.

רִשְׁעָה, f. constr. רִשְׁעַת, aff. רִשְׁעָתוֹ, i. q. רֶשַׁע. (a) *Wickedness*. (b) *Guilt, fault*. (a) Deut. ix. 4; Ezek. xviii. 20; Mal. i. 4, &c. (b) Deut. xxv. 2.

רֶשֶׁף, masc. pl. רְשָׁפִים, constr. רִשְׁפֵי, aff. רְשָׁפֶיהָ. Cogn. רצף, which see. *Burning*. (a) *A burning coal*. (b) *Lightning*. (c) בְּנֵי רֶשֶׁף, and קֶשֶׁת רִשְׁפֵי, *Ignited arrows*. (d) *A burning, wasting disease*. (e) *The heat of any strong passion*. (a) Cant. viii. 6. (b) Ps. lxxviii. 48; Hab. iii. 5. (c) Job v. 7, where see the note; Ps. lxxvi. 4. (d) Deut. xxxii. 24. (e) Cant. viii. 6. Some have supposed this word to signify *a bird*, pec. *a bird of prey*, and hence *any thing winged*, or *flying*. LXX. ὀρνέων, γυπὸς, περίπτερα, κράτη, πυρί. Vulg. *avis, potentias, igni, lampades, diabolus*.

רשׁשׁ, v. Cogn. רושׁ, and רצץ. Kal non occ.

Pih. pres. יְרַשֵּׁשׁ. *Reduced* a city, either to poverty, or in a military sense, Jer. v. 17.
Puh. רֻשַּׁשְׁנוּ. Pass. of Pih., Mal. i. 4.

רֶשֶׁת, f. aff. רִשְׁתּוֹ, רִשְׁתּוֹ, r. ירשׁ. (a) *A net.* (b) Metaph. *Any snare.* (c) *A net-work.* (a) Prov. i. 17. (b) Ps. lvii. 7; cxl. 6; Prov. xxix. 5, &c. (c) Exod. xxvii. 4, 5; xxxviii. 4. Also Infin. of יָרַשׁ.

רַתּוֹק, masc. r. רתק. *A chain,* Ezek. vii. 23.

רַתּוּקוֹת, pl. f. *Id.,* 1 Kings vi. 21.

רתח, m. pl. aff. וְתָחֶיהָ. Syr. ܪܬܚ, *fervefecit, ebullivit. Boiling,* Ezek. xxiv. 5.

רתח, v. Kal non occ.
Pih. Imp. רַתַּח. *Boil,* Ezek. xxiv. 5.
Puh. רֻתְּחוּ. Pass. of Pih. *Was heated, boiled; agitated,* Job xxx. 27.
Hiph. pres. יַרְתִּיחַ. *Caused to boil,* Job xli. 23.

רֹתֶם, masc. pl. רְתָמִים. Arab. رَتَم, *genista.* Spanish, *retama, Id. The broom,* 1 Kings xix. 4, 5; Job xxx. 4; Ps. cxx. 4. See Cels. Hierob., par. i. page 246.

רתם, v. only in Imp. רְתֹם. *Bind, yoke,* Mic. i. 13. Arab. اِرْتَم, *filum circa digitum ligavit.*

רתק, v. Kal non occ. Arab. رَتَق, *conjungendo partes fissas reparavit* rem. *Joined, bound.*
Niph. pres. יֵרָתֵק. Pass. of Kal, Eccl. xii. 6, *Keri.*
Puh. רֻתַּק, *Id.,* Nah. iii. 10.
רְתֻקוֹת, pl. f. *Chains,* Is. xl. 19.

רתת, m. Syr. ܪܬ, *tremuit. Trembling,* Hos. xiii. 1. See רְטָטּ.

שׁ

שׁ, *Sin,* distinguished from שׁ by the diacritical point, is pronounced as *s* in *son,* while the latter is sounded as *sh* in *shine.* It frequently interchanges with ס, which it resembles in sound, and occasionally with ו, and צ. The Syrians constantly substitute ܣ for this letter; the Arabs, on the contrary, generally use ش, for שׁ, and س, for ס and שׂ. As a numeral, ש (the diacritical point being omitted) stands for *three hundred.*

שָׂא, Imp. of נָשָׂא.

שְׂאֹר, masc. Chald. סְאֹר, *fermentum. Leaven,* Exod. xii. 15. 19; xiii. 7; Lev. ii. 11; Deut. xvi. 4.

שְׂאֵת, for שְׂאֵת, Infin. of נָשָׂא, which see.

שָׂבָךְ, m. pl. שְׂבָכִים. Cogn. סבך, which see. *Ornaments of net-work, or wreathing,* 1 Kings vii. 17.

שַׂבְּכָא, see סַבְּכָא.

שְׂבָכָה, fem. pl. שְׂבָכוֹת. (a) *Net work,* ornamenting the capitals of pillars. (b) *A lattice,* of a window. (c) *A net.* (a) 1 Kings vii. 17—42; 2 Kings xxv. 17, &c. (b) 2 Kings i. 2. (c) Job xviii. 8.

שָׂבֵעַ, m. constr. שְׂבַע, pl. שְׂבֵעִים f. שְׂבֵעָה. Arab. شَبِع, and Syr. ܣܒܥ, *satur fuit. Full, satisfied, surfeited.* [1] Abs., Gen. xxv. 8; Prov. xix. 23; xxvii. 7. [2] Of food, 1 Sam. ii. 5. [3] Of wealth, enjoyment, Deut. xxxiii. 23. [4] Of suffering, vexation, Job x. 15; xiv. 1. [5] Of years, Gen. xxxv. 29; 1 Chron. xxix. 28; Job xlii. 17.

שָׂבַע, v. pres. יִשְׂבַּע. Constr. abs. it. immed. it. med. בְּ. *Was full, satisfied, surfeited.* [1] Abs. [2] Of food. [3] Of drink. [4] Of wealth, enjoyment. [5] Of suffering, vexation. [6] Of years. [1] Ps. xvii. 15; Prov. xxx. 9; Is. ix. 19, &c. [2] Prov. xii. 11; xiv. 14; xxx. 22, &c. [3] Prov. xxx. 16; Jer. xlvi. 10; Amos iv. 8. [4] Ps. civ. 28; Eccl. i. 8; iv. 8, &c. [5] Job vii. 4; Ps. lxxxviii. 4; Prov. xxviii. 19, &c. [6] 1 Chron. xxxiii. 1; 2 Chron. xxiv. 15.
Infin. שָׂבוֹעַ, שְׂבֹעַ, Exod. xvi. 8; Joel ii. 27, &c.
Imp. שְׂבַע, Prov. xx. 13.
Pih. pres. in pause, יְשַׂבֵּעַ. *Satisfied,* Ezek. vii. 19.
Imp. aff. שַׂבְּעֵנוּ, Ps. xc. 14.
Hiph. הִשְׂבִּיעַ, pres. יַשְׂבִּיעַ. Causat. of Kal, Ps. lxxxi. 17; xci. 16; Is. lviii. 11, &c.

שבע (572) שגה

Infin. הַשְׂבִּיעַ, Job xxxviii. 27.
Part. מַשְׂבִּיעַ, Ps. ciii. 5; cxlv. 16.

שֶׂבַע, m. *Abundance*, Gen. xli. 29—53; Prov. iii. 10; Eccl. v. 11.

שֹׂבַע, m. aff. שָׂבְעֶךָ. *Fulness, sufficiency, abundance*, Exod. xvi. 3; Deut. xxv. 23; Ps. xvi. 11, &c.

שָׂבְעָה, f. aff. שָׂבְעָתֵךְ, *Id.*, Ruth ii. 18; Is. xxiii. 18; Ezek. xxxix. 19, &c.

שִׂבְעָה, fem. constr. שִׂבְעַת, *Id.*, Ezek. xvi. 49.

שָׂבַר, masc. aff. שִׂבְרוֹ. Arab. سَبَرَ, *exploravit* vulnus aliasve res. Syr. ܣܒܪ, *opinatus est*. Pah. *speravit*. *Hope, expectation*, Ps. cxix. 116; cxlvi. 5. See סבר.

שָׂבַר, v. *Looked at, examined*. Constr. med. בְּ.

Part. שֹׂבֵר, Neh. ii. 13. 15.
Pih. שִׂבַּרְתִּי, pres. יְשַׂבֵּר. *Looked to, hoped for*, or *in*. Med. לְ, אֶל, Ruth i. 13; Esth. ix. 1; Ps. civ. 27, &c.

שְׂגָא, v. Chald. pres. יִשְׂגֵּא. Syr. ܣܓܐ, *multiplicatus fuit, crevit*. *Increased, became great*, Ezra iv. 22; Dan. iii. 31; vi. 26.

Aph. pres. הַשְׂגִּיא. (a) *Made great, increased*, med. לְ. (b) *Declared great, magnified*, immed. (b) Job xxxvi. 24.
Part. מַשְׂגִּיא, (a) Job xii. 23.

שָׂגַב, v. שָׂגְבוּ, שָׂגְבָה. *Was high*. Metaph. *Was exalted in strength or security*, Deut. ii. 36; Job v. 16.

Niph. נִשְׂגַּב. (a) *Was lofty*, of a wall or city. (b) *Was secure*, within walls. (c) *Was exalted in praise*. (b) Prov. xviii. 10. (c) Is. ii. 11. 17.
Part. נִשְׂגָּב, f. נִשְׂגָּבָה. (a) Prov. xviii. 11; Is. xxvi. 5; xxx. 13.
Pih. pres. יְשַׂגֵּב. Constr. immed. (a) *Raised, placed in security*. (b) *Made powerful*. (a) Ps. lix. 2; xci. 14; cvii. 41, &c. (b) Is. ix. 10.
Puh. pres. יְשֻׂגַּב. Pass. of Pih., Prov. xxix. 25.
Hiph. pres. יַשְׂגִּיב. I. q. Pih., Job xxxvi. 22.

שָׂגַג, v. Pih. red. pres. תְּשַׂגְשֵׂגִי. According to some, *Fencest*, cogn. סוג, and סך. According to others, *Causest to in-*

crease, grow. Cogn. שׂגה, and שׂגא, Is. xvii. 11.

שָׂגָה, v. i. q. שׂגא, which see. Pres. יִשְׂגֶּה, Job viii. 7. 11; Ps. xcii. 13.
Hiph. הִשְׂגּוּ, Ps. lxxiii. 12.

שַׂגִּיא, Chald. masc. pl. f. שַׂגִּיאָן, r. שׂגא. (a) *Great*. (b) *Much, many*. (c) *Greatly*. (a) Dan. ii. 31; iv. 7. 9. Metaph. of God, Job xxxvi. 26; xxxvii. 23. (b) Ezra v. 11; Dan. ii. 6. 48; vii. 5. (c) Dan. ii. 12; v. 9, &c.

שָׂדַד, v. Pih. pres. יְשַׂדֵּד. *Harrowed*, Job xxxix. 10; Is. xxviii. 24; Hos. x. 11, al. non occ.

שָׂדֶה, masc. constr. שְׂדֵה, aff. שָׂדִי, שָׂדֵהוּ, pl. constr. שְׂדֵי, aff. שָׂדֵינוּ, שָׂדַי, it. pl. שָׂדוֹת, constr. שְׂדוֹת, aff. שְׂדוֹתֵינוּ, &c. (a) *The ground*. (b) *A field, a piece of ground*, pec. of *cultivated ground*. (c) *The open country*, as opposed to a town. (d) *A country, territory*. (a) Gen. ii. 5; iii. 18; Exod. ix. 22, &c. (b) Exod. xxii. 4; Lev. xxvii. 24; Num. xvi. 14; 1 Sam. xiv. 14, &c. (c) Gen. xxv. 27; 1 Sam. xx. 11; 2 Kings iv. 39, &c.

שָׂדַי, m. *Id.*, Ps. xcvi. 12; civ. 11; Is. lvi. 9, &c.

שְׂדֵרוֹת, pl. fem. *Ranks, rows*, 1 Kings vi. 9; 2 Kings xi. 8. 15; 2 Chron. xxiii. 14. See סדרים.

שֶׂה, masc. constr. שֵׂה, aff. שֵׂיוֹ, and שֵׂיֵהוּ. Arab. شَاةٌ, *ovis*. *A sheep* or *goat*, Exod. xii. 5; xxii. 9; Deut. xxii. 1; 1 Sam. xiv. 35, &c. It has no plural, the corresponding noun of multitude being צאן.

שָׂהֵד, masc. aff. שָׂהֲדִי. Arab. شَهِدَ, *præsens adfuit* rei; *testatus fuit*; شَاهِدٌ, *præsens*; *testis*. Syr. ܣܗܕ, *testatus fuit*. *A witness, an eye-witness*, Job xvi. 19.

שָׂהֲדוּתָא, Chald. f. i. q. Syr. ܣܗܕܘܬܐ, *Testimony, evidence*, Gen. xxxi. 47.

שַׂהֲרֹנִים, pl. masc. Syr. ܣܗܪܐ, *luna plena*. Arab. شَهْر, *luna*. Lit. *Small moons; crescent-shaped ornaments*, Judg. viii. 21. 26; Is. iii. 18. LXX. μηνίσκους. Vulg. *bullas; lunulas*. See Schrœd. de Vest. Mul.

שׂוֹא, Infin. of נשׂא.

שׁוֹב (573) שׂוֹם

שׂוֹבָךְ, masc. i. q. סְבָךְ. *Any thing entangled; entangled branches*, 2 Sam. xviii. 9.

שׁוּג, v. Niph. נָסוֹג, for נָסוּג. *Was driven back*, 2 Sam. i. 22. See סוּג.

שׂוּחַ, v. once, Gen. xxiv. 63. Arab. شَاحَ, r. شيح, *diligens fuit* in re suâ peragendâ. The interpretations are various. *To walk; to meditate; to busy himself*, i. e. for something. LXX. Ἀδολεσχῆσαι. Aquila, Ὁμιλῆσαι. Symm. Λαλῆσαι. Vulg. *ad meditandum*. See שׂיחַ.

שׂוּם, v. i. q. שׂמה.
Part. pl. constr. שָׂטֵי. *Those who turn aside to —*, Ps. xl. 5.

שׂוּךְ, v. pret. שָׂכָךְ. Cogn. סכך, סוג. Arab. شَوْك, *spina*. *Hedged, fenced*; properly, *with thorns*, Job i. 10.
Part. שָׂךְ, Hos. ii. 6.
Pih. pres. aff. תְּשֻׂכֵּנִי, *Id.*, Job x. 11.

שׂוֹךְ, m. aff. שׂוֹכֹה, and—

שׂוֹכָה, f. constr. שׂוֹכַת. Syr. ܣܘܟܠ, *ramus. A bough*, Judg. ix. 48, 49.

שׂוּם, and שׂים, v. pret. שָׂם, pres. יָשׂוּם (Exod. iv. 11), יָשִׂים, apoc. יָשֵׂם, יָשֶׂם. Constr. immed. Syr. ܣܡ, *statuit, constituit. Placed, appointed, rendered.* (a) *Placed, set*, [1] A thing. [2] A person. (b) *Set up*. (c) *Set in array*. (d) *Placed aside*. Phrr. (e) לַבּוֹ ש״, *Set his heart, considered*. (f) אֶל לֵב ש״, or עַל לֵב ש״, *Laid to heart, considered*. (g) פָּנָיו בְּ ש״, or אֶל, *Set his face against, or towards*. (h) ש״ עֵינָיו עַל, *Set his eyes upon*. (i) בְּאָזְנֵי ש״, *Told*. (k) בְּפִיו דְּבָרִים ש״, *Put words into his mouth*. (l) שֵׁם ש״, *Named*. (m) *Appointed*, [1] A thing. [2] A person. (n) *Rendered, made*; followed by two nouns, constr. of one, immed. and of the other immed. or med. לְ, or בְּ. (o) *Made, esteemed*, an object of confidence, &c. (p) *Shewed* mercy, pity, &c. (q) *Inflicted*. (r) *Ascribed*. (a), [1] Gen. vi. 16; xxviii. 18; Exod. xxvi. 35; 2 Kings iv. 29, &c. [2] Gen. xl. 15; Exod. xxxiii. 22; 2 Kings x. 24, &c. (b) Ps. lxxxix. 30; Jer. xliii. 10, &c. (e) Exod. ix. 21; Job i. 8, &c. (f) Is. xlvii. 7; lvii. 1; Jer. xii. 11, &c. (g) Lev. xx. 5. (h) Jer. xxiv. 6; Amos ix. 4, &c. (k) Exod. iv. 15; 2 Sam. xiv. 19; Is. li. 16, &c. (l) Judg. viii. 31; 2 Kings xvii. 34; Neh. ix. 7, &c. (m), [1] Exod. xv. 25; Job xxviii. 3; Ps. lxxviii. 5, &c. [2] Exod. xviii. 21; 2 Sam. xvii. 25; Ps. cv. 21, &c. (n) Gen. xlv. 9; Is. xiv. 17; xxi. 4; Joel i. 7; Zech. x. 3, &c. (o) Ps. xl. 5; xci. 9; Jer. xvii. 5, &c. (p) Is. xlvii. 6. (q) Exod. x. 2; xv. 26. (r) Is. xlii. 12.

Infin. abs. שׂוֹם, constr. שׂוּם, שׂים, aff. שׂוּמוֹ, Deut. xvii. 15; 1 Kings ix. 3; Job xx. 4; Prov. viii. 29, &c.
Imp. שִׂים, שִׂימָה, fem. שִׂימִי, pl. שִׂימוּ. (c) 1 Kings xx. 12. (d) 1 Sam. ix. 23. (i) Exod. vii. 14. (r) Josh. vii. 19; Ps. lxvi. 2, &c.
Part. שָׂם, pl. שָׂמִים, Is. v. 20; Zech. xii. 2, &c.
Part. pass. f. שׂוּמָה, 2 Sam. xiii. 32.
Hiph. Imp. f. הָשִׂימִי. *Place, set*, Ezek. xxi. 21.
Part. מֵשִׂים, Job iv. 20.
Hoph. pres. יוּשַׂם, Pass. of Hiph., Gen. xxiv. 33.

שׂוּם, Chald. v. pret. שָׂם. *Id. Placed, appointed*. (a) *Appointed* a person. (b) שֵׁם ש״, *Named*. (c) בָּל ש״, *Set his mind, endeavoured*. (d) מִטְעֵם ש״, [1] *Appointed, made a decree*. [2] *Placed consideration, regarded*. (a) Ezra v. 14. (b) Dan. v. 12. (c) vi. 15. (d), [1] iii. 10; [2] 12.
Imp. pl. שִׂימוּ, (d) Ezra iv. 21.
Peil. שִׂים, שָׂמַת for שׂוּמַת. Pass. (d) Ezra iv. 19; v. 17; Dan. iii. 29; vi. 18, &c.
Ithpe. pres. יִתְּשָׂם, Pass. *Was made, rendered, placed*, Ezra iv. 21; Dan. ii. 5.
Part. מִתְּשָׂם, Ezra v. 8.

שׂוּר, v. I. pres. apoc. יָשֻׂר. (a) *Was prince, ruled*, with עַל. (b) *Was powerful*, with אֶל. (a) Judg. ix. 22. (b) Hos. xii. 5.
Hiph. הֵשִׂירוּ, Causat. of Kal. *Appointed a prince* or *princes*, Hos. viii. 4. See שַׂר and שָׂרָה.
II. i. q. סוּר. *Retired, departed*.
Infin. aff. שׂוּרִי, Hos. ix. 12.
Hiph. pres. apoc. יָשַׂר, i. q. יָסַר. *Removed*, 1 Chron. xx. 3. *He brought and removed them into* some public works where they were compelled to labour with *saws*, &c. David setting the example, followed afterwards by Solomon, 1 Kings ix. 20—22. In the parallel passage, 2 Sam. xii. 31, instead of וַיָּשַׂר, we have וַיָּשֶׂם, which may be the true reading, the exegetical signification remaining the same.

שׁוּר

שׁוֹרָה, f. Arab. سُورَة, *linea vel strues lapidum in muro*. *A row; in rows*, Is. xxviii. 25, only. Vulg. *per ordinem*. Some take the word to be a participle f. of שָׂרָה, with the signification of *principal, best*.

שׂוֹשׂ, and שִׂישׂ, v. pret. שָׂשׂ, pres. יָשִׂישׂ. Constr. abs. it. med. בְּ, עַל. *Rejoiced, delighted, exulted, in, over*. Abs., Ps. xix. 6; Is. lxvi. 14; Lam. i. 21, &c. Med. בְּ, Ps. cxix. 14; Is. lxi. 10; lxv. 19, &c. Med. עַל, Deut. xxviii. 63; xxx. 9; Jer. xxxii. 41, &c. Immed. יָשִׂישׂוּ, for יָשִׂישׂוּ עֲלֵיהֶם, Is. xxxv. 1.

Infin. abs. שׂוֹשׂ, constr. שׂוּשׂ, Deut. xxx. 9; Is. lxi. 10.

Imp. f. שִׂישִׂי, Lam. iv. 21. Pl. שִׂישׂוּ, Is. lxv. 18; lxvi. 10.

Part. שָׂשׂ, Ps. cxix. 162; Is. lxiv. 4.

שִׂיחַ, m. aff. שִׂיחוֹ. *Purpose, design*, Amos iv. 13. See שִׂיחַ.

שָׂחָה, v. Syr. ܣܚܐ, *lavit, natavit*. *Swam*.

Infin. שָׂחוֹה, Is. xxv. 11.
Part. שָׂחֶה, *Ib*.
Hiph. pres. אַשְׂחֶה. *Caused to swim; overflowed*, Ps. vi. 7.

שָׂחוּ, m. for שָׂחֶה. *Swimming*. מֵי שׂ׳ *Waters of swimming*, i. e. to be crossed only by swimming, Ezek. xlvii. 5.

שָׂחַט, v. pres. אֶשְׂחַט. Chald. סְחַט, *compressit, expressit* humorem. *Pressed, crushed*, Gen. xl. 11, only.

שְׂחֹק, and שָׂחוֹק, m. i. q. צְחֹק. (a) *Laughter*. (b) *An object of laughter*. (c) *A subject of laughter*. (a) Job viii. 21; Ps. cxxvi. 1; Prov. xiv. 13, &c. (b) Job xii. 4; Lam. iii. 14; Jer. xlviii. 26, &c. (c) Prov. x. 23.

שָׂחַק, v. pres. יִשְׂחַק. (a) *Laughed*: abs. (b) *laughed at, derided*, or *disregarded*; med. בְּ, עַל, לְ. *Smiled upon, approved*: med. אֶל. (d) Perhaps *caused laughter*. (a) Prov. xxix. 9. (b) Med. בְּ, Prov. i. 26: med. עַל, Job xxx. 1; Ps. lii. 8; Lam. i. 7: med. לְ, Job v. 22; xxxix. 10; Ps. lix. 9, &c. (c) Job xxix. 24.

Infin. שְׂחֹק, שָׂחוֹק, (a) Eccl. iii. 4; (d) Judg. xvi. 27.

Pih. שִׂחַקְתִּי, pres. יְשַׂחֵק. (a) *Rejoiced, expressed joy*. (b) *Sported, played*. (c) *Played* with, med. בְּ. (d) *Played on an instrument*. (e) *Made sport, caused laughter*. (f) Probably *skirmished*. (b) Job xl. 20. (c) Job xl. 29. (d) 2 Sam. vi. 21. (e) Judg. xvi. 25. (f) 2 Sam. ii. 14.

Infin. שַׂחֵק, (b) Ps. civ. 26.
Part. מְשַׂחֵק, pl. מְשַׂחֲקִים, f. מְשַׂחֶקֶת, pl. מְשַׂחֲקוֹת, (a) Prov. viii. 30, 31; Jer. xv. 17; (b) Prov. xxvi. 19; Zech. viii. 5. (d) 1 Sam. xviii. 7.

Hiph. part. pl. מַשְׂחִיקִים. I. q. Pih. sign. (b) 2 Chron. xxx. 10.

שָׂטִים, m. pl. שָׂטִים. *Those who turn aside; backsliders*, Hos. v. 2. See שׂוּט.

שָׂטָה, v. שָׂטָה, pres. יִשְׂטֶה, apoc. יֵשְׂטְ. (a) *Went aside*; to or from a path. (b) *Went astray*. (a) Prov. vii. 25. (b) Num. v. 12. 19, 20. 22. Syr. ܣܛܐ, *Id*.

Imp. שְׂטֵה, (a) Prov. iv. 15.

שָׂטַם, v. pres. יִשְׂטֹם. Constr. immed. Arab. سطام, *acies gladii; acutiores et fervidiores hominum; repagulum portæ*. Syr. ܣܛܡ, *compedivit, vinxit*. ܣܛܡܐ, *chalybs*. *Acted fiercely, sharply, hardly towards; was under the influence of bitter feelings, hated*, Gen. xxvii. 41; xlix. 23; L. 15; Job xvi. 9; xxx. 21; Ps. lviii. 4.

שָׂטָן, m. Arab. شطن, *adversatus fuit à proposito reducens*. (a) *An adversary, opponent, impediment*. (b) הַשָּׂטָן, *The great adversary, the enemy of mankind, Satan*. (a) Num. xxii. 22. 32; 1 Sam. xxix. 4; 2 Sam. xix. 23; 1 Kings v. 4; xi. 14. 23. 25. (b) Job i. 6—12; ii. 1—7; Zech. iii. 1, 2. Without the article, 1 Chron. xxi. 1.

שָׂטַן, v. pres. aff. יִשְׂטְמוּנִי. Constr. immed. *Was an adversary to, opposed*, Ps. xxxviii. 21; cix. 4.

Infin. aff. שִׂטְנוֹ, Zech. iii. 1.
Part. pl. constr. שֹׂטְנֵי, aff. שֹׂטְנַי, Ps. lxxi. 13; cix. 20, 29.

שִׂטְנָה, f. *Opposition, accusation*, Ezra iv. 6, only.

שִׂיא, m. aff. שִׂיאוֹ, r. נשא. *Elevation, dignity*, Job xx. 6.

שִׂיב, m. aff. שִׂיבוֹ. Arab. شاب, r. شيب, *incanuit* caput. شَيْب, *cani-*

שׂיב (575) שׂכו

ties. *Whiteness* of the hair; *old age*, 1 Kings xiv. 4.

שִׂיב, v. pret. שַׂבְתִּי. *Was grey headed*, 1 Sam. xii. 2.
Part. שָׂב, Job xv. 10.

שִׂיבָה, f. constr. שֵׂיבַת, aff. שֵׂיבָתִי. *Whiteness of the hair; old age*, Gen. xv. 15; xlii. 38; xliv. 31, &c.

שִׂיב, m. r. שׂוּג. Probably *Retirement*, 1 Kings xviii. 27. Vulg. *in diversorio est.*

שִׂיד, m. Arab. شِيد, *res, quæ parieti inducitur, ut lutum, similisve res. Plastering; any kind of plaster; lime*, Deut. xxvii. 2. 4; Is. xxxiii. 12; Amos ii. 1.

שִׂיד, v. pret. שַׂדְתָּ. *Plastered*, Deut. xxvii. 2. 4.

שִׂיחָ, see שָׂחָ.

שִׂיחַ, m. aff. שִׂיחוֹ, pl. שִׂיחִים. Syr. ܣܚܐ, *virgultum*. Arab. شَح, *effudit aquam: profudit verba.* شِيش, r. شَاح, *diligens fuit, in re suâ peragendâ. Shooting forth, uttering.* (a) *A plant, bush.* (b) *Speech, message, business.* (c) *A complaint.* (d) *Sorrow.* (a) Gen. ii. 5; xxi. 15; Job xii. 8; xxx. 4. 7. (b) 1 Kings xviii. 27; 2 Kings ix. 11. (c) 1 Sam. i. 16; Job ix. 27; Ps. cxliii. 3, &c. (d) Job vii. 13.

שִׂיחַ, v. pres. יָשִׂיחַ. Constr. abs. it. med. בְּ of the subject. (a) *Spoke, uttered.* (b) *Talked with*, immed. (c) *Meditated.* (a) Job vii. 11; Ps. lv. 18; lxix. 13; cxlv. 5. (b) Prov. vi. 22. (c) Ps. lxxvii. 4. 7. 13; cxix. 15, &c.
Infin. שִׂיחַ, Ps. cxix. 148.
Imp. pl. שִׂיחוּ, Judg. v. 10; Ps. cv. 2.
Pih. pres. יְשׂוֹחֵחַ. (a) *Uttered, talked of*, med. אֵת. (b) *Meditated*, med. בְּ. (a) Is. lv. 8. (b) Ps. cxliii. 5.

שִׂיחָה, f. aff. שִׂיחָתִי. *Complaint, prayer, meditation*, Job xv. 4; Ps. cxix. 97. 99.

שִׂים, see שׂוּם.

שֵׂךְ, m. pl. שִׂכִּים. *Thorns*, Num. xxxiii. 55. See שׂוּךְ.

שָׂךְ, m. aff. שִׂכּוֹ. *A fence*, Lam. ii. 6.

שִׂכָּה, f. pl. שִׂכּוֹת. *Spears*, Job xl. 31, only. Arab. شَوْكَة, *arma eorumve cacumen.*

שִׂכְוִי, m. once. Arab. شَكْوَة, *uter.* Cogn. נסך. *A thunderstorm*, Job xxxviii. 36. See the note.

שְׂכִיוֹת, pl. f. once. Chald. סְכָה, *speculatus est, aspexit.* Syr. ܣܟܐ, *expectavit intendit, speravit.* Sam. סכי, *desideravit.* סכוי, *oculus, conspectus. Objects gazed on by the eye, or dwelt on by the mind*, Is. ii. 16.

שָׂכִין, masc. Arab. سِكِّين. Chald. סַכִּין. Syr. ܣܟܝܢܐ, *culter, gladius. A knife*, Prov. xxiii. 2, only.

שָׂכִיר, m. constr. שְׂכִיר, aff. שְׂכִירְךָ, pl. שְׂכִירָיו, r. שׂכר. *A hired person or thing.* Exod. xxii. 14; Lev. xxv. 6. 53; Deut. xxiv. 14; Jer. xlvi. 21.

שְׂכִירָה, f. *Hired; or the act of hiring*, Is. vii. 20.

שָׂכַךְ, v. pret. שַׂכֹּתִי. *Placed as a covering*, Exod. xxxiii. 22. See סכך.

שָׂכַל, and שָׂכֵל, m. aff. שִׂכְלוֹ. Chald. קבל, *intellexit, attendit, consideravit.* Arab. شكل, *similitudo; res conveniens et congruens; figura rei, aut imaginatæ, aut sensibus perceptæ.* (a) *Understanding, wisdom, skill.* (b) *Estimation, esteem.* (c) Probably *Signification.* (a) 1 Sam. xxv. 3; 1 Chron. xxii. 12; Ezra viii. 18, &c. (b) Prov. iii. 4. (c) Neh. viii. 8.

שָׂכַל, v. *Was wise, skilful*, 1 Sam. xviii. 30.
Pih. שִׂכֵּל. *Acted wisely, carefully, designedly* with regard to a thing, med. אֵת, Gen. xlviii. 14.
Hiph. הִשְׂכִּיל, pres. יַשְׂכִּיל. Constr. immed. it. med. אֵת, אֶל, בְּ, לְ, עַל. (a) *Examined the form of, looked at.* (b) *Reflected, considered.* (c) *Thought of, cared for.* (d) *Acted wisely, skilfully, was wise, skilful.* (e) *Prospered.* (f) *Made wise, taught.* (b) Job xxxiv. 27; Ps. lxiv. 10; cvi. 7; Dan. ix. 25, &c. (d) 1 Sam. xviii. 5; Ps. cxix. 99; Prov. xvii. 8, &c. (e) Josh. i. 7; Jer. x. 21. (f) Ps. xxxii. 8; Prov. xvi. 23.
Infin. הַשְׂכִּיל, הַשְׂכֵּל, aff. הַשְׂכִּילְךָ, Prov. i. 3; xxi. 11; Dan. ix. 22, &c. (a) Gen. iii. 6. נֶחְמָד לְהַשְׂכִּיל. LXX. ὡραῖον τοῦ κατανοῆσαι.
Imp. pl. הַשְׂכִּילוּ, Ps. ii. 10.
Part. מַשְׂכִּיל, pl. מַשְׂכִּילִים, constr. מַשְׂכִּילֵי,

שׂכל (576) שׂמא

f. מַשְׂכֶּלֶת, 1 Sam. xviii. 14; Prov. xix. 14; Dan. i. 4; xi. 33, &c. (c) Ps. xli. 2. In the titles of Pss. xxxii. xlii. xliv., &c.; מַשְׂכִּיל has been taken to mean *A didactic poem*.

שָׂכַל, v. Chald. *Id.* Ithpah. part. מִשְׂתַּכַּל. *Considered, looked at*, med. בְּ, Dan. vii. 8, only.

שִׂכְלוּת, f. i. q. סִכְלוּת. *Folly*, Eccl. i. 17, only.

שָׂכְלְתָנוּ, f. i. q. Syr. ܣܘܟܠܬܢܘ, *prudentia, intelligentia. Understanding, skill,* Dan. v. 11. 12. 14.

שָׂכַר, m. Arab. شَكَرَ, *præmio, mercede donavit. Reward, hire,* Prov. xi. 18; Is. xix. 10.

שָׂכָר, m. constr. שְׂכַר, aff. שְׂכָרִי. *Id.* Gen. xxx. 18; Num. xviii. 31; Deut. xv. 18, &c.

שָׂכַר, v. pres. יִשְׂכֹּר. Constr. immed. it. med. אֶת. (a) *Hired*. (b) *Bribed*. (a) Gen. xxx. 16; Judg. ix. 4; xviii. 4; 2 Chron. xxv. 6, &c. (b) Deut. xxiii. 5; Neh. ii. 12.
Infin. abs. שָׂכֹר, constr. שְׂכֹר, Gen. xxx. 16; 1 Chron. xix. 7.
Part. שֹׂכֵר, pl. שֹׂכְרִים, 2 Chron. xxiv. 12; Prov. xxvi. 10.
Part. pass. שָׂכוּר, Neh. vii. 13.
Niph. נִשְׂכְּרוּ. *Hired himself*, 1 Sam. ii. 5. Hith. part. מִשְׂתַּכֵּר. *Id.*, Hag. i. 6.

שְׂלָו, com. pl. שְׂלָוִים. Arab. سَلْوَى, *coturnix*. Syr. ܣܠܘܐ, *Id. A quail, quails,* Exod. xvi. 13; Num. xi. 31, 32; Ps. cv. 40. See Bochart. Hieroz., tom. ii. p. 92.

שַׂלְמָה, f. constr. שַׂלְמַת, aff. שַׂלְמָתוֹ, pl. שְׂלָמוֹת, aff. שַׂלְמֹתַי; i. q. שִׂמְלָה. (a) *The outer garment;* which [1] was loose, and [2] used to sleep in. (b) Pl. *Garments,* generally. (a) Exod. xxii. 8; Mic. ii. 8. [1] 1 Kings xi. 29, 30. [2] Exod. xxii. 25; Deut. xxiv. 13. (b) Josh. ix. 9. 13; 1 Kings x. 25; Job ix. 31, &c.

שְׂמֹאל, and שְׂמֹאול, m. aff. שְׂמֹאלִי, &c. Arab. شِمَال, *sinistrum latus.* (a) *The left hand.* (b) יַד־שׂ׳, *Id.* (c) שׂ׳ *On* or *to the left.* (d) הַשְּׂמֹאל, *Id.* (e) עַל שְׂמֹאל, *Id.* (f) עַל הַשְּׂמֹאל, *Id.* (g) מֵהַשְּׂמֹאול *On the left,* or *north.* See יָמִין. (h) *Id.* (a) Gen. xlviii. 13, 14; Dan. xii. 7, &c. (b) Judg. iii. 21; vii. 20; Ezek. xxxix. 3.

(c) Numb. xx. 17; xxii. 26; Job xxiii. 9. (d) Gen. xiii. 9. (e) Gen. xxiv. 49; 2 Kings xxiii. 8; Is. ix. 19, &c. (f) 2 Sam. ii. 19; 1 Chron. vi. 29. (g) Gen. xiv. 15; 1 Kings vii. 49; 2 Chron. iv. 6, &c. (h) 2 Chron. iii. 17; Ezek. i. 10. Hence—

שָׂמַאל, v. Hiph. pres. אַשְׂמְאִילָה. (a) *Went to the left,* Gen. xiii. 9; Is. xxx. 21. (b) *Used the left hand.*
Infin. הַשְׂמִיל, 2 Sam. xiv. 19.
Imp. f. הַשְׂמִילִי, Ezek. xxi. 21.
Part. pl. מַשְׂמְאִלִים, (b) 1 Chron. xii. 2.

שְׂמֹאלִי, m. שְׂמָאלִית, f. (a) *Belonging to the left; on the left.* (b) כַּף הַשְּׂמָאלִית. *The left hand* (palm). (c) צַד הַשְּׂמָאלִי. *The left side.* (a) 1 Kings vii 21; 2 Kings xi. 11; 2 Chron. iii. 18; xxxiii. 10. (b) Lev. xiv. 15, 16. 26, 27. (c) Ezek. iv. 4.

שָׂמֵחַ, m. pl. שְׂמֵחִים, constr. שִׂמְחֵי, and שִׂמְחֵי, f. שְׂמֵחָה. Arab. سَمْح, *beneficus, liberalis fuit.* (a) *Joyful.* (b) *Expressing joy.* (c) Constr. or med. לְ, *Rejoicing in* or *at.* (a) Deut. xvi. 15; Esth. v. 9; Ps. cxiii. 9, &c. — *of the heart,* Prov. xv. 13; xvii. 22; Eccl. ii. 10. (b) 1 Kings i. 40; 2 Kings xi. 14; 2 Chron. xxiii. 13, &c. (c) Ps. xxxv. 26; Prov. ii. 14; xvii. 5; Amos vi. 13.

שָׂמַח, v. pres. יִשְׂמַח. (a) *Was glad, joyful.* [1] Constr. abs. [2] med. בְּ, [3] עַל, [4] לְ, [5] אֶת, [6] מִן. (b) *Expressed joy.* (c) Metaph. of a light, *Burned brightly.* (a), [1] Exod. iv. 14; 1 Kings v. 21; Job xxxi. 25, &c. Of the heart, Ps. xvi. 9; xxxiii. 21; 1 Chron. xvi. 10, &c. [2] Judg. ix. 19; 1 Sam. ii. 1; Ps. xxxi. 8, &c. [3] Is. ix. 16; xxxix. 2; Jonah iv. 6. [4] Ps. xxxv. 19. 24; Mic. vii. 8, &c. (b) Deut. xii. 18; Neh. xii. 43; Jer. xxxi. 13, &c. (c) Prov. xiii. 9.
Infin. שְׂמֹחַ, Ps. cvi. 5, &c.
Imp. שְׂמַח, f. שִׂמְחִי, pl. שִׂמְחוּ. (a, 5) Is. lxvi. 10. (a, 6) Prov. v. 18; Judg. ix. 19; Zeph. iii. 14, &c.
Pih. שִׂמַּח, pres. יְשַׂמַּח. Causat. of Kal. Constr. immed. it. med. אֶת, of person, with בְּ, לְ, עַל, of subject, Deut. xxiv. 5; Ps. xxx. 2; Prov. x. 1; Jer. xx. 15; Lam. ii. 17, &c.
Infin. שַׂמֵּחַ, Jer. xx. 13.
Imp. שַׂמַּח, שַׂמְּחָה, Ps. lxxxvi. 4; xc. 15; Prov. xxvii. 11.

שמח (577) שנא

Part. מְשַׂמֵּחַ, pl. constr. מְשַׂמְּחֵי, Judg. ix. 13; Ps. xix. 9.
Hiph. הִשְׂמִיחַ, *Id.*, Ps. lxxxix. 43.

שִׂמְחָה, fem. constr. שִׂמְחַת, aff. שִׂמְחָתִי, שִׂמְחַתְכֶם, pl. שְׂמָחוֹת. (a) *Joy.* (b) *Any expression of joy, rejoicing;* pec. *a festival.* (c) *Merriment, pleasure.* Phrr. (d) שָׂמַח שִׂמְחָה. (e) ש״ עָשָׂה. (a) Esth. viii. 16; Ps. iv. 8; xxx. 12; Is. lxi. 7, &c. (b) Gen. xxxi. 27; Num. x. 10; 2 Sam. vi. 12; 2 Chron. xxx. 26, &c. (c) Prov. xiv. 13; xxi. 17; Eccl. ii. 1. 10; vii. 4. (d) 1 Kings i. 40; 1 Chron. xxix. 9; Neh. xii. 42, &c. (e) 2 Chron. xxx. 23; Neh. viii. 12; xii. 27.

שְׂמִיכָה, f. once, Judg. iv. 18. Sam. ܣܡܝܟܬܐ, *cervical.* Syr. ܡܣܟܒܐ, *accubitus.* LXX. ἐπιβολαίῳ. Vulg. *pallio. A coverlet.*

שִׂמְלָה, f. constr. שִׂמְלַת, aff. שִׂמְלָתוֹ, pl. שְׂמָלוֹת, aff. שִׂמְלוֹתָיו. Arab. شَمَلَ, *texit aliquem vestimento;* شَمْلَة, *vestimentum;* pec. *totum corpus involvens.* I. q. שַׂלְמָה. (a) *The loose outer garment,* used also to sleep in. (b) *Any cloth.* (c) *Collectively, Clothing.* (d) Pl. *Clothes,* generally. (a) Gen. ix. 29. (b) Judg. viii. 25; 1 Sam. xxi. 10. (c) Deut. x. 18; xxi. 13; Is. iii. 6, 7, &c. (d) Gen. xxxv. 2; xli. 14; Exod. xii. 34, &c.

שְׂמָמִית, fem. once, Prov. xxx. 28. According to some, *A spider;* but, according to Bochart. Hieroz., tom. i. page 1083, *A poisonous species of lizard.* So the LXX. καλαβώτης, and Vulg. *stellio.*

שָׂנֵא, v. יִשְׂנָא. Constr. immed. it. med. אֶת. Arab. شَنِئَ, *odit.* Syr. ܣܢܐ, *Id. Hated;* a word including every shade of *dislike* to a person or thing, together with the *expression of* that *dislike,* Gen. xxvi. 27; Deut. xii. 31; 2 Sam. xiii. 15. 22, &c.
Infin. abs. שָׂנֹא, constr. שְׂנֹא, שְׂנֹאת, Gen. xxxvii. 5; Judg. xv. 2; Prov. viii. 13, &c.
Imp. pl. שִׂנְאוּ, Ps. xcvii. 10.
Part. שׂנֵא, aff. שׂנְאוֹ, שׂנַאֲךָ, pl. constr. שׂנְאֵי, aff. שׂנְאַי, &c. *Hating;* an *enemy,* constr. immed. it. med. לְ, Exod. xviii. 21; xxiii. 5; Deut. iv. 42; Josh. xx. 5, &c.
Part. pass. pl. constr. שְׂנֻאֵי, f. שְׂנוּאָה, Gen. xxix. 31; 2 Sam. v. 5.
Niph. pres. יִשָּׂנֵא, Pass., Prov. xiv. 17. 20.
Pih. intens. or frequentative of Kal. Part.

aff. מְשַׂנְאוֹ, pl. constr. מְשַׂנְאֵי, aff. מְשַׂנְאַי, &c. *An enemy,* 2 Sam. xxii. 41; Job xxxi. 29; Ps. lxxxi. 16, &c.

שְׂנֵא, v. Chald. *Id.*
Part. pl. aff. שָׂנְאָיִךְ. *Thine enemies,* Dan. iv. 16.

שִׂנְאָה, f. constr. שִׂנְאַת, aff. שִׂנְאָתְךָ, שִׂנְאָתוֹ, שִׂנְאָתָם. *Hatred, dislike;* constr. with אֶת, or בְּ, of the object, Deut. i. 27; ix. 28; 2 Sam. xiii. 15; Ps. xxv. 19; Ezek. xxxv. 11, &c.

שְׂנִיאָה, i. q. שְׂנוּאָה, r. שׂנא. *Hated, disliked,* Deut. xxi. 15, only.

שָׂעִיר, m. constr. שְׂעִיר, pl. שְׂעִירִים, constr. שְׂעִירֵי, fem. שְׂעִירָה, constr. שְׂעִירַת, pl. שְׂעִירוֹת, r. שׂער. (a) *Hairy,* Gen. xxvii. 11. 23. (b) *A goat,* from its long hair, Lev. iv. 24; xvi. 9; Dan. viii. 21, &c. Always preceded by the fuller form, שְׂעִיר עִזִּים, or שְׂעִירַת עִזִּים, Gen. xxxvii. 3; Lev. iv. 23; Num. xv. 24, &c.: except in [1] Lev. xvii. 7; 2 Chron. xi. 15, where (pl.) spoken of as objects of idolatrous worship: and [2] Is. xiii. 21; xxxiv. 14, where they are said *to leap, skip, among ruins,* and *to call out to each other;* most probably *some species of wild goat.* (c) Pl. *Showers,* Deut. xxxii. 2. See שָׂעַר and שֵׂעָר.

שְׂעִפִּים, pl. m. aff. שְׂעִפַּי, i. q. סְעִפִּים. *Branches, branchings;* pec. of the mind, *thoughts, opinions,* Job iv. 13; xx. 2. See my notes.

שֵׂעָר, m. constr. שְׂעַר (once שַׂעַר, Is. vii. 20), aff. שְׂעָרוֹ. Arab. شَعَر, *crines.* Syr. ܣܥܪܐ, *Id. The hair,* pec. of the head, Gen. xxv. 25; Lev. xiv. 8; Num. vi. 5, &c. In 2 Kings i. 8, אִישׁ בַּעַל שֵׂעָר, i. q. אִישׁ לָבוּשׁ אַדֶּרֶת שֵׂעָר, *a man wearing a hairy robe.* See אַדֶּרֶת, p. 10.

שְׂעַר, masc. Chald. *Id.,* Dan. iii. 27; vii. 9.

שַׂעַר, m. (a) I. q. סַעַר. *A storm, tempest.* (b) *Shuddering, terror.* (a) Is. xxviii. 2. (b) Job xviii. 20; Ezek. xxvii. 35; xxxii. 10.

שָׂעַר, v. שָׂעִיר, pres. יִשְׂעֲרוּ. Constr. abs. it. immed. (a) *Shuddered.* (b) *Feared, dreaded, reverenced.* (c) *Swept, tore away as a tempest.* (a) Ezek. xxvii. 35; xxxii. 10. (b) Deut. xxxii. 17. (c) Ps. lviii. 10.

4 E

שָׂעַר (578) שָׂפָק

Imp. pl. שַׂעֲרוּ, (a) Jer. ii. 12.
Niph. נִשְׂעֲרָה. *A tempest raged,* Ps. L. 3.
Pih. pres. aff. יְשָׂעֲרֵנוּ, i. q. Kal, (c) Job xxvii. 21.
Hith. pres. יִשְׂתָּעֵר. *Raged like a tempest,* Dan. xi. 40.

שַׂעֲרָה, f. constr. שַׂעֲרַת, aff. שַׂעֲרָתוֹ, pl. constr. שַׂעֲרוֹת, i. q. שֵׂעָר. (a) *A hair.* (b) *The hair.* (a) Judg. xx. 16; Ps. xl. 13; lxix. 5. (b) 1 Sam. xiv. 47; 2 Sam. xiv. 11; 1 Kings i. 52.

שְׂעָרָה, f. i. q. סְעָרָה. *A tempest,* Job ix. 17; Nah. i. 3.

שְׂעֹרָה, f. pl. שְׂעֹרִים. Arab. شَعِير, *hordeum. Barley,* [1] in the sing. The plant. [2] In the plur. The grain. [1] Exod. ix. 31; Job xxxi. 40; Joel i. 11, &c. [2] Lev. xxvii. 16; Ruth ii. 17; 2 Sam. xvii. 28.

שָׂפָה, f. constr. שְׂפַת, aff. שְׂפָתוֹ, dual, שְׂפָתַיִם, constr. שִׂפְתֵי, aff. שְׂפָתַי, &c.; שִׂפְתוֹתֵיהֶם, pl. constr. שִׂפְתוֹת, aff. שִׂפְתוֹתָיו. Arab. شَفَة, *labium;* شَفَا, *extremitas et ora* rei cujusque. Syr. ܣܶܦܬܳܐ, *labium, extremitas.* (a) *A lip.* (b) *A language.* (c) *Speech, speaking, words.* (d) שְׂפָתַיִם אִישׁ, *A man of many words,* or *of much profession.* (e) *The brim of a vessel.* (f) *Shore of the sea.* (g) *A bank* of a river. (h) *An edge, edging.* (k) *A boundary, border* of a country. (a) Ps. xxii. 8; Prov. xv. 7; xxvi. 26, &c. (b) Gen. xi. 1; Ps. lxxxi. 6; Zeph. iii. 9, &c. (c) Ps. cxx. 2; Prov. xii. 19, &c. (d) Job xi. 2. (e) 1 Kings vii. 23; 2 Chron. iv. 2, &c. (f) Gen. xxii. 17; Exod. xiv. 30; Josh. xi. 4, &c. (g) Gen. xli. 3; Exod. ii. 3; Deut. ii. 36, &c. (h) Exod. xxvi. 4; xxviii. 26, &c. (k) Judg. vii. 22.

שָׂפַח, v. Kal non occ. See סָפַח.
Pih. שִׂפַּח. *Laid bare* the crown of the head, *struck with baldness,* Is. iii. 17.

שָׂפָם, m. aff. שְׂפָמוֹ. Probably from שָׂפָה, with the termination ־ָם. *The lower part of the face; the hair growing on it; the chin, the beard.* Only in the phrr. שָׂפָם עָטָה, *covered the chin or beard,* as a sign of mourning, Lev. xiii. 45; Ezek. xxiv. 17. 22; Mic. iii. 7: and עָשָׂה שְׂפָמוֹ, *trimmed his beard,* 2 Sam. xix. 25.

שָׂפַן, v. i. q. סָפַן. *Hid, concealed.*

Only in part. pass. pl. constr. שְׂפוּנֵי, *hidden things, treasures, stores,* Deut. xxxiii. 19.

שָׂפָק, m. *Clapping* of the hands, in contempt or exultation; *striking* hands in a bargain; *a bargain,* and, as a consequence of a good one, *wealth, abundance, sufficiency. Clapping of the hands* in contempt; *contempt,* Job xxxvi. 18. See סָפַק.

שָׂפַק, v. pres. יִשְׂפֹּק. (a) *Clapped* his hands in contempt. (b) *Was abundant, sufficient.* (a) Job xxvii. 23. (b) 1 Kings xx. 10.
Hiph. pres. שָׂפִיקוּ. Constr. med. בְּ. *Bargained with,* or *obtained wealth by,* Is. ii. 6.

שַׂק, m. aff. שַׂקִּי, pl. שַׂקִּים, aff. שַׂקֵּיהֶם. (a) *A coarse cloth made of hair, sackcloth;* worn as a mark of humiliation or mourning. (b) *A sack made of such cloth; a sack.* (a) Gen. xxxvii. 34; Job xvi. 15; Joel i. 8, &c. (b) Gen. xlii. 25. 27. 35; Josh. ix. 4. Æth. ሦቅ : *Id.* Comp. σάκκος, *saccus.*

שָׂקַד, v. Probably cogn. עקד. *Bound, tied.*
Niph. נִשְׂקַד, Pass., Lam. i. 14. But LXX. ἐγρηγορήθη. Vulg. vigilavit; as if נִשְׁקַד.

שָׂקַר, v. once. Syr. ܣܩܰܪ, *fucavit.* Chald. סְקַר, *intuitus est, aspexit; fucavit.* Pih. part. fem. pl. מְשַׂקְּרוֹת. According to some, *Staining* the eyes: others, *Rolling* the eyes *wantonly,* Is. iii. 16. LXX. ἐν νεύμασιν ὀφθαλμῶν. Vulg. *nutibus oculorum.*

שַׂר, m. pl. שָׂרִים, constr. שָׂרֵי, aff. שָׂרַי, &c. See שׂוּר. *A prince, ruler, chief, captain,* [1] Of an army. [2] Of any number of soldiers. [3] Of any number of men in a civil capacity. [4] Of any place. [1] Gen. xxi. 22; Josh. v. 14; 1 Sam. xxvi. 5, &c. [2] 1 Sam. xviii. 13; 1 Kings xvi. 9; 2 Kings i. 9, &c. [3] Gen. xl. 2; Exod. ii. 14; 1 Chron. xv. 5, &c. [4] Gen. xxxix. 21; 1 Kings xxii. 26; 2 Kings xxiii. 8, &c.

שָׂרַג, v. Kal non occ. Arab. شَرَج, *constrinxit clausitque, laqueolis invicem insertis, marsupium. Twisted, wove together.*
Puh. pres. in pause, יְשֹׂרָגוּ. *Were interwoven,* Job xl. 17.
Hith. pres. יִשְׂתָּרְגוּ, *Id.,* Lam. i. 14.

שָׂרַד, v. שָׂרְדִי, once, Josh. x. 20. Arab.

שָׂרד (579) שָׂרִי

شَرَدَ, *aufugit, vagatusque fuit.* Fled, escaped.

שָׂרָד, m. once, Is. xliv. 13. Bochart, after the Jewish interpreters, translates it *rubrica: Red ochre,* used in marking the form of the image, to determine the portion to be cut off. Gesenius compares the Arab. سِرَاذ, *instrumentum quo suitur,* and translates *stylus. A graver.* LXX. κόλλη. Vulg. *runcinâ.* The first is probably the true interpretation.

שְׂרָד, m. only in the phr. בִּגְדֵי שְׂרָד, Exod. xxxi. 10; xxxv. 19; xxxix. 1. 41. The LXX. translate τὰς στολὰς τὰς λειτουργικάς, as if the word were שרת; and similarly the Vulg. Gesenius takes the Arab. سَرَكَ, *contexuit conseruitque* loricam; سَرْك, *lorica;* and translates the word *knitting-work.* From Exod. xxxix. 1, it appears that these garments were of various colours; and, hence, comparing the preceding word, as well as the Samaritan שרדה, *variè picta, et colorata vestis,* it seems likely that *colour* is the true signification of this word, and *coloured dresses* the meaning of the phrase.

שָׂרָה, v. שָׂרִיתָ, i. q. שׂוּר. I. *Was a prince; prevailed* with, constr. med. אֶת, עַל, Gen. xxxii. 28; Hos. xii. 3, only.

שָׂרָה, f. of שַׂר, constr. שָׂרָתִי, pl. שָׂרוֹת, aff. שָׂרוֹתֶיהָ, שָׂרוֹתָיִךְ. *A princess, a lady of rank,* Judg. v. 29; 1 Kings xi. 3; Esth. i. 18; Is. xlix. 23. Metaph. Of a city, Lam. i. 1.

שְׂרוֹךְ, m. r. שׂוּךְ. *A shoe-latchet,* Gen. xiv. 23; Is. v. 27. Arab. شِرَاكٌ, *Id.*

שָׂרוּקִים, pl. m. aff. שָׂרוּקֶיהָ, r. שׂוּק. *The shoots, branches,* of a vine, Is. xvi. 8.

שָׂרַט, m. Arab. شَرَطَ, *fissuram incidit scalpello, scarificavit. Cutting; an incision,* Lev. xix. 28.

שׂרט, v. pres. יִשְׂרְטוּ. *Cut, made incisions,* Lev. xxi. 5.
Infin. abs. שָׂרוֹט, Zech. xii. 3.
Niph. pres. יִשָּׂרֵט. Pass. of Kal. *Was cut, cut to pieces; crushed,* Zech. xii. 3.

שָׂרֶמֶת, f. of שָׂרָם, Lev. xxi. 5.

שָׂרִיגִים, pl. m. aff. שָׂרִיגֶיהָ, r. שׂרג. *The shoots, branches* of a vine, Gen. xl. 10. 12; Joel i. 7.

שָׂרִיד, m. pl. שְׂרִידִים, constr. שְׂרִידֵי, aff. שְׂרִידָיו, r. שָׂרַד. (a) *One that escapes or is left* out of a number. (b) Collectively, *A remnant.* (c) Phr. הִשְׁאִיר שָׂרִיד, with a negation, *Left not one remaining.* (a) Josh. x. 20; Job xxvii. 15; Jer. xxxi. 2, &c. (b) Is. i. 9. (c) Num. xxi. 35; Josh. x. 28; 2 Kings x. 11, &c.

שְׂרִיקוֹת, pl. f. once, Is. xix. 9. Syr. ܣܪܩ, *pexuit.* Sam. סרק, *texuit. Combings.* עֹבְדֵי פִשְׁתִּים שְׂ׳, *those that comb the flax.* So LXX. and Vulg.

שׂרך, v. Kal non occ. Probably i. q. שׂרג. *Twisted, entangled.*
Pih. part. fem. מְשָׂרֶכֶת. Intens. of Kal. *Twisting, crossing repeatedly* her course, i. e. rambling in all directions, Jer. ii. 23.

שׂרע, v. Arab. شَرَعَ, *multum in altum sustulit* rem; أَشْرَعَ, *extremitatem protensam habens,* de naso. *Stretched out.* Only in part. pass. שָׂרוּעַ, *Stretched out, prolonged,* beyond due proportion, *having any monstrosity,* Lev. xxi. 18; xxii. 23. But LXX. ὠτότμητος.
Hiph. Infin. הִשְׂתָּרֵעַ. *To stretch himself out,* Is. xxviii. 20.

שְׂרַעַפִּים, pl. m. aff. שַׂרְעַפַּי, twice, Ps. xciv. 19; cxxxix. 23. Probably i. q. שְׂעִפִּים. *Thoughts.*

שָׂרַף, v. pres. יִשְׂרֹף. Constr. immed. it. med. אֶת, it. abs. (a) *Burned, consumed by fire.* (b) Abs. *Burned spices, &c.* at a funeral, with לְ, of the person. (c) *Baked bricks.* (a) Lev. iv. 21; xiii. 52; Jer. xxxvi. 29, &c. Followed by בְּאֵשׁ, Lev. viii. 17; Josh. xi. 9; Jer. xxi. 10, &c. (b) 2 Chron. xvi. 14; Jer. xxxiv. 5. (c) Gen. xi. 3.
Infin. abs. שָׂרֹף, constr. שְׂרֹף, aff. שָׂרְפוֹ, Judg. ix. 52; 2 Sam. xxiii. 7; Jer. vii. 31, &c.
Part. שֹׂרֵף, pl. שֹׂרְפִים, Lev. xvi. 28; Num xvii. 4, &c.
Part. pass. fem. שְׂרוּפָה, pl. שְׂרוּפוֹת, 1 Sam. xxx. 3; Is. i. 7, &c.
Niph. pres. יִשָּׂרֵף. Pass. of Kal. *Was burned,* Gen. xxxviii. 24; Lev. iv. 12, &c.
Puh. in pause, שֹׂרָף, *Id.,* Lev. x. 16.

שָׂרָף, m. pl. שְׂרָפִים. (a) *A species of*

שָׂרָף—שׂ (580) שׂ֫־ר—שָׁאַג

serpent, found in Arabia and Egypt; its bite was deadly; and it is called *flying*, probably from the great distance which it sprung. Possibly the *coluber cerastes* of Linn., Num. xxi. 7. 9; Deut. viii. 15; Is. xiv. 29; xxx. 6. (b) An angelic figure, having six wings, seen in a vision by the prophet Isaiah, Ib. vi. 2. 6. The etymology is uncertain; some take שָׂרָף, others the Arab.

شَرِيف, *nobilis, princeps*. There is nothing in the passage to guide our conjectures.

שְׂרֵפָה, f. constr. שְׂרֵפַת, r. שׂוּף. (a) *The act of burning; the fire* in which a thing is burning. (b) *A funeral-burning.* (a) Gen. xi. 3; Num. xix. 6; Amos iv. 11, &c. (b) 2 Chron. xvi. 14; xxi. 19.

שׂרֵק, m. and שׂרֵקָה, fem. *A species of vine*, of superior quality, apparently, Gen. xlix. 11; Is. v. 2; Jer. ii. 21.

שְׂרֻקִּים, pl. m. Of the colour of horses, probably *bay*, Zech. i. 8, only. Arab.

شَقْرَة, *rufus color.* See Hieroz., tom. i. p. 108.

שָׂרַר, v. pres. יָשֹׂר, i. q. שׂוּר. Constr. abs. it. med. עַל. *Acted as a prince, ruled*, Prov. viii. 16; Is. xxxii. 1.
Part. שֹׂרֵר. *Ruling, a ruler*, Esth. i. 22.
Hith. pres. הִשְׂתָּרֵר. *Made himself a prince*, assumed supremacy, Num. xvi. 13.
Infin. הִשְׂתָּרֵר, Ib.

שָׂשׂוֹן, m. constr. שְׂשׂוֹן, r. שׂוּשׂ. *Joy, rejoicing*, Ps. cv. 43; Is. xii. 3; Jer. xxxi. 13, &c. Joined with שִׂמְחָה, Ps. li. 10; Is. xxii. 13, &c.

שְׂתוֹ, see נָשָׂא.

שָׂתַם, v. i. q. סָתַם. *Shut up, shut out*, Lam. iii. 8, only.

שָׂתַר, v. Niph. pres. יִשָּׂתֵר, 1 Sam. v. 9, only. According to some, i. q. יִסָּתְרוּ. *Were concealed.* Others, comparing the Arab. شَذَر, *dissecuit, vulneravit; burst*, or *broke out.*

שׁ

שׁ, Shin, distinguished from שׂ by the diacritical point, is pronounced as *sh* in *shine*. It occasionally interchanges with ז and צ, and as a numeral stands for *three hundred*.

שֶׁ, שַׁ, (both followed by dagesh,) or שְׁ, an abbreviation of the relative pronoun אֲשֶׁר, and is prefixed to every part of speech. Its signification in every case is precisely the same as that which אֲשֶׁר would have, but it is seldom used except in the loftier style. For examples see Judg. v. 7; vii. 12; 1 Chron. xxvii. 27; Ps. cxxiv. 6; Eccl. i. 9; Cant. i. 6; Lam. iv. 9, &c.

שָׁאַב, v. pres. יִשְׁאַב. Arab. سَآب, and سَبّ, *potu satiatus fuit*. (a) *Drew* water. (b) *Drew* water. (a) 1 Sam. vii. 6; 2 Sam. xxiii. 16; 1 Chron. xi. 18; Is. xii. 3; (b) Gen. xxiv. 19, 20, 44; Ruth ii. 9.
Infin. שְׁאֹב, Gen. xxiv. 13, &c.
Imp. f. שַׁאֲבִי, Nah. iii. 14.

שָׁאַג, v. pres. יִשְׁאַג. Constr. abs. Arab. ثَاج, *vociferatum fuit* pecus; *balavit* ovis, capra. (a) *Roared*, of a lion. (b) Applied [1] To thunder. [2] To the voice of God denouncing calamity. [3] To the shouting of combatants. [4] To a loud cry of sorrow. (a) Is. v. 29; Jer. ii. 15; Hos. xi. 10, &c. (b), [1] Job xxxvii. 4. [2] Jer. xxv. 30; Joel iv. 16; Amos i. 2. [3] Ps. lxxiv. 4. [4] Ps. xxxviii. 9.
Infin. abs. שָׁאֹג, Jer. xxv. 30.
Part. שֹׁאֵג, pl. שֹׁאֲגִים, Judg. xiv. 5; Ps. civ. 21, &c.

שְׁאָגָה, f. constr. שַׁאֲגַת, aff. שַׁאֲגָתִי; pl. aff. שַׁאֲגוֹתַי. (a) *Roaring*, of a lion. (b) *A loud cry of sorrow.* (a) Job iv. 10; Is. v. 29; Ezek. xix. 7; Zech. xi. 3. (b) Job iii. 24; Ps. xxii. 2; xxxii. 3.

שָׁאָה, v. pret. שָׁאָה. Probably *Fell with a crash.* Hence, *Was desolate*, of a city, Is. vi. 11.
Niph. נִשְׁאָה. (a) *Was made desolate*, of a land, Is. vi. 11. (b) *Were dashed together*, of waters, Is. xvii. 12, 13.
Hiph. Infin. הַשְׁאוֹת. *To lay waste*, Is. xxxvii. 26.

שאו (581) שאל

Hith. part. מִשְׁתָּאֶה. According to some, *Being in confusion of mind and astonishment, with* לְ: but others make it synonymous with מִשְׁתָּעֶה, and translate, *Gazing* at her, Gen. xxiv. 21. LXX. κατεμάνθανεν αὐτὴν. Vulg. *contemplabatur eam.*

שְׁאוֹל, and שְׁאֹל, com. (a) *A grave*, generally a large subterraneous chamber or vault in which niches were hewn out to receive separate coffins: these were termed בָּתִּים, יַרְכְּתֵי בוֹר. (b) Hence, *The state of the dead*, or *a state of death, the grave*. (c) *Any great depth*. (a) Job xvii. 16; Ps. cxxxix. 8; cxli. 7; Is. xxxviii. 10, &c. (b) Job xxvi. 6; Ps. vi. 6; xvi. 10, &c. Applied to animals, Ps. xlix. 15. (c) Deut. xxxii. 22; Amos ix. 2. See my notes on Job xvii. 1; xxi. 13; xxvi. 6. With regard to the etymology of the word, it has usually been referred to שָׁאַל, because of its all devouring and ever craving character. Gesenius, however, proposes שׁעל, to which he assigns the idea of *hollowness*, and considers שְׁאוֹל, quasi שָׁעוֹל, *cavitas; locus cavus et subterraneus*.

שָׁאוֹן, m. constr. שְׁאוֹן, aff. שְׁאוֹנָהּ, r. שאה. *A tumultuous noise*. (a) *Shouting*, whether *in war* or *rejoicing*. (b) Phr. בְּנֵי שָׁאוֹן, *sons of shouting*, i. e. *shouters*. (c) *The noise of waves*. (d) *Desolation, ruin*. (a) Is. xxiv. 8; lxvi. 6; Jer. xxv. 31; Amos ii. 2, &c. (b) Jer. xlviii. 45. (c) Ps. lxv. 8; Is. xvii. 12, 13; Jer. li. 55. (d) Ps. xl. 3. Where LXX. ταλαιπωρίας. Vulg. *miseriæ*.

שְׁאָט, m. aff. שְׁאָטְךָ. *Contempt of* another, and *rejoicing over his misfortunes*, Ezek. xxv. 6. 15; xxxvi. 5. See שׁוט.

שְׁאִיָּה, f. r. שאה. *A crashing noise, destruction*, Is. xxiv. 12, only.

שָׁאַל, v. pres. יִשְׁאַל. Constr. abs. it. of the thing or subject, immed. אֶת, לְ: of the person, immed. med. אֶת, לְ, מִן. Arab. سَأَلَ, *interrogavit, rogavit*. Syr. ܫܐܠ, *Id. Asked*. (a) *Questioned, inquired*. (b) *Requested, prayed for, required*. (c) *Borrowed*. (d) Phrr. שׁ׳ לוֹ לְשָׁלוֹם, *Inquired respecting his welfare, saluted*. (e) שׁ׳ בֵּאלֹהִים, *Inquired of God*. (a) Gen. xliii. 7; xliv. 19; Deut. xiii. 14, &c. (b) Judg. v. 25; 1 Sam. ii. 20; 1 Kings iii. 10; Ps. xxi. 5, &c. Metaph. of the eyes, Eccl. ii. 10. (c) According to some, Exod. iii. 22; xi. 2;

xii. 35: but *requested, begged*, suits the context better. (d) Judg. xviii. 15; 1 Sam. x. 4; xvii. 22, &c. (e) 1 Sam. xiv. 39; xxii. 10; xxviii. 6, &c.

Infin. abs. שָׁאוֹל, constr. שְׁאֹל, Gen. xliii. 7; Josh. xv. 18, &c.

Imp. שְׁאַל, f. שַׁאֲלִי, pl. שַׁאֲלוּ, Deut. iv. 32; 1 Kings ii. 20; Ps. xxii. 6, &c.

Part. שֹׁאֵל, f. שֹׁאֶלֶת, שֹׁאֲלִים, Deut. x. 12; 1 Sam. viii. 10; 1 Kings ii. 20, &c.

Part. pass. שָׁאוּל, 1 Sam. i. 28. (c) 2 Kings vi. 5.

Niph. נִשְׁאַל. Probably *Requested leave of absence*, 1 Sam. xx. 6. 28; Neh. xii. 6.

Infin. נִשְׁאֹל, 1 Sam. xx. 6. 28.

Pih. שִׁאֵל, pres. יְשַׁאֵל. *Intensitive or frequentative of Kal*, 2 Sam. xx. 18; Ps. cix. 10.

Hiph. הִשְׁאַלְתִּי, pres. יַשְׁאִלוּ. *Gave in answer to a request, gave*, Exod. xii. 36; 1 Sam. i. 28.

שְׁאֵל, v. Chald. pres. aff. יִשְׁאֲלִנּוּן, *Id. Asked, inquired, required*, Ezra v. 9. 10; vii. 21; Dan. ii. 10.

Part. שָׁאֵל, Dan. ii. 11. 27.

שְׁאֵלָה, and שְׁאֵלָה, f. aff. שְׁאֵלָתִי, and שְׁאֵלָתְךָ, שְׁאֵלָתֵךְ, and שְׁאֵלָתְךָ, שְׁאֵלָתָם. *Asking; a request*: both *the act of requesting*, and *the thing requested*, Judg. viii. 24; 1 Sam. i. 17. 27; Esth. vii. 2, 3; Job vi. 8, &c.

שְׁאֵלָא, Chald. f. def. שְׁאֵלְתָּא. *A demand*, Dan. iv. 14.

שַׁאֲנָן, m. aff. שַׁאֲנַנְךָ, pl. שַׁאֲנַנִּים, f. שַׁאֲנַנּוֹת. Syr. ܫܐܢ, *placavit*. (a) *Quiet, tranquil, secure*. (b) *Wanton, luxurious*. (c) *Wantonness, pride*. (a) Is. xxxiii. 20. (b) Job xii. 5; Ps. cxxiii. 4; Amos vi. 1, &c. (c) 2 Kings xix. 28; Is. xxxvii. 29.

שַׁאֲנַן, v. pl. שַׁאֲנַנּוּ. *Was quiet, secure, wanton*, Job iii. 18; Prov. i. 33; Jer. xxx. 10; xlvi. 27; xlviii. 11.

שְׁאָסִיךָ, see שסה.

שָׁאַף, v. pres. יִשְׁאַף. Constr. abs. it immed. Arab. سَءَف, *vehementer sitivit*. Cogn. سَاف, r. سوف, *odoratus fuit rem*. (a) *Panted, gasped*. (b) *Panted for, desired eagerly*. (c) *Desired to swallow up, to destroy; swallowed up, destroyed*. (ε)

שָׁאַר (582) שְׁבוּ

Ps. cxix. 131. (b) Job v. 5; vii. 2; xxxvi. 20. (c) Ps. lvi. 23; Is. xlii. 14.
Infin. abs. שָׁאֹף, Ezek. xxxvi. 3.
Part. שֹׁאֵף, aff. שֹׁאֲפִי, pl. שֹׁאֲפִים, Ps. lvii. 4; Eccl. i. 5; Amos ii. 7; viii. 14.

שָׁאַר, v. Arab. سَئَرَ, *reliquus, residuus fuit. Remained out of a greater number, was left*, 1 Sam. xvi. 11.
Niph. נִשְׁאַר, pres. יִשָּׁאֵר. *Id*., Gen. vii. 23; xlvii. 18; Exod. viii. 27; Num. xiv. 26, &c.
Part. נִשְׁאָר, (once נֹאשָׁר, Ezek. ix. 8), f. נִשְׁאֶרֶת, and נִשְׁאָרָה: pl. נִשְׁאָרִים, f. נִשְׁאָרוֹת, Exod. x. 5; Lev. v. 9; Josh. xxiii. 4; 2 Kings xix. 30; Zech. xi. 9, &c.
Hiph. הִשְׁאִיר, pres. יַשְׁאִיר. Constr. immed. (a) *Allowed to remain, left*. (b) *Probably Had left*. (a) Exod. x. 12; Num. ix. 12; Josh. x. 28; 1 Kings xv. 29, &c. (b) Deut. xxviii. 55; Amos v. 3.
Infin. הַשְׁאִיר, once, Ezra ix. 8: usually הַשְׁאֵיר, Gram. art. 195. 16 : Num. xxi. 35; Deut. iii. 3; Josh. viii. 22, &c.

שְׁאָר, m. constr. id. *The remainder, remnant*, of persons or things, 1 Chron. xi. 8; Is. x. 20, 21; Mal. ii. 15, &c.

שְׁאָר, Chald. m. constr. id. and שְׁאָר, def. שְׁאָרָא. *Id*., Ezra iv. 7; vii. 18; Dan. vii. 7, &c.

שְׁאֵר, m. aff. שְׁאֵרִי. (a) *Flesh*. (b) *Any near relation* by blood or marriage. Comp. Arab. صِهْر, *cognatio*. (c) According to some, *Food*, generally; but more probably *A right or claim* of any kind *arising from marriage*. LXX. τὰ δέοντα. Vulg. *nuptias*. (a) Ps. lxxiii. 26; xcviii. 20. 26; Jer. li. 35; Mic. iii. 2, 3, &c. (b) Lev. xviii. 6. 12, 13; xxi. 2; xxv. 49, &c. (c) Exod. xxi. 10.

שַׁאֲרָה, f. once, Lev. xviii. 17. *A near relationship by blood or marriage; near relations*.

שְׁאֵרִית, f. (once שֵׁרִית, 1 Chron. xii. 38), aff. שְׁאֵרִיתוֹ, &c., i. q. שְׁאָר. *A remainder, remnant*, of person or things, Gen. xlv. 7; 2 Kings xix. 31; Is. xliv. 17, &c.

שְׁאֵת, f. r. שׁאה. *Desolation*, Lam. iii. 47, only.

שְׁבָבִים, pl. m. once, Hos. viii. 6. Chald. שְׁבַב, *fregit. Fragments*.

שָׁבָה, v. pres. apoc. יִשְׁבְּ. Arab. سَبَا, r. سَبَى, *captivum fecit*. Syr. ܫܒܐ,

Id. Constr. immed. it. med. אֶת. *Carried captive, took prisoners, carried off*, [1] Persons, [2] Cattle, or [3] Property of any kind. [1] Gen. xxxiv. 29; Num. xxi. 1; 1 Kings viii. 48, &c. [2] 1 Chron. v. 21; 2 Chron. xiv. 14. [3] 2 Chron. xxi. 17.
Infin. שְׁבוֹת, Obad. 11.
Imp. שְׁבֵה, Judg. v. 12.
Part. pl. שֹׁבִים, aff. שֹׁבֵיהֶם, 1 Kings viii. 46; Is. xiv. 2, &c.
Part. pass. pl. שְׁבוּיִם, f. שְׁבִיּוֹת, Gen. xxxi. 26; Is. lxi. 1.
Niph. נִשְׁבָּה, Pass. of Kal, Gen. xiv. 14; Exod. xxii. 9; 1 Sam. xxx. 3, &c.

שְׁבוּ, m. twice, Exod. xxviii. 19; xxxix. 12. *A precious stone, usually translated, An agate*. LXX. ἀχάτης. Vulg. *achates*.

שָׁבוּעַ, m. constr. שְׁבַע, dual שְׁבֻעַיִם, pl. שָׁבֻעִים, and שָׁבֻעוֹת, constr. שְׁבֻעוֹת, aff. שְׁבֻעֹתֵיכֶם, r. שָׁבַע. (a) *A week*. (b) *A space of seven years*. (c) חַג שָׁבֻעוֹת. *The feast of weeks*. (d) חַג שְׁבֻעוֹת יָמִים. *A feast of a week's duration*. (a) Gen. xxix. 27; Lev. xii. 5; Num. xxviii. 26, &c. (b) Dan. ix. 24—27; x. 2, 3. (d) Exod. xxxiv. 22; Deut. xvi. 10. 16; 2 Chron. viii. 13. (d) Ezek. xlv. 21.

שְׁבוּעָה, f. constr. שְׁבוּעַת, aff. שְׁבוּעָתוֹ, and שְׁבֻעָה, שְׁבֻעַת, שְׁבֻעָתוֹ, pl. שְׁבֻעוֹת, r. שבע. *An oath, or an engagement by oath*, Gen. xxiv. 8; xxvi. 3; Num. xxx. 3, &c. Phrr. בַּעֲלֵי שְׁבוּעָה לוֹ. *United to him by oath*, Neh. vi. 18. שְׁבֻעַת יְהוָֹה. *An oath appealing to the Lord*, Exod. xxii. 10; 2 Sam. xxi. 7; 1 Kings ii. 43, &c. See אָלָה, p. 30.

שְׁבוּת, and שְׁבִית, f. aff. שְׁבוּתְךָ, &c., r. שבה. (a) *Captivity*. (b) Phr. שָׁב אֶת־שְׁבוּת. *Turned the captivity of —*. [1] *Brought back from captivity*. [2] *Restored to former prosperity*. (a) Num. xxi. 29. (b), [1] Ps. xiv. 7; Jer. xxx. 3. 18; xxxiii. 11, &c. [2] Job xlii. 10; Ezek. xvi. 52, 53.

שׁבח, v. Kal non occ. Arab. I. سبح, *laudavit Deum*. II. سبخ, *otiosus fuit*. II. *Sedavit*.
Pih. שִׁבַּחְתִּי, pres. יְשַׁבַּח. Constr. immed. it. med. אֶת. I. (a) *Praised God, celebrated his works*. (b) *Pronounced happy, commended*. II. (c) *Quieted*. (d) *Restrained, kept back*. (a) Ps. lxiii. 4; cxlv. 4. (b) Eccl. viii. 15. (c) Ps. lxxxix. 10. (d) Prov. xxix. 11.

שבח (583) שבי

Imp. f. שַׁבְּחִי, pl. שַׁבְּחוּ, (a) Ps. cxvii. 1; cxlvii. 12.

Hiph. part. מַשְׁבִּיהַ. I. q. Pih. (c), Ps. lxv. 8.

Hith. Infin. הִשְׁתַּבֵּחַ, with בְּ. *To boast of, glory in,* 1 Chron. xvi. 35; Ps. cvi. 47.

שְׁבַח, v. Chald. Pah. שַׁבַּח. Constr. med. וֹ. *Praised,* Dan. iv. 31; v. 4. 23.

Part. מְשַׁבַּח, Dan. ii. 23; iv. 34.

שַׁבֵּחַ, m. *Praising.* Constr. med. אֶת, Eccl. iv. 2.

שֵׁבֶט, and שָׁבֶט, m. aff. שִׁבְטוֹ, pl. שְׁבָטִים, constr. שִׁבְטֵי, aff. שְׁבָטָיו, שִׁבְטֵיהֶם, &c. (a) *A staff,* of any kind. (b) *A shepherd's staff.* (c) *A dart or short spear.* (d) *A rod,* for punishment. Applied [1] To any calamity considered as a punishment. [2] To a person used as an instrument of punishment. (e) *A staff, used as an emblem of authority; a sceptre.* (f) *A tribe.* (a) 2 Sam. xxiii. 21; Is. xxviii. 26. (b) Lev. xxvii. 32; Ps. xxiii. 4; Mic. vii. 14. (c) 2 Sam. xviii. 14. (d) Prov. x. 13; xxii. 5; xxix. 15, &c. [1] Job xxi. 9; Ps. lxxxix. 33; Is. xi. 4, &c. [2] Is. x. 5. (e) Gen. xlix. 10; Ps. xlv. 7; Is. xiv. 5, &c. (f) Exod. xxviii. 21; Deut. iii. 13; Judg. xviii. 1, &c.

שְׁבַט, Chald. m. pl. constr. שִׁבְטֵי. Id. (f) Ezra vi. 17.

שְׁבָט, m. The eleventh month of the Jewish year, Zech. i. 7. See חֹדֶשׁ, p. 184. Syr. ܫܒܛ, Id.

שְׁבִי, in pause שֶׁבִי, m. aff. שִׁבְיוֹ, שִׁבְיְךָ, שִׁבְיָם, r. שבה. (a) *Captivity, the carrying off* of persons, cattle, or any spoil; also *their being carried off.* (b) Phrr. [1] הָלְכוּ בַשְּׁבִי or הָלְ"שׁ, *Went into captivity.* [2] לֻקְּחוּ בַשְּׁבִי, *Were taken captive.* (c) *Captives; spoil.* (d) *A captive.* (a) 2 Chron. xxix. 9; Ezra ix. 7; Ps. lxxviii. 61; Amos iv. 10, &c. (b), [1] Deut. xxviii. 41; Is. xlvi. 2; Jer. xxii. 22, &c. [2] Jer. xlviii. 46. (c) Num. xxi. 2; xxxi. 12; Is. xx. 4; Hab. i. 9, &c. (d) Exod. xii. 29.

שָׁבִיב, m. constr. שְׁבִיב. Arab. شَبَّ, *accendit.* شَبِيب, *ardor, flamma.* *A flame,* Job xviii. 5, only.

שְׁבִיב, Chald. m. def. שְׁבִיבָא, pl. שְׁבִיבִין. *Id.,* Dan. iii. 22; vii. 9.

שִׁבְיָה, f. of שְׁבִי, sign. (d), Is. lii. 2.

שִׁבְיָה, f. i. q. שְׁבִי, signn. (a) and (c). (a) Neh. iii. 36. (c) Deut. xxi. 11; xxxii. 42; 2 Chron. xxviii. 5, &c.

שְׁבִיל, m. aff. שְׁבִילְךָ, pl. constr. שְׁבִילֵי. Arab. سَبِيل, *via; modus, ratio.* Syr. ܫܒܝܠ, *direxit. A path; mode of conduct,* Ps. lxxvii. 20; Jer. xviii. 15, only.

שְׁבִיסִים, pl. m. once, Is. iii. 18. *Female ornaments,* but of what kind appears doubtful. LXX. τοὺς κοσύμβους. Aq. τελαμῶνας. These seem to have given to שׁבס the sense of *fastening,* or *wreathing.* Schrœder (De vestit. Mulier.) شُمَيْسَة, a diminutive of شَمْس, *sol; species monilis, ornamenti colli.* Either, *bands, fillets,* or, *Sun-like ornaments of the neck.*

שְׁבִיעִי, m. שְׁבִיעִית, f. r. שָׁבַע. *Seventh,* Gen. ii. 2; Josh. vi. 16, &c.

שְׁבִית, see שְׁבוּת.

שֹׁבֶל, m. once, Is. xlvii. 2. Arab. سَبَلَة, *crines qui supra mystacem sunt; pars faciei supra mentum: vestes.* أَسْبَلَ *profudit; emisit; laxavit, dimisit tegumentum.* إِزَار, *appellatum. Flowing down,* or *hanging loose* seems the primitive idea: hence interpreters have been divided between the significations *flowing; dishevelled hair,* &c.; and *a flowing, loose dress.* LXX. τὰς πολιάς. So also the Syriac. But Vulg. *humerum.*

שַׁבְלוּל, m. once, Ps. lviii. 9. *A snail;* so called, according to Bochart, from שׁבל *the path-maker,* or, as if שָׁב בְּלוּל, *dwelling in a winding house.* The interpretations, however, of this word have been exceedingly different. LXX. κηρός: so Theod. and Vulg. But Symm. χορίον; and Aquila, γῆς ἐντέρῳ. See Hieroz., tom. ii. p. 646.

שֹׁבֶל, fem. pl. constr. שֹׁבֲלֵי. *A branch,* Zech. iv. 12. So LXX. κλάδοι; but Vulg. *spicæ.*

שִׁבֹּלֶת, fem. pl. שִׁבֳּלִים. Arab. سُنْبُل, *pluvia; spica.* (a) *A stream* of water. (b) *An ear of corn.* (a) Ps. lxix. 3. 16; Is

שׁבע (584) שׁבע

xxvii. 12. (b) Sing. Job xxiv. 24: pl. Gen. xli. 5—27; Ruth ii. 2; Is. xvii. 5. The only other place where this word occurs is Judg. xii. 6, in which the sign. may be either the one or the other.

שֶׁבַע, masc. (and שְׁבַע, before another numeral), שִׁבְעָה, fem. constr. שִׁבְעַת. Arab. سَبْعٌ, and Syr. ܫܒܥ, septem. The numeral Seven. The resemblance between this word and the corresponding numerals in the Indo-Germanic languages can hardly be considered more than an accidental coincidence, and is of no more etymological importance than the identity of שְׂאָר, and the corresponding French word chair, which Castell has noted, Gen. v. 7. 26; xxxvii. 2; vii. 2; viii. 10, &c. In consequence of the institution of the Sabbath, this became a sacred number; and it is frequently as a round number, in consequence of that number of days so forming a marked and well defined period.

Dual, שִׁבְעָתַיִם. (a) Seven-fold, Gen. iv. 15. 24; Ps. lxxix. 12; Prov. vi. 31; Is. xxx. 26. (b) Seven times, Ps. xii. 7.

Pl. שִׁבְעִים. Seventy, Gen. v. 12. 31, &c.

שׁבע, v. Kal only in Part. pass. pl. constr. שְׁבֻעֵי, in the phr. שְׁבֻעֵי שְׁבוּעוֹת, bound by oaths, Ezek. xxi. 23.

Niph. נִשְׁבַּע, pres. יִשָּׁבַע, and יִשָּׁבֵעַ. (a) Swore. (b) The full construction is נִשְׁבַּע לוֹ בֵּאלֹהִים, followed either by the words of the oath or by a verb with לְ. (c) When God is said to swear, the construction is the same, omitting בֵּאלֹהִים, and sometimes substituting בְּנַפְשׁוֹ. (d) To swear by any being, or by his name, is used for to honour him. (e) נִשְׁבַּע לַיהוָֹה, Made a solemn vow to the Lord. (a) Abs., Gen. xxi. 31; 2 Chron. xv. 15, &c. (b) Josh. ix. 18; 1 Kings t. 17. 30; ii. 8, &c. (c) Gen. xxiv. 7; L. 24; Exod. xxxii. 13; Jer. li. 14, &c. (d) Deut. vi. 13; Jer. v. 7. (e) 2 Chron. xv. 14; Ps. cxxxii. 2.

Infin. הִשָּׁבֵעַ, and הִשָּׁבַע, Num. xxx. 3; Jer. vii. 9. (d) Jer. xii. 16.

Imp. הִשָּׁבְעָה, plur. הִשָּׁבְעוּ, Gen. xxi. 23; Josh. ii. 12, &c.

Part. נִשְׁבָּע, pl. נִשְׁבָּעִים, f. נִשְׁבָּעוֹת, Is. xix. 18; xlviii. 1; Zech. v. 4, &c.

Hiph. הִשְׁבִּיעַ, pres. יַשְׁבִּיעַ, apoc. יַשְׁבַּע. Causat. of Niph. Constr. immed. it. med. אֶת. (a) Caused to swear, imposed an oath on. (b) Adjured. (a) Gen. L. 5. 25; Exod. xiii. 19; Num. viii. 19, &c. (b) Cant. ii. 7; iii. 5, &c.

Infin. הַשְׁבִּיעַ, הַשְׁבֵּעַ, Exod. xiii. 19; 1 Sam. xiv. 28, &c.

Part. aff. מַשְׁבִּיעֲךָ, (b) 1 Kings xxii. 16; 2 Chron. xviii. 15.

שְׁבֻעָה, f. i. q. שְׁבוּעָה. Seven, Job xlii. 3, only.

שֵׂבֶץ, m. once, 2 Sam. i. 9. Arab. شَبَصٌ, asperitas; perplexio in arborum ramis. تَشَبَّصَ, perplexus fuit, de arboribus.

Syr. ܫܒܨ, confudit, miscuit. Twisting; entangling; perplexity. LXX. σκότος δεινόν. Aquila, ὁ σφιγκτῆς. Vulg. angustiæ.

שׁבץ, v. Kal non occ. Piḥ. שִׁבֵּץ. According to some, Quilted; others, wrought with checker-work; others, fastened, Exod. xxviii. 39. The signification is very doubtful. LXX. οἱ κοσυμβωτοί. Aquila, Symm. and Theod. αἱ συσφίγξεις. These take the word as a noun. Vulg. stringes.

Puḥ. part. pl. מְשֻׁבָּצִים. Fastened, set, Exod. xxviii. 20.

שׁבק, Chald. v. Syr. ܫܒܩ, reliquit. Left. Constr. immed.

Infin. מִשְׁבַּק, Dan. iv. 23.

Imp. pl. שְׁבֻקוּ, Dan. iv. 12. 20.

Ithpe. pres. תִּשְׁתְּבִק, Pass. Dan. ii. 44.

שֶׁבֶר, and שֵׁבֶר, m. aff. שִׁבְרִי, pl. שְׁבָרִים, aff. שְׁבָרֶיהָ. Arab. شَبَرَ, fregit; perdidit.

Syr. and Chald. Id. Arab. شِبْرٌ, spithama; شَبَرَ, donum; شَبَّرَ spithamis dimensus fuit; donavit. The two leading ideas are breaking, and apportioning. (a) Breaking, of a potter's vessel, wall, &c. (b) A fracture, an injury, to the person. (c) Vexation, sorrow. (d) Mischief, harm of any kind, calamity, ruin. (e) Provisions; corn. (f) Determination, decision; interpretation. (a) Is. xxx. 13, 14. (b) Lev. xxi. 18; xxiv. 20. Metaph. of a people, Is. xxx. 26; Jer. vi. 14; viii. 11, &c. (c) Prov. xv. 4; Is. lxv. 14. (d) Prov. xvi. 18; xvii. 19; xviii. 12; Is. xv. 5, &c. (e) Gen. xlii. 1, 2. 19; Exod. viii. 5; Neh. x. 32, &c. (f) Judg. vii. 15.

שָׁבַר, v. pres. יִשְׁבֹּר. Constr. immed. it. med. אֶת. (a) Broke, broke to pieces, a staff,

שָׁבַר (585) שָׁבַת

yoke, arm, ship, potter's vessel, &c. (b) *Tore*, as a wild beast. (c) Metaph. *Broke the heart.* (d) *Broke the power of, destroyed.* (e) *Quenched* thirst. (e) *Assigned, appointed.* (f) *Sold corn.* (g) *Bought corn.* (a) Is. xiv. 5; Jer. ii. 20; xix. 10; Ezek. xxvii. 26; xxx. 2, &c. (b) 1 Kings xiii. 26. 28. (c) Ps. lxix. 21. (d) Lev. xxvi. 19; Jer. xlviii. 38; Dan. xi. 26; Hos. ii. 20. (e) Job xxxviii. 10. See my notes. (f) Gen. xli. 56. (g) Gen. xliii. 4; Deut. ii. 6.

Infin. שְׁבֹר, aff. שִׁבְרִי, Gen. xix. 9; xlii. 7; Lev. xxvi. 26, &c.

Imp. שְׁבֹר, aff. שָׁבְרָם, pl. שִׁבְרוּ, Gen. xlii. 2; Ps. x. 19; Jer. xvii. 18, &c.

Part. שֹׁבֵר, pl. שֹׁבְרִים, Gen. xlvii. 14; Ps. xxix. 5, &c.

Part. pass. שָׁבוּר. (a) Abs. *With a broken limb*, Lev. xxii. 22. (b) שְׁבוּרֵי לֵב, *Brokenhearted*, Ps. cxlvii. 3.

Niph. נִשְׁבַּר, pres. יִשָּׁבֵר. Pass. of Kal, signn. (a), (b), (c), and (d). (a) Ps. xxxiv. 21; Is. xiv. 25; Jer. xlviii. 17, &c. (b) Exod. xxii. 9. 13. (c) Jer. xxiii. 9; Ezek. vi. 9. (d) 2 Chron. xiv. 12; Prov. vi. 15; Jer. xlviii. 14.

Infin. הִשָּׁבֵר, Jonah i. 14.

Part. נִשְׁבָּר, pl. נִשְׁבָּרִים, constr. נִשְׁבְּרֵי, fem. נִשְׁבָּרָה, and נִשְׁבֶּרֶת. (a) Jer. ii. 13. (b) Ezek. xxxiv. 4; Zech. xi. 16. (c) לֵב נִשְׁבָּר, Ps. li. 19: נִשְׁבְּרֵי לֵב, Ps. xxxiv. 19; Is. lxi. 1: רוּחַ נִשְׁבָּרָה, Ps. li. 19.

Pih. שִׁבֵּר (in pause, שִׁבֵּר), pres. יְשַׁבֵּר. Intensitive of Kal, sign. (a), Exod. ix. 25; 2 Chron. xxxiv. 4; Ps. xlvi. 10, &c.

Infin. שַׁבֵּר, Exod. xxiii. 24.

Part. מְשַׁבֵּר, 1 Kings xix. 11.

Hiph. pres. אַשְׁבִּיר. (a) *Caused to suffer labour-pains*, Is. lxvi. 9. See מַשְׁבֵּר. But LXX. ἔδωκα τὴν προσδοκίαν ταύτην, reading אֲשַׂבֵּר. (b) I. q. Kal. (f) *Sold corn*, Deut. ii. 28; Amos viii. 5, 6.

Part. מַשְׁבִּיר, (b) Gen. xlii. 6; Prov. xi. 26.

Hoph. הָשְׁבַּרְתִּי, Pass. of Kal, sign. (c) *I am broken-hearted*, Jer. viii. 21.

שִׁבָּרוֹן, m. constr. שִׁבְרוֹן. *Breaking.* (a) *Breaking* of the loins, and of violent pain or sorrow, Ezek. xxi. 11. (b) *Calamity, ruin*, Jer. xvii. 18.

שׁבשׁ, Chald. v. Peal non occ. See שָׁבַץ. *Entangling, perplexing.*

Ithpe. part. pl. מִשְׁתַּבְּשִׁין. *Perplexed*, Dan. v. 9, only.

שְׁבָת, Infin. of יָשַׁב, which see: f. aff. שִׁבְתִּי. (a) *Dwelling.* (b) *Sitting down.* (c) *Ceasing.* (d) *Ceasing from work.* (a) Gen. xix. 30; Exod. ii. 21; Num. xxxv. 2, &c. (b) Ps. cxxxvii. 2; cxxxix. 2, &c. (c) Prov. xx. 3. (d) Exod. xxi. 19.

שָׁבַת, v. pres. יִשְׁבֹּת, twice תִּשְׁבַּת, Lev. xxvi. 34; Neh. vi. 3. Constr. abs. it. med. מִן. Syr. ܫܒܬ, *quievit, cessavit.* Arab. سَبَتَ, *quievit, dormivit* vir. Cogn. ישׁב. (a) *Ceased*, [1] from being or doing any thing. [2] Abs. (b) *Rested.* (c) *Was interrupted*, of work. (d) *Ceased to exist, came to an end.* (a), [1] Gen. ii. 2, 3; Job xxxii. 1; Jer. xxxi. 36, &c. [2] Exod. xxiii. 12; xxxi. 17; xxxiv. 21, &c. (b) Lev. xxv. 2; xxvi. 34, 35, &c. (c) Neh. vi. 3. (d) Josh. v. 12; Is. xiv. 4; Lam. iii. 15, &c.

Niph. נִשְׁבַּת. I. q. Kal sign. (d), Is. xvii. 3; Ezek. vi. 6; xxx. 18; xxxiii. 28.

Hiph. הִשְׁבִּית, pres. יַשְׁבִּית, apoc. יַשְׁבֵּת. Causat. of Kal, signn. (a), (c), and (d). (a) Exod. v. 5; Josh. xxii. 25; Ezek. xxxiv. 10. (c) 2 Chron. xvi. 5; Neh. iv. 5. (d) Ruth iv. 14; 2 Kings xxiii. 5; Jer. xxxvi. 29, &c.

Infin. הַשְׁבִּית, Ps. viii. 3; Amos viii. 4.

Imp. pl. הַשְׁבִּיתוּ, Is. xxx. 11.

Part. מַשְׁבִּית, Ps. xlvi. 10; Jer. xvi. 9.

שַׁבָּת, m. constr. שַׁבַּת, aff. שַׁבַּתּוֹ, שַׁבַּתְּכֶם, pl. שַׁבָּתוֹת, constr. שַׁבְּתוֹת, aff. שַׁבְּתוֹתַי, &c. *A cessation, rest; a time of rest, Sabbath.* Exod. xvi. 25; xx. 10; Lev. xxiii. 15; xxv. 2; xxvi. 34, &c. Fully יוֹם הַשַּׁבָּת, Exod. xx. 8. 11; xxxi. 15; Jer. xxiv. 7, &c. Phrr. עָשָׂה אֶת־הַשַּׁבָּת, Exod. xxxi. 16. עָשָׂה אֶת־יוֹם הַשַּׁבָּת, Deut. v. 15. שֶׁבַע שַׁבְּתוֹת הַשָּׁנִים, *Seven Sabbaths of years*, Lev. xxv. 8. See my Sermon on —.

שַׁבָּתוֹן, m. *Cessation, rest; a time of rest*, Lev. xxiii. 24. 39; xxv. 5, &c.

שִׁבְתִּי, for שִׁבְתִּי, Infin. aff. of יָשַׁב, Ps. xxiii. 6: or it might be pret. of שׁוּב, in the sense of the cognate יָשַׁב.

שָׁגַב, v. i. q. שָׂגָה. Cogn. סוג. Syr. ܫܓܒ, *erravit ignoranter à viâ. Errec'*, abs., *committed* an error, Lev. v. 18.

Part. שֹׁגֵג, f. שֹׁגֶגֶת, Abs., Num. xv. 28; Job xii. 16; Ps. cxix. 67.

שְׁגָגָה, f. aff. שִׁגְגָתָם, שִׁגְגָתָם. *An error; an unintentional fault*, Lev. iv. 2; v. 18; Num. xv. 25, &c.

4 F

שגה (586) שגע

שָׁנָה, v. pres. יִשְׁגֶּה. *Erred; went astray; committed an error.* Constr. [1] Abs., 1 Sam. xxvi. 21; Job vi. 24; Ezek. xxxiv. 6, &c. [2] Med. מִן. In Prov. v. 19, it appears to signify, *was delighted*, med. בְּ. The same interpretation is applicable in the next verse, but the signification of *went astray* is equally suitable.
Infin. שְׁגוֹת, [2] Prov. xix. 27.
Part. שֹׁגֶה, pl. שֹׁגִים, [1] Ezek. xlv. 20. [2] Ps. cxviii. 21; cxix. 118.
Hiph. pres. aff. תַּשְׁגֵּנִי. Causat. of Kal. (a) *Allowed to err.* (b) *Caused to go astray.* (a) Ps. cxix. 10.
Part. מַשְׁגֶּה. (b) Deut. xxvii. 18; Job xii. 16; Prov. xxviii. 10.

שׁגח, v. Kal non. occ.
Hiph. הִשְׁגִּיחַ, pres. יַשְׁגִּיחוּ. *Looked*, med. אֶל, Ps. xxxiii. 14; Is. xiv. 16. Chald. *Id.*
Part. מַשְׁגִּיחַ. Abs., Cant. ii. 9.

שְׁגִיאוֹת, pl. f. once, Ps. xix. 13. *Errors.* r. שגא, for שגה.

שִׁגָּיוֹן, m. pl. שִׁגְיוֹנוֹת, Ps. vii. 1; Hab. iii. 1, only. Arab. شَجِيَ, *anxius mœstusve fuit.* Probably *Sorrow, distress; a psalm in such circumstances.*

שׁגל, v. pres. aff. יִשְׁגָּלֶנָּה. *Lay with a woman*, Deut. xxviii. 30.
Niph. pres. תִּשָּׁגַלְנָה, Pass. of Kal, Is. xiii. 16; Zech. xiv. 2.
Puh. שֻׁגְּלָה. *Id.*, Jer. iii. 2.
שֵׁגַל, f. *A king's wife; queen*, Neh. ii. 6; Ps. xlv. 10.
שֵׁגַל, Chald. f. pl. aff. שֵׁגְלָתֵהּ, *Id.*, Dan. v. 2, 3. 23.

שָׁגַם, "*propter delicta eorum*," Gesen. in v. שָׁגַג, Gen. vi. 3. But this ill suits the context. Better compd. of שׁ, i. q. אֲשֶׁר, and גַּם, p. 116, above.

שגע, v. Kal non occ. Arab. سَجَعَ, *locutus fuit rhythmicè; gemuit turtur.* ضَاجِع, *decumbens*, pec. *multum præ segnitie; stupidus.* شَجَعَ, *strenuitate, fortitudine vicit aliquem.*
Puh. part. מְשֻׁגָּע, pl. מְשֻׁגָּעִים. *Maddened, mad*, Deut. xxviii. 34; 1 Sam. xxi. 16. Applied contemptuously to prophets, 2 Kings ix. 11; Jer. xxix. 26; Hos. ix. 7.
Hith. Infin. הִשְׁתַּגֵּעַ. *To act like a madman*, 1 Sam. xxi. 16.

Part. מִשְׁתַּגֵּעַ, 1 Sam. xxi. 15.
שִׁגָּעוֹן, masc. *Madness, impetuosity*, Deut. xxviii. 28; 2 Kings ix. 20; Zech. xii. 4.

שֶׁגֶר, m. Arab. شَجَر, *copiâ, multitudine, abundavit.* Syr. ܫܓܪ, *misit, emisit.* *Offspring, progeny*, Exod. xiii. 12.
שֶׁגֶר, m. constr. שְׁגַר. *Id.*, Deut. vii. 13; xxviii. 4. 19. 51.

שַׁד, m. dual, שָׁדַיִם, constr. שְׁדֵי, aff. שָׁדָי, שְׁדֵיהֶן. Arab. ثَدْي, *mamma.* Syr. ܬܕܐ, *Id.* (a) Sing. *An animal's dug*, Lam. ii. 3. (b) Dual, *The breasts* of a woman, Ps. xxii. 10; Hos. ix. 14, &c.
שֹׁד, m. I. I. q. שַׁד. *The breast*, Job xxiv. 9; Is. lx. 16; lxvi. 11.
II. r. שדד. (a) *Violence; plundering.* (b) *Devastation; ruin.* (a) Job v. 21; Prov. xxi. 7; Is. xvi. 4, &c. (b) Is. xiii. 6; xxii. 4; Hos. vii. 13; Joel i. 15, &c.

שׁדד, v. pret. שָׁדְדוּ, and שָׁדוּ, pres. aff. יְשָׁדֵּם. Arab. شَدَّ, *impetum fecit in hostem*; شَدِيد, *vehemens, durus, validus.* Constr. immed. it. med. אֶת. *Attacked, invaded, plundered, laid waste, ruined*, Ps. xvii. 9; Prov. xi. 3; Ezek. xxxii. 12.
Infin. abs. שָׁדוֹד, constr. שְׁדוֹד, Jer. xlvii. 7; Mic. ii. 4.
Imp. pl. שָׁדְדוּ, Jer. xlix. 28.
Part. שֹׁדֵד, pl. שֹׁדְדִים, constr. שֹׁדְדֵי. *An invader, a plunderer*, Job xv. 21; Jer. xii. 12; Obad. 5, &c.
Part. pass. שָׁדוּד, f. שְׁדוּדָה, Judg. v. 27; Ps. cxxxvii 8, &c.
Niph. נָשַׁדְנוּ, Pass. of Kal, Mic. ii. 4.
Pih. pres. יְשַׁדֵּד, and יְשֹׁדֵד. Intensive of Kal. *Laid waste, ruined completely*, Prov. xxiv. 15; Hos. x. 2.
Part. מְשַׁדֵּד. *A destroyer*, Prov. xix. 26.
Puh. שֻׁדַּד, שֻׁדְּדָה, and שֻׁדָּדָה, Pass. of Pih. Is. xv. 1; Jer. iv. 20; Nah. iii. 7, &c.
Hoph. pres. יוּשַׁד, i. q. Puh., Is. xxxiii. 1; Hos. x. 14.

שְׁדָה, f. pl. שִׁדּוֹת, once, Eccl. ii. 8. These words have been interpreted in many different ways. The following are some of the cognate words which have been referred to. Arab. شَكَا, r. شدو, *cecinit*

שַׂדי (587) שָׂדף

vel modulatè recitavit carmen; سَبَّخَ, dominus; سَبَّا, domina; نَدَا, r. نَدَو, rigavit, madefecit. Syr. ܣܒܐ, semita, propositum. LXX. οἰνοχόον καὶ οἰνοχόας. Aquila, κυλίκιον καί κυλίκια. Sym. μέτρων σχήματα καὶ ἐπιθήματα. Vulg. *scyphos, et urceos in ministerio ad vinum fundendum.* Some, *A queen and ladies*; others, *cup-bearers*; others, *musicians*; others, taking the words in connexion with those immediately preceding, *a purpose and purposes*; *project and projects*; pleasures *of every kind.* Of these the first and last, which are adopted by Gesenius and Dathe respectively, appear the most probable.

שַׁדַּי, m. *The Almighty*, the name by which God was known to the Patriarchs. This title is sometimes used alone, Ruth i. 20; Job vi. 4. 14; viii. 3; Ps. lxviii. 15, &c.: and is sometimes preceded by אֵל, Gen. xvii. 1; xxviii. 3; Exod. vi. 3, &c. It appears to be of a plural form, Gram. art. 139. 6, but is joined to a singular verb. Comp. Arab. شَدِيد, *fortis, strenuus.*

שֵׁדִים, pl. m. used twice as a title of false gods, Deut. xxxii. 17; Ps. cvi. 37. According to some, *Destroyers*, from שׁוּד, i. q. שָׁדַד; according to others, *Lords*: compare Arab. سَيِّد, *dominus*, and Heb. בַּעַל. LXX. δαιμονίοις. Vulg. *dæmoniis.*

שַׁדִּין, for אֲשֶׁר דִּין, *That there is a judgment*, Job xix. 29.

שְׁדֵמָה, fem. once, Is. xxxvii. 27, for שְׁדֵפָה, which occurs in the parallel passage, 2 Kings xix. 26. *The blighting of corn; blighted corn.*

שַׁדְמוֹת, pl. f. constr. שַׁדְמוֹת. (a) *Fields*, 2 Kings xxiii. 4; Jer. xxxi. 40, Keri. (b) *Corn-fields*, Hab. iii. 17. (c) *Vineyards*, Deut. xxxii. 32; Is. xvi. 8. This word does not occur in the cognate dialects; but its signification is sufficiently clear from the context in each place.

שָׂדַף, v. only in Part. pass. pl. f. שְׁדוּפוֹת, and שְׁדֻפוֹת. *Blighted*, Gen. xli. 6. 23. 27. Arab. أَسْوَد, *niger.*

שְׁדֵפָה, f. *The blight* in corn, 2 Kings xix. 26, only.

שִׁדָּפוֹן, masc. *Id.*, Deut. xxviii. 22; 1 Kings v. 37; 2 Chron. vi. 28; Amos iv. 9; Hag. ii. 17.

שְׁדַר, Chald. v. only in Ithpa. part. מִשְׁתַּדַּר. *Exerting himself*, Dan. vi. 15, only. Syr. ܫܕܪ, *commovit.*

שֹׁהַם, m. Arab. سَهَم, *palluit.* Cogn. شَهَب, *cinereo colore præditus fuit.* A precious stone of some kind, usually interpreted *The onyx* or *sardonyx*, Gen. ii. 12; Exod. xxv. 7; Job xxviii. 16, &c.

שָׁוְא, m. once, שָׁו, Job xv. 31, Kethiv. Arab. سَا, r. سوأ, *malè fecit; malus fuit*; سُوء, *malum.* (a) *Evil; guilt.* (b) *Evil; calamity.* (c) *A thing of no value; worthlessness, vanity.* (d) *Falsehood.* (e) לַשָּׁוְא [1] *To no purpose.* [2] *Falsely.* (a) Job xi. 11; Ps. xxvi. 4. (b) Job vii. 3; xv. 31; Is. xxx. 28. (c) Ps. cxxvii. 2; Mal. iii. 14. (d) Ps. xii. 3; Ezek. xiii. 6—9; Hos. x. 4, &c. (e), [1] Jer. ii. 30; iv. 30; vi. 29, &c. [2] Exod. xx. 7; Deut. v. 11; Ps. xxiv. 4.

שׁוֹא, m. pl. aff. שֹׁאֲיהֶם, r. שׁאה. Either, *Their mischievous designs*, or *their ragings*, like a tempest, Ps. xxxv. 17.

שׁוֹאָה, f. constr. שׁוֹאַת, שֹׁאָה. (a) *A storm, sudden tempest.* (b) *Destruction, desolation.* (c) *A desolate place.* (a) Prov. i. 26; Ezek. xxxviii. 9. (b) Job xxx. 14; Ps. xxxv. 8; Is. xxvii. 11, &c. (c) Job xxx. 3; xxxviii. 27.

שׁוּב, v. pret. שָׁב, pres. יָשׁוּב, and יָשֵׁב, apoc. יָשֹׁב, and יָשָׁב. Syr. ܬܒ, *rediit; pænituit.* Arab. تَاب, r. توب, *conversus fuit à peccatis ad Deum; convertit se Deus ad homines propitius.* *Returned; turned himself*, — to, — from. (a) *Went or came back*, both of persons and things. [1] Abs. [2] *To a place or person*, med. אֶל, לְ, עַל. [3] *From a place or person*, med. מִן. (b) *Turned himself about.* (c) *Turned away from*, through fear. (d) *Returned to a state* med. אֶל, לְ, עַל. (e) *Returned to a course of life*, med. בְּ, לְ, עַל. (f) *Turned to God, returned* to a course of obedience to him, med. אֶל, עַד, בְּ, עַל. (g) *Went back from a course of life*, *retired* from an office, med. מִן. (h) *Went back* from God, med. מִן, מֵאַחֲרֵי. (i) *Changed his course of life*, abs. (k) Of

שׁוּב (588) שׁוּב

God, [1] *Changed his conduct, altered his dealings,* abs. [2] *Turned away from, disregarded,* med. מֵאַחֲרֵי. [3] *Returned to a people,* med. אֶל, לְ. [4] אֶת־שְׁבוּת "שׁ, *Turned back the captivity of; restored to prosperity.* [5] *Restored* prosperity, med. אֶת. (l) *Returned* to an action, *repeated* it; followed [1] by an Infin. with לְ; [2] by וְ, and a finite verb; [3] by a finite verb without וְ. (a), [1] Lev. xiv. 39; Josh. ii. 22; Jer. xlvi. 27, &c. [2] Med. אֶל, Exod. xxxiii. 11; Lev. xxv. 10; Dan. xi. 9, &c. Med. לְ, Gen. xviii. 33; 1 Sam. xxvi. 5; Jer. xxxvii. 7, &c. Med. עַל, Prov. xxvi. 11; Eccl. i. 6. [3] 1 Sam. xxiv. 2; 2 Sam. ii. 30; Jer. xliii. 5, &c. (b) 1 Chron. xxi. 10. (c) Med. מִפְּנֵי, Job xxxix. 22; Prov. xxx. 30. With אָחוֹר, Ps. lvi. 10. (d) Med. אֶל, Gen. iii. 19; Eccl. iii. 20. Med. לְ, Job xxxiii. 25. Med. עַל, Job xxxiv. 15. (e) Med. בְּ, Jer. viii. 6. Med. לְ, Ps. lxxxv. 9. Med. עַל, Jer. xi. 10. (f) Med. אֶל, 2 Kings xxiii. 25; Jer. iii. 7; Hos. vii. 10, &c. Med. עַד, Deut. iv. 30; xxx. 2; Is. ix. 12, &c. Med. בְּ, Hos. xii. 7. Med. עַל, 2 Chron. xv. 4; xxx. 9. (g) Num. viii. 25; 1 Kings xiii. 33; Ezek. iii. 19, &c. (h) Med. מִן, 1 Sam. xv. 11. Med. מֵאַחֲרֵי, Num. xiv. 43; xxxii. 15; Jer. iii. 19, &c. (i) Deut. xxx. 18; Prov. i. 23; Jer. xxxi. 18. (k), [1] Josh. xxiv. 20; Jer. xii. 15; Zech. viii. 15, &c. [2] Deut. xxxiii. 15; Jer. xxxii. 40. [3] Med. אֶל, Zech. i. 3; Mal. iii. 7. Med. לְ, Zech. i. 16. [4] Deut. xxx. 3; Jer. xxx. 18; Job xlii. 10, &c. [5] Nah. ii. 3. (l), [1] Deut. xxx. 9; Dan. x. 20; Hos. xi. 9, &c. [2] Eccl. iv. 1; ix. 11; Jer. xviii. 4, &c. [3] Gen. xxx. 31; Ezek. viii. 6. 13. 15, &c.

Infin. abs. שׁוֹב, constr. שׁוּב, aff. שׁוּבִי, Gen. xviii. 10; 1 Sam. xviii. 6; Ps. ix. 4, &c.

Imp. שׁוּב, f. שׁוּבִי, pl. שׁוּבוּ, f. שֹׁבְנָה, Gen. xvi. 9; xxxi. 3; xliii. 2; Ruth i. 8, &c.

Part. שָׁב, f. שָׁבָה, pl. שָׁבִים, Gen. xliii. 18; Ruth i. 22; 1 Sam. vii. 3. שָׁבֵי פֶשַׁע, *those who turn themselves from transgression,* Is. lix. 20. Aff. שָׁבֶיהָ, *Id.,* Is. i. 27.

Pih. שׁוֹבֵב, pres. יְשׁוֹבֵב. Causat. of Kal. (a) *Brought* or *led back.* (b) *Restored, gave back.* (c) *Led away, led astray.* (d) With נָפֶשׁ, *Refreshed.* (a) Ps. lx. 3; Jer. l. 19; Ezek. xxxviii. 4; xxxix. 2. (c) Is. xlvii. 10. (d) Ps. xxiii. 3.

Infin. שׁוֹבֵב, aff. שׁוֹבְבִי, (a) Is. xlix. 5; Ezek. xxxix. 27. (b) Mic. ii. 4.

Part. מְשׁוֹבֵב, (b) Is. lviii. 12.

Puh. Pass. of Pih. Part. f. מְשׁוֹבֶבֶת, Ezek. xxxviii. 8.

Hiph. הֵשִׁיב, pres. יָשִׁיב, apoc. יָשֵׁב, and יָשַׁב. Causat. of Kal. (a) *Brought back* things or persons. (b) *Restored* a person to a place. (c) *Restored* property. (d) *Made a return, requited.* (e) *Brought upon* a person, good or evil. (f) *Sent* as a tribute or atonement. (g) *Distributed, assigned.* (h) *Moved away, put aside.* (i) *Drove back, repelled, hindered.* (k) *Recalled, revoked* a declaration. (l) *Caused to turn* from sin. (m) *Withheld, withdrew* his hand or foot. (n) *Brought down, reduced.* (o), [1] *Answered,* constr. immed. [2] הֵשִׁיב אֹתוֹ דָּבָר, or [3] הֵשִׁיב אֵלָיו דָּבָר. (p) *Caused to answer.* Phrr. (q) אֶל־לִבּוֹ (or עַל) הֵשִׁיב, *Laid to heart, considered.* (r) הֵשִׁיב אֶת־פְּנֵי, *Turned away the face of;* [1] *Refused his request.* [2] *Drove back.* (s) הֵשִׁיב אֶת־שְׁבוּת, *Turned back the captivity of; restored to prosperity.* (a) Gen. xiv. 16; 1 Sam. xxx. 19; 2 Kings xiv. 28, &c. (b) Gen. xl. 13; xli. 13; Is. i. 26, &c. (c) Lev. v. 23; xxv. 27; Num. v. 7, &c. (d) 1 Sam. xxvi. 23; 2 Sam. xxii. 21; Ps. cxvi. 12, &c. (e) Deut. xxviii. 60; xxxii. 41; 2 Sam. xvi. 12, &c. (f) 1 Sam. vi. 8. 17; 2 Kings iii. 4; 2 Chron. xxvii. 5, &c. (g) Lev. xxvi. 26. (h) Gen. xxix. 3; Exod. xxxiv. 35. (i) Job ix. 12; xi. 10; Is. xiv. 27, &c. (k) Num. xxiii. 20. (l) Mal. ii. 6. (m) Josh. viii. 26; Is. lviii. 13; Ezek. xviii. 8, &c. (n) Job x. 9; xxx. 23; Ps. xc. 3, &c. (o), [1] Job xl. 4. [2] Num. xxii. 8; 2 Sam. xxiv. 13; Neh. ii. 20, &c. [3] Exod. xix. 8; 2 Chron. xxxiv. 16, &c. (p) Job xx. 2. (q) Deut. iv. 39; xxx. 1; 1 Kings viii. 47, &c. (r), [1] 1 Kings ii. 20; 2 Chron. vi. 42; Ps. cxxxii. 10, &c. [2] 2 Kings xviii. 24. (s) Jer. xxxii. 44; xxxiii. 11; xlix. 6.

Infin. abs. הָשֵׁב, constr. הָשִׁיב, and הָשֵׁב, aff. הֲשִׁיבוּ, Gen. xxxvii. 22; Exod. xxiii. 4; 1 Kings xii. 6; Ezek. xxi. 35.

Imp. הָשֵׁב, aff. הֲשִׁיבֵנִי, Gen. xx. 3. (o, 1) Job xxxiii. 32. Pl. הָשִׁיבוּ, *Turn* (yourselves), &c. *from sin,* Ezek. xviii. 30.

Part. מֵשִׁיב, pl. מְשִׁיבִים, constr. מְשִׁיבֵי, fem. constr. מְשִׁיבַת, Gen. xx. 7; Judg. xi. 9; Ps. xix. 8; Prov. xxvi. 16.

Hoph. הוּשַׁב, pres. יוּשַׁב. Pass. of Hiph. *Was returned, brought back,* Gen. xlii. 28; Exod. x. 8.

Part. מוּשָׁב, pl. מוּשָׁבִים, Gen. xlii. 28; xliii. 12; Jer. xxvii. 15.

שׁוּב (589) שׁוּח

שׁוֹבֵב, m. pl. שׁוֹבְבִים. *One who habitually turns aside; rebellious*, Is. lvii. 17; Jer. iii. 14. 22.

שׁוֹבֵב, m. שׁוֹבֵבָה, f. *Id.*, Jer. viii. 5; xxxi. 22; xlix. 4.

שׁוּבָה, f. *Returning;* pec. *returning to God*, Is. xxx. 15, only.

שׁוּד, v. pres. יָשׁוּד, i. q. שׁדד. *Attacked, laid waste*, Ps. xci. 6, only.

שָׁוָה, v. pres. יִשְׁוֶה. Constr. med. בְּ, לְ. Arab. سَوَى, *intendit, proposuit sibi rem;* سَوَى, *intentio, propositum;* سَوَى, *æqualitas, justitia;* سَوَى, *æqualis.* Syr. ܗܡܐ, *dignus, par fuit.* (a) *Was equal to, resembled.* (b) *Was of equal value* or *importance.* (c) *Was fitting, proper.* (d) *Was sufficient.* (a) Prov. xxvi. 4; Is. xl. 25. (b) Prov. iii. 15; viii. 11.

Part. שֹׁוֶה, (c) Esth. iii. 8. (d) Ib. v. 13. (b) Ib. vii. 4. *Were we to have been sold for slaves I should have been silent; for that calamity would not have been equal to the king's loss*, by our intended massacre.

Pih. שִׁוָּה, pres. יְשַׁוֶּה. (a) *Made level, smoothed.* (b) *Made similar,* with בְּ. (c) *Made himself like.* (d) Cogn. שׁית, *Placed.* (e) *Placed mentally; proposed* as an object. (f) *Produced* fruit. Comp. Æth. ⱦⱵⰒ: *maturuit:* ⰀⱵⰒⰒ: *maturescere fecit.* (a) Is. xxviii. 25. (b) Ps. cxxxi. 2. (c) Is. xxxviii. 13, unless written שִׁוִּיתִי, for שִׁוַּעְתִּי. (d) Ps. xxi. 6; lxxxix. 20. (e) Ps. xvi. 8; cxix. 30. (f) Hos. x. 1.

Part. מְשַׁוֶּה, (b) 2 Sam. xxii. 34; Ps. xviii. 34.

Hiph. שִׁוָּה. *Made* or *considered like, compared*, Is. xlvi. 5; Lam. ii. 13.

Niph. and Hith. combined, see Gram. art. 196. 3, part. f. נִשְׁתַּוָה. *Being,* i. e. *let her be, made* or *considered like*, Prov. xxvii. 15. Vulg. *comparatur.*

שׁוָה, Chald. *Id.*

Pah. שַׁוִּי. *Placed* or *made equal*, Dan. v. 21.

Ithpa. pres. יִשְׁתַּוֵּה. *Was made, rendered*, Dan. iii. 29.

שָׁוֶה, f. *What is equal and just; equity*, Job xxxiii. 27.

שׁוּח, v. pret. f. שָׁחָה. Cogn. שׁחח, from which indeed this form may be derived. Arab. سَاخَ, r. سوخ, *descendit et immersus fuit. Went down, sunk*, Ps. xliv. 26; Prov. ii. 18.

שׁוּחָה, f. *A pit,* pec. *one used as a snare*, Prov. xxii. 14; xxiii. 17; Jer. xviii. 20, &c.

שׁוֹט, masc. pl. שׁוֹטִים. Arab. سَوْط, *scutica, flagellum; calamitas.* (a) *A whip.* (b) Metaph. *A scourge, calamity.* (a) 1 Kings xii. 11. 14; Prov. xxvi. 3; Nah. iii. 2. (b) Job ix. 23; Is. x. 26; xxviii. 15. 18. In the last two of these passages the metaphor might more naturally be derived from the Æthiopic sign. of the word ⱷⰒⱤ: *fundere;* ⱵⰒⱤ: *effusio. An inundation.*

שׁוּט, v. I. Pret. שָׁט, pres. יָשׁוּט. Arab. سَاطَ, r. سوط, *commiscuit,* pec. *inter se movendo liquidiora; scuticâ percussit;* مِسْوَط, *instrumentum ligno constans, quo commiscentur res;* سَطَا, r. سطو, *impetum fecit; cum vehementiâ insultavit;* شَوْط, *longum fecit iter.* (a) Probably *Spread like water; went in various directions, went to and fro*, Num. xi. 8; 2 Sam. xxiv. 8. (b) *Struck*, pec. *struck into water, rowed.*

Infin. שׁוּט, שֻׁט, Job i. 7; ii. 2. In Job v. 21, שׁוֹט, בְּשׁוֹט, may be interpreted either, *In the running to and fro of the tongue;* or, taking سَطَا, as the cognate word, *In the attack, assault of the tongue.* Comp. Ps. lxxiii. 9.

Imp. שׁוּט, (a) 2 Sam. xxiv. 2. Part. pl. שָׁטִים. *Rowing; rowers*, Ezek. xxvii. 8. 26.

Pih. pres. יְשׁוֹטְטוּ. Frequentative of Kal, sign. (a), Dan. xii. 4; Amos viii. 12.

Imp. pl. שׁוֹטְטוּ, Jer. v. 1.

Part. pl. מְשׁוֹטְטִים, fem. מְשׁוֹטְטוֹת, 2 Chron. xvi. 9; Zech. iv. 10.

Hith. Imp. pl. f. הִשְׁתּוֹטַטְנָה, i. q. Pih., Jer. xlix. 3.

II. I. q. Syr. ܫܳܛ, *contempsit. Despised*, only in Part. pl. שָׁאטִים, f. שָׁאטוֹת, Ezek. xvi. 57; xxviii. 24. 26.

שׁוּלִים, pl. m. constr. שׁוּלֵי, aff. שׁוּלָיו. Cogn. Arab. ذَيْل, *postremum cujusque rei;*

שׁוּל (590) שׁוּף

lacinia vestis, syrma. The borders, skirts of a garment, a train, Exod. xxviii. 34; Is. vi. 1; Jer. xiii. 22, &c. See שׁוּל.

שׁוֹלָל, m. r. שׁלל. Spoil; applied to persons, captives, Job xii. 17. 19: as a captive, Mic. i. 8.

שׁוּמִים, pl. m. Arab. ثُوم, and Syr. ܬܘܡܐ, allium. Garlick, Num. xi. 5.

שׁוּעַ, m. aff. שׁוּעִי. A cry for help, Ps. v. 3. Hence—

שׁוּעַ, v. Pih. שִׁוַּעְתִּי, pres. יְשַׁוֵּעַ. Constr. abs. it. med. אֶל. Cried out for help, Job xxiv. 12; Ps. xxx. 3; Is. lviii. 9, &c.

Infin. aff. שַׁוְּעִי, Ps. xxviii. 2, &c.

Part. מְשַׁוֵּעַ, Job xxix. 12, &c.

שׁוּעַ, m. aff. שׁוּעֶךָ, for שׁוֹעַ, r. ישׁע. (a) Safety. (b) Affluence. (a) Job xxx. 24. (b) Ib. xxxvi. 19; Gram. art. 76.

שׁוֹעַ, m. for שׁוֹעַ, r. ישׁע. (a) Affluent. (b) Liberal. (a) Job xxxiv. 19. (b) Is. xxxii. 5.

שַׁוְעָה, f. constr. שַׁוְעַת, aff. שַׁוְעָתִי, i. q. שׁוּעַ. A cry for help, 1 Sam. v. 12; Ps. xviii. 7; xl. 2, &c.

שׁוּעָל, m. pl. שׁוּעָלִים. Arab. ثُعَال, and ثَعَلَب, vulpes. Syr. ܬܥܠܐ, Id. A fox, Judg. xv. 4; Neh. iii. 35; Ps. lxiii. 11, &c. Some suppose that in several passages we are rather to understand the jackal. Pers. شَغَال. Sans. शृगाल, srigála.

שׁוּף, v. pres. aff. יְשׁוּפֵנִי. Cogn. נשׁך, שׁאף. Arab. سَافَ, r. سوف, odoratus fuit atque ita exploravit rem; venatus fuit; سَيْف, ensis; سَاف, ense percussit; نَسَف, comminuit dispersitque; ventilavit flatu motuque frumentum; momordit. This word occurs only in three passages, Gen. iii. 15; * Job ix. 17; Ps. cxxxix. 11; and interpreters are much divided as to its precise signification. Watching, in order to injure, has been taken by some: by others, wounding, as the primitive idea conveyed by the word. The LXX. have τηρήσει, and τηρήσεις, in the first passage; ἐκτρίψῃ, in the second; and καταπατήσει, in the third. The Vulgate has conteret, insidiaberis, conteret, et conculcabunt. The Syr. has ܕܘܫ, ܬܕܘܫܝܘܗܝ, ܬܕܘܫܢܢܝ, and ܢܕܘܫ. Perhaps Struck, bruised, shattered, in Gen. iii. 15, and Job ix. 17. In Ps. cxxxix. 11, the word may be connected with נשׁף, and so, concealed may be the meaning; as the Auth. Vers. Symm. ἐπισκεπάσει.

שׁוֹפָר, m. constr. שׁוֹפַר, pl. שׁוֹפָרוֹת, constr. שׁוֹפְרוֹת, aff. שׁוֹפְרֹתֵיהֶם. A trumpet, a curved horn, Exod. xix. 16; Lev. xxv. 9; Judg. vii. 16, &c. LXX. σάλπιγξ, and κερατίνη. Arab. شَبُّور, Id. not سَبُّور, which Gesenius has: which mistake Winer has not only copied, but founded the etymology of the word upon it. The origin is uncertain.

שׁוֹק, f. dual, שׁוֹקַיִם, constr. שׁוֹקֵי, aff. שׁוֹקָיו. Arab. سَاق, crus. Syr. ܫܩܐ, Id. (a) A leg, of a man, Deut. xxviii. 35; Ps. cxlvii. 10; Prov. xxvi. 7; Cant. v. 15, &c. (b) Either, A leg, i. e. thigh, or a shoulder, of a sheep, Exod. xxix. 22. 27; Lev. vii. 32, 33, &c. That this was not the leg properly speaking, i. e. the shank, is manifest from 1 Sam. ix. 24, where it is given as the portion of the principal guest. The LXX. and Vulg. translate it shoulder.

שׁוּק, masc. pl. שְׁוָקִים. Arab. سُوق, forum, mercatus, et pro plateâ. Syr. ܫܘܩܐ, Id. A street, Prov. vii. 8; Eccl. xii. 4, 5; Cant. iii. 2.

שׁוּק, v. Kal non occ. Arab. سَاق, r. سوق, propulit, stimulavit. VII. Impulsus fuit; fluxit. Cogn. שׁקה, שׁקק. Probably Used the legs, ran, of animals; and hence, flowed, of liquids.

Hiph. הֵשִׁיק. (a) Caused to flow, caused to run over, Joel ii. 24. (b) Overflowed, Ib. iv. 13.

Pih. pres. aff. תְּשֹׁקְקֶהָ, i. q. Hiph. (a), Ps. lxv. 10; unless the true reading is תַּשְׁקֶהָ, Thou waterest it.

שׁוֹר, pl. aff. שׁוֹרֵיהֶם. Arab. سُور,

---

* The attempt that has been made gravely to justify a blunder of the Vulgate, which here reads ipsa instead of ipse, is a melancholy proof of the great neglect of the study of Hebrew in this country. Any one acquainted with the first elements of the grammar would see, that, to make the Vulgate correct, we must substitute תשופך, for ישופך, and תשופנה, for תשופנו.

שׁוּר

murus urbis. *A wall*, Gen. xlix. 22; 2 Sam. xxii. 30; Job xxiv. 11; and probably in Gen. xlix. 6, where the common reading is שׁוֹר.

שׁוּר, Chald. m. pl. def. שׁוּרַיָּא. *Id.*, Ezra iv. 12, 13; and, in verse 16, אֻשַּׁיָּא.

שׂוּר, m. pl. aff. שָׂרַי. Abstract for concr. *One who watches* with hatred; *an enemy*, Ps. xcii. 12. See שׁוּר, v.

שׁוֹר, m. but a generic term applied to both male and female. Arab. ثَوْرٌ, *taurus*. Chald. תּוֹר, *Id.* *An ox*, Exod. xxi. 28; xxii. 9; Lev. vii. 23, &c. Used as a noun of multitude, Gen. xxxii. 6, only; the usual term being בָּקָר. Aff. שׁוֹרִי, שׁוֹרְךָ: pl. שְׁוָרִים, Hos. xii. 12, only.

שׁוּר, v. pres. יָשׁוּר. Constr. abs. it. immed. Chald. סוּר, *inspexit, visitavit*. Arab. سَارَ, r. سير, *profectus fuit*. (a) *Viewed, beheld, perceived*. (b) *Watched*, for evil, as a beast of prey or a fowler. (c) *Watched*, for good; *looked after, cared for*. (d) Probably *Went*. (a) Num. xxiii. 9; Job xvii. 16; xxxv. 14. 29, &c. (b) Jer. v. 26; Hos. xiii. 7. (c) Hos. xiv. 9.

Imp. שׁוּר, (a) Job xxxv. 5.

Part. pl. f. aff. שָׁרוֹתַיִךְ, (d) *Thy travellers, carriers*, Ezek. xxvii. 25.

Pih. שׁוֹרֵר. Frequentative of Kal. *Contemplated*, Job xxxvi. 24.

שׁוֹשָׁן, and שׁוּשָׁן, m. pl. שׁוֹשַׁנִּים, it. שׁוֹשַׁנָּה, constr. שׁוֹשַׁנַּת. Pers. سُوسَن, سُوسَم, and سُوسَنَة; it. Arab. سُوس, سُوسَن, and سُوسَان, *lilium*; whence the Spanish *azucena*. (a) *The white lily*, Cant. ii. 1, 2. 16; iv. 5; v. 13, &c. (a) *An ornament resembling a lily*, 1 Kings vii. 19. 22. 26. (c) In the titles of Pss. xlv. lx. lxix. and lxxx.; but whether the name of *a musical instrument* bearing some resemblance to the form of a lily, or that of *a musical air*, as some suppose, cannot be determined. See Celsii Hierobot., tom. i. p. 383.

שׁוּרַת, v. see שִׁית.

שֵׁזֵב, v. Chald. i. q. Syr. ܫܘܙܒ, *eripuit, liberavit*.

Pah. שֵׁיזֵב, pres. יְשֵׁיזִב. Constr. immed. it.

שׁזף

med. לְ. *Delivered, rescued*, Dan. iii. 15. 17. 28.

Infin. aff. שֵׁיזָבוּתֵהּ, Dan. vi. 15. 17. 21.
Part. מְשֵׁיזִב, Dan. vi. 28.

שָׁזַף, v. only in the forms שְׁזָפַתּוּ, for שְׁזָפַתְהוּ, Job xx. 9; xxviii. 7, and שְׁזָפָתְנִי, Cant. i. 6. According to Castell, cogn. שָׂקַף, which seems doubtful, though the sign. of the latter verb will suit each passage. *Looked on, beheld, saw*. See my note on Job xx. 9.

שָׁזַר, v. Arab. شَزَرَ, *torsit* funem. مَشْزُورٌ, *valde contortus, de fune*. *Twisted*.

Part. Hoph. מָשְׁזָר. *Well twisted*, Exod. xxvi. 1; xxvii. 9; xxviii. 6, &c. LXX. κεκλωσμένος. Vulg. *retortus*.

שָׁחָה, m. r. שׁחח, once, Job xxii. 29, שַׁח עֵינַיִם. *Having downcast eyes, meek*.

שֹׁחַד, m. Syr. ܫܘܚܕܐ, *donavit*. *Giving*. (a) *A present*. (b) Pec. *A bribe*. (c) *Bribery*. (a) 1 Kings xv. 19; 2 Kings xvi. 8. (b) Exod. xxiii. 8; Deut. xvi. 19; Ps. xxvi. 10, &c. (c) Job xv. 34.

שָׁחַד, v. pres. תְּשַׁחֲדִי. *Gave presents to, bribed*. Med. אֶת, Ezek. xvi. 33.
Imp. pl. שַׁחֲדוּ; med. בְּעַד, Job vi. 22.

שָׁחָה, v. for שׁחח. *Bowed himself*. See שׁחח.

Imp. f. שְׁחִי, Is. li. 23.
Hiph. pres. aff. שַׁחֶנָּה. Causat. of Kal. Metaph., Prov. xii. 25.
Hith. הִשְׁתַּחֲוָה, pres. יִשְׁתַּחֲוֶה, apoc. יִשְׁתַּחוּ: Comp. Æth. ሰገደ፡ *expansus fuit*, de nube. *Prostrated himself*, as a mark of respect or reverence; *prostrated himself in worship, worshipped*. Constr. abs., Exod. xxxiii. 10; 2 Sam. xvi. 4; 2 Kings v. 18. It. with לְ, of the person or object of reverence or worship, Exod. xi. 18; xx. 5; Deut. iv. 19, &c.; or with לִפְנֵי, Gen. xxiii. 12; Deut. xxvi. 10; 2 Chron. xxv. 14, &c.; or with אֶל, Is. xlv. 14. It. with עַל, of the place, Gen. xlvi. 31; Is. lx. 14, &c.; or with אֶל, Ps. v. 8; or with לִפְנֵי, 2 Kings xviii. 22; 2 Chron. xxxii. 12, &c. The full form is וַיִּשְׁתַּחוּ לוֹ אַפַּיִם אַרְצָה, *He worships him* (falling) *on his face on the ground*, 2 Sam. xiv. 33; 1 Kings i. 23. This is equivalent to וַיִּשְׁתַּחוּ אַפָּיו אַרְצָה, Josh. v. 14; 2 Sam. i. 2; Job i. 20, &c.

Infin. הִשְׁתַּחֲוֺת, aff. הִשְׁתַּחֲוָיָתִי, of הִשְׁתַּחֲוָיָה, Gen. xxxvii. 10; 2 Kings v. 18, &c.

שחו (592) שחי

Imp. f. הִשְׁתַּחֲוִי, pl. הִשְׁתַּחֲווּ, Ps. xlv. 12; xcix. 5, &c.
Part. מִשְׁתַּחֲוֶה, pl. מִשְׁתַּחֲוִים, Gen. xxxvii. 9; 2 Kings xix. 37, &c. In Ezek. viii. 16, we have מִשְׁתַּחֲוִיתָם, which is probably an error for מִשְׁתַּחֲוִים.

שְׁחוֹר, m. r. שחר. *Blackness,* Lam. iv. 8.

שַׁחוּת, f. aff. שַׁחוּתוֹ, r. שחח. *A pit,* Prov. xxviii. 10.

שָׁחַח, v. pret. שַׁח, pres. יָשׁחַ. Constr. abs. (a) *Bowed himself, stooped,* either in sorrow, Ps. xxxv. 14; xxxviii. 7; or in ambush, Job xxxviii. 40; Ps. x. 10. (b) *Was brought low, was humbled,* Job ix. 13; Prov. xiv. 19; Is. ii. 11. 17, &c.
Infin. שְׁחוֹחַ, Is. lx. 14.
Niph. pres. יִשַּׁח. *Id.,* Eccl. xii. 4; Is. ii. 9; v. 15; xxix. 4.
Hiph. הֵשַׁח. Constr. immed. Causat. of Kal. *Brought low, humbled,* Is. xxv. 12; xxvi. 5.
Hith. pres. תִּשְׁתּוֹחַח, i. q. Kal with probably an intensitive signification, Ps. xlii. 7. 10. 12; xliii. 5.

שָׁחַט, v. pres. יִשְׁחַט. Constr. immed. it. med. אֶת. Arab. سَحَطَ, *mactavit; aquâ diluit vinum.* (a) *Slaughtered* an animal, [1] For food, [2] As a sacrifice. (b) *Slew* a person. (a), [1] 1 Sam. xiv. 34. [2] Lev. i. 5; xiv. 19. 25, &c. (b) 2 Kings x. 7; xxv. 7; Jer. lii. 10, &c.
Infin. abs. שָׁחוֹט, שָׁחֲטָה, constr. שְׁחֹט, aff. שָׁחֲטָם, Gen. xxii. 10; Is. xxii. 13; Ezek. xxiii. 39; Hos. v. 2, &c.
Imp. pl. שַׁחֲטוּ, Exod. xii. 21; 2 Chron. xxxv. 6.
Part. שׁוֹחֵט, pl. constr. שֹׁחֲטֵי, Is. lvii. 5; lxvi. 3.
Part. pass. שָׁחוּט, f. שְׁחוּטָה. (a) *Slaughtered,* Lev. xiv. 6. 51. (b) זָהָב שָׁחוּט, Probably *Alloyed gold;* as opposed to זָהָב סָגוּר, *Pure gold,* 1 Kings x. 16, 17; 2 Chron. ix. 15, 16.
Niph. pres. יִשָּׁחֵט. Pass. of Kal, Lev. vi. 25; Num. xi. 22.

שְׁחִיטָה, f. constr. שְׁחִיטַת. *The slaughtering* of animals for sacrifice, 2 Chron. xxx. 17.

שָׁחִין, m. Arab. سخن, *caluit, incaluit;* سُخْن, *calor febrilis. An inflammation,*

either local or general, *Any burning disease,* Exod. ix. 10; Lev. xiii. 18; 2 Kings xx. 7; Job ii. 7, &c.

שָׁחִיס, m. i. q. סָחִישׁ. *Spontaneous,* Is. xxxvii. 30, only.

שָׁחִיף, m. constr. שְׁחִיף. Arab. سَحَفَ, *tenuis, exiguus fuit;* سَحِيف, *levis, tenuis. A thin covering* of wood, Ezek. xli. 16.

שְׁחִית, f. pl. aff. שְׁחִיתוֹתָם. I. q. שַׁחוּת. *A pit,* Ps. cvii. 20; Lam. iv. 20.

שְׁחִיתָה, Chald. f. r. שחת. *A fault,* Dan. ii. 9; vi. 5.

שַׁחַל, m. *A lion,* Job iv. 10; Ps. xci. 13; Prov. xxvi. 13; Hos. v. 14, &c. Some derive the name from سَحَلَ, *rudit mulus,* and consider the word as equivalent to *the roarer.* Bochart, Hieroz., tom. i. p. 717, considers שַׁחַל as a variation of שַׁחַר, and supposes a kind of lion to be meant of a darker colour than ordinary, such as is said to have been found in Syria and India.

שְׁחֵלֶת, f. once, Exod. xxx. 34. Some kind of perfume, usually *Onyx.* So LXX. ὄνυχα, and Vulg. *onycha.* See Bochart. Hieroz., tom. i., p. 718.

שַׁחַף, m. *A bird;* according to Bochart, *A sea gull,* Lev. xi. 16; Deut. xiv. 15.

שַׁחֶפֶת, f. *A disease; Consumption,* Lev. xxvi. 16; Deut. xxviii. 22. Arab. سُحَاف, *tabes, phthisis.* But LXX. τὴν ψώραν.

שַׁחַץ, m. Arab. شَخَص, *elatus fuit;* شَخْص, *magno corpore præditus, et crassus fuit.* Probably *Greatness, power, haughtiness.* Only in the phr. בְּנֵי שַׁחַץ. *The mighty* or *fierce ones,* of animals, Job xxviii. 8; xli. 26.

שַׁחַק, m. pl. שְׁחָקִים. Arab. سَحَقَ, *fricando trivit, contrivit in pulverem;* سَحِقَ, and سَحَقَ, *procul et remotus fuit;* سَحَق, *nubes tenuis.* (a) *Dust.* (b) *A cloud.* (c) *The sky.* (a) Is. xl. 15. (b)

שָׂחַק (593) שָׁחַת

Job xxxv. 5; xxxvi. 28; Ps. lxxvii. 18, &c. (c) Ps. lxxxix. 7. 38.

שָׂחַק, v. שָׂחֲקָה, pres. aff. אֶשְׂחָקֶם. Constr. immed. *Reduced to dust, crushed, wasted away*, Exod. xxx. 36; Job xiv. 18; 2 Sam. xxii. 43; Ps. xviii. 43, al. non occ.

שָׁחַר, m. aff. שַׁחֲרָהּ. Arab. سَحَر, *primo diluculo fuit, fecit;* سَحَر, *tempus paulo ante auroram, primum diluculum.* Syr. ܫܚܪ, *denigravit;* ܫܚܪܐ, *tenebræ.* The primitive idea seems to be *darkness;* hence *the beginning and end of darkness, the dusk, the twilight,* both in the evening and morning, but especially the latter. (a) *The dawn,* Job xxxviii. 12; Amos iv. 13, &c. Phr. עָלָה הַשַּׁחַר. *The dawn began,* Gen. xix. 15; Josh. vi. 15; 1 Sam. ix. 26, &c. Metaph., Is. viii. 20. (b) Probably *Rise, origin,* Is. xlvii. 11; some, however, take the Arab. سِحْر, *magia, incantatio,* both here, and in viii. 20.

שָׁחֹר, m. pl. שְׁחֹרִים, f. שְׁחֹרָה, pl. שְׁחֹרוֹת. *Black,* Lev. xiii. 31. 37; Cant. i. 5; v. 11; Zech. vi. 2. 6.

שָׁחַר, v. (a) *Was* or *became black,* Job xxx. 30. (b) *Did a thing early in the morning;* pec. *sought early,* constr. immed. Part. שֹׁחֵר, (b) Prov. xi. 27.

Pih. שִׁחֵר, pres. יְשַׁחֵר. Constr. immed. it. med. אֶל, לְ. *Came to* or *sought early,* Job viii. 5; Ps. lxiii. 2; Prov. i. 28; Is. xxvi. 9, &c.

Infin. שַׁחֵר, Prov. vii. 15.

Part. pl. constr. מְשַׁחֲרֵי, aff. מְשַׁחֲרַי, Job xxiv. 5; Prov. viii. 17.

שַׁחֲרוּת, f. once, Eccl. xi. 10. According to some, *The dawn;* both youth and the dawn are vanity, i. e. equally fleeting. Others, *The dawn, the morning of life, youth.* lxx. ἄνοια. Vulg. *voluptas.*

שְׁחַרְחֹר, f. שְׁחַרְחֹרֶת, once, Cant. i. 6. Either *Very black* or *blackish;* most probably the former, see Gram. art. 169. 6.

שַׁחַת, f. aff. שַׁחְתָּם, r. שׁחה. (a) *A pit,* pec. *one used as a snare.* (b) *A dungeon.* (c) *A grave; the grave.* (d) *The filth of a dungeon; the corruption of the grave.* (e) *Destruction.* (a) Ps. vii. 16; x. 16; xxxv. 7; Ezek. xix. 4, &c. (b) Is. li. 14. (c) Ps. xxx. 10; xlix. 10. (d) Job ix. 31;

xvii. 15; Ps. xvi. 10. (e) Job xxxiii. 18; Ps. lv. 24, &c.

שָׁחַת, v. Kal non occ. Arab. سَحَت, *perdidit, eradicavit rem.* Syr. ܐܫܚܬ, *contraxit rubiginem;* ܫܘܚܬܐ, *ærugo, corruptio.*

Pih. שִׁחֵת, pres. יְשַׁחֵת. Constr. abs. it. immed.: it. med. אֶת, לְ. (a) *Acted corruptly.* (b) *Destroyed, ruined;* or *greatly injured.* (c) *Broke* a covenant. (d) שִׁחֵת רַחֲמָיו. *Destroyed his pity,* i. e. *laid it aside.* (a) Exod. xxxii. 7; Deut. ix. 12; xxxii. 5, &c. (b) Exod. xxi. 26; Num. xxxii. 15; 2 Kings xix. 12, &c. (c) Mal. ii. 8. (d) Amos i. 11.

Infin. שַׁחֵת, aff. שַׁחֶתְכֶם, שַׁחֶתְךָ, Gen. vi. 17; xix. 13; Ezek. v. 16, &c.

Imp. pl. in pause שַׁחֵתוּ, Jer. v. 10.

Niph. נִשְׁחַת, pres. יִשָּׁחֵת. Pass. of Pih. (a) *Was spoilt,* by rotting, Jer. xiii. 7: in making, Jer. xviii. 4. (b) *Was corrupted,* morally, Gen. vi. 11, 12. (c) *Was laid waste,* Exod. viii. 20.

Part. pl. f. נִשְׁחָתוֹת, (b) Ezek. ii. 44.

Hiph. הִשְׁחִית, pres. יַשְׁחִית, apoc. יַשְׁחֵת. Constr. immed. it. med. אֶת לְ. I. q. Pih. signn. (a) and (b). (a) Judg. ii. 19; Ps. liii. 2; Dan. viii. 24, &c. Fully, דַּרְכּוֹ ה׳, Gen. vi. 12. (b) Gen. xviii. 28. 31; Deut. xx. 19; Jer. xxxvi. 29, &c. In the titles of Pss. lvii., lviii., lix., and lxxv., אַל תַּשְׁחֵת may have denoted a certain musical air, named probably from some ancient composition which began with these words.

Infin. abs. הַשְׁחֵת, constr. הַשְׁחִית, Deut. xxxi. 29; 1 Sam. xxvi. 15, &c.

Part. pl. מַשְׁחִית, pl. מַשְׁחִיתִים. *Destroying,* Gen. xix. 14; Judg. xx. 42, &c. הַמַּשְׁחִית (a) *The destroyer,* Exod. xii. 23. (b) *The plunderers,* 1 Sam. xiii. 17.

Hoph. part. מָשְׁחָת. Pass. of Hiph. *Injured,* Mal. i. 14. *Polluted,* Prov. xxv. 26.

שִׁטָּה, f. (for שִׂנְטָה), pl. שִׁטִּים. Arab. سَنْط, *acacia. The Egyptian thorn; mimosa Nilotica* of Linn. from which Gum Arabic is obtained. Sing., Is. xli. 19, only. Pl. Exod. xxv. 5. 10. 13, &c. See Hierobot. tom. i., p. 498.

שָׂטַח, v. pret. aff. שְׁטָחוּם, pres. יִשְׁטַח. Constr. immed. Arab. سطح, *expandit.* Syr. ܫܛܚ, *Id.* *Spread abroad, strewed,* Num. xi. 32; 2 Sam. xvii. 19; Jer. viii. 2.

4 G

שׁמט (594) שׁיב

Infin. abs. שָׁמוֹט, Num. xi. 32. Part. שֹׁמֵט, with לְ. *Spreading abroad* (dwellings) *for* them, Job xii. 23.

Pih. שִׁמַּחְתִּי. Frequentative of Kal. *Spread abroad* the hands in prayer, Ps. lxxxviii. 10.

שׁוֹטֵט, m. i. q. שׁוֹט. *A whip, scourge,* Josh. xxiii. 13, only.

שֶׁטֶף, and שֵׁטֶף, m. *Washing away, overflowing, an inundation,* Job xxxviii. 25; Ps. xxxii. 6. Metaph., Prov. xxvii. 4; Dan. ix. 26; xi. 22; Nah. i. 8.

שָׁטַף, v. pres. יִשְׁטֹף. Constr. immed. (a) *Washed off* or *away.* (b) *Cleansed by washing.* (c) *Swept along* or *away,* of a torrent. (a) Ezek. xvi. 9. (b) Lev. xv. 11; 1 Kings xxii. 38. (c) Job xiv. 19; Ps. lxix. 3; Is. viii. 8, &c. Metaph., Dan. xi. 10. 26. 40. Part. שֹׁטֵף, pl. שֹׁטְפִים, *Overflowing,* Is. x. 22; xxviii. 2, &c. Metaph., of a horse in battle, Jer. viii. 6.

Niph. pres. יִשָּׁטֵף. Pass. of Kal, signn. (b) Lev. xv. 12. (c) Dan. xi. 22.

Puh. שֻׁטַּף. Pass. of Kal, sign. (b) Lev. vi. 21.

שׁוֹטֵר, m. pl. שֹׁטְרִים. Arab. سطر, *ordo seriesque* lapidum, arborum, hominum; سطر, *scripsit;* سَيْطَرَ, *præfectus fuit, rei curam habuit et adnotavit quæcunque ad rem gerendam spectarent. An officer, superintendent,* either civil or military. The name appears to refer either to the *orderly arrangement,* or to the *writing down,* and *enrolling* of persons and things. The LXX. render it γραμματεύς, and γραμματοεισαγωγεύς. Exod. v. 10. 14; Deut. i. 15; Josh. iii. 2; 2 Chron. xxvi. 11, &c. The application of the word appears to be of a very general character.

שְׁטַר, masc. Chald., Dan. vii. 5; where some read שְׂטַר. The former reading has been interpreted *Authority, sovereignty;* the latter, *Side.* Comp. Arab. شطر, *pars rei, pec. dimidia; latus.* Syr. ܣܛܪܐ, *latus,* once only.

שַׁי, m. *An offering, a present;* only in the phr. יוֹבִלוּ שַׁי. *They bring offerings,* Ps. lxviii. 30; lxxvi. 12; Is. xviii. 7. LXX. δῶρα. Vulg. *munera.* The etymology is uncertain. Comp. however the Arab. شيّ, *res.*

שִׁיבָה, I. f. constr. שִׁיבַת, once, Ps. cxxvi. 1: r. שׁוּב. *Returning; those who return.* In this place שָׁב שִׁיבַת, is used for the usual phr. שָׁב שְׁבוּת, *Brought back the captivity of—.* II. f. aff. שֵׂיבָתוֹ, r. יָשַׁב, *Residing, remaining,* 2 Sam. xix. 33, only.

שַׁיִט, m. *An oar, oars,* Is. xxxiii. 21. See שׁוּט.

שִׁילָה, and שֵׁלֹה, once, Gen. xlix. 10. Theologians are divided as to which of these forms ought to be taken; and then, as to how that preferred ought to be interpreted. 1st, As to the forms. According to Jahn (Heb. Bib. in loc.), the first, viz. שִׁילֹה, was unknown till about the middle of the tenth century. Up to that time, both Jews and Christians read, שֵׁלֹה. Of the centuries following also, forty codices read שֵׁלֹה (i. e. with reference to the collations of Kennicott and De Rossi), viz. five of the 12th century, twenty-two of the 13th, nine of the 14th, and four of the 15th. In two others of the 13th a marginal note gives שִׁלֹה; in one of the 16th the text has שִׁלֹה; in three of the 13th שִׁילֹה had been altered into שִׁילֹה. In one of the 13th again, שִׁילֹה, had been altered into שִׁלֹה. In three of the 13th, in one of the 14th, and one of the 15th, שִׁלֹה had been altered into שִׁילֹה. At length, however, most of the codices are for שִׁילֹה. The Greek of Venice, Σιλων; the Arab. of Erp.; and the Arab. Samaritan Commentary. The Targum of Jonathan is doubtful. The Vulgate seems to have read some form of שלח, for it has " qui mittendus est." It should seem, therefore, beyond doubt, that between the 10th and 16th centuries, the reading שִׁילֹה must have originated; and further, that very little reliance ought to be placed on the consideration of most Heb. MSS. being now in its favour. In earlier times, the contrary was evidently the fact; and this surely ought to determine the question in favour of שִׁלֹה.

As to its interpretation, Gesenius thinks that it is of little moment which reading is adopted; each having a form suitable enough to a proper name. All Jewish and Christian antiquity however took the form שִׁילֹה, as equivalent to לוֹ אֲשֶׁר. LXX. (1) τὰ ἀποκείμενα αὐτῷ; or, (2) ᾧ ἀπόκειται. Aquila, this last. Theod., i. q. LXX. 1. Sym. ᾧ ἀπόκειται. With Aquila Justin Martyr agrees, in his dialogue with Trypho, Epiphanius and Herodian, with LXX. (1). With this agrees Ezek. xxi. 32, עַד־בֹּא אֲשֶׁר־לוֹ הַמִּשְׁפָּט, which

(595)

appears to me to be a direct imitation of our passage in Genesis; and to this St. Paul's, ᾧ ἐπήγγελται (Gal. iii. 19) is probably an allusion. All the Targums, viz., of Onkelos, Jonathan, and Jerusalem, apply the place, moreover, directly to the Messiah. The passage may, therefore, be paraphrased thus:—The rod, or sceptre, of rule shall not depart from Judah, nor a Lawgiver, or executor, i. e. Ruler, from among his descendants, until he shall come whose it is (i. e. the rule), and to whom the obedience of the nations shall be rendered. Why we should recur here to a supposed proper name —which however has neither authority nor parallel in the Scriptures, and especially as this is directly opposed to the whole current of antiquity,—I must confess I cannot see; and, as the passage is much more obvious and clear without it,—whatever ingenuity it may otherwise have to boast,—the expedient is unworthy of adoption.

שִׁין, m. pl. aff. שֵׁינֵיהֶם, urine, 2 Kings xviii. 27; Is. xxxvi. 12. Syr. ܡܫܝܢ, minxit; ܡܫܝܢܐ, urina.

שִׁיצִיא, see יצא, Chald.

שִׁיר, m. aff. שִׁירוֹ, pl. שִׁירִים, aff. שִׁירָיו, &c. (a) Singing. (b) A song. (c) Instrumental music. (a) Eccl. vii. 5; Is. xxiii. 16; xxx. 29, &c. (b) Judg. v. 12; Ps. xxx. 1; xxxiii. 3; xcii. 1, &c. (c) 1 Chron. xvi. 42; 2 Chron. vii. 6; Amos vi. 5, &c.

שִׁיר, v. pret. שָׁר, pres. יָשִׁיר, apoc. יָשַׁר. (a) Sung. Constr. abs. it. immed. it. med. לְ, to, in praise of, or in prayer to. (b) Celebrated by singing, sung of; constr. immed. (a) Exod. xv. 1; Judg. v. 1; Ps. vii. 1, &c. (b) Ps. lix. 17; lxxxix. 2; ci. 1, &c.

Infin. only in the form לָשִׁיר, as if for לְהָשִׁיר, 1 Sam. xviii. 6.

Imp. pl. שִׁירוּ, Exod. xv. 21, &c.

Pih. pres. יְשׁוֹרֵר. Sounded, resounded, Zeph. ii. 14.

Part. מְשׁוֹרֵר, pl. מְשׁוֹרְרִים, f. מְשׁוֹרְרוֹת. Sounding, a singer, a musician, 1 Chron. vi. 18; xv. 16; 2 Chron. xxix. 28; Neh. vii. 67, &c.

Hoph. pres. יוּשַׁר. Pass. of Kal sign. (a) Is. xxvi. 1.

שִׁירָה, f. constr. שִׁירַת, pl. שִׁירוֹת. A song, Exod. xv. 1; Is. v. 1; Amos viii. 3, &c.

שַׁיִשׁ, m. Syr. ܫܝܫܐ, alabastrum. White marble, 1 Chron. xxix. 2, only. See שֵׁשׁ.

שִׁית, v. pret. שָׁת, pres. יָשִׁית, apoc. יָשֵׁת, יָשְׁת. Constr. immed. it. med. אֶת. I. q., שׂוּם. Set, placed, appointed, rendered. (a) Placed a thing or person. (b) Phrr. לִבּוֹ ש״, Set his heart upon, regarded, considered attentively, cared for. (c) פָּנָיו אֶל ש״, looked towards. (d) עִם יָדוֹ ש״, Assisted. (e) לְנֶגְדּוֹ ש״, Looked at, examined. (f) לְנֶגֶד עֵינָיו ש״, Looked at with approbation. (g) עֵצוֹת בְּנַפְשׁוֹ ש״, Deliberated anxiously. (h) עִם ש״, בְּ ש״, Ranked, classed with. (i) Put on ornaments. (k) Laid up treasure. (l) Appointed a person. (m) Appointed, fixed, a thing. (n) Appointed a limit, חֹק understood. (o) Imposed upon, required of. (p) Phr. עָלָיו חַטָּאת ש״, Laid sin on him, i. e. in its consequences, punished. (q) Rendered; constr. immed. and immed. or med. לְ, בְּ. (a) Gen. xxx. 40; xlvi. 4; Ps. xxx. 40, &c. (b) Exod. vii. 23; 1 Sam. iv. 20; Prov. xxiv. 32, &c. (c) Num. xxiv. 1. (d) Exod. xxiii. 1. (e) Ps. xc. 8. (f) Ps. ci. 3. (g) Ps. xiii. 3. (h) 2 Sam. xix. 29; Jer. iii. 19. (i) Exod. xxxiii. 4; Ps. xxi. 4. (l) Gen. xli. 33; 1 Kings xi. 34; Ps. xlv. 17, &c. (m) Job xiv. 13; Ps. civ. 20, &c. (n) Job xxxviii. 11. (o) Exod. xxi. 22. (p) Num. xii. 11. (q) Ps. lxxxviii. 9; Is. v. 6; Jer. xxii. 6; Hos. ii. 3, &c.

Infin. שִׁית, aff. שִׁיתִי, Exod. x. 1. (h) Job xxx. 1, &c.

Imp. שִׁית, f. שִׁיתִי, pl. שִׁיתוּ, Ps. xlviii. 14; Prov. xxvii. 23; Is. xvi. 3. (k) Job xxii. 24, &c.

Hoph. pres. יוּשַׁת. Pass. of Kal sign. (o) Exod. xxi. 30.

שִׁית, m. Putting on, wearing; a dress, Ps. lxxiii. 6; Prov. vii. 10.

שַׁיִת, m. aff. שִׁיתוֹ. Always joined with שָׁמִיר, and found only in Isaiah. From the passages in which these words occur, it appears that there were plants indigenous to Judea, and of very rapid growth there, so speedily occupying ground left out of cultivation as to render their extirpation almost hopeless. Usually Thorns, Is. v. 6; vii. 23—25; x. 17; xxvii. 4. LXX. ἄκανθα. Vulg. spinæ. The etymology is doubtful, as the word does not exist in any of the cognate dialects. Gesen. considers שָׁנָה as the original form, and שׁוּ as the primitive.

(596)

שָׁכַב, v. pres. יִשְׁכַּב. Syr. ܫܟܒ, Æth. ሰከበ : jacuit, cubavit. (a) *Lay down.* (b) Pec. *Lay down to sleep, slept.* (c) *Kept his bed.* (d) *Lay, of the slain.* (e) *Lay down in death.* (f) שׁ״עִם אֲבֹתָיו, *Lay, or slept with his fathers, died.* (g) Metaph., Of the heart, and nerves, *rested.* (h) *Lay* with a woman. [1] Med. אֶת, (אֹתָהּ). [2] Med. עִם. [3] Immed. (i) *Lay* with a man. [1] Med. אֶת. [2] Med. עִם. (a) Num. xxiii. 27; xxiv. 9; 2 Kings iv. 34. (b) Deut. xxiv. 13; 1 Sam. xxvi. 5; 2 Sam. xii. 16, &c. (c) 2 Sam. xiii. 6; Ps. xli. 9. (d) Ezek. xxxi. 18; xxxii. 21. (e) Job iii. 12; xiv. 12; Is. xiv. 8. (f) Gen. xlvii. 30; 2 Sam. vii. 12; 1 Kings xi. 21, &c. (g) Job xxx. 17; Eccl. ii. 23. (h), [1] Gen. xxvi. 10; Num. v. 13. 19, &c. [2] Exod. xxii. 16; Deut. xxii. 23. 25, &c. [3] Deut. xxviii. 30. (i), [1] Gen. xix. 33, 34. [2] Gen. xix. 32. 35.
Infin. abs. שָׁכֹב, constr. שְׁכַב, aff. שָׁכְבְּךָ, Lev. xv. 24; 1 Kings i. 21; Prov. vi. 22, &c.
Imp. שְׁכָב, שִׁכְבָה, f. שִׁכְבִי, Gen. xix. 34; xxxix. 7; 2 Sam. xiii. 5.
Part. שֹׁכֵב, f. שֹׁכֶבֶת, pl. שֹׁכְבִים, 1 Sam. xxvi. 6. (c) 2 Kings ix. 16. שֹׁכְבֵי קֶבֶר, *Those who lie in the grave,* Ps. lxxxviii. 6.
Hiph. הִשְׁכִּיב, pres. יַשְׁכִּיב. Constr. immed. (a) Causnt. of Kal. *Caused to lie, to lie down, placed.* (b) Either *Caused to rest, stopped,* or, *poured out, emptied.* Comp. Arab. سَكَبَ, *effudit* aquam. (a) 1 Kings iii. 21; xvii. 19; Hos. ii. 20. (b) Job xxxviii. 37.
Infin. הַשְׁכֵּב, 2 Sam. viii. 2. Probably *Casting a lot.*
Hoph. הָשְׁכַּב. Pass. of Hiph. *Was placed, was laid,* Ezek. xxxii. 32.
Part. מֻשְׁכָּב, 2 Kings iv. 32.

שְׁכָבָה, f. constr. שִׁכְבַת. (a) *The act of lying down,* or *lying with;* in the phr. שִׁכְבַת זֶרַע, Lev. xv. 16, &c. (b) *A layer* or *covering* of dew, Exod. xvi. 13, 14. In both of these applications the Arab. سَكَبَ, is taken by some, but this is unnecessary.

שְׁכֹבֶת, f. aff. שְׁכָבְתּוֹ, *Id.* sign. (a) Lev. xviii. 20. 23; xx. 9; Num. v. 20.

שְׁכוֹל, masc. r. שׁכל. (a) *Privation of children.* Metaph., Is. xlvii. 8, 9. (b) *Destitution,* Ps. xxxv. 12.

שַׁכּוּל, m. שַׁכֻּלָה, f. pl. שַׁכֻּלוֹת, r. שׁכל. (a) *Childless,* Jer. xviii. 21. (b) *Deprived of its young,* of a bear, 2 Sam. xvii. 8; Prov. xvii. 12; Hos. xiii. 8. (c) *Without young,* of a ewe, Cant. iv. 2; vi. 6.

שִׁכּוֹר, m. pl. שִׁכּוֹרִים, constr. שִׁכּוֹרֵי, fem. שִׁכֹּרָה. *One who is drunken, a drunkard,* 1 Sam. i. 13; xxv. 36; Is. xxviii. 1; Joel i. 5, &c.

שָׁכַח, v. for שָׁכֵחַ, pres. יִשְׁכַּח. Constr. immed. it. med. אֶת, it. מִן, before an Infin. (a) *Forgot.* (b) *Disregarded, neglected.* (a) Gen. xxvii. 45; xl. 23; Deut. iv. 9; Ps. cvi. 13, &c. (b) Deut. viii. 14; Ps. ix. 13; Prov. ii. 17, &c.
Infin. abs. שָׁכֹחַ, Deut. viii. 19.
Imp. f. שִׁכְחִי, Ps. xlv. 11.
Part. pl. constr. שֹׁכְחֵי, Job viii. 13; Ps. L. 22.
Niph. נִשְׁכַּח, pres. יִשָּׁכַח, and יִשָּׁכֵחַ. Pass. of Kal, (a) Gen. xli. 30; Deut. xxxi. 21; Eccl. ix. 5, &c. (b) Ps. ix. 19.
Part. נִשְׁכָּח, pl. נִשְׁכָּחִים, f. נִשְׁכָּחָה, and נִשְׁכַּחַת. *Forgotten,* Job xxviii. 4; Eccl. ii. 16; Is. xxiii. 15, 16.
Pih. שִׁכַּח. *Caused to be forgotten,* Lam. ii. 6.
Hiph. Infin. הַשְׁכִּיחַ. *To cause to forget,* Jer. xxiii. 27.
Hith. pres. יִשְׁתַּכְּחוּ, i. q. Niph., Eccl. viii. 10.

שִׁכְחָה, m. pl. שְׁכֵחִים, constr. שְׁכֵחֵי. *Forgetting, neglecting,* Ps. ix. 18; Is. lxv. 11.

שְׁכַח, Chald. v. Syr. ܐܫܟܚ, *invenit. Found.*
Ithpe. הִשְׁתְּכַח. *Was found, existed, was,* Ezra vi. 2; Dan. ii. 35; v. 11, &c.
Aph. הַשְׁכַּח, pres. יְהַשְׁכַּח. *Found, discovered,* Ezra iv. 19; Dan. ii. 25; vi. 6, &c.
Infin. sign. הַשְׁכָּחָה, Dan. vi. 5.

שָׁכַךְ, v. pret. f. in pause, שָׁכָכָה, pres. יָשֹׁךְ. Cogn. שׁחח. (a) *Stooped.* (b) *Lowered itself, abated.* (b) Of water, Gen. viii. 1 : of anger, Esth. vii. 10.
Infin. sign. (a) שֹׁךְ, Jer. v. 26 : sign. (b) שֹׁךְ, Esth. ii. 1.
Hiph. הִשְׁכִּתִּי. *Caused to abate, quieted,* Num. xvii. 20.

שָׁכַל, v. pret. שָׁכֹלְתִּי, and in pause, שָׁכָלְתִּי, pres. יְשַׁכֵּל. Constr. abs. it. immed. Arab. سَكِلَ, *orbatus vel orbus fuit* nato vel amico.

שכל (597) שכם

Became childless, Gen. xxvii. 45; xliii. 14; 1 Sam. xv. 33.
Part. pass. f. שְׁכוּלָה. *Deprived of children, childless*, Is. xlix. 21.
Pih. f. שִׁכֵּל, pres. יְשַׁכֵּל. Constr. immed. it. med. אֶת, it. abs. (a) *Made childless.* (b) *Stripped* a land *of inhabitants.* (c) *Destroyed,* of a sword. (d) *Lost their young,* pec. by abortion. (e) *Lost its fruit,* of a vine. (f) *Of a land, lost its inhabitants.* (a) Gen. xlii. 36; Lev. xxvi. 22; 1 Sam. xv. 33, &c. (b) Ezek. v. 17; xiv. 15. (c) Deut. xxxii. 25. (d) Gen. xxxi. 38; Job xxi. 10. (e) Mal. iii. 11. (f) Ezek. xxxvi. 14, 15.
Infin. aff. שַׁכְּלָם, (f) Ezek. xxxvi. 12.
Part. fem. מְשַׁכֵּלָה, and מְשַׁכֶּלֶת, (d) Exod. xxiii. 26. (f) 2 Kings ii. 19. 21; Ezek. xxxvi. 13.
Hiph. part. מַשְׁכִּיל. I. q. Pih. (f) Hos. ix. 14.

שִׁכֻּלִים, pl. m. aff. שִׁכֻּלָיִךְ. *The loss of children*, Is. xlix. 20.

שִׁכְלֵל, v. see כלל, Chald.

שְׁכֶם, m. in pause, שָׁכֶם, aff. שִׁכְמִי. (a) *A shoulder, the shoulders*, Gen. ix. 23; 1 Sam. ix. 2; Job xxxi. 36; Is. x. 2, &c. Phrr. (b) הִפְנָה שִׁכְמוֹ, *Turned his back, turned himself about*, 1 Sam. x. 9. (c) שְׁכֶם אֶחָד, *With one shoulder*, i. e. *with united efforts, with one mind*, Zeph. iii. 9. The metaphor is taken from two persons carrying together a burden on their shoulders. (d) Probably *A load,* i. e. as much as can be carried; thence *a portion*, Gen. xlviii. 22.

שכם, v. Kal non occ.
Hiph. הִשְׁכִּים, pres. יַשְׁכִּים, apoc. יַשְׁכֵּם. According to Ewald, whom Gesenius follows, the original meaning of this word was, *to place a load on the shoulder, to load*, pec. *to load beasts of burden preparatory to a journey;* hence *to prepare for a journey*. Comp. Æth. ሰከመ: *bajulavit*. (a) *Arose in the morning*, usually with בַּבֹּקֶר. (b) When joined to another verb, either with or without ו, it often should be translated, *as soon as he arose.* (c) *Came in the morning* to a place, with אֶל, or לְ. (a) 1 Sam. xv. 2; Job i. 5, &c. (b) Gen. xix. 2; xx. 8; Judg. xix. 9, &c. (c) Gen. xix. 27; Cant. vii. 13.
Infin. הַשְׁכֵּם, הַשְׁכִּים, Prov. xxvii. 14; אַשְׁכִּים after the Chaldee form, Jer. xxv. 3; used adverbially. (a) *In the morning*, 1 Sam. xvii. 16. (b) *Early, without delay*, Jer. vii. 13. 25; xi. 7, &c.
Imp. הַשְׁכֵּם, Exod. viii. 20; ix. 13; 1 Sam. xxix. 10.
Part. מַשְׁכִּים. (a) Adverbially, *In the morning*, Jer. v. 8. (b) מַשְׁכִּימֵי קוּם, *Rising early*, Ps. cxxvii. 2. (c) מַשְׁכִּימֵי בַבֹּקֶר, Id., Is. v. 11.

שִׁכְמָה, f. i. q. שְׁכֶם. *The shoulder, the shoulder-blade*, Job xxxi. 22. According to some the true reading is שִׁכְמָה, from שְׁכֶם.

שָׁכַן, and שָׁכֵן, v. pres. יִשְׁכֹּן. Constr. abs. it. immed. it. med. בְּ, עַל, עִם.
Arab. سَكَنَ, *quietus, tranquillus fuit; habitavit domum*. Syr. ܫܟܢ, *habitavit*. (a) *Lay down to rest*. (b) *Rested*. (c) *Rested*, of inanimate things. (d) *Continued*. (e) *Dwelt*: spoken [1] *Of God*. [2] *Of men*. [3] *Of animals*. [4] *Of judgment, wisdom*, &c. (f) *Inhabited* a land *in security*. (g) *Of a place, was inhabited*. (a) Deut. xxxiii. 20; Ps. xvi. 9. (b) Deut. v. 17; Ps. lv. 7; Prov. vii. 11. (c) Exod. xl. 35; Num. ix. 18; Josh. xxii. 19; Job xxxviii. 19, &c. (d) Ps. xciv. 17; cxx. 6. (e), [1] Exod. xxv. 8; Ps. lxviii. 17; Is. lvii. 15, &c. [2] Gen. xvi. 12; Exod. xxv. 8; Judg. v. 17, &c. [3] Is. xiii. 21; Ezek. xvii. 23; xxx. 13, &c. [4] Prov. viii. 12; Is. xxxii. 16, &c. (f) Prov. ii. 21; x. 30. (g) Is. xiii. 20; Jer. xxxiii. 15; xlvi. 26, &c.
Infin. constr. שְׁכֹן, aff. שָׁכְנִי, Gen. xxxv. 22; Deut. xii. 5, &c.
Imp. שְׁכֹן, pl. שִׁכְנוּ, Gen. xxvi. 2; Jer. xlviii. 28.
Part. שֹׁכֵן, and שֹׁכְנִי, fem. שֹׁכֶנֶת, for שֹׁכְנַת, pl שֹׁכְנִים, constr. שֹׁכְנֵי, aff. שֹׁכְנֵיהֶם. *Dwelling: an inhabitant*, Gen. xvi. 13; Deut. xxxiii. 16; Jer. li. 13, &c.
Part. pass. pl. constr. שֹׁכְנֵי בָאֳהָלִים שׁ״. *Settled in tents, dwelling in them*, Judg. viii. 11.
Pih. שִׁכֵּן, pres. אֲשַׁכְּנָה. Constr. immed. it. med. אֶת. Causat. of Kal. (a) *Caused to dwell*. (b) *Placed*. (c) Phr. שִׁמּוֹ, *Placed his name* there; *chose as his peculiar residence*. (a) Jer. vii. 3. 7. (b) Ps. lxxviii. 60.
Infin. שַׁכֵּן, (a) Num. xiv. 30. (c) Deut. xii. 11; xiv. 23, &c.
Hiph. הִשְׁכִּין, pres. apoc. יַשְׁכֵּן. Causat of Kal. (a) *Caused to dwell*. (b) *Fixed*,

שָׁכַן *placed.* (a) Job xi. 14; Ps. lxxviii. 55; Ezek. xxxii. 4. (b) Gen. iii. 24; Josh. xviii. 1.

שְׁכֵן, Chald. v. pres. pl. יִשְׁכְּנֻן, *Id.,* Dan. iv. 18.

Paḥ. שַׁכֵּן, i. q. Piḥ. (c) Ezra vi. 12.

שָׁכֵן, masc. aff. שְׁכֵנוֹ. *A dwelling,* Deut. xii. 5.

שָׁכֵן, m. constr. שְׁכַן, aff. שְׁכֵנוֹ, pl. aff. שְׁכֵנַי, &c. fem. aff. שְׁכֶנְתָּהּ, pl. שְׁכֵנוֹת. (a) *Dwelling,* habitually. (b) *An inhabitant.* (c) *A neighbour.* (d) *A neighbouring people.* (a) Deut. xxxiii. 12. (b) Is. xxxiii. 24; Jer. vi. 21; Hos. v. 10. (c) Exod. iii. 22; xii. 4; Ruth iv. 17; Ps. xxxi. 12. (d) Ps. xliv. 14; lxxix. 4; Jer. xii. 14, &c.

שֵׁכָר, v. Arab. سَكَر, *vinum, pec. potus ex dactylis et herbâ* كشوت, *appellatâ paratus;* سَكِر, *ebrius fuit.* (a) *Any exhilarating* or *intoxicating drink.* (b) *It is distinguished from* יַיִן, *with which it is often joined;* (c) *but which it includes.* (a) Num. vi. 3; Ps. lxix. 13; Prov. xxxi. 6, &c. (b) Lev. x. 9; Deut. xxix. 5; 1 Sam. i. 15, &c. (c) Num. xxviii. 7.

שָׁכַר, v. שָׁכְרוּ, pres. יִשְׁכַּר. Constr. abs. it. immed. of the drink. (a) *Drank* an exhilarating or intoxicating drink. (b) *Was exhilarated with drink.* (c) *Became intoxicated.* (d) *Became giddy* with astonishment or sorrow. (a) Is. xlix. 26. (b) Gen. xliii. 34. (c) Gen. ix. 21. Metaph., Lev. iv. 21; Nah. iii. 11. (d) Is. xxix. 9.

Infin. שָׁכְרָה, (b) Hag. i. 6.

Imp. pl. שִׁכְרוּ, (b) Metaph., Cant. v. 1. (c) Metaph., Jer. xxv. 27.

Part. pass. f. constr. שִׁכֻרַת, (d) Is. li. 21.

Piḥ. pres. יְשַׁכֵּר. Constr. immed. Causat. of Kal, signn. (b), (c), and (d). (b) 2 Sam. xi. 13. (d) Is. lxiii. 6.

Infin. שַׁכֵּר, (c) Hab. ii. 15.

Part. f. מְשַׁכְּרָה, (b) Metaph., Jer. li. 7.

Hiph. pres. הִשְׁכִּיר. I. q. Piḥ. (b) Metaph., Jer. li. 39. 57. (c) Metaph., Deut. xxxii. 42.

Imp. pl. aff. הַשְׁכִּירֻהוּ, (c) Metaph., Jer. xlviii. 26.

Hith. pres. f. תִּשְׁתַּכָּרִי. *Wilt thou make thyself drunk,* 1 Sam. i. 14.

שִׁכָּרוֹן, masc. *Drunkenness, giddiness.* Metaph., Ezek. xxiii. 33; xxxix. 19.

שַׁל, m. once, 2 Sam. vi. 7. *Fault, error:* r. שלה. LXX. προπετεία, ἐκνοίᾳ. Vulg. *temeritate.*

שֶׁל, i. q. אֲשֶׁר לְ. This combination occurs but seldom in the Scripture, though it is very common in Rabbinical Hebrew. כַּרְמִי שֶׁלִּי, *My* (own) *vineyard,* Cant. i. 6; viii. 12. בְּשֶׁלְּמִי, *On account of what belongs to whom?* i. e. *on account of whose conduct?* or, perhaps, *by what conduct of whom,* i. e. *who is the cause of it and what he has done?* Jonah i. 7. בְּשֶׁלִּי, *On account of what belongs to me,* i. e. *on account of what I have done,* Jonah i. 12. In Eccl. viii. 17, בְּשֶׁל אֲשֶׁר, is supposed by Gesenius, with some probability, to be a false reading for בְּגָל אֲשֶׁר.

שַׁלְאֲנָן, m. once, Job xxi. 23. Probably a compound of שלה, and שׁאן or שׁאֲנָן. *Wholly at rest.*

שָׁלַב, v. Kal non occ. Chald. שְׁלַב, *cohœsit, conjunctus fuit.* Paḥ. *conjunxit.* Puh. part. pl. f. מְשֻׁלָּבוֹת. *Joined together,* Exod. xxvi. 17; xxxvi. 22.

שְׁלַבִּים, pl. m. *Joinings, edges, borders,* 1 Kings vii. 28, 29. LXX. τῶν ἐξεχομένων. Vulg. *juncturas.*

שֶׁלֶג, masc. Arab. ثَلْج, *nix.* Syr. ܬܠܓܐ, *Id. Snow,* Exod. iv. 6; Job vi. 16; Ps. cxlvii. 16, &c.

שָׁלַג, v. only in Hiph. pres. תַּשְׁלֵג. Arab. ثلج, *ninxit cœlum;* ثلج, *quietus et tranquillus fuit* animus; *tranquillo, lœto fuit* animo. IV. *Lætitiâ affecit;* أَثْلَج, *victoria, bona fortuna.* Ps. lxviii. 15, בָּהּ תַּשְׁלֵג בְּצַלְמוֹן, *In it* (in that event) *thou givest snow,* i. e. comfort *in Salmon.* See my note on Job vi. 16.

שָׁלָה, v. for שָׁלַו, pret. שָׁלַוְתִּי, pl. שָׁלוּ, pres. pl. יִשְׁלָיוּ, apoc. יֶשֶׁל. Constr. abs. Arab. سَلَا, r. سلو, *tranquillus fuit.* (a) *Was prosperous, at ease, quiet, negligent.* (b) *Made prosperous, gave ease to.* (a) Job iii. 26; Ps. cxxii. 6; Jer. xii. 1, &c. (b) Job xxvii. 8: where see my note.

Niph. pres. יִשָּׁלוּ. *Became negligent,*

שלה (599) שלו

2 Chron. xxix. 11. LXX. μὴ διαλίπητε. Vulg. nolite negligere.

Hiph. pres. הַשְׁלָה. Either *Promised happiness to, flattered*, or,—taking the Chald. שָׁלָה, *erravit, aberravit,—deceived*, 2 Kings iv. 28. LXX. πλανήσεις. Vulg. *illudas*.

שָׁלֵה, Chald. m. *Prosperous, at ease*, Dan. iv. 1.

שָׁלֵה, Chald. for שְׁלִי, which see, Dan. iii. 29.

שַׁלְהֶבֶת, f. See לָהַב. Syr. ܫܠܗܒܬ, *inflammavit, accendit, combussit*. A *flame, destructive fire*, Job xv. 30; Ezek. xxi. 3. שַׁלְהֶבֶתְיָה, *Flame of the Lord*, i. e. *an intense flame*, Cant. viii. 6.

שְׁלוּ, masc. aff. שַׁלְוִי. *Prosperity*, Ps. xxx. 7, only.

שָׁלֵו, שָׁלִיו, and שָׁלֵיו, m. pl. constr. שַׁלְוֵי, f. שְׁלֵוָה. (a) *Prosperous, at ease*. (b) *Prosperity, ease*. (a) Job xvi. 12; xxi. 23; Ps. lxxiii. 12; Jer. xlix. 31; Zech. vii. 7, &c. (b) Job xx. 20.

שָׁלוּ, fem. Chald. *Negligence, failure*, Ezra iv. 22; vi. 9; Dan. vi. 5.

שַׁלְוָה, f. שָׁלַו, pl. aff. שַׁלְוֹתָיִךְ. *Prosperity, ease, quiet, negligence*, Ps. cxxii. 7; Prov. i. 32; Jer. xxii. 21, &c.

שְׁלוה, Chald. f. aff. שְׁלֵוְתָךְ, *Id.*, Dan. iv. 24.

שִׁלּוּחִים, pl. masc. aff. שִׁלּוּחֶיהָ, r. שׁלח. The act of *sending, sending away*. (a) The *divorce* of a wife, Exod. xviii. 2. (b) The *renunciation* of a claim, Mic. i. 14. (b) .*Presents*, pec. as a dowry, 1 Kings ix. 16.

שָׁלוֹם, m. constr. שְׁלוֹם, aff. שְׁלוֹמִי, &c. r. שלם. Cogn. שלה. Arab. سَلَام, *incolumitas, salus, pax*. Syr. ܫܠܡܐ, *salus*. *Peace*. (a) *Peace*, as opposed to war. (b) *Public quiet*, as opposed to civil dissensions. (c) *Prosperity*. (d) *Safety*. (e) *Soundness*, of body. (f) *Friendliness*, friendship. Phrr. (g) קְרָא אֲלֵיהֶם לְשָׁלוֹם, *Named to them peaceable proposals*. (h) עָנָם שָׁלוֹם, *Gave them a peaceable answer*. (i) עָשָׂה לָהֶם שָׁלוֹם, *Made peace with them*. (k) Used in friendly salutations and inquiries : [1] הֲשָׁלוֹם לוֹ, *Is he well?* or *Is it well with him?* [2] הֲשָׁלוֹם, *Is all well?* [3] שָׁאַל לָהֶם לְשָׁלוֹם, *Inquired after their welfare*. [4] שָׁאֲלָתָם־לוֹ בִשְׁמִי לְשָׁלוֹם, *Salute him in my name*. (l) Used in assurances of safety or friendship : [1] שָׁלוֹם לָךְ, *It is well with thee, there is no cause for thee to fear*. [2] לְךָ שָׁלוֹם, *Go in peace*. (m) Used elliptically, for לְךָ שָׁלוֹם, or בְּשָׁלוֹם. (n) אִישׁ שְׁלוֹמִי, *My friend*. (o) — אֱנוֹשׁ, *Id.* (p) Pl. מוּסַר שְׁלוֹמֵינוּ, *Chastisement of our peace*, i. e. procuring it. (q) שַׁלְמָיו, *His friends*. (r) וְלִשְׁלוֹמִים לְמוֹקֵשׁ, *And a snare to them when in security*. (a) Judg. iv. 17; 1 Sam. vii. 14; 1 Kings v. 12, &c. (b) Lev. xxvi. 6; Num. vi. 26; 2 Chron. xv. 5, &c. (c) Num. xxv. 12; 1 Kings ii. 33; Ps. lxxii. 7, &c. (d) Gen. xxvi. 29; 1 Sam. xx. 7. 21; 2 Sam. xviii. 29, &c. (e) Ps. xxxviii. 4. (f) Gen. xxxvii. 4; Ps. xxviii. 3; xxxiv. 15, &c. (g) Deut. xx. 10; Judg. xxi. 13. (h) Deut. xx. 11. (i) Josh. ix. 15. (k), [1] Gen. xxix. 6; 2 Kings iv. 26. [2] 2 Kings v. 21. [3] Gen. xliii. 27; 1 Sam. xvii. 22; xxx. 21, &c. [4] 1 Sam. xxv. 5. (l), [1] Gen. xliii. 23; Judg. vi. 24; xix. 20. [2] Exod. iv. 18; Judg. xviii. 6; 1 Sam. i. 17, &c. (m) 1 Sam. xvi. 4; xxv. 5; 2 Sam. xvii. 3, &c. (n) Ps. xli. 10. (o) Jer. xx. 10; xxxviii. 22. (p) Is. liii. 5. (q) Ps. lv. 21. (r) Ps. lxix. 23.

שִׁלּוֹם, see שָׁלָם.

שָׁלוֹשׁ, see שָׁלֹשׁ.

שֶׁלַח, masc. aff. שִׁלְחוֹ, pl. aff. שְׁלָחֶיךָ. *Sending, throwing*. (a) A *missile; a weapon* of any kind. Arab. سلْح, *arma*. (b) *Throwing aside; rejection, contempt*. (c) Pl. *Shoots; produce*. (a) 2 Chron. xxiii. 10; xxxii. 5; Joel ii. 8. (b) Job xxxiii. 18, where see my note; xxxvi. 12. (c) Cant. iv. 13. In Neh. iv. 17, אִישׁ שִׁלְחוֹ הַמַּיִם, cannot, I think, be the true reading. The LXX. have not the clause. The most probable reading seems to me to have been, בְיָדָם, or אִישׁ שִׁלְחוֹ בְּיָדָיִם —, each (having) *his weapon in their* (his) *hands*, or *hand*. See the preceding context.

שָׁלַח, v. pres. יִשְׁלַח. Constr. immed. it. med. אֶת. (a) *Sent*, [1] A person, or [2] *Thing;* with אֶל or לְ of the person to whom sent. (b) *Sent word, sent orders*, or *persons;* [1] With וְ, and another verb. [2] With לְ and an Infin. (c) בְּ דָּבָר, *Sent a message to*. (d) — without בְּ, *Id.*, with [1] אֶל. [2] עַל, [3] or לְ. (e) יָדוֹ, *Put forth his hand*. (f) בְּ יָדוֹ, *Laid his hand on*, to seize or injure. (g) שׁ׳ יָדוֹ אֶל, *Laid his hand on*, to injure. (h) שׁ׳ יָדוֹ עַל, *Laid his hand*

שלח (600) שלח

on, to seize, or support. (i) — without יָדוֹ, שׁ" אֶל, *Put forth his hand to.* (k) *Put forth, applied,* of any thing in the hand. (l) *Sent forth, shot out* arrows. (m) *Sent away.* (n) *Put forth, inflicted.* (a), [1] Gen. xlii. 4; Num. xiii. 16; Judg. xi. 17, &c. [2] Gen. xlv. 23; Neh. vi. 19; Ps. lxxviii. 25, &c. (b), [1] Gen. xxvii. 45; Job i. 4; Ps. cv. 20, &c. [2] Num. xvi. 12; 1 Sam. xxii. 11, &c. (c) Is. ix. 7. (d), [1] Gen. xxxviii. 25; 2 Sam. xix. 12; 2 Kings xiv. 9, &c. [2] 2 Chron. xxviii. 16. [3] 2 Chron. xvii. 7. (e) Gen. iii. 22; Exod. ix. 15; 2 Sam. xv. 5, &c. (f) Exod. xxii. 7; 1 Sam. xxvi. 9; Ps. lv. 21, &c. (g) Gen. xxii. 12; Exod. xxiv. 11; 2 Sam. xviii. 12, &c. (h) 1 Kings xiii. 4; 1 Chron. xiii. 10. (i) 2 Sam. vi. 6. (k) 1 Sam. xiv. 27. (l) 2 Sam. xxii. 15; Ps. xviii. 15. (n) Ps. cv. 28; cxi. 9; cxxxv. 9, &c. פִּיךָ שָׁלַחְתָּ בְרָעָה, *Didst order, commission thy mouth for evil*, Ps. L. 19.

Infin. abs. שָׁלֹחַ, const. שְׁלֹחַ, aff. שָׁלְחִי, Num. xxii. 15. 37; xxxii. 8. (k) Is. lviii. 9, &c.

Imp. שְׁלַח, שִׁלְחָה, pl. שִׁלְחוּ, Gen. xliii. 8. (d, 2) Jer. xxix. 31. (l) Ps. cxliv. 6. (k) Joel iv. 13. •(m) 2 Sam. xiii. 17.

Part. שֹׁלֵחַ, aff. שֹׁלְחִי, pl. שֹׁלְחִים, aff. שֹׁלְחָיו, 2 Sam. xxiv. 13; Job v. 10. (k) Ezek. viii. 17.

Part. pass. שָׁלוּחַ, f. שְׁלוּחָה, Gen. xxxii. 18; 1 Kings xiv. 6.

Niph. Infin. הִשָּׁלוֹחַ. *To be sent*, Esth. iii. 13.

Pih. שִׁלַּח, pres. יְשַׁלַּח, in pause יְשַׁלֵּחַ. Constr. immed. it. med. אֶת. (a) *Sent*, a person or thing. (b) *Sent away.* (c) *Allowed to depart, dismissed.* (d) *Set at liberty.* (e) חָפְשִׁי שׁ", *Id.* (f) הַחוּצָה שׁ", *Sent out, gave in marriage.* (g) *Sent away* a wife, *divorced* her. (h) *Sent, put* into a place. (i) יָדוֹ שׁ", *Put forth his hand.* (k) בָּאֵשׁ שׁ", *Set on fire.* (l) *Sent a calamity, inflicted* it; with בְּ, עַל, אַחֲרֵי. (m) *Caused.* (n) *Threw.* (o) *Threw off.* (p) מֵעַל פָּנָיו שׁ", *Cast out of his sight,* ceased to regard. (q) *Shot forth* branches, of a plant. (a) Gen. xxviii. 6; Exod. xxiii. 27; Jer. xxvii. 2, &c. (b) 1 Sam. xx. 22; 2 Sam. iii. 22; Job xxii. 9, &c. (c) Exod. v. 2; viii. 27; Judg. vii. 8, &c. (d) Gen. xliii. 14; Lev. xiv. 7; xvi. 22, &c. (e) Job xiii. 5; Jer. xxxiv. 14. 16, &c. (f) Judg. xii. 9. (g) Deut. xxiv. 4; Is. L. 1; Jer. iii. 8, &c. (h) Exod. xxii. 4. (i) Prov. xxxi. 19. (k)

Judg. i. 8; xx. 48; Ps. lxxiv. 7. (l) Lev. xxvi. 25; Jer. ix. 15; Ezek. v. 17, &c. (m) Prov. xvi. 28. (n) Jer. xxxviii. 11. (o) Job xxx. 11. (p) 1 Kings ix. 7. (q) Ps. lxxx. 12; Jer. xvii. 8; Ezek. xvii. 7, &c.

Infin. abs. שַׁלֵּחַ, constr. שַׁלַּח, aff. שַׁלְּחוֹ, Gen. viii. 10; Exod. xi. 1; Deut. xxii. 7, &c.

Imp. שַׁלַּח, pl. שַׁלְּחוּ, Exod. iv. 23. (n) Eccl. xi. 1.

Part. מְשַׁלֵּחַ, pl. מְשַׁלְּחִים, constr. מְשַׁלְּחֵי, Gen. xliii. 4; 1 Sam. vi. 3; Is. xxxii. 20, &c.

Puh. שֻׁלַּח, pres. יְשֻׁלַּח. Pass. of Pih. signn. (a), (c), (d), (g), and (n). (a) Judg. v. 15; Prov. xvii. 11; Dan. x. 11; Obad. 1. (c) Gen. xliv. 3. (g) Is. L. 1. (n) Job xviii. 8.

Part. מְשֻׁלָּח. *Left to himself, thrown out, neglected,* Prov. xxix. 16; Is. xvi. 2; xxvii. 10.

Hiph. הִשְׁלִיחַ, i. q. Pih. signn. (a) and (l). (l) With בְּ, Lev. xxvi. 22; Ezek. xiv. 12; Amos viii. 11.

Infin. הַשְׁלִיחַ, (a) 2 Kings xv. 37.

Part. מַשְׁלִיחַ, (l) Exod. viii. 21.

שְׁלַח, Chald. v. pres. יִשְׁלַח. (a) *Sent,* [1] A person or [2] Thing. (b) *Sent word, sent orders.* (c) יְדֵהּ שׁ", *Put forth his hand.* (a), [1] Dan. iii. 28; vi. 23. [2] Ezra iv. 11. 17; v. 6, 7. (b) Ezra iv. 14; v. 17; Dan. iii. 2, &c. (c) Ezra vi. 12.

Pehil, part. שְׁלִיחַ. Pass. signn. (a) Ezra vii. 14. (c) Dan. v. 24.

שִׁלְחוֹת, pl. f. aff. שִׁלְחוֹתֶיהָ, r. שלח. *Shoots, branches,* Is. xvi. 8, only.

שֻׁלְחָן, m. constr. שֻׁלְחַן, aff. שֻׁלְחָנִי, pl. שֻׁלְחָנוֹת, constr. שֻׁלְחֲנוֹת, r. שלח. *That on which food is set,* or *sent* to the guests; *a tray, table,* Exod. xxv. 23; 1 Sam. xx. 34; 1 Kings xiii. 20, &c. Phrr. שׁ" עָרַךְ, *Set out, provided a table*, Ps. xxiii. 5; lxxviii. 19; Is. lxv. 11, &c. הַפָּנִים שׁ", *The table of shew-bread,* Num. iv. 7. שֻׁלְחָנוֹ אֹכְלֵי, *Those who eat at his table,* 2 Sam. xix. 29; 1 Kings ii. 7.

שָׁלַט, v. pres. יִשְׁלַט. Syr. ܫܠܛ, *dominatus est.* Arab. سلط, *dominium, imperium;* تسلط, *dominium obtinuit.* Constr. med. בְּ, עַל. *Ruled, had* or *assumed power over,* Neh. v. 15; Esth. ix. 1; Eccl. ii. 19; viii. 9.

שלם (601) שלי

Infin. constr. שְׁלוֹם, Esth. ix. 1.
Hiph. הִשְׁלִיט, pres. יַשְׁלִיט. Constr. immed. (a) *Allowed to rule.* (b) *Gave authority to, permitted.* (a) Ps. cxix. 133. (b) Eccl. v. 18; vi. 2.

שְׁלֵם, Chald. v. pres. יִשְׁלַם. Constr. med. בְּ. *Id.* (a) *Ruled*, Dan. ii. 39; v. 7. 16. (b) *Had power over*, of fire, Dan. iii. 27. (c) *Seized*, of a lion, Dan. vi. 25.
Aph. pret. aff. הַשְׁלְטֵהּ. *Caused to rule*, Dan. ii. 38. 48.

שִׁלְטוֹן, m. *Power, authority,* Eccl. viii. 4. 8. Arab. سُلْطَان, *potestas*.

שִׁלְטוֹנִין, Chald. pl. constr. שִׁלְטוֹנֵי. *The authorities, rulers,* Dan. iii. 2, 3.

שְׁלָטִים, pl. m. constr. שִׁלְטֵי, aff. שִׁלְטֵיהֶם. A word variously translated, and of doubtful import. Arab. سَلَطَ, *durus;* سَلِيط, *acutus.* *Arms* of some kind, but whether offensive or defensive, appears uncertain, usually *Shields*, 2 Sam. viii. 7; 2 Kings xi. 10; Ezek. xxvii. 11, &c. LXX. ὅπλα, φαρέτρας, βολίδες, χλιδῶνας, κλοιούς, ἐρισούς. Sym. πανοπλίαν. Vulg. *arma, armatura, peltas, pharetras.*

שָׁלְטָן, Chald. m. constr. שָׁלְטָן, def. שָׁלְטָנָא, aff. שָׁלְטָנֵהּ, pl. def. שָׁלְטָנַיָּא. *Authority, sovereignty*, Dan. iii. 33; iv. 19; vii. 6, &c.

שַׁלֶּטֶת, see שַׁלִּיט.

שְׁלִי, m. in pause שָׁלִי, r. שׁלה. *Quiet.* בְּשֶׁלִי, *Quietly, privately*, 2 Sam. iii. 27, only.

שִׁלְיָה, f. aff. שִׁלְיָתָהּ, once, Deut. xxviii. 57. Arab. سلى, *membrana, quâ in utero fœtus involutus est. The after-birth.*

שַׁלְיוּ, see שָׁלֵו.

שַׁלִּיט, m. pl. שַׁלִּיטִים, f. שַׁלֶּטֶת, r. שׁלט. (a) *A ruler, one possessed of authority,* Gen. xlii. 6; Eccl. vii. 19; viii. 8; x. 5. (b) *Unrestrained, violent,* Ezek. xvi. 30.

שַׁלִּיט, Chald. m. def. שַׁלִּיטָא, pl. שַׁלִּיטִין. (a) I. q. Heb. (a), Dan. ii. 10. 15; iv. 23, &c. (b) *Permitted by authority, allowed, lawful,* Ezra vii. 24.

שָׁלִישׁ, m. aff. שָׁלִישׁוֹ, pl. שָׁלִישִׁים, aff. שָׁלִישָׁיו, r. שׁלשׁ. (a) *A measure,* probably the third part of an *Ephah,* and thus equivalent to a *Seah.* (b) *Used generically of any measure; By measures, abundantly.*

(c) *An officer of high rank,* probably *One, third in rank.* (d) *A peculiar class of soldiers so called,* but what was their precise character cannot be determined. (e) *A musical instrument;* according to some *a triangle;* others, *a harp with three strings.* (f) As an adj. *princely, excellent.* (a) Is. xl. 12. (b) Ps. lxxx. 6. (c) 2 Kings vii. 2; ix. 25; xv. 25, &c. (d) 1 Chron. xi. 11; xii. 19, &c. (e) 1 Sam. xviii. 6. (f) Prov. xx. 20.

שְׁלִישִׁי, m. שְׁלִישִׁיָּה, and שְׁלִישִׁית, f. pl. שְׁלִישִׁים, r. שׁלשׁ. (a) *Third,* Gen. i. 13; 1 Kings xviii. 1, &c. (b) *Of the third year,* Is. xv. 5; Jer. xlviii. 33. (c) In the fem. *A third part,* Num. xv. 6; xxviii. 14; Ezek. v. 2, &c. (d) Pl. *Chambers third in order, third stories,* Gen. vi. 16.

שָׁלַךְ, v. Kal non occ. Cogn. שׁלח.
Hiph. הִשְׁלִיךְ, pres. יַשְׁלִיךְ, apoc. יַשְׁלֵךְ. Constr. immed. (a) *Threw into,* אֶל; *on,* בְּ, עַל; *to,* לְ; *from,* מִן. (b) *Threw down.* (c) *Threw out, threw away.* (d) *Cast off,* as a plant its leaves. (e) *Expelled* a people. Phrr. אַחֲרָיו ה״, *Cast behind him, threw out of sight, disregarded.* (g) אַחֲרֵי גַוּ ה״, *Id.* (h) נָשׂוּא מִנֶּגֶד ה״, *Threw himself in the front, exposed himself.* (a) Num. xxxv. 20; Josh. x. 11; 2 Sam. xi. 21, &c. (b) Ps. cii. 11; Lam. ii. 1. (c) 2 Kings vii. 15; Ezek. xx. 8; Joel i. 7, &c. (d) Job xv. 33. (e) 2 Kings xiii. 23; xvii. 20; xxiv. 20, &c. (f) Ps. l. 17. (g) 1 Kings xiv. 8; Is. xxxviii. 17; Ezek. xxiii. 35. (h) Judg. ix. 17.
Infin. abs. הַשְׁלֵךְ, constr. הַשְׁלִיךְ, Eccl. iii. 5; Jer. xxii. 18, &c.
Imp. הַשְׁלֵךְ, f. הַשְׁלִיכִי, pl. הַשְׁלִיכוּ, Gen. xxxvii. 22; Exod. vii. 9; Jer. vii. 29, &c.
Part. מַשְׁלִיךְ, pl. constr. מַשְׁלִיכֵי, Is. xix. 8; Mic. ii. 5.
Hoph. הֻשְׁלַךְ, and הָשְׁלַךְ, pres. יֻשְׁלַךְ. Pass. of Hiph. (a) *Was thrown, down, out,* Is. xiv. 19; Jer. xxii. 28; Ezek. xix. 12, &c. (b) With עַל, *Was thrown upon,* for support, Ps. xxii. 11.
Part. מֻשְׁלָךְ, pl. מֻשְׁלָכִים, f. מֻשְׁלֶכֶת, 2 Sam. xx. 21; 1 Kings xiii. 24; Jer. xiv. 16, &c.

שָׁלָךְ, m. The name of a bird; according to Bochart, Hieroz., ii. p. 277, following the LXX. ὁ καταρράκτης, which appears to be the *Pelicanus Bassanus,* of Linn. *The Gannet,* Lev. xi. 17; Deut. xiv. 17.

4 H

שֶׁלֶךְ

שַׁלֶּכֶת, f. r. שׁלך. Either *The falling of leaves*, or *the felling* of a tree, Is. vi. 13, only.

שָׁלַל, v. pret. יְשָׁלוֹתָ, שָׁלְלוּ, שָׁלוּלוּ, יָשׁוֹלוּ. Constr. immed. Cogn. נשׁל. Arab. سَلّ, *eduxit, extraxit.* (a) *Plundered, spoiled.* (b) *Carried off* spoil. (c) *Scattered, let fall in carrying away.* (a) Ezek. xxxix. 10; Hab. ii. 8. (b) Ezek. xxvi. 12; xxix. 19. (c) Ruth ii. 16.

Infin. abs. שָׁלֹל, constr. שְׁלֹל, (b) Is. x. 6; Ezek. xxxviii. 12, 13. (c) Ruth ii. 16.

Part. pl. שֹׁלְלִים, aff. שֹׁלְלֵיהֶם, שֹׁלְלֶיהָ. (a) Jer. l. 10; Ezek. xxxix. 13; Zech. ii. 12.

Hith. אֶשְׁתּוֹלֲלוּ. A Chald. form for הִשְׁתּוֹלֲלוּ. *Were spoiled, plundered*, Ps. lxxvi. 6. But LXX. ἐταράχθησαν. Vulg. *turbati sunt.* Part. מִשְׁתּוֹלֵל, Is. lix. 15.

שָׁלָל, m. constr. שְׁלַל, aff. שְׁלָלָהּ. (a) *Spoil, plunder*. (b) Probably *Gain*. (c) שְׁלָלוֹ, *His spoil*. [1] His share of the spoil. [2] The spoil taken from him. (d) הָיְתָה לּוֹ נַפְשׁוֹ לְשָׁלָל, *His life was his share of the spoil*, i. e. he saved his life only. (e) לְצַוְּארֵי שָׁלָל, *Belonging to* (and taken from) *the necks of the spoiled*. (a) Gen. xlix. 27; Exod. xv. 9; Deut. xiii. 16, &c. (b) Prov. xxxi. 11. (c), [1] 1 Sam. xxx. 20. [2] Deut. xx. 14; Josh. xi. 14; Is. viii. 5, &c. (d) Jer. xxi. 9; xxxviii. 2; xxxix. 18, &c. (e) Judg. v. 30.

שָׁלֵם, m. pl. שְׁלֵמִים, f. שְׁלֵמָה, pl. שְׁלֵמוֹת. Arab. سَالِم, *incolumis, integer, vitii expers.* (a) *Perfect, complete, full.* Used of a building, *finished*, 2 Chron. viii. 16. Of weights and measures, Deut. xxv. 15; Prov. xi. 1. Metaph., of guilt, Gen. xv. 16. Of a reward, Ruth ii. 12. (b) לֵב שָׁלֵם, *A perfect heart, a heart fully engaged, without reserve or hypocrisy*, 1 Kings viii. 61; xv. 3; 2 Kings xx. 3, &c. (c) גָּלוּת שְׁלֵמָה, *A complete captivity*, of all the people, Amos i. 6, 9. (d) אֲבָנִים שְׁלֵמוֹת, *Rough, unwrought stones*, Deut. xxvii. 6; Josh. viii. 31. (e) אֶבֶן שְׁלֵמָה, *Stone fully prepared*, previously, 1 Kings vi. 7. But LXX. in these three places, ὁλοκλήρους. Vulg. *informibus et impolitis*, in the two former; and *dolatis atque perfectis*, in the last. (f) *Safe, in safety;* according to some, Gen. xxxiii. 18; but usually taken as a proper name. (g) *Peaceable*, Gen. xxxiv. 21. See שָׁלוֹם. (h)

שָׁלֵם

שְׁלֵמִים, in Nah. i. 12, is variously taken; some, *Perfect, having a perfect heart*, and *obeying fully;* others, *Complete, undiminished in numbers;* others, *At peace, and in security.*

שָׁלֵם, v. שָׁלְמוּ, pres. יִשְׁלָם. (a) From שָׁלוֹם. *Was at peace, was in security.* (b) From שָׁלֵם, *Was complete, was completed.* (a) Job ix. 4. (b) 1 Kings vii. 51; Is. lx. 20, &c.

Imp. in pause שְׁלָם, (a) Job xxii. 21.

Part. aff. שֹׁלְמִי. *One at peace with me*, Ps. vii. 8.

Part. pass. pl. constr. שְׁלֻמֵי. *Peaceable*, 2 Sam. xx. 19.

Pih. שִׁלַּם, pres. יְשַׁלֵּם. (a) *Completed.* (b) *Made complete by restitution, made restitution;* abs. (c) *Restored* a thing; immed. (d) *Gave in return* for a thing stolen or injured; immed. (e) *Requited, repaid*, either good or evil to a person; immed. of thing, and med. לְ of pers. it. immed. of pers. (f) *Performed* a vow. (g) *Restored* a person to a state of comfort. (a) 1 Kings ix. 25. (b) Exod. xxi. 34. (c) Lev. v. 24; 2 Sam. xii. 6; Joel ii. 25, &c. (d) Exod. xxi. 36; xxi. 2—14, &c. (e) Gen. xliv. 4; Judg. i. 7; Ruth ii. 12; Is. lxv. 6, &c. (f) Ps. xxii. 26; Prov. vii. 14; Is. xix. 21, &c. (g) Job viii. 6; Is. lvii. 18.

Infin. שַׁלֵּם, aff. שַׁלְּמוֹ, Exod. xxi. 36; Deut. xxiii. 22, &c.

Imp. שַׁלֵּם, f. שַׁלְּמִי, pl. שַׁלְּמוּ, Ps. lxxvi. 12; Eccl. v. 3; Nah. i. 15, &c.

Part. מְשַׁלֵּם, pl. מְשַׁלְּמִים, constr. מְשַׁלְּמֵי, Ps. xxxviii. 21; Is. lxvi. 6; Joel iv. 4, &c.

Puh. pres. יְשֻׁלַּם, Pass. of Pih. signn. (e) and (f). (e) Prov. xi. 31; xiii. 13; Jer. xviii. 20. (f) Ps. lxv. 2.

Part. מְשֻׁלָּם, Is. xlii. 19. *Made perfect, complete.* Comp. ch. vi. 7. See my Sermons and Dissertt. in loc.

Hiph. הִשְׁלִים; pres. יַשְׁלִים, apoc. יַשְׁלֵם. (a) *Made peace* with. (b) *Caused to be at peace* with. (c) *Completed, fulfilled.* (d) *Brought* a person *to an end*. (a) Med. אֶת, Josh. x. 1. 4; 2 Sam. x. 19. אֶל, Josh. xi. 19. עִם, Deut. xx. 12; 1 Kings xxii. 45; 1 Chron. xix. 19. (b) Med. אֶת, Prov. xvi. 7. (c) Job xxiii. 14; Is. xliv. 26. 28. (d) Is. xxxviii. 12, 13.

Hoph. הָשְׁלְמָה. Pass. of Hiph. sign. (b) Job v. 23; unless we take the Arab. أَسْلَمَ,

שלם (603) שלש

(pass. of اُسْلِمَ), *traditus fuit*, and translate, *Was delivered* to thee.

שָׁלֵם, m. pl. שְׁלָמִים, constr. שַׁלְמֵי, aff. שַׁלְמֵיכֶם, שַׁלְמֵינוּ. (a) *The offering of a sacrifice*, either as *the completion, performance of a vow*, or in acknowledgment of *peace, prosperity; a peace-offering, a thank-offering*, Amos v. 22. Pl. Exod. xxxii. 6, &c. Constr., [1] זֶבַח שְׁלָמִים, Lev. iii. 1—6. [2] וְזִבְחֵי שְׁלָמִים, Lev. xvii. 5. [3] זִבְחִים שְׁלָמִים, Exod. xxiv. 5. (b) *Any offering*, Judg. xx. 26; xxi. 4.

שָׁלֵם, m. *Retribution*, Deut. xxxii. 35, only.

שָׁלֻם, and שָׁלוּם, m. pl. שִׁלּוּמִים, *Id.* Is. xxxiv. 8; Hos. ix. 7; Mic. vii. 3.

שְׁלָם, Chald. m. def. שְׁלָמָא, aff. שְׁלָמְכוֹן, i. q. Heb. שָׁלוֹם. *Peace, prosperity*; it occurs only in salutations, Ezra iv. 17; v. 7; Dan. iii. 31; vi. 26.

שְׁלִם, Chald. v. *Completed*. Only in Part. pass. שְׁלִם, Ezra v. 16.

Aph. pret. aff. הַשְׁלְמָהּ. (a) *Brought to an end, terminated*. (b) *Restored*. (a) Dan. v. 26.

Imp. הַשְׁלֵם, (b) Ezra vii. 19.

שְׁלֻמָּה, f. constr. שֻׁלְמַת, i. q. שֻׁלֵּם, Ps. xci. 8, only.

שִׁלְמֹנִים, pl. m. *Recompenses*; either *Bribes* or *Penalties*, Is. i. 23, only.

שָׁלַף, v. pres. יִשְׁלֹף. Constr. immed. Arab. سَلَبَ, *eripuit vi; extraxit* gladium è vagina. (a) *Drew* a sword. (b) *Drew a sword*, abs. (c) *Drew out* a sword from a wound. (d) *Took off* a shoe. (e) *Plucked up grass*. (a) Judg. viii. 20; 1 Sam. xvii. 51. (b) Job xx. 25. (c) Judg. iii. 22. (d) Ruth iv. 7, 8. (e) Ps. cxxix. 6.

Imp. שְׁלֹף, (a) Judg. ix. 54, &c. Part. שֹׁלֵף חֶרֶב, pl. שֹׁלְפֵי חֶרֶב, *Drawing the sword, armed*, Judg. viii. 10; xx. 2. 25, &c. Part. pass. f. שְׁלוּפָה, *Drawn*, of a sword, Num. xxii. 23, &c.

שָׁלֹשׁ, and שָׁלוֹשׁ, m. constr. שְׁלָשׁ.— שְׁלֹשָׁה, f. constr. שְׁלֹשֶׁת, aff. שְׁלָשְׁתְּכֶם, שְׁלָשְׁתָּם.— Arab. ثَلَاثٌ, f. ثَلَاثَةٌ, *tres*. The numeral *Three*. Gen. v. 22; vi. 10; xi. 13; xxx. 36; Num. xii. 4; xxii. 32, &c. Pl. שְׁלֹשִׁים, *Thirty, thirtieth*, Gen. v. 3, &c. Hence—

שִׁלֵּשׁ, v. Pih. שִׁלֵּשָׁה, pres. pl. in pause יְשַׁלֵּשׁוּ. (a) *Divided into three equal parts*. (b) Abs. *Did a thing the third time*. (c) With a verb, *Did* a thing *on the third day*. (a) Deut. xix. 3. (b) 1 Kings xviii. 34. (c) 1 Sam. xx. 19.

Imp. pl. in pause שַׁלֵּשׁוּ, (b) 1 Kings xviii. 34.

Puh. part. מְשֻׁלָּשׁ, f. מְשֻׁלֶּשֶׁת, pl. מְשֻׁלָּשׁוֹת. (a) *Threefold*. (b) *Three-years-old*. (a) Eccl. iv. 12; Ezek. xlii. 6. (b) Gen. xv. 9.

שָׁלִישׁ, see שָׁלִישׁ.

שִׁלְשׁוֹם, and שִׁלְשֹׁם, compd. יוֹם + שָׁלְשָׁה. *Three days ago*. Always joined with תְּמוֹל or אֶתְמוֹל. Phrr. תְּמוֹל שִׁלְשׁוֹם, מִתְּמוֹל שִׁלְשׁוֹם, גַּם מִתְּמוֹל גַּם מִשִׁלְשֹׁם, *Both yesterday and the day before; heretofore, previously*, Gen. xxxi. 2; Deut. xix. 6; Exod. iv. 10, &c.

שִׁלֵּשִׁים, pl. m. *Posterity of the third generation, sons being reckoned as the first; great-grandchildren*, Exod. xx. 5; xxxiv. 7; Num. v. 9; Deut. xiv. 8. בְּנֵי שִׁלֵּשִׁים, *Grandchildren of grandchildren*, Gen. L. 23.

שָׁם, adv. Arab. ثَمَّ, *istic remotioris loci*. ثُمَّ, *tum, deinde*. Syr. ܬܡܢ, *ibi*. (a) *There*. (b) For שָׁמָּה, *Thither*. (c) שָׁם—שָׁם, *Here—there*. (d) אֲשֶׁר שָׁם, *Where*. (e) שָׁמָּה, [1] *Thither*, [2] *There*. (f) אֲשֶׁר שָׁמָּה, [1] *Whither*, [2] *Where*. (g) מִשָּׁם, *Thence*, from that place or thing. (h) אֲשֶׁר מִשָּׁם, *Whence*. (a) Gen. ii. 8. 12; Exod. viii. 18, &c. (b) Deut. i. 37; Judg. xviii. 3; 1 Sam. ii. 14, &c. (c) Is. xxviii 10. (d) Gen. ii. 11; Exod. xx. 18; 2 Sam. xv. 21, &c. (e), [1] Gen. xix. 20; Exod. xxvi. 33; Num. xxxv. 6, &c. [2] Ps. cxxii. 5; Is. xxxiv. 15; 1 Chron. iv. 41, &c. (f), [1] Gen. xx. 13; Num. xxxv. 25; Deut. xxx. 3, &c. [2] Ruth i. 7; 2 Kings xxiii. 8; Jer. xiii. 7. (g) Gen. ii. 16; 1 Sam. iv. 4, &c.; 1 Kings xvii. 13. (h) Gen. iii. 23; xxiv. 5; Deut. ix. 28, &c.

שֵׁם, m. constr. שֵׁם, sometimes with Mak. שֶׁם־, aff. שְׁמִי, שִׁמְךָ, שְׁמֵךְ, שִׁמְכֶם, pl. שֵׁמוֹת, constr. שְׁמוֹת, aff. שְׁמוֹתָם. Arab. اِسْم, Syr. ܫܡܐ. Æth. ሰም: *nomen*. (a) *A name*. (b) *Fame*. (c) *A great name, reputation*. (d) שֵׁם גָּדוֹל, *Id*. (e) אַנְשֵׁי שֵׁם,

Men of renown, distinguished men. (f) אַנְשֵׁי הַשֵּׁם, *Id.* (g) שְׁמוֹת "א, *Id.* (h) *A good name.* (i) שׁ" טוֹב, *Id.* (k) שׁ" רָע, *An evil name.* (l) בְּנֵי בְלִי שֵׁם, *The children of those without distinction.* (m) *Memory.* Phrr. [1] מָחָה שְׁמָם. [2] — הִשְׁמִיד. [3] — הִכְרִית, *Destroyed their remembrance.* (n) שֵׁם יְהֹוָה, *The name of the Lord,* i. e. *the Lord himself* as the object of praise or worship, reverence or confidence. (o) קָרָא שֵׁם יְהֹוָה, *Called on the name of the Lord, invoked him.* (p) קָרָא בְשֵׁם יְהֹוָה, *Id.* (q) הִלֵּל אֶת־שֵׁם יְהֹוָה, *Dishonoured the name of the Lord.* (r) לְמַעַן שֵׁם יְהֹוָה, *For the honour of the name of the Lord.* (a) Gen. ii. 11; xvi. 15; xxiv. 29, &c. (b) 1 Chron. xiv. 17. (c) Gen. xi. 4; 2 Sam. vii. 23; 1 Chron. xvii. 8, &c. (d) 2 Sam. vii. 9; 1 Chron. xvii. 8. (e) Num. xvi. 2. (f) Gen. vi. 4. (g) 1 Chron. v. 24. (h) Prov. xxii. 1. (i) Eccl. vii. 1. 3. (k) Deut. xxii. 14. 19; Neh. vi. 13. (l) Job xxx. 8. (m), [1] Deut. ix. 14; 2 Kings xiv. 27; Ps. ix. 6, &c. [2] 1 Sam. xxiv. 22. [3] Josh. vii. 9; Zech. xiii. 2. (n) Job i. 21; Ps. vii. 18; lxix. 31, &c. (o) Deut. xxxii. 3. (p) Gen. xiii. 4; Exod. xxxiii. 19; 1 Kings xviii. 24, &c. (q) Lev. xviii. 21; xix. 12; Ezek. xx. 39, &c. (r) Ps. xxv. 11; Is. xlviii. 9; Ezek. xx. 9, &c.

שֵׁם, Chald. m. aff. שְׁמֵהּ, pl. constr. שְׁמָהַת, aff. שְׁמָהָתְהוֹם, *A name,* Ezra v. 1. 4. 10; Dan. ii. 20, &c.

שׁמד, v. Kal non. occ.
Hiph. הִשְׁמִיד, pres. יַשְׁמִיד, apoc. יַשְׁמֵד.
Constr. immed. it. med. אֶת. *Destroyed,* [1] *Persons.* [2] *Things.* [1] 2 Kings xxi. 9; Ps. cvi. 34; Amos ii. 9, &c. [2] Lev. xxvi. 30; 1 Sam. xxiv. 21; Amos ii. 9, &c.
Infin. abs. הַשְׁמֵד, constr. הַשְׁמִיד, aff. הַשְׁמִידוֹ, Deut. ix. 8; Josh. xxiii. 15; Is. xiv. 23, &c.
Niph. נִשְׁמַד, pres. יִשָּׁמֵד. Pass. of Hiph. Judg. xxi. 16; Prov. xiv. 11; Ezek. xxxii. 12, &c.
Infin. הִשָּׁמֵד, aff. הִשָּׁמְדָם, Deut. iv. 26; vii. 23, &c.

שׁמד, Chald. v.
Aph. Infin. הַשְׁמָדָה. *To destroy,* Dan. vii. 26, only.

שַׁמָּה, see שֵׁם.

שַׁמָּה, f. pl. שַׁמּוֹת, r. שׁמם. (a) *Desolation.* (b) *Astonishment.* (c) *An object of astonishment.* (d) Phr. שָׂם אֶרֶץ לְשַׁמָּה, *Made a land desolate.* (a) Ps. xlvi. 9; liii. 19; Is. v. 9; xxiv. 12, &c. (b) Jer. viii. 21. (c) 2 Kings xxii. 19; Jer. v. 30; li. 37. (d) Is. xiii. 9; Jer. iv. 7; xviii. 16, &c. In Lev. xxvi. 43, בְּהָשַׁמָּה, should, probably, be pointed בְּהָשַׁמָּה, *in the desolation.* The LXX. ἐν τῷ ἐρημωθῆναι αὐτήν, taking apparently the Infin. of Niph., בְּהִשַׁמָּה, which, with the מֵהֶם, LXX. δι᾽ αὐτούς, following, bids fair for the true reading.

שְׁמוּעָה, and שֵׁמַע, f. constr. שִׁמְעַת, aff. שָׁמְעָתֵנוּ, pl. שְׁמֻעוֹת, r. שׁמע. *Any thing that is heard.* (a) *A report.* (b) *A message.* (a) 1 Sam. ii. 24; 2 Sam. xiii. 30; 1 Kings x. 7, &c. (b) Is. xxviii. 9. 19; liii. 1; Jer. xlix. 14, &c.

שׁמט, v. pret. שָׁמְטָה, pres. יִשְׁמְטוּ.
Constr. immed. it. med. כֵּן. Arab. سَمَطَ, *conticuit;* سَمَحَ, *dimisit debitorem;* ثَمَدَ, *cœnum tenue.* Syr. ܫܡܛ, *eduxit, evaginavit; evulsit. Gave up* his hold or claim on. (a) *Gave up* a debt. (b) *Left* the land *to itself.* (c) *Threw down.* (b) Exod. xxiii. 11; Jer. xvii. 4. (c) 2 Kings ix. 33. In 2 Sam. vi. 6, and 1 Chron. xiii. 9, שָׁמְטוּ הַבָּקָר, signifies, according to Bochart, *the oxen stuck fast:* comparing the Arab. سَمَطَ. LXX. περιέσπασεν αὐτὴν ὁ μόσχος, and ἐξέκλινεν αὐτήν. Vulg. *calcitrabant boves; bos lascíviens paululum inclinaverat eam.*
Infin. שְׁמוֹט, (a) Deut. xv. 2.
Imp. pl. שִׁמְטוּ, (c) 2 Kings ix. 33.
Niph. נִשְׁמְטוּ, Pass. of Kal. (c) *Was thrown down,* Ps. cxli. 6.
Hiph. pres. apoc. תַּשְׁמֵט. *Relaxed* his hand from, *gave up, forgave.* Deut. xv. 3.

שְׁמִטָּה, fem. *A relaxation, release, acquittal,* Deut. xv. 1, 2. שְׁנַת הַשְׁמִטָּה, *the year of release,* Deut. xv. 9; xxxi. 10.

שָׁמַיִם, pl. m. constr. שְׁמֵי, aff. שָׁמֶיךָ, שְׁמֵיכֶם, שָׁמָיו. Arab. سَمَاء, *cœlum;* سَمَا, *altus fuit.* Syr. ܫܡܝܐ, and Æth.
ሰማይ: *cœlum.* (a) *The heights;* heaven, *the sky.* (b) שְׁמֵי הַשָּׁמַיִם, *The heaven of heavens, the highest heavens.* (c) אֱלֹהֵי הַשָּׁמַיִם, *The God of heaven.* (d) הַשָּׁמַיְמָה, *Towards,* or *to, the sky.* (e) עַל הַשָּׁמַיִם, *Id.* (a) Gen. i. 1—30; Lev.

שמי (605) שמם

xxvi. 19; Deut. xxviii. 23; xxxiii. 28; Ps. xx. 7, &c. (b) Deut. x. 14; 1 Kings viii. 27; Ps. cxlviii. 4, &c. (c) Gen. xxiv. 3. 7; Neh. i. 4; Jonah i. 9, &c. (d) Gen. xv. 5; xxviii. 12; Exod. ix. 8, &c. (e) Exod. ix. 22, 23; x. 21, 22.

שָׁמַיִן, Chald. pl. m. def. שְׁמַיָּא, *Id.* (a) *Heaven, the sky.* (b) *The sovereign of heaven; God.* (c) אֱלָהּ שְׁמַיָּא, *The God of heaven.* (a) Dan. ii. 38; iv. 10. 20. 28, &c. (b) Dan. iv. 23. (c) Dan. ii. 18. 37. 44; iv. 20. 22, &c.

שְׁמִינִי, masc. שְׁמִינִית, fem. from שְׁמֹנֶה, *Eighth,* Exod. xxii. 29; Lev. xxv. 22, &c. עַל הַשְּׁמִינִית, *On the sheminith:* according to some, an instrument so called, and probably producing eight notes; others suppose the words refer to the pitch of the notes, 1 Chron. xv. 21; Ps. vi. 1; xii. 1.

שָׁמִיר, m. aff. שְׁמִירוֹ. Arab. سَمُر, *nomen plantæ; mimosæ unguiscati; arboris nomen; spinæ Ægyptiacæ;* سَامُور, *adamas.* (a) *A thorny shrub;* according to some, *spina Ægyptiaca,* Is. v. 6; vii. 23—25; ix. 17, &c. (b) *A diamond,* Jer. xvii. 1; Ezek. iii. 9; Zech. vii. 12.

שָׁמַם, v. pret. שָׁמְמָה, pres. אֶשֹּׁם, pl. יָשֹׁמוּ. Constr. abs. it. med. עַל. Cogn. ישׁם. (a) *Was desolate, was laid waste.* (b) *Was astonished.* (a) Lam. v. 18; Ezek. xxxv. 12. 15. (b) Lev. xxvi. 32; Job xvii. 17; Is. lii. 14, &c. (c) *Make desolate, ruin,* Is. xlii. 14.

Imp. pl. שֹׁמּוּ, (b) Jer. ii. 12.

Part. שֹׁמֵם, fem. שֹׁמֵמָה, pl. שֹׁמְמִים, and שֹׁמֵמִין, fem. שֹׁמֵמוֹת, constr. שֹׁמְמוֹת. (a) *Desolate,* Is. xlix. 8; Lam. iii. 11, &c. (b) Pl. f. *Desolate places,* Is. xlix. 19; lxi. 4; Dan. ix. 18. (c) *Solitary,* 2 Sam. xiii. 20; Is. liv. 1. (d) *Making desolate,* Dan. viii. 13.

Niph. pret. נָשַׁמּוּ, pres. יֵשֹׁם. I. q. Kal. (a) Lev. xxvi. 22; Is. xxxiii. 8; Lam. iv. 5, &c. (b) 1 Kings ix. 8; Job xviii. 20; Jer. iv. 9, &c.

Part. f. נְשַׁמָּה, pl. נְשַׁמּוֹת. *Desolate,* used of cities, countries, uncultivated lands, &c., Ps. lxix. 26; Is. liv. 3; Ezek. xxxii. 15, &c.

Pih. Part. מְשׁוֹמֵם. (a) *A desolater,* Dan. ix. 27; xi. 31. (b) Probably for מְשׁוֹמָם *Astonished,* Ezra ix. 3, 4.

Hiph. pret. הֲשִׁמּוֹתָ, pres. יָשֵׁם, aff. יְשִׁמֵּם. Causat. of Kal. Constr. immed. it. med. אֶת. (a) *Made desolate, laid waste.* (b) *Caused to wonder, astonished.* (c) *Was astonished.* (a) Lev. xxvi. 31; Job xvi. 7; Ezek. xxx. 12, &c. (b) Ezek. xxxii. 10.

Infin. הַשֵּׁמֵּם, Mic. vi. 13.

Imp. pl. הָשַׁמּוּ, (c) Job xxi. 5.

Part. מַשְׁמִים, (c) Ezek. iii. 15.

Hoph. pret. הָשַׁמָּה, Pass. of Hiph. *Was made desolate,* Lev. xxvi. 34, 35; 2 Chron. xxxvi. 21.

Hith. pres. יִשְׁתּוֹמֵם, once יְשׁוֹמֵם. (a) *Was desolate, disconsolate, of the heart.* (b) *Was astonished, wondered.* (c) *Destroyed himself.* (a) Ps. cxliii. 4. (b) Is. lix. 16; lxiii. 5; Dan. viii. 27. (c) Eccl. vii. 16. But LXX. μὴ ποτε ἐκπλαγῆς. Vulg. *ne obstupescas.*

שמם, Chald. v. *Id.*

Ithpe. pres. אֶשְׁתּוֹמֵם. *Was astonished,* Dan. iv. 6.

שָׁמֵם, m. שְׁמֵמָה, f. *Desolate,* Jer. xii. 11; Dan. ix. 17.

שְׁמָמָה, f. pl. constr. שִׁמְמוֹת. (a) *Desolation, the state of being desolate, uninhabited,* or *uncultivated; a desolate place.* (b) *Astonishment.* (a) Exod. xxiii. 29; Lev. xxvi. 33; Josh. viii. 28, &c. (b) Ezek. vii. 27.

שִׁמָמָה, f. pl. constr. שִׁמָמוֹת, *Id.,* Ezek. xxxv. 7. 9.

שִׁמָּמוֹן, m. *Astonishment, terror,* Ezek. iv. 16; xii. 19.

שֶׁמֶן, m. aff. שַׁמְנִי, שִׁמְנָה, pl. שְׁמָנִים, aff. שְׁמָנָיו. Arab. سَمِن, *pinguis et obesus fuit;* سَمْن, *butyrum. Fatness.* (a) *Oil.* (b) *Ointment.* (c) *Richness,* of food. (d) *Fertility.* (e) *Prosperity.* (a) Gen. xxviii. 18; Exod. xxvii. 20; Lev. ii. 1, &c. (b) Ps. cxxxiii. 2; Eccl. x. 1; Amos vi. 6, &c (c) Is. xxv. 6. (d) Is. v. 1; xxviii. 1. 4. (e) Is. x. 27. עֵץ שֶׁמֶן, variously rendered, *the wild olive tree, the fir, the citron tree;* but, according to Celsius, a generic term for *any tree of an oily* or *resinous nature,* 1 Kings vi. 23. 31, 32; Neh. viii. 15; Is. xli. 19.

שָׁמֵן, masc. שְׁמֵנָה, fem. *Fat,* adj. (a) *Plump,* of an animal. (b) *Robust, stout,* of a man. (c) *Nourishing,* of food. (d) *Rich,*

שמן (606) שמע

of pastures. (e) *Fertile.* (f) *Abundant, of provision.* (a) Num. xiii. 20; Ezek. xxxiv. 16. (b) Judg. iii. 29. (c) Is. xxx. 23. (d) Ezek. xxxiv. 14. (e) Neh. ix. 25. 35. (f) Gen. xlix. 20; Hab. i. 16.

שָׁמֵן, v. pret. שָׁמַנְתָּ, שָׁמְנוּ, pres. יִשְׁמַן. *Was fat; was prosperous,* Deut. xxxii. 15; Jer. v. 28.

Hiph. pres. יַשְׁמִינוּ. (a) *Produced fat; became fat.* (b) *Caused to be fat, dull, of the heart,* or *declared it to be so.* (a) Neh. ix. 25.

Imp. הַשְׁמֵן, (b) Is. vi. 10.

שְׁמֹנֶה, m. שְׁמֹנָה, f. constr. שְׁמֹנַת. Arab. ثَمَانٍ, octo. The numeral *Eight,* Gen. v. 4; xiv. 14; Num. ii. 24, &c.

Pl. שְׁמֹנִים, *Eighty, eightieth,* Gen. v. 25; 1 Kings vi. 1, &c.

שָׁמַע, in pause שָׁמֵעַ. Aff. שָׁמְעִי, שִׁמְעֲךָ, שִׁמְעָה, שָׁמְעָם. Arab. سَمِعَ, *audivit.* Syr. ܫܡܥ, Id. *Hearing.* (a) *The act of hearing.* (b) *Report, news, fame.* שִׁמְעֲךָ, *What is said of thee.* שֵׁמַע לִי, *A report heard by him.* (c) *Sound.* שֵׁמַע צִלְצְלֵי, *Cymbals of a* (loud) *sound.* (a) Job xlii. 8; Ps. xviii. 45. (b) Gen. xxix. 13; 1 Kings x. 1; Is. lxvi. 19; Hos. vii. 12, &c. (c) Ps. cl. 5.

שֵׁמַע, m. aff. שָׁמְעוֹ. *His fame,* Josh. vi. 27; ix. 9; Esth. ix. 4; Jer. vi. 24.

שָׁמַע, v. in pause, שָׁמֵעַ, Ps. xxii. 25, &c. pres. יִשְׁמַע. *Heard, hearkened.* (a) *Heard, a sound, person,* or *report.* Constr. [1] Abs. [2] Immed. or med. אֶת, of person or thing. [3] With כִּי. [4] With לֵאמֹר. (b) *Hearkened,* so as to grant, consent, or obey. Constr. [1] Abs. [2] Immed. or med. אֶת, of person or thing. [3] אֶל, אֶל דִּבְרֵי, אֶל קוֹל. [4] ?, לְקוֹל. [5] בְּ, בְּקוֹל. (c) *Understood.* (a), [1] 1 Sam. xiv. 27; Is. lxvi. 8; Jer. xviii. 13, &c. [2] Gen. xxiv. 52; 2 Sam. xiii. 21; Ezek. xxxiii. 5, &c. [3] Gen. xxix. 33; 1 Sam. xxiii. 10; 1 Kings v. 1, &c. [4] Exod. xxii. 11; 1 Sam. xiii. 4; 2 Sam. xix. 3, &c. (b), [1] Gen. xlii. 22; Judg. xi. 17; 2 Kings xiv. 11, &c. [2] Gen. xvii. 20; Exod. vi. 12; Ps. vi. 9; xxviii. 6, &c. [3] אֶל, Deut. iii. 26; 1 Kings viii. 30; xii. 15, &c. אֶל קוֹל, Gen. xxi. 16. אֶל דִּבְרֵי, Judg. xi. 28; 2 Chron. xxxv. 22. Jer. xxxvii. 2, &c. [4] ?,

2 Chron. x. 16; Neh. ix. 29; Hos. ix. 17, &c. לְקוֹל, Gen. iii. 17; Judg. ii. 20; Ps. lxxxi. 12, &c. [5] בְּ, Is. xlii. 24. בְּקוֹל, Gen. xxvi. 5; xxx. 6; Deut. i. 45, &c. (c) Gen. xli. 15; Deut. xxviii. 49.

Infin. abs. שָׁמוֹעַ, constr. שְׁמֹעַ, aff. שָׁמְעִי, שָׁמְעֵךְ, Exod. xv. 26; Num. xxx. 9; 2 Kings xxii. 19; Neh. i. 4, &c.

Infin. שְׁמֹעַ, שְׁמֹעָה, fem. שִׁמְעִי, pl. שִׁמְעוּ, fem. שְׁמַעְנָה, שְׁמַעַן, Gen. iv. 23; xxi. 12; xxxvii. 5; Job xxxii. 10, &c.

Part. שֹׁמֵעַ, aff. שֹׁמְעוֹ, fem. שֹׁמַעַת, pl. שֹׁמְעִים, constr. שֹׁמְעֵי, aff. שֹׁמְעָיו. (c) 1 Kings iii. 9; Gen. xviii. 10; Deut. iv. 12; 1 Sam. iii. 11; Ezek. xiii. 19, &c.

Niph. נִשְׁמַע, pres. יִשָּׁמַע. Pass. of Kal. (a) *Was heard.* (b) נִשְׁמַע בְּקוֹלָם, *Their voice was hearkened to,* by God. (c) *Was understood.* (a) Gen. xlv. 6; 1 Sam. i. 13; Is. lx. 18. נִשְׁמַע לוֹ, *It was heard by him,* Neh. vi. 1. 7. (b) 2 Chron. xxx. 27. (c) Job xxvi. 14.

Infin. הִשָּׁמַע, Esth. ii. 8.

Part. נִשְׁמָע, fem. נִשְׁמַעַת, pl. נִשְׁמָעִים, Neh. vi. 6; Eccl. ix. 16, 17; Jer. li. 47.

Pih. pres. שִׁמַּע. Causat. of Kal. *Caused to hear, summoned,* med. אֶת, 1 Sam. xv. 4; xxiii. 8.

Hiph. הִשְׁמִיעַ, pres. יַשְׁמִיעַ. Causat. of Kal. (a) *Caused to hear.* Constr. [1] Immed. of pers. [2] Immed. of pers. and thing. [3] Med. אֶת, of pers. and immed. of thing. [5] Med. אֶל, of pers. and immed. of thing. (b) *Caused to be heard.* Constr. immed. it. and med. אֶת. (c) *Caused himself to be heard,* abs. (d) *Proclaimed,* abs. (e) *Summoned,* med. אֶת. (a), [1] Judg. xiii. 23; Is. xliv. 8. [2] Ps. li. 10; Is. xliii. 9. [3] Deut. iv. 36; 1 Sam. ix. 27; Jer. xviii. 2. [4] 2 Kings vii. 6; Jer. xxiii. 22. [5] Ezek. xxxvi. 15. (b) Ps. lxxvi. 9; Is. xxx. 30; Jer. xlviii. 4, &c. (c) Neh. xii. 42. (d) Is. lxii. 11. (e) 1 Kings xv. 22.

Infin. הַשְׁמִיעַ, (c) 1 Chron. xv. 19; 2 Chron. v. 13.

Imp. aff. הַשְׁמִיעֵנִי, fem. aff. הַשְׁמִיעִינִי, pl. הַשְׁמִיעוּ, Ps. cxliii. 8; Cant. ii. 14; Jer. iv. 5.

Part. מַשְׁמִיעַ, pl. מַשְׁמִיעִים, 1 Chron. xv. 16; Is. xli. 26, &c.

שְׁמַע, Chald. v. pres. יִשְׁמַע, Id. *Heard.* Constr. [1] Abs. [2] Immed. [3] Med. עַל, *Concerning.* [2] Dan. iii. 5. 10. 15; vi. 15. [3] Ib. v. 14. 16.

Part. pl. שָׁמְעִין, [1] Dan. v. 23. [2] Ib. iii. 7.

שמץ (607) שמר

Ithpe. pres. יִשְׁתַּמְעוּן. *Obeyed*, med. לְ, Ib. vii. 27.

שֶׁמֶץ, masc. Arab. شَمَصَ, *propulit, impulit alacriter;* شَمَصَ, *festinanter locutus fuit. Hastening; saying or doing quickly. Any thing said or done quickly; a small portion, a hint,* Job iv. 12; xxvi. 14, only. LXX. ἐξαίσια ἐπὶ ἰκμάδα. Sym. ψιθυρισμόν, ψιθύρισμα. Vulg. *venas susurri; parvam stillam.*

שִׁמְצָה, fem. once, Exod. xxxii. 25. According to some, *Urging, urging to flight, routing; defeat:* others, *taunting; disgrace.* For the last, comp. Arab. شَمَعَ, *lusit, jocatus fuit.* LXX. ἐπίχαρμα. So Theod. Symm. κακωνυμίαν. Ἀλλ'. ὄνομα ῥύπου. Vulg. *ignominiam sordis.*

שָׁמַר, v. pres. יִשְׁמֹר. Arab. سَمَرَ, *noctem confabulando somno haud indulgens transegit.* Constr. immed. it. med. אֶת. *Kept, watched, preserved, observed.* (a) *Kept watch, kept watch over.* [1] Abs. [2] Immed. it. med. אֶת. [3] For good, עַל. [4] For evil, אֶל. (b) *Watched sheep,* abs. (c) *Guarded, preserved.* (d) *Kept in mind,* [1] A saying. [2] A feeling; *retained* it. (e) *Observed* a command, rule of life, institution, promise, &c. (f) *Attended to* an office. (g) *Took heed,* [1] To do, לְ, with Infin. [2] Abs. (h) *Watched,* for evil. (i) *Observed, noticed, remembered.* (k) *Regarded, reverenced.* (l) *Guarded himself against, avoided.* [1] Immed. [2] Med. מִן. (a), [2] Gen. xxx. 31; Jer. xxxi. 10. [3] Prov. vi. 22. (b) Hos. xii. 13. (c) Gen. xxviii. 20; 2 Sam. xxii. 22; Job x. 12, &c. (d), [1] Gen. xxxvii. 11. [2] 1 Kings iii. 6; Ps. lxxxix. 28; Amos i. 11. (e) Deut. vii. 2; 1 Kings viii. 24; xi. 10, &c. (f) Num. iii. 10; xviii. 7. (g), [1] Num. xxiii. 12; Deut. xvii. 10; 2 Kings x. 31, &c. (h) Ps. lvi. 7; cxxx. 3; Jer. viii. 7, &c. (i) Job x. 14. (l), [1] Ps. xvii. 4.

Infin. abs. שָׁמוֹר, constr. שְׁמֹר, aff. שָׁמְרִי, שָׁמְרוֹ, שָׁמְרָה. (a) Exod. xxii. 6. (h) 1 Sam. xix. 11. (k) Hos. iv. 10. &c.

Imp. שְׁמֹר, שָׁמְרָה, aff. שָׁמְרֵנִי, pl. שִׁמְרוּ. (c) 1 Kings xx. 39; Ps. xvi. 1. (g, 2) Deut. xii. 28. (i) Josh. vi. 18, &c.

Part. שֹׁמֵר, pl. שֹׁמְרִים. *Watching, keeping; one who keeps* or *guards,* Deut. vii. 9; 1 Sam. xvii. 20; Esth. ii. 3, &c. *A watchman,* abs., Is. xxi. 11, 12.

Part. pass. שָׁמוּר, fem. שְׁמֻרָה. *Kept, preserved, secured,* 1 Sam. ix. 24; 2 Sam. xxiii. 5; Eccl. v. 12.

Niph. נִשְׁמַר, pres. יִשָּׁמֵר. (a) *Was on his guard against, noticed, perceived,* med. בְּ. (b) *Was preserved, delivered.* (c) *Took heed,* [1] Abs. [2] לְנַפְשׁוֹ, *To himself.* [3] בְּרוּחוֹ, Id. (d) *Guarded himself, abstained,* [1] Med. מִן. [2] מִפְּנֵי. [3] בְּ. (a) 2 Sam. xx. 10. (b) 2 Kings vi. 10; Ps. xxxvii. 28; Hos. xii. 14. (c), [1] Deut. ii. 4. [2] Deut. iv. 15; Ezek. xiii. 11. [3] Mal. ii. 15, 16. (d), [1] Deut. xxiii. 10; Judg. xiii. 13; 1 Sam. xxi. 5. [2] Exod. xxiii. 13.

Imp. הִשָּׁמֵר. (a, 1) Is. vii. 4. (d, 2) Exod. xxiii. 21. הִשָּׁמֶר לְךָ, [1] *Beware,* abs., Deut. iv. 9. With מִן, and Infin., Gen. xxxi. 29; 2 Kings vi. 9. With Infin. only, Exod. xix. 12. With אֶל, and pres., Exod. x. 28; Job xxxvi. 21. With. פֶּן, and pres., Gen. xxiv. 6.

Pih. part. pl. מְשַׁמְּרִים, i. q. Kal. (k) Jonah ii. 9.

Hith. pres. יִשְׁתַּמֵּר. (a) *Kept, guarded himself,* med. מִן, 2 Sam. xxii. 24; Ps. xviii. 24. (b) *Was observed,* pass. of Kal. [e] Mic. vi. 16.

שָׁמְרָה, f. *A watch,* Ps. cxli. 3.

שְׁמֻרוֹת, pl. f. Id., Ps. lxxvii. 5.

שִׁמֻּרִים, pl. masc. *Observance* (of a festival), Exod. xii. 42.

שְׁמָרִים, pl. m. aff. שְׁמָרָיו, שִׁמְרֵיהֶם. *Things kept undisturbed in the same place or state.* (a) *The sediment* of things thus kept, *lees, dregs,* Ps. lxxv. 9; Jer. xlviii. 11; Zeph. i. 12. (b) *Wines long kept in the same vessel,* Is. xxv. 6.

שֶׁמֶשׁ, masc. usually, sometimes f. aff. שִׁמְשָׁה, שִׁמְשְׁךָ. Arab. شَمْس. Syr. ܫܡܫܐ, sol. (a) *The sun,* Gen. xv. 12; Josh. x. 12, &c. Metaph., of God, Ps. lxxxiv. 12. Phrr. זָרַח הַשֶּׁמֶשׁ, *The sun rose,* Gen. xxxii. 31; Exod. xxii. 2, &c. יָצָא ה׳, Id., Gen. xix. 23; Is. xiii. 10. בָּא הַשֶׁמֶשׁ set, Gen. xxviii. 11; Lev. xxii. 7, &c. תַּחַת ה׳, *Under the sun,* i. e. on the whole earth, Eccl. i. 9; ii. 11; iv. 1, &c. (b) Pl. aff. שִׁמְשֹׁתַיִךְ. Some, *Thy windows:*

שָׁמֵשׁ (608) שׁנה

others, *Thy pinnacles*, Is. liv. 12. LXX. ἐπάλξεις. Vulg. *propugnacula tua*.

שְׁמַשׁ, Chald. v. Paḥ. pres. aff. יְשַׁמְּשׁוּנֵהּ. Syr. ܫܰܡܶܫ, *ministravit*. *Attended, served*, Dan. vii. 10.

שֵׁן, c. aff. שִׁנּוֹ. Arab. سِنّ, *dens*. (a) *A tooth*. (b) *Ivory*. (c) *The ridge of a rock*. (d) שִׁנַּיִם, *The teeth*, either pl. or dual; probably *The two rows of teeth*. Constr. שִׁנֵּי, aff. שִׁנָּיו. (e) שְׁלֹשׁ הַשִּׁנַּיִם, *Having three teeth* or *prongs*. (a) Exod. xxi. 24; Prov. xxv. 19; Lam. ii. 16, &c. (b) 1 Kings x. 18; 2 Chron. ix. 17; Ps. xlv. 9, &c. (c) 1 Sam. xiv. 4, 5; Job xxxix. 28. (d) Gen. xlix. 12; Prov. x. 26; Amos iv. 6, &c. (e) 1 Sam. ii. 13.

שְׁנָא, v. pres. יִשְׁנֵא, for שָׁנָה. See שׁנה. Piḥ. שִׁנֵּא, for שִׁנָּה.
Puh. pres. יְשֻׁנֶּא, for יְשֻׁנֶּה.

שְׁנָא, Chald. v. pret. pl. שְׁנוֹ, pres. יִשְׁנֵא. I. q. Heb. שָׁנָה. (a) *Was changed*. (b) *Was different* from; med. מִן. (a) Dan. iii. 27; v. 6; vii. 28. (b) Ib. vii. 23, 24.

Part. f. שָׁנְיָה, pl. שָׁנְיָן, f. שָׁנְיָן, (a) Dan. v. 9. (b) Ib. vii. 3. 19.

Paḥ. pl. שַׁנִּיו, pres. pl. יְשַׁנּוֹן. (a) *Changed a command*, i. e. acted contrary to it. (b) *Made different*. (a) Dan. iii. 28. (b) Ib. v. 13.

Part. f. מְשַׁנְּיָה. *Different*, Dan. vii. 17.
Ithpa. אֶשְׁתַּנִּי, pres. יִשְׁתַּנֵּא. *Was changed*, Dan. ii. 9; iii. 19; vii. 28.
Aph. pres. יְהַשְׁנֵא. (a) *Changed*. (b) *Changed a command*. (b) Ezra vi. 11.
Infin. הַשְׁנָיָה. (a) Ezra vi. 12; Dan. vii. 25. (b) Dan. vi. 9. 16.
Part. מְהַשְׁנֵא. (a) Dan. ii. 21.

שְׁנָא, f. for שֵׁנָה. *Sleep*, Ps. cxxvii. 2.

שִׁנְאָן, m. once, Ps. lxviii. 18. According to Aben Ezra, whom Gesenius follows, *Repetition*, for שְׁנָן, r. שנה שִׁנְאָן אַלְפֵי. *Many thousands*. Others, take the word to be synonymous with שַׁאֲנָן, *Thousands of happy ones*. LXX. χιλιάδες εὐθηνούντων. Vulg. *millia lætantium*.

שָׁנָה, v. pres. יִשְׁנֶה. Arab. ثَنَّى, and Syr. ܬܢܳܐ, *iteravit*. (a) *Repeated an action*, *did it a second time*, [1] Abs. [2] Med. לְ, [3] Med. בְּ. (b) *Was different*. (c) *Was changed*. (d) *Changed a command*, *was disobedient*. (a), [1] 1 Kings xviii. 34;

Neh. xiii. 21; Job xxix. 22. [2] 1 Sam. xxvi. 8; 2 Sam. xx. 10. (c) Lam. iv. 1; Mal. iii. 6.

Imp. pl. שְׁנוּ. (a, 1) 1 Kings xviii. 34.
Part. שֹׁנֶה, pl. שׁוֹנִים, f. שׁוֹנוֹת. (a, 3) Prov. xvii. 9. (b) Esth. i. 7; iii. 8. (d) Prov. xxiv. 21.

Niph. Infin. הִשָּׁנוֹת. *Being repeated*, Gen. xli. 32.

Piḥ., שִׁנָּה, pres. יְשַׁנֶּה. Constr. immed. it. med. אֵת. (a) *Changed*. (b) *Violated* a promise, justice. (c) *Removed* a person to another place. (a) 1 Sam. xxi. 14; 2 Kings xxv. 29; Jer. lii. 33. (b) Ps. lxxxix. 35; Prov. xxxi. 5. (c) Esth. ii. 9.

Infin. שַׁנּוֹת, aff. שַׁנּוֹתוֹ. (a) Ps. xxxiv. 1; Jer. ii. 36.

Part. מְשַׁנֶּה. (a) Job xiv. 2.
Puḥ. pres. יְשֻׁנֶּא, for יְשֻׁנֶּה. Pass. of Piḥ. *Was changed*, Eccl. viii. 1.
Hith. pret. 2 f. הִשְׁתַּנִּית. *Changed, disguised himself*, 1 Kings xiv. 2.

שָׁנָה, f. constr. שְׁנַת, aff. שְׁנָתוֹ, dual שְׁנָתַיִם, pl. שָׁנִים, constr. שְׁנֵי, aff. שָׁנֵינוּ, שְׁנֵיהֶם, it. pl. constr. שְׁנוֹת, aff. שְׁנוֹתַי, &c.

Arab. سَنَة; and Syr. ܫܰܢܬܳܐ, *annus*. Probably *The repetition of the seasons*. (a) *A year*. (b) Meton., *The produce of a year*. Phrr. (c) שָׁנִים, *Years*, i. e. *several years*. (d) שָׁנָה בְשָׁנָה. *Year by year, annually*. (e) בִּשְׁנָתוֹ, *In its first year*. (f) בִּן־עֶשְׂרִים שָׁנָה, *Twenty years old*. (a) Gen. v. 3; vii. 11; xi. 10, &c. (b) Joel ii. 25. (c) 1 Sam. xxix. 3; 2 Chron. xviii. 2; Dan. xi. 6, &c. (d) Deut. xv. 20; 1 Sam. i. 7, &c. (e) Lev. xii. 6; xxiii. 12; Num. vi. 12, &c. (f) Lev. xxvii. 3; Num. i. 3, &c.

שְׁנָה, Chald. f. constr. שְׁנַת, pl. שְׁנִין, *Id*., Dan. vi. 1; vii. 1, &c.

שֵׁנָה, f. constr. שְׁנַת, aff. שְׁנָתוֹ, pl. שֵׁנוֹת, r. יָשֵׁן. (a) *Sleep*. (b) Probably *A dream*. (a) Gen. xxxi. 40; Esth. vi. 1; Prov. vi. 4. 10, &c. (b) Ps. xc. 5.

שֵׁנָה, Chald. f. aff. שִׁנְתֵּהּ, *Id*., Dan. vi. 19.

שֶׁנְהַבִּים, pl. m. twice, 1 Kings x. 22; 2 Chron. ix. 21. *Ivory*, according to the majority of interpreters: Bochart prefers *Elephants*. The etymology is doubtful. Gesenius adopts that proposed by Benary, (Annal. Litt., Berol. 1831, No. 96,) who derives the latter part of the word from the Sanscrit *ibha* इभ : *An elephant.*

שְׁנִי, m. constr. שְׁנִי, pl. שָׁנִים. Arab. سَنَا, *luxit, splenduit.* (a) *A bright colour;* pec. *the bright red colour* obtained from the תּוֹלַע. *Scarlet; any thing of a scarlet colour,* Gen. xxxviii. 28; Josh. ii. 18, &c. (b) שְׁנִי תוֹלַעַת, *Id.*, Lev. xiv. 4. 6; Num. xix. 6, &c. (c) תּוֹלַעַת שָׁנִי, and תּ"הַשָּׁנִי, *Id.*, Exod. xxviii. 5; Num. iv. 8, &c.

שֵׁנִי, m. שֵׁנִית, f. The ordinal *Second,* Gen. i. 8; iv. 19, &c. שֵׁנִית, *A second time,* Gen. xxii. 15; xli. 5, &c.

Pl. שְׁנִיִּם, [1] *Second in order,* Num. ii. 16. [2] *Chambers of a second story,* Gen. vi. 16.

שְׁנַיִם, m. constr. שְׁנֵי. The numeral *Two,* Gen. vi. 19; vii. 2, &c. Aff. שְׁנֵינוּ, שְׁנֵיכֶם, שְׁנֵיהֶם, *Both of us, of you, of them,* Gen. ii. 25; xxvii. 45; xxxi. 37, &c. שְׁנַיִם שְׁנַיִם, *Two and two, by pairs,* Gen. vii. 9. 15.

שְׁתַּיִם, f. (probably for שְׁנָתַיִם, and thus contracted that it may be distinguished from the dual of שָׁנָה, *A year.*) Constr. שְׁתֵּי, aff. שְׁתֵּיהֶם, and שְׁתֵּיהֶן, Gen. v. 18; xix. 30; Ruth i. 19; 1 Sam. xxv. 43, &c.

שְׁנֵים־עָשָׂר, m. שְׁתֵּים עֶשְׂרֵה, f. *Twelve, twelfth,* Exod. xxiv. 4; xxviii. 21, &c.

שְׁנִינָה, f. r. שׁנן. *A pointed saying, a taunt,* Deut. xxviii. 37; 1 Kings ix. 7; Jer. xxiv. 9.

שׁנן, v. pret. שִׁנּוֹתִי, שָׁנְנוּ. Arab. سَنَّ, *acuit* cultrum. Constr. immed. (a) *Sharpened,* a sword, Deut. xxii. 41. Metaph., The tongue, Ps. lxiv. 4; cxl. 4.

Part. pass. שָׁנוּן, plur. שְׁנוּנִים. *Sharpened, sharp,* of arrows, Ps. xlv. 6; Prov. xxv. 18, &c.

Pih. pret. שִׁנַּנְתָּ. *Taught assiduously.* Constr. immed. of thing, med. לְ, of pers. Deut. vi. 7.

Hith. pres. אֶשְׁתּוֹנָן. *Was wounded, pained acutely,* Ps. lxxiii. 21.

שׁנס, v. Kal non occ. Arab. شَنَصَ, and شَنَصَ, *adhæsit vel assiduè incubuit* rei. Chald. שְׁנַץ, *constrinxit.*

Pih. pres. שִׁנֵּס. *Girded* his loins, 1 Kings xviii. 46, only. LXX. συνέσφιγξε. Vulg. *accinctis.*

שְׁנָת, f. for שֵׁנָה. *Sleep,* Ps. cxxxii. 4, only.

שׂמה, v. pret. שָׂמוּ, pres. יִשְׂמֶה. Constr. immed. it. abs. *Plundered,* Ps. xliv. 11; Hos. xiii. 15.

Part. aff. שֹׂמֵהוּ, pl. שֹׂסִים, constr. שֹׁסֵי, aff. שׁוֹסֵינוּ, שֹׁסֵיהֶם, 1 Sam. xiv. 50; Is. xvii. 14, &c.

. Part. pass. שָׂסוּי, Is. xlii. 22.

Pih. שׁוֹסַתִּי, for שׁוֹסֵתִי, or שְׁסִיתִי, *Id.*, Is. x. 13.

שׁסס, v. pret. pl. aff. שְׁסָהוּ, pres. יָשֹׁסּוּ. *Id.*, Judg. ii. 14; 1 Sam. xvii. 53; Ps. lxxxix. 42.

Part. pl. aff. שֹׁאסַיִךְ, for שֹׁסְסַיִךְ, or שֹׁסַיִךְ, Jer. xxx. 16.

Niph. pl. נָשֹׁסּוּ, pres. יִשַּׁסּוּ. Pass., Is. xiii. 16; Zech. xiv. 2.

שֶׁסַע, m. Arab. شَسَعَ, *longiùs distitit;* شَاسِع, *distans, dissitus.* *Being distant; a separation, division* in a hoof, Lev. xi. 3. 7. 26; Deut. xiv. 6.

שׁסע, v. Part. שֹׁסַע, f. שֹׁסַעַת, with שֶׁסַע. *Having a division.*

Part. pass. f. שְׁסוּעָה. *Divided,* Deut. xiv. 7.

Pih. שִׁסַּע, pres. יְשַׁסַּע. Constr. immed. it. med. אֶת. (a) *Clove,* without dividing, Lev. i. 17. (b) *Tore asunder,* Judg. xiv. 6. (c) *Kept at a distance, withheld,* 1 Sam. xxiv. 7.

Infin. שַׁסַּע, (b) Judg. xiv. 6.

שׁסף, v. only in Pih. pres. יְשַׁסֵּף. Probably cogn. with שׁסע. *Cut down,* 1 Sam. xv. 33, only. LXX. ἔσφαξεν. Theod. ἐβασάνισεν. Aquila and Symm. διέσπασεν. Vulg. *in frusta concidit.* Syr. ܘܫܣܦ.

שָׁעָה, v. pres. יִשְׁעֶה, apoc. יֵשַׁע. *Looked regarded.* (a) *Looked at favourably, approved,* med. אֶל. (b) *Looked at with attention, attended,* med. בְּ. (c) *Looked to for help,* [1] Abs. [2] Med. עַל. [3] אֶל. [4] לְ. (d) *Looked away from, allowed a respite to,* med. מִן. (a) Gen. iv. 4, 5. (b) Exod. v. 9; Ps. cxix. 117. (c), [1] 2 Sam. xxii. 42. [2] Is. xvii. 7; xxxi. 1. [3] Is. xvii. 8. [4] Probably Is. xxxii. 3. See שׁעע. (d) Job vii. 19.

Imp. שְׁעֵה, pl. שְׁעוּ, (d) Job xiv. 6; Is. xxii. 4; xxix. 9.

Hiph. Imp. הָשַׁע. (a) I. q. Kal [d], Ps. xxxix. 14. (b) *Turned away* the eyes, Is. vi. 10. But see שׁעע.

4 I

שֵׁעָה

Hith. pres. תִּשְׁתָּע. *Looked about* with anxiety; *was alarmed*, Is. xli. 10. 23.

Hith. red. הִשְׁתַּעֲשִׁעוּ, *Id.*, Is. xxix. 9. See שׁעע.

שָׁעָה, Chald. def. שַׁעְתָּא. Arab. سَاعَة, and Syr. ܫܳܥܳܐ, *hora. An hour*, Dan. iv. 16. בַּהּ־שַׁעֲתָא, *Immediately*, Dan. iii. 6. 15; iv. 30; v. 5.

שַׁעֲטָה, f. constr. שַׁעֲטַת, once, Jer. xlvii. 3. Gesenius compares the Arab. شعط, II. *Contudit in partes, comminuit,* and translates, *The stamping* of the hoofs. Others take the Syr. ܫܥܛ, which is used to denote any progressive motion, whether flying, swimming, or walking, and translate *The progress* of the hoofs. Syr. ܒܫܥܛܐ ܕܦ̈ܪܣܬܗ.

שַׁעַטְנֵז, m. twice, Lev. xix. 19; Deut. xxii. 11. In the latter passage the word is explained by, a mixture *of wool and flax together.* Bochart considers it as compounded of שַׁעַט, and נֵז, the former being equivalent to the Arab. سَاطَ, r. سوط *commiscuit;* and the latter to the Chald. נוי, *fila contorsit. A mixed weaving, mixed cloth.*

שֹׁעַל, m. aff. שָׁעֳלֵי, pl. שְׁעָלִים, constr. שַׁעֲלֵי. Syr. ܫܘܥܠܐ, *pugillus.* (a) *The palm of the hand.* (b) *A handful.* (a) Is. xl. 12. (b) 1 Kings xx. 10; Ezek. xxx. 19.

שָׁעַן, v. Kal non occ.

Niph. נִשְׁעַן, pres. יִשָּׁעֵן. (a) *Leaned on*, med. עַל. (b) *Reclined*, abs. (c) *Touched* a boundary, med. לְ. (d) *Trusted in*, depended on, [1] Med. עַל. [2] אֶל. [3] בְּ. (e) *Was supported*, in prosperity, abs. (a) Judg. xvi. 26; Job viii. 15. (c) Num. xxi. 15. (d), [1] 2 Chron. xiii. 18; xvi. 7; Is. x. 20, &c. [2] Prov. iii. 5. [3] Is. l. 10. (e) Job xxiv. 23.

Infin. הִשָּׁעֵן, aff. הִשָּׁעֶנְךָ, הִשָּׁעֲנָם, 2 Chron. xvii. 7; Is. x. 20; Ezek. xxix. 7, &c.

Imp. pl. הִשָּׁעֵנוּ, (b) Gen. xvii. 4.

Part. נִשְׁעָן, 2 Kings v. 18, &c.

שָׁעַע, v. According to some cogn. Syr. ܫܥ, *linivit, occlusit.*

Imp. pl. שֹׁעוּ. Some, *Be blinded*, Is. xxix. 9. But this appears doubtful. It is more naturally derived from שׁוע, and so would signify, *Cry out for help.*

Hiph. Imp. הָשַׁע. Some, *Make blind*, immed., Is. vi. 10. But see שָׁעָה.

Pih. red. שִׁעֲשַׁע, pres. pl. יְשַׁעַשְׁעוּ. (a) *Delighted*, immed. (b) *Delighted himself in*, immed. (c) *Played*, of a child. (a) Ps. xciv. 19. (b) Ps. cxix. 70. (c) Is. xi. 8. Taking the sign. of שָׁעָה.

Puh. red. pres. pl. יְשָׁעֳשָׁע. *Was fondled*, as a child, Is. lxvi. 12.

Hith. red. pres. הִשְׁתַּעֲשַׁע, אֶשְׁתַּעֲשָׁע. *Delighted himself,* [1] Abs., Is. xxix. 9, according to some. [2] Med. בְּ, Ps. cxix. 16. 47.

שַׁעַר, m. usually, but sometimes f.—pl. שְׁעָרִים, constr. שַׁעֲרֵי, aff. שְׁעָרֶיהָ, שְׁעָרַיִךְ, שַׁעֲרֵיכֶם, &c. Arab. ثغر, *fregit*, ثغر, *separatus, divisus.* Syr. ܬܪܥ, *aperuit, secuit;* ܬܪܥܐ, ܬܘܪܥܐ, *porta ostium.* (a) *An opening, entrance, gate;* pec. *the gate* of a city. (b) *The city itself.* (c) *The gate of a city was the place for administering justice, and for any public business.* (d) *The people assembled at the gate.* (a) Josh. ii. 5; Job xxxviii. 17; Is. xlv. 1, &c. (b) Deut. xvi. 5; xvii. 2; xxviii. 52, &c. (c) Gen. xxiii. 10; xxxiv. 20; Deut. xxii. 24; Ps. cxxvii. 5, &c. (d) Ruth iii. 11.

שֹׁעֵר, m. pl. שֹׁעֲרִים, constr. שֹׁעֲרֵי. *One who has the custody of a gate; a porter*, 2 Kings vii. 10, 11; 2 Chron. xxiii. 4, &c.

שַׁעַר, v. once, Prov. xxiii. 7. Variously rendered. Arab. سِعْر, *pretium annonæ aliisve rebus impositum;* سَعَّر, *pretium constituit. Estimated the value*, abs. So Sym. εἰκάζων ἐν τῇ ψυχῇ αὐτοῦ. Vulg. *æstimat quod ignorat.*

שַׁעַר, m. pl. שְׁעָרִים. *Value; measure*, Gen. xxvi. 12, only.

שֹׁעָר, m. pl. שֹׁעָרִים, once, Jer. xxix. 17. תְּאֵנִים הַשֹּׁעָרִים, Theod. τὰ σῦκα τὰ σουαρείμ, as if denoting a peculiar kind of fig unfit for food. Vulg. *ficus malas;* and so Syr. ܬܐܢ̈ܐ ܒܝܫ̈ܬܐ. Castell, whom Gesen. follows, compares the verb שׁער, and translates *horrendi.* Possibly *Blighted figs.* Comp. Arab. سعر, *contagione infecit;* سعر, *vento fervido;* سموم, *appellato*

שָׁעַר (611) שָׁפַט

afflictus fuit vir; سَعِرَ, *contagium*; أَسْعَرُ, *macilentus*.

שַׁעֲרוּר, m. f. שַׁעֲרוּרָה, f. *Causing to shudder, horrible*, Jer. v. 30; xxiii. 14. LXX. φρικτά. Vulg. *mirabilia*.

שַׁעֲרוּרִי, m. שַׁעֲרוּרִיָה, f. *Id*., Jer. xviii. 13.

שַׁעֲשׁוּעִים, pl. m. aff. שַׁעֲשֻׁעַי, r. שׁעע. *Delight, source of delight*, Ps. cxix. 24; Prov. viii. 30; Is. v. 7, &c.

שָׁפָה, v. Kal non occ. Arab. شَفَا, *apparuit* nova luna, persona, &c. Probably *Became visible*, pec. *by ascending, rising.*
Niph. Part. נִשְׂפֶּה. *Conspicuous, lofty*, Is. xiii. 2.
Puh. pl. שֻׁפּוּ. *Were made to appear, became prominent*, Job xxxiii. 21.

שְׁפוֹט, m. r. שפט. *A judicial infliction*, 2 Chron. xx. 9, only.

שְׁפוּטִים, pl. m. *Judicial inflictions*, Ezek. xxiii. 10, only.

שְׁפוֹת, pl. f. constr. once, 2 Sam. xvii. 29, שְׁפוֹת בָּקָר. LXX. σαφὼθ βοῶν, leaving the word untranslated. Theod. γαλαθηνὰ μοσχάρια. Vulg. *pingues vitulos*. Syr. ܘܓܒܝܢ, *caseos bovinos*. Comp. Syr. ܚܦܐ, Pah. *purificavit, defæcavit*. Probably *Cheeses.*

שִׁפְחָה, f. constr. שִׁפְחַת, aff. שִׁפְחָתִי, pl. שְׁפָחוֹת, aff. שִׁפְחוֹתַי. *A female servant or slave*, Gen. xvi. 1, 2. 8; xx. 14; xxxii. 22, &c. The etymology is uncertain.

שָׁפַט, v. pres. יִשְׁפֹּט. Constr. immed. it. med. אֶת. (a) *Judged, administered justice.* (b) *Decided a cause.* (c) *Vindicated, defended the right of —.* (d) מִשְׁפָּט "ש, *Id*. (e) וּבֵין . . . . בֵּין "ש, and בְּ "ש, *Decided between —.* (f) *Punished.* (g) *Ruled.* (a) Abs., Gen. xix. 9; 1 Kings vii. 7, &c. Immed. it. med. אֶת of pers., Exod. xviii. 22; Lev. xix. 15, &c. צֶדֶק "ש, בְּצֶדֶק "ש, and מֵישָׁרִים "ש, Deut. i. 16; Ps. lviii. 2; xcvi. 13, &c. (b) Exod. xviii. 22. 26; 1 Kings iii. 28, &c. (c) 2 Sam. xviii. 31; Is. i. 23, &c. (d) Jer. viii. 28. (e) Gen. xvi. 5; Exod. xviii. 16; Ezek. xxxiv. 22, &c. (f) Ezek. vii. 3, med. בְּ; 2 Chron. xx. 12. (g) Judg. iii. 10; xvi. 31; 1 Sam. viii. 20, &c.
Infin. abs. שָׁפוֹט, constr. שְׁפֹט, aff. שָׁפְטֵנוּ, Gen. xix. 9; Ruth i. 1; 1 Sam. viii. 5, &c. In Job ix. 15, לִמְשֹׁפְטִי, is probably an error for לְשֹׁפְטִי = ־ִי + שֹׁפֵט + לְ. *For not*

judging me, i. e. *I would supplicate* (him) *not to judge me*.
Imp. שְׁפֹט, שָׁפְטָה, aff. שָׁפְטֵנִי, pl. שִׁפְטוּ, Ps. vii. 9; lxxxii. 8; Prov. xxxi. 9, &c.
Part. שֹׁפֵט, f. שֹׁפְטָה, pl. שֹׁפְטִים. *Judging; a judge, ruler*, Deut. xvi. 18; Judg. iv. 4; 1 Sam. iii. 13, &c.

Niph. נִשְׁפַּטְתִּי, pres. יִשָּׁפֵט. (a) *Was judged.* (b) *Had a controversy, reasoned with another, disputed.* (a) Ps. ix. 10. (b) Abs., Is. xliii. 26. Med. אֶת, Ezek. xvii. 20; xx. 35, 36. Med. עִם, Joel iv. 2. Med. לְ, Jer. xxv. 31.
Infin. הִשָּׁפֵט, aff. הִשָּׁפְטוֹ. Med. עִם, 2 Chron. xxii. 8; Ps. xxxvii. 33; cix. 7.
Part. נִשְׁפָּט, (b) Prov. xxix. 9, &c.

שְׁפָטִים, pl. masc. aff. שְׁפָטַי. *Judicial inflictions, judgments*, Exod. vii. 4; Prov. xix. 29, &c. Phr. בְּ שְׁפָטִים עָשָׂה, *inflicted judgments on*, Exod. xii. 12; Ezek. v. 10, &c.

שָׁפְטִין, Chald. pl. m. i. q. Heb. שֹׁפְטִים. *Judges*, Ezra vii. 25, only.

שְׁפִי, m. in pause, שֶׁפִי, pl. שְׁפָיִים, r. שפה. *An elevated and conspicuous place, having an extensive view*, Num. xxiii. 3; Is. xli. 18; Jer. iii. 2, &c.

שְׁפִיפֹן, m. once, Gen. xlix. 17. Syr. ܚܦ, and ܚܦܦ, *reptavit*. Arab. سَفَّ, *serpentis genus punctis nigris et albis distinctum*. Some kind of serpent, but the species cannot be determined. Vulg. *cerastes*. But LXX. ἐγκαθήμενος.

שַׁפִּיר, Chald. r. שפר. *Pleasing, beautiful, fine*, Dan. iv. 9. 18.

שָׁפַךְ, masc. Arab. سَفَكَ, *effudit, præsertim de sanguine*. *Pouring out*, of any liquid, dust, &c. *The place of pouring out*, of ashes, Lev. iv. 12, only.

שָׁפַךְ, v. pres. יִשְׁפֹּךְ. Constr. immed. it. med. אֶת. (a) *Poured out*, [1] Water. [2] Blood, of a sacrifice. [3] A libation. [4] Earth. (b) *Shed* blood. (c) *Threw up* a mound, by pouring out earth. (d) Metaph. *Uttered* a prayer. (e), [1] נֶפֶשׁ "ש, *Poured out his soul.* [2] לֵב "ש, *Poured out his heart.* (f) *Poured out* anger. (g) *Bestowed abundantly.* (a), [1] Exod. iv. 9; Amos v. 8. [2] Exod. xxix. 12; Lev. xvii. 13; Deut. xii. 16, &c. [3] Is. lvii. 6. [4] Lev. xiv. 41. (b) Gen. xxxvii. 22; 1 Kings ii.

שָׁפַךְ (612) שָׁפֵל

31; 2 Kings xxi. 16, &c. (c) 2 Kings xix. 32; Ezek. iv. 2; xxvi. 8, &c. (d) Ps. cii. 1; cxlii. 3. (e), [1] 1 Sam. i. 15; Ps. xlii. 5. (f) Lam. ii. 4; iv. 11; Ezek. xxii. 22, &c. (g) Ezek. xxxix. 29; Joel iii. 1, 2.

Infin. constr. שְׁפֹךְ, aff. שָׁפְכְּךָ, Is. lix. 7; Ezek. ix. 8, &c.

Imp. שְׁפֹךְ, fem. שִׁפְכִי, pl. שִׁפְכוּ, (e, 2) Ps. lxii. 9; Lam. ii. 19; Judg. vi. 20, &c.

Part. שֹׁפֵךְ, aff. שֹׁפְכוּ, fem. שֹׁפֶכֶת, pl. שֹׁפְכִים, f. שֹׁפְכוֹת, Prov. vi. 17; Lam. iv. 13; Ezek. xxii. 3, &c.

Part. pass. שָׁפוּךְ, fem. שְׁפוּכָה, Ps. lxxix. 10; Ezek. xx. 33, 34.

Niph. נִשְׁפַּךְ, pres. יִשָּׁפֵךְ. Pass. of Kal. *Was poured out, was shed*, Gen. ix. 6; 1 Kings xiii. 3; Lam. ii. 11, &c.

Infin. הִשָּׁפֵךְ, Ezek. xvi. 36.

Puh. שֻׁפַּךְ, (a) Pass. of Kal, Num. xxxv. 33; Zeph. i. 17. (b) *Slipped*, of footsteps, Ps. lxxiii. 2.

Hith. pres. יִשְׁתַּפֵּךְ, i. q. Niph., Job xxx. 16; Lam. iv. 1.

Infin. הִשְׁתַּפֵּךְ, Lam. ii. 12.

שָׁפְכָה, fem. *Membrum virile*, Deut. xxiii. 2, only.

שָׁפֵל, masc. aff. שְׁפָלֵנוּ. Arab. سَفَلَ, *inferus, humilis fuit. Being low*, either in place or rank. *A low place, a lowly condition*, Ps. cxxxvi. 23; Eccl. x. 6.

שָׁפָל, m. with ה paragogic, שְׁפֵלָה, Ezek. xxi. 31; constr. שְׁפַל, pl. שְׁפָלִים, fem. שְׁפֵלָה, constr. שִׁפְלַת. (a) *Low*. (b) *Low in rank* or *importance*. (c) שְׁפַל רוּחַ, *Humble in spirit*. (a) Of a spot, Lev. xiii. 20, 21. 26; xiv. 37. Of a tree, Ezek. xvii. 6. 24. Of a sound, Eccl. xii. 4. (b) 2 Sam. vi. 22; Job v. 11; Ezek. xvii. 14; xxi. 31, &c. (c) Prov. xvi. 18; xxix. 23.

שָׁפֵל, v. pres. יִשְׁפַּל. Constr. abs. (a) *Was low, was lowered*. (b) Metaph. *Was brought low, brought down, humbled*. (a) Is. xxxii. 19; xl. 4. (b) Is. ii. 9. 11; xxix. 4, &c.

Hiph. הִשְׁפִּיל, pres. יַשְׁפִּיל. Constr. immed. Causat. of Kal. (a) *Brought low; threw down*. (b) *Sent down*. (c) Metaph. *Cast down, humbled*. (a) Is. xxv. 12; xxvi. 5; Ezek. xvii. 24. (b) Is. lvii. 9. (c) Job xxii. 29; Is. xiii. 11; xxv. 11, &c. Abs., Ps. lxxviii. 8.

Infin. הַשְׁפִּיל, aff. הַשְׁפִּילְךָ, Prov. xxv. 7; Ezek. xxi. 26.

Imp. aff. הַשְׁפִּילֵהוּ, Job xl. 11. הַשְׁפִּילוּ שֵׁבוּ, *Humble (yourselves), sit*, i. e. *sit low* in the dust, Jer. xiii. 18.

Part. מַשְׁפִּיל, 1 Sam. ii. 7. Relat. מַשְׁפִּילִי, Ps. cxiii. 6.

שְׁפַל, Chald. m. *Low*, in rank, Dan. iv. 14.

שְׁפַל, Chald. v. Aph. הַשְׁפֵּלָה, pres. יְהַשְׁפֵּל. Constr. immed. *Humbled, brought low*, Dan. v. 22; vii. 24.

Infin. הַשְׁפָּלָה, Ib. iv. 34.

Part. מַשְׁפִּיל, Ib. v. 19.

שִׁפְלָה, f. i. q. שָׁפֵל, Is. xxxii. 19.

שְׁפֵלָה, f. aff. שִׁפְלָתוֹ. *A low* or *level country*. Always used with the article, and apparently as a proper name, Deut. i. 7; Josh. ix. 1; xi. 16, &c.

שִׁפְלוּת, f. *Lowness*, of the hands, i. e. their hanging down, their being inactive, Eccl. x. 18, only.

שָׁפָן, m. pl. שְׁפַנִּים. *The jerboa; dipus jaculus*, Linn., Lev. xi. 5; Deut. xiv. 7; Ps. civ. 18; Prov. xxx. 26. See Bochart. Hieroz., tom. i., p. 1001. The name is probably derived from the animal's *burrowing*. See ספן.

שָׁפַע, m. Syr. ܫܦܥ, *inundavit, profudit*; ܫܦܥܐ, *abundantia, copia*. *Overflowing; abundance*, Deut. xxxiii. 19.

שִׁפְעָה, f. constr. שִׁפְעַת. (a) *An overflowing*, of waters, *an inundation*. (b) *An abundance; a multitude*. (a) Job xxii. 11; xxxviii. 34. (b) 2 Kings ix. 17; Is. lx. 6; Ezek. xxvi. 10.

שֶׁפֶר, m. Syr. ܫܦܪ, *placuit, præclarus fuit*; ܫܘܦܪܐ, *pulchritudo*; ܫܦܝܪ, *pulcher*. *Pleasing; pleasantness, beauty*, Gen. xlix. 21, only.

שָׁפַר, v. pret. שָׁפְרָה. *Was pleasing; pleased*, med. עַל, Ps. xvi. 6, only.

שְׁפַר, Chald. v. pres. יִשְׁפַּר, *Id.*, Dan. iii. 32; iv. 24; vi. 2.

שִׁפְרָה, fem. i. q. שֶׁפֶר. *Beauty*, of the heavens, Job xxvi. 12: see my note.

שַׁפְרִיר, m. aff. שַׁפְרִירוֹ, once, Jer. xliii. 10. Apparently, *Some ornamental mark of royalty*. Probably *Royal canopy*. Syr. ܐܫܦܪ.

שַׁפְרַפָּר, *Canopy*. Chald. m. def. שַׁפְרַפָּרָא,

שפת (613) שׁקוּ

once, Dan. vi. 20. Syr. ܫܦܪܐ, *aurora. The dawn.*

שְׁפַת, v. pres. יִשְׁפּוֹת. Arab. ثَبَتَ, *stabilivit, fixit.* Constr. immed. *Fixed, placed,* Is. xxvi. 12; Ps. xxii. 16.

Imp. שְׁפֹת, 2 Kings iv. 38; Ezek. xxiv. 3.

שְׁפַתַיִם, m. dual, twice, Ps. lxviii. 14; Ezek. xl. 43. Arab. إِثْفِيَّة, *chytropus.* Probably some apparatus for supporting vessels for cooking. *Cooking vessels, pots.* See מִשְׁפְּתַיִם, and Appendix A.

שֶׁצֶף, m. i. q. שֶׁטֶף. *An overflowing,* Is. liv. 8, only.

שָׁק, Chald. pl. aff. שָׁקוֹהִי, i. q. Heb. שׁוֹק. *A leg.*

שָׁקַד, v. pres. יִשְׁקֹד. Constr. abs. it. med. עַל. Arab. شَقِدَ, *insomnis, vix dormiens.* (a) *Was sleepless, remained awake.* (b) *Watched, kept watch.* (c) *Watched for,* in order to effect. (a) Ps. cii. 8; cxxvii. 1. (b) Job xxi. 32; Jer. xxxi. 28. (c) Dan. ix. 14. Infin. constr. שְׁקֹד, Prov. viii. 34. Imp. pl. שִׁקְדוּ, Ezra viii. 29. Part. שֹׁקֵד, pl. constr. שֹׁקְדֵי, Jer. i. 12; viii. 6; xliv. 27. (c) Is. xxix. 20. Puh. part. plur. מְשֻׁקָּדִים. *Formed like almonds,* Exod. xxv. 33, 34; xxxvii. 19, 20. From—

שָׁקֵד, masc. pl. שְׁקֵדִים. (a) *An almond tree.* Said to be so named from its early blossoming. (b) *An almond.* (a) Eccl. xii. 5. (b) Gen. xliii. 11; Num. xvii. 23. LXX. κάρυα, ἀμύγδαλον. Aquila and Symm. ἀμύγδαλα. Vulg. *amydalas.* The word is not found in the cognate dialects.

שָׁקָה, v. Kal non occ. Arab. سَقَى, *rigavit, potum præbuit.* Æth. ሰቀየ: Id. Hiph. הִשְׁקָה, pres. יַשְׁקֶה, apoc. יַשְׁק. Constr. immed. it. med. אֶת. (a) *Made to drink.* (b) *Watered* the ground. (a), [1] Med. אֶת, or immed., Gen. xxiv. 46; xxix. 3; Num. xx. 8, &c. [2] Med. אֶת, or immed. of pers. and drink, Num. v. 24. 26; Jer. xxv. 15; xxxv. 2, &c. [3] Med. אֶת, or immed. of pers. and מִן, or בְּ, of drink, Ps. lxxx. 6; Ezek. xxxii. 6. (b) Gen. ii. 6; Deut. xi. 10; Joel iv. 18, &c. Infin. הַשְׁקוֹת, aff. הַשְׁקוֹתוֹ, Gen. xxiv. 19; Esth. i. 7, &c.

Imp. f. aff. הַשְׁקִינִי, pl. הַשְׁקוּ, Gen. xxiv. 43; xxix. 7, &c. Part. מַשְׁקֶה, Ps. civ. 13. See also p. 398. Niph. נִשְׁקָה, see שׁקע. Puh. pres. יְשֻׁקֶּה, Pass. of Hiph. *Was watered, refreshed,* Job xxi. 24.

שִׁקּוּי, m. pl. aff. שִׁקּוּיֵי, and שִׁקֻּיָי. (a) *Watering; refreshment.* (b) Plur. *Drink.* (a) Prov. iii. 8. (b) Ps. cii. 10; Hos. ii. 7.

שִׁקּוּץ, and שֶׁקֶץ, m. pl. שִׁקּוּצִים, constr. שִׁקּוּצֵי, aff. שִׁקּוּצָיו, r. שׁקץ. *An abomination, an object of detestation* or *disgust:* applied, [1] To idols. [2] To food, offered to idols. [3] To filth of any kind. [1] 1 Kings xi. 5. 7; 2 Kings xxiii. 13, &c. [2] Zech. ix. 7. [3] Nah. iii. 6.

שָׁקַט, m. Arab. سَقَطَ, *cecidit, decidit* è manu; سَكَتَ, *siluit, tacuit.* Syr. ܫܠܐ, *quievit, resedit. Rest, quiet,* pec. from war, 1 Chron. xxii. 9, only.

שָׁקַט, v. pres. יִשְׁקֹט. Constr. abs. *Rested.* (a) *Was quiet, undisturbed,* pec. of a country undisturbed by war. (b) *Ceased,* [1] Med. מִן. [2] Abs. (c) *Remained inactive.* (d) *Was silent.* (a) 2 Chron. xiii. 23; Job iii. 12; Jer. xxx. 10, &c. (b), [1] Josh. xi. 23; xiv. 15; 2 Kings xi. 20. [2] Jer. xlvii. 6, 7; Ezek. xvi. 42, &c. (c) Ps. lxxxiii. 2; Is. lxii. 1. (d) Ps. lxxvi. 9. Part. שֹׁקֵט, fem. שֹׁקֶטֶת, pl. שֹׁקְטִים, Judg. xviii. 7; Ezek. xxxviii. 11; Zech. i. 11, &c. Hiph. pres. יַשְׁקִיט, apoc. יַשְׁקֵט. Constr. abs. it. immed. it. med. לְ. (a) *Caused to rest,* or *cease.* (b) I. q. Kal [a]. (a) Job xxxiv. 29; Prov. xv. 18. Infin. הַשְׁקֵט, (a) Job xxxvii. 17; Ps. xciv. 13. (b) Is. xxxii. 17; lvii. 20, &c. Imp. הַשְׁקֵט, (b) Is. vii. 4.

שֶׁקֶל, m. pl. שְׁקָלִים, constr. שִׁקְלֵי. Arab. ثَقُلَ, *ponderosus fuit;* ثَقَّلَ, *gravitatem et pondus exploravit;* ثَقَلَ, *trutinavit nummum.* Syr. ܫܩܠ, *librando tulit, portavit;* ܫܩܠ, *pependit,* de pondere; *appendit. Weighing; a weight.* (a) *A certain weight,* used as a standard; *a shekel:* usually reckoned at *half an ounce.* (b) שֶׁקֶל הַקֹּדֶשׁ, *The shekel of the sanctuary,* which is stated to be twenty gerahs. (c) Probably *A silver coin* of that weight. (a) Gen. xxvi. 15; 1 Sam. xvii. 5; Amos viii. 5, &c. (b)

שָׁקַל (614) שָׁקַף

Exod. xxx. 13; xxxviii. 24, &c. (c) Neh. x. 33. רֶבַע שֶׁקֶל כֶּסֶף, either, *a coin weighing the fourth part of a shekel*, or, *a fourth part of the coin itself*, which possibly was divided by means of a cross, 1 Sam. ix. 8. שְׁקָלִים בְּאֶבֶן הַמֶּלֶךְ, *shekels by the king's standard*, 2 Sam. xiv. 26; but how this standard differed from that of the sanctuary does not appear.

שָׁקַל, v. pres. יִשְׁקֹל. Constr. immed. it. med. אֶת. (a) *Weighed*. (b) Pec. *Weighed money, or the precious metals in payment; paid*. (c) Metaph. *Examined, estimated, judged*. (a) 2 Sam. xiv. 26; Is. xl. 12. (b) Gen. xxiii. 16; Exod. xxii. 16; 1 Kings xx. 39, &c. (c) Job xxxi. 6.

Infin. abs. שָׁקוֹל, constr. שְׁקוֹל, (b) Esth. iv. 7. (c) Job vi. 2.

Part. שֹׁקֵל, (b) 2 Sam. xviii. 12. Abs., Is. xxxiii. 18. Some, *Paymaster, treasurer*. But LXX. οἱ συμβουλεύοντες. Vulg. *legis verba ponderans*.

Niph. נִשְׁקַל, pres. יִשָּׁקֵל. Pass. of Kal, (b) and (c). (b) Ezra viii. 33; Job xxviii. 15. (c) Job vi. 2.

שִׁקְמִים, pl. m. aff. שִׁקְמוֹתָם. *Sycamore trees*, i. e. fig-trees of a species peculiar to Egypt, Palestine, and Arabia. *Ficus sycomorus*, Linn. 1 Kings x. 27; 1 Chron. xxvii. 28; Ps. lxxviii. 47, &c. See בּוּלִים, and Celsii Hierobot., tom. i., p. 310.

שָׁקַע, v. pret. שָׁקְעָה, pres. תִּשְׁקַע. Constr. abs. (a) *Sunk*, in water. (b) *Was overflown*. (c) Of fire, *sunk down, abated*. (a) Jer. li. 64. (b) Amos ix. 5. (c) Num. xi. 2.

Niph. Keri, וְנִשְׁקְעָה (Kethiv, וְנִשְׁקָה). *Was overflown*, Amos viii. 8.

Hiph. pres. אַשְׁקִיעַ. Causat. of Kal. Constr. immed. (a) *Caused to sink, let down*. (b) *Caused to subside*. (a) Job xxxii. 34. (b) Ezek. xxxii. 14.

שְׁקַעֲרוּרֹת, pl. fem. once, Lev. xiv. 37. *Hollows, parts corroded*. LXX. κοιλάδας. Vulg. *valliculas*.

שְׁקֻפִים, m. once, 1 Kings vii. 5. Arab. سَقْف, *tectum domus*. *Covering; a coping*.

שָׁקַף, v. Kal non occ.

Niph. נִשְׁקַף. Probably *Looked over the parapet of a flat roof*. (a) *Looked, looked down*, מִן, — *through*, בְּעַד. (b) Metaph. of a place, *Lay towards*, עַל פְּנֵי. (c) Of a calamity, *Threatened*. (a) Judg. v. 28; Ps.

lxxxv. 12; Prov. vii. 6, &c. (b) Num. xxi. 20. (c) Jer. vi. 1.

Part. נִשְׁקָף, (b) Num. xxiii. 28; 1 Sam. xiii. 18.

Hiph. הִשְׁקִיף, pres. יַשְׁקִיף, apoc. יַשְׁקֵף. I. q. Niph. (a) Gen. xix. 28; Ps. xiv. 2; Lam. iii. 50, &c.

Imp. הַשְׁקִיפָה, Deut. xxvi. 15.

שְׁקֻפִים, pl. m. twice, 1 Kings vi. 4; vii. 4. *Coped; having copings*. See שָׁקַף. LXX. παρακυπτομένας, &c.

שֶׁקֶץ, m. *Abominating, detesting; an object of detestation and disgust*, used of unclean animals, Lev. vii. 21; xi. 10; Is. lxvi. 17, &c.

שָׁקַץ, v. Kal non occ.

Pih. שִׁקֵּץ, pres. יְשַׁקֵּץ. Constr. immed. it. med. אֶת. (a) *Regarded with disgust, considered as unclean*. (b) *Regarded with aversion*. (c) *Polluted*. (a) Deut. vii. 26; Lev. xi. 11, &c. (b) Ps. xxii. 25. (c) Lev. xi. 43; xx. 25.

Infin. שַׁקֵּץ, (a) Deut. vii. 26.

שִׁקּוּץ, see שִׁקּוּץ.

שָׁקַק, v. pres. יָשֹׁק. Cogn. שׁוּק. (a) *Ran to and fro*. (b) *Was eager, thirsty, hungry*. (a) Joel ii. 9.

Part. שׁוֹקֵק, (a) Is. xxxiii. 4. (b) Prov. xxviii. 15; Is. xxix. 8.

Hith. red. pres. יִשְׁתַּקְשְׁקוּן, i. q. Kal (a), Nah. ii. 5.

שֶׁקֶר, m. pl. שְׁקָרִים, constr. שִׁקְרֵיהֶם. Arab. شِقْر; and Syr. ܫܩܪܐ, *mendacium*; ܫܩܪ, *mentitus est*. (a) *Falsehood*. (b) עֵד שׁ׳. *A false witness*. (c) *A deceptive thing, a thing undeserving of confidence*. (d) *On false grounds*. (e) בְּשֶׁקֶר. *Falsely*. (f) לַשֶּׁקֶר, [1] *Id*. [2] *To no purpose*. (a) Exod. xxiii. 7; 2 Kings ix. 12; Prov. xii. 27, &c. (b) Exod. xx. 16; Deut. xix. 18; Prov. vi. 19, &c. (c) Jer. iii. 10. (f), [1] Lev. v. 24. [2] 1 Sam. xxv. 21.

שָׁקַר, v. pres. תִּשְׁקֹר. Med. לְ. *Acted falsely towards*, Gen. xxi. 23.

Pih. pret. שִׁקְּרוּ, pres. יְשַׁקֵּר. Constr. abs. it. med. בְּ. (a) *Uttered a falsehood*. (b) I. q. Kal. (a) Lev. xix. 11; 1 Sam. xxix. 29. (b) Ps. xliv. 18; lxxxix. 34; Is. lxiii. 8.

שֹׁקֶת, f. pl. constr. שִׁקֲתוֹת. r. שׁקה. *A drinking trough* for cattle, Gen. xxiv. 20; xxx. 38.

שַׂר, or שָׂרַח, pl. aff. שָׂרוֹחָתָי, i. q. שׁוּר. *A wall*, Jer. v. 10, only.

שֹׁר, m. aff. שָׁרְךָ. Arab. سُرّ, *pars umbilici quam obstetrix resecat. The navel*, Prov. iii. 8; Ezek. xvi. 4.

שְׂרָא, Chald. v. Syr. ܫܪܳܐ, *solvit quod ligatum fuit; habitavit, mansit*. Ethpe. *Solutus est.* (a) *Untied, loosened.* Metaph. *Solved.* (b) *Halted;* hence, *dwelt.* (b) Dan. ii. 22.
Infin. מִשְׁרֵא, (a) v. 16.
Part. pl. שָׁרַיִן. *Loose*, iii. 25.
Pah. pl. שָׁרִיו. (a) I. q. Kal [a] (b) *Began.* (a) Ezra v. 2.
Part. מְשָׁרֵא, (a) Dan. v. 12.
Ithpa. Pass.
Part. pl. מִשְׁתָּרַיִן. *Loose*, v. 6.

שָׂרַב, m. Syr. ܫܪܒ, *aruit.* (a) *Drought*, Is. xlix. 10. (b) According to some, *The mirage*, Is. xxxv. 7. Arab. سَرَاب, *vapor, qui meridiei tempore apparens in deserto, iter facientibus è longinquo aquæ speciem habet.*

שַׁרְבִיט, m. for שֵׁבֶט. *A sceptre*, Esth. iv. 11; v. 2; viii. 4.

שָׂרָה, v. pres. aff. יִשְׂרֶחוּ, i. q. Chald. שְׂרָא. *Loosened, set at liberty*, Job xxxvii. 3. Pih. pret. aff. שֵׁרִיתָךָ. *Id.*, Jer. xv. 11.

שֵׁרוֹת, pl. f. once, Is. iii. 19. Chald. שֵׁר, *catena, catenula; ornamentum, tam brachiorum (armillæ) quam pedum (periscelides) ex auro confectum. Chains; ornamental chains, bracelets.*

שִׁרְיָה, f. Arab. سَرِيَّة, *cuspis sagitta brevis et rotunda.* Syr. ܫܶܪܝܳܐ, *lorica.* Once, Job xli. 18. Usually *A coat of mail;* but, according to Bochart, *A kind of lance.* LXX. θώρακα. Vulg. *thorax.*

שִׁרְיוֹן, m. pl. שִׁרְיוֹנִים, and שִׁרְיוֹנוֹת. *A coat of mail*, 1 Sam. xvii. 5. 38; 2 Chron. xxvi. 14; Neh. iv. 10.

שִׁרְיָן, m. *Id.*, 1 Kings xxii. 34; 2 Chron. xviii. 33; Is. lix. 17.

שְׁרִיקוֹת, pl. f. r. שׁרק. *Whistling, piping, hissing*, Judg. v. 16; Jer. xviii. 16.

שָׁרִיר, m. pl. constr. שְׁרִירֵי. Chald. שְׁרִיר, *firmum, ratum.* ܫܰܪܺܝܪ, *confirmatus, comprobatus est. Firm; firmness*, Job xl. 16, only.

שְׁרִירוּת, f. always with לֵב. *Firmness, obstinacy* of heart, Deut. xxix. 19; Ps. lxxxi. 13; Jer. iii. 17, &c. Syr. ܫܰܪܺܝܪܽܘܬܳܐ, *veritas, firmitas.* Some comparing the Arab. شَرّ, *malè egit, malus fuit. Wickedness.*

שְׁרִית, see שְׁאֵרִית.

שְׂרְמוֹת, see שְׁדֵמָה.

שָׁרַץ, m. Æth. ሠረጸ: *germinavit, pullulavit;* ሠርጽ: *germen. Being numerous.* A generic term for *small animals*, whether insects, reptiles, or fishes, Gen. i. 20; Lev. v. 2; xi. 20, &c.

שָׁרַץ, v. pres. יִשְׁרֹץ. Constr. immed. it. abs. (a) *Became numerous.* (b) *Produced in great numbers.* (c) Usually, but not necessarily, *Moved, crept.* (a) Gen. viii. 17; Exod. i. 7; Ezek. xlvii. 9. (b) Gen. i. 20, 21; Exod. vii. 28; Ps. cv. 30. (c) Ezek. xlvii. 9.
Imp. pl. שִׁרְצוּ, (a) Gen. ix. 7.
Part. שֹׁרֵץ, f. שֹׁרֶצֶת, (c) Gen. vii. 21; Lev. xi. 29. 41—46.

שָׁרַק, v. pres. יִשְׁרֹק. Syr. ܫܪܰܩ, *sibilus. ܐܫܪܩ, sibilavit. Whistled, piped, hissed.* (a) *Called by whistling,* or *piping;* called, med. לְ. (b) *Hissed*, in contempt, [1] Abs. [2] Med. עַל. (a) Is. v. 26; vii. 18; Zech. x. 8. (b), [1] 1 Kings ix. 28; Lam. ii. 15, 16; Zeph. ii. 15. [2] Job xxvii. 23; Jer. xix. 8, &c.

שְׁרֵקָה, f. *Hissing; an object of hissing, contempt*, Jer. xxviii. 18; xix. 8; Mic. vi. 16, &c.

שָׁרַר, v. Syr. ܫܰܪ, *confirmatus est.* Ethp. *prævaluit.* Arab. شَرّ, *malum fecit.* III. *Adversatus fuit.* Kal non occ. except in Part. שׂוֹרֵר, pl. שׂוֹרְרִים, aff. שׂוֹרְרִי, Ps. v. 9; xxvii. 11, &c. *Adversary, enemy, &c.*

שָׁרַר, m. aff. שָׁרְרֵךְ, i. q. שֹׁר. *The navel*, Cant. vii. 3.

שֹׁרֶשׁ, m. aff. שָׁרְשׁוֹ, pl. constr. שָׁרְשֵׁי, aff. שָׁרָשָׁיו. Syr. ܫܶܪܫܳܐ, *radix.* (ε) *A root.* (b) *The lowest part* of a thing. [1] *The foot* of a mountain; [2] *The bottom* of the sea; [3] *The sole* of a foot. (c) *The origin, source.* (d) *Foundation, groundwork.* (e) *A shoot, sucker.* (a) 2 Kings xix. 30;

שרש (616) שש

Job viii. 17; xiv. 8, &c. (d), [1] Job xxviii. 9. [2] Ib. xxxvi. 30. [3] Ib. xiii. 27. (c) Judg. v. 14; Is. xiv. 29. (d) Job xix. 28; Prov. xii. 3. (e) Is. xi. 10; liii. 2.

שֵׁרֵשׁ, v. Piḥ. pret. aff. שֵׁרַשְׁךָ, pres. תְּשָׁרֵשׁ, Rooted up, immed., Job xxxi. 12; Ps. lii. 7.

Puh. שֹׁרַשׁ, pl. שֹׁרָשׁוּ, pres. pl. in pause יְשֹׁרָשׁוּ. (a) Was rooted up. (b) Became rooted, took root. (a) Job xxxi. 8. (b) Is. xl. 24; Jer. xii. 2.

Hiph. pres. apoc. יַשְׁרֵשׁ. (a) Took root. (b) Caused to take root. (b) Ps. lxxx. 12; Is. xxxvii. 6.

Part. מַשְׁרִישׁ, (a) Job v. 3.

שְׁרָשׁ, Chald. m. pl. aff. שָׁרְשׁוֹהִי, i. q. Heb. שֹׁרֶשׁ. A root, Dan. iv. 12. 20. 23.

שָׁרְשִׁי, Chald. f. for שְׁרִישׁוּ. Rooting up, banishment, Ezra vii. 26, only. LXX. εἰς παιδείαν. Vulg. in exilium. But Syr. [Syriac].

שַׁרְשְׁרוֹת, and שַׁרְשֶׁרֶת, pl. f. Arab. سِلْسِلَة, vinculum, catena. Chains, Exod. xxviii. 14. 22; xxxix. 15, &c.

שָׁרַת, v. Kal non occ.

Piḥ. שֵׁרֵת, pres. apoc. יְשָׁרֵת. (a) Waited on a person, as an attendant; constr. immed. it. med. אֶת. (b) Attended to a thing, med. לְ. (c) Performed the service of the sanctuary, [1] Abs. [2] בַּקֹּדֶשׁ. [3] אֶת יְהוָה. [4] לִפְנֵי יְהוָה. [5] Med. אֶת of the people in whose behalf the service is performed. (d) Worshipped, immed. (e) Of an animal, Became a sacrifice for, or Was in the power of—, immed. (a) Gen. xxxix. 4; Num. iii. 6; 1 Kings i. 4, &c. (b) Num. iv. 9. (c), [1] Num. iii. 31; iv. 14; 2 Kings xxv. 24, &c. [2] Num. iv. 12. [4] Deut. xviii. 7. [5] Ezek. xliv. 12. (e) Is. lx. 7.

Infin. שָׁרֵת, aff. שָׁרְתֵנִי, שָׁרְתוֹ, (c, 2) Exod. xxviii. 43; (c, 3) Deut. x. 8; (c, 4) Deut. xviii. 5. (d) Ezek. xx. 32.

Part. מְשָׁרֵת, aff. מְשָׁרְתוֹ, f. מְשָׁרַת, for מְשָׁרֶתֶת, pl. מְשָׁרְתִים, constr. מְשָׁרְתֵי, aff. מְשָׁרְתָיו, Num. xi. 28; 2 Sam. xiii. 17; 1 Kings i. 15, &c.

שָׁרֵת, m. The service of the sanctuary, Num. iv. 12; 2 Chron. xxiv. 14.

שִׂשָׂה, see שׂשׂ.

שֵׁשׁ, m. שִׁשָּׁה, f. constr. שֵׁשֶׁת. Arab. سِتّ, سِتَّة, sex. The numeral Six, Gen. vii. 6; xxx. 20; Exod. xvi. 26, &c. Pl. שִׁשִּׁים. Sixty, Gen. xxv. 26, &c.

שֵׁשׁ, m. (a) I. q. שַׁיִשׁ. White marble, Esth. i. 6. (b) A very fine kind of linen, used for the dresses of priests and persons of high rank, i. q. בּוּץ, Gen. xli. 42; Exod. xxviii. 40; Ezek. xvi. 10, &c. See Celsii Hierobot., tom. ii., p. 259.

שֵׁשֵׁא, v. Piḥ. pret. aff. שֵׁשֵׁאתִיךָ, Ezek. xxxix. 2, only. LXX. καθοδηγήσω σε. Vulg. educam te. Arab. شَصَّ, abiit.

IV. Removit. Æth. ሰውሰው : contr. ሰወ : v. አንሰወ : ambulavit. The signification is very doubtful. Probably Caused thee to walk, led thee.

שִׁשָּׁה, v. שִׁשִּׁיתָם, once, Ezek. xlv. 13. Divided into six parts, gave a sixth part of: r. שֵׁשׁ.

שִׁשִּׁי, m. שִׁשִּׁית, f. The ordinal, Sixth, Gen. i. 31; Exod. xxvi. 9, &c. In f. A sixth part, Ezek. iv. 11; xlv. 13; xlvi. 14.

שָׁשֵׁר, in pause, m. Arab. أَشَرَ, rubicundus. A red colouring matter, either Red ochre, or Red lead, Jer. xxii. 14; Ezek. xxiii. 14, only. LXX. ἐν μίλτῳ, ἐν γραφίδι. Vulg. sinopide; coloribus.

שֵׁת, f. pl. שָׁתוֹת, aff. שָׁתוֹתֵיהֶם, שָׁתוֹתֶיהָ. Arab. سَتّ, and إِسْت, pl. أَسْتَاه, and إِسْتَات, nates. See שִׁית. (a) The seat, posteriors. (b) Pl. Foundations. Metaph., Nobles, chiefs. (a) 2 Sam. x. 4; Is. xx. 4. (b) Ps. xi. 3; Is. xix. 10.

שֵׁת, and שִׁת, Chald. m. i. q. Heb. שֵׁשׁ. Six, Ezra vi. 15; Dan. iii. 1. Pl. שִׁתִּין. Sixty, Ezra vi. 3; Dan. iii. 1; vi. 1.

שָׁת, pret. of שִׁית, it. שָׁתָה. שַׁתִּי.

שָׁתָה, v. pres. יִשְׁתֶּה, apoc. יֵשְׁתְּ. Syr. ܐܫܬܝ, and Æth. ሰትየ : bibit. Cogn. שקה. Constr. immed. it. med. אֶת, it. abs. (a) Drank. (b) Metaph., Swallowed greedily, indulged. (c) Experienced. (d) Consumed. (e) Drank· the cup of wrath. (a) Gen. xliv. 5; Exod. xxxiv. 28; 2 Sam. xix. 36; Eccl. ii. 24, &c. (b) Job xxxiv. 7. (c) Job xxi. 20. (e) Jer. xxv. 26; xlix. 12.

שתה—ת (617) שתם—תאו

Infin. abs. שָׁתֹה, שָׁתוֹ, constr. שְׁתוֹת, שְׁתוֹת, aff. שְׁתוֹתוֹ, Exod. vii. 18; 1 Kings xiii. 23; Is. xxii. 13; Jer. xlix. 12, &c.
Imp. שְׁתֵה, pl. שְׁתוּ, Gen. xxiv. 14; Jer. xxxv. 5, &c.
Part. שֹׁתֶה, f. שֹׁתָה, pl. שֹׁתִים, constr. שֹׁתֵי, aff. שֹׁתָיו, (b) Job xv. 16. (c) Prov. xxvi. 6. (d) Job vi. 4; 1 Sam. xxx. 13, &c.
Niph. pres. יִשָּׁתֶה. Pass. of Kal. *Was drunk*, Lev. xi. 34.

שְׁתָה, or שְׁתָא, Chald. pret. pl. אִשְׁתִּיו with א euphonic, pres. יִשְׁתּוֹן, *Id. Drank*, Dan. v. 2—4.
Part. שָׁתֵין, pl. שָׁתַיִן, Dan. v. 1. 23.

שְׁתִי, m. (a) *Drinking*; r. שָׁתָה, Eccl. x. 17. (b) *The warp* of a web: r. שיה.
Comp. Arab. سَتا. *Id.*, Lev. xiii. 48—59.

שְׁתִיָּה, f. r. שָׁתָה. *Drinking*, Esth. i. 8.

שָׁתִיל, m. pl. constr. שְׁתִלֵי, r. שתל. *A plant, a shoot*, Ps. cxxviii. 3; only. Syr. ܫܬܠܐ, *stolo*.

שְׁתַיִם, see שְׁנַיִם.

שָׁתַל, v. pret. שְׁתַלְתִּי, pres. aff. אֶשְׁתָּלֶנּוּ.

Syr. ܫܬܠ, *plantavit* arborem. *Planted* a tree, Ezek. xvii. 22, 23.
Part. pass. שָׁתוּל, f. שְׁתוּלָה, pl. שְׁתוּלִים, Ps. i. 3; xcii. 14; Ezek. xvii. 8, &c.

שָׁתַם, only in the phr. שְׁתֻם הָעָיִן, Num. xxiv. 3. 15. The Vulg. takes the word as a part. pass. of סתם, i. q. סתם, — *cujus obturatus est oculus*. But the LXX. ὁ ἀληθινῶς ὁρῶν, as if for לוֹ הָעַיִן אֲשֶׁר אֹם, *Whose eye is perfect*.

שָׁתַן, v. only in the phr. מַשְׁתִּין בְּקִיר.
Syr. ܫܬܢ, *minxit*. According to Simonis this word is a contraction of מַשְׁתִּין, the root being שׁין. LXX. οὐροῦντα πρὸς τοῖχον, and so the other versions. The phrase itself has been variously interpreted of *males, children*, and *dogs*. The last seems most probable. 1 Sam. xxv. 22. 34; 1 Kings xiv. 10; xvi. 13; xxi. 21; 2 Kings ix. 8.

שָׁתַק, v. pres. יִשְׁתֹּק. Cogn. שקט. (a) *Became silent*, of the sea, Jonah i. 11, 12. (b) *Was at rest*, and in security. Ps. cvii. 30. (c) *Ceased*, of strife, Prov. xxvi. 20.

שָׁתַת, v. pl. שׁתוּ, see שׁיח.

ת

ת, *Taw*, or *Tav*, the twenty-second and last letter of the Hebrew alphabet, is sounded as *th* in *thin* when it has no dagesh, and as *t* in *tin* when it has one. As a numeral, it stands for *four hundred*, Gram. art. 4.

תָּא, m. pl. תָּאִים, constr. תָּאֵי, aff. תָּאָיו, it. pl. תָּאוֹת. Arab. نَوَى, *substitit, divertitque* aliquo in loco, n. a. نَوًى. Syr. ܬܘܢܐ, *thalamus*. *A room, chamber*, 1 Kings xiv. 28; 2 Chron. xii. 11; Ezek. xl. 7. 33. See Append. A.

תָּאַב, v. I. pret. תָּאַבְתִּי. Cogn. אבה, and אוה. *Desired, longed for*, med. ל, Ps. cxix. 40. 174.
II. Pih. part. מְתָאֵב, i. q. מְתָעֵב. *Abhorring*, med. אֵת, Amos vi. 8.

תַּאֲבָה, f. *Desire*, Ps. cxix. 20, only.

תָּאָה, v. Kal non occ.

Pih. pres. תְּתָאוּ. *Marked out, marked*, Num. xxxiv. 7, 8, See תוה.

תְּאוֹ, Deut. xiv. 5, and תוֹא, Is. li. 20. *The Egyptian antelope. Antelope Oryx*, Linn. See Bochart. Hieroz., tom. i. p. 974.
Comp. Arab. تَأَى, *præcessit et prævertit*.

תַּאֲוָה, f. constr. תַּאֲוַת, aff. תַּאֲוָתִי, תַּאֲוָתָם, r. אוה. (a) *Desire*. (b) *An object of desire*. (a) Num. xi. 4; Ps. cvi. 14; Prov. xxi. 26, &c. (b) Gen. iii. 7; Ps. xxi. 3; Prov. xiii. 12, &c.

תְּאוֹמִים, and תּוֹמִם, pl. masc. constr. תְּאוֹמֵי. Arab. تَوْءَم, *didymus*; تَوْءَم, *socium habuit in partu fratrem*. Syr. ܬܐܡܐ, *gemellus*. *Twins*, Gen. xxv. 24; xxxviii. 27; Cant. iv. 5.

תָּאָלָה, f. aff. תַּאֲלָתְךָ, r. אלה. *A curse*, Lam. iii. 65.

4 K

תאם, m. pl. constr. תְּאָמֵי. *Twins*, Cant. vii. 4.

תאם, v. *Was double*.
Part. plur. תֹּאֲמִים, Exod. xxvi. 24; xxxvi. 29.
Hiph. *Bore twins*.
Part. pl. f. מַתְאִימוֹת, Cant. iv. 2; vi. 6.

תְּאֵנָה, f. aff. תְּאֵנָתִי, &c. pl. תְּאֵנִים, constr. תְּאֵנֵי, aff. תְּאֵנֵיכֶם. Arab. تِين, coll. *ficus, fructus*. Syr. ܬܐܢܐ, *ficus, fructus et arbor*. (a) *A fig tree*. (b) Pl. *Figs*. (a) Gen. iii. 7; 1 Kings iv. 25; Prov. xxvii. 18, &c. (b) 2 Kings ii. 7; Is. xxxviii. 21; Jer. viii. 13, &c.

תאנה, f. aff. תַּאֲנָתָהּ, r. אנה: once, Jer. ii. 24. Variously rendered: *Periodical impulse; sexual impulse; impulse of anger*. Arab. أنى, *tempus fuit; tempestivum fuit; ad maturitatem pervenit; summo ardore ferbuit aqua calida*.

תְּאֵנָה, fem. once, Judg. xiv. 4. *An opportunity, or revenge*. See אנה. LXX. ἐκδίκησιν. Aquila, πρόφασιν. Ἀλλ' ἀνταπόδομα. Vulg. *occasionem*.

תַּאֲנִיָּה, f. syn. of אֲנִיָּה. *Suffering, pain*, Is. xxix. 2; Lam. ii. 5, only.

תְּאֻנִים, pl. m. r. אני. *Vexation, vanity, falsehood*, Ezek. xxiv. 12, only.

תֹּאַר, masc. aff. תָּאֳרוֹ, and תָּאֳרָם. Arab. تار, r. تور, *circumivit, conversus fuit*. See חור, *contour*. (a) *Form, personal appearance*. (b) *A handsome form; beauty*. (a) Gen. xli. 19; 1 Sam. xxviii. 14; Is. lii. 14; Lam. iv. 8, &c. Phr. יְפֵה ת", Gen. xxix. 17; xxxix. 6, &c. (b) 1 Sam. xvi. 18; Is. liii. 2.

תָּאַר, v. *Of a boundary, Turned, made a circuit*: but usually, *was formed, was drawn*, Josh. xv. 9. 11; xviii. 14. 17.
Pih. pres. aff. יְתָאֳרֵהוּ. *Formed, marked the form of*, Is. xliv. 13.

תְּאַשּׁוּר, m. *Some valuable or ornamental tree*: see אֶשֶׁר. According to Celsius, *the box tree*, Is. xli. 19; lx. 13. LXX. λεύκην, κέδρῳ. Vulg. *buxum; pinus*.

תֵּבָה, f. constr. תֵּבַת. Arab. تابوت, *arca*, pec. *feralis*. Probably *A chest* or *vessel of any kind*. Used only of Noah's ark, and of the vessel in which Moses was exposed, Gen. vi. 14, &c.; Exod. ii. 3.

תְּבוּאָה, f. constr. תְּבוּאַת, aff. תְּבוּאָתִי, pl. תְּבוּאוֹת, aff. תְּבוּאֹתֵיכֶם, r. בוא. (a) *Coming in, being stored up*. (b) *Income, revenue, profit*. (c) Pec. *Produce, fruit*, of the earth, the threshing floor, or the wine-press. (d) Metaph. *Fruit, effect*. (a) Ps. cvii. 37. (b) Prov. x. 16; xv. 6; Eccl. v. 9, &c. (c) Lev. xxiii. 39; xxv. 3; Deut. xiv. 22, &c. (d) Prov. xviii. 20.

תבון, m. aff. תְּבוּנָם, and—

תְּבוּנָה, fem. aff. תְּבוּנָתִי, pl. תְּבוּנוֹת, aff. תְּבוּנֹתֵיכֶם, r. בין, i. q. בִּינָה. *Understanding, discernment, prudence, skill*, Deut. xxxii. 28; Job xii. 13; Ps. cxxxvi. 5; Prov. v. 1; xxi. 30; Hos. xiii. 2, &c.

תבוסה, f. constr. תְּבוּסַת, once, 2 Chron. xxii. 7: r. בוס. *Trampling down; ruin*.

תָּבִיר, m. תְּבִירָה, f. Chald. *Liable to be broken, brittle*, Dan. ii. 42, only. Syr. ܬܒܪ, *fregit*.

תֵּבֵל, f. (a) *The world, the earth;* pec. *the inhabited parts of it*. (b) *Its inhabitants; mankind*. (a) 2 Sam. xxii. 16; Job xxxvii. 12; Ps. xxiv. 1; Is. xiv. 17. 21, &c. (b) Job xviii. 18; Ps. ix. 9; xcvi. 13, &c. The etymology is uncertain. Some derive it from יבל, and consider it properly to signify the *productive, fertile*, part of the earth's surface. See יבל. Syr. ܬܐܒܝܠ, *orbis habitabilis*. Pl. non occ.

תֶּבֶל, masc. Used of incestuous and unnatural intercourse, *Confusion*, i. e. a disregard of right and wrong, or of natural distinctions: r. בלל, Lev. xviii. 23; xx. 12, only. LXX. μυσαράν. Symm. ἄρρητον. Aquila, ἀπειρημένον. Vulg. *scelus*. Syr. ܬܘܒܠܐ.

תַּבְלִית, f. aff. תַּבְלִיתָם, r. בלה. *Destruction*, Is. x. 26.

תְּבַלֻּל, m. r. בלל. *Confusion, disorder; an injury* or *defect* in the eye, producing *confusion* or *indistinctness of vision*, Lev. xxi. 20, only. Aquila, ὑπόχυσις. LXX. πτίλλος. Vulg. *albuginem*.

תֶּבֶן, m. Arab. تِبن, *stramen, palea, Straw*, Gen. xxiv. 25; Exod. v. 7—18; Job xxi. 18, &c.

תבן (619) תו

תַּבְנִית, f. r. בנה. (a) *Building.* (b) *Model, pattern,* for building. (c) *Form, resemblance.* (a) Ps. cxliv. 12. (b) Exod. xxv. 9; 1 Chron. xxviii. 11; Ezek. xliii. 10, &c. (c) Deut. iv. 16—18; Josh. xxii. 28, &c.

תַּגְמוּל, m. pl. aff. תַּגְמוּלוֹהִי, r. גמל. *Retribution; kindness,* Ps. cxvi. 12, only.

תִגְרָה, f. constr. תִּגְרַת, r. גרה. *Attack; stroke,* Ps. xxxix. 11, only.

תִּדְהָר, masc. twice, Is. xli. 19; lx. 13. The name of a tree: according to some, *The pine;* others, *the Indian plane.* For the etymology, some compare the Arab. دَهْر, *perpetuitas;* others, زَهَر, *luxit, splenduit.* LXX. κυπάρισσον, πεύκη. Vulg. *ulmum; buxus.* See Hierobot., tom. ii. p. 271.

תְּדִירָא, Chald. f. r. דור. *A revolution.* בִּתְדִירָא, *continually,* Dan. vi. 17. 21.

תֹּהוּ, for תֹּהֶו, m. (a) *Emptiness.* (b) *A vain thing, a thing of nought, nothing.* (c) Adv. *In vain, to no purpose.* לְתֹהוּ, *Id.* (d) *Desolation.* (e) *A desert, wilderness.* (a) Gen. i. 2. (b) 1 Sam. xii. 21; Is. xliv. 9; lix. 4, &c. (c) Is. xlv. 19; xlix. 4. (d) Is. xxiv. 10; xxxiv. 11. (e) Job vi. 18; xii. 24; xxvi. 7, &c. Arab. تِيه, *desertum.*

תְּהוֹם, c. pl. תְּהוֹמוֹת, r. הום. (a) *The deep, the ocean;* from its tossing and roaring. (b) Fully, תְּהֹי רַבָּה, *Id.* (c) Pl. *Waves.* (a) Gen. i. 2; xlix. 25; Job xxviii. 14, &c. (b) Gen. vii. 11; Is. li. 10. (c) Exod. xv. 5. 8; Ps. xxxiii. 7.

תְּהִלָּה, fem. constr. תְּהִלַּת, aff. תְּהִלָּתִי, pl. תְּהִלּוֹת, r. הלל. (a) *Praise.* (b) *An object, a subject of praise.* (c) *A hymn of praise.* Pl. תְּהִלִּים, *the* (book of) *Psalms.* (a) Neh. xii. 46; Ps. xl. 4; c. 4, &c. (b) Deut. xxvi. 19; Is. lxii. 7. (c) Ps. cxlv. 1.

תָּהֳלָה, f. once, Job iv. 18. Arab. تَهَلٌ and تَهَلٌ, i. q. بَاطِل, *vanus; res vana. Folly, emptiness.* Sym. ματαιότητα. LXX. σκολιόν τι. Vulg. *pravitatem.* See הלל, No. III.

תַּהֲלֻכוֹת, pl. f. r. הלך. *Processions,* Neh. xii. 31, only.

תַּהְפֻּכוֹת, pl. f. r. הפך. *Perversion, perverseness,* Deut. xxxii. 20; Prov. ii. 11. 14; vi. 14, &c.

תָּו, m. Arab. تَوٌ, توى, *signum in animalis femore vel collo impressum crucis formâ.* A mark in the form of a cross, which was also the ancient form of the letter Taw, Ezek. ix. 4. Comp. Rev. vii. 3, &c. In Job xxxi. 35, we have תָּוִי, which some have taken as the same word in the sense of *my subscription, my mark* affixed to my pleadings. This certainly appears far fetched. Others consider תָּוִי as a contraction of תְּאָוִי, or תַּאֲוִי, which they suppose equivalent to תַּאֲוָתִי, *My desire.* If we suppose a primitive תוו having the sense of *to burn, to mark by burning, to brand;* and, Metaph. *to burn with desire, to desire,* the two significations of *a mark,* and *desire,* will be connected in a very simple manner. Comp. Æth. ኣተወ: *arsit.* See my note.

תּוֹא, see תְּאוֹ.

תוּב, Chald. v. pres. יְתוּב. I. q. Heb. שׁוּב. *Returned.* Med. עַל, Dan. iv. 31. 33. Aph. הֲתִיב, pres. יְתִיבוּן, and יַהֲתִבוּן. (a) *Returned, carried back.* (b) *Answered;* immed. of pers. or words. (a) Ezra vi. 5. (b) Ezra v. 5. 11; Dan. ii. 14.
Infin. aff. הֲתָבוּתִי, (b) Dan. iii. 16.

תּוֹדָה, f. constr. תּוֹדַת, pl. תּוֹדוֹת, r. ידה. (a) *Confession.* (b) *Praise, thanksgiving.* (c) *A company* or *chorus* of persons giving thanks. (d) Phr. "ת נְבַח, *Offered praise.* (e) "ת זֶבַח, *A sacrifice of thanksgiving.* (a) Josh. vii. 19; Ezra x. 11, &c. (b) Ps. xxvi. 7; Is. li. 3. (c) Neh. xii. 31. 38. 40. (d) Ps. L. 14. 23; cvii. 22; cxvi. 17. (e) Lev. vii. 12; xxii. 29; 2 Chron. xxxiii. 16, &c.

תְּוַהּ, Chald. v. Syr. ܬܘܗ, *stupuit, demiratus est.* Cogn. תמה, *Was astonished,* Dan. iii. 24, only.

תּוּחַ, v. Kal non occ. See פִּי.
Pih. pres. apoc. יְתָו. *Made marks, scrawled,* 1 Sam. xxi. 13.
Hiph. הִתְוִיתָ. *Set* a mark, *marked* with a cross, Ezek. ix. 4. In Ps. lxxviii. 41, הִתְווּ, is by some referred to this primitive, and translated, *Set bounds to, limited* the Holy One of Israel, i. e. presumed to dictate to Him. Others take the Syr. ܬܘܐ, *pænituit* and translate *Grieved.* LXX. παρώξυναν. Vulg. *exacerbaverunt.*

תּוֹחֶלֶת, f. aff. תּוֹחַלְתִּי, תּוֹחַלְתּוֹ, r. יחל.

Expectation, hope, Ps. xxxix. 8; Prov. x. 28; Lam. iii. 18, &c.

תָּוֶךְ, m. constr. תּוֹךְ, aff. תּוֹכִי, &c. (a) *The middle.* עַמּוּדֵי הַתָּוֶךְ, *The middle pillars,* Judg. xvi. 29. שַׁעַר הַתָּוֶךְ, *The middle gate,* Jer. xxxix. 3. (b) בְּתָוֶךְ, *In the middle,* Gen. xv. 10; Num. xxxv. 5, &c. (c) בְּתוֹךְ, *In the middle* or *midst of; among, within, through,* Gen. ix. 21; xviii. 24; xxiii. 10; Exod. xi. 4, &c. (d) מִתּוֹךְ, *From the midst of,* Gen. xix. 29; Exod. iii. 2, &c. (e) אֶל־תּוֹךְ, *Into the midst of,* Gen. xiv. 23; Num. xvii. 12, &c.

תּוֹדָה, see הֹד.

תּוֹכֵחָה, f. pl. תּוֹכָחוֹת, r. יכח. *Reproof, punishment,* 2 Kings xix. 3; Ps. cxlix. 7; Is. xxxvii. 3; Hos. v. 9.

תּוֹכַחַת, f. aff. תּוֹכַחְתִּי, תּוֹכַחְתּוֹ, pl. תּוֹכָחוֹת, constr. תּוֹכְחוֹת, r. יכח. (a) *An argument.* (b) *Reproof.* (c) Probably *Punishment.* (a) Job xiii. 6; xxiii. 4; Ps. xxxviii. 15. (b) Prov. x. 17; xii. 1; xiii. 18, &c. (c) Ps. xxxix. 12; lxxiii. 14; Prov. iii. 11.

תּוֹכִים, see תֻּכִּיִּים.

תּוֹלְדוֹת, pl. f. aff. תּוֹלְדֹתָי, תּוֹלְדֹתָם, r. ילד. (a) *Birth.* כְּתוֹלְדֹתָם, *According to their seniority,* Exod. xxviii. 10. (b) *Posterity,* Gen. v. 1; xi. 10; Num. iii. 1, &c. (c) Probably *History,* Gen. ii. 4; vi. 9.

תּוֹלָל, m. pl. aff. תּוֹלָלֵינוּ, once, Ps. cxxxvii. 3. Variously interpreted. (1) r. ילל. *Those who cause us to lament.* (2) Arab. تَلَّ, *stravit humi, prostravit; conjecit in malum.* IV. *Vinxit; manu duxit. Those who cast us down;* or, *Those who make up us captives.* (3) As if שׁוֹלָלֵינוּ, *Those who spoil us.* The first is perhaps the most natural. LXX. οἱ ἀπαγαγόντες ἡμᾶς. Ἀλλ᾽. οἱ καταλαζονευόμενοι ἡμῶν. Vulg. *qui abduxerunt nos.*

תּוֹלָע, m. pl. תּוֹלָעִים; תּוֹלֵעָה, and תּוֹלַעַת f. aff. תּוֹלַעְתָּם. Arab. تَلَّ, *longitudo colli;* تَلِيع, *procerus vir.* Syr. ܬܘܠܥܐ, and ܬܘܠܥܐ, *vermiculus, qui ex cocco nascitur.* (a) *A worm,* of any kind. (b) Pec. *The worm used in dyeing scarlet.* (c) *Scarlet, scarlet cloth.* (a) Exod. xvi. 20; Jonah iv. 7; Is. xiv. 11, &c. Metaph. Of a weak, helpless person, Ps. xxii. 7; Is. xli. 14. (b) Job xxv. 6. (c) Is. i. 18; Lam. iv. 5. Fully, [1] תּוֹלַעַת הַשָּׁנִי, Exod. xxviii. 5; xxxv. 25, &c. [2] שָׁנִי, Exod. xxv. 4; xxviii. 6, &c. [3] ת"ש, Lev. xiv. 4. 48, &c.

תּוֹמִים, see תְּאוֹמִים.

תּוֹעֵבָה, f. constr. תּוֹעֲבַת, pl. תּוֹעֵבוֹת, constr. תּוֹעֲבוֹת, aff. תּוֹעֲבוֹתָיו, &c. r. תעב. (a) *An abomination, an object of abhorrence.* (b) *An impure* or *detestable action.* (c) *Any thing causing a ceremonial pollution.* (d) *An idol.* (a) Lev. xviii. 22; xx. 13; Deut. vii. 25, &c. (b) Ezek. xxii. 11; xxxiii. 26; Mal. ii. 11, &c. (c) Gen. xliii. 32; xlvi. 34; Deut. xiv. 3. (d) Deut. vii. 26; 2 Kings xxiii. 13.

תּוֹעָה, f. r. תעה. *Error.* (a) *An erroneous* and *impious sentiment,* Is. xxxii. 6. (b) *Harm, failure,* Neh. iv. 2.

תּוֹעָפוֹת, pl. f. constr. תּוֹעֲפוֹת. Two etymologies are given. (a) Taking יָעֵף, and the Arab. وَجَفَ, *celeriter, cucurrit;* [1] *Swiftness,* Num. xxiii. 22; xxiv. 8. [2] *Wealth, treasures;* as being acquired by activity and fatigue, Job xxii. 25; Ps. xcv. 4. (b) Taking the Arab. يَفَع, *ascendit montem;* يَفَع, *collis;* [1] *Height,* Num. xxiii. 22; xxiv. 8; Ps. xcv. 4. [2] *Heaps,* Job xxii. 25.

תּוֹצָאוֹת, pl. f. constr. תּוֹצְאוֹת, aff. תּוֹצְאוֹתָם, r. יצא. *Going out.* (a) *Termination* of a territory or of a line of boundary. (b) *Escape.* (c) *Result.* (a) Num. xxxiv. 8; Josh. xv. 4, &c. (b) Ps. lxviii. 21. (c) Prov. iv. 23.

תּוֹר, and תֹּר, m. 1. (a) *The turtle dove:* the name being taken from the note of the bird as in the Latin *turtur,* and the Greek τρυγών. (b) Metaph. *Any beloved object.* (a) Gen. xv. 9; Lev. i. 14; v. 6, &c. (b) Ps. lxxiv. 19.

II. For תּוֹרָה. *Manner,* 1 Chron. xvii. 17; See 2 Sam. vii. 19.

III. Arab. تَار, r. نور, *circumivit, conversus fuit;* تَار, *tempus, vicis. Going* or *coming round.* (a) *A turn,* of persons or things succeeding each other. (b) Probably *An ornamental chain* or *band.* (a) Esth. ii. 12. 15. (b) Cant. i. 10, 11.

תור (621) תות

תוּר, v. pret. תַּרְתִּי, pres. יָתוּרוּ. *Went about*, or *round*. (a) *Travelled*, as a merchant, abs. (b) Went *round* a country, *examined* it, med. אֶת. (c) *Went over*, mentally, *investigated*. (d) *Thought of, purposed*. (e) *Looked out for, provided*. (f) *Went astray*. (b) Num. xiii. 2. 21. 32; xiv. 34. (d) Eccl. ii. 3. (e) Ezek. xx. 6. (f) Num. xv. 39.

Infin. תּוּר, (b) Num. xiii. 16, 17. (c) Eccl. i. 13; vii. 25. (e) Num. x. 33; Deut. i. 33.

Part. pl. תָּרִים. (a) *Travelling merchants*, 1 Kings x. 15; 2 Chron. ix. 14. (b) *Spies*, Num. xiv. 6.

Hiph. pres. יָתִיר. *Sent spies, sent to examine*, Judg. i. 23.

תּוֹר, Chald. m. pl. תּוֹרִין, i. q. Heb. שׁוֹר. *An ox*, Ezra vi. 9. 17; vii. 17; Dan. iv. 22, &c.

תּוֹרָה, f. constr. תּוֹרַת, aff. תּוֹרָתִי, pl. תּוֹרוֹת, aff. תּוֹרוֹתַי, &c. r. ירה. (a) *Instruction, direction*. (b) *A law, an enactment, a regulation*. (c) *The Law*: fully [1] תּוֹרַת יְהֹוָה, [2] תּ״ הָאֱלֹהִים; or [3] תּ״ מֹשֶׁה. (d) סֵפֶר הַתּוֹרָה, *The book of the Law*. (e) *Manner, rule of conduct*. (a) Job xxii. 22; Prov. i. 8; xiii. 14, &c. (b) Exod. xii. 49; Lev. vii. 7; Num. xv. 16, &c. (c) Deut. iv. 44; xvii. 19; xxxiii. 4, &c. [1] Exod. xiii. 9; 1 Chron. xxii. 12; 2 Chron. xii. 1, &c. [2] Josh. xxiv. 26; Neh. viii. 18; x. 29, &c. [3] Josh. viii. 31; xxiii. 6, &c. (d) Deut. xxxi. 26; Josh. i. 8; viii. 34, &c. (e) 2 Sam. vii. 19.

תּוֹשָׁב, m. aff. תּוֹשָׁבְךָ, pl. תּוֹשָׁבִים, constr. תּוֹשְׁבֵי, r. ישׁב. *An inhabitant*, pec. an inhabitant who is of another nation, *a settler, sojourner*, Exod. xii. 45; Lev. xxii. 10; Num. xxxv. 15, &c.

תּוּשִׁיָּה, f. Arab. وَسِيَ, *largitus est*; وَشِيَ, *multus fuit; coloravit pinxitve* pannum; *pulchrum reddidit*. IV. *Confecit rem: juvit restituitque ægrotum medicina; abundavit opibus* vir. وَأَشَاءَ, *Opulentia, abundantia* opum. Cogn. יֵשׁ, יָשַׁשׁ. (a) *Abundance, wealth*. (b) *Abundantly, entirely*. (c) *Security*. (d) *The means of security, wisdom*. (a) Job v. 12; vi. 13; xi. 6, &c. (b) Job xxx. 22. (c) Prov. ii. 7;

viii. 14; Mic. vi. 9. (d) Prov. iii. 21; Is. xxviii. 29. See my note on Job v. 12.

תּוֹתָח, m. once, Job xli. 21. Arab. وَقَتَ, *fuste percussit*; مِيتَخَة, *fustis. A club*. LXX. σφυρά. Vulg. *malleum*.

תזז, v. Kal non occ. Arab. تَازَ, r. تيز, *mortuus fuit*.

Hiph. הֵתַז. Probably *Left to wither, to die*, Is. xviii. 5. But LXX. ἀποκόψει. Vulg. *excutientur*.

תַּזְנוּת, f. aff. תַּזְנוּתָם, תַּזְנוּתָם, pl. aff. תַּזְנוּתַיִךְ, תַּזְנוּתָיהָ, r. זנה. *Whoredom*. Metaph. *Idolatry*, Ezek. xvi. 15—36; xxiii. 7—43.

תַּחְבֻּלוֹת, pl. f. aff. תַּחְבֻּלֹתָיו, r. חבל. Arab. حَبِلَ, *valdè versutus, gnarus, prudens*. (a) *Guidance, direction*. (b) *Rule of action*. (c) *Wisdom*. (a) Prov. xi. 14; xxiv. 6. (b) Prov. xii. 5. (c) Job xxxvii. 12; Prov. i. 5; xx. 18.

תְּחוֹת, Chald. aff. תְּחֹתוֹהִי, and תַּחְתּוֹהִי; i. q. Heb. תַּחַת. *Under*, Jer. x. 11; Dan. iv. 9. 11. 18; vii. 27.

תְּחִלָּה, f. constr. תְּחִלַּת, r. חלל. (a) *Beginning*. (b) בַּתְּחִלָּה, *At the first, formerly, before*. (a) Ruth i. 22; 2 Sam. xxi. 9; Prov. ix. 10, &c. (b) Gen. xiii. 3; Judg. i. 1; Dan. viii. 1, &c.

תַּחֲלֻאִים, pl. m. constr. תַּחֲלוּאֵי, aff. תַּחֲלֻאֶיהָ, תַּחֲלוּאָיִךְ, r. חלא, for חלה. *Diseases, pains of disease*, Deut. xxix. 21; 2 Chron. xxi. 19; Ps. ciii. 3; Jer. xiv. 18; xvi. 14.

תַּחְמָס, m. twice, Lev. xi. 16; Deut. xiv. 15. According to Bochart, Hieroz., tom. ii. p. 232, *The male ostrich*. LXX. Aquila and Theod., νυκτικόραξ. Vulg. *noctuam*.

תְּחִנָּה, f. constr. תְּחִנַּת, aff. תְּחִנָּתִי, תְּחִנָּתְכֶם, pl. aff. תְּחִנּוֹתֵיהֶם, r. חנן. (a) *Favour, mercy*. (b) *Prayer for favour or mercy, prayer*. (a) Josh. xi. 20; Ezra ix. 8. (b) 1 Kings viii. 30. 38; Ps. vi. 10; Jer. xxxvii. 20.

תַּחֲנוּנִים, pl. m. constr. תַּחֲנוּנֵי, aff. תַּחֲנוּנָי, r. חנן. *Prayers for favour or mercy, prayers, supplications*, Job xl. 27; Jer. ii. 21; Dan. ix. 17.

תַּחֲנוּנוֹת, pl. f. aff. תַּחֲנוּנוֹתַי. *Id.*, Ps. lxxxvi. 6.

תחרי (622) תחת

תַּחֲרָא, and תַּחֲרָא, Exod. xxviii. 32; xxxix. 23, only. Usually *A breastplate, corselet*. The meaning, however, is very uncertain. Syr. ܐܬܚܪܝ, *contendit, litigavit*. Aph. ܐܬܚܪܝ, *aptavit ad pugnam*.

תַּחַשׁ, m. pl. תְּחָשִׁים. In the phr. עוֹר תַּחַשׁ, pl. עוֹרֹת תְּחָשִׁים. (1) Some take it to be the name of an animal, *A badger*. The only reason for fixing on this animal being that the low Latin *taxus* resembles the Hebrew word. (2) Others consider the word to be the name of a colour, and with these agree the ancient versions. LXX. ὑακίνθινον. Aquila, Symm. Theod., ἰάνθινον. Vulg. *janthina*. Probably *Blue*, Exod. xxv. 5; xxxix. 34; Num. iv. 6—14; Ezek. xvi. 10.

תַּחַת, m. With pronouns it usually takes the pl. form of construction. תַּחְתַּי and תַּחְתֵּנִי, תַּחְתֶּיךָ, תַּחְתָּיו, תַּחְתֶּנָּה, and תַּחְתֵּיהֶן, תַּחְתֵּיכֶם, תַּחְתֵּיהֶם, and תַּחְתָּם, תַּחְתֵּינוּ. Arab. تَحْتُ, *quod inferius est, pars inferior*; تَحْتُ, sub. Æth. ታሕት: sub. ታሕት: *demisit*. (a) *The lower part* or *parts, what is under*. (b) *Under*, [1] With affix, or noun. [2] Abs. (c) *Instead of*, [1] *In the place of*, as a successor. [2] *In return for*, in payment. [3] *On account of*. (d) תַּחְתָּיו, *In his own place*. (e) מִתַּחַת, [1] *From under*. [2] *Under*. [3] *Under*, abs. (f) לְמִתַּחַת, *Under*. (g) אֶל־תַּחַת, *Id*. (h) תַּחַת אֲשֶׁר, [1] *Because*. [2] *Instead of*. (i) תַּחַת כִּי, *Because*. (a) Job xxviii. 5. (b), [1] Gen. vii. 19; xviii. 4; Exod. xvii. 12, &c. [2] Gen. xlix. 25; Deut. xxxiii. 13. (c), [1] Lev. xvi. 32; 1 Chron. vi. 10; Esth. ii. 17, &c. [2] Gen. xxx. 15; Exod. xxi. 37; 1 Sam. xxv. 21, &c. [3] 2 Sam. xix. 22; Job xxx. 14; Prov. xxx. 21, &c. (d) Exod. xvi. 29; Josh. v. 8; Job xl. 12. (e), [1] Exod. vi. 6; Prov. xxii. 27; Ezek. xlvii. 1, &c. [2] Job xxvi. 5. [3] Exod. xx. 4; Josh. ii. 11; Judg. vii. 8, &c. (f) Gen. i. 7; Exod. xxx. 4; Judg. iii. 16, &c. (g) 1 Sam. xxi. 4. (h), [1] 1 Sam. xxvi. 21; 2 Kings xxii. 17; Is. liii. 12, &c. [2] Deut. xxviii. 62. (i) Deut. iv. 37; Prov. i. 29.

תְּחֹת, Chald. aff. תְּחֹתוֹהִי. See תְּחוֹת.

תַּחְתּוֹן, m. pl. תַּחְתֹּנִים, f. pl. תַּחְתֹּנוֹת. Adj. *Under, lower*, Josh. xviii. 13; 1 Kings vi. 6; Is. xxii. 9, &c.

תַּחְתִּי, m. pl. תַּחְתִּים,—

תַּחְתִּית, and תַּחְתִּיָּה, f. pl. תַּחְתִּיּוֹת—Id. *Lower, lowest*. Pl. *Lowest parts* or *places*, Gen. vi. 16; Deut. xxxii. 22; Job xli. 15, &c.

תִּיכוֹן, m. תִּיכֹנָה, f. pl. תִּיכוֹנוֹת, r. תָּוֶךְ. Adj. *Middle*, in time or place, Exod. xxvi. 28; Judg. vii. 19; Ezek. xlii. 5, &c.

תֵּימָן, m. (f. Is. xliii. 6.) What lies on the right hand. See יָמֵי. (a) *The south*. (b) *The south wind*. (c) תֵּימָנָה, *Towards* or *on the south*. (a) Josh. xv. 1; Job ix. 9; xxxix. 26; Zech. vi. 6, &c. (b) Ps. lxxviii. 26; Cant. iv. 16. (c) Exod. xxvi. 16; Num. x. 6; Deut. iii. 27, &c.

תִּימָרוֹת, and תִּמָרוֹת, pl. constr. f. twice עָשָׁן תִּימְרוֹת. *Pillars of smoke*, Cant. iii. 6; Joel iii. 3. Apparently from תָּמָר, *A palm-tree*. LXX. στελέχη. Vulg. *virgula, vaporem*.

תִּירוֹשׁ, and תִּירֹשׁ, m. aff. תִּירֹשִׁי, &c. r. ירשׁ. *New wine*, so named, it is thought, from its *taking possession* of the mind; *wine, the juice of the grape*, Gen. xxvii. 28; Judg. ix. 13; Hos. ii. 11, &c. Syr. ܐܡܪܐ, *mustum*.

תַּיִשׁ, m. pl. תְּיָשִׁים. Arab. تَيْس, *hircus dorcadum, caprarum tam domesticarum quam montanarum*. *A he-goat*, Gen. xxx. 38; xxxii. 14; 2 Chron. xvii. 11; Prov. xxx. 31.

תֹּךְ, and תּוֹךְ, m. Arab. تَكّ, *stultus, mentis inops fuit; secuit; pedibus conculcavit donec confringeret rem*. Syr. ܬܟ, *læsit, damno affecit*; ܬܘܟܐ, *defectus, dolus; damnum*. Either, *Craft*, or *oppression*, Ps. x. 7; lv. 12; lxxii. 14. LXX. δόλου, τόκος. Vulg. *dolo, usura*.

תכה, v. Kal non occ. Arab. تَكَى, *qui multum recumbit*; اتّكى, *fecit ut inniteretur*. VIII. *Innixus fuit*. Puh. תֻּכּוּ. *Were seated, sat down*, Deut. xxxiii. 3, only. LXX. ὑπὸ σὲ εἰσί. Vulg. *appropinquant*.

תְּכוּנָה, f. תְּכוּנָתוֹ, r. כּוּן. Probably *Being*, thence *arrangement, appointment*.

תכי (623) תכן

(a) *Presence.* (b) *Arrangement* of a building. (c) *Furniture, stores.* (a) Job xxiii. 3. LXX. τέλος. Sym. ἕδρας. Vulg. *solium.* (b) Ezek. xliii. 11. Theod. ἑτοιμασίαν. Vulg. *fabricæ.* (c) Nah. ii. 9. LXX. ἑτοιμασίαν. Vulg. *divitiarum.*

תֻּכִּיִּים, and תּוּכִיִּים, m. pl. 1 Kings x. 22 ; 2 Chron. ix. 21, only. According to the majority of interpreters, *Peacocks;* some, however, suppose them to have been *Parrots.* For the former we have Pers. طَاوُس . Gr. ταῶς, *A peacock:* for the latter, Pers. طُوطِي , *A parrot;* dim. طُوطَكْ .

תְּכָכִים, pl. m. once, Prov. xxix. 13. See תֹּךְ. *Oppressions, injuries.* But LXX. δανειστοῦ. Vulg. *creditor.*

תִּכְלָה, f. once, Ps. cxix. 96 ; r. כלה. *Completeness, perfection.* לְכָל־תִּכְלָה, *To every thing however perfect.* LXX. συντελείας. Aquila, συντελέσει. Symm. κατασκευῆς. Vulg. *consummationis.* Michaelis, however, derives the word from Syr. ܬܘܟܠܐ, *confidit, fiduciam posuit:* and translates it by *Hope, confidence.*

תַּכְלִית, f. r. כלה. *Completion, ending.* (a) *Termination, extremity.* (b) *Boundary.* (c) *Completeness,* in degree, *perfection.* (a) Neh. iii. 21. (b) Job xxvi. 10 ; xxviii. 10. (c) Job xi. 7 ; Ps. cxxxix. 22.

תְּכֵלֶת, f. A colour ; supposed to be obtained from the *Helix Janthina ; Violet, blue,* and hence, *Any material dyed of this colour,* Exod. xxvi. 4 ; Num. iv. 6 ; Esth. viii. 15, &c. LXX. ὑακίνθινος. Vulg. *hyacinthinus.* See Hieroz., tom. ii. p. 720.

תֹּכֶן, m. Cogn. כון. (a) *Fixed quantity.* (b) *Measure, standard.* (a) Exod. v. 18 ; (b) Ezek. xlv. 11.

תכן, v. *Measured.* Metaph., *Examined, pondered.*

Part. תֹּכֵן, Prov. xvi. 2 ; xxi. 2 ; xxiv. 12. Niph. pret. נִתְכְּנוּ, pres. יִתָּכֵן. (a) *Was measured, examined.* (b) *Was of just measure, was fair, equal.* (a) 1 Sam. ii. 3. (b) Ezek. xviii. 25. 29 ; xxxiii. 17. 20.
Pih. תִּכֵּן. (a) *Measured.* (b) *Fixed.* (c) *Directed.* (a) Job xxviii. 25 ; Is. xl. 12. (b) Ps. lxxv. 4. (c) Is. xl. 13.

Puh. Pass. of Pih. Part. מְתֻכָּן. Of money, *Measured, weighed, reckoned,* 2 Kings xii. 12.

תָּכְנִית, f. *Measure, standard,* Ezek. xxviii. 12 ; xliii. 10.

תַּכְרִיךְ, m. Syr. ܟܢܰܒ, *involvit, operuit.* Chald. תַּכְרִיךְ, *involucrum, indumentum. A robe,* Esth. viii. 15, only.

תֵּל, m. aff. תִּלָּהּ, תִּלָּם, r. תלל. (a) *A heap,* pec. of ruins. (b) *A hill* or *mound.* (a) Deut. xiii. 17 ; Josh. viii. 28 ; Jer. xxx. 11 ; xlix. 2. (b) Josh. xi. 13. Arab. تَلّ, *collis, cumulus terræ.*

תלא, v. part. pass. pl. תְּלוּאִים, i. q., תְּלוּיִם, r. תלה, which see.

תְּלָאָה, f. r. לאה. *Weariness, trouble, vexation,* Exod. xviii. 8 ; Num. xx. 14 ; Neh. ix. 32, &c.

תַּלְאוּבוֹת, pl. f. Arab. لَابَ, r. لوب, *sitivit;* لَابَة, *locus lapidosus.* Cogn. להב. *Thirst, drought,* Hos. xiii. 5, only.

תִּלְבֹּשֶׁת, f. r. לבש. *Clothing,* Is. lix. 17, only.

תֶּלֶג, or תְּלִי, Chald. i. q. שֶׁלֶג. *Snow,* Dan. vii. 9, only.

תָּלָה, v. pres. aff. יִתְלֵם. Constr. med. אֶת, it. immed. Syr. ܬܠܐ, *'suspendit.* (a) *Hung, suspended.* (b) *Hung, executed.* (c) *Fully,* ח״י עַל־עֵץ, *Id.* (d) Metaph. *Made dependent.* (e) *Made uncertain, placed in suspense.* (a) 2 Sam. xxi. 12 ; Ps. cxxxvii. 2 ; Is. xxii. 24, &c. (b) Gen. xl. 22 ; xli. 13. (c) Gen. xli. 19 ; Deut. xxi. 22 ; Josh. viii. 29, &c.

Infin. constr. תְּלוֹת, Esth. vi. 4 ; Ezek. xv. 3.
Imp. pl. aff. תְּלוּי, Esth. vii. 9.
Part. תֹּלֶה, (d) Job xxvi. 7. See my note.
Part. pass. תָּלוּי, pl. תְּלוּיִם, it. תְּלוּאִים. (a) 2 Sam. xviii. 10 ; Cant. iv. 4. (c) Deut. xxi. 23 ; Josh. x. 26. (e) Deut. xxviii. 66 ; Hos. xi. 7.
Niph. pret. pl. נִתְלוּ, pres. יִתָּלוּ. Pass. of Kal. (b) Esth. ii. 22 ; Lam. v. 12.
Pih. pret. pl. תִּלּוּ. I. q., Kal (a) Ezek. xxvii. 10, 11.

תַּלְנוּת, pl. f. תְּלֻנֹּתַיִךְ, תְּלֻנֹּתָם, r. לון.

Murmurings, Exod. xvi. 7. 12; Num. xiv. 26; xvii. 25, 26.

תְּלִי, m. aff. תֶּלְיְךָ, r. תלה. Once, Gen. xxvii. 3. Usually interpreted, *A quiver*; but, by some, *A sword*. The word does not exist in either sense in the cognate languages. LXX. φαρέτραν. Vulg. *pharetram*. But Syr. ܬܡܒܬ.

תְּלִית, Chald. m. def. תְּלִיתָאה, or תְּלִיתָיָא, from תְּלָה. *Third*, Dan. ii. 39, only.

תלל, v. Arab. تَلَّ, *stravit humi, prostravit.* *Strewed on the ground, made a heap, formed a mound.* Only in Part. pass. תָּלוּל. *Raised*, as a mound, *lofty*, Ezek. xvii. 22, only.

תֶּלֶם, m. pl. constr. תַּלְמֵי, aff. תְּלָמֶיהָ. Arab. تَلْمٌ, *sulcus terræ vomere factus*. *A furrow*, Job xxxi. 38; xxxix. 10; Ps. lxv. 11; Hos. x. 4; xii. 12.

תַּלְמִיד, m. r. למד. *A learner*, 1 Chron. xxv. 8, only.

תלע, v. only in Puḥ. part. pl. מְתֻלָּעִים, *Clothed in scarlet*, Nah. ii. 4, only. See תּוֹלָע.

תַּלְפִּיּוֹת, pl. f. once, Cant. iv. 4. Variously rendered. (1) *Heights, lofty buildings, battlements.* Symm. ὕψη. Aquila, ἐπάλξεις. LXX. θαλπιώθ. Vulg. *propugnaculis*. (2) *A place for hanging weapons*; from תָּלָה, and פִּיּוֹת. (3) *Deadly things*, i. e. *Weapons*; from Arab. تَلِفَ, *periit*. IV. *Perdidit*. (4) Others take the same Arabic word and translate, לְתַלְפִּיּוֹת, *For the wanderers, for those who lose their way*, i. e. as a beacon. It is doubtful whether any one of these is the true interpretation.

תְּלָת, Chald. m. תְּלָתָא, and תְּלָתָה, f. aff. תְּלָתְהוֹן, i. q. Heb. שָׁלֹשׁ. *Three*, Ezra vi. 4; Dan. iii. 23; vii. 5. 24, &c. Pl. תְּלָתִין. *Thirty*, Dan. vi. 8. 13.

תְּלַת, Chald. m. def. תַּלְתָּא. *Third*, in rank, Dan. v. 16. 29.

תַּלְתִּי, Chald. *Id.*, Dan. v. 7.

תַּלְתַּלִּים, pl. m. once, Cant. v. 11. *Hanging, flowing*, of the hair. Comp. תָּלָה, and Arab. تَلْتَلَ, *commovit, agitavit.*

תֹּם, m. once תּוֹם, Prov. x. 9; aff. תֻּמִּי, תֻּמּוֹ, r. תמם. *Completeness.* (a) *Completeness, fulness*, in number or degree. (b) *Completeness* in character, *integrity*. (c) לְתֻמּוֹ, Variously rendered. [1] *With his full strength.* [2] *With all his skill*, with an accurate aim. [3] *In his integrity*, without any design to kill the king. (d) לְתֻמָּם, *In their integrity*, without any evil design. (e) Pl. תֻּמִּים, pl. תֻּמֶּיךָ, used only with אוּרִים, which see. (a) Job xxi. 23; Is. xlvii. 9. (b) Gen. xx. 5; Ps. xxv. 21; xxvi. 1, &c. (c) 1 Kings xxii. 34; 2 Chron. xviii. 33. LXX. εὐστόχως. Vulg. *in incertum*. (d) 2 Sam. xv. 11. (e) Exod. xxviii. 30; Lev. viii. 8; Deut. xxxiii. 8; Ezra ii. 62; Neh. vi. 65.

תָּם, m. (a) *One possessed of integrity, perfect, sound* in principle, *blameless*, Job i. 1; Ps. xxxvii. 37; Prov. xxix. 10, &c. (b) In Gen. xxv. 27, Jacob is said to be אִישׁ תָּם, apparently in contrast with the epithet אִישׁ יֹדֵעַ צַיִד, given to Esau; probably *Unacquainted with any arts.* Usually, however, interpreted as if a vicious character had been ascribed to Esau, and as if Jacob were free from his brother's faults; *perfect*. LXX. ἄπλαστος. Aquila, ἁπλοῦς. Symm. ἄμωμος. Vulg. *simplex*. (c) Fem. aff. תַּמָּתִי, *Blameless, perfect*, either in character or person, Cant. v. 2; vi. 9. (d) Pl. תַּמִּים apparently contr. for תְּאַמִּים, i. q. תְּאוֹמִים, *Double*, Exod. xxvi. 24; xxxvi. 39.

תֻּמָּה, f. constr. תֻּמַּת, aff. תֻּמָּתִי, תֻּמָּתְךָ, תֻּמָּתוֹ, i. q. תֹּם, sign. (b) Job ii. 3. 9; xxvii. 5; xxxi. 6; Prov. xi. 3.

תַּמָּה, Chald. i. q. Heb. שָׁמָּה, but used for שָׁם. *There*, Ezra v. 17; vi. 1. 6. 12.

תמה, v. pret. pl. in pause, תָּמָהוּ, pres. יִתְמְהוּ. Syr. ܬܡܗ, *miratus est.* (a) *Wondered, was astonished*, constr. abs. it. med. עַל, מִן. (b) *Looked with surprise on* another, med. אֶל. (a) Abs., Ps. xlviii. 6; Jer. iv. 9. Med. עַל, Eccl. v. 7. Med. מִן, Job xxvi. 11. (b) Gen. xliii. 33; Is. xiii. 8. Imp. pl. תִּמְהוּ, Is. xxix. 9; Hab. i. 5. Hith. pres. הִתַּמְּהוּ. I. q. Kal, (a) Hab. i. 5.

תִּמָּהוֹן, m. constr. irreg. תִּמְהוֹן. *Astonishment*, Deut. xxviii. 28; Zech. xii. 4.

תִּמְהִין, Chald. pl. m. def. תִּמְהַיָּא, aff. תִּמְהוֹהִי. *Wonders, miracles*, Dan. iii. 32. 33; vi. 21.

תְּמוֹל, i. q. אֶתְמוֹל, which see.

תְּמוּנָה, fem. constr. תְּמוּנַת, aff. תְּמוּנָתֶךָ. See מִין. *Resemblance, likeness, figure*, Exod. xx. 4; Deut. iv. 16; Ps. xvii. 15, &c.

תְּמוּרָה, f. aff. תְּמוּרָתוֹ, תְּמוּרָתָהּ, r. מור. (a) *What is given in return* or *exchange; an equivalent, a recompense.* (b) *Restitution.* (c) *An exchange, a transfer.* (a) Lev. xxvii. 10. 33; Job xv. 31; xxviii. 17. (b) Job xx. 18. (c) Ruth iv. 7.

תְּמוּתָה, f. i. q. מָוֶת. *Death :* only in the phr. בְּנֵי תְמוּתָה, *sons of death*, i. e. *those who are condemned to death*, Ps. lxxix. 11; cii. 21, only.

תָּמִיד, m. Cogn. מדד, and מור. (a) *Perpetuity.* (b) *Perpetual.* (c) Adv. *Continually.* Phrr. (d) לֶחֶם הַתָּמִיד, *The bread of perpetuity*, i. e. *the shewbread constantly placed in the Tabernacle.* (e) — עֹלַת, *The constant*, i. e. *daily offering.* (f) הַתָּמִיד, *Id.* (a) Exod. xxix. 42; xxx. 8; Num. iv. 7, &c. (b) Prov. xv. 15. (c) Exod. xxv. 30; Lev. xxiv. 4; 2 Sam. ix. 13, &c. (d) Num. iv. 7. (e) Num. xxviii. 10. 15; xxix. 6, &c. (f) Dan. viii. 11—13; xi. 31; xii. 11.

תָּמִים, masc. constr. תְּמִים, pl. תְּמִימִים, constr. תְּמִימֵי, f. תְּמִימָה, pl. תְּמִימֹת, r. תמם. (a) *Complete.* (b) *Whole, entire.* (c) *Perfect* in character. (d) *Free from fault.* (e) *Free from defect.* (f) *Integrity.* (a) Job xxxvi. 4; xxxvii. 16. (b) Lev. xv. 30; xxxiii. 15. (c) Gen. vi. 9; xvii. 1; Deut. xviii. 13, &c. (d) Ps. xviii. 31; xix. 8; ci. 2. (e) Exod. xii. 5; Lev. i. 3. 10; iv. 28, &c. (f) Josh. xxiv. 14; Judg. ix. 16. 19; Ps. lxxxiv. 12.

תמך, v. pret. תָּמְכָה, pres. יִתְמֹךְ. Constr. immed. it. med. בְּ. (a) *Took hold of.* (b) *Took hold of, and held up.* (c) *Held a sceptre.* (d) *Upheld, supported.* (e) *Obtained.* (f) *Apprehended, comprehended.* (g) *Arrived at, reached.* (a) Gen. xlviii. 17; Ps. xxxi. 19; Prov. xxviii. 17. (b) Exod. xvii. 12. (d) Abs., Job xxxvi. 17. Immed., Is. xli. 10. Med. בְּ, Ps. xli. 13; lxiii. 9; Is. xlii. 1. (e) Prov. xi. 16; xxix. 23. (f) Prov. iv. 4. (g) Prov. v. 5. Infin. abs. תָּמוֹךְ, constr. תְּמֹךְ, Ps. xvii. 15; Is. xxxiii. 15.

Part. תּוֹמֵךְ, and תּוֹמְכִי, pl. aff. תֹּמְכֶיהָ. (c) Amos i. 5. 8. (d) Ps. xvi. 5. (e) Prov. iii. 18.

תמם, v. pret. תַּם, תַּמּוּ, תַּמְנוּ, pres. יִתֹּם, יִתֹּם, תָּתֹם, in pause, אִיתָם. Arab. تَمَّ, *totus, integer, absolutus fuit; ad finem pervenit.* (a) *Was completed, was ended.* (b) *Was perfect*, in character; *upright.* (c) *Ceased.* (d) *Failed, came to an end.* (e) *Was consumed*, or *wasted away.* (f) *Finished*, constr. [1] Immed. [2] Med. לְ, with Infin. (g) *Consumed, destroyed*, immed. (a) 1 Sam. xvi. 11; Job xxxi. 40; Lam. iv. 22, &c. (b) Ps. xix. 14. (c) Ps. ix. 7; Is. xvi. 4. (d) Gen. xlvii. 15. 18; Ezek. xlvii. 12. (e) Lev. xxvi. 20; 2 Kings vii. 13; Jer. vi. 29, &c. (f), [1] Ps. lxiv. 7. [2] Deut. ii. 16; Josh. iii. 17; iv. 1. 11, &c. Infin. תֹּם, with Makkáph, תָּם־, aff. תֻּמִּי, תֻּמָּם, תֻּמָּם, (g) Jer. xxvii. 8; Lev. xxv. 29, &c.

Niph. pres. יִתַּמּוּ. I. q. Kal, (a) and (e). (a) Deut. xxxiv. 8; Ps. cii. 28. (e) Num. xiv. 35; Ps. civ. 35; Jer. xiv. 15, &c.

Hiph. pret. הֲתִמּוֹתִי, pres. יָתֵם. (a) I. q. Kal [f] and [g]. (b) *Declared perfect.* (c) According to some, *Took the sum of, counted.* (a), [f] 2 Sam. xx. 18. [g] Ezek. xxii. 15. (b) Job xxii. 3. (c) 2 Kings xxii. 4.

Infin. הָתֵם, aff. הֲתִימְךָ, [f] Is. xxxiii. 1; Dan. viii. 23; ix. 24.

Imp. הָתֵם, [g] Ezek. xxiv. 10.

Hith. pres. תִּתַּמָּם. *Showed himself perfect, acted uprightly*, 2 Sam. xxii. 26; Ps. xviii. 26.

תֵּמֶם, m. once, Ps. lviii. 9. *Melting, wasting away*, r. מסס.

תָּמָר, masc. pl. תְּמָרִים. Arab. تَمْر, *dactylus. A palm tree*, Exod. xv. 27; Ps. xcii. 13; Ezek. xl. 26, &c.

תֹּמֶר, m. *Id.*, Jer. x. 5, only.

תִּמֹרָה, fem. pl. תִּמֹרוֹת, and תִּמֹרִים, aff. תִּמֹרָיו. *An artificial palm tree*, 1 Kings vi. 29. 32. 35, 36; Ezek. xl. 22; xli. 18, 19.

תַּמְרוּק, masc. pl. constr. תַּמְרוּקֵי, aff. תַּמְרוּקֶיהָ, תַּמְרוּקֵיהֶן, r. מרק. *Cleansing, purification;* it. *the means of cleansing* or *purification*, Esth. ii. 3. 9. 12; Prov. xx. 30.

תַּמְרוּרִים, pl. m. r. מור. *Bitterness, bitter sorrow*, Hos. xii. 15; Jer. vi. 26; xxxi. 15. 21. In this last passage, however, many interpreters give the word the signi-

4 L

fication of *columns, pillars,* set up as landmarks; as if from תָּמָר.

תַּן, m. pl. תַּנִּים, and once תַּנִּין, Lam. iv. 3. Apparently a general term used for *any wild animal* of the desert. Some, however, confine the word to the *jackal,* and others to *the larger kinds of serpents.* LXX. Aquila and Sym. σειρῆνες. Vulg. *dracones,* Job xxx. 29; Ps. xliv. 20; Is. xiii. 22, &c.

תָּנָה, v. pres. pl. יִתְנוּ. Sam. תנה. Aph. אתנה, *dedit, donavit.* Cogn. נתן. *Made presents to, distributed gifts among; hired,* med. בְּ, Hos. viii. 10. Vulg. *mercede conduxerint.* E. μισθώσηται. But LXX. παραδοθήσονται, as if for יִתְּנוּ, used impersonally.

Pih. pres. pl. יְתַנּוּ. (a) *Ascribed praise to* a person, med. לְ. (b) *Celebrated* an action, immed. (b) Judg. v. 11.

Infin. תַּנּוֹת, (a) Judg. xi. 40. Comp. Arab. ثَنَّىٰ, *laudavit oratione aliquem.*

Hiph. הִתְנוּ. I. q. Kal, constr. immed., Hos. viii. 9.

תְּנוּאָה, f. aff. תְּנוּאָתִי, pl. תְּנוּאוֹת, r. נוא. (a) *Aversion; anger:* but some, *prohibition,* Num. xiv. 34. LXX. τὸν θυμὸν τῆς ὀργῆς μου. Vulg. *ultionem meam.* (b) Pl. *Things difficult to be borne, heavy things,* Job xxxiii. 10. See my note.

תְּנוּבָה, f. constr. תְּנוּבַת, aff. תְּנוּבָתִי, pl. תְּנוּבוֹת, r. נוב. *Produce, fruit,* Deut. xxxii. 13; Judg. ix. 11; Is. xxvii. 6; Lam. iv. 9; Ezek. xxxvi. 30.

תְּנוּךְ, masc. only in the phr. תְּנוּךְ אֹזֶן. *The extremity;* probably *lower part of the ear,* Exod. xxix. 20; Lev. viii. 23, 24; xiv. 14, &c.

תְּנוּמָה, fem. pl. תְּנוּמוֹת, r. נום. *Sleep, slumber,* Job xxxiii. 15; Ps. cxxxii. 4; Prov. vi. 4. 10; xxiv. 33.

תְּנוּפָה, f. constr. תְּנוּפַת, r. נוף. (a) *The lifting up* of the hand, either in beckoning or threatening, Is. xix. 16. (b) *Agitation, disturbance, tumult,* Is. xxx. 32. (c) *An offering,* Exod. xxix. 24; Lev. xxiii. 17; Num. vii. 20, &c.

תַּנּוּר, masc. pl. תַּנּוּרִים, aff. תַּנּוּרֶיךָ. *A furnace, an oven,* Gen. xv. 17; Exod. viii. 3; Neh. iii. 11, &c. Arab. تَنُّور, *fornax, clibanus.* Cogn. נור.

תַּנּוֹת, pl. fem. probably f. of תַּנִּים, Mal. i. 3.

תַּנְחוּמִים, pl. m. aff. תַּנְחֻמֶיךָ, תַּנְחוּמָיו, r. נחם. *Consolations, comforts,* Ps. xciv. 19; Is. lxvi. 11; Jer. xvi. 7.

תַּנְחוּמוֹת, pl. f. aff. תַּנְחוּמֹתֵיהֶם, *Id.,* Job xv. 11; xxi. 2.

תַּנִּים, (a) pl. of תַּן, which see. (b) For תַּנִּין, Ezek. xxix. 3; xxxii. 2.

תַּנִּין, masc. pl. תַּנִּינִים. Arab. تِنِّين, *serpens ingens, draco.* (a) *A serpent.* (b) *Any large animal* of the serpent kind. (c) Probably *A crocodile.* (d) *Any large marine animal.* (a) Exod. vii. 9, 10. 12; Deut. xxxii. 30; Ps. xci. 13. (b) Jer. li. 34. (c) Is. li. 9. (d) Gen. i. 21; Job vii. 12; Ps. lxxiv. 13, &c. Gesenius supposes that the leading idea of the primitive, תנן, or תן, is the same as that of the Sans. तन्, *extendere.* See my notes on Job, pp. 196. 427.

תִּנְיָן, Chald. fem. תִּנְיָנָה. *Second,* Dan. vii. 5. Syr. ܬܢܐ, *iteravit.*

תִּנְיָנוּת, Chald. *A second time,* Dan. ii. 7.

תִּנְשֶׁמֶת, fem. (a) *An unclean beast:* according to some, *The mole;* but Bochart (Hieroz., tom. i., p. 1078) makes it *the chameleon,* Lev. xi. 30, only. LXX. ἀσπάλαξ. Vulg. *talpa.* (b) *An unclean bird:* some, *the swan:* others, *the sea-gull:* but Bochart (Hieroz., tom. ii., p. 286), *the owl,* Lev. xi. 18; Deut. xiv. 16. LXX. πορφυρίωνα. Vulg. *cygnum.*

תָּעַב, v. Kal non occ. See תּוֹעֵבָה. Pih. pret. pl. aff. תִּעֲבוּנִי, pres. יְתַעֵב, and יְתָעֵב. Constr. immed. it. med. אֶת. (a) *Regarded with loathing, abhorred.* (b) *Rendered an object of loathing.* (c) *Excited loathing, was an object of abhorrence.* (a) Job xix. 19; xxx. 10; Ps. cxix. 163, &c. (b) Ezek. xvi. 25.

Infin. תַּעֵב, Deut. vii. 26.
Part. מְתָעֵב, pl. מְתַעֲבִים, (a) Mic. iii. 9. (c) Is. xlix. 9.

Niph. נִתְעָב, Pass. of Pih. (a) 1 Chron. xxi. 6.
Part. נִתְעָב, Job xv. 16; Is. xiv. 20.

Hiph. הִתְעַנָּב, pres. apoc. יַתְעֵב. *Acted abominably, committed a deed worthy of*

תעה (627) תעל

abhorrence, 1 Kings xxi. 26; Ezek. xvi. 52. Used adverbially, Ps. xiv. 1; liii. 2.

תָּעָה, v. pres. apoc. תַּעַט. I. q. טעה. Syr. ܠܥܐ, *erravit, periit*. Arab. طغي, *modum excessit*. (a) *Wandered, went astray*. (b) *Went astray*, morally. (c) *Staggered*, through drunkenness. (d) *Was in a state of confusion, disorder*, — of the heart. (a), [1] Abs., Job xxxviii. 41; Is. xxxv. 8, &c. [2] Immed. of place, Is. xvi. 8. [3] Med. בְּ, of place, Gen. xxi. 14; Prov. vii. 28, &c. (b), [1] Abs., Ps. lviii. 4; Prov. xiv. 22; Ezek. xlviii. 11. [2] Med. מֵעַל, Ezek. xliv. 10. [3] Med. מֵאַחֲרֵי, Ezek. xiv. 11. (c) Is. xxviii. 7. (d) Is. xxi. 4.

Infin. constr. תְּעוֹת, Ezek. xliv. 15; xlviii. 11.

Part. תֹּעֶה, Gen. xxxvii. 15; Exod. xxiii. 4, &c., תֹּעֵי לֵבָב, Ps. xcv. 10, תֹּעֵי רוּחַ, Is. xxix. 24.

Niph. (a) *Was led astray.* (b) *Was made to stagger.*

Infin. הִתָּעוֹת, (b) Is. xix. 14.

Part. נִתְעָה, (a) Job xv. 31.

Hiph. הִתְעָה, pres. יַתְעֶה, apoc. יַתַע. Causat. of Kal. (a) *Caused to wander.* (b) *Caused to go astray*, morally. (c) *Deceived, led astray.* (d) *Acted deceitfully.* (a) Gen. xx. 11; Job xii. 24; Jer. L. 6, &c. (b) 2 Chron. xxxiii. 9; Hos. iv. 12. (c) Is. xix. 13; Jer. xxiii. 13; Amos ii. 4. (d) Jer. xlii. 20.

Part. מַתְעֶה, pl. מַתְעִים, Prov. x. 17; Mic. iii. 5, &c.

תְּעוּדָה, fem. r. עוד. *An institution, appointment; a law, custom*, Ruth iv. 7; Is. iv. 17; viii. 20.

תְּעָלָה, f. constr. תְּעָלַת, pl. aff. תְּעָלֹתֶיהָ, r. עלה. (a) *A channel* for the passage of water, *conduit*. (b) Either, *An external application, a plaster*; or *a recovery, a getting up* after an illness. Gesenius takes the former: Castell the latter. Comp. Arab. علي. V. *Salva evasit, convaluit*, quasi *surrexit* à morbo mulier. (a) 1 Kings xviii. 32. 35; 2 Kings xx. 20; Job xxxviii. 25, &c. (b) Jer. xxx. 13; xlvi. 11.

תַּעֲלוּלִים, pl. m. aff. תַּעֲלֻלֵיהֶם, r. עלל. (a) *Children*, Is. vi. 4. (b) Some, *Mockeries, insults*; others, *vexations, calamities*, Is. lxvi. 4. LXX. ἐμπαίγματα. Vulg. *illusiones.*

תַּעֲלֻמָה, fem. pl. תַּעֲלֻמוֹת, r. עלם. *Any thing hidden* or *secret*, Job xi. 6; xxviii. 11; Ps. xliv. 22.

תַּעֲנוּג, m. pl. תַּעֲנוּגִים, aff. תַּעֲנוּגֶיךָ, תַּעֲנֻגֶיהָ, and תַּעֲנֻגוֹת, r. ענג. *Delight, pleasure, enjoyment, luxury*, Prov. xix. 10; Eccl. ii. 8; Cant. vii. 7; Mic. i. 16; ii. 9.

תַּעֲנִית, f. aff. תַּעֲנִיתִי, r. ענה. *Self-humiliation*, Ezra ix. 5, only.

תעע, v. Arab. تغي, *erupit in risum.* Cogn. תעה.

Pih. red. part. מְתַעְתֵּעַ. Either, *Mocking*, or *deceiving*, Gen. xxvii. 12.

Hiph. red. part. pl. מַתְעְתְּעִים. *Mocking*, med. בְּ, 2 Chron. xxxvi. 16.

תַּעֲצֻמוֹת, pl. f. r. עצם. *Strength*, Ps. lxviii. 36, only.

תַּעַר, masc. aff. תַּעְרְךָ, תַּעְרָהּ : probably r. ערה. (a) *A razor.* (b) תַּעַר הַסֹּפֵר, *A penknife.* (c) *The scabbard* of a sword. (a) Num. vi. 5; viii. 7; Ezek. v. 1, &c. (b) Jer. xxxvi. 23. (c) 1 Sam. xvii. 51; Jer. xlvii. 6; Ezek. xxi. 35, &c.

תַּעֲרֻבוֹת, pl. fem. r. ערב. See עֵרָבוֹן. *Security*, in a legal sense : only in the phr. בְּנֵי הַתַּ׳, *Hostages*, 2 Kings xiv. 14; 2 Chron. xxv. 24, only.

תַּעְתֻּעִים, pl. m. r. תעע. *Mockery*, or *deception, error*, Jer. x. 15; li. 18, only. LXX. ἐμπεπαιγμένα, μεμωκημένα. Vulg. *risu.*

תֹּף, masc. pl. תֻּפִּים, aff. תֻּפֵּךְ. Arab. دُفّ, *tympanum. A tambarine*, 1 Sam. x. 5; 2 Sam. vii. 5; Ezek. xxviii. 13, &c.

תִּפְאָרָה, and תִּפְאֶרֶת, fem. aff. תִּפְאַרְתִּי, &c. r. פאר. (a) *Beauty, ornament, splendour.* (b) *Honour, glory.* (c) *Boast, subject of glorying.* (a) Esth. i. 4; Is. xxviii. 5; Jer. xlviii. 17, &c. (b) Judg. iv. 9; Prov. iv. 9; Is. lxiii. 14, &c. (c) Ps. lxxviii. 61; Prov. xvii. 6; Is. lx. 19, &c.

תַּפּוּחַ, masc. pl. תַּפּוּחִים, constr. תַּפּוּחֵי. Arab. تُفَّاح, *malus* arbor; *malum, pomum.* (a) *An apple tree.* (b) *An apple.* (a) Cant. ii. 3; viii. 5; Joel i. 12. (a) Prov. xxv. 11; Cant. ii. 5; vii. 9.

תְּפוּצוֹת, pl. f. aff. תְּפוּצוֹתֵיכֶם, r. פוץ. *Dispersion, scattering*, Jer. xxv. 34, only.

תְּפִינִים, pl. m. constr. תְּפִינֵי, once, Lev.

תפל

iv. 14. According to Gesenius, from אפה. *Bakings, baked,* or *fried pieces.* LXX. ἐλικτά, ἐρικτά. *Pancakes,* or the like, from their resemblance in form to the חֹל.

תָּפֵל, masc. Arab. ثَفْل, *subsedit fæx aliudve crassamentum*. III. *Comedit frumentum aut legumina, lacte destitutus;* quod Arabi campestri grave est; ثُفْل, *turbidum vel crassamentum, quod in omni liquore in fundo est*; ذَاوِل, *Id.* it. *fimus, stercus. Any thing heavy* or *hard; sediment, refuse.* (a) *Curd.* (b) *Dung.* (c) Metaph. *Any thing harsh, unjust.* (a) Job vi. 6. (b) Ezek. xiii. 10, 11. 14, 15; xxii. 28. (c) Lam. ii. 14.

תִּפְלָה, f. *Heaviness, hardness, severity, injustice,* Job i. 22; xxiv. 12; Jer. xxiii. 13.

תְּפִלָּה, f. constr. תְּפִלַּת, aff. תְּפִלָּתִי, pl. תְּפִלּוֹת, r. פלל. (a) *Prayer; a prayer.* (b) *Intercession.* (c) *A hymn,* whether of praise or prayer. (a) 1 Kings viii. 28; Ps. iv. 2; xvii. 1, &c. (b) 2 Kings xix. 4; Is. xxxvii. 4. (c) Ps. lxxii. 20.

תפלצת, f. aff. תִּפְלַצְתְּךָ, r. פלץ. *Terror, great fear,* Jer. xlix. 16. *Thy terror;* either the object of thy terror, i. e. *thy idol,* or *the terror thou causedst,* i. e. *thy formidable character,* or *thy terror! (How great shall it be !)*

תפף, v. See חֹל. The word appears an ὀνοματοποιητικόν. Gesenius compares the Sans. तुप्, *ferire, occidere*. Part. f. pl. תוֹפֵפוֹת. *Striking the tambarine,* Ps. lxviii. 26.

Pih. part. f. pl. מְתֹפְפוֹת. *Striking their bosoms,* med. עַל, Nah. ii. 8.

תפר, v. pret. תָּפַרְתִּי, pres. יִתְפֹּר. Constr. immed. *Sewed,* Gen. iv. 7; Job xvi. 15. Infin. תְּפוֹר, Eccl. iii. 7. Pih. *Id.* Part. f. pl. מְתַפְּרוֹת, Ezek. xiii. 18.

תָּפַשׂ. v. pres. יִתְפֹּשׂ. Constr. immed. it. med. אֶת, בְּ. *Laid hold of, seized,* [1] A person, [2] A thing. (b) *Took* in war, [1] A city, or place, [2] A person. (c) *Kept possession of* a place; immed. (d) *Handled* an instrument or weapon. (e) Metaph., *Handled* the law. (f) *Carried on* war, *took* an active *part* in it. (g) *Enclosed.* (h) ת" שֵׁם אֱלֹהִים, *Handled* (irreverently) *the name of God, used* it in a falsehood, *perjured* himself. So LXX. and Vulg. (a), [1] Immed. Gen. xxxix. 12; Deut. xxii. 28, &c. Med. אֶת, Jer. xxvi. 8; xxxvii. 13. Med. בְּ, Is. iii. 6; Jer. xxxvii. 14. [2] Med. בְּ. Deut. ix. 17; 1 Kings xi. 30. (b), [1] Immed. 2 Kings xvi. 9; xviii. 13; Jer. xl. 10. Med. אֶת, 2 Kings xiv. 7. Med. בְּ, 2 Kings xiv. 13; 2 Chron. xxv. 23. (h) Prov. xxx. 9.

Infin. abs. תָּפוֹשׂ, constr. תְּפֹשׂ, aff. תָּפְשָׂה, (d) Ezek. xxx. 21; Deut. xx. 19; Jer. xxxiv. 3, &c.

Imp. pl. תִּפְשׂוּ, 1 Kings xviii. 40, &c. Part. תּוֹפֵשׂ, תֹּפֵשׂ, pl. constr. תֹּפְשֵׂי, (c) Jer. xlix. 16. (d) Gen. iv. 21; Jer. L. 16, &c. (e) Jer. ii. 8. (f) Num. xxxi. 37.

Part. pass. תָּפוּשׂ, (g) Hab. ii. 19.

Niph. נִתְפַּשׂ, pres. יִתָּפֵשׂ. Pass. of Kal, *Was taken, caught,* or *seized,* Num. v. 13; Ps. x. 2; Ezek. xix. 4, &c.

Infin. תָּפְשׂוֹ, Ezek. xxi. 28.

Pih. pres. יְתַפֵּשׂ. *Took hold;* abs., Prov. xxx. 28.

תֹּפֶת, f. Æth. ፐፍአ : *spuit, exspuit*. Arab. تُف, *adverbium detestandi et despicandi*; تَفَّفَ, *dixit* تُفّ, *in aliquem,* i. e. *repudiavit, detestatus fuit;* ثَفِىَ *vilis fuit. Detesting, despising, abhorring; an object of detestation,* Job xvii. 6, only.

תִּפְתָּיֵא, Chald. pl. def. According to some, *Officers of justice,* from Pers. تَفْتَن, تَافْتَن, *To burn;* so Castell. Others, *Chiefs of the law,* from Arab. فَتْوَى, *responsum à jurisconsulto datum.* But this is mere conjecture. Dan. iii. 2, 3, only. Vulg. *præfecti.* LXX. οἱ ἐπ' ἐξουσιῶν.

תִּקְוָה, f. constr. תִּקְוַת, aff. תִּקְוָתִי, &c., r. קוה. (a) *Hope, expectation.* (b) *A cord, thread.* (a) Job v. 16; Ps. lxii. 6; Prov. xi. 23, &c. (b) Josh. ii. 18. 21.

תְּקוּמָה, f. r. קום. *The power of standing* or *resisting,* Lev. xxvi. 37, only.

תְּקוֹמֵם, m. pl. aff. תְקוֹמְמָיו, r. קום. *An adversary, opponent,* Ps. cxxxix. 21, only.

תְּקוּפָה, f. constr. תְּקוּפַת, aff. תְּקוּפָתוֹ, pl. תְּקוּפוֹת, r. קוף, i. q. נקף. (a) *The going round,* of the sun. (b) *The coming round* of the year. (a) Ps. xix. 7. (b) Exod. xxxiv. 22; 1 Sam. i. 20; 2 Chron. xxiv. 23.

תָּקִיף, m. r. תקף. *Strong, powerful*, Eccl. vi. 10, only.

תַּקִּיף, Chald. pl. תַּקִּיפִין, f. תַּקִּיפָא, and תַּקִּיפָה, *Id.*, Dan. ii. 40. 42; iii. 53.

תקל, Chald. i. q. Heb. שׁקל. *Weighed.* Pehil, תְּקִילְתָּא. *Was weighed*, Dan. v. 27. Part. תְּקֵל, for תְּקִיל, Dan. v. 25.

תקן, v. cogn. חכן. *Was set in order, arranged; was straight.* Infin. תְּקֹן, Eccl. i. 15.
Pih. תִּקֵּן. (a) *Set in order.* (b) *Made straight.* (a) Eccl. xii. 9.
Infin. תַּקֵּן, (b) Eccl. vii. 13.

תקן, Chald. v. *Id.*
Hoph. הָתְקְנַת. *Was set in order, was established*, Dan. iv. 33, only.

תָּקַע, v. pres. יִתְקַע. Cogn. יקע. *Struck, fixed.* (a) *Struck* the hands. [1] In concluding a bargain. [2] In contempt. [3] joy. (b) *Thrust in* a weapon. (c) *Fixed, fastened.* (d) *Pitched* a tent. (e) *Threw into* the sea. (f) *Blew* a trumpet, med. בְּ, it. immed. (g) *Blew* an alarm, immed. (a), [1] Prov. vi. 1. [2] Nah. iii. 19. (b) Judg. iii. 21; 2 Sam. xviii. 14. (c) Judg. iv. 21; xvi. 14; 1 Sam. xxxi. 10, &c. (d) Gen. xxxi. 25. (e) Exod. vi. 19. (f), [1] Med. בְּ, Judg. vii. 18; 1 Sam. xiii. 3; Ezek. xxiii. 3. 6, &c. Immed., Judg. vii. 22. (g) Num. x. 5, 6.
Infin. abs. תָּקוֹעַ, constr. תְּקֹעַ, Josh. vi. 13; Judg. vii. 20; Is. xviii. 3.
Imp. pl. תִּקְעוּ, (a, 3) Ps. xlvii. 2. (d) Jer. vi. 3. (f, 2) Ps. lxxxi. 4; Jer. iv. 5; vi. 1, &c.
Part. תּוֹקֵעַ, pl. תּוֹקְעִים, constr. תֹּקְעֵי, (a, 1) Prov. xvii. 18; xxii. 25, 26 :· abs. xi. 15.
Part. pass. f. תְּקוּעָה, (c) Is. xxii. 25.
Niph. pres. יִתָּקַע, apoc. יִתָּקַע בְּשׁוֹפָר and שׁוֹפָר. *A trumpet is blown*, Is. xxvii. 13; Amos v. 6. (b) לִידֵי יִתָּקַע, *Strikes hands with me*, in concluding an agreement, Job xvii. 3.

תֶּקַע, m. *The blowing* of a trumpet, Ps. cl. 3, only.

תֹּקֶף, m. aff. תָּקְפּוֹ. Syr. ܬܩܦ, *prævaluit, invaluit.* Arab. ثَقَّفَ, *certavit et vicit ingenio, solertiâ. Strength, power, authority*, Exod. ix. 29; x. 2; Dan. xi. 17.

תְּקֹף, Chald. m. def. תָּקְפָּא, constr. תְּקָף. *Id.*, Dan. ii. 37; iv. 27.

תְּקֵף, v. pres. aff. יִתְקְמוּ. *Exerted power against, prevailed over;* constr. immed., Job xiv. 20; xv. 24; Eccl. iv. 12.

תְּקֵף, Chald. v. תָּקְפַת, תְּקִפְתְּ. (a) *Was strong*, Dan. iv. 8. 19. (b) *Was violent*, Ib. v. 20.
Pah. *Made strong, established a law.* Infin. תַּקָּפָה, Dan. vi. 8.

תָּר, see תּוֹר.

תַּרְבֻּגוּת, f. r. רבה, once, Num. xxxii. 14. *Some, A multitude; others, with more propriety, progeny, posterity.* LXX. σύντριμμα. Ἄλλοι, σύστρεμμα. Vulg. *incrementa et alumni.*

תַּרְבִּית, f. r. רבה. *Increase, usury*, Lev. xxv. 36; Prov. xxviii. 8; Ezek. xviii. 8. 13. 17; xxii. 12.

תרגם, v. Arab. تَرْجَم, *interpretatus fuit. Interpreted, translated.*
Part. pass. מְתֻרְגָּם, Ezra iv. 7, only.

תַּרְדֵּמָה, f. constr. תַּרְדֵּמַת, r. רדם. *A stupor, an unnatural drowsiness, a trance*, Gen. ii. 21; xv. 12; 1 Sam. xxvi. 12, &c.

תְּרוּמָה, f. constr. תְּרוּמַת, aff. תְּרוּמָתִי, pl. תְּרוּמוֹת, aff. תְּרוּמֹתָם, תְּרוּמֹתֵינוּ, r. רום. (a) *An offering, a contribution, gift.* (b) *An offering* to God. (c) *A sacrificial gift.* (a) Exod. xxv. 2, 3; Num. xxxi. 52, &c. (b) Exod. xxx. 13—15; xxxv. 5, &c. (c) Exod. xxix. 27, 28; Lev. vii. 32.

תְּרוּמִיָּה, f. *Id.*, Ezek. xlviii. 12.

תְּרוּעָה, f. constr. תְּרוּעַת, r. רוע. (a) *A shout, pec. of triumph or joy, shouting.* (b) *A warlike shout.* (c) *The sounding of a trumpet.* (a) Josh. vi. 5; 1 Sam. iv. 5; Job viii. 21, &c. (b) Job xxxix. 25; Jer. iv. 19; Amos i. 14, &c. (c) Lev. xxiii. 24; xxv. 9; Num. xxxi. 6.

תְּרוּפָה, f. once, Ezek. xlvii. 12: r. רוף, i. q. רפא. *Healing.* LXX. ὑγίειαν. Vulg. *medicinam.*

תִּרְזָה, f. once, Is. xliv. 14. *The name of a tree*, according to Celsius, Hierobot., ii., p. 269, *The Holly.* Vulg. *ilex.* Aquila and Symm. ἀγριοβάλανον. Comp. Arab. تَرَزَ, *durus fuit; aruit, riguit.*

תְּרֵין, Chald. m. constr. תְּרֵי, f. תַּרְתֵּי.

תרם (630) תשו

The numeral *Two*, Ezra iv. 17. 24; Dan. iv. 1. 26.

תָּרְמָה, f. r. רמה. *Deceit, craft,* Judg. ix. 31, only.

תַּרְמִית, f. aff. תַּרְמִיתָם, r. רמה. *Id.*, Ps. cxix. 118; Jer. viii. 5; xiv. 14; xxiii. 26; Zeph. iii. 13.

תֹּרֶן, m. aff. תָּרְנָם. *The mast* of a ship, Is. xxx. 17; xxxiii. 23; Ezek. xxvii. 5, only. The context and the ancient versions support this interpretation, but the etymology is uncertain.

תְּרַע, Chald. m. Syr. ܬܰܪܥܳܐ, *aperuit.* ܬܰܪܥܳܐ, *porta. An opening, entrance, gate,* Dan. ii. 49; iii. 26. Comp. Heb. שַׁעַר.

תרע, Chald. m. pl. def. תָּרָעַיָּא. *Doorkeepers, porters,* Ezra vii. 24, only.

תַּרְעֵלָה, f. r. רעל. *Trembling, staggering,* Ps. lx. 5; Is. li. 17. 22.

תְּרָפִים, pl. m. *Teraphim;* apparently figures of the human form, 1 Sam. xix. 13. 16; objects of worship, Gen. xxxi. 19. 30; consulted with regard to futurity, Ezek. xxi. 26; Zech. x. 2. The etymology of the word is doubtful. Possibly the meaning might originally be *Relics.* Comp. Æth. ተርፈ ፡ *reliquus, residuus fuit, superfuit.*

תַּרְשִׁישׁ, m. *A precious stone;* probably *The topaz,* Exod. xxviii. 20; xxxix. 13; Cant. v. 14; Ezek. i. 16, &c. But according to some, *Amber.* LXX. χρυσόλιθος.

תִּרְשָׁתָא, always with the article, הַתִּרְשָׁתָא. The title of the governor of Judea under the Persians, Ezra ii. 63; Neh. vii. 65. 70; viii. 9; x. 2. Gesenius derives the word from Pers. تُرْش, *Harsh.* A more natural etymology would be found in تَرَس, *Fear;* the governor being *the dreaded one.* All such derivations, however, are mere conjecture, and cannot be depended on.

תְּשׁוּמֶת, f. once, Lev. v. 21. Apparently, *A deposit.* R. שׂים. The LXX. however translate תְּשׂוּמֶת יָד, by κοινωνίας. Vulg. *creditum.*

תְּשֻׁאוֹת, pl. f. r. שׁוא, i. q. שׁאה. *Any loud noise, tumult, rumbling, shouting,* Job xxxvi. 29; xxxix. 7; Is. xxii. 2; Zech. iv. 7.

תַּשְׁבֵּץ, m. r. שׁבץ, once, Exod. xxviii. 4. Either, *Quilting,* or *embroidery;* more probably the latter. LXX. κοσσυμβωτόν. Vulg. *lineam strictam.*

תְּשׁוּבָה, f. constr. תְּשׁוּבַת, aff. תְּשׁוּבָתוֹ, pl. תְּשֻׁבוֹת, aff. תְּשׁוּבֹתֵיכֶם, r. שׁוב. *Returning.* (a) *The coming round,* or *return* of a season. (b) *The return* of a person in completing a circuit. (c) *An answer.* (a) 1 Sam. xi. 1; 1 Kings xx. 22. 26; 2 Chron. xxxvi. 10. (b) 1 Sam. vii. 17. (c) Job xxi. 34; xxxiv. 36.

תְּשׁוּעָה, f. constr. תְּשׁוּעַת, aff. תְּשׁוּעָתִי, r. ישׁע. I. q. יְשׁוּעָה. *Freedom, safety, salvation, deliverance,* 1 Sam. xi. 9; Ps. xxxvii. 39; Is. xlvi. 13, &c.

תְּשׁוּקָה, f. aff. תְּשׁוּקָתֵךְ, aff. תְּשׁוּקָתוֹ. Arab. شَوْق, *desiderium, propensio animi in rem, cupido. Desire,* Gen. iii. 16; iv. 7; Cant. vii. 11.

תְּשׁוּרָה, f. once, 1 Sam. ix. 7. Apparently, *A present.* Comp. Arab. سَارَ بِهِ, *eum adduxit.* LXX. πλεῖον. ΑΛΛ'. ὑπόστασιν. Vulg. *sportulam.*

תְּשִׁיעִי, m. תְּשִׁיעִית, f. *Ninth,* Num. vii. 60; 2 Kings xvii. 7, &c. From

תֵּשַׁע, m. constr. תְּשַׁע, תִּשְׁעָה, f. constr. תִּשְׁעַת. Arab. تِسْع, *novem.* The numeral *Nine,* Gen. v. 27; Num. xxxiv. 13; Josh. xix. 38, &c. Pl. תִּשְׁעִים. *Ninety,* Gen. v. 9, &c.

THE END.

PLAN AND SECTION OF SOLOMON'S TEMPLE,

SHOWING ALSO THE POSITION OF ITS FURNITURE, CHAMBERS &c.

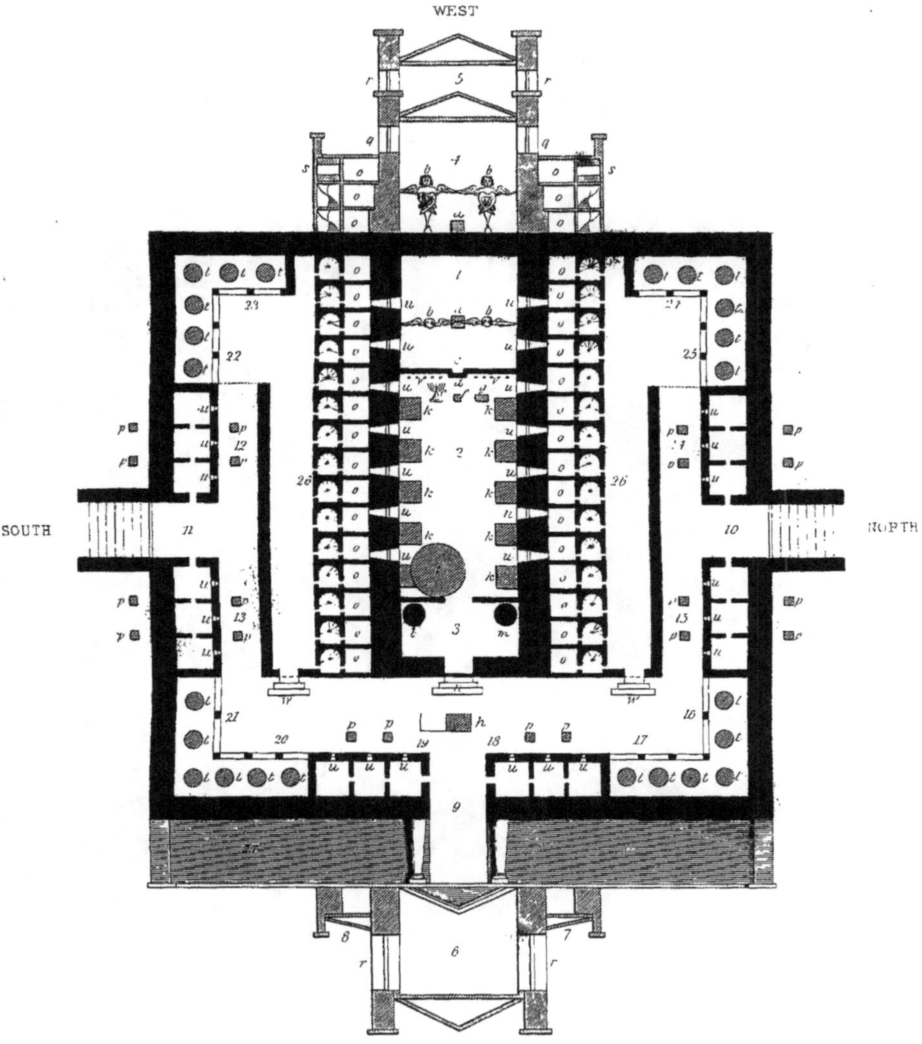

The great outer Court, bounded by a wall of 500 reeds on each of its sides, usually styled the Court of the Israelites, but at this time was common to them with the Proslytes of the Gentiles.

To face page 63.

London Duncan & Malcolm, Paternoster Row, 1840.

APPENDIX A.

A SHORT DESCRIPTION OF THE TEMPLE OF SOLOMON, WITH ITS APPURTENANCES, FURNITURE, &c.

THE object of the following plan and description of the Temple of Solomon is, merely to furnish the student, in the shortest and easiest way, with the form, proportions, position, &c. of the Temple, with those of its various parts, furniture, and the like. The foregoing pages will supply an interpretation generally of the terms used to represent these; but, as description is more likely to be misunderstood than picture, however rude, it has been thought advisable to add, by way of appendix, this plan and description; not, indeed, for the purpose of supplying a complete exhibition of the use of every technical term found in the several descriptions of the Temple: this would require a volume at least; but to append an easy and correct (it is hoped) conception of those parts, furniture, &c., which it is most desirable should be formed, at an early period of his progress, by the student of the Hebrew Bible. On the questions, as to the style of architecture adopted, the mass of wealth collected for the erection of the Temple, its duration, and final destruction, nothing will be said here. And, if it be found that the representations and descriptions given — as far as they do go — differ considerably from those found in larger and more complete works on the same subject, I have only to say, by way of apology, that the sole and real cause of this is, my having adhered to the Biblical accounts of this celebrated structure, in preference to those given by the Talmudists, Josephus, and their more immediate followers, whose main object seems to me to have been, to recommend their learned labours by descriptions, of this building and its furniture, far more splendid than those offered by the sacred writers themselves: on the faulty principle that, because He who is said to have made his residence in this holy house is the greatest of beings, that house must, therefore, have been the greatest and most splendid of buildings: a principle which seems at variance with the spirit of the Scripture, and certainly with the scriptural descriptions given of the Temple.

On the Temple, its Divisions, Courts, &c.

By the terms, הֵיכַל הַבַּיִת, הַבַּיִת, הֵיכַל, בֵּית אֱלֹהִים, בֵּית יְהוָה הַבַּיִת, הֵיכַל יְהוָה, *Temple*; בֵּית הָאֱלֹהִים, *House*; מִקְדָּשׁ, מִקְדַּשׁ יְהוָה, הַמִּקְדָּשׁ, בַּיִת, *Sanctuary*; and the like, is properly meant *the Temple* itself, but occasionally *the Temple together with its courts*. By מִקְדָּשׁ, is rather meant the *second court* or *enclosure:* and the same is true of the Ἱερόν of the New Testament. During the patriarchal times, בֵּית אֵל, or בֵּית אֱלֹהִים, seems to have been preferred, see Gen. xxviii. 17—22. From the times of Moses to those of Solomon, מִשְׁכַּן יְהוָה, מִשְׁכַּן אֹהֶל מוֹעֵד, מִשְׁכַּן הָעֵדוּת הַמִּשְׁכָּן, מִשְׁכַּן בֵּית הָאֱלֹהִים, and the like, were applied to the Tabernacle: rendered by the authors of the LXX. usually, ἡ σκηνή, σκηνὴ τοῦ μαρτυρίου, ἡ σκηνὴ κυρίου, &c.

The Temple had in its earliest times *two* enclosures; in later times *three*. Its first enclosure was bounded by a wall. (Ezek. xl. 5), one reed in breadth, and one in height; about thirteen feet, perhaps. The one reed *in breadth* probably comprehends the thickness of the wall, together with the breadth of the offices or small chambers attached to it, as given in the plan. The whole *length* and *breadth* of this *enclosure* or *court* was 100 cubits (Ib. vrr. 23. 27. 47; xli. 13, 14). It had three gates, the east, north, and south gate; to each of which there was an ascent of seven steps (xl. 22. 26; *eight* steps, reckoning inclusively, perhaps, as in some other cases, 31. 34. 37). The *second enclosure* contained, according to Ezekiel (xlii. 16, seq.), 500 reeds, both in *length* and *breadth;* which was, therefore, a square, as before.

Lamy, however, makes the wall which I have assigned to the first enclosure, a partition-wall between the second and third, viz. the court of the Israelites, and that of the Gentiles; while it is most probable that, at this period, no *third court* existed. That Lamy is wrong, it is, I think, evident from these considerations. 1st, Ezekiel says nothing about this larger enclosure until he has given all the measures of the first. (See chap. xlii. 15, seq.) That is, therefore, another and *distinct court*. 2d, In his account of the first court, it is evident that this wall and its measures are spoken of. (See chap. xl. 5.) At vr. 6, the eastern gate is mentioned as being in this wall: and vr. 7, the little chambers must have been attached to it. The same is true of many of the subsequent particulars. Again, at vr. 17, the *thirty* chambers mentioned must have been within this enclosure, and could be no other than those attached to the body of the Temple (chap. xli. 6): the terms *inner* and *outer* court, we shall presently consider.

In Ezekiel xl. 17, we find these *thirty chambers* (לְשָׁכוֹת) situated upon a *pavement* (רִצְפָה); and vr. 18, another *pavement*, over against the gates, termed the *lower pavement* (הָרִצְפָה הַתַּחְתֹּנָה). There were therefore two pavements in this court; one, *the higher* of the two, joining the sides of the Temple, and on which the chambers of the priests stood; another, against the gates and the small chambers attached to the wall, termed the *lower pavement*. We find again (vr. 17), that these pavements and chambers were in the same enclosure with the "*outer court*." The outer court, therefore, was not *without* this enclosure, as Lamy and others make it. And, again, this enclosure contained both an *outer and inner court*. We have seen that it contained an outer court. At vr. 19 a measurement is made from the forefront of the lower gate (הַשַּׁעַר הַתַּחְתֹּנָה), unto the forefront of the *inner court* (הֶחָצֵר הַפְּנִימִי), which I take to have extended from the entrance of the eastern gate to the west boundary wall. In vr. 17 we are told that there were chambers and a pavement made for the outer court; *thirty* chambers being upon the pavement. This pavement, as shown above, was the *higher* pavement; it appears here also to have been termed the *outer court* (הֶחָצֵר הַחִיצוֹנָה). The lower pavement, we have already seen, was termed the *inner court*. (Comp. ch. xlii. 4—14; xliv. 27).

These two courts, therefore, lay side by side. It also appears that the Temple stood on the *higher* pavement, from the circumstance that there was an ascent of steps from the lower pavement to it (xl. 49). A sort of fragment of this *higher pavement*, or *outer court*, will be seen in the plan, situated between the sheds of the boilers, and the chambers of the priests on each side of the Temple, and joining the extreme western boundary-wall. Each of these I take to have been termed the גִּזְרָה, *shred, strip*, or the like, Ezek. xli. 12—15; xlii. 1. 10. 13; styled by the LXX. τὸ ἀπόλοιπον, or διαστήμα. See Dict. p. 110.

In Ezek. xl. 23. 27. 44, also xliv. 17, we read of a *gate* of the inner court, or an *inner gate*; and chap. xl. 19, of *the lower gate*. (הַשַּׁעַר הַתַּחְתּוֹנָה) intimating that there was more than one in this court, and in this direction; whence it should seem that the porch to this entrance, and probably to the others, had two gates, an *inner* and an *outer gate*. If so, each of these porches was enclosed; each *inner gate* opening into the inner court, or part appropriated to the Levites: which, however, in the front of the Temple, was common to both the priests and Levites, and is termed, 2 Chron. iv. 9, *the great court* (הָעֲזָרָה הַגְּדוֹלָה), and the *court of the priests* (חָצַר הַכֹּהֲנִים). Once more; as the chambers attached to the sides of the Temple were assigned exclusively to the priests, so also was the *higher pavement*, or *outer* court; both were styled *Most Holy*, and therefore were inaccessible to the Levites. (Ezek. xliv. 13—15.) The distinctions of *inner* and *outer here* seem to have been made, the first with regard to the *outer enclosure* or *court* (ch. xliv. 19); the second, with reference to the Temple itself; or, it may be, as being beyond the wall separating it from that of the Levites, and termed *outer* on that account.

Having, then, so far determined the primary divisions of this first enclosure or court, with their terms; we may now proceed to point out its other particulars, according to the numbers laid down in the plan.

1. *The Holy of Holies, Most Holy place*, or *Oracle*. הַקֹּדֶשׁ, קֹדֶשׁ קָדָשִׁים, — בַּיִת, or הַדְּבִיר. LXX. τὸ ἅγιον, ἅγια ἁγίων, τὰ ἅγια τῶν ἁγίων, or δαβίρ. The measures of this were 20 cubits in length, breadth, and height, 1 Kings vi. 20; 2 Chron. iii. 8; Ezek. xli. 4.

(633)

2. *The Temple.* חַבַּיִת הַגָּדוֹל, הַהֵיכָל, as above. LXX. ναός, οἶκος, βασίλειον, θρόνος, &c.

3. *The Porch.* אוּלָם. LXX. κρηπίς, ναός. Twenty cubits by ten, 1 Kings vi. 3; 2 Chron. iii. 4; and, in this last place, 120 cubits high; so also the LXX. But, in all probability, some error in the numbers has crept in here.

4. Section of the *Most Holy Place*, or *Oracle.*

5. Section of *the Temple*, rising 10 cubits higher; its whole height being thirty cubits,* that of the Oracle twenty, 1 Kings vi. 2. 20, &c.

6. Section of *the Temple*, at its Eastern front, דֶּרֶךְ הַקָּדִים.

7. } Chambers of the priests as appearing
8. } above the Eastern boundary wall.

9. The *Eastern gate*, שַׁעַר אֲשֶׁר פָּנָיו דֶּרֶךְ הַקָּדִים, Ezek. xl. 6, &c. See LXX. It was ten cubits wide, thirteen high. There were steps (probably seven) up to it. מַעֲלוֹת, Ib. and vr. 11.

10. The *Northern gate*, with its eight steps, שַׁעַר הַצָּפוֹן שְׁמֹנֶה מַעֲלוֹת מַעֲלָיו, Ezek. xl. 37. But vr. 22, *seven* steps; reckoning exclusively, perhaps.

11. The *Southern gate* with its seven steps. וּמַעֲלוֹת שִׁבְעָה עֹלוֹתָיו, שַׁעַר דֶּרֶךְ הַדָּרוֹם, Ezek. xl. 24, 26.

12, 13, 14, 15. 18, 19. Chambers of the Levites, who were charged with various services as singers, washers of the sacrifices, &c. Ezek. xl. 38. 44; xliv. 11—15. These chambers are termed תָּאִים, constr. תָּאֵי, sing. תָּא, Ezek. xl. 7. 10; also vr. 12. תָּאוֹת. Arab. ثَوِيَّة, or ثَايَة, *mansio* (nocturna); r. ثوي. Cogn. redup. ثَانَ, *quievit*. Syr. ܬܘܢܐ, *thalamus.* LXX. θέειμ θεέ. These were erected against the boundary wall, and

with it are termed הַבִּנְיָן, Ezek. xl. 5, where we are told that the breadth of this *erection* was one *reed*, i. e. of six cubits and a span; giving about five cubits for the width of the chambers (Ib. vr. 7); and six and a span for their height. There were three of these chambers on each side of the gate (Ib. vr. 10, and so of every gate). Their measures were all alike (Ib). There was a border (גְּבוּל) in front of these, one cubit in width: a sort of stone base, perhaps intended to keep persons, &c., from touching and soiling the walls (Ib. vr. 12.) Each chamber was six cubits long (Ib.).

These chambers had, moreover, אֵילִם, i. e. *friezes*, or *entablatures* (see above), *one* cubit (in depth, apparently), and *sixty* in length; i. e. reaching over the whole system of these, with the sheds or boiling places attached to them, and encompassing likewise the porch of each gate (Ib. vr. 14); which will account for the whole length being sixty cubits.

They had also *splayed windows* (חַלּוֹנוֹת אֲטֻמוֹת), attached to their entablatures, looking towards the inner court (Ib. vr. 16.) And upon these entablatures were palm trees carved. (Ib.) The same was the case with all the chambers attached to the boundary wall of this court.

16, 17. 20, 21, 22, 23, 24, 25, seem to have been enclosed *sheds*, or *pent-houses*, such as to have presented the appearance of *porches*; and thence, apparently, they were termed אֵלַמּוֹת, i. q. אוּלָם, Ezek. xl. 16; xlvi. 20—24, &c. The Auth. Vers. styles these "*arches;*" things probably unknown at that time. With equal impropriety, perhaps, it renders אַיִל, by "*post.*" The LXX. ignorant, as it should seem, of what these terms meant, have given them in Greek letters just as they found them., viz., αἰλάμ (vr. 16), αἴθριον τοῦ αἰλάμ (vr. 14). Comp. the chapter throughout.

26. The *higher pavement*, or *Outer Court*, as noticed above, termed also מַהֲלַךְ עֶשֶׂר אַמּוֹת, *a walk of ten cubits* (Ezek. xlii. 4), and *Court of the Priests* (2 Chron. iii. 9), which was assigned exclusively to the priests, as it lay against their chambers, and was elevated, in some degree, above that appropriated to the Levites. Ezek. xli. 11, it is named מְקוֹם הַמֻּנָּח, as opposed, perhaps, to the lower pavement, on which *the work* of the Levites was carried on. On this pavement, and in front of the priests' chambers, was a wall of

---

* Josephus tells us, that another building, thirty cubits in height, was placed upon this, making sixty cubits in the whole; then, upon these, another also sixty cubits high, making the whole height of the Temple 120 cubits! A similar exaggeration is to be found in his myriads of vessels of gold used in the Temple service, while those of silver were double these numbers. It may be doubted, I think, whether such a writer is entitled to attention in any thing affecting his national vanity as a Jew.

fifty cubits in length, intended perhaps the more effectually to separate it from the lower pavement assigned to the Levites, but which, from its dimensions, would not cover the boiling-places at the west end (Ezek. xlii. 7). For in these (ch. xlvi. 19) it was the priests' office to boil the sacrifices. In the others, at the east end, the Levites probably officiated (Ib. vr. 24).

27. The boundary wall (חוֹמָה מָחוּץ לַבַּיִת, Ezek. xl. 5), as noticed above.

The Furniture, &c. of the Temple, and its Courts, as marked by letters in the Plan.

a. The Ark and *Mercy-seat*, two-and-a-half cubits long, one-and-a-half broad, and one-and-a-half high, Exod. xxv. 10; xxxvii. 6, הַכַּפֹּרֶת עַל־הָאָרוֹן מִלְמָעְלָה. LXX. τὸ ἱλαστήριον ἐπὶ τὴν κιβωτὸν ἄνωθεν.

b. The Cherubim, made of *resinous wood*, כְּרוּבִים עֲצֵי־שָׁמֶן, 1 Kings vi. 23. LXX. χερουβίμ. Josephus χερουβεῖς. πηχῶν ἑκάτερον τὸ ὕψος πέντε; five cubits high each. (Antiq. Jud. viii. c. iii. § iii.) He adds, τὰς δὲ χερουβεῖς οὐδεὶς ὁποῖαί τινες ἦσαν εἰπεῖν οὐδ᾽ εἰκάσαι δύναται. Comp. Heb. ix. 5. In 1 Kings l. c. however, these figures are said to be ten cubits in height. It is probable, however, that they stood upon a sort of *chariot*, which may account for this difference. In Ezek. i. 5, seq. they are particularly described.

c. The folding-doors of the Most Holy Place, four cubits wide, 1 Kings vi. 31. 34. Comp. Ezek. xli. 23, 24, דַּלְתוֹת עֲצֵי שָׁמֶן.

d. The Vail which hung in front of these, Exod. xxvi. 31, 32, הַפָּרֹכֶת. LXX. καταπέτασμα.

e. The Candlestick of gold, Exod. xxv. 31, &c., מְנֹרַת זָהָב. LXX. λυχνία ἐκ χρυσίου καθαροῦ.

f. The Golden Altar of Incense, Exod. xxx. 1; xl. 26; 1 Kings vi. 20, &c.; one cubit long, one broad, and two high, מִזְבֵּחַ מִקְטַר קְטֹרֶת. LXX. θυσιαστήριον θυμιάματος. But, Ezek. xli. 22, two cubits long, three high. The text, with Josephus, places this without the Vail: but Heb. ix. 4, within it. Termed *a table* apparently, Ezek. l. c. it. xliv. 16.

g. The Table with twelve cakes of shewbread, two cubits long, one broad, one-and-a-half high, Exod. xxv. 23. 30, &c., הַשֻּׁלְחָן. LXX. ἡ τράπεζα.

h. The Great Brazen Altar, מִזְבֵּחַ נְחֹשֶׁת, and מִזְבֵּחַ חָלָה, said to be five cubits long, five broad, and three high, Exod. xxxviii. 1, &c. But 2 Chron. iv. 1, twenty cubits long and broad, and ten high; and so Josephus, Antiq. viii. c. ii. § 7. LXX. θυσιαστήριον χαλκοῦν; θυσιαστήριον τῆς ὁλοκαυτώσεως. And Ezek. xliii. 15. 16. Twelve cubits long and broad, and four high. This was placed before the house, Ezek. xl. 47, לִפְנֵי הַבַּיִת. Comp. Exod. xxxviii. 30; xl. 6.

i. The Molten Sea, הַיָּם מוּצָק. LXX. ἡ θάλασσα χυτή. Ten cubits from brim to brim, and five high. See Captain T. M. Jervis's very interesting work, entitled, "Records of Ancient Science," Calcutta, 1835, on the measures of this vessel. The Jews, Lamy, &c., generally place it without the Temple, near the great altar. (Comp. Exod. xl. 7.) But in 2 Chron. iv. 10, it is expressly said that " he set the sea on the right side of the east (end), over against the south." נָתַן מִכֶּתֶף הַיְמָנִית קֵדְמָה וגו'. See LXX. Comp. 1 Kings vii. 39, where this is repeated, and where it also appears that it was placed together with the *lavers* and their *bases*. In 2 Kings xxv. 13, it is said to have been *within the house* of the Lord, with the *bases*. Comp. Jer. lii. 17.

k. Tables (שֻׁלְחָנוֹת) with *bases* and *lavers* of brass in which they washed the sacrifices, 1 Kings vii. 27—39; 2 Chron. iv. 6. 8. These *bases* are termed מְכֹנוֹת; by Josephus, μεχωνώθ. They stood upon wheels with their axles, each a cubit and a half high. The *lavers of brass*, כִּיּוֹרוֹת נְחֹשֶׁת, contained forty baths each. The *bases* were four cubits long, four broad, and three high. But, according to Josephus, five cubits long, four broad, and six high. These *tables* or, perhaps, *tablets*, were placed, apparently, as covers to the *lavers*, no particular use being assigned to them in the sacred text: and, as the *lavers* were placed on wheels, it is probable that they were rolled out on great sacrificial occasions, so as to be near the great brazen altar for the use of the priests in preparing the sacrifices.

l. ⎱ Two large brazen pillars, cast by
m. ⎰ Hiram, each twelve cubits in circumference; but, according to Josephus, eighteen. שְׁנֵי עַמּוּדִים נְחֹשֶׁת. LXX. τοὺς δύο στύλους τῷ αἰλὰμ τοῦ οἴκου, each eighteen cubits high, and fourteen in circumference, 1 Kings vii. 15—23. But, 2 Chron. iii. 15, seq., these pillars are said each to be thirty-five cubits high. They were set up in front of the Temple, one on the right hand

(635)

(south side), the other on the left. The former of these was named *Jakin*, (יָכִין), the latter *Boaz* (בֹּעַז). LXX. Ιαχούμ, Βολώξ. By Josephus, Ιαχίν, Βοάζ. The Jews, Lamy, and others, place these pillars in the front of the porch, and leave the porch open. It appears to me, however, that there were doors to the porch; and, if so, these pillars could not have been placed there.

n. Gates, or *folding-doors*, of the Temple, 1 Kings vi. 33—35, פֶּתַח הַהֵיכָל.—שְׁתֵּי דַלְתוֹת, שְׁנֵי צְלָעִים הַדֶּלֶת הָאַחַת וגו׳, Ezek. xli. 23, which, in vr. 25, are said to be of *thick wood to the front of the porch outward*, אֶל־פְּנֵי הָאוּלָם מֵחוּצָה. These appear to me, therefore, to have been the *doors* of the porch itself; and, if so, it must have been inclosed. See also Josephus, Antiq. (Ed. Hudson, p. 343), and Ezek. xl. 48, which gives six cubits for the width of these doors. In ch. xli. 2, we have for the breadth of the doors of the Temple (there *Tabernacle*) ten cubits. There must, therefore, have been folding doors to each. There were steps up to these gates, Ezek. xl. 49. According to the LXX. *ten.**

o. Thirty small chambers for the priests, fifteen being built on each side of the house, and of these there were three stories. To the two upper stories they ascended by *winding stairs* (לוּלִים), 1 Kings vi. 8;† and, for the purpose of giving space for these, the outer wall, in which they were placed, was five cubits in thickness, ch. xli. 9. Each higher chamber, too, as the walls of the house diminished in thickness at the distance of about every six cubits in height, was one cubit wider than the next below it, 1 Kings vi. 6; the lowest being five cubits square and high. Over these chambers were the narrow windows of the Temple, 1 Kings vi. 5—7; Ezek. xli. 6, 7; xlii. 5. These chambers are termed generally יָצִיעַ, and צְלָעוֹת, *a lying to*, or *ribs*, as buttresses, with reference to their position; but לְשָׁכוֹת, because, perhaps, *attached* to the house. They are also styled *holy*, Ezek. xlii. 13, because appropriated to the sacred uses of the priests. Those on the south side were occupied by the priests who had the charge of the house; those on the north, to those who had that of the altar, Ezek. xl. 45, 46.

p. Tables of stone, on which the animals for sacrifice were slaughtered, each one-and-a-half cubit in length and breadth, by one in height, Ezek. xl. 39—42, שֻׁלְחָנוֹת—אַבְנֵי גָזִית. LXX. τράπεζαι—λίθιναι λελαξευμέναι. There were eight of these to each gate (Ib. vr. 41).*

q. Narrow windows of the Most Holy Place, over the chambers.

r. Narrow windows of the Temple over the chambers.

s. Narrow windows to the upper story of the chambers. In the lower stories the light was obtained, perhaps, through the winding stairs.

t. Sheds or *porches*, in which the flesh of the sacrifices was boiled. See Num. 16, &c. above.

u. Chambers, תָּאִים, &c. See Num. 12, 13, &c., above, having narrow *splayed* windows (חַלּוֹנוֹת אֲטֻמוֹת, vr. 16). Also the *splayed windows* of the Temple.

v. Five candlesticks on each side of the Temple before the Oracle, 1 Kings vii. 49; 2 Chron. iv. 7, מְנֹרוֹת הַזָּהָב—הַמְּנֹרוֹת. LXX. λυχνίαι—λυχνίαι χρυσαῖ.

w. Steps with *entrance doors*, to the Court and chambers of the Priests, Ezek. xlii. 9. 12; xlvi. 19.

Such is an outline of the contents of the first *enclosure* or *Court*, as described by Ezekiel, &c. It has been noted above, from Ezek. xlii. 15, seq., that there was also an *outer space*, or *enclosure*, which had a boundary wall, Ezek. xlii. 20. According to Ezekiel, it was a square, each side of which measured 500 reeds. In Ezek. xliv. 19, this is expressly termed the *Outer Court*, (הֶחָצֵר הַחִיצוֹנָה), for there the people, who had access upon no occasion to the inner court, usually assembled. This, again, is termed (2 Chron. xx. 5) *the new court* (הֶחָצֵר הַחֲדָשָׁה), because, perhaps, it had been enclosed, or otherwise improved, by the then reigning King, Jehoshaphat. Other incidental notices might, perhaps, be found of this court; but nothing, certainly, that can justify the representations given of it by Villalpandus, Lamy, and others. Of a third *court*, or *enclosure*, usually styled *the Court of the Gentiles*, no mention whatever occurs in the

---

* Who read עָשׂוֹר, for אֲשֶׁר, here.
† Comp. Ezek. xli. 7.

* "*Within were hooks.*" Auth. Vers. (vr. 43). Heb. הַשְׁפַתַּיִם. Most probably, *channels*, a handbreadth each (טֹפַח), so set in the pavement round about the house as to carry off the rain, and other water, &c., as resulting from the sacrifices. Gesenius makes them a sort of stable. But, how these could be *a hand-breadth* only in measure, I cannot see.

Old Testament. It probably existed only from the times of Herod the Great.

Of the Second Enclosure, or Great Outer Court more particularly.

As we have no particular description given of this court, all we can say about it must necessarily be very general, and grounded, for the most part, on probabilities only. And, in the first place, as to its extent. The text of Ezekiel (xlii. 16—20) certainly gives 500 reeds for each of its sides, as marked in the plan: but, in all probability, this rests on the authority of erroneous readings only, for these reasons: I. Mount Moriah itself, on which the Temple stood, could not have contained an extent so great;. nor, in all probability did the whole city of Jerusalem. II. The rabbins themselves have, for some reason or other, assigned 500 cubits only to the measure of each side of this square or court. III. The Septuagint has (vr. 17) πήχεις πεντακοσίους, 500 cubits likewise: and again (vr. 20) πεντακοσίων πηχῶν εὖρος, the width of 500 cubits. In vr. 17, moreover, the textual reading of the Hebrew is חֲמֵשׁ אַמּוֹת, *five cubits;* which probably ought to be חֲמֵשׁ מֵאוֹת אַמּוֹת, *five hundred cubits.* And, if this may be relied on, אַמּוֹת ought to be understood in every other place; which, I have no doubt, was the intention of Ezekiel. This will make the whole practicable, and, at the same time, account sufficiently for the varieties of statement and readings, as noticed above.

This court, too, must have had its gates, and these were, perhaps, like those in the first, severally placed in the east, the north, and south sides of its boundary wall. It had, moreover, a western gate, as appears from 1 Chron. xxvi. 16. These again, probably, had their porches and chambers (אֻסְפִּים, 1 Chron. xxvi. 15), which may have been—as this court also was—much larger than those in the smaller, but superior, court. One of these porches—perhaps that belonging to the eastern gate—might have been termed "Solomon's," from the circumstance that at this gate the king usually entered (Ezek. xliv. 3). Attached to this, again, were probably the chambers or offices used in matters of public interest, as the Treasury (γαζοφυλάκιον, κορβανᾶν, Luke xxi. 1; Matt. xxvii. 6; 1 Chron. xxvi. 20. 24, אוֹצָרוֹת): certain chambers, also, assigned to the priests (Jer. xxxv. 2. 4); others, to the princes (Ib.), which appear to have been in a higher story. One of these priests, moreover, viz., Shallum, was a keeper of the gate. Ib., chap. xxxviii. 14, we read of a chamber in the "third," or "principal entry:" and in this the king discoursed with Jeremiah. That the treasury (γαζοφυλάκιον) was not in the first enclosure is evident from the circumstance that the people could not, in that case, have cast their contributions into it (Luke xxi. 1): that court being assigned exclusively to the priests and Levites. In one of these courts, Judas probably betrayed our Lord (Matt. xxvi. 14, &c.). In one of these, too, our Lord must, when a child, have disputed with the doctors (Luke ii. 46). In one of them, the Sanhedrim, or Council, must have condemned him (Luke xxii. 66), and intended to condemn Paul (Acts xxiii. 1, &c.). In this greater court, too, the prophets generally addressed the people, as also did our Lord on many occasions. Immediately before the eastern gate of the first court, in front of the great altar, and near the western extremity of this court, stood the king's pulpit (פִּיּוֹ, 2 Chron. vi. 12, 13; xxiii. 13), or pillar (עַמּוּד, 2 Kings xi. 14), which must have been in this court, otherwise it could not have been surrounded by the soldiers and people. Still, even this court is termed *the House of the Lord* (בֵּית יְהֹוָה, Ib. vr. 13), as it is *the Temple* (τὸ Ἱερόν) in the New Testament. In 1 Chron. xxiii. 28—32; xxiv., seq.; xxvi.; xxviii. 11—14, will be found David's distribution of the priests and Levites into courses, as also their several offices in and about the Temple.

It will be found, by referring to Exod. xxxvi., seq., that the Tabernacle, as erected by Moses, the Temple, as erected by Solomon, and the second Temple, as directed to be set up by Ezekiel, consisted generally of the same parts, measures, furniture, and vessels. In the Tabernacle, indeed, there were no side chambers for the priests, pillars named *Jakin* and *Boaz*, places in which to boil the sacrifices, small chambers (תָּאִים) for the Levites, &c. It had, however, its staves, rings, curtains, and some other things not found in the Temple. But these differences arose mainly from the circumstance that the Tabernacle was moveable, and a mere temporary erection; the Temple was not so. In the second Temple, too, some things, common to both the Tabernacle and Temple, were wanting, as the Cherubim, the

Ark of the Covenant, the Mercy-seat, the Golden Altar of Incense, the Urim and Thummim, and the Shekinah, or appearance of the Divine presence. For, although the first four of these are described in the directions of Ezekiel, it does not appear that they were ever set up. Some discrepancies, both as to things and measurements, will be found in each of the different descriptions of these: and hence the great obscurity in which this subject has generally been involved. Much of this difficulty, however, may have resulted from the ignorance and arrogance of the copyists, who,—as it is still the case in the East,—occasionally had no hesitation in amending what they thought amiss in the text: of which the book of Ezekiel, and particularly those parts of it which describe the Temple, may be considered as good specimens. After all, nevertheless, a tolerable correct notion of the Temple and its furniture, may, I think, be obtained; and such, without entering into the nicer particulars of its architecture, &c., I have here endeavoured to give. If, indeed, I have differed very greatly from others, and have, perhaps, erred in some instances—which in a subject of so much difficulty may be excusable—I have only to say, by way of defence, that I have done the best in my power to arrive at the truth, and have spared no pains, and, I trust, have been guided by no prejudiced opinions or views, in my endeavours to do this; and, I will add, when it shall be shown that I have erred, I shall be as ready to give up the notions I now hold, as I have to reject those of my predecessors in this question.

It is worthy of remark in this place, that, as certain services, offices and officers of the Christian Church, had their origin in those of primitive times, patriarchal as well as Jewish;[*]

---

[*] See my Third Letter to Dr. Pye Smith, p. 141, seq.

so also had the forms and general furniture of the Christian Churches themselves. If the reader will take the trouble to examine the plates given in the last volume of Bingham's "Antiquities of the Christian Church," or of Beveridge's edition of the Apostolical Canons, &c., he will find that the *Chancel*, or *Sanctuarium*, occupies the situation of the *Oracle*, or *Most Holy Place* in the Temple. The *Bema* (Lord's table), that of the *Ark* and *Mercy-seat*. The "*locus audientium*," that of the *Porch*: and that, as in the Temple—though not precisely in the same situation—the *Pastophoria* (see the LXX.) were the places of residence assigned to the priests; so were they in the primitive Churches. The enclosure of the whole, too, within certain precincts—as it is still the case in our cathedrals—which a very large portion of the nomenclature of places, offices, and officers,[*] afford other and very striking instances of coincidence in this respect. The Temple itself, too, as conceived by me at least, could not have exhibited either an appearance, or magnitude, differing much from many of our churches as they now are. The Temple of the Heavenly Jerusalem (comp. Gal. iv. 26), moreover, as described by John (Rev. xxi.), as the "Tabernacle of God with men"—if intended to be a description of the Christian Church, which I think cannot be denied—would lead us to believe that an analogy with the Temple would, to some extent at least, still be preserved. And such, in spirit and appointments, the Christian and Apostolic Church is.

---

[*] See Vitringa de Synagoga Vetera. The most approved writers and Tracts on the above subjects are, Lamy, "De Tabernaculo Fœderis," &c., Parisiis, 1720;.Calmet. Dictionary of the Bible, with Mr. Taylor's "Fragments." The Tracts, by Villalpandus, Capellus, &c., as prefixed to the London Polyglott; Lightfoot, on the Temple, &c., from which the names and titles of other writers and works will be learned.

(638)

APPENDIX B.

ENGLISH INDEX.

The numerals refer to the pages of the Dictionary; the letter *a* to the first column; *b* to the second.

Abase, 612 a.
Abate, 596 b, 614 a.
Abdomen, 208 b.
Abhor, 119 b, 167 b, 617 a, 626 b.
Abhorrence, 119 b, 620 b.
Abide, 276 a, 325 b.
Ability, 244 a, 292 a.
Abject, 612 a.
Able, 256 a, 288 b.
Be able, 256 a.
Abode, *n.* 585 b.
Abominable, 626 b.
Abomination, 613 b, 614 b, 620 b.
Above, 458 b.
Abound, 168 a, 578 b.
About, 435 b.
Abroad, 188 b.
Abrupt, 480 a.
Absent, 445 a.
Abstain, 413 b, 607 b.
Abundance, 10 a, 253 b, 260 b, 284 b, 348 b, 357 b, 548 a, 572 a, 612 b, 621 a.
Abundant, 547 b, 606 a.
Abundantly, 548 a, 621 a.
Accept, 428 b, 521 b.
Acceptable, 383 b.
Accepting, 387 a.
Accident, 151 a, 388 a, 489 b.
Accomplish, 464 b, 514 a.
Account, *n.* 7 a, 12 b, 128 b.
Accursed, 53 b.
Accusation, 574 b.
Accuse, 452 a.
Accuser, 574 b.
Accustom to, 329 b.
Acknowledge, 246 b, 420 a.
Acquaint, 439 b.
Acquaintance (person), 359 a.
Acquire, 383 a, 522 a, 532 a, 562 b.
Acquisition, 387 b, 532 a.
Acquit, 426 b, 510 a.
Acquittal, 509 b, 604 b.
Across, 448 a.
Action, 460 a, 497 b.
Adamant, 605 a.
Add, 262 b.
Adder, 49 a.

Adhere, 125 b.
Adjure, 584 b.
Admonish, 167 b, 264 b.
Adore, 431 a.
Adorn, 450 b, 457 a, 489 a.
Adversary, 13 a, 528 b, 574 b, 615 b, 628 b.
Adversity, 519 b.
Advice, 472 b.
Advise, 263 b, 264 b.
Adulterous, 169 a.
Adultery, 401 a; commit —, 401 a.
Afar, 559 a.
Affair, 126 a.
Affinity, contract —, 231 a.
Afflict, 199 a, 243 b, 311 b, 327 b, 406 a, 467 b, 503 a, 565 b.
Afflicted, 468 b.
Affliction, 243 b, 327 b, 381 a, 406 a, 468
Affluence, 590 a.
Affluent, 590 a.
Affright, *v.* 87 b, 215 a, 221 b, 231 b, 482 a.
Aforetime, 547 a.
Afraid, 270 a; be —, 270 a.
After, 21 a, 86 b.
After-birth, 601 a.
Aftermath, 332 a.
Afterwards, 21 a.
Again, 452 b.
Against, 458 b.
Agate, 582 b.
Age (generation), 134 b; of age, 85 b; old —, 176 a.
Aged, 176 a, 277 b.
Agitate, 412 a, 550 b.
Agitation, 158 a, 168 b, 174 b, 408 a, 626 a.
Agree, 17 b, 263 a.
Agreeable, 478 a.
Agreement, 94 a.
Air, *n.* 555 b.
Alarm, *v.* 87 b, 215 a, 482 a; *n.* 124 a.
Alas, 10 b, 19 b.
Alcove, 521 a.
Alienate, 420 a.
Alike, 396 a.

Alive, 193 b; keep —, 194 b.
All, 296 a.
Allow, 248 a, 417 b, 432 a.
Allowed, 601 a.
Almighty, 587 a.
Almond, 613 a; —tree, 324 a, 613 a.
Almost, 378 a.
Aloes, 11 a.
Alone, 19 b, 72 a.
Aloud, 525 b.
Already, 286 b.
Also, 47 b, 116 b.
Altar, 338 b, 348 b.
Alter, 346 b.
Amaze, 74 a.
Amazement, 74 a.
Ambassador, 326 a, 362 a, 513 b.
Ambuscader, 51 b.
Ambush, 335 b, 376 b.
Amend, 255 a.
Amethyst, 21 a.
Amiable, 421 b.
Amidst, 537 b.
Among, 80 a, 537 b, 620 a.
Amount, *n.* 444 a, 546 a.
Ample, 556 b.
Ancestor, 547 a.
Ancient, 487 b, 522 b, 523 b.
Ancle, 541 a.
Angel, 361 b.
Anger, *n.* 48 a, 87 b, 175 a, 205 a, b, 306 a, 448 b, 534 b, 550 b; *v.* 389 b.
Angle, 168 a, 387 b.
Angry, 175 b; be —, 45 a, 86 a, 175 a, 221 b, 448 a, 457 b, 535 a.
Animal, 193 b, 195 a, 424 a.
Anoint, 145 a, 394 b, 421 a, 437 a.
Anointed, *part.* 395 a.
Announce, 96 b, 365 a, 401 b.
Annoy, 430 b.
Anointing, *n.* 394 b.
Another, 21 b.
Answer, *v.* 467 b, 588 b, 619 b; *n.* 380 b, 630 b.
Ant, 420 b.

(639)

Antelope, 24 b, 264 a, 509 a, 617 b.
Antiquity, 450 a, 453 b, 523 a.
Anxiety, 124 a.
Any, any one, 26 a, 296 a.
Apart, 72 a; set —, 413 b.
Ape, 527 a.
Apothecary, 569 b.
Appear, 545 a.
Appearance, 190 a, 388 b, 457 b.
Appease, 308 b; be appeased, 556 a.
Apple, 627 b.
Appoint, 263 a, 370 b, 424 b, 432 a, 464 b, 499 a, 511 a, 526 a, 573 a, 585 a, 595 b; appointed time, 345 a.
Appointment, 219 a, 382 b.
Apportion, 204 a, 217 b, 414 a.
Apprehend, 625 a.
Approach, v. 407 a, 538 a.
Approbation, 568 a.
Approve, 494 b, 568 a, 574 a, 609 b.
Archer, 253 b, 347 a.
Argue, 255 b, 561 a.
Argument, 20 a, 362 a, 620 a.
Arise, 454 a, 459 a, 526 a, 527 b.
Ark, 53 a, 618 a.
Arm, n. 19 a, 177 a; v. 203 a, 439 b.
Arms, 431 a.
Army, 7 a, 195 b, 352 b, 431 a, 508 a.
Armoury, 431 a.
Around, 435 b.
Arrange, 431 b, 451 b, 480 b, 499 a.
Arrangement, 381 b, 382 b, 399 a, 480 a.
Arrive, 354 a, 383 a, 405 b, 625 a.
Arrow, 217 a, b.
Art, 226 a.
Artifice, 391 b, 419 b, 562 b.
Artificer, 40 b, 226 b, 227 b.
As, 299 b.
Ascend, 459 a.
Ascent, 379 b.
Ascribe, 432 a, 573 a.
Ashamed, be —, 77 a, 215 b, 299 a.
Ashes, 49 b, 145 a, 492 b.
Ask, 581 a.
Asleep, 277 b.
Asp, 458 b, 507 b.
Ass, 66 a, 206 a, 458 a; wild —, 479 a, 500 a.
Assault, v. 104 b.
Assay, 79 a.
Assemblage, 386 b.

Assemble, 104 b, 263 a, 303 a, 474 a, 517 b, 525 a, 536 b, 543 b.
Assembling, 388 a.
Assembly, 345 a, 386 b, 437 a, 450 b, 524 b.
Assign, 585 a.
Assist, 428 b, 456 a, 595 b.
Associate, n. 181 b, 303 a; v. 564 b, 568 a.
Astonish, 605 b.
Astonished, be —, 605 a, 619 b, 624 b.
Astonishment, 74 a, 154 b, *396 a, 604 a, 605 b, 624 b.
Astray, go —, 627 a.
Asylum, 386 b.
Athirst, 515 a.
Atone, 308 b.
Atonement, 307 b.
Attack, n. 619 a; v. 104 b, 405 a, 586 b, 589 a.
Attain, 429 b.
Attend, 18 b, 542 b, 607 a, 608 a, 609 b, 616 a.
Attention, 542 a.
Attentive, 542 a.
Aunt, 131 b.
Author, 2 a.
Authority, 393 b, 395 a, 396 a, 601 a, 629 a.
Autumn, 224 b.
Avaricious, 295 a.
Avenge, 427 a.
Avenger, 99 b.
Aversion, 626 a.
Avoid, 420 b, 607 a.
Awake, v. 269 b, 454 a, 527 b.
Awe, 564 b.
Awl, 392 a.
Axe, 121 b, 381 a, 539 a.
Axle, 444 b.

Babe, 253 a.
Back, n. 100 a, 107 a, 315 a, 481 b.
Backslider, 574 b.
Backsliding, n. 394 a; adj. 394 a.
Backwards, 20 a, 21 b.
Bad, 564 a.
Badness, 564 a.
Bag, 43 b, 259 a, 295 b, 521 b.
Bake, 48 a.
Baker, 48 a.
Balance, n. 335 a, 398 a.
Bald, 102 a, 540 a; be —, 391 a, 540 a.
Baldness, 102 a, 539 b.
Band (of men), 6 a, 180 a.
Bandage, 18 a.
Bank (of a river), 105 a, 578 a.
Banish, 408 a.

Banner, 130 a.
Banquet, n. 398 b.
Bar, n. 72 a, 93 a.
Barber, 112 b.
Bare, adj. 479 a, 512 b, 540 a; v. 227 a, 479 a, 482 a.
Barefoot, 255 a.
Bark, v. 402 a.
Barley, 578 a.
Barn, 122 a.
Barren, 475 b.
Base, n. 7 b, 9 a, 33 b, 358 a.
Basely, act —, 172 a.
Baseness, 97 a, 171 b.
Basilisk, 519 a.
Basis, 39 a, 301 b, 357 b.
Basket, 131 b, 238 a, 298 a, 440 a, b, 516 b.
Bason, 7 a, 112 b, 113 b, 306 a, 442 b.
Bastard, 366 a.
Bat, 457 a.
Bathe, 560 a.
Battle, n. 363 b, 431 a, 538 a.
Battlement, 381 a, 495 b.
Be, 151 a, 153 a.
Beam, n. 40 b, 527 b; weaver's —, 371 b.
Bean, 490 b.
Bear, n. 124 b.
Bear, v. carry, 242 b; bring forth, 428 b.
Beard, 176 a.
Beast, 87 a.
Beat, 137 a, 142 a, 157 a, 342 a; — out, 180 a; — small, 142 b, 315 b.
Beauty, 234 b, 265 b, 266 a, 612 b, 618 a, 627 b.
Beautify, 265 b.
Beautiful, 265 a, 611 b.
Because, 264 a, 622 a; — of, 330 a, 380 b, 447 a.
Beckon, 412 b.
Become, 151 a.
Bed, 267 b, 386 a, 395 b, 482 a.
Bee, 125 a.
Befal, 429 b.
Before, 331 b, 404 a, 419 a, 495 b, 521 b, 523 a.
Beg, 581 a.
Beget, 257 a.
Begin, 201 b, 515 b.
Beginning, 523 b, 547 a, 621 b.
Beguile, 430 a.
Behead, 481 b.
Behind, 20 a, 21 b, 86 b, 190 a.
Behold, int. 53 a, 146 b, 158 b, 159 b.
Behold, v. 420 a, 591 a.

Believe, 41 a.
Bell, *n.* 385 b, 498 a.
Bellows, 382 a.
Belly, 80 a, 110 b, 377 a.
Beloved, 11 b, 131 b, 246 b.
Belt, 18 a, 183 a.
Bend, 307 b, 452 b, 454 b.
Beneath, 622 a.
Benefit, *n.* 446 b.
Benevolence, 212 b.
Benign, 234 b.
Bequeath, 411 a.
Bereave, 597 a.
Berry, 120 b.
Beseech, 399 b.
Besides, 84 a, 84 b, 169 b, 452 b.
Besiege, 426 a, 512 a.
Betroth, 55 b.
Between, 80 a.
Bewail, 442 b.
Beware, 607 b.
Beyond, 448 a.
Bid, 42 a, 511 a.
Bier, 395 b.
Bind, 18 b, 47 a, 180 b, 214 a, 308 b, 475 b, 543 a, 571 b, 578 b; — about, 183 a; — up, 169 a, 182 a, 520 b.
Bird, 454 a, 518 b, 519 b.
Birth, 257 b, 344 a, 620 a; place of —, 344 a.
Bite, *v.* 430 b.
Bitter, 388 a, 391 b; be —, 392 a.
Bitterness, 366 b, 388 a, 390 a, 391 a, 392 b, 625 b.
Black, 523 b, 591 a; be —, 593 a.
Blackthorn, 22 a.
Blackness, 592 a.
Blameless, 624 b.
Blaspheme, 106 b, 225 a.
Blemish, *n.* 344 a.
Bless, 95 a.
Blessed, 92 a.
Blessing, *n.* 95 b.
Blight, *n.* 587 a, b; *v.* 587 a.
Blind, *adj.* 454 b; *v.* 454 b.
Blindness, 454 b.
Blood, 140 a.
Blossom, *n.* 424 b, 425 a, 513 a; *v.* 412 b.
Blot, *n.* 334 b; — out, 350 b.
Blow, *n.* 357 b, 406 a; *v.* 422 b, 430 b, 490 b; — a trumpet, 629 a.
Blue, 623 a.
Blush, *v.* 77 a, 215 b.
Blushing, *n.* 97 b.
Board, *n.* 541 b.
Boast, *n.* 627 b; *v.* 498 a, 583 a.

Body, 97 a, 107 a, 108 a, 473 b.
Boil, *v.* 97 a, 168 a, 571 a.
Boiling, *n.* 571 a.
Bolt, *n.* 373 b; *v.* 422 a.
Bond, fetter, 170 a, 344 b; obligation, 376 b.
Bondage, 446 b.
Bondman, 446 b.
Bondmaid, 611 a.
Bone, 121 b, 473 b.
Book, 443 b.
Booth, 439 a.
Booty, 77 b, 602 a.
Border, *n.* 374 a, 456 b, 533 b, 578 a, 590 a.
Bore, *v.* 426 a, 568 b.
Born, 258 a; be —, 257 b.
Borrow, 324 a, 581 a.
Bosom, 179 b, 196 a, 218 a.
Both, 609 a.
Bottle, 12 a, 403 a, 456 b.
Bottom, 541 b, 615 b.
Bough, 139 a, 573 a.
Bound, *n.* 102 b, 525 b; *adj.* 45 b.
Boundary, 101 b, 525 a, 578 a, 623 a.
Bow, *n.* 543; *v.* 416 a; — down, 307 b, 454 b, 591 b, 592 a; — himself down, 311 a.
Bowels, 377 a.
Bowl, 7 a, 112 b, 113 b, 373 b, 442 b, 443 a.
Bow-string, 357 a.
Box-tree, 618 a.
Boy, 256 b, 422 a.
Bracelet, 51 a, 515 b, 615 a.
Bramble, 143 a, 187 a, 441 b.
Branch, *n.* 72 a, 139 a, 172 b, 306 b, 354 a, 426 a, 442 a, 469 b, 489 a, 515 b.
Brand, *n.* 12 b.
Branding, *n.* 294 a.
Brass, 413 b, 415 b.
Brave, *adj.* 101 b.
Bray, 409 b.
Breach, *n.* 503 a.
Bread, 130 a, 326 b.
Breadth, 507 a, 558 b.
Break, 169 a, 315 b, 365 b, 503 b, 504 a, 566 a; — down, 162 a, 424 a, 433 a, 503 a; — forth, 503 a; — in pieces, 231 b, 503 a, 569 a, 584 b.
Breaker, 112 b, 394 a.
Breaking, 565 a, 584 b, 585 a.
Breast, 179 a, 190 a, 586 b.
Breath, 424 a, 431 a, 555 b.
Breathe, 424 b.
Breeches, 358 b.

Bribe, *v.* 576 a, 591 b; *n.* 591 b.
Bribery, 591 b.
Brick, 321 b.
Brick-kiln, 362 a.
Bride, 298 a.
Bridegroom, 231 a.
Bridle, *n.* 352 b, 398 b, 564 a; *v.* 84 a.
Bright, 512 b; be —, 15 b.
Brighten, 392 a.
Brightness, 167 b, 233 b, 512 b.
Brilliancy, 266 a.
Brim, 578 a.
Brimstone, 120 a.
Bring, 66 a, 75 b, 258 b, 428 b; — back, 413 b, 588 a; — down, 271 a, 302 b; — forth, 187 b, 257 a; — near, 407 a; — out, 266 b; — up, 459 a, 557 a.
Broad, 558 b.
Broider, 569 b.
Brook, *n.* 414 a, 493 a.
Broom, 571 b.
Broth, 392 a.
Brother, 19 a.
Brother-in-law, 242 b.
Brotherhood, 21 a.
Bruise, *n.* 352 b, 365 b; *v.* 236 b, 315 b, 379 a, 569 a.
Brutish, 87 b.
Bucket, 139 a.
Bud, *n.* 501 b; *v.* 501 b.
Buffalo, 546 a.
Build, 86 a.
Building, *n.* 336 b, 388 a, 447 b, 619 a.
Bull, 500 a.
Bullock, 449 b.
Bunch, 6 a.
Bundle, 36 b, 521 b.
Burden, *n.* 392 b, 417 a, 435 b, 436 a.
Burial, 521 b.
Burial-place, 521 b, 522 a.
Burn, *v.* 87 b, 139 b, 268 b, 269 a, 289 b, 579 b.
Burning, *n.* 87 b, 289 b, 346 b, 393 b, 570 b, 580 a; *adj.* 512 b.
Burnt-offering, 459 b.
Burst, 508 b, 510 b.
Bury, 522 b.
Bush, 575 a.
Business, 381 b, 447 b, 469 a, 575 a.
Busybody, 428 a, 562 a.
But, 96 a.
Butcher, *n.* 233 a.
Butler, 398 a.

(641)

Butt, 355 a, 382 a.
Butter, 205 a.
Buy, 309 b.
By-word, 396 a.

Cage, 298 a.
Cake, n. 199 b, 295 b, 377 b, 449 a, 518 b, 569 b.
Calamitous, 564 a.
Calamity, 24 a, 83 a, 228 a, 357 b, 392 b, 564 a, 565 a, 584 b, 585 a, 587 b, 589 b.
Caldron, 131 b, 529 b.
Calf, 90 a, 449 b; fatted —, 391 a.
Call, v. 536 a; — out, 563 b.
Camel, 118 a; young —, 82 b.
Camp, n. 48 a, 352 b.
Can, v. 256 a.
Canal, 12 a.
Candlestick, 372 a.
Cane, 531 b.
Canopy, 569 b.
Capable, 256 a.
Capacious, 558 b.
Capriciousness, 440 b.
Captain, 492 a, 578 b.
Captive, 46 a, 583 a; carry —, 582 b.
Captivity, 108 a, 113 b, 114 a, 582 b, 583 a; go into —, 113 a.
Carbuncle, 51 a.
Carcase, 382 b, 403 b, 489 b.
Care, n. 82 b.
Care for, 90 a, 595 b.
Carefully, 47 a.
Carpenter, 226 b.
Carry, 242 b, 428 b, 435 b, 562 a; — away, 428 b; — back, 588 b; — forth, 266 b; — on, 628 a.
Carrying, n. 392 b.
Cart, 449 b.
Carve, 219 a, b, 497 b, 506 b, 530 b.
Carving, n. 387 b, 506 a, 517 b.
Cassia, 522 b, 534 b.
Cast, 600 a, 601 b; — away, 176 b; — down, 271 a, 411 a; — forth, 235 b, 272 a; — out, 122 b; — up, 440 b.
Castle, 337 a.
Cataract, 516 b.
Catch, 270 a, 329 a.
Cattle, 87 a, 387 b.
Cause, n. 12 b, 128 b, 136 b; law-suit, 397 a; v. 600 a.
Cautious, 479 b.
Cave, 189 a, 381 b, 440 b.

Cease, 79 b, 184 a, 347 b, 410 b, 437 b, 447 b, 567 a, 585 b, 613 b, 617 b, 625 b.
Cedar, 53 b.
Ceiling, 443 a.
Celebrate, 246 a, 563 b, 595 a, 626 a.
Cell, 531 a.
Censer, 387 a.
Census, 382 b.
Certain, 290 a.
Certainly, 4 b, 28 a, 40 b, 569 a.
Cessation, 394 a, 490 b, 585 b.
Chaff, 112 b, 346 a, 454 b, 542 a.
Chain, n. 18 b, 415 b, 449 a, 571 a, 571 b, 615 a, 616 a.
Chalice, 102 b.
Chamber, 184 a, 333 b, 430 b, 460 a, 531 a, 617 a.
Chance, 388 a.
Change, n. (of clothes), 200 b; v. 159 b, 202 b, 260 b, 346 b, 435 a, 608 a.
Channel, 493 a.
Chaplet, 324 b.
Charcoal, 492 b.
Charge, n. 396 b; v. 499 a.
Chariot, 391 b, 449 b, 561 b, 562 a.
Charioteer, 562 a.
Charm, n. 327 b.
Chase, v. 553 b.
Chastise, 256 a, 262 b.
Chastisement, 344 b.
Cheek, 326 b, 569 b; —bone, 326 b.
Cheer, v. 442 a.
Cheerful, 576 b.
Cheese, 102 b.
Cherish, 179 b.
Cherub, 309 b.
Chest, 53 a, 618 a.
Chide, 119 b.
Chiding, n. 119 b.
Chief, n. 4 a, 405 a, 429 b, 436 a, 546 a, 578 b.
Child, 85 a, 238 b, 256 b, 453 a, 627 a.
Childhood, 422 a.
Childless, 480 a, 596 b.
Chilliness, 539 a.
Chin, 176 a.
Chirp, 519 a.
Choice, adj. 336 b; n. 568 b.
Choose, 79 a, 92 a, 96 a.
Chosen, 78 b.
Christ, 395 a.
Churning, n. 357 a.
Cinnamon, 532 a.
Circle, 186 b.

Circuit, 115 a, 435 b, 494 a, 628 b; make a —, 434 b.
Circular, 449 b.
Circumcise, 344 a, 420 b.
Circumcision, 344 a.
Cistern, 77 a, 100 b.
Citadel, 161 b, 384 b, 385 a.
City, 458 a, 529 a, 540 a.
Claim, 12 b.
Clap his hands, 350 a, 578 b.
Class, 499 b.
Clay, 208 b, 214 a, 236 b, 253 a, 363 b.
Clean, adj. 90 b, 233 b; v. 96 b, 170 b; be —, 233 b.
Cleanness, 90 b.
Cleanse, 234 a, 286 a, 427 a.
Cleansing, 233 b, 625 b.
Clear, adj. distinct, 512 b; free, 427 a.
Clearness, 233 b.
Cleave, adhere, 125 b; divide, 89 a, 503 b, 609 b.
Cleft, n. 98 a, 442 a.
Clod, 109 b.
Cloak, 71 b.
Close, v. 23 a, 436 a; adj. 539 b.
Cloth, 577 a.
Clothe, 322 a, 462 b.
Clothes, 577 a.
Clothing, n. 304 b, 362 a, 378 b, 577 a, 623 b.
Cloud, 430 a, 445 b, 469 a, 592 b.
Club, 621 b.
Cluster, of grapes, 58 a.
Coal, 569 a; burning —, 110 b, 570 b.
Coast, 101 b.
Coat, n. 338 b, 339 a.
Cock, 133 a.
Coffer, 53 a.
Coffin, 53 a.
Cold, n. 536 a; 539 a, b; adj. 536 a.
Collar, 469 b.
Collect, v. 46 b, 302 a, 303 a, 332 a, 522 a, 525 a, 543 b.
Collection, 47 a, 386 b, 522 a.
Colour, 457 b.
Column, 465 a.
Come, 66 a, 75 a; — back, 587 b; — down, 415 b; — forth, 266 a; — near, 407 a; — together, 522 a; — up, 459 a.
Comeliness, 618 a.
Comfort, n. 626 b; v. 411 a, 414 b.
Command, n. 335 a, 385 a, 510 b; v. 511 a.
Commemorate, 171 a.

4 N

(642)

Commend, 582 b.
Commerce, 438 b.
Commit, 482 b, 497 b.
Commotion, 158 a, 168 b, 174 b.
Companion, 181 b, 303 a, 564 a, 565 a.
Company (of persons), 180 a, 194 a.
Compare, 140 b, 396 a, 589 a.
Compasses, 351 a.
Compassion, have —, 188 b, 559 b.
Compel, 503 a.
Complain, 325 b.
Complaint, 575 a.
Complete, *adj.* 297 a, 602 a, 625 a; be —, 297 b, 602 b, 625 b; *v.* 88 b, 118 a, 297 b, 299 a, 602 b.
Completeness, 425 a, 623 a, 624 b.
Completion, 623 a.
Comply, 446 a.
Composition, 399 a.
Compound, *v.* 569 b.
Comprehend, 315 b, 625 a.
Compute, 227 b.
Conceal, 179 b, 237 b, 239 b, 292 b, 303 b, 445 a, 461 b, 519 a.
Concealed, *adj.* 48 b.
Concealment, 350 b, 445 a.
Concede, 248 a.
Conceive (be with child or with young), 161 a, 447 b.
Conception, 161 a.
Concerning, *prep.* 115 a, 458 b.
Concert, *v.* 173 a.
Conciliate, 199 a.
Conclude, 230 b.
Concubine, 327 b, 493 b.
Condemn, 570 b.
Condole, 410 a.
Conduct, *v.* 413 b.
Conduit, 627 a.
Confess, 247 a.
Confession, 619 b.
Confide, 41 a, 79 b, 213 a, 456 a.
Confidence, 79 b, 213 b, 305 a, 386 b.
Confine, 296 b.
Confinement, 296 b, 374 a.
Confirm, 41 b, 104 a, 464 b, 526 b.
Conflict, *n.* 538 a.
Confound, 83 b.
Confounded, be —, 299 a.
Confuse, 76 a, 83 b.
Confusion, 299 a, 336 a.
Congeal, 533 a.

Congregate, 474 a.
Congregation, 386 b, 388 a, 450 b.
Conquer, 408 b, 418 b.
Consecrate, 524 a.
Consecration, 361 b.
Consent, *v.* 17 b.
Consequently, 474 b.
Consider, 227 b, 420 a, 573 a, 575 b, 588 b.
Consideration, 437 a.
Consolation, 413 b, 415 a, 626 b.
Conspiracy, 543 a.
Conspire, 543 b.
Consternation, 83 a.
Constrain, 511 b.
Constitute, 370 b.
Construct, 567 a.
Consult, 264 b.
Consume, 87 b, 139 b, 374 a, 564 b, 625 b.
Be consumed, 625 b.
Consumption, 592 b.
Contain, 289 b.
Contemn, 75 b, 78 a, 154 b.
Contemplate, 591 a.
Contempt, 75 b, 143 a, 225 a, 529 b, 530 b, 599 b.
Contemptuously, 390 a.
Contend, 256 a.
Contention, 136 b, 339 b, 391 a.
Contest, *n.* 538 a.
Continual, 625 a.
Continually, 425 a, 449 b, 625 a.
Continue, 395 a, 464 a, 597 b.
Contract, *v.* 23 a.
Contribution, 629 b.
Contrite, 137 b, 585 a.
Controversy, 560 b.
Contusion, 352 b.
Convert, *v.* 159 b.
Convince, 255 b.
Convocation, 388 a.
Cook, *n.* 233 a; *v.* 97 a.
Coolness, 388 a.
Coping, 614 a.
Copper, 413 b, 415 b.
Copy, *n.* 396 b, 504 b.
Cord, 23 a, 180 a, 280 a, 357 a, 449 a, 507 a, 525 a, 628 b.
Coriander seed, 104 a.
Corn, 90 b, 130 a, 584 b.
Cornelian, 8 b.
Corner, 168 a, 387 b, 488 a, 495 a, b.
Corpse, 108 b, 489 b.
Corpulent, 605 b.
Correct, *v.* 262 b.
Correction, 376 b.

Correctness, 509 b.
Corrupt, *adj.* 33 b, 180 a, 403 a; *v.* 180 b, 593 b.
Corruptly, act —, 593 b.
Costly, 269 b.
Cotton, 505 b.
Couch, *n.* 267 b, 354 b, 386 a, 482 a.
Counsel, *n.* 345 b, 364 b, 437 a, 456 b, 472 b; *v.* 263 b, 264 b.
Count, *v.* 443 b.
Countenance, 495 b.
Country, 8 b, 55 a, 101 b, 340 a, 572 b.
Couple, *n.* 515 a.
Courage, 102 a.
Courageous, be —, 41 b.
Course, of life, 390 a.
Court, *n.* 217 b, 456 b.
Covenant, *n.* 40 b, 94 a, 451 a; break a —, 593 b.
Cover, 214 b, 215 a, 237 a, 239 b, 303 b, 308 a, 324 b, 439 a, 443 a, 456 b, 457 a, 462 b, 518 a, 569 a.
Covering, *n.* 304 b, 344 b, 358 b, 375 b, 445 b, 518 a.
Coverlet, 389 a, 577 a.
Covet, 12 b, 205 b.
Cowardice, 391 b.
Craft, 630 a.
Craftiness, 481 a.
Crane, 449 a.
Create, 91 b, 532 a.
Creator, 91 b.
Creature, 532 a.
Crib, 3 a.
Crime, 192 a, 505 a.
Crimson, 310 b.
Crooked, 475 b.
Crookedness, 476 b.
Crop, *n.* 534 b; of a bird, 389 a; *v.* 89 a, 332 b, 420 b.
Cross, *v.* 514 a.
Crow, *n.* 477 b.
Crowd, *n.* 439 a.
Crown, *n.* 315 a, 457 a, 519 a; of the head, 523 b; *v.* 457 a.
Crucible, 386 a, 460 a.
Cruel, 27 a, 480 a.
Cruelty, 27 b.
Crush, 454 a, 566 a, 568 b, 569 a, 574 a.
Crushing, *n.* 568 b.
Cry, *n.* 175 b, 401 b, 517 b 525 b, 540 a, 590 a; *v.* 81 b — out, 45 b, 175 b, 258 b 401 a, 517 b, 520 a, 536 a 563 b, 590 a.
Crying, *n.* 81 b; — out, 45 b
Crystal, 170 b.

(643)

Cubit, 39 a.
Cucumber, 388 a, 542 a.
Cud, 121 a.
Cummin, 300 b.
Cunning, adj. 479 a; n. 481 a.
Cunningly, act —, 481 a.
Cup, 45 b, 102 b, 291 a, 522 a.
Cupbearer, 398 a.
Curd, 628 a.
Cure, v. 566 b.
Curse, n. 336 a, 530 b, 617 b; v. 30 b, 55 b, 426 a, 521 a.
Cursed, 53 b.
Curtain, 273 a, 530 b.
Custody, 355 a.
Custom, 53 b, 143 b, 219 a, 397 a, 627 a.
Cut, v. 89 a, 98 b, 104 b, 110 b, 173 a, 193 a, 217 a, 219 b, 226 b, 493 b, 533 b, 579 a; — down, 312 a, 427 b, 535 a; — off, 88 a, 106 b, 109 b, 122 a, 312 a, 534 a, 535 a.
Cutting, n. 353 a.
Cymbals, 385 b, 514 b.
Cypress, 92 a.

Daily, 252 b.
Damsel, 422 b.
Dance, n. 351 a, 569 b; v. 188 a.
Dark, 188 a, 523 b; be —, 228 b.
Darken, 228 b.
Darkness, 49 a, 228 a, 335 b, 353 b, 431 a, 457 b, 459 b, 481 b, 524 a.
Dash, 353 a, 424 a.
Daub, v. 235 a.
Daughter, 97 b; — in-law, 298 a.
Dawn, n. 89 b, 394 b, 404 b, 431 a, 593 a, 613 a.
Day, 251 a.
Dead, 133 b.
Deadly, 564 a.
Deaf, 226 b; be —, 226 b.
Dear, 269 a, b.
Death, 347 b, 366 a, 625 a; put to —, 348 a.
Debase, 172 a, 302 b.
Debased, be —, 302 a.
Debt, 186 b, 393 b, 394 a, 430 b.
Decay, n. 73 b, 569 a.
Deceit, 391 b, 393 b, 563 a, 630 a.
Deceitful, 563 a.
Deceive, 162 b, 292 b, 430 a, 506 a, 562 b, 627 a.

Deception, 147 a.
Decide, 110 b, 219 b, 225 b, 561 a, 611 a.
Decision, 396 a, 397 a, 584 b.
Declare, 186 b, 404 a, b.
Declaration, 400 b.
Decline, v. 567 a.
Declivity, 347 a.
Decrease, v. 378 b.
Decree, n. 506 a, 528 b; v. 570 a.
Dedicate, 210 b, 394 b.
Dedication, 210 b.
Deep, n. 511 b, 619 a; adj. 465 b, 466 a.
Deepen, 466 a.
Defeat, n. 338 a; v. 418 b.
Defend, 561 a, 611 a.
Defer, 21 a.
Deficiency, 49 a, 214 a, b, 292 b.
Deficient, 213 b.
Defile, v. 237 b.
Defilement, 394 b.
Defraud, 475 a, 485 a.
Delay, n. 21 a; v. 341 b, 395 b.
Deliberation, 437 a.
Delicacies, 377 a.
Delicate, 451 a, 467 a.
Delicateness, 561 b.
Delight, n. 215 a, 229 b, 377 a, 467 a, 611 a, 627 b. v. 215 b, 555 a, 574 a, 610 b; — in, 229 b.
Delighting, adj. 215 b.
Deliver, 204 a, 278 a, 364 a, 425 b, 489 b, 591 b; — up, 384 a.
Deliverance, 160 a, 278 a, 489 b, 555 b, 630 b.
Delude, 162 b.
Deluge, 336 a.
Delusion, 342 b.
Demand, n. 581 b.
Den, 100 b, 189 a.
Deny, 292 b.
Denounce, 55 b.
Depart, 18 a, 155 b, 169 a, 324 a, 347 b, 410 a, 421 b, 437 b, 573 b.
Departure, 346 a.
Depend, 610 a.
Deposit, 499 b, 630 b.
Depress, 311 b.
Depth, 353 a, 380 b, 385 a, 465 b.
Deride, 325 b, 330 b, 331 a, 574 a.
Derision, 330 b.
Descend, 151 a, 271 a.
Descendant, 85 a.

Descent, 347 a.
Describe, 443 b.
Desert, n. 839 a, 478 b, 619 a; v. 423 a.
Design, n. 353 b.
Desire, n. 4 a, 12 b, 151 a, 205 a, 215 a, 229 b, 424 a, 564 a, 565 b, 617 a, b, 630 b; v. 12 b, 205 b, 215 b, 305 b, 581 b.
Desirable, 234 b, 352 a.
Desirous, 3 a, 4 a.
Desist, 184 a, 347 b, 567 a.
Desolate, v. 605 a; adj. 605 a, b; be —, 220 b, 277 b, 580 b, 605 a.
Desolation, 220 b, 394 a, 396 a, 581 a, 582 a, 604 a, 605 b, 619 a.
Despair, v. 242 a.
Despise, 75 b, 76 b, 78 a, 87 a, 401 a, 422 b, 529 b, 589 b.
Destitute, 4 a, 375 a, 481 b.
Destitution, 596 a.
Destroy, 2 b, 82 b, 84 a, 181 a, 214 a, 224 a, 292 b, 297 b, 350 b, 353 a, 433 a, 434 a, 438 a, 442 b, 447 b, 481 b, 534 a, 558 b, 581 b, 585 a, 593 b, 597 a, 604 a, 625 b.
Destruction, 2 b, 24 a, 83 a, 161 b, 228 a, 294 b, 492 b, 527 b, 558 b, 581 a, 587 b, 593 a, 618 b.
Detain, 474 a.
Determination, 173 a, 508 b, 584 b.
Determine, 172 b, 173 a, 225 b, 263 a, 297 b, 426 a.
Devastate, 84 a, 564 b.
Devastation, 77 a, 220 b, 586 b.
Device, 228 a, 345 b.
Devise, 227 b.
Devote, 224 a; — himself, 413 b.
Devour, 27 b, 84 a, 214 a, 327 a, 438 a.
Dew, 237 a.
Diadem, 315 a, 413 a, 457 a.
Diamond, 605 a.
Die, 348 a, 596 a.
Difficult, 284 b, 559 a.
Difficulty, 385 a, 519 b.
Dig, 215 b, 231 b, 309 b, 428 a, 506 b, 527 b.
Dignity, 149 a, 151 a, 384 a, 574 b.
Diminish, 214 b, 378 b, 530 b, 558 b, 567 a.
Dip, 233 a.

(644)

Direct, *v.* 279 a, 623 a.
Direction, 621 a, b.
Disagreeable, 564 a; be —, 392 a.
Discern, 80 b, 544 b.
Discernment, 80 b, 618 b.
Disciple, 330 a.
Discipline, 344 b, 376 b.
Discontinue, 184 a.
Discord, 339 b.
Discover, 383 b, 596 b.
Discourage, 410 a.
Discreet, 80 b.
Discretion, 80 b.
Disdain, 75 b.
Disease, 133 a, 200 a, 351 b, 621 b.
Diseased, 133 a; be —, 392 a.
Disentangle, 493 b.
Disgrace, *n.* 403 b, 479 b; *v.* 458 b.
Disguise, 608 b.
Disgust, 614 b.
Dish, 7 a, 442 b, 514 a.
Dislike, *n.* 577 b; *v.* 319 b, 577 a.
Dismiss, 600 a.
Dismount, 516 b.
Disobey, 389 b.
Dispel, 133 a.
Disperse, 78 a, 176 b, 412 b, 421 a, 424 a, 430 a, 490 b, 491 b.
Disperser, 382 b.
Dispersion, 627 b.
Displease, 221 b.
Displeasing, *adj.* 564 a.
Dispose, 290 b, 480 b.
Disposition, arrangement, 381 b; temper, 515 a.
Dispossess, 274 b.
Dispute, *n.* 339 b; *v.* 561 a, 611 b.
Disregard, *v.* 401 a, 430 a, 574 a, 588 a, 596 b, 601 b.
Dissemble, 72 a.
Dissimulation, 71 b.
Dissolve, 343 a, 374 a, 375 b.
Distaff, 295 b.
Distance, 390 b, 555 b, 559 a.
Distant, 390 b, 559 a; be —, 560 a.
Distinct, 512 b.
Distinction, 604 a.
Distinguish, 80 b.
Distress, *n.* 124 a, 511 b, 513 b; *v.* 511 b, 520 b.
Disturb, 139 a, 151 b, 410 b, 412 a, 550 b.
Disturbance, 626 a.
Divide, 72 b, 89 a, 110 b, 217 b, 431 b, 493 b, 503 b.

Divination, 387 b, 415 b, 532 b.
Divine, *v.* 415 b, 469 b, 532 b.
Diviner, 469 b.
Division, 217 b, 382 b, 493 b, 609 b.
Divorce, *n.* 310 a, 599 a; *v.* 600 a.
Do, 482 b.
Doctrine, 197 b, 344 b, 621 a.
Dog, 297 a.
Dominion, 366 b.
Door, 139 b, 506 b.
Door-post, 349 a.
Double, *v.* 307 b; *adj.* 396 b.
Doubling, *n.* 307 a.
Doubt, *n.* 560 b.
Dough, 88 b, 480 a.
Dove, 253 a.
Downwards, 354 b.
Dowry, 342 a.
Doze, 277 b.
Drag, *v.* 406 b.
Drain out, 384 b.
Draw, 395 a; — a sword, 561 a, 603 a; — water, 138 a, 580 a; — near, 538 a; — off, 433 b, 438 a; — out, 111 a, 394 a, 425 b.
Dread, *n.* 124 a, 230 a; *v.* 577 b.
Dreadful, 270 b.
Dream, *n.* 199 b, 201 b; *v.* 201 b.
Dregs, 607 b.
Dress, *n.* 595 b; *v.* 322 a.
Drink, *n.* 398 a, b, 613 b; *v.* 117 a, 434 b, 598 a, 616 b; strong —, 598 a; make to —, 613 a.
Drinking, *n.* 617 a.
Drive, 135 a, 142 a, 258 b, 408 a, 409 a; — about, 408 b; — away, 407 b; — out, 149 a, 240 a.
Driver, 562 a.
Driving, *n.* 371 a.
Dromedary, 310 b.
Drop, *n.* 6 b, 388 a, 417 b, 564 a; *v.* 413 a, 417 a, 481 b.
Dross, 439 a.
Drought, 220 b, 512 b, 513 a, 615 a, 623 b.
Drown, 233 a.
Drunkard, 596 a.
Drunken, 596 a.
Drunkenness, 598 b.
Dry, *adj.* 242 b, 512 b, 516 a; *v.* 221 a, 243 a; be —, 220 b, 226 a, 242 b.
Dry land, 243 a.

Dumb, 34 b; be —, 141 a, 226 b.
Dung, 60 a, 115 a, 141 b, 220 a, 504 b, 510 b, 518 b, 628 a.
Dungeon, 593 a.
Duration, 453 b.
During, 450 a.
Dusk, 431 a, 513 b.
Dust, 5 b, 471 a, 492 b, 592 b.
Duty, 219 a, 508 b.
Dwell, 108 b, 134 b, 276 a, 410 b, 597 b, 615 a.
Dwelling, *n.* 340 a, 347 b, 395 b, 410 b, 414 a, 439 a, 531 a, 585 b.

Each, 26 a, 296 a.
Eagle, 431 b.
Ear, 18 a; — of corn, 583 b.
Early, 593 a, 597 b; seek —, 593 a.
Earring, 413 a, 449 a.
Earth, 55 a, 208 b, 471 a, 618 b.
Earthenware, 226 a.
Earthquake, 566 a.
Ease, *n.* 599 a; *v.* 598 b.
East, 346 a, 350 a, 523 a, b; — wind, 523 a.
Easy, 530 a.
Eat, 27 b, 92 a, 327 a.
Ebony, 147 b.
Edge, 578 a; — of the sword, 490 a, 692 b.
Edict, 145 b, 335 a.
Edifice, 86 a, 388 a.
Educate, 106 a.
Effeminacy, 561 b.
Effeminate, 561 b.
Egg, 81 a.
Eight, 606 a.
Either, 11 b.
Elder, 105 a.
Elderly, 277 b.
Elegance, 209 b.
Elevation, 99 a.
Eleven, 486 a.
Embalm, 210 a.
Embassy, 362 a.
Embolden, 320 a.
Embrace, *v.* 181 b.
Embroider, 569 b.
Embroidery, 570 a.
Emerald, 21 a, 492 a.
Emerods, 470 b.
Eminence, 385 a.
Eminent, 557 a.
Emit, 432 a.
Employment, 446 b, 497 b, 498 a.
Empty, *adj.* 90 b, 561 a; *v.* 89 b, 479 a, 561 a.

(645)

Emptiness, 74 a, 77 a, 619 a.
Encamp, 209 b.
Enchanter, 22 a, 59 b, 327 b.
Enchantment, 532 b.
Enclose, 628 a.
Encompass, 315 a.
Encourage, 320 a, 428 b.
End, *n.* 437 b, 533 b, 534 a; *v.* 625 b.
Ending, *n.* 623 a.
Endure, 428 b, 435 b, 464 a.
Enemy, 13 a, 476 b, 519 b, 577 a, 615 b.
Engrave, 219 a, b, 314 a, 506 b.
Engraving, *n.* 506 a.
Enigma, 20 b, 194 b.
Enjoin, 452 a.
Enjoyment, 568 b, 627 b.
Enlarge, 548 b, 559 a.
Enlighten, 15 b, 167 b.
Enmity, 24 a.
Enough, 136 a, 547 b.
Enraged, be —, 175 b.
Enrich, 485 b.
Enrol, 314 a.
Ensign, 420 b.
Ensnare, 490 b.
Enter, 75 a.
Entice, 506 a.
Entice, 299 a, 625 a.
Entirely, 299 a, 425 a, 621 a.
Entrance, 70 b, 336 a, 506 b, 610 b, 630 a.
Entreat, 489 a.
Entry, 336 a.
Enumerate, 443 b.
Enumeration, 443 b.
Envy, *n.* 531 b; *v.* 531 a.
Envious, 564 a.
Epistle, 313 b, 359 b.
Equal, *v.* 589 a.
Equip, 203 a.
Equity, 397 a, 509 b, 510 a, 589 a.
Equivalent, *n.* 625 a.
Eradicate, 476 a.
Erect, *v.* 86 a, 176 a, b.
Err, 192 b, 585 b, 586 a.
Error, 394 a, 585 b, 586 a, 598 b, 620 b.
Escape, *v.* 324 a, 364 a, 411 b, 425 b, 494 a, 579 a; *n.* 382 b, 620 b.
Espousals, 298 a.
Espouse, 55 b.
Establish, 261 b, 290 b, 464 b, 527 a.
Esteem, *v.* 227 b, 573 a; *n.* 575 b.
Estimate, 614 a.
Estimation, 575 b.
Eternal, 449 b, 461 b.

Eternity, 449 b, 453 b.
Eunuch, 444 b.
Evening, 476 b.
Event, 388 a.
Ever, for —, 449 b, 461 b.
Everlasting, 462 a.
Every, 296 a.
Evidence, 572 b.
Evil, *n.* 565 a, 587 b; *adj.* 564 a; be —, 565 b.
Ewe, 559 b.
Exact, *v.* 407 a.
Exactor, 407 a.
Exalt, 101 a, 557 a.
Exalted, 390 a; be —, 572 a.
Examination, 499 b.
Examine, 79 a, 96 a, 499 a, 572 a, 595 b, 614 a, 621 a, 623 a.
Exceed, 447 b, 451 b.
Exceedingly, 334 a.
Excellence, 266 a, 280 b, 337 a, 348 b.
Excellent, 265 a, 279 b.
Except, *prep.* 13 b, 72 a, 84 b, 168 b, 569 a.
Exchange, *n.* 625 a; *v.* 260 b, 346 b.
Excite, 87 b, 121 a, 438 a, 454 a, 482 a.
Exclude, 519 a.
Excrement, 508 a.
Execute, 623 b.
Exempt, *adj.* 427 a.
Exile, 108 a.
Exist, 151 a, 153 a.
Expanse, 569 b.
Expect, 196 b, 254 b, 402 a, 517 b, 525 b.
Expectation, 305 a, 336 b, 386 b, 572 a, 620 a, 628 b.
Expel, 123 a, 133 a, 434 a, 601 b.
Expense, 424 a.
Experience, *n.* 340 b; *v.* 420 b.
Experiment, 79 a.
Expiate, 192 b, 308 a.
Expiation, 307 b.
Expire, 108 a, 422 b.
Explanation, 505 b.
Explain, 505 b, 507 b.
Exposure, 479 b.
Extend, 277 a, 548 b, 559 a.
Extensive, 558 b.
Extent, 339 a, 558 b.
Extinguish, 142 a, 285 b.
Extol, 557 a.
Extraordinary, 279 b.
Extremity, 49 a, 533 b, 534 a, 623 a.
Exult, 112 a, 134 a, 462 a, b, 574 a.
Exultation, 111 b.

Eye, 457 b; — brow, 100 a; — lid, 470 b.

Fabricate, 226 b.
Face, *n.* 495 b.
Fade, 403 a.
Fail, 184 a, 292 b, 387 b, 455 b, 625 b.
Failing, *adj.* 124 a.
Failure, 292 b, 599 a, 620 b.
Faint, *v.* 462 b.
Faintness, 124 a.
Fair, (beautiful,) 265 a.
Fairness, correctness, 509 b.
Faith, 39 b.
Faithful, 39 b, 40 b, 341 b.
Faithfulness, 425 a.
Fall, *n.* 382 b; *v.* 151 a, 423 a; — down, 423 a; — off, 430 b; — upon, 489 a, b, 514 a; let —, 602 a.
False, 292 a; — witness, 614 b.
Falsehood, 13 b, 292 a, b, 444 a, 587 b, 614 b; utter —, 614 b.
Falsely, 587 b, 614 b; act —, 614 b.
Fame, 603 b, 606 a.
Familiar, 33 a.
Family, 39 a, 81 b, 319 b, 397 a, 450 b, 531 a.
Famine, 564 b.
Famishing, *adj.* 564 b.
Fan, *n.* (for winnowing) 350 a, 560 b.
Far, 559 a.
Farther, 154 b.
Fashion, *v.* 268 b, 290 a, 512 a.
Fast, *n.* 511 b; *v.* 511 b.
Fasten, 562 b, 629 a.
Fat, *adj.* 92 b, 145 b, 239 b, 350 a, 391 a, 558 b, 605 b; be —, 606 a; *n.* 198 b.
Fatal, 564 a.
Father, 2 a; — in-law, 206 b, 231 a.
Fatherless, 279 b.
Fatigued, 243 b, 264 b.
Fatness, 145 a, 198 b, 396 b.
Fatten, 3 a, 145 a.
Fault, 570 b, 592 b, 598 b.
Faultless, 624 b.
Faulty, 570 b.
Favour, *n.* 209 b, 210 b, 212 b, 568 a, 621 b; *v.* 211 b, 568 a.
Fear, *n.* 25 a, 74 a, 196 a, 221 b, 230 a, 270 a, 337 b, 354 a, 491 b, 628 a; *v.* 109 a, 221 b, 244 a,

(646)

270 a, 481 b, 491 b, 577 b.
Fearful, 25 a, 135 b, 221 b, 270 b, 482 a.
Fearfulness, 381 b.
Feast, *n.* 27 b, 309 b, 326 b; *v.* 27 b.
Feather, 5 b.
Feeble, 40 b.
Feebleness, 567 b.
Feed, 3 a, 409 b, 564 b.
Feeding, *n.* 391 b.
Feel, 123 b, 261 a, 347 b, 398 b.
Feign, 420 a.
Fell, a tree, 423 b.
Fellow, 19 a.
Female, 426 b, 559 b.
Fence, *n.* 374 b, 393 a, 575 a; *v.* 106 b, 437 a, 573 a.
Ferment, *v.* 157 a, 207 b, 208 a, b.
Fertile, 606 a.
Fertility, 145 a, 605 b.
Festival, 182 a, 345 a, 577 a; keep a —, 182 b.
Fetter, *n.* 170 a, 286 a, 415 b, 436 b, 458 b, 513 a.
Fever, 523 a.
Few, 378 a.
Fewness, 378 b.
Fidelity, 40 b.
Field, 572 b, 587 a.
Fierce, 27 a.
Fig, 489 a, 618 a.
Fight, *v.* 327 a, 508 b.
Figure, *n.* 512 a, 625 a.
Fill, *v.* 360 b, 555 a; — up, 444 b.
Fillet, 50 a.
Filth, 438 b, 510 b.
Filthy, 237 a.
Filthiness, 510 b.
Find, 383 b, 596 b.
Fine, *v.* 470 a; *n.* 470 a.
Finger, 50 b; the little —, 528 a.
Finish, 88 b, 118 b, 297 b, 299 a, 625 b.
Finished, 297 a, 602 a.
Fir, 92 a.
Fire, 15 b, 56 a, 412 b; set on —, 600 a.
Firebrand, 12 b.
Firm, 209 a, 615 a.
Firmament, 569 b.
Firmness, 190 b, 424 b, 615 a, b.
First, 523 b, 547 a, 561 b.
First-born, 82 a.
First-fruits, 82 a.
Fish, *n.* 129 b; *v.* 131 a.
Fisherman, 131 a, 136 b.

Fishing, 131 a.
Fissure, 89 a, 98 a.
Fist, 7 a.
Five, 209 a.
Fix, 261 b, 290 b, 424 b, 526 b, 597 b, 613 a, 623 a, 629 a.
Flag, reed, 6 b; standard, 130 a.
Flame, *n.* 322 b, 583 a; *v.* 323 a.
Flashing, *adj.* 96 a.
Flatter, 301 b.
Flattering, 204 a.
Flax, 505 b.
Flea, 503 a.
Flee, 92 b, 407 b, 411 b, 579 a.
Fleece, *n.* 109 b.
Fleeing, *adj.* 92 b.
Fleet, *n.* 45 a.
Flesh, 97 a.
Flight, 371 b.
Flint, 202 b.
Float, *n.* 126 a, 567 b.
Flock, *n.* 391 b, 451 b, 508 a.
Flood, 336 a.
Floor, *n.* 569 a.
Flour, 441 a, 531 a.
Flourish, 491 a, 501 b, 513 a, 514 a, 515 b.
Flourishing, *adj.* 565 b.
Flow, 168 a, 511 b, 566 a, 590 b.
Flower, *n.* 425 b, 513 a, b; *v.* 513 a.
Flute, 414 a.
Flutter, 560 a.
Fly, *n.* 165 b; *v.* 124 a, 454 a.
Fodder, 83 b, 376 a.
Foe, 13 a.
Fold, *n.* 358 a.
Foliage, 459 b, 516 a.
Follow, 553 b.
Folly, 151 b, 403 b, 439 b, 507 a, 576 a, 619 a.
Food, 240 b, 349 a, 351 b, 358 b.
Fool, 13 a, 304 b, 439 b.
Foolish, 13 a, 156 b, 403 a, 507 a.
Foolishly, acted —, 403 a.
Foolishness, 13 a, 304 b, 305 a.
Foot, 551 a.
Footstep, 57 a, 386 a, 498 a.
Footstool, 148 b, 287 a.
Forbear, 54 b, 184 a.
Forbearance, 54 a.
Force, *n.* 191 a, 195 b; *v.* 133 a, 287 a.
Forehead, 385 b.
Foreign, 419 b.
Foreigner, 169 a, 366 a, 419 b, 459 a.

Foreskin, 480 b.
Forest, 265 a.
Foretel, 401 b.
Forget, 430 a, 596 b.
Forgetfulness, 430 b.
Forgive, 428 b, 440 a.
Forgiveness, 440 b.
Forgiving, *adj.* 440 b.
Fork, 349 b.
Form, *n.* 512 a, 618 a, 619 a; *v.* 91 b, 187 b, 268 b, 290 a, 497 b, 512 a.
Former, 523 b, 547 a, 561 b.
Formerly, 495 b, 547 a, 621 b.
Formidable, 25 a.
Fornication, 174 a.
Forsake, 411 a, 417 b, 423 b, 455 b, 560 b.
Fortification, 89 a, 195 b, 336 b.
Fortify, 88 a, 89 a.
Fortress, 384 b, 385 a.
Forwards, 419 b, 495 b.
Found, *v.* 261 b.
Foundation, 9 a, 262 a, 344 b, 357 b, 374 a, 615 b, 616 b.
Fountain, 336 a, 379 a, 387 a.
Four, 52 a.
Fowl, 454 a.
Fowler, 269 a.
Fox, 590 a.
Fracture, 564 a, 584 b.
Fragment, 148 b, 568 a, 582 a.
Frankincense, 321 b.
Fraud, 349 b, 475 b, 484 b.
Fraudulent, 484 b.
Free, *adj.* 216 a; *v.* 203 a, 278 a.
Freedom, 216 b, 277 a, 278 a, 630 b.
Freely, 210 b.
Freewill, 407 b.
Fresh, 194 a, 240 a, 326 a, 560 b.
Freshness, 274 a, 326 a.
Friend, 391 b, 561 a, 564 a, 565 a, 599 b.
Friendship, 599 a.
Fright, *n.* 83 a.
Fringe, *n.* 513 b.
Frog, 519 b.
Front, 495 b.
Frost, 539 b.
Fruit, 2 b, 8 b, 243 b, 418 a, 502 a, 618 b, 626 a; bear —, 501 a.
Fruitful, 145 b.
Frustrate, 410 a, 503 b.
Frying-pan, 350 b.

(647)

Fuel, 471 b.
Fugitive, *n.* 494 a.
Fulfil, 360 b, 568 a, 602 b.
Full, 361 a, 571 b, 602 a; be —, 360 b, 571 b.
Fuller, *n.* 286 a.
Fulness, 360 a, 572 a, 624 b.
Furnace, 291 a, 626 a.
Furrow, *n.* 104 b, 381 a, 624 a.
Fury, 205 b, 550 b.
Fuse, *v.* 176 b, 268 a.

Gain, *n.* 88 a; *v.* 88 a, 532 a, 562 b.
Gall, *n.* 366 b, 392 b.
Game, *n.* 512 b.
Garden, 118 b.
Garlick, 590 a.
Garment, 320 b, 378 b, 576 a, 577 a.
Garrison, 425 b.
Gasp, *v.* 581 b.
Gate, 506 b, 610 b, 630 a.
Gather, 89 a, 302 a, 303 a, 332 a, 522 a, 543 b.
Genealogy, 620 a.
Generation, 134 b.
Gentile, 107 b.
Gentle, 561 b; be —, 562 a.
Gently, 22 a.
Get, 324 a.
Giant, 422 b.
Giddiness, 565 b, 598 b.
Giddy, be —, 598 a.
Gift, 58 a, 67 a, 165 b, 342 a, 372 a, 393 a, 399 a, b, 429 b, 629 b.
Gin, 180 a, 491 b.
Gird, 19 a, 183 a, 203 a.
Girdle, 5 b, 183 a, 349 a.
Girl, 256 b, 422 b.
Give, 165 b, 248 a, 432 a; — up, 567 a; — way, 567 a.
Glad, 576 b; be —, 83 a, 183 b.
Gladden, 183 b.
Gladness, 183 b.
Glass, 170 b.
Glean, 460 b.
Gleaning, *n.* 460 b.
Glittering, *adj.* 96 a, 425 b.
Gloomily, 524 a.
Gloomy, 523 b.
Glorious, 9 a, 285 a.
Glory, *n.* 99 a, 105 b, 149 a, 151 a, b, 233 b, 269 b, 285 b, 337 a, 627 b; *v.* 156 b.
Gnash, 226 a.
Go, 155 a, 258 a; — about, 621 a; — aside, 416 a,

437 b, 574 b; — astray, 574 b; — away, 18 a, 437 b; — back, 587 b; — down, 271 a; — forth, 266 a; — in, 75 a; — near, 407 a; — out, 266 a; — round, 621 a; — up, 459 a.
Goad, *n.* 143 a, 365 b.
Goat, 455 a, 487 a, 508 a, 518 b, 572 b, 577 b, 622 b; scape —, 455 a.
Goblet, 442 b.
God, 24 a, 31 a.
Gold, 130 b, 167 a, 314 b.
Goldsmith, 520 b.
Good, *adj.* 234 b; *n.* 356 a; be —, 255 a.
Good tidings, 96 b.
Goodness, 213 a, 234 b.
Govern, 553 a, 564 b.
Government, 362 b, 393 b, 499 b.
Governor, 492 a, 534 b.
Grace, 209 b, 210 b, 422 a.
Gracious, 210 a, 213 b.
Grain, 500 b, 521 b, 561 a.
Granary, 337 b, 366 a.
Grandeur, 390 a.
Grape, 466 b.
Grasp, 531 a.
Grass, 83 b.
Grave, *n.* 581 a, 593 a.
Graven image, 497 a.
Graver, 456 b.
Grayheaded, 575 a.
Great, 8 a, 105 a, 286 a, 547 b, 572 b; be —, 105 b.
Greatness, 105 a, 389 a, 549 a.
Green, 560 b.
Greenness, 2 b, 274 a.
Grief, 243 b, 357 b, 472 a.
Grieve, 392 b, 414 b, 472 a.
Grievous, 44 b, 284 b.
Grind, 236 b; — small, 142 b.
Grinders, (teeth,) 399 a.
Groan, *n.* 409 b; *v.* 409 b.
Grope, 123 b, 261 a, 398 b.
Gross, 239 b.
Ground, *n.* 8 b, 572 b.
Groundwork, 615 b.
Grow, 459 a, 515 b, 549 a.
Growl, 147 b, 157 b.
Guard, *v.* 119 a, 417 b, 426 a, 607 a.
Guest, 536 b.
Guidance, 621 b.
Guide, *n.* 409 a; *v.* 413 b.
Guile, 391 b.
Guilt, 58 b, 453 b, 570 b, 587 b.
Guilty, 59 b, 570 b.
Gull, *n.* 592 b.

Habitation, 23 a, 166 a, 340 a, 357 b, 377 b, 386 b, 395 b, 410 b.
Haft, 424 b.
Hail, *n.* 29 b, 91 b.
Hailstones, 4 b.
Hair, 577 b, 578 a.
Hairy, 577 b.
Half, 217 b, 353 a.
Hallow, 524 a.
Halt, *adj.* 410 b; *v.* 615 a.
Hammer, *n.* 157 a, 386 b, 492 b.
Hand, 244 a, 306 a, 531 a.
Handbreadth, 239 a.
Handful, 509 a, 531 a, 610 a.
Handle, *n.* 424 b; *v.* 628 a.
Handmaid, 39 a; 611 a.
Handsome, 234 b, 265 a.
Hang, 212 a, 623 b; —down, 567 a.
Happen, 153 a, 537 a, 539 a.
Happiness, 234 b.
Happy, 60 a, 234 b; be —, 255 a.
Harass, 151 b.
Harbour, *n.* 351 a.
Hard, 92 b, 346 a, 542 b.
Harden, 533 a, 542 b.
Hard-hearted, 542 b.
Hardness, 543 a, 628 a.
Hare, 55 a.
Harlot, 56 b, 168 b.
Harm, *n.* 564 a, 620 b.
Harp, *n.* 529 b.
Harrow, *v.* 572 b.
Harsh, 455 a.
Harshness, 502 a.
Harvest, *n.* 534 b.
Haste, *n.* 196 b, 215 a; *v.* 14 b.
Hasten, *v.* 189 b, 342 b, 523 a, 558 a.
Hastily, 196 a.
Hatch, 89 a, 130 a.
Hate, *v.* 527 a, 574 b, 577 a.
Hatred, 393 a, 577 b.
Haughtily, 390 a, 577 b.
Haughtiness, 99 a, 100 b, 107 b, 167 a, 390 a, 557 b.
Haughty, 166 b, 250 b, 557 a; be —, 557 a.
Haven, 351 a.
Hawk, 424 b.
Hay, 229 b.
He, 149 b.
Head, 546 a.
Heal, 566 b.
Healing, *n.* 391 b, 567 a, 629 b.
Health, 567 a.
Heap, *n.* 105 b, 112 a, 244 a, 407 a, 457 a, 481 a, 509 a, 522 a, 623 b; *v.* 509 a.

(648)

Hear, 606 a.
Hearing, n. 162 a, 606 a.
Hearken, 606 a.
Heart, 82 b, 319 b.
Hearth, 346 b.
Heat, n. 205 a, b, 220 b, 222 a, 223 a; v. 17 b.
Heathen, 107 b.
Heaven, 604 b.
Heavily, 285 b.
Heaviness, 628 a.
Heavy, 284 b.
Hedge, n. 374 b; v. 573 a.
Hedgehog, 533 a.
Heed, v. 607 a.
Heel, 475 a.
Height, 100 b, 390 a, 527 a, 557 b.
Heir, 274 b.
Helmet, 289 b, 525 b.
Help, n. 456 a; v. 441 a, 456 a.
Helper, 456 a.
Herald, n. 310 a.
Herb, 482 a.
Herbage, 274 a.
Herd, n. 451 b.
Herdsman, 77, a.
Here, 490 a.
Hereafter, 353 b.
Heretofore, 603 b.
Heritage, 414 a.
Heron, 521 a.
Hew, 217 a, 497 b.
Hide, v. 179 b, 237 b, 461 b, 519 a.
Hiding-place, 350 b, 376 b, 439 a.
High, 100 b, 101 a, 390 a, 460 a, 557 a; be —, 101 a, 556 b, 572 a; Most High, 459 a, 460 a.
High place, 85 a, 393 a, 562 b.
Highway, 375 a.
Hill, 103 a, 623 b.
Hinderance, 381 a.
Hinge, n. 505 b, 513 b.
Hire, n. 576 a; v. 440 a, 576 a.
Hireling, 575 b.
Hiss, v. 615 b.
Hissing, n. 615 a, b.
History, 620 a.
Hither, 157 a, 159 a, 490 a.
Hoar frost, 307 a.
Hold, v. 20 b, 625 a; — out, 196 b.
Hole, 189 a.
Holiness, 524 a.
Hollow, adj. 402 a.
Holy, 233 b, 522 b, 523 a, 524 a.
Holly, 629 b.
Home, 81 a.

Home-born, 19 a.
Honey, 129 a, 265 a, 424 b.
Honey-comb, 511 b.
Honour, n. 149 a, 269 b, 509 a, 627 b; v. 149 a, 285 a.
Honourable, 269 b, 285 a.
Honoured, 269 a.
Hoof, 502 b.
Hook, 165 b, 439 a, 540 b.
Hope, n. 305 a, 336 b, 386 b, 572 a, 620 a, 628 b; v. 254 b, 525 b, 572 a.
Horn, 540 b.
Hornet, 520 b.
Horrible, 611 a.
Horror, 577 b.
Horse, n. 437 a, 504 b; post —, 562 b.
Horseman, 504 b, 562 a.
Host, 7 a.
Hostage, 627 b.
Hot, 204 b, 512 b; be —, 204 b, 221 b, 226 a, 254 b.
Hour, 610 a.
House, 81 a.
Household, 397 a.
Hover, 560 a.
Howl, 258 b.
Howling, n. 19 b.
Humble, v. 287 a, 302 b, 467 b, 592 a, 612 a; adj. 468 b, 612 a.
Humbled, be —, 302 a.
Humility, 468 b.
Hundred, 334 a.
Hunger, n. 307 b, 564 b; v. 564 b.
Hungry, 561 b, 564 b.
Hunt, v. 511 a.
Hunter, 513 a.
Hunting, n. 512 b.
Hurry, n. 215 a, 321 a; v. 74 a, 136 a, 189 b, 342 b.
Hurt, n. 180 a; v. 162 a.
Husband, 26 a, 87 a, 103 b.
Husbandman, 28 b.
Hut, 439 a.
Hyæna, 509 a.
Hymn, 172 b, 349 b, 628 a.
Hyssop, 18 a.

I, 44 b.
Ice, 539 b.
Idle, 473 a.
Idleness, 473 b.
Idol, 13 b, 34 a, 97 b, 192 b, 382 b, 471 b, 472 a, 497 a, 620 b.
Idolatrous, 168 b.
Idolatry, 13 b, 174 a.
If, 158 b.
Ignominy, 77 a, 97 b, 299 a.

Ignorance, 228 a.
Ignorant, 87 b, 507 a.
Ill, sick, 199 a.
Image, 382 b, 384 a, 393 a, 514 b.
Imagination, 172 a, 268 a, 393 a, 514 b.
Imagine, 140 b.
Immediately, 505 b.
Impatience, 535 a.
Impel, 407 a, 408 a, 428 b.
Impetuosity, 586 b.
Impiety, 212 a, 403 b, 570 b.
Impious, 403 a, 570 b.
Implement, 298 b.
Implore, 212 a.
Impose, 573 a, 595 b.
Imprison, 47 a.
Imprisonment, 396 b.
Impure, 237 a.
Impurity, 408 a.
Impute, 227 b.
Incantation, 327 b.
Incense, n. 387 a, 527 b, 528 b.
Incision, 579 a.
Inclination, 424 a.
Incline, 416 b.
Inclose, 436 a.
Inclosure, 217 b, 218 b, 374 a, 436 a.
Income, 618 b.
Inconstancy, 13 a.
Increase, n. 76 a, 318 b, 629 b; v. 410 a, 459 a, 548 b, 572 a.
Incurable, 44 b.
Indigenous, 19 a.
Indignant, 175 b; be —, 175 a, b.
Indignation, 175 a, 306 a.
Induce, 408 a, 438 a.
Infamy, 125 a.
Infant, 238 b, 453 a.
Infirm, 288 a; be —, 199 a, 288 b.
Inflame, 139 b, 323 a, 490 b.
Inflammation, 592 a.
Inflict, 432 a, 573 a.
Infliction, 406 a, b.
Influence, n. 395 a.
Inform, 247 a.
Inhabit, 347 b, 597 b.
Inhabitant, 597 b, 598 a, 621 a.
Inherit, 274 b.
Inheritance, 414 a.
Iniquity, 14 a, 453 a, b.
Injure, 137 a, 162 a, 180 b, 207 b, 299 b, 327 b, 379 a, 485 a.
Injury, 45 b, 73 b, 151 a, 180 a, 207 b, 354 a, 394 b,

(649)

413 a, 485 a, 505 a, 564 a, 565 a.
Injustice, 453 a, 570 b, 628 a.
Ink, 136 b.
Ink-horn, 532 b.
Inn, 362 b.
Inner, 496 a.
Innkeeper, 168 b.
Innocence, 170 b, 427 a.
Innocent, 427 a, 509 b; be —, 426 b.
Inquire, 90 a, 144 b, 220 a, 499 a, 581 a.
Inquiry, 90 a, 216 a, 219 b.
Insolence, 99 a, 167 a, 349 b, 554 a.
Insolent, 402 a, 502 a, 554 a.
Instability, 147 a.
Instant, *n.* 552 a.
Instead of, 622 a.
Instruct, 198 a, 272 a.
Instruction, 331 b, 621 a.
Instrument, 298 b.
Insult, *n.* 401 a; *v.* 325 b, 346 b, 512 b, 554 a.
Integrity, 278 a, 624 b, 625 a.
Intelligence, understanding, 80 b, 370 b.
Intend, 172 b.
Intent, *n.* 380 b.
Intention, 172 a.
Intercept, 329 a.
Intercession, 628 a.
Interest, *n.* 389 a, 393 b, 430 b.
Interior, *n.* 81 b.
Intermission, 159 b, 490 b.
Interpret, 505 b, 507 b, 629 b.
Interpretation, 505 b, 507 b.
Interpreter, 326 a.
Interval, 80 a, 559 a.
Intoxicated, be —, 598 a.
Intrepid, 101 b.
Inundation, 177 b, 594 a, 612 b.
Invade, 586 b.
Inventor, 2 a.
Invention, 349 b.
Invest, 456 b.
Investigate, 215 b, 216 a, 220 a.
Investigation, 216 a, 219 b.
Invite, 536 b.
Invoke, 604 a.
Inwards, *n.* 537 a.
Iron, 92 b, 501 b.
Irritate, 335 b.
Issue, *v.* 168 a.
Ivory, 608 a.

Jar, *n.* 287 b, 295 b, 403 a.
Jasper, 278 b.
Jaw, 365 b.

Jawbone, 326 b.
Jealous, 531 b, 532 a; be —, 531 a.
Jealousy, 531 b.
Jerboa, 458 a, 612 b.
Jew, 249 a.
Join, 181 b, 571 b, 598 b.
Joined, be —, 324 a.
Joiner, 374 a.
Joining, *n.* 182 a.
Joke, 512 b.
Journey, *n.* 143 b, 341 b, 375 b.
Joy, *n.* 183 b, 393 a, 577 a, 580 b.
Joyful, 576 b; be —, 576 b.
Judge, *n.* 136 b, 494 a, 534 b, 611 b; *v.* 134 a, 238 a, 494 b, 611 a, 614 a.
Judgment, 136 b, 238 a, 494 a, 611 b.
Juice, 398 b, 425 a.
Just, 509 b.
Justice, 397 a, 494 a, 509 b, 510 a; court of —, 397 a.
Justification, 509 b.
Justify, 510 a.

Keep, 607 a; — alive, 194 b; — back, 227 a, 373 a; — in mind, 607 a.
Key, 383 a.
Kick, *v.* 87 a.
Kid, 105 a, 508 a.
Kill, 161 a, 312 a, 406 a, 418 b, 528 a, 560 b, 568 b.
Killing, *n.* 568 b.
Kind, *n.* 173 b, 356 b; *adj.* 234 b.
Kindle, 139 b, 522 b.
Kindness, 212 b, 422 a, 619 a.
Kindred, 344 a.
King, 364 b.
Kingdom, 365 a, 366 b.
Kinsman, 99 b.
Kiss, *n.* 430 b; *v.* 431 a.
Kite, 545 b.
Knead, 326 a.
Kneading-trough, 394 a.
Knee, 95 a.
Kneel, 95 a.
Knife, 220 b, 335 a, 519 b, 575 b.
Knock, 142 a.
Knot, 6 a, 515 b.
Know, 246 b, 420 a.
Knowledge, 15 b, 80 b, 141 b, 142 a, 340 b, 370 b.
Known, make —, 113 a, 247 a.

Labour, *n.* 243 b, 381 a, b;

436 a, 465 a; *v.* 243 b, 446 a, 482 b.
Lace, *n.* 507 a.
Lack, *n.* 352 b; *v.* 214 b.
Lad, 422 a.
Ladder, 440 b.
Lade, 238 b.
Lady, 104 a, 579 a.
Lake, 259 a.
Lamb, 43 a, 237 a, 287 a, 309 a, 313 a, 508 a.
Lame, 497 a.
Lament, 4 a, 409 a, 442 b, 527 a.
Lamentation, 82 a, 259 a, 376 a, 390 b, 529 a.
Lamp, 331 b.
Lance, 210 b, 294 b.
Land, *n.* 8 b, 23 a, 55 a.
Language, 332 b, 578 a.
Languid, 124 a, 288 a.
Languor, 124 a, 535 a.
Lap, *n.* 95 a; *v.* 326 b.
Large, 547 b, 558 b.
Last, *adj.* 529 a.
Latter, 21 a; — state, 21 b.
Lattice, 223 b, 571 a.
Laugh, 512 b, 574 a.
Laughter, 512 b, 574 a.
Law, 145 b, 219 a, 451 a, 621 a, 627 a.
Lawful, 601 a.
Lawgiver, 219 b.
Lay, 428 b; — aside, 438 a; — hands on, 599 b; — hold of, 628 a; — on, 239 b; — up, 7 a, 51 a, 509 a, 519 a, 595 b; — wait, 509 b, 511 a; — waste, 509 b.
Layer, 392 a, 407 b, 596 a.
Lead, *n.* 45 a, 471 a; *v.* 144 a, 242 b, 258 b, 409 a, b, 413 b.
Leader, 33 b, 405 a, 425 a, 534 b.
Leaf, 459 b.
League, 93 a.
Lean, *adj.* 569 a; *v.* 441 a, 610 a.
Leanness, 558 b.
Leap, *v.* 112 a, 134 a, 138 a, 569 b.
Learn, 37 a, 329 b.
Learner, 624 a.
Learning, *n.* 345 a.
Leather, 454 b.
Leave, *v.* 280 b, 411 a, 417 b, 455 b, 582 a, 584 b.
Leaven, *n.* 571 a.
Leech, 459 b.
Leek, 218 a.
Lees, 607 b.

4 o

(650)

Left, *adj.* (not right) 576 a.
Leg, 311 a, 590 b, 613 a.
Lend, 324 a, 430 a, 447 a.
Length, 54 a.
Lengthen, 54 b, 395 a.
Lentiles, 451 b.
Leper, 520 a.
Leprosy, 520 b.
Lest, 495 a.
Let, — down, 614 a; — go, 567 a.
Letter, 313 b, 359 b, 431 b, 443 b, 506 a.
Level, *v.* 415 b, 440 b, 589 a.
Liar, 292 a.
Libation, 375 a, 421 a.
Liberal, 408 b, 590 a.
Liberality, 407 b, 408 b.
Liberty, 143 b, 216 b; set at —, 600 a.
Lick, 326 b, 332 b.
Lie, *n.* 72 b, 292 a; *v.* 292 a, b, 596 a.
Lie, — down, 550 a, 596 a, 597 b; — in wait, 51 b; — with, 549 b, 586 a, 596 a.
Life, 194 a, 195 a, 424 a, 431 a.
Lift up, 176 b, 412 a, 417 a, 428 b, 557 a.
Lifting up, *n.* 626 a.
Light, *n.* 14 b, 404 b, 409 a, 418 b, 428 a; *adj.* 529 b.
Lightness, 171 b.
Lightning, 56 a, 78 a, 96 a, 570 b.
Like, be — 140 b.
Liken, 140 b.
Likeness, 141 a, 625 a.
Lily, 181 a, 591 a.
Limb, 72 a.
Lime, 112 a.
Limit, *n.* 101 a, 533 b, 534 a; *v.* 102 b.
Line, 180 a, 187 a, 525 a.
Linen, 72 b, 76 b, 505 b, 616 b.
Lintel, 24 b, 398 a.
Lion, 54 a, 321 a, 329 a, 592 b; young —, 108 b, 307 a.
Lip, 578 a.
Listen, 542 b.
Little, 528 a; a —, 349 b, 378 a.
Littleness, 386 a.
Live, *v.* 194 b.
Livelihood, 424 a.
Lively, 193 b.
Liver, 284 b.
Living, *adj.* 193 b.
Lizard, 292 a, 508 a.

Lo, 159 a.
Load, *n.* 392 b, 416 b; *v.* 465 b.
Loaf, 295 b.
Loathe, 119 b, 319 b, 525 b, 527 a, 614 b, 626 b.
Loathing, 119 b.
Lock, *n.* 373 b; of hair, 513 b, 527 b.
Locust, 100 b, 107 a, 182 b, 213 b, 221 a, 440 b, 514 b.
Lodge, *v.* 325 b.
Lodging, 362 b.
Lofty, 100 b, 101 a, 557 a; be —, 98 b, 101 a, 556 b, 572 a.
Loftiness, 98 b, 99 a, 101 a.
Loins, 203 a, 225 b, 304 b, 399 b.
Long, *v.* 617 a.
Long-suffering, 54 a.
Look, *n.* 388 b, 457 b.
Look, *v.* 402 a, 517 b, 572 a, 586 a, 595 b, 609 b, 614 a.
Loop, *n.* 325 b, 540 b.
Loose, *adj.* 615 a; *v.* loosen, 506 b, 615 a.
Lord, 7 b, 87 a, 102 b, 388 b, the —, 249 a.
Lose, 2 b, 597 a.
Loss, 83 a, 413 a, 479 b.
Lot, 109 a, 203 b.
Loud, 557 a.
Love, *n.* 10 b, 131 a, 246 b, 449 a; *v.* 10 b, 179 b, 449 a, 559 b, 568 a.
Lovely, 10 b.
Low, *adj.* 612 a; be —, 612 a.
Lower, *v.* 592 a; *adj.* 622 b.
Lowly, 468 b.
Lowliness, 468 b.
Lucre, 88 a.
Luminary, 14 b, 334 b.
Lurk, 51 b.
Lust, *n.* 151 a.
Lute, 301 b.
Luxuriant, 444 a.
Luxurious, 451 a, 581 b.
Luxury, 627 b.
Lyre, 301 b.

Mace, (staff of authority,) 387 a.
Mad, 586 a.
Madness, 586 b.
Magician, 313 b.
Magistrate, 534 b.
Magnificence, 9 a, 105 b.
Magnificent, 9 a.
Magnify, 572 a.
Maid-servant, 39 a.
Maintain, 290 a.

Majestic, 8 a.
Majesty, 99 a, 100 b, 151 a, 169 b, 266 a, 285 b, 557 b.
Make, 91 b, 268 b, 446 b, 482 b, 497 b, 573 a.
Maker, 253 a.
Male, 170 b.
Man, 8 a, 26 a, 44 b, 103 b; young —, 422 a.
Manhood, 13 b.
Mankind, 97 a, 618 b.
Manna, 367 a.
Manner, 53 b, 143 b, 375 b, 377 a, 397 a, 620 b, 621 a.
Mantle, 71 b, 355 a, 378 b, 553 a.
Many, 547 b, 572 b.
Marble, 595 b, 616 b.
March, *n.* 375 b, 517 a.
Mare, 563 b.
Mark, *n.* 17 a, 619 b; butt, 355 a; *v.* 617 b, 619 b.
Market, 455 b.
Marriage, give in —, 359 a, 600 a.
Marry, 242 b.
Marrow, 350 a.
Marshal, *v.* 508 b.
Marvel, *v.* 624 b.
Mast, 630 a.
Master, 7 b, 87 a.
Mastich, 520 a.
Matter, 128 b.
Mature, *v.* 97 a.
Measure, *n.* 339 a, 393 a, 601 a, 623 a; *v.* 289 b, 339 a, 623 b.
Meat, 335 a.
Mediator, 326 a.
Medicine, 566 b.
Meditate, 140 b, 148 a, 227 b, 573 a, 575 a.
Meditation, 148 a.
Meek, 468 b, 591 b.
Meekness, 468 b.
Meet, *v.* 263 a, 489 a, b, 537 a, 539 a.
Meeting, *n.* 524 b, 540 a.
Melt, 176 b, 343 a, 375 b, 421 a, 432 a.
Melting, *n.* 162 b, 625 b.
Memorial, 17 a, 18 a, 137 b, 170 b, 171 b.
Memory, 138 a, 170 b, 604 a.
Mention, *v.* 171 a.
Merchandize, 374 b, 381 a, 387 a, 391 b, 455 b, 562 b.
Merchant, 562 b, 621 a.
Merciful, 559 a, 560 a.
Mercy, 560 a, 621 b.
Mercy-seat, 308 a.
Merriment, 577 a.

(651)

Message, 362 a, 575 a, 604 b.
Messenger, 362 a, 513 b.
Metropolis, 37 b.
Mid-day, 510 b.
Middle, *adj.* 620 a, 622 b; *n.* 320 a, 620 a.
Midst, 537 b, 620 a.
Midwife, 257 b.
Might, *n.* 26 b, 105 b, 195 b, 334 a, 455 a, b.
Mighty, 4 a, 24 a, 26 b, 49 a, 101 b, 190 b, 213 b, 286 a, 455 b, 488 a.
Milk, *n.* 198 a.
Mill, *n.* 236 a, 559 b.
Millstone, 493 b, 561 b.
Mind, *n.* 82 b, 340 b, 555 b.
Mineral, 4 b.
Miracle, 17 a, 382 b, 493 a, 624 b.
Mirage, 615 a.
Mire, 88 a, 236 b, 253 a.
Mirror, 389 a, 545 b.
Mischief, 565 a, 584 b.
Miserable, 4 a.
Misery, 3 a, 49 a, 228 a, 468 b.
Miss, a mark, 192 b; lose, 499 a.
Missile, 375 b, 599 b.
Missing, be —, 451 b.
Mist, 7 b.
Mistake, *n.* 394 a.
Mistress, 87 b, 104 a.
Mitre, 337 a.
Mix, 84 a, 374 b, 478 b.
Mixture, 348 b, 374 b.
Moan, *v.* 157 b.
Mock, 346 b, 530 b, 627 b.
Mockery, 627 b.
Model, *n.* 619 a.
Moist, 240 a, 326 a, 560 b.
Mole, 199 a, 626 b.
Molten-image, 375 a, 421 a.
Moment, 552 a.
Money, 305 a.
Month, 184 b, 273 a.
Monument, 171 b.
Moon, 273 a, 321 a; new —, 303 b.
Moor, heath, 381 a.
Moreover, 116 b.
Morning, 89 b; in the —, 597 b.
Morrow, 353 a.
Mortal, 44 b.
Mortar (for pounding), 340 a, 359 b.
Moth, 442 a, 484 b.
Mother, 37 b; —in-law, 206 a, 231 a.
Mound, 385 a, 407 a, 440 b, 513 a, 623 b.

Mount, *n.* 244 a.
Mountain, 160 a, 236 a.
Mourn, 4 a, 81 b, 258 b, 414 b.
Mournfully, 524 a.
Mourning, *n.* 4 a, 82 a.
Mouse, 458 a.
Mouth, 490 a.
Move, himself, 347 b.
Much, 547 b, 572 b.
Mud, 88 a, 236 b, 567 b.
Mule, 500 b.
Multiply, 548 b.
Multitude, 157 b, 352 b, 439 a, 473 b, 508 a, 524 b, 548 a, 612 b.
Murder, *n.* 568 b; *v.* 568 b.
Murderer, 568 b.
Murmur, *n.* 147 b, 624 a; *v.* 14 a, 147 b, 325 b, 552 a.
Music, 173 b, 405 b, 595 a.
Musician, 405 b, 595 a.
Muzzle, *v.* 214 a.
Myrrh, 388 b.
Myrtle, 148 b.

Nail, *n.* 375 b, 393 b, 519 b; — of the hand, 519 b.
Naked, 458 a, 479 a, b.
Nakedness, 378 a, 403 b, 458 a, 479 a, 480 a.
Name, *v.* 301 b, 426 a, 536 a, 573 a; *n.* 603 b.
Nard, 428 a.
Narrative, 7 a.
Narrow, 519 b.
Nation, 107 b, 319 b.
Nativity, 344 a.
Navel, 615 a, b.
Near, *prep.* 51 a, 344 a, 466 b; *adj.* 539 b.
Necessity, 228 a, 520 a.
Neck, 120 b, 481 b, 510 b, 512 a.
Necromancer, 22 a.
Need, *n.* 89 a, 352 b, 520 a.
Needy, 4 a.
Neglect, *v.* 417 b, 430 a, 451 b, 455 b, 596 b.
Negligence, 599 a.
Negligent, 599 a.
Neighbour, 564 b, 598 a.
Neigh, 510 b.
Neighing, *n.* 384 b.
Nerve, 111 a.
Nest, 531 a.
Net, 224 a, 358 b, 385 a, 571 a.
Nettle, *n.* 530 b, 531 a.
Net-work, 571 a.
Nevertheless, 13 b.
New, 186 a.
News, 606 a.

Night, 328 b.
Night-watch, 59 b.
Nine, 630 b.
Nitre, 433 b.
No, 318 a.
Noble, *adj.* 285 a; *n.* 220 a, 372 a, 504 b.
Noble-minded, 408 b.
Noble-mindedness, 408 b.
Noise, *n.* 566 a, 581 a.
Noon, 510 b.
Noose, *n.* 515 b.
North, 518 a, 576 a.
Nose, 47 b; — jewel, 413 a.
Nostrils, 47 b, 414 a.
Not, 25 a, 28 b, 82 b, 318 a; — yet, 240 a.
Nothing, 619 a.
Notice, *v.* 402 b, 607 a.
Nourish, 564 b.
Nourishing, 605 b.
Now, 486 b.
Nudity, 381 a, 480 a.
Number, *n.* 373 a, 376 a, 444 a; *v.* 370 b, 443 b, 499 a.
Numerous, 284 b; be —, 615 b.
Nurse, *n.* 261 b, 357 a, 373 b.
Nut, 6 a, 80 a.

Oak, 33 a.
Oar, 394 b, 594 b.
Oath, 30 a, 582 b.
Obdurate, 542 b.
Obey, 606 a.
Obeisance, do —, 591 b.
Object, *n.* (mark), 355 a, 575 b.
Obligation, 47 a, 376 b, 449 a.
Obscure, *adj.* 48 b.
Observance, 219 a, 396 b, 607 b.
Observe, 90 a, 177 a, 415 b, 426 a, 517 b, 544 a, 607 a.
Observation, 90 a.
Obstinacy, 543 b.
Obtain, 191 b, 324 a, 383 a, 428 b, 429 b, 625 a.
Occupation, 381 b.
Occurrence, 489 b.
Ocean, 619 a.
Odour, 561 a; be in bad —, 71 a.
Offence, 359 b.
Offend, 192 b.
Offensive, 564 a.
Offer, *v.* present an offering, 407 a, 412 a, 459 a, 538 b, 557 a.
Offering, *n.* 372 a, 374 b, 539 a, 594 a, 603 a, 626 a,

(652)

629 b; burnt —, 459 b; free-will —, 407 b; peace —, 603 a; sin —, 58 b.
Office, 499 b.
Officer, 500 a, 594 a.
Offspring, 258 a, 389 a, 502 a, 508 a, 586 b.
Oil, 267 b, 394 b, 605 b; — vat, 268 b.
Ointment, 392 a, 569 b, 605 b.
Old, 83 a, 176 a, 277 b; grow —, 83 a, 176 a; — age, 176 a, 575 b.
Olive, 170 a.
Olive-tree, 170 a.
Omit, 451 b.
On, 458 b.
Once, 498 a.
One, 19 b.
Only, *adj.* 19 b, 254 a; *adv.* 27 a, 569 a.
Onion, 88 a.
Onward, 154 b.
Onyx, 592 b.
Open, *v.* 113 a, 498 a, b, 499 b, 506 b.
Opening, *n.* 383 a, 610 b, 630 a.
Opinion, 141 b, 142 a.
Opponent, 574 b, 628 b.
Oppose, 561 a, 574 b.
Opposite, 344 a.
Opposition, 509 b, 574 b.
Oppress, 137 a, 236 b, 261 a, 327 b, 485 a, 566 a, 569 a.
Oppression, 327 b, 382 a, 390 a, 484 b, 485 a, 502 a.
Oppressive, 284 b, 295 a, 484 b.
Oppressor, 383 a, 563 b.
Or, 11 b.
Oracle, part of the temple, 125 a.
Order, *n.* 235 b, 381 b; *v.* 511 a; in order that, 330 a.
Origin, 387 a, 523 b, 615 b.
Orion, 304 b.
Ornament, *n.* 200 a, 451 a, 488 b, 509 a, 627 b.
Orphan, 279 b.
Osier, 477 b.
Ostrich, 264 a, 563 b, 621 b.
Other, 21 a.
Otherwise, 13 b, 31 a.
Outer, 196 a.
Outgoing, 346 a.
Outside, 188 b.
Outstretched, 416 b.
Outwards, 189 a.
Oven, 626 a.
Over, 379 a, 458 b.
Over-against, 344 a.
Overcome, 423 b.

Overflow, 168 a, 406 b, 490 b, 503 a, 566 a, 574 a, 590 b, 594 a.
Overflowing, *n.* 612 b, 613 a.
Overlay, 214 b, 512 a, 518 a, 569 a.
Overplus, 451 b.
Overpower, 566 a.
Oversee, 425 a.
Overseer, 425 a, 500 a.
Overtake, 429 b.
Overthrow, *n.* 342 a; *v.* 441 a.
Own, *v.* 532 a.
Ox, 90 a, 591 a, 621 a.

Pace, *n.* 551 a.
Pacify, 199 a.
Pain, *n.* 196 a, 200 a, 284 a, 357 a, 472 a, b; *v.* 243 b, 284 a; suffer —, 187 b.
Painful, 564 a.
Paint, *v.* 235 a.
Palace, 55 a, 81 a, 153 b, 161 b, 236 b.
Palate, 196 b.
Palm, of the hand, 306 a, 610 a; — tree, 625 b.
Pang, 180 b, 394 a, 513 b.
Pant, 581 b.
Panther, 420 b.
Parable, 396 a; utter —, 396 a.
Parapet, 381 a, 495 b.
Parched, *adj.* 457 b, 513 a; be —, 431 b.
Pardon, *v.* 428 b, 440 a.
Park, 500 b.
Parrot, 623 a.
Part, *n.* 72 a, 203 b, 217 b, 370 b, 373 b.
Partiality, 453 a.
Particle, 521 b.
Partridge, 537 b.
Party, 450 b.
Pass, *v.* 447 b, 450 b; — by, 202 b; — over, 447 b; *n.* 448 a.
Passage, *n.* 376 b, 448 a.
Passover, 497 a.
Pasture, *n.* 391 b, 565 a.
Pasturing, *n.* 391 b.
Patch, 237 a.
Path, 53 b, 375 a, 377 a, 432 a, 583 b.
Pattern, 619 a.
Pavement, 569 a.
Paw, *n.* 244 a.
Pay, *v.* 614 a.
Peace, 599 a, 603 a; be at —, 602 b.
Peacock, 623 a.
Pearl, 496 a.
Pedestal, 7 b.

Pedigree, 620 a.
Peel, 498 b.
Pelican, 521 a.
Pelt, 444 a.
Pen, 456 b; — knife, 627 b.
People, 333 b, 462 b.
Perceive, 80 b, 247 b, 402 a, 544 b, 591 a.
Perfect, *adj.* 602 a, 624 b, 625 a; be —, 625 a.
Perfection, 358 a, 425 a, 623 a.
Perfidious, 72 a.
Perfidy, 71 b, 72 a.
Perform, 446 b, 483 a, 497 b, 602 b.
Perfume, *n.* 96 b, 387 a, 392 a, 441 a, 569 b; *v.* 528 a, 569 b.
Perfumer, 569 b.
Perfuming, 569 b.
Perhaps, 13 b.
Perish, 2 b, 83 a, 348 a, 358 a, 423 a, 437 b, 442 b.
Perjure, 628 b.
Permission, 570 a.
Permit, 411 a, 601 a.
Perpetual, 625 a.
Perpetuity, 425 a, 625 a.
Perplex, 76 a, 585 a.
Perplexity, 336 a.
Persecute, 553 b.
Persevere, 324 a, 464 a.
Persist, 464 a.
Person, 424 a, 495 b.
Persuade, 506 a.
Perverse, 476 b, 507 b.
Perversion, 159 b, 619 a.
Perversely, act —, 379 b, 444 b, 452 b.
Perverseness, 326 a, 379 a, 440 b, 476 b, 509 b, 619 a.
Pervert, 416 b, 441 a, 452 b, 454 b.
Pestilence, 126 a, 338 a.
Pestle, 459 b.
Petition, 56 a, 87 a, 90 b.
Physician, 566 b.
Picture, *n.* 514 b.
Piece, *n.* 148 b, 431 b, 493 b, 505 b.
Pierce, 142 b, 201 a, 426 a, 427 b, 428 a, 568 b.
Piety, 213 a.
Pigeon, 253 a; young —, 107 b.
Pillar, 384 b, 385 a, 425 b, 465 a.
Pillow, *n.* 376 a.
Pin, *n.* 279 b.
Pine, *n.* 24 b, 31 a.
Pipe, *n.* 200 a; *v.* 201 b, 615 b.

(653)

Piping, n. 615 a.
Pit, 70 b, 100 b, 108 a, 492 a, 589 b, 592 a, b, 593 a.
Pitch, n. 175 b, 208 b, 307 b; v. — a tent, 11 a, 209 b, 308 a, 417 a, 629 a.
Pitcher, 287 b.
Pity, n. 413 b, 560 a; v. 188 b, 414 b, 559 b.
Pitiful, 559 a.
Place, n. 67 a, 301 b, 357 b, 386 b, 413 b; v. 411 a, 424 b, 432 a, 459 a, 499 a, 526 b, 562 a, 573 a, 595 b, 596 a, 597 b, 613 a.
Plague, n. 338 a.
Plain, n. 338 b, 357 a, 381 a, b.
Plaister, n. 112 a, 575 a; v. 235 a, 237 a, 575 a.
Plan, n. 399 a.
Plane-tree, 481 a.
Planets, 349 a.
Plank, 100 b, 541 b.
Plant, n. 354 b, 417 a, 515 b, 575 a, 617 a; v. 417 a, 617 b.
Plantation, 58 b, 417 a.
Plate, of metal, 491 b, 570 a.
Play, v. 574 a, 610 b.
Plead, 134 a, 255 b.
Pleasant, 398 b, 421 b; be —, 422 a.
Pleasantness, 422 a, 612 b.
Please, 612 b.
Pleasing, adj. 611 b.
Pleasure, 451 a, b, 467 a, 568 b, 577 a, 627 b.
Pledge, n. 180 b, 447 a, 478 b; v. 447 a, 478 a.
Pleiades, 295 a.
Plenty, 152 a, 558 b.
Plot, v. 261 b.
Plough, v. 226 b.
Ploughman, 28 b, 243 a.
Ploughshare, 65 b.
Pluck, v. 240 b; — off, 528 a; — out, 391 a; — up, 434 a.
Plumage, 513 a.
Plummet, 4 b.
Plump, 605 b.
Plunder, v. 425 b, 586 b, 602 a, 609 b.
Plundering, n. 586 b.
Plunge, v. 233 a.
Poison, n. 546 b.
Pole, 343 b.
Polish, v. 391 a, 392 a.
Polished, adj. 530 a.
Pollute, 99 b, 237 b, 593 b, 614 b.

Polluted, adj. 133 a, 237 a; be —, 237 b.
Pollution, 99 a.
Pomegranate, 563 a.
Pond, 6 b.
Ponder, 494 b, 623 a.
Pool, 6 b, 96 a.
Poor, 4 a, 138 a, 375 a, 468 b, 481 b, 561 b; be —, 275 a, 343 b, 558 a.
Poplar, 321 b.
Porch, 344 b, 374 a.
Porter, carrier, 436 a; doorkeeper, 610 b, 630 b.
Portion, n. 72 a, 98 b, 203 b, 217 b, 370 b, 373 b, 394 b, 414 a, b, 597 a.
Possess, 274 b, 414 a.
Possession, 20 b, 275 a, 347 a, 387 b, 414 a, 532 a; kept —, 628 a.
Possessor, 87 a.
Posterity, 620 a.
Pot, 131 b, 391 a, 439 a, 501 b.
Potentate, 102 b.
Potsherd, 226 a.
Potter, 492 a.
Poverty, 138 b, 375 a, 468 b, 561 b.
Pour, 176 b, 268 a, 406 b, 421 a, 432 a, 442 b, 479 a, 490 b, 561 a, 611 b.
Powder, n. 5 b.
Power, 13 b, 41 b, 101 b, 177 a, 214 a, 244 a, 292 a, 334 a, 455 a, 473 b, 601 a, 629 a.
Powerful, 8 a, 14 a, 24 a, 39 b, 121 b, 213 b, 256 a, 286 a, 473 a, 480 a, 629 a; be —, 41 b.
Practice, 497 b.
Practise, 497 b.
Praise, n. 154 b, 173 b, 455 a, 619 a, b; v. 156 b, 246 a, 582 b.
Pray, 86 b, 488 b, 494 b, 513 b, 581 a.
Prayer, 87 a, 393 b, 575 a, 621 b, 628 a.
Preach, 536 b.
Preacher, 525 a.
Precede, 523 a.
Precept, 128 b, 385 a, 450 b, 499 b, 510 b.
Precious, 234 b, 269 a, b.
Preciousness, 269 b.
Precocious, 82 a.
Preference, 392 b.
Pregnant, 161 a.
Prepare, 255 b, 290 b, 486 b, 524 a, 569 b.

Prepared, adj. 487 a.
Presence, 495 b.
Present, n. 95 b, 408 a, 591 b, 594 a, 599 a, 630 b; v. 538 b.
Preserve, 426 a, 607 a.
Preside, 425 a, 464 a.
President, 425 a.
Press, v. urge, 14 b, 37 a, 218 a, 499 a; squeeze, 379 a, 454 a, 574 a.
Pressure, 386 a.
Presume, 168 a.
Pretext, 459 b.
Prevail, 103 b, 456 a, 579 a.
Prevent, 296 b.
Previously, 603 b.
Prey, n. 240 a, 365 b, 384 b, 385 a, 396 b, 512 b.
Price, 342 a, 351 b, 358 b.
Pride, 98 b, 100 b, 101 a, 167 a, 492 a, 581 b.
Priest, 288 b; act as —, 289 a.
Priesthood, 289 a.
Primogeniture, 82 a.
Prince, 405 a, 408 b, 421 a, 429 b, 495 b, 534 b, 546 a, 558 b, 578 b.
Princess, 579 a.
Principal, 547 a.
Prison, 77 a, 296 b, 355 a, 374 a, 396 b, 436 b.
Prisoner, 46 a.
Privately, 601 a.
Privilege, 219 a.
Proceed, 155 a, 258 a.
Proceeding, n. 155 a, 386 a.
Procession, 619 a.
Proclamation, 540 a.
Proclaim, 175 b, 310 a, 536 b, 537 b, 606 b.
Produce, n. 8 b, 76 a, 121 a, 242 a, 418 a, 447 a, 502 b, 508 a, 599 b, 618 b, 626 a; v. 410 a, 432 a, 482 b, 515 b, 532 a.
Profane, adj. 201 a; v. 201 a; be —, 201 a.
Profit, n. 88 a, 253 b, 313 b, 618 b; v. 264 a.
Profound, 465 a.
Progeny, 178 a, 586 b.
Progress, 517 a.
Prohibit, 410 a.
Project, n. 353 b; v. 261 b.
Prolong, 54 b, 395 a.
Promise, v. 42 a.
Prong, 608 a.
Proof, 450 a, b.
Prop, n. 375 b.
Proper, be —, 589 a.
Property, 562 a.

(654)

Prophecy, 392 b, 393 a, 401 b.
Prophesy, 401 b.
Prophet, 402 b, 518 a, 545 a.
Prophetess, 402 b.
Propitiation, 307 b.
Proprietor, 7 b.
Prosper, 491 a, 514 a, 575 b.
Prosperity, 15 b, 234 b, 313 b, 428 a, 599 a, 603 a, 605 b.
Prosperous, 234 b, 421 b, 565 b, 599 a; be —, 439 a, 442 a, 598 b, 606 a.
Prostitute, 524 b.
Prostrate, v. 423 b, 591 b.
Protect, 119 a, 215 a, 439 b.
Protection, 513 b.
Protest, 452 a.
Protract, 395 b.
Proud, 100 b, 101 a, 166 b, 402 a, 492 a.
Provender, 376 a.
Proverb, 396 a.
Provide, 544 b, 621 a.
Providence, 499 b.
Province, 340 a.
Provision, 13 b, 240 b, 242 a, 326 b; provisions, 512 b, 513 a, 584 b.
Provoke, 531 a, 551 a.
Prowess, 102 a.
Prudence, 80 b, 437 a, 481 a, 618 b.
Prudent, 479 b.
Prudently, act —, 481 a.
Prune, 89 a, 173 a.
Pruning instrument, 349 b.
Psalm, 349 b, 619 a.
Publish, 71 a, 536 b.
Puff at, 490 b.
Pull off, 430 b.
Punish, 256 a, 427 a, 467 b, 494 b, 499 a, 611 a.
Punishment, 136 b, 397 a, 420 a, 427 b, 453 b, 499 b, 620 a.
Pupil, of the eye, 26 a, 71 b.
Purchase, n. 387 b; v. 309 b, 532 a.
Pure, 14 a, 90 b, 170 b, 233 b, 384 b, 520 b; be —, 170 b, 233 b, 426 b.
Purge, 433 b.
Purification, 233 b, 390 b, 625 b.
Purify, 170 b, 234 a, 520 b, 524 a.
Purity, 90 b, 170 b.
Purple, 52 b.
Purpose, n. 380 b, 565 b; v. 621 a.
Purse, 295 b.
Pursue, 511 a, 553 a.
Push, with horns, 405 a.

Put, 432 b, 573 a; — away, 347 b; — forth, 599 b; — on, 322 a, 599 b; — out, 142 a.
Putrify, 563 a.

Quadruped, 74 b.
Quail, n. 576 a.
Quantity, 399 a.
Quarrel, n. 560 b; v. 425 a, 561 a.
Queen, 102 b, 586 a.
Quench, 585 a.
Question, v. 581 a.
Quick, 341 b, 342 a.
Quickly, 9 b.
Quiet, adj. 133 b, 581 b, 613 b; be —, 598 b, 613 b; v. 582 b, 596 b; n. 371 a, 389 b, 555 b, 599 b.
Quietly, 601 a.
Quietness, 133 b, 141 a, 416 a.
Quit, v. 411 a.
Quiver, n. 59 b.
Quill, 5 b.

Race, a running, 390 a; people, 134 b.
Raft, 567 b.
Rage, n. 175 a, 565 b; v. 157 b, 578 a.
Raiment, 362 a.
Rain, n. 355 a; v. 355 a, 413 a; former —, 347 a; latter —, 365 b.
Rainbow, 544 b.
Raise, 101 a, 428 b, 454 a, 464 b, 526 b, 572 a.
Be raised, 556 a.
Ram, 24 b.
Range, n. 235 b.
Rank, n. 572 b.
Ransom, n. 490 a.
Rapine, 72 a, 110 a, 231 b.
Rare, 19 b, 269 b.
Rashness, 336 b.
Ratify, 104 a.
Rattling, n. 566 a.
Raven, 477 b.
Raw, 194 a, 400 b.
Razor, 347 a, 627 b.
Reach, 405 b, 429 a, 489 a, 625 a.
Read, v. 536 b.
Readily, 342 a.
Reading, n. 388 a.
Ready, 341 b, 342 a, 487 a; make —, 561 a.
Really, 300 b.
Reap, 535 b.
Rear, n. 475 a.
Rebel, v. 379 b, 389 b, 505 a.

Rebellion, 389 b, 391 a, 444 a, 505 a.
Rebellious, 389 b, 391 a, 589 a.
Rebuke, n. 119 b, 338 a; v. 119 b.
Recall, 588 b.
Receive, 332 b.
Recent, 186 a.
Recite, 467 a.
Reckon, 227 b, 443 b, 623 b.
Recline, 610 a.
Recognise, 247 a, 420 a.
Recompense, n. 603 a, 625 a; v. 118 a.
Record, n. 137 b, 138 a, 170 b, 171 b, 313 b, 443 b; v. 171 a.
Recount, v. 443 b.
Rectitude, 278 b.
Red, 8 b.
Redeem, 99 b, 489 b.
Redeemer, 99 b.
Redemption, 100 a, 489 b; — price, 307 b, 490 a.
Red-haired, 9 a.
Reduce, 139 a, 287 a.
Reed, 3 a, 6 b, 117 a, 531 b.
Refine, 520 b.
Refined, 14 a.
Refiner, 520 b.
Reflect, 575 b.
Refresh, 15 b, 442 a, 567 a, 588 a, 613 b.
Refreshment, 613 b.
Refuge, 352 b, 371 b, 376 b, 377 b, 387 a, 393 a, 455 a; take —, 452 b.
Refuse, v. 335 b, 588 b.
Regard, v. 246 b, 420 a, 542 b, 573 a, 595 b, 607 a, 609 b.
Region, 8 b, 115 a, 340 a.
Register, n. 313 b, 443 b; v. 314 a.
Reign, v. 474 a.
Reins, of the body, 298 b.
Reject, 87 a, 174 b, 176 b, 335 b, 401 a, b, 420 a, 452 a.
Rejection, 599 b.
Rejoice, 112 a, 183 b, 459 b, 462 a, b, 563 b, 574 b, 576 b.
Rejoicing, adj. 111 b, 459 b, 460 a; n. 393 a, 564 a, 577 a, 580 b.
Relation, 19 a, 99 b, 231 a.
Relationship, 100 a.
Relatives, 344 a.
Relax, 374 a.
Release, n. 604 b; v. 604 b.
Rely, 610 a.

(655)

Remain, 276 a, 280 a, 325 b, 464 a, 582 a.
Remainder, 280 a, 582 a.
Remedy, n. 391 b, 566 b.
Remember, 171 a, 607 a.
Remembrance, 604 a.
Remnant, 579 b, 582 a.
Remove, v. 347 b, 421 b, 433 b, 438 a, 447 b, 488 a, 557 a, 560 b, 573 b, 608 b.
Rend, 541 a.
Render, 432 a, 573 a, 595 b.
Renew, 186 a, 202 b.
Renown, 604 a.
Renunciation, 599 a.
Repair, v. 73 b, 445 a, 566 b.
Repairing, n. 53 a.
Repay, 118 a, 602 b.
Repeat, 262 b, 460 b, 588 a, 608 a.
Repent, 414 b, 587 b.
Report, n. 604 b, 606 a.
Reproach, n. 225 a, 401 a; v. 105 a, 225 a.
Reproof, 119 b, 620 a.
Reprove, 119 b, 452 a.
Reptile, 563 b.
Reputation, 603 b.
Request, n. 56 a, 581 b; v. 86 b, 90 b, 581 a.
Require, 581 a, 595 b.
Requite, 602 b.
Rescue, v. 425 b, 498 b, 503 b, 591 b.
Resemblance, 514 b, 619 a, 625 a.
Resemble, 140 b, 396 a, 589 a.
Reside, 108 b, 166 b, 276 a, 279 b.
Residence, 166 a, 337 b, 347 b, 377 b. 386 b.
Residue, 280 a.
Resolution, 508 b.
Resound, 565 b, 595 a.
Rest, n. 141 a, 371 a, 416 a, 585 b, 613 b; v. 410 b, 424 b, 552 b, 585 b, 597 b, 613 b.
Resting-place, 371 a, 389 b, 410 b.
Restitution, 625 a; make —, 602 b.
Restlessness, 408 a.
Restore, 186 a, 588 a, 602 b, 603 a.
Restrain, 182 a, 183 a, 227 a, 296 b, 474 a, 582 b.
Restraint, 381 a, 385 a, 386 a, 449 a, 474 a.
Result, n. 388 a, 437 b, 465 a, 502 a, 620 b.
Retain, 191 b, 607 a.
Retire, 573 b.

Retribution, 118 a, 603 a, 619 a.
Return, n. 589 a; v. 435 a, 587 b, 619 b.
Returning, n. 594 b, 630 b.
Reveal, 113 a.
Revelation, 190 a, b, 545 b.
Revenge, v. 427 a; n. 427 b.
Revenue, 618 b.
Reverence, v. 524 a, 577 b, 607 a; n. 346 b.
Revile, 530 a.
Reviling, n. 530 b.
Revoke, 588 b.
Revolution, 374 a.
Reward, n. 6 b, 351 b, 393 b, 502 a, 576 a; v. 118 a, 602 b.
Rib, 462 a, 514 b.
Rich, 284 b, 484 b, 605 b.
Riches, 485 b, 488 b.
Richness, 605 b.
Riddle, 194 b; propose —, 186 b.
Ride, 562 a.
Rider, 561 b, 562 a.
Ridge, 608 a.
Ridicule, n. 330 b, 512 b; v. 330 b, 331 a.
Riding, n. 562 a.
Right, n. 397 a; adj. 278 b; not left, 26 a.
Righteous, 278 b, 509 b.
Righteousness, 357 a, 509 b, 510 a.
Ring, n. 115 a, 233 a, 449 a; v. 563 b.
Ripen, 97 a, 118 a, 210 a.
Rise, 526 a.
Rising, n. 529 a.
River, 242 a, 409 b, 414 a.
Road, 53 b, 143 b, 375 a.
Roar, v. 157 b, 409 b, 422 a, 565 b, 580 b.
Roaring, n. 409 b, 550 b, 580 b.
Roast, 513 b, 529 b.
Rob, 193 b.
Robe, 10 a, 378 b, 623 b.
Robust, 605 b.
Rock, n. 306 b, 440 b, 512 a, 519 b.
Rod, 193 b, 354 a, 583 a.
Roll, v. 115 b.
Roof, n. 104 a, 527 b; v. 237 a.
Room, space, 386 b; chamber, 617 a.
Root, n. 615 b; take —, 616 a.
Root up, 476 a, 616 a.
Rope, 180 a, 354 a, 449 a.
Rottenness, 386 b, 569 a.

Round, adj. 449 b.
Rouse, 454 a.
Rout, v. 158 a, 408 b.
Row, n. 572 b, 574 a; v. 589 b.
Royalty, 362 b.
Rub bare, 391 a.
Ruby, 8 b, 287 b.
Ruddy, 8 b.
Ruin, v. 84 a, 89 a, 159 b, 231 b, 261 a, 297 b, 433 a, 481 b, 593 b, 605 a; n. 151 a, 161 b, 294 b, 313 b, 354 a, 382 b, 457 a, 581 a, 584 b, 585 a, 586 b.
Rule, n. 362 b, 365 a, 366 b, 396 a; v. 396 a, 474 a, 553 a, 573 b, 580 b, 600 b, 611 a.
Ruler, 366 b, 534 b, 578 b, 601 a, 611 b.
Rumbling, n. 566 a.
Run, 558 a; — over, 86 b; — through, 142 b; — to and fro, 614 b.
Running, n. 390 a.
Running to and fro, 398 a.
Rut, of a wheel, 377 a.

Sabbath, 585 b.
Sack, 43 b, 578 b.
Sackcloth, 578 b.
Sacred, 522 b.
Sacrifice, n. 166 a; v. 166 b.
Sad, 564 a.
Sadness, 306 a, 564 a.
Safe, 602 a.
Safety, 277 a, 278 a, 382 b, 387 a, 590 a, 599 a, 630 b.
Sail, n. 383 a, 420 b.
Sailor, 180 b, 363 b.
Sale, 366 b.
Salt, n. 363 a; adj. 363 b.
Salt, v. 363 a.
Saltpit, 359 a.
Salute, v. 599 a.
Salvation, 277 a, 278 a, 630 b.
Sanctify, 524 a.
Sanctuary, 386 b, 524 a.
Sand, 188 a.
Sandal, 422 a.
Sapphire, 443 a.
Satan, 574 b.
Satiate, 555 a.
Satisfied, 571 b.
Satisfy, 555 a, 568 a, 571 b.
Save, 278 a, 364 a.
Saviour, 278 a.
Saw, n. 338 a, 393 a; v. 122 b.
Saw, v. 122 b.
Say, 42 a.

(656)

Saying, *n.* 42 a, 128 b, 362 a.
Scab, 376 a.
Scabbard, 627 b.
Scale, *n.* of a fish, 542 a.
Scar, 180 a.
Scarce, 269 b.
Scarlet, 609 a, 620 a.
Scatter, 78 a, 178 b, 395 b, 406 b, 408 b, 417 b, 421 a, 490 b, 491 b, 504 a.
Scattering, 627 b.
Scent, *v.* 556 b.
Sceptre, 354 a, 583 a.
Science, 141 b, 142 a.
Scoffer, 331 a.
Scorn, *n.* 530 b, 565 b; *v.* 325 b, 331 a, 530 b.
Scorpion, 476 a.
Scourge, *n.* 589 b, 594 a.
Scrape, 120 b.
Scratch, 120 b.
Scrawl, 619 b.
Scribe, 443 b.
Scripture, 313 b.
Scrutinize, 426 a.
Sea, 259 a.
Sea-monster, 324 b.
Sea-shore, 188 b.
Sea-weed, 437 b.
Seal, *n.* 189 b, 231 a, 233 a, 456 a.
Seal, *v.* 230 b.
Search, *v.* 215 b, 216 a, 219 b; *n.* 216 a.
Season, *n.* 173 a, 486 b.
Seat, *n.* 347 b, 374 a, 562 a.
Second, 609 a.
Secret, *n.* 437 a, 558 b; 493 a.
Secretary, 443 b.
Secure, *adj.* 581 b; be —, 602 b.
Security, 387 a, 621 a.
Seduce, 506 a.
See, 190 a, 544 a.
Seed, 177 a, b.
Seed-time, 178 a.
Seek, 90 a, 144 b.
Seer, 545 a.
Seize, 20 b, 395 a, 601 a, 628 a.
Select, *v.* 96 a.
Self, 424 a, 473 b.
Sell, 359 a, 432 a.
Send, 599 b; — away, 600 a; — forth, 271 b, 600 a.
Sentence, *n.* 506 a.
Separate, *v.* 72 b, 96 a, 169 b, 500 b; *adj.* 72 b.
Separation, 609 b.
Sepulchres, 77 a, 522 a.
Series, 235 b.
Serpent, 415 a, 626 b.

Servant, 422 a, 446 b; maid —, 611 a.
Serve, 446 a, 494 a, 608 a.
Service, 446 b, 447 b, 508 b.
Servitude, 446 b, 459 a.
Set, 573 a, 595 b; — in order, 629 a; — up, 267 a, 424 b, 459 a, 526 b, 557 a, 573 a.
Set time, 345 a.
Settlement, 414 a.
Seven, 584 a.
Severity, 628 a.
Sew, *v.* 628 a.
Shade, 513 b.
Shadow, *n.* 513 b, 514 a, b.
Shake, 119 b, 412 a, 482 a, 550 b, 566 b.
Shaking, *n.* of the head, 371 a; trembling, 566 a.
Shame, *n.* 77 a, 97 b, 299 a, 403 b, 479 b; *v.* 215 b, 243 a, 299 b.
Share, *n.* 414 a.
Sharp, 183 a, 222 b, 609 a; be —, 225 b.
Sharpen, 183 b, 328 a, 609 a.
Shatter, 490 b.
Shave, 114 a, 540 a.
Sheaf, 36 b, 465 a, 466 b.
Shear, 109 b, 533 b.
Sheath, 408 b.
Shed, — blood, 611 b; — tears, 139 a.
Sheep, 508 a, 516 a, 559 b, 572 b.
Shekel, 613 b.
Shelter, *n.* 513 b.
Shepherd, 565 a.
Shew, *v.* 186 b, 255 b, 545 a.
Shield, *n.* 338 a, 516 a; *v.* 215 a.
Shine, 15 b, 156 b, 405 a, 540 b.
Ship, *n.* 45 a, 443 a, 512 b.
Shirt, 315 a.
Shoe, *n.* 422 a.
Shoe-latchet, 579 a.
Shoot, *n.* 72 a, 193 b, 271 b, 387 a, 417 a, 501 b, 515 b, 579 b, 599 b, 617 a; *v.* 548 a, 562 b, 600 a; — up, 515 b.
Shore, 188 b, 578 a.
Short, 535 a.
Shorten, 535 b.
Shortly, 539 b.
Shoulder, 177 a, 315 a, 597 a.
Shout, *n.* 152 b, 175 b, 563 b, 629 b; *v.* 467 a, 510 b, 511 a, 520 a, 536 a, 557 b, 563 b.

Shouting, *n.* 564 a, 581 a, 629 b.
Shower, *n.* 123 a, 549 a.
Shrine, of an idol, 63 a, 439 a.
Shrivel, *v.* 403 a.
Shudder, 577 b.
Shuddering, *n.* 577 b.
Shut, 23 b, 436 b, 440 a; — up, 426 a, 474 a, 580 b.
Sick, 133 a; be —, 199 a.
Sickle, 224 a, 337 b.
Sickness, 133 a, 200 a, 351 b.
Side, 273 b, 448 a, 509 a, 514 b.
Sjege, 385 a.
Sieve, 286 b.
Sigh, *n.* 44 b.
Sighing, *n.* 44 b.
Sight, 388 b, 457 b.
Sign, *n.* 345 b.
Signal, 393 a.
Signification, 575 b.
Silence, 34 a, 133 b, 141 a.
Silent, 34 b, 133 b, 613 b; be —, 140 b, 141 a, 228 a, 440 a, 516 a, 617 b.
Silly, 506 a.
Silver, 305 a.
Similitude, 141 a.
Sin, *n.* 13 b, 83 b, 192 a, b, 453 b; *v.* 192 b.
Sincere, 624 b.
Sincerity, 624 b.
Sinew, 111 a, 471 b.
Sing, 173 a, 563 b, 595 a.
Singer, 173 b, 595 a.
Singing, 563 b, 564 b, 595 a.
Singly, 254 a.
Singular, 19 b.
Sink, *v.* 589 b, 614 a; — down, 233 a, 413 a.
Sinner, 14 a.
Sister, 20 a; sister-in-law, 242 b.
Sit, 276 a, 279 b.
Six, 616 b.
Skill, 575 b, 576 a, 618 b.
Skilful, 341 b; be —, 575 b.
Skin, *n.* 112 b, 403 a, 454 b; for liquids, 12 a, 400 b, 403 a, 456 b; *v.* 505 a.
Skip, 138 a.
Skirmish, 574 b.
Skirt, *n.* 302 b, 590 a.
Skull, 112 b.
Sky, 569 b, 592 b, 604 b.
Slain, 201 a.
Slander, *v.* 333 b.
Slaughter, *n.* 160 b, 166 a, 232 b, 354 a, 357 b, 527 b, 568 b; *v.* 166 b, 568 b, 592 a.
Slaughtering, *n.* 592 a.

(657)

Slave, 446 b, 447 a.
Slavery, 447 a.
Slay, 161 a, 232 b, 528 a, 592 a.
Sleep, n. 608 a, b, 626 a; v. 277 b, 411 b, 596 a.
Sleepiness, 411 b.
Sleeping, 277 b.
Sleepless, be —, 613 a.
Sling, n. 530 b; v. 530 b.
Slinger, 530 b.
Slip, 612 a.
Slippery, 204 a.
Sloth, 473 b.
Slothful, 473 a; be —, 567 b.
Sluggish, 473 a.
Sluggishness, 411 b, 473 b.
Slumber, n. 626 a; v. 277 b.
Slumbering, 277 b.
Small, 142 b, 517 a, 519 b, 528 a, 535 a; be —, 528 a.
Smallness, 138 b, 517 a.
Smell, v. 556 b; n. 561 a.
Smile, v. 574 a.
Smite, 418 b.
Smith, 226 b.
Smoke, n. 484 b, 528 b; v. 485 a.
Smooth, adj. 204 a; v. 391 a, 589 a; be —, 204 a.
Snail, 583 b.
Snare, n. 180 a, 346 b, 364 b, 491 b, 515 b, 571 a; v. 270 a, 428 a.
Snatch, 231 b.
Sneezing, n. 457 a.
Snow, n. 598 b, 623 b.
Snuffers, 366 a.
So, 288 a.
Soap, 94 b, 433 b.
Sobbing, n. 44 b.
Soft, 561 b.
Softly, 22 a.
Softness, effeminacy, 391 b, 561 b.
Soil, n. 8 b.
Sojourn, v. 108 b.
Sojourner, 120 a, 121 a, 621 a.
Sojourning, n. 337 b.
Sole, of the foot, 306 a, 615 b.
Solitary, 72 b, 479 b, 605 a.
Solve, 615 a.
Some one, 19 b.
Somebody, 36 b.
Something, 126 a.
Son, 85 a, 90 b, 165; — in law, 231 a.
Song, 172 b, 173 b, 405 b, 563 b, 595 a.

Sorrow, n. 13 b, 49 a, 124 a, 243 b, 357 b, 390 a, 391 b, 409 b, 465 a, 575 a, 584 b; v. 14 a.
Sorrowful, 14 a.
Sort, 173 b.
Soul, 424 a, 555 b.
Sound, n. 525 b, 529 b, 606 a; adj. 624 b; v. 557 b, 595 a.
Soundness, 391 b, 399 a, 599 a.
Source, 546 a, 615 b.
South, 260 b, 404 a, 622 b.
Sovereign, n. 429 b.
Sovereignty, 413 a, 601 a.
Sow, v. 178 a.
Space, 386 b, 555 b.
Spacious, 556 b.
Span, n. 178 b.
Spare, 188 b, 206 b.
Spark, 294 b.
Sparrow, 518 b.
Speak, 128 a, 365 a, 467 a, 575 a.
Spear, 210 b, 294 b, 529 a, 563 a, 575 a.
Speech, 575 a, 578 a.
Spelt, 305 a.
Spice, n. 392 a.
Spider, 458 a.
Spikenard, 428 a.
Spill, 406 b.
Spine, 472 b.
Spinning-wheel, 494 a.
Spirit, 555 b; — of divination, 12 a.
Spit, v. 274 a, 570 a.
Spittle, 561 b, 569 a.
Splendid, 8 a.
Splendour, 169 b, 285 b, 627 b.
Spoil, n. 77 b, 200 b, 365 b, 450 a, 583 a, 590 a, 602 a; v. 78 a, 602 a.
Spokesman, 402 b.
Spontaneous, 592 b.
Sport, v. 512 b, 574 a.
Spot, n. 344 a.
Spotted, adj. 91 b.
Spread, 176 b, 416 a, 504 a, 505 a, 593 b.
Spreading, n. 383 a.
Spring, fountain, 336 a, 387 a, 457 b.
Sprinkle, 178 b, 412 a, b, 564 a.
Spurn, 78 a.
Spy, n. 621 a.
Square, 549 b.
Stable, n. 17 a, 53 b.
Staff, 343 b, 354 a, 531 b, 583 a.

Stagger, 313 a, 627 a.
Staggering, n. 630 a.
Stain, v. 233 a; n. 334 b.
Stalk, 531 b.
Stall, 3 a, 17 a, 53 b, 389 b, 567 b.
Stamp, v. 570 a.
Stand, v. 424 b, 464 a, 526 a; — fast, 267 a.
Standard, 130 a, 420 b, 623 a, b.
Standing, n. 380 a.
Standing corn, 530 b.
Star, 289 b.
Station, n. 301 b, 380 a, 384 a.
Statute, 219 a.
Staves, 72 a.
Steal, 118 b.
Steel-yard, 494 b.
Stem, 531 b.
Stench, 512 b.
Step, n. 155 a, 379 b, 386 a, 459 b, 504 b, 517 a; v. 504 b; — on, 144 a.
Stick, n. 354 a, 534 b.
Still, adv. 450 a, 452 b.
Sting, v. 504 a.
Stink, v. 71 a, 174 b.
Stir up, 454 a.
Stock, of a tree, 110 a.
Stomach, 521 a.
Stone, n. 4 b, 512 a; v. 441 a, 551 b.
Stoop, v. 592 a, 596 b.
Stop, 214 a.
Store-house, 46 a.
Stork, 213 b.
Storm, n. 577 b, 587 b.
Stout, 605 b.
Stove, 19 a.
Strange, 169 b, 419 b, 420 a.
Stranger, 169 a, 420 a.
Strangling, n. 352 b.
Straw, 618 b.
Stray, 2 b.
Stream, n. 242 b, 409 b, 413 a, 414 a, 493 a, 583 b.
Street, 559 a, 590 b.
Strength, 25 a, 177 a, 190 b, 191 a, 195 a, 214 a, 455 a, 473 b, 627 b, 629 a.
Strengthen, 41 b, 88 a, 103 b, 191 a, 292 a, 474 a, 526 b, 567 a.
Stretch, — out, 277 a, 398 b, 570 a; the hand, 395 a, 416 a, 504 a.
Strew, 267 b, 593 b.
Strife, 339 b, 391 a, 560 b.
Strike, 157 a, 350 b, 405 b, 406 a, 418 b, 560 b, 629 a.
String, 280 a.

4 P

(658)

Strip, v. 479 a; — off, 430 b, 505 a.
Stripe, 342 a.
Strive, contend, 561 a.
Stroke, 354 a, 357 b, 406 a.
Strong, 121 b, 190 b, 213 b, 455 a, 480 a, 629 a; be —, 191 a, 214 a, 456 a, 629 b.
Stronghold, 377 b.
Structure, 86 a.
Struggle, v. 507 b, 569 a.
Stubble, 542 a.
Stubborn, 444 b.
Stubbornness, 543 a.
Stumble, 313 a, 321 a, 489 b.
Stumbling, n. 359 b, 406 b.
Stumbling-block, 359 a.
Stupid, 87 b, 239 b, 284 b.
Stupor, 629 b.
Subdue, 89 a, 287 a, 553 a.
Subject, n. 396 b.
Sublimity, 99 a.
Submit, 567 b.
Subscribe, 614 a.
Subtle, 465 b.
Suburbs, 338 b.
Subversion, 159 b, 342 a.
Subvert, 159 b.
Succeed, 274 b, 514 a.
Success, 425 a.
Succour, n. 456 a.
Succour, v. 456 a.
Suck, v. 261 a, 384 b, 386 a.
Sucker, 426 a.
Suckle, 261 a, 453 a.
Suckling, 253 a, 453 a.
Suddenly, 505 b, 507 b.
Suddenness, 507 b.
Suffer, 44 a.
Suffice, 578 b.
Sufficiency, 136 a, 572 a.
Sufficient, be —, 589 a.
Suffocation, 352 b.
Suffuse, 83 b.
Suit, n. 480 a, 560 b.
Sulphur, 120 a.
Sum, n. 546 a.
Summer, 528 b, 529 a.
Summon, 175 b, 525 a, 536 b, 606 b.
Sun, 224 b, 607 b.
Supplication, 621 b.
Support, v. 290 a, 428 b, 435 b, 441 a, 442 a, 526 b, 567 a, 610 a, 625 a; n. 375 b, 397 a.
Supreme, 546 a.
Surbase, 456 b.
Sure, 290 a.
Surely, 28 a.
Surety, 478 b.
Surface, 495 b.

Surfeit, v. 571 b.
Surround, 315 a, 427 b, 434 b, 457 a, 512 a.
Suspend, 623 b.
Sustain, 290 a.
Swallow, n. 143 a, 437 a; v. 84 a, 581 b, 616 b.
Swarm, n. 450 b.
Swear, 30 b, 584 a.
Sweat, n. 174 b.
Sweep away, 122 b, 438 b.
Sweet, 398 b, 421 b; be —, 399 b.
Sweeten, 399 b.
Sweetness, 367 a, 398 b, 399 b.
Swift, 529 b.
Swim, 574 a.
Swine, 190 b.
Sword, 220 a.
Sycamore, 614 a.
Syriac, 55 a.

Tabernacle, 395 b.
Table, 600 b.
Tablet, 114 b, 324 b.
Tabret, 627 b.
Tail, 174 a.
Take, 20 b, 331 b, 414 b, 428 b, 521 b; — away, 332 a, 425 b, 428 b; — hold, 20 b, 395 a, 428 b, 625 a; — off, 603 a; — up, 557 a.
Talent, 295 b.
Talk, v. 443 b, 575 a.
Tall, 100 b, 101 a.
Tamarisk, 58 a.
Tambourine, 627 a.
Task, n. 435 b, 436 a; — master, 407 a.
Taste, n. 238 a; v. 238 a.
Taunt, n. 609 a.
Tax, n. 83 a, 373 b, 470 a; v. 470 a.
Teach, 37 a, 272 a, 329 b, 575 b.
Teacher, 347 a.
Tear, n. 141 b; v. 541 a, 585 a; — in pieces, 438 a, 503 b, 609 b.
Tell, 365 a, 404 b.
Tempest, 577 b, 578 a, 587 b.
Tempestuous, be —, 578 a.
Temple, 81 a, 153 b, 395 b; of the head, 569 b.
Tempt, 420 b.
Temptation, 374 b.
Ten, 483 b.
Tend, 409 a.
Tender, 467 a, 561 b; be —, 562 a.
Tenderness, 561 b.

Tendon, 471 b.
Tent, 11 a.
Terminate, 603 a.
Termination, 533 b, 620 b, 623 a.
Terrible, 270 b.
Terrify, 74 a, 87 b.
Terror, 74 a, 83 a, 88 a, 230 a, 337 b, 354 a, 381 b, 577 b, 605 b, 628 a.
Testimony, 450 a, 572 b.
Thanksgiving, 619 b.
Then, 8 a, 17 b.
Thence, 603 b.
There, 603 b, 624 b.
Therefore, 305 b, 323 a, 329 b.
These, 29 a, 31 a.
They, 157 a.
Thick, 449 a.
Thicket, 439 a.
Thickness, 447 a.
Thief, 118 b.
Thigh, 273 b, 492 a.
Thin, adj. 142 b, 569 a; beat —, 570 a.
Thing, 126 a.
Think, 140 b, 227 b.
Thirst, n. 515 a, 623 b; v. 515 a.
Thirsty, 515 a; be —, 614 b.
Thirty, 603 b.
This, 124 a, 137 a, 141 b, 150 a, 154 b, 167 a.
Thither, 603 b.
Thorn, 187 a, 439 a, 516 a, b, 527 b, 575 a.
Thoroughly, 425 a.
Thou, 66 a.
Thought, n. 349 b, 353 b.
Thousand, 37 a.
Thread, n. 187 a, 507 a, 527 b, 628 b.
Three, 603 a.
Threefold, 603 b.
Thresh, 10 b.
Threshing-floor, 9 a, 122 a.
Threshing-machine, 347 a.
Threshold, 383 a, 442 b.
Throat, 121 a, 330 b.
Throne, 303 b, 311 a.
Through, 620 a.
Throw, 562 b, 600 a, 601 b; — away, 601 b; — down, 423 b, 601 b; — in, 629 a; — off, 89 b, 600 a; — out, 601 b; — up, 440 b.
Thrust, — in, 629 a; — out, 149 a.
Thumb, 75 a.
Thunder, n. 525 b, 565 b; v. 565 b.
Thus, 288 a.

(659)

Tiara, 50 a.
Tidings, 604 b.
Tie, *v.* 47 a, 543 a, 562 b, 578 b; — up, 512 a, 520 b.
Till, *v.* 446 a.
Tillage, 446 b.
Timber, 471 b, 473 a.
Time, period, 173 a, 451 b, 486 b; turn, 498 a, 551 a.
Timid, 221 b, 561 b; be —, 562 a.
Tin, 72 b.
Tingle, 514 a.
Tithe, *n.* 382 a; *v.* 484 a.
To, 29 a, 316 a.
Toe, 50 b; great —, 75 a.
Together, 254 a.
Toil, *n.* 465 a.
Tomb, 522 a, 581 a.
Tongs, 366 a.
Tongue, 332 b, 333 b.
Tooth, 608 a.
Top, 546 a.
Topaz, 492 a.
Torch, 331 b.
Torrent, 48 b, 414 a.
Totter, 313 a, 343 b, 377 a.
Tottering, *n.* 343 b.
Touch, *v.* 398 b, 405 b.
Tow, *n.* 422 b.
Towards, 29 a, 316 a, 419 b, 448 a.
Tower, *n.* 337 a, 438 b, 520 a.
Town, 458 a, 540 a.
Track, *n.* 475 a.
Traffic, *n.* 374 b.
Train, *n.* 590 a; *v.* 330 a.
Trample, 76 b, 563 a, 567 b; — on, 87 a, 135 a.
Trampling, 336 a, 391 b, 618 b.
Trance, 629 b.
Tranquil, 581 b.
Transfer, *n.* 625 a.
Transgress, 202 b, 447 b, 505 a.
Transgression, 505 a.
Translate, 629 b.
Trap, 346 b, 364 b.
Travail, *n.* 465 a.
Travel, *v.* 54 a, 421 b.
Treacherous, 72 a.
Treachery, 71 b.
Tread, 76 b, 135 a, 144 a, 563 a; — down, 144 a; — out, 135 a.
Treading out, 137 a, 340 a.
Treason, 543 a.
Treasure, *n.* 14 b, 119 a, 354 b, 419 b, 499 b; *v.* 51 a, 509 a, 519 a.
Treasury, 14 b, 375 a.
Treat, 460 b.

Tree, 25 a, 471 b.
Tremble, 119 b, 221 b, 481 b, 550 b, 564 b, 566 a.
Trembling, *n.* 196 a, 221 b, 494 b, 551 a, 560 b, 564 b, 565 b, 566 a, 571 b, 630 a.
Trespass, *n.* 505 a; *v.* 447 b.
Trial, 79 a, 374 b.
Tribe, 194 a, 319 b, 354 b, 397 a, 583 a.
Tribute, 358 b, 373 b, 374 b, 392 b, 393 a.
Troop, 104 b.
Trouble, *n.* 386 a, 550 b, 623 b; *v.* 458 b.
Trough, 554 b, 614 b.
Trowsers, 444 a.
True, 278 b, 509 b, 543 a.
Truly, 301 a.
Trumpet, 218 b, 540 b, 590 b.
Trunk, of a tree, 110 a.
Trust, *v.* 213 a, 441 a, 525 b, 610 a; *n.* 336 b.
Truth, 43 a, 357 a, 425 a, 509 b, 510 a, 543 a.
Try, 79 a, 220 a, 420 b.
Tube, 346 a.
Tumor, 470 b.
Tumult, 341 b, 552 b, 565 b, 566 a, 626 a.
Turban, 385 b, 516 b.
Turn, *n.* time, 620 b; *v.* 169 a; — about, 434 b; — aside, 437 b; — away, 587 b; — back, 159 b, 587 b; — himself, 495 a, 587 b; — over, 159 b.
Turtle dove, 620 b.
Tutor, 40 b.
Twelve, 609 a.
Twenty, 484 a.
Twice, 498 a.
Twig, 387 a.
Twilight, 431 a, 593 a.
Twins, 617 b, 618 a.
Twist, 591 b.
Two, 609 a.
Tyranny, 554 a.

Unblameable, 624 b.
Uncircumcised, 481 a.
Uncircumcision, 480 b.
Uncle, 131 b.
Unclean, 133 a, 237 a.
Uncover, 113 a.
Under, 621 b, 622 a.
Understand, 80 b, 606 a.
Understanding, *n.* 370 b, 575 b, 576 a, 618 b.
Undertake, 420 b, 521 b.
Undeservedly, 210 b.
Unfair, 453 a.
Unfairness, 453 a.

Ungodliness, 212 a.
Ungodly, 212 a.
Unimportant, 561 b.
Unintelligible, 466 a.
Unite, 254 a.
Unjust, 453 a, 570 b.
Unleavened bread, 384 b.
Unless, 13 b, 31 a, 325 a.
Unlevel, 381 a.
Unrestrained, 601 a.
Unsearchable, 465 b.
Untie, 506 b, 615 a.
Until, 450 a.
Untimely birth, 423 a.
Unto, 450 a.
Unyielding, 190 b.
Upbraid, 225 a.
Uphold, 625 a.
Upon, 458 b.
Upper, 460 a.
Upright, 278 b.
Upwards, 379 b.
Urge, 14 b, 37 a, 135 a, 136 a, 438 a, 499 a, 511 b.
Urgent, 218 a, 415 a.
Usury, 629 b.
Utter, *v.* 404 a, 428 b, 490 b, 506 b, 575 a, 611 b.
Utterly, 297 a.

Vacillate, 377 a.
Vain, in —, 619 a; — thing, 619 a.
Vale, 466 a.
Valiant, 101 b.
Valley, 89 b, 111 a, 414 a, 466 a.
Valuable, 234 b, 358 b.
Value, *n.* 269 b, 358 b, 480 a; *v.* 440 a.
Vanity, 147 a, 587 b.
Vapour, 7 b, 430 a, 528 b.
Vary, 412 a.
Vast, 547 b.
Vat, 123 b, 268 b.
Vegetables, 178 b.
Vehemence, 191 a.
Vehicle, 562 a.
Veil, *n.* 273 a, 502 a, 515 b, 517 a, 553 a; *v.* 214 b, 319 b, 324 b, 374 b.
Vengeance, 427 b.
Venison, 512 b.
Venom, 546 b.
Very, 334 a.
Vessel, 298 b, 335 a, 403 a, 516 a, 518 b, 618 b.
Vex, 261 a, 319 b, 458 b, 520 a.
Vexation, 174 b, 306 a, 390 a, 465 a, 550 b, 584 b, 623 b.
View, *v.* 190 a, 544 a, 591 a; *n.* 389 a.

(660)

Vigorous, 193 b.
Vigour, 292 a, 326 a.
Village, 218 b, 308 a, 501 b.
Vindicate, 611 a.
Vine, 120 a.
Vinegar, 207 b.
Vineyard, 310 b.
Vintage, 88 a.
Violence, 72 a, 83 a, 177 a, 207 a, 586 b, commit —, 207 b.
Violent, 26 b, 480 a, 601 a; be —, 629 b.
Violet, adj. 623 a.
Viper, 49 b.
Virgin, 98 a, 461 a.
Virtue, 13 b.
Vision, 190 a, b, 351 a, 388 b, 389 a, 545 b.
Visit, 499 a, 544 b.
Voice, 525 b, 529 b.
Void, 90 b; become —, 89 b.
Vomit, n. 521 a, 528 b; v. 528 b.
Vow, n. 409 a; v. 408 b.
Vulture, 559 b.

Wages, 6 b, 351 b, 393 b, 497 b, 498 a.
Waggon, 377 a, 508 a.
Wail, v. 258 b.
Wailing, n. 259 a, 376 a.
Wait, 196 b, 254 b, 525 b; — on, 616 a.
Walk, v. 144 a, 155 a, 258 a, 517 a, 563 a; n. 341 b.
Walking stick, 387 a, 397 a.
Wall, n. 86 a, 106 b, 188 a, 196 a, 314 b, 529 a, 591 b, 615 a; v. 106 b.
Wander, v. 192 b, 407 b, 410 a, 412 a, 627 a.
Want, n. 214 a, 228 a, 307 b, 375 a; v. 214 b, 352 b.
Wanting, adj. 214 b.
Wanton, 581 b.
War, n. 327 a, 363 b, 538 a; v. 327 a.
Wardrobe, 336 a.
Ware, n. 381 a.
Warfare, 508 b.
Warlike, 103 b; be —, 103 b.
Warm, be —, 254 b.
Warn, 167 b, 452 a.
Warning, n. 17 a.
Warp, n. 617 a.
Wash, v. 286 a, 560 a, 594 b; — away, 594 a.
Washing, n. 560 a.
Wasp, 520 b.
Waste, v. 139 a, 297 b, 371 a,
387 b, 586 b; — away, 387 b, 403 a, 431 b.
Wasting, n. 535 a, 558 b.
Watch, v. 417 b, 426 a, 457 b, 517 b, 591 a, 607 a, 613 a; n. 59 b, 607 b.
Watcher, 458 a.
Watching, n. 396 b.
Watchman, 518 a, 607 b.
Watchtower, 386 a, 518 b, 519 a.
Water, n. 356 b; v. 613 a.
Watered, adj. 555 a.
Watering, n. 560 b, 613 b.
Wave, n. 112 a, 619 a.
Wax, n. 134 a.
Way, 53 b, 143 b, 155 a, 375 b, 377 a.
We, 44 b, 415 a.
Weak, 138 a, 288 a, 567 b; be —, 288 b.
Weaken, 139 a, 374 a, 410 a, 567 a.
Weakness, 535 a, 567 b.
Wealth, 13 b, 152 a, 242 a, 243 b, 286 a, 292 a, 362 a, 381 b, 387 b, 419 b, 438 b, 532 a, 562 a, 621 a.
Wean, 118 a.
Weapon, 220 a, 599 b.
Wear, 322 a, 428 b, 456 b.
Weariness, 465 a, 623 b.
Weary, adj. 243 b, 264 b, 457 b, 465 b; v. 319 b, 446 a; be —, 264 b, 319 a.
Weave, 52 b.
Weaver, 52 b.
Web, 52 a, 375 a.
Wedge, 333 a.
Week, 582 b.
Weep, 81 b.
Weeping, n. 4 a, 81 b, 141 b.
Weigh, 614 a, 623 b. 629 a.
Weight, 269 b, 284 b, 398 a.
Weighty, 284 b.
Welfare, 599 a.
Well, n. 70 b, 77 a, 100 b, 108 a, 379 a.
Well, adv. do —, 235 a, 255 a.
West, 381 a.
Western, 20 a, 21 a, 259 b.
Wet, v. 509 a.
Whale, 325 a.
What, 334 a, 340 b, 367 b.
Wheat, 193 a, 210 b.
Wheel, n. 14 b, 112 b, 377 a.
When, 43 b, 399 a.
Whence, 43 b.
Where, 23 b, 26 a, 43 b, 603 b.
Whey, 561 b.
Whether, 11 b.

While, 450 a.
Whip, n. 589 b, 594 a.
Whirlwind, 112 b, 437 b, 442 b.
Whisper, n. 327 b.
Whistle, v. 615 b.
Whistling, n. 615 a.
White, 321 a, 512 b.
Whiten, 321 b.
Whiteness, 321 b, 512 b; — of the hair, 575 a.
Whither, 43 b, 603 b.
Who, 60 b, 136 a, 367 b.
Whole, entire, 299 a, 625 a; n. 296 a.
Wholly, 254 a, 299 a, 425 a.
Whore, play the —, 174 a.
Whoredom, 174 a, b.
Why, 339 b.
Wicked, 392 b, 453 a, 564 a, 570 b.
Wickedness, 83 b, 192 a, 392 b, 565 a, 570 b.
Wide, 558 a; — place, 390 b.
Widow, 36 b.
Widower, 36 b.
Widowhood, 36 b.
Width, 558 b.
Wife, 56 b.
Wild-beast, 74 b.
Wilderness, 339 a, 513 a, 619 a.
Will, n. 215 a, 564 a, 565 a, 568 b.
Willing, 3 a, 215 b, 408 b; be —, 508 b.
Willow, 477 b.
Wind, n. 556 b.
Window, 52 a, 199 b, 289 a, 351 a, 510 b.
Wine, 208 a, 255 b, 434 b, 470 a, 622 b; — press, 491 a; — vat, 268 b.
Wing, n. 302 b.
Winter, n. 444 b.
Wipe out, 350 b.
Wisdom, 197 b, 370 b, 456 b, 575 b, 621 a, b.
Wise, 197 a; be —, 198 a, 575 b; — man, 196 b.
Wish, n. 565 a; v. 508 b.
With, 463 a.
Withdraw, 208 a, 413 b, 420 b, 503 b, 560 a, 567 a, 588 b.
Wither, 242 b, 531 a.
Withhold, 51 a, 183 a, 227 a, 292 b, 296 b, 373 a, 419 b, 567 a, 588 b, 609 b.
Within, 80 a, 81 b, 496 a, 620 a.
Without, outwards, 90 b,

(661)

188 b; wanting, 83 a, 84 a, 84 b.
Witness, *n.* 450 a, 572 b; bear —, 452 a; take to —, 452 a.
Woe! 13 a.
Wolf, 165 a.
Woman, 56 b.
Womb, 377 a, 559 b.
Wonder, *n.* 17 a, 345 b, 382 b, 624 b; *v.* 605 b, 624 b.
Wonder, *v.* 605 b, 624 b.
Wood, timber, 471 b, 473 a; forest, 226 b, 265 a.
Wool, 466 b, 516 a.
Word, 41 b, 126 a, 362 a.
Work, *n.* 362 a, 381 b, 382 b, 446 b, 447 b, 465 a, 497 b; *v.* 226 b, 446 a, 482 b, 497 b, 498 a.
Workman, 226 b.

World, 618 b.
Worm, *n.* 563 a, 620 a.
Wormwood, 331 a.
Worn out, 83 a.
Worship, *n.* 446 b, 447 b; *v.* 436 a, 446 a, 494 a, 591 b, 616 a.
Worth, *n.* 209 b.
Worthless, 403 a, 561 b.
Worthlessness, 403 b, 529 b, 587 b.
Would God, 20 b.
Wound, *n.* 357 b, 499 a; *v.* 406 a, 418 b, 499 a.
Wounded, 201 a.
Wrap, 516 b.
Wrath, 534 b.
Wreath, 324 b.
Wrestle, 5 b.
Wring out, 384 b.
Write, 314 a, 570 a.
Writer, 443 b.

Writing, *n.* 313 b, 314 a, 359 b, 443 b.
Wrong, *adj.* 564 a; *n.* 565 a; *v.* 207 b, 485 a, 565 b.
Wroth, be —, 535 a.

Yarn, 354 b.
Year, 608 b.
Yesterday, 43 a, 66 b.
Yielding, *n.* 391 b.
Yoke, *n.* 343 b, 459 a; *v.* 571 b.
You, 66 b.
Young, 517 a, 528 a, 561 b.
Younger, 517 a.
Youth, young person, 78 b, 422 a, 461 a, 507 a; time of life, 257 b, 421 b, 422 a, 459 b.

Zeal, 531 b.

(662)

APPENDIX C.

CORRECTIONS AND ADDITIONS.

By *a* joined with the numeral of the page is meant the first column; by *b* the second.

Page 1 a, *line* 4.—And elsewhere in the Æthiopic.

P. 2 a, *l.* 30.—אָב, — applied also to man, (a) *Father*, or (b) *Forefather*, or *ancestor*. (a) Gen. xliv. 19, 20; Num. iii. 24, &c. (b) 1 Kings xv. 11; 2 Kings xiv. 3; xv. 38; Is. xliii. 27. אָבִיךָ הָרִאשׁוֹן, *Thy first father*, Adam probably. Mostly pl. in this acceptation, Gen. xv. 15; Ps. xlv. 17, &c. Also constr. אֲבִי־, Gen. xvii. 4, 5, only.

P. 2 b, *l.* 49.—אֲבַדּוֹן, m.—pl. non. occ. r. אָבַד. (a) Gr. Ἀβαδδών, i. q. ἀπολλύων, Rev. ix. 11. *Utter destruction*, Job xxxi. 12. (b) Meton, i. q. שְׁאוֹל, Ib. xxvi. 6; xxviii. 22; Prov. xv. 11; Ps. lxxxviii. 12; al. non occ.

P. 8 a, *l.* 5.—Add אָרֵיב, m. r. אָרָב. Cogn. Heb. דאב, אנד. Arab. اَدَبَ, *punivit.* II. Conj. n. a. تَأدِيب, *castigated.* Gesen. Infin. of Hiph. for הַאֲדִיב. But this is unnecessary, as it might be a verbal noun of Kal. Once, 1 Sam. ii. 33. *Punish, chastise, vex.* LXX. καταρρεῖν.

P. 14 a, *l.* 12.—Add יִתְאוֹנֵן, Lam. iii. 39.

P. 16 b, *l.* 29.—This place, if any reliance may be placed on identity of signification in names, was *Mabug*; which, according to authorities cited by Asseman, Biblioth. Orient., tom. i., p. 328, was styled ܡܕܝܢܬܐ ܕܟܘܡܪܐ, *City of the Kūmrē*, or *priests;* which looks very like the χαμαρίνη, i. e. χαλδαίων πόλις, of Eupolemus, and the *Hierapolis* of the Greeks, which is also a name of this place, and presents but a free translation of the Syriac name just given.

P. 23 a, *l.* 17.—Add Part. אָמֻם, Prov. l. c. Pass. pl. masc. אֲמֻמִים, f. אֲמֻמוֹת *Splayed*, according to Jerome. Gesenius, "*fenestræ clathris cancellisve clausæ.*" In 1 Kings vi. 4, however, these windows are said to be שְׁקֻפִים אֲטֻמִים; and Ezek. xli. 16, מְכֻסּוֹת. Whence it should seem that they were *covered* or *closed* in some way. But if אֲטֻמִים signifies *splayed*, the other epithets might have been added to show, either that they were cancellated—as some have thought —or else were secured from the rain by something like our *Venetian blinds*, which will combine each signification. See LXX. and Appendix A.

P. 33 b, *l.* 35.—Add אֱלִי, Imp. f. r. אלה. Cogn. אלל, ילל, יָגֹן, Joel i. 8. *Cry, cry out.*

P. 41 a, *l.* 4.—Add תֵּאָמֵנָה, pl. f. pres. (See אָמֵן above). *Be protected, nursed*, Is. lx. 4.

P. 50 b, *l.* 12.—Add pl. Chald. f. אֶצְבְּעָן, Dan. v. 5. *Toes*, Ib. ii. 41, 42. Constr. אֶצְבְּעָת. Def. אֶצְבְּעָתָא.

P. 71 a, *l.* 20.—Add הֹבְאִישׁ, Is. xxx. 5, r. בּאשׁ, in the sense of בּוֹשׁ. See also יבשׁ, and Gram. art. 202. 3, note.

P. 77 a, *l.* 43.—After the " &c." add Hos. xiii. 15.

P. 87 a, *l.* 8, בְּעוּתִים.—Will be found page 88 a, line 8.

P. 87 b, *l.* 9.—Add בָּעַל, v. pres. יִבְעַל. Constr. immed. it. med. בְּ, לְ. (a) *Be, become, proprietor, possessor, lord*, in a feudal sense, Is. xxvi. 13; with לְ, 1 Chron. iv. 22. — of a wife, i. e. *a husband*, or *marry a wife*, Deut. xxi. 13; xxiv. 1, &c. Metaph. — a country, Is. lxii. 4; Jer. iii. 14; xxxi. 32. Gesenius prefers, here, Be weary of, reject ("*fastidivit, rejecit,*" with Syr. Rab. Jonah, Pococke, Porta Mosis, p. 5—10. LXX. ἠμέλησα αὐτῶν. Arab. بَعَلَ, with بِ, *fastidivit.*) The places, however, appear to me incapable of such sense. Part. pl. aff. בֹּעֲלַיִךְ, Is. liv. 5.

(663)

— pass. f. בְּעֻלָה, constr. בְּעֻלַת, Is. liv. 1; Gen. xx. 3, &c.

Niph. pres. fem. תִּבָּעֵל, Prov. xxx. 23. Metaph., Is. lxii. 4. *Be, become, married.*

P. 89 a, l. 25.—Add בַּעֲרוֹת, f. pl. Id., Jer. xiv. 1.

P. 109 a, l. 27.—Add Hos. vii. 14.

P. 143 b, l. 5.—Constr. as fem., Judg. xviii. 5; i. e. nom. taken as *a thing.* See Gram. artt. 216. 7; 220. 5.

P. 168 b, l. 17.—וּן, v. Kal. non occ. See וּנָה. Hoph. part. pl. מוּתָנִים. *Fed.* See also in its place.

Ithp. Chald. יִתְּוּן. *Is, may be, fed*, Dan. iv. 9, only.

P. 169 b, l. 4.—בָרוּ, add Ezek. xiv. 5.

P. 181 b, l. 32.—Add f. pl. aff. חַבְרֻבֹּתָיו. *His varieties; spots.* Arab. حَبَر, *vestis striata;* حَبَر, *color variegatus tunicæ.* Æth. ሐብረት : *variegata.* Once, Jer. xiii. 23.

P. 192 b, l. 7.—Chald., Ezra vi. 17. חַטַּיָּא, *Keri,* חַטָּיָא.

P. 193 b, l. 32.—רֳאִי. See רָאָה, p. 545.

P. 232 b, l. 3.—The v. מאמס, which should be here, will be found, p. 234 a, l. 31.

P. 249 a, l. 44.—Irenæus, ii. 26, should probably be lib. i., § vii., p. 20, of Grabe's edition; where see the note.

P. 264 a, l. 22.—Add יַעֲלֵי. See r. עלי.

P. 264 b, l. 5.—יֶעֱרוּ, whence pl. יְעֵרוּ, will be found under עור, p. 482; the pres. Pih. of which is the same with that of the cogn. עור.

P. 268 a, l. 25.—(יצק) Hiph. pres. pl. יַצִּקוּ. *They set up, placed,* with אֶת, 2 Sam. xv. 24. Aff. Josh. vii. 23. Cogn. יצג.

P. 270 a, l. 26.—Add יִרְאָה (before יָרֵאת), Ezek. i. 18.

P. 285 b, l. 19.—Add הִתְכַּבֵּד, Nah. iii. 15.

P. 287 a, l. 47.—Niph. once, Jer. xxxiv. 11. *Kethiv,* aff. יכבישום, i. q. Kal.

P. 308 a, l. 24.—Add Neh. vi. 2, and read כְּפָרִים, for כְּפִירִים, of the text; the (·) being in all probability a mere error of the copyists.

P. 309 b, l. 34.—Add Niph. pres. יָצְרָה. Pass. of Kal, Ps. xciv. 13.

P. 331 b, l. 28.—לָצוֹן, m.—pl. non occ. r. לוּץ. Cogn. לצץ. *Derision, scorn,* Prov. i. 22; Is. xxviii. 14; Prov. xxix. 8. אַנְשֵׁי לָצוֹן, i. q. לֵצִים, or לֹצְצִים.

P. 337 b, l. 39.—מְגִלָּה, f. constr. מְגִלַּת, r. גלל. Arab. مجلّه. Propr. A roll: thence *a volume,* or *book,* Jer. xxxvi. 6. 14, seq.; Ezek. ii. 9; iii. 1. 23; Ps. xl. 8. It Chald., Ezra vi. 2.

P. 387 b, l. 3.—Gesenius makes מִקְנֶה, fem., Exod. xxxiv. 19 (p. 1071). But this is unnecessary, the two preceding nominatives being taken as *one* whole thing. See Gram. art. 216. 2, seq.

P. 415 a, l. 23.—Lit. nostril: thence *Snorting,* Job xxxix. 20. See Hieroz., i., p. 123, seq.

P. 508 a, l. 12.—*Wild lotuses.* To the places cited, in my notes on Job xl. 21, 22, add Strabo, Edit. Casaubon, p. 565.

P. 546 a, l. 1, &c.—See the interesting extracts made on this subject by the late Mr. Taylor in his Fragments to Calmet., vol. iv., p. 611, Edit. 1838. "They (the unicorns) go together in herds like our wild buffaloes, and are very frequently to be met with on the borders of the Great Desert, about a month's journey from Lhassa (in Thibet), in that part of the country inhabited by the wandering Tartars." The horn " is twenty inches in length; at the root it is four inches and a half in circumference, and tapers to a point."

FURTHER CORRECTIONS AND ADDITIONS.

אָיַבְתִּי, r. איב, whence אֵיבָה, and אֹיֵב. *I will be enemy.* Before אֵיד, p. 24, once, Exod. xxiii. 22. LXX. ἐχθρεύσω.

אֲלָמִים, see מְאַלְּמִים, p. 34.

גִּזְבָּר, m. Chald. Syr. ܓܙܒܪܐ, *thesaurarius.* Pers. comp. گنج + بار. *Treasurer,* once, Ezra i. 8, p. 109, before גוה.

דמע, v. pret. non occ. pres. 2d pers. תִּדְמַע, r. דמע, p. 141. *Shed tears.* It.—Infin. דָּמֹעַ, *Shedding tears,* both in Jer. xiii. 17, only.

כָּעַס, v. pres. יִכְעַס, constr. abs. it. med. אֶל. Arab. cogn. كعص, *edit, comedit. Vexed, indignant, provoked,* Ezek. xvi. 42;

Ps. cxii. 10; Eccl. v. 16; Neh. iii. 33; 2 Chron. xvi. 10. See בַּעַס.
Infin. with לְ, לִכְעוֹס, Eccl. vii. 9, only.
Pih. pret. 3d pers. f. with aff. כִּעֲסָתָה, 1 Sam. i. 6. כִּעֲסוּנִי, trans. *She, they, vexed, made indignant,* Deut. xxxii. 21. It. med. בְּ, al. non occ.
Hiph. הִכְעִיס, pres. יַכְעִיס, apoc. יַכְעֵם, constr. abs. it. immed. it. med. אֶת, לִפְנֵי, it. immed. with בְּ, med. of the cause, i. q. Pih. *Vex, irritate,* &c. 1 Kings xv. 30; Hos. xii. 15; Deut. xxxii. 21; 1 Kings xxii. 54, &c.
Infin. הַכְעִיס, aff. הַכְעִסֵנִי, it. הַכְעִיסְכֶם, 1 Kings xvi. 13; 2 Kings xxii. 17; 2 Chron. xxxiv. 25, &c.
Part. pl. m. מַכְעִיסִים, 1 Kings xiv. 15; 2 Kings xxi. 15, &c.

מַדְמֵנָה, f. once, Is. xxv. 10. See דֹּמֶן, p. 141. Arab. مُتَدَمِّن, *fimo sordibusque inquinatus. A dunghill.*

מָעַד, p. 379, add. Puh. 3d pers. pl. m. מֹעָדוּ, Ezek. xxiii. 3, only. *Were bruised.*

עָנַד, v. pret. non occ. pres. אֶעֶנְדֶנּוּ. *I bind it,* Job xxxi. 36, only. See my notes. Arab. غُنْد, *difficultate magnâ pressit res.*
Imper. aff. עָנְדֵם. *Bind them,* synon. τοῦ, קָשַׁר, Prov. vi. 21, only.

עשׁת, see עָשֵׁת, p. 485, v. Kal. pret. עָשְׁתוּ, Jer. v. 28, with שָׁמְנוּ. *They shine,* as polished ivory, &c., once.
Hithp. יִתְעַשֵּׁת, Jonah i. 6, only, med. לְ, lit. *Become smooth, propitious.* LXX. διασώσῃ.

תּוּגָה, f. constr. תּוּגַת, r. יגה, p. 243. *Affliction, sorrow, sadness,* Ps. cxix. 28; Prov. x. 1; xiv. 13; xvii. 21, al. non occ.

ERRATA.

Page Line	Read	Page Line	Read	Page Line	Read
2 a, 15.	אָבִינוּ.	120 b, 45.	Ethp.	357 b, 20.	*Then.*
— b, 40.	אֲנִי.	126 a, 17.	דָּבָר.	371 b, 42.	*refugii.*
4 b, 41.	כִּים.	130 b, 35.	אַגֻּדָּה.	376 b, 23.	מָסֹרֶת.
— 42.	שָׁלְמָה.	153 a, 25.	לָבָן.	381 b, 31.	מַעֲשֶׂה.
5 a, 11.	אָזְנַיִם.	158 a, 14.	*rout.*	386 b, 40.	מִקְוָה.
13 a, 15.	אוֹיִבְךָ	173 a, 1.	נָעַם.	389 a, 36.	מַרְבַדִּים
17 b, 19.	*spakest.*	176 b, 27.	*septum fecit.*	390 b, 9.	ἑταιρεία τρυφητῶν.
21 b, 42.	Pehlavi.	192 a, 25.	אָחֹת׃	393 a, 35.	מַשְׁמָע.
22 a, 27.	לְאֹם עִמֶּךָ.	197 a, 36.	חָכָם.	394 a, 23.	מְצֻנֶּה.
35 b, 19.	Meninski.	199 a, 16.	פֶּסַח.	403 b, 9.	Verrere.
47 b, 7.	אֳסָרִי.	200 a, 26.	*mulierem.*	411 b, 4.	ὑμῶν.
49 a, 12.	الشمس.	211 a, 32.	*devourer.*	415 a, 21.	נַחֲרוּ.
		215 b, 45.	חֹטֶר.	425 b, 13.	אָן׃
— b, 40.	*Thy.*	238 a, 21.	מֵעַם.	432 a, 9.	on.
51 a, 38.	אֲקֻדָּה.	244 a, 22.	מִ֭י.		
— b, 32.	*Apparebo.*			440 b, 48.	صَلَف.
61 b, 42.	בַּעַל.	246 b, 10.	Spiritual.	458 a, 31.	עוּר.
73 a, 7.	בְּדֹלַח.	249 a, 54.	Drusius.	481 b, 35.	עָרוּךְ.
74 a, 4.	بَذَرَ. *Dispersed.*	253 b, 29.	יָרַה.	485 a, 9.	עָשָׁן.
83 b, 50.	Ps. xcii. 11.	265 a, 46.	יָפָה.	506 a, 5.	Is (for To).
89 a, 16.	רוּחַ.	269 b, 35.	יָקָר.	520 b, 3.	שׁוֹדֵד.
96 b, 3.	נָבָר.	289 a, 12.	כֹּהֵן.	560 b, 6.	לְלֶכֶת.
103 a, 23.	*third.*	301 a, 43.	אָכֵן.	574 a, 41.	(c) *Smiled, &c.*
110 a, 38.	גֵּם.	303 a, 36.	קִנְאָה.	584 a, 19.	*used as,* &c.
112 b, 13.	*Shaver.*	324 a, 25.	Gen. xxx. 37.	594 b, 50.	ὦ.
113 b, 38.	גֻּלָּה.	326 a, 18.	אָפֵן׃	595 a, 3.	ᾧ.
117 b, 17.	*longitudo.*	347 a, 17.	Varro.	604 b, 43.	مَحْبَل.
		350 b, 8.	יַגֵּעַ.		

www.ingramcontent.com/pod-product-compliance
Lightning Source LLC
Chambersburg PA
CBHW052039290426
44111CB00011B/1556